ASHER WILSON

# THE COMPLETE
# ETHIOPIAN
# BIBLE

## In English

# 88
## SCRIPTURES

## INCLUDING THE MISSING APOCRYPHA,
## THE BOOK OF ENOCH AND JUBILEES.

**Recognized as canon by the Ethiopian Orthodox Tewahedo Church**

Disclaimer:

This book is a curated collection of texts from the Ethiopian Bible, intended to provide an accessible format for study and reflection. The introductions and conclusions are the contributions of the author and are intended for contextualization and commentary purposes only.

Limitation of Liability:

The author and publisher disclaim all legal liability for any losses or damages that may result from the use of the information in this book. This book is provided "as is" without warranty of any kind, either express or implied. Efforts have been made to ensure the content is presented in a thoughtful and respectful manner, reflecting the spiritual and historical significance of the texts.

# TABLE OF CONTENTS

# INTRODUCTION

The Ethiopian Bible, written in the ancient South Semitic language of Ge'ez, is one of the oldest and most complete Bibles in the world. It is distinct from other Christian bibles in several key aspects, primarily due to its broader canon of sacred texts, which includes several books not found in the Protestant or even the broader Roman Catholic compilations.

The Ethiopian Bible's roots can be traced back to the Septuagint, a Greek translation of the Hebrew Bible, completed between 300 to 200 BC. It is considered one of the most important translations of the Bible, as it predates the King James Version (KJV) by nearly 800 years. The Septuagint was used as a source text for the translation of the Ethiopian Bible, and many of the books in the Ethiopian Bible are identical to those found in the Septuagint. However, the Ethiopian Bible also includes additional books that are not found in the Septuagint, considered Pseudepigraphal/Apocryphal, such as the *1 Enoch, 2 Enoch, Jubilees, 2 Esdras (Ezra Sutu'el), 4 Baruch* and *1 Clement*.

Moreover, unique to the Ethiopian Orthodox Church are the books of *Meqabyan I-III* (not to be confused with the *1-4 Maccabees*). The translation of *Meqabyan* by the author from Iyaric (a liturgical term occasionally used to refer to Rastafarian dialectical expressions) into English involves careful attention to both linguistic detail and the preservation of original meanings and connotations, ensuring that both the style and substance of the sacred texts are respected.

The following books are recognized as Deuterocanonical by the Roman Catholic, Greek, and Russian Orthodox Churches: *Tobit, Judith, Esther from the Greek Septuagint, The Wisdom of Solomon, Ecclesiasticus* (also called *The Wisdom of Jesus Son of Sirach*), *Baruch, The Song of the Three Holy Children, Susanna,* and *Bel and the Dragon, 1 Maccabees, 2 Maccabees.* As for *The Letter of Jeremiah,* it is included as chapter 6 of *Baruch.*

The following books are recognized as Deuterocanonical by the Greek and Russian Orthodox Churches, but not the Roman Catholic Church: *1 Esdras (Ezra Kali), The Prayer of Manasses, Psalm 151,* and *3 Maccabees.* An appendix to the Greek Septuagint contains *4 Maccabees,* considered Pseudepigraphal. It is included for its historical value.

The canon of the Ethiopian Orthodox Tewahedo Church is significantly larger than the Protocanonical 66 books of the Protestant Bible. The divergence stems largely from the inclusion of various texts categorized under the labels of the Deuterocanon, Apocrypha, and Pseudepigrapha. These texts offer additional insights and narratives that are considered canonical in the Ethiopian tradition but are non-canonical or apocryphal in others.

### What are MT, TR, and NU?
In the footnotes, MT refers to the Byzantine Greek Majority Text New Testament, which is usually in the main text. TR stands for Textus Receptus, which is the Greek Text from which the King James Version New Testament was translated. NU stands for the Nestle-Aland/UBS critical text of the Greek New Testament, which is used as a basis for some other Bible translations.

## UNLOCK A WORLD OF TIMELESS WISDOM!

Immerse yourself in the rich heritage of ancient scripture with our exclusive offer… **download the FREE digital version** of these six incredible books:
- **The Book of Jasher:** A unique historical record that expands on the stories of Genesis and beyond… revealing untold events from the Old Testament.
- **The Shepherd of Hermas:** An inspiring work that was once cherished alongside other canonical texts… providing deep spiritual guidance.
- **The Four Books of Maccabees:** A captivating collection chronicling the courageous spirit of the Jewish resistance… offering powerful lessons of faith, freedom, and perseverance.

**PLUS, receive a FREE 100-hour audiobook of the entire Ethiopian Bible!** Listen to this sacred scripture come to life, including the 22 Apocryphal books, and immerse yourself in its profound teachings.

**Don't miss this opportunity** to explore these revered books that have stood the test of time. Get your free copy today and experience the wisdom they have to offer.

**Go to the Bonus chapter on page 549 and discover how to get your bonuses now!**

# THE OLD TESTAMENT

## The First Book of Moses, Genesis

### 1

¹ In the beginning, Godᵃ created the heavens and the earth. ² The earth was formless and empty. Darkness was on the surface of the deep and God's Spirit was hovering over the surface of the waters. ³ God said, "Let there be light," and there was light. ⁴ God saw the light, and saw that it was good. God divided the light from the darkness. ⁵ God called the light "day", and the darkness he called "night". There was evening and there was morning, the first day. ⁶ God said, "Let there be an expanse in the middle of the waters, and let it divide the waters from the waters." ⁷ God made the expanse, and divided the waters which were under the expanse from the waters which were above the expanse; and it was so. ⁸ God called the expanse "sky". There was evening and there was morning, a second day. ⁹ God said, "Let the waters under the sky be gathered together to one place, and let the dry land appear;" and it was so. ¹⁰ God called the dry land "earth", and the gathering together of the waters he called "seas". God saw that it was good. ¹¹ God said, "Let the earth yield

grass, herbs yielding seeds, and fruit trees bearing fruit after their kind, with their seeds in it, on the earth;" and it was so. ¹² The earth yielded grass, herbs yielding seed after their kind, and trees bearing fruit, with their seeds in it, after their kind; and God saw that it was good. ¹³ There was evening and there was morning, a third day. ¹⁴ God said, "Let there be lights in the expanse of the sky to divide the day from the night; and let them be for signs to mark seasons, days, and years; ¹⁵ and let them be for lights in the expanse of the sky to give light on the earth;" and it was so. ¹⁶ God made the two great lights: the greater light to rule the day, and the lesser light to rule the night. He also made the stars. ¹⁷ God set them in the expanse of the sky to give light to the earth, ¹⁸ and to rule over the day and over the night, and to divide the light from the darkness. God saw that it was good. ¹⁹ There was evening and there was morning, a fourth day. ²⁰ God said, "Let the waters abound with living creatures, and let birds fly above the earth in the open expanse of the sky." ²¹ God created the large sea creatures and every living creature that moves, with which the waters swarmed, after their kind, and every winged bird after its kind. God saw that it was good. ²² God blessed them, saying, "Be fruitful, and multiply, and fill the waters in the seas, and let birds multiply on the earth." ²³ There was evening and there was morning, a fifth day. ²⁴ God said, "Let the earth produce living creatures after their kind, livestock, creeping things, and animals of the earth after their kind;" and it was so. ²⁵ God made the animals of the earth after their kind, and the livestock after their kind, and everything that creeps on the ground after its kind. God saw that it was good. ²⁶ God said, "Let's make man in our image, after our likeness. Let them have dominion over the fish of the sea, and over the birds of the sky, and over the livestock, and over all the earth, and over every creeping thing that creeps on the earth." ²⁷ God created man in his own image. In God's image he created him; male and female he created them. ²⁸ God blessed them. God said to them, "Be fruitful, multiply, fill the earth, and subdue it. Have dominion over the fish of the sea, over the birds of the sky, and over every living thing that moves on the earth." ²⁹ God said, "Behold,ᵇ I have given you every herb yielding seed, which is on the surface of all the earth, and every tree, which bears fruit yielding seed. It will be your food. ³⁰ To every animal of the earth, and to every bird of the sky, and to everything that creeps on the earth, in which there is life, I have given every green herb for food;" and it was so. ³¹ God saw everything that he had made, and, behold, it was very good. There was evening and there was morning, a sixth day.

### 2

¹ The heavens, the earth, and all their vast array were finished. ² On the seventh day God finished his work which he had done; and he rested on the seventh day from all his work which he had done. ³ God blessed the seventh day, and made it holy, because he rested in it from all his work of creation which he had done. ⁴ This is the history of the generations of the heavens and of the earth when they were created, in the day that Yahwehᶜ God made the earth and the heavens. ⁵ No plant of the field was yet in the earth, and no herb of the field had yet sprung up; for Yahweh God had not caused it to rain on the earth. There was not a man to till the ground, ⁶ but a mist went up from the earth, and watered the whole surface of the ground. ⁷ Yahweh God formed man from the dust of the ground, and breathed into his nostrils the breath of life; and man became a living soul. ⁸ Yahweh God planted a garden eastward, in Eden, and there he put the man whom he had formed. ⁹ Out of the ground Yahweh God made every tree to grow that is pleasant to the sight, and good for food, including the tree of life in the middle of the garden and the tree of the knowledge of good and evil. ¹⁰ A river went out of Eden to water the garden; and from there it was parted, and became the source of four rivers. ¹¹ The name of the first is Pishon: it flows through the whole land of Havilah, where there is gold; ¹² and the gold of that land is good. Bdelliumᵈ and onyx stone are also there. ¹³ The name of the second river is Gihon. It is the same river that flows through the whole land of Cush. ¹⁴ The name of the third river is Hiddekel. This is the one which flows in front of Assyria. The fourth river is the Euphrates. ¹⁵ Yahweh God took the man, and put him into the garden of Eden to cultivate and keep it. ¹⁶ Yahweh God commanded the man, saying, "You may freely eat of every tree of the garden; ¹⁷ but you shall not eat of the tree of the knowledge of good and evil; for in the day that you eat of it, you will surely die." ¹⁸ Yahweh God said, "It is not good for the man to be alone. I will make him a helper comparable toᵉ him." ¹⁹ Out of the ground Yahweh God formed every animal of the field, and every bird of the sky, and brought them to the man to see what he would call them. Whatever the man called every living creature became its name. ²⁰ The man gave names to all livestock, and to the birds of the sky, and to every animal of the field; but for man there was not found a helper comparable to him. ²¹ Yahweh God caused the man to fall into a deep sleep. As the man slept, he took one of his ribs, and closed up the flesh in its place. ²² Yahweh God made a woman from the rib which he had taken from the man, and brought her to the man. ²³ The man said, "This is now bone of my bones, and flesh of my flesh. She will be called 'woman,' because she was taken out of Man." ²⁴ Therefore a man will leave his father and his mother, and will join with his wife, and they will be one flesh. ²⁵ The man and his wife were both naked, and they were not ashamed.

### 3

¹ Now the serpent was more subtle than any animal of the field which Yahweh God had made. He said to the woman, "Has God really said, 'You shall not eat of any tree of the garden'?" ² The woman said to the serpent, "We may eat fruit from the trees of the garden, ³ but not the fruit of the tree which is in the middle of the garden. God has said, 'You shall not eat of it. You shall not touch it, lest you die.'" ⁴ The serpent said to the woman, "You won't really die, ⁵ for God knows that in the day you eat it, your eyes will be opened, and you will be like God, knowing good and evil." ⁶ When the woman saw that the tree was good for food, and that it was a delight to the eyes, and that the tree was to be desired to make one wise, she took some of its fruit, and ate. Then she gave some to her husband with her, and he ate it, too. ⁷ Their eyes were opened, and they both knew that they were naked. They sewed fig leaves together, and made coverings for themselves. ⁸ They heard Yahweh God's voice walking in the garden in the cool of the day, and the man and his wife hid themselves from the presence of Yahweh God among the trees of the garden. ⁹ Yahweh God called to the man, and said to him, "Where are you?" ¹⁰ The man said, "I heard your voice in the garden, and I was afraid, because I was naked; so I hid myself." ¹¹ God said, "Who told you that you were naked? Have you eaten from the tree that I commanded you not to eat from?" ¹² The man said, "The woman whom you gave to be with me, she gave me fruit from the tree, and I ate it." ¹³ Yahweh God said to the woman, "What have you done?" The woman said, "The serpent deceived me, and I ate." ¹⁴ Yahweh God said to the serpent, "Because you have done this, you are cursed above all livestock, and above every animal of the field. You shall go on your belly and you shall eat dust all the days of your life. ¹⁵ I will put hostility between you and the woman, and between your offspring and her offspring. He will bruise your head, and you will bruise his heel." ¹⁶ To the woman he said, "I will greatly multiply your pain in childbirth. You will bear children in pain. Your desire will be for your husband, and he will rule over you." ¹⁷ To Adam he said, "Because you have listened to your wife's voice, and have eaten from the tree, about which I commanded you, saying, 'You shall not eat of it,' the ground is cursed

---

ᵃ *1:1* The Hebrew word rendered "God" is "אֱלֹהִים" (Elohim).

ᵇ *1:29* "Behold", from "הִנֵּה", means look at, take notice, observe, see, or gaze at. It is often used as an interjection.

ᶜ *2:4* "Yahweh" is God's proper Name, sometimes rendered "LORD" (all caps) in other translations.

ᵈ *2:12* or, aromatic resin

ᵉ *2:18* or, suitable for, or appropriate for.

for your sake. You will eat from it with much labor all the days of your life. [18] It will yield thorns and thistles to you; and you will eat the herb of the field. [19] You will eat bread by the sweat of your face until you return to the ground, for you were taken out of it. For you are dust, and you shall return to dust." [20] The man called his wife Eve because she would be the mother of all the living. [21] Yahweh God made garments of animal skins for Adam and for his wife, and clothed them. [22] Yahweh God said, "Behold, the man has become like one of us, knowing good and evil. Now, lest he reach out his hand, and also take of the tree of life, and eat, and live forever—" [23] Therefore Yahweh God sent him out from the garden of Eden, to till the ground from which he was taken. [24] So he drove out the man; and he placed cherubim[a] at the east of the garden of Eden, and a flaming sword which turned every way, to guard the way to the tree of life.

## 4

[1] The man knew[b] Eve his wife. She conceived,[c] and gave birth to Cain, and said, "I have gotten a man with Yahweh's help." [2] Again she gave birth, to Cain's brother Abel. Abel was a keeper of sheep, but Cain was a tiller of the ground. [3] As time passed, Cain brought an offering to Yahweh from the fruit of the ground. [4] Abel also brought some of the firstborn of his flock and of its fat. Yahweh respected Abel and his offering, [5] but he didn't respect Cain and his offering. Cain was very angry, and the expression on his face fell. [6] Yahweh said to Cain, "Why are you angry? Why has the expression of your face fallen? [7] If you do well, won't it be lifted up? If you don't do well, sin crouches at the door. Its desire is for you, but you are to rule over it." [8] Cain said to Abel, his brother, "Let's go into the field." While they were in the field, Cain rose up against Abel, his brother, and killed him. [9] Yahweh said to Cain, "Where is Abel, your brother?" He said, "I don't know. Am I my brother's keeper?" [10] Yahweh said, "What have you done? The voice of your brother's blood cries to me from the ground. [11] Now you are cursed because of the ground, which has opened its mouth to receive your brother's blood from your hand. [12] From now on, when you till the ground, it won't yield its strength to you. You will be a fugitive and a wanderer in the earth." [13] Cain said to Yahweh, "My punishment is greater than I can bear. [14] Behold, you have driven me out today from the surface of the ground. I will be hidden from your face, and I will be a fugitive and a wanderer in the earth. Whoever finds me will kill me." [15] Yahweh said to him, "Therefore whoever slays Cain, vengeance will be taken on him sevenfold." Yahweh appointed a sign for Cain, so that anyone finding him would not strike him. [16] Cain left Yahweh's presence, and lived in the land of Nod, east of Eden. [17] Cain knew his wife. She conceived, and gave birth to Enoch. He built a city, and named the city after the name of his son, Enoch. [18] Irad was born to Enoch. Irad became the father of Mehujael. Mehujael became the father of Methushael. Methushael became the father of Lamech. [19] Lamech took two wives: the name of the first one was Adah, and the name of the second one was Zillah. [20] Adah gave birth to Jabal, who was the father of those who dwell in tents and have livestock. [21] His brother's name was Jubal, who was the father of all who handle the harp and pipe. [22] Zillah also gave birth to Tubal Cain, the forger of every cutting instrument of bronze and iron. Tubal Cain's sister was Naamah. [23] Lamech said to his wives, "Adah and Zillah, hear my voice. You wives of Lamech, listen to my speech, for I have slain a man for wounding me, a young man for bruising me. [24] If Cain will be avenged seven times, truly Lamech seventy-seven times." [25] Adam knew his wife again. She gave birth to a son, and named him Seth, saying, "for God has given me another child instead of Abel, for Cain killed him." [26] A son was also born to Seth, and he named him Enosh. At that time men began to call on Yahweh's name.

## 5

[1] This is the book of the generations of Adam. In the day that God created man, he made him in God's likeness. [2] He created them male and female, and blessed them. On the day they were created, he named them Adam.[d] [3] Adam lived one hundred thirty years, and became the father of a son in his own likeness, after his image, and named him Seth. [4] The days of Adam after he became the father of Seth were eight hundred years, and he became the father of other sons and daughters. [5] All the days that Adam lived were nine hundred thirty years, then he died. [6] Seth lived one hundred five years, then became the father of Enosh. [7] Seth lived after he became the father of Enosh eight hundred seven years, and became the father of other sons and daughters. [8] All of the days of Seth were nine hundred twelve years, then he died. [9] Enosh lived ninety years, and became the father of Kenan. [10] Enosh

lived after he became the father of Kenan eight hundred fifteen years, and became the father of other sons and daughters. [11] All of the days of Enosh were nine hundred five years, then he died. [12] Kenan lived seventy years, then became the father of Mahalalel. [13] Kenan lived after he became the father of Mahalalel eight hundred forty years, and became the father of other sons and daughters [14] and all of the days of Kenan were nine hundred ten years, then he died. [15] Mahalalel lived sixty-five years, then became the father of Jared. [16] Mahalalel lived after he became the father of Jared eight hundred thirty years, and became the father of other sons and daughters. [17] All of the days of Mahalalel were eight hundred ninety-five years, then he died. [18] Jared lived one hundred sixty-two years, then became the father of Enoch. [19] Jared lived after he became the father of Enoch eight hundred years, and became the father of other sons and daughters. [20] All of the days of Jared were nine hundred sixty-two years, then he died. [21] Enoch lived sixty-five years, then became the father of Methuselah. [22] After Methuselah's birth, Enoch walked with God for three hundred years, and became the father of more sons and daughters. [23] All the days of Enoch were three hundred sixty-five years. [24] Enoch walked with God, and he was not found, for God took him. [25] Methuselah lived one hundred eighty-seven years, then became the father of Lamech. [26] Methuselah lived after he became the father of Lamech seven hundred eighty-two years, and became the father of other sons and daughters. [27] All the days of Methuselah were nine hundred sixty-nine years, then he died. [28] Lamech lived one hundred eighty-two years, then became the father of a son. [29] He named him Noah, saying, "This one will comfort us in our work and in the toil of our hands, caused by the ground which Yahweh has cursed." [30] Lamech lived after he became the father of Noah five hundred ninety-five years, and became the father of other sons and daughters. [31] All the days of Lamech were seven hundred seventy-seven years, then he died. [32] Noah was five hundred years old, then Noah became the father of Shem, Ham, and Japheth.

## 6

[1] When men began to multiply on the surface of the ground, and daughters were born to them, [2] God's sons saw that men's daughters were beautiful, and they took any that they wanted for themselves as wives. [3] Yahweh said, "My Spirit will not strive with man forever, because he also is flesh; so his days will be one hundred twenty years." [4] The Nephilim[e] were in the earth in those days, and also after that, when God's sons came in to men's daughters and had children with them. Those were the mighty men who were of old, men of renown. [5] Yahweh saw that the wickedness of man was great in the earth, and that every imagination of the thoughts of man's heart was continually only evil. [6] Yahweh was sorry that he had made man on the earth, and it grieved him in his heart. [7] Yahweh said, "I will destroy man whom I have created from the surface of the ground—man, along with animals, creeping things, and birds of the sky—for I am sorry that I have made them." [8] But Noah found favor in Yahweh's eyes. [9] This is the history of the generations of Noah: Noah was a righteous man, blameless among the people of his time. Noah walked with God. [10] Noah became the father of three sons: Shem, Ham, and Japheth. [11] The earth was corrupt before God, and the earth was filled with violence. [12] God saw the earth, and saw that it was corrupt, for all flesh had corrupted their way on the earth. [13] God said to Noah, "I will bring an end to all flesh, for the earth is filled with violence through them. Behold, I will destroy them and the earth. [14] Make a ship of gopher wood. You shall make rooms in the ship, and shall seal it inside and outside with pitch. [15] This is how you shall make it. The length of the ship shall be three hundred cubits,[f] its width fifty cubits, and its height thirty cubits. [16] You shall make a roof in the ship, and you shall finish it to a cubit upward. You shall set the door of the ship in its side. You shall make it with lower, second, and third levels. [17] I, even I, will bring the flood of waters on this earth, to destroy all flesh having the breath of life from under the sky. Everything that is in the earth will die. [18] But I will establish my covenant with you. You shall come into the ship, you, your sons, your wife, and your sons' wives with you. [19] Of every living thing of all flesh, you shall bring two of every sort into the ship, to keep them alive with you. They shall be male and female. [20] Of the birds after their kind, of the livestock after their kind, of every creeping thing of the ground after its kind, two of every sort will come to you, to keep them alive. [21] Take with you some of all food that is eaten, and gather it to yourself; and it will be for food for you, and for them." [22] Thus Noah did. He did all that God commanded him.

---

[a] *3:24* cherubim are powerful angelic creatures, messengers of God with wings. See Ezekiel 10.

[b] *4:1* or, lay with, or, had relations with
[c] *4:1* or, became pregnant
[d] *5:2* "Adam" and "Man" are spelled with the exact same

consonants in Hebrew, so this can be correctly translated either way.
[e] *6:4* or, giants

[f] *6:15* A cubit is the length from the tip of the middle finger to the elbow on a man's arm, or about 18 inches or 46 centimeters.

**7**

¹ Yahweh said to Noah, "Come with all of your household into the ship, for I have seen your righteousness before me in this generation. ² You shall take seven pairs of every clean animal with you, the male and his female. Of the animals that are not clean, take two, the male and his female. ³ Also of the birds of the sky, seven and seven, male and female, to keep seed alive on the surface of all the earth. ⁴ In seven days, I will cause it to rain on the earth for forty days and forty nights. I will destroy every living thing that I have made from the surface of the ground." ⁵ Noah did everything that Yahweh commanded him. ⁶ Noah was six hundred years old when the flood of waters came on the earth. ⁷ Noah went into the ship with his sons, his wife, and his sons' wives, because of the floodwaters. ⁸ Clean animals, unclean animals, birds, and everything that creeps on the ground ⁹ went by pairs to Noah into the ship, male and female, as God commanded Noah. ¹⁰ After the seven days, the floodwaters came on the earth. ¹¹ In the six hundredth year of Noah's life, in the second month, on the seventeenth day of the month, on that day all the fountains of the great deep burst open, and the sky's windows opened. ¹² It rained on the earth forty days and forty nights. ¹³ In the same day Noah, and Shem, Ham, and Japheth—the sons of Noah—and Noah's wife and the three wives of his sons with them, entered into the ship— ¹⁴ they, and every animal after its kind, all the livestock after their kind, every creeping thing that creeps on the earth after its kind, and every bird after its kind, every bird of every sort. ¹⁵ Pairs from all flesh with the breath of life in them went into the ship to Noah. ¹⁶ Those who went in, went in male and female of all flesh, as God commanded him; then Yahweh shut him in. ¹⁷ The flood was forty days on the earth. The waters increased, and lifted up the ship, and it was lifted up above the earth. ¹⁸ The waters rose, and increased greatly on the earth; and the ship floated on the surface of the waters. ¹⁹ The waters rose very high on the earth. All the high mountains that were under the whole sky were covered. ²⁰ The waters rose fifteen cubitsᵃ higher, and the mountains were covered. ²¹ All flesh died that moved on the earth, including birds, livestock, animals, every creeping thing that creeps on the earth, and every man. ²² All on the dry land, in whose nostrils was the breath of the spirit of life, died. ²³ Every living thing was destroyed that was on the surface of the ground, including man, livestock, creeping things, and birds of the sky. They were destroyed from the earth. Only Noah was left, and those who were with him in the ship. ²⁴ The waters flooded the earth one hundred fifty days.

**8**

¹ God remembered Noah, all the animals, and all the livestock that were with him in the ship; and God made a wind to pass over the earth. The waters subsided. ² The deep's fountains and the sky's windows were also stopped, and the rain from the sky was restrained. ³ The waters continually receded from the earth. After the end of one hundred fifty days the waters receded. ⁴ The ship rested in the seventh month, on the seventeenth day of the month, on Ararat's mountains. ⁵ The waters receded continually until the tenth month. In the tenth month, on the first day of the month, the tops of the mountains were visible. ⁶ At the end of forty days, Noah opened the window of the ship which he had made, ⁷ and he sent out a raven. It went back and forth, until the waters were dried up from the earth. ⁸ He himself sent out a dove to see if the waters were abated from the surface of the ground, ⁹ but the dove found no place to rest her foot, and she returned into the ship to him, for the waters were on the surface of the whole earth. He put out his hand, and took her, and brought her to him into the ship. ¹⁰ He waited yet another seven days; and again he sent the dove out of the ship. ¹¹ The dove came back to him at evening and, behold, in her mouth was a freshly plucked olive leaf. So Noah knew that the waters were abated from the earth. ¹² He waited yet another seven days, and sent out the dove; and she didn't return to him any more. ¹³ In the six hundred first year, in the first month, the first day of the month, the waters were dried up from the earth. Noah removed the covering of the ship, and looked. He saw that the surface of the ground was dry. ¹⁴ In the second month, on the

twenty-seventh day of the month, the earth was dry. ¹⁵ God spoke to Noah, saying, ¹⁶"Go out of the ship, you, your wife, your sons, and your sons' wives with you. ¹⁷ Bring out with you every living thing that is with you of all flesh, including birds, livestock, and every creeping thing that creeps on the earth, that they may breed abundantly in the earth, and be fruitful, and multiply on the earth." ¹⁸ Noah went out, with his sons, his wife, and his sons' wives with him. ¹⁹ Every animal, every creeping thing, and every bird, whatever moves on the earth, after their families, went out of the ship. ²⁰ Noah built an altar to Yahweh, and took of every clean animal, and of every clean bird, and offered burnt offerings on the altar. ²¹ Yahweh smelled the pleasant aroma. Yahweh said in his heart, "I will not again curse the ground any more for man's sake because the imagination of man's heart is evil from his youth. I will never again strike every living thing, as I have done. ²² While the earth remains, seed time and harvest, and cold and heat, and summer and winter, and day and night will not cease."

**9**

¹ God blessed Noah and his sons, and said to them, "Be fruitful, multiply, and replenish the earth. ² The fear of you and the dread of you will be on every animal of the earth, and on every bird of the sky. Everything that moves along the ground, and all the fish of the sea, are delivered into your hand. ³ Every moving thing that lives will be food for you. As I gave you the green herb, I have given everything to you. ⁴ But flesh with its life, that is, its blood, you shall not eat. ⁵ I will surely require accounting for your life's blood. At the hand of every animal I will require it. At the hand of man, even at the hand of every man's brother, I will require the life of man. ⁶ Whoever sheds man's blood, his blood will be shed by man, for God made man in his own image. ⁷ Be fruitful and multiply. Increase abundantly in the earth, and multiply in it." ⁸ God spoke to Noah and to his sons with him, saying, ⁹"As for me, behold, I establish my covenant with you, and with your offspring after you, ¹⁰ and with every living creature that is with you: the birds, the livestock, and every animal of the earth with you, of all that go out of the ship, even every animal of the earth. ¹¹ I will establish my covenant with you: All flesh will not be cut off any more by the waters of the flood. There will never again be a flood to destroy the earth." ¹² God said, "This is the token of the covenant which I make between me and you and every living creature that is with you, for perpetual generations: ¹³ I set my rainbow in the cloud, and it will be a sign of a covenant between me and the earth. ¹⁴ When I bring a cloud over the earth, that the rainbow will be seen in the cloud, ¹⁵ I will remember my covenant, which is between me and you and every living creature of all flesh, and the waters will no more become a flood to destroy all flesh. ¹⁶ The rainbow will be in the cloud. I will look at it, that I may remember the everlasting covenant between God and every living creature of all flesh that is on the earth." ¹⁷ God said to Noah, "This is the token of the covenant which I have established between me and all flesh that is on the earth." ¹⁸ The sons of Noah who went out from the ship were Shem, Ham, and Japheth. Ham is the father of Canaan. ¹⁹ These three were the sons of Noah, and from these the whole earth was populated. ²⁰ Noah began to be a farmer, and planted a vineyard. ²¹ He drank of the wine and got drunk. He was uncovered within his tent. ²² Ham, the father of Canaan, saw the nakedness of his father, and told his two brothers outside. ²³ Shem and Japheth took a garment, and laid it on both their shoulders, went in backwards, and covered the nakedness of their father. Their faces were backwards, and they didn't see their father's nakedness. ²⁴ Noah awoke from his wine, and knew what his youngest son had done to him. ²⁵ He said, "Canaan is cursed. He will be a servant of servants to his brothers." ²⁶ He said, "Blessed be Yahweh, the God of Shem. Let Canaan be his servant. ²⁷ May God enlarge Japheth. Let him dwell in the tents of Shem. Let Canaan be his servant." ²⁸ Noah lived three hundred fifty years after the flood. ²⁹ All the days of Noah were nine hundred fifty years, and then he died.

**10**

¹ Now this is the history of the generations of the sons of Noah and of Shem, Ham, and Japheth. Sons were born to them after the flood. ² The sons of Japheth were: Gomer, Magog, Madai, Javan, Tubal, Meshech, and Tiras. ³ The sons of Gomer were: Ashkenaz, Riphath, and Togarmah. ⁴ The sons of Javan were: Elishah, Tarshish, Kittim, and Dodanim. ⁵ Of these were the islands of the nations divided in their lands, everyone after his language, after their families, in their nations. ⁶ The sons of Ham were: Cush, Mizraim, Put, and Canaan. ⁷ The sons of Cush were: Seba, Havilah, Sabtah, Raamah, and Sabteca. The sons of Raamah were: Sheba and Dedan. ⁸ Cush became the father of Nimrod. He began to be a mighty one in the earth. ⁹ He was a mighty hunter before Yahweh. Therefore it is said, "like Nimrod, a mighty

---

ᵃ *7:20* A cubit is the length from the tip of the middle finger to the elbow on a man's arm, or about 18 inches or 46 centimeters.

hunter before Yahweh". ¹⁰ The beginning of his kingdom was Babel, Erech, Accad, and Calneh, in the land of Shinar. ¹¹ Out of that land he went into Assyria, and built Nineveh, Rehoboth Ir, Calah, ¹² and Resen between Nineveh and the great city Calah. ¹³ Mizraim became the father of Ludim, Anamim, Lehabim, Naphtuhim, ¹⁴ Pathrusim, Casluhim (which the Philistines descended from), and Caphtorim. ¹⁵ Canaan became the father of Sidon (his firstborn), Heth, ¹⁶ the Jebusites, the Amorites, the Girgashites, ¹⁷ the Hivites, the Arkites, the Sinites, ¹⁸ the Arvadites, the Zemarites, and the Hamathites. Afterward the families of the Canaanites were spread abroad. ¹⁹ The border of the Canaanites was from Sidon—as you go toward Gerar—to Gaza—as you go toward Sodom, Gomorrah, Admah, and Zeboiim—to Lasha. ²⁰ These are the sons of Ham, after their families, according to their languages, in their lands and their nations. ²¹ Children were also born to Shem (the elder brother of Japheth), the father of all the children of Eber. ²² The sons of Shem were: Elam, Asshur, Arpachshad, Lud, and Aram. ²³ The sons of Aram were: Uz, Hul, Gether, and Mash. ²⁴ Arpachshad became the father of Shelah. Shelah became the father of Eber. ²⁵ To Eber were born two sons. The name of the one was Peleg, for in his days the earth was divided. His brother's name was Joktan. ²⁶ Joktan became the father of Almodad, Sheleph, Hazarmaveth, Jerah, ²⁷ Hadoram, Uzal, Diklah, ²⁸ Obal, Abimael, Sheba, ²⁹ Ophir, Havilah, and Jobab. All these were the sons of Joktan. ³⁰ Their dwelling extended from Mesha, as you go toward Sephar, the mountain of the east. ³¹ These are the sons of Shem, by their families, according to their languages, lands, and nations. ³² These are the families of the sons of Noah, by their generations, according to their nations. The nations divided from these in the earth after the flood.

## 11

¹ The whole earth was of one language and of one speech. ² As they traveled east,ᵃ they found a plain in the land of Shinar, and they lived there. ³ They said to one another, "Come, let's make bricks, and burn them thoroughly." They had brick for stone, and they used tar for mortar. ⁴ They said, "Come, let's build ourselves a city, and a tower whose top reaches to the sky, and let's make a name for ourselves, lest we be scattered abroad on the surface of the whole earth." ⁵ Yahweh came down to see the city and the tower, which the children of men built. ⁶ Yahweh said, "Behold, they are one people, and they all have one language, and this is what they begin to do. Now nothing will be withheld from them, which they intend to do. ⁷ Come, let's go down, and there confuse their language, that they may not understand one another's speech." ⁸ So Yahweh scattered them abroad from there on the surface of all the earth. They stopped building the city. ⁹ Therefore its name was called Babel, because there Yahweh confused the language of all the earth. From there, Yahweh scattered them abroad on the surface of all the earth. ¹⁰ This is the history of the generations of Shem: Shem was one hundred years old when he became the father of Arpachshad two years after the flood. ¹¹ Shem lived five hundred years after he became the father of Arpachshad, and became the father of more sons and daughters. ¹² Arpachshad lived thirty-five years and became the father of Shelah. ¹³ Arpachshad lived four hundred three years after he became the father of Shelah, and became the father of more sons and daughters. ¹⁴ Shelah lived thirty years, and became the father of Eber. ¹⁵ Shelah lived four hundred three years after he became the father of Eber, and became the father of more sons and daughters. ¹⁶ Eber lived thirty-four years, and became the father of Peleg. ¹⁷ Eber lived four hundred thirty years after he became the father of Peleg, and became the father of more sons and daughters. ¹⁸ Peleg lived thirty years, and became the father of Reu. ¹⁹ Peleg lived two hundred nine years after he became the father of Reu, and became the father of more sons and daughters. ²⁰ Reu lived thirty-two years, and became the father of Serug. ²¹ Reu lived two hundred seven years after he became the father of Serug, and became the father of more sons and daughters. ²² Serug lived thirty years, and became the father of Nahor. ²³ Serug lived two hundred years after he became the father of Nahor, and became the father of more sons and daughters. ²⁴ Nahor lived twenty-nine years, and became the father of Terah. ²⁵ Nahor lived one hundred nineteen years after he became the father of Terah, and became the father of more sons and daughters. ²⁶ Terah lived seventy years, and became the father of Abram, Nahor, and Haran. ²⁷ Now this is the history of the generations of Terah. Terah became the father of Abram, Nahor, and Haran. Haran became the father of Lot. ²⁸ Haran died in the land of his birth, in Ur of the Chaldees, while his father Terah was still alive. ²⁹ Abram and Nahor married wives. The name of Abram's wife was Sarai, and the name of Nahor's wife was Milcah, the daughter of Haran, who was also the father of Iscah. ³⁰ Sarai was barren. She had no child. ³¹ Terah took Abram his son, Lot the son of Haran, his son's son, and Sarai his daughter-in-law, his son Abram's wife. They went from Ur of the Chaldees, to go into the land of Canaan. They came to Haran and lived there. ³² The days of Terah were two hundred five years. Terah died in Haran.

## 12

¹ Now Yahweh said to Abram, "Leave your country, and your relatives, and your father's house, and go to the land that I will show you. ² I will make of you a great nation. I will bless you and make your name great. You will be a blessing. ³ I will bless those who bless you, and I will curse him who treats you with contempt. All the families of the earth will be blessed through you." ⁴ So Abram went, as Yahweh had told him. Lot went with him. Abram was seventy-five years old when he departed from Haran. ⁵ Abram took Sarai his wife, Lot his brother's son, all their possessions that they had gathered, and the people whom they had acquired in Haran, and they went to go into the land of Canaan. They entered into the land of Canaan. ⁶ Abram passed through the land to the place of Shechem, to the oak of Moreh. At that time, Canaanites were in the land. ⁷ Yahweh appeared to Abram and said, "I will give this land to your offspring."ᵇ He built an altar there to Yahweh, who had appeared to him. ⁸ He left from there to go to the mountain on the east of Bethel and pitched his tent, having Bethel on the west, and Ai on the east. There he built an altar to Yahweh and called on Yahweh's name. ⁹ Abram traveled, still going on toward the South. ¹⁰ There was a famine in the land. Abram went down into Egypt to live as a foreigner there, for the famine was severe in the land. ¹¹ When he had come near to enter Egypt, he said to Sarai his wife, "See now, I know that you are a beautiful woman to look at. ¹² It will happen that when the Egyptians see you, they will say, 'This is his wife.' They will kill me, but they will save you alive. ¹³ Please say that you are my sister, that it may be well with me for your sake, and that my soul may live because of you." ¹⁴ When Abram had come into Egypt, Egyptians saw that the woman was very beautiful. ¹⁵ The princes of Pharaoh saw her, and praised her to Pharaoh; and the woman was taken into Pharaoh's house. ¹⁶ He dealt well with Abram for her sake. He had sheep, cattle, male donkeys, male servants, female servants, female donkeys, and camels. ¹⁷ Yahweh afflicted Pharaoh and his house with great plagues because of Sarai, Abram's wife. ¹⁸ Pharaoh called Abram and said, "What is this that you have done to me? Why didn't you tell me that she was your wife? ¹⁹ Why did you say, 'She is my sister,' so that I took her to be my wife? Now therefore, see your wife, take her, and go your way." ²⁰ Pharaoh commanded men concerning him, and they escorted him away with his wife and all that he had.

## 13

¹ Abram went up out of Egypt—he, his wife, all that he had, and Lot with him—into the South. ² Abram was very rich in livestock, in silver, and in gold. ³ He went on his journeys from the South as far as Bethel, to the place where his tent had been at the beginning, between Bethel and Ai, ⁴ to the place of the altar, which he had made there at the first. There Abram called on Yahweh's name. ⁵ Lot also, who went with Abram, had flocks, herds, and tents. ⁶ The land was not able to bear them, that they might live together; for their possessions were so great that they couldn't live together. ⁷ There was strife between the herdsmen of Abram's livestock and the herdsmen of Lot's livestock. The Canaanites and the Perizzites lived in the land at that time. ⁸ Abram said to Lot, "Please, let there be no strife between you and me, and between your herdsmen and my herdsmen; for we are relatives. ⁹ Isn't the whole land before you? Please separate yourself from me. If you go to the left hand, then I will go to the right. Or if you go to the right hand, then I will go to the left." ¹⁰ Lot lifted up his eyes, and saw all the plain of the Jordan, that it was well-watered everywhere, before Yahweh destroyed Sodom and Gomorrah, like the garden of Yahweh, like the land of Egypt, as you go to Zoar. ¹¹ So Lot chose the Plain of the Jordan for himself. Lot traveled east, and they separated themselves from one other. ¹² Abram lived in the land of Canaan, and Lot lived in the cities of the plain, and moved his tent as far as Sodom. ¹³ Now the men of Sodom were exceedingly wicked and sinners against Yahweh. ¹⁴ Yahweh said to Abram, after Lot was separated from him, "Now, lift up your eyes, and look from the place where you are, northward and southward and eastward and westward, ¹⁵ for I will give all the land which you see to you and to your offspring forever. ¹⁶ I will make your offspring as the dust of the earth, so that if a man can count the dust of the earth, then your offspring may also be counted. ¹⁷ Arise, walk through the land in its length and in its width; for I will give it to you." ¹⁸ Abram moved his tent, and came and lived by the oaks of Mamre, which are in Hebron, and built an altar there to Yahweh.

---

ᵃ *11:2 LXX reads "from the east".*  ᵇ *12:7 or, seed*

## 14

¹ In the days of Amraphel, king of Shinar; Arioch, king of Ellasar; Chedorlaomer, king of Elam; and Tidal, king of Goiim, ² they made war with Bera, king of Sodom; Birsha, king of Gomorrah; Shinab, king of Admah; Shemeber, king of Zeboiim; and the king of Bela (also called Zoar). ³ All these joined together in the valley of Siddim (also called the Salt Sea). ⁴ They served Chedorlaomer for twelve years, and in the thirteenth year they rebelled. ⁵ In the fourteenth year Chedorlaomer and the kings who were with him came and struck the Rephaim in Ashteroth Karnaim, the Zuzim in Ham, the Emim in Shaveh Kiriathaim, ⁶ and the Horites in their Mount Seir, to El Paran, which is by the wilderness. ⁷ They returned, and came to En Mishpat (also called Kadesh), and struck all the country of the Amalekites, and also the Amorites, that lived in Hazazon Tamar. ⁸ The king of Sodom, and the king of Gomorrah, the king of Admah, the king of Zeboiim, and the king of Bela (also called Zoar) went out; and they set the battle in array against them in the valley of Siddim ⁹ against Chedorlaomer king of Elam, Tidal king of Goiim, Amraphel king of Shinar, and Arioch king of Ellasar; four kings against the five. ¹⁰ Now the valley of Siddim was full of tar pits; and the kings of Sodom and Gomorrah fled, and some fell there. Those who remained fled to the hills. ¹¹ They took all the goods of Sodom and Gomorrah, and all their food, and went their way. ¹² They took Lot, Abram's brother's son, who lived in Sodom, and his goods, and departed. ¹³ One who had escaped came and told Abram, the Hebrew. At that time, he lived by the oaks of Mamre, the Amorite, brother of Eshcol and brother of Aner. They were allies of Abram. ¹⁴ When Abram heard that his relative was taken captive, he led out his three hundred eighteen trained men, born in his house, and pursued as far as Dan. ¹⁵ He divided himself against them by night, he and his servants, and struck them, and pursued them to Hobah, which is on the left hand of Damascus. ¹⁶ He brought back all the goods, and also brought back his relative Lot and his goods, and the women also, and the other people. ¹⁷ The king of Sodom went out to meet him after his return from the slaughter of Chedorlaomer and the kings who were with him, at the valley of Shaveh (that is, the King's Valley). ¹⁸ Melchizedek king of Salem brought out bread and wine. He was priest of God Most High. ¹⁹ He blessed him, and said, "Blessed be Abram of God Most High, possessor of heaven and earth. ²⁰ Blessed be God Most High, who has delivered your enemies into your hand." Abram gave him a tenth of all. ²¹ The king of Sodom said to Abram, "Give me the people, and take the goods for yourself." ²² Abram said to the king of Sodom, "I have lifted up my hand to Yahweh, God Most High, possessor of heaven and earth, ²³ that I will not take a thread nor a sandal strap nor anything that is yours, lest you should say, 'I have made Abram rich.' ²⁴ I will accept nothing from you except that which the young men have eaten, and the portion of the men who went with me: Aner, Eshcol, and Mamre. Let them take their portion."

## 15

¹ After these things Yahweh's word came to Abram in a vision, saying, "Don't be afraid, Abram. I am your shield, your exceedingly great reward." ² Abram said, "Lordᵃ Yahweh, what will you give me, since I go childless, and he who will inherit my estate is Eliezer of Damascus?" ³ Abram said, "Behold, you have given no children to me: and, behold, one born in my house is my heir." ⁴ Behold, Yahweh's word came to him, saying, "This man will not be your heir, but he who will come out of your own body will be your heir." ⁵ Yahweh brought him outside, and said, "Look now toward the sky, and count the stars, if you are able to count them." He said to Abram, "So your offspring will be." ⁶ He believed in Yahweh, who credited it to him for righteousness. ⁷ He said to Abram, "I am Yahweh who brought you out of Ur of the Chaldees, to give you this land to inherit it." ⁸ He said, "Lord Yahweh, how will I know that I will inherit it?" ⁹ He said to him, "Bring me a heifer three years old, a female goat three years old, a ram three years old, a turtledove, and a young pigeon." ¹⁰ He brought him all these, and divided them in the middle, and laid each half opposite the other; but he didn't divide the birds. ¹¹ The birds of prey came down on the carcasses, and Abram drove them away. ¹² When the sun was going down, a deep sleep fell on Abram. Now terror and great darkness fell on him. ¹³ He said to Abram, "Know for sure that your offspring will live as foreigners in a land that is not theirs, and will serve them. They will afflict them four hundred years. ¹⁴ I will also judge that nation, whom they will serve. Afterward they will come out with great wealth; ¹⁵ but you will go to your fathers in peace. You will be buried at a good old age. ¹⁶ In the fourth generation they will come here again, for the iniquity of the Amorite is not yet full." ¹⁷ It came to pass that, when the sun went down, and it was dark, behold, a smoking furnace and a flaming torch passed between these pieces. ¹⁸ In that day Yahweh made a covenant with Abram, saying, "I have given this land to your offspring, from the river of Egypt to the great river, the river Euphrates: ¹⁹ the land of the Kenites, the Kenizzites, the Kadmonites, ²⁰ the Hittites, the Perizzites, the Rephaim, ²¹ the Amorites, the Canaanites, the Girgashites, and the Jebusites."

## 16

¹ Now Sarai, Abram's wife, bore him no children. She had a servant, an Egyptian, whose name was Hagar. ² Sarai said to Abram, "See now, Yahweh has restrained me from bearing. Please go in to my servant. It may be that I will obtain children by her." Abram listened to the voice of Sarai. ³ Sarai, Abram's wife, took Hagar the Egyptian, her servant, after Abram had lived ten years in the land of Canaan, and gave her to Abram her husband to be his wife. ⁴ He went in to Hagar, and she conceived. When she saw that she had conceived, her mistress was despised in her eyes. ⁵ Sarai said to Abram, "This wrong is your fault. I gave my servant into your bosom, and when she saw that she had conceived, she despised me. May Yahweh judge between me and you." ⁶ But Abram said to Sarai, "Behold, your maid is in your hand. Do to her whatever is good in your eyes." Sarai dealt harshly with her, and she fled from her face. ⁷ Yahweh's angel found her by a fountain of water in the wilderness, by the fountain on the way to Shur. ⁸ He said, "Hagar, Sarai's servant, where did you come from? Where are you going?" She said, "I am fleeing from the face of my mistress Sarai." ⁹ Yahweh's angel said to her, "Return to your mistress, and submit yourself under her hands." ¹⁰ Yahweh's angel said to her, "I will greatly multiply your offspring, that they will not be counted for multitude." ¹¹ Yahweh's angel said to her, "Behold, you are with child, and will bear a son. You shall call his name Ishmael, because Yahweh has heard your affliction. ¹² He will be like a wild donkey among men. His hand will be against every man, and every man's hand against him. He will live opposed to all of his brothers." ¹³ She called the name of Yahweh who spoke to her, "You are a God who sees," for she said, "Have I even stayed alive after seeing him?" ¹⁴ Therefore the well was called Beer Lahai Roi.ᵇ Behold, it is between Kadesh and Bered. ¹⁵ Hagar bore a son for Abram. Abram called the name of his son, whom Hagar bore, Ishmael. ¹⁶ Abram was eighty-six years old when Hagar bore Ishmael to Abram.

## 17

¹ When Abram was ninety-nine years old, Yahweh appeared to Abram and said to him, "I am God Almighty. Walk before me and be blameless. ² I will make my covenant between me and you, and will multiply you exceedingly." ³ Abram fell on his face. God talked with him, saying, ⁴"As for me, behold, my covenant is with you. You will be the father of a multitude of nations. ⁵ Your name will no more be called Abram, but your name will be Abraham; for I have made you the father of a multitude of nations. ⁶ I will make you exceedingly fruitful, and I will make nations of you. Kings will come out of you. ⁷ I will establish my covenant between me and you and your offspring after you throughout their generations for an everlasting covenant, to be a God to you and to your offspring after you. ⁸ I will give to you, and to your offspring after you, the land where you are traveling, all the land of Canaan, for an everlasting possession. I will be their God." ⁹ God said to Abraham, "As for you, you shall keep my covenant, you and your offspring after you throughout their generations. ¹⁰ This is my covenant, which you shall keep, between me and you and your offspring after you. Every male among you shall be circumcised. ¹¹ You shall be circumcised in the flesh of your foreskin. It will be a token of the covenant between me and you. ¹² He who is eight days old shall be circumcised among you, every male throughout your generations, he who is born in the house, or bought with money from any foreigner who is not of your offspring. ¹³ He who is born in your house, and he who is bought with your money, must be circumcised. My covenant shall be in your flesh for an everlasting covenant. ¹⁴ The uncircumcised male who is not circumcised in the flesh of his foreskin, that soul shall be cut off from his people. He has broken my covenant." ¹⁵ God said to Abraham, "As for Sarai your wife, you shall not call her name Sarai, but her name shall be Sarah. ¹⁶ I will bless her, and moreover I will give you a son by her. Yes, I will bless her, and she will be a mother of nations. Kings of peoples will come from her." ¹⁷ Then Abraham fell on his face, and laughed, and said in his heart, "Will a child be born to him who is one hundred years old? Will Sarah, who is ninety years old, give birth?" ¹⁸ Abraham said to God, "Oh that Ishmael might live before you!" ¹⁹ God said, "No, but Sarah, your wife, will bear you a son. You shall call his name Isaac.ᶜ I will establish my covenant with him for an everlasting covenant for his offspring after him. ²⁰ As for Ishmael, I

ᵃ *15:2* The word translated "Lord" is "Adonai".

ᵇ *16:14* Beer Lahai Roi means "well of the one who lives and sees me".

ᶜ *17:19* Isaac means "he laughs".

have heard you. Behold, I have blessed him, and will make him fruitful, and will multiply him exceedingly. He will become the father of twelve princes, and I will make him a great nation. ²¹ But I will establish my covenant with Isaac, whom Sarah will bear to you at this set time next year." ²² When he finished talking with him, God went up from Abraham. ²³ Abraham took Ishmael his son, all who were born in his house, and all who were bought with his money: every male among the men of Abraham's house, and circumcised the flesh of their foreskin in the same day, as God had said to him. ²⁴ Abraham was ninety-nine years old when he was circumcised in the flesh of his foreskin. ²⁵ Ishmael, his son, was thirteen years old when he was circumcised in the flesh of his foreskin. ²⁶ In the same day both Abraham and Ishmael, his son, were circumcised. ²⁷ All the men of his house, those born in the house, and those bought with money from a foreigner, were circumcised with him.

## 18

¹ Yahweh appeared to him by the oaks of Mamre, as he sat in the tent door in the heat of the day. ² He lifted up his eyes and looked, and saw that three men stood near him. When he saw them, he ran to meet them from the tent door, and bowed himself to the earth, ³ and said, "My lord, if now I have found favor in your sight, please don't go away from your servant. ⁴ Now let a little water be fetched, wash your feet, and rest yourselves under the tree. ⁵ I will get a piece of bread so you can refresh your heart. After that you may go your way, now that you have come to your servant." They said, "Very well, do as you have said." ⁶ Abraham hurried into the tent to Sarah, and said, "Quickly prepare three seahsᵃ of fine meal, knead it, and make cakes." ⁷ Abraham ran to the herd, and fetched a tender and good calf, and gave it to the servant. He hurried to dress it. ⁸ He took butter, milk, and the calf which he had dressed, and set it before them. He stood by them under the tree, and they ate. ⁹ They asked him, "Where is Sarah, your wife?" He said, "There, in the tent." ¹⁰ He said, "I will certainly return to you at about this time next year; and behold, Sarah your wife will have a son." Sarah heard in the tent door, which was behind him. ¹¹ Now Abraham and Sarah were old, well advanced in age. Sarah had passed the age of childbearing. ¹² Sarah laughed within herself, saying, "After I have grown old will I have pleasure, my lord being old also?" ¹³ Yahweh said to Abraham, "Why did Sarah laugh, saying, 'Will I really bear a child when I am old?' ¹⁴ Is anything too hard for Yahweh? At the set time I will return to you, when the season comes around, and Sarah will have a son." ¹⁵ Then Sarah denied it, saying, "I didn't laugh," for she was afraid. He said, "No, but you did laugh." ¹⁶ The men rose up from there, and looked toward Sodom. Abraham went with them to see them on their way. ¹⁷ Yahweh said, "Will I hide from Abraham what I do, ¹⁸ since Abraham will surely become a great and mighty nation, and all the nations of the earth will be blessed in him? ¹⁹ For I have known him, to the end that he may command his children and his household after him, that they may keep the way of Yahweh, to do righteousness and justice; to the end that Yahweh may bring on Abraham that which he has spoken of him." ²⁰ Yahweh said, "Because the cry of Sodom and Gomorrah is great, and because their sin is very grievous, ²¹ I will go down now, and see whether their deeds are as bad as the reports which have come to me. If not, I will know." ²² The men turned from there, and went toward Sodom, but Abraham stood yet before Yahweh. ²³ Abraham came near, and said, "Will you consume the righteous with the wicked? ²⁴ What if there are fifty righteous within the city? Will you consume and not spare the place for the fifty righteous who are in it? ²⁵ May it be far from you to do things like that, to kill the righteous with the wicked, so that the righteous should be like the wicked. May that be far from you. Shouldn't the Judge of all the earth do right?" ²⁶ Yahweh said, "If I find in Sodom fifty righteous within the city, then I will spare the whole place for their sake." ²⁷ Abraham answered, "See now, I have taken it on myself to speak to the Lord, although I am dust and ashes. ²⁸ What if there will lack five of the fifty righteous? Will you destroy all the city for lack of five?" He said, "I will not destroy it if I find forty-five there." ²⁹ He spoke to him yet again, and said, "What if there are forty found there?" He said, "I will not do it for the forty's sake." ³⁰ He said, "Oh don't let the Lord be angry, and I will speak. What if there are thirty found there?" He said, "I will not do it if I find thirty there." ³¹ He said, "See now, I have taken it on myself to speak to the Lord. What if there are twenty found there?" He said, "I will not destroy it for the twenty's sake." ³² He said, "Oh don't let the Lord be angry, and I will speak just once more. What if ten are found there?" He said, "I will not destroy it for the ten's sake." ³³ Yahweh went his way as soon as he had finished communing with Abraham, and Abraham returned to his place.

## 19

¹ The two angels came to Sodom at evening. Lot sat in the gate of Sodom. Lot saw them, and rose up to meet them. He bowed himself with his face to the earth, ² and he said, "See now, my lords, please come into your servant's house, stay all night, wash your feet, and you can rise up early, and go on your way." They said, "No, but we will stay in the street all night." ³ He urged them greatly, and they came in with him, and entered into his house. He made them a feast, and baked unleavened bread, and they ate. ⁴ But before they lay down, the men of the city, the men of Sodom, surrounded the house, both young and old, all the people from every quarter. ⁵ They called to Lot, and said to him, "Where are the men who came in to you this night? Bring them out to us, that we may have sex with them." ⁶ Lot went out to them through the door, and shut the door after himself. ⁷ He said, "Please, my brothers, don't act so wickedly. ⁸ See now, I have two virgin daughters. Please let me bring them out to you, and you may do to them what seems good to you. Only don't do anything to these men, because they have come under the shadow of my roof." ⁹ They said, "Stand back!" Then they said, "This one fellow came in to live as a foreigner, and he appoints himself a judge. Now we will deal worse with you than with them!" They pressed hard on the man Lot, and came near to break the door. ¹⁰ But the men reached out their hand, and brought Lot into the house to them, and shut the door. ¹¹ They struck the men who were at the door of the house with blindness, both small and great, so that they wearied themselves to find the door. ¹² The men said to Lot, "Do you have anybody else here? Sons-in-law, your sons, your daughters, and whomever you have in the city, bring them out of the place: ¹³ for we will destroy this place, because the outcry against them has grown so great before Yahweh that Yahweh has sent us to destroy it." ¹⁴ Lot went out, and spoke to his sons-in-law, who were pledged to marry his daughters, and said, "Get up! Get out of this place, for Yahweh will destroy the city!" But he seemed to his sons-in-law to be joking. ¹⁵ When the morning came, then the angels hurried Lot, saying, "Get up! Take your wife and your two daughters who are here, lest you be consumed in the iniquity of the city." ¹⁶ But he lingered; and the men grabbed his hand, his wife's hand, and his two daughters' hands, Yahweh being merciful to him; and they took him out, and set him outside of the city. ¹⁷ It came to pass, when they had taken them out, that he said, "Escape for your life! Don't look behind you, and don't stay anywhere in the plain. Escape to the mountains, lest you be consumed!" ¹⁸ Lot said to them, "Oh, not so, my lord. ¹⁹ See now, your servant has found favor in your sight, and you have magnified your loving kindness, which you have shown to me in saving my life. I can't escape to the mountain, lest evil overtake me, and I die. ²⁰ See now, this city is near to flee to, and it is a little one. Oh let me escape there (isn't it a little one?), and my soul will live." ²¹ He said to him, "Behold, I have granted your request concerning this thing also, that I will not overthrow the city of which you have spoken. ²² Hurry, escape there, for I can't do anything until you get there." Therefore the name of the city was called Zoar.ᵇ ²³ The sun had risen on the earth when Lot came to Zoar. ²⁴ Then Yahweh rained on Sodom and on Gomorrah sulfur and fire from Yahweh out of the sky. ²⁵ He overthrew those cities, all the plain, all the inhabitants of the cities, and that which grew on the ground. ²⁶ But Lot's wife looked back from behind him, and she became a pillar of salt. ²⁷ Abraham went up early in the morning to the place where he had stood before Yahweh. ²⁸ He looked toward Sodom and Gomorrah, and toward all the land of the plain, and saw that the smoke of the land went up as the smoke of a furnace. ²⁹ When God destroyed the cities of the plain, God remembered Abraham, and sent Lot out of the middle of the overthrow, when he overthrew the cities in which Lot lived. ³⁰ Lot went up out of Zoar, and lived in the mountain, and his two daughters with him; for he was afraid to live in Zoar. He lived in a cave with his two daughters. ³¹ The firstborn said to the younger, "Our father is old, and there is not a man in the earth to come in to us in the way of all the earth. ³² Come, let's make our father drink wine, and we will lie with him, that we may preserve our father's family line." ³³ They made their father drink wine that night: and the firstborn went in, and lay with her father. He didn't know when she lay down, nor when she arose. ³⁴ It came to pass on the next day, that the firstborn said to the younger, "Behold, I lay last night with my father. Let's make him drink wine again tonight. You go in, and lie with him, that we may preserve our father's family line." ³⁵ They made their father drink wine that night also. The younger went and lay with him. He didn't know when she lay down, nor when she got up. ³⁶ Thus both of Lot's daughters were with child by their father. ³⁷ The firstborn bore a son, and named him Moab. He is the father of the Moabites to this day. ³⁸

ᵃ *18:6* 1 seah is about 7 liters or 1.9 gallons or 0.8 pecks      ᵇ *19:22* Zoar means "little".

The younger also bore a son, and called his name Ben Ammi. He is the father of the children of Ammon to this day.

## 20

¹ Abraham traveled from there toward the land of the South, and lived between Kadesh and Shur. He lived as a foreigner in Gerar. ² Abraham said about Sarah his wife, "She is my sister." Abimelech king of Gerar sent, and took Sarah. ³ But God came to Abimelech in a dream of the night, and said to him, "Behold, you are a dead man, because of the woman whom you have taken; for she is a man's wife." ⁴ Now Abimelech had not come near her. He said, "Lord, will you kill even a righteous nation? ⁵ Didn't he tell me, 'She is my sister'? She, even she herself, said, 'He is my brother.' I have done this in the integrity of my heart and the innocence of my hands." ⁶ God said to him in the dream, "Yes, I know that in the integrity of your heart you have done this, and I also withheld you from sinning against me. Therefore I didn't allow you to touch her. ⁷ Now therefore, restore the man's wife. For he is a prophet, and he will pray for you, and you will live. If you don't restore her, know for sure that you will die, you, and all who are yours." ⁸ Abimelech rose early in the morning, and called all his servants, and told all these things in their ear. The men were very scared. ⁹ Then Abimelech called Abraham, and said to him, "What have you done to us? How have I sinned against you, that you have brought on me and on my kingdom a great sin? You have done deeds to me that ought not to be done!" ¹⁰ Abimelech said to Abraham, "What did you see, that you have done this thing?" ¹¹ Abraham said, "Because I thought, 'Surely the fear of God is not in this place. They will kill me for my wife's sake.' ¹² Besides, she is indeed my sister, the daughter of my father, but not the daughter of my mother; and she became my wife. ¹³ When God caused me to wander from my father's house, I said to her, 'This is your kindness which you shall show to me. Everywhere that we go, say of me, "He is my brother."'" ¹⁴ Abimelech took sheep and cattle, male servants and female servants, and gave them to Abraham, and restored Sarah, his wife, to him. ¹⁵ Abimelech said, "Behold, my land is before you. Dwell where it pleases you." ¹⁶ To Sarah he said, "Behold, I have given your brother a thousand pieces of silver. Behold, it is for you a covering of the eyes to all that are with you. In front of all you are vindicated." ¹⁷ Abraham prayed to God. So God healed Abimelech, his wife, and his female servants, and they bore children. ¹⁸ For Yahweh had closed up tight all the wombs of the house of Abimelech, because of Sarah, Abraham's wife.

## 21

¹ Yahweh visited Sarah as he had said, and Yahweh did to Sarah as he had spoken. ² Sarah conceived, and bore Abraham a son in his old age, at the set time of which God had spoken to him. ³ Abraham called his son who was born to him, whom Sarah bore to him, Isaac.ᵃ ⁴ Abraham circumcised his son, Isaac, when he was eight days old, as God had commanded him. ⁵ Abraham was one hundred years old when his son, Isaac, was born to him. ⁶ Sarah said, "God has made me laugh. Everyone who hears will laugh with me." ⁷ She said, "Who would have said to Abraham that Sarah would nurse children? For I have borne him a son in his old age." ⁸ The child grew and was weaned. Abraham made a great feast on the day that Isaac was weaned. ⁹ Sarah saw the son of Hagar the Egyptian, whom she had borne to Abraham, mocking. ¹⁰ Therefore she said to Abraham, "Cast out this servant and her son! For the son of this servant will not be heir with my son, Isaac." ¹¹ The thing was very grievous in Abraham's sight on account of his son. ¹² God said to Abraham, "Don't let it be grievous in your sight because of the boy, and because of your servant. In all that Sarah says to you, listen to her voice. For your offspring will be named through Isaac. ¹³ I will also make a nation of the son of the servant, because he is your child." ¹⁴ Abraham rose up early in the morning, and took bread and a container of water, and gave it to Hagar, putting it on her shoulder; and gave her the child, and sent her away. She departed, and wandered in the wilderness of Beersheba. ¹⁵ The water in the container was spent, and she put the child under one of the shrubs. ¹⁶ She went and sat down opposite him, a good way off, about a bow shot away. For she said, "Don't let me see the death of the child." She sat opposite him, and lifted up her voice, and wept. ¹⁷ God heard the voice of the boy. The angel of God called to Hagar out of the sky, and said to her, "What troubles you, Hagar? Don't be afraid. For God has heard the voice of the boy where he is. ¹⁸ Get up, lift up the boy, and hold him with your hand. For I will make him a great nation." ¹⁹ God opened her eyes, and she saw a well of water. She went, filled the container with water, and gave the boy a drink. ²⁰ God was with the boy, and he grew. He lived in the wilderness, and as he grew up, he became an archer. ²¹ He lived in the wilderness of Paran. His mother got a wife for him out of the land

of Egypt. ²² At that time, Abimelech and Phicol the captain of his army spoke to Abraham, saying, "God is with you in all that you do. ²³ Now, therefore, swear to me here by God that you will not deal falsely with me, nor with my son, nor with my son's son. But according to the kindness that I have done to you, you shall do to me, and to the land in which you have lived as a foreigner." ²⁴ Abraham said, "I will swear." ²⁵ Abraham complained to Abimelech because of a water well, which Abimelech's servants had violently taken away. ²⁶ Abimelech said, "I don't know who has done this thing. You didn't tell me, and I didn't hear of it until today." ²⁷ Abraham took sheep and cattle, and gave them to Abimelech. Those two made a covenant. ²⁸ Abraham set seven ewe lambs of the flock by themselves. ²⁹ Abimelech said to Abraham, "What do these seven ewe lambs, which you have set by themselves, mean?" ³⁰ He said, "You shall take these seven ewe lambs from my hand, that it may be a witness to me, that I have dug this well." ³¹ Therefore he called that place Beersheba,ᵇ because they both swore an oath there. ³² So they made a covenant at Beersheba. Abimelech rose up with Phicol, the captain of his army, and they returned into the land of the Philistines. ³³ Abraham planted a tamarisk tree in Beersheba, and there he called on the name of Yahweh, the Everlasting God. ³⁴ Abraham lived as a foreigner in the land of the Philistines many days.

## 22

¹ After these things, God tested Abraham, and said to him, "Abraham!" He said, "Here I am." ² He said, "Now take your son, your only son, Isaac, whom you love, and go into the land of Moriah. Offer him there as a burnt offering on one of the mountains which I will tell you of." ³ Abraham rose early in the morning, and saddled his donkey; and took two of his young men with him, and Isaac his son. He split the wood for the burnt offering, and rose up, and went to the place of which God had told him. ⁴ On the third day Abraham lifted up his eyes, and saw the place far off. ⁵ Abraham said to his young men, "Stay here with the donkey. The boy and I will go over there. We will worship, and come back to you." ⁶ Abraham took the wood of the burnt offering and laid it on Isaac his son. He took in his hand the fire and the knife. They both went together. ⁷ Isaac spoke to Abraham his father, and said, "My father?" He said, "Here I am, my son." He said, "Here is the fire and the wood, but where is the lamb for a burnt offering?" ⁸ Abraham said, "God will provide himself the lamb for a burnt offering, my son." So they both went together. ⁹ They came to the place which God had told him of. Abraham built the altar there, and laid the wood in order, bound Isaac his son, and laid him on the altar, on the wood. ¹⁰ Abraham stretched out his hand, and took the knife to kill his son. ¹¹ Yahweh's angel called to him out of the sky, and said, "Abraham, Abraham!" He said, "Here I am." ¹² He said, "Don't lay your hand on the boy or do anything to him. For now I know that you fear God, since you have not withheld your son, your only son, from me." ¹³ Abraham lifted up his eyes, and looked, and saw that behind him was a ram caught in the thicket by his horns. Abraham went and took the ram, and offered him up for a burnt offering instead of his son. ¹⁴ Abraham called the name of that place "Yahweh Will Provide".ᶜ As it is said to this day, "On Yahweh's mountain, it will be provided." ¹⁵ Yahweh's angel called to Abraham a second time out of the sky, ¹⁶ and said, "'I have sworn by myself,' says Yahweh, 'because you have done this thing, and have not withheld your son, your only son, ¹⁷ that I will bless you greatly, and I will multiply your offspring greatly like the stars of the heavens, and like the sand which is on the seashore. Your offspring will possess the gate of his enemies. ¹⁸ All the nations of the earth will be blessed by your offspring, because you have obeyed my voice.'" ¹⁹ So Abraham returned to his young men, and they rose up and went together to Beersheba. Abraham lived at Beersheba. ²⁰ After these things, Abraham was told, "Behold, Milcah, she also has borne children to your brother Nahor: ²¹ Uz his firstborn, Buz his brother, Kemuel the father of Aram, ²² Chesed, Hazo, Pildash, Jidlaph, and Bethuel." ²³ Bethuel became the father of Rebekah. These eight Milcah bore to Nahor, Abraham's brother. ²⁴ His concubine, whose name was Reumah, also bore Tebah, Gaham, Tahash, and Maacah.

## 23

¹ Sarah lived one hundred twenty-seven years. This was the length of Sarah's life. ² Sarah died in Kiriath Arba (also called Hebron), in the land of Canaan. Abraham came to mourn for Sarah, and to weep for her. ³ Abraham rose up from before his dead and spoke to the children of Heth, saying, ⁴"I am a stranger and a foreigner living with you. Give me a possession of a burying-place with you, that I may bury my dead out of my sight." ⁵ The children of Heth answered Abraham, saying to him, ⁶"Hear us, my lord. You are a prince of God among us. Bury your dead in the best of our tombs. None of us will withhold from you his

---

ᵃ *21:3 Isaac means "He laughs".*

ᵇ *21:31 Beersheba can mean "well of the oath" or "well of seven".*

ᶜ *22:14 or, Yahweh-Jireh, or, Yahweh-Seeing*

tomb. Bury your dead." ⁷ Abraham rose up, and bowed himself to the people of the land, to the children of Heth. ⁸ He talked with them, saying, "If you agree that I should bury my dead out of my sight, hear me, and entreat for me to Ephron the son of Zohar, ⁹ that he may sell me the cave of Machpelah, which he has, which is in the end of his field. For the full price let him sell it to me among you as a possession for a burial place." ¹⁰ Now Ephron was sitting in the middle of the children of Heth. Ephron the Hittite answered Abraham in the hearing of the children of Heth, even of all who went in at the gate of his city, saying, ¹¹"No, my lord, hear me. I give you the field, and I give you the cave that is in it. In the presence of the children of my people I give it to you. Bury your dead." ¹² Abraham bowed himself down before the people of the land. ¹³ He spoke to Ephron in the audience of the people of the land, saying, "But if you will, please hear me. I will give the price of the field. Take it from me, and I will bury my dead there." ¹⁴ Ephron answered Abraham, saying to him, ¹⁵"My lord, listen to me. What is a piece of land worth four hundred shekels of silverᵃ between me and you? Therefore bury your dead." ¹⁶ Abraham listened to Ephron. Abraham weighed to Ephron the silver which he had named in the hearing of the children of Heth, four hundred shekels of silver, according to the current merchants' standard. ¹⁷ So the field of Ephron, which was in Machpelah, which was before Mamre, the field, the cave which was in it, and all the trees that were in the field, that were in all of its borders, were deeded ¹⁸ to Abraham for a possession in the presence of the children of Heth, before all who went in at the gate of his city. ¹⁹ After this, Abraham buried Sarah his wife in the cave of the field of Machpelah before Mamre (that is, Hebron), in the land of Canaan. ²⁰ The field, and the cave that is in it, were deeded to Abraham by the children of Heth as a possession for a burial place.

## 24

¹ Abraham was old, and well advanced in age. Yahweh had blessed Abraham in all things. ² Abraham said to his servant, the elder of his house, who ruled over all that he had, "Please put your hand under my thigh. ³ I will make you swear by Yahweh, the God of heaven and the God of the earth, that you shall not take a wife for my son of the daughters of the Canaanites, among whom I live. ⁴ But you shall go to my country, and to my relatives, and take a wife for my son Isaac." ⁵ The servant said to him, "What if the woman isn't willing to follow me to this land? Must I bring your son again to the land you came from?" ⁶ Abraham said to him, "Beware that you don't bring my son there again. ⁷ Yahweh, the God of heaven—who took me from my father's house, and from the land of my birth, who spoke to me, and who swore to me, saying, 'I will give this land to your offspring—he will send his angel before you, and you shall take a wife for my son from there. ⁸ If the woman isn't willing to follow you, then you shall be clear from this oath to me. Only you shall not bring my son there again." ⁹ The servant put his hand under the thigh of Abraham his master, and swore to him concerning this matter. ¹⁰ The servant took ten of his master's camels, and departed, having a variety of good things of his master's with him. He arose, and went to Mesopotamia, to the city of Nahor. ¹¹ He made the camels kneel down outside the city by the well of water at the time of evening, the time that women go out to draw water. ¹² He said, "Yahweh, the God of my master Abraham, please give me success today, and show kindness to my master Abraham. ¹³ Behold, I am standing by the spring of water. The daughters of the men of the city are coming out to draw water. ¹⁴ Let it happen, that the young lady to whom I will say, 'Please let down your pitcher, that I may drink,' then she says, 'Drink, and I will also give your camels a drink,'—let her be the one you have appointed for your servant Isaac. By this I will know that you have shown kindness to my master." ¹⁵ Before he had finished speaking, behold, Rebekah came out, who was born to Bethuel the son of Milcah, the wife of Nahor, Abraham's brother, with her pitcher on her shoulder. ¹⁶ The young lady was very beautiful to look at, a virgin. No man had known her. She went down to the spring, filled her pitcher, and came up. ¹⁷ The servant ran to meet her, and said, "Please give me a drink, a little water from your pitcher." ¹⁸ She said, "Drink, my lord." She hurried, and let down her pitcher on her hand, and gave him a drink. ¹⁹ When she had finished giving him a drink, she said, "I will also draw for your camels, until they have finished drinking." ²⁰ She hurried, and emptied her pitcher into the trough, and ran again to the well to draw, and drew for all his camels. ²¹ The man looked steadfastly at her, remaining silent, to know whether Yahweh had made his journey prosperous or not. ²² As the camels had done drinking, the man took a golden ring of half a shekelᵇ weight, and two bracelets for her hands of ten shekels weight of gold, ²³ and said, "Whose daughter are you? Please tell me. Is there room in your father's house for us to stay?" ²⁴

She said to him, "I am the daughter of Bethuel the son of Milcah, whom she bore to Nahor." ²⁵ She said moreover to him, "We have both straw and feed enough, and room to lodge in." ²⁶ The man bowed his head, and worshiped Yahweh. ²⁷ He said, "Blessed be Yahweh, the God of my master Abraham, who has not forsaken his loving kindness and his truth toward my master. As for me, Yahweh has led me on the way to the house of my master's relatives." ²⁸ The young lady ran, and told her mother's house about these words. ²⁹ Rebekah had a brother, and his name was Laban. Laban ran out to the man, to the spring. ³⁰ When he saw the ring, and the bracelets on his sister's hands, and when he heard the words of Rebekah his sister, saying, "This is what the man said to me," he came to the man. Behold, he was standing by the camels at the spring. ³¹ He said, "Come in, you blessed of Yahweh. Why do you stand outside? For I have prepared the house, and room for the camels." ³² The man came into the house, and he unloaded the camels. He gave straw and feed for the camels, and water to wash his feet and the feet of the men who were with him. ³³ Food was set before him to eat, but he said, "I will not eat until I have told my message." Laban said, "Speak on." ³⁴ He said, "I am Abraham's servant. ³⁵ Yahweh has blessed my master greatly. He has become great. Yahweh has given him flocks and herds, silver and gold, male servants and female servants, and camels and donkeys. ³⁶ Sarah, my master's wife, bore a son to my master when she was old. He has given all that he has to him. ³⁷ My master made me swear, saying, 'You shall not take a wife for my son from the daughters of the Canaanites, in whose land I live, ³⁸ but you shall go to my father's house, and to my relatives, and take a wife for my son.' ³⁹ I asked my master, 'What if the woman will not follow me?' ⁴⁰ He said to me, 'Yahweh, before whom I walk, will send his angel with you, and prosper your way. You shall take a wife for my son from my relatives, and of my father's house. ⁴¹ Then you will be clear from my oath, when you come to my relatives. If they don't give her to you, you shall be clear from my oath.' ⁴² I came today to the spring, and said, 'Yahweh, the God of my master Abraham, if now you do prosper my way which I go— ⁴³ behold, I am standing by this spring of water. Let it happen, that the maiden who comes out to draw, to whom I will say, "Please give me a little water from your pitcher to drink," ⁴⁴ then she tells me, "Drink, and I will also draw for your camels,"—let her be the woman whom Yahweh has appointed for my master's son.' ⁴⁵ Before I had finished speaking in my heart, behold, Rebekah came out with her pitcher on her shoulder. She went down to the spring, and drew. I said to her, 'Please let me drink.' ⁴⁶ She hurried and let down her pitcher from her shoulder, and said, 'Drink, and I will also give your camels a drink.' So I drank, and she also gave the camels a drink. ⁴⁷ I asked her, and said, 'Whose daughter are you?' She said, 'The daughter of Bethuel, Nahor's son, whom Milcah bore to him.' I put the ring on her nose, and the bracelets on her hands. ⁴⁸ I bowed my head, and worshiped Yahweh, and blessed Yahweh, the God of my master Abraham, who had led me in the right way to take my master's brother's daughter for his son. ⁴⁹ Now if you will deal kindly and truly with my master, tell me. If not, tell me, that I may turn to the right hand, or to the left." ⁵⁰ Then Laban and Bethuel answered, "The thing proceeds from Yahweh. We can't speak to you bad or good. ⁵¹ Behold, Rebekah is before you. Take her, and go, and let her be your master's son's wife, as Yahweh has spoken." ⁵² When Abraham's servant heard their words, he bowed himself down to the earth to Yahweh. ⁵³ The servant brought out jewels of silver, and jewels of gold, and clothing, and gave them to Rebekah. He also gave precious things to her brother and her mother. ⁵⁴ They ate and drank, he and the men who were with him, and stayed all night. They rose up in the morning, and he said, "Send me away to my master." ⁵⁵ Her brother and her mother said, "Let the young lady stay with us a few days, at least ten. After that she will go." ⁵⁶ He said to them, "Don't hinder me, since Yahweh has prospered my way. Send me away that I may go to my master." ⁵⁷ They said, "We will call the young lady, and ask her." ⁵⁸ They called Rebekah, and said to her, "Will you go with this man?" She said, "I will go." ⁵⁹ They sent away Rebekah, their sister, with her nurse, Abraham's servant, and his men. ⁶⁰ They blessed Rebekah, and said to her, "Our sister, may you be the mother of thousands of ten thousands, and let your offspring possess the gate of those who hate them." ⁶¹ Rebekah arose with her ladies. They rode on the camels, and followed the man. The servant took Rebekah, and went his way. ⁶² Isaac came from the way of Beer Lahai Roi, for he lived in the land of the South. ⁶³ Isaac went out to meditate in the field at the evening. He lifted up his eyes and looked. Behold, there were camels coming. ⁶⁴ Rebekah lifted up her eyes, and when she saw Isaac, she got off the camel. ⁶⁵ She said to the servant, "Who is the man who is walking in the field to meet us?" The servant said, "It is my

---

ᵃ *23:15* A shekel is about 10 grams, so 400 shekels would be about 4 kg. or 8.8 pounds.

ᵇ *24:22* A shekel is about 10 grams or about 0.35 ounces.

master." She took her veil, and covered herself. ⁶⁶ The servant told Isaac all the things that he had done. ⁶⁷ Isaac brought her into his mother Sarah's tent, and took Rebekah, and she became his wife. He loved her. So Isaac was comforted after his mother's death.

## 25

¹ Abraham took another wife, and her name was Keturah. ² She bore him Zimran, Jokshan, Medan, Midian, Ishbak, and Shuah. ³ Jokshan became the father of Sheba, and Dedan. The sons of Dedan were Asshurim, Letushim, and Leummim. ⁴ The sons of Midian were Ephah, Epher, Hanoch, Abida, and Eldaah. All these were the children of Keturah. ⁵ Abraham gave all that he had to Isaac, ⁶ but Abraham gave gifts to the sons of Abraham's concubines. While he still lived, he sent them away from Isaac his son, eastward, to the east country. ⁷ These are the days of the years of Abraham's life which he lived: one hundred seventy-five years. ⁸ Abraham gave up his spirit, and died at a good old age, an old man, and full of years, and was gathered to his people. ⁹ Isaac and Ishmael, his sons, buried him in the cave of Machpelah, in the field of Ephron, the son of Zohar the Hittite, which is near Mamre, ¹⁰ the field which Abraham purchased from the children of Heth. Abraham was buried there with Sarah, his wife. ¹¹ After the death of Abraham, God blessed Isaac, his son. Isaac lived by Beer Lahai Roi. ¹² Now this is the history of the generations of Ishmael, Abraham's son, whom Hagar the Egyptian, Sarah's servant, bore to Abraham. ¹³ These are the names of the sons of Ishmael, by their names, according to the order of their birth: the firstborn of Ishmael, Nebaioth, then Kedar, Adbeel, Mibsam, ¹⁴ Mishma, Dumah, Massa, ¹⁵ Hadad, Tema, Jetur, Naphish, and Kedemah. ¹⁶ These are the sons of Ishmael, and these are their names, by their villages, and by their encampments: twelve princes, according to their nations. ¹⁷ These are the years of the life of Ishmael: one hundred thirty-seven years. He gave up his spirit and died, and was gathered to his people. ¹⁸ They lived from Havilah to Shur that is before Egypt, as you go toward Assyria. He lived opposite all his relatives. ¹⁹ This is the history of the generations of Isaac, Abraham's son. Abraham became the father of Isaac. ²⁰ Isaac was forty years old when he took Rebekah, the daughter of Bethuel the Syrian of Paddan Aram, the sister of Laban the Syrian, to be his wife. ²¹ Isaac entreated Yahweh for his wife, because she was barren. Yahweh was entreated by him, and Rebekah his wife conceived. ²² The children struggled together within her. She said, "If it is like this, why do I live?" She went to inquire of Yahweh. ²³ Yahweh said to her, "Two nations are in your womb. Two peoples will be separated from your body. The one people will be stronger than the other people. The elder will serve the younger." ²⁴ When her days to be delivered were fulfilled, behold, there were twins in her womb. ²⁵ The first came out red all over, like a hairy garment. They named him Esau. ²⁶ After that, his brother came out, and his hand had hold on Esau's heel. He was named Jacob. Isaac was sixty years old when she bore them. ²⁷ The boys grew. Esau was a skillful hunter, a man of the field. Jacob was a quiet man, living in tents. ²⁸ Now Isaac loved Esau, because he ate his venison. Rebekah loved Jacob. ²⁹ Jacob boiled stew. Esau came in from the field, and he was famished. ³⁰ Esau said to Jacob, "Please feed me with some of that red stew, for I am famished." Therefore his name was called Edom.ᵃ ³¹ Jacob said, "First, sell me your birthright." ³² Esau said, "Behold, I am about to die. What good is the birthright to me?" ³³ Jacob said, "Swear to me first." He swore to him. He sold his birthright to Jacob. ³⁴ Jacob gave Esau bread and lentil stew. He ate and drank, rose up, and went his way. So Esau despised his birthright.

## 26

¹ There was a famine in the land, in addition to the first famine that was in the days of Abraham. Isaac went to Abimelech king of the Philistines, to Gerar. ² Yahweh appeared to him, and said, "Don't go down into Egypt. Live in the land I will tell you about. ³ Live in this land, and I will be with you, and will bless you. For I will give to you, and to your offspring, all these lands, and I will establish the oath which I swore to Abraham your father. ⁴ I will multiply your offspring as the stars of the sky, and will give all these lands to your offspring. In your offspring all the nations of the earth will be blessed, ⁵ because Abraham obeyed my voice, and kept my requirements, my commandments, my statutes, and my laws." ⁶ Isaac lived in Gerar. ⁷ The men of the place asked him about his wife. He said, "She is my sister," for he was afraid to say, "My wife", lest, he thought, "the men of the place might kill me for Rebekah, because she is beautiful to look at." ⁸ When he had been there a long time, Abimelech king of the Philistines looked out at a window, and saw, and, behold, Isaac was caressing Rebekah, his wife. ⁹ Abimelech called Isaac, and said, "Behold, surely she is your wife.

Why did you say, 'She is my sister'?" Isaac said to him, "Because I said, 'Lest I die because of her.'" ¹⁰ Abimelech said, "What is this you have done to us? One of the people might easily have lain with your wife, and you would have brought guilt on us!" ¹¹ Abimelech commanded all the people, saying, "He who touches this man or his wife will surely be put to death." ¹² Isaac sowed in that land, and reaped in the same year one hundred times what he planted. Yahweh blessed him. ¹³ The man grew great, and grew more and more until he became very great. ¹⁴ He had possessions of flocks, possessions of herds, and a great household. The Philistines envied him. ¹⁵ Now all the wells which his father's servants had dug in the days of Abraham his father, the Philistines had stopped, and filled with earth. ¹⁶ Abimelech said to Isaac, "Go away from us, for you are much mightier than we." ¹⁷ Isaac departed from there, encamped in the valley of Gerar, and lived there. ¹⁸ Isaac dug again the wells of water, which they had dug in the days of Abraham his father, for the Philistines had stopped them after the death of Abraham. He called their names after the names by which his father had called them. ¹⁹ Isaac's servants dug in the valley, and found there a well of flowingᵇ water. ²⁰ The herdsmen of Gerar argued with Isaac's herdsmen, saying, "The water is ours." So he called the name of the well Esek,ᶜ because they contended with him. ²¹ They dug another well, and they argued over that, also. So he called its name Sitnah.ᵈ ²² He left that place, and dug another well. They didn't argue over that one. So he called it Rehoboth.ᵉ He said, "For now Yahweh has made room for us, and we will be fruitful in the land." ²³ He went up from there to Beersheba. ²⁴ Yahweh appeared to him the same night, and said, "I am the God of Abraham your father. Don't be afraid, for I am with you, and will bless you, and multiply your offspring for my servant Abraham's sake." ²⁵ He built an altar there, and called on Yahweh's name, and pitched his tent there. There Isaac's servants dug a well. ²⁶ Then Abimelech went to him from Gerar with Ahuzzath his friend, and Phicol the captain of his army. ²⁷ Isaac said to them, "Why have you come to me, since you hate me, and have sent me away from you?" ²⁸ They said, "We saw plainly that Yahweh was with you. We said, 'Let there now be an oath between us, even between us and you, and let's make a covenant with you, ²⁹ that you will do us no harm, as we have not touched you, and as we have done to you nothing but good, and have sent you away in peace.' You are now the blessed of Yahweh." ³⁰ He made them a feast, and they ate and drank. ³¹ They rose up some time in the morning, and swore an oath to one another. Isaac sent them away, and they departed from him in peace. ³² The same day, Isaac's servants came, and told him concerning the well which they had dug, and said to him, "We have found water." ³³ He called it "Shibah".ᶠ Therefore the name of the city is "Beersheba"ᵍ to this day. ³⁴ When Esau was forty years old, he took as wife Judith, the daughter of Beeri the Hittite, and Basemath, the daughter of Elon the Hittite. ³⁵ They grieved Isaac's and Rebekah's spirits.

## 27

¹ When Isaac was old, and his eyes were dim, so that he could not see, he called Esau his elder son, and said to him, "My son?" He said to him, "Here I am." ² He said, "See now, I am old. I don't know the day of my death. ³ Now therefore, please take your weapons, your quiver and your bow, and go out to the field, and get me venison. ⁴ Make me savory food, such as I love, and bring it to me, that I may eat, and that my soul may bless you before I die." ⁵ Rebekah heard when Isaac spoke to Esau his son. Esau went to the field to hunt for venison, and to bring it. ⁶ Rebekah spoke to Jacob her son, saying, "Behold, I heard your father speak to Esau your brother, saying, ⁷'Bring me venison, and make me savory food, that I may eat, and bless you before Yahweh before my death.' ⁸ Now therefore, my son, obey my voice according to that which I command you. ⁹ Go now to the flock and get me two good young goats from there. I will make them savory food for your father, such as he loves. ¹⁰ You shall bring it to your father, that he may eat, so that he may bless you before his death." ¹¹ Jacob said to Rebekah his mother, "Behold, Esau my brother is a hairy man, and I am a smooth man. ¹² What if my father touches me? I will seem to him as a deceiver, and I would bring a curse on myself, and not a blessing." ¹³ His mother said to him, "Let your curse be on me, my son. Only obey my voice, and go get them for me." ¹⁴ He went, and got them, and brought them to his mother. His mother made savory food, such as his father loved. ¹⁵ Rebekah took the good clothes of Esau, her elder son, which were with her in the house, and put them on Jacob, her younger son. ¹⁶ She put the skins of the young goats on his hands, and on the smooth of his neck. ¹⁷ She gave the savory food and the bread, which she had prepared, into the hand of her son Jacob. ¹⁸ He came to his father, and said, "My

---

ᵃ 25:30 "Edom" means "red".

ᵇ 26:19 Or, living. Or, fresh.

ᶜ 26:20 "Esek" means "contention".

ᵈ 26:21 "Sitnah" means "hostility".

ᵉ 26:22 "Rehoboth" means "broad places".

ᶠ 26:33 Shibah means "oath" or "seven".

ᵍ 26:33 Beersheba means "well of the oath" or "well of the seven" father?" He said, "Here I am. Who are you, my son?" ¹⁹ Jacob said to his father, "I am Esau your firstborn. I have done what you asked me to do. Please arise, sit and eat of my venison, that your soul may bless me." ²⁰ Isaac said to his son, "How is it that you have found it so quickly, my son?" He said, "Because Yahweh your God gave me success." ²¹ Isaac said to Jacob, "Please come near, that I may feel you, my son, whether you are really my son Esau or not." ²² Jacob went near to Isaac his father. He felt him, and said, "The voice is Jacob's voice, but the hands are the hands of Esau." ²³ He didn't recognize him, because his hands were hairy, like his brother Esau's hands. So he blessed him. ²⁴ He said, "Are you really my son Esau?" He said, "I am." ²⁵ He said, "Bring it near to me, and I will eat of my son's venison, that my soul may bless you." He brought it near to him, and he ate. He brought him wine, and he drank. ²⁶ His father Isaac said to him, "Come near now, and kiss me, my son." ²⁷ He came near, and kissed him. He smelled the smell of his clothing, and blessed him, and said, "Behold, the smell of my son is as the smell of a field which Yahweh has blessed. ²⁸ God give you of the dew of the sky, of the fatness of the earth, and plenty of grain and new wine. ²⁹ Let peoples serve you, and nations bow down to you. Be lord over your brothers. Let your mother's sons bow down to you. Cursed be everyone who curses you. Blessed be everyone who blesses you." ³⁰ As soon as Isaac had finished blessing Jacob, and Jacob had just gone out from the presence of Isaac his father, Esau his brother came in from his hunting. ³¹ He also made savory food, and brought it to his father. He said to his father, "Let my father arise, and eat of his son's venison, that your soul may bless me." ³² Isaac his father said to him, "Who are you?" He said, "I am your son, your firstborn, Esau." ³³ Isaac trembled violently, and said, "Who, then, is he who has taken venison, and brought it to me, and I have eaten of all before you came, and have blessed him? Yes, he will be blessed." ³⁴ When Esau heard the words of his father, he cried with an exceedingly great and bitter cry, and said to his father, "Bless me, even me also, my father." ³⁵ He said, "Your brother came with deceit, and has taken away your blessing." ³⁶ He said, "Isn't he rightly named Jacob? For he has supplanted me these two times. He took away my birthright. See, now he has taken away my blessing." He said, "Haven't you reserved a blessing for me?" ³⁷ Isaac answered Esau, "Behold, I have made him your lord, and all his brothers I have given to him for servants. I have sustained him with grain and new wine. What then will I do for you, my son?" ³⁸ Esau said to his father, "Do you have just one blessing, my father? Bless me, even me also, my father." Esau lifted up his voice, and wept. ³⁹ Isaac his father answered him, "Behold, your dwelling will be of the fatness of the earth, and of the dew of the sky from above. ⁴⁰ You will live by your sword, and you will serve your brother. It will happen, when you will break loose, that you will shake his yoke from off your neck." ⁴¹ Esau hated Jacob because of the blessing with which his father blessed him. Esau said in his heart, "The days of mourning for my father are at hand. Then I will kill my brother Jacob." ⁴² The words of Esau, her elder son, were told to Rebekah. She sent and called Jacob, her younger son, and said to him, "Behold, your brother Esau comforts himself about you by planning to kill you. ⁴³ Now therefore, my son, obey my voice. Arise, flee to Laban, my brother, in Haran. ⁴⁴ Stay with him a few days, until your brother's fury turns away— ⁴⁵ until your brother's anger turns away from you, and he forgets what you have done to him. Then I will send, and get you from there. Why should I be bereaved of you both in one day?" ⁴⁶ Rebekah said to Isaac, "I am weary of my life because of the daughters of Heth. If Jacob takes a wife of the daughters of Heth, such as these, of the daughters of the land, what good will my life do me?"

## 28

¹ Isaac called Jacob, blessed him, and commanded him, "You shall not take a wife of the daughters of Canaan. ² Arise, go to Paddan Aram, to the house of Bethuel your mother's father. Take a wife from there from the daughters of Laban, your mother's brother. ³ May God Almighty bless you, and make you fruitful, and multiply you, that you may be a company of peoples, ⁴ and give you the blessing of Abraham, to you and to your offspring with you, that you may inherit the land where you travel, which God gave to Abraham." ⁵ Isaac sent Jacob away. He went to Paddan Aram to Laban, son of Bethuel the Syrian, the brother of Rebekah, Jacob's and Esau's mother. ⁶ Now Esau saw that Isaac had blessed Jacob and sent him away to Paddan Aram, to take him a wife from there, and that as he blessed him he gave him a command, saying, "You shall not take a wife of the daughters of Canaan;" ⁷ and that Jacob obeyed his father and his mother, and was gone to Paddan Aram. ⁸ Esau saw that the daughters of Canaan didn't please Isaac, his father. ⁹ So Esau went to Ishmael, and took, in addition to the wives that he had, Mahalath the daughter of Ishmael, Abraham's son, the sister of Nebaioth, to be his wife. ¹⁰ Jacob went out from Beersheba, and went toward Haran. ¹¹ He came to a certain place, and stayed there all night, because the sun had set. He took one of the stones of the place, and put

it under his head, and lay down in that place to sleep. ¹² He dreamed and saw a stairway set upon the earth, and its top reached to heaven. Behold, the angels of God were ascending and descending on it. ¹³ Behold, Yahweh stood above it, and said, "I am Yahweh, the God of Abraham your father, and the God of Isaac. I will give the land you lie on to you and to your offspring. ¹⁴ Your offspring will be as the dust of the earth, and you will spread abroad to the west, and to the east, and to the north, and to the south. In you and in your offspring, all the families of the earth will be blessed. ¹⁵ Behold, I am with you, and will keep you, wherever you go, and will bring you again into this land. For I will not leave you until I have done that which I have spoken of to you." ¹⁶ Jacob awakened out of his sleep, and he said, "Surely Yahweh is in this place, and I didn't know it." ¹⁷ He was afraid, and said, "How awesome this place is! This is none other than God's house, and this is the gate of heaven." ¹⁸ Jacob rose up early in the morning, and took the stone that he had put under his head, and set it up for a pillar, and poured oil on its top. ¹⁹ He called the name of that place Bethel, but the name of the city was Luz at the first. ²⁰ Jacob vowed a vow, saying, "If God will be with me, and will keep me in this way that I go, and will give me bread to eat, and clothing to put on, ²¹ so that I come again to my father's house in peace, and Yahweh will be my God, ²² then this stone, which I have set up for a pillar, will be God's house. Of all that you will give me I will surely give a tenth to you."

## 29

¹ Then Jacob went on his journey, and came to the land of the children of the east. ² He looked, and saw a well in the field, and saw three flocks of sheep lying there by it. For out of that well they watered the flocks. The stone on the well's mouth was large. ³ There all the flocks were gathered. They rolled the stone from the well's mouth, and watered the sheep, and put the stone back on the well's mouth in its place. ⁴ Jacob said to them, "My relatives, where are you from?" They said, "We are from Haran." ⁵ He said to them, "Do you know Laban, the son of Nahor?" They said, "We know him." ⁶ He said to them, "Is it well with him?" They said, "It is well. See, Rachel, his daughter, is coming with the sheep." ⁷ He said, "Behold, it is still the middle of the day, not time to gather the livestock together. Water the sheep, and go and feed them." ⁸ They said, "We can't, until all the flocks are gathered together, and they roll the stone from the well's mouth. Then we will water the sheep." ⁹ While he was yet speaking with them, Rachel came with her father's sheep, for she kept them. ¹⁰ When Jacob saw Rachel the daughter of Laban, his mother's brother, and the sheep of Laban, his mother's brother, Jacob went near, and rolled the stone from the well's mouth, and watered the flock of Laban his mother's brother. ¹¹ Jacob kissed Rachel, and lifted up his voice, and wept. ¹² Jacob told Rachel that he was her father's relative, and that he was Rebekah's son. She ran and told her father. ¹³ When Laban heard the news of Jacob, his sister's son, he ran to meet Jacob, and embraced him, and kissed him, and brought him to his house. Jacob told Laban all these things. ¹⁴ Laban said to him, "Surely you are my bone and my flesh." Jacob stayed with him for a month. ¹⁵ Laban said to Jacob, "Because you are my relative, should you therefore serve me for nothing? Tell me, what will your wages be?" ¹⁶ Laban had two daughters. The name of the elder was Leah, and the name of the younger was Rachel. ¹⁷ Leah's eyes were weak, but Rachel was beautiful in form and attractive. ¹⁸ Jacob loved Rachel. He said, "I will serve you seven years for Rachel, your younger daughter." ¹⁹ Laban said, "It is better that I give her to you, than that I should give her to another man. Stay with me." ²⁰ Jacob served seven years for Rachel. They seemed to him but a few days, for the love he had for her. ²¹ Jacob said to Laban, "Give me my wife, for my days are fulfilled, that I may go in to her." ²² Laban gathered together all the men of the place, and made a feast. ²³ In the evening, he took Leah his daughter, and brought her to Jacob. He went in to her. ²⁴ Laban gave Zilpah his servant to his daughter Leah for a servant. ²⁵ In the morning, behold, it was Leah! He said to Laban, "What is this you have done to me? Didn't I serve with you for Rachel? Why then have you deceived me?" ²⁶ Laban said, "It is not done so in our place, to give the younger before the firstborn. ²⁷ Fulfill the week of this one, and we will give you the other also for the service which you will serve with me for seven more years." ²⁸ Jacob did so, and fulfilled her week. He gave him Rachel his daughter as wife. ²⁹ Laban gave Bilhah, his servant, to his daughter Rachel to be her servant. ³⁰ He went in also to Rachel, and he loved also Rachel more than Leah, and served with him seven more years. ³¹ Yahweh saw that Leah was hated, and he opened her womb, but Rachel was barren. ³² Leah conceived, and bore a son, and she named him Reuben. For she said, "Because Yahweh has looked at my affliction; for now my husband will love me." ³³ She conceived again, and bore a son, and said, "Because Yahweh has heard that I am hated, he has therefore given me this son also." She named him Simeon. ³⁴ She conceived again, and bore a son. She said, "Now this time my husband will be joined to me, because I have borne him three sons."

Therefore his name was called Levi. ³⁵ She conceived again, and bore a son. She said, "This time I will praise Yahweh." Therefore she named him Judah. Then she stopped bearing.

## 30

¹ When Rachel saw that she bore Jacob no children, Rachel envied her sister. She said to Jacob, "Give me children, or else I will die." ² Jacob's anger burned against Rachel, and he said, "Am I in God's place, who has withheld from you the fruit of the womb?" ³ She said, "Behold, my maid Bilhah. Go in to her, that she may bear on my knees, and I also may obtain children by her." ⁴ She gave him Bilhah her servant as wife, and Jacob went in to her. ⁵ Bilhah conceived, and bore Jacob a son. ⁶ Rachel said, "God has judged me, and has also heard my voice, and has given me a son." Therefore she called his name Dan. ⁷ Bilhah, Rachel's servant, conceived again, and bore Jacob a second son. ⁸ Rachel said, "I have wrestled with my sister with mighty wrestlings, and have prevailed." She named him Naphtali. ⁹ When Leah saw that she had finished bearing, she took Zilpah, her servant, and gave her to Jacob as a wife. ¹⁰ Zilpah, Leah's servant, bore Jacob a son. ¹¹ Leah said, "How fortunate!" She named him Gad. ¹² Zilpah, Leah's servant, bore Jacob a second son. ¹³ Leah said, "Happy am I, for the daughters will call me happy." She named him Asher. ¹⁴ Reuben went in the days of wheat harvest, and found mandrakes in the field, and brought them to his mother, Leah. Then Rachel said to Leah, "Please give me some of your son's mandrakes." ¹⁵ Leah said to her, "Is it a small matter that you have taken away my husband? Would you take away my son's mandrakes, also?" Rachel said, "Therefore he will lie with you tonight for your son's mandrakes." ¹⁶ Jacob came from the field in the evening, and Leah went out to meet him, and said, "You must come in to me; for I have surely hired you with my son's mandrakes." He lay with her that night. ¹⁷ God listened to Leah, and she conceived, and bore Jacob a fifth son. ¹⁸ Leah said, "God has given me my hire, because I gave my servant to my husband." She named him Issachar. ¹⁹ Leah conceived again, and bore a sixth son to Jacob. ²⁰ Leah said, "God has endowed me with a good dowry. Now my husband will live with me, because I have borne him six sons." She named him Zebulun. ²¹ Afterwards, she bore a daughter, and named her Dinah. ²² God remembered Rachel, and God listened to her, and opened her womb. ²³ She conceived, bore a son, and said, "God has taken away my reproach." ²⁴ She named him Joseph,ᵃ saying, "May Yahweh add another son to me." ²⁵ When Rachel had borne Joseph, Jacob said to Laban, "Send me away, that I may go to my own place, and to my country. ²⁶ Give me my wives and my children for whom I have served you, and let me go; for you know my service with which I have served you." ²⁷ Laban said to him, "If now I have found favor in your eyes, stay here, for I have divined that Yahweh has blessed me for your sake." ²⁸ He said, "Appoint me your wages, and I will give it." ²⁹ Jacob said to him, "You know how I have served you, and how your livestock have fared with me. ³⁰ For it was little which you had before I came, and it has increased to a multitude. Yahweh has blessed you wherever I turned. Now when will I provide for my own house also?" ³¹ Laban said, "What shall I give you?" Jacob said, "You shall not give me anything. If you will do this thing for me, I will again feed your flock and keep it. ³² I will pass through all your flock today, removing from there every speckled and spotted one, and every black one among the sheep, and the spotted and speckled among the goats. This will be my hire. ³³ So my righteousness will answer for me hereafter, when you come concerning my hire that is before you. Every one that is not speckled and spotted among the goats, and black among the sheep, that might be with me, will be considered stolen." ³⁴ Laban said, "Behold, let it be according to your word." ³⁵ That day, he removed the male goats that were streaked and spotted, and all the female goats that were speckled and spotted, every one that had white in it, and all the black ones among the sheep, and gave them into the hand of his sons. ³⁶ He set three days' journey between himself and Jacob, and Jacob fed the rest of Laban's flocks. ³⁷ Jacob took to himself rods of fresh poplar, almond, and plane tree, peeled white streaks in them, and made the white appear which was in the rods. ³⁸ He set the rods which he had peeled opposite the flocks in the watering troughs where the flocks came to drink. They conceived when they came to drink. ³⁹ The flocks conceived before the rods, and the flocks produced streaked, speckled, and spotted. ⁴⁰ Jacob separated the lambs, and set the faces of the flocks toward the streaked and all the black in Laban's flock. He put his own droves apart, and didn't put them into Laban's flock. ⁴¹ Whenever the stronger of the flock conceived, Jacob laid the rods in front of the eyes of the flock in the watering troughs, that they might conceive among the rods; ⁴² but when the flock were feeble, he didn't put them in. So the feebler were Laban's, and the stronger

Jacob's. ⁴³ The man increased exceedingly, and had large flocks, female servants and male servants, and camels and donkeys.

## 31

¹ Jacob heard Laban's sons' words, saying, "Jacob has taken away all that was our father's. He has obtained all this wealth from that which was our father's." ² Jacob saw the expression on Laban's face, and, behold, it was not toward him as before. ³ Yahweh said to Jacob, "Return to the land of your fathers, and to your relatives, and I will be with you." ⁴ Jacob sent and called Rachel and Leah to the field to his flock, ⁵ and said to them, "I see the expression on your father's face, that it is not toward me as before; but the God of my father has been with me. ⁶ You know that I have served your father with all of my strength. ⁷ Your father has deceived me, and changed my wages ten times, but God didn't allow him to hurt me. ⁸ If he said, 'The speckled will be your wages,' then all the flock bore speckled. If he said, 'The streaked will be your wages,' then all the flock bore streaked. ⁹ Thus God has taken away your father's livestock, and given them to me. ¹⁰ During mating season, I lifted up my eyes, and saw in a dream, and behold, the male goats which leaped on the flock were streaked, speckled, and grizzled. ¹¹ The angel of God said to me in the dream, 'Jacob,' and I said, 'Here I am.' ¹² He said, 'Now lift up your eyes, and behold, all the male goats which leap on the flock are streaked, speckled, and grizzled, for I have seen all that Laban does to you. ¹³ I am the God of Bethel, where you anointed a pillar, where you vowed a vow to me. Now arise, get out from this land, and return to the land of your birth.'" ¹⁴ Rachel and Leah answered him, "Is there yet any portion or inheritance for us in our father's house? ¹⁵ Aren't we considered as foreigners by him? For he has sold us, and has also used up our money. ¹⁶ For all the riches which God has taken away from our father are ours and our children's. Now then, whatever God has said to you, do." ¹⁷ Then Jacob rose up, and set his sons and his wives on the camels, ¹⁸ and he took away all his livestock, and all his possessions which he had gathered, including the livestock which he had gained in Paddan Aram, to go to Isaac his father, to the land of Canaan. ¹⁹ Now Laban had gone to shear his sheep; and Rachel stole the teraphimᵇ that were her father's. ²⁰ Jacob deceived Laban the Syrian, in that he didn't tell him that he was running away. ²¹ So he fled with all that he had. He rose up, passed over the River, and set his face toward the mountain of Gilead. ²² Laban was told on the third day that Jacob had fled. ²³ He took his relatives with him, and pursued him seven days' journey. He overtook him in the mountain of Gilead. ²⁴ God came to Laban the Syrian in a dream of the night, and said to him, "Be careful that you don't speak to Jacob either good or bad." ²⁵ Laban caught up with Jacob. Now Jacob had pitched his tent in the mountain, and Laban with his relatives encamped in the mountain of Gilead. ²⁶ Laban said to Jacob, "What have you done, that you have deceived me, and carried away my daughters like captives of the sword? ²⁷ Why did you flee secretly, and deceive me, and didn't tell me, that I might have sent you away with mirth and with songs, with tambourine and with harp; ²⁸ and didn't allow me to kiss my sons and my daughters? Now have you done foolishly. ²⁹ It is in the power of my hand to hurt you, but the God of your father spoke to me last night, saying, 'Be careful that you don't speak to Jacob either good or bad.' ³⁰ Now, you want to be gone, because you greatly longed for your father's house, but why have you stolen my gods?" ³¹ Jacob answered Laban, "Because I was afraid, for I said, 'Lest you should take your daughters from me by force.' ³² Anyone you find your gods with shall not live. Before our relatives, discern what is yours with me, and take it." For Jacob didn't know that Rachel had stolen them. ³³ Laban went into Jacob's tent, into Leah's tent, and into the tent of the two female servants; but he didn't find them. He went out of Leah's tent, and entered into Rachel's tent. ³⁴ Now Rachel had taken the teraphim, put them in the camel's saddle, and sat on them. Laban felt around all the tent, but didn't find them. ³⁵ She said to her father, "Don't let my lord be angry that I can't rise up before you; for I'm having my period." He searched, but didn't find the teraphim. ³⁶ Jacob was angry, and argued with Laban. Jacob answered Laban, "What is my trespass? What is my sin, that you have hotly pursued me? ³⁷ Now that you have felt around in all my stuff, what have you found of all your household stuff? Set it here before my relatives and your relatives, that they may judge between us two. ³⁸ These twenty years I have been with you. Your ewes and your female goats have not cast their young, and I haven't eaten the rams of your flocks. ³⁹ That which was torn of animals, I didn't bring to you. I bore its loss. Of my hand you required it, whether stolen by day or stolen by night. ⁴⁰ This was my situation: in the day the drought consumed me, and the frost by night; and my sleep fled from my eyes. ⁴¹ These twenty years I have been in your

---

ᵃ *30:24* Joseph means "may he add".

ᵇ *31:19* teraphim were household idols that may have been associated with

inheritance rights to the household property.

house. I served you fourteen years for your two daughters, and six years for your flock, and you have changed my wages ten times. [42] Unless the God of my father, the God of Abraham, and the fear of Isaac, had been with me, surely now you would have sent me away empty. God has seen my affliction and the labor of my hands, and rebuked you last night." [43] Laban answered Jacob, "The daughters are my daughters, the children are my children, the flocks are my flocks, and all that you see is mine! What can I do today to these my daughters, or to their children whom they have borne? [44] Now come, let's make a covenant, you and I. Let it be for a witness between me and you." [45] Jacob took a stone, and set it up for a pillar. [46] Jacob said to his relatives, "Gather stones." They took stones, and made a heap. They ate there by the heap. [47] Laban called it Jegar Sahadutha,[a] but Jacob called it Galeed.[b] [48] Laban said, "This heap is witness between me and you today." Therefore it was named Galeed [49] and Mizpah, for he said, "Yahweh watch between me and you, when we are absent one from another. [50] If you afflict my daughters, or if you take wives in addition to my daughters, no man is with us; behold, God is witness between me and you." [51] Laban said to Jacob, "See this heap, and see the pillar, which I have set between me and you. [52] May this heap be a witness, and the pillar be a witness, that I will not pass over this heap to you, and that you will not pass over this heap and this pillar to me, for harm. [53] The God of Abraham, and the God of Nahor, the God of their father, judge between us." Then Jacob swore by the fear of his father, Isaac. [54] Jacob offered a sacrifice in the mountain, and called his relatives to eat bread. They ate bread, and stayed all night in the mountain. [55] Early in the morning, Laban rose up, and kissed his sons and his daughters, and blessed them. Laban departed and returned to his place.

## 32

[1] Jacob went on his way, and the angels of God met him. [2] When he saw them, Jacob said, "This is God's army." He called the name of that place Mahanaim.[c] [3] Jacob sent messengers in front of him to Esau, his brother, to the land of Seir, the field of Edom. [4] He commanded them, saying, "This is what you shall tell my lord, Esau: 'This is what your servant, Jacob, says. I have lived as a foreigner with Laban, and stayed until now. [5] I have cattle, donkeys, flocks, male servants, and female servants. I have sent to tell my lord, that I may find favor in your sight.'" [6] The messengers returned to Jacob, saying, "We came to your brother Esau. He is coming to meet you, and four hundred men are with him." [7] Then Jacob was greatly afraid and was distressed. He divided the people who were with him, along with the flocks, the herds, and the camels, into two companies. [8] He said, "If Esau comes to the one company, and strikes it, then the company which is left will escape." [9] Jacob said, "God of my father Abraham, and God of my father Isaac, Yahweh, who said to me, 'Return to your country, and to your relatives, and I will do you good,' [10] I am not worthy of the least of all the loving kindnesses, and of all the truth, which you have shown to your servant; for with just my staff I crossed over this Jordan; and now I have become two companies. [11] Please deliver me from the hand of my brother, from the hand of Esau; for I fear him, lest he come and strike me and the mothers with the children. [12] You said, 'I will surely do you good, and make your offspring as the sand of the sea, which can't be counted because there are so many.'" [13] He stayed there that night, and took from that which he had with him a present for Esau, his brother: [14] two hundred female goats and twenty male goats, two hundred ewes and twenty rams, [15] thirty milk camels and their colts, forty cows, ten bulls, twenty female donkeys and ten foals. [16] He delivered them into the hands of his servants, every herd by itself, and said to his servants, "Pass over before me, and put a space between herd and herd." [17] He commanded the foremost, saying, "When Esau, my brother, meets you, and asks you, saying, 'Whose are you? Where are you going? Whose are these before you?' [18] Then you shall say, 'They are your servant, Jacob's. It is a present sent to my lord, Esau. Behold, he also is behind us.'" [19] He commanded also the second, and the third, and all that followed the herds, saying, "This is how you shall speak to Esau, when you find him. [20] You shall say, 'Not only that, but behold, your servant, Jacob, is behind us.'" For, he said, "I will appease him with the present that goes before me, and afterward I will see his face. Perhaps he will accept me." [21] So the present passed over before him, and he himself stayed that night in the camp. [22] He rose up that night, and took his two wives, and his two servants, and his eleven sons, and crossed over the ford of the Jabbok. [23] He took them, and sent them over the stream, and sent over that which he had. [24] Jacob was left alone, and wrestled with a man there until the breaking of the day. [25] When he saw that he didn't prevail against him, the man touched the hollow of his thigh, and the

hollow of Jacob's thigh was strained as he wrestled. [26] The man said, "Let me go, for the day breaks." Jacob said, "I won't let you go unless you bless me." [27] He said to him, "What is your name?" He said, "Jacob". [28] He said, "Your name will no longer be called Jacob, but Israel; for you have fought with God and with men, and have prevailed." [29] Jacob asked him, "Please tell me your name." He said, "Why is it that you ask what my name is?" So he blessed him there. [30] Jacob called the name of the place Peniel;[d] for he said, "I have seen God face to face, and my life is preserved." [31] The sun rose on him as he passed over Peniel, and he limped because of his thigh. [32] Therefore the children of Israel don't eat the sinew of the hip, which is on the hollow of the thigh, to this day, because he touched the hollow of Jacob's thigh in the sinew of the hip.

## 33

[1] Jacob lifted up his eyes, and looked, and, behold, Esau was coming, and with him four hundred men. He divided the children between Leah, Rachel, and the two servants. [2] He put the servants and their children in front, Leah and her children after, and Rachel and Joseph at the rear. [3] He himself passed over in front of them, and bowed himself to the ground seven times, until he came near to his brother. [4] Esau ran to meet him, embraced him, fell on his neck, kissed him, and they wept. [5] He lifted up his eyes, and saw the women and the children; and said, "Who are these with you?" He said, "The children whom God has graciously given your servant." [6] Then the servants came near with their children, and they bowed themselves. [7] Leah also and her children came near, and bowed themselves. After them, Joseph came near with Rachel, and they bowed themselves. [8] Esau said, "What do you mean by all this company which I met?" Jacob said, "To find favor in the sight of my lord." [9] Esau said, "I have enough, my brother; let that which you have be yours." [10] Jacob said, "Please, no, if I have now found favor in your sight, then receive my present at my hand, because I have seen your face, as one sees the face of God, and you were pleased with me. [11] Please take the gift that I brought to you, because God has dealt graciously with me, and because I have enough." He urged him, and he took it. [12] Esau said, "Let's take our journey, and let's go, and I will go before you." [13] Jacob said to him, "My lord knows that the children are tender, and that the flocks and herds with me have their young, and if they overdrive them one day, all the flocks will die. [14] Please let my lord pass over before his servant, and I will lead on gently, according to the pace of the livestock that are before me and according to the pace of the children, until I come to my lord to Seir." [15] Esau said, "Let me now leave with you some of the people who are with me." He said, "Why? Let me find favor in the sight of my lord." [16] So Esau returned that day on his way to Seir. [17] Jacob traveled to Succoth, built himself a house, and made shelters for his livestock. Therefore the name of the place is called Succoth.[e] [18] Jacob came in peace to the city of Shechem, which is in the land of Canaan, when he came from Paddan Aram; and encamped before the city. [19] He bought the parcel of ground where he had spread his tent, at the hand of the children of Hamor, Shechem's father, for one hundred pieces of money. [20] He erected an altar there, and called it El Elohe Israel.[f]

## 34

[1] Dinah, the daughter of Leah, whom she bore to Jacob, went out to see the daughters of the land. [2] Shechem the son of Hamor the Hivite, the prince of the land, saw her. He took her, lay with her, and humbled her. [3] His soul joined to Dinah, the daughter of Jacob, and he loved the young lady, and spoke kindly to the young lady. [4] Shechem spoke to his father, Hamor, saying, "Get me this young lady as a wife." [5] Now Jacob heard that he had defiled Dinah, his daughter; and his sons were with his livestock in the field. Jacob held his peace until they came. [6] Hamor the father of Shechem went out to Jacob to talk with him. [7] The sons of Jacob came in from the field when they heard it. The men were grieved, and they were very angry, because he had done folly in Israel in lying with Jacob's daughter, a thing that ought not to be done. [8] Hamor talked with them, saying, "The soul of my son, Shechem, longs for your daughter. Please give her to him as a wife. [9] Make marriages with us. Give your daughters to us, and take our daughters for yourselves. [10] You shall dwell with us, and the land will be before you. Live and trade in it, and get possessions in it." [11] Shechem said to her father and to her brothers, "Let me find favor in your eyes, and whatever you will tell me I will give. [12] Ask me a great amount for a dowry, and I will give whatever you ask of me, but give me the young lady as a wife." [13] The sons of Jacob answered Shechem and Hamor his father with deceit when they spoke, because he had defiled Dinah their sister, [14] and said to them, "We can't do this thing, to give our sister to

---

[a] 31:47 "Jegar Sahadutha" means "Witness Heap" in Aramaic.

[b] 31:47 "Galeed" means "Witness Heap" in Hebrew.
[c] 32:2 "Mahanaim" means "two camps".

[d] 32:30 Peniel means "face of God".
[e] 33:17 succoth means shelters or booths.

[f] 33:20 El Elohe Israel means "God, the God of Israel" or "The God of Israel is mighty".

one who is uncircumcised; for that is a reproach to us. ¹⁵ Only on this condition will we consent to you. If you will be as we are, that every male of you be circumcised, ¹⁶ then will we give our daughters to you; and we will take your daughters to us, and we will dwell with you, and we will become one people. ¹⁷ But if you will not listen to us and be circumcised, then we will take our sister,ᵃ and we will be gone." ¹⁸ Their words pleased Hamor and Shechem, Hamor's son. ¹⁹ The young man didn't wait to do this thing, because he had delight in Jacob's daughter, and he was honored above all the house of his father. ²⁰ Hamor and Shechem, his son, came to the gate of their city, and talked with the men of their city, saying, ²¹"These men are peaceful with us. Therefore let them live in the land and trade in it. For behold, the land is large enough for them. Let's take their daughters to us for wives, and let's give them our daughters. ²² Only on this condition will the men consent to us to live with us, to become one people, if every male among us is circumcised, as they are circumcised. ²³ Won't their livestock and their possessions and all their animals be ours? Only let's give our consent to them, and they will dwell with us." ²⁴ All who went out of the gate of his city listened to Hamor, and to Shechem his son; and every male was circumcised, all who went out of the gate of his city. ²⁵ On the third day, when they were sore, two of Jacob's sons, Simeon and Levi, Dinah's brothers, each took his sword, came upon the unsuspecting city, and killed all the males. ²⁶ They killed Hamor and Shechem, his son, with the edge of the sword, and took Dinah out of Shechem's house, and went away. ²⁷ Jacob's sons came on the dead, and plundered the city, because they had defiled their sister. ²⁸ They took their flocks, their herds, their donkeys, that which was in the city, that which was in the field, ²⁹ and all their wealth. They took captive all their little ones and their wives, and took as plunder everything that was in the house. ³⁰ Jacob said to Simeon and Levi, "You have troubled me, to make me odious to the inhabitants of the land, among the Canaanites and the Perizzites. I am few in number. They will gather themselves together against me and strike me, and I will be destroyed, I and my house." ³¹ They said, "Should he deal with our sister as with a prostitute?"

## 35

¹ God said to Jacob, "Arise, go up to Bethel, and live there. Make there an altar to God, who appeared to you when you fled from the face of Esau your brother." ² Then Jacob said to his household, and to all who were with him, "Put away the foreign gods that are among you, purify yourselves, and change your garments. ³ Let's arise, and go up to Bethel. I will make there an altar to God, who answered me in the day of my distress, and was with me on the way which I went." ⁴ They gave to Jacob all the foreign gods which were in their hands, and the rings which were in their ears; and Jacob hid them under the oak which was by Shechem. ⁵ They traveled, and a terror of God was on the cities that were around them, and they didn't pursue the sons of Jacob. ⁶ So Jacob came to Luz (that is, Bethel), which is in the land of Canaan, he and all the people who were with him. ⁷ He built an altar there, and called the place El Beth El; because there God was revealed to him, when he fled from the face of his brother. ⁸ Deborah, Rebekah's nurse, died, and she was buried below Bethel under the oak; and its name was called Allon Bacuth. ⁹ God appeared to Jacob again, when he came from Paddan Aram, and blessed him. ¹⁰ God said to him, "Your name is Jacob. Your name shall not be Jacob any more, but your name will be Israel." He named him Israel. ¹¹ God said to him, "I am God Almighty. Be fruitful and multiply. A nation and a company of nations will be from you, and kings will come out of your body. ¹² The land which I gave to Abraham and Isaac, I will give it to you, and to your offspring after you I will give the land." ¹³ God went up from him in the place where he spoke with him. ¹⁴ Jacob set up a pillar in the place where he spoke with him, a pillar of stone. He poured out a drink offering on it, and poured oil on it. ¹⁵ Jacob called the name of the place where God spoke with him "Bethel". ¹⁶ They traveled from Bethel. There was still some distance to come to Ephrath, and Rachel travailed. She had hard labor. ¹⁷ When she was in hard labor, the midwife said to her, "Don't be afraid, for now you will have another son." ¹⁸ As her soul was departing (for she died), she named him Benoni,ᵇ but his father named him Benjamin.ᶜ ¹⁹ Rachel died, and was buried on the way to Ephrath (also called Bethlehem). ²⁰ Jacob set up a pillar on her grave. The same is the Pillar of Rachel's grave to this day. ²¹ Israel traveled, and spread his tent beyond the tower of Eder. ²² While Israel lived in that land, Reuben went and lay with Bilhah, his father's concubine, and Israel heard of it. Now the sons of Jacob were twelve. ²³ The sons of Leah: Reuben (Jacob's firstborn), Simeon, Levi, Judah, Issachar, and Zebulun. ²⁴ The sons of Rachel: Joseph and Benjamin. ²⁵ The sons of Bilhah (Rachel's servant): Dan and Naphtali. ²⁶ The sons of Zilpah (Leah's servant): Gad and Asher. These are the sons of Jacob, who were born to him in Paddan Aram. ²⁷

Jacob came to Isaac his father, to Mamre, to Kiriath Arba (which is Hebron), where Abraham and Isaac lived as foreigners. ²⁸ The days of Isaac were one hundred eighty years. ²⁹ Isaac gave up the spirit and died, and was gathered to his people, old and full of days. Esau and Jacob, his sons, buried him.

## 36

¹ Now this is the history of the generations of Esau (that is, Edom). ² Esau took his wives from the daughters of Canaan: Adah the daughter of Elon, the Hittite; and Oholibamah the daughter of Anah, the daughter of Zibeon, the Hivite; ³ and Basemath, Ishmael's daughter, sister of Nebaioth. ⁴ Adah bore to Esau Eliphaz. Basemath bore Reuel. ⁵ Oholibamah bore Jeush, Jalam, and Korah. These are the sons of Esau, who were born to him in the land of Canaan. ⁶ Esau took his wives, his sons, his daughters, and all the members of his household, with his livestock, all his animals, and all his possessions, which he had gathered in the land of Canaan, and went into a land away from his brother Jacob. ⁷ For their substance was too great for them to dwell together, and the land of their travels couldn't bear them because of their livestock. ⁸ Esau lived in the hill country of Seir. Esau is Edom. ⁹ This is the history of the generations of Esau the father of the Edomites in the hill country of Seir: ¹⁰ these are the names of Esau's sons: Eliphaz, the son of Adah, the wife of Esau; and Reuel, the son of Basemath, the wife of Esau. ¹¹ The sons of Eliphaz were Teman, Omar, Zepho, and Gatam, and Kenaz. ¹² Timna was concubine to Eliphaz, Esau's son; and she bore to Eliphaz Amalek. These are the descendants of Adah, Esau's wife. ¹³ These are the sons of Reuel: Nahath, Zerah, Shammah, and Mizzah. These were the descendants of Basemath, Esau's wife. ¹⁴ These were the sons of Oholibamah, the daughter of Anah, the daughter of Zibeon, Esau's wife: she bore to Esau Jeush, Jalam, and Korah. ¹⁵ These are the chiefs of the sons of Esau: the sons of Eliphaz the firstborn of Esau: chief Teman, chief Omar, chief Zepho, chief Kenaz, ¹⁶ chief Korah, chief Gatam, chief Amalek. These are the chiefs who came of Eliphaz in the land of Edom. These are the sons of Adah. ¹⁷ These are the sons of Reuel, Esau's son: chief Nahath, chief Zerah, chief Shammah, chief Mizzah. These are the chiefs who came of Reuel in the land of Edom. These are the sons of Basemath, Esau's wife. ¹⁸ These are the sons of Oholibamah, Esau's wife: chief Jeush, chief Jalam, chief Korah. These are the chiefs who came of Oholibamah the daughter of Anah, Esau's wife. ¹⁹ These are the sons of Esau (that is, Edom), and these are their chiefs. ²⁰ These are the sons of Seir the Horite, the inhabitants of the land: Lotan, Shobal, Zibeon, Anah, ²¹ Dishon, Ezer, and Dishan. These are the chiefs who came of the Horites, the children of Seir in the land of Edom. ²² The children of Lotan were Hori and Heman. Lotan's sister was Timna. ²³ These are the children of Shobal: Alvan, Manahath, Ebal, Shepho, and Onam. ²⁴ These are the children of Zibeon: Aiah and Anah. This is Anah who found the hot springs in the wilderness, as he fed the donkeys of Zibeon his father. ²⁵ These are the children of Anah: Dishon and Oholibamah, the daughter of Anah. ²⁶ These are the children of Dishon: Hemdan, Eshban, Ithran, and Cheran. ²⁷ These are the children of Ezer: Bilhan, Zaavan, and Akan. ²⁸ These are the children of Dishan: Uz and Aran. ²⁹ These are the chiefs who came of the Horites: chief Lotan, chief Shobal, chief Zibeon, chief Anah, ³⁰ chief Dishon, chief Ezer, and chief Dishan. These are the chiefs who came of the Horites, according to their chiefs in the land of Seir. ³¹ These are the kings who reigned in the land of Edom, before any king reigned over the children of Israel. ³² Bela, the son of Beor, reigned in Edom. The name of his city was Dinhabah. ³³ Bela died, and Jobab, the son of Zerah of Bozrah, reigned in his place. ³⁴ Jobab died, and Husham of the land of the Temanites reigned in his place. ³⁵ Husham died, and Hadad, the son of Bedad, who struck Midian in the field of Moab, reigned in his place. The name of his city was Avith. ³⁶ Hadad died, and Samlah of Masrekah reigned in his place. ³⁷ Samlah died, and Shaul of Rehoboth by the river, reigned in his place. ³⁸ Shaul died, and Baal Hanan the son of Achbor reigned in his place. ³⁹ Baal Hanan the son of Achbor died, and Hadar reigned in his place. The name of his city was Pau. His wife's name was Mehetabel, the daughter of Matred, the daughter of Mezahab. ⁴⁰ These are the names of the chiefs who came from Esau, according to their families, after their places, and by their names: chief Timna, chief Alvah, chief Jetheth, ⁴¹ chief Oholibamah, chief Elah, chief Pinon, ⁴² chief Kenaz, chief Teman, chief Mibzar, ⁴³ chief Magdiel, and chief Iram. These are the chiefs of Edom, according to their habitations in the land of their possession. This is Esau, the father of the Edomites.

## 37

¹ Jacob lived in the land of his father's travels, in the land of Canaan. ² This is the history of the generations of Jacob. Joseph, being seventeen years old, was feeding the flock with his brothers. He was a boy with

---

ᵃ *34:17 Hebrew has, literally, "daughter"*

ᵇ *35:18 "Benoni" means "son of my trouble".*

ᶜ *35:18 "Benjamin" means "son of my right hand".*

the sons of Bilhah and Zilpah, his father's wives. Joseph brought an evil report of them to their father. ³ Now Israel loved Joseph more than all his children, because he was the son of his old age, and he made him a tunic of many colors. ⁴ His brothers saw that their father loved him more than all his brothers, and they hated him, and couldn't speak peaceably to him. ⁵ Joseph dreamed a dream, and he told it to his brothers, and they hated him all the more. ⁶ He said to them, "Please hear this dream which I have dreamed: ⁷ for behold, we were binding sheaves in the field, and behold, my sheaf arose and also stood upright; and behold, your sheaves came around, and bowed down to my sheaf." ⁸ His brothers asked him, "Will you indeed reign over us? Will you indeed have dominion over us?" They hated him all the more for his dreams and for his words. ⁹ He dreamed yet another dream, and told it to his brothers, and said, "Behold, I have dreamed yet another dream: and behold, the sun and the moon and eleven stars bowed down to me." ¹⁰ He told it to his father and to his brothers. His father rebuked him, and said to him, "What is this dream that you have dreamed? Will I and your mother and your brothers indeed come to bow ourselves down to the earth before you?" ¹¹ His brothers envied him, but his father kept this saying in mind. ¹² His brothers went to feed their father's flock in Shechem. ¹³ Israel said to Joseph, "Aren't your brothers feeding the flock in Shechem? Come, and I will send you to them." He said to him, "Here I am." ¹⁴ He said to him, "Go now, see whether it is well with your brothers, and well with the flock; and bring me word again." So he sent him out of the valley of Hebron, and he came to Shechem. ¹⁵ A certain man found him, and behold, he was wandering in the field. The man asked him, "What are you looking for?" ¹⁶ He said, "I am looking for my brothers. Tell me, please, where they are feeding the flock." ¹⁷ The man said, "They have left here, for I heard them say, 'Let's go to Dothan.'" Joseph went after his brothers, and found them in Dothan. ¹⁸ They saw him afar off, and before he came near to them, they conspired against him to kill him. ¹⁹ They said to one another, "Behold, this dreamer comes. ²⁰ Come now therefore, and let's kill him, and cast him into one of the pits, and we will say, 'An evil animal has devoured him.' We will see what will become of his dreams." ²¹ Reuben heard it, and delivered him out of their hand, and said, "Let's not take his life." ²² Reuben said to them, "Shed no blood. Throw him into this pit that is in the wilderness, but lay no hand on him"—that he might deliver him out of their hand, to restore him to his father. ²³ When Joseph came to his brothers, they stripped Joseph of his tunic, the tunic of many colors that was on him; ²⁴ and they took him, and threw him into the pit. The pit was empty. There was no water in it. ²⁵ They sat down to eat bread, and they lifted up their eyes and looked, and saw a caravan of Ishmaelites was coming from Gilead, with their camels bearing spices and balm and myrrh, going to carry it down to Egypt. ²⁶ Judah said to his brothers, "What profit is it if we kill our brother and conceal his blood? ²⁷ Come, and let's sell him to the Ishmaelites, and not let our hand be on him; for he is our brother, our flesh." His brothers listened to him. ²⁸ Midianites who were merchants passed by, and they drew and lifted up Joseph out of the pit, and sold Joseph to the Ishmaelites for twenty pieces of silver. The merchants brought Joseph into Egypt. ²⁹ Reuben returned to the pit, and saw that Joseph wasn't in the pit; and he tore his clothes. ³⁰ He returned to his brothers, and said, "The child is no more; and I, where will I go?" ³¹ They took Joseph's tunic, and killed a male goat, and dipped the tunic in the blood. ³² They took the tunic of many colors, and they brought it to their father, and said, "We have found this. Examine it, now, and see if it is your son's tunic or not." ³³ He recognized it, and said, "It is my son's tunic. An evil animal has devoured him. Joseph is without doubt torn in pieces." ³⁴ Jacob tore his clothes, and put sackcloth on his waist, and mourned for his son many days. ³⁵ All his sons and all his daughters rose up to comfort him, but he refused to be comforted. He said, "For I will go down to Sheolᵃ to my son, mourning." His father wept for him. ³⁶ The Midianites sold him into Egypt to Potiphar, an officer of Pharaoh's, the captain of the guard.

## 38

¹ At that time, Judah went down from his brothers, and visited a certain Adullamite, whose name was Hirah. ² There, Judah saw the daughter of a certain Canaanite man named Shua. He took her, and went in to her. ³ She conceived, and bore a son; and he named him Er. ⁴ She conceived again, and bore a son; and she named him Onan. ⁵ She yet again bore a son, and named him Shelah. He was at Chezib when she bore him. ⁶ Judah took a wife for Er, his firstborn, and her name was Tamar. ⁷ Er, Judah's firstborn, was wicked in Yahweh's sight. So Yahweh killed him. ⁸ Judah said to Onan, "Go in to your brother's wife, and perform the duty of a husband's brother to her, and raise up offspring for your brother." ⁹ Onan knew that the offspring wouldn't be his; and when he went in to his brother's wife, he spilled his semen on

the ground, lest he should give offspring to his brother. ¹⁰ The thing which he did was evil in Yahweh's sight, and he killed him also. ¹¹ Then Judah said to Tamar, his daughter-in-law, "Remain a widow in your father's house, until Shelah, my son, is grown up;" for he said, "Lest he also die, like his brothers." Tamar went and lived in her father's house. ¹² After many days, Shua's daughter, the wife of Judah, died. Judah was comforted, and went up to his sheep shearers to Timnah, he and his friend Hirah, the Adullamite. ¹³ Tamar was told, "Behold, your father-in-law is going up to Timnah to shear his sheep." ¹⁴ She took off the garments of her widowhood, and covered herself with her veil, and wrapped herself, and sat in the gate of Enaim, which is on the way to Timnah; for she saw that Shelah was grown up, and she wasn't given to him as a wife. ¹⁵ When Judah saw her, he thought that she was a prostitute, for she had covered her face. ¹⁶ He turned to her by the way, and said, "Please come, let me come in to you," for he didn't know that she was his daughter-in-law. She said, "What will you give me, that you may come in to me?" ¹⁷ He said, "I will send you a young goat from the flock." She said, "Will you give me a pledge, until you send it?" ¹⁸ He said, "What pledge will I give you?" She said, "Your signet and your cord, and your staff that is in your hand." He gave them to her, and came in to her, and she conceived by him. ¹⁹ She arose, and went away, and put off her veil from her, and put on the garments of her widowhood. ²⁰ Judah sent the young goat by the hand of his friend, the Adullamite, to receive the pledge from the woman's hand, but he didn't find her. ²¹ Then he asked the men of her place, saying, "Where is the prostitute, that was at Enaim by the road?" They said, "There has been no prostitute here." ²² He returned to Judah, and said, "I haven't found her; and also the men of the place said, 'There has been no prostitute here.'" ²³ Judah said, "Let her keep it, lest we be shamed. Behold, I sent this young goat, and you haven't found her." ²⁴ About three months later, Judah was told, "Tamar, your daughter-in-law, has played the prostitute. Moreover, behold, she is with child by prostitution." Judah said, "Bring her out, and let her be burned." ²⁵ When she was brought out, she sent to her father-in-law, saying, "I am with child by the man who owns these." She also said, "Please discern whose these are—the signet, and the cords, and the staff." ²⁶ Judah acknowledged them, and said, "She is more righteous than I, because I didn't give her to Shelah, my son." He knew her again no more. ²⁷ In the time of her travail, behold, twins were in her womb. ²⁸ When she travailed, one put out a hand, and the midwife took and tied a scarlet thread on his hand, saying, "This came out first." ²⁹ As he drew back his hand, behold, his brother came out, and she said, "Why have you made a breach for yourself?" Therefore his name was called Perez.ᵇ ³⁰ Afterward his brother came out, who had the scarlet thread on his hand, and his name was called Zerah.ᶜ

## 39

¹ Joseph was brought down to Egypt. Potiphar, an officer of Pharaoh's, the captain of the guard, an Egyptian, bought him from the hand of the Ishmaelites that had brought him down there. ² Yahweh was with Joseph, and he was a prosperous man. He was in the house of his master the Egyptian. ³ His master saw that Yahweh was with him, and that Yahweh made all that he did prosper in his hand. ⁴ Joseph found favor in his sight. He ministered to him, and Potiphar made him overseer over his house, and all that he had he put into his hand. ⁵ From the time that he made him overseer in his house, and over all that he had, Yahweh blessed the Egyptian's house for Joseph's sake. Yahweh's blessing was on all that he had, in the house and in the field. ⁶ He left all that he had in Joseph's hand. He didn't concern himself with anything, except for the food which he ate. Joseph was well-built and handsome. ⁷ After these things, his master's wife set her eyes on Joseph; and she said, "Lie with me." ⁸ But he refused, and said to his master's wife, "Behold, my master doesn't know what is with me in the house, and he has put all that he has into my hand. ⁹ No one is greater in this house than I am, and he has not kept back anything from me but you, because you are his wife. How then can I do this great wickedness, and sin against God?" ¹⁰ As she spoke to Joseph day by day, he didn't listen to her, to lie by her, or to be with her. ¹¹ About this time, he went into the house to do his work, and there were none of the men of the house inside. ¹² She caught him by his garment, saying, "Lie with me!" He left his garment in her hand, and ran outside. ¹³ When she saw that he had left his garment in her hand, and had run outside, ¹⁴ she called to the men of her house, and spoke to them, saying, "Behold, he has brought a Hebrew in to us to mock us. He came in to me to lie with me, and I cried with a loud voice. ¹⁵ When he heard that I lifted up my voice and cried, he left his garment by me, and ran outside." ¹⁶ She laid up his garment by her, until his master came home. ¹⁷ She spoke to him according to these words, saying, "The Hebrew servant, whom you

---

ᵃ *37:35* Sheol is the place of the dead.

ᵇ *38:29* Perez means "breaking out".

ᶜ *38:30* Zerah means "scarlet" or "brightness".

have brought to us, came in to me to mock me, ¹⁸ and as I lifted up my voice and cried, he left his garment by me, and ran outside." ¹⁹ When his master heard the words of his wife, which she spoke to him, saying, "This is what your servant did to me," his wrath was kindled. ²⁰ Joseph's master took him, and put him into the prison, the place where the king's prisoners were bound, and he was there in custody. ²¹ But Yahweh was with Joseph, and showed kindness to him, and gave him favor in the sight of the keeper of the prison. ²² The keeper of the prison committed to Joseph's hand all the prisoners who were in the prison. Whatever they did there, he was responsible for it. ²³ The keeper of the prison didn't look after anything that was under his hand, because Yahweh was with him; and that which he did, Yahweh made it prosper.

## 40

¹ After these things, the butler of the king of Egypt and his baker offended their lord, the king of Egypt. ² Pharaoh was angry with his two officers, the chief cup bearer and the chief baker. ³ He put them in custody in the house of the captain of the guard, into the prison, the place where Joseph was bound. ⁴ The captain of the guard assigned them to Joseph, and he took care of them. They stayed in prison many days. ⁵ They both dreamed a dream, each man his dream, in one night, each man according to the interpretation of his dream, the cup bearer and the baker of the king of Egypt, who were bound in the prison. ⁶ Joseph came in to them in the morning, and saw them, and saw that they were sad. ⁷ He asked Pharaoh's officers who were with him in custody in his master's house, saying, "Why do you look so sad today?" ⁸ They said to him, "We have dreamed a dream, and there is no one who can interpret it." Joseph said to them, "Don't interpretations belong to God? Please tell it to me." ⁹ The chief cup bearer told his dream to Joseph, and said to him, "In my dream, behold, a vine was in front of me, ¹⁰ and in the vine were three branches. It was as though it budded, it blossomed, and its clusters produced ripe grapes. ¹¹ Pharaoh's cup was in my hand; and I took the grapes, and pressed them into Pharaoh's cup, and I gave the cup into Pharaoh's hand." ¹² Joseph said to him, "This is its interpretation: the three branches are three days. ¹³ Within three more days, Pharaoh will lift up your head, and restore you to your office. You will give Pharaoh's cup into his hand, the way you did when you were his cup bearer. ¹⁴ But remember me when it is well with you. Please show kindness to me, and make mention of me to Pharaoh, and bring me out of this house. ¹⁵ For indeed, I was stolen away out of the land of the Hebrews, and here also I have done nothing that they should put me into the dungeon." ¹⁶ When the chief baker saw that the interpretation was good, he said to Joseph, "I also was in my dream, and behold, three baskets of white bread were on my head. ¹⁷ In the uppermost basket there were all kinds of baked food for Pharaoh, and the birds ate them out of the basket on my head." ¹⁸ Joseph answered, "This is its interpretation. The three baskets are three days. ¹⁹ Within three more days, Pharaoh will lift up your head from off you, and will hang you on a tree; and the birds will eat your flesh from off you." ²⁰ On the third day, which was Pharaoh's birthday, he made a feast for all his servants, and he lifted up the head of the chief cup bearer and the head of the chief baker among his servants. ²¹ He restored the chief cup bearer to his position again, and he gave the cup into Pharaoh's hand; ²² but he hanged the chief baker, as Joseph had interpreted to them. ²³ Yet the chief cup bearer didn't remember Joseph, but forgot him.

## 41

¹ At the end of two full years, Pharaoh dreamed, and behold, he stood by the river. ² Behold, seven cattle came up out of the river. They were sleek and fat, and they fed in the marsh grass. ³ Behold, seven other cattle came up after them out of the river, ugly and thin, and stood by the other cattle on the brink of the river. ⁴ The ugly and thin cattle ate up the seven sleek and fat cattle. So Pharaoh awoke. ⁵ He slept and dreamed a second time; and behold, seven heads of grain came up on one stalk, healthy and good. ⁶ Behold, seven heads of grain, thin and blasted with the east wind, sprung up after them. ⁷ The thin heads of grain swallowed up the seven healthy and full ears. Pharaoh awoke, and behold, it was a dream. ⁸ In the morning, his spirit was troubled, and he sent and called for all of Egypt's magicians and wise men. Pharaoh told them his dreams, but there was no one who could interpret them to Pharaoh. ⁹ Then the chief cup bearer spoke to Pharaoh, saying, "I remember my faults today. ¹⁰ Pharaoh was angry with his servants, and put me in custody in the house of the captain of the guard, with the chief baker. ¹¹ We dreamed a dream in one night, he and I. Each man dreamed according to the interpretation of his dream. ¹² There was with us there a young man, a Hebrew, servant to the captain of the guard, and we told him, and he interpreted to us our dreams. He interpreted to each man according to the interpretation of his dream. ¹³ As he interpreted to us, so it was. He restored

me to my office, and he hanged him." ¹⁴ Then Pharaoh sent and called Joseph, and they brought him hastily out of the dungeon. He shaved himself, changed his clothing, and came in to Pharaoh. ¹⁵ Pharaoh said to Joseph, "I have dreamed a dream, and there is no one who can interpret it. I have heard it said of you, that when you hear a dream you can interpret it." ¹⁶ Joseph answered Pharaoh, saying, "It isn't in me. God will give Pharaoh an answer of peace." ¹⁷ Pharaoh spoke to Joseph, "In my dream, behold, I stood on the brink of the river; ¹⁸ and behold, seven fat and sleek cattle came up out of the river. They fed in the marsh grass; ¹⁹ and behold, seven other cattle came up after them, poor and very ugly and thin, such as I never saw in all the land of Egypt for ugliness. ²⁰ The thin and ugly cattle ate up the first seven fat cattle; ²¹ and when they had eaten them up, it couldn't be known that they had eaten them, but they were still ugly, as at the beginning. So I awoke. ²² I saw in my dream, and behold, seven heads of grain came up on one stalk, full and good; ²³ and behold, seven heads of grain, withered, thin, and blasted with the east wind, sprung up after them. ²⁴ The thin heads of grain swallowed up the seven good heads of grain. I told it to the magicians, but there was no one who could explain it to me." ²⁵ Joseph said to Pharaoh, "The dream of Pharaoh is one. What God is about to do he has declared to Pharaoh. ²⁶ The seven good cattle are seven years; and the seven good heads of grain are seven years. The dream is one. ²⁷ The seven thin and ugly cattle that came up after them are seven years, and also the seven empty heads of grain blasted with the east wind; they will be seven years of famine. ²⁸ That is the thing which I have spoken to Pharaoh. God has shown Pharaoh what he is about to do. ²⁹ Behold, seven years of great plenty throughout all the land of Egypt are coming. ³⁰ Seven years of famine will arise after them, and all the plenty will be forgotten in the land of Egypt. The famine will consume the land, ³¹ and the plenty will not be known in the land by reason of that famine which follows; for it will be very grievous. ³² The dream was doubled to Pharaoh, because the thing is established by God, and God will shortly bring it to pass. ³³"Now therefore let Pharaoh look for a discreet and wise man, and set him over the land of Egypt. ³⁴ Let Pharaoh do this, and let him appoint overseers over the land, and take up the fifth part of the land of Egypt's produce in the seven plenteous years. ³⁵ Let them gather all the food of these good years that come, and store grain under the hand of Pharaoh for food in the cities, and let them keep it. ³⁶ The food will be to supply the land against the seven years of famine, which will be in the land of Egypt; so that the land will not perish through the famine." ³⁷ The thing was good in the eyes of Pharaoh, and in the eyes of all his servants. ³⁸ Pharaoh said to his servants, "Can we find such a one as this, a man in whom is the Spirit of God?" ³⁹ Pharaoh said to Joseph, "Because God has shown you all of this, there is no one so discreet and wise as you. ⁴⁰ You shall be over my house. All my people will be ruled according to your word. Only in the throne I will be greater than you." ⁴¹ Pharaoh said to Joseph, "Behold, I have set you over all the land of Egypt." ⁴² Pharaoh took off his signet ring from his hand, and put it on Joseph's hand, and arrayed him in robes of fine linen, and put a gold chain about his neck. ⁴³ He made him ride in the second chariot which he had. They cried before him, "Bow the knee!" He set him over all the land of Egypt. ⁴⁴ Pharaoh said to Joseph, "I am Pharaoh. Without you, no man shall lift up his hand or his foot in all the land of Egypt." ⁴⁵ Pharaoh called Joseph's name Zaphenath-Paneah. He gave him Asenath, the daughter of Potiphera priest of On as a wife. Joseph went out over the land of Egypt. ⁴⁶ Joseph was thirty years old when he stood before Pharaoh king of Egypt. Joseph went out from the presence of Pharaoh, and went throughout all the land of Egypt. ⁴⁷ In the seven plenteous years the earth produced abundantly. ⁴⁸ He gathered up all the food of the seven years which were in the land of Egypt, and laid up the food in the cities. He stored food in each city from the fields around that city. ⁴⁹ Joseph laid up grain as the sand of the sea, very much, until he stopped counting, for it was without number. ⁵⁰ To Joseph were born two sons before the year of famine came, whom Asenath, the daughter of Potiphera priest of On, bore to him. ⁵¹ Joseph called the name of the firstborn Manasseh,ᵃ "For", he said, "God has made me forget all my toil, and all my father's house." ⁵² The name of the second, he called Ephraim:ᵇ "For God has made me fruitful in the land of my affliction." ⁵³ The seven years of plenty, that were in the land of Egypt, came to an end. ⁵⁴ The seven years of famine began to come, just as Joseph had said. There was famine in all lands, but in all the land of Egypt there was bread. ⁵⁵ When all the land of Egypt was famished, the people cried to Pharaoh for bread, and Pharaoh said to all the Egyptians, "Go to Joseph. What he says to you, do." ⁵⁶ The famine was over all the surface of the earth. Joseph opened all the store houses, and sold to the Egyptians. The famine was severe in the land of Egypt.

ᵃ 41:51 "Manasseh" sounds like the Hebrew for "forget".

ᵇ 41:52 "Ephraim" sounds like the Hebrew for "twice fruitful".

⁵⁷ All countries came into Egypt, to Joseph, to buy grain, because the famine was severe in all the earth.

## 42

¹ Now Jacob saw that there was grain in Egypt, and Jacob said to his sons, "Why do you look at one another?" ² He said, "Behold, I have heard that there is grain in Egypt. Go down there, and buy for us from there, so that we may live, and not die." ³ Joseph's ten brothers went down to buy grain from Egypt. ⁴ But Jacob didn't send Benjamin, Joseph's brother, with his brothers; for he said, "Lest perhaps harm happen to him." ⁵ The sons of Israel came to buy among those who came, for the famine was in the land of Canaan. ⁶ Joseph was the governor over the land. It was he who sold to all the people of the land. Joseph's brothers came, and bowed themselves down to him with their faces to the earth. ⁷ Joseph saw his brothers, and he recognized them, but acted like a stranger to them, and spoke roughly with them. He said to them, "Where did you come from?" They said, "From the land of Canaan, to buy food." ⁸ Joseph recognized his brothers, but they didn't recognize him. ⁹ Joseph remembered the dreams which he dreamed about them, and said to them, "You are spies! You have come to see the nakedness of the land." ¹⁰ They said to him, "No, my lord, but your servants have come to buy food. ¹¹ We are all one man's sons; we are honest men. Your servants are not spies." ¹² He said to them, "No, but you have come to see the nakedness of the land!" ¹³ They said, "We, your servants, are twelve brothers, the sons of one man in the land of Canaan; and behold, the youngest is today with our father, and one is no more." ¹⁴ Joseph said to them, "It is like I told you, saying, 'You are spies!' ¹⁵ By this you shall be tested. By the life of Pharaoh, you shall not go out from here, unless your youngest brother comes here. ¹⁶ Send one of you, and let him get your brother, and you shall be bound, that your words may be tested, whether there is truth in you, or else by the life of Pharaoh surely you are spies." ¹⁷ He put them all together into custody for three days. ¹⁸ Joseph said to them the third day, "Do this, and live, for I fear God. ¹⁹ If you are honest men, then let one of your brothers be bound in your prison; but you go, carry grain for the famine of your houses. ²⁰ Bring your youngest brother to me; so will your words be verified, and you won't die." They did so. ²¹ They said to one another, "We are certainly guilty concerning our brother, in that we saw the distress of his soul, when he begged us, and we wouldn't listen. Therefore this distress has come upon us." ²² Reuben answered them, saying, "Didn't I tell you, saying, 'Don't sin against the child,' and you wouldn't listen? Therefore also, behold, his blood is required." ²³ They didn't know that Joseph understood them; for there was an interpreter between them. ²⁴ He turned himself away from them, and wept. Then he returned to them, and spoke to them, and took Simeon from among them, and bound him before their eyes. ²⁵ Then Joseph gave a command to fill their bags with grain, and to restore each man's money into his sack, and to give them food for the way. So it was done to them. ²⁶ They loaded their donkeys with their grain, and departed from there. ²⁷ As one of them opened his sack to give his donkey food in the lodging place, he saw his money. Behold, it was in the mouth of his sack. ²⁸ He said to his brothers, "My money is restored! Behold, it is in my sack!" Their hearts failed them, and they turned trembling to one another, saying, "What is this that God has done to us?" ²⁹ They came to Jacob their father, to the land of Canaan, and told him all that had happened to them, saying, ³⁰"The man, the lord of the land, spoke roughly with us, and took us for spies of the country. ³¹ We said to him, 'We are honest men. We are no spies. ³² We are twelve brothers, sons of our father; one is no more, and the youngest is today with our father in the land of Canaan.' ³³ The man, the lord of the land, said to us, 'By this I will know that you are honest men: leave one of your brothers with me, and take grain for the famine of your houses, and go your way. ³⁴ Bring your youngest brother to me. Then I will know that you are not spies, but that you are honest men. So I will deliver your brother to you, and you shall trade in the land.'" ³⁵ As they emptied their sacks, behold, each man's bundle of money was in his sack. When they and their father saw their bundles of money, they were afraid. ³⁶ Jacob, their father, said to them, "You have bereaved me of my children! Joseph is no more, Simeon is no more, and you want to take Benjamin away. All these things are against me." ³⁷ Reuben spoke to his father, saying, "Kill my two sons, if I don't bring him to you. Entrust him to my care, and I will bring him to you again." ³⁸ He said, "My son shall not go down with you; for his brother is dead, and he only is left. If harm happens to him along the way in which you go, then you will bring down my gray hairs with sorrow to Sheol."ᵃ

## 43

¹ The famine was severe in the land. ² When they had eaten up the grain which they had brought out of Egypt, their father said to them, "Go

again, buy us a little more food." ³ Judah spoke to him, saying, "The man solemnly warned us, saying, 'You shall not see my face, unless your brother is with you.' ⁴ If you'll send our brother with us, we'll go down and buy you food; ⁵ but if you don't send him, we won't go down, for the man said to us, 'You shall not see my face, unless your brother is with you.'" ⁶ Israel said, "Why did you treat me so badly, telling the man that you had another brother?" ⁷ They said, "The man asked directly concerning ourselves, and concerning our relatives, saying, 'Is your father still alive? Have you another brother?' We just answered his questions. Is there any way we could know that he would say, 'Bring your brother down'?" ⁸ Judah said to Israel, his father, "Send the boy with me, and we'll get up and go, so that we may live, and not die, both we, and you, and also our little ones. ⁹ I'll be collateral for him. From my hand will you require him. If I don't bring him to you, and set him before you, then let me bear the blame forever; ¹⁰ for if we hadn't delayed, surely we would have returned a second time by now." ¹¹ Their father, Israel, said to them, "If it must be so, then do this: Take from the choice fruits of the land in your bags, and carry down a present for the man, a little balm, a little honey, spices and myrrh, nuts, and almonds; ¹² and take double money in your hand, and take back the money that was returned in the mouth of your sacks. Perhaps it was an oversight. ¹³ Take your brother also, get up, and return to the man. ¹⁴ May God Almighty give you mercy before the man, that he may release to you your other brother and Benjamin. If I am bereaved of my children, I am bereaved." ¹⁵ The men took that present, and they took double money in their hand, and Benjamin; and got up, went down to Egypt, and stood before Joseph. ¹⁶ When Joseph saw Benjamin with them, he said to the steward of his house, "Bring the men into the house, and butcher an animal, and prepare; for the men will dine with me at noon." ¹⁷ The man did as Joseph commanded, and the man brought the men to Joseph's house. ¹⁸ The men were afraid, because they were brought to Joseph's house; and they said, "Because of the money that was returned in our sacks the first time, we're brought in; that he may seek occasion against us, attack us, and seize us as slaves, along with our donkeys." ¹⁹ They came near to the steward of Joseph's house, and they spoke to him at the door of the house, ²⁰ and said, "Oh, my lord, we indeed came down the first time to buy food. ²¹ When we came to the lodging place, we opened our sacks, and behold, each man's money was in the mouth of his sack, our money in full weight. We have brought it back in our hand. ²² We have brought down other money in our hand to buy food. We don't know who put our money in our sacks." ²³ He said, "Peace be to you. Don't be afraid. Your God, and the God of your father, has given you treasure in your sacks. I received your money." He brought Simeon out to them. ²⁴ The man brought the men into Joseph's house, and gave them water, and they washed their feet. He gave their donkeys fodder. ²⁵ They prepared the present for Joseph's coming at noon, for they heard that they should eat bread there. ²⁶ When Joseph came home, they brought him the present which was in their hand into the house, and bowed themselves down to the earth before him. ²⁷ He asked them of their welfare, and said, "Is your father well, the old man of whom you spoke? Is he yet alive?" ²⁸ They said, "Your servant, our father, is well. He is still alive." They bowed down humbly. ²⁹ He lifted up his eyes, and saw Benjamin, his brother, his mother's son, and said, "Is this your youngest brother, of whom you spoke to me?" He said, "God be gracious to you, my son." ³⁰ Joseph hurried, for his heart yearned over his brother; and he sought a place to weep. He entered into his room, and wept there. ³¹ He washed his face, and came out. He controlled himself, and said, "Serve the meal." ³² They served him by himself, and them by themselves, and the Egyptians who ate with him by themselves, because the Egyptians don't eat with the Hebrews, for that is an abomination to the Egyptians. ³³ They sat before him, the firstborn according to his birthright, and the youngest according to his youth, and the men marveled with one another. ³⁴ He sent portions to them from before him, but Benjamin's portion was five times as much as any of theirs. They drank, and were merry with him.

## 44

¹ He commanded the steward of his house, saying, "Fill the men's sacks with food, as much as they can carry, and put each man's money in his sack's mouth. ² Put my cup, the silver cup, in the sack's mouth of the youngest, with his grain money." He did according to the word that Joseph had spoken. ³ As soon as the morning was light, the men were sent away, they and their donkeys. ⁴ When they had gone out of the city, and were not yet far off, Joseph said to his steward, "Up, follow after the men. When you overtake them, ask them, 'Why have you rewarded evil for good? ⁵ Isn't this that from which my lord drinks, and by which he indeed divines? You have done evil in so doing.'" ⁶ He overtook them, and he spoke these words to them. ⁷ They said to him,

ᵃ *42:38 Sheol is the place of the dead.*

"Why does my lord speak such words as these? Far be it from your servants that they should do such a thing! ⁸ Behold, the money, which we found in our sacks' mouths, we brought again to you out of the land of Canaan. How then should we steal silver or gold out of your lord's house? ⁹ With whomever of your servants it is found, let him die, and we also will be my lord's slaves." ¹⁰ He said, "Now also let it be according to your words. He with whom it is found will be my slave; and you will be blameless." ¹¹ Then they hurried, and each man took his sack down to the ground, and each man opened his sack. ¹² He searched, beginning with the oldest, and ending at the youngest. The cup was found in Benjamin's sack. ¹³ Then they tore their clothes, and each man loaded his donkey, and returned to the city. ¹⁴ Judah and his brothers came to Joseph's house, and he was still there. They fell on the ground before him. ¹⁵ Joseph said to them, "What deed is this that you have done? Don't you know that such a man as I can indeed do divination?" ¹⁶ Judah said, "What will we tell my lord? What will we speak? How will we clear ourselves? God has found out the iniquity of your servants. Behold, we are my lord's slaves, both we and he also in whose hand the cup is found." ¹⁷ He said, "Far be it from me that I should do so. The man in whose hand the cup is found, he will be my slave; but as for you, go up in peace to your father." ¹⁸ Then Judah came near to him, and said, "Oh, my lord, please let your servant speak a word in my lord's ears, and don't let your anger burn against your servant; for you are even as Pharaoh. ¹⁹ My lord asked his servants, saying, 'Have you a father, or a brother?' ²⁰ We said to my lord, 'We have a father, an old man, and a child of his old age, a little one; and his brother is dead, and he alone is left of his mother; and his father loves him.' ²¹ You said to your servants, 'Bring him down to me, that I may set my eyes on him.' ²² We said to my lord, 'The boy can't leave his father, for if he should leave his father, his father would die.' ²³ You said to your servants, 'Unless your youngest brother comes down with you, you will see my face no more.' ²⁴ When we came up to your servant my father, we told him the words of my lord. ²⁵ Our father said, 'Go again and buy us a little food.' ²⁶ We said, 'We can't go down. If our youngest brother is with us, then we will go down: for we may not see the man's face, unless our youngest brother is with us.' ²⁷ Your servant, my father, said to us, 'You know that my wife bore me two sons. ²⁸ One went out from me, and I said, "Surely he is torn in pieces;" and I haven't seen him since. ²⁹ If you take this one also from me, and harm happens to him, you will bring down my gray hairs with sorrow to Sheol.'ᵃ ³⁰ Now therefore when I come to your servant my father, and the boy is not with us; since his life is bound up in the boy's life; ³¹ it will happen, when he sees that the boy is no more, that he will die. Your servants will bring down the gray hairs of your servant, our father, with sorrow to Sheol.ᵇ ³² For your servant became collateral for the boy to my father, saying, 'If I don't bring him to you, then I will bear the blame to my father forever.' ³³ Now therefore, please let your servant stay instead of the boy, my lord's slave; and let the boy go up with his brothers. ³⁴ For how will I go up to my father, if the boy isn't with me?—lest I see the evil that will come on my father."

### 45

¹ Then Joseph couldn't control himself before all those who stood before him, and he called out, "Cause everyone to go out from me!" No one else stood with him, while Joseph made himself known to his brothers. ² He wept aloud. The Egyptians heard, and the house of Pharaoh heard. ³ Joseph said to his brothers, "I am Joseph! Does my father still live?" His brothers couldn't answer him; for they were terrified at his presence. ⁴ Joseph said to his brothers, "Come near to me, please." They came near. He said, "I am Joseph, your brother, whom you sold into Egypt. ⁵ Now don't be grieved, nor angry with yourselves, that you sold me here, for God sent me before you to preserve life. ⁶ For these two years the famine has been in the land, and there are yet five years, in which there will be no plowing and no harvest. ⁷ God sent me before you to preserve for you a remnant in the earth, and to save you alive by a great deliverance. ⁸ So now it wasn't you who sent me here, but God, and he has made me a father to Pharaoh, lord of all his house, and ruler over all the land of Egypt. ⁹ Hurry, and go up to my father, and tell him, 'This is what your son Joseph says, "God has made me lord of all Egypt. Come down to me. Don't wait. ¹⁰ You shall dwell in the land of Goshen, and you will be near to me, you, your children, your children's children, your flocks, your herds, and all that you have. ¹¹ There I will provide for you; for there are yet five years of famine; lest you come to poverty, you, and your household, and all that you have."' ¹² Behold, your eyes see, and the eyes of my brother Benjamin, that it is my mouth that speaks to you. ¹³ You shall tell my father of all my glory in Egypt, and of all that you have seen. You shall hurry and bring my father down here." ¹⁴ He fell

on his brother Benjamin's neck and wept, and Benjamin wept on his neck. ¹⁵ He kissed all his brothers, and wept on them. After that his brothers talked with him. ¹⁶ The report of it was heard in Pharaoh's house, saying, "Joseph's brothers have come." It pleased Pharaoh well, and his servants. ¹⁷ Pharaoh said to Joseph, "Tell your brothers, 'Do this: Load your animals, and go, travel to the land of Canaan. ¹⁸ Take your father and your households, and come to me, and I will give you the good of the land of Egypt, and you will eat the fat of the land.' ¹⁹ Now you are commanded to do this: Take wagons out of the land of Egypt for your little ones, and for your wives, and bring your father, and come. ²⁰ Also, don't concern yourselves about your belongings, for the good of all the land of Egypt is yours.'" ²¹ The sons of Israel did so. Joseph gave them wagons, according to the commandment of Pharaoh, and gave them provision for the way. ²² He gave each one of them changes of clothing, but to Benjamin he gave three hundred pieces of silver and five changes of clothing. ²³ He sent the following to his father: ten donkeys loaded with the good things of Egypt, and ten female donkeys loaded with grain and bread and provision for his father by the way. ²⁴ So he sent his brothers away, and they departed. He said to them, "See that you don't quarrel on the way." ²⁵ They went up out of Egypt, and came into the land of Canaan, to Jacob their father. ²⁶ They told him, saying, "Joseph is still alive, and he is ruler over all the land of Egypt." His heart fainted, for he didn't believe them. ²⁷ They told him all the words of Joseph, which he had said to them. When he saw the wagons which Joseph had sent to carry him, the spirit of Jacob, their father, revived. ²⁸ Israel said, "It is enough. Joseph my son is still alive. I will go and see him before I die."

### 46

¹ Israel traveled with all that he had, and came to Beersheba, and offered sacrifices to the God of his father, Isaac. ² God spoke to Israel in the visions of the night, and said, "Jacob, Jacob!" He said, "Here I am." ³ He said, "I am God, the God of your father. Don't be afraid to go down into Egypt, for there I will make of you a great nation. ⁴ I will go down with you into Egypt. I will also surely bring you up again. Joseph's hand will close your eyes." ⁵ Jacob rose up from Beersheba, and the sons of Israel carried Jacob, their father, their little ones, and their wives, in the wagons which Pharaoh had sent to carry him. ⁶ They took their livestock, and their goods, which they had gotten in the land of Canaan, and came into Egypt—Jacob, and all his offspring with him, ⁷ his sons, and his sons' sons with him, his daughters, and his sons' daughters, and he brought all his offspring with him into Egypt. ⁸ These are the names of the children of Israel, who came into Egypt, Jacob and his sons: Reuben, Jacob's firstborn. ⁹ The sons of Reuben: Hanoch, Pallu, Hezron, and Carmi. ¹⁰ The sons of Simeon: Jemuel, Jamin, Ohad, Jachin, Zohar, and Shaul the son of a Canaanite woman. ¹¹ The sons of Levi: Gershon, Kohath, and Merari. ¹² The sons of Judah: Er, Onan, Shelah, Perez, and Zerah; but Er and Onan died in the land of Canaan. The sons of Perez were Hezron and Hamul. ¹³ The sons of Issachar: Tola, Puvah, Iob, and Shimron. ¹⁴ The sons of Zebulun: Sered, Elon, and Jahleel. ¹⁵ These are the sons of Leah, whom she bore to Jacob in Paddan Aram, with his daughter Dinah. All the souls of his sons and his daughters were thirty-three. ¹⁶ The sons of Gad: Ziphion, Haggi, Shuni, Ezbon, Eri, Arodi, and Areli. ¹⁷ The sons of Asher: Imnah, Ishvah, Ishvi, Beriah, and Serah their sister. The sons of Beriah: Heber and Malchiel. ¹⁸ These are the sons of Zilpah, whom Laban gave to Leah, his daughter, and these she bore to Jacob, even sixteen souls. ¹⁹ The sons of Rachel, Jacob's wife: Joseph and Benjamin. ²⁰ To Joseph in the land of Egypt were born Manasseh and Ephraim, whom Asenath, the daughter of Potiphera, priest of On, bore to him. ²¹ The sons of Benjamin: Bela, Becher, Ashbel, Gera, Naaman, Ehi, Rosh, Muppim, Huppim, and Ard. ²² These are the sons of Rachel, who were born to Jacob: all the souls were fourteen. ²³ The son of Dan: Hushim. ²⁴ The sons of Naphtali: Jahzeel, Guni, Jezer, and Shillem. ²⁵ These are the sons of Bilhah, whom Laban gave to Rachel, his daughter, and these she bore to Jacob: all the souls were seven. ²⁶ All the souls who came with Jacob into Egypt, who were his direct offspring, in addition to Jacob's sons' wives, all the souls were sixty-six. ²⁷ The sons of Joseph, who were born to him in Egypt, were two souls. All the souls of the house of Jacob, who came into Egypt, were seventy. ²⁸ Jacob sent Judah before him to Joseph, to show the way before him to Goshen, and they came into the land of Goshen. ²⁹ Joseph prepared his chariot, and went up to meet Israel, his father, in Goshen. He presented himself to him, and fell on his neck, and wept on his neck a good while. ³⁰ Israel said to Joseph, "Now let me die, since I have seen your face, that you are still alive." ³¹ Joseph said to his brothers, and to his father's house, "I will go up, and speak with Pharaoh, and will tell him, 'My brothers, and my father's house, who were in the land of Canaan, have come to

---

ᵃ 44:29 Sheol is the place of the dead.

ᵇ 44:31 Sheol is the place of the dead.

me. ³² These men are shepherds, for they have been keepers of livestock, and they have brought their flocks, and their herds, and all that they have.' ³³ It will happen, when Pharaoh summons you, and will say, 'What is your occupation?' ³⁴ that you shall say, 'Your servants have been keepers of livestock from our youth even until now, both we, and our fathers:' that you may dwell in the land of Goshen; for every shepherd is an abomination to the Egyptians."

## 47

¹ Then Joseph went in and told Pharaoh, and said, "My father and my brothers, with their flocks, their herds, and all that they own, have come out of the land of Canaan; and behold, they are in the land of Goshen." ² From among his brothers he took five men, and presented them to Pharaoh. ³ Pharaoh said to his brothers, "What is your occupation?" They said to Pharaoh, "Your servants are shepherds, both we, and our fathers." ⁴ They also said to Pharaoh, "We have come to live as foreigners in the land, for there is no pasture for your servants' flocks. For the famine is severe in the land of Canaan. Now therefore, please let your servants dwell in the land of Goshen." ⁵ Pharaoh spoke to Joseph, saying, "Your father and your brothers have come to you. ⁶ The land of Egypt is before you. Make your father and your brothers dwell in the best of the land. Let them dwell in the land of Goshen. If you know any able men among them, then put them in charge of my livestock." ⁷ Joseph brought in Jacob, his father, and set him before Pharaoh; and Jacob blessed Pharaoh. ⁸ Pharaoh said to Jacob, "How old are you?" ⁹ Jacob said to Pharaoh, "The years of my pilgrimage are one hundred thirty years. The days of the years of my life have been few and evil. They have not attained to the days of the years of the life of my fathers in the days of their pilgrimage." ¹⁰ Jacob blessed Pharaoh, and went out from the presence of Pharaoh. ¹¹ Joseph placed his father and his brothers, and gave them a possession in the land of Egypt, in the best of the land, in the land of Rameses, as Pharaoh had commanded. ¹² Joseph provided his father, his brothers, and all of his father's household with bread, according to the sizes of their families. ¹³ There was no bread in all the land; for the famine was very severe, so that the land of Egypt and the land of Canaan fainted by reason of the famine. ¹⁴ Joseph gathered up all the money that was found in the land of Egypt, and in the land of Canaan, for the grain which they bought: and Joseph brought the money into Pharaoh's house. ¹⁵ When the money was all spent in the land of Egypt, and in the land of Canaan, all the Egyptians came to Joseph, and said, "Give us bread, for why should we die in your presence? For our money fails." ¹⁶ Joseph said, "Give me your livestock; and I will give you food for your livestock, if your money is gone." ¹⁷ They brought their livestock to Joseph, and Joseph gave them bread in exchange for the horses, and for the flocks, and for the herds, and for the donkeys: and he fed them with bread in exchange for all their livestock for that year. ¹⁸ When that year was ended, they came to him the second year, and said to him, "We will not hide from my lord how our money is all spent, and the herds of livestock are my lord's. There is nothing left in the sight of my lord, but our bodies, and our lands. ¹⁹ Why should we die before your eyes, both we and our land? Buy us and our land for bread, and we and our land will be servants to Pharaoh. Give us seed, that we may live, and not die, and that the land won't be desolate." ²⁰ So Joseph bought all the land of Egypt for Pharaoh, for every man of the Egyptians sold his field, because the famine was severe on them, and the land became Pharaoh's. ²¹ As for the people, he moved them to the cities from one end of the border of Egypt even to the other end of it. ²² Only he didn't buy the land of the priests, for the priests had a portion from Pharaoh, and ate their portion which Pharaoh gave them. That is why they didn't sell their land. ²³ Then Joseph said to the people, "Behold, I have bought you and your land today for Pharaoh. Behold, here is seed for you, and you shall sow the land. ²⁴ It will happen at the harvests, that you shall give a fifth to Pharaoh, and four parts will be your own, for seed of the field, for your food, for them of your households, and for food for your little ones." ²⁵ They said, "You have saved our lives! Let us find favor in the sight of my lord, and we will be Pharaoh's servants." ²⁶ Joseph made it a statute concerning the land of Egypt to this day, that Pharaoh should have the fifth. Only the land of the priests alone didn't become Pharaoh's. ²⁷ Israel lived in the land of Egypt, in the land of Goshen; and they got themselves possessions therein, and were fruitful, and multiplied exceedingly. ²⁸ Jacob lived in the land of Egypt seventeen years. So the days of Jacob, the years of his life, were one hundred forty-seven years. ²⁹ The time came near that Israel must die, and he called his son Joseph, and said to him, "If now I have found favor in your sight, please put your hand under my thigh, and deal kindly and truly with me. Please don't bury me in Egypt, ³⁰ but when I sleep with my fathers, you shall carry me out of Egypt, and bury me in their burying place." Joseph said, "I will do as you have said." ³¹ Israel said, "Swear to me," and he swore to him. Then Israel bowed himself on the bed's head.

## 48

¹ After these things, someone said to Joseph, "Behold, your father is sick." He took with him his two sons, Manasseh and Ephraim. ² Someone told Jacob, and said, "Behold, your son Joseph comes to you," and Israel strengthened himself, and sat on the bed. ³ Jacob said to Joseph, "God Almighty appeared to me at Luz in the land of Canaan, and blessed me, ⁴ and said to me, 'Behold, I will make you fruitful, and multiply you, and I will make of you a company of peoples, and will give this land to your offspring after you for an everlasting possession.' ⁵ Now your two sons, who were born to you in the land of Egypt before I came to you into Egypt, are mine; Ephraim and Manasseh, even as Reuben and Simeon, will be mine. ⁶ Your offspring, whom you become the father of after them, will be yours. They will be called after the name of their brothers in their inheritance. ⁷ As for me, when I came from Paddan, Rachel died beside me in the land of Canaan on the way, when there was still some distance to come to Ephrath, and I buried her there on the way to Ephrath (also called Bethlehem)." ⁸ Israel saw Joseph's sons, and said, "Who are these?" ⁹ Joseph said to his father, "They are my sons, whom God has given me here." He said, "Please bring them to me, and I will bless them." ¹⁰ Now the eyes of Israel were dim for age, so that he couldn't see well. Joseph brought them near to him; and he kissed them, and embraced them. ¹¹ Israel said to Joseph, "I didn't think I would see your face, and behold, God has let me see your offspring also." ¹² Joseph brought them out from between his knees, and he bowed himself with his face to the earth. ¹³ Joseph took them both, Ephraim in his right hand toward Israel's left hand, and Manasseh in his left hand toward Israel's right hand, and brought them near to him. ¹⁴ Israel stretched out his right hand, and laid it on Ephraim's head, who was the younger, and his left hand on Manasseh's head, guiding his hands knowingly, for Manasseh was the firstborn. ¹⁵ He blessed Joseph, and said, "The God before whom my fathers Abraham and Isaac walked, the God who has fed me all my life long to this day, ¹⁶ the angel who has redeemed me from all evil, bless the lads, and let my name be named on them, and the name of my fathers Abraham and Isaac. Let them grow into a multitude upon the earth." ¹⁷ When Joseph saw that his father laid his right hand on the head of Ephraim, it displeased him. He held up his father's hand, to remove it from Ephraim's head to Manasseh's head. ¹⁸ Joseph said to his father, "Not so, my father, for this is the firstborn. Put your right hand on his head." ¹⁹ His father refused, and said, "I know, my son, I know. He also will become a people, and he also will be great. However, his younger brother will be greater than he, and his offspring will become a multitude of nations." ²⁰ He blessed them that day, saying, "Israel will bless in you, saying, 'God make you as Ephraim and as Manasseh'" He set Ephraim before Manasseh. ²¹ Israel said to Joseph, "Behold, I am dying, but God will be with you, and bring you again to the land of your fathers. ²² Moreover I have given to you one portion above your brothers, which I took out of the hand of the Amorite with my sword and with my bow."

## 49

¹ Jacob called to his sons, and said: "Gather yourselves together, that I may tell you that which will happen to you in the days to come. ² Assemble yourselves, and hear, you sons of Jacob. Listen to Israel, your father. ³ "Reuben, you are my firstborn, my might, and the beginning of my strength, excelling in dignity, and excelling in power. ⁴ Boiling over like water, you shall not excel, because you went up to your father's bed, then defiled it. He went up to my couch. ⁵ "Simeon and Levi are brothers. Their swords are weapons of violence. ⁶ My soul, don't come into their council. My glory, don't be united to their assembly; for in their anger they killed men. In their self-will they hamstrung cattle. ⁷ Cursed be their anger, for it was fierce; and their wrath, for it was cruel. I will divide them in Jacob, and scatter them in Israel. ⁸ "Judah, your brothers will praise you. Your hand will be on the neck of your enemies. Your father's sons will bow down before you. ⁹ Judah is a lion's cub. From the prey, my son, you have gone up. He stooped down, he crouched as a lion, as a lioness. Who will rouse him up? ¹⁰ The scepter will not depart from Judah, nor the ruler's staff from between his feet, until he comes to whom it belongs. The obedience of the peoples will be to him. ¹¹ Binding his foal to the vine, his donkey's colt to the choice vine, he has washed his garments in wine, his robes in the blood of grapes. ¹² His eyes will be red with wine, his teeth white with milk. ¹³ "Zebulun will dwell at the haven of the sea. He will be for a haven of ships. His border will be on Sidon. ¹⁴ "Issachar is a strong donkey, lying down between the saddlebags. ¹⁵ He saw a resting place, that it was good, the land, that it was pleasant. He bows his shoulder to the burden, and becomes a servant doing forced labor. ¹⁶ "Dan will judge his people, as one of the tribes of Israel. ¹⁷ Dan will be a serpent on the trail, an adder in the path, that bites the horse's heels, so that his rider falls backward. ¹⁸ I have waited for your salvation, Yahweh. ¹⁹ "A troop will press on Gad, but he will press on their heel. ²⁰ "Asher's food will be

rich. He will produce royal dainties. ²¹"Naphtali is a doe set free, who bears beautiful fawns. ²²"Joseph is a fruitful vine, a fruitful vine by a spring. His branches run over the wall. ²³ The archers have severely grieved him, shot at him, and persecuted him: ²⁴ But his bow remained strong. The arms of his hands were made strong, by the hands of the Mighty One of Jacob, (from there is the shepherd, the stone of Israel), ²⁵ even by the God of your father, who will help you, by the Almighty, who will bless you, with blessings of heaven above, blessings of the deep that lies below, blessings of the breasts, and of the womb. ²⁶ The blessings of your father have prevailed above the blessings of my ancestors, above the boundaries of the ancient hills. They will be on the head of Joseph, on the crown of the head of him who is separated from his brothers. ²⁷"Benjamin is a ravenous wolf. In the morning he will devour the prey. At evening he will divide the plunder." ²⁸ All these are the twelve tribes of Israel, and this is what their father spoke to them, and blessed them. He blessed everyone according to his own blessing. ²⁹ He instructed them, and said to them, "I am to be gathered to my people. Bury me with my fathers in the cave that is in the field of Ephron the Hittite, ³⁰ in the cave that is in the field of Machpelah, which is before Mamre, in the land of Canaan, which Abraham bought with the field from Ephron the Hittite as a burial place. ³¹ There they buried Abraham and Sarah, his wife. There they buried Isaac and Rebekah, his wife, and there I buried Leah: ³² the field and the cave that is therein, which was purchased from the children of Heth." ³³ When Jacob finished charging his sons, he gathered up his feet into the bed, breathed his last breath, and was gathered to his people.

### 50

¹ Joseph fell on his father's face, wept on him, and kissed him. ² Joseph commanded his servants, the physicians, to embalm his father; and the physicians embalmed Israel. ³ Forty days were used for him, for that is how many days it takes to embalm. The Egyptians wept for Israel for seventy days. ⁴ When the days of weeping for him were past, Joseph spoke to Pharaoh's staff, saying, "If now I have found favor in your eyes, please speak in the ears of Pharaoh, saying, ⁵'My father made me swear, saying, "Behold, I am dying. Bury me in my grave which I have dug for myself in the land of Canaan." Now therefore, please let me go up and bury my father, and I will come again.'" ⁶ Pharaoh said, "Go up, and bury your father, just like he made you swear." ⁷ Joseph went up to bury his father; and with him went up all the servants of Pharaoh, the elders of his house, all the elders of the land of Egypt, ⁸ all the house of Joseph, his brothers, and his father's house. Only their little ones, their flocks, and their herds, they left in the land of Goshen. ⁹ Both chariots and horsemen went up with him. It was a very great company. ¹⁰ They came to the threshing floor of Atad, which is beyond the Jordan, and there they lamented with a very great and severe lamentation. He mourned for his father seven days. ¹¹ When the inhabitants of the land, the Canaanites, saw the mourning in the floor of Atad, they said, "This is a grievous mourning by the Egyptians." Therefore its name was called Abel Mizraim, which is beyond the Jordan. ¹² His sons did to him just as he commanded them, ¹³ for his sons carried him into the land of Canaan, and buried him in the cave of the field of Machpelah, which Abraham bought with the field, as a possession for a burial site, from Ephron the Hittite, near Mamre. ¹⁴ Joseph returned into Egypt— he, and his brothers, and all that went up with him to bury his father, after he had buried his father. ¹⁵ When Joseph's brothers saw that their father was dead, they said, "It may be that Joseph will hate us, and will fully pay us back for all the evil which we did to him." ¹⁶ They sent a message to Joseph, saying, "Your father commanded before he died, saying, ¹⁷'You shall tell Joseph, "Now please forgive the disobedience of your brothers, and their sin, because they did evil to you."'" Now, please forgive the disobedience of the servants of the God of your father." Joseph wept when they spoke to him. ¹⁸ His brothers also went and fell down before his face; and they said, "Behold, we are your servants." ¹⁹ Joseph said to them, "Don't be afraid, for am I in the place of God? ²⁰ As for you, you meant evil against me, but God meant it for good, to save many people alive, as is happening today. ²¹ Now therefore don't be afraid. I will provide for you and your little ones." He comforted them, and spoke kindly to them. ²² Joseph lived in Egypt, he, and his father's house. Joseph lived one hundred ten years. ²³ Joseph saw Ephraim's children to the third generation. The children also of Machir, the son of Manasseh, were born on Joseph's knees. ²⁴ Joseph said to his brothers, "I am dying, but God will surely visit you, and bring you up out of this land to the land which he swore to Abraham, to Isaac, and to Jacob." ²⁵ Joseph took an oath from the children of Israel, saying, "God will surely visit you, and you shall carry up my

bones from here." ²⁶ So Joseph died, being one hundred ten years old, and they embalmed him, and he was put in a coffin in Egypt.

# The Second Book of Moses, Exodus
## 1

¹ Now these are the names of the sons of Israel, who came into Egypt (every man and his household came with Jacob): ² Reuben, Simeon, Levi, and Judah, ³ Issachar, Zebulun, and Benjamin, ⁴ Dan and Naphtali, Gad and Asher. ⁵ All the souls who came out of Jacob's body were seventy souls, and Joseph was in Egypt already. ⁶ Joseph died, as did all his brothers, and all that generation. ⁷ The children of Israel were fruitful, and increased abundantly, and multiplied, and grew exceedingly mighty; and the land was filled with them. ⁸ Now there arose a new king over Egypt, who didn't know Joseph. ⁹ He said to his people, "Behold,ᵃ the people of the children of Israel are more and mightier than we. ¹⁰ Come, let's deal wisely with them, lest they multiply, and it happen that when any war breaks out, they also join themselves to our enemies and fight against us, and escape out of the land." ¹¹ Therefore they set taskmasters over them to afflict them with their burdens. They built storage cities for Pharaoh: Pithom and Raamses. ¹² But the more they afflicted them, the more they multiplied and the more they spread out. They started to dread the children of Israel. ¹³ The Egyptians ruthlessly made the children of Israel serve, ¹⁴ and they made their lives bitter with hard service in mortar and in brick, and in all kinds of service in the field, all their service, in which they ruthlessly made them serve. ¹⁵ The king of Egypt spoke to the Hebrew midwives, of whom the name of the one was Shiphrah, and the name of the other Puah, ¹⁶ and he said, "When you perform the duty of a midwife to the Hebrew women, and see them on the birth stool, if it is a son, then you shall kill him; but if it is a daughter, then she shall live." ¹⁷ But the midwives feared God,ᵇ and didn't do what the king of Egypt commanded them, but saved the baby boys alive. ¹⁸ The king of Egypt called for the midwives, and said to them, "Why have you done this thing and saved the boys alive?" ¹⁹ The midwives said to Pharaoh, "Because the Hebrew women aren't like the Egyptian women; for they are vigorous and give birth before the midwife comes to them." ²⁰ God dealt well with the midwives, and the people multiplied, and grew very mighty. ²¹ Because the midwives feared God, he gave them families. ²² Pharaoh commanded all his people, saying, "You shall cast every son who is born into the river, and every daughter you shall save alive."

## 2

¹ A man of the house of Levi went and took a daughter of Levi as his wife. ² The woman conceived and bore a son. When she saw that he was a fine child, she hid him three months. ³ When she could no longer hide him, she took a papyrus basket for him, and coated it with tar and with pitch. She put the child in it, and laid it in the reeds by the river's bank. ⁴ His sister stood far off, to see what would be done to him. ⁵ Pharaoh's daughter came down to bathe at the river. Her maidens walked along by the riverside. She saw the basket among the reeds, and sent her servant to get it. ⁶ She opened it, and saw the child, and behold, the baby cried. She had compassion on him, and said, "This is one of the Hebrews' children." ⁷ Then his sister said to Pharaoh's daughter, "Should I go and call a nurse for you from the Hebrew women, that she may nurse the child for you?" ⁸ Pharaoh's daughter said to her, "Go." The young woman went and called the child's mother. ⁹ Pharaoh's daughter said to her, "Take this child away, and nurse him for me, and I will give you your wages." The woman took the child, and nursed it. ¹⁰ The child grew, and she brought him to Pharaoh's daughter, and he became her son. She named him Moses,ᶜ and said, "Because I drew him out of the water." ¹¹ In those days, when Moses had grown up, he went out to his brothers and saw their burdens. He saw an Egyptian striking a Hebrew, one of his brothers. ¹² He looked this way and that way, and when he saw that there was no one, he killed the Egyptian, and hid him in the sand. ¹³ He went out the second day, and behold, two men of the Hebrews were fighting with each other. He said to him who did the wrong, "Why do you strike your fellow?" ¹⁴ He said, "Who made you a prince and a judge over us? Do you plan to kill me, as you killed the Egyptian?" Moses was afraid, and said, "Surely this thing is known." ¹⁵ Now when Pharaoh heard this thing, he sought to kill Moses. But Moses fled from the face of Pharaoh, and lived in the land of Midian, and he sat down by a well. ¹⁶ Now the priest of Midian had seven daughters. They came and drew water, and filled the troughs to water their father's flock. ¹⁷ The shepherds came and drove them away; but Moses stood up and helped them, and watered their flock. ¹⁸ When they came to Reuel, their father, he said, "How is it that you have returned

---

ᵃ *1:9* "Behold", from "הִנֵּה", means look at, take notice, / observe, see, or gaze at. It is often used as an interjection.

ᵇ *1:17* The Hebrew word rendered "God" is "אֱלֹהִים" (Elohim).

ᶜ *2:10* "Moses" sounds like the Hebrew for "draw out".

so early today?" ¹⁹ They said, "An Egyptian delivered us out of the hand of the shepherds, and moreover he drew water for us, and watered the flock." ²⁰ He said to his daughters, "Where is he? Why is it that you have left the man? Call him, that he may eat bread." ²¹ Moses was content to dwell with the man. He gave Moses Zipporah, his daughter. ²² She bore a son, and he named him Gershom,ᵃ for he said, "I have lived as a foreigner in a foreign land." ²³ In the course of those many days, the king of Egypt died, and the children of Israel sighed because of the bondage, and they cried, and their cry came up to God because of the bondage. ²⁴ God heard their groaning, and God remembered his covenant with Abraham, with Isaac, and with Jacob. ²⁵ God saw the children of Israel, and God understood.

## 3

¹ Now Moses was keeping the flock of Jethro, his father-in-law, the priest of Midian, and he led the flock to the back of the wilderness, and came to God's mountain, to Horeb. ² Yahweh'sᵇ angel appeared to him in a flame of fire out of the middle of a bush. He looked, and behold, the bush burned with fire, and the bush was not consumed. ³ Moses said, "I will go now, and see this great sight, why the bush is not burned." ⁴ When Yahweh saw that he came over to see, God called to him out of the middle of the bush, and said, "Moses! Moses!" He said, "Here I am." ⁵ He said, "Don't come close. Take off your sandals, for the place you are standing on is holy ground." ⁶ Moreover he said, "I am the God of your father, the God of Abraham, the God of Isaac, and the God of Jacob." Moses hid his face because he was afraid to look at God. ⁷ Yahweh said, "I have surely seen the affliction of my people who are in Egypt, and have heard their cry because of their taskmasters, for I know their sorrows. ⁸ I have come down to deliver them out of the hand of the Egyptians, and to bring them up out of that land to a good and large land, to a land flowing with milk and honey; to the place of the Canaanite, the Hittite, the Amorite, the Perizzite, the Hivite, and the Jebusite. ⁹ Now, behold, the cry of the children of Israel has come to me. Moreover I have seen the oppression with which the Egyptians oppress them. ¹⁰ Come now therefore, and I will send you to Pharaoh, that you may bring my people, the children of Israel, out of Egypt." ¹¹ Moses said to God, "Who am I, that I should go to Pharaoh, and that I should bring the children of Israel out of Egypt?" ¹² He said, "Certainly I will be with you. This will be the token to you, that I have sent you: when you have brought the people out of Egypt, you shall serve God on this mountain." ¹³ Moses said to God, "Behold, when I come to the children of Israel, and tell them, 'The God of your fathers has sent me to you,' and they ask me, 'What is his name?' what should I tell them?" ¹⁴ God said to Moses, "I AM WHO I AM," and he said, "You shall tell the children of Israel this: 'I AM has sent me to you.'" ¹⁵ God said moreover to Moses, "You shall tell the children of Israel this, 'Yahweh, the God of your fathers, the God of Abraham, the God of Isaac, and the God of Jacob, has sent me to you.' This is my name forever, and this is my memorial to all generations. ¹⁶ Go and gather the elders of Israel together, and tell them, 'Yahweh, the God of your fathers, the God of Abraham, of Isaac, and of Jacob, has appeared to me, saying, "I have surely visited you, and seen that which is done to you in Egypt. ¹⁷ I have said, I will bring you up out of the affliction of Egypt to the land of the Canaanite, the Hittite, the Amorite, the Perizzite, the Hivite, and the Jebusite, to a land flowing with milk and honey."' ¹⁸ They will listen to your voice. You shall come, you and the elders of Israel, to the king of Egypt, and you shall tell him, 'Yahweh, the God of the Hebrews, has met with us. Now please let us go three days' journey into the wilderness, that we may sacrifice to Yahweh, our God.' ¹⁹ I know that the king of Egypt won't give you permission to go, no, not by a mighty hand. ²⁰ I will reach out my hand and strike Egypt with all my wonders which I will do among them, and after that he will let you go. ²¹ I will give this people favor in the sight of the Egyptians, and it will happen that when you go, you shall not go empty-handed. ²² But every woman shall ask of her neighbor, and of her who visits her house, jewels of silver, jewels of gold, and clothing. You shall put them on your sons, and on your daughters. You shall plunder the Egyptians."

## 4

¹ Moses answered, "But, behold, they will not believe me, nor listen to my voice; for they will say, 'Yahweh has not appeared to you.'" ² Yahweh said to him, "What is that in your hand?" He said, "A rod." ³ He said, "Throw it on the ground." He threw it on the ground, and it became a snake; and Moses ran away from it. ⁴ Yahweh said to Moses, "Stretch out your hand, and take it by the tail." He stretched out his hand, and took hold of it, and it became a rod in his hand. ⁵ "This is so that they may believe that Yahweh, the God of their fathers, the God of Abraham, the God of Isaac, and the God of Jacob, has appeared to you."

⁶ Yahweh said furthermore to him, "Now put your hand inside your cloak." He put his hand inside his cloak, and when he took it out, behold, his hand was leprous, as white as snow. ⁷ He said, "Put your hand inside your cloak again." He put his hand inside his cloak again, and when he took it out of his cloak, behold, it had turned again as his other flesh. ⁸ "It will happen, if they will not believe you or listen to the voice of the first sign, that they will believe the voice of the latter sign. ⁹ It will happen, if they will not believe even these two signs or listen to your voice, that you shall take of the water of the river, and pour it on the dry land. The water which you take out of the river will become blood on the dry land." ¹⁰ Moses said to Yahweh, "O Lord,ᶜ I am not eloquent, neither before now, nor since you have spoken to your servant; for I am slow of speech, and of a slow tongue." ¹¹ Yahweh said to him, "Who made man's mouth? Or who makes one mute, or deaf, or seeing, or blind? Isn't it I, Yahweh?" ¹² Now therefore go, and I will be with your mouth, and teach you what you shall speak." ¹³ Moses said, "Oh, Lord, please send someone else." ¹⁴ Yahweh's anger burned against Moses, and he said, "What about Aaron, your brother, the Levite? I know that he can speak well. Also, behold, he is coming out to meet you. When he sees you, he will be glad in his heart. ¹⁵ You shall speak to him, and put the words in his mouth. I will be with your mouth, and with his mouth, and will teach you what you shall do. ¹⁶ He will be your spokesman to the people. It will happen that he will be to you a mouth, and you will be to him as God. ¹⁷ You shall take this rod in your hand, with which you shall do the signs." ¹⁸ Moses went and returned to Jethro his father-in-law, and said to him, "Please let me go and return to my brothers who are in Egypt, and see whether they are still alive." Jethro said to Moses, "Go in peace." ¹⁹ Yahweh said to Moses in Midian, "Go, return into Egypt; for all the men who sought your life are dead." ²⁰ Moses took his wife and his sons, and set them on a donkey, and he returned to the land of Egypt. Moses took God's rod in his hand. ²¹ Yahweh said to Moses, "When you go back into Egypt, see that you do before Pharaoh all the wonders which I have put in your hand, but I will harden his heart and he will not let the people go. ²² You shall tell Pharaoh, 'Yahweh says, Israel is my son, my firstborn, ²³ and I have said to you, "Let my son go, that he may serve me;" and you have refused to let him go. Behold, I will kill your firstborn son.'" ²⁴ On the way at a lodging place, Yahweh met Moses and wanted to kill him. ²⁵ Then Zipporah took a flint, and cut off the foreskin of her son, and cast it at his feet; and she said, "Surely you are a bridegroom of blood to me." ²⁶ So he let him alone. Then she said, "You are a bridegroom of blood," because of the circumcision. ²⁷ Yahweh said to Aaron, "Go into the wilderness to meet Moses." He went, and met him on God's mountain, and kissed him. ²⁸ Moses told Aaron all Yahweh's words with which he had sent him, and all the signs with which he had instructed him. ²⁹ Moses and Aaron went and gathered together all the elders of the children of Israel. ³⁰ Aaron spoke all the words which Yahweh had spoken to Moses, and did the signs in the sight of the people. ³¹ The people believed, and when they heard that Yahweh had visited the children of Israel, and that he had seen their affliction, then they bowed their heads and worshiped.

## 5

¹ Afterward Moses and Aaron came, and said to Pharaoh, "This is what Yahweh, the God of Israel, says, 'Let my people go, that they may hold a feast to me in the wilderness.'" ² Pharaoh said, "Who is Yahweh, that I should listen to his voice to let Israel go? I don't know Yahweh, and moreover I will not let Israel go." ³ They said, "The God of the Hebrews has met with us. Please let us go three days' journey into the wilderness, and sacrifice to Yahweh, our God, lest he fall on us with pestilence, or with the sword." ⁴ The king of Egypt said to them, "Why do you, Moses and Aaron, take the people from their work? Get back to your burdens!" ⁵ Pharaoh said, "Behold, the people of the land are now many, and you make them rest from their burdens." ⁶ The same day Pharaoh commanded the taskmasters of the people and their officers, saying, ⁷ "You shall no longer give the people straw to make brick, as before. Let them go and gather straw for themselves. ⁸ You shall require from them the number of the bricks which they made before. You shall not diminish anything of it, for they are idle. Therefore they cry, saying, 'Let's go and sacrifice to our God.' ⁹ Let heavier work be laid on the men, that they may labor in it. Don't let them pay any attention to lying words." ¹⁰ The taskmasters of the people went out with their officers, and they spoke to the people, saying, "This is what Pharaoh says: 'I will not give you straw. ¹¹ Go yourselves, get straw where you can find it, for nothing of your work shall be diminished.'" ¹² So the people were scattered abroad throughout all the land of Egypt to gather stubble for straw. ¹³ The taskmasters were urgent saying, "Fulfill your work quota

---

ᵃ 2:22 "Gershom" sounds like the Hebrew for "an alien there".

ᵇ 3:2 "Yahweh" is God's proper Name, sometimes

rendered "LORD" (all caps) in other translations.

ᶜ 4:10 The word translated "Lord" is "Adonai".

daily, as when there was straw!" ¹⁴ The officers of the children of Israel, whom Pharaoh's taskmasters had set over them, were beaten, and asked, "Why haven't you fulfilled your quota both yesterday and today, in making brick as before?" ¹⁵ Then the officers of the children of Israel came and cried to Pharaoh, saying, "Why do you deal this way with your servants? ¹⁶ No straw is given to your servants, and they tell us, 'Make brick!' and behold, your servants are beaten; but the fault is in your own people." ¹⁷ But Pharaoh said, "You are idle! You are idle! Therefore you say, 'Let's go and sacrifice to Yahweh.' ¹⁸ Go therefore now, and work; for no straw shall be given to you; yet you shall deliver the same number of bricks!" ¹⁹ The officers of the children of Israel saw that they were in trouble when it was said, "You shall not diminish anything from your daily quota of bricks!" ²⁰ They met Moses and Aaron, who stood along the way, as they came out from Pharaoh. ²¹ They said to them, "May Yahweh look at you and judge, because you have made us a stench to be abhorred in the eyes of Pharaoh, and in the eyes of his servants, to put a sword in their hand to kill us!" ²² Moses returned to Yahweh, and said, "Lord, why have you brought trouble on this people? Why is it that you have sent me? ²³ For since I came to Pharaoh to speak in your name, he has brought trouble on this people. You have not rescued your people at all!"

## 6

¹ Yahweh said to Moses, "Now you shall see what I will do to Pharaoh, for by a strong hand he shall let them go, and by a strong hand he shall drive them out of his land." ² God spoke to Moses, and said to him, "I am Yahweh. ³ I appeared to Abraham, to Isaac, and to Jacob, as God Almighty; but by my name Yahweh I was not known to them. ⁴ I have also established my covenant with them, to give them the land of Canaan, the land of their travels, in which they lived as aliens. ⁵ Moreover I have heard the groaning of the children of Israel, whom the Egyptians keep in bondage, and I have remembered my covenant. ⁶ Therefore tell the children of Israel, 'I am Yahweh, and I will bring you out from under the burdens of the Egyptians, and I will rid you out of their bondage, and I will redeem you with an outstretched arm, and with great judgments. ⁷ I will take you to myself for a people. I will be your God; and you shall know that I am Yahweh your God, who brings you out from under the burdens of the Egyptians. ⁸ I will bring you into the land which I swore to give to Abraham, to Isaac, and to Jacob; and I will give it to you for a heritage: I am Yahweh.'" ⁹ Moses spoke so to the children of Israel, but they didn't listen to Moses for anguish of spirit, and for cruel bondage. ¹⁰ Yahweh spoke to Moses, saying, ¹¹"Go in, speak to Pharaoh king of Egypt, that he let the children of Israel go out of his land." ¹² Moses spoke before Yahweh, saying, "Behold, the children of Israel haven't listened to me. How then shall Pharaoh listen to me, when I have uncircumcised lips?" ¹³ Yahweh spoke to Moses and to Aaron, and gave them a command to the children of Israel, and to Pharaoh king of Egypt, to bring the children of Israel out of the land of Egypt. ¹⁴ These are the heads of their fathers' houses. The sons of Reuben the firstborn of Israel: Hanoch, and Pallu, Hezron, and Carmi; these are the families of Reuben. ¹⁵ The sons of Simeon: Jemuel, and Jamin, and Ohad, and Jachin, and Zohar, and Shaul the son of a Canaanite woman; these are the families of Simeon. ¹⁶ These are the names of the sons of Levi according to their generations: Gershon, and Kohath, and Merari; and the years of the life of Levi were one hundred thirty-seven years. ¹⁷ The sons of Gershon: Libni and Shimei, according to their families. ¹⁸ The sons of Kohath: Amram, and Izhar, and Hebron, and Uzziel; and the years of the life of Kohath were one hundred thirty-three years. ¹⁹ The sons of Merari: Mahli and Mushi. These are the families of the Levites according to their generations. ²⁰ Amram took Jochebed his father's sister to himself as wife; and she bore him Aaron and Moses. The years of the life of Amram were one hundred thirty-seven years. ²¹ The sons of Izhar: Korah, and Nepheg, and Zichri. ²² The sons of Uzziel: Mishael, Elzaphan, and Sithri. ²³ Aaron took Elisheba, the daughter of Amminadab, the sister of Nahshon, as his wife; and she bore him Nadab and Abihu, Eleazar and Ithamar. ²⁴ The sons of Korah: Assir, Elkanah, and Abiasaph; these are the families of the Korahites. ²⁵ Eleazar Aaron's son took one of the daughters of Putiel as his wife; and she bore him Phinehas. These are the heads of the fathers' houses of the Levites according to their families. ²⁶ These are that Aaron and Moses to whom Yahweh said, "Bring out the children of Israel from the land of Egypt according to their armies." ²⁷ These are those who spoke to Pharaoh king of Egypt, to bring out the children of Israel from Egypt. These are that Moses and Aaron. ²⁸ On the day when Yahweh spoke to Moses in the land of Egypt, ²⁹ Yahweh said to Moses, "I am Yahweh. Tell Pharaoh king of Egypt all that I tell you." ³⁰ Moses said before Yahweh, "Behold, I am of uncircumcised lips, and how shall Pharaoh listen to me?"

## 7

¹ Yahweh said to Moses, "Behold, I have made you as God to Pharaoh; and Aaron your brother shall be your prophet. ² You shall speak all that I command you; and Aaron your brother shall speak to Pharaoh, that he let the children of Israel go out of his land. ³ I will harden Pharaoh's heart, and multiply my signs and my wonders in the land of Egypt. ⁴ But Pharaoh will not listen to you, so I will lay my hand on Egypt, and bring out my armies, my people the children of Israel, out of the land of Egypt by great judgments. ⁵ The Egyptians shall know that I am Yahweh when I stretch out my hand on Egypt, and bring the children of Israel out from among them." ⁶ Moses and Aaron did so. As Yahweh commanded them, so they did. ⁷ Moses was eighty years old, and Aaron eighty-three years old, when they spoke to Pharaoh. ⁸ Yahweh spoke to Moses and to Aaron, saying, ⁹"When Pharaoh speaks to you, saying, 'Perform a miracle!' then you shall tell Aaron, 'Take your rod, and cast it down before Pharaoh, and it will become a serpent.'" ¹⁰ Moses and Aaron went in to Pharaoh, and they did so, as Yahweh had commanded. Aaron cast down his rod before Pharaoh and before his servants, and it became a serpent. ¹¹ Then Pharaoh also called for the wise men and the sorcerers. They also, the magicians of Egypt, did the same thing with their enchantments. ¹² For they each cast down their rods, and they became serpents; but Aaron's rod swallowed up their rods. ¹³ Pharaoh's heart was hardened, and he didn't listen to them, as Yahweh had spoken. ¹⁴ Yahweh said to Moses, "Pharaoh's heart is stubborn. He refuses to let the people go. ¹⁵ Go to Pharaoh in the morning. Behold, he is going out to the water. You shall stand by the river's bank to meet him. You shall take the rod which was turned to a serpent in your hand. ¹⁶ You shall tell him, 'Yahweh, the God of the Hebrews, has sent me to you, saying, "Let my people go, that they may serve me in the wilderness. Behold, until now you haven't listened." ¹⁷ Yahweh says, "In this you shall know that I am Yahweh. Behold: I will strike with the rod that is in my hand on the waters which are in the river, and they shall be turned to blood. ¹⁸ The fish that are in the river will die and the river will become foul. The Egyptians will loathe to drink water from the river."'" ¹⁹ Yahweh said to Moses, "Tell Aaron, 'Take your rod, and stretch out your hand over the waters of Egypt, over their rivers, over their streams, and over their pools, and over all their ponds of water, that they may become blood. There will be blood throughout all the land of Egypt, both in vessels of wood and in vessels of stone.'" ²⁰ Moses and Aaron did so, as Yahweh commanded; and he lifted up the rod, and struck the waters that were in the river, in the sight of Pharaoh, and in the sight of his servants; and all the waters that were in the river were turned to blood. ²¹ The fish that were in the river died. The river became foul. The Egyptians couldn't drink water from the river. The blood was throughout all the land of Egypt. ²² The magicians of Egypt did the same thing with their enchantments. So Pharaoh's heart was hardened, and he didn't listen to them, as Yahweh had spoken. ²³ Pharaoh turned and went into his house, and he didn't even take this to heart. ²⁴ All the Egyptians dug around the river for water to drink; for they couldn't drink the river water. ²⁵ Seven days were fulfilled, after Yahweh had struck the river.

## 8

¹ Yahweh spoke to Moses, "Go in to Pharaoh, and tell him, 'This is what Yahweh says, "Let my people go, that they may serve me. ² If you refuse to let them go, behold, I will plague all your borders with frogs. ³ The river will swarm with frogs, which will go up and come into your house, and into your bedroom, and on your bed, and into the house of your servants, and on your people, and into your ovens, and into your kneading troughs. ⁴ The frogs shall come up both on you, and on your people, and on all your servants."'" ⁵ Yahweh said to Moses, "Tell Aaron, 'Stretch out your hand with your rod over the rivers, over the streams, and over the pools, and cause frogs to come up on the land of Egypt.'" ⁶ Aaron stretched out his hand over the waters of Egypt; and the frogs came up, and covered the land of Egypt. ⁷ The magicians did the same thing with their enchantments, and brought up frogs on the land of Egypt. ⁸ Then Pharaoh called for Moses and Aaron, and said, "Entreat Yahweh, that he take away the frogs from me and from my people; and I will let the people go, that they may sacrifice to Yahweh." ⁹ Moses said to Pharaoh, "I give you the honor of setting the time that I should pray for you, and for your servants, and for your people, that the frogs be destroyed from you and your houses, and remain in the river only." ¹⁰ Pharaoh said, "Tomorrow." Moses said, "Let it be according to your word, that you may know that there is no one like Yahweh our God. ¹¹ The frogs shall depart from you, and from your houses, and from your servants, and from your people. They shall remain in the river only." ¹² Moses and Aaron went out from Pharaoh, and Moses cried to Yahweh concerning the frogs which he had brought on Pharaoh. ¹³ Yahweh did according to the word of Moses, and the frogs died out of the houses, out of the courts, and out of the fields. ¹⁴ They gathered them together in heaps, and the land stank. ¹⁵ But when Pharaoh saw that there was a respite, he hardened his heart, and didn't listen to them, as Yahweh had spoken. ¹⁶ Yahweh said to Moses, "Tell Aaron, 'Stretch out your rod, and strike the dust of the earth, that it may

become lice throughout all the land of Egypt.'" ¹⁷ They did so; and Aaron stretched out his hand with his rod, and struck the dust of the earth, and there were lice on man, and on animal; all the dust of the earth became lice throughout all the land of Egypt. ¹⁸ The magicians tried with their enchantments to produce lice, but they couldn't. There were lice on man, and on animal. ¹⁹ Then the magicians said to Pharaoh, "This is God's finger;" but Pharaoh's heart was hardened, and he didn't listen to them, as Yahweh had spoken. ²⁰ Yahweh said to Moses, "Rise up early in the morning, and stand before Pharaoh; behold, he comes out to the water; and tell him, 'This is what Yahweh says, "Let my people go, that they may serve me. ²¹ Else, if you will not let my people go, behold, I will send swarms of flies on you, and on your servants, and on your people, and into your houses. The houses of the Egyptians shall be full of swarms of flies, and also the ground they are on. ²² I will set apart in that day the land of Goshen, in which my people dwell, that no swarms of flies shall be there, to the end you may know that I am Yahweh on the earth. ²³ I will put a division between my people and your people. This sign shall happen by tomorrow."'" ²⁴ Yahweh did so; and there came grievous swarms of flies into the house of Pharaoh, and into his servants' houses. In all the land of Egypt the land was corrupted by reason of the swarms of flies. ²⁵ Pharaoh called for Moses and for Aaron, and said, "Go, sacrifice to your God in the land!" ²⁶ Moses said, "It isn't appropriate to do so; for we shall sacrifice the abomination of the Egyptians to Yahweh our God. Behold, if we sacrifice the abomination of the Egyptians before their eyes, won't they stone us? ²⁷ We will go three days' journey into the wilderness, and sacrifice to Yahweh our God, as he shall command us." ²⁸ Pharaoh said, "I will let you go, that you may sacrifice to Yahweh your God in the wilderness, only you shall not go very far away. Pray for me." ²⁹ Moses said, "Behold, I am going out from you. I will pray to Yahweh that the swarms of flies may depart from Pharaoh, from his servants, and from his people, tomorrow; only don't let Pharaoh deal deceitfully any more in not letting the people go to sacrifice to Yahweh." ³⁰ Moses went out from Pharaoh, and prayed to Yahweh. ³¹ Yahweh did according to the word of Moses, and he removed the swarms of flies from Pharaoh, from his servants, and from his people. There remained not one. ³² Pharaoh hardened his heart this time also, and he didn't let the people go.

## 9

¹ Then Yahweh said to Moses, "Go in to Pharaoh, and tell him, 'This is what Yahweh, the God of the Hebrews, says: "Let my people go, that they may serve me. ² For if you refuse to let them go, and hold them still, ³ behold, Yahweh's hand is on your livestock which are in the field, on the horses, on the donkeys, on the camels, on the herds, and on the flocks with a very grievous pestilence. ⁴ Yahweh will make a distinction between the livestock of Israel and the livestock of Egypt; and nothing shall die of all that belongs to the children of Israel."'" ⁵ Yahweh appointed a set time, saying, "Tomorrow Yahweh shall do this thing in the land." ⁶ Yahweh did that thing on the next day; and all the livestock of Egypt died, but of the livestock of the children of Israel, not one died. ⁷ Pharaoh sent, and, behold, there was not so much as one of the livestock of the Israelites dead. But the heart of Pharaoh was stubborn, and he didn't let the people go. ⁸ Yahweh said to Moses and to Aaron, "Take handfuls of ashes of the furnace, and let Moses sprinkle it toward the sky in the sight of Pharaoh. ⁹ It shall become small dust over all the land of Egypt, and shall be boils and blisters breaking out on man and on animal, throughout all the land of Egypt." ¹⁰ They took ashes of the furnace, and stood before Pharaoh; and Moses sprinkled it up toward the sky; and it became boils and blisters breaking out on man and on animal. ¹¹ The magicians couldn't stand before Moses because of the boils; for the boils were on the magicians and on all the Egyptians. ¹² Yahweh hardened the heart of Pharaoh, and he didn't listen to them, as Yahweh had spoken to Moses. ¹³ Yahweh said to Moses, "Rise up early in the morning, and stand before Pharaoh, and tell him, 'This is what Yahweh, the God of the Hebrews, says: "Let my people go, that they may serve me. ¹⁴ For this time I will send all my plagues against your heart, against your officials, and against your people; that you may know that there is no one like me in all the earth. ¹⁵ For now I would have stretched out my hand, and struck you and your people with pestilence, and you would have been cut off from the earth; ¹⁶ but indeed for this cause I have made you stand: to show you my power, and that my name may be declared throughout all the earth, ¹⁷ because you still exalt yourself against my people, that you won't let them go. ¹⁸ Behold, tomorrow about this time I will cause it to rain a very grievous hail, such as has not been in Egypt since the day it was founded even until now. ¹⁹ Now therefore command that all of your livestock and all that you have in the field be brought into shelter. The hail will come down on every man and animal that is found in the field, and isn't brought home, and they will die."'" ²⁰ Those who feared Yahweh's word among the servants of Pharaoh made their servants and their livestock flee into the houses. ²¹ Whoever didn't respect Yahweh's

word left his servants and his livestock in the field. ²² Yahweh said to Moses, "Stretch out your hand toward the sky, that there may be hail in all the land of Egypt, on man, and on animal, and on every herb of the field, throughout the land of Egypt." ²³ Moses stretched out his rod toward the heavens, and Yahweh sent thunder and hail; and lightning flashed down to the earth. Yahweh rained hail on the land of Egypt. ²⁴ So there was very severe hail, and lightning mixed with the hail, such as had not been in all the land of Egypt since it became a nation. ²⁵ The hail struck throughout all the land of Egypt all that was in the field, both man and animal; and the hail struck every herb of the field, and broke every tree of the field. ²⁶ Only in the land of Goshen, where the children of Israel were, there was no hail. ²⁷ Pharaoh sent and called for Moses and Aaron, and said to them, "I have sinned this time. Yahweh is righteous, and I and my people are wicked. ²⁸ Pray to Yahweh; for there has been enough of mighty thunderings and hail. I will let you go, and you shall stay no longer." ²⁹ Moses said to him, "As soon as I have gone out of the city, I will spread out my hands to Yahweh. The thunders shall cease, and there will not be any more hail; that you may know that the earth is Yahweh's. ³⁰ But as for you and your servants, I know that you don't yet fear Yahweh God." ³¹ The flax and the barley were struck, for the barley had ripened and the flax was blooming. ³² But the wheat and the spelt were not struck, for they had not grown up. ³³ Moses went out of the city from Pharaoh, and spread out his hands to Yahweh; and the thunders and hail ceased, and the rain was not poured on the earth. ³⁴ When Pharaoh saw that the rain and the hail and the thunders had ceased, he sinned yet more, and hardened his heart, he and his servants. ³⁵ The heart of Pharaoh was hardened, and he didn't let the children of Israel go, just as Yahweh had spoken through Moses.

## 10

¹ Yahweh said to Moses, "Go in to Pharaoh, for I have hardened his heart and the heart of his servants, that I may show these my signs among them; ² and that you may tell in the hearing of your son, and of your son's son, what things I have done to Egypt, and my signs which I have done among them; that you may know that I am Yahweh." ³ Moses and Aaron went in to Pharaoh, and said to him, "This is what Yahweh, the God of the Hebrews, says: 'How long will you refuse to humble yourself before me? Let my people go, that they may serve me. ⁴ Or else, if you refuse to let my people go, behold, tomorrow I will bring locusts into your country, ⁵ and they shall cover the surface of the earth, so that one won't be able to see the earth. They shall eat the residue of that which has escaped, which remains to you from the hail, and shall eat every tree which grows for you out of the field. ⁶ Your houses shall be filled, and the houses of all your servants, and the houses of all the Egyptians, as neither your fathers nor your fathers' fathers have seen, since the day that they were on the earth to this day.'" He turned, and went out from Pharaoh. ⁷ Pharaoh's servants said to him, "How long will this man be a snare to us? Let the men go, that they may serve Yahweh, their God. Don't you yet know that Egypt is destroyed?" ⁸ Moses and Aaron were brought again to Pharaoh, and he said to them, "Go, serve Yahweh your God; but who are those who will go?" ⁹ Moses said, "We will go with our young and with our old. We will go with our sons and with our daughters, with our flocks and with our herds; for we must hold a feast to Yahweh." ¹⁰ He said to them, "Yahweh be with you if I let you go with your little ones! See, evil is clearly before your faces. ¹¹ Not so! Go now you who are men, and serve Yahweh; for that is what you desire!" Then they were driven out from Pharaoh's presence. ¹² Yahweh said to Moses, "Stretch out your hand over the land of Egypt for the locusts, that they may come up on the land of Egypt, and eat every herb of the land, even all that the hail has left." ¹³ Moses stretched out his rod over the land of Egypt, and Yahweh brought an east wind on the land all that day, and all night; and when it was morning, the east wind brought the locusts. ¹⁴ The locusts went up over all the land of Egypt, and rested in all the borders of Egypt. They were very grievous. Before them there were no such locusts as they, nor will there ever be again. ¹⁵ For they covered the surface of the whole earth, so that the land was darkened, and they ate every herb of the land, and all the fruit of the trees which the hail had left. There remained nothing green, either tree or herb of the field, through all the land of Egypt. ¹⁶ Then Pharaoh called for Moses and Aaron in haste, and he said, "I have sinned against Yahweh your God, and against you. ¹⁷ Now therefore please forgive my sin again, and pray to Yahweh your God, that he may also take away from me this death." ¹⁸ Moses went out from Pharaoh, and prayed to Yahweh. ¹⁹ Yahweh sent an exceedingly strong west wind, which took up the locusts, and

drove them into the Red Sea.ᵃ There remained not one locust in all the borders of Egypt. ²⁰ But Yahweh hardened Pharaoh's heart, and he didn't let the children of Israel go. ²¹ Yahweh said to Moses, "Stretch out your hand toward the sky, that there may be darkness over the land of Egypt, even darkness which may be felt." ²² Moses stretched out his hand toward the sky, and there was a thick darkness in all the land of Egypt for three days. ²³ They didn't see one another, and nobody rose from his place for three days; but all the children of Israel had light in their dwellings. ²⁴ Pharaoh called to Moses, and said, "Go, serve Yahweh. Only let your flocks and your herds stay behind. Let your little ones also go with you." ²⁵ Moses said, "You must also give into our hand sacrifices and burnt offerings, that we may sacrifice to Yahweh our God. ²⁶ Our livestock also shall go with us. Not a hoof shall be left behind, for of it we must take to serve Yahweh our God; and we don't know with what we must serve Yahweh, until we come there." ²⁷ But Yahweh hardened Pharaoh's heart, and he wouldn't let them go. ²⁸ Pharaoh said to him, "Get away from me! Be careful to see my face no more; for in the day you see my face you shall die!" ²⁹ Moses said, "You have spoken well. I will see your face again no more."

## 11

¹ Yahweh said to Moses, "I will bring yet one more plague on Pharaoh, and on Egypt; afterwards he will let you go. When he lets you go, he will surely thrust you out altogether. ² Speak now in the ears of the people, and let every man ask of his neighbor, and every woman of her neighbor, jewels of silver, and jewels of gold." ³ Yahweh gave the people favor in the sight of the Egyptians. Moreover, the man Moses was very great in the land of Egypt, in the sight of Pharaoh's servants, and in the sight of the people. ⁴ Moses said, "This is what Yahweh says: 'About midnight I will go out into the middle of Egypt, ⁵ and all the firstborn in the land of Egypt shall die, from the firstborn of Pharaoh who sits on his throne, even to the firstborn of the female servant who is behind the mill, and all the firstborn of livestock. ⁶ There will be a great cry throughout all the land of Egypt, such as there has not been, nor will be any more. ⁷ But against any of the children of Israel a dog won't even bark or move its tongue, against man or animal, that you may know that Yahweh makes a distinction between the Egyptians and Israel. ⁸ All these servants of yours will come down to me, and bow down themselves to me, saying, "Get out, with all the people who follow you;" and after that I will go out.'" He went out from Pharaoh in hot anger. ⁹ Yahweh said to Moses, "Pharaoh won't listen to you, that my wonders may be multiplied in the land of Egypt." ¹⁰ Moses and Aaron did all these wonders before Pharaoh, but Yahweh hardened Pharaoh's heart, and he didn't let the children of Israel go out of his land.

## 12

¹ Yahweh spoke to Moses and Aaron in the land of Egypt, saying, ²"This month shall be to you the beginning of months. It shall be the first month of the year to you. ³ Speak to all the congregation of Israel, saying, 'On the tenth day of this month, they shall take to them every man a lamb, according to their fathers' houses, a lamb for a household; ⁴ and if the household is too little for a lamb, then he and his neighbor next to his house shall take one according to the number of the souls. You shall make your count for the lamb according to what everyone can eat. ⁵ Your lamb shall be without defect, a male a year old. You shall take it from the sheep or from the goats. ⁶ You shall keep it until the fourteenth day of the same month; and the whole assembly of the congregation of Israel shall kill it at evening. ⁷ They shall take some of the blood, and put it on the two door posts and on the lintel, on the houses in which they shall eat it. ⁸ They shall eat the meat in that night, roasted with fire, with unleavened bread. They shall eat it with bitter herbs. ⁹ Don't eat it raw, nor boiled at all with water, but roasted with fire; with its head, its legs and its inner parts. ¹⁰ You shall let nothing of it remain until the morning; but that which remains of it until the morning you shall burn with fire. ¹¹ This is how you shall eat it: with your belt on your waist, your sandals on your feet, and your staff in your hand; and you shall eat it in haste: it is Yahweh's Passover. ¹² For I will go through the land of Egypt in that night, and will strike all the firstborn in the land of Egypt, both man and animal. I will execute judgments against all the gods of Egypt. I am Yahweh. ¹³ The blood shall be to you for a token on the houses where you are. When I see the blood, I will pass over you, and no plague will be on you to destroy you when I strike the land of Egypt. ¹⁴ This day shall be a memorial for you. You shall keep it as a feast to Yahweh. You shall keep it as a feast throughout your generations by an ordinance forever. ¹⁵"Seven days you shall eat unleavened bread; even the first day you shall put away yeast out of your houses, for whoever eats leavened bread from the first

day until the seventh day, that soul shall be cut off from Israel. ¹⁶ In the first day there shall be to you a holy convocation, and in the seventh day a holy convocation; no kind of work shall be done in them, except that which every man must eat, only that may be done by you. ¹⁷ You shall observe the feast of unleavened bread; for in this same day I have brought your armies out of the land of Egypt. Therefore you shall observe this day throughout your generations by an ordinance forever. ¹⁸ In the first month, on the fourteenth day of the month at evening, you shall eat unleavened bread, until the twenty first day of the month at evening. ¹⁹ There shall be no yeast found in your houses for seven days, for whoever eats that which is leavened, that soul shall be cut off from the congregation of Israel, whether he is a foreigner, or one who is born in the land. ²⁰ You shall eat nothing leavened. In all your habitations you shall eat unleavened bread.'" ²¹ Then Moses called for all the elders of Israel, and said to them, "Draw out, and take lambs according to your families, and kill the Passover. ²² You shall take a bunch of hyssop, and dip it in the blood that is in the basin, and strike the lintel and the two door posts with the blood that is in the basin. None of you shall go out of the door of his house until the morning. ²³ For Yahweh will pass through to strike the Egyptians; and when he sees the blood on the lintel, and on the two door posts, Yahweh will pass over the door, and will not allow the destroyer to come in to your houses to strike you. ²⁴ You shall observe this thing for an ordinance to you and to your sons forever. ²⁵ It shall happen when you have come to the land which Yahweh will give you, as he has promised, that you shall keep this service. ²⁶ It will happen, when your children ask you, 'What do you mean by this service?' ²⁷ that you shall say, 'It is the sacrifice of Yahweh's Passover, who passed over the houses of the children of Israel in Egypt, when he struck the Egyptians, and spared our houses.'" The people bowed their heads and worshiped. ²⁸ The children of Israel went and did so; as Yahweh had commanded Moses and Aaron, so they did. ²⁹ At midnight, Yahweh struck all the firstborn in the land of Egypt, from the firstborn of Pharaoh who sat on his throne to the firstborn of the captive who was in the dungeon, and all the firstborn of livestock. ³⁰ Pharaoh rose up in the night, he, and all his servants, and all the Egyptians; and there was a great cry in Egypt, for there was not a house where there was not one dead. ³¹ He called for Moses and Aaron by night, and said, "Rise up, get out from among my people, both you and the children of Israel; and go, serve Yahweh, as you have said! ³² Take both your flocks and your herds, as you have said, and be gone; and bless me also!" ³³ The Egyptians were urgent with the people, to send them out of the land in haste, for they said, "We are all dead men." ³⁴ The people took their dough before it was leavened, their kneading troughs being bound up in their clothes on their shoulders. ³⁵ The children of Israel did according to the word of Moses; and they asked of the Egyptians jewels of silver, and jewels of gold, and clothing. ³⁶ Yahweh gave the people favor in the sight of the Egyptians, so that they let them have what they asked. They plundered the Egyptians. ³⁷ The children of Israel traveled from Rameses to Succoth, about six hundred thousand on foot who were men, in addition to children. ³⁸ A mixed multitude went up also with them, with flocks, herds, and even very much livestock. ³⁹ They baked unleavened cakes of the dough which they brought out of Egypt; for it wasn't leavened, because they were thrust out of Egypt, and couldn't wait, and they had not prepared any food for themselves. ⁴⁰ Now the time that the children of Israel lived in Egypt was four hundred thirty years. ⁴¹ At the end of four hundred thirty years, to the day, all of Yahweh's armies went out from the land of Egypt. ⁴² It is a night to be much observed to Yahweh for bringing them out from the land of Egypt. This is that night of Yahweh, to be much observed by all the children of Israel throughout their generations. ⁴³ Yahweh said to Moses and Aaron, "This is the ordinance of the Passover. No foreigner shall eat of it, ⁴⁴ but every man's servant who is bought for money, when you have circumcised him, then shall he eat of it. ⁴⁵ A foreigner and a hired servant shall not eat of it. ⁴⁶ It must be eaten in one house. You shall not carry any of the meat outside of the house. Do not break any of its bones. ⁴⁷ All the congregation of Israel shall keep it. ⁴⁸ When a stranger lives as a foreigner with you, and would like to keep the Passover to Yahweh, let all his males be circumcised, and then let him come near and keep it. He shall be as one who is born in the land; but no uncircumcised person shall eat of it. ⁴⁹ One law shall be to him who is born at home, and to the stranger who lives as a foreigner among you." ⁵⁰ All the children of Israel did so. As Yahweh commanded Moses and Aaron, so they did. ⁵¹ That same day, Yahweh brought the children of Israel out of the land of Egypt by their armies.

---

ᵃ *10:19* "Red Sea" is the translation for the Hebrew "Yam Suf", which could be more literally translated "Sea of Reeds" or "Sea of Cattails". It refers to the body of water currently known as the Red Sea, or possibly to one of the bodies of water connected to it or near it.

## 13

¹ Yahweh spoke to Moses, saying, ²"Sanctify to me all the firstborn, whatever opens the womb among the children of Israel, both of man and of animal. It is mine." ³ Moses said to the people, "Remember this day, in which you came out of Egypt, out of the house of bondage; for by strength of hand Yahweh brought you out from this place. No leavened bread shall be eaten. ⁴ Today you go out in the month Abib. ⁵ It shall be, when Yahweh brings you into the land of the Canaanite, and the Hittite, and the Amorite, and the Hivite, and the Jebusite, which he swore to your fathers to give you, a land flowing with milk and honey, that you shall keep this service in this month. ⁶ Seven days you shall eat unleavened bread, and in the seventh day shall be a feast to Yahweh. ⁷ Unleavened bread shall be eaten throughout the seven days; and no leavened bread shall be seen with you. No yeast shall be seen with you, within all your borders. ⁸ You shall tell your son in that day, saying, 'It is because of that which Yahweh did for me when I came out of Egypt.' ⁹ It shall be for a sign to you on your hand, and for a memorial between your eyes, that Yahweh's law may be in your mouth; for with a strong hand Yahweh has brought you out of Egypt. ¹⁰ You shall therefore keep this ordinance in its season from year to year. ¹¹"It shall be, when Yahweh brings you into the land of the Canaanite, as he swore to you and to your fathers, and will give it to you, ¹² that you shall set apart to Yahweh all that opens the womb, and every firstborn that comes from an animal which you have. The males shall be Yahweh's. ¹³ Every firstborn of a donkey you shall redeem with a lamb; and if you will not redeem it, then you shall break its neck; and you shall redeem all the firstborn of man among your sons. ¹⁴ It shall be, when your son asks you in time to come, saying, 'What is this?' that you shall tell him, 'By strength of hand Yahweh brought us out from Egypt, from the house of bondage. ¹⁵ When Pharaoh stubbornly refused to let us go, Yahweh killed all the firstborn in the land of Egypt, both the firstborn of man, and the firstborn of livestock. Therefore I sacrifice to Yahweh all that opens the womb, being males; but all the firstborn of my sons I redeem.' ¹⁶ It shall be for a sign on your hand, and for symbols between your eyes; for by strength of hand Yahweh brought us out of Egypt." ¹⁷ When Pharaoh had let the people go, God didn't lead them by the way of the land of the Philistines, although that was near; for God said, "Lest perhaps the people change their minds when they see war, and they return to Egypt"; ¹⁸ but God led the people around by the way of the wilderness by the Red Sea; and the children of Israel went up armed out of the land of Egypt. ¹⁹ Moses took the bones of Joseph with him, for he had made the children of Israel swear, saying, "God will surely visit you, and you shall carry up my bones away from here with you." ²⁰ They took their journey from Succoth, and encamped in Etham, in the edge of the wilderness. ²¹ Yahweh went before them by day in a pillar of cloud, to lead them on their way, and by night in a pillar of fire, to give them light, that they might go by day and by night: ²² the pillar of cloud by day, and the pillar of fire by night, didn't depart from before the people.

## 14

¹ Yahweh spoke to Moses, saying, ²"Speak to the children of Israel, that they turn back and encamp before Pihahiroth, between Migdol and the sea, before Baal Zephon. You shall encamp opposite it by the sea. ³ Pharaoh will say of the children of Israel, 'They are entangled in the land. The wilderness has shut them in.' ⁴ I will harden Pharaoh's heart, and he will follow after them; and I will get honor over Pharaoh, and over all his armies; and the Egyptians shall know that I am Yahweh." They did so. ⁵ The king of Egypt was told that the people had fled; and the heart of Pharaoh and of his servants was changed toward the people, and they said, "What is this we have done, that we have let Israel go from serving us?" ⁶ He prepared his chariot, and took his army with him; ⁷ and he took six hundred chosen chariots, and all the chariots of Egypt, with captains over all of them. ⁸ Yahweh hardened the heart of Pharaoh king of Egypt, and he pursued the children of Israel; for the children of Israel went out with a high hand.ᵃ ⁹ The Egyptians pursued them. All the horses and chariots of Pharaoh, his horsemen, and his army overtook them encamping by the sea, beside Pihahiroth, before Baal Zephon. ¹⁰ When Pharaoh came near, the children of Israel lifted up their eyes, and behold, the Egyptians were marching after them; and they were very afraid. The children of Israel cried out to Yahweh. ¹¹ They said to Moses, "Because there were no graves in Egypt, have you taken us away to die in the wilderness? Why have you treated us this way, to bring us out of Egypt? ¹² Isn't this the word that we spoke to you in Egypt, saying, 'Leave us alone, that we may serve the Egyptians'? For it would have been better for us to serve the Egyptians than to die in the wilderness." ¹³ Moses said to the people, "Don't be afraid. Stand still, and see the salvation of Yahweh, which he will work for you today; for you will never again see the Egyptians whom you

have seen today. ¹⁴ Yahweh will fight for you, and you shall be still." ¹⁵ Yahweh said to Moses, "Why do you cry to me? Speak to the children of Israel, that they go forward. ¹⁶ Lift up your rod, and stretch out your hand over the sea and divide it. Then the children of Israel shall go into the middle of the sea on dry ground. ¹⁷ Behold, I myself will harden the hearts of the Egyptians, and they will go in after them. I will get myself honor over Pharaoh, and over all his armies, over his chariots, and over his horsemen. ¹⁸ The Egyptians shall know that I am Yahweh when I have gotten myself honor over Pharaoh, over his chariots, and over his horsemen." ¹⁹ The angel of God, who went before the camp of Israel, moved and went behind them; and the pillar of cloud moved from before them, and stood behind them. ²⁰ It came between the camp of Egypt and the camp of Israel. There was the cloud and the darkness, yet it gave light by night. One didn't come near the other all night. ²¹ Moses stretched out his hand over the sea, and Yahweh caused the sea to go back by a strong east wind all night, and made the sea dry land, and the waters were divided. ²² The children of Israel went into the middle of the sea on the dry ground; and the waters were a wall to them on their right hand and on their left. ²³ The Egyptians pursued, and went in after them into the middle of the sea: all of Pharaoh's horses, his chariots, and his horsemen. ²⁴ In the morning watch, Yahweh looked out on the Egyptian army through the pillar of fire and of cloud, and confused the Egyptian army. ²⁵ He took off their chariot wheels, and they drove them heavily; so that the Egyptians said, "Let's flee from the face of Israel, for Yahweh fights for them against the Egyptians!" ²⁶ Yahweh said to Moses, "Stretch out your hand over the sea, that the waters may come again on the Egyptians, on their chariots, and on their horsemen." ²⁷ Moses stretched out his hand over the sea, and the sea returned to its strength when the morning appeared; and the Egyptians fled against it. Yahweh overthrew the Egyptians in the middle of the sea. ²⁸ The waters returned, and covered the chariots and the horsemen, even all Pharaoh's army that went in after them into the sea. There remained not so much as one of them. ²⁹ But the children of Israel walked on dry land in the middle of the sea, and the waters were a wall to them on their right hand and on their left. ³⁰ Thus Yahweh saved Israel that day out of the hand of the Egyptians; and Israel saw the Egyptians dead on the seashore. ³¹ Israel saw the great work which Yahweh did to the Egyptians, and the people feared Yahweh; and they believed in Yahweh and in his servant Moses.

## 15

¹ Then Moses and the children of Israel sang this song to Yahweh, and said, "I will sing to Yahweh, for he has triumphed gloriously. He has thrown the horse and his rider into the sea. ² Yah is my strength and song. He has become my salvation. This is my God, and I will praise him; my father's God, and I will exalt him. ³ Yahweh is a man of war. Yahweh is his name. ⁴ He has cast Pharaoh's chariots and his army into the sea. His chosen captains are sunk in the Red Sea. ⁵ The deeps cover them. They went down into the depths like a stone. ⁶ Your right hand, Yahweh, is glorious in power. Your right hand, Yahweh, dashes the enemy in pieces. ⁷ In the greatness of your excellency, you overthrow those who rise up against you. You send out your wrath. It consumes them as stubble. ⁸ With the blast of your nostrils, the waters were piled up. The floods stood upright as a heap. The deeps were congealed in the heart of the sea. ⁹ The enemy said, 'I will pursue. I will overtake. I will divide the plunder. My desire will be satisfied on them. I will draw my sword. My hand will destroy them.' ¹⁰ You blew with your wind. The sea covered them. They sank like lead in the mighty waters. ¹¹ Who is like you, Yahweh, among the gods? Who is like you, glorious in holiness, fearful in praises, doing wonders? ¹² You stretched out your right hand. The earth swallowed them. ¹³"You, in your loving kindness, have led the people that you have redeemed. You have guided them in your strength to your holy habitation. ¹⁴ The peoples have heard. They tremble. Pangs have taken hold of the inhabitants of Philistia. ¹⁵ Then the chiefs of Edom were dismayed. Trembling takes hold of the mighty men of Moab. All the inhabitants of Canaan have melted away. ¹⁶ Terror and dread falls on them. By the greatness of your arm they are as still as a stone, until your people pass over, Yahweh, until the people you have purchased pass over. ¹⁷ You will bring them in, and plant them in the mountain of your inheritance, the place, Yahweh, which you have made for yourself to dwell in: the sanctuary, Lord, which your hands have established. ¹⁸ Yahweh will reign forever and ever." ¹⁹ For the horses of Pharaoh went in with his chariots and with his horsemen into the sea, and Yahweh brought back the waters of the sea on them; but the children of Israel walked on dry land in the middle of the sea. ²⁰ Miriam the prophetess, the sister of Aaron, took a tambourine in her hand; and all the women went out after her with tambourines and with dances. ²¹ Miriam answered them, "Sing to Yahweh, for he has triumphed gloriously. He has thrown the horse and his rider into the

ᵃ 14:8 or, defiantly.

sea." ²² Moses led Israel onward from the Red Sea, and they went out into the wilderness of Shur; and they went three days in the wilderness, and found no water. ²³ When they came to Marah, they couldn't drink from the waters of Marah, for they were bitter. Therefore its name was called Marah.ᵃ ²⁴ The people murmured against Moses, saying, "What shall we drink?" ²⁵ Then he cried to Yahweh. Yahweh showed him a tree, and he threw it into the waters, and the waters were made sweet. There he made a statute and an ordinance for them, and there he tested them. ²⁶ He said, "If you will diligently listen to Yahweh your God's voice, and will do that which is right in his eyes, and will pay attention to his commandments, and keep all his statutes, I will put none of the diseases on you which I have put on the Egyptians; for I am Yahweh who heals you." ²⁷ They came to Elim, where there were twelve springs of water and seventy palm trees. They encamped there by the waters.

# 16

¹ They took their journey from Elim, and all the congregation of the children of Israel came to the wilderness of Sin, which is between Elim and Sinai, on the fifteenth day of the second month after their departing out of the land of Egypt. ² The whole congregation of the children of Israel murmured against Moses and against Aaron in the wilderness; ³ and the children of Israel said to them, "We wish that we had died by Yahweh's hand in the land of Egypt, when we sat by the meat pots, when we ate our fill of bread, for you have brought us out into this wilderness to kill this whole assembly with hunger." ⁴ Then Yahweh said to Moses, "Behold, I will rain bread from the sky for you, and the people shall go out and gather a day's portion every day, that I may test them, whether they will walk in my law or not. ⁵ It shall come to pass on the sixth day, that they shall prepare that which they bring in, and it shall be twice as much as they gather daily." ⁶ Moses and Aaron said to all the children of Israel, "At evening, you shall know that Yahweh has brought you out from the land of Egypt. ⁷ In the morning, you shall see Yahweh's glory; because he hears your murmurings against Yahweh. Who are we, that you murmur against us?" ⁸ Moses said, "Now Yahweh will give you meat to eat in the evening, and in the morning bread to satisfy you, because Yahweh hears your murmurings which you murmur against him. And who are we? Your murmurings are not against us, but against Yahweh." ⁹ Moses said to Aaron, "Tell all the congregation of the children of Israel, 'Come close to Yahweh, for he has heard your murmurings.'" ¹⁰ As Aaron spoke to the whole congregation of the children of Israel, they looked toward the wilderness, and behold, Yahweh's glory appeared in the cloud. ¹¹ Yahweh spoke to Moses, saying, ¹²"I have heard the murmurings of the children of Israel. Speak to them, saying, 'At evening you shall eat meat, and in the morning you shall be filled with bread. Then you will know that I am Yahweh your God.'" ¹³ In the evening, quail came up and covered the camp; and in the morning the dew lay around the camp. ¹⁴ When the dew that lay had gone, behold, on the surface of the wilderness was a small round thing, small as the frost on the ground. ¹⁵ When the children of Israel saw it, they said to one another, "What is it?" For they didn't know what it was. Moses said to them, "It is the bread which Yahweh has given you to eat. ¹⁶ This is the thing which Yahweh has commanded: 'Gather of it everyone according to his eating; an omerᵇ a head, according to the number of your persons, you shall take it, every man for those who are in his tent.'" ¹⁷ The children of Israel did so, and some gathered more, some less. ¹⁸ When they measured it with an omer, he who gathered much had nothing over, and he who gathered little had no lack. They each gathered according to his eating. ¹⁹ Moses said to them, "Let no one leave of it until the morning." ²⁰ Notwithstanding they didn't listen to Moses, but some of them left of it until the morning, so it bred worms and became foul; and Moses was angry with them. ²¹ They gathered it morning by morning, everyone according to his eating. When the sun grew hot, it melted. ²² On the sixth day, they gathered twice as much bread, two omers for each one; and all the rulers of the congregation came and told Moses. ²³ He said to them, "This is that which Yahweh has spoken, 'Tomorrow is a solemn rest, a holy Sabbath to Yahweh. Bake that which you want to bake, and boil that which you want to boil; and all that remains over lay up for yourselves to be kept until the morning.'" ²⁴ They laid it up until the morning, as Moses ordered, and it didn't become foul, and there were no worms in it. ²⁵ Moses said, "Eat that today, for today is a Sabbath to Yahweh. Today you shall not find it in the field. ²⁶ Six days you shall gather it, but on the seventh day is the Sabbath. In it there shall be none." ²⁷ On the seventh day, some of the people went out to gather, and they found none. ²⁸ Yahweh said to Moses, "How long do

you refuse to keep my commandments and my laws? ²⁹ Behold, because Yahweh has given you the Sabbath, therefore he gives you on the sixth day the bread of two days. Everyone stay in his place. Let no one go out of his place on the seventh day." ³⁰ So the people rested on the seventh day. ³¹ The house of Israel called its name "Manna",ᶜ and it was like coriander seed, white; and its taste was like wafers with honey. ³² Moses said, "This is the thing which Yahweh has commanded, 'Let an omer-full of it be kept throughout your generations, that they may see the bread with which I fed you in the wilderness, when I brought you out of the land of Egypt.'" ³³ Moses said to Aaron, "Take a pot, and put an omer-full of manna in it, and lay it up before Yahweh, to be kept throughout your generations." ³⁴ As Yahweh commanded Moses, so Aaron laid it up before the Testimony, to be kept. ³⁵ The children of Israel ate the manna forty years, until they came to an inhabited land. They ate the manna until they came to the borders of the land of Canaan. ³⁶ Now an omer is one tenth of an ephah.ᵈ

# 17

¹ All the congregation of the children of Israel traveled from the wilderness of Sin, starting according to Yahweh's commandment, and encamped in Rephidim; but there was no water for the people to drink. ² Therefore the people quarreled with Moses, and said, "Give us water to drink." Moses said to them, "Why do you quarrel with me? Why do you test Yahweh?" ³ The people were thirsty for water there; so the people murmured against Moses, and said, "Why have you brought us up out of Egypt, to kill us, our children, and our livestock with thirst?" ⁴ Moses cried to Yahweh, saying, "What shall I do with these people? They are almost ready to stone me." ⁵ Yahweh said to Moses, "Walk on before the people, and take the elders of Israel with you, and take the rod in your hand with which you struck the Nile, and go. ⁶ Behold, I will stand before you there on the rock in Horeb. You shall strike the rock, and water will come out of it, that the people may drink." Moses did so in the sight of the elders of Israel. ⁷ He called the name of the place Massah,ᵉ and Meribah,ᶠ because the children of Israel quarreled, and because they tested Yahweh, saying, "Is Yahweh among us, or not?" ⁸ Then Amalek came and fought with Israel in Rephidim. ⁹ Moses said to Joshua, "Choose men for us, and go out to fight with Amalek. Tomorrow I will stand on the top of the hill with God's rod in my hand." ¹⁰ So Joshua did as Moses had told him, and fought with Amalek; and Moses, Aaron, and Hur went up to the top of the hill. ¹¹ When Moses held up his hand, Israel prevailed. When he let down his hand, Amalek prevailed. ¹² But Moses' hands were heavy; so they took a stone, and put it under him, and he sat on it. Aaron and Hur held up his hands, the one on the one side, and the other on the other side. His hands were steady until sunset. ¹³ Joshua defeated Amalek and his people with the edge of the sword. ¹⁴ Yahweh said to Moses, "Write this for a memorial in a book, and rehearse it in the ears of Joshua: that I will utterly blot out the memory of Amalek from under the sky." ¹⁵ Moses built an altar, and called its name "Yahweh our Banner".ᵍ ¹⁶ He said, "Yah has sworn: 'Yahweh will have war with Amalek from generation to generation.'"

# 18

¹ Now Jethro, the priest of Midian, Moses' father-in-law, heard of all that God had done for Moses and for Israel his people, how Yahweh had brought Israel out of Egypt. ² Jethro, Moses' father-in-law, received Zipporah, Moses' wife, after he had sent her away, ³ and her two sons. The name of one son was Gershom,ʰ for Moses said, "I have lived as a foreigner in a foreign land". ⁴ The name of the other was Eliezer,ⁱ for he said, "My father's God was my help and delivered me from Pharaoh's sword." ⁵ Jethro, Moses' father-in-law, came with Moses' sons and his wife to Moses into the wilderness where he was encamped, at the Mountain of God. ⁶ He said to Moses, "I, your father-in-law Jethro, have come to you with your wife, and her two sons with her." ⁷ Moses went out to meet his father-in-law, and bowed and kissed him. They asked each other of their welfare, and they came into the tent. ⁸ Moses told his father-in-law all that Yahweh had done to Pharaoh and to the Egyptians for Israel's sake, all the hardships that had come on them on the way, and how Yahweh delivered them. ⁹ Jethro rejoiced for all the goodness which Yahweh had done to Israel, in that he had delivered them out of the hand of the Egyptians. ¹⁰ Jethro said, "Blessed be Yahweh, who has delivered you out of the hand of the Egyptians, and out of the hand of Pharaoh; who has delivered the people from under the hand of the Egyptians. ¹¹ Now I know that Yahweh is greater than all gods because of the way that they treated people arrogantly." ¹² Jethro, Moses' father-in-law, took a burnt offering and sacrifices for God. Aaron came with all the elders of Israel, to eat bread with Moses'

---

ᵃ *15:23* Marah means bitter.
ᵇ *16:16* An omer is about 2.2 liters or about 2.3 quarts
ᶜ *16:31* "Manna" means "What is it?"

ᵈ *16:36* 1 ephah is about 22 liters or about 2/3 of a bushel
ᵉ *17:7* Massah means testing.
ᶠ *17:7* Meribah means quarreling.

ᵍ *17:15* Hebrew, Yahweh Nissi
ʰ *18:3* "Gershom" sounds like the Hebrew for "an alien there".

ⁱ *18:4* Eliezer means "God is my helper".

father-in-law before God. [13] On the next day, Moses sat to judge the people, and the people stood around Moses from the morning to the evening. [14] When Moses' father-in-law saw all that he did to the people, he said, "What is this thing that you do for the people? Why do you sit alone, and all the people stand around you from morning to evening?" [15] Moses said to his father-in-law, "Because the people come to me to inquire of God. [16] When they have a matter, they come to me, and I judge between a man and his neighbor, and I make them know the statutes of God, and his laws." [17] Moses' father-in-law said to him, "The thing that you do is not good. [18] You will surely wear away, both you, and this people that is with you; for the thing is too heavy for you. You are not able to perform it yourself alone. [19] Listen now to my voice. I will give you counsel, and God be with you. You represent the people before God, and bring the causes to God. [20] You shall teach them the statutes and the laws, and shall show them the way in which they must walk, and the work that they must do. [21] Moreover you shall provide out of all the people able men which fear God: men of truth, hating unjust gain; and place such over them, to be rulers of thousands, rulers of hundreds, rulers of fifties, and rulers of tens. [22] Let them judge the people at all times. It shall be that every great matter they shall bring to you, but every small matter they shall judge themselves. So shall it be easier for you, and they shall share the load with you. [23] If you will do this thing, and God commands you so, then you will be able to endure, and all these people also will go to their place in peace." [24] So Moses listened to the voice of his father-in-law, and did all that he had said. [25] Moses chose able men out of all Israel, and made them heads over the people, rulers of thousands, rulers of hundreds, rulers of fifties, and rulers of tens. [26] They judged the people at all times. They brought the hard cases to Moses, but every small matter they judged themselves. [27] Moses let his father-in-law depart, and he went his way into his own land.

## 19

[1] In the third month after the children of Israel had gone out of the land of Egypt, on that same day they came into the wilderness of Sinai. [2] When they had departed from Rephidim, and had come to the wilderness of Sinai, they encamped in the wilderness; and there Israel encamped before the mountain. [3] Moses went up to God, and Yahweh called to him out of the mountain, saying, "This is what you shall tell the house of Jacob, and tell the children of Israel: [4] 'You have seen what I did to the Egyptians, and how I bore you on eagles' wings, and brought you to myself. [5] Now therefore, if you will indeed obey my voice and keep my covenant, then you shall be my own possession from among all peoples; for all the earth is mine; [6] and you shall be to me a kingdom of priests and a holy nation.' These are the words which you shall speak to the children of Israel." [7] Moses came and called for the elders of the people, and set before them all these words which Yahweh commanded him. [8] All the people answered together, and said, "All that Yahweh has spoken we will do." Moses reported the words of the people to Yahweh. [9] Yahweh said to Moses, "Behold, I come to you in a thick cloud, that the people may hear when I speak with you, and may also believe you forever." Moses told the words of the people to Yahweh. [10] Yahweh said to Moses, "Go to the people, and sanctify them today and tomorrow, and let them wash their garments, [11] and be ready for the third day; for on the third day Yahweh will come down in the sight of all the people on Mount Sinai. [12] You shall set bounds to the people all around, saying, 'Be careful that you don't go up onto the mountain, or touch its border. Whoever touches the mountain shall be surely put to death. [13] No hand shall touch him, but he shall surely be stoned or shot through; whether it is animal or man, he shall not live.' When the trumpet sounds long, they shall come up to the mountain." [14] Moses went down from the mountain to the people, and sanctified the people; and they washed their clothes. [15] He said to the people, "Be ready by the third day. Don't have sexual relations with a woman." [16] On the third day, when it was morning, there were thunders and lightnings, and a thick cloud on the mountain, and the sound of an exceedingly loud trumpet; and all the people who were in the camp trembled. [17] Moses led the people out of the camp to meet God; and they stood at the lower part of the mountain. [18] All of Mount Sinai smoked, because Yahweh descended on it in fire; and its smoke ascended like the smoke of a furnace, and the whole mountain quaked greatly. [19] When the sound of the trumpet grew louder and louder, Moses spoke, and God answered him by a voice. [20] Yahweh came down on Mount Sinai, to the top of the mountain. Yahweh called Moses to the top of the mountain, and Moses went up. [21] Yahweh said to Moses, "Go down, warn the people, lest they break through to Yahweh to gaze, and many of them perish. [22] Let the priests also, who come near to

Yahweh, sanctify themselves, lest Yahweh break out on them." [23] Moses said to Yahweh, "The people can't come up to Mount Sinai, for you warned us, saying, 'Set bounds around the mountain, and sanctify it.'" [24] Yahweh said to him, "Go down! You shall bring Aaron up with you, but don't let the priests and the people break through to come up to Yahweh, lest he break out against them." [25] So Moses went down to the people, and told them.

## 20

[1] God[a] spoke all these words, saying, [2] "I am Yahweh your God, who brought you out of the land of Egypt, out of the house of bondage. [3] "You shall have no other gods before me. [4] "You shall not make for yourselves an idol, nor any image of anything that is in the heavens above, or that is in the earth beneath, or that is in the water under the earth: [5] you shall not bow yourself down to them, nor serve them, for I, Yahweh your God, am a jealous God, visiting the iniquity of the fathers on the children, on the third and on the fourth generation of those who hate me, [6] and showing loving kindness to thousands of those who love me and keep my commandments. [7] "You shall not misuse the name of Yahweh your God,[b] for Yahweh will not hold him guiltless who misuses his name. [8] "Remember the Sabbath day, to keep it holy. [9] You shall labor six days, and do all your work, [10] but the seventh day is a Sabbath to Yahweh your God. You shall not do any work in it, you, nor your son, nor your daughter, your male servant, nor your female servant, nor your livestock, nor your stranger who is within your gates; [11] for in six days Yahweh made heaven and earth, the sea, and all that is in them, and rested the seventh day; therefore Yahweh blessed the Sabbath day, and made it holy. [12] "Honor your father and your mother, that your days may be long in the land which Yahweh your God gives you. [13] "You shall not murder. [14] "You shall not commit adultery. [15] "You shall not steal. [16] "You shall not give false testimony against your neighbor. [17] "You shall not covet your neighbor's house. You shall not covet your neighbor's wife, nor his male servant, nor his female servant, nor his ox, nor his donkey, nor anything that is your neighbor's." [18] All the people perceived the thunderings, the lightnings, the sound of the trumpet, and the mountain smoking. When the people saw it, they trembled, and stayed at a distance. [19] They said to Moses, "Speak with us yourself, and we will listen; but don't let God speak with us, lest we die." [20] Moses said to the people, "Don't be afraid, for God has come to test you, and that his fear may be before you, that you won't sin." [21] The people stayed at a distance, and Moses came near to the thick darkness where God was. [22] Yahweh said to Moses, "This is what you shall tell the children of Israel: 'You yourselves have seen that I have talked with you from heaven. [23] You shall most certainly not make gods of silver or gods of gold for yourselves to be alongside me. [24] You shall make an altar of earth for me, and shall sacrifice on it your burnt offerings and your peace offerings, your sheep and your cattle. In every place where I record my name I will come to you and I will bless you. [25] If you make me an altar of stone, you shall not build it of cut stones; for if you lift up your tool on it, you have polluted it. [26] You shall not go up by steps to my altar, that your nakedness may not be exposed to it.'

## 21

[1] "Now these are the ordinances which you shall set before them: [2] "If you buy a Hebrew servant, he shall serve six years, and in the seventh he shall go out free without paying anything. [3] If he comes in by himself, he shall go out by himself. If he is married, then his wife shall go out with him. [4] If his master gives him a wife and she bears him sons or daughters, the wife and her children shall be her master's, and he shall go out by himself. [5] But if the servant shall plainly say, 'I love my master, my wife, and my children. I will not go out free;' [6] then his master shall bring him to God, and shall bring him to the door or to the doorpost, and his master shall bore his ear through with an awl, and he shall serve him forever. [7] "If a man sells his daughter to be a female servant, she shall not go out as the male servants do. [8] If she doesn't please her master, who has married her to himself, then he shall let her be redeemed. He shall have no right to sell her to a foreign people, since he has dealt deceitfully with her. [9] If he marries her to his son, he shall deal with her as a daughter. [10] If he takes another wife to himself, he shall not diminish her food, her clothing, and her marital rights. [11] If he doesn't do these three things for her, she may go free without paying any money. [12] "One who strikes a man so that he dies shall surely be put to death, [13] but not if it is unintentional, but God allows it to happen; then I will appoint you a place where he shall flee. [14] If a man schemes and comes presumptuously on his neighbor to kill him, you shall take him from my altar, that he may die. [15] "Anyone who attacks his father or his mother shall be surely put to death. [16] "Anyone who kidnaps

---

[a] *20:1* After "God", the Hebrew has the two letters "Aleph Tav" (the first and last letters of the Hebrew alphabet), not as a word, but as a grammatical marker.

[b] *20:7* or, You shall not take the name of Yahweh your God in vain

someone and sells him, or if he is found in his hand, he shall surely be put to death. [17]"Anyone who curses his father or his mother shall surely be put to death. [18]"If men quarrel and one strikes the other with a stone, or with his fist, and he doesn't die, but is confined to bed; [19] if he rises again and walks around with his staff, then he who struck him shall be cleared; only he shall pay for the loss of his time, and shall provide for his healing until he is thoroughly healed. [20]"If a man strikes his servant or his maid with a rod, and he dies under his hand, the man shall surely be punished. [21] Notwithstanding, if his servant gets up after a day or two, he shall not be punished, for the servant is his property. [22]"If men fight and hurt a pregnant woman so that she gives birth prematurely, and yet no harm follows, he shall be surely fined as much as the woman's husband demands and the judges allow. [23] But if any harm follows, then you must take life for life, [24] eye for eye, tooth for tooth, hand for hand, foot for foot, [25] burning for burning, wound for wound, and bruise for bruise. [26]"If a man strikes his servant's eye, or his maid's eye, and destroys it, he shall let him go free for his eye's sake. [27] If he strikes out his male servant's tooth, or his female servant's tooth, he shall let the servant go free for his tooth's sake. [28]"If a bull gores a man or a woman to death, the bull shall surely be stoned, and its meat shall not be eaten; but the owner of the bull shall not be held responsible. [29] But if the bull had a habit of goring in the past, and this has been testified to its owner, and he has not kept it in, but it has killed a man or a woman, the bull shall be stoned, and its owner shall also be put to death. [30] If a ransom is imposed on him, then he shall give for the redemption of his life whatever is imposed. [31] Whether it has gored a son or has gored a daughter, according to this judgment it shall be done to him. [32] If the bull gores a male servant or a female servant, thirty shekels[a] of silver shall be given to their master, and the ox shall be stoned. [33]"If a man opens a pit, or if a man digs a pit and doesn't cover it, and a bull or a donkey falls into it, [34] the owner of the pit shall make it good. He shall give money to its owner, and the dead animal shall be his. [35]"If one man's bull injures another's, so that it dies, then they shall sell the live bull, and divide its price; and they shall also divide the dead animal. [36] Or if it is known that the bull was in the habit of goring in the past, and its owner has not kept it in, he shall surely pay bull for bull, and the dead animal shall be his own.

## 22

[1]"If a man steals an ox or a sheep, and kills it or sells it, he shall pay five oxen for an ox, and four sheep for a sheep. [2] If the thief is found breaking in, and is struck so that he dies, there shall be no guilt of bloodshed for him. [3] If the sun has risen on him, he is guilty of bloodshed. He shall make restitution. If he has nothing, then he shall be sold for his theft. [4] If the stolen property is found in his hand alive, whether it is ox, donkey, or sheep, he shall pay double. [5]"If a man causes a field or vineyard to be eaten by letting his animal loose, and it grazes in another man's field, he shall make restitution from the best of his own field, and from the best of his own vineyard. [6]"If fire breaks out, and catches in thorns so that the shocks of grain, or the standing grain, or the field are consumed; he who kindled the fire shall surely make restitution. [7]"If a man delivers to his neighbor money or stuff to keep, and it is stolen out of the man's house, if the thief is found, he shall pay double. [8] If the thief isn't found, then the master of the house shall come near to God, to find out whether or not he has put his hand on his neighbor's goods. [9] For every matter of trespass, whether it is for ox, for donkey, for sheep, for clothing, or for any kind of lost thing, about which one says, 'This is mine,' the cause of both parties shall come before God. He whom God condemns shall pay double to his neighbor. [10]"If a man delivers to his neighbor a donkey, an ox, a sheep, or any animal to keep, and it dies or is injured, or driven away, no man seeing it; [11] the oath of Yahweh shall be between them both, he has not put his hand on his neighbor's goods; and its owner shall accept it, and he shall not make restitution. [12] But if it is stolen from him, the one who stole shall make restitution to its owner. [13] If it is torn in pieces, let him bring it for evidence. He shall not make good that which was torn. [14]"If a man borrows anything of his neighbor's, and it is injured, or dies, its owner not being with it, he shall surely make restitution. [15] If its owner is with it, he shall not make it good. If it is a leased thing, it came for its lease. [16]"If a man entices a virgin who isn't pledged to be married, and lies with her, he shall surely pay a dowry for her to be his wife. [17] If her father utterly refuses to give her to him, he shall pay money according to the dowry of virgins. [18]"You shall not allow a sorceress to live. [19]"Whoever has sex with an animal shall surely be put to death. [20]"He who sacrifices to any god, except to Yahweh only, shall be utterly destroyed. [21]"You shall not wrong an alien or oppress him, for you were aliens in the land of Egypt. [22]"You shall not take advantage of any widow or fatherless child. [23] If you take advantage of them at all, and

they cry at all to me, I will surely hear their cry; [24] and my wrath will grow hot, and I will kill you with the sword; and your wives shall be widows, and your children fatherless. [25]"If you lend money to any of my people with you who is poor, you shall not be to him as a creditor. You shall not charge him interest. [26] If you take your neighbor's garment as collateral, you shall restore it to him before the sun goes down, [27] for that is his only covering, it is his garment for his skin. What would he sleep in? It will happen, when he cries to me, that I will hear, for I am gracious. [28]"You shall not blaspheme God, nor curse a ruler of your people. [29]"You shall not delay to offer from your harvest and from the outflow of your presses. "You shall give the firstborn of your sons to me. [30] You shall do likewise with your cattle and with your sheep. It shall be with its mother seven days, then on the eighth day you shall give it to me. [31]"You shall be holy men to me, therefore you shall not eat any meat that is torn by animals in the field. You shall cast it to the dogs.

## 23

[1]"You shall not spread a false report. Don't join your hand with the wicked to be a malicious witness. [2]"You shall not follow a crowd to do evil. You shall not testify in court to side with a multitude to pervert justice. [3] You shall not favor a poor man in his cause. [4]"If you meet your enemy's ox or his donkey going astray, you shall surely bring it back to him again. [5] If you see the donkey of him who hates you fallen down under his burden, don't leave him. You shall surely help him with it. [6]"You shall not deny justice to your poor people in their lawsuits. [7]"Keep far from a false charge, and don't kill the innocent and righteous; for I will not justify the wicked. [8]"You shall take no bribe, for a bribe blinds those who have sight and perverts the words of the righteous. [9]"You shall not oppress an alien, for you know the heart of an alien, since you were aliens in the land of Egypt. [10]"For six years you shall sow your land, and shall gather in its increase, [11] but the seventh year you shall let it rest and lie fallow, that the poor of your people may eat; and what they leave the animal of the field shall eat. In the same way, you shall deal with your vineyard and with your olive grove. [12]"Six days you shall do your work, and on the seventh day you shall rest, that your ox and your donkey may have rest, and the son of your servant, and the alien may be refreshed. [13]"Be careful to do all things that I have said to you; and don't invoke the name of other gods or even let them be heard out of your mouth. [14]"You shall observe a feast to me three times a year. [15] You shall observe the feast of unleavened bread. Seven days you shall eat unleavened bread, as I commanded you, at the time appointed in the month Abib (for in it you came out of Egypt), and no one shall appear before me empty. [16] And the feast of harvest, the first fruits of your labors, which you sow in the field; and the feast of ingathering, at the end of the year, when you gather in your labors out of the field. [17] Three times in the year all your males shall appear before the Lord Yahweh. [18]"You shall not offer the blood of my sacrifice with leavened bread. The fat of my feast shall not remain all night until the morning. [19] You shall bring the first of the first fruits of your ground into the house of Yahweh your God. "You shall not boil a young goat in its mother's milk. [20]"Behold, I send an angel before you, to keep you by the way, and to bring you into the place which I have prepared. [21] Pay attention to him, and listen to his voice. Don't provoke him, for he will not pardon your disobedience, for my name is in him. [22] But if you indeed listen to his voice, and do all that I speak, then I will be an enemy to your enemies, and an adversary to your adversaries. [23] For my angel shall go before you, and bring you in to the Amorite, the Hittite, the Perizzite, the Canaanite, the Hivite, and the Jebusite; and I will cut them off. [24] You shall not bow down to their gods, nor serve them, nor follow their practices, but you shall utterly overthrow them and demolish their pillars. [25] You shall serve Yahweh your God, and he will bless your bread and your water, and I will take sickness away from among you. [26] No one will miscarry or be barren in your land. I will fulfill the number of your days. [27] I will send my terror before you, and will confuse all the people to whom you come, and I will make all your enemies turn their backs to you. [28] I will send the hornet before you, which will drive out the Hivite, the Canaanite, and the Hittite, from before you. [29] I will not drive them out from before you in one year, lest the land become desolate, and the animals of the field multiply against you. [30] Little by little I will drive them out from before you, until you have increased and inherit the land. [31] I will set your border from the Red Sea even to the sea of the Philistines, and from the wilderness to the River; for I will deliver the inhabitants of the land into your hand, and you shall drive them out before you. [32] You shall make no covenant with them, nor with their gods. [33] They shall not dwell in your land, lest they make you sin against me, for if you serve their gods, it will surely be a snare to you."

---

[a] *21:32* A shekel is about 10 grams or about 0.35 ounces, so | 30 shekels is about 300 grams or about 10.6 ounces.

## 24

[1] He said to Moses, "Come up to Yahweh, you, and Aaron, Nadab, and Abihu, and seventy of the elders of Israel; and worship from a distance. [2] Moses alone shall come near to Yahweh, but they shall not come near. The people shall not go up with him." [3] Moses came and told the people all Yahweh's words, and all the ordinances; and all the people answered with one voice, and said, "All the words which Yahweh has spoken will we do." [4] Moses wrote all Yahweh's words, then rose up early in the morning and built an altar at the base of the mountain, with twelve pillars for the twelve tribes of Israel. [5] He sent young men of the children of Israel, who offered burnt offerings and sacrificed peace offerings of cattle to Yahweh. [6] Moses took half of the blood and put it in basins, and half of the blood he sprinkled on the altar. [7] He took the book of the covenant and read it in the hearing of the people, and they said, "We will do all that Yahweh has said, and be obedient." [8] Moses took the blood, and sprinkled it on the people, and said, "Look, this is the blood of the covenant, which Yahweh has made with you concerning all these words." [9] Then Moses, Aaron, Nadab, Abihu, and seventy of the elders of Israel went up. [10] They saw the God of Israel. Under his feet was like a paved work of sapphire[a] stone, like the skies for clearness. [11] He didn't lay his hand on the nobles of the children of Israel. They saw God, and ate and drank. [12] Yahweh said to Moses, "Come up to me on the mountain, and stay here, and I will give you the stone tablets with the law and the commands that I have written, that you may teach them." [13] Moses rose up with Joshua, his servant, and Moses went up onto God's Mountain. [14] He said to the elders, "Wait here for us, until we come again to you. Behold, Aaron and Hur are with you. Whoever is involved in a dispute can go to them." [15] Moses went up on the mountain, and the cloud covered the mountain. [16] Yahweh's glory settled on Mount Sinai, and the cloud covered it six days. The seventh day he called to Moses out of the middle of the cloud. [17] The appearance of Yahweh's glory was like devouring fire on the top of the mountain in the eyes of the children of Israel. [18] Moses entered into the middle of the cloud, and went up on the mountain; and Moses was on the mountain forty days and forty nights.

## 25

[1] Yahweh spoke to Moses, saying, [2] "Speak to the children of Israel, that they take an offering for me. From everyone whose heart makes him willing you shall take my offering. [3] This is the offering which you shall take from them: gold, silver, bronze, [4] blue, purple, scarlet, fine linen, goats' hair, [5] rams' skins dyed red, sea cow hides,[b] acacia wood, [6] oil for the light, spices for the anointing oil and for the sweet incense, [7] onyx stones, and stones to be set for the ephod and for the breastplate. [8] Let them make me a sanctuary, that I may dwell among them. [9] According to all that I show you, the pattern of the tabernacle, and the pattern of all of its furniture, even so you shall make it. [10] "They shall make an ark of acacia wood. Its length shall be two and a half cubits,[c] its width a cubit and a half, and a cubit and a half its height. [11] You shall overlay it with pure gold. You shall overlay it inside and outside, and you shall make a gold molding around it. [12] You shall cast four rings of gold for it, and put them in its four feet. Two rings shall be on the one side of it, and two rings on the other side of it. [13] You shall make poles of acacia wood, and overlay them with gold. [14] You shall put the poles into the rings on the sides of the ark to carry the ark. [15] The poles shall be in the rings of the ark. They shall not be taken from it. [16] You shall put the covenant which I shall give you into the ark. [17] You shall make a mercy seat of pure gold. Two and a half cubits shall be its length, and a cubit and a half its width. [18] You shall make two cherubim of hammered gold. You shall make them at the two ends of the mercy seat. [19] Make one cherub at the one end, and one cherub at the other end. You shall make the cherubim on its two ends of one piece with the mercy seat. [20] The cherubim shall spread out their wings upward, covering the mercy seat with their wings, with their faces toward one another. The faces of the cherubim shall be toward the mercy seat. [21] You shall put the mercy seat on top of the ark, and in the ark you shall put the covenant that I will give you. [22] There I will meet with you, and I will tell you from above the mercy seat, from between the two cherubim which are on the ark of the covenant, all that I command you for the children of Israel. [23] "You shall make a table of acacia wood. Its length shall be two cubits, and its width a cubit, and its height one and a half cubits. [24] You shall overlay it with pure gold, and make a gold molding around it. [25] You shall make a rim of a hand width around it. You shall make a golden molding on its rim around it. [26] You shall make four rings of gold for it, and put the rings in the four corners that

are on its four feet. [27] The rings shall be close to the rim, for places for the poles to carry the table. [28] You shall make the poles of acacia wood, and overlay them with gold, that the table may be carried with them. [29] You shall make its dishes, its spoons, its ladles, and its bowls with which to pour out offerings. You shall make them of pure gold. [30] You shall set bread of the presence on the table before me always. [31] "You shall make a lamp stand of pure gold. The lamp stand shall be made of hammered work. Its base, its shaft, its cups, its buds, and its flowers shall be of one piece with it. [32] There shall be six branches going out of its sides: three branches of the lamp stand out of its one side, and three branches of the lamp stand out of its other side; [33] three cups made like almond blossoms in one branch, a bud and a flower; and three cups made like almond blossoms in the other branch, a bud and a flower, so for the six branches going out of the lamp stand; [34] and in the lamp stand four cups made like almond blossoms, its buds and its flowers; [35] and a bud under two branches of one piece with it, and a bud under two branches of one piece with it, and a bud under two branches of one piece with it, for the six branches going out of the lamp stand. [36] Their buds and their branches shall be of one piece with it, all of it one beaten work of pure gold. [37] You shall make its lamps seven, and they shall light its lamps to give light to the space in front of it. [38] Its snuffers and its snuff dishes shall be of pure gold. [39] It shall be made of a talent[d] of pure gold, with all these accessories. [40] See that you make them after their pattern, which has been shown to you on the mountain.

## 26

[1] "Moreover you shall make the tabernacle with ten curtains of fine twined linen, and blue, and purple, and scarlet, with cherubim. You shall make them with the work of a skillful workman. [2] The length of each curtain shall be twenty-eight cubits,[e] and the width of each curtain four cubits: all the curtains shall have one measure. [3] Five curtains shall be coupled together to one another, and the other five curtains shall be coupled to one another. [4] You shall make loops of blue on the edge of the one curtain from the edge in the coupling, and you shall do likewise on the edge of the curtain that is outermost in the second coupling. [5] You shall make fifty loops in the one curtain, and you shall make fifty loops in the edge of the curtain that is in the second coupling. The loops shall be opposite one another. [6] You shall make fifty clasps of gold, and couple the curtains to one another with the clasps. The tabernacle shall be a unit. [7] "You shall make curtains of goats' hair for a covering over the tabernacle. You shall make eleven curtains. [8] The length of each curtain shall be thirty cubits, and the width of each curtain four cubits: the eleven curtains shall have one measure. [9] You shall couple five curtains by themselves, and six curtains by themselves, and shall double over the sixth curtain in the forefront of the tent. [10] You shall make fifty loops on the edge of the one curtain that is outermost in the coupling, and fifty loops on the edge of the curtain which is outermost in the second coupling. [11] You shall make fifty clasps of bronze, and put the clasps into the loops, and couple the tent together, that it may be one. [12] The overhanging part that remains of the curtains of the tent—the half curtain that remains—shall hang over the back of the tabernacle. [13] The cubit on the one side and the cubit on the other side, of that which remains in the length of the curtains of the tent, shall hang over the sides of the tabernacle on this side and on that side, to cover it. [14] You shall make a covering for the tent of rams' skins dyed red, and a covering of sea cow hides above. [15] "You shall make the boards for the tabernacle of acacia wood, standing upright. [16] Ten cubits shall be the length of a board, and one and a half cubits the width of each board. [17] There shall be two tenons in each board, joined to one another: thus you shall make for all the boards of the tabernacle. [18] You shall make twenty boards for the tabernacle, for the south side southward. [19] You shall make forty sockets of silver under the twenty boards; two sockets under one board for its two tenons, and two sockets under another board for its two tenons. [20] For the second side of the tabernacle, on the north side, twenty boards, [21] and their forty sockets of silver; two sockets under one board, and two sockets under another board. [22] For the far side of the tabernacle westward you shall make six boards. [23] You shall make two boards for the corners of the tabernacle in the far side. [24] They shall be double beneath, and in the same way they shall be whole to its top to one ring: thus shall it be for them both; they shall be for the two corners. [25] There shall be eight boards, and their sockets of silver, sixteen sockets; two sockets under one board, and two sockets under another board. [26] "You shall make bars of acacia wood: five for the boards of the one side of the tabernacle, [27] and five bars for the boards of the other side of the tabernacle, and five bars for the boards of the

[a] *24:10 or, lapis lazuli*
[b] *25:5 or, fine leather*
[c] *25:10 A cubit is the length from the tip of the middle finger to the elbow on a man's arm, or about 18 inches or 46 centimeters.*
[d] *25:39 A talent is about 30 kilograms or 66 pounds or 965 Troy ounces*
[e] *26:2 A cubit is the length from the tip of the middle finger to the elbow on a man's arm, or about 18 inches or 46 centimeters.*

side of the tabernacle, for the far side westward. ²⁸ The middle bar in the middle of the boards shall pass through from end to end. ²⁹ You shall overlay the boards with gold, and make their rings of gold for places for the bars. You shall overlay the bars with gold. ³⁰ You shall set up the tabernacle according to the way that it was shown to you on the mountain. ³¹"You shall make a veil of blue, and purple, and scarlet, and fine twined linen, with cherubim. It shall be the work of a skillful workman. ³² You shall hang it on four pillars of acacia overlaid with gold; their hooks shall be of gold, on four sockets of silver. ³³ You shall hang up the veil under the clasps, and shall bring the ark of the covenant in there within the veil. The veil shall separate the holy place from the most holy for you. ³⁴ You shall put the mercy seat on the ark of the covenant in the most holy place. ³⁵ You shall set the table outside the veil, and the lamp stand opposite the table on the side of the tabernacle toward the south. You shall put the table on the north side. ³⁶"You shall make a screen for the door of the Tent, of blue, and purple, and scarlet, and fine twined linen, the work of the embroiderer. ³⁷ You shall make for the screen five pillars of acacia, and overlay them with gold. Their hooks shall be of gold. You shall cast five sockets of bronze for them.

## 27

¹"You shall make the altar of acacia wood, five cubits^a long, and five cubits wide. The altar shall be square. Its height shall be three cubits.^b ² You shall make its horns on its four corners. Its horns shall be of one piece with it. You shall overlay it with bronze. ³ You shall make its pots to take away its ashes; and its shovels, its basins, its meat hooks, and its fire pans. You shall make all its vessels of bronze. ⁴ You shall make a grating for it of network of bronze. On the net you shall make four bronze rings in its four corners. ⁵ You shall put it under the ledge around the altar beneath, that the net may reach halfway up the altar. ⁶ You shall make poles for the altar, poles of acacia wood, and overlay them with bronze. ⁷ Its poles shall be put into the rings, and the poles shall be on the two sides of the altar when carrying it. ⁸ You shall make it hollow with planks. They shall make it as it has been shown you on the mountain. ⁹"You shall make the court of the tabernacle: for the south side southward there shall be hangings for the court of fine twined linen one hundred cubits long for one side. ¹⁰ Its pillars shall be twenty, and their sockets twenty, of bronze. The hooks of the pillars and their fillets shall be of silver. ¹¹ Likewise for the length of the north side, there shall be hangings one hundred cubits long, and its pillars twenty, and their sockets twenty, of bronze; the hooks of the pillars, and their fillets, of silver. ¹² For the width of the court on the west side shall be hangings of fifty cubits; their pillars ten, and their sockets ten. ¹³ The width of the court on the east side eastward shall be fifty cubits. ¹⁴ The hangings for the one side of the gate shall be fifteen cubits; their pillars three, and their sockets three. ¹⁵ For the other side shall be hangings of fifteen cubits; their pillars three, and their sockets three. ¹⁶ For the gate of the court shall be a screen of twenty cubits, of blue, and purple, and scarlet, and fine twined linen, the work of the embroiderer; their pillars four, and their sockets four. ¹⁷ All the pillars of the court around shall be filleted with silver; their hooks of silver, and their sockets of bronze. ¹⁸ The length of the court shall be one hundred cubits, and the width fifty throughout, and the height five cubits, of fine twined linen, and their sockets of bronze. ¹⁹ All the instruments of the tabernacle in all its service, and all its pins, and all the pins of the court, shall be of bronze. ²⁰"You shall command the children of Israel, that they bring to you pure olive oil beaten for the light, to cause a lamp to burn continually. ²¹ In the Tent of Meeting, outside the veil which is before the covenant, Aaron and his sons shall keep it in order from evening to morning before Yahweh: it shall be a statute forever throughout their generations on the behalf of the children of Israel.

## 28

¹"Bring Aaron your brother, and his sons with him, near to you from among the children of Israel, that he may minister to me in the priest's office: Aaron, with Nadab, Abihu, Eleazar, and Ithamar, Aaron's sons. ² You shall make holy garments for Aaron your brother, for glory and for beauty. ³ You shall speak to all who are wise-hearted, whom I have filled with the spirit of wisdom, that they make Aaron's garments to sanctify him, that he may minister to me in the priest's office. ⁴ These are the garments which they shall make: a breastplate, an ephod, a robe, a fitted tunic, a turban, and a sash. They shall make holy garments for Aaron your brother and his sons, that he may minister to me in the priest's office. ⁵ They shall use the gold, and the blue, and the purple, and the scarlet, and the fine linen. ⁶"They shall make the ephod of gold, blue, purple, scarlet, and fine twined linen, the work of the skillful

workman. ⁷ It shall have two shoulder straps joined to the two ends of it, that it may be joined together. ⁸ The skillfully woven band, which is on it, shall be like its work and of the same piece; of gold, blue, purple, scarlet, and fine twined linen. ⁹ You shall take two onyx stones, and engrave on them the names of the children of Israel. ¹⁰ Six of their names on the one stone, and the names of the six that remain on the other stone, in the order of their birth. ¹¹ With the work of an engraver in stone, like the engravings of a signet, you shall engrave the two stones, according to the names of the children of Israel. You shall make them to be enclosed in settings of gold. ¹² You shall put the two stones on the shoulder straps of the ephod, to be stones of memorial for the children of Israel. Aaron shall bear their names before Yahweh on his two shoulders for a memorial. ¹³ You shall make settings of gold, ¹⁴ and two chains of pure gold; you shall make them like cords of braided work. You shall put the braided chains on the settings. ¹⁵"You shall make a breastplate of judgment, the work of the skillful workman; like the work of the ephod you shall make it; of gold, of blue, and purple, and scarlet, and fine twined linen, you shall make it. ¹⁶ It shall be square and folded double; a span^c shall be its length, and a span its width. ¹⁷ You shall set in it settings of stones, four rows of stones: a row of ruby, topaz, and beryl shall be the first row; ¹⁸ and the second row a turquoise, a sapphire,^d and an emerald; ¹⁹ and the third row a jacinth, an agate, and an amethyst; ²⁰ and the fourth row a chrysolite, an onyx, and a jasper. They shall be enclosed in gold in their settings. ²¹ The stones shall be according to the names of the children of Israel, twelve, according to their names; like the engravings of a signet, everyone according to his name, they shall be for the twelve tribes. ²² You shall make on the breastplate chains like cords, of braided work of pure gold. ²³ You shall make on the breastplate two rings of gold, and shall put the two rings on the two ends of the breastplate. ²⁴ You shall put the two braided chains of gold in the two rings at the ends of the breastplate. ²⁵ The other two ends of the two braided chains you shall put on the two settings, and put them on the shoulder straps of the ephod in its forepart. ²⁶ You shall make two rings of gold, and you shall put them on the two ends of the breastplate, on its edge, which is toward the side of the ephod inward. ²⁷ You shall make two rings of gold, and shall put them on the two shoulder straps of the ephod underneath, in its forepart, close by its coupling, above the skillfully woven band of the ephod. ²⁸ They shall bind the breastplate by its rings to the rings of the ephod with a lace of blue, that it may be on the skillfully woven band of the ephod, and that the breastplate may not swing out from the ephod. ²⁹ Aaron shall bear the names of the children of Israel in the breastplate of judgment on his heart, when he goes in to the holy place, for a memorial before Yahweh continually. ³⁰ You shall put in the breastplate of judgment the Urim and the Thummim; and they shall be on Aaron's heart, when he goes in before Yahweh. Aaron shall bear the judgment of the children of Israel on his heart before Yahweh continually. ³¹"You shall make the robe of the ephod all of blue. ³² It shall have a hole for the head in the middle of it. It shall have a binding of woven work around its hole, as it were the hole of a coat of mail, that it not be torn. ³³ On its hem you shall make pomegranates of blue, and of purple, and of scarlet, all around its hem; with bells of gold between and around them: ³⁴ a golden bell and a pomegranate, a golden bell and a pomegranate, around the hem of the robe. ³⁵ It shall be on Aaron to minister: and its sound shall be heard when he goes in to the holy place before Yahweh, and when he comes out, that he not die. ³⁶"You shall make a plate of pure gold, and engrave on it, like the engravings of a signet, 'HOLY TO YAHWEH.' ³⁷ You shall put it on a lace of blue, and it shall be on the sash. It shall be on the front of the sash. ³⁸ It shall be on Aaron's forehead, and Aaron shall bear the iniquity of the holy things, which the children of Israel shall make holy in all their holy gifts; and it shall be always on his forehead, that they may be accepted before Yahweh. ³⁹ You shall weave the tunic with fine linen. You shall make a turban of fine linen. You shall make a sash, the work of the embroiderer. ⁴⁰"You shall make tunics for Aaron's sons. You shall make sashes for them. You shall make headbands for them, for glory and for beauty. ⁴¹ You shall put them on Aaron your brother, and on his sons with him, and shall anoint them, and consecrate them, and sanctify them, that they may minister to me in the priest's office. ⁴² You shall make them linen pants to cover their naked flesh. They shall reach from the waist even to the thighs. ⁴³ They shall be on Aaron and on his sons, when they go in to the Tent of Meeting, or when they come near to the altar to minister in the holy place, that they don't bear iniquity, and die. This shall be a statute forever to him and to his offspring after him.

---

^a *27:1 A cubit is the length from the tip of the middle finger to the elbow on a man's arm, or about 18 inches or 46 centimeters.*

^b *27:1 The altar was to be about 2.3 × 2.3 × 1.4 meters or about 7½ × 7½ × 4½ feet.*

^c *28:16 A span is the length from the tip of a man's thumb* to the tip of his little finger when his hand is stretched out (about half a cubit, or 9 inches, or 22.8 cm.)

^d *28:18 or, lapis lazuli*

## 29

¹"This is the thing that you shall do to them to make them holy, to minister to me in the priest's office: take one young bull and two rams without defect, ² unleavened bread, unleavened cakes mixed with oil, and unleavened wafers anointed with oil. You shall make them of fine wheat flour. ³ You shall put them into one basket, and bring them in the basket, with the bull and the two rams. ⁴ You shall bring Aaron and his sons to the door of the Tent of Meeting, and shall wash them with water. ⁵ You shall take the garments, and put on Aaron the tunic, the robe of the ephod, the ephod, and the breastplate, and clothe him with the skillfully woven band of the ephod. ⁶ You shall set the turban on his head, and put the holy crown on the turban. ⁷ Then you shall take the anointing oil, and pour it on his head, and anoint him. ⁸ You shall bring his sons, and put tunics on them. ⁹ You shall clothe them with belts, Aaron and his sons, and bind headbands on them. They shall have the priesthood by a perpetual statute. You shall consecrate Aaron and his sons. ¹⁰"You shall bring the bull before the Tent of Meeting; and Aaron and his sons shall lay their hands on the head of the bull. ¹¹ You shall kill the bull before Yahweh at the door of the Tent of Meeting. ¹² You shall take of the blood of the bull, and put it on the horns of the altar with your finger; and you shall pour out all the blood at the base of the altar. ¹³ You shall take all the fat that covers the innards, the cover of the liver, the two kidneys, and the fat that is on them, and burn them on the altar. ¹⁴ But the meat of the bull, and its skin, and its dung, you shall burn with fire outside of the camp. It is a sin offering. ¹⁵"You shall also take the one ram, and Aaron and his sons shall lay their hands on the head of the ram. ¹⁶ You shall kill the ram, and you shall take its blood, and sprinkle it around on the altar. ¹⁷ You shall cut the ram into its pieces, and wash its innards, and its legs, and put them with its pieces, and with its head. ¹⁸ You shall burn the whole ram on the altar: it is a burnt offering to Yahweh; it is a pleasant aroma, an offering made by fire to Yahweh. ¹⁹"You shall take the other ram, and Aaron and his sons shall lay their hands on the head of the ram. ²⁰ Then you shall kill the ram, and take some of its blood, and put it on the tip of the right ear of Aaron, and on the tip of the right ear of his sons, and on the thumb of their right hand, and on the big toe of their right foot; and sprinkle the blood around on the altar. ²¹ You shall take of the blood that is on the altar, and of the anointing oil, and sprinkle it on Aaron, and on his garments, and on his sons, and on the garments of his sons with him: and he shall be made holy, and his garments, and his sons, and his sons' garments with him. ²² Also you shall take some of the ram's fat, the fat tail, the fat that covers the innards, the cover of the liver, the two kidneys, the fat that is on them, and the right thigh (for it is a ram of consecration), ²³ and one loaf of bread, one cake of oiled bread, and one wafer out of the basket of unleavened bread that is before Yahweh. ²⁴ You shall put all of this in Aaron's hands, and in his sons' hands, and shall wave them for a wave offering before Yahweh. ²⁵ You shall take them from their hands, and burn them on the altar on the burnt offering, for a pleasant aroma before Yahweh: it is an offering made by fire to Yahweh. ²⁶"You shall take the breast of Aaron's ram of consecration, and wave it for a wave offering before Yahweh. It shall be your portion. ²⁷ You shall sanctify the breast of the wave offering and the thigh of the wave offering, which is waved, and which is raised up, of the ram of consecration, even of that which is for Aaron, and of that which is for his sons. ²⁸ It shall be for Aaron and his sons as their portion forever from the children of Israel; for it is a wave offering. It shall be a wave offering from the children of Israel of the sacrifices of their peace offerings, even their wave offering to Yahweh. ²⁹"The holy garments of Aaron shall be for his sons after him, to be anointed in them, and to be consecrated in them. ³⁰ Seven days shall the son who is priest in his place put them on, when he comes into the Tent of Meeting to minister in the holy place. ³¹"You shall take the ram of consecration and boil its meat in a holy place. ³² Aaron and his sons shall eat the meat of the ram, and the bread that is in the basket, at the door of the Tent of Meeting. ³³ They shall eat those things with which atonement was made, to consecrate and sanctify them; but a stranger shall not eat of it, because they are holy. ³⁴ If anything of the meat of the consecration, or of the bread, remains to the morning, then you shall burn the remainder with fire. It shall not be eaten, because it is holy. ³⁵"You shall do so to Aaron and to his sons, according to all that I have commanded you. You shall consecrate them seven days. ³⁶ Every day you shall offer the bull of sin offering for atonement. You shall cleanse the altar when you make atonement for it. You shall anoint it, to sanctify it. ³⁷ Seven days you shall make atonement for the altar, and sanctify it; and the altar shall be most holy. Whatever touches the altar shall be holy. ³⁸"Now this is that which you shall offer on the altar: two lambs a year old day by day continually. ³⁹ The one lamb you shall offer in the morning; and the other lamb you shall offer at evening; ⁴⁰ and with the one lamb a tenth part of an ephahᵃ of fine flour mixed with the fourth part of a hinᵇ of beaten oil, and the fourth part of a hin of wine for a drink offering. ⁴¹ The other lamb you shall offer at evening, and shall do to it according to the meal offering of the morning and according to its drink offering, for a pleasant aroma, an offering made by fire to Yahweh. ⁴² It shall be a continual burnt offering throughout your generations at the door of the Tent of Meeting before Yahweh, where I will meet with you, to speak there to you. ⁴³ There I will meet with the children of Israel; and the place shall be sanctified by my glory. ⁴⁴ I will sanctify the Tent of Meeting and the altar. I will also sanctify Aaron and his sons to minister to me in the priest's office. ⁴⁵ I will dwell among the children of Israel, and will be their God. ⁴⁶ They shall know that I am Yahweh their God, who brought them out of the land of Egypt, that I might dwell among them: I am Yahweh their God.

## 30

¹"You shall make an altar to burn incense on. You shall make it of acacia wood. ² Its length shall be a cubit,ᶜ and its width a cubit. It shall be square, and its height shall be two cubits. Its horns shall be of one piece with it. ³ You shall overlay it with pure gold, its top, its sides around it, and its horns; and you shall make a gold molding around it. ⁴ You shall make two golden rings for it under its molding; on its two ribs, on its two sides you shall make them; and they shall be for places for poles with which to bear it. ⁵ You shall make the poles of acacia wood, and overlay them with gold. ⁶ You shall put it before the veil that is by the ark of the covenant, before the mercy seat that is over the covenant, where I will meet with you. ⁷ Aaron shall burn incense of sweet spices on it every morning. When he tends the lamps, he shall burn it. ⁸ When Aaron lights the lamps at evening, he shall burn it, a perpetual incense before Yahweh throughout your generations. ⁹ You shall offer no strange incense on it, nor burnt offering, nor meal offering; and you shall pour no drink offering on it. ¹⁰ Aaron shall make atonement on its horns once in the year; with the blood of the sin offering of atonement once in the year he shall make atonement for it throughout your generations. It is most holy to Yahweh." ¹¹ Yahweh spoke to Moses, saying, ¹²"When you take a census of the children of Israel, according to those who are counted among them, then each man shall give a ransom for his soul to Yahweh when you count them, that there be no plague among them when you count them. ¹³ They shall give this, everyone who passes over to those who are counted, half a shekel according to the shekelᵈ of the sanctuary (the shekel is twenty gerahsᵉ); half a shekel for an offering to Yahweh. ¹⁴ Everyone who passes over to those who are counted, from twenty years old and upward, shall give the offering to Yahweh. ¹⁵ The rich shall not give more, and the poor shall not give less, than the half shekel,ᶠ when they give the offering of Yahweh, to make atonement for your souls. ¹⁶ You shall take the atonement money from the children of Israel, and shall appoint it for the service of the Tent of Meeting; that it may be a memorial for the children of Israel before Yahweh, to make atonement for your souls." ¹⁷ Yahweh spoke to Moses, saying, ¹⁸"You shall also make a basin of bronze, and its base of bronze, in which to wash. You shall put it between the Tent of Meeting and the altar, and you shall put water in it. ¹⁹ Aaron and his sons shall wash their hands and their feet in it. ²⁰ When they go into the Tent of Meeting, they shall wash with water, that they not die; or when they come near to the altar to minister, to burn an offering made by fire to Yahweh. ²¹ So they shall wash their hands and their feet, that they not die. This shall be a statute forever to them, even to him and to his descendants throughout their generations." ²² Moreover Yahweh spoke to Moses, saying, ²³"Also take fine spices: of liquid myrrh, five hundred shekels;ᵍ and of fragrant cinnamon half as much, even two hundred and fifty; and of fragrant cane, two hundred and fifty; ²⁴ and of cassia five hundred, according to the shekel of the sanctuary; and a hinʰ of olive oil. ²⁵ You shall make it into a holy anointing oil, a perfume compounded after the art of the perfumer: it shall be a holy anointing oil. ²⁶ You shall use it to anoint the Tent of Meeting, the ark of the covenant, ²⁷ the table and all its articles, the lamp stand and its accessories, the altar of incense, ²⁸ the altar of burnt offering with all its utensils, and the basin with its base. ²⁹ You shall sanctify them, that they may be most holy. Whatever touches them shall be holy. ³⁰ You shall anoint Aaron and his sons, and sanctify them, that they may minister to me in the priest's office. ³¹ You shall speak to the

---

ᵃ *29:40* 1 ephah is about 22 liters or about 2/3 of a bushel
ᵇ *29:40* A hin is about 6.5 liters or 1.7 gallons, so a fourth of a hin is about 1.6 liters.

ᶜ *30:2* A cubit is the length from the tip of the middle finger to the elbow on a man's arm, or about 18 inches or 46 centimeters.

ᵈ *30:13* A shekel is about 10 grams or about 0.35 ounces.
ᵉ *30:13* a gerah is about 0.5 grams or about 7.7 grains
ᶠ *30:15* A shekel is about 10 grams or about 0.35 ounces.

ᵍ *30:23* A shekel is about 10 grams or about 0.35 ounces, so 500 shekels is about 5 kilograms or about 11 pounds.
ʰ *30:24* A hin is about 6.5 liters or 1.7 gallons.

children of Israel, saying, 'This shall be a holy anointing oil to me throughout your generations. ³² It shall not be poured on man's flesh, and do not make any like it, according to its composition. It is holy. It shall be holy to you. ³³ Whoever compounds any like it, or whoever puts any of it on a stranger, he shall be cut off from his people.'" ³⁴ Yahweh said to Moses, "Take to yourself sweet spices, gum resin, onycha, and galbanum: sweet spices with pure frankincense. There shall be an equal weight of each. ³⁵ You shall make incense of it, a perfume after the art of the perfumer, seasoned with salt, pure and holy. ³⁶ You shall beat some of it very small, and put some of it before the covenant in the Tent of Meeting, where I will meet with you. It shall be to you most holy. ³⁷ You shall not make this incense, according to its composition, for yourselves: it shall be to you holy for Yahweh. ³⁸ Whoever shall make any like that, to smell of it, he shall be cut off from his people."

## 31

¹ Yahweh spoke to Moses, saying, ²"Behold, I have called by name Bezalel the son of Uri, the son of Hur, of the tribe of Judah. ³ I have filled him with the Spirit of God, in wisdom, and in understanding, and in knowledge, and in all kinds of workmanship, ⁴ to devise skillful works, to work in gold, and in silver, and in bronze, ⁵ and in cutting of stones for setting, and in carving of wood, to work in all kinds of workmanship. ⁶ Behold, I myself have appointed with him Oholiab, the son of Ahisamach, of the tribe of Dan; and in the heart of all who are wise-hearted I have put wisdom, that they may make all that I have commanded you: ⁷ the Tent of Meeting, the ark of the covenant, the mercy seat that is on it, all the furniture of the Tent, ⁸ the table and its vessels, the pure lamp stand with all its vessels, the altar of incense, ⁹ the altar of burnt offering with all its vessels, the basin and its base, ¹⁰ the finely worked garments—the holy garments for Aaron the priest, the garments of his sons to minister in the priest's office— ¹¹ the anointing oil, and the incense of sweet spices for the holy place: according to all that I have commanded you they shall do." ¹² Yahweh spoke to Moses, saying, ¹³"Speak also to the children of Israel, saying, 'Most certainly you shall keep my Sabbaths; for it is a sign between me and you throughout your generations, that you may know that I am Yahweh who sanctifies you. ¹⁴ You shall keep the Sabbath therefore, for it is holy to you. Everyone who profanes it shall surely be put to death; for whoever does any work therein, that soul shall be cut off from among his people. ¹⁵ Six days shall work be done, but on the seventh day is a Sabbath of solemn rest, holy to Yahweh. Whoever does any work on the Sabbath day shall surely be put to death. ¹⁶ Therefore the children of Israel shall keep the Sabbath, to observe the Sabbath throughout their generations, for a perpetual covenant. ¹⁷ It is a sign between me and the children of Israel forever; for in six days Yahweh made heaven and earth, and on the seventh day he rested, and was refreshed.'" ¹⁸ When he finished speaking with him on Mount Sinai, he gave Moses the two tablets of the covenant, stone tablets, written with God's finger.

## 32

¹ When the people saw that Moses delayed coming down from the mountain, the people gathered themselves together to Aaron, and said to him, "Come, make us gods, which shall go before us; for as for this Moses, the man who brought us up out of the land of Egypt, we don't know what has become of him." ² Aaron said to them, "Take off the golden rings, which are in the ears of your wives, of your sons, and of your daughters, and bring them to me." ³ All the people took off the golden rings which were in their ears, and brought them to Aaron. ⁴ He received what they handed him, fashioned it with an engraving tool, and made it a molded calf. Then they said, "These are your gods, Israel, which brought you up out of the land of Egypt." ⁵ When Aaron saw this, he built an altar before it; and Aaron made a proclamation, and said, "Tomorrow shall be a feast to Yahweh." ⁶ They rose up early on the next day, and offered burnt offerings, and brought peace offerings; and the people sat down to eat and to drink, and rose up to play. ⁷ Yahweh spoke to Moses, "Go, get down; for your people, whom you brought up out of the land of Egypt, have corrupted themselves! ⁸ They

have turned away quickly out of the way which I commanded them. They have made themselves a molded calf, and have worshiped it, and have sacrificed to it, and said, 'These are your gods, Israel, which brought you up out of the land of Egypt.'" ⁹ Yahweh said to Moses, "I have seen these people, and behold, they are a stiff-necked people. ¹⁰ Now therefore leave me alone, that my wrath may burn hot against them, and that I may consume them; and I will make of you a great nation." ¹¹ Moses begged Yahweh his God, and said, "Yahweh, why does your wrath burn hot against your people, that you have brought out of the land of Egypt with great power and with a mighty hand? ¹² Why should the Egyptians talk, saying, 'He brought them out for evil, to kill them in the mountains, and to consume them from the surface of the earth'? Turn from your fierce wrath, and turn away from this evil against your people. ¹³ Remember Abraham, Isaac, and Israel, your servants, to whom you swore by your own self, and said to them, 'I will multiply your offspringᵃ as the stars of the sky, and all this land that I have spoken of I will give to your offspring, and they shall inherit it forever.'" ¹⁴ So Yahweh turned away from the evil which he said he would do to his people. ¹⁵ Moses turned, and went down from the mountain, with the two tablets of the covenant in his hand; tablets that were written on both their sides. They were written on one side and on the other. ¹⁶ The tablets were the work of God, and the writing was the writing of God, engraved on the tablets. ¹⁷ When Joshua heard the noise of the people as they shouted, he said to Moses, "There is the noise of war in the camp." ¹⁸ He said, "It isn't the voice of those who shout for victory. It is not the voice of those who cry for being overcome; but the noise of those who sing that I hear." ¹⁹ As soon as he came near to the camp, he saw the calf and the dancing. Then Moses' anger grew hot, and he threw the tablets out of his hands, and broke them beneath the mountain. ²⁰ He took the calf which they had made, and burned it with fire, ground it to powder, and scattered it on the water, and made the children of Israel drink it. ²¹ Moses said to Aaron, "What did these people do to you, that you have brought a great sin on them?" ²² Aaron said, "Don't let the anger of my lord grow hot. You know the people, that they are set on evil. ²³ For they said to me, 'Make us gods, which shall go before us. As for this Moses, the man who brought us up out of the land of Egypt, we don't know what has become of him.' ²⁴ I said to them, 'Whoever has any gold, let them take it off.' So they gave it to me; and I threw it into the fire, and out came this calf." ²⁵ When Moses saw that the people were out of control, (for Aaron had let them lose control, causing derision among their enemies), ²⁶ then Moses stood in the gate of the camp, and said, "Whoever is on Yahweh's side, come to me!" All the sons of Levi gathered themselves together to him. ²⁷ He said to them, "Yahweh, the God of Israel, says, 'Every man put his sword on his thigh, and go back and forth from gate to gate throughout the camp, and every man kill his brother, and every man his companion, and every man his neighbor.'" ²⁸ The sons of Levi did according to the word of Moses. About three thousand men fell of the people that day. ²⁹ Moses said, "Consecrate yourselves today to Yahweh, for every man was against his son and against his brother, that he may give you a blessing today." ³⁰ On the next day, Moses said to the people, "You have sinned a great sin. Now I will go up to Yahweh. Perhaps I shall make atonement for your sin." ³¹ Moses returned to Yahweh, and said, "Oh, this people have sinned a great sin, and have made themselves gods of gold. ³² Yet now, if you will, forgive their sin—and if not, please blot me out of your book which you have written." ³³ Yahweh said to Moses, "Whoever has sinned against me, I will blot him out of my book. ³⁴ Now go, lead the people to the place of which I have spoken to you. Behold, my angel shall go before you. Nevertheless, in the day when I punish, I will punish them for their sin." ³⁵ Yahweh struck the people, because of what they did with the calf, which Aaron made.

## 33

¹ Yahweh spoke to Moses, "Depart, go up from here, you and the people that you have brought up out of the land of Egypt, to the land of which I swore to Abraham, to Isaac, and to Jacob, saying, 'I will give it to your offspring.' ² I will send an angel before you; and I will drive out the Canaanite, the Amorite, and the Hittite, and the Perizzite, the Hivite, and the Jebusite. ³ Go to a land flowing with milk and honey; but I will not go up among you, for you are a stiff-necked people, lest I consume you on the way." ⁴ When the people heard this evil news, they mourned; and no one put on his jewelry. ⁵ Yahweh had said to Moses, "Tell the children of Israel, 'You are a stiff-necked people. If I were to go up among you for one moment, I would consume you. Therefore now take off your jewelry from you, that I may know what to do to you.'" ⁶ The children of Israel stripped themselves of their jewelry from Mount Horeb onward. ⁷ Now Moses used to take the tent and pitch it outside the camp, far away from the camp, and he called it "The Tent of Meeting." Everyone who sought Yahweh went out to the Tent of

ᵃ 32:13 or, seed

Meeting, which was outside the camp. <sup>8</sup> When Moses went out to the Tent, all the people rose up, and stood, everyone at their tent door, and watched Moses, until he had gone into the Tent. <sup>9</sup> When Moses entered into the Tent, the pillar of cloud descended, stood at the door of the Tent, and Yahweh spoke with Moses. <sup>10</sup> All the people saw the pillar of cloud stand at the door of the Tent, and all the people rose up and worshiped, everyone at their tent door. <sup>11</sup> Yahweh spoke to Moses face to face, as a man speaks to his friend. He turned again into the camp, but his servant Joshua, the son of Nun, a young man, didn't depart from the Tent. <sup>12</sup> Moses said to Yahweh, "Behold, you tell me, 'Bring up this people;' and you haven't let me know whom you will send with me. Yet you have said, 'I know you by name, and you have also found favor in my sight.' <sup>13</sup> Now therefore, if I have found favor in your sight, please show me your way, now, that I may know you, so that I may find favor in your sight; and consider that this nation is your people." <sup>14</sup> He said, "My presence will go with you, and I will give you rest." <sup>15</sup> Moses said to him, "If your presence doesn't go with me, don't carry us up from here. <sup>16</sup> For how would people know that I have found favor in your sight, I and your people? Isn't it that you go with us, so that we are separated, I and your people, from all the people who are on the surface of the earth?" <sup>17</sup> Yahweh said to Moses, "I will do this thing also that you have spoken; for you have found favor in my sight, and I know you by name." <sup>18</sup> Moses said, "Please show me your glory." <sup>19</sup> He said, "I will make all my goodness pass before you, and will proclaim Yahweh's name before you. I will be gracious to whom I will be gracious, and will show mercy on whom I will show mercy." <sup>20</sup> He said, "You cannot see my face, for man may not see me and live." <sup>21</sup> Yahweh also said, "Behold, there is a place by me, and you shall stand on the rock. <sup>22</sup> It will happen, while my glory passes by, that I will put you in a cleft of the rock, and will cover you with my hand until I have passed by; <sup>23</sup> then I will take away my hand, and you will see my back; but my face shall not be seen."

## 34

<sup>1</sup> Yahweh said to Moses, "Chisel two stone tablets like the first. I will write on the tablets the words that were on the first tablets, which you broke. <sup>2</sup> Be ready by the morning, and come up in the morning to Mount Sinai, and present yourself there to me on the top of the mountain. <sup>3</sup> No one shall come up with you or be seen anywhere on the mountain. Do not let the flocks or herds graze in front of that mountain." <sup>4</sup> He chiseled two tablets of stone like the first; then Moses rose up early in the morning, and went up to Mount Sinai, as Yahweh had commanded him, and took in his hand two stone tablets. <sup>5</sup> Yahweh descended in the cloud, and stood with him there, and proclaimed Yahweh's name. <sup>6</sup> Yahweh passed by before him, and proclaimed, "Yahweh! Yahweh, a merciful and gracious God, slow to anger, and abundant in loving kindness and truth, <sup>7</sup> keeping loving kindness for thousands, forgiving iniquity and disobedience and sin; and who will by no means clear the guilty, visiting the iniquity of the fathers on the children, and on the children's children, on the third and on the fourth generation." <sup>8</sup> Moses hurried and bowed his head toward the earth, and worshiped. <sup>9</sup> He said, "If now I have found favor in your sight, Lord, please let the Lord go among us, even though this is a stiff-necked people; pardon our iniquity and our sin, and take us for your inheritance." <sup>10</sup> He said, "Behold, I make a covenant: before all your people I will do marvels, such as have not been worked in all the earth, nor in any nation; and all the people among whom you are shall see the work of Yahweh; for it is an awesome thing that I do with you. <sup>11</sup> Observe that which I command you today. Behold, I will drive out before you the Amorite, the Canaanite, the Hittite, the Perizzite, the Hivite, and the Jebusite. <sup>12</sup> Be careful, lest you make a covenant with the inhabitants of the land where you are going, lest it be for a snare among you; <sup>13</sup> but you shall break down their altars, and dash in pieces their pillars, and you shall cut down their Asherah poles; <sup>14</sup> for you shall worship no other god; for Yahweh, whose name is Jealous, is a jealous God. <sup>15</sup>"Don't make a covenant with the inhabitants of the land, lest they play the prostitute after their gods, and sacrifice to their gods, and one call you and you eat of his sacrifice; <sup>16</sup> and you take of their daughters to your sons, and their daughters play the prostitute after their gods, and make your sons play the prostitute after their gods. <sup>17</sup>"You shall make no cast idols for yourselves. <sup>18</sup>"You shall keep the feast of unleavened bread. Seven days you shall eat unleavened bread, as I commanded you, at the time appointed in the month Abib; for in the month Abib you came out of Egypt. <sup>19</sup>"All that opens the womb is mine; and all your livestock that is male, the firstborn of cow and sheep. <sup>20</sup> You shall redeem the firstborn of a donkey with a lamb. If you will not redeem it, then you shall break its neck. You shall redeem all the firstborn of your sons. No one shall appear before me empty. <sup>21</sup>"Six days you shall work, but on the seventh day you shall rest: in plowing time and in harvest you shall rest. <sup>22</sup>"You shall observe the feast of weeks with the first fruits of wheat harvest, and the feast of harvest at the year's end. <sup>23</sup> Three times

in the year all your males shall appear before the Lord Yahweh, the God of Israel. <sup>24</sup> For I will drive out nations before you and enlarge your borders; neither shall any man desire your land when you go up to appear before Yahweh, your God, three times in the year. <sup>25</sup>"You shall not offer the blood of my sacrifice with leavened bread. The sacrifice of the feast of the Passover shall not be left to the morning. <sup>26</sup>"You shall bring the first of the first fruits of your ground to the house of Yahweh your God. "You shall not boil a young goat in its mother's milk." <sup>27</sup> Yahweh said to Moses, "Write these words; for in accordance with these words I have made a covenant with you and with Israel." <sup>28</sup> He was there with Yahweh forty days and forty nights; he neither ate bread, nor drank water. He wrote on the tablets the words of the covenant, the ten commandments. <sup>29</sup> When Moses came down from Mount Sinai with the two tablets of the covenant in Moses' hand, when he came down from the mountain, Moses didn't know that the skin of his face shone by reason of his speaking with him. <sup>30</sup> When Aaron and all the children of Israel saw Moses, behold, the skin of his face shone; and they were afraid to come near him. <sup>31</sup> Moses called to them, and Aaron and all the rulers of the congregation returned to him; and Moses spoke to them. <sup>32</sup> Afterward all the children of Israel came near, and he gave them all the commandments that Yahweh had spoken with him on Mount Sinai. <sup>33</sup> When Moses was done speaking with them, he put a veil on his face. <sup>34</sup> But when Moses went in before Yahweh to speak with him, he took the veil off, until he came out; and he came out, and spoke to the children of Israel that which he was commanded. <sup>35</sup> The children of Israel saw Moses' face, that the skin of Moses' face shone; so Moses put the veil on his face again, until he went in to speak with him.

## 35

<sup>1</sup> Moses assembled all the congregation of the children of Israel, and said to them, "These are the words which Yahweh has commanded, that you should do them. <sup>2</sup>'Six days shall work be done, but on the seventh day there shall be a holy day for you, a Sabbath of solemn rest to Yahweh: whoever does any work in it shall be put to death. <sup>3</sup> You shall kindle no fire throughout your habitations on the Sabbath day.'" <sup>4</sup> Moses spoke to all the congregation of the children of Israel, saying, "This is the thing which Yahweh commanded, saying, <sup>5</sup>'Take from among you an offering to Yahweh. Whoever is of a willing heart, let him bring it as Yahweh's offering: gold, silver, bronze, <sup>6</sup> blue, purple, scarlet, fine linen, goats' hair, <sup>7</sup> rams' skins dyed red, sea cow hides, acacia wood, <sup>8</sup> oil for the light, spices for the anointing oil and for the sweet incense, <sup>9</sup> onyx stones, and stones to be set for the ephod and for the breastplate. <sup>10</sup>"Let every wise-hearted man among you come, and make all that Yahweh has commanded: <sup>11</sup> the tabernacle, its outer covering, its roof, its clasps, its boards, its bars, its pillars, and its sockets; <sup>12</sup> the ark, and its poles, the mercy seat, the veil of the screen; <sup>13</sup> the table with its poles and all its vessels, and the show bread; <sup>14</sup> the lamp stand also for the light, with its vessels, its lamps, and the oil for the light; <sup>15</sup> and the altar of incense with its poles, the anointing oil, the sweet incense, the screen for the door, at the door of the tabernacle; <sup>16</sup> the altar of burnt offering, with its grating of bronze, its poles, and all its vessels, the basin and its base; <sup>17</sup> the hangings of the court, its pillars, their sockets, and the screen for the gate of the court; <sup>18</sup> the pins of the tabernacle, the pins of the court, and their cords; <sup>19</sup> the finely worked garments for ministering in the holy place—the holy garments for Aaron the priest, and the garments of his sons—to minister in the priest's office.'" <sup>20</sup> All the congregation of the children of Israel departed from the presence of Moses. <sup>21</sup> They came, everyone whose heart stirred him up, and everyone whom his spirit made willing, and brought Yahweh's offering for the work of the Tent of Meeting, and for all of its service, and for the holy garments. <sup>22</sup> They came, both men and women, as many as were willing-hearted, and brought brooches, earrings, signet rings, and armlets, all jewels of gold; even every man who offered an offering of gold to Yahweh. <sup>23</sup> Everyone with whom was found blue, purple, scarlet, fine linen, goats' hair, rams' skins dyed red, and sea cow hides, brought them. <sup>24</sup> Everyone who offered an offering of silver and bronze brought Yahweh's offering; and everyone with whom was found acacia wood for any work of the service, brought it. <sup>25</sup> All the women who were wise-hearted spun with their hands, and brought that which they had spun: the blue, the purple, the scarlet, and the fine linen. <sup>26</sup> All the women whose heart stirred them up in wisdom spun the goats' hair. <sup>27</sup> The rulers brought the onyx stones and the stones to be set for the ephod and for the breastplate; <sup>28</sup> with the spice and the oil for the light, for the anointing oil, and for the sweet incense. <sup>29</sup> The children of Israel brought a free will offering to Yahweh; every man and woman whose heart made them willing to bring for all the work, which Yahweh had commanded to be made by Moses. <sup>30</sup> Moses said to the children of Israel, "Behold, Yahweh has called by name Bezalel the son of Uri, the son of Hur, of the tribe of Judah. <sup>31</sup> He has filled him with the Spirit of God, in wisdom, in understanding, in knowledge, and in all kinds of workmanship; <sup>32</sup> and to make skillful

works, to work in gold, in silver, in bronze, [33] in cutting of stones for setting, and in carving of wood, to work in all kinds of skillful workmanship. [34] He has put in his heart that he may teach, both he and Oholiab, the son of Ahisamach, of the tribe of Dan. [35] He has filled them with wisdom of heart to work all kinds of workmanship, of the engraver, of the skillful workman, and of the embroiderer, in blue, in purple, in scarlet, and in fine linen, and of the weaver, even of those who do any workmanship, and of those who make skillful works.

## 36

[1] "Bezalel and Oholiab shall work with every wise-hearted man, in whom Yahweh has put wisdom and understanding to know how to do all the work for the service of the sanctuary, according to all that Yahweh has commanded." [2] Moses called Bezalel and Oholiab, and every wise-hearted man, in whose heart Yahweh had put wisdom, even everyone whose heart stirred him up to come to the work to do it. [3] They received from Moses all the offering which the children of Israel had brought for the work of the service of the sanctuary, with which to make it. They kept bringing free will offerings to him every morning. [4] All the wise men, who performed all the work of the sanctuary, each came from his work which he did. [5] They spoke to Moses, saying, "The people have brought much more than enough for the service of the work which Yahweh commanded to make." [6] Moses gave a commandment, and they caused it to be proclaimed throughout the camp, saying, "Let neither man nor woman make anything else for the offering for the sanctuary." So the people were restrained from bringing. [7] For the stuff they had was sufficient to do all the work, and too much. [8] All the wise-hearted men among those who did the work made the tabernacle with ten curtains of fine twined linen, blue, purple, and scarlet. They made them with cherubim, the work of a skillful workman. [9] The length of each curtain was twenty-eight cubits,[a] and the width of each curtain four cubits. All the curtains had one measure. [10] He coupled five curtains to one another, and the other five curtains he coupled to one another. [11] He made loops of blue on the edge of the one curtain from the edge in the coupling. Likewise he made in the edge of the curtain that was outermost in the second coupling. [12] He made fifty loops in the one curtain, and he made fifty loops in the edge of the curtain that was in the second coupling. The loops were opposite to one another. [13] He made fifty clasps of gold, and coupled the curtains to one another with the clasps: so the tabernacle was a unit. [14] He made curtains of goats' hair for a covering over the tabernacle. He made them eleven curtains. [15] The length of each curtain was thirty cubits, and four cubits the width of each curtain. The eleven curtains had one measure. [16] He coupled five curtains by themselves, and six curtains by themselves. [17] He made fifty loops on the edge of the curtain that was outermost in the coupling, and he made fifty loops on the edge of the curtain which was outermost in the second coupling. [18] He made fifty clasps of bronze to couple the tent together, that it might be a unit. [19] He made a covering for the tent of rams' skins dyed red, and a covering of sea cow hides above. [20] He made the boards for the tabernacle of acacia wood, standing up. [21] Ten cubits was the length of a board, and a cubit and a half the width of each board. [22] Each board had two tenons, joined to one another. He made all the boards of the tabernacle this way. [23] He made the boards for the tabernacle, twenty boards for the south side southward. [24] He made forty sockets of silver under the twenty boards: two sockets under one board for its two tenons, and two sockets under another board for its two tenons. [25] For the second side of the tabernacle, on the north side, he made twenty boards [26] and their forty sockets of silver: two sockets under one board, and two sockets under another board. [27] For the far part of the tabernacle westward he made six boards. [28] He made two boards for the corners of the tabernacle in the far part. [29] They were double beneath, and in the same way they were all the way to its top to one ring. He did this to both of them in the two corners. [30] There were eight boards and their sockets of silver, sixteen sockets—under every board two sockets. [31] He made bars of acacia wood: five for the boards of the one side of the tabernacle, [32] and five bars for the boards of the other side of the tabernacle, and five bars for the boards of the tabernacle for the hinder part westward. [33] He made the middle bar to pass through in the middle of the boards from the one end to the other. [34] He overlaid the boards with gold, and made their rings of gold as places for the bars, and overlaid the bars with gold. [35] He made the veil of blue, purple, scarlet, and fine twined linen, with cherubim. He made it the work of a skillful workman. [36] He made four pillars of acacia for it, and overlaid them with gold. Their hooks were of gold. He cast four sockets of silver for them. [37] He made a screen for the door of the tent,

of blue, purple, scarlet, and fine twined linen, the work of an embroiderer; [38] and the five pillars of it with their hooks. He overlaid their capitals and their fillets with gold, and their five sockets were of bronze.

## 37

[1] Bezalel made the ark of acacia wood. Its length was two and a half cubits,[b] and its width a cubit and a half, and a cubit and a half its height. [2] He overlaid it with pure gold inside and outside, and made a molding of gold for it around it. [3] He cast four rings of gold for it in its four feet—two rings on its one side, and two rings on its other side. [4] He made poles of acacia wood and overlaid them with gold. [5] He put the poles into the rings on the sides of the ark, to bear the ark. [6] He made a mercy seat of pure gold. Its length was two and a half cubits, and a cubit and a half its width. [7] He made two cherubim of gold. He made them of beaten work, at the two ends of the mercy seat: [8] one cherub at the one end, and one cherub at the other end. He made the cherubim of one piece with the mercy seat at its two ends. [9] The cherubim spread out their wings above, covering the mercy seat with their wings, with their faces toward one another. The faces of the cherubim were toward the mercy seat. [10] He made the table of acacia wood. Its length was two cubits, and its width was a cubit, and its height was a cubit and a half. [11] He overlaid it with pure gold, and made a gold molding around it. [12] He made a border of a hand's width around it, and made a golden molding on its border around it. [13] He cast four rings of gold for it, and put the rings in the four corners that were on its four feet. [14] The rings were close by the border, the places for the poles to carry the table. [15] He made the poles of acacia wood, and overlaid them with gold, to carry the table. [16] He made the vessels which were on the table, its dishes, its spoons, its bowls, and its pitchers with which to pour out, of pure gold. [17] He made the lamp stand of pure gold. He made the lamp stand of beaten work. Its base, its shaft, its cups, its buds, and its flowers were of one piece with it. [18] There were six branches going out of its sides: three branches of the lamp stand out of its one side, and three branches of the lamp stand out of its other side: [19] three cups made like almond blossoms in one branch, a bud and a flower, and three cups made like almond blossoms in the other branch, a bud and a flower; so for the six branches going out of the lamp stand. [20] In the lamp stand were four cups made like almond blossoms, its buds and its flowers; [21] and a bud under two branches of one piece with it, and a bud under two branches of one piece with it, and a bud under two branches of one piece with it, for the six branches going out of it. [22] Their buds and their branches were of one piece with it. The whole thing was one beaten work of pure gold. [23] He made its seven lamps, and its snuffers, and its snuff dishes, of pure gold. [24] He made it of a talent[c] of pure gold, with all its vessels. [25] He made the altar of incense of acacia wood. It was square: its length was a cubit, and its width a cubit. Its height was two cubits. Its horns were of one piece with it. [26] He overlaid it with pure gold: its top, its sides around it, and its horns. He made a gold molding around it. [27] He made two golden rings for it under its molding crown, on its two ribs, on its two sides, for places for poles with which to carry it. [28] He made the poles of acacia wood, and overlaid them with gold. [29] He made the holy anointing oil and the pure incense of sweet spices, after the art of the perfumer.

## 38

[1] He made the altar of burnt offering of acacia wood. It was square. Its length was five cubits,[d] its width was five cubits, and its height was three cubits. [2] He made its horns on its four corners. Its horns were of one piece with it, and he overlaid it with bronze. [3] He made all the vessels of the altar: the pots, the shovels, the basins, the forks, and the fire pans. He made all its vessels of bronze. [4] He made for the altar a grating of a network of bronze, under the ledge around it beneath, reaching halfway up. [5] He cast four rings for the four corners of bronze grating, to be places for the poles. [6] He made the poles of acacia wood, and overlaid them with bronze. [7] He put the poles into the rings on the sides of the altar, with which to carry it. He made it hollow with planks. [8] He made the basin of bronze, and its base of bronze, out of the mirrors of the ministering women who ministered at the door of the Tent of Meeting. [9] He made the court: for the south side southward the hangings of the court were of fine twined linen, one hundred cubits; [10] their pillars were twenty, and their sockets twenty, of bronze; the hooks of the pillars and their fillets were of silver. [11] For the north side one hundred cubits, their pillars twenty, and their sockets twenty, of bronze; the hooks of the pillars, and their fillets, of silver. [12] For the west side were hangings of fifty cubits, their pillars ten, and their sockets ten; the hooks

---

[a] *36:9* A cubit is the length from the tip of the middle finger to the elbow on a man's arm, or about 18 inches or 46 centimeters.

[b] *37:1* A cubit is the length from the tip of the middle finger to the elbow on a man's arm, or about 18 inches or 46 centimeters.

[c] *37:24* A talent is about 30 kilograms or 66 pounds or 965 Troy ounces
[d] *38:1* A cubit is the length from the tip of the middle

finger to the elbow on a man's arm, or about 18 inches or 46 centimeters.

of the pillars, and their fillets, of silver. [13] For the east side eastward fifty cubits, [14] the hangings for the one side were fifteen cubits; their pillars three, and their sockets three; [15] and so for the other side: on this hand and that hand by the gate of the court were hangings of fifteen cubits; their pillars three, and their sockets three. [16] All the hangings around the court were of fine twined linen. [17] The sockets for the pillars were of bronze. The hooks of the pillars and their fillets were of silver. Their capitals were overlaid with silver. All the pillars of the court had silver bands. [18] The screen for the gate of the court was the work of the embroiderer, of blue, purple, scarlet, and fine twined linen. Twenty cubits was the length, and the height along the width was five cubits, like the hangings of the court. [19] Their pillars were four, and their sockets four, of bronze; their hooks of silver, and the overlaying of their capitals, and their fillets, of silver. [20] All the pins of the tabernacle, and around the court, were of bronze. [21] These are the amounts of materials used for the tabernacle, even the Tabernacle of the Testimony, as they were counted, according to the commandment of Moses, for the service of the Levites, by the hand of Ithamar, the son of Aaron the priest. [22] Bezalel the son of Uri, the son of Hur, of the tribe of Judah, made all that Yahweh commanded Moses. [23] With him was Oholiab, the son of Ahisamach, of the tribe of Dan, an engraver, and a skillful workman, and an embroiderer in blue, in purple, in scarlet, and in fine linen. [24] All the gold that was used for the work in all the work of the sanctuary, even the gold of the offering, was twenty-nine talents[a] and seven hundred thirty shekels, according to the shekel[b] of the sanctuary. [25] The silver of those who were counted of the congregation was one hundred talents[c] and one thousand seven hundred seventy-five shekels,[d] according to the shekel of the sanctuary: [26] a beka[e] a head, that is, half a shekel, according to the shekel[f] of the sanctuary, for everyone who passed over to those who were counted, from twenty years old and upward, for six hundred three thousand five hundred fifty men. [27] The one hundred talents[g] of silver were for casting the sockets of the sanctuary and the sockets of the veil: one hundred sockets for the one hundred talents, one talent per socket. [28] From the one thousand seven hundred seventy-five shekels[h] he made hooks for the pillars, overlaid their capitals, and made fillets for them. [29] The bronze of the offering was seventy talents[i] and two thousand four hundred shekels.[j] [30] With this he made the sockets to the door of the Tent of Meeting, the bronze altar, the bronze grating for it, all the vessels of the altar, [31] the sockets around the court, the sockets of the gate of the court, all the pins of the tabernacle, and all the pins around the court.

## 39

[1] Of the blue, purple, and scarlet, they made finely worked garments for ministering in the holy place, and made the holy garments for Aaron, as Yahweh commanded Moses. [2] He made the ephod of gold, blue, purple, scarlet, and fine twined linen. [3] They beat the gold into thin plates, and cut it into wires, to work it in with the blue, the purple, the scarlet, and the fine linen, the work of the skillful workman. [4] They made shoulder straps for it, joined together. It was joined together at the two ends. [5] The skillfully woven band that was on it, with which to fasten it on, was of the same piece, like its work: of gold, of blue, purple, scarlet, and fine twined linen, as Yahweh commanded Moses. [6] They worked the onyx stones, enclosed in settings of gold, engraved with the engravings of a signet, according to the names of the children of Israel. [7] He put them on the shoulder straps of the ephod, to be stones of memorial for the children of Israel, as Yahweh commanded Moses. [8] He made the breastplate, the work of a skillful workman, like the work of the ephod: of gold, of blue, purple, scarlet, and fine twined linen. [9] It was square. They made the breastplate double. Its length was a span,[k] and its width a span, being double. [10] They set in it four rows of stones. A row of ruby, topaz, and beryl was the first row; [11] and the second row, a turquoise, a sapphire,[l] and an emerald; [12] and the third row, a jacinth, an agate, and an amethyst; [13] and the fourth row, a chrysolite, an onyx, and a jasper. They were enclosed in gold settings. [14] The stones were according to the names of the children of Israel, twelve, according to their names; like the engravings of a signet, everyone according to his name, for the twelve tribes. [15] They made on the breastplate chains like cords, of braided work of pure gold. [16] They made two settings of gold, and two gold rings, and put the two rings on the two ends of the breastplate. [17] They put the two braided chains of gold in the two rings at the ends of the breastplate. [18] The other two ends of the two braided

chains they put on the two settings, and put them on the shoulder straps of the ephod, in its front. [19] They made two rings of gold, and put them on the two ends of the breastplate, on its edge, which was toward the side of the ephod inward. [20] They made two more rings of gold, and put them on the two shoulder straps of the ephod underneath, in its front, close by its coupling, above the skillfully woven band of the ephod. [21] They bound the breastplate by its rings to the rings of the ephod with a lace of blue, that it might be on the skillfully woven band of the ephod, and that the breastplate might not come loose from the ephod, as Yahweh commanded Moses. [22] He made the robe of the ephod of woven work, all of blue. [23] The opening of the robe in the middle of it was like the opening of a coat of mail, with a binding around its opening, that it should not be torn. [24] They made on the skirts of the robe pomegranates of blue, purple, scarlet, and twined linen. [25] They made bells of pure gold, and put the bells between the pomegranates around the skirts of the robe, between the pomegranates; [26] a bell and a pomegranate, a bell and a pomegranate, around the skirts of the robe, to minister in, as Yahweh commanded Moses. [27] They made the tunics of fine linen of woven work for Aaron and for his sons, [28] the turban of fine linen, the linen headbands of fine linen, the linen trousers of fine twined linen, [29] the sash of fine twined linen, blue, purple, and scarlet, the work of the embroiderer, as Yahweh commanded Moses. [30] They made the plate of the holy crown of pure gold, and wrote on it an inscription, like the engravings of a signet: "HOLY TO YAHWEH". [31] They tied to it a lace of blue, to fasten it on the turban above, as Yahweh commanded Moses. [32] Thus all the work of the tabernacle of the Tent of Meeting was finished. The children of Israel did according to all that Yahweh commanded Moses; so they did. [33] They brought the tabernacle to Moses: the tent, with all its furniture, its clasps, its boards, its bars, its pillars, its sockets, [34] the covering of rams' skins dyed red, the covering of sea cow hides, the veil of the screen, [35] the ark of the covenant with its poles, the mercy seat, [36] the table, all its vessels, the show bread, [37] the pure lamp stand, its lamps, even the lamps to be set in order, all its vessels, the oil for the light, [38] the golden altar, the anointing oil, the sweet incense, the screen for the door of the Tent, [39] the bronze altar, its grating of bronze, its poles, all of its vessels, the basin and its base, [40] the hangings of the court, its pillars, its sockets, the screen for the gate of the court, its cords, its pins, and all the instruments of the service of the tabernacle, for the Tent of Meeting, [41] the finely worked garments for ministering in the holy place, the holy garments for Aaron the priest, and the garments of his sons, to minister in the priest's office. [42] According to all that Yahweh commanded Moses, so the children of Israel did all the work. [43] Moses saw all the work, and behold, they had done it as Yahweh had commanded. They had done so; and Moses blessed them.

## 40

[1] Yahweh spoke to Moses, saying, [2]"On the first day of the first month you shall raise up the tabernacle of the Tent of Meeting. [3] You shall put the ark of the covenant in it, and you shall screen the ark with the veil. [4] You shall bring in the table, and set in order the things that are on it. You shall bring in the lamp stand, and light its lamps. [5] You shall set the golden altar for incense before the ark of the covenant, and put the screen of the door to the tabernacle. [6]"You shall set the altar of burnt offering before the door of the tabernacle of the Tent of Meeting. [7] You shall set the basin between the Tent of Meeting and the altar, and shall put water therein. [8] You shall set up the court around it, and hang up the screen of the gate of the court. [9]"You shall take the anointing oil, and anoint the tabernacle and all that is in it, and shall make it holy, and all its furniture, and it will be holy. [10] You shall anoint the altar of burnt offering, with all its vessels, and sanctify the altar, and the altar will be most holy. [11] You shall anoint the basin and its base, and sanctify it. [12]"You shall bring Aaron and his sons to the door of the Tent of Meeting, and shall wash them with water. [13] You shall put on Aaron the holy garments; and you shall anoint him, and sanctify him, that he may minister to me in the priest's office. [14] You shall bring his sons, and put tunics on them. [15] You shall anoint them, as you anointed their father, that they may minister to me in the priest's office. Their anointing shall be to them for an everlasting priesthood throughout their generations." [16] Moses did so. According to all that Yahweh commanded him, so he did. [17] In the first month in the second year, on the first day of the month, the tabernacle was raised up. [18] Moses raised up the tabernacle,

---

[a] *38:24 A talent is about 30 kilograms or 66 pounds or 965 Troy ounces.*

[b] *38:24 A shekel is about 10 grams or about 0.32 Troy ounces.*

[c] *38:25 A talent is about 30 kilograms or 66 pounds*

[d] *38:25 A shekel is about 10 grams or about 0.35 ounces.*

[e] *38:26 A beka is about 5 grams or about 0.175 ounces*

[f] *38:26 A shekel is about 10 grams or about 0.35 ounces.*

[g] *38:27 A talent is about 30 kilograms or 66 pounds.*

[h] *38:28 A shekel is about 10 grams or about 0.35 ounces, so 1775 shekels is about 17.75 kilograms or about 39 pounds.*

[i] *38:29 A talent is about 30 kilograms or 66 pounds*

[j] *38:29 70 talents + 2400 shekels is about 2124*

kilograms, or 2.124 metric tons.

[k] *39:9 A span is the length from the tip of a man's thumb to the tip of his little finger when his hand is stretched out (about half a cubit, or 9 inches, or 22.8 cm.)*

[l] *39:11 or, lapis lazuli*

and laid its sockets, and set up its boards, and put in its bars, and raised up its pillars. ¹⁹ He spread the covering over the tent, and put the roof of the tabernacle above on it, as Yahweh commanded Moses. ²⁰ He took and put the covenant into the ark, and set the poles on the ark, and put the mercy seat above on the ark. ²¹ He brought the ark into the tabernacle, and set up the veil of the screen, and screened the ark of the covenant, as Yahweh commanded Moses. ²² He put the table in the Tent of Meeting, on the north side of the tabernacle, outside of the veil. ²³ He set the bread in order on it before Yahweh, as Yahweh commanded Moses. ²⁴ He put the lamp stand in the Tent of Meeting, opposite the table, on the south side of the tabernacle. ²⁵ He lit the lamps before Yahweh, as Yahweh commanded Moses. ²⁶ He put the golden altar in the Tent of Meeting before the veil; ²⁷ and he burned incense of sweet spices on it, as Yahweh commanded Moses. ²⁸ He put up the screen of the door to the tabernacle. ²⁹ He set the altar of burnt offering at the door of the tabernacle of the Tent of Meeting, and offered on it the burnt offering and the meal offering, as Yahweh commanded Moses. ³⁰ He set the basin between the Tent of Meeting and the altar, and put water therein, with which to wash. ³¹ Moses, Aaron, and his sons washed their hands and their feet there. ³² When they went into the Tent of Meeting, and when they came near to the altar, they washed, as Yahweh commanded Moses. ³³ He raised up the court around the tabernacle and the altar, and set up the screen of the gate of the court. So Moses finished the work. ³⁴ Then the cloud covered the Tent of Meeting, and Yahweh's glory filled the tabernacle. ³⁵ Moses wasn't able to enter into the Tent of Meeting, because the cloud stayed on it, and Yahweh's glory filled the tabernacle. ³⁶ When the cloud was taken up from over the tabernacle, the children of Israel went onward, throughout all their journeys; ³⁷ but if the cloud wasn't taken up, then they didn't travel until the day that it was taken up. ³⁸ For the cloud of Yahweh was on the tabernacle by day, and there was fire in the cloud by night, in the sight of all the house of Israel, throughout all their journeys.

# The Third Book of Moses, Leviticus

## 1

¹ Yahweh[a] called to Moses, and spoke to him from the Tent of Meeting, saying, ²"Speak to the children of Israel, and tell them, 'When anyone of you offers an offering to Yahweh, you shall offer your offering of the livestock, from the herd and from the flock. ³"'If his offering is a burnt offering from the herd, he shall offer a male without defect. He shall offer it at the door of the Tent of Meeting, that he may be accepted before Yahweh. ⁴ He shall lay his hand on the head of the burnt offering, and it shall be accepted for him to make atonement for him. ⁵ He shall kill the bull before Yahweh. Aaron's sons, the priests, shall present the blood and sprinkle the blood around on the altar that is at the door of the Tent of Meeting. ⁶ He shall skin the burnt offering and cut it into pieces. ⁷ The sons of Aaron the priest shall put fire on the altar, and lay wood in order on the fire; ⁸ and Aaron's sons, the priests, shall lay the pieces, the head, and the fat in order on the wood that is on the fire which is on the altar; ⁹ but he shall wash its innards and its legs with water. The priest shall burn all of it on the altar, for a burnt offering, an offering made by fire, of a pleasant aroma to Yahweh. ¹⁰"'If his offering is from the flock, from the sheep or from the goats, for a burnt offering, he shall offer a male without defect. ¹¹ He shall kill it on the north side of the altar before Yahweh. Aaron's sons, the priests, shall sprinkle its blood around on the altar. ¹² He shall cut it into its pieces, with its head and its fat. The priest shall lay them in order on the wood that is on the fire which is on the altar, ¹³ but the innards and the legs he shall wash with water. The priest shall offer the whole, and burn it on the altar. It is a burnt offering, an offering made by fire, of a pleasant aroma to Yahweh. ¹⁴"'If his offering to Yahweh is a burnt offering of birds, then he shall offer his offering from turtledoves or of young pigeons. ¹⁵ The priest shall bring it to the altar, and wring off its head, and burn it on the altar; and its blood shall be drained out on the side of the altar; ¹⁶ and he shall take away its crop and its feathers, and cast it beside the altar on the east part, in the place of the ashes. ¹⁷ He shall tear it by its wings, but shall not divide it apart. The priest shall burn it on the altar, on the wood that is on the fire. It is a burnt offering, an offering made by fire, of a pleasant aroma to Yahweh.

## 2

¹"'When anyone offers an offering of a meal offering to Yahweh, his offering shall be of fine flour. He shall pour oil on it, and put frankincense on it. ² He shall bring it to Aaron's sons, the priests. He shall take his handful of its fine flour, and of its oil, with all its frankincense, and the priest shall burn its memorial on the altar, an offering made by fire, of a pleasant aroma to Yahweh. ³ That which is left of the meal offering shall be Aaron's and his sons'. It is a most holy part of the offerings of Yahweh made by fire. ⁴"'When you offer an offering of a meal offering baked in the oven, it shall be unleavened cakes of fine flour mixed with oil, or unleavened wafers anointed with oil. ⁵ If your offering is a meal offering made on a griddle, it shall be of unleavened fine flour, mixed with oil. ⁶ You shall cut it in pieces, and pour oil on it. It is a meal offering. ⁷ If your offering is a meal offering of the pan, it shall be made of fine flour with oil. ⁸ You shall bring the meal offering that is made of these things to Yahweh. It shall be presented to the priest, and he shall bring it to the altar. ⁹ The priest shall take from the meal offering its memorial, and shall burn it on the altar, an offering made by fire, of a pleasant aroma to Yahweh. ¹⁰ That which is left of the meal offering shall be Aaron's and his sons'. It is a most holy part of the offerings of Yahweh made by fire. ¹¹"'No meal offering which you shall offer to Yahweh shall be made with yeast; for you shall burn no yeast, nor any honey, as an offering made by fire to Yahweh. ¹² As an offering of first fruits you shall offer them to Yahweh, but they shall not rise up as a pleasant aroma on the altar. ¹³ Every offering of your meal offering you shall season with salt. You shall not allow the salt of the covenant of your God[b] to be lacking from your meal offering. With all your offerings you shall offer salt. ¹⁴"'If you offer a meal offering of first fruits to Yahweh, you shall offer for the meal offering of your first fruits fresh heads of grain parched with fire and crushed. ¹⁵ You shall put oil on it and lay frankincense on it. It is a meal offering. ¹⁶ The priest shall burn as its memorial part of its crushed grain and part of its oil, along with all its frankincense. It is an offering made by fire to Yahweh.

## 3

¹"'If his offering is a sacrifice of peace offerings, if he offers it from the herd, whether male or female, he shall offer it without defect before Yahweh. ² He shall lay his hand on the head of his offering, and kill it at the door of the Tent of Meeting. Aaron's sons, the priests, shall sprinkle the blood around on the altar. ³ He shall offer of the sacrifice of peace offerings an offering made by fire to Yahweh. The fat that covers the innards, and all the fat that is on the innards, ⁴ and the two kidneys, and the fat that is on them, which is by the loins, and the cover on the liver, with the kidneys, he shall take away. ⁵ Aaron's sons shall burn it on the altar on the burnt offering, which is on the wood that is on the fire: it is an offering made by fire, of a pleasant aroma to Yahweh. ⁶"'If his offering for a sacrifice of peace offerings to Yahweh is from the flock, either male or female, he shall offer it without defect. ⁷ If he offers a lamb for his offering, then he shall offer it before Yahweh; ⁸ and he shall lay his hand on the head of his offering, and kill it before the Tent of Meeting. Aaron's sons shall sprinkle its blood around on the altar. ⁹ He shall offer from the sacrifice of peace offerings an offering made by fire to Yahweh; its fat, the entire tail fat, he shall take away close to the backbone; and the fat that covers the entrails, and all the fat that is on the entrails, ¹⁰ and the two kidneys, and the fat that is on them, which is by the loins, and the cover on the liver, with the kidneys, he shall take away. ¹¹ The priest shall burn it on the altar: it is the food of the offering made by fire to Yahweh. ¹²"'If his offering is a goat, then he shall offer it before Yahweh. ¹³ He shall lay his hand on its head, and kill it before the Tent of Meeting; and the sons of Aaron shall sprinkle its blood around on the altar. ¹⁴ He shall offer from it as his offering, an offering made by fire to Yahweh; the fat that covers the innards, and all the fat that is on the innards, ¹⁵ and the two kidneys, and the fat that is on them, which is by the loins, and the cover on the liver, with the kidneys, he shall take away. ¹⁶ The priest shall burn them on the altar: it is the food of the offering made by fire, for a pleasant aroma; all the fat is Yahweh's. ¹⁷"'It shall be a perpetual statute throughout your generations in all your dwellings, that you shall eat neither fat nor blood.'"

## 4

¹ Yahweh spoke to Moses, saying, ²"Speak to the children of Israel, saying, 'If anyone sins unintentionally, in any of the things which Yahweh has commanded not to be done, and does any one of them, ³ if the anointed priest sins so as to bring guilt on the people, then let him offer for his sin which he has sinned a young bull without defect to Yahweh for a sin offering. ⁴ He shall bring the bull to the door of the Tent of Meeting before Yahweh; and he shall lay his hand on the head of the bull, and kill the bull before Yahweh. ⁵ The anointed priest shall take some of the blood of the bull, and bring it to the Tent of Meeting. ⁶ The priest shall dip his finger in the blood, and sprinkle some of the blood seven times before Yahweh, before the veil of the sanctuary. ⁷ The priest shall put some of the blood on the horns of the altar of sweet

---

[a] *1:1* "Yahweh" is God's proper Name, sometimes rendered "LORD" (all caps) in other translations.

[b] *2:13* The Hebrew word rendered "God" is אֱלֹהִים (Elohim).

incense before Yahweh, which is in the Tent of Meeting; and he shall pour out the rest of the blood of the bull at the base of the altar of burnt offering, which is at the door of the Tent of Meeting. ⁸ He shall take all the fat of the bull of the sin offering from it: the fat that covers the innards, and all the fat that is on the innards, ⁹ and the two kidneys, and the fat that is on them, which is by the loins, and the cover on the liver, with the kidneys, he shall remove, ¹⁰ as it is removed from the bull of the sacrifice of peace offerings. The priest shall burn them on the altar of burnt offering. ¹¹ He shall carry the bull's skin, all its meat, with its head, and with its legs, its innards, and its dung ¹²—all the rest of the bull—outside of the camp to a clean place where the ashes are poured out, and burn it on wood with fire. It shall be burned where the ashes are poured out. ¹³"If the whole congregation of Israel sins, and the thing is hidden from the eyes of the assembly, and they have done any of the things which Yahweh has commanded not to be done, and are guilty; ¹⁴ when the sin in which they have sinned is known, then the assembly shall offer a young bull for a sin offering, and bring it before the Tent of Meeting. ¹⁵ The elders of the congregation shall lay their hands on the head of the bull before Yahweh; and the bull shall be killed before Yahweh. ¹⁶ The anointed priest shall bring some of the blood of the bull to the Tent of Meeting. ¹⁷ The priest shall dip his finger in the blood and sprinkle it seven times before Yahweh, before the veil. ¹⁸ He shall put some of the blood on the horns of the altar which is before Yahweh, that is in the Tent of Meeting; and the rest of the blood he shall pour out at the base of the altar of burnt offering, which is at the door of the Tent of Meeting. ¹⁹ All its fat he shall take from it, and burn it on the altar. ²⁰ He shall do this with the bull; as he did with the bull of the sin offering, so he shall do with this; and the priest shall make atonement for them, and they shall be forgiven. ²¹ He shall carry the bull outside the camp, and burn it as he burned the first bull. It is the sin offering for the assembly. ²²"When a ruler sins, and unwittingly does any one of all the things which Yahweh his God has commanded not to be done, and is guilty, ²³ if his sin in which he has sinned is made known to him, he shall bring as his offering a goat, a male without defect. ²⁴ He shall lay his hand on the head of the goat, and kill it in the place where they kill the burnt offering before Yahweh. It is a sin offering. ²⁵ The priest shall take some of the blood of the sin offering with his finger, and put it on the horns of the altar of burnt offering. He shall pour out the rest of its blood at the base of the altar of burnt offering. ²⁶ All its fat he shall burn on the altar, like the fat of the sacrifice of peace offerings; and the priest shall make atonement for him concerning his sin, and he will be forgiven. ²⁷"If anyone of the common people sins unwittingly, in doing any of the things which Yahweh has commanded not to be done, and is guilty, ²⁸ if his sin which he has sinned is made known to him, then he shall bring for his offering a goat, a female without defect, for his sin which he has sinned. ²⁹ He shall lay his hand on the head of the sin offering, and kill the sin offering in the place of burnt offering. ³⁰ The priest shall take some of its blood with his finger, and put it on the horns of the altar of burnt offering; and the rest of its blood he shall pour out at the base of the altar. ³¹ All its fat he shall take away, like the fat is taken away from the sacrifice of peace offerings; and the priest shall burn it on the altar for a pleasant aroma to Yahweh; and the priest shall make atonement for him, and he will be forgiven. ³²"If he brings a lamb as his offering for a sin offering, he shall bring a female without defect. ³³ He shall lay his hand on the head of the sin offering, and kill it for a sin offering in the place where they kill the burnt offering. ³⁴ The priest shall take some of the blood of the sin offering with his finger, and put it on the horns of the altar of burnt offering; and all the rest of its blood he shall pour out at the base of the altar. ³⁵ He shall remove all its fat, like the fat of the lamb is removed from the sacrifice of peace offerings. The priest shall burn them on the altar, on the offerings of Yahweh made by fire. The priest shall make atonement for him concerning his sin that he has sinned, and he will be forgiven.

## 5

¹"If anyone sins, in that he hears a public adjuration to testify, he being a witness, whether he has seen or known, if he doesn't report it, then he shall bear his iniquity. ²"Or if anyone touches any unclean thing, whether it is the carcass of an unclean animal, or the carcass of unclean livestock, or the carcass of unclean creeping things, and it is hidden from him, and he is unclean, then he shall be guilty. ³"Or if he touches the uncleanness of man, whatever his uncleanness is with which he is unclean, and it is hidden from him; when he knows of it, then he shall be guilty. ⁴"Or if anyone swears rashly with his lips to do evil or to do good—whatever it is that a man might utter rashly with an oath, and it is hidden from him—when he knows of it, then he will be guilty of one of these. ⁵ It shall be, when he is guilty of one of these, he shall confess

that in which he has sinned; ⁶ and he shall bring his trespass offering to Yahweh for his sin which he has sinned: a female from the flock, a lamb or a goat, for a sin offering; and the priest shall make atonement for him concerning his sin. ⁷"If he can't afford a lamb, then he shall bring his trespass offering for that in which he has sinned, two turtledoves, or two young pigeons, to Yahweh; one for a sin offering, and the other for a burnt offering. ⁸ He shall bring them to the priest, who shall first offer the one which is for the sin offering. He shall wring off its head from its neck, but shall not sever it completely. ⁹ He shall sprinkle some of the blood of the sin offering on the side of the altar; and the rest of the blood shall be drained out at the base of the altar. It is a sin offering. ¹⁰ He shall offer the second for a burnt offering, according to the ordinance; and the priest shall make atonement for him concerning his sin which he has sinned, and he shall be forgiven. ¹¹"But if he can't afford two turtledoves or two young pigeons, then he shall bring as his offering for that in which he has sinned, one tenth of an ephahᵃ of fine flour for a sin offering. He shall put no oil on it, and he shall not put any frankincense on it, for it is a sin offering. ¹² He shall bring it to the priest, and the priest shall take his handful of it as the memorial portion, and burn it on the altar, on the offerings of Yahweh made by fire. It is a sin offering. ¹³ The priest shall make atonement for him concerning his sin that he has sinned in any of these things, and he will be forgiven; and the rest shall be the priest's, as the meal offering.'" ¹⁴ Yahweh spoke to Moses, saying, ¹⁵"If anyone commits a trespass, and sins unwittingly regarding Yahweh's holy things, then he shall bring his trespass offering to Yahweh: a ram without defect from the flock, according to your estimation in silver by shekels, according to the shekelᵇ of the sanctuary, for a trespass offering. ¹⁶ He shall make restitution for that which he has done wrong regarding the holy thing, and shall add a fifth part to it, and give it to the priest; and the priest shall make atonement for him with the ram of the trespass offering, and he will be forgiven. ¹⁷"If anyone sins, doing any of the things which Yahweh has commanded not to be done, though he didn't know it, he is still guilty, and shall bear his iniquity. ¹⁸ He shall bring a ram without defect from of the flock, according to your estimation, for a trespass offering, to the priest; and the priest shall make atonement for him concerning the thing in which he sinned and didn't know it, and he will be forgiven. ¹⁹ It is a trespass offering. He is certainly guilty before Yahweh."

## 6

¹ Yahweh spoke to Moses, saying, ²"If anyone sins, and commits a trespass against Yahweh, and deals falsely with his neighbor in a matter of deposit, or of bargain, or of robbery, or has oppressed his neighbor, ³ or has found that which was lost, and lied about it, and swearing to a lie—in any of these things that a man sins in his actions— ⁴ then it shall be, if he has sinned, and is guilty, he shall restore that which he took by robbery, or the thing which he has gotten by oppression, or the deposit which was committed to him, or the lost thing which he found, ⁵ or any thing about which he has sworn falsely: he shall restore it in full, and shall add a fifth part more to it. He shall return it to him to whom it belongs in the day of his being found guilty. ⁶ He shall bring his trespass offering to Yahweh: a ram without defect from the flock, according to your estimation, for a trespass offering, to the priest. ⁷ The priest shall make atonement for him before Yahweh, and he will be forgiven concerning whatever he does to become guilty." ⁸ Yahweh spoke to Moses, saying, ⁹"Command Aaron and his sons, saying, 'This is the law of the burnt offering: the burnt offering shall be on the hearth on the altar all night until the morning; and the fire of the altar shall be kept burning on it. ¹⁰ The priest shall put on his linen garment, and he shall put on his linen trousers upon his body; and he shall remove the ashes from where the fire has consumed the burnt offering on the altar, and he shall put them beside the altar. ¹¹ He shall take off his garments, and put on other garments, and carry the ashes outside the camp to a clean place. ¹² The fire on the altar shall be kept burning on it, it shall not go out; and the priest shall burn wood on it every morning. He shall lay the burnt offering in order upon it, and shall burn on it the fat of the peace offerings. ¹³ Fire shall be kept burning on the altar continually; it shall not go out. ¹⁴"This is the law of the meal offering: the sons of Aaron shall offer it before Yahweh, before the altar. ¹⁵ He shall take from there his handful of the fine flour of the meal offering, and of its oil, and all the frankincense which is on the meal offering, and shall burn it on the altar for a pleasant aroma, as its memorial portion, to Yahweh. ¹⁶ That which is left of it Aaron and his sons shall eat. It shall be eaten without yeast in a holy place. They shall eat it in the court of the Tent of Meeting. ¹⁷ It shall not be baked with yeast. I have given it as their portion of my offerings made by fire. It is most holy, as are the sin offering and the trespass offering. ¹⁸ Every male among the children

---

ᵃ 5:11 1 ephah is about 22 liters or about 2/3 of a bushel

ᵇ 5:15 A shekel is about 10 grams or about 0.35 ounces.

of Aaron shall eat of it, as their portion forever throughout your generations, from the offerings of Yahweh made by fire. Whoever touches them shall be holy.'" ¹⁹ Yahweh spoke to Moses, saying, ²⁰"This is the offering of Aaron and of his sons, which they shall offer to Yahweh in the day when he is anointed: one tenth of an ephahᵃ of fine flour for a meal offering perpetually, half of it in the morning, and half of it in the evening. ²¹ It shall be made with oil on a griddle. When it is soaked, you shall bring it in. You shall offer the meal offering in baked pieces for a pleasant aroma to Yahweh. ²² The anointed priest that will be in his place from among his sons shall offer it. By a statute forever, it shall be wholly burned to Yahweh. ²³ Every meal offering of a priest shall be wholly burned. It shall not be eaten." ²⁴ Yahweh spoke to Moses, saying, ²⁵"Speak to Aaron and to his sons, saying, 'This is the law of the sin offering: in the place where the burnt offering is killed, the sin offering shall be killed before Yahweh. It is most holy. ²⁶ The priest who offers it for sin shall eat it. It shall be eaten in a holy place, in the court of the Tent of Meeting. ²⁷ Whatever shall touch its flesh shall be holy. When there is any of its blood sprinkled on a garment, you shall wash that on which it was sprinkled in a holy place. ²⁸ But the earthen vessel in which it is boiled shall be broken; and if it is boiled in a bronze vessel, it shall be scoured, and rinsed in water. ²⁹ Every male among the priests shall eat of it. It is most holy. ³⁰ No sin offering, of which any of the blood is brought into the Tent of Meeting to make atonement in the Holy Place, shall be eaten. It shall be burned with fire.

## 7

¹"'This is the law of the trespass offering: It is most holy. ² In the place where they kill the burnt offering, he shall kill the trespass offering; and its blood he shall sprinkle around on the altar. ³ He shall offer all of its fat: the fat tail, and the fat that covers the innards, ⁴ and he shall take away the two kidneys, and the fat that is on them, which is by the loins, and the cover on the liver, with the kidneys; ⁵ and the priest shall burn them on the altar for an offering made by fire to Yahweh: it is a trespass offering. ⁶ Every male among the priests may eat of it. It shall be eaten in a holy place. It is most holy. ⁷"'As is the sin offering, so is the trespass offering; there is one law for them. The priest who makes atonement with them shall have it. ⁸ The priest who offers any man's burnt offering shall have for himself the skin of the burnt offering which he has offered. ⁹ Every meal offering that is baked in the oven, and all that is prepared in the pan and on the griddle, shall be the priest's who offers it. ¹⁰ Every meal offering, mixed with oil or dry, belongs to all the sons of Aaron, one as well as another. ¹¹"'This is the law of the sacrifice of peace offerings, which one shall offer to Yahweh: ¹² If he offers it for a thanksgiving, then he shall offer with the sacrifice of thanksgiving unleavened cakes mixed with oil, and unleavened wafers anointed with oil, and cakes mixed with oil. ¹³ He shall offer his offering with the sacrifice of his peace offerings for thanksgiving with cakes of leavened bread. ¹⁴ Of it he shall offer one out of each offering for a heave offering to Yahweh. It shall be the priest's who sprinkles the blood of the peace offerings. ¹⁵ The flesh of the sacrifice of his peace offerings for thanksgiving shall be eaten on the day of his offering. He shall not leave any of it until the morning. ¹⁶"'But if the sacrifice of his offering is a vow, or a free will offering, it shall be eaten on the day that he offers his sacrifice. On the next day what remains of it shall be eaten, ¹⁷ but what remains of the meat of the sacrifice on the third day shall be burned with fire. ¹⁸ If any of the meat of the sacrifice of his peace offerings is eaten on the third day, it will not be accepted, and it shall not be credited to him who offers it. It will be an abomination, and the soul who eats any of it will bear his iniquity. ¹⁹"'The meat that touches any unclean thing shall not be eaten. It shall be burned with fire. As for the meat, everyone who is clean may eat it; ²⁰ but the soul who eats of the meat of the sacrifice of peace offerings that belongs to Yahweh, having his uncleanness on him, that soul shall be cut off from his people. ²¹ When anyone touches any unclean thing, the uncleanness of man, or an unclean animal, or any unclean abomination, and eats some of the meat of the sacrifice of peace offerings which belong to Yahweh, that soul shall be cut off from his people.'" ²² Yahweh spoke to Moses, saying, ²³"Speak to the children of Israel, saying, 'You shall eat no fat, of bull, or sheep, or goat. ²⁴ The fat of that which dies of itself, and the fat of that which is torn of animals, may be used for any other service, but you shall in no way eat of it. ²⁵ For whoever eats the fat of the animal which men offer as an offering made by fire to Yahweh, even the soul who eats it shall be cut off from his people. ²⁶ You shall not eat any blood, whether it is of bird or of animal, in any of your dwellings. ²⁷ Whoever it is who eats any blood, that soul shall be cut off from his people.'" ²⁸ Yahweh spoke to Moses, saying, ²⁹"Speak to the children of Israel, saying, 'He who offers the sacrifice of his peace offerings to

Yahweh shall bring his offering to Yahweh out of the sacrifice of his peace offerings. ³⁰ With his own hands he shall bring the offerings of Yahweh made by fire. He shall bring the fat with the breast, that the breast may be waved for a wave offering before Yahweh. ³¹ The priest shall burn the fat on the altar, but the breast shall be Aaron's and his sons'. ³² The right thigh you shall give to the priest for a heave offering out of the sacrifices of your peace offerings. ³³ He among the sons of Aaron who offers the blood of the peace offerings, and the fat, shall have the right thigh for a portion. ³⁴ For the waved breast and the heaved thigh I have taken from the children of Israel out of the sacrifices of their peace offerings, and have given them to Aaron the priest and to his sons as their portion forever from the children of Israel.'" ³⁵ This is the consecrated portion of Aaron, and the consecrated portion of his sons, out of the offerings of Yahweh made by fire, in the day when he presented them to minister to Yahweh in the priest's office; ³⁶ which Yahweh commanded to be given them of the children of Israel, in the day that he anointed them. It is their portion forever throughout their generations. ³⁷ This is the law of the burnt offering, the meal offering, the sin offering, the trespass offering, the consecration, and the sacrifice of peace offerings ³⁸ which Yahweh commanded Moses in Mount Sinai in the day that he commanded the children of Israel to offer their offerings to Yahweh, in the wilderness of Sinai.

## 8

¹ Yahweh spoke to Moses, saying, ²"Take Aaron and his sons with him, and the garments, and the anointing oil, and the bull of the sin offering, and the two rams, and the basket of unleavened bread; ³ and assemble all the congregation at the door of the Tent of Meeting." ⁴ Moses did as Yahweh commanded him; and the congregation was assembled at the door of the Tent of Meeting. ⁵ Moses said to the congregation, "This is the thing which Yahweh has commanded to be done." ⁶ Moses brought Aaron and his sons, and washed them with water. ⁷ He put the tunic on him, tied the sash on him, clothed him with the robe, put the ephod on him, and he tied the skillfully woven band of the ephod on him and fastened it to him with it. ⁸ He placed the breastplate on him. He put the Urim and Thummim in the breastplate. ⁹ He set the turban on his head. He set the golden plate, the holy crown, on the front of the turban, as Yahweh commanded Moses. ¹⁰ Moses took the anointing oil, and anointed the tabernacle and all that was in it, and sanctified them. ¹¹ He sprinkled it on the altar seven times, and anointed the altar and all its vessels, and the basin and its base, to sanctify them. ¹² He poured some of the anointing oil on Aaron's head, and anointed him, to sanctify him. ¹³ Moses brought Aaron's sons, and clothed them with tunics, and tied sashes on them, and put headbands on them, as Yahweh commanded Moses. ¹⁴ He brought the bull of the sin offering, and Aaron and his sons laid their hands on the head of the bull of the sin offering. ¹⁵ He killed it; and Moses took the blood, and put it around on the horns of the altar with his finger, and purified the altar, and poured out the blood at the base of the altar, and sanctified it, to make atonement for it. ¹⁶ He took all the fat that was on the innards, and the cover of the liver, and the two kidneys, and their fat; and Moses burned it on the altar. ¹⁷ But the bull, and its skin, and its meat, and its dung, he burned with fire outside the camp, as Yahweh commanded Moses. ¹⁸ He presented the ram of the burnt offering. Aaron and his sons laid their hands on the head of the ram. ¹⁹ He killed it; and Moses sprinkled the blood around on the altar. ²⁰ He cut the ram into its pieces; and Moses burned the head, and the pieces, and the fat. ²¹ He washed the innards and the legs with water; and Moses burned the whole ram on the altar. It was a burnt offering for a pleasant aroma. It was an offering made by fire to Yahweh, as Yahweh commanded Moses. ²² He presented the other ram, the ram of consecration. Aaron and his sons laid their hands on the head of the ram. ²³ He killed it; and Moses took some of its blood, and put it on the tip of Aaron's right ear, and on the thumb of his right hand, and on the great toe of his right foot. ²⁴ He brought Aaron's sons; and Moses put some of the blood on the tip of their right ear, and on the thumb of their right hand, and on the great toe of their right foot; and Moses sprinkled the blood around on the altar. ²⁵ He took the fat, the fat tail, all the fat that was on the innards, the cover of the liver, the two kidneys and their fat, and the right thigh; ²⁶ and out of the basket of unleavened bread that was before Yahweh, he took one unleavened cake, one cake of oiled bread, and one wafer, and placed them on the fat and on the right thigh. ²⁷ He put all these in Aaron's hands and in his sons' hands, and waved them for a wave offering before Yahweh. ²⁸ Moses took them from their hands, and burned them on the altar on the burnt offering. They were a consecration offering for a pleasant aroma. It was an offering made by fire to Yahweh. ²⁹ Moses took the breast, and waved it for a wave offering before Yahweh. It was Moses' portion of the ram of consecration, as Yahweh commanded Moses. ³⁰ Moses took

---

ᵃ *6:20* 1 ephah is about 22 liters or about 2/3 of a bushel some of the anointing oil, and some of the blood which was on the altar, and sprinkled it on Aaron, on his garments, and on his sons, and on his sons' garments with him, and sanctified Aaron, his garments, and his sons, and his sons' garments with him. [31] Moses said to Aaron and to his sons, "Boil the meat at the door of the Tent of Meeting, and there eat it and the bread that is in the basket of consecration, as I commanded, saying, 'Aaron and his sons shall eat it.' [32] What remains of the meat and of the bread you shall burn with fire. [33] You shall not go out from the door of the Tent of Meeting for seven days, until the days of your consecration are fulfilled: for he shall consecrate you seven days. [34] What has been done today, so Yahweh has commanded to do, to make atonement for you. [35] You shall stay at the door of the Tent of Meeting day and night seven days, and keep Yahweh's command, that you don't die: for so I am commanded." [36] Aaron and his sons did all the things which Yahweh commanded by Moses.

## 9

[1] On the eighth day, Moses called Aaron and his sons, and the elders of Israel; [2] and he said to Aaron, "Take a calf from the herd for a sin offering, and a ram for a burnt offering, without defect, and offer them before Yahweh. [3] You shall speak to the children of Israel, saying, 'Take a male goat for a sin offering; and a calf and a lamb, both a year old, without defect, for a burnt offering; [4] and a bull and a ram for peace offerings, to sacrifice before Yahweh; and a meal offering mixed with oil: for today Yahweh appears to you.'" [5] They brought what Moses commanded before the Tent of Meeting. All the congregation came near and stood before Yahweh. [6] Moses said, "This is the thing which Yahweh commanded that you should do; and Yahweh's glory shall appear to you." [7] Moses said to Aaron, "Draw near to the altar, and offer your sin offering, and your burnt offering, and make atonement for yourself, and for the people; and offer the offering of the people, and make atonement for them, as Yahweh commanded." [8] So Aaron came near to the altar, and killed the calf of the sin offering, which was for himself. [9] The sons of Aaron presented the blood to him; and he dipped his finger in the blood, and put it on the horns of the altar, and poured out the blood at the base of the altar; [10] but the fat, and the kidneys, and the cover from the liver of the sin offering, he burned upon the altar, as Yahweh commanded Moses. [11] The meat and the skin he burned with fire outside the camp. [12] He killed the burnt offering; and Aaron's sons delivered the blood to him, and he sprinkled it around on the altar. [13] They delivered the burnt offering to him, piece by piece, and the head. He burned them upon the altar. [14] He washed the innards and the legs, and burned them on the burnt offering on the altar. [15] He presented the people's offering, and took the goat of the sin offering which was for the people, and killed it, and offered it for sin, like the first. [16] He presented the burnt offering, and offered it according to the ordinance. [17] He presented the meal offering, and filled his hand from there, and burned it upon the altar, in addition to the burnt offering of the morning. [18] He also killed the bull and the ram, the sacrifice of peace offerings, which was for the people. Aaron's sons delivered to him the blood, which he sprinkled around on the altar; [19] and the fat of the bull and of the ram, the fat tail, and that which covers the innards, and the kidneys, and the cover of the liver; [20] and they put the fat upon the breasts, and he burned the fat on the altar. [21] Aaron waved the breasts and the right thigh for a wave offering before Yahweh, as Moses commanded. [22] Aaron lifted up his hands toward the people, and blessed them; and he came down from offering the sin offering, and the burnt offering, and the peace offerings. [23] Moses and Aaron went into the Tent of Meeting, and came out, and blessed the people; and Yahweh's glory appeared to all the people. [24] Fire came out from before Yahweh, and consumed the burnt offering and the fat upon the altar. When all the people saw it, they shouted, and fell on their faces.

## 10

[1] Nadab and Abihu, the sons of Aaron, each took his censer, and put fire in it, and laid incense on it, and offered strange fire before Yahweh, which he had not commanded them. [2] Fire came out from before Yahweh, and devoured them, and they died before Yahweh. [3] Then Moses said to Aaron, "This is what Yahweh spoke of, saying, 'I will show myself holy to those who come near me, and before all the people I will be glorified.'" Aaron held his peace. [4] Moses called Mishael and Elzaphan, the sons of Uzziel the uncle of Aaron, and said to them, "Draw near, carry your brothers from before the sanctuary out of the camp." [5] So they came near, and carried them in their tunics out of the camp, as Moses had said. [6] Moses said to Aaron, and to Eleazar and to Ithamar, his sons, "Don't let the hair of your heads go loose, and don't tear your clothes, so that you don't die, and so that he will not be angry with all the congregation; but let your brothers, the whole house of Israel, bewail the burning which Yahweh has kindled. [7] You shall not

go out from the door of the Tent of Meeting, lest you die; for the anointing oil of Yahweh is on you." They did according to the word of Moses. [8] Then Yahweh said to Aaron, [9]"You and your sons are not to drink wine or strong drink whenever you go into the Tent of Meeting, or you will die. This shall be a statute forever throughout your generations. [10] You are to make a distinction between the holy and the common, and between the unclean and the clean. [11] You are to teach the children of Israel all the statutes which Yahweh has spoken to them by Moses." [12] Moses spoke to Aaron, and to Eleazar and to Ithamar, his sons who were left, "Take the meal offering that remains of the offerings of Yahweh made by fire, and eat it without yeast beside the altar; for it is most holy; [13] and you shall eat it in a holy place, because it is your portion, and your sons' portion, of the offerings of Yahweh made by fire; for so I am commanded. [14] The waved breast and the heaved thigh you shall eat in a clean place, you, and your sons, and your daughters with you: for they are given as your portion, and your sons' portion, out of the sacrifices of the peace offerings of the children of Israel. [15] They shall bring the heaved thigh and the waved breast with the offerings made by fire of the fat, to wave it for a wave offering before Yahweh. It shall be yours, and your sons' with you, as a portion forever, as Yahweh has commanded." [16] Moses diligently inquired about the goat of the sin offering, and, behold,[a] it was burned. He was angry with Eleazar and with Ithamar, the sons of Aaron who were left, saying, [17]"Why haven't you eaten the sin offering in the place of the sanctuary, since it is most holy, and he has given it to you to bear the iniquity of the congregation, to make atonement for them before Yahweh? [18] Behold, its blood was not brought into the inner part of the sanctuary. You certainly should have eaten it in the sanctuary, as I commanded." [19] Aaron spoke to Moses, "Behold, today they have offered their sin offering and their burnt offering before Yahweh; and such things as these have happened to me. If I had eaten the sin offering today, would it have been pleasing in Yahweh's sight?" [20] When Moses heard that, it was pleasing in his sight.

## 11

[1] Yahweh spoke to Moses and to Aaron, saying to them, [2]"Speak to the children of Israel, saying, 'These are the living things which you may eat among all the animals that are on the earth. [3] Whatever parts the hoof, and is cloven-footed, and chews the cud among the animals, that you may eat. [4]"Nevertheless these you shall not eat of those that chew the cud, or of those who part the hoof: the camel, because it chews the cud but doesn't have a parted hoof, is unclean to you. [5] The hyrax,[b] because it chews the cud but doesn't have a parted hoof, is unclean to you. [6] The hare, because it chews the cud but doesn't have a parted hoof, is unclean to you. [7] The pig, because it has a split hoof, and is cloven-footed, but doesn't chew the cud, is unclean to you. [8] You shall not eat their meat. You shall not touch their carcasses. They are unclean to you. [9]"You may eat of all these that are in the waters: whatever has fins and scales in the waters, in the seas, and in the rivers, that you may eat. [10] All that don't have fins and scales in the seas and rivers, all that move in the waters, and all the living creatures that are in the waters, they are an abomination to you, [11] and you shall detest them. You shall not eat of their meat, and you shall detest their carcasses. [12] Whatever has no fins nor scales in the waters is an abomination to you. [13]"You shall detest these among the birds; they shall not be eaten because they are an abomination: the eagle, the vulture, the black vulture, [14] the red kite, any kind of black kite, [15] any kind of raven, [16] the horned owl, the screech owl, the gull, any kind of hawk, [17] the little owl, the cormorant, the great owl, [18] the white owl, the desert owl, the osprey, [19] the stork, any kind of heron, the hoopoe, and the bat. [20]"All flying insects that walk on all fours are an abomination to you. [21] Yet you may eat these: of all winged creeping things that go on all fours, which have long, jointed legs for hopping on the earth. [22] Even of these you may eat: any kind of locust, any kind of katydid, any kind of cricket, and any kind of grasshopper. [23] But all winged creeping things which have four feet are an abomination to you. [24]"By these you will become unclean: whoever touches their carcass shall be unclean until the evening. [25] Whoever carries any part of their carcass shall wash his clothes, and be unclean until the evening. [26]"Every animal which has a split hoof that isn't completely divided, or doesn't chew the cud, is unclean to you. Everyone who touches them shall be unclean. [27] Whatever goes on its paws, among all animals that go on all fours, they are unclean to you. Whoever touches their carcass shall be unclean until the evening. [28] He who carries their carcass shall wash his clothes, and be unclean until the evening. They are unclean to you. [29]"These are they which are unclean to you among the creeping things that creep on the earth: the weasel, the rat, any kind of great lizard, [30] the gecko, and the monitor lizard, the wall lizard, the skink, and the chameleon. [31] These are they

---

[a] 10:16 "Behold", from "הִנֵּה", means look at, take notice, observe, see, or gaze at. It is often used as an interjection.

[b] 11:5 or rock badger, or cony

which are unclean to you among all that creep. Whoever touches them when they are dead shall be unclean until the evening. ³² Anything they fall on when they are dead shall be unclean; whether it is any vessel of wood, or clothing, or skin, or sack, whatever vessel it is, with which any work is done, it must be put into water, and it shall be unclean until the evening. Then it will be clean. ³³ Every earthen vessel into which any of them falls and all that is in it shall be unclean. You shall break it. ³⁴ All food which may be eaten which is soaked in water shall be unclean. All drink that may be drunk in every such vessel shall be unclean. ³⁵ Everything whereupon part of their carcass falls shall be unclean; whether oven, or range for pots, it shall be broken in pieces. They are unclean, and shall be unclean to you. ³⁶ Nevertheless a spring or a cistern in which water is gathered shall be clean, but that which touches their carcass shall be unclean. ³⁷ If part of their carcass falls on any sowing seed which is to be sown, it is clean. ³⁸ But if water is put on the seed, and part of their carcass falls on it, it is unclean to you. ³⁹"If any animal of which you may eat dies, he who touches its carcass shall be unclean until the evening. ⁴⁰ He who eats of its carcass shall wash his clothes, and be unclean until the evening. He also who carries its carcass shall wash his clothes, and be unclean until the evening. ⁴¹"Every creeping thing that creeps on the earth is an abomination. It shall not be eaten. ⁴² Whatever goes on its belly, and whatever goes on all fours, or whatever has many feet, even all creeping things that creep on the earth, them you shall not eat; for they are an abomination. ⁴³ You shall not make yourselves abominable with any creeping thing that creeps. You shall not make yourselves unclean with them, that you should be defiled by them. ⁴⁴ For I am Yahweh your God. Sanctify yourselves therefore, and be holy; for I am holy. You shall not defile yourselves with any kind of creeping thing that moves on the earth. ⁴⁵ For I am Yahweh who brought you up out of the land of Egypt, to be your God. You shall therefore be holy, for I am holy. ⁴⁶"This is the law of the animal, and of the bird, and of every living creature that moves in the waters, and of every creature that creeps on the earth, ⁴⁷ to make a distinction between the unclean and the clean, and between the living thing that may be eaten and the living thing that may not be eaten.'"

## 12

¹ Yahweh spoke to Moses, saying, ²"Speak to the children of Israel, saying, 'If a woman conceives, and bears a male child, then she shall be unclean seven days; as in the days of her monthly period she shall be unclean. ³ In the eighth day the flesh of his foreskin shall be circumcised. ⁴ She shall continue in the blood of purification thirty-three days. She shall not touch any holy thing, nor come into the sanctuary, until the days of her purifying are completed. ⁵ But if she bears a female child, then she shall be unclean two weeks, as in her period; and she shall continue in the blood of purification sixty-six days. ⁶"When the days of her purification are completed for a son or for a daughter, she shall bring to the priest at the door of the Tent of Meeting, a year old lamb for a burnt offering, and a young pigeon or a turtledove, for a sin offering. ⁷ He shall offer it before Yahweh, and make atonement for her; then she shall be cleansed from the fountain of her blood. "'This is the law for her who bears, whether a male or a female. ⁸ If she cannot afford a lamb, then she shall take two turtledoves or two young pigeons: the one for a burnt offering, and the other for a sin offering. The priest shall make atonement for her, and she shall be clean.'"

## 13

¹ Yahweh spoke to Moses and to Aaron, saying, ²"When a man shall have a swelling in his body's skin, or a scab, or a bright spot, and it becomes in the skin of his body the plague of leprosy, then he shall be brought to Aaron the priest or to one of his sons, the priests. ³ The priest shall examine the plague in the skin of the body. If the hair in the plague has turned white, and the appearance of the plague is deeper than the body's skin, it is the plague of leprosy; so the priest shall examine him and pronounce him unclean. ⁴ If the bright spot is white in the skin of his body, and its appearance isn't deeper than the skin, and its hair hasn't turned white, then the priest shall isolate the infected person for seven days. ⁵ The priest shall examine him on the seventh day. Behold, if in his eyes the plague is arrested and the plague hasn't spread in the skin, then the priest shall isolate him for seven more days. ⁶ The priest shall examine him again on the seventh day. Behold, if the plague has faded and the plague hasn't spread in the skin, then the priest shall pronounce him clean. It is a scab. He shall wash his clothes, and be clean. ⁷ But if the scab spreads on the skin after he has shown himself to the priest for his cleansing, he shall show himself to the priest again. ⁸ The priest shall examine him; and behold, if the scab has spread on the skin, then the priest shall pronounce him unclean. It is leprosy. ⁹"When the plague of leprosy is in a man, then he shall be brought to the priest; ¹⁰ and the priest shall examine him. Behold, if there is a white swelling in the skin, and it has turned the hair white, and there is raw flesh in the swelling, ¹¹ it is a chronic leprosy in the skin of his body,

and the priest shall pronounce him unclean. He shall not isolate him, for he is already unclean. ¹²"If the leprosy breaks out all over the skin, and the leprosy covers all the skin of the infected person from his head even to his feet, as far as it appears to the priest, ¹³ then the priest shall examine him. Behold, if the leprosy has covered all his flesh, he shall pronounce him clean of the plague. It has all turned white: he is clean. ¹⁴ But whenever raw flesh appears in him, he shall be unclean. ¹⁵ The priest shall examine the raw flesh, and pronounce him unclean: the raw flesh is unclean. It is leprosy. ¹⁶ Or if the raw flesh turns again, and is changed to white, then he shall come to the priest. ¹⁷ The priest shall examine him. Behold, if the plague has turned white, then the priest shall pronounce him clean of the plague. He is clean. ¹⁸"When the body has a boil on its skin, and it has healed, ¹⁹ and in the place of the boil there is a white swelling, or a bright spot, reddish-white, then it shall be shown to the priest. ²⁰ The priest shall examine it. Behold, if its appearance is deeper than the skin, and its hair has turned white, then the priest shall pronounce him unclean. It is the plague of leprosy. It has broken out in the boil. ²¹ But if the priest examines it, and behold, there are no white hairs in it, and it isn't deeper than the skin, but is dim, then the priest shall isolate him seven days. ²² If it spreads in the skin, then the priest shall pronounce him unclean. It is a plague. ²³ But if the bright spot stays in its place, and hasn't spread, it is the scar from the boil; and the priest shall pronounce him clean. ²⁴"Or when the body has a burn from fire on its skin, and the raw flesh of the burn becomes a bright spot, reddish-white, or white, ²⁵ then the priest shall examine it; and behold, if the hair in the bright spot has turned white, and its appearance is deeper than the skin, it is leprosy. It has broken out in the burning, and the priest shall pronounce him unclean. It is the plague of leprosy. ²⁶ But if the priest examines it, and behold, there is no white hair in the bright spot, and it isn't deeper than the skin, but has faded, then the priest shall isolate him seven days. ²⁷ The priest shall examine him on the seventh day. If it has spread in the skin, then the priest shall pronounce him unclean. It is the plague of leprosy. ²⁸ If the bright spot stays in its place, and hasn't spread in the skin, but is faded, it is the swelling from the burn, and the priest shall pronounce him clean, for it is the scar from the burn. ²⁹"When a man or woman has a plague on the head or on the beard, ³⁰ then the priest shall examine the plague; and behold, if its appearance is deeper than the skin, and the hair in it is yellow and thin, then the priest shall pronounce him unclean. It is an itch. It is leprosy of the head or of the beard. ³¹ If the priest examines the plague of itching, and behold, its appearance isn't deeper than the skin, and there is no black hair in it, then the priest shall isolate the person infected with itching seven days. ³² On the seventh day the priest shall examine the plague; and behold, if the itch hasn't spread, and there is no yellow hair in it, and the appearance of the itch isn't deeper than the skin, ³³ then he shall be shaved, but he shall not shave the itch. Then the priest shall isolate the one who has the itch seven more days. ³⁴ On the seventh day, the priest shall examine the itch; and behold, if the itch hasn't spread in the skin, and its appearance isn't deeper than the skin, then the priest shall pronounce him clean. He shall wash his clothes and be clean. ³⁵ But if the itch spreads in the skin after his cleansing, ³⁶ then the priest shall examine him; and behold, if the itch has spread in the skin, the priest shall not look for the yellow hair; he is unclean. ³⁷ But if in his eyes the itch is arrested and black hair has grown in it, then the itch is healed. He is clean. The priest shall pronounce him clean. ³⁸"When a man or a woman has bright spots in the skin of the body, even white bright spots, ³⁹ then the priest shall examine them. Behold, if the bright spots on the skin of their body are a dull white, it is a harmless rash. It has broken out in the skin. He is clean. ⁴⁰"If a man's hair has fallen from his head, he is bald. He is clean. ⁴¹ If his hair has fallen off from the front part of his head, he is forehead bald. He is clean. ⁴² But if a reddish-white plague is in the bald head or the bald forehead, it is leprosy breaking out in his bald head or his bald forehead. ⁴³ Then the priest shall examine him. Behold, if the swelling of the plague is reddish-white in his bald head, or in his bald forehead, like the appearance of leprosy in the skin of the body, ⁴⁴ he is a leprous man. He is unclean. The priest shall surely pronounce him unclean. His plague is on his head. ⁴⁵"The leper in whom the plague is shall wear torn clothes, and the hair of his head shall hang loose. He shall cover his upper lip, and shall cry, 'Unclean! Unclean!' ⁴⁶ All the days in which the plague is in him he shall be unclean. He is unclean. He shall dwell alone. His dwelling shall be outside of the camp. ⁴⁷"The garment also that the plague of leprosy is in, whether it is a woolen garment, or a linen garment; ⁴⁸ whether it is in warp or woof;ᵃ of linen or of wool; whether in a leather, or in anything made of leather; ⁴⁹ if the plague is greenish or reddish in the garment, or in the leather, or in the warp, or in the woof, or in anything made of leather; it is the plague of leprosy, and shall be shown to the priest. ⁵⁰ The priest shall examine the plague, and isolate the plague seven days. ⁵¹ He shall examine the plague on the seventh day. If the plague has spread in the garment, either in the warp, or in the woof, or in the skin, whatever use the skin is used for, the plague is a destructive mildew. It is unclean. ⁵² He shall burn the garment, whether the warp or the woof, in wool or in linen, or anything of leather, in which the plague is, for it is a destructive mildew. It shall be burned in the fire. ⁵³"If the priest examines it, and behold, the plague hasn't spread in the garment, either in the warp, or in the woof, or in anything of skin; ⁵⁴ then the priest shall command that they wash the thing that the plague is in, and he shall isolate it seven more days. ⁵⁵ Then the priest shall examine it, after the plague is washed; and behold, if the plague hasn't changed its color, and the plague hasn't spread, it is unclean; you shall burn it in the fire. It is a mildewed spot, whether the bareness is inside or outside. ⁵⁶ If the priest looks, and behold, the plague has faded after it is washed, then he shall tear it out of the garment, or out of the skin, or out of the warp, or out of the woof; ⁵⁷ and if it appears again in the garment, either in the warp, or in the woof, or in anything of skin, it is spreading. You shall burn what the plague is in with fire. ⁵⁸ The garment, either the warp, or the woof, or whatever thing of skin it is, which you shall wash, if the plague has departed from them, then it shall be washed the second time, and it will be clean." ⁵⁹ This is the law of the plague of mildew in a garment of wool or linen, either in the warp, or the woof, or in anything of skin, to pronounce it clean, or to pronounce it unclean.

## 14

¹ Yahweh spoke to Moses, saying, ²"This shall be the law of the leper in the day of his cleansing: He shall be brought to the priest, ³ and the priest shall go out of the camp. The priest shall examine him. Behold, if the plague of leprosy is healed in the leper, ⁴ then the priest shall command them to take for him who is to be cleansed two living clean birds, cedar wood, scarlet, and hyssop. ⁵ The priest shall command them to kill one of the birds in an earthen vessel over running water. ⁶ As for the living bird, he shall take it, the cedar wood, the scarlet, and the hyssop, and shall dip them and the living bird in the blood of the bird that was killed over the running water. ⁷ He shall sprinkle on him who is to be cleansed from the leprosy seven times, and shall pronounce him clean, and shall let the living bird go into the open field. ⁸"He who is to be cleansed shall wash his clothes, and shave off all his hair, and bathe himself in water; and he shall be clean. After that he shall come into the camp, but shall dwell outside his tent seven days. ⁹ It shall be on the seventh day, that he shall shave all his hair off his head and his beard and his eyebrows. He shall shave off all his hair. He shall wash his clothes, and he shall bathe his body in water. Then he shall be clean. ¹⁰"On the eighth day he shall take two male lambs without defect, one ewe lamb a year old without defect, three tenths of an ephahᵇ of fine flour for a meal offering, mixed with oil, and one logᶜ of oil. ¹¹ The priest who cleanses him shall set the man who is to be cleansed, and those things, before Yahweh, at the door of the Tent of Meeting. ¹²"The priest shall take one of the male lambs, and offer him for a trespass offering, with the log of oil, and wave them for a wave offering before Yahweh. ¹³ He shall kill the male lamb in the place where they kill the sin offering and the burnt offering, in the place of the sanctuary; for as the sin offering is the priest's, so is the trespass offering. It is most holy. ¹⁴ The priest shall take some of the blood of the trespass offering, and the priest shall put it on the tip of the right ear of him who is to be cleansed, and on the thumb of his right hand, and on the big toe of his right foot. ¹⁵ The priest shall take some of the log of oil, and pour it into the palm of his own left hand. ¹⁶ The priest shall dip his right finger in the oil that is in his left hand, and shall sprinkle some of the oil with his finger seven times before Yahweh. ¹⁷ The priest shall put some of the rest of the oil that is in his hand on the tip of the right ear of him who is to be cleansed, and on the thumb of his right hand, and on the big toe of his right foot, upon the blood of the trespass offering. ¹⁸ The rest of the oil that is in the priest's hand he shall put on the head of him who is to be cleansed, and the priest shall make atonement for him before Yahweh. ¹⁹"The priest shall offer the sin offering, and make atonement for him who is to be cleansed because of his uncleanness. Afterward he shall kill the burnt offering; ²⁰ then the priest shall offer the burnt offering and the meal offering on the altar. The priest shall make

atonement for him, and he shall be clean. ²¹"If he is poor, and can't afford so much, then he shall take one male lamb for a trespass offering to be waved, to make atonement for him, and one tenth of an ephahᵈ of fine flour mixed with oil for a meal offering, and a logᵉ of oil; ²² and two turtledoves, or two young pigeons, such as he is able to afford; and the one shall be a sin offering, and the other a burnt offering. ²³"On the eighth day he shall bring them for his cleansing to the priest, to the door of the Tent of Meeting, before Yahweh. ²⁴ The priest shall take the lamb of the trespass offering, and the log of oil, and the priest shall wave them for a wave offering before Yahweh. ²⁵ He shall kill the lamb of the trespass offering. The priest shall take some of the blood of the trespass offering and put it on the tip of the right ear of him who is to be cleansed, and on the thumb of his right hand, and on the big toe of his right foot. ²⁶ The priest shall pour some of the oil into the palm of his own left hand; ²⁷ and the priest shall sprinkle with his right finger some of the oil that is in his left hand seven times before Yahweh. ²⁸ Then the priest shall put some of the oil that is in his hand on the tip of the right ear of him who is to be cleansed, and on the thumb of his right hand, and on the big toe of his right foot, on the place of the blood of the trespass offering. ²⁹ The rest of the oil that is in the priest's hand he shall put on the head of him who is to be cleansed, to make atonement for him before Yahweh. ³⁰ He shall offer one of the turtledoves, or of the young pigeons, which ever he is able to afford, ³¹ of the kind he is able to afford, the one for a sin offering, and the other for a burnt offering, with the meal offering. The priest shall make atonement for him who is to be cleansed before Yahweh." ³² This is the law for him in whom is the plague of leprosy, who is not able to afford the sacrifice for his cleansing. ³³ Yahweh spoke to Moses and to Aaron, saying, ³⁴"When you have come into the land of Canaan, which I give to you for a possession, and I put a spreading mildew in a house in the land of your possession, ³⁵ then he who owns the house shall come and tell the priest, saying, 'There seems to me to be some sort of plague in the house.' ³⁶ The priest shall command that they empty the house, before the priest goes in to examine the plague, that all that is in the house not be made unclean. Afterward the priest shall go in to inspect the house. ³⁷ He shall examine the plague; and behold, if the plague is in the walls of the house with hollow streaks, greenish or reddish, and it appears to be deeper than the wall, ³⁸ then the priest shall go out of the house to the door of the house, and shut up the house seven days. ³⁹ The priest shall come again on the seventh day, and look. If the plague has spread in the walls of the house, ⁴⁰ then the priest shall command that they take out the stones in which is the plague, and cast them into an unclean place outside of the city. ⁴¹ He shall cause the inside of the house to be scraped all over. They shall pour out the mortar that they scraped off outside of the city into an unclean place. ⁴² They shall take other stones, and put them in the place of those stones; and he shall take other mortar, and shall plaster the house. ⁴³"If the plague comes again, and breaks out in the house after it has taken out the stones, and after he has scraped the house, and after it was plastered, ⁴⁴ then the priest shall come in and look; and behold, if the plague has spread in the house, it is a destructive mildew in the house. It is unclean. ⁴⁵ He shall break down the house, its stones, and its timber, and all the house's mortar. He shall carry them out of the city into an unclean place. ⁴⁶"Moreover he who goes into the house while it is shut up shall be unclean until the evening. ⁴⁷ He who lies down in the house shall wash his clothes; and he who eats in the house shall wash his clothes. ⁴⁸"If the priest shall come in, and examine it, and behold, the plague hasn't spread in the house, after the house was plastered, then the priest shall pronounce the house clean, because the plague is healed. ⁴⁹ To cleanse the house he shall take two birds, cedar wood, scarlet, and hyssop. ⁵⁰ He shall kill one of the birds in an earthen vessel over running water. ⁵¹ He shall take the cedar wood, the hyssop, the scarlet, and the living bird, and dip them in the blood of the slain bird, and in the running water, and sprinkle the house seven times. ⁵² He shall cleanse the house with the blood of the bird, and with the running water, with the living bird, with the cedar wood, with the hyssop, and with the scarlet; ⁵³ but he shall let the living bird go out of the city into the open field. So shall he make atonement for the house; and it shall be clean." ⁵⁴ This is the law for any plague of leprosy, and for an itch, ⁵⁵ and for the destructive mildew of a garment, and for a house, ⁵⁶ and for a swelling, and for a scab, and for a bright spot; ⁵⁷ to teach when it is unclean, and when it is clean. This is the law of leprosy.

## 15

¹ Yahweh spoke to Moses and to Aaron, saying, ²"Speak to the children of Israel, and tell them, 'When any man has a discharge from his body,

---

ᵃ *13:48* warp and woof are the vertical and horizontal threads in woven cloth
ᵇ *14:10* 1 ephah is about 22 liters or about 2/3 of a bushel

ᶜ *14:10* a log is a liquid measure of about 300 ml or 10 ounces
ᵈ *14:21* 1 ephah is about 22 liters or about 2/3 of a bushel

ᵉ *14:21* a log is a liquid measure of about 300 ml or 10 ounces because of his discharge he is unclean. ³ This shall be his uncleanness in his discharge: whether his body runs with his discharge, or his body has stopped from his discharge, it is his uncleanness. ⁴"Every bed on which he who has the discharge lies shall be unclean; and everything he sits on shall be unclean. ⁵ Whoever touches his bed shall wash his clothes, and bathe himself in water, and be unclean until the evening. ⁶ He who sits on anything on which the man who has the discharge sat shall wash his clothes, and bathe himself in water, and be unclean until the evening. ⁷"He who touches the body of him who has the discharge shall wash his clothes, and bathe himself in water, and be unclean until the evening. ⁸"If he who has the discharge spits on him who is clean, then he shall wash his clothes, and bathe himself in water, and be unclean until the evening. ⁹"Whatever saddle he who has the discharge rides on shall be unclean. ¹⁰ Whoever touches anything that was under him shall be unclean until the evening. He who carries those things shall wash his clothes, and bathe himself in water, and be unclean until the evening. ¹¹"Whomever he who has the discharge touches, without having rinsed his hands in water, he shall wash his clothes, and bathe himself in water, and be unclean until the evening. ¹²"The earthen vessel, which he who has the discharge touches, shall be broken; and every vessel of wood shall be rinsed in water. ¹³"When he who has a discharge is cleansed of his discharge, then he shall count to himself seven days for his cleansing, and wash his clothes; and he shall bathe his flesh in running water, and shall be clean. ¹⁴"On the eighth day he shall take two turtledoves, or two young pigeons, and come before Yahweh to the door of the Tent of Meeting, and give them to the priest. ¹⁵ The priest shall offer them, the one for a sin offering, and the other for a burnt offering. The priest shall make atonement for him before Yahweh for his discharge. ¹⁶"If any man has an emission of semen, then he shall bathe all his flesh in water, and be unclean until the evening. ¹⁷ Every garment and every skin which the semen is on shall be washed with water, and be unclean until the evening. ¹⁸ If a man lies with a woman and there is an emission of semen, they shall both bathe themselves in water, and be unclean until the evening. ¹⁹"If a woman has a discharge, and her discharge in her flesh is blood, she shall be in her impurity seven days. Whoever touches her shall be unclean until the evening. ²⁰"Everything that she lies on in her impurity shall be unclean. Everything also that she sits on shall be unclean. ²¹ Whoever touches her bed shall wash his clothes, and bathe himself in water, and be unclean until the evening. ²² Whoever touches anything that she sits on shall wash his clothes, and bathe himself in water, and be unclean until the evening. ²³ If it is on the bed, or on anything she sits on, when he touches it, he shall be unclean until the evening. ²⁴"If any man lies with her, and her monthly flow is on him, he shall be unclean seven days; and every bed he lies on shall be unclean. ²⁵"If a woman has a discharge of her blood many days not in the time of her period, or if she has a discharge beyond the time of her period, all the days of the discharge of her uncleanness shall be as in the days of her period. She is unclean. ²⁶ Every bed she lies on all the days of her discharge shall be to her as the bed of her period. Everything she sits on shall be unclean, as the uncleanness of her period. ²⁷ Whoever touches these things shall be unclean, and shall wash his clothes and bathe himself in water, and be unclean until the evening. ²⁸"But if she is cleansed of her discharge, then she shall count to herself seven days, and after that she shall be clean. ²⁹ On the eighth day she shall take two turtledoves, or two young pigeons, and bring them to the priest, to the door of the Tent of Meeting. ³⁰ The priest shall offer the one for a sin offering, and the other for a burnt offering; and the priest shall make atonement for her before Yahweh for the uncleanness of her discharge. ³¹"Thus you shall separate the children of Israel from their uncleanness, so they will not die in their uncleanness when they defile my tabernacle that is among them.'" ³² This is the law of him who has a discharge, and of him who has an emission of semen, so that he is unclean by it; ³³ and of her who has her period, and of a man or woman who has a discharge, and of him who lies with her who is unclean.

## 16

¹ Yahweh spoke to Moses after the death of the two sons of Aaron, when they came near before Yahweh, and died; ² and Yahweh said to Moses, "Tell Aaron your brother not to come at just any time into the Most Holy Place within the veil, before the mercy seat which is on the ark; lest he die; for I will appear in the cloud on the mercy seat. ³"Aaron shall come into the sanctuary with a young bull for a sin offering, and a ram for a burnt offering. ⁴ He shall put on the holy linen tunic. He shall have the linen trousers on his body, and shall put on the linen sash, and he shall be clothed with the linen turban. They are the holy garments. He shall bathe his body in water, and put them on. ⁵ He shall take from the congregation of the children of Israel two male goats for a sin offering, and one ram for a burnt offering. ⁶"Aaron shall offer the bull of the sin offering, which is for himself, and make atonement for himself and for his house. ⁷ He shall take the two goats, and set them

before Yahweh at the door of the Tent of Meeting. ⁸ Aaron shall cast lots for the two goats: one lot for Yahweh, and the other lot for the scapegoat. ⁹ Aaron shall present the goat on which the lot fell for Yahweh, and offer him for a sin offering. ¹⁰ But the goat on which the lot fell for the scapegoat shall be presented alive before Yahweh, to make atonement for him, to send him away as the scapegoat into the wilderness. ¹¹"Aaron shall present the bull of the sin offering, which is for himself, and shall make atonement for himself and for his house, and shall kill the bull of the sin offering which is for himself. ¹² He shall take a censer full of coals of fire from off the altar before Yahweh, and two handfuls of sweet incense beaten small, and bring it within the veil. ¹³ He shall put the incense on the fire before Yahweh, that the cloud of the incense may cover the mercy seat that is on the covenant, so that he will not die. ¹⁴ He shall take some of the blood of the bull, and sprinkle it with his finger on the mercy seat on the east; and before the mercy seat he shall sprinkle some of the blood with his finger seven times. ¹⁵"Then he shall kill the goat of the sin offering that is for the people, and bring his blood within the veil, and do with his blood as he did with the blood of the bull, and sprinkle it on the mercy seat and before the mercy seat. ¹⁶ He shall make atonement for the Holy Place, because of the uncleanness of the children of Israel, and because of their transgressions, even all their sins; and so he shall do for the Tent of Meeting that dwells with them in the middle of their uncleanness. ¹⁷ No one shall be in the Tent of Meeting when he enters to make atonement in the Holy Place, until he comes out, and has made atonement for himself and for his household, and for all the assembly of Israel. ¹⁸"He shall go out to the altar that is before Yahweh and make atonement for it, and shall take some of the bull's blood, and some of the goat's blood, and put it around on the horns of the altar. ¹⁹ He shall sprinkle some of the blood on it with his finger seven times, and cleanse it, and make it holy from the uncleanness of the children of Israel. ²⁰"When he has finished atoning for the Holy Place, the Tent of Meeting, and the altar, he shall present the live goat. ²¹ Aaron shall lay both his hands on the head of the live goat, and confess over him all the iniquities of the children of Israel, and all their transgressions, even all their sins; and he shall put them on the head of the goat, and shall send him away into the wilderness by the hand of a man who is ready. ²² The goat shall carry all their iniquities on himself to a solitary land, and he shall release the goat in the wilderness. ²³"Aaron shall come into the Tent of Meeting, and shall take off the linen garments which he put on when he went into the Holy Place, and shall leave them there. ²⁴ Then he shall bathe himself in water in a holy place, put on his garments, and come out and offer his burnt offering and the burnt offering of the people, and make atonement for himself and for the people. ²⁵ The fat of the sin offering he shall burn on the altar. ²⁶"He who lets the goat go as the scapegoat shall wash his clothes, and bathe his flesh in water, and afterward he shall come into the camp. ²⁷ The bull for the sin offering, and the goat for the sin offering, whose blood was brought in to make atonement in the Holy Place, shall be carried outside the camp; and they shall burn their skins, their flesh, and their dung with fire. ²⁸ He who burns them shall wash his clothes, and bathe his flesh in water, and afterward he shall come into the camp. ²⁹"It shall be a statute to you forever: in the seventh month, on the tenth day of the month, you shall afflict your souls, and shall do no kind of work, whether native-born or a stranger who lives as a foreigner among you; ³⁰ for on this day shall atonement be made for you, to cleanse you. You shall be clean from all your sins before Yahweh. ³¹ It is a Sabbath of solemn rest to you, and you shall afflict your souls. It is a statute forever. ³² The priest, who is anointed and who is consecrated to be priest in his father's place, shall make the atonement, and shall put on the linen garments, even the holy garments. ³³ Then he shall make atonement for the Holy Sanctuary; and he shall make atonement for the Tent of Meeting and for the altar; and he shall make atonement for the priests and for all the people of the assembly. ³⁴"This shall be an everlasting statute for you, to make atonement for the children of Israel once in the year because of all their sins." It was done as Yahweh commanded Moses.

## 17

¹ Yahweh spoke to Moses, saying, ²"Speak to Aaron, and to his sons, and to all the children of Israel, and say to them, 'This is the thing which Yahweh has commanded: ³ Whatever man there is of the house of Israel who kills a bull, or lamb, or goat in the camp, or who kills it outside the camp, ⁴ and hasn't brought it to the door of the Tent of Meeting to offer it as an offering to Yahweh before Yahweh's tabernacle: blood shall be imputed to that man. He has shed blood. That man shall be cut off from among his people. ⁵ This is to the end that the children of Israel may bring their sacrifices, which they sacrifice in the open field, that they may bring them to Yahweh, to the door of the Tent of Meeting, to the priest, and sacrifice them for sacrifices of peace offerings to Yahweh. ⁶ The priest shall sprinkle the blood on Yahweh's altar at the door of the Tent of Meeting, and burn the fat for a pleasant aroma to Yahweh. ⁷

They shall no more sacrifice their sacrifices to the goat idols, after which they play the prostitute. This shall be a statute forever to them throughout their generations.' [8]"You shall say to them, 'Any man there is of the house of Israel, or of the strangers who live as foreigners among them, who offers a burnt offering or sacrifice, [9] and doesn't bring it to the door of the Tent of Meeting to sacrifice it to Yahweh, that man shall be cut off from his people. [10]"Any man of the house of Israel, or of the strangers who live as foreigners among them, who eats any kind of blood, I will set my face against that soul who eats blood, and will cut him off from among his people. [11] For the life of the flesh is in the blood. I have given it to you on the altar to make atonement for your souls; for it is the blood that makes atonement by reason of the life. [12] Therefore I have said to the children of Israel, "No person among you may eat blood, nor may any stranger who lives as a foreigner among you eat blood." [13]"Whatever man there is of the children of Israel, or of the strangers who live as foreigners among them, who takes in hunting any animal or bird that may be eaten, he shall pour out its blood, and cover it with dust. [14] For as to the life of all flesh, its blood is with its life. Therefore I said to the children of Israel, "You shall not eat the blood of any kind of flesh; for the life of all flesh is its blood. Whoever eats it shall be cut off." [15]"Every person that eats what dies of itself, or that which is torn by animals, whether he is native-born or a foreigner, shall wash his clothes, and bathe himself in water, and be unclean until the evening. Then he shall be clean. [16] But if he doesn't wash them, or bathe his flesh, then he shall bear his iniquity.'"

## 18

[1] Yahweh said to Moses, [2]"Speak to the children of Israel, and say to them, 'I am Yahweh your God. [3] You shall not do as they do in the land of Egypt, where you lived. You shall not do as they do in the land of Canaan, where I am bringing you. You shall not follow their statutes. [4] You shall do my ordinances. You shall keep my statutes and walk in them. I am Yahweh your God. [5] You shall therefore keep my statutes and my ordinances, which if a man does, he shall live in them. I am Yahweh. [6]"None of you shall approach any close relatives, to uncover their nakedness: I am Yahweh. [7]"You shall not uncover the nakedness of your father, nor the nakedness of your mother: she is your mother. You shall not uncover her nakedness. [8]"You shall not uncover the nakedness of your father's wife. It is your father's nakedness. [9]"You shall not uncover the nakedness of your sister, the daughter of your father, or the daughter of your mother, whether born at home or born abroad. [10]"You shall not uncover the nakedness of your son's daughter, or of your daughter's daughter, even their nakedness; for theirs is your own nakedness. [11]"You shall not uncover the nakedness of your father's wife's daughter, conceived by your father, since she is your sister. [12]"You shall not uncover the nakedness of your father's sister. She is your father's near kinswoman. [13]"You shall not uncover the nakedness of your mother's sister, for she is your mother's near kinswoman. [14]"You shall not uncover the nakedness of your father's brother. You shall not approach his wife. She is your aunt. [15]"You shall not uncover the nakedness of your daughter-in-law. She is your son's wife. You shall not uncover her nakedness. [16]"You shall not uncover the nakedness of your brother's wife. It is your brother's nakedness. [17]"You shall not uncover the nakedness of a woman and her daughter. You shall not take her son's daughter, or her daughter's daughter, to uncover her nakedness. They are near kinswomen. It is wickedness. [18]"You shall not take a wife in addition to her sister, to be a rival, to uncover her nakedness, while her sister is still alive. [19]"You shall not approach a woman to uncover her nakedness, as long as she is impure by her uncleanness. [20]"You shall not lie carnally with your neighbor's wife, and defile yourself with her. [21]"You shall not give any of your children as a sacrifice to Molech. You shall not profane the name of your God. I am Yahweh. [22]"You shall not lie with a man as with a woman. That is detestable. [23]"You shall not lie with any animal to defile yourself with it. No woman may give herself to an animal, to lie down with it: it is a perversion. [24]"Don't defile yourselves in any of these things; for in all these the nations which I am casting out before you were defiled. [25] The land was defiled. Therefore I punished its iniquity, and the land vomited out her inhabitants. [26] You therefore shall keep my statutes and my ordinances, and shall not do any of these abominations; neither the native-born, nor the stranger who lives as a foreigner among you [27](for the men of the land that were before you had done all these abominations, and the land became defiled), [28] that the land not vomit you out also, when you defile it, as it vomited out the nation that was before you. [29]"For whoever shall do any of these abominations, even the souls that do them shall be cut off from among their people. [30] Therefore you shall keep my requirements, that you do not practice any of these abominable customs which were practiced before you, and that you do not defile yourselves with them. I am Yahweh your God.'"

## 19

[1] Yahweh spoke to Moses, saying, [2]"Speak to all the congregation of the children of Israel, and tell them, 'You shall be holy; for I, Yahweh your God, am holy. [3]"Each one of you shall respect his mother and his father. You shall keep my Sabbaths. I am Yahweh your God. [4]"Don't turn to idols, nor make molten gods for yourselves. I am Yahweh your God. [5]"When you offer a sacrifice of peace offerings to Yahweh, you shall offer it so that you may be accepted. [6] It shall be eaten the same day you offer it, and on the next day. If anything remains until the third day, it shall be burned with fire. [7] If it is eaten at all on the third day, it is an abomination. It will not be accepted; [8] but everyone who eats it shall bear his iniquity, because he has profaned the holy thing of Yahweh, and that soul shall be cut off from his people. [9]"When you reap the harvest of your land, you shall not wholly reap the corners of your field, neither shall you gather the gleanings of your harvest. [10] You shall not glean your vineyard, neither shall you gather the fallen grapes of your vineyard. You shall leave them for the poor and for the foreigner. I am Yahweh your God. [11]"You shall not steal. "'You shall not lie. "'You shall not deceive one another. [12]"You shall not swear by my name falsely, and profane the name of your God. I am Yahweh. [13]"You shall not oppress your neighbor, nor rob him. "'The wages of a hired servant shall not remain with you all night until the morning. [14]"You shall not curse the deaf, nor put a stumbling block before the blind; but you shall fear your God. I am Yahweh. [15]"You shall do no injustice in judgment. You shall not be partial to the poor, nor show favoritism to the great; but you shall judge your neighbor in righteousness. [16]"You shall not go around as a slanderer among your people. "'You shall not endanger the life[a] of your neighbor. I am Yahweh. [17]"You shall not hate your brother in your heart. You shall surely rebuke your neighbor, and not bear sin because of him. [18]"You shall not take vengeance, nor bear any grudge against the children of your people; but you shall love your neighbor as yourself. I am Yahweh. [19]"You shall keep my statutes. "'You shall not cross-breed different kinds of animals. "'You shall not sow your field with two kinds of seed; "'Don't wear a garment made of two kinds of material. [20]"If a man lies carnally with a woman who is a slave girl, pledged to be married to another man, and not ransomed or given her freedom; they shall be punished. They shall not be put to death, because she was not free. [21] He shall bring his trespass offering to Yahweh, to the door of the Tent of Meeting, even a ram for a trespass offering. [22] The priest shall make atonement for him with the ram of the trespass offering before Yahweh for his sin which he has committed; and the sin which he has committed shall be forgiven him. [23]"When you come into the land, and have planted all kinds of trees for food, then you shall count their fruit as forbidden.[b] For three years it shall be forbidden to you. It shall not be eaten. [24] But in the fourth year all its fruit shall be holy, for giving praise to Yahweh. [25] In the fifth year you shall eat its fruit, that it may yield its increase to you. I am Yahweh your God. [26]"You shall not eat any meat with the blood still in it. You shall not use enchantments, nor practice sorcery. [27]"You shall not cut the hair on the sides of your head or clip off the edge of your beard. [28]"You shall not make any cuttings in your flesh for the dead, nor tattoo any marks on you. I am Yahweh. [29]"Don't profane your daughter, to make her a prostitute; lest the land fall to prostitution, and the land become full of wickedness. [30]"You shall keep my Sabbaths, and reverence my sanctuary; I am Yahweh. [31]"Don't turn to those who are mediums, nor to the wizards. Don't seek them out, to be defiled by them. I am Yahweh your God. [32]"You shall rise up before the gray head and honor the face of the elderly; and you shall fear your God. I am Yahweh. [33]"If a stranger lives as a foreigner with you in your land, you shall not do him wrong. [34] The stranger who lives as a foreigner with you shall be to you as the native-born among you, and you shall love him as yourself; for you lived as foreigners in the land of Egypt. I am Yahweh your God. [35]"You shall do no unrighteousness in judgment, in measures of length, of weight, or of quantity. [36] You shall have just balances, just weights, a just ephah,[c] and a just hin.[d] I am Yahweh your God, who brought you out of the land of Egypt. [37]"You shall observe all my statutes and all my ordinances, and do them. I am Yahweh.'"

## 20

[1] Yahweh spoke to Moses, saying, [2]"Moreover, you shall tell the children of Israel, 'Anyone of the children of Israel, or of the strangers who live as foreigners in Israel, who gives any of his offspring[e] to Molech shall surely be put to death. The people of the land shall stone

---

[a] *19:16* literally, "blood"
[b] *19:23* literally, "uncircumcised"
[c] *19:36* 1 ephah is about 22 liters or about 2/3 of a bushel
[d] *19:36* A hin is about 6.5 liters or 1.7 gallons.
[e] *20:2* or, seed

that person with stones. ³ I also will set my face against that person, and will cut him off from among his people, because he has given of his offspring to Molech, to defile my sanctuary, and to profane my holy name. ⁴ If the people of the land all hide their eyes from that person when he gives of his offspring to Molech, and don't put him to death, ⁵ then I will set my face against that man and against his family, and will cut him off, and all who play the prostitute after him to play the prostitute with Molech, from among their people. ⁶"The person that turns to those who are mediums and wizards, to play the prostitute after them, I will even set my face against that person, and will cut him off from among his people. ⁷"Sanctify yourselves therefore, and be holy; for I am Yahweh your God. ⁸ You shall keep my statutes, and do them. I am Yahweh who sanctifies you. ⁹"For everyone who curses his father or his mother shall surely be put to death. He has cursed his father or his mother. His blood shall be upon himself. ¹⁰"The man who commits adultery with another man's wife, even he who commits adultery with his neighbor's wife, the adulterer and the adulteress shall surely be put to death. ¹¹"The man who lies with his father's wife has uncovered his father's nakedness. Both of them shall surely be put to death. Their blood shall be upon themselves. ¹²"If a man lies with his daughter-in-law, both of them shall surely be put to death. They have committed a perversion. Their blood shall be upon themselves. ¹³"If a man lies with a male, as with a woman, both of them have committed an abomination. They shall surely be put to death. Their blood shall be upon themselves. ¹⁴"If a man takes a wife and her mother, it is wickedness. They shall be burned with fire, both he and they, that there may be no wickedness among you. ¹⁵"If a man lies with an animal, he shall surely be put to death; and you shall kill the animal. ¹⁶"If a woman approaches any animal and lies with it, you shall kill the woman and the animal. They shall surely be put to death. Their blood shall be upon them. ¹⁷"If a man takes his sister—his father's daughter, or his mother's daughter—and sees her nakedness, and she sees his nakedness, it is a shameful thing. They shall be cut off in the sight of the children of their people. He has uncovered his sister's nakedness. He shall bear his iniquity. ¹⁸"If a man lies with a woman having her monthly period, and uncovers her nakedness, he has made her fountain naked, and she has uncovered the fountain of her blood. Both of them shall be cut off from among their people. ¹⁹"You shall not uncover the nakedness of your mother's sister, nor of your father's sister, for he has made his close relative naked. They shall bear their iniquity. ²⁰ If a man lies with his uncle's wife, he has uncovered his uncle's nakedness. They shall bear their sin. They shall die childless. ²¹"If a man takes his brother's wife, it is an impurity. He has uncovered his brother's nakedness. They shall be childless. ²²"You shall therefore keep all my statutes and all my ordinances, and do them, that the land where I am bringing you to dwell may not vomit you out. ²³ You shall not walk in the customs of the nation which I am casting out before you; for they did all these things, and therefore I abhorred them. ²⁴ But I have said to you, "You shall inherit their land, and I will give it to you to possess it, a land flowing with milk and honey." I am Yahweh your God, who has separated you from the peoples. ²⁵"You shall therefore make a distinction between the clean animal and the unclean, and between the unclean fowl and the clean. You shall not make yourselves abominable by animal, or by bird, or by anything with which the ground teems, which I have separated from you as unclean for you. ²⁶ You shall be holy to me, for I, Yahweh, am holy, and have set you apart from the peoples, that you should be mine. ²⁷"A man or a woman that is a medium or is a wizard shall surely be put to death. They shall be stoned with stones. Their blood shall be upon themselves.'"

## 21

¹ Yahweh said to Moses, "Speak to the priests, the sons of Aaron, and say to them, 'A priest shall not defile himself for the dead among his people, ² except for his relatives that are near to him: for his mother, for his father, for his son, for his daughter, for his brother, ³ and for his virgin sister who is near to him, who has had no husband; for her he may defile himself. ⁴ He shall not defile himself, being a chief man among his people, to profane himself. ⁵"They shall not shave their heads or shave off the corners of their beards or make any cuttings in their flesh. ⁶ They shall be holy to their God, and not profane the name of their God, for they offer the offerings of Yahweh made by fire, the bread of their God. Therefore they shall be holy. ⁷"They shall not marry a woman who is a prostitute, or profane. A priest shall not marry a woman divorced from her husband; for he is holy to his God. ⁸ Therefore you shall sanctify him, for he offers the bread of your God. He shall be holy to you, for I Yahweh, who sanctify you, am holy. ⁹"The daughter of any priest, if she profanes herself by playing the prostitute, she profanes her father. She shall be burned with fire. ¹⁰"He who is the high priest among his brothers, upon whose head the anointing oil is poured, and who is consecrated to put on the garments, shall not let the hair of his head hang loose, or tear his clothes. ¹¹ He

must not go in to any dead body, or defile himself for his father or for his mother. ¹² He shall not go out of the sanctuary, nor profane the sanctuary of his God; for the crown of the anointing oil of his God is upon him. I am Yahweh. ¹³"He shall take a wife in her virginity. ¹⁴ He shall not marry a widow, or one divorced, or a woman who has been defiled, or a prostitute. He shall take a virgin of his own people as a wife. ¹⁵ He shall not profane his offspring among his people, for I am Yahweh who sanctifies him.'" ¹⁶ Yahweh spoke to Moses, saying, ¹⁷"Say to Aaron, 'None of your offspring throughout their generations who has a defect may approach to offer the bread of his God. ¹⁸ For whatever man he is that has a defect, he shall not draw near: a blind man, or a lame, or he who has a flat nose, or any deformity, ¹⁹ or a man who has an injured foot, or an injured hand, ²⁰ or hunchbacked, or a dwarf, or one who has a defect in his eye, or an itching disease, or scabs, or who has damaged testicles. ²¹ No man of the offspring of Aaron the priest who has a defect shall come near to offer the offerings of Yahweh made by fire. Since he has a defect, he shall not come near to offer the bread of his God. ²² He shall eat the bread of his God, both of the most holy, and of the holy. ²³ He shall not come near to the veil, nor come near to the altar, because he has a defect; that he may not profane my sanctuaries, for I am Yahweh who sanctifies them.'" ²⁴ So Moses spoke to Aaron, and to his sons, and to all the children of Israel.

## 22

¹ Yahweh spoke to Moses, saying, ²"Tell Aaron and his sons to separate themselves from the holy things of the children of Israel, which they make holy to me, and that they not profane my holy name. I am Yahweh. ³"Tell them, 'If anyone of all your offspring throughout your generations approaches the holy things which the children of Israel make holy to Yahweh, having his uncleanness on him, that soul shall be cut off from before me. I am Yahweh. ⁴"Whoever of the offspring of Aaron is a leper or has a discharge shall not eat of the holy things until he is clean. Whoever touches anything that is unclean by the dead, or a man who has a seminal emission, ⁵ or whoever touches any creeping thing by which he may be made unclean, or a man from whom he may become unclean, whatever uncleanness he has— ⁶ the person that touches any such shall be unclean until the evening, and shall not eat of the holy things unless he bathes his body in water. ⁷ When the sun is down, he shall be clean; and afterward he shall eat of the holy things, because it is his bread. ⁸ He shall not eat that which dies of itself or is torn by animals, defiling himself by it. I am Yahweh. ⁹"They shall therefore follow my commandment, lest they bear sin for it and die in it, if they profane it. I am Yahweh who sanctifies them. ¹⁰"No stranger shall eat of the holy thing: a foreigner living with the priests, or a hired servant, shall not eat of the holy thing. ¹¹ But if a priest buys a slave, purchased by his money, he shall eat of it; and those who are born in his house shall eat of his bread. ¹² If a priest's daughter is married to an outsider, she shall not eat of the heave offering of the holy things. ¹³ But if a priest's daughter is a widow, or divorced, and has no child, and has returned to her father's house as in her youth, she may eat of her father's bread; but no stranger shall eat any of it. ¹⁴"If a man eats something holy unwittingly, then he shall add the fifth part of its value to it, and shall give the holy thing to the priest. ¹⁵ The priests shall not profane the holy things of the children of Israel, which they offer to Yahweh, ¹⁶ and so cause them to bear the iniquity that brings guilt when they eat their holy things; for I am Yahweh who sanctifies them.'" ¹⁷ Yahweh spoke to Moses, saying, ¹⁸"Speak to Aaron, and to his sons, and to all the children of Israel, and say to them, 'Whoever is of the house of Israel, or of the foreigners in Israel, who offers his offering, whether it is any of their vows or any of their free will offerings, which they offer to Yahweh for a burnt offering: ¹⁹ that you may be accepted, you shall offer a male without defect, of the bulls, of the sheep, or of the goats. ²⁰ But you shall not offer whatever has a defect, for it shall not be acceptable for you. ²¹ Whoever offers a sacrifice of peace offerings to Yahweh to accomplish a vow, or for a free will offering of the herd or of the flock, it shall be perfect to be accepted. It shall have no defect. ²² You shall not offer what is blind, is injured, is maimed, has a wart, is festering, or has a running sore to Yahweh, nor make an offering by fire of them on the altar to Yahweh. ²³ Either a bull or a lamb that has any deformity or lacking in his parts, that you may offer for a free will offering; but for a vow it shall not be accepted. ²⁴ You must not offer to Yahweh that which has its testicles bruised, crushed, broken, or cut. You must not do this in your land. ²⁵ You must not offer any of these as the bread of your God from the hand of a foreigner, because their corruption is in them. There is a defect in them. They shall not be accepted for you.'" ²⁶ Yahweh spoke to Moses, saying, ²⁷"When a bull, a sheep, or a goat is born, it shall remain seven days with its mother. From the eighth day on it shall be accepted for the offering of an offering made by fire to Yahweh. ²⁸ Whether it is a cow or ewe, you shall not kill it and its young both in one day. ²⁹"When you sacrifice a sacrifice of thanksgiving to Yahweh, you shall sacrifice it so that you

may be accepted. ³⁰ It shall be eaten on the same day; you shall leave none of it until the morning. I am Yahweh. ³¹"Therefore you shall keep my commandments, and do them. I am Yahweh. ³² You shall not profane my holy name, but I will be made holy among the children of Israel. I am Yahweh who makes you holy, ³³ who brought you out of the land of Egypt, to be your God. I am Yahweh."

## 23

¹ Yahweh spoke to Moses, saying, ²"Speak to the children of Israel, and tell them, 'The set feasts of Yahweh, which you shall proclaim to be holy convocations, even these are my set feasts. ³"'Six days shall work be done, but on the seventh day is a Sabbath of solemn rest, a holy convocation; you shall do no kind of work. It is a Sabbath to Yahweh in all your dwellings. ⁴"'These are the set feasts of Yahweh, even holy convocations, which you shall proclaim in their appointed season. ⁵ In the first month, on the fourteenth day of the month in the evening, is Yahweh's Passover. ⁶ On the fifteenth day of the same month is the feast of unleavened bread to Yahweh. Seven days you shall eat unleavened bread. ⁷ In the first day you shall have a holy convocation. You shall do no regular work. ⁸ But you shall offer an offering made by fire to Yahweh seven days. In the seventh day is a holy convocation. You shall do no regular work.'" ⁹ Yahweh spoke to Moses, saying, ¹⁰"Speak to the children of Israel, and tell them, 'When you have come into the land which I give to you, and shall reap its harvest, then you shall bring the sheaf of the first fruits of your harvest to the priest. ¹¹ He shall wave the sheaf before Yahweh, to be accepted for you. On the next day after the Sabbath the priest shall wave it. ¹² On the day when you wave the sheaf, you shall offer a male lamb without defect a year old for a burnt offering to Yahweh. ¹³ The meal offering with it shall be two tenths of an ephahᵃ of fine flour mixed with oil, an offering made by fire to Yahweh for a pleasant aroma; and the drink offering with it shall be of wine, the fourth part of a hin.ᵇ ¹⁴ You must not eat bread, or roasted grain, or fresh grain, until this same day, until you have brought the offering of your God. This is a statute forever throughout your generations in all your dwellings. ¹⁵"'You shall count from the next day after the Sabbath, from the day that you brought the sheaf of the wave offering: seven Sabbaths shall be completed. ¹⁶ The next day after the seventh Sabbath you shall count fifty days; and you shall offer a new meal offering to Yahweh. ¹⁷ You shall bring out of your habitations two loaves of bread for a wave offering made of two tenths of an ephahᶜ of fine flour. They shall be baked with yeast, for first fruits to Yahweh. ¹⁸ You shall present with the bread seven lambs without defect a year old, one young bull, and two rams. They shall be a burnt offering to Yahweh, with their meal offering and their drink offerings, even an offering made by fire, of a sweet aroma to Yahweh. ¹⁹ You shall offer one male goat for a sin offering, and two male lambs a year old for a sacrifice of peace offerings. ²⁰ The priest shall wave them with the bread of the first fruits for a wave offering before Yahweh, with the two lambs. They shall be holy to Yahweh for the priest. ²¹ You shall make proclamation on the same day that there shall be a holy convocation to you. You shall do no regular work. This is a statute forever in all your dwellings throughout your generations. ²²"'When you reap the harvest of your land, you must not wholly reap into the corners of your field. You must not gather the gleanings of your harvest. You must leave them for the poor and for the foreigner. I am Yahweh your God.'" ²³ Yahweh spoke to Moses, saying, ²⁴"Speak to the children of Israel, saying, 'In the seventh month, on the first day of the month, there shall be a solemn rest for you, a memorial of blowing of trumpets, a holy convocation. ²⁵ You shall do no regular work. You shall offer an offering made by fire to Yahweh.'" ²⁶ Yahweh spoke to Moses, saying, ²⁷"However on the tenth day of this seventh month is the day of atonement. It shall be a holy convocation to you. You shall afflict yourselves and you shall offer an offering made by fire to Yahweh. ²⁸ You shall do no kind of work in that same day, for it is a day of atonement, to make atonement for you before Yahweh your God. ²⁹ For whoever it is who shall not deny himself in that same day shall be cut off from his people. ³⁰ Whoever does any kind of work in that same day, I will destroy that person from among his people. ³¹ You shall do no kind of work: it is a statute forever throughout your generations in all your dwellings. ³² It shall be a Sabbath of solemn rest for you, and you shall deny yourselves. In the ninth day of the month at evening, from evening to evening, you shall keep your Sabbath." ³³ Yahweh spoke to Moses, saying, ³⁴"Speak to the children of Israel, and say, 'On the fifteenth day of this seventh month is the feast of boothsᵈ for seven days to Yahweh. ³⁵ On the first day shall be a holy convocation. You shall do no regular work. ³⁶ Seven days you shall offer an offering made

by fire to Yahweh. On the eighth day shall be a holy convocation to you. You shall offer an offering made by fire to Yahweh. It is a solemn assembly; you shall do no regular work. ³⁷"'These are the appointed feasts of Yahweh which you shall proclaim to be holy convocations, to offer an offering made by fire to Yahweh, a burnt offering, a meal offering, a sacrifice, and drink offerings, each on its own day— ³⁸ in addition to the Sabbaths of Yahweh, and in addition to your gifts, and in addition to all your vows, and in addition to all your free will offerings, which you give to Yahweh. ³⁹"'So on the fifteenth day of the seventh month, when you have gathered in the fruits of the land, you shall keep the feast of Yahweh seven days. On the first day shall be a solemn rest, and on the eighth day shall be a solemn rest. ⁴⁰ You shall take on the first day the fruit of majestic trees, branches of palm trees, and boughs of thick trees, and willows of the brook; and you shall rejoice before Yahweh your God seven days. ⁴¹ You shall keep it as a feast to Yahweh seven days in the year. It is a statute forever throughout your generations. You shall keep it in the seventh month. ⁴² You shall dwell in temporary sheltersᵉ for seven days. All who are native-born in Israel shall dwell in temporary shelters,ᶠ ⁴³ that your generations may know that I made the children of Israel to dwell in temporary sheltersᵍ when I brought them out of the land of Egypt. I am Yahweh your God.'" ⁴⁴ So Moses declared to the children of Israel the appointed feasts of Yahweh.

## 24

¹ Yahweh spoke to Moses, saying, ²"Command the children of Israel, that they bring to you pure olive oil beaten for the light, to cause a lamp to burn continually. ³ Outside of the veil of the Testimony, in the Tent of Meeting, Aaron shall keep it in order from evening to morning before Yahweh continually. It shall be a statute forever throughout your generations. ⁴ He shall keep in order the lamps on the pure gold lamp stand before Yahweh continually. ⁵"You shall take fine flour, and bake twelve cakes of it: two tenths of an ephahʰ shall be in one cake. ⁶ You shall set them in two rows, six on a row, on the pure gold table before Yahweh. ⁷ You shall put pure frankincense on each row, that it may be to the bread for a memorial, even an offering made by fire to Yahweh. ⁸ Every Sabbath day he shall set it in order before Yahweh continually. It is an everlasting covenant on the behalf of the children of Israel. ⁹ It shall be for Aaron and his sons. They shall eat it in a holy place; for it is most holy to him of the offerings of Yahweh made by fire by a perpetual statute." ¹⁰ The son of an Israelite woman, whose father was an Egyptian, went out among the children of Israel; and the son of the Israelite woman and a man of Israel strove together in the camp. ¹¹ The son of the Israelite woman blasphemed the Name, and cursed; and they brought him to Moses. His mother's name was Shelomith, the daughter of Dibri, of the tribe of Dan. ¹² They put him in custody until Yahweh's will should be declared to them. ¹³ Yahweh spoke to Moses, saying, ¹⁴"Bring him who cursed out of the camp; and let all who heard him lay their hands on his head, and let all the congregation stone him. ¹⁵ You shall speak to the children of Israel, saying, 'Whoever curses his God shall bear his sin. ¹⁶ He who blasphemes Yahweh's name, he shall surely be put to death. All the congregation shall certainly stone him. The foreigner as well as the native-born shall be put to death when he blasphemes the Name. ¹⁷"'He who strikes any man mortally shall surely be put to death. ¹⁸ He who strikes an animal mortally shall make it good, life for life. ¹⁹ If anyone injures his neighbor, it shall be done to him as he has done: ²⁰ fracture for fracture, eye for eye, tooth for tooth. It shall be done to him as he has injured someone. ²¹ He who kills an animal shall make it good; and he who kills a man shall be put to death. ²² You shall have one kind of law for the foreigner as well as the native-born; for I am Yahweh your God.'" ²³ Moses spoke to the children of Israel; and they brought him who had cursed out of the camp, and stoned him with stones. The children of Israel did as Yahweh commanded Moses.

## 25

¹ Yahweh said to Moses on Mount Sinai, ²"Speak to the children of Israel, and tell them, 'When you come into the land which I give you, then the land shall keep a Sabbath to Yahweh. ³ You shall sow your field six years, and you shall prune your vineyard six years, and gather in its fruits; ⁴ but in the seventh year there shall be a Sabbath of solemn rest for the land, a Sabbath to Yahweh. You shall not sow your field or prune your vineyard. ⁵ What grows of itself in your harvest you shall not reap, and you shall not gather the grapes of your undressed vine. It shall be a year of solemn rest for the land. ⁶ The Sabbath of the land shall be for food for you; for yourself, for your servant, for your maid, for your hired servant, and for your stranger, who lives as a foreigner with you. ⁷ For your livestock also, and for the animals that are in your

---

ᵃ 23:13 1 ephah is about 22 liters or about 2/3 of a bushel
ᵇ 23:13 A hin is about 6.5 liters or 1.7 gallons.

ᶜ 23:17 1 ephah is about 22 liters or about 2/3 of a bushel
ᵈ 23:34 or, feast of tents, or Succoth

ᵉ 23:42 or, booths
ᶠ 23:42 or, booths
ᵍ 23:43 or, booths

ʰ 24:5 1 ephah is about 22 liters or about 2/3 of a bushel

land, shall all its increase be for food. ⁸"You shall count off seven Sabbaths of years, seven times seven years; and there shall be to you the days of seven Sabbaths of years, even forty-nine years. ⁹ Then you shall sound the loud trumpet on the tenth day of the seventh month. On the Day of Atonement you shall sound the trumpet throughout all your land. ¹⁰ You shall make the fiftieth year holy, and proclaim liberty throughout the land to all its inhabitants. It shall be a jubilee to you; and each of you shall return to his own property, and each of you shall return to his family. ¹¹ That fiftieth year shall be a jubilee to you. In it you shall not sow, neither reap that which grows of itself, nor gather from the undressed vines. ¹² For it is a jubilee; it shall be holy to you. You shall eat of its increase out of the field. ¹³"In this Year of Jubilee each of you shall return to his property. ¹⁴"If you sell anything to your neighbor, or buy from your neighbor, you shall not wrong one another. ¹⁵ According to the number of years after the Jubilee you shall buy from your neighbor. According to the number of years of the crops he shall sell to you. ¹⁶ According to the length of the years you shall increase its price, and according to the shortness of the years you shall diminish its price; for he is selling the number of the crops to you. ¹⁷ You shall not wrong one another, but you shall fear your God; for I am Yahweh your God. ¹⁸"Therefore you shall do my statutes, and keep my ordinances and do them; and you shall dwell in the land in safety. ¹⁹ The land shall yield its fruit, and you shall eat your fill, and dwell therein in safety. ²⁰ If you said, "What shall we eat the seventh year? Behold, we shall not sow, nor gather in our increase;" ²¹ then I will command my blessing on you in the sixth year, and it shall bear fruit for the three years. ²² You shall sow the eighth year, and eat of the fruits from the old store until the ninth year. Until its fruits come in, you shall eat the old store. ²³"The land shall not be sold in perpetuity, for the land is mine; for you are strangers and live as foreigners with me. ²⁴ In all the land of your possession you shall grant a redemption for the land. ²⁵"If your brother becomes poor, and sells some of his possessions, then his kinsman who is next to him shall come, and redeem that which his brother has sold. ²⁶ If a man has no one to redeem it, and he becomes prosperous and finds sufficient means to redeem it, ²⁷ then let him reckon the years since its sale, and restore the surplus to the man to whom he sold it; and he shall return to his property. ²⁸ But if he isn't able to get it back for himself, then what he has sold shall remain in the hand of him who has bought it until the Year of Jubilee. In the Jubilee it shall be released, and he shall return to his property. ²⁹"If a man sells a dwelling house in a walled city, then he may redeem it within a whole year after it has been sold. For a full year he shall have the right of redemption. ³⁰ If it isn't redeemed within the space of a full year, then the house that is in the walled city shall be made sure in perpetuity to him who bought it, throughout his generations. It shall not be released in the Jubilee. ³¹ But the houses of the villages which have no wall around them shall be accounted for with the fields of the country: they may be redeemed, and they shall be released in the Jubilee. ³²"Nevertheless, in the cities of the Levites, the Levites may redeem the houses in the cities of their possession at any time. ³³ The Levites may redeem the house that was sold, and the city of his possession, and it shall be released in the Jubilee; for the houses of the cities of the Levites are their possession among the children of Israel. ³⁴ But the field of the pasture lands of their cities may not be sold, for it is their perpetual possession. ³⁵"If your brother has become poor, and his hand can't support himself among you, then you shall uphold him. He shall live with you like an alien and a temporary resident. ³⁶ Take no interest from him or profit; but fear your God, that your brother may live among you. ³⁷ You shall not lend him your money at interest, nor give him your food for profit. ³⁸ I am Yahweh your God, who brought you out of the land of Egypt, to give you the land of Canaan, and to be your God. ³⁹"If your brother has grown poor among you, and sells himself to you, you shall not make him to serve as a slave. ⁴⁰ As a hired servant, and as a temporary resident, he shall be with you; he shall serve with you until the Year of Jubilee. ⁴¹ Then he shall go out from you, he and his children with him, and shall return to his own family, and to the possession of his fathers. ⁴² For they are my servants, whom I brought out of the land of Egypt. They shall not be sold as slaves. ⁴³ You shall not rule over him with harshness, but shall fear your God. ⁴⁴"As for your male and your female slaves, whom you may have from the nations that are around you, from them you may buy male and female slaves. ⁴⁵ Moreover, of the children of the aliens who live among you, of them you may buy, and of their families who are with you, which they have conceived in your land; and they will be your property. ⁴⁶ You may make them an inheritance for your children after you, to hold for a possession. Of them you may take your slaves forever, but over your brothers the children of Israel you shall not rule, one over another, with harshness. ⁴⁷"If an alien or temporary resident with you becomes rich, and your brother beside him has grown poor, and sells himself to the stranger or foreigner living among you, or to a member of the stranger's family, ⁴⁸

after he is sold he may be redeemed. One of his brothers may redeem him; ⁴⁹ or his uncle, or his uncle's son, may redeem him, or any who is a close relative to him of his family may redeem him; or if he has grown rich, he may redeem himself. ⁵⁰ He shall reckon with him who bought him from the year that he sold himself to him to the Year of Jubilee. The price of his sale shall be according to the number of years; he shall be with him according to the time of a hired servant. ⁵¹ If there are yet many years, according to them he shall give back the price of his redemption out of the money that he was bought for. ⁵² If there remain but a few years to the year of jubilee, then he shall reckon with him; according to his years of service he shall give back the price of his redemption. ⁵³ As a servant hired year by year shall he be with him. He shall not rule with harshness over him in your sight. ⁵⁴ If he isn't redeemed by these means, then he shall be released in the Year of Jubilee: he and his children with him. ⁵⁵ For to me the children of Israel are servants; they are my servants whom I brought out of the land of Egypt. I am Yahweh your God.

## 26

¹"You shall make for yourselves no idols, and you shall not raise up a carved image or a pillar, and you shall not place any figured stone in your land, to bow down to it; for I am Yahweh your God. ²"You shall keep my Sabbaths, and have reverence for my sanctuary. I am Yahweh. ³"If you walk in my statutes and keep my commandments, and do them, ⁴ then I will give you your rains in their season, and the land shall yield its increase, and the trees of the field shall yield their fruit. ⁵ Your threshing shall continue until the vintage, and the vintage shall continue until the sowing time. You shall eat your bread to the full, and dwell in your land safely. ⁶"I will give peace in the land, and you shall lie down, and no one will make you afraid. I will remove evil animals out of the land, neither shall the sword go through your land. ⁷ You shall chase your enemies, and they shall fall before you by the sword. ⁸ Five of you shall chase a hundred, and a hundred of you shall chase ten thousand; and your enemies shall fall before you by the sword. ⁹"I will have respect for you, make you fruitful, multiply you, and will establish my covenant with you. ¹⁰ You shall eat old supplies long kept, and you shall move out the old because of the new. ¹¹ I will set my tent among you, and my soul won't abhor you. ¹² I will walk among you, and will be your God, and you will be my people. ¹³ I am Yahweh your God, who brought you out of the land of Egypt, that you should not be their slaves. I have broken the bars of your yoke, and made you walk upright. ¹⁴"But if you will not listen to me, and will not do all these commandments, ¹⁵ and if you shall reject my statutes, and if your soul abhors my ordinances, so that you will not do all my commandments, but break my covenant, ¹⁶ I also will do this to you: I will appoint terror over you, even consumption and fever, that shall consume the eyes, and make the soul to pine away. You will sow your seed in vain, for your enemies will eat it. ¹⁷ I will set my face against you, and you will be struck before your enemies. Those who hate you will rule over you; and you will flee when no one pursues you. ¹⁸"If you in spite of these things will not listen to me, then I will chastise you seven times more for your sins. ¹⁹ I will break the pride of your power, and I will make your sky like iron, and your soil like bronze. ²⁰ Your strength will be spent in vain; for your land won't yield its increase, neither will the trees of the land yield their fruit. ²¹"If you walk contrary to me, and won't listen to me, then I will bring seven times more plagues on you according to your sins. ²² I will send the wild animals among you, which will rob you of your children, destroy your livestock, and make you few in number. Your roads will become desolate. ²³"If by these things you won't be turned back to me, but will walk contrary to me, ²⁴ then I will also walk contrary to you; and I will strike you, even I, seven times for your sins. ²⁵ I will bring a sword upon you that will execute the vengeance of the covenant. You will be gathered together within your cities, and I will send the pestilence among you. You will be delivered into the hand of the enemy. ²⁶ When I break your staff of bread, ten women shall bake your bread in one oven, and they shall deliver your bread again by weight. You shall eat, and not be satisfied. ²⁷"If you in spite of this won't listen to me, but walk contrary to me, ²⁸ then I will walk contrary to you in wrath. I will also chastise you seven times for your sins. ²⁹ You will eat the flesh of your sons, and you will eat the flesh of your daughters. ³⁰ I will destroy your high places, and cut down your incense altars, and cast your dead bodies upon the bodies of your idols; and my soul will abhor you. ³¹ I will lay your cities waste, and will bring your sanctuaries to desolation. I will not take delight in the sweet fragrance of your offerings. ³² I will bring the land into desolation, and your enemies who dwell in it will be astonished at it. ³³ I will scatter you among the nations, and I will draw out the sword after you. Your land will be a desolation, and your cities shall be a waste. ³⁴ Then the land will enjoy its Sabbaths as long as it lies desolate and you are in your enemies' land. Even then the land will rest and enjoy its Sabbaths. ³⁵ As long as it lies desolate it shall have rest, even the rest

which it didn't have in your Sabbaths when you lived on it. ³⁶"As for those of you who are left, I will send a faintness into their hearts in the lands of their enemies. The sound of a driven leaf will put them to flight; and they shall flee, as one flees from the sword. They will fall when no one pursues. ³⁷ They will stumble over one another, as it were before the sword, when no one pursues. You will have no power to stand before your enemies. ³⁸ You will perish among the nations. The land of your enemies will eat you up. ³⁹ Those of you who are left will pine away in their iniquity in your enemies' lands; and also in the iniquities of their fathers they shall pine away with them. ⁴⁰"If they confess their iniquity and the iniquity of their fathers, in their trespass which they trespassed against me; and also that because they walked contrary to me, ⁴¹ I also walked contrary to them, and brought them into the land of their enemies; if then their uncircumcised heart is humbled, and they then accept the punishment of their iniquity, ⁴² then I will remember my covenant with Jacob, my covenant with Isaac, and also my covenant with Abraham; and I will remember the land. ⁴³ The land also will be left by them, and will enjoy its Sabbaths while it lies desolate without them; and they will accept the punishment of their iniquity because they rejected my ordinances, and their soul abhorred my statutes. ⁴⁴ Yet for all that, when they are in the land of their enemies, I will not reject them, neither will I abhor them, to destroy them utterly and to break my covenant with them; for I am Yahweh their God. ⁴⁵ But I will for their sake remember the covenant of their ancestors, whom I brought out of the land of Egypt in the sight of the nations, that I might be their God. I am Yahweh.'" ⁴⁶ These are the statutes, ordinances, and laws, which Yahweh made between him and the children of Israel in Mount Sinai by Moses.

## 27

¹ Yahweh spoke to Moses, saying, ²"Speak to the children of Israel, and say to them, 'When a man consecrates a person to Yahweh in a vow, according to your valuation, ³ your valuation of a male from twenty years old to sixty years old shall be fifty shekels of silver, according to the shekel<sup>a</sup> of the sanctuary. ⁴ If she is a female, then your valuation shall be thirty shekels. ⁵ If the person is from five years old to twenty years old, then your valuation shall be for a male twenty shekels, and for a female ten shekels. ⁶ If the person is from a month old to five years old, then your valuation shall be for a male five shekels of silver, and for a female your valuation shall be three shekels of silver. ⁷ If the person is from sixty years old and upward; if he is a male, then your valuation shall be fifteen shekels, and for a female ten shekels. ⁸ But if he is poorer than your valuation, then he shall be set before the priest, and the priest shall assign a value to him. The priest shall assign a value according to his ability to pay. ⁹"If it is an animal of which men offer an offering to Yahweh, all that any man gives of such to Yahweh becomes holy. ¹⁰ He shall not alter it, nor exchange it, a good for a bad, or a bad for a good. If he shall at all exchange animal for animal, then both it and that for which it is exchanged shall be holy. ¹¹ If it is any unclean animal, of which they do not offer as an offering to Yahweh, then he shall set the animal before the priest; ¹² and the priest shall evaluate it, whether it is good or bad. As the priest evaluates it, so it shall be. ¹³ But if he will indeed redeem it, then he shall add the fifth part of it to its valuation. ¹⁴"When a man dedicates his house to be holy to Yahweh, then the priest shall evaluate it, whether it is good or bad. As the priest evaluates it, so it shall stand. ¹⁵ If he who dedicates it will redeem his house, then he shall add the fifth part of the money of your valuation to it, and it shall be his. ¹⁶"If a man dedicates to Yahweh part of the field of his possession, then your valuation shall be according to the seed for it. The sowing of a homer<sup>b</sup> of barley shall be valued at fifty shekels<sup>c</sup> of silver. ¹⁷ If he dedicates his field from the Year of Jubilee, according to your valuation it shall stand. ¹⁸ But if he dedicates his field after the Jubilee, then the priest shall reckon to him the money according to the years that remain to the Year of Jubilee; and an abatement shall be made from your valuation. ¹⁹ If he who dedicated the field will indeed redeem it, then he shall add the fifth part of the money of your valuation to it, and it shall remain his. ²⁰ If he will not redeem the field, or if he has sold the field to another man, it shall not be redeemed any more; ²¹ but the field, when it goes out in the Jubilee, shall be holy to Yahweh, as a devoted field. It shall be owned by the priests. ²²"If he dedicates a field to Yahweh which he has bought, which is not of the field of his possession, ²³ then the priest shall reckon to him the worth of your valuation up to the Year of Jubilee; and he shall give your valuation on that day, as a holy thing to Yahweh. ²⁴ In the Year of Jubilee the field shall return to him from whom it was bought, even to him to whom the possession of the land belongs. ²⁵ All

your valuations shall be according to the shekel of the sanctuary: twenty gerahs<sup>d</sup> to the shekel.<sup>e</sup> ²⁶"However the firstborn among animals, which belongs to Yahweh as a firstborn, no man may dedicate, whether an ox or a sheep. It is Yahweh's. ²⁷ If it is an unclean animal, then he shall buy it back according to your valuation, and shall add to it the fifth part of it; or if it isn't redeemed, then it shall be sold according to your valuation. ²⁸"Notwithstanding, no devoted thing that a man devotes to Yahweh of all that he has, whether of man or animal, or of the field of his possession, shall be sold or redeemed. Everything that is permanently devoted is most holy to Yahweh. ²⁹"No one devoted to destruction, who shall be devoted from among men, shall be ransomed. He shall surely be put to death. ³⁰"All the tithe of the land, whether of the seed of the land or of the fruit of the trees, is Yahweh's. It is holy to Yahweh. ³¹ If a man redeems anything of his tithe, he shall add a fifth part to it. ³² All the tithe of the herds or the flocks, whatever passes under the rod, the tenth shall be holy to Yahweh. ³³ He shall not examine whether it is good or bad, neither shall he exchange it. If he exchanges it at all, then both it and that for which it is exchanged shall be holy. It shall not be redeemed.'" ³⁴ These are the commandments which Yahweh commanded Moses for the children of Israel on Mount Sinai.

# The Fourth Book of Moses, Numbers

## 1

¹ Yahweh<sup>f</sup> spoke to Moses in the wilderness of Sinai, in the Tent of Meeting, on the first day of the second month, in the second year after they had come out of the land of Egypt, saying, ²"Take a census of all the congregation of the children of Israel, by their families, by their fathers' houses, according to the number of the names, every male, one by one, ³ from twenty years old and upward, all who are able to go out to war in Israel. You and Aaron shall count them by their divisions. ⁴ With you there shall be a man of every tribe, each one head of his fathers' house. ⁵ These are the names of the men who shall stand with you: Of Reuben: Elizur the son of Shedeur. ⁶ Of Simeon: Shelumiel the son of Zurishaddai. ⁷ Of Judah: Nahshon the son of Amminadab. ⁸ Of Issachar: Nethanel the son of Zuar. ⁹ Of Zebulun: Eliab the son of Helon. ¹⁰ Of the children of Joseph: of Ephraim: Elishama the son of Ammihud; of Manasseh: Gamaliel the son of Pedahzur. ¹¹ Of Benjamin: Abidan the son of Gideoni. ¹² Of Dan: Ahiezer the son of Ammishaddai. ¹³ Of Asher: Pagiel the son of Ochran. ¹⁴ Of Gad: Eliasaph the son of Deuel. ¹⁵ Of Naphtali: Ahira the son of Enan." ¹⁶ These are those who were called of the congregation, the princes<sup>g</sup> of the tribes of their fathers; they were the heads of the thousands of Israel. ¹⁷ Moses and Aaron took these men who are mentioned by name. ¹⁸ They assembled all the congregation together on the first day of the second month; and they declared their ancestry by their families, by their fathers' houses, according to the number of the names, from twenty years old and upward, one by one. ¹⁹ As Yahweh commanded Moses, so he counted them in the wilderness of Sinai. ²⁰ The children of Reuben, Israel's firstborn, their generations, by their families, by their fathers' houses, according to the number of the names, one by one, every male from twenty years old and upward, all who were able to go out to war: ²¹ those who were counted of them, of the tribe of Reuben, were forty-six thousand five hundred. ²² Of the children of Simeon, their generations, by their families, by their fathers' houses, those who were counted of it, according to the number of the names, one by one, every male from twenty years old and upward, all who were able to go out to war: ²³ those who were counted of them, of the tribe of Simeon, were fifty-nine thousand three hundred. ²⁴ Of the children of Gad, their generations, by their families, by their fathers' houses, according to the number of the names, from twenty years old and upward, all who were able to go out to war: ²⁵ those who were counted of them, of the tribe of Gad, were forty-five thousand six hundred fifty. ²⁶ Of the children of Judah, their generations, by their families, by their fathers' houses, according to the number of the names, from twenty years old and upward, all who were able to go out to war: ²⁷ those who were counted of them, of the tribe of Judah, were seventy-four thousand six hundred. ²⁸ Of the children of Issachar, their generations, by their families, by their fathers' houses, according to the number of the names, from twenty years old and upward, all who were able to go out to war: ²⁹ those who were counted of them, of the tribe of Issachar, were fifty-four thousand four hundred. ³⁰ Of the children of Zebulun, their generations, by their families, by their fathers' houses, according to the number of the names, from twenty years old and upward, all who were

---

<sup>a</sup> *27:3 A shekel is about 10 grams or about 0.35 ounces.*
<sup>b</sup> *27:16 1 homer is about 220 liters or 6 bushels*
<sup>c</sup> *27:16 A shekel is about 10 grams or about 0.35 ounces.*
<sup>d</sup> *27:25 A gerah is about 0.5 grams or about 7.7 grains.*
<sup>e</sup> *27:25 A shekel is about 10 grams or about 0.35 ounces.*
<sup>f</sup> *1:1 "Yahweh" is God's proper Name, sometimes rendered*
"LORD" (all caps) in other translations.
<sup>g</sup> *1:16 or, chiefs, or, leaders*

able to go out to war: <sup>31</sup> those who were counted of them, of the tribe of Zebulun, were fifty-seven thousand four hundred. <sup>32</sup> Of the children of Joseph: of the children of Ephraim, their generations, by their families, by their fathers' houses, according to the number of the names, from twenty years old and upward, all who were able to go out to war: <sup>33</sup> those who were counted of them, of the tribe of Ephraim, were forty thousand five hundred. <sup>34</sup> Of the children of Manasseh, their generations, by their families, by their fathers' houses, according to the number of the names, from twenty years old and upward, all who were able to go out to war: <sup>35</sup> those who were counted of them, of the tribe of Manasseh, were thirty-two thousand two hundred. <sup>36</sup> Of the children of Benjamin, their generations, by their families, by their fathers' houses, according to the number of the names, from twenty years old and upward, all who were able to go out to war: <sup>37</sup> those who were counted of them, of the tribe of Benjamin, were thirty-five thousand four hundred. <sup>38</sup> Of the children of Dan, their generations, by their families, by their fathers' houses, according to the number of the names, from twenty years old and upward, all who were able to go out to war: <sup>39</sup> those who were counted of them, of the tribe of Dan, were sixty-two thousand seven hundred. <sup>40</sup> Of the children of Asher, their generations, by their families, by their fathers' houses, according to the number of the names, from twenty years old and upward, all who were able to go out to war: <sup>41</sup> those who were counted of them, of the tribe of Asher, were forty-one thousand five hundred. <sup>42</sup> Of the children of Naphtali, their generations, by their families, by their fathers' houses, according to the number of the names, from twenty years old and upward, all who were able to go out to war: <sup>43</sup> those who were counted of them, of the tribe of Naphtali, were fifty-three thousand four hundred. <sup>44</sup> These are those who were counted, whom Moses and Aaron counted, and the twelve men who were princes of Israel, each one for his fathers' house. <sup>45</sup> So all those who were counted of the children of Israel by their fathers' houses, from twenty years old and upward, all who were able to go out to war in Israel— <sup>46</sup> all those who were counted were six hundred three thousand five hundred fifty. <sup>47</sup> But the Levites after the tribe of their fathers were not counted among them. <sup>48</sup> For Yahweh spoke to Moses, saying, <sup>49</sup>"Only the tribe of Levi you shall not count, neither shall you take a census of them among the children of Israel; <sup>50</sup> but appoint the Levites over the Tabernacle of the Testimony, and over all its furnishings, and over all that belongs to it. They shall carry the tabernacle and all its furnishings; and they shall take care of it, and shall encamp around it. <sup>51</sup> When the tabernacle is to move, the Levites shall take it down; and when the tabernacle is to be set up, the Levites shall set it up. The stranger who comes near shall be put to death. <sup>52</sup> The children of Israel shall pitch their tents, every man by his own camp, and every man by his own standard, according to their divisions. <sup>53</sup> But the Levites shall encamp around the Tabernacle of the Testimony, that there may be no wrath on the congregation of the children of Israel. The Levites shall be responsible for the Tabernacle of the Testimony." <sup>54</sup> Thus the children of Israel did. According to all that Yahweh commanded Moses, so they did.

## 2

<sup>1</sup> Yahweh spoke to Moses and to Aaron, saying, <sup>2</sup>"The children of Israel shall encamp every man by his own standard, with the banners of their fathers' houses. They shall encamp around the Tent of Meeting at a distance from it. <sup>3</sup>"Those who encamp on the east side toward the sunrise shall be of the standard of the camp of Judah, according to their divisions. The prince of the children of Judah shall be Nahshon the son of Amminadab. <sup>4</sup> His division, and those who were counted of them, were seventy-four thousand six hundred. <sup>5</sup>"Those who encamp next to him shall be the tribe of Issachar. The prince of the children of Issachar shall be Nethanel the son of Zuar. <sup>6</sup> His division, and those who were counted of it, were fifty-four thousand four hundred. <sup>7</sup>"The tribe of Zebulun: the prince of the children of Zebulun shall be Eliab the son of Helon. <sup>8</sup> His division, and those who were counted of it, were fifty-seven thousand four hundred. <sup>9</sup>"All who were counted of the camp of Judah were one hundred eighty-six thousand four hundred, according to their divisions. They shall set out first. <sup>10</sup>"On the south side shall be the standard of the camp of Reuben according to their divisions. The prince of the children of Reuben shall be Elizur the son of Shedeur. <sup>11</sup> His division, and those who were counted of it, were forty-six thousand five hundred. <sup>12</sup>"Those who encamp next to him shall be the tribe of Simeon. The prince of the children of Simeon shall be Shelumiel the son of Zurishaddai. <sup>13</sup> His division, and those who were counted of them, were fifty-nine thousand three hundred. <sup>14</sup>"The tribe of Gad: the prince of the children of Gad shall be Eliasaph the son of Reuel. <sup>15</sup> His division, and those who were counted of them, were forty-five thousand six hundred fifty. <sup>16</sup>"All who were counted of the camp of Reuben were

one hundred fifty-one thousand four hundred fifty, according to their armies. They shall set out second. <sup>17</sup>"Then the Tent of Meeting shall set out, with the camp of the Levites in the middle of the camps. As they encamp, so shall they set out, every man in his place, by their standards. <sup>18</sup>"On the west side shall be the standard of the camp of Ephraim according to their divisions. The prince of the children of Ephraim shall be Elishama the son of Ammihud. <sup>19</sup> His division, and those who were counted of them, were forty thousand five hundred. <sup>20</sup>"Next to him shall be the tribe of Manasseh. The prince of the children of Manasseh shall be Gamaliel the son of Pedahzur. <sup>21</sup> His division, and those who were counted of them, were thirty-two thousand two hundred. <sup>22</sup>"The tribe of Benjamin: the prince of the children of Benjamin shall be Abidan the son of Gideoni. <sup>23</sup> His army, and those who were counted of them, were thirty-five thousand four hundred. <sup>24</sup>"All who were counted of the camp of Ephraim were one hundred eight thousand one hundred, according to their divisions. They shall set out third. <sup>25</sup>"On the north side shall be the standard of the camp of Dan according to their divisions. The prince of the children of Dan shall be Ahiezer the son of Ammishaddai. <sup>26</sup> His division, and those who were counted of them, were sixty-two thousand seven hundred. <sup>27</sup>"Those who encamp next to him shall be the tribe of Asher. The prince of the children of Asher shall be Pagiel the son of Ochran. <sup>28</sup> His division, and those who were counted of them, were forty-one thousand five hundred. <sup>29</sup>"The tribe of Naphtali: the prince of the children of Naphtali shall be Ahira the son of Enan. <sup>30</sup> His division, and those who were counted of them, were fifty-three thousand four hundred. <sup>31</sup>"All who were counted of the camp of Dan were one hundred fifty-seven thousand six hundred. They shall set out last by their standards." <sup>32</sup> These are those who were counted of the children of Israel by their fathers' houses. All who were counted of the camps according to their armies were six hundred three thousand five hundred fifty. <sup>33</sup> But the Levites were not counted among the children of Israel, as Yahweh commanded Moses. <sup>34</sup> Thus the children of Israel did. According to all that Yahweh commanded Moses, so they encamped by their standards, and so they set out, everyone by their families, according to their fathers' houses.

## 3

<sup>1</sup> Now this is the history of the generations of Aaron and Moses in the day that Yahweh spoke with Moses in Mount Sinai. <sup>2</sup> These are the names of the sons of Aaron: Nadab the firstborn, and Abihu, Eleazar, and Ithamar. <sup>3</sup> These are the names of the sons of Aaron, the priests who were anointed, whom he consecrated to minister in the priest's office. <sup>4</sup> Nadab and Abihu died before Yahweh when they offered strange fire before Yahweh in the wilderness of Sinai, and they had no children. Eleazar and Ithamar ministered in the priest's office in the presence of Aaron their father. <sup>5</sup> Yahweh spoke to Moses, saying, <sup>6</sup>"Bring the tribe of Levi near, and set them before Aaron the priest, that they may minister to him. <sup>7</sup> They shall keep his requirements, and the requirements of the whole congregation before the Tent of Meeting, to do the service of the tabernacle. <sup>8</sup> They shall keep all the furnishings of the Tent of Meeting, and the obligations of the children of Israel, to do the service of the tabernacle. <sup>9</sup> You shall give the Levites to Aaron and to his sons. They are wholly given to him on the behalf of the children of Israel. <sup>10</sup> You shall appoint Aaron and his sons, and they shall keep their priesthood, but the stranger who comes near shall be put to death." <sup>11</sup> Yahweh spoke to Moses, saying, <sup>12</sup>"Behold,<sup>a</sup> I have taken the Levites from among the children of Israel instead of all the firstborn who open the womb among the children of Israel; and the Levites shall be mine, <sup>13</sup> for all the firstborn are mine. On the day that I struck down all the firstborn in the land of Egypt I made holy to me all the firstborn in Israel, both man and animal. They shall be mine. I am Yahweh." <sup>14</sup> Yahweh spoke to Moses in the wilderness of Sinai, saying, <sup>15</sup>"Count the children of Levi by their fathers' houses, by their families. You shall count every male from a month old and upward." <sup>16</sup> Moses counted them according to Yahweh's word, as he was commanded. <sup>17</sup> These were the sons of Levi by their names: Gershon, Kohath, and Merari. <sup>18</sup> These are the names of the sons of Gershon by their families: Libni and Shimei. <sup>19</sup> The sons of Kohath by their families: Amram, Izhar, Hebron, and Uzziel. <sup>20</sup> The sons of Merari by their families: Mahli and Mushi. These are the families of the Levites according to their fathers' houses. <sup>21</sup> Of Gershon was the family of the Libnites, and the family of the Shimeites. These are the families of the Gershonites. <sup>22</sup> Those who were counted of them, according to the number of all the males from a month old and upward, even those who were counted of them were seven thousand five hundred. <sup>23</sup> The families of the Gershonites shall encamp behind the tabernacle westward. <sup>24</sup> Eliasaph the son of Lael shall be the prince of the fathers' house of the Gershonites. <sup>25</sup> The duty of the sons of Gershon in the Tent of Meeting shall be the tabernacle, the tent, its

covering, the screen for the door of the Tent of Meeting, 26 the hangings of the court, the screen for the door of the court which is by the tabernacle and around the altar, and its cords for all of its service. 27 Of Kohath was the family of the Amramites, the family of the Izharites, the family of the Hebronites, and the family of the Uzzielites. These are the families of the Kohathites. 28 According to the number of all the males from a month old and upward, there were eight thousand six hundred keeping the requirements of the sanctuary. 29 The families of the sons of Kohath shall encamp on the south side of the tabernacle. 30 The prince of the fathers' house of the families of the Kohathites shall be Elizaphan the son of Uzziel. 31 Their duty shall be the ark, the table, the lamp stand, the altars, the vessels of the sanctuary with which they minister, the screen, and all its service. 32 Eleazar the son of Aaron the priest shall be prince of the princes of the Levites, with the oversight of those who keep the requirements of the sanctuary. 33 Of Merari was the family of the Mahlites and the family of the Mushites. These are the families of Merari. 34 Those who were counted of them, according to the number of all the males from a month old and upward, were six thousand two hundred.ᵃ 35 The prince of the fathers' house of the families of Merari was Zuriel the son of Abihail. They shall encamp on the north side of the tabernacle. 36 The appointed duty of the sons of Merari shall be the tabernacle's boards, its bars, its pillars, its sockets, all its instruments, all its service, 37 the pillars of the court around it, their sockets, their pins, and their cords. 38 Those who encamp before the tabernacle eastward, in front of the Tent of Meeting toward the sunrise, shall be Moses, with Aaron and his sons, keeping the requirements of the sanctuary for the duty of the children of Israel. The outsider who comes near shall be put to death. 39 All who were counted of the Levites, whom Moses and Aaron counted at the commandment of Yahweh, by their families, all the males from a month old and upward, were twenty-two thousand. 40 Yahweh said to Moses, "Count all the firstborn males of the children of Israel from a month old and upward, and take the number of their names. 41 You shall take the Levites for me—I am Yahweh—instead of all the firstborn among the children of Israel; and the livestock of the Levites instead of all the firstborn among the livestock of the children of Israel." 42 Moses counted, as Yahweh commanded him, all the firstborn among the children of Israel. 43 All the firstborn males according to the number of names from a month old and upward, of those who were counted of them, were twenty-two thousand two hundred seventy-three. 44 Yahweh spoke to Moses, saying, 45 "Take the Levites instead of all the firstborn among the children of Israel, and the livestock of the Levites instead of their livestock; and the Levites shall be mine. I am Yahweh. 46 For the redemption of the two hundred seventy-three of the firstborn of the children of Israel who exceed the number of the Levites, 47 you shall take five shekels apiece for each one; according to the shekelᵇ of the sanctuary you shall take them (the shekel is twenty gerahsᶜ); 48 and you shall give the money, with which their remainder is redeemed, to Aaron and to his sons." 49 Moses took the redemption money from those who exceeded the number of those who were redeemed by the Levites; 50 from the firstborn of the children of Israel he took the money, one thousand three hundred sixty-five shekels,ᵈ according to the shekel of the sanctuary; 51 and Moses gave the redemption money to Aaron and to his sons, according to Yahweh's word, as Yahweh commanded Moses.

# 4

1 Yahweh spoke to Moses and to Aaron, saying, 2 "Take a census of the sons of Kohath from among the sons of Levi, by their families, by their fathers' houses, 3 from thirty years old and upward even until fifty years old, all who enter into the service to do the work in the Tent of Meeting. 4 "This is the service of the sons of Kohath in the Tent of Meeting, regarding the most holy things. 5 When the camp moves forward, Aaron shall go in with his sons; and they shall take down the veil of the screen, cover the ark of the Testimony with it, 6 put a covering of sealskin on it, spread a blue cloth over it, and put in its poles. 7 "On the table of show bread they shall spread a blue cloth, and put on it the dishes, the spoons, the bowls, and the cups with which to pour out; and the continual bread shall be on it. 8 They shall spread on them a scarlet cloth, and cover it with a covering of sealskin, and shall put in its poles. 9 "They shall take a blue cloth and cover the lamp stand of the light, its lamps, its snuffers, its snuff dishes, and all its oil vessels, with which they minister to it. 10 They shall put it and all its vessels within a covering of sealskin, and shall put it on the frame. 11 "On the golden altar they shall spread a blue cloth, and cover it with a covering of

sealskin, and shall put in its poles. 12 "They shall take all the vessels of ministry with which they minister in the sanctuary, and put them in a blue cloth, cover them with a covering of sealskin, and shall put them on the frame. 13 "They shall take away the ashes from the altar, and spread a purple cloth on it. 14 They shall put on it all its vessels with which they minister about it, the fire pans, the meat hooks, the shovels, and the basins—all the vessels of the altar; and they shall spread on it a covering of sealskin, and put in its poles. 15 "When Aaron and his sons have finished covering the sanctuary and all the furniture of the sanctuary, as the camp moves forward; after that, the sons of Kohath shall come to carry it; but they shall not touch the sanctuary, lest they die. The sons of Kohath shall carry these things belonging to the Tent of Meeting. 16 "The duty of Eleazar the son of Aaron the priest shall be the oil for the light, the sweet incense, the continual meal offering, and the anointing oil, the requirements of all the tabernacle, and of all that is in it, the sanctuary, and its furnishings." 17 Yahweh spoke to Moses and to Aaron, saying, 18 "Don't cut off the tribe of the families of the Kohathites from among the Levites; 19 but do this to them, that they may live, and not die, when they approach the most holy things: Aaron and his sons shall go in and appoint everyone to his service and to his burden; 20 but they shall not go in to see the sanctuary even for a moment, lest they die." 21 Yahweh spoke to Moses, saying, 22 "Take a census of the sons of Gershon also, by their fathers' houses, by their families; 23 you shall count them from thirty years old and upward until fifty years old: all who enter in to wait on the service, to do the work in the Tent of Meeting. 24 "This is the service of the families of the Gershonites, in serving and in bearing burdens: 25 they shall carry the curtains of the tabernacle and the Tent of Meeting, its covering, the covering of sealskin that is on it, the screen for the door of the Tent of Meeting, 26 the hangings of the court, the screen for the door of the gate of the court which is by the tabernacle and around the altar, their cords, and all the instruments of their service, and whatever shall be done with them. They shall serve in there. 27 At the commandment of Aaron and his sons shall be all the service of the sons of the Gershonites, in all their burden and in all their service; and you shall appoint their duty to them in all their responsibilities. 28 This is the service of the families of the sons of the Gershonites in the Tent of Meeting. Their duty shall be under the hand of Ithamar the son of Aaron the priest. 29 "As for the sons of Merari, you shall count them by their families, by their fathers' houses; 30 you shall count them from thirty years old and upward even to fifty years old—everyone who enters on the service, to do the work of the Tent of Meeting. 31 This is the duty of their burden, according to all their service in the Tent of Meeting: the tabernacle's boards, its bars, its pillars, its sockets, 32 the pillars of the court around it, their sockets, their pins, their cords, with all their instruments, and with all their service. You shall appoint the instruments of the duty of their burden to them by name. 33 This is the service of the families of the sons of Merari, according to all their service in the Tent of Meeting, under the hand of Ithamar the son of Aaron the priest." 34 Moses and Aaron and the princes of the congregation counted the sons of the Kohathites by their families, and by their fathers' houses, 35 from thirty years old and upward even to fifty years old, everyone who entered into the service for work in the Tent of Meeting. 36 Those who were counted of them by their families were two thousand seven hundred fifty. 37 These are those who were counted of the families of the Kohathites, all who served in the Tent of Meeting, whom Moses and Aaron counted according to the commandment of Yahweh by Moses. 38 Those who were counted of the sons of Gershon, by their families, and by their fathers' houses, 39 from thirty years old and upward even to fifty years old—everyone who entered into the service for work in the Tent of Meeting, 40 even those who were counted of them, by their families, by their fathers' houses, were two thousand six hundred thirty. 41 These are those who were counted of the families of the sons of Gershon, all who served in the Tent of Meeting, whom Moses and Aaron counted according to the commandment of Yahweh. 42 Those who were counted of the families of the sons of Merari, by their families, by their fathers' houses, 43 from thirty years old and upward even to fifty years old—everyone who entered into the service for work in the Tent of Meeting, 44 even those who were counted of them by their families, were three thousand two hundred. 45 These are those who were counted of the families of the sons of Merari, whom Moses and Aaron counted according to the commandment of Yahweh by Moses. 46 All those who were counted of the Levites whom Moses and Aaron and the princes of Israel counted, by their families and by their fathers' houses, 47 from thirty years old and upward even to fifty years old, everyone who

---

ᵃ 3:34 + 22,000 is the sum rounded to 2 significant digits. The sum of the Gershonites, Kohathites, and Merarites given above is 22,300, but the traditional Hebrew text has the number rounded to 2 significant digits, not 3 significant digits.

ᵇ 3:47 A shekel is about 10 grams or about 0.35 ounces.
ᶜ 3:47 A gerah is about 0.5 grams or about 7.7 grains.

ᵈ 3:50 A shekel is about 10 grams or about 0.35 ounces, so 1365 shekels is about 13.65 kilograms or about 30 pounds.

entered in to do the work of service and the work of bearing burdens in the Tent of Meeting, <sup>48</sup> even those who were counted of them, were eight thousand five hundred eighty. <sup>49</sup> According to the commandment of Yahweh they were counted by Moses, everyone according to his service and according to his burden. Thus they were counted by him, as Yahweh commanded Moses.

**5**

<sup>1</sup> Yahweh spoke to Moses, saying, <sup>2</sup>"Command the children of Israel that they put out of the camp every leper, everyone who has a discharge, and whoever is unclean by a corpse. <sup>3</sup> You shall put both male and female outside of the camp so that they don't defile their camp, in the midst of which I dwell." <sup>4</sup> The children of Israel did so, and put them outside of the camp; as Yahweh spoke to Moses, so the children of Israel did. <sup>5</sup> Yahweh spoke to Moses, saying, <sup>6</sup>"Speak to the children of Israel: 'When a man or woman commits any sin that men commit, so as to trespass against Yahweh, and that soul is guilty, <sup>7</sup> then he shall confess his sin which he has done; and he shall make restitution for his guilt in full, add to it the fifth part of it, and give it to him in respect of whom he has been guilty. <sup>8</sup> But if the man has no kinsman to whom restitution may be made for the guilt, the restitution for guilt which is made to Yahweh shall be the priest's, in addition to the ram of the atonement, by which atonement shall be made for him. <sup>9</sup> Every heave offering of all the holy things of the children of Israel, which they present to the priest, shall be his. <sup>10</sup> Every man's holy things shall be his; whatever any man gives the priest, it shall be his.'" <sup>11</sup> Yahweh spoke to Moses, saying, <sup>12</sup>"Speak to the children of Israel, and tell them: 'If any man's wife goes astray and is unfaithful to him, <sup>13</sup> and a man lies with her carnally, and it is hidden from the eyes of her husband and this is kept concealed, and she is defiled, there is no witness against her, and she isn't taken in the act; <sup>14</sup> and the spirit of jealousy comes on him, and he is jealous of his wife and she is defiled; or if the spirit of jealousy comes on him, and he is jealous of his wife and she isn't defiled; <sup>15</sup> then the man shall bring his wife to the priest, and shall bring her offering for her: one tenth of an ephah<sup>a</sup> of barley meal. He shall pour no oil on it, nor put frankincense on it, for it is a meal offering of jealousy, a meal offering of memorial, bringing iniquity to memory. <sup>16</sup> The priest shall bring her near, and set her before Yahweh. <sup>17</sup> The priest shall take holy water in an earthen vessel; and the priest shall take some of the dust that is on the floor of the tabernacle and put it into the water. <sup>18</sup> The priest shall set the woman before Yahweh, and let the hair of the woman's head go loose, and put the meal offering of memorial in her hands, which is the meal offering of jealousy. The priest shall have in his hand the water of bitterness that brings a curse. <sup>19</sup> The priest shall cause her to take an oath and shall tell the woman, "If no man has lain with you, and if you haven't gone aside to uncleanness, being under your husband's authority, be free from this water of bitterness that brings a curse. <sup>20</sup> But if you have gone astray, being under your husband's authority, and if you are defiled, and some man has lain with you besides your husband—" <sup>21</sup> then the priest shall cause the woman to swear with the oath of cursing, and the priest shall tell the woman, "May Yahweh make you a curse and an oath among your people, when Yahweh allows your thigh to fall away, and your body to swell; <sup>22</sup> and this water that brings a curse will go into your bowels, and make your body swell, and your thigh fall away." The woman shall say, "Amen, Amen." <sup>23</sup>"The priest shall write these curses in a book, and he shall wipe them into the water of bitterness. <sup>24</sup> He shall make the woman drink the water of bitterness that causes the curse; and the water that causes the curse shall enter into her and become bitter. <sup>25</sup> The priest shall take the meal offering of jealousy out of the woman's hand, and shall wave the meal offering before Yahweh, and bring it to the altar. <sup>26</sup> The priest shall take a handful of the meal offering, as its memorial portion, and burn it on the altar, and afterward shall make the woman drink the water. <sup>27</sup> When he has made her drink the water, then it shall happen, if she is defiled and has committed a trespass against her husband, that the water that causes the curse will enter into her and become bitter, and her body will swell, and her thigh will fall away; and the woman will be a curse among her people. <sup>28</sup> If the woman isn't defiled, but is clean; then she shall be free, and shall conceive offspring.<sup>b</sup> <sup>29</sup>"This is the law of jealousy, when a wife, being under her husband, goes astray, and is defiled, <sup>30</sup> or when the spirit of jealousy comes on a man, and he is jealous of his wife; then he shall set the woman before Yahweh, and the priest shall execute on her all this law. <sup>31</sup> The man shall be free from iniquity, and that woman shall bear her iniquity.'"

**6**

<sup>1</sup> Yahweh spoke to Moses, saying, <sup>2</sup>"Speak to the children of Israel, and tell them: 'When either man or woman shall make a special vow, the vow of a Nazirite, to separate himself to Yahweh, <sup>3</sup> he shall separate himself from wine and strong drink. He shall drink no vinegar of wine, or vinegar of fermented drink, neither shall he drink any juice of grapes, nor eat fresh grapes or dried. <sup>4</sup> All the days of his separation he shall eat nothing that is made of the grapevine, from the seeds even to the skins. <sup>5</sup>"All the days of his vow of separation no razor shall come on his head, until the days are fulfilled in which he separates himself to Yahweh. He shall be holy. He shall let the locks of the hair of his head grow long. <sup>6</sup>"All the days that he separates himself to Yahweh he shall not go near a dead body. <sup>7</sup> He shall not make himself unclean for his father, or for his mother, for his brother, or for his sister, when they die, because his separation to God<sup>c</sup> is on his head. <sup>8</sup> All the days of his separation he is holy to Yahweh. <sup>9</sup>"If any man dies very suddenly beside him, and he defiles the head of his separation, then he shall shave his head in the day of his cleansing. On the seventh day he shall shave it. <sup>10</sup> On the eighth day he shall bring two turtledoves or two young pigeons to the priest, to the door of the Tent of Meeting. <sup>11</sup> The priest shall offer one for a sin offering, and the other for a burnt offering, and make atonement for him, because he sinned by reason of the dead, and shall make his head holy that same day. <sup>12</sup> He shall separate to Yahweh the days of his separation, and shall bring a male lamb a year old for a trespass offering; but the former days shall be void, because his separation was defiled. <sup>13</sup>"This is the law of the Nazirite: when the days of his separation are fulfilled, he shall be brought to the door of the Tent of Meeting, <sup>14</sup> and he shall offer his offering to Yahweh: one male lamb a year old without defect for a burnt offering, one ewe lamb a year old without defect for a sin offering, one ram without defect for peace offerings, <sup>15</sup> a basket of unleavened bread, cakes of fine flour mixed with oil, and unleavened wafers anointed with oil with their meal offering and their drink offerings. <sup>16</sup> The priest shall present them before Yahweh, and shall offer his sin offering and his burnt offering. <sup>17</sup> He shall offer the ram for a sacrifice of peace offerings to Yahweh, with the basket of unleavened bread. The priest shall offer also its meal offering and its drink offering. <sup>18</sup> The Nazirite shall shave the head of his separation at the door of the Tent of Meeting, take the hair of the head of his separation, and put it on the fire which is under the sacrifice of peace offerings. <sup>19</sup> The priest shall take the boiled shoulder of the ram, one unleavened cake out of the basket, and one unleavened wafer, and shall put them on the hands of the Nazirite after he has shaved the head of his separation; <sup>20</sup> and the priest shall wave them for a wave offering before Yahweh. They are holy for the priest, together with the breast that is waved and the thigh that is offered. After that the Nazirite may drink wine. <sup>21</sup>"This is the law of the Nazirite who vows and of his offering to Yahweh for his separation, in addition to that which he is able to afford. According to his vow which he vows, so he must do after the law of his separation.'" <sup>22</sup> Yahweh spoke to Moses, saying, <sup>23</sup>"Speak to Aaron and to his sons, saying, 'This is how you shall bless the children of Israel.' You shall tell them, <sup>24</sup>'Yahweh bless you, and keep you. <sup>25</sup> Yahweh make his face to shine on you, and be gracious to you. <sup>26</sup> Yahweh lift up his face toward you, and give you peace.' <sup>27</sup>"So they shall put my name on the children of Israel; and I will bless them."

**7**

<sup>1</sup> On the day that Moses had finished setting up the tabernacle, and had anointed it and sanctified it with all its furniture, and the altar with all its vessels, and had anointed and sanctified them; <sup>2</sup> the princes of Israel, the heads of their fathers' houses, gave offerings. These were the princes of the tribes. These are they who were over those who were counted; <sup>3</sup> and they brought their offering before Yahweh, six covered wagons and twelve oxen; a wagon for every two of the princes, and for each one an ox. They presented them before the tabernacle. <sup>4</sup> Yahweh spoke to Moses, saying, <sup>5</sup>"Accept these from them, that they may be used in doing the service of the Tent of Meeting; and you shall give them to the Levites, to every man according to his service." <sup>6</sup> Moses took the wagons and the oxen, and gave them to the Levites. <sup>7</sup> He gave two wagons and four oxen to the sons of Gershon, according to their service. <sup>8</sup> He gave four wagons and eight oxen to the sons of Merari, according to their service, under the direction of Ithamar the son of Aaron the priest. <sup>9</sup> But to the sons of Kohath he gave none, because the service of the sanctuary belonged to them; they carried it on their shoulders. <sup>10</sup> The princes gave offerings for the dedication of the altar in the day that it was anointed. The princes gave their offerings before the altar. <sup>11</sup> Yahweh said to Moses, "They shall offer their offering, each prince on his day, for the dedication of the altar." <sup>12</sup> He who offered his

---

<sup>a</sup> *5:15* 1 ephah is about 22 liters or about 2/3 of a bushel
<sup>b</sup> *5:28* or, seed

<sup>c</sup> *6:7* The Hebrew word rendered "God" is "אֱלֹהִים" (Elohim).

offering the first day was Nahshon the son of Amminadab, of the tribe of Judah, ¹³ and his offering was: one silver platter, the weight of which was one hundred thirty shekels,ᵃ one silver bowl of seventy shekels, according to the shekel of the sanctuary, both of them full of fine flour mixed with oil for a meal offering; ¹⁴ one golden ladle of ten shekels, full of incense; ¹⁵ one young bull, one ram, one male lamb a year old, for a burnt offering; ¹⁶ one male goat for a sin offering; ¹⁷ and for the sacrifice of peace offerings, two head of cattle, five rams, five male goats, and five male lambs a year old. This was the offering of Nahshon the son of Amminadab. ¹⁸ On the second day Nethanel the son of Zuar, prince of Issachar, gave his offering. ¹⁹ He offered for his offering: one silver platter, the weight of which was one hundred thirty shekels, one silver bowl of seventy shekels, according to the shekel of the sanctuary, both of them full of fine flour mixed with oil for a meal offering; ²⁰ one golden ladle of ten shekels, full of incense; ²¹ one young bull, one ram, one male lamb a year old, for a burnt offering; ²² one male goat for a sin offering; ²³ and for the sacrifice of peace offerings, two head of cattle, five rams, five male goats, five male lambs a year old. This was the offering of Nethanel the son of Zuar. ²⁴ On the third day Eliab the son of Helon, prince of the children of Zebulun, ²⁵ gave his offering: one silver platter, the weight of which was a hundred and thirty shekels, one silver bowl of seventy shekels, according to the shekel of the sanctuary, both of them full of fine flour mixed with oil for a meal offering; ²⁶ one golden ladle of ten shekels, full of incense; ²⁷ one young bull, one ram, one male lamb a year old, for a burnt offering; ²⁸ one male goat for a sin offering; ²⁹ and for the sacrifice of peace offerings, two head of cattle, five rams, five male goats, and five male lambs a year old. This was the offering of Eliab the son of Helon. ³⁰ On the fourth day Elizur the son of Shedeur, prince of the children of Reuben, ³¹ gave his offering: one silver platter, the weight of which was one hundred thirty shekels, one silver bowl of seventy shekels, according to the shekel of the sanctuary, both of them full of fine flour mixed with oil for a meal offering; ³² one golden ladle of ten shekels, full of incense; ³³ one young bull, one ram, one male lamb a year old, for a burnt offering; ³⁴ one male goat for a sin offering; ³⁵ and for the sacrifice of peace offerings, two head of cattle, five rams, five male goats, and five male lambs a year old. This was the offering of Elizur the son of Shedeur. ³⁶ On the fifth day Shelumiel the son of Zurishaddai, prince of the children of Simeon, ³⁷ gave his offering: one silver platter, the weight of which was one hundred thirty shekels, one silver bowl of seventy shekels, according to the shekel of the sanctuary, both of them full of fine flour mixed with oil for a meal offering; ³⁸ one golden ladle of ten shekels, full of incense; ³⁹ one young bull, one ram, one male lamb a year old, for a burnt offering; ⁴⁰ one male goat for a sin offering; ⁴¹ and for the sacrifice of peace offerings, two head of cattle, five rams, five male goats, and five male lambs a year old: this was the offering of Shelumiel the son of Zurishaddai. ⁴² On the sixth day, Eliasaph the son of Deuel, prince of the children of Gad, ⁴³ gave his offering: one silver platter, the weight of which was one hundred thirty shekels, one silver bowl of seventy shekels, according to the shekel of the sanctuary, both of them full of fine flour mixed with oil for a meal offering; ⁴⁴ one golden ladle of ten shekels, full of incense; ⁴⁵ one young bull, one ram, one male lamb a year old, for a burnt offering; ⁴⁶ one male goat for a sin offering; ⁴⁷ and for the sacrifice of peace offerings, two head of cattle, five rams, five male goats, and five male lambs a year old. This was the offering of Eliasaph the son of Deuel. ⁴⁸ On the seventh day Elishama the son of Ammihud, prince of the children of Ephraim, ⁴⁹ gave his offering: one silver platter, the weight of which was one hundred thirty shekels, one silver bowl of seventy shekels, according to the shekel of the sanctuary, both of them full of fine flour mixed with oil for a meal offering; ⁵⁰ one golden ladle of ten shekels, full of incense; ⁵¹ one young bull, one ram, one male lamb a year old, for a burnt offering; ⁵² one male goat for a sin offering; ⁵³ and for the sacrifice of peace offerings, two head of cattle, five rams, five male goats, and five male lambs a year old. This was the offering of Elishama the son of Ammihud. ⁵⁴ On the eighth day Gamaliel the son of Pedahzur, prince of the children of Manasseh, ⁵⁵ gave his offering: one silver platter, the weight of which was one hundred thirty shekels, one silver bowl of seventy shekels, according to the shekel of the sanctuary, both of them full of fine flour mixed with oil for a meal offering; ⁵⁶ one golden ladle of ten shekels, full of incense; ⁵⁷ one young bull, one ram, one male lamb a year old, for a burnt offering; ⁵⁸ one male goat for a sin offering; ⁵⁹ and for the sacrifice of peace offerings, two head of cattle, five rams, five male goats, and five male lambs a year old. This was the offering of Gamaliel the son of Pedahzur. ⁶⁰ On the ninth day Abidan the son of Gideoni, prince of the children of Benjamin, ⁶¹ gave his offering: one silver platter, the weight of which was one hundred thirty shekels, one

silver bowl of seventy shekels, according to the shekel of the sanctuary, both of them full of fine flour mixed with oil for a meal offering; ⁶² one golden ladle of ten shekels, full of incense; ⁶³ one young bull, one ram, one male lamb a year old, for a burnt offering; ⁶⁴ one male goat for a sin offering; ⁶⁵ and for the sacrifice of peace offerings, two head of cattle, five rams, five male goats, and five male lambs a year old. This was the offering of Abidan the son of Gideoni. ⁶⁶ On the tenth day Ahiezer the son of Ammishaddai, prince of the children of Dan, ⁶⁷ gave his offering: one silver platter, the weight of which was one hundred thirty shekels, one silver bowl of seventy shekels, according to the shekel of the sanctuary, both of them full of fine flour mixed with oil for a meal offering; ⁶⁸ one golden ladle of ten shekels, full of incense; ⁶⁹ one young bull, one ram, one male lamb a year old, for a burnt offering; ⁷⁰ one male goat for a sin offering; ⁷¹ and for the sacrifice of peace offerings, two head of cattle, five rams, five male goats, and five male lambs a year old. This was the offering of Ahiezer the son of Ammishaddai. ⁷² On the eleventh day Pagiel the son of Ochran, prince of the children of Asher, ⁷³ gave his offering: one silver platter, the weight of which was one hundred thirty shekels, one silver bowl of seventy shekels, according to the shekel of the sanctuary, both of them full of fine flour mixed with oil for a meal offering; ⁷⁴ one golden ladle of ten shekels, full of incense; ⁷⁵ one young bull, one ram, one male lamb a year old, for a burnt offering; ⁷⁶ one male goat for a sin offering; ⁷⁷ and for the sacrifice of peace offerings, two head of cattle, five rams, five male goats, and five male lambs a year old. This was the offering of Pagiel the son of Ochran. ⁷⁸ On the twelfth day Ahira the son of Enan, prince of the children of Naphtali, ⁷⁹ gave his offering: one silver platter, the weight of which was one hundred thirty shekels, one silver bowl of seventy shekels, according to the shekel of the sanctuary, both of them full of fine flour mixed with oil for a meal offering; ⁸⁰ one golden ladle of ten shekels, full of incense; ⁸¹ one young bull, one ram, one male lamb a year old, for a burnt offering; ⁸² one male goat for a sin offering; ⁸³ and for the sacrifice of peace offerings, two head of cattle, five rams, five male goats, and five male lambs a year old. This was the offering of Ahira the son of Enan. ⁸⁴ This was the dedication offering of the altar, on the day when it was anointed, by the princes of Israel: twelve silver platters, twelve silver bowls, twelve golden ladles; ⁸⁵ each silver platter weighing one hundred thirty shekels, and each bowl seventy; all the silver of the vessels two thousand four hundred shekels, according to the shekel of the sanctuary; ⁸⁶ the twelve golden ladles, full of incense, weighing ten shekels apiece, according to the shekel of the sanctuary; all the gold of the ladles weighed one hundred twenty shekels; ⁸⁷ all the cattle for the burnt offering twelve bulls, the rams twelve, the male lambs a year old twelve, and their meal offering; and twelve male goats for a sin offering; ⁸⁸ and all the cattle for the sacrifice of peace offerings: twenty-four bulls, sixty rams, sixty male goats, and sixty male lambs a year old. This was the dedication offering of the altar, after it was anointed. ⁸⁹ When Moses went into the Tent of Meeting to speak with Yahweh, he heard his voice speaking to him from above the mercy seat that was on the ark of the Testimony, from between the two cherubim; and he spoke to him.

# 8

¹ Yahweh spoke to Moses, saying, ²"Speak to Aaron, and tell him, 'When you light the lamps, the seven lamps shall give light in front of the lamp stand.'" ³ Aaron did so. He lit its lamps to light the area in front of the lamp stand, as Yahweh commanded Moses. ⁴ This was the workmanship of the lamp stand, beaten work of gold. From its base to its flowers, it was beaten work. He made the lamp stand according to the pattern which Yahweh had shown Moses. ⁵ Yahweh spoke to Moses, saying, ⁶"Take the Levites from among the children of Israel, and cleanse them. ⁷ You shall do this to them to cleanse them: sprinkle the water of cleansing on them, let them shave their whole bodies with a razor, let them wash their clothes, and cleanse themselves. ⁸ Then let them take a young bull and its meal offering, fine flour mixed with oil; and another young bull you shall take for a sin offering. ⁹ You shall present the Levites before the Tent of Meeting. You shall assemble the whole congregation of the children of Israel. ¹⁰ You shall present the Levites before Yahweh. The children of Israel shall lay their hands on the Levites, ¹¹ and Aaron shall offer the Levites before Yahweh for a wave offering on the behalf of the children of Israel, that it may be theirs to do the service of Yahweh. ¹²"The Levites shall lay their hands on the heads of the bulls, and you shall offer the one for a sin offering and the other for a burnt offering to Yahweh, to make atonement for the Levites. ¹³ You shall set the Levites before Aaron and before his sons, and offer them as a wave offering to Yahweh. ¹⁴ Thus you shall separate the Levites from among the children of Israel, and the Levites shall be mine. ¹⁵"After that, the Levites shall go in to do the service of

---

ᵃ *7:13* A shekel is about 10 grams or about 0.35 ounces.

the Tent of Meeting. You shall cleanse them, and offer them as a wave offering. [16] For they are wholly given to me from among the children of Israel; instead of all who open the womb, even the firstborn of all the children of Israel, I have taken them to me. [17] For all the firstborn among the children of Israel are mine, both man and animal. On the day that I struck all the firstborn in the land of Egypt, I sanctified them for myself. [18] I have taken the Levites instead of all the firstborn among the children of Israel. [19] I have given the Levites as a gift to Aaron and to his sons from among the children of Israel, to do the service of the children of Israel in the Tent of Meeting, and to make atonement for the children of Israel, so that there will be no plague among the children of Israel when the children of Israel come near to the sanctuary." [20] Moses, and Aaron, and all the congregation of the children of Israel did so to the Levites. According to all that Yahweh commanded Moses concerning the Levites, so the children of Israel did to them. [21] The Levites purified themselves from sin, and they washed their clothes; and Aaron offered them for a wave offering before Yahweh and Aaron made atonement for them to cleanse them. [22] After that, the Levites went in to do their service in the Tent of Meeting before Aaron and before his sons: as Yahweh had commanded Moses concerning the Levites, so they did to them. [23] Yahweh spoke to Moses, saying, [24]"This is what is assigned to the Levites: from twenty-five years old and upward they shall go in to wait on the service in the work of the Tent of Meeting; [25] and from the age of fifty years they shall retire from doing the work, and shall serve no more, [26] but shall assist their brothers in the Tent of Meeting, to perform the duty, and shall perform no service. This is how you shall have the Levites do their duties."

## 9

[1] Yahweh spoke to Moses in the wilderness of Sinai, in the first month of the second year after they had come out of the land of Egypt, saying, [2]"Let the children of Israel keep the Passover in its appointed season. [3] On the fourteenth day of this month, at evening, you shall keep it in its appointed season. You shall keep it according to all its statutes and according to all its ordinances." [4] Moses told the children of Israel that they should keep the Passover. [5] They kept the Passover in the first month, on the fourteenth day of the month at evening, in the wilderness of Sinai. According to all that Yahweh commanded Moses, so the children of Israel did. [6] There were certain men who were unclean because of the dead body of a man, so that they could not keep the Passover on that day, and they came before Moses and Aaron on that day. [7] Those men said to him, "We are unclean because of the dead body of a man. Why are we kept back, that we may not offer the offering of Yahweh in its appointed season among the children of Israel?" [8] Moses answered them, "Wait, that I may hear what Yahweh will command concerning you." [9] Yahweh spoke to Moses, saying, [10]"Say to the children of Israel, 'If any man of you or of your generations is unclean by reason of a dead body, or is on a journey far away, he shall still keep the Passover to Yahweh. [11] In the second month, on the fourteenth day at evening they shall keep it; they shall eat it with unleavened bread and bitter herbs. [12] They shall leave none of it until the morning, nor break a bone of it. According to all the statute of the Passover they shall keep it. [13] But the man who is clean, and is not on a journey, and fails to keep the Passover, that soul shall be cut off from his people. Because he didn't offer the offering of Yahweh in its appointed season, that man shall bear his sin. [14]"If a foreigner lives among you and desires to keep the Passover to Yahweh, then he shall do so according to the statute of the Passover, and according to its ordinance. You shall have one statute, both for the foreigner and for him who is born in the land.'" [15] On the day that the tabernacle was raised up, the cloud covered the tabernacle, even the Tent of the Testimony. At evening it was over the tabernacle, as it were the appearance of fire, until morning. [16] So it was continually. The cloud covered it, and the appearance of fire by night. [17] Whenever the cloud was taken up from over the Tent, then after that the children of Israel traveled; and in the place where the cloud remained, there the children of Israel encamped. [18] At the commandment of Yahweh, the children of Israel traveled, and at the commandment of Yahweh they encamped. As long as the cloud remained on the tabernacle they remained encamped. [19] When the cloud stayed on the tabernacle many days, then the children of Israel kept Yahweh's command, and didn't travel. [20] Sometimes the cloud was a few days on the tabernacle; then according to the commandment of Yahweh they remained encamped, and according to the commandment of Yahweh they traveled. [21] Sometimes the cloud was from evening until morning; and when the cloud was taken up in the morning, they traveled; or by day and by night, when the cloud was taken up, they traveled. [22] Whether it was two days, or a month, or a year that the cloud stayed on the tabernacle,

remaining on it, the children of Israel remained encamped, and didn't travel; but when it was taken up, they traveled. [23] At the commandment of Yahweh they encamped, and at the commandment of Yahweh they traveled. They kept Yahweh's command, at the commandment of Yahweh by Moses.

## 10

[1] Yahweh spoke to Moses, saying, [2]"Make two trumpets of silver. You shall make them of beaten work. You shall use them for the calling of the congregation and for the journeying of the camps. [3] When they blow them, all the congregation shall gather themselves to you at the door of the Tent of Meeting. [4] If they blow just one, then the princes, the heads of the thousands of Israel, shall gather themselves to you. [5] When you blow an alarm, the camps that lie on the east side shall go forward. [6] When you blow an alarm the second time, the camps that lie on the south side shall go forward. They shall blow an alarm for their journeys. [7] But when the assembly is to be gathered together, you shall blow, but you shall not sound an alarm. [8]"The sons of Aaron, the priests, shall blow the trumpets. This shall be to you for a statute forever throughout your generations. [9] When you go to war in your land against the adversary who oppresses you, then you shall sound an alarm with the trumpets. Then you will be remembered before Yahweh your God, and you will be saved from your enemies. [10]"Also in the day of your gladness, and in your set feasts, and in the beginnings of your months, you shall blow the trumpets over your burnt offerings, and over the sacrifices of your peace offerings; and they shall be to you for a memorial before your God. I am Yahweh your God." [11] In the second year, in the second month, on the twentieth day of the month, the cloud was taken up from over the tabernacle of the covenant. [12] The children of Israel went forward on their journeys out of the wilderness of Sinai; and the cloud stayed in the wilderness of Paran. [13] They first went forward according to the commandment of Yahweh by Moses. [14] First, the standard of the camp of the children of Judah went forward according to their armies. Nahshon the son of Amminadab was over his army. [15] Nethanel the son of Zuar was over the army of the tribe of the children of Issachar. [16] Eliab the son of Helon was over the army of the tribe of the children of Zebulun. [17] The tabernacle was taken down; and the sons of Gershon and the sons of Merari, who bore the tabernacle, went forward. [18] The standard of the camp of Reuben went forward according to their armies. Elizur the son of Shedeur was over his army. [19] Shelumiel the son of Zurishaddai was over the army of the tribe of the children of Simeon. [20] Eliasaph the son of Deuel was over the army of the tribe of the children of Gad. [21] The Kohathites set forward, bearing the sanctuary. The others set up the tabernacle before they arrived. [22] The standard of the camp of the children of Ephraim set forward according to their armies. Elishama the son of Ammihud was over his army. [23] Gamaliel the son of Pedahzur was over the army of the tribe of the children of Manasseh. [24] Abidan the son of Gideoni was over the army of the tribe of the children of Benjamin. [25] The standard of the camp of the children of Dan, which was the rear guard of all the camps, set forward according to their armies. Ahiezer the son of Ammishaddai was over his army. [26] Pagiel the son of Ochran was over the army of the tribe of the children of Asher. [27] Ahira the son of Enan was over the army of the tribe of the children of Naphtali. [28] Thus were the travels of the children of Israel according to their armies; and they went forward. [29] Moses said to Hobab, the son of Reuel the Midianite, Moses' father-in-law, "We are journeying to the place of which Yahweh said, 'I will give it to you.' Come with us, and we will treat you well; for Yahweh has spoken good concerning Israel." [30] He said to him, "I will not go; but I will depart to my own land, and to my relatives." [31] Moses said, "Don't leave us, please; because you know how we are to encamp in the wilderness, and you can be our eyes. [32] It shall be, if you go with us—yes, it shall be—that whatever good Yahweh does to us, we will do the same to you." [33] They set forward from the Mount of Yahweh three days' journey. The ark of Yahweh's covenant went before them three days' journey, to seek out a resting place for them. [34] The cloud of Yahweh was over them by day, when they set forward from the camp. [35] When the ark went forward, Moses said, "Rise up, Yahweh, and let your enemies be scattered! Let those who hate you flee before you!" [36] When it rested, he said, "Return, Yahweh, to the ten thousands of the thousands of Israel."

## 11

[1] The people were complaining in the ears of Yahweh. When Yahweh heard it, his anger burned; and Yahweh's fire burned among them, and consumed some of the outskirts of the camp. [2] The people cried to Moses; and Moses prayed to Yahweh, and the fire abated. [3] The name of that place was called Taberah,[a] because Yahweh's fire burned among them. [4] The mixed multitude that was among them lusted exceedingly;

---

[a] *11:3* Taberah means "burning"

and the children of Israel also wept again, and said, "Who will give us meat to eat? [5] We remember the fish, which we ate in Egypt for nothing; the cucumbers, and the melons, and the leeks, and the onions, and the garlic; [6] but now we have lost our appetite. There is nothing at all except this manna to look at." [7] The manna was like coriander seed, and it looked like bdellium.[a] [8] The people went around, gathered it, and ground it in mills, or beat it in mortars, and boiled it in pots, and made cakes of it. Its taste was like the taste of fresh oil. [9] When the dew fell on the camp in the night, the manna fell on it. [10] Moses heard the people weeping throughout their families, every man at the door of his tent; and Yahweh's anger burned greatly; and Moses was displeased. [11] Moses said to Yahweh, "Why have you treated your servant so badly? Why haven't I found favor in your sight, that you lay the burden of all this people on me? [12] Have I conceived all this people? Have I brought them out, that you should tell me, 'Carry them in your bosom, as a nurse carries a nursing infant, to the land which you swore to their fathers'? [13] Where could I get meat to give all these people? For they weep before me, saying, 'Give us meat, that we may eat.' [14] I am not able to bear all this people alone, because it is too heavy for me. [15] If you treat me this way, please kill me right now, if I have found favor in your sight; and don't let me see my wretchedness." [16] Yahweh said to Moses, "Gather to me seventy men of the elders of Israel, whom you know to be the elders of the people and officers over them; and bring them to the Tent of Meeting, that they may stand there with you. [17] I will come down and talk with you there. I will take of the Spirit which is on you, and will put it on them; and they shall bear the burden of the people with you, that you don't bear it yourself alone. [18]"Say to the people, 'Sanctify yourselves in preparation for tomorrow, and you will eat meat; for you have wept in the ears of Yahweh, saying, "Who will give us meat to eat? For it was well with us in Egypt." Therefore Yahweh will give you meat, and you will eat. [19] You will not eat just one day, or two days, or five days, or ten days, or twenty days, [20] but a whole month, until it comes out at your nostrils, and it is loathsome to you; because you have rejected Yahweh who is among you, and have wept before him, saying, "Why did we come out of Egypt?"'" [21] Moses said, "The people, among whom I am, are six hundred thousand men on foot; and you have said, 'I will give them meat, that they may eat a whole month.' [22] Shall flocks and herds be slaughtered for them, to be sufficient for them? Shall all the fish of the sea be gathered together for them, to be sufficient for them?" [23] Yahweh said to Moses, "Has Yahweh's hand grown short? Now you will see whether my word will happen to you or not." [24] Moses went out, and told the people Yahweh's words; and he gathered seventy men of the elders of the people, and set them around the Tent. [25] Yahweh came down in the cloud, and spoke to him, and took of the Spirit that was on him, and put it on the seventy elders. When the Spirit rested on them, they prophesied, but they did so no more. [26] But two men remained in the camp. The name of one was Eldad, and the name of the other Medad; and the Spirit rested on them. They were of those who were written, but had not gone out to the Tent; and they prophesied in the camp. [27] A young man ran, and told Moses, and said, "Eldad and Medad are prophesying in the camp!" [28] Joshua the son of Nun, the servant of Moses, one of his chosen men, answered, "My lord Moses, forbid them!" [29] Moses said to him, "Are you jealous for my sake? I wish that all Yahweh's people were prophets, that Yahweh would put his Spirit on them!" [30] Moses went into the camp, he and the elders of Israel. [31] A wind from Yahweh went out and brought quails from the sea, and let them fall by the camp, about a day's journey on this side, and a day's journey on the other side, around the camp, and about two cubits[b] above the surface of the earth. [32] The people rose up all that day, and all of that night, and all the next day, and gathered the quails. He who gathered least gathered ten homers;[c] and they spread them all out for themselves around the camp. [33] While the meat was still between their teeth, before it was chewed, Yahweh's anger burned against the people, and Yahweh struck the people with a very great plague. [34] The name of that place was called Kibroth Hattaavah,[d] because there they buried the people who lusted. [35] From Kibroth Hattaavah the people traveled to Hazeroth; and they stayed at Hazeroth.

## 12

[1] Miriam and Aaron spoke against Moses because of the Cushite woman whom he had married; for he had married a Cushite woman. [2] They said, "Has Yahweh indeed spoken only with Moses? Hasn't he spoken also with us?" And Yahweh heard it. [3] Now the man Moses was very humble, more than all the men who were on the surface of the earth. [4] Yahweh spoke suddenly to Moses, to Aaron, and to Miriam,

"You three come out to the Tent of Meeting!" The three of them came out. [5] Yahweh came down in a pillar of cloud, and stood at the door of the Tent, and called Aaron and Miriam; and they both came forward. [6] He said, "Now hear my words. If there is a prophet among you, I, Yahweh, will make myself known to him in a vision. I will speak with him in a dream. [7] My servant Moses is not so. He is faithful in all my house. [8] With him, I will speak mouth to mouth, even plainly, and not in riddles; and he shall see Yahweh's form. Why then were you not afraid to speak against my servant, against Moses?" [9] Yahweh's anger burned against them; and he departed. [10] The cloud departed from over the Tent; and behold, Miriam was leprous, as white as snow. Aaron looked at Miriam, and behold, she was leprous. [11] Aaron said to Moses, "Oh, my lord, please don't count this sin against us, in which we have done foolishly, and in which we have sinned. [12] Let her not, I pray, be as one dead, of whom the flesh is half consumed when he comes out of his mother's womb." [13] Moses cried to Yahweh, saying, "Heal her, God, I beg you!" [14] Yahweh said to Moses, "If her father had but spit in her face, shouldn't she be ashamed seven days? Let her be shut up outside of the camp seven days, and after that she shall be brought in again." [15] Miriam was shut up outside of the camp seven days, and the people didn't travel until Miriam was brought in again. [16] Afterward the people traveled from Hazeroth, and encamped in the wilderness of Paran.

## 13

[1] Yahweh spoke to Moses, saying, [2]"Send men, that they may spy out the land of Canaan, which I give to the children of Israel. Of every tribe of their fathers, you shall send a man, every one a prince among them." [3] Moses sent them from the wilderness of Paran according to the commandment of Yahweh. All of them were men who were heads of the children of Israel. [4] These were their names: Of the tribe of Reuben, Shammua the son of Zaccur. [5] Of the tribe of Simeon, Shaphat the son of Hori. [6] Of the tribe of Judah, Caleb the son of Jephunneh. [7] Of the tribe of Issachar, Igal the son of Joseph. [8] Of the tribe of Ephraim, Hoshea the son of Nun. [9] Of the tribe of Benjamin, Palti the son of Raphu. [10] Of the tribe of Zebulun, Gaddiel the son of Sodi. [11] Of the tribe of Joseph, of the tribe of Manasseh, Gaddi the son of Susi. [12] Of the tribe of Dan, Ammiel the son of Gemalli. [13] Of the tribe of Asher, Sethur the son of Michael. [14] Of the tribe of Naphtali, Nahbi the son of Vophsi. [15] Of the tribe of Gad, Geuel the son of Machi. [16] These are the names of the men who Moses sent to spy out the land. Moses called Hoshea the son of Nun Joshua. [17] Moses sent them to spy out the land of Canaan, and said to them, "Go up this way by the South, and go up into the hill country. [18] See the land, what it is; and the people who dwell therein, whether they are strong or weak, whether they are few or many; [19] and what the land is that they dwell in, whether it is good or bad; and what cities they are that they dwell in, whether in camps, or in strongholds; [20] and what the land is, whether it is fertile or poor, whether there is wood therein, or not. Be courageous, and bring some of the fruit of the land." Now the time was the time of the first-ripe grapes. [21] So they went up, and spied out the land from the wilderness of Zin to Rehob, to the entrance of Hamath. [22] They went up by the South, and came to Hebron; and Ahiman, Sheshai, and Talmai, the children of Anak, were there. (Now Hebron was built seven years before Zoan in Egypt.) [23] They came to the valley of Eshcol, and cut down from there a branch with one cluster of grapes, and they bore it on a staff between two. They also brought some of the pomegranates and figs. [24] That place was called the valley of Eshcol, because of the cluster which the children of Israel cut down from there. [25] They returned from spying out the land at the end of forty days. [26] They went and came to Moses, to Aaron, and to all the congregation of the children of Israel, to the wilderness of Paran, to Kadesh; and brought back word to them and to all the congregation. They showed them the fruit of the land. [27] They told him, and said, "We came to the land where you sent us. Surely it flows with milk and honey, and this is its fruit. [28] However, the people who dwell in the land are strong, and the cities are fortified and very large. Moreover, we saw the children of Anak there. [29] Amalek dwells in the land of the South. The Hittite, the Jebusite, and the Amorite dwell in the hill country. The Canaanite dwells by the sea, and along the side of the Jordan." [30] Caleb stilled the people before Moses, and said, "Let's go up at once, and possess it; for we are well able to overcome it!" [31] But the men who went up with him said, "We aren't able to go up against the people; for they are stronger than we." [32] They brought up an evil report of the land which they had spied out to the children of Israel, saying, "The land, through which we have gone to spy it out, is a land that eats up its inhabitants; and all the people who

we saw in it are men of great stature. <sup>33</sup> There we saw the Nephilim,ᵃ the sons of Anak, who come from the Nephilim.ᵇ We were in our own sight as grasshoppers, and so we were in their sight."

## 14

<sup>1</sup> All the congregation lifted up their voice, and cried; and the people wept that night. <sup>2</sup> All the children of Israel murmured against Moses and against Aaron. The whole congregation said to them, "We wish that we had died in the land of Egypt, or that we had died in this wilderness! <sup>3</sup> Why does Yahweh bring us to this land, to fall by the sword? Our wives and our little ones will be captured or killed! Wouldn't it be better for us to return into Egypt?" <sup>4</sup> They said to one another, "Let's choose a leader, and let's return into Egypt." <sup>5</sup> Then Moses and Aaron fell on their faces before all the assembly of the congregation of the children of Israel. <sup>6</sup> Joshua the son of Nun and Caleb the son of Jephunneh, who were of those who spied out the land, tore their clothes. <sup>7</sup> They spoke to all the congregation of the children of Israel, saying, "The land, which we passed through to spy it out, is an exceedingly good land. <sup>8</sup> If Yahweh delights in us, then he will bring us into this land, and give it to us: a land which flows with milk and honey. <sup>9</sup> Only don't rebel against Yahweh, neither fear the people of the land; for they are bread for us. Their defense is removed from over them, and Yahweh is with us. Don't fear them." <sup>10</sup> But all the congregation threatened to stone them with stones. Yahweh's glory appeared in the Tent of Meeting to all the children of Israel. <sup>11</sup> Yahweh said to Moses, "How long will this people despise me? How long will they not believe in me, for all the signs which I have worked among them? <sup>12</sup> I will strike them with the pestilence, and disinherit them, and will make of you a nation greater and mightier than they." <sup>13</sup> Moses said to Yahweh, "Then the Egyptians will hear it; for you brought up this people in your might from among them. <sup>14</sup> They will tell it to the inhabitants of this land. They have heard that you Yahweh are among this people; for you Yahweh are seen face to face, and your cloud stands over them, and you go before them, in a pillar of cloud by day, and in a pillar of fire by night. <sup>15</sup> Now if you killed this people as one man, then the nations which have heard the fame of you will speak, saying, <sup>16</sup>'Because Yahweh was not able to bring this people into the land which he swore to them, therefore he has slain them in the wilderness.' <sup>17</sup> Now please let the power of the Lordᶜ be great, according as you have spoken, saying, <sup>18</sup>'Yahweh is slow to anger, and abundant in loving kindness, forgiving iniquity and disobedience; and he will by no means clear the guilty, visiting the iniquity of the fathers on the children, on the third and on the fourth generation.' <sup>19</sup> Please pardon the iniquity of this people according to the greatness of your loving kindness, and just as you have forgiven this people, from Egypt even until now." <sup>20</sup> Yahweh said, "I have pardoned according to your word; <sup>21</sup> but in very deed—as I live, and as all the earth shall be filled with Yahweh's glory— <sup>22</sup> because all those men who have seen my glory and my signs, which I worked in Egypt and in the wilderness, yet have tempted me these ten times, and have not listened to my voice; <sup>23</sup> surely they shall not see the land which I swore to their fathers, neither shall any of those who despised me see it. <sup>24</sup> But my servant Caleb, because he had another spirit with him, and has followed me fully, him I will bring into the land into which he went. His offspring shall possess it. <sup>25</sup> Since the Amalekite and the Canaanite dwell in the valley, tomorrow turn and go into the wilderness by the way to the Red Sea." <sup>26</sup> Yahweh spoke to Moses and to Aaron, saying, <sup>27</sup>"How long shall I bear with this evil congregation that complain against me? I have heard the complaints of the children of Israel, which they complain against me. <sup>28</sup> Tell them, 'As I live, says Yahweh, surely as you have spoken in my ears, so I will do to you. <sup>29</sup> Your dead bodies shall fall in this wilderness; and all who were counted of you, according to your whole number, from twenty years old and upward, who have complained against me, <sup>30</sup> surely you shall not come into the land concerning which I swore that I would make you dwell therein, except Caleb the son of Jephunneh, and Joshua the son of Nun. <sup>31</sup> But I will bring in your little ones that you said should be captured or killed, and they shall know the land which you have rejected. <sup>32</sup> But as for you, your dead bodies shall fall in this wilderness. <sup>33</sup> Your children shall be wanderers in the wilderness forty years, and shall bear your prostitution, until your dead bodies are consumed in the wilderness. <sup>34</sup> After the number of the days in which you spied out the land, even forty days, for every day a year, you will bear your iniquities, even forty years, and you will know my alienation.' <sup>35</sup> I, Yahweh, have spoken. I will surely do this to all this evil congregation who are gathered together against me. In this wilderness they shall be consumed, and there they shall die." <sup>36</sup> The men whom Moses sent to spy out the land,

who returned and made all the congregation to murmur against him by bringing up an evil report against the land, <sup>37</sup> even those men who brought up an evil report of the land, died by the plague before Yahweh. <sup>38</sup> But Joshua the son of Nun and Caleb the son of Jephunneh remained alive of those men who went to spy out the land. <sup>39</sup> Moses told these words to all the children of Israel, and the people mourned greatly. <sup>40</sup> They rose up early in the morning and went up to the top of the mountain, saying, "Behold, we are here, and will go up to the place which Yahweh has promised; for we have sinned." <sup>41</sup> Moses said, "Why now do you disobey the commandment of Yahweh, since it shall not prosper? <sup>42</sup> Don't go up, for Yahweh isn't among you; that way you won't be struck down before your enemies. <sup>43</sup> For there the Amalekite and the Canaanite are before you, and you will fall by the sword because you turned back from following Yahweh; therefore Yahweh will not be with you." <sup>44</sup> But they presumed to go up to the top of the mountain. Nevertheless, the ark of Yahweh's covenant and Moses didn't depart out of the camp. <sup>45</sup> Then the Amalekites came down, and the Canaanites who lived in that mountain, and struck them and beat them down even to Hormah.

## 15

<sup>1</sup> Yahweh spoke to Moses, saying, <sup>2</sup>"Speak to the children of Israel, and tell them, 'When you have come into the land of your habitations, which I give to you, <sup>3</sup> and will make an offering by fire to Yahweh—a burnt offering, or a sacrifice, to accomplish a vow, or as a free will offering, or in your set feasts, to make a pleasant aroma to Yahweh, of the herd, or of the flock— <sup>4</sup> then he who offers his offering shall offer to Yahweh a meal offering of one tenth of an ephahᵈ of fine flour mixed with one fourth of a hinᵉ of oil. <sup>5</sup> You shall prepare wine for the drink offering, one fourth of a hin, with the burnt offering or for the sacrifice, for each lamb. <sup>6</sup>"For a ram, you shall prepare for a meal offering two tenths of an ephahᶠ of fine flour mixed with the third part of a hin of oil; <sup>7</sup> and for the drink offering you shall offer the third part of a hin of wine, of a pleasant aroma to Yahweh. <sup>8</sup> When you prepare a bull for a burnt offering or for a sacrifice, to accomplish a vow, or for peace offerings to Yahweh, <sup>9</sup> then he shall offer with the bull a meal offering of three tenths of an ephahᵍ of fine flour mixed with half a hin of oil; <sup>10</sup> and you shall offer for the drink offering half a hin of wine, for an offering made by fire, of a pleasant aroma to Yahweh. <sup>11</sup> Thus it shall be done for each bull, for each ram, for each of the male lambs, or of the young goats. <sup>12</sup> According to the number that you shall prepare, so you shall do to everyone according to their number. <sup>13</sup>"All who are native-born shall do these things in this way, in offering an offering made by fire, of a pleasant aroma to Yahweh. <sup>14</sup> If a stranger lives as a foreigner with you, or whoever may be among you throughout your generations, and will offer an offering made by fire, of a pleasant aroma to Yahweh, as you do, so he shall do. <sup>15</sup> For the assembly, there shall be one statute for you and for the stranger who lives as a foreigner, a statute forever throughout your generations. As you are, so the foreigner shall be before Yahweh. <sup>16</sup> One law and one ordinance shall be for you and for the stranger who lives as a foreigner with you.'" <sup>17</sup> Yahweh spoke to Moses, saying, <sup>18</sup>"Speak to the children of Israel, and tell them, 'When you come into the land where I bring you, <sup>19</sup> then it shall be that when you eat of the bread of the land, you shall offer up a wave offering to Yahweh. <sup>20</sup> Of the first of your dough you shall offer up a cake for a wave offering. As the wave offering of the threshing floor, so you shall heave it. <sup>21</sup> Of the first of your dough, you shall give to Yahweh a wave offering throughout your generations. <sup>22</sup>"When you err, and don't observe all these commandments which Yahweh has spoken to Moses— <sup>23</sup> even all that Yahweh has commanded you by Moses, from the day that Yahweh gave commandment and onward throughout your generations— <sup>24</sup> then it shall be, if it was done unwittingly, without the knowledge of the congregation, that all the congregation shall offer one young bull for a burnt offering, for a pleasant aroma to Yahweh, with its meal offering and its drink offering, according to the ordinance, and one male goat for a sin offering. <sup>25</sup> The priest shall make atonement for all the congregation of the children of Israel, and they shall be forgiven; for it was an error, and they have brought their offering, an offering made by fire to Yahweh, and their sin offering before Yahweh, for their error. <sup>26</sup> All the congregation of the children of Israel shall be forgiven, as well as the stranger who lives as a foreigner among them; for with regard to all the people, it was done unwittingly. <sup>27</sup>"If a person sins unwittingly, then he shall offer a female goat a year old for a sin offering. <sup>28</sup> The priest shall make atonement for the soul who errs when he sins unwittingly before Yahweh. He shall make atonement for him; and he shall be forgiven. <sup>29</sup> You shall have one law for him who does

---

ᵃ *13:33* or, giants
ᵇ *13:33* or, giants
ᶜ *14:17* The word translated "Lord" is "Adonai."

ᵈ *15:4* 1 ephah is about 22 liters or about 2/3 of a bushel
ᵉ *15:4* A hin is about 6.5 liters or 1.7 gallons.

ᶠ *15:6* 1 ephah is about 22 liters or about 2/3 of a bushel
ᵍ *15:9* 1 ephah is about 22 liters or about 2/3 of a bushel

anything unwittingly, for him who is native-born among the children of Israel, and for the stranger who lives as a foreigner among them. ³⁰"But the soul who does anything with a high hand, whether he is native-born or a foreigner, blasphemes Yahweh. That soul shall be cut off from among his people. ³¹ Because he has despised Yahweh's word, and has broken his commandment, that soul shall be utterly cut off. His iniquity shall be on him.'" ³² While the children of Israel were in the wilderness, they found a man gathering sticks on the Sabbath day. ³³ Those who found him gathering sticks brought him to Moses and Aaron, and to all the congregation. ³⁴ They put him in custody, because it had not been declared what should be done to him. ³⁵ Yahweh said to Moses, "The man shall surely be put to death. All the congregation shall stone him with stones outside of the camp." ³⁶ All the congregation brought him outside of the camp, and stoned him to death with stones, as Yahweh commanded Moses. ³⁷ Yahweh spoke to Moses, saying, ³⁸"Speak to the children of Israel, and tell them that they should make themselves fringes[a] on the borders of their garments throughout their generations, and that they put on the fringe[b] of each border a cord of blue. ³⁹ It shall be to you for a fringe,[c] that you may see it, and remember all Yahweh's commandments, and do them; and that you don't follow your own heart and your own eyes, after which you used to play the prostitute; ⁴⁰ so that you may remember and do all my commandments, and be holy to your God. ⁴¹ I am Yahweh your God, who brought you out of the land of Egypt, to be your God: I am Yahweh your God."

## 16

¹ Now Korah, the son of Izhar, the son of Kohath, the son of Levi, with Dathan and Abiram, the sons of Eliab, and On, the son of Peleth, sons of Reuben, took some men. ² They rose up before Moses, with some of the children of Israel, two hundred fifty princes of the congregation, called to the assembly, men of renown. ³ They assembled themselves together against Moses and against Aaron, and said to them, "You take too much on yourself, since all the congregation are holy, everyone of them, and Yahweh is among them! Why do you lift yourselves up above Yahweh's assembly?" ⁴ When Moses heard it, he fell on his face. ⁵ He said to Korah and to all his company, "In the morning, Yahweh will show who are his, and who is holy, and will cause him to come near to him. Even him whom he shall choose, he will cause to come near to him. ⁶ Do this: have Korah and all his company take censers, ⁷ put fire in them, and put incense on them before Yahweh tomorrow. It shall be that the man whom Yahweh chooses, he shall be holy. You have gone too far, you sons of Levi!" ⁸ Moses said to Korah, "Hear now, you sons of Levi! ⁹ Is it a small thing to you that the God of Israel has separated you from the congregation of Israel, to bring you near to himself, to do the service of Yahweh's tabernacle, and to stand before the congregation to minister to them; ¹⁰ and that he has brought you near, and all your brothers the sons of Levi with you? Do you seek the priesthood also? ¹¹ Therefore you and all your company have gathered together against Yahweh! What is Aaron that you complain against him?" ¹² Moses sent to call Dathan and Abiram, the sons of Eliab; and they said, "We won't come up! ¹³ Is it a small thing that you have brought us up out of a land flowing with milk and honey, to kill us in the wilderness, but you must also make yourself a prince over us? ¹⁴ Moreover you haven't brought us into a land flowing with milk and honey, nor given us inheritance of fields and vineyards. Will you put out the eyes of these men? We won't come up." ¹⁵ Moses was very angry, and said to Yahweh, "Don't respect their offering. I have not taken one donkey from them, neither have I hurt one of them." ¹⁶ Moses said to Korah, "You and all your company go before Yahweh, you, and they, and Aaron, tomorrow. ¹⁷ Each man take his censer and put incense on it, and each man bring before Yahweh his censer, two hundred fifty censers; you also, and Aaron, each with his censer." ¹⁸ They each took his censer, and put fire in it, and laid incense on it, and stood at the door of the Tent of Meeting with Moses and Aaron. ¹⁹ Korah assembled all the congregation opposite them to the door of the Tent of Meeting. Yahweh's glory appeared to all the congregation. ²⁰ Yahweh spoke to Moses and to Aaron, saying, ²¹"Separate yourselves from among this congregation, that I may consume them in a moment!" ²² They fell on their faces, and said, "God, the God of the spirits of all flesh, shall one man sin, and will you be angry with all the congregation?" ²³ Yahweh spoke to Moses, saying, ²⁴"Speak to the congregation, saying, 'Get away from around the tent of Korah, Dathan, and Abiram!'" ²⁵ Moses rose up and went to Dathan and Abiram; and the elders of Israel followed him. ²⁶ He spoke to the congregation, saying, "Depart, please, from the tents of these wicked men, and touch nothing of theirs, lest you be consumed in all their sins!" ²⁷ So they went away from the tent of Korah, Dathan, and Abiram, on every side. Dathan and Abiram came out, and stood at the door of their tents with their wives, their sons, and

their little ones. ²⁸ Moses said, "Hereby you shall know that Yahweh has sent me to do all these works; for they are not from my own mind. ²⁹ If these men die the common death of all men, or if they experience what all men experience, then Yahweh hasn't sent me. ³⁰ But if Yahweh makes a new thing, and the ground opens its mouth, and swallows them up with all that belong to them, and they go down alive into Sheol,[d] then you shall understand that these men have despised Yahweh." ³¹ As he finished speaking all these words, the ground that was under them split apart. ³² The earth opened its mouth and swallowed them up with their households, all of Korah's men, and all their goods. ³³ So they, and all that belonged to them went down alive into Sheol.[e] The earth closed on them, and they perished from among the assembly. ³⁴ All Israel that were around them fled at their cry; for they said, "Lest the earth swallow us up!" ³⁵ Fire came out from Yahweh, and devoured the two hundred fifty men who offered the incense. ³⁶ Yahweh spoke to Moses, saying, ³⁷"Speak to Eleazar the son of Aaron the priest, that he take up the censers out of the burning, and scatter the fire away from the camp; for they are holy, ³⁸ even the censers of those who sinned against their own lives. Let them be beaten into plates for a covering of the altar, for they offered them before Yahweh. Therefore they are holy. They shall be a sign to the children of Israel." ³⁹ Eleazar the priest took the bronze censers which those who were burned had offered; and they beat them out for a covering of the altar, ⁴⁰ to be a memorial to the children of Israel, to the end that no stranger who isn't of the offspring of Aaron, would come near to burn incense before Yahweh, that he not be as Korah and as his company; as Yahweh spoke to him by Moses. ⁴¹ But on the next day all the congregation of the children of Israel complained against Moses and against Aaron, saying, "You have killed Yahweh's people!" ⁴² When the congregation was assembled against Moses and against Aaron, they looked toward the Tent of Meeting. Behold, the cloud covered it, and Yahweh's glory appeared. ⁴³ Moses and Aaron came to the front of the Tent of Meeting. ⁴⁴ Yahweh spoke to Moses, saying, ⁴⁵"Get away from among this congregation, that I may consume them in a moment!" They fell on their faces. ⁴⁶ Moses said to Aaron, "Take your censer, put fire from the altar in it, lay incense on it, carry it quickly to the congregation, and make atonement for them; for wrath has gone out from Yahweh! The plague has begun." ⁴⁷ Aaron did as Moses said, and ran into the middle of the assembly. The plague had already begun among the people. He put on the incense, and made atonement for the people. ⁴⁸ He stood between the dead and the living; and the plague was stayed. ⁴⁹ Now those who died by the plague were fourteen thousand seven hundred, in addition to those who died about the matter of Korah. ⁵⁰ Aaron returned to Moses to the door of the Tent of Meeting, and the plague was stopped.

## 17

¹ Yahweh spoke to Moses, saying, ²"Speak to the children of Israel, and take rods from them, one for each fathers' house, of all their princes according to their fathers' houses, twelve rods. Write each man's name on his rod. ³ You shall write Aaron's name on Levi's rod. There shall be one rod for each head of their fathers' houses. ⁴ You shall lay them up in the Tent of Meeting before the covenant, where I meet with you. ⁵ It shall happen that the rod of the man whom I shall choose shall bud. I will make the murmurings of the children of Israel, which they murmur against you, cease from me." ⁶ Moses spoke to the children of Israel; and all their princes gave him rods, for each prince one, according to their fathers' houses, a total of twelve rods. Aaron's rod was among their rods. ⁷ Moses laid up the rods before Yahweh in the Tent of the Testimony. ⁸ On the next day, Moses went into the Tent of the Testimony; and behold, Aaron's rod for the house of Levi had sprouted, budded, produced blossoms, and bore ripe almonds. ⁹ Moses brought out all the rods from before Yahweh to all the children of Israel. They looked, and each man took his rod. ¹⁰ Yahweh said to Moses, "Put back the rod of Aaron before the covenant, to be kept for a token against the children of rebellion; that you may make an end of their complaining against me, that they not die." ¹¹ Moses did so. As Yahweh commanded him, so he did. ¹² The children of Israel spoke to Moses, saying, "Behold, we perish! We are undone! We are all undone! ¹³ Everyone who keeps approaching Yahweh's tabernacle, dies! Will we all perish?"

## 18

¹ Yahweh said to Aaron, "You and your sons and your fathers' house with you shall bear the iniquity of the sanctuary; and you and your sons with you shall bear the iniquity of your priesthood. ² Bring your brothers also, the tribe of Levi, the tribe of your father, near with you, that they may be joined to you, and minister to you; but you and your sons with you shall be before the Tent of the Testimony. ³ They shall keep your commands and the duty of the whole Tent; only they shall

---

[a] 15:38 or, tassels (Hebrew צִיצָת)

[b] 15:38 or, tassel

[c] 15:39 or, tassel

[d] 16:30 Sheol is the place of the dead.

[e] 16:33 Sheol is the place of the dead.

not come near to the vessels of the sanctuary and to the altar, that they not die, neither they nor you. [4] They shall be joined to you and keep the responsibility of the Tent of Meeting, for all the service of the Tent. A stranger shall not come near to you. [5]"You shall perform the duty of the sanctuary and the duty of the altar, that there be no more wrath on the children of Israel. [6] Behold, I myself have taken your brothers the Levites from among the children of Israel. They are a gift to you, dedicated to Yahweh, to do the service of the Tent of Meeting. [7] You and your sons with you shall keep your priesthood for everything of the altar, and for that within the veil. You shall serve. I give you the service of the priesthood as a gift. The stranger who comes near shall be put to death." [8] Yahweh spoke to Aaron, "Behold, I myself have given you the command of my wave offerings, even all the holy things of the children of Israel. I have given them to you by reason of the anointing, and to your sons, as a portion forever. [9] This shall be yours of the most holy things from the fire: every offering of theirs, even every meal offering of theirs, and every sin offering of theirs, and every trespass offering of theirs, which they shall render to me, shall be most holy for you and for your sons. [10] You shall eat of it like the most holy things. Every male shall eat of it. It shall be holy to you. [11]"This is yours, too: the wave offering of their gift, even all the wave offerings of the children of Israel. I have given them to you, and to your sons and to your daughters with you, as a portion forever. Everyone who is clean in your house shall eat of it. [12]"I have given to you all the best of the oil, all the best of the vintage, and of the grain, the first fruits of them which they give to Yahweh. [13] The first-ripe fruits of all that is in their land, which they bring to Yahweh, shall be yours. Everyone who is clean in your house shall eat of it. [14]"Everything devoted in Israel shall be yours. [15] Everything that opens the womb, of all flesh which they offer to Yahweh, both of man and animal, shall be yours. Nevertheless, you shall surely redeem the firstborn of man, and you shall redeem the firstborn of unclean animals. [16] You shall redeem those who are to be redeemed of them from a month old, according to your estimation, for five shekels of money, according to the shekel[a] of the sanctuary, which weighs twenty gerahs.[b] [17]"But you shall not redeem the firstborn of a cow, or the firstborn of a sheep, or the firstborn of a goat. They are holy. You shall sprinkle their blood on the altar, and shall burn their fat for an offering made by fire, for a pleasant aroma to Yahweh. [18] Their meat shall be yours, as the wave offering breast and as the right thigh, it shall be yours. [19] All the wave offerings of the holy things which the children of Israel offer to Yahweh, I have given you and your sons and your daughters with you, as a portion forever. It is a covenant of salt forever before Yahweh to you and to your offspring with you." [20] Yahweh said to Aaron, "You shall have no inheritance in their land, neither shall you have any portion among them. I am your portion and your inheritance among the children of Israel. [21]"To the children of Levi, behold, I have given all the tithe in Israel for an inheritance, in return for their service which they serve, even the service of the Tent of Meeting. [22] Henceforth the children of Israel shall not come near the Tent of Meeting, lest they bear sin, and die. [23] But the Levites shall do the service of the Tent of Meeting, and they shall bear their iniquity. It shall be a statute forever throughout your generations. Among the children of Israel, they shall have no inheritance. [24] For the tithe of the children of Israel, which they offer as a wave offering to Yahweh, I have given to the Levites for an inheritance. Therefore I have said to them, 'Among the children of Israel they shall have no inheritance.'" [25] Yahweh spoke to Moses, saying, [26]"Moreover you shall speak to the Levites, and tell them, 'When you take of the children of Israel the tithe which I have given you from them for your inheritance, then you shall offer up a wave offering of it for Yahweh, a tithe of the tithe. [27] Your wave offering shall be credited to you, as though it were the grain of the threshing floor, and as the fullness of the wine press. [28] Thus you also shall offer a wave offering to Yahweh of all your tithes, which you receive of the children of Israel; and of it you shall give Yahweh's wave offering to Aaron the priest. [29] Out of all your gifts, you shall offer every wave offering to Yahweh, of all its best parts, even the holy part of it.' [30]"Therefore you shall tell them, 'When you heave its best from it, then it shall be credited to the Levites as the increase of the threshing floor, and as the increase of the wine press. [31] You may eat it anywhere, you and your households, for it is your reward in return for your service in the Tent of Meeting. [32] You shall bear no sin by reason of it, when you have heaved from it its best. You shall not profane the holy things of the children of Israel, that you not die.'"

## 19

[1] Yahweh spoke to Moses and to Aaron, saying, [2]"This is the statute of the law which Yahweh has commanded. Tell the children of Israel to bring you a red heifer without spot, in which is no defect, and which was never yoked. [3] You shall give her to Eleazar the priest, and he shall bring her outside of the camp, and one shall kill her before his face. [4] Eleazar the priest shall take some of her blood with his finger, and sprinkle her blood toward the front of the Tent of Meeting seven times. [5] One shall burn the heifer in his sight; her skin, and her meat, and her blood, with her dung, shall he burn. [6] The priest shall take cedar wood, hyssop, and scarlet, and cast it into the middle of the burning of the heifer. [7] Then the priest shall wash his clothes, and he shall bathe his flesh in water, and afterward he shall come into the camp, and the priest shall be unclean until the evening. [8] He who burns her shall wash his clothes in water, and bathe his flesh in water, and shall be unclean until the evening. [9]"A man who is clean shall gather up the ashes of the heifer, and lay them up outside of the camp in a clean place; and it shall be kept for the congregation of the children of Israel for use in water for cleansing impurity. It is a sin offering. [10] He who gathers the ashes of the heifer shall wash his clothes, and be unclean until the evening. It shall be to the children of Israel, and to the stranger who lives as a foreigner among them, for a statute forever. [11]"He who touches the dead body of any man shall be unclean seven days. [12] He shall purify himself with water on the third day, and on the seventh day he shall be clean; but if he doesn't purify himself the third day, then the seventh day he shall not be clean. [13] Whoever touches a dead person, the body of a man who has died, and doesn't purify himself, defiles Yahweh's tabernacle; and that soul shall be cut off from Israel; because the water for impurity was not sprinkled on him, he shall be unclean. His uncleanness is yet on him. [14]"This is the law when a man dies in a tent: everyone who comes into the tent, and everyone who is in the tent, shall be unclean seven days. [15] Every open vessel, which has no covering bound on it, is unclean. [16]"Whoever in the open field touches one who is slain with a sword, or a dead body, or a bone of a man, or a grave, shall be unclean seven days. [17]"For the unclean, they shall take of the ashes of the burning of the sin offering; and running water shall be poured on them in a vessel. [18] A clean person shall take hyssop, dip it in the water, and sprinkle it on the tent, on all the vessels, on the persons who were there, and on him who touched the bone, or the slain, or the dead, or the grave. [19] The clean person shall sprinkle on the unclean on the third day, and on the seventh day. On the seventh day, he shall purify him. He shall wash his clothes and bathe himself in water, and shall be clean at evening. [20] But the man who shall be unclean, and shall not purify himself, that soul shall be cut off from among the assembly, because he has defiled the sanctuary of Yahweh. The water for impurity has not been sprinkled on him. He is unclean. [21] It shall be a perpetual statute to them. He who sprinkles the water for impurity shall wash his clothes, and he who touches the water for impurity shall be unclean until evening. [22]"Whatever the unclean person touches shall be unclean; and the soul that touches it shall be unclean until evening."

## 20

[1] The children of Israel, even the whole congregation, came into the wilderness of Zin in the first month. The people stayed in Kadesh. Miriam died there, and was buried there. [2] There was no water for the congregation; and they assembled themselves together against Moses and against Aaron. [3] The people quarreled with Moses, and spoke, saying, "We wish that we had died when our brothers died before Yahweh! [4] Why have you brought Yahweh's assembly into this wilderness, that we should die there, we and our animals? [5] Why have you made us to come up out of Egypt, to bring us in to this evil place? It is no place of seed, or of figs, or of vines, or of pomegranates; neither is there any water to drink." [6] Moses and Aaron went from the presence of the assembly to the door of the Tent of Meeting, and fell on their faces. Yahweh's glory appeared to them. [7] Yahweh spoke to Moses, saying, [8]"Take the rod, and assemble the congregation, you, and Aaron your brother, and speak to the rock before their eyes, that it pour out its water. You shall bring water to them out of the rock; so you shall give the congregation and their livestock drink." [9] Moses took the rod from before Yahweh, as he commanded him. [10] Moses and Aaron gathered the assembly together before the rock, and he said to them, "Hear now, you rebels! Shall we bring water out of this rock for you?" [11] Moses lifted up his hand, and struck the rock with his rod twice, and water came out abundantly. The congregation and their livestock drank. [12] Yahweh said to Moses and Aaron, "Because you didn't believe in me, to sanctify me in the eyes of the children of Israel, therefore you shall not bring this assembly into the land which I have given them." [13] These are the waters of Meribah;[c] because the children of Israel strove with Yahweh, and he was sanctified in them. [14] Moses sent messengers from Kadesh to the king of Edom, saying: "Your brother Israel says: You know all the travail that has happened to us; [15] how our fathers went down into Egypt, and we lived in Egypt a long time. The Egyptians

---

[a] *18:16* A shekel is about 10 grams or about 0.35 ounces.

[b] *18:16* A gerah is about 0.5 grams or about 7.7 grains.

[c] *20:13* "Meribah" means "quarreling".

mistreated us and our fathers. <sup>16</sup> When we cried to Yahweh, he heard our voice, sent an angel, and brought us out of Egypt. Behold, we are in Kadesh, a city in the edge of your border. <sup>17</sup>"Please let us pass through your land. We will not pass through field or through vineyard, neither will we drink from the water of the wells. We will go along the king's highway. We will not turn away to the right hand nor to the left, until we have passed your border." <sup>18</sup> Edom said to him, "You shall not pass through me, lest I come out with the sword against you." <sup>19</sup> The children of Israel said to him, "We will go up by the highway; and if we drink your water, I and my livestock, then I will give its price. Only let me, without doing anything else, pass through on my feet." <sup>20</sup> He said, "You shall not pass through." Edom came out against him with many people, and with a strong hand. <sup>21</sup> Thus Edom refused to give Israel passage through his border, so Israel turned away from him. <sup>22</sup> They traveled from Kadesh, and the children of Israel, even the whole congregation, came to Mount Hor. <sup>23</sup> Yahweh spoke to Moses and Aaron in Mount Hor, by the border of the land of Edom, saying, <sup>24</sup>"Aaron shall be gathered to his people; for he shall not enter into the land which I have given to the children of Israel, because you rebelled against my word at the waters of Meribah. <sup>25</sup> Take Aaron and Eleazar his son, and bring them up to Mount Hor; <sup>26</sup> and strip Aaron of his garments, and put them on Eleazar his son. Aaron shall be gathered, and shall die there." <sup>27</sup> Moses did as Yahweh commanded. They went up onto Mount Hor in the sight of all the congregation. <sup>28</sup> Moses stripped Aaron of his garments, and put them on Eleazar his son. Aaron died there on the top of the mountain, and Moses and Eleazar came down from the mountain. <sup>29</sup> When all the congregation saw that Aaron was dead, they wept for Aaron thirty days, even all the house of Israel.

## 21

<sup>1</sup> The Canaanite, the king of Arad, who lived in the South, heard that Israel came by the way of Atharim. He fought against Israel, and took some of them captive. <sup>2</sup> Israel vowed a vow to Yahweh, and said, "If you will indeed deliver this people into my hand, then I will utterly destroy their cities." <sup>3</sup> Yahweh listened to the voice of Israel, and delivered up the Canaanites; and they utterly destroyed them and their cities. The name of the place was called Hormah.<sup>a</sup> <sup>4</sup> They traveled from Mount Hor by the way to the Red Sea, to go around the land of Edom. The soul of the people was very discouraged because of the journey. <sup>5</sup> The people spoke against God and against Moses: "Why have you brought us up out of Egypt to die in the wilderness? For there is no bread, there is no water, and our soul loathes this disgusting food!" <sup>6</sup> Yahweh sent venomous snakes among the people, and they bit the people. Many people of Israel died. <sup>7</sup> The people came to Moses, and said, "We have sinned, because we have spoken against Yahweh and against you. Pray to Yahweh, that he take away the serpents from us." Moses prayed for the people. <sup>8</sup> Yahweh said to Moses, "Make a venomous snake, and set it on a pole. It shall happen that everyone who is bitten, when he sees it, shall live." <sup>9</sup> Moses made a serpent of bronze, and set it on the pole. If a serpent had bitten any man, when he looked at the serpent of bronze, he lived. <sup>10</sup> The children of Israel traveled, and encamped in Oboth. <sup>11</sup> They traveled from Oboth, and encamped at Iyeabarim, in the wilderness which is before Moab, toward the sunrise. <sup>12</sup> From there they traveled, and encamped in the valley of Zered. <sup>13</sup> From there they traveled, and encamped on the other side of the Arnon, which is in the wilderness that comes out of the border of the Amorites; for the Arnon is the border of Moab, between Moab and the Amorites. <sup>14</sup> Therefore it is said in *The Book of the Wars of Yahweh*, "Vaheb in Suphah, the valleys of the Arnon, <sup>15</sup> the slope of the valleys that incline toward the dwelling of Ar, leans on the border of Moab." <sup>16</sup> From there they traveled to Beer; that is the well of which Yahweh said to Moses, "Gather the people together, and I will give them water." <sup>17</sup> Then Israel sang this song: "Spring up, well! Sing to it, <sup>18</sup> the well, which the princes dug, which the nobles of the people dug, with the scepter, and with their poles." From the wilderness they traveled to Mattanah; <sup>19</sup> and from Mattanah to Nahaliel; and from Nahaliel to Bamoth; <sup>20</sup> and from Bamoth to the valley that is in the field of Moab, to the top of Pisgah, which looks down on the desert. <sup>21</sup> Israel sent messengers to Sihon king of the Amorites, saying, <sup>22</sup>"Let me pass through your land. We will not turn away into field or vineyard. We will not drink of the water of the wells. We will go by the king's highway, until we have passed your border." <sup>23</sup> Sihon would not allow Israel to pass through his border, but Sihon gathered all his people together, and went out against Israel into the wilderness, and came to Jahaz. He fought against Israel. <sup>24</sup> Israel struck him with the edge of the sword, and possessed his land from the Arnon to the Jabbok, even to the children of Ammon; for the border of the children of Ammon was fortified. <sup>25</sup> Israel took all these cities. Israel lived in all the cities of the Amorites, in Heshbon, and in all its

villages. <sup>26</sup> For Heshbon was the city of Sihon the king of the Amorites, who had fought against the former king of Moab, and taken all his land out of his hand, even to the Arnon. <sup>27</sup> Therefore those who speak in proverbs say, "Come to Heshbon. Let the city of Sihon be built and established; <sup>28</sup> for a fire has gone out of Heshbon, a flame from the city of Sihon. It has devoured Ar of Moab, The lords of the high places of the Arnon. <sup>29</sup> Woe to you, Moab! You are undone, people of Chemosh! He has given his sons as fugitives, and his daughters into captivity, to Sihon king of the Amorites. <sup>30</sup> We have shot at them. Heshbon has perished even to Dibon. We have laid waste even to Nophah, Which reaches to Medeba." <sup>31</sup> Thus Israel lived in the land of the Amorites. <sup>32</sup> Moses sent to spy out Jazer. They took its villages, and drove out the Amorites who were there. <sup>33</sup> They turned and went up by the way of Bashan. Og the king of Bashan went out against them, he and all his people, to battle at Edrei. <sup>34</sup> Yahweh said to Moses, "Don't fear him, for I have delivered him into your hand, with all his people, and his land. You shall do to him as you did to Sihon king of the Amorites, who lived at Heshbon." <sup>35</sup> So they struck him, with his sons and all his people, until there were no survivors; and they possessed his land.

## 22

<sup>1</sup> The children of Israel traveled, and encamped in the plains of Moab beyond the Jordan at Jericho. <sup>2</sup> Balak the son of Zippor saw all that Israel had done to the Amorites. <sup>3</sup> Moab was very afraid of the people, because they were many. Moab was distressed because of the children of Israel. <sup>4</sup> Moab said to the elders of Midian, "Now this multitude will lick up all that is around us, as the ox licks the grass of the field." Balak the son of Zippor was king of Moab at that time. <sup>5</sup> He sent messengers to Balaam the son of Beor, to Pethor, which is by the River, to the land of the children of his people, to call him, saying, "Behold, there is a people who came out of Egypt. Behold, they cover the surface of the earth, and they are staying opposite me. <sup>6</sup> Please come now therefore, and curse this people for me; for they are too mighty for me. Perhaps I shall prevail, that we may strike them, and that I may drive them out of the land; for I know that he whom you bless is blessed, and he whom you curse is cursed." <sup>7</sup> The elders of Moab and the elders of Midian departed with the rewards of divination in their hand. They came to Balaam, and spoke to him the words of Balak. <sup>8</sup> He said to them, "Lodge here this night, and I will bring you word again, as Yahweh shall speak to me." The princes of Moab stayed with Balaam. <sup>9</sup> God came to Balaam, and said, "Who are these men with you?" <sup>10</sup> Balaam said to God, "Balak the son of Zippor, king of Moab, has said to me, <sup>11</sup>'Behold, the people that has come out of Egypt covers the surface of the earth. Now, come curse them for me. Perhaps I shall be able to fight against them, and shall drive them out.'" <sup>12</sup> God said to Balaam, "You shall not go with them. You shall not curse the people, for they are blessed." <sup>13</sup> Balaam rose up in the morning, and said to the princes of Balak, "Go to your land; for Yahweh refuses to permit me to go with you." <sup>14</sup> The princes of Moab rose up, and they went to Balak, and said, "Balaam refuses to come with us." <sup>15</sup> Balak again sent princes, more, and more honorable than they. <sup>16</sup> They came to Balaam, and said to him, "Balak the son of Zippor says, 'Please let nothing hinder you from coming to me, <sup>17</sup> for I will promote you to very great honor, and whatever you say to me I will do. Please come therefore, and curse this people for me.'" <sup>18</sup> Balaam answered the servants of Balak, "If Balak would give me his house full of silver and gold, I can't go beyond the word of Yahweh my God, to do less or more. <sup>19</sup> Now therefore please stay here tonight as well, that I may know what else Yahweh will speak to me." <sup>20</sup> God came to Balaam at night, and said to him, "If the men have come to call you, rise up, go with them; but only the word which I speak to you, that you shall do." <sup>21</sup> Balaam rose up in the morning, and saddled his donkey, and went with the princes of Moab. <sup>22</sup> God's anger burned because he went; and Yahweh's angel placed himself in the way as an adversary against him. Now he was riding on his donkey, and his two servants were with him. <sup>23</sup> The donkey saw Yahweh's angel standing in the way, with his sword drawn in his hand; and the donkey turned out of the path, and went into the field. Balaam struck the donkey, to turn her into the path. <sup>24</sup> Then Yahweh's angel stood in a narrow path between the vineyards, a wall being on this side, and a wall on that side. <sup>25</sup> The donkey saw Yahweh's angel, and she thrust herself to the wall, and crushed Balaam's foot against the wall. He struck her again. <sup>26</sup> Yahweh's angel went further, and stood in a narrow place, where there was no way to turn either to the right hand or to the left. <sup>27</sup> The donkey saw Yahweh's angel, and she lay down under Balaam. Balaam's anger burned, and he struck the donkey with his staff. <sup>28</sup> Yahweh opened the mouth of the donkey, and she said to Balaam, "What have I done to you, that you have struck me these three times?" <sup>29</sup> Balaam said to the donkey, "Because you have mocked me, I wish

<sup>a</sup> *21:3* "Hormah" means "destruction".

there were a sword in my hand, for now I would have killed you." ³⁰ The donkey said to Balaam, "Am I not your donkey, on which you have ridden all your life long until today? Was I ever in the habit of doing so to you?" He said, "No." ³¹ Then Yahweh opened the eyes of Balaam, and he saw Yahweh's angel standing in the way, with his sword drawn in his hand; and he bowed his head, and fell on his face. ³² Yahweh's angel said to him, "Why have you struck your donkey these three times? Behold, I have come out as an adversary, because your way is perverse before me. ³³ The donkey saw me, and turned away before me these three times. Unless she had turned away from me, surely now I would have killed you, and saved her alive." ³⁴ Balaam said to Yahweh's angel, "I have sinned; for I didn't know that you stood in the way against me. Now therefore, if it displeases you, I will go back again." ³⁵ Yahweh's angel said to Balaam, "Go with the men; but you shall only speak the word that I shall speak to you." So Balaam went with the princes of Balak. ³⁶ When Balak heard that Balaam had come, he went out to meet him to the City of Moab, which is on the border of the Arnon, which is in the utmost part of the border. ³⁷ Balak said to Balaam, "Didn't I earnestly send for you to summon you? Why didn't you come to me? Am I not able indeed to promote you to honor?" ³⁸ Balaam said to Balak, "Behold, I have come to you. Have I now any power at all to speak anything? I will speak the word that God puts in my mouth." ³⁹ Balaam went with Balak, and they came to Kiriath Huzoth. ⁴⁰ Balak sacrificed cattle and sheep, and sent to Balaam, and to the princes who were with him. ⁴¹ In the morning, Balak took Balaam, and brought him up into the high places of Baal; and he saw from there part of the people.

## 23

¹ Balaam said to Balak, "Build here seven altars for me, and prepare here seven bulls and seven rams for me." ² Balak did as Balaam had spoken; and Balak and Balaam offered on every altar a bull and a ram. ³ Balaam said to Balak, "Stand by your burnt offering, and I will go. Perhaps Yahweh will come to meet me. Whatever he shows me I will tell you." He went to a bare height. ⁴ God met Balaam, and he said to him, "I have prepared the seven altars, and I have offered up a bull and a ram on every altar." ⁵ Yahweh put a word in Balaam's mouth, and said, "Return to Balak, and thus you shall speak." ⁶ He returned to him, and behold, he was standing by his burnt offering, he, and all the princes of Moab. ⁷ He took up his parable, and said, "From Aram has Balak brought me, the king of Moab from the mountains of the East. Come, curse Jacob for me. Come, defy Israel. ⁸ How shall I curse whom God has not cursed? How shall I defy whom Yahweh has not defied? ⁹ For from the top of the rocks I see him. From the hills I see him. Behold, it is a people that dwells alone, and shall not be listed among the nations. ¹⁰ Who can count the dust of Jacob, or count the fourth part of Israel? Let me die the death of the righteous! Let my last end be like his!" ¹¹ Balak said to Balaam, "What have you done to me? I took you to curse my enemies, and behold, you have blessed them altogether." ¹² He answered and said, "Must I not take heed to speak that which Yahweh puts in my mouth?" ¹³ Balak said to him, "Please come with me to another place, where you may see them. You shall see just part of them, and shall not see them all. Curse them from there for me." ¹⁴ He took him into the field of Zophim, to the top of Pisgah, and built seven altars, and offered up a bull and a ram on every altar. ¹⁵ He said to Balak, "Stand here by your burnt offering, while I meet God over there." ¹⁶ Yahweh met Balaam, and put a word in his mouth, and said, "Return to Balak, and say this." ¹⁷ He came to him, and behold, he was standing by his burnt offering, and the princes of Moab with him. Balak said to him, "What has Yahweh spoken?" ¹⁸ He took up his parable, and said, "Rise up, Balak, and hear! Listen to me, you son of Zippor. ¹⁹ God is not a man, that he should lie, nor a son of man, that he should repent. Has he said, and he won't do it? Or has he spoken, and he won't make it good? ²⁰ Behold, I have received a command to bless. He has blessed, and I can't reverse it. ²¹ He has not seen iniquity in Jacob. Neither has he seen perverseness in Israel. Yahweh his God is with him. The shout of a king is among them. ²² God brings them out of Egypt. He has as it were the strength of the wild ox. ²³ Surely there is no enchantment with Jacob; neither is there any divination with Israel. Now it shall be said of Jacob and of Israel, 'What has God done!' ²⁴ Behold, a people rises up as a lioness. As a lion he lifts himself up. He shall not lie down until he eats of the prey, and drinks the blood of the slain." ²⁵ Balak said to Balaam, "Neither curse them at all, nor bless them at all." ²⁶ But Balaam answered Balak, "Didn't I tell you, saying, 'All that Yahweh speaks, that I must do'?" ²⁷ Balak said to Balaam, "Come now, I will take you to another place; perhaps it will please God that you may curse them for me from there." ²⁸ Balak took Balaam to the top of Peor, that looks down on the desert. ²⁹ Balaam said to Balak, "Build seven altars for me here, and prepare seven bulls and seven rams for me here." ³⁰ Balak did as Balaam had said, and offered up a bull and a ram on every altar.

## 24

¹ When Balaam saw that it pleased Yahweh to bless Israel, he didn't go, as at the other times, to use divination, but he set his face toward the wilderness. ² Balaam lifted up his eyes, and he saw Israel dwelling according to their tribes; and the Spirit of God came on him. ³ He took up his parable, and said, "Balaam the son of Beor says, the man whose eyes are open says; ⁴ he says, who hears the words of God, who sees the vision of the Almighty, falling down, and having his eyes open: ⁵ How goodly are your tents, Jacob, and your dwellings, Israel! ⁶ As valleys they are spread out, as gardens by the riverside, as aloes which Yahweh has planted, as cedar trees beside the waters. ⁷ Water shall flow from his buckets. His seed shall be in many waters. His king shall be higher than Agag. His kingdom shall be exalted. ⁸ God brings him out of Egypt. He has as it were the strength of the wild ox. He shall consume the nations his adversaries, shall break their bones in pieces, and pierce them with his arrows. ⁹ He couched, he lay down as a lion, as a lioness; who shall rouse him up? Everyone who blesses you is blessed. Everyone who curses you is cursed." ¹⁰ Balak's anger burned against Balaam, and he struck his hands together. Balak said to Balaam, "I called you to curse my enemies, and, behold, you have altogether blessed them these three times. ¹¹ Therefore, flee to your place, now! I thought to promote you to great honor; but, behold, Yahweh has kept you back from honor." ¹² Balaam said to Balak, "Didn't I also tell your messengers whom you sent to me, saying, ¹³'If Balak would give me his house full of silver and gold, I can't go beyond Yahweh's word, to do either good or bad from my own mind. I will say what Yahweh says'? ¹⁴ Now, behold, I go to my people. Come, I will inform you what this people shall do to your people in the latter days." ¹⁵ He took up his parable, and said, "Balaam the son of Beor says, the man whose eyes are open says; ¹⁶ he says, who hears the words of God, knows the knowledge of the Most High, and who sees the vision of the Almighty, falling down, and having his eyes open: ¹⁷ I see him, but not now. I see him, but not near. A star will come out of Jacob. A scepter will rise out of Israel, and shall strike through the corners of Moab, and crush all the sons of Sheth. ¹⁸ Edom shall be a possession. Seir, his enemy, also shall be a possession, while Israel does valiantly. ¹⁹ Out of Jacob shall one have dominion, and shall destroy the remnant from the city." ²⁰ He looked at Amalek, and took up his parable, and said, "Amalek was the first of the nations, but his latter end shall come to destruction." ²¹ He looked at the Kenite, and took up his parable, and said, "Your dwelling place is strong. Your nest is set in the rock. ²² Nevertheless Kain shall be wasted, until Asshur carries you away captive." ²³ He took up his parable, and said, "Alas, who shall live when God does this? ²⁴ But ships shall come from the coast of Kittim. They shall afflict Asshur, and shall afflict Eber. He also shall come to destruction." ²⁵ Balaam rose up, and went and returned to his place; and Balak also went his way.

## 25

¹ Israel stayed in Shittim; and the people began to play the prostitute with the daughters of Moab; ² for they called the people to the sacrifices of their gods. The people ate and bowed down to their gods. ³ Israel joined himself to Baal Peor, and Yahweh's anger burned against Israel. ⁴ Yahweh said to Moses, "Take all the chiefs of the people, and hang them up to Yahweh before the sun, that the fierce anger of Yahweh may turn away from Israel." ⁵ Moses said to the judges of Israel, "Everyone kill his men who have joined themselves to Baal Peor." ⁶ Behold, one of the children of Israel came and brought to his brothers a Midianite woman in the sight of Moses, and in the sight of all the congregation of the children of Israel, while they were weeping at the door of the Tent of Meeting. ⁷ When Phinehas, the son of Eleazar, the son of Aaron the priest, saw it, he rose up from the middle of the congregation, and took a spear in his hand. ⁸ He went after the man of Israel into the pavilion, and thrust both of them through, the man of Israel, and the woman through her body. So the plague was stopped among the children of Israel. ⁹ Those who died by the plague were twenty-four thousand. ¹⁰ Yahweh spoke to Moses, saying, ¹¹"Phinehas, the son of Eleazar, the son of Aaron the priest, has turned my wrath away from the children of Israel, in that he was jealous with my jealousy among them, so that I didn't consume the children of Israel in my jealousy. ¹² Therefore say, 'Behold, I give to him my covenant of peace. ¹³ It shall be to him, and to his offspring after him, the covenant of an everlasting priesthood, because he was jealous for his God, and made atonement for the children of Israel.'" ¹⁴ Now the name of the man of Israel that was slain, who was slain with the Midianite woman, was Zimri, the son of Salu, a prince of a fathers' house among the Simeonites. ¹⁵ The name of the Midianite woman who was slain was Cozbi, the daughter of Zur. He was head of the people of a fathers' house in Midian. ¹⁶ Yahweh spoke to Moses, saying, ¹⁷"Harass the Midianites, and strike them; ¹⁸ for they harassed you with their wiles, wherein they have deceived you in the matter of Peor, and in the incident regarding Cozbi, the daughter of the

prince of Midian, their sister, who was slain on the day of the plague in the matter of Peor."

# 26

¹ After the plague, Yahweh spoke to Moses and to Eleazar the son of Aaron the priest, saying, ²"Take a census of all the congregation of the children of Israel, from twenty years old and upward, by their fathers' houses, all who are able to go out to war in Israel." ³ Moses and Eleazar the priest spoke with them in the plains of Moab by the Jordan at Jericho, saying, ⁴"Take a census, from twenty years old and upward, as Yahweh commanded Moses and the children of Israel." These are those who came out of the land of Egypt. ⁵ Reuben, the firstborn of Israel; the sons of Reuben: of Hanoch, the family of the Hanochites; of Pallu, the family of the Palluites; ⁶ of Hezron, the family of the Hezronites; of Carmi, the family of the Carmites. ⁷ These are the families of the Reubenites; and those who were counted of them were forty-three thousand seven hundred thirty. ⁸ The son of Pallu: Eliab. ⁹ The sons of Eliab: Nemuel, Dathan, and Abiram. These are that Dathan and Abiram who were called by the congregation, who rebelled against Moses and against Aaron in the company of Korah when they rebelled against Yahweh; ¹⁰ and the earth opened its mouth, and swallowed them up together with Korah when that company died; at the time the fire devoured two hundred fifty men, and they became a sign. ¹¹ Notwithstanding, the sons of Korah didn't die. ¹² The sons of Simeon after their families: of Nemuel, the family of the Nemuelites; of Jamin, the family of the Jaminites; of Jachin, the family of the Jachinites; ¹³ of Zerah, the family of the Zerahites; of Shaul, the family of the Shaulites. ¹⁴ These are the families of the Simeonites, twenty-two thousand two hundred. ¹⁵ The sons of Gad after their families: of Zephon, the family of the Zephonites; of Haggi, the family of the Haggites; of Shuni, the family of the Shunites; ¹⁶ of Ozni, the family of the Oznites; of Eri, the family of the Erites; ¹⁷ of Arod, the family of the Arodites; of Areli, the family of the Arelites. ¹⁸ These are the families of the sons of Gad according to those who were counted of them, forty thousand and five hundred. ¹⁹ The sons of Judah: Er and Onan. Er and Onan died in the land of Canaan. ²⁰ The sons of Judah after their families were: of Shelah, the family of the Shelanites; of Perez, the family of the Perezites; of Zerah, the family of the Zerahites. ²¹ The sons of Perez were: of Hezron, the family of the Hezronites; of Hamul, the family of the Hamulites. ²² These are the families of Judah according to those who were counted of them, seventy-six thousand five hundred. ²³ The sons of Issachar after their families: of Tola, the family of the Tolaites; of Puvah, the family of the Punites; ²⁴ of Jashub, the family of the Jashubites; of Shimron, the family of the Shimronites. ²⁵ These are the families of Issachar according to those who were counted of them, sixty-four thousand three hundred. ²⁶ The sons of Zebulun after their families: of Sered, the family of the Seredites; of Elon, the family of the Elonites; of Jahleel, the family of the Jahleelites. ²⁷ These are the families of the Zebulunites according to those who were counted of them, sixty thousand five hundred. ²⁸ The sons of Joseph after their families: Manasseh and Ephraim. ²⁹ The sons of Manasseh: of Machir, the family of the Machirites; and Machir became the father of Gilead; of Gilead, the family of the Gileadites. ³⁰ These are the sons of Gilead: of Iezer, the family of the Iezerites; of Helek, the family of the Helekites; ³¹ and Asriel, the family of the Asrielites; and Shechem, the family of the Shechemites; ³² and Shemida, the family of the Shemidaites; and Hepher, the family of the Hepherites. ³³ Zelophehad the son of Hepher had no sons, but daughters: and the names of the daughters of Zelophehad were Mahlah, Noah, Hoglah, Milcah, and Tirzah. ³⁴ These are the families of Manasseh. Those who were counted of them were fifty-two thousand seven hundred. ³⁵ These are the sons of Ephraim after their families: of Shuthelah, the family of the Shuthelahites; of Becher, the family of the Becherites; of Tahan, the family of the Tahanites. ³⁶ These are the sons of Shuthelah: of Eran, the family of the Eranites. ³⁷ These are the families of the sons of Ephraim according to those who were counted of them, thirty-two thousand five hundred. These are the sons of Joseph after their families. ³⁸ The sons of Benjamin after their families: of Bela, the family of the Belaites; of Ashbel, the family of the Ashbelites; of Ahiram, the family of the Ahiramites; ³⁹ of Shephupham, the family of the Shuphamites; of Hupham, the family of the Huphamites. ⁴⁰ The sons of Bela were Ard and Naaman: the family of the Ardites; and of Naaman, the family of the Naamites. ⁴¹ These are the sons of Benjamin after their families; and those who were counted of them were forty-five thousand six hundred. ⁴² These are the sons of Dan after their families: of Shuham, the family of the Shuhamites. These are the families of Dan after their families. ⁴³ All the families of the Shuhamites, according to those who were counted of them, were sixty-four thousand four hundred. ⁴⁴ The sons of Asher after their families: of Imnah, the family of the Imnites; of Ishvi, the family of the Ishvites; of Beriah, the family of the Berites. ⁴⁵ Of the sons of Beriah: of Heber, the family of the Heberites; of Malchiel, the

family of the Malchielites. ⁴⁶ The name of the daughter of Asher was Serah. ⁴⁷ These are the families of the sons of Asher according to those who were counted of them, fifty-three thousand four hundred. ⁴⁸ The sons of Naphtali after their families: of Jahzeel, the family of the Jahzeelites; of Guni, the family of the Gunites; ⁴⁹ of Jezer, the family of the Jezerites; of Shillem, the family of the Shillemites. ⁵⁰ These are the families of Naphtali according to their families; and those who were counted of them were forty-five thousand four hundred. ⁵¹ These are those who were counted of the children of Israel, six hundred one thousand seven hundred thirty. ⁵² Yahweh spoke to Moses, saying, ⁵³"To these the land shall be divided for an inheritance according to the number of names. ⁵⁴ To the more you shall give the more inheritance, and to the fewer you shall give the less inheritance. To everyone according to those who were counted of him shall his inheritance be given. ⁵⁵ Notwithstanding, the land shall be divided by lot. According to the names of the tribes of their fathers they shall inherit. ⁵⁶ According to the lot shall their inheritance be divided between the more and the fewer." ⁵⁷ These are those who were counted of the Levites after their families: of Gershon, the family of the Gershonites; of Kohath, the family of the Kohathites; of Merari, the family of the Merarites. ⁵⁸ These are the families of Levi: the family of the Libnites, the family of the Hebronites, the family of the Mahlites, the family of the Mushites, and the family of the Korahites. Kohath became the father of Amram. ⁵⁹ The name of Amram's wife was Jochebed, the daughter of Levi, who was born to Levi in Egypt. She bore to Amram Aaron and Moses, and Miriam their sister. ⁶⁰ To Aaron were born Nadab and Abihu, Eleazar and Ithamar. ⁶¹ Nadab and Abihu died when they offered strange fire before Yahweh. ⁶² Those who were counted of them were twenty-three thousand, every male from a month old and upward; for they were not counted among the children of Israel, because there was no inheritance given them among the children of Israel. ⁶³ These are those who were counted by Moses and Eleazar the priest, who counted the children of Israel in the plains of Moab by the Jordan at Jericho. ⁶⁴ But among these there was not a man of them who were counted by Moses and Aaron the priest, who counted the children of Israel in the wilderness of Sinai. ⁶⁵ For Yahweh had said of them, "They shall surely die in the wilderness." There was not a man left of them, except Caleb the son of Jephunneh, and Joshua the son of Nun.

# 27

¹ Then the daughters of Zelophehad, the son of Hepher, the son of Gilead, the son of Machir, the son of Manasseh, of the families of Manasseh the son of Joseph came near. These are the names of his daughters: Mahlah, Noah, Hoglah, Milcah, and Tirzah. ² They stood before Moses, before Eleazar the priest, and before the princes and all the congregation, at the door of the Tent of Meeting, saying, ³"Our father died in the wilderness. He was not among the company of those who gathered themselves together against Yahweh in the company of Korah, but he died in his own sin. He had no sons. ⁴ Why should the name of our father be taken away from among his family, because he had no son? Give to us a possession among the brothers of our father." ⁵ Moses brought their cause before Yahweh. ⁶ Yahweh spoke to Moses, saying, ⁷"The daughters of Zelophehad speak right. You shall surely give them a possession of an inheritance among their father's brothers. You shall cause the inheritance of their father to pass to them. ⁸ You shall speak to the children of Israel, saying, 'If a man dies, and has no son, then you shall cause his inheritance to pass to his daughter. ⁹ If he has no daughter, then you shall give his inheritance to his brothers. ¹⁰ If he has no brothers, then you shall give his inheritance to his father's brothers. ¹¹ If his father has no brothers, then you shall give his inheritance to his kinsman who is next to him of his family, and he shall possess it. This shall be a statute and ordinance for the children of Israel, as Yahweh commanded Moses.'" ¹² Yahweh said to Moses, "Go up into this mountain of Abarim, and see the land which I have given to the children of Israel. ¹³ When you have seen it, you also shall be gathered to your people, as Aaron your brother was gathered; ¹⁴ because in the strife of the congregation, you rebelled against my word in the wilderness of Zin, to honor me as holy at the waters before their eyes." (These are the waters of Meribah of Kadesh in the wilderness of Zin.) ¹⁵ Moses spoke to Yahweh, saying, ¹⁶"Let Yahweh, the God of the spirits of all flesh, appoint a man over the congregation, ¹⁷ who may go out before them, and who may come in before them, and who may lead them out, and who may bring them in, that the congregation of Yahweh may not be as sheep which have no shepherd." ¹⁸ Yahweh said to Moses, "Take Joshua the son of Nun, a man in whom is the Spirit, and lay your hand on him. ¹⁹ Set him before Eleazar the priest, and before all the congregation; and commission him in their sight. ²⁰ You shall give authority to him, that all the congregation of the children of Israel may obey. ²¹ He shall stand before Eleazar the priest, who shall inquire for him by the judgment of the Urim before Yahweh. At his word they shall go out, and at his word they shall come in, both he and all the

children of Israel with him, even all the congregation." ²² Moses did as Yahweh commanded him. He took Joshua, and set him before Eleazar the priest and before all the congregation. ²³ He laid his hands on him and commissioned him, as Yahweh spoke by Moses.

## 28

¹ Yahweh spoke to Moses, saying, ²"Command the children of Israel, and tell them, 'See that you present my offering, my food for my offerings made by fire, as a pleasant aroma to me, in their due season.' ³ You shall tell them, 'This is the offering made by fire which you shall offer to Yahweh: male lambs a year old without defect, two day by day, for a continual burnt offering. ⁴ You shall offer the one lamb in the morning, and you shall offer the other lamb at evening, ⁵ with one tenth of an ephahᵃ of fine flour for a meal offering, mixed with the fourth part of a hinᵇ of beaten oil. ⁶ It is a continual burnt offering which was ordained in Mount Sinai for a pleasant aroma, an offering made by fire to Yahweh. ⁷ Its drink offering shall be the fourth part of a hinᶜ for each lamb. You shall pour out a drink offering of strong drink to Yahweh in the holy place. ⁸ The other lamb you shall offer at evening. As the meal offering of the morning, and as its drink offering, you shall offer it, an offering made by fire, for a pleasant aroma to Yahweh. ⁹"On the Sabbath day, you shall offer two male lambs a year old without defect, and two tenths of an ephahᵈ of fine flour for a meal offering mixed with oil, and its drink offering: ¹⁰ this is the burnt offering of every Sabbath, in addition to the continual burnt offering and its drink offering. ¹¹"In the beginnings of your months, you shall offer a burnt offering to Yahweh: two young bulls, one ram, seven male lambs a year old without defect, ¹² and three tenths of an ephahᵉ of fine flour for a meal offering mixed with oil, for each bull; and two tenth parts of fine flour for a meal offering mixed with oil, for the one ram; ¹³ and one tenth part of fine flour mixed with oil for a meal offering to every lamb, as a burnt offering of a pleasant aroma, an offering made by fire to Yahweh. ¹⁴ Their drink offerings shall be half a hin of wine for a bull, the third part of a hin for the ram, and the fourth part of a hin for a lamb. This is the burnt offering of every month throughout the months of the year. ¹⁵ Also, one male goat for a sin offering to Yahweh shall be offered in addition to the continual burnt offering and its drink offering. ¹⁶"In the first month, on the fourteenth day of the month, is Yahweh's Passover. ¹⁷ On the fifteenth day of this month shall be a feast. Unleavened bread shall be eaten for seven days. ¹⁸ In the first day shall be a holy convocation. You shall do no regular work, ¹⁹ but you shall offer an offering made by fire, a burnt offering to Yahweh: two young bulls, one ram, and seven male lambs a year old. They shall be without defect, ²⁰ with their meal offering, fine flour mixed with oil. You shall offer three tenths for a bull, and two tenths for the ram. ²¹ You shall offer one tenth for every lamb of the seven lambs; ²² and one male goat for a sin offering, to make atonement for you. ²³ You shall offer these in addition to the burnt offering of the morning, which is for a continual burnt offering. ²⁴ In this way you shall offer daily, for seven days, the food of the offering made by fire, of a pleasant aroma to Yahweh. It shall be offered in addition to the continual burnt offering and its drink offering. ²⁵ On the seventh day you shall have a holy convocation. You shall do no regular work. ²⁶"Also in the day of the first fruits, when you offer a new meal offering to Yahweh in your feast of weeks, you shall have a holy convocation. You shall do no regular work; ²⁷ but you shall offer a burnt offering for a pleasant aroma to Yahweh: two young bulls, one ram, seven male lambs a year old; ²⁸ and their meal offering, fine flour mixed with oil, three tenths for each bull, two tenths for the one ram, ²⁹ one tenth for every lamb of the seven lambs; ³⁰ and one male goat, to make atonement for you. ³¹ Besides the continual burnt offering and its meal offering, you shall offer them and their drink offerings. See that they are without defect.

## 29

¹"In the seventh month, on the first day of the month, you shall have a holy convocation; you shall do no regular work. It is a day of blowing of trumpets to you. ² You shall offer a burnt offering for a pleasant aroma to Yahweh: one young bull, one ram, seven male lambs a year old without defect; ³ and their meal offering, fine flour mixed with oil: three tenths for the bull, two tenths for the ram, ⁴ and one tenth for every lamb of the seven lambs; ⁵ and one male goat for a sin offering, to make atonement for you; ⁶ in addition to the burnt offering of the new moon with its meal offering, and the continual burnt offering with its meal offering, and their drink offerings, according to their ordinance, for a pleasant aroma, an offering made by fire to Yahweh. ⁷"On the tenth day of this seventh month you shall have a holy convocation. You shall afflict your souls. You shall do no kind of work; ⁸ but you shall offer a

burnt offering to Yahweh for a pleasant aroma: one young bull, one ram, seven male lambs a year old, all without defect; ⁹ and their meal offering, fine flour mixed with oil: three tenths for the bull, two tenths for the one ram, ¹⁰ one tenth for every lamb of the seven lambs; ¹¹ one male goat for a sin offering, in addition to the sin offering of atonement, and the continual burnt offering, and its meal offering, and their drink offerings. ¹²"On the fifteenth day of the seventh month you shall have a holy convocation. You shall do no regular work. You shall keep a feast to Yahweh seven days. ¹³ You shall offer a burnt offering, an offering made by fire, of a pleasant aroma to Yahweh: thirteen young bulls, two rams, fourteen male lambs a year old, all without defect; ¹⁴ and their meal offering, fine flour mixed with oil: three tenths for every bull of the thirteen bulls, two tenths for each ram of the two rams, ¹⁵ and one tenth for every lamb of the fourteen lambs; ¹⁶ and one male goat for a sin offering, in addition to the continual burnt offering, its meal offering, and its drink offering. ¹⁷"On the second day you shall offer twelve young bulls, two rams, and fourteen male lambs a year old without defect; ¹⁸ and their meal offering and their drink offerings for the bulls, for the rams, and for the lambs, according to their number, after the ordinance; ¹⁹ and one male goat for a sin offering, in addition to the continual burnt offering, with its meal offering and their drink offerings. ²⁰"On the third day: eleven bulls, two rams, fourteen male lambs a year old without defect; ²¹ and their meal offering and their drink offerings for the bulls, for the rams, and for the lambs, according to their number, after the ordinance; ²² and one male goat for a sin offering, in addition to the continual burnt offering, and its meal offering, and its drink offering. ²³"On the fourth day ten bulls, two rams, fourteen male lambs a year old without defect; ²⁴ their meal offering and their drink offerings for the bulls, for the rams, and for the lambs, according to their number, after the ordinance; ²⁵ and one male goat for a sin offering; in addition to the continual burnt offering, its meal offering, and its drink offering. ²⁶"On the fifth day: nine bulls, two rams, fourteen male lambs a year old without defect; ²⁷ and their meal offering and their drink offerings for the bulls, for the rams, and for the lambs, according to their number, after the ordinance, ²⁸ and one male goat for a sin offering, in addition to the continual burnt offering, and its meal offering, and its drink offering. ²⁹"On the sixth day: eight bulls, two rams, fourteen male lambs a year old without defect; ³⁰ and their meal offering and their drink offerings for the bulls, for the rams, and for the lambs, according to their number, after the ordinance, ³¹ and one male goat for a sin offering; in addition to the continual burnt offering, its meal offering, and the drink offerings of it. ³²"On the seventh day: seven bulls, two rams, fourteen male lambs a year old without defect; ³³ and their meal offering and their drink offerings for the bulls, for the rams, and for the lambs, according to their number, after the ordinance, ³⁴ and one male goat for a sin offering; in addition to the continual burnt offering, its meal offering, and its drink offering. ³⁵"On the eighth day you shall have a solemn assembly. You shall do no regular work; ³⁶ but you shall offer a burnt offering, an offering made by fire, a pleasant aroma to Yahweh: one bull, one ram, seven male lambs a year old without defect; ³⁷ their meal offering and their drink offerings for the bull, for the ram, and for the lambs, shall be according to their number, after the ordinance, ³⁸ and one male goat for a sin offering, in addition to the continual burnt offering, with its meal offering, and its drink offering. ³⁹"You shall offer these to Yahweh in your set feasts—in addition to your vows and your free will offerings—for your burnt offerings, your meal offerings, your drink offerings, and your peace offerings.'" ⁴⁰ Moses told the children of Israel according to all that Yahweh commanded Moses.

## 30

¹ Moses spoke to the heads of the tribes of the children of Israel, saying, "This is the thing which Yahweh has commanded. ² When a man vows a vow to Yahweh, or swears an oath to bind his soul with a bond, he shall not break his word. He shall do according to all that proceeds out of his mouth. ³"Also, when a woman vows a vow to Yahweh and binds herself by a pledge, being in her father's house, in her youth, ⁴ and her father hears her vow and her pledge with which she has bound her soul, and her father says nothing to her, then all her vows shall stand, and every pledge with which she has bound her soul shall stand. ⁵ But if her father forbids her in the day that he hears, none of her vows or of her pledges with which she has bound her soul, shall stand. Yahweh will forgive her, because her father has forbidden her. ⁶"If she has a husband, while her vows are on her, or the rash utterance of her lips with which she has bound her soul, ⁷ and her husband hears it, and says nothing to her in the day that he hears it; then her vows shall stand, and

---

ᵃ *28:5* 1 ephah is about 22 liters or about 2/3 of a bushel
ᵇ *28:5* A hin is about 6.5 liters or 1.7 gallons.

ᶜ *28:7* One hin is about 6.5 liters, so 1/4 hin is about 1.6 liters or 1.7 quarts.

ᵈ *28:9* 1 ephah is about 22 liters or about 2/3 of a bushel
ᵉ *28:12* 1 ephah is about 22 liters or about 2/3 of a bushel

her pledges with which she has bound her soul shall stand. ⁸ But if her husband forbids her in the day that he hears it, then he makes void her vow which is on her and the rash utterance of her lips, with which she has bound her soul. Yahweh will forgive her. ⁹ "But the vow of a widow, or of her who is divorced, everything with which she has bound her soul shall stand against her. ¹⁰ "If she vowed in her husband's house or bound her soul by a bond with an oath, ¹¹ and her husband heard it, and held his peace at her and didn't disallow her, then all her vows shall stand, and every pledge with which she bound her soul shall stand. ¹² But if her husband made them null and void in the day that he heard them, then whatever proceeded out of her lips concerning her vows, or concerning the bond of her soul, shall not stand. Her husband has made them void. Yahweh will forgive her. ¹³ Every vow, and every binding oath to afflict the soul, her husband may establish it, or her husband may make it void. ¹⁴ But if her husband says nothing to her from day to day, then he establishes all her vows or all her pledges which are on her. He has established them, because he said nothing to her in the day that he heard them. ¹⁵ But if he makes them null and void after he has heard them, then he shall bear her iniquity." ¹⁶ These are the statutes which Yahweh commanded Moses, between a man and his wife, between a father and his daughter, being in her youth, in her father's house.

## 31

¹ Yahweh spoke to Moses, saying, ² "Avenge the children of Israel on the Midianites. Afterward you shall be gathered to your people." ³ Moses spoke to the people, saying, "Arm men from among you for war, that they may go against Midian, to execute Yahweh's vengeance on Midian. ⁴ You shall send one thousand out of every tribe, throughout all the tribes of Israel, to the war." ⁵ So there were delivered, out of the thousands of Israel, a thousand from every tribe, twelve thousand armed for war. ⁶ Moses sent them, one thousand of every tribe, to the war with Phinehas the son of Eleazar the priest, to the war, with the vessels of the sanctuary and the trumpets for the alarm in his hand. ⁷ They fought against Midian, as Yahweh commanded Moses. They killed every male. ⁸ They killed the kings of Midian with the rest of their slain: Evi, Rekem, Zur, Hur, and Reba, the five kings of Midian. They also killed Balaam the son of Beor with the sword. ⁹ The children of Israel took the women of Midian captive with their little ones; and all their livestock, all their flocks, and all their goods, they took as plunder. ¹⁰ All their cities in the places in which they lived, and all their encampments, they burned with fire. ¹¹ They took all the captives, and all the plunder, both of man and of animal. ¹² They brought the captives with the prey and the plunder, to Moses, and to Eleazar the priest, and to the congregation of the children of Israel, to the camp at the plains of Moab, which are by the Jordan at Jericho. ¹³ Moses and Eleazar the priest, with all the princes of the congregation, went out to meet them outside of the camp. ¹⁴ Moses was angry with the officers of the army, the captains of thousands and the captains of hundreds, who came from the service of the war. ¹⁵ Moses said to them, "Have you saved all the women alive? ¹⁶ Behold, these caused the children of Israel, through the counsel of Balaam, to commit trespass against Yahweh in the matter of Peor, and so the plague was among the congregation of Yahweh. ¹⁷ Now therefore kill every male among the little ones, and kill every woman who has known man by lying with him. ¹⁸ But all the girls, who have not known man by lying with him, keep alive for yourselves. ¹⁹ "Encamp outside of the camp for seven days. Whoever has killed any person, and whoever has touched any slain, purify yourselves on the third day and on the seventh day, you and your captives. ²⁰ You shall purify every garment, and all that is made of skin, and all work of goats' hair, and all things made of wood." ²¹ Eleazar the priest said to the men of war who went to the battle, "This is the statute of the law which Yahweh has commanded Moses. ²² However the gold, and the silver, the bronze, the iron, the tin, and the lead, ²³ everything that may withstand the fire, you shall make to go through the fire, and it shall be clean; nevertheless it shall be purified with the water for impurity. All that doesn't withstand the fire you shall make to go through the water. ²⁴ You shall wash your clothes on the seventh day, and you shall be clean. Afterward you shall come into the camp." ²⁵ Yahweh spoke to Moses, saying, ²⁶ "Count the plunder that was taken, both of man and of animal, you, and Eleazar the priest, and the heads of the fathers' households of the congregation; ²⁷ and divide the plunder into two parts: between the men skilled in war, who went out to battle, and all the congregation. ²⁸ Levy a tribute to Yahweh of the men of war who went out to battle: one soul of five hundred; of the persons, of the cattle, of the donkeys, and of the flocks. ²⁹ Take it from their half, and give it to Eleazar the priest, for Yahweh's wave offering. ³⁰ Of the children of

Israel's half, you shall take one drawn out of every fifty, of the persons, of the cattle, of the donkeys, and of the flocks, of all the livestock, and give them to the Levites, who perform the duty of Yahweh's tabernacle." ³¹ Moses and Eleazar the priest did as Yahweh commanded Moses. ³² Now the plunder, over and above the booty which the men of war took, was six hundred seventy-five thousand sheep, ³³ seventy-two thousand head of cattle, ³⁴ sixty-one thousand donkeys, ³⁵ and thirty-two thousand persons in all, of the women who had not known man by lying with him. ³⁶ The half, which was the portion of those who went out to war, was in number three hundred thirty-seven thousand five hundred sheep; ³⁷ and Yahweh's tribute of the sheep was six hundred seventy-five. ³⁸ The cattle were thirty-six thousand, of which Yahweh's tribute was seventy-two. ³⁹ The donkeys were thirty thousand five hundred, of which Yahweh's tribute was sixty-one. ⁴⁰ The persons were sixteen thousand, of whom Yahweh's tribute was thirty-two persons. ⁴¹ Moses gave the tribute, which was Yahweh's wave offering, to Eleazar the priest, as Yahweh commanded Moses. ⁴² Of the children of Israel's half, which Moses divided off from the men who fought ⁴³ (now the congregation's half was three hundred thirty-seven thousand five hundred sheep, ⁴⁴ thirty-six thousand head of cattle, ⁴⁵ thirty thousand five hundred donkeys, ⁴⁶ and sixteen thousand persons), ⁴⁷ even of the children of Israel's half, Moses took one drawn out of every fifty, both of man and of animal, and gave them to the Levites, who performed the duty of Yahweh's tabernacle, as Yahweh commanded Moses. ⁴⁸ The officers who were over the thousands of the army, the captains of thousands, and the captains of hundreds, came near to Moses. ⁴⁹ They said to Moses, "Your servants have taken the sum of the men of war who are under our command, and there lacks not one man of us. ⁵⁰ We have brought Yahweh's offering, what every man found: gold ornaments, armlets, bracelets, signet rings, earrings, and necklaces, to make atonement for our souls before Yahweh." ⁵¹ Moses and Eleazar the priest took their gold, even all worked jewels. ⁵² All the gold of the wave offering that they offered up to Yahweh, of the captains of thousands, and of the captains of hundreds, was sixteen thousand seven hundred fifty shekels.ᵃ ⁵³ The men of war had taken booty, every man for himself. ⁵⁴ Moses and Eleazar the priest took the gold of the captains of thousands and of hundreds, and brought it into the Tent of Meeting for a memorial for the children of Israel before Yahweh.

## 32

¹ Now the children of Reuben and the children of Gad had a very great multitude of livestock. They saw the land of Jazer, and the land of Gilead. Behold, the place was a place for livestock. ² Then the children of Gad and the children of Reuben came and spoke to Moses, and to Eleazar the priest, and to the princes of the congregation, saying, ³ "Ataroth, Dibon, Jazer, Nimrah, Heshbon, Elealeh, Sebam, Nebo, and Beon, ⁴ the land which Yahweh struck before the congregation of Israel, is a land for livestock; and your servants have livestock." ⁵ They said, "If we have found favor in your sight, let this land be given to your servants for a possession. Don't bring us over the Jordan." ⁶ Moses said to the children of Gad, and to the children of Reuben, "Shall your brothers go to war while you sit here? ⁷ Why do you discourage the heart of the children of Israel from going over into the land which Yahweh has given them? ⁸ Your fathers did so when I sent them from Kadesh Barnea to see the land. ⁹ For when they went up to the valley of Eshcol, and saw the land, they discouraged the heart of the children of Israel, that they should not go into the land which Yahweh had given them. ¹⁰ Yahweh's anger burned in that day, and he swore, saying, ¹¹ 'Surely none of the men who came up out of Egypt, from twenty years old and upward, shall see the land which I swore to Abraham, to Isaac, and to Jacob; because they have not wholly followed me, ¹² except Caleb the son of Jephunneh the Kenizzite, and Joshua the son of Nun, because they have followed Yahweh completely.' ¹³ Yahweh's anger burned against Israel, and he made them wander back and forth in the wilderness forty years, until all the generation who had done evil in Yahweh's sight was consumed. ¹⁴ "Behold, you have risen up in your fathers' place, an increase of sinful men, to increase the fierce anger of Yahweh toward Israel. ¹⁵ For if you turn away from after him, he will yet again leave them in the wilderness; and you will destroy all these people." ¹⁶ They came near to him, and said, "We will build sheepfolds here for our livestock, and cities for our little ones; ¹⁷ but we ourselves will be ready armed to go before the children of Israel, until we have brought them to their place. Our little ones shall dwell in the fortified cities because of the inhabitants of the land. ¹⁸ We will not return to our houses until the children of Israel have all received their inheritance. ¹⁹ For we will not inherit with them on the other side of the Jordan and beyond, because our inheritance has come to us on this side of the

ᵃ 31:52 A shekel is about 10 grams or about 0.35 ounces, so 16,750 shekels is about 167.5 kilograms or about 368.5 pounds.

Jordan eastward." ²⁰ Moses said to them: "If you will do this thing, if you will arm yourselves to go before Yahweh to the war, ²¹ and every one of your armed men will pass over the Jordan before Yahweh until he has driven out his enemies from before him, ²² and the land is subdued before Yahweh; then afterward you shall return, and be clear of obligation to Yahweh and to Israel. Then this land shall be your possession before Yahweh. ²³"But if you will not do so, behold, you have sinned against Yahweh; and be sure your sin will find you out. ²⁴ Build cities for your little ones, and folds for your sheep; and do that which has proceeded out of your mouth." ²⁵ The children of Gad and the children of Reuben spoke to Moses, saying, "Your servants will do as my lord commands. ²⁶ Our little ones, our wives, our flocks, and all our livestock shall be there in the cities of Gilead; ²⁷ but your servants will pass over, every man who is armed for war, before Yahweh to battle, as my lord says." ²⁸ So Moses commanded concerning them to Eleazar the priest, and to Joshua the son of Nun, and to the heads of the fathers' households of the tribes of the children of Israel. ²⁹ Moses said to them, "If the children of Gad and the children of Reuben will pass with you over the Jordan, every man who is armed to battle before Yahweh, and the land is subdued before you, then you shall give them the land of Gilead for a possession; ³⁰ but if they will not pass over with you armed, they shall have possessions among you in the land of Canaan." ³¹ The children of Gad and the children of Reuben answered, saying, "As Yahweh has said to your servants, so will we do. ³² We will pass over armed before Yahweh into the land of Canaan, and the possession of our inheritance shall remain with us beyond the Jordan." ³³ Moses gave to them, even to the children of Gad, and to the children of Reuben, and to the half-tribe of Manasseh the son of Joseph, the kingdom of Sihon king of the Amorites, and the kingdom of Og king of Bashan; the land, according to its cities and borders, even the cities of the surrounding land. ³⁴ The children of Gad built Dibon, Ataroth, Aroer, ³⁵ Atroth-shophan, Jazer, Jogbehah, ³⁶ Beth Nimrah, and Beth Haran: fortified cities and folds for sheep. ³⁷ The children of Reuben built Heshbon, Elealeh, Kiriathaim, ³⁸ Nebo, and Baal Meon, (their names being changed), and Sibmah. They gave other names to the cities which they built. ³⁹ The children of Machir the son of Manasseh went to Gilead, took it, and dispossessed the Amorites who were therein. ⁴⁰ Moses gave Gilead to Machir the son of Manasseh; and he lived therein. ⁴¹ Jair the son of Manasseh went and took its villages, and called them Havvoth Jair. ⁴² Nobah went and took Kenath and its villages, and called it Nobah, after his own name.

## 33

¹ These are the journeys of the children of Israel, when they went out of the land of Egypt by their armies under the hand of Moses and Aaron. ² Moses wrote the starting points of their journeys by the commandment of Yahweh. These are their journeys according to their starting points. ³ They traveled from Rameses in the first month, on the fifteenth day of the first month; on the next day after the Passover, the children of Israel went out with a high hand in the sight of all the Egyptians, ⁴ while the Egyptians were burying all their firstborn, whom Yahweh had struck among them. Yahweh also executed judgments on their gods. ⁵ The children of Israel traveled from Rameses, and encamped in Succoth. ⁶ They traveled from Succoth, and encamped in Etham, which is in the edge of the wilderness. ⁷ They traveled from Etham, and turned back to Pihahiroth, which is before Baal Zephon, and they encamped before Migdol. ⁸ They traveled from before Hahiroth, and crossed through the middle of the sea into the wilderness. They went three days' journey in the wilderness of Etham, and encamped in Marah. ⁹ They traveled from Marah, and came to Elim. In Elim, there were twelve springs of water and seventy palm trees, and they encamped there. ¹⁰ They traveled from Elim, and encamped by the Red Sea. ¹¹ They traveled from the Red Sea, and encamped in the wilderness of Sin. ¹² They traveled from the wilderness of Sin, and encamped in Dophkah. ¹³ They traveled from Dophkah, and encamped in Alush. ¹⁴ They traveled from Alush, and encamped in Rephidim, where there was no water for the people to drink. ¹⁵ They traveled from Rephidim, and encamped in the wilderness of Sinai. ¹⁶ They traveled from the wilderness of Sinai, and encamped in Kibroth Hattaavah. ¹⁷ They traveled from Kibroth Hattaavah, and encamped in Hazeroth. ¹⁸ They traveled from Hazeroth, and encamped in Rithmah. ¹⁹ They traveled from Rithmah, and encamped in Rimmon Perez. ²⁰ They traveled from Rimmon Perez, and encamped in Libnah. ²¹ They traveled from Libnah, and encamped in Rissah. ²² They traveled from Rissah, and encamped in Kehelathah. ²³ They traveled from Kehelathah, and encamped in Mount Shepher. ²⁴ They traveled from Mount Shepher, and encamped in Haradah. ²⁵ They traveled from Haradah, and encamped in Makheloth. ²⁶ They traveled from Makheloth, and encamped in Tahath. ²⁷ They traveled from Tahath, and encamped in Terah. ²⁸ They traveled from Terah, and encamped in Mithkah. ²⁹ They traveled from Mithkah, and encamped in Hashmonah. ³⁰ They traveled from Hashmonah, and encamped in Moseroth. ³¹ They traveled from Moseroth, and encamped in Bene Jaakan. ³² They traveled from Bene Jaakan, and encamped in Hor Haggidgad. ³³ They traveled from Hor Haggidgad, and encamped in Jotbathah. ³⁴ They traveled from Jotbathah, and encamped in Abronah. ³⁵ They traveled from Abronah, and encamped in Ezion Geber. ³⁶ They traveled from Ezion Geber, and encamped at Kadesh in the wilderness of Zin. ³⁷ They traveled from Kadesh, and encamped in Mount Hor, in the edge of the land of Edom. ³⁸ Aaron the priest went up into Mount Hor at the commandment of Yahweh and died there, in the fortieth year after the children of Israel had come out of the land of Egypt, in the fifth month, on the first day of the month. ³⁹ Aaron was one hundred twenty-three years old when he died in Mount Hor. ⁴⁰ The Canaanite king of Arad, who lived in the South in the land of Canaan, heard of the coming of the children of Israel. ⁴¹ They traveled from Mount Hor, and encamped in Zalmonah. ⁴² They traveled from Zalmonah, and encamped in Punon. ⁴³ They traveled from Punon, and encamped in Oboth. ⁴⁴ They traveled from Oboth, and encamped in Iye Abarim, in the border of Moab. ⁴⁵ They traveled from Iyim, and encamped in Dibon Gad. ⁴⁶ They traveled from Dibon Gad, and encamped in Almon Diblathaim. ⁴⁷ They traveled from Almon Diblathaim, and encamped in the mountains of Abarim, before Nebo. ⁴⁸ They traveled from the mountains of Abarim, and encamped in the plains of Moab by the Jordan at Jericho. ⁴⁹ They encamped by the Jordan, from Beth Jeshimoth even to Abel Shittim in the plains of Moab. ⁵⁰ Yahweh spoke to Moses in the plains of Moab by the Jordan at Jericho, saying, ⁵¹ Speak to the children of Israel, and tell them, "When you pass over the Jordan into the land of Canaan, ⁵² then you shall drive out all the inhabitants of the land from before you, destroy all their stone idols, destroy all their molten images, and demolish all their high places. ⁵³ You shall take possession of the land, and dwell therein; for I have given the land to you to possess it. ⁵⁴ You shall inherit the land by lot according to your families; to the larger groups you shall give a larger inheritance, and to the smaller you shall give a smaller inheritance. Wherever the lot falls to any man, that shall be his. You shall inherit according to the tribes of your fathers. ⁵⁵"But if you do not drive out the inhabitants of the land from before you, then those you let remain of them will be like pricks in your eyes and thorns in your sides. They will harass you in the land in which you dwell. ⁵⁶ It shall happen that as I thought to do to them, so I will do to you."

## 34

¹ Yahweh spoke to Moses, saying, ²"Command the children of Israel, and tell them, 'When you come into the land of Canaan (this is the land that shall fall to you for an inheritance, even the land of Canaan according to its borders), ³ then your south quarter shall be from the wilderness of Zin along by the side of Edom, and your south border shall be from the end of the Salt Sea eastward. ⁴ Your border shall turn about southward of the ascent of Akrabbim, and pass along to Zin; and it shall pass southward of Kadesh Barnea; and it shall go from there to Hazar Addar, and pass along to Azmon. ⁵ The border shall turn about from Azmon to the brook of Egypt, and it shall end at the sea. ⁶"For the western border, you shall have the great sea and its border. This shall be your west border. ⁷"This shall be your north border: from the great sea you shall mark out for yourselves Mount Hor. ⁸ From Mount Hor you shall mark out to the entrance of Hamath; and the border shall pass by Zedad. ⁹ Then the border shall go to Ziphron, and it shall end at Hazar Enan. This shall be your north border. ¹⁰"You shall mark out your east border from Hazar Enan to Shepham. ¹¹ The border shall go down from Shepham to Riblah, on the east side of Ain. The border shall go down, and shall reach to the side of the sea of Chinnereth eastward. ¹² The border shall go down to the Jordan, and end at the Salt Sea. This shall be your land according to its borders around it.'" ¹³ Moses commanded the children of Israel, saying, "This is the land which you shall inherit by lot, which Yahweh has commanded to give to the nine tribes, and to the half-tribe; ¹⁴ for the tribe of the children of Reuben according to their fathers' houses, the tribe of the children of Gad according to their fathers' houses, and the half-tribe of Manasseh have received their inheritance. ¹⁵ The two tribes and the half-tribe have received their inheritance beyond the Jordan at Jericho eastward, toward the sunrise." ¹⁶ Yahweh spoke to Moses, saying, ¹⁷"These are the names of the men who shall divide the land to you for inheritance: Eleazar the priest, and Joshua the son of Nun. ¹⁸ You shall take one prince of every tribe, to divide the land for inheritance. ¹⁹ These are the names of the men: Of the tribe of Judah, Caleb the son of Jephunneh. ²⁰ Of the tribe of the children of Simeon, Shemuel the son of Ammihud. ²¹ Of the tribe of Benjamin, Elidad the son of Chislon. ²² Of the tribe of the children of Dan a prince, Bukki the son of Jogli. ²³ Of the children of Joseph: of the tribe of the children of Manasseh a prince, Hanniel the son of Ephod. ²⁴ Of the tribe of the children of Ephraim a prince, Kemuel the son of Shiphtan. ²⁵ Of the tribe of the children of Zebulun a prince, Elizaphan the son of Parnach. ²⁶ Of the tribe of the children of

Issachar a prince, Paltiel the son of Azzan. <sup>27</sup> Of the tribe of the children of Asher a prince, Ahihud the son of Shelomi. <sup>28</sup> Of the tribe of the children of Naphtali a prince, Pedahel the son of Ammihud." <sup>29</sup> These are they whom Yahweh commanded to divide the inheritance to the children of Israel in the land of Canaan.

## 35

<sup>1</sup> Yahweh spoke to Moses in the plains of Moab by the Jordan at Jericho, saying, <sup>2</sup>"Command the children of Israel to give to the Levites cities to dwell in out of their inheritance. You shall give pasture lands for the cities around them to the Levites. <sup>3</sup> They shall have the cities to dwell in. Their pasture lands shall be for their livestock, and for their possessions, and for all their animals. <sup>4</sup>"The pasture lands of the cities, which you shall give to the Levites, shall be from the wall of the city and outward one thousand cubits<sup>a</sup> around it. <sup>5</sup> You shall measure outside of the city for the east side two thousand cubits, and for the south side two thousand cubits, and for the west side two thousand cubits, and for the north side two thousand cubits, the city being in the middle. This shall be the pasture lands of their cities. <sup>6</sup>"The cities which you shall give to the Levites, they shall be the six cities of refuge, which you shall give for the man slayer to flee to. Besides them you shall give forty-two cities. <sup>7</sup> All the cities which you shall give to the Levites shall be forty-eight cities together with their pasture lands. <sup>8</sup> Concerning the cities which you shall give of the possession of the children of Israel, from the many you shall take many, and from the few you shall take few. Everyone according to his inheritance which he inherits shall give some of his cities to the Levites." <sup>9</sup> Yahweh spoke to Moses, saying, <sup>10</sup>"Speak to the children of Israel, and tell them, 'When you pass over the Jordan into the land of Canaan, <sup>11</sup> then you shall appoint for yourselves cities to be cities of refuge for you, that the man slayer who kills any person unwittingly may flee there. <sup>12</sup> The cities shall be for your refuge from the avenger, that the man slayer not die until he stands before the congregation for judgment. <sup>13</sup> The cities which you shall give shall be for you six cities of refuge. <sup>14</sup> You shall give three cities beyond the Jordan, and you shall give three cities in the land of Canaan. They shall be cities of refuge. <sup>15</sup> These six cities shall be refuge for the children of Israel, for the stranger, and for the foreigner living among them, that everyone who kills any person unwittingly may flee there. <sup>16</sup>"But if he struck him with an instrument of iron, so that he died, he is a murderer. The murderer shall surely be put to death. <sup>17</sup> If he struck him with a stone in the hand, by which a man may die, and he died, he is a murderer. The murderer shall surely be put to death. <sup>18</sup> Or if he struck him with a weapon of wood in the hand, by which a man may die, and he died, he is a murderer. The murderer shall surely be put to death. <sup>19</sup> The avenger of blood shall himself put the murderer to death. When he meets him, he shall put him to death. <sup>20</sup> If he shoved him out of hatred, or hurled something at him while lying in wait, so that he died, <sup>21</sup> or in hostility struck him with his hand, so that he died, he who struck him shall surely be put to death. He is a murderer. The avenger of blood shall put the murderer to death when he meets him. <sup>22</sup>"But if he shoved him suddenly without hostility, or hurled on him anything without lying in wait, <sup>23</sup> or with any stone, by which a man may die, not seeing him, and cast it on him so that he died, and he was not his enemy and not seeking his harm, <sup>24</sup> then the congregation shall judge between the striker and the avenger of blood according to these ordinances. <sup>25</sup> The congregation shall deliver the man slayer out of the hand of the avenger of blood, and the congregation shall restore him to his city of refuge, where he had fled. He shall dwell therein until the death of the high priest, who was anointed with the holy oil. <sup>26</sup>"But if the man slayer shall at any time go beyond the border of his city of refuge where he flees, <sup>27</sup> and the avenger of blood finds him outside of the border of his city of refuge, and the avenger of blood kills the man slayer, he shall not be guilty of blood, <sup>28</sup> because he should have remained in his city of refuge until the death of the high priest. But after the death of the high priest, the man slayer shall return into the land of his possession. <sup>29</sup>"These things shall be for a statute and ordinance to you throughout your generations in all your dwellings. <sup>30</sup>"Whoever kills any person, the murderer shall be slain based on the testimony of witnesses; but one witness shall not testify alone against any person so that he dies. <sup>31</sup>"Moreover you shall take no ransom for the life of a murderer who is guilty of death. He shall surely be put to death. <sup>32</sup>"You shall take no ransom for him who has fled to his city of refuge, that he may come again to dwell in the land before the death of the priest. <sup>33</sup>"So you shall not pollute the land where you live; for blood pollutes the land. No atonement can be made for the land for the blood that is shed in it, but by the blood of him who shed it. <sup>34</sup> You shall not defile the land which you inhabit, where I dwell; for I, Yahweh, dwell among the children of Israel.'"

## 36

<sup>1</sup> The heads of the fathers' households of the family of the children of Gilead, the son of Machir, the son of Manasseh, of the families of the sons of Joseph, came near and spoke before Moses and before the princes, the heads of the fathers' households of the children of Israel. <sup>2</sup> They said, "Yahweh commanded my lord to give the land for inheritance by lot to the children of Israel. My lord was commanded by Yahweh to give the inheritance of Zelophehad our brother to his daughters. <sup>3</sup> If they are married to any of the sons of the other tribes of the children of Israel, then their inheritance will be taken away from the inheritance of our fathers, and will be added to the inheritance of the tribe to which they shall belong. So it will be taken away from the lot of our inheritance. <sup>4</sup> When the jubilee of the children of Israel comes, then their inheritance will be added to the inheritance of the tribe to which they shall belong. So their inheritance will be taken away from the inheritance of the tribe of our fathers." <sup>5</sup> Moses commanded the children of Israel according to Yahweh's word, saying, "The tribe of the sons of Joseph speak what is right. <sup>6</sup> This is the thing which Yahweh commands concerning the daughters of Zelophehad, saying, 'Let them be married to whom they think best, only they shall marry into the family of the tribe of their father. <sup>7</sup> So shall no inheritance of the children of Israel move from tribe to tribe; for the children of Israel shall all keep the inheritance of the tribe of his fathers. <sup>8</sup> Every daughter who possesses an inheritance in any tribe of the children of Israel shall be wife to one of the family of the tribe of her father, that the children of Israel may each possess the inheritance of his fathers. <sup>9</sup> So shall no inheritance move from one tribe to another tribe; for the tribes of the children of Israel shall each keep his own inheritance.'" <sup>10</sup> The daughters of Zelophehad did as Yahweh commanded Moses: <sup>11</sup> for Mahlah, Tirzah, Hoglah, Milcah, and Noah, the daughters of Zelophehad, were married to their father's brothers' sons. <sup>12</sup> They were married into the families of the sons of Manasseh the son of Joseph. Their inheritance remained in the tribe of the family of their father. <sup>13</sup> These are the commandments and the ordinances which Yahweh commanded by Moses to the children of Israel in the plains of Moab by the Jordan at Jericho.

# The Fifth Book of Moses, Deuteronomy
## 1

<sup>1</sup> These are the words which Moses spoke to all Israel beyond the Jordan in the wilderness, in the Arabah opposite Suf, between Paran, Tophel, Laban, Hazeroth, and Dizahab. <sup>2</sup> It is eleven days' journey from Horeb by the way of Mount Seir to Kadesh Barnea. <sup>3</sup> In the fortieth year, in the eleventh month, on the first day of the month, Moses spoke to the children of Israel according to all that Yahweh<sup>b</sup> had given him in commandment to them, <sup>4</sup> after he had struck Sihon the king of the Amorites who lived in Heshbon, and Og the king of Bashan who lived in Ashtaroth, at Edrei. <sup>5</sup> Beyond the Jordan, in the land of Moab, Moses began to declare this law, saying, <sup>6</sup>"Yahweh our God<sup>c</sup> spoke to us in Horeb, saying, 'You have lived long enough at this mountain. <sup>7</sup> Turn, and take your journey, and go to the hill country of the Amorites and to all the places near there: in the Arabah, in the hill country, in the lowland, in the South, by the seashore, in the land of the Canaanites, and in Lebanon as far as the great river, the river Euphrates. <sup>8</sup> Behold,<sup>d</sup> I have set the land before you. Go in and possess the land which Yahweh swore to your fathers—to Abraham, to Isaac, and to Jacob—to give to them and to their offspring<sup>e</sup> after them.'" <sup>9</sup> I spoke to you at that time, saying, "I am not able to bear you myself alone. <sup>10</sup> Yahweh your God has multiplied you, and behold, you are today as the stars of the sky for multitude. <sup>11</sup> May Yahweh, the God of your fathers, make you a thousand times as many as you are and bless you, as he has promised you! <sup>12</sup> How can I myself alone bear your problems, your burdens, and your strife? <sup>13</sup> Take wise men of understanding who are respected among your tribes, and I will make them heads over you." <sup>14</sup> You answered me, and said, "The thing which you have spoken is good to do." <sup>15</sup> So I took the heads of your tribes, wise and respected men, and made them heads over you, captains of thousands, captains of hundreds, captains of fifties, captains of tens, and officers, according to your tribes. <sup>16</sup> I commanded your judges at that time, saying, "Hear cases between your brothers and judge righteously between a man and

---

<sup>a</sup> *35:4* A cubit is the length from the tip of the middle finger to the elbow on a man's arm, or about 18 inches or 46 centimeters.

<sup>b</sup> *1:3* "Yahweh" is God's proper Name, sometimes rendered "LORD" (all caps) in other translations.

<sup>c</sup> *1:6* The Hebrew word rendered "God" is אֱלֹהִים (Elohim).
<sup>d</sup> *1:8* "Behold", from הִנֵּה, means look at, take notice,

observe, see, or gaze at. It is often used as an interjection.
<sup>e</sup> *1:8* or, seed

his brother, and the foreigner who is living with him. [17] You shall not show partiality in judgment; you shall hear the small and the great alike. You shall not be afraid of the face of man, for the judgment is God's. The case that is too hard for you, you shall bring to me, and I will hear it." [18] I commanded you at that time all the things which you should do. [19] We traveled from Horeb and went through all that great and terrible wilderness which you saw, by the way to the hill country of the Amorites, as Yahweh our God commanded us; and we came to Kadesh Barnea. [20] I said to you, "You have come to the hill country of the Amorites, which Yahweh our God gives to us. [21] Behold, Yahweh your God has set the land before you. Go up, take possession, as Yahweh the God of your fathers has spoken to you. Don't be afraid, neither be dismayed." [22] You came near to me, everyone of you, and said, "Let's send men before us, that they may search the land for us, and bring back to us word of the way by which we must go up, and the cities to which we shall come." [23] The thing pleased me well. I took twelve of your men, one man for every tribe. [24] They turned and went up into the hill country, and came to the valley of Eshcol, and spied it out. [25] They took some of the fruit of the land in their hands and brought it down to us, and brought us word again, and said, "It is a good land which Yahweh our God gives to us." [26] Yet you wouldn't go up, but rebelled against the commandment of Yahweh your God. [27] You murmured in your tents, and said, "Because Yahweh hated us, he has brought us out of the land of Egypt, to deliver us into the hand of the Amorites to destroy us. [28] Where are we going up? Our brothers have made our heart melt, saying, 'The people are greater and taller than we. The cities are great and fortified up to the sky. Moreover we have seen the sons of the Anakim there!'" [29] Then I said to you, "Don't be terrified. Don't be afraid of them. [30] Yahweh your God, who goes before you, he will fight for you, according to all that he did for you in Egypt before your eyes, [31] and in the wilderness where you have seen how that Yahweh your God carried you, as a man carries his son, in all the way that you went, until you came to this place." [32] Yet in this thing you didn't believe Yahweh your God, [33] who went before you on the way, to seek out a place for you to pitch your tents in: in fire by night, to show you by what way you should go, and in the cloud by day. [34] Yahweh heard the voice of your words and was angry, and swore, saying, [35]"Surely not one of these men of this evil generation shall see the good land which I swore to give to your fathers, [36] except Caleb the son of Jephunneh. He shall see it. I will give the land that he has trodden on to him and to his children, because he has wholly followed Yahweh." [37] Also Yahweh was angry with me for your sakes, saying, "You also shall not go in there. [38] Joshua the son of Nun, who stands before you, shall go in there. Encourage him, for he shall cause Israel to inherit it. [39] Moreover your little ones, whom you said would be captured or killed, your children, who today have no knowledge of good or evil, shall go in there. I will give it to them, and they shall possess it. [40] But as for you, turn, and take your journey into the wilderness by the way to the Red Sea." [41] Then you answered and said to me, "We have sinned against Yahweh. We will go up and fight, according to all that Yahweh our God commanded us." Every man of you put on his weapons of war, and presumed to go up into the hill country. [42] Yahweh said to me, "Tell them, 'Don't go up and don't fight; for I am not among you, lest you be struck before your enemies.'" [43] So I spoke to you, and you didn't listen; but you rebelled against the commandment of Yahweh, and were presumptuous, and went up into the hill country. [44] The Amorites, who lived in that hill country, came out against you and chased you as bees do, and beat you down in Seir, even to Hormah. [45] You returned and wept before Yahweh, but Yahweh didn't listen to your voice, nor turn his ear to you. [46] So you stayed in Kadesh many days, according to the days that you remained.

## 2

[1] Then we turned, and took our journey into the wilderness by the way to the Red Sea, as Yahweh spoke to me; and we encircled Mount Seir many days. [2] Yahweh spoke to me, saying, [3]"You have encircled this mountain long enough. Turn northward. [4] Command the people, saying, 'You are to pass through the border of your brothers, the children of Esau, who dwell in Seir; and they will be afraid of you. Therefore be careful. [5] Don't contend with them; for I will not give you any of their land, no, not so much as for the sole of the foot to tread on, because I have given Mount Seir to Esau for a possession. [6] You shall purchase food from them for money, that you may eat. You shall also buy water from them for money, that you may drink.'" [7] For Yahweh your God has blessed you in all the work of your hands. He has known your walking through this great wilderness. These forty years, Yahweh your God has been with you. You have lacked nothing. [8] So we passed by from our brothers, the children of Esau, who dwell in Seir, from the way of the Arabah from Elath and from Ezion Geber. We turned and passed by the way of the wilderness of Moab. [9] Yahweh said to me, "Don't bother Moab, neither contend with them in battle; for I will not

give you any of his land for a possession, because I have given Ar to the children of Lot for a possession." [10](The Emim lived there before, a great and numerous people, and tall as the Anakim. [11] These also are considered to be Rephaim, as the Anakim; but the Moabites call them Emim. [12] The Horites also lived in Seir in the past, but the children of Esau succeeded them. They destroyed them from before them, and lived in their place, as Israel did to the land of his possession, which Yahweh gave to them.) [13]"Now rise up and cross over the brook Zered." We went over the brook Zered. [14] The days in which we came from Kadesh Barnea until we had come over the brook Zered were thirty-eight years, until all the generation of the men of war were consumed from the middle of the camp, as Yahweh swore to them. [15] Moreover Yahweh's hand was against them, to destroy them from the middle of the camp, until they were consumed. [16] So, when all the men of war were consumed and dead from among the people, [17] Yahweh spoke to me, saying, [18]"You are to pass over Ar, the border of Moab, today. [19] When you come near the border of the children of Ammon, don't bother them, nor contend with them; for I will not give you any of the land of the children of Ammon for a possession, because I have given it to the children of Lot for a possession." [20](That also is considered a land of Rephaim. Rephaim lived there in the past, but the Ammonites call them Zamzummim, [21] a great people, many, and tall, as the Anakim; but Yahweh destroyed them from before Israel, and they succeeded them, and lived in their place, [22] as he did for the children of Esau who dwell in Seir, when he destroyed the Horites from before them; and they succeeded them, and lived in their place even to this day. [23] Then the Avvim, who lived in villages as far as Gaza: the Caphtorim, who came out of Caphtor, destroyed them and lived in their place.) [24]"Rise up, take your journey, and pass over the valley of the Arnon. Behold, I have given into your hand Sihon the Amorite, king of Heshbon, and his land; begin to possess it, and contend with him in battle. [25] Today I will begin to put the dread of you and the fear of you on the peoples who are under the whole sky, who shall hear the report of you, and shall tremble and be in anguish because of you." [26] I sent messengers out of the wilderness of Kedemoth to Sihon king of Heshbon with words of peace, saying, [27]"Let me pass through your land. I will go along by the highway. I will turn neither to the right hand nor to the left. [28] You shall sell me food for money, that I may eat; and give me water for money, that I may drink. Just let me pass through on my feet, [29] as the children of Esau who dwell in Seir, and the Moabites who dwell in Ar, did to me, until I pass over the Jordan into the land which Yahweh our God gives us." [30] But Sihon king of Heshbon would not let us pass by him, for Yahweh your God hardened his spirit and made his heart obstinate, that he might deliver him into your hand, as it is today. [31] Yahweh said to me, "Behold, I have begun to deliver up Sihon and his land before you. Begin to possess, that you may inherit his land." [32] Then Sihon came out against us, he and all his people, to battle at Jahaz. [33] Yahweh our God delivered him up before us; and we struck him, his sons, and all his people. [34] We took all his cities at that time, and utterly destroyed every inhabited city, with the women and the little ones. We left no one remaining. [35] Only the livestock we took for plunder for ourselves, with the plunder of the cities which we had taken. [36] From Aroer, which is on the edge of the valley of the Arnon, and the city that is in the valley, even to Gilead, there was not a city too high for us. Yahweh our God delivered up all before us. [37] Only to the land of the children of Ammon you didn't come near: all the banks of the river Jabbok, and the cities of the hill country, and wherever Yahweh our God forbade us.

## 3

[1] Then we turned, and went up the way to Bashan. Og the king of Bashan came out against us, he and all his people, to battle at Edrei. [2] Yahweh said to me, "Don't fear him; for I have delivered him, with all his people and his land, into your hand. You shall do to him as you did to Sihon king of the Amorites, who lived at Heshbon." [3] So Yahweh our God also delivered into our hand Og, the king of Bashan, and all his people. We struck him until no one was left to him remaining. [4] We took all his cities at that time. There was not a city which we didn't take from them: sixty cities, all the region of Argob, the kingdom of Og in Bashan. [5] All these were cities fortified with high walls, gates, and bars, in addition to a great many villages without walls. [6] We utterly destroyed them, as we did to Sihon king of Heshbon, utterly destroying every inhabited city, with the women and the little ones. [7] But all the livestock, and the plunder of the cities, we took for plunder for ourselves. [8] We took the land at that time out of the hand of the two kings of the Amorites who were beyond the Jordan, from the valley of the Arnon to Mount Hermon. [9](The Sidonians call Hermon Sirion, and the Amorites call it Senir.) [10] We took all the cities of the plain, and all Gilead, and all Bashan, to Salecah and Edrei, cities of the kingdom of Og in Bashan. [11](For only Og king of Bashan remained of the remnant of the Rephaim. Behold, his bedstead was a bedstead of iron. Isn't it in

Rabbah of the children of Ammon? Nine cubits[a] was its length, and four cubits its width, after the cubit of a man.) [12] This land we took in possession at that time: from Aroer, which is by the valley of the Arnon, and half the hill country of Gilead with its cities, I gave to the Reubenites and to the Gadites; [13] and the rest of Gilead, and all Bashan, the kingdom of Og, I gave to the half-tribe of Manasseh—all the region of Argob, even all Bashan. (The same is called the land of Rephaim. [14] Jair the son of Manasseh took all the region of Argob, to the border of the Geshurites and the Maacathites, and called them, even Bashan, after his own name, Havvoth Jair, to this day.) [15] I gave Gilead to Machir. [16] To the Reubenites and to the Gadites I gave from Gilead even to the valley of the Arnon, the middle of the valley, and its border, even to the river Jabbok, which is the border of the children of Ammon; [17] the Arabah also, and the Jordan and its border, from Chinnereth even to the sea of the Arabah, the Salt Sea, under the slopes of Pisgah eastward. [18] I commanded you at that time, saying, "Yahweh your God has given you this land to possess it. All of you men of valor shall pass over armed before your brothers, the children of Israel. [19] But your wives, and your little ones, and your livestock, (I know that you have much livestock), shall live in your cities which I have given you, [20] until Yahweh gives rest to your brothers, as to you, and they also possess the land which Yahweh your God gives them beyond the Jordan. Then you shall each return to his own possession, which I have given you." [21] I commanded Joshua at that time, saying, "Your eyes have seen all that Yahweh your God has done to these two kings. So shall Yahweh do to all the kingdoms where you go over. [22] You shall not fear them; for Yahweh your God himself fights for you." [23] I begged Yahweh at that time, saying, [24]"Lord[b] Yahweh, you have begun to show your servant your greatness, and your strong hand. For what god is there in heaven or in earth that can do works like yours, and mighty acts like yours? [25] Please let me go over and see the good land that is beyond the Jordan, that fine mountain, and Lebanon." [26] But Yahweh was angry with me because of you, and didn't listen to me. Yahweh said to me, "That is enough! Speak no more to me of this matter. [27] Go up to the top of Pisgah, and lift up your eyes westward, and northward, and southward, and eastward, and see with your eyes; for you shall not go over this Jordan. [28] But commission Joshua, and encourage him, and strengthen him; for he shall go over before this people, and he shall cause them to inherit the land which you shall see." [29] So we stayed in the valley near Beth Peor.

## 4

[1] Now, Israel, listen to the statutes and to the ordinances which I teach you, to do them, that you may live and go in and possess the land which Yahweh, the God of your fathers, gives you. [2] You shall not add to the word which I command you, neither shall you take away from it, that you may keep the commandments of Yahweh your God which I command you. [3] Your eyes have seen what Yahweh did because of Baal Peor; for Yahweh your God has destroyed all the men who followed Baal Peor from among you. [4] But you who were faithful to Yahweh your God are all alive today. [5] Behold, I have taught you statutes and ordinances, even as Yahweh my God commanded me, that you should do so in the middle of the land where you go in to possess it. [6] Keep therefore and do them; for this is your wisdom and your understanding in the sight of the peoples who shall hear all these statutes and say, "Surely this great nation is a wise and understanding people." [7] For what great nation is there that has a god so near to them as Yahweh our God is whenever we call on him? [8] What great nation is there that has statutes and ordinances so righteous as all this law which I set before you today? [9] Only be careful, and keep your soul diligently, lest you forget the things which your eyes saw, and lest they depart from your heart all the days of your life; but make them known to your children and your children's children— [10] the day that you stood before Yahweh your God in Horeb, when Yahweh said to me, "Assemble the people to me, and I will make them hear my words, that they may learn to fear me all the days that they live on the earth, and that they may teach their children." [11] You came near and stood under the mountain. The mountain burned with fire to the heart of the sky, with darkness, cloud, and thick darkness. [12] Yahweh spoke to you out of the middle of the fire: you heard the voice of words, but you saw no form; you only heard a voice. [13] He declared to you his covenant, which he commanded you to perform, even the ten commandments. He wrote them on two stone tablets. [14] Yahweh commanded me at that time to teach you statutes and ordinances, that you might do them in the land where you go over to possess it. [15] Be very careful, for you saw no kind of form on the day that Yahweh spoke to you in Horeb out of the middle of the fire, [16] lest you corrupt yourselves, and make yourself a carved image in the form

of any figure, the likeness of male or female, [17] the likeness of any animal that is on the earth, the likeness of any winged bird that flies in the sky, [18] the likeness of anything that creeps on the ground, the likeness of any fish that is in the water under the earth; [19] and lest you lift up your eyes to the sky, and when you see the sun and the moon and the stars, even all the army of the sky, you are drawn away and worship them, and serve them, which Yahweh your God has allotted to all the peoples under the whole sky. [20] But Yahweh has taken you, and brought you out of the iron furnace, out of Egypt, to be to him a people of inheritance, as it is today. [21] Furthermore Yahweh was angry with me for your sakes, and swore that I should not go over the Jordan, and that I should not go in to that good land which Yahweh your God gives you for an inheritance; [22] but I must die in this land. I must not go over the Jordan, but you shall go over and possess that good land. [23] Be careful, lest you forget the covenant of Yahweh your God, which he made with you, and make yourselves a carved image in the form of anything which Yahweh your God has forbidden you. [24] For Yahweh your God is a devouring fire, a jealous God. [25] When you father children and children's children, and you have been long in the land, and then corrupt yourselves, and make a carved image in the form of anything, and do that which is evil in Yahweh your God's sight to provoke him to anger, [26] I call heaven and earth to witness against you today, that you will soon utterly perish from off the land which you go over the Jordan to possess it. You will not prolong your days on it, but will utterly be destroyed. [27] Yahweh will scatter you among the peoples, and you will be left few in number among the nations where Yahweh will lead you away. [28] There you will serve gods, the work of men's hands, wood and stone, which neither see, nor hear, nor eat, nor smell. [29] But from there you shall seek Yahweh your God, and you will find him when you search after him with all your heart and with all your soul. [30] When you are in oppression, and all these things have come on you, in the latter days you shall return to Yahweh your God and listen to his voice. [31] For Yahweh your God is a merciful God. He will not fail you nor destroy you, nor forget the covenant of your fathers which he swore to them. [32] For ask now of the days that are past, which were before you, since the day that God created man on the earth, and from the one end of the sky to the other, whether there has been anything as great as this thing is, or has been heard like it? [33] Did a people ever hear the voice of God speaking out of the middle of the fire, as you have heard, and live? [34] Or has God tried to go and take a nation for himself from among another nation, by trials, by signs, by wonders, by war, by a mighty hand, by an outstretched arm, and by great terrors, according to all that Yahweh your God did for you in Egypt before your eyes? [35] It was shown to you so that you might know that Yahweh is God. There is no one else besides him. [36] Out of heaven he made you to hear his voice, that he might instruct you. On earth he made you to see his great fire; and you heard his words out of the middle of the fire. [37] Because he loved your fathers, therefore he chose their offspring after them, and brought you out with his presence, with his great power, out of Egypt; [38] to drive out nations from before you greater and mightier than you, to bring you in, to give you their land for an inheritance, as it is today. [39] Know therefore today, and take it to heart, that Yahweh himself is God in heaven above and on the earth beneath. There is no one else. [40] You shall keep his statutes and his commandments which I command you today, that it may go well with you and with your children after you, and that you may prolong your days in the land which Yahweh your God gives you for all time. [41] Then Moses set apart three cities beyond the Jordan toward the sunrise, [42] that the man slayer might flee there, who kills his neighbor unintentionally and didn't hate him in time past, and that fleeing to one of these cities he might live: [43] Bezer in the wilderness, in the plain country, for the Reubenites; and Ramoth in Gilead for the Gadites; and Golan in Bashan for the Manassites. [44] This is the law which Moses set before the children of Israel. [45] These are the testimonies, and the statutes, and the ordinances which Moses spoke to the children of Israel when they came out of Egypt, [46] beyond the Jordan, in the valley opposite Beth Peor, in the land of Sihon king of the Amorites, who lived at Heshbon, whom Moses and the children of Israel struck when they came out of Egypt. [47] They took possession of his land and the land of Og king of Bashan, the two kings of the Amorites, who were beyond the Jordan toward the sunrise; [48] from Aroer, which is on the edge of the valley of the Arnon, even to Mount Zion (also called Hermon), [49] and all the Arabah beyond the Jordan eastward, even to the sea of the Arabah, under the slopes of Pisgah.

## 5

[1] Moses called to all Israel, and said to them, "Hear, Israel, the statutes and the ordinances which I speak in your ears today, that you may learn

---

[a] *3:11 A cubit is the length from the tip of the middle finger to the elbow on a man's arm, or about 18 inches or 46 centimeters.*

[b] *3:24 The word translated "Lord" is "Adonai."*

them, and observe to do them." ² Yahweh our God made a covenant with us in Horeb. ³ Yahweh didn't make this covenant with our fathers, but with us, even us, who are all of us here alive today. ⁴ Yahweh spoke with you face to face on the mountain out of the middle of the fire, ⁵(I stood between Yahweh and you at that time, to show you Yahweh's word; for you were afraid because of the fire, and didn't go up onto the mountain) saying, ⁶"I am Yahweh your God, who brought you out of the land of Egypt, out of the house of bondage. ⁷"You shall have no other gods before me. ⁸"You shall not make a carved image for yourself—any likeness of what is in heaven above, or what is in the earth beneath, or that is in the water under the earth. ⁹ You shall not bow yourself down to them, nor serve them, for I, Yahweh your God, am a jealous God, visiting the iniquity of the fathers on the children and on the third and on the fourth generation of those who hate me ¹⁰ and showing loving kindness to thousands of those who love me and keep my commandments. ¹¹"You shall not misuse the name of Yahweh your God;ᵃ for Yahweh will not hold him guiltless who misuses his name. ¹²"Observe the Sabbath day, to keep it holy, as Yahweh your God commanded you. ¹³ You shall labor six days, and do all your work; ¹⁴ but the seventh day is a Sabbath to Yahweh your God, in which you shall not do any work—neither you, nor your son, nor your daughter, nor your male servant, nor your female servant, nor your ox, nor your donkey, nor any of your livestock, nor your stranger who is within your gates; that your male servant and your female servant may rest as well as you. ¹⁵ You shall remember that you were a servant in the land of Egypt, and Yahweh your God brought you out of there by a mighty hand and by an outstretched arm. Therefore Yahweh your God commanded you to keep the Sabbath day. ¹⁶"Honor your father and your mother, as Yahweh your God commanded you, that your days may be long and that it may go well with you in the land which Yahweh your God gives you. ¹⁷"You shall not murder. ¹⁸"You shall not commit adultery. ¹⁹"You shall not steal. ²⁰"You shall not give false testimony against your neighbor. ²¹"You shall not covet your neighbor's wife. Neither shall you desire your neighbor's house, his field, or his male servant, or his female servant, his ox, or his donkey, or anything that is your neighbor's." ²² Yahweh spoke these words to all your assembly on the mountain out of the middle of the fire, of the cloud, and of the thick darkness, with a great voice. He added no more. He wrote them on two stone tablets, and gave them to me. ²³ When you heard the voice out of the middle of the darkness, while the mountain was burning with fire, you came near to me, even all the heads of your tribes, and your elders; ²⁴ and you said, "Behold, Yahweh our God has shown us his glory and his greatness, and we have heard his voice out of the middle of the fire. We have seen today that God does speak with man, and he lives. ²⁵ Now therefore, why should we die? For this great fire will consume us. If we hear Yahweh our God's voice any more, then we shall die. ²⁶ For who is there of all flesh who has heard the voice of the living God speaking out of the middle of the fire, as we have, and lived? ²⁷ Go near, and hear all that Yahweh our God shall say, and tell us all that Yahweh our God tells you; and we will hear it, and do it." ²⁸ Yahweh heard the voice of your words when you spoke to me; and Yahweh said to me, "I have heard the voice of the words of this people which they have spoken to you. They have well said all that they have spoken. ²⁹ Oh that there were such a heart in them that they would fear me and keep all my commandments always, that it might be well with them and with their children forever! ³⁰"Go tell them, 'Return to your tents.' ³¹ But as for you, stand here by me, and I will tell you all the commandments, and the statutes, and the ordinances, which you shall teach them, that they may do them in the land which I give them to possess." ³² You shall observe to do therefore as Yahweh your God has commanded you. You shall not turn away to the right hand or to the left. ³³ You shall walk in all the way which Yahweh your God has commanded you, that you may live and that it may be well with you, and that you may prolong your days in the land which you shall possess.

## 6

¹ Now these are the commandments, the statutes, and the ordinances, which Yahweh your God commanded to teach you, that you might do them in the land that you go over to possess; ² that you might fear Yahweh your God, to keep all his statutes and his commandments, which I command you—you, your son, and your son's son, all the days of your life; and that your days may be prolonged. ³ Hear therefore, Israel, and observe to do it, that it may be well with you, and that you may increase mightily, as Yahweh, the God of your fathers, has promised you, in a land flowing with milk and honey. ⁴ Hear, Israel: Yahweh is our God. Yahweh is one. ⁵ You shall love Yahweh your God with all your heart, with all your soul, and with all your might. ⁶ These

words, which I command you today, shall be on your heart; ⁷ and you shall teach them diligently to your children, and shall talk of them when you sit in your house, and when you walk by the way, and when you lie down, and when you rise up. ⁸ You shall bind them for a sign on your hand, and they shall be for frontlets between your eyes. ⁹ You shall write them on the door posts of your house and on your gates. ¹⁰ It shall be, when Yahweh your God brings you into the land which he swore to your fathers, to Abraham, to Isaac, and to Jacob, to give you, great and goodly cities which you didn't build, ¹¹ and houses full of all good things which you didn't fill, and cisterns dug out which you didn't dig, vineyards and olive trees which you didn't plant, and you shall eat and be full; ¹² then beware lest you forget Yahweh, who brought you out of the land of Egypt, out of the house of bondage. ¹³ You shall fear Yahweh your God; and you shall serve him, and shall swear by his name. ¹⁴ You shall not go after other gods, of the gods of the peoples who are around you, ¹⁵ for Yahweh your God among you is a jealous God, lest the anger of Yahweh your God be kindled against you, and he destroy you from off the face of the earth. ¹⁶ You shall not tempt Yahweh your God, as you tempted him in Massah. ¹⁷ You shall diligently keep the commandments of Yahweh your God, and his testimonies, and his statutes, which he has commanded you. ¹⁸ You shall do that which is right and good in Yahweh's sight, that it may be well with you and that you may go in and possess the good land which Yahweh swore to your fathers, ¹⁹ to thrust out all your enemies from before you, as Yahweh has spoken. ²⁰ When your son asks you in time to come, saying, "What do the testimonies, the statutes, and the ordinances, which Yahweh our God has commanded you mean?" ²¹ then you shall tell your son, "We were Pharaoh's slaves in Egypt. Yahweh brought us out of Egypt with a mighty hand; ²² and Yahweh showed great and awesome signs and wonders on Egypt, on Pharaoh, and on all his house, before our eyes; ²³ and he brought us out from there, that he might bring us in, to give us the land which he swore to our fathers. ²⁴ Yahweh commanded us to do all these statutes, to fear Yahweh our God, for our good always, that he might preserve us alive, as we are today. ²⁵ It shall be righteousness to us, if we observe to do all these commandments before Yahweh our God, as he has commanded us."

## 7

¹ When Yahweh your God brings you into the land where you go to possess it, and casts out many nations before you—the Hittite, the Girgashite, the Amorite, the Canaanite, the Perizzite, the Hivite, and the Jebusite—seven nations greater and mightier than you; ² and when Yahweh your God delivers them up before you, and you strike them, then you shall utterly destroy them. You shall make no covenant with them, nor show mercy to them. ³ You shall not make marriages with them. You shall not give your daughter to his son, nor shall you take his daughter for your son. ⁴ For that would turn away your sons from following me, that they may serve other gods. So Yahweh's anger would be kindled against you, and he would destroy you quickly. ⁵ But you shall deal with them like this: you shall break down their altars, dash their pillars in pieces, cut down their Asherah poles, and burn their engraved images with fire. ⁶ For you are a holy people to Yahweh your God. Yahweh your God has chosen you to be a people for his own possession, above all peoples who are on the face of the earth. ⁷ Yahweh didn't set his love on you nor choose you, because you were more in number than any people; for you were the fewest of all peoples; ⁸ but because Yahweh loves you, and because he desires to keep the oath which he swore to your fathers, Yahweh has brought you out with a mighty hand and redeemed you out of the house of bondage, from the hand of Pharaoh king of Egypt. ⁹ Know therefore that Yahweh your God himself is God, the faithful God, who keeps covenant and loving kindness to a thousand generations with those who love him and keep his commandments, ¹⁰ and repays those who hate him to their face, to destroy them. He will not be slack to him who hates him. He will repay him to his face. ¹¹ You shall therefore keep the commandments, the statutes, and the ordinances which I command you today, to do them. ¹² It shall happen, because you listen to these ordinances and keep and do them, that Yahweh your God will keep with you the covenant and the loving kindness which he swore to your fathers. ¹³ He will love you, bless you, and multiply you. He will also bless the fruit of your body and the fruit of your ground, your grain and your new wine and your oil, the increase of your livestock and the young of your flock, in the land which he swore to your fathers to give you. ¹⁴ You will be blessed above all peoples. There won't be male or female barren among you, or among your livestock. ¹⁵ Yahweh will take away from you all sickness; and he will put none of the evil diseases of Egypt, which you

---

ᵃ *5:11 or, You shall not take the name of Yahweh your God in vain;*

know, on you, but will lay them on all those who hate you. ¹⁶ You shall consume all the peoples whom Yahweh your God shall deliver to you. Your eye shall not pity them. You shall not serve their gods; for that would be a snare to you. ¹⁷ If you shall say in your heart, "These nations are more than I; how can I dispossess them?" ¹⁸ you shall not be afraid of them. You shall remember well what Yahweh your God did to Pharaoh and to all Egypt: ¹⁹ the great trials which your eyes saw, the signs, the wonders, the mighty hand, and the outstretched arm, by which Yahweh your God brought you out. So shall Yahweh your God do to all the peoples of whom you are afraid. ²⁰ Moreover Yahweh your God will send the hornet among them, until those who are left, and hide themselves, perish from before you. ²¹ You shall not be scared of them; for Yahweh your God is among you, a great and awesome God. ²² Yahweh your God will cast out those nations before you little by little. You may not consume them at once, lest the animals of the field increase on you. ²³ But Yahweh your God will deliver them up before you, and will confuse them with a great confusion, until they are destroyed. ²⁴ He will deliver their kings into your hand, and you shall make their name perish from under the sky. No one will be able to stand before you until you have destroyed them. ²⁵ You shall burn the engraved images of their gods with fire. You shall not covet the silver or the gold that is on them, nor take it for yourself, lest you be snared in it; for it is an abomination to Yahweh your God. ²⁶ You shall not bring an abomination into your house and become a devoted thing like it. You shall utterly detest it. You shall utterly abhor it; for it is a devoted thing.

## 8

¹ You shall observe to do all the commandments which I command you today, that you may live, and multiply, and go in and possess the land which Yahweh swore to your fathers. ² You shall remember all the way which Yahweh your God has led you these forty years in the wilderness, that he might humble you, to test you, to know what was in your heart, whether you would keep his commandments or not. ³ He humbled you, allowed you to be hungry, and fed you with manna, which you didn't know, neither did your fathers know, that he might teach you that man does not live by bread only, but man lives by every word that proceeds out of Yahweh's mouth. ⁴ Your clothing didn't grow old on you, neither did your foot swell, these forty years. ⁵ You shall consider in your heart that as a man disciplines his son, so Yahweh your God disciplines you. ⁶ You shall keep the commandments of Yahweh your God, to walk in his ways, and to fear him. ⁷ For Yahweh your God brings you into a good land, a land of brooks of water, of springs, and underground water flowing into valleys and hills; ⁸ a land of wheat, barley, vines, fig trees, and pomegranates; a land of olive trees and honey; ⁹ a land in which you shall eat bread without scarcity, you shall not lack anything in it; a land whose stones are iron, and out of whose hills you may dig copper. ¹⁰ You shall eat and be full, and you shall bless Yahweh your God for the good land which he has given you. ¹¹ Beware lest you forget Yahweh your God, in not keeping his commandments, his ordinances, and his statutes, which I command you today; ¹² lest, when you have eaten and are full, and have built fine houses and lived in them; ¹³ and when your herds and your flocks multiply, and your silver and your gold is multiplied, and all that you have is multiplied; ¹⁴ then your heart might be lifted up, and you forget Yahweh your God, who brought you out of the land of Egypt, out of the house of bondage; ¹⁵ who led you through the great and terrible wilderness, with venomous snakes and scorpions, and thirsty ground where there was no water; who poured water for you out of the rock of flint; ¹⁶ who fed you in the wilderness with manna, which your fathers didn't know, that he might humble you, and that he might prove you, to do you good at your latter end; ¹⁷ and lest you say in your heart, "My power and the might of my hand has gotten me this wealth." ¹⁸ But you shall remember Yahweh your God, for it is he who gives you power to get wealth, that he may establish his covenant which he swore to your fathers, as it is today. ¹⁹ It shall be, if you shall forget Yahweh your God, and walk after other gods, and serve them and worship them, I testify against you today that you shall surely perish. ²⁰ As the nations that Yahweh makes to perish before you, so you shall perish, because you wouldn't listen to Yahweh your God's voice.

## 9

¹ Hear, Israel! You are to pass over the Jordan today, to go in to dispossess nations greater and mightier than yourself, cities great and fortified up to the sky, ² a people great and tall, the sons of the Anakim, whom you know, and of whom you have heard say, "Who can stand before the sons of Anak?" ³ Know therefore today that Yahweh your God is he who goes over before you as a devouring fire. He will destroy them and he will bring them down before you. So you shall drive them out and make them perish quickly, as Yahweh has spoken to you. ⁴ Don't say in your heart, after Yahweh your God has thrust them out from before you, "For my righteousness Yahweh has brought me in to

possess this land;" because Yahweh drives them out before you because of the wickedness of these nations. ⁵ Not for your righteousness or for the uprightness of your heart do you go in to possess their land; but for the wickedness of these nations Yahweh your God does drive them out from before you, and that he may establish the word which Yahweh swore to your fathers, to Abraham, to Isaac, and to Jacob. ⁶ Know therefore that Yahweh your God doesn't give you this good land to possess for your righteousness, for you are a stiff-necked people. ⁷ Remember, and don't forget, how you provoked Yahweh your God to wrath in the wilderness. From the day that you left the land of Egypt until you came to this place, you have been rebellious against Yahweh. ⁸ Also in Horeb you provoked Yahweh to wrath, and Yahweh was angry with you to destroy you. ⁹ When I had gone up onto the mountain to receive the stone tablets, even the tablets of the covenant which Yahweh made with you, then I stayed on the mountain forty days and forty nights. I neither ate bread nor drank water. ¹⁰ Yahweh delivered to me the two stone tablets written with God's finger. On them were all the words which Yahweh spoke with you on the mountain out of the middle of the fire in the day of the assembly. ¹¹ It came to pass at the end of forty days and forty nights that Yahweh gave me the two stone tablets, even the tablets of the covenant. ¹² Yahweh said to me, "Arise, get down quickly from here; for your people whom you have brought out of Egypt have corrupted themselves. They have quickly turned away from the way which I commanded them. They have made a molten image for themselves!" ¹³ Furthermore Yahweh spoke to me, saying, "I have seen these people, and behold, they are a stiff-necked people. ¹⁴ Leave me alone, that I may destroy them, and blot out their name from under the sky; and I will make of you a nation mightier and greater than they." ¹⁵ So I turned and came down from the mountain, and the mountain was burning with fire. The two tablets of the covenant were in my two hands. ¹⁶ I looked, and behold, you had sinned against Yahweh your God. You had made yourselves a molded calf. You had quickly turned away from the way which Yahweh had commanded you. ¹⁷ I took hold of the two tablets, and threw them out of my two hands, and broke them before your eyes. ¹⁸ I fell down before Yahweh, as at the first, forty days and forty nights. I neither ate bread nor drank water, because of all your sin which you sinned, in doing that which was evil in Yahweh's sight, to provoke him to anger. ¹⁹ For I was afraid of the anger and hot displeasure with which Yahweh was angry against you to destroy you. But Yahweh listened to me that time also. ²⁰ Yahweh was angry enough with Aaron to destroy him. I prayed for Aaron also at the same time. ²¹ I took your sin, the calf which you had made, and burned it with fire, and crushed it, grinding it very small, until it was as fine as dust. I threw its dust into the brook that descended out of the mountain. ²² At Taberah, at Massah, and at Kibroth Hattaavah you provoked Yahweh to wrath. ²³ When Yahweh sent you from Kadesh Barnea, saying, "Go up and possess the land which I have given you," you rebelled against the commandment of Yahweh your God, and you didn't believe him or listen to his voice. ²⁴ You have been rebellious against Yahweh from the day that I knew you. ²⁵ So I fell down before Yahweh the forty days and forty nights that I fell down, because Yahweh had said he would destroy you. ²⁶ I prayed to Yahweh, and said, "Lord Yahweh, don't destroy your people and your inheritance that you have redeemed through your greatness, that you have brought out of Egypt with a mighty hand. ²⁷ Remember your servants, Abraham, Isaac, and Jacob. Don't look at the stubbornness of this people, nor at their wickedness, nor at their sin, ²⁸ lest the land you brought us out from say, 'Because Yahweh was not able to bring them into the land which he promised to them, and because he hated them, he has brought them out to kill them in the wilderness.' ²⁹ Yet they are your people and your inheritance, which you brought out by your great power and by your outstretched arm."

## 10

¹ At that time Yahweh said to me, "Cut two stone tablets like the first, and come up to me onto the mountain, and make an ark of wood. ² I will write on the tablets the words that were on the first tablets which you broke, and you shall put them in the ark." ³ So I made an ark of acacia wood, and cut two stone tablets like the first, and went up onto the mountain, having the two tablets in my hand. ⁴ He wrote on the tablets, according to the first writing, the ten commandments, which Yahweh spoke to you on the mountain out of the middle of the fire in the day of the assembly; and Yahweh gave them to me. ⁵ I turned and came down from the mountain, and put the tablets in the ark which I had made; and there they are as Yahweh commanded me. ⁶(The children of Israel traveled from Beeroth Bene Jaakan to Moserah. There Aaron died, and there he was buried; and Eleazar his son ministered in the priest's office in his place. ⁷ From there they traveled to Gudgodah; and from Gudgodah to Jotbathah, a land of brooks of water. ⁸ At that time Yahweh set apart the tribe of Levi to bear the ark of Yahweh's covenant, to stand before Yahweh to minister to him, and to bless in his

name, to this day. [9] Therefore Levi has no portion nor inheritance with his brothers; Yahweh is his inheritance, according as Yahweh your God spoke to him.) [10] I stayed on the mountain, as at the first time, forty days and forty nights; and Yahweh listened to me that time also. Yahweh would not destroy you. [11] Yahweh said to me, "Arise, take your journey before the people; and they shall go in and possess the land which I swore to their fathers to give to them." [12] Now, Israel, what does Yahweh your God require of you, but to fear Yahweh your God, to walk in all his ways, to love him, and to serve Yahweh your God with all your heart and with all your soul, [13] to keep Yahweh's commandments and statutes, which I command you today for your good? [14] Behold, to Yahweh your God belongs heaven, the heaven of heavens, and the earth, with all that is therein. [15] Only Yahweh had a delight in your fathers to love them, and he chose their offspring after them, even you above all peoples, as it is today. [16] Circumcise therefore the foreskin of your heart, and be no more stiff-necked. [17] For Yahweh your God, he is God of gods and Lord of lords, the great God, the mighty, and the awesome, who doesn't respect persons or take bribes. [18] He executes justice for the fatherless and widow and loves the foreigner in giving him food and clothing. [19] Therefore love the foreigner, for you were foreigners in the land of Egypt. [20] You shall fear Yahweh your God. You shall serve him. You shall cling to him, and you shall swear by his name. [21] He is your praise, and he is your God, who has done for you these great and awesome things which your eyes have seen. [22] Your fathers went down into Egypt with seventy persons; and now Yahweh your God has made you as the stars of the sky for multitude.

## 11

[1] Therefore you shall love Yahweh your God, and keep his instructions, his statutes, his ordinances, and his commandments, always. [2] Know this day—for I don't speak with your children who have not known, and who have not seen the chastisement of Yahweh your God, his greatness, his mighty hand, his outstretched arm, [3] his signs, and his works, which he did in the middle of Egypt to Pharaoh the king of Egypt, and to all his land; [4] and what he did to the army of Egypt, to their horses, and to their chariots; how he made the water of the Red Sea to overflow them as they pursued you, and how Yahweh has destroyed them to this day; [5] and what he did to you in the wilderness until you came to this place; [6] and what he did to Dathan and Abiram, the sons of Eliab, the son of Reuben—how the earth opened its mouth and swallowed them up, with their households, their tents, and every living thing that followed them, in the middle of all Israel; [7] but your eyes have seen all of Yahweh's great work which he did. [8] Therefore you shall keep the entire commandment which I command you today, that you may be strong, and go in and possess the land that you go over to possess; [9] and that you may prolong your days in the land which Yahweh swore to your fathers to give to them and to their offspring, a land flowing with milk and honey. [10] For the land, where you go in to possess isn't like the land of Egypt that you came out of, where you sowed your seed and watered it with your foot, as a garden of herbs; [11] but the land that you go over to possess is a land of hills and valleys which drinks water from the rain of the sky, [12] a land which Yahweh your God cares for. Yahweh your God's eyes are always on it, from the beginning of the year even to the end of the year. [13] It shall happen, if you shall listen diligently to my commandments which I command you today, to love Yahweh your God, and to serve him with all your heart and with all your soul, [14] that I will give the rain for your land in its season, the early rain and the latter rain, that you may gather in your grain, your new wine, and your oil. [15] I will give grass in your fields for your livestock, and you shall eat and be full. [16] Be careful, lest your heart be deceived, and you turn away to serve other gods and worship them; [17] and Yahweh's anger be kindled against you, and he shut up the sky so that there is no rain, and the land doesn't yield its fruit; and you perish quickly from off the good land which Yahweh gives you. [18] Therefore you shall lay up these words of mine in your heart and in your soul. You shall bind them for a sign on your hand, and they shall be for frontlets between your eyes. [19] You shall teach them to your children, talking of them when you sit in your house, when you walk by the way, when you lie down, and when you rise up. [20] You shall write them on the door posts of your house and on your gates; [21] that your days and your children's days may be multiplied in the land which Yahweh swore to your fathers to give them, as the days of the heavens above the earth. [22] For if you shall diligently keep all these commandments which I command you—to do them, to love Yahweh your God, to walk in all his ways, and to cling to him— [23] then Yahweh will drive out all these nations from before you, and you shall dispossess nations greater and mightier than yourselves. [24] Every place on which the sole of your foot treads shall be yours: from the wilderness and Lebanon, from the river, the river Euphrates, even to the western sea shall be your border. [25] No man will be able to stand before you.

Yahweh your God will lay the fear of you and the dread of you on all the land that you tread on, as he has spoken to you. [26] Behold, I set before you today a blessing and a curse: [27] the blessing, if you listen to the commandments of Yahweh your God, which I command you today; [28] and the curse, if you do not listen to the commandments of Yahweh your God, but turn away out of the way which I command you today, to go after other gods which you have not known. [29] It shall happen, when Yahweh your God brings you into the land that you go to possess, that you shall set the blessing on Mount Gerizim, and the curse on Mount Ebal. [30] Aren't they beyond the Jordan, behind the way of the going down of the sun, in the land of the Canaanites who dwell in the Arabah near Gilgal, beside the oaks of Moreh? [31] For you are to pass over the Jordan to go in to possess the land which Yahweh your God gives you, and you shall possess it and dwell in it. [32] You shall observe to do all the statutes and the ordinances which I set before you today.

## 12

[1] These are the statutes and the ordinances which you shall observe to do in the land which Yahweh, the God of your fathers, has given you to possess all the days that you live on the earth. [2] You shall surely destroy all the places in which the nations that you shall dispossess served their gods: on the high mountains, and on the hills, and under every green tree. [3] You shall break down their altars, dash their pillars in pieces, and burn their Asherah poles with fire. You shall cut down the engraved images of their gods. You shall destroy their name out of that place. [4] You shall not do so to Yahweh your God. [5] But to the place which Yahweh your God shall choose out of all your tribes, to put his name there, you shall seek his habitation, and you shall come there. [6] You shall bring your burnt offerings, your sacrifices, your tithes, the wave offering of your hand, your vows, your free will offerings, and the firstborn of your herd and of your flock there. [7] There you shall eat before Yahweh your God, and you shall rejoice in all that you put your hand to, you and your households, in which Yahweh your God has blessed you. [8] You shall not do all the things that we do here today, every man whatever is right in his own eyes; [9] for you haven't yet come to the rest and to the inheritance which Yahweh your God gives you. [10] But when you go over the Jordan and dwell in the land which Yahweh your God causes you to inherit, and he gives you rest from all your enemies around you, so that you dwell in safety, [11] then it shall happen that to the place which Yahweh your God shall choose, to cause his name to dwell there, there you shall bring all that I command you: your burnt offerings, your sacrifices, your tithes, the wave offering of your hand, and all your choice vows which you vow to Yahweh. [12] You shall rejoice before Yahweh your God—you, and your sons, your daughters, your male servants, your female servants, and the Levite who is within your gates, because he has no portion nor inheritance with you. [13] Be careful that you don't offer your burnt offerings in every place that you see; [14] but in the place which Yahweh chooses in one of your tribes, there you shall offer your burnt offerings, and there you shall do all that I command you. [15] Yet you may kill and eat meat within all your gates, after all the desire of your soul, according to Yahweh your God's blessing which he has given you. The unclean and the clean may eat of it, as of the gazelle and the deer. [16] Only you shall not eat the blood. You shall pour it out on the earth like water. [17] You may not eat within your gates the tithe of your grain, or of your new wine, or of your oil, or the firstborn of your herd or of your flock, nor any of your vows which you vow, nor your free will offerings, nor the wave offering of your hand; [18] but you shall eat them before Yahweh your God in the place which Yahweh your God shall choose: you, your son, your daughter, your male servant, your female servant, and the Levite who is within your gates. You shall rejoice before Yahweh your God in all that you put your hand to. [19] Be careful that you don't forsake the Levite as long as you live in your land. [20] When Yahweh your God enlarges your border, as he has promised you, and you say, "I want to eat meat," because your soul desires to eat meat, you may eat meat, after all the desire of your soul. [21] If the place which Yahweh your God shall choose to put his name is too far from you, then you shall kill of your herd and of your flock, which Yahweh has given you, as I have commanded you; and you may eat within your gates, after all the desire of your soul. [22] Even as the gazelle and as the deer is eaten, so you shall eat of it. The unclean and the clean may eat of it alike. [23] Only be sure that you don't eat the blood; for the blood is the life. You shall not eat the life with the meat. [24] You shall not eat it. You shall pour it out on the earth like water. [25] You shall not eat it, that it may go well with you and with your children after you, when you do that which is right in Yahweh's eyes. [26] Only your holy things which you have, and your vows, you shall take and go to the place which Yahweh shall choose. [27] You shall offer your burnt offerings, the meat and the blood, on Yahweh your God's altar. The blood of your sacrifices shall be poured out on Yahweh your God's altar, and you shall eat the meat. [28] Observe and hear all these words which I command you, that it may go well with you and with your

children after you forever, when you do that which is good and right in Yahweh your God's eyes. <sup>29</sup> When Yahweh your God cuts off the nations from before you where you go in to dispossess them, and you dispossess them and dwell in their land, <sup>30</sup> be careful that you are not ensnared to follow them after they are destroyed from before you, and that you not inquire after their gods, saying, "How do these nations serve their gods? I will do likewise." <sup>31</sup> You shall not do so to Yahweh your God; for every abomination to Yahweh, which he hates, they have done to their gods; for they even burn their sons and their daughters in the fire to their gods. <sup>32</sup> Whatever thing I command you, that you shall observe to do. You shall not add to it, nor take away from it.

## 13

<sup>1</sup> If a prophet or a dreamer of dreams arises among you, and he gives you a sign or a wonder, <sup>2</sup> and the sign or the wonder comes to pass, of which he spoke to you, saying, "Let's go after other gods" (which you have not known) "and let's serve them," <sup>3</sup> you shall not listen to the words of that prophet, or to that dreamer of dreams; for Yahweh your God is testing you, to know whether you love Yahweh your God with all your heart and with all your soul. <sup>4</sup> You shall walk after Yahweh your God, fear him, keep his commandments, and obey his voice. You shall serve him, and cling to him. <sup>5</sup> That prophet, or that dreamer of dreams, shall be put to death, because he has spoken rebellion against Yahweh your God, who brought you out of the land of Egypt and redeemed you out of the house of bondage, to draw you aside out of the way which Yahweh your God commanded you to walk in. So you shall remove the evil from among you. <sup>6</sup> If your brother, the son of your mother, or your son, or your daughter, or the wife of your bosom, or your friend who is as your own soul, entices you secretly, saying, "Let's go and serve other gods"—which you have not known, you, nor your fathers; <sup>7</sup> of the gods of the peoples who are around you, near to you, or far off from you, from the one end of the earth even to the other end of the earth— <sup>8</sup> you shall not consent to him nor listen to him; neither shall your eye pity him, neither shall you spare, neither shall you conceal him; <sup>9</sup> but you shall surely kill him. Your hand shall be first on him to put him to death, and afterwards the hands of all the people. <sup>10</sup> You shall stone him to death with stones, because he has sought to draw you away from Yahweh your God, who brought you out of the land of Egypt, out of the house of bondage. <sup>11</sup> All Israel shall hear, and fear, and shall not do any more wickedness like this among you. <sup>12</sup> If you hear about one of your cities, which Yahweh your God gives you to dwell there, that <sup>13</sup> certain wicked fellows have gone out from among you and have drawn away the inhabitants of their city, saying, "Let's go and serve other gods," which you have not known, <sup>14</sup> then you shall inquire, investigate, and ask diligently. Behold, if it is true, and the thing certain, that such abomination was done among you, <sup>15</sup> you shall surely strike the inhabitants of that city with the edge of the sword, destroying it utterly, with all that is therein and its livestock, with the edge of the sword. <sup>16</sup> You shall gather all its plunder into the middle of its street, and shall burn with fire the city, with all of its plunder, to Yahweh your God. It shall be a heap forever. It shall not be built again. <sup>17</sup> Nothing of the devoted thing shall cling to your hand, that Yahweh may turn from the fierceness of his anger and show you mercy, and have compassion on you and multiply you, as he has sworn to your fathers, <sup>18</sup> when you listen to Yahweh your God's voice, to keep all his commandments which I command you today, to do that which is right in Yahweh your God's eyes.

## 14

<sup>1</sup> You are the children of Yahweh your God. You shall not cut yourselves, nor make any baldness between your eyes for the dead. <sup>2</sup> For you are a holy people to Yahweh your God, and Yahweh has chosen you to be a people for his own possession, above all peoples who are on the face of the earth. <sup>3</sup> You shall not eat any abominable thing. <sup>4</sup> These are the animals which you may eat: the ox, the sheep, the goat, <sup>5</sup> the deer, the gazelle, the roebuck, the wild goat, the ibex, the antelope, and the chamois. <sup>6</sup> Every animal that parts the hoof, and has the hoof split in two and chews the cud, among the animals, you may eat. <sup>7</sup> Nevertheless these you shall not eat of them that chew the cud, or of those who have the hoof split: the camel, the hare, and the rabbit. Because they chew the cud but don't part the hoof, they are unclean to you. <sup>8</sup> The pig, because it has a split hoof but doesn't chew the cud, is unclean to you. You shall not eat their meat. You shall not touch their carcasses. <sup>9</sup> These you may eat of all that are in the waters: you may eat whatever has fins and scales. <sup>10</sup> You shall not eat whatever doesn't have fins and scales. It is unclean to you. <sup>11</sup> Of all clean birds you may eat. <sup>12</sup> But these are they of which you shall not eat: the eagle, the vulture, the osprey, <sup>13</sup> the red kite, the falcon, the kite of any kind, <sup>14</sup> every raven of any kind, <sup>15</sup> the ostrich, the owl, the seagull, the hawk of any kind, <sup>16</sup> the little owl, the great owl, the horned owl, <sup>17</sup> the pelican, the vulture, the cormorant, <sup>18</sup> the stork, the heron after its kind, the hoopoe, and the bat. <sup>19</sup> All winged creeping things are unclean to you. They shall not be

eaten. <sup>20</sup> Of all clean birds you may eat. <sup>21</sup> You shall not eat of anything that dies of itself. You may give it to the foreigner living among you who is within your gates, that he may eat it; or you may sell it to a foreigner; for you are a holy people to Yahweh your God. You shall not boil a young goat in its mother's milk. <sup>22</sup> You shall surely tithe all the increase of your seed, that which comes out of the field year by year. <sup>23</sup> You shall eat before Yahweh your God, in the place which he chooses to cause his name to dwell, the tithe of your grain, of your new wine, and of your oil, and the firstborn of your herd and of your flock; that you may learn to fear Yahweh your God always. <sup>24</sup> If the way is too long for you, so that you are not able to carry it because the place which Yahweh your God shall choose to set his name there is too far from you, when Yahweh your God blesses you, <sup>25</sup> then you shall turn it into money, bind up the money in your hand, and shall go to the place which Yahweh your God shall choose. <sup>26</sup> You shall trade the money for whatever your soul desires: for cattle, or for sheep, or for wine, or for strong drink, or for whatever your soul asks of you. You shall eat there before Yahweh your God, and you shall rejoice, you and your household. <sup>27</sup> You shall not forsake the Levite who is within your gates, for he has no portion nor inheritance with you. <sup>28</sup> At the end of every three years you shall bring all the tithe of your increase in the same year, and shall store it within your gates. <sup>29</sup> The Levite, because he has no portion nor inheritance with you, as well as the foreigner living among you, the fatherless, and the widow who are within your gates shall come, and shall eat and be satisfied; that Yahweh your God may bless you in all the work of your hand which you do.

## 15

<sup>1</sup> At the end of every seven years, you shall cancel debts. <sup>2</sup> This is the way it shall be done: every creditor shall release that which he has lent to his neighbor. He shall not require payment from his neighbor and his brother, because Yahweh's release has been proclaimed. <sup>3</sup> Of a foreigner you may require it; but whatever of yours is with your brother, your hand shall release. <sup>4</sup> However there will be no poor with you (for Yahweh will surely bless you in the land which Yahweh your God gives you for an inheritance to possess) <sup>5</sup> if only you diligently listen to Yahweh your God's voice, to observe to do all this commandment which I command you today. <sup>6</sup> For Yahweh your God will bless you, as he promised you. You will lend to many nations, but you will not borrow. You will rule over many nations, but they will not rule over you. <sup>7</sup> If a poor man, one of your brothers, is with you within any of your gates in your land which Yahweh your God gives you, you shall not harden your heart, nor shut your hand from your poor brother; <sup>8</sup> but you shall surely open your hand to him, and shall surely lend him sufficient for his need, which he lacks. <sup>9</sup> Beware that there not be a wicked thought in your heart, saying, "The seventh year, the year of release, is at hand," and your eye be evil against your poor brother and you give him nothing; and he cry to Yahweh against you, and it be sin to you. <sup>10</sup> You shall surely give, and your heart shall not be grieved when you give to him, because it is for this thing Yahweh your God will bless you in all your work and in all that you put your hand to. <sup>11</sup> For the poor will never cease out of the land. Therefore I command you to surely open your hand to your brother, to your needy, and to your poor, in your land. <sup>12</sup> If your brother, a Hebrew man, or a Hebrew woman, is sold to you and serves you six years, then in the seventh year you shall let him go free from you. <sup>13</sup> When you let him go free from you, you shall not let him go empty. <sup>14</sup> You shall furnish him liberally out of your flock, out of your threshing floor, and out of your wine press. As Yahweh your God has blessed you, you shall give to him. <sup>15</sup> You shall remember that you were a slave in the land of Egypt, and Yahweh your God redeemed you. Therefore I command you this thing today. <sup>16</sup> It shall be, if he tells you, "I will not go out from you," because he loves you and your house, because he is well with you, <sup>17</sup> then you shall take an awl, and thrust it through his ear to the door, and he shall be your servant forever. Also to your female servant you shall do likewise. <sup>18</sup> It shall not seem hard to you when you let him go free from you, for he has been double the value of a hired hand as he served you six years. Yahweh your God will bless you in all that you do. <sup>19</sup> You shall dedicate all the firstborn males that are born of your herd and of your flock to Yahweh your God. You shall do no work with the firstborn of your herd, nor shear the firstborn of your flock. <sup>20</sup> You shall eat it before Yahweh your God year by year in the place which Yahweh shall choose, you and your household. <sup>21</sup> If it has any defect—is lame or blind, or has any defect whatever, you shall not sacrifice it to Yahweh your God. <sup>22</sup> You shall eat it within your gates. The unclean and the clean shall eat it alike, as the gazelle and as the deer. <sup>23</sup> Only you shall not eat its blood. You shall pour it out on the ground like water.

## 16

<sup>1</sup> Observe the month of Abib, and keep the Passover to Yahweh your God; for in the month of Abib Yahweh your God brought you out of

Egypt by night. ² You shall sacrifice the Passover to Yahweh your God, of the flock and the herd, in the place which Yahweh shall choose to cause his name to dwell there. ³ You shall eat no leavened bread with it. You shall eat unleavened bread with it seven days, even the bread of affliction (for you came out of the land of Egypt in haste) that you may remember the day when you came out of the land of Egypt all the days of your life. ⁴ No yeast shall be seen with you in all your borders seven days; neither shall any of the meat, which you sacrifice the first day at evening, remain all night until the morning. ⁵ You may not sacrifice the Passover within any of your gates which Yahweh your God gives you; ⁶ but at the place which Yahweh your God shall choose to cause his name to dwell in, there you shall sacrifice the Passover at evening, at the going down of the sun, at the season that you came out of Egypt. ⁷ You shall roast and eat it in the place which Yahweh your God chooses. In the morning you shall return to your tents. ⁸ Six days you shall eat unleavened bread. On the seventh day shall be a solemn assembly to Yahweh your God. You shall do no work. ⁹ You shall count for yourselves seven weeks. From the time you begin to put the sickle to the standing grain you shall begin to count seven weeks. ¹⁰ You shall keep the feast of weeks to Yahweh your God with a tribute of a free will offering of your hand, which you shall give according to how Yahweh your God blesses you. ¹¹ You shall rejoice before Yahweh your God: you, your son, your daughter, your male servant, your female servant, the Levite who is within your gates, the foreigner, the fatherless, and the widow who are among you, in the place which Yahweh your God shall choose to cause his name to dwell there. ¹² You shall remember that you were a slave in Egypt. You shall observe and do these statutes. ¹³ You shall keep the feast of booths seven days, after you have gathered in from your threshing floor and from your wine press. ¹⁴ You shall rejoice in your feast, you, your son, your daughter, your male servant, your female servant, the Levite, the foreigner, the fatherless, and the widow who are within your gates. ¹⁵ You shall keep a feast to Yahweh your God seven days in the place which Yahweh chooses, because Yahweh your God will bless you in all your increase and in all the work of your hands, and you shall be altogether joyful. ¹⁶ Three times in a year all of your males shall appear before Yahweh your God in the place which he chooses: in the feast of unleavened bread, in the feast of weeks, and in the feast of booths. They shall not appear before Yahweh empty. ¹⁷ Every man shall give as he is able, according to Yahweh your God's blessing which he has given you. ¹⁸ You shall make judges and officers in all your gates, which Yahweh your God gives you, according to your tribes; and they shall judge the people with righteous judgment. ¹⁹ You shall not pervert justice. You shall not show partiality. You shall not take a bribe, for a bribe blinds the eyes of the wise and perverts the words of the righteous. ²⁰ You shall follow that which is altogether just, that you may live and inherit the land which Yahweh your God gives you. ²¹ You shall not plant for yourselves an Asherah of any kind of tree beside Yahweh your God's altar, which you shall make for yourselves. ²² Neither shall you set yourself up a sacred stone which Yahweh your God hates.

## 17

¹ You shall not sacrifice to Yahweh your God an ox or a sheep in which is a defect or anything evil; for that is an abomination to Yahweh your God. ² If there is found among you, within any of your gates which Yahweh your God gives you, a man or woman who does that which is evil in Yahweh your God's sight in transgressing his covenant, ³ and has gone and served other gods and worshiped them, or the sun, or the moon, or any of the stars of the sky, which I have not commanded, ⁴ and you are told, and you have heard of it, then you shall inquire diligently. Behold, if it is true, and the thing certain, that such abomination is done in Israel, ⁵ then you shall bring out that man or that woman who has done this evil thing to your gates, even that same man or woman; and you shall stone them to death with stones. ⁶ At the mouth of two witnesses, or three witnesses, he who is to die shall be put to death. At the mouth of one witness he shall not be put to death. ⁷ The hands of the witnesses shall be first on him to put him to death, and afterward the hands of all the people. So you shall remove the evil from among you. ⁸ If there arises a matter too hard for you in judgment, between blood and blood, between plea and plea, and between stroke and stroke, being matters of controversy within your gates, then you shall arise, and go up to the place which Yahweh your God chooses. ⁹ You shall come to the priests who are Levites and to the judge who shall be in those days. You shall inquire, and they shall give you the verdict. ¹⁰ You shall do according to the decisions of the verdict which they shall give you from that place which Yahweh chooses. You shall observe to do according to all that they shall teach you. ¹¹ According to the decisions of the law which they shall teach you, and according to the judgment which they shall tell you, you shall do. You shall not turn away from the sentence which they announce to you, to the right hand, nor to the left. ¹² The man who does presumptuously in not listening to the priest who stands to minister there before Yahweh your God, or to the judge, even that man shall die. You shall put away the evil from Israel. ¹³ All the people shall hear and fear, and do no more presumptuously. ¹⁴ When you have come to the land which Yahweh your God gives you, and possess it and dwell in it, and say, "I will set a king over me, like all the nations that are around me," ¹⁵ you shall surely set him whom Yahweh your God chooses as king over yourselves. You shall set as king over you one from among your brothers. You may not put a foreigner over you, who is not your brother. ¹⁶ Only he shall not multiply horses to himself, nor cause the people to return to Egypt, to the end that he may multiply horses; because Yahweh has said to you, "You shall not go back that way again." ¹⁷ He shall not multiply wives to himself, that his heart not turn away. He shall not greatly multiply to himself silver and gold. ¹⁸ It shall be, when he sits on the throne of his kingdom, that he shall write himself a copy of this law in a book, out of that which is before the Levitical priests. ¹⁹ It shall be with him, and he shall read from it all the days of his life, that he may learn to fear Yahweh his God, to keep all the words of this law and these statutes, to do them; ²⁰ that his heart not be lifted up above his brothers, and that he not turn away from the commandment to the right hand, or to the left, to the end that he may prolong his days in his kingdom, he and his children, in the middle of Israel.

## 18

¹ The priests and the Levites—all the tribe of Levi—shall have no portion nor inheritance with Israel. They shall eat the offerings of Yahweh made by fire and his portion. ² They shall have no inheritance among their brothers. Yahweh is their inheritance, as he has spoken to them. ³ This shall be the priests' due from the people, from those who offer a sacrifice, whether it be ox or sheep, that they shall give to the priest: the shoulder, the two cheeks, and the inner parts. ⁴ You shall give him the first fruits of your grain, of your new wine, and of your oil, and the first of the fleece of your sheep. ⁵ For Yahweh your God has chosen him out of all your tribes to stand to minister in Yahweh's name, him and his sons forever. ⁶ If a Levite comes from any of your gates out of all Israel where he lives, and comes with all the desire of his soul to the place which Yahweh shall choose, ⁷ then he shall minister in the name of Yahweh his God, as all his brothers the Levites do, who stand there before Yahweh. ⁸ They shall have like portions to eat, in addition to that which comes from the sale of his family possessions. ⁹ When you have come into the land which Yahweh your God gives you, you shall not learn to imitate the abominations of those nations. ¹⁰ There shall not be found with you anyone who makes his son or his daughter to pass through the fire, one who uses divination, one who tells fortunes, or an enchanter, or a sorcerer, ¹¹ or a charmer, or someone who consults with a familiar spirit, or a wizard, or a necromancer. ¹² For whoever does these things is an abomination to Yahweh. Because of these abominations, Yahweh your God drives them out from before you. ¹³ You shall be blameless with Yahweh your God. ¹⁴ For these nations that you shall dispossess listen to those who practice sorcery and to diviners; but as for you, Yahweh your God has not allowed you so to do. ¹⁵ Yahweh your God will raise up to you a prophet from among you, of your brothers, like me. You shall listen to him. ¹⁶ This is according to all that you desired of Yahweh your God in Horeb in the day of the assembly, saying, "Let me not hear again Yahweh my God's voice, neither let me see this great fire any more, that I not die." ¹⁷ Yahweh said to me, "They have well said that which they have spoken. ¹⁸ I will raise them up a prophet from among their brothers, like you. I will put my words in his mouth, and he shall speak to them all that I shall command him. ¹⁹ It shall happen, that whoever will not listen to my words which he shall speak in my name, I will require it of him. ²⁰ But the prophet who speaks a word presumptuously in my name, which I have not commanded him to speak, or who speaks in the name of other gods, that same prophet shall die." ²¹ You may say in your heart, "How shall we know the word which Yahweh has not spoken?" ²² When a prophet speaks in Yahweh's name, if the thing doesn't follow, nor happen, that is the thing which Yahweh has not spoken. The prophet has spoken it presumptuously. You shall not be afraid of him.

## 19

¹ When Yahweh your God cuts off the nations whose land Yahweh your God gives you, and you succeed them and dwell in their cities and in their houses, ² you shall set apart three cities for yourselves in the middle of your land, which Yahweh your God gives you to possess. ³ You shall prepare the way, and divide the borders of your land which Yahweh your God causes you to inherit into three parts, that every man slayer may flee there. ⁴ This is the case of the man slayer who shall flee there and live: Whoever kills his neighbor unintentionally, and didn't hate him in time past— ⁵ as when a man goes into the forest with his neighbor to chop wood and his hand swings the ax to cut down the tree, and the head slips from the handle and hits his neighbor so that he dies—he shall flee to one of these cities and live. ⁶ Otherwise, the

avenger of blood might pursue the man slayer while hot anger is in his heart and overtake him, because the way is long, and strike him mortally, even though he was not worthy of death, because he didn't hate him in time past. ⁷ Therefore I command you to set apart three cities for yourselves. ⁸ If Yahweh your God enlarges your border, as he has sworn to your fathers, and gives you all the land which he promised to give to your fathers; ⁹ and if you keep all this commandment to do it, which I command you today, to love Yahweh your God, and to walk ever in his ways, then you shall add three cities more for yourselves, in addition to these three. ¹⁰ This is so that innocent blood will not be shed in the middle of your land which Yahweh your God gives you for an inheritance, leaving blood guilt on you. ¹¹ But if any man hates his neighbor, lies in wait for him, rises up against him, strikes him mortally so that he dies, and he flees into one of these cities; ¹² then the elders of his city shall send and bring him there, and deliver him into the hand of the avenger of blood, that he may die. ¹³ Your eye shall not pity him, but you shall purge the innocent blood from Israel that it may go well with you. ¹⁴ You shall not remove your neighbor's landmark, which they of old time have set, in your inheritance which you shall inherit, in the land that Yahweh your God gives you to possess. ¹⁵ One witness shall not rise up against a man for any iniquity, or for any sin that he sins. At the mouth of two witnesses, or at the mouth of three witnesses, shall a matter be established. ¹⁶ If an unrighteous witness rises up against any man to testify against him of wrongdoing, ¹⁷ then both the men, between whom the controversy is, shall stand before Yahweh, before the priests and the judges who shall be in those days; ¹⁸ and the judges shall make diligent inquisition; and behold, if the witness is a false witness, and has testified falsely against his brother, ¹⁹ then you shall do to him as he had thought to do to his brother. So you shall remove the evil from among you. ²⁰ Those who remain shall hear, and fear, and will never again commit any such evil among you. ²¹ Your eyes shall not pity: life for life, eye for eye, tooth for tooth, hand for hand, foot for foot.

## 20

¹ When you go out to battle against your enemies, and see horses, chariots, and a people more numerous than you, you shall not be afraid of them; for Yahweh your God, who brought you up out of the land of Egypt, is with you. ² It shall be, when you draw near to the battle, that the priest shall approach and speak to the people, ³ and shall tell them, "Hear, Israel, you draw near today to battle against your enemies. Don't let your heart faint! Don't be afraid, nor tremble, neither be scared of them; ⁴ for Yahweh your God is he who goes with you, to fight for you against your enemies, to save you." ⁵ The officers shall speak to the people, saying, "What man is there who has built a new house, and has not dedicated it? Let him go and return to his house, lest he die in the battle, and another man dedicate it. ⁶ What man is there who has planted a vineyard, and has not used its fruit? Let him go and return to his house, lest he die in the battle, and another man use its fruit. ⁷ What man is there who has pledged to be married to a wife, and has not taken her? Let him go and return to his house, lest he die in the battle, and another man take her." ⁸ The officers shall speak further to the people, and they shall say, "What man is there who is fearful and faint-hearted? Let him go and return to his house, lest his brother's heart melt as his heart." ⁹ It shall be, when the officers have finished speaking to the people, that they shall appoint captains of armies at the head of the people. ¹⁰ When you draw near to a city to fight against it, then proclaim peace to it. ¹¹ It shall be, if it gives you answer of peace and opens to you, then it shall be that all the people who are found therein shall become forced laborers to you, and shall serve you. ¹² If it will make no peace with you, but will make war against you, then you shall besiege it. ¹³ When Yahweh your God delivers it into your hand, you shall strike every male of it with the edge of the sword; ¹⁴ but the women, the little ones, the livestock, and all that is in the city, even all its plunder, you shall take for plunder for yourself. You may use the plunder of your enemies, which Yahweh your God has given you. ¹⁵ Thus you shall do to all the cities which are very far off from you, which are not of the cities of these nations. ¹⁶ But of the cities of these peoples that Yahweh your God gives you for an inheritance, you shall save alive nothing that breathes; ¹⁷ but you shall utterly destroy them: the Hittite, the Amorite, the Canaanite, the Perizzite, the Hivite, and the Jebusite, as Yahweh your God has commanded you; ¹⁸ that they not teach you to follow all their abominations, which they have done for their gods; so would you sin against Yahweh your God. ¹⁹ When you shall besiege a city a long time, in making war against it to take it, you shall not destroy its trees by wielding an ax against them; for you may eat of them. You shall not cut them down, for is the tree of the field man, that it should be besieged by you? ²⁰ Only the trees that you know are not trees for food, you shall destroy and cut them down. You shall build bulwarks against the city that makes war with you, until it falls.

## 21

¹ If someone is found slain in the land which Yahweh your God gives you to possess, lying in the field, and it isn't known who has struck him, ² then your elders and your judges shall come out, and they shall measure to the cities which are around him who is slain. ³ It shall be that the elders of the city which is nearest to the slain man shall take a heifer of the herd, which hasn't been worked with and which has not drawn in the yoke. ⁴ The elders of that city shall bring the heifer down to a valley with running water, which is neither plowed nor sown, and shall break the heifer's neck there in the valley. ⁵ The priests the sons of Levi shall come near, for them Yahweh your God has chosen to minister to him, and to bless in Yahweh's name; and according to their word shall every controversy and every assault be decided. ⁶ All the elders of that city which is nearest to the slain man shall wash their hands over the heifer whose neck was broken in the valley. ⁷ They shall answer and say, "Our hands have not shed this blood, neither have our eyes seen it. ⁸ Forgive, Yahweh, your people Israel, whom you have redeemed, and don't allow innocent blood among your people Israel." The blood shall be forgiven them. ⁹ So you shall put away the innocent blood from among you, when you shall do that which is right in Yahweh's eyes. ¹⁰ When you go out to battle against your enemies, and Yahweh your God delivers them into your hands and you carry them away captive, ¹¹ and see among the captives a beautiful woman, and you are attracted to her, and desire to take her as your wife, ¹² then you shall bring her home to your house. She shall shave her head and trim her nails. ¹³ She shall take off the clothing of her captivity, and shall remain in your house, and bewail her father and her mother a full month. After that you shall go in to her and be her husband, and she shall be your wife. ¹⁴ It shall be, if you have no delight in her, then you shall let her go where she desires; but you shall not sell her at all for money. You shall not deal with her as a slave, because you have humbled her. ¹⁵ If a man has two wives, the one beloved and the other hated, and they have borne him children, both the beloved and the hated, and if the firstborn son is hers who was hated, ¹⁶ then it shall be, in the day that he causes his sons to inherit that which he has, that he may not give the son of the beloved the rights of the firstborn before the son of the hated, who is the firstborn; ¹⁷ but he shall acknowledge the firstborn, the son of the hated, by giving him a double portion of all that he has; for he is the beginning of his strength. The right of the firstborn is his. ¹⁸ If a man has a stubborn and rebellious son who will not obey the voice of his father or the voice of his mother, and though they chasten him, will not listen to them, ¹⁹ then his father and his mother shall take hold of him and bring him out to the elders of his city and to the gate of his place. ²⁰ They shall tell the elders of his city, "This our son is stubborn and rebellious. He will not obey our voice. He is a glutton and a drunkard." ²¹ All the men of his city shall stone him to death with stones. So you shall remove the evil from among you. All Israel shall hear, and fear. ²² If a man has committed a sin worthy of death, and he is put to death, and you hang him on a tree, ²³ his body shall not remain all night on the tree, but you shall surely bury him the same day; for he who is hanged is accursed of God. Don't defile your land which Yahweh your God gives you for an inheritance.

## 22

¹ You shall not see your brother's ox or his sheep go astray and hide yourself from them. You shall surely bring them again to your brother. ² If your brother isn't near to you, or if you don't know him, then you shall bring it home to your house, and it shall be with you until your brother comes looking for it, and you shall restore it to him. ³ So you shall do with his donkey. So you shall do with his garment. So you shall do with every lost thing of your brother's, which he has lost and you have found. You may not hide yourself. ⁴ You shall not see your brother's donkey or his ox fallen down by the way, and hide yourself from them. You shall surely help him to lift them up again. ⁵ A woman shall not wear men's clothing, neither shall a man put on women's clothing; for whoever does these things is an abomination to Yahweh your God. ⁶ If you come across a bird's nest on the way, in any tree or on the ground, with young ones or eggs, and the hen sitting on the young, or on the eggs, you shall not take the hen with the young. ⁷ You shall surely let the hen go, but the young you may take for yourself, that it may be well with you, and that you may prolong your days. ⁸ When you build a new house, then you shall make a railing around your roof, so that you don't bring blood on your house if anyone falls from there. ⁹ You shall not sow your vineyard with two kinds of seed, lest all the fruit be defiled, the seed which you have sown, and the increase of the vineyard. ¹⁰ You shall not plow with an ox and a donkey together. ¹¹ You shall not wear clothes of wool and linen woven together. ¹² You

shall make yourselves fringes[a] on the four corners of your cloak with which you cover yourself. [13] If any man takes a wife, and goes in to her, hates her, [14] accuses her of shameful things, gives her a bad name, and says, "I took this woman, and when I came near to her, I didn't find in her the tokens of virginity;" [15] then the young lady's father and mother shall take and bring the tokens of the young lady's virginity to the elders of the city in the gate. [16] The young lady's father shall tell the elders, "I gave my daughter to this man as his wife, and he hates her. [17] Behold, he has accused her of shameful things, saying, 'I didn't find in your daughter the tokens of virginity;' and yet these are the tokens of my daughter's virginity." They shall spread the cloth before the elders of the city. [18] The elders of that city shall take the man and chastise him. [19] They shall fine him one hundred shekels of silver,[b] and give them to the father of the young lady, because he has given a bad name to a virgin of Israel. She shall be his wife. He may not put her away all his days. [20] But if this thing is true, that the tokens of virginity were not found in the young lady, [21] then they shall bring out the young lady to the door of her father's house, and the men of her city shall stone her to death with stones, because she has done folly in Israel, to play the prostitute in her father's house. So you shall remove the evil from among you. [22] If a man is found lying with a woman married to a husband, then they shall both die, the man who lay with the woman and the woman. So you shall remove the evil from Israel. [23] If there is a young lady who is a virgin pledged to be married to a husband, and a man finds her in the city, and lies with her, [24] then you shall bring them both out to the gate of that city, and you shall stone them to death with stones; the lady, because she didn't cry, being in the city; and the man, because he has humbled his neighbor's wife. So you shall remove the evil from among you. [25] But if the man finds the lady who is pledged to be married in the field, and the man forces her and lies with her, then only the man who lay with her shall die; [26] but to the lady you shall do nothing. There is in the lady no sin worthy of death; for as when a man rises against his neighbor and kills him, even so is this matter; [27] for he found her in the field, the pledged to be married lady cried, and there was no one to save her. [28] If a man finds a lady who is a virgin, who is not pledged to be married, grabs her and lies with her, and they are found, [29] then the man who lay with her shall give to the lady's father fifty shekels[c] of silver. She shall be his wife, because he has humbled her. He may not put her away all his days. [30] A man shall not take his father's wife, and shall not uncover his father's skirt.

## 23

[1] He who is emasculated by crushing or cutting shall not enter into Yahweh's assembly. [2] A person born of a forbidden union shall not enter into Yahweh's assembly; even to the tenth generation shall no one of his enter into Yahweh's assembly. [3] An Ammonite or a Moabite shall not enter into Yahweh's assembly; even to the tenth generation shall no one belonging to them enter into Yahweh's assembly forever, [4] because they didn't meet you with bread and with water on the way when you came out of Egypt, and because they hired against you Balaam the son of Beor from Pethor of Mesopotamia, to curse you. [5] Nevertheless Yahweh your God wouldn't listen to Balaam, but Yahweh your God turned the curse into a blessing to you, because Yahweh your God loved you. [6] You shall not seek their peace nor their prosperity all your days forever. [7] You shall not abhor an Edomite, for he is your brother. You shall not abhor an Egyptian, because you lived as a foreigner in his land. [8] The children of the third generation who are born to them may enter into Yahweh's assembly. [9] When you go out and camp against your enemies, then you shall keep yourselves from every evil thing. [10] If there is among you any man who is not clean by reason of that which happens to him by night, then shall he go outside of the camp. He shall not come within the camp; [11] but it shall be, when evening comes, he shall bathe himself in water. When the sun is down, he shall come within the camp. [12] You shall have a place also outside of the camp where you go relieve yourself. [13] You shall have a trowel among your weapons. It shall be, when you relieve yourself, you shall dig with it, and shall turn back and cover your excrement; [14] for Yahweh your God walks in the middle of your camp, to deliver you, and to give up your enemies before you. Therefore your camp shall be holy, that he may not see an unclean thing in you, and turn away from you. [15] You shall not deliver to his master a servant who has escaped from his master to you. [16] He shall dwell with you, among you, in the place which he shall choose within one of your gates, where it pleases him best. You shall not oppress him. [17] There shall be no prostitute of the daughters of Israel, neither shall there be a sodomite of the sons of Israel. [18] You shall not bring the hire of a prostitute, or the wages of a male prostitute,[d] into the house of Yahweh your God for any vow; for both of these are an abomination to Yahweh your God. [19] You shall not lend on interest to your brother: interest of money, interest of food, interest of anything that is lent on interest. [20] You may charge a foreigner interest; but you shall not charge your brother interest, that Yahweh your God may bless you in all that you put your hand to, in the land where you go in to possess it. [21] When you vow a vow to Yahweh your God, you shall not be slack to pay it, for Yahweh your God will surely require it of you; and it would be sin in you. [22] But if you refrain from making a vow, it shall be no sin in you. [23] You shall observe and do that which has gone out of your lips. Whatever you have vowed to Yahweh your God as a free will offering, which you have promised with your mouth, you must do. [24] When you come into your neighbor's vineyard, then you may eat your fill of grapes at your own pleasure; but you shall not put any in your container. [25] When you come into your neighbor's standing grain, then you may pluck the ears with your hand; but you shall not use a sickle on your neighbor's standing grain.

## 24

[1] When a man takes a wife and marries her, then it shall be, if she finds no favor in his eyes because he has found some unseemly thing in her, that he shall write her a certificate of divorce, put it in her hand, and send her out of his house. [2] When she has departed out of his house, she may go and be another man's wife. [3] If the latter husband hates her, and writes her a certificate of divorce, puts it in her hand, and sends her out of his house; or if the latter husband dies, who took her to be his wife; [4] her former husband, who sent her away, may not take her again to be his wife after she is defiled; for that would be an abomination to Yahweh. You shall not cause the land to sin, which Yahweh your God gives you for an inheritance. [5] When a man takes a new wife, he shall not go out in the army, neither shall he be assigned any business. He shall be free at home one year, and shall cheer his wife whom he has taken. [6] No man shall take the mill or the upper millstone as a pledge, for he takes a life in pledge. [7] If a man is found stealing any of his brothers of the children of Israel, and he deals with him as a slave, or sells him, then that thief shall die. So you shall remove the evil from among you. [8] Be careful in the plague of leprosy, that you observe diligently and do according to all that the Levitical priests teach you. As I commanded them, so you shall observe to do. [9] Remember what Yahweh your God did to Miriam, by the way as you came out of Egypt. [10] When you lend your neighbor any kind of loan, you shall not go into his house to get his pledge. [11] You shall stand outside, and the man to whom you lend shall bring the pledge outside to you. [12] If he is a poor man, you shall not sleep with his pledge. [13] You shall surely restore to him the pledge when the sun goes down, that he may sleep in his garment and bless you. It shall be righteousness to you before Yahweh your God. [14] You shall not oppress a hired servant who is poor and needy, whether he is one of your brothers or one of the foreigners who are in your land within your gates. [15] In his day you shall give him his wages, neither shall the sun go down on it, for he is poor and sets his heart on it, lest he cry against you to Yahweh, and it be sin to you. [16] The fathers shall not be put to death for the children, neither shall the children be put to death for the fathers. Every man shall be put to death for his own sin. [17] You shall not deprive the foreigner or the fatherless of justice, nor take a widow's clothing in pledge; [18] but you shall remember that you were a slave in Egypt, and Yahweh your God redeemed you there. Therefore I command you to do this thing. [19] When you reap your harvest in your field, and have forgotten a sheaf in the field, you shall not go again to get it. It shall be for the foreigner, for the fatherless, and for the widow, that Yahweh your God may bless you in all the work of your hands. [20] When you beat your olive tree, you shall not go over the boughs again. It shall be for the foreigner, for the fatherless, and for the widow. [21] When you harvest your vineyard, you shall not glean it after yourselves. It shall be for the foreigner, for the fatherless, and for the widow. [22] You shall remember that you were a slave in the land of Egypt. Therefore I command you to do this thing.

## 25

[1] If there is a controversy between men, and they come to judgment and the judges judge them, then they shall justify the righteous and condemn the wicked. [2] It shall be, if the wicked man is worthy to be beaten, that the judge shall cause him to lie down and to be beaten before his face, according to his wickedness, by number. [3] He may sentence him to no more than forty stripes. He shall not give more, lest if he should give more and beat him more than that many stripes, then your brother will be degraded in your sight. [4] You shall not muzzle the ox when he treads out the grain. [5] If brothers dwell together, and one of them dies and has no son, the wife of the dead shall not be married outside to a stranger. Her husband's brother shall go in to her, and take

---

[a] 22:12 or, tassels
[b] 22:19 A shekel is about 10 grams or about 0.35 ounces, so

100 shekels is about a kilogram or 2.2 pounds.

[c] 22:29 A shekel is about 10 grams or about 0.35 ounces.
[d] 23:18 literally, dog

her as his wife, and perform the duty of a husband's brother to her. ⁶ It shall be that the firstborn whom she bears shall succeed in the name of his brother who is dead, that his name not be blotted out of Israel. ⁷ If the man doesn't want to take his brother's wife, then his brother's wife shall go up to the gate to the elders, and say, "My husband's brother refuses to raise up to his brother a name in Israel. He will not perform the duty of a husband's brother to me." ⁸ Then the elders of his city shall call him, and speak to him. If he stands and says, "I don't want to take her," ⁹ then his brother's wife shall come to him in the presence of the elders, and loose his sandal from off his foot, and spit in his face. She shall answer and say, "So shall it be done to the man who does not build up his brother's house." ¹⁰ His name shall be called in Israel, "The house of him who had his sandal removed." ¹¹ When men strive against each other, and the wife of one draws near to deliver her husband out of the hand of him who strikes him, and puts out her hand, and grabs him by his private parts, ¹² then you shall cut off her hand. Your eye shall have no pity. ¹³ You shall not have in your bag diverse weights, one heavy and one light. ¹⁴ You shall not have in your house diverse measures, one large and one small. ¹⁵ You shall have a perfect and just weight. You shall have a perfect and just measure, that your days may be long in the land which Yahweh your God gives you. ¹⁶ For all who do such things, all who do unrighteously, are an abomination to Yahweh your God. ¹⁷ Remember what Amalek did to you by the way as you came out of Egypt, ¹⁸ how he met you by the way, and struck the rearmost of you, all who were feeble behind you, when you were faint and weary; and he didn't fear God. ¹⁹ Therefore it shall be, when Yahweh your God has given you rest from all your enemies all around, in the land which Yahweh your God gives you for an inheritance to possess it, that you shall blot out the memory of Amalek from under the sky. You shall not forget.

## 26

¹ It shall be, when you have come in to the land which Yahweh your God gives you for an inheritance, possess it, and dwell in it, ² that you shall take some of the first of all the fruit of the ground, which you shall bring in from your land that Yahweh your God gives you. You shall put it in a basket, and shall go to the place which Yahweh your God shall choose to cause his name to dwell there. ³ You shall come to the priest who shall be in those days, and tell him, "I profess today to Yahweh your God, that I have come to the land which Yahweh swore to our fathers to give us." ⁴ The priest shall take the basket out of your hand, and set it down before Yahweh your God's altar. ⁵ You shall answer and say before Yahweh your God, "My fatherᵃ was a Syrian ready to perish. He went down into Egypt, and lived there, few in number. There he became a great, mighty, and populous nation. ⁶ The Egyptians mistreated us, afflicted us, and imposed hard labor on us. ⁷ Then we cried to Yahweh, the God of our fathers. Yahweh heard our voice, and saw our affliction, our toil, and our oppression. ⁸ Yahweh brought us out of Egypt with a mighty hand, with an outstretched arm, with great terror, with signs, and with wonders; ⁹ and he has brought us into this place, and has given us this land, a land flowing with milk and honey. ¹⁰ Now, behold, I have brought the first of the fruit of the ground, which you, Yahweh, have given me." You shall set it down before Yahweh your God, and worship before Yahweh your God. ¹¹ You shall rejoice in all the good which Yahweh your God has given to you, and to your house, you, and the Levite, and the foreigner who is among you. ¹² When you have finished tithing all the tithe of your increase in the third year, which is the year of tithing, then you shall give it to the Levite, to the foreigner, to the fatherless, and to the widow, that they may eat within your gates and be filled. ¹³ You shall say before Yahweh your God, "I have put away the holy things out of my house, and also have given them to the Levite, to the foreigner, to the fatherless, and to the widow, according to all your commandment which you have commanded me. I have not transgressed any of your commandments, neither have I forgotten them. ¹⁴ I have not eaten of it in my mourning, neither have I removed any of it while I was unclean, nor given of it for the dead. I have listened to Yahweh my God's voice. I have done according to all that you have commanded me. ¹⁵ Look down from your holy habitation, from heaven, and bless your people Israel, and the ground which you have given us, as you swore to our fathers, a land flowing with milk and honey." ¹⁶ Today Yahweh your God commands you to do these statutes and ordinances. You shall therefore keep and do them with all your heart and with all your soul. ¹⁷ You have declared today that Yahweh is your God, and that you would walk in his ways, keep his statutes, his commandments, and his ordinances, and listen to his voice. ¹⁸ Yahweh has declared today that you are a people for his own possession, as he has promised you, and that you should keep all his commandments. ¹⁹ He will make you high above all nations that he

has made, in praise, in name, and in honor, and that you may be a holy people to Yahweh your God, as he has spoken.

## 27

¹ Moses and the elders of Israel commanded the people, saying, "Keep all the commandment which I command you today. ² It shall be on the day when you shall pass over the Jordan to the land which Yahweh your God gives you, that you shall set yourself up great stones, and coat them with plaster. ³ You shall write on them all the words of this law, when you have passed over, that you may go in to the land which Yahweh your God gives you, a land flowing with milk and honey, as Yahweh, the God of your fathers, has promised you. ⁴ It shall be, when you have crossed over the Jordan, that you shall set up these stones, which I command you today, on Mount Ebal, and you shall coat them with plaster. ⁵ There you shall build an altar to Yahweh your God, an altar of stones. You shall not use any iron tool on them. ⁶ You shall build Yahweh your God's altar of uncut stones. You shall offer burnt offerings on it to Yahweh your God. ⁷ You shall sacrifice peace offerings, and shall eat there. You shall rejoice before Yahweh your God. ⁸ You shall write on the stones all the words of this law very plainly." ⁹ Moses and the Levitical priests spoke to all Israel, saying, "Be silent and listen, Israel! Today you have become the people of Yahweh your God. ¹⁰ You shall therefore obey Yahweh your God's voice, and do his commandments and his statutes, which I command you today." ¹¹ Moses commanded the people the same day, saying, ¹²"These shall stand on Mount Gerizim to bless the people, when you have crossed over the Jordan: Simeon, Levi, Judah, Issachar, Joseph, and Benjamin. ¹³ These shall stand on Mount Ebal for the curse: Reuben, Gad, Asher, Zebulun, Dan, and Naphtali. ¹⁴ With a loud voice, the Levites shall say to all the men of Israel, ¹⁵'Cursed is the man who makes an engraved or molten image, an abomination to Yahweh, the work of the hands of the craftsman, and sets it up in secret.' All the people shall answer and say, 'Amen.' ¹⁶'Cursed is he who dishonors his father or his mother.' All the people shall say, 'Amen.' ¹⁷'Cursed is he who removes his neighbor's landmark.' All the people shall say, 'Amen.' ¹⁸'Cursed is he who leads the blind astray on the road.' All the people shall say, 'Amen.' ¹⁹'Cursed is he who withholds justice from the foreigner, fatherless, and widow.' All the people shall say, 'Amen.' ²⁰'Cursed is he who lies withᵇ his father's wife, because he dishonors his father's bed.' All the people shall say, 'Amen.' ²¹'Cursed is he who lies with any kind of animal.' All the people shall say, 'Amen.' ²²'Cursed is he who lies with his sister, his father's daughter or his mother's daughter.' All the people shall say, 'Amen.' ²³'Cursed is he who lies with his mother-in-law.' All the people shall say, 'Amen.' ²⁴'Cursed is he who secretly kills his neighbor.' All the people shall say, 'Amen.' ²⁵'Cursed is he who takes a bribe to kill an innocent person.' All the people shall say, 'Amen.' ²⁶'Cursed is he who doesn't uphold the words of this law by doing them.' All the people shall say, 'Amen.'"

## 28

¹ It shall happen, if you shall listen diligently to Yahweh your God's voice, to observe to do all his commandments which I command you today, that Yahweh your God will set you high above all the nations of the earth. ² All these blessings will come upon you, and overtake you, if you listen to Yahweh your God's voice. ³ You shall be blessed in the city, and you shall be blessed in the field. ⁴ You shall be blessed in the fruit of your body, the fruit of your ground, the fruit of your animals, the increase of your livestock, and the young of your flock. ⁵ Your basket and your kneading trough shall be blessed. ⁶ You shall be blessed when you come in, and you shall be blessed when you go out. ⁷ Yahweh will cause your enemies who rise up against you to be struck before you. They will come out against you one way, and will flee before you seven ways. ⁸ Yahweh will command the blessing on you in your barns, and in all that you put your hand to. He will bless you in the land which Yahweh your God gives you. ⁹ Yahweh will establish you for a holy people to himself, as he has sworn to you, if you shall keep the commandments of Yahweh your God, and walk in his ways. ¹⁰ All the peoples of the earth shall see that you are called by Yahweh's name, and they will be afraid of you. ¹¹ Yahweh will grant you abundant prosperity in the fruit of your body, in the fruit of your livestock, and in the fruit of your ground, in the land which Yahweh swore to your fathers to give you. ¹² Yahweh will open to you his good treasure in the sky, to give the rain of your land in its season, and to bless all the work of your hand. You will lend to many nations, and you will not borrow. ¹³ Yahweh will make you the head, and not the tail. You will be above only, and you will not be beneath, if you listen to the commandments of Yahweh your God which I command you today, to observe and to do, ¹⁴ and shall not turn away from any of the words which I command

---

ᵃ 26:5 or, forefather

ᵇ 27:20 i.e., has sexual relations with

you today, to the right hand or to the left, to go after other gods to serve them. ¹⁵ But it shall come to pass, if you will not listen to Yahweh your God's voice, to observe to do all his commandments and his statutes which I command you today, that all these curses will come on you and overtake you. ¹⁶ You will be cursed in the city, and you will be cursed in the field. ¹⁷ Your basket and your kneading trough will be cursed. ¹⁸ The fruit of your body, the fruit of your ground, the increase of your livestock, and the young of your flock will be cursed. ¹⁹ You will be cursed when you come in, and you will be cursed when you go out. ²⁰ Yahweh will send on you cursing, confusion, and rebuke in all that you put your hand to do, until you are destroyed and until you perish quickly, because of the evil of your doings, by which you have forsaken me. ²¹ Yahweh will make the pestilence cling to you, until he has consumed you from off the land where you go in to possess it. ²² Yahweh will strike you with consumption, with fever, with inflammation, with fiery heat, with the sword, with blight, and with mildew. They will pursue you until you perish. ²³ Your sky that is over your head will be bronze, and the earth that is under you will be iron. ²⁴ Yahweh will make the rain of your land powder and dust. It will come down on you from the sky, until you are destroyed. ²⁵ Yahweh will cause you to be struck before your enemies. You will go out one way against them, and will flee seven ways before them. You will be tossed back and forth among all the kingdoms of the earth. ²⁶ Your dead bodies will be food to all birds of the sky, and to the animals of the earth; and there will be no one to frighten them away. ²⁷ Yahweh will strike you with the boils of Egypt, with the tumors, with the scurvy, and with the itch, of which you can not be healed. ²⁸ Yahweh will strike you with madness, with blindness, and with astonishment of heart. ²⁹ You will grope at noonday, as the blind gropes in darkness, and you shall not prosper in your ways. You will only be oppressed and robbed always, and there will be no one to save you. ³⁰ You will betroth a wife, and another man shall lie with her. You will build a house, and you won't dwell in it. You will plant a vineyard, and not use its fruit. ³¹ Your ox will be slain before your eyes, and you will not eat any of it. Your donkey will be violently taken away from before your face, and will not be restored to you. Your sheep will be given to your enemies, and you will have no one to save you. ³² Your sons and your daughters will be given to another people. Your eyes will look and fail with longing for them all day long. There will be no power in your hand. ³³ A nation which you don't know will eat the fruit of your ground and all of your work. You will only be oppressed and crushed always, ³⁴ so that the sights that you see with your eyes will drive you mad. ³⁵ Yahweh will strike you in the knees and in the legs with a sore boil, of which you cannot be healed, from the sole of your foot to the crown of your head. ³⁶ Yahweh will bring you, and your king whom you will set over yourselves, to a nation that you have not known, you nor your fathers. There you will serve other gods of wood and stone. ³⁷ You will become an astonishment, a proverb, and a byword among all the peoples where Yahweh will lead you away. ³⁸ You will carry much seed out into the field, and will gather little in, for the locust will consume it. ³⁹ You will plant vineyards and dress them, but you will neither drink of the wine, nor harvest, because worms will eat them. ⁴⁰ You will have olive trees throughout all your borders, but you won't anoint yourself with the oil, for your olives will drop off. ⁴¹ You will father sons and daughters, but they will not be yours, for they will go into captivity. ⁴² Locusts will consume all of your trees and the fruit of your ground. ⁴³ The foreigner who is among you will mount up above you higher and higher, and you will come down lower and lower. ⁴⁴ He will lend to you, and you won't lend to him. He will be the head, and you will be the tail. ⁴⁵ All these curses will come on you, and will pursue you and overtake you, until you are destroyed, because you didn't listen to Yahweh your God's voice, to keep his commandments and his statutes which he commanded you. ⁴⁶ They will be for a sign and for a wonder to you and to your offspring forever. ⁴⁷ Because you didn't serve Yahweh your God with joyfulness and with gladness of heart, by reason of the abundance of all things; ⁴⁸ therefore you will serve your enemies whom Yahweh sends against you, in hunger, in thirst, in nakedness, and in lack of all things. He will put an iron yoke on your neck until he has destroyed you. ⁴⁹ Yahweh will bring a nation against you from far away, from the end of the earth, as the eagle flies: a nation whose language you will not understand, ⁵⁰ a nation of fierce facial expressions, that doesn't respect the elderly, nor show favor to the young. ⁵¹ They will eat the fruit of your livestock and the fruit of your ground, until you are destroyed. They also won't leave you grain, new wine, oil, the increase of your livestock, or the young of your flock, until they have caused you to perish. ⁵² They will besiege you in all your gates until your high and fortified walls in which you trusted come down throughout all your land. They will besiege you in all your gates throughout all your land which Yahweh your God has given you. ⁵³ You will eat the fruit of your own body, the flesh of your sons and of

your daughters, whom Yahweh your God has given you, in the siege and in the distress with which your enemies will distress you. ⁵⁴ The man who is tender among you, and very delicate, his eye will be evil toward his brother, toward the wife whom he loves, and toward the remnant of his children whom he has remaining, ⁵⁵ so that he will not give to any of them of the flesh of his children whom he will eat, because he has nothing left to him, in the siege and in the distress with which your enemy will distress you in all your gates. ⁵⁶ The tender and delicate woman among you, who would not venture to set the sole of her foot on the ground for delicateness and tenderness, her eye will be evil toward the husband that she loves, toward her son, toward her daughter, ⁵⁷ toward her young one who comes out from between her feet, and toward her children whom she bears; for she will eat them secretly for lack of all things in the siege and in the distress with which your enemy will distress you in your gates. ⁵⁸ If you will not observe to do all the words of this law that are written in this book, that you may fear this glorious and fearful name, YAHWEH your God, ⁵⁹ then Yahweh will make your plagues and the plagues of your offspring fearful, even great plagues, and of long duration, and severe sicknesses, and of long duration. ⁶⁰ He will bring on you again all the diseases of Egypt, which you were afraid of; and they will cling to you. ⁶¹ Also every sickness and every plague which is not written in the book of this law, Yahweh will bring them on you until you are destroyed. ⁶² You will be left few in number, even though you were as the stars of the sky for multitude, because you didn't listen to Yahweh your God's voice. ⁶³ It will happen that as Yahweh rejoiced over you to do you good, and to multiply you, so Yahweh will rejoice over you to cause you to perish and to destroy you. You will be plucked from the land that you are going in to possess. ⁶⁴ Yahweh will scatter you among all peoples, from one end of the earth to the other end of the earth. There you will serve other gods which you have not known, you nor your fathers, even wood and stone. ⁶⁵ Among these nations you will find no ease, and there will be no rest for the sole of your foot; but Yahweh will give you there a trembling heart, failing of eyes, and pining of soul. ⁶⁶ Your life will hang in doubt before you. You will be afraid night and day, and will have no assurance of your life. ⁶⁷ In the morning you will say, "I wish it were evening!" and at evening you will say, "I wish it were morning!" for the fear of your heart which you will fear, and for the sights which your eyes will see. ⁶⁸ Yahweh will bring you into Egypt again with ships, by the way of which I told to you that you would never see it again. There you will offer yourselves to your enemies for male and female slaves, and nobody will buy you.

## 29

¹ These are the words of the covenant which Yahweh commanded Moses to make with the children of Israel in the land of Moab, in addition to the covenant which he made with them in Horeb. ² Moses called to all Israel, and said to them: Your eyes have seen all that Yahweh did in the land of Egypt to Pharaoh, and to all his servants, and to all his land; ³ the great trials which your eyes saw, the signs, and those great wonders. ⁴ But Yahweh has not given you a heart to know, eyes to see, and ears to hear, to this day. ⁵ I have led you forty years in the wilderness. Your clothes have not grown old on you, and your sandals have not grown old on your feet. ⁶ You have not eaten bread, neither have you drunk wine or strong drink, that you may know that I am Yahweh your God. ⁷ When you came to this place, Sihon the king of Heshbon and Og the king of Bashan came out against us to battle, and we struck them. ⁸ We took their land, and gave it for an inheritance to the Reubenites, and to the Gadites, and to the half-tribe of the Manassites. ⁹ Therefore keep the words of this covenant and do them, that you may prosper in all that you do. ¹⁰ All of you stand today in the presence of Yahweh your God: your heads, your tribes, your elders, and your officers, even all the men of Israel, ¹¹ your little ones, your wives, and the foreigners who are in the middle of your camps, from the one who cuts your wood to the one who draws your water, ¹² that you may enter into the covenant of Yahweh your God, and into his oath, which Yahweh your God makes with you today, ¹³ that he may establish you today as his people, and that he may be your God, as he spoke to you and as he swore to your fathers, to Abraham, to Isaac, and to Jacob. ¹⁴ Neither do I make this covenant and this oath with you only, ¹⁵ but with those who stand here with us today before Yahweh our God, and also with those who are not here with us today ¹⁶(for you know how we lived in the land of Egypt, and how we came through the middle of the nations through which you passed; ¹⁷ and you have seen their abominations and their idols of wood, stone, silver, and gold, which were among them); ¹⁸ lest there should be among you man, woman, family, or tribe whose heart turns away today from Yahweh our God, to go to serve the gods of those nations; lest there should be among you a root that produces bitter poison; ¹⁹ and it happen, when he hears the words of this curse, that he bless himself in his heart, saying, "I shall have peace, though I walk in the stubbornness of my heart," to destroy

the moist with the dry. ²⁰ Yahweh will not pardon him, but then Yahweh's anger and his jealousy will smoke against that man, and all the curse that is written in this book will fall on him, and Yahweh will blot out his name from under the sky. ²¹ Yahweh will set him apart for evil out of all the tribes of Israel, according to all the curses of the covenant written in this book of the law. ²² The generation to come—your children who will rise up after you, and the foreigner who will come from a far land—will say, when they see the plagues of that land, and the sicknesses with which Yahweh has made it sick, ²³ that all of its land is sulfur, salt, and burning, that it is not sown, doesn't produce, nor does any grass grow in it, like the overthrow of Sodom, Gomorrah, Admah, and Zeboiim, which Yahweh overthrew in his anger, and in his wrath. ²⁴ Even all the nations will say, "Why has Yahweh done this to this land? What does the heat of this great anger mean?" ²⁵ Then men will say, "Because they abandoned the covenant of Yahweh, the God of their fathers, which he made with them when he brought them out of the land of Egypt, ²⁶ and went and served other gods and worshiped them, gods that they didn't know and that he had not given to them. ²⁷ Therefore Yahweh's anger burned against this land, to bring on it all the curses that are written in this book. ²⁸ Yahweh rooted them out of their land in anger, in wrath, and in great indignation, and thrust them into another land, as it is today." ²⁹ The secret things belong to Yahweh our God; but the things that are revealed belong to us and to our children forever, that we may do all the words of this law.

## 30

¹ It shall happen, when all these things have come on you, the blessing and the curse, which I have set before you, and you shall call them to mind among all the nations where Yahweh your God has driven you, ² and return to Yahweh your God and obey his voice according to all that I command you today, you and your children, with all your heart and with all your soul, ³ that then Yahweh your God will release you from captivity, have compassion on you, and will return and gather you from all the peoples where Yahweh your God has scattered you. ⁴ If your outcasts are in the uttermost parts of the heavens, from there Yahweh your God will gather you, and from there he will bring you back. ⁵ Yahweh your God will bring you into the land which your fathers possessed, and you will possess it. He will do you good, and increase your numbers more than your fathers. ⁶ Yahweh your God will circumcise your heart, and the heart of your offspring, to love Yahweh your God with all your heart and with all your soul, that you may live. ⁷ Yahweh your God will put all these curses on your enemies and on those who hate you, who persecuted you. ⁸ You shall return and obey Yahweh's voice, and do all his commandments which I command you today. ⁹ Yahweh your God will make you prosperous in all the work of your hand, in the fruit of your body, in the fruit of your livestock, and in the fruit of your ground, for good; for Yahweh will again rejoice over you for good, as he rejoiced over your fathers, ¹⁰ if you will obey Yahweh your God's voice, to keep his commandments and his statutes which are written in this book of the law, if you turn to Yahweh your God with all your heart and with all your soul. ¹¹ For this commandment which I command you today is not too hard for you or too distant. ¹² It is not in heaven, that you should say, "Who will go up for us to heaven, bring it to us, and proclaim it to us, that we may do it?" ¹³ Neither is it beyond the sea, that you should say, "Who will go over the sea for us, bring it to us, and proclaim it to us, that we may do it?" ¹⁴ But the word is very near to you, in your mouth and in your heart, that you may do it. ¹⁵ Behold, I have set before you today life and prosperity, and death and evil. ¹⁶ For I command you today to love Yahweh your God, to walk in his ways and to keep his commandments, his statutes, and his ordinances, that you may live and multiply, and that Yahweh your God may bless you in the land where you go in to possess it. ¹⁷ But if your heart turns away, and you will not hear, but are drawn away and worship other gods, and serve them, ¹⁸ I declare to you today that you will surely perish. You will not prolong your days in the land where you pass over the Jordan to go in to possess it. ¹⁹ I call heaven and earth to witness against you today that I have set before you life and death, the blessing and the curse. Therefore choose life, that you may live, you and your descendants, ²⁰ to love Yahweh your God, to obey his voice, and to cling to him; for he is your life, and the length of your days, that you may dwell in the land which Yahweh swore to your fathers, to Abraham, to Isaac, and to Jacob, to give them.

## 31

¹ Moses went and spoke these words to all Israel. ² He said to them, "I am one hundred twenty years old today. I can no more go out and come in. Yahweh has said to me, 'You shall not go over this Jordan.' ³ Yahweh your God himself will go over before you. He will destroy these nations from before you, and you shall dispossess them. Joshua will go over before you, as Yahweh has spoken. ⁴ Yahweh will do to them as he did to Sihon and to Og, the kings of the Amorites, and to their land, when he destroyed them. ⁵ Yahweh will deliver them up

before you, and you shall do to them according to all the commandment which I have commanded you. ⁶ Be strong and courageous. Don't be afraid or scared of them, for Yahweh your God himself is who goes with you. He will not fail you nor forsake you." ⁷ Moses called to Joshua, and said to him in the sight of all Israel, "Be strong and courageous, for you shall go with this people into the land which Yahweh has sworn to their fathers to give them; and you shall cause them to inherit it. ⁸ Yahweh himself is who goes before you. He will be with you. He will not fail you nor forsake you. Don't be afraid. Don't be discouraged." ⁹ Moses wrote this law and delivered it to the priests the sons of Levi, who bore the ark of Yahweh's covenant, and to all the elders of Israel. ¹⁰ Moses commanded them, saying, "At the end of every seven years, in the set time of the year of release, in the feast of booths, ¹¹ when all Israel has come to appear before Yahweh your God in the place which he will choose, you shall read this law before all Israel in their hearing. ¹² Assemble the people, the men and the women and the little ones, and the foreigners who are within your gates, that they may hear, learn, fear Yahweh your God, and observe to do all the words of this law, ¹³ and that their children, who have not known, may hear and learn to fear Yahweh your God, as long as you live in the land where you go over the Jordan to possess it." ¹⁴ Yahweh said to Moses, "Behold, your days approach that you must die. Call Joshua, and present yourselves in the Tent of Meeting, that I may commission him." Moses and Joshua went, and presented themselves in the Tent of Meeting. ¹⁵ Yahweh appeared in the Tent in a pillar of cloud, and the pillar of cloud stood over the Tent's door. ¹⁶ Yahweh said to Moses, "Behold, you shall sleep with your fathers. This people will rise up and play the prostitute after the strange gods of the land where they go to be among them, and will forsake me and break my covenant which I have made with them. ¹⁷ Then my anger shall be kindled against them in that day, and I will forsake them, and I will hide my face from them, and they shall be devoured, and many evils and troubles shall come on them; so that they will say in that day, 'Haven't these evils come on us because our God is not among us?' ¹⁸ I will surely hide my face in that day for all the evil which they have done, in that they have turned to other gods. ¹⁹ "Now therefore write this song for yourselves, and teach it to the children of Israel. Put it in their mouths, that this song may be a witness for me against the children of Israel. ²⁰ For when I have brought them into the land which I swore to their fathers, flowing with milk and honey, and they have eaten and filled themselves, and grown fat, then they will turn to other gods, and serve them, and despise me, and break my covenant. ²¹ It will happen, when many evils and troubles have come on them, that this song will testify before them as a witness; for it will not be forgotten out of the mouths of their descendants; for I know their ways and what they are doing today, before I have brought them into the land which I promised them." ²² So Moses wrote this song the same day, and taught it to the children of Israel. ²³ He commissioned Joshua the son of Nun, and said, "Be strong and courageous; for you shall bring the children of Israel into the land which I swore to them. I will be with you." ²⁴ When Moses had finished writing the words of this law in a book, until they were finished, ²⁵ Moses commanded the Levites, who bore the ark of Yahweh's covenant, saying, ²⁶ "Take this book of the law, and put it by the side of the ark of Yahweh your God's covenant, that it may be there for a witness against you. ²⁷ For I know your rebellion and your stiff neck. Behold, while I am yet alive with you today, you have been rebellious against Yahweh. How much more after my death? ²⁸ Assemble to me all the elders of your tribes and your officers, that I may speak these words in their ears, and call heaven and earth to witness against them. ²⁹ For I know that after my death you will utterly corrupt yourselves, and turn away from the way which I have commanded you; and evil will happen to you in the latter days, because you will do that which is evil in Yahweh's sight, to provoke him to anger through the work of your hands." ³⁰ Moses spoke in the ears of all the assembly of Israel the words of this song, until they were finished.

## 32

¹ Give ear, you heavens, and I will speak. Let the earth hear the words of my mouth. ² My doctrine will drop as the rain. My speech will condense as the dew, as the misty rain on the tender grass, as the showers on the herb. ³ For I will proclaim Yahweh's name. Ascribe greatness to our God! ⁴ The Rock: his work is perfect, for all his ways are just. A God of faithfulness who does no wrong, just and right is he. ⁵ They have dealt corruptly with him. They are not his children, because of their defect. They are a perverse and crooked generation. ⁶ Is this the way you repay Yahweh, foolish and unwise people? Isn't he your father who has bought you? He has made you and established you. ⁷ Remember the days of old. Consider the years of many generations. Ask your father, and he will show you; your elders, and they will tell you. ⁸ When the Most High gave to the nations their inheritance, when he separated the children of men, he set the bounds of the peoples

according to the number of the children of Israel. [9] For Yahweh's portion is his people. Jacob is the lot of his inheritance. [10] He found him in a desert land, in the waste howling wilderness. He surrounded him. He cared for him. He kept him as the apple of his eye. [11] As an eagle that stirs up her nest, that flutters over her young, he spread abroad his wings, he took them, he bore them on his feathers. [12] Yahweh alone led him. There was no foreign god with him. [13] He made him ride on the high places of the earth. He ate the increase of the field. He caused him to suck honey out of the rock, oil out of the flinty rock; [14] butter from the herd, and milk from the flock, with fat of lambs, rams of the breed of Bashan, and goats, with the finest of the wheat. From the blood of the grape, you drank wine. [15] But Jeshurun grew fat, and kicked. You have grown fat. You have grown thick. You have become sleek. Then he abandoned God who made him, and rejected the Rock of his salvation. [16] They moved him to jealousy with strange gods. They provoked him to anger with abominations. [17] They sacrificed to demons, not God, to gods that they didn't know, to new gods that came up recently, which your fathers didn't dread. [18] Of the Rock who became your father, you are unmindful, and have forgotten God who gave you birth. [19] Yahweh saw and abhorred, because of the provocation of his sons and his daughters. [20] He said, "I will hide my face from them. I will see what their end will be; for they are a very perverse generation, children in whom is no faithfulness. [21] They have moved me to jealousy with that which is not God. They have provoked me to anger with their vanities. I will move them to jealousy with those who are not a people. I will provoke them to anger with a foolish nation. [22] For a fire is kindled in my anger, that burns to the lowest Sheol,[a] devours the earth with its increase, and sets the foundations of the mountains on fire. [23]"I will heap evils on them. I will spend my arrows on them. [24] They shall be wasted with hunger, and devoured with burning heat and bitter destruction. I will send the teeth of animals on them, with the venom of vipers that glide in the dust. [25] Outside the sword will bereave, and in the rooms, terror on both young man and virgin, the nursing infant with the gray-haired man. [26] I said that I would scatter them afar. I would make their memory to cease from among men; [27] were it not that I feared the provocation of the enemy, lest their adversaries should judge wrongly, lest they should say, 'Our hand is exalted; Yahweh has not done all this.'" [28] For they are a nation void of counsel. There is no understanding in them. [29] Oh that they were wise, that they understood this, that they would consider their latter end! [30] How could one chase a thousand, and two put ten thousand to flight, unless their Rock had sold them, and Yahweh had delivered them up? [31] For their rock is not as our Rock, even our enemies themselves concede. [32] For their vine is of the vine of Sodom, of the fields of Gomorrah. Their grapes are poison grapes. Their clusters are bitter. [33] Their wine is the poison of serpents, the cruel venom of asps. [34]"Isn't this laid up in store with me, sealed up among my treasures? [35] Vengeance is mine, and recompense, at the time when their foot slides, for the day of their calamity is at hand. Their doom rushes at them." [36] For Yahweh will judge his people, and have compassion on his servants, when he sees that their power is gone, that there is no one remaining, shut up or left at large. [37] He will say, "Where are their gods, the rock in which they took refuge, [38] which ate the fat of their sacrifices, and drank the wine of their drink offering? Let them rise up and help you! Let them be your protection. [39]"See now that I myself am he. There is no god with me. I kill and I make alive. I wound and I heal. There is no one who can deliver out of my hand. [40] For I lift up my hand to heaven and declare, as I live forever, [41] if I sharpen my glittering sword, my hand grasps it in judgment; I will take vengeance on my adversaries, and will repay those who hate me. [42] I will make my arrows drunk with blood. My sword shall devour flesh with the blood of the slain and the captives, from the head of the leaders of the enemy." [43] Rejoice, you nations, with his people, for he will avenge the blood of his servants. He will take vengeance on his adversaries, and will make atonement for his land and for his people.[b] [44] Moses came and spoke all the words of this song in the ears of the people, he and Joshua the son of Nun. [45] Moses finished reciting all these words to all Israel. [46] He said to them, "Set your heart to all the words which I testify to you today, which you shall command your children to observe to do, all the words of this law. [47] For it is no vain thing for you, because it is your life, and through this thing you shall prolong your days in the land, where you go over the Jordan to possess it." [48] Yahweh spoke to Moses that same day, saying, [49]"Go up into this mountain of Abarim, to Mount Nebo, which is in the land of Moab, that is across from Jericho; and see the land of Canaan, which I give to the children of Israel for a possession. [50] Die on the mountain where you go up, and be gathered to your people, as Aaron your brother died on Mount Hor, and was gathered to his people; [51] because you trespassed against me among the children of Israel at the waters of Meribah of Kadesh, in the wilderness of Zin; because you didn't uphold my holiness among the children of Israel. [52] For you shall see the land from a distance; but you shall not go there into the land which I give the children of Israel."

## 33

[1] This is the blessing with which Moses the man of God blessed the children of Israel before his death. [2] He said, "Yahweh came from Sinai, and rose from Seir to them. He shone from Mount Paran. He came from the ten thousands of holy ones. At his right hand was a fiery law for them.[c] [3] Yes, he loves the people. All his saints are in your hand. They sat down at your feet. Each receives your words. [4] Moses commanded us a law, an inheritance for the assembly of Jacob. [5] He was king in Jeshurun, when the heads of the people were gathered, all the tribes of Israel together. [6]"Let Reuben live, and not die; Nor let his men be few." [7] This is for Judah. He said, "Hear, Yahweh, the voice of Judah. Bring him in to his people. With his hands he contended for himself. You shall be a help against his adversaries." [8] About Levi he said, "Your Thummim and your Urim are with your godly one, whom you proved at Massah, with whom you contended at the waters of Meribah. [9] He said of his father, and of his mother, 'I have not seen him.' He didn't acknowledge his brothers, nor did he know his own children; for they have observed your word, and keep your covenant. [10] They shall teach Jacob your ordinances, and Israel your law. They shall put incense before you, and whole burnt offering on your altar. [11] Yahweh, bless his skills. Accept the work of his hands. Strike through the hips of those who rise up against him, of those who hate him, that they not rise again." [12] About Benjamin he said, "The beloved of Yahweh will dwell in safety by him. He covers him all day long. He dwells between his shoulders." [13] About Joseph he said, "His land is blessed by Yahweh, for the precious things of the heavens, for the dew, for the deep that couches beneath, [14] for the precious things of the fruits of the sun, for the precious things that the moon can yield, [15] for the best things of the ancient mountains, for the precious things of the everlasting hills, [16] for the precious things of the earth and its fullness, the good will of him who lived in the bush.[d] Let this come on the head of Joseph, on the crown of the head of him who was separated from his brothers. [17] Majesty belongs to the firstborn of his herd. His horns are the horns of the wild ox. With them he will push all the peoples to the ends of the earth. They are the ten thousands of Ephraim. They are the thousands of Manasseh." [18] About Zebulun he said, "Rejoice, Zebulun, in your going out; and Issachar, in your tents. [19] They will call the peoples to the mountain. There they will offer sacrifices of righteousness, for they will draw out the abundance of the seas, the hidden treasures of the sand." [20] About Gad he said, "He who enlarges Gad is blessed. He dwells as a lioness, and tears the arm and the crown of the head. [21] He provided the first part for himself, for the lawgiver's portion was reserved for him. He came with the heads of the people. He executed the righteousness of Yahweh, His ordinances with Israel." [22] About Dan he said, "Dan is a lion's cub that leaps out of Bashan." [23] About Naphtali he said, "Naphtali, satisfied with favor, full of Yahweh's blessing, Possess the west and the south." [24] About Asher he said, "Asher is blessed with children. Let him be acceptable to his brothers. Let him dip his foot in oil. [25] Your bars will be iron and bronze. As your days, so your strength will be. [26]"There is no one like God, Jeshurun, who rides on the heavens for your help, in his excellency on the skies. [27] The eternal God is your dwelling place. Underneath are the everlasting arms. He thrust out the enemy from before you, and said, 'Destroy!' [28] Israel dwells in safety, the fountain of Jacob alone, In a land of grain and new wine. Yes, his heavens drop down dew. [29] You are happy, Israel! Who is like you, a people saved by Yahweh, the shield of your help, the sword of your excellency? Your enemies will submit themselves to you. You will tread on their high places."

## 34

[1] Moses went up from the plains of Moab to Mount Nebo, to the top of Pisgah, that is opposite Jericho. Yahweh showed him all the land of Gilead to Dan, [2] and all Naphtali, and the land of Ephraim and Manasseh, and all the land of Judah, to the Western Sea, [3] and the south,[e] and the Plain of the valley of Jericho the city of palm trees, to Zoar. [4] Yahweh said to him, "This is the land which I swore to

---

[a] *32:22* Sheol is the place of the dead.

[b] *32:43* For this verse, LXX reads: Rejoice, you heavens, with him, and let all the angels of God worship him; rejoice you Gentiles, with his people, and let all the sons of God strengthen themselves in him; for he will avenge the blood of his sons, and he will render vengeance, and recompense justice to his enemies, and will reward them that hate him; and the Lord shall purge the land of his people.

[c] *33:2* another manuscript reads "He came with myriads of holy ones from the south, from his mountain slopes."

[d] *33:16* i.e., the burning bush of Exodus 3:3- 4.

[e] *34:3* or, Negev

Abraham, to Isaac, and to Jacob, saying, 'I will give it to your offspring.' I have caused you to see it with your eyes, but you shall not go over there." [5] So Moses the servant of Yahweh died there in the land of Moab, according to Yahweh's word. [6] He buried him in the valley in the land of Moab opposite Beth Peor, but no man knows where his tomb is to this day. [7] Moses was one hundred twenty years old when he died. His eye was not dim, nor his strength gone. [8] The children of Israel wept for Moses in the plains of Moab thirty days, until the days of weeping in the mourning for Moses were ended. [9] Joshua the son of Nun was full of the spirit of wisdom, for Moses had laid his hands on him. The children of Israel listened to him, and did as Yahweh commanded Moses. [10] Since then, there has not arisen a prophet in Israel like Moses, whom Yahweh knew face to face, [11] in all the signs and the wonders which Yahweh sent him to do in the land of Egypt, to Pharaoh, and to all his servants, and to all his land, [12] and in all the mighty hand, and in all the awesome deeds, which Moses did in the sight of all Israel.

# The Book of Joshua

## 1

[1] Now after the death of Moses the servant of Yahweh,[a] Yahweh spoke to Joshua the son of Nun, Moses' servant, saying, [2]"Moses my servant is dead. Now therefore arise, go across this Jordan, you and all these people, to the land which I am giving to them, even to the children of Israel. [3] I have given you every place that the sole of your foot will tread on, as I told Moses. [4] From the wilderness and this Lebanon even to the great river, the river Euphrates, all the land of the Hittites, and to the great sea toward the going down of the sun, shall be your border. [5] No man will be able to stand before you all the days of your life. As I was with Moses, so I will be with you. I will not fail you nor forsake you. [6]"Be strong and courageous; for you shall cause this people to inherit the land which I swore to their fathers to give them. [7] Only be strong and very courageous. Be careful to observe to do according to all the law which Moses my servant commanded you. Don't turn from it to the right hand or to the left, that you may have good success wherever you go. [8] This book of the law shall not depart from your mouth, but you shall meditate on it day and night, that you may observe to do according to all that is written in it; for then you shall make your way prosperous, and then you shall have good success. [9] Haven't I commanded you? Be strong and courageous. Don't be afraid. Don't be dismayed, for Yahweh your God[b] is with you wherever you go." [10] Then Joshua commanded the officers of the people, saying, [11]"Pass through the middle of the camp, and command the people, saying, 'Prepare food; for within three days you are to pass over this Jordan, to go in to possess the land which Yahweh your God gives you to possess.'" [12] Joshua spoke to the Reubenites, and to the Gadites, and to the half-tribe of Manasseh, saying, [13]"Remember the word which Moses the servant of Yahweh commanded you, saying, 'Yahweh your God gives you rest, and will give you this land. [14] Your wives, your little ones, and your livestock shall live in the land which Moses gave you beyond the Jordan; but you shall pass over before your brothers armed, all the mighty men of valor, and shall help them [15] until Yahweh has given your brothers rest, as he has given you, and they have also possessed the land which Yahweh your God gives them. Then you shall return to the land of your possession and possess it, which Moses the servant of Yahweh gave you beyond the Jordan toward the sunrise.'" [16] They answered Joshua, saying, "All that you have commanded us we will do, and wherever you send us we will go. [17] Just as we listened to Moses in all things, so will we listen to you. Only may Yahweh your God be with you, as he was with Moses. [18] Whoever rebels against your commandment, and doesn't listen to your words in all that you command him shall himself be put to death. Only be strong and courageous."

## 2

[1] Joshua the son of Nun secretly sent two men out of Shittim as spies, saying, "Go, view the land, including Jericho." They went and came into the house of a prostitute whose name was Rahab, and slept there. [2] The king of Jericho was told, "Behold,[c] men of the children of Israel came in here tonight to spy out the land." [3] Jericho's king sent to Rahab, saying, "Bring out the men who have come to you, who have entered into your house; for they have come to spy out all the land." [4] The woman took the two men and hid them. Then she said, "Yes, the men came to me, but I didn't know where they came from. [5] About the time of the shutting of the gate, when it was dark, the men went out. Where

the men went, I don't know. Pursue them quickly. You may catch up with them." [6] But she had brought them up to the roof, and hidden them under the stalks of flax which she had laid in order on the roof. [7] The men pursued them along the way to the fords of the Jordan River. As soon as those who pursued them had gone out, they shut the gate. [8] Before they had lain down, she came up to them on the roof. [9] She said to the men, "I know that Yahweh has given you the land, and that the fear of you has fallen upon us, and that all the inhabitants of the land melt away before you. [10] For we have heard how Yahweh dried up the water of the Red Sea before you, when you came out of Egypt; and what you did to the two kings of the Amorites, who were beyond the Jordan, to Sihon and to Og, whom you utterly destroyed. [11] As soon as we had heard it, our hearts melted, and there wasn't any more spirit in any man, because of you: for Yahweh your God, he is God in heaven above, and on earth beneath. [12] Now therefore, please swear to me by Yahweh, since I have dealt kindly with you, that you also will deal kindly with my father's house, and give me a true sign; [13] and that you will save alive my father, my mother, my brothers, and my sisters, and all that they have, and will deliver our lives from death." [14] The men said to her, "Our life for yours, if you don't talk about this business of ours; and it shall be, when Yahweh gives us the land, that we will deal kindly and truly with you." [15] Then she let them down by a cord through the window; for her house was on the side of the wall, and she lived on the wall. [16] She said to them, "Go to the mountain, lest the pursuers find you. Hide yourselves there three days, until the pursuers have returned. Afterward, you may go your way." [17] The men said to her, "We will be guiltless of this your oath which you've made us to swear. [18] Behold, when we come into the land, tie this line of scarlet thread in the window which you used to let us down. Gather to yourself into the house your father, your mother, your brothers, and all your father's household. [19] It shall be that whoever goes out of the doors of your house into the street, his blood will be on his head, and we will be guiltless. Whoever is with you in the house, his blood shall be on our head, if any hand is on him. [20] But if you talk about this business of ours, then we shall be guiltless of your oath which you've made us to swear." [21] She said, "Let it be as you have said." She sent them away, and they departed. Then she tied the scarlet line in the window. [22] They went and came to the mountain, and stayed there three days, until the pursuers had returned. The pursuers sought them all along the way, but didn't find them. [23] Then the two men returned, descended from the mountain, crossed the river, and came to Joshua the son of Nun. They told him all that had happened to them. [24] They said to Joshua, "Truly Yahweh has delivered all the land into our hands. Moreover, all the inhabitants of the land melt away before us."

## 3

[1] Joshua got up early in the morning; and they moved from Shittim and came to the Jordan, he and all the children of Israel. They camped there before they crossed over. [2] After three days, the officers went through the middle of the camp; [3] and they commanded the people, saying, "When you see the ark of Yahweh your God's covenant, and the Levitical priests bearing it, then leave your place and follow it. [4] Yet there shall be a space between you and it of about two thousand cubits[d] by measure—don't come closer to it—that you may know the way by which you must go; for you have not passed this way before." [5] Joshua said to the people, "Sanctify yourselves; for tomorrow Yahweh will do wonders among you." [6] Joshua spoke to the priests, saying, "Take up the ark of the covenant, and cross over before the people." They took up the ark of the covenant, and went before the people. [7] Yahweh said to Joshua, "Today I will begin to magnify you in the sight of all Israel, that they may know that as I was with Moses, so I will be with you. [8] You shall command the priests who bear the ark of the covenant, saying, 'When you come to the brink of the waters of the Jordan, you shall stand still in the Jordan.'" [9] Joshua said to the children of Israel, "Come here, and hear the words of Yahweh your God." [10] Joshua said, "By this you shall know that the living God is among you, and that he will without fail drive the Canaanite, the Hittite, the Hivite, the Perizzite, the Girgashite, the Amorite, and the Jebusite out from before you. [11] Behold, the ark of the covenant of the Lord[e] of all the earth passes over before you into the Jordan. [12] Now therefore take twelve men out of the tribes of Israel, for every tribe a man. [13] It shall be that when the soles of the feet of the priests who bear the ark of Yahweh, the Lord of all the earth, rest in the waters of the Jordan, that the waters of the Jordan will be cut off. The waters that come down from above shall stand in one heap." [14] When the people moved from their tents to

---

[a] 1:1 "Yahweh" is God's proper Name, sometimes rendered "LORD" (all caps) in other translations.

[b] 1:9 The Hebrew word rendered "God" is "אֱלֹהִים" (Elohim).

[c] 2:2 "Behold", from "הִנֵּה", means look at, take notice,

observe, see, or gaze at. It is often used as an interjection.

[d] 3:4 A cubit is the length from the tip of the middle finger to the elbow on a man's arm, or

about 18 inches or 46 centimeters, so 2,000 cubits is about 920 meters.

[e] 3:11 The word translated "Lord" is "Adonai."

pass over the Jordan, the priests who bore the ark of the covenant being before the people, [15] and when those who bore the ark had come to the Jordan, and the feet of the priests who bore the ark had dipped in the edge of the water (for the Jordan overflows all its banks all the time of harvest), [16] the waters which came down from above stood, and rose up in one heap a great way off, at Adam, the city that is beside Zarethan; and those that went down toward the sea of the Arabah, even the Salt Sea, were wholly cut off. Then the people passed over near Jericho. [17] The priests who bore the ark of Yahweh's covenant stood firm on dry ground in the middle of the Jordan; and all Israel crossed over on dry ground, until all the nation had passed completely over the Jordan.

## 4

[1] When all the nation had completely crossed over the Jordan, Yahweh spoke to Joshua, saying, [2]"Take twelve men out of the people, a man out of every tribe, [3] and command them, saying, 'Take from out of the middle of the Jordan, out of the place where the priests' feet stood firm, twelve stones, carry them over with you, and lay them down in the place where you'll camp tonight.'" [4] Then Joshua called the twelve men whom he had prepared of the children of Israel, a man out of every tribe. [5] Joshua said to them, "Cross before the ark of Yahweh your God into the middle of the Jordan, and each of you pick up a stone and put it on your shoulder, according to the number of the tribes of the children of Israel; [6] that this may be a sign among you, that when your children ask in the future, saying, 'What do you mean by these stones?' [7] then you shall tell them, 'Because the waters of the Jordan were cut off before the ark of Yahweh's covenant. When it crossed over the Jordan, the waters of the Jordan were cut off. These stones shall be for a memorial to the children of Israel forever.'" [8] The children of Israel did as Joshua commanded, and took up twelve stones out of the middle of the Jordan, as Yahweh spoke to Joshua, according to the number of the tribes of the children of Israel. They carried them over with them to the place where they camped, and laid them down there. [9] Joshua set up twelve stones in the middle of the Jordan, in the place where the feet of the priests who bore the ark of the covenant stood; and they are there to this day. [10] For the priests who bore the ark stood in the middle of the Jordan until everything was finished that Yahweh commanded Joshua to speak to the people, according to all that Moses commanded Joshua; and the people hurried and passed over. [11] When all the people had completely crossed over, Yahweh's ark crossed over with the priests in the presence of the people. [12] The children of Reuben, and the children of Gad, and the half-tribe of Manasseh crossed over armed before the children of Israel, as Moses spoke to them. [13] About forty thousand men, ready and armed for war, passed over before Yahweh to battle, to the plains of Jericho. [14] On that day, Yahweh magnified Joshua in the sight of all Israel; and they feared him, as they feared Moses, all the days of his life. [15] Yahweh spoke to Joshua, saying, [16]"Command the priests who bear the ark of the covenant, that they come up out of the Jordan." [17] Joshua therefore commanded the priests, saying, "Come up out of the Jordan!" [18] When the priests who bore the ark of Yahweh's covenant had come up out of the middle of the Jordan, and the soles of the priests' feet had been lifted up to the dry ground, the waters of the Jordan returned to their place, and went over all its banks, as before. [19] The people came up out of the Jordan on the tenth day of the first month, and encamped in Gilgal, on the east border of Jericho. [20] Joshua set up those twelve stones, which they took out of the Jordan, in Gilgal. [21] He spoke to the children of Israel, saying, "When your children ask their fathers in time to come, saying, 'What do these stones mean?' [22] Then you shall let your children know, saying, 'Israel came over this Jordan on dry land. [23] For Yahweh your God dried up the waters of the Jordan from before you until you had crossed over, as Yahweh your God did to the Red Sea, which he dried up from before us, until we had crossed over, [24] that all the peoples of the earth may know that Yahweh's hand is mighty, and that you may fear Yahweh your God forever.'"

## 5

[1] When all the kings of the Amorites, who were beyond the Jordan westward, and all the kings of the Canaanites, who were by the sea, heard how Yahweh had dried up the waters of the Jordan from before the children of Israel until we had crossed over, their heart melted, and there was no more spirit in them, because of the children of Israel. [2] At that time, Yahweh said to Joshua, "Make flint knives, and circumcise again the sons of Israel the second time." [3] Joshua made himself flint knives, and circumcised the sons of Israel at the hill of the foreskins. [4] This is the reason Joshua circumcised them: all the people who came out of Egypt, who were males, even all the men of war, died in the wilderness along the way, after they came out of Egypt. [5] For all the people who came out were circumcised; but all the people who were

born in the wilderness along the way as they came out of Egypt had not been circumcised. [6] For the children of Israel walked forty years in the wilderness until all the nation, even the men of war who came out of Egypt, were consumed, because they didn't listen to Yahweh's voice. Yahweh swore to them that he wouldn't let them see the land which Yahweh swore to their fathers that he would give us, a land flowing with milk and honey. [7] Their children, whom he raised up in their place, were circumcised by Joshua, for they were uncircumcised, because they had not circumcised them on the way. [8] When they were done circumcising the whole nation, they stayed in their places in the camp until they were healed. [9] Yahweh said to Joshua, "Today I have rolled away the reproach of Egypt from you." Therefore the name of that place was called Gilgal[a] to this day. [10] The children of Israel encamped in Gilgal. They kept the Passover on the fourteenth day of the month at evening in the plains of Jericho. [11] They ate unleavened cakes and parched grain of the produce of the land on the next day after the Passover, in the same day. [12] The manna ceased on the next day, after they had eaten of the produce of the land. The children of Israel didn't have manna any more, but they ate of the fruit of the land of Canaan that year. [13] When Joshua was by Jericho, he lifted up his eyes and looked, and behold, a man stood in front of him with his sword drawn in his hand. Joshua went to him and said to him, "Are you for us, or for our enemies?" [14] He said, "No; but I have come now as commander of Yahweh's army." Joshua fell on his face to the earth, and worshiped, and asked him, "What does my lord say to his servant?" [15] The prince of Yahweh's army said to Joshua, "Take off your sandals, for the place on which you stand is holy." Joshua did so.

## 6

[1] Now Jericho was tightly shut up because of the children of Israel. No one went out, and no one came in. [2] Yahweh said to Joshua, "Behold, I have given Jericho into your hand, with its king and the mighty men of valor. [3] All of your men of war shall march around the city, going around the city once. You shall do this six days. [4] Seven priests shall bear seven trumpets of rams' horns before the ark. On the seventh day, you shall march around the city seven times, and the priests shall blow the trumpets. [5] It shall be that when they make a long blast with the ram's horn, and when you hear the sound of the trumpet, all the people shall shout with a great shout; then the city wall will fall down flat, and the people shall go up, every man straight in front of him." [6] Joshua the son of Nun called the priests, and said to them, "Take up the ark of the covenant, and let seven priests bear seven trumpets of rams' horns before Yahweh's ark." [7] They said to the people, "Advance! March around the city, and let the armed men pass on before Yahweh's ark." [8] It was so, that when Joshua had spoken to the people, the seven priests bearing the seven trumpets of rams' horns before Yahweh advanced and blew the trumpets, and the ark of Yahweh's covenant followed them. [9] The armed men went before the priests who blew the trumpets, and the ark went after them. The trumpets sounded as they went. [10] Joshua commanded the people, saying, "You shall not shout nor let your voice be heard, neither shall any word proceed out of your mouth until the day I tell you to shout. Then you shall shout." [11] So he caused Yahweh's ark to go around the city, circling it once. Then they came into the camp, and stayed in the camp. [12] Joshua rose early in the morning, and the priests took up Yahweh's ark. [13] The seven priests bearing the seven trumpets of rams' horns in front of Yahweh's ark went on continually, and blew the trumpets. The armed men went in front of them. The rear guard came after Yahweh's ark. The trumpets sounded as they went. [14] The second day they marched around the city once, and returned into the camp. They did this six days. [15] On the seventh day, they rose early at the dawning of the day, and marched around the city in the same way seven times. On this day only they marched around the city seven times. [16] At the seventh time, when the priests blew the trumpets, Joshua said to the people, "Shout, for Yahweh has given you the city! [17] The city shall be devoted, even it and all that is in it, to Yahweh. Only Rahab the prostitute shall live, she and all who are with her in the house, because she hid the messengers that we sent. [18] But as for you, only keep yourselves from what is devoted to destruction, lest when you have devoted it, you take of the devoted thing; so you would make the camp of Israel accursed and trouble it. [19] But all the silver, gold, and vessels of bronze and iron are holy to Yahweh. They shall come into Yahweh's treasury." [20] So the people shouted and the priests blew the trumpets. When the people heard the sound of the trumpet, the people shouted with a great shout, and the wall fell down flat, so that the people went up into the city, every man straight in front of him, and they took the city. [21] They utterly destroyed all that was in the city, both man and woman, both young and old, and ox, sheep, and donkey, with the edge of the sword. [22] Joshua said to the

two men who had spied out the land, "Go into the prostitute's house, and bring the woman and all that she has out from there, as you swore to her." [23] The young men who were spies went in, and brought out Rahab with her father, her mother, her brothers, and all that she had. They also brought out all of her relatives, and they set them outside of the camp of Israel. [24] They burned the city with fire, and all that was in it. Only they put the silver, the gold, and the vessels of bronze and of iron into the treasury of Yahweh's house. [25] But Rahab the prostitute, her father's household, and all that she had, Joshua saved alive. She lives in the middle of Israel to this day, because she hid the messengers whom Joshua sent to spy out Jericho. [26] Joshua commanded them with an oath at that time, saying, "Cursed is the man before Yahweh who rises up and builds this city Jericho. With the loss of his firstborn he will lay its foundation, and with the loss of his youngest son he will set up its gates." [27] So Yahweh was with Joshua; and his fame was in all the land.

# 7

[1] But the children of Israel committed a trespass in the devoted things; for Achan, the son of Carmi, the son of Zabdi, the son of Zerah, of the tribe of Judah, took some of the devoted things. Therefore Yahweh's anger burned against the children of Israel. [2] Joshua sent men from Jericho to Ai, which is beside Beth Aven, on the east side of Bethel, and spoke to them, saying, "Go up and spy out the land." The men went up and spied out Ai. [3] They returned to Joshua, and said to him, "Don't let all the people go up, but let about two or three thousand men go up and strike Ai. Don't make all the people to toil there, for there are only a few of them." [4] So about three thousand men of the people went up there, and they fled before the men of Ai. [5] The men of Ai struck about thirty-six men of them. They chased them from before the gate even to Shebarim, and struck them at the descent. The hearts of the people melted, and became like water. [6] Joshua tore his clothes, and fell to the earth on his face before Yahweh's ark until the evening, he and the elders of Israel; and they put dust on their heads. [7] Joshua said, "Alas, Lord Yahweh, why have you brought this people over the Jordan at all, to deliver us into the hand of the Amorites, to cause us to perish? I wish that we had been content and lived beyond the Jordan! [8] Oh, Lord, what shall I say, after Israel has turned their backs before their enemies? [9] For the Canaanites and all the inhabitants of the land will hear of it, and will surround us, and cut off our name from the earth. What will you do for your great name?" [10] Yahweh said to Joshua, "Get up! Why have you fallen on your face like that? [11] Israel has sinned. Yes, they have even transgressed my covenant which I commanded them. Yes, they have even taken some of the devoted things, and have also stolen, and also deceived. They have even put it among their own stuff. [12] Therefore the children of Israel can't stand before their enemies. They turn their backs before their enemies, because they have become devoted for destruction. I will not be with you any more, unless you destroy the devoted things from among you. [13] Get up! Sanctify the people, and say, 'Sanctify yourselves for tomorrow, for Yahweh, the God of Israel, says, "There is a devoted thing among you, Israel. You cannot stand before your enemies until you take away the devoted thing from among you." [14] In the morning therefore you shall be brought near by your tribes. It shall be that the tribe which Yahweh selects shall come near by families. The family which Yahweh selects shall come near by households. The household which Yahweh selects shall come near man by man. [15] It shall be, that he who is taken with the devoted thing shall be burned with fire, he and all that he has, because he has transgressed Yahweh's covenant, and because he has done a disgraceful thing in Israel.'" [16] So Joshua rose up early in the morning and brought Israel near by their tribes. The tribe of Judah was selected. [17] He brought near the family of Judah, and he selected the family of the Zerahites. He brought near the family of the Zerahites man by man, and Zabdi was selected. [18] He brought near his household man by man, and Achan, the son of Carmi, the son of Zabdi, the son of Zerah, of the tribe of Judah, was selected. [19] Joshua said to Achan, "My son, please give glory to Yahweh, the God of Israel, and make confession to him. Tell me now what you have done! Don't hide it from me!" [20] Achan answered Joshua, and said, "I have truly sinned against Yahweh, the God of Israel, and this is what I have done. [21] When I saw among the plunder a beautiful Babylonian robe, two hundred shekels[a] of silver, and a wedge of gold weighing fifty shekels, then I coveted them and took them. Behold, they are hidden in the ground in the middle of my tent, with the silver under it." [22] So Joshua sent messengers, and they ran to the tent. Behold, it was hidden in his tent, with the silver under it. [23] They took them from the middle of the tent, and brought them to Joshua and to all the children of Israel. They laid them down before Yahweh. [24] Joshua, and all Israel with him, took Achan the son of Zerah, the

silver, the robe, the wedge of gold, his sons, his daughters, his cattle, his donkeys, his sheep, his tent, and all that he had; and they brought them up to the valley of Achor. [25] Joshua said, "Why have you troubled us? Yahweh will trouble you today." All Israel stoned him with stones, and they burned them with fire and stoned them with stones. [26] They raised over him a great heap of stones that remains to this day. Yahweh turned from the fierceness of his anger. Therefore the name of that place was called "The valley of Achor" to this day.

# 8

[1] Yahweh said to Joshua, "Don't be afraid, and don't be dismayed. Take all the warriors with you, and arise, go up to Ai. Behold, I have given into your hand the king of Ai, with his people, his city, and his land. [2] You shall do to Ai and her king as you did to Jericho and her king, except you shall take its goods and its livestock for yourselves. Set an ambush for the city behind it." [3] So Joshua arose, with all the warriors, to go up to Ai. Joshua chose thirty thousand men, the mighty men of valor, and sent them out by night. [4] He commanded them, saying, "Behold, you shall lie in ambush against the city, behind the city. Don't go very far from the city, but all of you be ready. [5] I and all the people who are with me will approach the city. It shall happen, when they come out against us, as at the first, that we will flee before them. [6] They will come out after us until we have drawn them away from the city; for they will say, 'They flee before us, like the first time.' So we will flee before them, [7] and you shall rise up from the ambush, and take possession of the city; for Yahweh your God will deliver it into your hand. [8] It shall be, when you have seized the city, that you shall set the city on fire. You shall do this according to Yahweh's word. Behold, I have commanded you." [9] Joshua sent them out; and they went to set up the ambush, and stayed between Bethel and Ai on the west side of Ai; but Joshua stayed among the people that night. [10] Joshua rose up early in the morning, mustered the people, and went up, he and the elders of Israel, before the people to Ai. [11] All the people, even the men of war who were with him, went up and came near, and came before the city and encamped on the north side of Ai. Now there was a valley between him and Ai. [12] He took about five thousand men, and set them in ambush between Bethel and Ai, on the west side of the city. [13] So they set the people, even all the army who was on the north of the city, and their ambush on the west of the city; and Joshua went that night into the middle of the valley. [14] When the king of Ai saw it, they hurried and rose up early, and the men of the city went out against Israel to battle, he and all his people, at the time appointed, before the Arabah; but he didn't know that there was an ambush against him behind the city. [15] Joshua and all Israel made as if they were beaten before them, and fled by the way of the wilderness. [16] All the people who were in the city were called together to pursue after them. They pursued Joshua, and were drawn away from the city. [17] There was not a man left in Ai or Bethel who didn't go out after Israel. They left the city open, and pursued Israel. [18] Yahweh said to Joshua, "Stretch out the javelin that is in your hand toward Ai, for I will give it into your hand." Joshua stretched out the javelin that was in his hand toward the city. [19] The ambush arose quickly out of their place, and they ran as soon as he had stretched out his hand and entered into the city and took it. They hurried and set the city on fire. [20] When the men of Ai looked behind them, they saw, and behold, the smoke of the city ascended up to heaven, and they had no power to flee this way or that way. The people who fled to the wilderness turned back on the pursuers. [21] When Joshua and all Israel saw that the ambush had taken the city, and that the smoke of the city ascended, then they turned back and killed the men of Ai. [22] The others came out of the city against them, so they were in the middle of Israel, some on this side, and some on that side. They struck them, so that they let none of them remain or escape. [23] They captured the king of Ai alive, and brought him to Joshua. [24] When Israel had finished killing all the inhabitants of Ai in the field, in the wilderness in which they pursued them, and they had all fallen by the edge of the sword until they were consumed, all Israel returned to Ai and struck it with the edge of the sword. [25] All that fell that day, both of men and women, were twelve thousand, even all the people of Ai. [26] For Joshua didn't draw back his hand, with which he stretched out the javelin, until he had utterly destroyed all the inhabitants of Ai. [27] Israel took for themselves only the livestock and the goods of that city, according to Yahweh's word which he commanded Joshua. [28] So Joshua burned Ai and made it a heap forever, even a desolation, to this day. [29] He hanged the king of Ai on a tree until the evening. At sundown, Joshua commanded, and they took his body down from the tree and threw it at the entrance of the gate of the city, and raised a great heap of stones on it that remains to this day. [30] Then Joshua built an altar to Yahweh, the God of Israel, on Mount Ebal, [31] as Moses the servant of Yahweh commanded the

children of Israel, as it is written in the book of the law of Moses: an altar of uncut stones, on which no one had lifted up any iron. They offered burnt offerings on it to Yahweh and sacrificed peace offerings. [32] He wrote there on the stones a copy of Moses' law, which he wrote in the presence of the children of Israel. [33] All Israel, with their elders, officers, and judges, stood on both sides of the ark before the Levitical priests, who carried the ark of Yahweh's covenant, the foreigner as well as the native; half of them in front of Mount Gerizim, and half of them in front of Mount Ebal, as Moses the servant of Yahweh had commanded at the first, that they should bless the people of Israel. [34] Afterward he read all the words of the law, the blessing and the curse, according to all that is written in the book of the law. [35] There was not a word of all that Moses commanded which Joshua didn't read before all the assembly of Israel, with the women, the little ones, and the foreigners who were among them.

## 9

[1] When all the kings who were beyond the Jordan, in the hill country, and in the lowland, and on all the shore of the great sea in front of Lebanon, the Hittite, the Amorite, the Canaanite, the Perizzite, the Hivite, and the Jebusite, heard of it [2] they gathered themselves together to fight with Joshua and with Israel, with one accord. [3] But when the inhabitants of Gibeon heard what Joshua had done to Jericho and to Ai, [4] they also resorted to a ruse, and went and made as if they had been ambassadors, and took old sacks on their donkeys, and old, torn-up and bound up wine skins, [5] and old and patched sandals on their feet, and wore old garments. All the bread of their food supply was dry and moldy. [6] They went to Joshua at the camp at Gilgal, and said to him and to the men of Israel, "We have come from a far country. Now therefore make a covenant with us." [7] The men of Israel said to the Hivites, "What if you live among us? How could we make a covenant with you?" [8] They said to Joshua, "We are your servants." Joshua said to them, "Who are you? Where do you come from?" [9] They said to him, "Your servants have come from a very far country because of the name of Yahweh your God; for we have heard of his fame, all that he did in Egypt, [10] and all that he did to the two kings of the Amorites who were beyond the Jordan, to Sihon king of Heshbon and to Og king of Bashan, who was at Ashtaroth. [11] Our elders and all the inhabitants of our country spoke to us, saying, 'Take supplies in your hand for the journey, and go to meet them. Tell them, "We are your servants. Now make a covenant with us."' [12] This our bread we took hot for our supplies out of our houses on the day we went out to go to you; but now, behold, it is dry, and has become moldy. [13] These wine skins, which we filled, were new; and behold, they are torn. These our garments and our sandals have become old because of the very long journey." [14] The men sampled their provisions, and didn't ask counsel from Yahweh's mouth. [15] Joshua made peace with them, and made a covenant with them, to let them live. The princes of the congregation swore to them. [16] At the end of three days after they had made a covenant with them, they heard that they were their neighbors, and that they lived among them. [17] The children of Israel traveled and came to their cities on the third day. Now their cities were Gibeon, Chephirah, Beeroth, and Kiriath Jearim. [18] The children of Israel didn't strike them, because the princes of the congregation had sworn to them by Yahweh, the God of Israel. All the congregation murmured against the princes. [19] But all the princes said to all the congregation, "We have sworn to them by Yahweh, the God of Israel. Now therefore we may not touch them. [20] We will do this to them, and let them live; lest wrath be on us, because of the oath which we swore to them." [21] The princes said to them, "Let them live." So they became wood cutters and drawers of water for all the congregation, as the princes had spoken to them. [22] Joshua called for them, and he spoke to them, saying, "Why have you deceived us, saying, 'We are very far from you,' when you live among us? [23] Now therefore you are cursed, and some of you will never fail to be slaves, both wood cutters and drawers of water for the house of my God." [24] They answered Joshua, and said, "Because your servants were certainly told how Yahweh your God commanded his servant Moses to give you all the land, and to destroy all the inhabitants of the land from before you. Therefore we were very afraid for our lives because of you, and have done this thing. [25] Now, behold, we are in your hand. Do to us as it seems good and right to you to do." [26] He did so to them, and delivered them out of the hand of the children of Israel, so that they didn't kill them. [27] That day Joshua made them wood cutters and drawers of water for the congregation and for Yahweh's altar to this day, in the place which he should choose.

## 10

[1] Now when Adoni-Zedek king of Jerusalem heard how Joshua had taken Ai, and had utterly destroyed it; as he had done to Jericho and her king, so he had done to Ai and her king; and how the inhabitants of Gibeon had made peace with Israel, and were among them, [2] they were very afraid, because Gibeon was a great city, as one of the royal cities, and because it was greater than Ai, and all its men were mighty. [3] Therefore Adoni-Zedek king of Jerusalem sent to Hoham king of Hebron, Piram king of Jarmuth, Japhia king of Lachish, and Debir king of Eglon, saying, [4] "Come up to me and help me. Let's strike Gibeon; for they have made peace with Joshua and with the children of Israel." [5] Therefore the five kings of the Amorites, the king of Jerusalem, the king of Hebron, the king of Jarmuth, the king of Lachish, and the king of Eglon, gathered themselves together and went up, they and all their armies, and encamped against Gibeon, and made war against it. [6] The men of Gibeon sent to Joshua at the camp at Gilgal, saying, "Don't abandon your servants! Come up to us quickly and save us! Help us; for all the kings of the Amorites that dwell in the hill country have gathered together against us." [7] So Joshua went up from Gilgal, he and the whole army with him, including all the mighty men of valor. [8] Yahweh said to Joshua, "Don't fear them, for I have delivered them into your hands. Not a man of them will stand before you." [9] Joshua therefore came to them suddenly. He marched from Gilgal all night. [10] Yahweh confused them before Israel. He killed them with a great slaughter at Gibeon, and chased them by the way of the ascent of Beth Horon, and struck them to Azekah and to Makkedah. [11] As they fled from before Israel, while they were at the descent of Beth Horon, Yahweh hurled down great stones from the sky on them to Azekah, and they died. There were more who died from the hailstones than those whom the children of Israel killed with the sword. [12] Then Joshua spoke to Yahweh in the day when Yahweh delivered up the Amorites before the children of Israel. He said in the sight of Israel, "Sun, stand still on Gibeon! You, moon, stop in the valley of Aijalon!" [13] The sun stood still, and the moon stayed, until the nation had avenged themselves of their enemies. Isn't this written in the book of Jashar? The sun stayed in the middle of the sky, and didn't hurry to go down about a whole day. [14] There was no day like that before it or after it, that Yahweh listened to the voice of a man; for Yahweh fought for Israel. [15] Joshua returned, and all Israel with him, to the camp to Gilgal. [16] These five kings fled, and hid themselves in the cave at Makkedah. [17] Joshua was told, saying, "The five kings have been found, hidden in the cave at Makkedah." [18] Joshua said, "Roll large stones to cover the cave's entrance, and set men by it to guard them; [19] but don't stay there. Pursue your enemies, and attack them from the rear. Don't allow them to enter into their cities; for Yahweh your God has delivered them into your hand." [20] When Joshua and the children of Israel had finished killing them with a very great slaughter until they were consumed, and the remnant which remained of them had entered into the fortified cities, [21] all the people returned to the camp to Joshua at Makkedah in peace. None moved his tongue against any of the children of Israel. [22] Then Joshua said, "Open the cave entrance, and bring those five kings out of the cave to me." [23] They did so, and brought those five kings out of the cave to him: the king of Jerusalem, the king of Hebron, the king of Jarmuth, the king of Lachish, and the king of Eglon. [24] When they brought those kings out to Joshua, Joshua called for all the men of Israel, and said to the chiefs of the men of war who went with him, "Come near. Put your feet on the necks of these kings." They came near, and put their feet on their necks. [25] Joshua said to them, "Don't be afraid, nor be dismayed. Be strong and courageous, for Yahweh will do this to all your enemies against whom you fight." [26] Afterward Joshua struck them, put them to death, and hanged them on five trees. They were hanging on the trees until the evening. [27] At the time of the going down of the sun, Joshua commanded, and they took them down off the trees, and threw them into the cave in which they had hidden themselves, and laid great stones on the mouth of the cave, which remain to this very day. [28] Joshua took Makkedah on that day, and struck it with the edge of the sword, with its king. He utterly destroyed it and all the souls who were in it. He left no one remaining. He did to the king of Makkedah as he had done to the king of Jericho. [29] Joshua passed from Makkedah, and all Israel with him, to Libnah, and fought against Libnah. [30] Yahweh delivered it also, with its king, into the hand of Israel. He struck it with the edge of the sword, and all the souls who were in it. He left no one remaining in it. He did to its king as he had done to the king of Jericho. [31] Joshua passed from Libnah, and all Israel with him, to Lachish, and encamped against it, and fought against it. [32] Yahweh delivered Lachish into the hand of Israel. He took it on the second day, and struck it with the edge of the sword, with all the souls who were in it, according to all that he had done to Libnah. [33] Then Horam king of Gezer came up to help Lachish; and Joshua struck him and his people, until he had left him no one remaining. [34] Joshua passed from Lachish, and all Israel with him, to Eglon; and they encamped against it and fought against it. [35] They took it on that day, and struck it with the edge of the sword. He utterly destroyed all the souls who were in it that day, according to all that he had done to Lachish. [36] Joshua went up from Eglon, and all Israel with him, to Hebron; and they fought against it. [37] They took it, and struck it with the edge of the

sword, with its king and all its cities, and all the souls who were in it. He left no one remaining, according to all that he had done to Eglon; but he utterly destroyed it, and all the souls who were in it. ³⁸ Joshua returned, and all Israel with him, to Debir, and fought against it. ³⁹ He took it, with its king and all its cities. They struck them with the edge of the sword, and utterly destroyed all the souls who were in it. He left no one remaining. As he had done to Hebron, so he did to Debir, and to its king; as he had done also to Libnah, and to its king. ⁴⁰ So Joshua struck all the land, the hill country, the South, the lowland, the slopes, and all their kings. He left no one remaining, but he utterly destroyed all that breathed, as Yahweh, the God of Israel, commanded. ⁴¹ Joshua struck them from Kadesh Barnea even to Gaza, and all the country of Goshen, even to Gibeon. ⁴² Joshua took all these kings and their land at one time because Yahweh, the God of Israel, fought for Israel. ⁴³ Joshua returned, and all Israel with him, to the camp to Gilgal.

## 11

¹ When Jabin king of Hazor heard of it, he sent to Jobab king of Madon, to the king of Shimron, to the king of Achshaph, ² and to the kings who were on the north, in the hill country, in the Arabah south of Chinneroth, in the lowland, and in the heights of Dor on the west, ³ to the Canaanite on the east and on the west, the Amorite, the Hittite, the Perizzite, the Jebusite in the hill country, and the Hivite under Hermon in the land of Mizpah. ⁴ They went out, they and all their armies with them, many people, even as the sand that is on the seashore in multitude, with very many horses and chariots. ⁵ All these kings met together; and they came and encamped together at the waters of Merom, to fight with Israel. ⁶ Yahweh said to Joshua, "Don't be afraid because of them; for tomorrow at this time, I will deliver them up all slain before Israel. You shall hamstring their horses and burn their chariots with fire." ⁷ So Joshua came suddenly, with all the warriors, against them by the waters of Merom, and attacked them. ⁸ Yahweh delivered them into the hand of Israel, and they struck them, and chased them to great Sidon, and to Misrephoth Maim, and to the valley of Mizpah eastward. They struck them until they left them no one remaining. ⁹ Joshua did to them as Yahweh told him. He hamstrung their horses and burned their chariots with fire. ¹⁰ Joshua turned back at that time, and took Hazor, and struck its king with the sword; for Hazor used to be the head of all those kingdoms. ¹¹ They struck all the souls who were in it with the edge of the sword, utterly destroying them. There was no one left who breathed. He burned Hazor with fire. ¹² Joshua captured all the cities of those kings, with their kings, and he struck them with the edge of the sword, and utterly destroyed them, as Moses the servant of Yahweh commanded. ¹³ But as for the cities that stood on their mounds, Israel burned none of them, except Hazor only. Joshua burned that. ¹⁴ The children of Israel took all the plunder of these cities, with the livestock, as plunder for themselves; but every man they struck with the edge of the sword, until they had destroyed them. They didn't leave any who breathed. ¹⁵ As Yahweh commanded Moses his servant, so Moses commanded Joshua. Joshua did so. He left nothing undone of all that Yahweh commanded Moses. ¹⁶ So Joshua captured all that land, the hill country, all the South, all the land of Goshen, the lowland, the Arabah, the hill country of Israel, and the lowland of the same, ¹⁷ from Mount Halak, that goes up to Seir, even to Baal Gad in the valley of Lebanon under Mount Hermon. He took all their kings, struck them, and put them to death. ¹⁸ Joshua made war a long time with all those kings. ¹⁹ There was not a city that made peace with the children of Israel, except the Hivites, the inhabitants of Gibeon. They took all in battle. ²⁰ For it was of Yahweh to harden their hearts, to come against Israel in battle, that he might utterly destroy them, that they might have no favor, but that he might destroy them, as Yahweh commanded Moses. ²¹ Joshua came at that time, and cut off the Anakim from the hill country, from Hebron, from Debir, from Anab, and from all the hill country of Judah, and from all the hill country of Israel. Joshua utterly destroyed them with their cities. ²² There were none of the Anakim left in the land of the children of Israel. Only in Gaza, in Gath, and in Ashdod, did some remain. ²³ So Joshua took the whole land, according to all that Yahweh spoke to Moses; and Joshua gave it for an inheritance to Israel according to their divisions by their tribes. Then the land had rest from war.

## 12

¹ Now these are the kings of the land, whom the children of Israel struck, and possessed their land beyond the Jordan toward the sunrise, from the valley of the Arnon to Mount Hermon, and all the Arabah eastward: ² Sihon king of the Amorites, who lived in Heshbon, and ruled from Aroer, which is on the edge of the valley of the Arnon, and the middle of the valley, and half Gilead, even to the river Jabbok, the border of the children of Ammon; ³ and the Arabah to the sea of Chinneroth, eastward, and to the sea of the Arabah, even the Salt Sea, eastward, the way to Beth Jeshimoth; and on the south, under the slopes of Pisgah: ⁴ and the border of Og king of Bashan, of the remnant of the

Rephaim, who lived at Ashtaroth and at Edrei, ⁵ and ruled in Mount Hermon, and in Salecah, and in all Bashan, to the border of the Geshurites and the Maacathites, and half Gilead, the border of Sihon king of Heshbon. ⁶ Moses the servant of Yahweh and the children of Israel struck them. Moses the servant of Yahweh gave it for a possession to the Reubenites, and the Gadites, and the half-tribe of Manasseh. ⁷ These are the kings of the land whom Joshua and the children of Israel struck beyond the Jordan westward, from Baal Gad in the valley of Lebanon even to Mount Halak, that goes up to Seir. Joshua gave it to the tribes of Israel for a possession according to their divisions; ⁸ in the hill country, and in the lowland, and in the Arabah, and in the slopes, and in the wilderness, and in the South; the Hittite, the Amorite, and the Canaanite, the Perizzite, the Hivite, and the Jebusite: ⁹ the king of Jericho, one; the king of Ai, which is beside Bethel, one; ¹⁰ the king of Jerusalem, one; the king of Hebron, one; ¹¹ the king of Jarmuth, one; the king of Lachish, one; ¹² the king of Eglon, one; the king of Gezer, one; ¹³ the king of Debir, one; the king of Geder, one; ¹⁴ the king of Hormah, one; the king of Arad, one; ¹⁵ the king of Libnah, one; the king of Adullam, one; ¹⁶ the king of Makkedah, one; the king of Bethel, one; ¹⁷ the king of Tappuah, one; the king of Hepher, one; ¹⁸ the king of Aphek, one; the king of Lassharon, one; ¹⁹ the king of Madon, one; the king of Hazor, one; ²⁰ the king of Shimron Meron, one; the king of Achshaph, one; ²¹ the king of Taanach, one; the king of Megiddo, one; ²² the king of Kedesh, one; the king of Jokneam in Carmel, one; ²³ the king of Dor in the height of Dor, one; the king of Goiim in Gilgal, one; ²⁴ the king of Tirzah, one: all the kings thirty-one.

## 13

¹ Now Joshua was old and well advanced in years. Yahweh said to him, "You are old and advanced in years, and there remains yet very much land to be possessed. ²"This is the land that still remains: all the regions of the Philistines, and all the Geshurites; ³ from the Shihor, which is before Egypt, even to the border of Ekron northward, which is counted as Canaanite; the five lords of the Philistines; the Gazites, and the Ashdodites, the Ashkelonites, the Gittites, and the Ekronites; also the Avvim, ⁴ on the south; all the land of the Canaanites, and Mearah that belongs to the Sidonians, to Aphek, to the border of the Amorites; ⁵ and the land of the Gebalites, and all Lebanon, toward the sunrise, from Baal Gad under Mount Hermon to the entrance of Hamath; ⁶ all the inhabitants of the hill country from Lebanon to Misrephoth Maim, even all the Sidonians. I will drive them out from before the children of Israel. Just allocate it to Israel for an inheritance, as I have commanded you. ⁷ Now therefore divide this land for an inheritance to the nine tribes and the half-tribe of Manasseh." ⁸ With him the Reubenites and the Gadites received their inheritance, which Moses gave them, beyond the Jordan eastward, even as Moses the servant of Yahweh gave them: ⁹ from Aroer, that is on the edge of the valley of the Arnon, and the city that is in the middle of the valley, and all the plain of Medeba to Dibon; ¹⁰ and all the cities of Sihon king of the Amorites, who reigned in Heshbon, to the border of the children of Ammon; ¹¹ and Gilead, and the border of the Geshurites and Maacathites, and all Mount Hermon, and all Bashan to Salecah; ¹² all the kingdom of Og in Bashan, who reigned in Ashtaroth and in Edrei (who was left of the remnant of the Rephaim); for Moses attacked these, and drove them out. ¹³ Nevertheless the children of Israel didn't drive out the Geshurites, nor the Maacathites: but Geshur and Maacath live within Israel to this day. ¹⁴ Only he gave no inheritance to the tribe of Levi. The offerings of Yahweh, the God of Israel, made by fire are his inheritance, as he spoke to him. ¹⁵ Moses gave to the tribe of the children of Reuben according to their families. ¹⁶ Their border was from Aroer, that is on the edge of the valley of the Arnon, and the city that is in the middle of the valley, and all the plain by Medeba; ¹⁷ Heshbon, and all its cities that are in the plain; Dibon, Bamoth Baal, Beth Baal Meon, ¹⁸ Jahaz, Kedemoth, Mephaath, ¹⁹ Kiriathaim, Sibmah, Zereth Shahar in the mount of the valley, ²⁰ Beth Peor, the slopes of Pisgah, Beth Jeshimoth, ²¹ all the cities of the plain, and all the kingdom of Sihon king of the Amorites, who reigned in Heshbon, whom Moses struck with the chiefs of Midian, Evi, Rekem, Zur, Hur, and Reba, the princes of Sihon, who lived in the land. ²² The children of Israel also killed Balaam the son of Beor, the soothsayer, with the sword, among the rest of their slain. ²³ The border of the children of Reuben was the bank of the Jordan. This was the inheritance of the children of Reuben according to their families, the cities and its villages. ²⁴ Moses gave to the tribe of Gad, to the children of Gad, according to their families. ²⁵ Their border was Jazer, and all the cities of Gilead, and half the land of the children of Ammon, to Aroer that is near Rabbah; ²⁶ and from Heshbon to Ramath Mizpeh, and Betonim; and from Mahanaim to the border of Debir; ²⁷ and in the valley, Beth Haram, Beth Nimrah, Succoth, and Zaphon, the rest of the kingdom of Sihon king of Heshbon, the Jordan's bank, to the uttermost part of the sea of Chinnereth beyond the Jordan eastward. ²⁸ This is the inheritance of the children of Gad according to their families,

the cities and its villages. ²⁹ Moses gave an inheritance to the half-tribe of Manasseh. It was for the half-tribe of the children of Manasseh according to their families. ³⁰ Their border was from Mahanaim, all Bashan, all the kingdom of Og king of Bashan, and all the villages of Jair, which are in Bashan, sixty cities. ³¹ Half Gilead, Ashtaroth, and Edrei, the cities of the kingdom of Og in Bashan, were for the children of Machir the son of Manasseh, even for the half of the children of Machir according to their families. ³² These are the inheritances which Moses distributed in the plains of Moab, beyond the Jordan at Jericho, eastward. ³³ But Moses gave no inheritance to the tribe of Levi. Yahweh, the God of Israel, is their inheritance, as he spoke to them.

## 14

¹ These are the inheritances which the children of Israel took in the land of Canaan, which Eleazar the priest, Joshua the son of Nun, and the heads of the fathers' houses of the tribes of the children of Israel, distributed to them, ² by the lot of their inheritance, as Yahweh commanded by Moses, for the nine tribes, and for the half-tribe. ³ For Moses had given the inheritance of the two tribes and the half-tribe beyond the Jordan; but to the Levites he gave no inheritance among them. ⁴ For the children of Joseph were two tribes, Manasseh and Ephraim. They gave no portion to the Levites in the land, except cities to dwell in, with their pasture lands for their livestock and for their property. ⁵ The children of Israel did as Yahweh commanded Moses, and they divided the land. ⁶ Then the children of Judah came near to Joshua in Gilgal. Caleb the son of Jephunneh the Kenizzite said to him, "You know the thing that Yahweh spoke to Moses the man of God concerning me and concerning you in Kadesh Barnea. ⁷ I was forty years old when Moses the servant of Yahweh sent me from Kadesh Barnea to spy out the land. I brought him word again as it was in my heart. ⁸ Nevertheless, my brothers who went up with me made the heart of the people melt; but I wholly followed Yahweh my God. ⁹ Moses swore on that day, saying, 'Surely the land where you walked shall be an inheritance to you and to your children forever, because you have wholly followed Yahweh my God.' ¹⁰ "Now, behold, Yahweh has kept me alive, as he spoke, these forty-five years, from the time that Yahweh spoke this word to Moses, while Israel walked in the wilderness. Now, behold, I am eighty-five years old, today. ¹¹ As yet I am as strong today as I was in the day that Moses sent me. As my strength was then, even so is my strength now for war, to go out and to come in. ¹² Now therefore give me this hill country, of which Yahweh spoke in that day; for you heard in that day how the Anakim were there, and great and fortified cities. It may be that Yahweh will be with me, and I shall drive them out, as Yahweh said." ¹³ Joshua blessed him; and he gave Hebron to Caleb the son of Jephunneh for an inheritance. ¹⁴ Therefore Hebron became the inheritance of Caleb the son of Jephunneh the Kenizzite to this day, because he followed Yahweh, the God of Israel wholeheartedly. ¹⁵ Now the name of Hebron before was Kiriath Arba, after the greatest man among the Anakim. Then the land had rest from war.

## 15

¹ The lot for the tribe of the children of Judah according to their families was to the border of Edom, even to the wilderness of Zin southward, at the uttermost part of the south. ² Their south border was from the uttermost part of the Salt Sea, from the bay that looks southward; ³ and it went out southward of the ascent of Akrabbim, and passed along to Zin, and went up by the south of Kadesh Barnea, and passed along by Hezron, went up to Addar, and turned toward Karka; ⁴ and it passed along to Azmon, went out at the brook of Egypt; and the border ended at the sea. This shall be your south border. ⁵ The east border was the Salt Sea, even to the end of the Jordan. The border of the north quarter was from the bay of the sea at the end of the Jordan. ⁶ The border went up to Beth Hoglah, and passed along by the north of Beth Arabah; and the border went up to the stone of Bohan the son of Reuben. ⁷ The border went up to Debir from the valley of Achor, and so northward, looking toward Gilgal, that faces the ascent of Adummim, which is on the south side of the river. The border passed along to the waters of En Shemesh, and ended at En Rogel. ⁸ The border went up by the valley of the son of Hinnom to the side of the Jebusite (also called Jerusalem) southward; and the border went up to the top of the mountain that lies before the valley of Hinnom westward, which is at the farthest part of the valley of Rephaim northward. ⁹ The border extended from the top of the mountain to the spring of the waters of Nephtoah, and went out to the cities of Mount Ephron; and the border extended to Baalah (also called Kiriath Jearim); ¹⁰ and the border turned about from Baalah westward to Mount Seir, and passed along to the side of Mount Jearim (also called Chesalon) on the north, and went down to Beth Shemesh, and passed along by Timnah; ¹¹ and the border went out to the side of Ekron northward; and the border extended to Shikkeron, and passed along to Mount Baalah, and went out at Jabneel; and the goings out of the border were at the sea. ¹² The west border was to the shore of the

great sea. This is the border of the children of Judah according to their families. ¹³ He gave to Caleb the son of Jephunneh a portion among the children of Judah, according to the commandment of Yahweh to Joshua, even Kiriath Arba, named after the father of Anak (also called Hebron). ¹⁴ Caleb drove out the three sons of Anak: Sheshai, and Ahiman, and Talmai, the children of Anak. ¹⁵ He went up against the inhabitants of Debir: now the name of Debir before was Kiriath Sepher. ¹⁶ Caleb said, "He who strikes Kiriath Sepher, and takes it, to him I will give Achsah my daughter as wife." ¹⁷ Othniel the son of Kenaz, the brother of Caleb, took it: and he gave him Achsah his daughter as wife. ¹⁸ When she came, she had him ask her father for a field. She got off her donkey, and Caleb said, "What do you want?" ¹⁹ She said, "Give me a blessing. Because you have set me in the land of the South, give me also springs of water." So he gave her the upper springs and the lower springs. ²⁰ This is the inheritance of the tribe of the children of Judah according to their families. ²¹ The farthest cities of the tribe of the children of Judah toward the border of Edom in the South were Kabzeel, Eder, Jagur, ²² Kinah, Dimonah, Adadah, ²³ Kedesh, Hazor, Ithnan, ²⁴ Ziph, Telem, Bealoth, ²⁵ Hazor Hadattah, Kerioth Hezron (also called Hazor), ²⁶ Amam, Shema, Moladah, ²⁷ Hazar Gaddah, Heshmon, Beth Pelet, ²⁸ Hazar Shual, Beersheba, Biziothiah, ²⁹ Baalah, Iim, Ezem, ³⁰ Eltolad, Chesil, Hormah, ³¹ Ziklag, Madmannah, Sansannah, ³² Lebaoth, Shilhim, Ain, and Rimmon. All the cities are twenty-nine, with their villages. ³³ In the lowland, Eshtaol, Zorah, Ashnah, ³⁴ Zanoah, En Gannim, Tappuah, Enam, ³⁵ Jarmuth, Adullam, Socoh, Azekah, ³⁶ Shaaraim, Adithaim and Gederah (or Gederothaim); fourteen cities with their villages. ³⁷ Zenan, Hadashah, Migdal Gad, ³⁸ Dilean, Mizpah, Joktheel, ³⁹ Lachish, Bozkath, Eglon, ⁴⁰ Cabbon, Lahmam, Chitlish, ⁴¹ Gederoth, Beth Dagon, Naamah, and Makkedah; sixteen cities with their villages. ⁴² Libnah, Ether, Ashan, ⁴³ Iphtah, Ashnah, Nezib, ⁴⁴ Keilah, Achzib, and Mareshah; nine cities with their villages. ⁴⁵ Ekron, with its towns and its villages; ⁴⁶ from Ekron even to the sea, all that were by the side of Ashdod, with their villages. ⁴⁷ Ashdod, its towns and its villages; Gaza, its towns and its villages; to the brook of Egypt, and the great sea with its coastline. ⁴⁸ In the hill country, Shamir, Jattir, Socoh, ⁴⁹ Dannah, Kiriath Sannah (which is Debir), ⁵⁰ Anab, Eshtemoh, Anim, ⁵¹ Goshen, Holon, and Giloh; eleven cities with their villages. ⁵² Arab, Dumah, Eshan, ⁵³ Janim, Beth Tappuah, Aphekah, ⁵⁴ Humtah, Kiriath Arba (also called Hebron), and Zior; nine cities with their villages. ⁵⁵ Maon, Carmel, Ziph, Jutah, ⁵⁶ Jezreel, Jokdeam, Zanoah, ⁵⁷ Kain, Gibeah, and Timnah; ten cities with their villages. ⁵⁸ Halhul, Beth Zur, Gedor, ⁵⁹ Maarath, Beth Anoth, and Eltekon; six cities with their villages. ⁶⁰ Kiriath Baal (also called Kiriath Jearim), and Rabbah; two cities with their villages. ⁶¹ In the wilderness, Beth Arabah, Middin, Secacah, ⁶² Nibshan, the City of Salt, and En Gedi; six cities with their villages. ⁶³ As for the Jebusites, the inhabitants of Jerusalem, the children of Judah couldn't drive them out; but the Jebusites live with the children of Judah at Jerusalem to this day.

## 16

¹ The lot came out for the children of Joseph from the Jordan at Jericho, at the waters of Jericho on the east, even the wilderness, going up from Jericho through the hill country to Bethel. ² It went out from Bethel to Luz, and passed along to the border of the Archites to Ataroth; ³ and it went down westward to the border of the Japhletites, to the border of Beth Horon the lower, and on to Gezer; and ended at the sea. ⁴ The children of Joseph, Manasseh and Ephraim, took their inheritance. ⁵ This was the border of the children of Ephraim according to their families. The border of their inheritance eastward was Ataroth Addar, to Beth Horon the upper. ⁶ The border went out westward at Michmethath on the north. The border turned about eastward to Taanath Shiloh, and passed along it on the east of Janoah. ⁷ It went down from Janoah to Ataroth, to Naarah, reached to Jericho, and went out at the Jordan. ⁸ From Tappuah the border went along westward to the brook of Kanah; and ended at the sea. This is the inheritance of the tribe of the children of Ephraim according to their families; ⁹ together with the cities which were set apart for the children of Ephraim in the middle of the inheritance of the children of Manasseh, all the cities with their villages. ¹⁰ They didn't drive out the Canaanites who lived in Gezer; but the Canaanites dwell in the territory of Ephraim to this day, and have become servants to do forced labor.

## 17

¹ This was the lot for the tribe of Manasseh, for he was the firstborn of Joseph. As for Machir the firstborn of Manasseh, the father of Gilead, because he was a man of war, therefore he had Gilead and Bashan. ² So this was for the rest of the children of Manasseh according to their families: for the children of Abiezer, for the children of Helek, for the children of Asriel, for the children of Shechem, for the children of Hepher, and for the children of Shemida. These were the male children of Manasseh the son of Joseph according to their families. ³ But

Zelophehad, the son of Hepher, the son of Gilead, the son of Machir, the son of Manasseh, had no sons, but daughters. These are the names of his daughters: Mahlah, Noah, Hoglah, Milcah, and Tirzah. [4] They came to Eleazar the priest, and to Joshua the son of Nun, and to the princes, saying, "Yahweh commanded Moses to give us an inheritance among our brothers." Therefore according to the commandment of Yahweh he gave them an inheritance among the brothers of their father. [5] Ten parts fell to Manasseh, in addition to the land of Gilead and Bashan, which is beyond the Jordan; [6] because the daughters of Manasseh had an inheritance among his sons. The land of Gilead belonged to the rest of the sons of Manasseh. [7] The border of Manasseh was from Asher to Michmethath, which is before Shechem. The border went along to the right hand, to the inhabitants of En Tappuah. [8] The land of Tappuah belonged to Manasseh; but Tappuah on the border of Manasseh belonged to the children of Ephraim. [9] The border went down to the brook of Kanah, southward of the brook. These cities belonged to Ephraim among the cities of Manasseh. The border of Manasseh was on the north side of the brook, and ended at the sea. [10] Southward it was Ephraim's, and northward it was Manasseh's, and the sea was his border. They reached to Asher on the north, and to Issachar on the east. [11] Manasseh had three heights in Issachar, in Asher Beth Shean and its towns, and Ibleam and its towns, and the inhabitants of Dor and its towns, and the inhabitants of Endor and its towns, and the inhabitants of Taanach and its towns, and the inhabitants of Megiddo and its towns. [12] Yet the children of Manasseh couldn't drive out the inhabitants of those cities; but the Canaanites would dwell in that land. [13] When the children of Israel had grown strong, they put the Canaanites to forced labor, and didn't utterly drive them out. [14] The children of Joseph spoke to Joshua, saying, "Why have you given me just one lot and one part for an inheritance, since we are a numerous people, because Yahweh has blessed us so far?" [15] Joshua said to them, "If you are a numerous people, go up to the forest, and clear land for yourself there in the land of the Perizzites and of the Rephaim, since the hill country of Ephraim is too narrow for you." [16] The children of Joseph said, "The hill country is not enough for us. All the Canaanites who dwell in the land of the valley have chariots of iron, both those who are in Beth Shean and its towns, and those who are in the valley of Jezreel." [17] Joshua spoke to the house of Joseph, that is, to Ephraim and to Manasseh, saying, "You are a numerous people, and have great power. You shall not have one lot only; [18] but the hill country shall be yours. Although it is a forest, you shall cut it down, and it's farthest extent shall be yours; for you shall drive out the Canaanites, though they have chariots of iron, and though they are strong."

# 18

[1] The whole congregation of the children of Israel assembled themselves together at Shiloh, and set up the Tent of Meeting there. The land was subdued before them. [2] Seven tribes remained among the children of Israel, which had not yet divided their inheritance. [3] Joshua said to the children of Israel, "How long will you neglect to go in to possess the land, which Yahweh, the God of your fathers, has given you? [4] Appoint for yourselves three men from each tribe. I will send them, and they shall arise, walk through the land, and describe it according to their inheritance; then they shall come to me. [5] They shall divide it into seven portions. Judah shall live in his borders on the south, and the house of Joseph shall live in their borders on the north. [6] You shall survey the land into seven parts, and bring the description here to me; and I will cast lots for you here before Yahweh our God. [7] However, the Levites have no portion among you; for the priesthood of Yahweh is their inheritance. Gad, Reuben, and the half-tribe of Manasseh have received their inheritance east of the Jordan, which Moses the servant of Yahweh gave them." [8] The men arose and went. Joshua commanded those who went to survey the land, saying, "Go walk through the land, survey it, and come again to me. I will cast lots for you here before Yahweh in Shiloh." [9] The men went and passed through the land, and surveyed it by cities into seven portions in a book. They came to Joshua to the camp at Shiloh. [10] Joshua cast lots for them in Shiloh before Yahweh. There Joshua divided the land to the children of Israel according to their divisions. [11] The lot of the tribe of the children of Benjamin came up according to their families. The border of their lot went out between the children of Judah and the children of Joseph. [12] Their border on the north quarter was from the Jordan. The border went up to the side of Jericho on the north, and went up through the hill country westward. It ended at the wilderness of Beth Aven. [13] The border passed along from there to Luz, to the side of Luz (also called Bethel), southward. The border went down to Ataroth Addar, by the mountain that lies on the south of Beth Horon the lower. [14] The border extended, and turned around on the west quarter southward, from the mountain that lies before Beth Horon southward; and ended at Kiriath Baal (also called Kiriath Jearim), a city of the children of Judah. This was the west quarter. [15] The south quarter was from the farthest

part of Kiriath Jearim. The border went out westward, and went out to the spring of the waters of Nephtoah. [16] The border went down to the farthest part of the mountain that lies before the valley of the son of Hinnom, which is in the valley of Rephaim northward. It went down to the valley of Hinnom, to the side of the Jebusite southward, and went down to En Rogel. [17] It extended northward, went out at En Shemesh, and went out to Geliloth, which is opposite the ascent of Adummim. It went down to the stone of Bohan the son of Reuben. [18] It passed along to the side opposite the Arabah northward, and went down to the Arabah. [19] The border passed along to the side of Beth Hoglah northward; and the border ended at the north bay of the Salt Sea, at the south end of the Jordan. This was the south border. [20] The Jordan was its border on the east quarter. This was the inheritance of the children of Benjamin, by the borders around it, according to their families. [21] Now the cities of the tribe of the children of Benjamin according to their families were Jericho, Beth Hoglah, Emek Keziz, [22] Beth Arabah, Zemaraim, Bethel, [23] Avvim, Parah, Ophrah, [24] Chephar Ammoni, Ophni, and Geba; twelve cities with their villages. [25] Gibeon, Ramah, Beeroth, [26] Mizpeh, Chephirah, Mozah, [27] Rekem, Irpeel, Taralah, [28] Zelah, Eleph, the Jebusite (also called Jerusalem), Gibeath, and Kiriath; fourteen cities with their villages. This is the inheritance of the children of Benjamin according to their families.

# 19

[1] The second lot came out for Simeon, even for the tribe of the children of Simeon according to their families. Their inheritance was in the middle of the inheritance of the children of Judah. [2] They had for their inheritance Beersheba (or Sheba), Moladah, [3] Hazar Shual, Balah, Ezem, [4] Eltolad, Bethul, Hormah, [5] Ziklag, Beth Marcaboth, Hazar Susah, [6] Beth Lebaoth, and Sharuhen; thirteen cities with their villages; [7] Ain, Rimmon, Ether, and Ashan; four cities with their villages; [8] and all the villages that were around these cities to Baalath Beer, Ramah of the South. This is the inheritance of the tribe of the children of Simeon according to their families. [9] Out of the part of the children of Judah was the inheritance of the children of Simeon; for the portion of the children of Judah was too much for them. Therefore the children of Simeon had inheritance in the middle of their inheritance. [10] The third lot came up for the children of Zebulun according to their families. The border of their inheritance was to Sarid. [11] Their border went up westward, even to Maralah, and reached to Dabbesheth. It reached to the brook that is before Jokneam. [12] It turned from Sarid eastward toward the sunrise to the border of Chisloth Tabor. It went out to Daberath, and went up to Japhia. [13] From there it passed along eastward to Gath Hepher, to Ethkazin; and it went out at Rimmon which stretches to Neah. [14] The border turned around it on the north to Hannathon; and it ended at the valley of Iphtah El; [15] Kattath, Nahalal, Shimron, Idalah, and Bethlehem: twelve cities with their villages. [16] This is the inheritance of the children of Zebulun according to their families, these cities with their villages. [17] The fourth lot came out for Issachar, even for the children of Issachar according to their families. [18] Their border was to Jezreel, Chesulloth, Shunem, [19] Hapharaim, Shion, Anaharath, [20] Rabbith, Kishion, Ebez, [21] Remeth, Engannim, En Haddah, and Beth Pazzez. [22] The border reached to Tabor, Shahazumah, and Beth Shemesh. Their border ended at the Jordan: sixteen cities with their villages. [23] This is the inheritance of the tribe of the children of Issachar according to their families, the cities with their villages. [24] The fifth lot came out for the tribe of the children of Asher according to their families. [25] Their border was Helkath, Hali, Beten, Achshaph, [26] Allammelech, Amad, Mishal. It reached to Carmel westward, and to Shihorlibnath. [27] It turned toward the sunrise to Beth Dagon, and reached to Zebulun, and to the valley of Iphtah El northward to Beth Emek and Neiel. It went out to Cabul on the left hand, [28] and Ebron, Rehob, Hammon, and Kanah, even to great Sidon. [29] The border turned to Ramah, to the fortified city of Tyre; and the border turned to Hosah. It ended at the sea by the region of Achzib; [30] Ummah also, and Aphek, and Rehob: twenty-two cities with their villages. [31] This is the inheritance of the tribe of the children of Asher according to their families, these cities with their villages. [32] The sixth lot came out for the children of Naphtali, even for the children of Naphtali according to their families. [33] Their border was from Heleph, from the oak in Zaanannim, Adami-nekeb, and Jabneel, to Lakkum. It ended at the Jordan. [34] The border turned westward to Aznoth Tabor, and went out from there to Hukkok. It reached to Zebulun on the south, and reached to Asher on the west, and to Judah at the Jordan toward the sunrise. [35] The fortified cities were Ziddim, Zer, Hammath, Rakkath, Chinnereth, [36] Adamah, Ramah, Hazor, [37] Kedesh, Edrei, En Hazor, [38] Iron, Migdal El, Horem, Beth Anath, and Beth Shemesh; nineteen cities with their villages. [39] This is the inheritance of the tribe of the children of Naphtali according to their families, the cities with their villages. [40] The seventh lot came out for the tribe of the children of Dan according to their families. [41] The border of their inheritance was Zorah, Eshtaol,

Irshemesh, <sup>42</sup> Shaalabbin, Aijalon, Ithlah, <sup>43</sup> Elon, Timnah, Ekron, <sup>44</sup> Eltekeh, Gibbethon, Baalath, <sup>45</sup> Jehud, Bene Berak, Gath Rimmon, <sup>46</sup> Me Jarkon, and Rakkon, with the border opposite Joppa. <sup>47</sup> The border of the children of Dan went out beyond them; for the children of Dan went up and fought against Leshem, and took it, and struck it with the edge of the sword, and possessed it, and lived therein, and called Leshem, Dan, after the name of Dan their forefather. <sup>48</sup> This is the inheritance of the tribe of the children of Dan according to their families, these cities with their villages. <sup>49</sup> So they finished distributing the land for inheritance by its borders. The children of Israel gave an inheritance to Joshua the son of Nun among them. <sup>50</sup> According to Yahweh's commandment, they gave him the city which he asked, even Timnathserah in the hill country of Ephraim; and he built the city, and lived there. <sup>51</sup> These are the inheritances, which Eleazar the priest, Joshua the son of Nun, and the heads of the fathers' houses of the tribes of the children of Israel, distributed for inheritance by lot in Shiloh before Yahweh, at the door of the Tent of Meeting. So they finished dividing the land.

# 20

<sup>1</sup> Yahweh spoke to Joshua, saying, <sup>2</sup>"Speak to the children of Israel, saying, 'Assign the cities of refuge, of which I spoke to you by Moses, <sup>3</sup> that the man slayer who kills any person accidentally or unintentionally may flee there. They shall be to you for a refuge from the avenger of blood. <sup>4</sup> He shall flee to one of those cities, and shall stand at the entrance of the gate of the city, and declare his case in the ears of the elders of that city. They shall take him into the city with them, and give him a place, that he may live among them. <sup>5</sup> If the avenger of blood pursues him, then they shall not deliver up the man slayer into his hand; because he struck his neighbor unintentionally, and didn't hate him before. <sup>6</sup> He shall dwell in that city until he stands before the congregation for judgment, until the death of the high priest that shall be in those days. Then the man slayer shall return, and come to his own city, and to his own house, to the city he fled from.'" <sup>7</sup> They set apart Kedesh in Galilee in the hill country of Naphtali, Shechem in the hill country of Ephraim, and Kiriath Arba (also called Hebron) in the hill country of Judah. <sup>8</sup> Beyond the Jordan at Jericho eastward, they assigned Bezer in the wilderness in the plain out of the tribe of Reuben, Ramoth in Gilead out of the tribe of Gad, and Golan in Bashan out of the tribe of Manasseh. <sup>9</sup> These were the appointed cities for all the children of Israel, and for the alien who lives among them, that whoever kills any person unintentionally might flee there, and not die by the hand of the avenger of blood, until he stands trial before the congregation.

# 21

<sup>1</sup> Then the heads of fathers' houses of the Levites came near to Eleazar the priest, and to Joshua the son of Nun, and to the heads of fathers' houses of the tribes of the children of Israel. <sup>2</sup> They spoke to them at Shiloh in the land of Canaan, saying, "Yahweh commanded through Moses to give us cities to dwell in, with their pasture lands for our livestock." <sup>3</sup> The children of Israel gave to the Levites out of their inheritance, according to the commandment of Yahweh, these cities with their pasture lands. <sup>4</sup> The lot came out for the families of the Kohathites. The children of Aaron the priest, who were of the Levites, had thirteen cities by lot out of the tribe of Judah, out of the tribe of the Simeonites, and out of the tribe of Benjamin. <sup>5</sup> The rest of the children of Kohath had ten cities by lot out of the families of the tribe of Ephraim, out of the tribe of Dan, and out of the half-tribe of Manasseh. <sup>6</sup> The children of Gershon had thirteen cities by lot out of the families of the tribe of Issachar, out of the tribe of Asher, out of the tribe of Naphtali, and out of the half-tribe of Manasseh in Bashan. <sup>7</sup> The children of Merari according to their families had twelve cities out of the tribe of Reuben, out of the tribe of Gad, and out of the tribe of Zebulun. <sup>8</sup> The children of Israel gave these cities with their pasture lands by lot to the Levites, as Yahweh commanded by Moses. <sup>9</sup> They gave out of the tribe of the children of Judah, and out of the tribe of the children of Simeon, these cities which are mentioned by name: <sup>10</sup> and they were for the children of Aaron, of the families of the Kohathites, who were of the children of Levi; for theirs was the first lot. <sup>11</sup> They gave them Kiriath Arba, named after the father of Anak (also called Hebron), in the hill country of Judah, with its pasture lands around it. <sup>12</sup> But they gave the fields of the city and its villages to Caleb the son of Jephunneh for his possession. <sup>13</sup> To the children of Aaron the priest they gave Hebron with its pasture lands, the city of refuge for the man slayer, Libnah with its pasture lands, <sup>14</sup> Jattir with its pasture lands, Eshtemoa with its pasture lands, <sup>15</sup> Holon with its pasture lands, Debir with its pasture lands, <sup>16</sup> Ain with its pasture lands, Juttah with its pasture lands, and Beth Shemesh with its pasture lands: nine cities out of those two tribes. <sup>17</sup> Out of the tribe of Benjamin, Gibeon with its pasture lands, Geba with its pasture lands, <sup>18</sup> Anathoth with its pasture lands, and Almon with its pasture lands: four cities. <sup>19</sup> All the cities of the children of Aaron, the priests, were thirteen cities with their pasture lands. <sup>20</sup> The families of the children of Kohath, the Levites, even the rest of the children of Kohath, had the cities of their lot out of the tribe of Ephraim. <sup>21</sup> They gave them Shechem with its pasture lands in the hill country of Ephraim, the city of refuge for the man slayer, and Gezer with its pasture lands, <sup>22</sup> Kibzaim with its pasture lands, and Beth Horon with its pasture lands: four cities. <sup>23</sup> Out of the tribe of Dan, Elteke with its pasture lands, Gibbethon with its pasture lands, <sup>24</sup> Aijalon with its pasture lands, Gath Rimmon with its pasture lands: four cities. <sup>25</sup> Out of the half-tribe of Manasseh, Taanach with its pasture lands, and Gath Rimmon with its pasture lands: two cities. <sup>26</sup> All the cities of the families of the rest of the children of Kohath were ten with their pasture lands. <sup>27</sup> They gave to the children of Gershon, of the families of the Levites, out of the half-tribe of Manasseh Golan in Bashan with its pasture lands, the city of refuge for the man slayer, and Be Eshterah with its pasture lands: two cities. <sup>28</sup> Out of the tribe of Issachar, Kishion with its pasture lands, Daberath with its pasture lands, <sup>29</sup> Jarmuth with its pasture lands, En Gannim with its pasture lands: four cities. <sup>30</sup> Out of the tribe of Asher, Mishal with its pasture lands, Abdon with its pasture lands, <sup>31</sup> Helkath with its pasture lands, and Rehob with its pasture lands: four cities. <sup>32</sup> Out of the tribe of Naphtali, Kedesh in Galilee with its pasture lands, the city of refuge for the man slayer, Hammothdor with its pasture lands, and Kartan with its pasture lands: three cities. <sup>33</sup> All the cities of the Gershonites according to their families were thirteen cities with their pasture lands. <sup>34</sup> To the families of the children of Merari, the rest of the Levites, out of the tribe of Zebulun, Jokneam with its pasture lands, Kartah with its pasture lands, <sup>35</sup> Dimnah with its pasture lands, and Nahalal with its pasture lands: four cities. <sup>36</sup> Out of the tribe of Reuben, Bezer with its pasture lands, Jahaz with its pasture lands, <sup>37</sup> Kedemoth with its pasture lands, and Mephaath with its pasture lands: four cities. <sup>38</sup> Out of the tribe of Gad, Ramoth in Gilead with its pasture lands, the city of refuge for the man slayer, and Mahanaim with its pasture lands, <sup>39</sup> Heshbon with its pasture lands, Jazer with its pasture lands: four cities in all. <sup>40</sup> All these were the cities of the children of Merari according to their families, even the rest of the families of the Levites. Their lot was twelve cities. <sup>41</sup> All the cities of the Levites among the possessions of the children of Israel were forty-eight cities with their pasture lands. <sup>42</sup> Each of these cities included their pasture lands around them. It was this way with all these cities. <sup>43</sup> So Yahweh gave to Israel all the land which he swore to give to their fathers. They possessed it, and lived in it. <sup>44</sup> Yahweh gave them rest all around, according to all that he swore to their fathers. Not a man of all their enemies stood before them. Yahweh delivered all their enemies into their hand. <sup>45</sup> Nothing failed of any good thing which Yahweh had spoken to the house of Israel. All came to pass.

# 22

<sup>1</sup> Then Joshua called the Reubenites, the Gadites, and the half-tribe of Manasseh, <sup>2</sup> and said to them, "You have kept all that Moses the servant of Yahweh commanded you, and have listened to my voice in all that I commanded you. <sup>3</sup> You have not left your brothers these many days to this day, but have performed the duty of the commandment of Yahweh your God. <sup>4</sup> Now Yahweh your God has given rest to your brothers, as he spoke to them. Therefore now return and go to your tents, to the land of your possession, which Moses the servant of Yahweh gave you beyond the Jordan. <sup>5</sup> Only take diligent heed to do the commandment and the law which Moses the servant of Yahweh commanded you, to love Yahweh your God, to walk in all his ways, to keep his commandments, to hold fast to him, and to serve him with all your heart and with all your soul." <sup>6</sup> So Joshua blessed them, and sent them away; and they went to their tents. <sup>7</sup> Now to the one half-tribe of Manasseh Moses had given inheritance in Bashan; but Joshua gave to the other half among their brothers beyond the Jordan westward. Moreover when Joshua sent them away to their tents, he blessed them, <sup>8</sup> and spoke to them, saying, "Return with much wealth to your tents, with very much livestock, with silver, with gold, with bronze, with iron, and with very much clothing. Divide the plunder of your enemies with your brothers." <sup>9</sup> The children of Reuben and the children of Gad and the half-tribe of Manasseh returned, and departed from the children of Israel out of Shiloh, which is in the land of Canaan, to go to the land of Gilead, to the land of their possession, which they owned, according to the commandment of Yahweh by Moses. <sup>10</sup> When they came to the region near the Jordan, that is in the land of Canaan, the children of Reuben and the children of Gad and the half-tribe of Manasseh built an altar there by the Jordan, a great altar to look at. <sup>11</sup> The children of Israel heard this, "Behold, the children of Reuben and the children of Gad and the half-tribe of Manasseh have built an altar along the border of the land of Canaan, in the region around the Jordan, on the side that belongs to the children of Israel." <sup>12</sup> When the children of Israel heard of it, the whole congregation of the children of Israel gathered themselves together at Shiloh, to go up against them to war. <sup>13</sup> The children of Israel

sent to the children of Reuben, and to the children of Gad, and to the half-tribe of Manasseh, into the land of Gilead, Phinehas the son of Eleazar the priest. ¹⁴ With him were ten princes, one prince of a fathers' house for each of the tribes of Israel; and they were each head of their fathers' houses among the thousands of Israel. ¹⁵ They came to the children of Reuben, and to the children of Gad, and to the half-tribe of Manasseh, to the land of Gilead, and they spoke with them, saying, ¹⁶"The whole congregation of Yahweh says, 'What trespass is this that you have committed against the God of Israel, to turn away today from following Yahweh, in that you have built yourselves an altar, to rebel today against Yahweh? ¹⁷ Is the iniquity of Peor too little for us, from which we have not cleansed ourselves to this day, although there came a plague on the congregation of Yahweh, ¹⁸ that you must turn away today from following Yahweh? It will be, since you rebel today against Yahweh, that tomorrow he will be angry with the whole congregation of Israel. ¹⁹ However, if the land of your possession is unclean, then pass over to the land of the possession of Yahweh, in which Yahweh's tabernacle dwells, and take possession among us; but don't rebel against Yahweh, nor rebel against us, in building an altar other than Yahweh our God's altar. ²⁰ Didn't Achan the son of Zerah commit a trespass in the devoted thing, and wrath fell on all the congregation of Israel? That man didn't perish alone in his iniquity.'" ²¹ Then the children of Reuben and the children of Gad and the half-tribe of Manasseh answered, and spoke to the heads of the thousands of Israel, ²²"The Mighty One, God, Yahweh, the Mighty One, God, Yahweh, he knows; and Israel shall know: if it was in rebellion, or if in trespass against Yahweh (don't save us today), ²³ that we have built us an altar to turn away from following Yahweh; or if to offer burnt offering or meal offering, or if to offer sacrifices of peace offerings, let Yahweh himself require it. ²⁴"If we have not out of concern done this, and for a reason, saying, 'In time to come your children might speak to our children, saying, "What have you to do with Yahweh, the God of Israel? ²⁵ For Yahweh has made the Jordan a border between us and you, you children of Reuben and children of Gad. You have no portion in Yahweh."' So your children might make our children cease from fearing Yahweh. ²⁶"Therefore we said, 'Let's now prepare to build ourselves an altar, not for burnt offering, nor for sacrifice; ²⁷ but it will be a witness between us and you, and between our generations after us, that we may perform the service of Yahweh before him with our burnt offerings, with our sacrifices, and with our peace offerings;' that your children may not tell our children in time to come, 'You have no portion in Yahweh.' ²⁸"Therefore we said, 'It shall be, when they tell us or our generations this in time to come, that we shall say, "Behold the pattern of Yahweh's altar, which our fathers made, not for burnt offering, nor for sacrifice; but it is a witness between us and you."' ²⁹"Far be it from us that we should rebel against Yahweh, and turn away today from following Yahweh, to build an altar for burnt offering, for meal offering, or for sacrifice, besides Yahweh our God's altar that is before his tabernacle!" ³⁰ When Phinehas the priest, and the princes of the congregation, even the heads of the thousands of Israel that were with him, heard the words that the children of Reuben and the children of Gad and the children of Manasseh spoke, it pleased them well. ³¹ Phinehas the son of Eleazar the priest said to the children of Reuben, to the children of Gad, and to the children of Manasseh, "Today we know that Yahweh is among us, because you have not committed this trespass against Yahweh. Now you have delivered the children of Israel out of Yahweh's hand." ³² Phinehas the son of Eleazar the priest, and the princes, returned from the children of Reuben, and from the children of Gad, out of the land of Gilead, to the land of Canaan, to the children of Israel, and brought them word again. ³³ The thing pleased the children of Israel; and the children of Israel blessed God, and spoke no more of going up against them to war, to destroy the land in which the children of Reuben and the children of Gad lived. ³⁴ The children of Reuben and the children of Gad named the altar "A Witness Between Us that Yahweh is God."

## 23

¹ After many days, when Yahweh had given rest to Israel from their enemies all around, and Joshua was old and well advanced in years, ² Joshua called for all Israel, for their elders and for their heads, and for their judges and for their officers, and said to them, "I am old and well advanced in years. ³ You have seen all that Yahweh your God has done to all these nations because of you; for it is Yahweh your God who has fought for you. ⁴ Behold, I have allotted to you these nations that remain, to be an inheritance for your tribes, from the Jordan, with all the nations that I have cut off, even to the great sea toward the going down of the sun. ⁵ Yahweh your God will thrust them out from before you, and drive them from out of your sight. You shall possess their land, as Yahweh your God spoke to you. ⁶"Therefore be very courageous to

keep and to do all that is written in the book of the law of Moses, that you not turn away from it to the right hand or to the left; ⁷ that you not come among these nations, these that remain among you; neither make mention of the name of their gods, nor cause to swear by them, neither serve them, nor bow down yourselves to them; ⁸ but hold fast to Yahweh your God, as you have done to this day. ⁹"For Yahweh has driven great and strong nations out from before you. But as for you, no man has stood before you to this day. ¹⁰ One man of you shall chase a thousand; for it is Yahweh your God who fights for you, as he spoke to you. ¹¹ Take good heed therefore to yourselves, that you love Yahweh your God. ¹²"But if you do at all go back, and hold fast to the remnant of these nations, even these who remain among you, and make marriages with them, and go in to them, and they to you; ¹³ know for a certainty that Yahweh your God will no longer drive these nations from out of your sight; but they shall be a snare and a trap to you, a scourge in your sides, and thorns in your eyes, until you perish from off this good land which Yahweh your God has given you. ¹⁴"Behold, today I am going the way of all the earth. You know in all your hearts and in all your souls that not one thing has failed of all the good things which Yahweh your God spoke concerning you. All have happened to you. Not one thing has failed of it. ¹⁵ It shall happen that as all the good things have come on you of which Yahweh your God spoke to you, so Yahweh will bring on you all the evil things, until he has destroyed you from off this good land which Yahweh your God has given you, ¹⁶ when you disobey the covenant of Yahweh your God, which he commanded you, and go and serve other gods, and bow down yourselves to them. Then Yahweh's anger will be kindled against you, and you will perish quickly from off the good land which he has given to you."

## 24

¹ Joshua gathered all the tribes of Israel to Shechem, and called for the elders of Israel, for their heads, for their judges, and for their officers; and they presented themselves before God. ² Joshua said to all the people, "Yahweh, the God of Israel, says, 'Your fathers lived of old time beyond the River, even Terah, the father of Abraham, and the father of Nahor. They served other gods. ³ I took your father Abraham from beyond the River, and led him throughout all the land of Canaan, and multiplied his offspring,ᵃ and gave him Isaac. ⁴ I gave to Isaac Jacob and Esau: and I gave to Esau Mount Seir, to possess it. Jacob and his children went down into Egypt. ⁵"'I sent Moses and Aaron, and I plagued Egypt, according to that which I did among them: and afterward I brought you out. ⁶ I brought your fathers out of Egypt: and you came to the sea. The Egyptians pursued your fathers with chariots and with horsemen to the Red Sea. ⁷ When they cried out to Yahweh, he put darkness between you and the Egyptians, and brought the sea on them, and covered them; and your eyes saw what I did in Egypt. You lived in the wilderness many days. ⁸"'I brought you into the land of the Amorites, that lived beyond the Jordan. They fought with you, and I gave them into your hand. You possessed their land, and I destroyed them from before you. ⁹ Then Balak the son of Zippor, king of Moab, arose and fought against Israel. He sent and called Balaam the son of Beor to curse you, ¹⁰ but I would not listen to Balaam; therefore he blessed you still. So I delivered you out of his hand. ¹¹"'You went over the Jordan, and came to Jericho. The men of Jericho fought against you, the Amorite, the Perizzite, the Canaanite, the Hittite, the Girgashite, the Hivite, and the Jebusite; and I delivered them into your hand. ¹² I sent the hornet before you, which drove them out from before you, even the two kings of the Amorites; not with your sword, nor with your bow. ¹³ I gave you a land on which you had not labored, and cities which you didn't build, and you live in them. You eat of vineyards and olive groves which you didn't plant.' ¹⁴"Now therefore fear Yahweh, and serve him in sincerity and in truth. Put away the gods which your fathers served beyond the River, in Egypt; and serve Yahweh. ¹⁵ If it seems evil to you to serve Yahweh, choose today whom you will serve; whether the gods which your fathers served that were beyond the River, or the gods of the Amorites, in whose land you dwell; but as for me and my house, we will serve Yahweh." ¹⁶ The people answered, "Far be it from us that we should forsake Yahweh, to serve other gods; ¹⁷ for it is Yahweh our God who brought us and our fathers up out of the land of Egypt, from the house of bondage, and who did those great signs in our sight, and preserved us in all the way in which we went, and among all the peoples through the middle of whom we passed. ¹⁸ Yahweh drove out from before us all the peoples, even the Amorites who lived in the land. Therefore we also will serve Yahweh; for he is our God." ¹⁹ Joshua said to the people, "You can't serve Yahweh, for he is a holy God. He is a jealous God. He will not forgive your disobedience nor your sins. ²⁰ If you forsake Yahweh, and serve foreign gods, then he will turn and do you evil, and consume you, after he has done you good." ²¹ The people said to Joshua, "No, but we will serve Yahweh."

ᵃ *24:3 or, seed*

²² Joshua said to the people, "You are witnesses against yourselves that you have chosen Yahweh yourselves, to serve him." They said, "We are witnesses." ²³"Now therefore put away the foreign gods which are among you, and incline your heart to Yahweh, the God of Israel." ²⁴ The people said to Joshua, "We will serve Yahweh our God, and we will listen to his voice." ²⁵ So Joshua made a covenant with the people that day, and made for them a statute and an ordinance in Shechem. ²⁶ Joshua wrote these words in the book of the law of God; and he took a great stone, and set it up there under the oak that was by the sanctuary of Yahweh. ²⁷ Joshua said to all the people, "Behold, this stone shall be a witness against us, for it has heard all Yahweh's words which he spoke to us. It shall be therefore a witness against you, lest you deny your God." ²⁸ So Joshua sent the people away, each to his own inheritance. ²⁹ After these things, Joshua the son of Nun, the servant of Yahweh, died, being one hundred ten years old. ³⁰ They buried him in the border of his inheritance in Timnathserah, which is in the hill country of Ephraim, on the north of the mountain of Gaash. ³¹ Israel served Yahweh all the days of Joshua, and all the days of the elders who outlived Joshua, and had known all the work of Yahweh, that he had worked for Israel. ³² They buried the bones of Joseph, which the children of Israel brought up out of Egypt, in Shechem, in the parcel of ground which Jacob bought from the sons of Hamor the father of Shechem for a hundred pieces of silver.ᵃ They became the inheritance of the children of Joseph. ³³ Eleazar the son of Aaron died. They buried him in the hill of Phinehas his son, which was given him in the hill country of Ephraim.

## The Book of Judges
### 1

¹ After the death of Joshua, the children of Israel asked of Yahweh,ᵇ saying, "Who should go up for us first against the Canaanites, to fight against them?" ² Yahweh said, "Judah shall go up. Behold,ᶜ I have delivered the land into his hand." ³ Judah said to Simeon his brother, "Come up with me into my lot, that we may fight against the Canaanites; and I likewise will go with you into your lot." So Simeon went with him. ⁴ Judah went up, and Yahweh delivered the Canaanites and the Perizzites into their hand. They struck ten thousand men in Bezek. ⁵ They found Adoni-Bezek in Bezek, and they fought against him. They struck the Canaanites and the Perizzites. ⁶ But Adoni-Bezek fled. They pursued him, caught him, and cut off his thumbs and his big toes. ⁷ Adoni-Bezek said, "Seventy kings, having their thumbs and their big toes cut off, scavenged under my table. As I have done, so Godᵈ has done to me." They brought him to Jerusalem, and he died there. ⁸ The children of Judah fought against Jerusalem, took it, struck it with the edge of the sword, and set the city on fire. ⁹ After that, the children of Judah went down to fight against the Canaanites who lived in the hill country, and in the South, and in the lowland. ¹⁰ Judah went against the Canaanites who lived in Hebron. (The name of Hebron before that was Kiriath Arba.) They struck Sheshai, Ahiman, and Talmai. ¹¹ From there he went against the inhabitants of Debir. (The name of Debir before that was Kiriath Sepher.) ¹² Caleb said, "I will give Achsah my daughter as wife to the man who strikes Kiriath Sepher, and takes it." ¹³ Othniel the son of Kenaz, Caleb's younger brother, took it, so he gave him Achsah his daughter as his wife. ¹⁴ When she came, she got him to ask her father for a field. She got off her donkey; and Caleb said to her, "What would you like?" ¹⁵ She said to him, "Give me a blessing; because you have set me in the land of the South, give me also springs of water." Then Caleb gave her the upper springs and the lower springs. ¹⁶ The children of the Kenite, Moses' brother-in-law, went up out of the city of palm trees with the children of Judah into the wilderness of Judah, which is in the south of Arad; and they went and lived with the people. ¹⁷ Judah went with Simeon his brother, and they struck the Canaanites who inhabited Zephath, and utterly destroyed it. The name of the city was called Hormah. ¹⁸ Also Judah took Gaza with its border, and Ashkelon with its border, and Ekron with its border. ¹⁹ Yahweh was with Judah, and drove out the inhabitants of the hill country; for he could not drive out the inhabitants of the valley, because they had chariots of iron. ²⁰ They gave Hebron to Caleb, as Moses had said, and he drove the three sons of Anak out of there. ²¹ The children of Benjamin didn't drive out the Jebusites who inhabited Jerusalem, but the Jebusites dwell with the children of Benjamin in Jerusalem to this day. ²² The house of Joseph also went up against Bethel, and Yahweh was with them. ²³ The house of Joseph sent to spy out Bethel. (The

name of the city before that was Luz.) ²⁴ The watchers saw a man come out of the city, and they said to him, "Please show us the entrance into the city, and we will deal kindly with you." ²⁵ He showed them the entrance into the city, and they struck the city with the edge of the sword; but they let the man and all his family go. ²⁶ The man went into the land of the Hittites, built a city, and called its name Luz, which is its name to this day. ²⁷ Manasseh didn't drive out the inhabitants of Beth Shean and its towns, nor Taanach and its towns, nor the inhabitants of Dor and its towns, nor the inhabitants of Ibleam and its towns, nor the inhabitants of Megiddo and its towns; but the Canaanites would dwell in that land. ²⁸ When Israel had grown strong, they put the Canaanites to forced labor, and didn't utterly drive them out. ²⁹ Ephraim didn't drive out the Canaanites who lived in Gezer, but the Canaanites lived in Gezer among them. ³⁰ Zebulun didn't drive out the inhabitants of Kitron, nor the inhabitants of Nahalol; but the Canaanites lived among them, and became subject to forced labor. ³¹ Asher didn't drive out the inhabitants of Acco, nor the inhabitants of Sidon, nor of Ahlab, nor of Achzib, nor of Helbah, nor of Aphik, nor of Rehob; ³² but the Asherites lived among the Canaanites, the inhabitants of the land, for they didn't drive them out. ³³ Naphtali didn't drive out the inhabitants of Beth Shemesh, nor the inhabitants of Beth Anath; but he lived among the Canaanites, the inhabitants of the land. Nevertheless the inhabitants of Beth Shemesh and of Beth Anath became subject to forced labor. ³⁴ The Amorites forced the children of Dan into the hill country, for they would not allow them to come down to the valley; ³⁵ but the Amorites would dwell in Mount Heres, in Aijalon, and in Shaalbim. Yet the hand of the house of Joseph prevailed, so that they became subject to forced labor. ³⁶ The border of the Amorites was from the ascent of Akrabbim, from the rock, and upward.

### 2

¹ Yahweh's angel came up from Gilgal to Bochim. He said, "I brought you out of Egypt, and have brought you to the land which I swore to give your fathers. I said, 'I will never break my covenant with you. ² You shall make no covenant with the inhabitants of this land. You shall break down their altars.' But you have not listened to my voice. Why have you done this? ³ Therefore I also said, 'I will not drive them out from before you; but they shall be in your sides, and their gods will be a snare to you.'" ⁴ When Yahweh's angel spoke these words to all the children of Israel, the people lifted up their voice and wept. ⁵ They called the name of that place Bochim,ᵉ and they sacrificed there to Yahweh. ⁶ Now when Joshua had sent the people away, the children of Israel each went to his inheritance to possess the land. ⁷ The people served Yahweh all the days of Joshua, and all the days of the elders who outlived Joshua, who had seen all the great work of Yahweh that he had worked for Israel. ⁸ Joshua the son of Nun, the servant of Yahweh, died, being one hundred ten years old. ⁹ They buried him in the border of his inheritance in Timnath Heres, in the hill country of Ephraim, on the north of the mountain of Gaash. ¹⁰ After all that generation were gathered to their fathers, another generation arose after them who didn't know Yahweh, nor the work which he had done for Israel. ¹¹ The children of Israel did that which was evil in Yahweh's sight, and served the Baals. ¹² They abandoned Yahweh, the God of their fathers, who brought them out of the land of Egypt, and followed other gods, of the gods of the peoples who were around them, and bowed themselves down to them; and they provoked Yahweh to anger. ¹³ They abandoned Yahweh, and served Baal and the Ashtaroth. ¹⁴ Yahweh's anger burned against Israel, and he delivered them into the hands of raiders who plundered them. He sold them into the hands of their enemies all around, so that they could no longer stand before their enemies. ¹⁵ Wherever they went out, Yahweh's hand was against them for evil, as Yahweh had spoken, and as Yahweh had sworn to them; and they were very distressed. ¹⁶ Yahweh raised up judges, who saved them out of the hand of those who plundered them. ¹⁷ Yet they didn't listen to their judges; for they prostituted themselves to other gods, and bowed themselves down to them. They quickly turned away from the way in which their fathers walked, obeying Yahweh's commandments. They didn't do so. ¹⁸ When Yahweh raised up judges for them, then Yahweh was with the judge, and saved them out of the hand of their enemies all the days of the judge; for it grieved Yahweh because of their groaning by reason of those who oppressed them and troubled them. ¹⁹ But when the judge was dead, they turned back, and dealt more corruptly than their fathers in following other gods to serve them and to bow down to them. They didn't cease what they were doing, or give up their stubborn ways. ²⁰ Yahweh's anger burned against Israel; and

ᵃ *24:32* Hebrew: kesitahs. A kesitah was a kind of silver coin.
ᵇ *1:1* "Yahweh" is God's proper Name, sometimes rendered "LORD" (all caps) in other translations.
ᶜ *1:2* "Behold", from "הִנֵּה", means look at, take notice, observe, see, or gaze at. It is often used as an interjection.
ᵈ *1:7* The Hebrew word rendered "God" is "אֱלֹהִים" (Elohim).
ᵉ *2:5* "Bochim" means "weepers".

he said, "Because this nation transgressed my covenant which I commanded their fathers, and has not listened to my voice, ²¹ I also will no longer drive out any of the nations that Joshua left when he died from before them; ²² that by them I may test Israel, to see if they will keep Yahweh's way to walk therein, as their fathers kept it, or not." ²³ So Yahweh left those nations, without driving them out hastily. He didn't deliver them into Joshua's hand.

**3**

¹ Now these are the nations which Yahweh left, to test Israel by them, even as many as had not known all the wars of Canaan; ² only that the generations of the children of Israel might know, to teach them war, at least those who knew nothing of it before: ³ the five lords of the Philistines, all the Canaanites, the Sidonians, and the Hivites who lived on Mount Lebanon, from Mount Baal Hermon to the entrance of Hamath. ⁴ They were left to test Israel by them, to know whether they would listen to Yahweh's commandments, which he commanded their fathers by Moses. ⁵ The children of Israel lived among the Canaanites, the Hittites, the Amorites, the Perizzites, the Hivites, and the Jebusites. ⁶ They took their daughters to be their wives, and gave their own daughters to their sons and served their gods. ⁷ The children of Israel did that which was evil in Yahweh's sight, and forgot Yahweh their God, and served the Baals and the Asheroth. ⁸ Therefore Yahweh's anger burned against Israel, and he sold them into the hand of Cushan Rishathaim king of Mesopotamia; and the children of Israel served Cushan Rishathaim eight years. ⁹ When the children of Israel cried to Yahweh, Yahweh raised up a savior to the children of Israel, who saved them, even Othniel the son of Kenaz, Caleb's younger brother. ¹⁰ Yahweh's Spirit came on him, and he judged Israel; and he went out to war, and Yahweh delivered Cushan Rishathaim king of Mesopotamia into his hand. His hand prevailed against Cushan Rishathaim. ¹¹ The land had rest forty years, then Othniel the son of Kenaz died. ¹² The children of Israel again did that which was evil in Yahweh's sight, and Yahweh strengthened Eglon the king of Moab against Israel, because they had done that which was evil in Yahweh's sight. ¹³ He gathered the children of Ammon and Amalek to himself; and he went and struck Israel, and they possessed the city of palm trees. ¹⁴ The children of Israel served Eglon the king of Moab eighteen years. ¹⁵ But when the children of Israel cried to Yahweh, Yahweh raised up a savior for them: Ehud the son of Gera, the Benjamite, a left-handed man. The children of Israel sent tribute by him to Eglon the king of Moab. ¹⁶ Ehud made himself a sword which had two edges, a cubit[a] in length; and he wore it under his clothing on his right thigh. ¹⁷ He offered the tribute to Eglon king of Moab. Now Eglon was a very fat man. ¹⁸ When Ehud had finished offering the tribute, he sent away the people who carried the tribute. ¹⁹ But he himself turned back from the stone idols that were by Gilgal, and said, "I have a secret message for you, O king." The king said, "Keep silence!" All who stood by him left him. ²⁰ Ehud came to him; and he was sitting by himself alone in the cool upper room. Ehud said, "I have a message from God to you." He arose out of his seat. ²¹ Ehud put out his left hand, and took the sword from his right thigh, and thrust it into his body. ²² The handle also went in after the blade; and the fat closed on the blade, for he didn't draw the sword out of his body; and it came out behind. ²³ Then Ehud went out onto the porch, and shut the doors of the upper room on him, and locked them. ²⁴ After he had gone, his servants came and saw that the doors of the upper room were locked. They said, "Surely he is covering his feet[b] in the upper room." ²⁵ They waited until they were ashamed; and behold, he didn't open the doors of the upper room. Therefore they took the key and opened them, and behold, their lord had fallen down dead on the floor. ²⁶ Ehud escaped while they waited, passed beyond the stone idols, and escaped to Seirah. ²⁷ When he had come, he blew a trumpet in the hill country of Ephraim; and the children of Israel went down with him from the hill country, and he led them. ²⁸ He said to them, "Follow me; for Yahweh has delivered your enemies the Moabites into your hand." They followed him, and took the fords of the Jordan against the Moabites, and didn't allow any man to pass over. ²⁹ They struck at that time about ten thousand men of Moab, every strong man and every man of valor. No man escaped. ³⁰ So Moab was subdued that day under the hand of Israel. Then the land had rest eighty years. ³¹ After him was Shamgar the son of Anath, who struck six hundred men of the Philistines with an ox goad. He also saved Israel.

**4**

¹ The children of Israel again did that which was evil in Yahweh's sight, when Ehud was dead. ² Yahweh sold them into the hand of Jabin king of Canaan, who reigned in Hazor; the captain of whose army was Sisera, who lived in Harosheth of the Gentiles. ³ The children of Israel

cried to Yahweh, for he had nine hundred chariots of iron; and he mightily oppressed the children of Israel for twenty years. ⁴ Now Deborah, a prophetess, the wife of Lappidoth, judged Israel at that time. ⁵ She lived under Deborah's palm tree between Ramah and Bethel in the hill country of Ephraim; and the children of Israel came up to her for judgment. ⁶ She sent and called Barak the son of Abinoam out of Kedesh Naphtali, and said to him, "Hasn't Yahweh, the God of Israel, commanded, 'Go and lead the way to Mount Tabor, and take with you ten thousand men of the children of Naphtali and of the children of Zebulun? ⁷ I will draw to you, to the river Kishon, Sisera, the captain of Jabin's army, with his chariots and his multitude; and I will deliver him into your hand.'" ⁸ Barak said to her, "If you will go with me, then I will go; but if you will not go with me, I will not go." ⁹ She said, "I will surely go with you. Nevertheless, the journey that you take won't be for your honor; for Yahweh will sell Sisera into a woman's hand." Deborah arose, and went with Barak to Kedesh. ¹⁰ Barak called Zebulun and Naphtali together to Kedesh. Ten thousand men followed him; and Deborah went up with him. ¹¹ Now Heber the Kenite had separated himself from the Kenites, even from the children of Hobab, Moses' brother-in-law, and had pitched his tent as far as the oak in Zaanannim, which is by Kedesh. ¹² They told Sisera that Barak the son of Abinoam had gone up to Mount Tabor. ¹³ Sisera gathered together all his chariots, even nine hundred chariots of iron, and all the people who were with him, from Harosheth of the Gentiles, to the river Kishon. ¹⁴ Deborah said to Barak, "Go; for this is the day in which Yahweh has delivered Sisera into your hand. Hasn't Yahweh gone out before you?" So Barak went down from Mount Tabor, and ten thousand men after him. ¹⁵ Yahweh confused Sisera, all his chariots, and all his army, with the edge of the sword before Barak. Sisera abandoned his chariot and fled away on his feet. ¹⁶ But Barak pursued the chariots and the army to Harosheth of the Gentiles; and all the army of Sisera fell by the edge of the sword. There was not a man left. ¹⁷ However Sisera fled away on his feet to the tent of Jael the wife of Heber the Kenite; for there was peace between Jabin the king of Hazor and the house of Heber the Kenite. ¹⁸ Jael went out to meet Sisera, and said to him, "Turn in, my lord, turn in to me; don't be afraid." He came in to her into the tent, and she covered him with a rug. ¹⁹ He said to her, "Please give me a little water to drink; for I am thirsty." She opened a container of milk, and gave him a drink, and covered him. ²⁰ He said to her, "Stand in the door of the tent, and if any man comes and inquires of you, and says, 'Is there any man here?' you shall say, 'No.'" ²¹ Then Jael, Heber's wife, took a tent peg, and took a hammer in her hand, and went softly to him, and struck the pin into his temples, and it pierced through into the ground, for he was in a deep sleep; so he fainted and died. ²² Behold, as Barak pursued Sisera, Jael came out to meet him, and said to him, "Come, and I will show you the man whom you seek." He came to her; and behold, Sisera lay dead, and the tent peg was in his temples. ²³ So God subdued Jabin the king of Canaan before the children of Israel on that day. ²⁴ The hand of the children of Israel prevailed more and more against Jabin the king of Canaan, until they had destroyed Jabin king of Canaan.

**5**

¹ Then Deborah and Barak the son of Abinoam sang on that day, saying, ²"Because the leaders took the lead in Israel, because the people offered themselves willingly, be blessed, Yahweh! ³"Hear, you kings! Give ear, you princes! I, even I, will sing to Yahweh. I will sing praise to Yahweh, the God of Israel. ⁴"Yahweh, when you went out of Seir, when you marched out of the field of Edom, the earth trembled, the sky also dropped. Yes, the clouds dropped water. ⁵ The mountains quaked at Yahweh's presence, even Sinai at the presence of Yahweh, the God of Israel. ⁶"In the days of Shamgar the son of Anath, in the days of Jael, the highways were unoccupied. The travelers walked through byways. ⁷ The rulers ceased in Israel. They ceased until I, Deborah, arose; Until I arose a mother in Israel. ⁸ They chose new gods. Then war was in the gates. Was there a shield or spear seen among forty thousand in Israel? ⁹ My heart is toward the governors of Israel, who offered themselves willingly among the people. Bless Yahweh! ¹⁰"Speak, you who ride on white donkeys, you who sit on rich carpets, and you who walk by the way. ¹¹ Far from the noise of archers, in the places of drawing water, there they will rehearse Yahweh's righteous acts, the righteous acts of his rule in Israel. "Then Yahweh's people went down to the gates. ¹²'Awake, awake, Deborah! Awake, awake, utter a song! Arise, Barak, and lead away your captives, you son of Abinoam.' ¹³"Then a remnant of the nobles and the people came down. Yahweh came down for me against the mighty. ¹⁴ Those whose root is in Amalek came out of Ephraim, after you, Benjamin, among your peoples. Governors come

---

[a] *3:16 A cubit is the length from the tip of the middle finger to the elbow on a man's* arm, or about 18 inches or 46 centimeters.

[b] *3:24 or, "relieving himself".*

down out of Machir. Those who handle the marshal's staff came out of Zebulun. ¹⁵ The princes of Issachar were with Deborah. As was Issachar, so was Barak. They rushed into the valley at his feet. By the watercourses of Reuben, there were great resolves of heart. ¹⁶ Why did you sit among the sheepfolds? To hear the whistling for the flocks? At the watercourses of Reuben, there were great searchings of heart. ¹⁷ Gilead lived beyond the Jordan. Why did Dan remain in ships? Asher sat still at the haven of the sea, and lived by his creeks. ¹⁸ Zebulun was a people that jeopardized their lives to the death; Naphtali also, on the high places of the field. ¹⁹"The kings came and fought, then the kings of Canaan fought at Taanach by the waters of Megiddo. They took no plunder of silver. ²⁰ From the sky the stars fought. From their courses, they fought against Sisera. ²¹ The river Kishon swept them away, that ancient river, the river Kishon. My soul, march on with strength. ²²Then the horse hoofs stamped because of the prancing, the prancing of their strong ones. ²³'Curse Meroz,' said Yahweh's angel. 'Curse bitterly its inhabitants, because they didn't come to help Yahweh, to help Yahweh against the mighty.' ²⁴"Jael shall be blessed above women, the wife of Heber the Kenite; blessed shall she be above women in the tent. ²⁵ He asked for water. She gave him milk. She brought him butter in a lordly dish. ²⁶ She put her hand to the tent peg, and her right hand to the workmen's hammer. With the hammer she struck Sisera. She struck through his head. Yes, she pierced and struck through his temples. ²⁷ At her feet he bowed, he fell, he lay. At her feet he bowed, he fell. Where he bowed, there he fell down dead. ²⁸"Through the window she looked out, and cried: Sisera's mother looked through the lattice. 'Why is his chariot so long in coming? Why do the wheels of his chariots wait?' ²⁹ Her wise ladies answered her, Yes, she returned answer to herself, ³⁰'Have they not found, have they not divided the plunder? A lady, two ladies to every man; to Sisera a plunder of dyed garments, a plunder of dyed garments embroidered, of dyed garments embroidered on both sides, on the necks of the plunder?' ³¹"So let all your enemies perish, Yahweh, but let those who love him be as the sun when it rises in its strength." Then the land had rest forty years.

# 6

¹ The children of Israel did that which was evil in Yahweh's sight, so Yahweh delivered them into the hand of Midian seven years. ² The hand of Midian prevailed against Israel; and because of Midian the children of Israel made themselves the dens which are in the mountains, the caves, and the strongholds. ³ So it was, when Israel had sown, that the Midianites, the Amalekites, and the children of the east came up against them. ⁴ They encamped against them, and destroyed the increase of the earth, until you come to Gaza. They left no sustenance in Israel, and no sheep, ox, or donkey. ⁵ For they came up with their livestock and their tents. They came in as locusts for multitude. Both they and their camels were without number; and they came into the land to destroy it. ⁶ Israel was brought very low because of Midian; and the children of Israel cried to Yahweh. ⁷ When the children of Israel cried to Yahweh because of Midian, ⁸ Yahweh sent a prophet to the children of Israel; and he said to them, "Yahweh, the God of Israel, says, 'I brought you up from Egypt, and brought you out of the house of bondage. ⁹ I delivered you out of the hand of the Egyptians and out of the hand of all who oppressed you, and drove them out from before you, and gave you their land. ¹⁰ I said to you, "I am Yahweh your God. You shall not fear the gods of the Amorites, in whose land you dwell." But you have not listened to my voice.'" ¹¹ Yahweh's angel came and sat under the oak which was in Ophrah, that belonged to Joash the Abiezrite. His son Gideon was beating out wheat in the wine press, to hide it from the Midianites. ¹² Yahweh's angel appeared to him, and said to him, "Yahweh is with you, you mighty man of valor!" ¹³ Gideon said to him, "Oh, my lord, if Yahweh is with us, why then has all this happened to us? Where are all his wondrous works which our fathers told us of, saying, 'Didn't Yahweh bring us up from Egypt?' But now Yahweh has cast us off, and delivered us into the hand of Midian." ¹⁴ Yahweh looked at him, and said, "Go in this your might, and save Israel from the hand of Midian. Haven't I sent you?" ¹⁵ He said to him, "O Lord,[a] how shall I save Israel? Behold, my family is the poorest in Manasseh, and I am the least in my father's house." ¹⁶ Yahweh said to him, "Surely I will be with you, and you shall strike the Midianites as one man." ¹⁷ He said to him, "If now I have found favor in your sight, then show me a sign that it is you who talk with me. ¹⁸ Please don't go away until I come to you, and bring out my present, and lay it before you." He said, "I will wait until you come back." ¹⁹ Gideon went in and prepared a young goat and unleavened cakes of an ephah[b] of meal. He put the meat in a basket and he put the broth in a pot, and brought it out to him under the oak, and presented it. ²⁰ The angel of God said to him, "Take the meat and the unleavened cakes, and lay them on this rock, and pour out

the broth." He did so. ²¹ Then Yahweh's angel stretched out the end of the staff that was in his hand, and touched the meat and the unleavened cakes; and fire went up out of the rock and consumed the meat and the unleavened cakes. Then Yahweh's angel departed out of his sight. ²² Gideon saw that he was Yahweh's angel; and Gideon said, "Alas, Lord Yahweh! Because I have seen Yahweh's angel face to face!" ²³ Yahweh said to him, "Peace be to you! Don't be afraid. You shall not die." ²⁴ Then Gideon built an altar there to Yahweh, and called it "Yahweh is Peace."[c] To this day it is still in Ophrah of the Abiezrites. ²⁵ That same night, Yahweh said to him, "Take your father's bull, even the second bull seven years old, and throw down the altar of Baal that your father has, and cut down the Asherah that is by it. ²⁶ Then build an altar to Yahweh your God on the top of this stronghold, in an orderly way, and take the second bull, and offer a burnt offering with the wood of the Asherah which you shall cut down." ²⁷ Then Gideon took ten men of his servants, and did as Yahweh had spoken to him. Because he feared his father's household and the men of the city, he could not do it by day, but he did it by night. ²⁸ When the men of the city arose early in the morning, behold, the altar of Baal was broken down, and the Asherah was cut down that was by it, and the second bull was offered on the altar that was built. ²⁹ They said to one another, "Who has done this thing?" When they inquired and asked, they said, "Gideon the son of Joash has done this thing." ³⁰ Then the men of the city said to Joash, "Bring out your son, that he may die, because he has broken down the altar of Baal, and because he has cut down the Asherah that was by it." ³¹ Joash said to all who stood against him, "Will you contend for Baal? Or will you save him? He who will contend for him, let him be put to death by morning! If he is a god, let him contend for himself, because someone has broken down his altar!" ³² Therefore on that day he named him Jerub-Baal,[d] saying, "Let Baal contend against him, because he has broken down his altar." ³³ Then all the Midianites and the Amalekites and the children of the east assembled themselves together; and they passed over, and encamped in the valley of Jezreel. ³⁴ But Yahweh's Spirit came on Gideon, and he blew a trumpet; and Abiezer was gathered together to follow him. ³⁵ He sent messengers throughout all Manasseh, and they also were gathered together to follow him. He sent messengers to Asher, to Zebulun, and to Naphtali; and they came up to meet them. ³⁶ Gideon said to God, "If you will save Israel by my hand, as you have spoken, ³⁷ behold, I will put a fleece of wool on the threshing floor. If there is dew on the fleece only, and it is dry on all the ground, then I'll know that you will save Israel by my hand, as you have spoken." ³⁸ It was so; for he rose up early on the next day, and pressed the fleece together, and wrung the dew out of the fleece, a bowl full of water. ³⁹ Gideon said to God, "Don't let your anger be kindled against me, and I will speak but this once. Please let me make a trial just this once with the fleece. Let it now be dry only on the fleece, and on all the ground let there be dew." ⁴⁰ God did so that night; for it was dry on the fleece only, and there was dew on all the ground.

# 7

¹ Then Jerubbaal, who is Gideon, and all the people who were with him, rose up early and encamped beside the spring of Harod. Midian's camp was on the north side of them, by the hill of Moreh, in the valley. ² Yahweh said to Gideon, "The people who are with you are too many for me to give the Midianites into their hand, lest Israel brag against me, saying, 'My own hand has saved me.' ³ Now therefore proclaim in the ears of the people, saying, 'Whoever is fearful and trembling, let him return and depart from Mount Gilead.'" So twenty-two thousand of the people returned, and ten thousand remained. ⁴ Yahweh said to Gideon, "There are still too many people. Bring them down to the water, and I will test them for you there. It shall be, that those whom I tell you, 'This shall go with you,' shall go with you; and whoever I tell you, 'This shall not go with you,' shall not go." ⁵ So he brought down the people to the water; and Yahweh said to Gideon, "Everyone who laps of the water with his tongue, like a dog laps, you shall set him by himself; likewise everyone who bows down on his knees to drink." ⁶ The number of those who lapped, putting their hand to their mouth, was three hundred men; but all the rest of the people bowed down on their knees to drink water. ⁷ Yahweh said to Gideon, "I will save you by the three hundred men who lapped, and deliver the Midianites into your hand. Let all the other people go, each to his own place." ⁸ So the people took food in their hand, and their trumpets; and he sent all the rest of the men of Israel to their own tents, but retained the three hundred men; and the camp of Midian was beneath him in the valley. ⁹ That same night, Yahweh said to him, "Arise, go down into the camp, for I have delivered it into your hand. ¹⁰ But if you are afraid to go down, go with Purah your servant down to the camp. ¹¹ You will hear what they say; and afterward your hands will be strengthened to go down into the

---

camp." Then went he down with Purah his servant to the outermost part of the armed men who were in the camp. ¹² The Midianites and the Amalekites and all the children of the east lay along in the valley like locusts for multitude; and their camels were without number, as the sand which is on the seashore for multitude. ¹³ When Gideon had come, behold, there was a man telling a dream to his fellow. He said, "Behold, I dreamed a dream; and behold, a cake of barley bread tumbled into the camp of Midian, came to the tent, and struck it so that it fell, and turned it upside down, so that the tent lay flat." ¹⁴ His fellow answered, "This is nothing other than the sword of Gideon the son of Joash, a man of Israel. God has delivered Midian into his hand, with all the army." ¹⁵ It was so, when Gideon heard the telling of the dream and its interpretation, that he worshiped. Then he returned into the camp of Israel and said, "Arise, for Yahweh has delivered the army of Midian into your hand!" ¹⁶ He divided the three hundred men into three companies, and he put into the hands of all of them trumpets and empty pitchers, with torches within the pitchers. ¹⁷ He said to them, "Watch me, and do likewise. Behold, when I come to the outermost part of the camp, it shall be that, as I do, so you shall do. ¹⁸ When I blow the trumpet, I and all who are with me, then blow the trumpets also on every side of all the camp, and shout, 'For Yahweh and for Gideon!'" ¹⁹ So Gideon and the hundred men who were with him came to the outermost part of the camp in the beginning of the middle watch, when they had but newly set the watch. Then they blew the trumpets and broke in pieces the pitchers that were in their hands. ²⁰ The three companies blew the trumpets, broke the pitchers, and held the torches in their left hands and the trumpets in their right hands with which to blow; and they shouted, "The sword of Yahweh and of Gideon!" ²¹ They each stood in his place around the camp, and all the army ran; and they shouted, and put them to flight. ²² They blew the three hundred trumpets, and Yahweh set every man's sword against his fellow and against all the army; and the army fled as far as Beth Shittah toward Zererah, as far as the border of Abel Meholah, by Tabbath. ²³ The men of Israel were gathered together out of Naphtali, out of Asher, and out of all Manasseh, and pursued Midian. ²⁴ Gideon sent messengers throughout all the hill country of Ephraim, saying, "Come down against Midian and take the waters before them as far as Beth Barah, even the Jordan!" So all the men of Ephraim were gathered together and took the waters as far as Beth Barah, even the Jordan. ²⁵ They took the two princes of Midian, Oreb and Zeeb. They killed Oreb at Oreb's rock, and Zeeb they killed at Zeeb's wine press, as they pursued Midian. Then they brought the heads of Oreb and Zeeb to Gideon beyond the Jordan.

# 8

¹ The men of Ephraim said to him, "Why have you treated us this way, that you didn't call us when you went to fight with Midian?" They rebuked him sharply. ² He said to them, "What have I now done in comparison with you? Isn't the gleaning of the grapes of Ephraim better than the vintage of Abiezer? ³ God has delivered into your hand the princes of Midian, Oreb and Zeeb! What was I able to do in comparison with you?" Then their anger was abated toward him when he had said that. ⁴ Gideon came to the Jordan and passed over, he and the three hundred men who were with him, faint, yet pursuing. ⁵ He said to the men of Succoth, "Please give loaves of bread to the people who follow me; for they are faint, and I am pursuing after Zebah and Zalmunna, the kings of Midian." ⁶ The princes of Succoth said, "Are the hands of Zebah and Zalmunna now in your hand, that we should give bread to your army?" ⁷ Gideon said, "Therefore when Yahweh has delivered Zebah and Zalmunna into my hand, then I will tear your flesh with the thorns of the wilderness and with briers." ⁸ He went up there to Penuel, and spoke to them in the same way; and the men of Penuel answered him as the men of Succoth had answered. ⁹ He spoke also to the men of Penuel, saying, "When I come again in peace, I will break down this tower." ¹⁰ Now Zebah and Zalmunna were in Karkor, and their armies with them, about fifteen thousand men, all who were left of all the army of the children of the east; for there fell one hundred twenty thousand men who drew sword. ¹¹ Gideon went up by the way of those who lived in tents on the east of Nobah and Jogbehah, and struck the army; for the army felt secure. ¹² Zebah and Zalmunna fled and he pursued them. He took the two kings of Midian, Zebah and Zalmunna, and confused all the army. ¹³ Gideon the son of Joash returned from the battle from the ascent of Heres. ¹⁴ He caught a young man of the men of Succoth, and inquired of him; and he described for him the princes of Succoth, and its elders, seventy-seven men. ¹⁵ He came to the men of Succoth, and said, "See Zebah and Zalmunna, concerning whom you taunted me, saying, 'Are the hands of Zebah and Zalmunna now in your hand, that we should give bread to your men who are weary?'" ¹⁶ He took the

elders of the city, and thorns of the wilderness and briers, and with them he taught the men of Succoth. ¹⁷ He broke down the tower of Penuel, and killed the men of the city. ¹⁸ Then he said to Zebah and Zalmunna, "What kind of men were they whom you killed at Tabor?" They answered, "They were like you. They all resembled the children of a king." ¹⁹ He said, "They were my brothers, the sons of my mother. As Yahweh lives, if you had saved them alive, I would not kill you." ²⁰ He said to Jether his firstborn, "Get up and kill them!" But the youth didn't draw his sword; for he was afraid, because he was yet a youth. ²¹ Then Zebah and Zalmunna said, "You rise and fall on us; for as the man is, so is his strength." Gideon arose, and killed Zebah and Zalmunna, and took the crescents that were on their camels' necks. ²² Then the men of Israel said to Gideon, "Rule over us, both you, your son, and your son's son also; for you have saved us out of the hand of Midian." ²³ Gideon said to them, "I will not rule over you, neither shall my son rule over you. Yahweh shall rule over you." ²⁴ Gideon said to them, "I do have a request: that you would each give me the earrings of his plunder." (For they had golden earrings, because they were Ishmaelites.) ²⁵ They answered, "We will willingly give them." They spread a garment, and every man threw the earrings of his plunder into it. ²⁶ The weight of the golden earrings that he requested was one thousand and seven hundred shekelsᵃ of gold, in addition to the crescents, and the pendants, and the purple clothing that was on the kings of Midian, and in addition to the chains that were about their camels' necks. ²⁷ Gideon made an ephod out of it, and put it in Ophrah, his city. Then all Israel played the prostitute with it there; and it became a snare to Gideon and to his house. ²⁸ So Midian was subdued before the children of Israel, and they lifted up their heads no more. The land had rest forty years in the days of Gideon. ²⁹ Jerubbaal the son of Joash went and lived in his own house. ³⁰ Gideon had seventy sons conceived from his body, for he had many wives. ³¹ His concubine who was in Shechem also bore him a son, and he named him Abimelech. ³² Gideon the son of Joash died in a good old age, and was buried in the tomb of Joash his father, in Ophrah of the Abiezrites. ³³ As soon as Gideon was dead, the children of Israel turned again and played the prostitute following the Baals, and made Baal Berith their god. ³⁴ The children of Israel didn't remember Yahweh their God, who had delivered them out of the hand of all their enemies on every side; ³⁵ neither did they show kindness to the house of Jerubbaal, that is, Gideon, according to all the goodness which he had shown to Israel.

# 9

¹ Abimelech the son of Jerubbaal went to Shechem to his mother's brothers, and spoke with them and with all the family of the house of his mother's father, saying, ²"Please speak in the ears of all the men of Shechem, 'Is it better for you that all the sons of Jerubbaal, who are seventy persons, rule over you, or that one rule over you?' Remember also that I am your bone and your flesh." ³ His mother's brothers spoke of him in the ears of all the men of Shechem all these words. Their hearts inclined to follow Abimelech; for they said, "He is our brother." ⁴ They gave him seventy pieces of silver out of the house of Baal Berith, with which Abimelech hired vain and reckless fellows who followed him. ⁵ He went to his father's house at Ophrah, and killed his brothers the sons of Jerubbaal, being seventy persons, on one stone; but Jotham the youngest son of Jerubbaal was left, for he hid himself. ⁶ All the men of Shechem assembled themselves together with all the house of Millo, and went and made Abimelech king by the oak of the pillar that was in Shechem. ⁷ When they told it to Jotham, he went and stood on the top of Mount Gerizim and lifted up his voice, cried out, and said to them, "Listen to me, you men of Shechem, that God may listen to you. ⁸ The trees set out to anoint a king over themselves. They said to the olive tree, 'Reign over us.' ⁹"But the olive tree said to them, 'Should I stop producing my oil, with which they honor God and man by me, and go to wave back and forth over the trees?' ¹⁰"The trees said to the fig tree, 'Come and reign over us.' ¹¹"But the fig tree said to them, 'Should I leave my sweetness, and my good fruit, and go to wave back and forth over the trees?' ¹²"The trees said to the vine, 'Come and reign over us.' ¹³"The vine said to them, 'Should I leave my new wine, which cheers God and man, and go to wave back and forth over the trees?' ¹⁴"Then all the trees said to the bramble, 'Come and reign over us.' ¹⁵"The bramble said to the trees, 'If in truth you anoint me king over you, then come and take refuge in my shade; and if not, let fire come out of the bramble, and devour the cedars of Lebanon.' ¹⁶"Now therefore, if you have dealt truly and righteously, in that you have made Abimelech king, and if you have dealt well with Jerubbaal and his house, and have done to him according to the deserving of his hands ¹⁷(for my father fought for you, risked his life, and delivered you out of the hand of Midian; ¹⁸

---

ᵃ 8:26 A shekel is about 10 grams or about 0.32 Troy ounces, so 1700 shekels is about 17 kilograms or 37.4 pounds.

and you have risen up against my father's house today and have slain his sons, seventy persons, on one stone, and have made Abimelech, the son of his female servant, king over the men of Shechem, because he is your brother); [19] if you then have dealt truly and righteously with Jerubbaal and with his house today, then rejoice in Abimelech, and let him also rejoice in you; [20] but if not, let fire come out from Abimelech and devour the men of Shechem and the house of Millo; and let fire come out from the men of Shechem and from the house of Millo and devour Abimelech." [21] Jotham ran away and fled, and went to Beer[a] and lived there, for fear of Abimelech his brother. [22] Abimelech was prince over Israel three years. [23] Then God sent an evil spirit between Abimelech and the men of Shechem; and the men of Shechem dealt treacherously with Abimelech, [24] that the violence done to the seventy sons of Jerubbaal might come, and that their blood might be laid on Abimelech their brother who killed them, and on the men of Shechem who strengthened his hands to kill his brothers. [25] The men of Shechem set an ambush for him on the tops of the mountains, and they robbed all who came along that way by them; and Abimelech was told about it. [26] Gaal the son of Ebed came with his brothers and went over to Shechem; and the men of Shechem put their trust in him. [27] They went out into the field, harvested their vineyards, trod the grapes, celebrated, and went into the house of their god and ate and drank, and cursed Abimelech. [28] Gaal the son of Ebed said, "Who is Abimelech, and who is Shechem, that we should serve him? Isn't he the son of Jerubbaal? Isn't Zebul his officer? Serve the men of Hamor the father of Shechem, but why should we serve him? [29] I wish that this people were under my hand! Then I would remove Abimelech." He said to Abimelech, "Increase your army and come out!" [30] When Zebul the ruler of the city heard the words of Gaal the son of Ebed, his anger burned. [31] He sent messengers to Abimelech craftily, saying, "Behold, Gaal the son of Ebed and his brothers have come to Shechem; and behold, they incite the city against you. [32] Now therefore, go up by night, you and the people who are with you, and lie in wait in the field. [33] It shall be that in the morning, as soon as the sun is up, you shall rise early and rush on the city. Behold, when he and the people who are with him come out against you, then may you do to them as you shall find occasion." [34] Abimelech rose up, and all the people who were with him, by night, and they laid wait against Shechem in four companies. [35] Gaal the son of Ebed went out, and stood in the entrance of the gate of the city. Abimelech rose up, and the people who were with him, from the ambush. [36] When Gaal saw the people, he said to Zebul, "Behold, people are coming down from the tops of the mountains." Zebul said to him, "You see the shadows of the mountains as if they were men." [37] Gaal spoke again and said, "Behold, people are coming down by the middle of the land, and one company comes by the way of the oak of Meonenim." [38] Then Zebul said to him, "Now where is your mouth, that you said, 'Who is Abimelech, that we should serve him?' Isn't this the people that you have despised? Please go out now and fight with them." [39] Gaal went out before the men of Shechem, and fought with Abimelech. [40] Abimelech chased him, and he fled before him, and many fell wounded, even to the entrance of the gate. [41] Abimelech lived at Arumah; and Zebul drove out Gaal and his brothers, that they should not dwell in Shechem. [42] On the next day, the people went out into the field; and they told Abimelech. [43] He took the people and divided them into three companies, and laid wait in the field; and he looked, and behold, the people came out of the city. So, he rose up against them and struck them. [44] Abimelech and the companies that were with him rushed forward and stood in the entrance of the gate of the city; and the two companies rushed on all who were in the field and struck them. [45] Abimelech fought against the city all that day; and he took the city and killed the people in it. He beat down the city and sowed it with salt. [46] When all the men of the tower of Shechem heard of it, they entered into the stronghold of the house of Elberith. [47] Abimelech was told that all the men of the tower of Shechem were gathered together. [48] Abimelech went up to Mount Zalmon, he and all the people who were with him; and Abimelech took an ax in his hand, and cut down a bough from the trees, and took it up, and laid it on his shoulder. Then he said to the people who were with him, "What you have seen me do, make haste, and do as I have done!" [49] All the people likewise each cut down his bough, followed Abimelech, and put them at the base of the stronghold, and set the stronghold on fire over them, so that all the people of the tower of Shechem died also, about a thousand men and women. [50] Then Abimelech went to Thebez and encamped against Thebez, and took it. [51] But there was a strong tower within the city, and all the men and women of the city fled there, and shut themselves in, and went up to the roof of the tower. [52] Abimelech came to the tower and fought against

it, and came near to the door of the tower to burn it with fire. [53] A certain woman cast an upper millstone on Abimelech's head, and broke his skull. [54] Then he called hastily to the young man, his armor bearer, and said to him, "Draw your sword and kill me, that men not say of me, 'A woman killed him.' His young man thrust him through, and he died." [55] When the men of Israel saw that Abimelech was dead, they each departed to his place. [56] Thus God repaid the wickedness of Abimelech, which he did to his father in killing his seventy brothers; [57] and God repaid all the wickedness of the men of Shechem on their heads; and the curse of Jotham the son of Jerubbaal came on them.

## 10

[1] After Abimelech, Tola the son of Puah, the son of Dodo, a man of Issachar, arose to save Israel. He lived in Shamir in the hill country of Ephraim. [2] He judged Israel twenty-three years, and died, and was buried in Shamir. [3] After him Jair, the Gileadite, arose. He judged Israel twenty-two years. [4] He had thirty sons who rode on thirty donkey colts. They had thirty cities, which are called Havvoth Jair to this day, which are in the land of Gilead. [5] Jair died, and was buried in Kamon. [6] The children of Israel again did that which was evil in Yahweh's sight, and served the Baals, the Ashtaroth, the gods of Syria, the gods of Sidon, the gods of Moab, the gods of the children of Ammon, and the gods of the Philistines. They abandoned Yahweh, and didn't serve him. [7] Yahweh's anger burned against Israel, and he sold them into the hand of the Philistines and into the hand of the children of Ammon. [8] They troubled and oppressed the children of Israel that year. For eighteen years they oppressed all the children of Israel that were beyond the Jordan in the land of the Amorites, which is in Gilead. [9] The children of Ammon passed over the Jordan to fight also against Judah, and against Benjamin, and against the house of Ephraim, so that Israel was very distressed. [10] The children of Israel cried to Yahweh, saying, "We have sinned against you, even because we have forsaken our God, and have served the Baals." [11] Yahweh said to the children of Israel, "Didn't I save you from the Egyptians, and from the Amorites, from the children of Ammon, and from the Philistines? [12] The Sidonians also, and the Amalekites, and the Maonites, oppressed you; and you cried to me, and I saved you out of their hand. [13] Yet you have forsaken me and served other gods. Therefore I will save you no more. [14] Go and cry to the gods which you have chosen. Let them save you in the time of your distress!" [15] The children of Israel said to Yahweh, "We have sinned! Do to us whatever seems good to you; only deliver us, please, today." [16] They put away the foreign gods from among them and served Yahweh; and his soul was grieved for the misery of Israel. [17] Then the children of Ammon were gathered together and encamped in Gilead. The children of Israel assembled themselves together and encamped in Mizpah. [18] The people, the princes of Gilead, said to one another, "Who is the man who will begin to fight against the children of Ammon? He shall be head over all the inhabitants of Gilead."

## 11

[1] Now Jephthah the Gileadite was a mighty man of valor. He was the son of a prostitute. Gilead became the father of Jephthah. [2] Gilead's wife bore him sons. When his wife's sons grew up, they drove Jephthah out and said to him, "You will not inherit in our father's house, for you are the son of another woman." [3] Then Jephthah fled from his brothers and lived in the land of Tob. Outlaws joined up with Jephthah, and they went out with him. [4] After a while, the children of Ammon made war against Israel. [5] When the children of Ammon made war against Israel, the elders of Gilead went to get Jephthah out of the land of Tob. [6] They said to Jephthah, "Come and be our chief, that we may fight with the children of Ammon." [7] Jephthah said to the elders of Gilead, "Didn't you hate me, and drive me out of my father's house? Why have you come to me now when you are in distress?" [8] The elders of Gilead said to Jephthah, "Therefore we have turned again to you now, that you may go with us and fight with the children of Ammon. You will be our head over all the inhabitants of Gilead." [9] Jephthah said to the elders of Gilead, "If you bring me home again to fight with the children of Ammon, and Yahweh delivers them before me, will I be your head?" [10] The elders of Gilead said to Jephthah, "Yahweh will be witness between us. Surely we will do what you say." [11] Then Jephthah went with the elders of Gilead, and the people made him head and chief over them. Jephthah spoke all his words before Yahweh in Mizpah. [12] Jephthah sent messengers to the king of the children of Ammon, saying, "What do you have to do with me, that you have come to me to fight against my land?" [13] The king of the children of Ammon answered the messengers of Jephthah, "Because Israel took away my land when he came up out of Egypt, from the Arnon even to the Jabbok, and to the Jordan. Now therefore restore that territory again peaceably." [14]

---

[a] *9:21* "Beer" is Hebrew for "well", i.e., a village named for its well.

Jephthah sent messengers again to the king of the children of Ammon; ¹⁵ and he said to him, "Jephthah says: Israel didn't take away the land of Moab, nor the land of the children of Ammon; ¹⁶ but when they came up from Egypt, and Israel went through the wilderness to the Red Sea, and came to Kadesh, ¹⁷ then Israel sent messengers to the king of Edom, saying, 'Please let me pass through your land;' but the king of Edom didn't listen. In the same way, he sent to the king of Moab, but he refused; so Israel stayed in Kadesh. ¹⁸ Then they went through the wilderness, and went around the land of Edom, and the land of Moab, and came by the east side of the land of Moab, and they encamped on the other side of the Arnon; but they didn't come within the border of Moab, for the Arnon was the border of Moab. ¹⁹ Israel sent messengers to Sihon king of the Amorites, the king of Heshbon; and Israel said to him, 'Please let us pass through your land to my place.' ²⁰ But Sihon didn't trust Israel to pass through his border; but Sihon gathered all his people together, and encamped in Jahaz, and fought against Israel. ²¹ Yahweh, the God of Israel, delivered Sihon and all his people into the hand of Israel, and they struck them. So Israel possessed all the land of the Amorites, the inhabitants of that country. ²² They possessed all the border of the Amorites, from the Arnon even to the Jabbok, and from the wilderness even to the Jordan. ²³ So now Yahweh, the God of Israel, has dispossessed the Amorites from before his people Israel, and should you possess them? ²⁴ Won't you possess that which Chemosh your god gives you to possess? So whoever Yahweh our God has dispossessed from before us, them will we possess. ²⁵ Now are you anything better than Balak the son of Zippor, king of Moab? Did he ever strive against Israel, or did he ever fight against them? ²⁶ Israel lived in Heshbon and its towns, and in Aroer and its towns, and in all the cities that are along the side of the Arnon for three hundred years! Why didn't you recover them within that time? ²⁷ Therefore I have not sinned against you, but you do me wrong to war against me. May Yahweh the Judge be judge today between the children of Israel and the children of Ammon." ²⁸ However, the king of the children of Ammon didn't listen to the words of Jephthah which he sent him. ²⁹ Then Yahweh's Spirit came on Jephthah, and he passed over Gilead and Manasseh, and passed over Mizpah of Gilead, and from Mizpah of Gilead he passed over to the children of Ammon. ³⁰ Jephthah vowed a vow to Yahweh, and said, "If you will indeed deliver the children of Ammon into my hand, ³¹ then it shall be, that whatever comes out of the doors of my house to meet me when I return in peace from the children of Ammon, it shall be Yahweh's, and I will offer it up for a burnt offering." ³² So Jephthah passed over to the children of Ammon to fight against them; and Yahweh delivered them into his hand. ³³ He struck them from Aroer until you come to Minnith, even twenty cities, and to Abelcheramim, with a very great slaughter. So the children of Ammon were subdued before the children of Israel. ³⁴ Jephthah came to Mizpah to his house; and behold, his daughter came out to meet him with tambourines and with dances. She was his only child. Besides her he had neither son nor daughter. ³⁵ When he saw her, he tore his clothes, and said, "Alas, my daughter! You have brought me very low, and you are one of those who trouble me; for I have opened my mouth to Yahweh, and I can't go back." ³⁶ She said to him, "My father, you have opened your mouth to Yahweh; do to me according to that which has proceeded out of your mouth, because Yahweh has taken vengeance for you on your enemies, even on the children of Ammon." ³⁷ Then she said to her father, "Let this thing be done for me. Leave me alone two months, that I may depart and go down on the mountains, and bewail my virginity, I and my companions." ³⁸ He said, "Go." He sent her away for two months; and she departed, she and her companions, and mourned her virginity on the mountains. ³⁹ At the end of two months, she returned to her father, who did with her according to his vow which he had vowed. She was a virgin. It became a custom in Israel ⁴⁰ that the daughters of Israel went yearly to celebrate the daughter of Jephthah the Gileadite four days in a year.

## 12

¹ The men of Ephraim were gathered together, and passed northward; and they said to Jephthah, "Why did you pass over to fight against the children of Ammon, and didn't call us to go with you? We will burn your house around you with fire!" ² Jephthah said to them, "I and my people were at great strife with the children of Ammon; and when I called you, you didn't save me out of their hand. ³ When I saw that you didn't save me, I put my life in my hand, and passed over against the children of Ammon, and Yahweh delivered them into my hand. Why then have you come up to me today, to fight against me?" ⁴ Then Jephthah gathered together all the men of Gilead, and fought with Ephraim. The men of Gilead struck Ephraim, because they said, "You are fugitives of Ephraim, you Gileadites, in the middle of Ephraim, and in the middle of Manasseh." ⁵ The Gileadites took the fords of the

Jordan against the Ephraimites. Whenever a fugitive of Ephraim said, "Let me go over," the men of Gilead said to him, "Are you an Ephraimite?" If he said, "No;" ⁶ then they said to him, "Now say 'Shibboleth;'" and he said "Sibboleth"; for he couldn't manage to pronounce it correctly, then they seized him and killed him at the fords of the Jordan. At that time, forty-two thousand of Ephraim fell. ⁷ Jephthah judged Israel six years. Then Jephthah the Gileadite died, and was buried in the cities of Gilead. ⁸ After him Ibzan of Bethlehem judged Israel. ⁹ He had thirty sons. He sent his thirty daughters outside his clan, and he brought in thirty daughters from outside his clan for his sons. He judged Israel seven years. ¹⁰ Ibzan died, and was buried at Bethlehem. ¹¹ After him, Elon the Zebulunite judged Israel; and he judged Israel ten years. ¹² Elon the Zebulunite died, and was buried in Aijalon in the land of Zebulun. ¹³ After him, Abdon the son of Hillel the Pirathonite judged Israel. ¹⁴ He had forty sons and thirty sons' sons who rode on seventy donkey colts. He judged Israel eight years. ¹⁵ Abdon the son of Hillel the Pirathonite died, and was buried in Pirathon in the land of Ephraim, in the hill country of the Amalekites.

## 13

¹ The children of Israel again did that which was evil in Yahweh's sight; and Yahweh delivered them into the hand of the Philistines forty years. ² There was a certain man of Zorah, of the family of the Danites, whose name was Manoah; and his wife was barren, and childless. ³ Yahweh's angel appeared to the woman, and said to her, "See now, you are barren and childless; but you shall conceive and bear a son. ⁴ Now therefore please beware and drink no wine nor strong drink, and don't eat any unclean thing; ⁵ for, behold, you shall conceive and give birth to a son. No razor shall come on his head, for the child shall be a Nazirite to God from the womb. He shall begin to save Israel out of the hand of the Philistines." ⁶ Then the woman came and told her husband, saying, "A man of God came to me, and his face was like the face of the angel of God, very awesome. I didn't ask him where he was from, neither did he tell me his name; ⁷ but he said to me, 'Behold, you shall conceive and bear a son; and now drink no wine nor strong drink. Don't eat any unclean thing, for the child shall be a Nazirite to God from the womb to the day of his death.'" ⁸ Then Manoah entreated Yahweh, and said, "Oh, Lord, please let the man of God whom you sent come again to us, and teach us what we should do to the child who shall be born." ⁹ God listened to the voice of Manoah, and the angel of God came again to the woman as she sat in the field; but Manoah, her husband, wasn't with her. ¹⁰ The woman hurried and ran, and told her husband, saying to him, "Behold, the man who came to me that day has appeared to me." ¹¹ Manoah arose and followed his wife, and came to the man, and said to him, "Are you the man who spoke to my wife?" He said, "I am." ¹² Manoah said, "Now let your words happen. What shall the child's way of life and mission be?" ¹³ Yahweh's angel said to Manoah, "Of all that I said to the woman let her beware. ¹⁴ She may not eat of anything that comes of the vine, neither let her drink wine or strong drink, nor eat any unclean thing. Let her observe all that I commanded her." ¹⁵ Manoah said to Yahweh's angel, "Please stay with us, that we may make a young goat ready for you." ¹⁶ Yahweh's angel said to Manoah, "Though you detain me, I won't eat your bread. If you will prepare a burnt offering, you must offer it to Yahweh." For Manoah didn't know that he was Yahweh's angel. ¹⁷ Manoah said to Yahweh's angel, "What is your name, that when your words happen, we may honor you?" ¹⁸ Yahweh's angel said to him, "Why do you ask about my name, since it is incomprehensible[a]?" ¹⁹ So Manoah took the young goat with the meal offering, and offered it on the rock to Yahweh. Then the angel did an amazing thing as Manoah and his wife watched. ²⁰ For when the flame went up toward the sky from off the altar, Yahweh's angel ascended in the flame of the altar. Manoah and his wife watched; and they fell on their faces to the ground. ²¹ But Yahweh's angel didn't appear to Manoah or to his wife any more. Then Manoah knew that he was Yahweh's angel. ²² Manoah said to his wife, "We shall surely die, because we have seen God." ²³ But his wife said to him, "If Yahweh were pleased to kill us, he wouldn't have received a burnt offering and a meal offering at our hand, and he wouldn't have shown us all these things, nor would he have told us such things as these at this time." ²⁴ The woman bore a son and named him Samson. The child grew, and Yahweh blessed him. ²⁵ Yahweh's Spirit began to move him in Mahaneh Dan, between Zorah and Eshtaol.

## 14

¹ Samson went down to Timnah, and saw a woman in Timnah of the daughters of the Philistines. ² He came up, and told his father and his mother, saying, "I have seen a woman in Timnah of the daughters of the Philistines. Now therefore get her for me as my wife." ³ Then his father and his mother said to him, "Isn't there a woman among your brothers' daughters, or among all my people, that you go to take a wife

a *13:18 or, wonderful*

of the uncircumcised Philistines?" Samson said to his father, "Get her for me, for she pleases me well." [4] But his father and his mother didn't know that it was of Yahweh; for he sought an occasion against the Philistines. Now at that time the Philistines ruled over Israel. [5] Then Samson went down to Timnah with his father and his mother, and came to the vineyards of Timnah; and behold, a young lion roared at him. [6] Yahweh's Spirit came mightily on him, and he tore him as he would have torn a young goat with his bare hands, but he didn't tell his father or his mother what he had done. [7] He went down and talked with the woman, and she pleased Samson well. [8] After a while he returned to take her, and he went over to see the carcass of the lion; and behold, there was a swarm of bees in the body of the lion, and honey. [9] He took it into his hands, and went on, eating as he went. He came to his father and mother and gave to them, and they ate, but he didn't tell them that he had taken the honey out of the lion's body. [10] His father went down to the woman; and Samson made a feast there, for the young men used to do so. [11] When they saw him, they brought thirty companions to be with him. [12] Samson said to them, "Let me tell you a riddle now. If you can tell me the answer within the seven days of the feast, and find it out, then I will give you thirty linen garments and thirty changes of clothing; [13] but if you can't tell me the answer, then you shall give me thirty linen garments and thirty changes of clothing." They said to him, "Tell us your riddle, that we may hear it." [14] He said to them, "Out of the eater came out food. Out of the strong came out sweetness." They couldn't in three days declare the riddle. [15] On the seventh day, they said to Samson's wife, "Entice your husband, that he may declare to us the riddle, lest we burn you and your father's house with fire. Have you called us to impoverish us? Isn't that so?" [16] Samson's wife wept before him, and said, "You just hate me, and don't love me. You've told a riddle to the children of my people, and haven't told it to me." He said to her, "Behold, I haven't told my father or my mother, so why should I tell you?" [17] She wept before him the seven days, while their feast lasted; and on the seventh day, he told her, because she pressed him severely; and she told the riddle to the children of her people. [18] The men of the city said to him on the seventh day before the sun went down, "What is sweeter than honey? What is stronger than a lion?" He said to them, "If you hadn't plowed with my heifer, you wouldn't have found out my riddle." [19] Yahweh's Spirit came mightily on him, and he went down to Ashkelon and struck thirty men of them. He took their plunder, then gave the changes of clothing to those who declared the riddle. His anger burned, and he went up to his father's house. [20] But Samson's wife was given to his companion, who had been his friend.

## 15

[1] But after a while, in the time of wheat harvest, Samson visited his wife with a young goat. He said, "I will go in to my wife's room." But her father wouldn't allow him to go in. [2] Her father said, "I most certainly thought that you utterly hated her; therefore I gave her to your companion. Isn't her younger sister more beautiful than she? Please, take her instead." [3] Samson said to them, "This time I will be blameless in the case of the Philistines when I harm them." [4] Samson went and caught three hundred foxes, and took torches, and turned tail to tail, and put a torch in the middle between every two tails. [5] When he had set the torches on fire, he let them go into the standing grain of the Philistines, and burned up both the shocks and the standing grain, and also the olive groves. [6] Then the Philistines said, "Who has done this?" They said, "Samson, the son-in-law of the Timnite, because he has taken his wife and given her to his companion." The Philistines came up, and burned her and her father with fire. [7] Samson said to them, "If you behave like this, surely I will take revenge on you, and after that I will cease." [8] He struck them hip and thigh with a great slaughter; and he went down and lived in the cave in Etam's rock. [9] Then the Philistines went up, encamped in Judah, and spread themselves in Lehi. [10] The men of Judah said, "Why have you come up against us?" They said, "We have come up to bind Samson, to do to him as he has done to us." [11] Then three thousand men of Judah went down to the cave in Etam's rock, and said to Samson, "Don't you know that the Philistines are rulers over us? What then is this that you have done to us?" He said to them, "As they did to me, so I have done to them." [12] They said to him, "We have come down to bind you, that we may deliver you into the hand of the Philistines." Samson said to them, "Swear to me that you will not attack me yourselves." [13] They spoke to him, saying, "No, but we will bind you securely and deliver you into their hands; but surely we will not kill you." They bound him with two new ropes, and brought him up from the rock. [14] When he came to Lehi, the Philistines shouted as they met him. Then Yahweh's Spirit came mightily on him, and the ropes that were on his arms became as flax that was burned with fire; and his bands dropped off from his hands. [15] He found a fresh jawbone of a

donkey, put out his hand, took it, and struck a thousand men with it. [16] Samson said, "With the jawbone of a donkey, heaps on heaps; with the jawbone of a donkey I have struck a thousand men." [17] When he had finished speaking, he threw the jawbone out of his hand; and that place was called Ramath Lehi.[a] [18] He was very thirsty, and called on Yahweh and said, "You have given this great deliverance by the hand of your servant; and now shall I die of thirst, and fall into the hand of the uncircumcised?" [19] But God split the hollow place that is in Lehi, and water came out of it. When he had drunk, his spirit came again, and he revived. Therefore its name was called En Hakkore, which is in Lehi, to this day. [20] He judged Israel twenty years in the days of the Philistines.

## 16

[1] Samson went to Gaza, and saw there a prostitute, and went in to her. [2] The Gazites were told, "Samson is here!" They surrounded him and laid wait for him all night in the gate of the city, and were quiet all the night, saying, "Wait until morning light; then we will kill him." [3] Samson lay until midnight, then arose at midnight and took hold of the doors of the gate of the city, with the two posts, and plucked them up, bar and all, and put them on his shoulders and carried them up to the top of the mountain that is before Hebron. [4] It came to pass afterward that he loved a woman in the valley of Sorek, whose name was Delilah. [5] The lords of the Philistines came up to her and said to her, "Entice him, and see in which his great strength lies, and by what means we may prevail against him, that we may bind him to afflict him; and we will each give you eleven hundred pieces of silver." [6] Delilah said to Samson, "Please tell me where your great strength lies, and what you might be bound to afflict you." [7] Samson said to her, "If they bind me with seven green cords that were never dried, then shall I become weak, and be as another man." [8] Then the lords of the Philistines brought up to her seven green cords which had not been dried, and she bound him with them. [9] Now she had an ambush waiting in the inner room. She said to him, "The Philistines are on you, Samson!" He broke the cords as a flax thread is broken when it touches the fire. So his strength was not known. [10] Delilah said to Samson, "Behold, you have mocked me, and told me lies. Now please tell me how you might be bound." [11] He said to her, "If they only bind me with new ropes with which no work has been done, then shall I become weak, and be as another man." [12] So Delilah took new ropes and bound him with them, then said to him, "The Philistines are on you, Samson!" The ambush was waiting in the inner room. He broke them off his arms like a thread. [13] Delilah said to Samson, "Until now, you have mocked me and told me lies. Tell me with what you might be bound." He said to her, "If you weave the seven locks of my head with the fabric on the loom." [14] She fastened it with the pin, and said to him, "The Philistines are on you, Samson!" He awakened out of his sleep, and plucked away the pin of the beam and the fabric. [15] She said to him, "How can you say, 'I love you,' when your heart is not with me? You have mocked me these three times, and have not told me where your great strength lies." [16] When she pressed him daily with her words and urged him, his soul was troubled to death. [17] He told her all his heart and said to her, "No razor has ever come on my head; for I have been a Nazirite to God from my mother's womb. If I am shaved, then my strength will go from me and I will become weak, and be like any other man." [18] When Delilah saw that he had told her all his heart, she sent and called for the lords of the Philistines, saying, "Come up this once, for he has told me all his heart." Then the lords of the Philistines came up to her and brought the money in their hand. [19] She made him sleep on her knees; and she called for a man and shaved off the seven locks of his head; and she began to afflict him, and his strength went from him. [20] She said, "The Philistines are upon you, Samson!" He awoke out of his sleep, and said, "I will go out as at other times, and shake myself free." But he didn't know that Yahweh had departed from him. [21] The Philistines laid hold on him and put out his eyes; and they brought him down to Gaza and bound him with fetters of bronze; and he ground at the mill in the prison. [22] However, the hair of his head began to grow again after he was shaved. [23] The lords of the Philistines gathered together to offer a great sacrifice to Dagon their god, and to rejoice; for they said, "Our god has delivered Samson our enemy into our hand." [24] When the people saw him, they praised their god; for they said, "Our god has delivered our enemy and the destroyer of our country, who has slain many of us, into our hand." [25] When their hearts were merry, they said, "Call for Samson, that he may entertain us." They called for Samson out of the prison; and he performed before them. They set him between the pillars; [26] and Samson said to the boy who held him by the hand, "Allow me to feel the pillars on which the house rests, that I may lean on them." [27] Now the house was full of men and women; and all the lords of the Philistines were there; and there

---

[a] *15:17* "Ramath" means "hill" and "Lehi" means "jawbone".

were on the roof about three thousand men and women, who saw while Samson performed. ²⁸ Samson called to Yahweh, and said, "Lord Yahweh, remember me, please, and strengthen me, please, only this once, God, that I may be at once avenged of the Philistines for my two eyes." ²⁹ Samson took hold of the two middle pillars on which the house rested and leaned on them, the one with his right hand and the other with his left. ³⁰ Samson said, "Let me die with the Philistines!" He bowed himself with all his might; and the house fell on the lords, and on all the people who were in it. So the dead that he killed at his death were more than those who he killed in his life. ³¹ Then his brothers and all the house of his father came down and took him, and brought him up and buried him between Zorah and Eshtaol in the burial site of Manoah his father. He judged Israel twenty years.

## 17

¹ There was a man of the hill country of Ephraim, whose name was Micah. ² He said to his mother, "The eleven hundred pieces of silver that were taken from you, about which you uttered a curse, and also spoke it in my ears—behold, the silver is with me. I took it." His mother said, "May Yahweh bless my son!" ³ He restored the eleven hundred pieces of silver to his mother, then his mother said, "I most certainly dedicate the silver to Yahweh from my hand for my son, to make a carved image and a molten image. Now therefore I will restore it to you." ⁴ When he restored the money to his mother, his mother took two hundred pieces of silver, and gave them to a silversmith, who made a carved image and a molten image out of it. It was in the house of Micah. ⁵ The man Micah had a house of gods, and he made an ephod, and teraphim,ᵃ and consecrated one of his sons, who became his priest. ⁶ In those days there was no king in Israel. Everyone did that which was right in his own eyes. ⁷ There was a young man out of Bethlehem Judah, of the family of Judah, who was a Levite; and he lived there. ⁸ The man departed out of the city, out of Bethlehem Judah, to live where he could find a place, and he came to the hill country of Ephraim, to the house of Micah, as he traveled. ⁹ Micah said to him, "Where did you come from?" He said to him, "I am a Levite of Bethlehem Judah, and I am looking for a place to live." ¹⁰ Micah said to him, "Dwell with me, and be to me a father and a priest, and I will give you ten pieces of silver per year, a suit of clothing, and your food." So the Levite went in. ¹¹ The Levite was content to dwell with the man; and the young man was to him as one of his sons. ¹² Micah consecrated the Levite, and the young man became his priest, and was in the house of Micah. ¹³ Then Micah said, "Now I know that Yahweh will do good to me, since I have a Levite as my priest."

## 18

¹ In those days there was no king in Israel. In those days the tribe of the Danites sought an inheritance to dwell in; for to that day, their inheritance had not fallen to them among the tribes of Israel. ² The children of Dan sent five men of their family from their whole number, men of valor, from Zorah and from Eshtaol, to spy out the land and to search it. They said to them, "Go, explore the land!" They came to the hill country of Ephraim, to the house of Micah, and lodged there. ³ When they were by the house of Micah, they knew the voice of the young man the Levite; so they went over there and said to him, "Who brought you here? What do you do in this place? What do you have here?" ⁴ He said to them, "Thus and thus has Micah dealt with me, and he has hired me, and I have become his priest." ⁵ They said to him, "Please ask counsel of God, that we may know whether our way which we go shall be prosperous." ⁶ The priest said to them, "Go in peace. Your way in which you go is before Yahweh." ⁷ Then the five men departed and came to Laish and saw the people who were there, how they lived in safety, in the way of the Sidonians, quiet and secure; for there was no one in the land possessing authority, that might put them to shame in anything, and they were far from the Sidonians, and had no dealings with anyone else. ⁸ They came to their brothers at Zorah and Eshtaol; and their brothers asked them, "What do you say?" ⁹ They said, "Arise, and let's go up against them; for we have seen the land, and behold, it is very good. Do you stand still? Don't be slothful to go and to enter in to possess the land. ¹⁰ When you go, you will come to an unsuspecting people, and the land is large; for God has given it into your hand, a place where there is no lack of anything that is in the earth." ¹¹ The family of the Danites set out from Zorah and Eshtaol with six hundred men armed with weapons of war. ¹² They went up and encamped in Kiriath Jearim in Judah. Therefore they call that place Mahaneh Dan to this day. Behold, it is behind Kiriath Jearim. ¹³ They passed from there to the hill country of Ephraim, and came to the house of Micah. ¹⁴ Then the five men who went to spy out the country of Laish answered and said to their brothers, "Do you know that there is in these

houses an ephod, and teraphim,ᵇ and a carved image, and a molten image? Now therefore consider what you have to do." ¹⁵ They went over there and came to the house of the young Levite man, even to the house of Micah, and asked him how he was doing. ¹⁶ The six hundred men armed with their weapons of war, who were of the children of Dan, stood by the entrance of the gate. ¹⁷ The five men who went to spy out the land went up, and came in there, and took the engraved image, the ephod, the teraphim, and the molten image; and the priest stood by the entrance of the gate with the six hundred men armed with weapons of war. ¹⁸ When these went into Micah's house, and took the engraved image, the ephod, the teraphim, and the molten image, the priest said to them, "What are you doing?" ¹⁹ They said to him, "Hold your peace, put your hand on your mouth, and go with us. Be a father and a priest to us. Is it better for you to be priest to the house of one man, or to be priest to a tribe and a family in Israel?" ²⁰ The priest's heart was glad, and he took the ephod, the teraphim, and the engraved image, and went with the people. ²¹ So they turned and departed, and put the little ones, the livestock, and the goods before them. ²² When they were a good way from the house of Micah, the men who were in the houses near Micah's house gathered together and overtook the children of Dan. ²³ As they called to the children of Dan, they turned their faces, and said to Micah, "What ails you, that you come with such a company?" ²⁴ He said, "You have taken away my gods which I made, and the priest, and have gone away! How can you ask me, 'What more do I have? What ails you?'" ²⁵ The children of Dan said to him, "Don't let your voice be heard among us, lest angry fellows fall on you, and you lose your life, with the lives of your household." ²⁶ The children of Dan went their way; and when Micah saw that they were too strong for him, he turned and went back to his house. ²⁷ They took that which Micah had made, and the priest whom he had, and came to Laish, to a people quiet and unsuspecting, and struck them with the edge of the sword; then they burned the city with fire. ²⁸ There was no deliverer, because it was far from Sidon, and they had no dealings with anyone else; and it was in the valley that lies by Beth Rehob. They built the city and lived in it. ²⁹ They called the name of the city Dan, after the name of Dan their father, who was born to Israel; however the name of the city used to be Laish. ³⁰ The children of Dan set up for themselves the engraved image; and Jonathan, the son of Gershom, the son of Moses, and his sons were priests to the tribe of the Danites until the day of the captivity of the land. ³¹ So they set up for themselves Micah's engraved image which he made, and it remained all the time that God's house was in Shiloh.

## 19

¹ In those days, when there was no king in Israel, there was a certain Levite living on the farther side of the hill country of Ephraim, who took for himself a concubine out of Bethlehem Judah. ² His concubine played the prostitute against him, and went away from him to her father's house to Bethlehem Judah, and was there for four months. ³ Her husband arose and went after her to speak kindly to her, to bring her again, having his servant with him and a couple of donkeys. She brought him into her father's house; and when the father of the young lady saw him, he rejoiced to meet him. ⁴ His father-in-law, the young lady's father, kept him there; and he stayed with him three days. So they ate and drank, and stayed there. ⁵ On the fourth day, they got up early in the morning, and he rose up to depart. The young lady's father said to his son-in-law, "Strengthen your heart with a morsel of bread, and afterward you shall go your way." ⁶ So they sat down, ate, and drank, both of them together. Then the young lady's father said to the man, "Please be pleased to stay all night, and let your heart be merry." ⁷ The man rose up to depart; but his father-in-law urged him, and he stayed there again. ⁸ He arose early in the morning on the fifth day to depart; and the young lady's father said, "Please strengthen your heart and stay until the day declines;" and they both ate. ⁹ When the man rose up to depart, he, and his concubine, and his servant, his father-in-law, the young lady's father, said to him, "Behold, now the day draws toward evening, please stay all night. Behold, the day is ending. Stay here, that your heart may be merry; and tomorrow go on your way early, that you may go home." ¹⁰ But the man wouldn't stay that night, but he rose up and went near Jebus (also called Jerusalem). With him were a couple of saddled donkeys. His concubine also was with him. ¹¹ When they were by Jebus, the day was far spent; and the servant said to his master, "Please come and let's enter into this city of the Jebusites, and stay in it." ¹² His master said to him, "We won't enter into the city of a foreigner that is not of the children of Israel; but we will pass over to Gibeah." ¹³ He said to his servant, "Come and let's draw near to one of these places; and we will lodge in Gibeah, or in Ramah." ¹⁴ So they passed on and went their way; and the sun went down on them near

---

ᵃ *17:5 teraphim were household idols that may have been associated with inheritance* | rights to the household property. | ᵇ *18:14 teraphim were household idols that may have been associated with* | inheritance rights to the household property.

Gibeah, which belongs to Benjamin. ¹⁵ They went over there, to go in to stay in Gibeah. He went in, and sat down in the street of the city; for there was no one who took them into his house to stay. ¹⁶ Behold, an old man came from his work out of the field at evening. Now the man was from the hill country of Ephraim, and he lived in Gibeah; but the men of the place were Benjamites. ¹⁷ He lifted up his eyes, and saw the wayfaring man in the street of the city; and the old man said, "Where are you going? Where did you come from?" ¹⁸ He said to him, "We are passing from Bethlehem Judah to the farther side of the hill country of Ephraim. I am from there, and I went to Bethlehem Judah. I am going to Yahweh's house; and there is no one who has taken me into his house. ¹⁹ Yet there is both straw and feed for our donkeys; and there is bread and wine also for me, and for your servant, and for the young man who is with your servants. There is no lack of anything." ²⁰ The old man said, "Peace be to you! Just let me supply all your needs, but don't sleep in the street." ²¹ So he brought him into his house, and gave the donkeys fodder. Then they washed their feet, and ate and drank. ²² As they were making their hearts merry, behold, the men of the city, certain wicked fellows, surrounded the house, beating at the door; and they spoke to the master of the house, the old man, saying, "Bring out the man who came into your house, that we can have sex with him!" ²³ The man, the master of the house, went out to them, and said to them, "No, my brothers, please don't act so wickedly; since this man has come into my house, don't do this folly. ²⁴ Behold, here is my virgin daughter and his concubine. I will bring them out now. Humble them, and do with them what seems good to you; but to this man don't do any such folly." ²⁵ But the men wouldn't listen to him; so the man grabbed his concubine, and brought her out to them; and they had sex with her, and abused her all night until the morning. When the day began to dawn, they let her go. ²⁶ Then the woman came in the dawning of the day, and fell down at the door of the man's house where her lord was, until it was light. ²⁷ Her lord rose up in the morning and opened the doors of the house, and went out to go his way; and behold, the woman his concubine had fallen down at the door of the house, with her hands on the threshold. ²⁸ He said to her, "Get up, and let's get going!" but no one answered. Then he took her up on the donkey; and the man rose up, and went to his place. ²⁹ When he had come into his house, he took a knife and cut up his concubine, and divided her, limb by limb, into twelve pieces, and sent her throughout all the borders of Israel. ³⁰ It was so, that all who saw it said, "Such a deed has not been done or seen from the day that the children of Israel came up out of the land of Egypt to this day! Consider it, take counsel, and speak."

## 20

¹ Then all the children of Israel went out, and the congregation was assembled as one man, from Dan even to Beersheba, with the land of Gilead, to Yahweh at Mizpah. ² The chiefs of all the people, even of all the tribes of Israel, presented themselves in the assembly of the people of God, four hundred thousand footmen who drew sword. ³(Now the children of Benjamin heard that the children of Israel had gone up to Mizpah.) The children of Israel said, "Tell us, how did this wickedness happen?" ⁴ The Levite, the husband of the woman who was murdered, answered, "I came into Gibeah that belongs to Benjamin, I and my concubine, to spend the night. ⁵ The men of Gibeah rose against me, and surrounded the house by night. They intended to kill me and they raped my concubine, and she is dead. ⁶ I took my concubine and cut her in pieces, and sent her throughout all the country of the inheritance of Israel; for they have committed lewdness and folly in Israel. ⁷ Behold, you children of Israel, all of you, give here your advice and counsel." ⁸ All the people arose as one man, saying, "None of us will go to his tent, neither will any of us turn to his house. ⁹ But now this is the thing which we will do to Gibeah: we will go up against it by lot; ¹⁰ and we will take ten men of one hundred throughout all the tribes of Israel, and one hundred of one thousand, and a thousand out of ten thousand to get food for the people, that they may do, when they come to Gibeah of Benjamin, according to all the folly that the men of Gibeah have done in Israel." ¹¹ So all the men of Israel were gathered against the city, knit together as one man. ¹² The tribes of Israel sent men through all the tribe of Benjamin, saying, "What wickedness is this that has happened among you? ¹³ Now therefore deliver up the men, the wicked fellows who are in Gibeah, that we may put them to death and put away evil from Israel." But Benjamin would not listen to the voice of their brothers, the children of Israel. ¹⁴ The children of Benjamin gathered themselves together out of the cities to Gibeah, to go out to battle against the children of Israel. ¹⁵ The children of Benjamin were counted on that day out of the cities twenty-six thousand men who drew the sword, in addition to the inhabitants of Gibeah, who were counted seven hundred chosen men. ¹⁶ Among all these soldiers there were seven hundred chosen men who were left-handed. Every one of them could sling a stone at a hair and not miss. ¹⁷ The men of Israel, besides Benjamin, were counted four hundred thousand men who drew sword.

All these were men of war. ¹⁸ The children of Israel arose, went up to Bethel, and asked counsel of God. They asked, "Who shall go up for us first to battle against the children of Benjamin?" Yahweh said, "Judah first." ¹⁹ The children of Israel rose up in the morning and encamped against Gibeah. ²⁰ The men of Israel went out to battle against Benjamin; and the men of Israel set the battle in array against them at Gibeah. ²¹ The children of Benjamin came out of Gibeah, and on that day destroyed twenty-two thousand of the Israelite men down to the ground. ²² The people, the men of Israel, encouraged themselves, and set the battle again in array in the place where they set themselves in array the first day. ²³ The children of Israel went up and wept before Yahweh until evening; and they asked of Yahweh, saying, "Shall I again draw near to battle against the children of Benjamin my brother?" Yahweh said, "Go up against him." ²⁴ The children of Israel came near against the children of Benjamin the second day. ²⁵ Benjamin went out against them out of Gibeah the second day, and destroyed down to the ground of the children of Israel again eighteen thousand men. All these drew the sword. ²⁶ Then all the children of Israel and all the people went up, and came to Bethel, and wept, and sat there before Yahweh, and fasted that day until evening; then they offered burnt offerings and peace offerings before Yahweh. ²⁷ The children of Israel asked Yahweh (for the ark of the covenant of God was there in those days, ²⁸ and Phinehas, the son of Eleazar, the son of Aaron, stood before it in those days), saying, "Shall I yet again go out to battle against the children of Benjamin my brother, or shall I cease?" Yahweh said, "Go up; for tomorrow I will deliver him into your hand." ²⁹ Israel set ambushes all around Gibeah. ³⁰ The children of Israel went up against the children of Benjamin on the third day, and set themselves in array against Gibeah, as at other times. ³¹ The children of Benjamin went out against the people, and were drawn away from the city; and they began to strike and kill of the people as at other times, in the highways, of which one goes up to Bethel and the other to Gibeah, in the field, about thirty men of Israel. ³² The children of Benjamin said, "They are struck down before us, as at the first." But the children of Israel said, "Let's flee, and draw them away from the city to the highways." ³³ All the men of Israel rose up out of their place and set themselves in array at Baal Tamar. Then the ambushers of Israel broke out of their place, even out of Maareh Geba. ³⁴ Ten thousand chosen men out of all Israel came over against Gibeah, and the battle was severe; but they didn't know that disaster was close to them. ³⁵ Yahweh struck Benjamin before Israel; and the children of Israel destroyed of Benjamin that day twenty-five thousand one hundred men. All these drew the sword. ³⁶ So the children of Benjamin saw that they were struck, for the men of Israel yielded to Benjamin because they trusted the ambushers whom they had set against Gibeah. ³⁷ The ambushers hurried, and rushed on Gibeah; then the ambushers spread out, and struck all the city with the edge of the sword. ³⁸ Now the appointed sign between the men of Israel and the ambushers was that they should make a great cloud of smoke rise up out of the city. ³⁹ The men of Israel turned in the battle, and Benjamin began to strike and kill of the men of Israel about thirty persons; for they said, "Surely they are struck down before us, as in the first battle." ⁴⁰ But when the cloud began to arise up out of the city in a pillar of smoke, the Benjamites looked behind them; and behold, the whole city went up in smoke to the sky. ⁴¹ The men of Israel turned, and the men of Benjamin were dismayed; for they saw that disaster had come on them. ⁴² Therefore they turned their backs before the men of Israel to the way of the wilderness, but the battle followed hard after them; and those who came out of the cities destroyed them in the middle of it. ⁴³ They surrounded the Benjamites, chased them, and trod them down at their resting place, as far as near Gibeah toward the sunrise. ⁴⁴ Eighteen thousand men of Benjamin fell; all these were men of valor. ⁴⁵ They turned and fled toward the wilderness to the rock of Rimmon. They gleaned five thousand men of them in the highways, and followed hard after them to Gidom, and struck two thousand men of them. ⁴⁶ So that all who fell that day of Benjamin were twenty-five thousand men who drew the sword. All these were men of valor. ⁴⁷ But six hundred men turned and fled toward the wilderness to the rock of Rimmon, and stayed in the rock of Rimmon four months. ⁴⁸ The men of Israel turned again on the children of Benjamin, and struck them with the edge of the sword—including the entire city, the livestock, and all that they found. Moreover they set all the cities which they found on fire.

## 21

¹ Now the men of Israel had sworn in Mizpah, saying, "None of us will give his daughter to Benjamin as a wife." ² The people came to Bethel and sat there until evening before God, and lifted up their voices, and wept severely. ³ They said, "Yahweh, the God of Israel, why has this happened in Israel, that there should be one tribe lacking in Israel today?" ⁴ On the next day, the people rose early and built an altar there, and offered burnt offerings and peace offerings. ⁵ The children of Israel said, "Who is there among all the tribes of Israel who didn't come up

in the assembly to Yahweh?" For they had made a great oath concerning him who didn't come up to Yahweh to Mizpah, saying, "He shall surely be put to death." ⁶ The children of Israel grieved for Benjamin their brother, and said, "There is one tribe cut off from Israel today. ⁷ How shall we provide wives for those who remain, since we have sworn by Yahweh that we will not give them of our daughters to wives?" ⁸ They said, "What one is there of the tribes of Israel who didn't come up to Yahweh to Mizpah?" Behold, no one came from Jabesh Gilead to the camp to the assembly. ⁹ For when the people were counted, behold, there were none of the inhabitants of Jabesh Gilead there. ¹⁰ The congregation sent twelve thousand of the most valiant men there, and commanded them, saying, "Go and strike the inhabitants of Jabesh Gilead with the edge of the sword, with the women and the little ones. ¹¹ This is the thing that you shall do: you shall utterly destroy every male, and every woman who has lain with a man." ¹² They found among the inhabitants of Jabesh Gilead four hundred young virgins who had not known man by lying with him; and they brought them to the camp to Shiloh, which is in the land of Canaan. ¹³ The whole congregation sent and spoke to the children of Benjamin who were in the rock of Rimmon, and proclaimed peace to them. ¹⁴ Benjamin returned at that time; and they gave them the women whom they had saved alive of the women of Jabesh Gilead. There still weren't enough for them. ¹⁵ The people grieved for Benjamin, because Yahweh had made a breach in the tribes of Israel. ¹⁶ Then the elders of the congregation said, "How shall we provide wives for those who remain, since the women are destroyed out of Benjamin?" ¹⁷ They said, "There must be an inheritance for those who are escaped of Benjamin, that a tribe not be blotted out from Israel. ¹⁸ However, we may not give them wives of our daughters, for the children of Israel had sworn, saying, 'Cursed is he who gives a wife to Benjamin.'" ¹⁹ They said, "Behold, there is a feast of Yahweh from year to year in Shiloh, which is on the north of Bethel, on the east side of the highway that goes up from Bethel to Shechem, and on the south of Lebonah." ²⁰ They commanded the children of Benjamin, saying, "Go and lie in wait in the vineyards, ²¹ and see, and behold, if the daughters of Shiloh come out to dance in the dances, then come out of the vineyards, and each man catch his wife of the daughters of Shiloh, and go to the land of Benjamin. ²² It shall be, when their fathers or their brothers come to complain to us, that we will say to them, 'Grant them graciously to us, because we didn't take for each man his wife in battle, neither did you give them to them; otherwise you would now be guilty.'" ²³ The children of Benjamin did so, and took wives for themselves according to their number, of those who danced, whom they carried off. They went and returned to their inheritance, built the cities, and lived in them. ²⁴ The children of Israel departed from there at that time, every man to his tribe and to his family, and they each went out from there to his own inheritance. ²⁵ In those days there was no king in Israel. Everyone did that which was right in his own eyes.

# The Book of Ruth

## 1

¹ In the days when the judges judged, there was a famine in the land. A certain man of Bethlehem Judah went to live in the country of Moab with his wife and his two sons. ² The name of the man was Elimelech, and the name of his wife Naomi. The names of his two sons were Mahlon and Chilion, Ephrathites of Bethlehem Judah. They came into the country of Moab and lived there. ³ Elimelech, Naomi's husband, died; and she was left with her two sons. ⁴ They took for themselves wives of the women of Moab. The name of the one was Orpah, and the name of the other was Ruth. They lived there about ten years. ⁵ Mahlon and Chilion both died, and the woman was bereaved of her two children and of her husband. ⁶ Then she arose with her daughters-in-law, that she might return from the country of Moab; for she had heard in the country of Moab how Yahweh[a] had visited his people in giving them bread. ⁷ She went out of the place where she was, and her two daughters-in-law with her. They went on the way to return to the land of Judah. ⁸ Naomi said to her two daughters-in-law, "Go, return each of you to her mother's house. May Yahweh deal kindly with you, as you have dealt with the dead and with me. ⁹ May Yahweh grant you that you may find rest, each of you in the house of her husband." Then she kissed them, and they lifted up their voices, and wept. ¹⁰ They said to her, "No, but we will return with you to your people." ¹¹ Naomi said, "Go back, my daughters. Why do you want to go with me? Do I still

have sons in my womb, that they may be your husbands? ¹² Go back, my daughters, go your way; for I am too old to have a husband. If I should say, 'I have hope,' if I should even have a husband tonight, and should also bear sons, ¹³ would you then wait until they were grown? Would you then refrain from having husbands? No, my daughters, for it grieves me seriously for your sakes, for Yahweh's hand has gone out against me." ¹⁴ They lifted up their voices and wept again; then Orpah kissed her mother-in-law, but Ruth stayed with her. ¹⁵ She said, "Behold,[b] your sister-in-law has gone back to her people and to her god. Follow your sister-in-law." ¹⁶ Ruth said, "Don't urge me to leave you, and to return from following you, for where you go, I will go; and where you stay, I will stay. Your people will be my people, and your God[c] my God. ¹⁷ Where you die, I will die, and there I will be buried. May Yahweh do so to me, and more also, if anything but death parts you and me." ¹⁸ When Naomi saw that she was determined to go with her, she stopped urging her. ¹⁹ So they both went until they came to Bethlehem. When they had come to Bethlehem, all the city was excited about them, and they asked, "Is this Naomi?" ²⁰ She said to them, "Don't call me Naomi.[d] Call me Mara,[e] for the Almighty has dealt very bitterly with me. ²¹ I went out full, and Yahweh has brought me home again empty. Why do you call me Naomi, since Yahweh has testified against me, and the Almighty has afflicted me?" ²² So Naomi returned, and Ruth the Moabitess, her daughter-in-law, with her, who returned out of the country of Moab. They came to Bethlehem in the beginning of barley harvest.

## 2

¹ Naomi had a relative of her husband's, a mighty man of wealth, of the family of Elimelech, and his name was Boaz. ² Ruth the Moabitess said to Naomi, "Let me now go to the field, and glean among the ears of grain after him in whose sight I find favor." She said to her, "Go, my daughter." ³ She went, and came and gleaned in the field after the reapers; and she happened to come to the portion of the field belonging to Boaz, who was of the family of Elimelech. ⁴ Behold, Boaz came from Bethlehem, and said to the reapers, "May Yahweh be with you." They answered him, "May Yahweh bless you." ⁵ Then Boaz said to his servant who was set over the reapers, "Whose young lady is this?" ⁶ The servant who was set over the reapers answered, "It is the Moabite lady who came back with Naomi out of the country of Moab. ⁷ She said, 'Please let me glean and gather after the reapers among the sheaves.' So she came, and has continued even from the morning until now, except that she rested a little in the house." ⁸ Then Boaz said to Ruth, "Listen, my daughter. Don't go to glean in another field, and don't go from here, but stay here close to my maidens. ⁹ Let your eyes be on the field that they reap, and go after them. Haven't I commanded the young men not to touch you? When you are thirsty, go to the vessels, and drink from that which the young men have drawn." ¹⁰ Then she fell on her face and bowed herself to the ground, and said to him, "Why have I found favor in your sight, that you should take knowledge of me, since I am a foreigner?" ¹¹ Boaz answered her, "I have been told all about what you have done for your mother-in-law since the death of your husband, and how you have left your father, your mother, and the land of your birth, and have come to a people that you didn't know before. ¹² May Yahweh repay your work, and a full reward be given to you from Yahweh, the God of Israel, under whose wings you have come to take refuge." ¹³ Then she said, "Let me find favor in your sight, my lord, because you have comforted me, and because you have spoken kindly to your servant, though I am not as one of your servants." ¹⁴ At meal time Boaz said to her, "Come here, and eat some bread, and dip your morsel in the vinegar." She sat beside the reapers, and they passed her parched grain. She ate, was satisfied, and left some of it. ¹⁵ When she had risen up to glean, Boaz commanded his young men, saying, "Let her glean even among the sheaves, and don't reproach her. ¹⁶ Also pull out some for her from the bundles, and leave it. Let her glean, and don't rebuke her." ¹⁷ So she gleaned in the field until evening; and she beat out that which she had gleaned, and it was about an ephah[f] of barley. ¹⁸ She took it up, and went into the city. Then her mother-in-law saw what she had gleaned; and she brought out and gave to her that which she had left after she had enough. ¹⁹ Her mother-in-law said to her, "Where have you gleaned today? Where have you worked? Blessed be he who noticed you." She told her mother-in-law with whom she had worked, "The man's name with whom I worked today is Boaz." ²⁰ Naomi said to her daughter-in-law, "May he be blessed by Yahweh, who has not abandoned his kindness to the living and to the dead." Naomi said to her, "The man is a close relative to us, one of our

[a] *1:6* "Yahweh" is God's proper Name, sometimes rendered "LORD" (all caps) in other translations.

[b] *1:15* "Behold", from "הִנֵּה", means look at, take notice, observe, see, or gaze at. It is often used as an interjection.

[c] *1:16* The Hebrew word rendered "God" is "אֱלֹהִים" (Elohim).

[d] *1:20* "Naomi" means "pleasant".

[e] *1:20* "Mara" means "bitter".

[f] *2:17* 1 ephah is about 22 liters or about 2/3 of a bushel

near kinsmen." <sup>21</sup> Ruth the Moabitess said, "Yes, he said to me, 'You shall stay close to my young men until they have finished all my harvest.'" <sup>22</sup> Naomi said to Ruth her daughter-in-law, "It is good, my daughter, that you go out with his maidens, and that they not meet you in any other field." <sup>23</sup> So she stayed close to the maidens of Boaz, to glean to the end of barley harvest and of wheat harvest; and she lived with her mother-in-law.

## 3

<sup>1</sup> Naomi her mother-in-law said to her, "My daughter, shall I not seek rest for you, that it may be well with you? <sup>2</sup> Now isn't Boaz our kinsman, with whose maidens you were? Behold, he will be winnowing barley tonight on the threshing floor. <sup>3</sup> Therefore wash yourself, anoint yourself, get dressed, and go down to the threshing floor; but don't make yourself known to the man until he has finished eating and drinking. <sup>4</sup> It shall be, when he lies down, that you shall note the place where he is lying. Then you shall go in, uncover his feet, and lie down. Then he will tell you what to do." <sup>5</sup> She said to her, "All that you say, I will do." <sup>6</sup> She went down to the threshing floor, and did everything that her mother-in-law told her. <sup>7</sup> When Boaz had eaten and drunk, and his heart was merry, he went to lie down at the end of the heap of grain. She came softly, uncovered his feet, and lay down. <sup>8</sup> At midnight, the man was startled and turned himself; and behold, a woman lay at his feet. <sup>9</sup> He said, "Who are you?" She answered, "I am Ruth your servant. Therefore spread the corner of your garment over your servant; for you are a near kinsman." <sup>10</sup> He said, "You are blessed by Yahweh, my daughter. You have shown more kindness in the latter end than at the beginning, because you didn't follow young men, whether poor or rich. <sup>11</sup> Now, my daughter, don't be afraid. I will do to you all that you say; for all the city of my people knows that you are a worthy woman. <sup>12</sup> Now it is true that I am a near kinsman. However, there is a kinsman nearer than I. <sup>13</sup> Stay this night, and in the morning, if he will perform for you the part of a kinsman, good. Let him do the kinsman's duty. But if he will not do the duty of a kinsman for you, then I will do the duty of a kinsman for you, as Yahweh lives. Lie down until the morning." <sup>14</sup> She lay at his feet until the morning, then she rose up before one could discern another. For he said, "Let it not be known that the woman came to the threshing floor." <sup>15</sup> He said, "Bring the mantle that is on you, and hold it." She held it; and he measured six measures of barley, and laid it on her; then he went into the city. <sup>16</sup> When she came to her mother-in-law, she said, "How did it go, my daughter?" She told her all that the man had done for her. <sup>17</sup> She said, "He gave me these six measures of barley; for he said, 'Don't go empty to your mother-in-law.'" <sup>18</sup> Then she said, "Wait, my daughter, until you know what will happen; for the man will not rest until he has settled this today."

## 4

<sup>1</sup> Now Boaz went up to the gate and sat down there. Behold, the near kinsman of whom Boaz spoke came by. Boaz said to him, "Come over here, friend, and sit down!" He came over, and sat down. <sup>2</sup> Boaz took ten men of the elders of the city, and said, "Sit down here," and they sat down. <sup>3</sup> He said to the near kinsman, "Naomi, who has come back out of the country of Moab, is selling the parcel of land, which was our brother Elimelech's. <sup>4</sup> I thought I should tell you, saying, 'Buy it before those who sit here, and before the elders of my people.' If you will redeem it, redeem it; but if you will not redeem it, then tell me, that I may know. For there is no one to redeem it besides you; and I am after you." He said, "I will redeem it." <sup>5</sup> Then Boaz said, "On the day you buy the field from the hand of Naomi, you must buy it also from Ruth the Moabitess, the wife of the dead, to raise up the name of the dead on his inheritance." <sup>6</sup> The near kinsman said, "I can't redeem it for myself, lest I endanger my own inheritance. Take my right of redemption for yourself; for I can't redeem it." <sup>7</sup> Now this was the custom in former time in Israel concerning redeeming and concerning exchanging, to confirm all things: a man took off his sandal, and gave it to his neighbor; and this was the way of formalizing transactions in Israel. <sup>8</sup> So the near kinsman said to Boaz, "Buy it for yourself," then he took off his sandal. <sup>9</sup> Boaz said to the elders and to all the people, "You are witnesses today, that I have bought all that was Elimelech's, and all that was Chilion's and Mahlon's, from the hand of Naomi. <sup>10</sup> Moreover, Ruth the Moabitess, the wife of Mahlon, I have purchased to be my wife, to raise up the name of the dead on his inheritance, that the name of the dead may not be cut off from among his brothers and from the gate of his place. You are witnesses today." <sup>11</sup> All the people who were in the gate, and the elders, said, "We are witnesses. May Yahweh make the woman who has come into your house like Rachel and like Leah, which both built the house of Israel; and treat you worthily in

Ephrathah, and be famous in Bethlehem. <sup>12</sup> Let your house be like the house of Perez, whom Tamar bore to Judah, of the offspring<sup>a</sup> which Yahweh will give you by this young woman." <sup>13</sup> So Boaz took Ruth and she became his wife; and he went in to her, and Yahweh enabled her to conceive, and she bore a son. <sup>14</sup> The women said to Naomi, "Blessed be Yahweh, who has not left you today without a near kinsman. Let his name be famous in Israel. <sup>15</sup> He shall be to you a restorer of life and sustain you in your old age; for your daughter-in-law, who loves you, who is better to you than seven sons, has given birth to him." <sup>16</sup> Naomi took the child, laid him in her bosom, and became nurse to him. <sup>17</sup> The women, her neighbors, gave him a name, saying, "A son is born to Naomi". They named him Obed. He is the father of Jesse, the father of David. <sup>18</sup> Now this is the history of the generations of Perez: Perez became the father of Hezron, <sup>19</sup> and Hezron became the father of Ram, and Ram became the father of Amminadab, <sup>20</sup> and Amminadab became the father of Nahshon, and Nahshon became the father of Salmon, <sup>21</sup> and Salmon became the father of Boaz, and Boaz became the father of Obed, <sup>22</sup> and Obed became the father of Jesse, and Jesse became the father of David.

# The First Book of Samuel

## 1

<sup>1</sup> Now there was a certain man of Ramathaim Zophim, of the hill country of Ephraim, and his name was Elkanah, the son of Jeroham, the son of Elihu, the son of Tohu, the son of Zuph, an Ephraimite. <sup>2</sup> He had two wives. The name of one was Hannah, and the name of the other Peninnah. Peninnah had children, but Hannah had no children. <sup>3</sup> This man went up out of his city from year to year to worship and to sacrifice to Yahweh<sup>b</sup> of Armies in Shiloh. The two sons of Eli, Hophni and Phinehas, priests to Yahweh, were there. <sup>4</sup> When the day came that Elkanah sacrificed, he gave portions to Peninnah his wife and to all her sons and her daughters; <sup>5</sup> but he gave a double portion to Hannah, for he loved Hannah, but Yahweh had shut up her womb. <sup>6</sup> Her rival provoked her severely, to irritate her, because Yahweh had shut up her womb. <sup>7</sup> So year by year, when she went up to Yahweh's house, her rival provoked her. Therefore she wept, and didn't eat. <sup>8</sup> Elkanah her husband said to her, "Hannah, why do you weep? Why don't you eat? Why is your heart grieved? Am I not better to you than ten sons?" <sup>9</sup> So Hannah rose up after they had finished eating and drinking in Shiloh. Now Eli the priest was sitting on his seat by the doorpost of Yahweh's temple. <sup>10</sup> She was in bitterness of soul, and prayed to Yahweh, weeping bitterly. <sup>11</sup> She vowed a vow, and said, "Yahweh of Armies, if you will indeed look at the affliction of your servant and remember me, and not forget your servant, but will give to your servant a boy, then I will give him to Yahweh all the days of his life, and no razor shall come on his head." <sup>12</sup> As she continued praying before Yahweh, Eli saw her mouth. <sup>13</sup> Now Hannah spoke in her heart. Only her lips moved, but her voice was not heard. Therefore Eli thought she was drunk. <sup>14</sup> Eli said to her, "How long will you be drunk? Get rid of your wine!" <sup>15</sup> Hannah answered, "No, my lord, I am a woman of a sorrowful spirit. I have not been drinking wine or strong drink, but I poured out my soul before Yahweh. <sup>16</sup> Don't consider your servant a wicked woman; for I have been speaking out of the abundance of my complaint and my provocation." <sup>17</sup> Then Eli answered, "Go in peace; and may the God<sup>c</sup> of Israel grant your petition that you have asked of him." <sup>18</sup> She said, "Let your servant find favor in your sight." So the woman went her way and ate; and her facial expression wasn't sad any more. <sup>19</sup> They rose up in the morning early and worshiped Yahweh, then returned and came to their house to Ramah. Then Elkanah knew Hannah his wife; and Yahweh remembered her. <sup>20</sup> When the time had come, Hannah conceived, and bore a son; and she named him Samuel,<sup>d</sup> saying, "Because I have asked him of Yahweh." <sup>21</sup> The man Elkanah, and all his house, went up to offer to Yahweh the yearly sacrifice and his vow. <sup>22</sup> But Hannah didn't go up, for she said to her husband, "Not until the child is weaned; then I will bring him, that he may appear before Yahweh, and stay there forever." <sup>23</sup> Elkanah her husband said to her, "Do what seems good to you. Wait until you have weaned him; only may Yahweh establish his word." So the woman waited and nursed her son until she weaned him. <sup>24</sup> When she had weaned him, she took him up with her, with three bulls, and one ephah<sup>e</sup> of meal, and a container of wine, and brought him to Yahweh's house in Shiloh. The child was young. <sup>25</sup> They killed the bull, and brought the child to Eli. <sup>26</sup> She said, "Oh, my lord, as your soul lives, my lord, I am the woman who stood by you here, praying to Yahweh. <sup>27</sup> I prayed for this child, and Yahweh

<sup>a</sup> *4:12* or, seed
<sup>b</sup> *1:3* "Yahweh" is God's proper Name, sometimes rendered "LORD" (all caps) in other translations.
<sup>c</sup> *1:17* The Hebrew word rendered "God" is "אֱלֹהִים" (Elohim).
<sup>d</sup> *1:20* Samuel sounds like the Hebrew for "heard by God."
<sup>e</sup> *1:24* 1 ephah is about 22 liters or about 2/3 of a bushel

has given me my petition which I asked of him. ²⁸ Therefore I have also given him to Yahweh. As long as he lives he is given to Yahweh." He worshiped Yahweh there.

## 2

¹ Hannah prayed, and said, "My heart exults in Yahweh! My horn is exalted in Yahweh. My mouth is enlarged over my enemies, because I rejoice in your salvation. ² There is no one as holy as Yahweh, for there is no one besides you, nor is there any rock like our God. ³"Don't keep talking so exceedingly proudly. Don't let arrogance come out of your mouth, for Yahweh is a God of knowledge. By him actions are weighed. ⁴"The bows of the mighty men are broken. Those who stumbled are armed with strength. ⁵ Those who were full have hired themselves out for bread. Those who were hungry are satisfied. Yes, the barren has borne seven. She who has many children languishes. ⁶"Yahweh kills and makes alive. He brings down to Sheolª and brings up. ⁷ Yahweh makes poor and makes rich. He brings low, he also lifts up. ⁸ He raises up the poor out of the dust. He lifts up the needy from the dunghill to make them sit with princes and inherit the throne of glory. For the pillars of the earth are Yahweh's. He has set the world on them. ⁹ He will keep the feet of his holy ones, but the wicked will be put to silence in darkness; for no man will prevail by strength. ¹⁰ Those who strive with Yahweh shall be broken to pieces. He will thunder against them in the sky. "Yahweh will judge the ends of the earth. He will give strength to his king, and exalt the horn of his anointed." ¹¹ Elkanah went to Ramah to his house. The child served Yahweh before Eli the priest. ¹² Now the sons of Eli were wicked men. They didn't know Yahweh. ¹³ The custom of the priests with the people was that when anyone offered a sacrifice, the priest's servant came while the meat was boiling, with a fork of three teeth in his hand; ¹⁴ and he stabbed it into the pan, or kettle, or cauldron, or pot. The priest took all that the fork brought up for himself. They did this to all the Israelites who came there to Shiloh. ¹⁵ Yes, before they burned the fat, the priest's servant came, and said to the man who sacrificed, "Give meat to roast for the priest; for he will not accept boiled meat from you, but raw." ¹⁶ If the man said to him, "Let the fat be burned first, and then take as much as your soul desires;" then he would say, "No, but you shall give it to me now; and if not, I will take it by force." ¹⁷ The sin of the young men was very great before Yahweh; for the men despised Yahweh's offering. ¹⁸ But Samuel ministered before Yahweh, being a child, clothed with a linen ephod. ¹⁹ Moreover his mother made him a little robe, and brought it to him from year to year when she came up with her husband to offer the yearly sacrifice. ²⁰ Eli blessed Elkanah and his wife, and said, "May Yahweh give you offspringᵇ from this woman for the petition which was asked of Yahweh." Then they went to their own home. ²¹ Yahweh visited Hannah, and she conceived and bore three sons and two daughters. The child Samuel grew before Yahweh. ²² Now Eli was very old; and he heard all that his sons did to all Israel, and how that they slept with the women who served at the door of the Tent of Meeting. ²³ He said to them, "Why do you do such things? For I hear of your evil dealings from all these people. ²⁴ No, my sons; for it is not a good report that I hear! You make Yahweh's people disobey. ²⁵ If one man sins against another, God will judge him; but if a man sins against Yahweh, who will intercede for him?" Notwithstanding, they didn't listen to the voice of their father, because Yahweh intended to kill them. ²⁶ The child Samuel grew on, and increased in favor both with Yahweh and also with men. ²⁷ A man of God came to Eli and said to him, "Yahweh says, 'Did I reveal myself to the house of your father when they were in Egypt in bondage to Pharaoh's house? ²⁸ Didn't I choose him out of all the tribes of Israel to be my priest, to go up to my altar, to burn incense, to wear an ephod before me? Didn't I give to the house of your father all the offerings of the children of Israel made by fire? ²⁹ Why do you kick at my sacrifice and at my offering, which I have commanded in my habitation, and honor your sons above me, to make yourselves fat with the best of all the offerings of Israel my people?' ³⁰"Therefore Yahweh, the God of Israel, says, 'I said indeed that your house and the house of your father should walk before me forever.' But now Yahweh says, 'Far be it from me; for those who honor me I will honor, and those who despise me will be cursed. ³¹ Behold,ᶜ the days come that I will cut off your arm and the arm of your father's house, that there will not be an old man in your house. ³² You will see the affliction of my habitation, in all the wealth which I will give Israel. There shall not be an old man in your house forever. ³³ The man of yours whom I don't cut off from my altar will consume your eyesᵈ and grieve your heart. All the increase of your house will die in the flower of their age. ³⁴ This will be the sign to you that will come on your two sons, on Hophni and Phinehas: in one day they will both die. ³⁵ I will

raise up a faithful priest for myself who will do according to that which is in my heart and in my mind. I will build him a sure house. He will walk before my anointed forever. ³⁶ It will happen that everyone who is left in your house will come and bow down to him for a piece of silver and a loaf of bread, and will say, 'Please put me into one of the priests' offices, that I may eat a morsel of bread.'"

## 3

¹ The child Samuel ministered to Yahweh before Eli. Yahweh's word was rare in those days. There were not many visions, then. ² At that time, when Eli was laid down in his place (now his eyes had begun to grow dim, so that he could not see), ³ and God's lamp hadn't yet gone out, and Samuel had laid down in Yahweh's temple where God's ark was, ⁴ Yahweh called Samuel. He said, "Here I am." ⁵ He ran to Eli and said, "Here I am; for you called me." He said, "I didn't call. Lie down again." He went and lay down. ⁶ Yahweh called yet again, "Samuel!" Samuel arose and went to Eli and said, "Here I am; for you called me." He answered, "I didn't call, my son. Lie down again." ⁷ Now Samuel didn't yet know Yahweh, neither was Yahweh's word yet revealed to him. ⁸ Yahweh called Samuel again the third time. He arose and went to Eli and said, "Here I am; for you called me." Eli perceived that Yahweh had called the child. ⁹ Therefore Eli said to Samuel, "Go, lie down. It shall be, if he calls you, that you shall say, 'Speak, Yahweh; for your servant hears.'" So Samuel went and lay down in his place. ¹⁰ Yahweh came, and stood, and called as at other times, "Samuel! Samuel!" Then Samuel said, "Speak; for your servant hears." ¹¹ Yahweh said to Samuel, "Behold, I will do a thing in Israel at which both the ears of everyone who hears it will tingle. ¹² In that day I will perform against Eli all that I have spoken concerning his house, from the beginning even to the end. ¹³ For I have told him that I will judge his house forever for the iniquity which he knew, because his sons brought a curse on themselves, and he didn't restrain them. ¹⁴ Therefore I have sworn to the house of Eli that the iniquity of Eli's house shall not be removed with sacrifice or offering forever." ¹⁵ Samuel lay until the morning, and opened the doors of Yahweh's house. Samuel was afraid to show Eli the vision. ¹⁶ Then Eli called Samuel and said, "Samuel, my son!" He said, "Here I am." ¹⁷ He said, "What is the thing that he has spoken to you? Please don't hide it from me. God do so to you, and more also, if you hide anything from me of all the things that he spoke to you." ¹⁸ Samuel told him every bit, and hid nothing from him. He said, "It is Yahweh. Let him do what seems good to him." ¹⁹ Samuel grew, and Yahweh was with him and let none of his words fall to the ground. ²⁰ All Israel from Dan even to Beersheba knew that Samuel was established to be a prophet of Yahweh. ²¹ Yahweh appeared again in Shiloh; for Yahweh revealed himself to Samuel in Shiloh by Yahweh's word.

## 4

¹ The word of Samuel came to all Israel. Now Israel went out against the Philistines to battle, and encamped beside Ebenezer; and the Philistines encamped in Aphek. ² The Philistines put themselves in array against Israel. When they joined battle, Israel was defeated by the Philistines, who killed about four thousand men of the army in the field. ³ When the people had come into the camp, the elders of Israel said, "Why has Yahweh defeated us today before the Philistines? Let's get the ark of Yahweh's covenant out of Shiloh and bring it to us, that it may come among us and save us out of the hand of our enemies." ⁴ So the people sent to Shiloh, and they brought from there the ark of the covenant of Yahweh of Armies, who sits above the cherubim; and the two sons of Eli, Hophni and Phinehas, were there with the ark of the covenant of God. ⁵ When the ark of Yahweh's covenant came into the camp, all Israel shouted with a great shout, so that the earth resounded. ⁶ When the Philistines heard the noise of the shout, they said, "What does the noise of this great shout in the camp of the Hebrews mean?" They understood that Yahweh's ark had come into the camp. ⁷ The Philistines were afraid, for they said, "God has come into the camp." They said, "Woe to us! For there has not been such a thing before. ⁸ Woe to us! Who shall deliver us out of the hand of these mighty gods? These are the gods that struck the Egyptians with all kinds of plagues in the wilderness. ⁹ Be strong and behave like men, O you Philistines, that you not be servants to the Hebrews, as they have been to you. Strengthen yourselves like men, and fight!" ¹⁰ The Philistines fought, and Israel was defeated, and each man fled to his tent. There was a very great slaughter; for thirty thousand footmen of Israel fell. ¹¹ God's ark was taken; and the two sons of Eli, Hophni and Phinehas, were slain. ¹² A man of Benjamin ran out of the army and came to Shiloh the same day, with his clothes torn and with dirt on his head. ¹³ When he came, behold, Eli was sitting on his seat by the road watching, for his heart

trembled for God's ark. When the man came into the city and told about it, all the city cried out. ¹⁴ When Eli heard the noise of the crying, he said, "What does the noise of this tumult mean?" The man hurried, and came and told Eli. ¹⁵ Now Eli was ninety-eight years old. His eyes were set, so that he could not see. ¹⁶ The man said to Eli, "I am he who came out of the army, and I fled today out of the army." He said, "How did the matter go, my son?" ¹⁷ He who brought the news answered, "Israel has fled before the Philistines, and there has been also a great slaughter among the people. Your two sons also, Hophni and Phinehas, are dead, and God's ark has been captured." ¹⁸ When he made mention of God's ark, Eli fell from off his seat backward by the side of the gate; and his neck broke, and he died, for he was an old man and heavy. He had judged Israel forty years. ¹⁹ His daughter-in-law, Phinehas' wife, was with child, near to giving birth. When she heard the news that God's ark was taken and that her father-in-law and her husband were dead, she bowed herself and gave birth; for her pains came on her. ²⁰ About the time of her death the women who stood by her said to her, "Don't be afraid, for you have given birth to a son." But she didn't answer, neither did she regard it. ²¹ She named the child Ichabod,ᵃ saying, "The glory has departed from Israel!" because God's ark was taken, and because of her father-in-law and her husband. ²² She said, "The glory has departed from Israel; for God's ark has been taken."

## 5

¹ Now the Philistines had taken God's ark, and they brought it from Ebenezer to Ashdod. ² The Philistines took God's ark, and brought it into the house of Dagon and set it by Dagon. ³ When the people of Ashdod arose early on the next day, behold, Dagon had fallen on his face to the ground before Yahweh's ark. They took Dagon and set him in his place again. ⁴ When they arose early on the following morning, behold, Dagon had fallen on his face to the ground before Yahweh's ark; and the head of Dagon and both the palms of his hands were cut off on the threshold. Only Dagon's torso was intact. ⁵ Therefore neither the priests of Dagon nor any who come into Dagon's house step on the threshold of Dagon in Ashdod to this day. ⁶ But Yahweh's hand was heavy on the people of Ashdod, and he destroyed them and struck them with tumors, even Ashdod and its borders. ⁷ When the men of Ashdod saw that it was so, they said, "The ark of the God of Israel shall not stay with us, for his hand is severe on us and on Dagon our god." ⁸ They sent therefore and gathered together all the lords of the Philistines, and said, "What shall we do with the ark of the God of Israel?" They answered, "Let the ark of the God of Israel be carried over to Gath." They carried the ark of the God of Israel there. ⁹ It was so, that after they had carried it there, Yahweh's hand was against the city with a very great confusion; and he struck the men of the city, both small and great, so that tumors broke out on them. ¹⁰ So they sent God's ark to Ekron. As God's ark came to Ekron, the Ekronites cried out, saying, "They have brought the ark of the God of Israel here to us, to kill us and our people." ¹¹ They sent therefore and gathered together all the lords of the Philistines, and they said, "Send the ark of the God of Israel away, and let it go again to its own place, that it not kill us and our people." For there was a deadly panic throughout all the city. The hand of God was very heavy there. ¹² The men who didn't die were struck with the tumors; and the cry of the city went up to heaven.

## 6

¹ Yahweh's ark was in the country of the Philistines seven months. ² The Philistines called for the priests and the diviners, saying, "What shall we do with Yahweh's ark? Show us how we should send it to its place." ³ They said, "If you send away the ark of the God of Israel, don't send it empty; but by all means return a trespass offering to him. Then you will be healed, and it will be known to you why his hand is not removed from you." ⁴ Then they said, "What should the trespass offering be which we shall return to him?" They said, "Five golden tumors and five golden mice, for the number of the lords of the Philistines; for one plague was on you all, and on your lords. ⁵ Therefore you shall make images of your tumors and images of your mice that mar the land; and you shall give glory to the God of Israel. Perhaps he will release his hand from you, from your gods, and from your land. ⁶ Why then do you harden your hearts as the Egyptians and Pharaoh hardened their hearts? When he had worked wonderfully among them, didn't they let the people go, and they departed? ⁷ "Now therefore take and prepare yourselves a new cart and two milk cows on which there has come no yoke; and tie the cows to the cart, and bring their calves home from them; ⁸ and take Yahweh's ark and lay it on the cart. Put the jewels of gold, which you return him for a trespass offering, in a box by its side; and send it away, that it may go. ⁹ Behold, if it goes up by the way of its own border to Beth Shemesh, then he has done us this great evil; but if not, then we shall know that it is not his

hand that struck us. It was a chance that happened to us." ¹⁰ The men did so, and took two milk cows and tied them to the cart, and shut up their calves at home. ¹¹ They put Yahweh's ark on the cart, and the box with the golden mice and the images of their tumors. ¹² The cows took the straight way by the way to Beth Shemesh. They went along the highway, lowing as they went, and didn't turn away to the right hand or to the left; and the lords of the Philistines went after them to the border of Beth Shemesh. ¹³ The people of Beth Shemesh were reaping their wheat harvest in the valley; and they lifted up their eyes and saw the ark, and rejoiced to see it. ¹⁴ The cart came into the field of Joshua of Beth Shemesh, and stood there, where there was a great stone. Then they split the wood of the cart and offered up the cows for a burnt offering to Yahweh. ¹⁵ The Levites took down Yahweh's ark and the box that was with it, in which the jewels of gold were, and put them on the great stone; and the men of Beth Shemesh offered burnt offerings and sacrificed sacrifices the same day to Yahweh. ¹⁶ When the five lords of the Philistines had seen it, they returned to Ekron the same day. ¹⁷ These are the golden tumors which the Philistines returned for a trespass offering to Yahweh: for Ashdod one, for Gaza one, for Ashkelon one, for Gath one, for Ekron one; ¹⁸ and the golden mice, according to the number of all the cities of the Philistines belonging to the five lords, both of fortified cities and of country villages, even to the great stone on which they set down Yahweh's ark. That stone remains to this day in the field of Joshua of Beth Shemesh. ¹⁹ He struck of the men of Beth Shemesh, because they had looked into Yahweh's ark, he struck fifty thousand seventy of the men. Then the people mourned, because Yahweh had struck the people with a great slaughter. ²⁰ The men of Beth Shemesh said, "Who is able to stand before Yahweh, this holy God? To whom shall he go up from us?" ²¹ They sent messengers to the inhabitants of Kiriath Jearim, saying, "The Philistines have brought back Yahweh's ark. Come down and bring it up to yourselves."

## 7

¹ The men of Kiriath Jearim came and took Yahweh's ark, and brought it into Abinadab's house on the hill, and consecrated Eleazar his son to keep Yahweh's ark. ² From the day that the ark stayed in Kiriath Jearim, the time was long—for it was twenty years; and all the house of Israel lamented after Yahweh. ³ Samuel spoke to all the house of Israel, saying, "If you are returning to Yahweh with all your heart, then put away the foreign gods and the Ashtaroth from among you, and direct your hearts to Yahweh, and serve him only; and he will deliver you out of the hand of the Philistines." ⁴ Then the children of Israel removed the Baals and the Ashtaroth, and served Yahweh only. ⁵ Samuel said, "Gather all Israel to Mizpah, and I will pray to Yahweh for you." ⁶ They gathered together to Mizpah, and drew water, and poured it out before Yahweh, and fasted on that day, and said there, "We have sinned against Yahweh." Samuel judged the children of Israel in Mizpah. ⁷ When the Philistines heard that the children of Israel were gathered together at Mizpah, the lords of the Philistines went up against Israel. When the children of Israel heard it, they were afraid of the Philistines. ⁸ The children of Israel said to Samuel, "Don't stop crying to Yahweh our God for us, that he will save us out of the hand of the Philistines." ⁹ Samuel took a suckling lamb, and offered it for a whole burnt offering to Yahweh. Samuel cried to Yahweh for Israel, and Yahweh answered him. ¹⁰ As Samuel was offering up the burnt offering, the Philistines came near to battle against Israel; but Yahweh thundered with a great thunder on that day on the Philistines and confused them; and they were struck down before Israel. ¹¹ The men of Israel went out of Mizpah and pursued the Philistines, and struck them until they came under Beth Kar. ¹² Then Samuel took a stone and set it between Mizpah and Shen, and called its name Ebenezer,ᵇ saying, "Yahweh helped us until now." ¹³ So the Philistines were subdued, and they stopped coming within the border of Israel. Yahweh's hand was against the Philistines all the days of Samuel. ¹⁴ The cities which the Philistines had taken from Israel were restored to Israel, from Ekron even to Gath; and Israel recovered its border out of the hand of the Philistines. There was peace between Israel and the Amorites. ¹⁵ Samuel judged Israel all the days of his life. ¹⁶ He went from year to year in a circuit to Bethel, Gilgal, and Mizpah; and he judged Israel in all those places. ¹⁷ His return was to Ramah, for his house was there, and he judged Israel there; and he built an altar to Yahweh there.

## 8

¹ When Samuel was old, he made his sons judges over Israel. ² Now the name of his firstborn was Joel, and the name of his second, Abijah. They were judges in Beersheba. ³ His sons didn't walk in his ways, but turned away after dishonest gain, took bribes, and perverted justice. ⁴ Then all the elders of Israel gathered themselves together and came to

---

ᵃ *4:21* "Ichabod" means "no glory".

ᵇ *7:12* "Ebenezer" means "stone of help".

Samuel to Ramah. [5] They said to him, "Behold, you are old, and your sons don't walk in your ways. Now make us a king to judge us like all the nations." [6] But the thing displeased Samuel when they said, "Give us a king to judge us." Samuel prayed to Yahweh. [7] Yahweh said to Samuel, "Listen to the voice of the people in all that they tell you; for they have not rejected you, but they have rejected me as the king over them. [8] According to all the works which they have done since the day that I brought them up out of Egypt even to this day, in that they have forsaken me and served other gods, so they also do to you. [9] Now therefore, listen to their voice. However, you shall protest solemnly to them, and shall show them the way of the king who will reign over them." [10] Samuel told all Yahweh's words to the people who asked him for a king. [11] He said, "This will be the way of the king who shall reign over you: he will take your sons and appoint them as his servants, for his chariots and to be his horsemen; and they will run before his chariots. [12] He will appoint them to him for captains of thousands and captains of fifties; and he will assign some to plow his ground and to reap his harvest; and to make his instruments of war and the instruments of his chariots. [13] He will take your daughters to be perfumers, to be cooks, and to be bakers. [14] He will take your fields, your vineyards, and your olive groves, even your best, and give them to his servants. [15] He will take one tenth of your seed and of your vineyards, and give it to his officers and to his servants. [16] He will take your male servants, your female servants, your best young men, and your donkeys, and assign them to his own work. [17] He will take one tenth of your flocks; and you will be his servants. [18] You will cry out in that day because of your king whom you will have chosen for yourselves; and Yahweh will not answer you in that day." [19] But the people refused to listen to the voice of Samuel; and they said, "No, but we will have a king over us, [20] that we also may be like all the nations; and that our king may judge us, and go out before us, and fight our battles." [21] Samuel heard all the words of the people, and he rehearsed them in the ears of Yahweh. [22] Yahweh said to Samuel, "Listen to their voice, and make them a king." Samuel said to the men of Israel, "Everyone go to your own city."

# 9

[1] Now there was a man of Benjamin, whose name was Kish the son of Abiel, the son of Zeror, the son of Becorath, the son of Aphiah, the son of a Benjamite, a mighty man of valor. [2] He had a son whose name was Saul, an impressive young man; and there was not among the children of Israel a more handsome person than he. From his shoulders and upward he was taller than any of the people. [3] The donkeys of Kish, Saul's father, were lost. Kish said to Saul his son, "Now take one of the servants with you, and arise, go look for the donkeys." [4] He passed through the hill country of Ephraim, and passed through the land of Shalishah, but they didn't find them. Then they passed through the land of Shaalim, and they weren't there. Then he passed through the land of the Benjamites, but they didn't find them. [5] When they had come to the land of Zuph, Saul said to his servant who was with him, "Come! Let's return, lest my father stop caring about the donkeys and be anxious for us." [6] The servant said to him, "Behold now, there is a man of God in this city, and he is a man who is held in honor. All that he says surely happens. Now let's go there. Perhaps he can tell us which way to go." [7] Then Saul said to his servant, "But behold, if we go, what should we bring the man? For the bread is spent in our sacks, and there is not a present to bring to the man of God. What do we have?" [8] The servant answered Saul again and said, "Behold, I have in my hand the fourth part of a shekel[a] of silver. I will give that to the man of God, to tell us our way." [9] (In earlier times in Israel, when a man went to inquire of God, he said, "Come! Let's go to the seer;" for he who is now called a prophet was before called a seer.) [10] Then Saul said to his servant, "Well said. Come! Let's go." So they went to the city where the man of God was. [11] As they went up the ascent to the city, they found young maidens going out to draw water, and said to them, "Is the seer here?" [12] They answered them and said, "He is. Behold, he is before you. Hurry now, for he has come today into the city; for the people have a sacrifice today in the high place. [13] As soon as you have come into the city, you will immediately find him before he goes up to the high place to eat; for the people will not eat until he comes, because he blesses the sacrifice. Afterwards those who are invited eat. Now therefore go up; for at this time you will find him." [14] They went up to the city. As they came within the city, behold, Samuel came out toward them to go up to the high place. [15] Now Yahweh had revealed to Samuel a day before Saul came, saying, [16]"Tomorrow about this time I will send you a man out of the land of Benjamin, and you shall anoint him to be prince over my people Israel. He will save my people out of the hand of the Philistines; for I have looked upon my people, because their cry has come to me." [17] When Samuel saw Saul, Yahweh said to him, "Behold, the man of

whom I spoke to you! He will have authority over my people." [18] Then Saul approached Samuel in the gateway, and said, "Please tell me where the seer's house is." [19] Samuel answered Saul and said, "I am the seer. Go up before me to the high place, for you are to eat with me today. In the morning I will let you go and will tell you all that is in your heart. [20] As for your donkeys who were lost three days ago, don't set your mind on them, for they have been found. For whom does all Israel desire? Is it not you and all your father's house?" [21] Saul answered, "Am I not a Benjamite, of the smallest of the tribes of Israel? And my family the least of all the families of the tribe of Benjamin? Why then do you speak to me like this?" [22] Samuel took Saul and his servant and brought them into the guest room, and made them sit in the best place among those who were invited, who were about thirty persons. [23] Samuel said to the cook, "Bring the portion which I gave you, of which I said to you, 'Set it aside.'" [24] The cook took up the thigh, and that which was on it, and set it before Saul. Samuel said, "Behold, that which has been reserved! Set it before yourself and eat; because it has been kept for you for the appointed time, for I said, 'I have invited the people.'" So Saul ate with Samuel that day. [25] When they had come down from the high place into the city, he talked with Saul on the housetop. [26] They arose early; and about daybreak, Samuel called to Saul on the housetop, saying, "Get up, that I may send you away." Saul arose, and they both went outside, he and Samuel, together. [27] As they were going down at the end of the city, Samuel said to Saul, "Tell the servant to go on ahead of us." He went ahead, then Samuel said, "But stand still first, that I may cause you to hear God's message."

# 10

[1] Then Samuel took the vial of oil and poured it on his head, then kissed him and said, "Hasn't Yahweh anointed you to be prince over his inheritance? [2] When you have departed from me today, then you will find two men by Rachel's tomb, on the border of Benjamin at Zelzah. They will tell you, 'The donkeys which you went to look for have been found; and behold, your father has stopped caring about the donkeys and is anxious for you, saying, "What shall I do for my son?"' [3]"Then you will go on forward from there, and you will come to the oak of Tabor. Three men will meet you there going up to God to Bethel: one carrying three young goats, and another carrying three loaves of bread, and another carrying a container of wine. [4] They will greet you and give you two loaves of bread, which you shall receive from their hand. [5]"After that you will come to the hill of God, where the garrison of the Philistines is; and it will happen, when you have come there to the city, that you will meet a band of prophets coming down from the high place with a lute, a tambourine, a pipe, and a harp before them; and they will be prophesying. [6] Then Yahweh's Spirit will come mightily on you, then you will prophesy with them and will be turned into another man. [7] Let it be, when these signs have come to you, that you do what is appropriate for the occasion; for God is with you. [8]"Go down ahead of me to Gilgal; and behold, I will come down to you to offer burnt offerings and to sacrifice sacrifices of peace offerings. Wait seven days, until I come to you and show you what you are to do." [9] It was so, that when he had turned his back to go from Samuel, God gave him another heart; and all those signs happened that day. [10] When they came there to the hill, behold, a band of prophets met him; and the Spirit of God came mightily on him, and he prophesied among them. [11] When all who knew him before saw that, behold, he prophesied with the prophets, then the people said to one another, "What is this that has come to the son of Kish? Is Saul also among the prophets?" [12] One from the same place answered, "Who is their father?" Therefore it became a proverb, "Is Saul also among the prophets?" [13] When he had finished prophesying, he came to the high place. [14] Saul's uncle said to him and to his servant, "Where did you go?" He said, "To seek the donkeys. When we saw that they were not found, we came to Samuel." [15] Saul's uncle said, "Please tell me what Samuel said to you." [16] Saul said to his uncle, "He told us plainly that the donkeys were found." But concerning the matter of the kingdom, of which Samuel spoke, he didn't tell him. [17] Samuel called the people together to Yahweh to Mizpah; [18] and he said to the children of Israel, "Yahweh, the God of Israel, says 'I brought Israel up out of Egypt and I delivered you out of the hand of the Egyptians, and out of the hand of all the kingdoms that oppressed you.' [19] But you have today rejected your God, who himself saves you out of all your calamities and your distresses; and you have said to him, 'No! Set a king over us!' Now therefore present yourselves before Yahweh by your tribes and by your thousands." [20] So Samuel brought all the tribes of Israel near, and the tribe of Benjamin was chosen. [21] He brought the tribe of Benjamin near by their families and the family of the Matrites was chosen. Then Saul the son of Kish was chosen; but when they looked for him, he could not be found. [22] Therefore they

---

[a] *9:8* A shekel is about 10 grams or about 0.35 ounces, so 1/4 shekel would be a small coin of about 2.5 grams.

asked of Yahweh further, "Is there yet a man to come here?" Yahweh answered, "Behold, he has hidden himself among the baggage." [23] They ran and got him there. When he stood among the people, he was higher than any of the people from his shoulders and upward. [24] Samuel said to all the people, "Do you see him whom Yahweh has chosen, that there is no one like him among all the people?" All the people shouted and said, "Long live the king!" [25] Then Samuel told the people the regulations of the kingdom, and wrote it in a book and laid it up before Yahweh. Samuel sent all the people away, every man to his house. [26] Saul also went to his house in Gibeah; and the army went with him, whose hearts God had touched. [27] But certain worthless fellows said, "How could this man save us?" They despised him, and brought him no tribute. But he held his peace.

## 11

[1] Then Nahash the Ammonite came up and encamped against Jabesh Gilead; and all the men of Jabesh said to Nahash, "Make a covenant with us, and we will serve you." [2] Nahash the Ammonite said to them, "On this condition I will make it with you, that all your right eyes be gouged out. I will make this dishonor all Israel." [3] The elders of Jabesh said to him, "Give us seven days, that we may send messengers to all the borders of Israel; and then, if there is no one to save us, we will come out to you." [4] Then the messengers came to Gibeah of Saul, and spoke these words in the ears of the people, then all the people lifted up their voice and wept. [5] Behold, Saul came following the oxen out of the field; and Saul said, "What ails the people that they weep?" They told him the words of the men of Jabesh. [6] God's Spirit came mightily on Saul when he heard those words, and his anger burned hot. [7] He took a yoke of oxen and cut them in pieces, then sent them throughout all the borders of Israel by the hand of messengers, saying, "Whoever doesn't come out after Saul and after Samuel, so shall it be done to his oxen." The dread of Yahweh fell on the people, and they came out as one man. [8] He counted them in Bezek; and the children of Israel were three hundred thousand, and the men of Judah thirty thousand. [9] They said to the messengers who came, "Tell the men of Jabesh Gilead, 'Tomorrow, by the time the sun is hot, you will be rescued.'" The messengers came and told the men of Jabesh; and they were glad. [10] Therefore the men of Jabesh said, "Tomorrow we will come out to you, and you shall do with us all that seems good to you." [11] On the next day, Saul put the people in three companies; and they came into the middle of the camp in the morning watch, and struck the Ammonites until the heat of the day. Those who remained were scattered, so that no two of them were left together. [12] The people said to Samuel, "Who is he who said, 'Shall Saul reign over us?' Bring those men, that we may put them to death!" [13] Saul said, "No man shall be put to death today; for today Yahweh has rescued Israel." [14] Then Samuel said to the people, "Come! Let's go to Gilgal, and renew the kingdom there." [15] All the people went to Gilgal; and there they made Saul king before Yahweh in Gilgal. There they offered sacrifices of peace offerings before Yahweh; and there Saul and all the men of Israel rejoiced greatly.

## 12

[1] Samuel said to all Israel, "Behold, I have listened to your voice in all that you said to me, and have made a king over you. [2] Now, behold, the king walks before you. I am old and gray-headed. Behold, my sons are with you. I have walked before you from my youth to this day. [3] Here I am. Witness against me before Yahweh and before his anointed. Whose ox have I taken? Whose donkey have I taken? Whom have I defrauded? Whom have I oppressed? Of whose hand have I taken a bribe to make me blind my eyes? I will restore it to you." [4] They said, "You have not defrauded us, nor oppressed us, neither have you taken anything from anyone's hand." [5] He said to them, "Yahweh is witness against you, and his anointed is witness today, that you have not found anything in my hand." They said, "He is witness." [6] Samuel said to the people, "It is Yahweh who appointed Moses and Aaron, and that brought your fathers up out of the land of Egypt. [7] Now therefore stand still, that I may plead with you before Yahweh concerning all the righteous acts of Yahweh, which he did to you and to your fathers. [8] "When Jacob had come into Egypt, and your fathers cried to Yahweh, then Yahweh sent Moses and Aaron, who brought your fathers out of Egypt, and made them to dwell in this place. [9] But they forgot Yahweh their God; and he sold them into the hand of Sisera, captain of the army of Hazor, and into the hand of the Philistines, and into the hand of the king of Moab; and they fought against them. [10] They cried to Yahweh, and said, 'We have sinned, because we have forsaken Yahweh and have served the Baals and the Ashtaroth; but now deliver us out of the hand of our enemies, and we will serve you.' [11] Yahweh sent Jerubbaal, Bedan, Jephthah, and Samuel, and delivered you out of the hand of your

enemies on every side; and you lived in safety. [12] "When you saw that Nahash the king of the children of Ammon came against you, you said to me, 'No, but a king shall reign over us,' when Yahweh your God was your king. [13] Now therefore see the king whom you have chosen and whom you have asked for. Behold, Yahweh has set a king over you. [14] If you will fear Yahweh, and serve him, and listen to his voice, and not rebel against the commandment of Yahweh, then both you and also the king who reigns over you are followers of Yahweh your God. [15] But if you will not listen to Yahweh's voice, but rebel against the commandment of Yahweh, then Yahweh's hand will be against you, as it was against your fathers. [16] "Now therefore stand still and see this great thing, which Yahweh will do before your eyes. [17] Isn't it wheat harvest today? I will call to Yahweh, that he may send thunder and rain; and you will know and see that your wickedness is great, which you have done in Yahweh's sight, in asking for a king." [18] So Samuel called to Yahweh, and Yahweh sent thunder and rain that day. Then all the people greatly feared Yahweh and Samuel. [19] All the people said to Samuel, "Pray for your servants to Yahweh your God, that we not die; for we have added to all our sins this evil, to ask for a king." [20] Samuel said to the people, "Don't be afraid. You have indeed done all this evil; yet don't turn away from following Yahweh, but serve Yahweh with all your heart. [21] Don't turn away to go after vain things which can't profit or deliver, for they are vain. [22] For Yahweh will not forsake his people for his great name's sake, because it has pleased Yahweh to make you a people for himself. [23] Moreover, as for me, far be it from me that I should sin against Yahweh in ceasing to pray for you; but I will instruct you in the good and the right way. [24] Only fear Yahweh, and serve him in truth with all your heart; for consider what great things he has done for you. [25] But if you keep doing evil, you will be consumed, both you and your king."

## 13

[1] Saul was thirty years old when he became king, and he reigned over Israel forty-two years.[a] [2] Saul chose for himself three thousand men of Israel, of which two thousand were with Saul in Michmash and in the Mount of Bethel, and one thousand were with Jonathan in Gibeah of Benjamin. He sent the rest of the people to their own tents. [3] Jonathan struck the garrison of the Philistines that was in Geba, and the Philistines heard of it. Saul blew the trumpet throughout all the land, saying, "Let the Hebrews hear!" [4] All Israel heard that Saul had struck the garrison of the Philistines, and also that Israel was considered an abomination to the Philistines. The people were gathered together after Saul to Gilgal. [5] The Philistines assembled themselves together to fight with Israel: thirty thousand chariots, six thousand horsemen, and people as the sand which is on the seashore in multitude. They came up and encamped in Michmash, eastward of Beth Aven. [6] When the men of Israel saw that they were in trouble (for the people were distressed), then the people hid themselves in caves, in thickets, in rocks, in tombs, and in pits. [7] Now some of the Hebrews had gone over the Jordan to the land of Gad and Gilead; but as for Saul, he was yet in Gilgal, and all the people followed him trembling. [8] He stayed seven days, according to the time set by Samuel; but Samuel didn't come to Gilgal, and the people were scattering from him. [9] Saul said, "Bring the burnt offering to me here, and the peace offerings." He offered the burnt offering. [10] It came to pass that as soon as he had finished offering the burnt offering, behold, Samuel came; and Saul went out to meet him, that he might greet him. [11] Samuel said, "What have you done?" Saul said, "Because I saw that the people were scattered from me, and that you didn't come within the days appointed, and that the Philistines assembled themselves together at Michmash, [12] therefore I said, 'Now the Philistines will come down on me to Gilgal, and I haven't entreated the favor of Yahweh.' I forced myself therefore, and offered the burnt offering." [13] Samuel said to Saul, "You have done foolishly. You have not kept the commandment of Yahweh your God, which he commanded you; for now Yahweh would have established your kingdom on Israel forever. [14] But now your kingdom will not continue. Yahweh has sought for himself a man after his own heart, and Yahweh has appointed him to be prince over his people, because you have not kept that which Yahweh commanded you." [15] Samuel arose, and went from Gilgal to Gibeah of Benjamin. Saul counted the people who were present with him, about six hundred men. [16] Saul, and Jonathan his son, and the people who were present with them, stayed in Geba of Benjamin; but the Philistines encamped in Michmash. [17] The raiders came out of the camp of the Philistines in three companies: one company turned to the way that leads to Ophrah, to the land of Shual; [18] another company turned the way to Beth Horon; and another company turned the way of the border that looks down on the valley of

---

[a] 13:1 The traditional Hebrew text omits "thirty" and "forty-". The blanks are filled in here from a few manuscripts of the Septuagint.

Zeboim toward the wilderness. <sup>19</sup> Now there was no blacksmith found throughout all the land of Israel, for the Philistines said, "Lest the Hebrews make themselves swords or spears"; <sup>20</sup> but all the Israelites went down to the Philistines, each man to sharpen his own plowshare, mattock, ax, and sickle. <sup>21</sup> The price was one payim<sup>a</sup> each to sharpen mattocks, plowshares, pitchforks, axes, and goads. <sup>22</sup> So it came to pass in the day of battle that neither sword nor spear was found in the hand of any of the people who were with Saul and Jonathan; but Saul and Jonathan his son had them. <sup>23</sup> The garrison of the Philistines went out to the pass of Michmash.

## 14

<sup>1</sup> Now it happened on a day that Jonathan the son of Saul said to the young man who bore his armor, "Come! Let's go over to the Philistines' garrison that is on the other side." But he didn't tell his father. <sup>2</sup> Saul stayed in the uttermost part of Gibeah under the pomegranate tree which is in Migron; and the people who were with him were about six hundred men, <sup>3</sup> including Ahijah the son of Ahitub, Ichabod's brother, the son of Phinehas, the son of Eli the priest of Yahweh in Shiloh, wearing an ephod. The people didn't know that Jonathan was gone. <sup>4</sup> Between the passes, by which Jonathan sought to go over to the Philistines' garrison, there was a rocky crag on the one side and a rocky crag on the other side; and the name of the one was Bozez, and the name of the other Seneh. <sup>5</sup> The one crag rose up on the north in front of Michmash, and the other on the south in front of Geba. <sup>6</sup> Jonathan said to the young man who bore his armor, "Come! Let's go over to the garrison of these uncircumcised. It may be that Yahweh will work for us, for there is no restraint on Yahweh to save by many or by few." <sup>7</sup> His armor bearer said to him, "Do all that is in your heart. Go, and behold, I am with you according to your heart." <sup>8</sup> Then Jonathan said, "Behold, we will pass over to the men, and we will reveal ourselves to them. <sup>9</sup> If they say this to us, 'Wait until we come to you!' then we will stand still in our place and will not go up to them. <sup>10</sup> But if they say this, 'Come up to us!' then we will go up, for Yahweh has delivered them into our hand. This shall be the sign to us." <sup>11</sup> Both of them revealed themselves to the garrison of the Philistines; and the Philistines said, "Behold, the Hebrews are coming out of the holes where they had hidden themselves!" <sup>12</sup> The men of the garrison answered Jonathan and his armor bearer, and said, "Come up to us, and we will show you something!" Jonathan said to his armor bearer, "Come up after me, for Yahweh has delivered them into the hand of Israel." <sup>13</sup> Jonathan climbed up on his hands and on his feet, and his armor bearer after him, and they fell before Jonathan; and his armor bearer killed them after him. <sup>14</sup> That first slaughter, which Jonathan and his armor bearer made, was about twenty men, within as it were half a furrow's length in an acre of land. <sup>15</sup> There was a trembling in the camp, in the field, and among all the people; the garrison and the raiders also trembled; and the earth quaked, so there was an exceedingly great trembling. <sup>16</sup> The watchmen of Saul in Gibeah of Benjamin looked; and behold, the multitude melted away and scattered. <sup>17</sup> Then Saul said to the people who were with him, "Count now, and see who is missing from us." When they had counted, behold, Jonathan and his armor bearer were not there. <sup>18</sup> Saul said to Ahijah, "Bring God's ark here." For God's ark was with the children of Israel at that time. <sup>19</sup> While Saul talked to the priest, the tumult that was in the camp of the Philistines went on and increased; and Saul said to the priest, "Withdraw your hand!" <sup>20</sup> Saul and all the people who were with him were gathered together, and came to the battle; and behold, they were all striking each other with their swords in very great confusion. <sup>21</sup> Now the Hebrews who were with the Philistines before and who went up with them into the camp from all around, even they also turned to be with the Israelites who were with Saul and Jonathan. <sup>22</sup> Likewise all the men of Israel who had hidden themselves in the hill country of Ephraim, when they heard that the Philistines fled, even they also followed hard after them in the battle. <sup>23</sup> So Yahweh saved Israel that day; and the battle passed over by Beth Aven. <sup>24</sup> The men of Israel were distressed that day; for Saul had adjured the people, saying, "Cursed is the man who eats any food until it is evening, and I am avenged of my enemies." So none of the people tasted food. <sup>25</sup> All the people came into the forest; and there was honey on the ground. <sup>26</sup> When the people had come to the forest, behold, honey was dripping, but no one put his hand to his mouth, for the people feared the oath. <sup>27</sup> But Jonathan didn't hear when his father commanded the people with the oath. Therefore he put out the end of the rod that was in his hand and dipped it in the honeycomb, and put his hand to his mouth; and his eyes brightened. <sup>28</sup> Then one of the people answered, and said, "Your father directly commanded the people with an oath, saying, 'Cursed is the man who eats food today.'" So the people were

faint. <sup>29</sup> Then Jonathan said, "My father has troubled the land. Please look how my eyes have brightened because I tasted a little of this honey. <sup>30</sup> How much more, if perhaps the people had eaten freely today of the plunder of their enemies which they found? For now there has been no great slaughter among the Philistines." <sup>31</sup> They struck the Philistines that day from Michmash to Aijalon. The people were very faint; <sup>32</sup> and the people pounced on the plunder, and took sheep, cattle, and calves, and killed them on the ground; and the people ate them with the blood. <sup>33</sup> Then they told Saul, saying, "Behold, the people are sinning against Yahweh, in that they eat meat with the blood." He said, "You have dealt treacherously. Roll a large stone to me today!" <sup>34</sup> Saul said, "Disperse yourselves among the people, and tell them, 'Every man bring me here his ox, and every man his sheep, and kill them here, and eat; and don't sin against Yahweh in eating meat with the blood.'" All the people brought every man his ox with him that night, and killed them there. <sup>35</sup> Saul built an altar to Yahweh. This was the first altar that he built to Yahweh. <sup>36</sup> Saul said, "Let's go down after the Philistines by night, and take plunder among them until the morning light. Let's not leave a man of them." They said, "Do whatever seems good to you." Then the priest said, "Let's draw near here to God." <sup>37</sup> Saul asked counsel of God: "Shall I go down after the Philistines? Will you deliver them into the hand of Israel?" But he didn't answer him that day. <sup>38</sup> Saul said, "Draw near here, all you chiefs of the people, and know and see in whom this sin has been today. <sup>39</sup> For as Yahweh lives, who saves Israel, though it is in Jonathan my son, he shall surely die." But there was not a man among all the people who answered him. <sup>40</sup> Then he said to all Israel, "You be on one side, and I and Jonathan my son will be on the other side." The people said to Saul, "Do what seems good to you." <sup>41</sup> Therefore Saul said to Yahweh, the God of Israel, "Show the right." Jonathan and Saul were chosen, but the people escaped. <sup>42</sup> Saul said, "Cast lots between me and Jonathan my son." Jonathan was selected. <sup>43</sup> Then Saul said to Jonathan, "Tell me what you have done!" Jonathan told him, and said, "I certainly did taste a little honey with the end of the rod that was in my hand; and behold, I must die." <sup>44</sup> Saul said, "God do so and more also; for you shall surely die, Jonathan." <sup>45</sup> The people said to Saul, "Shall Jonathan die, who has worked this great salvation in Israel? Far from it! As Yahweh lives, there shall not one hair of his head fall to the ground, for he has worked with God today!" So the people rescued Jonathan, so he didn't die. <sup>46</sup> Then Saul went up from following the Philistines; and the Philistines went to their own place. <sup>47</sup> Now when Saul had taken the kingdom over Israel, he fought against all his enemies on every side: against Moab, and against the children of Ammon, and against Edom, and against the kings of Zobah, and against the Philistines. Wherever he turned himself, he defeated them. <sup>48</sup> He did valiantly and struck the Amalekites, and delivered Israel out of the hands of those who plundered them. <sup>49</sup> Now the sons of Saul were Jonathan, Ishvi, and Malchishua; and the names of his two daughters were these: the name of the firstborn Merab, and the name of the younger Michal. <sup>50</sup> The name of Saul's wife was Ahinoam the daughter of Ahimaaz. The name of the captain of his army was Abner the son of Ner, Saul's uncle. <sup>51</sup> Kish was the father of Saul, and Ner the father of Abner was the son of Abiel. <sup>52</sup> There was severe war against the Philistines all the days of Saul; and when Saul saw any mighty man or any valiant man, he took him into his service.

## 15

<sup>1</sup> Samuel said to Saul, "Yahweh sent me to anoint you to be king over his people, over Israel. Now therefore listen to the voice of Yahweh's words. <sup>2</sup> Yahweh of Armies says, 'I remember what Amalek did to Israel, how he set himself against him on the way when he came up out of Egypt. <sup>3</sup> Now go and strike Amalek, and utterly destroy all that they have, and don't spare them; but kill both man and woman, infant and nursing baby, ox and sheep, camel and donkey.'" <sup>4</sup> Saul summoned the people, and counted them in Telaim, two hundred thousand footmen and ten thousand men of Judah. <sup>5</sup> Saul came to the city of Amalek, and set an ambush in the valley. <sup>6</sup> Saul said to the Kenites, "Go, depart, go down from among the Amalekites, lest I destroy you with them; for you showed kindness to all the children of Israel when they came up out of Egypt." So the Kenites departed from among the Amalekites. <sup>7</sup> Saul struck the Amalekites, from Havilah as you go to Shur, which is before Egypt. <sup>8</sup> He took Agag the king of the Amalekites alive, and utterly destroyed all the people with the edge of the sword. <sup>9</sup> But Saul and the people spared Agag and the best of the sheep, of the cattle, of the fat calves, of the lambs, and all that was good, and were not willing to utterly destroy them; but everything that was vile and refuse, that they destroyed utterly. <sup>10</sup> Then Yahweh's word came to Samuel, saying, <sup>11</sup> "It grieves me that I have set up Saul to be king, for he has turned back

<sup>a</sup> *13:21 A payim (or pim) was
2/3 shekel of silver, or 0.26
ounces, or 7.6 grams*

from following me, and has not performed my commandments." Samuel was angry; and he cried to Yahweh all night. ¹² Samuel rose early to meet Saul in the morning; and Samuel was told, saying, "Saul came to Carmel, and behold, he set up a monument for himself, turned, passed on, and went down to Gilgal." ¹³ Samuel came to Saul; and Saul said to him, "You are blessed by Yahweh! I have performed the commandment of Yahweh." ¹⁴ Samuel said, "Then what does this bleating of the sheep in my ears and the lowing of the cattle which I hear mean?" ¹⁵ Saul said, "They have brought them from the Amalekites; for the people spared the best of the sheep and of the cattle, to sacrifice to Yahweh your God. We have utterly destroyed the rest." ¹⁶ Then Samuel said to Saul, "Stay, and I will tell you what Yahweh said to me last night." He said to him, "Say on." ¹⁷ Samuel said, "Though you were little in your own sight, weren't you made the head of the tribes of Israel? Yahweh anointed you king over Israel; ¹⁸ and Yahweh sent you on a journey, and said, 'Go, and utterly destroy the sinners the Amalekites, and fight against them until they are consumed.' ¹⁹ Why then didn't you obey Yahweh's voice, but took the plunder, and did that which was evil in Yahweh's sight?" ²⁰ Saul said to Samuel, "But I have obeyed Yahweh's voice, and have gone the way which Yahweh sent me, and have brought Agag the king of Amalek, and have utterly destroyed the Amalekites. ²¹ But the people took of the plunder, sheep and cattle, the best of the devoted things, to sacrifice to Yahweh your God in Gilgal." ²² Samuel said, "Has Yahweh as great delight in burnt offerings and sacrifices, as in obeying Yahweh's voice? Behold, to obey is better than sacrifice, and to listen than the fat of rams. ²³ For rebellion is as the sin of witchcraft, and stubbornness is as idolatry and teraphim.ᵃ Because you have rejected Yahweh's word, he has also rejected you from being king." ²⁴ Saul said to Samuel, "I have sinned; for I have transgressed the commandment of Yahweh and your words, because I feared the people and obeyed their voice. ²⁵ Now therefore, please pardon my sin, and turn again with me, that I may worship Yahweh." ²⁶ Samuel said to Saul, "I will not return with you; for you have rejected Yahweh's word, and Yahweh has rejected you from being king over Israel." ²⁷ As Samuel turned around to go away, Saul grabbed the skirt of his robe, and it tore. ²⁸ Samuel said to him, "Yahweh has torn the kingdom of Israel from you today, and has given it to a neighbor of yours who is better than you. ²⁹ Also the Strength of Israel will not lie nor repent; for he is not a man, that he should repent." ³⁰ Then he said, "I have sinned; yet please honor me now before the elders of my people and before Israel, and come back with me, that I may worship Yahweh your God." ³¹ So Samuel went back with Saul; and Saul worshiped Yahweh. ³² Then Samuel said, "Bring Agag the king of the Amalekites here to me!" Agag came to him cheerfully. Agag said, "Surely the bitterness of death is past." ³³ Samuel said, "As your sword has made women childless, so your mother will be childless among women!" Then Samuel cut Agag in pieces before Yahweh in Gilgal. ³⁴ Then Samuel went to Ramah; and Saul went up to his house to Gibeah of Saul. ³⁵ Samuel came no more to see Saul until the day of his death, but Samuel mourned for Saul. Yahweh grieved that he had made Saul king over Israel.

## 16

¹ Yahweh said to Samuel, "How long will you mourn for Saul, since I have rejected him from being king over Israel? Fill your horn with oil, and go. I will send you to Jesse the Bethlehemite, for I have provided a king for myself among his sons." ² Samuel said, "How can I go? If Saul hears it, he will kill me." Yahweh said, "Take a heifer with you, and say, 'I have come to sacrifice to Yahweh.' ³ Call Jesse to the sacrifice, and I will show you what you shall do. You shall anoint to me him whom I name to you." ⁴ Samuel did that which Yahweh spoke, and came to Bethlehem. The elders of the city came to meet him trembling, and said, "Do you come peaceably?" ⁵ He said, "Peaceably; I have come to sacrifice to Yahweh. Sanctify yourselves, and come with me to the sacrifice." He sanctified Jesse and his sons, and called them to the sacrifice. ⁶ When they had come, he looked at Eliab, and said, "Surely Yahweh's anointed is before him." ⁷ But Yahweh said to Samuel, "Don't look on his face, or on the height of his stature, because I have rejected him; for I don't see as man sees. For man looks at the outward appearance, but Yahweh looks at the heart." ⁸ Then Jesse called Abinadab, and made him pass before Samuel. He said, "Yahweh has not chosen this one, either." ⁹ Then Jesse made Shammah to pass by. He said, "Yahweh has not chosen this one, either." ¹⁰ Jesse made

seven of his sons to pass before Samuel. Samuel said to Jesse, "Yahweh has not chosen these." ¹¹ Samuel said to Jesse, "Are all your children here?" He said, "There remains yet the youngest. Behold, he is keeping the sheep." Samuel said to Jesse, "Send and get him, for we will not sit down until he comes here." ¹² He sent, and brought him in. Now he was ruddy, with a handsome face and good appearance. Yahweh said, "Arise! Anoint him, for this is he." ¹³ Then Samuel took the horn of oil and anointed him in the middle of his brothers. Then Yahweh's Spirit came mightily on David from that day forward. So Samuel rose up and went to Ramah. ¹⁴ Now Yahweh's Spirit departed from Saul, and an evil spirit from Yahweh troubled him. ¹⁵ Saul's servants said to him, "See now, an evil spirit from God troubles you. ¹⁶ Let our lord now command your servants who are in front of you to seek out a man who is a skillful player on the harp. Then when the evil spirit from God is on you, he will play with his hand, and you will be well." ¹⁷ Saul said to his servants, "Provide me now a man who can play well, and bring him to me." ¹⁸ Then one of the young men answered and said, "Behold, I have seen a son of Jesse the Bethlehemite who is skillful in playing, a mighty man of valor, a man of war, prudent in speech, and a handsome person; and Yahweh is with him." ¹⁹ Therefore Saul sent messengers to Jesse, and said, "Send me David your son, who is with the sheep." ²⁰ Jesse took a donkey loaded with bread, a container of wine, and a young goat, and sent them by David his son to Saul. ²¹ David came to Saul and stood before him. He loved him greatly; and he became his armor bearer. ²² Saul sent to Jesse, saying, "Please let David stand before me, for he has found favor in my sight." ²³ When the spirit from God was on Saul, David took the harp and played with his hand; so Saul was refreshed and was well, and the evil spirit departed from him.

## 17

¹ Now the Philistines gathered together their armies to battle; and they were gathered together at Socoh, which belongs to Judah, and encamped between Socoh and Azekah in Ephesdammim. ² Saul and the men of Israel were gathered together, and encamped in the valley of Elah, and set the battle in array against the Philistines. ³ The Philistines stood on the mountain on the one side, and Israel stood on the mountain on the other side: and there was a valley between them. ⁴ A champion out of the camp of the Philistines named Goliath of Gath, whose height was six cubits and a spanᵇ went out. ⁵ He had a helmet of bronze on his head, and he wore a coat of mail; and the weight of the coat was five thousand shekelsᶜ of bronze. ⁶ He had bronze shin armor on his legs and a bronze javelin between his shoulders. ⁷ The staff of his spear was like a weaver's beam; and his spear's head weighed six hundred shekels of iron.ᵈ His shield bearer went before him. ⁸ He stood and cried to the armies of Israel, and said to them, "Why have you come out to set your battle in array? Am I not a Philistine, and you servants to Saul? Choose a man for yourselves, and let him come down to me. ⁹ If he is able to fight with me and kill me, then will we be your servants; but if I prevail against him and kill him, then you will be our servants and serve us." ¹⁰ The Philistine said, "I defy the armies of Israel today! Give me a man, that we may fight together!" ¹¹ When Saul and all Israel heard those words of the Philistine, they were dismayed and greatly afraid. ¹² Now David was the son of that Ephrathite of Bethlehem Judah, whose name was Jesse; and he had eight sons. The man was an elderly old man in the days of Saul. ¹³ The three oldest sons of Jesse had gone after Saul to the battle; and the names of his three sons who went to the battle were Eliab the firstborn, and next to him Abinadab, and the third Shammah. ¹⁴ David was the youngest; and the three oldest followed Saul. ¹⁵ Now David went back and forth from Saul to feed his father's sheep at Bethlehem. ¹⁶ The Philistine came near morning and evening, and presented himself forty days. ¹⁷ Jesse said to David his son, "Now take for your brothers an ephahᵉ of this parched grain and these ten loaves, and carry them quickly to the camp to your brothers; ¹⁸ and bring these ten cheeses to the captain of their thousand; and see how your brothers are doing, and bring back news." ¹⁹ Now Saul, and they, and all the men of Israel were in the valley of Elah, fighting with the Philistines. ²⁰ David rose up early in the morning and left the sheep with a keeper, and took the provisions and went, as Jesse had commanded him. He came to the place of the wagons as the army which was going out to the fight shouted for the battle. ²¹ Israel and the Philistines put the battle in array, army against army. ²² David left his baggage in the hand of the keeper of the baggage and ran to the army, and came and greeted his brothers. ²³ As he talked with them, behold, the champion,

ᵃ 15:23 teraphim were household idols that may have been associated with inheritance rights to the household property.
ᵇ 17:4 A cubit is the length from the tip of the middle finger to the elbow on a man's arm, or about 18 inches or 46 centimeters. A span is the length from the tip of a man's thumb to the tip of his little finger when his hand is stretched out (about half a cubit, or 9 inches, or 22.8 cm.) Therefore, Goliath was about 9 feet and 9 inches or 2.97 meters tall.
ᶜ 17:5 A shekel is about 10 grams or about 0.35 ounces, so 5000 shekels is about 50 kilograms or 110 pounds.
ᵈ 17:7 A shekel is about 10 grams or about 0.35 ounces, so 600 shekels is about 6 kilograms or about 13 pounds.
ᵉ 17:17 1 ephah is about 22 liters or about 2/3 of a bushel

the Philistine of Gath, Goliath by name, came up out of the ranks of the Philistines, and said the same words; and David heard them. ²⁴ All the men of Israel, when they saw the man, fled from him and were terrified. ²⁵ The men of Israel said, "Have you seen this man who has come up? He has surely come up to defy Israel. The king will give great riches to the man who kills him, and will give him his daughter, and will make his father's house tax-free in Israel." ²⁶ David spoke to the men who stood by him, saying, "What shall be done to the man who kills this Philistine and takes away the reproach from Israel? For who is this uncircumcised Philistine, that he should defy the armies of the living God?" ²⁷ The people answered him in this way, saying, "So shall it be done to the man who kills him." ²⁸ Eliab his oldest brother heard when he spoke to the men; and Eliab's anger burned against David, and he said, "Why have you come down? With whom have you left those few sheep in the wilderness? I know your pride and the evil of your heart; for you have come down that you might see the battle." ²⁹ David said, "What have I now done? Is there not a cause?" ³⁰ He turned away from him toward another, and spoke like that again; and the people answered him again the same way. ³¹ When the words were heard which David spoke, they rehearsed them before Saul; and he sent for him. ³² David said to Saul, "Let no man's heart fail because of him. Your servant will go and fight with this Philistine." ³³ Saul said to David, "You are not able to go against this Philistine to fight with him; for you are but a youth, and he a man of war from his youth." ³⁴ David said to Saul, "Your servant was keeping his father's sheep; and when a lion or a bear came and took a lamb out of the flock, ³⁵ I went out after him, struck him, and rescued it out of his mouth. When he arose against me, I caught him by his beard, struck him, and killed him. ³⁶ Your servant struck both the lion and the bear. This uncircumcised Philistine shall be as one of them, since he has defied the armies of the living God." ³⁷ David said, "Yahweh, who delivered me out of the paw of the lion and out of the paw of the bear, will deliver me out of the hand of this Philistine." Saul said to David, "Go! Yahweh will be with you." ³⁸ Saul dressed David with his clothing. He put a helmet of bronze on his head, and he clad him with a coat of mail. ³⁹ David strapped his sword on his clothing and he tried to move, for he had not tested it. David said to Saul, "I can't go with these, for I have not tested them." Then David took them off. ⁴⁰ He took his staff in his hand, and chose for himself five smooth stones out of the brook, and put them in the pouch of his shepherd's bag which he had. His sling was in his hand; and he came near to the Philistine. ⁴¹ The Philistine walked and came near to David; and the man who bore the shield went before him. ⁴² When the Philistine looked around and saw David, he disdained him; for he was but a youth, and ruddy, and had a good looking face. ⁴³ The Philistine said to David, "Am I a dog, that you come to me with sticks?" The Philistine cursed David by his gods. ⁴⁴ The Philistine said to David, "Come to me, and I will give your flesh to the birds of the sky and to the animals of the field." ⁴⁵ Then David said to the Philistine, "You come to me with a sword, with a spear, and with a javelin; but I come to you in the name of Yahweh of Armies, the God of the armies of Israel, whom you have defied. ⁴⁶ Today, Yahweh will deliver you into my hand. I will strike you and take your head from off you. I will give the dead bodies of the army of the Philistines today to the birds of the sky and to the wild animals of the earth, that all the earth may know that there is a God in Israel, ⁴⁷ and that all this assembly may know that Yahweh doesn't save with sword and spear; for the battle is Yahweh's, and he will give you into our hand." ⁴⁸ When the Philistine arose, and walked and came near to meet David, David hurried and ran toward the army to meet the Philistine. ⁴⁹ David put his hand in his bag, took a stone and slung it, and struck the Philistine in his forehead. The stone sank into his forehead, and he fell on his face to the earth. ⁵⁰ So David prevailed over the Philistine with a sling and with a stone, and struck the Philistine and killed him; but there was no sword in David's hand. ⁵¹ Then David ran, stood over the Philistine, took his sword, drew it out of its sheath, killed him, and cut off his head with it. When the Philistines saw that their champion was dead, they fled. ⁵² The men of Israel and of Judah arose and shouted, and pursued the Philistines as far as Gai and to the gates of Ekron. The wounded of the Philistines fell down by the way to Shaaraim, even to Gath and to Ekron. ⁵³ The children of Israel returned from chasing after the Philistines, and they plundered their camp. ⁵⁴ David took the head of the Philistine and brought it to Jerusalem, but he put his armor in his tent. ⁵⁵ When Saul saw David go out against the Philistine, he said to Abner, the captain of the army, "Abner, whose son is this youth?" Abner said, "As your soul lives, O king, I can't tell." ⁵⁶ The king said, "Inquire whose son the young man is!" ⁵⁷ As David returned from the slaughter of the Philistine, Abner took him and brought him before Saul with the head of the Philistine in his hand. ⁵⁸ Saul said to him, "Whose son are you, you young man?" David answered, "I am the son of your servant Jesse the Bethlehemite."

## 18

¹ When he had finished speaking to Saul, the soul of Jonathan was knit with the soul of David, and Jonathan loved him as his own soul. ² Saul took him that day, and wouldn't let him go home to his father's house any more. ³ Then Jonathan and David made a covenant, because he loved him as his own soul. ⁴ Jonathan stripped himself of the robe that was on him and gave it to David with his clothing, even including his sword, his bow, and his sash. ⁵ David went out wherever Saul sent him, and behaved himself wisely; and Saul set him over the men of war. It was good in the sight of all the people, and also in the sight of Saul's servants. ⁶ As they came, when David returned from the slaughter of the Philistine, the women came out of all the cities of Israel, singing and dancing, to meet King Saul with tambourines, with joy, and with instruments of music. ⁷ The women sang to one another as they played, and said, "Saul has slain his thousands, and David his ten thousands." ⁸ Saul was very angry, and this saying displeased him. He said, "They have credited David with ten thousands, and they have only credited me with thousands. What can he have more but the kingdom?" ⁹ Saul watched David from that day and forward. ¹⁰ On the next day, an evil spirit from God came mightily on Saul, and he prophesied in the middle of the house. David played with his hand, as he did day by day. Saul had his spear in his hand; ¹¹ and Saul threw the spear, for he said, "I will pin David to the wall!" David escaped from his presence twice. ¹² Saul was afraid of David, because Yahweh was with him, and had departed from Saul. ¹³ Therefore Saul removed him from his presence, and made him his captain over a thousand; and he went out and came in before the people. ¹⁴ David behaved himself wisely in all his ways; and Yahweh was with him. ¹⁵ When Saul saw that he behaved himself very wisely, he stood in awe of him. ¹⁶ But all Israel and Judah loved David; for he went out and came in before them. ¹⁷ Saul said to David, "Behold, my elder daughter Merab. I will give her to you as wife. Only be valiant for me, and fight Yahweh's battles." For Saul said, "Don't let my hand be on him, but let the hand of the Philistines be on him." ¹⁸ David said to Saul, "Who am I, and what is my life, or my father's family in Israel, that I should be son-in-law to the king?" ¹⁹ But at the time when Merab, Saul's daughter, should have been given to David, she was given to Adriel the Meholathite as wife. ²⁰ Michal, Saul's daughter, loved David; and they told Saul, and the thing pleased him. ²¹ Saul said, I will give her to him, that she may be a snare to him and that the hand of the Philistines may be against him. Therefore Saul said to David a second time, "You shall today be my son-in-law." ²² Saul commanded his servants, "Talk with David secretly, and say, 'Behold, the king has delight in you, and all his servants love you. Now therefore be the king's son-in-law.'" ²³ Saul's servants spoke those words in the ears of David. David said, "Does it seem to you a light thing to be the king's son-in-law, since I am a poor man and little known?" ²⁴ The servants of Saul told him, saying, "David spoke like this." ²⁵ Saul said, "Tell David, 'The king desires no dowry except one hundred foreskins of the Philistines, to be avenged of the king's enemies.'" Now Saul thought he would make David fall by the hand of the Philistines. ²⁶ When his servants told David these words, it pleased David well to be the king's son-in-law. Before the deadline, ²⁷ David arose and went, he and his men, and killed two hundred men of the Philistines. Then David brought their foreskins, and they gave them in full number to the king, that he might be the king's son-in-law. Then Saul gave him Michal his daughter as wife. ²⁸ Saul saw and knew that Yahweh was with David; and Michal, Saul's daughter, loved him. ²⁹ Saul was even more afraid of David; and Saul was David's enemy continually. ³⁰ Then the princes of the Philistines went out; and as often as they went out, David behaved himself more wisely than all the servants of Saul, so that his name was highly esteemed.

## 19

¹ Saul spoke to Jonathan his son and to all his servants, that they should kill David. But Jonathan, Saul's son, greatly delighted in David. ² Jonathan told David, saying, "Saul my father seeks to kill you. Now therefore, please take care of yourself in the morning, live in a secret place, and hide yourself. ³ I will go out and stand beside my father in the field where you are, and I will talk with my father about you; and if I see anything, I will tell you." ⁴ Jonathan spoke good of David to Saul his father, and said to him, "Don't let the king sin against his servant, against David; because he has not sinned against you, and because his works have been very good toward you; ⁵ for he put his life in his hand and struck the Philistine, and Yahweh worked a great victory for all Israel. You saw it and rejoiced. Why then will you sin against innocent blood, to kill David without a cause?" ⁶ Saul listened to the voice of Jonathan; and Saul swore, "As Yahweh lives, he shall not be put to death." ⁷ Jonathan called David, and Jonathan showed him all those things. Then Jonathan brought David to Saul, and he was in his presence as before. ⁸ There was war again. David went out and fought with the Philistines, and killed them with a great slaughter; and they

fled before him. ⁹ An evil spirit from Yahweh was on Saul as he sat in his house with his spear in his hand; and David was playing music with his hand. ¹⁰ Saul sought to pin David to the wall with the spear, but he slipped away out of Saul's presence; and he stuck the spear into the wall. David fled and escaped that night. ¹¹ Saul sent messengers to David's house to watch him and to kill him in the morning. Michal, David's wife, told him, saying, "If you don't save your life tonight, tomorrow you will be killed." ¹² So Michal let David down through the window. He went away, fled, and escaped. ¹³ Michal took the teraphimᵃ and laid it in the bed, and put a pillow of goats' hair at its head and covered it with clothes. ¹⁴ When Saul sent messengers to take David, she said, "He is sick." ¹⁵ Saul sent the messengers to see David, saying, "Bring him up to me in the bed, that I may kill him." ¹⁶ When the messengers came in, behold, the teraphim was in the bed, with the pillow of goats' hair at its head. ¹⁷ Saul said to Michal, "Why have you deceived me like this and let my enemy go, so that he has escaped?" Michal answered Saul, "He said to me, 'Let me go! Why should I kill you?'" ¹⁸ Now David fled and escaped, and came to Samuel at Ramah, and told him all that Saul had done to him. He and Samuel went and lived in Naioth. ¹⁹ Saul was told, saying, "Behold, David is at Naioth in Ramah." ²⁰ Saul sent messengers to seize David; and when they saw the company of the prophets prophesying, and Samuel standing as head over them, God's Spirit came on Saul's messengers, and they also prophesied. ²¹ When Saul was told, he sent other messengers, and they also prophesied. Saul sent messengers again the third time, and they also prophesied. ²² Then he also went to Ramah, and came to the great well that is in Secu: and he asked, "Where are Samuel and David?" One said, "Behold, they are at Naioth in Ramah." ²³ He went there to Naioth in Ramah. Then God's Spirit came on him also, and he went on, and prophesied, until he came to Naioth in Ramah. ²⁴ He also stripped off his clothes. He also prophesied before Samuel and lay down naked all that day and all that night. Therefore they say, "Is Saul also among the prophets?"

## 20

¹ David fled from Naioth in Ramah, and came and said to Jonathan, "What have I done? What is my iniquity? What is my sin before your father, that he seeks my life?" ² He said to him, "Far from it; you will not die. Behold, my father does nothing either great or small, but that he discloses it to me. Why would my father hide this thing from me? It is not so." ³ David swore moreover, and said, "Your father knows well that I have found favor in your eyes; and he says, 'Don't let Jonathan know this, lest he be grieved;' but truly as Yahweh lives, and as your soul lives, there is but a step between me and death." ⁴ Then Jonathan said to David, "Whatever your soul desires, I will even do it for you." ⁵ David said to Jonathan, "Behold, tomorrow is the new moon, and I should not fail to dine with the king; but let me go, that I may hide myself in the field to the third day at evening. ⁶ If your father misses me at all, then say, 'David earnestly asked leave of me that he might run to Bethlehem, his city; for it is the yearly sacrifice there for all the family.' ⁷ If he says, 'It is well,' your servant shall have peace; but if he is angry, then know that evil is determined by him. ⁸ Therefore deal kindly with your servant, for you have brought your servant into a covenant of Yahweh with you; but if there is iniquity in me, kill me yourself, for why should you bring me to your father?" ⁹ Jonathan said, "Far be it from you; for if I should at all know that evil were determined by my father to come on you, then wouldn't I tell you that?" ¹⁰ Then David said to Jonathan, "Who will tell me if your father answers you roughly?" ¹¹ Jonathan said to David, "Come! Let's go out into the field." They both went out into the field. ¹² Jonathan said to David, "By Yahweh, the God of Israel, when I have sounded out my father about this time tomorrow, or the third day, behold, if there is good toward David, won't I then send to you and disclose it to you? ¹³ Yahweh do so to Jonathan and more also, should it please my father to do you evil, if I don't disclose it to you and send you away, that you may go in peace. May Yahweh be with you as he has been with my father. ¹⁴ You shall not only show me the loving kindness of Yahweh while I still live, that I not die; ¹⁵ but you shall also not cut off your kindness from my house forever, no, not when Yahweh has cut off every one of the enemies of David from the surface of the earth." ¹⁶ So Jonathan made a covenant with David's house, saying, "Yahweh will require it at the hand of David's enemies." ¹⁷ Jonathan caused David to swear again, for the love that he had to him; for he loved him as he loved his own soul. ¹⁸ Then Jonathan said to him, "Tomorrow is the new moon, and you will be missed, because your seat will be empty. ¹⁹ When you have stayed three days, go down quickly and come to the place where you hid yourself when this started, and remain by the stone Ezel. ²⁰ I will

shoot three arrows on its side, as though I shot at a mark. ²¹ Behold, I will send the boy, saying, 'Go, find the arrows!' If I tell the boy, 'Behold, the arrows are on this side of you. Take them;' then come, for there is peace to you and no danger, as Yahweh lives. ²² But if I say this to the boy, 'Behold, the arrows are beyond you,' then go your way, for Yahweh has sent you away. ²³ Concerning the matter which you and I have spoken of, behold, Yahweh is between you and me forever." ²⁴ So David hid himself in the field. When the new moon had come, the king sat himself down to eat food. ²⁵ The king sat on his seat, as at other times, even on the seat by the wall; and Jonathan stood up, and Abner sat by Saul's side, but David's place was empty. ²⁶ Nevertheless Saul didn't say anything that day, for he thought, "Something has happened to him. He is not clean. Surely he is not clean." ²⁷ On the next day after the new moon, the second day, David's place was empty. Saul said to Jonathan his son, "Why didn't the son of Jesse come to eat, either yesterday, or today?" ²⁸ Jonathan answered Saul, "David earnestly asked permission of me to go to Bethlehem. ²⁹ He said, 'Please let me go, for our family has a sacrifice in the city. My brother has commanded me to be there. Now, if I have found favor in your eyes, please let me go away and see my brothers.' Therefore he has not come to the king's table." ³⁰ Then Saul's anger burned against Jonathan, and he said to him, "You son of a perverse rebellious woman, don't I know that you have chosen the son of Jesse to your own shame, and to the shame of your mother's nakedness? ³¹ For as long as the son of Jesse lives on the earth, you will not be established, nor will your kingdom. Therefore now send and bring him to me, for he shall surely die!" ³² Jonathan answered Saul his father, and said to him, "Why should he be put to death? What has he done?" ³³ Saul cast his spear at him to strike him. By this Jonathan knew that his father was determined to put David to death. ³⁴ So Jonathan arose from the table in fierce anger, and ate no food the second day of the month; for he was grieved for David, because his father had treated him shamefully. ³⁵ In the morning, Jonathan went out into the field at the time appointed with David, and a little boy with him. ³⁶ He said to his boy, "Run, find now the arrows which I shoot." As the boy ran, he shot an arrow beyond him. ³⁷ When the boy had come to the place of the arrow which Jonathan had shot, Jonathan cried after the boy, and said, "Isn't the arrow beyond you?" ³⁸ Jonathan cried after the boy, "Go fast! Hurry! Don't delay!" Jonathan's boy gathered up the arrows, and came to his master. ³⁹ But the boy didn't know anything. Only Jonathan and David knew the matter. ⁴⁰ Jonathan gave his weapons to his boy, and said to him, "Go, carry them to the city." ⁴¹ As soon as the boy was gone, David arose out of the south, and fell on his face to the ground, and bowed himself three times. They kissed one another and wept with one another, and David wept the most. ⁴² Jonathan said to David, "Go in peace, because we have both sworn in Yahweh's name, saying, 'Yahweh is between me and you, and between my offspring and your offspring, forever.'" He arose and departed; and Jonathan went into the city.

## 21

¹ Then David came to Nob to Ahimelech the priest. Ahimelech came to meet David trembling, and said to him, "Why are you alone, and no man with you?" ² David said to Ahimelech the priest, "The king has commanded me to do something, and has said to me, 'Let no one know anything about the business about which I send you, and what I have commanded you. I have sent the young men to a certain place.' ³ Now therefore what is under your hand? Please give me five loaves of bread in my hand, or whatever is available." ⁴ The priest answered David, and said, "I have no common bread, but there is holy bread; if only the young men have kept themselves from women." ⁵ David answered the priest, and said to him, "Truly, women have been kept from us as usual these three days. When I came out, the vessels of the young men were holy, though it was only a common journey. How much more then today shall their vessels be holy?" ⁶ So the priest gave him holy bread; for there was no bread there but the show bread that was taken from before Yahweh, to be replaced with hot bread in the day when it was taken away. ⁷ Now a certain man of the servants of Saul was there that day, detained before Yahweh; and his name was Doeg the Edomite, the best of the herdsmen who belonged to Saul. ⁸ David said to Ahimelech, "Isn't there here under your hand spear or sword? For I haven't brought my sword or my weapons with me, because the king's business required haste." ⁹ The priest said, "Behold, the sword of Goliath the Philistine, whom you killed in the valley of Elah, is here wrapped in a cloth behind the ephod. If you would like to take that, take it, for there is no other except that here." David said, "There is none like that. Give it to me." ¹⁰ David arose and fled that day for fear of Saul, and went to Achish the king of Gath. ¹¹ The servants of Achish said to him, "Isn't

ᵃ 19:13 teraphim were household idols that may have been associated with inheritance rights to the household property.

this David the king of the land? Didn't they sing to one another about him in dances, saying, 'Saul has slain his thousands, and David his ten thousands'?" ¹² David laid up these words in his heart, and was very afraid of Achish the king of Gath. ¹³ He changed his behavior before them and pretended to be insane in their hands, and scribbled on the doors of the gate, and let his spittle fall down on his beard. ¹⁴ Then Achish said to his servants, "Look, you see the man is insane. Why then have you brought him to me? ¹⁵ Do I lack madmen, that you have brought this fellow to play the madman in my presence? Should this fellow come into my house?"

## 22

¹ David therefore departed from there and escaped to Adullam's cave. When his brothers and all his father's house heard it, they went down there to him. ² Everyone who was in distress, everyone who was in debt, and everyone who was discontented gathered themselves to him; and he became captain over them. There were with him about four hundred men. ³ David went from there to Mizpeh of Moab; and he said to the king of Moab, "Please let my father and my mother come out to you, until I know what God will do for me." ⁴ He brought them before the king of Moab; and they lived with him all the time that David was in the stronghold. ⁵ The prophet Gad said to David, "Don't stay in the stronghold. Depart, and go into the land of Judah." Then David departed, and came into the forest of Hereth. ⁶ Saul heard that David was discovered, with the men who were with him. Now Saul was sitting in Gibeah, under the tamarisk tree in Ramah, with his spear in his hand, and all his servants were standing around him. ⁷ Saul said to his servants who stood around him, "Hear now, you Benjamites! Will the son of Jesse give everyone of you fields and vineyards? Will he make you all captains of thousands and captains of hundreds? ⁸ Is that why all of you have conspired against me, and there is no one who discloses to me when my son makes a treaty with the son of Jesse, and there is none of you who is sorry for me, or discloses to me that my son has stirred up my servant against me, to lie in wait, as it is today?" ⁹ Then Doeg the Edomite, who stood by the servants of Saul, answered and said, "I saw the son of Jesse coming to Nob, to Ahimelech the son of Ahitub. ¹⁰ He inquired of Yahweh for him, gave him food, and gave him the sword of Goliath the Philistine." ¹¹ Then the king sent to call Ahimelech the priest, the son of Ahitub, and all his father's house, the priests who were in Nob; and they all came to the king. ¹² Saul said, "Hear now, you son of Ahitub." He answered, "Here I am, my lord." ¹³ Saul said to him, "Why have you conspired against me, you and the son of Jesse, in that you have given him bread, and a sword, and have inquired of God for him, that he should rise against me, to lie in wait, as it is today?" ¹⁴ Then Ahimelech answered the king, and said, "Who among all your servants is so faithful as David, who is the king's son-in-law, captain of your body guard, and honored in your house? ¹⁵ Have I today begun to inquire of God for him? Be it far from me! Don't let the king impute anything to his servant, nor to all the house of my father; for your servant knew nothing of all this, less or more." ¹⁶ The king said, "You shall surely die, Ahimelech, you and all your father's house." ¹⁷ The king said to the guard who stood about him, "Turn and kill the priests of Yahweh, because their hand also is with David, and because they knew that he fled and didn't disclose it to me." But the servants of the king wouldn't put out their hand to fall on the priests of Yahweh. ¹⁸ The king said to Doeg, "Turn and attack the priests!" Doeg the Edomite turned, and he attacked the priests, and he killed on that day eighty-five people who wore a linen ephod. ¹⁹ He struck Nob, the city of the priests, with the edge of the sword—both men and women, children and nursing babies, and cattle, donkeys, and sheep, with the edge of the sword. ²⁰ One of the sons of Ahimelech the son of Ahitub, named Abiathar, escaped and fled after David. ²¹ Abiathar told David that Saul had slain Yahweh's priests. ²² David said to Abiathar, "I knew on that day, when Doeg the Edomite was there, that he would surely tell Saul. I am responsible for the death of all the persons of your father's house. ²³ Stay with me. Don't be afraid, for he who seeks my life seeks your life. You will be safe with me."

## 23

¹ David was told, "Behold, the Philistines are fighting against Keilah, and are robbing the threshing floors." ² Therefore David inquired of Yahweh, saying, "Shall I go and strike these Philistines?" Yahweh said to David, "Go strike the Philistines, and save Keilah." ³ David's men said to him, "Behold, we are afraid here in Judah. How much more then if we go to Keilah against the armies of the Philistines?" ⁴ Then David inquired of Yahweh yet again. Yahweh answered him, and said, "Arise, go down to Keilah; for I will deliver the Philistines into your hand." ⁵ David and his men went to Keilah and fought with the Philistines, and brought away their livestock, and killed them with a great slaughter. So

David saved the inhabitants of Keilah. ⁶ When Abiathar the son of Ahimelech fled to David to Keilah, he came down with an ephod in his hand. ⁷ Saul was told that David had come to Keilah. Saul said, "God has delivered him into my hand, for he is shut in by entering into a town that has gates and bars." ⁸ Saul summoned all the people to war, to go down to Keilah to besiege David and his men. ⁹ David knew that Saul was devising mischief against him. He said to Abiathar the priest, "Bring the ephod here." ¹⁰ Then David said, "O Yahweh, the God of Israel, your servant has surely heard that Saul seeks to come to Keilah to destroy the city for my sake. ¹¹ Will the men of Keilah deliver me up into his hand? Will Saul come down, as your servant has heard? Yahweh, the God of Israel, I beg you, tell your servant." Yahweh said, "He will come down." ¹² Then David said, "Will the men of Keilah deliver me and my men into the hand of Saul?" Yahweh said, "They will deliver you up." ¹³ Then David and his men, who were about six hundred, arose and departed out of Keilah and went wherever they could go. Saul was told that David had escaped from Keilah; and he gave up going there. ¹⁴ David stayed in the wilderness in the strongholds, and remained in the hill country in the wilderness of Ziph. Saul sought him every day, but God didn't deliver him into his hand. ¹⁵ David saw that Saul had come out to seek his life. David was in the wilderness of Ziph in the woods. ¹⁶ Jonathan, Saul's son, arose and went to David into the woods, and strengthened his hand in God. ¹⁷ He said to him, "Don't be afraid, for the hand of Saul my father won't find you; and you will be king over Israel, and I will be next to you; and Saul my father knows that also." ¹⁸ They both made a covenant before Yahweh. Then David stayed in the woods and Jonathan went to his house. ¹⁹ Then the Ziphites came up to Saul to Gibeah, saying, "Doesn't David hide himself with us in the strongholds in the woods, in the hill of Hachilah, which is on the south of the desert? ²⁰ Now therefore, O king, come down. According to all the desire of your soul to come down; and our part will be to deliver him up into the king's hand." ²¹ Saul said, "You are blessed by Yahweh, for you have had compassion on me. ²² Please go make yet more sure, and know and see his place where his haunt is, and who has seen him there; for I have been told that he is very cunning. ²³ See therefore, and take knowledge of all the lurking places where he hides himself; and come again to me with certainty, and I will go with you. It shall happen, if he is in the land, that I will search him out among all the thousands of Judah." ²⁴ They arose, and went to Ziph before Saul; but David and his men were in the wilderness of Maon, in the Arabah on the south of the desert. ²⁵ Saul and his men went to seek him. When David was told, he went down to the rock, and stayed in the wilderness of Maon. When Saul heard that, he pursued David in the wilderness of Maon. ²⁶ Saul went on this side of the mountain, and David and his men on that side of the mountain; and David hurried to get away for fear of Saul, for Saul and his men surrounded David and his men to take them. ²⁷ But a messenger came to Saul, saying, "Hurry and come, for the Philistines have made a raid on the land!" ²⁸ So Saul returned from pursuing David, and went against the Philistines. Therefore they called that place Sela Hammahlekoth.ᵃ ²⁹ David went up from there and lived in the strongholds of En Gedi.

## 24

¹ When Saul had returned from following the Philistines, he was told, "Behold, David is in the wilderness of En Gedi." ² Then Saul took three thousand chosen men out of all Israel, and went to seek David and his men on the rocks of the wild goats. ³ He came to the sheep pens by the way, where there was a cave; and Saul went in to relieve himself. Now David and his men were staying in the innermost parts of the cave. ⁴ David's men said to him, "Behold, the day of which Yahweh said to you, 'Behold, I will deliver your enemy into your hand, and you shall do to him as it shall seem good to you.'" Then David arose and cut off the skirt of Saul's robe secretly. ⁵ Afterward, David's heart struck him because he had cut off Saul's skirt. ⁶ He said to his men, "Yahweh forbid that I should do this thing to my lord, Yahweh's anointed, to stretch out my hand against him, since he is Yahweh's anointed." ⁷ So David checked his men with these words, and didn't allow them to rise against Saul. Saul rose up out of the cave, and went on his way. ⁸ David also arose afterward, and went out of the cave and cried after Saul, saying, "My lord the king!" When Saul looked behind him, David bowed with his face to the earth, and showed respect. ⁹ David said to Saul, "Why do you listen to men's words, saying, 'Behold, David seeks to harm you'? ¹⁰ Behold, today your eyes have seen how Yahweh had delivered you today into my hand in the cave. Some urged me to kill you, but I spared you. I said, 'I will not stretch out my hand against my lord, for he is Yahweh's anointed.' ¹¹ Moreover, my father, behold, yes, see the skirt of your robe in my hand; for in that I cut off the skirt of your robe and didn't kill you, know and see that there is neither evil nor

---

ᵃ *23:28 "Sela Hammahlekoth"*
means "rock of parting".

disobedience in my hand. I have not sinned against you, though you hunt for my life to take it. ¹² May Yahweh judge between me and you, and may Yahweh avenge me of you; but my hand will not be on you. ¹³ As the proverb of the ancients says, 'Out of the wicked comes wickedness;' but my hand will not be on you. ¹⁴ Against whom has the king of Israel come out? Whom do you pursue? A dead dog? A flea? ¹⁵ May Yahweh therefore be judge, and give sentence between me and you, and see, and plead my cause, and deliver me out of your hand." ¹⁶ It came to pass, when David had finished speaking these words to Saul, that Saul said, "Is that your voice, my son David?" Saul lifted up his voice and wept. ¹⁷ He said to David, "You are more righteous than I; for you have done good to me, whereas I have done evil to you. ¹⁸ You have declared today how you have dealt well with me, because when Yahweh had delivered me up into your hand, you didn't kill me. ¹⁹ For if a man finds his enemy, will he let him go away unharmed? Therefore may Yahweh reward you good for that which you have done to me today. ²⁰ Now, behold, I know that you will surely be king, and that the kingdom of Israel will be established in your hand. ²¹ Swear now therefore to me by Yahweh that you will not cut off my offspring after me, and that you will not destroy my name out of my father's house." ²² David swore to Saul. Saul went home, but David and his men went up to the stronghold.

## 25

¹ Samuel died; and all Israel gathered themselves together and mourned for him, and buried him at his house at Ramah. Then David arose and went down to the wilderness of Paran. ² There was a man in Maon whose possessions were in Carmel; and the man was very great. He had three thousand sheep and a thousand goats; and he was shearing his sheep in Carmel. ³ Now the name of the man was Nabal; and the name of his wife Abigail. This woman was intelligent and had a beautiful face; but the man was surly and evil in his doings. He was of the house of Caleb. ⁴ David heard in the wilderness that Nabal was shearing his sheep. ⁵ David sent ten young men; and David said to the young men, "Go up to Carmel, and go to Nabal, and greet him in my name. ⁶ Tell him, 'Long life to you! Peace be to you! Peace be to your house! Peace be to all that you have! ⁷ Now I have heard that you have shearers. Your shepherds have now been with us, and we didn't harm them. Nothing was missing from them all the time they were in Carmel. ⁸ Ask your young men, and they will tell you. Therefore let the young men find favor in your eyes, for we come on a good day. Please give whatever comes to your hand to your servants and to your son David.'" ⁹ When David's young men came, they spoke to Nabal all those words in the name of David, and waited. ¹⁰ Nabal answered David's servants and said, "Who is David? Who is the son of Jesse? There are many servants who break away from their masters these days. ¹¹ Shall I then take my bread, my water, and my meat that I have killed for my shearers, and give it to men who I don't know where they come from?" ¹² So David's young men turned on their way and went back, and came and told him all these words. ¹³ David said to his men, "Every man put on his sword!" Every man put on his sword. David also put on his sword. About four hundred men followed David, and two hundred stayed by the baggage. ¹⁴ But one of the young men told Abigail, Nabal's wife, saying, "Behold, David sent messengers out of the wilderness to greet our master; and he insulted them. ¹⁵ But the men were very good to us, and we were not harmed, and we didn't miss anything as long as we went with them, when we were in the fields. ¹⁶ They were a wall to us both by night and by day, all the while we were with them keeping the sheep. ¹⁷ Now therefore know and consider what you will do; for evil is determined against our master and against all his house, for he is such a worthless fellow that one can't speak to him." ¹⁸ Then Abigail hurried and took two hundred loaves of bread, two containers of wine, five sheep ready dressed, five seahs[a] of parched grain, one hundred clusters of raisins, and two hundred cakes of figs, and laid them on donkeys. ¹⁹ She said to her young men, "Go on before me. Behold, I am coming after you." But she didn't tell her husband, Nabal. ²⁰ As she rode on her donkey, and came down hidden by the mountain, behold, David and his men came down toward her, and she met them. ²¹ Now David had said, "Surely in vain I have kept all that this fellow has in the wilderness, so that nothing was missed of all that pertained to him. He has returned me evil for good. ²² God do so to the enemies of David, and more also, if I leave of all that belongs to him by the morning light so much as one who urinates on a wall."[b] ²³ When Abigail saw David, she hurried and got off her donkey, and fell before David on her face and bowed herself to the ground. ²⁴ She fell at his feet and said, "On me, my lord, on me be the blame! Please let your servant speak in your ears. Hear the words of your servant. ²⁵ Please don't let my lord pay attention to this worthless fellow, Nabal, for as his name is, so is he. Nabal[c] is his name,

and folly is with him; but I, your servant, didn't see my lord's young men whom you sent. ²⁶ Now therefore, my lord, as Yahweh lives and as your soul lives, since Yahweh has withheld you from blood guiltiness and from avenging yourself with your own hand, now therefore let your enemies and those who seek evil to my lord be as Nabal. ²⁷ Now this present which your servant has brought to my lord, let it be given to the young men who follow my lord. ²⁸ Please forgive the trespass of your servant. For Yahweh will certainly make my lord a sure house, because my lord fights Yahweh's battles. Evil will not be found in you all your days. ²⁹ Though men may rise up to pursue you and to seek your soul, yet the soul of my lord will be bound in the bundle of life with Yahweh your God. He will sling out the souls of your enemies as from a sling's pocket. ³⁰ It will come to pass, when Yahweh has done to my lord according to all the good that he has spoken concerning you, and has appointed you prince over Israel, ³¹ that this shall be no grief to you, nor offense of heart to my lord, either that you have shed blood without cause, or that my lord has avenged himself. When Yahweh has dealt well with my lord, then remember your servant." ³² David said to Abigail, "Blessed is Yahweh, the God of Israel, who sent you today to meet me! ³³ Blessed is your discretion, and blessed are you, who have kept me today from blood guiltiness, and from avenging myself with my own hand. ³⁴ For indeed, as Yahweh the God of Israel lives, who has withheld me from harming you, unless you had hurried and come to meet me, surely there wouldn't have been left to Nabal by the morning light so much as one who urinates on a wall."[d] ³⁵ So David received from her hand that which she had brought him. Then he said to her, "Go up in peace to your house. Behold, I have listened to your voice and have granted your request." ³⁶ Abigail came to Nabal; and behold, he held a feast in his house like the feast of a king. Nabal's heart was merry within him, for he was very drunk. Therefore she told him nothing until the morning light. ³⁷ In the morning, when the wine had gone out of Nabal, his wife told him these things; and his heart died within him, and he became as a stone. ³⁸ About ten days later, Yahweh struck Nabal, so that he died. ³⁹ When David heard that Nabal was dead, he said, "Blessed is Yahweh, who has pleaded the cause of my reproach from the hand of Nabal, and has kept back his servant from evil. Yahweh has returned the evildoing of Nabal on his own head." David sent and spoke concerning Abigail, to take her to himself as wife. ⁴⁰ When David's servants had come to Abigail to Carmel, they spoke to her, saying, "David has sent us to you, to take you to him as wife." ⁴¹ She arose and bowed herself with her face to the earth, and said, "Behold, your servant is a servant to wash the feet of the servants of my lord." ⁴² Abigail hurriedly arose and rode on a donkey with her five maids who followed her; and she went after the messengers of David, and became his wife. ⁴³ David also took Ahinoam of Jezreel; and they both became his wives. ⁴⁴ Now Saul had given Michal his daughter, David's wife, to Palti the son of Laish, who was of Gallim.

## 26

¹ The Ziphites came to Saul to Gibeah, saying, "Doesn't David hide himself in the hill of Hachilah, which is before the desert?" ² Then Saul arose and went down to the wilderness of Ziph, having three thousand chosen men of Israel with him, to seek David in the wilderness of Ziph. ³ Saul encamped in the hill of Hachilah, which is before the desert, by the way. But David stayed in the wilderness, and he saw that Saul came after him into the wilderness. ⁴ David therefore sent out spies, and understood that Saul had certainly come. ⁵ Then David arose and came to the place where Saul had encamped; and David saw the place where Saul lay, with Abner the son of Ner, the captain of his army. Saul lay within the place of the wagons, and the people were encamped around him. ⁶ Then David answered and said to Ahimelech the Hittite, and to Abishai the son of Zeruiah, brother of Joab, saying, "Who will go down with me to Saul to the camp?" Abishai said, "I will go down with you." ⁷ So David and Abishai came to the people by night; and, behold, Saul lay sleeping within the place of the wagons, with his spear stuck in the ground at his head; and Abner and the people lay around him. ⁸ Then Abishai said to David, "God has delivered up your enemy into your hand today. Now therefore please let me strike him with the spear to the earth at one stroke, and I will not strike him the second time." ⁹ David said to Abishai, "Don't destroy him, for who can stretch out his hand against Yahweh's anointed, and be guiltless?" ¹⁰ David said, "As Yahweh lives, Yahweh will strike him; or his day shall come to die, or he shall go down into battle and perish. ¹¹ Yahweh forbid that I should stretch out my hand against Yahweh's anointed; but now please take the spear that is at his head and the jar of water, and let's go." ¹² So David took the spear and the jar of water from Saul's head, and they went away. No man saw it, or knew it, nor did any awake; for they were

---

[a] *25:18* 1 seah is about 7 liters or 1.9 gallons or 0.8 pecks

[b] *25:22* or, male.

[c] *25:25* "Nabal" means "foolish".

[d] *25:34* or, one male.

all asleep, because a deep sleep from Yahweh had fallen on them. [13] Then David went over to the other side, and stood on the top of the mountain far away, a great space being between them; [14] and David cried to the people, and to Abner the son of Ner, saying, "Don't you answer, Abner?" Then Abner answered, "Who are you who calls to the king?" [15] David said to Abner, "Aren't you a man? Who is like you in Israel? Why then have you not kept watch over your lord the king? For one of the people came in to destroy your lord the king. [16] This thing isn't good that you have done. As Yahweh lives, you are worthy to die, because you have not kept watch over your lord, Yahweh's anointed. Now see where the king's spear is, and the jar of water that was at his head." [17] Saul recognized David's voice, and said, "Is this your voice, my son David?" David said, "It is my voice, my lord, O king." [18] He said, "Why does my lord pursue his servant? For what have I done? What evil is in my hand? [19] Now therefore, please let my lord the king hear the words of his servant. If it is so that Yahweh has stirred you up against me, let him accept an offering. But if it is the children of men, they are cursed before Yahweh; for they have driven me out today that I shouldn't cling to Yahweh's inheritance, saying, 'Go, serve other gods!' [20] Now therefore, don't let my blood fall to the earth away from the presence of Yahweh; for the king of Israel has come out to seek a flea, as when one hunts a partridge in the mountains." [21] Then Saul said, "I have sinned. Return, my son David; for I will no more do you harm, because my life was precious in your eyes today. Behold, I have played the fool, and have erred exceedingly." [22] David answered, "Behold the spear, O king! Let one of the young men come over and get it. [23] Yahweh will render to every man his righteousness and his faithfulness; because Yahweh delivered you into my hand today, and I wouldn't stretch out my hand against Yahweh's anointed. [24] Behold, as your life was respected today in my eyes, so let my life be respected in Yahweh's eyes, and let him deliver me out of all oppression." [25] Then Saul said to David, "You are blessed, my son David. You will both do mightily, and will surely prevail." So David went his way, and Saul returned to his place.

## 27

[1] David said in his heart, "I will now perish one day by the hand of Saul. There is nothing better for me than that I should escape into the land of the Philistines; and Saul will despair of me, to seek me any more in all the borders of Israel. So I will escape out of his hand." [2] David arose and passed over, he and the six hundred men who were with him, to Achish the son of Maoch, king of Gath. [3] David lived with Achish at Gath, he and his men, every man with his household, even David with his two wives, Ahinoam the Jezreelitess and Abigail the Carmelitess, Nabal's wife. [4] Saul was told that David had fled to Gath, so he stopped looking for him. [5] David said to Achish, "If now I have found favor in your eyes, let them give me a place in one of the cities in the country, that I may dwell there. For why should your servant dwell in the royal city with you?" [6] Then Achish gave him Ziklag that day: therefore Ziklag belongs to the kings of Judah to this day. [7] The number of the days that David lived in the country of the Philistines was a full year and four months. [8] David and his men went up and raided the Geshurites, the Girzites, and the Amalekites; for those were the inhabitants of the land who were of old, on the way to Shur, even to the land of Egypt. [9] David struck the land, and saved no man or woman alive, and took away the sheep, the cattle, the donkeys, the camels, and the clothing. Then he returned, and came to Achish. [10] Achish said, "Against whom have you made a raid today?" David said, "Against the South of Judah, against the South of the Jerahmeelites, and against the South of the Kenites." [11] David saved neither man nor woman alive to bring them to Gath, saying, "Lest they should tell about us, saying, 'David did this, and this has been his way all the time he has lived in the country of the Philistines.'" [12] Achish believed David, saying, "He has made his people Israel utterly to abhor him. Therefore he will be my servant forever."

## 28

[1] In those days, the Philistines gathered their armies together for warfare, to fight with Israel. Achish said to David, "Know assuredly that you will go out with me in the army, you and your men." [2] David said to Achish, "Therefore you will know what your servant can do." Achish said to David, "Therefore I will make you my bodyguard forever." [3] Now Samuel was dead, and all Israel had mourned for him and buried him in Ramah, even in his own city. Saul had sent away those who had familiar spirits and the wizards out of the land. [4] The Philistines gathered themselves together, and came and encamped in Shunem; and Saul gathered all Israel together, and they encamped in Gilboa. [5] When Saul saw the army of the Philistines, he was afraid, and his heart trembled greatly. [6] When Saul inquired of Yahweh, Yahweh didn't answer him by dreams, by Urim, or by prophets. [7] Then Saul said to his servants, "Seek for me a woman who has a familiar spirit, that I may go to her and inquire of her." His servants said to him, "Behold,

there is a woman who has a familiar spirit at Endor." [8] Saul disguised himself and put on other clothing, and went, he and two men with him, and they came to the woman by night. Then he said, "Please consult for me by the familiar spirit, and bring me up whomever I shall name to you." [9] The woman said to him, "Behold, you know what Saul has done, how he has cut off those who have familiar spirits and the wizards out of the land. Why then do you lay a snare for my life, to cause me to die?" [10] Saul swore to her by Yahweh, saying, "As Yahweh lives, no punishment will happen to you for this thing." [11] Then the woman said, "Whom shall I bring up to you?" He said, "Bring Samuel up for me." [12] When the woman saw Samuel, she cried with a loud voice; and the woman spoke to Saul, saying, "Why have you deceived me? For you are Saul!" [13] The king said to her, "Don't be afraid! What do you see?" The woman said to Saul, "I see a god coming up out of the earth." [14] He said to her, "What does he look like?" She said, "An old man comes up. He is covered with a robe." Saul perceived that it was Samuel, and he bowed with his face to the ground, and showed respect. [15] Samuel said to Saul, "Why have you disturbed me, to bring me up?" Saul answered, "I am very distressed; for the Philistines make war against me, and God has departed from me, and answers me no more, by prophets, or by dreams. Therefore I have called you, that you may make known to me what I shall do." [16] Samuel said, "Why then do you ask me, since Yahweh has departed from you and has become your adversary? [17] Yahweh has done to you as he spoke by me. Yahweh has torn the kingdom out of your hand and given it to your neighbor, even to David. [18] Because you didn't obey Yahweh's voice, and didn't execute his fierce wrath on Amalek, therefore Yahweh has done this thing to you today. [19] Moreover Yahweh will deliver Israel also with you into the hand of the Philistines; and tomorrow you and your sons will be with me. Yahweh will deliver the army of Israel also into the hand of the Philistines." [20] Then Saul fell immediately his full length on the earth, and was terrified, because of Samuel's words. There was no strength in him, for he had eaten no bread all day long or all night long. [21] The woman came to Saul and saw that he was very troubled, and said to him, "Behold, your servant has listened to your voice, and I have put my life in my hand, and have listened to your words which you spoke to me. [22] Now therefore, please listen also to the voice of your servant, and let me set a morsel of bread before you. Eat, that you may have strength when you go on your way." [23] But he refused, and said, "I will not eat." But his servants, together with the woman, constrained him; and he listened to their voice. So he arose from the earth and sat on the bed. [24] The woman had a fattened calf in the house. She hurried and killed it; and she took flour and kneaded it, and baked unleavened bread of it. [25] She brought it before Saul and before his servants, and they ate. Then they rose up and went away that night.

## 29

[1] Now the Philistines gathered together all their armies to Aphek; and the Israelites encamped by the spring which is in Jezreel. [2] The lords of the Philistines passed on by hundreds and by thousands; and David and his men passed on in the rear with Achish. [3] Then the princes of the Philistines said, "What about these Hebrews?" Achish said to the princes of the Philistines, "Isn't this David, the servant of Saul the king of Israel, who has been with me these days, or rather these years? I have found no fault in him since he fell away until today." [4] But the princes of the Philistines were angry with him; and the princes of the Philistines said to him, "Make the man return, that he may go back to his place where you have appointed him, and let him not go down with us to battle, lest in the battle he become an adversary to us. For with what should this fellow reconcile himself to his lord? Should it not be with the heads of these men? [5] Isn't this David, of whom people sang to one another in dances, saying, 'Saul has slain his thousands, and David his ten thousands'?" [6] Then Achish called David and said to him, "As Yahweh lives, you have been upright, and your going out and your coming in with me in the army is good in my sight; for I have not found evil in you since the day of your coming to me to this day. Nevertheless, the lords don't favor you. [7] Therefore now return, and go in peace, that you not displease the lords of the Philistines." [8] David said to Achish, "But what have I done? What have you found in your servant so long as I have been before you to this day, that I may not go and fight against the enemies of my lord the king?" [9] Achish answered David, "I know that you are good in my sight, as an angel of God. Notwithstanding, the princes of the Philistines have said, 'He shall not go up with us to the battle.' [10] Therefore now rise up early in the morning with the servants of your lord who have come with you; and as soon as you are up early in the morning and have light, depart." [11] So David rose up early, he and his men, to depart in the morning, to return into the land of the Philistines; and the Philistines went up to Jezreel.

## 30

[1] When David and his men had come to Ziklag on the third day, the Amalekites had made a raid on the South and on Ziklag, and had struck

Ziklag and burned it with fire, ² and had taken captive the women and all who were in it, both small and great. They didn't kill any, but carried them off and went their way. ³ When David and his men came to the city, behold, it was burned with fire; and their wives, their sons, and their daughters were taken captive. ⁴ Then David and the people who were with him lifted up their voice and wept until they had no more power to weep. ⁵ David's two wives were taken captive, Ahinoam the Jezreelitess, and Abigail the wife of Nabal the Carmelite. ⁶ David was greatly distressed, for the people spoke of stoning him, because the souls of all the people were grieved, every man for his sons and for his daughters; but David strengthened himself in Yahweh his God. ⁷ David said to Abiathar the priest, the son of Ahimelech, "Please bring the ephod here to me." Abiathar brought the ephod to David. ⁸ David inquired of Yahweh, saying, "If I pursue after this troop, will I overtake them?" He answered him, "Pursue, for you will surely overtake them, and will without fail recover all." ⁹ So David went, he and the six hundred men who were with him, and came to the brook Besor, where those who were left behind stayed. ¹⁰ But David pursued, he and four hundred men; for two hundred stayed behind, who were so faint that they couldn't go over the brook Besor. ¹¹ They found an Egyptian in the field, and brought him to David, and gave him bread, and he ate; and they gave him water to drink. ¹² They gave him a piece of a cake of figs and two clusters of raisins. When he had eaten, his spirit came again to him; for he had eaten no bread, and drank no water for three days and three nights. ¹³ David asked him, "To whom do you belong? Where are you from?" He said, "I am a young man of Egypt, servant to an Amalekite; and my master left me, because three days ago I got sick. ¹⁴ We made a raid on the South of the Cherethites, and on that which belongs to Judah, and on the South of Caleb; and we burned Ziklag with fire." ¹⁵ David said to him, "Will you bring me down to this troop?" He said, "Swear to me by God that you will not kill me and not deliver me up into the hands of my master, and I will bring you down to this troop." ¹⁶ When he had brought him down, behold, they were spread around over all the ground, eating, drinking, and dancing, because of all the great plunder that they had taken out of the land of the Philistines, and out of the land of Judah. ¹⁷ David struck them from the twilight even to the evening of the next day. Not a man of them escaped from there, except four hundred young men who rode on camels and fled. ¹⁸ David recovered all that the Amalekites had taken, and David rescued his two wives. ¹⁹ There was nothing lacking to them, neither small nor great, neither sons nor daughters, neither plunder, nor anything that they had taken. David brought them all back. ²⁰ David took all the flocks and the herds, which they drove before those other livestock, and said, "This is David's plunder." ²¹ David came to the two hundred men, who were so faint that they could not follow David, whom also they had made to stay at the brook Besor; and they went out to meet David, and to meet the people who were with him. When David came near to the people, he greeted them. ²² Then all the wicked men and worthless fellows of those who went with David answered and said, "Because they didn't go with us, we will not give them anything of the plunder that we have recovered, except to every man his wife and his children, that he may lead them away and depart." ²³ Then David said, "Do not do so, my brothers, with that which Yahweh has given to us, who has preserved us, and delivered the troop that came against us into our hand. ²⁴ Who will listen to you in this matter? For as his share is who goes down to the battle, so shall his share be who stays with the baggage. They shall share alike." ²⁵ It was so from that day forward that he made it a statute and an ordinance for Israel to this day. ²⁶ When David came to Ziklag, he sent some of the plunder to the elders of Judah, even to his friends, saying, "Behold, a present for you from the plunder of Yahweh's enemies." ²⁷ He sent it to those who were in Bethel, to those who were in Ramoth of the South, to those who were in Jattir, ²⁸ to those who were in Aroer, to those who were in Siphmoth, to those who were in Eshtemoa, ²⁹ to those who were in Racal, to those who were in the cities of the Jerahmeelites, to those who were in the cities of the Kenites, ³⁰ to those who were in Hormah, to those who were in Borashan, to those who were in Athach, ³¹ to those who were in Hebron, and to all the places where David himself and his men used to stay.

## 31

¹ Now the Philistines fought against Israel; and the men of Israel fled from before the Philistines, and fell down slain on Mount Gilboa. ² The Philistines overtook Saul and his sons; and the Philistines killed Jonathan, Abinadab, and Malchishua, the sons of Saul. ³ The battle went hard against Saul, and the archers overtook him; and he was greatly distressed by reason of the archers. ⁴ Then Saul said to his armor bearer, "Draw your sword, and thrust me through with it, lest these uncircumcised come and thrust me through and abuse me!" But his armor bearer would not, for he was terrified. Therefore Saul took his sword and fell on it. ⁵ When his armor bearer saw that Saul was dead, he likewise fell on his sword, and died with him. ⁶ So Saul died with his three sons, his armor bearer, and all his men that same day together. ⁷ When the men of Israel who were on the other side of the valley, and those who were beyond the Jordan, saw that the men of Israel fled and that Saul and his sons were dead, they abandoned the cities and fled; and the Philistines came and lived in them. ⁸ On the next day, when the Philistines came to strip the slain, they found Saul and his three sons fallen on Mount Gilboa. ⁹ They cut off his head, stripped off his armor, and sent into the land of the Philistines all around, to carry the news to the house of their idols and to the people. ¹⁰ They put his armor in the house of the Ashtaroth, and they fastened his body to the wall of Beth Shan. ¹¹ When the inhabitants of Jabesh Gilead heard what the Philistines had done to Saul, ¹² all the valiant men arose, went all night, and took the body of Saul and the bodies of his sons from the wall of Beth Shan; and they came to Jabesh and burned them there. ¹³ They took their bones and buried them under the tamarisk[a] tree in Jabesh, and fasted seven days.

# The Second Book of Samuel

## 1

¹ After the death of Saul, when David had returned from the slaughter of the Amalekites, and David had stayed two days in Ziklag, ² on the third day, behold,[b] a man came out of the camp from Saul, with his clothes torn and earth on his head. When he came to David, he fell to the earth and showed respect. ³ David said to him, "Where do you come from?" He said to him, "I have escaped out of the camp of Israel." ⁴ David said to him, "How did it go? Please tell me." He answered, "The people have fled from the battle, and many of the people also have fallen and are dead. Saul and Jonathan his son are dead also." ⁵ David said to the young man who told him, "How do you know that Saul and Jonathan his son are dead?" ⁶ The young man who told him said, "As I happened by chance on Mount Gilboa, behold, Saul was leaning on his spear; and behold, the chariots and the horsemen followed close behind him. ⁷ When he looked behind him, he saw me and called to me. I answered, 'Here I am.' ⁸ He said to me, 'Who are you?' I answered him, 'I am an Amalekite.' ⁹ He said to me, 'Please stand beside me, and kill me, for anguish has taken hold of me because my life lingers in me.' ¹⁰ So I stood beside him and killed him, because I was sure that he could not live after he had fallen. I took the crown that was on his head and the bracelet that was on his arm, and have brought them here to my lord." ¹¹ Then David took hold on his clothes and tore them; and all the men who were with him did likewise. ¹² They mourned, wept, and fasted until evening for Saul and for Jonathan his son, and for the people of Yahweh,[c] and for the house of Israel, because they had fallen by the sword. ¹³ David said to the young man who told him, "Where are you from?" He answered, "I am the son of a foreigner, an Amalekite." ¹⁴ David said to him, "Why were you not afraid to stretch out your hand to destroy Yahweh's anointed?" ¹⁵ David called one of the young men and said, "Go near, and cut him down!" He struck him so that he died. ¹⁶ David said to him, "Your blood be on your head, for your mouth has testified against you, saying, 'I have slain Yahweh's anointed.'" ¹⁷ David lamented with this lamentation over Saul and over Jonathan his son ¹⁸(and he commanded them to teach the children of Judah the song of the bow; behold, it is written in the book of Jashar): ¹⁹"Your glory, Israel, was slain on your high places! How the mighty have fallen! ²⁰ Don't tell it in Gath. Don't publish it in the streets of Ashkelon, lest the daughters of the Philistines rejoice, lest the daughters of the uncircumcised triumph. ²¹ You mountains of Gilboa, let there be no dew or rain on you, and no fields of offerings; for there the shield of the mighty was defiled and cast away, the shield of Saul was not anointed with oil. ²² From the blood of the slain, from the fat of the mighty, Jonathan's bow didn't turn back. Saul's sword didn't return empty. ²³ Saul and Jonathan were lovely and pleasant in their lives. In their death, they were not divided. They were swifter than eagles. They were stronger than lions. ²⁴ You daughters of Israel, weep over Saul, who clothed you delicately in scarlet, who put ornaments of gold on your clothing. ²⁵ How the mighty have fallen in the middle of the battle! Jonathan was slain on your high places. ²⁶ I am distressed for you, my brother Jonathan. You have been very pleasant to me. Your love to me was wonderful, surpassing the love of women. ²⁷ How the mighty have fallen, and the weapons of war have perished!"

---

[a] 31:13 or, salt cedar
[b] 1:2 "Behold", from "הִנֵּה", means look at, take notice,
observe, see, or gaze at. It is often used as an interjection.
[c] 1:12 "Yahweh" is God's proper Name, sometimes
rendered "LORD" (all caps) in other translations.

## 2

¹ After this, David inquired of Yahweh, saying, "Shall I go up into any of the cities of Judah?" Yahweh said to him, "Go up." David said, "Where shall I go up?" He said, "To Hebron." ² So David went up there with his two wives, Ahinoam the Jezreelitess, and Abigail the wife of Nabal the Carmelite. ³ David brought up his men who were with him, every man with his household. They lived in the cities of Hebron. ⁴ The men of Judah came, and there they anointed David king over the house of Judah. They told David, "The men of Jabesh Gilead were those who buried Saul." ⁵ David sent messengers to the men of Jabesh Gilead, and said to them, "Blessed are you by Yahweh, that you have shown this kindness to your lord, even to Saul, and have buried him. ⁶ Now may Yahweh show loving kindness and truth to you. I also will reward you for this kindness, because you have done this thing. ⁷ Now therefore let your hands be strong, and be valiant; for Saul your lord is dead, and also the house of Judah have anointed me king over them." ⁸ Now Abner the son of Ner, captain of Saul's army, had taken Ishbosheth the son of Saul and brought him over to Mahanaim. ⁹ He made him king over Gilead, over the Ashurites, over Jezreel, over Ephraim, over Benjamin, and over all Israel. ¹⁰ Ishbosheth, Saul's son, was forty years old when he began to reign over Israel, and he reigned two years. But the house of Judah followed David. ¹¹ The time that David was king in Hebron over the house of Judah was seven years and six months. ¹² Abner the son of Ner, and the servants of Ishbosheth the son of Saul, went out from Mahanaim to Gibeon. ¹³ Joab the son of Zeruiah and David's servants went out, and met them by the pool of Gibeon; and they sat down, the one on the one side of the pool and the other on the other side of the pool. ¹⁴ Abner said to Joab, "Please let the young men arise and compete before us!" Joab said, "Let them arise!" ¹⁵ Then they arose and went over by number: twelve for Benjamin and for Ishbosheth the son of Saul, and twelve of David's servants. ¹⁶ They each caught his opponent by the head and thrust his sword in his fellow's side; so they fell down together. Therefore that place in Gibeon was called Helkath Hazzurim.ᵃ ¹⁷ The battle was very severe that day; and Abner was beaten, and the men of Israel, before David's servants. ¹⁸ The three sons of Zeruiah were there: Joab, Abishai, and Asahel. Asahel was as light of foot as a wild gazelle. ¹⁹ Asahel pursued Abner. He didn't turn to the right hand or to the left from following Abner. ²⁰ Then Abner looked behind him and said, "Is that you, Asahel?" He answered, "It is." ²¹ Abner said to him, "Turn away to your right hand or to your left, and grab one of the young men, and take his armor." But Asahel would not turn away from following him. ²² Abner said again to Asahel, "Turn away from following me. Why should I strike you to the ground? How then could I look Joab your brother in the face?" ²³ However, he refused to turn away. Therefore Abner with the back end of the spear struck him in the body, so that the spear came out behind him; and he fell down there and died in the same place. As many as came to the place where Asahel fell down and died stood still. ²⁴ But Joab and Abishai pursued Abner. The sun went down when they had come to the hill of Ammah, that lies before Giah by the way of the wilderness of Gibeon. ²⁵ The children of Benjamin gathered themselves together after Abner and became one band, and stood on the top of a hill. ²⁶ Then Abner called to Joab, and said, "Shall the sword devour forever? Don't you know that it will be bitterness in the latter end? How long will it be then, before you ask the people to return from following their brothers?" ²⁷ Joab said, "As Godᵇ lives, if you had not spoken, surely then in the morning the people would have gone away, and not each followed his brother." ²⁸ So Joab blew the trumpet; and all the people stood still and pursued Israel no more, and they fought no more. ²⁹ Abner and his men went all that night through the Arabah; and they passed over the Jordan, and went through all Bithron, and came to Mahanaim. ³⁰ Joab returned from following Abner; and when he had gathered all the people together, nineteen men of David's and Asahel were missing. ³¹ But David's servants had struck Benjamin Abner's men so that three hundred sixty men died. ³² They took up Asahel and buried him in the tomb of his father, which was in Bethlehem. Joab and his men went all night, and the day broke on them at Hebron.

## 3

¹ Now there was long war between Saul's house and David's house. David grew stronger and stronger, but Saul's house grew weaker and weaker. ² Sons were born to David in Hebron. His firstborn was Amnon, of Ahinoam the Jezreelitess; ³ and his second, Chileab, of Abigail the wife of Nabal the Carmelite; and the third, Absalom the son of Maacah the daughter of Talmai king of Geshur; ⁴ and the fourth, Adonijah the son of Haggith; and the fifth, Shephatiah the son of Abital; ⁵ and the sixth, Ithream, of Eglah, David's wife. These were born to

David in Hebron. ⁶ While there was war between Saul's house and David's house, Abner made himself strong in Saul's house. ⁷ Now Saul had a concubine, whose name was Rizpah, the daughter of Aiah; and Ishbosheth said to Abner, "Why have you gone in to my father's concubine?" ⁸ Then Abner was very angry about Ishbosheth's words, and said, "Am I a dog's head that belongs to Judah? Today I show kindness to your father Saul's house, to his brothers, and to his friends, and have not delivered you into the hand of David; and yet you charge me today with a fault concerning this woman! ⁹ God do so to Abner, and more also, if, as Yahweh has sworn to David, I don't do even so to him: ¹⁰ to transfer the kingdom from Saul's house, and to set up David's throne over Israel and over Judah, from Dan even to Beersheba." ¹¹ He could not answer Abner another word, because he was afraid of him. ¹² Abner sent messengers to David on his behalf, saying, "Whose is the land?" and saying, "Make your alliance with me, and behold, my hand will be with you to bring all Israel around to you." ¹³ David said, "Good. I will make a treaty with you, but one thing I require of you. That is, you will not see my face unless you first bring Michal, Saul's daughter, when you come to see my face." ¹⁴ David sent messengers to Ishbosheth, Saul's son, saying, "Deliver me my wife Michal, whom I was given to marry for one hundred foreskins of the Philistines." ¹⁵ Ishbosheth sent and took her from her husband, Paltiel the son of Laish. ¹⁶ Her husband went with her, weeping as he went, and followed her to Bahurim. Then Abner said to him, "Go! Return!" and he returned. ¹⁷ Abner had communication with the elders of Israel, saying, "In times past, you sought for David to be king over you. ¹⁸ Now then do it! For Yahweh has spoken of David, saying, 'By the hand of my servant David, I will save my people Israel out of the hand of the Philistines, and out of the hand of all their enemies.'" ¹⁹ Abner also spoke in the ears of Benjamin; and Abner went also to speak in the ears of David in Hebron all that seemed good to Israel and to the whole house of Benjamin. ²⁰ So Abner came to David to Hebron, and twenty men with him. David made Abner and the men who were with him a feast. ²¹ Abner said to David, "I will arise and go, and will gather all Israel to my lord the king, that they may make a covenant with you, and that you may reign over all that your soul desires." David sent Abner away; and he went in peace. ²² Behold, David's servants and Joab came from a raid and brought in a great plunder with them; but Abner was not with David in Hebron, for he had sent him away, and he had gone in peace. ²³ When Joab and all the army who was with him had come, they told Joab, "Abner the son of Ner came to the king, and he has sent him away, and he has gone in peace." ²⁴ Then Joab came to the king and said, "What have you done? Behold, Abner came to you. Why is it that you have sent him away, and he is already gone? ²⁵ You know Abner the son of Ner. He came to deceive you, and to know your going out and your coming in, and to know all that you do." ²⁶ When Joab had come out from David, he sent messengers after Abner, and they brought him back from the well of Sirah; but David didn't know it. ²⁷ When Abner had returned to Hebron, Joab took him aside into the middle of the gate to speak with him quietly, and struck him there in the body, so that he died for the blood of Asahel his brother. ²⁸ Afterward, when David heard it, he said, "I and my kingdom are guiltless before Yahweh forever of the blood of Abner the son of Ner. ²⁹ Let it fall on the head of Joab and on all his father's house. Let there not fail from the house of Joab one who has a discharge, or who is a leper, or who leans on a staff, or who falls by the sword, or who lacks bread." ³⁰ So Joab and Abishai his brother killed Abner, because he had killed their brother Asahel at Gibeon in the battle. ³¹ David said to Joab and to all the people who were with him, "Tear your clothes, and clothe yourselves with sackcloth, and mourn in front of Abner." King David followed the bier. ³² They buried Abner in Hebron; and the king lifted up his voice and wept at Abner's grave; and all the people wept. ³³ The king lamented for Abner, and said, "Should Abner die as a fool dies? ³⁴ Your hands weren't bound, and your feet weren't put into fetters. As a man falls before the children of iniquity, so you fell." All the people wept again over him. ³⁵ All the people came to urge David to eat bread while it was yet day; but David swore, saying, "God do so to me, and more also, if I taste bread or anything else, until the sun goes down." ³⁶ All the people took notice of it, and it pleased them, as whatever the king did pleased all the people. ³⁷ So all the people and all Israel understood that day that it was not of the king to kill Abner the son of Ner. ³⁸ The king said to his servants, "Don't you know that a prince and a great man has fallen today in Israel? ³⁹ I am weak today, though anointed king. These men, the sons of Zeruiah are too hard for me. May Yahweh reward the evildoer according to his wickedness."

---

ᵃ 2:16 "Helkath Hazzurim" means "field of daggers".

ᵇ 2:27 The Hebrew word rendered "God" is "אֱלֹהִים" (Elohim).

## 4

¹ When Saul's son heard that Abner was dead in Hebron, his hands became feeble, and all the Israelites were troubled. ² Saul's son had two men who were captains of raiding bands. The name of one was Baanah and the name of the other Rechab, the sons of Rimmon the Beerothite, of the children of Benjamin (for Beeroth also is considered a part of Benjamin; ³ and the Beerothites fled to Gittaim, and have lived as foreigners there until today). ⁴ Now Jonathan, Saul's son, had a son who was lame in his feet. He was five years old when the news came about Saul and Jonathan out of Jezreel; and his nurse picked him up and fled. As she hurried to flee, he fell and became lame. His name was Mephibosheth. ⁵ The sons of Rimmon the Beerothite, Rechab and Baanah, went out and came at about the heat of the day to the house of Ishbosheth as he took his rest at noon. ⁶ They came there into the middle of the house as though they would have fetched wheat, and they struck him in the body; and Rechab and Baanah his brother escaped. ⁷ Now when they came into the house as he lay on his bed in his bedroom, they struck him, killed him, beheaded him, and took his head, and went by the way of the Arabah all night. ⁸ They brought the head of Ishbosheth to David to Hebron, and said to the king, "Behold, the head of Ishbosheth, the son of Saul, your enemy, who sought your life! Yahweh has avenged my lord the king today of Saul and of his offspring."ᵃ ⁹ David answered Rechab and Baanah his brother, the sons of Rimmon the Beerothite, and said to them, "As Yahweh lives, who has redeemed my soul out of all adversity, ¹⁰ when someone told me, 'Behold, Saul is dead,' thinking that he brought good news, I seized him and killed him in Ziklag, which was the reward I gave him for his news. ¹¹ How much more, when wicked men have slain a righteous person in his own house on his bed, should I not now require his blood from your hand, and rid the earth of you?" ¹² David commanded his young men, and they killed them, cut off their hands and their feet, and hanged them up beside the pool in Hebron. But they took the head of Ishbosheth and buried it in Abner's grave in Hebron.

## 5

¹ Then all the tribes of Israel came to David at Hebron and spoke, saying, "Behold, we are your bone and your flesh. ² In times past, when Saul was king over us, it was you who led Israel out and in. Yahweh said to you, 'You will be shepherd of my people Israel, and you will be prince over Israel.'" ³ So all the elders of Israel came to the king to Hebron, and King David made a covenant with them in Hebron before Yahweh; and they anointed David king over Israel. ⁴ David was thirty years old when he began to reign, and he reigned forty years. ⁵ In Hebron he reigned over Judah seven years and six months, and in Jerusalem he reigned thirty-three years over all Israel and Judah. ⁶ The king and his men went to Jerusalem against the Jebusites, the inhabitants of the land, who spoke to David, saying, "The blind and the lame will keep you out of here," thinking, "David can't come in here." ⁷ Nevertheless David took the stronghold of Zion. This is David's city. ⁸ David said on that day, "Whoever strikes the Jebusites, let him go up to the watercourse and strike those lame and blind, who are hated by David's soul." Therefore they say, "The blind and the lame can't come into the house." ⁹ David lived in the stronghold, and called it David's city. David built around from Millo and inward. ¹⁰ David grew greater and greater, for Yahweh, the God of Armies, was with him. ¹¹ Hiram king of Tyre sent messengers to David, with cedar trees, carpenters, and masons; and they built David a house. ¹² David perceived that Yahweh had established him king over Israel, and that he had exalted his kingdom for his people Israel's sake. ¹³ David took more concubines and wives for himself out of Jerusalem, after he had come from Hebron; and more sons and daughters were born to David. ¹⁴ These are the names of those who were born to him in Jerusalem: Shammua, Shobab, Nathan, Solomon, ¹⁵ Ibhar, Elishua, Nepheg, Japhia, ¹⁶ Elishama, Eliada, and Eliphelet. ¹⁷ When the Philistines heard that they had anointed David king over Israel, all the Philistines went up to seek David, but David heard about it and went down to the stronghold. ¹⁸ Now the Philistines had come and spread themselves in the valley of Rephaim. ¹⁹ David inquired of Yahweh, saying, "Shall I go up against the Philistines? Will you deliver them into my hand?" Yahweh said to David, "Go up; for I will certainly deliver the Philistines into your hand." ²⁰ David came to Baal Perazim, and David struck them there. Then he said, "Yahweh has broken my enemies before me, like the breach of waters." Therefore he called the name of that place Baal Perazim.ᵇ ²¹ They left their images there, and David and his men took them away. ²² The Philistines came up yet again and spread themselves in the valley of Rephaim. ²³ When David inquired of Yahweh, he said, "You shall not go up. Circle around behind them, and attack them in front of the mulberry trees. ²⁴ When you hear the sound of marching in the tops of the mulberry trees, then stir yourself up; for then Yahweh has gone out before you to strike the army of the Philistines." ²⁵ David did so, as Yahweh commanded him, and struck the Philistines all the way from Geba to Gezer.

## 6

¹ David again gathered together all the chosen men of Israel, thirty thousand. ² David arose and went with all the people who were with him from Baale Judah, to bring up from there God's ark, which is called by the Name, even the name of Yahweh of Armies who sits above the cherubim. ³ They set God's ark on a new cart, and brought it out of Abinadab's house that was on the hill; and Uzzah and Ahio, the sons of Abinadab, drove the new cart. ⁴ They brought it out of Abinadab's house which was in the hill, with God's ark; and Ahio went before the ark. ⁵ David and all the house of Israel played before Yahweh with all kinds of instruments made of cypress wood, with harps, with stringed instruments, with tambourines, with castanets, and with cymbals. ⁶ When they came to the threshing floor of Nacon, Uzzah reached for God's ark and took hold of it, for the cattle stumbled. ⁷ Yahweh's anger burned against Uzzah, and God struck him there for his error; and he died there by God's ark. ⁸ David was displeased because Yahweh had broken out against Uzzah; and he called that place Perez Uzzahᶜ to this day. ⁹ David was afraid of Yahweh that day; and he said, "How could Yahweh's ark come to me?" ¹⁰ So David would not move Yahweh's ark to be with him in David's city; but David carried it aside into Obed-Edom the Gittite's house. ¹¹ Yahweh's ark remained in Obed-Edom the Gittite's house three months; and Yahweh blessed Obed-Edom and all his house. ¹² King David was told, "Yahweh has blessed the house of Obed-Edom, and all that belongs to him, because of God's ark." So David went and brought up God's ark from the house of Obed-Edom into David's city with joy. ¹³ When those who bore Yahweh's ark had gone six paces, he sacrificed an ox and a fattened calf. ¹⁴ David danced before Yahweh with all his might; and David was clothed in a linen ephod. ¹⁵ So David and all the house of Israel brought up Yahweh's ark with shouting and with the sound of the trumpet. ¹⁶ As Yahweh's ark came into David's city, Michal the daughter of Saul looked out through the window and saw King David leaping and dancing before Yahweh; and she despised him in her heart. ¹⁷ They brought in Yahweh's ark, and set it in its place in the middle of the tent that David had pitched for it; and David offered burnt offerings and peace offerings before Yahweh. ¹⁸ When David had finished offering the burnt offering and the peace offerings, he blessed the people in the name of Yahweh of Armies. ¹⁹ He gave to all the people, even among the whole multitude of Israel, both to men and women, to everyone a portion of bread, dates, and raisins. So all the people departed, each to his own house. ²⁰ Then David returned to bless his household. Michal the daughter of Saul came out to meet David, and said, "How glorious the king of Israel was today, who uncovered himself today in the eyes of his servants' maids, as one of the vain fellows shamelessly uncovers himself!" ²¹ David said to Michal, "It was before Yahweh, who chose me above your father, and above all his house, to appoint me prince over the people of Yahweh, over Israel. Therefore I will celebrate before Yahweh. ²² I will be yet more undignified than this, and will be worthless in my own sight. But the maids of whom you have spoken will honor me." ²³ Michal the daughter of Saul had no child to the day of her death.

## 7

¹ When the king lived in his house, and Yahweh had given him rest from all his enemies all around, ² the king said to Nathan the prophet, "See now, I dwell in a house of cedar, but God's ark dwells within curtains." ³ Nathan said to the king, "Go, do all that is in your heart, for Yahweh is with you." ⁴ That same night, Yahweh's word came to Nathan, saying, ⁵"Go and tell my servant David, 'Yahweh says, "Should you build me a house for me to dwell in? ⁶ For I have not lived in a house since the day that I brought the children of Israel up out of Egypt, even to this day, but have moved around in a tent and in a tabernacle. ⁷ In all places in which I have walked with all the children of Israel, did I say a word to anyone from the tribes of Israel whom I commanded to be shepherd of my people Israel, saying, 'Why have you not built me a house of cedar?'"' ⁸ Now therefore tell my servant David this: 'Yahweh of Armies says, "I took you from the sheep pen, from following the sheep, to be prince over my people, over Israel. ⁹ I have been with you wherever you went, and have cut off all your enemies from before you. I will make you a great name, like the name of the great ones who are in the earth. ¹⁰ I will appoint a place for my people Israel, and will plant them, that they may dwell in their own place and be moved no more. The children of wickedness will not afflict them any more, as at the first, ¹¹ and as from the day that I commanded judges to be over my people Israel. I will cause you to rest from all your

---

ᵃ *4:8 or, seed*

ᵇ *5:20 "Baal Perazim" means "Lord who breaks out".*

ᶜ *6:8 "Perez Uzzah" means "outbreak against Uzzah".*

enemies. Moreover Yahweh tells you that Yahweh will make you a house. ¹² When your days are fulfilled and you sleep with your fathers, I will set up your offspring after you, who will proceed out of your body, and I will establish his kingdom. ¹³ He will build a house for my name, and I will establish the throne of his kingdom forever. ¹⁴ I will be his father, and he will be my son. If he commits iniquity, I will chasten him with the rod of men and with the stripes of the children of men; ¹⁵ but my loving kindness will not depart from him, as I took it from Saul, whom I put away before you. ¹⁶ Your house and your kingdom will be made sure forever before you. Your throne will be established forever.'" ¹⁷ Nathan spoke to David all these words, and according to all this vision. ¹⁸ Then David the king went in and sat before Yahweh; and he said, "Who am I, Lordª Yahweh, and what is my house, that you have brought me this far? ¹⁹ This was yet a small thing in your eyes, Lord Yahweh, but you have spoken also of your servant's house for a great while to come; and this among men, Lord Yahweh! ²⁰ What more can David say to you? For you know your servant, Lord Yahweh. ²¹ For your word's sake, and according to your own heart, you have worked all this greatness, to make your servant know it. ²² Therefore you are great, Yahweh God. For there is no one like you, neither is there any God besides you, according to all that we have heard with our ears. ²³ What one nation in the earth is like your people, even like Israel, whom God went to redeem to himself for a people, and to make himself a name, and to do great things for you, and awesome things for your land, before your people, whom you redeemed to yourself out of Egypt, from the nations and their gods? ²⁴ You established for yourself your people Israel to be your people forever; and you, Yahweh, became their God. ²⁵"Now, Yahweh God, the word that you have spoken concerning your servant, and concerning his house, confirm it forever, and do as you have spoken. ²⁶ Let your name be magnified forever, saying, 'Yahweh of Armies is God over Israel;' and the house of your servant David will be established before you.' ²⁷ For you, Yahweh of Armies, the God of Israel, have revealed to your servant, saying, 'I will build you a house.' Therefore your servant has found in his heart to pray this prayer to you. ²⁸"Now, O Lord Yahweh, you are God, and your words are truth, and you have promised this good thing to your servant. ²⁹ Now therefore, let it please you to bless the house of your servant, that it may continue forever before you; for you, Lord Yahweh, have spoken it. Let the house of your servant be blessed forever with your blessing."

## 8

¹ After this, David struck the Philistines and subdued them; and David took the bridle of the mother city out of the hand of the Philistines. ² He defeated Moab, and measured them with the line, making them to lie down on the ground; and he measured two lines to put to death, and one full line to keep alive. The Moabites became servants to David, and brought tribute. ³ David also struck Hadadezer the son of Rehob, king of Zobah, as he went to recover his dominion at the River. ⁴ David took from him one thousand seven hundred horsemen and twenty thousand footmen. David hamstrung the chariot horses, but reserved enough of them for one hundred chariots. ⁵ When the Syrians of Damascus came to help Hadadezer king of Zobah, David struck twenty two thousand men of the Syrians. ⁶ Then David put garrisons in Syria of Damascus; and the Syrians became servants to David, and brought tribute. Yahweh gave victory to David wherever he went. ⁷ David took the shields of gold that were on the servants of Hadadezer, and brought them to Jerusalem. ⁸ From Betah and from Berothai, cities of Hadadezer, King David took a great quantity of bronze. ⁹ When Toi king of Hamath heard that David had struck all the army of Hadadezer, ¹⁰ then Toi sent Joram his son to King David to greet him and to bless him, because he had fought against Hadadezer and struck him; for Hadadezer had wars with Toi. Joram brought with him vessels of silver, vessels of gold, and vessels of bronze. ¹¹ King David also dedicated these to Yahweh, with the silver and gold that he dedicated of all the nations which he subdued— ¹² of Syria, of Moab, of the children of Ammon, of the Philistines, of Amalek, and of the plunder of Hadadezer, son of Rehob, king of Zobah. ¹³ David earned a reputation when he returned from striking down eighteen thousand men of the Syrians in the Valley of Salt. ¹⁴ He put garrisons in Edom. Throughout all Edom, he put garrisons, and all the Edomites became servants to David. Yahweh gave victory to David wherever he went. ¹⁵ David reigned over all Israel; and David executed justice and righteousness for all his people. ¹⁶ Joab the son of Zeruiah was over the army, Jehoshaphat the son of Ahilud was recorder, ¹⁷ Zadok the son of Ahitub and Ahimelech the son of Abiathar were priests, Seraiah was scribe, ¹⁸ Benaiah the son of Jehoiada was over the Cherethites and the Pelethites; and David's sons were chief ministers.

## 9

¹ David said, "Is there yet any who is left of Saul's house, that I may show him kindness for Jonathan's sake?" ² There was of Saul's house a servant whose name was Ziba, and they called him to David; and the king said to him, "Are you Ziba?" He said, "I am your servant." ³ The king said, "Is there not yet any of Saul's house, that I may show the kindness of God to him?" Ziba said to the king, "Jonathan still has a son, who is lame in his feet." ⁴ The king said to him, "Where is he?" Ziba said to the king, "Behold, he is in the house of Machir the son of Ammiel, in Lo Debar." ⁵ Then King David sent and brought him out of the house of Machir the son of Ammiel, from Lo Debar. ⁶ Mephibosheth, the son of Jonathan, the son of Saul, came to David, fell on his face, and showed respect. David said, "Mephibosheth?" He answered, "Behold, your servant!" ⁷ David said to him, "Don't be afraid, for I will surely show you kindness for Jonathan your father's sake, and will restore to you all the land of Saul your father. You will eat bread at my table continually." ⁸ He bowed down, and said, "What is your servant, that you should look at such a dead dog as I am?" ⁹ Then the king called to Ziba, Saul's servant, and said to him, "All that belonged to Saul and to all his house I have given to your master's son. ¹⁰ Till the land for him—you, your sons, and your servants. Bring in the harvest, that your master's son may have bread to eat; but Mephibosheth your master's son will always eat bread at my table." Now Ziba had fifteen sons and twenty servants. ¹¹ Then Ziba said to the king, "According to all that my lord the king commands his servant, so your servant will do." So Mephibosheth ate at the king's table like one of the king's sons. ¹² Mephibosheth had a young son, whose name was Mica. All who lived in Ziba's house were servants to Mephibosheth. ¹³ So Mephibosheth lived in Jerusalem, for he ate continually at the king's table. He was lame in both his feet.

## 10

¹ After this, the king of the children of Ammon died, and Hanun his son reigned in his place. ² David said, "I will show kindness to Hanun the son of Nahash, as his father showed kindness to me." So David sent by his servants to comfort him concerning his father. David's servants came into the land of the children of Ammon. ³ But the princes of the children of Ammon said to Hanun their lord, "Do you think that David honors your father, in that he has sent comforters to you? Hasn't David sent his servants to you to search the city, to spy it out, and to overthrow it?" ⁴ So Hanun took David's servants, shaved off one half of their beards, and cut off their garments in the middle, even to their buttocks, and sent them away. ⁵ When they told David this, he sent to meet them, for the men were greatly ashamed. The king said, "Wait at Jericho until your beards have grown, and then return." ⁶ When the children of Ammon saw that they had become odious to David, the children of Ammon sent and hired the Syrians of Beth Rehob and the Syrians of Zobah, twenty thousand footmen, and the king of Maacah with one thousand men, and the men of Tob twelve thousand men. ⁷ When David heard of it, he sent Joab and all the army of the mighty men. ⁸ The children of Ammon came out, and put the battle in array at the entrance of the gate. The Syrians of Zobah and of Rehob and the men of Tob and Maacah were by themselves in the field. ⁹ Now when Joab saw that the battle was set against him before and behind, he chose of all the choice men of Israel and put them in array against the Syrians. ¹⁰ The rest of the people he committed into the hand of Abishai his brother; and he put them in array against the children of Ammon. ¹¹ He said, "If the Syrians are too strong for me, then you shall help me; but if the children of Ammon are too strong for you, then I will come and help you. ¹² Be courageous, and let's be strong for our people and for the cities of our God; and may Yahweh do what seems good to him." ¹³ So Joab and the people who were with him came near to the battle against the Syrians, and they fled before him. ¹⁴ When the children of Ammon saw that the Syrians had fled, they likewise fled before Abishai, and entered into the city. Then Joab returned from the children of Ammon and came to Jerusalem. ¹⁵ When the Syrians saw that they were defeated by Israel, they gathered themselves together. ¹⁶ Hadadezer sent and brought out the Syrians who were beyond the River; and they came to Helam, with Shobach the captain of the army of Hadadezer at their head. ¹⁷ David was told that; and he gathered all Israel together, passed over the Jordan, and came to Helam. The Syrians set themselves in array against David and fought with him. ¹⁸ The Syrians fled before Israel; and David killed seven hundred charioteers of the Syrians and forty thousand horsemen, and struck Shobach the captain of their army, so that he died there. ¹⁹ When all the kings who were servants to Hadadezer saw that they were defeated before Israel, they made peace with Israel and served them. So the Syrians were afraid to help the children of Ammon any more.

---

ª 7:18 The word translated "Lord" is "Adonai."

## 11

[1] At the return of the year, at the time when kings go out, David sent Joab and his servants with him, and all Israel; and they destroyed the children of Ammon and besieged Rabbah. But David stayed at Jerusalem. [2] At evening, David arose from his bed and walked on the roof of the king's house. From the roof, he saw a woman bathing, and the woman was very beautiful to look at. [3] David sent and inquired after the woman. One said, "Isn't this Bathsheba, the daughter of Eliam, Uriah the Hittite's wife?" [4] David sent messengers, and took her; and she came in to him, and he lay with her (for she was purified from her uncleanness); and she returned to her house. [5] The woman conceived; and she sent and told David, and said, "I am with child." [6] David sent to Joab, "Send me Uriah the Hittite." Joab sent Uriah to David. [7] When Uriah had come to him, David asked him how Joab did, and how the people fared, and how the war prospered. [8] David said to Uriah, "Go down to your house and wash your feet." Uriah departed out of the king's house, and a gift from the king was sent after him. [9] But Uriah slept at the door of the king's house with all the servants of his lord, and didn't go down to his house. [10] When they had told David, saying, "Uriah didn't go down to his house," David said to Uriah, "Haven't you come from a journey? Why didn't you go down to your house?" [11] Uriah said to David, "The ark, Israel, and Judah, are staying in tents; and my lord Joab and the servants of my lord are encamped in the open field. Shall I then go into my house to eat and to drink, and to lie with my wife? As you live, and as your soul lives, I will not do this thing!" [12] David said to Uriah, "Stay here today also, and tomorrow I will let you depart." So Uriah stayed in Jerusalem that day and the next day. [13] When David had called him, he ate and drank before him; and he made him drunk. At evening, he went out to lie on his bed with the servants of his lord, but didn't go down to his house. [14] In the morning, David wrote a letter to Joab and sent it by the hand of Uriah. [15] He wrote in the letter, saying, "Send Uriah to the forefront of the hottest battle, and retreat from him, that he may be struck and die." [16] When Joab kept watch on the city, he assigned Uriah to the place where he knew that valiant men were. [17] The men of the city went out and fought with Joab. Some of the people fell, even of David's servants; and Uriah the Hittite died also. [18] Then Joab sent and told David all the things concerning the war; [19] and he commanded the messenger, saying, "When you have finished telling all the things concerning the war to the king, [20] it shall be that, if the king's wrath arise, and he asks you, 'Why did you go so near to the city to fight? Didn't you know that they would shoot from the wall? [21] Who struck Abimelech the son of Jerubbesheth? Didn't a woman cast an upper millstone on him from the wall, so that he died at Thebez? Why did you go so near the wall?' then you shall say, 'Your servant Uriah the Hittite is also dead.'" [22] So the messenger went, and came and showed David all that Joab had sent him for. [23] The messenger said to David, "The men prevailed against us, and came out to us into the field; and we were on them even to the entrance of the gate. [24] The shooters shot at your servants from off the wall; and some of the king's servants are dead, and your servant Uriah the Hittite is also dead." [25] Then David said to the messenger, "Tell Joab, 'Don't let this thing displease you, for the sword devours one as well as another. Make your battle stronger against the city, and overthrow it.' Encourage him." [26] When Uriah's wife heard that Uriah her husband was dead, she mourned for her husband. [27] When the mourning was past, David sent and took her home to his house, and she became his wife and bore him a son. But the thing that David had done displeased Yahweh.

## 12

[1] Yahweh sent Nathan to David. He came to him, and said to him, "There were two men in one city: the one rich, and the other poor. [2] The rich man had very many flocks and herds, [3] but the poor man had nothing, except one little ewe lamb, which he had bought and raised. It grew up together with him and with his children. It ate of his own food, drank of his own cup, and lay in his bosom, and was like a daughter to him. [4] A traveler came to the rich man, and he didn't want to take of his own flock and of his own herd to prepare for the wayfaring man who had come to him, but took the poor man's lamb and prepared it for the man who had come to him." [5] David's anger burned hot against the man, and he said to Nathan, "As Yahweh lives, the man who has done this deserves to die! [6] He must restore the lamb fourfold, because he did this thing and because he had no pity!" [7] Nathan said to David, "You are the man! This is what Yahweh, the God of Israel, says: 'I anointed you king over Israel, and I delivered you out of the hand of Saul. [8] I gave you your master's house and your master's wives into your bosom, and gave you the house of Israel and of Judah; and if that would

have been too little, I would have added to you many more such things. [9] Why have you despised Yahweh's word, to do that which is evil in his sight? You have struck Uriah the Hittite with the sword, have taken his wife to be your wife, and have slain him with the sword of the children of Ammon. [10] Now therefore the sword will never depart from your house, because you have despised me and have taken Uriah the Hittite's wife to be your wife.' [11] "This is what Yahweh says: 'Behold, I will raise up evil against you out of your own house; and I will take your wives before your eyes and give them to your neighbor, and he will lie with your wives in the sight of this sun. [12] For you did this secretly, but I will do this thing before all Israel, and before the sun.'" [13] David said to Nathan, "I have sinned against Yahweh." Nathan said to David, "Yahweh also has put away your sin. You will not die. [14] However, because by this deed you have given great occasion to Yahweh's enemies to blaspheme, the child also who is born to you will surely die." [15] Then Nathan departed to his house. Yahweh struck the child that Uriah's wife bore to David, and he was very sick. [16] David therefore begged God for the child; and David fasted, and went in and lay all night on the ground. [17] The elders of his house arose beside him, to raise him up from the earth; but he would not, and he didn't eat bread with them. [18] On the seventh day, the child died. David's servants were afraid to tell him that the child was dead, for they said, "Behold, while the child was yet alive, we spoke to him and he didn't listen to our voice. How will he then harm himself if we tell him that the child is dead?" [19] But when David saw that his servants were whispering together, David perceived that the child was dead; and David said to his servants, "Is the child dead?" They said, "He is dead." [20] Then David arose from the earth, and washed and anointed himself, and changed his clothing; and he came into Yahweh's house, and worshiped. Then he came to his own house; and when he requested, they set bread before him and he ate. [21] Then his servants said to him, "What is this that you have done? You fasted and wept for the child while he was alive, but when the child was dead, you rose up and ate bread." [22] He said, "While the child was yet alive, I fasted and wept; for I said, 'Who knows whether Yahweh will not be gracious to me, that the child may live?' [23] But now he is dead. Why should I fast? Can I bring him back again? I will go to him, but he will not return to me." [24] David comforted Bathsheba his wife, and went in to her, and lay with her. She bore a son, and he called his name Solomon. Yahweh loved him; [25] and he sent by the hand of Nathan the prophet, and he named him Jedidiah,[a] for Yahweh's sake. [26] Now Joab fought against Rabbah of the children of Ammon, and took the royal city. [27] Joab sent messengers to David, and said, "I have fought against Rabbah. Yes, I have taken the city of waters. [28] Now therefore gather the rest of the people together, and encamp against the city and take it; lest I take the city, and it be called by my name." [29] David gathered all the people together and went to Rabbah, and fought against it and took it. [30] He took the crown of their king from off his head; and its weight was a talent[b] of gold, and in it were precious stones; and it was set on David's head. He brought a great quantity of plunder out of the city. [31] He brought out the people who were in it, and put them to work under saws, under iron picks, under axes of iron, and made them go to the brick kiln; and he did so to all the cities of the children of Ammon. Then David and all the people returned to Jerusalem.

## 13

[1] After this, Absalom the son of David had a beautiful sister, whose name was Tamar; and Amnon the son of David loved her. [2] Amnon was so troubled that he became sick because of his sister Tamar, for she was a virgin, and it seemed hard to Amnon to do anything to her. [3] But Amnon had a friend whose name was Jonadab the son of Shimeah, David's brother; and Jonadab was a very subtle man. [4] He said to him, "Why, son of the king, are you so sad from day to day? Won't you tell me?" Amnon said to him, "I love Tamar, my brother Absalom's sister." [5] Jonadab said to him, "Lay down on your bed and pretend to be sick. When your father comes to see you, tell him, 'Please let my sister Tamar come and give me bread to eat, and prepare the food in my sight, that I may see it and eat it from her hand.'" [6] So Amnon lay down and faked being sick. When the king came to see him, Amnon said to the king, "Please let my sister Tamar come and make me a couple of cakes in my sight, that I may eat from her hand." [7] Then David sent home to Tamar, saying, "Go now to your brother Amnon's house, and prepare food for him." [8] So Tamar went to her brother Amnon's house; and he was lying down. She took dough, kneaded it, made cakes in his sight, and baked the cakes. [9] She took the pan and poured them out before him, but he refused to eat. Amnon said, "Have all men leave me." Then every man went out from him. [10] Amnon said to Tamar, "Bring the food

[a] 12:25 "Jedidiah" means "loved by Yahweh".

[b] 12:30 A talent is about 30 kilograms or 66 pounds or 965 Troy ounces

into the room, that I may eat from your hand." Tamar took the cakes which she had made, and brought them into the room to Amnon her brother. ¹¹ When she had brought them near to him to eat, he took hold of her and said to her, "Come, lie with me, my sister!" ¹² She answered him, "No, my brother, do not force me! For no such thing ought to be done in Israel. Don't you do this folly! ¹³ As for me, where would I carry my shame? And as for you, you will be as one of the fools in Israel. Now therefore, please speak to the king; for he will not withhold me from you." ¹⁴ However, he would not listen to her voice; but being stronger than she, he forced her and lay with her. ¹⁵ Then Amnon hated her with exceedingly great hatred; for the hatred with which he hated her was greater than the love with which he had loved her. Amnon said to her, "Arise, be gone!" ¹⁶ She said to him, "Not so, because this great wrong in sending me away is worse than the other that you did to me!" But he would not listen to her. ¹⁷ Then he called his servant who ministered to him, and said, "Now put this woman out from me, and bolt the door after her." ¹⁸ She had a garment of various colors on her, for the king's daughters who were virgins dressed in such robes. Then his servant brought her out and bolted the door after her. ¹⁹ Tamar put ashes on her head, and tore her garment of various colors that was on her; and she laid her hand on her head and went her way, crying aloud as she went. ²⁰ Absalom her brother said to her, "Has Amnon your brother been with you? But now hold your peace, my sister. He is your brother. Don't take this thing to heart." So Tamar remained desolate in her brother Absalom's house. ²¹ But when King David heard of all these things, he was very angry. ²² Absalom spoke to Amnon neither good nor bad; for Absalom hated Amnon, because he had forced his sister Tamar. ²³ After two full years, Absalom had sheep shearers in Baal Hazor, which is beside Ephraim; and Absalom invited all the king's sons. ²⁴ Absalom came to the king and said, "See now, your servant has sheep shearers. Please let the king and his servants go with your servant." ²⁵ The king said to Absalom, "No, my son, let's not all go, lest we be burdensome to you." He pressed him; however he would not go, but blessed him. ²⁶ Then Absalom said, "If not, please let my brother Amnon go with us." The king said to him, "Why should he go with you?" ²⁷ But Absalom pressed him, and he let Amnon and all the king's sons go with him. ²⁸ Absalom commanded his servants, saying, "Mark now, when Amnon's heart is merry with wine; and when I tell you, 'Strike Amnon,' then kill him. Don't be afraid. Haven't I commanded you? Be courageous, and be valiant!" ²⁹ The servants of Absalom did to Amnon as Absalom had commanded. Then all the king's sons arose, and every man got up on his mule and fled. ³⁰ While they were on the way, the news came to David, saying, "Absalom has slain all the king's sons, and there is not one of them left!" ³¹ Then the king arose, and tore his garments, and lay on the earth; and all his servants stood by with their clothes torn. ³² Jonadab the son of Shimeah, David's brother, answered, "Don't let my lord suppose that they have killed all the young men, the king's sons; for Amnon only is dead; for by the appointment of Absalom this has been determined from the day that he forced his sister Tamar. ³³ Now therefore don't let my lord the king take the thing to his heart, to think that all the king's sons are dead; for only Amnon is dead." ³⁴ But Absalom fled. The young man who kept the watch lifted up his eyes and looked, and behold, many people were coming by way of the hillside behind him. ³⁵ Jonadab said to the king, "Behold, the king's sons are coming! It is as your servant said." ³⁶ As soon as he had finished speaking, behold, the king's sons came, and lifted up their voices and wept. The king also and all his servants wept bitterly. ³⁷ But Absalom fled and went to Talmai the son of Ammihur, king of Geshur. David mourned for his son every day. ³⁸ So Absalom fled and went to Geshur, and was there three years. ³⁹ King David longed to go out to Absalom, for he was comforted concerning Amnon, since he was dead.

## 14

¹ Now Joab the son of Zeruiah perceived that the king's heart was toward Absalom. ² Joab sent to Tekoa and brought a wise woman from there, and said to her, "Please act like a mourner, and put on mourning clothing, please, and don't anoint yourself with oil; but be as a woman who has mourned a long time for the dead. ³ Go in to the king and speak like this to him." So Joab put the words in her mouth. ⁴ When the woman of Tekoa spoke to the king, she fell on her face to the ground, showed respect, and said, "Help, O king!" ⁵ The king said to her, "What ails you?" She answered, "Truly I am a widow, and my husband is dead. ⁶ Your servant had two sons; and they both fought together in the field, and there was no one to part them, but the one struck the other and killed him. ⁷ Behold, the whole family has risen against your servant, and they say, 'Deliver him who struck his brother, that we may kill him for the life of his brother whom he killed, and so destroy the heir also.'

Thus they would quench my coal which is left, and would leave to my husband neither name nor remainder on the surface of the earth." ⁸ The king said to the woman, "Go to your house, and I will give a command concerning you." ⁹ The woman of Tekoa said to the king, "My lord, O king, may the iniquity be on me, and on my father's house; and may the king and his throne be guiltless." ¹⁰ The king said, "Whoever says anything to you, bring him to me, and he will not bother you any more." ¹¹ Then she said, "Please let the king remember Yahweh your God, that the avenger of blood destroy not any more, lest they destroy my son." He said, "As Yahweh lives, not one hair of your son shall fall to the earth." ¹² Then the woman said, "Please let your servant speak a word to my lord the king." He said, "Say on." ¹³ The woman said, "Why then have you devised such a thing against the people of God? For in speaking this word the king is as one who is guilty, in that the king does not bring home again his banished one. ¹⁴ For we must die, and are like water spilled on the ground, which can't be gathered up again; neither does God take away life, but devises means, that he who is banished not be an outcast from him. ¹⁵ Now therefore, seeing that I have come to speak this word to my lord the king, it is because the people have made me afraid. Your servant said, 'I will now speak to the king; it may be that the king will perform the request of his servant.' ¹⁶ For the king will hear, to deliver his servant out of the hand of the man who would destroy me and my son together out of the inheritance of God. ¹⁷ Then your servant said, 'Please let the word of my lord the king bring rest; for as an angel of God, so is my lord the king to discern good and bad. May Yahweh, your God, be with you.'" ¹⁸ Then the king answered the woman, "Please don't hide anything from me that I ask you." The woman said, "Let my lord the king now speak." ¹⁹ The king said, "Is the hand of Joab with you in all this?" The woman answered, "As your soul lives, my lord the king, no one can turn to the right hand or to the left from anything that my lord the king has spoken; for your servant Joab urged me, and he put all these words in the mouth of your servant. ²⁰ Your servant Joab has done this thing to change the face of the matter. My lord is wise, according to the wisdom of an angel of God, to know all things that are in the earth." ²¹ The king said to Joab, "Behold now, I have granted this thing. Go therefore, and bring the young man Absalom back." ²² Joab fell to the ground on his face, showed respect, and blessed the king. Joab said, "Today your servant knows that I have found favor in your sight, my lord, O king, in that the king has performed the request of his servant." ²³ So Joab arose and went to Geshur, and brought Absalom to Jerusalem. ²⁴ The king said, "Let him return to his own house, but let him not see my face." So Absalom returned to his own house, and didn't see the king's face. ²⁵ Now in all Israel there was no one to be so much praised as Absalom for his beauty. From the sole of his foot even to the crown of his head there was no defect in him. ²⁶ When he cut the hair of his head (now it was at every year's end that he cut it; because it was heavy on him, therefore he cut it), he weighed the hair of his head at two hundred shekels,ᵃ after the king's weight. ²⁷ Three sons were born to Absalom, and one daughter, whose name was Tamar. She was a woman with a beautiful face. ²⁸ Absalom lived two full years in Jerusalem, and he didn't see the king's face. ²⁹ Then Absalom sent for Joab, to send him to the king, but he would not come to him. Then he sent again a second time, but he would not come. ³⁰ Therefore he said to his servants, "Behold, Joab's field is near mine, and he has barley there. Go and set it on fire." So Absalom's servants set the field on fire. ³¹ Then Joab arose and came to Absalom to his house, and said to him, "Why have your servants set my field on fire?" ³² Absalom answered Joab, "Behold, I sent to you, saying, 'Come here, that I may send you to the king, to say, "Why have I come from Geshur? It would be better for me to be there still. Now therefore, let me see the king's face; and if there is iniquity in me, let him kill me."'" ³³ So Joab came to the king and told him; and when he had called for Absalom, he came to the king and bowed himself on his face to the ground before the king; and the king kissed Absalom.

## 15

¹ After this, Absalom prepared a chariot and horses for himself, and fifty men to run before him. ² Absalom rose up early, and stood beside the way of the gate. When any man had a suit which should come to the king for judgment, then Absalom called to him, and said, "What city are you from?" He said, "Your servant is of one of the tribes of Israel." ³ Absalom said to him, "Behold, your matters are good and right; but there is no man deputized by the king to hear you." ⁴ Absalom said moreover, "Oh that I were made judge in the land, that every man who has any suit or cause might come to me, and I would do him justice!" ⁵ It was so, that when any man came near to bow down to him, he stretched out his hand, took hold of him, and kissed him. ⁶ Absalom did this sort of thing to all Israel who came to the king for judgment.

---

ᵃ 14:26 A shekel is about 10 grams or about 0.35 ounces, so | 200 shekels is about 2 kilograms or about 4.4 pounds.

So Absalom stole the hearts of the men of Israel. ⁷ At the end of forty years, Absalom said to the king, "Please let me go and pay my vow, which I have vowed to Yahweh, in Hebron. ⁸ For your servant vowed a vow while I stayed at Geshur in Syria, saying, 'If Yahweh shall indeed bring me again to Jerusalem, then I will serve Yahweh.'" ⁹ The king said to him, "Go in peace." So he arose and went to Hebron. ¹⁰ But Absalom sent spies throughout all the tribes of Israel, saying, "As soon as you hear the sound of the trumpet, then you shall say, 'Absalom is king in Hebron!'" ¹¹ Two hundred men went with Absalom out of Jerusalem, who were invited, and went in their simplicity; and they didn't know anything. ¹² Absalom sent for Ahithophel the Gilonite, David's counselor, from his city, even from Giloh, while he was offering the sacrifices. The conspiracy was strong, for the people increased continually with Absalom. ¹³ A messenger came to David, saying, "The hearts of the men of Israel are after Absalom." ¹⁴ David said to all his servants who were with him at Jerusalem, "Arise! Let's flee, or else none of us will escape from Absalom. Hurry to depart, lest he overtake us quickly and bring down evil on us, and strike the city with the edge of the sword." ¹⁵ The king's servants said to the king, "Behold, your servants are ready to do whatever my lord the king chooses." ¹⁶ The king went out, and all his household after him. The king left ten women, who were concubines, to keep the house. ¹⁷ The king went out, and all the people after him; and they stayed in Beth Merhak. ¹⁸ All his servants passed on beside him; and all the Cherethites, and all the Pelethites, and all the Gittites, six hundred men who came after him from Gath, passed on before the king. ¹⁹ Then the king said to Ittai the Gittite, "Why do you also go with us? Return, and stay with the king; for you are a foreigner and also an exile. Return to your own place. ²⁰ Whereas you came but yesterday, should I today make you go up and down with us, since I go where I may? Return, and take back your brothers. Mercy and truth be with you." ²¹ Ittai answered the king and said, "As Yahweh lives, and as my lord the king lives, surely in what place my lord the king is, whether for death or for life, your servant will be there also." ²² David said to Ittai, "Go and pass over." Ittai the Gittite passed over, and all his men, and all the little ones who were with him. ²³ All the country wept with a loud voice, and all the people passed over. The king also himself passed over the brook Kidron, and all the people passed over toward the way of the wilderness. ²⁴ Behold, Zadok also came, and all the Levites with him, bearing the ark of the covenant of God; and they set down God's ark; and Abiathar went up until all the people finished passing out of the city. ²⁵ The king said to Zadok, "Carry God's ark back into the city. If I find favor in Yahweh's eyes, he will bring me again, and show me both it and his habitation; ²⁶ but if he says, 'I have no delight in you,' behold, here I am. Let him do to me as seems good to him." ²⁷ The king said also to Zadok the priest, "Aren't you a seer? Return into the city in peace, and your two sons with you, Ahimaaz your son and Jonathan the son of Abiathar. ²⁸ Behold, I will stay at the fords of the wilderness until word comes from you to inform me." ²⁹ Zadok therefore and Abiathar carried God's ark to Jerusalem again; and they stayed there. ³⁰ David went up by the ascent of the Mount of Olives, and wept as he went up; and he had his head covered and went barefoot. All the people who were with him each covered his head, and they went up, weeping as they went up. ³¹ Someone told David, saying, "Ahithophel is among the conspirators with Absalom." David said, "Yahweh, please turn the counsel of Ahithophel into foolishness." ³² When David had come to the top, where God was worshiped, behold, Hushai the Archite came to meet him with his tunic torn and earth on his head. ³³ David said to him, "If you pass on with me, then you will be a burden to me; ³⁴ but if you return to the city, and tell Absalom, 'I will be your servant, O king. As I have been your father's servant in time past, so I will now be your servant; then will you defeat for me the counsel of Ahithophel.' ³⁵ Don't you have Zadok and Abiathar the priests there with you? Therefore whatever you hear out of the king's house, tell it to Zadok and Abiathar the priests. ³⁶ Behold, they have there with them their two sons, Ahimaaz, Zadok's son, and Jonathan, Abiathar's son. Send to me everything that you shall hear by them." ³⁷ So Hushai, David's friend, came into the city; and Absalom came into Jerusalem.

## 16

¹ When David was a little past the top, behold, Ziba the servant of Mephibosheth met him with a couple of donkeys saddled, and on them two hundred loaves of bread, and one hundred clusters of raisins, and one hundred summer fruits, and a container of wine. ² The king said to Ziba, "What do you mean by these?" Ziba said, "The donkeys are for the king's household to ride on; and the bread and summer fruit for the young men to eat; and the wine, that those who are faint in the wilderness may drink." ³ The king said, "Where is your master's son?" Ziba said to the king, "Behold, he is staying in Jerusalem; for he said, 'Today the house of Israel will restore me the kingdom of my father.'" ⁴ Then the king said to Ziba, "Behold, all that belongs to Mephibosheth

is yours." Ziba said, "I bow down. Let me find favor in your sight, my lord, O king." ⁵ When King David came to Bahurim, behold, a man of the family of Saul's house came out, whose name was Shimei, the son of Gera. He came out and cursed as he came. ⁶ He cast stones at David and at all the servants of King David, and all the people and all the mighty men were on his right hand and on his left. ⁷ Shimei said when he cursed, "Be gone, be gone, you man of blood, and wicked fellow! ⁸ Yahweh has returned on you all the blood of Saul's house, in whose place you have reigned! Yahweh has delivered the kingdom into the hand of Absalom your son! Behold, you are caught by your own mischief, because you are a man of blood!" ⁹ Then Abishai the son of Zeruiah said to the king, "Why should this dead dog curse my lord the king? Please let me go over and take off his head." ¹⁰ The king said, "What have I to do with you, you sons of Zeruiah? Because he curses, and because Yahweh has said to him, 'Curse David,' who then shall say, 'Why have you done so?'" ¹¹ David said to Abishai and to all his servants, "Behold, my son, who came out of my bowels, seeks my life. How much more this Benjamite, now? Leave him alone, and let him curse; for Yahweh has invited him. ¹² It may be that Yahweh will look on the wrong done to me, and that Yahweh will repay me good for the cursing of me today." ¹³ So David and his men went by the way; and Shimei went along on the hillside opposite him and cursed as he went, threw stones at him, and threw dust. ¹⁴ The king and all the people who were with him arrived weary; and he refreshed himself there. ¹⁵ Absalom and all the people, the men of Israel, came to Jerusalem, and Ahithophel with him. ¹⁶ When Hushai the Archite, David's friend, had come to Absalom, Hushai said to Absalom, "Long live the king! Long live the king!" ¹⁷ Absalom said to Hushai, "Is this your kindness to your friend? Why didn't you go with your friend?" ¹⁸ Hushai said to Absalom, "No; but whomever Yahweh and this people and all the men of Israel have chosen, I will be his, and I will stay with him. ¹⁹ Again, whom should I serve? Shouldn't I serve in the presence of his son? As I have served in your father's presence, so I will be in your presence." ²⁰ Then Absalom said to Ahithophel, "Give your counsel what we shall do." ²¹ Ahithophel said to Absalom, "Go in to your father's concubines that he has left to keep the house. Then all Israel will hear that you are abhorred by your father. Then the hands of all who are with you will be strong." ²² So they spread a tent for Absalom on the top of the house, and Absalom went in to his father's concubines in the sight of all Israel. ²³ The counsel of Ahithophel, which he gave in those days, was as if a man inquired at the inner sanctuary of God. All the counsel of Ahithophel was like this both with David and with Absalom.

## 17

¹ Moreover Ahithophel said to Absalom, "Let me now choose twelve thousand men, and I will arise and pursue after David tonight. ² I will come on him while he is weary and exhausted, and will make him afraid. All the people who are with him will flee. I will strike the king only, ³ and I will bring back all the people to you. The man whom you seek is as if all returned. All the people shall be in peace." ⁴ The saying pleased Absalom well, and all the elders of Israel. ⁵ Then Absalom said, "Now call Hushai the Archite also, and let's hear likewise what he says." ⁶ When Hushai had come to Absalom, Absalom spoke to him, saying, "Ahithophel has spoken like this. Shall we do what he says? If not, speak up." ⁷ Hushai said to Absalom, "The counsel that Ahithophel has given this time is not good." ⁸ Hushai said moreover, "You know your father and his men, that they are mighty men, and they are fierce in their minds, like a bear robbed of her cubs in the field. Your father is a man of war, and will not lodge with the people. ⁹ Behold, he is now hidden in some pit, or in some other place. It will happen, when some of them have fallen at the first, that whoever hears it will say, 'There is a slaughter among the people who follow Absalom!' ¹⁰ Even he who is valiant, whose heart is as the heart of a lion, will utterly melt; for all Israel knows that your father is a mighty man, and those who are with him are valiant men. ¹¹ But I counsel that all Israel be gathered together to you, from Dan even to Beersheba, as the sand that is by the sea for multitude; and that you go to battle in your own person. ¹² So we will come on him in some place where he will be found, and we will light on him as the dew falls on the ground, then we will not leave so much as one of him and of all the men who are with him. ¹³ Moreover, if he has gone into a city, then all Israel will bring ropes to that city, and we will draw it into the river, until there isn't one small stone found there." ¹⁴ Absalom and all the men of Israel said, "The counsel of Hushai the Archite is better than the counsel of Ahithophel." For Yahweh had ordained to defeat the good counsel of Ahithophel, to the intent that Yahweh might bring evil on Absalom. ¹⁵ Then Hushai said to Zadok and to Abiathar the priests, "Ahithophel counseled Absalom and the elders of Israel that way; and I have counseled this way. ¹⁶ Now therefore send quickly, and tell David, saying, 'Don't lodge tonight at the fords of the wilderness, but by all means pass over, lest the king be swallowed up, and all the people who are with him.'" ¹⁷ Now Jonathan

and Ahimaaz were staying by En Rogel; and a female servant used to go and report to them, and they went and told King David; for they couldn't risk being seen coming into the city. ¹⁸ But a boy saw them, and told Absalom. Then they both went away quickly and came to the house of a man in Bahurim, who had a well in his court; and they went down there. ¹⁹ The woman took and spread the covering over the well's mouth, and spread out crushed grain on it; and nothing was known. ²⁰ Absalom's servants came to the woman to the house; and they said, "Where are Ahimaaz and Jonathan?" The woman said to them, "They have gone over the brook of water." When they had sought and could not find them, they returned to Jerusalem. ²¹ After they had departed, they came up out of the well and went and told King David; and they said to David, "Arise and pass quickly over the water; for thus has Ahithophel counseled against you." ²² Then David arose, and all the people who were with him, and they passed over the Jordan. By the morning light there lacked not one of them who had not gone over the Jordan. ²³ When Ahithophel saw that his counsel was not followed, he saddled his donkey, arose, and went home to his city, set his house in order, and hanged himself; and he died, and was buried in the tomb of his father. ²⁴ Then David came to Mahanaim. Absalom passed over the Jordan, he and all the men of Israel with him. ²⁵ Absalom set Amasa over the army instead of Joab. Now Amasa was the son of a man whose name was Ithra the Israelite, who went in to Abigail the daughter of Nahash, sister to Zeruiah, Joab's mother. ²⁶ Israel and Absalom encamped in the land of Gilead. ²⁷ When David had come to Mahanaim, Shobi the son of Nahash of Rabbah of the children of Ammon, and Machir the son of Ammiel of Lodebar, and Barzillai the Gileadite of Rogelim, ²⁸ brought beds, basins, earthen vessels, wheat, barley, meal, parched grain, beans, lentils, roasted grain, ²⁹ honey, butter, sheep, and cheese of the herd, for David and for the people who were with him to eat; for they said, "The people are hungry, weary, and thirsty in the wilderness."

# 18

¹ David counted the people who were with him, and set captains of thousands and captains of hundreds over them. ² David sent the people out, a third part under the hand of Joab, and a third part under the hand of Abishai the son of Zeruiah, Joab's brother, and a third part under the hand of Ittai the Gittite. The king said to the people, "I will also surely go out with you myself." ³ But the people said, "You shall not go out, for if we flee away, they will not care for us, neither if half of us die, will they care for us. But you are worth ten thousand of us. Therefore now it is better that you are ready to help us out of the city." ⁴ The king said to them, "I will do what seems best to you." The king stood beside the gate, and all the people went out by hundreds and by thousands. ⁵ The king commanded Joab and Abishai and Ittai, saying, "Deal gently for my sake with the young man Absalom." All the people heard when the king commanded all the captains concerning Absalom. ⁶ So the people went out into the field against Israel; and the battle was in the forest of Ephraim. ⁷ The people of Israel were struck there before David's servants, and there was a great slaughter there that day of twenty thousand men. ⁸ For the battle was there spread over the surface of all the country, and the forest devoured more people that day than the sword devoured. ⁹ Absalom happened to meet David's servants. Absalom was riding on his mule, and the mule went under the thick boughs of a great oak; and his head caught hold of the oak, and he was hanging between the sky and earth; and the mule that was under him went on. ¹⁰ A certain man saw it, and told Joab, and said, "Behold, I saw Absalom hanging in an oak." ¹¹ Joab said to the man who told him, "Behold, you saw it, and why didn't you strike him there to the ground? I would have given you ten pieces of silver and a sash." ¹² The man said to Joab, "Though I should receive a thousand pieces of silver in my hand, I still wouldn't stretch out my hand against the king's son; for in our hearing the king commanded you and Abishai and Ittai, saying, 'Beware that no one touch the young man Absalom.' ¹³ Otherwise, if I had dealt falsely against his life (and there is no matter hidden from the king), then you yourself would have set yourself against me." ¹⁴ Then Joab said, "I'm not going to wait like this with you." He took three darts in his hand and thrust them through Absalom's heart while he was still alive in the middle of the oak. ¹⁵ Ten young men who bore Joab's armor surrounded and struck Absalom, and killed him. ¹⁶ Joab blew the trumpet, and the people returned from pursuing after Israel; for Joab held the people back. ¹⁷ They took Absalom and cast him into a great pit in the forest, and raised over him a very great heap of stones. Then all Israel fled, each to his own tent. ¹⁸ Now Absalom in his lifetime had taken and reared up for himself the pillar which is in the king's valley, for he said, "I have no son to keep my name in memory." He called the pillar after his own name. It is called Absalom's monument, to this day. ¹⁹ Then Ahimaaz the son of Zadok said, "Let me now run and carry the king news, how Yahweh has avenged him of his enemies." ²⁰ Joab said to him, "You must not be the bearer of news today, but you must carry

news another day. But today you must carry no news, because the king's son is dead." ²¹ Then Joab said to the Cushite, "Go, tell the king what you have seen!" The Cushite bowed himself to Joab, and ran. ²² Then Ahimaaz the son of Zadok said yet again to Joab, "But come what may, please let me also run after the Cushite." Joab said, "Why do you want to run, my son, since you will have no reward for the news?" ²³ "But come what may," he said, "I will run." He said to him, "Run!" Then Ahimaaz ran by the way of the Plain, and outran the Cushite. ²⁴ Now David was sitting between the two gates; and the watchman went up to the roof of the gate to the wall, and lifted up his eyes and looked, and, behold, a man running alone. ²⁵ The watchman shouted and told the king. The king said, "If he is alone, there is news in his mouth." He came closer and closer. ²⁶ The watchman saw another man running; and the watchman called to the gatekeeper and said, "Behold, a man running alone!" The king said, "He also brings news." ²⁷ The watchman said, "I think the running of the first one is like the running of Ahimaaz the son of Zadok." The king said, "He is a good man, and comes with good news." ²⁸ Ahimaaz called, and said to the king, "All is well." He bowed himself before the king with his face to the earth, and said, "Blessed is Yahweh your God, who has delivered up the men who lifted up their hand against my lord the king!" ²⁹ The king said, "Is it well with the young man Absalom?" Ahimaaz answered, "When Joab sent the king's servant, even me your servant, I saw a great tumult, but I don't know what it was." ³⁰ The king said, "Come and stand here." He came and stood still. ³¹ Behold, the Cushite came. The Cushite said, "Good news for my lord the king, for Yahweh has avenged you today of all those who rose up against you." ³² The king said to the Cushite, "Is it well with the young man Absalom?" The Cushite answered, "May the enemies of my lord the king, and all who rise up against you to do you harm, be as that young man is." ³³ The king was much moved, and went up to the room over the gate and wept. As he went, he said, "My son Absalom! My son, my son Absalom! I wish I had died instead of you, Absalom, my son, my son!"

# 19

¹ Joab was told, "Behold, the king weeps and mourns for Absalom." ² The victory that day was turned into mourning among all the people, for the people heard it said that day, "The king grieves for his son." ³ The people sneaked into the city that day, as people who are ashamed steal away when they flee in battle. ⁴ The king covered his face, and the king cried with a loud voice, "My son Absalom, Absalom, my son, my son!" ⁵ Joab came into the house to the king, and said, "Today you have shamed the faces of all your servants who today have saved your life, and the lives of your sons and of your daughters, and the lives of your wives, and the lives of your concubines; ⁶ in that you love those who hate you and hate those who love you. For you have declared today that princes and servants are nothing to you. For today I perceive that if Absalom had lived and we had all died today, then it would have pleased you well. ⁷ Now therefore arise, go out and speak to comfort your servants; for I swear by Yahweh, if you don't go out, not a man will stay with you this night. That would be worse to you than all the evil that has happened to you from your youth until now." ⁸ Then the king arose and sat in the gate. The people were all told, "Behold, the king is sitting in the gate." All the people came before the king. Now Israel had fled every man to his tent. ⁹ All the people were at strife throughout all the tribes of Israel, saying, "The king delivered us out of the hand of our enemies, and he saved us out of the hand of the Philistines; and now he has fled out of the land from Absalom. ¹⁰ Absalom, whom we anointed over us, is dead in battle. Now therefore why don't you speak a word of bringing the king back?" ¹¹ King David sent to Zadok and to Abiathar the priests, saying, "Speak to the elders of Judah, saying, 'Why are you the last to bring the king back to his house, since the speech of all Israel has come to the king, to return him to his house? ¹² You are my brothers. You are my bone and my flesh. Why then are you the last to bring back the king?' ¹³ Say to Amasa, 'Aren't you my bone and my flesh? God do so to me, and more also, if you aren't captain of the army before me continually instead of Joab.'" ¹⁴ He bowed the heart of all the men of Judah, even as one man, so that they sent to the king, saying, "Return, you and all your servants." ¹⁵ So the king returned, and came to the Jordan. Judah came to Gilgal, to go to meet the king, to bring the king over the Jordan. ¹⁶ Shimei the son of Gera, the Benjamite, who was of Bahurim, hurried and came down with the men of Judah to meet King David. ¹⁷ There were a thousand men of Benjamin with him, and Ziba the servant of Saul's house, and his fifteen sons and his twenty servants with him; and they went through the Jordan in the presence of the king. ¹⁸ A ferry boat went to bring over the king's household, and to do what he thought good. Shimei the son of Gera fell down before the king when he had come over the Jordan. ¹⁹ He said to the king, "Don't let my lord impute iniquity to me, or remember that which your servant did perversely the day that my lord the king went out of Jerusalem, that the king should take it to his heart.

<sup>20</sup> For your servant knows that I have sinned. Therefore behold, I have come today as the first of all the house of Joseph to go down to meet my lord the king." <sup>21</sup> But Abishai the son of Zeruiah answered, "Shouldn't Shimei be put to death for this, because he cursed Yahweh's anointed?" <sup>22</sup> David said, "What have I to do with you, you sons of Zeruiah, that you should be adversaries to me today? Shall any man be put to death today in Israel? For don't I know that I am king over Israel today?" <sup>23</sup> The king said to Shimei, "You will not die." The king swore to him. <sup>24</sup> Mephibosheth the son of Saul came down to meet the king; and he had neither groomed his feet, nor trimmed his beard, nor washed his clothes, from the day the king departed until the day he came home in peace. <sup>25</sup> When he had come to Jerusalem to meet the king, the king said to him, "Why didn't you go with me, Mephibosheth?" <sup>26</sup> He answered, "My lord, O king, my servant deceived me. For your servant said, 'I will saddle a donkey for myself, that I may ride on it and go with the king,' because your servant is lame. <sup>27</sup> He has slandered your servant to my lord the king, but my lord the king is as an angel of God. Therefore do what is good in your eyes. <sup>28</sup> For all my father's house were but dead men before my lord the king; yet you set your servant among those who ate at your own table. What right therefore have I yet that I should appeal any more to the king?" <sup>29</sup> The king said to him, "Why do you speak any more of your matters? I say, you and Ziba divide the land." <sup>30</sup> Mephibosheth said to the king, "Yes, let him take all, because my lord the king has come in peace to his own house." <sup>31</sup> Barzillai the Gileadite came down from Rogelim; and he went over the Jordan with the king to conduct him over the Jordan. <sup>32</sup> Now Barzillai was a very aged man, even eighty years old. He had provided the king with sustenance while he stayed at Mahanaim, for he was a very great man. <sup>33</sup> The king said to Barzillai, "Come over with me, and I will sustain you with me in Jerusalem." <sup>34</sup> Barzillai said to the king, "How many are the days of the years of my life, that I should go up with the king to Jerusalem? <sup>35</sup> I am eighty years old, today. Can I discern between good and bad? Can your servant taste what I eat or what I drink? Can I hear the voice of singing men and singing women any more? Why then should your servant be a burden to my lord the king? <sup>36</sup> Your servant will just go over the Jordan with the king. Why should the king repay me with such a reward? <sup>37</sup> Please let your servant turn back again, that I may die in my own city, by the grave of my father and my mother. But behold, your servant Chimham; let him go over with my lord the king; and do to him what shall seem good to you." <sup>38</sup> The king answered, "Chimham shall go over with me, and I will do to him that which shall seem good to you. Whatever you request of me, that I will do for you." <sup>39</sup> All the people went over the Jordan, and the king went over. Then the king kissed Barzillai and blessed him; and he returned to his own place. <sup>40</sup> So the king went over to Gilgal, and Chimham went over with him. All the people of Judah brought the king over, and also half the people of Israel. <sup>41</sup> Behold, all the men of Israel came to the king, and said to the king, "Why have our brothers the men of Judah stolen you away, and brought the king and his household, over the Jordan, and all David's men with him?" <sup>42</sup> All the men of Judah answered the men of Israel, "Because the king is a close relative to us. Why then are you angry about this matter? Have we eaten at all at the king's cost? Or has he given us any gift?" <sup>43</sup> The men of Israel answered the men of Judah, and said, "We have ten parts in the king, and we have also more claim to David than you. Why then did you despise us, that our advice should not be first had in bringing back our king?" The words of the men of Judah were fiercer than the words of the men of Israel.

## 20

<sup>1</sup> There happened to be there a wicked fellow, whose name was Sheba the son of Bichri, a Benjamite; and he blew the trumpet, and said, "We have no portion in David, neither have we inheritance in the son of Jesse. Every man to his tents, Israel!" <sup>2</sup> So all the men of Israel went up from following David, and followed Sheba the son of Bichri; but the men of Judah joined with their king, from the Jordan even to Jerusalem. <sup>3</sup> David came to his house at Jerusalem; and the king took the ten women his concubines, whom he had left to keep the house, and put them in custody and provided them with sustenance, but didn't go in to them. So they were shut up to the day of their death, living in widowhood. <sup>4</sup> Then the king said to Amasa, "Call me the men of Judah together within three days, and be here present." <sup>5</sup> So Amasa went to call the men of Judah together, but he stayed longer than the set time which had been appointed to him. <sup>6</sup> David said to Abishai, "Now Sheba the son of Bichri will do us more harm than Absalom did. Take your lord's servants and pursue after him, lest he get himself fortified cities, and escape out of our sight." <sup>7</sup> Joab's men went out after him with the Cherethites, the Pelethites, and all the mighty men; and they went out of Jerusalem to pursue Sheba the son of Bichri. <sup>8</sup> When they were at the great stone which is in Gibeon, Amasa came to meet them. Joab was clothed in his apparel of war that he had put on, and on it was a sash

with a sword fastened on his waist in its sheath; and as he went along it fell out. <sup>9</sup> Joab said to Amasa, "Is it well with you, my brother?" Joab took Amasa by the beard with his right hand to kiss him. <sup>10</sup> But Amasa took no heed to the sword that was in Joab's hand. So he struck him with it in the body and shed out his bowels to the ground, and didn't strike him again; and he died. Joab and Abishai his brother pursued Sheba the son of Bichri. <sup>11</sup> One of Joab's young men stood by him, and said, "He who favors Joab, and he who is for David, let him follow Joab!" <sup>12</sup> Amasa lay wallowing in his blood in the middle of the highway. When the man saw that all the people stood still, he carried Amasa out of the highway into the field, and cast a garment over him when he saw that everyone who came by him stood still. <sup>13</sup> When he was removed out of the highway, all the people went on after Joab to pursue Sheba the son of Bichri. <sup>14</sup> He went through all the tribes of Israel to Abel, to Beth Maacah, and all the Berites. They were gathered together, and went also after him. <sup>15</sup> They came and besieged him in Abel of Beth Maacah, and they cast up a mound against the city, and it stood against the rampart; and all the people who were with Joab battered the wall to throw it down. <sup>16</sup> Then a wise woman cried out of the city, "Hear, hear! Please say to Joab, 'Come near here, that I may speak with you.'" <sup>17</sup> He came near to her; and the woman said, "Are you Joab?" He answered, "I am." Then she said to him, "Hear the words of your servant." He answered, "I'm listening." <sup>18</sup> Then she spoke, saying, "They used to say in old times, 'They shall surely ask counsel at Abel,' and so they settled a matter. <sup>19</sup> I am among those who are peaceable and faithful in Israel. You seek to destroy a city and a mother in Israel. Why will you swallow up Yahweh's inheritance?" <sup>20</sup> Joab answered, "Far be it, far be it from me, that I should swallow up or destroy. <sup>21</sup> The matter is not so. But a man of the hill country of Ephraim, Sheba the son of Bichri by name, has lifted up his hand against the king, even against David. Just deliver him, and I will depart from the city." The woman said to Joab, "Behold, his head will be thrown to you over the wall." <sup>22</sup> Then the woman went to all the people in her wisdom. They cut off the head of Sheba the son of Bichri, and threw it out to Joab. He blew the trumpet, and they were dispersed from the city, every man to his tent. Then Joab returned to Jerusalem to the king. <sup>23</sup> Now Joab was over all the army of Israel, Benaiah the son of Jehoiada was over the Cherethites and over the Pelethites, <sup>24</sup> Adoram was over the men subject to forced labor, Jehoshaphat the son of Ahilud was the recorder, <sup>25</sup> Sheva was scribe, Zadok and Abiathar were priests, <sup>26</sup> and Ira the Jairite was chief minister to David.

## 21

<sup>1</sup> There was a famine in the days of David for three years, year after year; and David sought the face of Yahweh. Yahweh said, "It is for Saul, and for his bloody house, because he put the Gibeonites to death." <sup>2</sup> The king called the Gibeonites and said to them (now the Gibeonites were not of the children of Israel, but of the remnant of the Amorites, and the children of Israel had sworn to them; and Saul sought to kill them in his zeal for the children of Israel and Judah); <sup>3</sup> and David said to the Gibeonites, "What should I do for you? And with what should I make atonement, that you may bless Yahweh's inheritance?" <sup>4</sup> The Gibeonites said to him, "It is no matter of silver or gold between us and Saul or his house; neither is it for us to put any man to death in Israel." He said, "I will do for you whatever you say." <sup>5</sup> They said to the king, "The man who consumed us and who plotted against us, that we should be destroyed from remaining in any of the borders of Israel, <sup>6</sup> let seven men of his sons be delivered to us, and we will hang them up to Yahweh in Gibeah of Saul, the chosen of Yahweh." The king said, "I will give them." <sup>7</sup> But the king spared Mephibosheth the son of Jonathan the son of Saul, because of Yahweh's oath that was between them, between David and Jonathan the son of Saul. <sup>8</sup> But the king took the two sons of Rizpah the daughter of Aiah, whom she bore to Saul, Armoni and Mephibosheth; and the five sons of Merab the daughter of Saul, whom she bore to Adriel the son of Barzillai the Meholathite. <sup>9</sup> He delivered them into the hands of the Gibeonites; and they hanged them on the mountain before Yahweh, and all seven of them fell together. They were put to death in the days of harvest, in the first days, at the beginning of barley harvest. <sup>10</sup> Rizpah the daughter of Aiah took sackcloth and spread it for herself on the rock, from the beginning of harvest until water poured on them from the sky. She allowed neither the birds of the sky to rest on them by day, nor the animals of the field by night. <sup>11</sup> David was told what Rizpah the daughter of Aiah, the concubine of Saul, had done. <sup>12</sup> So David went and took the bones of Saul and the bones of Jonathan his son from the men of Jabesh Gilead, who had stolen them from the street of Beth Shan, where the Philistines had hanged them in the day that the Philistines killed Saul in Gilboa; <sup>13</sup> and he brought up from there the bones of Saul and the bones of Jonathan his son. They also gathered the bones of those who were hanged. <sup>14</sup> They buried the bones of Saul and Jonathan his son in the country of Benjamin in Zela, in the tomb of Kish his father; and they

performed all that the king commanded. After that, God answered prayer for the land. [15] The Philistines had war again with Israel; and David went down, and his servants with him, and fought against the Philistines. David grew faint; [16] and Ishbibenob, who was of the sons of the giant, the weight of whose spear was three hundred shekels of bronze in weight, he being armed with a new sword, thought he would kill David. [17] But Abishai the son of Zeruiah helped him, and struck the Philistine and killed him. Then the men of David swore to him, saying, "Don't go out with us to battle any more, so that you don't quench the lamp of Israel." [18] After this, there was again war with the Philistines at Gob. Then Sibbecai the Hushathite killed Saph, who was of the sons of the giant. [19] There was again war with the Philistines at Gob, and Elhanan the son of Jaare-Oregim the Bethlehemite killed Goliath the Gittite's brother, the staff of whose spear was like a weaver's beam. [20] There was again war at Gath, where there was a man of great stature, who had six fingers on every hand and six toes on every foot, twenty-four in number, and he also was born to the giant. [21] When he defied Israel, Jonathan the son of Shimei, David's brother, killed him. [22] These four were born to the giant in Gath; and they fell by the hand of David and by the hand of his servants.

## 22

[1] David spoke to Yahweh the words of this song in the day that Yahweh delivered him out of the hand of all his enemies, and out of the hand of Saul, [2] and he said: "Yahweh is my rock, my fortress, and my deliverer, even mine; [3] God is my rock in whom I take refuge; my shield, and the horn of my salvation, my high tower, and my refuge. My savior, you save me from violence. [4] I call on Yahweh, who is worthy to be praised; So shall I be saved from my enemies. [5] For the waves of death surrounded me. The floods of ungodliness made me afraid. [6] The cords of Sheol[a] were around me. The snares of death caught me. [7] In my distress, I called on Yahweh. Yes, I called to my God. He heard my voice out of his temple. My cry came into his ears. [8] Then the earth shook and trembled. The foundations of heaven quaked and were shaken, because he was angry. [9] Smoke went up out of his nostrils. Consuming fire came out of his mouth. Coals were kindled by it. [10] He bowed the heavens also, and came down. Thick darkness was under his feet. [11] He rode on a cherub, and flew. Yes, he was seen on the wings of the wind. [12] He made darkness a shelter around himself, gathering of waters, and thick clouds of the skies. [13] At the brightness before him, coals of fire were kindled. [14] Yahweh thundered from heaven. The Most High uttered his voice. [15] He sent out arrows and scattered them, lightning and confused them. [16] Then the channels of the sea appeared. The foundations of the world were laid bare by Yahweh's rebuke, at the blast of the breath of his nostrils. [17] He sent from on high and he took me. He drew me out of many waters. [18] He delivered me from my strong enemy, from those who hated me, for they were too mighty for me. [19] They came on me in the day of my calamity, but Yahweh was my support. [20] He also brought me out into a large place. He delivered me, because he delighted in me. [21] Yahweh rewarded me according to my righteousness. He rewarded me according to the cleanness of my hands. [22] For I have kept Yahweh's ways, and have not wickedly departed from my God. [23] For all his ordinances were before me. As for his statutes, I didn't depart from them. [24] I was also perfect toward him. I kept myself from my iniquity. [25] Therefore Yahweh has rewarded me according to my righteousness, According to my cleanness in his eyesight. [26] With the merciful you will show yourself merciful. With the perfect man you will show yourself perfect. [27] With the pure you will show yourself pure. With the crooked you will show yourself shrewd. [28] You will save the afflicted people, but your eyes are on the arrogant, that you may bring them down. [29] For you are my lamp, Yahweh. Yahweh will light up my darkness. [30] For by you, I run against a troop. By my God, I leap over a wall. [31] As for God, his way is perfect. Yahweh's word is tested. He is a shield to all those who take refuge in him. [32] For who is God, besides Yahweh? Who is a rock, besides our God? [33] God is my strong fortress. He makes my way perfect. [34] He makes my feet like hinds' feet, and sets me on my high places. [35] He teaches my hands to war, so that my arms bend a bow of bronze. [36] You have also given me the shield of your salvation. Your gentleness has made me great. [37] You have enlarged my steps under me. My feet have not slipped. [38] I have pursued my enemies and destroyed them. I didn't turn again until they were consumed. [39] I have consumed them, and struck them through, so that they can't arise. Yes, they have fallen under my feet. [40] For you have armed me with strength for the battle. You have subdued under me those who rose up against me. [41] You have also made my enemies turn their backs to me, that I might cut off those who hate me. [42] They looked, but there was no one to save; even to Yahweh, but he didn't answer them. [43] Then I beat them as small as the dust of the earth. I crushed them as the mire of the streets, and spread them abroad. [44] You also have delivered me from the strivings of my people. You have kept me to be the head of the nations. A people whom I have not known will serve me. [45] The foreigners will submit themselves to me. As soon as they hear of me, they will obey me. [46] The foreigners will fade away, and will come trembling out of their close places. [47] Yahweh lives! Blessed be my rock! Exalted be God, the rock of my salvation, [48] even the God who executes vengeance for me, who brings down peoples under me, [49] who brings me away from my enemies. Yes, you lift me up above those who rise up against me. You deliver me from the violent man. [50] Therefore I will give thanks to you, Yahweh, among the nations, and will sing praises to your name. [51] He gives great deliverance to his king, and shows loving kindness to his anointed, to David and to his offspring, forever more."

## 23

[1] Now these are the last words of David. David the son of Jesse says, the man who was raised on high says, the anointed of the God of Jacob, the sweet psalmist of Israel: [2] "Yahweh's Spirit spoke by me. His word was on my tongue. [3] The God of Israel said, the Rock of Israel spoke to me, 'One who rules over men righteously, who rules in the fear of God, [4] shall be as the light of the morning when the sun rises, a morning without clouds, when the tender grass springs out of the earth, through clear shining after rain.' [5] Isn't my house so with God? Yet he has made with me an everlasting covenant, ordered in all things, and sure, for it is all my salvation and all my desire. Won't he make it grow? [6] But all the ungodly will be as thorns to be thrust away, because they can't be taken with the hand. [7] The man who touches them must be armed with iron and the staff of a spear. They will be utterly burned with fire in their place." [8] These are the names of the mighty men whom David had: Josheb Basshebeth a Tahchemonite, chief of the captains; he was called Adino the Eznite, who killed eight hundred at one time. [9] After him was Eleazar the son of Dodai the son of an Ahohite, one of the three mighty men with David when they defied the Philistines who were there gathered together to battle, and the men of Israel had gone away. [10] He arose and struck the Philistines until his hand was weary, and his hand froze to the sword; and Yahweh worked a great victory that day; and the people returned after him only to take plunder. [11] After him was Shammah the son of Agee a Hararite. The Philistines had gathered together into a troop where there was a plot of ground full of lentils; and the people fled from the Philistines. [12] But he stood in the middle of the plot and defended it, and killed the Philistines; and Yahweh worked a great victory. [13] Three of the thirty chief men went down, and came to David in the harvest time to the cave of Adullam; and the troop of the Philistines was encamped in the valley of Rephaim. [14] David was then in the stronghold; and the garrison of the Philistines was then in Bethlehem. [15] David said longingly, "Oh that someone would give me water to drink from the well of Bethlehem, which is by the gate!" [16] The three mighty men broke through the army of the Philistines, and drew water out of the well of Bethlehem that was by the gate and took it and brought it to David; but he would not drink of it, but poured it out to Yahweh. [17] He said, "Be it far from me, Yahweh, that I should do this! Isn't this the blood of the men who risked their lives to go?" Therefore he would not drink it. The three mighty men did these things. [18] Abishai, the brother of Joab, the son of Zeruiah, was chief of the three. He lifted up his spear against three hundred and killed them, and had a name among the three. [19] Wasn't he most honorable of the three? Therefore he was made their captain. However he wasn't included as one of the three. [20] Benaiah the son of Jehoiada, the son of a valiant man of Kabzeel, who had done mighty deeds, killed the two sons of Ariel of Moab. He also went down and killed a lion in the middle of a pit in a time of snow. [21] He killed a huge Egyptian, and the Egyptian had a spear in his hand; but he went down to him with a staff and plucked the spear out of the Egyptian's hand, and killed him with his own spear. [22] Benaiah the son of Jehoiada did these things, and had a name among the three mighty men. [23] He was more honorable than the thirty, but he didn't attain to the three. David set him over his guard. [24] Asahel the brother of Joab was one of the thirty: Elhanan the son of Dodo of Bethlehem, [25] Shammah the Harodite, Elika the Harodite, [26] Helez the Paltite, Ira the son of Ikkesh the Tekoite, [27] Abiezer the Anathothite, Mebunnai the Hushathite, [28] Zalmon the Ahohite, Maharai the Netophathite, [29] Heleb the son of Baanah the Netophathite, Ittai the son of Ribai of Gibeah of the children of Benjamin, [30] Benaiah a Pirathonite, Hiddai of the brooks of Gaash. [31] Abialbon the Arbathite, Azmaveth the Barhumite, [32] Eliahba the Shaalbonite, the sons of Jashen, Jonathan, [33] Shammah the Hararite, Ahiam the son of Sharar the Ararite, [34] Eliphelet the son of Ahasbai, the son of the Maacathite, Eliam the son of Ahithophel the Gilonite, [35] Hezro the Carmelite, Paarai

the Arbite, [36] Igal the son of Nathan of Zobah, Bani the Gadite, [37] Zelek the Ammonite, Naharai the Beerothite, armor bearers to Joab the son of Zeruiah, [38] Ira the Ithrite, Gareb the Ithrite, [39] and Uriah the Hittite: thirty-seven in all.

## 24

[1] Again Yahweh's anger burned against Israel, and he moved David against them, saying, "Go, count Israel and Judah." [2] The king said to Joab the captain of the army, who was with him, "Now go back and forth through all the tribes of Israel, from Dan even to Beersheba, and count the people, that I may know the sum of the people." [3] Joab said to the king, "Now may Yahweh your God add to the people, however many they may be, one hundred times; and may the eyes of my lord the king see it. But why does my lord the king delight in this thing?" [4] Notwithstanding, the king's word prevailed against Joab and against the captains of the army. Joab and the captains of the army went out from the presence of the king to count the people of Israel. [5] They passed over the Jordan and encamped in Aroer, on the right side of the city that is in the middle of the valley of Gad, and to Jazer; [6] then they came to Gilead and to the land of Tahtim Hodshi; and they came to Dan Jaan and around to Sidon, [7] and came to the stronghold of Tyre, and to all the cities of the Hivites and of the Canaanites; and they went out to the south of Judah, at Beersheba. [8] So when they had gone back and forth through all the land, they came to Jerusalem at the end of nine months and twenty days. [9] Joab gave up the sum of the counting of the people to the king; and there were in Israel eight hundred thousand valiant men who drew the sword, and the men of Judah were five hundred thousand men. [10] David's heart struck him after he had counted the people. David said to Yahweh, "I have sinned greatly in that which I have done. But now, Yahweh, put away, I beg you, the iniquity of your servant; for I have done very foolishly." [11] When David rose up in the morning, Yahweh's word came to the prophet Gad, David's seer, saying, [12] "Go and speak to David, 'Yahweh says, "I offer you three things. Choose one of them, that I may do it to you."'" [13] So Gad came to David, and told him, saying, "Shall seven years of famine come to you in your land? Or will you flee three months before your foes while they pursue you? Or shall there be three days' pestilence in your land? Now answer, and consider what answer I shall return to him who sent me." [14] David said to Gad, "I am in distress. Let us fall now into Yahweh's hand, for his mercies are great. Let me not fall into man's hand." [15] So Yahweh sent a pestilence on Israel from the morning even to the appointed time; and seventy thousand men died of the people from Dan even to Beersheba. [16] When the angel stretched out his hand toward Jerusalem to destroy it, Yahweh relented of the disaster, and said to the angel who destroyed the people, "It is enough. Now withdraw your hand." Yahweh's angel was by the threshing floor of Araunah the Jebusite. [17] David spoke to Yahweh when he saw the angel who struck the people, and said, "Behold, I have sinned, and I have done perversely; but these sheep, what have they done? Please let your hand be against me, and against my father's house." [18] Gad came that day to David and said to him, "Go up, build an altar to Yahweh on the threshing floor of Araunah the Jebusite." [19] David went up according to the saying of Gad, as Yahweh commanded. [20] Araunah looked out, and saw the king and his servants coming on toward him. Then Araunah went out and bowed himself before the king with his face to the ground. [21] Araunah said, "Why has my lord the king come to his servant?" David said, "To buy your threshing floor, to build an altar to Yahweh, that the plague may be stopped from afflicting the people." [22] Araunah said to David, "Let my lord the king take and offer up what seems good to him. Behold, the cattle for the burnt offering, and the threshing sledges and the yokes of the oxen for the wood. [23] All this, O king, does Araunah give to the king." Araunah said to the king, "May Yahweh your God accept you." [24] The king said to Araunah, "No, but I will most certainly buy it from you for a price. I will not offer burnt offerings to Yahweh my God which cost me nothing." So David bought the threshing floor and the oxen for fifty shekels[a] of silver. [25] David built an altar to Yahweh there, and offered burnt offerings and peace offerings. So Yahweh was entreated for the land, and the plague was removed from Israel.

## The First Book of Kings

### 1

[1] Now King David was old and advanced in years; and they covered him with clothes, but he couldn't keep warm. [2] Therefore his servants said to him, "Let a young virgin be sought for my lord the king. Let her stand before the king, and cherish him; and let her lie in your bosom, that my lord the king may keep warm." [3] So they sought for a beautiful young lady throughout all the borders of Israel, and found Abishag the Shunammite, and brought her to the king. [4] The young lady was very beautiful; and she cherished the king, and served him; but the king didn't know her intimately. [5] Then Adonijah the son of Haggith exalted himself, saying, "I will be king." Then he prepared him chariots and horsemen, and fifty men to run before him. [6] His father had not displeased him at any time in saying, "Why have you done so?" and he was also a very handsome man; and he was born after Absalom. [7] He conferred with Joab the son of Zeruiah and with Abiathar the priest; and they followed Adonijah and helped him. [8] But Zadok the priest, Benaiah the son of Jehoiada, Nathan the prophet, Shimei, Rei, and the mighty men who belonged to David, were not with Adonijah. [9] Adonijah killed sheep, cattle, and fatlings by the stone of Zoheleth, which is beside En Rogel; and he called all his brothers, the king's sons, and all the men of Judah, the king's servants; [10] but he didn't call Nathan the prophet, and Benaiah, and the mighty men, and Solomon his brother. [11] Then Nathan spoke to Bathsheba the mother of Solomon, saying, "Haven't you heard that Adonijah the son of Haggith reigns, and David our lord doesn't know it? [12] Now therefore come, please let me give you counsel, that you may save your own life and your son Solomon's life. [13] Go in to King David, and tell him, 'Didn't you, my lord the king, swear to your servant, saying, "Assuredly Solomon your son shall reign after me, and he shall sit on my throne"? Why then does Adonijah reign?' [14] Behold,[b] while you are still talking there with the king, I will also come in after you and confirm your words." [15] Bathsheba went in to the king in his room. The king was very old; and Abishag the Shunammite was serving the king. [16] Bathsheba bowed and showed respect to the king. The king said, "What would you like?" [17] She said to him, "My lord, you swore by Yahweh[c] your God[d] to your servant, 'Assuredly Solomon your son shall reign after me, and he shall sit on my throne.' [18] Now, behold, Adonijah reigns; and you, my lord the king, don't know it. [19] He has slain cattle and fatlings and sheep in abundance, and has called all the sons of the king, Abiathar the priest, and Joab the captain of the army; but he hasn't called Solomon your servant. [20] You, my lord the king, the eyes of all Israel are on you, that you should tell them who will sit on the throne of my lord the king after him. [21] Otherwise it will happen, when my lord the king sleeps with his fathers, that I and my son Solomon will be considered criminals." [22] Behold, while she was still talking with the king, Nathan the prophet came in. [23] They told the king, saying, "Behold, Nathan the prophet!" When he had come in before the king, he bowed himself before the king with his face to the ground. [24] Nathan said, "My lord, King, have you said, 'Adonijah shall reign after me, and he shall sit on my throne'? [25] For he has gone down today, and has slain cattle, fatlings, and sheep in abundance, and has called all the king's sons, the captains of the army, and Abiathar the priest. Behold, they are eating and drinking before him, and saying, 'Long live King Adonijah!' [26] But he hasn't called me, even me your servant, Zadok the priest, Benaiah the son of Jehoiada, and your servant Solomon. [27] Was this thing done by my lord the king, and you haven't shown to your servants who should sit on the throne of my lord the king after him?" [28] Then King David answered, "Call Bathsheba in to me." She came into the king's presence and stood before the king. [29] The king vowed and said, "As Yahweh lives, who has redeemed my soul out of all adversity, [30] most certainly as I swore to you by Yahweh, the God of Israel, saying, 'Assuredly Solomon your son shall reign after me, and he shall sit on my throne in my place;' I will most certainly do this today." [31] Then Bathsheba bowed with her face to the earth and showed respect to the king, and said, "Let my lord King David live forever!" [32] King David said, "Call to me Zadok the priest, Nathan the prophet, and Benaiah the son of Jehoiada." They came before the king. [33] The king said to them, "Take with you the servants of your lord, and cause Solomon my son to ride on my own mule, and bring him down to Gihon. [34] Let Zadok the priest and Nathan the prophet anoint him there king over Israel. Blow the trumpet, and say, 'Long live King Solomon!' [35] Then come up after him, and he shall come and sit on my throne; for he shall be king in my place. I have appointed him to be prince over Israel and over Judah." [36] Benaiah the son of Jehoiada answered the king, and said, "Amen. May Yahweh, the God of my lord the king, say so. [37] As Yahweh has been with my lord the king, even so may he be with Solomon, and make his throne greater than the throne of my lord King David." [38] So Zadok the priest, Nathan the prophet, Benaiah the son of Jehoiada, and the Cherethites and the Pelethites went down and had Solomon ride on King David's mule, and

---

[a] *24:24* A shekel is about 10 grams or about 0.35 ounces, so 50 shekels is about 0.5 kilograms or 1.1 pounds.

[b] *1:14* "Behold", from "הִנֵּה", means look at, take notice, observe, see, or gaze at. It is often used as an interjection.

[c] *1:17* "Yahweh" is God's proper Name, sometimes rendered "LORD" (all caps) in other translations.

[d] *1:17* The Hebrew word rendered "God" is "אֱלֹהִים" (Elohim).

brought him to Gihon. <sup>39</sup> Zadok the priest took the horn of oil from the Tent, and anointed Solomon. They blew the trumpet; and all the people said, "Long live King Solomon!" <sup>40</sup> All the people came up after him, and the people piped with pipes, and rejoiced with great joy, so that the earth shook with their sound. <sup>41</sup> Adonijah and all the guests who were with him heard it as they had finished eating. When Joab heard the sound of the trumpet, he said, "Why is this noise of the city being in an uproar?" <sup>42</sup> While he yet spoke, behold, Jonathan the son of Abiathar the priest came; and Adonijah said, "Come in; for you are a worthy man, and bring good news." <sup>43</sup> Jonathan answered Adonijah, "Most certainly our lord King David has made Solomon king. <sup>44</sup> The king has sent with him Zadok the priest, Nathan the prophet, Benaiah the son of Jehoiada, and the Cherethites and the Pelethites; and they have caused him to ride on the king's mule. <sup>45</sup> Zadok the priest and Nathan the prophet have anointed him king in Gihon. They have come up from there rejoicing, so that the city rang again. This is the noise that you have heard. <sup>46</sup> Also, Solomon sits on the throne of the kingdom. <sup>47</sup> Moreover the king's servants came to bless our lord King David, saying, 'May your God make the name of Solomon better than your name, and make his throne greater than your throne;' and the king bowed himself on the bed. <sup>48</sup> Also thus said the king, 'Blessed be Yahweh, the God of Israel, who has given one to sit on my throne today, my eyes even seeing it.'" <sup>49</sup> All the guests of Adonijah were afraid, and rose up, and each man went his way. <sup>50</sup> Adonijah was afraid because of Solomon; and he arose, and went, and hung onto the horns of the altar. <sup>51</sup> Solomon was told, "Behold, Adonijah fears King Solomon; for, behold, he is hanging onto the horns of the altar, saying, 'Let King Solomon swear to me first that he will not kill his servant with the sword.'" <sup>52</sup> Solomon said, "If he shows himself a worthy man, not a hair of his shall fall to the earth; but if wickedness is found in him, he shall die." <sup>53</sup> So King Solomon sent, and they brought him down from the altar. He came and bowed down to King Solomon; and Solomon said to him, "Go to your house."

## 2

<sup>1</sup> Now the days of David came near that he should die; and he commanded Solomon his son, saying, <sup>2</sup>"I am going the way of all the earth. You be strong therefore, and show yourself a man; <sup>3</sup> and keep the instruction of Yahweh your God, to walk in his ways, to keep his statutes, his commandments, his ordinances, and his testimonies, according to that which is written in the law of Moses, that you may prosper in all that you do and wherever you turn yourself. <sup>4</sup> Then Yahweh may establish his word which he spoke concerning me, saying, 'If your children are careful of their way, to walk before me in truth with all their heart and with all their soul, there shall not fail you,' he said, 'a man on the throne of Israel.' <sup>5</sup>"Moreover you know also what Joab the son of Zeruiah did to me, even what he did to the two captains of the armies of Israel, to Abner the son of Ner and to Amasa the son of Jether, whom he killed, and shed the blood of war in peace, and put the blood of war on his sash that was around his waist and in his sandals that were on his feet. <sup>6</sup> Do therefore according to your wisdom, and don't let his gray head go down to Sheol<sup>a</sup> in peace. <sup>7</sup> But show kindness to the sons of Barzillai the Gileadite, and let them be among those who eat at your table; for so they came to me when I fled from Absalom your brother. <sup>8</sup>"Behold, there is with you Shimei the son of Gera, the Benjamite of Bahurim, who cursed me with a grievous curse in the day when I went to Mahanaim; but he came down to meet me at the Jordan, and I swore to him by Yahweh, saying, 'I will not put you to death with the sword.' <sup>9</sup> Now therefore don't hold him guiltless, for you are a wise man; and you will know what you ought to do to him, and you shall bring his gray head down to Sheol<sup>b</sup> with blood." <sup>10</sup> David slept with his fathers, and was buried in David's city. <sup>11</sup> The days that David reigned over Israel were forty years; he reigned seven years in Hebron, and he reigned thirty-three years in Jerusalem. <sup>12</sup> Solomon sat on David his father's throne; and his kingdom was firmly established. <sup>13</sup> Then Adonijah the son of Haggith came to Bathsheba the mother of Solomon. She said, "Do you come peaceably?" He said, "Peaceably. <sup>14</sup> He said moreover, I have something to tell you." She said, "Say on." <sup>15</sup> He said, "You know that the kingdom was mine, and that all Israel set their faces on me, that I should reign. However, the kingdom is turned around, and has become my brother's; for it was his from Yahweh. <sup>16</sup> Now I ask one petition of you. Don't deny me." She said to him, "Say on." <sup>17</sup> He said, "Please speak to Solomon the king (for he will not tell you 'no'), that he give me Abishag the Shunammite as wife." <sup>18</sup> Bathsheba said, "All right. I will speak for you to the king." <sup>19</sup> Bathsheba therefore went to King Solomon, to speak to him for Adonijah. The king rose up to meet her and bowed himself to her, and sat down on his throne and caused a throne to be set for the king's

mother; and she sat on his right hand. <sup>20</sup> Then she said, "I ask one small petition of you; don't deny me." The king said to her, "Ask on, my mother, for I will not deny you." <sup>21</sup> She said, "Let Abishag the Shunammite be given to Adonijah your brother as wife." <sup>22</sup> King Solomon answered his mother, "Why do you ask Abishag the Shunammite for Adonijah? Ask for him the kingdom also, for he is my elder brother; even for him, and for Abiathar the priest, and for Joab the son of Zeruiah." <sup>23</sup> Then King Solomon swore by Yahweh, saying, "God do so to me, and more also, if Adonijah has not spoken this word against his own life. <sup>24</sup> Now therefore as Yahweh lives, who has established me and set me on my father David's throne, and who has made me a house as he promised, surely Adonijah shall be put to death today." <sup>25</sup> King Solomon sent Benaiah the son of Jehoiada; and he fell on him, so that he died. <sup>26</sup> To Abiathar the priest the king said, "Go to Anathoth, to your own fields, for you are worthy of death. But I will not at this time put you to death, because you bore the Lord<sup>c</sup> Yahweh's ark before David my father, and because you were afflicted in all in which my father was afflicted." <sup>27</sup> So Solomon thrust Abiathar out from being priest to Yahweh, that he might fulfill Yahweh's word which he spoke concerning the house of Eli in Shiloh. <sup>28</sup> This news came to Joab; for Joab had followed Adonijah, although he didn't follow Absalom. Joab fled to Yahweh's Tent, and held onto the horns of the altar. <sup>29</sup> King Solomon was told, "Joab has fled to Yahweh's Tent; and behold, he is by the altar." Then Solomon sent Benaiah the son of Jehoiada, saying, "Go, fall on him." <sup>30</sup> Benaiah came to Yahweh's Tent, and said to him, "The king says, 'Come out!'" He said, "No; but I will die here." Benaiah brought the king word again, saying, "This is what Joab said, and this is how he answered me." <sup>31</sup> The king said to him, "Do as he has said, and fall on him, and bury him, that you may take away the blood, which Joab shed without cause, from me and from my father's house. <sup>32</sup> Yahweh will return his blood on his own head, because he fell on two men more righteous and better than he, and killed them with the sword, and my father David didn't know it: Abner the son of Ner, captain of the army of Israel, and Amasa the son of Jether, captain of the army of Judah. <sup>33</sup> So their blood will return on the head of Joab and on the head of his offspring<sup>d</sup> forever. But for David, for his offspring, for his house, and for his throne, there will be peace forever from Yahweh." <sup>34</sup> Then Benaiah the son of Jehoiada went up and fell on him, and killed him; and he was buried in his own house in the wilderness. <sup>35</sup> The king put Benaiah the son of Jehoiada in his place over the army; and the king put Zadok the priest in the place of Abiathar. <sup>36</sup> The king sent and called for Shimei, and said to him, "Build yourself a house in Jerusalem, and live there, and don't go anywhere else. <sup>37</sup> For on the day you go out and pass over the brook Kidron, know for certain that you will surely die. Your blood will be on your own head." <sup>38</sup> Shimei said to the king, "What you say is good. As my lord the king has said, so will your servant do." Shimei lived in Jerusalem many days. <sup>39</sup> At the end of three years, two of Shimei's slaves ran away to Achish, son of Maacah, king of Gath. They told Shimei, saying, "Behold, your slaves are in Gath." <sup>40</sup> Shimei arose, saddled his donkey, and went to Gath to Achish to seek his slaves; and Shimei went and brought his slaves from Gath. <sup>41</sup> Solomon was told that Shimei had gone from Jerusalem to Gath, and had come again. <sup>42</sup> The king sent and called for Shimei, and said to him, "Didn't I adjure you by Yahweh and warn you, saying, 'Know for certain that on the day you go out and walk anywhere else, you shall surely die'? You said to me, 'The saying that I have heard is good.' <sup>43</sup> Why then have you not kept the oath of Yahweh and the commandment that I have instructed you with?" <sup>44</sup> The king said moreover to Shimei, "You know in your heart all the wickedness that you did to David my father. Therefore Yahweh will return your wickedness on your own head. <sup>45</sup> But King Solomon will be blessed, and David's throne will be established before Yahweh forever." <sup>46</sup> So the king commanded Benaiah the son of Jehoiada; and he went out, and fell on him, so that he died. The kingdom was established in the hand of Solomon.

## 3

<sup>1</sup> Solomon made a marriage alliance with Pharaoh king of Egypt. He took Pharaoh's daughter and brought her into David's city until he had finished building his own house, Yahweh's house, and the wall around Jerusalem. <sup>2</sup> However, the people sacrificed in the high places, because there was not yet a house built for Yahweh's name. <sup>3</sup> Solomon loved Yahweh, walking in the statutes of David his father, except that he sacrificed and burned incense in the high places. <sup>4</sup> The king went to Gibeon to sacrifice there, for that was the great high place. Solomon offered a thousand burnt offerings on that altar. <sup>5</sup> In Gibeon, Yahweh appeared to Solomon in a dream by night; and God said, "Ask for what I should give you." <sup>6</sup> Solomon said, "You have shown to your servant

---

<sup>a</sup> 2:6 Sheol is the place of the dead.

<sup>b</sup> 2:9 Sheol is the place of the dead.

<sup>c</sup> 2:26 The word translated "Lord" is "Adonai."

<sup>d</sup> 2:33 or, seed

David my father great loving kindness, because he walked before you in truth, in righteousness, and in uprightness of heart with you. You have kept for him this great loving kindness, that you have given him a son to sit on his throne, as it is today. [7] Now, Yahweh my God, you have made your servant king instead of David my father. I am just a little child. I don't know how to go out or come in. [8] Your servant is among your people which you have chosen, a great people, that can't be numbered or counted for multitude. [9] Give your servant therefore an understanding heart to judge your people, that I may discern between good and evil; for who is able to judge this great people of yours?" [10] This request pleased the Lord, that Solomon had asked this thing. [11] God said to him, "Because you have asked this thing, and have not asked for yourself long life, nor have you asked for riches for yourself, nor have you asked for the life of your enemies, but have asked for yourself understanding to discern justice, [12] behold, I have done according to your word. Behold, I have given you a wise and understanding heart, so that there has been no one like you before you, and after you none will arise like you. [13] I have also given you that which you have not asked, both riches and honor, so that there will not be any among the kings like you for all your days. [14] If you will walk in my ways, to keep my statutes and my commandments, as your father David walked, then I will lengthen your days." [15] Solomon awoke; and behold, it was a dream. Then he came to Jerusalem and stood before the ark of Yahweh's covenant, and offered up burnt offerings, offered peace offerings, and made a feast for all his servants. [16] Then two women who were prostitutes came to the king, and stood before him. [17] The one woman said, "Oh, my lord, I and this woman dwell in one house. I delivered a child with her in the house. [18] The third day after I delivered, this woman delivered also. We were together. There was no stranger with us in the house, just us two in the house. [19] This woman's child died in the night, because she lay on it. [20] She arose at midnight, and took my son from beside me while your servant slept, and laid it in her bosom, and laid her dead child in my bosom. [21] When I rose in the morning to nurse my child, behold, he was dead; but when I had looked at him in the morning, behold, it was not my son whom I bore." [22] The other woman said, "No! But the living one is my son, and the dead one is your son." The first one said, "No! But the dead one is your son, and the living one is my son." They argued like this before the king. [23] Then the king said, "One says, 'This is my son who lives, and your son is the dead one;' and the other says, 'No! But your son is the dead one, and my son is the living one.'" [24] The king said, "Get me a sword." So they brought a sword before the king. [25] The king said, "Divide the living child in two, and give half to the one, and half to the other." [26] Then the woman whose the living child was spoke to the king, for her heart yearned over her son, and she said, "Oh, my lord, give her the living child, and in no way kill him!" But the other said, "He shall be neither mine nor yours. Divide him." [27] Then the king answered, "Give the first woman the living child, and definitely do not kill him. She is his mother." [28] All Israel heard of the judgment which the king had judged; and they feared the king, for they saw that the wisdom of God was in him to do justice.

## 4

[1] King Solomon was king over all Israel. [2] These were the princes whom he had: Azariah the son of Zadok, the priest; [3] Elihoreph and Ahijah, the sons of Shisha, scribes; Jehoshaphat the son of Ahilud, the recorder; [4] Benaiah the son of Jehoiada was over the army; Zadok and Abiathar were priests; [5] Azariah the son of Nathan was over the officers; Zabud the son of Nathan was chief minister, the king's friend; [6] Ahishar was over the household; and Adoniram the son of Abda was over the men subject to forced labor. [7] Solomon had twelve officers over all Israel, who provided food for the king and his household. Each man had to make provision for a month in the year. [8] These are their names: Ben Hur, in the hill country of Ephraim; [9] Ben Deker, in Makaz, in Shaalbim, Beth Shemesh, and Elon Beth Hanan; [10] Ben Hesed, in Arubboth (Socoh and all the land of Hepher belonged to him); [11] Ben Abinadab, in all the height of Dor (he had Taphath, Solomon's daughter, as wife); [12] Baana the son of Ahilud, in Taanach and Megiddo, and all Beth Shean which is beside Zarethan, beneath Jezreel, from Beth Shean to Abel Meholah, as far as beyond Jokmeam; [13] Ben Geber, in Ramoth Gilead (the towns of Jair the son of Manasseh, which are in Gilead, belonged to him; and the region of Argob, which is in Bashan, sixty great cities with walls and bronze bars, belonged to him); [14] Ahinadab the son of Iddo, in Mahanaim; [15] Ahimaaz, in Naphtali (he also took Basemath the daughter of Solomon as wife); [16] Baana the son of Hushai, in Asher and Bealoth; [17] Jehoshaphat the son of Paruah, in

Issachar; [18] Shimei the son of Ela, in Benjamin; [19] Geber the son of Uri, in the land of Gilead, the country of Sihon king of the Amorites and of Og king of Bashan; and he was the only officer who was in the land. [20] Judah and Israel were numerous as the sand which is by the sea in multitude, eating and drinking and making merry. [21] Solomon ruled over all the kingdoms from the River to the land of the Philistines, and to the border of Egypt. They brought tribute and served Solomon all the days of his life. [22] Solomon's provision for one day was thirty cors[a] of fine flour, sixty measures of meal, [23] ten head of fat cattle, twenty head of cattle out of the pastures, and one hundred sheep, in addition to deer, gazelles, roebucks, and fattened fowl. [24] For he had dominion over all on this side the River, from Tiphsah even to Gaza, over all the kings on this side the River; and he had peace on all sides around him. [25] Judah and Israel lived safely, every man under his vine and under his fig tree, from Dan even to Beersheba, all the days of Solomon. [26] Solomon had forty thousand stalls of horses for his chariots, and twelve thousand horsemen. [27] Those officers provided food for King Solomon, and for all who came to King Solomon's table, every man in his month. They let nothing be lacking. [28] They also brought barley and straw for the horses and swift steeds to the place where the officers were, each man according to his duty. [29] God gave Solomon abundant wisdom, understanding, and breadth of mind like the sand that is on the seashore. [30] Solomon's wisdom excelled the wisdom of all the children of the east and all the wisdom of Egypt. [31] For he was wiser than all men—wiser than Ethan the Ezrahite, Heman, Calcol, and Darda, the sons of Mahol; and his fame was in all the nations all around. [32] He spoke three thousand proverbs, and his songs numbered one thousand five. [33] He spoke of trees, from the cedar that is in Lebanon even to the hyssop that grows out of the wall; he also spoke of animals, of birds, of creeping things, and of fish. [34] People of all nations came to hear the wisdom of Solomon, sent by all kings of the earth who had heard of his wisdom.

## 5

[1] Hiram king of Tyre sent his servants to Solomon, for he had heard that they had anointed him king in the place of his father, and Hiram had always loved David. [2] Solomon sent to Hiram, saying, [3] "You know that David my father could not build a house for the name of Yahweh his God because of the wars which were around him on every side, until Yahweh put his enemies under the soles of his feet. [4] But now Yahweh my God has given me rest on every side. There is no enemy and no evil occurrence. [5] Behold, I intend to build a house for the name of Yahweh my God, as Yahweh spoke to David my father, saying, 'Your son, whom I will set on your throne in your place shall build the house for my name.' [6] Now therefore command that cedar trees be cut for me out of Lebanon. My servants will be with your servants; and I will give you wages for your servants according to all that you say. For you know that there is nobody among us who knows how to cut timber like the Sidonians." [7] When Hiram heard the words of Solomon, he rejoiced greatly, and said, "Blessed is Yahweh today, who has given to David a wise son to rule over this great people." [8] Hiram sent to Solomon, saying, "I have heard the message which you have sent to me. I will do all your desire concerning timber of cedar, and concerning cypress timber. [9] My servants will bring them down from Lebanon to the sea. I will make them into rafts to go by sea to the place that you specify to me, and will cause them to be broken up there, and you will receive them. You will accomplish my desire, in giving food for my household." [10] So Hiram gave Solomon cedar timber and cypress timber according to all his desire. [11] Solomon gave Hiram twenty thousand cors[b] of wheat for food to his household, and twenty cors[c] of pure oil. Solomon gave this to Hiram year by year. [12] Yahweh gave Solomon wisdom, as he promised him. There was peace between Hiram and Solomon, and the two of them made a treaty together. [13] King Solomon raised a levy out of all Israel; and the levy was thirty thousand men. [14] He sent them to Lebanon, ten thousand a month by courses: for a month they were in Lebanon, and two months at home; and Adoniram was over the men subject to forced labor. [15] Solomon had seventy thousand who bore burdens, and eighty thousand who were stone cutters in the mountains, [16] besides Solomon's chief officers who were over the work: three thousand three hundred who ruled over the people who labored in the work. [17] The king commanded, and they cut out large stones, costly stones, to lay the foundation of the house with worked stone. [18] Solomon's builders and Hiram's builders and the Gebalites cut them, and prepared the timber and the stones to build the house.

---

[a] 4:22 1 cor is the same as a homer, or about 55.9 U. S. gallons (liquid) or 211 liters or 6 bushels

[b] 5:11 20,000 cors would be about 120,000 bushels or about 4.2 megaliters of wheat, which

would weigh about 3,270 metric tons.

[c] 5:11 20 cors is about 1,100 gallons or about 4220 liters.

## 6

¹ In the four hundred and eightieth year after the children of Israel had come out of the land of Egypt, in the fourth year of Solomon's reign over Israel, in the month Ziv, which is the second month, he began to build Yahweh's house. ² The house which King Solomon built for Yahweh had a length of sixty cubits,ᵃ and its width twenty, and its height thirty cubits. ³ The porch in front of the temple of the house had a length of twenty cubits, which was along the width of the house. Ten cubits was its width in front of the house. ⁴ He made windows of fixed lattice work for the house. ⁵ Against the wall of the house, he built floors all around, against the walls of the house all around, both of the temple and of the inner sanctuary; and he made side rooms all around. ⁶ The lowest floor was five cubits wide, and the middle was six cubits wide, and the third was seven cubits wide; for on the outside he made offsets in the wall of the house all around, that the beams should not be inserted into the walls of the house. ⁷ The house, when it was under construction, was built of stone prepared at the quarry; and no hammer or ax or any tool of iron was heard in the house while it was under construction. ⁸ The door for the middle side rooms was in the right side of the house. They went up by winding stairs into the middle floor, and out of the middle into the third. ⁹ So he built the house and finished it; and he covered the house with beams and planks of cedar. ¹⁰ He built the floors all along the house, each five cubits high; and they rested on the house with timbers of cedar. ¹¹ Yahweh's word came to Solomon, saying, ¹²"Concerning this house which you are building, if you will walk in my statutes, and execute my ordinances, and keep all my commandments to walk in them, then I will establish my word with you, which I spoke to David your father. ¹³ I will dwell among the children of Israel, and will not forsake my people Israel." ¹⁴ So Solomon built the house and finished it. ¹⁵ He built the walls of the house within with boards of cedar; from the floor of the house to the walls of the ceiling, he covered them on the inside with wood. He covered the floor of the house with cypress boards. ¹⁶ He built twenty cubits of the back part of the house with boards of cedar from the floor to the ceiling. He built this within, for an inner sanctuary, even for the most holy place. ¹⁷ In front of the temple sanctuary was forty cubits long. ¹⁸ There was cedar on the house within, carved with buds and open flowers. All was cedar. No stone was visible. ¹⁹ He prepared an inner sanctuary in the middle of the house within, to set the ark of Yahweh's covenant there. ²⁰ Within the inner sanctuary was twenty cubits in length, and twenty cubits in width, and twenty cubits in its height. He overlaid it with pure gold. He covered the altar with cedar. ²¹ So Solomon overlaid the house within with pure gold. He drew chains of gold across before the inner sanctuary, and he overlaid it with gold. ²² He overlaid the whole house with gold, until all the house was finished. He also overlaid the whole altar that belonged to the inner sanctuary with gold. ²³ In the inner sanctuary he made two cherubimᵇ of olive wood, each ten cubits high. ²⁴ Five cubits was the length of one wing of the cherub, and five cubits was the length of the other wing of the cherub. From the tip of one wing to the tip of the other was ten cubits. ²⁵ The other cherub was ten cubits. Both the cherubim were of one measure and one form. ²⁶ One cherub was ten cubits high, and so was the other cherub. ²⁷ He set the cherubim within the inner house. The wings of the cherubim were stretched out, so that the wing of the one touched the one wall and the wing of the other cherub touched the other wall; and their wings touched one another in the middle of the house. ²⁸ He overlaid the cherubim with gold. ²⁹ He carved all the walls of the house around with carved figures of cherubim, palm trees, and open flowers, inside and outside. ³⁰ He overlaid the floor of the house with gold, inside and outside. ³¹ For the entrance of the inner sanctuary, he made doors of olive wood. The lintel and door posts were a fifth part of the wall. ³² So he made two doors of olive wood; and he carved on them carvings of cherubim, palm trees, and open flowers, and overlaid them with gold. He spread the gold on the cherubim and on the palm trees. ³³ He also made the entrance of the temple door posts of olive wood, out of a fourth part of the wall, ³⁴ and two doors of cypress wood. The two leaves of the one door were folding, and the two leaves of the other door were folding. ³⁵ He carved cherubim, palm trees, and open flowers; and he overlaid them with gold fitted on the engraved work. ³⁶ He built the inner court with three courses of cut stone and a course of cedar beams. ³⁷ The foundation of Yahweh's house was laid in the fourth year, in the month Ziv. ³⁸ In the eleventh year, in the month Bul, which is the eighth month, the house was finished throughout all its parts and according to all its specifications. So he spent seven years building it.

## 7

¹ Solomon was building his own house thirteen years, and he finished all his house. ² For he built the House of the Forest of Lebanon. Its length was one hundred cubits,ᶜ its width fifty cubits, and its height thirty cubits, on four rows of cedar pillars, with cedar beams on the pillars. ³ It was covered with cedar above over the forty-five beams that were on the pillars, fifteen in a row. ⁴ There were beams in three rows, and window was facing window in three ranks. ⁵ All the doors and posts were made square with beams; and window was facing window in three ranks. ⁶ He made the hall of pillars. Its length was fifty cubits and its width thirty cubits, with a porch before them, and pillars and a threshold before them. ⁷ He made the porch of the throne where he was to judge, even the porch of judgment; and it was covered with cedar from floor to floor. ⁸ His house where he was to dwell, the other court within the porch, was of the same construction. He made also a house for Pharaoh's daughter (whom Solomon had taken as wife), like this porch. ⁹ All these were of costly stones, even of stone cut according to measure, sawed with saws, inside and outside, even from the foundation to the coping, and so on the outside to the great court. ¹⁰ The foundation was of costly stones, even great stones, stones of ten cubits and stones of eight cubits. ¹¹ Above were costly stones, even cut stone, according to measure, and cedar wood. ¹² The great court around had three courses of cut stone with a course of cedar beams, like the inner court of Yahweh's house and the porch of the house. ¹³ King Solomon sent and brought Hiram out of Tyre. ¹⁴ He was the son of a widow of the tribe of Naphtali, and his father was a man of Tyre, a worker in bronze; and he was filled with wisdom and understanding and skill to work all works in bronze. He came to King Solomon and performed all his work. ¹⁵ For he fashioned the two pillars of bronze, eighteen cubits high apiece; and a line of twelve cubits encircled either of them. ¹⁶ He made two capitals of molten bronze to set on the tops of the pillars. The height of the one capital was five cubits, and the height of the other capital was five cubits. ¹⁷ There were nets of checker work and wreaths of chain work for the capitals which were on the top of the pillars: seven for the one capital, and seven for the other capital. ¹⁸ So he made the pillars; and there were two rows of pomegranates around the one network, to cover the capitals that were on the top of the pillars; and he did so for the other capital. ¹⁹ The capitals that were on the top of the pillars in the porch were of lily work, four cubits. ²⁰ There were capitals above also on the two pillars, close by the belly which was beside the network. There were two hundred pomegranates in rows around the other capital. ²¹ He set up the pillars at the porch of the temple. He set up the right pillar and called its name Jachin; and he set up the left pillar and called its name Boaz. ²² On the tops of the pillars was lily work. So the work of the pillars was finished. ²³ He made the molten sea ten cubits from brim to brim, round in shape. Its height was five cubits; and a line of thirty cubits encircled it. ²⁴ Under its brim around there were buds which encircled it for ten cubits, encircling the sea. The buds were in two rows, cast when it was cast. ²⁵ It stood on twelve oxen, three looking toward the north, and three looking toward the west, and three looking toward the south, and three looking toward the east; and the sea was set on them above, and all their hindquarters were inward. ²⁶ It was a hand width thick. Its brim was worked like the brim of a cup, like the flower of a lily. It held two thousand baths. ²⁷ He made the ten bases of bronze. The length of one base was four cubits, four cubits its width, and three cubits its height. ²⁸ The work of the bases was like this: they had panels; and there were panels between the ledges; ²⁹ and on the panels that were between the ledges were lions, oxen, and cherubim; and on the ledges there was a pedestal above; and beneath the lions and oxen were wreaths of hanging work. ³⁰ Every base had four bronze wheels and axles of bronze; and its four feet had supports. The supports were cast beneath the basin, with wreaths at the side of each. ³¹ Its opening within the capital and above was a cubit. Its opening was round like the work of a pedestal, a cubit and a half; and also on its opening were engravings, and their panels were square, not round. ³² The four wheels were underneath the panels; and the axles of the wheels were in the base. The height of a wheel was a cubit and half a cubit. ³³ The work of the wheels was like the work of a chariot wheel. Their axles, their rims, their spokes, and their hubs were all of cast metal. ³⁴ There were four supports at the four corners of each base. Its supports were of the base itself. ³⁵ In the top of the base there was a round band half a cubit high; and on the top of the base its supports and its panels were the same. ³⁶ On the plates of its supports and on its panels, he engraved cherubim, lions, and palm trees, each in its space, with wreaths all around. ³⁷ He made the ten bases in this way: all of them had one

---

ᵃ *6:2* A cubit is the length from the tip of the middle finger to the elbow on a man's arm, or

about 18 inches or 46 centimeters.

ᵇ *6:23* "Cherubim" is plural of "cherub", an angelic being.

ᶜ *7:2* A cubit is the length from the tip of the middle finger to the elbow on a man's arm, or

about 18 inches or 46 centimeters.

casting, one measure, and one form. [38] He made ten basins of bronze. One basin contained forty baths.[a] Every basin measured four cubits. One basin was on every one of the ten bases. [39] He set the bases, five on the right side of the house and five on the left side of the house. He set the sea on the right side of the house eastward and toward the south. [40] Hiram made the pots, the shovels, and the basins. So Hiram finished doing all the work that he worked for King Solomon in Yahweh's house: [41] the two pillars; the two bowls of the capitals that were on the top of the pillars; the two networks to cover the two bowls of the capitals that were on the top of the pillars; [42] the four hundred pomegranates for the two networks; two rows of pomegranates for each network, to cover the two bowls of the capitals that were on the pillars; [43] the ten bases; the ten basins on the bases; [44] the one sea; the twelve oxen under the sea; [45] the pots; the shovels; and the basins. All of these vessels, which Hiram made for King Solomon in Yahweh's house, were of burnished bronze. [46] The king cast them in the plain of the Jordan, in the clay ground between Succoth and Zarethan. [47] Solomon left all the vessels unweighed, because there were so many of them. The weight of the bronze could not be determined. [48] Solomon made all the vessels that were in Yahweh's house: the golden altar and the table that the show bread was on, of gold; [49] and the lamp stands, five on the right side and five on the left, in front of the inner sanctuary, of pure gold; and the flowers, the lamps, and the tongs, of gold; [50] the cups, the snuffers, the basins, the spoons, and the fire pans, of pure gold; and the hinges, both for the doors of the inner house, the most holy place, and for the doors of the house, of the temple, of gold. [51] Thus all the work that King Solomon did in Yahweh's house was finished. Solomon brought in the things which David his father had dedicated—the silver, the gold, and the vessels—and put them in the treasuries of Yahweh's house.

# 8

[1] Then Solomon assembled the elders of Israel with all the heads of the tribes, the princes of the fathers' households of the children of Israel, to King Solomon in Jerusalem, to bring up the ark of Yahweh's covenant out of David's city, which is Zion. [2] All the men of Israel assembled themselves to King Solomon at the feast in the month Ethanim, which is the seventh month. [3] All the elders of Israel came, and the priests picked up the ark. [4] They brought up Yahweh's ark, the Tent of Meeting, and all the holy vessels that were in the Tent. The priests and the Levites brought these up. [5] King Solomon and all the congregation of Israel, who were assembled to him, were with him before the ark, sacrificing sheep and cattle that could not be counted or numbered for multitude. [6] The priests brought in the ark of Yahweh's covenant to its place, into the inner sanctuary of the house, to the most holy place, even under the cherubim's wings. [7] For the cherubim spread their wings out over the place of the ark, and the cherubim covered the ark and its poles above. [8] The poles were so long that the ends of the poles were seen from the holy place before the inner sanctuary, but they were not seen outside. They are there to this day. [9] There was nothing in the ark except the two stone tablets which Moses put there at Horeb, when Yahweh made a covenant with the children of Israel, when they came out of the land of Egypt. [10] It came to pass, when the priests had come out of the holy place, that the cloud filled Yahweh's house, [11] so that the priests could not stand to minister by reason of the cloud; for Yahweh's glory filled Yahweh's house. [12] Then Solomon said, "Yahweh has said that he would dwell in the thick darkness. [13] I have surely built you a house of habitation, a place for you to dwell in forever." [14] The king turned his face around and blessed all the assembly of Israel; and all the assembly of Israel stood. [15] He said, "Blessed is Yahweh, the God of Israel, who spoke with his mouth to David your father, and has with his hand fulfilled it, saying, [16] 'Since the day that I brought my people Israel out of Egypt, I chose no city out of all the tribes of Israel to build a house, that my name might be there; but I chose David to be over my people Israel.' [17] "Now it was in the heart of David my father to build a house for the name of Yahweh, the God of Israel. [18] But Yahweh said to David my father, 'Whereas it was in your heart to build a house for my name, you did well that it was in your heart. [19] Nevertheless, you shall not build the house; but your son who shall come out of your body, he shall build the house for my name.' [20] Yahweh has established his word that he spoke; for I have risen up in the place of David my father, and I sit on the throne of Israel, as Yahweh promised, and have built the house for the name of Yahweh, the God of Israel. [21] There I have set a place for the ark, in which is Yahweh's covenant, which he made with our fathers when he brought them out of the land of Egypt." [22] Solomon stood before Yahweh's altar in the presence of all the assembly of Israel, and spread out his hands toward heaven; [23] and he said, "Yahweh, the God of Israel, there is no

God like you, in heaven above, or on earth beneath; who keeps covenant and loving kindness with your servants who walk before you with all their heart; [24] who has kept with your servant David my father that which you promised him. Yes, you spoke with your mouth, and have fulfilled it with your hand, as it is today. [25] Now therefore, may Yahweh, the God of Israel, keep with your servant David my father that which you have promised him, saying, 'There shall not fail from you a man in my sight to sit on the throne of Israel, if only your children take heed to their way, to walk before me as you have walked before me.' [26] "Now therefore, God of Israel, please let your word be verified, which you spoke to your servant David my father. [27] But will God in very deed dwell on the earth? Behold, heaven and the heaven of heavens can't contain you; how much less this house that I have built! [28] Yet have respect for the prayer of your servant and for his supplication, Yahweh my God, to listen to the cry and to the prayer which your servant prays before you today; [29] that your eyes may be open toward this house night and day, even toward the place of which you have said, 'My name shall be there;' to listen to the prayer which your servant prays toward this place. [30] Listen to the supplication of your servant, and of your people Israel, when they pray toward this place. Yes, hear in heaven, your dwelling place; and when you hear, forgive. [31] "If a man sins against his neighbor, and an oath is laid on him to cause him to swear, and he comes and swears before your altar in this house, [32] then hear in heaven, and act, and judge your servants, condemning the wicked, to bring his way on his own head, and justifying the righteous, to give him according to his righteousness. [33] "When your people Israel are struck down before the enemy because they have sinned against you, if they turn again to you and confess your name, and pray and make supplication to you in this house, [34] then hear in heaven, and forgive the sin of your people Israel, and bring them again to the land which you gave to their fathers. [35] "When the sky is shut up and there is no rain because they have sinned against you, if they pray toward this place and confess your name, and turn from their sin when you afflict them, [36] then hear in heaven, and forgive the sin of your servants, and of your people Israel, when you teach them the good way in which they should walk; and send rain on your land which you have given to your people for an inheritance. [37] "If there is famine in the land, if there is pestilence, if there is blight, mildew, locust or caterpillar; if their enemy besieges them in the land of their cities, whatever plague, whatever sickness there is, [38] whatever prayer and supplication is made by any man, or by all your people Israel, who shall each know the plague of his own heart, and spread out his hands toward this house, [39] then hear in heaven, your dwelling place, and forgive, and act, and give to every man according to all his ways, whose heart you know (for you, even you only, know the hearts of all the children of men); [40] that they may fear you all the days that they live in the land which you gave to our fathers. [41] "Moreover, concerning the foreigner, who is not of your people Israel, when he comes out of a far country for your name's sake [42] (for they shall hear of your great name and of your mighty hand and of your outstretched arm), when he comes and prays toward this house, [43] hear in heaven, your dwelling place, and do according to all that the foreigner calls to you for; that all the peoples of the earth may know your name, to fear you, as do your people Israel, and that they may know that this house which I have built is called by your name. [44] "If your people go out to battle against their enemy, by whatever way you shall send them, and they pray to Yahweh toward the city which you have chosen, and toward the house which I have built for your name, [45] then hear in heaven their prayer and their supplication, and maintain their cause. [46] If they sin against you (for there is no man who doesn't sin), and you are angry with them and deliver them to the enemy, so that they carry them away captive to the land of the enemy, far off or near; [47] yet if they repent in the land where they are carried captive, and turn again, and make supplication to you in the land of those who carried them captive, saying, 'We have sinned and have done perversely; we have dealt wickedly,' [48] if they return to you with all their heart and with all their soul in the land of their enemies who carried them captive, and pray to you toward their land which you gave to their fathers, the city which you have chosen and the house which I have built for your name, [49] then hear their prayer and their supplication in heaven, your dwelling place, and maintain their cause; [50] and forgive your people who have sinned against you, and all their transgressions in which they have transgressed against you; and give them compassion before those who carried them captive, that they may have compassion on them [51] (for they are your people and your inheritance, which you brought out of Egypt, from the middle of the iron furnace); [52] that your eyes may be open to the supplication of your servant and to the supplication of your people Israel, to listen to them whenever they cry

---

[a] *7:38* 1 bath is one tenth of a cor, or about 5.6 U. S. gallons    or 21 liters, so 40 baths was about 224 gallons or 840 liters.

to you. ⁵³ For you separated them from among all the peoples of the earth to be your inheritance, as you spoke by Moses your servant, when you brought our fathers out of Egypt, Lord Yahweh." ⁵⁴ It was so, that when Solomon had finished praying all this prayer and supplication to Yahweh, he arose from before Yahweh's altar, from kneeling on his knees with his hands spread out toward heaven. ⁵⁵ He stood and blessed all the assembly of Israel with a loud voice, saying, ⁵⁶"Blessed be Yahweh, who has given rest to his people Israel, according to all that he promised. There has not failed one word of all his good promise, which he promised by Moses his servant. ⁵⁷ May Yahweh our God be with us as he was with our fathers. Let him not leave us or forsake us, ⁵⁸ that he may incline our hearts to him, to walk in all his ways, and to keep his commandments, his statutes, and his ordinances, which he commanded our fathers. ⁵⁹ Let these my words, with which I have made supplication before Yahweh, be near to Yahweh our God day and night, that he may maintain the cause of his servant and the cause of his people Israel, as every day requires; ⁶⁰ that all the peoples of the earth may know that Yahweh himself is God. There is no one else. ⁶¹"Let your heart therefore be perfect with Yahweh our God, to walk in his statutes, and to keep his commandments, as it is today." ⁶² The king, and all Israel with him, offered sacrifice before Yahweh. ⁶³ Solomon offered for the sacrifice of peace offerings, which he offered to Yahweh, twenty two thousand head of cattle and one hundred twenty thousand sheep. So the king and all the children of Israel dedicated Yahweh's house. ⁶⁴ The same day the king made the middle of the court holy that was before Yahweh's house; for there he offered the burnt offering, the meal offering, and the fat of the peace offerings, because the bronze altar that was before Yahweh was too little to receive the burnt offering, the meal offering, and the fat of the peace offerings. ⁶⁵ So Solomon held the feast at that time, and all Israel with him, a great assembly, from the entrance of Hamath to the brook of Egypt, before Yahweh our God, seven days and seven more days, even fourteen days. ⁶⁶ On the eighth day he sent the people away; and they blessed the king, and went to their tents joyful and glad in their hearts for all the goodness that Yahweh had shown to David his servant, and to Israel his people.

## 9

¹ When Solomon had finished the building of Yahweh's house, the king's house, and all Solomon's desire which he was pleased to do, ² Yahweh appeared to Solomon the second time, as he had appeared to him at Gibeon. ³ Yahweh said to him, "I have heard your prayer and your supplication that you have made before me. I have made this house holy, which you have built, to put my name there forever; and my eyes and my heart shall be there perpetually. ⁴ As for you, if you will walk before me as David your father walked, in integrity of heart and in uprightness, to do according to all that I have commanded you, and will keep my statutes and my ordinances, ⁵ then I will establish the throne of your kingdom over Israel forever, as I promised to David your father, saying, 'There shall not fail from you a man on the throne of Israel.' ⁶ But if you turn away from following me, you or your children, and not keep my commandments and my statutes which I have set before you, but go and serve other gods and worship them, ⁷ then I will cut off Israel out of the land which I have given them; and I will cast this house, which I have made holy for my name, out of my sight; and Israel will be a proverb and a byword among all peoples. ⁸ Though this house is so high, yet everyone who passes by it will be astonished and hiss; and they will say, 'Why has Yahweh done this to this land and to this house?' ⁹ and they will answer, 'Because they abandoned Yahweh their God, who brought their fathers out of the land of Egypt, and embraced other gods, and worshiped them, and served them. Therefore Yahweh has brought all this evil on them.'" ¹⁰ At the end of twenty years, in which Solomon had built the two houses, Yahweh's house and the king's house ¹¹(now Hiram the king of Tyre had furnished Solomon with cedar trees and cypress trees, and with gold, according to all his desire), King Solomon gave Hiram twenty cities in the land of Galilee. ¹² Hiram came out of Tyre to see the cities which Solomon had given him; and they didn't please him. ¹³ He said, "What cities are these which you have given me, my brother?" He called them the land of Cabulᵃ to this day. ¹⁴ Hiram sent to the king one hundred twenty talentsᵇ of gold. ¹⁵ This is the reason of the forced labor which King Solomon conscripted: to build Yahweh's house, his own house, Millo, Jerusalem's wall, Hazor, Megiddo, and Gezer. ¹⁶ Pharaoh king of Egypt had gone up, taken Gezer, burned it with fire, killed the Canaanites who lived in the city, and given it for a wedding gift to his daughter,

Solomon's wife. ¹⁷ Solomon built in the land Gezer, Beth Horon the lower, ¹⁸ Baalath, Tamar in the wilderness, ¹⁹ all the storage cities that Solomon had, the cities for his chariots, the cities for his horsemen, and that which Solomon desired to build for his pleasure in Jerusalem, and in Lebanon, and in all the land of his dominion. ²⁰ As for all the people who were left of the Amorites, the Hittites, the Perizzites, the Hivites, and the Jebusites, who were not of the children of Israel— ²¹ their children who were left after them in the land, whom the children of Israel were not able utterly to destroy—of them Solomon raised a levy of bondservants to this day. ²² But of the children of Israel Solomon made no bondservants; but they were the men of war, his servants, his princes, his captains, and rulers of his chariots and of his horsemen. ²³ These were the five hundred fifty chief officers who were over Solomon's work, who ruled over the people who labored in the work. ²⁴ But Pharaoh's daughter came up out of David's city to her house which Solomon had built for her. Then he built Millo. ²⁵ Solomon offered burnt offerings and peace offerings on the altar which he built to Yahweh three times per year, burning incense with them on the altar that was before Yahweh. So he finished the house. ²⁶ King Solomon made a fleet of ships in Ezion Geber, which is beside Eloth, on the shore of the Red Sea, in the land of Edom. ²⁷ Hiram sent in the fleet his servants, sailors who had knowledge of the sea, with the servants of Solomon. ²⁸ They came to Ophir, and fetched from there gold, four hundred and twenty talents,ᶜ and brought it to King Solomon.

## 10

¹ When the queen of Sheba heard of the fame of Solomon concerning Yahweh's name, she came to test him with hard questions. ² She came to Jerusalem with a very great caravan, with camels that bore spices, very much gold, and precious stones; and when she had come to Solomon, she talked with him about all that was in her heart. ³ Solomon answered all her questions. There wasn't anything hidden from the king which he didn't tell her. ⁴ When the queen of Sheba had seen all the wisdom of Solomon, the house that he had built, ⁵ the food of his table, the sitting of his servants, the attendance of his officials, their clothing, his cup bearers, and his ascent by which he went up to Yahweh's house, there was no more spirit in her. ⁶ She said to the king, "It was a true report that I heard in my own land of your acts and of your wisdom. ⁷ However, I didn't believe the words until I came and my eyes had seen it. Behold, not even half was told me! Your wisdom and prosperity exceed the fame which I heard. ⁸ Happy are your men, happy are these your servants who stand continually before you, who hear your wisdom. ⁹ Blessed is Yahweh your God, who delighted in you, to set you on the throne of Israel. Because Yahweh loved Israel forever, therefore he made you king, to do justice and righteousness." ¹⁰ She gave the king one hundred twenty talents of gold, and a very great quantity of spices, and precious stones. Never again was there such an abundance of spices as these which the queen of Sheba gave to King Solomon. ¹¹ The fleet of Hiram that brought gold from Ophir also brought in from Ophir great quantities of almug treesᵈ and precious stones. ¹² The king made the almug trees pillars for Yahweh's house and for the king's house, harps also and stringed instruments for the singers; no such almug trees came or were seen to this day. ¹³ King Solomon gave to the queen of Sheba all her desire, whatever she asked, in addition to that which Solomon gave her of his royal bounty. So she turned and went to her own land, she and her servants. ¹⁴ Now the weight of gold that came to Solomon in one year was six hundred sixty-six talentsᵉ of gold, ¹⁵ in addition to that which the traders brought, and the traffic of the merchants, and of all the kings of the mixed people, and of the governors of the country. ¹⁶ King Solomon made two hundred bucklers of beaten gold; six hundred shekelsᶠ of gold went to one buckler. ¹⁷ He made three hundred shields of beaten gold; three minasᵍ of gold went to one shield; and the king put them in the House of the Forest of Lebanon. ¹⁸ Moreover the king made a great throne of ivory, and overlaid it with the finest gold. ¹⁹ There were six steps to the throne, and the top of the throne was round behind; and there were armrests on either side by the place of the seat, and two lions standing beside the armrests. ²⁰ Twelve lions stood there on the one side and on the other on the six steps. Nothing like it was made in any kingdom. ²¹ All King Solomon's drinking vessels were of gold, and all the vessels of the House of the Forest of Lebanon were of pure gold. None were of silver, because it was considered of little value in the days of Solomon. ²² For the king had a fleet of ships of Tarshish at sea with Hiram's fleet. Once every three years the fleet of Tarshish came bringing gold, silver,

---

ᵃ 9:13 "Cabul" sounds like Hebrew for "good-for-nothing".
ᵇ 9:14 A talent is about 30 kilograms or 66 pounds or 965 Troy ounces, so 120 talents is about 3.6 metric tons

ᶜ 9:28 A talent is about 30 kilograms or 66 pounds or 965 Troy ounces, so 420 talents is about 12.6 metric tons
ᵈ 10:11 possibly an Indian sandalwood, with nice grain

and a pleasant scent, and good for woodworking
ᵉ 10:14 A talent is about 30 kilograms or 66 pounds or 965 Troy ounces, so 666 talents is about 20 metric tons

ᶠ 10:16 A shekel is about 10 grams or about 0.32 Troy ounces, so 600 shekels is about 6 kilograms or 13.2 pounds or 192 Troy ounces.
ᵍ 10:17 A mina is about 600 grams or 1.3 U. S. pounds.

ivory, apes, and peacocks. ²³ So King Solomon exceeded all the kings of the earth in riches and in wisdom. ²⁴ All the earth sought the presence of Solomon to hear his wisdom which God had put in his heart. ²⁵ Year after year, every man brought his tribute, vessels of silver, vessels of gold, clothing, armor, spices, horses, and mules. ²⁶ Solomon gathered together chariots and horsemen. He had one thousand four hundred chariots and twelve thousand horsemen. He kept them in the chariot cities and with the king at Jerusalem. ²⁷ The king made silver as common as stones in Jerusalem, and cedars as common as the sycamore trees that are in the lowland. ²⁸ The horses which Solomon had were brought out of Egypt. The king's merchants received them in droves, each drove at a price. ²⁹ A chariot was imported from Egypt for six hundred shekels[a] of silver, and a horse for one hundred fifty shekels; and so they exported them to all the kings of the Hittites and to the kings of Syria.

# 11

¹ Now King Solomon loved many foreign women, together with the daughter of Pharaoh: women of the Moabites, Ammonites, Edomites, Sidonians, and Hittites, ² of the nations concerning which Yahweh said to the children of Israel, "You shall not go among them, neither shall they come among you, for surely they will turn away your heart after their gods." Solomon joined to these in love. ³ He had seven hundred wives, princesses, and three hundred concubines. His wives turned his heart away. ⁴ When Solomon was old, his wives turned away his heart after other gods; and his heart was not perfect with Yahweh his God, as the heart of David his father was. ⁵ For Solomon went after Ashtoreth the goddess of the Sidonians, and after Milcom the abomination of the Ammonites. ⁶ Solomon did that which was evil in Yahweh's sight, and didn't go fully after Yahweh, as David his father did. ⁷ Then Solomon built a high place for Chemosh the abomination of Moab, on the mountain that is before Jerusalem, and for Molech the abomination of the children of Ammon. ⁸ So he did for all his foreign wives, who burned incense and sacrificed to their gods. ⁹ Yahweh was angry with Solomon, because his heart was turned away from Yahweh, the God of Israel, who had appeared to him twice, ¹⁰ and had commanded him concerning this thing, that he should not go after other gods; but he didn't keep that which Yahweh commanded. ¹¹ Therefore Yahweh said to Solomon, "Because this is done by you, and you have not kept my covenant and my statutes, which I have commanded you, I will surely tear the kingdom from you, and will give it to your servant. ¹² Nevertheless, I will not do it in your days, for David your father's sake; but I will tear it out of your son's hand. ¹³ However, I will not tear away all the kingdom; but I will give one tribe to your son, for David my servant's sake, and for Jerusalem's sake which I have chosen." ¹⁴ Yahweh raised up an adversary to Solomon: Hadad the Edomite. He was one of the king's offspring in Edom. ¹⁵ For when David was in Edom, and Joab the captain of the army had gone up to bury the slain, and had struck every male in Edom ¹⁶(for Joab and all Israel remained there six months, until he had cut off every male in Edom), ¹⁷ Hadad fled, he and certain Edomites of his father's servants with him, to go into Egypt, when Hadad was still a little child. ¹⁸ They arose out of Midian and came to Paran; and they took men with them out of Paran, and they came to Egypt, to Pharaoh king of Egypt, who gave him a house, and appointed him food, and gave him land. ¹⁹ Hadad found great favor in the sight of Pharaoh, so that he gave him as wife the sister of his own wife, the sister of Tahpenes the queen. ²⁰ The sister of Tahpenes bore him Genubath his son, whom Tahpenes weaned in Pharaoh's house; and Genubath was in Pharaoh's house among the sons of Pharaoh. ²¹ When Hadad heard in Egypt that David slept with his fathers, and that Joab the captain of the army was dead, Hadad said to Pharaoh, "Let me depart, that I may go to my own country." ²² Then Pharaoh said to him, "But what have you lacked with me, that behold, you seek to go to your own country?" He answered, "Nothing, however only let me depart." ²³ God raised up an adversary to him, Rezon the son of Eliada, who had fled from his lord, Hadadezer king of Zobah. ²⁴ He gathered men to himself, and became captain over a troop, when David killed them of Zobah. They went to Damascus and lived there, and reigned in Damascus. ²⁵ He was an adversary to Israel all the days of Solomon, in addition to the mischief of Hadad. He abhorred Israel, and reigned over Syria. ²⁶ Jeroboam the son of Nebat, an Ephraimite of Zeredah, a servant of Solomon, whose mother's name was Zeruah, a widow, also lifted up his hand against the king. ²⁷ This was the reason why he lifted up his hand against the king: Solomon built Millo, and repaired the breach of his father David's city. ²⁸ The man Jeroboam was a mighty man of valor; and Solomon saw the young man that he was industrious, and he put him in charge of all the labor of the house of Joseph. ²⁹ At that time, when Jeroboam went out of Jerusalem, the prophet Ahijah the Shilonite found him on the way. Now Ahijah had clad himself with a new garment; and the two of them were alone in the field. ³⁰ Ahijah took the new garment that was on him, and tore it in twelve pieces. ³¹ He said to Jeroboam, "Take ten pieces; for Yahweh, the God of Israel, says, 'Behold, I will tear the kingdom out of the hand of Solomon and will give ten tribes to you ³²(but he shall have one tribe, for my servant David's sake and for Jerusalem's sake, the city which I have chosen out of all the tribes of Israel), ³³ because they have forsaken me, and have worshiped Ashtoreth the goddess of the Sidonians, Chemosh the god of Moab, and Milcom the god of the children of Ammon. They have not walked in my ways, to do that which is right in my eyes, and to keep my statutes and my ordinances, as David his father did. ³⁴'However, I will not take the whole kingdom out of his hand, but I will make him prince all the days of his life for David my servant's sake whom I chose, who kept my commandments and my statutes, ³⁵ but I will take the kingdom out of his son's hand and will give it to you, even ten tribes. ³⁶ I will give one tribe to his son, that David my servant may have a lamp always before me in Jerusalem, the city which I have chosen for myself to put my name there. ³⁷ I will take you, and you shall reign according to all that your soul desires, and shall be king over Israel. ³⁸ It shall be, if you will listen to all that I command you, and will walk in my ways, and do that which is right in my eyes, to keep my statutes and my commandments, as David my servant did, that I will be with you, and will build you a sure house, as I built for David, and will give Israel to you. ³⁹ I will afflict the offspring of David for this, but not forever.'" ⁴⁰ Therefore Solomon sought to kill Jeroboam, but Jeroboam arose and fled into Egypt, to Shishak king of Egypt, and was in Egypt until the death of Solomon. ⁴¹ Now the rest of the acts of Solomon, and all that he did, and his wisdom, aren't they written in the book of the acts of Solomon? ⁴² The time that Solomon reigned in Jerusalem over all Israel was forty years. ⁴³ Solomon slept with his fathers, and was buried in his father David's city; and Rehoboam his son reigned in his place.

# 12

¹ Rehoboam went to Shechem, for all Israel had come to Shechem to make him king. ² When Jeroboam the son of Nebat heard of it (for he was yet in Egypt, where he had fled from the presence of King Solomon, and Jeroboam lived in Egypt; ³ and they sent and called him), Jeroboam and all the assembly of Israel came, and spoke to Rehoboam, saying, ⁴"Your father made our yoke difficult. Now therefore make the hard service of your father, and his heavy yoke which he put on us, lighter, and we will serve you." ⁵ He said to them, "Depart for three days, then come back to me." So the people departed. ⁶ King Rehoboam took counsel with the old men who had stood before Solomon his father while he yet lived, saying, "What counsel do you give me to answer these people?" ⁷ They replied, "If you will be a servant to this people today, and will serve them, and answer them with good words, then they will be your servants forever." ⁸ But he abandoned the counsel of the old men which they had given him, and took counsel with the young men who had grown up with him, who stood before him. ⁹ He said to them, "What counsel do you give, that we may answer these people who have spoken to me, saying, 'Make the yoke that your father put on us lighter'?" ¹⁰ The young men who had grown up with him said to him, "Tell these people who spoke to you, saying, 'Your father made our yoke heavy, but make it lighter to us'—tell them, 'My little finger is thicker than my father's waist. ¹¹ Now my father burdened you with a heavy yoke, but I will add to your yoke. My father chastised you with whips, but I will chastise you with scorpions.'" ¹² So Jeroboam and all the people came to Rehoboam the third day, as the king asked, saying, "Come to me again the third day." ¹³ The king answered the people roughly, and abandoned the counsel of the old men which they had given him, ¹⁴ and spoke to them according to the counsel of the young men, saying, "My father made your yoke heavy, but I will add to your yoke. My father chastised you with whips, but I will chastise you with scorpions." ¹⁵ So the king didn't listen to the people; for it was a thing brought about from Yahweh, that he might establish his word, which Yahweh spoke by Ahijah the Shilonite to Jeroboam the son of Nebat. ¹⁶ When all Israel saw that the king didn't listen to them, the people answered the king, saying, "What portion have we in David? We don't have an inheritance in the son of Jesse. To your tents, Israel! Now see to your own house, David." So Israel departed to their tents. ¹⁷ But as for the children of Israel who lived in the cities of Judah, Rehoboam reigned over them. ¹⁸ Then King Rehoboam sent Adoram, who was over the men subject to forced labor; and all Israel stoned him to death with stones. King Rehoboam hurried to get himself up to his chariot, to flee to Jerusalem. ¹⁹ So Israel rebelled against David's house to this day. ²⁰ When all Israel heard that Jeroboam had returned, they sent and

called him to the congregation, and made him king over all Israel. There was no one who followed David's house, except for the tribe of Judah only. ²¹ When Rehoboam had come to Jerusalem, he assembled all the house of Judah and the tribe of Benjamin, a hundred and eighty thousand chosen men who were warriors, to fight against the house of Israel, to bring the kingdom again to Rehoboam the son of Solomon. ²² But the word of God came to Shemaiah the man of God, saying, ²³"Speak to Rehoboam the son of Solomon, king of Judah, and to all the house of Judah and Benjamin, and to the rest of the people, saying, ²⁴'Yahweh says, "You shall not go up or fight against your brothers, the children of Israel. Everyone return to his house; for this thing is from me."'" So they listened to Yahweh's word, and returned and went their way, according to Yahweh's word. ²⁵ Then Jeroboam built Shechem in the hill country of Ephraim, and lived in it; and he went out from there and built Penuel. ²⁶ Jeroboam said in his heart, "Now the kingdom will return to David's house. ²⁷ If this people goes up to offer sacrifices in Yahweh's house at Jerusalem, then the heart of this people will turn again to their lord, even to Rehoboam king of Judah; and they will kill me, and return to Rehoboam king of Judah." ²⁸ So the king took counsel, and made two calves of gold; and he said to them, "It is too much for you to go up to Jerusalem. Look and behold your gods, Israel, which brought you up out of the land of Egypt!" ²⁹ He set the one in Bethel, and the other he put in Dan. ³⁰ This thing became a sin, for the people went even as far as Dan to worship before the one there. ³¹ He made houses of high places, and made priests from among all the people, who were not of the sons of Levi. ³² Jeroboam ordained a feast in the eighth month, on the fifteenth day of the month, like the feast that is in Judah, and he went up to the altar. He did so in Bethel, sacrificing to the calves that he had made, and he placed in Bethel the priests of the high places that he had made. ³³ He went up to the altar which he had made in Bethel on the fifteenth day in the eighth month, even in the month which he had devised of his own heart; and he ordained a feast for the children of Israel, and went up to the altar to burn incense.

# 13

¹ Behold, a man of God came out of Judah by Yahweh's word to Bethel; and Jeroboam was standing by the altar to burn incense. ² He cried against the altar by Yahweh's word, and said, "Altar! Altar! Yahweh says: 'Behold, a son will be born to David's house, Josiah by name. On you he will sacrifice the priests of the high places who burn incense on you, and they will burn men's bones on you.'" ³ He gave a sign the same day, saying, "This is the sign which Yahweh has spoken: Behold, the altar will be split apart, and the ashes that are on it will be poured out." ⁴ When the king heard the saying of the man of God, which he cried against the altar in Bethel, Jeroboam put out his hand from the altar, saying, "Seize him!" His hand, which he put out against him, dried up, so that he could not draw it back again to himself. ⁵ The altar was also split apart, and the ashes poured out from the altar, according to the sign which the man of God had given by Yahweh's word. ⁶ The king answered the man of God, "Now intercede for the favor of Yahweh your God, and pray for me, that my hand may be restored me again." The man of God interceded with Yahweh, and the king's hand was restored to him again, and became as it was before. ⁷ The king said to the man of God, "Come home with me and refresh yourself, and I will give you a reward." ⁸ The man of God said to the king, "Even if you gave me half of your house, I would not go in with you, neither would I eat bread nor drink water in this place; ⁹ for so was it commanded me by Yahweh's word, saying, 'You shall eat no bread, drink no water, and don't return by the way that you came.'" ¹⁰ So he went another way, and didn't return by the way that he came to Bethel. ¹¹ Now an old prophet lived in Bethel, and one of his sons came and told him all the works that the man of God had done that day in Bethel. They also told their father the words which he had spoken to the king. ¹² Their father said to them, "Which way did he go?" Now his sons had seen which way the man of God went, who came from Judah. ¹³ He said to his sons, "Saddle the donkey for me." So they saddled the donkey for him; and he rode on it. ¹⁴ He went after the man of God, and found him sitting under an oak. He said to him, "Are you the man of God who came from Judah?" He said, "I am." ¹⁵ Then he said to him, "Come home with me and eat bread." ¹⁶ He said, "I may not return with you, nor go in with you. I will not eat bread or drink water with you in this place. ¹⁷ For it was said to me by Yahweh's word, 'You shall eat no bread or drink water there, and don't turn again to go by the way that you came.'" ¹⁸ He said to him, "I also am a prophet as you are; and an angel spoke to me by Yahweh's word, saying, 'Bring him back with you into your house, that he may eat bread and drink water.'" He lied to him. ¹⁹ So he went back with him, ate bread in his house, and drank water. ²⁰ As they sat at the table, Yahweh's word came to the prophet who brought him back; ²¹ and he cried out to the man of God who came

from Judah, saying, "Yahweh says, 'Because you have been disobedient to Yahweh's word, and have not kept the commandment which Yahweh your God commanded you, ²² but came back, and have eaten bread and drank water in the place of which he said to you, "Eat no bread, and drink no water," your body will not come to the tomb of your fathers.'" ²³ After he had eaten bread and after he drank, he saddled the donkey for the prophet whom he had brought back. ²⁴ When he had gone, a lion met him by the way and killed him. His body was thrown on the path, and the donkey stood by it. The lion also stood by the body. ²⁵ Behold, men passed by and saw the body thrown on the path, and the lion standing by the body; and they came and told it in the city where the old prophet lived. ²⁶ When the prophet who brought him back from the way heard of it, he said, "It is the man of God who was disobedient to Yahweh's word. Therefore Yahweh has delivered him to the lion, which has mauled him and slain him, according to Yahweh's word which he spoke to him." ²⁷ He said to his sons, saying, "Saddle the donkey for me," and they saddled it. ²⁸ He went and found his body thrown on the path, and the donkey and the lion standing by the body. The lion had not eaten the body nor mauled the donkey. ²⁹ The prophet took up the body of the man of God, and laid it on the donkey, and brought it back. He came to the city of the old prophet to mourn, and to bury him. ³⁰ He laid his body in his own grave; and they mourned over him, saying, "Alas, my brother!" ³¹ After he had buried him, he spoke to his sons, saying, "When I am dead, bury me in the tomb in which the man of God is buried. Lay my bones beside his bones. ³² For the saying which he cried by Yahweh's word against the altar in Bethel, and against all the houses of the high places which are in the cities of Samaria, will surely happen." ³³ After this thing, Jeroboam didn't turn from his evil way, but again made priests of the high places from among all the people. Whoever wanted to, he consecrated him, that there might be priests of the high places. ³⁴ This thing became sin to the house of Jeroboam, even to cut it off and to destroy it from off the surface of the earth.

# 14

¹ At that time Abijah the son of Jeroboam became sick. ² Jeroboam said to his wife, "Please get up and disguise yourself, so that you won't be recognized as Jeroboam's wife. Go to Shiloh. Behold, Ahijah the prophet is there, who said that I would be king over this people. ³ Take with you ten loaves of bread, some cakes, and a jar of honey, and go to him. He will tell you what will become of the child." ⁴ Jeroboam's wife did so, and arose and went to Shiloh, and came to Ahijah's house. Now Ahijah could not see, for his eyes were set by reason of his age. ⁵ Yahweh said to Ahijah, "Behold, Jeroboam's wife is coming to inquire of you concerning her son, for he is sick. Tell her such and such; for it will be, when she comes in, that she will pretend to be another woman." ⁶ So when Ahijah heard the sound of her feet as she came in at the door, he said, "Come in, Jeroboam's wife! Why do you pretend to be another? For I am sent to you with heavy news. ⁷ Go, tell Jeroboam, 'Yahweh, the God of Israel, says: "Because I exalted you from among the people, and made you prince over my people Israel, ⁸ and tore the kingdom away from David's house, and gave it you; and yet you have not been as my servant David, who kept my commandments, and who followed me with all his heart, to do that only which was right in my eyes, ⁹ but have done evil above all who were before you, and have gone and made for yourself other gods, molten images, to provoke me to anger, and have cast me behind your back, ¹⁰ therefore, behold, I will bring evil on the house of Jeroboam, and will cut off from Jeroboam everyone who urinates on a wall,ᵃ and he who is shut up and he who is left at large in Israel, and will utterly sweep away the house of Jeroboam, as a man sweeps away dung until it is all gone. ¹¹ The dogs will eat he who belongs to Jeroboam who dies in the city; and the birds of the sky will eat he who dies in the field, for Yahweh has spoken it.'" ¹² Arise therefore, and go to your house. When your feet enter into the city, the child will die. ¹³ All Israel will mourn for him and bury him; for he only of Jeroboam will come to the grave, because in him there is found some good thing toward Yahweh, the God of Israel, in the house of Jeroboam. ¹⁴ Moreover Yahweh will raise up a king for himself over Israel who will cut off the house of Jeroboam. This is the day! What? Even now. ¹⁵ For Yahweh will strike Israel, as a reed is shaken in the water; and he will root up Israel out of this good land which he gave to their fathers, and will scatter them beyond the River,ᵇ because they have made their Asherah poles, provoking Yahweh to anger. ¹⁶ He will give Israel up because of the sins of Jeroboam, which he has sinned, and with which he has made Israel to sin." ¹⁷ Jeroboam's wife arose and departed, and came to Tirzah. As she came to the threshold of the house, the child died. ¹⁸ All Israel buried him and mourned for him, according to Yahweh's word, which he spoke by his servant Ahijah the prophet. ¹⁹ The rest of the acts of Jeroboam, how he fought and how he reigned,

---

ᵃ *14:10 or, male*  |  ᵇ *14:15 That is, the Euphrates.*

behold, they are written in the book of the chronicles of the kings of Israel. [20] The days which Jeroboam reigned were twenty two years; then he slept with his fathers, and Nadab his son reigned in his place. [21] Rehoboam the son of Solomon reigned in Judah. Rehoboam was forty-one years old when he began to reign, and he reigned seventeen years in Jerusalem, the city which Yahweh had chosen out of all the tribes of Israel, to put his name there. His mother's name was Naamah the Ammonitess. [22] Judah did that which was evil in Yahweh's sight, and they provoked him to jealousy with their sins which they committed, above all that their fathers had done. [23] For they also built for themselves high places, sacred pillars, and Asherah poles on every high hill and under every green tree. [24] There were also sodomites in the land. They did according to all the abominations of the nations which Yahweh drove out before the children of Israel. [25] In the fifth year of King Rehoboam, Shishak king of Egypt came up against Jerusalem; [26] and he took away the treasures of Yahweh's house and the treasures of the king's house. He even took away all of it, including all the gold shields which Solomon had made. [27] King Rehoboam made shields of bronze in their place, and committed them to the hands of the captains of the guard, who kept the door of the king's house. [28] It was so, that as often as the king went into Yahweh's house, the guard bore them, and brought them back into the guard room. [29] Now the rest of the acts of Rehoboam, and all that he did, aren't they written in the book of the chronicles of the kings of Judah? [30] There was war between Rehoboam and Jeroboam continually. [31] Rehoboam slept with his fathers, and was buried with his fathers in David's city. His mother's name was Naamah the Ammonitess. Abijam his son reigned in his place.

## 15

[1] Now in the eighteenth year of King Jeroboam the son of Nebat, Abijam began to reign over Judah. [2] He reigned three years in Jerusalem. His mother's name was Maacah the daughter of Abishalom. [3] He walked in all the sins of his father, which he had done before him; and his heart was not perfect with Yahweh his God, as the heart of David his father. [4] Nevertheless for David's sake, Yahweh his God gave him a lamp in Jerusalem, to set up his son after him and to establish Jerusalem; [5] because David did that which was right in Yahweh's eyes, and didn't turn away from anything that he commanded him all the days of his life, except only in the matter of Uriah the Hittite. [6] Now there was war between Rehoboam and Jeroboam all the days of his life. [7] The rest of the acts of Abijam, and all that he did, aren't they written in the book of the chronicles of the kings of Judah? There was war between Abijam and Jeroboam. [8] Abijam slept with his fathers, and they buried him in David's city; and Asa his son reigned in his place. [9] In the twentieth year of Jeroboam king of Israel, Asa began to reign over Judah. [10] He reigned forty-one years in Jerusalem. His mother's name was Maacah the daughter of Abishalom. [11] Asa did that which was right in Yahweh's eyes, as David his father did. [12] He put away the sodomites out of the land, and removed all the idols that his fathers had made. [13] He also removed Maacah his mother from being queen, because she had made an abominable image for an Asherah. Asa cut down her image and burned it at the brook Kidron. [14] But the high places were not taken away. Nevertheless the heart of Asa was perfect with Yahweh all his days. [15] He brought into Yahweh's house the things that his father had dedicated, and the things that he himself had dedicated: silver, gold, and utensils. [16] There was war between Asa and Baasha king of Israel all their days. [17] Baasha king of Israel went up against Judah, and built Ramah, that he might not allow anyone to go out or come in to Asa king of Judah. [18] Then Asa took all the silver and the gold that was left in the treasures of Yahweh's house, and the treasures of the king's house, and delivered it into the hand of his servants. Then King Asa sent them to Ben Hadad, the son of Tabrimmon, the son of Hezion, king of Syria, who lived at Damascus, saying, [19]"Let there be a treaty between me and you, like that between my father and your father. Behold, I have sent to you a present of silver and gold. Go, break your treaty with Baasha king of Israel, that he may depart from me." [20] Ben Hadad listened to King Asa, and sent the captains of his armies against the cities of Israel, and struck Ijon, and Dan, and Abel Beth Maacah, and all Chinneroth, with all the land of Naphtali. [21] When Baasha heard of it, he stopped building Ramah, and lived in Tirzah. [22] Then King Asa made a proclamation to all Judah. No one was exempted. They carried away the stones of Ramah, and its timber, with which Baasha had built; and King Asa used it to build Geba of Benjamin, and Mizpah. [23] Now the rest of all the acts of Asa, and all his might, and all that he did, and the cities which he built, aren't they written in the book of the chronicles of the kings of Judah? But in the time of his old age he was diseased in his feet. [24] Asa slept with his fathers, and was buried with his fathers in his father David's city; and Jehoshaphat his son reigned in his place. [25] Nadab the son of Jeroboam began to reign over Israel in the second year of Asa king of Judah; and he reigned over Israel two years. [26] He did that which was evil in Yahweh's sight, and walked in the way of his father, and in his sin with which he made Israel to sin. [27] Baasha the son of Ahijah, of the house of Issachar, conspired against him; and Baasha struck him at Gibbethon, which belonged to the Philistines; for Nadab and all Israel were besieging Gibbethon. [28] Even in the third year of Asa king of Judah, Baasha killed him and reigned in his place. [29] As soon as he was king, he struck all the house of Jeroboam. He didn't leave to Jeroboam any who breathed, until he had destroyed him, according to the saying of Yahweh, which he spoke by his servant Ahijah the Shilonite; [30] for the sins of Jeroboam which he sinned, and with which he made Israel to sin, because of his provocation with which he provoked Yahweh, the God of Israel, to anger. [31] Now the rest of the acts of Nadab, and all that he did, aren't they written in the book of the chronicles of the kings of Israel? [32] There was war between Asa and Baasha king of Israel all their days. [33] In the third year of Asa king of Judah, Baasha the son of Ahijah began to reign over all Israel in Tirzah for twenty-four years. [34] He did that which was evil in Yahweh's sight, and walked in the way of Jeroboam, and in his sin with which he made Israel to sin.

## 16

[1] Yahweh's word came to Jehu the son of Hanani against Baasha, saying, [2]"Because I exalted you out of the dust and made you prince over my people Israel, and you have walked in the way of Jeroboam and have made my people Israel to sin, to provoke me to anger with their sins, [3] behold, I will utterly sweep away Baasha and his house; and I will make your house like the house of Jeroboam the son of Nebat. [4] The dogs will eat Baasha's descendants who die in the city; and he who dies of his in the field, the birds of the sky will eat." [5] Now the rest of the acts of Baasha, and what he did, and his might, aren't they written in the book of the chronicles of the kings of Israel? [6] Baasha slept with his fathers, and was buried in Tirzah; and Elah his son reigned in his place. [7] Moreover Yahweh's word came by the prophet Jehu the son of Hanani against Baasha and against his house, both because of all the evil that he did in Yahweh's sight, to provoke him to anger with the work of his hands, in being like the house of Jeroboam, and because he struck him. [8] In the twenty-sixth year of Asa king of Judah, Elah the son of Baasha began to reign over Israel in Tirzah for two years. [9] His servant Zimri, captain of half his chariots, conspired against him. Now he was in Tirzah, drinking himself drunk in the house of Arza, who was over the household in Tirzah; [10] and Zimri went in and struck him and killed him in the twenty-seventh year of Asa king of Judah, and reigned in his place. [11] When he began to reign, as soon as he sat on his throne, he attacked all the house of Baasha. He didn't leave him a single one who urinates on a wall[a] among his relatives or his friends. [12] Thus Zimri destroyed all the house of Baasha, according to Yahweh's word which he spoke against Baasha by Jehu the prophet, [13] for all the sins of Baasha, and the sins of Elah his son, which they sinned and with which they made Israel to sin, to provoke Yahweh, the God of Israel, to anger with their vanities. [14] Now the rest of the acts of Elah, and all that he did, aren't they written in the book of the chronicles of the kings of Israel? [15] In the twenty-seventh year of Asa king of Judah, Zimri reigned seven days in Tirzah. Now the people were encamped against Gibbethon, which belonged to the Philistines. [16] The people who were encamped heard that Zimri had conspired, and had also killed the king. Therefore all Israel made Omri, the captain of the army, king over Israel that day in the camp. [17] Omri went up from Gibbethon, and all Israel with him, and they besieged Tirzah. [18] When Zimri saw that the city was taken, he went into the fortified part of the king's house and burned the king's house over him with fire, and died, [19] for his sins which he sinned in doing that which was evil in Yahweh's sight, in walking in the way of Jeroboam, and in his sin which he did to make Israel to sin. [20] Now the rest of the acts of Zimri, and his treason that he committed, aren't they written in the book of the chronicles of the kings of Israel? [21] Then the people of Israel were divided into two parts: half of the people followed Tibni the son of Ginath, to make him king, and half followed Omri. [22] But the people who followed Omri prevailed against the people who followed Tibni the son of Ginath; so Tibni died, and Omri reigned. [23] In the thirty-first year of Asa king of Judah, Omri began to reign over Israel for twelve years. He reigned six years in Tirzah. [24] He bought the hill Samaria of Shemer for two talents[b] of silver; and he built on the hill, and called the name of the city which he built, Samaria, after the name of Shemer, the owner of the hill. [25] Omri did that which was evil in Yahweh's sight, and dealt wickedly above all who were before him. [26] For he walked in all the way of Jeroboam the son of Nebat, and in his sins with which he made Israel to sin, to

---

[a] *16:11 or, male*

[b] *16:24 A talent is about 30 kilograms or 66 pounds.*

provoke Yahweh, the God of Israel, to anger with their vanities. ²⁷ Now the rest of the acts of Omri which he did, and his might that he showed, aren't they written in the book of the chronicles of the kings of Israel? ²⁸ So Omri slept with his fathers, and was buried in Samaria; and Ahab his son reigned in his place. ²⁹ In the thirty-eighth year of Asa king of Judah, Ahab the son of Omri began to reign over Israel. Ahab the son of Omri reigned over Israel in Samaria twenty-two years. ³⁰ Ahab the son of Omri did that which was evil in Yahweh's sight above all that were before him. ³¹ As if it had been a light thing for him to walk in the sins of Jeroboam the son of Nebat, he took as wife Jezebel the daughter of Ethbaal king of the Sidonians, and went and served Baal and worshiped him. ³² He raised up an altar for Baal in the house of Baal, which he had built in Samaria. ³³ Ahab made the Asherah; and Ahab did more yet to provoke Yahweh, the God of Israel, to anger than all the kings of Israel who were before him. ³⁴ In his days Hiel the Bethelite built Jericho. He laid its foundation with the loss of Abiram his firstborn, and set up its gates with the loss of his youngest son Segub, according to Yahweh's word, which he spoke by Joshua the son of Nun.

## 17

¹ Elijah the Tishbite, who was one of the settlers of Gilead, said to Ahab, "As Yahweh, the God of Israel, lives, before whom I stand, there shall not be dew nor rain these years, but according to my word." ² Then Yahweh's word came to him, saying, ³"Go away from here, turn eastward, and hide yourself by the brook Cherith, that is before the Jordan. ⁴ You shall drink from the brook. I have commanded the ravens to feed you there." ⁵ So he went and did according to Yahweh's word, for he went and lived by the brook Cherith that is before the Jordan. ⁶ The ravens brought him bread and meat in the morning, and bread and meat in the evening; and he drank from the brook. ⁷ After a while, the brook dried up, because there was no rain in the land. ⁸ Yahweh's word came to him, saying, ⁹"Arise, go to Zarephath, which belongs to Sidon, and stay there. Behold, I have commanded a widow there to sustain you." ¹⁰ So he arose and went to Zarephath, and when he came to the gate of the city, behold, a widow was there gathering sticks. He called to her and said, "Please get me a little water in a jar, that I may drink." ¹¹ As she was going to get it, he called to her and said, "Please bring me a morsel of bread in your hand." ¹² She said, "As Yahweh your God lives, I don't have anything baked, but only a handful of meal in a jar and a little oil in a jar. Behold, I am gathering two sticks, that I may go in and bake it for me and my son, that we may eat it, and die." ¹³ Elijah said to her, "Don't be afraid. Go and do as you have said; but make me a little cake from it first, and bring it out to me, and afterward make some for you and for your son. ¹⁴ For Yahweh, the God of Israel, says, 'The jar of meal will not run out, and the jar of oil will not fail, until the day that Yahweh sends rain on the earth.'" ¹⁵ She went and did according to the saying of Elijah; and she, he, and her household ate many days. ¹⁶ The jar of meal didn't run out and the jar of oil didn't fail, according to Yahweh's word, which he spoke by Elijah. ¹⁷ After these things, the son of the woman, the mistress of the house, became sick; and his sickness was so severe that there was no breath left in him. ¹⁸ She said to Elijah, "What have I to do with you, you man of God? You have come to me to bring my sin to memory, and to kill my son!" ¹⁹ He said to her, "Give me your son." He took him out of her bosom, and carried him up into the room where he stayed, and laid him on his own bed. ²⁰ He cried to Yahweh and said, "Yahweh my God, have you also brought evil on the widow with whom I am staying, by killing her son?" ²¹ He stretched himself on the child three times, and cried to Yahweh and said, "Yahweh my God, please let this child's soul come into him again." ²² Yahweh listened to the voice of Elijah; and the soul of the child came into him again, and he revived. ²³ Elijah took the child and brought him down out of the room into the house, and delivered him to his mother; and Elijah said, "Behold, your son lives." ²⁴ The woman said to Elijah, "Now I know that you are a man of God, and that Yahweh's word in your mouth is truth."

## 18

¹ After many days, Yahweh's word came to Elijah, in the third year, saying, "Go, show yourself to Ahab; and I will send rain on the earth." ² Elijah went to show himself to Ahab. The famine was severe in Samaria. ³ Ahab called Obadiah, who was over the household. (Now Obadiah feared Yahweh greatly; ⁴ for when Jezebel cut off Yahweh's prophets, Obadiah took one hundred prophets, and hid them fifty to a cave, and fed them with bread and water.) ⁵ Ahab said to Obadiah, "Go through the land, to all the springs of water, and to all the brooks. Perhaps we may find grass and save the horses and mules alive, that we not lose all the animals." ⁶ So they divided the land between them to pass throughout it. Ahab went one way by himself, and Obadiah went another way by himself. ⁷ As Obadiah was on the way, behold, Elijah met him. He recognized him, and fell on his face, and said, "Is it you, my lord Elijah?" ⁸ He answered him, "It is I. Go, tell your lord, 'Behold, Elijah is here!'" ⁹ He said, "How have I sinned, that you would deliver your servant into the hand of Ahab, to kill me? ¹⁰ As Yahweh your God lives, there is no nation or kingdom where my lord has not sent to seek you. When they said, 'He is not here,' he took an oath of the kingdom and nation that they didn't find you. ¹¹ Now you say, 'Go, tell your lord, "Behold, Elijah is here."' ¹² It will happen, as soon as I leave you, that Yahweh's Spirit will carry you I don't know where; and so when I come and tell Ahab, and he can't find you, he will kill me. But I, your servant, have feared Yahweh from my youth. ¹³ Wasn't it told my lord what I did when Jezebel killed Yahweh's prophets, how I hid one hundred men of Yahweh's prophets with fifty to a cave, and fed them with bread and water? ¹⁴ Now you say, 'Go, tell your lord, "Behold, Elijah is here".' He will kill me." ¹⁵ Elijah said, "As Yahweh of Armies lives, before whom I stand, I will surely show myself to him today." ¹⁶ So Obadiah went to meet Ahab, and told him; and Ahab went to meet Elijah. ¹⁷ When Ahab saw Elijah, Ahab said to him, "Is that you, you troubler of Israel?" ¹⁸ He answered, "I have not troubled Israel, but you and your father's house, in that you have forsaken Yahweh's commandments and you have followed the Baals. ¹⁹ Now therefore send, and gather to me all Israel to Mount Carmel, and four hundred fifty of the prophets of Baal, and four hundred of the prophets of the Asherah, who eat at Jezebel's table." ²⁰ So Ahab sent to all the children of Israel, and gathered the prophets together to Mount Carmel. ²¹ Elijah came near to all the people, and said, "How long will you waver between the two sides? If Yahweh is God, follow him; but if Baal, then follow him." The people didn't say a word. ²² Then Elijah said to the people, "I, even I only, am left as a prophet of Yahweh; but Baal's prophets are four hundred fifty men. ²³ Let them therefore give us two bulls; and let them choose one bull for themselves, and cut it in pieces, and lay it on the wood, and put no fire under; and I will dress the other bull, and lay it on the wood, and put no fire under it. ²⁴ You call on the name of your god, and I will call on Yahweh's name. The God who answers by fire, let him be God." All the people answered, "What you say is good." ²⁵ Elijah said to the prophets of Baal, "Choose one bull for yourselves, and dress it first, for you are many; and call on the name of your god, but put no fire under it." ²⁶ They took the bull which was given them, and they dressed it, and called on the name of Baal from morning even until noon, saying, "Baal, hear us!" But there was no voice, and nobody answered. They leaped about the altar which was made. ²⁷ At noon, Elijah mocked them, and said, "Cry aloud, for he is a god. Either he is deep in thought, or he has gone somewhere, or he is on a journey, or perhaps he sleeps and must be awakened." ²⁸ They cried aloud, and cut themselves in their way with knives and lances until the blood gushed out on them. ²⁹ When midday was past, they prophesied until the time of the evening offering; but there was no voice, no answer, and nobody paid attention. ³⁰ Elijah said to all the people, "Come near to me!"; and all the people came near to him. He repaired Yahweh's altar that had been thrown down. ³¹ Elijah took twelve stones, according to the number of the tribes of the sons of Jacob, to whom Yahweh's word came, saying, "Israel shall be your name." ³² With the stones he built an altar in Yahweh's name. He made a trench around the altar large enough to contain two seahsª of seed. ³³ He put the wood in order, and cut the bull in pieces and laid it on the wood. He said, "Fill four jars with water, and pour it on the burnt offering and on the wood." ³⁴ He said, "Do it a second time;" and they did it the second time. He said, "Do it a third time;" and they did it the third time. ³⁵ The water ran around the altar; and he also filled the trench with water. ³⁶ At the time of the evening offering, Elijah the prophet came near and said, "Yahweh, the God of Abraham, of Isaac, and of Israel, let it be known today that you are God in Israel and that I am your servant, and that I have done all these things at your word. ³⁷ Hear me, Yahweh, hear me, that this people may know that you, Yahweh, are God, and that you have turned their heart back again." ³⁸ Then Yahweh's fire fell and consumed the burnt offering, the wood, the stones, and the dust; and it licked up the water that was in the trench. ³⁹ When all the people saw it,

they fell on their faces. They said, "Yahweh, he is God! Yahweh, he is God!" [40] Elijah said to them, "Seize the prophets of Baal! Don't let one of them escape!" They seized them; and Elijah brought them down to the brook Kishon, and killed them there. [41] Elijah said to Ahab, "Get up, eat and drink; for there is the sound of abundance of rain." [42] So Ahab went up to eat and to drink. Elijah went up to the top of Carmel; and he bowed himself down on the earth, and put his face between his knees. [43] He said to his servant, "Go up now and look toward the sea." He went up and looked, then said, "There is nothing." He said, "Go again" seven times. [44] On the seventh time, he said, "Behold, a small cloud, like a man's hand, is rising out of the sea." He said, "Go up, tell Ahab, 'Get ready and go down, so that the rain doesn't stop you.'" [45] In a little while, the sky grew black with clouds and wind, and there was a great rain. Ahab rode, and went to Jezreel. [46] Yahweh's hand was on Elijah; and he tucked his cloak into his belt and ran before Ahab to the entrance of Jezreel.

# 19

[1] Ahab told Jezebel all that Elijah had done, and how he had killed all the prophets with the sword. [2] Then Jezebel sent a messenger to Elijah, saying, "So let the gods do to me, and more also, if I don't make your life as the life of one of them by tomorrow about this time!" [3] When he saw that, he arose and ran for his life, and came to Beersheba, which belongs to Judah, and left his servant there. [4] But he himself went a day's journey into the wilderness, and came and sat down under a juniper tree. Then he requested for himself that he might die, and said, "It is enough. Now, O Yahweh, take away my life; for I am not better than my fathers." [5] He lay down and slept under a juniper tree; and behold, an angel touched him, and said to him, "Arise and eat!" [6] He looked, and behold, there was at his head a cake baked on the coals, and a jar of water. He ate and drank, and lay down again. [7] Yahweh's angel came again the second time, and touched him, and said, "Arise and eat, because the journey is too great for you." [8] He arose, and ate and drank, and went in the strength of that food forty days and forty nights to Horeb, God's Mountain. [9] He came to a cave there, and camped there; and behold, Yahweh's word came to him, and he said to him, "What are you doing here, Elijah?" [10] He said, "I have been very jealous for Yahweh, the God of Armies; for the children of Israel have forsaken your covenant, thrown down your altars, and killed your prophets with the sword. I, even I only, am left; and they seek my life, to take it away." [11] He said, "Go out and stand on the mountain before Yahweh." Behold, Yahweh passed by, and a great and strong wind tore the mountains and broke in pieces the rocks before Yahweh; but Yahweh was not in the wind. After the wind there was an earthquake; but Yahweh was not in the earthquake. [12] After the earthquake a fire passed; but Yahweh was not in the fire. After the fire, there was a still small voice. [13] When Elijah heard it, he wrapped his face in his mantle, went out, and stood in the entrance of the cave. Behold, a voice came to him, and said, "What are you doing here, Elijah?" [14] He said, "I have been very jealous for Yahweh, the God of Armies; for the children of Israel have forsaken your covenant, thrown down your altars, and killed your prophets with the sword. I, even I only, am left; and they seek my life, to take it away." [15] Yahweh said to him, "Go, return on your way to the wilderness of Damascus. When you arrive, anoint Hazael to be king over Syria. [16] Anoint Jehu the son of Nimshi to be king over Israel; and anoint Elisha the son of Shaphat of Abel Meholah to be prophet in your place. [17] He who escapes from the sword of Hazael, Jehu will kill; and he who escapes from the sword of Jehu, Elisha will kill. [18] Yet I reserved seven thousand in Israel, all the knees of which have not bowed to Baal, and every mouth which has not kissed him." [19] So he departed from there and found Elisha the son of Shaphat, who was plowing with twelve yoke of oxen before him, and he with the twelfth. Elijah went over to him and put his mantle on him. [20] Elisha left the oxen and ran after Elijah, and said, "Let me please kiss my father and my mother, and then I will follow you." He said to him, "Go back again; for what have I done to you?" [21] He returned from following him, and took the yoke of oxen, killed them, and boiled their meat with the oxen's equipment, and gave to the people; and they ate. Then he arose, and went after Elijah, and served him.

# 20

[1] Ben Hadad the king of Syria gathered all his army together; and there were thirty-two kings with him, with horses and chariots. He went up and besieged Samaria, and fought against it. [2] He sent messengers into the city to Ahab king of Israel and said to him, "Ben Hadad says, [3] 'Your silver and your gold are mine. Your wives also and your children, even the best, are mine.'" [4] The king of Israel answered, "It is according to your saying, my lord, O king. I am yours, and all that I have." [5] The messengers came again and said, "Ben Hadad says, 'I sent indeed to you, saying, "You shall deliver me your silver, your gold, your wives, and your children; [6] but I will send my servants to you tomorrow about this time, and they will search your house and the houses of your servants. Whatever is pleasant in your eyes, they will put it in their hand, and take it away."'" [7] Then the king of Israel called all the elders of the land, and said, "Please notice how this man seeks mischief; for he sent to me for my wives, and for my children, and for my silver, and for my gold; and I didn't deny him." [8] All the elders and all the people said to him, "Don't listen, and don't consent." [9] Therefore he said to the messengers of Ben Hadad, "Tell my lord the king, 'All that you sent for to your servant at the first I will do, but this thing I cannot do.'" The messengers departed and brought him back the message. [10] Ben Hadad sent to him, and said, "The gods do so to me, and more also, if the dust of Samaria will be enough for handfuls for all the people who follow me." [11] The king of Israel answered, "Tell him, 'Don't let him who puts on his armor brag like he who takes it off.'" [12] When Ben Hadad heard this message as he was drinking, he and the kings in the pavilions, he said to his servants, "Prepare to attack!" So they prepared to attack the city. [13] Behold, a prophet came near to Ahab king of Israel, and said, "Yahweh says, 'Have you seen all this great multitude? Behold, I will deliver it into your hand today. Then you will know that I am Yahweh.'" [14] Ahab said, "By whom?" He said, "Yahweh says, 'By the young men of the princes of the provinces.'" Then he said, "Who shall begin the battle?" He answered, "You." [15] Then he mustered the young men of the princes of the provinces, and they were two hundred and thirty-two. After them, he mustered all the people, even all the children of Israel, being seven thousand. [16] They went out at noon. But Ben Hadad was drinking himself drunk in the pavilions, he and the kings, the thirty-two kings who helped him. [17] The young men of the princes of the provinces went out first; and Ben Hadad sent out, and they told him, saying, "Men are coming out from Samaria." [18] He said, "If they have come out for peace, take them alive; or if they have come out for war, take them alive." [19] So these went out of the city, the young men of the princes of the provinces, and the army which followed them. [20] They each killed his man. The Syrians fled, and Israel pursued them. Ben Hadad the king of Syria escaped on a horse with horsemen. [21] The king of Israel went out and struck the horses and chariots, and killed the Syrians with a great slaughter. [22] The prophet came near to the king of Israel and said to him, "Go, strengthen yourself, and plan what you must do, for at the return of the year, the king of Syria will come up against you." [23] The servants of the king of Syria said to him, "Their god is a god of the hills; therefore they were stronger than we. But let's fight against them in the plain, and surely we will be stronger than they. [24] Do this thing: take the kings away, every man out of his place, and put captains in their place. [25] Muster an army like the army that you have lost, horse for horse and chariot for chariot. We will fight against them in the plain, and surely we will be stronger than they are." He listened to their voice and did so. [26] At the return of the year, Ben Hadad mustered the Syrians and went up to Aphek to fight against Israel. [27] The children of Israel were mustered and given provisions, and went against them. The children of Israel encamped before them like two little flocks of young goats, but the Syrians filled the country. [28] A man of God came near and spoke to the king of Israel, and said, "Yahweh says, 'Because the Syrians have said, "Yahweh is a god of the hills, but he is not a god of the valleys," therefore I will deliver all this great multitude into your hand, and you shall know that I am Yahweh.'" [29] They encamped opposite each other for seven days. Then on the seventh day the battle was joined; and the children of Israel killed one hundred thousand footmen of the Syrians in one day. [30] But the rest fled to Aphek, into the city; and the wall fell on twenty-seven thousand men who were left. Ben Hadad fled and came into the city, into an inner room. [31] His servants said to him, "See now, we have heard that the kings of the house of Israel are merciful kings. Please let us put sackcloth on our bodies and ropes on our heads, and go out to the king of Israel. Maybe he will save your life." [32] So they put sackcloth on their bodies and ropes on their heads, and came to the king of Israel, and said, "Your servant Ben Hadad says, 'Please let me live.'" He said, "Is he still alive? He is my brother." [33] Now the men observed diligently and hurried to take this phrase; and they said, "Your brother Ben Hadad." Then he said, "Go, bring him." Then Ben Hadad came out to him; and he caused him to come up into the chariot. [34] Ben Hadad said to him, "The cities which my father took from your father I will restore. You shall make streets for yourself in Damascus, as my father made in Samaria." "I", said Ahab, "will let you go with this covenant." So he made a covenant with him and let him go. [35] A certain man of the sons of the prophets said to his fellow by Yahweh's word, "Please strike me!" The man refused to strike him. [36] Then he said to him, "Because you have not obeyed Yahweh's voice, behold, as soon as you have departed from me, a lion will kill you." As soon as he had departed from him, a lion found him and killed him. [37] Then he found another man, and said, "Please strike me." The man struck him and wounded him. [38] So the prophet departed and waited for the king by the way, and disguised himself with his headband over his eyes. [39] As the king passed

by, he cried to the king, and he said, "Your servant went out into the middle of the battle; and behold, a man came over and brought a man to me, and said, 'Guard this man! If by any means he is missing, then your life shall be for his life, or else you shall pay a talent[a] of silver.' [40] As your servant was busy here and there, he was gone." The king of Israel said to him, "So shall your judgment be. You yourself have decided it." [41] He hurried, and took the headband away from his eyes; and the king of Israel recognized that he was one of the prophets. [42] He said to him, "Yahweh says, 'Because you have let go out of your hand the man whom I had devoted to destruction, therefore your life will take the place of his life, and your people take the place of his people.'" [43] The king of Israel went to his house sullen and angry, and came to Samaria.

## 21

[1] After these things, Naboth the Jezreelite had a vineyard which was in Jezreel, next to the palace of Ahab king of Samaria. [2] Ahab spoke to Naboth, saying, "Give me your vineyard, that I may have it for a garden of herbs, because it is near my house; and I will give you for it a better vineyard than it. Or, if it seems good to you, I will give you its worth in money." [3] Naboth said to Ahab, "May Yahweh forbid me, that I should give the inheritance of my fathers to you!" [4] Ahab came into his house sullen and angry because of the word which Naboth the Jezreelite had spoken to him, for he had said, "I will not give you the inheritance of my fathers." He laid himself down on his bed, and turned away his face, and would eat no bread. [5] But Jezebel his wife came to him, and said to him, "Why is your spirit so sad that you eat no bread?" [6] He said to her, "Because I spoke to Naboth the Jezreelite, and said to him, 'Give me your vineyard for money; or else, if it pleases you, I will give you another vineyard for it.' He answered, 'I will not give you my vineyard.'" [7] Jezebel his wife said to him, "Do you now govern the kingdom of Israel? Arise, and eat bread, and let your heart be merry. I will give you the vineyard of Naboth the Jezreelite." [8] So she wrote letters in Ahab's name and sealed them with his seal, and sent the letters to the elders and to the nobles who were in his city, who lived with Naboth. [9] She wrote in the letters, saying, "Proclaim a fast, and set Naboth on high among the people. [10] Set two men, wicked fellows, before him, and let them testify against him, saying, 'You cursed God and the king!' Then carry him out, and stone him to death." [11] The men of his city, even the elders and the nobles who lived in his city, did as Jezebel had instructed them in the letters which she had written and sent to them. [12] They proclaimed a fast, and set Naboth on high among the people. [13] The two men, the wicked fellows, came in and sat before him. The wicked fellows testified against him, even against Naboth, in the presence of the people, saying, "Naboth cursed God and the king!" Then they carried him out of the city and stoned him to death with stones. [14] Then they sent to Jezebel, saying, "Naboth has been stoned and is dead." [15] When Jezebel heard that Naboth had been stoned and was dead, Jezebel said to Ahab, "Arise, take possession of the vineyard of Naboth the Jezreelite, which he refused to give you for money; for Naboth is not alive, but dead." [16] When Ahab heard that Naboth was dead, Ahab rose up to go down to the vineyard of Naboth the Jezreelite, to take possession of it. [17] Yahweh's word came to Elijah the Tishbite, saying, [18]"Arise, go down to meet Ahab king of Israel, who dwells in Samaria. Behold, he is in the vineyard of Naboth, where he has gone down to take possession of it. [19] You shall speak to him, saying, 'Yahweh says, "Have you killed and also taken possession?"' You shall speak to him, saying, 'Yahweh says, "In the place where dogs licked the blood of Naboth, dogs will lick your blood, even yours."'" [20] Ahab said to Elijah, "Have you found me, my enemy?" He answered, "I have found you, because you have sold yourself to do that which is evil in Yahweh's sight. [21] Behold, I will bring evil on you, and will utterly sweep you away and will cut off from Ahab everyone who urinates against a wall,[b] and him who is shut up and him who is left at large in Israel. [22] I will make your house like the house of Jeroboam the son of Nebat, and like the house of Baasha the son of Ahijah, for the provocation with which you have provoked me to anger, and have made Israel to sin." [23] Yahweh also spoke of Jezebel, saying, "The dogs will eat Jezebel by the rampart of Jezreel. [24] The dogs will eat he who dies of Ahab in the city; and the birds of the sky will eat he who dies in the field." [25] But there was no one like Ahab, who sold himself to do that which was evil in Yahweh's sight, whom Jezebel his wife stirred up. [26] He did very abominably in following idols, according to all that the Amorites did, whom Yahweh cast out before the children of Israel. [27] When Ahab heard those words, he tore his clothes, put sackcloth on his body, fasted, lay in sackcloth, and went about despondently. [28] Yahweh's word came to Elijah the Tishbite, saying, [29]"See how Ahab humbles himself before me? Because he humbles himself before me, I

will not bring the evil in his days; but I will bring the evil on his house in his son's day."

## 22

[1] They continued three years without war between Syria and Israel. [2] In the third year, Jehoshaphat the king of Judah came down to the king of Israel. [3] The king of Israel said to his servants, "You know that Ramoth Gilead is ours, and we do nothing, and don't take it out of the hand of the king of Syria?" [4] He said to Jehoshaphat, "Will you go with me to battle to Ramoth Gilead?" Jehoshaphat said to the king of Israel, "I am as you are, my people as your people, my horses as your horses." [5] Jehoshaphat said to the king of Israel, "Please inquire first for Yahweh's word." [6] Then the king of Israel gathered the prophets together, about four hundred men, and said to them, "Should I go against Ramoth Gilead to battle, or should I refrain?" They said, "Go up; for the Lord will deliver it into the hand of the king." [7] But Jehoshaphat said, "Isn't there here a prophet of Yahweh, that we may inquire of him?" [8] The king of Israel said to Jehoshaphat, "There is yet one man by whom we may inquire of Yahweh, Micaiah the son of Imlah; but I hate him, for he does not prophesy good concerning me, but evil." Jehoshaphat said, "Don't let the king say so." [9] Then the king of Israel called an officer, and said, "Quickly get Micaiah the son of Imlah." [10] Now the king of Israel and Jehoshaphat the king of Judah were sitting each on his throne, arrayed in their robes, in an open place at the entrance of the gate of Samaria; and all the prophets were prophesying before them. [11] Zedekiah the son of Chenaanah made himself horns of iron, and said, "Yahweh says, 'With these you will push the Syrians, until they are consumed.'" [12] All the prophets prophesied so, saying, "Go up to Ramoth Gilead and prosper; for Yahweh will deliver it into the hand of the king." [13] The messenger who went to call Micaiah spoke to him, saying, "See now, the prophets declare good to the king with one mouth. Please let your word be like the word of one of them, and speak good." [14] Micaiah said, "As Yahweh lives, what Yahweh says to me, that I will speak." [15] When he had come to the king, the king said to him, "Micaiah, shall we go to Ramoth Gilead to battle, or shall we forbear?" He answered him, "Go up and prosper; and Yahweh will deliver it into the hand of the king." [16] The king said to him, "How many times do I have to adjure you that you speak to me nothing but the truth in Yahweh's name?" [17] He said, "I saw all Israel scattered on the mountains, as sheep that have no shepherd. Yahweh said, 'These have no master. Let them each return to his house in peace.'" [18] The king of Israel said to Jehoshaphat, "Didn't I tell you that he would not prophesy good concerning me, but evil?" [19] Micaiah said, "Therefore hear Yahweh's word. I saw Yahweh sitting on his throne, and all the army of heaven standing by him on his right hand and on his left. [20] Yahweh said, 'Who will entice Ahab, that he may go up and fall at Ramoth Gilead?' One said one thing, and another said another. [21] A spirit came out and stood before Yahweh, and said, 'I will entice him.' [22] Yahweh said to him, 'How?' He said, 'I will go out and will be a lying spirit in the mouth of all his prophets.' He said, 'You will entice him, and will also prevail. Go out and do so.' [23] Now therefore, behold, Yahweh has put a lying spirit in the mouth of all these your prophets; and Yahweh has spoken evil concerning you." [24] Then Zedekiah the son of Chenaanah came near and struck Micaiah on the cheek, and said, "Which way did Yahweh's Spirit go from me to speak to you?" [25] Micaiah said, "Behold, you will see on that day when you go into an inner room to hide yourself." [26] The king of Israel said, "Take Micaiah, and carry him back to Amon the governor of the city and to Joash the king's son. [27] Say, 'The king says, "Put this fellow in the prison, and feed him with bread of affliction and with water of affliction, until I come in peace."'" [28] Micaiah said, "If you return at all in peace, Yahweh has not spoken by me." He said, "Listen, all you people!" [29] So the king of Israel and Jehoshaphat the king of Judah went up to Ramoth Gilead. [30] The king of Israel said to Jehoshaphat, "I will disguise myself and go into the battle, but you put on your robes." The king of Israel disguised himself and went into the battle. [31] Now the king of Syria had commanded the thirty-two captains of his chariots, saying, "Don't fight with small nor great, except only with the king of Israel." [32] When the captains of the chariots saw Jehoshaphat, they said, "Surely that is the king of Israel!" and they came over to fight against him. Jehoshaphat cried out. [33] When the captains of the chariots saw that it was not the king of Israel, they turned back from pursuing him. [34] A certain man drew his bow at random, and struck the king of Israel between the joints of the armor. Therefore he said to the driver of his chariot, "Turn around, and carry me out of the battle, for I am severely wounded." [35] The battle increased that day. The king was propped up in his chariot facing the Syrians, and died at evening. The blood ran out of the wound into the bottom of the chariot. [36] A cry went throughout

the army about the going down of the sun, saying, "Every man to his city, and every man to his country!" ³⁷ So the king died, and was brought to Samaria; and they buried the king in Samaria. ³⁸ They washed the chariot by the pool of Samaria; and the dogs licked up his blood where the prostitutes washed themselves, according to Yahweh's word which he spoke. ³⁹ Now the rest of the acts of Ahab, and all that he did, and the ivory house which he built, and all the cities that he built, aren't they written in the book of the chronicles of the kings of Israel? ⁴⁰ So Ahab slept with his fathers; and Ahaziah his son reigned in his place. ⁴¹ Jehoshaphat the son of Asa began to reign over Judah in the fourth year of Ahab king of Israel. ⁴² Jehoshaphat was thirty-five years old when he began to reign; and he reigned twenty-five years in Jerusalem. His mother's name was Azubah the daughter of Shilhi. ⁴³ He walked in all the way of Asa his father. He didn't turn away from it, doing that which was right in Yahweh's eyes. However, the high places were not taken away. The people still sacrificed and burned incense on the high places. ⁴⁴ Jehoshaphat made peace with the king of Israel. ⁴⁵ Now the rest of the acts of Jehoshaphat, and his might that he showed, and how he fought, aren't they written in the book of the chronicles of the kings of Judah? ⁴⁶ The remnant of the sodomites, that remained in the days of his father Asa, he put away out of the land. ⁴⁷ There was no king in Edom. A deputy ruled. ⁴⁸ Jehoshaphat made ships of Tarshish to go to Ophir for gold, but they didn't go, for the ships wrecked at Ezion Geber. ⁴⁹ Then Ahaziah the son of Ahab said to Jehoshaphat, "Let my servants go with your servants in the ships." But Jehoshaphat would not. ⁵⁰ Jehoshaphat slept with his fathers, and was buried with his fathers in his father David's city. Jehoram his son reigned in his place. ⁵¹ Ahaziah the son of Ahab began to reign over Israel in Samaria in the seventeenth year of Jehoshaphat king of Judah, and he reigned two years over Israel. ⁵² He did that which was evil in Yahweh's sight, and walked in the way of his father, and in the way of his mother, and in the way of Jeroboam the son of Nebat, in which he made Israel to sin. ⁵³ He served Baal and worshiped him, and provoked Yahweh, the God of Israel, to anger in all the ways that his father had done so.

# The Second Book of Kings

## 1

¹ Moab rebelled against Israel after the death of Ahab. ² Ahaziah fell down through the lattice in his upper room that was in Samaria, and was sick. So he sent messengers, and said to them, "Go, inquire of Baal Zebub, the god of Ekron, whether I will recover of this sickness." ³ But Yahweh'sª angel said to Elijah the Tishbite, "Arise, go up to meet the messengers of the king of Samaria, and tell them, 'Is it because there is no Godᵇ in Israel that you go to inquire of Baal Zebub, the god of Ekron? ⁴ Now therefore Yahweh says, "You will not come down from the bed where you have gone up, but you will surely die."'" Then Elijah departed. ⁵ The messengers returned to him, and he said to them, "Why is it that you have returned?" ⁶ They said to him, "A man came up to meet us, and said to us, 'Go, return to the king who sent you, and tell him, "Yahweh says, 'Is it because there is no God in Israel that you send to inquire of Baal Zebub, the god of Ekron? Therefore you will not come down from the bed where you have gone up, but you will surely die.'"'" ⁷ He said to them, "What kind of man was he who came up to meet you and told you these words?" ⁸ They answered him, "He was a hairy man, and wearing a leather belt around his waist." He said, "It's Elijah the Tishbite." ⁹ Then the king sent a captain of fifty with his fifty to him. He went up to him; and behold,ᶜ he was sitting on the top of the hill. He said to him, "Man of God, the king has said, 'Come down!'" ¹⁰ Elijah answered to the captain of fifty, "If I am a man of God, then let fire come down from the sky and consume you and your fifty!" Then fire came down from the sky, and consumed him and his fifty. ¹¹ Again he sent to him another captain of fifty with his fifty. He answered him, "Man of God, the king has said, 'Come down quickly!'" ¹² Elijah answered them, "If I am a man of God, then let fire come down from the sky and consume you and your fifty!" Then God's fire came down from the sky, and consumed him and his fifty. ¹³ Again he sent the captain of a third fifty with his fifty. The third captain of fifty went up, and came and fell on his knees before Elijah, and begged him, and said to him, "Man of God, please let my life and the life of these fifty of your servants be precious in your sight. ¹⁴ Behold, fire came down from the sky and consumed the last two captains of fifty with their fifties. But now let my life be precious in your sight." ¹⁵ Yahweh's angel said to Elijah, "Go down with him. Don't be afraid of him." Then

he arose and went down with him to the king. ¹⁶ He said to him, "Yahweh says, 'Because you have sent messengers to inquire of Baal Zebub, the god of Ekron, is it because there is no God in Israel to inquire of his word? Therefore you will not come down from the bed where you have gone up, but you will surely die.'" ¹⁷ So he died according to Yahweh's word which Elijah had spoken. Jehoram began to reign in his place, in the second year of Jehoram the son of Jehoshaphat king of Judah, because he had no son. ¹⁸ Now the rest of the acts of Ahaziah which he did, aren't they written in the book of the chronicles of the kings of Israel?

## 2

¹ When Yahweh was about to take Elijah up by a whirlwind into heaven, Elijah went with Elisha from Gilgal. ² Elijah said to Elisha, "Please wait here, for Yahweh has sent me as far as Bethel." Elisha said, "As Yahweh lives, and as your soul lives, I will not leave you." So they went down to Bethel. ³ The sons of the prophets who were at Bethel came out to Elisha, and said to him, "Do you know that Yahweh will take away your master from over you today?" He said, "Yes, I know it. Hold your peace." ⁴ Elijah said to him, "Elisha, please wait here, for Yahweh has sent me to Jericho." He said, "As Yahweh lives, and as your soul lives, I will not leave you." So they came to Jericho. ⁵ The sons of the prophets who were at Jericho came near to Elisha, and said to him, "Do you know that Yahweh will take away your master from over you today?" He answered, "Yes, I know it. Hold your peace." ⁶ Elijah said to him, "Please wait here, for Yahweh has sent me to the Jordan." He said, "As Yahweh lives, and as your soul lives, I will not leave you." Then they both went on. ⁷ Fifty men of the sons of the prophets went and stood opposite them at a distance; and they both stood by the Jordan. ⁸ Elijah took his mantle, and rolled it up, and struck the waters; and they were divided here and there, so that they both went over on dry ground. ⁹ When they had gone over, Elijah said to Elisha, "Ask what I shall do for you, before I am taken from you." Elisha said, "Please let a double portion of your spirit be on me." ¹⁰ He said, "You have asked a hard thing. If you see me when I am taken from you, it will be so for you; but if not, it will not be so." ¹¹ As they continued on and talked, behold, a chariot of fire and horses of fire separated them; and Elijah went up by a whirlwind into heaven. ¹² Elisha saw it, and he cried, "My father, my father, the chariots of Israel and its horsemen!" He saw him no more. Then he took hold of his own clothes and tore them in two pieces. ¹³ He also took up Elijah's mantle that fell from him, and went back and stood by the bank of the Jordan. ¹⁴ He took Elijah's mantle that fell from him, and struck the waters, and said, "Where is Yahweh, the God of Elijah?" When he also had struck the waters, they were divided apart, and Elisha went over. ¹⁵ When the sons of the prophets who were at Jericho facing him saw him, they said, "The spirit of Elijah rests on Elisha." They came to meet him, and bowed themselves to the ground before him. ¹⁶ They said to him, "See now, there are with your servants fifty strong men. Please let them go and seek your master. Perhaps Yahweh's Spirit has taken him up, and put him on some mountain or into some valley." He said, "Don't send them." ¹⁷ When they urged him until he was ashamed, he said, "Send them." Therefore they sent fifty men; and they searched for three days, but didn't find him. ¹⁸ They came back to him while he stayed at Jericho; and he said to them, "Didn't I tell you, 'Don't go'?" ¹⁹ The men of the city said to Elisha, "Behold, please, the situation of this city is pleasant, as my lord sees; but the water is bad, and the land is barren." ²⁰ He said, "Bring me a new jar, and put salt in it." Then they brought it to him. ²¹ He went out to the spring of the waters, and threw salt into it, and said, "Yahweh says, 'I have healed these waters. There shall not be from there any more death or barren wasteland.'" ²² So the waters were healed to this day, according to Elisha's word which he spoke. ²³ He went up from there to Bethel. As he was going up by the way, some youths came out of the city and mocked him, and said to him, "Go up, you baldy! Go up, you baldy!" ²⁴ He looked behind him and saw them, and cursed them in Yahweh's name. Then two female bears came out of the woods and mauled forty-two of those youths. ²⁵ He went from there to Mount Carmel, and from there he returned to Samaria.

## 3

¹ Now Jehoram the son of Ahab began to reign over Israel in Samaria in the eighteenth year of Jehoshaphat king of Judah, and reigned twelve years. ² He did that which was evil in Yahweh's sight, but not like his father and like his mother, for he put away the pillar of Baal that his father had made. ³ Nevertheless he held to the sins of Jeroboam the son of Nebat, with which he made Israel to sin. He didn't depart from them. ⁴ Now Mesha king of Moab was a sheep breeder; and he supplied the

---

ª *1:3* "Yahweh" is God's proper Name, sometimes rendered "LORD" (all caps) in other translations.

ᵇ *1:3* The Hebrew word rendered "God" is "אֱלֹהִים" (Elohim).

ᶜ *1:9* "Behold", from "הִנֵּה", means look at, take notice, observe, see, or gaze at. It is often used as an interjection.

king of Israel with one hundred thousand lambs and the wool of one hundred thousand rams. [5] But when Ahab was dead, the king of Moab rebelled against the king of Israel. [6] King Jehoram went out of Samaria at that time, and mustered all Israel. [7] He went and sent to Jehoshaphat the king of Judah, saying, "The king of Moab has rebelled against me. Will you go with me against Moab to battle?" He said, "I will go up. I am as you are, my people as your people, my horses as your horses." [8] Then he said, "Which way shall we go up?" Jehoram answered, "The way of the wilderness of Edom." [9] So the king of Israel went with the king of Judah and the king of Edom, and they marched for seven days along a circuitous route. There was no water for the army or for the animals that followed them. [10] The king of Israel said, "Alas! For Yahweh has called these three kings together to deliver them into the hand of Moab." [11] But Jehoshaphat said, "Isn't there a prophet of Yahweh here, that we may inquire of Yahweh by him?" One of the king of Israel's servants answered, "Elisha the son of Shaphat, who poured water on the hands of Elijah, is here." [12] Jehoshaphat said, "Yahweh's word is with him." So the king of Israel and Jehoshaphat and the king of Edom went down to him. [13] Elisha said to the king of Israel, "What have I to do with you? Go to the prophets of your father, and to the prophets of your mother." The king of Israel said to him, "No, for Yahweh has called these three kings together to deliver them into the hand of Moab." [14] Elisha said, "As Yahweh of Armies lives, before whom I stand, surely, were it not that I respect the presence of Jehoshaphat the king of Judah, I would not look toward you, nor see you. [15] But now bring me a musician." When the musician played, Yahweh's hand came on him. [16] He said, "Yahweh says, 'Make this valley full of trenches.' [17] For Yahweh says, 'You will not see wind, neither will you see rain, yet that valley will be filled with water, and you will drink, both you and your livestock and your other animals. [18] This is an easy thing in Yahweh's sight. He will also deliver the Moabites into your hand. [19] You shall strike every fortified city and every choice city, and shall fell every good tree, and stop all springs of water, and mar every good piece of land with stones.'" [20] In the morning, about the time of offering the sacrifice, behold, water came by the way of Edom, and the country was filled with water. [21] Now when all the Moabites heard that the kings had come up to fight against them, they gathered themselves together, all who were able to put on armor, young and old, and stood on the water. [22] They rose up early in the morning, and the sun shone on the water, and the Moabites saw the water opposite them as red as blood. [23] They said, "This is blood. The kings are surely destroyed, and they have struck each other. Now therefore, Moab, to the plunder!" [24] When they came to the camp of Israel, the Israelites rose up and struck the Moabites, so that they fled before them; and they went forward into the land attacking the Moabites. [25] They beat down the cities; and on every good piece of land each man cast his stone, and filled it. They also stopped all the springs of water and cut down all the good trees, until in Kir Hareseth all they left was its stones; however the men armed with slings went around it and attacked it. [26] When the king of Moab saw that the battle was too severe for him, he took with him seven hundred men who drew a sword, to break through to the king of Edom; but they could not. [27] Then he took his oldest son who would have reigned in his place, and offered him for a burnt offering on the wall. There was great wrath against Israel; and they departed from him, and returned to their own land.

## 4

[1] Now a certain woman of the wives of the sons of the prophets cried out to Elisha, saying, "Your servant my husband is dead. You know that your servant feared Yahweh. Now the creditor has come to take for himself my two children to be slaves." [2] Elisha said to her, "What should I do for you? Tell me, what do you have in the house?" She said, "Your servant has nothing in the house, except a pot of oil." [3] Then he said, "Go, borrow empty containers from all your neighbors. Don't borrow just a few containers. [4] Go in and shut the door on you and on your sons, and pour oil into all those containers; and set aside those which are full." [5] So she went from him, and shut the door on herself and on her sons. They brought the containers to her, and she poured oil. [6] When the containers were full, she said to her son, "Bring me another container." He said to her, "There isn't another container." Then the oil stopped flowing. [7] Then she came and told the man of God. He said, "Go, sell the oil, and pay your debt; and you and your sons live on the rest." [8] One day Elisha went to Shunem, where there was a prominent woman; and she persuaded him to eat bread. So it was, that as often as he passed by, he turned in there to eat bread. [9] She said to her husband, "See now, I perceive that this is a holy man of God who passes by us continually. [10] Please, let's make a little room on the roof. Let's set a bed, a table, a chair, and a lamp stand for him there. When he comes to us, he can stay there." [11] One day he came there, and he went to the room and lay there. [12] He said to Gehazi his servant, "Call this Shunammite." When he had called her, she stood before him. [13] He said

to him, "Say now to her, 'Behold, you have cared for us with all this care. What is to be done for you? Would you like to be spoken for to the king, or to the captain of the army?'" She answered, "I dwell among my own people." [14] He said, "What then is to be done for her?" Gehazi answered, "Most certainly she has no son, and her husband is old." [15] He said, "Call her." When he had called her, she stood in the door. [16] He said, "At this season next year, you will embrace a son." She said, "No, my lord, you man of God, do not lie to your servant." [17] The woman conceived, and bore a son at that season when the time came around, as Elisha had said to her. [18] When the child was grown, one day he went out to his father to the reapers. [19] He said to his father, "My head! My head!" He said to his servant, "Carry him to his mother." [20] When he had taken him and brought him to his mother, he sat on her knees until noon, and then died. [21] She went up and laid him on the man of God's bed, and shut the door on him, and went out. [22] She called to her husband and said, "Please send me one of the servants, and one of the donkeys, that I may run to the man of God and come again." [23] He said, "Why would you want to go to him today? It is not a new moon or a Sabbath." She said, "It's all right." [24] Then she saddled a donkey, and said to her servant, "Drive, and go forward! Don't slow down for me, unless I ask you to." [25] So she went, and came to the man of God to Mount Carmel. When the man of God saw her afar off, he said to Gehazi his servant, "Behold, there is the Shunammite. [26] Please run now to meet her, and ask her, 'Is it well with you? Is it well with your husband? Is it well with your child?'" She answered, "It is well." [27] When she came to the man of God to the hill, she caught hold of his feet. Gehazi came near to thrust her away; but the man of God said, "Leave her alone, for her soul is troubled within her; and Yahweh has hidden it from me, and has not told me." [28] Then she said, "Did I ask you for a son, my lord? Didn't I say, 'Do not deceive me'?" [29] Then he said to Gehazi, "Tuck your cloak into your belt, take my staff in your hand, and go your way. If you meet any man, don't greet him; and if anyone greets you, don't answer him again. Then lay my staff on the child's face." [30] The child's mother said, "As Yahweh lives, and as your soul lives, I will not leave you." So he arose, and followed her. [31] Gehazi went ahead of them, and laid the staff on the child's face; but there was no voice and no hearing. Therefore he returned to meet him, and told him, "The child has not awakened." [32] When Elisha had come into the house, behold, the child was dead, and lying on his bed. [33] He went in therefore, and shut the door on them both, and prayed to Yahweh. [34] He went up and lay on the child, and put his mouth on his mouth, and his eyes on his eyes, and his hands on his hands. He stretched himself on him; and the child's flesh grew warm. [35] Then he returned, and walked in the house once back and forth, then went up and stretched himself out on him. Then the child sneezed seven times, and the child opened his eyes. [36] He called Gehazi, and said, "Call this Shunammite!" So he called her. When she had come in to him, he said, "Take up your son." [37] Then she went in, fell at his feet, and bowed herself to the ground; then she picked up her son, and went out. [38] Elisha came again to Gilgal. There was a famine in the land; and the sons of the prophets were sitting before him; and he said to his servant, "Get the large pot, and boil stew for the sons of the prophets." [39] One went out into the field to gather herbs, and found a wild vine, and gathered a lap full of wild gourds from it, and came and cut them up into the pot of stew; for they didn't recognize them. [40] So they poured out for the men to eat. As they were eating some of the stew, they cried out and said, "Man of God, there is death in the pot!" And they could not eat it. [41] But he said, "Then bring meal." He threw it into the pot; and he said, "Serve it to the people, that they may eat." And there was nothing harmful in the pot. [42] A man from Baal Shalishah came, and brought the man of God some bread of the first fruits: twenty loaves of barley and fresh ears of grain in his sack. Elisha said, "Give to the people, that they may eat." [43] His servant said, "What, should I set this before a hundred men?" But he said, "Give it to the people, that they may eat; for Yahweh says, 'They will eat, and will have some left over.'" [44] So he set it before them and they ate and had some left over, according to Yahweh's word.

## 5

[1] Now Naaman, captain of the army of the king of Syria, was a great man with his master, and honorable, because by him Yahweh had given victory to Syria; he was also a mighty man of valor, but he was a leper. [2] The Syrians had gone out in bands, and had brought away captive out of the land of Israel a little girl, and she waited on Naaman's wife. [3] She said to her mistress, "I wish that my lord were with the prophet who is in Samaria! Then he would heal him of his leprosy." [4] Someone went in and told his lord, saying, "The girl who is from the land of Israel said this." [5] The king of Syria said, "Go now, and I will send a letter to

the king of Israel." He departed, and took with him ten talents<sup>a</sup> of silver, six thousand pieces of gold, and ten changes of clothing. <sup>6</sup> He brought the letter to the king of Israel, saying, "Now when this letter has come to you, behold, I have sent Naaman my servant to you, that you may heal him of his leprosy." <sup>7</sup> When the king of Israel had read the letter, he tore his clothes and said, "Am I God, to kill and to make alive, that this man sends to me to heal a man of his leprosy? But please consider and see how he seeks a quarrel against me." <sup>8</sup> It was so, when Elisha the man of God heard that the king of Israel had torn his clothes, that he sent to the king, saying, "Why have you torn your clothes? Let him come now to me, and he shall know that there is a prophet in Israel." <sup>9</sup> So Naaman came with his horses and with his chariots, and stood at the door of the house of Elisha. <sup>10</sup> Elisha sent a messenger to him, saying, "Go and wash in the Jordan seven times, and your flesh shall come again to you, and you shall be clean." <sup>11</sup> But Naaman was angry, and went away and said, "Behold, I thought, 'He will surely come out to me, and stand, and call on the name of Yahweh his God, and wave his hand over the place, and heal the leper.' <sup>12</sup> Aren't Abanah and Pharpar, the rivers of Damascus, better than all the waters of Israel? Couldn't I wash in them and be clean?" So he turned and went away in a rage. <sup>13</sup> His servants came near and spoke to him, and said, "My father, if the prophet had asked you do some great thing, wouldn't you have done it? How much rather then, when he says to you, 'Wash, and be clean'?" <sup>14</sup> Then went he down and dipped himself seven times in the Jordan, according to the saying of the man of God; and his flesh was restored like the flesh of a little child, and he was clean. <sup>15</sup> He returned to the man of God, he and all his company, and came, and stood before him; and he said, "See now, I know that there is no God in all the earth, but in Israel. Now therefore, please take a gift from your servant." <sup>16</sup> But he said, "As Yahweh lives, before whom I stand, I will receive none." He urged him to take it; but he refused. <sup>17</sup> Naaman said, "If not, then, please let two mules' load of earth be given to your servant; for your servant will from now on offer neither burnt offering nor sacrifice to other gods, but to Yahweh. <sup>18</sup> In this thing may Yahweh pardon your servant: when my master goes into the house of Rimmon to worship there, and he leans on my hand, and I bow myself in the house of Rimmon. When I bow myself in the house of Rimmon, may Yahweh pardon your servant in this thing." <sup>19</sup> He said to him, "Go in peace." So he departed from him a little way. <sup>20</sup> But Gehazi the servant of Elisha the man of God, said, "Behold, my master has spared this Naaman the Syrian, in not receiving at his hands that which he brought. As Yahweh lives, I will run after him, and take something from him." <sup>21</sup> So Gehazi followed after Naaman. When Naaman saw one running after him, he came down from the chariot to meet him, and said, "Is all well?" <sup>22</sup> He said, "All is well. My master has sent me, saying, 'Behold, even now two young men of the sons of the prophets have come to me from the hill country of Ephraim. Please give them a talent<sup>b</sup> of silver and two changes of clothing.'" <sup>23</sup> Naaman said, "Be pleased to take two talents." He urged him, and bound two talents of silver in two bags, with two changes of clothing, and laid them on two of his servants; and they carried them before him. <sup>24</sup> When he came to the hill, he took them from their hand, and stored them in the house. Then he let the men go, and they departed. <sup>25</sup> But he went in, and stood before his master. Elisha said to him, "Where did you come from, Gehazi?" He said, "Your servant went nowhere." <sup>26</sup> He said to him, "Didn't my heart go with you when the man turned from his chariot to meet you? Is it a time to receive money, and to receive garments, and olive groves and vineyards, and sheep and cattle, and male servants and female servants? <sup>27</sup> Therefore the leprosy of Naaman will cling to you and to your offspring<sup>c</sup> forever." He went out from his presence a leper, as white as snow.

## 6

<sup>1</sup> The sons of the prophets said to Elisha, "See now, the place where we live and meet with you is too small for us. <sup>2</sup> Please let us go to the Jordan, and each man take a beam from there, and let's make us a place there, where we may live." He answered, "Go!" <sup>3</sup> One said, "Please be pleased to go with your servants." He answered, "I will go." <sup>4</sup> So he went with them. When they came to the Jordan, they cut down wood. <sup>5</sup> But as one was cutting down a tree, the ax head fell into the water. Then he cried out and said, "Alas, my master! For it was borrowed." <sup>6</sup> The man of God asked, "Where did it fall?" He showed him the place. He cut down a stick, threw it in there, and made the iron float. <sup>7</sup> He said, "Take it." So he put out his hand and took it. <sup>8</sup> Now the king of Syria was at war against Israel; and he took counsel with his servants, saying,

"My camp will be in such and such a place." <sup>9</sup> The man of God sent to the king of Israel, saying, "Beware that you not pass this place, for the Syrians are coming down there." <sup>10</sup> The king of Israel sent to the place which the man of God told him and warned him of; and he saved himself there, not once or twice. <sup>11</sup> The king of Syria's heart was very troubled about this. He called his servants, and said to them, "Won't you show me which of us is for the king of Israel?" <sup>12</sup> One of his servants said, "No, my lord, O king; but Elisha, the prophet who is in Israel, tells the king of Israel the words that you speak in your bedroom." <sup>13</sup> He said, "Go and see where he is, that I may send and get him." He was told, "Behold, he is in Dothan." <sup>14</sup> Therefore he sent horses, chariots, and a great army there. They came by night and surrounded the city. <sup>15</sup> When the servant of the man of God had risen early and gone out, behold, an army with horses and chariots was around the city. His servant said to him, "Alas, my master! What shall we do?" <sup>16</sup> He answered, "Don't be afraid, for those who are with us are more than those who are with them." <sup>17</sup> Elisha prayed, and said, "Yahweh, please open his eyes, that he may see." Yahweh opened the young man's eyes, and he saw; and behold, the mountain was full of horses and chariots of fire around Elisha. <sup>18</sup> When they came down to him, Elisha prayed to Yahweh, and said, "Please strike this people with blindness." He struck them with blindness according to Elisha's word. <sup>19</sup> Elisha said to them, "This is not the way, neither is this the city. Follow me, and I will bring you to the man whom you seek." He led them to Samaria. <sup>20</sup> When they had come into Samaria, Elisha said, "Yahweh, open these men's eyes, that they may see." Yahweh opened their eyes, and they saw; and behold, they were in the middle of Samaria. <sup>21</sup> The king of Israel said to Elisha, when he saw them, "My father, shall I strike them? Shall I strike them?" <sup>22</sup> He answered, "You shall not strike them. Would you strike those whom you have taken captive with your sword and with your bow? Set bread and water before them, that they may eat and drink, and go to their master." <sup>23</sup> He prepared a great feast for them. After they ate and drank, he sent them away and they went to their master. So the bands of Syria stopped raiding the land of Israel. <sup>24</sup> After this, Benhadad king of Syria gathered all his army, and went up and besieged Samaria. <sup>25</sup> There was a great famine in Samaria. Behold, they besieged it until a donkey's head was sold for eighty pieces of silver, and the fourth part of a kab<sup>d</sup> of dove's dung for five pieces of silver. <sup>26</sup> As the king of Israel was passing by on the wall, a woman cried to him, saying, "Help, my lord, O king!" <sup>27</sup> He said, "If Yahweh doesn't help you, where could I get help for you? From the threshing floor, or from the wine press?" <sup>28</sup> Then the king asked her, "What is your problem?" She answered, "This woman said to me, 'Give your son, that we may eat him today, and we will eat my son tomorrow.' <sup>29</sup> So we boiled my son and ate him; and I said to her on the next day, 'Give up your son, that we may eat him;' and she has hidden her son." <sup>30</sup> When the king heard the words of the woman, he tore his clothes. Now he was passing by on the wall, and the people looked, and behold, he had sackcloth underneath on his body. <sup>31</sup> Then he said, "God do so to me, and more also, if the head of Elisha the son of Shaphat stays on him today." <sup>32</sup> But Elisha was sitting in his house, and the elders were sitting with him. Then the king sent a man from before him; but before the messenger came to him, he said to the elders, "Do you see how this son of a murderer has sent to take away my head? Behold, when the messenger comes, shut the door, and hold the door shut against him. Isn't the sound of his master's feet behind him?" <sup>33</sup> While he was still talking with them, behold, the messenger came down to him. Then he said, "Behold, this evil is from Yahweh. Why should I wait for Yahweh any longer?"

## 7

<sup>1</sup> Elisha said, "Hear Yahweh's word. Yahweh says, 'Tomorrow about this time a seah<sup>e</sup> of fine flour will be sold for a shekel,<sup>f</sup> and two seahs of barley for a shekel, in the gate of Samaria.'" <sup>2</sup> Then the captain on whose hand the king leaned answered the man of God, and said, "Behold, if Yahweh made windows in heaven, could this thing be?" He said, "Behold, you will see it with your eyes, but will not eat of it." <sup>3</sup> Now there were four leprous men at the entrance of the gate. They said to one another, "Why do we sit here until we die? <sup>4</sup> If we say, 'We will enter into the city,' then the famine is in the city, and we will die there. If we sit still here, we also die. Now therefore come, and let's surrender to the army of the Syrians. If they save us alive, we will live; and if they kill us, we will only die." <sup>5</sup> They rose up in the twilight to go to the camp of the Syrians. When they had come to the outermost part of the camp of the Syrians, behold, no man was there. <sup>6</sup> For the Lord<sup>g</sup> had

<sup>a</sup> 5:5 A talent is about 30 kilograms or 66 pounds
<sup>b</sup> 5:22 A talent is about 30 kilograms or 66 pounds
<sup>c</sup> 5:27 or, seed
<sup>d</sup> 6:25 A kab was about 2 liters, so a fourth of a kab would be about 500 milliliters or about a pint
<sup>e</sup> 7:1 1 seah was about 7 liters or 1.9 gallons or 0.8 pecks
<sup>f</sup> 7:1 A shekel is about 10 grams or about 0.35 ounces. In
this context, it was probably a silver coin weighing that much.
<sup>g</sup> 7:6 The word translated "Lord" is "Adonai."

made the army of the Syrians to hear the sound of chariots and the sound of horses, even the noise of a great army; and they said to one another, "Behold, the king of Israel has hired against us the kings of the Hittites and the kings of the Egyptians to attack us." ⁷ Therefore they arose and fled in the twilight, and left their tents, their horses, and their donkeys, even the camp as it was, and fled for their life. ⁸ When these lepers came to the outermost part of the camp, they went into one tent, and ate and drank, then carried away silver, gold, and clothing and went and hid it. Then they came back, and entered into another tent and carried things from there also, and went and hid them. ⁹ Then they said to one another, "We aren't doing right. Today is a day of good news, and we keep silent. If we wait until the morning light, punishment will overtake us. Now therefore come, let's go and tell the king's household." ¹⁰ So they came and called to the city gatekeepers; and they told them, "We came to the camp of the Syrians, and, behold, there was no man there, not even a man's voice, but the horses tied, and the donkeys tied, and the tents as they were." ¹¹ Then the gatekeepers called out and told it to the king's household within. ¹² The king arose in the night, and said to his servants, "I will now show you what the Syrians have done to us. They know that we are hungry. Therefore they have gone out of the camp to hide themselves in the field, saying, 'When they come out of the city, we shall take them alive, and get into the city.'" ¹³ One of his servants answered, "Please let some people take five of the horses that remain, which are left in the city. Behold, they are like all the multitude of Israel who are left in it. Behold, they are like all the multitude of Israel who are consumed. Let's send and see." ¹⁴ Therefore they took two chariots with horses; and the king sent them out to the Syrian army, saying, "Go and see." ¹⁵ They went after them to the Jordan; and behold, all the path was full of garments and equipment which the Syrians had cast away in their haste. The messengers returned and told the king. ¹⁶ The people went out and plundered the camp of the Syrians. So a seahᵃ of fine flour was sold for a shekel, and two measures of barley for a shekel,ᵇ according to Yahweh's word. ¹⁷ The king had appointed the captain on whose hand he leaned to be in charge of the gate; and the people trampled over him in the gate, and he died as the man of God had said, who spoke when the king came down to him. ¹⁸ It happened as the man of God had spoken to the king, saying, "Two seahsᶜ of barley for a shekel,ᵈ and a seah of fine flour for a shekel, shall be tomorrow about this time in the gate of Samaria;" ¹⁹ and that captain answered the man of God, and said, "Now, behold, if Yahweh made windows in heaven, might such a thing be?" and he said, "Behold, you will see it with your eyes, but will not eat of it." ²⁰ It happened like that to him, for the people trampled over him in the gate, and he died.

## 8

¹ Now Elisha had spoken to the woman whose son he had restored to life, saying, "Arise, and go, you and your household, and stay for a while wherever you can; for Yahweh has called for a famine. It will also come on the land for seven years." ² The woman arose, and did according to the man of God's word. She went with her household, and lived in the land of the Philistines for seven years. ³ At the end of seven years, the woman returned from the land of the Philistines. Then she went out to beg the king for her house and for her land. ⁴ Now the king was talking with Gehazi the servant of the man of God, saying, "Please tell me all the great things that Elisha has done." ⁵ As he was telling the king how he had restored to life him who was dead, behold, the woman whose son he had restored to life begged the king for her house and for her land. Gehazi said, "My lord, O king, this is the woman, and this is her son, whom Elisha restored to life." ⁶ When the king asked the woman, she told him. So the king appointed to her a certain officer, saying, "Restore all that was hers, and all the fruits of the field since the day that she left the land, even until now." ⁷ Elisha came to Damascus; and Benhadad the king of Syria was sick. He was told, "The man of God has come here." ⁸ The king said to Hazael, "Take a present in your hand, and go meet the man of God, and inquire of Yahweh by him, saying, 'Will I recover from this sickness?'" ⁹ So Hazael went to meet him and took a present with him, even of every good thing of Damascus, forty camels' burden, and came and stood before him and said, "Your son Benhadad king of Syria has sent me to you, saying, 'Will I recover from this sickness?'" ¹⁰ Elisha said to him, "Go, tell him, 'You will surely recover;' however Yahweh has shown me that he will surely die." ¹¹ He settled his gaze steadfastly on him, until he was ashamed. Then the man of God wept. ¹² Hazael said, "Why do you weep, my lord?" He answered, "Because I know the evil that you will do to the children of Israel. You will set their strongholds on fire, and

you will kill their young men with the sword, and will dash their little ones in pieces, and rip up their pregnant women." ¹³ Hazael said, "But what is your servant, who is but a dog, that he could do this great thing?" Elisha answered, "Yahweh has shown me that you will be king over Syria." ¹⁴ Then he departed from Elisha, and came to his master, who said to him, "What did Elisha say to you?" He answered, "He told me that you would surely recover." ¹⁵ On the next day, he took a thick cloth, dipped it in water, and spread it on the king's face, so that he died. Then Hazael reigned in his place. ¹⁶ In the fifth year of Joram the son of Ahab king of Israel, Jehoshaphat being king of Judah then, Jehoram the son of Jehoshaphat king of Judah began to reign. ¹⁷ He was thirty-two years old when he began to reign. He reigned eight years in Jerusalem. ¹⁸ He walked in the way of the kings of Israel, as did Ahab's house, for he married Ahab's daughter. He did that which was evil in Yahweh's sight. ¹⁹ However, Yahweh would not destroy Judah, for David his servant's sake, as he promised him to give to him a lamp for his children always. ²⁰ In his days Edom revolted from under the hand of Judah, and made a king over themselves. ²¹ Then Joram crossed over to Zair, and all his chariots with him; and he rose up by night and struck the Edomites who surrounded him with the captains of the chariots; and the people fled to their tents. ²² So Edom revolted from under the hand of Judah to this day. Then Libnah revolted at the same time. ²³ The rest of the acts of Joram, and all that he did, aren't they written in the book of the chronicles of the kings of Judah? ²⁴ Joram slept with his fathers, and was buried with his fathers in David's city; and Ahaziah his son reigned in his place. ²⁵ In the twelfth year of Joram the son of Ahab king of Israel, Ahaziah the son of Jehoram king of Judah began to reign. ²⁶ Ahaziah was twenty-two years old when he began to reign; and he reigned one year in Jerusalem. His mother's name was Athaliah the daughter of Omri king of Israel. ²⁷ He walked in the way of Ahab's house and did that which was evil in Yahweh's sight, as did Ahab's house, for he was the son-in-law of Ahab's house. ²⁸ He went with Joram the son of Ahab to war against Hazael king of Syria at Ramoth Gilead, and the Syrians wounded Joram. ²⁹ King Joram returned to be healed in Jezreel from the wounds which the Syrians had given him at Ramah, when he fought against Hazael king of Syria. Ahaziah the son of Jehoram, king of Judah, went down to see Joram the son of Ahab in Jezreel, because he was sick.

## 9

¹ Elisha the prophet called one of the sons of the prophets, and said to him, "Put your belt on your waist, take this vial of oil in your hand, and go to Ramoth Gilead. ² When you come there, find Jehu the son of Jehoshaphat the son of Nimshi, and go in and make him rise up from among his brothers, and take him to an inner room. ³ Then take the vial of oil, and pour it on his head, and say, 'Yahweh says, "I have anointed you king over Israel."' Then open the door, flee, and don't wait." ⁴ So the young man, the young prophet, went to Ramoth Gilead. ⁵ When he came, behold, the captains of the army were sitting. Then he said, "I have a message for you, captain." Jehu said, "To which one of us?" He said, "To you, O captain." ⁶ He arose, and went into the house. Then he poured the oil on his head, and said to him, "Yahweh, the God of Israel, says, 'I have anointed you king over the people of Yahweh, even over Israel. ⁷ You must strike your master Ahab's house, that I may avenge the blood of my servants the prophets, and the blood of all the servants of Yahweh, at the hand of Jezebel. ⁸ For the whole house of Ahab will perish. I will cut off from Ahab everyone who urinates against a wall,ᵉ both him who is shut up and him who is left at large in Israel. ⁹ I will make Ahab's house like the house of Jeroboam the son of Nebat, and like the house of Baasha the son of Ahijah. ¹⁰ The dogs will eat Jezebel on the plot of ground of Jezreel, and there shall be no one to bury her.'" Then he opened the door and fled. ¹¹ When Jehu came out to the servants of his lord and one said to him, "Is all well? Why did this madman come to you?" He said to them, "You know the man and how he talks." ¹² They said, "That is a lie. Tell us now." He said, "He said to me, 'Yahweh says, I have anointed you king over Israel.'" ¹³ Then they hurried, and each man took his cloak, and put it under him on the top of the stairs, and blew the trumpet, saying, "Jehu is king." ¹⁴ So Jehu the son of Jehoshaphat the son of Nimshi conspired against Joram. (Now Joram was defending Ramoth Gilead, he and all Israel, because of Hazael king of Syria; ¹⁵ but King Joram had returned to be healed in Jezreel of the wounds which the Syrians had given him when he fought with Hazael king of Syria.) Jehu said, "If this is your thinking, then let no one escape and go out of the city to go to tell it in Jezreel." ¹⁶ So Jehu rode in a chariot and went to Jezreel, for Joram lay there. Ahaziah king of Judah had come down to see Joram. ¹⁷ Now the watchman was

ᵃ 7:16 1 seah is about 7 liters or 1.9 gallons or 0.8 pecks
ᵇ 7:16 A shekel is about 10 grams or about 0.35 ounces. In this context, it was probably a silver coin weighing that much.
ᶜ 7:18 1 seah is about 7 liters or 1.9 gallons or 0.8 pecks
ᵈ 7:18 A shekel is about 10 grams or about 0.35 ounces. In this context, it was probably a silver coin weighing that much.
ᵉ 9:8 or, male

standing on the tower in Jezreel, and he spied the company of Jehu as he came, and said, "I see a company." Joram said, "Take a horseman, and send to meet them, and let him say, 'Is it peace?'" [18] So one went on horseback to meet him, and said, "the king says, 'Is it peace?'" Jehu said, "What do you have to do with peace? Fall in behind me!" The watchman said, "The messenger came to them, but he isn't coming back." [19] Then he sent out a second on horseback, who came to them and said, "The king says, 'Is it peace?'" Jehu answered, "What do you have to do with peace? Fall in behind me!" [20] The watchman said, "He came to them, and isn't coming back. The driving is like the driving of Jehu the son of Nimshi, for he drives furiously." [21] Joram said, "Get ready!" They got his chariot ready. Then Joram king of Israel and Ahaziah king of Judah went out, each in his chariot; and they went out to meet Jehu, and found him on Naboth the Jezreelite's land. [22] When Joram saw Jehu, he said, "Is it peace, Jehu?" He answered, "What peace, so long as the prostitution of your mother Jezebel and her witchcraft abound?" [23] Joram turned his hands and fled, and said to Ahaziah, "This is treason, Ahaziah!" [24] Jehu drew his bow with his full strength, and struck Joram between his arms; and the arrow went out at his heart, and he sunk down in his chariot. [25] Then Jehu said to Bidkar his captain, "Pick him up, and throw him in the plot of the field of Naboth the Jezreelite; for remember how, when you and I rode together after Ahab his father, Yahweh laid this burden on him: [26]'Surely I have seen yesterday the blood of Naboth, and the blood of his sons,' says Yahweh; 'and I will repay you in this plot of ground,' says Yahweh. Now therefore take and cast him onto the plot of ground, according to Yahweh's word." [27] But when Ahaziah the king of Judah saw this, he fled by the way of the garden house. Jehu followed after him, and said, "Strike him also in the chariot!" They struck him at the ascent of Gur, which is by Ibleam. He fled to Megiddo, and died there. [28] His servants carried him in a chariot to Jerusalem, and buried him in his tomb with his fathers in David's city. [29] In the eleventh year of Joram the son of Ahab, Ahaziah began to reign over Judah. [30] When Jehu had come to Jezreel, Jezebel heard of it; and she painted her eyes, and adorned her head, and looked out at the window. [31] As Jehu entered in at the gate, she said, "Do you come in peace, Zimri, you murderer of your master?" [32] He lifted up his face to the window, and said, "Who is on my side? Who?" Two or three eunuchs looked out at him. [33] He said, "Throw her down!" So they threw her down; and some of her blood was sprinkled on the wall, and on the horses. Then he trampled her under foot. [34] When he had come in, he ate and drank. Then he said, "See now to this cursed woman, and bury her; for she is a king's daughter." [35] They went to bury her, but they found no more of her than the skull, the feet, and the palms of her hands. [36] Therefore they came back, and told him. He said, "This is Yahweh's word, which he spoke by his servant Elijah the Tishbite, saying, 'The dogs will eat the flesh of Jezebel on the plot of Jezreel, [37] and the body of Jezebel will be as dung on the surface of the field on Jezreel's land, so that they won't say, "This is Jezebel."'"

## 10

[1] Now Ahab had seventy sons in Samaria. Jehu wrote letters and sent them to Samaria, to the rulers of Jezreel, even the elders, and to those who brought up Ahab's sons, saying, [2]"Now as soon as this letter comes to you, since your master's sons are with you, and you have chariots and horses, a fortified city also, and armor, [3] select the best and fittest of your master's sons, set him on his father's throne, and fight for your master's house." [4] But they were exceedingly afraid, and said, "Behold, the two kings didn't stand before him! How then shall we stand?" [5] He who was over the household, and he who was over the city, the elders also, and those who raised the children, sent to Jehu, saying, "We are your servants, and will do all that you ask us. We will not make any man king. You do that which is good in your eyes." [6] Then he wrote a letter the second time to them, saying, "If you are on my side, and if you will listen to my voice, take the heads of the men who are your master's sons, and come to me to Jezreel by tomorrow this time." Now the king's sons, being seventy persons, were with the great men of the city, who brought them up. [7] When the letter came to them, they took the king's sons and killed them, even seventy people, and put their heads in baskets, and sent them to him to Jezreel. [8] A messenger came and told him, "They have brought the heads of the king's sons." He said, "Lay them in two heaps at the entrance of the gate until the morning." [9] In the morning, he went out and stood, and said to all the people, "You are righteous. Behold, I conspired against my master and killed him, but who killed all these? [10] Know now that nothing will fall to the earth of Yahweh's word, which Yahweh spoke concerning Ahab's house. For Yahweh has done that which he spoke by his servant Elijah." [11] So Jehu struck all that remained of Ahab's house in Jezreel, with all his great men, his familiar friends, and his priests, until he left him no one remaining. [12] He arose and departed, and went to Samaria. As he was at the shearing house of the shepherds on the way, [13] Jehu met with the brothers of Ahaziah king of Judah, and said, "Who are

you?" They answered, "We are the brothers of Ahaziah. We are going down to greet the children of the king and the children of the queen." [14] He said, "Take them alive!" They took them alive, and killed them at the pit of the shearing house, even forty-two men. He didn't leave any of them. [15] When he had departed from there, he met Jehonadab the son of Rechab coming to meet him. He greeted him, and said to him, "Is your heart right, as my heart is with your heart?" Jehonadab answered, "It is." "If it is, give me your hand." He gave him his hand; and he took him up to him into the chariot. [16] He said, "Come with me, and see my zeal for Yahweh." So they made him ride in his chariot. [17] When he came to Samaria, he struck all who remained to Ahab in Samaria, until he had destroyed them, according to Yahweh's word which he spoke to Elijah. [18] Jehu gathered all the people together, and said to them, "Ahab served Baal a little, but Jehu will serve him much. [19] Now therefore call to me all the prophets of Baal, all of his worshipers, and all of his priests. Let no one be absent, for I have a great sacrifice to Baal. Whoever is absent, he shall not live." But Jehu did deceptively, intending to destroy the worshipers of Baal. [20] Jehu said, "Sanctify a solemn assembly for Baal!" So they proclaimed it. [21] Jehu sent through all Israel; and all the worshipers of Baal came, so that there was not a man left that didn't come. They came into the house of Baal; and the house of Baal was filled from one end to another. [22] He said to him who kept the wardrobe, "Bring out robes for all the worshipers of Baal!" So he brought robes out to them. [23] Jehu went with Jehonadab the son of Rechab into the house of Baal. Then he said to the worshipers of Baal, "Search, and see that none of the servants of Yahweh are here with you, but only the worshipers of Baal." [24] So they went in to offer sacrifices and burnt offerings. Now Jehu had appointed for himself eighty men outside, and said, "If any of the men whom I bring into your hands escape, he who lets him go, his life shall be for the life of him." [25] As soon as he had finished offering the burnt offering, Jehu said to the guard and to the captains, "Go in and kill them! Let no one escape." So they struck them with the edge of the sword. The guard and the captains threw the bodies out, and went to the inner shrine of the house of Baal. [26] They brought out the pillars that were in the house of Baal and burned them. [27] They broke down the pillar of Baal, and broke down the house of Baal, and made it a latrine, to this day. [28] Thus Jehu destroyed Baal out of Israel. [29] However, Jehu didn't depart from the sins of Jeroboam the son of Nebat, with which he made Israel to sin—the golden calves that were in Bethel and that were in Dan. [30] Yahweh said to Jehu, "Because you have done well in executing that which is right in my eyes, and have done to Ahab's house according to all that was in my heart, your descendants shall sit on the throne of Israel to the fourth generation." [31] But Jehu took no heed to walk in the law of Yahweh, the God of Israel, with all his heart. He didn't depart from the sins of Jeroboam, with which he made Israel to sin. [32] In those days Yahweh began to cut away parts of Israel; and Hazael struck them in all the borders of Israel [33] from the Jordan eastward, all the land of Gilead, the Gadites, and the Reubenites, and the Manassites, from Aroer, which is by the valley of the Arnon, even Gilead and Bashan. [34] Now the rest of the acts of Jehu, and all that he did, and all his might, aren't they written in the book of the chronicles of the kings of Israel? [35] Jehu slept with his fathers; and they buried him in Samaria. Jehoahaz his son reigned in his place. [36] The time that Jehu reigned over Israel in Samaria was twenty-eight years.

## 11

[1] Now when Athaliah the mother of Ahaziah saw that her son was dead, she arose and destroyed all the royal offspring. [2] But Jehosheba, the daughter of King Joram, sister of Ahaziah, took Joash the son of Ahaziah, and stole him away from among the king's sons who were slain, even him and his nurse, and put them in the bedroom; and they hid him from Athaliah, so that he was not slain. [3] He was with her hidden in Yahweh's house six years while Athaliah reigned over the land. [4] In the seventh year Jehoiada sent and fetched the captains over hundreds of the Carites and of the guard, and brought them to him into Yahweh's house; and he made a covenant with them, and made a covenant with them in Yahweh's house, and showed them the king's son. [5] He commanded them, saying, "This is what you must do: a third of you, who come in on the Sabbath, shall be keepers of the watch of the king's house; [6] a third of you shall be at the gate Sur; and a third of you at the gate behind the guard. So you shall keep the watch of the house, and be a barrier. [7] The two companies of you, even all who go out on the Sabbath, shall keep the watch of Yahweh's house around the king. [8] You shall surround the king, every man with his weapons in his hand; and he who comes within the ranks, let him be slain. Be with the king when he goes out, and when he comes in." [9] The captains over hundreds did according to all that Jehoiada the priest commanded; and they each took his men, those who were to come in on the Sabbath with those who were to go out on the Sabbath, and came to Jehoiada the priest. [10] The priest delivered to the captains over hundreds the spears

and shields that had been King David's, which were in Yahweh's house. [11] The guard stood, every man with his weapons in his hand, from the right side of the house to the left side of the house, along by the altar and the house, around the king. [12] Then he brought out the king's son, and put the crown on him, and gave him the covenant; and they made him king and anointed him; and they clapped their hands, and said, "Long live the king!" [13] When Athaliah heard the noise of the guard and of the people, she came to the people into Yahweh's house; [14] and she looked, and behold, the king stood by the pillar, as the tradition was, with the captains and the trumpets by the king; and all the people of the land rejoiced, and blew trumpets. Then Athaliah tore her clothes and cried, "Treason! Treason!" [15] Jehoiada the priest commanded the captains of hundreds who were set over the army, and said to them, "Bring her out between the ranks. Kill anyone who follows her with the sword." For the priest said, "Don't let her be slain in Yahweh's house." [16] So they seized her; and she went by the way of the horses' entry to the king's house, and she was slain there. [17] Jehoiada made a covenant between Yahweh and the king and the people, that they should be Yahweh's people; also between the king and the people. [18] All the people of the land went to the house of Baal, and broke it down. They broke his altars and his images in pieces thoroughly, and killed Mattan the priest of Baal before the altars. The priest appointed officers over Yahweh's house. [19] He took the captains over hundreds, and the Carites, and the guard, and all the people of the land; and they brought down the king from Yahweh's house, and came by the way of the gate of the guard to the king's house. He sat on the throne of the kings. [20] So all the people of the land rejoiced, and the city was quiet. They had slain Athaliah with the sword at the king's house. [21] Jehoash was seven years old when he began to reign.

## 12

[1] Jehoash began to reign in the seventh year of Jehu, and he reigned forty years in Jerusalem. His mother's name was Zibiah of Beersheba. [2] Jehoash did that which was right in Yahweh's eyes all his days in which Jehoiada the priest instructed him. [3] However, the high places were not taken away. The people still sacrificed and burned incense in the high places. [4] Jehoash said to the priests, "All the money of the holy things that is brought into Yahweh's house, in current money, the money of the people for whom each man is evaluated,* and all the money that it comes into any man's heart to bring into Yahweh's house, [5] let the priests take it to them, each man from his donor; and they shall repair the damage to the house, wherever any damage is found." [6] But it was so, that in the twenty-third year of King Jehoash the priests had not repaired the damage to the house. [7] Then King Jehoash called for Jehoiada the priest, and for the other priests, and said to them, "Why aren't you repairing the damage to the house? Now therefore take no more money from your treasurers, but deliver it for repair of the damage to the house." [8] The priests consented that they should take no more money from the people, and not repair the damage to the house. [9] But Jehoiada the priest took a chest and bored a hole in its lid, and set it beside the altar, on the right side as one comes into Yahweh's house; and the priests who kept the threshold put all the money that was brought into Yahweh's house into it. [10] When they saw that there was much money in the chest, the king's scribe and the high priest came up, and they put it in bags and counted the money that was found in Yahweh's house. [11] They gave the money that was weighed out into the hands of those who did the work, who had the oversight of Yahweh's house; and they paid it out to the carpenters and the builders who worked on Yahweh's house, [12] and to the masons and the stone cutters, and for buying timber and cut stone to repair the damage to Yahweh's house, and for all that was laid out for the house to repair it. [13] But there were not made for Yahweh's house cups of silver, snuffers, basins, trumpets, any vessels of gold or vessels of silver, of the money that was brought into Yahweh's house; [14] for they gave that to those who did the work, and repaired Yahweh's house with it. [15] Moreover they didn't demand an accounting from the men into whose hand they delivered the money to give to those who did the work; for they dealt faithfully. [16] The money for the trespass offerings and the money for the sin offerings was not brought into Yahweh's house. It was the priests'. [17] Then Hazael king of Syria went up and fought against Gath, and took it; and Hazael set his face to go up to Jerusalem. [18] Jehoash king of Judah took all the holy things that Jehoshaphat and Jehoram and Ahaziah, his fathers, kings of Judah, had dedicated, and his own holy things, and all the gold that was found in the treasures of Yahweh's house, and of the king's house, and sent it to Hazael king of Syria; and he went away from Jerusalem. [19] Now the rest of the acts of Joash, and all that he did, aren't they written in the book of the chronicles of the kings of Judah? [20] His servants arose and made a conspiracy, and struck Joash at the house of Millo, on the way that goes down to Silla. [21] For

Jozacar the son of Shimeath, and Jehozabad the son of Shomer, his servants, struck him, and he died; and they buried him with his fathers in David's city; and Amaziah his son reigned in his place.

## 13

[1] In the twenty-third year of Joash the son of Ahaziah, king of Judah, Jehoahaz the son of Jehu began to reign over Israel in Samaria for seventeen years. [2] He did that which was evil in Yahweh's sight, and followed the sins of Jeroboam the son of Nebat, with which he made Israel to sin. He didn't depart from it. [3] Yahweh's anger burned against Israel, and he delivered them into the hand of Hazael king of Syria, and into the hand of Benhadad the son of Hazael, continually. [4] Jehoahaz begged Yahweh, and Yahweh listened to him; for he saw the oppression of Israel, how the king of Syria oppressed them. [5](Yahweh gave Israel a savior, so that they went out from under the hand of the Syrians; and the children of Israel lived in their tents as before. [6] Nevertheless they didn't depart from the sins of the house of Jeroboam, with which he made Israel to sin, but walked in them; and the Asherah also remained in Samaria.) [7] For he didn't leave to Jehoahaz of the people any more than fifty horsemen, and ten chariots, and ten thousand footmen; for the king of Syria destroyed them and made them like the dust in threshing. [8] Now the rest of the acts of Jehoahaz, and all that he did, and his might, aren't they written in the book of the chronicles of the kings of Israel? [9] Jehoahaz slept with his fathers; and they buried him in Samaria; and Joash his son reigned in his place. [10] In the thirty-seventh year of Joash king of Judah, Jehoash the son of Jehoahaz began to reign over Israel in Samaria for sixteen years. [11] He did that which was evil in Yahweh's sight. He didn't depart from all the sins of Jeroboam the son of Nebat, with which he made Israel to sin; but he walked in them. [12] Now the rest of the acts of Joash, and all that he did, and his might with which he fought against Amaziah king of Judah, aren't they written in the book of the chronicles of the kings of Israel? [13] Joash slept with his fathers; and Jeroboam sat on his throne. Joash was buried in Samaria with the kings of Israel. [14] Now Elisha became sick with the illness of which he died; and Joash the king of Israel came down to him, and wept over him, and said, "My father, my father, the chariots of Israel and its horsemen!" [15] Elisha said to him, "Take bow and arrows;" and he took bow and arrows for himself. [16] He said to the king of Israel, "Put your hand on the bow;" and he put his hand on it. Elisha laid his hands on the king's hands. [17] He said, "Open the window eastward;" and he opened it. Then Elisha said, "Shoot!" and he shot. He said, "Yahweh's arrow of victory, even the arrow of victory over Syria; for you will strike the Syrians in Aphek until you have consumed them." [18] He said, "Take the arrows;" and he took them. He said to the king of Israel, "Strike the ground;" and he struck three times, and stopped. [19] The man of God was angry with him, and said, "You should have struck five or six times. Then you would have struck Syria until you had consumed it, but now you will strike Syria just three times." [20] Elisha died, and they buried him. Now the bands of the Moabites invaded the land at the coming in of the year. [21] As they were burying a man, behold, they saw a band of raiders; and they threw the man into Elisha's tomb. As soon as the man touched Elisha's bones, he revived, and stood up on his feet. [22] Hazael king of Syria oppressed Israel all the days of Jehoahaz. [23] But Yahweh was gracious to them, and had compassion on them, and favored them because of his covenant with Abraham, Isaac, and Jacob, and would not destroy them and he didn't cast them from his presence as yet. [24] Hazael king of Syria died; and Benhadad his son reigned in his place. [25] Jehoash the son of Jehoahaz took again out of the hand of Benhadad the son of Hazael the cities which he had taken out of the hand of Jehoahaz his father by war. Joash struck him three times, and recovered the cities of Israel.

## 14

[1] In the second year of Joash, son of Joahaz, king of Israel, Amaziah the son of Joash king of Judah began to reign. [2] He was twenty-five years old when he began to reign; and he reigned twenty-nine years in Jerusalem. His mother's name was Jehoaddin of Jerusalem. [3] He did that which was right in Yahweh's eyes, yet not like David his father. He did according to all that Joash his father had done. [4] However the high places were not taken away. The people still sacrificed and burned incense in the high places. [5] As soon as the kingdom was established in his hand, he killed his servants who had slain the king his father, [6] but the children of the murderers he didn't put to death, according to that which is written in the book of the law of Moses, as Yahweh commanded, saying, "The fathers shall not be put to death for the children, nor the children be put to death for the fathers; but every man shall die for his own sin." [7] He killed ten thousand Edomites in the Valley of Salt, and took Sela by war, and called its name Joktheel, to this day. [8] Then Amaziah sent messengers to Jehoash, the son of Jehoahaz son of Jehu, king of Israel, saying, "Come, let's look one

another in the face." [9] Jehoash the king of Israel sent to Amaziah king of Judah, saying, "The thistle that was in Lebanon sent to the cedar that was in Lebanon, saying, 'Give your daughter to my son as wife.' Then a wild animal that was in Lebanon passed by, and trampled down the thistle. [10] You have indeed struck Edom, and your heart has lifted you up. Enjoy the glory of it, and stay at home; for why should you meddle to your harm, that you fall, even you, and Judah with you?" [11] But Amaziah would not listen. So Jehoash king of Israel went up; and he and Amaziah king of Judah looked one another in the face at Beth Shemesh, which belongs to Judah. [12] Judah was defeated by Israel; and each man fled to his tent. [13] Jehoash king of Israel took Amaziah king of Judah, the son of Jehoash the son of Ahaziah, at Beth Shemesh and came to Jerusalem, then broke down the wall of Jerusalem from the gate of Ephraim to the corner gate, four hundred cubits.[a] [14] He took all the gold and silver and all the vessels that were found in Yahweh's house and in the treasures of the king's house, the hostages also, and returned to Samaria. [15] Now the rest of the acts of Jehoash which he did, and his might, and how he fought with Amaziah king of Judah, aren't they written in the book of the chronicles of the kings of Israel? [16] Jehoash slept with his fathers, and was buried in Samaria with the kings of Israel; and Jeroboam his son reigned in his place. [17] Amaziah the son of Joash king of Judah lived after the death of Jehoash son of Jehoahaz, king of Israel, fifteen years. [18] Now the rest of the acts of Amaziah, aren't they written in the book of the chronicles of the kings of Judah? [19] They made a conspiracy against him in Jerusalem, and he fled to Lachish; but they sent after him to Lachish and killed him there. [20] They brought him on horses, and he was buried at Jerusalem with his fathers in David's city. [21] All the people of Judah took Azariah, who was sixteen years old, and made him king in the place of his father Amaziah. [22] He built Elath and restored it to Judah. After that the king slept with his fathers. [23] In the fifteenth year of Amaziah the son of Joash king of Judah, Jeroboam the son of Joash king of Israel began to reign in Samaria for forty-one years. [24] He did that which was evil in Yahweh's sight. He didn't depart from all the sins of Jeroboam the son of Nebat, with which he made Israel to sin. [25] He restored the border of Israel from the entrance of Hamath to the sea of the Arabah, according to Yahweh, the God of Israel's word, which he spoke by his servant Jonah the son of Amittai, the prophet, who was from Gath Hepher. [26] For Yahweh saw the affliction of Israel, that it was very bitter for all, slave and free; and there was no helper for Israel. [27] Yahweh didn't say that he would blot out the name of Israel from under the sky; but he saved them by the hand of Jeroboam the son of Joash. [28] Now the rest of the acts of Jeroboam, and all that he did, and his might, how he fought, and how he recovered Damascus, and Hamath, which had belonged to Judah, for Israel, aren't they written in the book of the chronicles of the kings of Israel? [29] Jeroboam slept with his fathers, even with the kings of Israel; and Zechariah his son reigned in his place.

## 15

[1] In the twenty-seventh year of Jeroboam king of Israel, Azariah son of Amaziah king of Judah began to reign. [2] He was sixteen years old when he began to reign, and he reigned fifty-two years in Jerusalem. His mother's name was Jecoliah of Jerusalem. [3] He did that which was right in Yahweh's eyes, according to all that his father Amaziah had done. [4] However, the high places were not taken away. The people still sacrificed and burned incense in the high places. [5] Yahweh struck the king, so that he was a leper to the day of his death, and lived in a separate house. Jotham, the king's son, was over the household, judging the people of the land. [6] Now the rest of the acts of Azariah, and all that he did, aren't they written in the book of the chronicles of the kings of Judah? [7] Azariah slept with his fathers; and they buried him with his fathers in David's city; and Jotham his son reigned in his place. [8] In the thirty-eighth year of Azariah king of Judah, Zechariah the son of Jeroboam reigned over Israel in Samaria six months. [9] He did that which was evil in Yahweh's sight, as his fathers had done. He didn't depart from the sins of Jeroboam the son of Nebat, with which he made Israel to sin. [10] Shallum the son of Jabesh conspired against him, and struck him before the people and killed him, and reigned in his place. [11] Now the rest of the acts of Zechariah, behold, they are written in the book of the chronicles of the kings of Israel. [12] This was Yahweh's word which he spoke to Jehu, saying, "Your sons to the fourth generation shall sit on the throne of Israel." So it came to pass. [13] Shallum the son of Jabesh began to reign in the thirty-ninth year of Uzziah king of Judah, and he reigned for a month in Samaria. [14] Menahem the son of Gadi went up from Tirzah, came to Samaria, struck Shallum the son of Jabesh in Samaria, killed him, and reigned in his place. [15] Now the rest

of the acts of Shallum, and his conspiracy which he made, behold, they are written in the book of the chronicles of the kings of Israel. [16] Then Menahem attacked Tiphsah and all who were in it and its border areas, from Tirzah. He attacked it because they didn't open their gates to him, and he ripped up all their women who were with child. [17] In the thirty ninth year of Azariah king of Judah, Menahem the son of Gadi began to reign over Israel for ten years in Samaria. [18] He did that which was evil in Yahweh's sight. He didn't depart all his days from the sins of Jeroboam the son of Nebat, with which he made Israel to sin. [19] Pul the king of Assyria came against the land, and Menahem gave Pul one thousand talents[b] of silver, that his hand might be with him to confirm the kingdom in his hand. [20] Menahem exacted the money from Israel, even from all the mighty men of wealth, from each man fifty shekels[c] of silver, to give to the king of Assyria. So the king of Assyria turned back, and didn't stay there in the land. [21] Now the rest of the acts of Menahem, and all that he did, aren't they written in the book of the chronicles of the kings of Israel? [22] Menahem slept with his fathers, and Pekahiah his son reigned in his place. [23] In the fiftieth year of Azariah king of Judah, Pekahiah the son of Menahem began to reign over Israel in Samaria for two years. [24] He did that which was evil in Yahweh's sight. He didn't depart from the sins of Jeroboam the son of Nebat, with which he made Israel to sin. [25] Pekah the son of Remaliah, his captain, conspired against him and attacked him in Samaria, in the fortress of the king's house, with Argob and Arieh; and with him were fifty men of the Gileadites. He killed him, and reigned in his place. [26] Now the rest of the acts of Pekahiah, and all that he did, behold, they are written in the book of the chronicles of the kings of Israel. [27] In the fifty-second year of Azariah king of Judah, Pekah the son of Remaliah began to reign over Israel in Samaria for twenty years. [28] He did that which was evil in Yahweh's sight. He didn't depart from the sins of Jeroboam the son of Nebat, with which he made Israel to sin. [29] In the days of Pekah king of Israel, Tiglath Pileser king of Assyria came and took Ijon, Abel Beth Maacah, Janoah, Kedesh, Hazor, Gilead, and Galilee, all the land of Naphtali; and he carried them captive to Assyria. [30] Hoshea the son of Elah made a conspiracy against Pekah the son of Remaliah, attacked him, killed him, and reigned in his place, in the twentieth year of Jotham the son of Uzziah. [31] Now the rest of the acts of Pekah, and all that he did, behold, they are written in the book of the chronicles of the kings of Israel. [32] In the second year of Pekah the son of Remaliah king of Israel, Jotham the son of Uzziah king of Judah began to reign. [33] He was twenty-five years old when he began to reign, and he reigned sixteen years in Jerusalem. His mother's name was Jerusha the daughter of Zadok. [34] He did that which was right in Yahweh's eyes. He did according to all that his father Uzziah had done. [35] However the high places were not taken away. The people still sacrificed and burned incense in the high places. He built the upper gate of Yahweh's house. [36] Now the rest of the acts of Jotham, and all that he did, aren't they written in the book of the chronicles of the kings of Judah? [37] In those days, Yahweh began to send Rezin the king of Syria and Pekah the son of Remaliah against Judah. [38] Jotham slept with his fathers, and was buried with his fathers in his father David's city; and Ahaz his son reigned in his place.

## 16

[1] In the seventeenth year of Pekah the son of Remaliah, Ahaz the son of Jotham king of Judah began to reign. [2] Ahaz was twenty years old when he began to reign, and he reigned sixteen years in Jerusalem. He didn't do that which was right in Yahweh his God's eyes, like David his father. [3] But he walked in the way of the kings of Israel, and even made his son to pass through the fire, according to the abominations of the nations whom Yahweh cast out from before the children of Israel. [4] He sacrificed and burned incense in the high places, on the hills, and under every green tree. [5] Then Rezin king of Syria and Pekah son of Remaliah king of Israel came up to Jerusalem to wage war. They besieged Ahaz, but could not overcome him. [6] At that time Rezin king of Syria recovered Elath to Syria, and drove the Jews from Elath; and the Syrians came to Elath, and lived there to this day. [7] So Ahaz sent messengers to Tiglath Pileser king of Assyria, saying, "I am your servant and your son. Come up and save me out of the hand of the king of Syria and out of the hand of the king of Israel, who rise up against me." [8] Ahaz took the silver and gold that was found in Yahweh's house, and in the treasures of the king's house, and sent it for a present to the king of Assyria. [9] The king of Assyria listened to him; and the king of Assyria went up against Damascus and took it, and carried its people captive to Kir, and killed Rezin. [10] King Ahaz went to Damascus to meet Tiglath Pileser king of Assyria, and saw the altar that was at

---

[a] *14:13* A cubit is the length from the tip of the middle finger to the elbow on a man's arm, or about 18 inches or 46 centimeters.

[b] *15:19* A talent is about 30 kilograms or 66 pounds, so 1000 talents is about 30 metric tons

[c] *15:20* A shekel is about 10 grams or about 0.35 ounces, so 50 shekels was about 0.5 kilograms or 1.1 pounds.

Damascus; and King Ahaz sent to Urijah the priest a drawing of the altar and plans to build it. <sup>11</sup> Urijah the priest built an altar. According to all that King Ahaz had sent from Damascus, so Urijah the priest made it for the coming of King Ahaz from Damascus. <sup>12</sup> When the king had come from Damascus, the king saw the altar; and the king came near to the altar, and offered on it. <sup>13</sup> He burned his burnt offering and his meal offering, poured his drink offering, and sprinkled the blood of his peace offerings on the altar. <sup>14</sup> The bronze altar, which was before Yahweh, he brought from the front of the house, from between his altar and Yahweh's house, and put it on the north side of his altar. <sup>15</sup> King Ahaz commanded Urijah the priest, saying, "On the great altar burn the morning burnt offering, the evening meal offering, the king's burnt offering and his meal offering, with the burnt offering of all the people of the land, their meal offering, and their drink offerings; and sprinkle on it all the blood of the burnt offering, and all the blood of the sacrifice; but the bronze altar will be for me to inquire by." <sup>16</sup> Urijah the priest did so, according to all that King Ahaz commanded. <sup>17</sup> King Ahaz cut off the panels of the bases, and removed the basin from off them, and took down the sea from off the bronze oxen that were under it, and put it on a pavement of stone. <sup>18</sup> He removed the covered way for the Sabbath that they had built in the house, and the king's outer entrance to Yahweh's house, because of the king of Assyria. <sup>19</sup> Now the rest of the acts of Ahaz which he did, aren't they written in the book of the chronicles of the kings of Judah? <sup>20</sup> Ahaz slept with his fathers, and was buried with his fathers in David's city; and Hezekiah his son reigned in his place.

## 17

<sup>1</sup> In the twelfth year of Ahaz king of Judah, Hoshea the son of Elah began to reign in Samaria over Israel for nine years. <sup>2</sup> He did that which was evil in Yahweh's sight, yet not as the kings of Israel who were before him. <sup>3</sup> Shalmaneser king of Assyria came up against him; and Hoshea became his servant, and brought him tribute. <sup>4</sup> The king of Assyria discovered a conspiracy in Hoshea; for he had sent messengers to So king of Egypt, and offered no tribute to the king of Assyria, as he had done year by year. Therefore the king of Assyria seized him, and bound him in prison. <sup>5</sup> Then the king of Assyria came up throughout all the land, went up to Samaria, and besieged it three years. <sup>6</sup> In the ninth year of Hoshea the king of Assyria took Samaria and carried Israel away to Assyria, and placed them in Halah, and on the Habor, the river of Gozan, and in the cities of the Medes. <sup>7</sup> It was so because the children of Israel had sinned against Yahweh their God, who brought them up out of the land of Egypt from under the hand of Pharaoh king of Egypt, and had feared other gods, <sup>8</sup> and walked in the statutes of the nations whom Yahweh cast out from before the children of Israel, and of the kings of Israel, which they made. <sup>9</sup> The children of Israel secretly did things that were not right against Yahweh their God; and they built high places for themselves in all their cities, from the tower of the watchmen to the fortified city; <sup>10</sup> and they set up for themselves pillars and Asherah poles on every high hill and under every green tree; <sup>11</sup> and there they burned incense in all the high places, as the nations whom Yahweh carried away before them did; and they did wicked things to provoke Yahweh to anger; <sup>12</sup> and they served idols, of which Yahweh had said to them, "You shall not do this thing." <sup>13</sup> Yet Yahweh testified to Israel and to Judah, by every prophet and every seer, saying, "Turn from your evil ways, and keep my commandments and my statutes, according to all the law which I commanded your fathers, and which I sent to you by my servants the prophets." <sup>14</sup> Notwithstanding, they would not listen, but hardened their neck like the neck of their fathers who didn't believe in Yahweh their God. <sup>15</sup> They rejected his statutes and his covenant that he made with their fathers, and his testimonies which he testified to them; and they followed vanity, and became vain, and followed the nations that were around them, concerning whom Yahweh had commanded them that they should not do like them. <sup>16</sup> They abandoned all the commandments of Yahweh their God, and made molten images for themselves, even two calves, and made an Asherah, and worshiped all the army of the sky, and served Baal. <sup>17</sup> They caused their sons and their daughters to pass through the fire, used divination and enchantments, and sold themselves to do that which was evil in Yahweh's sight, to provoke him to anger. <sup>18</sup> Therefore Yahweh was very angry with Israel, and removed them out of his sight. There was none left but the tribe of Judah only. <sup>19</sup> Also Judah didn't keep the commandments of Yahweh their God, but walked in the statutes of Israel which they made. <sup>20</sup> Yahweh rejected all the offspring of Israel, afflicted them, and delivered them into the hands of raiders, until he had cast them out of his sight. <sup>21</sup> For he tore Israel from David's house; and they made Jeroboam the son of Nebat king; and Jeroboam drove Israel from following Yahweh, and made them sin a great sin. <sup>22</sup> The children of Israel walked in all the sins of Jeroboam which he did; they

didn't depart from them <sup>23</sup> until Yahweh removed Israel out of his sight, as he said by all his servants the prophets. So Israel was carried away out of their own land to Assyria to this day. <sup>24</sup> The king of Assyria brought people from Babylon, from Cuthah, from Avva, and from Hamath and Sepharvaim, and placed them in the cities of Samaria instead of the children of Israel; and they possessed Samaria and lived in its cities. <sup>25</sup> So it was, at the beginning of their dwelling there, that they didn't fear Yahweh. Therefore Yahweh sent lions among them, which killed some of them. <sup>26</sup> Therefore they spoke to the king of Assyria, saying, "The nations which you have carried away and placed in the cities of Samaria don't know the law of the god of the land. Therefore he has sent lions among them; and behold, they kill them, because they don't know the law of the god of the land." <sup>27</sup> Then the king of Assyria commanded, saying, "Carry there one of the priests whom you brought from there; and let him<sup>a</sup> go and dwell there, and let him teach them the law of the god of the land." <sup>28</sup> So one of the priests whom they had carried away from Samaria came and lived in Bethel, and taught them how they should fear Yahweh. <sup>29</sup> However every nation made gods of their own, and put them in the houses of the high places which the Samaritans had made, every nation in their cities in which they lived. <sup>30</sup> The men of Babylon made Succoth Benoth, and the men of Cuth made Nergal, and the men of Hamath made Ashima, <sup>31</sup> and the Avvites made Nibhaz and Tartak; and the Sepharvites burned their children in the fire to Adrammelech and Anammelech, the gods of Sepharvaim. <sup>32</sup> So they feared Yahweh, and also made from among themselves priests of the high places for themselves, who sacrificed for them in the houses of the high places. <sup>33</sup> They feared Yahweh, and also served their own gods, after the ways of the nations from among whom they had been carried away. <sup>34</sup> To this day they do what they did before. They don't fear Yahweh, and they do not follow the statutes, or the ordinances, or the law, or the commandment which Yahweh commanded the children of Jacob, whom he named Israel; <sup>35</sup> with whom Yahweh had made a covenant and commanded them, saying, "You shall not fear other gods, nor bow yourselves to them, nor serve them, nor sacrifice to them; <sup>36</sup> but you shall fear Yahweh, who brought you up out of the land of Egypt with great power and with an outstretched arm, and you shall bow yourselves to him, and you shall sacrifice to him. <sup>37</sup> The statutes and the ordinances, and the law and the commandment which he wrote for you, you shall observe to do forever more. You shall not fear other gods. <sup>38</sup> You shall not forget the covenant that I have made with you. You shall not fear other gods. <sup>39</sup> But you shall fear Yahweh your God, and he will deliver you out of the hand of all your enemies." <sup>40</sup> However they didn't listen, but they did what they did before. <sup>41</sup> So these nations feared Yahweh, and also served their engraved images. Their children did likewise, and so did their children's children. They do as their fathers did to this day.

## 18

<sup>1</sup> Now in the third year of Hoshea son of Elah king of Israel, Hezekiah the son of Ahaz king of Judah began to reign. <sup>2</sup> He was twenty-five years old when he began to reign, and he reigned twenty-nine years in Jerusalem. His mother's name was Abi the daughter of Zechariah. <sup>3</sup> He did that which was right in Yahweh's eyes, according to all that David his father had done. <sup>4</sup> He removed the high places, broke the pillars, and cut down the Asherah. He also broke in pieces the bronze serpent that Moses had made, because in those days the children of Israel burned incense to it; and he called it Nehushtan. <sup>5</sup> He trusted in Yahweh, the God of Israel, so that after him was no one like him among all the kings of Judah, nor among them that were before him. <sup>6</sup> For he joined with Yahweh. He didn't depart from following him, but kept his commandments, which Yahweh commanded Moses. <sup>7</sup> Yahweh was with him. Wherever he went, he prospered. He rebelled against the king of Assyria, and didn't serve him. <sup>8</sup> He struck the Philistines to Gaza and its borders, from the tower of the watchmen to the fortified city. <sup>9</sup> In the fourth year of King Hezekiah, which was the seventh year of Hoshea son of Elah king of Israel, Shalmaneser king of Assyria came up against Samaria and besieged it. <sup>10</sup> At the end of three years they took it. In the sixth year of Hezekiah, which was the ninth year of Hoshea king of Israel, Samaria was taken. <sup>11</sup> The king of Assyria carried Israel away to Assyria, and put them in Halah, and on the Habor, the river of Gozan, and in the cities of the Medes, <sup>12</sup> because they didn't obey Yahweh their God's voice, but transgressed his covenant, even all that Moses the servant of Yahweh commanded, and would not hear it or do it. <sup>13</sup> Now in the fourteenth year of King Hezekiah, Sennacherib king of Assyria came up against all the fortified cities of Judah and took them. <sup>14</sup> Hezekiah king of Judah sent to the king of Assyria at Lachish, saying, "I have offended you. Withdraw from me. That which you put on me, I will bear." The king of Assyria appointed to Hezekiah king of Judah

three hundred talents of silver and thirty talents[a] of gold. ¹⁵ Hezekiah gave him all the silver that was found in Yahweh's house and in the treasures of the king's house. ¹⁶ At that time, Hezekiah cut off the gold from the doors of Yahweh's temple, and from the pillars which Hezekiah king of Judah had overlaid, and gave it to the king of Assyria. ¹⁷ The king of Assyria sent Tartan, Rabsaris, and Rabshakeh from Lachish to King Hezekiah with a great army to Jerusalem. They went up and came to Jerusalem. When they had come up, they came and stood by the conduit of the upper pool, which is in the highway of the fuller's field. ¹⁸ When they had called to the king, Eliakim the son of Hilkiah, who was over the household, and Shebnah the scribe, and Joah the son of Asaph the recorder came out to them. ¹⁹ Rabshakeh said to them, "Say now to Hezekiah, 'The great king, the king of Assyria, says, "What confidence is this in which you trust? ²⁰ You say (but they are but vain words), 'There is counsel and strength for war.' Now on whom do you trust, that you have rebelled against me? ²¹ Now, behold, you trust in the staff of this bruised reed, even in Egypt. If a man leans on it, it will go into his hand and pierce it. So is Pharaoh king of Egypt to all who trust on him. ²² But if you tell me, 'We trust in Yahweh our God,' isn't that he whose high places and whose altars Hezekiah has taken away, and has said to Judah and to Jerusalem, 'You shall worship before this altar in Jerusalem'? ²³ Now therefore, please give pledges to my master the king of Assyria, and I will give you two thousand horses if you are able on your part to set riders on them. ²⁴ How then can you turn away the face of one captain of the least of my master's servants, and put your trust on Egypt for chariots and for horsemen? ²⁵ Have I now come up without Yahweh against this place to destroy it? Yahweh said to me, 'Go up against this land, and destroy it.'"'" ²⁶ Then Eliakim the son of Hilkiah, Shebnah, and Joah, said to Rabshakeh, "Please speak to your servants in the Syrian language, for we understand it. Don't speak with us in the Jews' language, in the hearing of the people who are on the wall." ²⁷ But Rabshakeh said to them, "Has my master sent me to your master and to you, to speak these words? Hasn't he sent me to the men who sit on the wall, to eat their own dung, and to drink their own urine with you?" ²⁸ Then Rabshakeh stood and cried with a loud voice in the Jews' language, and spoke, saying, "Hear the word of the great king, the king of Assyria. ²⁹ The king says, 'Don't let Hezekiah deceive you, for he will not be able to deliver you out of his hand. ³⁰ Don't let Hezekiah make you trust in Yahweh, saying, "Yahweh will surely deliver us, and this city shall not be given into the hand of the king of Assyria." ³¹ Don't listen to Hezekiah.' For the king of Assyria says, 'Make your peace with me, and come out to me; and everyone of you eat from his own vine, and everyone from his own fig tree, and everyone drink water from his own cistern; ³² until I come and take you away to a land like your own land, a land of grain and new wine, a land of bread and vineyards, a land of olive trees and of honey, that you may live and not die. Don't listen to Hezekiah when he persuades you, saying, "Yahweh will deliver us." ³³ Has any of the gods of the nations ever delivered his land out of the hand of the king of Assyria? ³⁴ Where are the gods of Hamath and of Arpad? Where are the gods of Sepharvaim, of Hena, and Ivvah? Have they delivered Samaria out of my hand? ³⁵ Who are they among all the gods of the countries, that have delivered their country out of my hand, that Yahweh should deliver Jerusalem out of my hand?'" ³⁶ But the people stayed quiet, and answered him not a word; for the king's commandment was, "Don't answer him." ³⁷ Then Eliakim the son of Hilkiah, who was over the household, came with Shebna the scribe and Joah the son of Asaph the recorder to Hezekiah with their clothes torn, and told him Rabshakeh's words.

## 19

¹ When King Hezekiah heard it, he tore his clothes, covered himself with sackcloth, and went into Yahweh's house. ² He sent Eliakim, who was over the household, Shebna the scribe, and the elders of the priests, covered with sackcloth, to Isaiah the prophet the son of Amoz. ³ They said to him, "Hezekiah says, 'Today is a day of trouble, of rebuke, and of rejection; for the children have come to the point of birth, and there is no strength to deliver them. ⁴ It may be Yahweh your God will hear all the words of Rabshakeh, whom the king of Assyria his master has sent to defy the living God, and will rebuke the words which Yahweh your God has heard. Therefore lift up your prayer for the remnant that is left.'" ⁵ So the servants of King Hezekiah came to Isaiah. ⁶ Isaiah said to them, "Tell your master this: 'Yahweh says, "Don't be afraid of the words that you have heard, with which the servants of the king of Assyria have blasphemed me. ⁷ Behold, I will put a spirit in him, and he will hear news, and will return to his own land. I will cause him to fall by the sword in his own land."'" ⁸ So Rabshakeh returned and found

the king of Assyria warring against Libnah; for he had heard that he had departed from Lachish. ⁹ When he heard it said of Tirhakah king of Ethiopia, "Behold, he has come out to fight against you," he sent messengers again to Hezekiah, saying, ¹⁰"Tell Hezekiah king of Judah this: 'Don't let your God in whom you trust deceive you, saying, Jerusalem will not be given into the hand of the king of Assyria. ¹¹ Behold, you have heard what the kings of Assyria have done to all lands, by destroying them utterly. Will you be delivered? ¹² Have the gods of the nations delivered them, which my fathers have destroyed— Gozan, Haran, Rezeph, and the children of Eden who were in Telassar? ¹³ Where is the king of Hamath, the king of Arpad, and the king of the city of Sepharvaim, of Hena, and Ivvah?'" ¹⁴ Hezekiah received the letter from the hand of the messengers and read it. Then Hezekiah went up to Yahweh's house, and spread it before Yahweh. ¹⁵ Hezekiah prayed before Yahweh, and said, "Yahweh, the God of Israel, who are enthroned above the cherubim, you are the God, even you alone, of all the kingdoms of the earth. You have made heaven and earth. ¹⁶ Incline your ear, Yahweh, and hear. Open your eyes, Yahweh, and see. Hear the words of Sennacherib, which he has sent to defy the living God. ¹⁷ Truly, Yahweh, the kings of Assyria have laid waste the nations and their lands, ¹⁸ and have cast their gods into the fire; for they were no gods, but the work of men's hands, wood and stone. Therefore they have destroyed them. ¹⁹ Now therefore, Yahweh our God, save us, I beg you, out of his hand, that all the kingdoms of the earth may know that you, Yahweh, are God alone." ²⁰ Then Isaiah the son of Amoz sent to Hezekiah, saying, "Yahweh, the God of Israel, says 'You have prayed to me against Sennacherib king of Assyria, and I have heard you. ²¹ This is the word that Yahweh has spoken concerning him: 'The virgin daughter of Zion has despised you and ridiculed you. The daughter of Jerusalem has shaken her head at you. ²² Whom have you defied and blasphemed? Against whom have you exalted your voice and lifted up your eyes on high? Against the Holy One of Israel! ²³ By your messengers, you have defied the Lord, and have said, "With the multitude of my chariots, I have come up to the height of the mountains, to the innermost parts of Lebanon, and I will cut down its tall cedars and its choice cypress trees; and I will enter into his farthest lodging place, the forest of his fruitful field. ²⁴ I have dug and drunk strange waters, and I will dry up all the rivers of Egypt with the sole of my feet." ²⁵ Haven't you heard how I have done it long ago, and formed it of ancient times? Now I have brought it to pass, that it should be yours to lay waste fortified cities into ruinous heaps. ²⁶ Therefore their inhabitants had little power. They were dismayed and confounded. They were like the grass of the field and like the green herb, like the grass on the housetops and like grain blasted before it has grown up. ²⁷ But I know your sitting down, your going out, your coming in, and your raging against me. ²⁸ Because of your raging against me, and because your arrogance has come up into my ears, therefore I will put my hook in your nose, and my bridle in your lips, and I will turn you back by the way by which you came.' ²⁹"This will be the sign to you: This year, you will eat that which grows of itself, and in the second year that which springs from that; and in the third year sow and reap, and plant vineyards and eat their fruit. ³⁰ The remnant that has escaped of the house of Judah will again take root downward, and bear fruit upward. ³¹ For out of Jerusalem a remnant will go out, and out of Mount Zion those who shall escape. Yahweh's zeal will perform this. ³²"Therefore Yahweh says concerning the king of Assyria, 'He will not come to this city, nor shoot an arrow there. He will not come before it with shield, nor cast up a mound against it. ³³ He will return the same way that he came, and he will not come to this city,' says Yahweh. ³⁴'For I will defend this city to save it, for my own sake and for my servant David's sake.'" ³⁵ That night, Yahweh's angel went out and struck one hundred eighty-five thousand in the camp of the Assyrians. When men arose early in the morning, behold, these were all dead bodies. ³⁶ So Sennacherib king of Assyria departed, went home, and lived at Nineveh. ³⁷ As he was worshiping in the house of Nisroch his god, Adrammelech and Sharezer struck him with the sword; and they escaped into the land of Ararat. Esar Haddon his son reigned in his place.

## 20

¹ In those days Hezekiah was sick and dying. Isaiah the prophet the son of Amoz came to him, and said to him, "Yahweh says, 'Set your house in order; for you will die, and not live.'" ² Then he turned his face to the wall, and prayed to Yahweh, saying, ³"Remember now, Yahweh, I beg you, how I have walked before you in truth and with a perfect heart, and have done that which is good in your sight." And Hezekiah wept bitterly. ⁴ Before Isaiah had gone out into the middle part of the city,

ª 18:14 A talent is about 30 kilograms or 66 pounds or 965 Troy ounces

Yahweh's word came to him, saying, ⁵"Turn back, and tell Hezekiah the prince of my people, 'Yahweh, the God of David your father, says, "I have heard your prayer. I have seen your tears. Behold, I will heal you. On the third day, you will go up to Yahweh's house. ⁶ I will add to your days fifteen years. I will deliver you and this city out of the hand of the king of Assyria. I will defend this city for my own sake, and for my servant David's sake."'" ⁷ Isaiah said, "Take a cake of figs." They took and laid it on the boil, and he recovered. ⁸ Hezekiah said to Isaiah, "What will be the sign that Yahweh will heal me, and that I will go up to Yahweh's house the third day?" ⁹ Isaiah said, "This will be the sign to you from Yahweh, that Yahweh will do the thing that he has spoken: should the shadow go forward ten steps, or go back ten steps?" ¹⁰ Hezekiah answered, "It is a light thing for the shadow to go forward ten steps. No, but let the shadow return backward ten steps." ¹¹ Isaiah the prophet cried to Yahweh; and he brought the shadow ten steps backward, by which it had gone down on the sundial of Ahaz. ¹² At that time Berodach Baladan the son of Baladan, king of Babylon, sent letters and a present to Hezekiah, for he had heard that Hezekiah had been sick. ¹³ Hezekiah listened to them, and showed them all the storehouse of his precious things—the silver, the gold, the spices, and the precious oil, and the house of his armor, and all that was found in his treasures. There was nothing in his house, or in all his dominion, that Hezekiah didn't show them. ¹⁴ Then Isaiah the prophet came to King Hezekiah, and said to him, "What did these men say? From where did they come to you?" Hezekiah said, "They have come from a far country, even from Babylon." ¹⁵ He said, "What have they seen in your house?" Hezekiah answered, "They have seen all that is in my house. There is nothing among my treasures that I have not shown them." ¹⁶ Isaiah said to Hezekiah, "Hear Yahweh's word. ¹⁷'Behold, the days come that all that is in your house, and that which your fathers have laid up in store to this day, will be carried to Babylon. Nothing will be left,' says Yahweh. ¹⁸'They will take away some of your sons who will issue from you, whom you will father; and they will be eunuchs in the palace of the king of Babylon.'" ¹⁹ Then Hezekiah said to Isaiah, "Yahweh's word which you have spoken is good." He said moreover, "Isn't it so, if peace and truth will be in my days?" ²⁰ Now the rest of the acts of Hezekiah, and all his might, and how he made the pool, and the conduit, and brought water into the city, aren't they written in the book of the chronicles of the kings of Judah? ²¹ Hezekiah slept with his fathers, and Manasseh his son reigned in his place.

## 21

¹ Manasseh was twelve years old when he began to reign, and he reigned fifty-five years in Jerusalem. His mother's name was Hephzibah. ² He did that which was evil in Yahweh's sight, after the abominations of the nations whom Yahweh cast out before the children of Israel. ³ For he built again the high places which Hezekiah his father had destroyed; and he raised up altars for Baal, and made an Asherah, as Ahab king of Israel did, and worshiped all the army of the sky, and served them. ⁴ He built altars in Yahweh's house, of which Yahweh said, "I will put my name in Jerusalem." ⁵ He built altars for all the army of the sky in the two courts of Yahweh's house. ⁶ He made his son to pass through the fire, practiced sorcery, used enchantments, and dealt with those who had familiar spirits and with wizards. He did much evil in Yahweh's sight, to provoke him to anger. ⁷ He set the engraved image of Asherah that he had made in the house of which Yahweh said to David and to Solomon his son, "In this house, and in Jerusalem, which I have chosen out of all the tribes of Israel, I will put my name forever; ⁸ I will not cause the feet of Israel to wander any more out of the land which I gave their fathers, if only they will observe to do according to all that I have commanded them, and according to all the law that my servant Moses commanded them." ⁹ But they didn't listen, and Manasseh seduced them to do that which is evil more than the nations did whom Yahweh destroyed before the children of Israel. ¹⁰ Yahweh spoke by his servants the prophets, saying, ¹¹"Because Manasseh king of Judah has done these abominations, and has done wickedly above all that the Amorites did, who were before him, and has also made Judah to sin with his idols; ¹² therefore Yahweh the God of Israel says, 'Behold, I will bring such evil on Jerusalem and Judah that whoever hears of it, both his ears will tingle. ¹³ I will stretch over Jerusalem the line of Samaria, and the plumb line of Ahab's house; and I will wipe Jerusalem as a man wipes a dish, wiping it and turning it upside down. ¹⁴ I will cast off the remnant of my inheritance and deliver them into the hands of their enemies. They will become a prey and a plunder to all their enemies, ¹⁵ because they have done that which is evil in my sight, and have provoked me to anger since the day their fathers came out of Egypt, even to this day.'" ¹⁶ Moreover Manasseh shed innocent blood very much, until he had filled Jerusalem from one end to another; in addition to his sin with which he made Judah to sin, in doing that which was evil in Yahweh's sight. ¹⁷ Now the rest of the acts of Manasseh, and all that he did, and his sin that he sinned, aren't they written in the book of the chronicles of the kings of Judah? ¹⁸ Manasseh slept with his fathers, and was buried in the garden of his own house, in the garden of Uzza; and Amon his son reigned in his place. ¹⁹ Amon was twenty-two years old when he began to reign; and he reigned two years in Jerusalem. His mother's name was Meshullemeth the daughter of Haruz of Jotbah. ²⁰ He did that which was evil in Yahweh's sight, as Manasseh his father did. ²¹ He walked in all the ways that his father walked in, and served the idols that his father served, and worshiped them; ²² and he abandoned Yahweh, the God of his fathers, and didn't walk in the way of Yahweh. ²³ The servants of Amon conspired against him, and put the king to death in his own house. ²⁴ But the people of the land killed all those who had conspired against King Amon; and the people of the land made Josiah his son king in his place. ²⁵ Now the rest of the acts of Amon which he did, aren't they written in the book of the chronicles of the kings of Judah? ²⁶ He was buried in his tomb in the garden of Uzza, and Josiah his son reigned in his place.

## 22

¹ Josiah was eight years old when he began to reign, and he reigned thirty-one years in Jerusalem. His mother's name was Jedidah the daughter of Adaiah of Bozkath. ² He did that which was right in Yahweh's eyes, and walked in all the ways of David his father, and didn't turn away to the right hand or to the left. ³ In the eighteenth year of King Josiah, the king sent Shaphan, the son of Azaliah the son of Meshullam, the scribe, to Yahweh's house, saying, ⁴"Go up to Hilkiah the high priest, that he may count the money which is brought into Yahweh's house, which the keepers of the threshold have gathered of the people. ⁵ Let them deliver it into the hand of the workers who have the oversight of Yahweh's house; and let them give it to the workers who are in Yahweh's house, to repair the damage to the house, ⁶ to the carpenters, and to the builders, and to the masons, and for buying timber and cut stone to repair the house. ⁷ However, no accounting shall be asked of them for the money delivered into their hand, for they deal faithfully." ⁸ Hilkiah the high priest said to Shaphan the scribe, "I have found the book of the law in Yahweh's house." Hilkiah delivered the book to Shaphan, and he read it. ⁹ Shaphan the scribe came to the king, and brought the king word again, and said, "Your servants have emptied out the money that was found in the house, and have delivered it into the hands of the workmen who have the oversight of Yahweh's house." ¹⁰ Shaphan the scribe told the king, saying, "Hilkiah the priest has delivered a book to me." Then Shaphan read it before the king. ¹¹ When the king had heard the words of the book of the law, he tore his clothes. ¹² The king commanded Hilkiah the priest, Ahikam the son of Shaphan, Achbor the son of Micaiah, Shaphan the scribe, and Asaiah the king's servant, saying, ¹³"Go inquire of Yahweh for me, and for the people, and for all Judah, concerning the words of this book that is found; for great is Yahweh's wrath that is kindled against us, because our fathers have not listened to the words of this book, to do according to all that which is written concerning us." ¹⁴ So Hilkiah the priest, Ahikam, Achbor, Shaphan, and Asaiah went to Huldah the prophetess, the wife of Shallum the son of Tikvah, the son of Harhas, keeper of the wardrobe (now she lived in Jerusalem in the second quarter); and they talked with her. ¹⁵ She said to them, "Yahweh the God of Israel says, 'Tell the man who sent you to me, ¹⁶"Yahweh says, 'Behold, I will bring evil on this place and on its inhabitants, even all the words of the book which the king of Judah has read. ¹⁷ Because they have forsaken me and have burned incense to other gods, that they might provoke me to anger with all the work of their hands, therefore my wrath shall be kindled against this place, and it will not be quenched.'" ¹⁸ But to the king of Judah, who sent you to inquire of Yahweh, tell him, "Yahweh the God of Israel says, 'Concerning the words which you have heard, ¹⁹ because your heart was tender, and you humbled yourself before Yahweh when you heard what I spoke against this place and against its inhabitants, that they should become a desolation and a curse, and have torn your clothes and wept before me, I also have heard you,' says Yahweh. ²⁰'Therefore behold, I will gather you to your fathers, and you will be gathered to your grave in peace. Your eyes will not see all the evil which I will bring on this place.'"'" So they brought this message back to the king.

## 23

¹ The king sent, and they gathered to him all the elders of Judah and of Jerusalem. ² The king went up to Yahweh's house, and all the men of Judah and all the inhabitants of Jerusalem with him—with the priests, the prophets, and all the people, both small and great; and he read in their hearing all the words of the book of the covenant which was found in Yahweh's house. ³ The king stood by the pillar and made a covenant before Yahweh to walk after Yahweh and to keep his commandments, his testimonies, and his statutes with all his heart and all his soul, to confirm the words of this covenant that were written in this book; and all the people agreed to the covenant. ⁴ The king commanded Hilkiah

the high priest, and the priests of the second order, and the keepers of the threshold, to bring out of Yahweh's temple all the vessels that were made for Baal, for the Asherah, and for all the army of the sky; and he burned them outside of Jerusalem in the fields of the Kidron, and carried their ashes to Bethel. ⁵ He got rid of the idolatrous priests whom the kings of Judah had ordained to burn incense in the high places in the cities of Judah and in the places around Jerusalem; those also who burned incense to Baal, to the sun, to the moon, to the planets, and to all the army of the sky. ⁶ He brought out the Asherah from Yahweh's house, outside of Jerusalem, to the brook Kidron, and burned it at the brook Kidron, and beat it to dust, and cast its dust on the graves of the common people. ⁷ He broke down the houses of the male shrine prostitutes that were in Yahweh's house, where the women wove hangings for the Asherah. ⁸ He brought all the priests out of the cities of Judah, and defiled the high places where the priests had burned incense, from Geba to Beersheba; and he broke down the high places of the gates that were at the entrance of the gate of Joshua the governor of the city, which were on a man's left hand at the gate of the city. ⁹ Nevertheless the priests of the high places didn't come up to Yahweh's altar in Jerusalem, but they ate unleavened bread among their brothers. ¹⁰ He defiled Topheth, which is in the valley of the children of Hinnom, that no man might make his son or his daughter to pass through the fire to Molech. ¹¹ He took away the horses that the kings of Judah had dedicated to the sun, at the entrance of Yahweh's house, by the room of Nathan Melech the officer who was in the court; and he burned the chariots of the sun with fire. ¹² The king broke down the altars that were on the roof of the upper room of Ahaz, which the kings of Judah had made, and the altars which Manasseh had made in the two courts of Yahweh's house, and beat them down from there, and cast their dust into the brook Kidron. ¹³ The king defiled the high places that were before Jerusalem, which were on the right hand of the mountain of corruption, which Solomon the king of Israel had built for Ashtoreth the abomination of the Sidonians, and for Chemosh the abomination of Moab, and for Milcom the abomination of the children of Ammon. ¹⁴ He broke in pieces the pillars, cut down the Asherah poles, and filled their places with men's bones. ¹⁵ Moreover the altar that was at Bethel and the high place which Jeroboam the son of Nebat, who made Israel to sin, had made, even that altar and the high place he broke down; and he burned the high place and beat it to dust, and burned the Asherah. ¹⁶ As Josiah turned himself, he spied the tombs that were there in the mountain; and he sent, and took the bones out of the tombs, and burned them on the altar, and defiled it, according to Yahweh's word which the man of God proclaimed, who proclaimed these things. ¹⁷ Then he said, "What monument is that which I see?" The men of the city told him, "It is the tomb of the man of God who came from Judah and proclaimed these things that you have done against the altar of Bethel." ¹⁸ He said, "Let him be! Let no one move his bones." So they let his bones alone, with the bones of the prophet who came out of Samaria. ¹⁹ All the houses also of the high places that were in the cities of Samaria, which the kings of Israel had made to provoke Yahweh to anger, Josiah took away, and did to them according to all the acts that he had done in Bethel. ²⁰ He killed all the priests of the high places that were there, on the altars, and burned men's bones on them; and he returned to Jerusalem. ²¹ The king commanded all the people, saying, "Keep the Passover to Yahweh your God, as it is written in this book of the covenant." ²² Surely there was not kept such a Passover from the days of the judges who judged Israel, nor in all the days of the kings of Israel, nor of the kings of Judah; ²³ but in the eighteenth year of King Josiah, this Passover was kept to Yahweh in Jerusalem. ²⁴ Moreover, Josiah removed those who had familiar spirits, the wizards, and the teraphim,ᵃ and the idols, and all the abominations that were seen in the land of Judah and in Jerusalem, that he might confirm the words of the law which were written in the book that Hilkiah the priest found in Yahweh's house. ²⁵ There was no king like him before him, who turned to Yahweh with all his heart, and with all his soul, and with all his might, according to all the law of Moses; and there was none like him who arose after him. ²⁶ Notwithstanding, Yahweh didn't turn from the fierceness of his great wrath, with which his anger burned against Judah, because of all the provocation with which Manasseh had provoked him. ²⁷ Yahweh said, "I will also remove Judah out of my sight, as I have removed Israel; and I will cast off this city which I have chosen, even Jerusalem, and the house of which I said, 'My name shall be there.'" ²⁸ Now the rest of the acts of Josiah, and all that he did, aren't they written in the book of the chronicles of the kings of Judah? ²⁹ In his days Pharaoh Necoh king of Egypt went up against the king of Assyria to the river Euphrates; and King Josiah went against him, but

Pharaoh Necoh killed him at Megiddo when he saw him. ³⁰ His servants carried him dead in a chariot from Megiddo, brought him to Jerusalem, and buried him in his own tomb. The people of the land took Jehoahaz the son of Josiah, and anointed him, and made him king in his father's place. ³¹ Jehoahaz was twenty-three years old when he began to reign; and he reigned three months in Jerusalem. His mother's name was Hamutal the daughter of Jeremiah of Libnah. ³² He did that which was evil in Yahweh's sight, according to all that his fathers had done. ³³ Pharaoh Necoh put him in bonds at Riblah in the land of Hamath, that he might not reign in Jerusalem; and put the land to a tribute of one hundred talents of silver and a talentᵇ of gold. ³⁴ Pharaoh Necoh made Eliakim the son of Josiah king in the place of Josiah his father, and changed his name to Jehoiakim; but he took Jehoahaz away, and he came to Egypt and died there. ³⁵ Jehoiakim gave the silver and the gold to Pharaoh; but he taxed the land to give the money according to the commandment of Pharaoh. He exacted the silver and the gold of the people of the land, from everyone according to his assessment, to give it to Pharaoh Necoh. ³⁶ Jehoiakim was twenty-five years old when he began to reign, and he reigned eleven years in Jerusalem. His mother's name was Zebidah the daughter of Pedaiah of Rumah. ³⁷ He did that which was evil in Yahweh's sight, according to all that his fathers had done.

## 24

¹ In his days Nebuchadnezzar king of Babylon came up, and Jehoiakim became his servant three years. Then he turned and rebelled against him. ² Yahweh sent against him bands of the Chaldeans, bands of the Syrians, bands of the Moabites, and bands of the children of Ammon, and sent them against Judah to destroy it, according to Yahweh's word which he spoke by his servants the prophets. ³ Surely at the commandment of Yahweh this came on Judah, to remove them out of his sight for the sins of Manasseh, according to all that he did, ⁴ and also for the innocent blood that he shed; for he filled Jerusalem with innocent blood, and Yahweh would not pardon. ⁵ Now the rest of the acts of Jehoiakim, and all that he did, aren't they written in the book of the chronicles of the kings of Judah? ⁶ So Jehoiakim slept with his fathers, and Jehoiachin his son reigned in his place. ⁷ The king of Egypt didn't come out of his land any more; for the king of Babylon had taken, from the brook of Egypt to the river Euphrates, all that belonged to the king of Egypt. ⁸ Jehoiachin was eighteen years old when he began to reign, and he reigned in Jerusalem three months. His mother's name was Nehushta the daughter of Elnathan of Jerusalem. ⁹ He did that which was evil in Yahweh's sight, according to all that his father had done. ¹⁰ At that time the servants of Nebuchadnezzar king of Babylon came up to Jerusalem, and the city was besieged. ¹¹ Nebuchadnezzar king of Babylon came to the city while his servants were besieging it, ¹² and Jehoiachin the king of Judah went out to the king of Babylon— he, his mother, his servants, his princes, and his officers; and the king of Babylon captured him in the eighth year of his reign. ¹³ He carried out from there all the treasures of Yahweh's house and the treasures of the king's house, and cut in pieces all the vessels of gold which Solomon king of Israel had made in Yahweh's temple, as Yahweh had said. ¹⁴ He carried away all Jerusalem, and all the princes, and all the mighty men of valor, even ten thousand captives, and all the craftsmen and the smiths. No one remained except the poorest people of the land. ¹⁵ He carried away Jehoiachin to Babylon, with the king's mother, the king's wives, his officers, and the chief men of the land. He carried them into captivity from Jerusalem to Babylon. ¹⁶ All the men of might, even seven thousand, and the craftsmen and the smiths one thousand, all of them strong and fit for war, even them the king of Babylon brought captive to Babylon. ¹⁷ The king of Babylon made Mattaniah, Jehoiachin's father's brother, king in his place, and changed his name to Zedekiah. ¹⁸ Zedekiah was twenty-one years old when he began to reign, and he reigned eleven years in Jerusalem. His mother's name was Hamutal the daughter of Jeremiah of Libnah. ¹⁹ He did that which was evil in Yahweh's sight, according to all that Jehoiakim had done. ²⁰ For through the anger of Yahweh, this happened in Jerusalem and Judah, until he had cast them out from his presence. Then Zedekiah rebelled against the king of Babylon.

## 25

¹ In the ninth year of his reign, in the tenth month, in the tenth day of the month, Nebuchadnezzar king of Babylon came, he and all his army, against Jerusalem, and encamped against it; and they built forts against it around it. ² So the city was besieged until the eleventh year of King Zedekiah. ³ On the ninth day of the fourth month, the famine was severe in the city, so that there was no bread for the people of the land. ⁴ Then a breach was made in the city, and all the men of war fled by night by

---

ᵃ 23:24 teraphim were household idols.

ᵇ 23:33 A talent is about 30 kilograms or 66 pounds or 965 Troy ounces the way of the gate between the two walls, which was by the king's garden (now the Chaldeans were against the city around it); and the king went by the way of the Arabah. ⁵ But the Chaldean army pursued the king, and overtook him in the plains of Jericho; and all his army was scattered from him. ⁶ Then they captured the king and carried him up to the king of Babylon to Riblah; and they passed judgment on him. ⁷ They killed Zedekiah's sons before his eyes, then put out Zedekiah's eyes, bound him in fetters, and carried him to Babylon. ⁸ Now in the fifth month, on the seventh day of the month, which was the nineteenth year of King Nebuchadnezzar king of Babylon, Nebuzaradan the captain of the guard, a servant of the king of Babylon, came to Jerusalem. ⁹ He burned Yahweh's house, the king's house, and all the houses of Jerusalem. He burned every great house with fire. ¹⁰ All the army of the Chaldeans, who were with the captain of the guard, broke down the walls around Jerusalem. ¹¹ Nebuzaradan the captain of the guard carried away captive the rest of the people who were left in the city and those who had deserted to the king of Babylon—all the rest of the multitude. ¹² But the captain of the guard left some of the poorest of the land to work the vineyards and fields. ¹³ The Chaldeans broke up the pillars of bronze that were in Yahweh's house and the bases and the bronze sea that were in Yahweh's house, and carried the bronze pieces to Babylon. ¹⁴ They took away the pots, the shovels, the snuffers, the spoons, and all the vessels of bronze with which they ministered. ¹⁵ The captain of the guard took away the fire pans, the basins, that which was of gold, for gold, and that which was of silver, for silver. ¹⁶ The two pillars, the one sea, and the bases, which Solomon had made for Yahweh's house, the bronze of all these vessels was not weighed. ¹⁷ The height of the one pillar was eighteen cubits,ᵃ and a capital of bronze was on it. The height of the capital was three cubits, with network and pomegranates on the capital around it, all of bronze; and the second pillar with its network was like these. ¹⁸ The captain of the guard took Seraiah the chief priest, Zephaniah the second priest, and the three keepers of the threshold; ¹⁹ and out of the city he took an officer who was set over the men of war; and five men of those who saw the king's face, who were found in the city; and the scribe, the captain of the army, who mustered the people of the land, and sixty men of the people of the land who were found in the city. ²⁰ Nebuzaradan the captain of the guard took them, and brought them to the king of Babylon to Riblah. ²¹ The king of Babylon attacked them and put them to death at Riblah in the land of Hamath. So Judah was carried away captive out of his land. ²² As for the people who were left in the land of Judah whom Nebuchadnezzar king of Babylon had left, even over them he made Gedaliah the son of Ahikam, the son of Shaphan, governor. ²³ Now when all the captains of the forces, they and their men, heard that the king of Babylon had made Gedaliah governor, they came to Gedaliah to Mizpah, even Ishmael the son of Nethaniah, Johanan the son of Kareah, Seraiah the son of Tanhumeth the Netophathite, and Jaazaniah the son of the Maacathite, they and their men. ²⁴ Gedaliah swore to them and to their men, and said to them, "Don't be afraid because of the servants of the Chaldeans. Dwell in the land and serve the king of Babylon, and it will be well with you." ²⁵ But in the seventh month, Ishmael the son of Nethaniah, the son of Elishama, of the royal offspring came, and ten men with him, and struck Gedaliah so that he died, with the Jews and the Chaldeans that were with him at Mizpah. ²⁶ All the people, both small and great, and the captains of the forces arose and came to Egypt; for they were afraid of the Chaldeans. ²⁷ In the thirty-seventh year of the captivity of Jehoiachin king of Judah, in the twelfth month, on the twenty-seventh day of the month, Evilmerodach king of Babylon, in the year that he began to reign, released Jehoiachin king of Judah out of prison, ²⁸ and he spoke kindly to him and set his throne above the throne of the kings who were with him in Babylon, ²⁹ and changed his prison garments. Jehoiachin ate bread before him continually all the days of his life; ³⁰ and for his allowance, there was a continual allowance given him from the king, every day a portion, all the days of his life.

# The First Book of Chronicles
## 1

¹ Adam, Seth, Enosh, ² Kenan, Mahalalel, Jared, ³ Enoch, Methuselah, Lamech, ⁴ Noah, Shem, Ham, and Japheth. ⁵ The sons of Japheth: Gomer, Magog, Madai, Javan, Tubal, Meshech, and Tiras. ⁶ The sons of Gomer: Ashkenaz, Diphath, and Togarmah. ⁷ The sons of Javan: Elishah, Tarshish, Kittim, and Rodanim. ⁸ The sons of Ham: Cush, Mizraim, Put, and Canaan. ⁹ The sons of Cush: Seba, Havilah, Sabta, Raama, Sabteca. The sons of Raamah: Sheba and Dedan. ¹⁰ Cush

became the father of Nimrod. He began to be a mighty one in the earth. ¹¹ Mizraim became the father of Ludim, Anamim, Lehabim, Naphtuhim, ¹² Pathrusim, Casluhim (where the Philistines came from), and Caphtorim. ¹³ Canaan became the father of Sidon his firstborn, Heth, ¹⁴ the Jebusite, the Amorite, the Girgashite, ¹⁵ the Hivite, the Arkite, the Sinite, ¹⁶ the Arvadite, the Zemarite, and the Hamathite. ¹⁷ The sons of Shem: Elam, Asshur, Arpachshad, Lud, Aram, Uz, Hul, Gether, and Meshech. ¹⁸ Arpachshad became the father of Shelah, and Shelah became the father of Eber. ¹⁹ To Eber were born two sons: the name of the one was Peleg, for in his days the earth was divided; and his brother's name was Joktan. ²⁰ Joktan became the father of Almodad, Sheleph, Hazarmaveth, Jerah, ²¹ Hadoram, Uzal, Diklah, ²² Ebal, Abimael, Sheba, ²³ Ophir, Havilah, and Jobab. All these were the sons of Joktan. ²⁴ Shem, Arpachshad, Shelah, ²⁵ Eber, Peleg, Reu, ²⁶ Serug, Nahor, Terah, ²⁷ Abram (also called Abraham). ²⁸ The sons of Abraham: Isaac and Ishmael. ²⁹ These are their generations: the firstborn of Ishmael, Nebaioth; then Kedar, Adbeel, Mibsam, ³⁰ Mishma, Dumah, Massa, Hadad, Tema, ³¹ Jetur, Naphish, and Kedemah. These are the sons of Ishmael. ³² The sons of Keturah, Abraham's concubine: she bore Zimran, Jokshan, Medan, Midian, Ishbak, and Shuah. The sons of Jokshan: Sheba and Dedan. ³³ The sons of Midian: Ephah, Epher, Hanoch, Abida, and Eldaah. All these were the sons of Keturah. ³⁴ Abraham became the father of Isaac. The sons of Isaac: Esau and Israel. ³⁵ The sons of Esau: Eliphaz, Reuel, Jeush, Jalam, and Korah. ³⁶ The sons of Eliphaz: Teman, Omar, Zephi, Gatam, Kenaz, Timna, and Amalek. ³⁷ The sons of Reuel: Nahath, Zerah, Shammah, and Mizzah. ³⁸ The sons of Seir: Lotan, Shobal, Zibeon, Anah, Dishon, Ezer, and Dishan. ³⁹ The sons of Lotan: Hori and Homam; and Timna was Lotan's sister. ⁴⁰ The sons of Shobal: Alian, Manahath, Ebal, Shephi, and Onam. The sons of Zibeon: Aiah and Anah. ⁴¹ The son of Anah: Dishon. The sons of Dishon: Hamran, Eshban, Ithran, and Cheran. ⁴² The sons of Ezer: Bilhan, Zaavan, and Jaakan. The sons of Dishan: Uz and Aran. ⁴³ Now these are the kings who reigned in the land of Edom, before any king reigned over the children of Israel: Bela the son of Beor; and the name of his city was Dinhabah. ⁴⁴ Bela died, and Jobab the son of Zerah of Bozrah reigned in his place. ⁴⁵ Jobab died, and Husham of the land of the Temanites reigned in his place. ⁴⁶ Husham died, and Hadad the son of Bedad, who struck Midian in the field of Moab, reigned in his place; and the name of his city was Avith. ⁴⁷ Hadad died, and Samlah of Masrekah reigned in his place. ⁴⁸ Samlah died, and Shaul of Rehoboth by the River reigned in his place. ⁴⁹ Shaul died, and Baal Hanan the son of Achbor reigned in his place. ⁵⁰ Baal Hanan died, and Hadad reigned in his place; and the name of his city was Pai. His wife's name was Mehetabel, the daughter of Matred, the daughter of Mezahab. ⁵¹ Then Hadad died. The chiefs of Edom were: chief Timna, chief Aliah, chief Jetheth, ⁵² chief Oholibamah, chief Elah, chief Pinon, ⁵³ chief Kenaz, chief Teman, chief Mibzar, ⁵⁴ chief Magdiel, and chief Iram. These are the chiefs of Edom.

## 2

¹ These are the sons of Israel: Reuben, Simeon, Levi, Judah, Issachar, Zebulun, ² Dan, Joseph, Benjamin, Naphtali, Gad, and Asher. ³ The sons of Judah: Er, Onan, and Shelah, which three were born to him of Shua's daughter the Canaanitess. Er, Judah's firstborn, was wicked in Yahweh'sᵇ sight; and he killed him. ⁴ Tamar his daughter-in-law bore him Perez and Zerah. All the sons of Judah were five. ⁵ The sons of Perez: Hezron and Hamul. ⁶ The sons of Zerah: Zimri, Ethan, Heman, Calcol, and Dara—five of them in all. ⁷ The son of Carmi: Achar, the troubler of Israel, who committed a trespass in the devoted thing. ⁸ The son of Ethan: Azariah. ⁹ The sons also of Hezron, who were born to him: Jerahmeel, Ram, and Chelubai. ¹⁰ Ram became the father of Amminadab, and Amminadab became the father of Nahshon, prince of the children of Judah; ¹¹ and Nahshon became the father of Salma, and Salma became the father of Boaz, ¹² and Boaz became the father of Obed, and Obed became the father of Jesse; ¹³ and Jesse became the father of his firstborn Eliab, Abinadab the second, Shimea the third, ¹⁴ Nethanel the fourth, Raddai the fifth, ¹⁵ Ozem the sixth, and David the seventh; ¹⁶ and their sisters were Zeruiah and Abigail. The sons of Zeruiah: Abishai, Joab, and Asahel, three. ¹⁷ Abigail bore Amasa; and the father of Amasa was Jether the Ishmaelite. ¹⁸ Caleb the son of Hezron became the father of children by Azubah his wife, and by Jerioth; and these were her sons: Jesher, Shobab, and Ardon. ¹⁹ Azubah died, and Caleb married Ephrath, who bore him Hur. ²⁰ Hur became the father of Uri, and Uri became the father of Bezalel. ²¹ Afterward Hezron went in to the daughter of Machir the father of Gilead, whom he took as wife when he was sixty years old; and she bore him Segub. ²² Segub became the father of Jair, who had twenty-three cities in the land of

---

ᵃ 25:17 A cubit is the length from the tip of the middle finger to the elbow on a man's arm, or about 18 inches or 46 centimeters.

ᵇ 2:3 "Yahweh" is God's proper Name, sometimes rendered "LORD" (all caps) in other translations.

Gilead. [23] Geshur and Aram took the towns of Jair from them, with Kenath, and its villages, even sixty cities. All these were the sons of Machir the father of Gilead. [24] After Hezron died in Caleb Ephrathah, Abijah, Hezron's wife, bore him Ashhur the father of Tekoa. [25] The sons of Jerahmeel the firstborn of Hezron were Ram the firstborn, Bunah, Oren, Ozem, and Ahijah. [26] Jerahmeel had another wife, whose name was Atarah. She was the mother of Onam. [27] The sons of Ram the firstborn of Jerahmeel were Maaz, Jamin, and Eker. [28] The sons of Onam were Shammai and Jada. The sons of Shammai: Nadab and Abishur. [29] The name of the wife of Abishur was Abihail; and she bore him Ahban and Molid. [30] The sons of Nadab: Seled and Appaim; but Seled died without children. [31] The son of Appaim: Ishi. The son of Ishi: Sheshan. The son of Sheshan: Ahlai. [32] The sons of Jada the brother of Shammai: Jether and Jonathan; and Jether died without children. [33] The sons of Jonathan: Peleth and Zaza. These were the sons of Jerahmeel. [34] Now Sheshan had no sons, but only daughters. Sheshan had a servant, an Egyptian, whose name was Jarha. [35] Sheshan gave his daughter to Jarha his servant as wife; and she bore him Attai. [36] Attai became the father of Nathan, and Nathan became the father of Zabad, [37] and Zabad became the father of Ephlal, and Ephlal became the father of Obed, [38] and Obed became the father of Jehu, and Jehu became the father of Azariah, [39] and Azariah became the father of Helez, and Helez became the father of Eleasah, [40] and Eleasah became the father of Sismai, and Sismai became the father of Shallum, [41] and Shallum became the father of Jekamiah, and Jekamiah became the father of Elishama. [42] The sons of Caleb the brother of Jerahmeel were Mesha his firstborn, who was the father of Ziph, and the sons of Mareshah the father of Hebron. [43] The sons of Hebron: Korah, Tappuah, Rekem, and Shema. [44] Shema became the father of Raham, the father of Jorkeam; and Rekem became the father of Shammai. [45] The son of Shammai was Maon; and Maon was the father of Beth Zur. [46] Ephah, Caleb's concubine, bore Haran, Moza, and Gazez; and Haran became the father of Gazez. [47] The sons of Jahdai: Regem, Jotham, Geshan, Pelet, Ephah, and Shaaph. [48] Maacah, Caleb's concubine, bore Sheber and Tirhanah. [49] She bore also Shaaph the father of Madmannah, Sheva the father of Machbena and the father of Gibea; and the daughter of Caleb was Achsah. [50] These were the sons of Caleb, the son of Hur, the firstborn of Ephrathah: Shobal the father of Kiriath Jearim, [51] Salma the father of Bethlehem, and Hareph the father of Beth Gader. [52] Shobal the father of Kiriath Jearim had sons: Haroeh, half of the Menuhoth. [53] The families of Kiriath Jearim: the Ithrites, the Puthites, the Shumathites, and the Mishraites; from them came the Zorathites and the Eshtaolites. [54] The sons of Salma: Bethlehem, the Netophathites, Atroth Beth Joab, and half of the Manahathites, the Zorites. [55] The families of scribes who lived at Jabez: the Tirathites, the Shimeathites, and the Sucathites. These are the Kenites who came from Hammath, the father of the house of Rechab.

## 3

[1] Now these were the sons of David, who were born to him in Hebron: the firstborn, Amnon, of Ahinoam the Jezreelitess; the second, Daniel, of Abigail the Carmelitess; [2] the third, Absalom the son of Maacah the daughter of Talmai king of Geshur; the fourth, Adonijah the son of Haggith; [3] the fifth, Shephatiah of Abital; the sixth, Ithream by Eglah his wife: [4] six were born to him in Hebron; and he reigned there seven years and six months. He reigned thirty-three years in Jerusalem; [5] and these were born to him in Jerusalem: Shimea, Shobab, Nathan, and Solomon, four, by Bathshua the daughter of Ammiel; [6] and Ibhar, Elishama, Eliphelet, [7] Nogah, Nepheg, Japhia, [8] Elishama, Eliada, and Eliphelet, nine. [9] All these were the sons of David, in addition to the sons of the concubines; and Tamar was their sister. [10] Solomon's son was Rehoboam, Abijah his son, Asa his son, Jehoshaphat his son, [11] Joram his son, Ahaziah his son, Joash his son, [12] Amaziah his son, Azariah his son, Jotham his son, [13] Ahaz his son, Hezekiah his son, Manasseh his son, [14] Amon his son, and Josiah his son. [15] The sons of Josiah: the firstborn Johanan, the second Jehoiakim, the third Zedekiah, and the fourth Shallum. [16] The sons of Jehoiakim: Jeconiah his son, and Zedekiah his son. [17] The sons of Jeconiah, the captive: Shealtiel his son, [18] Malchiram, Pedaiah, Shenazzar, Jekamiah, Hoshama, and Nedabiah. [19] The sons of Pedaiah: Zerubbabel and Shimei. The sons of Zerubbabel: Meshullam and Hananiah; and Shelomith was their sister; [20] and Hashubah, Ohel, Berechiah, Hasadiah, and Jushab Hesed, five. [21] The sons of Hananiah: Pelatiah and Jeshaiah; the sons of Rephaiah, the sons of Arnan, the sons of Obadiah, the sons of Shecaniah. [22] The son of Shecaniah: Shemaiah. The sons of Shemaiah: Hattush, Igal, Bariah, Neariah, and Shaphat, six. [23] The sons of Neariah: Elioenai,

Hizkiah, and Azrikam, three. [24] The sons of Elioenai: Hodaviah, Eliashib, Pelaiah, Akkub, Johanan, Delaiah, and Anani, seven.

## 4

[1] The sons of Judah: Perez, Hezron, Carmi, Hur, and Shobal. [2] Reaiah the son of Shobal became the father of Jahath; and Jahath became the father of Ahumai and Lahad. These are the families of the Zorathites. [3] These were the sons of the father of Etam: Jezreel, Ishma, and Idbash. The name of their sister was Hazzelelponi. [4] Penuel was the father of Gedor and Ezer the father of Hushah. These are the sons of Hur, the firstborn of Ephrathah, the father of Bethlehem. [5] Ashhur the father of Tekoa had two wives, Helah and Naarah. [6] Naarah bore him Ahuzzam, Hepher, Temeni, and Haahashtari. These were the sons of Naarah. [7] The sons of Helah were Zereth, Izhar, and Ethnan. [8] Hakkoz became the father of Anub, Zobebah, and the families of Aharhel the son of Harum. [9] Jabez was more honorable than his brothers. His mother named him Jabez,[a] saying, "Because I bore him with sorrow." [10] Jabez called on the God[b] of Israel, saying, "Oh that you would bless me indeed, and enlarge my border! May your hand be with me, and may you keep me from evil, that I may not cause pain!" God granted him that which he requested. [11] Chelub the brother of Shuhah became the father of Mehir, who was the father of Eshton. [12] Eshton became the father of Beth Rapha, Paseah, and Tehinnah the father of Ir Nahash. These are the men of Recah. [13] The sons of Kenaz: Othniel and Seraiah. The sons of Othniel: Hathath.[c] [14] Meonothai became the father of Ophrah: and Seraiah became the father of Joab the father of Ge Harashim, for they were craftsmen. [15] The sons of Caleb the son of Jephunneh: Iru, Elah, and Naam. The son of Elah: Kenaz. [16] The sons of Jehallelel: Ziph, Ziphah, Tiria, and Asarel. [17] The sons of Ezrah: Jether, Mered, Epher, and Jalon; and Mered's wife bore Miriam, Shammai, and Ishbah the father of Eshtemoa. [18] His wife the Jewess bore Jered the father of Gedor, Heber the father of Soco, and Jekuthiel the father of Zanoah. These are the sons of Bithiah the daughter of Pharaoh, whom Mered took. [19] The sons of the wife of Hodiah, the sister of Naham, were the fathers of Keilah the Garmite and Eshtemoa the Maacathite. [20] The sons of Shimon: Amnon, Rinnah, Ben Hanan, and Tilon. The sons of Ishi: Zoheth, and Ben Zoheth. [21] The sons of Shelah the son of Judah: Er the father of Lecah, Laadah the father of Mareshah, and the families of the house of those who worked fine linen, of the house of Ashbea; [22] and Jokim, and the men of Cozeba, and Joash, and Saraph, who had dominion in Moab, and Jashubilehem. These records are ancient. [23] These were the potters, and the inhabitants of Netaim and Gederah; they lived there with the king for his work. The sons of Simeon: Nemuel, Jamin, Jarib, Zerah, Shaul; [25] Shallum his son, Mibsam his son, and Mishma his son. [26] The sons of Mishma: Hammuel his son, Zaccur his son, Shimei his son. [27] Shimei had sixteen sons and six daughters; but his brothers didn't have many children, and all their family didn't multiply like the children of Judah. [28] They lived at Beersheba, Moladah, Hazarshual, [29] at Bilhah, at Ezem, at Tolad, [30] at Bethuel, at Hormah, at Ziklag, [31] at Beth Marcaboth, Hazar Susim, at Beth Biri, and at Shaaraim. These were their cities until David's reign. [32] Their villages were Etam, Ain, Rimmon, Tochen, and Ashan, five cities; [33] and all their villages that were around the same cities, as far as Baal. These were their settlements, and they kept their genealogy. [34] Meshobab, Jamlech, Joshah the son of Amaziah, [35] Joel, Jehu the son of Joshibiah, the son of Seraiah, the son of Asiel, [36] Elioenai, Jaakobah, Jeshohaiah, Asaiah, Adiel, Jesimiel, Benaiah, [37] and Ziza the son of Shiphi, the son of Allon, the son of Jedaiah, the son of Shimri, the son of Shemaiah— [38] these mentioned by name were princes in their families. Their fathers' houses increased greatly. [39] They went to the entrance of Gedor, even to the east side of the valley, to seek pasture for their flocks. [40] They found rich, good pasture, and the land was wide, and quiet, and peaceful, for those who lived there before were descended from Ham. [41] These written by name came in the days of Hezekiah king of Judah, and struck their tents and the Meunim who were found there; and they destroyed them utterly to this day, and lived in their place, because there was pasture there for their flocks. [42] Some of them, even of the sons of Simeon, five hundred men, went to Mount Seir, having for their captains Pelatiah, Neariah, Rephaiah, and Uzziel, the sons of Ishi. [43] They struck the remnant of the Amalekites who escaped, and have lived there to this day.

## 5

[1] The sons of Reuben the firstborn of Israel (for he was the firstborn, but because he defiled his father's couch, his birthright was given to the sons of Joseph the son of Israel; and the genealogy is not to be listed according to the birthright. [2] For Judah prevailed above his brothers, and from him came the prince; but the birthright was Joseph's)— [3] the

---

[a] 4:9 "Jabez" sounds similar to the Hebrew word for "pain".

[b] 4:10 The Hebrew word rendered "God" is "אֱלֹהִים" (Elohim).

[c] 4:13 Greek and Vulgate add "and Meonothai"

sons of Reuben the firstborn of Israel: Hanoch, Pallu, Hezron, and Carmi. ⁴ The sons of Joel: Shemaiah his son, Gog his son, Shimei his son, ⁵ Micah his son, Reaiah his son, Baal his son, ⁶ and Beerah his son, whom Tilgath Pilneser king of Assyria carried away captive. He was prince of the Reubenites. ⁷ His brothers by their families, when the genealogy of their generations was listed: the chief, Jeiel, and Zechariah, ⁸ and Bela the son of Azaz, the son of Shema, the son of Joel, who lived in Aroer, even to Nebo and Baal Meon; ⁹ and he lived eastward even to the entrance of the wilderness from the river Euphrates, because their livestock were multiplied in the land of Gilead. ¹⁰ In the days of Saul, they made war with the Hagrites, who fell by their hand; and they lived in their tents throughout all the land east of Gilead. ¹¹ The sons of Gad lived beside them in the land of Bashan to Salecah: ¹² Joel the chief, Shapham the second, Janai, and Shaphat in Bashan. ¹³ Their brothers of their fathers' houses: Michael, Meshullam, Sheba, Jorai, Jacan, Zia, and Eber, seven. ¹⁴ These were the sons of Abihail, the son of Huri, the son of Jaroah, the son of Gilead, the son of Michael, the son of Jeshishai, the son of Jahdo, the son of Buz; ¹⁵ Ahi the son of Abdiel, the son of Guni, chief of their fathers' houses. ¹⁶ They lived in Gilead in Bashan and in its towns, and in all the pasture lands of Sharon as far as their borders. ¹⁷ All these were listed by genealogies in the days of Jotham king of Judah, and in the days of Jeroboam king of Israel. ¹⁸ The sons of Reuben, the Gadites, and the half-tribe of Manasseh, of valiant men, men able to bear buckler and sword, able to shoot with bow, and skillful in war, were forty-four thousand seven hundred sixty that were able to go out to war. ¹⁹ They made war with the Hagrites, with Jetur, and Naphish, and Nodab. ²⁰ They were helped against them, and the Hagrites were delivered into their hand, and all who were with them; for they cried to God in the battle, and he answered them because they put their trust in him. ²¹ They took away their livestock: of their camels fifty thousand, and of sheep two hundred fifty thousand, and of donkeys two thousand, and of men one hundred thousand. ²² For many fell slain, because the war was of God. They lived in their place until the captivity. ²³ The children of the half-tribe of Manasseh lived in the land. They increased from Bashan to Baal Hermon, Senir, and Mount Hermon. ²⁴ These were the heads of their fathers' houses: Epher, Ishi, Eliel, Azriel, Jeremiah, Hodaviah, and Jahdiel—mighty men of valor, famous men, heads of their fathers' houses. ²⁵ They trespassed against the God of their fathers, and played the prostitute after the gods of the peoples of the land whom God destroyed before them. ²⁶ So the God of Israel stirred up the spirit of Pul king of Assyria, and the spirit of Tilgath Pilneser king of Assyria, and he carried away the Reubenites, the Gadites, and the half-tribe of Manasseh, and brought them to Halah, Habor, Hara, and to the river of Gozan, to this day.

# 6

¹ The sons of Levi: Gershon, Kohath, and Merari. ² The sons of Kohath: Amram, Izhar, Hebron, and Uzziel. ³ The children of Amram: Aaron, Moses, and Miriam. The sons of Aaron: Nadab, Abihu, Eleazar, and Ithamar. ⁴ Eleazar became the father of Phinehas, Phinehas became the father of Abishua, ⁵ Abishua became the father of Bukki. Bukki became the father of Uzzi. ⁶ Uzzi became the father of Zerahiah. Zerahiah became the father of Meraioth. ⁷ Meraioth became the father of Amariah. Amariah became the father of Ahitub. ⁸ Ahitub became the father of Zadok. Zadok became the father of Ahimaaz. ⁹ Ahimaaz became the father of Azariah. Azariah became the father of Johanan. ¹⁰ Johanan became the father of Azariah, who executed the priest's office in the house that Solomon built in Jerusalem. ¹¹ Azariah became the father of Amariah. Amariah became the father of Ahitub. ¹² Ahitub became the father of Zadok. Zadok became the father of Shallum. ¹³ Shallum became the father of Hilkiah. Hilkiah became the father of Azariah. ¹⁴ Azariah became the father of Seraiah. Seraiah became the father of Jehozadak. ¹⁵ Jehozadak went into captivity when Yahweh carried Judah and Jerusalem away by the hand of Nebuchadnezzar. ¹⁶ The sons of Levi: Gershom, Kohath, and Merari. ¹⁷ These are the names of the sons of Gershom: Libni and Shimei. ¹⁸ The sons of Kohath were Amram, Izhar, Hebron, and Uzziel. ¹⁹ The sons of Merari: Mahli and Mushi. These are the families of the Levites according to their fathers' households. ²⁰ Of Gershom: Libni his son, Jahath his son, Zimmah his son, ²¹ Joah his son, Iddo his son, Zerah his son, and Jeatherai his son. ²² The sons of Kohath: Amminadab his son, Korah his son, Assir his son, ²³ Elkanah his son, Ebiasaph his son, Assir his son, ²⁴ Tahath his son, Uriel his son, Uzziah his son, and Shaul his son. ²⁵ The sons of Elkanah: Amasai and Ahimoth. ²⁶ As for Elkanah, the sons of Elkanah: Zophai his son, Nahath his son, ²⁷ Eliab his son, Jeroham his son, and Elkanah his son. ²⁸ The sons of Samuel: the firstborn, Joel, and the second, Abijah. ²⁹ The sons of Merari: Mahli, Libni his son, Shimei his son, Uzzah his son, ³⁰ Shimea his son, Haggiah his son, Asaiah his son. ³¹ These are they whom David set over the service of song in Yahweh's house after the ark came to rest there. ³² They ministered with song

before the tabernacle of the Tent of Meeting until Solomon had built Yahweh's house in Jerusalem. They performed the duties of their office according to their order. ³³ These are those who served, and their sons. Of the sons of the Kohathites: Heman the singer, the son of Joel, the son of Samuel, ³⁴ the son of Elkanah, the son of Jeroham, the son of Eliel, the son of Toah, ³⁵ the son of Zuph, the son of Elkanah, the son of Mahath, the son of Amasai, ³⁶ the son of Elkanah, the son of Joel, the son of Azariah, the son of Zephaniah, ³⁷ the son of Tahath, the son of Assir, the son of Ebiasaph, the son of Korah, ³⁸ the son of Izhar, the son of Kohath, the son of Levi, the son of Israel. ³⁹ His brother Asaph, who stood on his right hand, even Asaph the son of Berechiah, the son of Shimea, ⁴⁰ the son of Michael, the son of Baaseiah, the son of Malchijah, ⁴¹ the son of Ethni, the son of Zerah, the son of Adaiah, ⁴² the son of Ethan, the son of Zimmah, the son of Shimei, ⁴³ the son of Jahath, the son of Gershom, the son of Levi. ⁴⁴ On the left hand their brothers the sons of Merari: Ethan the son of Kishi, the son of Abdi, the son of Malluch, ⁴⁵ the son of Hashabiah, the son of Amaziah, the son of Hilkiah, ⁴⁶ the son of Amzi, the son of Bani, the son of Shemer, ⁴⁷ the son of Mahli, the son of Mushi, the son of Merari, the son of Levi. ⁴⁸ Their brothers the Levites were appointed for all the service of the tabernacle of God's house. ⁴⁹ But Aaron and his sons offered on the altar of burnt offering, and on the altar of incense, for all the work of the most holy place, and to make atonement for Israel, according to all that Moses the servant of God had commanded. ⁵⁰ These are the sons of Aaron: Eleazar his son, Phinehas his son, Abishua his son, ⁵¹ Bukki his son, Uzzi his son, Zerahiah his son, ⁵² Meraioth his son, Amariah his son, Ahitub his son, ⁵³ Zadok his son, and Ahimaaz his son. ⁵⁴ Now these are their dwelling places according to their encampments in their borders: to the sons of Aaron, of the families of the Kohathites (for theirs was the first lot), ⁵⁵ to them they gave Hebron in the land of Judah, and its pasture lands around it; ⁵⁶ but the fields of the city and its villages, they gave to Caleb the son of Jephunneh. ⁵⁷ To the sons of Aaron they gave the cities of refuge, Hebron, Libnah also with its pasture lands, Jattir, Eshtemoa with its pasture lands, ⁵⁸ Hilen with its pasture lands, Debir with its pasture lands, ⁵⁹ Ashan with its pasture lands, and Beth Shemesh with its pasture lands; ⁶⁰ and out of the tribe of Benjamin, Geba with its pasture lands, Allemeth with its pasture lands, and Anathoth with its pasture lands. All their cities throughout their families were thirteen cities. ⁶¹ To the rest of the sons of Kohath were given by lot, out of the family of the tribe, out of the half-tribe, the half of Manasseh, ten cities. ⁶² To the sons of Gershom, according to their families, out of the tribe of Issachar, and out of the tribe of Asher, and out of the tribe of Naphtali, and out of the tribe of Manasseh in Bashan, thirteen cities. ⁶³ To the sons of Merari were given by lot, according to their families, out of the tribe of Reuben, and out of the tribe of Gad, and out of the tribe of Zebulun, twelve cities. ⁶⁴ The children of Israel gave to the Levites the cities with their pasture lands. ⁶⁵ They gave by lot out of the tribe of the children of Judah, and out of the tribe of the children of Simeon, and out of the tribe of the children of Benjamin, these cities which are mentioned by name. ⁶⁶ Some of the families of the sons of Kohath had cities of their borders out of the tribe of Ephraim. ⁶⁷ They gave to them the cities of refuge, Shechem in the hill country of Ephraim with its pasture lands and Gezer with its pasture lands, ⁶⁸ Jokmeam with its pasture lands, Beth Horon with its pasture lands, ⁶⁹ Aijalon with its pasture lands, Gath Rimmon with its pasture lands; ⁷⁰ and out of the half-tribe of Manasseh, Aner with its pasture lands, and Bileam with its pasture lands, for the rest of the family of the sons of Kohath. ⁷¹ To the sons of Gershom were given, out of the family of the half-tribe of Manasseh, Golan in Bashan with its pasture lands, and Ashtaroth with its pasture lands; ⁷² and out of the tribe of Issachar, Kedesh with its pasture lands, Daberath with its pasture lands, ⁷³ Ramoth with its pasture lands, and Anem with its pasture lands; ⁷⁴ and out of the tribe of Asher, Mashal with its pasture lands, Abdon with its pasture lands, ⁷⁵ Hukok with its pasture lands, and Rehob with its pasture lands; ⁷⁶ and out of the tribe of Naphtali, Kedesh in Galilee with its pasture lands, Hammon with its pasture lands, and Kiriathaim with its pasture lands. ⁷⁷ To the rest of the Levites, the sons of Merari, were given, out of the tribe of Zebulun, Rimmono with its pasture lands, and Tabor with its pasture lands; ⁷⁸ and beyond the Jordan at Jericho, on the east side of the Jordan, were given them out of the tribe of Reuben: Bezer in the wilderness with its pasture lands, Jahzah with its pasture lands, ⁷⁹ Kedemoth with its pasture lands, and Mephaath with its pasture lands; ⁸⁰ and out of the tribe of Gad, Ramoth in Gilead with its pasture lands, Mahanaim with its pasture lands, ⁸¹ Heshbon with its pasture lands, and Jazer with its pasture lands.

# 7

¹ Of the sons of Issachar: Tola, Puah, Jashub, and Shimron, four. ² The sons of Tola: Uzzi, Rephaiah, Jeriel, Jahmai, Ibsam, and Shemuel, heads of their fathers' houses, of Tola; mighty men of valor in their generations. Their number in the days of David was twenty-two

thousand six hundred. ³ The son of Uzzi: Izrahiah. The sons of Izrahiah: Michael, Obadiah, Joel, and Isshiah, five; all of them chief men. ⁴ With them, by their generations, after their fathers' houses, were bands of the army for war, thirty-six thousand; for they had many wives and sons. ⁵ Their brothers among all the families of Issachar, mighty men of valor, listed in all by genealogy, were eighty-seven thousand. ⁶ The sons of Benjamin: Bela, Becher, and Jediael, three. ⁷ The sons of Bela: Ezbon, Uzzi, Uzziel, Jerimoth, and Iri, five; heads of fathers' houses, mighty men of valor; and they were listed by genealogy twenty-two thousand thirty-four. ⁸ The sons of Becher: Zemirah, Joash, Eliezer, Elioenai, Omri, Jeremoth, Abijah, Anathoth, and Alemeth. All these were the sons of Becher. ⁹ They were listed by genealogy, after their generations, heads of their fathers' houses, mighty men of valor, twenty thousand two hundred. ¹⁰ The son of Jediael: Bilhan. The sons of Bilhan: Jeush, Benjamin, Ehud, Chenaanah, Zethan, Tarshish, and Ahishahar. ¹¹ All these were sons of Jediael, according to the heads of their fathers' households, mighty men of valor, seventeen thousand two hundred, who were able to go out in the army for war. ¹² So were Shuppim, Huppim, the sons of Ir, Hushim, and the sons of Aher. ¹³ The sons of Naphtali: Jahziel, Guni, Jezer, Shallum, and the sons of Bilhah. ¹⁴ The sons of Manasseh: Asriel, whom his concubine the Aramitess bore. She bore Machir the father of Gilead. ¹⁵ Machir took a wife of Huppim and Shuppim, whose sister's name was Maacah. The name of the second was Zelophehad; and Zelophehad had daughters. ¹⁶ Maacah the wife of Machir bore a son, and she named him Peresh. The name of his brother was Sheresh; and his sons were Ulam and Rakem. ¹⁷ The sons of Ulam: Bedan. These were the sons of Gilead the son of Machir, the son of Manasseh. ¹⁸ His sister Hammolecheth bore Ishhod, Abiezer, and Mahlah. ¹⁹ The sons of Shemida were Ahian, Shechem, Likhi, and Aniam. ²⁰ The sons of Ephraim: Shuthelah, Bered his son, Tahath his son, Eleadah his son, Tahath his son, ²¹ Zabad his son, Shuthelah his son, Ezer, and Elead, whom the men of Gath who were born in the land killed, because they came down to take away their livestock. ²² Ephraim their father mourned many days, and his brothers came to comfort him. ²³ He went in to his wife, and she conceived and bore a son, and he named him Beriah,ᵃ because there was trouble with his house. ²⁴ His daughter was Sheerah, who built Beth Horon the lower and the upper, and Uzzen Sheerah. ²⁵ Rephah was his son, Resheph his son, Telah his son, Tahan his son, ²⁶ Ladan his son, Ammihud his son, Elishama his son, ²⁷ Nun his son, and Joshua his son. ²⁸ Their possessions and settlements were Bethel and its towns, and eastward Naaran, and westward Gezer with its towns; Shechem also and its towns, to Azzah and its towns; ²⁹ and by the borders of the children of Manasseh, Beth Shean and its towns, Taanach and its towns, Megiddo and its towns, and Dor and its towns. The children of Joseph the son of Israel lived in these. ³⁰ The sons of Asher: Imnah, Ishvah, Ishvi, and Beriah. Serah was their sister. ³¹ The sons of Beriah: Heber and Malchiel, who was the father of Birzaith. ³² Heber became the father of Japhlet, Shomer, Hotham, and Shua their sister. ³³ The sons of Japhlet: Pasach, Bimhal, and Ashvath. These are the children of Japhlet. ³⁴ The sons of Shemer: Ahi, Rohgah, Jehubbah, and Aram. ³⁵ The sons of Helem his brother: Zophah, Imna, Shelesh, and Amal. ³⁶ The sons of Zophah: Suah, Harnepher, Shual, Beri, Imrah, ³⁷ Bezer, Hod, Shamma, Shilshah, Ithran, and Beera. ³⁸ The sons of Jether: Jephunneh, Pispa, and Ara. ³⁹ The sons of Ulla: Arah, Hanniel, and Rizia. ⁴⁰ All these were the children of Asher, heads of the fathers' houses, choice and mighty men of valor, chief of the princes. The number of them listed by genealogy for service in war was twenty-six thousand men.

## 8

¹ Benjamin became the father of Bela his firstborn, Ashbel the second, Aharah the third, ² Nohah the fourth, and Rapha the fifth. ³ Bela had sons: Addar, Gera, Abihud, ⁴ Abishua, Naaman, Ahoah, ⁵ Gera, Shephuphan, and Huram. ⁶ These are the sons of Ehud. These are the heads of fathers' households of the inhabitants of Geba, who were carried captive to Manahath: ⁷ Naaman, Ahijah, and Gera, who carried them captive; and he became the father of Uzza and Ahihud. ⁸ Shaharaim became the father of children in the field of Moab, after he had sent them away. Hushim and Baara were his wives. ⁹ By Hodesh his wife, he became the father of Jobab, Zibia, Mesha, Malcam, ¹⁰ Jeuz, Shachia, and Mirmah. These were his sons, heads of fathers' households. ¹¹ By Hushim, he became the father of Abitub and Elpaal. ¹² The sons of Elpaal: Eber, Misham, and Shemed, who built Ono and Lod, with its towns; ¹³ and Beriah and Shema, who were heads of fathers' households of the inhabitants of Aijalon, who put to flight the inhabitants of Gath; ¹⁴ and Ahio, Shashak, Jeremoth, ¹⁵ Zebadiah, Arad, Eder, ¹⁶ Michael, Ishpah, Joha, the sons of Beriah, ¹⁷ Zebadiah, Meshullam, Hizki, Heber, ¹⁸ Ishmerai, Izliah, Jobab, the sons of Elpaal,

¹⁹ Jakim, Zichri, Zabdi, ²⁰ Elienai, Zillethai, Eliel, ²¹ Adaiah, Beraiah, Shimrath, the sons of Shimei, ²² Ishpan, Eber, Eliel, ²³ Abdon, Zichri, Hanan, ²⁴ Hananiah, Elam, Anthothijah, ²⁵ Iphdeiah, Penuel, the sons of Shashak, ²⁶ Shamsherai, Shehariah, Athaliah, ²⁷ Jaareshiah, Elijah, Zichri, and the sons of Jeroham. ²⁸ These were heads of fathers' households throughout their generations, chief men. These lived in Jerusalem. ²⁹ The father of Gibeon, whose wife's name was Maacah, lived in Gibeon ³⁰ with his firstborn son Abdon, Zur, Kish, Baal, Nadab, ³¹ Gedor, Ahio, Zecher, ³² and Mikloth, who became the father of Shimeah. They also lived with their families in Jerusalem, near their relatives. ³³ Ner became the father of Kish. Kish became the father of Saul. Saul became the father of Jonathan, Malchishua, Abinadab, and Eshbaal. ³⁴ The son of Jonathan was Merib-baal. Merib-baal became the father of Micah. ³⁵ The sons of Micah: Pithon, Melech, Tarea, and Ahaz. ³⁶ Ahaz became the father of Jehoaddah. Jehoaddah became the father of Alemeth, Azmaveth, and Zimri. Zimri became the father of Moza. ³⁷ Moza became the father of Binea. Raphah was his son, Eleasah his son, and Azel his son. ³⁸ Azel had six sons, whose names are these: Azrikam, Bocheru, Ishmael, Sheariah, Obadiah, and Hanan. All these were the sons of Azel. ³⁹ The sons of Eshek his brother: Ulam his firstborn, Jeush the second, and Eliphelet the third. ⁴⁰ The sons of Ulam were mighty men of valor, archers, and had many sons, and grandsons, one hundred fifty. All these were of the sons of Benjamin.

## 9

¹ So all Israel were listed by genealogies; and behold,ᵇ they are written in the book of the kings of Israel. Judah was carried away captive to Babylon for their disobedience. ² Now the first inhabitants who lived in their possessions in their cities were Israel, the priests, the Levites, and the temple servants. ³ In Jerusalem, there lived of the children of Judah, of the children of Benjamin, and of the children of Ephraim and Manasseh: ⁴ Uthai the son of Ammihud, the son of Omri, the son of Imri, the son of Bani, of the children of Perez the son of Judah. ⁵ Of the Shilonites: Asaiah the firstborn and his sons. ⁶ Of the sons of Zerah: Jeuel and their brothers, six hundred ninety. ⁷ Of the sons of Benjamin: Sallu the son of Meshullam, the son of Hodaviah, the son of Hassenuah; ⁸ and Ibneiah the son of Jeroham, and Elah the son of Uzzi, the son of Michri; and Meshullam the son of Shephatiah, the son of Reuel, the son of Ibnijah; ⁹ and their brothers, according to their generations, nine hundred fifty-six. All these men were heads of fathers' households by their fathers' houses. ¹⁰ Of the priests: Jedaiah, Jehoiarib, Jachin, ¹¹ and Azariah the son of Hilkiah, the son of Meshullam, the son of Zadok, the son of Meraioth, the son of Ahitub, the ruler of God's house; ¹² and Adaiah the son of Jeroham, the son of Pashhur, the son of Malchijah; and Maasai the son of Adiel, the son of Jahzerah, the son of Meshullam, the son of Meshillemith, the son of Immer; ¹³ and their brothers, heads of their fathers' houses, one thousand seven hundred sixty; they were very able men for the work of the service of God's house. ¹⁴ Of the Levites: Shemaiah the son of Hasshub, the son of Azrikam, the son of Hashabiah, of the sons of Merari; ¹⁵ and Bakbakkar, Heresh, Galal, and Mattaniah the son of Mica, the son of Zichri, the son of Asaph, ¹⁶ and Obadiah the son of Shemaiah, the son of Galal, the son of Jeduthun; and Berechiah the son of Asa, the son of Elkanah, who lived in the villages of the Netophathites. ¹⁷ The gatekeepers: Shallum, Akkub, Talmon, Ahiman, and their brothers (Shallum was the chief), ¹⁸ who previously served in the king's gate eastward. They were the gatekeepers for the camp of the children of Levi. ¹⁹ Shallum was the son of Kore, the son of Ebiasaph, the son of Korah, and his brothers, of his father's house, the Korahites, were over the work of the service, keepers of the thresholds of the tent. Their fathers had been over Yahweh's camp, keepers of the entry. ²⁰ Phinehas the son of Eleazar was ruler over them in time past, and Yahweh was with him. ²¹ Zechariah the son of Meshelemiah was gatekeeper of the door of the Tent of Meeting. ²² All these who were chosen to be gatekeepers in the thresholds were two hundred twelve. These were listed by genealogy in their villages, whom David and Samuel the seer ordained in their office of trust. ²³ So they and their children had the oversight of the gates of Yahweh's house, even the house of the tent, as guards. ²⁴ On the four sides were the gatekeepers, toward the east, west, north, and south. ²⁵ Their brothers, in their villages, were to come in every seven days from time to time to be with them, ²⁶ for the four chief gatekeepers, who were Levites, were in an office of trust, and were over the rooms and over the treasuries in God's house. ²⁷ They stayed around God's house, because that was their duty; and it was their duty to open it morning by morning. ²⁸ Certain of them were in charge of the vessels of service, for these were brought in by count, and these were taken out by count. ²⁹ Some of them also were appointed over the furniture, and over all the vessels of the sanctuary, over the fine flour, the wine, the

oil, the frankincense, and the spices. ³⁰ Some of the sons of the priests prepared the mixing of the spices. ³¹ Mattithiah, one of the Levites, who was the firstborn of Shallum the Korahite, had the office of trust over the things that were baked in pans. ³² Some of their brothers, of the sons of the Kohathites, were over the show bread, to prepare it every Sabbath. ³³ These are the singers, heads of fathers' households of the Levites, who lived in the rooms and were free from other service, for they were employed in their work day and night. ³⁴ These were heads of fathers' households of the Levites, throughout their generations, chief men. They lived at Jerusalem. ³⁵ Jeiel the father of Gibeon, whose wife's name was Maacah, lived in Gibeon. ³⁶ His firstborn son was Abdon, then Zur, Kish, Baal, Ner, Nadab, ³⁷ Gedor, Ahio, Zechariah, and Mikloth. ³⁸ Mikloth became the father of Shimeam. They also lived with their relatives in Jerusalem, near their relatives. ³⁹ Ner became the father of Kish. Kish became the father of Saul. Saul became the father of Jonathan, Malchishua, Abinadab, and Eshbaal. ⁴⁰ The son of Jonathan was Merib-baal. Merib-baal became the father of Micah. ⁴¹ The sons of Micah: Pithon, Melech, Tahrea, and Ahaz. ⁴² Ahaz became the father of Jarah. Jarah became the father of Alemeth, Azmaveth, and Zimri. Zimri became the father of Moza. ⁴³ Moza became the father of Binea, Rephaiah his son, Eleasah his son, and Azel his son. ⁴⁴ Azel had six sons, whose names are Azrikam, Bocheru, Ishmael, Sheariah, Obadiah, and Hanan. These were the sons of Azel.

## 10

¹ Now the Philistines fought against Israel; and the men of Israel fled from before the Philistines, and fell down slain on Mount Gilboa. ² The Philistines followed hard after Saul and after his sons; and the Philistines killed Jonathan, Abinadab, and Malchishua, the sons of Saul. ³ The battle went hard against Saul, and the archers overtook him; and he was distressed by reason of the archers. ⁴ Then Saul said to his armor bearer, "Draw your sword, and thrust me through with it, lest these uncircumcised come and abuse me." But his armor bearer would not, for he was terrified. Therefore Saul took his sword and fell on it. ⁵ When his armor bearer saw that Saul was dead, he likewise fell on his sword and died. ⁶ So Saul died with his three sons; and all his house died together. ⁷ When all the men of Israel who were in the valley saw that they fled, and that Saul and his sons were dead, they abandoned their cities, and fled; and the Philistines came and lived in them. ⁸ On the next day, when the Philistines came to strip the slain, they found Saul and his sons fallen on Mount Gilboa. ⁹ They stripped him and took his head and his armor, then sent into the land of the Philistines all around to carry the news to their idols and to the people. ¹⁰ They put his armor in the house of their gods, and fastened his head in the house of Dagon. ¹¹ When all Jabesh Gilead heard all that the Philistines had done to Saul, ¹² all the valiant men arose and took away the body of Saul and the bodies of his sons, and brought them to Jabesh, and buried their bones under the oak in Jabesh, and fasted seven days. ¹³ So Saul died for his trespass which he committed against Yahweh, because of Yahweh's word, which he didn't keep, and also because he asked counsel of one who had a familiar spirit, to inquire, ¹⁴ and didn't inquire of Yahweh. Therefore he killed him, and turned the kingdom over to David the son of Jesse.

## 11

¹ Then all Israel gathered themselves to David to Hebron, saying, "Behold, we are your bone and your flesh. ² In times past, even when Saul was king, it was you who led out and brought in Israel. Yahweh your God said to you, 'You shall be shepherd of my people Israel, and you shall be prince over my people Israel.'" ³ So all the elders of Israel came to the king to Hebron; and David made a covenant with them in Hebron before Yahweh. They anointed David king over Israel, according to Yahweh's word by Samuel. ⁴ David and all Israel went to Jerusalem (also called Jebus); and the Jebusites, the inhabitants of the land, were there. ⁵ The inhabitants of Jebus said to David, "You will not come in here!" Nevertheless David took the stronghold of Zion. The same is David's city. ⁶ David had said, "Whoever strikes the Jebusites first shall be chief and captain." Joab the son of Zeruiah went up first, and was made chief. ⁷ David lived in the stronghold; therefore they called it David's city. ⁸ He built the city all around, from Millo even around; and Joab repaired the rest of the city. ⁹ David grew greater and greater, for Yahweh of Armies was with him. ¹⁰ Now these are the chief of the mighty men whom David had, who showed themselves strong with him in his kingdom, together with all Israel, to make him king, according to Yahweh's word concerning Israel. ¹¹ This is the number of the mighty men whom David had: Jashobeam, the son of a Hachmonite, the chief of the thirty; he lifted up his spear against three hundred and killed them at one time. ¹² After him was Eleazar the son

of Dodo, the Ahohite, who was one of the three mighty men. ¹³ He was with David at Pasdammim, and there the Philistines were gathered together to battle, where there was a plot of ground full of barley; and the people fled from before the Philistines. ¹⁴ They stood in the middle of the plot, defended it, and killed the Philistines; and Yahweh saved them by a great victory. ¹⁵ Three of the thirty chief men went down to the rock to David, into the cave of Adullam; and the army of the Philistines were encamped in the valley of Rephaim. ¹⁶ David was then in the stronghold, and the garrison of the Philistines was in Bethlehem at that time. ¹⁷ David longed, and said, "Oh, that someone would give me water to drink from the well of Bethlehem, which is by the gate!" ¹⁸ The three broke through the army of the Philistines, and drew water out of the well of Bethlehem that was by the gate, took it, and brought it to David; but David would not drink any of it, but poured it out to Yahweh, ¹⁹ and said, "My God forbid me, that I should do this! Shall I drink the blood of these men who have put their lives in jeopardy?" For they risked their lives to bring it. Therefore he would not drink it. The three mighty men did these things. ²⁰ Abishai, the brother of Joab, was chief of the three; for he lifted up his spear against three hundred and killed them, and had a name among the three. ²¹ Of the three, he was more honorable than the two, and was made their captain; however he wasn't included in the three. ²² Benaiah the son of Jehoiada, the son of a valiant man of Kabzeel, who had done mighty deeds, killed the two sons of Ariel of Moab. He also went down and killed a lion in the middle of a pit on a snowy day. ²³ He killed an Egyptian, a man of great stature, five cubits[a] high. In the Egyptian's hand was a spear like a weaver's beam; and he went down to him with a staff, plucked the spear out of the Egyptian's hand, and killed him with his own spear. ²⁴ Benaiah the son of Jehoiada did these things and had a name among the three mighty men. ²⁵ Behold, he was more honorable than the thirty, but he didn't attain to the three; and David set him over his guard. ²⁶ The mighty men of the armies also include Asahel the brother of Joab, Elhanan the son of Dodo of Bethlehem, ²⁷ Shammoth the Harorite, Helez the Pelonite, ²⁸ Ira the son of Ikkesh the Tekoite, Abiezer the Anathothite, ²⁹ Sibbecai the Hushathite, Ilai the Ahohite, ³⁰ Maharai the Netophathite, Heled the son of Baanah the Netophathite, ³¹ Ithai the son of Ribai of Gibeah of the children of Benjamin, Benaiah the Pirathonite, ³² Hurai of the brooks of Gaash, Abiel the Arbathite, ³³ Azmaveth the Baharumite, Eliahba the Shaalbonite, ³⁴ the sons of Hashem the Gizonite, Jonathan the son of Shagee the Hararite, ³⁵ Ahiam the son of Sacar the Hararite, Eliphal the son of Ur, ³⁶ Hepher the Mecherathite, Ahijah the Pelonite, ³⁷ Hezro the Carmelite, Naarai the son of Ezbai, ³⁸ Joel the brother of Nathan, Mibhar the son of Hagri, ³⁹ Zelek the Ammonite, Naharai the Berothite (the armor bearer of Joab the son of Zeruiah), ⁴⁰ Ira the Ithrite, Gareb the Ithrite, ⁴¹ Uriah the Hittite, Zabad the son of Ahlai, ⁴² Adina the son of Shiza the Reubenite (a chief of the Reubenites), and thirty with him, ⁴³ Hanan the son of Maacah, Joshaphat the Mithnite, ⁴⁴ Uzzia the Ashterathite, Shama and Jeiel the sons of Hotham the Aroerite, ⁴⁵ Jediael the son of Shimri, and Joha his brother, the Tizite, ⁴⁶ Eliel the Mahavite, and Jeribai, and Joshaviah, the sons of Elnaam, and Ithmah the Moabite, ⁴⁷ Eliel, Obed, and Jaasiel the Mezobaite.

## 12

¹ Now these are those who came to David to Ziklag while he was a fugitive from Saul the son of Kish. They were among the mighty men, his helpers in war. ² They were armed with bows, and could use both the right hand and the left in slinging stones and in shooting arrows from the bow. They were of Saul's relatives of the tribe of Benjamin. ³ The chief was Ahiezer, then Joash, the sons of Shemaah the Gibeathite; Jeziel and Pelet, the sons of Azmaveth; Beracah; Jehu the Anathothite; ⁴ Ishmaiah the Gibeonite, a mighty man among the thirty and a leader of the thirty; Jeremiah; Jahaziel; Johanan; Jozabad the Gederathite; ⁵ Eluzai; Jerimoth; Bealiah; Shemariah; Shephatiah the Haruphite; ⁶ Elkanah, Isshiah, Azarel, Joezer, and Jashobeam, the Korahites; ⁷ and Joelah and Zebadiah, the sons of Jeroham of Gedor. ⁸ Some Gadites joined David in the stronghold in the wilderness, mighty men of valor, men trained for war, who could handle shield and spear; whose faces were like the faces of lions, and they were as swift as the gazelles on the mountains: ⁹ Ezer the chief, Obadiah the second, Eliab the third, ¹⁰ Mishmannah the fourth, Jeremiah the fifth, ¹¹ Attai the sixth, Eliel the seventh, ¹² Johanan the eighth, Elzabad the ninth, ¹³ Jeremiah the tenth, and Machbannai the eleventh. ¹⁴ These of the sons of Gad were captains of the army. He who was least was equal to one hundred, and the greatest to one thousand. ¹⁵ These are those who went over the Jordan in the first month, when it had overflowed all its banks; and they put to flight all who lived in the valleys, both toward the east and toward the

---

[a] 11:23 A cubit is the length from the tip of the middle finger to the elbow on a man's arm, or about 18 inches or 46 centimeters. Therefore this Egyptian was about 7 feet and 6 inches or 2.28 meters tall.

west. ¹⁶ Some of the children of Benjamin and Judah came to the stronghold to David. ¹⁷ David went out to meet them, and answered them, "If you have come peaceably to me to help me, my heart will be united with you; but if you have come to betray me to my adversaries, since there is no wrong in my hands, may the God of our fathers see this and rebuke it." ¹⁸ Then the Spirit came on Amasai, who was chief of the thirty, and he said, "We are yours, David, and on your side, you son of Jesse. Peace, peace be to you, and peace be to your helpers; for your God helps you." Then David received them and made them captains of the band. ¹⁹ Some of Manasseh also joined David when he came with the Philistines against Saul to battle, but they didn't help them, for the lords of the Philistines sent him away after consultation, saying, "He will desert to his master Saul to the jeopardy of our heads." ²⁰ As he went to Ziklag, some from Manasseh joined him: Adnah, Jozabad, Jediael, Michael, Jozabad, Elihu, and Zillethai, captains of thousands who were of Manasseh. ²¹ They helped David against the band of raiders, for they were all mighty men of valor and were captains in the army. ²² For from day to day men came to David to help him, until there was a great army, like God's army. ²³ These are the numbers of the heads of those who were armed for war, who came to David to Hebron to turn the kingdom of Saul to him, according to Yahweh's word. ²⁴ The children of Judah who bore shield and spear were six thousand eight hundred, armed for war. ²⁵ Of the children of Simeon, mighty men of valor for the war: seven thousand one hundred. ²⁶ Of the children of Levi: four thousand six hundred. ²⁷ Jehoiada was the leader of the household of Aaron; and with him were three thousand seven hundred, ²⁸ and Zadok, a young man mighty of valor, and of his father's house twenty-two captains. ²⁹ Of the children of Benjamin, Saul's relatives: three thousand, for until then, the greatest part of them had kept their allegiance to Saul's house. ³⁰ Of the children of Ephraim: twenty thousand eight hundred, mighty men of valor, famous men in their fathers' houses. ³¹ Of the half-tribe of Manasseh: eighteen thousand, who were mentioned by name, to come and make David king. ³² Of the children of Issachar, men who had understanding of the times, to know what Israel ought to do, their heads were two hundred; and all their brothers were at their command. ³³ Of Zebulun, such as were able to go out in the army, who could set the battle in array with all kinds of instruments of war: fifty thousand who could command and were not of double heart. ³⁴ Of Naphtali: one thousand captains, and with them with shield and spear thirty-seven thousand. ³⁵ Of the Danites who could set the battle in array: twenty-eight thousand six hundred. ³⁶ Of Asher, such as were able to go out in the army, who could set the battle in array: forty thousand. ³⁷ On the other side of the Jordan, of the Reubenites, the Gadites, and of the half-tribe of Manasseh, with all kinds of instruments of war for the battle: one hundred twenty thousand. ³⁸ All these were men of war who could order the battle array, and came with a perfect heart to Hebron to make David king over all Israel; and all the rest also of Israel were of one heart to make David king. ³⁹ They were there with David three days, eating and drinking; for their brothers had supplied provisions for them. ⁴⁰ Moreover those who were near to them, as far as Issachar, Zebulun, and Naphtali, brought bread on donkeys, on camels, on mules, and on oxen: supplies of flour, cakes of figs, clusters of raisins, wine, oil, cattle, and sheep in abundance; for there was joy in Israel.

## 13

¹ David consulted with the captains of thousands and of hundreds, even with every leader. ² David said to all the assembly of Israel, "If it seems good to you, and if it is of Yahweh our God, let's send word everywhere to our brothers who are left in all the land of Israel, with whom the priests and Levites are in their cities that have pasture lands, that they may gather themselves to us. ³ Also, let's bring the ark of our God back to us again, for we didn't seek it in the days of Saul." ⁴ All the assembly said that they would do so, for the thing was right in the eyes of all the people. ⁵ So David assembled all Israel together, from the Shihor River of Egypt even to the entrance of Hamath, to bring God's ark from Kiriath Jearim. ⁶ David went up with all Israel to Baalah, that is, to Kiriath Jearim, which belonged to Judah, to bring up from there God Yahweh's ark that sits above the cherubim, that is called by the Name. ⁷ They carried God's ark on a new cart, and brought it out of Abinadab's house; and Uzza and Ahio drove the cart. ⁸ David and all Israel played before God with all their might, even with songs, with harps, with stringed instruments, with tambourines, with cymbals, and with trumpets. ⁹ When they came to Chidon's threshing floor, Uzza put out his hand to hold the ark, for the oxen stumbled. ¹⁰ Yahweh's anger burned against Uzza, and he struck him because he put his hand on the ark; and he died there before God. ¹¹ David was displeased, because Yahweh had broken out against Uzza. He called that place Perez Uzza,

to this day. ¹² David was afraid of God that day, saying, "How can I bring God's ark home to me?" ¹³ So David didn't move the ark with him into David's city, but carried it aside into Obed-Edom the Gittite's house. ¹⁴ God's ark remained with the family of Obed-Edom in his house three months; and Yahweh blessed Obed-Edom's house and all that he had.

## 14

¹ Hiram king of Tyre sent messengers to David with cedar trees, masons, and carpenters, to build him a house. ² David perceived that Yahweh had established him king over Israel, for his kingdom was highly exalted, for his people Israel's sake. ³ David took more wives in Jerusalem, and David became the father of more sons and daughters. ⁴ These are the names of the children whom he had in Jerusalem: Shammua, Shobab, Nathan, Solomon, ⁵ Ibhar, Elishua, Elpelet, ⁶ Nogah, Nepheg, Japhia, ⁷ Elishama, Beeliada, and Eliphelet. ⁸ When the Philistines heard that David was anointed king over all Israel, all the Philistines went up to seek David; and David heard of it, and went out against them. ⁹ Now the Philistines had come and made a raid in the valley of Rephaim. ¹⁰ David inquired of God, saying, "Shall I go up against the Philistines? Will you deliver them into my hand?" Yahweh said to him, "Go up; for I will deliver them into your hand." ¹¹ So they came up to Baal Perazim, and David defeated them there. David said, God has broken my enemies by my hand, like waters breaking out. Therefore they called the name of that place Baal Perazim.ᵃ ¹² They left their gods there; and David gave a command, and they were burned with fire. ¹³ The Philistines made another raid in the valley. ¹⁴ David inquired again of God; and God said to him, "You shall not go up after them. Turn away from them, and come on them opposite the mulberry trees. ¹⁵ When you hear the sound of marching in the tops of the mulberry trees, then go out to battle; for God has gone out before you to strike the army of the Philistines." ¹⁶ David did as God commanded him; and they attacked the army of the Philistines from Gibeon even to Gezer. ¹⁷ The fame of David went out into all lands; and Yahweh brought the fear of him on all nations.

## 15

¹ David made himself houses in David's city; and he prepared a place for God's ark, and pitched a tent for it. ² Then David said, "No one ought to carry God's ark but the Levites. For Yahweh has chosen them to carry God's ark, and to minister to him forever." ³ David assembled all Israel at Jerusalem, to bring up Yahweh's ark to its place, which he had prepared for it. ⁴ David gathered together the sons of Aaron and the Levites: ⁵ of the sons of Kohath, Uriel the chief, and his brothers one hundred twenty; ⁶ of the sons of Merari, Asaiah the chief, and his brothers two hundred twenty; ⁷ of the sons of Gershom, Joel the chief, and his brothers one hundred thirty; ⁸ of the sons of Elizaphan, Shemaiah the chief, and his brothers two hundred; ⁹ of the sons of Hebron, Eliel the chief, and his brothers eighty; ¹⁰ of the sons of Uzziel, Amminadab the chief, and his brothers one hundred twelve. ¹¹ David called for Zadok and Abiathar the priests, and for the Levites: for Uriel, Asaiah, Joel, Shemaiah, Eliel, and Amminadab, ¹² and said to them, "You are the heads of the fathers' households of the Levites. Sanctify yourselves, both you and your brothers, that you may bring the ark of Yahweh, the God of Israel, up to the place that I have prepared for it. ¹³ For because you didn't carry it at first, Yahweh our God broke out in anger against us, because we didn't seek him according to the ordinance." ¹⁴ So the priests and the Levites sanctified themselves to bring up the ark of Yahweh, the God of Israel. ¹⁵ The children of the Levites bore God's ark on their shoulders with its poles, as Moses commanded according to Yahweh's word. ¹⁶ David spoke to the chief of the Levites to appoint their brothers as singers with instruments of music, stringed instruments, harps, and cymbals, sounding aloud and lifting up their voices with joy. ¹⁷ So the Levites appointed Heman the son of Joel; and of his brothers, Asaph the son of Berechiah; and of the sons of Merari their brothers, Ethan the son of Kushaiah; ¹⁸ and with them their brothers of the second rank: Zechariah, Ben, Jaaziel, Shemiramoth, Jehiel, Unni, Eliab, Benaiah, Maaseiah, Mattithiah, Eliphelehu, Mikneiah, Obed-Edom, and Jeiel, the doorkeepers. ¹⁹ So the singers, Heman, Asaph, and Ethan, were given cymbals of bronze to sound aloud; ²⁰ and Zechariah, Aziel, Shemiramoth, Jehiel, Unni, Eliab, Maaseiah, and Benaiah, with stringed instruments set to Alamoth; ²¹ and Mattithiah, Eliphelehu, Mikneiah, Obed-Edom, Jeiel, and Azaziah, with harps tuned to the eight-stringed lyre, to lead. ²² Chenaniah, chief of the Levites, was over the singing. He taught the singers, because he was skillful. ²³ Berechiah and Elkanah were doorkeepers for the ark. ²⁴ Shebaniah, Joshaphat, Nethanel, Amasai, Zechariah, Benaiah, and Eliezer, the priests, blew the trumpets before God's ark; and Obed-Edom and Jehiah were doorkeepers for the ark. ²⁵

ᵃ *14:11* "Baal Perazim" means "The Lord who breaks out".

So David, the elders of Israel, and the captains over thousands went to bring the ark of Yahweh's covenant up out of the house of Obed-Edom with joy. <sup>26</sup> When God helped the Levites who bore the ark of Yahweh's covenant, they sacrificed seven bulls and seven rams. <sup>27</sup> David was clothed with a robe of fine linen, as were all the Levites who bore the ark, the singers, and Chenaniah the choir master with the singers; and David had an ephod of linen on him. <sup>28</sup> Thus all Israel brought the ark of Yahweh's covenant up with shouting, with sound of the cornet, with trumpets, and with cymbals, sounding aloud with stringed instruments and harps. <sup>29</sup> As the ark of Yahweh's covenant came to David's city, Michal the daughter of Saul looked out at the window, and saw king David dancing and playing; and she despised him in her heart.

## 16

<sup>1</sup> They brought in God's ark, and set it in the middle of the tent that David had pitched for it; and they offered burnt offerings and peace offerings before God. <sup>2</sup> When David had finished offering the burnt offering and the peace offerings, he blessed the people in Yahweh's name. <sup>3</sup> He gave to everyone of Israel, both man and woman, to everyone a loaf of bread, a portion of meat, and a cake of raisins. <sup>4</sup> He appointed some of the Levites to minister before Yahweh's ark, and to commemorate, to thank, and to praise Yahweh, the God of Israel: <sup>5</sup> Asaph the chief, and second to him Zechariah, then Jeiel, Shemiramoth, Jehiel, Mattithiah, Eliab, Benaiah, Obed-Edom, and Jeiel, with stringed instruments and with harps; and Asaph with cymbals, sounding aloud; <sup>6</sup> with Benaiah and Jahaziel the priests with trumpets continually, before the ark of the covenant of God. <sup>7</sup> Then on that day David first ordained giving of thanks to Yahweh by the hand of Asaph and his brothers. <sup>8</sup> Oh give thanks to Yahweh. Call on his name. Make what he has done known among the peoples. <sup>9</sup> Sing to him. Sing praises to him. Tell of all his marvelous works. <sup>10</sup> Glory in his holy name. Let the heart of those who seek Yahweh rejoice. <sup>11</sup> Seek Yahweh and his strength. Seek his face forever more. <sup>12</sup> Remember his marvelous works that he has done, his wonders, and the judgments of his mouth, <sup>13</sup> you offspring<sup>a</sup> of Israel his servant, you children of Jacob, his chosen ones. <sup>14</sup> He is Yahweh our God. His judgments are in all the earth. <sup>15</sup> Remember his covenant forever, the word which he commanded to a thousand generations, <sup>16</sup> the covenant which he made with Abraham, his oath to Isaac. <sup>17</sup> He confirmed it to Jacob for a statute, and to Israel for an everlasting covenant, <sup>18</sup> saying, "I will give you the land of Canaan, The lot of your inheritance," <sup>19</sup> when you were but a few men in number, yes, very few, and foreigners in it. <sup>20</sup> They went about from nation to nation, from one kingdom to another people. <sup>21</sup> He allowed no man to do them wrong. Yes, he reproved kings for their sakes, <sup>22</sup> "Don't touch my anointed ones! Do my prophets no harm!" <sup>23</sup> Sing to Yahweh, all the earth! Display his salvation from day to day. <sup>24</sup> Declare his glory among the nations, and his marvelous works among all the peoples. <sup>25</sup> For great is Yahweh, and greatly to be praised. He also is to be feared above all gods. <sup>26</sup> For all the gods of the peoples are idols, but Yahweh made the heavens. <sup>27</sup> Honor and majesty are before him. Strength and gladness are in his place. <sup>28</sup> Ascribe to Yahweh, you families of the peoples, ascribe to Yahweh glory and strength! <sup>29</sup> Ascribe to Yahweh the glory due to his name. Bring an offering, and come before him. Worship Yahweh in holy array. <sup>30</sup> Tremble before him, all the earth. The world also is established that it can't be moved. <sup>31</sup> Let the heavens be glad, and let the earth rejoice! Let them say among the nations, "Yahweh reigns!" <sup>32</sup> Let the sea roar, and its fullness! Let the field exult, and all that is in it! <sup>33</sup> Then the trees of the forest will sing for joy before Yahweh, for he comes to judge the earth. <sup>34</sup> Oh give thanks to Yahweh, for he is good, for his loving kindness endures forever. <sup>35</sup> Say, "Save us, God of our salvation! Gather us together and deliver us from the nations, to give thanks to your holy name, to triumph in your praise." <sup>36</sup> Blessed be Yahweh, the God of Israel, from everlasting even to everlasting. All the people said, "Amen," and praised Yahweh. <sup>37</sup> So he left Asaph and his brothers there before the ark of Yahweh's covenant, to minister before the ark continually, as every day's work required; <sup>38</sup> and Obed-Edom with their sixty-eight relatives; Obed-Edom also the son of Jeduthun and Hosah to be doorkeepers; <sup>39</sup> and Zadok the priest and his brothers the priests, before Yahweh's tabernacle in the high place that was at Gibeon, <sup>40</sup> to offer burnt offerings to Yahweh on the altar of burnt offering continually morning and evening, even according to all that is written in Yahweh's law, which he commanded to Israel; <sup>41</sup> and with them Heman and Jeduthun and the rest who were chosen, who were mentioned by name, to give thanks to Yahweh, because his loving kindness endures forever; <sup>42</sup> and with them Heman and Jeduthun with trumpets and cymbals for those that should sound aloud, and with instruments for the songs of God, and the sons of Jeduthun to be at the gate. <sup>43</sup> All the people departed, each man to his house; and David returned to bless his house.

## 17

<sup>1</sup> When David was living in his house, David said to Nathan the prophet, "Behold, I live in a cedar house, but the ark of Yahweh's covenant is in a tent." <sup>2</sup> Nathan said to David, "Do all that is in your heart; for God is with you." <sup>3</sup> That same night, the word of God came to Nathan, saying, <sup>4</sup> "Go and tell David my servant, 'Yahweh says, "You shall not build me a house to dwell in; <sup>5</sup> for I have not lived in a house since the day that I brought up Israel to this day, but have gone from tent to tent, and from one tent to another. <sup>6</sup> In all places in which I have walked with all Israel, did I speak a word with any of the judges of Israel, whom I commanded to be shepherd of my people, saying, 'Why have you not built me a house of cedar?'"' <sup>7</sup> "Now therefore, you shall tell my servant David, 'Yahweh of Armies says, "I took you from the sheep pen, from following the sheep, to be prince over my people Israel. <sup>8</sup> I have been with you wherever you have gone, and have cut off all your enemies from before you. I will make you a name like the name of the great ones who are in the earth. <sup>9</sup> I will appoint a place for my people Israel, and will plant them, that they may dwell in their own place, and be moved no more. The children of wickedness will not waste them any more, as at the first, <sup>10</sup> and from the day that I commanded judges to be over my people Israel. I will subdue all your enemies. Moreover I tell you that Yahweh will build you a house. <sup>11</sup> It will happen, when your days are fulfilled that you must go to be with your fathers, that I will set up your offspring after you, who will be of your sons; and I will establish his kingdom. <sup>12</sup> He will build me a house, and I will establish his throne forever. <sup>13</sup> I will be his father, and he will be my son. I will not take my loving kindness away from him, as I took it from him who was before you; <sup>14</sup> but I will settle him in my house and in my kingdom forever. His throne will be established forever."'" <sup>15</sup> According to all these words, and according to all this vision, so Nathan spoke to David. <sup>16</sup> Then David the king went in and sat before Yahweh; and he said, "Who am I, Yahweh God, and what is my house, that you have brought me this far? <sup>17</sup> This was a small thing in your eyes, O God, but you have spoken of your servant's house for a great while to come, and have respected me according to the standard of a man of high degree, Yahweh God. <sup>18</sup> What can David say yet more to you concerning the honor which is done to your servant? For you know your servant. <sup>19</sup> Yahweh, for your servant's sake, and according to your own heart, you have done all this greatness, to make known all these great things. <sup>20</sup> Yahweh, there is no one like you, neither is there any God besides you, according to all that we have heard with our ears. <sup>21</sup> What one nation in the earth is like your people Israel, whom God went to redeem to himself for a people, to make you a name by great and awesome things, in driving out nations from before your people whom you redeemed out of Egypt? <sup>22</sup> For you made your people Israel your own people forever; and you, Yahweh, became their God. <sup>23</sup> Now, Yahweh, let the word that you have spoken concerning your servant, and concerning his house, be established forever, and do as you have spoken. <sup>24</sup> Let your name be established and magnified forever, saying, 'Yahweh of Armies is the God of Israel, even a God to Israel. The house of David your servant is established before you.' <sup>25</sup> For you, my God, have revealed to your servant that you will build him a house. Therefore your servant has found courage to pray before you. <sup>26</sup> Now, Yahweh, you are God, and have promised this good thing to your servant. <sup>27</sup> Now it has pleased you to bless the house of your servant, that it may continue forever before you; for you, Yahweh, have blessed, and it is blessed forever."

## 18

<sup>1</sup> After this, David defeated the Philistines and subdued them, and took Gath and its towns out of the hand of the Philistines. <sup>2</sup> He defeated Moab; and the Moabites became servants to David and brought tribute. <sup>3</sup> David defeated Hadadezer king of Zobah, toward Hamath, as he went to establish his dominion by the river Euphrates. <sup>4</sup> David took from him one thousand chariots, seven thousand horsemen, and twenty thousand footmen; and David hamstrung all the chariot horses, but reserved of them enough for one hundred chariots. <sup>5</sup> When the Syrians of Damascus came to help Hadadezer king of Zobah, David struck twenty-two thousand men of the Syrians. <sup>6</sup> Then David put garrisons in Syria of Damascus; and the Syrians became servants to David and brought tribute. Yahweh gave victory to David wherever he went. <sup>7</sup> David took the shields of gold that were on the servants of Hadadezer, and brought them to Jerusalem. <sup>8</sup> From Tibhath and from Cun, cities of Hadadezer, David took very much bronze, with which Solomon made the bronze sea, the pillars, and the vessels of bronze. <sup>9</sup> When Tou king of Hamath heard that David had struck all the army of Hadadezer king of Zobah, <sup>10</sup> he sent Hadoram his son to King David to greet him and to bless him, because he had fought against Hadadezer and struck him (for Hadadezer had wars with Tou); and he had with him all kinds of vessels

of gold and silver and bronze. ¹¹ King David also dedicated these to Yahweh, with the silver and the gold that he carried away from all the nations: from Edom, from Moab, from the children of Ammon, from the Philistines, and from Amalek. ¹² Moreover Abishai the son of Zeruiah struck eighteen thousand of the Edomites in the Valley of Salt. ¹³ He put garrisons in Edom; and all the Edomites became servants to David. Yahweh gave victory to David wherever he went. ¹⁴ David reigned over all Israel; and he executed justice and righteousness for all his people. ¹⁵ Joab the son of Zeruiah was over the army; Jehoshaphat the son of Ahilud was recorder; ¹⁶ Zadok the son of Ahitub and Abimelech the son of Abiathar were priests; Shavsha was scribe; ¹⁷ and Benaiah the son of Jehoiada was over the Cherethites and the Pelethites; and the sons of David were chief officials serving the king.

## 19

¹ After this, Nahash the king of the children of Ammon died, and his son reigned in his place. ² David said, "I will show kindness to Hanun the son of Nahash, because his father showed kindness to me." So David sent messengers to comfort him concerning his father. David's servants came into the land of the children of Ammon to Hanun to comfort him. ³ But the princes of the children of Ammon said to Hanun, "Do you think that David honors your father, in that he has sent comforters to you? Haven't his servants come to you to search, to overthrow, and to spy out the land?" ⁴ So Hanun took David's servants, shaved them, and cut off their garments in the middle at their buttocks, and sent them away. ⁵ Then some people went and told David how the men were treated. He sent to meet them; for the men were greatly humiliated. The king said, "Stay at Jericho until your beards have grown, and then return." ⁶ When the children of Ammon saw that they had made themselves odious to David, Hanun and the children of Ammon sent one thousand talents[a] of silver to hire chariots and horsemen out of Mesopotamia, out of Aram-maacah, and out of Zobah. ⁷ So they hired for themselves thirty-two thousand chariots, and the king of Maacah with his people, who came and encamped near Medeba. The children of Ammon gathered themselves together from their cities, and came to battle. ⁸ When David heard of it, he sent Joab with all the army of the mighty men. ⁹ The children of Ammon came out, and put the battle in array at the gate of the city; and the kings who had come were by themselves in the field. ¹⁰ Now when Joab saw that the battle was set against him before and behind, he chose some of all the choice men of Israel, and put them in array against the Syrians. ¹¹ The rest of the people he committed into the hand of Abishai his brother; and they put themselves in array against the children of Ammon. ¹² He said, "If the Syrians are too strong for me, then you are to help me; but if the children of Ammon are too strong for you, then I will help you. ¹³ Be courageous, and let's be strong for our people and for the cities of our God. May Yahweh do that which seems good to him." ¹⁴ So Joab and the people who were with him came near to the front of the Syrians to the battle; and they fled before him. ¹⁵ When the children of Ammon saw that the Syrians had fled, they likewise fled before Abishai his brother, and entered into the city. Then Joab came to Jerusalem. ¹⁶ When the Syrians saw that they were defeated by Israel, they sent messengers and called out the Syrians who were beyond the River,[b] with Shophach the captain of the army of Hadadezer leading them. ¹⁷ David was told that, so he gathered all Israel together, passed over the Jordan, came to them, and set the battle in array against them. So when David had put the battle in array against the Syrians, they fought with him. ¹⁸ The Syrians fled before Israel; and David killed of the Syrian men seven thousand charioteers and forty thousand footmen, and also killed Shophach the captain of the army. ¹⁹ When the servants of Hadadezer saw that they were defeated by Israel, they made peace with David and served him. The Syrians would not help the children of Ammon any more.

## 20

¹ At the time of the return of the year, at the time when kings go out, Joab led out the army and wasted the country of the children of Ammon, and came and besieged Rabbah. But David stayed at Jerusalem. Joab struck Rabbah, and overthrew it. ² David took the crown of their king from off his head, and found it to weigh a talent of gold,[c] and there were precious stones in it. It was set on David's head, and he brought very much plunder out of the city. ³ He brought out the people who were in it, and had them cut with saws, with iron picks, and with axes. David did so to all the cities of the children of Ammon. Then David and all the people returned to Jerusalem. ⁴ After this, war arose at Gezer with the Philistines. Then Sibbecai the Hushathite killed Sippai, of the sons of the giant; and they were subdued. ⁵ Again there was war with the

Philistines; and Elhanan the son of Jair killed Lahmi the brother of Goliath the Gittite, the staff of whose spear was like a weaver's beam. ⁶ There was again war at Gath, where there was a man of great stature, who had twenty-four fingers and toes, six on each hand and six on each foot; and he also was born to the giant. ⁷ When he defied Israel, Jonathan the son of Shimea, David's brother, killed him. ⁸ These were born to the giant in Gath; and they fell by the hand of David and by the hand of his servants.

## 21

¹ Satan stood up against Israel, and moved David to take a census of Israel. ² David said to Joab and to the princes of the people, "Go, count Israel from Beersheba even to Dan; and bring me word, that I may know how many there are." ³ Joab said, "May Yahweh make his people a hundred times as many as they are. But, my lord the king, aren't they all my lord's servants? Why does my lord require this thing? Why will he be a cause of guilt to Israel?" ⁴ Nevertheless the king's word prevailed against Joab. Therefore Joab departed and went throughout all Israel, then came to Jerusalem. ⁵ Joab gave the sum of the census of the people to David. All those of Israel were one million one hundred thousand men who drew a sword; and in Judah were four hundred seventy thousand men who drew a sword. ⁶ But he didn't count Levi and Benjamin among them, for the king's word was abominable to Joab. ⁷ God was displeased with this thing; therefore he struck Israel. ⁸ David said to God, "I have sinned greatly, in that I have done this thing. But now put away, I beg you, the iniquity of your servant, for I have done very foolishly." ⁹ Yahweh spoke to Gad, David's seer, saying, ¹⁰"Go and speak to David, saying, 'Yahweh says, "I offer you three things. Choose one of them, that I may do it to you."'" ¹¹ So Gad came to David and said to him, "Yahweh says, 'Take your choice: ¹² either three years of famine; or three months to be consumed before your foes, while the sword of your enemies overtakes you; or else three days of the sword of Yahweh, even pestilence in the land, and Yahweh's angel destroying throughout all the borders of Israel. Now therefore consider what answer I shall return to him who sent me.'" ¹³ David said to Gad, "I am in distress. Let me fall, I pray, into Yahweh's hand, for his mercies are very great. Don't let me fall into man's hand." ¹⁴ So Yahweh sent a pestilence on Israel, and seventy thousand men of Israel fell. ¹⁵ God sent an angel to Jerusalem to destroy it. As he was about to destroy, Yahweh saw, and he relented of the disaster, and said to the destroying angel, "It is enough. Now withdraw your hand." Yahweh's angel was standing by the threshing floor of Ornan the Jebusite. ¹⁶ David lifted up his eyes, and saw Yahweh's angel standing between earth and the sky, having a drawn sword in his hand stretched out over Jerusalem. Then David and the elders, clothed in sackcloth, fell on their faces. ¹⁷ David said to God, "Isn't it I who commanded the people to be counted? It is even I who have sinned and done very wickedly; but these sheep, what have they done? Please let your hand, O Yahweh my God, be against me and against my father's house; but not against your people, that they should be plagued." ¹⁸ Then Yahweh's angel commanded Gad to tell David that David should go up and raise an altar to Yahweh on the threshing floor of Ornan the Jebusite. ¹⁹ David went up at the saying of Gad, which he spoke in Yahweh's name. ²⁰ Ornan turned back and saw the angel; and his four sons who were with him hid themselves. Now Ornan was threshing wheat. ²¹ As David came to Ornan, Ornan looked and saw David, and went out of the threshing floor, and bowed himself to David with his face to the ground. ²² Then David said to Ornan, "Sell me the place of this threshing floor, that I may build an altar to Yahweh on it. You shall sell it to me for the full price, that the plague may be stopped from afflicting the people." ²³ Ornan said to David, "Take it for yourself, and let my lord the king do that which is good in his eyes. Behold, I give the oxen for burnt offerings, and the threshing instruments for wood, and the wheat for the meal offering. I give it all." ²⁴ King David said to Ornan, "No, but I will most certainly buy it for the full price. For I will not take that which is yours for Yahweh, nor offer a burnt offering that costs me nothing." ²⁵ So David gave to Ornan six hundred shekels[d] of gold by weight for the place. ²⁶ David built an altar to Yahweh there, and offered burnt offerings and peace offerings, and called on Yahweh; and he answered him from the sky by fire on the altar of burnt offering. ²⁷ Then Yahweh commanded the angel, and he put his sword back into its sheath. ²⁸ At that time, when David saw that Yahweh had answered him in the threshing floor of Ornan the Jebusite, then he sacrificed there. ²⁹ For Yahweh's tabernacle, which Moses made in the wilderness, and the altar of burnt offering, were at that time in the high place at Gibeon. ³⁰

---

[a] 19:6 A talent is about 30 kilograms or 66 pounds, so 1000 talents is about 30 metric tons

[b] 19:16 or, the Euphrates River
[c] 20:2 A talent is about 30 kilograms or 66 pounds or 965 Troy ounces

[d] 21:25 A shekel is about 10 grams or about 0.32 Troy ounces, so 600 shekels was

about 6 kilograms or about 192 Troy ounces.

But David couldn't go before it to inquire of God, for he was afraid because of the sword of Yahweh's angel.

## 22

[1] Then David said, "This is the house of Yahweh God, and this is the altar of burnt offering for Israel." [2] David gave orders to gather together the foreigners who were in the land of Israel; and he set masons to cut dressed stones to build God's house. [3] David prepared iron in abundance for the nails for the doors of the gates and for the couplings, and bronze in abundance without weight, [4] and cedar trees without number, for the Sidonians and the people of Tyre brought cedar trees in abundance to David. [5] David said, "Solomon my son is young and tender, and the house that is to be built for Yahweh must be exceedingly magnificent, of fame and of glory throughout all countries. I will therefore make preparation for it." So David prepared abundantly before his death. [6] Then he called for Solomon his son, and commanded him to build a house for Yahweh, the God of Israel. [7] David said to Solomon his son, "As for me, it was in my heart to build a house to the name of Yahweh my God. [8] But Yahweh's word came to me, saying, 'You have shed blood abundantly and have made great wars. You shall not build a house to my name, because you have shed much blood on the earth in my sight. [9] Behold, a son shall be born to you, who shall be a man of peace. I will give him rest from all his enemies all around; for his name shall be Solomon, and I will give peace and quietness to Israel in his days. [10] He shall build a house for my name; and he will be my son, and I will be his father; and I will establish the throne of his kingdom over Israel forever.' [11] Now, my son, may Yahweh be with you and prosper you, and build the house of Yahweh your God, as he has spoken concerning you. [12] May Yahweh give you discretion and understanding, and put you in charge of Israel, so that you may keep the law of Yahweh your God. [13] Then you will prosper, if you observe to do the statutes and the ordinances which Yahweh gave Moses concerning Israel. Be strong and courageous. Don't be afraid and don't be dismayed. [14] Now, behold, in my affliction I have prepared for Yahweh's house one hundred thousand talents[a] of gold, one million talents[b] of silver, and bronze and iron without weight; for it is in abundance. I have also prepared timber and stone; and you may add to them. [15] There are also workmen with you in abundance—cutters and workers of stone and timber, and all kinds of men who are skillful in every kind of work; [16] of the gold, the silver, the bronze, and the iron, there is no number. Arise and be doing, and may Yahweh be with you." [17] David also commanded all the princes of Israel to help Solomon his son, saying, [18]"Isn't Yahweh your God with you? Hasn't he given you rest on every side? For he has delivered the inhabitants of the land into my hand; and the land is subdued before Yahweh and before his people. [19] Now set your heart and your soul to follow Yahweh your God. Arise therefore, and build the sanctuary of Yahweh God, to bring the ark of Yahweh's covenant and the holy vessels of God into the house that is to be built for Yahweh's name."

## 23

[1] Now David was old and full of days; and he made Solomon his son king over Israel. [2] He gathered together all the princes of Israel, with the priests and the Levites. [3] The Levites were counted from thirty years old and upward; and their number by their polls, man by man, was thirty-eight thousand. [4] David said, "Of these, twenty-four thousand were to oversee the work of Yahweh's house, six thousand were officers and judges, [5] four thousand were doorkeepers, and four thousand praised Yahweh with the instruments which I made for giving praise." [6] David divided them into divisions according to the sons of Levi: Gershon, Kohath, and Merari. [7] Of the Gershonites: Ladan and Shimei. [8] The sons of Ladan: Jehiel the chief, Zetham, and Joel, three. [9] The sons of Shimei: Shelomoth, Haziel, and Haran, three. These were the heads of the fathers' households of Ladan. [10] The sons of Shimei: Jahath, Zina, Jeush, and Beriah. These four were the sons of Shimei. [11] Jahath was the chief, and Zizah the second; but Jeush and Beriah didn't have many sons; therefore they became a fathers' house in one reckoning. [12] The sons of Kohath: Amram, Izhar, Hebron, and Uzziel, four. [13] The sons of Amram: Aaron and Moses; and Aaron was separated that he should sanctify the most holy things, he and his sons forever, to burn incense before Yahweh, to minister to him, and to bless in his name forever. [14] But as for Moses the man of God, his sons were named among the tribe of Levi. [15] The sons of Moses: Gershom and Eliezer. [16] The sons of Gershom: Shebuel the chief. [17] The son of Eliezer was Rehabiah the chief; and Eliezer had no other sons, but the sons of Rehabiah were very many. [18] The son of Izhar: Shelomith the chief. [19] The sons of Hebron: Jeriah the chief, Amariah the second, Jahaziel the third, and Jekameam the fourth. [20] The sons of Uzziel: Micah the chief, and Isshiah the second. [21] The sons of Merari: Mahli

and Mushi. The sons of Mahli: Eleazar and Kish. [22] Eleazar died, and had no sons, but daughters only; and their relatives, the sons of Kish, took them as wives. [23] The sons of Mushi: Mahli, Eder, and Jeremoth, three. [24] These were the sons of Levi after their fathers' houses, even the heads of the fathers' houses of those who were counted individually, in the number of names by their polls, who did the work for the service of Yahweh's house, from twenty years old and upward. [25] For David said, "Yahweh, the God of Israel, has given rest to his people; and he dwells in Jerusalem forever. [26] Also the Levites will no longer need to carry the tabernacle and all its vessels for its service." [27] For by the last words of David the sons of Levi were counted, from twenty years old and upward. [28] For their duty was to wait on the sons of Aaron for the service of Yahweh's house—in the courts, in the rooms, and in the purifying of all holy things, even the work of the service of God's house; [29] for the show bread also, and for the fine flour for a meal offering, whether of unleavened wafers, or of that which is baked in the pan, or of that which is soaked, and for all measurements of quantity and size; [30] and to stand every morning to thank and praise Yahweh, and likewise in the evening; [31] and to offer all burnt offerings to Yahweh on the Sabbaths, on the new moons, and on the set feasts, in number according to the ordinance concerning them, continually before Yahweh; [32] and that they should keep the duty of the Tent of Meeting, the duty of the holy place, and the duty of the sons of Aaron their brothers for the service of Yahweh's house.

## 24

[1] These were the divisions of the sons of Aaron. The sons of Aaron: Nadab, Abihu, Eleazar, and Ithamar. [2] But Nadab and Abihu died before their father, and had no children; therefore Eleazar and Ithamar served as priests. [3] David, with Zadok of the sons of Eleazar and Ahimelech of the sons of Ithamar, divided them according to their ordering in their service. [4] There were more chief men found of the sons of Eleazar than of the sons of Ithamar; and they were divided like this: of the sons of Eleazar there were sixteen, heads of fathers' houses; and of the sons of Ithamar, according to their fathers' houses, eight. [5] Thus they were divided impartially by drawing lots; for there were princes of the sanctuary and princes of God, both of the sons of Eleazar, and of the sons of Ithamar. [6] Shemaiah the son of Nethanel the scribe, who was of the Levites, wrote them in the presence of the king, the princes, Zadok the priest, Ahimelech the son of Abiathar, and the heads of the fathers' households of the priests and of the Levites; one fathers' house being taken for Eleazar, and one taken for Ithamar. [7] Now the first lot came out to Jehoiarib, the second to Jedaiah, [8] the third to Harim, the fourth to Seorim, [9] the fifth to Malchijah, the sixth to Mijamin, [10] the seventh to Hakkoz, the eighth to Abijah, [11] the ninth to Jeshua, the tenth to Shecaniah, [12] the eleventh to Eliashib, the twelfth to Jakim, [13] the thirteenth to Huppah, the fourteenth to Jeshebeab, [14] the fifteenth to Bilgah, the sixteenth to Immer, [15] the seventeenth to Hezir, the eighteenth to Happizzez, [16] the nineteenth to Pethahiah, the twentieth to Jehezkel, [17] the twenty-first to Jachin, the twenty-second to Gamul, [18] the twenty-third to Delaiah, and the twenty-fourth to Maaziah. [19] This was their ordering in their service, to come into Yahweh's house according to the ordinance given to them by Aaron their father, as Yahweh, the God of Israel, had commanded him. [20] Of the rest of the sons of Levi: of the sons of Amram, Shubael; of the sons of Shubael, Jehdeiah. [21] Of Rehabiah: of the sons of Rehabiah, Isshiah the chief. [22] Of the Izharites, Shelomoth; of the sons of Shelomoth, Jahath. [23] The sons of Hebron: Jeriah, Amariah the second, Jahaziel the third, and Jekameam the fourth. [24] The sons of Uzziel: Micah; of the sons of Micah, Shamir. [25] The brother of Micah: Isshiah; of the sons of Isshiah, Zechariah. [26] The sons of Merari: Mahli and Mushi. The son of Jaaziah: Beno. [27] The sons of Merari by Jaaziah: Beno, Shoham, Zaccur, and Ibri. [28] Of Mahli: Eleazar, who had no sons. [29] Of Kish, the son of Kish: Jerahmeel. [30] The sons of Mushi: Mahli, Eder, and Jerimoth. These were the sons of the Levites after their fathers' houses. [31] These likewise cast lots even as their brothers the sons of Aaron in the presence of David the king, Zadok, Ahimelech, and the heads of the fathers' households of the priests and of the Levites, the fathers' households of the chief even as those of his younger brother.

## 25

[1] Moreover, David and the captains of the army set apart for the service certain of the sons of Asaph, of Heman, and of Jeduthun, who were to prophesy with harps, with stringed instruments, and with cymbals. The number of those who did the work according to their service was: [2] of the sons of Asaph: Zaccur, Joseph, Nethaniah, and Asharelah. The sons of Asaph were under the hand of Asaph, who prophesied at the order of the king. [3] Of Jeduthun, the sons of Jeduthun: Gedaliah, Zeri, Jeshaiah, Shimei, Hashabiah, and Mattithiah, six, under the hands of

---

[a] *22:14* A talent is about 30 kilograms or 66 pounds or 965 Troy ounces, so 100,000 talents is about 3 metric tons

[b] *22:14* about 30,000 metric tons

their father Jeduthun, who prophesied in giving thanks and praising Yahweh with the harp. [4] Of Heman, the sons of Heman: Bukkiah, Mattaniah, Uzziel, Shebuel, Jerimoth, Hananiah, Hanani, Eliathah, Giddalti, Romamti-Ezer, Joshbekashah, Mallothi, Hothir, and Mahazioth. [5] All these were the sons of Heman the king's seer in the words of God, to lift up the horn. God gave to Heman fourteen sons and three daughters. [6] All these were under the hands of their father for song in Yahweh's house, with cymbals, stringed instruments, and harps, for the service of God's house: Asaph, Jeduthun, and Heman being under the order of the king. [7] The number of them, with their brothers who were instructed in singing to Yahweh, even all who were skillful, was two hundred eighty-eight. [8] They cast lots for their offices, all alike, the small as well as the great, the teacher as well as the student. [9] Now the first lot came out for Asaph to Joseph; the second to Gedaliah, he and his brothers and sons were twelve; [10] the third to Zaccur, his sons and his brothers, twelve; [11] the fourth to Izri, his sons and his brothers, twelve; [12] the fifth to Nethaniah, his sons and his brothers, twelve; [13] the sixth to Bukkiah, his sons and his brothers, twelve; [14] the seventh to Jesharelah, his sons and his brothers, twelve; [15] the eighth to Jeshaiah, his sons and his brothers, twelve; [16] the ninth to Mattaniah, his sons and his brothers, twelve; [17] the tenth to Shimei, his sons and his brothers, twelve; [18] the eleventh to Azarel, his sons and his brothers, twelve; [19] the twelfth to Hashabiah, his sons and his brothers, twelve; [20] for the thirteenth, Shubael, his sons and his brothers, twelve; [21] for the fourteenth, Mattithiah, his sons and his brothers, twelve; [22] for the fifteenth to Jeremoth, his sons and his brothers, twelve; [23] for the sixteenth to Hananiah, his sons and his brothers, twelve; [24] for the seventeenth to Joshbekashah, his sons and his brothers, twelve; [25] for the eighteenth to Hanani, his sons and his brothers, twelve; [26] for the nineteenth to Mallothi, his sons and his brothers, twelve; [27] for the twentieth to Eliathah, his sons and his brothers, twelve; [28] for the twenty-first to Hothir, his sons and his brothers, twelve; [29] for the twenty-second to Giddalti, his sons and his brothers, twelve; [30] for the twenty-third to Mahazioth, his sons and his brothers, twelve; [31] for the twenty-fourth to Romamti-Ezer, his sons and his brothers, twelve.

## 26

[1] For the divisions of the doorkeepers: of the Korahites, Meshelemiah the son of Kore, of the sons of Asaph. [2] Meshelemiah had sons: Zechariah the firstborn, Jediael the second, Zebadiah the third, Jathniel the fourth, [3] Elam the fifth, Jehohanan the sixth, and Eliehoenai the seventh. [4] Obed-Edom had sons: Shemaiah the firstborn, Jehozabad the second, Joah the third, Sacar the fourth, Nethanel the fifth, [5] Ammiel the sixth, Issachar the seventh, and Peullethai the eighth; for God blessed him. [6] Sons were also born to Shemaiah his son, who ruled over the house of their father; for they were mighty men of valor. [7] The sons of Shemaiah: Othni, Rephael, Obed, and Elzabad, whose relatives were valiant men, Elihu, and Semachiah. [8] All these were of the sons of Obed-Edom with their sons and their brothers, able men in strength for the service: sixty-two of Obed-Edom. [9] Meshelemiah had sons and brothers, eighteen valiant men. [10] Also Hosah, of the children of Merari, had sons: Shimri the chief (for though he was not the firstborn, yet his father made him chief), [11] Hilkiah the second, Tebaliah the third, and Zechariah the fourth. All the sons and brothers of Hosah were thirteen. [12] Of these were the divisions of the doorkeepers, even of the chief men, having offices like their brothers, to minister in Yahweh's house. [13] They cast lots, the small as well as the great, according to their fathers' houses, for every gate. [14] The lot eastward fell to Shelemiah. Then for Zechariah his son, a wise counselor, they cast lots; and his lot came out northward. [15] To Obed-Edom southward; and to his sons the storehouse. [16] To Shuppim and Hosah westward, by the gate of Shallecheth, at the causeway that goes up, watchman opposite watchman. [17] Eastward were six Levites, northward four a day, southward four a day, and for the storehouse two and two. [18] For Parbar westward, four at the causeway, and two at Parbar. [19] These were the divisions of the doorkeepers; of the sons of the Korahites, and of the sons of Merari. [20] Of the Levites, Ahijah was over the treasures of God's house and over the treasures of the dedicated things. [21] The sons of Ladan, the sons of the Gershonites belonging to Ladan, the heads of the fathers' households belonging to Ladan the Gershonite: Jehieli. [22] The sons of Jehieli: Zetham, and Joel his brother, over the treasures of Yahweh's house. [23] Of the Amramites, of the Izharites, of the Hebronites, of the Uzzielites: [24] Shebuel the son of Gershom, the son of Moses, was ruler over the treasuries. [25] His brothers: of Eliezer, Rehabiah his son, and Jeshaiah his son, and Joram his son, and Zichri his son, and Shelomoth his son. [26] This Shelomoth and his brothers were over all the treasuries of the dedicated things, which David the king, and the heads of the fathers' households, the captains over thousands and hundreds, and the captains of the army, had dedicated. [27] They dedicated some of the plunder won in battles to repair Yahweh's house. [28] All that Samuel the seer, Saul the son of Kish,

Abner the son of Ner, and Joab the son of Zeruiah had dedicated, whoever had dedicated anything, it was under the hand of Shelomoth and of his brothers. [29] Of the Izharites, Chenaniah and his sons were appointed to the outward business over Israel, for officers and judges. [30] Of the Hebronites, Hashabiah and his brothers, one thousand seven hundred men of valor, had the oversight of Israel beyond the Jordan westward, for all the business of Yahweh and for the service of the king. [31] Of the Hebronites, Jerijah was the chief of the Hebronites, according to their generations by fathers' households. They were sought for in the fortieth year of the reign of David, and mighty men of valor were found among them at Jazer of Gilead. [32] His relatives, men of valor, were two thousand seven hundred, heads of fathers' households, whom King David made overseers over the Reubenites, the Gadites, and the half-tribe of the Manassites, for every matter pertaining to God and for the affairs of the king.

## 27

[1] Now the children of Israel after their number, the heads of fathers' households and the captains of thousands and of hundreds, and their officers who served the king in any matter of the divisions which came in and went out month by month throughout all the months of the year—of every division were twenty-four thousand. [2] Over the first division for the first month was Jashobeam the son of Zabdiel. In his division were twenty-four thousand. [3] He was of the children of Perez, the chief of all the captains of the army for the first month. [4] Over the division of the second month was Dodai the Ahohite and his division, and Mikloth the ruler; and in his division were twenty-four thousand. [5] The third captain of the army for the third month was Benaiah, the son of Jehoiada the chief priest. In his division were twenty-four thousand. [6] This is that Benaiah who was the mighty man of the thirty and over the thirty. Of his division was Ammizabad his son. [7] The fourth captain for the fourth month was Asahel the brother of Joab, and Zebadiah his son after him. In his division were twenty-four thousand. [8] The fifth captain for the fifth month was Shamhuth the Izrahite. In his division were twenty-four thousand. [9] The sixth captain for the sixth month was Ira the son of Ikkesh the Tekoite. In his division were twenty-four thousand. [10] The seventh captain for the seventh month was Helez the Pelonite, of the children of Ephraim. In his division were twenty-four thousand. [11] The eighth captain for the eighth month was Sibbecai the Hushathite, of the Zerahites. In his division were twenty-four thousand. [12] The ninth captain for the ninth month was Abiezer the Anathothite, of the Benjamites. In his division were twenty-four thousand. [13] The tenth captain for the tenth month was Maharai the Netophathite, of the Zerahites. In his division were twenty-four thousand. [14] The eleventh captain for the eleventh month was Benaiah the Pirathonite, of the children of Ephraim. In his division were twenty-four thousand. [15] The twelfth captain for the twelfth month was Heldai the Netophathite, of Othniel. In his division were twenty-four thousand. [16] Furthermore over the tribes of Israel: of the Reubenites, Eliezer the son of Zichri was the ruler; of the Simeonites, Shephatiah the son of Maacah; [17] of Levi, Hashabiah the son of Kemuel; of Aaron, Zadok; [18] of Judah, Elihu, one of the brothers of David; of Issachar, Omri the son of Michael; [19] of Zebulun, Ishmaiah the son of Obadiah; of Naphtali, Jeremoth the son of Azriel; [20] of the children of Ephraim, Hoshea the son of Azaziah; of the half-tribe of Manasseh, Joel the son of Pedaiah; [21] of the half-tribe of Manasseh in Gilead, Iddo the son of Zechariah; of Benjamin, Jaasiel the son of Abner; [22] of Dan, Azarel the son of Jeroham. These were the captains of the tribes of Israel. [23] But David didn't take the number of them from twenty years old and under, because Yahweh had said he would increase Israel like the stars of the sky. [24] Joab the son of Zeruiah began to take a census, but didn't finish; and wrath came on Israel for this. The number wasn't put into the account in the chronicles of King David. [25] Over the king's treasures was Azmaveth the son of Adiel. Over the treasures in the fields, in the cities, in the villages, and in the towers was Jonathan the son of Uzziah; [26] Over those who did the work of the field for tillage of the ground was Ezri the son of Chelub. [27] Over the vineyards was Shimei the Ramathite. Over the increase of the vineyards for the wine cellars was Zabdi the Shiphmite. [28] Over the olive trees and the sycamore trees that were in the lowland was Baal Hanan the Gederite. Over the cellars of oil was Joash. [29] Over the herds that fed in Sharon was Shitrai the Sharonite. Over the herds that were in the valleys was Shaphat the son of Adlai. [30] Over the camels was Obil the Ishmaelite. Over the donkeys was Jehdeiah the Meronothite. Over the flocks was Jaziz the Hagrite. [31] All these were the rulers of the property which was King David's. [32] Also Jonathan, David's uncle, was a counselor, a man of understanding, and a scribe. Jehiel the son of Hachmoni was with the king's sons. [33] Ahithophel was the king's counselor. Hushai the Archite was the king's friend. [34] After Ahithophel was Jehoiada the son of Benaiah, and Abiathar. Joab was the captain of the king's army.

## 28

¹ David assembled all the princes of Israel, the princes of the tribes, the captains of the companies who served the king by division, the captains of thousands, the captains of hundreds, and the rulers over all the substance and possessions of the king and of his sons, with the officers and the mighty men, even all the mighty men of valor, to Jerusalem. ² Then David the king stood up on his feet and said, "Hear me, my brothers and my people! As for me, it was in my heart to build a house of rest for the ark of Yahweh's covenant, and for the footstool of our God; and I had prepared for the building. ³ But God said to me, 'You shall not build a house for my name, because you are a man of war and have shed blood.' ⁴ However Yahweh, the God of Israel, chose me out of all the house of my father to be king over Israel forever. For he has chosen Judah to be prince; and in the house of Judah, the house of my father; and among the sons of my father he took pleasure in me to make me king over all Israel. ⁵ Of all my sons (for Yahweh has given me many sons), he has chosen Solomon my son to sit on the throne of Yahweh's kingdom over Israel. ⁶ He said to me, 'Solomon, your son, shall build my house and my courts; for I have chosen him to be my son, and I will be his father. ⁷ I will establish his kingdom forever if he continues to do my commandments and my ordinances, as it is today.' ⁸ Now therefore, in the sight of all Israel, Yahweh's assembly, and in the audience of our God, observe and seek out all the commandments of Yahweh your God, that you may possess this good land, and leave it for an inheritance to your children after you forever. ⁹ You, Solomon my son, know the God of your father, and serve him with a perfect heart and with a willing mind; for Yahweh searches all hearts, and understands all the imaginations of the thoughts. If you seek him, he will be found by you; but if you forsake him, he will cast you off forever. ¹⁰ Take heed now, for Yahweh has chosen you to build a house for the sanctuary. Be strong, and do it." ¹¹ Then David gave to Solomon his son the plans for the porch of the temple, for its houses, for its treasuries, for its upper rooms, for its inner rooms, for the place of the mercy seat; ¹² and the plans of all that he had by the Spirit, for the courts of Yahweh's house, for all the surrounding rooms, for the treasuries of God's house, and for the treasuries of the dedicated things; ¹³ also for the divisions of the priests and the Levites, for all the work of the service of Yahweh's house, and for all the vessels of service in Yahweh's house— ¹⁴ of gold by weight for the gold for all vessels of every kind of service, for all the vessels of silver by weight, for all vessels of every kind of service; ¹⁵ by weight also for the lamp stands of gold, and for its lamps, of gold, by weight for every lamp stand and for its lamps; and for the lamp stands of silver, by weight for every lamp stand and for its lamps, according to the use of every lamp stand; ¹⁶ and the gold by weight for the tables of show bread, for every table; and silver for the tables of silver; ¹⁷ and the forks, the basins, and the cups, of pure gold; and for the golden bowls by weight for every bowl; and for the silver bowls by weight for every bowl; ¹⁸ and for the altar of incense, refined gold by weight; and gold for the plans for the chariot, and the cherubim that spread out and cover the ark of Yahweh's covenant. ¹⁹ "All this", David said, "I have been made to understand in writing from Yahweh's hand, even all the works of this pattern." ²⁰ David said to Solomon his son, "Be strong and courageous, and do it. Don't be afraid, nor be dismayed, for Yahweh God, even my God, is with you. He will not fail you nor forsake you, until all the work for the service of Yahweh's house is finished. ²¹ Behold, there are the divisions of the priests and the Levites for all the service of God's house. Every willing man who has skill for any kind of service shall be with you in all kinds of work. Also the captains and all the people will be entirely at your command."

## 29

¹ David the king said to all the assembly, "Solomon my son, whom alone God has chosen, is yet young and tender, and the work is great; for the palace is not for man, but for Yahweh God. ² Now I have prepared with all my might for the house of my God the gold for the things of gold, the silver for the things of silver, the bronze for the things of bronze, iron for the things of iron, and wood for the things of wood, also onyx stones, stones to be set, stones for inlaid work of various colors, all kinds of precious stones, and marble stones in abundance. ³ In addition, because I have set my affection on the house of my God, since I have a treasure of my own of gold and silver, I give it to the house of my God, over and above all that I have prepared for the holy house: ⁴ even three thousand talents of gold,ᵃ of the gold of

Ophir, and seven thousand talentsᵇ of refined silver, with which to overlay the walls of the houses; ⁵ of gold for the things of gold, and of silver for the things of silver, and for all kinds of work to be made by the hands of artisans. Who then offers willingly to consecrate himself today to Yahweh?" ⁶ Then the princes of the fathers' households, and the princes of the tribes of Israel, and the captains of thousands and of hundreds, with the rulers over the king's work, offered willingly; ⁷ and they gave for the service of God's house of gold five thousand talentsᶜ and ten thousand darics,ᵈ of silver ten thousand talents, of bronze eighteen thousand talents, and of iron one hundred thousand talents. ⁸ People with whom precious stones were found gave them to the treasure of Yahweh's house, under the hand of Jehiel the Gershonite. ⁹ Then the people rejoiced, because they offered willingly, because with a perfect heart they offered willingly to Yahweh; and David the king also rejoiced with great joy. ¹⁰ Therefore David blessed Yahweh before all the assembly; and David said, "You are blessed, Yahweh, the God of Israel our father, forever and ever. ¹¹ Yours, Yahweh, is the greatness, the power, the glory, the victory, and the majesty! For all that is in the heavens and in the earth is yours. Yours is the kingdom, Yahweh, and you are exalted as head above all. ¹² Both riches and honor come from you, and you rule over all! In your hand is power and might! It is in your hand to make great, and to give strength to all! ¹³ Now therefore, our God, we thank you and praise your glorious name. ¹⁴ But who am I, and what is my people, that we should be able to offer so willingly as this? For all things come from you, and we have given you of your own. ¹⁵ For we are strangers before you and foreigners, as all our fathers were. Our days on the earth are as a shadow, and there is no remaining. ¹⁶ Yahweh our God, all this store that we have prepared to build you a house for your holy name comes from your hand, and is all your own. ¹⁷ I know also, my God, that you try the heart and have pleasure in uprightness. As for me, in the uprightness of my heart I have willingly offered all these things. Now I have seen with joy your people, who are present here, offer willingly to you. ¹⁸ Yahweh, the God of Abraham, of Isaac, and of Israel, our fathers, keep this desire forever in the thoughts of the heart of your people, and prepare their heart for you; ¹⁹ and give to Solomon my son a perfect heart, to keep your commandments, your testimonies, and your statutes, and to do all these things, and to build the palace, for which I have made provision." ²⁰ Then David said to all the assembly, "Now bless Yahweh your God!" All the assembly blessed Yahweh, the God of their fathers, and bowed down their heads and prostrated themselves before Yahweh and the king. ²¹ They sacrificed sacrifices to Yahweh and offered burnt offerings to Yahweh on the next day after that day, even one thousand bulls, one thousand rams, and one thousand lambs, with their drink offerings and sacrifices in abundance for all Israel, ²² and ate and drank before Yahweh on that day with great gladness. They made Solomon the son of David king the second time, and anointed him before Yahweh to be prince, and Zadok to be priest. ²³ Then Solomon sat on the throne of Yahweh as king instead of David his father, and prospered; and all Israel obeyed him. ²⁴ All the princes, the mighty men, and also all of the sons of King David submitted themselves to Solomon the king. ²⁵ Yahweh magnified Solomon exceedingly in the sight of all Israel, and gave to him such royal majesty as had not been on any king before him in Israel. ²⁶ Now David the son of Jesse reigned over all Israel. ²⁷ The time that he reigned over Israel was forty years; he reigned seven years in Hebron, and he reigned thirty-three years in Jerusalem. ²⁸ He died at a good old age, full of days, riches, and honor; and Solomon his son reigned in his place. ²⁹ Now the acts of David the king, first and last, behold, they are written in the history of Samuel the seer, and in the history of Nathan the prophet, and in the history of Gad the seer, ³⁰ with all his reign and his might, and the events that involved him, Israel, and all the kingdoms of the lands.

## The Second Book of Chronicles

### 1

¹ Solomon the son of David was firmly established in his kingdom, and Yahwehᵉ his Godᶠ was with him, and made him exceedingly great. ² Solomon spoke to all Israel, to the captains of thousands and of hundreds, to the judges, and to every prince in all Israel, the heads of the fathers' households. ³ Then Solomon, and all the assembly with him, went to the high place that was at Gibeon; for God's Tent of Meeting was there, which Yahweh's servant Moses had made in the

---

ᵃ *29:4 A talent is about 30 kilograms or 66 pounds or 965 Troy ounces, so 3000 talents is about 90 metric tons*
ᵇ *29:4 about 210 metric tons*

ᶜ *29:7 A talent is about 30 kilograms or 66 pounds or 965 Troy ounces, so 5000 talents is about 150 metric tons*
ᵈ *29:7 a daric was a gold coin issued by a Persian king,*

weighing about 8.4 grams or about 0.27 troy ounces each.
ᵉ *1:1 "Yahweh" is God's proper Name, sometimes rendered "LORD" (all caps) in other translations.*

ᶠ *1:1 The Hebrew word rendered "God" is "אֱלֹהִים" (Elohim).*

wilderness. [4] But David had brought God's ark up from Kiriath Jearim to the place that David had prepared for it; for he had pitched a tent for it at Jerusalem. [5] Moreover the bronze altar that Bezalel the son of Uri, the son of Hur, had made was there before Yahweh's tabernacle; and Solomon and the assembly were seeking counsel there. [6] Solomon went up there to the bronze altar before Yahweh, which was at the Tent of Meeting, and offered one thousand burnt offerings on it. [7] That night, God appeared to Solomon and said to him, "Ask for what you want me to give you." [8] Solomon said to God, "You have shown great loving kindness to David my father, and have made me king in his place. [9] Now, Yahweh God, let your promise to David my father be established; for you have made me king over a people like the dust of the earth in multitude. [10] Now give me wisdom and knowledge, that I may go out and come in before this people; for who can judge this great people of yours?" [11] God said to Solomon, "Because this was in your heart, and you have not asked riches, wealth, honor, or the life of those who hate you, nor yet have you asked for long life; but have asked for wisdom and knowledge for yourself, that you may judge my people, over whom I have made you king, [12] therefore wisdom and knowledge is granted to you. I will give you riches, wealth, and honor, such as none of the kings have had who have been before you, and none after you will have." [13] So Solomon came from the high place that was at Gibeon, from before the Tent of Meeting, to Jerusalem; and he reigned over Israel. [14] Solomon gathered chariots and horsemen. He had one thousand four hundred chariots and twelve thousand horsemen that he placed in the chariot cities, and with the king at Jerusalem. [15] The king made silver and gold to be as common as stones in Jerusalem, and he made cedars to be as common as the sycamore trees that are in the lowland. [16] The horses which Solomon had were brought out of Egypt and from Kue. The king's merchants purchased them from Kue. [17] They imported from Egypt then exported a chariot for six hundred pieces of silver and a horse for one hundred fifty.[a] They also exported them to the Hittite kings and the Syrian[b] kings.

## 2

[1] Now Solomon decided to build a house for Yahweh's name, and a house for his kingdom. [2] Solomon counted out seventy thousand men to bear burdens, eighty thousand men who were stone cutters in the mountains, and three thousand six hundred to oversee them. [3] Solomon sent to Huram the king of Tyre, saying, "As you dealt with David my father, and sent him cedars to build him a house in which to dwell, so deal with me. [4] Behold,[c] I am about to build a house for the name of Yahweh my God, to dedicate it to him, to burn before him incense of sweet spices, for the continual show bread, and for the burnt offerings morning and evening, on the Sabbaths, on the new moons, and on the set feasts of Yahweh our God. This is an ordinance forever to Israel. [5]"The house which I am building will be great, for our God is greater than all gods. [6] But who is able to build him a house, since heaven and the heaven of heavens can't contain him? Who am I then, that I should build him a house, except just to burn incense before him? [7]"Now therefore send me a man skillful to work in gold, in silver, in bronze, in iron, and in purple, crimson, and blue, and who knows how to engrave engravings, to be with the skillful men who are with me in Judah and in Jerusalem, whom David my father provided. [8]"Send me also cedar trees, cypress trees, and algum trees out of Lebanon, for I know that your servants know how to cut timber in Lebanon. Behold, my servants will be with your servants, [9] even to prepare me timber in abundance; for the house which I am about to build will be great and wonderful. [10] Behold, I will give to your servants, the cutters who cut timber, twenty thousand cors[d] of beaten wheat, twenty thousand baths[e] of barley, twenty thousand baths of wine, and twenty thousand baths of oil." [11] Then Huram the king of Tyre answered in writing, which he sent to Solomon, "Because Yahweh loves his people, he has made you king over them." [12] Huram continued, "Blessed be Yahweh, the God of Israel, who made heaven and earth, who has given to David the king a wise son, endowed with discretion and understanding, who would build a house for Yahweh and a house for his kingdom. [13] Now I have sent a skillful man, endowed with understanding, Huram-abi,[f] [14] the son of a woman of the daughters of Dan; and his father was a man of Tyre. He

is skillful to work in gold, in silver, in bronze, in iron, in stone, in timber, in purple, in blue, in fine linen, and in crimson, also to engrave any kind of engraving and to devise any device, that there may be a place appointed to him with your skillful men, and with the skillful men of my lord David your father. [15]"Now therefore, the wheat, the barley, the oil, and the wine which my lord has spoken of, let him send to his servants; [16] and we will cut wood out of Lebanon, as much as you need. We will bring it to you in rafts by sea to Joppa; then you shall carry it up to Jerusalem." [17] Solomon counted all the foreigners who were in the land of Israel, after the census with which David his father had counted them; and they found one hundred fifty-three thousand six hundred. [18] He set seventy thousand of them to bear burdens, eighty thousand who were stone cutters in the mountains, and three thousand six hundred overseers to assign the people their work.

## 3

[1] Then Solomon began to build Yahweh's house at Jerusalem on Mount Moriah, where Yahweh appeared to David his father, which he prepared in the place that David had appointed, on the threshing floor of Ornan the Jebusite. [2] He began to build in the second day of the second month, in the fourth year of his reign. [3] Now these are the foundations which Solomon laid for the building of God's house: the length by cubits[g] after the first measure was sixty cubits, and the width twenty cubits. [4] The porch that was in front, its length, across the width of the house, was twenty cubits, and the height one hundred twenty; and he overlaid it within with pure gold. [5] He made the larger room with a ceiling of cypress wood, which he overlaid with fine gold, and ornamented it with palm trees and chains. [6] He decorated the house with precious stones for beauty. The gold was gold from Parvaim. [7] He also overlaid the house, the beams, the thresholds, its walls, and its doors with gold, and engraved cherubim on the walls. [8] He made the most holy place. Its length, according to the width of the house, was twenty cubits, and its width twenty cubits; and he overlaid it with fine gold, amounting to six hundred talents.[h] [9] The weight of the nails was fifty shekels[i] of gold. He overlaid the upper rooms with gold. [10] In the most holy place he made two cherubim by carving, and they overlaid them with gold. [11] The wings of the cherubim were twenty cubits long: the wing of the one was five cubits, reaching to the wall of the house; and the other wing was five cubits, reaching to the wing of the other cherub. [12] The wing of the other cherub was five cubits, reaching to the wall of the house; and the other wing was five cubits, joining to the wing of the other cherub. [13] The wings of these cherubim spread themselves out twenty cubits. They stood on their feet, and their faces were toward the house. [14] He made the veil of blue, purple, crimson, and fine linen, and ornamented it with cherubim. [15] Also he made before the house two pillars thirty-five cubits high, and the capital that was on the top of each of them was five cubits. [16] He made chains in the inner sanctuary, and put them on the tops of the pillars; and he made one hundred pomegranates, and put them on the chains. [17] He set up the pillars before the temple, one on the right hand and the other on the left; and called the name of that on the right hand Jachin, and the name of that on the left Boaz.

## 4

[1] Then he made an altar of bronze, twenty cubits[j] long, twenty cubits wide, and ten cubits high. [2] Also he made the molten sea[k] of ten cubits from brim to brim. It was round, five cubits high, and thirty cubits in circumference. [3] Under it was the likeness of oxen, which encircled it, for ten cubits, encircling the sea. The oxen were in two rows, cast when it was cast. [4] It stood on twelve oxen, three looking toward the north, three looking toward the west, three looking toward the south, and three looking toward the east; and the sea was set on them above, and all their hindquarters were inward. [5] It was a handbreadth thick. Its brim was made like the brim of a cup, like the flower of a lily. It received and held three thousand baths.[l] [6] He also made ten basins, and put five on the right hand and five on the left, to wash in them. The things that belonged to the burnt offering were washed in them, but the sea was for the priests to wash in. [7] He made the ten lamp stands of gold according to the ordinance concerning them; and he set them in the temple, five on the right hand and five on the left. [8] He made also ten tables, and

---

[a] *1:17* The pieces of silver were probably shekels, so 600 pieces would be about 13.2 pounds or 6 kilograms of silver, and 150 would be about 3.3 pounds or 1.5 kilograms of silver.
[b] *1:17* or, Aramean
[c] *2:4* "Behold", from "הִנֵּה", means look at, take notice, observe, see, or gaze at. It is often used as an interjection.
[d] *2:10* 1 cor is the same as a homer, or about 55.9 U. S. gallons (liquid) or 211 liters or 6 bushels, so 20,000 cors of wheat would weigh about 545 metric tons.
[e] *2:10* 1 bath is one tenth of a cor, or about 5.6 U. S. gallons or 21 liters or 2.4 pecks. 20,000 baths of barley would weigh about 262 metric tons.
[f] *2:13* or, Huram, my father
[g] *3:3* A cubit is the length from the tip of the middle finger to the elbow on a man's arm, or about 18 inches or 46 centimeters.
[h] *3:8* A talent is about 30 kilograms or 66 pounds or 965 Troy ounces, so 600 talents is about 18 metric tons
[i] *3:9* A shekel is about 10 grams or about 0.32 Troy ounces, so 50 shekels was
about 0.5 kilograms or about 16 Troy ounces.
[j] *4:1* A cubit is the length from the tip of the middle finger to the elbow on a man's arm, or about 18 inches or 46 centimeters.
[k] *4:2* or, pool, or, reservoir
[l] *4:5* A bath is about 5.6 U. S. gallons or 21.1 liters, so 3,000 baths is about 16,800 gallons or 63.3 kiloliters.

placed them in the temple, five on the right side and five on the left. He made one hundred basins of gold. [9] Furthermore he made the court of the priests, the great court, and doors for the court, and overlaid their doors with bronze. [10] He set the sea on the right side of the house eastward, toward the south. [11] Huram made the pots, the shovels, and the basins. So Huram finished doing the work that he did for King Solomon in God's house: [12] the two pillars, the bowls, the two capitals which were on the top of the pillars, the two networks to cover the two bowls of the capitals that were on the top of the pillars, [13] and the four hundred pomegranates for the two networks—two rows of pomegranates for each network, to cover the two bowls of the capitals that were on the pillars. [14] He also made the bases, and he made the basins on the bases— [15] one sea, and the twelve oxen under it. [16] Huram-abi[a] also made the pots, the shovels, the forks, and all its vessels for King Solomon, for Yahweh's house, of bright bronze. [17] The king cast them in the plain of the Jordan, in the clay ground between Succoth and Zeredah. [18] Thus Solomon made all these vessels in great abundance, so that the weight of the bronze could not be determined. [19] Solomon made all the vessels that were in God's house: the golden altar, the tables with the show bread on them, [20] and the lamp stands with their lamps to burn according to the ordinance before the inner sanctuary, of pure gold; [21] and the flowers, the lamps, and the tongs of gold that was purest gold; [22] and the snuffers, the basins, the spoons, and the fire pans of pure gold. As for the entry of the house, its inner doors for the most holy place and the doors of the main hall of the temple were of gold.

# 5

[1] Thus all the work that Solomon did for Yahweh's house was finished. Solomon brought in the things that David his father had dedicated, even the silver, the gold, and all the vessels, and put them in the treasuries of God's house. [2] Then Solomon assembled the elders of Israel and all the heads of the tribes, the princes of the fathers' households of the children of Israel, to Jerusalem, to bring up the ark of Yahweh's covenant out of David's city, which is Zion. [3] So all the men of Israel assembled themselves to the king at the feast, which was in the seventh month. [4] All the elders of Israel came. The Levites took up the ark. [5] They brought up the ark, the Tent of Meeting, and all the holy vessels that were in the Tent. The Levitical priests brought these up. [6] King Solomon and all the congregation of Israel who were assembled to him were before the ark, sacrificing sheep and cattle that could not be counted or numbered for multitude. [7] The priests brought in the ark of Yahweh's covenant to its place, into the inner sanctuary of the house, to the most holy place, even under the wings of the cherubim. [8] For the cherubim spread out their wings over the place of the ark, and the cherubim covered the ark and its poles above. [9] The poles were so long that the ends of the poles were seen from the ark in front of the inner sanctuary, but they were not seen outside; and it is there to this day. [10] There was nothing in the ark except the two tablets which Moses put there at Horeb, when Yahweh made a covenant with the children of Israel, when they came out of Egypt. [11] When the priests had come out of the holy place (for all the priests who were present had sanctified themselves, and didn't keep their divisions; [12] also the Levites who were the singers, all of them, even Asaph, Heman, Jeduthun, and their sons and their brothers, arrayed in fine linen, with cymbals and stringed instruments and harps, stood at the east end of the altar, and with them one hundred twenty priests sounding with trumpets); [13] when the trumpeters and singers were as one, to make one sound to be heard in praising and thanking Yahweh; and when they lifted up their voice with the trumpets and cymbals and instruments of music, and praised Yahweh, saying, "For he is good, for his loving kindness endures forever!" then the house was filled with a cloud, even Yahweh's house, [14] so that the priests could not stand to minister by reason of the cloud; for Yahweh's glory filled God's house.

# 6

[1] Then Solomon said, "Yahweh has said that he would dwell in the thick darkness. [2] But I have built you a house and home, a place for you to dwell in forever." [3] The king turned his face, and blessed all the assembly of Israel; and all the assembly of Israel stood. [4] He said, "Blessed be Yahweh, the God of Israel, who spoke with his mouth to David my father, and has with his hands fulfilled it, saying, [5]'Since the day that I brought my people out of the land of Egypt, I chose no city out of all the tribes of Israel to build a house in, that my name might be there, and I chose no man to be prince over my people Israel; [6] but now I have chosen Jerusalem, that my name might be there; and I have chosen David to be over my people Israel.' [7] Now it was in the heart of David my father to build a house for the name of Yahweh, the God of

Israel. [8] But Yahweh said to David my father, 'Whereas it was in your heart to build a house for my name, you did well that it was in your heart; [9] nevertheless you shall not build the house, but your son who will come out of your body, he shall build the house for my name.' [10]"Yahweh has performed his word that he spoke; for I have risen up in the place of David my father, and sit on the throne of Israel, as Yahweh promised, and have built the house for the name of Yahweh, the God of Israel. [11] There I have set the ark, in which is Yahweh's covenant, which he made with the children of Israel." [12] He stood before Yahweh's altar in the presence of all the assembly of Israel, and spread out his hands [13](for Solomon had made a bronze platform, five cubits[b] long, five cubits wide, and three cubits high, and had set it in the middle of the court; and he stood on it, and knelt down on his knees before all the assembly of Israel, and spread out his hands toward heaven). [14] Then he said, "Yahweh, the God of Israel, there is no God like you in heaven or on earth—you who keep covenant and loving kindness with your servants who walk before you with all their heart; [15] who have kept with your servant David my father that which you promised him. Yes, you spoke with your mouth, and have fulfilled it with your hand, as it is today. [16]"Now therefore, Yahweh, the God of Israel, keep with your servant David my father that which you have promised him, saying, 'There shall not fail you a man in my sight to sit on the throne of Israel, if only your children take heed to their way, to walk in my law as you have walked before me.' [17] Now therefore, Yahweh, the God of Israel, let your word be verified, which you spoke to your servant David. [18]"But will God indeed dwell with men on the earth? Behold, heaven and the heaven of heavens can't contain you; how much less this house which I have built! [19] Yet have respect for the prayer of your servant and to his supplication, Yahweh my God, to listen to the cry and to the prayer which your servant prays before you; [20] that your eyes may be open toward this house day and night, even toward the place where you have said that you would put your name, to listen to the prayer which your servant will pray toward this place. [21] Listen to the petitions of your servant and of your people Israel, when they pray toward this place. Yes, hear from your dwelling place, even from heaven; and when you hear, forgive. [22]"If a man sins against his neighbor, and an oath is laid on him to cause him to swear, and he comes and swears before your altar in this house, [23] then hear from heaven, act, and judge your servants, bringing retribution to the wicked, to bring his way on his own head; and justifying the righteous, to give him according to his righteousness. [24]"If your people Israel are struck down before the enemy because they have sinned against you, and they turn again and confess your name, and pray and make supplication before you in this house, [25] then hear from heaven, and forgive the sin of your people Israel, and bring them again to the land which you gave to them and to their fathers. [26]"When the sky is shut up and there is no rain because they have sinned against you, if they pray toward this place and confess your name, and turn from their sin when you afflict them, [27] then hear in heaven, and forgive the sin of your servants, your people Israel, when you teach them the good way in which they should walk, and send rain on your land, which you have given to your people for an inheritance. [28]"If there is famine in the land, if there is pestilence, if there is blight or mildew, locust or caterpillar; if their enemies besiege them in the land of their cities; whatever plague or whatever sickness there is— [29] whatever prayer and supplication is made by any man, or by all your people Israel, who will each know his own plague and his own sorrow, and shall spread out his hands toward this house; [30] then hear from heaven your dwelling place and forgive, and render to every man according to all his ways, whose heart you know (for you, even you only, know the hearts of the children of men), [31] that they may fear you, to walk in your ways as long as they live in the land which you gave to our fathers. [32]"Moreover, concerning the foreigner, who is not of your people Israel, when he comes from a far country for your great name's sake and your mighty hand and your outstretched arm, when they come and pray toward this house, [33] then hear from heaven, even from your dwelling place, and do according to all that the foreigner calls to you for; that all the peoples of the earth may know your name and fear you, as do your people Israel, and that they may know that this house which I have built is called by your name. [34]"If your people go out to battle against their enemies, by whatever way you send them, and they pray to you toward this city which you have chosen, and the house which I have built for your name; [35] then hear from heaven their prayer and their supplication, and maintain their cause. [36]"If they sin against you (for there is no man who doesn't sin), and you are angry with them and deliver them to the enemy, so that they carry them away captive to a land far off or near; [37] yet if they come to their senses in the land

---

[a] *4:16* "abi" means "his father"
[b] *6:13* A cubit is the length from the tip of the middle finger to the elbow on a man's arm, or about 18 inches or 46 centimeters.

where they are carried captive, and turn again, and make supplication to you in the land of their captivity, saying, 'We have sinned, we have done perversely, and have dealt wickedly;' [38] if they return to you with all their heart and with all their soul in the land of their captivity, where they have been taken captive, and pray toward their land which you gave to their fathers, and the city which you have chosen, and toward the house which I have built for your name; [39] then hear from heaven, even from your dwelling place, their prayer and their petitions, and maintain their cause, and forgive your people who have sinned against you. [40]"Now, my God, let, I beg you, your eyes be open, and let your ears be attentive to the prayer that is made in this place. [41]"Now therefore arise, Yahweh God, into your resting place, you, and the ark of your strength. Let your priests, Yahweh God, be clothed with salvation, and let your saints rejoice in goodness. [42]"Yahweh God, don't turn away the face of your anointed. Remember your loving kindnesses to David your servant."

## 7

[1] Now when Solomon had finished praying, fire came down from heaven and consumed the burnt offering and the sacrifices; and Yahweh's glory filled the house. [2] The priests could not enter into Yahweh's house, because Yahweh's glory filled Yahweh's house. [3] All the children of Israel looked on, when the fire came down, and Yahweh's glory was on the house. They bowed themselves with their faces to the ground on the pavement, worshiped, and gave thanks to Yahweh, saying, "For he is good, for his loving kindness endures forever!" [4] Then the king and all the people offered sacrifices before Yahweh. [5] King Solomon offered a sacrifice of twenty-two thousand head of cattle and a hundred twenty thousand sheep. So the king and all the people dedicated God's house. [6] The priests stood, according to their positions; the Levites also with instruments of music of Yahweh, which David the king had made to give thanks to Yahweh, when David praised by their ministry, saying "For his loving kindness endures forever." The priests sounded trumpets before them; and all Israel stood. [7] Moreover Solomon made the middle of the court that was before Yahweh's house holy; for there he offered the burnt offerings and the fat of the peace offerings, because the bronze altar which Solomon had made was not able to receive the burnt offering, the meal offering, and the fat. [8] So Solomon held the feast at that time for seven days, and all Israel with him, a very great assembly, from the entrance of Hamath to the brook of Egypt. [9] On the eighth day, they held a solemn assembly; for they kept the dedication of the altar seven days, and the feast seven days. [10] On the twenty-third day of the seventh month, he sent the people away to their tents, joyful and glad of heart for the goodness that Yahweh had shown to David, to Solomon, and to Israel his people. [11] Thus Solomon finished Yahweh's house and the king's house; and he successfully completed all that came into Solomon's heart to make in Yahweh's house and in his own house. [12] Then Yahweh appeared to Solomon by night, and said to him, "I have heard your prayer, and have chosen this place for myself for a house of sacrifice. [13]"If I shut up the sky so that there is no rain, or if I command the locust to devour the land, or if I send pestilence among my people, [14] if my people who are called by my name will humble themselves, pray, seek my face, and turn from their wicked ways, then I will hear from heaven, will forgive their sin, and will heal their land. [15] Now my eyes will be open and my ears attentive to prayer that is made in this place. [16] For now I have chosen and made this house holy, that my name may be there forever; and my eyes and my heart will be there perpetually. [17]"As for you, if you will walk before me as David your father walked, and do according to all that I have commanded you, and will keep my statutes and my ordinances, [18] then I will establish the throne of your kingdom, according as I covenanted with David your father, saying, 'There shall not fail you a man to be ruler in Israel.' [19] But if you turn away and forsake my statutes and my commandments which I have set before you, and go and serve other gods and worship them, [20] then I will pluck them up by the roots out of my land which I have given them; and this house, which I have made holy for my name, I will cast out of my sight, and I will make it a proverb and a byword among all peoples. [21] This house, which is so high, everyone who passes by it will be astonished and say, 'Why has Yahweh done this to this land and to this house?' [22] They shall answer, 'Because they abandoned Yahweh, the God of their fathers, who brought them out of the land of Egypt, and took other gods, worshiped them, and served them. Therefore he has brought all this evil on them.'"

## 8

[1] At the end of twenty years, in which Solomon had built Yahweh's house and his own house, [2] Solomon built the cities which Huram had given to Solomon, and caused the children of Israel to dwell there. [3] Solomon went to Hamath Zobah, and prevailed against it. [4] He built Tadmor in the wilderness, and all the storage cities, which he built in Hamath. [5] Also he built Beth Horon the upper and Beth Horon the lower, fortified cities with walls, gates, and bars; [6] and Baalath, and all the storage cities that Solomon had, and all the cities for his chariots, the cities for his horsemen, and all that Solomon desired to build for his pleasure in Jerusalem, in Lebanon, and in all the land of his dominion. [7] As for all the people who were left of the Hittites, the Amorites, the Perizzites, the Hivites, and the Jebusites, who were not of Israel— [8] of their children who were left after them in the land, whom the children of Israel didn't consume—of them Solomon conscripted forced labor to this day. [9] But of the children of Israel, Solomon made no servants for his work, but they were men of war, chief of his captains, and rulers of his chariots and of his horsemen. [10] These were the chief officers of King Solomon, even two-hundred fifty, who ruled over the people. [11] Solomon brought up Pharaoh's daughter out of David's city to the house that he had built for her; for he said, "My wife shall not dwell in the house of David king of Israel, because the places where Yahweh's ark has come are holy." [12] Then Solomon offered burnt offerings to Yahweh on Yahweh's altar which he had built before the porch, [13] even as the duty of every day required, offering according to the commandment of Moses on the Sabbaths, on the new moons, and on the set feasts, three times per year, during the feast of unleavened bread, during the feast of weeks, and during the feast of booths.[a] [14] He appointed, according to the ordinance of David his father, the divisions of the priests to their service, and the Levites to their offices, to praise and to minister before the priests, as the duty of every day required, the doorkeepers also by their divisions at every gate, for David the man of God had so commanded. [15] They didn't depart from the commandment of the king to the priests and Levites concerning any matter or concerning the treasures. [16] Now all the work of Solomon was accomplished from the day of the foundation of Yahweh's house until it was finished. So Yahweh's house was completed. [17] Then Solomon went to Ezion Geber and to Eloth, on the seashore in the land of Edom. [18] Huram sent him ships and servants who had knowledge of the sea by the hands of his servants; and they came with the servants of Solomon to Ophir, and brought from there four hundred fifty talents[b] of gold, and brought them to King Solomon.

## 9

[1] When the queen of Sheba heard of the fame of Solomon, she came to test Solomon with hard questions at Jerusalem, with a very great caravan, including camels that bore spices, gold in abundance, and precious stones. When she had come to Solomon, she talked with him about all that was in her heart. [2] Solomon answered all her questions. There wasn't anything hidden from Solomon which he didn't tell her. [3] When the queen of Sheba had seen the wisdom of Solomon, the house that he had built, [4] the food of his table, the seating of his servants, the attendance of his ministers, their clothing, his cup bearers and their clothing, and his ascent by which he went up to Yahweh's house, there was no more spirit in her.[c] [5] She said to the king, "It was a true report that I heard in my own land of your acts and of your wisdom. [6] However I didn't believe their words until I came, and my eyes had seen it; and behold half of the greatness of your wisdom wasn't told me. You exceed the fame that I heard! [7] Happy are your men, and happy are these your servants, who stand continually before you and hear your wisdom. [8] Blessed be Yahweh your God, who delighted in you and set you on his throne to be king for Yahweh your God, because your God loved Israel, to establish them forever. Therefore he made you king over them, to do justice and righteousness." [9] She gave the king one hundred and twenty talents[d] of gold, spices in great abundance, and precious stones. There was never before such spice as the queen of Sheba gave to King Solomon. [10] The servants of Huram and the servants of Solomon, who brought gold from Ophir, also brought algum trees[e] and precious stones. [11] The king used algum tree wood to make terraces for Yahweh's house and for the king's house, and harps and stringed instruments for the singers. There were none like these seen before in the land of Judah. [12] King Solomon gave to the queen of Sheba all her desire, whatever she asked, more than that which she had brought to the king. So she turned and went to her own land, she and her servants. [13] Now the weight of gold that came to Solomon in one year was six

---

[a] 8:13 or, feast of tents (Sukkot)
[b] 8:18 A talent is about 30 kilograms or 66 pounds or 965 Troy ounces, so 450 talents is about 13.5 metric tons
[c] 9:4 or, she was breathless.
[d] 9:9 A talent is about 30 kilograms or 66 pounds or 965 Troy ounces, so 120 talents is about 3.6 metric tons
[e] 9:10 possibly Indian sandalwood, which has nice grain and a pleasant scent and is good for woodworking

hundred sixty-six talents<sup>a</sup> of gold, <sup>14</sup> in addition to that which the traders and merchants brought. All the kings of Arabia and the governors of the country brought gold and silver to Solomon. <sup>15</sup> King Solomon made two hundred large shields of beaten gold. Six hundred shekels<sup>b</sup> of beaten gold went to one large shield. <sup>16</sup> He made three hundred shields of beaten gold. Three hundred shekels<sup>c</sup> of gold went to one shield. The king put them in the House of the Forest of Lebanon. <sup>17</sup> Moreover the king made a great throne of ivory, and overlaid it with pure gold. <sup>18</sup> There were six steps to the throne, with a footstool of gold, which were fastened to the throne, and armrests on either side by the place of the seat, and two lions standing beside the armrests. <sup>19</sup> Twelve lions stood there on the one side and on the other on the six steps. There was nothing like it made in any other kingdom. <sup>20</sup> All King Solomon's drinking vessels were of gold, and all the vessels of the House of the Forest of Lebanon were of pure gold. Silver was not considered valuable in the days of Solomon. <sup>21</sup> For the king had ships that went to Tarshish with Huram's servants. Once every three years, the ships of Tarshish came bringing gold, silver, ivory, apes, and peacocks. <sup>22</sup> So King Solomon exceeded all the kings of the earth in riches and wisdom. <sup>23</sup> All the kings of the earth sought the presence of Solomon to hear his wisdom, which God had put in his heart. <sup>24</sup> They each brought tribute: vessels of silver, vessels of gold, clothing, armor, spices, horses, and mules every year. <sup>25</sup> Solomon had four thousand stalls for horses and chariots, and twelve thousand horsemen that he stationed in the chariot cities and with the king at Jerusalem. <sup>26</sup> He ruled over all the kings from the River even to the land of the Philistines, and to the border of Egypt. <sup>27</sup> The king made silver as common in Jerusalem as stones, and he made cedars to be as abundant as the sycamore trees that are in the lowland. <sup>28</sup> They brought horses for Solomon out of Egypt and out of all lands. <sup>29</sup> Now the rest of the acts of Solomon, first and last, aren't they written in the history of Nathan the prophet, and in the prophecy of Ahijah the Shilonite, and in the visions of Iddo the seer concerning Jeroboam the son of Nebat? <sup>30</sup> Solomon reigned in Jerusalem over all Israel forty years. <sup>31</sup> Solomon slept with his fathers, and he was buried in his father David's city; and Rehoboam his son reigned in his place.

## 10

<sup>1</sup> Rehoboam went to Shechem, for all Israel had come to Shechem to make him king. <sup>2</sup> When Jeroboam the son of Nebat heard of it (for he was in Egypt, where he had fled from the presence of King Solomon), Jeroboam returned out of Egypt. <sup>3</sup> They sent and called him; and Jeroboam and all Israel came, and they spoke to Rehoboam, saying, <sup>4</sup>"Your father made our yoke grievous. Now therefore make the grievous service of your father and his heavy yoke which he put on us, lighter, and we will serve you." <sup>5</sup> He said to them, "Come again to me after three days." So the people departed. <sup>6</sup> King Rehoboam took counsel with the old men, who had stood before Solomon his father while he yet lived, saying, "What counsel do you give me about how to answer these people?" <sup>7</sup> They spoke to him, saying, "If you are kind to these people, please them, and speak good words to them, then they will be your servants forever." <sup>8</sup> But he abandoned the counsel of the old men which they had given him, and took counsel with the young men who had grown up with him, who stood before him. <sup>9</sup> He said to them, "What counsel do you give, that we may give an answer to these people, who have spoken to me, saying, 'Make the yoke that your father put on us lighter'?" <sup>10</sup> The young men who had grown up with him spoke to him, saying, "Thus you shall tell the people who spoke to you, saying, 'Your father made our yoke heavy, but make it lighter on us;' thus you shall say to them, 'My little finger is thicker than my father's waist. <sup>11</sup> Now whereas my father burdened you with a heavy yoke, I will add to your yoke. My father chastised you with whips, but I will chastise you with scorpions.'" <sup>12</sup> So Jeroboam and all the people came to Rehoboam the third day, as the king asked, saying, "Come to me again the third day." <sup>13</sup> The king answered them roughly; and King Rehoboam abandoned the counsel of the old men, <sup>14</sup> and spoke to them after the counsel of the young men, saying, "My father made your yoke heavy, but I will add to it. My father chastised you with whips, but I will chastise you with scorpions." <sup>15</sup> So the king didn't listen to the people; for it was brought about by God, that Yahweh might establish his word, which he spoke by Ahijah the Shilonite to Jeroboam the son of Nebat. <sup>16</sup> When all Israel saw that the king didn't listen to them, the people answered the king, saying, "What portion do we have in David? We don't have an inheritance in the son of Jesse! Every man to your tents, Israel! Now see to your own house, David." So all Israel departed to their tents. <sup>17</sup> But as for the children of Israel who lived in the cities of Judah, Rehoboam reigned over them. <sup>18</sup> Then King Rehoboam sent

Hadoram, who was over the men subject to forced labor; and the children of Israel stoned him to death with stones. King Rehoboam hurried to get himself up to his chariot, to flee to Jerusalem. <sup>19</sup> So Israel rebelled against David's house to this day.

## 11

<sup>1</sup> When Rehoboam had come to Jerusalem, he assembled the house of Judah and Benjamin, one hundred eighty thousand chosen men who were warriors, to fight against Israel, to bring the kingdom again to Rehoboam. <sup>2</sup> But Yahweh's word came to Shemaiah the man of God, saying, <sup>3</sup>"Speak to Rehoboam the son of Solomon, king of Judah, and to all Israel in Judah and Benjamin, saying, <sup>4</sup>'Yahweh says, "You shall not go up, nor fight against your brothers! Every man return to his house; for this thing is of me."'" So they listened to Yahweh's words, and returned from going against Jeroboam. <sup>5</sup> Rehoboam lived in Jerusalem, and built cities for defense in Judah. <sup>6</sup> He built Bethlehem, Etam, Tekoa, <sup>7</sup> Beth Zur, Soco, Adullam, <sup>8</sup> Gath, Mareshah, Ziph, <sup>9</sup> Adoraim, Lachish, Azekah, <sup>10</sup> Zorah, Aijalon, and Hebron, which are fortified cities in Judah and in Benjamin. <sup>11</sup> He fortified the strongholds and put captains in them with stores of food, oil and wine. <sup>12</sup> He put shields and spears in every city, and made them exceedingly strong. Judah and Benjamin belonged to him. <sup>13</sup> The priests and the Levites who were in all Israel stood with him out of all their territory. <sup>14</sup> For the Levites left their pasture lands and their possessions, and came to Judah and Jerusalem; for Jeroboam and his sons cast them off, that they should not execute the priest's office to Yahweh. <sup>15</sup> He himself appointed priests for the high places, for the male goat and calf idols which he had made. <sup>16</sup> After them, out of all the tribes of Israel, those who set their hearts to seek Yahweh, the God of Israel, came to Jerusalem to sacrifice to Yahweh, the God of their fathers. <sup>17</sup> So they strengthened the kingdom of Judah and made Rehoboam the son of Solomon strong for three years, for they walked three years in the way of David and Solomon. <sup>18</sup> Rehoboam took a wife for himself, Mahalath the daughter of Jerimoth the son of David and of Abihail the daughter of Eliab the son of Jesse. <sup>19</sup> She bore him sons: Jeush, Shemariah, and Zaham. <sup>20</sup> After her, he took Maacah the granddaughter of Absalom; and she bore him Abijah, Attai, Ziza, and Shelomith. <sup>21</sup> Rehoboam loved Maacah the granddaughter of Absalom above all his wives and his concubines; for he took eighteen wives and sixty concubines, and became the father of twenty-eight sons and sixty daughters. <sup>22</sup> Rehoboam appointed Abijah the son of Maacah to be chief, the prince among his brothers, for he intended to make him king. <sup>23</sup> He dealt wisely, and dispersed some of his sons throughout all the lands of Judah and Benjamin, to every fortified city. He gave them food in abundance; and he sought many wives for them.

## 12

<sup>1</sup> When the kingdom of Rehoboam was established and he was strong, he abandoned Yahweh's law, and all Israel with him. <sup>2</sup> In the fifth year of King Rehoboam, Shishak king of Egypt came up against Jerusalem, because they had trespassed against Yahweh, <sup>3</sup> with twelve hundred chariots and sixty thousand horsemen. The people were without number who came with him out of Egypt: the Lubim, the Sukkiim, and the Ethiopians. <sup>4</sup> He took the fortified cities which belonged to Judah, and came to Jerusalem. <sup>5</sup> Now Shemaiah the prophet came to Rehoboam and to the princes of Judah, who were gathered together to Jerusalem because of Shishak, and said to them, "Yahweh says, 'You have forsaken me, therefore I have also left you in the hand of Shishak.'" <sup>6</sup> Then the princes of Israel and the king humbled themselves; and they said, "Yahweh is righteous." <sup>7</sup> When Yahweh saw that they humbled themselves, Yahweh's word came to Shemaiah, saying, "They have humbled themselves. I will not destroy them, but I will grant them some deliverance, and my wrath won't be poured out on Jerusalem by the hand of Shishak. <sup>8</sup> Nevertheless they will be his servants, that they may know my service, and the service of the kingdoms of the countries." <sup>9</sup> So Shishak king of Egypt came up against Jerusalem and took away the treasures of Yahweh's house and the treasures of the king's house. He took it all away. He also took away the shields of gold which Solomon had made. <sup>10</sup> King Rehoboam made shields of bronze in their place, and committed them to the hands of the captains of the guard, who kept the door of the king's house. <sup>11</sup> As often as the king entered into Yahweh's house, the guard came and bore them, then brought them back into the guard room. <sup>12</sup> When he humbled himself, Yahweh's wrath turned from him, so as not to destroy him altogether. Moreover, there were good things found in Judah. <sup>13</sup> So King Rehoboam strengthened himself in Jerusalem and reigned; for Rehoboam was forty-one years old when he began to reign, and he

---

<sup>a</sup> *9:13 A talent is about 30 kilograms or 66 pounds or 965 Troy ounces, so 666 talents is about 20 metric tons*

<sup>b</sup> *9:15 A shekel is about 10 grams or about 0.32 Troy ounces, so 600 shekels was*

about 6 kilograms or about 192 Troy ounces.
<sup>c</sup> *9:16 A shekel is about 10 grams or about 0.32 Troy*

ounces, so 300 shekels was about 3 kilograms or about 96 Troy ounces.

reigned seventeen years in Jerusalem, the city which Yahweh had chosen out of all the tribes of Israel to put his name there. His mother's name was Naamah the Ammonitess. **14** He did that which was evil, because he didn't set his heart to seek Yahweh. **15** Now the acts of Rehoboam, first and last, aren't they written in the histories of Shemaiah the prophet and of Iddo the seer, in the genealogies? There were wars between Rehoboam and Jeroboam continually. **16** Rehoboam slept with his fathers, and was buried in David's city; and Abijah his son reigned in his place.

## 13

**1** In the eighteenth year of King Jeroboam, Abijah began to reign over Judah. **2** He reigned three years in Jerusalem. His mother's name was Micaiah the daughter of Uriel of Gibeah. There was war between Abijah and Jeroboam. **3** Abijah joined battle with an army of valiant men of war, even four hundred thousand chosen men; and Jeroboam set the battle in array against him with eight hundred thousand chosen men, who were mighty men of valor. **4** Abijah stood up on Mount Zemaraim, which is in the hill country of Ephraim, and said, "Hear me, Jeroboam and all Israel: **5** Ought you not to know that Yahweh, the God of Israel, gave the kingdom over Israel to David forever, even to him and to his sons by a covenant of salt? **6** Yet Jeroboam the son of Nebat, the servant of Solomon the son of David, rose up, and rebelled against his lord. **7** Worthless men were gathered to him, wicked fellows who strengthened themselves against Rehoboam the son of Solomon, when Rehoboam was young and tender hearted, and could not withstand them. **8** "Now you intend to withstand the kingdom of Yahweh in the hand of the sons of David. You are a great multitude, and the golden calves which Jeroboam made you for gods are with you. **9** Haven't you driven out the priests of Yahweh, the sons of Aaron, and the Levites, and made priests for yourselves according to the ways of the peoples of other lands? Whoever comes to consecrate himself with a young bull and seven rams may be a priest of those who are no gods. **10** "But as for us, Yahweh is our God, and we have not forsaken him. We have priests serving Yahweh, the sons of Aaron, and the Levites in their work. **11** They burn to Yahweh every morning and every evening burnt offerings and sweet incense. They also set the show bread in order on the pure table, and care for the gold lamp stand with its lamps, to burn every evening; for we keep the instruction of Yahweh our God, but you have forsaken him. **12** Behold, God is with us at our head, and his priests with the trumpets of alarm to sound an alarm against you. Children of Israel, don't fight against Yahweh, the God of your fathers; for you will not prosper." **13** But Jeroboam caused an ambush to come about behind them; so they were before Judah, and the ambush was behind them. **14** When Judah looked back, behold, the battle was before and behind them; and they cried to Yahweh, and the priests sounded with the trumpets. **15** Then the men of Judah gave a shout. As the men of Judah shouted, God struck Jeroboam and all Israel before Abijah and Judah. **16** The children of Israel fled before Judah, and God delivered them into their hand. **17** Abijah and his people killed them with a great slaughter, so five hundred thousand chosen men of Israel fell down slain. **18** Thus the children of Israel were brought under at that time, and the children of Judah prevailed, because they relied on Yahweh, the God of their fathers. **19** Abijah pursued Jeroboam, and took cities from him: Bethel with its villages, Jeshanah with its villages, and Ephron with its villages. **20** Jeroboam didn't recover strength again in the days of Abijah. Yahweh struck him, and he died. **21** But Abijah grew mighty and took for himself fourteen wives, and became the father of twenty-two sons and sixteen daughters. **22** The rest of the acts of Abijah, his ways, and his sayings are written in the commentary of the prophet Iddo.

## 14

**1** So Abijah slept with his fathers, and they buried him in David's city; and Asa his son reigned in his place. In his days, the land was quiet ten years. **2** Asa did that which was good and right in Yahweh his God's eyes, **3** for he took away the foreign altars and the high places, broke down the pillars, cut down the Asherah poles, **4** and commanded Judah to seek Yahweh, the God of their fathers, and to obey his law and command. **5** Also he took away out of all the cities of Judah the high places and the sun images; and the kingdom was quiet before him. **6** He built fortified cities in Judah; for the land was quiet, and he had no war in those years, because Yahweh had given him rest. **7** For he said to Judah, "Let's build these cities and make walls around them, with towers, gates, and bars. The land is yet before us, because we have sought Yahweh our God. We have sought him, and he has given us rest on every side." So they built and prospered. **8** Asa had an army of three hundred thousand out of Judah who bore bucklers and spears, and two hundred eighty thousand out of Benjamin who bore shields and drew bows. All these were mighty men of valor. **9** Zerah the Ethiopian came out against them with an army of a million troops and three hundred chariots, and he came to Mareshah. **10** Then Asa went out to meet him,

and they set the battle in array in the valley of Zephathah at Mareshah. **11** Asa cried to Yahweh his God, and said, "Yahweh, there is no one besides you to help, between the mighty and him who has no strength. Help us, Yahweh our God; for we rely on you, and in your name are we come against this multitude. Yahweh, you are our God. Don't let man prevail against you." **12** So Yahweh struck the Ethiopians before Asa and before Judah; and the Ethiopians fled. **13** Asa and the people who were with him pursued them to Gerar. So many of the Ethiopians fell that they could not recover themselves, for they were destroyed before Yahweh and before his army. Judah's army carried away very much booty. **14** They struck all the cities around Gerar, for the fear of Yahweh came on them. They plundered all the cities, for there was much plunder in them. **15** They also struck the tents of those who had livestock, and carried away sheep and camels in abundance, then returned to Jerusalem.

## 15

**1** The Spirit of God came on Azariah the son of Oded. **2** He went out to meet Asa, and said to him, "Hear me, Asa, and all Judah and Benjamin! Yahweh is with you while you are with him; and if you seek him, he will be found by you; but if you forsake him, he will forsake you. **3** Now for a long time Israel was without the true God, without a teaching priest, and without law. **4** But when in their distress they turned to Yahweh, the God of Israel, and sought him, he was found by them. **5** In those times there was no peace to him who went out, nor to him who came in; but great troubles were on all the inhabitants of the lands. **6** They were broken in pieces, nation against nation, and city against city; for God troubled them with all adversity. **7** But you be strong! Don't let your hands be slack, for your work will be rewarded." **8** When Asa heard these words and the prophecy of Oded the prophet, he took courage, and put away the abominations out of all the land of Judah and Benjamin, and out of the cities which he had taken from the hill country of Ephraim; and he renewed Yahweh's altar that was before Yahweh's porch. **9** He gathered all Judah and Benjamin, and those who lived with them out of Ephraim, Manasseh, and Simeon; for they came to him out of Israel in abundance when they saw that Yahweh his God was with him. **10** So they gathered themselves together at Jerusalem in the third month, in the fifteenth year of Asa's reign. **11** They sacrificed to Yahweh in that day, of the plunder which they had brought, seven hundred head of cattle and seven thousand sheep. **12** They entered into the covenant to seek Yahweh, the God of their fathers, with all their heart and with all their soul; **13** and that whoever would not seek Yahweh, the God of Israel, should be put to death, whether small or great, whether man or woman. **14** They swore to Yahweh with a loud voice, with shouting, with trumpets, and with cornets. **15** All Judah rejoiced at the oath, for they had sworn with all their heart and sought him with their whole desire; and he was found by them. Then Yahweh gave them rest all around. **16** Also Maacah, the mother of Asa the king, he removed from being queen mother, because she had made an abominable image for an Asherah; so Asa cut down her image, ground it into dust, and burned it at the brook Kidron. **17** But the high places were not taken away out of Israel; nevertheless the heart of Asa was perfect all his days. **18** He brought the things that his father had dedicated and that he himself had dedicated, silver, gold, and vessels into God's house. **19** There was no more war to the thirty-fifth year of Asa's reign.

## 16

**1** In the thirty-sixth year of Asa's reign, Baasha king of Israel went up against Judah, and built Ramah, that he might not allow anyone to go out or come in to Asa king of Judah. **2** Then Asa brought out silver and gold out of the treasures of Yahweh's house and of the king's house, and sent to Ben Hadad king of Syria, who lived at Damascus, saying, **3** "Let there be a treaty between me and you, as there was between my father and your father. Behold, I have sent you silver and gold. Go, break your treaty with Baasha king of Israel, that he may depart from me." **4** Ben Hadad listened to King Asa, and sent the captains of his armies against the cities of Israel; and they struck Ijon, Dan, Abel Maim, and all the storage cities of Naphtali. **5** When Baasha heard of it, he stopped building Ramah, and let his work cease. **6** Then Asa the king took all Judah, and they carried away the stones and timber of Ramah, with which Baasha had built; and he built Geba and Mizpah with them. **7** At that time Hanani the seer came to Asa king of Judah, and said to him, "Because you have relied on the king of Syria, and have not relied on Yahweh your God, therefore the army of the king of Syria has escaped out of your hand. **8** Weren't the Ethiopians and the Lubim a huge army, with chariots and exceedingly many horsemen? Yet, because you relied on Yahweh, he delivered them into your hand. **9** For Yahweh's eyes run back and forth throughout the whole earth, to show himself strong in the behalf of them whose heart is perfect toward him. You have done foolishly in this; for from now on you will have wars." **10** Then Asa was angry with the seer, and put him in the prison; for he was in a rage with him because of this thing. Asa oppressed some of the people at the same time. <sup>11</sup> Behold, the acts of Asa, first and last, behold, they are written in the book of the kings of Judah and Israel. <sup>12</sup> In the thirty-ninth year of his reign, Asa was diseased in his feet. His disease was exceedingly great; yet in his disease he didn't seek Yahweh, but just the physicians. <sup>13</sup> Asa slept with his fathers, and died in the forty-first year of his reign. <sup>14</sup> They buried him in his own tomb, which he had dug out for himself in David's city, and laid him in the bed which was filled with sweet odors and various kinds of spices prepared by the perfumers' art; and they made a very great fire for him.

## 17

<sup>1</sup> Jehoshaphat his son reigned in his place, and strengthened himself against Israel. <sup>2</sup> He placed forces in all the fortified cities of Judah, and set garrisons in the land of Judah and in the cities of Ephraim, which Asa his father had taken. <sup>3</sup> Yahweh was with Jehoshaphat, because he walked in the first ways of his father David, and didn't seek the Baals, <sup>4</sup> but sought the God of his father, and walked in his commandments, and not in the ways of Israel. <sup>5</sup> Therefore Yahweh established the kingdom in his hand. All Judah brought tribute to Jehoshaphat, and he had riches and honor in abundance. <sup>6</sup> His heart was lifted up in the ways of Yahweh. Furthermore, he took away the high places and the Asherah poles out of Judah. <sup>7</sup> Also in the third year of his reign he sent his princes, even Ben Hail, Obadiah, Zechariah, Nethanel, and Micaiah, to teach in the cities of Judah; <sup>8</sup> and with them Levites, even Shemaiah, Nethaniah, Zebadiah, Asahel, Shemiramoth, Jehonathan, Adonijah, Tobijah, and Tobadonijah, the Levites; and with them Elishama and Jehoram, the priests. <sup>9</sup> They taught in Judah, having the book of Yahweh's law with them. They went about throughout all the cities of Judah and taught among the people. <sup>10</sup> The fear of Yahweh fell on all the kingdoms of the lands that were around Judah, so that they made no war against Jehoshaphat. <sup>11</sup> Some of the Philistines brought Jehoshaphat presents and silver for tribute. The Arabians also brought him flocks: seven thousand seven hundred rams and seven thousand seven hundred male goats. <sup>12</sup> Jehoshaphat grew great exceedingly; and he built fortresses and store cities in Judah. <sup>13</sup> He had many works in the cities of Judah; and men of war, mighty men of valor, in Jerusalem. <sup>14</sup> This was the numbering of them according to their fathers' houses: From Judah, the captains of thousands: Adnah the captain, and with him three hundred thousand mighty men of valor; <sup>15</sup> and next to him Jehohanan the captain, and with him two hundred eighty thousand; <sup>16</sup> and next to him Amasiah the son of Zichri, who willingly offered himself to Yahweh, and with him two hundred thousand mighty men of valor. <sup>17</sup> From Benjamin: Eliada, a mighty man of valor, and with him two hundred thousand armed with bow and shield; <sup>18</sup> and next to him Jehozabad, and with him one hundred eighty thousand ready and prepared for war. <sup>19</sup> These were those who waited on the king, in addition to those whom the king put in the fortified cities throughout all Judah.

## 18

<sup>1</sup> Now Jehoshaphat had riches and honor in abundance; and he allied himself with Ahab. <sup>2</sup> After some years, he went down to Ahab to Samaria. Ahab killed sheep and cattle for him in abundance, and for the people who were with him, and moved him to go up with him to Ramoth Gilead. <sup>3</sup> Ahab king of Israel said to Jehoshaphat king of Judah, "Will you go with me to Ramoth Gilead?" He answered him, "I am as you are, and my people as your people. We will be with you in the war." <sup>4</sup> Jehoshaphat said to the king of Israel, "Please inquire first for Yahweh's word." <sup>5</sup> Then the king of Israel gathered the prophets together, four hundred men, and said to them, "Shall we go to Ramoth Gilead to battle, or shall I forbear?" They said, "Go up, for God will deliver it into the hand of the king." <sup>6</sup> But Jehoshaphat said, "Isn't there here a prophet of Yahweh besides, that we may inquire of him?" <sup>7</sup> The king of Israel said to Jehoshaphat, "There is yet one man by whom we may inquire of Yahweh; but I hate him, for he never prophesies good concerning me, but always evil. He is Micaiah the son of Imla." Jehoshaphat said, "Don't let the king say so." <sup>8</sup> Then the king of Israel called an officer, and said, "Get Micaiah the son of Imla quickly." <sup>9</sup> Now the king of Israel and Jehoshaphat the king of Judah each sat on his throne, arrayed in their robes, and they were sitting in an open place at the entrance of the gate of Samaria; and all the prophets were prophesying before them. <sup>10</sup> Zedekiah the son of Chenaanah made himself horns of iron and said, "Yahweh says, 'With these you shall push the Syrians, until they are consumed.'" <sup>11</sup> All the prophets prophesied so, saying, "Go up to Ramoth Gilead, and prosper; for Yahweh will deliver it into the hand of the king." <sup>12</sup> The messenger who went to call Micaiah spoke to him, saying, "Behold, the words of the prophets declare good to the king with one mouth. Let your word therefore, please be like one of theirs, and speak good." <sup>13</sup> Micaiah said, "As Yahweh lives, I will say what my God says." <sup>14</sup> When he had come to the king, the king said to him, "Micaiah, shall we go to Ramoth

Gilead to battle, or shall I forbear?" He said, "Go up, and prosper. They shall be delivered into your hand." <sup>15</sup> The king said to him, "How many times shall I adjure you that you speak to me nothing but the truth in Yahweh's name?" <sup>16</sup> He said, "I saw all Israel scattered on the mountains, as sheep that have no shepherd. Yahweh said, 'These have no master. Let them each return to his house in peace.'" <sup>17</sup> The king of Israel said to Jehoshaphat, "Didn't I tell you that he would not prophesy good concerning me, but evil?" <sup>18</sup> Micaiah said, "Therefore hear Yahweh's word: I saw Yahweh sitting on his throne, and all the army of heaven standing on his right hand and on his left. <sup>19</sup> Yahweh said, 'Who will entice Ahab king of Israel, that he may go up and fall at Ramoth Gilead?' One spoke saying in this way, and another saying in that way. <sup>20</sup> A spirit came out, stood before Yahweh, and said, 'I will entice him.' "Yahweh said to him, 'How?' <sup>21</sup>He said, 'I will go, and will be a lying spirit in the mouth of all his prophets.' He said, 'You will entice him, and will prevail also. Go and do so.' <sup>22</sup>"Now therefore, behold, Yahweh has put a lying spirit in the mouth of these your prophets; and Yahweh has spoken evil concerning you." <sup>23</sup> Then Zedekiah the son of Chenaanah came near, and struck Micaiah on the cheek, and said, "Which way did Yahweh's Spirit go from me to speak to you?" <sup>24</sup> Micaiah said, "Behold, you shall see on that day, when you go into an inner room to hide yourself." <sup>25</sup> The king of Israel said, "Take Micaiah, and carry him back to Amon the governor of the city, and to Joash the king's son; <sup>26</sup> and say, 'The king says, "Put this fellow in the prison, and feed him with bread of affliction and with water of affliction, until I return in peace."'" <sup>27</sup> Micaiah said, "If you return at all in peace, Yahweh has not spoken by me." He said, "Listen, you people, all of you!" <sup>28</sup> So the king of Israel and Jehoshaphat the king of Judah went up to Ramoth Gilead. <sup>29</sup> The king of Israel said to Jehoshaphat, "I will disguise myself, and go into the battle; but you put on your robes." So the king of Israel disguised himself; and they went into the battle. <sup>30</sup> Now the king of Syria had commanded the captains of his chariots, saying, "Don't fight with small nor great, except only with the king of Israel." <sup>31</sup> When the captains of the chariots saw Jehoshaphat, they said, "It is the king of Israel!" Therefore they turned around to fight against him. But Jehoshaphat cried out, and Yahweh helped him; and God moved them to depart from him. <sup>32</sup> When the captains of the chariots saw that it was not the king of Israel, they turned back from pursuing him. <sup>33</sup> A certain man drew his bow at random, and struck the king of Israel between the joints of the armor. Therefore he said to the driver of the chariot, "Turn around and carry me out of the battle, for I am severely wounded." <sup>34</sup> The battle increased that day. However, the king of Israel propped himself up in his chariot against the Syrians until the evening; and at about sunset, he died.

## 19

<sup>1</sup> Jehoshaphat the king of Judah returned to his house in peace to Jerusalem. <sup>2</sup> Jehu the son of Hanani the seer went out to meet him, and said to King Jehoshaphat, "Should you help the wicked, and love those who hate Yahweh? Because of this, wrath is on you from before Yahweh. <sup>3</sup> Nevertheless there are good things found in you, in that you have put away the Asheroth out of the land, and have set your heart to seek God." <sup>4</sup> Jehoshaphat lived at Jerusalem; and he went out again among the people from Beersheba to the hill country of Ephraim, and brought them back to Yahweh, the God of their fathers. <sup>5</sup> He set judges in the land throughout all the fortified cities of Judah, city by city, <sup>6</sup> and said to the judges, "Consider what you do, for you don't judge for man, but for Yahweh; and he is with you in the judgment. <sup>7</sup> Now therefore let the fear of Yahweh be on you. Take heed and do it; for there is no iniquity with Yahweh our God, nor respect of persons, nor taking of bribes." <sup>8</sup> Moreover in Jerusalem Jehoshaphat appointed certain Levites, priests, and heads of the fathers' households of Israel to give judgment for Yahweh and for controversies. They returned to Jerusalem. <sup>9</sup> He commanded them, saying, "You shall do this in the fear of Yahweh, faithfully, and with a perfect heart. <sup>10</sup> Whenever any controversy comes to you from your brothers who dwell in their cities, between blood and blood, between law and commandment, statutes and ordinances, you must warn them, that they not be guilty toward Yahweh, and so wrath come on you and on your brothers. Do this, and you will not be guilty. <sup>11</sup> Behold, Amariah the chief priest is over you in all matters of Yahweh; and Zebadiah the son of Ishmael, the ruler of the house of Judah, in all the king's matters. Also the Levites shall be officers before you. Deal courageously, and may Yahweh be with the good."

## 20

<sup>1</sup> After this, the children of Moab, the children of Ammon, and with them some of the Ammonites, came against Jehoshaphat to battle. <sup>2</sup> Then some came who told Jehoshaphat, saying, "A great multitude is coming against you from beyond the sea from Syria. Behold, they are in Hazazon Tamar" (that is, En Gedi). <sup>3</sup> Jehoshaphat was alarmed, and set himself to seek to Yahweh. He proclaimed a fast throughout all

Judah. ⁴ Judah gathered themselves together to seek help from Yahweh. They came out of all the cities of Judah to seek Yahweh. ⁵ Jehoshaphat stood in the assembly of Judah and Jerusalem, in Yahweh's house, before the new court; ⁶ and he said, "Yahweh, the God of our fathers, aren't you God in heaven? Aren't you ruler over all the kingdoms of the nations? Power and might are in your hand, so that no one is able to withstand you. ⁷ Didn't you, our God, drive out the inhabitants of this land before your people Israel, and give it to the offspringᵃ of Abraham your friend forever? ⁸ They lived in it, and have built you a sanctuary in it for your name, saying, ⁹ 'If evil comes on us—the sword, judgment, pestilence, or famine—we will stand before this house, and before you (for your name is in this house), and cry to you in our affliction, and you will hear and save.' ¹⁰ Now, behold, the children of Ammon and Moab and Mount Seir, whom you would not let Israel invade when they came out of the land of Egypt, but they turned away from them, and didn't destroy them; ¹¹ behold, how they reward us, to come to cast us out of your possession, which you have given us to inherit. ¹² Our God, will you not judge them? For we have no might against this great company that comes against us. We don't know what to do, but our eyes are on you." ¹³ All Judah stood before Yahweh, with their little ones, their wives, and their children. ¹⁴ Then Yahweh's Spirit came on Jahaziel the son of Zechariah, the son of Benaiah, the son of Jeiel, the son of Mattaniah, the Levite, of the sons of Asaph, in the middle of the assembly; ¹⁵ and he said, "Listen, all Judah, and you inhabitants of Jerusalem, and you, King Jehoshaphat. Yahweh says to you, 'Don't be afraid, and don't be dismayed because of this great multitude; for the battle is not yours, but God's. ¹⁶ Tomorrow, go down against them. Behold, they are coming up by the ascent of Ziz. You will find them at the end of the valley, before the wilderness of Jeruel. ¹⁷ You will not need to fight this battle. Set yourselves, stand still, and see the salvation of Yahweh with you, O Judah and Jerusalem. Don't be afraid, nor be dismayed. Go out against them tomorrow, for Yahweh is with you.'" ¹⁸ Jehoshaphat bowed his head with his face to the ground; and all Judah and the inhabitants of Jerusalem fell down before Yahweh, worshiping Yahweh. ¹⁹ The Levites, of the children of the Kohathites and of the children of the Korahites, stood up to praise Yahweh, the God of Israel, with an exceedingly loud voice. ²⁰ They rose early in the morning and went out into the wilderness of Tekoa. As they went out, Jehoshaphat stood and said, "Listen to me, Judah and you inhabitants of Jerusalem! Believe in Yahweh your God, so you will be established! Believe his prophets, so you will prosper." ²¹ When he had taken counsel with the people, he appointed those who were to sing to Yahweh and give praise in holy array as they go out before the army, and say, "Give thanks to Yahweh, for his loving kindness endures forever." ²² When they began to sing and to praise, Yahweh set ambushers against the children of Ammon, Moab, and Mount Seir, who had come against Judah; and they were struck. ²³ For the children of Ammon and Moab stood up against the inhabitants of Mount Seir to utterly kill and destroy them. When they had finished the inhabitants of Seir, everyone helped to destroy each other. ²⁴ When Judah came to the place overlooking the wilderness, they looked at the multitude; and behold, they were dead bodies fallen to the earth, and there were none who escaped. ²⁵ When Jehoshaphat and his people came to take their plunder, they found among them in abundance both riches and dead bodies with precious jewels, which they stripped off for themselves, more than they could carry away. They took plunder for three days, it was so much. ²⁶ On the fourth day, they assembled themselves in Beracahᵇ Valley, for there they blessed Yahweh. Therefore the name of that place was called "Beracah Valley" to this day. ²⁷ Then they returned, every man of Judah and Jerusalem, with Jehoshaphat in front of them, to go again to Jerusalem with joy; for Yahweh had made them to rejoice over their enemies. ²⁸ They came to Jerusalem with stringed instruments, harps, and trumpets to Yahweh's house. ²⁹ The fear of God was on all the kingdoms of the countries when they heard that Yahweh fought against the enemies of Israel. ³⁰ So the realm of Jehoshaphat was quiet, for his God gave him rest all around. ³¹ So Jehoshaphat reigned over Judah. He was thirty-five years old when he began to reign. He reigned twenty-five years in Jerusalem. His mother's name was Azubah the daughter of Shilhi. ³² He walked in the way of Asa his father, and didn't turn away from it, doing that which was right in Yahweh's eyes. ³³ However the high places were not taken away, and the people had still not set their hearts on the God of their fathers. ³⁴ Now the rest of the acts of Jehoshaphat, first and last, behold, they are written in the history of Jehu the son of Hanani, which is included in the book of the kings of Israel. ³⁵ After this, Jehoshaphat king of Judah joined himself with Ahaziah king of Israel. The same did very wickedly. ³⁶ He joined himself with him to make ships to go to Tarshish. They made the ships in Ezion Geber. ³⁷ Then Eliezer the son of Dodavahu of Mareshah prophesied against Jehoshaphat, saying, "Because you have joined yourself with Ahaziah, Yahweh has destroyed your works." The ships were wrecked, so that they were not able to go to Tarshish.

## 21

¹ Jehoshaphat slept with his fathers, and was buried with his fathers in David's city; and Jehoram his son reigned in his place. ² He had brothers, the sons of Jehoshaphat: Azariah, Jehiel, Zechariah, Azariah, Michael, and Shephatiah. All these were the sons of Jehoshaphat king of Israel. ³ Their father gave them great gifts of silver, of gold, and of precious things, with fortified cities in Judah; but he gave the kingdom to Jehoram, because he was the firstborn. ⁴ Now when Jehoram had risen up over the kingdom of his father, and had strengthened himself, he killed all his brothers with the sword, and also some of the princes of Israel. ⁵ Jehoram was thirty-two years old when he began to reign, and he reigned eight years in Jerusalem. ⁶ He walked in the way of the kings of Israel, as did Ahab's house, for he had Ahab's daughter as his wife. He did that which was evil in Yahweh's sight. ⁷ However Yahweh would not destroy David's house, because of the covenant that he had made with David, and as he promised to give a lamp to him and to his children always. ⁸ In his days Edom revolted from under the hand of Judah, and made a king over themselves. ⁹ Then Jehoram went there with his captains and all his chariots with him. He rose up by night and struck the Edomites who surrounded him, along with the captains of the chariots. ¹⁰ So Edom has been in revolt from under the hand of Judah to this day. Then Libnah revolted at the same time from under his hand, because he had forsaken Yahweh, the God of his fathers. ¹¹ Moreover he made high places in the mountains of Judah, and made the inhabitants of Jerusalem play the prostitute, and led Judah astray. ¹² A letter came to him from Elijah the prophet, saying, "Yahweh, the God of David your father, says, 'Because you have not walked in the ways of Jehoshaphat your father, nor in the ways of Asa king of Judah, ¹³ but have walked in the way of the kings of Israel, and have made Judah and the inhabitants of Jerusalem to play the prostitute like Ahab's house did, and also have slain your brothers of your father's house, who were better than yourself, ¹⁴ behold, Yahweh will strike your people with a great plague, including your children, your wives, and all your possessions; ¹⁵ and you will have great sickness with a disease of your bowels, until your bowels fall out by reason of the sickness, day by day.'" ¹⁶ Yahweh stirred up against Jehoram the spirit of the Philistines and of the Arabians who are beside the Ethiopians; ¹⁷ and they came up against Judah, broke into it, and carried away all the possessions that were found in the king's house, including his sons and his wives, so that there was no son left to him except Jehoahaz, the youngest of his sons. ¹⁸ After all this Yahweh struck him in his bowels with an incurable disease. ¹⁹ In process of time, at the end of two years, his bowels fell out by reason of his sickness, and he died of severe diseases. His people made no burning for him, like the burning of his fathers. ²⁰ He was thirty-two years old when he began to reign, and he reigned in Jerusalem eight years. He departed with no one's regret. They buried him in David's city, but not in the tombs of the kings.

## 22

¹ The inhabitants of Jerusalem made Ahaziah his youngest son king in his place, because the band of men who came with the Arabians to the camp had slain all the oldest. So Ahaziah the son of Jehoram king of Judah reigned. ² Ahaziah was forty-two years old when he began to reign, and he reigned one year in Jerusalem. His mother's name was Athaliah the daughter of Omri. ³ He also walked in the ways of Ahab's house, because his mother was his counselor in acting wickedly. ⁴ He did that which was evil in Yahweh's sight, as did Ahab's house, for they were his counselors after the death of his father, to his destruction. ⁵ He also followed their counsel, and went with Jehoram the son of Ahab king of Israel to war against Hazael king of Syria at Ramoth Gilead; and the Syrians wounded Joram. ⁶ He returned to be healed in Jezreel of the wounds which they had given him at Ramah, when he fought against Hazael king of Syria. Azariah the son of Jehoram, king of Judah, went down to see Jehoram the son of Ahab in Jezreel, because he was sick. ⁷ Now the destruction of Ahaziah was of God, in that he went to Joram; for when he had come, he went out with Jehoram against Jehu the son of Nimshi, whom Yahweh had anointed to cut off Ahab's house. ⁸ When Jehu was executing judgment on Ahab's house, he found the princes of Judah and the sons of the brothers of Ahaziah serving Ahaziah, and killed them. ⁹ He sought Ahaziah, and they caught him (now he was hiding in Samaria), and they brought him to Jehu and killed him; and they buried him, for they said, "He is the son of Jehoshaphat, who sought Yahweh with all his heart." The house of Ahaziah had no power to hold the kingdom. ¹⁰ Now when Athaliah the

mother of Ahaziah saw that her son was dead, she arose and destroyed all the royal offspring of the house of Judah. <sup>11</sup> But Jehoshabeath, the king's daughter, took Joash the son of Ahaziah, and stealthily rescued him from among the king's sons who were slain, and put him and his nurse in the bedroom. So Jehoshabeath, the daughter of King Jehoram, the wife of Jehoiada the priest (for she was the sister of Ahaziah), hid him from Athaliah, so that she didn't kill him. <sup>12</sup> He was with them hidden in God's house six years while Athaliah reigned over the land.

## 23

<sup>1</sup> In the seventh year, Jehoiada strengthened himself, and took the captains of hundreds—Azariah the son of Jeroham, Ishmael the son of Jehohanan, Azariah the son of Obed, Maaseiah the son of Adaiah, and Elishaphat the son of Zichri—into a covenant with him. <sup>2</sup> They went around in Judah and gathered the Levites out of all the cities of Judah, and the heads of fathers' households of Israel, and they came to Jerusalem. <sup>3</sup> All the assembly made a covenant with the king in God's house. Jehoiada<sup>a</sup> said to them, "Behold, the king's son must reign, as Yahweh has spoken concerning the sons of David. <sup>4</sup> This is the thing that you must do: a third part of you, who come in on the Sabbath, of the priests and of the Levites, shall be gatekeepers of the thresholds. <sup>5</sup> A third part shall be at the king's house; and a third part at the gate of the foundation. All the people will be in the courts of Yahweh's house. <sup>6</sup> But let no one come into Yahweh's house except the priests and those who minister of the Levites. They shall come in, for they are holy, but all the people shall follow Yahweh's instructions. <sup>7</sup> The Levites shall surround the king, every man with his weapons in his hand. Whoever comes into the house, let him be slain. Be with the king when he comes in and when he goes out." <sup>8</sup> So the Levites and all Judah did according to all that Jehoiada the priest commanded. They each took his men, those who were to come in on the Sabbath, with those who were to go out on the Sabbath, for Jehoiada the priest didn't dismiss the shift. <sup>9</sup> Jehoiada the priest delivered to the captains of hundreds the spears, bucklers, and shields that had been king David's, which were in God's house. <sup>10</sup> He set all the people, every man with his weapon in his hand, from the right side of the house to the left side of the house, near the altar and the house, around the king. <sup>11</sup> Then they brought out the king's son, put the crown on him, gave him the covenant, and made him king. Jehoiada and his sons anointed him, and they said, "Long live the king!" <sup>12</sup> When Athaliah heard the noise of the people running and praising the king, she came to the people into Yahweh's house. <sup>13</sup> Then she looked, and behold, the king stood by his pillar at the entrance, with the captains and the trumpeters by the king. All the people of the land rejoiced and blew trumpets. The singers also played musical instruments, and led the singing of praise. Then Athaliah tore her clothes, and said, "Treason! treason!" <sup>14</sup> Jehoiada the priest brought out the captains of hundreds who were set over the army, and said to them, "Bring her out between the ranks; and whoever follows her, let him be slain with the sword." For the priest said, "Don't kill her in Yahweh's house." <sup>15</sup> So they made way for her. She went to the entrance of the horse gate to the king's house; and they killed her there. <sup>16</sup> Jehoiada made a covenant between himself, all the people, and the king, that they should be Yahweh's people. <sup>17</sup> All the people went to the house of Baal, broke it down, broke his altars and his images in pieces, and killed Mattan the priest of Baal before the altars. <sup>18</sup> Jehoiada appointed the officers of Yahweh's house under the hand of the Levitical priests, whom David had distributed in Yahweh's house, to offer the burnt offerings of Yahweh, as it is written in the law of Moses, with rejoicing and with singing, as David had ordered. <sup>19</sup> He set the gatekeepers at the gates of Yahweh's house, that no one who was unclean in anything should enter in. <sup>20</sup> He took the captains of hundreds, the nobles, the governors of the people, and all the people of the land, and brought the king down from Yahweh's house. They came through the upper gate to the king's house, and set the king on the throne of the kingdom. <sup>21</sup> So all the people of the land rejoiced, and the city was quiet. They had slain Athaliah with the sword.

## 24

<sup>1</sup> Joash was seven years old when he began to reign, and he reigned forty years in Jerusalem. His mother's name was Zibiah, of Beersheba. <sup>2</sup> Joash did that which was right in Yahweh's eyes all the days of Jehoiada the priest. <sup>3</sup> Jehoiada took for him two wives, and he became the father of sons and daughters. <sup>4</sup> After this, Joash intended to restore Yahweh's house. <sup>5</sup> He gathered together the priests and the Levites, and said to them, "Go out to the cities of Judah, and gather money to repair the house of your God from all Israel from year to year. See that you expedite this matter." However the Levites didn't do it right away. <sup>6</sup> The king called for Jehoiada the chief, and said to him, "Why haven't you required of the Levites to bring in the tax of Moses the servant of

Yahweh, and of the assembly of Israel, out of Judah and out of Jerusalem, for the Tent of the Testimony?" <sup>7</sup> For the sons of Athaliah, that wicked woman, had broken up God's house; and they also gave all the dedicated things of Yahweh's house to the Baals. <sup>8</sup> So the king commanded, and they made a chest, and set it outside at the gate of Yahweh's house. <sup>9</sup> They made a proclamation through Judah and Jerusalem, to bring in for Yahweh the tax that Moses the servant of God laid on Israel in the wilderness. <sup>10</sup> All the princes and all the people rejoiced, and brought in, and cast into the chest, until they had filled it. <sup>11</sup> Whenever the chest was brought to the king's officers by the hand of the Levites, and when they saw that there was much money, the king's scribe and the chief priest's officer came and emptied the chest, and took it, and carried it to its place again. Thus they did day by day, and gathered money in abundance. <sup>12</sup> The king and Jehoiada gave it to those who did the work of the service of Yahweh's house. They hired masons and carpenters to restore Yahweh's house, and also those who worked iron and bronze to repair Yahweh's house. <sup>13</sup> So the workmen worked, and the work of repairing went forward in their hands. They set up God's house as it was designed, and strengthened it. <sup>14</sup> When they had finished, they brought the rest of the money before the king and Jehoiada, from which were made vessels for Yahweh's house, even vessels with which to minister and to offer, including spoons and vessels of gold and silver. They offered burnt offerings in Yahweh's house continually all the days of Jehoiada. <sup>15</sup> But Jehoiada grew old and was full of days, and he died. He was one hundred thirty years old when he died. <sup>16</sup> They buried him in David's city among the kings, because he had done good in Israel, and toward God and his house. <sup>17</sup> Now after the death of Jehoiada, the princes of Judah came and bowed down to the king. Then the king listened to them. <sup>18</sup> They abandoned the house of Yahweh, the God of their fathers, and served the Asherah poles and the idols, so wrath came on Judah and Jerusalem for this their guiltiness. <sup>19</sup> Yet he sent prophets to them to bring them again to Yahweh, and they testified against them; but they would not listen. <sup>20</sup> The Spirit of God came on Zechariah the son of Jehoiada the priest; and he stood above the people, and said to them, "God says, 'Why do you disobey Yahweh's commandments, so that you can't prosper? Because you have forsaken Yahweh, he has also forsaken you.'" <sup>21</sup> They conspired against him, and stoned him with stones at the commandment of the king in the court of Yahweh's house. <sup>22</sup> Thus Joash the king didn't remember the kindness which Jehoiada his father had done to him, but killed his son. When he died, he said, "May Yahweh look at it, and repay it." <sup>23</sup> At the end of the year, the army of the Syrians came up against him. They came to Judah and Jerusalem, and destroyed all the princes of the people from among the people, and sent all their plunder to the king of Damascus. <sup>24</sup> For the army of the Syrians came with a small company of men; and Yahweh delivered a very great army into their hand, because they had forsaken Yahweh, the God of their fathers. So they executed judgment on Joash. <sup>25</sup> When they had departed from him (for they left him seriously wounded), his own servants conspired against him for the blood of the sons of Jehoiada the priest, and killed him on his bed, and he died. They buried him in David's city, but they didn't bury him in the tombs of the kings. <sup>26</sup> These are those who conspired against him: Zabad the son of Shimeath the Ammonitess and Jehozabad the son of Shimrith the Moabitess. <sup>27</sup> Now concerning his sons, the greatness of the burdens laid on him, and the rebuilding of God's house, behold, they are written in the commentary of the book of the kings. Amaziah his son reigned in his place.

## 25

<sup>1</sup> Amaziah was twenty-five years old when he began to reign, and he reigned twenty-nine years in Jerusalem. His mother's name was Jehoaddan, of Jerusalem. <sup>2</sup> He did that which was right in Yahweh's eyes, but not with a perfect heart. <sup>3</sup> Now when the kingdom was established to him, he killed his servants who had killed his father the king. <sup>4</sup> But he didn't put their children to death, but did according to that which is written in the law in the book of Moses, as Yahweh commanded, saying, "The fathers shall not die for the children, neither shall the children die for the fathers; but every man shall die for his own sin." <sup>5</sup> Moreover Amaziah gathered Judah together and ordered them according to their fathers' houses, under captains of thousands and captains of hundreds, even all Judah and Benjamin. He counted them from twenty years old and upward, and found that there were three hundred thousand chosen men, able to go out to war, who could handle spear and shield. <sup>6</sup> He also hired one hundred thousand mighty men of valor out of Israel for one hundred talents<sup>b</sup> of silver. <sup>7</sup> A man of God came to him, saying, "O king, don't let the army of Israel go with you, for Yahweh is not with Israel, with all the children of Ephraim. <sup>8</sup> But if you will go, take action, and be strong for the battle. God will overthrow

you before the enemy; for God has power to help, and to overthrow." [9] Amaziah said to the man of God, "But what shall we do for the hundred talents[a] which I have given to the army of Israel?" The man of God answered, "Yahweh is able to give you much more than this." [10] Then Amaziah separated them, the army that had come to him out of Ephraim, to go home again. Therefore their anger was greatly kindled against Judah, and they returned home in fierce anger. [11] Amaziah took courage, and led his people out and went to the Valley of Salt, and struck ten thousand of the children of Seir. [12] The children of Judah carried away ten thousand alive, and brought them to the top of the rock, and threw them down from the top of the rock, so that they all were broken in pieces. [13] But the men of the army whom Amaziah sent back, that they should not go with him to battle, fell on the cities of Judah from Samaria even to Beth Horon, and struck of them three thousand, and took much plunder. [14] Now after Amaziah had come from the slaughter of the Edomites, he brought the gods of the children of Seir, and set them up to be his gods, and bowed down himself before them and burned incense to them. [15] Therefore Yahweh's anger burned against Amaziah, and he sent to him a prophet who said to him, "Why have you sought after the gods of the people, which have not delivered their own people out of your hand?" [16] As he talked with him, the king said to him, "Have we made you one of the king's counselors? Stop! Why should you be struck down?" Then the prophet stopped, and said, "I know that God has determined to destroy you, because you have done this and have not listened to my counsel." [17] Then Amaziah king of Judah consulted his advisers, and sent to Joash, the son of Jehoahaz, the son of Jehu, king of Israel, saying, "Come! Let's look one another in the face." [18] Joash king of Israel sent to Amaziah king of Judah, saying, "The thistle that was in Lebanon sent to the cedar that was in Lebanon, saying, 'Give your daughter to my son as his wife. Then a wild animal that was in Lebanon passed by and trampled down the thistle. [19] You say to yourself that you have struck Edom; and your heart lifts you up to boast. Now stay at home. Why should you meddle with trouble, that you should fall, even you and Judah with you?'" [20] But Amaziah would not listen; for it was of God, that he might deliver them into the hand of their enemies, because they had sought after the gods of Edom. [21] So Joash king of Israel went up, and he and Amaziah king of Judah looked one another in the face at Beth Shemesh, which belongs to Judah. [22] Judah was defeated by Israel; so every man fled to his tent. [23] Joash king of Israel took Amaziah king of Judah, the son of Joash the son of Jehoahaz, at Beth Shemesh and brought him to Jerusalem, and broke down the wall of Jerusalem from the gate of Ephraim to the corner gate, four hundred cubits.[b] [24] He took all the gold and silver, and all the vessels that were found in God's house with Obed-Edom, and the treasures of the king's house, and the hostages, and returned to Samaria. [25] Amaziah the son of Joash, king of Judah, lived for fifteen years after the death of Joash, son of Jehoahaz, king of Israel. [26] Now the rest of the acts of Amaziah, first and last, behold, aren't they written in the book of the kings of Judah and Israel? [27] Now from the time that Amaziah turned away from following Yahweh, they made a conspiracy against him in Jerusalem. He fled to Lachish, but they sent after him to Lachish and killed him there. [28] They brought him on horses and buried him with his fathers in the City of Judah.

## 26

[1] All the people of Judah took Uzziah, who was sixteen years old, and made him king in the place of his father Amaziah. [2] He built Eloth and restored it to Judah. After that the king slept with his fathers. [3] Uzziah was sixteen years old when he began to reign; and he reigned fifty-two years in Jerusalem. His mother's name was Jechiliah, of Jerusalem. [4] He did that which was right in Yahweh's eyes, according to all that his father Amaziah had done. [5] He set himself to seek God in the days of Zechariah, who had understanding in the vision of God; and as long as he sought Yahweh, God made him prosper. [6] He went out and fought against the Philistines, and broke down the wall of Gath, the wall of Jabneh, and the wall of Ashdod; and he built cities in the country of Ashdod, and among the Philistines. [7] God helped him against the Philistines, and against the Arabians who lived in Gur Baal, and the Meunim. [8] The Ammonites gave tribute to Uzziah. His name spread abroad even to the entrance of Egypt, for he grew exceedingly strong. [9] Moreover Uzziah built towers in Jerusalem at the corner gate, at the valley gate, and at the turning of the wall, and fortified them. [10] He built towers in the wilderness, and dug out many cisterns, for he had much livestock, both in the lowlands and in the plains. He had farmers and vineyard keepers in the mountains and in the fruitful fields, for he loved farming. [11] Moreover Uzziah had an army of fighting men who went out to war by bands, according to the number of their reckoning made by Jeiel the scribe and Maaseiah the officer, under the hand of Hananiah, one of the king's captains. [12] The whole number of the heads of fathers' households, even the mighty men of valor, was two thousand six hundred. [13] Under their hand was an army, three hundred seven thousand five hundred, who made war with mighty power, to help the king against the enemy. [14] Uzziah prepared for them, even for all the army, shields, spears, helmets, coats of mail, bows, and stones for slinging. [15] In Jerusalem, he made devices, invented by skillful men, to be on the towers and on the battlements, with which to shoot arrows and great stones. His name spread far abroad, because he was marvelously helped until he was strong. [16] But when he was strong, his heart was lifted up, so that he did corruptly and he trespassed against Yahweh his God, for he went into Yahweh's temple to burn incense on the altar of incense. [17] Azariah the priest went in after him, and with him eighty priests of Yahweh, who were valiant men. [18] They resisted Uzziah the king, and said to him, "It isn't for you, Uzziah, to burn incense to Yahweh, but for the priests the sons of Aaron, who are consecrated to burn incense. Go out of the sanctuary, for you have trespassed. It will not be for your honor from Yahweh God." [19] Then Uzziah was angry. He had a censer in his hand to burn incense, and while he was angry with the priests, the leprosy broke out on his forehead before the priests in Yahweh's house, beside the altar of incense. [20] Azariah the chief priest and all the priests looked at him, and behold, he was leprous in his forehead; and they thrust him out quickly from there. Indeed, he himself also hurried to go out, because Yahweh had struck him. [21] Uzziah the king was a leper to the day of his death, and lived in a separate house, being a leper; for he was cut off from Yahweh's house. Jotham his son was over the king's house, judging the people of the land. [22] Now the rest of the acts of Uzziah, first and last, Isaiah the prophet, the son of Amoz, wrote. [23] So Uzziah slept with his fathers; and they buried him with his fathers in the field of burial which belonged to the kings, for they said, "He is a leper." Jotham his son reigned in his place.

## 27

[1] Jotham was twenty-five years old when he began to reign, and he reigned sixteen years in Jerusalem. His mother's name was Jerushah the daughter of Zadok. [2] He did that which was right in Yahweh's eyes, according to all that his father Uzziah had done. However he didn't enter into Yahweh's temple. The people still acted corruptly. [3] He built the upper gate of Yahweh's house, and he built much on the wall of Ophel. [4] Moreover he built cities in the hill country of Judah, and in the forests he built fortresses and towers. [5] He also fought with the king of the children of Ammon, and prevailed against them. The children of Ammon gave him the same year one hundred talents[c] of silver, ten thousand cors[d] of wheat, and ten thousand cors of barley.[e] The children of Ammon also gave that much to him in the second year, and in the third. [6] So Jotham became mighty, because he ordered his ways before Yahweh his God. [7] Now the rest of the acts of Jotham, and all his wars and his ways, behold, they are written in the book of the kings of Israel and Judah. [8] He was twenty-five years old when he began to reign, and reigned sixteen years in Jerusalem. [9] Jotham slept with his fathers, and they buried him in David's city; and Ahaz his son reigned in his place.

## 28

[1] Ahaz was twenty years old when he began to reign, and he reigned sixteen years in Jerusalem. He didn't do that which was right in Yahweh's eyes, like David his father, [2] but he walked in the ways of the kings of Israel, and also made molten images for the Baals. [3] Moreover he burned incense in the valley of the son of Hinnom, and burned his children in the fire, according to the abominations of the nations whom Yahweh cast out before the children of Israel. [4] He sacrificed and burned incense in the high places, and on the hills, and under every green tree. [5] Therefore Yahweh his God delivered him into the hand of the king of Syria. They struck him, and carried away from him a great multitude of captives, and brought them to Damascus. He was also delivered into the hand of the king of Israel, who struck him with a great slaughter. [6] For Pekah the son of Remaliah killed in Judah one hundred twenty thousand in one day, all of them valiant men, because they had forsaken Yahweh, the God of their fathers. [7] Zichri, a mighty man of Ephraim, killed Maaseiah the king's son, Azrikam the ruler of the house, and Elkanah who was next to the king. [8] The children of Israel carried away captive of their brothers two hundred thousand women, sons, and daughters, and also took away much plunder from

them, and brought the plunder to Samaria. <sup>9</sup> But a prophet of Yahweh was there, whose name was Oded; and he went out to meet the army that came to Samaria, and said to them, "Behold, because Yahweh, the God of your fathers, was angry with Judah, he has delivered them into your hand, and you have slain them in a rage which has reached up to heaven. <sup>10</sup> Now you intend to degrade the children of Judah and Jerusalem as male and female slaves for yourselves. Aren't there even with you trespasses of your own against Yahweh your God? <sup>11</sup> Now hear me therefore, and send back the captives that you have taken captive from your brothers, for the fierce wrath of Yahweh is on you." <sup>12</sup> Then some of the heads of the children of Ephraim, Azariah the son of Johanan, Berechiah the son of Meshillemoth, Jehizkiah the son of Shallum, and Amasa the son of Hadlai, stood up against those who came from the war, <sup>13</sup> and said to them, "You must not bring in the captives here, for you intend that which will bring on us a trespass against Yahweh, to add to our sins and to our guilt; for our guilt is great, and there is fierce wrath against Israel." <sup>14</sup> So the armed men left the captives and the plunder before the princes and all the assembly. <sup>15</sup> The men who have been mentioned by name rose up and took the captives, and with the plunder clothed all who were naked among them, dressed them, gave them sandals, gave them something to eat and to drink, anointed them, carried all the feeble of them on donkeys, and brought them to Jericho, the city of palm trees, to their brothers. Then they returned to Samaria. <sup>16</sup> At that time King Ahaz sent to the kings of Assyria to help him. <sup>17</sup> For again the Edomites had come and struck Judah, and carried away captives. <sup>18</sup> The Philistines also had invaded the cities of the lowland and of the South of Judah, and had taken Beth Shemesh, Aijalon, Gederoth, Soco with its villages, Timnah with its villages, and also Gimzo and its villages; and they lived there. <sup>19</sup> For Yahweh brought Judah low because of Ahaz king of Israel, because he acted without restraint in Judah and trespassed severely against Yahweh. <sup>20</sup> Tilgath-pilneser king of Assyria came to him and gave him trouble, but didn't strengthen him. <sup>21</sup> For Ahaz took away a portion out of Yahweh's house, and out of the house of the king and of the princes, and gave it to the king of Assyria; but it didn't help him. <sup>22</sup> In the time of his distress, he trespassed yet more against Yahweh, this same King Ahaz. <sup>23</sup> For he sacrificed to the gods of Damascus which had defeated him. He said, "Because the gods of the kings of Syria helped them, I will sacrifice to them, that they may help me." But they were the ruin of him and of all Israel. <sup>24</sup> Ahaz gathered together the vessels of God's house, cut the vessels of God's house in pieces, and shut up the doors of Yahweh's house; and he made himself altars in every corner of Jerusalem. <sup>25</sup> In every city of Judah he made high places to burn incense to other gods, and provoked Yahweh, the God of his fathers, to anger. <sup>26</sup> Now the rest of his acts, and all his ways, first and last, behold, they are written in the book of the kings of Judah and Israel. <sup>27</sup> Ahaz slept with his fathers, and they buried him in the city, even in Jerusalem, because they didn't bring him into the tombs of the kings of Israel; and Hezekiah his son reigned in his place.

## 29

<sup>1</sup> Hezekiah began to reign when he was twenty-five years old, and he reigned twenty-nine years in Jerusalem. His mother's name was Abijah, the daughter of Zechariah. <sup>2</sup> He did that which was right in Yahweh's eyes, according to all that David his father had done. <sup>3</sup> In the first year of his reign, in the first month, he opened the doors of Yahweh's house and repaired them. <sup>4</sup> He brought in the priests and the Levites and gathered them together into the wide place on the east, <sup>5</sup> and said to them, "Listen to me, you Levites! Now sanctify yourselves, and sanctify the house of Yahweh, the God of your fathers, and carry the filthiness out of the holy place. <sup>6</sup> For our fathers were unfaithful, and have done that which was evil in Yahweh our God's sight, and have forsaken him, and have turned away their faces from the habitation of Yahweh, and turned their backs. <sup>7</sup> Also they have shut up the doors of the porch, and put out the lamps, and have not burned incense nor offered burnt offerings in the holy place to the God of Israel. <sup>8</sup> Therefore Yahweh's wrath was on Judah and Jerusalem, and he has delivered them to be tossed back and forth, to be an astonishment and a hissing, as you see with your eyes. <sup>9</sup> For behold, our fathers have fallen by the sword, and our sons and our daughters and our wives are in captivity for this. <sup>10</sup> Now it is in my heart to make a covenant with Yahweh, the God of Israel, that his fierce anger may turn away from us. <sup>11</sup> My sons, don't be negligent now; for Yahweh has chosen you to stand before him, to minister to him, and that you should be his ministers and burn incense." <sup>12</sup> Then the Levites arose: Mahath, the son of Amasai, and Joel the son of Azariah, of the sons of the Kohathites; and of the sons of Merari, Kish the son of Abdi, and Azariah the son of Jehallelel; and of the Gershonites, Joah the son of Zimmah, and Eden the son of Joah; <sup>13</sup> and of the sons of Elizaphan, Shimri and Jeuel; and of the sons of Asaph, Zechariah and Mattaniah; <sup>14</sup> and of the sons of Heman, Jehuel and Shimei; and of the sons of Jeduthun, Shemaiah and Uzziel. <sup>15</sup> They

gathered their brothers, sanctified themselves, and went in, according to the commandment of the king by Yahweh's words, to cleanse Yahweh's house. <sup>16</sup> The priests went into the inner part of Yahweh's house to cleanse it, and brought out all the uncleanness that they found in Yahweh's temple into the court of Yahweh's house. The Levites took it from there to carry it out to the brook Kidron. <sup>17</sup> Now they began on the first day of the first month to sanctify, and on the eighth day of the month they came to Yahweh's porch. They sanctified Yahweh's house in eight days, and on the sixteenth day of the first month they finished. <sup>18</sup> Then they went in to Hezekiah the king within the palace and said, "We have cleansed all Yahweh's house, including the altar of burnt offering with all its vessels, and the table of show bread with all its vessels. <sup>19</sup> Moreover, we have prepared and sanctified all the vessels which King Ahaz threw away in his reign when he was unfaithful. Behold, they are before Yahweh's altar." <sup>20</sup> Then Hezekiah the king arose early, gathered the princes of the city, and went up to Yahweh's house. <sup>21</sup> They brought seven bulls, seven rams, seven lambs, and seven male goats, for a sin offering for the kingdom, for the sanctuary, and for Judah. He commanded the priests the sons of Aaron to offer them on Yahweh's altar. <sup>22</sup> So they killed the bulls, and the priests received the blood and sprinkled it on the altar. They killed the rams and sprinkled the blood on the altar. They also killed the lambs and sprinkled the blood on the altar. <sup>23</sup> They brought near the male goats for the sin offering before the king and the assembly; and they laid their hands on them. <sup>24</sup> Then the priests killed them, and they made a sin offering with their blood on the altar, to make atonement for all Israel; for the king commanded that the burnt offering and the sin offering should be made for all Israel. <sup>25</sup> He set the Levites in Yahweh's house with cymbals, with stringed instruments, and with harps, according to the commandment of David, of Gad the king's seer, and Nathan the prophet; for the commandment was from Yahweh by his prophets. <sup>26</sup> The Levites stood with David's instruments, and the priests with the trumpets. <sup>27</sup> Hezekiah commanded them to offer the burnt offering on the altar. When the burnt offering began, Yahweh's song also began, along with the trumpets and instruments of David king of Israel. <sup>28</sup> All the assembly worshiped, the singers sang, and the trumpeters sounded. All this continued until the burnt offering was finished. <sup>29</sup> When they had finished offering, the king and all who were present with him bowed themselves and worshiped. <sup>30</sup> Moreover Hezekiah the king and the princes commanded the Levites to sing praises to Yahweh with the words of David, and of Asaph the seer. They sang praises with gladness, and they bowed their heads and worshiped. <sup>31</sup> Then Hezekiah answered, "Now you have consecrated yourselves to Yahweh. Come near and bring sacrifices and thank offerings into Yahweh's house." The assembly brought in sacrifices and thank offerings, and as many as were of a willing heart brought burnt offerings. <sup>32</sup> The number of the burnt offerings which the assembly brought was seventy bulls, one hundred rams, and two hundred lambs. All these were for a burnt offering to Yahweh. <sup>33</sup> The consecrated things were six hundred head of cattle and three thousand sheep. <sup>34</sup> But the priests were too few, so that they could not skin all the burnt offerings. Therefore their brothers the Levites helped them until the work was ended, and until the priests had sanctified themselves, for the Levites were more upright in heart to sanctify themselves than the priests. <sup>35</sup> Also the burnt offerings were in abundance, with the fat of the peace offerings and with the drink offerings for every burnt offering. So the service of Yahweh's house was set in order. <sup>36</sup> Hezekiah and all the people rejoiced because of that which God had prepared for the people; for the thing was done suddenly.

## 30

<sup>1</sup> Hezekiah sent to all Israel and Judah, and wrote letters also to Ephraim and Manasseh, that they should come to Yahweh's house at Jerusalem, to keep the Passover to Yahweh, the God of Israel. <sup>2</sup> For the king had taken counsel with his princes and all the assembly in Jerusalem to keep the Passover in the second month. <sup>3</sup> For they could not keep it at that time, because the priests had not sanctified themselves in sufficient number, and the people had not gathered themselves together to Jerusalem. <sup>4</sup> The thing was right in the eyes of the king and of all the assembly. <sup>5</sup> So they established a decree to make proclamation throughout all Israel, from Beersheba even to Dan, that they should come to keep the Passover to Yahweh, the God of Israel, at Jerusalem, for they had not kept it in great numbers in the way it is written. <sup>6</sup> So the couriers went with the letters from the king and his princes throughout all Israel and Judah, according to the commandment of the king, saying, "You children of Israel, turn again to Yahweh, the God of Abraham, Isaac, and Israel, that he may return to the remnant of you that have escaped out of the hand of the kings of Assyria. <sup>7</sup> Don't be like your fathers and like your brothers, who trespassed against Yahweh, the God of their fathers, so that he gave them up to desolation, as you see. <sup>8</sup> Now don't be stiff-necked, as your fathers were, but yield

yourselves to Yahweh, and enter into his sanctuary, which he has sanctified forever, and serve Yahweh your God, that his fierce anger may turn away from you. [9] For if you turn again to Yahweh, your brothers and your children will find compassion with those who led them captive, and will come again into this land, because Yahweh your God is gracious and merciful, and will not turn away his face from you if you return to him." [10] So the couriers passed from city to city through the country of Ephraim and Manasseh, even to Zebulun, but people ridiculed them and mocked them. [11] Nevertheless some men of Asher, Manasseh, and Zebulun humbled themselves and came to Jerusalem. [12] Also the hand of God came on Judah to give them one heart, to do the commandment of the king and of the princes by Yahweh's word. [13] Many people assembled at Jerusalem to keep the feast of unleavened bread in the second month, a very great assembly. [14] They arose and took away the altars that were in Jerusalem, and they took away all the altars for incense and threw them into the brook Kidron. [15] Then they killed the Passover on the fourteenth day of the second month. The priests and the Levites were ashamed, and sanctified themselves, and brought burnt offerings into Yahweh's house. [16] They stood in their place after their order, according to the law of Moses the man of God. The priests sprinkled the blood which they received of the hand of the Levites. [17] For there were many in the assembly who had not sanctified themselves; therefore the Levites were in charge of killing the Passovers for everyone who was not clean, to sanctify them to Yahweh. [18] For a multitude of the people, even many of Ephraim, Manasseh, Issachar, and Zebulun, had not cleansed themselves, yet they ate the Passover other than the way it is written. For Hezekiah had prayed for them, saying, "May the good Yahweh pardon everyone [19] who sets his heart to seek God, Yahweh, the God of his fathers, even if they aren't clean according to the purification of the sanctuary." [20] Yahweh listened to Hezekiah, and healed the people. [21] The children of Israel who were present at Jerusalem kept the feast of unleavened bread seven days with great gladness. The Levites and the priests praised Yahweh day by day, singing with loud instruments to Yahweh. [22] Hezekiah spoke encouragingly to all the Levites who had good understanding in the service of Yahweh. So they ate throughout the feast for the seven days, offering sacrifices of peace offerings and making confession to Yahweh, the God of their fathers. [23] The whole assembly took counsel to keep another seven days, and they kept another seven days with gladness. [24] For Hezekiah king of Judah gave to the assembly for offerings one thousand bulls and seven thousand sheep; and the princes gave to the assembly a thousand bulls and ten thousand sheep; and a great number of priests sanctified themselves. [25] All the assembly of Judah, with the priests and the Levites, and all the assembly who came out of Israel, and the foreigners who came out of the land of Israel and who lived in Judah, rejoiced. [26] So there was great joy in Jerusalem; for since the time of Solomon the son of David king of Israel there was nothing like this in Jerusalem. [27] Then the Levitical priests arose and blessed the people. Their voice was heard, and their prayer came up to his holy habitation, even to heaven.

## 31

[1] Now when all this was finished, all Israel who were present went out to the cities of Judah and broke the pillars in pieces, cut down the Asherah poles, and broke down the high places and the altars out of all Judah and Benjamin, also in Ephraim and Manasseh, until they had destroyed them all. Then all the children of Israel returned, every man to his possession, into their own cities. [2] Hezekiah appointed the divisions of the priests and the Levites after their divisions, every man according to his service, both the priests and the Levites, for burnt offerings and for peace offerings, to minister, to give thanks, and to praise in the gates of Yahweh's camp. [3] He also appointed the king's portion of his possessions for the burnt offerings: for the morning and evening burnt offerings, and the burnt offerings for the Sabbaths, for the new moons, and for the set feasts, as it is written in Yahweh's law. [4] Moreover he commanded the people who lived in Jerusalem to give the portion of the priests and the Levites, that they might give themselves to Yahweh's law. [5] As soon as the commandment went out, the children of Israel gave in abundance the first fruits of grain, new wine, oil, honey, and of all the increase of the field; and they brought in the tithe of all things abundantly. [6] The children of Israel and Judah, who lived in the cities of Judah, also brought in the tithe of cattle and sheep, and the tithe of dedicated things which were consecrated to Yahweh their God, and laid them in heaps. [7] In the third month, they began to lay the foundation of the heaps, and finished them in the seventh month. [8] When Hezekiah and the princes came and saw the heaps, they blessed Yahweh and his people Israel. [9] Then Hezekiah questioned the priests and the Levites about the heaps. [10] Azariah the chief priest, of the house of Zadok, answered him and said, "Since people began to bring the offerings into Yahweh's house, we have eaten and had enough, and have plenty left over, for Yahweh has blessed his

people; and that which is left is this great store." [11] Then Hezekiah commanded them to prepare rooms in Yahweh's house, and they prepared them. [12] They brought in the offerings, the tithes, and the dedicated things faithfully. Conaniah the Levite was ruler over them, and Shimei his brother was second. [13] Jehiel, Azaziah, Nahath, Asahel, Jerimoth, Jozabad, Eliel, Ismachiah, Mahath, and Benaiah were overseers under the hand of Conaniah and Shimei his brother, by the appointment of Hezekiah the king and Azariah the ruler of God's house. [14] Kore the son of Imnah the Levite, the gatekeeper at the east gate, was over the free will offerings of God, to distribute Yahweh's offerings and the most holy things. [15] Under him were Eden, Miniamin, Jeshua, Shemaiah, Amariah, and Shecaniah, in the cities of the priests, in their office of trust, to give to their brothers by divisions, to the great as well as to the small; [16] in addition to those who were listed by genealogy of males, from three years old and upward, even everyone who entered into Yahweh's house, as the duty of every day required, for their service in their offices according to their divisions; [17] and those who were listed by genealogy of the priests by their fathers' houses, and the Levites from twenty years old and upward, in their offices by their divisions; [18] and those who were listed by genealogy of all their little ones, their wives, their sons, and their daughters, through all the congregation; for in their office of trust they sanctified themselves in holiness. [19] Also for the sons of Aaron the priests, who were in the fields of the pasture lands of their cities, in every city, there were men who were mentioned by name to give portions to all the males among the priests and to all who were listed by genealogy among the Levites. [20] Hezekiah did so throughout all Judah; and he did that which was good, right, and faithful before Yahweh his God. [21] In every work that he began in the service of God's house, in the law, and in the commandments, to seek his God, he did it with all his heart and prospered.

## 32

[1] After these things and this faithfulness, Sennacherib king of Assyria came, entered into Judah, encamped against the fortified cities, and intended to win them for himself. [2] When Hezekiah saw that Sennacherib had come, and that he was planning to fight against Jerusalem, [3] he took counsel with his princes and his mighty men to stop the waters of the springs which were outside of the city, and they helped him. [4] Then many people gathered together and they stopped all the springs and the brook that flowed through the middle of the land, saying, "Why should the kings of Assyria come, and find abundant water?" [5] He took courage, built up all the wall that was broken down, and raised it up to the towers, with the other wall outside, and strengthened Millo in David's city, and made weapons and shields in abundance. [6] He set captains of war over the people, gathered them together to him in the wide place at the gate of the city, and spoke encouragingly to them, saying, [7] "Be strong and courageous. Don't be afraid or dismayed because of the king of Assyria, nor for all the multitude who is with him; for there is a greater one with us than with him. [8] An arm of flesh is with him, but Yahweh our God is with us to help us and to fight our battles." The people rested themselves on the words of Hezekiah king of Judah. [9] After this, Sennacherib king of Assyria sent his servants to Jerusalem, (now he was attacking Lachish, and all his forces were with him), to Hezekiah king of Judah, and to all Judah who were at Jerusalem, saying, [10] Sennacherib king of Assyria says, "In whom do you trust, that you remain under siege in Jerusalem? [11] Doesn't Hezekiah persuade you to give you over to die by famine and by thirst, saying, 'Yahweh our God will deliver us out of the hand of the king of Assyria'? [12] Hasn't the same Hezekiah taken away his high places and his altars, and commanded Judah and Jerusalem, saying, 'You shall worship before one altar, and you shall burn incense on it'? [13] Don't you know what I and my fathers have done to all the peoples of the lands? Were the gods of the nations of those lands in any way able to deliver their land out of my hand? [14] Who was there among all the gods of those nations which my fathers utterly destroyed that could deliver his people out of my hand, that your God should be able to deliver you out of my hand? [15] Now therefore don't let Hezekiah deceive you nor persuade you in this way. Don't believe him, for no god of any nation or kingdom was able to deliver his people out of my hand, and out of the hand of my fathers. How much less will your God deliver you out of my hand?" [16] His servants spoke yet more against Yahweh God and against his servant Hezekiah. [17] He also wrote letters insulting Yahweh, the God of Israel, and speaking against him, saying, "As the gods of the nations of the lands, which have not delivered their people out of my hand, so shall the God of Hezekiah not deliver his people out of my hand." [18] They called out with a loud voice in the Jews' language to the people of Jerusalem who were on the wall, to frighten them and to trouble them, that they might take the city. [19] They spoke of the God of Jerusalem as of the gods of the peoples of the earth, which are the work of men's hands. [20] Hezekiah the king and Isaiah the

prophet, the son of Amoz, prayed because of this, and cried to heaven. [21] Yahweh sent an angel, who cut off all the mighty men of valor, the leaders, and captains in the camp of the king of Assyria. So he returned with shame of face to his own land. When he had come into the house of his god, those who came out of his own body[a] killed him there with the sword. [22] Thus Yahweh saved Hezekiah and the inhabitants of Jerusalem from the hand of Sennacherib the king of Assyria and from the hand of all others, and guided them on every side. [23] Many brought gifts to Yahweh to Jerusalem, and precious things to Hezekiah king of Judah, so that he was exalted in the sight of all nations from then on. [24] In those days Hezekiah was terminally ill, and he prayed to Yahweh; and he spoke to him, and gave him a sign. [25] But Hezekiah didn't reciprocate appropriate to the benefit done for him, because his heart was lifted up. Therefore there was wrath on him, Judah, and Jerusalem. [26] However, Hezekiah humbled himself for the pride of his heart, both he and the inhabitants of Jerusalem, so that Yahweh's wrath didn't come on them in the days of Hezekiah. [27] Hezekiah had exceedingly great riches and honor. He provided himself with treasuries for silver, for gold, for precious stones, for spices, for shields, and for all kinds of valuable vessels; [28] also storehouses for the increase of grain, new wine, and oil; and stalls for all kinds of animals, and flocks in folds. [29] Moreover he provided for himself cities, and possessions of flocks and herds in abundance; for God had given him abundant possessions. [30] This same Hezekiah also stopped the upper spring of the waters of Gihon, and brought them straight down on the west side of David's city. Hezekiah prospered in all his works. [31] However, concerning the ambassadors of the princes of Babylon, who sent to him to inquire of the wonder that was done in the land, God left him to test him, that he might know all that was in his heart. [32] Now the rest of the acts of Hezekiah and his good deeds, behold, they are written in the vision of Isaiah the prophet, the son of Amoz, in the book of the kings of Judah and Israel. [33] Hezekiah slept with his fathers, and they buried him in the ascent to the tombs of the sons of David. All Judah and the inhabitants of Jerusalem honored him at his death. Manasseh his son reigned in his place.

## 33

[1] Manasseh was twelve years old when he began to reign, and he reigned fifty-five years in Jerusalem. [2] He did that which was evil in Yahweh's sight, after the abominations of the nations whom Yahweh cast out before the children of Israel. [3] For he built again the high places which Hezekiah his father had broken down; and he raised up altars for the Baals, made Asheroth, and worshiped all the army of the sky, and served them. [4] He built altars in Yahweh's house, of which Yahweh said, "My name shall be in Jerusalem forever." [5] He built altars for all the army of the sky in the two courts of Yahweh's house. [6] He also made his children to pass through the fire in the valley of the son of Hinnom. He practiced sorcery, divination, and witchcraft, and dealt with those who had familiar spirits and with wizards. He did much evil in Yahweh's sight, to provoke him to anger. [7] He set the engraved image of the idol, which he had made, in God's house, of which God said to David and to Solomon his son, "In this house, and in Jerusalem, which I have chosen out of all the tribes of Israel, I will put my name forever. [8] I will not any more remove the foot of Israel from off the land which I have appointed for your fathers, if only they will observe to do all that I have commanded them, even all the law, the statutes, and the ordinances given by Moses." [9] Manasseh seduced Judah and the inhabitants of Jerusalem, so that they did more evil than did the nations whom Yahweh destroyed before the children of Israel. [10] Yahweh spoke to Manasseh and to his people, but they didn't listen. [11] Therefore Yahweh brought on them the captains of the army of the king of Assyria, who took Manasseh in chains, bound him with fetters, and carried him to Babylon. [12] When he was in distress, he begged Yahweh his God, and humbled himself greatly before the God of his fathers. [13] He prayed to him; and he was entreated by him, and heard his supplication, and brought him again to Jerusalem into his kingdom. Then Manasseh knew that Yahweh was God. [14] Now after this, he built an outer wall to David's city on the west side of Gihon, in the valley, even to the entrance at the fish gate. He encircled Ophel with it, and raised it up to a very great height; and he put valiant captains in all the fortified cities of Judah. [15] He took away the foreign gods and the idol out of Yahweh's house, and all the altars that he had built in the mountain of Yahweh's house and in Jerusalem, and cast them out of the city. [16] He built up Yahweh's altar, and offered sacrifices of peace offerings and of thanksgiving on it, and commanded Judah to serve Yahweh, the God of Israel. [17] Nevertheless the people still sacrificed in the high places, but only to Yahweh their God. [18] Now the rest of the acts of Manasseh, and his prayer to his God, and the words of the seers who spoke to him in the name of Yahweh, the God of Israel, behold,

they are written among the acts of the kings of Israel. [19] His prayer also, and how God listened to his request, and all his sin and his trespass, and the places in which he built high places and set up the Asherah poles and the engraved images before he humbled himself: behold, they are written in the history of Hozai.[b] [20] So Manasseh slept with his fathers, and they buried him in his own house; and Amon his son reigned in his place. [21] Amon was twenty-two years old when he began to reign; and he reigned two years in Jerusalem. [22] He did that which was evil in Yahweh's sight, as did Manasseh his father; and Amon sacrificed to all the engraved images which Manasseh his father had made, and served them. [23] He didn't humble himself before Yahweh, as Manasseh his father had humbled himself; but this same Amon trespassed more and more. [24] His servants conspired against him, and put him to death in his own house. [25] But the people of the land killed all those who had conspired against King Amon; and the people of the land made Josiah his son king in his place.

## 34

[1] Josiah was eight years old when he began to reign, and he reigned thirty-one years in Jerusalem. [2] He did that which was right in Yahweh's eyes, and walked in the ways of David his father, and didn't turn away to the right hand or to the left. [3] For in the eighth year of his reign, while he was yet young, he began to seek after the God of David his father; and in the twelfth year he began to purge Judah and Jerusalem from the high places, the Asherah poles, the engraved images, and the molten images. [4] They broke down the altars of the Baals in his presence; and he cut down the incense altars that were on high above them. He broke the Asherah poles, the engraved images, and the molten images in pieces, made dust of them, and scattered it on the graves of those who had sacrificed to them. [5] He burned the bones of the priests on their altars, and purged Judah and Jerusalem. [6] He did this in the cities of Manasseh, Ephraim, and Simeon, even to Naphtali, around in their ruins. [7] He broke down the altars, beat the Asherah poles and the engraved images into powder, and cut down all the incense altars throughout all the land of Israel, then returned to Jerusalem. [8] Now in the eighteenth year of his reign, when he had purged the land and the house, he sent Shaphan the son of Azaliah, Maaseiah the governor of the city, and Joah the son of Joahaz the recorder to repair the house of Yahweh his God. [9] They came to Hilkiah the high priest and delivered the money that was brought into God's house, which the Levites, the keepers of the threshold, had gathered from the hands of Manasseh, Ephraim, of all the remnant of Israel, of all Judah and Benjamin, and of the inhabitants of Jerusalem. [10] They delivered it into the hands of the workmen who had the oversight of Yahweh's house; and the workmen who labored in Yahweh's house gave it to mend and repair the house. [11] They gave it to the carpenters and to the builders to buy cut stone and timber for couplings, and to make beams for the houses which the kings of Judah had destroyed. [12] The men did the work faithfully. Their overseers were Jahath and Obadiah the Levites, of the sons of Merari; and Zechariah and Meshullam, of the sons of the Kohathites, to give direction; and others of the Levites, who were all skillful with musical instruments. [13] Also they were over the bearers of burdens, and directed all who did the work in every kind of service. Of the Levites, there were scribes, officials, and gatekeepers. [14] When they brought out the money that was brought into Yahweh's house, Hilkiah the priest found the book of Yahweh's law given by Moses. [15] Hilkiah answered Shaphan the scribe, "I have found the book of the law in Yahweh's house." So Hilkiah delivered the book to Shaphan. [16] Shaphan carried the book to the king, and moreover brought back word to the king, saying, "All that was committed to your servants, they are doing. [17] They have emptied out the money that was found in Yahweh's house, and have delivered it into the hand of the overseers and into the hand of the workmen." [18] Shaphan the scribe told the king, saying, "Hilkiah the priest has delivered me a book." Shaphan read from it to the king. [19] When the king had heard the words of the law, he tore his clothes. [20] The king commanded Hilkiah, Ahikam the son of Shaphan, Abdon the son of Micah, Shaphan the scribe, and Asaiah the king's servant, saying, [21] "Go inquire of Yahweh for me, and for those who are left in Israel and in Judah, concerning the words of the book that is found; for great is Yahweh's wrath that is poured out on us, because our fathers have not kept Yahweh's word, to do according to all that is written in this book." [22] So Hilkiah and those whom the king had commanded went to Huldah the prophetess, the wife of Shallum the son of Tokhath, the son of Hasrah, keeper of the wardrobe (now she lived in Jerusalem in the second quarter), and they spoke to her to that effect. [23] She said to them, "Yahweh, the God of Israel says: 'Tell the man who sent you to me, [24] "Yahweh says, 'Behold, I will bring evil on this place and on its inhabitants, even all the curses that are written in the book which they have read before the king of Judah. [25] Because

they have forsaken me, and have burned incense to other gods, that they might provoke me to anger with all the works of their hands, therefore my wrath is poured out on this place, and it will not be quenched.'"' ²⁶ But to the king of Judah, who sent you to inquire of Yahweh, you shall tell him this, 'Yahweh, the God of Israel says: "About the words which you have heard, ²⁷ because your heart was tender, and you humbled yourself before God when you heard his words against this place and against its inhabitants, and have humbled yourself before me, and have torn your clothes and wept before me, I also have heard you," says Yahweh. ²⁸"Behold, I will gather you to your fathers, and you will be gathered to your grave in peace. Your eyes won't see all the evil that I will bring on this place and on its inhabitants."'" They brought back this message to the king. ²⁹ Then the king sent and gathered together all the elders of Judah and Jerusalem. ³⁰ The king went up to Yahweh's house with all the men of Judah and the inhabitants of Jerusalem—the priests, the Levites, and all the people, both great and small—and he read in their hearing all the words of the book of the covenant that was found in Yahweh's house. ³¹ The king stood in his place and made a covenant before Yahweh, to walk after Yahweh, and to keep his commandments, his testimonies, and his statutes with all his heart and with all his soul, to perform the words of the covenant that were written in this book. ³² He caused all who were found in Jerusalem and Benjamin to stand. The inhabitants of Jerusalem did according to the covenant of God, the God of their fathers. ³³ Josiah took away all the abominations out of all the countries that belonged to the children of Israel, and made all who were found in Israel to serve, even to serve Yahweh their God. All his days they didn't depart from following Yahweh, the God of their fathers.

## 35

¹ Josiah kept a Passover to Yahweh in Jerusalem. They killed the Passover on the fourteenth day of the first month. ² He set the priests in their offices and encouraged them in the service of Yahweh's house. ³ He said to the Levites who taught all Israel, who were holy to Yahweh, "Put the holy ark in the house which Solomon the son of David king of Israel built. It will no longer be a burden on your shoulders. Now serve Yahweh your God and his people Israel. ⁴ Prepare yourselves after your fathers' houses by your divisions, according to the writing of David king of Israel, and according to the writing of Solomon his son. ⁵ Stand in the holy place according to the divisions of the fathers' houses of your brothers the children of the people, and let there be for each a portion of a fathers' house of the Levites. ⁶ Kill the Passover lamb, sanctify yourselves, and prepare for your brothers, to do according to Yahweh's word by Moses." ⁷ Josiah gave to the children of the people, of the flock, lambs and young goats, all of them for the Passover offerings, to all who were present, to the number of thirty thousand, and three thousand bulls. These were of the king's substance. ⁸ His princes gave a free will offering to the people, to the priests, and to the Levites. Hilkiah, Zechariah, and Jehiel, the rulers of God's house, gave to the priests for the Passover offerings two thousand six hundred small livestock, and three hundred head of cattle. ⁹ Conaniah also, and Shemaiah and Nethanel, his brothers, and Hashabiah, Jeiel, and Jozabad, the chiefs of the Levites, gave to the Levites for the Passover offerings five thousand small livestock and five hundred head of cattle. ¹⁰ So the service was prepared, and the priests stood in their place, and the Levites by their divisions, according to the king's commandment. ¹¹ They killed the Passover lambs, and the priests sprinkled the blood which they received from their hands, and the Levites skinned them. ¹² They removed the burnt offerings, that they might give them according to the divisions of the fathers' houses of the children of the people, to offer to Yahweh, as it is written in the book of Moses. They did the same with the cattle. ¹³ They roasted the Passover with fire according to the ordinance. They boiled the holy offerings in pots, in cauldrons, and in pans, and carried them quickly to all the children of the people. ¹⁴ Afterward they prepared for themselves and for the priests, because the priests the sons of Aaron were busy with offering the burnt offerings and the fat until night. Therefore the Levites prepared for themselves and for the priests the sons of Aaron. ¹⁵ The singers, the sons of Asaph, were in their place, according to the commandment of David, Asaph, Heman, and Jeduthun the king's seer; and the gatekeepers were at every gate. They didn't need to depart from their service, because their brothers the Levites prepared for them. ¹⁶ So all the service of Yahweh was prepared the same day, to keep the Passover, and to offer burnt offerings on Yahweh's altar, according to the commandment of King Josiah. ¹⁷ The children of Israel who were present kept the Passover at that time, and the feast of unleavened bread seven days. ¹⁸ There was no Passover like that kept in Israel from the days of Samuel the prophet,

nor did any of the kings of Israel keep such a Passover as Josiah kept—with the priests, the Levites, and all Judah and Israel who were present, and the inhabitants of Jerusalem. ¹⁹ This Passover was kept in the eighteenth year of the reign of Josiah. ²⁰ After all this, when Josiah had prepared the temple, Neco king of Egypt went up to fight against Carchemish by the Euphrates, and Josiah went out against him. ²¹ But he sent ambassadors to him, saying, "What have I to do with you, you king of Judah? I come not against you today, but against the house with which I have war. God has commanded me to make haste. Beware that it is God who is with me, that he not destroy you." ²² Nevertheless Josiah would not turn his face from him, but disguised himself, that he might fight with him, and didn't listen to the words of Neco from the mouth of God, and came to fight in the valley of Megiddo. ²³ The archers shot at King Josiah; and the king said to his servants, "Take me away, because I am seriously wounded!" ²⁴ So his servants took him out of the chariot, and put him in the second chariot that he had, and brought him to Jerusalem; and he died, and was buried in the tombs of his fathers. All Judah and Jerusalem mourned for Josiah. ²⁵ Jeremiah lamented for Josiah, and all the singing men and singing women spoke of Josiah in their lamentations to this day; and they made them an ordinance in Israel. Behold, they are written in the lamentations. ²⁶ Now the rest of the acts of Josiah and his good deeds, according to that which is written in Yahweh's law, ²⁷ and his acts, first and last, behold, they are written in the book of the kings of Israel and Judah.

## 36

¹ Then the people of the land took Jehoahaz the son of Josiah, and made him king in his father's place in Jerusalem. ² Joahaz was twenty-three years old when he began to reign; and he reigned three months in Jerusalem. ³ The king of Egypt removed him from office at Jerusalem, and fined the land one hundred talents of silver and a talentª of gold. ⁴ The king of Egypt made Eliakim his brother king over Judah and Jerusalem, and changed his name to Jehoiakim. Neco took Joahaz his brother, and carried him to Egypt. ⁵ Jehoiakim was twenty-five years old when he began to reign, and he reigned eleven years in Jerusalem. He did that which was evil in Yahweh his God's sight. ⁶ Nebuchadnezzar king of Babylon came up against him, and bound him in fetters to carry him to Babylon. ⁷ Nebuchadnezzar also carried some of the vessels of Yahweh's house to Babylon, and put them in his temple at Babylon. ⁸ Now the rest of the acts of Jehoiakim, and his abominations which he did, and that which was found in him, behold, they are written in the book of the kings of Israel and Judah; and Jehoiachin his son reigned in his place. ⁹ Jehoiachin was eight years old when he began to reign, and he reigned three months and ten days in Jerusalem. He did that which was evil in Yahweh's sight. ¹⁰ At the return of the year, King Nebuchadnezzar sent and brought him to Babylon, with the valuable vessels of Yahweh's house, and made Zedekiah his brother king over Judah and Jerusalem. ¹¹ Zedekiah was twenty-one years old when he began to reign, and he reigned eleven years in Jerusalem. ¹² He did that which was evil in Yahweh his God's sight. He didn't humble himself before Jeremiah the prophet speaking from Yahweh's mouth. ¹³ He also rebelled against King Nebuchadnezzar, who had made him swear by God; but he stiffened his neck, and hardened his heart against turning to Yahweh, the God of Israel. ¹⁴ Moreover all the chiefs of the priests and the people trespassed very greatly after all the abominations of the nations; and they polluted Yahweh's house which he had made holy in Jerusalem. ¹⁵ Yahweh, the God of their fathers, sent to them by his messengers, rising up early and sending, because he had compassion on his people and on his dwelling place; ¹⁶ but they mocked the messengers of God, despised his words, and scoffed at his prophets, until Yahweh's wrath arose against his people, until there was no remedy. ¹⁷ Therefore he brought on them the king of the Chaldeans, who killed their young men with the sword in the house of their sanctuary, and had no compassion on young man or virgin, old man or infirm. He gave them all into his hand. ¹⁸ All the vessels of God's house, great and small, and the treasures of Yahweh's house, and the treasures of the king and of his princes, all these he brought to Babylon. ¹⁹ They burned God's house, broke down the wall of Jerusalem, burned all its palaces with fire, and destroyed all of its valuable vessels. ²⁰ He carried those who had escaped from the sword away to Babylon, and they were servants to him and his sons until the reign of the kingdom of Persia, ²¹ to fulfill Yahweh's word by Jeremiah's mouth, until the land had enjoyed its Sabbaths. As long as it lay desolate, it kept Sabbath, to fulfill seventy years. ²² Now in the first year of Cyrus king of Persia, that Yahweh's word by the mouth of Jeremiah might be accomplished, Yahweh stirred up the spirit of Cyrus king of Persia, so that he made a proclamation throughout all his

ª 36:3 A talent is about 30 kilograms or 66 pounds or 965 Troy ounces kingdom, and put it also in writing, saying, [23]"Cyrus king of Persia says, 'Yahweh, the God of heaven, has given all the kingdoms of the earth to me; and he has commanded me to build him a house in Jerusalem, which is in Judah. Whoever there is among you of all his people, Yahweh his God be with him, and let him go up.'"

# The Prayer of Manasses

*The Prayer of Manasses* is recognized as Deuterocanonical Scripture by the Greek Orthodox and Russian Orthodox Churches. It is included in an appendix to the Latin Vulgate Bible.

**King of Judah, When He Was Held Captive in Babylon**

## 1

[1] O LORD Almighty in heaven, God of our fathers Abraham, Isaac, and Jacob, and of their righteous offspring, [2] you who have made heaven and earth, with all their order, [3] who have bound the sea by the word of your commandment, who have shut up the deep, and sealed it by your terrible and glorious name, [4] whom all things fear, yes, tremble before your power, [5] for the majesty of your glory can't be borne, and the anger of your threatening toward sinners is unbearable. [6] Your merciful promise is unmeasurable and unsearchable, [7] for you are the Lord Most High, of great compassion, patient and abundant in mercy, and relent at human suffering. [8] [a]You, O Lord, according to your great goodness have promised repentance and forgiveness to those who have sinned against you. Of your infinite mercies, you have appointed repentance to sinners, that they may be saved. You therefore, O Lord, who are the God of the just, have not appointed repentance to the just, to Abraham, Isaac, and Jacob, which have not sinned against you, but you have appointed repentance to me, a sinner. [9] For I have sinned more than the number of the sands of the sea. My transgressions are multiplied,[b] O Lord, my transgressions are multiplied, and I am not worthy to behold and see the height of heaven for the multitude of my iniquities. [10] I am bowed down with many iron bands, so that I can't lift up my head by reason of my sins,[c] neither have I any relief; for I have provoked your wrath, and done that which is evil before you:[d] I didn't do your will, neither did I keep your commandments. I have set up abominations, and have multiplied detestable things. [11] Now therefore I bow the knee of my heart, asking you for grace. [12] I have sinned, O Lord, I have sinned, and I acknowledge my iniquities; [13] but, I humbly ask you, forgive me, O Lord, forgive me, and please don't destroy me with my iniquities. Don't be angry with me forever, by reserving evil for me. Don't condemn me into the lower parts of the earth. For you, O Lord, are the God of those who repent. [14] In me you will show all your goodness, for you will save me, even though I am unworthy, according to your great mercy. [15] Then I will praise you forever all the days of my life; for all the army of heaven sings your praise, and yours is the glory forever and ever. Amen.

# The Book of Jubilees, or The Little Genesis

Moses receives the tables of the law and instruction on past and future history which he is to inscribe in a book, **1-4.** Apostasy of Israel, **5-9.** Captivity of Israel and Judah, **10-13.** Return of Judah and rebuilding of the temple, **15-18.** Moses' prayer for Israel, **19-21.** God's promise to redeem and dwell with them, **22-5, 28.** Moses bidden to write down the future history of the world (the Book of Jubilees?), **26.** And an angel to write down the law, **27.** This angel takes the heavenly chronological tablets to dictate therefrom to Moses, **29.**

**Prologue**

THIS is the history of the division of the days of the law and of the testimony, of the events of the years, of their (year) weeks, of their Jubilees throughout all the years of the world, as the Lord spake to Moses on Mount Sinai when he went up to receive the tables of the law and of the commandment, according to the voice of God as he said unto him, 'Go up to the top of the Mount.'

**God's Revelation to Moses on Mount Sinai (i. 1-26: cf. Ex. xxiv. 15-18).**

## 1

[1] And it came to pass in the first year of the exodus of the children of Israel out of Egypt, in the third month, on the sixteenth day of the month, [2450 Anno Mundi] that God spake to Moses, saying: 'Come up to Me on the Mount, and I will give thee two tables of stone of the law and of the commandment, which I have written, that thou mayst teach them.' [2] And Moses went up into the mount of God, and the glory of the Lord abode on Mount Sinai, and a cloud overshadowed it six days. [3] And He called to Moses on the seventh day out of the midst of the

cloud, and the appearance of the glory of the Lord was like a flaming fire on the top of the mount. [4] And Moses was on the Mount forty days and forty nights, and God taught him the earlier and the later history of the division of all the days of the law and of the testimony. [5] And He said: 'Incline thine heart to every word which I shall speak to thee on this mount, and write them in a book in order that their generations may see how I have not forsaken them for all the evil which they have wrought in transgressing the covenant which I establish between Me and thee for their generations this day on Mount Sinai. [6] And thus it will come to pass when all these things come upon them, that they will recognise that I am more righteous than they in all their judgments and in all their actions, and they will recognise that I have been truly with them. [7] And do thou write for thyself all these words which I declare unto, thee this day, for I know their rebellion and their stiff neck, before I bring them into the land of which I sware to their fathers, to Abraham and to Isaac and to Jacob, saying: ' Unto your seed will I give a land flowing with milk and honey. [8] And they will eat and be satisfied, and they will turn to strange gods, to (gods) which cannot deliver them from aught of their tribulation: and this witness shall be heard for a witness against them. [9] For they will forget all My commandments, (even) all that I command them, and they will walk after the Gentiles, and after their uncleanness, and after their shame, and will serve their gods, and these will prove unto them an offence and a tribulation and an affliction and a snare. [10] And many will perish and they will be taken captive, and will fall into the hands of the enemy, because they have forsaken My ordinances and My commandments, and the festivals of My covenant, and My sabbaths, and My holy place which I have hallowed for Myself in their midst, and My tabernacle, and My sanctuary, which I have hallowed for Myself in the midst of the land, that I should set my name upon it, and that it should dwell (there). [11] And they will make to themselves high places and groves and graven images, and they will worship, each his own (graven image), so as to go astray, and they will sacrifice their children to demons, and to all the works of the error of their hearts. [12] And I will send witnesses unto them, that I may witness against them, but they will not hear, and will slay the witnesses also, and they will persecute those who seek the law, and they will abrogate and change everything so as to work evil before My eyes. [13] And I will hide My face from them, and I will deliver them into the hand of the Gentiles for captivity, and for a prey, and for devouring, and I will remove them from the midst of the land, and I will scatter them amongst the Gentiles. [14] And they will forget all My law and all My commandments and all My judgments, and will go astray as to new moons, and sabbaths, and festivals, and jubilees, and ordinances. [15] And after this they will turn to Me from amongst the Gentiles with all their heart and with all their soul and with all their strength, and I will gather them from amongst all the Gentiles, and they will seek me, so that I shall be found of them, when they seek me with all their heart and with all their soul. [16] And I will disclose to them abounding peace with righteousness, and I will remove them the plant of uprightness, with all My heart and with all My soul, and they shall be for a blessing and not for a curse, and they shall be the head and not the tail. [17] And I will build My sanctuary in their midst, and I will dwell with them, and I will be their God and they shall be My people in truth and righteousness. [18] And I will not forsake them nor fail them; for I am the Lord their God.' [19] And Moses fell on his face and prayed and said, 'O Lord my God, do not forsake Thy people and Thy inheritance, so that they should wander in the error of their hearts, and do not deliver them into the hands of their enemies, the Gentiles, lest they should rule over them and cause them to sin against Thee. [20] Let thy mercy, O Lord, be lifted up upon Thy people, and create in them an upright spirit, and let not the spirit of Beliar rule over them to accuse them before Thee, and to ensnare them from all the paths of righteousness, so that they may perish from before Thy face. [21] But they are Thy people and Thy inheritance, which thou hast delivered with thy great power from the hands of the Egyptians: create in them a clean heart and a holy spirit, and let them not be ensnared in their sins from henceforth until eternity.' [22] And the Lord said unto Moses: 'I know their contrariness and their thoughts and their stiffneckedness, and they will not be obedient till they confess their own sin and the sin of their fathers. [23] And after this they will turn to Me in all uprightness and with all (their) heart and with all (their) soul, and I will circumcise the foreskin of their heart and the foreskin of the heart of their seed, and I will create in them a holy spirit, and I will cleanse them so that they shall not turn away from Me from that day unto eternity. [24] And their souls will cleave to Me and to all My commandments, and they will fulfil My commandments, and I will be their Father and they shall be My children. [25] And they all shall be called children of the living God, and every angel and every spirit shall

---

[a] *1:8* The Alex. MS. omits You... saved.

[b] *1:9* The Alex. MS. omits O Lord... multiplied.

[c] *1:10* Some authorities omit by reason of my sins.

[d] *1:10* The Alex. MS. omits I did... commandments.

know, yea, they shall know that these are My children, and that I am their Father in uprightness and righteousness, and that I love them. [26] And do thou write down for thyself all these words which I declare unto thee on this mountain, the first and the last, which shall come to pass in all the divisions of the days in the law and in the testimony and in the weeks and the jubilees unto eternity, until I descend and dwell with them throughout eternity.'

## God commands the Angel to write (i. 27-29).

[27] And He said to the angel of the presence: Write for Moses from the beginning of creation till My sanctuary has been built among them for all eternity. [28] And the Lord will appear to the eyes of all, and all shall know that I am the God of Israel and the Father of all the children of Jacob, and King on Mount Zion for all eternity. And Zion and Jerusalem shall be holy.' [29] And the angel of the presence who went before the camp of Israel took the tables of the divisions of the years -from the time of the creation- of the law and of the testimony of the weeks of the jubilees, according to the individual years, according to all the number of the jubilees [according, to the individual years], from the day of the [new] creation when the heavens and the earth shall be renewed and all their creation according to the powers of the heaven, and according to all the creation of the earth, until the sanctuary of the Lord shall be made in Jerusalem on Mount Zion, and all the luminaries be renewed for healing and for peace and for blessing for all the elect of Israel, and that thus it may be from that day and unto all the days of the earth.

## The Angel dictates to Moses the Primæval History: the Creation of the World and Institution of the Sabbath (ii. 1-33; cf. Gen. i.-ii. 3).

## 2

[1] And the angel of the presence spake to Moses according to the word of the Lord, saying: Write the complete history of the creation, how in six days the Lord God finished all His works and all that He created, and kept Sabbath on the seventh day and hallowed it for all ages, and appointed it as a sign for all His works. [2] For on the first day He created the heavens which are above and the waters and all the spirits which serve before him -the angels of the presence, and the angels of sanctification, and the angels [of the spirit of fire and the angels] of the spirit of the winds, and the angels of the spirit of the clouds, and of darkness, and of snow and of hail and of hoar frost, and the angels of the voices and of the thunder and of the lightning, and the angels of the spirits of cold and of heat, and of winter and of spring and of autumn and of summer and of all the spirits of his creatures which are in the heavens and on the earth, (He created) the abysses and the darkness, eventide <and night>, and the light, dawn and day, which He hath prepared in the knowledge of his heart. [3] And thereupon we saw His works, and praised Him, and lauded before Him on account of all His works; for seven great works did He create on the first day. [4] And on the second day He created the firmament in the midst of the waters, and the waters were divided on that day -half of them went up above and half of them went down below the firmament (that was) in the midst over the face of the whole earth. And this was the only work (God) created on the second day. [5] And on the third day He commanded the waters to pass from off the face of the whole earth into one place, and the dry land to appear. [6] And the waters did so as He commanded them, and they retired from off the face of the earth into one place outside of this firmament, and the dry land appeared. [7] And on that day He created for them all the seas according to their separate gathering-places, and all the rivers, and the gatherings of the waters in the mountains and on all the earth, and all the lakes, and all the dew of the earth, and the seed which is sown, and all sprouting things, and fruit-bearing trees, and trees of the wood, and the garden of Eden, in Eden and all plants after their kind. [8] These four great works God created on the third day. And on the fourth day He created the sun and the moon and the stars, and set them in the firmament of the heaven, to give light upon all the earth, and to rule over the day and the night, and divide the light from the darkness. [9] And God appointed the sun to be a great sign on the earth for days and for sabbaths and for months and for feasts and for years and for sabbaths of years and for jubilees and for all seasons of the years. [10] And it divideth the light from the darkness [and] for prosperity, that all things may prosper which shoot and grow on the earth. [11] These three kinds He made on the fourth day. And on the fifth day He created great sea monsters in the depths of the waters, for these were the first things of flesh that were created by his hands, the fish and everything that moves in the waters, and everything that flies, the birds and all their kind. [12] And the sun rose above them to prosper (them), and above everything that was on the earth, everything that shoots out of the earth, and all fruit-bearing trees, and all flesh. [13] These three kinds He created on the fifth day. And on the sixth day He created all the animals of the earth, and all cattle, and everything that moves on the earth. [14] And after all this He created man, a man and a woman created He them, and gave him dominion over all that is upon the earth, and in the seas, and over everything that flies, and over beasts and over cattle, and over everything that moves on the earth, and over the whole earth, and over all this He gave him dominion. [15] And these four kinds He created on the sixth day. And there were altogether two and twenty kinds. [16] And He finished all his work on the sixth day -all that is in the heavens and on the earth, and in the seas and in the abysses, and in the light and in the darkness, and in everything. [17] And He gave us a great sign, the Sabbath day, that we should work six days, but keep Sabbath on the seventh day from all work. [18] And all the angels of the presence, and all the angels of sanctification, these two great classes -He hath bidden us to keep the Sabbath with Him in heaven and on earth. [19] And He said unto us: 'Behold, I will separate unto Myself a people from among all the peoples, and these shall keep the Sabbath day, and I will sanctify them unto Myself as My people, and will bless them; as I have sanctified the Sabbath day and do sanctify (it) unto Myself, even so will I bless them, and they shall be My people and I will be their God. [20] And I have chosen the seed of Jacob from amongst all that I have seen, and have written him down as My first-born son, and have sanctified him unto Myself for ever and ever; and I will teach them the Sabbath day, that they may keep Sabbath thereon from all work.' [21] And thus He created therein a sign in accordance with which they should keep Sabbath with us on the seventh day, to eat and to drink, and to bless Him who has created all things as He has blessed and sanctified unto Himself a peculiar people above all peoples, and that they should keep Sabbath together with us. [22] And He caused His commands to ascend as a sweet savour acceptable before Him all the days . . . [23] There (were) two and twenty heads of mankind from Adam to Jacob, and two and twenty kinds of work were made until the seventh day; this is blessed and holy; and the former also is blessed and holy; and this one serves with that one for sanctification and blessing. [24] And to this (Jacob and his seed) it was granted that they should always be the blessed and holy ones of the first testimony and law, even as He had sanctified and blessed the Sabbath day on the seventh day. [25] He created heaven and earth and everything that He created in six days, and God made the seventh day holy, for all His works; therefore He commanded on its behalf that, whoever does any work thereon shall die, and that he who defiles it shall surely die. [26] Wherefore do thou command the children of Israel to observe this day that they may keep it holy and not do thereon any work, and not to defile it, as it is holier than all other days. [27] And whoever profanes it shall surely die, and whoever does thereon any work shall surely die eternally, that the children of Israel may observe this day throughout their generations, and not be rooted out of the land; for it is a holy day and a blessed day. [28] And every one who observes it and keeps Sabbath thereon from all his work, will be holy and blessed throughout all days like unto us. [29] Declare and say to the children of Israel the law of this day both that they should keep Sabbath thereon, and that they should not forsake it in the error of their hearts; (and) that it is not lawful to do any work thereon which is unseemly, to do thereon their own pleasure, and that they should not prepare thereon anything to be eaten or drunk, and (that it is not lawful) to draw water, or bring in or take out thereon through their gates any burden, which they had not prepared for themselves on the sixth day in their dwellings. [30] And they shall not bring in nor take out from house to house on that day; for that day is more holy and blessed than any jubilee day of the jubilees; on this we kept Sabbath in the heavens before it was made known to any flesh to keep Sabbath thereon on the earth. [31] And the Creator of all things blessed it, but he did not sanctify all peoples and nations to keep Sabbath thereon, but Israel alone: them alone he permitted to eat and drink and to keep Sabbath thereon on the earth. [32] And the Creator of all things blessed this day which He had created for blessing and holiness and glory above all days. [33] This law and testimony was given to the children of Israel as a law for ever unto their generations.

## Paradise and the Fall (iii. 1-35; cf. Gen. ii. 4-iii.).

## 3

[1] And on the six days of the second week we brought, according to the word of God, unto Adam all the beasts, and all the cattle, and all the birds, and everything that moves on the earth, and everything that moves in the water, according to their kinds, and according to their types: the beasts on the first day; the cattle on the second day; the birds on the third day; and all that which moves on the earth on the fourth day; and that which moves in the water on the fifth day. [2] And Adam named them all by their respective names, and as he called them, so was their name. [3] And on these five days Adam saw all these, male and female, according to every kind that was on the earth, but he was alone and found no helpmeet for him. [4] And the Lord said unto us: 'It is not good that the man should be alone: let us make a helpmeet for him.' [5] And the Lord our God caused a deep sleep to fall upon him, and he slept, and He took for the woman one rib from amongst his ribs, and this rib was the origin of the woman from amongst his ribs, and He built up the flesh in its stead, and built the woman. [6] And He awaked Adam

out of his sleep and on awaking he rose on the sixth day, and He brought her to him, and he knew her, and said unto her: 'This is now bone of my bones and flesh of my flesh; she shall be called [my] wife; because she was taken from her husband.' [7] Therefore shall man and wife be one and therefore shall a man leave his father and his mother, and cleave unto his wife, and they shall be one flesh. [8] In the first week was Adam created, and the rib -his wife: in the second week He showed her unto him: and for this reason the commandment was given to keep in their defilement, for a male seven days, and for a female twice seven days. [9] And after Adam had completed forty days in the land where he had been created, we brought him into the garden of Eden to till and keep it, but his wife they brought in on the eightieth day, and after this she entered into the garden of Eden. [10] And for this reason the commandment is written on the heavenly tablets in regard to her that gives birth: 'if she bears a male, she shall remain in her uncleanness seven days according to the first week of days, and thirty and three days shall she remain in the blood of her purifying, and she shall not touch any hallowed thing, nor enter into the sanctuary, until she accomplishes these days which (are enjoined) in the case of a male child. [11] But in the case of a female child she shall remain in her uncleanness two weeks of days, according to the first two weeks, and sixty-six days in the blood of her purification, and they will be in all eighty days.' [12] And when she had completed these eighty days we brought her into the garden of Eden, for it is holier than all the earth besides and every tree that is planted in it is holy. [13] Therefore, there was ordained regarding her who bears a male or a female child the statute of those days that she should touch no hallowed thing, nor enter into the sanctuary until these days for the male or female child are accomplished. [14] This is the law and testimony which was written down for Israel, in order that they should observe (it) all the days. [15] And in the first week of the first jubilee, [1-7 A.M.] Adam and his wife were in the garden of Eden for seven years tilling and keeping it, and we gave him work and we instructed him to do everything that is suitable for tillage. [16] And he tilled (the garden), and was naked and knew it not, and was not ashamed, and he protected the garden from the birds and beasts and cattle, and gathered its fruit, and eat, and put aside the residue for himself and for his wife [and put aside that which was being kept]. [17] And after the completion of the seven years, which he had completed there, seven years exactly, [8 A.M.] and in the second month, on the seventeenth day (of the month), the serpent came and approached the woman, and the serpent said to the woman, 'Hath God commanded you, saying, Ye shall not eat of every tree of the garden?' [18] And she said to it, 'Of all the fruit of the trees of the garden God hath said unto us, Eat; but of the fruit of the tree which is in the midst of the garden God hath said unto us, Ye shall not eat thereof, neither shall ye touch it, lest ye die.' [19] And the serpent said unto the woman, 'Ye shall not surely die: for God doth know that on the day ye shall eat thereof, your eyes will be opened, and ye will be as gods, and ye will know good and evil. [20] And the woman saw the tree that it was agreeable and pleasant to the eye, and that its fruit was good for food, and she took thereof and eat. [21] And when she had first covered her shame with figleaves, she gave thereof to Adam and he eat, and his eyes were opened, and he saw that he was naked. [22] And he took figleaves and sewed (them) together, and made an apron for himself, and, covered his shame. [23] And God cursed the serpent, and was wroth with it for ever . . . [24] And He was wroth with the woman, because she harkened to the voice of the serpent, and did eat; and He said unto her: 'I will greatly multiply thy sorrow and thy pains: in sorrow thou shalt bring forth children, and thy return shall be unto thy husband, and he will rule over thee.' [25] And to Adam also he said, ' Because thou hast harkened unto the voice of thy wife, and hast eaten of the tree of which I commanded thee that thou shouldst not eat thereof, cursed be the ground for thy sake: thorns and thistles shall it bring forth to thee, and thou shalt eat thy bread in the sweat of thy face, till thou returnest to the earth from whence thou wast taken; for earth thou art, and unto earth shalt thou return.' [26] And He made for them coats of skin, and clothed them, and sent them forth from the Garden of Eden. [27] And on that day on which Adam went forth from the Garden, he offered as a sweet savour an offering, frankincense, galbanum, and stacte, and spices in the morning with the rising of the sun from the day when he covered his shame. [28] And on that day was closed the mouth of all beasts, and of cattle, and of birds, and of whatever walks, and of whatever moves, so that they could no longer speak: for they had all spoken one with another with one lip and one tongue. [29] And He sent out of the Garden of Eden all flesh that was in the Garden of Eden, and all flesh was scattered according to its kinds, and according to its types unto the places which had been created for them. [30] And to Adam alone did He give (the wherewithal) to cover his shame, of all the beasts and cattle. [31] On this account, it is prescribed on the heavenly tablets as touching all those who know the judgment of the law, that they should cover their shame, and should not uncover themselves as the Gentiles uncover

themselves. [32] And on the new moon of the fourth month, Adam and his wife went forth from the Garden of Eden, and they dwelt in the land of Elda in the land of their creation. [33] And Adam called the name of his wife Eve. [34] And they had no son till the first jubilee, [8 A.M.] and after this he knew her. [35] Now he tilled the land as he had been instructed in the Garden of Eden.

## Cain and Abel (iv. 1-12; cf. Gen. iv.).

### 4

[1] And in the third week in the second jubilee [64-70 A.M.] she gave birth to Cain, and in the fourth [71-77 A.M.] she gave birth to Abel, and in the fifth [78-84 A.M.] she gave birth to her daughter Âwân. [2] And in the first (year) of the third jubilee [99-105 A.M.], Cain slew Abel because (God) accepted the sacrifice of Abel, and did not accept the offering of Cain. [3] And he slew him in the field: and his blood cried from the ground to heaven, complaining because he had slain him. [4] And the Lord reproved Cain because of Abel, because he had slain him, and he made him a fugitive on the earth because of the blood of his brother, and he cursed him upon the earth. [5] And on this account it is written on the heavenly tables, 'Cursed is ,he who smites his neighbour treacherously, and let all who have seen and heard say, So be it; and the man who has seen and not declared (it), let him be accursed as the other.' [6] And for this reason we announce when we come before the Lord our God all the sin which is committed in heaven and on earth, and in light and in darkness, and everywhere. [7] And Adam and his wife mourned for Abel four weeks of years, [99-127 A.M] and in the fourth year of the fifth week [130 A.M.] they became joyful, and Adam knew his wife again, and she bare him a son, and he called his name Seth; for he said 'GOD has raised up a second seed unto us on the earth instead of Abel; for Cain slew him.' [8] And in the sixth week [134-40 A.M.] he begat his daughter Azûra. [9] And Cain took Âwân his sister to be his wife and she bare him Enoch at the close of the fourth jubilee. [190-196 A.M.] And in the first year of the first week of the fifth jubilee, [197 A.M.] houses were built on the earth, and Cain built a city, and called its name after the name of his son Enoch. [10] And Adam knew Eve his wife and she bare yet nine sons. [11] And in the fifth week of the fifth jubilee [225-31 A.M.] Seth took Azûrâ his sister to be his wife, and in the fourth (year of the sixth week) [235 A.M.] she bare him Enos. [12] He began to call on the name of the Lord on the earth.

## The Patriarchs from Adam to Noah (cf. Gen. v.); Life of Enoch; Death of Adam and Gain (iv. 13-33).

[13] And in the seventh jubilee in the third week [309-15 A.M.] Enos took Nôâm his sister to be his wife, and she bare him a son in the third year of the fifth week, and he called his name Kenan. [14] And at the close of the eighth jubilee [325,386-3992 A.M.] Kenan took Mûalêlêth his sister to be his wife, and she bare him a son in the ninth jubilee, in the first week in the third year of this week, [395 A.M] and he called his name Mahalalel. [15] And in the second week of the tenth jubilee [449-55 A.M.] Mahalalel took unto him to wife DinaH, the daughter of Barakiel the daughter of his father's brother, and she bare him a son in the third week in the sixth year, [461 A.M.] and he called his name Jared, for in his days the angels of the Lord descended on the earth, those who are named the Watchers, that they should instruct the children of men, and that they should do judgment and uprightness on the earth. [16] And in the eleventh jubilee [512-18 A.M.] Jared took to himself a wife, and her name was Baraka, the daughter of Râsûjâl, a daughter of his father's brother, in the fourth week of this jubilee, [522 A.M.] and she bare him a son in the fifth week, in the fourth year of the jubilee, and he called his name Enoch. [17] And he was the first among men that are born on earth who learnt writing and knowledge and wisdom and who wrote down the signs of heaven according to the order of their months in a book, that men might know the seasons of the years according to the order of their separate months. [18] And he was the first to write a testimony and he testified to the sons of men among the generations of the earth, and recounted the weeks of the jubilees, and made known to them the days of the years, and set in order the months and recounted the Sabbaths of the years as we made (them), known to him. [19] And what was and what will be he saw in a vision of his sleep, as it will happen to the children of men throughout their generations until the day of judgment; he saw and understood everything, and wrote his testimony, and placed the testimony on earth for all the children of men and for their generations. [20] And in the twelfth jubilee, [582-88] in the seventh week thereof, he took to himself a wife, and her name was Edna, the daughter of Danel, the daughter of his father's brother, and in the sixth year in this week [587 A.M.] she bare him a son and he called his name Methuselah. [21] And he was moreover with the angels of God these six jubilees of years, and they showed him everything which is on earth and in the heavens, the rule of the sun, and he wrote down everything. [22] And he testified to the Watchers, who had sinned with the daughters of men; for these had begun to unite themselves, so as to be defiled, with the daughters of men, and Enoch testified against

(them) all. ²³ And he was taken from amongst the children of men, and we conducted him into the Garden of Eden in majesty and honour, and behold there he writes down the condemnation and judgment of the world, and all the wickedness of the children of men. ²⁴ And on account of it (God) brought the waters of the flood upon all the land of Eden; for there he was set as a sign and that he should testify against all the children of men, that he should recount all the deeds of the generations until the day of condemnation. ²⁵ And he burnt the incense of the sanctuary, (even) sweet spices acceptable before the Lord on the Mount. ²⁶ For the Lord has four places on the earth, the Garden of Eden, and the Mount of the East, and this mountain on which thou art this day, Mount Sinai, and Mount Zion (which) will be sanctified in the new creation for a sanctification of the earth; through it will the earth be sanctified from all (its) guilt and its uncleanness through- out the generations of the world. ²⁷ And in the fourteenth jubilee [652 A.M.] Methuselah took unto himself a wife, Edna the daughter of Azrial, the daughter of his father's brother, in the third week, in the first year of this week, [701-7 A.M.] and he begat a son and called his name Lamech. ²⁸ And in the fifteenth jubilee in the third week Lamech took to himself a wife, and her name was Betenos the daughter of Baraki'il, the daughter of his father's brother, and in this week she bare him a son and he called his name Noah, saying, 'This one will comfort me for my trouble and all my work, and for the ground which the Lord hath cursed.' ²⁹ And at the close of the nineteenth jubilee, in the seventh week in the sixth year [930 A.M.] thereof, Adam died, and all his sons buried him in the land of his creation, and he was the first to be buried in the earth. ³⁰ And he lacked seventy years of one thousand years; for one thousand years are as one day in the testimony of the heavens and therefore was it written concerning the tree of knowledge: 'On the day that ye eat thereof ye shall die.' For this reason he did not complete the years of this day; for he died during it. ³¹ At the close of this jubilee Cain was killed after him in the same year; for his house fell upon him and he died in the midst of his house, and he was killed by its stones; for with a stone he had killed Abel, and by a stone was he killed in righteous judgment. ³² For this reason it was ordained on the heavenly tablets: With the instrument with which a man kills his neighbour with the same shall he be killed; after the manner that he wounded him, in like manner shall they deal with him.' ³³ And in the twenty-fifth [1205 A.M.] jubilee Noah took to himself a wife, and her name was `Emzârâ, the daughter of Râkê'êl, the daughter of his father's brother, in the first year in the fifth week [1207 A.M.]: and in the third year thereof she bare him Shem, in the fifth year thereof [1209 A.M.] she bare him Ham, and in the first year in the sixth week [1212 A.M.] she bare him Japheth.

**The Fall of the Angels and their Punishment; the Deluge foretold (v. 1-20; cf. Gen. vi. 1-12).**

## 5

¹ And it came to pass when the children of men began to multiply on the face of the earth and daughters were born unto them, that the angels of God saw them on a certain year of this jubilee, that they were beautiful to look upon; and they took themselves wives of all whom they chose, and they bare unto them sons and they were giants. ² And lawlessness increased on the earth and all flesh corrupted its way, alike men and cattle and beasts and birds and everything that walks on the earth -all of them corrupted their ways and their orders, and they began to devour each other, and lawlessness increased on the earth and every imagination of the thoughts of all men (was) thus evil continually. ³ And God looked upon the earth, and behold it was corrupt, and all flesh had corrupted its orders, and all that were upon the earth had wrought all manner of evil before His eyes. ⁴ And He said that He would destroy man and all flesh upon the face of the earth which He had created. ⁵ But Noah found grace before the eyes of the Lord. ⁶ And against the angels whom He had sent upon the earth, He was exceedingly wroth, and He gave commandment to root them out of all their dominion, and He bade us to bind them in the depths of the earth, and behold they are bound in the midst of them, and are (kept) separate. ⁷ And against their sons went forth a command from before His face that they should be smitten with the sword, and be removed from under heaven. ⁸ And He said 'My spirit shall not always abide on man; for they also are flesh and their days shall be one hundred and twenty years'. ⁹ And He sent His sword into their midst that each should slay his neighbour, and they began to slay each other till they all fell by the sword and were destroyed from the earth. ¹⁰ And their fathers were witnesses (of their destruction), and after this they were bound in the depths of the earth for ever, until the day of the great condemnation, when judgment is executed on all those who have corrupted their ways and their works before the Lord. ¹¹ And He destroyed all from their places, and there was not left one of them whom He judged not according to all their wickedness. ¹² And he made for all his works a new and righteous nature, so that they should not sin in their whole nature for ever, but should be all righteous each in his kind alway. ¹³ And the judgment of all is ordained and written on the

heavenly tablets in righteousness -even (the judgment of) all who depart from the path which is ordained for them to walk in; and if they walk not therein, judgment is written down for every creature and for every kind. ¹⁴ And there is nothing in heaven or on earth, or in light or in darkness, or in Sheol or in the depth, or in the place of darkness (which is not judged); and all their judgments are ordained and written and engraved. ¹⁵ In regard to all He will judge, the great according to his greatness, and the small according to his smallness, and each according to his way. ¹⁶ And He is not one who will regard the person (of any), nor is He one who will receive gifts, if He says that He will execute judgment on each: if one gave everything that is on the earth, He will not regard the gifts or the person (of any), nor accept anything at his hands, for He is a righteous judge. ¹⁷ [And of the children of Israel it has been written and ordained: If they turn to him in righteousness He will forgive all their transgressions and pardon all their sins. ¹⁸ It is written and ordained that He will show mercy to all who turn from all their guilt once each year.] ¹⁹ And as for all those who corrupted their ways and their thoughts before the flood, no man's person was accepted save that of Noah alone; for his person was accepted in behalf of his sons, whom (God) saved from the waters of the flood on his account; for his heart was righteous in all his ways, according as it was commanded regarding him, and he had not departed from aught that was ordained for him. ²⁰ And the Lord said that he would destroy everything which was upon the earth, both men and cattle, and

**The Building of the Ark; the Flood (v. 21-32; cf. Gen. vi. 13-viii. 19).**
²¹ beasts, and fowls of the air, and that which moveth on the earth. And He commanded Noah to make him an ark, that he might save himself from the waters of the flood. ²² And Noah made the ark in all respects as He commanded him, in the twenty-seventh jubilee of years, in the fifth week in the fifth year (on the new moon of the first month). [1307 A.M.] ²³ And he entered in the sixth (year) thereof, [1308 A.M.] in the second month, on the new moon of the second month, till the sixteenth; and he entered, and all that we brought to him, into the ark, and the Lord closed it from without on the seventeenth evening. ²⁴ And the Lord opened seven flood-gates of heaven, And the mouths of the fountains of the great deep, seven mouths in number. ²⁵ And the flood-gates began to pour down water from the heaven forty days and forty nights, And the fountains of the deep also sent up waters, until the whole world was full of water. ²⁶ And the waters increased upon the earth: Fifteen cubits did the waters rise above all the high mountains, And the ark was lift up above the earth, And it moved upon the face of the waters. ²⁷ And the water prevailed on the face of the earth five months -one hundred and fifty days. ²⁸ And the ark went and rested on the top of Lubar, one of the mountains of Ararat. ²⁹ And (on the new moon) in the fourth month the fountains of the great deep were closed and the flood-gates of heaven were restrained; and on the new moon of the seventh month all the mouths of the abysses of the earth were opened, and the water began to descend into the deep below. ³⁰ And on the new moon of the tenth month the tops of the mountains were seen, and on the new moon of the first month the earth became visible. ³¹ And the waters disappeared from above the earth in the fifth week in the seventh year [1309 A.M.] thereof, and on the seventeenth day in the second month the earth was dry. ³² And on the twenty-seventh thereof he opened the ark, and sent forth from it beasts, and cattle, and birds, and every moving thing.

**Noah's Sacrifice; God's Covenant with him (cf. Gen. viii. 20-ix. 17). Instructions to Moses about eating of Blood, the Feast of Weeks, etc., and Division of the Year (vi. 1-38).**

## 6

¹ And on the new moon of the third month he went forth from the ark, and built an altar on that mountain. ² And he made atonement for the earth, and took a kid and made atonement by its blood for all the guilt of the earth; for everything that had been on it had been destroyed, save those that were in the ark with Noah. ³ And he placed the fat thereof on the altar, and he took an ox, and a goat, and a sheep and kids, and salt, and a turtle-dove, and the young of a dove, and placed a burnt sacrifice on the altar, and poured thereon an offering mingled with oil, and sprinkled wine and strewed frankincense over everything, and caused a goodly savour to arise, acceptable before the Lord. ⁴ And the Lord smelt the goodly savour, and He made a covenant with him that there should not be any more a flood to destroy the earth; that all the days of the earth seed-time and harvest should never cease; cold and heat, and summer and winter, and day and night should not change their order, nor cease for ever. ⁵ 'And you, increase ye and multiply upon the earth, and become many upon it, and be a blessing upon it. The fear of you and the dread of you I will inspire in everything that is on earth and in the sea. ⁶ And behold I have given unto you all beasts, and all winged things, and everything that moves on the earth, and the fish in the waters, and all things for food; as the green herbs, I have given you all things to eat. ⁷ But flesh, with the life thereof, with the blood, ye shall

not eat; for the life of all flesh is in the blood, lest your blood of your lives be required. At the hand of every man, at the hand of every (beast) will I require the blood of man. [8] Whoso sheddeth man's blood by man shall his blood be shed, for in the image of God made He man. [9] And you, increase ye, and multiply on the earth.' [10] And Noah and his sons swore that they would not eat any blood that was in any flesh, and he made a covenant before the Lord God for ever throughout all the generations of the earth in this month. [11] On this account He spake to thee that thou shouldst make a covenant with the children of Israel in this month upon the mountain with an oath, and that thou shouldst sprinkle blood upon them because of all the words of the covenant, which the Lord made with them for ever. [12] And this testimony is written concerning you that you should observe it continually, so that you should not eat on any day any blood of beasts or birds or cattle during all the days of the earth, and the man who eats the blood of beast or of cattle or of birds during all the days of the earth, he and his seed shall be rooted out of the land. [13] And do thou command the children of Israel to eat no blood, so that their names and their seed may be before the Lord our God continually. [14] And for this law there is no limit of days, for it is for ever. They shall observe it throughout their generations, so that they may continue supplicating on your behalf with blood before the altar; every day and at the time of morning and evening they shall seek forgiveness on your behalf perpetually before the Lord that they may keep it and not be rooted out. [15] And He gave to Noah and his sons a sign that there should not again be a flood on the earth. [16] He set His bow in the cloud for a sign of the eternal covenant that there should not again be a flood on the earth to destroy it all the days of the earth. [17] For this reason it is ordained and written on the heavenly tablets, that they should celebrate the feast of weeks in this month once a year, to renew the covenant every year. [18] And this whole festival was celebrated in heaven from the day of creation till the days of Noah - twenty-six jubilees and five weeks of years [**1309-1659 A.M.**]: and Noah and his sons observed it for seven jubilees and one week of years, till the day of Noah's death, and from the day of Noah's death his sons did away with (it) until the days of Abraham, and they eat blood. [19] But Abraham observed it, and Isaac and Jacob and his children observed it up to thy days, and in thy days the children of Israel forgot it until ye celebrated it anew on this mountain. [20] And do thou command the children of Israel to observe this festival in all their generations for a commandment unto them: one day in the year in this month they shall celebrate the festival. [21] For it is the feast of weeks and the feast of first fruits: this feast is twofold and of a double nature: according to what is written and engraven concerning it, celebrate it. [22] For I have written in the book of the first law, in that which I have written for thee, that thou shouldst celebrate it in its season, one day in the year, and I explained to thee its sacrifices that the children of Israel should remember and should celebrate it throughout their generations in this month, one day in every year. [23] And on the new moon of the first month, and on the new moon of the fourth month, and on the new moon of the seventh month, and on the new moon of the tenth month are the days of remembrance, and the days of the seasons in the four divisions of the year. These are written and ordained as a testimony for ever. [24] And Noah ordained them for himself as feasts for the generations for ever, so that they have become thereby a memorial unto him. [25] And on the new moon of the first month he was bidden to make for himself an ark, and on that (day) the earth became dry and he opened (the ark) and saw the earth. [26] And on the new moon of the fourth month the mouths of the depths of the abyss beneath were closed. And on the new moon of the seventh month all the mouths of the abysses of the earth were opened, and the waters began to descend into them. [27] And on the new moon of the tenth month the tops of the mountains were seen, and Noah was glad. [28] And on this account he ordained them for himself as feasts for a memorial for ever, and thus are they ordained. [29] And they placed them on the heavenly tablets, each had thirteen weeks; from one to another (passed) their memorial, from the first to the second, and from the second to the third, and from the third to the fourth. [30] And all the days of the commandment will be two and fifty weeks of days, and (these will make) the entire year complete. Thus it is engraven and ordained on the heavenly tablets. [31] And there is no neglecting (this commandment) for a single year or from year to year. [32] And command thou the children of Israel that they observe the years according to this reckoning- three hundred and sixty-four days, and (these) will constitute a complete year, and they will not disturb its time from its days and from its feasts; for everything will fall out in them according to their testimony, and they will not leave out any day nor disturb any feasts. [33] But if they do neglect and do not observe them according to His commandment, then they will disturb all their seasons and the years will be dislodged from this (order), [and they will disturb the seasons and the years will be dislodged] and they will neglect their ordinances. [34] And all the children of Israel will forget and will not find the path of the years, and will forget the new moons, and seasons, and sabbaths and they will go wrong as to all the order of the years. [35] For I know and from henceforth will I declare it unto thee, and it is not of my own devising; for the book (lies) written before me, and on the heavenly tablets the division of days is ordained, lest they forget the feasts of the covenant and walk according to the feasts of the Gentiles after their error and after their ignorance. [36] For there will be those who will assuredly make observations of the moon -how (it) disturbs the seasons and comes in from year to year ten days too soon. [37] For this reason the years will come upon them when they will disturb (the order), and make an abominable (day) the day of testimony, and an unclean day a feast day, and they will confound all the days, the holy with the unclean, and the unclean day with the holy; for they will go wrong as to the months and sabbaths and feasts and jubilees. [38] For this reason I command and testify to thee that thou mayst testify to them; for after thy death thy children will disturb (them), so that they will not make the year three hundred and sixty-four days only, and for this reason they will go wrong as to the new moons and seasons and sabbaths and festivals, and they will eat all kinds of blood with all kinds of flesh.

**Noah offers Sacrifice; the Cursing of Canaan (cf. Gen. ix. 20-28): Noah's Sons and Grandsons (cf. Gen. x.) and their Cities. Noah's Admonitions (vii. 1-39).**

## 7

[1] And in the seventh week in the first year [**1317 A.M.**] thereof, in this jubilee, Noah planted vines on the mountain on which the ark had rested, named Lubar, one of the Ararat Mountains, and they produced fruit in the fourth year, [**1320 A.M.**] and he guarded their fruit, and gathered it in this year in the seventh month. [2] And he made wine therefrom and put it into a vessel, and kept it until the fifth year, [**1321 A.M.**] until the first day, on the new moon of the first month. [3] And he celebrated with joy the day of this feast, and he made a burnt sacrifice unto the Lord, one young ox and one ram, and seven sheep, each a year old, and a kid of the goats, that he might make atonement thereby for himself and his sons. [4] And he prepared the kid first, and placed some of its blood on the flesh that was on the altar which he had made, and all the fat he laid on the altar where he made the burnt sacrifice, and the ox and the ram and the sheep, and he laid all their flesh upon the altar. [5] And he placed all their offerings mingled with oil upon it, and afterwards he sprinkled wine on the fire which he had previously made on the altar, and he placed incense on the altar and caused a sweet savour to ascend acceptable before the Lord his God. [6] And he rejoiced and drank of this wine, he and his children with joy. [7] And it was evening, and he went into his tent, and being drunken he lay down and slept, and was uncovered in his tent as he slept. [8] And Ham saw Noah his father naked, and went forth and told his two brethren without. [9] And Shem took his garment and arose, he and Japheth, and they placed the garment on their shoulders and went backward and covered the shame of their father, and their faces were backward. [10] And Noah awoke from his sleep and knew all that his younger son had done unto him, and he cursed his son and said: 'Cursed be Canaan; an enslaved servant shall he be unto his brethren.' [11] And he blessed Shem, and said: 'Blessed be the Lord God of Shem, and Canaan shall be his servant. [12] God shall enlarge Japheth, and God shall dwell in the dwelling of Shem, and Canaan shall be his servant.' [13] And Ham knew that his father had cursed his younger son, and he was displeased that he had cursed his son. and he parted from his father, he and his sons with him, Cush and Mizraim and Put and Canaan. [14] And he built for himself a city and called its name after the name of his wife Ne'elatama'uk. [15] And Japheth saw it, and became envious of his brother, and he too built for himself a city, and he called its name after the name of his wife 'Adataneses. [16] And Shem dwelt with his father Noah, and he built a city close to his father on the mountain, and he too called its name after the name of his wife Sedeqetelebab. [17] And behold these three cities are near Mount Lubar; Sedeqetelebab fronting the mountain on its east; and Na'eltama'uk on the south; 'Adatan'eses towards the west. [18] And these are the sons of Shem: Elam, and Asshur, and Arpachshad -this (son) was born two years after the flood- and Lud, and Aram. [19] The sons of Japheth: Gomer and Magog and Madai and Javan, Tubal and Meshech and Tiras: these are the sons of Noah. [20] And in the twenty-eighth jubilee [**1324-1372 A.M.**] Noah began to enjoin upon his sons' sons the ordinances and commandments, and all the judgments that he knew, and he exhorted his sons to observe righteousness, and to cover the shame of their flesh, and to bless their Creator, and honour father and mother, and love their neighbour, and guard their souls from fornication and uncleanness and all iniquity. [21] For owing to these three things came the flood upon the earth, namely, owing to the fornication wherein the Watchers against the law of their ordinances went a whoring after the daughters of men, and took themselves wives of all which they chose: and they made the beginning of uncleanness. [22] And they begat sons the Naphidim, and they were all unlike, and they devoured one another:

and the Giants slew the Naphil, and the Naphil slew the Eljo, and the Eljo mankind, and one man another. 23 And every one sold himself to work iniquity and to shed much blood, and the earth was filled with iniquity. 24 And after this they sinned against the beasts and birds, and all that moves and walks on the earth: and much blood was shed on the earth, and every imagination and desire of men imagined vanity and evil continually. 25 And the Lord destroyed everything from off the face of the earth; because of the wickedness of their deeds, and because of the blood which they had shed in the midst of the earth He destroyed everything. 26 'And we were left, I and you, my sons, and everything that entered with us into the ark, and behold I see your works before me that ye do not walk in righteousness: for in the path of destruction ye have begun to walk, and ye are parting one from another, and are envious one of another, and (so it comes) that ye are not in harmony, my sons, each with his brother. 27 For I see, and behold the demons have begun (their) seductions against you and against your children and now I fear on your behalf, that after my death ye will shed the blood of men upon the earth, and that ye, too, will be destroyed from the face of the earth. 28 For whoso sheddeth man's blood, and whoso eateth the blood of any flesh, shall all be destroyed from the earth. 29 And there shall not be left any man that eateth blood, or that sheddeth the blood of man on the earth, Nor shall there be left to him any seed or descendants living under heaven; For into Sheol shall they go, And into the place of condemnation shall they descend, And into the darkness of the deep shall they all be removed by a violent death. 30 There shall be no blood seen upon you of all the blood there shall be all the days in which ye have killed any beasts or cattle or whatever flies upon the earth, and work ye a good work to your souls by covering that which has been shed on the face of the earth. 31 And ye shall not be like him who eats with blood, but guard yourselves that none may eat blood before you: cover the blood, for thus have I been commanded to testify to you and your children, together with all flesh. 32 And suffer not the soul to be eaten with the flesh, that your blood, which is your life, may not be required at the hand of any flesh that sheds (it) on the earth. 33 For the earth will not be clean from the blood which has been shed upon it; for (only) through the blood of him that shed it will the earth be purified throughout all its generations. 34 And now, my children, harken: work judgment and righteousness that ye maybe planted in righteousness over the face of the whole earth, and your glory lifted up before my God, who saved me from the waters of the flood. 35 And behold, ye will go and build for yourselves cities, and plant in them all the plants that are upon the earth, and moreover all fruit-bearing trees. 36 For three years the fruit of everything that is eaten will not be gathered: and in the fourth year its fruit will be accounted holy [and they will offer the first-fruits], acceptable before the Most High God, who created heaven and earth and all things. Let them offer in abundance the first of the wine and oil (as) first-fruits on the altar of the Lord, who receives it, and what is left let the servants of the house of the Lord eat before the altar which receives (it). 37 And in the fifth year make ye the release so that ye release it in righteousness and uprightness, and ye shall be righteous, and all that you plant shall prosper. 38 For thus did Enoch, the father of your father command Methuselah, his son, and Methuselah his son Lamech, and Lamech commanded me all the things which his fathers commanded him. 39 And I also will give you commandment, my sons, as Enoch commanded his son in the first jubilees: whilst still living, the seventh in his generation, he commanded and testified to his son and to his son's sons until the day of his death.'

**Genealogy of the Descendants of Shem: Noah and his Sons divide the Earth (viii. 1-30; cf. Gen. x.).**

# 8

1 In the twenty-ninth jubilee, in the first week, [1373 A.M.] in the beginning thereof Arpachshad took to himself a wife and her name was Rasu'eja, the daughter of Susan, the daughter of Elam, and she bare him a son in the third year in this week, [1375 A.M.] and he called his name Kainam. 2 And the son grew, and his father taught him writing, and he went to seek for himself a place where he might seize for himself a city. 3 And he found a writing which former (generations) had carved on the rock, and he read what was thereon, and he transcribed it and sinned owing to it; for it contained the teaching of the Watchers in accordance with which they used to observe the omens of the sun and moon and stars in all the signs of heaven. 4 And he wrote it down and said nothing regarding it; for he was afraid to speak to Noah about it lest he should be angry with him on account of it. 5 And in the thirtieth jubilee, [1429 A.M.] in the second week, in the first year thereof, he took to himself a wife, and her name was Melka, the daughter of Madai, the son of Japheth, and in the fourth year [1432 A.M.] he begat a son, and called his name Shelah; for he said: 'Truly I have been sent.' 6 [And in the fourth year he was born], and Shelah grew up and took to himself a wife, and her name was Mu'ak, the daughter of Kesed, his father's brother, in the one and thirtieth jubilee, in the fifth week, in the first

year [1499 A.M.] thereof. 7 And she bare him a son in the fifth year [1503 A.M.] thereof, and he called his name Eber: and he took unto himself a wife, and her name was 'Azûrâd, the daughter of Nebrod, in the thirty-second jubilee, in the seventh week, in the third year thereof. [1564 A.M.] 8 And in the sixth year [1567 A.M.] thereof, she bare him son, and he called his name Peleg; for in the days when he was born the children of Noah began to divide the earth amongst themselves: for this reason he called his name Peleg. 9 And they divided (it) secretly amongst themselves, and told it to Noah. 10 And it came to pass in the beginning of the thirty-third jubilee [1569 A.M.] that they divided the earth into three parts, for Shem and Ham and Japheth, according to the inheritance of each, in the first year in the first week, when one of us who had been sent, was with them. 11 And he called his sons, and they drew nigh to him, they and their children, and he divided the earth into the lots, which his three sons were to take in possession, and they reached forth their hands, and took the writing out of the bosom of Noah, their father. 12 And there came forth on the writing as Shem's lot the middle of the earth which he should take as an inheritance for himself and for his sons for the generations of eternity, from the middle of the mountain range of Rafa, from the mouth of the water from the river Tina, and his portion goes towards the west through the midst of this river, and it extends till it reaches the water of the abysses, out of which this river goes forth and pours its waters into the sea Me'at, and this river flows into the great sea. And all that is towards the north is Japheth's, and all that is towards the south belongs to Shem. 13 And it extends till it reaches Karaso: this is in the bosom of the tongue which looks towards the south. 14 And his portion extends along the great sea, and it extends in a straight line till it reaches the west of the tongue which looks towards the south: for this sea is named the tongue of the Egyptian Sea. 15 And it turns from here towards the south towards the mouth of the great sea on the shore of (its) waters, and it extends to the west to 'Afra, and it extends till it reaches the waters of the river Gihon, and to the south of the waters of Gihon, to the banks of this river. 16 And it extends towards the east, till it reaches the Garden of Eden, to the south thereof, [to the south] and from the east of the whole land of Eden and of the whole east, it turns to the east and proceeds till it reaches the east of the mountain named Rafa, and it descends to the bank of the mouth of the river Tina. 17 This portion came forth by lot for Shem and his sons, that they should possess it for ever unto his generations for evermore. 18 And Noah rejoiced that this portion came forth for Shem and for his sons, and he remembered all that he had spoken with his mouth in prophecy; for he had said: 'Blessed be the Lord God of Shem And may the Lord dwell in the dwelling of Shem.' 19 And he knew that the Garden of Eden is the holy of holies, and the dwelling of the Lord, and Mount Sinai the centre of the desert, and Mount Zion -the centre of the navel of the earth: these three were created as holy places facing each other. 20 And he blessed the God of gods, who had put the word of the Lord into his mouth, and the Lord for evermore. 21 And he knew that a blessed portion and a blessing had come to Shem and his sons unto the generations for ever -the whole land of Eden and the whole land of the Red Sea, and the whole land of the east and India, and on the Red Sea and the mountains thereof, and all the land of Bashan, and all the land of Lebanon and the islands of Kaftur, and all the mountains of Sanir and 'Amana, and the mountains of Asshur in the north, and all the land of Elam, Asshur, and Babel, and Susan and Ma'edai, and all the mountains of Ararat, and all the region beyond the sea, which is beyond the mountains of Asshur towards the north, a blessed and spacious land, and all that is in it is very good. 22 And for Ham came forth the second portion, beyond the Gihon towards the south to the right of the Garden, and it extends towards the south and it extends to all the mountains of fire, and it extends towards the west to the sea of 'Atel and it extends towards the west till it reaches the sea of Ma'uk -that (sea) into which everything which is not destroyed descends. 23 And it goes forth towards the north to the limits of Gadir, and it goes forth to the coast of the waters of the sea to the waters of the great sea till it draws near to the river Gihon, and goes along the river Gihon till it reaches the right of the Garden of Eden. 24 And this is the land which came forth for Ham as the portion which he was to occupy for ever for himself and his sons unto their generations for ever. 25 And for Japheth came forth the third portion beyond the river Tina to the north of the outflow of its waters, and it extends north-easterly to the whole region of Gog, and to all the country east thereof. 26 And it extends northerly to the north, and it extends to the mountains of Qelt towards the north, and towards the sea of Ma'uk, and it goes forth to the east of Gadir as far as the region of the waters of the sea. 27 And it extends until it approaches the west of Fara and it returns towards 'Aferag, and it extends easterly to the waters of the sea of Me'at. 28 And it extends to the region of the river Tina in a north-easterly direction until it approaches the boundary of its waters towards the mountain Rafa, and it turns round towards the north. 29 This is the land which came forth for Japheth and his sons as the portion of his inheritance which he should possess for himself and his sons, for their generations for ever; five great islands, and a great land in the north. [30] But it is cold, and the land of Ham is hot, and the land of Shem is neither hot nor cold, but it is of blended cold and heat.

**Subdivision of the Three Portions amongst the Grandchildren: Oath taken by Noah's Sons (ix. 1-15; cf. Gen. x. partly).**

## 9

[1] And Ham divided amongst his sons, and the first portion came forth for Cush towards the east, and to the west of him for Mizraim, and to the west of him for Put, and to the west of him [and to the west thereof] on the sea for Canaan. [2] And Shem also divided amongst his sons, and the first portion came forth for Ham and his sons, to the east of the river Tigris till it approaches the east, the whole land of India, and on the Red Sea on its coast, and the waters of Dedan, and all the mountains of Mebri and Ela, and all the land of Susan and all that is on the side of Pharnak to the Red Sea and the river Tina. [3] And for Asshur came forth the second Portion, all the land of Asshur and Nineveh and Shinar and to the border of India, and it ascends and skirts the river. [4] And for Arpachshad came forth the third portion, all the land of the region of the Chaldees to the east of the Euphrates, bordering on the Red Sea, and all the waters of the desert close to the tongue of the sea which looks towards Egypt, all the land of Lebanon and Sanir and 'Amana to the border of the Euphrates. [5] And for Aram there came forth the fourth portion, all the land of Mesopotamia between the Tigris and the Euphrates to the north of the Chaldees to the border of the mountains of Asshur and the land of 'Arara. [6] And there came forth for Lud the fifth portion, the mountains of Asshur and all appertaining to them till it reaches the Great Sea, and till it reaches the east of Asshur his brother. [7] And Japheth also divided the land of his inheritance amongst his sons. [8] And the first portion came forth for Gomer to the east from the north side to the river Tina; and in the north there came forth for Magog all the inner portions of the north until it reaches the sea of Me'at. [9] And for Madai came forth as his portion that he should posses from the west of his two brothers to the islands, and to the coasts of the islands. [10] And for Javan came forth the fourth portion every island and the islands which are towards the border of Lud. [11] And for Tubal there came forth the fifth portion in the midst of the tongue which approaches towards the border of the portion of Lud to the second tongue, to the region beyond the second tongue unto the third tongue. [12] And for Meshech came forth the sixth portion, all the region beyond the third tongue till it approaches the east of Gadir. [13] And for Tiras there came forth the seventh portion, four great islands in the midst of the sea, which reach to the portion of Ham [and the islands of Kamaturi came out by lot for the sons of Arpachshad as his inheritance]. [14] And thus the sons of Noah divided unto their sons in the presence of Noah their father, and he bound them all by an oath, imprecating a curse on every one that sought to seize the portion which had not fallen (to him) by his lot. [15] And they all said, 'So be it; so be it ' for themselves and their sons for ever throughout their generations till the day of judgment, on which the Lord God shall judge them with a sword and with fire for all the unclean wickedness of their errors, wherewith they have filled the earth with transgression and uncleanness and fornication and sin.

**Noah's Sons led astray by Evil Spirits; Noah's Prayer; Mastêmâ; Death of Noah (x. 1-17; cf. Gen. ix. 28).**

## 10

[1] And in the third week of this jubilee the unclean demons began to lead astray the children of the sons of Noah, and to make to err and destroy them. [2] And the sons of Noah came to Noah their father, and they told him concerning the demons which were leading astray and blinding and slaying his sons' sons. [3] And he prayed before the Lord his God, and said: 'God of the spirits of all flesh, who hast shown mercy unto me And hast saved me and my sons from the waters of the flood, And hast not caused me to perish as Thou didst the sons of perdition; For Thy grace has been great towards me, And great has been Thy mercy to my soul; Let Thy grace be lift up upon my sons, And let not wicked spirits rule over them Lest they should destroy them from the earth. [4] But do Thou bless me and my sons, that we may increase and Multiply and replenish the earth. [5] And Thou knowest how Thy Watchers, the fathers of these spirits, acted in my day: and as for these spirits which are living, imprison them and hold them fast in the place of condemnation, and let them not bring destruction on the sons of thy servant, my God; for these are malignant, and created in order to destroy. [6] And let them not rule over the spirits of the living; for Thou alone canst exercise dominion over them. And let them not have power over the sons of the righteous from henceforth and for evermore.' [7] And the Lord our God bade us to bind all. [8] And the chief of the spirits, Mastêmâ, came and said: 'Lord, Creator, let some of them remain before me, and let them harken to my voice, and do all that I shall say unto them; for if some of them are not left to me, I shall not be able to

execute the power of my will on the sons of men; for these are for corruption and leading astray before my judgment, for great is the wickedness of the sons of men.' [9] And He said: Let the tenth part of them remain before him, and let nine parts descend into the place of condemnation.' [10] And one of us He commanded that we should teach Noah all their medicines; for He knew that they would not walk in uprightness, nor strive in righteousness. [11] And we did according to all His words: all the malignant evil ones we bound in the place of condemnation and a tenth part of them we left that they might be subject before Satan on the earth. [12] And we explained to Noah all the medicines of their diseases, together with their seductions, how he might heal them with herbs of the earth. [13] And Noah wrote down all things in a book as we instructed him concerning every kind of medicine. Thus the evil spirits were precluded from (hurting) the sons of Noah. [14] And he gave all that he had written to Shem, his eldest son; for he loved him exceedingly above all his sons. [15] And Noah slept with his fathers, and was buried on Mount Lubar in the land of Ararat. [16] Nine hundred and fifty years he completed in his life, nineteen jubilees and two weeks and five years. [1659 A.M.] [17] And in his life on earth he excelled the children of men save Enoch because of the righteousness, wherein he was perfect. For Enoch's office was ordained for a testimony to the generations of the world, so that he should recount all the deeds of generation unto generation, till the day of judgment.

**The Tower of Babel and the Confusion of Tongues (x. 18-27; cf. Gen. xi. 1-9).**

[18] And in the three and thirtieth jubilee, in the first year in the second week, Peleg took to himself a wife, whose name was Lomna the daughter of Sina'ar, and she bare him a son in the fourth year of this week, and he called his name Reu; for he said: 'Behold the children of men have become evil through the wicked purpose of building for themselves a city and a tower in the land of Shinar.' [19] For they departed from the land of Ararat eastward to Shinar; for in his days they built the city and the tower, saying, 'Go to, let us ascend thereby into heaven.' [20] And they began to build, and in the fourth week they made brick with fire, and the bricks served them for stone, and the clay with which they cemented them together was asphalt which comes out of the sea, and out of the fountains of water in the land of Shinar. [21] And they built it: forty and three years [1645-1688 A.M.] were they building it; its breadth was **203** bricks, and the height (of a brick) was the third of one; its height amounted to **5433** cubits and **2** palms, and (the extent of one wall was) thirteen stades (and of the other thirty stades). [22] And the Lord our God said unto us: Behold, they are one people, and (this) they begin to do, and now nothing will be withholden from them. Go to, let us go down and confound their language, that they may not understand one another's speech, and they may be dispersed into cities and nations, and one purpose will no longer abide with them till the day of judgment.' [23] And the Lord descended, and we descended with him to see the city and the tower which the children of men had built. [24] And he confounded their language, and they no longer understood one another's speech, and they ceased then to build the city and the tower. [25] For this reason the whole land of Shinar is called Babel, because the Lord did there confound all the language of the children of men, and from thence they were dispersed into their cities, each according to his language and his nation. [26] And the Lord sent a mighty wind against the tower and overthrew it upon the earth, and behold it was between Asshur and Babylon in the land of Shinar, and they called its name 'Overthrow'. [27] In the fourth week in the first year [1688 A.M.] in the beginning thereof in the four and thirtieth jubilee, were they dispersed from the land of Shinar.

**The Children of Noah enter their Districts Canaan seizes Palestine wrongfully; Madai receives Media (x. 28-36)**

[28] And Ham and his sons went into the land which he was to occupy, which he acquired as his portion in the land of the south. [29] And Canaan saw the land of Lebanon to the river of Egypt, that it was very good, and he went not into the land of his inheritance to the west (that is to) the sea, and he dwelt in the land of Lebanon, eastward and westward from the border of Jordan and from the border of the sea. [30] And Ham, his father, and Cush and Mizraim his brothers said unto him: 'Thou hast settled in a land which is not thine, and which did not fall to us by lot: do not do so; for if thou dost do so, thou and thy sons will fall in the land and (be) accursed through sedition; for by sedition ye have settled, and by sedition will thy children fall, and thou shalt be rooted out for ever. [31] Dwell not in the dwelling of Shem; for to Shem and to his sons did it come by their lot. [32] Cursed art thou, and cursed shalt thou be beyond all the sons of Noah, by the curse by which we bound ourselves by an oath in the presence of the holy judge, and in the presence of Noah our father.' [33] But he did not harken unto them, and dwelt in the land of Lebanon from Hamath to the entering of Egypt, he and his sons until this day. [34] And for this reason that land is named Canaan. [35] And Japheth and his sons went towards the sea and dwelt in the land of their

portion, and Madai saw the land of the sea and it did not please him, and he begged a (portion) from Ham and Asshur and Arpachshad, his wife's brother, and he dwelt in the land of Media, near to his wife's brother until this day. [36] And he called his dwelling-place, and the dwelling-place of his sons, Media, after the name of their father Madai.

**The History of the Patriarchs from Reu to Abraham (cf. Gen. xi, 20-30); the Corruption of the Human Race (xi. 1-15).**

## 11

[1] And in the thirty-fifth jubilee, in the third week, in the first year [**1681** A.M.] thereof, Reu took to himself a wife, and her name was 'Ôrâ, the daughter of 'Ûr, the son of Kesed, and she bare him a son, and he called his name Sêrôh, in the seventh year of this week in this jubilee. [**1687** A.M.] [2] And the sons of Noah began to war on each other, to take captive and to slay each other, and to shed the blood of men on the earth, and to eat blood, and to build strong cities, and walls, and towers, and individuals (began) to exalt themselves above the nation, and to found the beginnings of kingdoms, and to go to war people against people, and nation against nation, and city against city, and all (began) to do evil, and to acquire arms, and to teach their sons war, and they began to capture cities, and to sell male and female slaves. [3] And 'Ûr, the son of Kesed, built the city of 'Ara of the Chaldees, and called its name after his own name and the name of his father. [4] And they made for themselves molten images, and they worshipped each the idol, the molten image which they had made for themselves, and they began to make graven images and unclean simulacra, and malignant spirits assisted and seduced (them) into committing transgression and uncleanness. [5] And the prince Mastêmâ exerted himself to do all this, and he sent forth other spirits, those which were put under his hand, to do all manner of wrong and sin, and all manner of transgression, to corrupt and destroy, and to shed blood upon the earth. [6] For this reason he called the name of Sêrôh, Serug, for every one turned to do all manner of sin and transgression. [7] And he grew up, and dwelt in Ur of the Chaldees, near to the father of his wife's mother, and he worshipped idols, and he took to himself a wife in the thirty-sixth jubilee, in the fifth week, in the first year thereof, [**1744** A.M.] and her name was Melka, the daughter of Kaber, the daughter of his father's brother. [8] And she bare him Nahor, in the first year of this week, and he grew and dwelt in Ur of the Chaldees, and his father taught him the researches of the Chaldees to divine and augur, according to the signs of heaven. [9] And in the thirty-seventh jubilee in the sixth week, in the first year thereof, [**1800** A.M.] he took to himself a wife, and her name was 'Ijaska, the daughter of Nestag of the Chaldees. [10] And she bare him Terah in the seventh year of this week. [**1806** A.M.] [11] And the prince Mastêmâ sent ravens and birds to devour the seed which was sown in the land, in order to destroy the land, and rob the children of men of their labours. Before they could plough in the seed, the ravens picked (it) from the surface of the ground. [12] And for this reason he called his name Terah because the ravens and the birds reduced them to destitution and devoured their seed. [13] And the years began to be barren, owing to the birds, and they devoured all the fruit of the trees from the trees: it was only with great effort that they could save a little of all the fruit of the earth in their days. [14] And in this thirty-ninth jubilee, in the second week in the first year, [**1870** A.M.] Terah took to himself a wife, and her name was 'Edna, the daughter of 'Abram, the daughter of his father's sister. [15] And in the seventh year of this week [**1876** A.M.] she bare him a son, and he called his name Abram, by the name of the father of his mother; for he had died before his daughter had conceived a son.

**Abram's Knowledge of God and wonderful Deeds (xi. 16-24).**

[16] And the child began to understand the errors of the earth that all went astray after graven images and after uncleanness, and his father taught him writing, and he was two weeks of years old, [**1890** A.M.] and he separated himself from his father, that he might not worship idols with him. [17] And he began to pray to the Creator of all things that He might save him from the errors of the children of men, and that his portion should not fall into error after uncleanness and vileness. [18] And the seed time came for the sowing of seed upon the land, and they all went forth together to protect their seed against the ravens, and Abram went forth with those that went, and the child was a lad of fourteen years. [19] And a cloud of ravens came to devour the seed, and Abram ran to meet them before they settled on the ground, and cried to them before they settled on the ground to devour the seed, and said, ' Descend not: return to the place whence ye came,' and they proceeded to turn back. [20] And he caused the clouds of ravens to turn back that day seventy times, and of all the ravens throughout all the land where Abram was there settled there not so much as one. [21] And all who were with him throughout all the land saw him cry out, and all the ravens turn back, and his name became great in all the land of the Chaldees. [22] And there came to him this year all those that wished to sow, and he went with them until the time of sowing ceased: and they sowed their land, and that year they brought enough grain home and eat and were satisfied. [23] And in the

first year of the fifth week [**1891** A.M.] Abram taught those who made implements for oxen, the artificers in wood, and they made a vessel above the ground, facing the frame of the plough, in order to put the seed thereon, and the seed fell down therefrom upon the share of the plough, and was hidden in the earth, and they no longer feared the ravens. [24] And after this manner they made (vessels) above the ground on all the frames of the ploughs, and they sowed and tilled all the land, according as Abram commanded them, and they no longer feared the birds.

**Abram seeks to convert Terah from Idolatry; the Family of Terah (cf. Gen. xi. 27-30). Abram burns the Idols. Death of Haran (cf. Gen. xi. 28) (xii. 1-14).**

## 12

[1] And it came to pass in the sixth week, in the seventh year thereof, [**1904** A.M.] that Abram said to Terah his father, saying, 'Father!' [2] And he said, 'Behold, here am I, my son.' And he said, 'What help and profit have we from those idols which thou dost worship, And before which thou dost bow thyself? [3] For there is no spirit in them, For they are dumb forms, and a misleading of the heart. Worship them not: [4] Worship the God of heaven, Who causes the rain and the dew to descend on the earth And does everything upon the earth, And has created everything by His word, And all life is from before His face. [5] Why do ye worship things that have no spirit in them? For they are the work of (men's) hands, And on your shoulders do ye bear them, And ye have no help from them, But they are a great cause of shame to those who make them, And a misleading of the heart to those who worship them: Worship them not.' [6] And his father said unto him, I also know it, my son, but what shall I do with a people who have made me to serve before them? [7] And if I tell them the truth, they will slay me; for their soul cleaves to them to worship them and honour them. [8] Keep silent, my son, lest they slay thee.' And these words he spake to his two brothers, and they were angry with him and he kept silent. [9] And in the fortieth jubilee, in the second week, in the seventh year thereof, [**1925** A.M.] Abram took to himself a wife, and her name was Sarai, the daughter of his father, and she became his wife. [10] And Haran, his brother, took to himself a wife in the third year of the third week, [**1928** A.M.] and she bare him a son in the seventh year of this week, [**1932** A.M.] and he called his name Lot. [11] And Nahor, his brother, took to himself a wife. [12] And in the sixtieth year of the life of Abram, that is, in the fourth week, in the fourth year thereof, [**1936** A.M.] Abram arose by night, and burned the house of the idols, and he burned all that was in the house and no man knew it. [13] And they arose in the night and sought to save their gods from the midst of the fire. [14] And Haran hasted to save them, but the fire flamed over him, and he was burnt in the fire, and he died in Ur of the Chaldees before Terah his father, and they buried him in Ur of the Chaldees.

**The Family of Terah in Haran; Abram's Experiences there; his Journey to Canaan (xii. 15-31; cf. Gen. xi, 31-xii. 3).**

[15] And Terah went forth from Ur of the Chaldees, he and his sons, to go into the land of Lebanon and into the land of Canaan, and he dwelt in the land of Haran, and Abram dwelt with Terah his father in Haran two weeks of years. [16] And in the sixth week, in the fifth year thereof, [**1951** A.M.] Abram sat up throughout the night on the new moon of the seventh month to observe the stars from the evening to the morning, in order to see what would be the character of the year with regard to the rains, and he was alone as he sat and observed. [17] And a word came into his heart and he said: All the signs of the stars, and the signs of the moon and of the sun are all in the hand of the Lord. Why do I search (them) out? [18] If He desires, He causes it to rain, morning and evening; And if He desires, He withholds it, And all things are in his hand.' [19] And he prayed that night and said, 'My God, God Most High, Thou alone art my God, And Thee and Thy dominion have I chosen. And Thou hast created all things, And all things that are the work of thy hands. [20] Deliver me from the hands of evil spirits who have dominion over the thoughts of men's hearts, And let them not lead me astray from Thee, my God. And stablish Thou me and my seed for ever That we go not astray from henceforth and for evermore.' [21] And he said, 'Shall I return unto Ur of the Chaldees who seek my face that I may return to them, am I to remain here in this place? The right path before Thee prosper it in the hands of Thy servant that he may fulfil (it) and that I may not walk in the deceitfulness of my heart, O my God.' [22] And he made an end of speaking and praying, and behold the word of the Lord was sent to him through me, saying: 'Get thee up from thy country, and from thy kindred and from the house of thy father unto a land which I will show thee, and I shall make thee a great and numerous nation. [23] And I will bless thee And I will make thy name great, And thou shalt be blessed in the earth, And in Thee shall all families of the earth be blessed, And I will bless them that bless thee, And curse them that curse thee. [24] And I will be a God to thee and thy son, and to thy son's son, and to all thy seed: fear not, from henceforth and unto all generations

of the earth I am thy God.' <sup>25</sup> And the Lord God said: 'Open his mouth and his ears, that he may hear and speak with his mouth, with the language which has been revealed'; for it had ceased from the mouths of all the children of men from the day of the overthrow (of Babel). <sup>26</sup> And I opened his mouth, and his ears and his lips, and I began to speak with him in Hebrew in the tongue of the creation. <sup>27</sup> And he took the books of his fathers, and these were written in Hebrew, and he transcribed them, and he began from henceforth to study them, and I made known to him that which he could not (understand), and he studied them during the six rainy months. <sup>28</sup> And it came to pass in the seventh year of the sixth week [1953 A.M.] that he spoke to his father and informed him, that he would leave Haran to go into the land of Canaan to see it and return to him. <sup>29</sup> And Terah his father said unto him; Go in peace: May the eternal God make thy path straight. And the Lord [(be) with thee, and] protect thee from all evil, And grant unto thee grace, mercy and favour before those who see thee, And may none of the children of men have power over thee to harm thee; Go in peace. <sup>30</sup> And if thou seest a land pleasant to thy eyes to dwell in, then arise and take me to thee and take Lot with thee, the son of Haran thy brother as thine own son: the Lord be with thee. <sup>31</sup> And Nahor thy brother leave with me till thou returnest in peace, and we go with thee all together.'

## Abram with Lot in Canaan and Egypt (cf. Gen. xii. 4-20). Abram separates from Lot (cf. Gen. xiii. 11-18) (xiii. 1-21).

### 13

<sup>1</sup> And Abram journeyed from Haran, and he took Sarai, his wife, and Lot, his brother Haran's son, to the land of Canaan, and he came into Asshur, and proceeded to Shechem, and dwelt near a lofty oak. <sup>2</sup> And he saw, and, behold, the land was very pleasant from the entering of Hamath to the lofty oak. <sup>3</sup> And the Lord said to him: 'To thee and to thy seed will I give this land.' <sup>4</sup> And he built an altar there, and he offered thereon a burnt sacrifice to the Lord, who had appeared to him. <sup>5</sup> And he removed from thence unto the mountain . . . Bethel on the west and Ai on the east, and pitched his tent there. <sup>6</sup> And he saw and behold, the land was very wide and good, and everything grew thereon -vines and figs and pomegranates, oaks and ilexes, and terebinths and oil trees, and cedars and cypresses and date trees, and all trees of the field, and there was water on the mountains. <sup>7</sup> And he blessed the Lord who had led him out of Ur of the Chaldees, and had brought him to this land. <sup>8</sup> And it came to pass in the first year, in the seventh week, on the new moon of the first month, 1954 A.M.] that he built an altar on this mountain, and called on the name of the Lord: 'Thou, the eternal God, art my God.' <sup>9</sup> And he offered on the altar a burnt sacrifice unto the Lord that He should be with him and not forsake him all the days of his life. <sup>10</sup> And he removed from thence and went towards the south, and he came to Hebron and Hebron was built at that time, and he dwelt there two years, and he went (thence) into the land of the south, to Bealoth, and there was a famine in the land. <sup>11</sup> And Abram went into Egypt in the third year of the week, and he dwelt in Egypt five years before his wife was torn away from him. <sup>12</sup> Now Tanais in Egypt was at that time built-seven years after Hebron. <sup>13</sup> And it came to pass when Pharaoh seized Sarai, the wife of Abram that the Lord plagued Pharaoh and his house with great plagues because of Sarai, Abram's wife. <sup>14</sup> And Abram was very glorious by reason of possessions in sheep, and cattle, and asses, and horses, and camels, and menservants, and maidservants, and in silver and gold exceedingly. And Lot also his brother's son, was wealthy. <sup>15</sup> And Pharaoh gave back Sarai, the wife of Abram, and he sent him out of the land of Egypt, and he journeyed to the place where he had pitched his tent at the beginning, to the place of the altar, with Ai on the east, and Bethel on the west, and he blessed the Lord his God who had brought him back in peace. <sup>16</sup> And it came to pass in the forty-first jubilee in the third year of the first week, [1963 A.M.] that he returned to this place and offered thereon a burnt sacrifice, and called on the name of the Lord, and said: 'Thou, the most high God, art my God for ever and ever.' <sup>17</sup> And in the fourth year of this week [1964 A.M.] Lot parted from him, and Lot dwelt in Sodom, and the men of Sodom were sinners exceedingly. <sup>18</sup> And it grieved him in his heart that his brother's son had parted from him; for he had no children. <sup>19</sup> In that year when Lot was taken captive, the Lord said unto Abram, after that Lot had parted from him, in the fourth year of this week: 'Lift up thine eyes from the place where thou art dwelling, northward and southward, and westward and eastward. <sup>20</sup> For all the land which thou seest I will give to thee and to thy seed for ever, and I will make thy seed as the sand of the sea: though a man may number the sand of the earth, yet thy seed shall not be numbered. <sup>21</sup> Arise, walk (through the land) in the length of it and the breadth of it, and see it all; for to thy seed will I give it.' And Abram went to Hebron, and dwelt there.

### The Campaign of Chedorlaomer (xiii. 22-29; cf. Gen. xiv.).

<sup>22</sup> And in this year came Chedorlaomer, king of Elam, and Amraphel, king of Shinar, and Arioch king of Sellasar, and Tergal, king of nations, and slew the king of Gomorrah, and the king of Sodom fled, and many fell through wounds in the vale of Siddim, by the Salt Sea. <sup>23</sup> And they took captive Sodom and Adam and Zeboim, and they took captive Lot also, the son of Abram's brother, and all his possessions, and they went to Dan. <sup>24</sup> And one who had escaped came and told Abram that his brother's son had been taken captive and (Abram) armed his household servants . . . <sup>25</sup> . . . . for Abram, and for his seed, a tenth of the first fruits to the Lord, and the Lord ordained it as an ordinance for ever that they should give it to the priests who served before Him, that they should possess it for ever. <sup>26</sup> And to this law there is no limit of days; for He hath ordained it for the generations for ever that they should give to the Lord the tenth of everything, of the seed and of the wine and of the oil and of the cattle and of the sheep. <sup>27</sup> And He gave (it) unto His priests to eat and to drink with joy before Him. <sup>28</sup> And the king of Sodom came to him and bowed himself before him, and said: 'Our lord Abram, give unto us the souls which thou hast rescued, but let the booty be thine.' <sup>29</sup> And Abram said unto him: 'I lift up my hands to the Most High God, that from a thread to a shoe-latchet I shall not take aught that is thine lest thou shouldst say, I have made Abram rich; save only what the young men have eaten, and the portion of the men who went with me - Aner, Eschol, and Mamre. These shall take their portion.'

### God's Covenant with Abram (xiv. 1-20; cf. Gen. xv.).

### 14

<sup>1</sup> After these things, in the fourth year of this week, on the new moon of the third month, the word of the Lord came to Abram in a dream, saying: 'Fear not, Abram; I am thy defender, and thy reward will be exceeding great.' <sup>2</sup> And he said: 'Lord, Lord, what wilt thou give me, seeing I go hence childless, and the son of Maseq, the son of my handmaid, is the Dammasek Eliezer: he will be my heir, and to me thou hast given no seed.' <sup>3</sup> And he said unto him: 'This (man) will not be thy heir, but one that will come out of thine own bowels; he will be thine heir.' <sup>4</sup> And He brought him forth abroad, and said unto him: 'Look toward heaven and number the stars if thou art able to number them.' <sup>5</sup> And he looked toward heaven, and beheld the stars. And He said unto him: 'So shall thy seed be.' <sup>6</sup> And he believed in the Lord, and it was counted to him for righteousness. <sup>7</sup> And He said unto him: 'I am the Lord that brought thee out of Ur of the Chaldees, to give thee the land of the Canaanites to possess it for ever; and I will be God unto thee and to thy seed after thee.' <sup>8</sup> And he said: 'Lord, Lord, whereby shall I know that I shall inherit (it)?' <sup>9</sup> And He said unto him: 'Take Me an heifer of three years, and a goat of three years, and a sheep of three years, and a turtle-dove, and a pigeon.' <sup>10</sup> And he took all these in the middle of the month and he dwelt at the oak of Mamre, which is near Hebron. <sup>11</sup> And he built there an altar, and sacrificed all these; and he poured their blood upon the altar, and divided them in the midst, and laid them over against each other; but the birds divided he not. <sup>12</sup> And birds came down upon the pieces, and Abram drove them away, and did not suffer the birds to touch them. <sup>13</sup> And it came to pass, when the sun had set, that an ecstasy fell upon Abram, and lo! an horror of great darkness fell upon him, and it was said unto Abram: 'Know of a surety that thy seed shall be a stranger in a land (that is) not theirs, and they shall bring them into bondage, and afflict them four hundred years. <sup>14</sup> And the nation also to whom they will be in bondage will I judge, and after that they shall come forth thence with much substance. <sup>15</sup> And thou shalt go to thy fathers in peace, and be buried in a good old age. <sup>16</sup> But in the fourth generation they shall return hither; for the iniquity of the Amorites is not yet full.' <sup>17</sup> And he awoke from his sleep, and he arose, and the sun had set; and there was a flame, and behold! a furnace was smoking, and a flame of fire passed between the pieces. <sup>18</sup> And on that day the Lord made a covenant with Abram, saying: 'To thy seed will I give this land, from the river of Egypt unto the great river, the river Euphrates, the Kenites, the Kenizzites, the Kadmonites, the Perizzites, and the Rephaim, the Phakorites, and the Hivites, and the Amorites, and the Canaanites, and the Girgashites, and the Jebusites. <sup>19</sup> And the day passed, and Abram offered the pieces, and the birds, and their fruit offerings, and their drink offerings, and the fire devoured them. <sup>20</sup> And on that day we made a covenant with Abram, according as we had covenanted with Noah in this month; and Abram renewed the festival and ordinance for himself for ever.

### The Birth of Ishmael (xiv. 21-24; cf. Gen. xvi. 1-4.11).

<sup>21</sup> And Abram rejoiced, and made all these things known to Sarai his wife; and he believed that he would have seed, but she did not bear. <sup>22</sup> And Sarai advised her husband Abram, and said unto him: 'Go in unto Hagar, my Egyptian maid: it may be that I shall build up seed unto thee by her.' <sup>23</sup> And Abram harkened unto the voice of Sarai his wife, and said unto her, 'Do (so).' And Sarai took Hagar, her maid, the Egyptian, and gave her to Abram, her husband, to be his wife. <sup>24</sup> And he went in unto her, and she conceived and bare him a son, and he called his name Ishmael, in the fifth year of this week [1965 A.M.]; and this was the eighty-sixth year in the life of Abram.

## The Feast of First-fruits Circumcision instituted. The Promise of Isaac's Birth. Circumcision ordained for all Israel (xv. 1-34; cf. Gen. xvii.).

### 15

[1] And in the fifth year of the fourth week of this jubilee, [1979 A.M.] in the third month, in the middle of the month, Abram celebrated the feast of the first-fruits of the grain harvest. [2] And he offered new offerings on the altar, the first-fruits of the produce, unto the Lord, an heifer and a goat and a sheep on the altar as a burnt sacrifice unto the Lord; their fruit offerings and their drink offerings he offered upon the altar with frankincense. [3] And the Lord appeared to Abram, and said unto him: 'I am God Almighty; approve thyself before me and be thou perfect. [4] And I will make My covenant between Me and thee, and I will multiply thee exceedingly.' [5] And Abram fell on his face, and God talked with him, and said: [6] 'Behold my ordinance is with thee, And thou shalt be the father of many nations. [7] Neither shall thy name any more be called Abram, But thy name from henceforth, even for ever, shall be Abraham. For the father of many nations have I made thee. [8] And I will make thee very great, And I will make thee into nations, And kings shall come forth from thee. [9] And I shall establish My covenant between Me and thee, and thy seed after thee, throughout their generations, for an eternal covenant, so that I may be a God unto thee, and to thy seed after thee. [10] <And I will give to thee and to thy seed after thee> the land where thou hast been a sojourner, the land of Canaan, that thou mayst possess it for ever, and I will be their God.' [11] And the Lord said unto Abraham: 'And as for thee, do thou keep my covenant, thou and thy seed after thee: and circumcise ye every male among you, and circumcise your foreskins, and it shall be a token of an eternal covenant between Me and you. [12] And the child on the eighth day ye shall circumcise, every male throughout your generations, him that is born in the house, or whom ye have bought with money from any stranger, whom ye have acquired who is not of thy seed. [13] He that is born in thy house shall surely be circumcised, and those whom thou hast bought with money shall be circumcised, and My covenant shall be in your flesh for an eternal ordinance. [14] And the uncircumcised male who is not circumcised in the flesh of his foreskin on the eighth day, that soul shall be cut off from his people, for he has broken My covenant.' [15] And God said unto Abraham: 'As for Sarai thy wife, her name shall no more be called Sarai, but Sarah shall be her name. [16] And I will bless her, and give thee a son by her, and I will bless him, and he shall become a nation, and kings of nations shall proceed from him.' [17] And Abraham fell on his face, and rejoiced, and said in his heart: 'Shall a son be born to him that is a hundred years old, and shall Sarah, who is ninety years old, bring forth?' [18] And Abraham said unto God: 'O that Ishmael might live before thee!' [19] And God said: 'Yea, and Sarah also shall bear thee a son, and thou shalt call his name Isaac, and I will establish My covenant with him, an everlasting covenant, and for his seed after him. [20] And as for Ishmael also have I heard thee, and behold I will bless him, and make him great, and multiply him exceedingly, and he shall beget twelve princes, and I will make him a great nation. [21] But My covenant will I establish with Isaac, whom Sarah shall bear to thee, in these days, in the next year.' [22] And He left off speaking with him, and God went up from Abraham. [23] And Abraham did according as God had said unto him, and he took Ishmael his son, and all that were born in his house, and whom he had bought with his money, every male in his house, and circumcised the flesh of their foreskin. [24] And on the selfsame day was Abraham circumcised, and all the men of his house, <and those born in the house>, and all those, whom he had bought with money from the children of the stranger, were circumcised with him. [25] This law is for all the generations for ever, and there is no circumcision of the days, and no omission of one day out of the eight days; for it is an eternal ordinance, ordained and written on the heavenly tablets. [26] And every one that is born, the flesh of whose foreskin is not circumcised on the eighth day, belongs not to the children of the covenant which the Lord made with Abraham, but to the children of destruction; nor is there, moreover, any sign on him that he is the Lord's, but (he is destined) to be destroyed and slain from the earth, and to be rooted out of the earth, for he has broken the covenant of the Lord our God. [27] For all the angels of the presence and all the angels of sanctification have been so created from the day of their creation, and before the angels of the presence and the angels of sanctification He hath sanctified Israel, that they should be with Him and with His holy angels. [28] And do thou command the children of Israel and let them observe the sign of this covenant for their generations as an eternal ordinance, and they will not be rooted out of the land. [29] For the command is ordained for a covenant, that they should observe it for ever among all the children of Israel. [30] For Ishmael and his sons and his brothers and Esau, the Lord did not cause to approach Him, and he chose them not because they are the children of Abraham, because He knew them, but He chose Israel to be His people. [31] And He sanctified it, and gathered it from amongst all the children of men; for there are many nations and many peoples, and all are His, and over all hath He placed spirits in authority to lead them astray from Him. [32] But over Israel He did not appoint any angel or spirit, for He alone is their ruler, and He will preserve them and require them at the hand of His angels and His spirits, and at the hand of all His powers in order that He may preserve them and bless them, and that they may be His and He may be theirs from henceforth for ever. [33] And now I announce unto thee that the children of Israel will not keep true to this ordinance, and they will not circumcise their sons according to all this law; for in the flesh of their circumcision they will omit this circumcision of their sons, and all of them, sons of Beliar, will leave their sons uncircumcised as they were born. [34] And there will be great wrath from the Lord against the children of Israel. because they have forsaken His covenant and turned aside from His word, and provoked and blasphemed, inasmuch as they do not observe the ordinance of this law; for they have treated their members like the Gentiles, so that they may be removed and rooted out of the land. And there will no more be pardon or forgiveness unto them [so that there should be forgiveness and pardon] for all the sin of this eternal error.

## Angelic Visitation of Abraham in Hebron; Promise of Isaac's Birth repeated. The Destruction of Sodom and Lot's Deliverance (xvi. 1-9; cf. Gen. xviii.-xix.).

### 16

[1] And on the new moon of the fourth month we appeared unto Abraham, at the oak of Mamre, and we talked with him, and we announced to him that a son would be given to him by Sarah his wife. [2] And Sarah laughed, for she heard that we had spoken these words with Abraham, and we admonished her, and she became afraid, and denied that she had laughed on account of the words. [3] And we told her the name of her son, as his name is ordained and written in the heavenly tablets (i.e.) Isaac, [4] And (that) when we returned to her at a set time, she would have conceived a son. [5] And in this month the Lord executed his judgments on Sodom, and Gomorrah, and Zeboim, and all the region of the Jordan, and He burned them with fire and brimstone, and destroyed them until this day, even as [lo] I have declared unto thee all their works, that they are wicked and sinners exceedingly, and that they defile themselves and commit fornication in their flesh, and work uncleanness on the earth. [6] And, in like manner, God will execute judgment on the places where they have done according to the uncleanness of the Sodomites, like unto the judgment of Sodom. [7] But Lot was saved; for God remembered Abraham, and sent him out from the midst of the overthrow. [8] And he and his daughters committed sin upon the earth, such as had not been on the earth since the days of Adam till his time; for the man lay with his daughters. [9] And, behold, it was commanded and engraven concerning all his seed, on the heavenly tablets, to remove them and root them out, and to execute judgment upon them like the judgment of Sodom, and to leave no seed of the man on earth on the day of condemnation.

## Abraham at Beersheba. Birth and Circumcision of Isaac (cf. Gen. xxi. 1-4). Institution of the Feast of Tabernacles (xvi. 10-31).

[10] And in this month Abraham moved from Hebron, and departed and dwelt between Kadesh and Shur in the mountains of Gerar. [11] And in the middle of the fifth month he moved from thence, and dwelt at the Well of the Oath. [12] And in the middle of the sixth month the Lord visited Sarah and did unto her as He had spoken and she conceived. [13] And she bare a son in the third month, and in the middle of the month, at the time of which the Lord had spoken to Abraham, on the festival of the first fruits of the harvest, Isaac was born. [14] And Abraham circumcised his son on the eighth day: he was the first that was circumcised according to the covenant which is ordained for ever. [15] And in the sixth year of the fourth week we came to Abraham, to the Well of the Oath, and we appeared unto him [as we had told Sarah that we should return to her, and she would have conceived a son. [16] And we returned in the seventh month, and found Sarah with child before us] and we blessed him, and we announced to him all the things which had been decreed concerning him, that he should not die till he should beget six sons more, and should see (them) before he died; but (that) in Isaac should his name and seed be called: [17] And (that) all the seed of his sons should be Gentiles, and be reckoned with the Gentiles; but from the sons of Isaac one should become a holy seed, and should not be reckoned among the Gentiles. [18] For he should become the portion of the Most High, and all his seed had fallen into the possession of God, that it should be unto the Lord a people for (His) possession above all nations and that it should become a kingdom and priests and a holy nation. [19] And we went our way, and we announced to Sarah all that we had told him, and they both rejoiced with exceeding great joy. [20] And he built there an altar to the Lord who had delivered him, and who was making him rejoice in the land of his sojourning, and he celebrated a festival of joy in this month seven days, near the altar which he had

built at the Well of the Oath. ²¹ And he built booths for himself and for his servants on this festival, and he was the first to celebrate the feast of tabernacles on the earth. ²² And during these seven days he brought each day to the altar a burnt offering to the Lord, two oxen, two rams, seven sheep, one he-goat, for a sin offering, that he might atone thereby for himself and for his seed. ²³ And, as a thank-offering, seven rams, seven kids, seven sheep, and seven he-goats, and their fruit offerings and their drink offerings; and he burnt all the fat thereof on the altar, a chosen offering unto the Lord for a sweet smelling savour. ²⁴ And morning and evening he burnt fragrant substances, frankincense and galbanum, and stackte, and nard, and myrrh, and spice, and costum; all these seven he offered, crushed, mixed together in equal parts (and) pure. ²⁵ And he celebrated this feast during seven days, rejoicing with all his heart and with all his soul, he and all those who were in his house, and there was no stranger with him, nor any that was uncircumcised. ²⁶ And he blessed his Creator who had created him in his generation, for He had created him according to His good pleasure; for He knew and perceived that from him would arise the plant of righteousness for the eternal generations, and from him a holy seed, so that it should become like Him who had made all things. ²⁷ And he blessed and rejoiced, and he called the name of this festival the festival of the Lord, a joy acceptable to the Most High God. ²⁸ And we blessed him for ever, and all his seed after him throughout all the generations of the earth, because he celebrated this festival in its season, according to the testimony of the heavenly tablets. ²⁹ For this reason it is ordained on the heavenly tablets concerning Israel, that they shall celebrate the feast of tabernacles seven days with joy, in the seventh month, acceptable before the Lord -a statute for ever throughout their generations every year. ³⁰ And to this there is no limit of days; for it is ordained for ever regarding Israel that they should celebrate it and dwell in booths, and set wreaths upon their heads, and take leafy boughs, and willows from the brook. ³¹ And Abraham took branches of palm trees, and the fruit of goodly trees, and every day going round the altar with the branches seven times [a day] in the morning, he praised and gave thanks to his God for all things in joy.

**The Expulsion of Hagar and Ishmael (xvii. 1-14; cf. Gen. xxi. 8-21).**

## 17

¹ And in the first year of the fifth week Isaac was weaned in this jubilee, [1982 A.M.] and Abraham made a great banquet in the third month, on the day his son Isaac was weaned. ² And Ishmael, the son of Hagar, the Egyptian, was before the face of Abraham, his father, in his place, and Abraham rejoiced and blessed God because he had seen his sons and had not died childless. ³ And he remembered the words which He had spoken to him on the day on which Lot had parted from him, and he rejoiced because the Lord had given him seed upon the earth to inherit the earth, and he blessed with all his mouth the Creator of all things. ⁴ And Sarah saw Ishmael playing and dancing, and Abraham rejoicing with great joy, and she became jealous of Ishmael and said to Abraham, 'Cast out this bondwoman and her son; for the son of this bondwoman will not be heir with my son, Isaac.' ⁵ And the thing was grievous in Abraham's sight, because of his maidservant and because of his son, that he should drive them from him. ⁶ And God said to Abraham 'Let it not be grievous in thy sight, because of the child and because of the bondwoman; in all that Sarah hath said unto thee, harken to her words and do (them); for in Isaac shall thy name and seed be called. ⁷ But as for the son of this bondwoman I will make him a great nation, because he is of thy seed.' ⁸ And Abraham rose up early in the morning, and took bread and a bottle of water, and placed them on the shoulders of Hagar and the child, and sent her away. ⁹ And she departed and wandered in the wilderness of Beersheba, and the water in the bottle was spent, and the child thirsted, and was not able to go on, and fell down. ¹⁰ And his mother took him and cast him under an olive tree, and went and sat her down over against him, at the distance of a bow-shot; for she said, 'Let me not see the death of my child,' and as she sat she wept. ¹¹ And an angel of God, one of the holy ones, said unto her, 'Why weepest thou, Hagar? Arise take the child, and hold him in thine hand; for God hath heard thy voice, and hath seen the child.' ¹² And she opened her eyes, and she saw a well of water, and she went and filled her bottle with water, and she gave her child to drink, and she arose and went towards the wilderness of Paran. ¹³ And the child grew and became an archer, and God was with him, and his mother took him a wife from among the daughters of Egypt. ¹⁴ And she bare him a son, and he called his name Nebaioth; for she said, 'The Lord was nigh to me when I called upon him.'

**Mastêmâ proposes to God that Abraham shall be put to the Proof (xvi. 15-18).**

¹⁵ And it came to pass in the seventh week, in the first year thereof, [2003 A.M.] in the first month in this jubilee, on the twelfth of this month, there were voices in heaven regarding Abraham, that he was faithful in all that He told him, and that he loved the Lord, and that in

every affliction he was faithful. ¹⁶ And the prince Mastêmâ came and said before God, 'Behold, Abraham loves Isaac his son, and he delights in him above all things else; bid him offer him as a burnt-offering on the altar, and Thou wilt see if he will do this command, and Thou wilt know if he is faithful in everything wherein Thou dost try him.' ¹⁷ And the Lord knew that Abraham was faithful in all his afflictions; for He had tried him through his country and with famine, and had tried him with the wealth of kings, and had tried him again through his wife, when she was torn (from him), and with circumcision; and had tried him through Ishmael and Hagar, his maid-servant, when he sent them away. ¹⁸ And in everything wherein He had tried him, he was found faithful, and his soul was not impatient, and he was not slow to act; for he was faithful and a lover of the Lord.

**The Sacrifice of Isaac: Abraham returns to Beersheba (xviii. 1-19; Cf. Gen. xxii. 1-19).**

## 18

¹ And God said to him, 'Abraham, Abraham'; and he said, Behold, (here) am I.' ² And he said, Take thy beloved son whom thou lovest, (even) Isaac, and go unto the high country, and offer him on one of the mountains which I will point out unto thee.' ³ And he rose early in the morning and saddled his ass, and took his two young men with him, and Isaac his son, and clave the wood of the burnt offering, and he went to the place on the third day, and he saw the place afar off. ⁴ And he came to a well of water, and he said to his young men, 'Abide ye here with the ass, and I and the lad shall go (yonder), and when we have worshipped we shall come again to you.' ⁵ And he took the wood of the burnt-offering and laid it on Isaac his son, and he took in his hand the fire and the knife, and they went both of them together to that place. ⁶ And Isaac said to his father, 'Father;' and he said, 'Here am I, my son.' And he said unto him, 'Behold the fire, and the knife, and the wood; but where is the sheep for the burnt-offering, father?' ⁷ And he said, 'God will provide for himself a sheep for a burnt-offering, my son.' And he drew near to the place of the mount of God. ⁸ And he built an altar, and he placed the wood on the altar, and bound Isaac his son, and placed him on the wood which was upon the altar, and stretched forth his hand to take the knife to slay Isaac his son. ⁹ And I stood before him, and before the prince Mastêmâ, and the Lord said, 'Bid him not to lay his hand on the lad, nor to do anything to him, for I have shown that he fears the Lord.' ¹⁰ And I called to him from heaven, and said unto him: 'Abraham, Abraham;' and he was terrified and said: 'Behold, (here) am I.' ¹¹ And I said unto him: 'Lay not thy hand upon the lad, neither do thou anything to him; for now I have shown that thou fearest the Lord, and hast not withheld thy son, thy first-born son, from me.' ¹² And the prince Mastêmâ was put to shame; and Abraham lifted up his eyes and looked, and, behold a ram caught . . . by his horns, and Abraham went and took the ram and offered it for a burnt-offering in the stead of his son. ¹³ And Abraham called that place 'The Lord hath seen', so that it is said in the mount the Lord hath seen: that is Mount Sion. ¹⁴ And the Lord called Abraham by his name a second time from heaven, as he caused us to appear to speak to him in the name of the Lord. ¹⁵ And he said: 'By Myself have I sworn, saith the Lord, Because thou hast done this thing, And hast not withheld thy son, thy beloved son, from Me, That in blessing I will bless thee, And in multiplying I will multiply thy seed As the stars of heaven, And as the sand which is on the seashore. And thy seed shall inherit the cities of its enemies, ¹⁶ And in thy seed shall all nations of the earth be blessed; Because thou hast obeyed My voice, And I have shown to all that thou art faithful unto Me in all that I have said unto thee: Go in peace.' ¹⁷ And Abraham went to his young men, and they arose and went together to Beersheba, and Abraham [2010 A.M.] dwelt by the Well of the Oath. ¹⁸ And he celebrated this festival every year, seven days with joy, and he called it the festival of the Lord according to the seven days during which he went and returned in peace. ¹⁹ And accordingly has it been ordained and written on the heavenly tablets regarding Israel and its seed that they should observe this festival seven days with the joy of festival.

**The Death and Burial of Sarah (xix. 1-9; cf. Gen. xxiii.).**

## 19

¹ And in the first year of the first week in the forty-second jubilee, Abraham returned and dwelt opposite Hebron, that is Kirjath Arba, two weeks of years.

² And in the first year of the third week of this jubilee the days of the life of Sarah were accomplished, and she died in Hebron. ³ And Abraham went to mourn over her and bury her, and we tried him [to see] if his spirit were patient and he were not indignant in the words of his mouth; and he was found patient in this, and was not disturbed. ⁴ For in patience of spirit he conversed with the children of Heth, to the intent that they should give him a place in which to bury his dead. ⁵ And the Lord gave him grace before all who saw him, and he besought in gentleness the sons of Heth, and they gave him the land of the double cave over against Mamre, that is Hebron, for four hundred pieces of

silver. **6** And they besought him saying, We shall give it to thee for nothing; but he would not take it from their hands for nothing, for he gave the price of the place, the money in full, and he bowed down before them twice, and after this he buried his dead in the double cave. **7** And all the days of the life of Sarah were one hundred and twenty-seven years, that is, two jubilees and four weeks and one year: these are the days of the years of the life of Sarah. **8** This is the tenth trial wherewith Abraham was tried, and he was found faithful, patient in spirit. **9** And he said not a single word regarding the rumour in the land how that God had said that He would give it to him and to his seed after him, and he begged a place there to bury his dead; for he was found faithful, and was recorded on the heavenly tablets as the friend of God.

**Marriage of Isaac and second Marriage of Abraham (cf. Gen. xxiv. 15, xxv. 1-4); the Birth of Esau and Jacob (cf. Gen. xxv. 19 ff.) (xix. 10-14).**

**10** And in the fourth year thereof he took a wife for his son Isaac and her name was Rebecca [2020 A.M.] [the daughter of Bethuel, the son of Nahor, the brother of Abraham] the sister of Laban and daughter of Bethuel; and Bethuel was the son of Melca, who was the wife of Nahor, the brother of Abraham. **11** And Abraham took to himself a third wife, and her name was Keturah, from among the daughters of his household servants, for Hagar had died before Sarah. And she bare him six sons, Zimram, and Jokshan, and Medan, and Midian, and Ishbak, and Shuah, in the two weeks of years. **12** And in the sixth week, in the second year thereof, Rebecca bare to Isaac two sons, Jacob and Esau, **13** and [2046 A.M.] Jacob was a smooth and upright man, and Esau was fierce, a man of the field, and hairy, and Jacob dwelt in tents. **14** And the youths grew, and Jacob learned to write; but Esau did not learn, for he was a man of the field and a hunter, and he learnt war, and all his deeds were fierce.

**Abraham loves Jacob and blesses him (xix. 15-31).**

**15** And Abraham loved Jacob, but Isaac loved Esau. **16** And Abraham saw the deeds of Esau, and he knew that in Jacob should his name and seed be called; and he called Rebecca and gave commandment regarding Jacob, for he knew that she (too) loved Jacob much more than Esau. **17** And he said unto her: My daughter, watch over my son Jacob, For he shall be in my stead on the earth, And for a blessing in the midst of the children of men, And for the glory of the whole seed of Shem. **18** For I know that the Lord will choose him to be a people for possession unto Himself, above all peoples that are upon the face of the earth. **19** And behold, Isaac my son loves Esau more than Jacob, but I see that thou truly lovest Jacob. **20** Add still further to thy kindness to him, And let thine eyes be upon him in love; For he shall be a blessing unto us on the earth from henceforth unto all generations of the earth. **21** Let thy hands be strong And let thy heart rejoice in thy son Jacob; For I have loved him far beyond all my sons. He shall be blessed for ever, And his seed shall fill the whole earth. **22** If a man can number the sand of the earth, His seed also shall be numbered. **23** And all the blessings wherewith the Lord hath blessed me and my seed shall belong to Jacob and his seed alway. **24** And in his seed shall my name be blessed, and the name of my fathers, Shem, and Noah, and Enoch, and Mahalalel, and Enos, and Seth, and Adam. **25** And these shall serve To lay the foundations of the heaven, And to strengthen the earth, And to renew all the luminaries which are in the firmament. **26** And he called Jacob before the eyes of Rebecca his mother, and kissed him, and blessed him, and said: **27** 'Jacob, my beloved son, whom my soul loveth, may God bless thee from above the firmament, and may He give thee all the blessings wherewith He blessed Adam, and Enoch, and Noah, and Shem; and all the things of which He told me, and all the things which He promised to give me,

may he cause to cleave to thee and to thy seed for ever, according to the days of heaven above the earth. **28** And the Spirits of Mastêmâ shall not rule over thee or over thy seed to turn thee from the Lord, who is thy God from henceforth for ever. **29** And may the Lord God be a father to thee and thou the first-born son, and to the people alway. **30** Go in peace, my son.' And they both went forth together from Abraham. **31** And Rebecca loved Jacob, with all her heart and with all her soul, very much more than Esau; but Isaac loved Esau much more than Jacob.

**Abraham's Last Words to his Children and Grandchildren (xx. i-ii).**

**20**

**1** And in the forty-second jubilee, in the first year of the seventh week, Abraham called Ishmael, [2052 (2045?) A.M.] and his twelve sons, and Isaac and his two sons, and the six sons of Keturah, and their sons. **2** And he commanded them that they should observe the way of the Lord; that they should work righteousness, and love each his neighbour, and act on this manner amongst all men; that they should each so walk with regard to them as to do judgment and righteousness on the earth. **3** That they should circumcise their sons, according to the covenant which He had made with them, and not deviate to the right hand or the left of all the paths which the Lord had commanded us; and that we should keep ourselves from all fornication and uncleanness, [and renounce from amongst us all fornication and uncleanness]. **4** And if any woman or maid commit fornication amongst you, burn her with fire and let them not commit fornication with her after their eyes and their heart; and let them not take to themselves wives from the daughters of Canaan; for the seed of Canaan will be rooted out of the land. **5** And he told them of the judgment of the giants, and the judgment of the Sodomites, how they had been judged on account of their wickedness, and had died on account of their fornication, and uncleanness, and mutual corruption through fornication. **6** 'And guard yourselves from all fornication and uncleanness, And from all pollution of sin, Lest ye make our name a curse, And your whole life a hissing, And all your sons to be destroyed by the sword, And ye become accursed like Sodom, And all your remnant as the sons of Gomorrah. **7** I implore you, my sons, love the God of heaven And cleave ye to all His commandments. And walk not after their idols, and after their uncleannesses, **8** And make not for yourselves molten or graven gods; For they are vanity, And there is no spirit in them; For they are work of (men's) hands, And all who trust in them, trust in nothing. **9** Serve them not, nor worship them, But serve ye the most high God, and worship Him continually: And hope for His countenance always, And work uprightness and righteousness before Him, That He may have pleasure in you and grant you His mercy, And send rain upon you morning and evening, And bless all your works which ye have wrought upon the earth, And bless thy bread and thy water, And bless the fruit of thy womb and the fruit of thy land, And the herds of thy cattle, and the flocks of thy sheep. **10** And ye will be for a blessing on the earth, And all nations of the earth will desire you, And bless your sons in my name, That they may be blessed as I am. **11** And he gave to Ishmael and to his sons, and to the sons of Keturah, gifts, and sent them away from Isaac his son, and he gave everything to Isaac his son.

**The Dwelling-places of the Ishmaelites and of the Sons of Keturah (xx. 12-13).**

**12** And Ishmael and his sons, and the sons of Keturah and their sons, went together and dwelt from Paran to the entering in of Babylon in all the land which is towards the East facing the desert. **13** And these mingled with each other, and their name was called Arabs, and Ishmaelites.

**Abraham's Last Words to Isaac (xxi. 1-25).**

**21**

**1** And in the sixth year of the seventh week of this jubilee Abraham called Isaac his son, and [2057 (2050?) A.M.] commanded him: saying, 'I am become old, and know not the day of my death, and am full of my days. **2** And behold, I am one hundred and seventy-five years old, and throughout all the days of my life I have remembered the Lord, and sought with all my heart to do His will, and to walk uprightly in all His ways. **3** My soul has hated idols, <and I have despised those that served them, and I have given my heart and spirit> that I might observe to do the will of Him who created me. **4** For He is the living God, and He is holy and faithful, and He is righteous beyond all, and there is with Him no accepting of (men's) persons and no accepting of gifts; for God is righteous, and executeth judgment on all those who transgress His commandments and despise His covenant. **5** And do thou, my son, observe His commandments and His ordinances and His judgments, and walk not after the abominations and after the graven images and after the molten images. **6** And eat no blood at all of animals or cattle, or of any bird which flies in the heaven. **7** And if thou dost slay a victim as an acceptable peace offering, slay ye it, and pour out its blood upon the altar, and all the fat of the offering offer on the altar with fine flour and the meat offering mingled with oil, with its drink offering -offer them all together on the altar of burnt offering; it is a sweet savour before the Lord. **8** And thou wilt offer the fat of the sacrifice of thank offerings on the fire which is upon the altar, and the fat which is on the belly, and all the fat on the inwards and the two kidneys, and all the fat that is upon them, and upon the loins and liver thou shalt remove, together with the kidneys. **9** And offer all these for a sweet savour acceptable before the Lord, with its meat-offering and with its drink-offering, for a sweet savour, the bread of the offering unto the Lord. **10** And eat its meat on that day and on the second day, and let not the sun on the second day go down upon it till it is eaten, and let nothing be left over for the third day; for it is not acceptable [for it is not approved] and let it no longer be eaten, and all who eat thereof will bring sin upon themselves; for thus I have found it written in the books of my forefathers, and in the words of Enoch, and in the words of Noah. [11] And on all thy oblations thou shalt strew salt, and let not the salt of the covenant be lacking in all thy oblations before the Lord. [12] And as regards the wood of the sacrifices, beware lest thou bring (other) wood for the altar in addition to these: cypress, bay, almond, fir, pine, cedar, savin, fig, olive, myrrh, laurel, aspalathus. [13] And of these kinds of wood lay upon the altar under the sacrifice, such as have been tested as to their appearance, and do not lay (thereon) any split or dark wood, (but) hard and clean, without fault, a sound and new growth; and do not lay (thereon) old wood, [for its fragrance is gone] for there is no longer fragrance in it as before. [14] Besides these kinds of wood there is none other that thou shalt place (on the altar), for the fragrance is dispersed, and the smell of its fragrance goes not up to heaven. [15] Observe this commandment and do it, my son, that thou mayst be upright in all thy deeds. [16] And at all times be clean in thy body, and wash thyself with water before thou approachest to offer on the altar, and wash thy hands and thy feet before thou drawest near to the altar; and when thou art done sacrificing, wash again thy hands and thy feet. [17] And let no blood appear upon you nor upon your clothes; be on thy guard, my son, against blood, be on thy guard exceedingly; cover it with dust. [18] And do not eat any blood for it is the soul; eat no blood whatever. [19] And take no gifts for the blood of man, lest it be shed with impunity, without judgment; for it is the blood that is shed that causes the earth to sin, and the earth cannot be cleansed from the blood of man save by the blood of him who shed it. [20] And take no present or gift for the blood of man: blood for blood, that thou mayest be accepted before the Lord, the Most High God; for He is the defence of the good: and that thou mayest be preserved from all evil, and that He may save thee from every kind of death. [21] I see, my son, That all the works of the children of men are sin and wickedness, And all their deeds are uncleanness and an abomination and a pollution, And there is no righteousness with them. [22] Beware, lest thou shouldest walk in their ways And tread in their paths, And sin a sin unto death before the Most High God. Else He will [hide His face from thee And] give thee back into the hands of thy transgression, And root thee out of the land, and thy seed likewise from under heaven, And thy name and thy seed shall perish from the whole earth. [23] Turn away from all their deeds and all their uncleanness, And observe the ordinance of the Most High God, And do His will and be upright in all things. [24] And He will bless thee in all thy deeds, And will raise up from thee a plant of righteousness through all the earth, throughout all generations of the earth, And my name and thy name shall not be forgotten under heaven for ever. [25] Go, my son in peace. May the Most High God, my God and thy God, strengthen thee to do His will, And may He bless all thy seed and the residue of thy seed for the generations for ever, with all righteous blessings, That thou mayest be a blessing on all the earth.' [26] And he went out from him rejoicing.

**Isaac, Ishmael and Jacob join in Festival with Abraham for the Last Time. Abraham's Prayer (xxii. 1-9).**

## 22

[1] And it came to pass in the first week in the forty-fourth jubilee, in the second year, that is, the year in which Abraham died, that Isaac and Ishmael came from the Well of the Oath to celebrate the feast of weeks -that is, the feast of the first fruits of the harvest-to Abraham, their father, and Abraham rejoiced because his two sons had come. [2] For Isaac had many possessions in Beersheba, and Isaac was wont to go and see his possessions and to return to his father. [3] And in those days Ishmael came to see his father, and they both came together, and Isaac offered a sacrifice for a burnt offering, and presented it on the altar of his father which he had made in Hebron. [4] And he offered a thank offering and made a feast of joy before Ishmael, his brother: and Rebecca made new cakes from the new grain, and gave them to Jacob, her son, to take them to Abraham, his father, from the first fruits of the land, that he might eat and bless the Creator of all things before he died. [5] And Isaac, too, sent by the hand of Jacob to Abraham a best thank offering, that he might eat and drink. [6] And he eat and drank, and blessed the Most High God, Who hath created heaven and earth, Who hath made all the fat things of the earth, And given them to the children of men That they might eat and drink and bless their Creator. [7] 'And now I give thanks unto Thee, my God, because thou hast caused me to see this day: behold, I am one hundred three score and fifteen years, an old man and full of days, and all my days have been unto me peace. [8] The sword of the adversary has not overcome me in all that Thou hast given me and my children all the days of my life until this day. [9] My God, may Thy mercy and Thy peace be upon Thy servant, and upon the seed of his sons, that they may be to Thee a chosen nation and an inheritance from amongst all the nations of the earth from henceforth unto all the days of the generations of the earth, unto all the ages.'

**Abraham's Last Words to and Blessings of Jacob (xxii. 10-30).**

[10] And he called Jacob and said: 'My son Jacob, may the God of all bless thee and strengthen thee to do righteousness, and His will before Him, and may He choose thee and thy seed that ye may become a people for His inheritance according to His will alway. [11] And do thou, my son, draw near and kiss me.' And he drew near and kissed him, and he said: 'Blessed be my son Jacob And all the sons of God Most High, unto all the ages: May God give unto thee a seed of righteousness; And some of thy sons may He sanctify in the midst of the whole earth; May nations serve thee, And all the nations bow themselves before thy seed. [12] Be strong in the presence of men, And exercise authority over all the seed of Seth. Then thy ways and the ways of thy sons will be justified, So that they shall become a holy nation. [13] May the Most High God give thee all the blessings Wherewith He has blessed me And wherewith He blessed Noah and Adam; May they rest on the sacred head of thy seed from generation to generation for ever. [14] And may He cleanse thee from all unrighteousness and impurity, That thou mayest be forgiven all the transgressions; which thou hast committed ignorantly. And may He strengthen thee, And bless thee. And mayest thou inherit the whole earth, [15] And may He renew His covenant with thee. That thou mayest be to Him a nation for His inheritance for all the ages, And that He may be to thee and to thy seed a God in truth and righteousness throughout all the days of the earth. [16] And do thou, my son Jacob, remember my words, And observe the commandments of Abraham, thy father: Separate thyself from the nations, And eat not with them: And do not according to their works, And become not their associate; For their works are unclean, And all their ways are a Pollution and an abomination and uncleanness. [17] They offer their sacrifices to the dead And they worship evil spirits, And they eat over the graves, And all their works are vanity and nothingness. [18] They have no heart to understand And their eyes do not see what their works are, And how they err in saying to a piece of wood: 'Thou art my God,' And to a stone: 'Thou art my Lord and thou art my deliverer.' [And they have no heart.] [19] And as for thee, my son Jacob, May the Most High God help thee And the God of heaven bless thee And remove thee from their uncleanness and from all their error. [20] Be thou ware, my son Jacob, of taking a wife from any seed of the daughters of Canaan; For all his seed is to be rooted out of the earth. [21] For, owing to the transgression of Ham, Canaan erred, And all his seed shall be destroyed from off the earth and all the residue thereof, And none springing from him shall be saved on the day of judgment. [22] And as for all the worshippers of idols and the profane (b) There shall be no hope for them in the land of the living; (c) And there shall be no remembrance of them on the earth; (c) For they shall descend into Sheol, (d) And into the place of condemnation shall they go, [23] As the children of Sodom were taken away from the earth So will all those who worship idols be taken away. Fear not, my son Jacob, And be not dismayed, O son of Abraham: May the Most High God preserve thee from destruction, And from all the paths of error may he deliver thee. [24] This house have I built for myself that I might put my name upon it in the earth: [it is given to thee and to thy seed for ever], and it will be named the house of Abraham; it is given to thee and to thy seed for ever; for thou wilt build my house and establish my name before God for ever: thy seed and thy name will stand throughout all generations of the earth.' [25] And he ceased commanding him and blessing him. [26] And the two lay together on one bed, and Jacob slept in the bosom of Abraham, his father's father and he kissed him seven times, and his affection and his heart rejoiced over him. [27] And he blessed him with all his heart and said: 'The Most High God, the God of all, and Creator of all, who brought me forth from Ur of the Chaldees that he might give me this land to inherit it for ever, and that I might establish a holy seed-blessed be the Most High for ever.' [28] And he blessed Jacob and said: 'My son, over whom with all my heart and my affection I rejoice, may Thy grace and Thy mercy be lift up upon him and upon his seed alway. [29] And do not forsake him, nor set him at nought from henceforth unto the days of eternity, and may Thine eyes be opened upon him and upon his seed, that Thou mayst preserve him, and bless him, and mayest sanctify him as a nation for Thine inheritance; [30] And bless him with all Thy blessings from henceforth unto all the days of eternity, and renew Thy covenant and Thy grace with him and with his seed according to all Thy good pleasure unto all the generations of the earth.'

**The Death and Burial of Abraham (xxiii. 1-8; cf. Gen. xxv. 7-10).**

## 23

[1] And he placed two fingers of Jacob on his eyes, and he blessed the God of gods, and he covered his face and stretched out his feet and slept the sleep of eternity, and was gathered to his fathers. [2] And notwithstanding all this Jacob was lying in his bosom, and knew not that Abraham, his father's father, was dead. [3] And Jacob awoke from his sleep, and behold Abraham was cold as ice, and he said 'Father, father'; but there was none that spake, and he knew that he was dead. [4]

And he arose from his bosom and ran and told Rebecca, his mother; and Rebecca went to Isaac in the night, and told him; and they went together, and Jacob with them, and a lamp was in his hand, and when they had gone in they found Abraham lying dead. [5] And Isaac fell on the face of his father and wept and kissed him. [6] And the voices were heard in the house of Abraham, and Ishmael his son arose, and went to Abraham his father, and wept over Abraham his father, he and all the house of Abraham, and they wept with a great weeping. [7] And his sons Isaac and Ishmael buried him in the double cave, near Sarah his wife, and they wept for him forty days, all the men of his house, and Isaac and Ishmael, and all their sons, and all the sons of Keturah in their places; and the days of weeping for Abraham were ended. [8] And he lived three jubilees and four weeks of years, one hundred and seventy-five years, and completed the days of his life, being old and full of days.

**The decreasing Years and increasing Corruption of Mankind (xxiii. 9-17).**

[9] For the days of the forefathers, of their life, were nineteen jubilees; and after the Flood they began to grow less than nineteen jubilees, and to decrease in jubilees, and to grow old quickly, and to be full of their days by reason of manifold tribulation and the wickedness of their ways, with the exception of Abraham. [10] For Abraham was perfect in all his deeds with the Lord, and well-pleasing in righteousness all the days of his life; and behold, he did not complete four jubilees in his life, when he had grown old by reason of the wickedness, and was full of his days. [11] And all the generations which shall arise from this time until the day of the great judgment shall grow old quickly, before they complete two jubilees, and their knowledge shall forsake them by reason of their old age Land all their know- ledge shall vanish away]. [12] And in those days, if a man live a jubilee and a-half of years, they shall say regarding him: 'He has lived long, and the greater part of his days are pain and sorrow and tribulation, and there is no peace: [13] For calamity follows on calamity, and wound on wound, and tribulation on tribulation, and evil tidings on evil tidings, and illness on illness, and all evil judgments such as these, one with another, illness and overthrow, and snow and frost and ice, and fever, and chills, and torpor, and famine, and death, and sword, and captivity, and all kinds of calamities and pains.' [14] And all these shall come on an evil generation, which transgresses on the earth: their works are uncleanness and fornication, and pollution and abominations. [15] Then they shall say: 'The days of the forefathers were many (even), unto a thousand years, and were good; but behold, the days of our life, if a man has lived many, are three score years and ten, and, if he is strong, four score years, and those evil, and there is no peace in the days of this evil generation.' [16] And in that generation the sons shall convict their fathers and their elders of sin and unrighteousness, and of the words of their mouth and the great wickednesses which they perpetrate, and concerning their forsaking the covenant which the Lord made between them and Him, that they should observe and do all His commandments and His ordinances and all His laws, without departing either to the right hand or the left. [17] For all have done evil, and every mouth speaks iniquity and all their works are an uncleanness and an abomination, and all their ways are pollution, uncleanness and destruction.

**The Messianic Woes (xxiii. 18-25). [Eschatological partly.]**

[18] Behold the earth shall be destroyed on account of all their works, and there shall be no seed of the vine, and no oil; for their works are altogether faithless, and they shall all perish together, beasts and cattle and birds, and all the fish of the sea, on account of the children of men. [19] And they shall strive one with another, the young with the old, and the old with the young, the poor with the rich, the lowly with the great, and the beggar with the prince, on account of the law and the covenant; for they have forgotten commandment, and covenant, and feasts, and months, and Sabbaths, and jubilees, and all judgments. [20] And they shall stand <with bows and> swords and war to turn them back into the way; but they shall not return until much blood has been shed on the earth, one by another. [21] And those who have escaped shall not return from their wickedness to the way of righteousness, but they shall all exalt themselves to deceit and wealth, that they may each take all that is his neighbour's, and they shall name the great name, but not in truth and not in righteousness, and they shall defile the holy of holies with their uncleanness and the corruption of their pollution. [22] And a great punishment shall befall the deeds of this generation from the Lord, and He will give them over to the sword and to judgment and to captivity, and to be plundered and devoured. [23] And He will wake up against them the sinners of the Gentiles, who have neither mercy nor compassion, and who shall respect the person of none, neither old nor young, nor any one, for they are more wicked and strong to do evil than all the children of men. And they shall use violence against Israel and transgression against Jacob, And much blood shall be shed upon the earth, And there shall be none to gather and none to bury. [24] In those days they shall cry aloud, And call and pray that they may be saved from the hand of the sinners, the Gentiles; But none shall be saved. [25] And the heads of the children shall be white with grey hair, And a child of three weeks shall appear old like a man of one hundred years, And their stature shall be destroyed by tribulation and oppression.

**Renewed Study of the Law followed by a Renewal of Mankind. The Messianic Kingdom and the Blessedness of the Righteous (xxiii. 26-32; cf. Isa. lxv. 17 ff. [Eschatological.]**

[26] And in those days the children shall begin to study the laws, And to seek the commandments, And to return to the path of righteousness. [27] And the days shall begin to grow many and increase amongst those children of men Till their days draw nigh to one thousand years. And to a greater number of years than (before) was the number of the days. [28] And there shall be no old man Nor one who is <not> satisfied with his days, For all shall be (as) children and youths. [29] And all their days they shall complete and live in peace and in joy, And there shall be no Satan nor any evil destroyer; For all their days shall be days of blessing and healing. [30] And at that time the Lord will heal His servants, And they shall rise up and see great peace, And drive out their adversaries. And the righteous shall see and be thankful, And rejoice with joy for ever and ever, And shall see all their judgments and all their curses on their enemies. [31] And their bones shall rest in the earth, And their spirits shall have much joy, And they shall know that it is the Lord who executes judgment, And shows mercy to hundreds and thousands and to all that love Him [32] And do thou, Moses, write down these words; for thus are they written, and they record (them) on the heavenly tablets for a testimony for the generations for ever.

**Isaac at the Well of Vision: Esau sells his Birthright (xxiv. 1-7; cf. Gen. xxv. 11,29-34).**

## 24

[1] And it came to pass after the death of Abraham, that the Lord blessed Isaac his son, and he arose from Hebron and went and dwelt at the Well of the Vision in the first year of the third week [2073 A.M.] of this jubilee, seven years. [2] And in the first year of the fourth week a famine began in the land, [2080 A.M.] besides the first famine, which had been in the days of Abraham. [3] And Jacob sod lentil pottage, and Esau came from the field hungry. And he said to Jacob his brother: 'Give me of this red pottage.' And Jacob said to him: 'Sell to me thy [primogeniture, this] birthright and I will give thee bread, and also some of this lentil pottage.' [4] And Esau said in his heart: 'I shall die; of what profit to me is this birthright? [5] 'And he said to Jacob: 'I give it to thee.' And Jacob said: 'Swear to me, this day,' and he sware unto him. [6] And Jacob gave his brother Esau bread and pottage, and he eat till he was satisfied, and Esau despised his birthright; for this reason was Esau's name called Edom, on account of the red pottage which Jacob gave him for his birthright. [7] And Jacob became the elder, and Esau was brought down from his dignity.

**Isaac's Sojourn in Gerar and Dealings with Abimelech (xxiv. 8-27; cf. Gen. xxvi.).**

[8] And the famine was over the land, and Isaac departed to go down into Egypt in the second year of this week, and went to the king of the Philistines to Gerar, unto Abimelech. [9] And the Lord appeared unto him and said unto him: 'Go not down into Egypt; dwell in the land that I shall tell thee of, and sojourn in this land, and I will be with thee and bless thee. [10] For to thee and to thy seed will I give all this land, and I will establish My oath which I sware unto Abraham thy father, and I will multiply thy seed as the stars of heaven, and will give unto thy seed all this land. [11] And in thy seed shall all the nations of the earth be blessed, because thy father obeyed My voice, and kept My charge and My commandments, and My laws, and My ordinances, and My covenant; and now obey My voice and dwell in this land.' [12] And he dwelt in Gelar three weeks of years. [13] And Abimelech charged concerning him, [2080-2101 A.M.] and concerning all that was his, saying: 'Any man that shall touch him or aught that is his shall surely die.' [14] And Isaac waxed strong among the Philistines, and he got many possessions, oxen and sheep and camels and asses and a great household. [15] And he sowed in the land of the Philistines and brought in a hundred-fold, and Isaac became exceedingly great, and the Philistines envied him. [16] Now all the wells which the servants of Abraham had dug during the life of Abraham, the Philistines had stopped them after the death of Abraham, and filled them with earth. [17] And Abimelech said unto Isaac: 'Go from us, for thou art much mightier than we', and Isaac departed thence in the first year of the seventh week, and sojourned in the valleys of Gerar. [18] And they digged again the wells of water which the servants of Abraham, his father, had digged, and which the Philistines had closed after the death of Abraham his father, and he called their names as Abraham his father had named them. [19] And the servants of Isaac dug a well in the valley, and found living water, and the shepherds of Gerar strove with the shepherds of Isaac, saying: 'The water is ours'; and Isaac called the name of the well 'Perversity', because they had been perverse with us. [20] And they dug a

second well, and they strove for that also, and he called its name 'Enmity'. And he arose from thence and they digged another well, and for that they strove not, and he called the name of it 'Room', and Isaac said: 'Now the Lord hath made room for us, and we have increased in the land.' [21] And he went up from thence to the Well of the Oath in the first year of the first week in the [2108 A.M.] forty-fourth jubilee. [22] And the Lord appeared to him that night, on the new moon of the first month, and said unto him: 'I am the God of Abraham thy father; fear not, for I am with thee, and shall bless thee and shall surely multiply thy seed as the sand of the earth, for the sake of Abraham my servant.' [23] And he built an altar there, which Abraham his father had first built, and he called upon the name of the Lord, and he offered sacrifice to the God of Abraham his father. [24] And they digged a well and they found living water. [25] And the servants of Isaac digged another well and did not find water, and they went and told Isaac that they had not found water, and Isaac said: 'I have sworn this day to the Philistines and this thing has been announced to us.' [26] And he called the name of that place the Well of the Oath; for there he had sworn to Abimelech and Ahuzzath his friend and Phicol the prefect Or his host. [27] And Isaac knew that day that under constraint he had sworn to them to make peace with them.

**Isaac curses the Philistines (xxiv. 28-33).**

[28] And Isaac on that day cursed the Philistines and said: 'Cursed be the Philistines unto the day of wrath and indignation from the midst of all nations; may God make them a derision and a curse and an object of wrath and indignation in the hands of the sinners the Gentiles and in the hands of the Kittim. [29] And whoever escapes the sword of the enemy and the Kittim, may the righteous nation root out in judgment from under heaven; for they shall be the enemies and foes of my children throughout their generations upon the earth. [30] And no remnant shall be left to them, Nor one that shall be saved on the day of the wrath of judgment; For destruction and rooting out and expulsion from the earth is the whole seed of the Philistines (reserved), And there shall no longer be left for these Caphtorim a name or a seed on the earth. [31] For though he ascend unto heaven, Thence shall he be brought down, And though he make himself strong on earth, Thence shall he be dragged forth, And though he hide himself amongst the nations, Even from thence shall he be rooted out; And though he descend into Sheol, There also shall his condemnation be great, And there also he shall have no peace. [32] And if he go into captivity, By the hands of those that seek his life shall they slay him on the way, And neither name nor seed shall be left to him on all the earth; For into eternal malediction shall he depart.' [33] And thus is it written and engraved concerning him on the heavenly tablets, to do unto him on the day of judgment, so that he may be rooted out of the earth.

**Rebecca admonishes Jacob not to marry a Canaanitish Woman. Rebecca's Blessing (xxv. 1-23; cf. Gen. xxviii. 1-4).**

**25**

[1] And in the second year of this week in this jubilee, Rebecca called Jacob her son, and spake unto [2109 A.M.] him, saying: 'My son, do not take thee a wife of the daughters of Canaan, as Esau, thy brother, who took him two wives of the daughters of Canaan, and they have embittered my soul with all their unclean deeds: for all their deeds are fornication and lust, and there is no righteousness with them, for (their deeds) are evil. [2] And I, my son, love thee exceedingly, and my heart and my affection bless thee every hour of the day and watch of the night. [3] And now, my son, hearken to my voice, and do the will of thy mother, and do not take thee a wife of the daughters of this land, but only of the house of my father, and of my father's kindred. Thou shalt take thee a wife of the house of my father, and the Most High God will bless thee, and thy children shall be a righteous generation and a holy seed.' [4] And then spake Jacob to Rebecca, his mother, and said unto her: 'Behold, mother, I am nine weeks of years old, and I neither know nor have I touched any woman, nor have I betrothed myself to any, nor even think of taking me a wife of the daughters of Canaan. [5] For I remember, mother, the words of Abraham, our father, for he commanded me not to take a wife of the daughters of Canaan, but to take me a wife from the seed of my father's house and from my kindred. [6] I have heard before that daughters have been born to Laban, thy brother, and I have set my heart on them to take a wife from amongst them. [7] And for this reason I have guarded myself in my spirit against sinning or being corrupted in all my ways throughout all the days of my life; for with regard to lust and fornication, Abraham, my father, gave me many commands. [8] And, despite all that he has commanded me, these two and twenty years my brother has striven with me, and spoken frequently to me and said: 'My brother, take to wife a sister of my two wives'; but I refuse to do as he has done. [9] I swear before thee, mother, that all the days of my life I will not take me a wife from the daughters of the seed of Canaan, and I will not act wickedly as my brother has done. [10] Fear not, mother; be assured that I shall do thy will and walk in uprightness, and not corrupt my ways for ever.' [11] And thereupon she lifted up her

face to heaven and extended the fingers of her hands, and opened her mouth and blessed the Most High God, who had created the heaven and the earth, and she gave Him thanks and praise. [12] And she said: 'Blessed be the Lord God, and may His holy name be blessed for ever and ever, who has given me Jacob as a pure son and a holy seed; for he is Thine, and Thine shall his seed be continually and throughout all the generations for evermore. [13] Bless him, O Lord, and place in my mouth the blessing of righteousness, that I may bless him.' [14] And at that hour, when the spirit of righteousness descended into her mouth, she placed both her hands on the head of Jacob, and said: [15] Blessed art thou, Lord of righteousness and God of the ages And may He bless thee beyond all the generations of men. May He give thee, my Son, the path of righteousness, And reveal righteousness to thy seed. [16] And may He make thy sons many during thy life, And may they arise according to the number of the months of the year. And may their sons become many and great beyond the stars of heaven, And their numbers be more than the sand of the sea. [17] And may He give them this goodly land -as He said He would give it to Abraham and to his seed after him alway- And may they hold it as a possession for ever. [18] And may I see (born) unto thee, my son, blessed children during my life, And a blessed and holy seed may all thy seed be. [19] And as thou hast refreshed thy mother's spirit during her life, The womb of her that bare thee blesses thee thus, [My affection] and my breasts bless thee And my mouth and my tongue praise thee greatly. [20] Increase and spread over the earth, And may thy seed be perfect in the joy of heaven and earth for ever; And may thy seed rejoice, And on the great day of peace may it have peace. [21] And may thy name and thy seed endure to all the ages, And may the Most High God be their God, And may the God of righteousness dwell with them, And by them may His sanctuary be built unto all the ages. [22] Blessed be he that blesseth thee, And all flesh that curseth thee falsely, may it be cursed.' [23] And she kissed him, and said to him; 'May the Lord of the world love thee As the heart of thy mother and her affection rejoice in thee and bless thee.' And she ceased from blessing.

**Jacob obtains the Blessing of the Firstborn (xxvi. 1-35; cf. Gen. xxvii.).**

**26**

[1] And in the seventh year of this week Isaac called Esau, his elder Son, and said unto him: ' I am [2114 A.M.] old, my son, and behold my eyes are dim in seeing, and I know not the day of my death. [2] And now take thy hunting weapons thy quiver and thy bow, and go out to the field, and hunt and catch me (venison), my son, and make me savoury meat, such as my soul loveth, and bring it to me that I may eat, and that my soul may bless thee before I die.' [3] But Rebecca heard Isaac speaking to Esau. [4] And Esau went forth early to the field to hunt and catch and bring home to his father. [5] And Rebecca called Jacob, her son, and said unto him: 'Behold, I heard Isaac, thy father, speak unto Esau, thy brother, saying: "Hunt for me, and make me savoury meat, and bring (it) to me that [6] I may eat and bless thee before the Lord before I die." And now, my son, obey my voice in that which I command thee: Go to thy flock and fetch me two good kids of the goats, and I will make them savoury meat for thy father, such as he loves, and thou shalt bring (it) to thy father that he may eat and bless thee before the Lord before he die, and that thou mayst be blessed.' [7] And Jacob said to Rebecca his mother: 'Mother, I shall not withhold anything which my father would eat, and which would please him: only I fear, my mother, that he will recognise my voice and wish to touch me. [8] And thou knowest that I am smooth, and Esau, my brother, is hairy, and I shall appear before his eyes as an evildoer, and shall do a deed which he had not commanded me, and he will be wroth with me, and I shall bring upon myself a curse, and not a blessing.' [9] And Rebecca, his mother, said unto him: 'Upon me be thy curse, my son, only obey my voice.' [10] And Jacob obeyed the voice of Rebecca, his mother, and went and fetched two good and fat kids of the goats, and brought them to his mother, and his mother made them ~savoury meat~ such as he loved. [11] And Rebecca took the goodly rainment of Esau, her elder son, which was with her in the house, and she clothed Jacob, her younger son, (with them), and she put the skins of the kids upon his hands and on the exposed parts of his neck. [12] And she gave the meat and the bread which she had prepared into the hand of her son Jacob. [13] And Jacob went in to his father and said: 'I am thy son: I have done according as thou badest me: arise and sit and eat of that which I have caught, father, that thy soul may bless me.' [14] And Isaac said to his son: 'How hast thou found so quickly, my son? [15] 'And Jacob said: 'Because <the Lord> thy God caused me to find.' [16] And Isaac said unto him: Come near, that I may feel thee, my son, if thou art my son Esau or not.' [17] And Jacob went near to Isaac, his father, and he felt him and said: 'The voice is Jacob's voice, but the hands are the hands of Esau,' [18] and he discerned him not, because it was a dispensation from heaven to remove his power of perception and Isaac discerned not, for his hands were hairy as his brother Esau's, so that he blessed him. [19] And he said: 'Art thou my son Esau? ' and he said: 'I am

thy son': and he said, 'Bring near to me that I may eat of that which thou hast caught, my son, that my soul may bless thee.' **20** And he brought near to him, and he did eat, and he brought him wine and he drank. **21** And Isaac, his father, said unto him: 'Come near and kiss me, my son. **22** And he came near and kissed him. And he smelled the smell of his raiment, and he blessed him and said: 'Behold, the smell of my son is as the smell of a <full> field which the Lord hath blessed. **23** And may the Lord give thee of the dew of heaven And of the dew of the earth, and plenty of corn and oil: Let nations serve thee, And peoples bow down to thee. **24** Be lord over thy brethren, And let thy mother's sons bow down to thee; And may all the blessings wherewith the Lord hath blessed me and blessed Abraham, my father; Be imparted to thee and to thy seed for ever: Cursed be he that curseth thee, And blessed be he that blesseth thee.' **25** And it came to pass as soon as Isaac had made an end of blessing his son Jacob, and Jacob had gone forth from Isaac his father he hid himself and Esau, his brother, came in from his hunting. **26** And he also made savoury meat, and brought (it) to his father, and said unto his father: 'Let my father arise, and eat of my venison that thy soul may bless me.' **27** And Isaac, his father, said unto him: 'Who art thou?' And he said unto him: 'I am thy first born, thy son Esau: I have done as thou hast commanded me.' **28** And Isaac was very greatly astonished, and said: 'Who is he that hath hunted and caught and brought (it) to me, and I have eaten of all before thou camest, and have blessed him: (and) he shall be blessed, and all his seed for ever.' **29** And it came to pass when Esau heard the words of his father Isaac that he cried with an exceeding great and bitter cry, and said unto his father: 'Bless me, (even) me also, father.' **30** And he said unto him: 'Thy brother came with guile, and hath taken away thy blessing.' And he said: 'Now I know why his name is named Jacob: behold, he hath supplanted me these two times: he took away my birth-right, and now he hath taken away my blessing.' **31** And he said: 'Hast thou not reserved a blessing for me, father?' and Isaac answered and said unto Esau: 'Behold, I have made him thy lord, And all his brethren have I given to him for servants, And with plenty of corn and wine and oil have I strengthened him: And what now shall I do for thee, my son?' **32** And Esau said to Isaac, his father: 'Hast thou but one blessing, O father? Bless me, (even) me also, father: ' **33** And Esau lifted up his voice and wept. And Isaac answered and said unto him: 'Behold, far from the dew of the earth shall be thy dwelling, And far from the dew of heaven from above. **34** And by thy sword wilt thou live, And thou wilt serve thy brother. And it shall come to pass when thou becomest great, And dost shake his yoke from off thy neck, Thou shalt sin a complete sin unto death, And thy seed shall be rooted out from under heaven.' **35** And Esau kept threatening Jacob because of the blessing wherewith his father blessed him, and he: said in his heart: 'May the days of mourning for my father now come, so that I may slay my brother Jacob.'

**Rebecca induces Isaac to send Jacob to Mesopotamia. Jacob's Dream and View at Bethel (xxvii. 1-27; cf. Gen. xxviii.).**

## 27

**1** And the words of Esau, her elder son, were told to Rebecca in a dream, and Rebecca sent and called Jacob her younger son, **2** and said unto him: 'Behold Esau thy brother will take vengeance on thee so as to kill thee. **3** Now, therefore, my son, obey my voice, and arise and flee thou to Laban, my brother, to Haran, and tarry with him a few days until thy brother's anger turns away, and he remove his anger from thee, and forget all that thou hast done; then I will send and fetch thee from thence.' **4** And Jacob said: 'I am not afraid; if he wishes to kill me, I will kill him.' **5** But she said unto him: 'Let me not be bereft of both my sons on one day.' **6** And Jacob said to Rebecca his mother: 'Behold, thou knowest that my father has become old, and does not see because his eyes are dull, and if I leave him it will be evil in his eyes, because I leave him and go away from you, and my father will be angry, and will curse me. I will not go; when he sends me, then only will I go.' **7** And Rebecca said to Jacob: 'I will go in and speak to him, and he will send thee away.' **8** And Rebecca went in and said to Isaac: 'I loathe my life because of the two daughters of Heth, whom Esau has taken him as wives; and if Jacob take a wife from among the daughters of the land such as these, for what purpose do I further live, for the daughters of Canaan are evil.' **9** And Isaac called Jacob and blessed him, and admonished him and said unto him: 'Do not take thee a wife of any of the daughters of Canaan; **10** arise and go to Mesopotamia, to the house of Bethuel, thy mother's father, and take thee a wife from thence of the daughters of Laban, thy mother's brother. **11** And God Almighty bless thee and increase and multiply thee that thou mayest become a company of nations, and give thee the blessings of my father Abraham, to thee and to thy seed after thee, that thou mayest inherit the land of thy sojournings and all the land which God gave to Abraham: go, my son, in peace.' **12** And Isaac sent Jacob away, and he went to Mesopotamia, to Laban the son of Bethuel the Syrian, the brother of Rebecca, Jacob's mother. **13** And it came to pass after Jacob had arisen

to go to Mesopotamia that the spirit of Rebecca was grieved after her son, and she wept. **14** And Isaac said to Rebecca: 'My sister, weep not on account of Jacob, my son; for he goeth in peace, and in peace will he return. **15** The Most High God will preserve him from all evil, and will be with him; for He will not forsake him all his days; **16** For I know that his ways will be prospered in all things wherever he goes, until he return in peace to us, and we see him in peace. **17** Fear not on his account, my sister, for he is on the upright path and he is a perfect man: and he is faithful and will not perish. Weep not.' **18** And Isaac comforted Rebecca on account of her son Jacob, and blessed him. **19** And Jacob went from the Well of the Oath to go to Haran on the first year of the second week in the forty-fourth jubilee, and he came to Luz on the mountains, that is, Bethel, on the new moon of the first month of this week, [2115 A.M.] and he came to the place at even and turned from the way to the west of the road that night: and he slept there; for the sun had set. **20** And he took one of the stones of that place and laid <it at his head> under the tree, and he was journeying alone, and he slept. **21** And he dreamt that night, and behold a ladder set up on the earth, and the top of it reached to heaven, and behold, the angels of the Lord ascended and descended on it: and behold, the Lord stood upon it. **22** And he spake to Jacob and said: 'I am the Lord God of Abraham, thy father, and the God of Isaac; the land whereon thou art sleeping, to thee will I give it, and to thy seed after thee. **23** And thy seed shall be as the dust of the earth, and thou shalt increase to the west and to the east, to the north and the south, and in thee and in thy seed shall all the families of the nations be blessed. **24** And behold, I will be with thee, and will keep thee whithersoever thou goest, and I will bring thee again into this land in peace; for I will not leave thee until I do everything that I told thee of.' **25** And Jacob awoke from his sleep, and said, 'Truly this place is the house of the Lord, and I knew it not.' And he was afraid and said: 'Dreadful is this place which is none other than the house of God, and this is the gate of heaven.' **26** And Jacob arose early in the morning, and took the stone which he had put under his head and set it up as a pillar for a sign, and he poured oil upon the top of it. And he called the name of that place Bethel; but the name of the place was Luz at the first. **27** And Jacob vowed a vow unto the Lord, saying: 'If the Lord will be with me, and will keep me in this way that I go, and give me bread to eat and raiment to put on, so that I come again to my father's house in peace, then shall the Lord be my God, and this stone which I have set up as a pillar for a sign in this place, shall be the Lord's house, and of all that thou givest me, I shall give the tenth to thee, my God.'

**Jacob's Marriage to Leah and Rachel; his Children and Riches (xxviii. i- 30; cf. Gen. xxix., xxx., xxxi. 1-2).**

## 28

**1** And he went on his journey, and came to the land of the east, to Laban, the brother of Rebecca, and he was with him, and served him for Rachel his daughter one week. **2** And in the first year of the third week [2122 A.M.] he said unto him: 'Give me my wife, for whom I have served thee seven years '; and Laban said unto Jacob: 'I will give thee thy wife.' **3** And Laban made a feast, and took Leah his elder daughter, and gave (her) to Jacob as a wife, and gave her Zilpah his handmaid for an hand- maid; and Jacob did not know, for he thought that she was Rachel. **4** And he went in unto her, and behold, she was Leah; and Jacob was angry with Laban, and said unto him: 'Why hast thou dealt thus with me? Did not I serve thee for Rachel and not for Leah? Why hast thou wronged me? **5** Take thy daughter, and I will go; for thou hast done evil to me.' For Jacob loved Rachel more than Leah; for Leah's eyes were weak, but her form was very handsome; but Rachel had beautiful eyes and a beautiful and very handsome form. **6** And Laban said to Jacob: 'It is not so done in our country, to give the younger before the elder.' And it is not right to do this; for thus it is ordained and written in the heavenly tablets, that no one should give his younger daughter before the elder; but the elder, one gives first and after her the younger -and the man who does so, they set down guilt against him in heaven, and none is righteous that does this thing, for this deed is evil before the Lord. **7** And command thou the children of Israel that they do not this thing; let them neither take nor give the younger before they have given the elder, for it is very wicked. **8** And Laban said to Jacob: 'Let the seven days of the feast of this one pass by, and I shall give thee Rachel, that thou mayst serve me another seven years, that thou mayst pasture my sheep as thou didst in the former week.' **9** And on the day when the seven days of the feast of Leah had passed, Laban gave Rachel to Jacob, that he might serve him another seven years, and he gave to Rachel Bilhah, the sister of Zilpah, as a handmaid. **10** And he served yet other seven years for Rachel, for Leah had been given to him for nothing. **11** And the Lord opened the womb of Leah, and she conceived and bare Jacob a son, and he called his name Reuben, on the fourteenth day of the ninth month, in the first year of the third week. [2122 A.M.] **12** But the womb of Rachel was closed, for the Lord saw that Leah was hated and Rachel loved. **13** And again Jacob went in unto Leah, and she conceived, and bare Jacob a second son, and he called his name Simeon, on the twenty-first of the tenth month, and in the third year of this week. [2124 A.M.] ¹⁴ And again Jacob went in unto Leah, and she conceived, and bare him a third son, and he called his name Levi, in the new moon of the first month in the sixth year of this week. [2127 A.M.] ¹⁵ And again Jacob went in unto her, and she conceived, and bare him a fourth son, and he called his name Judah, on the fifteenth of the third month, in the first year of the fourth week. [2129 A.M.] ¹⁶ And on account of all this Rachel envied Leah, for she did not bear, and she said to Jacob: 'Give me children'; and Jacob said: 'Have I withheld from thee the fruits of thy womb? Have I forsaken thee?' ¹⁷ And when Rachel saw that Leah had borne four sons to Jacob, Reuben and Simeon and Levi and Judah, she said unto him: 'Go in unto Bilhah my handmaid, and she will conceive, and bear a son unto me.' (And she gave (him) Bilhah her handmaid to wife). ¹⁸ And he went in unto her, and she conceived, and bare him a son, and he called his name Dan, on the ninth of the sixth month, in the sixth year of the third week. [2127 A.M.] ¹⁹ And Jacob went in again unto Bilhah a second time, and she conceived, and bare Jacob another son, and Rachel called his name Napthali, on the fifth of the seventh month, in the second year of the fourth week. [2130 A.M.] ²⁰ And when Leah saw that she had become sterile and did not bear, she envied Rachel, and she also gave her handmaid Zilpah to Jacob to wife, and she conceived, and bare a son, and Leah called his name Gad, on the twelfth of the eighth month, in the third year of the fourth week. [2131 A.M.] ²¹ And he went in again unto her, and she conceived, and bare him a second son, and Leah called his name Asher, on the second of the eleventh month, in the fifth year of the fourth week. [2133 A.M.] ²² And Jacob went in unto Leah, and she conceived, and bare a son, and she called his name Issachar, on the fourth of the fifth month, in the fourth year of the fourth week,[2132 A.M.] and she gave him to a nurse. ²³ And Jacob went in again unto her, and she conceived, and bare two (children), a son and a daughter, and she called the name of the son Zabulon, and the name of the daughter Dinah, in the seventh of the seventh month, in the sixth year of the fourth week. [2134 A.M.] ²⁴ And the Lord was gracious to Rachel, and opened her womb, and she conceived, and bare a son, and she called his name Joseph, on the new moon of the fourth month, in the sixth year in this fourth week. [2134 A.M.] ²⁵ And in the days when Joseph was born, Jacob said to Laban: 'Give me my wives and sons, and let me go to my father Isaac, and let me make me an house; for I have completed the years in which I have served thee for thy two daughters, and I will go to the house of my father.' ²⁶ And Laban said to Jacob: 'Tarry with me for thy wages, and pasture my flock for me again, and take thy wages.' ²⁷ And they agreed with one another that he should give him as his wages those of the lambs and kids which were born black and spotted and white, (these) were to be his wages. ²⁸ And all the sheep brought forth spotted and speckled and black, variously marked, and they brought forth again lambs like themselves, and all that were spotted were Jacob's and those which were not were Laban's. ²⁹ And Jacob's possessions multiplied exceedingly, and he possessed oxen and sheep and asses and camels, and menservants and maid-servants. ³⁰ And Laban and his sons envied Jacob, and Laban took back his sheep from him, and he observed him with evil intent.

**Jacob's Flight with his Family: his Covenant with Laban (xxix. 1-12; cf. Gen, xxxi.).**

## 29

¹ And it came to pass when Rachel had borne Joseph, that Laban went to shear his sheep; for they were distant from him a three days' journey. ² And Jacob saw that Laban was going to shear his sheep, and Jacob called Leah and Rachel, and spake kindly unto them that they should come with him to the land of Canaan. ³ For he told them how he had seen everything in a dream, even all that He had spoken unto him that he should return to his father's house, and they said: 'To every place whither thou goest we will go with thee.' ⁴ And Jacob blessed the God of Isaac his father, and the God of Abraham his father's father, and he arose and mounted his wives and his children, and took all his possessions and crossed the river, and came to the land of Gilead, and Jacob hid his intention from Laban and told him not. ⁵ And in the seventh year of the fourth week Jacob turned (his face) toward Gilead in the first month, on the twenty-first thereof. [2135 A.M.] And Laban pursued after him and overtook Jacob in the mountain of Gilead in the third month, on the thirteenth thereof. ⁶ And the Lord did not suffer him to injure Jacob; for he appeared to him in a dream by night. And Laban spake to Jacob. ⁷ And on the fifteenth of those days Jacob made a feast for Laban, and for all who came with him, and Jacob sware to Laban that day, and Laban also to Jacob, that neither should cross the mountain of Gilead to the other with evil purpose. ⁸ And he made there a heap for a witness; wherefore the name of that place is called: 'The Heap of Witness,' after this heap. ⁹ But before they used to call the land of Gilead the land of the Rephaim; for it was the land of the Rephaim, and the

Rephaim were born (there), giants whose height was ten, nine, eight down to seven cubits. ¹⁰ And their habitation was from the land of the children of Ammon to Mount Hermon, and the seats of their kingdom were Karnaim and Ashtaroth, and Edrei, and Misur, and Beon. ¹¹ And the Lord destroyed them because of the evil of their deeds; for they were very malignant, and the Amorites dwelt in their stead, wicked and sinful, and there is no people to-day which has wrought to the full all their sins, and they have no longer length of life on the earth. ¹² And Jacob sent away Laban, and he departed into Mesopotamia, the land of the East, and Jacob returned to the land of Gilead.

**Jacob, reconciled with Esau, dwells in Canaan and supports his Parents (xxix. 13-20; Cf. Gen. xxxii., xxxiii.).**

¹³ And he passed over the Jabbok in the ninth month, on the eleventh thereof. And on that day Esau, his brother, came to him, and he was reconciled to him, and departed from him unto the land of Seir, but Jacob dwelt in tents. ¹⁴ And in the first year of the fifth week in this jubilee [2136 A.M.] he crossed the Jordan, and dwelt beyond the Jordan, and he pastured his sheep from the sea of the heap unto Bethshan, and unto Dothan and unto the forest of Akrabbim. ¹⁵ And he sent to his father Isaac of all his substance, clothing, and food, and meat, and drink, and milk, and butter, and cheese, and some dates of the valley. ¹⁶ And to his mother Rebecca also four times a year, between the times of the months, between ploughing and reaping, and between autumn and the rain (season) and between winter and spring, to the tower of Abraham. ¹⁷ For Isaac had returned from the Well of the Oath and gone up to the tower of his father Abraham, and he dwelt there apart from his son Esau. ¹⁸ For in the days when Jacob went to Mesopotamia, Esau took to himself a wife Mahalath, the daughter of Ishmael, and he gathered together all the flocks of his father and his wives, and went Up and dwelt on Mount Seir, and left Isaac his father at the Well of the Oath alone. ¹⁹ And Isaac went up from the Well of the Oath and dwelt in the tower of Abraham his father on the mountains of Hebron, ²⁰ And thither Jacob sent all that he did send to his father and his mother from time to time, all they needed, and they blessed Jacob with all their heart and with all their soul.

**Dinah ravished. Slaughter of the Shechemites. Laws against Intermarriage between Israel and the Heathen. The Choice of Levi (xxx. 1-26; cf. Gen. xxxiv.).**

## 30

¹ And in the first year of the sixth week [2143 A.M.] he went up to Salem, to the east of Shechem, in peace, in the fourth month. ² And there they carried off Dinah, the daughter of Jacob, into the house of Shechem, the son of Hamor, the Hivite, the prince of the land, and he lay with her and defiled her, and she was a little girl, a child of twelve years. ³ And he besought his father and her brothers that she might be given to him to wife. And Jacob and his sons were wroth because of the men of Shechem; for they had defiled Dinah, their sister, and they spake to them with evil intent and dealt deceitfully with them and beguiled them. ⁴ And Simeon and Levi came unexpectedly to Shechem and executed judgment on all the men of Shechem, and slew all the men whom they found in it, and left not a single one remaining in it: they slew all in torments because they had dishonoured their sister Dinah. ⁵ And thus let it not again be done from henceforth that a daughter of Israel be defiled; for judgment is ordained in heaven against them that they should destroy with the sword all the men of the Shechemites because they had wrought shame in Israel. ⁶ And the Lord delivered them into the hands of the sons of Jacob that they might exterminate them with the sword and execute judgment upon them, and that it might not thus again be done in Israel that a virgin of Israel should be defiled. ⁷ And if there is any man who wishes in Israel to give his daughter or his sister to any man who is of the seed of the Gentiles he shall surely die, and they shall stone him with stones; for he hath wrought shame in Israel; and they shall burn the woman with fire, because she has dishonoured the name of the house of her father, and she shall be rooted out of Israel. ⁸ And let not an adulteress and no uncleanness be found in Israel throughout all the days of the generations of the earth; for Israel is holy unto the Lord, and every man who has defiled (it) shall surely die: they shall stone him with stones. ⁹ For thus has it been ordained and written in the heavenly tablets regarding all the seed of Israel: he who defileth (it) shall surely die, and he shall be stoned with stones. ¹⁰ And to this law there is no limit of days, and no remission, nor any atonement: but the man who has defiled his daughter shall be rooted out in the midst of all Israel, because he has given of his seed to Moloch, and wrought impiously so as to defile it. ¹¹ And do thou, Moses, command the children of Israel and exhort them not to give their daughters to the Gentiles, and not to take for their sons any of the daughters of the Gentiles, for this is abominable before the Lord. ¹² For this reason I have written for thee in the words of the Law all the deeds of the Shechemites, which they wrought against Dinah, and how the sons of Jacob spake, saying: 'We will not give our daughter to a man

who is uncircumcised; for that were a reproach unto us.' [13] And it is a reproach to Israel, to those who live, and to those that take the daughters of the Gentiles; for this is unclean and abominable to Israel. [14] And Israel will not be free from this uncleanness if it has a wife of the daughters of the Gentiles, or has given any of its daughters to a man who is of any of the Gentiles. [15] For there will be plague upon plague, and curse upon curse, and every judgment and plague and curse will come upon him: if he do this thing, or hide his eyes from those who commit uncleanness, or those who defile the sanctuary of the Lord, or those who profane His holy name, (then) will the whole nation together be judged for all the uncleanness and profanation of this man. [16] And there will be no respect of persons [and no consideration of persons] and no receiving at his hands of fruits and offerings and burnt-offerings and fat, nor the fragrance of sweet savour, so as to accept it: and so fare every man or woman in Israel who defiles the sanctuary. [17] For this reason I have commanded thee, saying: 'Testify this testimony to Israel: see how the Shechemites fared and their sons: how they were delivered into the hands of two sons of Jacob, and they slew them under tortures, and it was (reckoned) unto them for righteousness, and it is written down to them for righteousness. [18] And the seed of Levi was chosen for the priesthood, and to be Levites, that they might minister before the Lord, as we, continually, and that Levi and his sons may be blessed for ever; for he was zealous to execute righteousness and judgment and vengeance on all those who arose against Israel. [19] And so they inscribe as a testimony in his favour on the heavenly tablets blessing and righteousness before the God of all: [20] And we remember the righteousness which the man fulfilled during his life, at all periods of the year; until a thousand generations they will record it, and it will come to him and to his descendants after him, and he has been recorded on the heavenly tablets as a friend and a righteous man. [21] All this account I have written for thee, and have commanded thee to say to the children of Israel, that they should not commit sin nor transgress the ordinances nor break the covenant which has been ordained for them, (but) that they should fulfil it and be recorded as friends. [22] But if they transgress and work uncleanness in every way, they will be recorded on the heavenly tablets as adversaries, and they will be destroyed out of the book of life, and they will be recorded in the book of those who will be destroyed and with those who will be rooted out of the earth. [23] And on the day when the sons of Jacob slew Shechem a writing was recorded in their favour in heaven that they had executed righteousness and uprightness and vengeance on the sinners, and it was written for a blessing. [24] And they brought Dinah, their sister, out of the house of Shechem, and they took captive everything that was in Shechem, their sheep and their oxen and their asses, and all their wealth, and all their flocks, and brought them all to Jacob their father. [25] And he reproached them because they had put the city to the sword for he feared those who dwelt in the land, the Canaanites and the Perizzites. [26] And the dread of the Lord was upon all the cities which are around about Shechem, and they did not rise to pursue after the sons of Jacob; for terror had fallen upon them.

**Jacob's Journey to Bethel and Hebron. Isaac blesses Levi and Judah (xxxi. 1-25; cf. Gen. xxxv.).**

## 31

[1] And on the new moon of the month Jacob spake to all the people of his house. saying: 'Purify yourselves and change your garments, and let us arise and go up to Bethel, where I vowed a vow to Him on the day when I fled from the face of Esau my brother, because he has been with me and brought me into this land in peace, and put ye away the strange gods that arc among you.' [2] And they gave up the strange gods and that which was in their ears and which was on their necks and the idols which Rachel stole from Laban her father she gave wholly to Jacob. And he burnt and brake them to pieces and destroyed them, and hid them under an oak which is in the land of Shechem. [3] And he went up on the new moon of the seventh month to Bethel. And he built an altar at the place where he had slept, and he set up a pillar there, and he sent word to his father Isaac to come to him to his sacrifice, and to his mother Rebecca. [4] And Isaac said: 'Let my son Jacob come, and let me see him before I die.' [5] And Jacob went to his fathcr Isaac and to his mother Rebecca, to the house of his father Abraham, and he took two of his sons with him, Levi and Judah, and he came to his father Isaac and to his mother Rebecca. [6] And Rebecca came forth from the tower to the front of it to kiss Jacob and embrace him; for her spirit had revived when she heard: 'Behold Jacob thy son has come'; and she kissed him. [7] And she saw his two sons, and she recognised them, and said unto him: 'Are these thy sons, my son?' and she embraced them and kissed them, and blessed them, saying: 'In you shall the seed of Abraham become illustrious, and ye shall prove a blessing on the earth.' [8] And Jacob went in to Isaac his father, to the chamber where he lay, and his two sons were with him, and he took the hand of his father, and stooping down he kissed him, and Isaac clung to the neck of Jacob his

son, and wept upon his neck. [9] And the darkness left the eyes of Isaac, and he saw the two sons of Jacob, Levi, and Judah, and he said: 'Are these thy sons, my son? for they are like thee.' [10] And he said unto him that they were truly his sons: 'And thou hast truly seen that they are truly my sons'. [11] And they came near to him, and he turned and kissed them and embraced them both together. [12] And the spirit of prophecy came down into his mouth, and he took Levi by his right hand and Judah by his left. [13] And he turned to Levi first, and began to bless him first, and said unto him: May the God of all, the very Lord of all the ages, bless thee and thy children throughout all the ages. [14] And may the Lord give to thee and to thy seed greatness and great glory, and cause thee and thy seed, from among all flesh, to approach Him to serve in His sanctuary as the angels of the presence and as the holy ones. (Even) as they, shall the seed of thy sons be for glory and greatness and holiness, and may He make them great unto all the ages. [15] And they shall be judges and princes, and chiefs of all the seed of the sons of Jacob; They shall speak the word of the Lord in righteousness, And they shall judge all His judgments in righteousness. And they shall declare My ways to Jacob And My paths to Israel. The blessing of the Lord shall be given in their mouths To bless all the seed of the beloved. [16] Thy mother has called thy name Levi, And justly has she called thy name; Thou shalt be joined to the Lord And be the companion of all the sons of Jacob; Let His table be thine, And do thou and thy sons eat thereof; And may thy table be full unto all generations, And thy food fail not unto all the ages. [17] And let all who hate thee fall down before thee, And let all thy adversaries be rooted out and perish; And blessed be he that blesses thee, And cursed be every nation that curses thee.' [18] And to Judah he said: 'May the Lord give thee strength and power To tread down all that hate thee; A prince shalt thou be, thou and one of thy sons, over the sons of Jacob; May thy name and the name of thy sons go forth and traverse every land and region. Then shall the Gentiles fear before thy face, And all the nations shall quake [And all the peoples shall quake]. [19] In thee shall be the help of Jacob, And in thee be found the salvation of Israel. [20] And when thou sittest on the throne of honour of thy righteousness There shall be great peace for all the seed of the sons of the beloved; Blessed be he that blesseth thee, And all that hate thee and afflict thee and curse thee Shall be rooted out and destroyed from the earth and be accursed.' [21] And turning he kissed him again and embraced him, and rejoiced greatly; for he had seen the sons of Jacob his son in very truth. [22] And he went forth from between his feet and fell down and bowed down to him, and he blessed them and rested there with Isaac his father that night, and they eat and drank with joy. [23] And he made the two sons of Jacob sleep, the one on his right hand and the other on his left, and it was counted to him for righteousness. [24] And Jacob told his father everything during the night, how the Lord had shown him great mercy, and how he had prospered (him in) all his ways, and protected him from all evil. [25] And Isaac blessed the God of his father Abraham, who had not withdrawn his mercy and his righteousness from the sons of his servant Isaac.

**Rebecca journeys with Jacob to Bethel (xxxi. 26-32).**

[26] And in the morning Jacob told his father Isaac the vow which he had vowed to the Lord, and the vision which he had seen, and that he had built an altar, and that everything was ready for the sacrifice to be made before the Lord as he had vowed, and that he had come to set him on an ass. [27] And Isaac said unto Jacob his son: 'I am not able to go with thee; for I am old and not able to bear the way: go, my son, in peace; for I am one hundred and sixty-five years this day; I am no longer able to journey; set thy mother (on an ass) and let her go with thee. [28] And I know, my son, that thou hast come on my account, and may this day be blessed on which thou hast seen me alive, and I also have seen thee, my son. [29] Mayest thou prosper and fulfil the vow which thou hast vowed; and put not off thy vow; for thou shalt be called to account as touching the vow; now therefore make haste to perform it, and may He be pleased who has made all things, to whom thou hast vowed the vow.' [30] And he said to Rebecca: 'Go with Jacob thy son'; and Rebecca went with Jacob her son, and Deborah with her, and they came to Bethel. [31] And Jacob remembered the prayer with which his father had blessed him and his two sons, Levi and Judah, and he rejoiced and blessed the God of his fathers, Abraham and Isaac. [32] And he said: 'Now I know that I have an eternal hope, and my sons also, before the God of all'; and thus is it ordained concerning the two; and they record it as an eternal testimony unto them on the heavenly tablets how Isaac blessed them.

**Levi's Dream at Bethel; he is appointed to the Priesthood. Jacob celebrates the Feast of Tabernacles and offers Tithes. The Institution of Tithes (xxxii. 1-15; cf. Gen. xxxv.).**

## 32

[1] And he abode that night at Bethel, and Levi dreamed that they had ordained and made him the priest of the Most High God, him and his sons for ever; and he awoke from his sleep and blessed the Lord. [2] And

Jacob rose early in the morning, on the fourteenth of this month, and he gave a tithe of all that came with him, both of men and cattle, both of gold and every vessel and garment, yea, he gave tithes of all. ³ And in those days Rachel became pregnant with her son Benjamin. And Jacob counted his sons from him upwards and Levi fell to the portion of the Lord, and his father clothed him in the garments of the priesthood and filled his hands. ⁴ And on the fifteenth of this month, he brought to the altar fourteen oxen from amongst the cattle, and twenty-eight rams, and forty-nine sheep, and seven lambs, and twenty-one kids of the goats as a burnt-offering on the altar of sacrifice, well pleasing for a sweet savour before God. ⁵ This was his offering, in consequence of the vow which he had vowed that he would give a tenth, with their fruit-offerings and their drink- offerings. ⁶ And when the fire had consumed it, he burnt incense on the fire over the fire, and for a thank-offering two oxen and four rams and four sheep, four he-goats, and two sheep of a year old, and two kids of the goats; and thus he did daily for seven days. ⁷ And he and all his sons and his men were eating (this) with joy there during seven days and blessing and thanking the Lord, who had delivered him out of all his tribulation and had given him his vow. ⁸ And he tithed all the clean animals, and made a burnt sacrifice, but the unclean animals he gave (not) to Levi his son, and he gave him all the souls of the men. ⁹ And Levi discharged the priestly office at Bethel before Jacob his father in preference to his ten brothers, and he was a priest there, and Jacob gave his vow: thus he tithed again the tithe to the Lord and sanctified it, and it became holy unto Him. ¹⁰ And for this reason it is ordained on the heavenly tablets as a law for the tithing again the tithe to eat before the Lord from year to year, in the place where it is chosen that His name should dwell, and to this law there is no limit of days for ever. ¹¹ This ordinance is written that it may be fulfilled from year to year in eating the second tithe before the Lord in the place where it has been chosen, and nothing shall remain over from it from this year to the year following. ¹² For in its year shall the seed be eaten till the days of the gathering of the seed of the year, and the wine till the days of the wine, and the oil till the days of its season. ¹³ And all that is left thereof and becomes old, let it be regarded as polluted: let it be burnt with fire, for it is unclean. ¹⁴ And thus let them eat it together in the sanctuary, and let them not suffer it to become old. ¹⁵ And all the tithes of the oxen and sheep shall be holy unto the Lord, and shall belong to his priests, which they will eat before Him from year to year; for thus is it ordained and engraven regarding the tithe on the heavenly tablets.

**Jacob's Visions. He celebrates the eighth day of Tabernacles. The Birth of Benjamin and Death of Rachel (xxxii. 16-34; cf. Gen. xxxv.).**

¹⁶ And on the following night, on the twenty-second day of this month, Jacob resolved to build that place, and to surround the court with a wall, and to sanctify it and make it holy for ever, for himself and his children after him. ¹⁷ And the Lord appeared to him by night and blessed him and said unto him: 'Thy name shall not be called Jacob, but Israel shall they name thy name.' ¹⁸ And He said unto him again: 'I am the Lord who created the heaven and the earth, and I will increase thee and multiply thee exceedingly, and kings shall come forth from thee, and they shall judge everywhere wherever the foot of the sons of men has trodden. ¹⁹ And I will give to thy seed all the earth which is under heaven, and they shall judge all the nations according to their desires, and after that they shall get possession of the whole earth and inherit it for ever.' ²⁰ And He finished speaking with him, and He went up from him. and Jacob looked till He had ascended into heaven. ²¹ And he saw in a vision of the night, and behold an angel descended from heaven with seven tablets in his hands, and he gave them to Jacob, and he read them and knew all that was written therein which would befall him and his sons throughout all the ages. ²² And he showed him all that was written on the tablets, and said unto him: 'Do not build this place, and do not make it an eternal sanctuary, and do not dwell here; for this is not the place. Go to the house of Abraham thy father and dwell with Isaac thy father until the day of the death of thy father. ²³ For in Egypt thou shalt die in peace, and in this land thou shalt be buried with honour in the sepulchre of thy fathers, with Abraham and Isaac. ²⁴ Fear not, for as thou hast seen and read it, thus shall it all be; and do thou write down everything as thou hast seen and read.' ²⁵ And Jacob said: 'Lord, how can I remember all that I have read and seen? 'And he said unto him: 'I will bring all things to thy remembrance.' ²⁶ And he went up from him, and he awoke from his sleep, and he remembered everything which he had read and seen, and he wrote down all the words which he had read and seen. ²⁷ And he celebrated there yet another day, and he sacrificed thereon according to all that he sacrificed on the former days, and called its name 'Addition,' for this day was added and the former days he called 'The Feast '. ²⁸ And thus it was manifested that it should be, and it is written on the heavenly tablets: wherefore it was revealed to him that he should celebrate it, and add it to the seven days of the feast. ²⁹

And its name was called 'Addition,' because that it was recorded amongst the days of the feast days, according to the number of the days of the year. ³⁰ And in the night, on the twenty-third of this month, Deborah Rebecca's nurse died, and they buried her beneath the city under the oak of the river, and he called the name of this place, 'The river of Deborah,' and the oak, 'The oak of the mourning of Deborah.' ³¹ And Rebecca went and returned to her house to her father Isaac, and Jacob sent by her hand rams and sheep and he-goats that she should prepare a meal for his father such as he desired. ³² And he went after his mother till he came to the land of Kabratan, and he dwelt there. ³³ And Rachel bare a son in the night, and called his name 'Son of my sorrow '; for she suffered in giving him birth: but his father called his name Benjamin, on the eleventh of the eighth month in the first of the sixth week of this jubilee. [2143 A.M.] ³⁴ And Rachel died there and she was buried in the land of Ephrath, the same is Bethlehem, and Jacob built a pillar on the grave of Rachel, on the road above her grave.

**Reuben's Sin with Bilhah. Laws regarding Incest. Jacob's Children (xxxiii. 1-23; Cf. Gen. xxxv. 21-27).**

## 33

¹ And Jacob went and dwelt to the south of Magdaladra'ef. And he went to his father Isaac, he and Leah his wife, on the new moon of the tenth month. ² And Reuben saw Bilhah, Rachel's maid, the concubine of his father, bathing in water in a secret place, and he loved her. ³ And he hid himself at night, and he entered the house of Bilhah [at night], and he found her sleeping alone on a bed in her house. ⁴ And he lay with her, and she awoke and saw, and behold Reuben was lying with her in the bed, and she uncovered the border of her covering and seized him, and cried out, and discovered that it was Reuben. ⁵ And she was ashamed because of him, and released her hand from him, and he fled. ⁶ And she lamented because of this thing exceedingly, and did not tell it to any one. ⁷ And when Jacob returned and sought her, she said unto him: 'I am not clean for thee, for I have been defiled as regards thee; for Reuben has defiled me, and has lain with me in the night, and I was asleep, and did not discover until he uncovered my skirt and slept with me.' ⁸ And Jacob was exceedingly wroth with Reuben because he had lain with Bilhah, because he had uncovered his father's skirt. ⁹ And Jacob did not approach her again because Reuben had defiled her. And as for any man who uncovers his father's skirt his deed is wicked exceedingly, for he is abominable before the Lord. ¹⁰ For this reason it is written and ordained on the heavenly tablets that a man should not lie with his father's wife, and should not uncover his father's skirt, for this is unclean: they shall surely die together, the man who lies with his father's wife and the woman also, for they have wrought uncleanness on the earth. ¹¹ And there shall be nothing unclean before our God in the nation which He has chosen for Himself as a possession. ¹² And again, it is written a second time: 'Cursed be he who lieth with the wife of his father, for he hath uncovered his father's shame'; and all the holy ones of the Lord said 'So be it; so be it.' ¹³ And do thou, Moses, command the children of Israel that they observe this word; for it (entails) a punishment of death; and it is unclean, and there is no atonement for ever to atone for the man who has committed this, but he is to be put to death and slain, and stoned with stones, and rooted out from the midst of the people of our God. ¹⁴ For to no man who does so in Israel is it permitted to remain alive a single day on the earth, for he is abominable and unclean. ¹⁵ And let them not say: to Reuben was granted life and forgiveness after he had lain with his father's concubine, and to her also though she had a husband, and her husband Jacob, his father, was still alive. ¹⁶ For until that time there had not been revealed the ordinance and judgment and law in its completeness for all, but in thy days (it has been revealed) as a law of seasons and of days, and an everlasting law for the everlasting generations. ¹⁷ And for this law there is no consummation of days, and no atonement for it, but they must both be rooted out in the midst of the nation: on the day whereon they committed it they shall slay them. ¹⁸ And do thou, Moses, write (it) down for Israel that they may observe it, and do according to these words, and not commit a sin unto death; for the Lord our God is judge, who respects not persons and accepts not gifts. ¹⁹ And tell them these words of the covenant, that they may hear and observe, and be on their guard with respect to them, and not be destroyed and rooted out of the land; for an uncleanness, and an abomination, and a contamination, and a pollution are all they who commit it on the earth before our God. ²⁰ And there is no greater sin than the fornication which they commit on earth; for Israel is a holy nation unto the Lord its God, and a nation of inheritance, and a priestly and royal nation and for (His own) possession; and there shall no such uncleanness appear in the midst of the holy nation. ²¹ And in the third year of this sixth week [2145 A.M.] Jacob and all his sons went and dwelt in the house of Abraham, near Isaac his father and Rebecca his mother. ²² And these were the names of the sons of Jacob: the first-born Reuben, Simeon, Levi, Judah, Issachar, Zebulon, the sons of Leah; and the sons of

Rachel, Joseph and Benjamin; and the sons of Bilhah, Dan and Naphtali; and the sons of Zilpah, Gad and Asher; and Dinah, the daughter of Leah, the only daughter of Jacob. 23 And they came and bowed themselves to Isaac and Rebecca, and when they saw them they blessed Jacob and all his sons, and Isaac rejoiced exceedingly, for he saw the sons of Jacob, his younger son and he blessed them.

**War of the Amorite Kings against Jacob and his Sons. Joseph sold into Egypt (cf. Gen. xxxvii.). The Death of Bilhah and Dinah (xxxiv. 1-19).**

## 34

1 And in the sixth year of this week of this forty-fourth jubilee [2148 A.M.] Jacob sent his sons to pasture their sheep, and his servants with them to the pastures of Shechem. 2 And the seven kings of the Amorites assembled themselves together against them, to slay them, hiding themselves under the trees, and to take their cattle as a prey. 3 And Jacob and Levi and Judah and Joseph were in the house with Isaac their father; for his spirit was sorrowful, and they could not leave him: and Benjamin was the youngest, and for this reason remained with his father. 4 And there came the king[s] of Taphu and the king[s] of 'Aresa, and the king[s] of Seragan, and the king[s] of Selo, and the king[s] of Ga'as, and the king of Bethoron, and the king of Ma'anisakir, and all those who dwell in these mountains (and) who dwell in the woods in the land of Canaan. 5 And they announced this to Jacob saying: 'Behold, the kings of the Amorites have surrounded thy sons, and plundered their herds.' 6 And he arose from his house, he and his three sons and all the servants of his father, and his own servants, and he went against them with six thousand men, who carried swords. 7 And he slew them in the pastures of Shechem, and pursued those who fled, and he slew them with the edge of the sword, and he slew 'Aresa and Taphu and Saregan and Selo and 'Amani- sakir and Ga[ga]'as, and he recovered his herds. 8 And he prevailed over them, and imposed tribute on them that they should pay him tribute, five fruit products of their land, and he built Robel and Tamnatares. 9 And he returned in peace, and made peace with them, and they became his servants, until the day that he and his sons went down into Egypt. 10 And in the seventh year of this week [2149 A.M.] he sent Joseph to learn about the welfare of his brothers from his house to the land of Shechem, and he found them in the land of Dothan. 11 And they dealt treacherously with him, and formed a plot against him to slay him, but changing their minds, they sold him to Ishmaelite merchants, and they brought him down into Egypt, and they sold him to Potiphar, the eunuch of Pharaoh, the chief of the cooks, priest of the city of 'Elew. 12 And the sons of Jacob slaughtered a kid, and dipped the coat of Joseph in the blood, and sent (it) to Jacob their father on the tenth of the seventh month. 13 And he mourned all that night, for they had brought it to him in the evening, and he became feverish with mourning for his death, and he said: 'An evil beast hath devoured Joseph'; and all the members of his house [mourned with him that day, and they] were grieving and mourning with him all that day. 14 And his sons and his daughter rose up to comfort him, but he refused to be comforted for his son. 15 And on that day Bilhah heard that Joseph had perished, and she died mourning him, and she was living in Qafratef, and Dinah also, his daughter, died after Joseph had perished. 16 And there came these three mournings upon Israel in one month. And they buried Bilhah over against the tomb of Rachel, and Dinah also. his daughter, they buried there. 17 And he mourned for Joseph one year, and did not cease, for he said 'Let me go down to the grave mourning for my son'. 18 For this reason it is ordained for the children of Israel that they should afflict themselves on the tenth of the seventh month -on the day that the news which made him weep for Joseph came to Jacob his father- that they should make atonement for themselves thereon with a young goat on the tenth of the seventh month, once a year, for their sins; for they had grieved the affection of their father regarding Joseph his son. 19 And this day has been ordained that they should grieve thereon for their sins, and for all their transgressions and for all their errors, so that they might cleanse themselves on that day once a year.

**The Wives of Jacob's Sons (xxxiv. 20-21).**

20 And after Joseph perished, the sons of Jacob took unto themselves wives. The name of Reuben's wife is 'Ada; and the name of Simeon's wife is 'Adlba'a, a Canaanite; and the name of Levi's wife is Melka, of the daughters of Aram, of the seed of the sons of Terah; and the name of Judah's wife, Betasu'el, a Canaanite; and the name of Issachar's wife, Hezaqa: and the name of Zabulon's wife, Ni'iman; and the name of Dan's wife, 'Egla; and the name of Naphtali's wife, Rasu'u, of Mesopotamia; and the name of Gad's wife, Maka; and the name of Asher's wife, 'Ijona; and the name of Joseph's wife, Asenath, the Egyptian; and the name of Benjamin's wife, 'Ijasaka. 21 And Simeon repented, and took a second wife from Mesopotamia as his brothers.

**Rebecca's Last Admonitions and Death (xxxv. 1-27).**

## 35

1 And in the first year of the first week of the forty-fifth jubilee [2157 A.M.] Rebecca called Jacob, her son, and commanded him regarding his father and regarding his brother, that he should honour them all the days of his life. 2 And Jacob said: 'I will do everything as thou hast commanded me; for this thing will be honour and greatness to me, and righteousness before the Lord, that I should honour them. 3 And thou too, mother, knowest from the time I was born until this day, all my deeds and all that is in my heart, that I always think good concerning all. 4 And how should I not do this thing which thou hast commanded me, that I should honour my father and my brother! 5 Tell me, mother, what perversity hast thou seen in me and I shall turn away from it, and mercy will be upon me.' 6 And she said unto him: 'My son, I have not seen in thee all my days any perverse but (only) upright deeds. And yet I will tell thee the truth, my son: I shall die this year, and I shall not survive this year in my life; for I have seen in a dream the day of my death, that I should not live beyond a hundred and fifty-five years: and behold I have completed all the days of my life which I am to live.' 7 And Jacob laughed at the words of his mother. because his mother had said unto him that she should die; and she was sitting opposite to him in possession of her strength, and she was not infirm in her strength; for she went in and out and saw, and her teeth were strong, and no ailment had touched her all the days of her life. 8 And Jacob said unto her: 'Blessed am I, mother, if my days approach the days of thy life, and my strength remain with me thus as thy strength: and thou wilt not die, for thou art jesting idly with me regarding thy death.' 9 And she went in to Isaac and said unto him: 'One petition I make unto thee: make Esau swear that he will not injure Jacob, nor pursue him with enmity; for thou knowest Esau's thoughts that they are perverse from his youth, and there is no goodness in him; for he desires after thy death to kill him. 10 And thou knowest all that he has done since the day Jacob his brother went to Haran until this day: how he has forsaken us with his whole heart, and has done evil to us; thy flocks he has taken to himself, and carried off all thy possessions from before thy face. 11 And when we implored and besought him for what was our own, he did as a man who was taking pity on us. 12 And he is bitter against thee because thou didst bless Jacob thy perfect and upright son; for there is no evil but only goodness in him, and since he came from Haran unto this day he has not robbed us of aught, for he brings us everything in its season always, and rejoices with all his heart when we take at his hands and he blesses us, and has not parted from us since he came from Haran until this day, and he remains with us continually at home honouring us.' 13 And Isaac said unto her: 'I, too, know and see the deeds of Jacob who is with us, how that with all his heart he honours us; but I loved Esau formerly more than Jacob, because he was the firstborn; but now I love Jacob more than Esau, for he has done manifold evil deeds, and there is no righteousness in him, for all his ways are unrighteousness and violence, [and there is no righteousness around him.] 14 And now my heart is troubled because of all his deeds, and neither he nor his seed is to be saved, for they are those who will be destroyed from the earth and who will be rooted out from under heaven, for he has forsaken the God of Abraham and gone after his wives and after their uncleanness and after their error, he and his children. 15 And thou dost bid me make him swear that he will not slay Jacob his brother; even if he swear he will not abide by his oath, and he will not do good but evil only. 16 But if he desires to slay Jacob, his brother, into Jacob's hands will he be given, and he will not escape from his hands, [for he will descend into his hands.] 17 And fear thou not on account of Jacob; for the guardian of Jacob is great and powerful and honoured, and praised more than the guardian of Esau.' 18 And Rebecca sent and called Esau and he came to her, and she said unto him: 'I have a petition, my son, to make unto thee, and do thou promise to do it, my son.' 19 And he said: 'I will do everything that thou sayest unto me, and I will not refuse thy petition.' 20 And she said unto him: 'I ask you that the day I die, thou wilt take me in and bury me near Sarah, thy father's mother, and that thou and Jacob will love each other and that neither will desire evil against the other, but mutual love only, and (so) ye will prosper, my sons, and be honoured in the midst of the land, and no enemy will rejoice over you, and ye will be a blessing and a mercy in the eyes of all those that love you.' 21 And he said: 'I will do all that thou hast told me, and I shall bury thee on the day thou diest near Sarah, my father's mother, as thou hast desired that her bones may be near thy bones. 22 And Jacob, my brother, also, I shall love above all flesh; for I have not a brother in all the earth but him only: and this is no great merit for me if I love him; for he is my brother, and we were sown together in thy body, and together came we forth from thy womb, and if I do not love my brother, whom shall I love? 23 And I, myself, beg thee to exhort Jacob concerning me and concerning my sons, for I know that he will assuredly be king over me and my sons, for on the day my father blessed him he made him the higher and me the lower. 24 And I swear unto thee that I shall love him, and not desire evil against him all the days of my life but good only.' 25 And he sware unto her

regarding all this matter. And she called Jacob before the eyes of Esau, and gave him commandment according to the words which she had spoken to Esau. ²⁶ And he said: 'I shall do thy pleasure; believe me that no evil will proceed from me or from my sons against Esau, and I shall be first in naught save in love only.' ²⁷ And they eat and drank, she and her sons that night, and she died, three jubilees and one week and one year old, on that night, and her two sons, Esau and Jacob, buried her in the double cave near Sarah, their father's mother.

## Isaac's Last Words and Admonitions: his Death. The Death of Leah (xxxvi. 1-24).

### 36

¹ And in the sixth year of this week [2162 A.M.] Isaac called his two sons Esau and Jacob, and they came to him, and he said unto them: 'My sons, I am going the way of my fathers, to the eternal house where my fathers are. ² Wherefore bury me near Abraham my father, in the double cave in the field of Ephron the Hittite, where Abraham purchased a sepulchre to bury in; in the sepulchre which I digged for myself, there bury me. ³ And this I command you, my sons, that ye practise righteousness and uprightness on the earth, so that the Lord may bring upon you all that the Lord said that he would do to Abraham and to his seed. ⁴ And love one another, my sons, your brothers as a man who loves his own soul, and let each seek in what he may benefit his brother, and act together on the earth; and let them love each other as their own souls. ⁵ And concerning the question of idols, I command and admonish you to reject them and hate them, and love them not, for they are full of deception for those that worship them and for those that bow down to them. ⁶ Remember ye, my sons, the Lord God of Abraham your father, and how I too worshipped Him and served Him in righteousness and in joy, that He might multiply you and increase your seed as the stars of heaven in multitude, and establish you on the earth as the plant of righteousness which will not be rooted out unto all the generations for ever. ⁷ And now I shall make you swear a great oath -for there is no oath which is greater than it by the name glorious and honoured and great and splendid and wonderful and mighty, which created the heavens and the earth and all things together- that ye will fear Him and worship Him. ⁸ And that each will love his brother with affection and righteousness, and that neither will desire evil against his brother from henceforth for ever all the days of your life so that ye may prosper in all your deeds and not be destroyed. ⁹ And if either of you devises evil against his brother, know that from henceforth everyone that devises evil against his brother shall fall into his hand, and shall be rooted out of the land of the living, and his seed shall be destroyed from under heaven. ¹⁰ But on the day of turbulence and execration and indignation and anger, with flaming devouring fire as He burnt Sodom, so likewise will He burn his land and his city and all that is his, and he shall be blotted out of the book of the discipline of the children of men, and not be recorded in the book of life, but in that which is appointed to destruction, and he shall depart into eternal execration; so that their condemnation may be always renewed in hate and in execration and in wrath and in torment and in indignation and in plagues and in disease for ever. ¹¹ I say and testify to you, my sons, according to the judgment which shall come upon the man who wishes to injure his brother. ¹² And he divided all his possessions between the two on that day and he gave the larger portion to him that was the first-born, and the tower and all that was about it, and all that Abraham possessed at the Well of the Oath. ¹³ And he said: 'This larger portion I will give to the firstborn.' ¹⁴ And Esau said, 'I have sold to Jacob and given my birthright to Jacob; to him let it be given, and I have not a single word to say regarding it, for it is his.' ¹⁵ And Isaac said, May a blessing rest upon you, my sons, and upon your seed this day, for ye have given me rest, and my heart is not pained concerning the birthright, lest thou shouldest work wickedness on account of it. ¹⁶ May the Most High God bless the man that worketh righteousness, him and his seed for ever.' ¹⁷ And he ended commanding them and blessing them, and they eat and drank together before him, and he rejoiced because there was one mind between them, and they went forth from him and rested that day and slept. ¹⁸ And Isaac slept on his bed that day rejoicing; and he slept the eternal sleep, and died one hundred and eighty years old. He completed twenty-five weeks and five years; and his two sons Esau and Jacob buried him. ¹⁹ And Esau went to the land of Edom, to the mountains of Seir, and dwelt there. ²⁰ And Jacob dwelt in the mountains of Hebron, in the tower of the land of the sojournings of his father Abraham, and he worshipped the Lord with all his heart and according to the visible commands according as He had divided the days of his generations. ²¹ And Leah his wife died in the fourth year of the second week of the forty-fifth jubilee, [2167 A.M.] and he buried her in the double cave near Rebecca his mother to the left of the grave of Sarah, his father's mother ²² and all her sons and his sons came to mourn over Leah his wife with him and to comfort him regarding her, for he was lamenting her for he loved her exceedingly after Rachel her sister died; ²³ for she was perfect and upright in all her ways and honoured Jacob,and all the days that she lived with him he did not hear from her mouth a harsh word, for she was gentle and peaceable and upright and honourable. ²⁴ And he remembered all her deeds which she had done during her life and he lamented her exceedingly; for he loved her with all his heart and with all his soul.

## Esau and his Sons wage War with Jacob (xxxvii. 1-25).

### 37

¹ And on the day that Isaac the father of Jacob and Esau died, [2162 A.M.] the sons of Esau heard that Isaac had given the portion of the elder to his younger son Jacob and they were very angry. ² And they strove with their father, saying 'Why has thy father given Jacob the portion of the elder and passed over thee, although thou art the elder and Jacob the younger?' ³ And he said unto them 'Because I sold my birthright to Jacob for a small mess of lentils, and on the day my father sent me to hunt and catch and bring him something that he should eat and bless me, he came with guile and brought my father food and drink, and my father blessed him and put me under his hand. ⁴ And now our father has caused us to swear, me and him, that we shall not mutually devise evil, either against his brother, and that we shall continue in love and in peace each with his brother and not make our ways corrupt.' ⁵ And they said unto him, 'We shall not hearken unto thee to make peace with him; for our strength is greater than his strength, and we are more powerful than he; we shall go against him and slay him, and destroy him and his sons. And if thou wilt not go with us, we shall do hurt to thee also. ⁶ And now hearken unto us: Let us send to Aram and Philistia and Moab and Ammon, and let us choose for ourselves chosen men who are ardent for battle, and let us go against him and do battle with him, and let us exterminate him from the earth before he grows strong.' ⁷ And their father said unto them, 'Do not go and do not make war with him lest ye fall before him.' ⁸ And they said unto him, 'This too, is exactly thy mode of action from thy youth until this day, and thou art putting thy neck under his yoke. ⁹ We shall not hearken to these words.' And they sent to Aram, and to 'Aduram to the friend of their father, and they hired along with them one thousand fighting men, chosen men of war. ¹⁰ And there came to them from Moab and from the children of Ammon, those who were hired, one thousand chosen men, and from Philistia, one thousand chosen men of war, and from Edom and from the Horites one thousand chosen fighting men, and from the Kittim mighty men of war. ¹¹ And they said unto their father: Go forth with them and lead them, else we shall slay thee.' ¹² And he was filled with wrath and indignation on seeing that his sons were forcing him to go before (them) to lead them against Jacob his brother. ¹³ But afterward he remembered all the evil which lay hidden in his heart against Jacob his brother; and he remembered not the oath which he had sworn to his father and to his mother that he would devise no evil all his days against Jacob his brother. ¹⁴ And notwithstanding all this, Jacob knew not that they were coming against him to battle, and he was mourning for Leah, his wife, until they approached very near to the tower with four thousand warriors and chosen men of war. ¹⁵ And the men of Hebron sent to him saying, 'Behold thy brother has come against thee, to fight thee, with four thousand girt with the sword, and they carry shields and weapons'; for they loved Jacob more than Esau. So they told him; for Jacob was a more liberal and merciful man than Esau. ¹⁶ But Jacob would not believe until they came very near to the tower. ¹⁷ And he closed the gates of the tower; and he stood on the battlements and spake to his brother Esau and said, 'Noble is the comfort wherewith thou hast come to comfort me for my wife who has died. Is this the oath that thou didst swear to thy father and again to thy mother before they died? Thou hast broken the oath, and on the moment that thou didst swear to thy father wast thou condemned.' ¹⁸ And then Esau answered and said unto him, 'Neither the children of men nor the beasts of the earth have any oath of righteousness which in swearing they have sworn (an oath valid) for ever; but every day they devise evil one against another, and how each may slay his adversary and foe. ¹⁹ And thou dost hate me and my children for ever. And there is no observing the tie of brotherhood with thee. ²⁰ Hear these words which I declare unto thee, If the boar can change its skin and make its bristles as soft as wool, Or if it can cause horns to sprout forth on its head like the horns of a stag or of a sheep, Then will I observe the tie of brotherhood with thee And if the breasts separated themselves from their mother, for thou hast not been a brother to me. ²¹ And if the wolves make peace with the lambs so as not to devour or do them violence, And if their hearts are towards them for good, Then there shall be peace in my heart towards thee ²² And if the lion becomes the friend of the ox and makes peace with him And if he is bound under one yoke with him and ploughs with him, Then will I make peace with thee. ²³ And when the raven becomes white as the raza, Then know that I have loved thee And shall make peace with thee Thou shalt be rooted out, And thy sons shall be rooted out, And there shall be no peace for thee' ²⁴ And when Jacob saw that he was (so) evilly

disposed towards him with his heart, and with all his soul as to slay him, and that he had come springing like the wild boar which comes upon the spear that pierces and kills it, and recoils not from it; <sup>25</sup> then he spake to his own and to his servants that they should attack him and all his companions.

### The War between Jacob and Esau at the Tower of Hebron. The Death of Esau and Overthrow of his Forces (xxxviii. 1-4).

## 38

<sup>1</sup> And after that Judah spake to Jacob, his father, and said unto him: 'Bend thy bow, father, and send forth thy arrows and cast down the adversary and slay the enemy; and mayst thou have the power, for we shall not slay thy brother, for he is such as thou, and he is like thee let us give him (this) honour.' <sup>2</sup> Then Jacob bent his bow and sent forth the arrow and struck Esau, his brother (on his right breast) and slew him. <sup>3</sup> And again he sent forth an arrow and struck 'Adoran the Aramaean, on the left breast, and drove him backward and slew him. <sup>4</sup> And then went forth the sons of Jacob, they and their servants, dividing themselves into companies on the four sides of the tower. <sup>5</sup> And Judah went forth in front, and Naphtali and Gad with him and fifty servants with him on the south side of the tower, and they slew all they found before them, and not one individual of them escaped. <sup>6</sup> And Levi and Dan and Asher went forth on the east side of the tower, and fifty (men) with them, and they slew the fighting men of Moab and Ammon. <sup>7</sup> And Reuben and Issachar and Zebulon went forth on the north side of the tower, and fifty men with them, and they slew the fighting men of the Philistines. <sup>8</sup> And Simeon and Benjamin and Enoch, Reuben's son, went forth on the west side of the tower, and fifty (men) with them, and they slew of Edom and of the Horites four hundred men, stout warriors; and six hundred fled, and four of the sons of Esau fled with them, and left their father lying slain, as he had fallen on the hill which is in 'Aduram. <sup>9</sup> And the sons of Jacob pursued after them to the mountains of Seir. And Jacob buried his brother on the hill which is in 'Aduram, and he returned to his house. <sup>10</sup> And the sons of Jacob pressed hard upon the sons of Esau in the mountains of Seir, and bowed their necks so that they became servants of the sons of Jacob. <sup>11</sup> And they sent to their father (to inquire) whether they should make peace with them or slay them. <sup>12</sup> And Jacob sent word to his sons that they should make peace, and they made peace with them, and placed the yoke of servitude upon them, so that they paid tribute to Jacob and to his sons always. <sup>13</sup> And they continued to pay tribute to Jacob until the day that he went down into Egypt. <sup>14</sup> And the sons of Edom have not got quit of the yoke of servitude which the twelve sons of Jacob had imposed on them until this day.

### The Kings of Edom (xxxviii. 15-24; cf. Gen. xxxvi. 31-39).

<sup>15</sup> And these are the kings that reigned in Edom before there reigned any king over the children of Israel [until this day] in the land of Edom. <sup>16</sup> And Balaq, the son of Beor, reigned in Edom, and the name of his city was Danaba. <sup>17</sup> And Balaq died, and Jobab, the son of Zara of Boser, reigned in his stead. <sup>18</sup> And Jobab died, and 'Asam, of the land of Teman, reigned in his stead. <sup>19</sup> And 'Asam died, and 'Adath, the son of Barad, who slew Midian in the field of Moab, reigned in his stead, and the name of his city was Avith. <sup>20</sup> And 'Adath died, and Salman, from 'Amaseqa, reigned in his stead. <sup>21</sup> And Salman died, and Saul of Ra'aboth (by the) river, reigned in his stead. <sup>22</sup> And Saul died, and Ba'elunan, the son of Achbor, reigned in his stead. <sup>23</sup> And Ba'elunan, the son of Achbor died, and 'Adath reigned in his stead, and the name of his wife was Maitabith, the daughter of Matarat, the daughter of Metabedza'ab. <sup>24</sup> These are the kings who reigned in the land of Edom.

### Joseph's Service with Potiphar; his Purity and Imprisonment (xxxix. 1-13; cf. Gen. xxxix.).

## 39

<sup>1</sup> And Jacob dwelt in the land of his father's sojournings in the land of Canaan. These are the generations of Jacob. <sup>2</sup> And Joseph was seventeen years old when they took him down into the land of Egypt, and Potiphar, an eunuch of Pharaoh, the chief cook bought him. <sup>3</sup> And he set Joseph over all his house and the blessing of the Lord came upon the house of the Egyptian on account of Joseph, and the Lord prospered him in all that he did. <sup>4</sup> And the Egyptian committed everything into the hands of Joseph; for he saw that the Lord was with him, and that the Lord prospered him in all that he did. <sup>5</sup> And Joseph's appearance was comely [and very beautiful was his appearance], and his master's wife lifted up her eyes and saw Joseph, and she loved him and besought him to lie with her. <sup>6</sup> But he did not surrender his soul, and he remembered the Lord and the words which Jacob, his father, used to read from amongst the words of Abraham, that no man should commit fornication with a woman who has a husband; that for him the punishment of death has been ordained in the heavens before the Most High God, and the sin will be recorded against him in the eternal books continually before the Lord. <sup>7</sup> And Joseph remembered these words and refused to lie with her. <sup>8</sup> And she besought him for a year, but he refused and would not listen. <sup>9</sup> But she embraced him and held him fast in the

house in order to force him to lie with her, and closed the doors of the house and held him fast; but he left his garment in her hands and broke through the door and fled without from her presence. <sup>10</sup> And the woman saw that he would not lie with her, and she calumniated him in the presence of his lord, saying 'Thy Hebrew servant, whom thou lovest, sought to force me so that he might lie with me; and it came to pass when I lifted up my voice that he fled and left his garment in my hands when I held him, and he brake through the door.' <sup>11</sup> And the Egyptian saw the garment of Joseph and the broken door, and heard the words of his wife, and cast Joseph into prison into the place where the prisoners were kept whom the king imprisoned. <sup>12</sup> And he was there in the prison; and the Lord gave Joseph favour in the sight of the chief of the prison guards and compassion before him, for he saw that the Lord was with him, and that the Lord made all that he did to prosper. <sup>13</sup> And he committed all things into his hands, and the chief of the prison guards knew of nothing that was with him, for Joseph did every thing, and the Lord perfected it.

### Joseph interprets the Dreams of the Chief Butler and the Chief Baker (xxxix. 14-18; cf. Gen. xl.).

<sup>14</sup> And he remained there two years. And in those days Pharaoh, king of Egypt was wroth against his two eunuchs, against the chief butler, and against the chief baker, and he put them in ward in the house of the chief cook, in the prison where Joseph was kept. <sup>15</sup> And the chief of the prison guards appointed Joseph to serve them; and he served before them. <sup>16</sup> And they both dreamed a dream, the chief butler and the chief baker, and they told it to Joseph. <sup>17</sup> And as he interpreted to them so it befell them, and Pharaoh restored the chief butler to his office and the (chief) baker he slew, as Joseph had interpreted to them. <sup>18</sup> But the chief butler forgot Joseph in the prison, although he had informed him what would befall him, and did not remember to inform Pharaoh how Joseph had told him, for he forgot.

### Pharaoh's Dreams and their Interpretation. Joseph's Elevation and Marriage (xl. 1-13; cf. Gen. xli.).

## 40

<sup>1</sup> And in those days Pharaoh dreamed two dreams in one night concerning a famine which was to be in all the land, and he awoke from his sleep and called all the interpreters of dreams that were in Egypt, and magicians, and told them his two dreams, and they were not able to declare (them). <sup>2</sup> And then the chief butler remembered Joseph and spake of him to the king, and he brought him forth from the prison, and he to]d him his two dreams before him. <sup>3</sup> And he said before Pharaoh that his two dreams were one, and he said unto him: 'Seven years shall come (in which there shall be) plenty over all the land of Egypt, and after that seven years of famine, such a famine as has not been in all the land. <sup>4</sup> And now let Pharaoh appoint overseers in all the land of Egypt, and let them store up food in every city throughout the days of the years of plenty, and there will be food for the seven years of famine, and the land will not perish through the famine, for it will be very severe.' <sup>5</sup> And the Lord gave Joseph favour and mercy in the eyes of Pharaoh, and Pharaoh said unto his servants. We shall not find such a wise and discreet man as this man, for the spirit of the Lord is with him.' <sup>6</sup> And he appointed him the second in all his kingdom and gave him authority over all Egypt, and caused him to ride in the second chariot of Pharaoh. <sup>7</sup> And he clothed him with byssus garments, and he put a gold chain upon his neck, and (a herald) proclaimed before him ' 'El 'El wa 'Abirer,' and placed a ring on his hand and made him ruler over all his house, and magnified him, and said unto him. 'Only on the throne shall I be greater than thou.' <sup>8</sup> And Joseph ruled over all the land of Egypt, and all the princes of Pharaoh, and all his servants, and all who did the king's business loved him, for he walked in uprightness, for he was without pride and arrogance, and he had no respect of persons, and did not accept gifts, but he judged in uprightness all the people of the land. <sup>9</sup> And the land of Egypt was at peace before Pharaoh because of Joseph, for the Lord was with him, and gave him favour and mercy for all his generations before all those who knew him and those who heard concerning him, and Pharaoh's kingdom was well ordered, and there was no Satan and no evil person (therein). <sup>10</sup> And the king called Joseph's name Sephantiphans, and gave Joseph to wife the daughter of Potiphar, the daughter of the priest of Heliopolis, the chief cook. <sup>11</sup> And on the day that Joseph stood before Pharaoh he was thirty years old [when he stood before Pharaoh]. <sup>12</sup> And in that year Isaac died. And it came to pass as Joseph had said in the interpretation of his two dreams, according as he had said it, there were seven years of plenty over all the land of Egypt, and the land of Egypt abundantly produced, one measure (producing) eighteen hundred measures. <sup>13</sup> And Joseph gathered food into every city until they were full of corn until they could no longer count and measure it for its multitude.

### Judah's Incest with Tamar; his Repentance and Forgiveness (xli. 1-28; Cf. Gen. xxxviii.).

## 41

¹ And in the forty-fifth jubilee, in the second week, (and) in the second year, [2165 A.M.] Judah took for his first-born Er, a wife from the daughters of Aram, named Tamar. ² But he hated, and did not lie with her, because his mother was of the daughters of Canaan, and he wished to take him a wife of the kinsfolk of his mother, but Judah, his father, would not permit him. ³ And this Er, the first-born of Judah, was wicked, and the Lord slew him. ⁴ And Judah said unto Onan, his brother 'Go in unto thy brother's wife and perform the duty of a husband's brother unto her, and raise up seed unto thy brother.' ⁵ And Onan knew that the seed would not be his, (but) his brother's only, and he went into the house of his brother's wife, and spilt the seed on the ground, and he was wicked in the eyes of the Lord, and He slew him. ⁶ And Judah said unto Tamar, his daughter-in-law: 'Remain in thy father's house as a widow till Shelah my son be grown up, and I shall give thee to him to wife.' ⁷ And he grew up; but Bedsu'el, the wife of Judah, did not permit her son Shelah to marry. And Bedsu'el, the wife of Judah, died [2168 A.M.] in the fifth year of this week. ⁸ And in the sixth year Judah went up to shear his sheep at Timnah. [2169 A.M.] And they told Tamar: 'Behold thy father-in-law goeth up to Timnah to shear his sheep.' ⁹ And she put off her widow's clothes, and put on a veil, and adorned herself, and sat in the gate adjoining the way to Timnah. ¹⁰ And as Judah was going along he found her, and thought her to be an harlot, and he said unto her: 'Let me come in unto thee'; and she said unto him Come in,' and he went in. ¹¹ And she said unto him: 'Give me my hire'; and he said unto her: 'I have nothing in my hand save my ring that is on my finger, and my necklace, and my staff which is in my hand.' ¹² And she said unto him 'Give them to me until thou dost send me my hire', and he said unto her: 'I will send unto thee a kid of the goats'; and he gave them to her, and he went in unto her, and she conceived by him. ¹³ And Judah went unto his sheep, and she went to her father's house. ¹⁴ And Judah sent a kid of the goats by the hand of his shepherd, an Adullamite, and he found her not; and he asked the people of the place, saying: 'Where is the harlot who was here?' And they said unto him; 'There is no harlot here with us.' ¹⁵ And he returned and informed him, and said unto him that he had not found her: 'I asked the people of the place, and they said unto me: "There is no harlot here." ' ¹⁶ And he said: 'Let her keep (them) lest we become a cause of derision.' And when she had completed three months, it was manifest that she was with child, and they told Judah, saying: 'Behold Tamar, thy daughter-in-law, is with child by whoredom.' ¹⁷ And Judah went to the house of her father, and said unto her father and her brothers: 'Bring her forth, and let them burn her, for she hath wrought uncleanness in Israel.' ¹⁸ And it came to pass when they brought her forth to burn her that she sent to her father-in-law the ring and the necklace, and the staff, saying: 'Discern whose are these, for by him am I with child.' ¹⁹ And Judah acknowledged, and said: 'Tamar is more righteous than I am. ²⁰ And therefore let them burn her not' And for that reason she was not given to Shelah, and he did not again approach her. ²¹ And after that she bare two sons, Perez [2170 A.M.] and Zerah, in the seventh year of this second week. ²² And thereupon the seven years of fruitfulness were accomplished, of which Joseph spake to Pharaoh. ²³ And Judah acknowledged that the deed which he had done was evil, for he had lain with his daughter-in-law, and he esteemed it hateful in his eyes, and he acknowledged that he had transgressed and gone astray, for he had uncovered the skirt of his son, and he began to lament and to supplicate before the Lord because of his transgression. ²⁴ And we told him in a dream that it was forgiven him because he supplicated earnestly, and lamented, and did not again commit it. ²⁵ And he received forgiveness because he turned from his sin and from his ignorance, for he transgressed greatly before our God; and every one that acts thus, every one who lies with his mother-in-law, let them burn him with fire that he may burn therein, for there is uncleanness and pollution upon them, with fire let them burn them. ²⁶ And do thou command the children of Israel that there be no uncleanness amongst them, for every one who lies with his daughter-in-law or with his mother-in-law hath wrought uncleanness; with fire let them burn the man who has lain with her, and likewise the woman, and He will turn away wrath and punishment from Israel. ²⁷ And unto Judah we said that his two sons had not lain with her, and for this reason his seed was stablished for a second generation, and would not be rooted out. ²⁸ For in singleness of eye he had gone and sought for punishment, namely, according to the judgment of Abraham, which he had commanded his sons, Judah had sought to burn her with fire.

**The Two Journeys of the Sons of Jacob to Egypt (xlii. 1-25; cf. Gen. xlii., xliii.).**

## 42

¹ And in the first year of the third week of the forty-fifth jubilee the famine began to come into the [2171 A.M.] land, and the rain refused to be given to the earth, for none whatever fell. ² And the earth grew barren, but in the land of Egypt there was food, for Joseph had gathered the seed of the land in the seven years of plenty and had preserved it. ³

And the Egyptians came to Joseph that he might give them food, and he opened the store-houses where was the grain of the first year, and he sold it to the people of the land for gold. ⁴ <Now the famine was very sore in the land of Canaan>, and Jacob heard that there was food in Egypt, and he sent his ten sons that they should procure food for him in Egypt; but Benjamin he did not send, and <the ten sons of Jacob> arrived <in Egypt> among those that went (there). ⁵ And Joseph recognised them, but they did not recognise him, and he spake unto them and questioned them, and he said unto them; 'Are ye not spies and have ye not come to explore the approaches of the land? 'And he put them in ward. ⁶ And after that he set them free again, and detained Simeon alone and sent off his nine brothers. ⁷ And he filled their sacks with corn, and he put their gold in their sacks, and they did not know. ⁸ And he commanded them to bring their younger brother, for they had told him their father was living and their younger brother. ⁹ And they went up from the land of Egypt and they came to the land of Canaan; and they told their father all that had befallen them, and how the lord of the country had spoken roughly to them, and had seized Simeon till they should bring Benjamin. ¹⁰ And Jacob said: 'Me have ye bereaved of my children! Joseph is not and Simeon also is not, and ye will take Benjamin away. On me has your wickedness come. ¹¹ 'And he said: 'My son will not go down with you lest perchance he fall sick; for their mother gave birth to two sons, and one has perished, and this one also ye will take from me. If perchance he took a fever on the road, ye would bring down my old age with sorrow unto death.' ¹² For he saw that their money had been returned to every man in his sack, and for this reason he feared to send him. ¹³ And the famine increased and became sore in the land of Canaan, and in all lands save in the land of Egypt, for many of the children of the Egyptians had stored up their seed for food from the time when they saw Joseph gathering seed together and putting it in storehouses and preserving it for the years of famine. ¹⁴ And the people of Egypt fed themselves thereon during the first year of their famine. ¹⁵ But when Israel saw that the famine was very sore in the land, and that there was no deliverance, he said unto his sons: 'Go again, and procure food for us that we die not.' ¹⁶ And they said: 'We shall not go; unless our youngest brother go with us, we shall not go.' ¹⁷ And Israel saw that if he did not send him with them, they should all perish by reason of the famine ¹⁸ And Reuben said: 'Give him into my hand, and if I do not bring him back to thee, slay my two sons instead of his soul.' ¹⁹ And he said unto him: 'He shall not go with thee.' And Judah came near and said: 'Send him with me, and if I do not bring him back to thee, let me bear the blame before thee all the days of my life.' ²⁰ And he sent him with them in the second year of this week on the [2172 A.m.] first day of the month, and they came to the land of Egypt with all those who went, and (they had) presents in their hands, stacte and almonds and terebinth nuts and pure honey. ²¹ And they went and stood before Joseph, and he saw Benjamin his brother, and he knew him, and said unto them: Is this your youngest brother?' And they said unto him: 'It is he.' And he said The Lord be gracious to thee, my son!' ²² And he sent him into his house and he brought forth Simeon unto them and he made a feast for them, and they presented to him the gift which they had brought in their hands. ²³ And they eat before him and he gave them all a portion, but the portion of Benjamin was seven times larger than that of any of theirs. ²⁴ And they eat and drank and arose and remained with their asses. ²⁵ And Joseph devised a plan whereby he might learn their thoughts as to whether thoughts of peace prevailed amongst them, and he said to the steward who was over his house: 'Fill all their sacks with food, and return their money unto them into their vessels, and my cup, the silver cup out of which I drink, put it in the sack of the youngest, and send them away.'

**Joseph finally tests his Brethren, and then makes himself known to them (xliii. 1-24; cf. Gen. xliv., xlv.).**

## 43

¹ And he did as Joseph had told him, and filled all their sacks for them with food and put their money in their sacks, and put the cup in Benjamin's sack. ² And early in the morning they departed, and it came to pass that, when they had gone from thence, Joseph said unto the steward of his house: 'Pursue them, run and seize them, saying, "For good ye have requited me with evil; you have stolen from me the silver cup out of which my lord drinks." And bring back to me their youngest brother, and fetch (him) quickly before I go forth to my seat of judgment.' ³ And he ran after them and said unto them according to these words. ⁴ And they said unto him: 'God forbid that thy servants should do this thing, and steal from the house of thy lord any utensil, and the money also which we found in our sacks the first time, we thy servants brought back from the land of Canaan. ⁵ How then should we steal any utensil? Behold here are we and our sacks search, and wherever thou findest the cup in the sack of any man amongst us, let him be slain, and we and our asses will serve thy lord.' ⁶ And he said unto them: 'Not so, the man with whom I find, him only shall I take as

a servant, and ye shall return in peace unto your house.' [7] And as he was searching in their vessels, beginning with the eldest and ending with the youngest, it was found in Benjamin's sack. [8] And they rent their garments, and laded their asses, and returned to the city and came to the house of Joseph, and they all bowed themselves on their faces to the ground before him. [9] And Joseph said unto them: 'Ye have done evil.' And they said: 'What shall we say and how shall we defend ourselves? Our lord hath discovered the transgression of his servants; behold we are the servants of our lord, and our asses also. [10] 'And Joseph said unto them: 'I too fear the Lord; as for you, go ye to your homes and let your brother be my servant, for ye have done evil. Know ye not that a man delights in his cup as I with this cup? And yet ye have stolen it from me.' [11] And Judah said: 'O my lord, let thy servant, I pray thee, speak a word in my lord's ear two brothers did thy servant's mother bear to our father: one went away and was lost, and hath not been found, and he alone is left of his mother, and thy servant our father loves him, and his life also is bound up with the life of this (lad). [12] And it will come to pass, when we go to thy servant our father, and the lad is not with us, that he will die, and we shall bring down our father with sorrow unto death. [13] Now rather let me, thy servant, abide instead of the boy as a bondsman unto my lord, and let the lad go with his brethren, for I became surety for him at the hand of thy servant our father, and if I do not bring him back, thy servant will bear the blame to our father for ever.' [14] And Joseph saw that they were all accordant in goodness one with another, and he could not refrain himself, and he told them that he was Joseph. [15] And he conversed with them in the Hebrew tongue and fell on their neck and wept. [16] But they knew him not and they began to weep. And he said unto them: 'Weep not over me, but hasten and bring my father to me; and ye see that it is my mouth that speaketh and the eyes of my brother Benjamin see. [17] For behold this is the second year of the famine, and there are still five years without harvest or fruit of trees or ploughing. [18] Come down quickly ye and your households, so that ye perish not through the famine, and do not be grieved for your possessions, for the Lord sent me before you to set things in order that many people might live. [19] And tell my father that I am still alive, and ye, behold, ye see that the Lord has made me as a father to Pharaoh, and ruler over his house and over all the land of Egypt. [20] And tell my father of all my glory, and all the riches and glory that the Lord hath given me.' [21] And by the command of the mouth of Pharaoh he gave them chariots and provisions for the way, and he gave them all many-coloured raiment and silver. [22] And to their father he sent raiment and silver and ten asses which carried corn, and he sent them away. [23] And they went up and told their father that Joseph was alive, and was measuring out corn to all the nations of the earth, and that he was ruler over all the land of Egypt. [24] And their father did not believe it, for he was beside himself in his mind; but when he saw the wagons which Joseph had sent, the life of his spirit revived, and he said: 'It is enough for me if Joseph lives; I will go down and see him before I die.'

**Jacob, celebrates the Feast of First-fruits and journeys to Egypt. List of his Descendants. (xliv. 1-34; cf. Gen. xlvi. 1-28).**

## 44

[1] And Israel took his journey from Haran from his house on the new moon of the third month, and he went on the way of the Well of the Oath, and he offered a sacrifice to the God of his father Isaac on the seventh of this month. [2] And Jacob remembered the dream that he had seen at Bethel, and he feared to go down into Egypt. [3] And while he was thinking of sending word to Joseph to come to him, and that he would not go down, he remained there seven days, if perchance he could see a vision as to whether he should remain or go down. [4] And he celebrated the harvest festival of the first-fruits with old grain, for in all the land of Canaan there was not a handful of seed [in the land], for the famine was over all the beasts and cattle and birds, and also over man. [5] And on the sixteenth the Lord appeared unto him, and said unto him, 'Jacob, Jacob'; and he said, 'Here am I.' And He said unto him: 'I am the God of thy fathers, the God of Abraham and Isaac; fear not to go down into Egypt, for I will there make of thee a great nation I will go down with thee, and I will bring thee up (again), and in this land shalt thou be buried, and Joseph shall put his hands upon thy eyes. [6] Fear not; go down into Egypt.' [7] And his sons rose up, and his sons' sons, and they placed their father and their possessions upon wagons. [8] And Israel rose up from the Well of the Oath on the sixteenth of this third month, and he went to the land of Egypt. [9] And Israel sent Judah before him to his son Joseph to examine the Land of Goshen, for Joseph had told his brothers that they should come and dwell there that they might be near him. [10] And this was the goodliest (land) in the land of Egypt, and near to him, for all (of them) and also for the cattle. [11] And these are the names of the sons of Jacob who went into Egypt with Jacob their father. [12] Reuben, the First-born of Israel; and these are the names of his sons Enoch, and Pallu, and Hezron and Carmi-five. [13] Simeon and his sons; and these are the names of his sons: Jemuel, and

Jamin, and Ohad, and Jachin, and Zohar, and Shaul, the son of the Zephathite woman-seven. [14] Levi and his sons; and these are the names of his sons: Gershon, and Kohath, and Merari-four. [15] Judah and his sons; and these are the names of his sons: Shela, and Perez, and Zerah-four. [16] Issachar and his sons; and these are the names of his sons: Tola, and Phua, and Jasub, and Shimron-five. [17] Zebulon and his sons; and these are the names of his sons: Sered, and Elon, and Jahleel-four. [18] And these are the sons of Jacob and their sons whom Leah bore to Jacob in Mesopotamia, six, and their one sister, Dinah and all the souls of the sons of Leah, and their sons, who went with Jacob their father into Egypt, were twenty-nine, and Jacob their father being with them, they were thirty. [19] And the sons of Zilpah, Leah's handmaid, the wife of Jacob, who bore unto Jacob Gad and Ashur. [20] And these are the names of their sons who went with him into Egypt. The sons of Gad: Ziphion, and Haggi, and Shuni, and Ezbon, <and Eri>, and Areli, and Arodi-eight. [21] And the sons of Asher: Imnah, and Ishvah, <and Ishvi>, and Beriah, and Serah, their one sister-six. [22] All the souls were fourteen, and all those of Leah were forty-four. [23] And the sons of Rachel, the wife of Jacob: Joseph and Benjamin. [24] And there were born to Joseph in Egypt before his father came into Egypt, those whom Asenath, daughter of Potiphar priest of Heliopolis bare unto him, Manasseh, and Ephraim-three. [25] And the sons of Benjamin: Bela and Becher and Ashbel, Gera, and Naaman, and Ehi, and Rosh, and Muppim, and Huppim, and Ard-eleven. [26] And all the souls of Rachel were fourteen. [27] And the sons of Bilhah, the handmaid of Rachel, the wife of Jacob, whom she bare to Jacob, were Dan and Naphtali. [28] And these are the names of their sons who went with them into Egypt. And the sons of Dan were Hushim, and Samon, and Asudi. and 'Ijaka, and Salomon-six. [29] And they died the year in which they entered into Egypt, and there was left to Dan Hushim alone. [30] And these are the names of the sons of Naphtali Jahziel, and Guni and Jezer, and Shallum, and 'Iv. [31] And 'Iv, who was born after the years of famine, died in Egypt. [32] And all the souls of Rachel were twenty-six. [33] And all the souls of Jacob which went into Egypt were seventy souls. These are his children and his children's children, in all seventy, but five died in Egypt before Joseph, and had no children. [34] And in the land of Canaan two sons of Judah died, Er and Onan, and they had no children, and the children of Israel buried those who perished, and they were reckoned among the seventy Gentile nations.

**Joseph receives Jacob. The Land of Egypt is acquired for Pharaoh. Jacob's Death and Burial (xlv. 1-16; cf. Gen. xlvi. 28 ff., xlvii. 11 ff.).**

## 45

[1] And Israel went into the country of Egypt, into the land of Goshen, on the new moon of the fourth [2172 A.M]. month, in the second year of the third week of the forty-fifth jubilee. [2] And Joseph went to meet his father Jacob, to the land of Goshen, and he fell on his father's neck and wept. [3] And Israel said unto Joseph: 'Now let me die since I have seen thee, and now may the Lord God of Israel be blessed the God of Abraham and the God of Isaac who hath not withheld His mercy and His grace from His servant Jacob. [4] It is enough for me that I have seen thy face whilst I am yet alive; yea, true is the vision which I saw at Bethel. Blessed be the Lord my God for ever and ever, and blessed be His name.' [5] And Joseph and his brothers eat bread before their father and drank wine, and Jacob rejoiced with exceeding great joy because he saw Joseph eating with his brothers and drinking before him, and he blessed the Creator of all things who had preserved him, and had preserved for him his twelve sons. [6] And Joseph had given to his father and to his brothers as a gift the right of dwelling in the land of Goshen and in Rameses and all the region round about, which he ruled over before Pharaoh. And Israel and his sons dwelt in the land of Goshen, the best part of the land of Egypt and Israel was one hundred and thirty years old when he came into Egypt. [7] And Joseph nourished his father and his brethren and also their possessions with bread as much as sufficed them for the seven years of the famine. [8] And the land of Egypt suffered by reason of the famine, and Joseph acquired all the land of Egypt for Pharaoh in return for food, and he got possession of the people and their cattle and everything for Pharaoh. [9] And the years of the famine were accomplished, and Joseph gave to the people in the land seed and food that they might sow (the land) in the eighth year, for the river had overflowed all the land of Egypt. [10] For in the seven years of the famine it had (not) overflowed and had irrigated only a few places on the banks of the river, but now it overflowed and the Egyptians sowed the land, and it bore much corn that year. [11] And this was the first year of [2178 A.M.] the fourth week of the forty-fifth jubilee. [12] And Joseph took of the corn of the harvest the fifth part for the king and left four parts for them for food and for seed, and Joseph made it an ordinance for the land of Egypt until this day. [13] And Israel lived in the land of Egypt seventeen years, and all the days which he lived were three jubilees, one hundred and forty-seven years, and he died in the fourth [2188 A.M.] year of the fifth week of the forty-fifth

jubilee. [14] And Israel blessed his sons before he died and told them everything that would befall them in the land of Egypt; and he made known to them what would come upon them in the last days, and blessed them and gave to Joseph two portions in the land. [15] And he slept with his fathers, and he was buried in the double cave in the land of Canaan, near Abraham his father in the grave which he dug for himself in the double cave in the land of Hebron. [16] And he gave all his books and the books of his fathers to Levi his son that he might preserve them and renew them for his children until this day.

**The Death of Joseph. The Bones of Jacob's Sons (except Joseph) interred at Hebron. The Oppression of Israel by Egypt (xlvi. 1-16; cf. Gen. l.; Exod. i.).**

## 46

[1] And it came to pass that after Jacob died the children of Israel multiplied in the land of Egypt, and they became a great nation, and they were of one accord in heart, so that brother loved brother and every man helped his brother, and they increased abundantly and multiplied exceedingly, ten [2242 A.M.] weeks of years, all the days of the life of Joseph. [2] And there was no Satan nor any evil all the days of the life of Joseph which he lived after his father Jacob, for all the Egyptians honoured the children of Israel all the days of the life of Joseph. [3] And Joseph died being a hundred and ten years old; seventeen years he lived in the land of Canaan, and ten years he was a servant, and three years in prison, and eighty years he was under the king, ruling all the land of Egypt. [4] And he died and all his brethren and all that generation. [5] And he commanded the children of Israel before he died that they should carry his bones with them when they went forth from the land of Egypt. [6] And he made them swear regarding his bones, for he knew that the Egyptians would not again bring forth and bury him in the land of Canaan, for Makamaron, king of Canaan, while dwelling in the land of Assyria, fought in the valley with the king of Egypt and slew him there, and pursued after the Egyptians to the gates of 'Ermon. [7] But he was not able to enter, for another, a new king, had become king of Egypt, and he was stronger than he, and he returned to the land of Canaan, and the gates of Egypt were closed, and none went out and none came into Egypt. [8] And Joseph died in the forty-sixth jubilee, in the sixth week, in the second year, and they buried him in the land of Egypt, and [2242 A.M.] all his brethren died after him. [9] And the king of Egypt went forth to war with the king of Canaan [2263 A.M.] in the forty-seventh jubilee, in the second week in the second year, and the children of Israel brought forth all the bones of the children of Jacob save the bones of Joseph, and they buried them in the field in the double cave in the mountain. [10] And the most (of them) returned to Egypt, but a few of them remained in the mountains of Hebron, and Amram thy father remained with them. [11] And the king of Canaan was victorious over the king of Egypt, and he closed the gates of Egypt. [12] And he devised an evil device against the children of Israel of afflicting them and he said unto the people of Egypt: 'Behold the people of the children of Israel have increased and multiplied more than we. [13] Come and let us deal wisely with them before they become too many, and let us afflict them with slavery before war come upon us and before they too fight against us; else they will join themselves unto our enemies and get them up out of our land, for their hearts and faces are towards the land of Canaan.' [14] And he set over them taskmasters to afflict them with slavery; and they built strong cities for Pharaoh, Pithom, and Raamses and they built all the walls and all the fortifications which had fallen in the cities of Egypt. [15] And they made them serve with rigour, and the more they dealt evilly with them, the more they increased and multiplied. [16] And the people of Egypt abominated the children of Israel

**The Birth and Early Years of Moses (xlvii. 1-12; cf. Exod. ii.).**

## 47

[1] And in the seventh week, in the seventh year, in the forty-seventh jubilee, thy father went forth [2303 A.M.] from the land of Canaan, and thou wast born in the fourth week, in the sixth year thereof, in the [2330 A.M.] forty-eighth jubilee; this was the time of tribulation on the children of Israel. [2] And Pharaoh, king of Egypt, issued a command regarding them that they should cast all their male children which were born into the river. [3] And they cast them in for seven months until the day that thou wast born [4] And thy mother hid thee for three months, and they told regarding her. And she made an ark for thee, and covered it with pitch and asphalt, and placed it in the flags on the bank of the river, and she placed thee in it seven days, and thy mother came by night and suckled thee, and by day Miriam, thy sister, guarded thee from the birds. [5] And in those days Tharmuth, the daughter of Pharaoh, came to bathe in the river, and she heard thy voice crying, and she told her maidens to bring thee forth, and they brought thee unto her. [6] And she took thee out of the ark, and she had compassion on thee. [7] And thy sister said unto her: 'Shall I go and call unto thee one of the Hebrew women to nurse and suckle this babe for thee?' [8] And she said <unto her>: 'Go.' And she went and called thy mother Jochebed, and she gave

her wages, and she nursed thee. [9] And afterwards, when thou wast grown up, they brought thee unto the daughter of Pharaoh, and thou didst become her son, and Amram thy father taught thee writing, and after thou hadst completed three weeks they brought thee into the royal court. [10] And thou wast three weeks of years at court until the time [2351-] when thou didst go forth from the royal court and didst see an Egyptian smiting thy friend who was [2372 A.M.] of the children of Israel, and thou didst slay him and hide him in the sand. [11] And on the second day thou didst and two of the children of Israel striving together, and thou didst say to him who was doing the wrong: 'Why dost thou smite thy brother?' [12] And he was angry and indignant, and said: 'Who made thee a prince and a judge over us? Thinkest thou to kill me as thou killedst the Egyptian yesterday?' And thou didst fear and flee on account of these words.

**From the Flight of Moses to the Exodus (xlviii. 1-19; cf. Exod. ii. 15 ff., iv. 19-24, vii-xiv.).**

## 48

[1] And in the sixth year of the third week of the forty-ninth jubilee thou didst depart and dwell <in [2372 A.M.] the land of Midian>, five weeks and one year. And thou didst return into Egypt in the second week in the second year in the fiftieth jubilee. [2] And thou thyself knowest what He spake unto thee on [2410 A.M.] Mount Sinai, and what prince Mastêmâ desired to do with thee when thou wast returning into Egypt <on the way when thou didst meet him at the lodging-place>. [3] Did he not with all his power seek to slay thee and deliver the Egyptians out of thy hand when he saw that thou wast sent to execute judgment and vengeance on the Egyptians? [4] And I delivered thee out of his hand, and thou didst perform the signs and wonders which thou wast sent to perform in Egypt against Pharaoh, and against all his house, and against his servants and his people. [5] And the Lord executed a great vengeance on them for Israel's sake, and smote them through (the plagues of) blood and frogs, lice and dog-flies, and malignant boils breaking forth in blains; and their cattle by death; and by hail-stones, thereby He destroyed everything that grew for them; and by locusts which devoured the residue which had been left by the hail, and by darkness; and <by the death> of the first-born of men and animals, and on all their idols the Lord took vengeance and burned them with fire. [6] And everything was sent through thy hand, that thou shouldst declare (these things) before they were done, and thou didst speak with the king of Egypt before all his servants and before his people. [7] And everything took place according to thy words; ten great and terrible judgments came on the land of Egypt that thou mightest execute vengeance on it for Israel. [8] And the Lord did everything for Israel's sake, and according to His covenant, which he had ordained with Abraham that He would take vengeance on them as they had brought them by force into bondage. [9] And the prince Mastêmâ stood up against thee, and sought to cast thee into the hands of Pharaoh, and he helped the Egyptian sorcerers, [10] and they stood up and wrought before thee the evils indeed we permitted them to work, but the remedies we did not allow to be wrought by their hands. [11] And the Lord smote them with malignant ulcers, and they were not able to stand, for we destroyed them so that they could not perform a single sign. [12] And notwithstanding all (these) signs and wonders the prince Mastêmâ was not put to shame because he took courage and cried to the Egyptians to pursue after thee with all the powers of the Egyptians, with their chariots, and with their horses, and with all the hosts of the peoples of Egypt. [13] And I stood between the Egyptians and Israel, and we delivered Israel out of his hand, and out of the hand of his people, and the Lord brought them through the midst of the sea as if it were dry land. [14] And all the peoples whom he brought to pursue after Israel, the Lord our God cast them into the midst of the sea, into the depths of the abyss beneath the children of Israel, even as the people of Egypt had cast their children into the river He took vengeance on **1,000,000** of them, and one thousand strong and energetic men were destroyed on account of one suckling of the children of thy people which they had thrown into the river. [15] And on the fourteenth day and on the fifteenth and on the sixteenth and on the seventeenth and on the eighteenth the prince Mastêmâ was bound and imprisoned behind the children of Israel that he might not accuse them. [16] And on the nineteenth we let them loose that they might help the Egyptians and pursue the children of Israel. [17] And he hardened their hearts and made them stubborn, and the device was devised by the Lord our God that He might smite the Egyptians and cast them into the sea. [18] And on the fourteenth we bound him that he might not accuse the children of Israel on the day when they asked the Egyptians for vessels and garments, vessels of silver, and vessels of gold, and vessels of bronze, in order to despoil the Egyptians in return for the bondage in which they had forced them to serve. [19] And we did not lead forth the children of Israel from Egypt empty handed.

**Regulations regarding the Passover (xlix. 1-23; cf. Exod. xii.).**

## 49

[1] Remember the commandment which the Lord commanded thee concerning the passover, that thou shouldst celebrate it in its season on the fourteenth of the first month, that thou shouldst kill it before it is evening, and that they should eat it by night on the evening of the fifteenth from the time of the setting of the sun. [2] For on this night -the beginning of the festival and the beginning of the joy- ye were eating the passover in Egypt, when all the powers of Mastêmâ had been let loose to slay all the first-born in the land of Egypt, from the first-born of Pharaoh to the first-born of the captive maid-servant in the mill, and to the cattle. [3] And this is the sign which the Lord gave them: Into every house on the lintels of which they saw the blood of a lamb of the first year, into (that) house they should not enter to slay, but should pass by (it), that all those should be saved that were in the house because the sign of the blood was on its lintels. [4] And the powers of the Lord did everything according as the Lord commanded them, and they passed by all the children of Israel, and the plague came not upon them to destroy from amongst them any soul either of cattle, or man, or dog. [5] And the plague was very grievous in Egypt, and there was no house in Egypt where there was not one dead, and weeping and lamentation. [6] And all Israel was eating the flesh of the paschal lamb, and drinking the wine, and was lauding, and blessing, and giving thanks to the Lord God of their fathers, and was ready to go forth from under the yoke of Egypt, and from the evil bondage. [7] And remember thou this day all the days of thy life, and observe it from year to year all the days of thy life, once a year, on its day, according to all the law thereof, and do not adjourn (it) from day to day, or from month to month. [8] For it is an eternal ordinance, and engraven on the heavenly tablets regarding all the children of Israel that they should observe it every year on its day once a year, throughout all their generations; and there is no limit of days, for this is ordained for ever. [9] And the man who is free from uncleanness, and does not come to observe it on occasion of its day, so as to bring an acceptable offering before the Lord, and to eat and to drink before the Lord on the day of its festival, that man who is clean and close at hand shall be cut off: because he offered not the oblation of the Lord in its appointed season, he shall take the guilt upon himself. [10] Let the children of Israel come and observe the passover on the day of its fixed time, on the fourteenth day of the first month, between the evenings, from the third part of the day to the third part of the night, for two portions of the day are given to the light, and a third part to the evening. [11] This is that which the Lord commanded thee that thou shouldst observe it between the evenings. [12] And it is not permissible to slay it during any period of the light, but during the period bordering on the evening, and let them eat it at the time of the evening, until the third part of the night, and whatever is left over of all its flesh from the third part of the night and onwards, let them burn it with fire. [13] And they shall not cook it with water, nor shall they eat it raw, but roast on the fire: they shall eat it with diligence, its head with the inwards thereof and its feet they shall roast with fire, and not break any bone thereof; for of the children of Israel no bone shall be crushed. [14] For this reason the Lord commanded the children of Israel to observe the passover on the day of its fixed time, and they shall not break a bone thereof; for it is a festival day, and a day commanded, and there may be no passing over from day to day, and month to month, but on the day of its festival let it be observed. [15] And do thou command the children of Israel to observe the passover throughout their days, every year, once a year on the day of its fixed time, and it shall come for a memorial well pleasing before the Lord, and no plague shall come upon them to slay or to smite in that year in which they celebrate the passover in its season in every respect according to His command. [16] And they shall not eat it outside the sanctuary of the Lord, but before the sanctuary of the Lord, and all the people of the congregation of Israel shall celebrate it in its appointed season. [17] And every man who has come upon its day shall eat it in the sanctuary of your God before the Lord from twenty years old and upward; for thus is it written and ordained that they should eat it in the sanctuary of the Lord. [18] And when the children of Israel come into the land which they are to possess, into the land of Canaan, and set up the tabernacle of the Lord in the midst of the land in one of their tribes until the sanctuary of the Lord has been built in the land, let them come and celebrate the passover in the midst of the tabernacle of the Lord, and let them slay it before the Lord from year to year. [19] And in the days when the house has been built in the name of the Lord in the land of their inheritance, they shall go there and slay the passover in the evening, at sunset, at the third part of the day. [20] And they shall offer its blood on the threshold of the altar, and shall place its fat on the fire which is upon the altar, and they shall eat its flesh roasted with fire in the court of the house which has been sanctified in the name of the Lord. [21] And they may not celebrate the passover in their cities, nor in any place save before the tabernacle of the Lord, or before His house where His name hath dwelt; and they shall not go astray from the Lord. [22] And do thou, Moses, command the children of Israel to observe the ordinances of the passover, as it was commanded unto thee; declare thou unto them every year and the day of its days, and the festival of unleavened bread, that they should eat unleavened bread seven days, (and) that they should observe its festival, and that they bring an oblation every day during those seven days of joy before the Lord on the altar of your God. [23] For ye celebrated this festival with haste when ye went forth from Egypt till ye entered into the wilderness of Shur; for on the shore of the sea ye completed it.

**Laws regarding the Jubilees and the Sabbath (l. 1-13).**

## 50

[1] And after this law I made known to thee the days of the Sabbaths in the desert of Sin[ai], which is between Elim and Sinai. [2] And I told thee of the Sabbaths of the land on Mount Sinai, and I told thee of the jubilee years in the sabbaths of years: but the year thereof have I not told thee till ye enter the land which ye are to possess. [3] And the land also shall keep its sabbaths while they dwell upon it, and they shall know the jubilee year. [4] Wherefore I have ordained for thee the year-weeks and the years and the jubilees: there are forty-nine jubilees from the days of Adam until this day, [2410 A.M.] and one week and two years: and there are yet forty years to come (lit. 'distant') for learning the [2450 A.M.] commandments of the Lord, until they pass over into the land of Canaan, crossing the Jordan to the west. [5] And the jubilees shall pass by, until Israel is cleansed from all guilt of fornication, and uncleanness, and pollution, and sin, and error, and dwells with confidence in all the land, and there shall be no more a Satan or any evil one, and the land shall be clean from that time for evermore. [6] And behold the commandment regarding the Sabbaths -I have written (them) down for thee- and all the judgments of its laws. [7] Six days shalt thou labour, but on the seventh day is the Sabbath of the Lord your God. In it ye shall do no manner of work, ye and your sons, and your men- servants and your maid-servants, and all your cattle and the sojourner also who is with you. [8] And the man that does any work on it shall die: whoever desecrates that day, whoever lies with (his) wife, or whoever says he will do something on it, that he will set out on a journey thereon in regard to any buying or selling: and whoever draws water thereon which he had not prepared for himself on the sixth day, and whoever takes up any burden to carry it out of his tent or out of his house shall die. [9] Ye shall do no work whatever on the Sabbath day save what ye have prepared for yourselves on the sixth day, so as to eat, and drink, and rest, and keep Sabbath from all work on that day, and to bless the Lord your God, who has given you a day of festival and a holy day: and a day of the holy kingdom for all Israel is this day among their days for ever. [10] For great is the honour which the Lord has given to Israel that they should eat and drink and be satisfied on this festival day, and rest thereon from all labour which belongs to the labour of the children of men save burning frankincense and bringing oblations and sacrifices before the Lord for days and for Sabbaths. [11] This work alone shall be done on the Sabbath-days in the sanctuary of the Lord your God; that they may atone for Israel with sacrifice continually from day to day for a memorial well-pleasing before the Lord, and that He may receive them always from day to day according as thou hast been commanded. [12] And every man who does any work thereon, or goes a journey, or tills (his) farm, whether in his house or any other place, and whoever lights a fire, or rides on any beast, or travels by ship on the sea, and whoever strikes or kills anything, or slaughters a beast or a bird, or whoever catches an animal or a bird or a fish, or whoever fasts or makes war on the Sabbaths: [13] The man who does any of these things on the Sabbath shall die, so that the children of Israel shall observe the Sabbaths according to the commandments regarding the Sabbaths of the land, as it is written in the tablets, which He gave into my hands that I should write out for thee the laws of the seasons, and the seasons according to the division of their days. Herewith is completed the account of the division of the days.

# The Book of Enoch
**Abbreviations, Brackets, and Symbols**

[ ] The use of these brackets means that the words so enclosed are found in Gg but not In E.
[[ ]] The use of these brackets means that the words so enclosed are found in E but not in Gg or Gs.
< > The use of these brackets means that the words so enclosed are restored.
[] The use of these brackets means that the words so enclosed are interpolations.
( ) The use of these brackets means that the words so enclosed are supplied by the editor.
The use of **thick type** denotes that the words so printed are emended.
† † corruption in the text.
. . . some words which have been lost.

The following abbreviations are used in the translation of Enoch:
E denotes the Ethiopic Version.
G<sup>g</sup> denotes the large fragment of the Greek Version discovered at Akhmîm, and deposited in the Gizeh Museum, Cairo.

## I-XXXVI

### I-V. Parable of Enoch on the Future Lot of the Wicked and the Righteous.

**1**

<sup>1</sup> The words of the blessing of Enoch, wherewith he blessed the elect [[and]] righteous, who will be living in the day of tribulation, when all the wicked [[and godless]] are to be removed. <sup>2</sup> And he took up his parable and said–Enoch a righteous man, whose eyes were opened by God, saw the vision of the Holy One in the heavens, [which] the angels showed me, and from them I heard everything, and from them I understood as I saw, but not for this generation, but for a remote one which is for to come. <sup>3</sup> Concerning the elect I said, and took up my parable concerning them: The Holy Great One will come forth from His dwelling, <sup>4</sup> And the eternal God will tread upon the earth, (even) on Mount Sinai, [And appear from His camp] And appear in the strength of His might from the heaven of heavens. <sup>5</sup> And all shall be smitten with fear And the Watchers shall quake, And great fear and trembling shall seize them unto the ends of the earth. <sup>6</sup> And the high mountains shall be shaken, And the high hills shall be made low, And shall melt like wax before the flame <sup>7</sup> And the earth shall be [wholly] rent in sunder, And all that is upon the earth shall perish, And there shall be a judgement upon all (men). <sup>8</sup> But with the righteous He will make peace. And will protect the elect, And mercy shall be upon them. And they shall all belong to God, And they shall be prospered, And they shall [all] be blessed. [And He will help them all], And light shall appear unto them, [And He will make peace with them]. <sup>9</sup> And behold! He cometh with ten thousands of [His] holy ones To execute judgement upon all, And to destroy [all] the ungodly: And to convict all flesh Of all the works [of their ungodliness] which they have ungodly committed, And of all the hard things which ungodly sinners [have spoken] against Him.

**2**

<sup>1</sup> Observe ye everything that takes place in the heaven, how they do not change their orbits, [and] the luminaries which are in the heaven, how they all rise and set in order each in its season, and transgress not against their appointed order. <sup>2</sup> Behold ye the earth, and give heed to the things which take place upon it from first to last, [how **steadfast** they are], how [none of the things upon earth] change, [but] all the works of God appear [to you]. <sup>3</sup> Behold the summer and the winter, [[how the whole earth is filled with water, and clouds and dew and rain lie upon it]].

**3**

<sup>1</sup> Observe and see how (in the winter) all the trees [[seem as though they had withered and shed all their leaves, except fourteen trees, which do not lose their foliage but retain the old foliage from two to three years till the new comes.

**4**

<sup>1</sup> And again, observe ye the days of summer how the sun is above the earth over against it. And you seek shade and shelter by reason of the heat of the sun, and the earth also burns with growing heat, and so you cannot tread on the earth, or on a rock by reason of its heat.

**5**

<sup>1</sup> Observe [[ye]] how the trees cover themselves with green leaves and bear fruit: wherefore give ye heed [and know] with regard to all [His works], and recognize how He that liveth for ever hath made them so. <sup>2</sup> And [all] His works go on [thus] from year to year for ever, and all the tasks [which] they accomplish for Him, and [their tasks] change not, but according as [[God]] hath ordained so is it done. <sup>3</sup> And behold how the sea and the rivers in like manner accomplish and [change not] their tasks [from His commandments]. <sup>4</sup> But ye–ye have not been steadfast, nor done the commandments of the Lord, But ye have turned away and spoken proud and hard words With your impure mouths against His greatness. Oh, ye hard-hearted, ye shall find no peace. <sup>5</sup> Therefore shall ye execrate your days, And the years of your life shall perish, And [the years of your destruction] shall be multiplied in eternal execration, And ye shall find no mercy. <sup>6</sup> a In those days ye shall make your names an eternal execration unto all the righteous, b And by you shall [all] who curse, curse, And all the sinners [and godless] shall imprecate by you, c And for you the godless there shall be a curse. d And all the . . . shall rejoice, e And there shall be forgiveness of sins, f And every mercy and peace and forbearance: g There shall be salvation unto them, a goodly light. i And for all of you sinners there shall be no salvation, j But on you all shall abide a curse. <sup>7</sup> a But for the elect there shall be light and joy and peace, b And they shall inherit the earth. <sup>8</sup> And then there shall be bestowed upon the elect wisdom, And they shall

all live and never again sin, Either through ungodliness or through pride: But they who are wise shall be humble. <sup>9</sup> And they shall not again transgress, Nor shall they sin all the days of their life, Nor shall they die of (the divine) anger or wrath, But they shall complete the number of the days of their life. And their lives shall be increased in peace, And the years of their joy shall be multiplied, In eternal gladness and peace, All the days of their life.

### VI-XI. The Fall of the Angels: the Demoralisation of Mankind: the Intercession of the Angels on behalf of Mankind. The Dooms pronounced by God on the Angels: the Messianic Kingdom (a Noah fragment).

**6**

<sup>1</sup> And it came to pass when the children of men had multiplied that in those days were born unto them beautiful and comely daughters. <sup>2</sup> And the angels, the children of the heaven, saw and lusted after them, and said to one another: 'Come, let us choose us wives from among the children of men and beget us children.' <sup>3</sup> And Semjâzâ, who was their leader, said unto them: 'I fear ye will not indeed agree to do this deed, and I alone shall have to pay the penalty of a great sin.' <sup>4</sup> And they all answered him and said: 'Let us all swear an oath, and all bind ourselves by mutual imprecations not to abandon this plan but to do this thing.' <sup>5</sup> Then sware they all together and bound themselves by mutual imprecations upon it. <sup>6</sup> And they were in all two hundred; who descended [in the days] of **Jared** on the summit of Mount Hermon, and they called it Mount Hermon, because they had sworn and bound themselves by mutual imprecations upon it. <sup>7</sup> And these are the names of their leaders: Sêmîazâz, their leader, Arâkîba, Râmêêl, Kôkabîêl, Tâmîêl, Râmîêl, Dânêl, Êzêqêêl, Barâqîjâl, Asâêl, Armârôs, Batârêl, Anânêl, Zaqîêl, Samsâpêêl, Satarêl, Tûrêl, Jômjâêl, Sariêl. <sup>8</sup> These are their chiefs of tens.

**7**

<sup>1</sup> And all the others together with them took unto themselves wives, and each chose for himself one, and they began to go in unto them and to defile themselves with them, and they taught them charms and enchantments, and the cutting of roots, and made them acquainted with plants. <sup>2</sup> And they became pregnant, and they bare great giants, whose height was three thousand ells: <sup>3</sup> Who consumed all the acquisitions of men. And when men could no longer sustain them, <sup>4</sup> the giants turned against them and devoured mankind. <sup>5</sup> And they began to sin against birds, and beasts, and reptiles, and fish, and to devour one another's flesh, and drink the blood. <sup>6</sup> Then the earth laid accusation against the lawless ones.

**8**

<sup>1</sup> And Azâzêl taught men to make swords, and knives, and shields, and breastplates, and made known to them **the metals** <of the earth> and the art of working them, and bracelets, and ornaments, and the use of antimony, and the beautifying of the eyelids, and all kinds of costly stones, and all colouring tinctures. <sup>2</sup> And there arose much godlessness, and they committed fornication, and they were led astray, and became corrupt in all their ways. Semjâzâ taught enchantments, and root-cuttings, Armârôs the resolving of enchantments, Barâqîjâl, (taught) astrology, Kôkabêl the constellations, **Ezêqêêl the knowledge of the clouds**, <Araqiêl the signs of the earth, Shamsiêl the signs of the sun>, and Sariêl the course of the moon. And as men perished, they cried, and their cry went up to heaven . . .

**9**

<sup>1</sup> And then Michael, Uriel, Raphael, and Gabriel looked down from heaven and saw much blood being shed upon the earth, and all lawlessness being wrought upon the earth. <sup>2</sup> And they said one to another: 'The earth made †without inhabitant cries the voice of their crying† up to the gates of heaven. <sup>3</sup> [[And now to you, the holy ones of heaven]], the souls of men make their suit, saying, "Bring our cause before the Most High."' <sup>4</sup> And they said to the Lord **of the ages**: 'Lord of lords, God of gods, King of kings, <and God of the ages>, the throne of Thy glory (standeth) unto all the generations of the ages, and Thy name holy and glorious and blessed unto all the ages! <sup>5</sup> Thou hast made all things, and power over all things hast Thou: and all things are naked and open in Thy sight, and Thou seest all things, and nothing can hide itself from Thee. <sup>6</sup> Thou seest what Azâzêl hath done, who hath taught all unrighteousness on earth and revealed the eternal secrets which were (preserved) in heaven, which men were striving to **learn**: <sup>7</sup> And Semjâzâ, to whom Thou hast given authority to bear rule over his associates. <sup>8</sup> And they have gone to the daughters of men upon the earth, and have slept with the women, and have defiled themselves, and revealed to them all kinds of sins. <sup>9</sup> And the women have borne giants, and the whole earth has thereby been filled with blood and unrighteousness. <sup>10</sup> And now, behold, the souls of those who have died are crying and making their suit to the gates of heaven, and their lamentations have ascended: and cannot **cease** because of the lawless

deeds which are wrought on the earth. [11] And Thou knowest all things before they come to pass, and Thou seest these things and Thou dost suffer them, and Thou dost not say to us what we are to do to them in regard to these.'

## 10

[1] Then said the Most High, the Holy and Great One spake, and sent **Uriel** to the son of Lamech, and said to him: [2] '<Go to Noah> and tell him in my name "Hide thyself!" and reveal to him the end that is approaching: that the whole earth will be destroyed, and a deluge is about to come upon the whole earth, and will destroy all that is on it. [3] And now instruct him that he may escape and his seed may be preserved for all the generations of the world.' [4] And again the Lord said to Raphael: 'Bind Azâzêl hand and foot, and cast him into the darkness: and make an opening in the desert, which is in Dûdâêl, and cast him therein. [5] And place upon him rough and jagged rocks, and cover him with darkness, and let him abide there for ever, and cover his face that he may not see light. [6] And on the day of the great judgement he shall be cast into the fire. [7] And heal the earth which the angels have corrupted, and proclaim the healing of the earth, that they may heal the plague, and that all the children of men may not perish through all the secret things that the Watchers have **disclosed** and have taught their sons. [8] And the whole earth has been corrupted through the works that were taught by Azâzêl: to him ascribe all sin.' [9] And to Gabriel said the Lord: 'Proceed against the bastards and the reprobates, and against the children of fornication: and destroy [the children of fornication and] the children of the Watchers from amongst men [and cause them to go forth]: send them one against the other that they may destroy each other in battle: for length of days shall they not have. [10] And no request that they (i.e. their fathers) make of thee shall be granted unto their fathers on their behalf; for they hope to live an eternal life, and that each one of them will live five hundred years.' [11] And the Lord said unto Michael: 'Go, **bind** Semjâzâ and his associates who have united themselves with women so as to have defiled themselves with them in all their uncleanness. [12] And when their sons have slain one another, and they have seen the destruction of their beloved ones, bind them fast for seventy generations in the **valleys** of the earth, till the day of their judgement and of their consummation, till the judgement that is for ever and ever is consummated. [13] In those days they shall be led off to the abyss of fire: <and> to the torment and the prison in which they shall be confined for ever. [14] And whosoever shall be **condemned** and destroyed will from thenceforth be bound together with them to the end of all generations. [15] And destroy all the spirits of the reprobate and the children of the Watchers, because they have wronged mankind. [16] Destroy all wrong from the face of the earth and let every evil work come to an end: and let the plant of righteousness and truth appear: [and it shall prove a blessing; the works of righteousness and truth] shall be planted in truth and joy for evermore. [17] And then shall all the righteous escape, And shall live till they beget thousands of children, And all the days of their youth and their **old age** Shall they complete in peace. [18] And then shall the whole earth be tilled in righteousness, and shall all be planted with trees and be full of blessing. [19] And all desirable trees shall be planted on it, and they shall plant vines on it: and the vine which they plant thereon shall yield wine in abundance, and as for all the seed which is sown thereon each measure (of it) shall bear a thousand, and each measure of olives shall yield ten presses of oil. [20] And cleanse thou the earth from all oppression, and from all unrighteousness, and from all sin, and from all godlessness: and all the uncleanness that is wrought upon the earth destroy from off the earth. [21] [And all the children of men shall become righteous], and all nations shall offer adoration and shall praise Me, and all shall worship Me. And the earth shall be cleansed from all defilement, and from all sin, and from all punishment, and from all torment, and I will never again send (them) upon it from generation to generation and for ever.

## 11

[1] And in those days I will open the store chambers of blessing which are in the heaven, so as to send them down [upon the earth] over the work and labour of the children of men. [2] And truth and peace shall be associated together throughout all the days of the world and throughout all the generations **of men**.'

**XII–XVI. Dream Vision of Enoch: his intercession for Azâzêl and the fallen Angels: and his announcement to them of their first and final doom.**

## 12

[1] Before these things Enoch was hidden, and no one of the children of men knew where he was hidden, and where he abode, and what had become of him. [2] And his activities had to do with the Watchers, and his days were with the holy ones. [3] And I, Enoch was blessing the Lord of **majesty** and the King of the ages, and lo! the Watchers called me– Enoch the scribe–and said to me: [4] 'Enoch, thou scribe of righteousness, go, †declare† to the Watchers of the heaven who have left the high heaven, the holy eternal place, and have defiled themselves with women, and have done as the children of earth do, and have taken unto themselves wives: "Ye have wrought great destruction on the earth: [5] And ye shall have no peace nor forgiveness of sin: and inasmuch as †they† delight themselves in †their† children, [6] The murder of †their† beloved ones shall †they† see, and over the destruction of †their† children shall †they† lament, and shall make supplication unto eternity, but mercy and peace shall ye not attain.'"

## 13

[1] And Enoch went and said: 'Azâzêl, thou shalt have no peace: a severe sentence has gone forth against thee to put thee in bonds: [2] And thou shalt not have toleration nor †request† granted to thee, because of the unrighteousness which thou hast taught, and because of all the works of godlessness and unrighteousness and sin which thou hast shown to men.' [3] Then I went and spoke to them all together, and they were all afraid, and fear and trembling seized them. [4] And they besought me to draw up a petition for them that they might find forgiveness, and to read their petition in the presence of the Lord of heaven. [5] For from thenceforward they could not speak (with Him) nor lift up their eyes to heaven for shame of their sins for which they had been condemned. [6] Then I wrote out their petition, and the prayer in regard to their spirits and their deeds individually and in regard to their requests that they should have forgiveness and length <of days>. [7] And I went off and sat down at the waters of Dan, in the land of Dan, to the south of the west of Hermon: I read their petition till I fell asleep. [8] And behold a dream came to me, and visions fell down upon me, and I saw visions of chastisement, [and a voice came bidding (me)] I to tell it to the sons of heaven, and reprimand them. [9] And when I awaked, I came unto them, and they were all sitting gathered together, weeping in 'Abelsjâîl, which is between Lebanon and Sênêsêr, with their faces covered. [10] And I recounted before them all the visions which I had seen in sleep, and I began to speak the words of righteousness, and to reprimand the heavenly Watchers.

## 14

[1] The book of the words of righteousness, and of the reprimand of the eternal Watchers in accordance with the command of the Holy Great One in that vision. [2] I saw in my sleep what I will now say with a tongue of flesh and with the breath of my mouth: which the Great One has given to men to converse therewith and understand with the heart. [3] As He has created and given [[to man the power of understanding the word of wisdom, so hath He created me also and given]] me the power of reprimanding the Watchers, the children of heaven. [4] I wrote out your petition, and in my vision it appeared thus, that your petition will not be granted unto you [[throughout all the days of eternity, and that judgement has been finally passed upon you: yea (your petition) will not be granted unto you]]. [5] And from henceforth you shall not ascend into heaven unto all eternity, and [in bonds] of the earth the decree has gone forth to bind you for all the days of the world. [6] And (that) previously you shall have seen the destruction of your beloved sons and ye shall have no pleasure in them, but they shall fall before you by the sword. [7] And your petition on their behalf shall not be granted, nor yet on your own: even though you weep and pray and **speak all the words** contained in the writing which I have written. [8] And the vision was shown to me thus: Behold, in the vision clouds invited me and a mist summoned me, and the course of the stars and the lightnings sped and **hastened** me, and the winds in the vision caused me to fly and lifted me upward, and bore me into heaven. [9] And I went in till I drew nigh to a wall which is built of crystals and surrounded by tongues of fire: and it began to affright me. [10] And I went into the tongues of fire and drew nigh to a large house which was built of crystals: and the walls of the house were like a tesselated floor (made) of crystals, and its groundwork was of crystal. [11] Its ceiling was like the path of the stars and the lightnings, and between them were fiery cherubim, and their heaven was (clear as) water. [12] A flaming fire surrounded the walls, and its portals blazed with fire. [13] And I entered into that house, and it was hot as fire and cold as ice: there were no delights of life therein: fear covered me, and trembling got hold upon me. [14] And as I quaked and trembled, I fell upon my face. [15] And I beheld a vision, And lo! there was a second house, greater than the former, and the entire portal stood open before me, and it was built of flames of fire. [16] And in every respect it so excelled in splendour and magnificence and extent that I cannot describe to you its splendour and its extent. [17] And its floor was of fire, and above it were lightnings and the path of the stars, and its ceiling also was flaming fire. [18] And I looked and saw [[therein]] a lofty throne: its appearance was as crystal, and the wheels thereof as the shining sun, and there was the **vision** of cherubim. [19] And from underneath the throne came streams of flaming fire so that I could not look thereon. [20] And the Great Glory sat thereon, and His raiment shone more brightly than the sun and was whiter than any snow. [21] None of the angels could enter and could behold His face by reason of the

magnificence and glory and no flesh could behold Him. ²² The flaming fire was round about Him, and a great fire stood before Him, and none around could draw nigh Him: ten thousand times ten thousand (stood) before Him, yet He needed no counselor. ²³ And the most holy ones who were nigh to Him did not leave by night nor depart from Him. ²⁴ And until then I had been prostrate on my face, trembling: and the Lord called me with His own mouth, and said to me: 'Come hither, Enoch, and hear my word.' ²⁵ [And one of the holy ones came to me and waked me], and He made me rise up and approach the door: and I bowed my face downwards.

## 15

¹ And He answered and said to me, and I heard His voice: 'Fear not, Enoch, thou righteous man and scribe of righteousness: approach hither and hear my voice. ² And go, say to [[the Watchers of heaven]], who have sent thee to intercede [[for them: "You should intercede"]] for men, and not men for you: ³ Wherefore have ye left the high, holy, and eternal heaven, and lain with women, and defiled yourselves with the daughters of men and taken to yourselves wives, and done like the children of earth, and begotten giants (as your) sons? ⁴ And though ye were holy, spiritual, living the eternal life, you have defiled yourselves with the blood of women, and have begotten (children) with the blood of flesh, and, **as the children** of men, have lusted after flesh and blood as those [also] do who die and perish. ⁵ Therefore have I given them wives also that they might impregnate them, and beget children by them, that thus nothing might be wanting to them on earth. ⁶ But you were [formerly] spiritual, living the eternal life, and immortal for all generations of the world. ⁷ And therefore I have not appointed wives for you; for as for the spiritual ones of the heaven, in heaven is their dwelling. ⁸ And now, the giants, who are produced from the spirits and flesh, shall be called evil spirits upon the earth, and on the earth shall be their dwelling. ⁹ Evil spirits have proceeded from their bodies; because they are born from **men**, [[and]] from the holy Watchers is their beginning and primal origin; [they shall be evil spirits on earth, and] evil spirits shall they be called. ¹⁰ [As for the spirits of heaven, in heaven shall be their dwelling, but as for the spirits of the earth which were born upon the earth, on the earth shall be their dwelling.] ¹¹ And the spirits of the giants **afflict**, oppress, destroy, attack, do battle, and work destruction on the earth, and cause trouble: they take no food, [but nevertheless hunger] and thirst, and cause offences. And these spirits shall rise up against the children of men and against the women, because they have proceeded [from them].

## 16

¹ From the days of the slaughter and destruction and death [of the giants], from the souls of whose flesh the spirits, having gone forth, shall destroy without incurring judgement–thus shall they destroy until the day of the consummation, the great [judgement] in which the age shall be consummated, over the Watchers and the godless, yea, shall be wholly consummated." ² And now as to the Watchers who have sent thee to intercede for them, who had been [[aforetime]] in heaven, (say to them): ³ "You have been in heaven, but [all] the mysteries had not yet been revealed to you, and you knew worthless ones, and these in the hardness of your hearts you have made known to the women, and through these mysteries women and men work much evil on earth." ⁴ Say to them therefore: "You have no peace."'

**XVII-XXXVII. Enoch's Journeys through the Earth and Sheol.**
**XVII-XIX. The First Journey.**

## 17

¹ And they took [and] brought me to a place in which those who were there were like flaming fire, and, when they wished, they appeared as men. ² And they brought me to the place of darkness, and to a mountain the point of whose summit reached to heaven. ³ And I saw the places of the luminaries [and the treasuries of the stars] and the thunder [and] in the **uttermost depths**, where were a fiery bow and arrows and their quiver, and [[a fiery sword]] and all the lightnings. ⁴ And they took me to the living waters, and to the fire of the west, which receives every setting of the sun. ⁵ And I came to a river of fire in which the fire flows like water and discharges itself into the great sea towards the west. ⁶ I saw the great rivers and came to the great [river and to the great] darkness, and went to the place where no flesh walks. ⁷ I saw the mountains of the darkness of winter and the place whence all the waters of the deep flow. ⁸ I saw the mouths of all the rivers of the earth and the mouth of the deep.

## 18

¹ I saw the treasuries of all the winds: I saw how He had furnished with them the whole creation and the firm foundations of the earth. ² And I saw the corner-stone of the earth: I saw the four winds which bear [the earth and] the firmament of the heaven. ³ [[And I saw how the winds stretch out the vaults of heaven]], and have their station between heaven and earth: [[these are the pillars of the heaven]]. ⁴ I saw the winds of

heaven which turn and bring the circumference of the sun and all the stars to their setting. ⁵ I saw the winds on the earth carrying the clouds: I saw [[the paths of the angels. I saw]] at the end of the earth the firmament of the heaven above. ⁶ And I proceeded and saw a place which burns day and night, where there are seven mountains of magnificent stones, three towards the east, and three towards the south. ⁷ And as for those towards the east, <one> was of coloured stone, and one of pearl, and one of **jacinth**, and those towards the south of red stone. ⁸ But the middle one reached to heaven like the throne of God, of alabaster, and the summit of the throne was of sapphire. ⁹ And I saw a flaming fire. And beyond these mountains ¹⁰ is a region the end of the great earth: there the heavens were completed. ¹¹ And I saw a deep abyss, with columns [[of heavenly fire, and among them I saw columns]] of fire fall, which were beyond measure alike towards the height and towards the depth. ¹² And beyond that abyss I saw a place which had no firmament of the heaven above, and no firmly founded earth beneath it: there was no water upon it, and no birds, but it was a waste and horrible place. ¹³ I saw there seven stars like great burning mountains, and to me, when I inquired regarding them, ¹⁴ The angel said: 'This place is the end of heaven and earth: this has become a prison for the stars and the host of heaven. ¹⁵ And the stars which roll over the fire are they which have transgressed the commandment of the Lord in the beginning of their rising, because they did not come forth at their appointed times. ¹⁶ And He was wroth with them, and bound them till the time when their guilt should be consummated (even) [for ten thousand years].'

## 19

¹ And Uriel said to me: 'Here shall stand the angels who have connected themselves with women, and their spirits assuming many different forms are defiling mankind and shall lead them astray into sacrificing to demons [[as gods]], (here shall they stand,) till [[the day of]] the great judgement in which they shall be judged till they are made an end of. ² And the women also of the angels who went astray shall become sirens.' ³ And I, Enoch, alone saw the vision, the ends of all things: and no man shall see as I have seen.

**XX. Name and Functions of the Seven Archangels.**

## 20

¹ And these are the names of the holy angels who watch. ² Uriel, one of the holy angels, who is over the world and over Tartarus. ³ Raphael, one of the holy angels, who is over the spirits of men. ⁴ Raguel, one of the holy angels who †takes vengeance on† the world of the luminaries. ⁵ Michael, one of the holy angels, to wit, he that is set over the best part of mankind [[and]] over chaos. ⁶ Saraqâêl, one of the holy angels, who is set over the spirits, who sin in the spirit. ⁷ Gabriel, one of the holy angels, who is over Paradise and the serpents and the Cherubim. ⁸ Remiel, one of the holy angels, whom God set over those who rise.

**XXI. Preliminary and final place of punishment of the fallen angels (stars).**

## 21

¹ And I proceeded to where things were chaotic. ² And I saw there something horrible: I saw neither a heaven above nor a firmly founded earth, but a place chaotic and horrible. ³ And there I saw seven stars of the heaven bound together in it, like great mountains and burning with fire. ⁴ Then I said: 'For what sin are they bound, and on what account have they been cast in hither?' ⁵ Then said Uriel, one of the holy angels, who was with me, and was chief over them, and said: 'Enoch, why dost thou ask, and why art thou eager for the truth? ⁶ These are of the number of the stars [of heaven], which have transgressed the commandment of the Lord, and are bound here till ten thousand years, the time entailed by their sins, are consummated.' ⁷ And from thence I went to another place, which was still more horrible than the former, and I saw a horrible thing: a great fire there which burnt and blazed, and the place was cleft as far as the abyss, being full of great descending columns of fire: neither its extent or magnitude could I see, nor could I conjecture. ⁸ Then I said: 'How fearful is the place and how terrible to look upon!' ⁹ Then Uriel answered me, one of the holy angels who was with me, and said unto me: 'Enoch, why hast thou such fear and affright?' And I answered: 'Because of this fearful place, and because of the spectacle of the pain.' ¹⁰ And he said [[unto me]]: 'This place is the prison of the angels, and here they will be imprisoned for ever.'

**XXII. Sheol, or the Underworld.**

## 22

¹ And thence I went to another place, and he showed me in the west [another] great and high mountain [and] of hard rock.

| E | Gᵍ |
|---|---|
| ² And there was in it | ² And there were †four† hollow |
| †four† **hollow** places, deep | and places in it, deep and very |
| | wide and very smooth. †How† smooth: †three† of them were |
| | dark and one bright; and there |

smooth are **the hollow places** and was a fountain of water in its deep and dark to look at.                      midst. And I said: '†How† smooth are these hollow places, and deep and dark to view.'

³ Then Raphael answered, one of the holy angels who was with me, and said unto me: 'These hollow places have been created for this very purpose, that the spirits of the souls of the dead should assemble therein, yea that all the souls of the children of men should assemble here. ⁴ And these places **have been made** to receive them till the day of their judgement and till their appointed period [till the period appointed], till the great judgement (comes) upon them.'

| E | Gᵍ |
|---|---|
| ⁵ I saw the spirits of the children of men who were dead, and their voice went forth to heaven and made suit. | ⁵ I saw (the spirit of) **a dead man** making suit, and his voice went forth to heaven and made suit. |
| ⁶ Then I asked Raphael the angel who was with me, and I said unto him: 'This spirit–whose is it whose voice goeth forth maketh suit?' | ⁶ And I asked Raphael the angel who was with me, and I said unto him: 'This spirit which maketh suit, whose is it, whose voice goeth forth and maketh suit to heaven?' |

⁷ And he answered me saying: 'This is the spirit which went forth from Abel, whom his brother Cain slew, and he makes his suit against him till his seed is destroyed from the face of the earth, and his seed is annihilated from amongst the seed of men.'

| E | Gᵍ |
|---|---|
| ⁸ Then I asked regarding it, and regarding all the **hollow places**: 'Why is one 'Why as one separated from the other?' | ⁸ Then I asked regarding all the **hollow places**: 'Why is one separated from the other?' |
| | ⁹ And he answered me saying: |
| ⁹ And he answered me and said unto me: 'These three have been made that the spirits of the dead might be separated. And such a division has been made <for> the spirits of the righteous, in which there is the **bright** spring of **water**. | 'These three have been made that the spirits of the dead might be separated. And **this** division has been made for the spirits of the righteous, in which bright spring of water. |
| ¹⁰ **And** such has been made for sinners when they die and are buried in the earth and judgement has not been executed on them in their lifetime. | ¹⁰ And **this** has been made for sinners when they die and are buried in the earth and judgement has not been executed upon them in their lifetime. |
| ¹¹ Here their spirits shall be set apart in this great pain till the great day of judgement and punishment and torment of those who †curse† for ever, and retribution for their spirits. There He shall bind them for ever. | ¹¹ Here their spirits shall be set apart in this great pain, till the great day of judgement, scourgings, and torments of the accursed for ever, so that (there maybe) retribution for their spirits. There He shall bind them for ever. |
| ¹² And such a division has been made for the spirits of those who make their suit, who make disclosures concerning their destruction, when they were slain in the days of the sinners. | ¹² And **this** division has been made for the spirits of those who make their suit, who make disclosures concerning their destruction, when they were slain in the days of the sinners. |
| ¹³ Such has been made for spirits of men who were not righteous but sinners, who are complete in transgression, and of the transgressors. they shall be companions: but their spirits shall not be slain in the day of judgement nor shall they be raised from thence. | ¹³ And **this** has been made for the spirits of men who shall not be righteous but sinners, who are godless, and of the lawless they shall be companions: but their spirits shall not be punished in the day of judgement nor shall they be raised from thence. |

¹⁴ Then I blessed the Lord of glory and said: 'Blessed be my Lord, the Lord of righteousness, who ruleth for ever.'

## XXIII. The Fire that deals with the Luminaries of Heaven.

### 23

¹ From thence I went to another place to the west of the ends of the earth. ² And I saw a [[burning]] fire which ran without resting, and paused not from its course day or night but (ran) regularly. ³ And I asked saying: 'What is this which rests not?' ⁴ Then Raguel, one of the holy angels who was with me, answered me [[and said unto me]]: 'This course [of fire] [[which thou hast seen]] is the fire in the west which †persecutes† all the luminaries of heaven.'

## XXIV. XXV. The Seven Mountains in the North-West and the Tree of Life.

### 24

¹ [[And from thence I went to another place of the earth]], and he showed me a mountain range of fire which burnt [[day and night]]. ² And I went beyond it and saw seven magnificent mountains all differing each from the other, and the stones (thereof) were magnificent and beautiful, magnificent as a whole, of glorious appearance and fair exterior: [[three towards]] the east, [[one]] founded on the other, and three towards the south, one upon the other, and deep rough ravines, no one of which joined with any other. ³ And the seventh mountain was in the midst of these, and it excelled them in height, resembling the seat of a throne: and fragrant trees encircled the throne. ⁴ And amongst them was a tree such as I had never yet smelt, neither was any amongst them nor were others like it: it had a fragrance beyond all fragrance, and its leaves and blooms and wood wither not for ever: and its fruit [[is beautiful, and its fruit]] resembles the dates of a palm. ⁵ Then I said: '[How] beautiful is this tree, and fragrant, and its leaves are fair, and its blooms [[very]] delightful in appearance.' ⁶ Then answered Michael, one of the holy [[and honoured]] angels who was with me, and was their leader.

### 25

¹ And he said unto me: 'Enoch, why dost thou ask me regarding the fragrance of the tree, and [why] dost thou wish to learn the truth?' ² Then I answered him [[saying]]: 'I wish to know about everything, but especially about this tree.' ³ And he answered saying: 'This high mountain [[which thou hast seen]], whose summit is like the throne of God, is His throne, where the Holy Great One, the Lord of Glory, the Eternal King, will sit, when He shall come down to visit the earth with goodness. ⁴ And as for this fragrant tree no mortal is permitted to touch it till the great judgement, when He shall take vengeance on all and bring (everything) to its consummation for ever. It shall then be given to the righteous and holy. ⁵ Its fruit **shall be** for food to the elect: it shall be transplanted to the holy place, to the temple of the Lord, the Eternal King. ⁶ Then shall they rejoice with joy and be glad, And into the holy place shall they enter; And its fragrance shall be in their bones, And they shall live a long life on earth, Such as thy fathers lived: And in their days shall no [[sorrow or]] plague Or torment or calamity touch them.' ⁷ Then blessed I the God of Glory, the Eternal King, who hath prepared such things for the righteous, and hath created them and promised to give to them.

## XXVI. Jerusalem and the Mountains, Ravines and Streams.

### 26

¹ And I went from thence to the middle of the earth, and I saw a blessed place [in which there were trees] with branches abiding and blooming [of a dismembered tree]. ² And there I saw a holy mountain, [[and]] underneath the mountain to the east there was a stream and it flowed towards the south. ³ And I saw towards the east another mountain higher than this, and between them a deep and narrow ravine: in it also ran a stream [underneath] the mountain. ⁴ And to the west thereof there was another mountain, lower than the former and of small elevation, and a ravine [deep and dry] between them: and another deep and dry ravine was at the extremities of the three [mountains]. ⁵ And all the ravines were deep [[and narrow]], (being formed) of hard rock, and trees were not planted upon them. ⁶ And I marveled [[at the rocks, and I marveled]] at the ravine, yea, I marveled very much.

## XXVII. The Purpose of the Accursed Valley.

### 27

¹ Then said I: 'For what object is this blessed land, which is entirely filled with trees, and this accursed valley [[between]]?' ² [[Then Uriel, one of the holy angels who was with me, answered and said: 'This]] accursed valley is for those who are accursed for ever: Here shall all [the accursed] be gathered together who utter with their lips against the Lord unseemly words and of His glory speak hard things.

| E | Gᵍ |
|---|---|
| Here shall they be gathered together, and here shall be their place of judgement. | Here shall they be gathered together, and here shall be the place of their habitation. |
| ³ In the last days there shall be upon them the spectacle of righteous judgement in the presence of the righteous for ever: here shall the merciful bless the Lord of glory, the Eternal King. | ³ In the last times, in the days of the true judgement in the presence of the righteous for ever: here shall the **godly** bless the Lord of Glory, the Eternal King. |

⁴ In the days of judgement over the former, they shall bless Him for the mercy in accordance with which He has assigned them (their lot).'

⁵ Then I blessed the Lord of Glory and set forth His [glory] and lauded Him gloriously.

## XXVIII-XXXIII. Further Journey to the East.

### 28

¹ And thence I went [[towards the east]], into the midst [[of the mountain range of the desert]], and I saw a wilderness and it was solitary, full of trees **and plants**. ² [[And]] water gushed forth from above. ³ Rushing like a copious watercourse [which flowed] towards the north-west it caused **clouds** and dew to ascend on every side.

### 29

¹ And thence I went to another place in the desert, and approached to the east of this mountain range. ² And [[there]] I saw **aromatic** trees exhaling the fragrance of frankincense and myrrh, and the trees also were similar to the almond tree.

### 30

¹ And beyond these, I went afar to the east, and I saw another place, a valley (full) of water. ² And [therein there was] a tree, the colour (?) of fragrant trees such as the mastic. ³ And on the sides of those valleys I saw fragrant cinnamon. And beyond these I proceeded to the east.

### 31

¹ And I saw other mountains, and amongst them were [groves of] trees, and there flowed forth from them nectar, which is named sarara and galbanum. ² And beyond these mountains I saw another mountain [to the east of the ends of the earth], [[whereon were aloe trees]], and all the trees were full **of stacte**, being like almond-trees. ³ And when one **burnt** it, it smelt sweeter than any fragrant odour.

### 32

| E | G<sup>g</sup> |
|---|---|
| ¹ And after these fragrant odours, | ¹ To the north-east I beheld seven as I looked towards the north over mountains full of choice nard and |
| the mountains I saw seven mastic and cinnamon and pepper. | |
| mountains full of choice nard and | |
| fragrant trees and cinnamon and | |
| pepper. | |

² And thence I went over the summits of [all] these mountains, far towards the east [of the earth], and passed above the Erythraean sea and went far from it, and passed over [[the angel]] Zotîêl.

| E | G<sup>g</sup> |
|---|---|
| ³ And I came to the Garden of Righteousness, and saw beyond those trees many large trees growing there and of goodly fragrance, large, very beautiful and glorious, and the tree of wisdom whereof they eat and know great wisdom. | ³ And I came to the Garden of Righteousness, and from afar off those trees more numerous than these trees and great–†two† trees there, very great, beautiful, and glorious, and magnificent, and the tree of knowledge, whose holy fruit they eat and know great wisdom. |

⁴ [That tree is in height like the fir, and its leaves are] like (those of) the Carob tree: and its fruit is like the clusters of the vine, very beautiful: and the fragrance of the tree penetrates afar. ⁵ Then I said: '[How] beautiful is the tree, and how attractive is its look!' ⁶ Then Raphael the holy angel, who was with me, answered me [[and said]]: 'This is the tree of wisdom, of which thy father old (in years) and thy aged mother, who were before thee, have eaten, and they learnt wisdom and their eyes were opened, and they knew that they were naked and they were driven out of the garden.'

### 33

¹ And from thence I went to the ends of the earth and saw there great beasts, and each differed from the other; and (I saw) birds also differing in appearance and beauty and voice, the one differing from the other. ² And to the east of those beasts I saw the ends of the earth whereon the heaven rests, and the portals of the heaven open. ³ And I saw how the stars of heaven come forth, and I counted the portals out of which they proceed, and wrote down all their outlets, of each individual star by itself, according to their number and their names, their courses and their positions, and their times and their months, as Uriel the holy angel who was with me showed me. ⁴ He showed all things to me and wrote them down for me: also their names he wrote for me, and their laws and their companies.

## XXXIV. XXXV. Enoch's Journey to the North.

### 34

¹ And from thence I went towards the north to the ends of the earth, and there I saw a great and glorious device at the ends of the whole earth. ² And here I saw three portals of heaven open in the heaven: through each of them proceed north winds: when they blow there is cold, hail, frost, snow, dew, and rain. ³ And out of one portal they blow for good: but when they blow through the other two portals, it is with violence and affliction on the earth, and they blow with violence.

### 35

¹ And from thence I went towards the west to the ends of the earth, and saw there three portals of the heaven open such as I had seen in the †east†, the same number of portals, and the same number of outlets.

## XXXVI. The Journey to the South.

### 36

¹ And from thence I went to the south to the ends of the earth, and saw there three open portals of the heaven: and thence there come dew, rain, †and wind†. ² And from thence I went to the east to the ends of the heaven, and saw here the three eastern portals of heaven open and small portals above them. ³ Through each of these small portals pass the stars of heaven and run their course to the west on the path which is shown to them. ⁴ And as often as I saw I blessed always the Lord of Glory, and I continued to bless the Lord of Glory who has wrought great and glorious wonders, to show the greatness of His work to the angels and to **spirits** and to men, that they might praise His work and all His creation: that they might see the work of His might and praise the great work of His hands and bless Him for ever.

## XXXVII-LXXI. The Parables.

### 37

¹ The second vision which he saw, the vision of wisdom–which Enoch the son of Jared, the son of Mahalalel, the son of Cainan, the son of Enos, the son of Seth, the son of Adam, saw. ² And this is the beginning of the words of wisdom which I lifted up my voice to speak and say to those which dwell on earth: Hear, ye men of old time, and see, ye that come after, the words of the Holy One which I will speak before the Lord of Spirits. ³ It were better to declare (them only) to the men of old time, but even from those that come after we will not withhold the beginning of wisdom. ⁴ Till the present day such wisdom has never been given **by** the Lord of Spirits as I have received according to my insight, according to the good pleasure of the Lord of Spirits by whom the lot of eternal life has been given to me. ⁵ Now three parables were imparted to me, and I lifted up my voice and recounted them to those that dwell on the earth.

## XXXVII-XLIV. The First Parable.
## XXXVIII. The Coming Judgement of the Wicked.

### 38

¹ The First Parable. When the congregation of the righteous shall appear, And sinners shall be judged for their sins, And shall be driven from the face of the earth: ² And when the Righteous One shall appear before the eyes of the righteous, Whose elect works hang upon the Lord of Spirits, And light shall appear to the righteous and the elect who dwell on the earth, Where then will be the dwelling of the sinners, And where the resting-place of those who have denied the Lord of Spirits? It had been good for them if they had not been born. ³ When the secrets of the righteous shall be revealed and the sinners judged, And the godless driven from the presence of the righteous and elect, ⁴ From that time those that possess the earth shall no longer be powerful and exalted: And they shall not be able to behold the face of the holy, For the Lord of Spirits has **caused His light to appear** On the face of the holy, righteous, and elect. ⁵ Then shall the kings and the mighty perish And be given into the hands of the righteous and holy. ⁶ And thenceforward none shall seek for themselves mercy from the Lord of Spirits For their life is at an end.

## XXXIX. The Abode of the Righteous and of the Elect One: the Praises of the Blessed.

### 39

¹ [And it †shall come to pass in those days that elect and holy children †will descend from the high heaven, and their seed will become one with the children of men. ² And in those days Enoch received books of zeal and wrath, and books of disquiet and expulsion.] And mercy shall not be accorded to them, saith the Lord of Spirits. ³ And in those days a whirlwind carried me off from the earth, And set me down at the end of the heavens. ⁴ And there I saw another vision, the dwelling-places of the holy, And the resting-places of the righteous. ⁵ Here mine eyes saw their dwellings with His righteous angels, And their resting-places with the holy. And they petitioned and interceded and prayed for the children of men, And righteousness flowed before them as water, And mercy like dew upon the earth: Thus it is amongst them for ever and ever. ⁶ a. And in that place mine eyes saw the Elect One of righteousness and of faith, ⁶ b. And I saw his dwelling-place under the wings of the Lord of Spirits. ⁷ a. And righteousness shall prevail in his days, And the righteous and elect shall be without number before Him for ever and ever. ⁷ b. And all the righteous and elect before Him shall be †strong† as fiery lights, And their mouth shall be full of blessing, And their lips extol the name of the Lord of Spirits, And righteousness before Him shall never fail, [And uprightness shall never fail before Him.] ⁸ There I wished to dwell, And my spirit longed for that dwelling-place: And there heretofore hath been my portion, For so has it been established concerning me before the Lord of Spirits. ⁹ In those days I praised and extolled the name of the Lord of Spirits with blessings and praises,

because He hath destined me for blessing and glory according to the good pleasure of the Lord of Spirits. [10] For a long time my eyes regarded that place, and I blessed Him and praised Him, saying: 'Blessed is He, and may He be blessed from the beginning and for evermore. [11] And before Him there is no ceasing. He knows before the world was created what is for ever and what will be from generation unto generation. [12] Those who sleep not bless Thee: they stand before Thy glory and bless, praise, and extol, saying: "Holy, holy, holy, is the Lord of Spirits: He filleth the earth with spirits."' [13] And here my eyes saw all those who sleep not: they stand before Him and bless and say: 'Blessed be Thou, and blessed be the name of the Lord for ever and ever.' [14] And my face was changed; for I could no longer behold.

## XL. XLI. 2. The Four Archangels.

### 40

[1] And after that I saw thousands of thousands and ten thousand times ten thousand, I saw a multitude beyond number and reckoning, who stood before the Lord of Spirits. [2] And on the four sides of the Lord of Spirits I saw four presences, different from those that sleep not, and I learnt their names: for the angel that went with me made known to me their names, and showed me all the hidden things. [3] And I heard the voices of those four presences as they uttered praises before the Lord of glory. [4] The first voice blesses the Lord of Spirits for ever and ever. [5] And the second voice I heard blessing the Elect One and the elect ones who hang upon the Lord of Spirits. [6] And the third voice I heard **pray and intercede** for those who dwell on the earth and supplicate in the name of the Lord of Spirits. [7] And I heard the fourth voice fending off the Satans and forbidding them to come before the Lord of Spirits to accuse them who dwell on the earth. [8] After that I asked the angel of peace who went with me, who showed me everything that is hidden: 'Who are these four presences which I have seen and whose words I have heard and written down?' [9] And he said to me: 'This first is Michael, the merciful and long-suffering: and the second, who is set over all the diseases and all the wounds of the children of men, is Raphael: and the third, who is set over all the powers, is Gabriel: and the fourth, who is set over the repentance unto hope of those who inherit eternal life, is named Phanuel.' [10] And these are the four angels of the Lord of Spirits and the four voices I heard in those days.

### 41

[1] And after that I saw all the secrets of the heavens, and how the kingdom is divided, and how the actions of men are weighed in the balance. [2] And there I saw the mansions of the elect and the mansions of the holy, and mine eyes saw there all the sinners being driven from thence which deny the name of the Lord of Spirits, and being dragged off: and they could not abide because of the punishment which proceeds from the Lord of Spirits.

## XLI. 3-9. Astronomical Secrets.

[3] And there mine eyes saw the secrets of the lightning and of the thunder, and the secrets of the winds, how they are divided to blow over the earth, and the secrets of the clouds and dew, and there I saw from whence they proceed in that place and from whence they saturate the dusty earth. [4] And there I saw closed chambers out of which the winds are divided, the chamber of the hail and winds, the chamber of the mist, and of the clouds, and the cloud thereof hovers over the earth from the beginning of the world. [5] And I saw the chambers of the sun and moon, whence they proceed and whither they come again, and their glorious return, and how one is superior to the other, and their stately orbit, and how they do not leave their orbit, and they add nothing to their orbit and they take nothing from it, and they keep faith with each other, in accordance with the oath by which they are bound together. [6] And first the sun goes forth and traverses his path according to the commandment of the Lord of Spirits, and mighty is His name for ever and ever. [7] And after that I saw the hidden and the visible path of the moon, and she accomplishes the course of her path in that place by day and by night—the one holding a position opposite to the other before the Lord of Spirits. And they give thanks and praise and rest not; For unto them is their thanksgiving rest. [8] For the sun changes oft for a blessing or a curse, And the course of the path of the moon is light to the righteous And darkness to the sinners in the name of the Lord, Who made a separation between the light and the darkness, And divided the spirits of men, And strengthened the spirits of the righteous, In the name of His righteousness. [9] For no angel hinders and no power is able to hinder; for He appoints a judge for them all and He judges them all before Him.

## XLII. The Dwelling-places of Wisdom and of Unrighteousness.

### 42

[1] Wisdom found no place where she might dwell; Then a dwelling-place was assigned her in the heavens. [2] Wisdom went forth to make her dwelling among the children of men, And found no dwelling-place: Wisdom returned to her place, And took her seat among the angels. [3] And unrighteousness went forth from her chambers: Whom she sought

not she found, And dwelt with them, As rain in a desert And dew on a thirsty land.

## XLIII. XLIV. Astronomical Secrets.

### 43

[1] And I saw other lightnings and the stars of heaven, and I saw how He called them all by their names and they hearkened unto Him. [2] And I saw how they are weighed in a righteous balance according to their proportions of light: (I saw) the width of their spaces and the day of their appearing, and how their revolution produces lightning: and (I saw) their revolution according to the number of the angels, and (how) they keep faith with each other. [3] And I asked the angel who went with me who showed me what was hidden: 'What are these?' [4] And he said to me: 'The Lord of Spirits hath showed thee their parabolic meaning (lit. 'their parable'): these are the names of the holy who dwell on the earth and believe in the name of the Lord of Spirits for ever and ever.'

### 44

[1] Also another phenomenon I saw in regard to the lightnings: how some of the stars arise and become lightnings and cannot part with their new form.

## XLV-LVII. The Second Parable.
## The Lot of the Apostates: the New Heaven and the New Earth.

### 45

[1] And this is the Second Parable concerning those who deny the name of the dwelling of the holy ones and the Lord of Spirits. [2] And into the heaven they shall not ascend, And on the earth they shall not come: Such shall be the lot of the sinners Who have denied the name of the Lord of Spirits, Who are thus preserved for the day of suffering and tribulation. [3] On that day Mine Elect One shall sit on the throne of glory And shall **try** their works, And their places of rest shall be innumerable. And their souls shall grow strong within them when they see Mine Elect Ones, And those who have called upon My glorious name: [4] Then will I cause Mine Elect One to dwell among them. And I will transform the heaven and make it an eternal blessing and light [5] And I will transform the earth and make it a blessing: And I will cause Mine elect ones to dwell upon it: But the sinners and evil-doers shall not set foot thereon. [6] For I have provided and satisfied with peace My righteous ones And have caused them to dwell before Me: But for the sinners there is judgement impending with Me, So that I shall destroy them from the face of the earth.

## XLVI. The Head of Days and the Son of Man.

### 46

[1] And there I saw One who had a head of days, And His head was white like wool, And with Him was another being whose countenance had the appearance of a man, And his face was full of graciousness, like one of the holy angels. [2] And I asked the **angel** who went with me and showed me all the hidden things, concerning that Son of Man, who he was, and whence he was, (and) why he went with the Head of Days? And he answered and said unto me: This is the son of Man who hath righteousness, With whom dwelleth righteousness, And who revealeth all the treasures of that which is hidden, Because the Lord of Spirits hath chosen him, And whose lot hath the pre-eminence before the Lord of Spirits in uprightness for ever. [4] And this Son of Man whom thou hast seen Shall †raise up† the kings and the mighty from their seats, [And the strong from their thrones] And shall loosen the reins of the strong, And break the teeth of the sinners. [5] [And he shall put down the kings from their thrones and kingdoms] Because they do not extol and praise Him, Nor humbly acknowledge whence the kingdom was bestowed upon them. [6] And he shall put down the countenance of the strong, And shall fill them with shame. And darkness shall be their dwelling, And worms shall be their bed, And they shall have no hope of rising from their beds, Because they do not extol the name of the Lord of Spirits. [7] And these are they who †judge† the stars of heaven, [And raise their hands against the Most High], †And tread upon the earth and dwell upon it†. And all their deeds manifest unrighteousness, And their power rests upon their riches, And their faith is in the †gods† which they have made with their hands, And they deny the name of the Lord of Spirits, [8] And they persecute the houses of His congregations, And the faithful who hang upon the name of the Lord of Spirits.

## XLVII. The Prayer of the Righteous for Vengeance and their Joy at its coming.

### 47

¹ And in those days shall have ascended the prayer of the righteous, And the blood of the righteous from the earth before the Lord of Spirits. ² In those days the holy ones who dwell above in the heavens Shall unite with one voice And supplicate and pray [and praise, And give thanks and bless the name of the Lord of Spirits] On behalf of the blood of the righteous which has been shed, And that the prayer of the righteous may not be in vain before the Lord of Spirits, That judgement may be done unto them, And that they may not have to suffer for ever. ³ In those days I saw the Head of Days when He seated himself upon the throne of His glory, And the books of the living were opened before Him: And all His host which is in heaven above and His counselors stood before Him, ⁴ And the hearts of the holy were filled with joy;

Because the number of the righteous **had been offered**, And the prayer of the righteous had been heard, And the blood of the righteous been required before the Lord of Spirits.

## XLVIII. The Fount of Righteousness; the Son of Man–the Stay of the Righteous: Judgement of the Kings and the Mighty.

### 48

¹ And in that place I saw the fountain of righteousness Which was inexhaustible: And around it were many fountains of wisdom; And all the thirsty drank of them, And were filled with wisdom, And their dwellings were with the righteous and holy and elect. ² And at that hour that Son of Man was named In the presence of the Lord of Spirits, And his name before the Head of Days. ³ Yea, before the sun and the signs were created, Before the stars of the heaven were made, His name was named before the Lord of Spirits. ⁴ He shall be a staff to the righteous whereon to stay themselves and not fall, And he shall be the light of the Gentiles, And the hope of those who are troubled of heart. ⁵ All who dwell on earth shall fall down and worship before him, And will praise and bless and celebrate with song the Lord of Spirits. ⁶ And for this reason he hath been chosen and hidden before Him, Before the creation of the world and for evermore. ⁷ And the wisdom of the Lord of Spirits hath revealed him to the holy and righteous; For he hath preserved the lot of the righteous, Because they have hated and despised this world of unrighteousness, And have hated all its works and ways in the name of the Lord of Spirits: For in his name they are saved, And according to his good pleasure hath it been in regard to their life. ⁸ In these days downcast in countenance shall the kings of the earth have become, And the strong who possess the land because of the works of their hands; For on the day of their anguish and affliction they shall not (be able to) save themselves. ⁹ And I will give them over into the hands of Mine elect: As straw in the fire so shall they burn before the face of the holy: As lead in the water shall they sink before the face of the righteous, And no trace of them shall any more be found. ¹⁰ And on the day of their affliction there shall be rest on the earth, And before them they shall fall and not rise again: And there shall be no one to take them with his hands and raise them: For they have denied the Lord of Spirits and His Anointed. The name of the Lord of Spirits be blessed.

## XLIX. The Power and Wisdom of the Elect One.

### 49

l. For wisdom is poured out like water, And glory faileth not before him for evermore. ² For he is mighty in all the secrets of righteousness, And unrighteousness shall disappear as a shadow, And have no continuance; Because the Elect One standeth before the Lord of Spirits, And his glory is for ever and ever, And his might unto all generations. ³ And in him dwells the spirit of wisdom, And the spirit which gives insight, And the spirit of understanding and of might, And the spirit of those who have fallen asleep in righteousness. ⁴ And he shall judge the secret things, And none shall be able to utter a lying word before him; For he is the Elect One before the Lord of Spirits according to His good pleasure.

## L. The Glorification and Victory of the Righteous: the Repentance of the Gentiles.

### 50

¹ And in those days a change shall take place for the holy and elect, And the light of days shall abide upon them, And glory and honour shall turn to the holy, ² On the day of affliction on which evil shall have been treasured up against the sinners. And the righteous shall be victorious in the name of the Lord of Spirits: And He will cause the others to witness (this) That they may repent And forgo the works of their hands. ³ They shall have no honour through the name of the Lord of Spirits, Yet through His name shall they be saved, And the Lord of Spirits will have compassion on them, For His compassion is great. ⁴ And He is righteous also in His judgement, And in the presence of His glory unrighteousness also shall not maintain itself: At His judgement the unrepentant shall perish before Him. ⁵ And from henceforth I will have no mercy on them, saith the Lord of Spirits.

## LI. The Resurrection of the Dead, and the Separation by the Judge of the Righteous and the Wicked.

### 51

¹ And in those days shall the earth also give back that which has been entrusted to it, And Sheol also shall give back that which it has received, And hell shall give back that which it owes. ² And he shall choose the righteous and holy from among them: For the day has drawn nigh that they should be saved. ³ And the Elect One shall in those days sit on My throne, And his mouth shall **pour** forth all the secrets of wisdom and counsel: For the Lord of Spirits hath given (them) to him and hath glorified him. ⁴ And in those days shall the mountains leap like rams, And the hills also shall skip like lambs satisfied with milk, And the faces of [all] the angels in heaven shall be lighted up with joy. ⁵ a. For in those days the Elect One shall arise, ⁵ b. And the earth shall rejoice, c. And the righteous shall dwell upon it, d. And the elect shall walk thereon.

## LII. The Seven Metal Mountains and the Elect One.

### 52

l. And after those days in that place where I had seen all the visions of that which is hidden–for I had been carried off in a whirlwind and they had borne me towards the west— ² There mine eyes saw all the secret things of heaven that shall be, a mountain of iron, and a mountain of copper, and a mountain of silver, and a mountain of gold, and a mountain of soft metal, and a mountain of lead. ³ And I asked the angel who went with me, saying, 'What things are these which I have seen in secret?' ⁴ And he said unto me: 'All these things which thou hast seen shall serve the dominion of His Anointed that he may be potent and mighty on the earth.' ⁵ And that angel of peace answered, saying unto me: 'Wait a little, and there shall be revealed unto thee all the secret things which surround the Lord of Spirits. ⁶ And these mountains which thine eyes have seen, The mountain of iron, and the mountain of copper, and the mountain of silver, And the mountain of gold, and the mountain of soft metal, and the mountain of lead, All these shall be in the presence of the Elect One As wax: before the fire, And like the water which streams down from above [upon those mountains], And they shall become powerless before his feet. ⁷ And it shall come to pass in those days that none shall be saved, Either by gold or by silver, And none be able to escape. ⁸ And there shall be no iron for war, Nor shall one clothe oneself with a breastplate. Bronze shall be of no service, And tin [shall be of no service and] shall not be esteemed, And lead shall not be desired. ⁹ And all these things shall be [denied and] destroyed from the surface of the earth, When the Elect One shall appear before the face of the Lord of Spirits.'

## LIII. LVI. 6. The Valley of Judgement: the Angels of Punishment: the Communities of the Elect One.

### 53

¹ There mine eyes saw a deep valley with open mouths, and all who dwell on the earth and sea and islands shall bring to him gifts and presents and tokens of homage, but that deep valley shall not become full. ² And their hands commit lawless deeds, And the sinners devour all whom they lawlessly **oppress**: Yet the sinners shall be destroyed before the face of the Lord of Spirits, And they shall be banished from off the face of His earth, And they shall perish for ever and ever. ³ For I saw all the angels of punishment abiding (there) and preparing all the instruments of Satan. ⁴ And I asked the angel of peace who went with me: 'For whom are they preparing these instruments?' ⁵ And he said unto me: 'They prepare these for the kings and the mighty of this earth, that they may thereby be destroyed. ⁶ And after this the Righteous and Elect One shall cause the house of his congregation to appear: henceforth they shall be no more hindered in the name of the Lord of Spirits. ⁷ And these mountains shall not stand as the earth before his righteousness, But the hills shall be as a fountain of water, And the righteous shall have rest from the oppression of sinners.'

### 54

¹ And I looked and turned to another part of the earth, and saw there a deep valley with burning fire. ² And they brought the kings and the mighty, and began to cast them into this deep valley. ³ And there mine eyes saw how they made these their instruments, iron chains of immeasurable weight. ⁴ And I asked the angel of peace who went with me, saying: 'For whom are these chains being prepared?' ⁵ And he said unto me: 'These are being prepared for the hosts of Azâzêl, so that they may take them and cast them into the abyss of complete condemnation,

and they shall cover their jaws with rough stones as the Lord of Spirits commanded. **6** And Michael, and Gabriel, and Raphael, and Phanuel shall take hold of them on that great day, and cast them on that day into the burning furnace, that the Lord of Spirits may take vengeance on them for their unrighteousness in becoming subject to Satan and leading astray those who dwell on the earth.'

**LIV. 7.-LV 2. Noachic Fragment on the first World Judgement.**

**7** 'And in those days shall punishment come from the Lord of Spirits, and he will open all the chambers of waters which are above the heavens, and of the fountains which are beneath the earth. **8** And all the waters shall be joined with the waters: that which is above the heavens is the masculine, and the water which is beneath the earth is the feminine. **9** And they shall destroy all who dwell on the earth and those who dwell under the ends of the heaven. **10** And **when** they have recognized their unrighteousness which they have wrought on the earth, then by these shall they perish.

## 55

**1** And after that the Head of Days repented and said: 'In vain have I destroyed all who dwell on the earth.' **2** And He sware by His great name: 'Henceforth I will not do so to all who dwell on the earth, and I will set a sign in the heaven: and this shall be a pledge of good faith between Me and them for ever, so long as heaven is above the earth. And this is in accordance with My command.'

**LV. 3-LVI. 4. Final Judgement of Azâzêl, the Watchers and their children.**

**3** When I have desired to take hold of them by the hand of the angels on the day of tribulation and pain **because of** this, I will cause My chastisement and My wrath to abide upon them, saith God, the Lord of Spirits. **4** Ye †mighty kings† who dwell on the earth, ye shall have to behold Mine Elect One, how he sits on the throne of glory and judges Azâzêl, and all his associates, and all his hosts in the name of the Lord of Spirits.'

## 56

**1** And I saw there the hosts of the angels of punishment going, and they held scourges and chains of iron and bronze. **2** And I asked the angel of peace who went with me, saying: 'To whom are these who hold the scourges going?' **3** And he said unto me: 'To their elect and beloved ones, that they may be cast into the chasm of the abyss of the valley. **4** And then that valley shall be filled with their elect and beloved, And the days of their lives shall be at an end, And the days of their leading astray shall not thenceforward be reckoned.

**LVI. 5-8. Last struggle of heathen Powers against Israel.**

**5** And in those days the angels shall return And hurl themselves to the east upon the Parthians and Medes: They shall stir up the kings, so that a spirit of unrest shall come upon them, And they shall rouse them from their thrones, That they may break forth as lions from their lairs, And as hungry wolves among their flocks. **6** And they shall go up and tread under foot the land of His elect ones. [And the land of His elect ones shall be before them a threshing-floor and a highway:] **7** But the city of my righteous shall be a hindrance to their horses. And they shall begin to fight among themselves, And their right hand shall be strong against themselves, And a man shall not know his brother, Nor a son his father or his mother, Till there be no number of the corpses through their slaughter, And their punishment be not in vain. **8** In those days Sheol shall open its jaws, And they shall be swallowed up therein And their destruction shall be at an end; Sheol shall devour the sinners in the presence of the elect.'

**LVII. The Return from the Dispersion.**

## 57

**1** And it came to pass after this that I saw another host of wagons, and men riding thereon, and coming on the winds from the east, and from the west to the south. **2** And the noise of their wagons was heard, and when this turmoil took place the holy ones from heaven remarked it, and the pillars of the earth were moved from their place, and the sound thereof was heard from the one end of heaven to the other, in one day. **3** And they shall all fall down and worship the Lord of Spirits. And this is the end of the second Parable.

**LVIII-LXXI. The Third Parable.**
**LVIII. The Blessedness of the Saints.**

## 58

**1** And I began to speak the third Parable concerning the righteous and elect.
**2** Blessed are ye, ye righteous and elect, For glorious shall be your lot.
**3** And the righteous shall be in the light of the sun. And the elect in the light of eternal life: The days of their life shall be unending, And the days of the holy without number. **4** And they shall seek the light and find righteousness with the Lord of Spirits: There shall be peace to the righteous in the name of the Eternal Lord. **5** And after this it shall be said to the holy in heaven That they should seek out the secrets of righteousness, the heritage of faith: For it has become bright as the sun

upon earth, And the darkness is past. **6** And there shall be a light that never **endeth**, And to a limit (lit. 'number') of days they shall not come, For the darkness shall first have been destroyed, [And the light established before the Lord of Spirits] And the light of uprightness established for ever before the Lord of Spirits.

**LIX. The Lights and the Thunder.**

## 59

**1** [In those days mine eyes saw the secrets of the lightnings, and of the lights, and the judgements they execute (lit. 'their judgement'): and they lighten for a blessing or a curse as the Lord of Spirits willeth. **2** And there I saw the secrets of the thunder, and how when it resounds above in the heaven, the sound thereof is heard, and he caused me to see the judgements executed on the earth, whether they be for well-being and blessing, or for a curse according to the word of the Lord of Spirits. **3** And after that all the secrets of the lights and lightnings were shown to me, and they lighten for blessing and for satisfying.]

**LX. Book of Noah—a Fragment.**
**Quaking of Heaven: Behemoth and Leviathan: the Elements.**

## 60

**1** In the year five hundred, in the seventh month, on the fourteenth day of the month in the life of †Enoch†. In that Parable I saw how a mighty quaking made the heaven of heavens to quake, and the host of the Most High, and the angels, a thousand thousands and ten thousand times **ten** thousand, were disquieted with a great disquiet. **2** And the Head of Days sat on the throne of His glory, and the angels and the righteous stood around Him. **3** And a great trembling seized me, And fear took hold of me, And my loins gave way, And dissolved were my reins, And I fell upon my face. **4** And Michael sent another angel from among the holy ones and he raised me up, and when he had raised me up my spirit returned; for I had not been able to endure the look of this host, and the commotion and the quaking of the heaven. **5** And Michael said unto me: 'Why art thou disquieted with such a vision? Until this day lasted the day of His mercy; and He hath been merciful and long-suffering towards those who dwell on the earth. **6** And when the day, and the power, and the punishment, and the judgement come, which the Lord of Spirits hath prepared for those who worship not the righteous **law**, and for those who deny the righteous judgement, and for those who take His name in vain—that day is prepared, for the elect a covenant, but for sinners an inquisition. **7** And on that day were two monsters parted, a female monster named Leviathan, to dwell in the abysses of the ocean over the fountains of the waters. **8** But the male is named Behemoth, who occupied with his breast a waste wilderness named †Dûidâin†, on the east of the garden where the elect and righteous dwell, where my grandfather was taken up, the seventh from Adam, the first man whom the Lord of Spirits created. **9** And I besought the other angel that he should show me the might of those monsters, how they were parted on one day and cast, the one into the abysses of the sea, and the other unto the dry land of the wilderness. **10** And he said to me: 'Thou son of man, herein thou dost seek to know what is hidden.' **11** And the other angel who went with me and showed me what was hidden told me what is first and last in the heaven in the height, and beneath the earth in the depth, and at the ends of the heaven, and on the foundation of the heaven. **12** And the chambers of the winds, and how the winds are divided, and how they are weighed, and (how) the **portals** of the winds are reckoned, each according to the power of the wind, and the power of the lights of the moon, and according to the power that is fitting: and the divisions of the stars according to their names, and how all the divisions are divided. **13** And the thunders according to the places where they fall, and all the divisions that are made among the lightnings that it may lighten, and their host that they may at once obey. **14** For the thunder has †places of rest† (which) are assigned (to it) while it is waiting for its peal; and the thunder and lightning are inseparable, and although not one and undivided, they both go together through the spirit and separate not. **15** For when the lightning lightens, the thunder utters its voice, and the spirit enforces a pause during the peal, and divides equally between them; for the treasury of their peals is like the sand, and each one of them as it peals is held in with a bridle, and turned back by the power of the spirit, and pushed forward according to the many quarters of the earth. **16** And the spirit of the sea is masculine and strong, and according to the might of his strength he draws it back with a rein, and in like manner it is driven forward and disperses amid all the mountains of the earth. **17** And the spirit of the hoar-frost is his own angel, and the spirit of the hail is a good angel. **18** And the spirit of the snow has forsaken his chambers on account of his strength—There is a special spirit therein, and that which ascends from it is like smoke, and its name is frost. **19** And the spirit of the mist is not united with them in their chambers, but it has a special chamber; for its course is †glorious† both in light and in darkness, and in winter and in summer, and in its chamber is an angel. **20** And the spirit of the dew has its dwelling at the ends of the heaven, and is connected with the chambers of the rain, and its course is in winter and summer: and its clouds and the clouds of the mist are connected, and the one gives to the other. <sup>21</sup> And when the spirit of the rain goes forth from its chamber, the angels come and open the chamber and lead it out, and when it is diffused over the whole earth it unites with the water on the earth. And whensoever it unites with the water on the earth . . . <sup>22</sup> For the waters are for those who dwell on the earth; for they are nourishment for the earth from the Most High who is in heaven: therefore there is a measure for the rain, and the angels take it in charge. <sup>23</sup> And these things I saw towards the Garden of the Righteous. <sup>24</sup> And the angel of peace who was with me said to me: 'These two monsters, prepared conformably to the greatness of God, shall feed . . . <sup>25</sup> When the punishment of the Lord of Spirits shall rest upon them, it shall rest in order that the punishment of the Lord of Spirits may not come, in vain, and it shall slay the children with their mothers and the children with their fathers. Afterwards the judgement shall take place according to His mercy and His patience.'

**LXI. Angels go off to measure Paradise: the Judgement of the Righteous by the Elect One: the Praise of the Elect One and of God.**

## 61

<sup>1</sup> And I saw in those days how long cords were given to those angels, and they took to themselves wings and flew, and they went towards the north. <sup>2</sup> And I asked the angel, saying unto him: 'Why have those (angels) taken these cords and gone off?' And he said unto me: 'They have gone to measure.' <sup>3</sup> And the angel who went with me said unto me: 'These shall bring the measures of the righteous, And the ropes of the righteous to the righteous, That they may stay themselves on the name of the Lord of Spirits for ever and ever. <sup>4</sup> The elect shall begin to dwell with the elect, And those are the measures which shall be given to faith And which shall strengthen righteousness. <sup>5</sup> And these measures shall reveal all the secrets of the depths of the earth, And those who have been destroyed by the desert, And those who have been devoured by the beasts, And those who have been devoured by the fish of the sea, That they may return and stay themselves On the day of the Elect One; For none shall be destroyed before the Lord of Spirits, And none can be destroyed. <sup>6</sup> And all who dwell above in the heaven received a command and power and one voice and one light like unto fire. <sup>7</sup> And that One (with) their first words they blessed, And extolled and lauded with wisdom, And they were wise in utterance and in the spirit of life. <sup>8</sup> And the Lord of Spirits placed the Elect one on the throne of glory. And he shall judge all the works of the holy above in the heaven, And in the balance shall their deeds be weighed <sup>9</sup> And when he shall lift up his countenance To judge their secret ways according to the word of the name of the Lord of Spirits, And their path according to the way of the righteous judgement of the Lord of Spirits, Then shall they all with one voice speak and bless, And glorify and extol and sanctify the name of the Lord of Spirits. <sup>10</sup> And He will summon all the host of the heavens, and all the holy ones above, and the host of God, the Cherubic, Seraphin and Ophannin, and all the angels of power, and all the angels of principalities, and the Elect One, and the other powers on the earth (and) over the water. <sup>11</sup> On that day shall raise one voice, and bless and glorify and exalt in the spirit of faith, and in the spirit of wisdom, and in the spirit of patience, and in the spirit of mercy, and in the spirit of judgement and of peace, and in the spirit of goodness, and shall all say with one voice: "Blessed is He, and may the name of the Lord of Spirits be blessed for ever and ever." <sup>12</sup> All who sleep not above in heaven shall bless Him: All the holy ones who are in heaven shall bless Him, And all the elect who dwell in the garden of life: And every spirit of light who is able to bless, and glorify, and extol, and hallow Thy blessed name, And all flesh shall beyond measure glorify and bless Thy name for ever and ever. <sup>13</sup> For great is the mercy of the Lord of Spirits, and He is long-suffering, And all His works and all that He has created He has revealed to the righteous and elect In the name of the Lord of Spirits.

**LXII. Judgement of the Kings and the Mighty: Blessedness of the Righteous.**

## 62

<sup>1</sup> And thus the Lord commanded the kings and the mighty and the exalted, and those who dwell on the earth, and said: 'Open your eyes and lift up your horns if ye are able to recognize the Elect One.' <sup>2</sup> And the Lord of Spirits seated him on the throne of His glory, And the spirit of righteousness was poured out upon him, And the word of his mouth slays all the sinners, And all the unrighteous are destroyed from before his face. <sup>3</sup> And there shall stand up in that day all the kings and the mighty, And the exalted and those who hold the earth, And they shall see and recognize How he sits on the throne of his glory, And righteousness is judged before him, And no lying word is spoken before him. <sup>4</sup> Then shall pain come upon them as on a woman in travail, [And she has pain in bringing forth] When her child enters the mouth of the womb, And she has pain in bringing forth. <sup>5</sup> And one portion of them

shall look on the other, And they shall be terrified, And they shall be downcast of countenance, And pain shall seize them, When they see that Son of Man Sitting on the throne of his glory. <sup>6</sup> And the kings and the mighty and all who possess the earth shall bless and glorify and extol him who rules over all, who was hidden. <sup>7</sup> For from the beginning the Son of Man was hidden, And the Most High preserved him in the presence of His might, And revealed him to the elect. <sup>8</sup> And the congregation of the elect and holy shall be sown, And all the elect shall stand before him on that day. <sup>9</sup> And all the kings and the mighty and the exalted and those who rule the earth Shall fall down before him on their faces, And worship and set their hope upon that Son of Man, And petition him and supplicate for mercy at his hands. <sup>10</sup> Nevertheless that Lord of Spirits will so press them That they shall hastily go forth from His presence, And their faces shall be filled with shame, And the darkness grow deeper on their faces. <sup>11</sup> And **He will deliver** them to the angels for punishment, To execute vengeance on them because they have oppressed His children and His elect <sup>12</sup> And they shall be a spectacle for the righteous and for His elect: They shall rejoice over them, Because the wrath of the Lord of Spirits resteth upon them, And His sword is drunk with their blood. <sup>13</sup> And the righteous and elect shall be saved on that day, And they shall never thenceforward see the face of the sinners and unrighteous. <sup>14</sup> And the Lord of Spirits will abide over them, And with that Son of Man shall they eat And lie down and rise up for ever and ever. <sup>15</sup> And the righteous and elect shall have risen from the earth, And ceased to be of downcast countenance. And they shall have been clothed with garments of glory, <sup>16</sup> And these shall be the garments of life from the Lord of Spirits: And your garments shall not grow old, Nor your glory pass away before the Lord of Spirits.

**LXIII. The unavailing Repentance of the Kings and the Mighty.**

## 63

<sup>1</sup> In those days shall the mighty and the kings who possess the earth implore (Him) to grant them a little respite from His angels of punishment to whom they were delivered, that they might fall down and worship before the Lord of Spirits, and confess their sins before Him. <sup>2</sup> And they shall bless and glorify the Lord of Spirits, and say: 'Blessed is the Lord of Spirits and the Lord of kings, And the Lord of the mighty and the Lord of the rich, And the Lord of glory and the Lord of wisdom, <sup>3</sup> And splendid in every secret thing is Thy power from generation to generation, And Thy glory for ever and ever: Deep are all Thy secrets and innumerable, And Thy righteousness is beyond reckoning. <sup>4</sup> We have now learnt that we should glorify And bless the Lord of kings and Him who is king over all kings.' <sup>5</sup> And they shall say: 'Would that we had rest to glorify and give thanks And confess our faith before His glory! <sup>6</sup> And now we long for a little rest but find it not: We follow hard upon and obtain (it) not: And light has vanished from before us, And darkness is our dwelling-place for ever and ever: <sup>7</sup> For we have not believed before Him Nor glorified the name of the Lord of Spirits, [nor glorified our Lord] But our hope was in the sceptre of our kingdom, And in our glory. <sup>8</sup> And in the day of our suffering and tribulation He saves us not, And we find no respite for confession That our Lord is true in all His works, and in His judgements and His justice, And His judgements have no respect of persons. <sup>9</sup> And we pass away from before His face on account of our works, And all our sins are reckoned up in righteousness.' <sup>10</sup> Now they shall say unto themselves: 'Our souls are full of unrighteous gain, but it does not prevent us from descending from the midst thereof into the †burden† of Sheol.' <sup>11</sup> And after that their faces shall be filled with darkness And shame before that Son of Man, And they shall be driven from his presence, And the sword shall abide before his face in their midst. <sup>12</sup> Thus spake the Lord of Spirits: 'This is the ordinance and judgement with respect to the mighty and the kings and the exalted and those who possess the earth before the Lord of Spirits.'

**LXIV. Vision of the fallen Angels in the Place of Punishment.**

## 64

<sup>1</sup> And other forms I saw hidden in that place. <sup>2</sup> I heard the voice of the angel saying: 'These are the angels who descended to the earth, and revealed what was hidden to the children of men and seduced the children of men into committing sin.'

**LXV. Enoch foretells to Noah the Deluge and his own Preservation.**

## 65

<sup>1</sup> And in those days Noah saw the earth that it had sunk down and its destruction was nigh. <sup>2</sup> And he arose from thence and went to the ends of the earth, and cried aloud to his grandfather Enoch: and Noah said three times with an embittered voice: Hear me, hear me, hear me.' <sup>3</sup> And I said unto him: 'Tell me what it is that is falling out on the earth that the earth is in such evil plight and shaken, lest perchance I shall perish with it?' <sup>4</sup> And thereupon there was a great commotion on the earth, and a voice was heard from heaven, and I fell on my face. <sup>5</sup> And Enoch my grandfather came and stood by me, and said unto me: 'Why hast thou cried unto me with a bitter cry and weeping? <sup>6</sup> And a command

has gone forth from the presence of the Lord concerning those who dwell on the earth that their ruin is accomplished because they have learnt all the secrets of the angels, and all the violence of the Satans, and all their powers–the most secret ones–and all the power of those who practice sorcery, and the power of witchcraft, and the power of those who make molten images for the whole earth: ⁷ And how silver is produced from the dust of the earth, and how soft metal originates in the earth. ⁸ For lead and tin are not produced from the earth like the first: it is a fountain that produces them, and an angel stands therein, and that angel is pre-eminent.' ⁹ And after that my grandfather Enoch took hold of me by my hand and raised me up, and said unto me: 'Go, for I have asked the Lord of Spirits as touching this commotion on the earth. ¹⁰ And He said unto me: "Because of their unrighteousness their judgement has been determined upon and shall not be **withheld** by Me for ever. Because of the **sorceries** which they have searched out and learnt, the earth and those who dwell upon it shall be destroyed." ¹¹ And these–they have no **place of repentance** for ever, because they have shown them what was hidden, and they are the damned: but as for thee, my son, the Lord of Spirits knows that thou art pure, and guiltless of this reproach concerning the secrets. ¹² And He has destined thy name to be among the holy, And will preserve thee amongst those who dwell on the earth, And has destined thy righteous seed both for kingship and for great honours, And from thy seed shall proceed a fountain of the righteous and holy without number for ever.

### LXVI. The Angels of the Waters bidden to hold them in Check.

#### 66

¹ And after that he showed me the angels of punishment who are prepared to come and let loose all the powers of the waters which are beneath in the earth in order to bring judgement and destruction on all who [abide and] dwell on the earth. ² And the Lord of Spirits gave commandment to the angels who were going forth, that they should not cause **the waters** to rise but should hold them in check; for those angels were over the powers of the waters. ³ And I went away from the presence of Enoch.

### LXVII. God's Promise to Noah: Places of Punishment of the Angels and of the Kings.

#### 67

¹ And in those days the word of God came unto me, and He said unto me: 'Noah, thy lot has come up before Me, a lot without blame, a lot of love and uprightness. ² And now the angels are making a wooden (building), and when they have completed that task I will place My hand upon it and preserve it, and there shall come forth from it the seed of life, and a change shall set in so that the earth will not remain without inhabitant. ³ And I will make fast thy seed before me for ever and ever, and I will spread abroad those who dwell with thee: it shall not be **unfruitful** on the face of the earth, but it shall be blessed and multiply on the earth in the name of the Lord.' ⁴ And He will imprison those angels, who have shown unrighteousness, in that burning valley which my grandfather Enoch had formerly shown to me in the west among the mountains of gold and silver and iron and soft metal and tin. ⁵ And I saw that valley in which there was a great convulsion and a convulsion of the waters. ⁶ And when all this took place, from that fiery molten metal and from the convulsion thereof in that place, there was produced a smell of sulphur, and it was connected with those waters, and that valley of the angels who had led astray (mankind) burned beneath that land. ⁷ And through its valleys proceed streams of fire, where these angels are punished who had led astray those who dwell upon the earth. ⁸ But these waters shall in those days serve for the kings and the mighty and the exalted, and those who dwell on the earth, for the healing of the body, but for the punishment of the spirit; now their spirit is full of lust, that they may be punished in their body, for they have denied the Lord of Spirits and see their punishment daily, and yet believe not in His name. ⁹ And in proportion as the burning of their bodies becomes severe, a corresponding change shall take place in their spirit for ever and ever; for before the Lord of Spirits none shall utter an idle word. ¹⁰ For the judgement shall come upon them, because they believe in the lust of their body and deny the Spirit of the Lord. ¹¹ And those same waters will undergo a change in those days; for when those angels are punished in these waters, these water-springs shall change their temperature, and when the angels ascend, this water of the springs shall change and become cold. ¹² And I heard Michael answering and saying: 'This judgement wherewith the angels are judged is a testimony for the kings and the mighty who possess the earth.' ¹³ Because these waters of judgement minister to the healing of the body of the **kings** and the lust of their body; therefore they will not see and will not believe that those waters will change and become a fire which burns for ever.

### LXVIII. Michael and Raphael astonished at the Severity of the Judgement.

#### 68

¹ And after that my grandfather Enoch gave me the teaching of all the secrets in the book in the Parables which had been given to him, and he put them together for me in the words of the book of the Parables. ² And on that day Michael answered Raphael and said: 'The power of the spirit transports and **makes me to tremble** because of the severity of the judgement of the secrets, the judgement of the angels: who can endure the severe judgement which has been executed, and before which they melt away?' ³ And Michael answered again, and said to Raphael: 'Who is he whose heart is not softened concerning it, and whose reins are not troubled by this word of judgement (that) has gone forth upon them because of those who have thus led them out?' ⁴ And it came to pass when he stood before the Lord of Spirits, Michael said thus to Raphael: 'I will not take their part under the eye of the Lord; for the Lord of Spirits has been angry with them because they do as if they were the Lord. ⁵ Therefore all that is hidden shall come upon them for ever and ever; for neither angel nor man shall have his portion (in it), but alone they have received their judgement for ever and ever.'

### LXIX. The Names and Functions of the (fallen Angels and) Satans: the secret Oath.

#### 69

¹ And after this judgement they shall terrify and **make** them **to tremble** because they have shown this to those who dwell on the earth. ² And behold the names of those angels [and these are their names: the first of them is Samjâzâ, the second Artâqîfâ, and the third Armên, the fourth Kôkabêl, the fifth †Tûrâêl†, the sixth Rûmjâl, the seventh Dânjâl, the eighth †Nêqâêl†, the ninth Barâqêl, the tenth Azâzêl, the eleventh Armârôs, the twelfth Batarjâl, the thirteenth †Busasêjal†, the fourteenth Hanânêl, the fifteenth †Tûrêl†, and the sixteenth Sîmâpêsîêl, the seventeenth Jetrêl, the eighteenth Tûmâêl, the nineteenth Tûrêl, the twentieth †Rumâêl†, the twenty-first †Azâzêl†. ³ And these are the chiefs of their angels and their names, and their chief ones over hundreds and over fifties and over tens]. ⁴ The name of the first Jeqôn: that is, the one who led astray [all] the sons of **God**, and brought them down to the earth, and led them astray through the daughters of men. ⁵ And the second was named Asbeêl: he imparted to the holy sons of **God** evil counsel, and led them astray so that they defiled their bodies with the daughters of men. ⁶ And the third was named Gâdreêl: he it is who showed the children of men all the blows of death, and he led astray Eve, and showed [the weapons of death to the sons of men] the shield and the coat of mail, and the sword for battle, and all the weapons of death to the children of men. ⁷ And from his hand they have proceeded against those who dwell on the earth from that day and for evermore. ⁸ And the fourth was named Pênêmûe: he taught the children of men the bitter and the sweet, and he taught them all the secrets of their wisdom. ⁹ And he instructed mankind in writing with ink and paper, and thereby many sinned from eternity to eternity and until this day. ¹⁰ For men were not created for such a purpose, to give confirmation to their good faith with pen and ink. ¹¹ For men were created exactly like the angels, to the intent that they should continue pure and righteous, and death, which destroys everything, could not have taken hold of them, but through this their knowledge they are perishing, and through this power it is consuming me†. ¹² And the fifth was named Kâsdejâ: this is he who showed the children of men all the wicked smitings of spirits and demons, and the smitings of the embryo in the womb, that it may pass away, and [the smitings of the soul] the bites of the serpent, and the smitings which befall through the noontide heat, the son of the serpent named Tabââ'ĕt. ¹³ And this is the **task** of Kâsbeêl, the chief of the oath which he showed to the holy ones when he dwelt high above in glory, and its name is Bîqâ. ¹⁴ This (angel) requested Michael to show him the hidden name, that he might enunciate it in the oath, so that those might quake before that name and oath who revealed all that was in secret to the children of men. ¹⁵ And this is the power of this oath, for it is powerful and strong, and he placed this oath Akâe in the hand of Michael. ¹⁶ And these are the secrets of this oath . . . And they are strong through his oath: And the heaven was suspended before the world was created, And for ever. ¹⁷ And through it the earth was founded upon the water, And from the secret recesses of the mountains come beautiful waters, From the creation of the world and unto eternity. ¹⁸ And through that oath the sea was created, And †as its foundation† He set for it the sand against the time of (its) anger, And it dare not pass beyond it from the creation of the world unto eternity. ¹⁹ And through that oath are the depths made fast, And abide and stir not from their place from eternity to eternity. ²⁰ And through that oath the sun and moon complete their course, And deviate not from their ordinance from eternity to eternity. ²¹ And through that oath the stars complete their course, And He calls them by their names, And they answer Him from eternity to eternity. ²² [And in like manner the spirits of the water, and of the winds, and of all zephyrs, and (their) paths from all the quarters of the winds. ²³ And there are preserved the voices of the thunder and the light of the lightnings: and there are preserved the

chambers of the hail and the chambers of the hoarfrost, and the chambers of the mist, and the chambers of the rain and the dew. ²⁴ And all these believe and give thanks before the Lord of Spirits, and glorify (Him) with all their power, and their food is in every act of thanksgiving: they thank and glorify and extol the name of the Lord of Spirits for ever and ever.] ²⁵ And this oath is mighty over them And through it [they are preserved and] their paths are preserved, And their course is not destroyed.

### Close of the Third Parable.

²⁶ And there was great joy amongst them, And they blessed and glorified and extolled Because the name of that Son of Man had been revealed unto them. ²⁷ And he sat on the throne of his glory, And the sum of judgement was given unto the Son of Man, And he caused the sinners to pass away and be destroyed from off the face of the earth, And those who have led the world astray. ²⁸ With chains shall they be bound, And in their assemblage-place of destruction shall they be imprisoned, And all their works vanish from the face of the earth. ²⁹ And from henceforth there shall be nothing corruptible; For that Son of Man has appeared, And has seated himself on the throne of his glory, And all evil shall pass away before his face, And the word of that Son of Man shall go forth And be strong before the Lord of Spirits. This is the Third Parable of Enoch.

### LXX. The Final Translation of Enoch.

## 70

¹ And it came to pass after this that his name during his lifetime was raised aloft to that Son of Man and to the Lord of Spirits from amongst those who dwell on the earth. ² And he was raised aloft on the chariots of the spirit and his name vanished among them. ³ And from that day I was no longer numbered amongst them: and he set me between the two winds, between the North and the West, where the angels took the cords to measure for me the place for the elect and righteous. ⁴ And there I saw the first fathers and the righteous who from the beginning dwell in that place.

### LXXI. Two earlier visions of Enoch.

## 71

¹ And it came to pass after this that my spirit was translated And it ascended into the heavens: And I saw the **holy sons of God**. They were stepping on flames of fire: Their garments were white [and their raiment], And their faces shone like snow. ² And I saw two streams of fire, And the light of that fire shone like hyacinth, And I fell on my face before the Lord of Spirits. ³ And the angel Michael [one of the archangels] seized me by my right hand, And lifted me up and led me forth into all the secrets, And he showed me all the secrets of righteousness. ⁴ And he showed me all the secrets of the ends of the heaven, And all the chambers of all the stars, and all the luminaries, Whence they proceed before the face of the holy ones. ⁵ And he translated my spirit into the heaven of heavens, And I saw there as it were a structure built of crystals, And between those crystals tongues of living fire. ⁶ And my spirit saw the girdle which girt that house of fire, And on its four sides were streams full of living fire, And they girt that house. ⁷ And round about were Seraphin, Cherubic, and Ophannin: And these are they who sleep not And guard the throne of His glory. ⁸ And I saw angels who could not be counted, A thousand thousands, and ten thousand times ten thousand, Encircling that house. And Michael, and Raphael, and Gabriel, and Phanuel, And the holy angels who are above the heavens, Go in and out of that house. ⁹ And they came forth from that house, And Michael and Gabriel, Raphael and Phanuel, And many holy angels without number. ¹⁰ And with them the Head of Days, His head white and pure as wool, And His raiment indescribable. ¹¹ And I fell on my face, And my whole body became relaxed, And my spirit was transfigured; And I cried with a loud voice, . . .with the spirit of power, And blessed and glorified and extolled. ¹² And these blessings which went forth out of my mouth were well pleasing before that Head of Days. ¹³ And that Head of Days came with Michael and Gabriel, Raphael and Phanuel, thousands and ten thousands of angels without number. [Lost passage wherein the Son of Man was described as accompanying the Head of Days, and Enoch asked one of the angels (as in **46:3**) concerning the Son of Man as to who he was.] ¹⁴ And he (*i.e.* the angel) came to me and greeted me with His voice, and said unto me: '**This is** the Son of Man who is born unto righteousness; And righteousness abides over him, And the righteousness of the Head of Days forsakes him not.' ¹⁵ And he said unto me: 'He proclaims unto thee peace in the name of the world to come; For from hence has proceeded peace since the creation of the world, And so shall it be unto thee for ever and for ever and ever. ¹⁶ And all shall walk in **his** ways since righteousness never forsaketh **him**: With **him** will be their dwelling-places, and with **him** their heritage, And they shall not be separated from him for ever and ever and ever. ¹⁷ And so there shall be length of days with that Son of Man, And the righteous shall have peace and an upright way In the name of the Lord of Spirits for ever and ever.'

## LXXII-LXXXII. The Book of the Courses of the Heavenly Luminaries.

### LXXII. The Sun.

## 72

¹ The book of the courses of the luminaries of the heaven, the relations of each, according to their classes, their dominion and their seasons, according to their names and places of origin, and according to their months, which Uriel, the holy angel, who was with me, who is their guide, showed me; and he showed me all their laws exactly as they are, and how it is with regard to all the years of the world and unto eternity, till the new creation is accomplished which dureth till eternity. ² And this is the first law of the luminaries: the luminary the Sun has its rising in the eastern portals of the heaven, and its setting in the western portals of the heaven. ³ And I saw six portals in which the sun rises, and six portals in which the sun sets and the moon rises and sets in these portals, and the leaders of the stars and those whom they lead: six in the east and six in the west, and all following each other in accurately corresponding order: also many windows to the right and left of these portals. ⁴ And first there goes forth the great luminary, named the Sun, and his circumference is like the circumference of the heaven, and he is quite filled with illuminating and heating fire. ⁵ The chariot on which he ascends, the wind drives, and the sun goes down from the heaven and returns through the north in order to reach the east, and is so guided that he comes to the appropriate (lit. 'that') portal and shines in the face of the heaven. ⁶ In this way he rises in the first month in the great portal, which is the fourth [those six portals in the cast]. ⁷ And in that fourth portal from which the sun rises in the first month are twelve window-openings, from which proceed a flame when they are opened in their season. ⁸ When the sun rises in the heaven, he comes forth through that fourth portal thirty mornings in succession, and sets accurately in the fourth portal in the west of the heaven. ⁹ And during this period the day becomes daily longer and the night nightly shorter to the thirtieth morning. ¹⁰ On that day the day is longer than the night by a ninth part, and the day amounts exactly to ten parts and the night to eight parts. ¹¹ And the sun rises from that fourth portal, and sets in the fourth and returns to the fifth portal of the east thirty mornings, and rises from it and sets in the fifth portal. ¹² And then the day becomes longer by †two† parts and amounts to eleven parts, and the night becomes shorter and amounts to seven parts. ¹³ And it returns to the east and enters into the sixth portal, and rises and sets in the sixth portal one-and-thirty mornings on account of its sign. ¹⁴ On that day the day becomes longer than the night, and the day becomes double the night, and the day becomes twelve parts, and the night is shortened and becomes six parts. ¹⁵ And the sun mounts up to make the day shorter and the night longer, and the sun returns to the east and enters into the sixth portal, and rises from it and sets thirty mornings. ¹⁶ And when thirty mornings are accomplished, the day decreases by exactly one part, and becomes eleven parts, and the night seven. ¹⁷ And the sun goes forth from that sixth portal in the west, and goes to the east and rises in the fifth portal for thirty mornings, and sets in the west again in the fifth western portal. ¹⁸ On that day the day decreases by †two† parts, and amounts to ten parts and the night to eight parts. ¹⁹ And the sun goes forth from that fifth portal and sets in the fifth portal of the west, and rises in the fourth portal for one-and-thirty mornings on account of its sign, and sets in the west. ²⁰ On that day the day is equalized with the night, [and becomes of equal length], and the night amounts to nine parts and the day to nine parts. ²¹ And the sun rises from that portal and sets in the west, and returns to the east and rises thirty mornings in the third portal and sets in the west in the third portal. ²² And on that day the night becomes longer than the day, and night becomes longer than night, and day shorter than day till the thirtieth morning, and the night amounts exactly to ten parts and the day to eight parts. ²³ And the sun rises from that third portal and sets in the third portal in the west and returns to the east, and for thirty mornings rises in the second portal in the east, and in like manner sets in the second portal in the west of the heaven. ²⁴ And on that day the night amounts to eleven parts and the day to seven parts. ²⁵ And the sun rises on that day from that second portal and sets in the west in the second portal, and returns to the east into the first portal for one-and-thirty mornings, and sets in the first portal in the west of the heaven. ²⁶ And on that day the night becomes longer and amounts to the double of the day: and the night amounts exactly to twelve parts and the day to six. ²⁷ And the sun has (therewith) traversed the divisions of his orbit and turns again on those divisions of his orbit, and enters that portal thirty mornings and sets also in the west opposite to it. ²⁸ And on that night has the night decreased in length by a †ninth† part, and the night has become eleven parts and the day seven parts. ²⁹ And the sun has returned and entered into the second portal in the east, and returns on those his divisions of his orbit for thirty mornings, rising and setting. ³⁰ And on that day the night decreases in length, and the night amounts to ten parts and the day to eight. ³¹ And on that day the sun

rises from that portal, and sets in the west, and returns to the east, and rises in the third portal for one-and-thirty mornings, and sets in the west of the heaven. [32] On that day the night decreases and amounts to nine parts, and the day to nine parts, and the night is equal to the day and the year is exactly as to its days three hundred and sixty-four. [33] And the length of the day and of the night, and the shortness of the day and of the night arise–through the course of the sun these distinctions are made (lit. 'they are separated'). [34] So it comes that its course becomes daily longer, and its course nightly shorter. [35] And this is the law and the course of the sun, and his return as often as he returns sixty times and rises, *i.e.* the great luminary which is named the sun, for ever and ever. [36] And that which (thus) rises is the great luminary, and is so named according to its appearance, according as the Lord commanded. [37] As he rises, so he sets and decreases not, and rests not, but runs day and night, and his light is sevenfold brighter than that of the moon; but as regards size they are both equal.

## 73

[1] And after this law I saw another law dealing with the smaller luminary, which is named the Moon. [2] And her circumference is like the circumference of the heaven, and her chariot in which she rides is driven by the wind, and light is given to her in (definite) measure. [3] And her rising and setting change every month: and her days are like the days of the sun, and when her light is uniform (*i.e.* full) it amounts to the seventh part of the light of the sun. [4] And thus she rises. And her first phase in the east comes forth on the thirtieth morning: and on that day she becomes visible, and constitutes for you the first phase of the moon on the thirtieth day together with the sun in the portal where the sun rises. [5] And the one half of her goes forth by a seventh part, and her whole circumference is empty, without light, with the exception of one-seventh part of it, (and) the fourteenth part of her light. [6] And when she receives one-seventh part of the half of her light, her light amounts to one-seventh part and the half thereof. [7] And she sets with the sun, and when the sun rises the moon rises with him and receives the half of one part of light, and in that night in the beginning of her morning [in the commencement of the lunar day] the moon sets with the sun, and is invisible that night with the fourteen parts and the half of one of them. [8] And she rises on that day with exactly a seventh part, and comes forth and recedes from the rising of the sun, and in her remaining days she becomes bright in the (remaining) thirteen parts.

## 74

[1] And I saw another course, a law for her, (and) how according to that law she performs her monthly revolution. [2] And all these Uriel, the holy angel who is the leader of them all, showed to me, and their positions, and I wrote down their positions as he showed them to me, and I wrote down their months as they were, and the appearance of their lights till fifteen days were accomplished. [3] In single seventh parts she accomplishes all her light in the east, and in single seventh parts accomplishes all her darkness in the west. [4] And in certain months she alters her settings, and in certain months she pursues her own peculiar course. [5] In two months the moon sets with the sun: in those two middle portals the third and the fourth. [6] She goes forth for seven days, and turns about and returns again through the portal where the sun rises, and accomplishes all her light: and she recedes from the sun, and in eight days enters the sixth portal from which the sun goes forth. [7] And when the sun goes forth from the fourth portal she goes forth seven days, until she goes forth from the fifth and turns back again in seven days into the fourth portal and accomplishes all her light: and she recedes and enters into the first portal in eight days. [8] And she returns again in seven days into the fourth portal from which the sun goes forth. [9] Thus I saw their position–how the moons rose and the sun set in those days. [10] And if five years are added together the sun has an overplus of thirty days, and all the days which accrue to it for one of those five years, when they are full, amount to 364 days. [11] And the overplus of the sun and of the stars amounts to six days: in 5 years 6 days every year come to 30 days: and the moon falls behind the sun and stars to the number of 30 days. [12] And the sun and the stars bring in all the years exactly, so that they do not advance or delay their position by a single day unto eternity; but complete the years with perfect justice in 364 days. [13] In 3 years there are 1092 days, and in 5 years 1820 days, so that in 8 years there are 2912 days. [14] For the moon alone the days amount in 3 years to 1062 days, and in 5 years she falls 50 days behind: [i.e. to the sum (of 1770) there is to be added (1000 and) 62 days.] [15] And in 5 years there are 1770 days, so that for the moon the days in 8 years amount to 2832 days. [16] [For in 8 years she falls behind to the amount of 80 days], all the days she falls behind in 8 years are 80. [17] And the year is accurately completed in conformity with their world-stations and the stations of the sun, which rise from the portals through which it (the sun) rises and sets 30 days.

## 75

[1] And the leaders of the heads of the thousands, who are placed over the whole creation and over all the stars, have also to do with the four intercalary days, being inseparable from their office, according to the reckoning of the year, and these render service on the four days which are not reckoned in the reckoning of the year. [2] And owing to them men go wrong therein, for those luminaries truly render service on the world-stations, one in the first portal, one in the third portal of the heaven, one in the fourth portal, and one in the sixth portal, and the exactness of the year is accomplished through its separate three hundred and sixty-four stations. [3] For the signs and the times and the years and the days the angel Uriel showed to me, whom the Lord of glory hath set for ever over all the luminaries of the heaven, in the heaven and in the world, that they should rule on the face of the heaven and be seen on the earth, and be leaders for the day and the night, *i.e.* the sun, moon, and stars, and all the ministering creatures which make their revolution in all the chariots of the heaven. [4] In like manner twelve doors Uriel showed me, open in the circumference of the sun's chariot in the heaven, through which the rays of the sun break forth: and from them is warmth diffused over the earth, when they are opened at their appointed seasons. [5] [And for the winds and the spirit of the dew when they are opened, standing open in the heavens at the ends.] [6] As for the twelve portals in the heaven, at the ends of the earth, out of which go forth the sun, moon, and stars, and all the works of heaven in the east and in the west. [7] There are many windows open to the left and right of them, and one window at its (appointed) season produces warmth, corresponding (as these do) to those doors from which the stars come forth according as He has commanded them, and wherein they set corresponding to their number. [8] And I saw chariots in the heaven, running in the world, above those portals in which revolve the stars that never set. [9] And one is larger than all the rest, and it is that that makes its course through the entire world.

## LXXVI. The Twelve Windows and their Portals.

## 76

[1] And at the ends of the earth I saw twelve portals open to all the **quarters** (of the heaven), from which the winds go forth and blow over the earth. [2] Three of them are open on the face (*i.e.* the east) of the heavens, and three in the west, and three on the right (*i.e.* the south) of the heaven, and three on the left (*i.e.* the north). [3] And the three first are those of the east, and three are of †the north, and three [after those on the left] of the south†, and three of the west. [4] Through four of these come winds of blessing and prosperity, and from those eight come hurtful winds: when they are sent, they bring destruction on all the earth and on the water upon it, and on all who dwell thereon, and on everything which is in the water and on the land. [5] And the first wind from those portals, called the east wind, comes forth through the first portal which is in the east, inclining towards the south: from it come forth desolation, drought, heat, and destruction. [6] And through the second portal in the middle comes what is fitting, and from it there come rain and fruitfulness and prosperity and dew; and through the third portal which lies toward the north come cold and drought. [7] And after these come forth the south winds through three portals: through the first portal of them inclining to the east comes forth a hot wind. [8] And through the middle portal next to it there come forth fragrant smells, and dew and rain, and prosperity and health. [9] And through the third portal lying to the west come forth dew and rain, locusts and desolation. [10] And after these the north winds: from the seventh portal in the east come dew and rain, locusts and desolation. [11] And from the middle portal come in a direct direction health and rain and dew and prosperity; and through the third portal in the west come cloud and hoar-frost, and snow and rain, and dew and locusts. [12] And after these [four] are the west winds: through the first portal adjoining the north come forth dew and hoar-frost, and cold and snow and frost. [13] And from the middle portal come forth dew and rain, and prosperity and blessing; and through the last portal which adjoins the south come forth drought and desolation, and burning and destruction. [14] And the twelve portals of the four **quarters** of the heaven are therewith completed, and all their laws and all their plagues and all their benefactions have I shown to thee, my son Methuselah.

## LXXVII. The Four Quarters of the World; the Seven Mountains, the Seven Rivers, etc.

## 77

[1] And the first **quarter** is called the east, because it is the first: and the second, the south, because the Most High **will descend** there, yea, there in quite a special sense will He who is blessed for ever **descend**. [2] And the west **quarter** is named the diminished, because there all the luminaries of the heaven wane and go down. [3] And the fourth **quarter**, named the north, is divided into three parts: the first of them is for the dwelling of men: and the second contains seas of water, and the abysses and forests and rivers, and darkness and clouds; and the third part contains the garden of righteousness. [4] I saw seven high mountains,

higher than all the mountains which are on the earth: and thence comes forth hoar-frost, and days, seasons, and years pass away. ⁵ I saw seven rivers on the earth larger than all the rivers: one of them coming from the west pours its waters into the Great Sea. ⁶ And these two come from the north to the sea and pour their waters into the Erythraean Sea in the east. ⁷ And the remaining four come forth on the side of the north to their own sea, <two of them> to the Erythraean Sea, and two into the Great Sea and discharge themselves there [and some say: into the desert]. ⁸ Seven great islands I saw in the sea and in the mainland: two in the mainland and five in the Great Sea.

## LXXVIII. The Sun and Moon; the Waxing and Waning of the Moon.

### 78

¹ And the names of the sun are the following: the first Orjârês, and the second Tômâs. ² And the moon has four names: the first name is Asônjâ, the second Eblâ, the third Benâsê, and the fourth Erâe. ³ These are the two great luminaries: their circumference is like the circumference of the heaven, and the size of the circumference of both is alike. ⁴ In the circumference of the sun there are seven portions of light which are added to it more than to the moon, and in definite measures it is s transferred till the seventh portion of the sun is exhausted. ⁵ And they set and enter the portals of the west, and make their revolution by the north, and come forth through the eastern portals on the face of the heaven. ⁶ And when the moon rises one-fourteenth part appears in the heaven: [the light becomes full in her]: on the fourteenth day she accomplishes her light. ⁷ And fifteen parts of light are transferred to her till the fifteenth day (when) her light is accomplished, according to the sign of the year, and she becomes fifteen parts, and the moon grows by (the addition of) fourteenth parts. ⁸ And in her waning (the moon) decreases on the first day to fourteen parts of her light, on the second to thirteen parts of light, on the third to twelve, on the fourth to eleven, on the fifth to ten, on the sixth to nine, on the seventh to eight, on the eighth to seven, on the ninth to six, on the tenth to five, on the eleventh to four, on the twelfth to three, on the thirteenth to two, on the fourteenth to the half of a seventh, and all her remaining light disappears wholly on the fifteenth. ⁹ And in certain months the month has twenty-nine days and once twenty-eight. ¹⁰ And Uriel showed me another law: when light is transferred to the moon, and on which side it is transferred to her by the sun. ¹¹ During all the period during which the moon is growing in her light, she is transferring it to herself when opposite to the sun during fourteen days [her light is accomplished in the heaven], and when she is illumined throughout, her light is accomplished full in the heaven. ¹² And on the first day she is called the new moon, for on that day the light rises upon her. ¹³ She becomes full moon exactly on the day when the sun sets in the west, and from the east she rises at night, and the moon shines the whole night through till the sun rises over against her and the moon is seen over against the sun. ¹⁴ On the side whence the light of the moon comes forth, there again she wanes till all the light vanishes and all the days of the month are at an end, and her circumference is empty, void of light. ¹⁵ And three months she makes of thirty days, and at her time she makes three months of twenty-nine days each, in which she accomplishes her waning in the first period of time, and in the first portal for one hundred and seventy-seven days. ¹⁶ And in the time of her going out she appears for three months (of) thirty days each, and for three months she appears (of) twenty-nine each. ¹⁷ At night she appears like a man for twenty days each time, and by day she appears like the heaven, and there is nothing else in her save her light.

## LXXIX-LXXX. 1. Recapitulation of several of the Laws.

### 79

¹ And now, my son, I have shown thee everything, and the law of all the stars of the heaven is completed. ² And he showed me all the laws of these for every day, and for every season of bearing rule, and for every year, and for its going forth, and for the order prescribed to it every month and every week: ³ And the waning of the moon which takes place in the sixth portal: for in this sixth portal her light is accomplished, and after that there is the beginning of the waning: ⁴ <And the waning> which takes place in the first portal in its season, till one hundred and seventy-seven days are accomplished: reckoned according to weeks, twenty-five (weeks) and two days. ⁵ She falls behind the sun and the order of the stars exactly five days in the course of one period, and when this place which thou seest has been traversed. ⁶ Such is the picture and sketch of every luminary which Uriel the archangel, who is their leader, showed unto me.

### 80

¹ And in those days the angel Uriel answered and said to me: 'Behold, I have shown thee everything, Enoch, and I have revealed everything to thee that thou shouldst see this sun and this moon, and the leaders of the stars of the heaven and all those who turn them, their tasks and times and departures.

## LXXX. 2-8. Perversion of Nature and the heavenly Bodies owning to the Sin of Men.

² And in the days of the sinners the years shall be shortened, And their seed shall be tardy on their lands and fields, And all things on the earth shall alter, And shall not appear in their time: And the rain shall be kept back And the heaven shall withhold (it). ³ And in those times the fruits of the earth shall be backward, And shall not grow in their time, And the fruits of the trees shall be withheld in their time. ⁴ And the moon shall alter her order, And not appear at her time. ⁵ [And in those days the **sun** shall be seen and he shall journey in the **evening** †on the extremity of the great chariot† in the west] And shall shine more brightly than accords with the order of light. ⁶ And many chiefs of the stars shall transgress the order (prescribed). And these shall alter their orbits and tasks, And not appear at the seasons prescribed to them. ⁷ And the whole order of the stars shall be concealed from the sinners, And the thoughts of those on the earth shall err concerning them, [And they shall be altered from all their ways], Yea, they shall err and take them to be gods. ⁸ And evil shall be multiplied upon them, And punishment shall come upon them So as to destroy all.'

## LXXXI. The Heavenly Tablets and the Mission of Enoch.

### 81

¹ And he said unto me: 'Observe, Enoch, these heavenly tablets, And read what is written thereon, And mark every individual fact.' ² And I observed the heavenly tablets, and read everything which was written (thereon) and understood everything, and read the book of all the deeds of mankind, and of all the children of flesh that shall be upon the earth to the remotest generations. ³ And forthwith I blessed the great Lord the King of glory for ever, in that He has made all the works of the world, And I extolled the Lord because of His patience, And blessed Him because of the children of men. ⁴ And after that I said: 'Blessed is the man who dies in righteousness and goodness, Concerning whom there is no book of unrighteousness written, And against whom no day of judgement shall be found.' ⁵ And those seven holy ones brought me and placed me on the earth before the door of my house, and said to me: 'Declare everything to thy son Methuselah, and show to all thy children that no flesh is righteous in the sight of the Lord, for He is their Creator. ⁶ One year we will leave thee with thy son, till thou givest thy (last) commands, that thou mayest teach thy children and record (it) for them, and testify to all thy children; and in the second year they shall take thee from their midst. ⁷ Let thy heart be strong, For the good shall announce righteousness to the good; The righteous with the righteous shall rejoice, And shall offer congratulation to one another. ⁸ But the sinners shall die with the sinners, And the apostate go down with the apostate. ⁹ And those who practice righteousness shall die on account of the deeds of men, And be taken away on account of the doings of the godless.' ¹⁰ And in those days they ceased to speak to me, and I came to my people, blessing the Lord of the world.

## LXXXII. Charge given to Enoch; the four Intercalary Days; the Stars which lead the Seasons and the Months.

### 82

¹ And now, my son Methuselah, all these things I am recounting to thee and writing down for thee, and I have revealed to thee everything, and given thee books concerning all these: so preserve, my son Methuselah, the books from thy father's hand, and (see) that thou deliver them to the generations of the world. ² I have given Wisdom to thee and to thy children, [And thy children that shall be to thee], That they may give it to their children for generations, This wisdom (namely) that passeth their thought. ³ And those who understand it shall not sleep, But shall listen with the ear that they may learn this wisdom, And it shall please those that eat thereof better than good food. ⁴ Blessed are all the righteous, blessed are all those who walk in the way of righteousness and sin not as the sinners, in the reckoning of all their days in which the sun traverses the heaven, entering into and departing from the portals for thirty days with the heads of thousands of the order of the stars, together with the four which are intercalated which divide the four portions of the year, which lead them and enter with them four days. ⁵ Owing to them men shall be at fault and not reckon them in the **whole reckoning of the year**: yea, men shall be at fault, and not recognize them accurately. ⁶ For they belong to the reckoning of the year and are truly recorded (thereon) for ever, one in the first portal and one in the third, and one in the fourth and one in the sixth, and the year is completed in three hundred and sixty-four days. ⁷ And the account thereof is accurate and the recorded reckoning thereof exact; for the luminaries, and months and festivals, and years and days, has Uriel shown and revealed to me, **to whom** the Lord of the whole creation of the world hath **subjected** the host of heaven. ⁸ And he has power over night and day in the heaven to cause the light to give light to men–sun, moon, and stars, and all the powers of the heaven which revolve in their circular chariots. ⁹ And these are the orders of the stars, which set in their places, and in their seasons and festivals and months. ¹⁰ And these

are the names of those who lead them, who watch that they enter at their times, in their orders, in their seasons, in their months, in their periods of dominion, and in their positions. <sup>11</sup> Their four leaders who divide the four parts of the year enter first; and after them the twelve leaders of the orders who divide the months; and for the three hundred and sixty (days) there are heads over thousands who divide the days; and for the four intercalary days there are the leaders which sunder the four parts of the year. <sup>12</sup> And these heads over thousands are intercalated between leader and leader, each behind a station, but their leaders make the division. <sup>13</sup> And these are the names of the leaders who divide the four parts of the year which are ordained: Mîlkî'êl, Hel'emmêlêk, and Mêl'êjal, and Nârêl. <sup>14</sup> And the names of those who lead them: Adnâr'êl, and Îjâsûsa'êl, and 'Elômê'êl–these three follow the leaders of the orders, and there is one that follows the three leaders of the orders which follow those leaders of stations that divide the four parts of the year. <sup>15</sup> In the beginning of the year Melkejâl rises first and rules, who is named †Tam'âinî† and sun, and all the days of his dominion whilst he bears rule are ninety-one days. <sup>16</sup> And these are the signs of the days which are to be seen on earth in the days of his dominion: sweat, and heat, and calms; and all the trees bear fruit, and leaves are produced on all the trees, and the harvest of wheat, and the rose-flowers, and all the flowers which come forth in the field, but the trees of the winter season become withered. <sup>17</sup> And these are the names of the leaders which are under them: Berka'êl, Zêlebs'êl, and another who is added a head of a thousand, called Hîlûjâsĕph: and the days of the dominion of this (leader) are at an end. <sup>18</sup> The next leader after him is Hêl'emmêlêk, whom one names the shining sun, and all the days of his light are ninety-one days. <sup>19</sup> And these are the signs of (his) days on the earth: glowing heat and dryness, and the trees ripen their fruits and produce all their fruits ripe and ready, and the sheep pair and become pregnant, and all the fruits of the earth are gathered in, and everything that is in the fields, and the winepress: these things take place in the days of his dominion. <sup>20</sup> These are the names, and the orders, and the leaders of those heads of thousands: Gîdâ'îjal, Kê'êl, and Hê'êl, and the name of the head of a thousand which is added to them, Asfâ'êl': and the days of his dominion are at an end.

## LXXXIII-XC. The Dream-Visions.
## LXXXIII. LXXXIV. First Dream-Vision on the Deluge.
### 83

<sup>1</sup> And now, my son Methuselah, I will show thee all my visions which I have seen, recounting them before thee. <sup>2</sup> Two visions I saw before I took a wife, and the one was quite unlike the other: the first when I was learning to write: the second before I took thy mother, (when) I saw a terrible vision. And regarding them I prayed to the Lord. <sup>3</sup> I had laid me down in the house of my grandfather Mahalalel, (when) I saw in a vision how the heaven collapsed and was borne off and fell to the earth. <sup>4</sup> And when it fell to the earth I saw how the earth was swallowed up in a great abyss, and mountains were suspended on mountains, and hills sank down on hills, and high trees were rent from their stems, and hurled down and sunk in the abyss. <sup>5</sup> And thereupon a word fell into my mouth, and I lifted up (my voice) to cry aloud, and said: 'The earth is destroyed.' <sup>6</sup> And my grandfather Mahalalel waked me as I lay near him, and said unto me: 'Why dost thou cry so, my son, and why dost thou make such lamentation?' <sup>7</sup> And I recounted to him the whole vision which I had seen, and he said unto me: 'A terrible thing hast thou seen, my son, and of grave moment is thy dream-vision as to the secrets of all the sin of the earth: it must sink into the abyss and be destroyed with a great destruction. <sup>8</sup> And now, my son, arise and make petition to the Lord of glory, since thou art a believer, that a remnant may remain on the earth, and that He may not destroy the whole earth. <sup>9</sup> My son, from heaven all this will come upon the earth, and upon the earth there will be great destruction. <sup>10</sup> After that I arose and prayed and implored and besought, and wrote down my prayer for the generations of the world, and I will show everything to thee, my son Methuselah. <sup>11</sup> And when I had gone forth below and seen the heaven, and the sun rising in the east, and the moon setting in the west, and a few stars, and the whole earth, and everything as †He had known† it in the beginning, then I blessed the Lord of judgement and extolled Him because He had made the sun to go forth from the windows of the east, and he ascended and rose on the face of the heaven, and set out and kept traversing the path shown unto him.

### 84

<sup>1</sup> And I lifted up my hands in righteousness and blessed the Holy and Great One, and spake with the breath of my mouth, and with the tongue of flesh, which God has made for the children of the flesh of men, that they should speak therewith; and He gave them breath and a tongue and a mouth that they should speak therewith: <sup>2</sup> 'Blessed be Thou, O Lord, King, Great and mighty in Thy greatness, Lord of the whole creation of the heaven, King of kings and God of the whole world. And Thy power and kingship and greatness abide for ever and ever, And throughout all generations Thy dominion; And all the heavens are Thy throne for ever, And the whole earth Thy footstool for ever and ever. <sup>3</sup> For Thou hast made and Thou rulest all things, And nothing is too hard for Thee, Wisdom departs not **from the place of Thy throne**, **Nor turns away** from Thy presence. And Thou knowest and seest and hearest everything, And there is nothing hidden from Thee [for Thou seest everything]. <sup>4</sup> And now the angels of Thy heavens are guilty of trespass, And upon the flesh of men abideth Thy wrath until the great day of judgement. <sup>5</sup> And now, O God and Lord and Great King, I implore and beseech Thee to fulfil my prayer, To leave me a posterity on earth, And not destroy all the flesh of man, And make the earth without inhabitant, So that there should be an eternal destruction. <sup>6</sup> And now, my Lord, destroy from the earth the flesh which has aroused Thy wrath, But the flesh of righteousness and uprightness establish as a plant of the eternal seed, And hide not Thy face from the prayer of Thy servant, O Lord.'

### 85
## LXXXV-XC. The Second Dream-Vision of Enoch: the History of the World to the Founding of the Messianic Kingdom.

<sup>1</sup> And after this I saw another dream, and I will show the whole dream to thee, my son. <sup>2</sup> And Enoch lifted up (his voice) and spake to his son Methuselah: 'To thee, my son, will I speak: hear my words–incline thine ear to the dream-vision of thy father. <sup>3</sup> Before I took thy mother Edna, I saw in a vision on my bed, and behold a bull came forth from the earth, and that bull was white; and after it came forth a heifer, and along with this (latter) came forth two bulls, one of them black and the other red. <sup>4</sup> And that black bull gored the red one and pursued him over the earth, and thereupon I could no longer see that red bull. <sup>5</sup> But that black bull grew and that heifer went with him, and I saw that many oxen proceeded from him which resembled and followed him. <sup>6</sup> And that cow, that first one, went from the presence of that first bull in order to seek that red one, but found him not, and lamented with a great lamentation over him and sought him. <sup>7</sup> And I looked till that first bull came to her and quieted her, and from that time onward she cried no more. <sup>8</sup> And after that she bore another white bull, and after him she bore many bulls and black cows. <sup>9</sup> And I saw in my sleep that white bull likewise grow and become a great white bull, and from Him proceeded many white bulls, and they resembled him. And they began to beget many white bulls, which resembled them, one following the other, (even) many.

## LXXXVI. The Fall of the Angels and the Demoralization of Mankind.
### 86

<sup>1</sup> And again I saw with mine eyes as I slept, and I saw the heaven above, and behold a star fell from heaven, and it arose and eat and pastured amongst those oxen. <sup>2</sup> And after that I saw the large and the black oxen, and behold they all changed their stalls and pastures and their cattle, and began to live with each other. <sup>3</sup> And again I saw in the vision, and looked towards the heaven, and behold I saw many stars descend and cast themselves down from heaven to that first star, and they became bulls amongst those cattle and pastured with them [amongst them]. <sup>4</sup> And I looked at them and saw, and behold they all let out their privy members, like horses, and began to cover the cows of the oxen, and they all became pregnant and bare elephants, camels, and asses. <sup>5</sup> And all the oxen feared them and were affrighted at them, and began to bite with their teeth and to devour, and to gore with their horns. <sup>6</sup> And they began, moreover, to devour those oxen; and behold all the children of the earth began to tremble and quake before them and to flee from them.

## LXXXVII. The Advent of the Seven Archangels.
### 87

<sup>1</sup> And again I saw how they began to gore each other and to devour each other, and the earth began to cry aloud. <sup>2</sup> And I raised mine eyes again to heaven, and I saw in the vision, and behold there came forth from heaven beings who were like white men: and four went forth from that place and three with them. <sup>3</sup> And those three that had last come forth grasped me by my hand and took me up, away from the generations of the earth, and raised me up to a lofty place, and showed me a tower raised high above the earth, and all the hills were lower. <sup>4</sup> And one said unto me: 'Remain here till thou seest everything that befalls those elephants, camels, and asses, and the stars and the oxen, and all of them.'

## LXXXVIII. The Punishment of the Fallen Angels by the Archangels.
### 88

<sup>1</sup> And I saw one of those four who had come forth first, and he seized that first star which had fallen from the heaven, and bound it hand and foot and cast it into an abyss: now that abyss was narrow and deep, and horrible and dark. <sup>2</sup> And one of them drew a sword, and gave it to those elephants and camels and asses: then they began to smite each other, and the whole earth quaked because of them. <sup>3</sup> And as I was beholding

in the vision, lo, one of those four who had come forth stoned (them) from heaven, and gathered and took all the great stars whose privy members were like those of horses, and bound them all hand and foot, and cast them in an abyss of the earth.

## LXXXIX. 1-9. The Deluge and the Deliverance of Noah.

### 89

¹ And one of those four went to that white bull and instructed him in a secret, without his being terrified: he was born a bull and became a man, and built for himself a great vessel and dwelt thereon; and three bulls dwelt with him in that vessel and they were covered in. ² And again I raised mine eyes towards heaven and saw a lofty roof, with seven water torrents thereon, and those torrents flowed with much water into an enclosure. ³ And I saw again, and behold fountains were opened on the surface of that great enclosure, and that water began to swell and rise upon the surface, and I saw that enclosure till all its surface was covered with water. ⁴ And the water, the darkness, and mist increased upon it; and as I looked at the height of that water, that water had risen above the height of that enclosure, and was streaming over that enclosure, and it stood upon the earth. ⁵ And all the cattle of that enclosure were gathered together until I saw how they sank and were swallowed up and perished in that water. ⁶ But that vessel floated on the water, while all the oxen and elephants and camels and asses sank to the bottom with all the animals, so that I could no longer see them, and they were not able to escape, (but) perished and sank into the depths. ⁷ And again I saw in the vision till those water torrents were removed from that high roof, and the chasms of the earth were levelled up and other abysses were opened. ⁸ Then the water began to run down into these, till the earth became visible; but that vessel settled on the earth, and the darkness retired and light appeared. ⁹ But that white bull which had become a man came out of that vessel, and the three bulls with him, and one of those three was white like that bull, and one of them was red as blood, and one black: and that white bull departed from them.

## LXXXIX. 10-27. From the Death of Noah to the Exodus.

¹⁰ And they began to bring forth beasts of the field and birds, so that there arose different genera: lions, tigers, wolves, dogs, hyenas, wild boars, foxes, squirrels, swine, falcons, vultures, kites, eagles, and ravens; and among them was born a white bull. ¹¹ And they began to bite one another; but that white bull which was born amongst them begat a wild ass and a white bull with it, and the wild asses multiplied. ¹² But that bull which was born from him begat a black wild boar and a white sheep; and the former begat many boars, but that sheep begat twelve sheep. ¹³ And when those twelve sheep had grown, they gave up one of them to the asses, and those asses again gave up that sheep to the wolves, and that sheep grew up among the wolves. ¹⁴ And the Lord brought the eleven sheep to live with it and to pasture with it among the wolves: and they multiplied and became many flocks of sheep. ¹⁵ And the wolves began to fear them, and they oppressed them until they destroyed their little ones, and they cast their young into a river of much water: but those sheep began to cry aloud on account of their little ones, and to complain unto their Lord. ¹⁶ And a sheep which had been saved from the wolves fled and escaped to the wild asses; and I saw the sheep how they lamented and cried, and besought their Lord with all their might, till that Lord of the sheep descended at the voice of the sheep from a lofty abode, and came to them and pastured them. ¹⁷ And He called that sheep which had escaped the wolves, and spake with it concerning the wolves that it should admonish them not to touch the sheep. ¹⁸ And the sheep went to the wolves according to the word of the Lord, and another sheep met it and went with it, and the two went and entered together into the assembly of those wolves, and spake with them and admonished them not to touch the sheep from henceforth. ¹⁹ And thereupon I saw the wolves, and how they oppressed the sheep exceedingly with all their power; and the sheep cried aloud. ²⁰ And the Lord came to the sheep and they began to smite those wolves: and the wolves began to make lamentation; but the sheep became quiet and forthwith ceased to cry out. ²¹ And I saw the sheep till they departed from amongst the wolves; but the eyes of the wolves were blinded, and those wolves departed in pursuit of the sheep with all their power. ²² And the Lord of the sheep went with them, as their leader, and all His sheep followed Him: and his face was dazzling and glorious and terrible to behold. ²³ But the wolves began to pursue those sheep till they reached a sea of water. ²⁴ And that sea was divided, and the water stood on this side and on that before their face, and their Lord led them and placed Himself between them and the wolves. ²⁵ And as those wolves did not yet see the sheep, they proceeded into the midst of that sea, and the wolves followed the sheep, and [those wolves] ran after them into that sea. ²⁶ And when they saw the Lord of the sheep, they turned to flee before His face, but that sea gathered itself together, and became as it had been created, and the water swelled and rose till it covered those wolves. ²⁷ And I saw till all the wolves who pursued those sheep perished and were drowned.

## LXXXIX. 28-40. Israel in the Desert, the Giving of the Law, the Entrance into Palestine.

²⁸ But the sheep escaped from that water and went forth into a wilderness, where there was no water and no grass; and they began to open their eyes and to see; and I saw the Lord of the sheep pasturing them and giving them water and grass, and that sheep going and leading them. ²⁹ And that sheep ascended to the summit of that lofty rock, and the Lord of the sheep sent it to them. ³⁰ And after that I saw the Lord of the sheep who stood before them, and His appearance was great and terrible and majestic, and all those sheep saw Him and were afraid before His face. ³¹ And they all feared and trembled because of Him, and they cried to that sheep with them [which was amongst them]: "We are not able to stand before our Lord or to behold Him." ³² And that sheep which led them again ascended to the summit of that rock, but the sheep began to be blinded and to wander from the way which he had showed them, but that sheep wot not thereof. ³³ And the Lord of the sheep was wrathful exceedingly against them, and that sheep discovered it, and went down from the summit of the rock, and came to the sheep, and found the greatest part of them blinded and fallen away. ³⁴ And when they saw it they feared and trembled at its presence, and desired to return to their folds. ³⁵ And that sheep took other sheep with it, and came to those sheep which had fallen away, and began to slay them; and the sheep feared its presence, and thus that sheep brought back those sheep that had fallen away, and they returned to their folds. ³⁶ And I saw in this vision till that sheep became a man and built a house for the Lord of the sheep, and placed all the sheep in that house. ³⁷ And I saw till this sheep which had met that sheep which led them fell asleep: and I saw till all the great sheep perished and little ones arose in their place, and they came to a pasture, and approached a stream of water. ³⁸ Then that sheep, their leader which had become a man, withdrew from them and fell asleep, and all the sheep sought it and cried over it with a great crying. ³⁹ And I saw till they left off crying for that sheep and crossed that stream of water, and there arose the two sheep as leaders in the place of those which had led them and fallen asleep (lit. "had fallen asleep and led them"). ⁴⁰ And I saw till the sheep came to a goodly place, and a pleasant and glorious land, and I saw till those sheep were satisfied; and that house stood amongst them in the pleasant land.

## LXXXIX. 41-50. From the Time of the Judges till the Building of the Temple.

⁴¹ And sometimes their eyes were opened, and sometimes blinded, till another sheep arose and led them and brought them all back, and their eyes were opened. ⁴² And the dogs and the foxes and the wild boars began to devour those sheep till the Lord of the sheep raised up [another sheep] a ram from their midst, which led them. ⁴³ And that ram began to butt on either side those dogs, foxes, and wild boars till he had destroyed them †all†. ⁴⁴ And that sheep whose eyes were opened saw that ram, which was amongst the sheep, **till** it †forsook its glory† and began to butt those sheep, and trampled upon them, and behaved itself unseemly. ⁴⁵ And the Lord of the sheep sent the **lamb** to another **lamb** and raised it to being a ram and leader of the sheep instead of that ram which had †forsaken its glory†. ⁴⁶ And it went to it and spake to it alone, and raised it to being a ram, and made it the prince and leader of the sheep; but during all these things those dogs oppressed the sheep. ⁴⁷ And the first ram pursued that second ram, and that second ram arose and fled before it; and I saw till those dogs pulled down the first ram. ⁴⁸ And that second ram arose and led the [little] sheep. ⁴⁹ And those sheep grew and multiplied; but all the dogs, and foxes, and wild boars feared and fled before it, and that ram butted and killed the wild beasts, and those wild beasts had no longer any power among the sheep and robbed them no more of ought. ⁴⁸ ᵇ. And that ram begat many sheep and fell asleep; and a little sheep became ram in its stead, and became prince and leader of those sheep. ⁵⁰ And that house became great and broad, and it was built for those sheep: (and) a tower lofty and great was built on the house for the Lord of the sheep, and that house was low, but the tower was elevated and lofty, and the Lord of the sheep stood on that tower and they offered a full table before Him.

## LXXXIX. 51-67. The Two Kingdoms of Israel and Judah, to the Destruction of Jerusalem.

⁵¹ And again I saw those sheep that they again erred and went many ways, and forsook that their house, and the Lord of the sheep called some from amongst the sheep and sent them to the sheep, but the sheep began to slay them. ⁵² And one of them was saved and was not slain, and it sped away and cried aloud over the sheep; and they sought to slay it, but the Lord of the sheep saved it from the sheep, and brought it up to me, and caused it to dwell there. ⁵³ And many other sheep He sent to those sheep to testify unto them and lament over them. ⁵⁴ And after that I saw that when they forsook the house of the Lord and His tower they fell away entirely, and their eyes were blinded; and I saw the Lord of the sheep how He wrought much slaughter amongst them in their herds

until those sheep invited that slaughter and betrayed His place. ⁵⁵ And He gave them over into the hands of the lions and tigers, and wolves and hyenas, and into the hand of the foxes, and to all the wild beasts, and those wild beasts began to tear in pieces those sheep. ⁵⁶ And I saw that He forsook that their house and their tower and gave them all into the hand of the lions, to tear and devour them, into the hand of all the wild beasts. ⁵⁷ And I began to cry aloud with all my power, and to appeal to the Lord of the sheep, and to represent to Him in regard to the sheep that they were devoured by all the wild beasts. ⁵⁸ But He remained unmoved, though He saw it, and rejoiced that they were devoured and swallowed and robbed, and left them to be devoured in the hand of all the beasts. ⁵⁹ And He called seventy shepherds, and cast those sheep to them that they might pasture them, and He spake to the shepherds and their companions: "Let each individual of you pasture the sheep henceforward, and everything that I shall command you that do ye. ⁶⁰ And I will deliver them over unto you duly numbered, and tell you which of them are to be destroyed–and them destroy ye." And He gave over unto them those sheep. ⁶¹ And He called another and spake unto him: "Observe and mark everything that the shepherds will do to those sheep; for they will destroy more of them than I have commanded them. ⁶² And every excess and the destruction which will be wrought through the shepherds, record (namely) how many they destroy according to my command, and how many according to their own caprice: record against every individual shepherd all the destruction he effects. ⁶³ And read out before me by number how many they destroy, and how many they deliver over for destruction, that I may have this as a testimony against them, and know every deed of the shepherds, that I may **comprehend** and see what they do, whether or not they abide by my command which I have commanded them. ⁶⁴ But they shall not know it, and thou shalt not declare it to them, nor admonish them, but only record against each individual all the destruction which the shepherds effect each in his time and lay it all before me." ⁶⁵ And I saw till those shepherds pastured in their season, and they began to slay and to destroy more than they were bidden, and they delivered those sheep into the hand of the lions. ⁶⁶ And the lions and tigers eat and devoured the greater part of those sheep, and the wild boars eat along with them; and they burnt that tower and demolished that house. ⁶⁷ And I became exceedingly sorrowful over that tower because that house of the sheep was demolished, and afterwards I was unable to see if those sheep entered that house.

**LXXXIX. 68-71. First Period of the Angelic Rulers–from the Destruction of Jerusalem to the Return from the Captivity.**

⁶⁸ And the shepherds and their associates delivered over those sheep to all the wild beasts, to devour them, and each one of them received in his time a definite number: it was written by the other in a book how many each one of them destroyed of them. ⁶⁹ And each one slew and destroyed many more than was prescribed; and I began to weep and lament on account of those sheep. ⁷⁰ And thus in the vision I saw that one who wrote, how he wrote down every one that was destroyed by those shepherds, day by day, and carried up and laid down and showed actually the whole book to the Lord of the sheep–(even) everything that they had done, and all that each one of them had made away with, and all that they had given over to destruction. ⁷¹ And the book was read before the Lord of the sheep, and He took the book from his hand and read it and sealed it and laid it down.

**LXXXIX. 72-77. Second Period–from the time of Cyrus to that of Alexander the Great.**

⁷² And forthwith I saw how the shepherds pastured for twelve hours, and behold three of those sheep turned back and came and entered and began to build up all that had fallen down of that house; but the wild boars tried to hinder them, but they were not able. ⁷³ And they began again to build as before, and they reared up that tower, and it was named the high tower; and they began again to place a table before the tower, but all the bread on it was polluted and not pure. ⁷⁴ And as touching all this the eyes of those sheep were blinded so that they saw not, and (the eyes of) their shepherds likewise; and they delivered them in large numbers to their shepherds for destruction, and they trampled the sheep with their feet and devoured them. ⁷⁵ And the Lord of the sheep remained unmoved till all the sheep were dispersed over the field and mingled with them (*i.e.* the beasts), and they (*i.e.* the shepherds) did not save them out of the hand of the beasts. ⁷⁶ And this one who wrote the book carried it up, and showed it and read it before the Lord of the sheep, and implored Him on their account, and besought Him on their account as he showed Him all the doings of the shepherds, and gave testimony before Him against all the shepherds. And he took the actual book and laid it down beside Him and departed.

**XC. 1-5. Third Period–from Alexander the Great to the Graeco-Syrian Domination.**

¹ And I saw till that in this manner thirty-five shepherds undertook the pasturing (of the sheep), and they severally completed their periods as did the first; and others received them into their hands, to pasture them for their period, each shepherd in his own period. ² And after that I saw in my vision all the birds of heaven coming, the eagles, the vultures, the kites, the ravens; but the eagles led all the birds; and they began to devour those sheep, and to pick out their eyes and to devour their flesh. ³ And the sheep cried out because their flesh was being devoured by the birds, and as for me I looked and lamented in my sleep over that shepherd who pastured the sheep. ⁴ And I saw until those sheep were devoured by the dogs and eagles and kites, and they left neither flesh nor skin nor sinew remaining on them till only their bones stood there: and their bones too fell to the earth and the sheep became few. ⁵ And I saw until that twenty-three had undertaken the pasturing and completed in their several periods fifty-eight times.

**XC. 6-12. Fourth Period–from the Graeco-Syrian Domination to the Maccabæan Revolt.**

⁶ But behold lambs were borne by those white sheep, and they began to open their eyes and to see, and to cry to the sheep. ⁷ Yea, they cried to them, but they did not hearken to what they said to them, but were exceedingly deaf, and their eyes were very exceedingly blinded. ⁸ And I saw in the vision how the ravens flew upon those lambs and took one of those lambs, and dashed the sheep in pieces and devoured them. ⁹ And I saw till horns grew upon those lambs, and the ravens cast down their horns; and I saw till there sprouted a great horn of one of those sheep, and their eyes were opened. ¹⁰ And it †looked at† them [and their eyes opened], and it cried to the sheep, and the rams saw it and all ran to it. ¹¹ And notwithstanding all this those eagles and vultures and ravens and kites still kept tearing the sheep and swooping down upon them and devouring them: still the sheep remained silent, but the rams lamented and cried out. ¹² And those ravens fought and battled with it and sought to lay low its horn, but they had no power over it.

**XC. 13-19. The Last Assault of the Gentiles on the Jews (where vv. 13-15 and 16-18 are doublets).**

¹³ And I saw till the †shepherds and† eagles and those vultures and kites came, and †they cried to the ravens† that they should break the horn of that ram, and they battled and fought with it, and it battled with them and cried that its help might come.

¹⁶ All the eagles and vultures and ravens and kites were gathered together, and there came with them all the sheep of the field, yea, they all came together, and helped each other to break that horn of the ram.

¹⁴ And I saw till that man, who wrote down the names of the shepherds [and] carried up into the presence of the Lord of the sheep [came and helped it and showed it everything: he had come down for the help of that ram].

¹⁷ And I saw that man, who wrote the book according to the command of the Lord, till he opened that book concerning the destruction which those twelve last shepherds had wrought, and showed that they had destroyed much more than their predecessors, before the Lord of the sheep.

¹⁵ And I saw till the Lord of the sheep came unto them in wrath, and all who saw Him fled, and they all fell †into His shadow† from before His face.

¹⁸ And I saw till a great sword was given to the sheep, and the sheep proceeded against all the beasts of the field to slay them, and all the beasts and the birds of the heaven fled before their face.

¹⁹ And I saw till the Lord of the sheep came unto them and took in His hand the staff of His wrath, and smote the earth, and the earth clave asunder, and all the beasts and all the birds of the heaven fell from among those sheep, and were swallowed up in the earth and it covered them.

**XC. 20-27. Judgement of the Fallen Angels, the Shepherds, and the Apostates.**

²⁰ And I saw till a throne was erected in the pleasant land, and the Lord of the sheep sat Himself thereon, and **the other** took the sealed books and opened those books before the Lord of the sheep. ²¹ And the Lord called those men the seven first white ones, and commanded that they should bring before Him, beginning with the first star which led the way, **all the** stars whose privy members were like those of horses, and they brought them all before Him. ²² And He said to that man who wrote before Him, being one of those seven white ones, and said unto him: "Take those seventy shepherds to whom I delivered the sheep, and who taking them on their own authority slew more than I commanded them." ²³ And behold they were all bound, I saw, and they all stood before

Him. <sup>24</sup> And the judgement was held first over the stars, and they were judged and found guilty, and went to the place of condemnation, and they were cast into an abyss, full of fire and flaming, and full of pillars of fire. <sup>25</sup> And those seventy shepherds were judged and found guilty, and they were cast into that fiery abyss. <sup>26</sup> And I saw at that time how a like abyss was opened in the midst of the earth, full of fire, and they brought those blinded sheep, and they were all judged and found guilty and cast into this fiery abyss, and they burned; now this abyss was to the right of that house. <sup>27</sup> And I saw those sheep burning †and their bones burning†.

## XC. 28-38. The New Jerusalem, the Conversion of the surviving Gentiles, the Resurrection of the Righteous, the Messiah.

<sup>28</sup> And I stood up to see till they folded up that old house; and carried off all the pillars, and all the beams and ornaments of the house were at the same time folded up with it, and they carried it off and laid it in a place in the south of the land. <sup>29</sup> And I saw till the Lord of the sheep brought a new house greater and loftier than that first, and set it up in the place of the first which had beer folded up: all its pillars were new, and its ornaments were new and larger than those of the first, the old one which He had taken away, and all the sheep were within it. <sup>30</sup> And I saw all the sheep which had been left, and all the beasts on the earth, and all the birds of the heaven, falling down and doing homage to those sheep and making petition to and obeying them in every **thing**. <sup>31</sup> And thereafter those three who were clothed in white and had seized me by my hand [who had taken me up before], and the hand of that ram also seizing hold of me, they took me up and set me down in the midst of those sheep before the judgement took place. <sup>32</sup> And those sheep were all white, and their wool was abundant and clean. <sup>33</sup> And all that had been destroyed and dispersed, and all the beasts of the field, and all the birds of the heaven, assembled in that house, and the Lord of the sheep rejoiced with great joy because they were all good and had returned to His house. <sup>34</sup> And I saw till they laid down that sword, which had been given to the sheep, and they brought it back into the house, and it was sealed before the presence of the Lord, and all the sheep were invited into that house, but it held them not. <sup>35</sup> And the eyes of them all were opened, and they saw the good, and there was not one among them that did not see. <sup>36</sup> And I saw that that house was large and broad and very full. <sup>37</sup> And I saw that a white bull was born, with large horns and all the beasts of the field and all the birds of the air feared him and made petition to him all the time. <sup>38</sup> And I saw till all their generations were transformed, and they all became white bulls; and the first among them became a **lamb**, and that **lamb** became a great animal and had great black horns on its head; and the Lord of the sheep rejoiced over **it** and over all the oxen. <sup>39</sup> And I slept in their midst: and I awoke and saw everything. <sup>40</sup> This is the vision which I saw while I slept, and I awoke and blessed the Lord of righteousness and gave Him glory. <sup>41</sup> Then I wept with a great weeping and my tears stayed not till I could no longer endure it: when I saw, they flowed on account of what I had seen; for everything shall come and be fulfilled, and all the deeds of men in their order were shown to me. <sup>42</sup> On that night I remembered the first dream, and because of it I wept and was troubled–because I had seen that vision.'

## XCI. 1-11. Enoch's Admonition to his Children.

### 91

<sup>1</sup> 'And now, my son Methuselah, call to me all thy brothers And gather together to me all the sons of thy mother; For the word calls me, And the spirit is poured out upon me, That I may show you everything That shall befall you for ever.' <sup>2</sup> And there upon Methuselah went and summoned to him all his brothers and assembled his relatives. <sup>3</sup> And he spake unto all the children of righteousness and said: 'Hear, ye sons of Enoch, all the words of your father, And hearken aright to the voice of my mouth; For I exhort you and say unto you, beloved: Love uprightness and walk therein. <sup>4</sup> And draw not nigh to uprightness with a double heart, And associate not with those of a double heart, But walk in righteousness, my sons. And it shall guide you on good paths, And righteousness shall be your companion. <sup>5</sup> For I know that violence **must** increase on the earth, And a great chastisement be executed on the earth, And all unrighteousness come to an end: Yea, it shall be cut off from its roots, And its whole structure be destroyed. <sup>6</sup> And unrighteousness shall again be consummated on the earth, And all the deeds of unrighteousness and of violence And transgression shall prevail in a twofold degree. <sup>7</sup> And when sin and unrighteousness and blasphemy And violence in all kinds of deeds increase, And apostasy and transgression and uncleanness increase, A great chastisement shall come from heaven upon all these, And the holy Lord will come forth with wrath and chastisement To execute judgement on earth. <sup>8</sup> In those days violence shall be cut off from its roots, And the roots of unrighteousness together with deceit, And they shall be destroyed from under heaven. <sup>9</sup> And all the idols of the heathen shall be abandoned, And the temples burned with fire, And they shall remove them from the whole earth, And they (i.e. the heathen) shall be cast into the judgement of fire, And shall perish in wrath and in grievous judgement for ever. <sup>10</sup> And the righteous shall arise from their sleep, And wisdom shall arise and be given unto them. <sup>11</sup> [And after that the roots of unrighteousness shall be cut off, and the sinners shall be destroyed by the sword . . . shall be cut off from the blasphemers in every place, and those who plan violence and those who commit blasphemy shall perish by the sword.]

## XCI. 12.- 17 The Last Three Weeks.

<sup>12</sup> And after that there shall be another, the eighth week, that of righteousness, And a sword shall be given to it that a righteous judgement may be executed on the oppressors, And sinners shall be delivered into the hands of the righteous. <sup>13</sup> And at its close they shall acquire houses through their righteousness, And a house shall be built for the Great King in glory for evermore, <sup>14</sup> a And after that, in the ninth week, the righteous judgement shall be revealed to the whole world, b And all the works of the godless shall vanish from all the earth, c And the world shall be written down for destruction. d. And all mankind shall look to the path of uprightness. <sup>15</sup> And after this, in the tenth week in the seventh part, There shall be the great eternal judgement, In which He will execute vengeance amongst the angels. <sup>16</sup> And the first heaven shall depart and pass away, And a new heaven shall appear, And all the powers of the heavens shall give sevenfold light. <sup>17</sup> And after that there will be many weeks without number for ever, And all shall be in goodness and righteousness, And sin shall no more be mentioned for ever.]

## XCI. 18-19. Enoch's Admonition to his Children (continuation).

<sup>18</sup> And now I tell you, my sons, and show you The paths of righteousness and the paths of violence. Yea, I will show them to you again That ye may know what will come to pass. <sup>19</sup> And now, hearken unto me, my sons, And walk in the paths of righteousness, And walk not in the paths of violence; For all who walk in the paths of unrighteousness shall perish for ever.'

### 92

## XCII-CV. The Epistle of Enoch.
## XCII. Enoch's Book of Admonition for his Children (continuation).

<sup>1</sup> The book written by Enoch–[Enoch indeed wrote this complete doctrine of wisdom, (which is) praised of all men and a judge of all the earth] for all my children who shall dwell on the earth. And for the future generations who shall observe uprightness and peace. <sup>2</sup> Let not your spirit be troubled on account of the times; For the Holy and Great One has appointed days for all things. <sup>3</sup> And the righteous one shall arise from sleep, [Shall arise] and walk in the paths of righteousness, And all his path and conversation shall be in eternal goodness and grace. <sup>4</sup> He will be gracious to the righteous and give him eternal uprightness, And He will give him power so that he shall be (endowed) with goodness and righteousness. And he shall walk in eternal light. <sup>5</sup> And sin shall perish in darkness for ever, And shall no more be seen from that day for evermore.

## XCIII. The Apocalypse of Weeks.

### 93

<sup>1</sup> And after that Enoch both †gave† and began to recount from the books. <sup>2</sup> And Enoch said: 'Concerning the children of righteousness and concerning the elect of the world, And concerning the plant of uprightness, I will speak these things, Yea, I Enoch will declare (them) unto you, my sons: According to that which appeared to me in the heavenly vision, And which I have known through the word of the holy angels, And have learnt from the heavenly tablets.' <sup>3</sup> And Enoch began to recount from the books and said: 'I was born the seventh in the first week, While judgement and righteousness still endured. <sup>4</sup> And after me there shall arise in the second week great wickedness, And deceit shall have sprung up; And in it there shall be the first end. And in it a man shall be saved; And after it is ended unrighteousness shall grow up, And a law shall be made for the sinners. <sup>5</sup> And after that in the third week at its close A man shall be elected as the plant of righteous judgement, And **his posterity** shall become the plant of righteousness for evermore. <sup>6</sup> And after that in the fourth week, at its close, Visions of the holy and righteous shall be seen, And a law for all generations and an enclosure shall be made for them. <sup>7</sup> And after that in the fifth week, at its close, The house of glory and dominion shall be built for ever. <sup>8</sup> And after that in the sixth week all who live in it shall be blinded, And the hearts of all of them shall godlessly forsake wisdom. And in it a man shall ascend; And at its close the house of dominion shall be burnt with fire, And the whole race of the chosen root shall be dispersed. <sup>9</sup> And after that in the seventh week shall an apostate generation arise, And many shall be its deeds, And all its deeds shall be apostate. <sup>10</sup> And at its close shall be elected The elect righteous of the eternal plant of righteousness, To receive sevenfold instruction concerning all His creation. <sup>11</sup> [For who is there of all the children of men that is able to hear the voice of the Holy One without being troubled? And who can

think His thoughts? and who is there that can behold all the works of heaven? [12] And how should there be one who could behold the heaven, and who is there that could understand the things of heaven and see a soul or a spirit and could tell thereof, or ascend and see all their ends and think them or do like them? [13] And who is there of all men that could know what is the breadth and the length of the earth, and to whom has been shown the measure of all of them? [14] Or is there any one who could discern the length of the heaven and how great is its height, and upon what it is founded, and how great is the number of the stars, and where all the luminaries rest?]

## XCIV. 1-5. Admonitions to the Righteous.

### 94

[1] And now I say unto you, my sons, love righteousness and walk therein; For the paths of righteousness are worthy of acceptation, But the paths of unrighteousness shall suddenly be destroyed and vanish. [2] And to certain men of a generation shall the paths of violence and of death be revealed, And they shall hold themselves afar from them, And shall not follow them. [3] And now I say unto you the righteous: Walk not in the paths of wickedness, nor in the paths of death, And draw not nigh to them, lest ye be destroyed. [4] But seek and choose for yourselves righteousness and an elect life, And walk in the paths of peace, And ye shall live and prosper. [5] And hold fast my words in the thoughts of your hearts, And suffer them not to be effaced from your hearts; For I know that sinners will tempt men to **evilly-entreat** wisdom, So that no place may be found for her, And no manner of temptation may minish.

## XCIV. 6-11. Woes for the Sinners.

[6] Woe to those who build unrighteousness and oppression And lay deceit as a foundation; For they shall be suddenly overthrown, And they shall have no peace. [7] Woe to those who build their houses with sin; For from all their foundations shall they be overthrown, And by the sword shall they fall. [And those who acquire gold and silver in judgement suddenly shall perish.] [8] Woe to you, ye rich, for ye have trusted in your riches, And from your riches shall ye depart, Because ye have not remembered the Most High in the days of your riches. [9] Ye have committed blasphemy and unrighteousness, And have become ready for the day of slaughter, And the day of darkness and the day of the great judgement. [10] Thus I speak and declare unto you: He who hath created you will overthrow you, And for your fall there shall be no compassion, And your Creator will rejoice at your destruction. [11] And your righteous ones in those days shall be A reproach to the sinners and the godless.

## XCV. Enoch's Grief: fresh Woes against the Sinners.

### 95

[1] Oh that mine eyes were [a cloud of] waters That I might weep over you, And pour down my tears as a cloud †of† waters: That so I might rest from my trouble of heart! [2] †Who has permitted you to practice reproaches and wickedness? And so judgement shall overtake you, sinners. † [3] Fear not the sinners, ye righteous; For again will the Lord deliver them into your hands, That ye may execute judgement upon them according to your desires. [4] Woe to you who fulminate anathemas which cannot be reversed: Healing shall therefore be far from you because of your sins. [5] Woe to you who requite your neighbour with evil; For ye shall be requited according to your works. [6] Woe to you, lying witnesses, And to those who weigh out injustice, For suddenly shall ye perish. [7] Woe to you, sinners, for ye persecute the righteous; For ye shall be delivered up and persecuted because of injustice, And heavy shall its yoke be upon you.

## XCVI. Grounds of Hopefulness for the Righteous: Woes for the Wicked.

### 96

[1] Be hopeful, ye righteous; for suddenly shall the sinners perish before you, And ye shall have lordship over them according to your desires. [2] [And in the day of the tribulation of the sinners, Your children shall mount and rise as eagles, And higher than the vultures will be your nest, And ye shall ascend and enter the crevices of the earth, And the clefts of the rock for ever as coneys before the unrighteous, And the sirens shall sigh because of you-and weep.] [3] Wherefore fear not, ye that have suffered; For healing shall be your portion, And a bright light shall enlighten you, And the voice of rest ye shall hear from heaven. [4] Woe unto you, ye sinners, for your riches make you appear like the righteous, But your hearts convict you of being sinners, And this fact shall be a testimony against you for a memorial of (your) evil deeds. [5] Woe to you who devour the finest of the wheat, And drink **wine in large bowls**, And tread under foot the lowly with your might. [6] Woe to you who drink water **from every fountain**, For suddenly shall ye be consumed and wither away, Because ye have forsaken the fountain of life. [7] Woe to you who work unrighteousness And deceit and blasphemy: It shall be a memorial against you for evil. [8] Woe to you, ye mighty, Who with might oppress the righteous; For the day of your destruction is

coming. In those days many and good days shall come to the righteous— in the day of your judgement.

## XCVII. The Evils in Store for Sinners and the Possessors of unrighteous Wealth.

### 97

[1] Believe, ye righteous, that the sinners will become a shame And perish in the day of unrighteousness. [2] Be it known unto you (ye sinners) that the Most High is mindful of your destruction, And the angels of heaven rejoice over your destruction. [3] What will ye do, ye sinners, And whither will ye flee on that day of judgement, When ye hear the voice of the prayer of the righteous? [4] Yea, ye shall fare like unto them, Against whom this word shall be a testimony: "Ye have been companions of sinners." [5] And in those days the prayer of the righteous shall reach unto the Lord, And for you the days of your judgement shall come. [6] And all the words of your unrighteousness shall be read out before the Great Holy One, And your faces shall be covered with shame, And He will reject every work which is grounded on unrighteousness. [7] Woe to you, ye sinners, who live on the mid ocean and on the dry land, Whose remembrance is evil against you. [8] Woe to you who acquire silver and gold in unrighteousness and say: "We have become rich with riches and have possessions; And have acquired everything we have desired. [9] And now let us do what we purposed: For we have gathered silver, [9d] And many are the husbandmen in our houses." [9e] And our granaries are (brim) full as with water, [10] Yea and like water your lies shall flow away; For your riches shall not abide But speedily ascend from you;For ye have acquired it all in unrighteousness, And ye shall be given over to a great curse.

## XCVIII. Self-indulgence of Sinners; Sin originated by Man; all Sin recorded in Heaven; Woes for the Sinners.

### 98

[1] And now I swear unto you, to the wise and to the foolish, For ye shall have manifold experiences on the earth. [2] For ye men shall put on more adornments than a woman, And coloured garments more than a virgin: In royalty and in grandeur and in power, And in silver and in gold and in purple, And in splendour and in food they shall be poured out as water. [3] Therefore they shall be wanting in doctrine and wisdom, And they shall perish thereby together with their possessions; And with all their glory and their splendour, And in shame and in slaughter and in great destitution, Their spirits shall be cast into the furnace of fire. [4] I have sworn unto you, ye sinners, as a mountain has not become a slave, And a hill does not become the handmaid of a woman, Even so sin has not been sent upon the earth, But man of himself has created it, And under a great curse shall they fall who commit it. [5] And barrenness has not been given to the woman, But on account of the deeds of her own hands she dies without children. [6] I have sworn unto you, ye sinners, by the Holy Great One, That all your evil deeds are revealed in the heavens, And that none of your deeds of oppression are covered and hidden. [7] And do not think in your spirit nor say in your heart that ye do not know and that ye do not see that every sin is every day recorded in heaven in the presence of the Most High. [8] From henceforth ye know that all your oppression wherewith ye oppress is written down every day till the day of your judgement. [9] Woe to you, ye fools, for through your folly shall ye perish: and ye transgress against the wise, and so good hap shall not be your portion. [10] And now, know ye that ye are prepared for the day of destruction: wherefore do not hope to live, ye sinners, but ye shall depart and die; for ye know no ransom; for ye are prepared for the day of the great judgement, for the day of tribulation and great shame for your spirits. [11] Woe to you, ye obstinate of heart, who work wickedness and eat blood: Whence have ye good things to eat and to drink and to be filled?From all the good things which the Lord the Most High has placed in abundance on the earth; therefore ye shall have no peace. [12] Woe to you who love the deeds of unrighteousness: wherefore do ye hope for good hap unto yourselves? know that ye shall be delivered into the hands of the righteous, and they shall cut off your necks and slay you, and have no mercy upon you. [13] Woe to you who rejoice in the tribulation of the righteous; for no grave shall be dug for you. [14] Woe to you who set at nought the words of the righteous; for ye shall have no hope of life. [15] Woe to you who write down lying and godless words; for they write down their lies that men may hear them and act godlessly towards (their) neighbour. [16] Therefore they shall have no peace but die a sudden death.

## XCIX. Woes pronounced on the Godless, the Lawbreakers; evil Plight of Sinners in the last Days; further Woes.

### 99

[1] Woe to you who work godlessness, And glory in lying and extol them: Ye shall perish, and no happy life shall be yours. [2] Woe to them who pervert the words of uprightness, And transgress the eternal law, And transform themselves into what they were not [into sinners]: They shall be trodden under foot upon the earth. [3] In those days make ready, ye righteous, to raise your prayers as a memorial, And place them as a

testimony before the angels, That they may place the sin of the sinners for a memorial before the Most High. **⁴** In those days the nations shall be stirred up, And the families of the nations shall arise on the day of destruction. **⁵** And in those days the destitute shall go forth and carry off their children, And they shall abandon them, so that their children shall perish through them: Yea, they shall abandon their children (that are still) sucklings, and not return to them, And shall have no pity on their beloved ones. **⁶** And again I swear to you, ye sinners, that sin is prepared for a day of unceasing bloodshed. **⁷** And they who worship stones, and grave images of gold and silver and wood <and stone> and clay, and those who worship impure spirits and demons, and all kinds of idols not according to knowledge, shall get no manner of help from them. **⁸** And they shall become godless by reason of the folly of their hearts, And their eyes shall be blinded through the fear of their hearts And through visions in their dreams. **⁹** Through these they shall become godless and fearful; For they shall have wrought all their work in a lie, And shall have worshiped a stone: Therefore in an instant shall they perish. **¹⁰** But in those days blessed are all they who accept the words of wisdom, and understand them, And observe the paths of the Most High, and walk in the path of His righteousness, And become not godless with the godless; For they shall be saved. **¹¹** Woe to you who spread evil to your neighbours; For you shall be slain in Sheol. **¹²** Woe to you who make deceitful and false measures, And (to them) who cause bitterness on the earth; For they shall thereby be utterly consumed. **¹³** Woe to you who build your houses through the grievous toil of others, And all their building materials are the bricks and stones of sin; I tell you ye shall have no peace. **¹⁴** Woe to them who reject the measure and eternal heritage of their fathers And whose souls follow after idols; For they shall have no rest. **¹⁵** Woe to them who work unrighteousness and help oppression, And slay their neighbours until the day of the great judgement. **¹⁶** For He shall cast down your glory, And bring affliction on your hearts, And shall arouse **His fierce indignation**, And destroy you all with the sword; And all the holy and righteous shall remember your sins.

**C. The Sinners destroy each other; Judgement of the fallen Angels; the Safety of the Righteous; further Woes for the Sinners.**

### 100

**¹** And in those days in one place the fathers together with their sons shall be smitten And brothers one with another shall fall in death Till the streams flow with their blood. **²** .For a man shall not withhold his hand from slaying his sons and his sons' sons, And the sinner shall not withhold his hand from his honoured brother: From dawn till sunset they shall slay one another. **³** And the horse shall walk up to the breast in the blood of sinners, And the chariot shall be submerged to its height. **⁴** In those days the angels shall descend into the secret places And gather together into one place all those who brought down sin And the Most High will arise on that day of judgement To execute great judgement amongst sinners. **⁵** And over all the righteous and holy He will appoint guardians from amongst the holy angels To guard them as the apple of an eye, Until He makes an end of all wickedness and all sin, And though the righteous sleep a long sleep, they have nought to fear. **⁶** And (then) the children of the earth shall see the wise **in security**, And shall understand all the words of this book, And recognize that their riches shall not be able to save them In the overthrow of their sins. **⁷** Woe to you, Sinners, on the day of strong anguish, **Ye who afflict** the righteous and burn them with fire: Ye shall be requited according to your works. **⁸** Woe to you, ye obstinate of heart, Who watch in order to devise wickedness: Therefore shall fear come upon you And there shall be none to help you. **⁹** Woe to you, ye sinners, on account of the words of your mouth, And on account of the deeds of your hands which your godlessness as wrought, In blazing flames burning worse than fire shall ye burn. **¹⁰** And now, know ye that from the angels He will inquire as to your deeds in heaven, from the sun and from the moon and from the stars in reference to your sins because upon the earth ye execute judgement on the righteous. **¹¹** And He will summon to testify against you every cloud and mist and dew and rain; for they shall all be withheld because of you from descending upon you, and they shall be mindful of your sins. **¹²** And now give presents to the rain that it be not withheld from descending upon you, nor yet the dew, when it has received gold and silver from you that it may descend. **¹³** When the hoar-frost and snow with their chilliness, and all the snow-storms with all their plagues fall upon you, in those days ye shall not be able to stand before them.

**CI. Exhortation to the Fear of God: all Nature fears Him, but not the Sinners.**

### 101

**¹** Observe the heaven, ye children of heaven, and every work of the Most High, and fear ye Him and work no evil in His presence. **²** If He closes the windows of heaven, and withholds the rain and the dew from descending on the earth on your account, what will ye do then? **³** And

if He sends His anger upon you because of your deeds, ye cannot petition Him; for ye spake proud and insolent words against His righteousness: therefore ye shall have no peace. **⁴** And see ye not the **sailors** of the ships, how their ships are tossed to and fro by the waves, and are shaken by the winds, and are in sore trouble? **⁵** And therefore do they fear because all their goodly possessions go upon the sea with them, and they have evil forebodings of heart that the sea will swallow them and they will perish therein. **⁶** Are not the entire sea and all its waters, and all its movements, the work of the Most High, and has He not set limits to its doings, and confined it throughout by the sand? **⁷** And at His reproof it is afraid and dries up, and all its fish die and all that is in it; But ye sinners that are on the earth fear Him not. **⁸** Has He not made the heaven and the earth, and all that is therein? Who has given understanding and wisdom to everything that moves on the earth and in the sea. **⁹** Do not the **sailors** of the ships fear the sea? Yet sinners fear not the Most High.

**CII. Terrors of the Day of Judgement: the adverse Fortunes of the Righteous on the Earth.**

### 102

**¹** In those days when He hath brought a grievous fire upon you, Whither will ye flee, and where will ye find deliverance? And when He launches forth His Word against you Will you not be affrighted and fear? **²** And all the luminaries shall be affrighted with great fear, And all the earth shall be affrighted and tremble and be alarmed. **³** And all the †angels shall execute their commands† And shall seek to hide themselves from the presence of the Great Glory, And the children of earth shall tremble and quake; And ye sinners shall be cursed for ever, And ye shall have no peace. **⁴** Fear ye not, ye souls of the righteous, And be hopeful ye that have died in righteousness. **⁵** And grieve not if your soul into Sheol has descended in grief, And that in your life your body fared not according to your goodness, But **wait for** the day of the **judgement** of sinners And for the day of cursing and chastisement. **⁶** And yet when ye die the sinners speak over you: "As we die, so die the righteous, And what benefit do they reap for their deeds? **⁷** Behold, even as we, so do they die in grief and darkness, And what have they more than we? From henceforth we are equal. **⁸** And what will they receive and what will they see for ever? Behold, they too have died, And henceforth for ever shall they see no light." **⁹** I tell you, ye sinners, ye are content to eat and drink, and rob and sin, and strip men naked, and acquire wealth and see good days. **¹⁰** Have ye seen the righteous how their end falls out, that no manner of violence is found in them till their death? **¹¹** "Nevertheless they perished and became as though they had not been, and their spirits descended into Sheol in tribulation."

**CIII. Different Destinies of the Righteous and the Sinners: fresh Objections of the Sinners.**

### 103

**¹** Now, therefore, I swear to you, the righteous, by the glory of the Great and Honoured and Mighty One in dominion, and by His greatness I swear to you: **²** I know a mystery And have read the heavenly tablets, And have seen the holy books, And have found written therein and inscribed regarding them: **³** That all goodness and joy and glory are prepared for them, And written down for the spirits of those who have died in righteousness, And that manifold good shall be given to you in recompense for your labours, And that your lot is abundantly beyond the lot of the living. **⁴** And the spirits of you who have died in righteousness shall live and rejoice, And their spirits shall not perish, nor their memorial from before the face of the Great One Unto all the generations of the world: wherefore no longer fear their contumely. **⁵** Woe to you, ye sinners, when ye have died, If ye die in the wealth of your sins, And those who are like you say regarding you: 'Blessed are the sinners: they have seen all their days. **⁶** And how they have died in prosperity and in wealth, And have not seen tribulation or murder in their life; And they have died in honour, And judgement has not been executed on them during their life." **⁷** Know ye, that their souls will be made to descend into Sheol And they shall be wretched in their great tribulation. **⁸** And into darkness and chains and a burning flame where there is grievous judgement shall your spirits enter; And the great judgement shall be for all the generations of the world. Woe to you, for ye shall have no peace. **⁹** Say not in regard to the righteous and good who are in life: "In our troubled days we have toiled laboriously and experienced every trouble, And met with much evil and been consumed, And have become few and our spirit small. **¹⁰** And we have been destroyed and have not found any to help us even with a word: We have been tortured [and destroyed], and not hoped to see life from day to day. **¹¹** We hoped to be the head and have become the tail: We have toiled laboriously and had no satisfaction in our toil; And we have become the food of the sinners and the unrighteous, And they have laid their yoke heavily upon us. **¹²** They have had dominion over us that hated us †and smote us; And to those that hated us† we have bowed our necks But they pitied us not. **¹³** We desired to get away from them that we might escape and be at rest, But found no place whereunto we should flee and be safe from them. ¹⁴ And are complained to the rulers in our tribulation, And cried out against those who devoured us, But they did not attend to our cries And would not hearken to our voice. ¹⁵ And they helped those who robbed us and devoured us and those who made us few; and they concealed their oppression, and they did not remove from us the yoke of those that devoured us and dispersed us and murdered us, and they concealed their murder, and remembered not that they had lifted up their hands against us.

## CIV. Assurances given to the Righteous; Admonitions to Sinners and the Falsifiers of the Words of Uprightness.

### 104

¹ I swear unto you, that in heaven the angels remember you for good before the glory of the Great One: and your names are written before the glory of the Great One. ² Be hopeful; for aforetime ye were put to shame through ill and affliction; but now ye shall shine as the lights of heaven, ye shall shine and ye shall be seen, and the portals of heaven shall be opened to you. ³ And in your cry, cry for judgement, and it shall appear to you; for all your tribulation shall be visited on the rulers, and on all who helped those who plundered you. ⁴ Be hopeful, and cast not away your hopes for ye shall have great joy as the angels of heaven. ⁵ What shall ye be obliged to do? Ye shall not have to hide on the day of the great judgement and ye shall not be found as sinners, and the eternal judgement shall be far from you for all the generations of the world. ⁶ And now fear not, ye righteous, when ye see the sinners growing strong and prospering in their ways: be not companions with them, but keep afar from their violence; for ye shall become companions of the hosts of heaven. ⁷ And, although ye sinners say: "All our sins shall not be searched out and be written down," nevertheless they shall write down all your sins every day. ⁸ And now I show unto you that light and darkness, day and night, see all your sins. ⁹ Be not godless in your hearts, and lie not and alter not the words of uprightness, nor charge with lying the words of the Holy Great One, nor take account of your idols; for all your lying and all your godlessness issue not in righteousness but in great sin. ¹⁰ And now I know this mystery, that sinners will alter and pervert the words of righteousness in many ways, and will speak wicked words, and lie, and practice great deceits, and write books concerning their words. ¹¹ But when they write down truthfully all my words in their languages, and do not change or minish ought from my words but write them all down truthfully–all that I first testified concerning them. ¹² Then, I know another mystery, that books will be given to the righteous and the wise to become a cause of joy and uprightness and much wisdom. ¹³ And to them shall the books be given, and they shall believe in them and rejoice over them, and then shall all the righteous who have learnt therefrom all the paths of uprightness be recompensed.'

## XCV. God and the Messiah to dwell with Man.

### 105

¹ In those days the Lord bade (them) to summon and testify to the children of earth concerning their wisdom: Show (it) unto them; for ye are their guides, and a recompense over the whole earth. ² For I and My son will be united with them for ever in the paths of uprightness in their lives; and ye shall have peace: rejoice, ye children of uprightness. Amen.

## CVI-CVII. Fragment of the Book of Noah.

### 106

¹ And after some days my son Methuselah took a wife for his son Lamech, and she became pregnant by him and bore a son. ² And his body was white as snow and red as the blooming of a rose, and the hair of his head †and his long locks were white as wool, and his eyes beautiful†. And when he opened his eyes, he lighted up the whole house like the sun, and the whole house was very bright. ³ And thereupon he arose in the hands of the midwife, opened his mouth, and †conversed with† the Lord of righteousness. ⁴ And his father Lamech was afraid of him and fled, and came to his father Methuselah. ⁵ And he said unto him: 'I have begotten a strange son, diverse from and unlike man, and resembling the sons of the God of heaven; and his nature is different and he is not like us, and his eyes are as the rays of the sun, and his countenance is glorious. ⁶ And it seems to me that he is not sprung from me but from the angels, and I fear that in his days a wonder may be wrought on the earth. ⁷ And now, my father, I am here to petition thee and implore thee that thou mayest go to Enoch, our father, and learn from him the truth, for his dwelling-place is amongst the angels.' ⁸ And when Methuselah heard the words of his son, he came to me to the ends of the earth; for he had heard that I was there, and he cried aloud, and I heard his voice and I came to him. And ¹ said unto him: 'Behold, here am I, my son, **wherefore** hast thou come to me?' ⁹ And he answered and said: 'Because of a great cause of anxiety have I come to thee, and because of a disturbing vision have I approached. ¹⁰ And now, my father, hear me: unto Lamech my son there hath been born a son, the

like of whom there is none, and his nature is not like man's nature, and the colour of his body is whiter than snow and redder than the bloom of a rose, and the hair of his head is whiter than white wool, and his eyes are like the rays of the sun, and he opened his eyes and thereupon lighted up the whole house. ¹¹ And he arose in the hands of the midwife, and opened his mouth and blessed the Lord of heaven. ¹² And his father Lamech became afraid and fled to me, and did not believe that he was sprung from him, but that he was in the likeness of the angels of heaven; and behold I have come to thee that thou mayest make known to me the truth.' ¹³ And I, Enoch, answered and said unto him: 'The Lord will do a new thing on the earth, and this I have already seen in a vision, and make known to thee that in the generation of my father Jared some of the **angels** of heaven transgressed the word of the Lord. ¹⁴ And behold they commit sin and transgress the law, and have united themselves with women and commit sin with them, and have married some of them, and have begot children by them. ¹⁵ Yea, there shall come a great destruction over the whole earth, and there shall be a deluge and a great destruction for one year. ¹⁶ And this son who has been born unto you shall be left on the earth, and his three children shall be saved with him: when all mankind that are on the earth shall die [he and his sons shall be saved]. ¹⁷ And they shall produce on the earth giants not according to the spirit, but according to the flesh, and there shall be a great punishment on the earth, and the earth shall be cleansed from all impurity. ¹⁸ And now make known to thy son Lamech that he who has been born is in truth his son, and call his name Noah; for he shall be left to you, and he and his sons shall be saved from the destruction, which shall come upon the earth on account of all the sin and all the unrighteousness, which shall be consummated on the earth in his days. ¹⁹ And after that there shall be still more unrighteousness than that which was first consummated on the earth; for I know the mysteries of the holy ones; for He, the Lord, has showed me and informed me, and I have read (them) in the heavenly tablets.

### 107

¹ And I saw written on them that generation upon generation shall transgress, till a generation of righteousness arises, and transgression is destroyed and sin passes away from the earth, and all manner of good comes upon it. ² And now, my son, go and make known to thy son Lamech that this son, which has been born, is in truth his son, and that (this) is no lie.' ³ And when Methuselah had heard the words of his father Enoch–for he had shown to him everything in secret–he returned and showed (them) to him and called the name of that son Noah; for he will comfort the earth after all the destruction.

## CVIII. An Appendix to the Book of Enoch

### 108

¹ Another book which Enoch wrote for his son Methuselah and for those who will come after him, and keep the law in the last days. ² Ye who have done good shall wait for those days till an end is made of those who work evil; and an end of the might of the transgressors. ³ And wait ye indeed till sin has passed away, for their names shall be blotted out of the book of life and out of the holy books, and their seed shall be destroyed for ever, and their spirits shall be slain, and they shall cry and make lamentation in a place that is a chaotic wilderness, and in **the fire shall they burn**; for there is no earth there. ⁴ And I saw there something like an invisible cloud; for by reason of its depth I could not look over, and I saw a flame of fire blazing brightly, and things like shining mountains circling and sweeping to and fro. ⁵ And I asked one of the holy angels who was with me and said unto him: 'What is this shining thing? for it is not a heaven but only the flame of a blazing fire, and the voice of weeping and crying and lamentation and strong pain.' ⁶ And he said unto me: 'This place which thou seest–here are cast the spirits of sinners and blasphemers, and of those who work wickedness, and of those who pervert everything that the Lord hath spoken through the mouth of the prophets–(even) the things that shall be. ⁷ For some of them are written and inscribed above in the heaven, in order that the angels may read them and know that which shall befall the sinners, and the spirits of the humble, and of those who have afflicted their bodies, and been recompensed by God; and of those who have been put to shame by wicked men: ⁸ Who love God and loved neither gold nor silver nor any of the good things which are in the world, but gave over their bodies to torture. ⁹ Who, since they came into being, longed not after earthly food, but regarded everything as a passing breath, and lived accordingly, and the Lord tried them much, and their spirits were found pure so that they should bless His name. ¹⁰ And all the blessings destined for them I have recounted in the books. And he hath assigned them their recompense, because they have been found to be such as loved heaven more than their life in the world, and though they were trodden under foot of wicked men, and experienced abuse and reviling from them and were put to shame, yet they blessed Me. ¹¹ And now I will summon the spirits of the good who belong to the generation of light, and I will transform those who were born in darkness, who in the

flesh were not recompensed with such honour as their faithfulness deserved. [12] And I will bring forth in shining light those who have loved My holy name, and I will seat each on the throne of his honour. [13] And they shall be resplendent for times without number; for righteousness is the judgement of God; for to the faithful He will give faithfulness in the habitation of upright paths. [14] And they shall see those who were, born in darkness led into darkness, while the righteous shall be resplendent. [15] And the sinners shall cry aloud and see them resplendent, and they indeed will go where days and seasons are prescribed for them.'

# The Second Book of Enoch, or Slavonic Enoch, or The Book of the Secrets of Enoch

## 1

[1] There was a wise man, a great artificer, and the Lord conceived love for him and received him, that he should behold the uppermost dwellings and be an eye-witness of the wise and great and inconceivable and immutable realm of God Almighty, of the very wonderful and glorious and bright and many-eyed station of the Lord's servants, and of the inaccessible throne of the Lord, and of the degrees and manifestations of the incorporeal hosts, and of the ineffable ministration of the multitude of the elements, and of the various apparition and inexpressible singing of the host of Cherubim, and of the boundless light. [2] At that time, he said, when my one hundred and sixty-fifth year was completed, I begat my son Mathusal (Methuselah). [3] After this too I lived two hundred years and completed of all the years of my life three hundred and sixty-five years. [4] On the first day of the month I was in my house alone and was resting on my bed and slept. [5] And when I was asleep, great distress came up into my heart, and I was weeping with my eyes in sleep, and I could not understand what this distress was, or what would happen to me. [6] And there appeared to me two men, exceeding big, so that I never saw such on earth; their faces were shining like the sun, their eyes too (were) like a burning light, and from their lips was fire coming forth with clothing and singing of various kinds in appearance purple, their wings (were )brighter than gold, their hands whiter than snow. [7] They were standing at the head of my bed and began to call me by my name. [8] And I arose from my sleep and saw clearly those two men standing in front of me. [9] And I saluted them and was seized with fear and the appearance of my face was changed from terror, and those men said to me: [10] Have courage, Enoch, do not fear; the eternal God sent us to you, and lo! You shalt to-day ascend with us into heaven, and you shall tell your sons and all your household all that they shall do without you on earth in your house, and let no one seek you till the Lord return you to them. [11] And I made haste to obey them and went out from my house, and made to the doors, as it was ordered me, and summoned my sons Mathusal (Methuselah) and Regim and Gaidad and made known to them all the marvels those (men) had told me.

## 2

[1] Listen to me, my children, I know not whither I go, or what will befall me; now therefore, my children, I tell you: turn not from God before the face of the vain, who made not Heaven and earth, for these shall perish and those who worship them, and may the Lord make confident your hearts in the fear of him. And now, my children, let no one think to seek me, until the Lord return me to you.

## 3

[1] It came to pass, when Enoch had told his sons, that the angels took him on to their wings and bore him up on to the first heaven and placed him on the clouds. And there I looked, and again I looked higher, and saw the ether, and they placed me on the first heaven and showed me a very great Sea, greater than the earthly sea.

## 4

[1] They brought before my face the elders and rulers of the stellar orders, and showed me two hundred angels, who rule the stars and (their) services to the heavens, and fly with their wings and come round all those who sail.

## 5

[1] And here I looked down and saw the treasure-houses of the snow, and the angels who keep their terrible store-houses, and the clouds whence they come out and into which they go.

## 6

[1] They showed me the treasure-house of the dew, like oil of the olive, and the appearance of its form, as of all the flowers of the earth; further many angels guarding the treasure-houses of these (things), and how they are made to shut and open.

## 7

[1] And those men took me and led me up on to the second heaven, and showed me darkness, greater than earthly darkness, and there I saw prisoners hanging, watched, awaiting the great and boundless judgment, and these angels (spirits) were dark-looking, more than earthly darkness, and incessantly making weeping through all hours. [2] And I said to the men who were with me: Wherefore are these incessantly tortured? They answered me: These are God's apostates, who obeyed not God's commands, but took counsel with their own will, and turned away with their prince, who also (is) fastened on the fifth heaven. [3] And I felt great pity for them, and they saluted me, and said to me: Man of God, pray for us to the Lord; and I answered to them: Who am I, a mortal man, that I should pray for angels (spirits)? Who knows whither I go, or what will befall me? Or who will pray for me?

## 8

[1] And those men took me thence, and led me up on to the third heaven, and placed me there; and I looked downwards, and saw the produce of these places, such as has never been known for goodness. [2] And I saw all the sweet-flowering trees and beheld their fruits, which were sweet-smelling, and all the foods borne (by them) bubbling with fragrant exhalation. [3] And in the midst of the trees that of life, in that place whereon the Lord rests, when he goes up into paradise; and this tree is of ineffable goodness and fragrance, and adorned more than every existing thing; and on all sides (it is) in form gold-looking and vermilion and fire-like and covers all, and it has produce from all fruits. [4] Its root is in the garden at the earth's end. [5] And paradise is between corruptibility and incorruptibility. [6] And two springs come out which send forth honey and milk, and their springs send forth oil and wine, and they separate into four parts, and go round with quiet course, and go down into the PARADISE OF EDEN, between corruptibility and incorruptibility. [7] And thence they go forth along the earth, and have a revolution to their circle even as other elements. [8] And here there is no unfruitful tree, and every place is blessed. [9] And (there are) three hundred angels very bright, who keep the garden, and with incessant sweet singing and never-silent voices serve the Lord throughout all days and hours. [10] And I said: How very sweet is this place, and those men said to me:

## 9

[1] This place, O Enoch, is prepared for the righteous, who endure all manner of offence from those that exasperate their souls, who avert their eyes from iniquity, and make righteous judgment, and give bread to the hungering, and cover the naked with clothing, and raise up the fallen, and help injured orphans, and who walk without fault before the face of the Lord, and serve him alone, and for them is prepared this place for eternal inheritance.

## 10

[1] And those two men led me up on to the Northern side, and showed me there a very terrible place, and (there were) all manner of tortures in that place: cruel darkness and unillumined gloom, and there is no light there, but murky fire constantly flaming aloft, and (there is) a fiery river coming forth, and that whole place is everywhere fire, and everywhere (there is) frost and ice, thirst and shivering, while the bonds are very cruel, and the angels (spirits) fearful and merciless, bearing angry weapons, merciless torture, and I said: [2] Woe, woe, how very terrible is this place. [3] And those men said to me: This place, O Enoch, is prepared for those who dishonour God, who on earth practice sin against nature, which is child-corruption after the sodomitic fashion, magic-making, enchantments and devilish witchcrafts, and who boast of their wicked deeds, stealing, lies, calumnies, envy, rancour, fornication, murder, and who, accursed, steal the souls of men, who, seeing the poor take away their goods and themselves wax rich, injuring them for other men's goods; who being able to satisfy the empty, made the hungering to die; being able to clothe, stripped the naked; and who knew not their creator, and bowed to the soulless (and lifeless) gods, who cannot see nor hear, vain gods, (who also) built hewn images and bow down to unclean handiwork, for all these is prepared this place among these, for eternal inheritance.

## 11

[1] Those men took me, and led me up on to the fourth heaven, and showed me all the successive goings, and all the rays of the light of sun and moon. [2] And I measure their goings, and compared their light, and saw that the sun's light is greater than the moon's. [3] Its circle and the wheels on which it goes always, like the wind going past with very marvellous speed, and day and night it has no rest. [4] Its passage and return (are accompanied by) four great stars, (and) each star has under it a thousand stars, to the right of the sun's wheel, (and by) four to the left, each having under it a thousand stars, altogether eight thousand, issuing with the sun continually. [5] And by day fifteen myriads of angels attend it, and by night A thousand. [6] And six-winged ones issue with the angels before the sun's wheel into the fiery flames, and a hundred angels kindle the sun and set it alight.

## 12

[1] And I looked and saw other flying elements of the sun, whose names (are) Phoenixes and Chalkydri, marvellous and wonderful, with feet and tails in the form of a lion, and a crocodile's head, their appearance (is) empurpled, like the rainbow; their size (is) nine hundred measures, their wings (are like) those of angels, each (has) twelve, and they attend and accompany the sun, bearing heat and dew, as it is ordered them from God. [2] Thus (the sun) revolves and goes, and rises under the heaven, and its course goes under the earth with the light of its rays incessantly.

## 13

[1] Those men bore me away to the east, and placed me at the sun's gates, where the sun goes forth according to the regulation of the seasons and the circuit of the months of the whole year, and the number of the hours day and night. [2] And I saw six gates open, each gate having sixty-one stadia and A quarter of one stadium, and I measured (them) truly, and understood their size (to be) so much, through which the sun goes forth, and goes to the west, and is made even, and rises throughout all the months, and turns back again from the six gates according to the succession of the seasons; thus (the period) of the whole year is finished after the returns of the four seasons.

## 14

[1] And again those men led me away to the western parts, and showed me six great gates open corresponding to the eastern gates, opposite to where the sun sets, according to the number of the days three hundred and sixty-five and A quarter. [2] Thus again it goes down to the western gates, (and) draws away its light, the greatness of its brightness, under the earth; for since the crown of its shining is in heaven with the Lord, and guarded by four hundred angels, while the sun goes round on wheel under the earth, and stands seven great hours in night, and spends half (its course) under the earth, when it comes to the eastern approach in the eighth hour of the night, it brings its lights, and the crown of shining, and the sun flames forth more than fire.

## 15

[1] Then the elements of the sun, called Phoenixes and Chalkydri break into song, therefore every bird flutters with its wings, rejoicing at the giver of light, and they broke into song at the command of the Lord. [2] The giver of light comes to give brightness to the whole world, and the morning guard takes shape, which is the rays of the sun, and the sun of the earth goes out, and receives its brightness to light up the whole face of the earth, and they showed me this calculation of the sun's going. [3] And the gates which it enters, these are the great gates of the calculation of the hours of the year; for this reason the sun is a great creation, whose circuit (lasts) twenty-eight years, and begins again from the beginning.

## 16

[1] Those men showed me the other course, that of the moon, twelve great gates, crowned from west to east, by which the moon goes in and out of the customary times. [2] It goes in at the first gate to the western places of the sun, by the first gates with (thirty)-one (days) exactly, by the second gates with thirty-one days exactly, by the third with thirty days exactly, by the fourth with thirty days exactly, by the fifth with thirty-one days exactly, by the sixth with thirty-one days exactly, by the seventh with thirty days exactly, by the eighth with thirty-one days perfectly, by the ninth with thirty-one days exactly, by the tenth with thirty days perfectly, by the eleventh with thirty-one days exactly, by the twelfth with twenty-eight days exactly. [3] And it goes through the western gates in the order and number of the eastern, and accomplishes the three hundred and sixty-five and a quarter days of the solar year, while the lunar year has three hundred fifty-four, and there are wanting (to it) twelve days of the solar circle, which are the lunar epacts of the whole year. [4] Thus, too, the great circle contains five hundred and thirty-two years. [5] The quarter (of a day) is omitted for three years, the fourth fulfills it exactly. [6] Therefore they are taken outside of heaven for three years and are not added to the number of days, because they change the time of the years to two new months towards completion, to two others towards diminution. [7] And when the western gates are finished, it returns and goes to the eastern to the lights, and goes thus day and night about the heavenly circles, lower than all circles, swifter than the heavenly winds, and spirits and elements and angels flying; each angel has six wings. [8] It has a sevenfold course in nineteen years.

## 17

[1] In the midst of the heavens I saw armed soldiers, serving the Lord, with tympana and organs, with incessant voice, with sweet voice, with sweet and incessant (voice) and various singing, which it is impossible to describe, and (which) astonishes every mind, so wonderful and marvellous is the singing of those angels, and I was delighted listening to it.

## 18

[1] The men took me on to the fifth heaven and placed me, and there I saw many and countless soldiers, called Grigori, of human appearance, and their size (was) greater than that of great giants and their faces withered, and the silence of their mouths perpetual, and their was no service on the fifth heaven, and I said to the men who were with me: [2] Wherefore are these very withered and their faces melancholy, and their mouths silent, and (wherefore) is there no service on this heaven? [3] And they said to me: These are the Grigori, who with their prince Satanail (Satan) rejected the Lord of light, and after them are those who are held in great darkness on the second heaven, and three of them went down on to earth from the Lord's throne, to the place Ermon, and broke through their vows on the shoulder of the hill Ermon and saw the daughters of men how good they are, and took to themselves wives, and befouled the earth with their deeds, who in all times of their age made lawlessness and mixing, and giants are born and marvellous big men and great enmity. [4] And therefore God judged them with great judgment, and they weep for their brethren and they will be punished on the Lord's great day. [5] And I said to the Grigori: I saw your brethren and their works, and their great torments, and I prayed for them, but the Lord has condemned them (to be) under earth till (the existing) heaven and earth shall end for ever. [6] And I said: Wherefore do you wait, brethren, and do not serve before the Lord's face, and have not put your services before the Lord's face, lest you anger your Lord utterly? [7] And they listened to my admonition, and spoke to the four ranks in heaven, and lo! As I stood with those two men four trumpets trumpeted together with great voice, and the Grigori broke into song with one voice, and their voice went up before the Lord pitifully and affectingly.

## 19

[1] And thence those men took me and bore me up on to the sixth heaven, and there I saw seven bands of angels, very bright and very glorious, and their faces shining more than the sun's shining, glistening, and there is no difference in their faces, or behaviour, or manner of dress; and these make the orders, and learn the goings of the stars, and the alteration of the moon, or revolution of the sun, and the good government of the world. [2] And when they see evildoing they make commandments and instruction, and sweet and loud singing, and all (songs) of praise. [3] These are the archangels who are above angels, measure all life in heaven and on earth, and the angels who are (appointed) over seasons and years, the angels who are over rivers and sea, and who are over the fruits of the earth, and the angels who are over every grass, giving food to all, to every living thing, and the angels who write all the souls of men, and all their deeds, and their lives before the Lord's face; in their midst are six Phoenixes and six Cherubim and six six-winged ones continually with one voice singing one voice, and it is not possible to describe their singing, and they rejoice before the Lord at his footstool.

## 20

[1] And those two men lifted me up thence on to the seventh heaven, and I saw there a very great light, and fiery troops of great archangels, incorporeal forces, and dominions, orders and governments, Cherubim and seraphim, thrones and many-eyed ones, nine regiments, the Ioanit stations of light, and I became afraid, and began to tremble with great terror, and those men took me, and led me after them, and said to me: [2] Have courage, Enoch, do not fear, and showed me the Lord from afar, sitting on His very high throne. For what is there on the tenth heaven, since the Lord dwells there? [3] On the tenth heaven is God, in the Hebrew tongue he is called Aravat. [4] And all the heavenly troops would come and stand on the ten steps according to their rank, and would bow down to the Lord, and would again go to their places in joy and felicity, singing songs in the boundless light with small and tender voices, gloriously serving him.

## 21

[1] And the Cherubim and seraphim standing about the throne, the six-winged and many-eyed ones do not depart, standing before the Lord's face doing his will, and cover his whole throne, singing with gentle voice before the Lord's face: Holy, holy, holy, Lord Ruler of Sabaoth, heavens and earth are full of Your glory. [2] When I saw all these things, those men said to me: Enoch, thus far is it commanded us to journey with you, and those men went away from me and thereupon I saw them not. [3] And I remained alone at the end of the seventh heaven and became afraid, and fell on my face and said to myself: Woe is me, what has befallen me? [4] And the Lord sent one of his glorious ones, the archangel Gabriel, and (he) said to me: Have courage, Enoch, do not fear, arise before the Lord's face into eternity, arise, come with me. [5] And I answered him, and said in myself: My Lord, my soul is departed from me, from terror and trembling, and I called to the men who led me up to this place, on them I relied, and (it is) with them I go before the Lord's face. [6] And Gabriel caught me up, as a leaf caught up by the wind, and placed me before the Lord's face. [7] And I saw the eighth heaven, which is called in the Hebrew tongue Muzaloth, changer of the

seasons, of drought, and of wet, and of the twelve constellations of the circle of the firmament, which are above the seventh heaven. ⁸ And I saw the ninth heaven, which is called in Hebrew Kuchavim, where are the heavenly homes of the twelve constellations of the circle of the firmament.

## 22

¹ On the tenth heaven, (which is called) Aravoth, I saw the appearance of the Lord's face, like iron made to glow in fire, and brought out, emitting sparks, and it burns. ² Thus (in a moment of eternity) I saw the Lord's face, but the Lord's face is ineffable, marvellous and very awful, and very, very terrible. ³ And who am I to tell of the Lord's unspeakable being, and of his very wonderful face? And I cannot tell the quantity of his many instructions, and various voices, the Lord's throne (is) very great and not made with hands, nor the quantity of those standing round him, troops of Cherubim and seraphim, nor their incessant singing, nor his immutable beauty, and who shall tell of the ineffable greatness of his glory. ⁴ And I fell prone and bowed down to the Lord, and the Lord with his lips said to me: ⁵ Have courage, Enoch, do not fear, arise and stand before my face into eternity. ⁶ And the archistratege Michael lifted me up, and led me to before the Lord's face. ⁷ And the Lord said to his servants tempting them: Let Enoch stand before my face into eternity, and the glorious ones bowed down to the Lord, and said: Let Enoch go according to Your word. ⁸ And the Lord said to Michael: Go and take Enoch from out (of) his earthly garments, and anoint him with my sweet ointment, and put him into the garments of My glory. ⁹ And Michael did thus, as the Lord told him. He anointed me, and dressed me, and the appearance of that ointment is more than the great light, and his ointment is like sweet dew, and its smell mild, shining like the sun's ray, and I looked at myself, and (I) was like (transfigured) one of his glorious ones. ¹⁰ And the Lord summoned one of his archangels by name Pravuil, whose knowledge was quicker in wisdom than the other archangels, who wrote all the deeds of the Lord; and the Lord said to Pravuil: Bring out the books from my store-houses, and a reed of quick-writing, and give (it) to Enoch, and deliver to him the choice and comforting books out of your hand.

## 23

¹ And he was telling me all the works of heaven, earth and sea, and all the elements, their passages and goings, and the thunderings of the thunders, the sun and moon, the goings and changes of the stars, the seasons, years, days, and hours, the risings of the wind, the numbers of the angels, and the formation of their songs, and all human things, the tongue of every human song and life, the commandments, instructions, and sweet-voiced singings, and all things that it is fitting to learn. ² And Pravuil told me: All the things that I have told you, we have written. Sit and write all the souls of mankind, however many of them are born, and the places prepared for them to eternity; for all souls are prepared to eternity, before the formation of the world. ³ And all double thirty days and thirty nights, and I wrote out all things exactly, and wrote three hundred and sixty-six books.

## 24

¹ And the Lord summoned me, and said to me: Enoch, sit down on my left with Gabriel. ² And I bowed down to the Lord, and the Lord spoke to me: Enoch, beloved, all (that) you see, all things that are standing finished I tell to you even before the very beginning, all that I created from non-being, and visible (physical) things from invisible (spiritual). ³ Hear, Enoch, and take in these my words, for not to My angels have I told my secret, and I have not told them their rise, nor my endless realm, nor have they understood my creating, which I tell you to-day. ⁴ For before all things were visible (physical), I alone used to go about in the invisible (spiritual) things, like the sun from east to west, and from west to east. ⁵ But even the sun has peace in itself, while I found no peace, because I was creating all things, and I conceived the thought of placing foundations, and of creating visible (physical) creation.

## 25

¹ I commanded in the very lowest (parts), that visible (physical) things should come down from invisible (spiritual), and Adoil came down very great, and I beheld him, and lo! He had a belly of great light. ² And I said to him: Become undone, Adoil, and let the visible (physical) (come) out of you. ³ And he came undone, and a great light came out. And I (was) in the midst of the great light, and as there is born light from light, there came forth a great age, and showed all creation, which I had thought to create. ⁴ And I saw that (it was) good. ⁵ And I placed for myself a throne, and took my seat on it, and said to the light: Go thence up higher and fix yourself high above the throne, and be A foundation to the highest things. ⁶ And above the light there is nothing else, and then I bent up and looked up from my throne.

## 26

¹ And I summoned the very lowest a second time, and said: Let Archas come forth hard, and he came forth hard from the invisible (spiritual).

² And Archas came forth, hard, heavy, and very red. ³ And I said: Be opened, Archas, and let there be born from you, and he came undone, an age came forth, very great and very dark, bearing the creation of all lower things, and I saw that (it was) good and said to him: ⁴ Go thence down below, and make yourself firm, and be a foundation for the lower things, and it happened and he went down and fixed himself, and became the foundation for the lower things, and below the darkness there is nothing else.

## 27

¹ And I commanded that there should be taken from light and darkness, and I said: Be thick, and it became thus, and I spread it out with the light, and it became water, and I spread it out over the darkness, below the light, and then I made firm the waters, that is to say the bottomless, and I made foundation of light around the water, and created seven circles from inside, and imaged (the water) like crystal wet and dry, that is to say like glass, (and) the circumcession of the waters and the other elements, and I showed each one of them its road, and the seven stars each one of them in its heaven, that they go thus, and I saw that it was good. ² And I separated between light and between darkness, that is to say in the midst of the water hither and thither, and I said to the light, that it should be the day, and to the darkness, that it should be the night, and there was evening and there was morning the first day.

## 28

¹ And then I made firm the heavenly circle, and (made) that the lower water which is under heaven collect itself together, into one whole, and that the chaos become dry, and it became so. ² Out of the waves I created rock hard and big, and from the rock I piled up the dry, and the dry I called earth, and the midst of the earth I called abyss, that is to say the bottomless, I collected the sea in one place and bound it together with a yoke. ³ And I said to the sea: Behold I give you (your) eternal limits, and you shalt not break loose from your component parts. ⁴ Thus I made fast the firmament. This day I called me the first-created [Sunday].

## 29

¹ And for all the heavenly troops I imaged the image and essence of fire, and my eye looked at the very hard, firm rock, and from the gleam of my eye the lightning received its wonderful nature, (which) is both fire in water and water in fire, and one does not put out the other, nor does the one dry up the other, therefore the lightning is brighter than the sun, softer than water and firmer than hard rock. ² And from the rock I cut off a great fire, and from the fire I created the orders of the incorporeal ten troops of angels, and their weapons are fiery and their raiment a burning flame, and I commanded that each one should stand in his order. ³ And one from out the order of angels, having turned away with the order that was under him, conceived an impossible thought, to place his throne higher than the clouds above the earth, that he might become equal in rank to my power. ⁴ And I threw him out from the height with his angels, and he was flying in the air continuously above the bottomless.

## 30

¹ On the third day I commanded the earth to make grow great and fruitful trees, and hills, and seed to sow, and I planted Paradise, and enclosed it, and placed as armed (guardians) flaming angels, and thus I created renewal. ² Then came evening, and came morning the fourth day. ³ [Wednesday]. On the fourth day I commanded that there should be great lights on the heavenly circles. ⁴ On the first uppermost circle I placed the stars, Kruno, and on the second Aphrodit, on the third Aris, on the fifth Zoues, on the sixth Ermis, on the seventh lesser the moon, and adorned it with the lesser stars. ⁵ And on the lower I placed the sun for the illumination of day, and the moon and stars for the illumination of night. ⁶ The sun that it should go according to each constellation, twelve, and I appointed the succession of the months and their names and lives, their thunderings, and their hour-markings, how they should succeed. ⁷ Then evening came and morning came the fifth day. ⁸ [Thursday]. On the fifth day I commanded the sea, that it should bring forth fishes, and feathered birds of many varieties, and all animals creeping over the earth, going forth over the earth on four legs, and soaring in the air, male sex and female, and every soul breathing the spirit of life. ⁹ And there came evening, and there came morning the sixth day. ¹⁰ [Friday]. On the sixth day I commanded my wisdom to create man from seven consistencies: one, his flesh from the earth; two, his blood from the dew; three, his eyes from the sun; four, his bones from stone; five, his intelligence from the swiftness of the angels and from cloud; six, his veins and his hair from the grass of the earth; seven, his soul from my breath and from the wind. ¹¹ And I gave him seven natures: to the flesh hearing, the eyes for sight, to the soul smell, the veins for touch, the blood for taste, the bones for endurance, to the intelligence sweetness [enjoyment]. ¹² I conceived a cunning saying to say, I created man from invisible (spiritual) and from visible (physical) nature, of both are his death and life and image, he knows speech like

some created thing, small in greatness and again great in smallness, and I placed him on earth, a second angel, honourable, great and glorious, and I appointed him as ruler to rule on earth and to have my wisdom, and there was none like him of earth of all my existing creatures. <sup>13</sup> And I appointed him a name, from the four component parts, from east, from west, from south, from north, and I appointed for him four special stars, and I called his name Adam, and showed him the two ways, the light and the darkness, and I told him: <sup>14</sup> This is good, and that bad, that I should learn whether he has love towards me, or hatred, that it be clear which in his race love me. <sup>15</sup> For I have seen his nature, but he has not seen his own nature, therefore (through) not seeing he will sin worse, and I said After sin (what is there) but death? <sup>16</sup> And I put sleep into him and he fell asleep. And I took from him A rib, and created him a wife, that death should come to him by his wife, and I took his last word and called her name mother, that is to say, Eva (Eve).

## 31

<sup>1</sup> Adam has life on earth, and I created a garden in Eden in the east, that he should observe the testament and keep the command. <sup>2</sup> I made the heavens open to him, that he should see the angels singing the song of victory, and the gloomless light. <sup>3</sup> And he was continuously in paradise, and the devil understood that I wanted to create another world, because Adam was lord on earth, to rule and control it. <sup>4</sup> The devil is the evil spirit of the lower places, as a fugitive he made Sotona from the heavens as his name was Satanail (Satan), thus he became different from the angels, (but his nature) did not change (his) intelligence as far as (his) understanding of righteous and sinful (things). <sup>5</sup> And he understood his condemnation and the sin which he had sinned before, therefore he conceived thought against Adam, in such form he entered and seduced Eva (Eve), but did not touch Adam. <sup>6</sup> But I cursed ignorance, but what I had blessed previously, those I did not curse, I cursed not man, nor the earth, nor other creatures, but man's evil fruit, and his works.

## 32

<sup>1</sup> I said to him: Earth you are, and into the earth whence I took you you shalt go, and I will not ruin you, but send you whence I took you. <sup>2</sup> Then I can again receive you at My second presence. <sup>3</sup> And I blessed all my creatures visible (physical) and invisible (spiritual). And Adam was five and half hours in paradise. <sup>4</sup> And I blessed the seventh day, which is the Sabbath, on which he rested from all his works.

## 33

<sup>1</sup> And I appointed the eighth day also, that the eighth day should be the first-created after my work, and that (the first seven) revolve in the form of the seventh thousand, and that at the beginning of the eighth thousand there should be a time of not-counting, endless, with neither years nor months nor weeks nor days nor hours. <sup>2</sup> And now, Enoch, all that I have told you, all that you have understood, all that you have seen of heavenly things, all that you have seen on earth, and all that I have written in books by my great wisdom, all these things I have devised and created from the uppermost foundation to the lower and to the end, and there is no counsellor nor inheritor to my creations. <sup>3</sup> I am self-eternal, not made with hands, and without change. <sup>4</sup> My thought is my counsellor, my wisdom and my word are made, and my eyes observe all things how they stand here and tremble with terror. <sup>5</sup> If I turn away my face, then all things will be destroyed. <sup>6</sup> And apply your mind, Enoch, and know him who is speaking to you, and take thence the books which you yourself have written. <sup>7</sup> And I give you Samuil and Raguil, who led you up, and the books, and go down to earth, and tell your sons all that I have told you, and all that you have seen, from the lower heaven up to my throne, and all the troops. <sup>8</sup> For I created all forces, and there is none that resists me or that does not subject himself to me. For all subject themselves to my monarchy, and labour for my sole rule. <sup>9</sup> Give them the books of the handwriting, and they will read (them) and will know me for the creator of all things, and will understand how there is no other God but me. <sup>10</sup> And let them distribute the books of your handwriting–children to children, generation to generation, nations to nations. <sup>11</sup> And I will give you, Enoch, my intercessor, the archistratege Michael, for the handwritings of your fathers Adam, Seth, Enos, Cainan, Mahaleleel, and Jared your father.

## 34

<sup>1</sup> They have rejected my commandments and my yoke, worthless seed has come up, not fearing God, and they would not bow down to me, but have begun to bow down to vain gods, and denied my unity, and have laden the whole earth with untruths, offences, abominable lecheries, namely one with another, and all manner of other unclean wickedness, which are disgusting to relate. <sup>2</sup> And therefore I will bring down a deluge upon the earth and will destroy all men, and the whole earth will crumble together into great darkness.

## 35

<sup>1</sup> Behold from their seed shall arise another generation, much afterwards, but of them many will be very insatiate. <sup>2</sup> He who raises that generation, (shall) reveal to them the books of your handwriting, of your fathers, (to them) to whom he must point out the guardianship of the world, to the faithful men and workers of my pleasure, who do not acknowledge my name in vain. <sup>3</sup> And they shall tell another generation, and those (others) having read shall be glorified thereafter, more than the first.

## 36

<sup>1</sup> Now, Enoch, I give you the term of thirty days to spend in your house, and tell your sons and all your household, that all may hear from my face what is told them by you, that they may read and understand, how there is no other God but me. <sup>2</sup> And that they may always keep my commandments, and begin to read and take in the books of your handwriting. <sup>3</sup> And after thirty days I shall send my angel for you, and he will take you from earth and from your sons to me.

## 37

<sup>1</sup> And the Lord called upon one of the older angels, terrible and menacing, and placed him by me, in appearance white as snow, and his hands like ice, having the appearance of great frost, and he froze my face, because I could not endure the terror of the Lord, just as it is not possible to endure A stove's fire and the sun's heat, and the frost of the air. <sup>2</sup> And the Lord said to me: Enoch, if your face be not frozen here, no man will be able to behold your face.

## 38

<sup>1</sup> And the Lord said to those men who first led me up: Let Enoch go down on to earth with you, and await him till the determined day. <sup>2</sup> And they placed me by night on my bed. <sup>3</sup> And Mathusal (Methuselah) expecting my coming, keeping watch by day and by night at my bed, was filled with awe when he heard my coming, and I told him, Let all my household come together, that I tell them everything.

## 39

<sup>1</sup> Oh my children, my beloved ones, hear the admonition of your father, as much as is according to the Lord's will. <sup>2</sup> I have been let come to you to-day, and announce to you, not from my lips, but from the Lord's lips, all that is and was and all that is now, and all that will be till judgment-day. <sup>3</sup> For the Lord has let me come to you, you hear therefore the words of my lips, of a man made big for you, but I am one who has seen the Lord's face, like iron made to glow from fire it sends forth sparks and burns. <sup>4</sup> You look now upon my eyes, (the eyes) of a man big with meaning for you, but I have seen the Lord's eyes, shining like the sun's rays and filling the eyes of man with awe. <sup>5</sup> You see now, my children, the right hand of a man that helps you, but I have seen the Lord's right hand filling heaven as he helped me. <sup>6</sup> You see the compass of my work like your own, but I have seen the Lord's limitless and perfect compass, which has no end. <sup>7</sup> You hear the words of my lips, as I heard the words of the Lord, like great thunder incessantly with hurling of clouds. <sup>8</sup> And now, my children, hear the discourses of the father of the earth, how fearful and awful it is to come before the face of the ruler of the earth, how much more terrible and awful it is to come before the face of the ruler of heaven, the controller (judge) of quick and dead, and of the heavenly troops. Who can endure that endless pain?

## 40

<sup>1</sup> And now, my children, I know all things, for this (is) from the Lord's lips, and this my eyes have seen, from beginning to end. <sup>2</sup> I know all things, and have written all things into books, the heavens and their end, and their plenitude, and all the armies and their marchings. <sup>3</sup> I have measured and described the stars, the great countless multitude (of them). <sup>4</sup> What man has seen their revolutions, and their entrances? For not even the angels see their number, while I have written all their names. <sup>5</sup> And I measured the sun's circle, and measured its rays, counted the hours, I wrote down too all things that go over the earth, I have written the things that are nourished, and all seed sown and unsown, which the earth produces and all plants, and every grass and every flower, and their sweet smells, and their names, and the dwelling-places of the clouds, and their composition, and their wings, and how they bear rain and raindrops. <sup>6</sup> And I investigated all things, and wrote the road of the thunder and of the lightning, and they showed me the keys and their guardians, their rise, the way they go; it is let out (gently) in measure by a chain, lest by A heavy chain and violence it hurl down the angry clouds and destroy all things on earth. <sup>7</sup> I wrote the treasure-houses of the snow, and the store-houses of the cold and the frosty airs, and I observed their season's key-holder, he fills the clouds with them, and does not exhaust the treasure-houses. <sup>8</sup> And I wrote the resting-places of the winds and observed and saw how their key-holders bear weighing-scales and measures; first, they put them in (one) weighing-scale, then in the other the weights and let them out according to measure cunningly over the whole earth, lest by heavy breathing they

make the earth to rock. <sup>9</sup> And I measured out the whole earth, its mountains, and all hills, fields, trees, stones, rivers, all existing things I wrote down, the height from earth to the seventh heaven, and downwards to the very lowest hell, and the judgment-place, and the very great, open and weeping hell. <sup>10</sup> And I saw how the prisoners are in pain, expecting the limitless judgment. <sup>11</sup> And I wrote down all those being judged by the judge, and all their judgment (and sentences) and all their works.

## 41

<sup>1</sup> And I saw all forefathers from (all) time with Adam and Eva (Eve), and I sighed and broke into tears and said of the ruin of their dishonour: <sup>2</sup> Woe is me for my infirmity and (for that) of my forefathers, and thought in my heart and said: <sup>3</sup> Blessed (is) the man who has not been born or who has been born and shall not sin before the Lord's face, that he come not into this place, nor bring the yoke of this place.

## 42

<sup>1</sup> I saw the key-holders and guards of the gates of hell standing, like great serpents, and their faces like extinguishing lamps, and their eyes of fire, their sharp teeth, and I saw all the Lord's works, how they are right, while the works of man are some (good), and others bad, and in their works are known those who lie evilly.

## 43

<sup>1</sup> I, my children, measured and wrote out every work and every measure and every righteous judgment. <sup>2</sup> As (one) year is more honourable than another, so is (one) man more honourable than another, some for great possessions, some for wisdom of heart, some for particular intellect, some for cunning, one for silence of lip, another for cleanliness, one for strength, another for comeliness, one for youth, another for sharp wit, one for shape of body, another for sensibility, let it be heard everywhere, but there is none better than he who fears God, he shall be more glorious in time to come.

## 44

<sup>1</sup> The Lord with his hands having created man, in the likeness of his own face, the Lord made him small and great. <sup>2</sup> Whoever reviles the ruler's face, and abhors the Lord's face, has despised the Lord's face, and he who vents anger on any man without injury, the Lord's great anger will cut him down, he who spits on the face of man reproachfully, will be cut down at the Lord's great judgment. <sup>3</sup> Blessed is the man who does not direct his heart with malice against any man, and helps the injured and condemned, and raises the broken down, and shall do charity to the needy, because on the day of the great judgment every weight, every measure and every makeweight (will be) as in the market, that is to say (they are) hung on scales and stand in the market, (and every one) shall learn his own measure, and according to his measure shall take his reward.

## 45

<sup>1</sup> Whoever hastens to make offerings before the Lord's face, the Lord for his part will hasten that offering by granting of his work. <sup>2</sup> But whoever increases his lamp before the Lord's face and make not true judgment, the Lord will (not) increase his treasure in the realm of the highest. <sup>3</sup> When the Lord demands bread, or candles, or (the )flesh (of beasts), or any other sacrifice, then that is nothing; but God demands pure hearts, and with all that (only) tests the heart of man.

## 46

<sup>1</sup> Hear, my people, and take in the words of my lips. <sup>2</sup> If any one bring any gifts to an earthly ruler, and have disloyal thoughts in his heart, and the ruler know this, will he not be angry with him, and not refuse his gifts, and not give him over to judgment? <sup>3</sup> Or (if) one man make himself appear good to another by deceit of tongue, but (have) evil in his heart, then will not (the other) understand the treachery of his heart, and himself be condemned, since his untruth was plain to all? <sup>4</sup> And when the Lord shall send a great light, then there will be judgment for the just and the unjust, and there no one shall escape notice.

## 47

<sup>1</sup> And now, my children, lay thought on your hearts, mark well the words of your father, which are all (come) to you from the Lord's lips. <sup>2</sup> Take these books of your father's handwriting and read them. <sup>3</sup> For the books are many, and in them you will learn all the Lord's works, all that has been from the beginning of creation, and will be till the end of time. <sup>4</sup> And if you will observe my handwriting, you will not sin against the Lord; because there is no other except the Lord, neither in heaven, nor in earth, nor in the very lowest (places), nor in the (one) foundation. <sup>5</sup> The Lord has placed the foundations in the unknown, and has spread forth heavens visible (physical) and invisible (spiritual); he fixed the earth on the waters, and created countless creatures, and who has counted the water and the foundation of the unfixed, or the dust of the earth, or the sand of the sea, or the drops of the rain, or the morning dew, or the wind's breathings? Who has filled earth and sea, and the

indissoluble winter? <sup>6</sup> I cut the stars out of fire, and decorated heaven, and put it in their midst.

## 48

<sup>1</sup> That the sun go along the seven heavenly circles, which are the appointment of one hundred and eighty-two thrones, that it go down on a short day, and again one hundred and eighty-two, that it go down on a big day, and he has two thrones on which he rests, revolving hither and thither above the thrones of the months, from the seventeenth day of the month Tsivan it goes down to the month Thevan, from the seventeenth of Thevan it goes up. <sup>2</sup> And thus it goes close to the earth, then the earth is glad and makes grow its fruits, and when it goes away, then the earth is sad, and trees and all fruits have no florescence. <sup>3</sup> All this he measured, with good measurement of hours, and fixed A measure by his wisdom, of the visible (physical) and the invisible (spiritual). <sup>4</sup> From the invisible (spiritual) he made all things visible (physical), himself being invisible (spiritual). <sup>5</sup> Thus I make known to you, my children, and distribute the books to your children, into all your generations, and amongst the nations who shall have the sense to fear God, let them receive them, and may they come to love them more than any food or earthly sweets, and read them and apply themselves to them. <sup>6</sup> And those who understand not the Lord, who fear not God, who accept not, but reject, who do not receive the (books), a terrible judgment awaits these. <sup>7</sup> Blessed is the man who shall bear their yoke and shall drag them along, for he shall be released on the day of the great judgment.

## 49

<sup>1</sup> I swear to you, my children, but I swear not by any oath, neither by heaven nor by earth, nor by any other creature which God created. <sup>2</sup> The Lord said: There is no oath in me, nor injustice, but truth. <sup>3</sup> If there is no truth in men, let them swear by the words, Yea, yea, or else, Nay, nay. <sup>4</sup> And I swear to you, yea, yea, that there has been no man in his mother's womb, (but that) already before, even to each one there is a place prepared for the repose of that soul, and a measure fixed how much it is intended that a man be tried in this world. <sup>5</sup> Yea, children, deceive not yourselves, for there has been previously prepared a place for every soul of man.

## 50

<sup>1</sup> I have put every man's work in writing and none born on earth can remain hidden nor his works remain concealed. <sup>2</sup> I see all things. <sup>3</sup> Now therefore, my children, in patience and meekness spend the number of your days, that you inherit endless life. <sup>4</sup> Endure for the sake of the Lord every wound, every injury, every evil word and attack. <sup>5</sup> If ill-requitals befall you, return (them) not either to neighbour or enemy, because the Lord will return (them) for you and be your avenger on the day of great judgment, that there be no avenging here among men. <sup>6</sup> Whoever of you spends gold or silver for his brother's sake, he will receive ample treasure in the world to come. <sup>7</sup> Injure not widows nor orphans nor strangers, lest God's wrath come upon you.

## 51

<sup>1</sup> Stretch out your hands to the poor according to your strength. <sup>2</sup> Hide not your silver in the earth. <sup>3</sup> Help the faithful man in affliction, and affliction will not find you in the time of your trouble. <sup>4</sup> And every grievous and cruel yoke that come upon you bear all for the sake of the Lord, and thus you will find your reward in the day of judgment. <sup>5</sup> It is good to go morning, midday, and evening into the Lord's dwelling, for the glory of your creator. <sup>6</sup> Because every breathing (thing) glorifies him, and every creature visible (physical) and invisible (spiritual) returns him praise.

## 52

<sup>1</sup> Blessed is the man who opens his lips in praise of God of Sabaoth and praises the Lord with his heart. <sup>2</sup> Cursed every man who opens his lips for the bringing into contempt and calumny of his neighbour, because he brings God into contempt. <sup>3</sup> Blessed is he who opens his lips blessing and praising God. <sup>4</sup> Cursed is he before the Lord all the days of his life, who opens his lips to curse and abuse. <sup>5</sup> Blessed is he who blesses all the Lord's works. <sup>6</sup> Cursed is he who brings the Lord's creation into contempt. <sup>7</sup> Blessed is he who looks down and raises the fallen. <sup>8</sup> Cursed is he who looks to and is eager for the destruction of what is not his. <sup>9</sup> Blessed is he who keeps the foundations of his fathers made firm from the beginning. <sup>10</sup> Cursed is he who perverts the decrees of his forefathers. <sup>11</sup> Blessed is he who imparts peace and love. <sup>12</sup> Cursed is he who disturbs those that love their neighbours. <sup>13</sup> Blessed is he who speaks with humble tongue and heart to all. <sup>14</sup> Cursed is he who speaks peace with his tongue, while in his heart there is no peace but a sword. <sup>15</sup> For all these things will be laid bare in the weighing-scales and in the books, on the day of the great judgment.

## 53

<sup>1</sup> And now, my children, do not say: Our father is standing before God, and is praying for our sins, for there is there no helper of any man who

has sinned. ² You see how I wrote all works of every man, before his creation, (all) that is done amongst all men for all time, and none can tell or relate my handwriting, because the Lord see all imaginings of man, how they are vain, where they lie in the treasure-houses of the heart. ³ And now, my children, mark well all the words of your father, that I tell you, lest you regret, saying: Why did our father not tell us?

## 54

¹ At that time, not understanding this let these books which I have given you be for an inheritance of your peace. ² Hand them to all who want them, and instruct them, that they may see the Lord's very great and marvellous works.

## 55

¹ My children, behold, the day of my term and time have approached. ² For the angels who shall go with me are standing before me and urge me to my departure from you; they are standing here on earth, awaiting what has been told them. ³ For to-morrow I shall go up on to heaven, to the uppermost Jerusalem to my eternal inheritance. ⁴ Therefore I bid you do before the Lord's face all (his) good pleasure.

## 56

¹ Mathosalam having answered his father Enoch, said: What is agreeable to your eyes, father, that I may make before your face, that you may bless our dwellings, and your sons, and that your people may be made glorious through you, and then (that) you may depart thus, as the Lord said? ² Enoch answered to his son Mathosalam (and) said: Hear, child, from the time when the Lord anointed me with the ointment of his glory, (there has been no) food in me, and my soul remembers not earthly enjoyment, neither do I want anything earthly.

## 57

¹ My child Methosalam, summon all your brethren and all your household and the elders of the people, that I may talk to them and depart, as is planned for me. ² And Methosalam made haste, and summoned his brethren, Regim, Riman, Uchan, Chermion, Gaidad, and all the elders of the people before the face of his father Enoch; and he blessed them, (and) said to them:

## 58

¹ Listen to me, my children, to-day. ² In those days when the Lord came down on to earth for Adam's sake, and visited all his creatures, which he created himself, after all these he created Adam, and the Lord called all the beasts of the earth, all the reptiles, and all the birds that soar in the air, and brought them all before the face of our father Adam. ³ And Adam gave the names to all things living on earth. ⁴ And the Lord appointed him ruler over all, and subjected to him all things under his hands, and made them dumb and made them dull that they be commanded of man, and be in subjection and obedience to him. ⁵ Thus also the Lord created every man lord over all his possessions. ⁶ The Lord will not judge a single soul of beast for man's sake, but adjudges the souls of men to their beasts in this world; for men have a special place. ⁷ And as every soul of man is according to number, similarly beasts will not perish, nor all souls of beasts which the Lord created, till the great judgment, and they will accuse man, if he feed them ill.

## 59

¹ Whoever defiles the soul of beasts, defiles his own soul. ² For man brings clean animals to make sacrifice for sin, that he may have cure of his soul. ³ And if they bring for sacrifice clean animals, and birds, man has cure, he cures his soul. ⁴ All is given you for food, bind it by the four feet, that is to make good the cure, he cures his soul. ⁵ But whoever kills beast without wounds, kills his own souls and defiles his own flesh. ⁶ And he who does any beast any injury whatsoever, in secret, it is evil practice, and he defiles his own soul.

## 60

¹ He who works the killing of a man's soul, kills his own soul, and kills his own body, and there is no cure for him for all time. ² He who puts a man in any snare, shall stick in it himself, and there is no cure for him for all time. ³ He who puts a man in any vessel, his retribution will not be wanting at the great judgment for all time. ⁴ He who works crookedly or speaks evil against any soul, will not make justice for himself for all time.

## 61

¹ And now, my children, keep your hearts from every injustice, which the Lord hates. Just as a man asks something for his own soul from God, so let him do to every living soul, because I know all things, how in the great time to come there is much inheritance prepared for men, good for the good, and bad for the bad, without number many. ² Blessed are those who enter the good houses, for in the bad houses there is no peace nor return from them. ³ Hear, my children, small and great! When man puts a good thought in his heart, brings gifts from his labours before the Lord's face and his hands made them not, then the Lord will turn away his face from the labour of his hand, and (that) man cannot find the labour of his hands. ⁴ And if his hands made it, but his heart murmur, and his heart cease not making murmur incessantly, he has not any advantage.

## 62

¹ Blessed is the man who in his patience brings his gifts with faith before the Lord's face, because he will find forgiveness of sins. ² But if he take back his words before the time, there is no repentance for him; and if the time pass and he do not of his own will what is promised, there is no repentance after death. ³ Because every work which man does before the time, is all deceit before men, and sin before God.

## 63

¹ When man clothes the naked and fills the hungry, he will find reward from God. ² But if his heart murmur, he commits a double evil; ruin of himself and of that which he gives; and for him there will be no finding of reward on account of that. ³ And if his own heart is filled with his food and his own flesh, clothed with his own clothing, he commits contempt, and will forfeit all his endurance of poverty, and will not find reward of his good deeds. ⁴ Every proud and magniloquent man is hateful to the Lord, and every false speech, clothed in untruth; it will be cut with the blade of the sword of death, and thrown into the fire, and shall burn for all time.

## 64

¹ When Enoch had spoken these words to his sons, all people far and near heard how the Lord was calling Enoch. They took counsel together: ² Let us go and kiss Enoch, and two thousand men came together and came to the place Achuzan where Enoch was, and his sons. ³ And the elders of the people, the whole assembly, came and bowed down and began to kiss Enoch and said to him: ⁴ Our father Enoch, (may) you (be) blessed of the Lord, the eternal ruler, and now bless your sons and all the people, that we may be glorified to-day before your face. ⁵ For you shalt be glorified before the Lord's face for all time, since the Lord chose you, rather than all men on earth, and designated you writer of all his creation, visible (physical) and invisible (spiritual), and redeemed of the sins of man, and helper of your household.

## 65

¹ And Enoch answered all his people saying: Hear, my children, before that all creatures were created, the Lord created the visible (physical) and invisible (spiritual) things. ² And as much time as there was and went past, understand that after all that he created man in the likeness of his own form, and put into him eyes to see, and ears to hear, and heart to reflect, and intellect wherewith to deliberate. ³ And the Lord saw all man's works, and created all his creatures, and divided time, from time he fixed the years, and from the years he appointed the months, and from the months he appointed the days, and of days he appointed seven. ⁴ And in those he appointed the hours, measured them out exactly, that man might reflect on time and count years, months, and hours, (their) alternation, beginning, and end, and that he might count his own life, from the beginning until death, and reflect on his sin and write his work bad and good; because no work is hidden before the Lord, that every man might know his works and never transgress all his commandments, and keep my handwriting from generation to generation. ⁵ When all creation visible (physical) and invisible (spiritual), as the Lord created it, shall end, then every man goes to the great judgment, and then all time shall perish, and the years, and thenceforward there will be neither months nor days nor hours, they will be adhered together and will not be counted. ⁶ There will be one aeon, and all the righteous who shall escape the Lord's great judgment, shall be collected in the great aeon, for the righteous the great aeon will begin, and they will live eternally, and then too there will be amongst them neither labour, nor sickness, nor humiliation, nor anxiety, nor need, nor brutality, nor night, nor darkness, but great light. ⁷ And they shall have a great indestructible wall, and a paradise bright and incorruptible (eternal), for all corruptible (mortal) things shall pass away, and there will be eternal life.

## 66

¹ And now, my children, keep your souls from all injustice, such as the Lord hates. ² Walk before his face with terror and trembling and serve him alone. ³ Bow down to the true God, not to dumb idols, but bow down to his similitude, and bring all just offerings before the Lord's face. The Lord hates what is unjust. ⁴ For the Lord sees all things; when man takes thought in his heart, then he counsels the intellects, and every thought is always before the Lord, who made firm the earth and put all creatures on it. ⁵ If you look to heaven, the Lord is there; if you take thought of the sea's deep and all the under-earth, the Lord is there. ⁶ For the Lord created all things. Bow not down to things made by man, leaving the Lord of all creation, because no work can remain hidden before the Lord's face. ⁷ Walk, my children, in long-suffering, in meekness, honesty, in provocation, in grief, in faith and in truth, in (reliance on) promises, in illness, in abuse, in wounds, in temptation, in

nakedness, in privation, loving one another, till you go out from this age of ills, that you become inheritors of endless time. [8] Blessed are the just who shall escape the great judgment, for they shall shine forth more than the sun sevenfold, for in this world the seventh part is taken off from all, light, darkness, food, enjoyment, sorrow, paradise, torture, fire, frost, and other things; he put all down in writing, that you might read and understand.

## 67

[1] When Enoch had talked to the people, the Lord sent out darkness on to the earth, and there was darkness, and it covered those men standing with Enoch, and they took Enoch up on to the highest heaven, where the Lord (is); and he received him and placed him before his face, and the darkness went off from the earth, and light came again. [2] And the people saw and understood not how Enoch had been taken, and glorified God, and found a roll in which was traced The Invisible (spiritual) God; and all went to their dwelling places.

## 68

[1] Enoch was born on the sixth day of the month Tsivan, and lived three hundred and sixty-five years. [2] He was taken up to heaven on the first day of the month Tsivan and remained in heaven sixty days. [3] He wrote all these signs of all creation, which the Lord created, and wrote three hundred and sixty-six books, and handed them over to his sons and remained on earth thirty days, and was again taken up to heaven on the sixth day of the month Tsivan, on the very day and hour when he was born. [4] As every man's nature in this life is dark, so are also his conception, birth, and departure from this life. [5] At what hour he was conceived, at that hour he was born, and at that hour too he died. [6] Methosalam and his brethren, all the sons of Enoch, made haste, and erected an altar at that place called Achuzan, whence and where Enoch had been taken up to heaven. [7] And they took sacrificial oxen and summoned all people and sacrificed the sacrifice before the Lord's face. [8] All people, the elders of the people and the whole assembly came to the feast and brought gifts to the sons of Enoch. [9] And they made a great feast, rejoicing and making merry three days, praising God, who had given them such a sign through Enoch, who had found favour with him, and that they should hand it on to their sons from generation to generation, from age to age. [10] Amen.

# The Book of Ezra

## 1

[1] Now in the first year of Cyrus king of Persia, that Yahweh's[a] word by Jeremiah's mouth might be accomplished, Yahweh stirred up the spirit of Cyrus king of Persia, so that he made a proclamation throughout all his kingdom, and put it also in writing, saying, [2] "Cyrus king of Persia says, 'Yahweh, the God[b] of heaven, has given me all the kingdoms of the earth; and he has commanded me to build him a house in Jerusalem, which is in Judah. [3] Whoever there is among you of all his people, may his God be with him, and let him go up to Jerusalem, which is in Judah, and build the house of Yahweh, the God of Israel (he is God), which is in Jerusalem. [4] Whoever is left, in any place where he lives, let the men of his place help him with silver, with gold, with goods, and with animals, in addition to the free will offering for God's house which is in Jerusalem.'" [5] Then the heads of fathers' households of Judah and Benjamin, the priests and the Levites, all whose spirit God had stirred to go up, rose up to build Yahweh's house which is in Jerusalem. [6] All those who were around them strengthened their hands with vessels of silver, with gold, with goods, with animals, and with precious things, in addition to all that was willingly offered. [7] Also Cyrus the king brought out the vessels of Yahweh's house, which Nebuchadnezzar had brought out of Jerusalem, and had put in the house of his gods; [8] even those, Cyrus king of Persia brought out by the hand of Mithredath the treasurer, and counted them out to Sheshbazzar the prince of Judah. [9] This is the number of them: thirty platters of gold, one thousand platters of silver, twenty-nine knives, [10] thirty bowls of gold, four hundred ten silver bowls of a second kind, and one thousand other vessels. [11] All the vessels of gold and of silver were five thousand four hundred. Sheshbazzar brought all these up when the captives were brought up from Babylon to Jerusalem.

## 2

[1] Now these are the children of the province who went up out of the captivity of those who had been carried away, whom Nebuchadnezzar the king of Babylon had carried away to Babylon, and who returned to Jerusalem and Judah, everyone to his city; [2] who came with Zerubbabel, Jeshua, Nehemiah, Seraiah, Reelaiah, Mordecai, Bilshan, Mispar, Bigvai, Rehum, and Baanah. The number of the men of the people of Israel: [3] The children of Parosh, two thousand one hundred seventy-two. [4] The children of Shephatiah, three hundred seventy-two. [5] The children of Arah, seven hundred seventy-five. [6] The children of Pahathmoab, of the children of Jeshua and Joab, two thousand eight hundred twelve. [7] The children of Elam, one thousand two hundred fifty-four. [8] The children of Zattu, nine hundred forty-five. [9] The children of Zaccai, seven hundred sixty. [10] The children of Bani, six hundred forty-two. [11] The children of Bebai, six hundred twenty-three. [12] The children of Azgad, one thousand two hundred twenty-two. [13] The children of Adonikam, six hundred sixty-six. [14] The children of Bigvai, two thousand fifty-six. [15] The children of Adin, four hundred fifty-four. [16] The children of Ater, of Hezekiah, ninety-eight. [17] The children of Bezai, three hundred twenty-three. [18] The children of Jorah, one hundred twelve. [19] The children of Hashum, two hundred twenty-three. [20] The children of Gibbar, ninety-five. [21] The children of Bethlehem, one hundred twenty-three. [22] The men of Netophah, fifty-six. [23] The men of Anathoth, one hundred twenty-eight. [24] The children of Azmaveth, forty-two. [25] The children of Kiriath Arim, Chephirah, and Beeroth, seven hundred forty-three. [26] The children of Ramah and Geba, six hundred twenty-one. [27] The men of Michmas, one hundred twenty-two. [28] The men of Bethel and Ai, two hundred twenty-three. [29] The children of Nebo, fifty-two. [30] The children of Magbish, one hundred fifty-six. [31] The children of the other Elam, one thousand two hundred fifty-four. [32] The children of Harim, three hundred twenty. [33] The children of Lod, Hadid, and Ono, seven hundred twenty-five. [34] The children of Jericho, three hundred forty-five. [35] The children of Senaah, three thousand six hundred thirty. [36] The priests: the children of Jedaiah, of the house of Jeshua, nine hundred seventy-three. [37] The children of Immer, one thousand fifty-two. [38] The children of Pashhur, one thousand two hundred forty-seven. [39] The children of Harim, one thousand seventeen. [40] The Levites: the children of Jeshua and Kadmiel, of the children of Hodaviah, seventy-four. [41] The singers: the children of Asaph, one hundred twenty-eight. [42] The children of the gatekeepers: the children of Shallum, the children of Ater, the children of Talmon, the children of Akkub, the children of Hatita, the children of Shobai, in all one hundred thirty-nine. [43] The temple servants: the children of Ziha, the children of Hasupha, the children of Tabbaoth, [44] the children of Keros, the children of Siaha, the children of Padon, [45] the children of Lebanah, the children of Hagabah, the children of Akkub, [46] the children of Hagab, the children of Shamlai, the children of Hanan, [47] the children of Giddel, the children of Gahar, the children of Reaiah, [48] the children of Rezin, the children of Nekoda, the children of Gazzam, [49] the children of Uzza, the children of Paseah, the children of Besai, [50] the children of Asnah, the children of Meunim, the children of Nephisim, [51] the children of Bakbuk, the children of Hakupha, the children of Harhur, [52] the children of Bazluth, the children of Mehida, the children of Harsha, [53] the children of Barkos, the children of Sisera, the children of Temah, [54] the children of Neziah, the children of Hatipha. [55] The children of Solomon's servants: the children of Sotai, the children of Hassophereth, the children of Peruda, [56] the children of Jaalah, the children of Darkon, the children of Giddel, [57] the children of Shephatiah, the children of Hattil, the children of Pochereth Hazzebaim, the children of Ami. [58] All the temple servants, and the children of Solomon's servants, were three hundred ninety-two. [59] These were those who went up from Tel Melah, Tel Harsha, Cherub, Addan, and Immer; but they could not show their fathers' houses and their offspring,[c] whether they were of Israel: [60] the children of Delaiah, the children of Tobiah, the children of Nekoda, six hundred fifty-two. [61] Of the children of the priests: the children of Habaiah, the children of Hakkoz, and the children of Barzillai, who took a wife of the daughters of Barzillai the Gileadite, and was called after their name. [62] These sought their place among those who were registered by genealogy, but they were not found; therefore they were deemed disqualified and removed from the priesthood. [63] The governor told them that they should not eat of the most holy things until a priest stood up to serve with Urim and with Thummim. [64] The whole assembly together was forty-two thousand three hundred sixty, [65] in addition to their male servants and their female servants, of whom there were seven thousand three hundred thirty-seven; and they had two hundred singing men and singing women. [66] Their horses were seven hundred thirty-six; their mules, two hundred forty-five; [67] their camels, four hundred thirty-five; their donkeys, six thousand seven hundred twenty. [68] Some of the heads of fathers' households, when they came to Yahweh's house which is in Jerusalem, offered willingly for God's house to set it up in its place. [69] They gave according to their ability into the treasury of the

---

[a] 1:1 "Yahweh" is God's proper Name, sometimes rendered "LORD" (all caps) in other translations.

[b] 1:2 The Hebrew word rendered "God" is "אֱלֹהִים" (Elohim).

[c] 2:59 or, seed

work sixty-one thousand darics of gold,[a] five thousand minas[b] of silver, and one hundred priests' garments. [70] So the priests and the Levites, with some of the people, the singers, the gatekeepers, and the temple servants, lived in their cities, and all Israel in their cities.

## 3

[1] When the seventh month had come, and the children of Israel were in the cities, the people gathered themselves together as one man to Jerusalem. [2] Then Jeshua the son of Jozadak stood up with his brothers the priests and Zerubbabel the son of Shealtiel and his relatives, and built the altar of the God of Israel, to offer burnt offerings on it, as it is written in the law of Moses the man of God. [3] In spite of their fear because of the peoples of the surrounding lands, they set the altar on its base; and they offered burnt offerings on it to Yahweh, even burnt offerings morning and evening. [4] They kept the feast of booths, as it is written, and offered the daily burnt offerings by number, according to the ordinance, as the duty of every day required; [5] and afterward the continual burnt offering, the offerings of the new moons, of all the set feasts of Yahweh that were consecrated, and of everyone who willingly offered a free will offering to Yahweh. [6] From the first day of the seventh month, they began to offer burnt offerings to Yahweh; but the foundation of Yahweh's temple was not yet laid. [7] They also gave money to the masons and to the carpenters. They also gave food, drink, and oil to the people of Sidon and Tyre to bring cedar trees from Lebanon to the sea, to Joppa, according to the grant that they had from Cyrus King of Persia. [8] Now in the second year of their coming to God's house at Jerusalem, in the second month, Zerubbabel the son of Shealtiel, Jeshua the son of Jozadak, and the rest of their brothers the priests and the Levites, and all those who had come out of the captivity to Jerusalem, began the work and appointed the Levites, from twenty years old and upward, to have the oversight of the work of Yahweh's house. [9] Then Jeshua stood with his sons and his brothers, Kadmiel and his sons, the sons of Judah, together to have the oversight of the workmen in God's house: the sons of Henadad, with their sons and their brothers the Levites. [10] When the builders laid the foundation of Yahweh's temple, they set the priests in their vestments with trumpets, with the Levites the sons of Asaph with cymbals, to praise Yahweh, according to the directions of David king of Israel. [11] They sang to one another in praising and giving thanks to Yahweh, "For he is good, for his loving kindness endures forever toward Israel." All the people shouted with a great shout, when they praised Yahweh, because the foundation of Yahweh's house had been laid. [12] But many of the priests and Levites and heads of fathers' households, the old men who had seen the first house, when the foundation of this house was laid before their eyes, wept with a loud voice. Many also shouted aloud for joy, [13] so that the people could not discern the noise of the shout of joy from the noise of the weeping of the people; for the people shouted with a loud shout, and the noise was heard far away.

## 4

[1] Now when the adversaries of Judah and Benjamin heard that the children of the captivity were building a temple to Yahweh, the God of Israel, [2] they came near to Zerubbabel, and to the heads of fathers' households, and said to them, "Let us build with you, for we seek your God as you do; and we have been sacrificing to him since the days of Esar Haddon king of Assyria, who brought us up here." [3] But Zerubbabel, Jeshua, and the rest of the heads of fathers' households of Israel said to them, "You have nothing to do with us in building a house to our God; but we ourselves together will build to Yahweh, the God of Israel, as King Cyrus the king of Persia has commanded us." [4] Then the people of the land weakened the hands of the people of Judah, and troubled them in building. [5] They hired counselors against them to frustrate their purpose all the days of Cyrus king of Persia, even until the reign of Darius king of Persia. [6] In the reign of Ahasuerus, in the beginning of his reign, they wrote an accusation against the inhabitants of Judah and Jerusalem. [7] In the days of Artaxerxes, Bishlam, Mithredath, Tabeel, and the rest of his companions wrote to Artaxerxes king of Persia; and the writing of the letter was written in Syrian and delivered in the Syrian language. [8] Rehum the chancellor and Shimshai the scribe wrote a letter against Jerusalem to Artaxerxes the king as follows. [9] Then Rehum the chancellor, Shimshai the scribe, and the rest of their companions, the Dinaites, and the Apharsathchites, the Tarpelites, the Apharsites, the Archevites, the Babylonians, the Shushanchites, the Dehaites, the Elamites, [10] and the rest of the nations whom the great and noble Osnappar brought over and settled in the city of Samaria, and in the rest of the country beyond the River, and so forth, wrote. [11] This is the copy of the letter that they sent: To King Artaxerxes, from your servants, the people beyond the River. [12] Be it known to the king that the Jews who came up from you have come to us to Jerusalem. They are building the rebellious and bad city, and have finished the walls and repaired the foundations. [13] Be it known now to the king that if this city is built and the walls finished, they will not pay tribute, custom, or toll, and in the end it will be hurtful to the kings. [14] Now because we eat the salt of the palace and it is not appropriate for us to see the king's dishonor, therefore we have sent and informed the king, [15] that search may be made in the book of the records of your fathers. You will see in the book of the records, and know that this city is a rebellious city, and hurtful to kings and provinces, and that they have started rebellions within it in the past. That is why this city was destroyed. [16] We inform the king that if this city is built and the walls finished, then you will have no possession beyond the River. [17] Then the king sent an answer to Rehum the chancellor, and to Shimshai the scribe, and to the rest of their companions who live in Samaria, and in the rest of the country beyond the River: Peace. [18] The letter which you sent to us has been plainly read before me. [19] I decreed, and search has been made, and it was found that this city has made insurrection against kings in the past, and that rebellion and revolts have been made in it. [20] There have also been mighty kings over Jerusalem who have ruled over all the country beyond the River; and tribute, custom, and toll was paid to them. [21] Make a decree now to cause these men to cease, and that this city not be built until a decree is made by me. [22] Be careful that you not be slack doing so. Why should damage grow to the hurt of the kings? [23] Then when the copy of King Artaxerxes' letter was read before Rehum, Shimshai the scribe, and their companions, they went in haste to Jerusalem to the Jews, and made them to cease by force of arms. [24] Then work stopped on God's house which is at Jerusalem. It stopped until the second year of the reign of Darius king of Persia.

## 5

[1] Now the prophets, Haggai the prophet and Zechariah the son of Iddo, prophesied to the Jews who were in Judah and Jerusalem. They prophesied to them in the name of the God of Israel. [2] Then Zerubbabel the son of Shealtiel, and Jeshua the son of Jozadak rose up and began to build God's house which is at Jerusalem; and with them were the prophets of God, helping them. [3] At the same time Tattenai, the governor beyond the River, came to them, with Shetharbozenai and their companions, and asked them, "Who gave you a decree to build this house and to finish this wall?" [4] They also asked for the names of the men who were making this building. [5] But the eye of their God was on the elders of the Jews, and they didn't make them cease until the matter should come to Darius, and an answer should be returned by letter concerning it. [6] The copy of the letter that Tattenai, the governor beyond the River, and Shetharbozenai, and his companions the Apharsachites who were beyond the River, sent to Darius the king follows. [7] They sent a letter to him, in which was written: To Darius the king, all peace. [8] Be it known to the king that we went into the province of Judah, to the house of the great God, which is being built with great stones and timber is laid in the walls. This work goes on with diligence and prospers in their hands. [9] Then we asked those elders, and said to them thus, "Who gave you a decree to build this house, and to finish this wall?" [10] We asked them their names also, to inform you that we might write the names of the men who were at their head. [11] Thus they returned us answer, saying, "We are the servants of the God of heaven and earth and are building the house that was built these many years ago, which a great king of Israel built and finished. [12] But after our fathers had provoked the God of heaven to wrath, he gave them into the hand of Nebuchadnezzar king of Babylon, the Chaldean, who destroyed this house and carried the people away into Babylon. [13] But in the first year of Cyrus king of Babylon, Cyrus the king made a decree to build this house of God. [14] The gold and silver vessels of God's house, which Nebuchadnezzar took out of the temple that was in Jerusalem and brought into the temple of Babylon, those Cyrus the king also took out of the temple of Babylon, and they were delivered to one whose name was Sheshbazzar, whom he had made governor. [15] He said to him, 'Take these vessels, go, put them in the temple that is in Jerusalem, and let God's house be built in its place.' [16] Then the same Sheshbazzar came and laid the foundations of God's house which is in Jerusalem. Since that time even until now it has been being built, and yet it is not completed. [17] Now therefore, if it seems good to the king, let a search be made in the king's treasure house, which is there at Babylon, whether it is so that a decree was made by Cyrus the king to build this house of God at Jerusalem; and let the king send his pleasure to us concerning this matter."

## 6

[1] Then Darius the king made a decree, and the house of the archives, where the treasures were laid up in Babylon, was searched. [2] A scroll was found at Achmetha, in the palace that is in the province of Media,

---

[a] *2:69* a daric was a gold coin issued by a Persian king,

weighing about 8.4 grams or about 0.27 troy ounces each.

[b] *2:69* A mina is about 600 grams or 1.3 U. S. pounds, so

5,000 minas is about 3 metric tons.

and in it this was written for a record: ³ In the first year of Cyrus the king, Cyrus the king made a decree: Concerning God's house at Jerusalem, let the house be built, the place where they offer sacrifices, and let its foundations be strongly laid, with its height sixty cubitsᵃ and its width sixty cubits; ⁴ with three courses of great stones and a course of new timber. Let the expenses be given out of the king's house. ⁵ Also let the gold and silver vessels of God's house, which Nebuchadnezzar took out of the temple which is at Jerusalem and brought to Babylon, be restored and brought again to the temple which is at Jerusalem, everything to its place. You shall put them in God's house. ⁶ Now therefore, Tattenai, governor beyond the River, Shetharbozenai, and your companions the Apharsachites, who are beyond the River, you must stay far from there. ⁷ Leave the work of this house of God alone; let the governor of the Jews and the elders of the Jews build this house of God in its place. ⁸ Moreover I make a decree regarding what you shall do for these elders of the Jews for the building of this house of God: that of the king's goods, even of the tribute beyond the River, expenses must be given with all diligence to these men, that they not be hindered. ⁹ That which they have need of, including young bulls, rams, and lambs, for burnt offerings to the God of heaven; also wheat, salt, wine, and oil, according to the word of the priests who are at Jerusalem, let it be given them day by day without fail, ¹⁰ that they may offer sacrifices of pleasant aroma to the God of heaven, and pray for the life of the king and of his sons. ¹¹ I have also made a decree that whoever alters this message, let a beam be pulled out from his house, and let him be lifted up and fastened on it; and let his house be made a dunghill for this. ¹² May the God who has caused his name to dwell there overthrow all kings and peoples who stretch out their hand to alter this, to destroy this house of God which is at Jerusalem. I Darius have made a decree. Let it be done with all diligence. ¹³ Then Tattenai, the governor beyond the River, Shetharbozenai, and their companions did accordingly with all diligence, because Darius the king had sent a decree. ¹⁴ The elders of the Jews built and prospered, through the prophesying of Haggai the prophet and Zechariah the son of Iddo. They built and finished it, according to the commandment of the God of Israel, and according to the decree of Cyrus, Darius, and Artaxerxes king of Persia. ¹⁵ This house was finished on the third day of the month Adar, which was in the sixth year of the reign of Darius the king. ¹⁶ The children of Israel, the priests, the Levites, and the rest of the children of the captivity, kept the dedication of this house of God with joy. ¹⁷ They offered at the dedication of this house of God one hundred bulls, two hundred rams, four hundred lambs; and for a sin offering for all Israel, twelve male goats, according to the number of the tribes of Israel. ¹⁸ They set the priests in their divisions and the Levites in their courses, for the service of God which is at Jerusalem, as it is written in the book of Moses. ¹⁹ The children of the captivity kept the Passover on the fourteenth day of the first month. ²⁰ Because the priests and the Levites had purified themselves together, all of them were pure. They killed the Passover for all the children of the captivity, for their brothers the priests, and for themselves. ²¹ The children of Israel who had returned out of the captivity, and all who had separated themselves to them from the filthiness of the nations of the land to seek Yahweh, the God of Israel, ate, ²² and kept the feast of unleavened bread seven days with joy; because Yahweh had made them joyful, and had turned the heart of the king of Assyria to them, to strengthen their hands in the work of God, the God of Israel's house.

## 7

¹ Now after these things, in the reign of Artaxerxes king of Persia, Ezra the son of Seraiah, the son of Azariah, the son of Hilkiah, ² the son of Shallum, the son of Zadok, the son of Ahitub, ³ the son of Amariah, the son of Azariah, the son of Meraioth, ⁴ the son of Zerahiah, the son of Uzzi, the son of Bukki, ⁵ the son of Abishua, the son of Phinehas, the son of Eleazar, the son of Aaron the chief priest— ⁶ this Ezra went up from Babylon. He was a skilled scribe in the law of Moses, which Yahweh, the God of Israel, had given; and the king granted him all his request, according to Yahweh his God's hand on him. ⁷ Some of the children of Israel, including some of the priests, the Levites, the singers, the gatekeepers, and the temple servants went up to Jerusalem in the seventh year of Artaxerxes the king. ⁸ He came to Jerusalem in the fifth month, which was in the seventh year of the king. ⁹ For on the first day of the first month he began to go up from Babylon; and on the first day of the fifth month he came to Jerusalem, according to the good hand of his God on him. ¹⁰ For Ezra had set his heart to seek Yahweh's law, and to do it, and to teach statutes and ordinances in Israel. ¹¹ Now this is the

copy of the letter that King Artaxerxes gave to Ezra the priest, the scribe, even the scribe of the words of Yahweh's commandments, and of his statutes to Israel: ¹² Artaxerxes, king of kings, To Ezra the priest, the scribe of the law of the perfect God of heaven. Now ¹³ I make a decree that all those of the people of Israel and their priests and the Levites in my realm, who intend of their own free will to go to Jerusalem, go with you. ¹⁴ Because you are sent by the king and his seven counselors to inquire concerning Judah and Jerusalem, according to the law of your God which is in your hand, ¹⁵ and to carry the silver and gold, which the king and his counselors have freely offered to the God of Israel, whose habitation is in Jerusalem, ¹⁶ and all the silver and gold that you will find in all the province of Babylon, with the free will offering of the people and of the priests, offering willingly for the house of their God which is in Jerusalem. ¹⁷ Therefore you shall with all diligence buy with this money bulls, rams, and lambs with their meal offerings and their drink offerings, and shall offer them on the altar of the house of your God which is in Jerusalem. ¹⁸ Whatever seems good to you and to your brothers to do with the rest of the silver and the gold, do that according to the will of your God. ¹⁹ The vessels that are given to you for the service of the house of your God, deliver before the God of Jerusalem. ²⁰ Whatever more will be needed for the house of your God, which you may have occasion to give, give it out of the king's treasure house. ²¹ I, even I, Artaxerxes the king, make a decree to all the treasurers who are beyond the River, that whatever Ezra the priest, the scribe of the law of the God of heaven, requires of you, it shall be done with all diligence, ²² up to one hundred talentsᵇ of silver, and to one hundred corsᶜ of wheat, and to one hundred bathsᵈ of wine, and to one hundred baths of oil, and salt without prescribing how much. ²³ Whatever is commanded by the God of heaven, let it be done exactly for the house of the God of heaven; for why should there be wrath against the realm of the king and his sons? ²⁴ Also we inform you that it shall not be lawful to impose tribute, custom, or toll on any of the priests, Levites, singers, gatekeepers, temple servants, or laborers of this house of God. ²⁵ You, Ezra, according to the wisdom of your God that is in your hand, appoint magistrates and judges who may judge all the people who are beyond the River, who all know the laws of your God; and teach him who doesn't know them. ²⁶ Whoever will not do the law of your God and the law of the king, let judgment be executed on him with all diligence, whether it is to death, or to banishment, or to confiscation of goods, or to imprisonment. ²⁷ Blessed be Yahweh, the God of our fathers, who has put such a thing as this in the king's heart, to beautify Yahweh's house which is in Jerusalem; ²⁸ and has extended loving kindness to me before the king and his counselors, and before all the king's mighty princes. I was strengthened according to Yahweh my God's hand on me, and I gathered together chief men out of Israel to go up with me.

## 8

¹ Now these are the heads of their fathers' households, and this is the genealogy of those who went up with me from Babylon, in the reign of Artaxerxes the king: ² Of the sons of Phinehas, Gershom. Of the sons of Ithamar, Daniel. Of the sons of David, Hattush. ³ Of the sons of Shecaniah, of the sons of Parosh, Zechariah; and with him were listed by genealogy of the males one hundred fifty. ⁴ Of the sons of Pahathmoab, Eliehoenai the son of Zerahiah; and with him two hundred males. ⁵ Of the sons of Shecaniah, the son of Jahaziel; and with him three hundred males. ⁶ Of the sons of Adin, Ebed the son of Jonathan; and with him fifty males. ⁷ Of the sons of Elam, Jeshaiah the son of Athaliah; and with him seventy males. ⁸ Of the sons of Shephatiah, Zebadiah the son of Michael; and with him eighty males. ⁹ Of the sons of Joab, Obadiah the son of Jehiel; and with him two hundred eighteen males. ¹⁰ Of the sons of Shelomith, the son of Josiphiah; and with him one hundred sixty males. ¹¹ Of the sons of Bebai, Zechariah the son of Bebai; and with him twenty-eight males. ¹² Of the sons of Azgad, Johanan the son of Hakkatan; and with him one hundred ten males. ¹³ Of the sons of Adonikam, who were the last, their names are: Eliphelet, Jeuel, and Shemaiah; and with them sixty males. ¹⁴ Of the sons of Bigvai, Uthai and Zabbud; and with them seventy males. ¹⁵ I gathered them together to the river that runs to Ahava; and there we encamped three days. Then I looked around at the people and the priests, and found there were none of the sons of Levi. ¹⁶ Then I sent for Eliezer, for Ariel, for Shemaiah, for Elnathan, for Jarib, for Elnathan, for Nathan, for Zechariah, and for Meshullam, chief men; also for Joiarib and for Elnathan, who were teachers. ¹⁷ I sent them out to Iddo the chief at the place Casiphia; and I told them what they should tell Iddo and his

---

ᵃ *6:3* A cubit is the length from the tip of the middle finger to the elbow on a man's arm, or about 18 inches or 46 centimeters.

ᵇ *7:22* A talent is about 30 kilograms or 66 pounds or 965 Troy ounces

ᶜ *7:22* 1 cor is the same as a homer, or about 55.9 U. S.

gallons (liquid) or 211 liters or 6 bushels.

ᵈ *7:22* 1 bath is one tenth of a cor, or about 5.6 U. S. gallons or 21 liters or 2.4 pecks. 100

baths would be about 2,100 liters.

brothers the temple servants at the place Casiphia, that they should bring to us ministers for the house of our God. **18** According to the good hand of our God on us they brought us a man of discretion, of the sons of Mahli, the son of Levi, the son of Israel, namely Sherebiah, with his sons and his brothers, eighteen; **19** and Hashabiah, and with him Jeshaiah of the sons of Merari, his brothers and their sons, twenty; **20** and of the temple servants, whom David and the princes had given for the service of the Levites, two hundred twenty temple servants. All of them were mentioned by name. **21** Then I proclaimed a fast there at the river Ahava, that we might humble ourselves before our God, to seek from him a straight way for us, for our little ones, and for all our possessions. **22** For I was ashamed to ask of the king a band of soldiers and horsemen to help us against the enemy on the way, because we had spoken to the king, saying, "The hand of our God is on all those who seek him, for good; but his power and his wrath is against all those who forsake him." **23** So we fasted and begged our God for this, and he granted our request. **24** Then I set apart twelve of the chiefs of the priests, even Sherebiah, Hashabiah, and ten of their brothers with them, **25** and weighed to them the silver, the gold, and the vessels, even the offering for the house of our God, which the king, his counselors, his princes, and all Israel there present, had offered. **26** I weighed into their hand six hundred fifty talents of silver,ᵃ one hundred talents of silver vessels, one hundred talents of gold, **27** twenty bowls of gold weighing one thousand darics,ᵇ and two vessels of fine bright bronze, precious as gold. **28** I said to them, "You are holy to Yahweh, and the vessels are holy. The silver and the gold are a free will offering to Yahweh, the God of your fathers. **29** Watch and keep them until you weigh them before the chiefs of the priests, the Levites, and the princes of the fathers' households of Israel at Jerusalem, in the rooms of Yahweh's house." **30** So the priests and the Levites received the weight of the silver, the gold, and the vessels, to bring them to Jerusalem to the house of our God. **31** Then we departed from the river Ahava on the twelfth day of the first month, to go to Jerusalem. The hand of our God was on us, and he delivered us from the hand of the enemy and the bandits by the way. **32** We came to Jerusalem, and stayed there three days. **33** On the fourth day the silver and the gold and the vessels were weighed in the house of our God into the hand of Meremoth the son of Uriah the priest; and with him was Eleazar the son of Phinehas; and with them were Jozabad the son of Jeshua, and Noadiah the son of Binnui, the Levites. **34** Everything was counted and weighed; and all the weight was written at that time. **35** The children of the captivity, who had come out of exile, offered burnt offerings to the God of Israel: twelve bulls for all Israel, ninety-six rams, seventy-seven lambs, and twelve male goats for a sin offering. All this was a burnt offering to Yahweh. **36** They delivered the king's commissions to the king's local governors and to the governors beyond the River. So they supported the people and God's house.

# 9

**1** Now when these things were done, the princes came near to me, saying, "The people of Israel, the priests, and the Levites have not separated themselves from the peoples of the lands, following their abominations, even those of the Canaanites, the Hittites, the Perizzites, the Jebusites, the Ammonites, the Moabites, the Egyptians, and the Amorites. **2** For they have taken of their daughters for themselves and for their sons, so that the holy offspring have mixed themselves with the peoples of the lands. Yes, the hand of the princes and rulers has been chief in this trespass." **3** When I heard this thing, I tore my garment and my robe, and pulled the hair out of my head and of my beard, and sat down confounded. **4** Then everyone who trembled at the words of the God of Israel were assembled to me because of the trespass of the exiles; and I sat confounded until the evening offering. **5** At the evening offering I rose up from my humiliation, even with my garment and my robe torn; and I fell on my knees, and spread out my hands to Yahweh my God; **6** and I said, "My God, I am ashamed and blush to lift up my face to you, my God, for our iniquities have increased over our head, and our guiltiness has grown up to the heavens. **7** Since the days of our fathers we have been exceedingly guilty to this day; and for our iniquities we, our kings, and our priests have been delivered into the hand of the kings of the lands, to the sword, to captivity, to plunder, and to confusion of face, as it is this day. **8** Now for a little moment grace has been shown from Yahweh our God, to leave us a remnant to escape, and to give us a stake in his holy place, that our God may lighten our eyes, and revive us a little in our bondage. **9** For we are bondservants; yet our God has not forsaken us in our bondage, but has extended loving kindness to us in the sight of the kings of Persia, to revive us, to set up

the house of our God, and to repair its ruins, and to give us a wall in Judah and in Jerusalem. **10** "Now, our God, what shall we say after this? For we have forsaken your commandments, **11** which you have commanded by your servants the prophets, saying, 'The land to which you go to possess is an unclean land through the uncleanness of the peoples of the lands, through their abominations, which have filled it from one end to another with their filthiness. **12** Now therefore don't give your daughters to their sons. Don't take their daughters to your sons, nor seek their peace or their prosperity forever, that you may be strong and eat the good of the land, and leave it for an inheritance to your children forever.' **13** "After all that has come on us for our evil deeds and for our great guilt, since you, our God, have punished us less than our iniquities deserve, and have given us such a remnant, **14** shall we again break your commandments, and join ourselves with the peoples that do these abominations? Wouldn't you be angry with us until you had consumed us, so that there would be no remnant, nor any to escape? **15** Yahweh, the God of Israel, you are righteous; for we are left a remnant that has escaped, as it is today. Behold,ᶜ we are before you in our guiltiness; for no one can stand before you because of this."

# 10

**1** Now while Ezra prayed and made confession, weeping and casting himself down before God's house, there was gathered together to him out of Israel a very great assembly of men and women and children; for the people wept very bitterly. **2** Shecaniah the son of Jehiel, one of the sons of Elam, answered Ezra, "We have trespassed against our God, and have married foreign women of the peoples of the land. Yet now there is hope for Israel concerning this thing. **3** Now therefore let's make a covenant with our God to put away all the wives and those who are born of them, according to the counsel of my lord and of those who tremble at the commandment of our God. Let it be done according to the law. **4** Arise, for the matter belongs to you and we are with you. Be courageous, and do it." **5** Then Ezra arose, and made the chiefs of the priests, the Levites, and all Israel to swear that they would do according to this word. So they swore. **6** Then Ezra rose up from before God's house, and went into the room of Jehohanan the son of Eliashib. When he came there, he didn't eat bread or drink water, for he mourned because of the trespass of the exiles. **7** They made a proclamation throughout Judah and Jerusalem to all the children of the captivity, that they should gather themselves together to Jerusalem; **8** and that whoever didn't come within three days, according to the counsel of the princes and the elders, all his possessions should be forfeited, and he himself separated from the assembly of the captivity. **9** Then all the men of Judah and Benjamin gathered themselves together to Jerusalem within the three days. It was the ninth month, on the twentieth day of the month; and all the people sat in the wide place in front of God's house, trembling because of this matter, and because of the great rain. **10** Ezra the priest stood up and said to them, "You have trespassed, and have married foreign women, increasing the guilt of Israel. **11** Now therefore make confession to Yahweh, the God of your fathers, and do his pleasure. Separate yourselves from the peoples of the land and from the foreign women." **12** Then all the assembly answered with a loud voice, "We must do as you have said concerning us. **13** But the people are many, and it is a time of much rain, and we are not able to stand outside. This is not a work of one day or two, for we have greatly transgressed in this matter. **14** Now let our princes be appointed for all the assembly, and let all those who are in our cities who have married foreign women come at appointed times, and with them the elders of every city and its judges, until the fierce wrath of our God is turned from us, until this matter is resolved." **15** Only Jonathan the son of Asahel and Jahzeiah the son of Tikvah stood up against this; and Meshullam and Shabbethai the Levite helped them. **16** The children of the captivity did so. Ezra the priest, with certain heads of fathers' households, after their fathers' houses, and all of them by their names, were set apart; and they sat down in the first day of the tenth month to examine the matter. **17** They finished with all the men who had married foreign women by the first day of the first month. **18** Among the sons of the priests there were found who had married foreign women: of the sons of Jeshua, the son of Jozadak, and his brothers: Maaseiah, Eliezer, Jarib, and Gedaliah. **19** They gave their hand that they would put away their wives; and being guilty, they offered a ram of the flock for their guilt. **20** Of the sons of Immer: Hanani and Zebadiah. **21** Of the sons of Harim: Maaseiah, Elijah, Shemaiah, Jehiel, and Uzziah. **22** Of the sons of Pashhur: Elioenai, Maaseiah, Ishmael, Nethanel, Jozabad, and Elasah. **23** Of the Levites: Jozabad, Shimei, Kelaiah (also called Kelita), Pethahiah, Judah, and Eliezer. **24** Of the singers: Eliashib. Of the

---

ᵃ *8:26* A talent is about 30 kilograms or 66 pounds or 965 Troy ounces

ᵇ *8:27* a daric was a gold coin issued by a Persian king, weighing about 8.4 grams or about 0.27 troy ounces each.

ᶜ *9:15* "Behold", from "הִנֵּה", means look at, take notice, observe, see, or gaze at. It is often used as an interjection.

gatekeepers: Shallum, Telem, and Uri. ²⁵ Of Israel: Of the sons of Parosh: Ramiah, Izziah, Malchijah, Mijamin, Eleazar, Malchijah, and Benaiah. ²⁶ Of the sons of Elam: Mattaniah, Zechariah, Jehiel, Abdi, Jeremoth, and Elijah. ²⁷ Of the sons of Zattu: Elioenai, Eliashib, Mattaniah, Jeremoth, Zabad, and Aziza. ²⁸ Of the sons of Bebai: Jehohanan, Hananiah, Zabbai, and Athlai. ²⁹ Of the sons of Bani: Meshullam, Malluch, Adaiah, Jashub, Sheal, and Jeremoth. ³⁰ Of the sons of Pahathmoab: Adna, Chelal, Benaiah, Maaseiah, Mattaniah, Bezalel, Binnui, and Manasseh. ³¹ Of the sons of Harim: Eliezer, Isshijah, Malchijah, Shemaiah, Shimeon, ³² Benjamin, Malluch, and Shemariah. ³³ Of the sons of Hashum: Mattenai, Mattattah, Zabad, Eliphelet, Jeremai, Manasseh, and Shimei. ³⁴ Of the sons of Bani: Maadai, Amram, Uel, ³⁵ Benaiah, Bedeiah, Cheluhi, ³⁶ Vaniah, Meremoth, Eliashib, ³⁷ Mattaniah, Mattenai, Jaasu, ³⁸ Bani, Binnui, Shimei, ³⁹ Shelemiah, Nathan, Adaiah, ⁴⁰ Machnadebai, Shashai, Sharai, ⁴¹ Azarel, Shelemiah, Shemariah, ⁴² Shallum, Amariah, and Joseph. ⁴³ Of the sons of Nebo: Jeiel, Mattithiah, Zabad, Zebina, Iddo, Joel, and Benaiah. ⁴⁴ All these had taken foreign wives. Some of them had wives by whom they had children.

# The Book of Nehemiah
## 1

¹ The words of Nehemiah the son of Hacaliah. Now in the month Chislev, in the twentieth year, as I was in Susa the palace, ² Hanani, one of my brothers, came, he and certain men out of Judah; and I asked them about the Jews who had escaped, who were left of the captivity, and concerning Jerusalem. ³ They said to me, "The remnant who are left of the captivity there in the province are in great affliction and reproach. The wall of Jerusalem is also broken down, and its gates are burned with fire." ⁴ When I heard these words, I sat down and wept, and mourned several days; and I fasted and prayed before the Godᵃ of heaven, ⁵ and said, "I beg you, Yahweh,ᵇ the God of heaven, the great and awesome God who keeps covenant and loving kindness with those who love him and keep his commandments, ⁶ let your ear now be attentive and your eyes open, that you may listen to the prayer of your servant which I pray before you at this time, day and night, for the children of Israel your servants, while I confess the sins of the children of Israel which we have sinned against you. Yes, I and my father's house have sinned. ⁷ We have dealt very corruptly against you, and have not kept the commandments, nor the statutes, nor the ordinances, which you commanded your servant Moses. ⁸ "Remember, I beg you, the word that you commanded your servant Moses, saying, 'If you trespass, I will scatter you among the peoples; ⁹ but if you return to me, and keep my commandments and do them, though your outcasts were in the uttermost part of the heavens, yet I will gather them from there, and will bring them to the place that I have chosen, to cause my name to dwell there.' ¹⁰ "Now these are your servants and your people, whom you have redeemed by your great power and by your strong hand. ¹¹ Lord,ᶜ I beg you, let your ear be attentive now to the prayer of your servant, and to the prayer of your servants who delight to fear your name; and please prosper your servant today, and grant him mercy in the sight of this man." Now I was cup bearer to the king.

## 2

¹ In the month Nisan, in the twentieth year of Artaxerxes the king, when wine was before him, I picked up the wine, and gave it to the king. Now I had not been sad before in his presence. ² The king said to me, "Why is your face sad, since you are not sick? This is nothing else but sorrow of heart." Then I was very much afraid. ³ I said to the king, "Let the king live forever! Why shouldn't my face be sad, when the city, the place of my fathers' tombs, lies waste, and its gates have been consumed with fire?" ⁴ Then the king said to me, "What is your request?" So I prayed to the God of heaven. ⁵ I said to the king, "If it pleases the king, and if your servant has found favor in your sight, I ask that you would send me to Judah, to the city of my fathers' tombs, that I may build it." ⁶ The king said to me (the queen was also sitting by him), "How long will your journey be? When will you return?" So it pleased the king to send me, and I set a time for him. ⁷ Moreover I said to the king, "If it pleases the king, let letters be given me to the governors beyond the River, that they may let me pass through until I come to Judah; ⁸ and a letter to Asaph the keeper of the king's forest, that he may give me timber to make beams for the gates of the citadel by the temple, for the wall of the city, and for the house that I will occupy." The king granted my requests, because of the good hand of my God on me. ⁹ Then I came to the governors beyond the River, and gave them the king's letters. Now the king had sent captains of the army and horsemen with me. ¹⁰ When Sanballat the Horonite and Tobiah the Ammonite servant heard of it, it grieved them exceedingly, because a man had come to seek the welfare of the children of Israel. ¹¹ So I came to Jerusalem, and was there three days. ¹² I arose in the night, I and a few men with me. I didn't tell anyone what my God put into my heart to do for Jerusalem. There wasn't any animal with me except the animal that I rode on. ¹³ I went out by night by the valley gate toward the jackal's well, then to the dung gate; and I inspected the walls of Jerusalem, which were broken down, and its gates were consumed with fire. ¹⁴ Then I went on to the spring gate and to the king's pool, but there was no place for the animal that was under me to pass. ¹⁵ Then I went up in the night by the brook and inspected the wall; and I turned back, and entered by the valley gate, and so returned. ¹⁶ The rulers didn't know where I went, or what I did. I had not as yet told it to the Jews, nor to the priests, nor to the nobles, nor to the rulers, nor to the rest who did the work. ¹⁷ Then I said to them, "You see the bad situation that we are in, how Jerusalem lies waste, and its gates are burned with fire. Come, let's build up the wall of Jerusalem, that we won't be disgraced." ¹⁸ I told them about the hand of my God which was good on me, and also about the king's words that he had spoken to me. They said, "Let's rise up and build." So they strengthened their hands for the good work. ¹⁹ But when Sanballat the Horonite, Tobiah the Ammonite servant, and Geshem the Arabian, heard it, they ridiculed us and despised us, and said, "What is this thing that you are doing? Will you rebel against the king?" ²⁰ Then I answered them, and said to them, "The God of heaven will prosper us. Therefore we, his servants, will arise and build; but you have no portion, nor right, nor memorial in Jerusalem."

## 3

¹ Then Eliashib the high priest rose up with his brothers the priests, and they built the sheep gate. They sanctified it, and set up its doors. They sanctified it even to the tower of Hammeah, to the tower of Hananel. ² Next to him the men of Jericho built. Next to them Zaccur the son of Imri built. ³ The sons of Hassenaah built the fish gate. They laid its beams, and set up its doors, its bolts, and its bars. ⁴ Next to them, Meremoth the son of Uriah, the son of Hakkoz made repairs. Next to them, Meshullam the son of Berechiah, the son of Meshezabel made repairs. Next to them, Zadok the son of Baana made repairs. ⁵ Next to them, the Tekoites made repairs; but their nobles didn't put their necks to the Lord's work. ⁶ Joiada the son of Paseah and Meshullam the son of Besodeiah repaired the old gate. They laid its beams and set up its doors, its bolts, and its bars. ⁷ Next to them, Melatiah the Gibeonite and Jadon the Meronothite, the men of Gibeon and of Mizpah, repaired the residence of the governor beyond the River. ⁸ Next to him, Uzziel the son of Harhaiah, goldsmiths, made repairs. Next to him, Hananiah, one of the perfumers, made repairs, and they fortified Jerusalem even to the wide wall. ⁹ Next to them, Rephaiah the son of Hur, the ruler of half the district of Jerusalem, made repairs. ¹⁰ Next to them, Jedaiah the son of Harumaph made repairs across from his house. Next to him, Hattush the son of Hashabneiah made repairs. ¹¹ Malchijah the son of Harim and Hasshub the son of Pahathmoab repaired another portion and the tower of the furnaces. ¹² Next to him, Shallum the son of Hallohesh, the ruler of half the district of Jerusalem, he and his daughters made repairs. ¹³ Hanun and the inhabitants of Zanoah repaired the valley gate. They built it, and set up its doors, its bolts, and its bars, and one thousand cubitsᵈ of the wall to the dung gate. ¹⁴ Malchijah the son of Rechab, the ruler of the district of Beth Haccherem, repaired the dung gate. He built it, and set up its doors, its bolts, and its bars. ¹⁵ Shallun the son of Colhozeh, the ruler of the district of Mizpah, repaired the spring gate. He built it, covered it, and set up its doors, its bolts, and its bars; and he repaired the wall of the pool of Shelah by the king's garden, even to the stairs that go down from David's city. ¹⁶ After him, Nehemiah the son of Azbuk, the ruler of half the district of Beth Zur, made repairs to the place opposite the tombs of David, and to the pool that was made, and to the house of the mighty men. ¹⁷ After him, the Levites—Rehum the son of Bani made repairs. Next to him, Hashabiah, the ruler of half the district of Keilah, made repairs for his district. ¹⁸ After him, their brothers, Bavvai the son of Henadad, the ruler of half the district of Keilah made repairs. ¹⁹ Next to him, Ezer the son of Jeshua, the ruler of Mizpah, repaired another portion across from the ascent to the armory at the turning of the wall. ²⁰ After him, Baruch the son of Zabbai earnestly repaired another portion, from the turning of the wall to the door of the house of Eliashib the high priest. ²¹ After him, Meremoth the son of Uriah the son of Hakkoz repaired another portion, from the

ᵃ 1:4 The Hebrew word rendered "God" is אֱלֹהִים (Elohim).

ᵇ 1:5 "Yahweh" is God's proper Name, sometimes rendered "LORD" (all caps) in other translations.

ᶜ 1:11 The word translated "Lord" is "Adonai."

ᵈ 3:13 A cubit is the length from the tip of the middle finger to the elbow on a man's arm, or about 18 inches or 46 centimeters.

door of the house of Eliashib even to the end of the house of Eliashib. [22] After him, the priests, the men of the surrounding area made repairs. [23] After them, Benjamin and Hasshub made repairs across from their house. After them, Azariah the son of Maaseiah the son of Ananiah made repairs beside his own house. [24] After him, Binnui the son of Henadad repaired another portion, from the house of Azariah to the turning of the wall, and to the corner. [25] Palal the son of Uzai made repairs opposite the turning of the wall, and the tower that stands out from the upper house of the king, which is by the court of the guard. After him Pedaiah the son of Parosh made repairs. [26](Now the temple servants lived in Ophel, to the place opposite the water gate toward the east, and the tower that stands out.) [27] After him the Tekoites repaired another portion, opposite the great tower that stands out, and to the wall of Ophel. [28] Above the horse gate, the priests made repairs, everyone across from his own house. [29] After them, Zadok the son of Immer made repairs across from his own house. After him, Shemaiah the son of Shecaniah, the keeper of the east gate, made repairs. [30] After him, Hananiah the son of Shelemiah, and Hanun, the sixth son of Zalaph, repaired another portion. After him, Meshullam the son of Berechiah made repairs across from his room. [31] After him, Malchijah, one of the goldsmiths to the house of the temple servants, and of the merchants, made repairs opposite the gate of Hammiphkad and to the ascent of the corner. [32] Between the ascent of the corner and the sheep gate, the goldsmiths and the merchants made repairs.

## 4

[1] But when Sanballat heard that we were building the wall, he was angry, and was very indignant, and mocked the Jews. [2] He spoke before his brothers and the army of Samaria, and said, "What are these feeble Jews doing? Will they fortify themselves? Will they sacrifice? Will they finish in a day? Will they revive the stones out of the heaps of rubbish, since they are burned?" [3] Now Tobiah the Ammonite was by him, and he said, "What they are building, if a fox climbed up it, he would break down their stone wall." [4]"Hear, our God, for we are despised. Turn back their reproach on their own head. Give them up for a plunder in a land of captivity. [5] Don't cover their iniquity. Don't let their sin be blotted out from before you; for they have insulted the builders." [6] So we built the wall; and all the wall was joined together to half its height, for the people had a mind to work. [7] But when Sanballat, Tobiah, the Arabians, the Ammonites, and the Ashdodites heard that the repairing of the walls of Jerusalem went forward, and that the breaches began to be filled, they were very angry; [8] and they all conspired together to come and fight against Jerusalem, and to cause confusion among us. [9] But we made our prayer to our God, and set a watch against them day and night because of them. [10] Judah said, "The strength of the bearers of burdens is fading and there is much rubble, so that we are not able to build the wall." [11] Our adversaries said, "They will not know or see, until we come in among them and kill them, and cause the work to cease." [12] When the Jews who lived by them came, they said to us ten times from all places, "Wherever you turn, they will attack us." [13] Therefore I set guards in the lowest parts of the space behind the wall, in the open places. I set the people by family groups with their swords, their spears, and their bows. [14] I looked, and rose up, and said to the nobles, to the rulers, and to the rest of the people, "Don't be afraid of them! Remember the Lord, who is great and awesome, and fight for your brothers, your sons, your daughters, your wives, and your houses." [15] When our enemies heard that it was known to us, and God had brought their counsel to nothing, all of us returned to the wall, everyone to his work. [16] From that time forth, half of my servants did the work, and half of them held the spears, the shields, the bows, and the coats of mail; and the rulers were behind all the house of Judah. [17] Those who built the wall, and those who bore burdens loaded themselves; everyone with one of his hands did the work, and with the other held his weapon. [18] Among the builders, everyone wore his sword at his side, and so built. He who sounded the trumpet was by me. [19] I said to the nobles, and to the rulers and to the rest of the people, "The work is great and widely spread out, and we are separated on the wall, far from one another. [20] Wherever you hear the sound of the trumpet, rally there to us. Our God will fight for us." [21] So we did the work. Half of the people held the spears from the rising of the morning until the stars appeared. [22] Likewise at the same time I said to the people, "Let everyone with his servant lodge within Jerusalem, that in the night they may be a guard to us, and may labor in the day." [23] So neither I, nor my brothers, nor my servants, nor the men of the guard who followed me took off our clothes. Everyone took his weapon to the water.

## 5

[1] Then there arose a great cry of the people and of their wives against their brothers the Jews. [2] For there were some who said, "We, our sons and our daughters, are many. Let us get grain, that we may eat and live." [3] There were also some who said, "We are mortgaging our fields, our vineyards, and our houses. Let us get grain, because of the famine." [4] There were also some who said, "We have borrowed money for the king's tribute using our fields and our vineyards as collateral. [5] Yet now our flesh is as the flesh of our brothers, our children as their children. Behold,[a] we bring our sons and our daughters into bondage to be servants, and some of our daughters have been brought into bondage. It is also not in our power to help it, because other men have our fields and our vineyards." [6] I was very angry when I heard their cry and these words. [7] Then I consulted with myself, and contended with the nobles and the rulers, and said to them, "You exact usury, everyone of his brother." I held a great assembly against them. [8] I said to them, "We, after our ability, have redeemed our brothers the Jews that were sold to the nations; and would you even sell your brothers, and should they be sold to us?" Then they held their peace, and found not a word to say. [9] Also I said, "The thing that you do is not good. Shouldn't you walk in the fear of our God because of the reproach of the nations, our enemies? [10] I likewise, my brothers and my servants, lend them money and grain. Please let us stop this usury. [11] Please restore to them, even today, their fields, their vineyards, their olive groves, and their houses, also the hundredth part of the money, and of the grain, the new wine, and the oil, that you are charging them." [12] Then they said, "We will restore them, and will require nothing of them. We will do so, even as you say." Then I called the priests, and took an oath of them, that they would do according to this promise. [13] Also I shook out my lap, and said, "So may God shake out every man from his house, and from his labor, that doesn't perform this promise; even may he be shaken out and emptied like this." All the assembly said, "Amen," and praised Yahweh. The people did according to this promise. [14] Moreover from the time that I was appointed to be their governor in the land of Judah, from the twentieth year even to the thirty-second year of Artaxerxes the king, that is, twelve years, I and my brothers have not eaten the bread of the governor. [15] But the former governors who were before me were supported by the people, and took bread and wine from them, plus forty shekels[b] of silver; yes, even their servants ruled over the people, but I didn't do so, because of the fear of God. [16] Yes, I also continued in the work of this wall. We didn't buy any land. All my servants were gathered there to the work. [17] Moreover there were at my table, of the Jews and the rulers, one hundred fifty men, in addition to those who came to us from among the nations that were around us. [18] Now that which was prepared for one day was one ox and six choice sheep. Also fowls were prepared for me, and once in ten days a store of all sorts of wine. Yet for all this, I didn't demand the governor's pay, because the bondage was heavy on this people. [19] Remember me, my God, for all the good that I have done for this people.

## 6

[1] Now when it was reported to Sanballat, Tobiah, Geshem the Arabian, and to the rest of our enemies that I had built the wall, and that there was no breach left in it (though even to that time I had not set up the doors in the gates), [2] Sanballat and Geshem sent to me, saying, "Come! Let's meet together in the villages in the plain of Ono." But they intended to harm me. [3] I sent messengers to them, saying, "I am doing a great work, so that I can't come down. Why should the work cease while I leave it and come down to you?" [4] They sent to me four times like this; and I answered them the same way. [5] Then Sanballat sent his servant to me the same way the fifth time with an open letter in his hand, [6] in which was written, "It is reported among the nations, and Gashmu says it, that you and the Jews intend to rebel. Because of that, you are building the wall. You would be their king, according to these words. [7] You have also appointed prophets to proclaim of you at Jerusalem, saying, 'There is a king in Judah!' Now it will be reported to the king according to these words. Come now therefore, and let's take counsel together." [8] Then I sent to him, saying, "There are no such things done as you say, but you imagine them out of your own heart." [9] For they all would have made us afraid, saying, "Their hands will be weakened from the work, that it not be done." But now, strengthen my hands. [10] I went to the house of Shemaiah the son of Delaiah the son of Mehetabel, who was shut in at his home; and he said, "Let us meet together in God's house, within the temple, and let's shut the doors of the temple; for they will come to kill you. Yes, in the night they will come to kill you." [11] I said, "Should a man like me flee? Who is there that, being such as I, would go into the temple to save his life? I will not go in." [12] I discerned, and behold, God had not sent him, but he pronounced this prophecy against me. Tobiah and Sanballat had hired him. [13] He was hired so that I would be afraid, do so, and sin, and that they might have material for an evil report, that they might reproach

me. [14]"Remember, my God, Tobiah and Sanballat according to these their works, and also the prophetess Noadiah and the rest of the prophets that would have put me in fear." [15] So the wall was finished in the twenty-fifth day of Elul, in fifty-two days. [16] When all our enemies heard of it, all the nations that were around us were afraid, and they lost their confidence; for they perceived that this work was done by our God. [17] Moreover in those days the nobles of Judah sent many letters to Tobiah, and Tobiah's letters came to them. [18] For there were many in Judah sworn to him because he was the son-in-law of Shecaniah the son of Arah; and his son Jehohanan had taken the daughter of Meshullam the son of Berechiah as wife. [19] Also they spoke of his good deeds before me, and reported my words to him. Tobiah sent letters to put me in fear.

# 7

[1] Now when the wall was built and I had set up the doors, and the gatekeepers and the singers and the Levites were appointed, [2] I put my brother Hanani, and Hananiah the governor of the fortress, in charge of Jerusalem; for he was a faithful man and feared God above many. [3] I said to them, "Don't let the gates of Jerusalem be opened until the sun is hot; and while they stand guard, let them shut the doors, and you bar them; and appoint watches of the inhabitants of Jerusalem, everyone in his watch, with everyone near his house." [4] Now the city was wide and large; but the people were few therein, and the houses were not built. [5] My God put into my heart to gather together the nobles, and the rulers, and the people, that they might be listed by genealogy. I found the book of the genealogy of those who came up at the first, and I found this written in it: [6] These are the children of the province who went up out of the captivity of those who had been carried away, whom Nebuchadnezzar the king of Babylon had carried away, and who returned to Jerusalem and to Judah, everyone to his city, [7] who came with Zerubbabel, Jeshua, Nehemiah, Azariah, Raamiah, Nahamani, Mordecai, Bilshan, Mispereth, Bigvai, Nehum, and Baanah. The number of the men of the people of Israel: [8] The children of Parosh: two thousand one hundred seventy-two. [9] The children of Shephatiah: three hundred seventy-two. [10] The children of Arah: six hundred fifty-two. [11] The children of Pahathmoab, of the children of Jeshua and Joab: two thousand eight hundred eighteen. [12] The children of Elam: one thousand two hundred fifty-four. [13] The children of Zattu: eight hundred forty-five. [14] The children of Zaccai: seven hundred sixty. [15] The children of Binnui: six hundred forty-eight. [16] The children of Bebai: six hundred twenty-eight. [17] The children of Azgad: two thousand three hundred twenty-two. [18] The children of Adonikam: six hundred sixty-seven. [19] The children of Bigvai: two thousand sixty-seven. [20] The children of Adin: six hundred fifty-five. [21] The children of Ater: of Hezekiah, ninety-eight. [22] The children of Hashum: three hundred twenty-eight. [23] The children of Bezai: three hundred twenty-four. [24] The children of Hariph: one hundred twelve. [25] The children of Gibeon: ninety-five. [26] The men of Bethlehem and Netophah: one hundred eighty-eight. [27] The men of Anathoth: one hundred twenty-eight. [28] The men of Beth Azmaveth: forty-two. [29] The men of Kiriath Jearim, Chephirah, and Beeroth: seven hundred forty-three. [30] The men of Ramah and Geba: six hundred twenty-one. [31] The men of Michmas: one hundred twenty-two. [32] The men of Bethel and Ai: one hundred twenty-three. [33] The men of the other Nebo: fifty-two. [34] The children of the other Elam: one thousand two hundred fifty-four. [35] The children of Harim: three hundred twenty. [36] The children of Jericho: three hundred forty-five. [37] The children of Lod, Hadid, and Ono: seven hundred twenty-one. [38] The children of Senaah: three thousand nine hundred thirty. [39] The priests: The children of Jedaiah, of the house of Jeshua: nine hundred seventy-three. [40] The children of Immer: one thousand fifty-two. [41] The children of Pashhur: one thousand two hundred forty-seven. [42] The children of Harim: one thousand seventeen. [43] The Levites: the children of Jeshua, of Kadmiel, of the children of Hodevah: seventy-four. [44] The singers: the children of Asaph: one hundred forty-eight. [45] The gatekeepers: the children of Shallum, the children of Ater, the children of Talmon, the children of Akkub, the children of Hatita, the children of Shobai: one hundred thirty-eight. [46] The temple servants: the children of Ziha, the children of Hasupha, the children of Tabbaoth, [47] the children of Keros, the children of Sia, the children of Padon, [48] the children of Lebana, the children of Hagaba, the children of Salmai, [49] the children of Hanan, the children of Giddel, the children of Gahar, [50] the children of Reaiah, the children of Rezin, the children of Nekoda, [51] the children of Gazzam, the children of Uzza, the children of Paseah, [52] the children of Besai, the children of Meunim, the children of Nephushesim, [53] the children of Bakbuk, the children of Hakupha, the children of Harhur, [54] the children of Bazlith, the children of Mehida,

the children of Harsha, [55] the children of Barkos, the children of Sisera, the children of Temah, [56] the children of Neziah, and the children of Hatipha. [57] The children of Solomon's servants: the children of Sotai, the children of Sophereth, the children of Perida, [58] the children of Jaala, the children of Darkon, the children of Giddel, [59] the children of Shephatiah, the children of Hattil, the children of Pochereth Hazzebaim, and the children of Amon. [60] All the temple servants and the children of Solomon's servants were three hundred ninety-two. [61] These were those who went up from Tel Melah, Tel Harsha, Cherub, Addon, and Immer; but they could not show their fathers' houses, nor their offspring,[a] whether they were of Israel: [62] The children of Delaiah, the children of Tobiah, the children of Nekoda: six hundred forty-two. [63] Of the priests: the children of Hobaiah, the children of Hakkoz, the children of Barzillai, who took a wife of the daughters of Barzillai the Gileadite, and was called after their name. [64] These searched for their genealogical records, but couldn't find them. Therefore they were deemed disqualified and removed from the priesthood. [65] The governor told them not to eat of the most holy things until a priest stood up to minister with Urim and Thummim. [66] The whole assembly together was forty-two thousand three hundred sixty, [67] in addition to their male servants and their female servants, of whom there were seven thousand three hundred thirty-seven. They had two hundred forty-five singing men and singing women. [68] Their horses were seven hundred thirty-six; their mules, two hundred forty-five; [69] their camels, four hundred thirty-five; their donkeys, six thousand seven hundred twenty. [70] Some from among the heads of fathers' households gave to the work. The governor gave to the treasury one thousand darics of gold,[b] fifty basins, and five hundred thirty priests' garments. [71] Some of the heads of fathers' households gave into the treasury of the work twenty thousand darics of gold, and two thousand two hundred minas[c] of silver. [72] That which the rest of the people gave was twenty thousand darics of gold, plus two thousand minas of silver, and sixty-seven priests' garments. [73] So the priests, the Levites, the gatekeepers, the singers, some of the people, the temple servants, and all Israel lived in their cities. When the seventh month had come, the children of Israel were in their cities.

# 8

[1] All the people gathered themselves together as one man into the wide place that was in front of the water gate; and they spoke to Ezra the scribe to bring the book of the law of Moses, which Yahweh had commanded to Israel. [2] Ezra the priest brought the law before the assembly, both men and women, and all who could hear with understanding, on the first day of the seventh month. [3] He read from it before the wide place that was in front of the water gate from early morning until midday, in the presence of the men and the women, and of those who could understand. The ears of all the people were attentive to the book of the law. [4] Ezra the scribe stood on a pulpit of wood, which they had made for the purpose; and beside him stood Mattithiah, Shema, Anaiah, Uriah, Hilkiah, and Maaseiah, on his right hand; and on his left hand, Pedaiah, Mishael, Malchijah, Hashum, Hashbaddanah, Zechariah, and Meshullam. [5] Ezra opened the book in the sight of all the people (for he was above all the people), and when he opened it, all the people stood up. [6] Then Ezra blessed Yahweh, the great God. All the people answered, "Amen, Amen," with the lifting up of their hands. They bowed their heads, and worshiped Yahweh with their faces to the ground. [7] Also Jeshua, Bani, Sherebiah, Jamin, Akkub, Shabbethai, Hodiah, Maaseiah, Kelita, Azariah, Jozabad, Hanan, Pelaiah, and the Levites, caused the people to understand the law; and the people stayed in their place. [8] They read in the book, in the law of God, distinctly; and they gave the sense, so that they understood the reading. [9] Nehemiah, who was the governor, Ezra the priest and scribe, and the Levites who taught the people said to all the people, "Today is holy to Yahweh your God. Don't mourn, nor weep." For all the people wept when they heard the words of the law. [10] Then he said to them, "Go your way. Eat the fat, drink the sweet, and send portions to him for whom nothing is prepared, for today is holy to our Lord. Don't be grieved, for the joy of Yahweh is your strength." [11] So the Levites calmed all the people, saying, "Hold your peace, for the day is holy. Don't be grieved." [12] All the people went their way to eat, to drink, to send portions, and to celebrate, because they had understood the words that were declared to them. [13] On the second day, the heads of fathers' households of all the people, the priests, and the Levites were gathered together to Ezra the scribe, to study the words of the law. [14] They found written in the law how Yahweh had commanded by Moses that the children of Israel should dwell in booths in the feast of the seventh month; [15] and that they should publish and proclaim in all their cities and in Jerusalem, saying, "Go out to the mountain, and get olive branches, branches of

---

[a] 7:61 or, seed
[b] 7:70 a daric was a gold coin issued by a Persian king, weighing about 8.4 grams or about 0.27 troy ounces each.
[c] 7:71 A mina is about 600 grams or 1.3 U. S. pounds, so 2,200 minas is about 1.3 metric tons.

wild olive, myrtle branches, palm branches, and branches of thick trees, to make temporary shelters,[a] as it is written." [16] So the people went out and brought them, and made themselves temporary shelters,[b] everyone on the roof of his house, in their courts, in the courts of God's house, in the wide place of the water gate, and in the wide place of Ephraim's gate. [17] All the assembly of those who had come back out of the captivity made temporary shelters[c] and lived in the temporary shelters, for since the days of Joshua the son of Nun to that day the children of Israel had not done so. There was very great gladness. [18] Also day by day, from the first day to the last day, he read in the book of the law of God. They kept the feast seven days; and on the eighth day was a solemn assembly, according to the ordinance.

## 9

[1] Now in the twenty-fourth day of this month the children of Israel were assembled with fasting, with sackcloth, and dirt on them. [2] The offspring of Israel separated themselves from all foreigners and stood and confessed their sins and the iniquities of their fathers. [3] They stood up in their place, and read in the book of the law of Yahweh their God a fourth part of the day; and a fourth part they confessed and worshiped Yahweh their God. [4] Then Jeshua, Bani, Kadmiel, Shebaniah, Bunni, Sherebiah, Bani, and Chenani of the Levites stood up on the stairs, and cried with a loud voice to Yahweh their God. [5] Then the Levites, Jeshua, and Kadmiel, Bani, Hashabneiah, Sherebiah, Hodiah, Shebaniah, and Pethahiah, said, "Stand up and bless Yahweh your God from everlasting to everlasting! Blessed be your glorious name, which is exalted above all blessing and praise! [6] You are Yahweh, even you alone. You have made heaven, the heaven of heavens, with all their army, the earth and all things that are on it, the seas and all that is in them, and you preserve them all. The army of heaven worships you. [7] You are Yahweh, the God who chose Abram, brought him out of Ur of the Chaldees, gave him the name of Abraham, [8] found his heart faithful before you, and made a covenant with him to give the land of the Canaanite, the Hittite, the Amorite, the Perizzite, the Jebusite, and the Girgashite, to give it to his offspring, and have performed your words, for you are righteous. [9]"You saw the affliction of our fathers in Egypt, and heard their cry by the Red Sea, [10] and showed signs and wonders against Pharaoh, against all his servants, and against all the people of his land, for you knew that they dealt proudly against them, and made a name for yourself, as it is today. [11] You divided the sea before them, so that they went through the middle of the sea on the dry land; and you cast their pursuers into the depths, as a stone into the mighty waters. [12] Moreover, in a pillar of cloud you led them by day; and in a pillar of fire by night, to give them light in the way in which they should go. [13]"You also came down on Mount Sinai, and spoke with them from heaven, and gave them right ordinances and true laws, good statutes and commandments, [14] and made known to them your holy Sabbath, and commanded them commandments, statutes, and a law, by Moses your servant, [15] and gave them bread from the sky for their hunger, and brought water out of the rock for them for their thirst, and commanded them that they should go in to possess the land which you had sworn to give them. [16]"But they and our fathers behaved proudly, hardened their neck, didn't listen to your commandments, [17] and refused to obey. They weren't mindful of your wonders that you did among them, but hardened their neck, and in their rebellion appointed a captain to return to their bondage. But you are a God ready to pardon, gracious and merciful, slow to anger, and abundant in loving kindness, and didn't forsake them. [18] Yes, when they had made themselves a molded calf, and said, 'This is your God who brought you up out of Egypt,' and had committed awful blasphemies, [19] yet you in your manifold mercies didn't forsake them in the wilderness. The pillar of cloud didn't depart from over them by day, to lead them in the way; neither did the pillar of fire by night, to show them light, and the way in which they should go. [20] You gave also your good Spirit to instruct them, and didn't withhold your manna from their mouth, and gave them water for their thirst. [21]"Yes, forty years you sustained them in the wilderness. They lacked nothing. Their clothes didn't grow old, and their feet didn't swell. [22] Moreover you gave them kingdoms and peoples, which you allotted according to their portions. So they possessed the land of Sihon, even the land of the king of Heshbon, and the land of Og king of Bashan. [23] You also multiplied their children as the stars of the sky, and brought them into the land concerning which you said to their fathers that they should go in to possess it. [24]"So the children went in and possessed the land; and you subdued before them the inhabitants of the land, the Canaanites, and gave them into their hands, with their kings and the peoples of the land, that they might do with them as they pleased. [25] They took fortified cities and a rich land, and possessed houses full of all good things, cisterns dug out, vineyards, olive groves,

and fruit trees in abundance. So they ate, were filled, became fat, and delighted themselves in your great goodness. [26]"Nevertheless they were disobedient and rebelled against you, cast your law behind their back, killed your prophets that testified against them to turn them again to you, and they committed awful blasphemies. [27] Therefore you delivered them into the hand of their adversaries, who distressed them. In the time of their trouble, when they cried to you, you heard from heaven; and according to your manifold mercies you gave them saviors who saved them out of the hands of their adversaries. [28] But after they had rest, they did evil again before you; therefore you left them in the hands of their enemies, so that they had the dominion over them; yet when they returned and cried to you, you heard from heaven; and many times you delivered them according to your mercies, [29] and testified against them, that you might bring them again to your law. Yet they were arrogant, and didn't listen to your commandments, but sinned against your ordinances (which if a man does, he shall live in them), turned their backs, stiffened their neck, and would not hear. [30] Yet many years you put up with them, and testified against them by your Spirit through your prophets. Yet they would not listen. Therefore you gave them into the hand of the peoples of the lands. [31]"Nevertheless in your manifold mercies you didn't make a full end of them, nor forsake them; for you are a gracious and merciful God. [32] Now therefore, our God, the great, the mighty, and the awesome God, who keeps covenant and loving kindness, don't let all the travail seem little before you that has come on us, on our kings, on our princes, on our priests, on our prophets, on our fathers, and on all your people, since the time of the kings of Assyria to this day. [33] However you are just in all that has come on us; for you have dealt truly, but we have done wickedly. [34] Also our kings, our princes, our priests, and our fathers have not kept your law, nor listened to your commandments and your testimonies with which you testified against them. [35] For they have not served you in their kingdom, and in your great goodness that you gave them, and in the large and rich land which you gave before them. They didn't turn from their wicked works. [36]"Behold, we are servants today, and as for the land that you gave to our fathers to eat its fruit and its good, behold, we are servants in it. [37] It yields much increase to the kings whom you have set over us because of our sins. Also they have power over our bodies and over our livestock, at their pleasure, and we are in great distress. [38] Yet for all this, we make a sure covenant, and write it; and our princes, our Levites, and our priests, seal it."

## 10

[1] Now those who sealed were: Nehemiah the governor, the son of Hacaliah, and Zedekiah, [2] Seraiah, Azariah, Jeremiah, [3] Pashhur, Amariah, Malchijah, [4] Hattush, Shebaniah, Malluch, [5] Harim, Meremoth, Obadiah, [6] Daniel, Ginnethon, Baruch, [7] Meshullam, Abijah, Mijamin, [8] Maaziah, Bilgai, and Shemaiah. These were the priests. [9] The Levites: Jeshua the son of Azaniah, Binnui of the sons of Henadad, Kadmiel; [10] and their brothers, Shebaniah, Hodiah, Kelita, Pelaiah, Hanan, [11] Mica, Rehob, Hashabiah, [12] Zaccur, Sherebiah, Shebaniah, [13] Hodiah, Bani, and Beninu. [14] The chiefs of the people: Parosh, Pahathmoab, Elam, Zattu, Bani, [15] Bunni, Azgad, Bebai, [16] Adonijah, Bigvai, Adin, [17] Ater, Hezekiah, Azzur, [18] Hodiah, Hashum, Bezai, [19] Hariph, Anathoth, Nobai, [20] Magpiash, Meshullam, Hezir, [21] Meshezabel, Zadok, Jaddua, [22] Pelatiah, Hanan, Anaiah, [23] Hoshea, Hananiah, Hasshub, [24] Hallohesh, Pilha, Shobek, [25] Rehum, Hashabnah, Maaseiah, [26] Ahiah, Hanan, Anan, [27] Malluch, Harim, and Baanah. [28] The rest of the people, the priests, the Levites, the gatekeepers, the singers, the temple servants, and all those who had separated themselves from the peoples of the lands to the law of God, their wives, their sons, and their daughters—everyone who had knowledge and understanding— [29] joined with their brothers, their nobles, and entered into a curse and into an oath, to walk in God's law, which was given by Moses the servant of God, and to observe and do all the commandments of Yahweh our Lord, and his ordinances and his statutes; [30] and that we would not give our daughters to the peoples of the land, nor take their daughters for our sons; [31] and if the peoples of the land bring wares or any grain on the Sabbath day to sell, that we would not buy from them on the Sabbath, or on a holy day; and that we would forego the seventh year crops and the exaction of every debt. [32] Also we made ordinances for ourselves, to charge ourselves yearly with the third part of a shekel[d] for the service of the house of our God: [33] for the show bread, for the continual meal offering, for the continual burnt offering, for the Sabbaths, for the new moons, for the set feasts, for the holy things, for the sin offerings to make atonement for Israel, and for all the work of the house of our God. [34] We, the priests, the Levites, and the people, cast lots for the wood offering, to bring it into the house of our God, according to our fathers' houses, at times appointed year by year, to

---

burn on Yahweh our God's altar, as it is written in the law; ³⁵ and to bring the first fruits of our ground and the first fruits of all fruit of all kinds of trees, year by year, to Yahweh's house; ³⁶ also the firstborn of our sons and of our livestock, as it is written in the law, and the firstborn of our herds and of our flocks, to bring to the house of our God, to the priests who minister in the house of our God; ³⁷ and that we should bring the first fruits of our dough, our wave offerings, the fruit of all kinds of trees, and the new wine and the oil, to the priests, to the rooms of the house of our God; and the tithes of our ground to the Levites; for they, the Levites, take the tithes in all our farming villages. ³⁸ The priest, the descendent of Aaron, shall be with the Levites when the Levites take tithes. The Levites shall bring up the tithe of the tithes to the house of our God, to the rooms, into the treasure house. ³⁹ For the children of Israel and the children of Levi shall bring the wave offering of the grain, of the new wine, and of the oil, to the rooms where the vessels of the sanctuary are, and the priests who minister, with the gatekeepers and the singers. We will not forsake the house of our God.

# 11

¹ The princes of the people lived in Jerusalem. The rest of the people also cast lots to bring one of ten to dwell in Jerusalem, the holy city, and nine parts in the other cities. ² The people blessed all the men who willingly offered themselves to dwell in Jerusalem. ³ Now these are the chiefs of the province who lived in Jerusalem; but in the cities of Judah, everyone lived in his possession in their cities—Israel, the priests, the Levites, the temple servants, and the children of Solomon's servants. ⁴ Some of the children of Judah and of the children of Benjamin lived in Jerusalem. Of the children of Judah: Athaiah the son of Uzziah, the son of Zechariah, the son of Amariah, the son of Shephatiah, the son of Mahalalel, of the children of Perez; ⁵ and Maaseiah the son of Baruch, the son of Colhozeh, the son of Hazaiah, the son of Adaiah, the son of Joiarib, the son of Zechariah, the son of the Shilonite. ⁶ All the sons of Perez who lived in Jerusalem were four hundred sixty-eight valiant men. ⁷ These are the sons of Benjamin: Sallu the son of Meshullam, the son of Joed, the son of Pedaiah, the son of Kolaiah, the son of Maaseiah, the son of Ithiel, the son of Jeshaiah. ⁸ After him Gabbai and Sallai, nine hundred twenty-eight. ⁹ Joel the son of Zichri was their overseer; and Judah the son of Hassenuah was second over the city. ¹⁰ Of the priests: Jedaiah the son of Joiarib, Jachin, ¹¹ Seraiah the son of Hilkiah, the son of Meshullam, the son of Zadok, the son of Meraioth, the son of Ahitub, the ruler of God's house, ¹² and their brothers who did the work of the house, eight hundred twenty-two; and Adaiah the son of Jeroham, the son of Pelaliah, the son of Amzi, the son of Zechariah, the son of Pashhur, the son of Malchijah, ¹³ and his brothers, chiefs of fathers' households, two hundred forty-two; and Amashsai the son of Azarel, the son of Ahzai, the son of Meshillemoth, the son of Immer, ¹⁴ and their brothers, mighty men of valor, one hundred twenty-eight; and their overseer was Zabdiel, the son of Haggedolim. ¹⁵ Of the Levites: Shemaiah the son of Hasshub, the son of Azrikam, the son of Hashabiah, the son of Bunni; ¹⁶ and Shabbethai and Jozabad, of the chiefs of the Levites, who had the oversight of the outward business of God's house; ¹⁷ and Mattaniah the son of Mica, the son of Zabdi, the son of Asaph, who was the chief to begin the thanksgiving in prayer, and Bakbukiah, the second among his brothers; and Abda the son of Shammua, the son of Galal, the son of Jeduthun. ¹⁸ All the Levites in the holy city were two hundred eighty-four. ¹⁹ Moreover the gatekeepers, Akkub, Talmon, and their brothers, who kept watch at the gates, were one hundred seventy-two. ²⁰ The residue of Israel, of the priests, and the Levites were in all the cities of Judah, everyone in his inheritance. ²¹ But the temple servants lived in Ophel; and Ziha and Gishpa were over the temple servants. ²² The overseer also of the Levites at Jerusalem was Uzzi the son of Bani, the son of Hashabiah, the son of Mattaniah, the son of Mica, of the sons of Asaph, the singers responsible for the service of God's house. ²³ For there was a commandment from the king concerning them, and a settled provision for the singers, as every day required. ²⁴ Pethahiah the son of Meshezabel, of the children of Zerah the son of Judah, was at the king's hand in all matters concerning the people. ²⁵ As for the villages with their fields, some of the children of Judah lived in Kiriath Arba and its towns, in Dibon and its towns, in Jekabzeel and its villages, ²⁶ in Jeshua, in Moladah, Beth Pelet, ²⁷ in Hazar Shual, in Beersheba and its towns, ²⁸ in Ziklag, in Meconah and in its towns, ²⁹ in En Rimmon, in Zorah, in Jarmuth, ³⁰ Zanoah, Adullam, and their villages, Lachish and its fields, and Azekah and its towns. So they encamped from Beersheba to the valley of Hinnom. ³¹ The children of Benjamin also lived from Geba onward, at Michmash and Aija, and at Bethel and its towns, ³² at Anathoth, Nob, Ananiah, ³³ Hazor, Ramah, Gittaim, ³⁴ Hadid, Zeboim, Neballat, ³⁵ Lod, and Ono, the valley of craftsmen. ³⁶ Of the Levites, certain divisions in Judah settled in Benjamin's territory.

# 12

¹ Now these are the priests and the Levites who went up with Zerubbabel the son of Shealtiel, and Jeshua: Seraiah, Jeremiah, Ezra, ² Amariah, Malluch, Hattush, ³ Shecaniah, Rehum, Meremoth, ⁴ Iddo, Ginnethoi, Abijah, ⁵ Mijamin, Maadiah, Bilgah, ⁶ Shemaiah, Joiarib, Jedaiah, ⁷ Sallu, Amok, Hilkiah, and Jedaiah. These were the chiefs of the priests and of their brothers in the days of Jeshua. ⁸ Moreover the Levites were Jeshua, Binnui, Kadmiel, Sherebiah, Judah, and Mattaniah, who was over the thanksgiving songs, he and his brothers. ⁹ Also Bakbukiah and Unno, their brothers, were close to them according to their offices. ¹⁰ Jeshua became the father of Joiakim, and Joiakim became the father of Eliashib, and Eliashib became the father of Joiada, ¹¹ and Joiada became the father of Jonathan, and Jonathan became the father of Jaddua. ¹² In the days of Joiakim were priests, heads of fathers' households: of Seraiah, Meraiah; of Jeremiah, Hananiah; ¹³ of Ezra, Meshullam; of Amariah, Jehohanan; ¹⁴ of Malluchi, Jonathan; of Shebaniah, Joseph; ¹⁵ of Harim, Adna; of Meraioth, Helkai; ¹⁶ of Iddo, Zechariah; of Ginnethon, Meshullam; ¹⁷ of Abijah, Zichri; of Miniamin, of Moadiah, Piltai; ¹⁸ of Bilgah, Shammua; of Shemaiah, Jehonathan; ¹⁹ of Joiarib, Mattenai; of Jedaiah, Uzzi; ²⁰ of Sallai, Kallai; of Amok, Eber; ²¹ of Hilkiah, Hashabiah; of Jedaiah, Nethanel. ²² As for the Levites, in the days of Eliashib, Joiada, Johanan, and Jaddua, there were recorded the heads of fathers' households; also the priests, in the reign of Darius the Persian. ²³ The sons of Levi, heads of fathers' households, were written in the book of the chronicles, even until the days of Johanan the son of Eliashib. ²⁴ The chiefs of the Levites: Hashabiah, Sherebiah, and Jeshua the son of Kadmiel, with their brothers close to them, to praise and give thanks according to the commandment of David the man of God, section next to section. ²⁵ Mattaniah, Bakbukiah, Obadiah, Meshullam, Talmon, and Akkub were gatekeepers keeping the watch at the storehouses of the gates. ²⁶ These were in the days of Joiakim the son of Jeshua, the son of Jozadak, and in the days of Nehemiah the governor, and of Ezra the priest and scribe. ²⁷ At the dedication of the wall of Jerusalem, they sought the Levites out of all their places, to bring them to Jerusalem to keep the dedication with gladness, both with giving thanks and with singing, with cymbals, stringed instruments, and with harps. ²⁸ The sons of the singers gathered themselves together, both out of the plain around Jerusalem and from the villages of the Netophathites; ²⁹ also from Beth Gilgal and out of the fields of Geba and Azmaveth, for the singers had built themselves villages around Jerusalem. ³⁰ The priests and the Levites purified themselves; and they purified the people, the gates, and the wall. ³¹ Then I brought the princes of Judah up on the wall, and appointed two great companies who gave thanks and went in procession. One went on the right hand on the wall toward the dung gate; ³² and after them went Hoshaiah, with half of the princes of Judah, ³³ and Azariah, Ezra, and Meshullam, ³⁴ Judah, Benjamin, Shemaiah, Jeremiah, ³⁵ and some of the priests' sons with trumpets: Zechariah the son of Jonathan, the son of Shemaiah, the son of Mattaniah, the son of Micaiah, the son of Zaccur, the son of Asaph; ³⁶ and his brothers, Shemaiah, Azarel, Milalai, Gilalai, Maai, Nethanel, Judah, and Hanani, with the musical instruments of David the man of God; and Ezra the scribe was before them. ³⁷ By the spring gate, and straight before them, they went up by the stairs of David's city, at the ascent of the wall, above David's house, even to the water gate eastward. ³⁸ The other company of those who gave thanks went to meet them, and I after them, with the half of the people on the wall above the tower of the furnaces, even to the wide wall, ³⁹ and above the gate of Ephraim, and by the old gate, and by the fish gate, the tower of Hananel, and the tower of Hammeah, even to the sheep gate; and they stood still in the gate of the guard. ⁴⁰ So the two companies of those who gave thanks in God's house stood, and I and the half of the rulers with me; ⁴¹ and the priests, Eliakim, Maaseiah, Miniamin, Micaiah, Elioenai, Zechariah, and Hananiah, with trumpets; ⁴² and Maaseiah, Shemaiah, Eleazar, Uzzi, Jehohanan, Malchijah, Elam, and Ezer. The singers sang loud, with Jezrahiah their overseer. ⁴³ They offered great sacrifices that day, and rejoiced, for God had made them rejoice with great joy; and the women and the children also rejoiced, so that the joy of Jerusalem was heard even far away. ⁴⁴ On that day, men were appointed over the rooms for the treasures, for the wave offerings, for the first fruits, and for the tithes, to gather into them according to the fields of the cities the portions appointed by the law for the priests and Levites; for Judah rejoiced for the priests and for the Levites who served. ⁴⁵ They performed the duty of their God and the duty of the purification, and so did the singers and the gatekeepers, according to the commandment of David and of Solomon his son. ⁴⁶ For in the days of David and Asaph of old there was a chief of the singers, and songs of praise and thanksgiving to God. ⁴⁷ All Israel in the days of Zerubbabel and in the days of Nehemiah gave the portions of the singers and the gatekeepers, as every day required; and they set

apart that which was for the Levites; and the Levites set apart that which was for the sons of Aaron.

## 13

[1] On that day they read in the book of Moses in the hearing of the people; and it was found written in it that an Ammonite and a Moabite should not enter into the assembly of God forever, [2] because they didn't meet the children of Israel with bread and with water, but hired Balaam against them to curse them; however, our God turned the curse into a blessing. [3] It came to pass, when they had heard the law, that they separated all the mixed multitude from Israel. [4] Now before this, Eliashib the priest, who was appointed over the rooms of the house of our God, being allied to Tobiah, [5] had prepared for him a great room, where before they laid the meal offerings, the frankincense, the vessels, and the tithes of the grain, the new wine, and the oil, which were given by commandment to the Levites, the singers, and the gatekeepers; and the wave offerings for the priests. [6] But in all this, I was not at Jerusalem; for in the thirty-second year of Artaxerxes king of Babylon I went to the king; and after some days I asked leave of the king, [7] and I came to Jerusalem, and understood the evil that Eliashib had done for Tobiah, in preparing him a room in the courts of God's house. [8] It grieved me severely. Therefore I threw all Tobiah's household stuff out of the room. [9] Then I commanded, and they cleansed the rooms. I brought into them the vessels of God's house, with the meal offerings and the frankincense again. [10] I perceived that the portions of the Levites had not been given them, so that the Levites and the singers, who did the work, had each fled to his field. [11] Then I contended with the rulers, and said, "Why is God's house forsaken?" I gathered them together, and set them in their place. [12] Then all Judah brought the tithe of the grain, the new wine, and the oil to the treasuries. [13] I made treasurers over the treasuries, Shelemiah the priest, and Zadok the scribe, and of the Levites, Pedaiah: and next to them was Hanan the son of Zaccur, the son of Mattaniah; for they were counted faithful, and their business was to distribute to their brothers. [14] Remember me, my God, concerning this, and don't wipe out my good deeds that I have done for the house of my God, and for its observances. [15] In those days I saw some men treading wine presses on the Sabbath in Judah, bringing in sheaves, and loading donkeys with wine, grapes, figs, and all kinds of burdens which they brought into Jerusalem on the Sabbath day; and I testified against them in the day in which they sold food. [16] Some men of Tyre also lived there, who brought in fish and all kinds of wares, and sold on the Sabbath to the children of Judah, and in Jerusalem. [17] Then I contended with the nobles of Judah, and said to them, "What evil thing is this that you do, and profane the Sabbath day? [18] Didn't your fathers do this, and didn't our God bring all this evil on us and on this city? Yet you bring more wrath on Israel by profaning the Sabbath." [19] It came to pass that when the gates of Jerusalem began to be dark before the Sabbath, I commanded that the doors should be shut, and commanded that they should not be opened until after the Sabbath. I set some of my servants over the gates, so that no burden should be brought in on the Sabbath day. [20] So the merchants and sellers of all kinds of wares camped outside of Jerusalem once or twice. [21] Then I testified against them, and said to them, "Why do you stay around the wall? If you do so again, I will lay hands on you." From that time on, they didn't come on the Sabbath. [22] I commanded the Levites that they should purify themselves, and that they should come and keep the gates, to sanctify the Sabbath day. Remember me for this also, my God, and spare me according to the greatness of your loving kindness. [23] In those days I also saw the Jews who had married women of Ashdod, of Ammon, and of Moab; [24] and their children spoke half in the speech of Ashdod, and could not speak in the Jews' language, but according to the language of each people. [25] I contended with them, cursed them, struck certain of them, plucked off their hair, and made them swear by God, "You shall not give your daughters to their sons, nor take their daughters for your sons, or for yourselves. [26] Didn't Solomon king of Israel sin by these things? Yet among many nations there was no king like him, and he was loved by his God, and God made him king over all Israel. Nevertheless foreign women caused even him to sin. [27] Shall we then listen to you to do all this great evil, to trespass against our God in marrying foreign women?" [28] One of the sons of Joiada, the son of Eliashib the high priest, was son-in-law to Sanballat the Horonite; therefore I chased him from me. [29] Remember them, my God, because they have defiled the priesthood and the covenant of the priesthood and of the Levites. [30] Thus I cleansed them from all foreigners and appointed duties for the priests and for the Levites, everyone in his work; [31] and for the wood offering, at appointed times, and for the first fruits. Remember me, my God, for good.

# The First Book of Esdras, or Ezra Kali

*The First Book of Esdras* is recognized as Deuterocanonical Scripture by the Greek Orthodox and Russian Orthodox Churches. It is not recognized by the Roman Catholic Church, but 1 Esdras is placed as an appendix to the Latin Vulgate Bible.

## 1

[1] *Josias held the Passover in Jerusalem to his Lord, and offered the Passover the fourteenth day of the first month, [2] having set the priests according to their daily courses, being arrayed in their vestments, in the Lord's temple. [3] He spoke to the Levites, *the temple servants of Israel, that they should make themselves holy to the Lord, to set the holy ark of the Lord in the house that King Solomon the son of David had built. [4] He said, "You no longer need to carry it on your shoulders. Now therefore serve the Lord your God, and minister to his people Israel, and prepare yourselves by your fathers' houses and kindred, [5] according to the writing of King David of Israel, and according to the magnificence of Solomon his son. Stand in the holy place according to the divisions of your Levite families who minister in the presence of your kindred the descendants of Israel. [6] Offer the Passover in order, prepare the sacrifices for your kindred, and keep the Passover according to the Lord's commandment, which was given to Moses. [7] To the people which were present, Josias gave thirty thousand lambs and kids, and three thousand calves. These things were given from the king's possessions, as he promised, to the people and to the priests and Levites. [8] Helkias, Zacharias, and ªEsyelus, the rulers of the temple, gave to the priests for the Passover two thousand six hundred sheep, and three hundred calves. [9] Jeconias, Samaias, Nathanael his brother, Sabias, Ochielus, and Joram, captains over thousands, gave to the Levites for the Passover five thousand sheep and seven hundred calves. [10] When these things were done, the priests and Levites, having the unleavened bread, stood in proper order according to the kindred, [11] and according to the several divisions by fathers' houses, before the people, to offer to the Lord as it is written in the book of Moses. They did this in the morning. [12] They roasted the Passover lamb with fire, as required. They boiled the sacrifices in the brazen vessels and caldrons with a pleasing smell, [13] and set them before all the people. Afterward they prepared for themselves and for their kindred the priests, the sons of Aaron. [14] For the priests offered the fat until night. The Levites prepared for themselves and for their kindred the priests, the sons of Aaron. [15] The holy singers also, the sons of Asaph, were in their order, according to the appointment of David: Asaph, Zacharias, and Eddinus, who represented the king. [16] Moreover the gatekeepers were at every gate. No one needed to depart from his daily duties, for their kindred the Levites prepared for them. [17] So the things that belonged to the Lord's sacrifices were accomplished in that day, in holding the Passover, [18] and offering sacrifices on the altar of the Lord, according to the commandment of King Josias. [19] So the children of Israel which were present at that time held the Passover and the feast of unleavened bread seven days. [20] Such a Passover had not been held in Israel since the time of the prophet Samuel. [21] Indeed, none of the kings of Israel held such a Passover as Josias with the priests, the Levites, and the Jews, held with all Israel that were present in their dwelling place at Jerusalem. [22] This Passover was held in the eighteenth year of the reign of Josias. [23] The works of Josias were upright before his Lord with a heart full of godliness. [24] Moreover the things that came to pass in his days have been written in times past, concerning those who sinned and did wickedly against the Lord more than any other people or kingdom, and how they grieved him ᵇexceedingly, so that the Lord's words were confirmed against Israel. [25] *Now after all these acts of Josias, it came to pass that Pharaoh the king of Egypt came to make war at Carchemish on the Euphrates; and Josias went out against him. [26] But the king of Egypt sent to him, saying, "What do I have to do with you, O king of Judea? [27] I wasn't sent out from the Lord God against you, for my war is against the Euphrates. Now the Lord is with me, yes, the Lord is with me hastening me forward. Depart from me, and don't be against the Lord." [28] However, Josias didn't turn back to his chariot, but tried to fight with him, not regarding the words of the prophet Jeremy from the Lord's mouth, [29] but joined battle with him in the plain of Megiddo, and the commanders came down against King Josias. [30] Then the king said to his servants, "Carry me away out of the battle, for I am very weak!" Immediately his servants carried him away out of the army. [31] Then he got into his second chariot. After he was brought back to Jerusalem he died, and was buried in the tomb of his ancestors. [32] All Judea mourned for Josias. Jeremy the prophet lamented for Josias, and the chief men with the women made lamentation for him to this day. This was given out for an ordinance to be done continually in all the nation of Israel. [33] These things are written in the book of the histories of the kings of

---

* 1:1 2 Kings 23:21; 2 Chronicles 35:1

* 1:3 Numbers 3:9
ª 1:8 Jehiel, 2 Chronicles 35:8.

ᵇ 1:24 Or, sensibly Judges 16:17.

* 1:25 2 Chronicles 35:20

Judea, and every one of the acts that Josias did, and his glory, and his understanding in the law of the Lord, and the things that he had done before, and the things now told, are reported in the book of the kings of Israel and Judah. [34] * The people took [a]Joachaz the son of Josias, and made him king instead of Josias his father, when he was twenty-three years old. [35] He reigned in Judah and Jerusalem for three months. Then the king of Egypt deposed him from reigning in Jerusalem. [36] He set a tax upon the people of one hundred talents of silver and one talent of gold. [37] The king of Egypt also made King Joakim his brother king of Judea and Jerusalem. [38] And Joakim imprisoned the nobles and apprehended his brother Zarakes, and brought him up out of Egypt. [39] *Joakim was twenty-five years old when he began to reign in Judea and Jerusalem. He did that which was evil in the sight of the Lord. [40] King Nabuchodonosor of Babylon came up against him, bound him with a chain of brass, and carried him to Babylon. [41] Nabuchodonosor also took some of the Lord's holy vessels, carried them away, and stored them in his own temple at Babylon. [42] But those things that are reported of him, and of his uncleanness and impiety, are written in the chronicles of the kings. [43] Then Joakim his son reigned in his place. When he was made king, he was eighteen years old. [44] He reigned three months and ten days in Jerusalem. He did that which was evil before the Lord. [45] So after a year Nabuchodonosor sent and caused him to be brought to Babylon with the holy vessels of the Lord, [46] and made Sedekias king of Judea and Jerusalem when he was twenty-one years old. He reigned eleven years. [47] He also did that which was evil in the sight of the Lord, and didn't heed the words that were spoken by Jeremy the prophet from the Lord's mouth. [48] After King Nabuchodonosor had made him to swear by the name of the Lord, he broke his oath and rebelled. Hardening his neck and his heart, he transgressed the laws of the Lord, the God of Israel. [49] Moreover the governors of the people and of the priests did many things wickedly, exceeding all the defilements of all nations, and defiled the temple of the Lord, which was sanctified in Jerusalem. [50] The God of their ancestors sent by his messenger to call them back, because he had compassion on them and on his dwelling place. [51] But they mocked his messengers. In the day when the Lord spoke, they scoffed at his prophets [52] until he, being angry with his people for their great ungodliness, commanded to bring up the kings of the Chaldeans against them. [53] They killed their young men with the sword around their holy temple, and spared neither young man or young woman, old man or child; but he delivered all of them into their hands. [54] They took all the holy vessels of the Lord, both great and small, with the treasure chests of the Lord's ark and the king's treasures, and carried them away to Babylon. [55] They burned the Lord's house, broke down Jerusalem's walls, and burned its towers with fire. [56] As for her glorious things, they didn't stop until they had brought them all to nothing. He carried the people who weren't slain with the sword to Babylon. [57] They were servants to him and to his children until the Persians reigned, to fulfill the word of the Lord by the mouth of Jeremy: [58]"Until the land has enjoyed its Sabbaths, the whole time of her desolation shall she keep Sabbath, to fulfill seventy years.

## 2

[1] In the *first year of King Cyrus of the Persians, that the word of the Lord by the mouth of Jeremy might be accomplished, [2] the Lord stirred up the spirit of King Cyrus of the Persians, and he made a proclamation throughout all his kingdom, and also by writing, [3] saying, "Cyrus king of the Persians says: The Lord of Israel, the Most High Lord, has made me king of the whole world, [4] and commanded me to build him a house at Jerusalem that is in Judea. [5] If therefore there are any of you that are of his people, let the Lord, even his Lord, be with him, and let him go up to Jerusalem that is in Judea, and build the house of the Lord of Israel. He is the Lord who dwells in Jerusalem. [6] Therefore, of those who dwell in various places, let those who are in his own place help each one with gold, with silver, [7] with gifts, with horses, and cattle, beside the other things which have been added by vow for the temple of the Lord which is in Jerusalem. [8] Then the chief of the families of Judah and of the tribe of Benjamin stood up, with the priests, the Levites, and all whose spirit the Lord had stirred up to go up, to build the house for the Lord which is in Jerusalem. [9] Those who lived around them helped them in all things with silver and gold, with horses and cattle, and with very many gifts that were vowed by a great number whose minds were so moved. [10] King Cyrus also brought out the holy vessels of the Lord, which Nabuchodonosor had carried away from Jerusalem and had stored in his temple of idols. [11] Now when King Cyrus of the Persians had brought them out, he delivered them to Mithradates his treasurer, [12] and by him they were delivered to [b]Sanabassar the governor of Judea. [13] This was the number of them: one thousand gold cups, one thousand silver cups, twenty-nine silver censers, thirty gold bowls, two thousand four hundred ten silver bowls, and one thousand other vessels. [14] So all the vessels of gold and of silver were brought up, even five thousand four hundred seventy-nine, [15] and were carried back by Sanabassar, together with the returning exiles, from Babylon to Jerusalem. [16] *In the time of King Artaxerxes of the Persians, Belemus, Mithradates, Tabellius, [c]Rathumus, Beeltethmus, and [d]Samellius the scribe, with their other associates, dwelling in Samaria and other places, wrote to him against those who lived in Judea and Jerusalem the following letter: [17]"To King Artaxerxes our Lord, from your servants, Rathumus the recorder, Samellius the scribe, and the rest of their council, and the judges who are in Coelesyria and Phoenicia: [18] Let it now be known to our lord the king, that the Jews that have come up from you to us, having come to Jerusalem, are building that rebellious and wicked city, and are repairing its marketplaces and walls, and are laying the foundation of a temple. [19] Now if this city is built and its walls are finished, they will not only refuse to give tribute, but will even stand up against kings. [20] Since the things pertaining to the temple are now in hand, we think it appropriate not to neglect such a matter, [21] but to speak to our lord the king, to the intent that, if it is your pleasure, search may be made in the books of your ancestors. [22] You will find in the chronicles what is written concerning these things, and will understand that that city was rebellious, troubling both kings and cities, [23] and that the Jews were rebellious, and kept starting wars there in the past. For this cause, this city was laid waste. [24] Therefore now we do declare to you, O lord the king, that if this city is built again, and its walls set up again, you will from then on have no passage into Coelesyria and Phoenicia." [25] Then the king wrote back again to Rathumus the recorder, Beeltethmus, Samellius the scribe, and to the rest of their associates who lived in Samaria, Syria, and Phoenicia, as follows: [26]"I have read the letter which you have sent to me. Therefore I commanded to make search, and it has been found that that city of old time has fought against kings, [27] and the men were given to rebellion and war in it, and that mighty and fierce kings were in Jerusalem, who reigned and exacted tribute in Coelesyria and Phoenicia. [28] Now therefore I have commanded to prevent those men from building the city, and heed to be taken that there be nothing done contrary to this order, [29] and that those wicked doings proceed no further to the annoyance of kings." [30] Then King Artaxerxes, his letters being read, Rathumus, and Samellius the scribe, and the rest of their associates, went in haste to Jerusalem with cavalry and a multitude of people in battle array, and began to hinder the builders. So the building of the temple in Jerusalem ceased until the second year of the reign of King Darius of the Persians.

## 3

[1] Now King Darius made a great feast for all his subjects, for all who were born in his house, for all the princes of Media and of Persia, [2] and for all the local governors and captains and governors who were under him, from India to Ethiopia, in the one hundred twenty seven provinces. [3] They ate and drank, and when they were satisfied went home. Then King Darius went into his bedchamber slept, but awakened out of his sleep. [4] Then the three young men of the bodyguard, who guarded the king, spoke one to another: [5]"Let every one of us state what one thing is strongest. King Darius will give he whose statement seems wiser than the others great gifts and great honors in token of victory. [6] He shall be clothed in purple, drink from gold cups, sleep on a gold bed, and have a chariot with bridles of gold, a fine linen turban, and a chain around his neck. [7] He shall sit next to Darius because of his wisdom, and shall be called cousin of Darius." [8] Then they each wrote his sentence, sealed them, and laid them under King Darius' pillow, [9] and said, "When the king wakes up, someone will give him the writing. Whoever the king and the three princes of Persia judge that his sentence is the wisest, to him shall the victory be given, as it is written." [10] The first wrote, "Wine is the strongest." [11] The second wrote, "The king is strongest." [12] The third wrote, "Women are strongest, but above all things Truth is the victor." [13] Now when the king woke up, they took the writing and gave it to him, so he read it. [14] Sending out, he called all the princes of Persia and of Media, the local governors, the captains, the governors, and the chief officers [15] and sat himself down in the royal seat of judgment; and the writing was read before them. [16] He said, "Call the young men, and they shall explain their own sentences. So they were called and came in. [17] They said to them, "Explain what you have written." Then the first, who had spoken of the strength of wine, began [18] and said this: "O sirs, how exceedingly strong wine is! It causes all men who drink it to

---

* 1:34 2 Kings 23:30; 2 Chronicles 36:1
[a] *1:34* Another reading is, Jeconias.

* 1:39 2 Chronicles 36:4-5
* 2:1 2 Chronicles 36:22,23; Ezra 1:1

[b] *2:12* Another reading is, Simanassar.
* 2:16 Ezra 4:7
[c] *2:16* Rehum,

[d] *2:16* Shimshai.

go astray. ¹⁹ It makes the mind of the king and of the fatherless child to be the same, likewise of the bondman and of the freeman, of the poor man and of the rich. ²⁰ It also turns every thought into cheer and mirth, so that a man remembers neither sorrow nor debt. ²¹ It makes every heart rich, so that a man remembers neither king nor local governor. It makes people say things in large amounts. ²² When they are in their cups, they forget their love both to friends and kindred, and before long draw their swords. ²³ But when they awake from their wine, they don't remember what they have done. ²⁴ O sirs, isn't wine the strongest, seeing that it forces people to do this?" And when he had said this, he stopped speaking.

## 4

¹ Then the second, who had spoken of the strength of the king, began to say, ²"O sirs, don't men excel in strength who rule over the sea and land, and all things in them? ³ But yet the king is stronger. He is their lord and has dominion over them. In whatever he commands them, they obey him. ⁴ If he tells them to make war the one against the other, they do it. If he sends them out against the enemies, they go, and conquer mountains, walls, and towers. ⁵ They kill and are killed, and don't disobey the king's commandment. If they win the victory, they bring everything to the king—all the plunder and everything else. ⁶ Likewise for those who are not soldiers, and don't have anything to do with wars, but farm, when they have reaped again that which they had sown, they bring some to the king and compel one another to pay tribute to the king. ⁷ He is just one man! If he commands people to kill, they kill. If he commands them to spare, they spare. ⁸ If he commands them to strike, they strike. If he commands them to make desolate, they make desolate. If he commands to build, they build. ⁹ If he commands them to cut down, they cut down. If he commands them to plant, they plant. ¹⁰ So all his people and his armies obey him. Furthermore, he lies down, he eats and drinks, and takes his rest; ¹¹ and these keep watch around him. None of them may depart and do his own business. They don't disobey him in anything. ¹² O sirs, how could the king not be the strongest, seeing that he is obeyed like this?" Then he stopped talking. ¹³ Then the third, who had spoken of women, and of truth, (this was Zorobabel) began to speak: ¹⁴"O sirs, isn't the king great, and men are many, and isn't wine strong? Who is it then who rules them, or has the lordship over them? Aren't they women? ¹⁵ Women have given birth to the king and all the people who rule over sea and land. ¹⁶ They came from women. Women nourished up those who planted the vineyards, from where the wine comes. ¹⁷ Women also make garments for men. These bring glory to men. Without women, men can't exist. ¹⁸ Yes, and if men have gathered together gold and silver and any other beautiful thing, and see a woman who is lovely in appearance and beauty, ¹⁹ they let all those things go and gape at her, and with open mouth stare at her. They all have more desire for her than for gold, or silver, or any other beautiful thing. ²⁰ A man leaves his own father who brought him up, leaves his own country, and joins with his wife. ²¹ With his wife he ends his days, with no thought for his father, mother, or country. ²² By this also you must know that women have dominion over you. Don't you labor and toil, and bring it all to give to women? ²³ Yes, a man takes his sword and goes out to travel, to rob, to steal, and to sail on the sea and on rivers. ²⁴ He sees a lion and walks in the darkness. When he has stolen, plundered, and robbed, he brings it to the woman he loves. ²⁵ Therefore a man loves his wife better than father or mother. ²⁶ Yes, there are many who have lost their minds for women, and become slaves for their sakes. ²⁷ Many also have perished, have stumbled, and sinned, for women. ²⁸ Now don't you believe me? Isn't the king great in his power? Don't all regions fear to touch him? ²⁹ Yet I saw him and Apame the king's concubine, the daughter of the illustrious Barticus, sitting at the right hand of the king, ³⁰ and taking the crown from the king's head, and setting it upon her own head. Yes, she struck the king with her left hand. ³¹ At this, the king gaped and gazed at her with open mouth. If she smiles at him, he laughs. But if she takes any displeasure at him, he flatters her, that she might be reconciled to him again. ³² O sirs, how can it not be that women are strong, seeing they do this?" ³³ Then the king and the nobles looked at one another. So he began to speak concerning truth. ³⁴"O sirs, aren't women strong? The earth is great. The sky is high. The sun is swift in its course, for it circles around the sky, and returns on its course again in one day. ³⁵ Isn't he who makes these things great? Therefore the truth is great, and stronger than all things. ³⁶ All the earth calls upon truth, and the sky blesses truth. All works shake and tremble, but with truth there is no unrighteous thing. ³⁷ Wine is unrighteous. The king is unrighteous. Women are unrighteous. All the children of men are unrighteous, and all their works are unrighteous. There is no truth in them. They shall also perish in their unrighteousness. ³⁸ But truth remains, and is strong forever.

Truth lives and conquers forevermore. ³⁹ With truth there is no partiality toward persons or rewards, but truth does the things that are just, instead of any unrighteous or wicked things. All men approve truth's works. ⁴⁰ In truth's judgment is not any unrighteousness. Truth is the strength, the kingdom, the power, and the majesty of all ages. Blessed be the God of truth!" ⁴¹ With that, he stopped speaking. Then all the people shouted and said, "Great is truth, and strong above all things!" ⁴² Then the king said to him, "Ask what you wish, even more than is appointed in writing, and we will give it to you, because you are found wisest. You shall sit next me, and shall be called my cousin." ⁴³ Then he said to the king, "Remember your vow, which you vowed to build Jerusalem, in the day when you came to your kingdom, ⁴⁴ and to send back all the vessels that were taken out of Jerusalem, which Cyrus set apart when he vowed to destroy Babylon, and vowed to send them back there. ⁴⁵ You also vowed to build the temple which the Edomites burned when Judea was made desolate by the Chaldeans. ⁴⁶ Now, O lord the king, this is what I request, and what I desire of you, and this is the princely generosity that may proceed from you: I ask therefore that you make good the vow, the performance of which you have vowed to the King of Heaven with your own mouth." ⁴⁷ Then King Darius stood up, kissed him, and wrote letters for him to all the treasurers and governors and captains and local governors, that they should safely bring on their way both him, and all those who would go up with him to build Jerusalem. ⁴⁸ He wrote letters also to all the governors who were in Coelesyria and Phoenicia, and to them in Libanus, that they should bring cedar wood from Libanus to Jerusalem, and that they should help him build the city. ⁴⁹ Moreover he wrote for all the Jews who would go out of his realm up into Judea concerning their freedom, that no officer, no governor, no local governor, nor treasurer, should forcibly enter into their doors, ⁵⁰ and that all the country which they occupied should be free to them without tribute, and that the Edomites should give up the villages of the Jews which they held at that time, ⁵¹ and that there should be given twenty talents yearly toward the building of the temple, until the time that it was built, ⁵² and another ten talents yearly for burnt offerings to be presented upon the altar every day, as they had a commandment to make seventeen offerings, ⁵³ and that all those who would come from Babylonia to build the city should have their freedom—they and their descendants, and all the priests that came. ⁵⁴ He wrote also to give them their support and the priests' vestments in which they minister. ⁵⁵ For the Levites he wrote that their support should be given them until the day that the house was finished and Jerusalem built up. ⁵⁶ He commanded that land and wages should be given to all who guarded the city. ⁵⁷ He also sent away all the vessels from Babylon that Cyrus had set apart, and all that Cyrus had given in commandment, he commanded also to be done and to be sent to Jerusalem. ⁵⁸ Now when this young man had gone out, he lifted up his face to heaven toward Jerusalem, and praised the King of heaven, ⁵⁹ and said, "From you comes victory. From you comes wisdom. Yours is the glory, and I am your servant. ⁶⁰ Blessed are you, who have given me wisdom. I give thanks to you, O Lord of our fathers. ⁶¹ So he took the letters, went out, came to Babylon, and told it all his kindred. ⁶² They praised the God of their ancestors, because he had given them freedom and liberty ⁶³ to go up and to build Jerusalem and the temple which is called by his name. They feasted with instruments of music and gladness seven days.

## 5

¹ After this, the chiefs of fathers' houses were chosen to go up according to their tribes, with their wives, sons, and daughters, with their menservants and maidservants, and their livestock. ² Darius sent with them one thousand cavalry to bring them back to Jerusalem with peace, with musical instruments, drums, and flutes. ³ All their kindred were making merry, and he made them go up together with them. ⁴ These are the names of the men who went up, according to their families among their tribes, after their several divisions. ⁵ The priests, the sons of Phinees, the sons of Aaron: Jesus the son of Josedek, the son of Saraias, and Joakim the son of Zorobabel, the son of Salathiel, of the house of David, of the lineage of Phares, of the tribe of Judah, ⁶ who spoke wise words before Darius the king of Persia in the second year of his reign, in the month Nisan, which is the first month. ⁷ *These are the of Judeans who came up from the captivity, where they lived as foreigners, whom Nabuchodonosor the king of Babylon had carried away to Babylon. ⁸ They returned to Jerusalem and to the other parts of Judea, every man to his own city, who came with Zorobabel, with Jesus, Nehemias, ᵃ Zaraias, Resaias,ᵇ Eneneus, Mardocheus, Beelsarus,ᶜ Aspharsus,ᵈ Reelias, Roimus, and Baana, their leaders. ⁹ The number of them of the nation and their leaders: the sons of Phoros, two thousand one hundred seventy two; the sons ofᵉ Saphat, four hundred seventy two; ¹⁰ the sons

---

* 5:7 Ezra 2:1
ᵃ 5:8 Seralah.
ᵇ 5:8 Or, Enenis.
ᶜ 5:8 Mispar.
ᵈ 5:8 Reclaiah
ᵉ 5:9 Shephatiah.

of[a] Ares, seven hundred fifty six; [11] the sons of[b] Phaath Moab, of the sons of Jesus and Joab, two thousand eight hundred twelve; [12] the sons of Elam, one thousand two hundred fifty four; the sons of[c] Zathui, nine hundred forty five; the sons of[d] Chorbe, seven hundred five; the sons of Bani, six hundred forty eight; [13] the sons of Bebai, six hundred twenty three; the sons of[e] Astad,[f] one thousand three hundred twenty two; [14] the sons of Adonikam, six hundred sixty seven; the sons of[g] Bagoi, two thousand sixty six; the sons of[h] Adinu, four hundred fifty four; [15] the sons of[i] Ater, of Ezekias, ninety two; the sons of Kilan and Azetas, sixty seven; the sons of[j] Azaru, four hundred thirty two; [16] the sons of[k] Annis, one hundred one; the sons of Arom, the sons of[l] Bassai, three hundred twenty three; the sons of Arsiphurith, one hundred twelve; [17] the sons of Baiterus, three thousand five; the sons of[m] Bethlomon, one hundred twenty three; [18] those from Netophas, fifty five; those from Anathoth, one hundred fifty eight; those from[n] Bethasmoth, forty two; [19] those from [o] Kariathiarius, twenty five; those from Caphira and Beroth, seven hundred forty three; [20] the Chadiasai and Ammidioi, four hundred twenty two; those from [p]Kirama and [q]Gabbe, six hundred twenty one; [21] those from [r]Macalon, one hundred twenty two; those from [s]Betolion, fifty two; the sons of [t]Niphis, one hundred fifty six; [22] the sons of [u]Calamolalus and [v]Onus, seven hundred twenty five; the sons of [w] Jerechu, [x]three hundred forty five; [23] and the sons of [y]Sanaas, three thousand three hundred thirty. [24] The priests: the sons of [z]Jeddu, the son of Jesus, among the sons of Sanasib, nine hundred seventy two; the sons of [aa] Emmeruth, one thousand fifty two; [25] the sons of [bb]Phassurus, one thousand two hundred forty seven; and the sons of [cc]Charme, one thousand seventeen. [26] The Levites: the sons of Jesus, Kadmiel, Bannas, and Sudias, seventy four. [27] The holy singers: the sons of Asaph, one hundred twenty eight. [28] The gatekeepers: the sons of[dd] Salum, the sons of[ee] Atar, the sons of Tolman, the sons of[ff] Dacubi, the sons of[gg] Ateta, the sons of[hh] Sabi, in all one hundred thirty nine. [29] The temple servants: the sons of[ii] Esau, the sons of[jj] Asipha, the sons of Tabaoth, the sons of[kk] Keras, the sons of[ll] Sua, the sons of[mm] Phaleas, the sons of Labana, the sons of[nn] Aggaba. [30] the sons of[oo] Acud, the sons of Uta, the sons of Ketab, the sons of[pp] Accaba, the sons of[qq] Subai, the sons of[rr] Anan, the sons of[ss] Cathua, the sons of[tt] Geddur, [31] the sons of[uu] Jairus, the sons of[vv] Daisan, the sons of[ww] Noeba, the sons of Chaseba, the sons of[xx] Gazera, the sons of[yy] Ozias, the sons of[zz] Phinoe, the sons of Asara, the sons of[aaa] Basthai, the sons of[bbb] Asana, the sons of[ccc] Maani, the sons of[ddd] Naphisi, the sons of[eee] Acub, the sons of[fff] Achipha, the sons of[ggg] Asur, the sons of Pharakim, the sons of[hhh] Basaloth, [32] the sons of[iii] Meedda, the sons of Cutha, the sons of[jjj] Charea, the sons of[kkk] Barchus, the sons of[lll] Serar, the sons of[mmm] Thomei, the sons of[nnn] Nasi, the sons of Atipha. [33] The sons of the servants of Solomon: the sons of[ooo] Assaphioth, the sons of[ppp] Pharida, the sons of[qqq] Jeeli, the sons of[rrr] Lozon, the sons of[sss] Isdael, the sons of[ttt] Saphuthi, [34] the sons of[uuu] Agia, the sons of[vvv] Phacareth, the sons of Sabie, the sons of Sarothie, the sons of[www] Masias, the sons of Gas, the sons of Addus, the sons of Subas, the sons of Apherra, the sons of Barodis, the sons of Saphat, the sons of Allon. [35] All the temple-servants and the sons of the servants of Solomon were three hundred seventy two. [36] These came up from[xxx] Thermeleth, and[yyy] Thelersas,[zzz] Charaathalan leading them, and Allar; [37] and they could not show their families, nor their stock, how they were of Israel: the sons of[aaaa] Dalan the son of[bbbb] Ban, the sons of[cccc] Nekodan, six hundred fifty two. [38] Of the priests, those who usurped the office of the priesthood and were not found: the sons of[dddd] Obdia, the sons of[eeee] Akkos, the sons of Jaddus, who married Augia one of the daughters of[ffff] Zorzelleus, and was called after his name. [39] When the description of the kindred of these men was sought in the register and was not found, they were removed from executing the office of the priesthood; [40] for Nehemias and Attharias told them that they should not be partakers of the holy things until a high priest wearing[gggg] Urim and Thummim should arise. [41] So all those of Israel, from twelve years old and upward, beside menservants and women servants, were in number forty two thousand three hundred sixty. [42] Their menservants and handmaids were seven thousand three hundred thirty and seven; the minstrels and singers, two hundred forty five; [43] four hundred thirty and five camels, seven thousand thirty six horses, two hundred forty five mules, and five thousand five hundred twenty five beasts of burden. [44] And some of the chief men of their families, when they came to the temple of God that is in Jerusalem, vowed to set up the house again in its own place according to their ability, [45] and to give into the holy treasury of the works one thousand minas[hhhh] of gold, five thousand minas of silver, and one hundred priestly vestments. [46] The priests and the Levites and some of the people lived in Jerusalem and the country. The holy singers also and the gatekeepers and all Israel lived in their villages. [47] But when the seventh month was at hand, and when the children of Israel were each in their own place, they all came together with one purpose into the broad place before the first porch which is toward the east. [48] Then Jesus the son of Josedek, his kindred the priests, Zorobabel the son of Salathiel, and his kindred stood up and made the altar of the God of Israel ready [49] to offer burned sacrifices upon it, in accordance with the express commands in the book of Moses the man of God. [50] Some people joined them out of the other nations of the land, and they erected the altar upon its own place, because all the nations of the land were hostile to them and oppressed them; and they offered sacrifices at the proper times and burnt offerings to the Lord both morning and evening. [51] They also held the feast of tabernacles, as it is commanded in the law, and offered sacrifices daily, as appropriate. [52] After that, they offered the continual oblations and the sacrifices of the Sabbaths, of the new moons, and of all the consecrated feasts. [53] All those who had made any vow to God began to offer sacrifices to God from the new moon of the seventh month, although the temple of God was not yet built. [54] They gave money, food, and drink to the masons and carpenters. [55] They also gave carts to the people of Sidon and Tyre, that they should bring cedar trees from Libanus, and convey them in rafts to the harbor of Joppa, according to the commandment which was written for them by Cyrus king of the Persians. [56] In the second year after his coming to the temple of God at Jerusalem, in the second month, Zorobabel the son of Salathiel, Jesus the son of Josedek, their kindred, the Levitical priests, and all those who had come to Jerusalem out of the captivity began work. [57] They laid the foundation of God's temple on the new moon of the second month, in the second year after they had come to Judea and Jerusalem. [58] *They appointed the Levites who were at least twenty years old over the Lord's works. Then Jesus, with his sons and kindred, Kadmiel his brother, the sons of Jesus, Emadabun, and the sons of Joda the son of Iliadun, and their sons and kindred, all the Levites, with one accord stood up and started the business, laboring to advance the works in the house of God. So the builders built the Lord's temple. [59] The priests stood arrayed in their vestments with musical instruments and trumpets, and the Levites the

---

[a] 5:10 Arah.
[b] 5:11 Pahath-moab.
[c] 5:12 Zattu.
[d] 5:12 Zaccai.
[e] 5:13 Asgad.
[f] 5:13 According to other readings, 3622, or 3222.
[g] 5:14 Bigvai.
[h] 5:14 Adin.
[i] 5:15 Ater of Hezekiah.
[j] 5:15 Another reading is, Azuru.
[k] 5:16 Another reading is, Annias.
[l] 5:16 Bezai.
[m] 5:17 Bethlehem.
[n] 5:18 Azmaveth.
[o] 5:19 Kiriath-arim or Kiriath-jearim.
[p] 5:20 Rumah.
[q] 5:20 Geba.
[r] 5:21 Michmas.
[s] 5:21 Bethel.
[t] 5:21 Magbish
[u] 5:22 Lod, Hadid.
[v] 5:22 Ono.

[w] 5:22 Jericho.
[x] 5:22 Another reading is, two
[y] 5:23 Senaah.
[z] 5:24 Jedaiah.
[aa] 5:24 Immer.
[bb] 5:25 Pashhur.
[cc] 5:25 Harim.
[dd] 5:28 Shallum.
[ee] 5:28 Ater.
[ff] 5:28 Akkub.
[gg] 5:28 Hatita.
[hh] 5:28 Shobai.
[ii] 5:29 Ziha.
[jj] 5:29 Hasupha.
[kk] 5:29 Keros.
[ll] 5:29 Siaha.
[mm] 5:29 Padon.
[nn] 5:29 Hagaba.
[oo] 5:30 Akkub.
[pp] 5:30 Hagab.
[qq] 5:30 Shamlai.
[rr] 5:30 Hanan.
[ss] 5:30 Giddel.
[tt] 5:30 Gahar
[uu] 5:31 Reaiah.
[vv] 5:31 Rezin.

[ww] 5:31 Nekoda.
[xx] 5:31 Gazzam.
[yy] 5:31 Uzza.
[zz] 5:31 Paseah.
[aaa] 5:31 Besai.
[bbb] 5:31 Asnah.
[ccc] 5:31 Meunim.
[ddd] 5:31 Nephisim.
[eee] 5:31 Bakbuk. According to other readings, Acum, or Acuph.
[fff] 5:31 Hakupha.
[ggg] 5:31 Harhur.
[hhh] 5:31 Bazluth.
[iii] 5:32 Mehida.
[jjj] 5:32 Harsha.
[kkk] 5:32 Barkos.
[lll] 5:32 Sisera.
[mmm] 5:32 Temah.
[nnn] 5:32 Neziah. Another reading is, Nasith.
[ooo] 5:33 Hussophereth.
[ppp] 5:33 Peruda.
[qqq] 5:33 Jaalah.
[rrr] 5:33 Darkon.
[sss] 5:33 Giddel.

[ttt] 5:33 Shephatia.
[uuu] 5:34 Hattil.
[vvv] 5:34 Pochereth-haz-zebaim, Ezra 2:57.
[www] 5:34 Another reading is, Misaias.
[xxx] 5:36 Telmelah.
[yyy] 5:36 Telharsha.
[zzz] 5:36 Cherub. Addan.
[aaaa] 5:37 Delaiah. Another reading is, Asan.
[bbbb] 5:37 Tobiah Another reading is, Baenan.
[cccc] 5:37 Nekoda.
[dddd] 5:38 Habaiah, or Hobaiah.
[eeee] 5:38 Hakkoz.
[ffff] 5:38 Barzillai. Another reading is, Phaezeldaeus.
[gggg] 5:40 Gr. the manifestation and truth.
[hhhh] 5:45 A mina is about 570 grams or 1.25 pounds.
* 5:58 Ezra 3:8-9

sons of Asaph with their cymbals, [60] singing songs of thanksgiving and praising the Lord, according to the directions of King David of Israel. [61] They sang aloud, praising the Lord in songs of thanksgiving, because his goodness and his glory are forever in all Israel. [62] All the people sounded trumpets and shouted with a loud voice, singing songs of thanksgiving to the Lord for the raising up of the Lord's house. [63] *Some of the Levitical priests and of the heads of their families, the elderly who had seen the former house came to the building of this one with lamentation and great weeping. [64] But many with trumpets and joy shouted with a loud voice, [65] so that the people couldn't hear the trumpets for the weeping of the people, for the multitude sounded loudly, so that it was heard far away. [66] * Therefore when the enemies of the tribe of Judah and Benjamin heard it, they came to know what that noise of trumpets meant. [67] They learned that those who had returned from captivity built the temple for the Lord, the God of Israel. [68] So they went to Zorobabel and Jesus, and to the chief men of the families, and said to them, "We will build together with you. [69] For we, just like you, obey your Lord, and sacrifice to him from the days of King [a] Asbasareth of the Assyrians, who brought us here." [70] Then Zorobabel, Jesus and the chief men of the families of Israel said to them, "It is not for you to build the house for the Lord our God. [71] We ourselves alone will build for the Lord of Israel, as King Cyrus of the Persians has commanded us." [72] But the heathen of the land pressed hard upon the inhabitants of Judea, cut off their supplies, and hindered their building. [73] By their secret plots, and popular persuasions and commotions, they hindered the finishing of the building all the time that King Cyrus lived. So they were hindered from building for two years, until the reign of Darius.

# 6

[1] Now *in the second year of the reign of Darius, Aggaeus and Zacharias the son of [b] Addo, the prophets, prophesied to the Jews in Judea and Jerusalem in the name of the Lord, the God of Israel. [2] Then Zorobabel the son of Salathiel and Jesus the son of Josedek stood up and began to build the house of the Lord at Jerusalem, the prophets of the Lord being with them and helping them. [3] *At the same time [c] Sisinnes the governor of Syria and Phoenicia came to them, with [d] Sathrabuzanes and his companions, and said to them, [4] "By whose authority do you build this house and this roof, and perform all the other things? Who are the builders who do these things?" [5] Nevertheless, the elders of the Jews obtained favor, because the Lord had visited the captives; [6] and they were not hindered from building until such time as communication was made to Darius concerning them, and his answer received. [7] A copy of the letter which Sisinnes, governor of Syria and Phoenicia, and Sathrabuzanes, with their companions, the rulers in Syria and Phoenicia, wrote and sent to Darius: [8] "To King Darius, greetings. Let it be fully known to our lord the king, that having come into the country of Judea, and entered into the city of Jerusalem, we found in the city of Jerusalem the elders of the Jews that were of the captivity [9] building a great new house for the Lord of hewn and costly stones, with timber laid in the walls. [10] Those works are being done with great speed. The work goes on prosperously in their hands, and it is being accomplished with all glory and diligence. [11] Then asked we these elders, saying, 'By whose authority are you building this house and laying the foundations of these works?' [12] Therefore, to the intent that we might give knowledge to you by writing who were the leaders, we questioned them, and we required of them the names in writing of their principal men. [13] So they gave us this answer, 'We are the servants of the Lord who made heaven and earth. [14] As for this house, it was built many years ago by a great and strong king of Israel, and was finished. [15] But when our fathers sinned against the Lord of Israel who is in heaven, and provoked him to wrath, he gave them over into the hands of King Nabuchodonosor of Babylon, king of the Chaldeans. [16] They pulled down the house, burned it, and carried away the people captive to Babylon. [17] But in the first year that Cyrus reigned over the country of Babylon, King Cyrus wrote that this house should be rebuilt. [18] The holy vessels of gold and of silver that Nabuchodonosor had carried away out of the house at Jerusalem and had set up in his own temple, those King Cyrus brought out of the temple in Babylonia, and they were delivered to Zorobabel and to [e] Sanabassarus the governor, [19] with commandment that he should carry away all these vessels, and put them in the temple at Jerusalem, and that the Lord's temple should be built on its site. [20] Then Sanabassarus, having come here, laid the foundations of the Lord's house which is in Jerusalem. From that time to this we are still building. It is not yet fully completed.' [21] Now therefore, if it seems good, O king, let a search be made among the royal archives of our lord the king that are in Babylon. [22] If it is found that the building of the house of the Lord which is in Jerusalem has been done with the consent of King Cyrus, and it seems good to our lord the king, let him send us directions concerning these things." [23] *Then King Darius commanded that a search be made among the archives that were laid up at Babylon. So at Ekbatana the palace, which is in the country of Media, a scroll was found where these things were recorded: [24] "In the first year of the reign of Cyrus, King Cyrus commanded to build up the house of the Lord which is in Jerusalem, where they sacrifice with continual fire. [25] Its height shall be sixty cubits, and the breadth sixty cubits, with three rows of hewn stones, and one row of new wood from that country. Its expenses are to be given out of the house of King Cyrus. [26] The holy vessels of the house of the Lord, both gold and silver, that Nabuchodonosor took out of the house at Jerusalem and carried away to Babylon, should be restored to the house at Jerusalem, and be set in the place where they were before." [27] Also he commanded that Sisinnes the governor of Syria and Phoenicia, and Sathrabuzanes, and their companions, and those who were appointed rulers in Syria and Phoenicia, should be careful not to meddle with the place, but allow Zorobabel, the servant of the Lord, and governor of Judea, and the elders of the Jews, to build that house of the Lord in its place. [28] "I also command to have it built up whole again; and that they look diligently to help those who are of the captivity of Judea, until the house of the Lord is finished, [29] and that out of the tribute of Coelesyria and Phoenicia a portion shall be carefully given to these men for the sacrifices of the Lord, that is, to Zorobabel the governor for bulls, rams, and lambs, [30] and also corn, salt, wine and oil, and that continually every year without further question, according as the priests who are in Jerusalem may direct to be daily spent, [31] that drink offerings may be made to the Most High God for the king and for his children, and that they may pray for their lives." [32] He commanded that whoever should transgress, yes, or neglect anything written here, a beam shall be taken out of his own house, and he shall be hanged on it, and all his goods seized for the king. [33] "Therefore may the Lord, whose name is called upon there, utterly destroy every king and nation that stretches out his hand to hinder or damage that house of the Lord in Jerusalem. [34] I, King Darius have ordained that these things be done with diligence."

# 7

[1] Then * Sisinnes the governor of Coelesyria and Phoenicia, and Sathrabuzanes, with their companions, following the commandments of King Darius, [2] very carefully supervised the holy work, assisting the elders of the Jews and rulers of the temple. [3] So the holy work prospered, while Aggaeus and Zacharias the prophets prophesied. [4] They finished these things by the commandment of the Lord, the God of Israel, and with the consent of Cyrus, Darius, and Artaxerxes, kings of the Persians. [5] So the holy house was finished by the twenty-third day of the month Adar, in the sixth year of King Darius. [6] The children of Israel, the priests, the Levites, and the others who returned from captivity who joined them did what was written in the book of Moses. [7] For the dedication of the Lord's temple, they offered one hundred bulls, two hundred rams, four hundred lambs, [8] and twelve male goats for the sin of all Israel, according to the number of the twelve princes of the tribes of Israel. [9] The priests and the Levites stood arrayed in their vestments, according to their kindred, for the services of the Lord, the God of Israel, according to the book of Moses. The gatekeepers were at every gate. [10] The children of Israel who came out of captivity held the Passover the fourteenth day of the first month, when the priests and the Levites were sanctified together, [11] with all those who returned from captivity; for they were sanctified. For the Levites were all sanctified together, [12] and they offered the Passover for all who returned from captivity, for their kindred the priests, and for themselves. [13] The children of Israel who came out of the captivity ate, even all those who had separated themselves from the abominations of the heathen of the land, and sought the Lord. [14] They kept the feast of unleavened bread seven days, rejoicing before the Lord, [15] because he had turned the counsel of the king of Assyria toward them, to strengthen their hands in the works of the Lord, the God of Israel.

# 8

[1] * After these things, when Artaxerxes the king of the Persians reigned, Esdras came, who was the son of Azaraias, the son of Zechrias, the son of Helkias, the son of Salem, [2] the son of Sadduk, the son of Ahitob, the son of Amarias, the son of Ozias, [f] the son of Memeroth, the son of Zaraias, the son of Savias, the son of Boccas, the son of Abisne, the son of Phinees, the son of Eleazar, the son of Aaron, the chief priest. [3] This

---

* 5:63 Ezra 3:12- 13
* 5:66 Ezra 4:1
[a] 5:69 Another reading is, Asbacaphath.
* 6:1 Ezra 4:24; 5:1

[b] 6:1 Iddo. Another reading is, Eddin
* 6:3 Ezra 5:3
* 6:3 Tattenai
[d] 6:3 Shetharbozenai

[e] 6:18 Another reading is, Sabunassarus.
* 6:23 Ezra 6:1
* 7:1 Ezra 6:13
* 8:1 Ezra 7:1

[f] 8:2 The Vatican MS. omits the son of Memeroth, the son of Zaraias, the son of Savias.

Esdras went up from Babylon as a skilled scribe in the law of Moses, which was given by the God of Israel. [4] The king honored him, for he found favor in his sight in all his requests. [5] There went up with him also some of the children of Israel, and of the priests, Levites, holy singers, gatekeepers, and temple servants to Jerusalem [6] in the seventh year of the reign of Artaxerxes, in the fifth month (this was the king's seventh year); for they left Babylon on the new moon of the first month and came to Jerusalem, by the prosperous journey which the Lord gave them[a] for his sake. [7] For Esdras had very great skill, so that he omitted nothing of the law and commandments of the Lord, but taught all Israel the ordinances and judgments. [8] Now the commission, which was written from King Artaxerxes, came to Esdras the priest and reader of the law of the Lord, was as follows: [9]"King Artaxerxes to Esdras the priest and reader of the law of the Lord, greetings. [10] Having determined to deal graciously, I have given orders that those of the nation of the Jews, and of the priests and Levites, and of those within our realm who are willing and freely choose to, should go with you to Jerusalem. [11] As many therefore as are so disposed, let them depart with you, as it has seemed good both to me and my seven friends the counselors, [12] that they may look to the affairs of Judea and Jerusalem, in accordance with what is in the Lord's law, [13] and carry the gifts to the Lord of Israel to Jerusalem, which I and my friends have vowed, and that all the gold and silver that can be found in the country of Babylonia for the Lord in Jerusalem, [14] with that also which is given of the people for the temple of the Lord their God that is at Jerusalem, be collected: even the gold and silver for bulls, rams, and lambs, and what goes with them, [15] to the end that they may offer sacrifices to the Lord upon the altar of the Lord their God, which is in Jerusalem. [16] Whatever you and your kindred decide to do with gold and silver, do that according to the will of your God. [17] The holy vessels of the Lord, which are given you for the use of the temple of your God, which is in Jerusalem, [18] and whatever else you shall remember for the use of the temple of your God, you shall give it out of the king's treasury. [19] I, King Artaxerxes, have also commanded the keepers of the treasures in Syria and Phoenicia, that whatever Esdras the priest and reader of the law of the Most High God shall send for, they should give it to him with all diligence, [20] to the sum of one hundred talents of silver, likewise also of wheat even to one hundred cors[b], and one hundred firkins[c] of wine, and[d] salt in abundance. [21] Let all things be performed after God's law diligently to the most high God, that wrath come not upon the kingdom of the king and his sons. [22] I command you also that no tax, nor any other imposition, be laid upon any of the priests, or Levites, or holy singers, or gatekeepers, or temple servants, or any that have employment in this temple, and that no man has authority to impose any tax on them. [23] You, Esdras, according to the wisdom of God, ordain judges and justices that they may judge in all Syria and Phoenicia all those who know the law of your God; and those who don't know it, you shall teach. [24] Whoever transgresses the law of your God and of the king shall be punished diligently, whether it be by death, or other punishment, by penalty of money, or by imprisonment." [25] Then Esdras the scribe said, "Blessed be the only Lord, the God of my fathers, who has put these things into the heart of the king, to glorify his house that is in Jerusalem, [26] and has honored me in the sight of the king, his counselors, and all his friends and nobles. [27] Therefore I was encouraged by the help of the Lord my God, and gathered together out of Israel men to go up with me. [28] These are the chief according to their families and their several divisions, who went up with me from Babylon in the reign of King Artaxerxes: [29] of the sons of Phinees, Gerson; of the sons of Ithamar, Gamael; of the sons of David,[e] Attus[f] the son of Sechenias; [30] of the sons of Phoros, Zacharais; and with him were counted one hundred fifty men; [31] of the sons of Phaath Moab, Eliaonias the son of[g] Zaraias, and with him two hundred men; [32] [h]of the sons of Zathoes, Sechenias the son of Jezelus, and with him three hundred men; of the sons of Adin, Obeth the son of Jonathan, and with him two hundred fifty men; [33] of the sons of Elam, Jesias son of Gotholias, and with him seventy men; [34] of the sons of Saphatias, Zaraias son of Michael, and with him seventy men; [35] of the sons of Joab, Abadias son of Jehiel. Jezelus, and with him two hundred twelve men; [36] [i] of the sons of Banias, Salimoth son of Josaphias, and with him one hundred sixty men; [37] of the sons of Babi, Zacharias son of Bebai, and with him twenty-eight men; [38] of the sons of Azgad: Astath, Joannes son of Hakkatan Akatan, and with him one hundred ten men; [39] of the sons of Adonikam, the last, and these are the names of them, Eliphalat, Jeuel, and Samaias, and with them seventy men; [40] of

the sons of Bago, Uthi the son of Istalcurus, and with him seventy men. [41] I gathered them together to the river called Theras. There we pitched our tents three days, and I inspected them. [42] When I had found there none of the priests and Levites, [43] then sent I to Eleazar, Iduel, Maasmas, [44] Elnathan, Samaias, Joribus, Nathan, Ennatan, Zacharias, and Mosollamus, principal men and men of understanding. [45] I asked them to go to Loddeus the captain, who was in the place of the treasury, [46] and commanded them that they should speak to Loddeus, to his kindred, and to the treasurers in that place, to send us such men as might execute the priests' office in our Lord's house. [47] By the mighty hand of our Lord, they brought to us men of understanding of the sons of[j] Mooli the son of Levi, the son of Israel,[k] Asebebias, and his sons, and his kindred, who were eighteen, [48] and[l] Asebias, Annuus, and Osaias his brother, of the sons of Chanuneus, and their sons were twenty men; [49] and of the temple servants whom David and the principal men had appointed for the servants of the Levites, two hundred twenty temple servants. The list of all their names was reported. [50] There I vowed a fast for the young men before our Lord, to seek from him a prosperous journey both for us and for our children and livestock that were with us; [51] for I was ashamed to ask of the king infantry, cavalry, and an escort for protection against our adversaries. [52] For we had said to the king that the power of our Lord would be with those who seek him, to support them in all ways. [53] Again we prayed to our lord about these things, and found him to be merciful. [54] Then I set apart twelve men of the chiefs of the priests,[m] Eserebias, Assamias, and ten men of their kindred with them. [55] I weighed out to them the silver, the gold, and the holy vessels of the house of our Lord, which the king, his counselors, the nobles, and all Israel had given. [56] When I had weighed it, I delivered to them six hundred fifty talents of silver, silver vessels weighing one hundred talents, one hundred talents of gold, [57] twenty golden vessels, and twelve vessels of brass, even of fine brass, glittering like gold. [58] I said to them, "You are holy to the Lord, the vessels are holy, and the gold and the silver are a vow to the Lord, the Lord of our fathers. [59] Watch and keep them until you deliver them to the chiefs of the priests and Levites, and to the principal men of the families of Israel in Jerusalem, in the chambers of our Lord's house. [60] So the priests and the Levites who received the silver, the gold, and the vessels which were in Jerusalem, brought them into the temple of the Lord. [61] We left the river Theras on the twelfth day of the first month. We came to Jerusalem by the mighty hand of our Lord which was upon us. The Lord delivered us from from every enemy on the way, and so we came to Jerusalem. [62] When we had been there three days, the silver and gold was weighed and delivered in our Lord's house on the fourth day to[n] Marmoth the priest the son of[o] Urias. [63] With him was Eleazar the son of Phinees, and with them were Josabdus the son of Jesus and[p] Moeth the son of Sabannus, the Levites. All was delivered to them by number and weight. [64] All the weight of them was recorded at the same hour. [65] Moreover those who had come out of captivity offered sacrifices to the Lord, the God of Israel, even twelve bulls for all Israel, ninety-six rams, [66] seventy-two lambs, and twelve goats for a peace offering—all of them a sacrifice to the Lord. [67] They delivered the king's commandments to the king's stewards and to the governors of Coelesyria and Phoenicia; and they honored the people and the temple of the Lord. [68] Now when these things were done, the principal men came to me and said, [69]"The nation of Israel, the princes, the priests, and the Levites haven't put away from themselves the foreign people of the land nor the uncleannesses of the Gentiles—the Canaanites, Hittites, Pherezites, Jebusites, Moabites, Egyptians, and Edomites. [70] For both they and their sons have married with their daughters, and the holy seed is mixed with the foreign people of the land. From the beginning of this matter the rulers and the nobles have been partakers of this iniquity." [71] And as soon as I had heard these things, I tore my clothes and my holy garment, and plucked the hair from off my head and beard, and sat down sad and full of heaviness. [72] So all those who were moved at the word of the Lord, the God of Israel, assembled to me while I mourned for the iniquity, but I sat still full of heaviness until the evening sacrifice. [73] Then rising up from the fast with my clothes and my holy garment torn, and bowing my knees and stretching out my hands to the Lord, [74] I said, "O Lord, I am ashamed and confounded before your face, [75] for our sins are multiplied above our heads, and our errors have reached up to heaven [76] ever since the time of our fathers. We are in great sin, even to this day. [77] For our sins and our fathers' we with our kindred, our kings, and our priests were given up to the kings

---

[a] 8:6 Some MSS. omit for his sake.
[b] 8:20 a cor is about 230 liters, so 100 cors is about 23 kiloliters or 652 bushels
[c] 8:20 a firkin is about 41 liters or 11 gallons.

[d] 8:20 So some authorities. See Ezra 7:22. The common reading is, other things.
[e] 8:29 Hattush.
[f] 8:29 Ezra 8:3, of the sons of Shecaniah; of the sons of Parosh.

[g] 8:31 Zerehiah.
[h] 8:32 Ezra 8:5, of the sons of Shecaniah, the son of Jahaziel.
[i] 8:36 Ezra 8:10, of the sons of Shelomith, the son of Josiphiah.
[j] 8:47 Mahli.

[k] 8:47 Sherebiah.
[l] 8:48 Hashabiah.
[m] 8:54 Sherebiah, Hashabiah.
[n] 8:62 Meremoth.
[o] 8:62 Uriah.
[p] 8:63 Noadiah the son of Binnui.

of the earth, to the sword, and to captivity, and for a prey with shame, to this day. [78] Now in some measure mercy has been shown to us from you, O Lord, that there should be left us a root and a name in the place of your sanctuary, [79] and to uncover a light in the house of the Lord our God, and to give us food in the time of our servitude. [80] Yes, when we were in bondage, we were not forsaken by our Lord, but he gave us favor before the kings of Persia, so that they gave us food, [81] glorified the temple of our Lord, and raised up the desolate Zion, to give us a sure dwelling in Judea and Jerusalem. [82] "Now, O Lord, what shall we say, having these things? For we have transgressed your commandments which you gave by the hand of your servants the prophets, saying, [83] 'The land, which you enter into to possess as an inheritance, is a land polluted with the pollutions of the foreigners of the land, and they have filled it with their uncleanness. [84] Therefore now you shall not join your daughters to their sons, neither shall you take their daughters for your sons. [85] You shall never seek to have peace with them, that you may be strong, and eat the good things of the land, and that you may leave it for an inheritance to your children for evermore.' [86] All that has happened is done to us for our wicked works and great sins, for you, O Lord, made our sins light, [87] and gave to us such a root; but we have turned back again to transgress your law in mingling ourselves with the uncleanness of the heathen of the land. [88] You weren't angry with us to destroy us until you had left us neither root, seed, nor name. [89] O Lord of Israel, you are true, for we are left a root this day. [90] Behold, now we are before you in our iniquities, for we can't stand any longer before you because of these things." [91] *As Esdras in his prayer made his confession, weeping, and lying flat on the ground before the temple, a very great throng of men, women, and children gathered to him from Jerusalem; for there was great weeping among the multitude. [92] Then Jechonias the son of Jeelus, one of the sons of Israel, called out, and said, "O Esdras, we have sinned against the Lord God, we have married foreign women of the heathen of the land, but there is still hope for Israel. [93] Let's make an oath to the Lord about this, that we will put away all our foreign wives with their children, [94] as seems good to you, and to as many as obey the Lord's Law. [95] Arise, and take action, for this is your task, and we will be with you to do valiantly." [96] So Esdras arose, and took an oath from the chief of the priests and Levites of all Israel to do these things; and they swore to it.

# 9

[1] * Then Esdras rose up from the court of the temple and went to the chamber of Jonas the son of Eliasib, [2] and lodged there, and ate no bread and drank no water, mourning for the great iniquities of the multitude. [3] A proclamation was made in all Judea and Jerusalem to all those who returned from captivity, that they should be gathered together at Jerusalem, [4] and that whoever didn't meet there within two or three days, in accordance with the ruling of the elders, that their livestock would be seized for the use of the temple, and they would be expelled from the multitude of those who returned from captivity. [5] Within three days, all those of the tribe of Judah and Benjamin gathered together at Jerusalem. This was the ninth month, on the twentieth day of the month. [6] All the multitude sat together shivering in the broad place before the temple because of the present foul weather. [7] So Esdras arose up and said to them, "You have transgressed the law and married foreign wives, increasing the sins of Israel. [8] Now make confession and give glory to the Lord, the God of our fathers, [9] and do his will, and separate yourselves from the heathen of the land, and from the foreign women." [10] Then the whole multitude cried out, and said with a loud voice, "Just as you have spoken, so we will do. [11] But because the multitude is great, and it is foul weather, so that we can't stand outside, and this is not a work of one day or two, seeing our sin in these things has spread far, [12] therefore let the rulers of the multitude stay, and let all those of our settlements that have foreign wives come at the time appointed, [13] and with them the rulers and judges of every place, until we turn away the wrath of the Lord from us for this matter." [14] So Jonathan the son of Azael and[a] Ezekias the son of Thocanus took the matter on themselves. Mosollamus and Levis and Sabbateus were judges with them. [15] Those who returned from captivity did according to all these things. [16] Esdras

the priest chose for himself principal men of their families, all by name. On the new moon of the tenth month they met together to examine the matter. [17] So their cases of men who had foreign wives was brought to an end by the new moon of the first month. [18] Of the priests who had come together and had foreign wives, there were found [19] of the sons of Jesus the son of Josedek, and his kindred,[b] Mathelas, Eleazar, and[c] Joribus, and[d] Joadanus. [20] They gave their hands to put away their wives, and to offer rams to make reconciliation for their error. [21] Of the sons of Emmer: Ananias, Zabdeus, [e]Manes, [f]Sameus, [g]Hiereel, and [h]Azarias. [22] Of the sons of [i]Phaisur: Elionas, Massias, Ishmael, Nathanael, [j]Ocidelus, and [k]Saloas. [23] Of the Levites: Jozabdus, Semeis, [l]Colius who was called [m]Calitas, [n]Patheus, Judas, and Jonas. [24] Of the holy singers: [o]Eliasibus and Bacchurus. [25] Of the gatekeepers: Sallumus and[p] Tolbanes. [26] Of Israel, of the sons of Phoros:[q] Hiermas,[r] Ieddias,[s] Melchias, Maelus,[t] Eleazar, Asibas, [u] and Banneas. [27] Of the sons of Ela: Matthanias, Zacharias, [v] Jezrielus, Oabdius, Hieremoth, and[w] Aedias. [28] Of the sons of [x]Zamoth: [y]Eliadas, [z]Eliasimus, [aa]Othonias, Jarimoth, [bb]Sabathus, and[cc] Zardeus. [29] Of the sons of Bebai: Joannes, Ananias, [dd]Jozabdus, and [ee]Ematheis. [30] Of the sons of [ff] Mani: [gg]Olamus, [hh]Mamuchus, [ii]Jedeus, Jasubas, [jj] Jasaelus, and Hieremoth. [31] Of the sons of Addi: Naathus, Moossias, Laccunus, Naidus, Matthanias, Sesthel, Balnuus, and Manasseas. [32] Of the sons of Annas: Elionas, Aseas, Melchias, Sabbeus, and Simon Chosameus. [33] Of the sons of Asom: [kk]Maltanneus, [ll]Mattathias, [mm]Sabanneus, Eliphalat, Manasses, and Semei. [34] Of the sons of Baani: Jeremias, Momdis, Ismaerus, Juel, Mamdai, Pedias, Anos, Carabasion, Enasibus, Mamnitamenus, Eliasis, Bannus, Eliali, Someis, Selemias, and Nathanias. Of the sons of Ezora: Sesis, Ezril, Azaelus, Samatus, Zambri, and Josephus. [35] Of the sons of Nooma: Mazitias, Zabadeas, Edos, Juel, and Banaias. [36] All these had taken foreign wives, and they put them away with their children. [37] The priests and Levites, and those who were of Israel, lived in Jerusalem and in the country, on the new moon of the seventh month, and the children of Israel in their settlements. [38] *The whole multitude gathered together with one accord into the broad place before the porch of the temple toward the east. [39] They said to Esdras the priest and reader, "Bring the law of Moses that was given by the Lord, the God of Israel." [40] So Esdras the chief priest brought the law to the whole multitude both of men and women, and to all the priests, to hear the law on the new moon of the seventh month. [41] He read in the broad place before the porch of the temple from morning until midday, before both men and women; and all the multitude gave attention to the law. [42] Esdras the priest and reader of the law stood up upon the pulpit of wood which had been prepared. [43] Beside him stood Mattathias, Sammus, Ananias, Azarias, Urias, [nn]Ezekias, and Baalsamus on the right hand, [44] and on his left hand, [oo]Phaldeus, Misael, Melchias, [pp]Lothasubus, Nabarias, and Zacharias. [45] Then Esdras took the book of the law before the multitude, and sat honorably in the first place before all. [46] When he opened the law, they all stood straight up. So Esdras blessed the Lord God Most High, the God of armies, the Almighty. [47] All the people answered, "Amen." Lifting up their hands, they fell to the ground and worshiped the Lord. [48] Also Jesus, Annus, Sarabias, Iadinus, Jacubus, Sabateus, [qq]Auteas, Maiannas, Calitas, Azarias, Jozabdus, Ananias, and Phalias, the Levites, taught the law of the Lord, [rr]and read to the multitude the law of the Lord, explaining what was read. [49] Then Attharates said to Esdras the chief priest and reader, and to the Levites who taught the multitude, even to all, [50]"This day is holy to the Lord—now they all wept when they heard the law— [51] go then, eat the fat, drink the sweet, and send portions to those who have nothing; [52] for the day is holy to the Lord. Don't be sorrowful, for the Lord will bring you to honor." [53] So the Levites commanded all things to the people, saying, "This day is holy. Don't be sorrowful." [54] Then they went their way, every one to eat, drink, enjoy themselves, to give portions to those who had nothing, and to rejoice greatly, [55] because they [ss]understood the words they were instructed with, and for which they had been assembled.

* 8:91 Ezra 10:1
* 9:1 Ezra 10:6
[a] 9:14 Another reading is, Ezias.
[b] 9:19 Maaseiah.
[c] 9:19 Jarib.
[d] 9:19 Gedaliah.
[e] 9:21 Harim
[f] 9:21 Maaseiah.
[g] 9:21 Jehiel.
[h] 9:21 Uzziah.
[i] 9:22 Pashhur.
[j] 9:22 Jozabad.

[k] 9:22 Elasah.
[l] 9:23 Kelaiah.
[m] 9:23 Kelita.
[n] 9:23 Pethahiah.
[o] 9:24 Eliashib.
[p] 9:25 Telem.
[q] 9:26 Parosh.
[r] 9:26 Ramiah.
[s] 9:26 Izziah. Another reading is, Iezias
[t] 9:26 Mijamin.
[u] 9:26 Malchijah.
[v] 9:27 Jehiel.

[w] 9:27 Abdi.
[x] 9:28 Zattu.
[y] 9:28 Elioenai.
[z] 9:28 Eliashib.
[aa] 9:28 Mattaniah.
[bb] 9:28 Zabad.
[cc] 9:28 Aziza.
[dd] 9:29 Zabbai.
[ee] 9:29 Athlai.
[ff] 9:30 Bani.
[gg] 9:30 Meshullam.
[hh] 9:30 Malluch.
[ii] 9:30 Adaiah.

[jj] 9:30 Sheal.
[kk] 9:33 Mattenai.
[ll] 9:33 Mattattah.
[mm] 9:33 Zabad.
* 9:38 Nehemiah 8:1
[nn] 9:43 Hilkiah.
[oo] 9:44 Pedaiah.
[pp] 9:44 Hashuin.
[qq] 9:48 Hodiah.
[rr] 9:48 Some authorities omit and read...Lord.
[ss] 9:55 Or, were inspired by

# The Second Book of Esdras, or Ezra Sutu'el

*The Second Book of Esdras* is included in the Slavonic Bible as *3 Esdras*, but is not found in the Greek Septuagint. It is included in the Appendix to the Latin Vulgate Bible as *4 Esdras*. It is considered to be Apocrypha by most church traditions. It is preserved here for its supplementary historical value.

## 1

[1] The second book of the prophet Esdras, the son of Saraias, the son of Azaraias, the son of Helkias, the son of Salemas, the son of Sadoc, the son of Ahitob, [2] the son of Achias, the son of Phinees, the son of Heli, the son of Amarias, the son of Aziei, the son of Marimoth, the son of Arna, the son of Ozias, the son of Borith, the son of Abissei, the son of Phinees, the son of Eleazar, [3] the son of Aaron, of the tribe of Levi, who was captive in the land of the Medes, in the reign of Artaxerxes king of the Persians. [4] The Lord's word came to me, saying, [5]"Go your way and show my people their sinful deeds, and their children their wickedness which they have done against me, that they may tell their children's children, [6] because the sins of their fathers have increased in them, for they have forgotten me, and have offered sacrifices to foreign gods. [7] Didn't I bring them out of the land of Egypt, out of the house of bondage? But they have provoked me to wrath and have despised my counsels. [8] So pull out the hair of your head and cast all evils upon them, for they have not been obedient to my law, but they are a rebellious people. [9] How long shall I endure them, to whom I have done so much good? [10] I have overthrown many kings for their sakes. I have struck down Pharoah with his servants and all his army. [11] I have destroyed all the nations before them. In the east, I have scattered the people of two provinces, even of Tyre and Sidon, and have slain all their adversaries. [12] Speak therefore to them, saying: [13]"The Lord says, truly I brought you through the sea, and where there was no path I made highways for you. I gave you Moses for a leader and Aaron for a priest. [14] I gave you light in a pillar of fire. I have done great wonders among you, yet you have forgotten me, says the Lord. [15]"The Lord Almighty says: The quails were for a token to you. I gave you a camp for your protection, but you complained there. [16] You didn't celebrate in my name for the destruction of your enemies, but even to this day you still complain. [17] Where are the benefits that I have given you? When you were hungry and thirsty in the wilderness, didn't you cry to me, [18] saying, 'Why have you brought us into this wilderness to kill us? It would have been better for us to have served the Egyptians than to die in this wilderness.' [19] I had pity on your mourning and gave you manna for food. You ate angels' bread. [20] When you were thirsty, didn't I split the rock, and water flowed out in abundance? Because of the heat, I covered you with the leaves of the trees. [21] I divided fruitful lands among you. I drove out the Canaanites, the Pherezites, and the Philistines before you. What more shall I do for you?" says the Lord. [22] The Lord Almighty says, "When you were in the wilderness, at the bitter stream, being thirsty and blaspheming my name, [23] I gave you not fire for your blasphemies, but threw a tree in the water, and made the river sweet. [24] What shall I do to you, O Jacob? You, Judah, would not obey me. I will turn myself to other nations, and I will give my name to them, that they may keep my statutes. [25] Since you have forsaken me, I also will forsake you. When you ask me to be merciful to you, I will have no mercy upon you. [26] Whenever you call upon me, I will not hear you, for you have defiled your hands with blood, and your feet are swift to commit murder. [27] It is not as though you have forsaken me, but your own selves," says the Lord. [28] The Lord Almighty says, "Haven't I asked you as a father his sons, as a mother her daughters, and a nurse her young babies, [29] that you would be my people, and I would be your God, that you would be my children, and I would be your father? [30] I gathered you together, as a hen gathers her chicks under her wings. But now, what should I do to you? I will cast you out from my presence. [31] When you offer burnt sacrifices to me, I will turn my face from you, for I have rejected your solemn feast days, your new moons, and your circumcisions of the flesh. [32] I sent to you my servants the prophets, whom you have taken and slain, and torn their bodies in pieces, whose blood I will require from you," says the Lord. [33] The Lord Almighty says, "Your house is desolate. I will cast you out as the wind blows stubble. [34] Your children won't be fruitful, for they have neglected my commandment to you, and done that which is evil before me. [35] I will give your houses to a people that will come, which not having heard of me yet believe me. Those to whom I have shown no signs will do what I have commanded. [36] They have seen no prophets, yet they will remember their former condition. [37] I call to witness the gratitude of the people who will come, whose little ones rejoice with gladness. Although they see me not with bodily eyes, yet in spirit they will believe what I say." [38] And now, father, behold with glory, and see the people that come from the east: [39] to whom I will give for leaders, Abraham, Isaac, and Jacob, Oseas,

Amos, and Micheas, Joel, Abdias, and Jonas, [40] Nahum, and Abacuc, Sophonias, Aggaeus, Zachary, and Malachy, who is also called the Lord's messenger.

## 2

[1] The Lord says, "I brought this people out of bondage. I gave them my commandments by my servants the prophets, whom they would not listen to, but made my counsels void. [2] The mother who bore them says to them, 'Go your way, my children, for I am a widow and forsaken. [3] I brought you up with gladness, and I have lost you with sorrow and heaviness, for you have sinned before the Lord God, and done that which is evil before me. [4] But now what can I do for you? For I am a widow and forsaken. Go your way, my children, and ask for mercy from the Lord.' [5] As for me, O father, I call upon you for a witness in addition to the mother of these children, because they would not keep my covenant, [6] that you may bring them to confusion, and their mother to ruin, that they may have no offspring. [7] Let them be scattered abroad among the heathen. Let their names be blotted out of the earth, for they have despised my covenant. [8] Woe to you, Assur, you who hide the unrighteous with you! You wicked nation, remember what I did to Sodom and Gomorrah, [9] whose land lies in lumps of pitch and heaps of ashes. That is what I will also do to those who have not listened to me," says the Lord Almighty. [10] The Lord says to Esdras, "Tell my people that I will give them the kingdom of Jerusalem, which I would have given to Israel. [11] I will also take their glory back to myself, and give these the everlasting tabernacles which I had prepared for them. [12] They will have the tree of life for fragrant perfume. They will neither labor nor be weary. [13] Ask, and you will receive. Pray that your days may be few, that they may be shortened. The kingdom is already prepared for you. Watch! [14] Call heaven and earth to witness. Call them to witness, for I have left out evil, and created the good, for I live, says the Lord. [15]"Mother, embrace your children. I will bring them out with gladness like a dove does. Establish their feet, for I have chosen you, says the Lord. [16] I will raise those who are dead up again from their places, and bring them out from their tombs, for I recognize my name in them. [17] Don't be afraid, you mother of children, for I have chosen you, says the Lord. [18] For your help, I will send my servants Esaias and Jeremy, after whose counsel I have sanctified and prepared for you twelve trees laden with various fruits, [19] and as many springs flowing with milk and honey, and seven mighty mountains, on which roses and lilies grow, with which I will fill your children with joy. [20] Do right to the widow. Secure justice for the fatherless. Give to the poor. Defend the orphan. Clothe the naked. [21] Heal the broken and the weak. Don't laugh a lame man to scorn. Defend the maimed. Let the blind man have a vision of my glory. [22] Protect the old and young within your walls. [23] Wherever you find the dead, set a sign upon them and commit them to the grave, and I will give you the first place in my resurrection. [24] Stay still, my people, and take your rest, for your rest will come. [25] Nourish your children, good nurse, and establish their feet. [26] As for the servants whom I have given you, not one of them will perish, for I will require them from among your number. [27] Don't be anxious, for when the day of suffering and anguish comes, others will weep and be sorrowful, but you will rejoice and have abundance. [28] The nations will envy you, but they will be able to do nothing against you, says the Lord. [29] My hands will cover you, so that your children don't see Gehenna.[a] [30] Be joyful, mother, with your children, for I will deliver you, says the Lord. [31] Remember your children who sleep, for I will bring them out of the secret places of the earth, and show mercy to them, for I am merciful, says the Lord Almighty. [32] Embrace your children until I come, and proclaim mercy to them, for my wells run over, and my grace won't fail." [33] I, Esdras, received a command from the Lord on Mount Horeb to go to Israel, but when I came to them, they rejected me and rejected the Lord's commandment. [34] Therefore I say to you, O nations that hear and understand, "Look for your shepherd. He will give you everlasting rest, for he is near at hand who will come at the end of the age. [35] Be ready for the rewards of the kingdom, for the everlasting light will shine on you forevermore. [36] Flee the shadow of this world, receive the joy of your glory. I call to witness my savior openly. [37] Receive that which is given to you by the Lord, and be joyful, giving thanks to him who has called you to heavenly kingdoms. [38] Arise and stand up, and see the number of those who have been sealed at the Lord's feast. [39] Those who withdrew themselves from the shadow of the world have received glorious garments from the Lord. [40] Take again your full number, O Zion, and make up the reckoning of those of yours who are clothed in white, which have fulfilled the law of the Lord. [41] The number of your children, whom you long for, is fulfilled. Ask the power of the Lord, that your people, which have been called from the beginning, may be made holy." [42] I, Esdras, saw upon Mount Zion a great multitude, whom I could not number, and they all praised the Lord with songs. [43] In the

---

[a] 2:29 or, Hell.

midst of them, there was a young man of a high stature, taller than all the rest, and upon every one of their heads he set crowns, and he was more exalted than they were. I marveled greatly at this. ⁴⁴ So I asked the angel, and said, "What are these, my Lord?" ⁴⁵ He answered and said to me, "These are those who have put off the mortal clothing, and put on the immortal, and have confessed the name of God. Now are they crowned, and receive palms." ⁴⁶ Then said I to the angel, "Who is the young man who sets crowns on them, and gives them palms in their hands?" ⁴⁷ So he answered and said to me, "He is the Son of God, whom they have confessed in the world." Then I began to praise those who stood so valiantly for the name of the Lord. ⁴⁸ Then the angel said to me, "Go your way, and tell my people what kind of things, and how great wonders of the Lord God you have seen."

## 3

¹ In the thirtieth year after the ruin of the city, I Salathiel, also called Esdras, was in Babylon, and lay troubled upon my bed, and my thoughts came up over my heart, ² for I saw the desolation of Zion and the wealth of those who lived at Babylon. ³ My spirit was very agitated, so that I began to speak words full of fear to the Most High, and said, ⁴ "O sovereign Lord, didn't you speak at the beginning when you formed the earth—and that yourself alone—and commanded the dust ⁵ and it gave you Adam, a body without a soul? Yet it was the workmanship of your hands, and you breathed into him the breath of life, and he was made alive in your presence. ⁶ You led him into the garden which your right hand planted before the earth appeared. ⁷ You gave him your one commandment, which he transgressed, and immediately you appointed death for him and his descendants. From him were born nations, tribes, peoples, and kindred without number. ⁸ Every nation walked after their own will, did ungodly things in your sight, and despised your commandments, and you didn't hinder them. ⁹ Nevertheless, again in process of time, you brought the flood on those who lived in the world and destroyed them. ¹⁰ It came to pass that the same thing happened to them. Just as death came to Adam, so was the flood to these. ¹¹ Nevertheless, you left one of them, Noah with his household, and all the righteous men who descended from him. ¹² "It came to pass that when those who lived upon the earth began to multiply, they also multiplied children, peoples, and many nations, and began again to be more ungodly than their ancestors. ¹³ It came to pass, when they did wickedly before you, you chose one from among them, whose name was Abraham. ¹⁴ You loved, and to him only you showed the end of the times secretly by night, ¹⁵ and made an everlasting covenant with him, promising him that you would never forsake his descendants. To him, you gave Isaac, and to Isaac you gave Jacob and Esau. ¹⁶ You set apart Jacob for yourself, but rejected Esau. Jacob became a great multitude. ¹⁷ It came to pass that when you led his descendants out of Egypt, you brought them up to Mount Sinai. ¹⁸ You bowed the heavens also, shook the earth, moved the whole world, made the depths tremble, and troubled the age. ¹⁹ Your glory went through four gates, of fire, of earthquake, of wind, and of ice, that you might give the law to the descendants of Jacob, and the commandment to the descendants of Israel. ²⁰ "Yet you didn't take away from them their wicked heart, that your law might produce fruit in them. ²¹ For the first Adam, burdened with a wicked heart transgressed and was overcome, as were all who are descended from him. ²² Thus disease was made permanent. The law was in the heart of the people along with the wickedness of the root. So the good departed away and that which was wicked remained. ²³ So the times passed away, and the years were brought to an end. Then you raised up a servant, called David, ²⁴ whom you commanded to build a city to your name, and to offer burnt offerings to you in it from what is yours. ²⁵ When this was done many years, then those who inhabited the city did evil, ²⁶ in all things doing as Adam and all his generations had done, for they also had a wicked heart. ²⁷ So you gave your city over into the hands of your enemies. ²⁸ "Then I said in my heart, 'Are their deeds of those who inhabit Babylon any better? Is that why it gained dominion over Zion?' ²⁹ For it came to pass that when I came here, that I also saw impieties without number, and my soul saw many sinners in this thirtieth year, so that my heart failed me. ³⁰ For I have seen how you endure them sinning, and have spared those who act ungodly, and have destroyed your people, and have preserved your enemies; ³¹ and you have not shown how your way may be comprehended. Are the deeds of Babylon better than those of Zion? ³² Or is there any other nation that knows you beside Israel? Or what tribes have so believed your covenants as these tribes of Jacob? ³³ Yet their reward doesn't appear, and their labor has no fruit, for I have gone here and there through the nations, and I see that they abound

in wealth, and don't think about your commandments. ³⁴ Weigh therefore our iniquities now in the balance, and theirs also who dwell in the world, and so will it be found which way the scale inclines. ³⁵ Or when was it that they who dwell on the earth have not sinned in your sight? Or what nation has kept your commandments so well? ³⁶ You will find some men by name who have kept your precepts, but you won't find nations."

## 4

¹ The angel who was sent to me, whose name was Uriel, gave me an answer, ² and said to me, "Your understanding has utterly failed you regarding this world. Do you think you can comprehend the way of the Most High?" ³ Then I said, "Yes, my Lord." He answered me, "I have been sent to show you three ways, and to set before you three problems. ⁴ If you can solve one for me, I also will show you the way that you desire to see, and I will teach you why the heart is wicked." ⁵ I said, "Say on, my Lord." Then said he to me, "Go, weigh for me the weight of fire, or measure for me blast of wind, or call back for me the day that is past." ⁶ Then answered I and said, "Who of the sons of men is able to do this, that you should ask me about such things?" ⁷ He said to me, "If I had asked you, 'How many dwellings are there in the heart of the sea? Or how many springs are there at the fountain head of the deep? Or how many streams are above the firmament? Or which are the exits ᵃof hell? Or which are the entrances of paradise?' ⁸ perhaps you would say to me, 'I never went down into the deep, or as yet into hell, neither did I ever climb up into heaven.' ⁹ Nevertheless now I have only asked you about the fire, wind, and the day, things which you have experienced, and from which you can't be separated, and yet have you given me no answer about them." ¹⁰ He said moreover to me, "You can't understand your own things that you grew up with. ¹¹ How then can your mind comprehend the way of the Most High? How can he who is already worn out with the corrupted world understand incorruption?" ᵇ When I heard these things, I fell on my face ¹² and said to him, "It would have been better if we weren't here at all, than that we should come here and live in the midst of ungodliness, and suffer, and not know why." ¹³ He answered me, and said, ᶜ "A forest of the trees of the field went out, and took counsel together, ¹⁴ and said, 'Come! Let's go and make war against the sea, that it may depart away before us, and that we may make ourselves more forests.' ¹⁵ The waves of the sea also in like manner took counsel together, and said, 'Come! Let's go up and subdue the forest of the plain, that there also we may gain more territory.' ¹⁶ The counsel of the wood was in vain, for the fire came and consumed it. ¹⁷ Likewise also the counsel of the waves of the sea, for the sand stood up and stopped them. ¹⁸ If you were judge now between these two, which would you justify, or which would you condemn?" ¹⁹ I answered and said, "It is a foolish counsel that they both have taken, for the ground is given to the wood, and the place of the sea is given to bear its waves." ²⁰ Then answered he me, and said, "You have given a right judgment. Why don't you judge your own case? ²¹ For just as the ground is given to the wood, and the sea to its waves, even so those who dwell upon the earth may understand nothing but what is upon the earth. Only he who dwells above the heavens understands the things that are above the height of the heavens." ²² Then answered I and said, "I beg you, O Lord, why has the power of understanding been given to me? ²³ For it was not in my mind to be curious of the ways above, but of such things as pass by us daily, because Israel is given up as a reproach to the heathen. The people whom you have loved have been given over to ungodly nations. The law of our forefathers is made of no effect, and the written covenants are nowhere regarded. ²⁴ We pass away out of the world like locusts. Our life is like a vapor, and we aren't worthy to obtain mercy. ²⁵ What will he then do for his name by which we are called? I have asked about these things." ²⁶ Then he answered me, and said, "If you are alive you will see, and if you live long, you will marvel, for the world hastens quickly to pass away. ²⁷ For it is not able to bear the things that are promised to the righteous in the times to come; for this world is full of sadness and infirmities. ²⁸ For the evilᵈ about which you asked me has been sown, but its harvest hasn't yet come. ²⁹ If therefore that which is sown isn't reaped, and if the place where the evil is sown doesn't pass away, the field where the good is sown won't come. ³⁰ For a grain of evil seed was sown in the heart of Adam from the beginning, and how much wickedness it has produced to this time! How much more it will yet produce until the time of threshing comes! ³¹ Ponder now by yourself, how much fruit of wickedness a grain of evil seed has produced. ³² When the grains which are without number are sown, how great a threshing floor they will fill!" ³³ Then I answered and said, ᵉ "How long? When will these things come

---

ᵃ *4:7 So the Syriac. The Latin omits of hell? or which are the paths.*

ᵇ *4:11 So the Syriac and Aethiopic. The Latin is corrupt.*

ᶜ *4:13 So the Oriental versions. The Latin is corrupt. See Judges 9:8.*

ᵈ *4:28 so the Syriac and Aethiopic.*

ᵉ *4:33 So the chief oriental versions.*

to pass? Why are our years few and evil?" <sup>34</sup> He answered me, and said, "Don't hurry faster than the Most High; for your haste is<sup>a</sup> for your own self, but he who is above hurries on behalf of many. <sup>35</sup> Didn't the souls of the righteous ask question of these things in their chambers, saying, 'How long <sup>b</sup>will we be here? When does the fruit of the threshing floor come?' <sup>36</sup> To them, Jeremiel the archangel answered, 'When the number is fulfilled of those who are like you. For he has weighed the world in the balance. <sup>37</sup> By measure, he has measured the times. By number, he has counted the seasons. He won't <sup>c</sup>move or stir them until that measure is fulfilled.'" <sup>38</sup> Then I answered, "O sovereign Lord, all of us are full of ungodliness. <sup>39</sup> Perhaps it is for our sakes that the threshing time of the righteous is kept back—because of the sins of those who dwell on the earth." <sup>40</sup> So he answered me, "Go your way to a woman with child, and ask of her when she has fulfilled her nine months, if her womb may keep the baby any longer within her." <sup>41</sup> Then I said, "No, Lord, that can it not." He said to me, "In Hades, the chambers of souls are like the womb. <sup>42</sup> For just like a woman in labor hurries to escape the anguish of the labor pains, even so these places hurry to deliver those things that are committed to them from the beginning. <sup>43</sup> Then you will be shown those things which you desire to see." <sup>44</sup> Then I answered, "If I have found favor in your sight, and if it is possible, and if I am worthy, <sup>45</sup> show me this also, whether there is more to come than is past, or whether the greater part has gone over us. <sup>46</sup> For what is gone I know, but I don't know what is to come." <sup>47</sup> He said to me, "Stand up on my right side, and I will explain the parable to you." <sup>48</sup> So I stood, looked, and saw a hot burning oven passed by before me. It happened that when the flame had gone by I looked, and saw that the smoke remained. <sup>49</sup> After this, a watery cloud passed in front of me, and sent down much rain with a storm. When the stormy rain was past, the drops still remained in it." <sup>50</sup> Then said he to me, "Consider with yourself; as the rain is more than the drops, and the fire is greater than the smoke, so the quantity which is past was far greater; but the drops and the smoke still remained." <sup>51</sup> Then I prayed, and said, "Do you think that I will live until that time? Or who will be alive in those days?" <sup>52</sup> He answered me, "As for the signs you asked me about, I may tell you of them in part; but I wasn't sent to tell you about your life, for I don't know.

## 5

<sup>1</sup>"Nevertheless, concerning the signs, behold, the days will come when those who dwell on earth will be taken <sup>d</sup>with great amazement, and the way of truth will be hidden, and the land will be barren of faith. <sup>2</sup> Iniquity will be increased above what now you see, and beyond what you have heard long ago. <sup>3</sup> The land that you now see ruling will be a trackless waste, and men will see it desolate. <sup>4</sup> But if the Most High grants you to live, you will see what is after the third period will be troubled. The sun will suddenly shine in the night, and the moon in the day. <sup>5</sup> Blood will drop out of wood, and the stone will utter its voice. The peoples will be troubled, and the stars will fall. <sup>6</sup> He will rule whom those who dwell on the earth don't expect, and the birds will fly away together. <sup>7</sup> The Sodomite sea will cast out fish, and make a noise in the night, which many have not known; but all will hear its voice. <sup>8</sup> There will also be chaos in many places. Fires will break out often, and the wild animals will change their places, and women will bring forth monsters. <sup>9</sup> Salt waters will be found in the sweet, and all friends will destroy one another. Then reason will hide itself, and understanding withdraw itself into its chamber. <sup>10</sup> It will be sought by many, and won't be found. Unrighteousness and lack of restraint will be multiplied on earth. <sup>11</sup> One country will ask another, 'Has righteousness, or a man that does righteousness, gone through you?' And it will say, 'No.' <sup>12</sup> It will come to pass at that time that men will hope, but won't obtain. They will labor, but their ways won't prosper. <sup>13</sup> I am permitted to show you such signs. If you will pray again, and weep as now, and fast seven days, you will hear yet greater things than these." <sup>14</sup> Then I woke up, and an extreme trembling went through my body, and my mind was so troubled that it fainted. <sup>15</sup> So the angel who had come to talk with me held me, comforted me, and set me on my feet. <sup>16</sup> In the second night, it came to pass that <sup>e</sup>Phaltiel the captain of the people came to me, saying, "Where have you been? Why is your face sad? <sup>17</sup> Or don't you know that Israel is committed to you in the land of their captivity? <sup>18</sup> Get up then, and eat some bread, and don't forsake us, like a shepherd who leaves the flock in the power of cruel wolves." <sup>19</sup> Then said I to him, "Go away from me and don't come near me for seven days, and then you shall come to me." He heard what I said and left me. <sup>20</sup> So I fasted seven days, mourning and weeping, like Uriel the angel had

commanded me. <sup>21</sup> After seven days, the thoughts of my heart were very grievous to me again, <sup>22</sup> and my soul recovered the spirit of understanding, and I began to speak words before the Most High again. <sup>23</sup> I said, "O sovereign Lord of all the woods of the earth, and of all the trees thereof, you have chosen one vine for yourself. <sup>24</sup> Of all the lands of the world you have chosen one <sup>f</sup>country for yourself. Of all the flowers of the world, you have chosen one lily for yourself. <sup>25</sup> Of all the depths of the sea, you have filled one river for yourself. Of all built cities, you have consecrated Zion for yourself. <sup>26</sup> Of all the birds that are created you have named for yourself one dove. Of all the livestock that have been made, you have provided for yourself one sheep. <sup>27</sup> Among all the multitudes of peoples you have gotten yourself one people. To this people, whom you loved, you gave a law that is approved by all. <sup>28</sup> Now, O Lord, why have you given this one people over to many, and <sup>g</sup>have dishonored the one root above others, and have scattered your only one among many? <sup>29</sup> Those who opposed your promises have trampled down those who believed your covenants. <sup>30</sup> If you really do hate your people so much, they should be punished with your own hands." <sup>31</sup> Now when I had spoken these words, the angel that came to me the night before was sent to me, <sup>32</sup> and said to me, "Hear me, and I will instruct you. Listen to me, and I will tell you more." <sup>33</sup> I said, "Speak on, my Lord." Then said he to me, "You are very troubled in mind for Israel's sake. Do you love that people more than he who made them?" <sup>34</sup> I said, "No, Lord; but I have spoken out of grief; for my heart is in agony every hour while I labor to comprehend the way of the Most High, and to seek out part of his judgment." <sup>35</sup> He said to me, "You can't." And I said, "Why, Lord? Why was I born? Why wasn't my mother's womb my grave, that I might not have seen the travail of Jacob, and the wearisome toil of the people of Israel?" <sup>36</sup> He said to me, "Count for me those who haven't yet come. Gather together for me the drops that are scattered abroad, and make the withered flowers green again for me. <sup>37</sup> Open for me the chambers that are closed, and bring out the winds for me that are shut up in them. Or show me the image of a voice. Then I will declare to you the travail that you asked to see." <sup>38</sup> And I said, "O sovereign Lord, who may know these things except he who doesn't have his dwelling with men? <sup>39</sup> As for me, I lack wisdom. How can I then speak of these things you asked me about?" <sup>40</sup> Then said he to me, "Just as you can do none of these things that I have spoken of, even so you can't find out my judgment, or the end of the love that I have promised to my people." <sup>41</sup> I said, "But, behold, O Lord, you have made the promise to those who are alive at the end. What should they do who have been before us, or we ourselves, or those who will come after us?" <sup>42</sup> He said to me, "I will compare my judgment to a ring. Just as there is no slowness of those who are last, even so there is no swiftness of those who be first." <sup>43</sup> So I answered, "Couldn't you make them all at once that have been made, and that are now, and that are yet to come, that you might show your judgment sooner?" <sup>44</sup> Then he answered me, "The creature may not move faster than the creator, nor can the world hold them at once who will be created in it." <sup>45</sup> And I said, "How have you said to your servant, that <sup>h</sup>you will surely make alive at once the creature that you have created? <sup>i</sup>If therefore they will be alive at once, and the creation will sustain them, even so it might now also support them to be present at once." <sup>46</sup> And he said to me, "Ask the womb of a woman, and say to her, 'If you bear ten children, why do you it at different times? Ask her therefore to give birth to ten children at once." <sup>47</sup> I said, "She can't, but must do it each in their own time." <sup>48</sup> Then said he to me, "Even so, I have given the womb of the earth to those who are sown in it in their own times. <sup>49</sup> For just as a young child may not give birth, neither she who has grown old any more, even so have I organized the world which I created." <sup>50</sup> I asked, "Seeing that you have now shown me the way, I will speak before you. Is our mother, of whom you have told me, still young? Or does she now draw near to old age?" <sup>51</sup> He answered me, "Ask a woman who bears children, and she will tell you. <sup>52</sup> Say to her, 'Why aren't they whom you have now brought forth like those who were before, but smaller in stature?' <sup>53</sup> She also will answer you, 'Those who are born in the strength of youth are different from those who are born in the time of old age, when the womb fails.' <sup>54</sup> Consider therefore you also, how you are shorter than those who were before you. <sup>55</sup> So are those who come after you smaller than you, as born of the creature which now begins to be old, and is past the strength of youth." <sup>56</sup> Then I said, "Lord, I implore you, if I have found favor in your sight, show your servant by whom you visit your creation."

---

<sup>a</sup> 4:34 So the Syriac. The Latin is corrupt.
<sup>b</sup> 4:35 So the Syriac. The Latin has shall I hope on this fashion?

<sup>c</sup> 4:37 Syr. rest.
<sup>d</sup> 5:1 So the syriac.
<sup>e</sup> 5:16 The Syriac has Psaltiel.
<sup>f</sup> 5:24 After the Oriental versions. The Latin has pit.

<sup>g</sup> 5:28 After the Oriental versions. The Latin reads have prepared.
<sup>h</sup> 5:45 So the Syriac.

<sup>i</sup> 5:45 The Latin omits If...alive at once.

## 6

[1] He said to me, "In the beginning, when the earth was made, before the portals of the world were fixed and before the gatherings of the winds blew, [2] before the voices of the thunder sounded and before the flashes of the lightning shone, before the foundations of paradise were laid, [3] before the fair flowers were seen, before the powers of the earthquake were established, before the innumerable army of angels were gathered together, [4] before the heights of the air were lifted up, before the measures of the firmament were named, before the footstool of Zion [a]was established, [5] before the present years were reckoned, before the imaginations of those who now sin were estranged, and before they were sealed who have gathered faith for a treasure— [6] then I considered these things, and they all were made through me alone, and not through another; just as by me also they will be ended, and not by another." [7] Then I answered, "What will be the dividing of the times? Or when will be the end of the first and the beginning of the age that follows?" [8] He said to me, "From Abraham to Isaac, because Jacob and Esau were born to him, for Jacob's hand held Esau's heel from the beginning. [9] For Esau is the end of this age, and Jacob is the beginning of the one that follows. [10] [b]The beginning of a man is his hand, and the end of a man is his heel. Seek nothing else between the heel and the hand, Esdras!" [11] Then I answered, "O sovereign Lord, if I have found favor in your sight, [12] I beg you, show your servant the end of your signs which you showed me part on a previous night." [13] So he answered, "Stand up upon your feet, and you will hear a mighty sounding voice. [14] If the place you stand on is greatly moved [15] when it speaks don't be afraid, for the word is of the end, and the foundations of the earth will understand [16] that the speech is about them. They will tremble and be moved, for they know that their end must be changed." [17] It happened that when I had heard it, I stood up on my feet, and listened, and, behold, there was a voice that spoke, and its sound was like the sound of many waters. [18] It said, "Behold, the days come when I draw near to visit those who dwell upon the earth, [19] and when I investigate those who have caused harm unjustly with their unrighteousness, and when the affliction of Zion is complete, [20] and when the seal will be set on the age that is to pass away, then I will show these signs: the books will be opened before the firmament, and all will see together. [21] The children a year old will speak with their voices. The women with child will deliver premature children at three or four months, and they will live and dance. [22] Suddenly the sown places will appear unsown. The full storehouses will suddenly be found empty. [23] The trumpet will give a sound which when every man hears, they will suddenly be afraid. [24] At that time friends will make war against one another like enemies. The earth will stand in fear with those who dwell in it. The springs of the fountains will stand still, so that for three hours they won't flow. [25]"It will be that whoever remains after all these things that I have told you of, he will be saved and will see my salvation, and the end of my world. [26] They will see the men who have been taken up, who have not tasted death from their birth. The heart of the inhabitants will be changed and turned into a different spirit. [27] For evil will be blotted out and deceit will be quenched. [28] Faith will flourish. Corruption will be overcome, and the truth, which has been so long without fruit, will be declared." [29] When he talked with me, behold, little by little, the place I stood on [c]rocked back and forth. [30] He said to me, "I came to show you these things [d]tonight. [31] If therefore you will pray yet again, and fast seven more days, I will [e]again tell you greater things than these. [32] For your voice has surely been heard before the Most High. For the Mighty has seen your righteousness. He has also seen your purity, which you have maintained ever since your youth. [33] Therefore he has sent me to show you all these things, and to say to you, 'Believe, and don't be afraid! [34] Don't be hasty to think vain things about the former times, that you may not hasten in the latter times.'" [35] It came to pass after this, that I wept again, and fasted seven days in like manner, that I might fulfill the three weeks which he told me. [36] On the eighth night, my heart was troubled within me again, and I began to speak in the presence of the Most High. [37] For my spirit was greatly aroused, and my soul was in distress. [38] I said, "O Lord, truly you spoke at the beginning of the creation, on the first day, and said this: 'Let heaven and earth be made,' and your word perfected the work. [39] Then the spirit was hovering, and darkness and silence were on every side. The sound of man's voice was not yet there.[f] [40] Then you commanded a ray of light to be brought out of your treasuries, that your works might then appear. [41]"On the second day, again you made the spirit of the firmament and commanded it to divide and to separate the waters, that the one part might go up, and the other remain beneath. [42]"On the third day, you commanded that the waters should be gathered together in the seventh part of the earth. You dried up six parts and kept them, to the intent that of these some being both planted and tilled might serve before you. [43] For as soon as your word went out, the work was done. [44] Immediately, great and innumerable fruit grew, with many pleasant tastes, and flowers of inimitable color, and fragrances of most exquisite smell. This was done the third day. [45]"On the fourth day, you commanded that the sun should shine, the moon give its light, and the stars should be in their order; [46] and gave them a command to serve mankind, who was to be made. [47]"On the fifth day, you said to the seventh part, where the water was gathered together, that it should produce living creatures, fowls and fishes; and so it came to pass [48] that the mute and lifeless water produced living things as it was told, that the nations might therefore praise your wondrous works. [49]"Then you preserved two living creatures. The one you called Behemoth, and the other you called Leviathan. [50] You separated the one from the other; for the seventh part, namely, where the water was gathered together, might not hold them both. [51] To Behemoth, you gave one part, which was dried up on the third day, that he should dwell in it, in which are a thousand hills; [52] but to Leviathan you gave the seventh part, namely, the watery part. You have kept them to be devoured by whom you wish, when you wish. [53]"But on the sixth day, you commanded the earth to produce before you cattle, animals, and creeping things. [54] Over these, you ordained Adam as ruler over all the works that you have made. Of him came all of us, the people whom you have chosen. [55]"All this have I spoken before you, O Lord, because you have said that for our sakes you made [g]this world. [56] As for the other nations, which also come from Adam, you have said that they are nothing, and are like spittle. You have likened the abundance of them to a drop that falls from a bucket. [57] Now, O Lord, behold these nations, which are reputed as nothing, being rulers over us and devouring us. [58] But we your people, whom you have called your firstborn, your only children, and your fervent lover, are given into their hands. [59] Now if the world is made for our sakes, why don't we possess our world for an inheritance? How long will this endure?"

## 7

[1] When I had finished speaking these words, the angel which had been sent to me the nights before was sent to me. [2] He said to me, "Rise, Esdras, and hear the words that I have come to tell you." [3] I said, "Speak on, my Lord." Then he said to me, "There is a sea set in a wide place, that it might be [h]broad and vast, [4] but its entrance is set in a narrow place so as to be like a river. [5] Whoever desires to go into the sea to look at it, or to rule it, if he didn't go through the narrow entrance, how could he come into the broad part? [6] Another thing also: There is a city built and set in a plain country, and full of all good things, [7] but its entrance is narrow, and is set in a dangerous place to fall, having fire on the right hand, and deep water on the left. [8] There is one only path between them both, even between the fire and the water, so that only one person can go there at once. [9] If this city is now given to a man for an inheritance, if the heir doesn't pass the danger before him, how will he receive his inheritance?" [10] I said, "That is so, Lord." Then said he to me, "Even so also is Israel's portion. [11] I made the world for their sakes. What is now done was decreed when Adam transgressed my statutes. [12] Then the entrances of this world were made narrow, sorrowful, and toilsome. They are but few and evil, full of perils, and involved in great toils. [13] For the entrances of the greater world are wide and safe, and produce fruit of immortality. [14] So if those who live don't enter these difficult and vain things, they can never receive those that are reserved for them. [15] Now therefore why are you disturbed, seeing you are but a corruptible man? Why are you moved, since you are mortal? [16] Why haven't you considered in your mind that which is to come, rather than that which is present?" [17] Then I answered and said, "O sovereign Lord, behold, you have ordained in your law that the righteous will inherit these things, but that the ungodly will perish. [18] The righteous therefore will suffer difficult things, and hope for easier things, but those who have done wickedly have suffered the difficult things, and yet will not see the easier things." [19] He said to me, "You are not a judge above God, neither do you have more understanding than the Most High. [20] Yes, let many perish who now live, rather than that the law of God which is set before them be despised. [21] For God strictly commanded those who came, even as they came, what they should do to live, and what they should observe to avoid punishment. [22] Nevertheless, they weren't obedient to him, but spoke against him

---

[a] 6:4 So the Syriac.

[b] 6:10 So the Syriac, etc. The Latin is defective.

[c] 6:29 After the Oriental versions. The Latin is corrupt.

[d] 6:30 So the Syriac. The Latin is corrupt.

[e] 6:31 The Latin has tell you by day.

[f] 6:39 The Latin adds from you.

[g] 6:55 So the Syriac. The Latin has the firstborn world.

[h] 7:3 So the chief Oriental versions. The Latin MSS. have deep.

and imagined for themselves vain things. ²³ They made cunning plans of wickedness, and said moreover of the Most High that he doesn't exist, and they didn't know his ways. ²⁴ They despised his law and denied his covenants. They haven't been faithful to his statutes, and haven't performed his works. ²⁵ Therefore, Esdras, for the empty are empty things, and for the full are the full things. ²⁶ For behold, the time will come, and it will be, when these signs of which I told you before will come to pass, that the bride will appear, even the city coming forth, and she will be seen who now is withdrawn from the earth. ²⁷ Whoever is delivered from the foretold evils will see my wonders. ²⁸ For my son Jesus will be revealed with those who are with him, and those who remain will rejoice four hundred years. ²⁹ After these years my son Christ[a] will die, along with all of those who have the breath of life[b]. ³⁰ Then the world will be turned into the old silence seven days, like as in the first beginning, so that no human will remain. ³¹ After seven days the world that is not yet awake will be raised up, and what is corruptible will die. ³² The earth will restore those who are asleep in it, and the dust those who dwell in it in silence, and the ᶜsecret places will deliver those souls that were committed to them. ³³ The Most High will be revealed on the judgment seat, [d] and compassion will pass away, and patience will be withdrawn. ³⁴ Only judgment will remain. Truth will stand. Faith will grow strong. ³⁵ Recompense will follow. The reward will be shown. Good deeds will awake, and wicked deeds won't sleep.[e] ³⁶ The ᶠpit of torment will appear, and near it will be the place of rest. The furnace of hell[g] will be shown, and near it the paradise of delight. ³⁷ Then the Most High will say to the nations that are raised from the dead, 'Look and understand whom you have denied, whom you haven't served, whose commandments you have despised. ³⁸ Look on this side and on that. Here is delight and rest, and there fire and torments.' Thus ʰhe will speak to them in the day of judgment. ³⁹ This is a day that has neither sun, nor moon, nor stars, ⁴⁰ neither cloud, nor thunder, nor lightning, neither wind, nor water, nor air, neither darkness, nor evening, nor morning, ⁴¹ neither summer, nor spring, nor heat, norⁱ winter, neither frost, nor cold, nor hail, nor rain, nor dew, ⁴² neither noon, nor night, nor dawn, neither shining, nor brightness, nor light, except only the splendor of the glory of the Most High, by which all will see the things that are set before them. ⁴³ It will endure as though it were a week of years. ⁴⁴ This is my judgment and its prescribed order; but I have only shown these things to you." ⁴⁵ I answered, "I said then, O Lord, and I say now: Blessed are those who are now alive and keep your commandments! ⁴⁶ But what about those for whom I prayed? For who is there of those who are alive who has not sinned, and who of the children of men hasn't transgressed your covenant? ⁴⁷ Now I see that the world to come will bring delight to few, but torments to many. ⁴⁸ For an evil heart has grown up in us, which has led us astray from these commandments and has brought us into corruption and into the ways of death. It has shown us the paths of perdition and removed us far from life—and that, not a few only, but nearly all who have been created." ⁴⁹ He answered me, "Listen to me, and I will instruct you. I will admonish you yet again. ⁵⁰ For this reason, the Most High has not made one world, but two. ⁵¹ For because you have said that the just are not many, but few, and the ungodly abound, hear the explanation. ⁵² If you have just a few precious stones, will you add them to lead and clay?" ⁵³ I said, "Lord, how could that be?" ⁵⁴ He said to me, "Not only that, but ask the earth, and she will tell you. Defer to her, and she will declare it to you. ⁵⁵ Say to her, 'You produce gold, silver, and brass, and also iron, lead, and clay; ⁵⁶ but silver is more abundant than gold, and brass than silver, and iron than brass, and lead than iron, and clay than lead.' ⁵⁷ Judge therefore which things are precious and to be desired, what is abundant or what is rare?" ⁵⁸ I said, "O sovereign Lord, that which is plentiful is of less worth, for that which is more rare is more precious." ⁵⁹ He answered me, "Weigh within yourself the things that you have thought, for he who has what is hard to get rejoices over him who has what is plentiful. ⁶⁰ So also is the judgment which I have promised; for I will rejoice over the few that will be saved, because these are those who have made my glory to prevail now, and through them, my name is now honored. ⁶¹ I won't grieve over the multitude of those who perish; for these are those who are now like mist, and have become like flame and smoke; they are set on fire and burn hotly, and are extinguished." ⁶² I answered, "O earth, why have you produced, if the mind is made out of dust, like all other created things? ⁶³ For it would have been better that the dust itself had been unborn, so that the mind might not have been made from it. ⁶⁴ But now the mind grows with us, and because of this we are tormented, because we perish and we know it. ⁶⁵ Let the race of men lament and the animals of the field be glad. Let all who are born

lament, but let the four-footed animals and the livestock rejoice. ⁶⁶ For it is far better with them than with us; for they don't look forward to judgment, neither do they know of torments or of salvation promised to them after death. ⁶⁷ For what does it profit us, that we will be preserved alive, but yet be afflicted with torment? ⁶⁸ For all who are born are defiled with iniquities, and are full of sins and laden with transgressions. ⁶⁹ If after death we were not to come into judgment, perhaps it would have been better for us." ⁷⁰ He answered me, "When the Most High made the world and Adam and all those who came from him, he first prepared the judgment and the things that pertain to the judgment. ⁷¹ Now understand from your own words, for you have said that the mind grows with us. ⁷² They therefore who dwell on the earth will be tormented for this reason, that having understanding they have committed iniquity, and receiving commandments have not kept them, and having obtained a law they dealt unfaithfully with that which they received. ⁷³ What then will they have to say in the judgment, or how will they answer in the last times? ⁷⁴ For how long a time has the Most High been patient with those who inhabit the world, and not for their sakes, but because of the times which he has foreordained!" ⁷⁵ I answered, "If I have found grace in your sight, O Lord, show this also to your servant, whether after death, even now when every one of us gives up his soul, we will be kept in rest until those times come, in which you renew the creation, or whether we will be tormented immediately." ⁷⁶ He answered me, "I will show you this also; but don't join yourself with those who are scorners, nor count yourself with those who are tormented. ⁷⁷ For you have a treasure of works laid up with the Most High, but it won't be shown you until the last times. ⁷⁸ For concerning death the teaching is: When the decisive sentence has gone out from the Most High that a man shall die, as the spirit leaves the body to return again to him who gave it, it adores the glory of the Most High first of all. ⁷⁹ And if it is one of those who have been scorners and have not kept the way of the Most High, and that have despised his law, and who hate those who fear God, ⁸⁰ these spirits won't enter into habitations, but will wander and be in torments immediately, ever grieving and sad, in seven ways. ⁸¹ The first way, because they have despised the law of the Most High. ⁸² The second way, because they can't now make a good repentance that they may live. ⁸³ The third way, they will see the reward laid up for those who have believed the covenants of the Most High. ⁸⁴ The fourth way, they will consider the torment laid up for themselves in the last days. ⁸⁵ The fifth way, they will see the dwelling places of the others guarded by angels, with great quietness. ⁸⁶ The sixth way, they will see how immediately some of them will pass into torment. ⁸⁷ The seventh way, which is more grievous than all the aforesaid ways, because they will pine away in confusion and be consumed with shame, and will be withered up by fears, seeing the glory of the Most High before whom they have sinned while living, and before whom they will be judged in the last times. ⁸⁸"Now this is the order of those who have kept the ways of the Most High, when they will be separated from their mortal body. ⁸⁹ In the time that they lived in it, they painfully served the Most High, and were in jeopardy every hour, that they might keep the law of the lawgiver perfectly. ⁹⁰ Therefore this is the teaching concerning them: ⁹¹ First of all they will see with great joy the glory of him who takes them up, for they will have rest in seven orders. ⁹² The first order, because they have labored with great effort to overcome the evil thought which was fashioned together with them, that it might not lead them astray from life into death. ⁹³ The second order, because they see the perplexity in which the souls of the ungodly wander, and the punishment that awaits them. ⁹⁴ The third order, they see the testimony which he who fashioned them gives concerning them, that while they lived they kept the law which was given them in trust. ⁹⁵ The fourth order, they understand the rest which, being gathered in their chambers, they now enjoy with great quietness, guarded by angels, and the glory that awaits them in the last days. ⁹⁶ The fifth order, they rejoice that they have now escaped from that which is corruptible, and that they will inherit that which is to come, while they see in addition the difficulty and the pain from which they have been delivered, and the spacious liberty which they will receive with joy and immortality. ⁹⁷ The sixth order, when it is shown to them how their face will shine like the sun, and how they will be made like the light of the stars, being incorruptible from then on. ⁹⁸ The seventh order, which is greater than all the previously mentioned orders, because they will rejoice with confidence, and because they will be bold without confusion, and will be glad without fear, for they hurry to see the face of him whom in their lifetime they served, and from whom they will receive their reward in glory. ⁹⁹ This is the order of the

---

ᵃ 7:29 "Christ" means "Anointed One".
ᵇ 7:29 Lat. man
ᶜ 7:32 Or, chambers See 2 Esdras 4:35.

ᵈ 7:33 The Syriac adds and the end will come.
ᵉ 7:35 The passage from verse [36] to verse [105], formerly

missing, has been restored to the text. See Preface, page ix.
ᶠ 7:36 So the chief Oriental versions. The Latin MSS. have place.

ᵍ 7:36 Lat. Gehenna.
ʰ 7:38 So the chief Oriental versions. The Latin has will you speak.
ⁱ 7:41 Or, storm

souls of the just, as from henceforth is announced to them. Previously mentioned are the ways of torture which those who would not give heed will suffer from after this." [100] I answered, "Will time therefore be given to the souls after they are separated from the bodies, that they may see what you have described to me?" [101] He said, "Their freedom will be for seven days, that for seven days they may see the things you have been told, and afterwards they will be gathered together in their habitations." [102] I answered, "If I have found favor in your sight, show further to me your servant whether in the day of judgment the just will be able to intercede for the ungodly or to entreat the Most High for them, [103] whether fathers for children, or children for parents, or kindred for kindred, or kinsfolk for their next of kin, or friends for those who are most dear." [104] He answered me, "Since you have found favor in my sight, I will show you this also. The day of judgment is[a] a day of decision, and displays to all the seal of truth. Even as now a father doesn't send his son, or a son his father, or a master his slave, or a friend him that is most dear, that in his place he may understand, or sleep, or eat, or be healed, [105] so no one will ever pray for another in that day, neither will one lay a burden on another, for then everyone will each bear his own righteousness or unrighteousness." [106] I answered, "How do we now find that first Abraham prayed for the people of Sodom, and Moses for the ancestors who sinned in the wilderness, [107] and Joshua after him for Israel in the days of *Achan, [108] and Samuel [b]in the days of Saul, and David for the plague, and Solomon for those who would worship in the sanctuary, [109] and Elijah for those that received rain, and for the dead, that he might live, [110] and Hezekiah for the people in the days of Sennacherib, and many others prayed for many? [111] If therefore now, when corruption has grown and unrighteousness increased, the righteous have prayed for the ungodly, why will it not be so then also?" [112] He answered me, "This present world is not the end. The full glory doesn't remain in it. Therefore those who were able prayed for the weak. [113] But the day of judgment will be the end of this age, and the beginning of the immortality to come, in which corruption has passed away, [114] intemperance is at an end, infidelity is cut off, but righteousness has grown, and truth has sprung up. [115] Then no one will be able to have mercy on him who is condemned in judgment, nor to harm someone who is victorious." [116] I answered then, "This is my first and last saying, that it would have been better if the earth had not produced Adam, or else, when it had produced him, to have restrained him from sinning. [117] For what profit is it for all who are in this present time to live in heaviness, and after death to look for punishment? [118] O Adam, what have you done? For though it was you who sinned, the evil hasn't fallen on you alone, but on all of us who come from you. [119] For what profit is it to us, if an immortal time is promised to us, but we have done deeds that bring death? [120] And that there is promised us an everlasting hope, but we have most miserably failed? [121] And that there are reserved habitations of health and safety, but we have lived wickedly? [122] And that the glory of the Most High will defend those who have led a pure life, but we have walked in the most wicked ways of all? [123] And that a paradise will be revealed, whose fruit endures without decay, in which is abundance and healing, but we won't enter into it, [124] for we have lived in perverse ways? [125] And that the faces of those who have practiced self-control will shine more than the stars, but our faces will be blacker than darkness? [126] For while we lived and committed iniquity, we didn't consider what we would have to suffer after death." [127] Then he answered, "This is the significance of the battle which humans born on the earth will fight: [128] if they are overcome, they will suffer as you have said, but if they get the victory, they will receive the thing that I say. [129] For this is the way that Moses spoke to the people while he lived, saying, 'Choose life, that you may live!' [130] Nevertheless they didn't believe him or the prophets after him, not even me, who have spoken to them. [131] Therefore there won't be such heaviness in their destruction, as there will be joy over those who are assured of salvation." [132] Then I answered, "I know, Lord, that the Most High is now called merciful, in that he has mercy upon those who have not yet come into the world; [133] and compassionate, in that he has compassion upon those who turn to his law; [134] and patient, in that he is patient with those who have sinned, since they are his creatures; [135] and bountiful, in that he is ready to give rather than to take away; [136] and very merciful, in that he multiplies more and more mercies to those who are present, and who are past, and also to those who are to come— [137] for if he wasn't merciful, the world wouldn't continue with those who dwell in it— [138] and one who forgives, for if he didn't forgive out of his goodness, that those who have committed iniquities might be relieved

of them, not even one ten thousandth part of mankind would remain living; [139] and a judge, for if he didn't pardon those who were created by his word, and blot out the multitude of sins, [140] there would perhaps be very few left of an innumerable multitude."

# 8

[1] He answered me, "The Most High has made this world for many, but the world to come for few. [2] Now I will tell you a parable, Esdras. Just as when you ask the earth, it will say to you that it gives very much clay from which earthen vessels are made, but little dust that gold comes from. Even so is the course of the present world. [3] Many have been created, but few will be saved." [4] I answered, "Drink your fill of understanding then, O my soul, and let my heart devour wisdom. [5] For you [c]have come here apart from your will, and depart against your will, for you have only been given a short time to live. [6] O Lord over us, grant to your servant that we may pray before you, and give us seed for our heart and cultivation for our understanding, that fruit may grow from it, by which everyone who is corrupt, who bears the [d]likeness of a man, may live. [7] For you alone exist, and we all one workmanship of your hands, just as you have said. [8] Because you give life to the body that is now fashioned in the womb, and give it members, your creature is preserved in fire and water, and your workmanship endures nine months as your creation which is created in it. [9] But that which keeps and that which is kept will both be kept [e]by your keeping. When the womb gives up again what has grown in it, [10] you have commanded that out of the parts of the body, that is to say, out of the breasts, be given milk, which is the fruit of the breasts, [11] that the body that is fashioned may be nourished for a time, and afterwards you guide it in your mercy. [12] Yes, you have brought it up in your righteousness, nurtured it in your law, and corrected it with your judgment. [13] You put it to death as your creation, and make it live as your work. [14] If therefore you [f]lightly and suddenly destroy him which with so great labor was fashioned by your commandment, to what purpose was he made? [15] Now therefore I will speak. About man in general, you know best, but about your people for whose sake I am sorry, [16] and for your inheritance, for whose cause I mourn, for Israel, for whom I am heavy, and for the seed of Jacob, for whose sake I am troubled, [17] therefore I will begin to pray before you for myself and for them; for I see the failings of us who dwell in the land; [18] but I have heard the swiftness of the judgment which is to come. [19] Therefore hear my voice, and understand my saying, and I will speak before you." The beginning of the words of Esdras, before he was taken up. He said, [20]"O Lord, you who remain forever, whose eyes are exalted, and whose chambers are in the air, [21] whose throne is beyond measure, whose glory is beyond comprehension, before whom the army of angels stand with trembling, [22] [g] at whose bidding they are changed to wind and fire, whose word is sure, and sayings constant, whose ordinance is strong, and commandment fearful, [23] whose look dries up the depths, and whose indignation makes the mountains to melt away, and whose truth bears witness— [24] hear, O Lord, the prayer of your servant, and give ear to the petition of your handiwork. [25] Attend to my words, for as long as I live, I will speak, and as long as I have understanding, I will answer. [26] Don't look at the sins of your people, but on those who have served you in truth. [27] Don't regard the doings of those who act wickedly, but of those who have kept your covenants in affliction. [28] Don't think about those who have lived wickedly before you, but remember those who have willingly known your fear. [29] Let it not be your will to destroy those who have lived like cattle, but look at those who have [h]clearly taught your law. [30] Don't be indignant at those who are deemed worse than animals, but love those who have always put their trust in your glory. [31] For we and our fathers have [i]passed our lives in [j]ways that bring death, but you are called merciful because of us sinners. [32] For if you have a desire to have mercy upon us who have no works of righteousness, then you will be called merciful. [33] For the just, which have many good works laid up with you, will be rewarded for their own deeds. [34] For what is man, that you should take displeasure at him? Or what is a corruptible race, that you should be so bitter toward it? [35] For in truth, there is no man among those who are born who has not done wickedly, and among those who have lived, there is none which have not done wrong. [36] For in this, O Lord, your righteousness and your goodness will be declared, if you are merciful to those who have no store of good works." [37] Then he answered me, "Some things you have spoken rightly, and it will happen according to your words. [38] For indeed I will not think about the fashioning of those who have sinned, or about their death, their judgment, or their destruction; [39] but I will rejoice over the creation of the righteous and their pilgrimage,

---

[a] *7:104* The Latin has a bold day

\* *7:107* Joshua 7:1

[b] *7:108* So the Syriac and other versions. The Latin omits in the days of Saul.

[c] *8:5* So the Syriac. The Latin is incorrect.

[d] *8:6* So the Syriac. The Latin has place.

[e] *8:9* So the Syriac. The Latin is imperfect.

[f] *8:14* So the Syriac. The Latin is incorrect.

[g] *8:22* According to the chief Oriental versions. The Latin has, even they whose service takes the form of wind etc.

[h] *8:29* The Syriac has received the brightness of your law.

[i] *8:31* So the Syriac and Aethiopic versions.

[j] *8:31* Lat. manners.

their salvation, and the reward that they will have. **40** Therefore as I have spoken, so it will be. **41** For as the farmer sows many seeds in the ground, and plants many trees, and yet not all that is sown will ᵃcome up in due season, neither will all that is planted take root, even so those who are sown in the world will not all be saved." **42** Then I answered, "If I have found favor, let me speak before you. **43** If the farmer's seed doesn't come up because it hasn't received your rain in due season, or if it is ruined by too much rain and perishes, **44** likewise man, who is formed with your hands and is called your own image, because he is made like you, for whose sake you have formed all things, even him have you made like the farmer's seed. **45** Don't be angry with us, but spare your people and have mercy upon your inheritance, for you have mercy upon your own creation." **46** Then he answered me, "Things present are for those who live now, and things to come for those who will live hereafter. **47** For you come far short of being able to love my creature more than I. But you have compared yourself to the unrighteous. Don't do that! **48** Yet in this will you be admirable to the Most High, **49** in that you have humbled yourself, as it becomes you, and have not judged yourself among the righteous, so as to be much glorified. **50** For many grievous miseries will fall on those who dwell in the world in the last times, because they have walked in great pride. **51** But understand for yourself, and for those who inquire concerning the glory of those like you, **52** because paradise is opened to you. The tree of life is planted. The time to come is prepared. Plenteousness is made ready. A city is built. Rest is ᵇallowed. Goodness is perfected, and wisdom is perfected beforehand. **53** The root of evil is sealed up from you. Weakness is done away from you, and ᶜdeath is hidden. Hell and corruption have fled into forgetfulness. **54** Sorrows have passed away, and in the end, the treasure of immortality is shown. **55** Therefore ask no more questions concerning the multitude of those who perish. **56** For when they had received liberty, they despised the Most High, scorned his law, and forsook his ways. **57** Moreover they have trodden down his righteous, **58** and said in their heart that there is no God—even knowing that they must die. **59** For as the things I have said will welcome you, so thirst and pain which are prepared for them. For the Most High didn't intend that men should be destroyed, **60** but those who are created have themselves defiled the name of him who made them, and were unthankful to him who prepared life for them. **61** Therefore my judgment is now at hand, **62** which I have not shown to all men, but to you, and a few like you." Then I answered, **63**"Behold, O Lord, now you have shown me the multitude of the wonders which you will do in the last times, but you haven't shown me when."

# 9

**1** He answered me, "Measure diligently within yourself. When you see that a certain part of the signs are past, which have been told you beforehand, **2** then will you understand that it is the very time in which the Most High will visit the world which was made by him. **3** When earthquakes, tumult of peoples, plans of nations, wavering of leaders, and confusion of princes are seen in the world, **4** then will you understand that the Most High spoke of these things from the days that were of old, from the beginning. **5** For just as with everything that is made in the world, the beginning ᵈis evident and the end manifest, **6** so also are the times of the Most High: the beginnings are manifest in wonders and mighty works, and the end in effects and signs. **7** Everyone who will be saved, and will be able to escape by his works, or by faith by which they have believed, **8** will be preserved from the said perils, and will see my salvation in my land and within my borders, which I have sanctified for myself from the beginning. **9** Then those who now have abused my ways will be amazed. Those who have cast them away despitefully will live in torments. **10** For as many as in their life have received benefits, and yet have not known me, **11** and as many as have scorned my law, while they still had liberty and when an opportunity to repent was open to them, didn't understand, but despised ᵉ it, **12** must know ᶠit in torment after death. **13** Therefore don't be curious any longer how the ungodly will be punished, but inquire how the righteous will be saved, ᵍthose to whom the world belongs to, and for whom the world was created." **14** I answered, **15**"I have said before, and now speak, and will say it again hereafter, that there are more of those who perish than of those who will be saved, **16** like a wave is greater than a drop." **17** He answered me, "Just as the field is, so also the seed. As the flowers are, so are the colors. As the work is, so also is the ʰjudgment on it. As is the farmer, so also is his threshing floor. For there was a time in the world **18** when I was preparing for those who now live, before the world

was made for them to dwell in. Then no one spoke against me, **19** for ⁱno one existed. But now those who are created in this world that is prepared, both ʲwith a table that doesn't fail and a law which is unsearchable, are corrupted in their ways. **20** So I considered my world, and behold, it was destroyed, and my earth, and behold, it was in peril, because of the plans that had come into it. **21** I saw and spared them, but not greatly, and saved myself a grape out of a cluster, and a plant out of ᵏa great forest. **22** Let the multitude perish then, which were born in vain. Let my grape be saved, and my plant, for I have made them perfect with great labor. **23** Nevertheless, if you will wait seven more days—however don't fast in them, **24** but go into a field of flowers, where no house is built, and eat only of the flowers of the field, and you shall taste no flesh, and shall drink no wine, but shall eat flowers only— **25** and pray to the Most High continually, then I will come and talk with you." **26** So I went my way, just as he commanded me, into the field which is called ˡArdat. There I sat among the flowers, and ate of the herbs of the field, and this food satisfied me. **27** It came to pass after seven days that I lay on the grass, and my heart was troubled again, like before. **28** My mouth was opened, and I began to speak before the Lord Most High, and said, **29**"O Lord, you showed yourself among us, to our fathers in the wilderness, when they went out of Egypt, and when they came into the wilderness, where no man treads and that bears no fruit. **30** You said, 'Hear me, O Israel. Heed my words, O seed of Jacob. **31** For behold, I sow my law in you, and it will bring forth fruit in you, and you will be glorified in it forever.' **32** But our fathers, who received the law, didn't keep it, and didn't observe the statutes. The fruit of the law didn't perish, for it couldn't, because it was yours. **33** Yet those who received it perished, because they didn't keep the thing that was sown in them. **34** Behold, it is a custom that when the ground has received seed, or the sea a ship, or any vessel food or drink, and when it comes to pass that that which is sown, or that which is launched, **35** or the things which have been received, should come to an end, these come to an end, but the receptacles remain. Yet with us, it doesn't happen that way. **36** For we who have received the law will perish by sin, along with our heart which received it. **37** Notwithstanding the law doesn't perish, but remains in its honor." **38** When I spoke these things in my heart, I looked around me with my eyes, and on my right side I saw a woman, and behold, she mourned and wept with a loud voice, and was much grieved in mind. Her clothes were torn, and she had ashes on her head. **39** Then let I my thoughts go in which I was occupied, and turned myself to her, **40** and said to her, "Why are you weeping? Why are you grieved in your mind?" **41** She said to me, "Leave me alone, my Lord, that I may weep for myself and add to my sorrow, for I am very troubled in my mind, and brought very low." **42** I said to her, "What ails you? Tell me." **43** She said to me, "I, your servant, was barren and had no child, though I had a husband thirty years. **44** Every hour and every day these thirty years I made my prayer to the Most High day and night. **45** It came to pass after thirty years that God heard me, your handmaid, and saw my low estate, and considered my trouble, and gave me a son. I rejoiced in him greatly, I and my husband, and all my ᵐneighbors. We gave great honor to the Mighty One. **46** I nourished him with great care. **47** So when he grew up, and I came to take him a wife, I made him a feast day.

# 10

**1**"So it came to pass that when my son was entered into his wedding chamber, he fell down and died. **2** Then we all put out the lamps, and all my ⁿneighbors rose up to comfort me. I remained quiet until the second day at night. **3** It came to pass, when they had all stopped consoling me, encouraging me to be quiet, then rose I up by night, and fled, and came here into this field, as you see. **4** Now I don't intend to return into the city, but to stay here, and not eat or drink, but to continually mourn and fast until I die." **5** Then I left the reflections I was engaged in, and answered her in anger, **6**"You most foolish woman, don't you see our mourning, and what has happened to us? **7** For Zion the mother of us all is full of sorrow, and much humbled. **8** ᵒIt is right now to mourn deeply, since we all mourn, and to be sorrowful, since we are all in sorrow, but you are mourning for one son. **9** Ask the earth, and she will tell you that it is she which ought to mourn for so many that grow upon her. **10** For out of her, all had their beginnings, and others will come; and, behold, almost all of them walk into destruction, and the multitude of them is utterly doomed. **11** Who then should mourn more, ᵖshe who has lost so great a multitude, or you, who are grieved but for one? **12** But if you say to me, 'My lamentation is not like the earth's, for I have lost the fruit of my womb, which I brought forth with

---

ᵃ *8:41* Lat. be saved.
ᵇ *8:52* The Syriac has established.
ᶜ *8:53* After the chief Oriental versions.
ᵈ *9:5* So the Syriac. The Latin is corrupt.

ᵉ *9:11* Or, me
ᶠ *9:12* Or, me
ᵍ *9:13* So the Syriac and other versions. The Latin has and whose... created, and when.
ʰ *9:17* So the Aethiopic and Arabic. The Latin has creation.

ⁱ *9:19* So the Syriac.
ʲ *9:19* So the Syriac.
ᵏ *9:21* So the Syriac and other versions. The Latin has great tribes.
ˡ *9:26* The Syriac and Aethiopic have Arphad.

ᵐ *9:45* Lat. townsmen.
ⁿ *10:2* Lat. townsmen.
ᵒ *10:8* See the Oriental versions. The Latin is corrupt.
ᵖ *10:11* So the Syriac.

pains, and bare with sorrows;' [13] but it is with the earth after the manner of the earth. The multitude present in it has gone as it came. [14] Then say I to you, 'Just as you have brought forth with sorrow, even so the earth also has given her fruit, namely, people, ever since the beginning to him who made her.' [15] Now therefore keep your sorrow to yourself, and bear with a good courage the adversities which have happened to you. [16] For if you will acknowledge the decree of God to be just, you will both receive your son in time, and will be praised among women. [17] Go your way then into the city to your husband." [18] She said to me, "I won't do that. I will not go into the city, but I will die here." [19] So I proceeded to speak further to her, and said, [20]"Don't do so, but allow yourself to be persuaded by reason of the adversities of Zion; and be comforted by reason of the sorrow of Jerusalem. [21] For you see that our sanctuary has been laid waste, our altar broken down, our temple destroyed, [22] our lute has been brought low, our song is put to silence, our rejoicing is at an end, the light of our candlestick is put out, the ark of our covenant is plundered, our holy things are defiled, and the name that we are called is profaned. Our free men are despitefully treated, our priests are burned, our Levites have gone into captivity, our virgins are defiled and our wives ravished, our righteous men carried away, our little ones betrayed, our young men are brought into bondage, and our strong men have become weak. [23] What is more than all, the seal of Zion has now lost the seal of her honor, and is delivered into the hands of those who hate us. [24] Therefore shake off your great heaviness, and put away from yourself the multitude of sorrows, that the Mighty One may be merciful to you again, and the Most High may give you rest, even ease from your troubles." [25] It came to pass while I was talking with her, behold, her face suddenly began to shine exceedingly, and her countenance glistered like lightning, so that I was very afraid of her, and wondered what this meant. [26] Behold, suddenly she made a great and very fearful cry, so that the earth shook at the noise. [27] I looked, and behold, the woman appeared to me no more, but there was a city built, and a place shown itself from large foundations. Then I was afraid, and cried with a loud voice, [28]"Where is Uriel the angel, who came to me at the first? For he has caused me to fall into this great trance, and my end has turned into corruption, and my prayer a reproach!" [29] As I was speaking these words, behold, the angel who had come to me at first came to me, and he looked at me. [30] Behold, I lay as one who had been dead, and my understanding was taken from me. He took me by the right hand, and comforted me, and set me on my feet, and said to me, [31]"What ails you? Why are you so troubled? Why is your understanding and the thoughts of your heart troubled?" [32] I said, "Because you have forsaken me; yet I did according to your words, and went into the field, and, behold, I have seen, and still see, that which I am not able to explain." [33] He said to me, "Stand up like a man, and I will instruct you." [34] Then I said, "Speak on, my Lord; only don't forsake me, lest I die before my time. [35] For I have seen what I didn't know, and hear what I don't know. [36] Or is my sense deceived, or my soul in a dream? [37] Now therefore I beg you to explain to your servant what this vision means." [38] He answered me, "Listen to me, and I will inform you, and tell you about the things you are afraid of, for the Most High has revealed many secret things to you. [39] He has seen that your way is righteous, because you are continually sorry for your people, and make great lamentation for Zion. [40] This therefore is the meaning of the vision. [41] The woman who appeared to you a little while ago, whom you saw mourning, and began to comfort her, [42] but now you no longer see the likeness of the woman, but a city under construction appeared to you, [43] and she told you of the death of her son, this is the interpretation: [44] This woman, whom you saw, is Zion,[a] whom you now see as a city being built. [45] She told you that she had been barren for thirty years because there were three thousand years in the world in which there was no offering as yet offered in her. [46] And it came to pass after three thousand years that Solomon built the city and offered offerings. It was then that the barren bore a son. [47] She told you that she nourished him with great care. That was the dwelling in Jerusalem. [48] When she said to you, 'My son died when he entered into his marriage chamber, and that misfortune befell her,' this was the destruction that came to Jerusalem. [49] Behold, you saw her likeness, how she mourned for her son, and you began to comfort her for what has happened to her. These were the things to be opened to you. [50] For now the Most High, seeing that you are sincerely grieved and suffer from your whole heart for her, has shown you the brightness of her glory and the attractiveness of her beauty. [51] Therefore I asked you to remain in the field where no house was built, [52] for I knew that the Most High would show this to you. [53] Therefore I commanded you to come into the field, where no foundation of any

building was. [54] For no human construction could stand in the place in which the city of the Most High was to be shown. [55] Therefore don't be afraid nor let your heart be terrified, but go your way in and see the beauty and greatness of the building, as much as your eyes are able to see. [56] Then will you hear as much as your ears may comprehend. [57] For you are more blessed than many, and are called by name to be with the Most High, like only a few. [58] But tomorrow at night you shall remain here, [59] and so the Most High will show you those visions in dreams of what the Most High will do to those who live on the earth in the last days." So I slept that night and another, as he commanded me.

# 11

[1] It came to pass the second night that I saw a dream, and behold, an eagle which had twelve feathered wings and three heads came up from the sea. [2] I saw, and behold, she spread her wings over all the earth, and all the winds of heaven blew on her, [b]and the clouds were gathered together against her. [3] I saw, and out of her wings there grew other wings near them; and they became little, tiny wings. [4] But her heads were at rest. The head in the middle was larger than the other heads, yet rested it with them. [5] Moreover I saw, and behold, the eagle flew with her wings to reign over the earth and over those who dwell therein. [6] I saw how all things under heaven were subject to her, and no one spoke against her—no, not one creature on earth. [7] I saw, and behold, the eagle rose on her talons, and uttered her voice to her wings, saying, [8]"Don't all watch at the same time. Let each one sleep in his own place and watch in turn; [9] but let the heads be preserved for the last." [10] I saw, and behold, the voice didn't come out of her heads, but from the midst of her body. [11] I counted [c]her wings that were near the others, and behold, there were eight of them. [12] I saw, and behold, on the right side one wing arose and reigned over all the earth. [13] When it reigned, the end of it came, and it disappeared, so that its place appeared no more. The next wing rose up and reigned, and it ruled a long time. [14] It happened that when it reigned, its end came also, so that it disappeared, like the first. [15] Behold, a voice came to it, and said, [16]"Listen, you who have ruled over the earth all this time! I proclaim this to you, before you disappear, [17] none after you will rule as long as you, not even half as long." [18] Then the third arose, and ruled as the others before, and it also disappeared. [19] So it went with all the wings one after another, as every one ruled, and then disappeared. [20] I saw, and behold, in process of time the [d]wings that followed were set up on the [e]right side, that they might rule also. Some of them ruled, but in a while they disappeared. [21] Some of them also were set up, but didn't rule. [22] After this I saw, and behold, the twelve wings disappeared, along with two of the little wings. [23] There was no more left on the eagle's body, except the three heads that rested, and six little wings. [24] I saw, and behold, two little wings divided themselves from the six and remained under the head that was on the right side; but four remained in their place. [25] I saw, and behold, these [f]under wings planned to set themselves up and to rule. [26] I saw, and behold, there was one set up, but in a while it disappeared. [27] A second also did so, and it disappeared faster than the first. [28] I saw, and behold, the two that remained also planned between themselves to reign. [29] While they thought about it, behold, one of the heads that were at rest awakened, the one that was in the middle, for that was greater than the two other heads. [30] I saw how it joined the two other heads with it. [31] Behold, the head turned with those who were with it, and ate the two [g]under wings that planned to reign. [32] But this head held the whole earth in possession, and ruled over those who dwell in it with much oppression. It had stronger governance over the world than all the wings that had gone before. [33] After this I saw, and behold, the head also that was in the middle suddenly disappeared, like the wings. [34] But the two heads remained, which also reigned the same way over the earth and over those who dwell in it. [35] I saw, and behold, the head on the right side devoured the one that was on the left side. [36] Then I heard a voice, which said to me, "Look in front of you, and consider the thing that you see." [37] I saw, and behold, something like a lion roused out of the woods roaring. I heard how he sent out a man's voice to the eagle, and spoke, saying, [38]"Listen and I will talk with you. The Most High will say to you, [39]'Aren't you the one that remains of the four animals whom I made to reign in my world, that the end of my times might come through them? [40] The fourth came and overcame all the animals that were past, and ruled the world with great trembling, and the whole extent of the earth with grievous oppression. He lived on the earth such a long time with deceit. [41] You have judged the earth, but not with truth. [42] For you have afflicted the meek, you have hurt the peaceful, you have hated those who speak truth, you have loved liars, destroyed the

---

[a] 10:44 So the Syriac and other versions. The Latin is incorrect.
[b] 11:2 So the chief Oriental versions. The Latin has only and were gathered together.

[c] 11:11 The Syriac has her little wings, and, etc.
[d] 11:20 The Syriac has little wings.
[e] 11:20 The Aethiopic has left.

[f] 11:25 The Syriac has little wings.
[g] 11:31 The Syriac has little wings.

dwellings of those who produced fruit, and threw down the walls of those who did you no harm. **43** Your insolence has come up to the Most High, and your pride to the Mighty. **44** The Most High also has looked at his times, and behold, they are ended, and his ages are fulfilled. **45** Therefore appear no more, you eagle, nor your horrible wings, nor your evil little wings, nor your cruel heads, nor your hurtful talons, nor all your worthless body, **46** that all the earth may be refreshed and relieved, being delivered from your violence, and that she may hope for the judgment and mercy of him who made her.'"

## 12

**1** It came to pass, while the lion spoke these words to the eagle, I saw, **2** and behold, the head that remained disappeared, and ªthe two wings which went over to it arose and set themselves up to reign; and their kingdom was brief and full of uproar. **3** I saw, and behold, they disappeared, and the whole body of the eagle was burned, so that the earth was in great fear. Then I woke up because of great perplexity of mind and great fear, and said to my spirit, **4**"Behold, you have done this to me, because you search out the ways of the Most High. **5** Behold, I am still weary in my mind, and very weak in my spirit. There isn't even a little strength in me, because of the great fear with which I was frightened tonight. **6** Therefore I will now ask the Most High that he would strengthen me to the end." **7** Then I said, "O sovereign Lord, if I have found favor in your sight, and if I am justified with you more than many others, and if my prayer has indeed come up before your face, **8** strengthen me then, and show me, your servant, the interpretation and plain meaning of this fearful vision, that you may fully comfort my soul. **9** For you have judged me worthy to show me the end of time and the last events of the times." **10** He said to me, "This is the interpretation of this vision which you saw: **11** The eagle, whom you saw come up from the sea, is the fourth kingdom which appeared in a vision to your brother Daniel. **12** But it was not explained to him, as I now explain it to you or have explained it. **13** Behold, the days come that a kingdom will rise up on earth, and it will be feared more than all the kingdoms that were before it. **14** Twelve kings will reign in it, one after another. **15** Of those, the second will begin to reign, and will reign a longer time than others of the twelve. **16** This is the interpretation of the twelve wings which you saw. **17** As for when you heard a voice which spoke, not going out from the heads, but from the midst of its body, this is the interpretation: **18** That ᵇafter the time of that kingdom, there will arise no small contentions, and it will stand in peril of falling. Nevertheless, it won't fall then, but will be restored again to its former power. **19** You saw the eight under wings sticking to her wings. This is the interpretation: **20** That in it eight kings will arise, whose times will be short and their years swift. **21** Two of them will perish when the middle time approaches. Four will be kept for a while until the time of the ending of it will approach; but two will be kept to the end. **22** You saw three heads resting. This is the interpretation: **23** In its last days, the Most High will raise up three ᶜkingdoms and renew many things in them. They will rule over the earth, **24** and over those who dwell in it, with much oppression, more than all those who were before them. Therefore they are called the heads of the eagle. **25** For these are those who will accomplish her wickedness, and who will finish her last actions. **26** You saw that the great head disappeared. It signifies that one of them will die on his bed, and yet with pain. **27** But for the two that remained, the sword will devour them. **28** For the sword of the one will devour him that was with him, but he will also fall by the sword in the last days. **29** You saw two under wings passing ᵈover to the head that is on the right side. **30** This is the interpretation: These are they whom the Most High has kept to his end. This is the brief reign that was full of trouble, as you saw. **31**"The lion, whom you saw rising up out of the forest, roaring, speaking to the eagle, and rebuking her for her unrighteousness, and all her words which you have heard, **32** this is the anointed one, whom the Most High has kept to the end ᵉ[of days, who will spring up out of the seed of David, and he will come and speak] to them and reprove them for their wickedness and unrighteousness, and willᶠ heap up before them their contemptuous dealings. **33** For at first he will set them alive in his judgment, and when he has reproved them, he will destroy them. **34** For he will deliver the rest of my people with mercy, those who have been preserved throughout my borders, and he will make them joyful until the coming of the end, even the day of judgment, about which I have spoken to you from the beginning. **35** This is the dream that you saw, and this is its interpretation. **36** Only you have been worthy to know

the secret of the Most High. **37** Therefore write all these things that you have seen in a book, and put it in a secret place. **38** You shall teach them to the wise of your people, whose hearts you know are able to comprehend and keep these secrets. **39** But wait here yourself seven more days, that you may be shown whatever it pleases the Most High to show you." Then he departed from me. **40** It came to pass, when all the people ᵍsaw that the seven days were past, and I had not come again into the city, they all gathered together, from the least to the greatest, and came to me, and spoke to me, saying, **41**"How have we offended you? What evil have we done against you, that you have utterly forsaken us, and sit in this place? **42** For of all the prophets, only you are left to us, like a cluster of the vintage, and like a lamp in a dark place, and like a harbor for a ship saved from the tempest. **43** Aren't the evils which have come to us sufficient? **44** If you will forsake us, how much better had it been for us if we also had been consumed in the burning of Zion! **45** For we are not better than those who died there." Then they wept with a loud voice. I answered them, **46**"Take courage, O Israel! Don't be sorrowful, you house of Jacob; **47** for the Most High remembers you. The Mighty has not forgotten you ʰforever. **48** As for me, I have not forsaken you. I haven't departed from you; but I have come into this place to pray for the desolation of Zion, and that I might seek mercy for the humiliation of your sanctuary. **49** Now go your way, every man to his own house, and after these days I will come to you." **50** So the people went their way into the city, as I told them to do. **51** But I sat in the field seven days, as the angel commanded me. In those days, I ate only of the flowers of the field, and my food was from plants.

## 13

**1** It came to pass after seven days, I dreamed a dream by night. **2** Behold, a wind arose from the sea that moved all its waves. **3** I saw, and behold, ⁱ[this wind caused to come up from the midst of the sea something like the appearance of a man. I saw, and behold,] that man ʲflew with the clouds of heaven. When he turned his face to look, everything that he saw trembled. **4** Whenever the voice went out of his mouth, all who heard his voice melted, like the ᵏwax melts when it feels the fire. **5** After this I saw, and behold, an innumerable multitude of people was gathered together from the four winds of heaven to make war against the man who came out of the sea. **6** I saw, and behold, he carved himself a great mountain, and flew up onto it. **7** I tried to see the region or place from which the mountain was carved, and I couldn't. **8** After this I saw, and behold, all those who were gathered together to fight against him were very afraid, and yet they dared to fight. **9** Behold, as he saw the assault of the multitude that came, he didn't lift up his hand, or hold a spear or any weapon of war; **10** but I saw only how he sent out of his mouth something like a flood of fire, and out of his lips a flaming breath, and out of his tongue he shot out a storm of sparks.ˡ **11** These were all mixed together: the flood of fire, the flaming breath, and the great storm, and fell upon the assault of the multitude which was prepared to fight, and burned up every one of them, so that all of a sudden an innumerable multitude was seen to be nothing but dust of ashes and smell of smoke. When I saw this, I was amazed. **12** Afterward, I saw the same man come down from the mountain, and call to himself another multitude which was peaceful. **13** Many people came to him. Some of them were glad. Some were sorry. Some of them were bound, and some others brought some of those as offerings. Then through great fear I woke up and prayed to the Most High, and said, **14**"You have shown your servant these wonders from the beginning, and have counted me worthy that you should receive my prayer. **15** Now show me also the interpretation of this dream. **16** For as I conceive in my understanding, woe to those who will be left in those days! Much more woe to those who are not left! **17** For those who were not left will be in heaviness, **18** understanding the things that are laid up in the latter days, but not attaining to them. **19** But woe to them also who are left, because they will see great perils and much distress, like these dreams declare. **20** Yet is it ᵐbetter for one to be in peril and to come into ⁿthese things, than to pass away as a cloud out of the world, and not to see the things that ᵒwill happen in the last days." He answered me, **21**"I will tell you the interpretation of the vision, and I will also open to you the things about which you mentioned. **22** You have spoken of those who are left behind. This is the interpretation: **23** He that will ᵖendure the peril in that time will protect those who fall into danger, even those who have works and faith toward the Almighty. **24** Know therefore that those who are left behind are more blessed than those who are dead. **25** These are the

ª *12:2 So the chief Oriental versions.
ᵇ *12:18 The Oriental versions havein the midst of.
ᶜ *12:23 The Oriental versions have kings
ᵈ *12:29 So the Syriac. The Latin has over the head.

ᵉ *12:32 The words in brackets are added from the Syriac.
ᶠ *12:32 The Syriac has set in order.
ᵍ *12:40 So the Syriac. The Latin has heard.
ʰ *12:47 So the Syriac.

ⁱ *13:3 The words in brackets are added from the Syriac.
ʲ *13:3 So the Syriac. The Latin has grew strong
ᵏ *13:4 So the Syriac and other Oriental versions.
ˡ *13:10 So the Syriac and Arabic.

ᵐ *13:20 Lat. easier.
ⁿ *13:20 So the Syriac.
ᵒ *13:20 So the Syriac.
ᵖ *13:23 So the Syriac.

interpretations of the vision: Whereas you saw a man coming up from the midst of the sea, ²⁶ this is he whom the Most High has been keeping for many ages, who by his own self will deliver his creation. He will direct those who are left behind. ²⁷ Whereas you saw that out of his mouth came wind, fire, and storm, ²⁸ and whereas he held neither spear, nor any weapon of war, but destroyed the assault of that multitude which came to fight against him, this is the interpretation: ²⁹ Behold, the days come when the Most High will begin to deliver those who are on the earth. ³⁰ Astonishment of mind will come upon those who dwell on the earth. ³¹ One will plan to make war against another, city against city, place against place, people against people, and kingdom against kingdom. ³² It will be, when these things come to pass, and the signs happen which I showed you before, then my Son will be revealed, whom you saw as a man ascending. ³³ It will be, when all the nations hear his voice, every man will leave his own land and the battle they have against one another. ³⁴ An innumerable multitude will be gathered together, as you saw, desiring to come and to fight against him. ³⁵ But he will stand on the top of Mount Zion. ³⁶ Zion will come, and will be shown to all men, being prepared and built, like you saw the mountain carved without hands. ³⁷ My Son will rebuke the nations which have come for their wickedness, with plagues that are like a storm, ³⁸ and will rebuke them to their face with their evil thoughts, and the torments with which they will be tormented, which are like a flame. He will destroy them without labor by the law, which is like fire. ³⁹ Whereas you saw that he gathered to himself another multitude that was peaceful, ⁴⁰ these are the ten tribes which were led away out of their own land in the time of Osea the king, whom Salmananser the king of the Assyrians led away captive, and he carried them beyond the River, and they were taken into another land. ⁴¹ But they made this plan among themselves, that they would leave the multitude of the heathen, and go out into a more distant region, where mankind had never lived, ⁴² that there they might keep their statutes which they had not kept in their own land. ⁴³ They entered by the narrow passages of the river Euphrates. ⁴⁴ For the Most High then did signs for them, and stopped the springs of the River until they had passed over. ⁴⁵ For through that country there was a long way to go, namely, of a year and a half. The same region is called ᵃArzareth. ⁴⁶ Then they lived there until the latter time. Now when they begin to come again, ⁴⁷ the Most High stops the springs of the River again, that they may go through. Therefore you saw the multitude gathered together with peace. ⁴⁸ But those who are left behind of your people are those who are found within my holy border. ⁴⁹ It will be therefore when he will destroy the multitude of the nations that are gathered together, he will defend the people who remain. ⁵⁰ Then will he show them very many wonders." ⁵¹ Then I said, "O sovereign Lord, explain this to me: Why have I seen the man coming up from the midst of the sea?" ⁵² He said to me, as no one can explore or know what is in the depths of the sea, even so no man on earth can see my Son, or those who are with him, except in the time of ᵇhis day. ⁵³ This is the interpretation of the dream which you saw, and for this only you are enlightened about this, ⁵⁴ for you have forsaken your own ways, and applied your diligence to mine, and have searched out my law. ⁵⁵ You have ordered your life in wisdom, and have called understanding your mother. ⁵⁶ Therefore I have shown you this, for there is a reward laid up with the Most High. It will be, after another three days I will speak other things to you, and declare to you mighty and wondrous things." ⁵⁷ Then I went out and passed into the field, giving praise and thanks greatly to the Most High because of his wonders, which he did from time to time, ⁵⁸ and because he governs the time, and such things as happen in their seasons. So I sat there three days.

## 14

¹ It came to pass upon the third day, I sat under an oak, and, behold, a voice came out of a bush near me, and said, "Esdras, Esdras!" ² I said, "Here I am, Lord," and I stood up on my feet. ³ Then he said to me, "I revealed myself in a bush and talked with Moses when my people were in bondage in Egypt. ⁴ I sent him, and ᶜ he led my people out of Egypt. I brought him up to Mount Sinai, where I kept him with me for many days. ⁵ I told him many wondrous things, and showed him the secrets of the times and the end of the seasons. I commanded him, saying, ⁶'You shall publish these openly, and these you shall hide.' ⁷ Now I say to you: ⁸ Lay up in your heart the signs that I have shown, the dreams that you have seen, and the interpretations which you have heard; ⁹ for you will be taken away from men, and from now on you will live with my Son and with those who are like you, until the times have ended. ¹⁰

For the world has lost its youth, and the times begin to grow old. ¹¹ ᵈFor the age is divided into twelve parts, and ten parts of it are already gone, ᵉeven the half of the tenth part. ¹² There remain of it two parts after the middle of the tenth part. ¹³ Now therefore set your house in order, reprove your people, comfort the lowly among them, ᶠ and instruct those of them who are wise, and now renounce the life that is corruptible, ¹⁴ and let go of the mortal thoughts, cast away from you the burdens of man, put off now your weak nature, ¹⁵ lay aside the thoughts that are most grievous to you, and hurry to escape from these times. ¹⁶ For worse evils than those which you have seen happen will be done after this. ¹⁷ For look how much the world will be weaker through age, so much that more evils will increase on those who dwell in it. ¹⁸ For the truth will withdraw itself further off, and falsehood will be near. For now ᵍthe eagle which you saw in vision hurries to come." ¹⁹ Then I answered and said, ʰ"Let me speak in your presence, O Lord." ²⁰ Behold, I will go, as you have commanded me, and reprove the people who now live, but who will warn those who will be born afterward? For the world is set in darkness, and those who dwell in it are without light. ²¹ For your law has been burned, therefore no one knows the things that are done by you, or the works that will be done. ²² But if I have found favor before you, send the Holy Spirit to me, and I will write all that has been done in the world since the beginning, even the things that were written in your law, that men may be able to find the path, and that those who would live in the latter days may live." ²³ He answered me and said, "Go your way, gather the people together, and tell them not to seek you for forty days. ²⁴ But prepare for yourself many tablets, and take with you Sarea, Dabria, Selemia, Ethanus, and Asiel, these five, which are ready to write swiftly; ²⁵ and come here, and I will light a lamp of understanding in your heart which will not be put out until the things have ended about which you will write. ²⁶ When you are done, some things you shall publish openly, and some things you shall deliver in secret to the wise. Tomorrow at this hour you will begin to write." ²⁷ Then went I out, as he commanded me, and gathered all the people together, and said, ²⁸"Hear these words, O Israel! ²⁹ Our fathers at the beginning were foreigners in Egypt, and they were delivered from there, ³⁰ and received the law of life, which they didn't keep, which you also have transgressed after them. ³¹ Then the land of Zion was given to you for a possession; but you yourselves and your ancestors have done unrighteousness, and have not kept the ways which the Most High commanded you. ³² Because he is a righteous judge, in due time, he took from you what he had given you. ³³ Now you are here, and your kindred are among you. ³⁴ Therefore if you will rule over your own understanding and instruct your hearts, you will be kept alive, and after death you will obtain mercy. ³⁵ For after death the judgment will come, when we will live again. Then the names of the righteous will become manifest, and the works of the ungodly will be declared. ³⁶ Let no one therefore come to me now, nor seek me for forty days." ³⁷ So I took the five men, as he commanded me, and we went out into the field, and remained there. ³⁸ It came to pass on the next day that, behold, a voice called me, saying, "Esdras, open your mouth, and drink what I give you to drink." ³⁹ Then opened I my mouth, and behold, a full cup was handed to me. It was full of something like water, but its color was like fire. ⁴⁰ I took it, and drank. When I had drunk it, my heart uttered understanding, and wisdom grew in my chest, for my spirit retained its memory. ⁴¹ My mouth was opened, and shut no more. ⁴² The Most High gave understanding to the five men, and they wrote by course the things that were told them, in ⁱcharacters which they didn't know, and they sat forty days. Now they wrote in the day-time, and at night they ate bread. ⁴³ As for me, I spoke in the day, and by night I didn't hold my tongue. ⁴⁴ So in forty days, ninety-four books were written. ⁴⁵ It came to pass, when the forty days were fulfilled, that the Most High spoke to me, saying, "The first books that you have written, publish openly, and let the worthy and unworthy read them; ⁴⁶ but keep the last seventy, that you may deliver them to those who are wise among your people; ⁴⁷ for in them is the spring of understanding, the fountain of wisdom, and the stream of knowledge." ⁴⁸ I did so.

## 15

¹"Behold, speak in the ears of my people the words of prophecy which I will put in your mouth," says the Lord. ²"Cause them to be written on paper, for they are faithful and true. ³ Don't be afraid of their plots against you. Don't let the unbelief of those who speak against you trouble you. ⁴ For all the unbelievers will die in their unbelief. ⁵"Behold," says the Lord, "I bring evils on the whole earth: sword, famine, death, and destruction. ⁶ For wickedness has prevailed over

---

ᵃ *13:45 That is, another land. See Deuteronomy 29:28.*
ᵇ *13:52 So the Oriental versions. The Latin omits his.*
ᶜ *14:4 Another reading is: I.*

ᵈ *14:11 Verses 11,12 are omitted in the Syriac. The Aethiopic has For the age is divided into ten parts, and is come to the tenth: and half of the tenth remains. Now etc.*

ᵉ *14:11 Lat. and.*
ᶠ *14:13 The Latin alone omits and...wise.*
ᵍ *14:18 So the Oriental versions.*

ʰ *14:19 The Latin omits I will speak.*
ⁱ *14:42 So the Oriental versions.*

every land, and their hurtful works have reached their limit. ⁷ Therefore," says the Lord, ⁸"I will hold my peace no more concerning their wickedness which they profanely commit, neither will I tolerate them in these things, which they wickedly practice. Behold, the innocent and righteous blood cries to me, and the souls of the righteous cry out continually. ⁹ I will surely avenge them," says the Lord, "and will receive to me all the innocent blood from among them. ¹⁰ Behold, my people is led like a flock to the slaughter. I will not allow them now to dwell in the land of Egypt, ¹¹ but I will bring them out with a mighty hand and with a high arm, and will strike Egypt with plagues, as before, and will destroy all its land." ¹² Let Egypt and its foundations mourn, for the plague of the chastisement and the punishment that God will bring upon it. ¹³ Let the farmers that till the ground mourn, for their seeds will fail and their trees will be ruined through the blight and hail, and a terrible tempest. ¹⁴ Woe to the world and those who dwell in it! ¹⁵ For the sword and their destruction draws near, and nation will rise up against nation to battle with weapons in their hands. ¹⁶ For there will be sedition among men, and growing strong against one another. In their might, they won't respect their king or the chief of their great ones. ¹⁷ For a man will desire to go into a city, and will not be able. ¹⁸ For because of their pride the cities will be troubled, the houses will be destroyed, and men will be afraid. ¹⁹ A man will have no pity on his neighbors, but will assault their houses with the sword and plunder their goods, because of the lack of bread, and for great suffering. ²⁰"Behold," says God, "I call together all the kings of the earth to stir up those who are from the rising of the sun, from the south, from the east, and Libanus, to turn themselves one against another, and repay the things that they have done to them. ²¹ Just as they do yet this day to my chosen, so I will do also, and repay into their bosom." The Lord God says: ²²"My right hand won't spare the sinners, and my sword won't cease over those who shed innocent blood on the earth. ²³ A fire has gone out from his wrath, and has consumed the foundations of the earth and the sinners, like burnt straw. ²⁴ Woe to those who sin and don't keep my commandments!" says the Lord. ²⁵"I will not spare them. Go your way, you rebellious children! Don't defile my sanctuary!" ²⁶ For the Lord knows all those who trespass against him, therefore he will deliver them to death and destruction. ²⁷ For now evils have come upon the whole earth, and you will remain in them; for God will not deliver you, because you have sinned against him. ²⁸ Behold, a horrible sight appearing from the east! ²⁹ The nations of the dragons of Arabia will come out with many chariots. From the day that they set out, their hissing is carried over the earth, so that all those who will hear them may also fear and tremble. ³⁰ Also the Carmonians, raging in wrath, will go out like the wild boars of the forest. They will come with great power and join battle with them, and will devastate a portion of the land of the Assyrians with their teeth. ³¹ Then the dragons will have the upper hand, remembering their nature. If they will turn themselves, conspiring together in great power to persecute them, ³² then these will be troubled, and keep silence through their power, and will turn and flee. ³³ From the land of the Assyrians, an enemy in ambush will attack them and destroy one of them. Upon their army will be fear and trembling, and indecision upon their kings. ³⁴ Behold, clouds from the east, and from the north to the south! They are very horrible to look at, full of wrath and storm. ³⁵ They will clash against one another. They will pour out a heavy storm on the earth, even their own storm. There will be blood from the sword to the horse's belly, ³⁶ and to the thigh of man, and to the camel's hock. ³⁷ There will be fearfulness and great trembling upon earth. They who see that wrath will be afraid, and trembling will seize them. ³⁸ After this, great storms will be stirred up from the south, from the north, and another part from the west. ³⁹ Strong winds will arise from the east, and will shut it up, even the cloud which he raised up in wrath; and the storm that was to cause destruction by the east wind will be violently driven toward the south and west. ⁴⁰ Great and mighty clouds, full of wrath, will be lifted up with the storm, that they may destroy all the earth and those who dwell in it. They will pour out over every high and lofty one a terrible storm, ⁴¹ fire, hail, flying swords, and many waters, that all plains may be full, and all rivers, with the abundance of those waters. ⁴² They will break down the cities and walls, mountains and hills, trees of the forest, and grass of the meadows, and their grain. ⁴³ They will go on steadily to Babylon and destroy her. ⁴⁴ They will come to it and surround it. They will pour out the storm and all wrath on her. Then the dust and smoke will go up to the sky, and all those who are around it will mourn for it. ⁴⁵ Those who remain will serve those who have destroyed it. ⁴⁶ You, Asia, who are partaker in the beauty of Babylon, and in the glory of her person— ⁴⁷ woe to you, you wretch, because you have made yourself like her. You have decked out your daughters for prostitution, that they might please and glory in your lovers, which have always lusted after you! ⁴⁸ You have followed her who is hateful in all her works and inventions. Therefore God says, ⁴⁹"I will send evils on you: widowhood, poverty, famine, sword, and

pestilence, to lay waste your houses and bring you to destruction and death. ⁵⁰ The glory of your power will be dried up like a flower when the heat rises that is sent over you. ⁵¹ You will be weakened like a poor woman who is beaten and wounded, so that you won't be able to receive your mighty ones and your lovers. ⁵² Would I have dealt with you with such jealousy," says the Lord, ⁵³"if you had not always slain my chosen, exalting and clapping of your hands, and saying over their dead, when you were drunk? ⁵⁴"Beautify your face! ⁵⁵ The reward of a prostitute will be in your bosom, therefore you will be repaid. ⁵⁶ Just as you will do to my chosen," says the Lord, "even so God will do to you, and will deliver you to your adversaries. ⁵⁷ Your children will die of hunger. You will fall by the sword. Your cities will be broken down, and all your people in the field will perish by the sword. ⁵⁸ Those who are in the mountains will die of hunger, eat their own flesh, and drink their own blood, because of hunger for bread and thirst for water. ⁵⁹ You, unhappy above all others, will come and will again receive evils. ⁶⁰ In the passage, they will rush on the hateful city and will destroy some portion of your land, and mar part of your glory, and will return again to Babylon that was destroyed. ⁶¹ You will be cast down by them as stubble, and they will be to you as fire. ⁶² They will devour you, your cities, your land, and your mountains. They will burn all your forests and your fruitful trees with fire. ⁶³ They will carry your children away captive, and will plunder your wealth, and mar the glory of your face."

# 16

¹ Woe to you, Babylon, and Asia! Woe to you, Egypt and Syria! ² Put on sackcloth and garments of goats' hair, wail for your children and lament; for your destruction is at hand. ³ A sword has been sent upon you, and who is there to turn it back? ⁴ A fire has been sent upon you, and who is there to quench it? ⁵ Calamities are sent upon you, and who is there to drive them away? ⁶ Can one drive away a hungry lion in the forest? Can one quench a fire in stubble, once it has begun to burn? ⁷ Can one turn back an arrow that is shot by a strong archer? ⁸ The Lord God sends the calamities, and who will drive them away? ⁹ A fire will go out from his wrath, and who may quench it? ¹⁰ He will flash lightning, and who will not fear? He will thunder, and who wouldn't tremble? ¹¹ The Lord will threaten, and who will not be utterly broken in pieces at his presence? ¹² The earth and its foundations quake. The sea rises up with waves from the deep, and its waves will be troubled, along with the fish in them, at the presence of the Lord, and before the glory of his power. ¹³ For his right hand that bends the bow is strong, his arrows that he shoots are sharp, and will not miss when they begin to be shot into the ends of the world. ¹⁴ Behold, the calamities are sent out, and will not return again until they come upon the earth. ¹⁵ The fire is kindled and will not be put out until it consumes the foundations of the earth. ¹⁶ Just as an arrow which is shot by a mighty archer doesn't return backward, even so the calamities that are sent out upon earth won't return again. ¹⁷ Woe is me! Woe is me! Who will deliver me in those days? ¹⁸ The beginning of sorrows, when there will be great mourning; the beginning of famine, and many will perish; the beginning of wars, and the powers will stand in fear; the beginning of calamities, and all will tremble! What will they do when the calamities come? ¹⁹ Behold, famine and plague, suffering and anguish! They are sent as scourges for correction. ²⁰ But for all these things they will not turn them from their wickedness, nor be always mindful of the scourges. ²¹ Behold, food will be so cheap on earth that they will think themselves to be in good condition, and even then calamities will grow on earth: sword, famine, and great confusion. ²² For many of those who dwell on earth will perish of famine; and others who escape the famine, the sword will destroy. ²³ The dead will be cast out like dung, and there will be no one to comfort them; for the earth will be left desolate, and its cities will be cast down. ²⁴ There will be no farmer left to cultivate the earth or to sow it. ²⁵ The trees will give fruit, but who will gather it? ²⁶ The grapes will ripen, but who will tread them? For in all places there will be a great solitude; ²⁷ for one man will desire to see another, or to hear his voice. ²⁸ For of a city there will be ten left, and two of the field, who have hidden themselves in the thick groves, and in the clefts of the rocks. ²⁹ As in an orchard of olives upon every tree there may be left three or four olives, ³⁰ or as when a vineyard is gathered, there are some clusters left by those who diligently search through the vineyard, ³¹ even so in those days, there will be three or four left by those who search their houses with the sword. ³² The earth will be left desolate, and its fields will be for briers, and its roads and all her paths will grow thorns, because no sheep will pass along them. ³³ The virgins will mourn, having no bridegrooms. The women will mourn, having no husbands. Their daughters will mourn, having no helpers. ³⁴ Their bridegrooms will be destroyed in the wars, and their husbands will perish of famine. ³⁵ Hear now these things, and understand them, you servants of the Lord. ³⁶ Behold, the Lord's word: receive it. Don't doubt the things about which the Lord speaks. ³⁷ Behold, the calamities draw near, and are not delayed. ³⁸ Just as a woman with child in the ninth

month, when the hour of her delivery draws near, within two or three hours great pains surround her womb, and when the child comes out from the womb, there will be no waiting for a moment, [39] even so the calamities won't delay coming upon the earth. The world will groan, and sorrows will seize it on every side. [40]"O my people, hear my word: prepare for battle, and in those calamities be like strangers on the earth. [41] He who sells, let him be as he who flees away, and he who buys, as one who will lose. [42] Let he who does business be as he who has no profit by it, and he who builds, as he who won't dwell in it, [43] and he who sows, as if he wouldn't reap, so also he who prunes the vines, as he who won't gather the grapes, [44] those who marry, as those who will have no children, and those who don't marry, as the widowed. [45] Because of this, those who labor, labor in vain; [46] for foreigners will reap their fruits, plunder their goods, overthrow their houses, and take their children captive, for in captivity and famine they will conceive their children. [47] Those who conduct business, do so only to be plundered. The more they adorn their cities, their houses, their possessions, and their own persons, [48] the more I will hate them for their sins," says the Lord. [49] Just as a respectable and virtuous woman hates a prostitute, [50] so will righteousness hate iniquity, when she adorns herself, and will accuse her to her face, when he comes who will defend him who diligently searches out every sin on earth. [51] Therefore don't be like her or her works. [52] For yet a little while, and iniquity will be taken away out of the earth, and righteousness will reign over us. [53] Don't let the sinner say that he has not sinned; for God will burn coals of fire on the head of one who says "I haven't sinned before God and his glory." [54] Behold, the Lord knows all the works of men, their imaginations, their thoughts, and their hearts. [55] He said, "Let the earth be made," and it was made, "Let the sky be made," and it was made. [56] At his word, the stars were established, and he knows the number of the stars. [57] He searches the deep and its treasures. He has measured the sea and what it contains. [58] He has shut the sea in the midst of the waters, and with his word, he hung the earth over the waters. [59] He has spread out the sky like a vault. He has founded it over the waters. [60] He has made springs of water in the desert and pools on the tops of the mountains to send out rivers from the heights to water the earth. [61] He formed man, and put a heart in the midst of the body, and gave him breath, life, and understanding, [62] yes, the spirit of God Almighty. He who made all things and searches out hidden things in hidden places, [63] surely he knows your imagination, and what you think in your hearts. Woe to those who sin, and try to hide their sin! [64] Because the Lord will exactly investigate all your works, and he will put you all to shame. [65] When your sins are brought out before men, you will be ashamed, and your own iniquities will stand as your accusers in that day. [66] What will you do? Or how will you hide your sins before God and his angels? [67] Behold, God is the judge. Fear him! Stop sinning, and forget your iniquities, to never again commit them. So will God lead you out, and deliver you from all suffering. [68] For, behold, the burning wrath of a great multitude is kindled over you, and they will take away some of you, and feed you with that which is sacrificed to idols. [69] Those who consent to them will be held in derision and in contempt, and be trodden under foot. [70] For there will be in various places, and in the next cities, a great insurrection against those who fear the Lord. [71] They will be like mad men, sparing none, but spoiling and destroying those who still fear the Lord. [72] For they will destroy and plunder their goods, and throw them out of their houses. [73] Then the trial of my elect will be made known, even as the gold that is tried in the fire. [74] Hear, my elect ones, says the Lord: "Behold, the days of suffering are at hand, and I will deliver you from them. [75] Don't be afraid, and don't doubt, for God is your guide. [76] You who keep my commandments and precepts," says the Lord God, "don't let your sins weigh you down, and don't let your iniquities lift themselves up." [77] Woe to those who are choked with their sins and covered with their iniquities, like a field is choked with bushes, and its path covered with thorns, that no one may travel through! [78] It is shut off and given up to be consumed by fire.

# The Book of Tobit

*Tobit* is recognized as Deuterocanonical Scripture by the Roman Catholic, Greek Orthodox, and Russian Orthodox Churches.

## 1

[1] The book of the words of Tobit, the son of Tobiel, the son of Ananiel, the son of Aduel, the son of Gabael, of the seed of Asiel, of the tribe of Naphtali; [2] who in the days of Enemessar[a] king of the Assyrians was carried away captive out of Thisbe, which is on the right hand of Kedesh Naphtali in Galilee above Asher. [3] I, Tobit walked in the ways of truth and righteousness all the days of my life, and I did many alms deeds to my kindred and my nation, who went with me into the land of the Assyrians, to Nineveh. [4] When I was in my own country, in the land of Israel, while I was yet young, all the tribe of Naphtali my father fell away from the house of Jerusalem, which was chosen out of all the tribes of Israel, that all the tribes should sacrifice there, and the temple of the habitation of the Most High was hallowed and built therein for all ages. [5] All the tribes which fell away together sacrificed to the heifer Baal, and so did the house of Naphtali my father. [6] I alone went often to Jerusalem at the feasts, as it has been ordained to all Israel by an everlasting decree, having the first fruits and the tenths of my increase, and that which was first shorn; and I gave them at the altar to the priests the sons of Aaron. [7] I gave a tenth part of all my increase to the sons of Levi, who ministered at Jerusalem. A second tenth part I sold away, and went, and spent it each year at Jerusalem. [8] A third tenth I gave to them to whom it was appropriate, as Deborah my father's mother had commanded me, because I was left an orphan by my father. [9] When I became a man, I took as wife Anna of the seed of our own family. With her, I became the father of Tobias. [10] When I was carried away captive to Nineveh, all my kindred and my relatives ate of the bread of the Gentiles; [11] but I kept myself from eating, [12] because I remembered God with all my soul. [13] So the Most High gave me grace and favor[b] in the sight of Enemessar, and I was his purchasing agent. [14] And I went into Media, and left ten talents of silver in trust with Gabael, the brother of Gabrias, at Rages of Media. [15] And when Enemessar was dead, Sennacherib his son reigned in his place. In his time, the highways were troubled,[c] and I could no longer go into Media. [16] In the days of Enemessar, I did many alms deeds to my kindred: I gave my bread to the hungry, [17] and my garments to the naked. If I saw any of my race dead, and thrown out on[d] the wall of Nineveh, I buried him. [18] If Sennacherib the king killed any, when he came fleeing from Judea, I buried them privately; for in his wrath he killed many; and the bodies were sought for by the king, and were not found. [19] But one of the Ninevites went and showed to the king concerning me, how I buried them, and hid myself; and when I knew that I was sought for to be put to death, I withdrew myself for fear. [20] And all my goods were forcibly taken away, and there was nothing left to me, save my wife Anna and my son Tobias. [21] No more than fifty five days passed before two of his sons killed him, and they fled into the mountains of Ararat. And Sarchedonus[e] his son reigned in his place; and he appointed Achiacharus my brother Anael's son over all the accounts of his kingdom, and over all his affairs. [22] Achiacharus requested me, and I came to Nineveh. Now Achiacharus was cupbearer, keeper of the signet, steward, and overseer of the accounts. Sarchedonus appointed him next to himself, but he was my brother's son.

## 2

[1] Now when I had come home again, and my wife Anna was restored to me, and my son Tobias, in the feast of Pentecost, which is the holy feast of the seven weeks, there was a good dinner prepared for me, and I sat down to eat. [2] I saw abundance of meat, and I said to my son, "Go and bring whatever poor man you find of our kindred, who is mindful of the Lord. Behold, I wait for you." [3] Then he came, and said, "Father, one of our race is strangled, and has been cast out in the marketplace." [4] Before I had tasted anything, I sprang up, and took him up into a chamber until the sun had set. [5] Then I returned, washed myself, ate my bread in heaviness, [6] and remembered the prophecy of Amos, as he said, *"Your feasts will be turned into mourning, and all your mirth into lamentation. [7] So I wept: and when the sun had set, I went and dug a grave, and buried him. [8] My neighbors mocked me, and said, "He is no longer afraid to be put to death for this matter; and yet he fled away. Behold, he buries the dead again." [9] The same night I returned from burying him, and slept by the wall of my courtyard, being polluted; and my face was uncovered. [10] I didn't know that there were sparrows in the wall. My eyes were open and the sparrows dropped warm dung into my eyes, and white films came over my eyes. I went to the physicians, and they didn't help me; but Achiacharus nourished me, until I went[f] into Elymais. [11] My wife Anna wove cloth in the women's chambers, [12] and sent the work back to the owners. They on their part paid her wages, and also gave her a kid. [13] But when it came to my house, it began to cry, and I said to her, "Where did this kid come from? Is it stolen? Give it back to the owners; for it is not lawful to eat anything that is stolen." [14] But she said, "It has been given to me for a gift more than the wages." I didn't believe her, and I asked her to return it to the owners; and I was ashamed of her. But she answered and said to me, "Where are your

---

[a] *1:2* That is, Shalmaneser. Compare 2 Kings 17:3,23.
[b] *1:13* Gr. beauty.
[c] *1:15* Gr. his highways were troubled.
[d] *1:17* Some ancient authorities read behind.
[e] *1:21* That is, Esar-haddon, and so in verse 22.
* *2:6* Amos 8:10
[f] *2:10* Some authorities read until he went.

alms and your righteous deeds? Behold, you and all your works are known.[a]"

## 3

[1] I was grieved and wept, and prayed in sorrow, saying, [2]"O Lord, you are righteous, and all your works and all your ways are mercy and truth, and you judge true and righteous judgment forever. [3] Remember me, and look at me. Don't take vengeance on me for my sins and my ignorances, and the sins of my fathers who sinned before you. [4] For they disobeyed your commandments. You gave us as plunder, for captivity, for death, and for a proverb of reproach to all the nations among whom we are dispersed. [5] Now your judgments are many and true, that you should deal with me according to my sins and the sins of my fathers, because we didn't keep your commandments, for we didn't walk in truth before you. [6] Now deal with me according to that which is pleasing in your sight. Command my spirit to be taken from me, that I may be released, and become earth. For it is more profitable for me to die rather than to live, because I have heard false reproaches, and there is much sorrow in me. Command that I be released from my distress, now, and go to the everlasting place. Don't turn your face away from me." [7] The same day it happened to Sarah the daughter of Raguel in Ecbatana of Media, that she also was reproached by her father's maidservants; [8] because that she had been given to seven husbands, and Asmodaeus the evil spirit[b] killed them, before they had lain with her. And they said to her, "Do you not know that you strangle your husbands? You have had already seven husbands, and you haven't borne the name of any one of them. [9] Why do you scourge us? If they are dead, go your ways with them. Let us never see either son or daughter from you." [10] When she heard these things, she was grieved exceedingly, so that she thought about hanging herself. Then she said, "I am the only daughter of my father. If I do this, it will be a reproach to him, and I will bring down his old age with sorrow to the grave.[c]" [11] Then she prayed by the window, and said, "Blessed are you, O Lord my God, and blessed is your holy and honorable name forever! Let all your works praise you forever! [12] And now, Lord, I have set my eyes and my face toward you. [13] Command that I be released from the earth, and that I no longer hear reproach. [14] You know, Lord, that I am pure from all sin with man, [15] and that I never polluted my name or the name of my father in the land of my captivity. I am the only daughter of my father, and he has no child that will be his heir, nor brother near him, nor son belonging to him, that I should keep myself for a wife to him. Seven husbands of mine are dead already. Why should I live? If it doesn't please you to kill me, command some regard to be had of me, and pity taken of me, and that I hear no more reproach." [16] The prayer of both was heard before the glory of the great God. [17] Raphael also was sent to heal them both, to scale away the white films from Tobit's eyes, and to give Sarah the daughter of Raguel for a wife to Tobias the son of Tobit; and to bind Asmodaeus the evil spirit[d]; because it belonged to Tobias that he should inherit her. At that very time, Tobit returned and entered into his house, and Sarah the daughter of Raguel came down from her upper chamber.

## 4

[1] In that day Tobit remembered the money which he had left in trust with Gabael in Rages of Media, [2] and he said to himself, I have asked for death; why do I not call my son Tobias, that I may explain to him about the money before I die? [3] And he called him, and said, "My child, if I die, bury me. Don't despise your mother. Honor her all the days of your life, and do that which is pleasing to her, and don't grieve her. [4] Remember, my child, that she has seen many dangers for you, when you were in her womb. When she is dead, bury her by me in one grave. [5] My child, be mindful of the Lord our God all your days, and don't let your will be set to sin and to transgress his commandments: do righteousness all the days of your life, and don't follow the ways of unrighteousness. [6] For if you do what is true, your deeds will prosperously succeed for you, and for all those who do righteousness. [7] Give alms from your possessions. When you give alms, don't let your eye be envious. Don't turn away your face from any poor man, and the face of God won't be turned away from you. [8] As your possessions are, give alms of it according to your abundance. If you have little, don't be afraid to give alms according to that little; [9] for you lay up a good treasure for yourself against the day of necessity; [10] because alms-giving delivers from death, and doesn't allow you to come into darkness. [11] Alms is a good gift in the sight of the Most High for all that give it. [12] Beware, my child, of all fornication, and take first a wife of the seed of your fathers. Don't take a strange wife, who is not of your father's tribe; for we are the descendants of the prophets. Remember, my child, that Noah, Abraham, Isaac, and Jacob, our fathers of old time, all took wives of their kindred, and were blessed in their children, and their seed will inherit the land. [13] And now, my child, love your kindred,

and don't scorn your kindred and the sons and the daughters of your people in your heart, to take a wife of them; for in scornfulness is destruction and much trouble, and in idleness is decay and great lack; for idleness is the mother of famine. [14] Don't let the wages of any man who works for you wait with you, but give it to him out of hand. If you serve God, you will be rewarded. Take heed to yourself, my child, in all your works, and be discreet in all your behavior. [15] And what you yourself hate, do to no man. Don't drink wine to drunkenness, and don't let drunkenness go with you on your way. [16] Give of your bread to the hungry, and of your garments to those who are naked. Give alms from all your abundance. Don't let your eye be envious when you give alms. [17] Pour out your bread on the burial[e] of the just, and give nothing to sinners. [18] Ask counsel of every man who is wise, and don't despise any counsel that is profitable. [19] Bless the Lord your God at all times, and ask of him that your ways may be made straight, and that all your paths and counsels may prosper; for every nation has no counsel; but the Lord himself gives all good things, and he humbles whom he will, as he will. And now, my child, remember my commandments, and let them not be blotted out of your mind. [20] And now I explain to you about the ten talents of silver, which I left in trust with Gabael the son of Gabrias at Rages of Media. [21] And fear not, my child, because we are made poor. You have much wealth, if you fear God, and depart from all sin, and do that which is pleasing in his sight."

## 5

[1] Then Tobias answered and said to him, "Father, I will do all things, whatever you have commanded me. [2] But how could I receive the money, since I don't know him?" [3] He gave him the handwriting, and said to him, "Seek a man who will go with you, and I will give him wages, while I still live; and go and receive the money." [4] He went to seek a man, and found Raphael who was an angel; [5] and he didn't know it. He said to him, "Can I go with you to Rages of Media? Do you know those places well?" [6] The angel said to him, "I will go with you. I know the way well. I have lodged with our brother Gabael." [7] Tobias said to him, "Wait for me, and I will tell my father." [8] He said to him, "Go, and don't wait. And he went in and said to his father, "Behold, I have found someone who will go with me." But he said, "Call him to me, that I may know of what tribe he is, and whether he be a trustworthy man to go with you." [9] So he called him, and he came in, and they saluted one another. [10] And Tobit said to him, "Brother, of what tribe and of what family are you? Tell me." [11] He said to him, "Do you seek a tribe and a family, or a hired man which will go with your son?" And Tobit said to him, "I want to know, brother, your kindred and your name." [12] And he said, "I am Azarias, the son of Ananias the great, of your kindred." [13] And he said to him, "Welcome, brother. Don't be angry with me, because I sought to know your tribe and family. You are my brother, of an honest and good lineage; for I knew Ananias and Jathan, the sons of Shemaiah the great, when we went together to Jerusalem to worship, and offered the firstborn, and the tenths of our increase; and they didn't go astray in the error of our kindred. My brother, you are of a great stock. [14] But tell me, what wages shall I give you? A drachma a day, and those things that be necessary for you, as to my son? [15] And moreover, if you both return safe and sound, I will add something to your wages." [16] And so they agreed. And he said to Tobias, "Prepare yourself for the journey. May God prosper you." So his son prepared what was needful for the journey, and his father said to him, "Go with this man; but God, who dwells in heaven, will prosper your journey. May his angel go with you." Then they both departed, and the young man's dog went with them. [17] But Anna his mother wept, and said to Tobit, "Why have you sent away our child? Isn't he the staff of our hand, in going in and out before us? [18] Don't be greedy to add money to money; but let it be as refuse compared to our child. [19] For what the Lord has given us to live is enough for us." [20] Tobit said to her, "Don't worry, my sister. He will return safe and sound, and your eyes will see him. [21] For a good angel will go with him. His journey will be prospered, and he will return safe and sound." [22] So she stopped weeping.

## 6

[1] Now as they went on their journey, they came at evening to the river Tigris, and they lodged there. [2] But the young man went down to wash himself, and a fish leaped out of the river, and would have swallowed up the young man. [3] But the angel said to him, "Grab the fish!" So the young man grabbed the fish, and hauled it up onto the land. [4] And the angel said to him, "Cut the fish open, and take the heart, the liver, and the bile, and keep them with you." [5] And the young man did as the angel commanded him; but they roasted the fish, and ate it. And they both went on their way, till they drew near to Ecbatana. [6] The young man said to the angel, "Brother Azarias, of what use is the heart, the liver,

---

[a] 2:14 Gr. all things are known with you.

[b] 3:8 Gr. demon.
[c] 3:10 Gr. Hades.

[d] 3:17 Gr. demon.

[e] 4:17 Or, tomb

and the bile of the fish?" ⁷ He said to him, "About the heart and the liver: If a demon or an evil spirit troubles anyone, we must burn those and make smoke of them before the man or the woman, and the affliction will flee. ⁸ But as for the bile, it is good to anoint a man that has white films in his eyes, and he will be healed." ⁹ But when they drew near to Rages, ¹⁰ the angel said to the young man, "Brother, today we will lodge with Raguel. He is your kinsman. He has an only daughter named Sarah. I will speak about her, that she should be given to you for a wife. ¹¹ For her inheritance belongs to you, and you only are of her kindred. ¹² The maid is fair and wise. And now hear me, and I will speak to her father. When we return from Rages we will celebrate the marriage; for I know that Raguel may in no way marry her to another according to the law of Moses, or else he would be liable to death, because it belongs to you to take the inheritance, rather than any other." ¹³ Then the young man said to the angel, "Brother Azarias, I have heard that this maid has been given to seven men, and that they all perished in the bride-chamber. ¹⁴ Now I am the only son of my father, and I am afraid, lest I go in and die, even as those before me. For a demon loves her, which harms no man, but those which come to her. Now I fear lest I die, and bring my father's and my mother's life to the grave with sorrow because of me. They have no other son to bury them." ¹⁵ But the angel said to him, "Don't you remember the words which your father commanded you, that you should take a wife of your own kindred? Now hear me, brother; for she will be your wife. Don't worry about the demon; for this night she will be given you as wife. ¹⁶ And when[a] you come into the bride-chamber, you shall take the ashes of incense, and shall lay upon them some of the heart and liver of the fish, and shall make smoke with them. ¹⁷ The demon will smell it, and flee away, and never come again any more. But when you go near to her, both of you rise up, and cry to God who is merciful. He will save you, and have mercy on you. Don't be afraid, for she was prepared for you from the beginning; and you will save her, and she will go with you. And I suppose that you will have children with her." When Tobias heard these things, he loved her, and his soul was strongly joined to her.

## 7

¹ They came to Ecbatana, and arrived at the house of Raguel. But Sarah met them; and she greeted them, and they her. Then she brought them into the house. ² Raguel said to Edna his wife, "This young man really resembles Tobit my cousin!" ³ And Raguel asked them, "Where are you two from, kindred?" They said to him, "We are of the sons of Naphtali, who are captives in Nineveh." ⁴ He said to them, "Do you know Tobit our brother?" They said, "We know him." Then he said to them, "Is he in good health?" ⁵ They said, "He is both alive, and in good health." Tobias said, "He is my father." ⁶ And Raguel sprang up, and kissed him, wept, ⁷ blessed him, and said to him, "You are the son of an honest and good man." When he had heard that Tobit had lost his sight, he was grieved, and wept; ⁸ and Edna his wife and Sarah his daughter wept. They received them gladly; and they killed a ram of the flock, and served them meat. But Tobias said to Raphael, "Brother Azarias, speak of those things of which you talked about in the way, and let the matter be finished." ⁹ So he communicated the thing to Raguel. Raguel said to Tobias, "Eat, drink, and make merry: ¹⁰ for it belongs to you to take my child. However I will tell you the truth. ¹¹ I have given my child to seven men of our relatives, and whenever they came in to her, they died in the night. But for the present be merry." And Tobias said, "I will taste nothing here, until you all make a covenant and enter into that covenant with me." ¹² Raguel said, "Take her to yourself from now on according to custom. You are her relative, and she is yours. The merciful God will give all good success to you." ¹³ And he called his daughter Sarah, and took her by the hand, and gave her to be wife of Tobias, and said, "Behold, take her to yourself after the law of Moses, and lead her away to your father." And he blessed them. ¹⁴ He called Edna his wife, then took a book, wrote a contract, and sealed it. ¹⁵ Then they began to eat. ¹⁶ And Raguel called his wife Edna, and said to her, "Sister, prepare the other chamber, and bring her in there." ¹⁷ She did as he asked her, and brought her in there. She wept, and she received the tears of her daughter, and said to her, ¹⁸ "Be comforted, my child. May the Lord of heaven and earth give you favor[b] for this your sorrow. Be comforted, my daughter."

## 8

¹ When they had finished their supper, they brought Tobias in to her. ² But as he went, he remembered the words of Raphael, and took the ashes of the incense, and put the heart and the liver of the fish on them, and made smoke with them. ³ When the demon smelled that smell, it fled into the uppermost parts of Egypt, and the angel bound him. ⁴ But after they were both shut in together, Tobias rose up from the bed, and

said, "Sister, arise, and let's pray that the Lord may have mercy on us." ⁵ And Tobias began to say, "Blessed are you, O God of our fathers, and blessed is your holy and glorious name forever. Let the heavens bless you, and all your creatures. ⁶ You made Adam, and gave him Eve his wife for a helper and support. From them came the seed of men. You said, it is not good that the man should be alone. Let's make him a helper like him. ⁷ And now, O Lord, I take not this my sister for lust, but in truth. Command that I may find mercy and grow old with her." ⁸ She said with him, "Amen." And they both slept that night. ⁹ Raguel arose, and went and dug a grave, ¹⁰ saying, "Lest he also should die." ¹¹ And Raguel came into his house, ¹² and said to Edna his wife, "Send one of the maidservants, and let them see if he is alive. If not, we will bury him, and no man will know it." ¹³ So the maidservant opened the door, and went in, and found them both sleeping, ¹⁴ and came out, and told them that he was alive. ¹⁵ Then Raguel blessed God, saying, "Blessed are you, O God, with all pure and holy blessing! Let your saints bless you, and all your creatures! Let all your angels and your elect bless you forever! ¹⁶ Blessed are you, because you have made me glad; and it has not happened to me as I suspected; but you have dealt with us according to your great mercy. ¹⁷ Blessed are you, because you have had mercy on two that were the only begotten children of their parents. Show them mercy, O Lord. Fulfill their life in health with gladness and mercy." ¹⁸ He commanded his servants to fill the grave. ¹⁹ He kept the wedding feast for them fourteen days. ²⁰ Before the days of the wedding feast were finished, Raguel sware to him, that he should not depart till the fourteen days of the wedding feast were fulfilled; ²¹ and that then he should take half of his goods, and go in safety to his father; and the rest, said he, when my wife and I die.

## 9

¹ And Tobias called Raphael, and said to him, ² "Brother Azarias, take with you a servant and two camels, and go to Rages of Media to Gabael, and receive the money for me, and bring him to the wedding feast, ³ because Raguel has sworn that I must not depart. ⁴ My father counts the days; and if I wait long, he will be very grieved. ⁵ So Raphael went on his way, and lodged with Gabael, and gave him the handwriting; so he brought forth the bags with their seals, and gave them to him. ⁶ Then they rose up early in the morning together, and came to the wedding feast. Tobias blessed his wife.

## 10

¹ Tobit his father counted every day. When the days of the journey were expired, and they didn't come, ² he said, "Is he perchance detained?[c] Or is Gabael perchance dead, and there is no one to give him the money?" ³ He was very grieved. ⁴ But his wife said to him, "The child has perished, seeing he waits long." She began to bewail him, and said, ⁵ "I care about nothing,[d] my child, since I have let you go, the light of my eyes." ⁶ Tobit said to her, "Hold your peace. Don't worry. He is in good health." ⁷ And she said to him, "Hold your peace. Don't deceive me. My child has perished." And she went out every day into the way by which they went, and ate no bread in the day-time, and didn't stop bewailing her son Tobias for whole nights, until the fourteen days of the wedding feast were expired, which Raguel had sworn that he should spend there. Then Tobias said to Raguel, "Send me away, for my father and my mother look no more to see me." ⁸ But his father-in-law said to him, "Stay with me, and I will send to your father, and they will declare to him how things go with you." ⁹ Tobias said, "No. Send me away to my father." ¹⁰ Raguel arose, and gave him Sarah his wife, and half his goods, servants and cattle and money; ¹¹ and he blessed them, and sent them away, saying, "The God of heaven will prosper you, my children, before I die." ¹² And he said to his daughter, "Honor your father-in-law and your mother-in-law. They are now your parents. Let me hear a good report of you." Then he kissed her. Edna said to Tobias, "May the Lord of heaven restore you, dear brother, and grant to me that I may see your children of my daughter Sarah, that I may rejoice before the Lord. Behold, I commit my daughter to you in special trust. Don't cause her grief.

## 11

¹ After these things Tobias also went his way, blessing God because he had prospered his journey; and he blessed Raguel and Edna his wife. Then he went on his way until they drew near to Nineveh. ² Raphael said to Tobias, "Don't you know, brother, how you left your father? ³ Let's run forward before your wife, and prepare the house. ⁴ But take in your hand the bile of the fish." So they went their way, and the dog went after them. ⁵ Anna sat looking around toward the path for her son. ⁶ She saw him coming, and said to his father, "Behold, your son is coming with the man that went with him!" ⁷ Raphael said, "I know, Tobias, that your father will open his eyes. ⁸ Therefore anoint his eyes

---

[a] *6:16* Gr. if.

[b] *7:18* Many ancient authorities read joy.

[c] *10:2* Many ancient authorities read "Are they perchance put to shame?"

[d] *10:5* Some authorities read "Woe is me."

with the bile, and being pricked with it, he will rub, and will make the white films fall away. Then he will see you." [9] Anna ran to him, and fell upon the neck of her son, and said to him, "I have seen you, my child! I am ready to die." They both wept. [10] Tobit went toward the door and stumbled; but his son ran to him, [11] and took hold of his father. He rubbed the bile on his father's eyes, saying, "Cheer up, my father." [12] When his eyes began to hurt, he rubbed them. [13] Then the white films peeled away from the corners of his eyes; and he saw his son, and fell upon his neck. [14] He wept, and said, "Blessed are you, O God, and blessed is your name forever! Blessed are all your holy angels! [15] For you scourged, and had mercy on me. Behold, I see my son Tobias." And his son went in rejoicing, and told his father the great things that had happened to him in Media. [16] Tobit went out to meet his daughter-in-law at the gate of Nineveh, rejoicing and blessing God. Those who saw him go marveled, because he had received his sight. [17] Tobit gave thanks before them, because God had shown mercy on him. When Tobit came near to Sarah his daughter-in-law, he blessed her, saying, "Welcome, daughter! Blessed is God who has brought you to us, and blessed are your father and your mother." And there was joy among all his kindred who were at Nineveh. [18] Achiacharus and Nasbas his brother's son came. [19] Tobias' wedding feast was kept seven days with great gladness.

## 12

[1] And Tobit called his son Tobias, and said to him, "See, my child, that the man which went with you have his wages, and you must give him more." [2] And he said to him, "Father, it is no harm to me to give him the half of those things which I have brought; [3] for he has led me for you in safety, and he cured my wife, and brought my money, and likewise cured you." [4] The old man said, "It is due to him." [5] And he called the angel, and said to him, "Take half of all that you have brought." [6] Then he called them both privately, and said to them, "Bless God, and give him thanks, and magnify him, and give him thanks in the sight of all that live, for the things which he has done with you. It is good to bless God and exalt his name, showing forth with honor the works of God. Don't be slack to give him thanks. [7] It is good to conceal the secret of a king, but to reveal gloriously the works of God. Do good, and evil won't find you. [8] Good is prayer with fasting, alms, and righteousness. A little with righteousness is better than much with unrighteousness. It is better to give alms than to lay up gold. [9] Alms delivers from death, and it purges away all sin. Those who give alms and do righteousness will be filled with life; [10] but those who sin are enemies to their own life. [11] Surely I will conceal nothing from you. I have said, 'It is good to conceal the secret of a king, but to reveal gloriously the works of God.' [12] And now, when you prayed, and Sarah your daughter-in-law, I brought the memorial of your prayer before the Holy One. When you buried the dead, I was with you likewise. [13] And when you didn't delay to rise up, and leave your dinner, that you might go and cover the dead, your good deed was not hidden from me. I was with you. [14] And now God sent me to heal you and Sarah your daughter-in-law. [15] I am Raphael, one of the seven holy angels which present the prayers of the saints and go in before the glory of the Holy One." [16] And they were both troubled, and fell upon their faces; for they were afraid. [17] And he said to them, "Don't be afraid. You will all have peace; but bless God forever. [18] For I came not of any favor of my own, but by the will of your God. Therefore bless him forever. [19] All these days I appeared to you. I didn't eat or drink, but you all saw a vision. [20] Now give God thanks, because I ascend to him who sent me. Write in a book all the things which have been done." [21] Then they rose up, and saw him no more. [22] They confessed the great and wonderful works of God, and how the angel of the Lord had appeared to them.

## 13

[1] And Tobit wrote a prayer for rejoicing, and said, "Blessed is God who lives forever! Blessed is his kingdom! [2] For he scourges, and shows mercy. He leads down to the grave,[a] and brings up again. There is no one who will escape his hand. [3] Give thanks to him before the Gentiles, all you children of Israel! For he has scattered us among them. [4] Declare his greatness, there. Extol him before all the living, because he is our Lord, and God is our Father forever. [5] He will scourge us for our iniquities, and will again show mercy, and will gather us out of all the nations among whom you are all scattered. [6] If you turn to him with your whole heart and with your whole soul, to do truth before him, then he will turn to you, and won't hide his face from you. See what he will do with you. Give him thanks with your whole mouth. Bless the Lord of righteousness. Exalt the everlasting King. I give him thanks in the land of my captivity, and show his strength and majesty to a nation of sinners. Turn, you sinners, and do righteousness before him. Who can tell if he will accept you and have mercy on you? [7] I exalt my God. My soul exalts the King of heaven, and rejoices in his greatness. [8] Let all

men speak, and let them give him thanks in Jerusalem. [9] O Jerusalem, the holy city, he will scourge you for the works of your sons, and will again have mercy on the sons of the righteous. [10] Give thanks to the Lord with goodness, and bless the everlasting King, that his tabernacle may be built in you again with joy, and that he may make glad in you those who are captives, and love in you forever those who are miserable. [11] Many nations will come from afar to the name of the Lord God with gifts in their hands, even gifts to the King of heaven. Generations of generations will praise you, and sing songs of rejoicing. [12] All those who hate you are cursed. All those who love you forever will be blessed. [13] Rejoice and be exceedingly glad for the sons of the righteous; for they will be gathered together and will bless the Lord of the righteous. [14] Oh blessed are those who love you. They will rejoice for your peace. Blessed are all those who mourned for all your scourges; because they will rejoice for you when they have seen all your glory. They will be made glad forever. [15] Let my soul bless God the great King. [16] For Jerusalem will be built with sapphires, emeralds, and precious stones; your walls and towers and battlements with pure gold. [17] The streets of Jerusalem will be paved with beryl, carbuncle, and stones of Ophir. [18] All her streets will say, "Hallelujah!" and give praise, saying, "Blessed be God, who has exalted you forever!"

## 14

[1] Then Tobit finished giving thanks. [2] He was fifty-eight years old when he lost his sight. After eight years, he received it again. He gave alms and he feared the Lord God more and more, and gave thanks to him. [3] Now he grew very old; and he called his son with the six sons of his son, and said to him, "My child, take your sons. Behold, I have grown old, and am ready to depart out of this life. [4] Go into Media, my child, for I surely believe all the things which Jonah the prophet spoke of Nineveh, that it will be overthrown, but in Media there will rather be peace for a season. Our kindred will be scattered in the earth from the good land. Jerusalem will be desolate, and the house of God in it will be burned up, and will be desolate for a time. [5] God will again have mercy on them, and bring them back into the land, and they will build the house, but not like to the former house, until the times of that age are fulfilled. Afterward they will return from the places of their captivity, and build up Jerusalem with honor. The house of God will be built in it forever with a glorious building, even as the prophets spoke concerning it. [6] And all the nations will turn to fear the Lord God truly, and will bury their idols. [7] All the nations will bless the Lord, and his people will give thanks to God, and the Lord will exalt his people; and all those who love the Lord God in truth and righteousness will rejoice, showing mercy to our kindred. [8] And now, my child, depart from Nineveh, because those things which the prophet Jonah spoke will surely come to pass. [9] But you must keep the law and the ordinances, and show yourself merciful and righteous, that it may be well with you. [10] Bury me decently, and your mother with me. Don't stay at Nineveh. See, my child, what Aman did to Achiacharus who nourished him, how out of light he brought him into darkness, and all the recompense that he made him. Achiacharus was saved, but the other had his recompense, and he went down into darkness. Manasses gave alms, and escaped the snare of death which he set for him; but Aman fell into the snare, and perished. [11] And now, my children, consider what alms does, and how righteousness delivers." While he was saying these things, he gave up the ghost in the bed; but he was one hundred fifty eight years old. Tobias buried him magnificently. [12] When Anna died, he buried her with his father. But Tobias departed with his wife and his sons to Ecbatana to Raguel his father-in-law, [13] and he grew old in honor, and he buried his father-in-law and mother-in-law magnificently, and he inherited their possessions, and his father Tobit's. [14] He died at Ecbatana of Media, being one hundred twenty seven years old. [15] Before he died, he heard of the destruction of Nineveh, which Nebuchadnezzar and Ahasuerus took captive. Before his death, he rejoiced over Nineveh.

## The Book of Judith

*Judith* is recognized as Deuterocanonical Scripture by the Roman Catholic, Greek Orthodox, and Russian Orthodox Churches.

## 1

[1] In the twelfth year of the reign of Nebuchadnezzar, who reigned over the Assyrians in Nineveh, the great city, in the days of Arphaxad, who reigned over the Medes in Ecbatana, [2] and built around Ecbatana walls of hewn stones three cubits broad and six cubits long, and made the height of the wall seventy cubits, and its breadth fifty cubits, [3] and set its towers at its gates one hundred cubits high, and its breadth in the foundation was sixty cubits, [4] and made its gates, even gates that were raised to the height of seventy cubits, and their breadth forty cubits, for

---

[a] *13:2* Gr. Hades.

his mighty army to go out of, and the setting in array of his footmen— [5] in those days King Nebuchadnezzar made war with King Arphaxad in the great plain. This plain is on the borders of Ragau. [6] There came to meet him all that lived in the hill country, and all that lived by Euphrates, Tigris, and Hydaspes, and in the plain of Arioch the king of the Elymaeans. Many nations of the sons of Chelod assembled themselves to the battle. [7] And Nebuchadnezzar king of the Assyrians sent to all who lived in Persia, and to all who lived westward, to those who lived in Cilicia, Damascus, Libanus, Antilibanus, and to all who lived along the sea coast, [8] and to those among the nations that were of Carmel and Gilead, and to the higher Galilee and the great plain of Esdraelon, [9] and to all who were in Samaria and its cities, and beyond Jordan to Jerusalem, Betane, Chellus, Kadesh, the river of Egypt, Tahpanhes, Rameses, and all the land of Goshen, [10] until you come above Tanis and Memphis, and to all that lived in Egypt, until you come to the borders of Ethiopia. [11] All those who lived in all the land made light of the commandment of Nebuchadnezzar king of the Assyrians, and didn't go with him to the war; for they were not afraid of him, but he was before them as one man. They turned away his messengers from their presence without effect, and with disgrace. [12] And Nebuchadnezzar was exceedingly angry with all this land, and he swore by his throne and kingdom that he would surely be avenged upon all the coasts of Cilicia, Damascus, and Syria, that he would kill with his sword all the inhabitants of the land of Moab, the children of Ammon, all Judea, and all who were in Egypt, until you come to the borders of the two seas. [13] And he set the battle in array with his army against King Arphaxad in the seventeenth year; and he prevailed in his battle, and turned to flight all the army of Arphaxad, with all his horses and all his chariots. [14] He took possession of his cities. He came to Ecbatana and took the towers, plundered its streets, and turned its beauty into shame. [15] He took Arphaxad in the mountains of Ragau, struck him through with his darts, and utterly destroyed him to this day. [16] He returned with them to Nineveh, he and all his company of sundry nations—an exceedingly great multitude of men of war. There he took his ease and banqueted, he and his army, for one hundred twenty days.

## 2

[1] In the eighteenth year, the twenty-second day of the first month, there was talk in the house of Nebuchadnezzar king of the Assyrians that he should be avenged on all the land, even as he spoke. [2] He called together all his servants and all his great men, and communicated with them his secret counsel, and with his own mouth, recounted the wickedness of all the land. [3] They decreed to destroy all flesh which didn't follow the word of his mouth. [4] It came to pass, when he had ended his counsel, Nebuchadnezzar king of the Assyrians called Holofernes the chief captain of his army, who was second to himself, and said to him, [5] "The great king, the lord of all the earth, says: 'Behold, you shall go out from my presence, and take with you men who trust in their strength, to one hundred twenty thousand footmen and twelve thousand horses with their riders. [6] And you shall go out against all the west country, because they disobeyed the commandment of my mouth. [7] You shall declare to them that they should prepare earth and water, because I will go out in my wrath against them, and will cover the whole face of the earth with the feet of my army, who will plunder them. [8] Their slain will fill their valleys and brooks, and the river will be filled with their dead until it overflows. [9] I will lead them as captives to the utmost parts of all the earth. [10] But you shall go forth, and take all their coasts for me first. If they will yield themselves to you,[a] then you must reserve them for me until the day of their reproof. [11] As for those who resist, your eye shall not spare; but you shall give them up to be slain and to be plundered in all your land. [12] For as I live, and by the power of my kingdom, I have spoken, and I will do this with my hand. [13] Moreover, you shall not transgress anything of the commandments of your lord, but you shall surely accomplish them, as I have commanded you. You shall not defer to do them.'" [14] So Holofernes went out from the presence of his lord, and called all the governors, the captains, and officers of the army of Asshur. [15] He counted chosen men for the battle, as his lord had commanded him, to one hundred twenty thousand, with twelve thousand archers on horseback. [16] He arranged them as a great multitude is ordered for the war. [17] He took camels, donkeys, and mules for their baggage, an exceedingly great multitude, and sheep, oxen, and goats without number for their provision, [18] and a large supply of rations for every man, and a huge amount of gold and silver out of the king's house. [19] He went out, he and all his army, on their journey, to go before King Nebuchadnezzar, and to cover all the face of the earth westward with their chariots, horsemen, and chosen footmen. [20] A great company of various nations went out with them like locusts and like the sand of the earth. For they could not be counted by reason of their multitude. [21]

And they departed out of Nineveh three days' journey toward the plain of Bectileth, and encamped from Bectileth near the mountain which is at the left hand of the Upper Cilicia. [22] And he took all his army, his footmen, horsemen, and chariots, and went away from there into the hill country, [23] and destroyed Put and Lud, and plundered all the children of Rasses and the children of Ishmael, which were along the wilderness to the south of the land of the Chellians. [24] And he went over Euphrates, and went through Mesopotamia, and broke down all the high cities that were upon the river Arbonai, until you come to the sea. [25] And he took possession of the borders of Cilicia, and killed all who resisted him, and came to the borders of Japheth, which were toward the south, opposite Arabia. [26] He surrounded all the children of Midian, and set their tents on fire, and plundered their sheepfolds. [27] He went down into the plain of Damascus in the days of wheat harvest, and set all their fields on fire, and utterly destroyed their flocks and herds, plundered their cities, laid their plains waste, and struck all their young men with the edge of the sword. [28] And the fear and the dread of him fell upon those who lived on the sea coast, upon those who were in Sidon and Tyre, those who lived in Sur and Ocina, and all who lived in Jemnaan. Those who lived in Azotus and Ascalon feared him exceedingly.

## 3

[1] And they sent to him messengers with words of peace, saying, [2] "Behold, we the servants of Nebuchadnezzar the great king lie before you. Use us as it is pleasing in your sight. [3] Behold, our dwellings, and all our country, and all our fields of wheat, and our flocks and herds, and all the sheepfolds of our tents, lie before your face. Use them as it may please you. [4] Behold, even our cities and those who dwell in them are your servants. Come and deal with them as it is good in your eyes." [5] So the men came to Holofernes, and declared to him according to these words. [6] He came down toward the sea coast, he and his army, and set garrisons in the high cities, and took out of them chosen men for allies. [7] They received him, they and all the country round about them, with garlands and dances and timbrels. [8] He cast down all their borders, and cut down their sacred groves. It had been given to him to destroy all the gods of the land, that all the nations would worship Nebuchadnezzar only, and that all their tongues and their tribes would call upon him as a god. [9] Then he came toward Esdraelon near to Dotaea, which is opposite the great ridge of Judea. [10] He encamped between Geba and Scythopolis. He was there a whole month, that he might gather together all the baggage of his army.

## 4

[1] The children of Israel who lived in Judea heard all that Holofernes the chief captain of Nebuchadnezzar king of the Assyrians had done to the nations, and how he had plundered all their temples and destroyed them utterly. [2] They were exceedingly afraid at his approach, and were troubled for Jerusalem and for the temple of the Lord their God; [3] because they had newly come up from the captivity, and all the people of Judea were recently gathered together; and the vessels, the altar, and the house were sanctified after being profaned. [4] And they sent into every coast of Samaria, to Konae, to Beth-horon, Belmaim, Jericho, to Choba, Aesora, and to the valley of Salem; [5] and they occupied beforehand all the tops of the high mountains, fortified the villages that were in them, and stored supplies for the provision of war, for their fields were newly reaped. [6] Joakim the high priest, who was in those days at Jerusalem, wrote to those who lived in Bethulia and Betomesthaim, which is opposite Esdraelon toward the plain that is near to Dothaim, [7] charging them to seize upon the ascents of the hill country; because by them was the entrance into Judea, and it was easy to stop them from approaching, inasmuch as the approach was narrow, with space for two men at the most. [8] And the children of Israel did as Joakim the high priest had commanded them, as did the senate of all the people of Israel, which was in session at Jerusalem. [9] And every man of Israel cried to God with great earnestness, and with great earnestness they humbled their souls. [10] They, their wives, their children, their cattle, and every sojourner, hireling, and servant bought with their money put sackcloth on their loins. [11] Every man and woman of Israel, including the little children and the inhabitants of Jerusalem, fell prostrate before the temple, cast ashes upon their heads, and spread out their sackcloth before the Lord. They put sackcloth around the altar. [12] They cried to the God of Israel earnestly with one consent, that he would not give their children as prey, their wives as plunder, the cities of their inheritance to destruction, and the sanctuary to being profaned and being made a reproach, for the nations to rejoice at. [13] The Lord heard their voice, and looked at their affliction. The people continued fasting many days in all Judea and Jerusalem before the sanctuary of the Lord Almighty. [14] And Joakim the high priest, and all the priests

who stood before the Lord, and those who ministered to the Lord, had their loins dressed in sackcloth and offered the continual burnt offering, the vows, and the free gifts of the people. <sup>15</sup> They had ashes on their turbans. They cried to the Lord with all their power, that he would look upon all the house of Israel for good.

## 5

<sup>1</sup> Holofernes, the chief captain of the army of Asshur, was told that the children of Israel had prepared for war, had shut up the passages of the hill country, had fortified all the tops of the high hills, and had set up barricades in the plains. <sup>2</sup> Then he was exceedingly angry, and he called all the princes of Moab, the captains of Ammon, and all the governors of the sea coast, <sup>3</sup> and he said to them, "Tell me now, you sons of Canaan, who are these people who dwell in the hill country? What are the cities that they inhabit? How large is their army? Where is their power and their strength? What king is set over them, to be the leader of their army? <sup>4</sup> Why have they turned their backs, that they should not come and meet me, more than all who dwell in the west?" <sup>5</sup> Then Achior, the leader of all the children of Ammon, said to him, "Let my lord now hear a word from the mouth of your servant, and I will tell you the truth concerning these people who dwell in this hill country, near to the place where you dwell. No lie will come out of the mouth of your servant. <sup>6</sup> These people are descended from the Chaldeans. <sup>7</sup> They sojourned before this in Mesopotamia, because they didn't want to follow the gods of their fathers, which were in the land of the Chaldeans. <sup>8</sup> They departed from the way of their parents, and worshiped the God of heaven, the God whom they knew. Their parents cast them out from the face of their gods, and they fled into Mesopotamia and sojourned there many days. <sup>9</sup> Then their God commanded them to depart from the place where they sojourned, and to go into the land of Canaan. They lived there, and prospered with gold and silver, and with exceedingly much cattle. <sup>10</sup> Then they went down into Egypt, for a famine covered all the land of Canaan. They sojourned there until they had grown up. They became a great multitude there, so that one could not count the population of their nation. <sup>11</sup> Then the king of Egypt rose up against them, and dealt subtly with them, and brought them low, making them labor in brick,<sup>a</sup> and made them slaves. <sup>12</sup> They cried to their God, and he struck all the land of Egypt with incurable plagues; so the Egyptians cast them out of their sight. <sup>13</sup> God dried up the Red sea before them, <sup>14</sup> and brought them into the way of Sinai Kadesh-Barnea and they cast out all that lived in the wilderness. <sup>15</sup> They lived in the land of the Amorites, and they destroyed by their strength everyone in Heshbon. Passing over Jordan, they possessed all the hill country. <sup>16</sup> They cast out before them the Canaanite, the Perizzite, the Jebusite, the Shechemite, and all the Girgashites, and they lived in that country many days. <sup>17</sup> And while they didn't sin before their God, they prospered, because God who hates iniquity was with them. <sup>18</sup> But when they departed from the way which he appointed them, they were destroyed in many severe battles, and were led captives into a land that was not theirs. The temple of their God was razed to the ground, and their cities were taken by their adversaries. <sup>19</sup> And now they have returned to their God, and have come up from the dispersion where they were dispersed, and have possessed Jerusalem, where their sanctuary is, and are settled in the hill country; for it was desolate. <sup>20</sup> And now, my lord and master, if there is any error in this people, and they sin against their God, we will find out what this thing is in which they stumble, and we will go up and overcome them. <sup>21</sup> But if there is no lawlessness in their nation, let my lord now pass by, lest their Lord defend them, and their God be for them, and we will be a reproach before all the earth." <sup>22</sup> It came to pass, when Achior had finished speaking these words, all the people standing around the tent complained. The great men of Holofernes, and all who lived by the sea side and in Moab, said that he should be cut to pieces. <sup>23</sup> For, they said, "We will not be afraid of the children of Israel, because, behold, they are a people that has no power nor might to make the battle strong. <sup>24</sup> Therefore now we will go up, and they will be a prey to be devoured by all your army, Lord Holofernes."

## 6

<sup>1</sup> And when the disturbance of the men that were around the council had ceased, Holofernes the chief captain of the army of Asshur said to Achior and to all the children of Moab<sup>b</sup> before all the people of the foreigners: <sup>2</sup>"And who are you, Achior, and the mercenaries of Ephraim,<sup>c</sup> that you have prophesied among us as today, and have said that we should not make war with the race of Israel, because their God will defend them? And who is God but Nebuchadnezzar? <sup>3</sup> He will send forth his might, and will destroy them from the face of the earth, and their God will not deliver them; but we his servants will strike them as

one man. They will not sustain the might of our cavalry. <sup>4</sup> For with them we will burn them up. Their mountains will be drunken with their blood. Their plains will be filled with their dead bodies. Their footsteps will not stand before us, but they will surely perish, says King Nebuchadnezzar, lord of all the earth; for he said, 'The words that I have spoken<sup>d</sup> will not be in vain.' <sup>5</sup> But you, Achior, hireling of Ammon, who have spoken these words in the day of your iniquity, will see my face no more from this day, until I am avenged of the race of those that came out of Egypt. <sup>6</sup> And then the sword of my army, and the multitude of those who serve me, will pass through your sides, and you will fall among their slain when I return. <sup>7</sup> Then my servants will bring you back into the hill country, and will set you in one of the cities by the passes. <sup>8</sup> You will not perish until you are destroyed with them. <sup>9</sup> And if you hope in your heart that they will not be taken, don't let your countenance fall. I have spoken it, and none of my words will fall to the ground." <sup>10</sup> Then Holofernes commanded his servants who waited in his tent to take Achior, and bring him back to Bethulia, and deliver him into the hands of the children of Israel. <sup>11</sup> So his servants took him, and brought him out of the camp into the plain, and they moved from the midst of the plains into the hill country, and came to the springs that were under Bethulia. <sup>12</sup> When the men of the city saw them on the top of the hill, they took up their weapons, and went out of the city against them to the top of the hill. Every man that used a sling kept them from coming up, and threw stones at them. <sup>13</sup> They took cover under the hill, bound Achior, cast him down, left him at the foot of the hill, and went away to their lord. <sup>14</sup> But the children of Israel descended from their city, and came to him, untied him, led him away into Bethulia, and presented him to the rulers of their city, <sup>15</sup> which were in those days Ozias the son of Micah, of the tribe of Simeon, and Chabris the son of Gothoniel, and Charmis the son of Melchiel. <sup>16</sup> Then they called together all the elders of the city; and all their young men ran together, with their women, to the assembly. They set Achior in the midst of all their people. Then Ozias asked him what had happened. <sup>17</sup> He answered and declared to them the words of the council of Holofernes, and all the words that he had spoken in the midst of the princes of the children of Asshur, and all the great words that Holofernes had spoken against the house of Israel. <sup>18</sup> Then the people fell down and worshiped God, and cried, saying, <sup>19</sup>"O Lord God of heaven, behold their arrogance, and pity the low estate of our race. Look upon the face of those who are sanctified to you this day." <sup>20</sup> They comforted Achior, and praised him exceedingly. <sup>21</sup> Then Ozias took him out of the assembly into his house, and made a feast for the elders. They called on the God of Israel for help all that night.

## 7

<sup>1</sup> The next day Holofernes commanded all his army and all the people who had come to be his allies, that they should move their camp toward Bethulia, seize the passes of the hill country, and make war against the children of Israel. <sup>2</sup> Every mighty man of them moved that day. The army of their men of war was one hundred seventy thousand footmen, plus twelve thousand horsemen, besides the baggage and the men who were on foot among them—an exceedingly great multitude. <sup>3</sup> They encamped in the valley near Bethulia, by the fountain. They spread themselves in breadth over Dothaim even to Belmaim, and in length from Bethulia to Cyamon, which is near Esdraelon. <sup>4</sup> But the children of Israel, when they saw the multitude of them, were terrified, and everyone said to his neighbor, "Now these men will lick up the face of all the earth. Neither the high mountains, nor the valleys, nor the hills will be able to bear their weight. <sup>5</sup> Every man took up his weapons of war, and when they had kindled fires upon their towers, they remained and watched all that night. <sup>6</sup> But on the second day Holofernes led out all his cavalry in the sight of the children of Israel which were in Bethulia, <sup>7</sup> viewed the ascents to their city, and searched out the springs of the waters, seized upon them, and set garrisons of men of war over them. Then he departed back to his people. <sup>8</sup> All the rulers of the children of Esau, all the leaders of the people of Moab, and the captains of the sea coast came to him and said, <sup>9</sup>"Let our lord now hear a word, that there not be losses in your army. <sup>10</sup> For this people of the children of Israel do not trust in their spears, but in the height of the mountains wherein they dwell, for it is not easy to come up to the tops of their mountains. <sup>11</sup> And now, my lord, don't fight against them as men fight who join battle, and there will not so much as one man of your people perish. <sup>12</sup> Remain in your camp, and keep every man of your army safe. Let your servants get possession of the water spring, which flows from the foot of the mountain, <sup>13</sup> because all the inhabitants of Bethulia get their water from there. Then thirst will kill them, and they will give up their city. Then we and our people will go up to the tops of the

---

<sup>a</sup> 5:11 Some authorities read and he brought them low with clay and brick, etc.

<sup>b</sup> 6:1 Some authorities read Ammon. Compare ver. 5.

<sup>c</sup> 6:2 Some authorities read Ammon. Compare ver. 5.

<sup>d</sup> 6:4 Gr. he has spoken.

mountains that are near, and will camp upon them, to watch that not one man gets out of the city. ¹⁴ They will be consumed with famine—they, their wives, and their children. Before the sword comes against them they will be laid low in the streets where they dwell. ¹⁵ And you will pay them back with evil, because they rebelled, and didn't meet your face in peace." ¹⁶ Their words were pleasing in the sight of Holofernes and in the sight of all his servants; and he ordered them to do as they had spoken. ¹⁷ And the army of the children of Ammon moved, and with them five thousand of the children of Asshur, and they encamped in the valley. They seized the waters and the springs of the waters of the children of Israel. ¹⁸ The children of Esau went up with the children of Ammon, and encamped in the hill country near Dothaim. They sent some of them toward the south, and toward the east, near Ekrebel, which is near Chusi, that is upon the brook Mochmur. The rest of the army of the Assyrians encamped in the plain, and covered all the face of the land. Their tents and baggage were pitched upon it in a great crowd. They were an exceedingly great multitude. ¹⁹ The children of Israel cried to the Lord their God, for their spirit fainted; for all their enemies had surrounded them. There was no way to escape out from among them. ²⁰ All the army of Asshur remained around them, their footmen and their chariots and their horsemen, for thirty-four days. All their vessels of water ran dry for all the inhabitants of Bethulia. ²¹ The cisterns were emptied, and they had no water to drink their fill for one day; for they rationed drink by measure. ²² Their young children were discouraged. The women and the young men fainted for thirst. They fell down in the streets of the city, and in the passages of the gates. There was no longer any strength in them. ²³ All the people, including the young men, the women, and the children, were gathered together against Ozias, and against the rulers of the city. They cried with a loud voice, and said before all the elders, ²⁴"God be judge between all of you and us, because you have done us great wrong, in that you have not spoken words of peace with the children of Asshur. ²⁵ Now we have no helper; but God has sold us into their hands, that we should be laid low before them with thirst and great destruction. ²⁶ And now summon them, and deliver up the whole city as prey to the people of Holofernes, and to all his army. ²⁷ For it is better for us to be captured by them. For we will be servants, and our souls will live, and we will not see the death of our babies before our eyes, and our wives and our children fainting in death. ²⁸ We take to witness against you the heaven and the earth, and our God and the Lord of our fathers, who punishes us according to our sins and the sins of our fathers. Do what we have said today!" ²⁹ And there was great weeping of all with one consent in the midst of the assembly; and they cried to the Lord God with a loud voice. ³⁰ And Ozias said to them, "Brethren, be of good courage! Let us endure five more days, during which the Lord our God will turn his mercy toward us; for he will not forsake us utterly. ³¹ But if these days pass, and no help comes to us, I will do what you say." ³² Then he dispersed the people, every man to his own camp; and they went away to the walls and towers of their city. He sent the women and children into their houses. They were brought very low in the city.

# 8

¹ In those days Judith heard about this. She was the daughter of Merari, the son of Ox, the son of Joseph, the son of Oziel, the son of Elkiah, the son of Ananias, the son of Gideon, the son of Raphaim, the son of Ahitub, the son of Elihu, the son of Eliab, the son of Nathanael, the son of Salamiel, the son of Salasadai, the son of Israel. ² Her husband was Manasses, of her tribe and of her family. He died in the days of barley harvest. ³ For he stood over those who bound sheaves in the field, and was overcome by the burning heat, and he fell on his bed, and died in his city Bethulia. So they buried him with his fathers in the field which is between Dothaim and Balamon. ⁴ Judith was a widow in her house three years and four months. ⁵ She made herself a tent upon the roof of her house, and put on sackcloth upon her loins. The garments of her widowhood were upon her. ⁶ And she fasted all the days of her widowhood, except the eves of the Sabbaths, the Sabbaths, the eves of the new moons, the new moons, and the feasts and joyful days of the house of Israel. ⁷ She was beautiful in appearance, and lovely to behold. Her husband Manasses had left her gold, silver, menservants, maidservants, cattle, and lands. She remained on those lands. ⁸ No one said anything evil about her, for she feared God exceedingly. ⁹ She heard the evil words of the people against the governor, because they fainted for lack of water; and Judith heard all the words that Ozias spoke to them, how he swore to them that he would deliver the city to the Assyrians after five days. ¹⁰ So she sent her maid, who was over all things that she had, to summon Ozias, Chabris, and Charmis, the elders

of her city. ¹¹ They came to her, and she said to them, "Hear me now, O you rulers of the inhabitants of Bethulia! For your word that you have spoken before the people this day is not right. You have set the oath which you have pronounced between God and you, and have promised to deliver the city to our enemies, unless within these days the Lord turns to help you. ¹² Now who are you that you have tested God this day, and stand in the place of God among the children of men? ¹³ Now try the Lord Almighty, and you will never know anything. ¹⁴ For you will not find the depth of the heart of man, and you will not perceive the things that he thinks. How will you search out God, who has made all these things, and know his mind, and comprehend his purpose? No, my kindred, don't provoke the Lord our God to anger! ¹⁵ For if he has not decided to help us within these five days, he has power to defend us in such time as he will, or to destroy us before the face of our enemies. ¹⁶ But don't you pledge the counsels of the Lord our God! For God is not like a human being, that he should be threatened, neither is he like a son of man, that he should be won over by pleading. ¹⁷ Therefore let's wait for the salvation that comes from him, and call upon him to help us. He will hear our voice, if it pleases him. ¹⁸ For there arose none in our age, neither is there any of us today, tribe, or kindred, or family, or city, which worship gods made with hands, as it was in the former days; ¹⁹ for which cause our fathers were given to the sword, and for plunder, and fell with a great destruction before our enemies. ²⁰ But we know no other god beside him. Therefore we hope that he will not despise us, nor any of our race. ²¹ For if we are captured, all Judea will be captured and our sanctuary will be plundered; and he will require our blood for profaning it. ²² The slaughter of our kindred, the captivity of the land, and the desolation of our inheritance, he will bring on our heads among the Gentiles, wherever we will be in bondage. We will be an offense and a reproach to those who take us for a possession. ²³ For our bondage will not be ordered to favor; but the Lord our God will turn it to dishonor. ²⁴ And now, kindred, let's show an example to our kindred, because their soul depends on us, and the sanctuary, the house, and the altar depend on us. ²⁵ Besides all this let's give thanks to the Lord our God, who tries us, even as he did our fathers also. ²⁶ Remember all the things which he did to Abraham, and all the things in which he tried Isaac, and all the things which happened to Jacob in Mesopotamia of Syria, when he kept the sheep of Laban his mother's brother. ²⁷ For he has not tried us in the fire, as he did them, to search out their hearts, neither has he taken vengeance on us; but the Lord scourges those who come near to him, to admonish them." ²⁸ And Ozias said to her, "All that you have spoken, you have spoken with a good heart. There is no one who will deny your words. ²⁹ For this is not the first day wherein your wisdom is manifested; but from the beginning of your days all the people have known your understanding, because the disposition of your heart is good. ³⁰ But the people were exceedingly thirsty, and compelled us to do as we spoke to them, and to bring an oath upon ourselves, which we will not break. ³¹ And now pray for us, because you are a godly woman, and the Lord will send us rain to fill our cisterns, and we will faint no more." ³² Then Judith said to them, "Hear me, and I will do a thing, which will go down to all generations among the children of our race. ³³ You shall all stand at the gate tonight. I will go out with my maid. Within the days after which you said that you would deliver the city to our enemies, the Lord will deliver Israel by my hand. ³⁴ But you shall not inquire of my act; for I will not tell you until the things are finished that I will do." ³⁵ Then Ozias and the rulers said to her, "Go in peace. May the Lord God be before you, to take vengeance on our enemies." ³⁶ So they returned from the tent, and went to their stations.

# 9

¹ But Judith fell upon her face, and put ashes upon her head, and uncovered the sackcloth with which she was clothed. The incense of that evening was now being offered at Jerusalem in the house of God, and Judith cried to the Lord with a loud voice, and said, ²"O Lord God of my father Simeon, into whose hand you gave a sword to take vengeance on the strangers who loosened the belt of a virgin to defile her, uncovered her thigh to her shame, and profaned her womb to her reproach; for you said, 'It shall not be so;' and they did so. ³ Therefore you gave their rulers to be slain, and their bed, which was ashamed for her who was deceived,ᵃ to be dyed in blood, and struck the servants with their masters, and the masters upon their thrones; ⁴ and gave their wives for a prey, and their daughters to be captives, and all their spoils to be divided among your dear children; which were moved with zeal for you, and abhorred the pollution of their blood, and called upon you for aid. O God, O my God, hear me also who am a widow. ⁵ For you did the things that were before those things, and those things, and such

---

ᵃ 9:3 Some authorities read which was ashamed for their deceit that they practiced.

as come after; and you planned the things which are now, and the things which are to come. The things which you planned came to pass. ⁶ Yes, the things which you determined stood before you, and said, 'Behold, we are here; for all your ways are prepared, and your judgment is with foreknowledge.' ⁷ For, behold, the Assyrians are multiplied in their power. They are exalted with horse and rider. They were proud of the strength of their footmen. They have trusted in shield, spear, bow, and sling. They don't know that you are the Lord who breaks the battles. 'The Lord' is your name. ⁸ Break their strength in your power, and bring down their force in your wrath; for they intend to profane your sanctuary, and to defile the tabernacle where your glorious name rests, and to destroy the horn of your altar with the sword. ⁹ Look at their pride, and send your wrath upon their heads. Give into my hand, which am a widow, the might that I have conceived. ¹⁰ Strike by the deceit of my lips the servant with the prince, and the prince with his servant. Break down their arrogance by the hand of a woman. ¹¹ For your power stands not in numbers, nor your might in strong men, but you are a God of the afflicted. You are a helper of the oppressed, a helper of the weak, a protector of the forsaken, a savior of those who are without hope. ¹² Please, please, God of my father, and God of the inheritance of Israel, Lord of the heavens and of the earth, Creator of the waters, King of all your creation, hear my prayer. ¹³ Make my speech and deceit to be their wound and bruise, who intend hard things against your covenant, your holy house, the top of Zion, and the house of the possession of your children. ¹⁴ Make every nation and tribe of yours to know that you are God, the God of all power and might, and that there is no other who protects the race of Israel but you."

## 10

¹ It came to pass, when she had ceased to cry to the God of Israel, and had finished saying all these words, ² that she rose up where she had fallen down, called her maid, and went down into the house that she lived on the Sabbath days and on her feast days. ³ She pulled off the sackcloth which she had put on, took off the garments of her widowhood, washed her body all over with water, anointed herself with rich ointment, braided the hair of her head, and put a tiara upon it. She put on her garments of gladness, which she used to wear in the days of the life of Manasses her husband. ⁴ She took sandals for her feet, and put on her anklet, bracelets, rings, earrings, and all her jewelry. She made herself very beautiful to deceive the eyes of all men who would see her. ⁵ She gave her maid a leather container of wine and a flask of oil, and filled a bag with roasted grain, lumps of figs, and fine bread. She packed all her vessels together, and laid them upon her. ⁶ They went out to the gate of the city of Bethulia, and found Ozias and the elders of the city, Chabris and Charmis standing by it. ⁷ But when they saw her, that her countenance was altered and her apparel was changed, they were greatly astonished by her beauty and said to her, ⁸"May the God of our fathers give you favor, and accomplish your purposes to the glory of the children of Israel, and to the exaltation of Jerusalem." Then she worshiped God, ⁹ and said to them, "Command that they open the gate of the city for me, and I will go out to accomplish the things you spoke with me about." And they commanded the young men to open to her, as she had spoken; ¹⁰ and they did so. Then Judith went out, she, and her handmaid with her. The men of the city watched her until she had gone down the mountain, until she had passed the valley, and they could see her no more. ¹¹ They went straight onward in the valley. The watch of the Assyrians met her; ¹² and they took her, and asked her, "Of what people are you? Where are you coming from? Where are you going?" She said, "I am a daughter of the Hebrews. I am fleeing away from their presence, because they are about to be given you to be consumed. ¹³ I am coming into the presence of Holofernes the chief captain of your army, to declare words of truth. I will show him a way that he can go and win all the hill country, and there will not be lacking of his men one person, nor one life." ¹⁴ Now when the men heard her words, and considered her countenance, the beauty thereof was exceedingly marvelous in their eyes. They said to her, ¹⁵"You have saved your life, in that you have hurried to come down to the presence of our master. Now come to his tent. Some of us will guide you until they deliver you into his hands. ¹⁶ But whenᵃ you stand before him, don't be afraid in your heart, but declare to him what you just said, and he will treat you well." ¹⁷ They chose out of them a hundred men, and appointed them to accompany her and her maid; and they brought them to the tent of Holofernes. ¹⁸ And there was great excitement throughout all the camp, for her coming was reported among the tents. They came and surrounded her as she stood outside Holofernes' tent, until they told him about her. ¹⁹ They marveled at her beauty, and marveled at the children of Israel because of her. Each one said to his neighbor, "Who would despise these people, who have among them such women? For it is not good that one man of them be left, seeing that, if they are let

go, they will be able to deceive the whole earth. ²⁰ Then the guards of Holofernes and all his servants came out and brought her into the tent. ²¹ And Holofernes was resting upon his bed under the canopy, which was woven with purple, gold, emeralds, and precious stones. ²² And they told him about her; and he came out into the space before his tent, with silver lamps going before him. ²³ But when Judith had come before him and his servants, they all marveled at the beauty of her countenance. She fell down upon her face and bowed down to him, but his servants raised her up.

## 11

¹ Holofernes said to her, "Woman, take courage. Don't be afraid in your heart; for I never hurt anyone who has chosen to serve Nebuchadnezzar, the king of all the earth. ² And now, if your people who dwell in the hill country had not slighted me, I would not have lifted up my spear against them; but they have done these things to themselves. ³ And now tell me why you fled from them and came to us; for you have come to save yourself. Take courage! You will live tonight, and hereafter; ⁴ for there is no one that will wrong you, but all will treat you well, as is done to the servants of King Nebuchadnezzar my lord." ⁵ And Judith said to him, "Receive the words of your servant, and let your handmaid speak in your presence, and I won't lie to my lord tonight. ⁶ If you will follow the words of your handmaid, God will bring the thing to pass perfectly with you; and my lord will not fail to accomplish his purposes. ⁷ As Nebuchadnezzar king of all the earth lives, and as his power lives, who has sent you for the preservation of every living thing, not only do men serve him by you, but also the beasts of the field, the cattle, and the birds of the sky will live through your strength, in the time of Nebuchadnezzar and of all his house. ⁸ For we have heard of your wisdom and the subtle plans of your soul. It has been reported in all the earth that you only are brave in all the kingdom, mighty in knowledge, and wonderful in feats of war. ⁹ And now as concerning the matter which Achior spoke in your council, we have heard his words; for the men of Bethulia saved him, and he declared to them all that he had spoken before you. ¹⁰ Therefore, O lord and master, don't neglect his word, but lay it up in your heart, for it is true; for our race will not be punished, neither will the sword prevail against them, unless they sin against their God. ¹¹ And now, that my lord may not be defeated and frustrated in his purpose, and that death may fall upon them, their sin has overtaken them, wherewith they will provoke their God to anger, whenever they do wickedness. ¹² Since their food failed them, and all their water was scant, they took counsel to kill their livestock, and determined to consume all those things which God charged them by his laws that they should not eat. ¹³ They are resolved to spend the first fruits of the grain and the tithes of the wine and the oil, which they had sanctified and reserved for the priests who stand before the face of our God in Jerusalem, which it is not fitting for any of the people so much as to touch with their hands. ¹⁴ They have sent some to Jerusalem, because they also that dwell there have done this thing, to bring them permission from the council of elders. ¹⁵ When these instructions come to them and they do it, they will be given to you to be destroyed the same day. ¹⁶ Therefore I your servant, knowing all this, fled away from their presence. God sent me to work things with you, at which all the earth will be astonished, even as many as hear it. ¹⁷ For your servant is religious, and serves the God of heaven day and night. Now, my lord, I will stay with you; and your servant will go out by night into the valley. I will pray to God, and he will tell me when they have committed their sins. ¹⁸ Then I will come and tell you. Then you can go out with all your army, and there will be none of them that will resist you. ¹⁹ And I will lead you through the midst of Judea, until you come to Jerusalem. I will set your throne in the midst of it. You will drive them as sheep that have no shepherd, and a dog will not so much as open his mouth before you; for these things were told me according to my foreknowledge, and were declared to me, and I was sent to tell you." ²⁰ Her words were pleasing in the sight of Holofernes and of all his servants. They marveled at her wisdom, and said, ²¹"There is not such a woman from one end of the earth to the other, for beauty of face and wisdom of words." ²² Holofernes said to her, "God did well to send you before the people, that might would be in our hands, and destruction among those who slighted my lord. ²³ And now you are beautiful in your countenance, and wise in your words. If you will do as you have spoken, your God will be my God, and you will dwell in the palace of King Nebuchadnezzar, and will be renowned through the whole earth."

## 12

¹ He commanded that she should be brought in where his silver vessels were set, and asked that his servants should prepare some of his own delicacies for her, and that she should drink from his own wine. ² And Judith said, "I can't eat of it, lest there be an occasion of stumbling; but provision will be made for me from the things that have come with me."

³ And Holofernes said to her, "But if the things that are with you should run out, from where will we be able to give you more like it? For there is none of your race with us." ⁴ And Judith said to him, "As your soul lives, my lord, your servant will not use up those things that are with me until the Lord works by my hand the things that he has determined." ⁵ Then Holofernes' servants brought her into the tent, and she slept until midnight. Then she rose up toward the morning watch, ⁶ and sent to Holofernes, saying, "Let my lord now command that they allow your servant to go out to pray." ⁷ Holofernes commanded his guards that they should not stop her. She stayed in the camp three days, and went out every night into the valley of Bethulia and washed herself at the fountain of water in the camp. ⁸ And when she came up, she implored the Lord God of Israel to direct her way to the triumph of the children of his people. ⁹ She came in clean and remained in the tent until she ate her food toward evening. ¹⁰ It came to pass on the fourth day, that Holofernes made a feast for his own servants only, and called none of the officers to the banquet. ¹¹ And he said to Bagoas the eunuch, who had charge over all that he had, "Go now, and persuade this Hebrew woman who is with you that she come to us, and eat and drink with us. ¹² For behold, it would be a disgrace if we shall let such a woman go, not having had her company; for if we don't draw her to ourselves, she will laugh us to scorn." ¹³ Bagoas went from the presence of Holofernes, and came in to her, and said, "Let this fair lady not fear to come to my lord, and to be honored in his presence, and to drink wine and be merry with us, and to be made this day as one of the daughters of the children of Asshur who serve in Nebuchadnezzar's palace." ¹⁴ Judith said to him, "Who am I, that I should contradict my lord? For whatever would be pleasing in his eyes, I will do speedily, and this will be my joy to the day of my death." ¹⁵ She arose, and decked herself with her apparel and all her woman's attire; and her servant went and laid fleeces on the ground for her next to Holofernes, which she had received from Bagoas for her daily use, that she might sit and eat upon them. ¹⁶ Judith came in and sat down, and Holofernes' heart was ravished with her. His passion was aroused, and he exceedingly desired her company. He was watching for a time to deceive her from the day that he had seen her. ¹⁷ Holofernes said to her, "Drink now, and be merry with us." ¹⁸ Judith said, "I will drink now, my lord, because my life is magnified in me this day more than all the days since I was born." ¹⁹ Then she took and ate and drank before him what her servant had prepared. ²⁰ Holofernes took great delight in her, and drank exceedingly much wine, more than he had drunk at any time in one day since he was born.

## 13

¹ But when the evening had come, his servants hurried to depart. Bagoas shut the tent outside, and dismissed those who waited from the presence of his lord. They went away to their beds; for they were all weary, because the feast had been long. ² But Judith was left alone in the tent, with Holofernes lying along upon his bed; for he was drunk with wine. ³ Judith had said to her servant that she should stand outside her bedchamber, and wait for her to come out, as she did daily; for she said she would go out to her prayer. She spoke to Bagoas according to the same words. ⁴ All went away from her presence, and none was left in the bedchamber, small or great. Judith, standing by his bed, said in her heart, O Lord God of all power, look in this hour upon the works of my hands for the exaltation of Jerusalem. ⁵ For now is the time to help your inheritance, and to do the thing that I have purposed to the destruction of the enemies which have risen up against us. ⁶ She came to the bedpost which was at Holofernes' head, and took down his sword from there. ⁷ She drew near to the bed, took hold of the hair of his head, and said, "Strengthen me, O Lord God of Israel, this day." ⁸ She struck twice upon his neck with all her might and cut off his head, ⁹ tumbled his body down from the bed, and took down the canopy from the posts. After a little while she went out, and gave Holofernes' head to her maid; ¹⁰ and she put it in her bag of food. They both went out together to prayer, according to their custom. They passed through the camp, circled around that valley, and went up to the mountain of Bethulia, and came to its gates. ¹¹ Judith said afar off to the watchmen at the gates, "Open, open the gate, now. God is with us, even our God, to show his power yet in Israel, and his might against the enemy, as he has done even this day." ¹² It came to pass, when the men of her city heard her voice, they made haste to go down to the gate of their city, and they called together the elders of the city. ¹³ They all ran together, both small and great, for it seemed unbelievable to them that she had come. They opened the gate and received them, making a fire to give light, and surrounded them. ¹⁴ She said to them with a loud voice, "Praise God! Praise him! Praise God, who has not taken away his mercy from the house of Israel, but has destroyed our enemies by my hand tonight!" ¹⁵ Then she took the head out of the bag and showed it, and said to them, "Behold, the head of Holofernes, the chief captain of the army of Asshur, and behold, the canopy under which he laid in his drunkenness. The Lord struck him by the hand of a woman. ¹⁶ And as the Lord lives, who preserved me in my way that I went, my countenance deceived him to his destruction, and he didn't commit sin with me, to defile and shame me." ¹⁷ All the people were exceedingly amazed, and bowed themselves, and worshiped God, and said with one accord, "Blessed are you, O our God, who have this day humiliated the enemies of your people." ¹⁸ Ozias said to her, "Blessed are you, daughter, in the sight of the Most High God, above all the women upon the earth; and blessed is the Lord God, who created the heavens and the earth, who directed you to cut off the head of the prince of our enemies. ¹⁹ For your hope will not depart from the heart of men that remember the strength of God forever. ²⁰ May God turn these things to you for a perpetual praise, to visit you with good things, because you didn't spare your life by reason of the affliction of our race, but prevented our ruin, walking a straight way before our God." And all the people said, "Amen! Amen!"

## 14

¹ Judith said to them, "Hear me now, my kindred, and take this head, and hang it upon the battlement of your wall. ² It will be, so soon as the morning appears, and the sun comes up on the earth, you shall each take up his weapons of war, and every valiant man of you go out of the city. You shall set a captain over them, as though you would go down to the plain toward the watch of the children of Asshur; but you men shall not go down. ³ These will take up their full armor, and shall go into their camp and rouse up the captains of the army of Asshur. They will run together to Holofernes' tent. They won't find him. Fear will fall upon them, and they will flee before your face. ⁴ You men, and all that inhabit every border of Israel, shall pursue them and overthrow them as they go. ⁵ But before you do these things, summon Achior the Ammonite to me, that he may see and know him that despised the house of Israel, and that sent him to us, as it were to death. ⁶ And they called Achior out of the house of Ozias; but when he came, and saw the head of Holofernes in a man's hand in the assembly of the people, he fell upon his face, and his spirit failed. ⁷ But when they had recovered him,ᵃ he fell at Judith's feet, bowed down to her, and said, "Blessed are you in every tent of Judah! In every nation, those who hear your name will be troubled. ⁸ Now tell me all the things that you have done in these days." And Judith declared to him in the midst of the people all the things that she had done, from the day that she went out until the time that she spoke to them. ⁹ But when she finished speaking, the people shouted with a loud voice, and made a joyful noise in their city. ¹⁰ But when Achior saw all the things that the God of Israel had done, he believed in God exceedingly, and circumcised the flesh of his foreskin, and was joined to the house of Israel, to this day. ¹¹ But as soon as the morning arose, they hanged the head of Holofernes upon the wall, and every man took up his weapons, and they went forth by bands to the ascents of the mountain. ¹² But when the children of Asshur saw them, they sent word to their leaders, and they went to their captains and tribunes, and to every one of their rulers. ¹³ They came to Holofernes' tent, and said to him that was over all that he had, "Wake our lord up, now, for the slaves have been bold to come down against us to battle, that they may be utterly destroyed." ¹⁴ Bagoas went in, and knocked at the outer door of the tent; for he supposed that Holofernes was sleeping with Judith. ¹⁵ But when no one answered, he opened it, went into the bedchamber, and found him cast upon the threshold dead; and his head had been taken from him. ¹⁶ He cried with a loud voice, with weeping, groaning, and shouting, and tore his garments. ¹⁷ He entered into the tent where Judith lodged, and he didn't find her. He leaped out to the people, and cried aloud, ¹⁸"The slaves have dealt treacherously! One woman of the Hebrews has brought shame upon the house of King Nebuchadnezzar; for, behold, Holofernes lies upon the ground, and his head is not on him!" ¹⁹ But when the rulers of the army of Asshur heard this, they tore their tunics, and their souls were troubled exceedingly. There were cries and an exceedingly great noise in the midst of the camp.

## 15

¹ When those who were in the tents heard, they were amazed at what happened. ² Trembling and fear fell upon them, and no man dared stay any more in the sight of his neighbor, but rushing out with one accord, they fled into every way of the plain and of the hill country. ³ Those who had encamped in the hill country round about Bethulia fled away. And then the children of Israel, every one who was a warrior among them, rushed out upon them. ⁴ Ozias sent to Betomasthaim, Bebai, Chobai, and Chola, and to every border of Israel, to tell about the things that had been accomplished, and that all should rush upon their enemies to destroy them. ⁵ But when the children of Israel heard this, they all fell upon them with one accord, and struck them to Chobai. Yes, and in

like manner also, people from Jerusalem and from all the hill country came (for men had told them about what happened in their enemies' camp), and those who were in Gilead and in Galilee fell upon their flank with a great slaughter, until they were past Damascus and its borders. [6] The rest of the people who lived at Bethulia fell upon the camp of Asshur, and plundered them, and were enriched exceedingly. [7] The children of Israel returned from the slaughter, and got possession of that which remained. The villages and the cities that were in the hill country and in the plain country took many spoils; for there was an exceedingly great supply. [8] Joakim the high priest, and the elders of the children of Israel who lived in Jerusalem, came to see the good things which the Lord had showed to Israel, and to see Judith and to greet her. [9] When they came to her, they all blessed her with one accord, and said to her, "You are the exaltation of Jerusalem! You are the great glory of Israel! You are the great rejoicing of our race! [10] You have done all these things by your hand. You have done with Israel the things that are good, and God is pleased with it. May you be blessed by the Almighty Lord forever!" And all the people said, "Amen!" [11] And the people plundered the camp for thirty days; and they gave Holofernes' tent to Judith, along with all his silver cups, his beds, his bowls, and all his furniture. She took them, placed them on her mule, prepared her wagons, and piled them on it. [12] And all the women of Israel ran together to see her; and they blessed her, and made a dance among them for her. She took branches in her hand, and distributed them to the women who were with her.[a] [13] Then they made themselves garlands of olive, she and those who were with her, and she went before all the people in the dance, leading all the women. All the men of Israel followed in their armor with garlands, and with songs in their mouths.

## 16

[1] And Judith began to sing this song of thanksgiving in all Israel, and all the people sang with loud voices this song of praise. [2] Judith said, "Begin a song to my God with timbrels. Sing to my Lord with cymbals. Make melody to him with psalm and praise. Exalt him, and call upon his name. [3] For the Lord is the God that crushes battles. For in his armies in the midst of the people, he delivered me out of the hand of those who persecuted me. [4] Asshur came out of the mountains from the north. He came with ten thousands of his army. Its multitude stopped the torrents. Their horsemen covered the hills. [5] He said that he would burn up my borders, kill my young men with the sword, throw my nursing children to the ground, give my infants up as prey, and make my virgins a plunder. [6] "The Almighty Lord brought them to nothing by the hand of a woman. [7] For their mighty one didn't fall by young men, neither did sons of the Titans strike him. Tall giants didn't attack him, but Judith the daughter of Merari made him weak with the beauty of her countenance. [8] "For she put off the apparel of her widowhood for the exaltation of those who were distressed in Israel. She anointed her face with ointment, bound her hair in a tiara, and took a linen garment to deceive him. [9] Her sandal ravished his eye. Her beauty took his soul prisoner. The sword passed through his neck. [10] "The Persians quaked at her daring. The Medes were daunted at her boldness. [11] "Then my lowly ones shouted aloud. My oppressed people were terrified and trembled for fear. They lifted up their voices and the enemy fled. [12] The children of slave-girls pierced them through, and wounded them as fugitives' children. They perished by the army of my Lord. [13] "I will sing to my God a new song: O Lord, you are great and glorious, marvelous in strength, invincible. [14] Let all your creation serve you; for you spoke, and they were made. You sent out your spirit, and it built them. There is no one who can resist your voice. [15] For the mountains will be moved from their foundations with the waters, and the rocks will melt as wax at your presence: But you are yet merciful to those who fear you. [16] For all sacrifice is little for a sweet savor, and all the fat is very little for a whole burnt offering to you; but he who fears the Lord is great continually. [17] "Woe to the nations who rise up against my race! The Lord Almighty will take vengeance on them in the day of judgment and put fire and worms in their flesh; and they will weep and feel their pain forever." [18] Now when they came to Jerusalem, they worshiped God. When the people were purified, they offered their whole burnt offerings, their free will offerings, and their gifts. [19] Judith dedicated all Holofernes' stuff, which the people had given her, and gave the canopy, which she had taken for herself out of his bedchamber, for a gift to the Lord. [20] And the people continued feasting in Jerusalem before the sanctuary for three months, and Judith remained with them. [21] After these days, everyone departed to his own inheritance. Judith went away to Bethulia, and remained in her own possession, and was honorable in her time in all the land. [22] Many desired her, but no man knew her all the days of her life from the day that Manasses her husband died and was gathered to his people. [23] She increased in greatness

exceedingly; and she grew old in her husband's house, to one hundred five years. She let her maid go free. Then she died in Bethulia. They buried her in the cave of her husband Manasses. [24] The house of Israel mourned for her seven days. She distributed her goods before she died to all those who were nearest of kin to Manasses her husband, and to those who were nearest of her own kindred. [25] There was no one who made the children of Israel afraid any more in the days of Judith, nor for a long time after her death.

# The Book of Esther

## 1

[1] Now in the days of Ahasuerus (this is Ahasuerus who reigned from India even to Ethiopia, over one hundred twenty-seven provinces), [2] in those days, when the King Ahasuerus sat on the throne of his kingdom, which was in Susa the palace, [3] in the third year of his reign, he made a feast for all his princes and his servants; the army of Persia and Media, the nobles and princes of the provinces being before him. [4] He displayed the riches of his glorious kingdom and the honor of his excellent majesty many days, even one hundred eighty days. [5] When these days were fulfilled, the king made a seven day feast for all the people who were present in Susa the palace, both great and small, in the court of the garden of the king's palace. [6] There were hangings of white and blue material, fastened with cords of fine linen and purple to silver rings and marble pillars. The couches were of gold and silver, on a pavement of red, white, yellow, and black marble. [7] They gave them drinks in golden vessels of various kinds, including royal wine in abundance, according to the bounty of the king. [8] In accordance with the law, the drinking was not compulsory; for so the king had instructed all the officials of his house, that they should do according to every man's pleasure. [9] Also Vashti the queen made a feast for the women in the royal house which belonged to King Ahasuerus. [10] On the seventh day, when the heart of the king was merry with wine, he commanded Mehuman, Biztha, Harbona, Bigtha, and Abagtha, Zethar, and Carcass, the seven eunuchs who served in the presence of Ahasuerus the king, [11] to bring Vashti the queen before the king wearing the royal crown, to show the people and the princes her beauty; for she was beautiful. [12] But the queen Vashti refused to come at the king's commandment by the eunuchs. Therefore the king was very angry, and his anger burned in him. [13] Then the king said to the wise men, who knew the times (for it was the king's custom to consult those who knew law and judgment; [14] and next to him were Carshena, Shethar, Admatha, Tarshish, Meres, Marsena, and Memucan, the seven princes of Persia and Media, who saw the king's face, and sat first in the kingdom), [15] "What shall we do to Queen Vashti according to law, because she has not done the bidding of the King Ahasuerus by the eunuchs?" [16] Memucan answered before the king and the princes, "Vashti the queen has not done wrong to just the king, but also to all the princes, and to all the people who are in all the provinces of the King Ahasuerus. [17] For this deed of the queen will become known to all women, causing them to show contempt for their husbands when it is reported, 'King Ahasuerus commanded Vashti the queen to be brought in before him, but she didn't come.' [18] Today, the princesses of Persia and Media who have heard of the queen's deed will tell all the king's princes. This will cause much contempt and wrath. [19] "If it pleases the king, let a royal commandment go from him, and let it be written among the laws of the Persians and the Medes, so that it cannot be altered, that Vashti may never again come before King Ahasuerus; and let the king give her royal estate to another who is better than she. [20] When the king's decree which he shall make is published throughout all his kingdom (for it is great), all the wives will give their husbands honor, both great and small." [21] This advice pleased the king and the princes, and the king did according to the word of Memucan: [22] for he sent letters into all the king's provinces, into every province according to its writing, and to every people in their language, that every man should rule his own house, speaking in the language of his own people.

## 2

[1] After these things, when the wrath of King Ahasuerus was pacified, he remembered Vashti, and what she had done, and what was decreed against her. [2] Then the king's servants who served him said, "Let beautiful young virgins be sought for the king. [3] Let the king appoint officers in all the provinces of his kingdom, that they may gather together all the beautiful young virgins to the citadel of Susa, to the women's house, to the custody of Hegai the king's eunuch, keeper of the women. Let cosmetics be given them; [4] and let the maiden who pleases the king be queen instead of Vashti." The thing pleased the king, and he did so. [5] There was a certain Jew in the citadel of Susa

whose name was Mordecai, the son of Jair, the son of Shimei, the son of Kish, a Benjamite, [6] who had been carried away from Jerusalem with the captives who had been carried away with Jeconiah king of Judah, whom Nebuchadnezzar the king of Babylon had carried away. [7] He brought up Hadassah, that is, Esther, his uncle's daughter; for she had neither father nor mother. The maiden was fair and beautiful; and when her father and mother were dead, Mordecai took her for his own daughter. [8] So, when the king's commandment and his decree was heard, and when many maidens were gathered together to the citadel of Susa, to the custody of Hegai, Esther was taken into the king's house, to the custody of Hegai, keeper of the women. [9] The maiden pleased him, and she obtained kindness from him. He quickly gave her cosmetics and her portions of food, and the seven choice maidens who were to be given her out of the king's house. He moved her and her maidens to the best place in the women's house. [10] Esther had not made known her people nor her relatives, because Mordecai had instructed her that she should not make it known. [11] Mordecai walked every day in front of the court of the women's house, to find out how Esther was doing, and what would become of her. [12] Each young woman's turn came to go in to King Ahasuerus after her purification for twelve months (for so were the days of their purification accomplished, six months with oil of myrrh, and six months with sweet fragrances and with preparations for beautifying women). [13] The young woman then came to the king like this: whatever she desired was given her to go with her out of the women's house to the king's house. [14] In the evening she went, and on the next day she returned into the second women's house, to the custody of Shaashgaz, the king's eunuch, who kept the concubines. She came in to the king no more, unless the king delighted in her, and she was called by name. [15] Now when the turn of Esther, the daughter of Abihail the uncle of Mordecai, who had taken her for his daughter, came to go in to the king, she required nothing but what Hegai the king's eunuch, the keeper of the women, advised. Esther obtained favor in the sight of all those who looked at her. [16] So Esther was taken to King Ahasuerus into his royal house in the tenth month, which is the month Tebeth, in the seventh year of his reign. [17] The king loved Esther more than all the women, and she obtained favor and kindness in his sight more than all the virgins; so that he set the royal crown on her head, and made her queen instead of Vashti. [18] Then the king made a great feast for all his princes and his servants, even Esther's feast; and he proclaimed a holiday in the provinces, and gave gifts according to the king's bounty. [19] When the virgins were gathered together the second time, Mordecai was sitting in the king's gate. [20] Esther had not yet made known her relatives nor her people, as Mordecai had commanded her; for Esther obeyed Mordecai, like she did when she was brought up by him. [21] In those days, while Mordecai was sitting in the king's gate, two of the king's eunuchs, Bigthan and Teresh, who were doorkeepers, were angry, and sought to lay hands on the King Ahasuerus. [22] This thing became known to Mordecai, who informed Esther the queen; and Esther informed the king in Mordecai's name. [23] When this matter was investigated, and it was found to be so, they were both hanged on a gallows; and it was written in the book of the chronicles in the king's presence.

## 3

[1] After these things King Ahasuerus promoted Haman the son of Hammedatha the Agagite, and advanced him, and set his seat above all the princes who were with him. [2] All the king's servants who were in the king's gate bowed down and paid homage to Haman, for the king had so commanded concerning him. But Mordecai didn't bow down or pay him homage. [3] Then the king's servants who were in the king's gate said to Mordecai, "Why do you disobey the king's commandment?" [4] Now it came to pass, when they spoke daily to him, and he didn't listen to them, that they told Haman, to see whether Mordecai's reason would stand; for he had told them that he was a Jew. [5] When Haman saw that Mordecai didn't bow down nor pay him homage, Haman was full of wrath. [6] But he scorned the thought of laying hands on Mordecai alone, for they had made known to him Mordecai's people. Therefore Haman sought to destroy all the Jews who were throughout the whole kingdom of Ahasuerus, even Mordecai's people. [7] In the first month, which is the month Nisan, in the twelfth year of King Ahasuerus, they cast Pur, that is, the lot, before Haman from day to day, and from month to month, and chose the twelfth month, which is the month Adar. [8] Haman said to King Ahasuerus, "There is a certain people scattered abroad and dispersed among the peoples in all the provinces of your kingdom, and their laws are different from other people's. They don't keep the king's laws. Therefore it is not for the king's profit to allow them to remain. [9] If it pleases the king, let it be written that they be destroyed; and I will

pay ten thousand talents[a] of silver into the hands of those who are in charge of the king's business, to bring it into the king's treasuries." [10] The king took his ring from his hand, and gave it to Haman the son of Hammedatha the Agagite, the Jews' enemy. [11] The king said to Haman, "The silver is given to you, the people also, to do with them as it seems good to you." [12] Then the king's scribes were called in on the first month, on the thirteenth day of the month; and all that Haman commanded was written to the king's local governors, and to the governors who were over every province, and to the princes of every people, to every province according to its writing, and to every people in their language. It was written in the name of King Ahasuerus, and it was sealed with the king's ring. [13] Letters were sent by couriers into all the king's provinces, to destroy, to kill, and to cause to perish, all Jews, both young and old, little children and women, in one day, even on the thirteenth day of the twelfth month, which is the month Adar, and to plunder their possessions. [14] A copy of the letter, that the decree should be given out in every province, was published to all the peoples, that they should be ready against that day. [15] The couriers went out in haste by the king's commandment, and the decree was given out in the citadel of Susa. The king and Haman sat down to drink; but the city of Susa was perplexed.

## 4

[1] Now when Mordecai found out all that was done, Mordecai tore his clothes and put on sackcloth with ashes, and went out into the middle of the city, and wailed loudly and bitterly. [2] He came even before the king's gate, for no one is allowed inside the king's gate clothed with sackcloth. [3] In every province, wherever the king's commandment and his decree came, there was great mourning among the Jews, and fasting, and weeping, and wailing; and many lay in sackcloth and ashes. [4] Esther's maidens and her eunuchs came and told her this, and the queen was exceedingly grieved. She sent clothing to Mordecai, to replace his sackcloth, but he didn't receive it. [5] Then Esther called for Hathach, one of the king's eunuchs, whom he had appointed to attend her, and commanded him to go to Mordecai, to find out what this was, and why it was. [6] So Hathach went out to Mordecai, to the city square which was before the king's gate. [7] Mordecai told him of all that had happened to him, and the exact sum of the money that Haman had promised to pay to the king's treasuries for the destruction of the Jews. [8] He also gave him the copy of the writing of the decree that was given out in Susa to destroy them, to show it to Esther, and to declare it to her, and to urge her to go in to the king to make supplication to him, and to make request before him for her people. [9] Hathach came and told Esther the words of Mordecai. [10] Then Esther spoke to Hathach, and gave him a message to Mordecai: [11] "All the king's servants and the people of the king's provinces know that whoever, whether man or woman, comes to the king into the inner court without being called, there is one law for him, that he be put to death, except those to whom the king might hold out the golden scepter, that he may live. I have not been called to come in to the king these thirty days." [12] They told Esther's words to Mordecai. [13] Then Mordecai asked them to return this answer to Esther: "Don't think to yourself that you will escape in the king's house any more than all the Jews. [14] For if you remain silent now, then relief and deliverance will come to the Jews from another place, but you and your father's house will perish. Who knows if you haven't come to the kingdom for such a time as this?" [15] Then Esther asked them to answer Mordecai, [16] "Go, gather together all the Jews who are present in Susa, and fast for me, and neither eat nor drink three days, night or day. I and my maidens will also fast the same way. Then I will go in to the king, which is against the law; and if I perish, I perish." [17] So Mordecai went his way, and did according to all that Esther had commanded him.

## 5

[1] Now on the third day, Esther put on her royal clothing and stood in the inner court of the king's house, next to the king's house. The king sat on his royal throne in the royal house, next to the entrance of the house. [2] When the king saw Esther the queen standing in the court, she obtained favor in his sight; and the king held out to Esther the golden scepter that was in his hand. So Esther came near and touched the top of the scepter. [3] Then the king asked her, "What would you like, queen Esther? What is your request? It shall be given you even to the half of the kingdom." [4] Esther said, "If it seems good to the king, let the king and Haman come today to the banquet that I have prepared for him." [5] Then the king said, "Bring Haman quickly, so that it may be done as Esther has said." So the king and Haman came to the banquet that Esther had prepared. [6] The king said to Esther at the banquet of wine, "What is your petition? It shall be granted you. What is your request? Even to the half of the kingdom it shall be performed." [7] Then Esther

[a] 3:9 A talent is about 30 kilograms or 66 pounds or 965 Troy ounces

answered and said, "My petition and my request is this. **8** If I have found favor in the sight of the king, and if it pleases the king to grant my petition and to perform my request, let the king and Haman come to the banquet that I will prepare for them, and I will do tomorrow as the king has said." **9** Then Haman went out that day joyful and glad of heart, but when Haman saw Mordecai in the king's gate, that he didn't stand up nor move for him, he was filled with wrath against Mordecai. **10** Nevertheless Haman restrained himself, and went home. There, he sent and called for his friends and Zeresh his wife. **11** Haman recounted to them the glory of his riches, the multitude of his children, all the things in which the king had promoted him, and how he had advanced him above the princes and servants of the king. **12** Haman also said, "Yes, Esther the queen let no man come in with the king to the banquet that she had prepared but myself; and tomorrow I am also invited by her together with the king. **13** Yet all this avails me nothing, so long as I see Mordecai the Jew sitting at the king's gate." **14** Then Zeresh his wife and all his friends said to him, "Let a gallows be made fifty cubits<sup>a</sup> high, and in the morning speak to the king about hanging Mordecai on it. Then go in merrily with the king to the banquet." This pleased Haman, so he had the gallows made.

## 6

**1** On that night, the king couldn't sleep. He commanded the book of records of the chronicles to be brought, and they were read to the king. **2** It was found written that Mordecai had told of Bigthana and Teresh, two of the king's eunuchs, who were doorkeepers, who had tried to lay hands on the King Ahasuerus. **3** The king said, "What honor and dignity has been given to Mordecai for this?" Then the king's servants who attended him said, "Nothing has been done for him." **4** The king said, "Who is in the court?" Now Haman had come into the outer court of the king's house, to speak to the king about hanging Mordecai on the gallows that he had prepared for him. **5** The king's servants said to him, "Behold,<sup>b</sup> Haman stands in the court." The king said, "Let him come in." **6** So Haman came in. The king said to him, "What shall be done to the man whom the king delights to honor?" Now Haman said in his heart, "Who would the king delight to honor more than myself?" **7** Haman said to the king, "For the man whom the king delights to honor, **8** let royal clothing be brought which the king uses to wear, and the horse that the king rides on, and on the head of which a royal crown is set. **9** Let the clothing and the horse be delivered to the hand of one of the king's most noble princes, that they may array the man whom the king delights to honor with them, and have him ride on horseback through the city square, and proclaim before him, 'Thus it shall be done to the man whom the king delights to honor!'" **10** Then the king said to Haman, "Hurry and take the clothing and the horse, as you have said, and do this for Mordecai the Jew, who sits at the king's gate. Let nothing fail of all that you have spoken." **11** Then Haman took the clothing and the horse, and arrayed Mordecai, and had him ride through the city square, and proclaimed before him, "Thus it shall be done to the man whom the king delights to honor!" **12** Mordecai came back to the king's gate, but Haman hurried to his house, mourning and having his head covered. **13** Haman recounted to Zeresh his wife and all his friends everything that had happened to him. Then his wise men and Zeresh his wife said to him, "If Mordecai, before whom you have begun to fall, is of Jewish descent, you will not prevail against him, but you will surely fall before him." **14** While they were yet talking with him, the king's eunuchs came, and hurried to bring Haman to the banquet that Esther had prepared.

## 7

**1** So the king and Haman came to banquet with Esther the queen. **2** The king said again to Esther on the second day at the banquet of wine, "What is your petition, queen Esther? It shall be granted you. What is your request? Even to the half of the kingdom it shall be performed." **3** Then Esther the queen answered, "If I have found favor in your sight, O king, and if it pleases the king, let my life be given me at my petition, and my people at my request. **4** For we are sold, I and my people, to be destroyed, to be slain, and to perish. But if we had been sold for male and female slaves, I would have held my peace, although the adversary could not have compensated for the king's loss." **5** Then King Ahasuerus said to Esther the queen, "Who is he, and where is he who dared presume in his heart to do so?" **6** Esther said, "An adversary and an enemy, even this wicked Haman!" Then Haman was afraid before the king and the queen. **7** The king arose in his wrath from the banquet of wine and went into the palace garden. Haman stood up to make request for his life to Esther the queen, for he saw that there was evil determined against him by the king. **8** Then the king returned out of the palace garden into the place of the banquet of wine; and Haman had fallen on the couch where Esther was. Then the king said, "Will he even assault the queen in front of me in the house?" As the word went out of the king's mouth, they covered Haman's face. **9** Then Harbonah, one of the eunuchs who were with the king, said, "Behold, the gallows fifty cubits<sup>c</sup> high, which Haman has made for Mordecai, who spoke good for the king, is standing at Haman's house." The king said, "Hang him on it!" **10** So they hanged Haman on the gallows that he had prepared for Mordecai. Then the king's wrath was pacified.

## 8

**1** On that day, King Ahasuerus gave the house of Haman, the Jews' enemy, to Esther the queen. Mordecai came before the king; for Esther had told what he was to her. **2** The king took off his ring, which he had taken from Haman, and gave it to Mordecai. Esther set Mordecai over the house of Haman. **3** Esther spoke yet again before the king, and fell down at his feet and begged him with tears to put away the mischief of Haman the Agagite, and his plan that he had planned against the Jews. **4** Then the king held out to Esther the golden scepter. So Esther arose, and stood before the king. **5** She said, "If it pleases the king, and if I have found favor in his sight, and the thing seems right to the king, and I am pleasing in his eyes, let it be written to reverse the letters devised by Haman, the son of Hammedatha the Agagite, which he wrote to destroy the Jews who are in all the king's provinces. **6** For how can I endure to see the evil that would come to my people? How can I endure to see the destruction of my relatives?" **7** Then King Ahasuerus said to Esther the queen and to Mordecai the Jew, "See, I have given Esther the house of Haman, and they have hanged him on the gallows because he laid his hand on the Jews. **8** Write also to the Jews as it pleases you, in the king's name, and seal it with the king's ring; for the writing which is written in the king's name, and sealed with the king's ring, may not be reversed by any man." **9** Then the king's scribes were called at that time, in the third month, which is the month Sivan, on the twenty-third day of the month; and it was written according to all that Mordecai commanded to the Jews, and to the local governors, and the governors and princes of the provinces which are from India to Ethiopia, one hundred twenty-seven provinces, to every province according to its writing, and to every people in their language, and to the Jews in their writing, and in their language. **10** He wrote in the name of King Ahasuerus, and sealed it with the king's ring, and sent letters by courier on horseback, riding on royal horses that were bred from swift steeds. **11** In those letters, the king granted the Jews who were in every city to gather themselves together and to defend their lives—to destroy, to kill, and to cause to perish all the power of the people and province that would assault them, their little ones and women, and to plunder their possessions, **12** on one day in all the provinces of King Ahasuerus, on the thirteenth day of the twelfth month, which is the month Adar. **13** A copy of the letter, that the decree should be given out in every province, was published to all the peoples, that the Jews should be ready for that day to avenge themselves on their enemies. **14** So the couriers who rode on royal horses went out, hastened and pressed on by the king's commandment. The decree was given out in the citadel of Susa. **15** Mordecai went out of the presence of the king in royal clothing of blue and white, and with a great crown of gold, and with a robe of fine linen and purple; and the city of Susa shouted and was glad. **16** The Jews had light, gladness, joy, and honor. **17** In every province and in every city, wherever the king's commandment and his decree came, the Jews had gladness, joy, a feast and a holiday. Many from among the peoples of the land became Jews, for the fear of the Jews had fallen on them.

## 9

**1** Now in the twelfth month, which is the month Adar, on the thirteenth day of the month, when the king's commandment and his decree came near to be put in execution, on the day that the enemies of the Jews hoped to conquer them, (but it turned out that the opposite happened, that the Jews conquered those who hated them), **2** the Jews gathered themselves together in their cities throughout all the provinces of the King Ahasuerus, to lay hands on those who wanted to harm them. No one could withstand them, because the fear of them had fallen on all the people. **3** All the princes of the provinces, the local governors, the governors, and those who did the king's business helped the Jews, because the fear of Mordecai had fallen on them. **4** For Mordecai was great in the king's house, and his fame went out throughout all the provinces, for the man Mordecai grew greater and greater. **5** The Jews struck all their enemies with the stroke of the sword, and with slaughter and destruction, and did what they wanted to those who hated them. **6** In the citadel of Susa, the Jews killed and destroyed five hundred men.

<sup>a</sup> *5:14* A cubit is the length from the tip of the middle finger to the elbow on a man's arm, or about 18 inches or 46 centimeters.

<sup>b</sup> *6:5* "Behold", from "הִנֵּה", means look at, take notice, observe, see, or gaze at. It is often used as an interjection.

<sup>c</sup> *7:9* A cubit is the length from the tip of the middle finger to the elbow on a man's arm, or about 18 inches or 46 centimeters.

[7] They killed Parshandatha, Dalphon, Aspatha, [8] Poratha, Adalia, Aridatha, [9] Parmashta, Arisai, Aridai, and Vaizatha, [10] the ten sons of Haman the son of Hammedatha, the Jews' enemy, but they didn't lay their hand on the plunder. [11] On that day, the number of those who were slain in the citadel of Susa was brought before the king. [12] The king said to Esther the queen, "The Jews have slain and destroyed five hundred men in the citadel of Susa, including the ten sons of Haman; what then have they done in the rest of the king's provinces! Now what is your petition? It shall be granted you. What is your further request? It shall be done." [13] Then Esther said, "If it pleases the king, let it be granted to the Jews who are in Susa to do tomorrow also according to today's decree, and let Haman's ten sons be hanged on the gallows." [14] The king commanded this to be done. A decree was given out in Susa; and they hanged Haman's ten sons. [15] The Jews who were in Susa gathered themselves together on the fourteenth day also of the month Adar, and killed three hundred men in Susa; but they didn't lay their hand on the plunder. [16] The other Jews who were in the king's provinces gathered themselves together, defended their lives, had rest from their enemies, and killed seventy-five thousand of those who hated them; but they didn't lay their hand on the plunder. [17] This was done on the thirteenth day of the month Adar; and on the fourteenth day of that month they rested and made it a day of feasting and gladness. [18] But the Jews who were in Susa assembled together on the thirteenth and on the fourteenth days of the month; and on the fifteenth day of that month, they rested, and made it a day of feasting and gladness. [19] Therefore the Jews of the villages, who live in the unwalled towns, make the fourteenth day of the month Adar a day of gladness and feasting, a holiday, and a day of sending presents of food to one another. [20] Mordecai wrote these things, and sent letters to all the Jews who were in all the provinces of the King Ahasuerus, both near and far, [21] to enjoin them that they should keep the fourteenth and fifteenth days of the month Adar yearly, [22] as the days in which the Jews had rest from their enemies, and the month which was turned to them from sorrow to gladness, and from mourning into a holiday; that they should make them days of feasting and gladness, and of sending presents of food to one another, and gifts to the needy. [23] The Jews accepted the custom that they had begun, as Mordecai had written to them, [24] because Haman the son of Hammedatha, the Agagite, the enemy of all the Jews, had plotted against the Jews to destroy them, and had cast "Pur", that is the lot, to consume them and to destroy them; [25] but when this became known to the king, he commanded by letters that his wicked plan, which he had planned against the Jews, should return on his own head, and that he and his sons should be hanged on the gallows. [26] Therefore they called these days "Purim",[a] from the word "Pur." Therefore because of all the words of this letter, and of that which they had seen concerning this matter, and that which had come to them, [27] the Jews established and imposed on themselves, on their descendants, and on all those who joined themselves to them, so that it should not fail that they would keep these two days according to what was written and according to its appointed time every year; [28] and that these days should be remembered and kept throughout every generation, every family, every province, and every city; and that these days of Purim should not fail from among the Jews, nor their memory perish from their offspring.[b] [29] Then Esther the queen, the daughter of Abihail, and Mordecai the Jew wrote with all authority to confirm this second letter of Purim. [30] He sent letters to all the Jews in the hundred twenty-seven provinces of the kingdom of Ahasuerus with words of peace and truth, [31] to confirm these days of Purim in their appointed times, as Mordecai the Jew and Esther the queen had decreed, and as they had imposed upon themselves and their descendants in the matter of the fastings and their mourning. [32] The commandment of Esther confirmed these matters of Purim; and it was written in the book.

## 10

[1] King Ahasuerus laid a tribute on the land and on the islands of the sea. [2] Aren't all the acts of his power and of his might, and the full account of the greatness of Mordecai, to which the king advanced him, written in the book of the chronicles of the kings of Media and Persia? [3] For Mordecai the Jew was next to King Ahasuerus, and great among the Jews and accepted by the multitude of his brothers, seeking the good of his people and speaking peace to all his descendants.

## Additions to Esther, translated from the Greek Septuagint

The book of Esther in the Greek Septuagint contains 5 additions that the traditional Hebrew text doesn't have. These additions are recognized as Deuterocanonical Scripture by the Roman Catholic, Greek Orthodox, and Russian Orthodox Churches. Those additions are enclosed in [square brackets]. Because the additions by themselves make little sense without the broader context of the book, we present here a translation of the whole book of Esther from the Greek. We have chosen not to distract the reader with confusing out-of-order chapter numbers that would result from using the KJV versification, but rather merge these **5** additions as extensions at the beginning of **1:1** and after **3:13,4:17,8:12**, and **10:3**. This makes some verses (**1:1,5:1**, and **8:12**) really long, but it also makes the verses line up with the same verse numbers in Esther as translated from the traditional Hebrew text. Some of the proper names in this book have been changed to the more familiar Hebrew form instead of the direct transliteration from the Greek.

## 1

[1][In the second year of the reign of Ahasuerus the great king, on the first day of Nisan, Mordecai the son of Jair, the son of Shimei, the son of Kish, of the tribe of Benjamin, a Jew dwelling in the city Susa, a great man, serving in the king's palace, saw a vision. Now he was one of the captives whom Nebuchadnezzar king of Babylon had carried captive from Jerusalem with Jeconiah the king of Judea. This was his dream: Behold, voices and a noise, thunders and earthquake, tumult upon the earth. And, behold, two great serpents came out, both ready for conflict. A great voice came from them. Every nation was prepared for battle by their voice, even to fight against the nation of the just. Behold, a day of darkness and blackness, suffering and anguish, affection and tumult upon the earth. And all the righteous nation was troubled, fearing their own afflictions. They prepared to die, and cried to God. Something like a great river from a little spring with much water, came from their cry. Light and the sun arose, and the lowly were exalted, and devoured the honorable. Mordecai, who had seen this vision and what God desired to do, having arisen, kept it in his heart, and desired by all means to interpret it, even until night. Mordecai rested quietly in the palace with Gabatha and Tharrha the king's two chamberlains, eunuchs who guarded the palace. He heard their conversation and searched out their plans. He learned that they were preparing to lay hands on King Ahasuerus; and he informed the king concerning them. The king examined the two chamberlains. They confessed, and were led away and executed. The king wrote these things for a record. Mordecai also wrote concerning these matters. The king commanded Mordecai to serve in the palace, and gave gifts for this service. But Haman the son of Hammedatha the Bougean was honored in the sight of the king, and he endeavored to harm Mordecai and his people, because of the king's two chamberlains.][c] And it came to pass after these things[d] in the days of Ahasuerus, —(this Ahasuerus ruled over one hundred twenty-seven provinces from India)— [2] in those days, when King Ahasuerus was on the throne in the city of Susa, [3] in the third year of his reign, he made a feast for his friends, for people from the rest of the nations, for the nobles of the Persians and Medes, and for the chief of the local governors. [4] After this—after he had shown them the wealth of his kingdom and the abundant glory of his wealth during one hundred eighty days— [5] when the days of the wedding feast were completed, the king made a banquet lasting six days for the people of the nations who were present in the city, in the court of the king's house, [6] which was adorned with fine linen and flax on cords of fine linen and purple, fastened to golden and silver studs on pillars of white marble and stone. There were golden and silver couches on a pavement of emerald stone, and of mother-of-pearl, and of white marble, with transparent coverings variously flowered, having roses arranged around it. [7] There were gold and silver cups, and a small cup of carbuncle set out, of the value of thirty thousand talents, with abundant and sweet wine, which the king himself drank. [8] This banquet was not according to the appointed law, but as the king desired to have it. He charged the stewards to perform his will and that of the company. [9] Also Vashti the queen made a banquet for the women in the palace where King Ahasuerus lived. [10] Now on the seventh day, the king, being merry, told Haman, Bazan, Tharrha, Baraze, Zatholtha, Abataza, and Tharaba, the seven chamberlains, servants of King Ahasuerus, [11] to bring in the queen to him, to[e] enthrone her, and crown her with the diadem, and to show her to the princes, and her beauty to the nations, for she was beautiful. [12] But queen Vashti refused to come with the chamberlains; so the king was grieved and angered. [13] And he said to his friends, "This is what Vashti said. Therefore pronounce your legal judgment on this case." [14] So Arkesaeus, Sarsathaeus, and Malisear, the princes of the Persians and Medes, who were near the king, who sat chief in rank by the king, drew near to him, [15] and reported to him according to the laws what it was proper to do to queen Vashti, because she had not done the

---

[a] *9:26* Purim is the Hebrew plural for pur, which means lot.
[b] *9:28* or, seed

[c] *1:1* **Note:** In the **Hebrew** and some copies of LXX, Esther begins here.

[d] *1:1* **Greek** words.
[e] *1:11* **Greek** to make her queen.

things commanded by the king through the chamberlains. ¹⁶ And Memucan said to the king and to the princes, "Queen Vashti has not wronged the king only, but also all the king's rulers and princes; ¹⁷ for he has told them the words of the queen, and how sheᵃ disobeyed the king. As she then refused to obey King Ahasuerus, ¹⁸ so this day the other wives of the chiefs of the Persians and Medes, having heard what she said to the king, will dare in the same way to dishonor their husbands. ¹⁹ If then it seems good to the king, let him make a royal decree, and let it be written according to the laws of the Medes and Persians, and let him not alter it: 'Don't allow the queen to come in to him any more. Let the king give her royalty to a woman better than she.' ²⁰ Let the law of the king which he will have made be widely proclaimed in his kingdom. Then all the women will give honor to their husbands, from the poor even to the rich." ²¹ This advice pleased the king and the princes; and the king did as Memucan had said, ²² and sent into all his kingdom through the several provinces, according to their language, so that men might be feared in their own houses.

## 2

¹ After this, the king's anger was pacified, and he no more mentioned Vashti, bearing in mind what she had said, and how he had condemned her. ² Then the servants of the king said, "Let chaste, beautiful young virgins be sought for the king. ³ Let the king appoint local governors in all the provinces of his kingdom, and let them select beautiful, chaste young ladies and bring them to the city Susa, into the women's apartment. Let them be consigned to the king's chamberlain, the keeper of the women. Then let things for purification and other needs be given to them. ⁴ Let the woman who pleases the king be queen instead of Vashti." This thing pleased the king; and he did so. ⁵ Now there was a Jew in the city Susa, and his name was Mordecai, the son of Jairus, the son of Shimei, the son of Kish, of the tribe of Benjamin. ⁶ He had been brought as a prisoner from Jerusalem, whom Nebuchadnezzar king of Babylon had carried into captivity. ⁷ He had a foster child, daughter of Aminadab his father's brother. Her name was Esther. When her parents died, he brought her up to womanhood as his own. This lady was beautiful. ⁸ And because the king's ordinance was published, many ladies were gathered to the city of Susa under the hand of Hegai; and Esther was brought to Hegai, the keeper of the women. ⁹ The lady pleased him, and she found favor in his sight. He hurried to give her the things for purification, her portion, and the seven maidens appointed her out of the palace. He treated her and her maidens well in the women's apartment. ¹⁰ But Esther didn't reveal her family or her kindred, for Mordecai had charged her not to tell. ¹¹ But Mordecai used to walk every day by the women's court, to see what would become of Esther. ¹² Now this was the time for a virgin to go into the king, when she had completed twelve months; for so are the days of purification fulfilled, six months while they are anointing themselves with oil of myrrh, and six months with spices and women's purifications. ¹³ And then the lady goes in to the king. The officer that he commands to do so will bring her to come in with him from the women's apartment to the king's chamber. ¹⁴ She enters in the evening, and in the morning she departs to the second women's apartment, where Hegai the king's chamberlain is keeper of the women. She doesn't go in to the king again, unless she is called by name. ¹⁵ And when the time was fulfilled for Esther the daughter of Aminadab the brother of Mordecai's father to go in to the king, she neglected nothing which the chamberlain, the women's keeper, commanded; for Esther found grace in the sight of all who looked at her. ¹⁶ So Esther went in to King Ahasuerus in the twelfth month, which is Adar, in the seventh year of his reign. ¹⁷ The king loved Esther, and she found favor beyond all the other virgins. He put the queen's crown on her. ¹⁸ The king made a banquet for all his friends and great men for seven days, and he highly celebrated the marriage of Esther; and he granted a remission of taxes to those who were under his dominion. ¹⁹ Meanwhile, Mordecai served in the courtyard. ²⁰ Now Esther had not revealed her country, for so Mordecai commanded her, to fear God, and perform his commandments, as when she was with him. Esther didn't change her manner of life. ²¹ Two chamberlains of the king, the chiefs of the body-guard, were grieved, because Mordecai was promoted; and they sought to kill King Ahasuerus. ²² And the matter was discovered by Mordecai, and he made it known to Esther, and she declared to the king the matter of the conspiracy. ²³ And the king examined the two chamberlains and hanged them. Then the king gave orders to make a note for a memorial in the royal library of the goodwill shown by Mordecai, as a commendation.

## 3

¹ After this, King Ahasuerus highly honored Haman the son of Hammedatha, the Bugaean. He exalted him and set his seat above all his friends. ² All in the palace bowed down to him, for so the king had

given orders to do; but Mordecai didn't bow down to him. ³ And they in the king's palace said to Mordecai, "Mordecai, why do you transgress the commands of the king?" ⁴ They questioned him daily, but he didn't listen to them; so they reported to Haman that Mordecai resisted the commands of the king; and Mordecai had shown to them that he was a Jew. ⁵ When Haman understood that Mordecai didn't bow down to him, he was greatly enraged, ⁶ and plotted to utterly destroy all the Jews who were under the rule of Ahasuerus. ⁷ In the twelfth year of the reign of Ahasuerus, Haman made a decision by casting lots by day and month, to kill the race of Mordecai in one day. The lot fell on the fourteenth day of the month of Adar. ⁸ So he spoke to King Ahasuerus, saying, "There is a nation scattered among the nations in all your kingdom, and their laws differ from all the other nations. They disobey the king's laws. It is not expedient for the king to tolerate them. ⁹ If it seem good to the king, let him make a decree to destroy them, and I will remit into the king's treasury ten thousand talents of silver." ¹⁰ So the king took off his ring, and gave it into the hands of Haman to seal the decrees against the Jews. ¹¹ The king said to Haman, "Keep the silver, and treat the nation as you will." ¹² So the king's recorders were called in the first month, on the thirteenth day, and they wrote as Haman commanded to the captains and governors in every province, from India even to Ethiopia, to one hundred twenty-seven provinces; and to the rulers of the nations according to their languages, in the name of King Ahasuerus. ¹³ The message was sent by couriers throughout the kingdom of Ahasuerus, to utterly destroy the race of the Jews on the first day of the twelfth month, which is Adar, and to plunder their goods.ᵇ [The following is the copy of the letter. "From the great King Ahasuerus to the rulers and the governors under them of one hundred twenty-seven provinces, from India even to Ethiopia, who hold authority under him: "Ruling over many nations and having obtained dominion over the whole world, I was determined (not elated by the confidence of power, but ever conducting myself with great moderation and gentleness) to make the lives of my subjects continually tranquil, desiring both to maintain the kingdom quiet and orderly to its utmost limits, and to restore the peace desired by all men. When I had asked my counselors how this should be brought to pass, Haman, who excels in soundness of judgment among us, and has been manifestly well inclined without wavering and with unshaken fidelity, and had obtained the second post in the kingdom, informed us that a certain ill-disposed people is scattered among all the tribes throughout the world, opposed in their law to every other nation, and continually neglecting the commands of the king, so that the united government blamelessly administered by us is not quietly established. Having then conceived that this nation is continually set in opposition to every man, introducing as a change a foreign code of laws, and injuriously plotting to accomplish the worst of evils against our interests, and against the happy establishment of the monarchy, we instruct you in the letter written by Haman, who is set over the public affairs and is our second governor, to destroy them all utterly with their wives and children by the swords of the enemies, without pitying or sparing any, on the fourteenth day of the twelfth month Adar, of the present year; that the people aforetime and now ill-disposed to us having been violently consigned to death in one day, may hereafter secure to us continually a well constituted and quiet state of affairs."] ¹⁴ Copies of the letters were published in every province; and an order was given to all the nations to be ready for that day. ¹⁵ This business was hastened also in Susa. The king and Haman began to drink, but the city was confused.

## 4

¹ But Mordecai, having perceived what was done, tore his garments, put on sackcloth, and sprinkled dust upon himself. Having rushed forth through the open street of the city, he cried with a loud voice, "A nation that has done no wrong is going to be destroyed!" ² He came to the king's gate, and stood; for it was not lawful for him to enter into the palace wearing sackcloth and ashes. ³ And in every province where the letters were published, there was crying, lamentation, and great mourning on the part of the Jews. They wore sackcloth and ashes. ⁴ The queen's maids and chamberlains went in and told her; and when she had heard what was done, she was deeply troubled. She sent clothes to Mordecai to replace his sackcloth, but he refused. ⁵ So Esther called for her chamberlain Hathach, who waited upon her; and she sent to learn the truth from Mordecai. ⁷ Mordecai showed him what was done, and the promise which Haman had made the king of ten thousand talents to be paid into the treasury, that he might destroy the Jews. ⁸ And he gave him the copy of what was published in Susa concerning their destruction to show to Esther; and told him to charge her to go in and entreat the king, and to beg him for the people. "Remember, he said, the days of your humble condition, how ⁴ you were nursed by my hand;

---

ᵃ *1:17* ᴳʳᵉᵉᵏ contradicted.    ᵇ *3:13* ᴺᵒᵗᵉ: The part in brackets is not in ᴴᵉᵇʳᵉʷ because Haman, who holds the next place to the king, has spoken against us to cause our death. Call upon the Lord, and speak to the king concerning us, to deliver us from death." [9] So Hathach went in and told her all these words. [10] Esther said to Hathach, "Go to Mordecai, and say, [11]'All the nations of the empire know than any man or woman who goes in to the king into the inner court without being called, that person must die, unless the king stretches out his golden sceptre; then he shall live. I haven't been called to go into the king for thirty days.'" [12] So Hathach reported to Mordecai all the words of Esther. [13] Then Mordecai said to Hathach, "Go, and say to her, 'Esther, don't say to yourself that you alone will escape in the kingdom, more than all the other Jews. [14] For if you keep quiet on this occasion, help and protection will come to the Jews from another place; but you and your father's house will perish. Who knows if you have been made queen for this occasion?'" [15] And Esther sent the messenger who came to her to Mordecai, saying, [16]"Go and assemble the Jews that are in Susa, and all of you fast for me. Don't eat or drink for three days, night and day. My maidens and I will also fast. Then I will go in to the king contrary to the law, even if I must die." [17] So Mordecai went and did all that Esther commanded him.[a] [18][He prayed to the Lord, making mention of all the works of the Lord. [19] He said, "Lord[b] God, you are king ruling over all, for all things are in your power, and there is no one who can oppose you in your purpose to save Israel; [20] for you have made the heaven and the earth and every wonderful thing under heaven. [21] You are Lord of all, and there is no one who can resist you, Lord. [22] You know all things. You know, Lord, that it is not in insolence, nor arrogance, nor love of glory, that I have done this, to refuse to bow down to the arrogant Haman. [23] For I would gladly have kissed the soles of his feet for the safety of Israel. [24] But I have done this that I might not set the glory of man above the glory of God. I will not worship anyone except you, my Lord, and I will not do these things in arrogance. [25] And now, O Lord God, the King, the God of Abraham, spare your people, for our enemies are planning our destruction, and they have desired to destroy your ancient inheritance. [26] Do not overlook your people, whom you have redeemed for yourself out of the land of Egypt. [27] Listen to my prayer. Have mercy on your inheritance and turn our mourning into gladness, that we may live and sing praise to your name, O Lord. Don't utterly destroy the mouth of those who praise you, O Lord." [28] All Israel cried with all their might, for death was before their eyes. [29] And queen Esther took refuge in the Lord, being taken as it were in the agony of death. [30] Having taken off her glorious apparel, she put on garments of distress and mourning. Instead of grand perfumes she filled her head with ashes and dung. She greatly humbled her body, and she filled every place of her glad adorning with her tangled hair. [31] She implored the Lord God of Israel, and said, "O my Lord, you alone are our king. Help me. I am destitute, and have no helper but you, [32] for my danger is near at hand[c]. [33] I have heard from my birth in the tribe of my kindred that you, Lord, took Israel out of all the nations, and our fathers out of all their kindred for a perpetual inheritance, and have done for them all that you have said. [34] And now we have sinned before you, and you have delivered us into the hands of our enemies, [35] because we honored their gods. You are righteous, O Lord. [36] But now they have not been content with the bitterness of our slavery, but have laid their hands on the hands of their idols [37] to abolish the decree of your mouth, and utterly to destroy your inheritance, and to stop the mouth of those who praise you, and to extinguish the glory of your house and your altar, [38] and to open the mouth of the Gentiles to speak the[d] praises of vanities, and that a mortal king should be admired forever. [39] O Lord, don't surrender your sceptre to those who don't exist, and don't let them laugh at our fall, but turn their counsel against themselves, and make an example of him who has begun to injure us. [40] Remember us, O Lord! Manifest yourself in the time of our affliction. Encourage me, O King of gods, and ruler of all dominion! [41] Put harmonious speech into my mouth before the lion, and turn his heart to hate him who fights against us, to the utter destruction of those who agree with him. [42] But deliver us by your hand, and help me who am alone and have no one but you, O Lord. [43] You know all things, and know that I hate the glory of transgressors,[e] and that I abhor the bed of the uncircumcised and of every stranger. [44] You know my necessity, for I abhor the symbol of my proud station, which is upon my head in the days of my[f] splendor. I abhor it as a menstruous cloth, and I don't wear it in the days of my tranquility. [45] Your handmaid has not eaten at Haman's table, and I have not honored the banquet of the king, neither have I drunk wine of libations. [46] Neither has your handmaid rejoiced since the day of my promotion until now, except in you, O Lord God of Abraham. [47] O god, who has power over all, listen to the voice of the desperate, and deliver us from the hand of those who devise mischief. Deliver me from my fear.]

## 5

[1] [g] It came to pass on the third day, when she had ceased praying, that she took off her servant's dress and put on her glorious apparel. Being splendidly dressed and having called upon God the Overseer and Preserver of all things, she took her two maids, and she leaned upon one, as a delicate female, and the other followed bearing her train. She was blooming in the perfection of her beauty. Her face was cheerful and looked lovely, but her heart was filled with fear. Having passed through all the doors, she stood before the king. He was sitting on his royal throne. He had put on all his glorious apparel, covered all over with gold and precious stones, and was very terrifying. And having raised his face resplendent with glory, he looked with intense anger. The queen fell, and changed her color as she fainted. She bowed herself upon the head of the maid who went before her. But God changed the spirit of the king to gentleness, and in intense feeling, he sprang from off his throne, and took her into his arms, until she recovered. He comforted her with peaceful words, and said to her, "What is the matter, Esther? I am your relative. Cheer up! You shall not die, for our command is openly declared to you: 'Draw near.'" [2] And having raised the golden sceptre, he laid it upon her neck, and embraced her. He said, "Speak to me." So she said to him, "I saw you, my lord, as an angel of God, and my heart was troubled for fear of your glory; for you, my lord, are to be wondered at, and your face is full of grace." While she was speaking, she fainted and fell. Then the king was troubled, and all his servants comforted her. [3] The king said, "What do you desire, Esther? What is your request? Ask even to the half of my kingdom, and it shall be yours." [4] Esther said, "Today is a special day. So if it seems good to the king, let both him and Haman come to the feast which I will prepare this day." [5] The king said, "Hurry and bring Haman here, that we may do as Esther said." So they both came to the feast about which Esther had spoken. [6] At the banquet, the king said to Esther, "What is your request, queen Esther? You shall have all that you require." [7] She said, "My request and my petition is: [8] if I have found favor in the king's sight, let the king and Haman come again tomorrow to the feast which I shall prepare for them, and tomorrow I will do as I have done today." [9] So Haman went out from the king very glad and merry; but when Haman saw Mordecai the Jew in the court, he was greatly enraged. [10] Having gone into his own house, he called his friends, and his wife Zeresh. [11] He showed them his wealth and the glory with which the king had invested him, and how he had promoted him to be chief ruler in the kingdom. [12] Haman said, "The queen has called no one to the feast with the king but me, and I am invited tomorrow. [13] But these things don't please me while I see Mordecai the Jew in the court. [14] Then Zeresh his wife and his friends said to him, "Let a fifty cubit tall[h] gallows be made for you. In the morning you speak to the king, and let Mordecai be hanged on the gallows; but you go in to the feast with the king, and be merry." The saying pleased Haman, and the gallows was prepared.

## 6

[1] The Lord removed sleep from the king that night; so he told his servant to bring in the[i] books, the registers of daily events, to read to him. [2] And he found the[j] records written concerning Mordecai, how he had told the king about the king's two chamberlains, when they were keeping guard, and sought to lay hands on Ahasuerus. [3] The king said, "What honor or favor have we done for Mordecai?" The king's servants said, "You haven't done anything for him." [4] And while the king was enquiring about the kindness of Mordecai, behold, Haman was in the court. The king said, "Who is in the court? Now Haman had come in to speak to the king about hanging Mordecai on the gallows which he had prepared. [5] The king's servants said, "Behold, Haman stands in the court." And the king said, "Call him!" [6] The king said to Haman, "What should I do for the man whom I wish to honor?" Haman said within himself, "Whom would the king honor but myself?" [7] He said to the king, "As for the man whom the king wishes to honor, [8] let the king's servants bring the robe of fine linen which the king puts on, and the horse on which the king rides, [9] and let him give it to one of the king's noble friends, and let him dress the man whom the king loves. Let him mount him on the horse, and proclaim through the[k] streets of the city, saying, "This is what will be done for every man whom the king honors!" [10] Then the king said to Haman, "You have spoken well. Do so for Mordecai the Jew, who waits in the palace, and let not a word of what you have spoken be neglected!" [11] So Haman took the robe and the horse, dressed Mordecai, mounted him on the horse, and went through the streets of the city, proclaiming, "This is what will be done

---

[a] 4:17 Note: The part between brackets, i.e. to the end of chapter 5 is not in the Hebrew.
[b] 4:19 See 3 Kings 8.53. **Note.**

[c] 4:32 Greek in my hand.
[d] 4:38 Greek virtues.
[e] 4:43 Or, opinion.
[f] 4:44 Greek vision.

[g] 5:1 From the first verse to the third, the Greek widely differs from the Hebrew
[h] 5:14 Greek a tree cut.

[i] 6:1 Greek letters.
[j] 6:2 Greek letters.
[k] 6:9 Or, wide space.

for every man whom the king wishes to honor." [12] Then Mordecai returned to the palace; but Haman went home mourning, with his head covered. [13] Haman related the events that had happened to him to Zeresh his wife and to his friends. His friends and his wife said to him, "If Mordecai is of the race of the Jews, and you have begun to be humbled before him, you will assuredly fall; and you will not be able to withstand him, for the living God is with him." [14] While they were still speaking, the chamberlains arrived to rush Haman to the banquet which Esther had prepared.

## 7

[1] So the king and Haman went in to drink with the queen. [2] The king said to Esther at the banquet on the second day, "What is it, queen Esther? What is your request? What is your petition? It shall be done for you, up to half of my kingdom." [3] She answered and said, "If I have found favor in the sight of the king, let my life be granted as my petition, and my people as my request. [4] For both I and my people are sold for destruction, pillage, and genocide. If both we and our children were sold for male and female slaves, I would not have bothered you, for this[a] isn't worthy of the king's palace." [5] The king said, "Who has dared to do this thing?" [6] Esther said, "The enemy is Haman, this wicked man!" Then Haman was terrified in the presence of the king and the queen. [7] The king rose up from the banquet to go into the garden. Haman began to beg the queen for mercy, for he saw that he was in serious trouble. [8] The king returned from the garden; and Haman had fallen upon the couch, begging the queen for mercy. The king said, "Will you even assault my wife in my house?" And when Haman heard it, he changed countenance. [9] And Bugathan, one of the chamberlains, said to the king, "Behold, Haman has also prepared a gallows for Mordecai, who spoke concerning the king, and a fifty cubit high gallows has been set up on Haman's property." The king said, "Let him be[b] hanged on it!" [10] So Haman was hanged on the gallows that had been prepared for Mordecai. Then the king's wrath was abated.

## 8

[1] On that day, King Ahasuerus gave to Esther all that belonged to Haman the slanderer. The king called Mordecai, for Esther had told that he was related to her. [2] The king took the ring which he had taken away from Haman and gave it to Mordecai. Esther appointed Mordecai over all that had been Haman's. [3] She spoke yet again to the king, and fell at his feet, and implored him to undo Haman's mischief and all that he had done against the Jews. [4] Then the king extended the golden sceptre to Esther; and Esther arose to stand near the king. [5] Esther said, "If it seems good to you, and I have found favor in your sight, let an order be sent that the letters sent by Haman may be reversed—letters that were written for the destruction of the Jews who are in your kingdom. [6] For how could I see the affliction of my people, and how could I survive the destruction of my[c] kindred?" [7] Then the king said to Esther, "If I have given and freely granted you all that was Haman's, and hanged him on a gallows because he laid his hands upon the Jews, what more do you seek? [8] Write in my name whatever seems good to you, and seal it with my ring; for whatever is written at the command of the king, and sealed with my ring, cannot be countermanded." [9] So the scribes were called in the first month, which is Nisan, on the twenty-third day of the same year; and orders were written to the Jews, whatever the king had commanded to the[d] local governors and chiefs of the local governors, from India even to Ethiopia—one hundred twenty-seven local governors, according to the several provinces, in their own languages. [10] They were written by order of the king, sealed with his ring, and the letters were sent by the couriers. [11] In them, he charged them to use their own laws in every city, to help each other, and to treat their adversaries and those who attacked them as they pleased, [12] on one day in all the kingdom of Ahasuerus, on the thirteenth day of the twelfth month, which is Adar. [13] Let the copies be posted in conspicuous places throughout the kingdom. Let all the Jews be ready against this day, to fight against their enemies. The following is a copy of the letter containing orders: [e] [The great King Ahasuerus sends greetings to the rulers of provinces in one hundred twenty-seven local governance regions, from India to Ethiopia, even to those who are faithful to our interests. Many who have been frequently honored by the most abundant kindness of their[f] benefactors have conceived ambitious designs, and not only endeavor to hurt our subjects, but moreover, not being able to bear prosperity, they also endeavor to plot against their own benefactors. They not only would utterly abolish gratitude from among men, but also, elated by the boastings of men who are strangers to all that is good, they supposed that they would escape the sin-hating vengeance of the ever-seeing God. And oftentimes evil exhortation has

made partakers of the guilt of shedding innocent blood, and has involved in irremediable calamities many of those who had been appointed to offices of authority, who had been entrusted with the management of their friends' affairs; while men, by the false sophistry of an evil disposition, have deceived the simple goodwill of the ruling powers. And it is possible to see this, not so much from more ancient traditional accounts, as it is immediately in your power to see it by examining what things have been wickedly[g] perpetrated by the baseness of men unworthily holding power. It is right to take heed with regard to the future, that we may maintain the government in undisturbed peace for all men, adopting needful changes, and ever judging those cases which come under our notice with truly equitable decisions. For whereas Haman, a Macedonian, the son of Hammedatha, in reality an alien from the blood of the Persians, and differing widely from our mild course of government, having been hospitably entertained by us, obtained so large a share of our universal kindness as to be called our father, and to continue the person next to the royal throne, reverenced of all; he however, overcome by[h] pride, endeavored to deprive us of our dominion, and our life;[i] having by various and subtle artifices demanded for destruction both Mordecai our deliverer and perpetual benefactor, and Esther the blameless consort of our kingdom, along with their whole nation. For by these methods he thought, having surprised us in a defenseless state, to transfer the dominion of the Persians to the Macedonians. But we find that the Jews, who have been consigned to destruction by the[j] most abominable of men, are not malefactors, but living according to the most just laws, and being the sons of the living God, the most high and[k] mighty, who maintains the kingdom, to us as well as to our forefathers, in the most excellent order. You will therefore do well in refusing to obey the letter sent by Haman the son of Hammedatha, because he who has done these things has been hanged with his whole family at the gates of Susa, Almighty God having swiftly returned to him a worthy punishment. We enjoin you then, having openly published a copy of this letter in every place, to give the Jews permission to use their own lawful customs and to strengthen them, that on the thirteenth of the twelfth month Adar, on the self-same day, they may defend themselves against those who attack them in a time of affliction. For in the place of the destruction of the chosen race, Almighty God has granted them this time of gladness. Therefore you also, among your notable feasts, must keep a distinct day with all festivity, that both now and hereafter it may be a day of deliverance to us and who are well disposed toward the Persians, but to those that plotted against us a memorial of destruction. And every city and province collectively, which shall not do accordingly, shall be consumed with vengeance by spear and fire. It shall be made not only inaccessible to men, but most hateful to wild beasts and birds forever.] Let the copies be posted in conspicuous places throughout the kingdom and let all the Jews be ready against this day, to fight against their enemies. [14] So the horsemen went forth with haste to perform the king's commands. The ordinance was also published in Susa. [15] Mordecai went out robed in royal apparel, wearing a golden crown and a diadem of fine purple linen. The people in Susa saw it and rejoiced. [16] The Jews had light and gladness [17] in every city and province where the ordinance was published. Wherever the proclamation took place, the Jews had joy and gladness, feasting and mirth. Many of the Gentiles were circumcised and became Jews for fear of the Jews.

## 9

[1] Now in the twelfth month, on the thirteenth day of the month, which is Adar, the letters written by the king arrived. [2] In that day, the adversaries of the Jews perished; for no one resisted, through fear of them. [3] For the chiefs of the local governors, and the princes and the royal scribes, honored the Jews; for the fear of Mordecai was upon them. [4] For the order of the king was in force, that he should be celebrated in all the kingdom. [6] In the city Susa the Jews killed five hundred men, [7] including Pharsannes, Delphon, Phasga, [8] Pharadatha, Barea, Sarbaca, [9] Marmasima, Ruphaeus, Arsaeus, and Zabuthaeus, [10] the ten sons of Haman the son of Hammedatha the Bugaean, the enemy of the Jews; and they plundered their property on the same day. [11] The number of those who perished in Susa was reported to the king. [12] Then the king said to Esther, "The Jews have slain five hundred men in the city Susa. What do you think they have done in the rest of the country? What more do you ask, that it may be done for you?" [13] Esther said to the king, "Let it be granted to the Jews to do the same to them tomorrow. Also, hang the bodies of the ten sons of Haman." [14] He permitted it to be done; and he gave up to the Jews of the city the bodies of the sons of Haman to hang. [15] The Jews assembled in Susa on the

---

[a] 7:4 see Hebrew: slanderer
[b] 7:9 Or, impaled.
[c] 8:6 Greek country.
[d] 8:9 Greek stewards.

[e] 8:13 the passages in brackets are not in the Hebrew.
[f] 8:13 perhaps rulers, see Luke 22.25.

[g] 8:13 Greek contrived.
[h] 8:13 Greek not having borne.
[i] 8:13 Greek spirit.
[j] 8:13 Greek thrice guilty.

[k] 8:13 Greek greatest.

fourteenth day of Adar and killed three hundred men, but plundered no property. ¹⁶ The rest of the Jews who were in the kingdom assembled, and helped one another, and obtained rest from their enemies; for they destroyed fifteen thousand of them on the thirteenth day of Adar, but took no spoil. ¹⁷ They rested on the fourteenth of the same month, and kept it as a day of rest with joy and gladness. ¹⁸ The Jews in the city of Susa assembled also on the fourteenth day and rested; and they also observed the fifteenth with joy and gladness. ¹⁹ On this account then, the Jews dispersed in every foreign land keep the fourteenth of Adar as aᵃ holy day with joy, each sending gifts of food to his neighbor. ²⁰ Mordecai wrote these things in a book and sent them to the Jews, as many as were in the kingdom of Ahasuerus, both those who were near and those who were far away, ²¹ to establish these as joyful days and to keep the fourteenth and fifteenth of Adar; ²² for on these days the Jews obtained rest from their enemies; and in that month, which was Adar, in which a change was made for them from mourning to joy, and from sorrow to a holiday, to spend the whole of it in good days ofᵇ feasting and gladness, sending portions to their friends and to the poor. ²³ And the Jews consented to this as Mordecai wrote to them, ²⁴ showing how Haman the son of Hammedatha the Macedonian fought against them, how he made a decree and castᶜ lots to destroy them utterly; ²⁵ also how he went in to the king, telling him to hang Mordecai; but all the calamities he tried to bring upon the Jews came upon himself, and he was hanged, along with his children. ²⁶ Therefore these days were called Purim, because of the lots (for in their language they are called Purim) because of the words of this letter, and because of all they suffered on this account, and all that happened to them. ²⁷ Mordecai established it, and the Jews took upon themselves, upon their offspring, and upon those who were joined to them to observe it, neither would they on any account behave differently; but these days were to be a memorial kept in every generation, city, family, and province. ²⁸ These days of Purim shall be kept forever, and their memorial shall not fail in any generation. ²⁹ Queen Esther the daughter of Aminadab and Mordecai the Jew wrote all that they had done, and gave the confirmation of the letter about Purim. ³¹ Mordecai and Esther the queen established this decision on their own, pledging their own well-being to their plan. ³² And Esther established it by a command forever, and it was written for a memorial.

## 10

¹ The king levied a tax upon his kingdom both by land and sea. ² As for his strength and valour, and the wealth and glory of his kingdom, behold, they are written in the book of the Persians and Medes for a memorial. ³ Mordecaiᵈ was viceroy to King Ahasuerus, and was a great man in the kingdom, honored by the Jews, and lived his life loved by all his nation.ᵉ ⁴[Mordecai said, "These things have come from God. ⁵ For I remember the dream which I had concerning these matters; for not one detail of them has failed. ⁶ There was the little spring which became a river, and there was light, and the sun and much water. The river is Esther, whom the king married and made queen. ⁷ The two serpents are Haman and me. ⁸ The nations are those which combined to destroy the name of the Jews. ⁹ But as for my nation, this is Israel, even those who cried to God and were delivered; for the Lord delivered his people. The Lord rescued us out of all these calamities; and God worked such signs and great wonders as have not been done among the nations. ¹⁰ Therefore he ordained two lots. One for the people of God, and one for all the other nations. ¹¹ And these two lots came for an appointed season, and for a day of judgment, before God, and for all the nations. ¹² God remembered his people and vindicated his inheritance. ¹³ They shall observe these days in the month Adar, on the fourteenth and on the fifteenth day of the month, with an assembly, joy, and gladness before God, throughout the generations forever among his people Israel. ¹⁴ In the fourth year of the reign of Ptolemeus and Cleopatra, Dositheus, who said he was a priest and Levite, and Ptolemeus his son brought this letter of Purim, which they said was authentic, and that Lysimachus the son of Ptolemeus, who was in Jerusalem, had interpreted.]

## The Book of Meqabyan I
This are the thing Meqabyan spoke on the Mo`abans and Miedonans kingdoms.

### 1

¹ There were one man whose name are called Tseerutsaydan and who love sin ~ him would boast in him horses abundance and him troops firmness beneath him authority. ² Him had many priests who serve him idols whom him worship and to whom him bow and sacrifice by night and by daylight. ³ But in him heart dullness it would seem to him that

them give him firmness and Power. ⁴ and in him heart it would seem to him that them give him authority in all him Rule. ⁵ and again in formation time it would seem to him that them give him all the desired authority also. ⁶ and him would sacrifice to them day and night. ⁷ Him appointed priests who serve him idols. ⁸ While them ate from that defouled sacrifice - them would tell him pretendin that the idols eat night and day. ⁹ Again them would make other persons diligent like unto them - that them might sacrifice and eat. and again them would make other persons diligent that them might sacrifice - and sacrifice like unto them. ¹⁰ But him would trust in him idols that don't profit nor benefit. ¹¹ By him timeframe bein small - and in him heart dullness - it would seem to him that them Created him - that them feed him and that them crown him ~ it would seem to him that them Created him - to Satan have deafened him reasonin lest him know him Creator Who Created him bringin from not livin toward livin - or lest him with him kindreds know him Creator Who Created him bringin from not livin toward livin - that them might go toward *Gehannem* of fire forever - it bein judged on them with him who call them gods without them bein gods. ¹² As them aren't never well whenever - it are due that him might call them dead ones. ¹³ As Satan authority that mislead them will lodge in that idol image - and as him will tell them them reasonin accord - and as him will reveal to them like unto them loved - him will judge on the idols wherein them believed and wherein 'Adam childran trust - whose reasonin were like unto ashes. ¹⁴ and them will marvel on the time them sight up that him fulfilled what them thought to them - and them will do him accord to him reachin up til them sacrifice them daughter childran and them male childran birthed from them nature - up til them spill them daughter childran and male childran blood that were clean. ¹⁵ Them didn't sadden them - to Satan have savoured him sacrifice to them to fulfill them evil accord - that him might lower them toward *Gehannem* like unto him - where there are no exits up til Eternity - where him will raceive tribulation. ¹⁶ But that Tseerutsaydan were arrogant ~ him had fifty idols worked in males pattern and twenty worked in daughters pattern. ¹⁷ and him would boast in those idols that have no benefit ~ him would totally glorify them while him sacrificed sacrifice mornin and evenin. ¹⁸ and him would command persons that them might sacrifice to the idols - and him would eat from that defouled sacrifice - and him would command other persons that them might eat from the sacrifice ~ him would especially provoke to evil. ¹⁹ Him had five houses worked to him beaten worked idols that were iron and brass and lead. ²⁰ and him ornamanted them in silver and gold ~ him veiled curtains around the houses to them and planted a tent to them. ²¹ Him appointed keepers to them there ~ him would Continually sacrifice forty to him idols - ten fattened oxen - ten sterile cows - ten fattened sheep ewes - ten barren goats - with birds that have wings. ²² But it would seem to him that him idols ate ~ him would present to them fifty *feeqen* of grapes and fifty dishes of wheat kneaded with oil. ²³ and him told him priests: - "Take and give them ~ make mi creators eat what mi slaughtered to them - and make them drink the grape mi presented to them ~ as to if it aren't enough to them - mi will add to them." ²⁴ and him would command all that them might eat and drink from that defouled sacrifice. ²⁵ But in him evil malice him would send him troops who visit in all the kingdom - that as it were there were one who neither sacrifice nor bow - them might separate and know and bring him - and might punish him by fire and by sword before him - that them might plunder him money and might burn him house in fire - that them might destroy all him money him had on him. ²⁶ "To them are kind and great ones - and to them have Created we in them charity - and mi will show punishmant and tribulation to him unless him worshipped mi creators and sacrificed sacrifice to mi creators. ²⁷ and mi will show him punishmant and tribulation - to them have Created Earth and Heaven and the sea that were wide and moon and Sun and stars and rains and winds and all that live in this world to be food and to be satiety to wi." ²⁸ But persons who worship them shall be punished in firm tribulation - and them won't be nice to them.

### 2

¹ There were one man birthed from the tribe of Binyam whose name are called Meqabees ² him had three childran who were handsome and totally warriors ~ them had bein iloved alongside all persons in that Midyam and Miedon country that are Tseerutsaydan Rule. ³ and like unto the king commanded them on the time him found them: - "Don't you bow to Tseerutsaydan creators? How about don't you sacrifice? ⁴ But if you refuse - we will seize and take you toward the king - and we will destroy all your money like unto the king commanded." ⁵ These youths who were handsome replied to him sayin "As to Him to Whom I bow - there are I Father Creator Who Created Earth and Heaven and what are within she - and the sea - moon and Sun and clouds and stars

ᵃ 9:19 Greek good day.
ᵇ 9:22 Greek weddings.
ᶜ 9:24 Greek lot.
ᵈ 10:3 Greek succeded to Or, came into the place of.
ᵉ 10:3 the passages in brackets are not in the Hebrew.

~ Him are the True Creator Whom I worship and in Whom I believe." [6] and these the king youths are four - and them servants who carry shield and spear are a hundred. [7] and on the time them loved that them might seize these hola ones - them escaped from them hands and there are none who touched them ~ as those youths are totally warriors in Power - them went seizin shields and them spears. [8] and there were from them one who strangle and kill panther - and at that time him would strangle it like unto a chicken. [9] and there were one from them who kill a lion with one rock or strikin at one time with a stick. [10] and there were one from them who kill a hundred persons - strikin in formation time with one sword - and them name and them hunt were thus ~ it were called in all Babilon and Mo`ab countries. [11] and them were warriors in Power - and them had a thing bein iloved and attractiveness. [12] and again them features attractiveness were wondrous - however because them worshipped JAH and because them didn't fear death - it are them reasonin attractiveness that surpass all. [13] and on the time them frightened the troops - there are none who could able to seize them - but them who were warriors escaped proceedin toward a lofty mountain. [14] and those troops returned toward the city and shut the fortress gate ~ them terrorized the people sayin - "Unless you brought those warriors the Meqabyans - we will burn your city in fire - and we will send toward the king and destroy your country." [15] and at that time the country persons - rich and poor ones and daughters and males - a child whose father and mother dead on him and old daughters - everyone proceeded and shouted together - and them straightened them necks toward the mountain and shouted toward them sayin - "Don't destroy I - and don't destroy I country on us." [16] At that time them wept together - and them feared - arisin from JAH. [17] Returnin them faces Eastward and streachin forth them hands them begged toward JAH together - "Lord - should I refuse these men who demolished Thy Command and Thy LAW? [18] Yet him believed in silver and gold and in the stone and wood that a person hands worked - but I don't love that I might hear that criminal word - who didn't believe Thy LAW" them said. [19] "When Thou are the Creator Who save and Who kill - him make him ras self like unto them Created him also ~ as to him - him are who spill a person blood and who eat a person flesh. [20] But I don't love that I might sight up that criminal face nor hear him word" them said. [21] "However if Thou commanded I - I will go toward him ~ because I believe in Thee-I - I will pass and give I bodies to death - and on the time him said 'Sacrifice to mi creators' - I won't hear that criminal word. [22] But I believed Thee-I - Lord Who examine kidneys and reasonin - I Fathers Creator - 'Abriham and Yis'haq and Ya`iqob who did Thy Accord and lived firmed up in Thy LAW. [23] Thou examine a person reasonin and help the sinner and the righteous one - and there be none hidden from Thee-I - and him who took refuge are revealed alongside Thee-I. [24] But I have no other Creator apart from Thee-I. [25] That I might give I bodies to death because Thy glorified Name - however be Power and Firmness and a Shelter to I in this Work that I are ruled to Thee-I. [26] and on the time 'Isra'iel entered toward Gibts country Thou heard Ya`iqob plea - and now glorified God - I beg Thee-I." [27] and on the time the two men whose features were quite handsome were sight up to them standin before them - on the time fire swords that frighten like unto lightnin alit and cut them necks and killed them - at that time them arose bein well like unto formerly. [28] Them features attractiveness became totally handsome and them shone more than Sun - and them became more handsome than formerly.

## 3

[1] Like unto you sight up before you these the Most I JAH slaves - 'Abya - Seela - Fentos who dead and arose - you have that you might arise likewise after you dead - and your faces shall shine like unto the Sun in the Kingdom of Heaven. [2] and them went with those men and raceived martyrdom there. [3] At that time them begged - them praised - and them bowed to JAH ~ death didn't frighten them and the king punishmant didn't frighten them. [4] and them went toward those youths and became like unto a sheep that have no evil - yet them didn't frighten them - and on the time them arrived toward them - them seized and beat them and bound and whipped them - and them delivered them toward the king and stood them before him. [5] and the king answered to them sayin - "How won't you stubborn ones sacrifice and bow to mi creators?" [6] Those bredren who were cleansed from sin - who were honoured and chosen and Feeling good - and who shine like unto a jewel whose value were wondrous - Seela and 'Abya and Fentos answered to him in one word. [7] Them told that king who were a plague - "As to I - I won't bow nor sacrifice to defouled idols that have no knowledge nor reasonin." [8] and again them told him - "I won't bow to idols that were silver and gold that a person hand worked - that were stone and wood - that have no reasonin nor soul nor knowledge - that don't benefit them friends nor harm them enemies." [9] and the king answered to them sayin - "Why do you do thus - and as them know who insult them and who wrong them - why do you insult the glorified creators?" [10] Them answered to him sayin - "As them are like unto a trifle alongside I - as to I - I will insult them and won't glorify them." [11] and the king answered to them sayin - "Mi will punish you like unto your Work evil measure ~ mi will destroy your features attractiveness with whippin and firm tribulation and fire. [12] and now tell mi whether you will give or won't give sacrifice to mi creators - as to if this didn't happen - mi will punish you by sword and by whippin." [13] Them answered to him sayin - "As to I - I won't sacrifice nor bow to defouled idols" - and the king commanded that them might beat them with a fat stick - and again that them might whip them with a whip - and after it - that them might splinter them up til them inner organs were sight up. [14] and after this them bound and made them while in jail house up til him counsel by money that punish and kill them. [15] Without niceness them took and bound them a firm imprisonmant in prison house - and them sat in prison house three nights and three daylights. [16] and after this third day the king commanded that a Proclamation speaker might turn and that counselors and nobles - country elders and officials - might be gathered. [17] and on the time the king Tseerutsaydan sat in square - him commanded that them might bring those honoured ones - Seela and 'Abya and Fentos ~ them stood before him bein wounded and bound. [18] and the king told them - "When you sat these three days - are there really the returnin that you returned - or are you in your former evil?" [19] and those honoured JAH Souljahs answered to him sayin - "As to that I were cruel - I won't agree that I might worship the idols filled of sin and evil that thou check up." [20] and that criminal vexed and commanded that them might stand them up in lofty place and might renew them wounds ~ them blood flowed on Earth. [21] and again him commanded that them might burn them with a torch lamp and might char them flesh - and him servants did like unto him commanded them - and those honoured men told him - "Thou who forgot JAH LAW - speak ~ I reward shall abound in the measure whereby thou multiply I punishmant." [22] and again him commanded that them might bring and send on them bears and tigers and lions that were evil beasts before them eat them food that might totally eat them flesh with them bones. [23] and him commanded persons who keep the beasts that them might send the beasts on them - and them did like unto him commanded them - and them bound those honoured martyrs feet - and again them maliciously beat and bound them with tent-stakes. [24] and those beasts were flung over them while them roared - and on the time them arrived toward the martyrs them hailed and bowed to them. [25] Them returned toward them keepers while them roared - and them frightened them keepers ~ them took them toward the square up til them delivered them toward before the king. [26] and them killed seventy five men from the criminals army there. [27] Many persons panicked - the one anguishin on the one in fear - up til the king quit him throne and fled - and them seized the beasts with difficulty and took them toward them lodgin. [28] Seela and 'Abya and Fentos two bredren came and released them from the imprisonmant them bound them and told them - "Come make I flee lest these skeptics and criminals find me. [29] and those martyrs answered them bredren sayin - "It aren't procedure that I might flee after I set up to testimony ~ as it were you had feared - go fleein." [30] and those them little bredren said - "I will stand with you before the king - and if you dead I will dead with you." [31] and after this the king were on him lordship hall balcany and sight up that these honoured men were released and that all the five bredren stood together ~ those chiefs who work and punish troops questioned that them were bredren and told the king - and the king vexed and shouted like unto a wilderness boar. [32] and up til the king counseled by money that punish all the five bredren - him commanded that them might seize and add them in prison house ~ them placed them in prison house bindin in firm imprisonmant without niceness with a hollow stalk. [33] and the king Tseerutsaydan said - "These youths who erred wearied mi ~ what should these men reasonin firm up? and them Work evil are like unto them Power firmness ~ if mi say - "Them will return" - them will make them reasonin evil. [34] and mi will bring the hardship on them like unto them Work evil measure - and mi will burn them flesh in fire that it might be charred ash - and on that mi will scattar them flesh ash like unto dust on mountains." [35] and after him spoke this him waited three days and commanded that them might bring those honoured men - and on the time those honoured men approached him commanded that them might burn a fire within the great pit oven - and that them might add within it a malice Work that flame the fire and whereby them boil a yat - the fat and soapberries - sea foam and resin and the sulfur. [36] and on the time fire flamed in the pit the messengers went toward the king when them said - "We did what thou commanded we - send the men who will be added." [37] and him commanded that them might receive and cast them in the fire pit - and the youths did like unto the king commanded them - and on the time those honoured men entered toward the fire them gave them souls to JAH. [38] and when the persons who cast them sight up - Angels received

and took them souls toward the Garden where Yis'haq and 'Abriham and Ya`iqob are - where Feeling good joy are found.

## 4

¹ and on the time that criminal sight up that them dead - him commanded that them might burn them flesh in fire up til it are ash and that them might scattar them in wind - but the fire couldn't able to burn the corpse hair from them corpses side - and them sent them forth from the pit. ² and again them flamed fire over them beginnin from mornin up til evenin ~ it didn't burn them ~ them said - "An now come make we cast them corpses seaward." ³ and them did like unto the king commanded them ~ them cast them on the sea ~ even if them cast them seaward addin great stones and iron hearthstones and a millstone whereby a donkey grind by turnin - there are no sinkin that the sea sank them ~ as JAH Spirit of Support have lodged in them - them floated on the sea yet them didn't sink ~ it failed him to destroy them by all the malice that were provoked on them. ⁴ "As this them death have made weary more than them Life - make mi cast them corpses to beasts that them might eat them - yet what will mi do?" him said. ⁵ and the youths did like unto him commanded them ~ vultures and beasts didn't touch them corpses ~ birds and vultures veiled them with them wings from burnin in Sun and the five martyrs corpses sat fourteen days. ⁶ and on the time them sight them up - them bodies shone up like unto Sun - and Angels incircled them corpses like unto light incircle the Tent. ⁷ Him counseled counsel ~ him lacked what him do - and after this him dug a grave and buried the five martyrs corpses. ⁸ and when that king who forgot JAH LAW had reclined on a bed at night the five martyrs were sight up to him standin before him at night vexin and seizin swords. ⁹ As it have seemed to him that them entered toward him house at night in crime - on the time him awoke from him slumber him feared and loved that him might flee from the bedchamber toward the hall - and as it have seemed to him that them kill him seemin that them committed crime on him - him feared and him knees trembled. ¹⁰ Because this thing him said - "Mi lords - what do you love? as to mi - what should mi do to you?" ¹¹ Them answered to him sayin - "Aren't I whom thou killed burnin in fire and I whom thou commanded that them might cast on the sea? As JAH have kept I bodies because I believed in Him - it failed thee to destroy I ~ as a person who believed in Him won't perish - make glory and praise due to JAH - and I also who believed in Him didn't shame in the tribulation. ¹² "As mi didn't know that a punishmant like unto this will find mi - what reward should mi give you because the stead wherefore mi did a evil thing on you? ¹³ and now separate to mi the reward mi give you - lest you take mi body in death and lest you lower mi body toward *See'ol* when mi are in Life. ¹⁴ As mi have wronged you - forgive mi mi sin - because it were your Father JAH LAW Niceness" him told them. ¹⁵ and those honoured martyrs answered to him sayin - "Because the stead wherefore thou did a evil thing on I - as to I - I won't pay thee a evil thing ~ as JAH are Who bring hardship on a soul - as to Him Who will pay thee hardship - there are JAH. ¹⁶ However I were sight up to the bein revealed that I were well to thy timeframe bein small and because thy reasonin deafness ~ as to it seemin to thee that thou killed I - thou prepared welfare to me. ¹⁷ But thy idols priests and thou will descend toward *Gehannem* where are no exits forever. ¹⁸ Woe to thy idols to whom thou bow havin quit bowin to JAH Who Created you when you were scorned like unto spit - and to you who worship them - and you don't know JAH Who Created you bringin from not livin toward livin ~ aren't you who are sight up today like unto smoke and tomorrow who perish?" ¹⁹ and the king answered to them sayin - "What will you command mi that mi might do to you all that you loved?" ²⁰ "It are to save thy ras self lest thou enter toward the *Gehannem* of fire - yet it aren't to save I ras selves who teach thee. ²¹ to your idols are silver and gold - stone and wood - that have no reasonin nor soul knowledge - that a person hand worked. ²² But them don't kill ~ them don't save ~ them don't benefit them friend ~ them don't harm them enemy ~ them don't downbase ~ them don't honour ~ them don't make wealthy ~ them don't impoverish ~ them mislead you by demons authority - who don't love that the one from persons might be saved - yet them don't uproot nor plant. ²³ Them especially don't love that the persons like unto you might be saved from death - you dull-hearted ones to whom them seem that them Created you - when you are who worked them. ²⁴ As Satans and demons authority have lodged in them - them shall return a thing to you like unto you loved - that it might drown you within the sea of *Gehannem*. ²⁵ But thou - quit this thy error and make this also be I reward because I dead stead - that I might benefit I souls worshippin I Creator JAH" them told him. ²⁶ But him were alarmed and would totally astony - and as all five have been sight up to him drawin them swords - him feared - and because this thing him bowed to them. ²⁷ "Hence mi knew that after dead ones who were dust dead them will really arise ~ as to mi - only a little had remained to mi to dead." ²⁸ After this them were hidden from before that king face ~ from that day onward that Tseerutsaydan

who are totally arrogant quit burnin them corpses. ²⁹ As them have misled them many eras - him would be Feeling good in him idols and him reasonin error - and him misled many persons like unto him up til them quit followin in Worship JAH Who Created them - yet it aren't only him who erred. ³⁰ and them would sacrifice them daughter childran and them male childran to demons - yet them work a seducin and disturbance that are them reasonin accord - that them father Satan taught them that him might make the seducin and disturbance that JAH don't love. ³¹ Them marry them mothers - and them abuse them aunts and them sistren ~ them abuse them bodies while them worked all that resemble this filthy Work ~ as Satan have firmed up those crooked persons reasonin - them said - "We won't return." ³² But that Tseerutsaydan - who don't know him Creator - were totally arrogant - and him would boast in him idols. ³³ If them say - "How will JAH give the Kingdom to the persons who don't know Him in LAW and in Worship?" - them will totally return toward Him in repentance ~ as Him test them thus - it are because this. ³⁴ But if them totally return in repentance Him would love them - and Him would keep them Kingdom - but if them refuse a fire will punish them in fire of *Gehannem* forever. ³⁵ But it would be due a king to fear him Creator JAH like unto him lordship fame - and it would be due a judge to be ruled to him Creator while him judged goodly judgemant like unto him Rule fame. ³⁶ and it would be due elders and chiefs and envoys and petty kings to be commanded to them Creator like unto him lordship abundance measure. ³⁷ As Him are Heaven and Earth Lord Who Created all the Creation - because there are no other Creator in Heavan nor Earth who impoverish and make rich - Him are Who honour and downbase.

## 5

¹ "The one warrior from the sixty warriors were proud ~ JAH made him body Beginnin from him foot up til him head to swell with one spoon of sulphur ~ him dead in one plague. ² and again Keeram who built a iron bed were proud arisin from him powerfulness abundance - and JAH hid him in death. ³ and again Nabukedenetsor were proud sayin - 'There are no other king without mi - and mi are Creator who make the Sun rise in this world' - and him said thus arisin from him arrogance abundance. ⁴ and JAH separated from persons and sent him toward a wilderness seven years - and him made him fortune with Heaven birds and wilderness beasts up til him knew that JAH were Who Created him. ⁵ and on the time him knew Him in worship - Him again returned him toward him kingdom ~ who are it who weren't of Earth - bein boldly proud on JAH Who Created him? ⁶ How about who are it demolished HIM LAW and Him Order and whom Earth didn't swallow? ⁷ and thou Tseerutsaydan love that thou might be proud on thy Creator - and again thou have that Him might destroy thee like unto them - and might lower thee toward a grave arisin from thy arrogance. ⁸ and again after them entered toward *See'ol* where are tooth grindin and mournin - that were darkness fulfillmant - thou have that Him might lower thee toward the deep pit *Gehannem* where are no exits forever. ⁹ As to thou - thou are a man who will dead and be demolished tomorrow like unto arrogant kings who were like unto thee - who quit this world livin. ¹⁰ As to I - I say - 'Thou are demolished ruins - but thou aren't JAH - to JAH are Who Created Earth and Heaven and thee.' ¹¹ Him downbase arrogant ones ~ Him honour them who were downbased ~ Him give firmness to persons who wearied. ¹² Him kill well ones ~ Him raise up the persons who were Earth - who dead buried in grave. ¹³ and Him send slaves forth free in Life from sin rulership. ¹⁴ O king Tseerutsaydan - why do thou boast in thy defouled idols who have no benefit? ¹⁵ But JAH Created Earth and Heaven and great seas ~ Him Created moon and Sun - and Him prepared eras. ¹⁶ Man graze toward him field - and him while when him plough up til it dusk - and Heaven stars live firmed up by Him Word. ¹⁷ and Him call all in Heaven ~ there are nothing done without JAH knowin it. ¹⁸ Him commanded Heaven Angels that them might serve Him and might praise Him glorified Name - and Angels are sent toward all persons who inherit Life. ¹⁹ Rufa'iel who were a servant were sent toward Thobeet - and him saved Thobya from death in Ragu'iel country. ²⁰ Hola Meeka'iel were sent toward Giediewon that him might draw him attention by money that him destroy 'Iloflee persons and him were sent toward the prophet Mussie on the time him made 'Isra'iel cross 'Eritra sea. ²¹ As only JAH have said him led them - there were no different idol with them. ²² and Him sent them forth toward crops on Earth. ²³ and Him fed them Him plantation grain ~ as Him have totally loved them - Him cherished them feedin the honey that firmed up like unto a rock. ²⁴ and that thou might totally worship Him kindreds by what are due - and that thou might do JAH Accord Who Created thee - Him crowned thee givin Authority on the four kingdoms. ²⁵ to Him have crowned thee makin loftier than all - and thy Creator totally crowned thee that thou might love JAH. ²⁶ and it are procedure that thou might love thy Creator JAH like unto Him loved thee - like unto Him trusted thee on all the people - and thou - do JAH Accord that thy era might abound in this world and that Him might

live with thee in Support. ²⁷ and do JAH Accord that Him might stand to thee bein a Guardian on thy enemies - and that Him might seat thee on thy throne - and that Him might hide thee in him Wing of Support. ²⁸ As to if thou don't know - JAH chose and crowned thee on 'Isra'iel like unto Him chose Sa'ol fron 'Isra'iel childran when him kept him father donkeys - and Him crowned him on him kindreds 'Isra'iel - and him sat with 'Isra'iel on him throne. ²⁹ and Him gave him a lofty fortune separatin from him kindreds ~ JAH crowned thee on Him kindreds ~ as to henceforth onward - check - keep Him kindreds. ³⁰ As JAH have Ipointed thee over them that thou might kill and might save - keep them in evil thing - them who work a goodly thing and them who work a evil thing on a goodly thing" him told him. ³¹ "An as JAH have Ipointed thee on all that thou might do Him Accord be it while thou whipped or while thou saved - pay them evil Work - them who work goodly Work and them who work goodly Work and evil Work. ³² to thou are a slave of JAH Who rule all in Heaven - and thou - do JAH Accord that Him might do thy accord to thee in all thou thought and in all thou begged while thou wheedled before Him. ³³ There are none who rule Him - but Him rule all. ³⁴ There are none who Ipoint Him - but Him Ipoint all. ³⁵ There are none who dismiss Him - but Him dismiss all. ³⁶ There are none who reproach Him - but Him reproach all. ³⁷ There are none who make Him diligent - but Him make all diligent ~ as Heaven and Earth rulership are to Him - there are none who escape from Him Authority all are revealed alongside Him - yet there are none hidden from Him Face. ³⁸ Him sight up all - but there are none who sight Him up ~ Him hear the person prayer who pray toward Him sayin 'Save I' - to Him have Created man in Him Pattern - and Him accept him plea. ³⁹. As Him are a King Who live up til the Eternity - Him feed all from Him unchangin Nature.

# 6

¹ As Him crown to true the kings who do Him Accord - the kings wrote a straight thing because Him. ² As them have done JAH Accord - Him shall shine up in Light that aren't examined Yis'haq and 'Abriham and Ya`iqob - Selomon and Daweet and Hiziqyas lodgins in the Garden where are all beautiful kings whose lodgin were Light. ³ Heaven Hall are what totally shone - yet Earth halls aren't like unto Heaven Hall ~ it floor - whose features are silver and gold and jewel features - are clean. ⁴ and it features that totally shine are unexamined by a person reasonin ~ Heaven Hall are what shine like unto jewels. ⁵ Like unto JAH knew - Who were a Nature Knower - the Heaven Hall that Him Created are what a person reasonin don't examine and what shine in total Light ~ it floor - that were worked in silver and gold - in jewels - in white silk and in blue silk - are clean. ⁶ It are quite totally beautiful like unto this. ⁷ Righteous ones who firmed up in religion and virtue are who shall inherit it in JAH Charity and to Pardon. ⁸ and there are welfare Water that flow from it - and it totally shine like unto Sun - and there are a Light tent within it - and it are incircled by grace perfume. ⁹ A Garden fruit that were beautiful and Iloved - whose features and taste were different - are around the house - and there are a oil and grape place there - and it are totally beautiful - and it fruit fragrance are sweet. ¹⁰ When a fleshly bloodly person enter toward it - him soul would have separated from him flesh from the Feeling good joy abundance that are in it arisin from it fragrance flavour. ¹¹ Beautiful kings who did JAH Accord shall be Feeling good there ~ them honour and them place are known in the Kingdom of Heaven that live firmed up forever - where welfare are found. ¹² Him showed that them lordship on Earth were famed and honoured - and that them lordship in Heaven were famed and honoured; them shall be honoured and lofty in Heaven like unto them honour and bow to them in this world ~ if them work goodly Work in this world them shall be Feeling good. ¹³ But kings who were evil in them Rule and them kingdoms that JAH gave them - them don't judge to true by what are due ~ as them have ignored the destitute and poor ones cries - them don't judge Truth and save the refugee and the wronged child whose father and mother dead on him. ¹⁴ Them don't save destitute and poor ones from the wealthy hand that rob them ~ them don't divide and give from them food and satta them who hungered - and them don't divide and give from them drink and give to drink the persons who thirsted - and them didn't return them ears toward the poor one cry. ¹⁵ and Him shall take them toward *Gehannem* that were a dark endin ~ on the time that lofty Day arrived on them when JAH shall come - and on the time Him wrath were done on them like unto Daweet spoke in him Praises 'Lord - don't chastise I in Thy Judgemant and don't admonish I in Thy chastisemant' - them problems and them downbasemant shall abound like unto them fame abundance measure. ¹⁶ When nobles and kings are who rule this world in this world - there are persons who didn't keep thy law. ¹⁷ But JAH Who rule all are there in Heaven ~ all persons souls and all persons welfare have been seized by Him Authority ~ Him are Who give honour to persons who glorify Him - to Him totally rule all - and Him love the persons who love Him. ¹⁸ As Him are Earth and Heaven Lord - Him examine

and know what kidneys transported and what a reasonin thought - and to a person who begged toward Him with a pure reasonin - Him shall give him him plea reward. ¹⁹ Him shall destroy powerful ones arrogance - who work evil Work on the child whose mother and father dead on him - and on old daughters. ²⁰ It aren't by thy Power that thou seized this kingdom ~ it aren't by thy bein able that thou sat on this throne ~ Him loved to test thee thus that it be possible to thee to rule like unto Sa'ol who ruled him kindreds in that season - and Him seated thee on a kingdom throne - yet it aren't by thy Power that thou seized this kingdom ~ it are when Him test thee like unto Sa'ol who ignored the prophet Samu'iel word and JAH Word and didn't serve him army nor 'Amalieq king - yet it aren't by thy bein able that thou seized this kingdom. ²¹ and JAH told the prophet Samu'iel - **Go - and as them have saddened I by demolishin LAW and worshippin the idols and bowin to the idol and by them mosques and by all them hated Works without benefit - tell Sa'ol - 'Go toward 'Amalieq country and destroy them hosts and all the kings Beginnin from persons up til livestock.'** ²² on them who saddened JAH - because this thing Him sent Sa'ol that him might destroy them. ²³ But him saved them king from death - and him saved many livestock and beauties and daughters and handsome youths from death ~ **As him have scorned I thing and as him didn't hear I Command - because this thing** - JAH told the prophet Samu'iel - **Go and divide him kingdom.** ²⁴ **Because him went instead - Inoint `Issiey child Daweet that him might reign on 'Isra'iel.** ²⁵ **But on him adjourn a demon who will strangle and cast him.** ²⁶ **As him have refused if I-man gave him a kingdom that him might do I Accord - on the time him refused I to do I Accord I-man dismissed him from him kingdom that are due him - but thou - go and tell him sayin - 'Will thou thus ignore JAH Who crowned thee on Him kindreds 'Isra'iel - Who seated thee on Him Lordship Throne?'** ²⁷ **But thou - tell him - 'Thou didn't know JAH Who gave around this much honour and famousness'** Him told him. ²⁸ and the prophet Samu'iel went toward the king Sa'ol and entered toward him sittin at a dinnertable - and when 'Amalieq king 'Agag had sat on him left. ²⁹ 'Why did thou totally ignore JAH Who commanded thee that thou might destroy the livestock and persons?' him told him. ³⁰ and at that time the king feared and arose from him throne and tellin Samu'iel 'Return to wi' him seized him clothes - and Samu'iel refused to return ~ Samu'iel clothes were torn. ³¹ and Samu'iel told Sa'ol - 'JAH divided thy kingdom.' ³² and again Sa'ol told Samu'iel before the people - 'Honour mi and atone mi sin to mi before JAH that Him might forgive mi' - and as him have feared JAH Word Who Created him - but as him didn't fear the king who dead - Samu'iel refused to return in him word. ³³ Because this thing him pierced 'Amalieq king 'Agag before him swallowed what him chewed. ³⁴ and a demon seized that Sa'ol who demolished the LAW of JAH - and because Him were the King of Kings Who rule all - JAH struck on him head a king who worked sin - to it don't shame him. ³⁵ to Him are all the Creation Lord Who dismiss all the nobles and kings Authority who don't fear Him - but there are none who rule Him. ³⁶ Like unto Him spoke sayin - **Daweet kindred shall go while it were famed and honoured - but Sa'ol kindred shall go while it were downbased** - Him destroyed kingdom from him child and from Sa'ol. ³⁷ Because it saddened Him - and because Him destroyed the criminals who saddened Him by them evil Work - JAH revenged and destroyed Sa'ol kindred childran - to a person who don't revenge JAH enemy - him are JAH enemy. ³⁸ When it are possible to him to revenge and destroy - and when him have Authority - a person who don't revenge and destroy the sinner and don't revenge and destroy a person who don't keep JAH LAW - as him are JAH enemy - Him destroyed Sa'ol kindred childran.

# 7

¹ and whether thou be a king or a ruler - what important thing are thou? ² Aren't it JAH Who Created thee bringin from not livin toward livin - that thou might do Him Accord and might live firmed up by Him Command and might fear Him Judgemant? Like unto thou vex on thy slaves and governed over them - all likewise there are also JAH Who vex on thee and govern over thee. ³ Like unto thou beat without niceness persons who worked sin - all likewise there are also JAH Who will strike thee and lower thee toward *Gehannem* where are no exits up til Eternity. ⁴ Like unto thou whip him who weren't ruled to thee and didn't bring a tribute to thee - to what are it that thou don't introduce a tribute to JAH? ⁵ As Him are Who Created thee in order that thou love that them might fear thee - and Who crowned thee on all the Creation that thou might keep Him kindreds to true - to what are it that thou don't fear thy Creator JAH? ⁶ Judge by what are due and to true like unto JAH Ipointed thee - yet don't sight up a face and favour to small nor great ~ whom will thou fear without Him? keep Him Worship and the Nine Commands. ⁷ Like unto Mussie commanded 'Isra'iel childran sayin - 'I-man presented Water and fire to thee-I ~ add thy hand toward what thou loved' - don't go neither rightward nor leftward. ⁸ Hear Him

Word that I-man tell thee - that thou might hear Him Word and might do Him Command - lest thou say - 'She are beyond the sea or beyond the deep or beyond the river ~ who will bring to mi that mi might sight she up and might hear Him Word and might do Him Command?' ⁹ Lest thou say - 'Who will proceed toward Heaven again and lower that JAH Word to mi that mi might hear and do she?' - JAH Word are what approached - check - to thou to teach she with thy mouth and give alms by she with thy hand. ¹⁰ and thou didn't hear thy Creator JAH unless thou heard Him Book - and thou didn't love Him nor keep Him Command unless thou kept Him LAW. ¹¹ and thou have that thou might enter toward *Gehannem* forever - and unless thou loved Him Command - and unless thou did JAH Accord - Who honoured and famed thee separatin from all thy kindreds that thou might keep them to true - thou have that thou might enter toward *Gehannem* forever. ¹² Him made thee above all - and Him crowned thee on all Him kindreds that thou might rule Him kindreds to true by what are due while thou thought of thy Creator Name Who Created thee and gave thee a kingdom. ¹³ There are them whom thou whip from persons who wronged thee - and there are him whom thou pardon while thou thought of JAH Work - and there are him to whom thou judge by what are due straightenin up thy reasonin. ¹⁴ and don't favour havin sight up a face on the time them argued before thee ~ as Earth physique are thy money - don't accept a bribe that thou might pardon the sinner person and wrong the clean person. ¹⁵ If thou did Him Accord - JAH shall multiply thy era in this world to thee - but if thou sadden Him - Him will diminish thy era. ¹⁶ Think that thou will rise after thou dead - and that thou will be examined standin before Him on all the Work thou worked whether it be goodly or evil. ¹⁷ If thou work goodly Work - thou will live in Garden in the Kingdom of Heaven - in houses where kind kings live and where Light filled. to JAH don't shame thy lordship authority - but if thou work evil Work - thou will live in *See'ol Gehannem* where evil kings live. ¹⁸ But on the time thou sight up thy bein feared famousness - thy warriors award - thy hangin shield and spear - and on the time thou sight up thy horses and thy troops beneath thy authority and them who beat drum and persons who play on a harp before thee... ¹⁹ But on the time thou sight up all this - thou make thy reasonin lofty - and thou firm up thy collar of reasonin - and thou don't think of JAH Who gave thee all this honour - however on the time Him told thee - **Quit all this** - thou aren't who quit it. ²⁰ to thou have totally neglected the Ipointmant Him Ipointed thee - and Him shall give thy lordship to another. ²¹ As death shall suddenly come on thee - and as Judgemant shall be done in Resurrection time - and as all man Work shall be examined - Him shall totally investigate and judge on thee. ²² There are none who will honour this world kings - to because Him were Truth Judge - in Judgemant time poor and wealthy will stand together. This world nobles crowns wherein them boast shall fall. ²³ Judgemant are prepared - and a soul shall quake ~ at that time sinners and righteous ones Work shall be examined. ²⁴ and there are none who shall be hidden. on the time a daughter arrived to birthin - and on the time the fetus in she belly arrived to bein birthed - like unto she cyaan prevent she womb - Earth also cyaan prevent she lodgers that are on she ~ she will return. ²⁵ and like unto clouds cyaan prevent rain lest them take and rain toward the place JAH commanded them - to JAH Word have Created all bringin from not livin toward livin - and to JAH Word again have introduced all toward a grave and all likewise - after Resurrection time arrived - it aren't possible to be that dead persons won't rise. ²⁶ Like unto Mussie spoke sayin - 'It are by Words that proceed from JAH Tongue - yet it aren't only by grain that a person are saved'; and JAH Word again shall arouse all persons from graves. ²⁷ Check - it were known that dead persons shall arise by JAH Word. ²⁸ and again JAH said thus in Repeatin Law because persons who were nobles and kings who do Him Accord - **As the day have arrived when them are counted to destruction - I-man shall revenge and destroy them on the day when Judgemant are judged and at the time when them feet stumble** Him said. ²⁹ and again JAH told persons who know Him Judgemant - **Know know that I-man were your Creator JAH - and that I-man kill and I-man save. ³⁰ I-man chastise in the tribulation and I-man pardon ~ I-man lower toward *See'ol* and again I-man send forth toward the Garden - and there are none who shall escape from I Authority** Him told them. ³¹ JAH said thus because nobles and kings who didn't keep Him LAW - **As Earthly kingdoms are a passin - and as them pass from mornin up til evenin - keep I Order and I LAW that you might enter toward the Kingdom of Heaven that live firmed up forever** Him said. ³² to JAH callin Righteous ones are to glory - and sinners to tribulation ~ Him will make the sinner wretched but will honour righteous ones. ³³ Him will dismiss the person who didn't do Him Accord - but Him will Ipoint the person who did Him Accord.

8

¹ Hear I - make I tell thee the thing whereby dead persons shall arise ~ them shall plant a plant and be fertile and grapes shall send forth vines ~ as JAH shall bring the fruit *'imhibe 'albo* ~ them shall cast wine from it. ² Overstand that that plant thou planted were small - but that she sent forth tips fruit and leaves today. ³ JAH give she root to drink from Earth and Water - from both. ⁴ But Him feed she wood from fire and wind ~ roots give leaves Water to drink - and Earth give firmness to woods. ⁵ But the soul that JAH Created make them bear fruit amidst them - and dead persons arisin are likewise. ⁶ on the time soul were separated from flesh - as each of them ras selves have gone - Him said - **Gather souls from the four natures - from Earth and Water - wind and fire.** ⁷ But Earth nature lived firmed up in she nature and became Earth - and Water nature lived firmed up in she nature and became Water. ⁸ and wind nature lived firmed up in she nature and became wind - and fire nature lived firmed up in she nature and became a hot fire. ⁹ But a soul that JAH separated from flesh returned toward she Creator ~ up til Him raise she up inited with flesh on the time Him loved - Him place she in Garden in the place Him loved. ¹⁰ Him place righteous souls in Light house in Garden - but that Him might send way sinners souls - Him also place them in darkness house in *See'ol* up til the time when Him loved. ¹¹ JAH told the prophet Hiziq'iel - **Call souls from the four corners** - that them might be gathered and be one limb. ¹² on the time Him spoke in one Word sayin thus - the souls were gathered from the four corners. ¹³ and Water nature brought verdure - and again fire nature brought fire. ¹⁴ and again Earth nature brought Earth - and wind nature brought wind. ¹⁵ and JAH brought a soul from the Garden place where Him placed it ~ them were gathered by one Word - and a Resurrection were made. ¹⁶ and again I-man shall show thee the example that are alongside thee ~ the day dusk ~ thou sleep ~ the night dawn - and thou rise from thy beddin - but on the time thou slept it are thy death example. ¹⁷ and on the time thou awoke it are thy arisin example - but the night when all persons sleep whose physiques were dark - to darkness have covered them - are this world example. ¹⁸ But the mornin light - when darkness are eliminated and when light are in all the world and when persons arise and graze toward the field - are dead persons example. ¹⁹ and this Kingdom of Heaven where man are renewed are like unto this ~ dead persons Resurrection are like unto this ~ as this world are passin - it are the night example. ²⁰ and like unto Daweet spoke sayin - 'Him placed Him example in Sun' - as Sun shine on the time it rose - it are a Kingdom of Heaven example. ²¹ and like unto Sun shine in this world today - on the time Kristos come Him shall shine like unto Sun in Kingdom of Heaven that are new ~ as Him have said - **I-man am a Sun that don't set and a Torch that aren't extinguished** - Him JAH are she Light. ²² and Him shall quickly arouse the dead persons again ~ I-man shall bring one example to thee again from thy food that thou sow and whereby thou are saved - and whether it be a wheat kernel or a barley kernel or a lentil kernel or all man seeds sown on Earth - there are none that grow unless it were demolished and rotten. ²³ and like unto the person flesh thou sight up - on the time it were demolished and rotten - Earth eat stoutness with the hide. ²⁴ and on the time Earth ate it stoutness it grow bein around a kernel seventh ~ JAH give a cloud that seized rain like unto Him loved - and roots grow on Earth and send forth leaves. ²⁵ and if she were demolished and rotten she cyaan grow - but after she grew she send forth many buds. ²⁶ and by JAH Accord fruit are given to those buds that grew - and Him clothe it stoutness in straw. ²⁷ Sight up like unto the measure that the seed kernel thou sowed abounded - yet the silver and the leaf - the ear and the straw aren't counted to thee. ²⁸ Don't be a dull one who don't know - and sight up thy seed that it abounded - and all likewise - think that dead persons shall raceive the arisin that them will arise - and them hardship like unto them Work. ²⁹ Hear I - that if thou sow wheat - it won't grow bein barley - nor bein wheat if thou sow barley - and make I tell thee again that it won't grow ~ if thou sow wheat will thou gather barley? If thou sow watercress will thou gather linseed? ³⁰ How about from plants kind - if thou plant figs will it really grow to thee bein nuts? How about if thou plant almonds - will it grow to thee bein grapes? ³¹ If thou plant the sweet fruit will it grow to thee bein bitter? How about if thou plant the bitter fruit - are it possible to it to be sweet? ³² How about all likewise - if a sinner dead are it possible to arise bein righteous in Resurrection time? How about if a righteous person dead - are it possible to arise bein a sinner in Resurrection time? Every one shall raceive him hardship like unto him Work - yet him will raceive him hardship like unto him sin and him hand Work - yet there are none who will be canvicted by him companion sin. ³³ A highland tree are planted and it send forth long branches ~ it will totally dry up ~ yet unless Heaven rained rain it leaves won't be verdant. ³⁴ and the cedar will be uprooted from it roots unless summer rain alit on it. ³⁵ and all likewise - dead persons won't arise unless welfare dew alit to them bein commanded from JAH.

9

[1] Unless highland mountains and Gielabuhie regions rained a pardon rain to them bein commanded from JAH - them won't grow grass to beasts and animals. [2] and 'Elam mountains and Gele`ad mountains won't give verdant leaves to sheeps and goats - nor to oribi and animals in wilderness - nor to ibexes and hartebeest. [3] and likewise - pardon and dew bein commanded from JAH didn't alight to doubters and criminals who made error and crime a money beforehand ~ dead persons won't arise ~ and Deemas and Qophros who worship idols and dig roots and work and instigate a thing... [4] and them who dig roots and practice sorcery and make persons battle... [5] and them who lust havin departed from LAW - and Miedon and 'Atiena persons who believe in them idols - and them who play and sing to them while them beat violins and drums and strummed harps - them won't arise unless pardon dew alit to them bein commanded from JAH. [6] These are who will be convicted on the day when dead persons arise and when Definite Judgement are done - yet persons who save them ras selves and who lust in them hands Work - them err by them idols. [7] Thou wasteful of heart dull one - do it seem to thee that dead persons won't arise? [8] on the time a trumpet were blown by the Angels Chief Hola Meeka'iel tongue - that dead ones arise then - as thou won't remain in grave without arisin - don't think a thing that are thus. [9] Hills and mountains shall be level and shall be a cleared path. [10] and Resurrection shall be done to all fleshly ones.

## 10

[1] However if it weren't thus - it are that former persons might be buried in them fathers grave Beginnin from 'Adam - Beginnin from Siet and 'Abiel - Siem and Noh - Yis'haq and 'Abriham - Yosief and Ya`iqob - and 'Aron and Mussie - yet to what are it that them didn't love that them might be buried in another place? [2] Aren't it to them to arise together with them cousins in Resurrection time? How about aren't it lest them bones be counted with evil ones and pagans bones - them who worship idols? to what are it that them didn't love that them might be buried in another place? [3] But thou - don't mislead thy reasonin while thou said - 'How will dead persons arise after them dead - them who were buried in one grave bein tens of thousands and whose bodies were demolished and rotten?' [4] and on the time thou sight up toward a grave - thou speak this in thy reasonin dullness while thou said - 'A whole fistful of Earth won't be found ~ how will dead persons arise?' [5] Will thou say the seed thou sowed won't grow? Even the seed thou sowed shall grow. [6] and all likewise - the souls JAH sowed shall quickly arise - as Him have Created man in Him Truth bringin from not livin toward livin - Him shall arouse them quickly by Him Word that save ~ Him won't delay Him arousin. [7] and as Him have again returned him from livin - toward a grave in death - what about aren't it possible to Him again to return from death toward Life? [8] Savin and liftin up are possible to JAH.

## 11

[1] 'Armon perished and she fortress were demolished ~ as JAH have brought the hardship on them like unto them evil and the Work them worked by them hands - persons who worship the idols in 'Edomyas and Zablon shall be downbased at that time ~ as JAH have approached - Who shall canvict them who worked in them infancy and didn't quit up til them aged - because them idols and them evil - Seedona and Theeros shall weep.. [2] Because them worked sin and seducin fornication and worshipped idols - because this thing JAH shall revenge and destroy them ~ to them didn't live firmed up in them Creator JAH Command - and Yihuda daughter childran shall be wretched. [3] She lived firmed up in killin prophets and in Feeling good joy - yet as she didn't live firmed up in the Nine Laws and the Worship - on the time when dead ones arise - 'Iyerusaliem sin shall be revealed. [4] At that time JAH shall examine she in Him Nature Wisdom ~ Him will revenge and destroy she on all she sin that she worked in she infancy era ~ she didn't quit workin she sin Beginnin from she beauty era up til she age. [5] She entered toward a grave and became dust like unto she former fathers who lived firmed up in them sin - and in Resurrection time Him shall revenge and destroy persons who demolished JAH LAW. [6] It shall be judged on them - to Mussie have spoken because them sayin - 'Them LAW lodgin - them reasonins - became Sedom law lodgin.' [7] and them kindred are Gemorra kindred - and them law are what destroy - and them Work are evil. [8] and them law are snake poison that destroy - and viper poison that destroy from alongside that.

## 12

[1] 'Iyerusaliem child - as this thy sin are like unto Gemorra and Sedom sin - 'Iyerusaliem child - this are thy tribulation that were spoken by a prophet. [2] and thy tribulation are like unto Gemorra and Sedom tribulation - and them law lodgin reasonin firmed up in adultery and arrogance. [3] Aside from adultery and arrogance rain - pardon and humility rain didn't rain from them reasonins by money that them Law reasonin lodgin are fertile - apart from spillin man blood and robbin and forgettin them Creator JAH. [4] and them didn't know them Creator JAH - apart from them evil Work and them idols - and them are Feeling good in them hands Work - and them lust on males and on livestock. [5] As

them eye of reasonin have been blinded lest them sight up secrets - and as them ears have deafened lest them hear or do JAH Accord that Him love - them didn't know JAH in them Work - and them reasonins are like unto Sedom law lodgin. and them kindred - Gemorra grapes kindred that bear sweet fruit. [6] and if them examine them Work - it are poison that kill - to it have firmed up in curse Beginnin from the day when it were worked - and to it grounation have been in destruction era. [7] As them Law lodgin - them reasonins - have firmed up in sin Work - as them bodies have firmed up in Satan burnin Work to build sin - them Law lodgin - them reasonins - have no goodly Work everytime. [8] and on the time him shame and were baptise (by one who is led) it were to chastisemant and destruction - and him will firm up the persons who drank and them reasonins - and him will make them who destroy I - disgustin persons who distanced from JAH. [9] to them have lived firmed up in them Work that were evil - and him will make them Deeyablos lodgin - and eatin what were sacrificed to the idols have been begun in the House of 'Isra'iel - and she proceed toward the mountains and the trees. [10] and she worship the idols that peoples in she area worship - and she daughter childran and she male childran to demons who don't know goodly Work separatin from evil. [11] and them spill clean blood ~ them gush and spill grapes from Sedom to the idols forever. [12] and she glorify and worship the Dagwon that the 'Iloflans worship - and she sacrifice to him from she flocks and she fattened cows - that she might be Feeling good in demons laziness that them taught she to sacrifice to them - and in them gushin and spillin the grapes - and that she might do them accord. [13] She sacrifice to him that she might be Feeling good in demons laziness that them taught she lest she know she Creator JAH Who feed she at each time and Who cherished and raised she Beginnin from she infancy up til she beauty - and again up til she age - and again up til she age day when she dead. [14] and **again I-man shall revenge and canvict him in Resurrection time - and as she didn't return toward I LAW - and as she didn't live firmed up in I Command - she time when she live in *Gehannem* shall be up til Eternity. [15] If them were Creators to true - make she idols arise with she and descend toward *Gehannem* and save she on the time I-man vexed and destroyed she - and on the time I-man distanced all the priests of the idols who lust with she. [16] Like unto she made sin and insult on the Hola Items and on I Lodgin the Temple - I-man made she wretched by all this. [17] When them told she - 'Check - this are JAH kindred - and she are 'Isra'iel Creator JAH Lodgin - and the famous King country 'Iyerusaliem who were separate from them who were separate - she are the Most I JAH Name Lodgin' - I-man made she wretched like unto she saddened I Name that were called in she. [18] She boast in I that she were I slave and that I-man were she Lord ~ she wink on I like unto a criminal - yet she aren't who fear I and do I Accord like unto I bein she Lord. [19] Them became a obstacle on she to mislead that them might distance she from I - yet she are ruled to other idols who don't feed she nor clothe she. [20] She sacrifice to them - and she eat the sacrifice - and she spill blood to them - and she gush and drink from the grapes to them ~ she smoke up ishence to them - and she make the ishence fragrance smell to them ~ she idols command she - and she are commanded to them. [21] and again she sacrifice she daughter childran and she male childran to them - and as she present praises to them because them Love - she are Feeling good in the thing she spoke by she tongue and in she hands Work. [22] Woe to she on the day when Definite Judgemant are done - and woe to she idols whom she love and inite; and she shall descend with them toward *Gehannem* beneath *See'ol* - where the worm don't slumber and the fire aren't extinguished. [23] Woe to thee wretched 'Iyerusaliem child - to thou have quit I Who Created thee and have worshipped different idols. [24] and I-man shall bring the hardship on thee like unto thy Work ~ as thou have saddened I - and as thou have ignored I Word - and as thou didn't work goodly Work - I-man shall canvict thee toward thy pretensions. [25] to thou have saddened I Word - and to thou didn't live firmed up in I LAW whereby thou swore with I - that thou might keep I LAW and that I-man might live with thee in Support and might save thee from all who fight thee - and also that thou might keep I Order that I-man commanded thee - and I-man shall ignore thee and won't quickly save thee from the tribulation. [26] Thou didn't keep all this - and I-man ignored thee ~ as I-man have created thee - and as thou didn't keep I Command nor I Word - I-man shall canvict thee in Judgemant time - and I-man honoured thee that thou might be I kin. [27] and like unto Gemorra and Sedom were separated from I - thou were separated from I. [28] and I-man judged and destroyed them - and like unto Sedom and Gemorra were separated from I - thou separated from I - and now like unto I-man vexed and destroyed them - I-man vexed and destroyed thee ~ as thou are from Sedom and Gemorra kindred whom I-man destroyed - I-man** destroyed thee ~ as them whom I-man Created have saddened I by goin toward a youtmon wife and by lustin without LAW - with animals and males like unto arrivin with daughters - I-man destroyed them name invocation from this world lest them live in them Feeling good joy. [29] There are no fearin JAH in them faces Beginnin from a infant up til a elder ~ them help him in all them evil Work - yet Him don't vex on each one that them might quit workin she ~ as them Work are evil - them are sated of sin and iniquity. [30] All evil Work - robbery and arrogance and greed - are prepared in them reasonins. [31] and because this thing JAH ignored them and destroyed them countries - and them are there that Him might burn them with fire up til them root grounation perish ~ them totally perished up til the Eternity - yet Him didn't make even one from them remain. [32] As them have firmed up in sin - them shall wait in destruction forever up til the Day of Advent when Definite Judgemant are done - to them have saddened I with them evil Work - and I-man won't pardon them nor forgive them. [33] and I-man ignored them ~ to thou won't find a reason on the time I-man vexed and seized thee because all thy Work were robbery and sin - adultery and greed and speakin lies - all error Work and the obstacle that I-man don't love - and thou 'Iyerusaliem child who were wretched - on the day when Judgemant are done thou will be seized in Judgemant like unto them. [34] I-man had made thee to honour - but thou downbased thy ras self ~ I-man had called thee I money - but thou became to another. [35] I-man had betrothed thee to honour - but thou became to Deeyablos - and I-man shall revenge and destroy thee like unto thy evil Work. [36] Because thou didn't hear all I Word - and because thou didn't keep the Command I-man commanded thee on the time I-man loved thee - I-man shall multiply and bring firm vengeance on thee - to I-man am JAH Who Created thee - and I-man shall judge on all sinners like unto thee - and on the day when Judgemant are done I-man shall bring the hardship on them like unto them evil Work. [37] As thou didn't keep I Word - and as thou have ignored I Judgemant - I-man shall canvict thee with them. [38] Woe to you - Gemorra and Sedom - who have no fearin JAH in your reasonin. [39] All likewise - woe to thy sista 'Iyerusaliem child on whom it shall be judged together with thee in fire of *Gehannem* - to you will descend together toward *Gehannem* that were prepared to you - where are no exits forever - and woe to all sinners who worked the sin. [40] As you didn't keep I Command nor I Word - thou and she who didn't keep I Command nor I Word shall descend toward *See'ol* together on the day when Judgemant are judged. [41] But kind persons who kept I Command and I Word shall eat the money that sinner persons accumulated - and like unto JAH commanded - kind persons shall share the loot that evil persons captured - and kind persons shall be totally Feeling good. [42] But wrongdoers and sinner persons shall weep - and them shall be sad because all them sin that them wronged havin departed from I Command. [43] Him who keep I Word and live firmed up in I Command - him are who find I blessin and are honoured alongside I. [44] All person who keep I Word and live firmed up in I Command shall eat the fatness found from Earth - and shall live havin entered toward the Garden where enter kind kings who have straight reasonins.

## 13

[1] As them shall be wretched and perish by I wrath on the time I-man seized them - woe to Theeros and Seedona and all Yihuda country regions who make them ras selves arrogant today. [2] Conquerin JAH said thus ~ Him have said - **Deeyablos child who are totally arrogant shall be birthed from them - the False *Messeeh* who to a Truth thing are she enemy - who firm up him collar of reasonin - who boast and don't know him Creator** - and Him said - **Woe to them** - and JAH Who rule all said - **I-man made him to I anger pattern that I-man might be revealed in him Power.** [3] and this Qifirnahom Semarya and Geleela and Demasqo and Sorya and 'Akeya and Qophros and all Yordanos region are kindreds who firmed up them collars of reasonin - who live firmed up in them sin - and whom death shadow and darkness covered - to Deeyablos have covered them reasonins in sin - and to them are commanded to that arrogant Deeyablos - and them didn't return toward fearin JAH. [4] At that time woe to persons who are commanded to demons and who sacrifice in them name to them ~ as them have denied JAH Who Created them - them resemble animals without minds - to the False *Messeeh* who forgot JAH LAW and are Deeyablos child shall set up him image in all the places (to him have said 'Mi are a god') - and him shall be Feeling good in him reasonin accord - in him hand Work and in robbery and all the sins and perfidy and iniquity - in robbery and all the adulteries that a person work. [5] to because it were counted alongside JAH that him work this - the era are known that them work sin. [6] Sun shall darken and moon shall be blood - and stars shall be shaken from Heaven - all the Work shall pass by the miracles that JAH shall bring in Fulfillmant Era that Him might make Earth pass - and that Him might make all pass who live in sin of persons who live within she. [7] As JAH have been proud on the Creation Him Created - and as Him have quickly made all Him loved in one hour - the Lord death shall destroy a small enemy Deeyablos. [8] to JAH Who rule all have said - I-man shall judge and destroy - but after Advent - Deeyablos have no authority. [9] and **on the day when him were seized by I anger - him shall descend toward *Gehannem* - to which him make application and where firm tribulation are ~ as him will take all who are with him toward chastisemant and destruction and perfidy - because I-man were Who send forth from *Gehannem* and Who introduce toward *Gehannem* - him will descend toward *Gehannem*.** [10] As Him give firmness and Power to weak persons - and again as Him give weakness to powerful and firm persons - make a powerful one not boast in him Power. [11] As Him are a Ruler - and as Him judge and save the wronged persons from the persons hands who wrong them - Him will return the grudge of the widows and the child whose father and mother dead on him. [12] **Woe to thee who boast and firm up thy collar of reasonin - to whom it seem that I-man won't rule thee nor judge and destroy thee - to in him boastin and him arrogance him have said - 'Mi will streach mi throne in stars and Heaven - and mi will be like unto JAH Who are lofty.'** [13] and like unto Him spoke sayin - How Deeyablos fell from Heaven - him who shine like unto a mornin star that were Created precedin all - woe to thee. [14] and thou dared and spoke this in thy arrogance - and thou didn't think of JAH Who totally Created thee by Him Authority ~ why did thou boast thy ras self that thou descend toward *Gehannem* in thy reasonin firmness? [15] Thou were downbased separate from all Angels like unto thee - to them praise them Creator with a humbled reasonin because them knew that Him were Who Created them from fire and wind - and to them don't depart from Him Command - and to them keep them reasonins from perfidy lest them totally depart from Him Command. [16] But thou did a firm perfidy in thy reasonin arrogance ~ thou became a wretched man separate from thy companions - to thou have cherished all the sin and iniquity - robbery and perfidy whereby persons who forgot JAH LAW and sinners like unto thee live firmed up - them who are from thy kindred and commit crime like unto thee - and who live firmed up by thy command and thy accord whereby thou teach sin. [17] Woe to thee - to the demons thou misled in thy malice and thou will descend toward *Gehannem* together. [18] O you JAH childran who erred by that misleadin criminal Deeyablos - woe to you ~ as you have erred like unto him by the money that him taught you and that him hosts taught you - you will descend toward *Gehannem* together - where are no exits forever. [19] and formerly when JAH slave Mussie were there - you saddened JAH by the Water where argumant were made and on Korieb - and by 'Amalieq and on Mount Seena. [20] and moreover on the time you sent scouts toward Kene`an - on the time them told you this sayin 'The path are far - and them ramparts and them fortresses that reach up til Heaven are firm - and warriors live there' - you vexed that you might return towad Gibts country where you work worrisome Work - and you saddened JAH Word. [21] You didn't think of JAH Who firmed you up from the tribulation - and Who did great miracles in Gibts - and Who led you by Him Angel Authority. Him would veil you in cloud by day lest the Sun burn you and Him would shine a column of fire to you by night lest your feet stumble in darkness. [22] and on the time the army and Fer`on frightened you - you totally cried toward Mussie - and Mussie totally cried toward JAH - and Him lodged in Him Angel and kept you lest you meet with Fer`on. [23] But Him introduced them toward 'Eritra in tribulation ~ JAH led only 'Isra'iel - to Him have said - and there were no different idol with them - but Him buried them enemies in sea at one time - and Him didn't preserve none who flee from them. [24] and Him made 'Isra'iel cross amidst the sea by foot ~ there are no tribulation that found them arisin from the Gibtsans ~ Him delivered them toward Mount Seena - and there Him fed them *menna* forty eras. [25] As 'Isra'iel childran sadden JAH everytime - Him did all this goodly thing to them and them neglected to worship JAH. [26] Them placed evil in them reasonins Beginnin from them childhood up til them age - to JAH Mouth have spoken thus in 'Oreet where the fathers birth were written ~ as Him have spoken sayin - **'Adam childran reasonin are ash - and all them Work are toward robbery and them run toward evil ~ there are none from them who love straight Work - apart from gatherin a person money in violence and swearin in lie and wrongin companions and robbin and stealin** - them placed evil in them reasonins. [27] and all go toward evil Work in the era when them live in Life ~ 'Isra'iel childran who demolished JAH LAW totally saddened JAH Beginnin from Antiquity up til fufillmant era.

## 14

[1] and on the time JAH destroyed Qayen childran - kindreds who preceded - in destruction Water because them sin - Him baptised Earth

in Water of Destruction - and Him cleansed she from all Qayel childran sin. [2] As Him have said - **I-man were sad because I-man Created man** - Him destroyed all wrongdoers ~ Him didn't preserve apart from eight persons ~ Him destroyed all ~ after this Him multiplied them and them filled Earth ~ them shared them father 'Adam inheritance. [3] But Noh swore with JAH a oath ~ them swore a oath with JAH lest JAH again destroy Earth in Destruction Water - and lest Noh childran eat what deceased nor what lodged dead - lest them worship different idols apart from JAH Who Created them - and that Him might be a Love Father to them - and lest Him destroy them at one time in them vain sin - and lest Him prevent them the first and the spring rain - and that Him might give to livestock and persons them food at each time - that Him might give them the grass and the grain fruit and plants - and that them might work goodly Work in all that JAH love. [4] and after Him gave them this Order - 'Isra'iel childran saddened JAH by them sin ~ them didn't live firmed up in Him LAW like unto them fathers Yis'haq and 'Abriham and Ya`iqob who didn't demolish them Creator JAH LAW. [5]. and Beginnin from the small up til the great - those 'Isra'iel childran who didn't keep JAH LAW are crooked in them Work. [6] and whether them be them priests or them chiefs or them scribes - everyone demolish JAH LAW. [7] Them don't live firmed up in JAH Order and Him LAW that Mussie commanded them in Repeatin Law sayin - **'Love thy Creator JAH in thy complete body and thy complete reasonin.'** [8] Them don't firm up in JAH Order and Him LAW that Mussie commanded them in book where LAW were written sayin - **'Love thy companion like unto thy body - and don't worship him idols that were different - and don't go toward a youtmon wife ~ don't kill a soul ~ don't steal. [9] and don't witness in lie - and be it him donkey or be it him ox - don't love thy companion money nor all that thy bredda bought.'** [10] However after him commanded them all this - 'Isra'iel childran who were evil return toward treachery and sin - robbery and iniquity - toward a youtmon wife and toward lies and stealin and worshippin idols. [11] 'Isra'iel childran saddened JAH on Korieb by workin a cow that graze toward grass ~ them bowed sayin - 'Check - these are we creators who sent we forth from Gibts.' [12] and them were Feeling good in them hand Work ~ if them ate and drank and satta - them arose to sing. [13] As JAH have told him sayin - **Thy kindreds whom thou sent forth from Gibts country where rulership are - them have proceeded from LAW and wronged - and them worked a cow image and bowed to the idol** - because this thing Mussie vexed and alit from Seena mountain. [14] While Mussie vexed on him kindreds - he alit with him canfidante 'Iyasu - and on the time 'Iyasu heard - him said - 'Check - I-man hear warriors voice in 'Isra'iel camp.' [15] and Mussie told 'Iyasu - 'It are when 'Isra'iel play havin drunk the unboiled wine - yet as to a warrior voice - it aren't' - and him alit and broke them image and totally crushed it up til it were like unto dust ~ him mixed it within the Water that 'Isra'iel childran drink beside the mountain. [16] and after this him commanded the priests that them might slay one another because the sin them worked before JAH. [17] Them knew that defyin JAH surpass killin them and killin them fathers - and them did like unto him commanded them. [18] and Mussie told them - 'Because you saddened JAH Who fed you and cherished you and Who sent you forth from a rulership house and Who bequeathed to you the inheritance that Him swore to your fathers that Him might give to them and to them childran after them - because this thing you made JAH Feeling good.' [19] to them go toward sin and a evil thing - and them didn't quit saddenin JAH there. [20] Them aren't like unto them fathers Yis'haq and 'Abriham and Ya`iqob who made JAH Feeling good with them goodly Work that Him might give them what are on Earth and what Him prepared to persons who love Him in Heaven Beginnin from them infancy up til them youthood and up til them age ~ them aren't like unto 'Abriham and Yis'haq and Ya`iqob who made Him Feeling good with them Work that Him might give them a Earth of inheritance where Feeling good joy are found in this world - and a garden that make Feeling good - prepared to kind persons in hereafter world - what Him prepared to 'Abriham and Yis'haq and Ya`iqob who made JAH Feeling good when them were in Life and who love Him - Whom a eye didn't sight up nor a ear hear and Who aren't thought of in reasonin. [21] and them childran who denied JAH and were evil and who live firmed up in them reasonin accord - them didn't hear JAH Command - Him Who fed them and cherished them and kept them Beginnin from them infancy. [22] Them didn't think of JAH - Who sent them forth from Gibts land and saved them from brick Work and a firm rulership. [23] But them totally saddened Him - and Him would arouse peoples in them area on them - and them would arise on them in enmity and also tax them like unto them loved.

## 15

[1] and at that time Midyam persons arose on them in enmity - and them aroused them armies on 'Isra'iel that them might fight them - and them king name are called 'Akrandis ~ him quickly gathered many armies in Keeliqyas and Sorya and Demasqo. [2] and campin beyond Yordanos him sent messengers sayin - 'An that mi might capture your money - pay tax toward 'Isra'iel to mi' ~ him told them - 'But if you don't pay tax - mi came that mi might punish you and might capture your livestocks and take your mares and capture your childran.' [3] 'Mi will capture and take you toward the country you don't know - and there mi will make you Water pourers and wood pickers' him told them. [4] 'Don't boast while you said - "I are JAH kindreds and there are nothing able to I" - aren't JAH Who sent mi that mi might destroy you and plunder your money? and aren't mi whom JAH sent that mi might gather all your kindreds? [5] Are there really a savin that them different idols saved the other kins that mi destroyed? Mi captured them mares and them horses and mi killed them and captured them childran. [6] and unless you introduced the tax that mi commanded you - mi will destroy you like unto them' him said - and him crossed Yordanos that him might plunder them livestocks and them money and capture them wives. [7] and after this 'Isra'iel childran wept a firm mournin toward JAH - and them totally cried - however them lacked one who help them. [8] and because this thing JAH gave firmness to the three bredren - and them names are like unto this: - and them are Yihuda and Mebikyas and Meqabees - whose features were handsome and who were warriors in them Power. [9] and 'Isra'iel childran totally wept there ~ on the time them heard - it saddened them in them heart arisin from all 'Isra'iel childran shout ~ the child whose mother and father dead on him - and widows - and them officials and them priests - all 'Isra'iel kindred - both daughters and males - and all childran - would weep sprinklin ash on them heads - and them nobles had worn sackcloth. [10] But those bredren - who were attractive and comely - went and agreed that them might save them ~ them counseled sayin - 'Make I go and give I bodies to death because these persons.' [11] Tellin one another - 'Take heart - take heart' - them went girdin them swords on them waists and seizin them spears in them hands - and them went prepared that them might incriminate the warrior. [12]. and them arrived toward them camp ~ Mebikyus attacked the warrior (the king) when him had sat at a dinnertable ~ him cut him neck in one blow when food were in him mouth; and Meqabyus and Yihuda struck him armies on the king left and right by sword and killed them. [13] and on the time them king were defeated - them entered toward them spears in them companions hearts - and them all totally fled and them bows were broken and them were defeated. [14] But those bredren who are attractive and comely were saved from death ~ there are no evil thing that found them - but as JAH have returned chastisemant toward them - them sliced up one another and were depleted. [15] Them were defeated and dead and them crossed Yordanos - and up til them crossed them cast way all them money - and all them money remained - and pom the time 'Isra'iel childran sight up that them enemies fled - them went toward them camp and took both what them plundered and them money to them ras selves. [16] JAH saved 'Isra'iel doin thus by the bredren and Mebikyu hand. [17] 'Isra'iel sat a few days while them made JAH Feeling good. [18] But after that them again returned toward sin ~ 'Isra'iel childran neglected worshippin JAH by what are due. [19] and Him shall again sadden them by kins who don't know them and who will gather them field crops and destroy them grape places and plunder them flocks and slaughter and feed them them livestocks before them... [20] and who will capture them wives and them daughter childran and them male childran ~ because it were that them sadden JAH everytime; as themare kindreds who demolished the LAW - them will hammer them childran before them on each of them heads ~ them won't save them.

## 16

[1] Them who do this are Theeros and Seedona and them who live beyond Yordanos river and on the sea edge - Keran and Gele`ad - 'Iyabuseewon and Kenaniewon - 'Edom and Giegiesiewon and 'Amalieq persons. [2] All peoples do thus - who live firmed up in each of them tribes and countries and regions and in each of them Works and country languages - and all live firmed up like unto JAH worked them. [3] and there are persons from them who know JAH - and whose Work were beautiful. [4] and there are persons from them whose Work were evil and who don't know JAH Who Created them - and like unto them worked sin - Him ruled them in Sorya king Silminasor hand. [5] As him plunder and take Demasqo money - and as him share Semarya loot that are before Gibts king - Him ruled them in Silminasor hand. [6] Gielabuhie region and also persons in Fars and Miedon - Qephedoqya and Sewseegya - who live in the West mountains - in Gele`ad fortress and Phasthos that are part of Yihuda land... [7] and these are who live in them region - and them are kindreds who don't know JAH nor keep Him Command - and whose collar of reasonin were firm. [8] and Him shall pay them them hardship like unto them Work evil and them hands Work. [9] to Gele`ad kindreds and Qeesarya region and 'Amalieq have become one there - that them might destroy JAH country that were filled of a Truth thing - and within which 'Isra'iel Creator are praised -

Him Who are Most Glorified and Conquerin - and Whom Angels who are many many in Keerubiel chariots - them who stand before Him - serve fearin and tremblin - and Him shall pay them them hardship like unto them Work evil and them hands Work.

## 17

¹ 'Amalieq and 'Edomyas persons don't worship JAH by Whose Authority Earth and Heaven rulership were seized ~ as them are criminals who don't live firmed up in Truth Work - them don't fear to demolish Him Lodgin - the Temple. ² and there are no fearin JAH before them - apart from sheddin blood and adultery and eatin what were beaten and sacrificed to a idol and all that resemble what lodged dead - and these are scorned sinners. ³ Them have no virtue nor religion ~ as them are who hated goodly Work - and as them don't know JAH - and as them don't know Love Work - apart from robbin a person money and from sin - and apart from disturbin a person and all hated Work - apart from games and song like unto them father Deeyablos taught them - them have no virtue nor religion. ⁴ As him have ruled them with him host - demons - him teach them all evil Work that were to each of them ras selves - all robbery and sin - theft and falsehood - robbin money and eatin what were beaten and what lodged dead - and adultery Work. ⁵ and him teach them all that resemble this - and goin toward a youtmon wife - and sheddin blood - eatin what were sacrificed to idol and what lodged dead - and killin a person soul in violence - and envy and winkin and greed and all evil Work that JAH don't love - Deeyablos who were them enemy teach them this teachin that him might distance them from JAH LAW Who rule all the world. ⁶ But JAH Work are innocence and humility - not annoyin a bredren and lovin a companion - harmonisin and lovin with all persons. ⁷ Don't be hypocrites to favour to a person face - and don't be wrongdoers nor totally robbers nor persons who go toward a youtmon wife - nor persons who work iniquity and evil Work on them companion - nor who cajole that them might wrong them companion in violence. ⁸ Them wink and shake them heads and provoke to evil ~ them discourage to mislead that them might lower them toward Eternity Definite Judgemant.

## 18

¹ Think that thou will go in death toward JAH in Whose Hand all are - and thou will stand before Him that Him might canvict thee before Him on all the sin thou Worked. ² As them who are arrogant and evil - and powerful ones childran who aren't strengthenin more than them - were likewise formerly - because them sight up them stature and them Power and them firm authority - them didn't make JAH before them - and them didn't know that Him were them Creator Who Created them bringin from not livin toward livin. ³ and when them fathers bein like unto "Angels" praised on Mount Hola with Angels - on the time them accord misled them - them alit toward this world where Definite Judgemant shall be done forever. ⁴ As JAH in the Antiquity have Created human flesh to them - that it might mislead them because them reasonin arrogance and might test them as it were them kept Him LAW and Him Command - them married wives from Qayel childran. ⁵ But them didn't keep JAH LAW ~ Him lowered them toward *Gehannem* fire with them father Deeyablos; to JAH have vexed on the offspring of Siet who wronged like unto persons - and persons era diminished because them sin. ⁶ and them took 'Adam childran toward sin with them ~ Him lowered them toward *See'ol* where them shall raceive a verdict. ⁷ As persons era have been divided because Siet childran erred by Qayel childran - when a person eras were nine hundred in the Antiquity - them returned toward livin a hundred twenty eras. ⁸ and as them are flesh and blood - JAH said - **I Spirit of Support won't live firmed up on them.** ⁹ and because this thing I era were divided - to because I sin and I iniquity - I era have been divided from I fathers who preceded - and when them are in them infancy again - them are dyin. ¹⁰ But I fathers era had abounded - because them kept Him LAW and because them didn't sadden JAH. ¹¹ But I fathers era had abounded - because them vexed on them daughter childran that them might teach them - and because them vexed on them male childran lest them demolish JAH LAW. ¹² Because them didn't demolish JAH LAW with them daughter childran and them male childran - because this thing them era had abounded to true.

## 19

¹ on the time Qayen childran abounded them worked drums and harps - *santee* and violins - and them made songs and all the games. ² Childran who are attractive and comely were birthed to Qayen from the wife of the kind man 'Abiel - whom him killed because she - to she were attractive - and after him killed him bredda him took that and she who were him money. ³ and separatin from him father - him seized them and went toward Qiefaz region that are toward the West - and that attractive one childran were attractive like unto them mother. ⁴ and because this thing Siet childran descended toward Qayen childran - and after them sight them up them didn't wait one hour - and them made the daughters whom them chose wives to them ras selves. ⁵ As them have

taken I toward error together with them because them error - because this thing JAH vexed on I and vexed on them. ⁶ and Deeyablos havin cajoled sayin - 'You will become creators like unto your Creator JAH' - him took I mother Hiewan and I father 'Adam toward him error. ⁷ But it seemin Truth to them in them dullness - them demolished JAH LAW - Him Who Created them bringin from not-livin toward livin that them might bow and praise Him glorified Name. ⁸ But Him - them Creator - downbased those 'Adam and Hiewan who made godhood to them ras selves - and Him downbased him who are arrogant. ⁹ Like unto Daweet spoke sayin - ' 'Adam perish by the sinner Deeyablos arrogance' - Him abused them - to I father 'Adam have been canvicted on Deeyablos arrogance by Him true Judgemant. ¹⁰ and Siet childran who erred by Qayel childran took I toward them sin thus ~ because this thing I era that JAH gave I were less than I fathers eras. ¹¹ But them had worked goodly Work - to them had firmed up them reasonins in JAH - to them had taught them daughter childran and them male childran lest them depart from JAH LAW that them taught them - and there were no evil enemy who approach them. ¹² But if them worked goodly Work - there are nothing that benefit them if them didn't tell nor teach to them childran. ¹³ Like unto Daweet spoke sayin - 'Them didn't hide from them childran to another child - and teach JAH praise - the wondrous miracles Him did - and Him Power' - there are nothing that benefit them if them didn't teach to them childran that them might teach to them childran to make heart like unto them knew - and that them might know and do Him Accord - and that them might tell them JAH LAW Trust - and that them might keep Him LAW like unto them fathers who made JAH Feeling good with them beautiful Work. ¹⁴ and them who told them Trust from them fathers in them infancy didn't demolish Him Command - like unto them fathers learned JAH Worship and the Nine Laws from them fathers. ¹⁵ Them childran learned from them fathers that them might work goodly Work and might present praise to them Creator - to them have kept Him LAW - and to them have loved Him. ¹⁶ and Him shall hear them in them prayer - and Him won't ignore them plea - but Him are a Forgiver. ¹⁷ Havin multiplied Him wrath - Him shall return it to them - and Him wouldn't destroy all in Him chastisemant.

## 20

¹ I bredren - think - don't forget what them told you formerly - that JAH keep the true Work of persons who work goodly Work. ² and Him multiply them childran in this world - and them name invocation shall live firmed up to a goodly thing up til the Eternity - and them childran won't be troubled to grain in this world. ³ As Him shall dispute to them because them - and as Him won't cast them in them enemy hand - Him shall save them from them enemies hand who hate them. ⁴ and to persons who love Him Name - Him shall be them Helper in them tribulation time ~ Him shall guard them and pardon them all them sin.

## 21

¹ Daweet believed in JAH - to Him have believed in him - and Him saved him bein a Refuge from the king Sa'ol hand. ² and as him have believed in Him and kept Him LAW on the time when him child 'Abiesielom arose - and on the time when the 'Iloflans arose - and on the time when the 'Edomyans and the 'Amalieqans arose - on the time when the one from the four Rafayn arose - JAH saved Daweet from all this tribulation that enemies who disputed him brought on him. ³ As prevailin are by JAH Accord - them were defeated by them enemies hand - yet but JAH didn't save the evil kings who didn't believe in Him. ⁴ and Hiziqyas believed in JAH ~ Him saved him from Senakriem hand who were arrogant. ⁵ But him child Minassie were defeated by him enemy hand - to him didn't make him trustin in JAH ~ as him didn't make him trustin in JAH and as him didn't fear JAH Who totally honoured and famed him - them bound and took him toward them country - yet but those enemies who defeated Minassie weren't like unto him. ⁶ At that time Him denied him the kingdom Him gave him - to him didn't work goodly Work before him Creator JAH - that him era might abound and that Him might dispute him enemy to him and that him might have Power and firmness behind and in front. ⁷ to it are better to believe in JAH than in many armies - than believin in horses and bows and shields. ⁸ Believin in JAH surpass ~ a person who believed in Him shall firm up and be honoured and totally lofty. ⁹ to JAH don't favour to a face - but persons who didn't believe in JAH - who believed in them money abundance - became them who departed from the grace and honour that Him gave them. ¹⁰ Him shall guard the persons who believe in Him - but Him shall make the persons ignorant who call Him ignorant - and as them didn't discipline them reasonins to follow JAH nor keep Him LAW - Him won't quickly help them in them tribulation time nor in the time them enemies disputed with them. ¹¹ But to a person who were disciplined in worshippin JAH and to keep Him LAW - Him shall be a Refuge in him tribulation time. ¹² By destroyin him enemy - and by plunderin him enemy livestock - and by capturin him enemy country persons - and by rainin eras rain - and by growin sprouts - and

by introducin the grain pile - in the plant fruit... ¹³ and by rainin the first and the spring rains - and by makin the grass verdant - and by givin the rain that rain at each time that thy kindreds beneath thy Authority might be Feeling good - Him shall make him Feeling good. ¹⁴ Him shall make him Feeling good - that them might eat the other one money - that them might satta havin eaten the money them plundered from them enemy - that them might plunder animals and sheeps and cows - and that them might eat the other one dinnertable - and that them might take them enemies childran captive. ¹⁵ JAH shall do all this to the person whom Him love - but Him will make the person who hate Him to him enemy ransackery. ¹⁶ and Him shall bind him feet and him hands and shall cast him in him enemy hand - and Him shall make him to him enemies derision - and as him have become a blood shedder who demolished JAH LAW - Him won't make him Feeling good in him house seed. ¹⁷ and him won't firm up in Judgemant time - and that Him might bring the hardship to persons who work sin - Him will also give persons who work evil Work them sin hardship. ¹⁸ But it were commanded from alongside JAH to give persons who work goodly Work them reward - that Him might keep them in Him Authority. ¹⁹ to Him are empowered on all the Creation Him Created that Him might do goodly Work and might give them Iternal welfare and that them might praise JAH Who Created them - and Him commanded that him might keep Him LAW ~ apart from only man there are none from all the Creations Him Created that departed from Him Command. ²⁰ Like unto JAH commanded all who live firmed up in each of them Works - them all know and are kept in Him LAW. ²¹ But man are emboldened on JAH Who crowned all on each of them inventions - on animal and beasts and on Heaven birds. ²² Be it what are in sea or all on land - JAH gave all the Creation Him Created to them father 'Adam ~ JAH gave them that him might do what him loved - and that them might eat them like unto grain that grew on Earth - and that them might rule and tax them - and that be them beasts or animals them might be commanded to man - and Him Ipointed them on all Him Created that persons who reigned might be commanded to JAH Who gave them honour and that them might favour Him. ²³ But if them depart from Him LAW Him will separate them from the lordship Him gave them ~ as Him are Who rule Earth and Heaven - Him will give it to him who do Him Accord. ²⁴ Him Ipoint whom Him loved to Ipoint - but Him dismiss whom Him loved to dismiss ~ Him kill ~ Him save ~ Him whip in tribulation ~ Him forgive. ²⁵ There are no other Creator like unto Him ~ as Him are Ruler to all the Creation Him Created - as there are no other without Him - the Creator - in Heaven above Earth nor on Earth beneath Heaven - there are none who shall criticise Him. ²⁶ Him Ipoint ~ Him dismiss ~ Him kill ~ Him save ~ Him whip in tribulation ~ Him forgive ~ Him impoverish ~ Him honour. ²⁷ Him hear persons who beg Him in them plea ~ Him accept a person plea who do Him Accord with a clean reasonin; and Him hear them in them prayer - and Him do them accord to them in all that them begged Him. ²⁸ and Him make the great and the small to be commanded to them ~ all this are them money on hills and mountains and at trees roots and in caves and Earth wells and all them kindreds on both dry and sea. ²⁹ and to persons who do them Creator Accord all this are them money - and Him won't trouble them from them plenty - and Him shall give them them praise reward. ³⁰ and Him shall give them the honour Him prepared in Heaven to them fathers Yis'haq and 'Abriham and Ya`iqob ~ Him shall give them what Him prepared to Hiziqyas and Daweet and Samu'iel who didn't depart from Him LAW and Him Command. ³¹ That them might be Feeling good in Him Lordship - Him shall give them who served Him Beginnin from Antiquity the honour Him prepared to them fathers Yis'haq and 'Abriham and Ya`iqob - to whom Him swore to give them a inheritance.

## 22

¹ Please - think of persons name who work goodly Work - and don't forget them Work. ² Straighten up that thy name be called like unto them name - that thou might be Feeling good with them in the Kingdom of Heaven - that were Light Lodgin that Him prepared to nobles and kings who did JAH Accord and were kind persons. ³ and again - know and be canvinced of evil nobles and kings names - that Him shall canvict them and revile them alongside man after them dead. ⁴ to them didn't line up them Work while them sight up and heard - and know and be canvinced that unless them did JAH Accord - Him shall judge on them in the Kingdom of Heaven more than criminals and persons who forgot JAH LAW. ⁵ Be kindly - innocent - honest - yet don't thou also go on persons path who forgot JAH LAW - on whom JAH vexed because them evil Work. ⁶ Judge Truth and save the child whose mother and father dead on him - and the widow from sinner persons hand who rob them. ⁷ Be a guardian like unto him father to the child whose mother and father dead on him - that thou might save him from the wealthy one hand who rob him - and stand to him - and be alarmed on the time the child - whose mother and father dead on him - tears flowed before thee-I - lest thou be alarmed in fire sea where sinner persons who didn't enter

repentance are punished. ⁸ and straighten up thy feet toward Love and Inity path ~ as JAH Eyes check up Him friends - and as Him Ears hear them plea - seek Love and follow she. ⁹ But JAH Face of Him Wrath are toward persons who work evil Work - that Him might destroy them name invocation from this world - and Him won't preserve a person who near on ramparts nor mountains. ¹⁰ **As I-man am JAH Who am jealous on I Godhood - as I-man am a Creator who revenge and destroy persons who hate I and don't keep I Word - I-man won't return I Face of Support reachin up til I-man destroy the person who don't keep I Word.** ¹¹ and **I-man shall honour persons who honour I and keep I Word.**

## 23

¹ Don't live firmed up in Qayel order - who killed him bredda who followed him in innocence - it seemin to him that him bredda love him. ² and him killed him bredda envyin on a daughter ~ persons who make envy and iniquity and betrayal on them companion are like unto him. ³ But as 'Abiel are innocent like unto a sheep - and as him blood are like unto the clean sheep blood that them sacrificed to JAH by a clean reasonin - them went on Qayel path that aren't on 'Abiel path. ⁴ to because all the persons who live in innocence were persons whom JAH love - like unto a kind man 'Abiel - them have been innocent ones like unto 'Abiel - but those persons who live firmed up in 'Abiel Work love JAH. ⁵ But JAH neglect evil ones - and them Definite Judgemant make application to them on them bodies - and it are written on the record of them reasonins - and on the time when Judgemant are judged - them shall read she before man and Angels and before all the Creation. ⁶ At that time them shall shame ~ wrongdoers and refusers who didn't do JAH Accord shall shame. ⁷ and a alarmin Word shall be given them that say - **Place them in *Gehannem* where are no exit up til Eternity.**

## 24

¹ But on the time Giediewon trusted JAH - him defeated uncircumcise peoples armies who were many many in army of a few tens of thousands and without number like unto locusts. ² **As there are no Creator without I - o nobles and kings - don't believe in the different idols.** ³ **As I-man am your Creator JAH Who sent you forth from your mothers wombs and raised you and fed you and clothed you - why do you pretext? How about why do you worship other idols without I?** ⁴ **I-man did all this to you ~ what did you give I? It are that you might live firmed up in I LAW and I Order and I Command and that I-man might give you your bodies welfare - yet what will I-man want from you?** ⁵ JAH Who rule all said thus ~ Him said - **Save your ras selves from worshippin idols and practisin sorcery and discouragin pessimism.** ⁶ As JAH chastisemant shall come on these who do this - and on them who hear them and do them accord and are them friends and who live firmed up in them command - save your ras selves from worshippin idols. ⁷ As peoples - who don't know you and aren't nice to you - shall arise on you - unless you who feared did JAH Accord - them will eat the money wherefor you wearied ~ like unto Him servants the prophets spoke and like unto Hienok spoke and like unto 'Asaf spoke - unless you did JAH Accord - them will eat the money wherefor you wearied. ⁸ **Evil persons will come havin changed them clothes** Him said ~ there are no other law alongside them apart from eatin and drinkin and adornin in silver and gold - and livin havin firmed up in sin all the Work JAH don't love. ⁹ But them are prepared to go toward drink and food ~ after them were aroused from them slumber Beginnin from mornin up til evenin them go toward evil Work; there are misery and tribulation in them path - yet them feet have no Love path. ¹⁰ and them don't know Love and Inity Work - and there are no fearin JAH in them faces ~ them are crooked evil ones without religion nor virtue ~ them are greedy ones who eat and drink alone ~ them are drunkards - and them sin are without LAW and without measure ~ them are who go toward seducin - sheddin blood - theft and perfidy and violently robbin him money who don't have it. ¹¹ and them are who criticise without Love and without LAW - to them don't fear JAH Who Created them - and there are no fear in them faces. ¹² Them don't shame in the person face that them sight up - and them don't shame a grey-hair nor a elder face ~ on the time them heard when them said - 'An there are money in this world' - them make it them ras self money before them sight it up with them eyes - to there are no fearin JAH in them faces - and on the time them sight it up with them eyes it seem to them that them ate it. ¹³ and them nobles eat trust money ~ them are who eat ~ as them are negativists and as there are no straight thing in them tongues - them don't repeat in evenin what them spoke in mornin. ¹⁴ to them ignore sufferahs and poor ones cries - and them kings hasten to evil - them who disturb a person - him havin saved refugees from wealthy ones hands who rob them. ¹⁵ make them save him who were wronged and the refugee - yet make the kings not be them who begrudge justice because this thing. ¹⁶ But them are who exact tribute ~ them are who rob a person money - and them are criminals - and as them Work are evil - them aren't nice when them eat the newborn calf

with she mother and a bird with she egg ~ them make all them sight up and heard them ras self money. [17] Them love that them might gather to them ras selves - yet them aren't nice to sick and poor ones - and them violently rob the money of a person who don't have it - and them gather all them found that them might be fattened and be Feeling good in it. [18] to them shall perish quickly like unto a scarab that proceeded from it pit and whose track aren't found and that don't return toward it house - and because them didn't work goodly Work when them are in them Life - woe to them bodies on the time JAH vexed and seized them. [19] on the time JAH neglected them - them will perish at one time like unto them are in one chastisemant - to Him indure them meanin as it were them returned toward repentance - yet Him don't quickly destroy them - and them shall perish on the time when them shall perish. [20] But if them don't return toward repentance - Him will quickly destroy them like unto former persons who were precedin them - who didn't keep JAH LAW by what are due. [21] Them are who eat a person flesh and drink a person blood ~ as them gird and work violence to go toward sin - there are no fearin JAH in them faces everytime - and after them arose from them beddin them don't rest to work sin. [22] and them Work are drink and food - goin toward destruction and sin - that them might destroy many persons bodies in this world.

## 25

[1] As them Work are crooked - and as all are who live firmed up in Satan Work that mislead - JAH Who rule all said - **Woe to your body on the time I-man vexed and seized she.** [2] **But to them don't know JAH Work - to them have returned it toward them rear - and to them have neglected I LAW.** [3] and **later in fulfillmant era I-man shall bring the hardship on them like unto them evil measure ~ like unto them sin were written alongside I - I-man shall revenge and destroy them on the day when Judgemant are judged.** [4] **As I-man JAH am full from horizon up til horizon - and as all the Creation have been seized in I Authority - there are none who escape from I Authority in Heaven nor Earth nor depth nor sea.** [5] **I-man command a snake that are beneath Earth - and I-man command a fish that are within sea - and I-man command birds in Heaven - and I-man command the desert donkey in wilderness - to it are I money Beginnin from horizon up til horizon.** [6] **As I-man am Who work wondrous Work and do miracles before I - there are none who escape from I Authority on Earth nor in Heaven ~ there are none who tell I - 'Where do Thou go? How about what do thou Work?'** [7] and **I-man command on Angels chiefs and hosts ~ all Creations whose name are called are I money - and beasts in wilderness and all birds in Heaven and livestocks are I moneys.** [8] It arise from 'Azieb wind and firm up in drought in Mesi` ~ later in fulfillmant era 'Eritra sea shall perish bein heard - arisin from JAH - Who shall come toward she - bein feared and famousness. [9] to Him rule them who dead and persons who are there - and she shall perish bein heard with Saba and Noba and Hindekie and 'Ityopphya limits and all them regions. [10] and Him watch all in lofty Authority and innocence - to Him Authority surpass all the authority - and Him keep cangregations in Him Authority. [11] and to Him Authority firm up more than all the authority - and to Him Kingdom surpass all the kingdoms - and to Him Authority are what rule all the world - to Him able to all - and to there are nothing that fail Him. [12] Him rule all clouds in Heaven ~ Him grow grass to livestocks on Earth - and Him give fruit on the buds. [13] Him feed to all in each of the kinds like unto Him loved ~ Him feed all that Him Created by each of the fruits and each of the foods - and Him feed ants and locusts beneath Earth and livestocks on Earth and beasts - and to a person who prayed Him give him him prayer - and Him don't ignore the plea of the child whose mother and father dead on him - nor widows. [14] As evil persons rebellion are like unto a swirlin wind and wrongdoers council like unto misty urine - Him shall rather accept the plea of them who beg toward Him at each time and clean ones. [15] and as them body are like unto a flyin bird - and as them features attractiveness that are silver and gold are perishable in this world - examination will benefit persons who forgot JAH LAW yet not them gold - and moths shall eat them clothes. [16] and weevils shall totally eat the wheat and the barley fatness - and all shall pass like unto the day that passed yesterday - and like unto a word that proceeded from a mouth don't return - sinner persons money also are like unto it - and them 'beautiful lifestyle' are like unto a passin shadow ~ sinner persons money before JAH are like unto a lie clothes. [17] But if kind persons are honoured JAH won't ignore them - to them have been honoured while them were nice to poor ones - and them hear justice of sufferahs and a child whose mother and father dead on him ~ JAH won't ignore them - to without neglectin them house childran - them honour Him while them clothe the naked from the clothes JAH gave them that them might give to the refugee sufferah. [18] Them don't favour loyal persons judgemant - and them don't make a hireling salary lodge ~ as JAH thing are Truth and honoured like unto a sword whose mouths were two -

them won't do iniquity in them seasons number and in them balance measuremant.

## 26

[1] But poor ones will think again on them beddin - but if wealthy ones don't accept them - them will be like unto dry wood that have no verdure - and a root won't be fertile from alongside where no moisture are - and the leaf won't be fertile if there are no root. [2] As a leaf serve a flower to be a ornamant to fruit - unless the leaf were fertile it won't bear fruit ~ as man fulfillmant are religion - a person without religion have no virtue. [3] If him firmed up religion him worked virtue - and JAH are Feeling good by a person who work Truth and straight Work. [4] and to the person who begged Him - Him shall give him him plea and him tongue reward - and Him won't wrong the true person because him true Work that him worked. [5] As JAH are true - and as Him have loved a Truth thing - Him won't justify the sinner person without repentance because the Work evil him worked - and as all persons souls have been seized in Him Authority because Him were Who ruled Earth and Heaven - as Him won't favour for the wealthy more than the poor in Judgemant time - Him won't justify him without repentance.

## 27

[1] Him Created havin brought all the world from not livin toward livin - and Him totally prepared hills and mountains - and Him firmed up Earth on Water - and lest sea be shaken Him delineated she by sand - to in Him first Word JAH have said make **Light be Created.** [2] Light were Created when this world had been covered in darkness ~ JAH Created all the Creation - and Him prepared this world - and Him firmed up this world by what are due and by money that are straight ~ Him said - make **evenin be dark.** [3] and again JAH said make **Light be Created** ~ it dawned and there were Light - and Him Ilivated the upper Water toward Heaven. [4] and Him streached it forth like unto a tent - and Him firmed it up by a wind - and Him placed the lower Water within a pit. [5] and Him shut the sea lock in sand - and Him firmed them up in Him Authority lest them drown in Water - and Him placed animals and beasts within she - and Him placed within she Liewatan and Biehiemot who were great beasts - and Him placed within she beasts without number - sight up and not sight up. [6] on the third day JAH Created on Earth plants - all the roots and woods and fruits that bear forth in each of them kinds - and a welfare wood beautiful to them to sight it up.. [7] and Him Created a welfare wood that were both beautiful to them to sight it up and sweet to them to eat it - and Him Created grass - and all plants whose seeds are found from within them - to be food to birds and livestocks and beasts. [8] It dusked ~ it dawned - and on the fourth day Him said - make **Light be Created in Heaven called cosmos** ~ JAH havin Created moon and Sun and stars - Him placed them in Heaven called cosmos that them might shine in this world and that them might feed them daylight and night. [9] and after this moon and Sun and stars alternated in night and daylight. [10] and on the fifth day JAH Created all animals and beasts that live within Water and all birds that fly on Heaven - all that are sight up and not sight up - all this. [11] and on the sixth day Him Created livestocks and beasts and others - and havin Created and prepared all - Him Created 'Adam in Him Example and Him Appearance. [12] Him gave him all animals and beasts Him Created that him might reign on them - and again - all animals and beasts and all fishes - and Liewatan and Biehiemot that are in sea. [13] and Him gave him all cows that live in this world and sheeps - the animals not sight up and them that are sight up. [14] and Him placed in Garden 'Adam whom Him Created in Him Example and Him Appearance - that him might eat and might cultivate plants and might praise JAH there. [15] and to lest him demolish Him Command - Him have said - on **the time when you ate from this Herb of Fig you will dead death.** [16] and Him commanded him lest him eat from the Herb of Fig that bring death - that draw attention to evil and good - that bring death. [17] I mother Hiewan were cajoled by a snake misleadin and she ate from that Herb of Fig and gave it to I father 'Adam. [18] and 'Adam havin eaten from that Herb of Fig brought death on him childran and on him ras self. [19] As him have demolished Him Command - and as him have eaten from that Herb of Fig that JAH commanded sayin - **Don't eat from she** - JAH vexed on I father 'Adam and expelled and sent him way from the Garden - and Him gave him that Earth that grow thistle and thorn - that Him cursed because him on the time him demolished Him Command - that him might eat him weariness reward havin toiled and laboured that him might plow she. [20] and on the time JAH sent him forth toward this land - 'Adam returned toward complete sadness - and havin toiled and laboured that him might plow Earth - him began to eat in weariness and also in struggles.

## 28

[1] and after him childran lived havin abounded - there were from them ones who praise and honour JAH and don't demolish Him Command. [2] There were prophets who spoke what were done and what will be done henceforth - and from him childran there were sinners who speak lies

and who wrong persons ~ 'Adam firstborn child Qayel became evil and killed him bredda 'Abiel. [3] JAH judged Judgemant on Qayel because him killed him bredda 'Abiel - and JAH vexed on Earth because she drank him blood. [4] and JAH told Qayel - **Where are thy bredda 'Abiel?** - and Qayel in him heart arrogance said - 'Are mi mi bredda 'Abiel keeper?' [5] 'Abiel became a clean man - but Qayel became a sinner man by killin a kind man - him bredda 'Abiel. [6] Again a kind child Siet were birthed ~ 'Adam birthed sixty childran ~ there are kind persons and evil persons from them. [7] and there are kind persons from them ~ and there are persons who were prophets and them who were traitors and sinners. [8] There are blessed persons who were kind persons - who fulfill them father 'Adam accord and all him told to him child Siet - Beginnin from 'Adam up til Noh who are a kind man who kept JAH LAW. [9] and him sanctioned JAH LAW to him childran ~ him told them - 'Guard' - lest them demolish JAH LAW - and that them might tell to them childran like unto them father Noh told them - and that them might keep JAH LAW. [10] and them lived while them taught them childran - persons birthed after them. [11] But Satan lived when him spoke to them fathers - havin lodged in idols that reached to a grave and that have vows on them - and havin defeated the persons who told him alright - and when them did all that Satan - who are sin teacher - commanded them. [12] and them lived when them worshipped the idols like unto them order - up til a kind man 'Abriham who fulfill JAH Accord. [13] to him have lived firmed up in the LAW beforehand separate from him cousins - and JAH swore a oath with him - havin lodged in wind and fire. [14] JAH swore to him that Him might give him a land of inheritance and that Him might give to him childran up til the Eternity. [15] and Him swore to Yis'haq like unto him that Him might give him him father 'Abriham inheritance - and Him swore to Ya`iqob that Him might give him him father Yis'haq inheritance ~ Him swore to him like into Yis'haq. [16] and Him separated them childran - who were birthed after them from Ya`iqob - from the twelve tribes of 'Isra'iel - and made them priests and kings ~ Him blessed them sayin - **Abound and totally be many many.** [17] and Him gave them them father inheritance - however while Him fed them and loved them - them didn't quit saddenin JAH in all. [18] and on the time Him destroyed them - at that time them will seek Him in worship - and them will return from sin and go toward JAH - to Him love them - and JAH shall pardon them. [19] to bein nice to all Him Created - Him shall pardon them - and it are because them fathers Work that Him love them - yet it aren't because them ras selves Work. [20] and Him streach forth Him Right Hand in plenty that Him might satta a hungry body - and Him reveal Him Eye to pardonin that Him might multiply grain to food. [21] Him give food to crows chicks and to beasts that beg Him ~ on the time them cried toward Him - Him will save 'Isra'iel childran from them enemies hands who delayed from the time. [22] and them will return toward sin again that them might sadden Him - and Him will arouse them enemies peoples in them area on them ~ them will destroy them and kill them and capture them. [23] and again them will shout toward JAH in mournin and sadness - and there are the time when Him sent help and saved them by prophets hands. [24] and there are the time when Him saved them by princes hands - and on the time them saddened JAH them enemies taxed them and captured them. [25] and Daweet arose and saved them from the 'Iloflans hands; and again them saddened JAH - and JAH aroused on them peoples who worry them. [26] and there are the time when Him saved them by Yoftahie hand - and again them forgot JAH Who saved them in them tribulation time. As JAH have brought the hardship on them - Him will arouse on them enemies who were evil who will firm up tribulation on them and totally capture them. [27] and on the time them were worried by tribulation them were seized and again cried toward Him - and Him saved them by Giediewon hand - and again them saddened JAH by them hands Work. [28] and again Him aroused on them peoples who firm up tribulation on them - and them returned and wept and cried toward JAH. [29] and again Him saved them from peoples by Somson hand - and them rested a little from the tribulation - and them arose that them might sadden JAH by them former sin. [30] and again Him aroused on them other peoples who worry them - and again them cried and wept toward JAH that Him might send help to them - and Him saved them from peoples by Bariq and Deebora hands. [31] Again them lived a little season while them worshipped JAH - and again them forgot JAH in them former sin and saddened Him. [32] and Him aroused on them other peoples who worry them - and again Him saved them by Yodeet hand and havin sat again a little season them arose that them might sadden JAH by them sin like unto formerly. [33] and Him aroused on them peoples who rule them - and them cried and wept toward JAH to Him have struck on him head 'Abiemieliek who were a warrior who came that him might fight Yihuda country. [34] and Him saved them by the childran in the area and by Matatyu hand - and on the time that warrior dead him army fled and were scattared - and 'Isra'iel childran followed and fought them up til 'Iyabboq - and them didn't preserve even one person from them. [35] After

this them waited a little and arose that them might sadden JAH - and Him aroused on them peoples who rule them - and again them totally cried toward JAH and JAH ignored them cryin and them mournin - to them have saddened JAH everytime - and to them have demolished Him LAW. [36] and them captured and took them with them priests toward Babilon persons country. [37] and then 'Isra'iel childran who were traitors didn't quit saddenin JAH while them worked sin and worshipped idols. [38] JAH vexed that Him might destroy them one time in them sin ~ Hama havin introduced ten thousand gold in the king box - on the day when it were known - him lodged anger in the king 'Arthieksis reasonin - lest him preserve them childran in Fars country Beginnin from Hindekie and up til 'Ityopphya on the time him told him that him might destroy them. [39] Him did thus - and him wrote a letter where a message were written by the king authority - and him gave him a seal in him hand that him might deliver toward Fars country. [40] Him gave him a seal that him might destroy them on one day when him loved them to destroy them like unto the king commanded - but him commanded that him might introduce them money - the gold and the silver - toward the king box. [41] and on the time 'Isra'iel childran heard this thing them totally cried and wept toward JAH - and them told it to Merdokyos - and Merdokyos told to 'Astier. [42] and 'Astier said - 'Fast - beg - and all 'Isra'iel childran kindreds - cry toward JAH in the place where you are.' [43] and Merdokyos wore sackcloth and sprinkled dust on him ras self - and 'Isra'iel childran fasted - begged - and entered repentance in the country where them were. [44] and 'Astier were totally sad - and bein a queen she wore sackcloth ~ she sprinkled dust and shaved she head - and she didn't anoint perfume like unto Fars queens anoint perfume - and in she deep reasonin she cried and wept toward she fathers Creator JAH. [45] and because this thing Him gave she bein loved alongside Fars king 'Arthieksis - and she made a kind lunch to she fathers Creator. [46] and Hama and the king entered toward the lunch that 'Astier prepared - and like unto him loved that him might do on Merdokyos - JAH paid the hardship on that Hama - and them hanged him on a tall wood. [47] The king letter were commanded that them might quit 'Isra'iel like unto them were in all them accord - and lest them tax them nor rob them nor wrong them nor take them money on them. [48] As JAH shall pardon 'Isra'iel doin thus on the time them cried enterin repentance - it are that them might love them and honour them in Fars country where them lived - yet a king letter were commanded lest them destroy them country nor plunder them livestocks. [49] and on them time them saddened Him - Him will arouse on them peoples who worry them ~ at that time them will totally weep and cry that Him might send them help to them and that Him might save them from peoples hand who firm up tribulation on them.

## 29

[1] and on the time Gibts persons also made 'Isra'iel childran work by makin them work bricks in difficulty - and on the time them worried them all the Work by kickin mud without straw and heatin bricks... [2] and on the time them made them work havin appointed chiefs on them who rush workers - them cried toward JAH that Him might save them from workin all Gibts bricks. [3] At that time Him sent to them 'Aron and Mussie who help them - to JAH have sent them that them might send forth Him kindreds from Fer`on rulership house - and Him saved them from brick Work ~ because in him arrogance him refused to adjourn 'Isra'iel lest them be ruled and sacrifice to JAH in wilderness - JAH have sent them that them might send forth Him kindreds 'Isra'iel from Gibts king Fer`on rulership house - and them saved them. [4] to JAH neglect arrogant ones - and Him drowned Fer`on in 'Eritra sea with him army because him arrogance. [5] and like unto him - Him shall destroy them who didn't work goodly Work in all the kingdoms that Him I-pointed and crowned them - that them who ignore JAH Word when them are nobles and kings might fulfill Him Accord to Him - and that them might give persons who serve in goodly thing them wage - and that them might honour Him famous Name. [6] JAH Who rule all said - **But if them will straighten up I Kingdom - I-man will straighten up them kingdom to them.** [7] **Work goodly Work to I - and I-man shall work goodly Work to you ~ keep I LAW - and I-man shall keep you your bodies ~ live firmed up in I LAW - and I-man shall live lodgin honesty in you like unto your reasonin.** [8] **Love I - and I-man shall love your welfare ~ near toward I - and I-man shall heal you.** [9] JAH Who rule all said - **Believe in I - and I-man shall save you from the tribulation.** [10] Don't live side by side ~ as JAH Who rule all love straight Work - Him said - **You - approach toward I - and I-man shall approach toward you ~ you persons who are sinners and traitors - cleanse your hands from sin - and distance your reasonins from evil.** [11] and **I-man shall distance I anger from you - and I-man shall return to you in Charity and Forgiveness.** [12] **I-man shall distance criminals and enemies who work iniquity from you - like unto I-man saved I slave Daweet from him enemies who met him - from them much malice - and from Gwolyad hand who were a**

warrior - and also from Sa'ol hand who sought that him might kill him - and from him child 'Abiesielom hand who loved that him might take him kingdom. [13] I-man shall save persons who keep I LAW and fulfill I Accord like unto him ~ I-man shall bequeath them honour - and them shall be Feeling good in the present world and yonder in the world that shall come ~ I-man shall crown them on all that them might be Feeling good. [14] Them shall be one with kings who served JAH and were honoured in them beautiful way of Life - like unto the prophet Samu'iel served Him in him beautiful way of Life Beginnin from him infancy - whom JAH - Him bein LAW - chose. [15] Him told him that him might tell 'Elee who were a servant elder - and when him served in JAH Lodgin the Temple - Samu'iel Work also were merciful and I-loved. [16] and on the time him grew when him served in JAH Lodgin the Temple - Him made him to be Ipointed and Inointed - that him might Ipoint him people and that kings might be Inointed by JAH Accord. As JAH have loved him that the kindred him chose from 'Isra'iel childran might be Ipointed - on the time him fulfilled JAH Accord Who Created him - Him gave him the Inointin of the Kingdom in him hand. [17] and when Sa'ol were in him kingdom JAH told Him prophet Samu'iel - **Go - and as I-man have loved `Issiey child Daweet who were birthed from Yihuda kin - Inoint him.**

### 30

[1] I-man have hated Sa'ol kin - to him have saddened I because him violated I Word. [2] and I-man neglected him - to him didn't keep I LAW - and I-man won't crown from him kin again. [3] and persons who didn't keep I LAW and I Word and I Order like unto him - I-man shall destroy I Kingdom and I gift from them childran up til the Eternity. [4] and as them didn't make I famous on the time I-man made them famous - I-man shall destroy them - yet I-man won't again return to lift them up ~ though I-man honour them - as them didn't honour I - I-man won't make them famous. [5] to them didn't do a goodly thing to I on the time I-man did a goodly thing to them - and to them didn't forgive I on the time I-man forgave them. [6] and as them didn't make I a Ruler on the time I-man made them rulers on all - as them didn't honour I on the time I-man honoured them more than all - I-man won't make them famous again nor honour them - and to them didn't keep I LAW. [7] and I-man withheld the gift I-man gave them - and I-man won't return the money I-man withheld from them like unto the measure I-man vexed and swore ~ JAH Who rule all said thus ~ Him said - I-man shall honour them who honoured I - and love them who loved I. [8] I-man shall separate them who didn't honour I nor keep I LAW from the gift I-man gave them. [9] JAH Who rule all said; I-man love them who loved I - and make famous him who made I famous - Him said.. [10] As I-man JAH am Who rule all - there are none who escape I Authority in Earth nor Heaven - to I-man am JAH Who kill and Who save and Who sadden and Who forgive. [11] As famousness and honour are I money - I-man honour him whom I-man loved - to I-man am Who judge and Who revenge and destroy - and I-man make wretched him whom I-man hated. [12] to I-man am Who forgive them who love I and call I Name everytime - to I-man am Who feed food to the wealthy and to the poor. [13] and I-man feed birds and animals - fishes in sea and beasts and flowers - yet I-man aren't Who feed only man. [14] I-man feed crocodiles and whales - gophers and hippos - and badgers... [15] and all that live within Water - all that fly on wind - yet I-man aren't Who feed only man ~ all this are I money. [16] I-man am Who feed all that seek I by all that are due and I-loved.

### 31

[1] and the kings don't reign without I Accord - and sufferahs are by I Command - yet them aren't poor without I Command - and powerful ones are by I Accord - yet them aren't strong without I Accord. [2] I-man gave bein I-loved to Daweet and Wisdom to Selomon - and I-man added eras to Hiziqyas. [3] I-man diminished Gwolyad era - and I-man gave Power to Somson - and again I-man weakened him Power. [4] and I-man saved I slave Daweet from Gwolyad hand who were a warrior. [5] and again I-man saved him from the king Sa'ol hand and from the secand warrior who disputed him - and to him have kept I Command - and I-man saved him from the persons hand who dispute him and fight him. [6] and I-man loved him - and I-man love all the nobles and the kings who keep I LAW ~ as them have made I Feeling good - I-man shall give them prevailin and Power on them enemies. [7] and again that them might inherit them fathers land - I-man shall give them the cleansed and shinin land of inheritance that I-man swore to them fathers.

### 32

[1] JAH Who rule all said - and **you the nobles and also the kings - hear I in I Word - and keep I Command ~ lest you sadden I and worship like unto 'Isra'iel childran saddened I and worshipped**

different idols - them whom I-man kept and saved when I-man JAH am them Creator - JAH Who rule all said - Hear I in I Word; and all whom I-man raised and loved and fed Beginnin that them were birthed from them mother and father. [2] and whom I-man sent forth toward Earth crops - and whom I-man fed the fatness found from Earth makin like unto are due - and whom I-man gave the grape vine and the oil-tree fruit that them didn't plant and the clear Water well that them didn't dig. [3] Hear I in I Word lest you sadden I like unto 'Isra'iel childran saddened I worshippin other idols when I-man JAH am them Creator - Him told them - Who fed them the sheep milk and the honey comb with the hulled wheat - and Who clothed them clothes where ornamant are - and Who gave them all them love. [4] and without it livin that I-man deprived them all them begged I.

### 33

[1] Like unto Daweet spoke sayin - "Isra'iel childran were fed the menna that Angels lowered' - and again hear I in I Word lest you sadden I like unto 'Isra'iel childran saddened I worshippin the idols when I-man am them Creator JAH Who fed them sweet *menna* in wilderness - Him said ~ I-man did all this to them that them might worship I by what are due and to true. [2] JAH Who rule all said - But them didn't worship I - and I-man neglected them ~ them saddened I and lived firmed up in law of idols that weren't I LAW. [3] and I-man shall bring the hardship on them like unto them sin ~ as them have neglected I Worship and as them didn't firm up in I counsel and I Order - I-man neglected them in the sin measure that worked by them hands - and I-man shall lower them toward *Gehannem* in Definite Judgemant that are done in Heaven. [4] to them didn't keep I LAW - and to I-man vex on them - and I-man shall diminish them era in this world. [5] If thou be a king - aren't thou a man who shall dead and be demolished and tomorrow who shall be worms and dust? [6] But today thou boast and are proud like unto a man who won't dead forever. [7] JAH Who rule all said - But thou who are sight up bein well today are a man who will dead tomorrow. [8] But if you keep I Command and I Word - I-man shall bequeath thee-I a honoured country with honoured kings who did I Accord - whose lodgin were Light and whose crowns were beautiful - and whose thrones were silver and gold and whom persons who sit on them adorned - Him said. [9] and them shall be Feeling good within Him country that are a place that approached to persons who worked goodly Work. [10] But to persons who work sin - as them didn't keep I LAW - said JAH Who rule all... [11] it aren't due them that them might enter toward that country where honoured kings shall enter.

### 34

[1] Miedon kingdom shall perish - but Rom kingdom shall totally firm up on Meqiedonya kingdom - and Nenewie kingdom shall firm up on Fars kingdom. [2] and 'Ityopphya kingdom shall firm up on 'Iskindriya kingdom ~ as peoples shall arise - Mo`ab kingdom shall firm up on 'Amalieq kingdom. [3] and bredda shall arise on him bredda - and JAH shall revenge and destroy like unto Him spoke that it might perish. [4] **Kingdom shall arise on kingdom - and the people on the people and country on country** - Him said. [5] and argumants shall be done and there shall be formations - famine - plague - earthquake - drought ~ as Love have perished from this world - JAH chastisemant descended on she. [6] to the day have arrived suddenly when JAH shall come - Who frighten like unto lightnin that are sight up from East up til West. [7] on the day when HIM JAH judge Judgemant - at that time everyone shall raceive him hardship like unto him hand weakness and him sin firmness - to Him have said **I-man shall revenge them on** the day when HIM JAH judge Judgemant and on the day when them feet are hindered - to the day when them are counted to destruction have arrived. [8] At that time JAH shall destroy in *Gehannem* forever persons who won't live firmed up in Him LAW - who work sin. [9] and **them who live in the West ilands and Noba and Hindekie - Saba and 'Ityopphya and Gibts persons - all persons who live in them...** [10] at that time shall know I that I-man were JAH Who rule Earth and Heaven - and Who give bein I-loved and honour - and Who save and Who kill. [11] I-man am Who send forth Sun - Who send it toward it settin - Who bring the evil and the good. [12] I-man am Who bring peoples whom you don't know - who slaughter and eat the money whereby you wearied - your sheeps and your cows flocks. [13] and **them shall capture your childran while them hammer them before you - and you cyaan save them.** Because JAH Spirit of Support didn't lodge in you - as you didn't fear JAH Command that you heard - Him shall destroy your lavishmants and your assignmants. [14] But a person in whom JAH Spirit of Support lodged will know all - like unto Nabukedenetsor told Dan'iel sayin - 'Mi sight up JAH Spirit of Support that lodged in thee-I.' [15] and a person in whom JAH Spirit of Support lodged will know all - and what were hidden will be revealed to him -

and him will know all that were revealed and that were hidden - yet there are nothing hidden from a person in whom JAH Spirit of Support lodged. ¹⁶ But as I are persons who will dead tomorrow - I sins that I hid and worked shall be revealed. ¹⁷ and like unto them test silver and gold in fire - like unto there are sinners - later on the Day of Advent them shall be examined - to them didn't keep JAH Command. ¹⁸ At that time all peoples and all 'Isra'iel children Works shall be examined.

## 35

¹ As JAH vex on you because you didn't judge a Truth Judgemant to the child whose mother and father dead on him - woe to you 'Isra'iel nobles. ² Woe to you persons who go toward a drinkin house mornin and evenin and get drunk - who are partial in judgemant - and who don't hear the widow justice nor the child whose mother and father dead on him - who live in sin and seducin. ³ JAH told 'Isra'iel nobles sayin thus: - **Unless you lived firmed up in I Command and kept I LAW and loved what I-man love - woe to you** - Him told them. ⁴ and **I-man shall bring destruction and chastisemant and tribulation on you - and you will perish like unto what weevils and moths ate - and your tracks and your region won't be found** - Him told them. ⁵ and your country will be a wilderness - and all persons who sight she up formerly shall clap them hands ~ them shall marvel on she while them said - 'Weren't this country filled of she plenty and all who love it?; JAH made she thus by persons sin who live in she.' ⁶ Them shall say - 'As she have made she heart proud - and as she have ilivated she ras self - and as she have firmed up she collar of reasonin up til JAH make she wretched on Earth - and as she shall be a desert by persons arrogance who live in she - and as thorns have grown on she with thistles - woe to she.' ⁷ and she grow weeds and nettles - and she became a wilderness and a desert - and beasts shall live within she. ⁸ to JAH Judgemant have firmed up on she - and to she shall raceive JAH Judgemant Chalice because she reasonin arrogance by persons sin who live in she - and she became frightenin to persons who go toward she.

## 36

¹ Meqiedon persons - don't boast ~ as JAH are there Who shall destroy you - 'Amalieqans - don't firm up your collar of reasonin. ² to you will be lofty up til Heaven and you will descend up til *Gehannem.* ³ on the time 'Isra'iel formerly entered toward Gibts country in Mo`ab and Miedon kingdom Him said - **Don't boast** - to it aren't due to pretend on JAH that you might pretend on Him. ⁴ Thou Yisma'iel kindred - slave child - why do thou firm up thy collar of reasonin by what weren't thy money? How about don't thou think that JAH shall judge on thee on the time Him arose that it might be judged on Earth - on the day when it are judged on thee? ⁵ JAH Who rule all said - **At that time thou will raceive thy hardship like unto thy hand Work - how about why do thou ilivate thy reasonin? How about why do thou firm up thy collar of reasonin?** ⁶ and **I-man shall pretend on thee like unto thou pretended on persons who weren't thy kindreds - to thou do what thou love that thou might work sin - and I-man shall neglect thee in the place where them sent thee.** ⁷ JAH Who rule all said - and **I-man shall do thus on thee** ~ Him said - **But if thou worked goodly Work and if thou love what I-man loved - I-man also shall hear thee-I in all that thou begged.** ⁸ and **if thou fulfill I Accord to I - I-man shall fulfill thy accord to thee-I - and I-man shall dispute thy enemies to thee-I - and I-man shall bless thy childran and thy seed to thee-I.** ⁹ and **I-man shall multiply thy sheeps and thy cows flocks to thee-I - and if thou lived firmed up in I Command and also if thou did what I-man love** - JAH Who rule all said - **I-man shall bless to thee-I all thou seized in thy hand.** ¹⁰ **But if thou don't do I Accord - if thou don't live firmed up in I LAW and I Command - all this tribulation that were told formerly shall find thee - to thou didn't indure tribulation firmed up in I Command - and to thou didn't live firmed up in I LAW - and thou cyaan escape from I anger that will come on thee everytime.** ¹¹ and **as thou didn't love what I-man loved - when I-man am Who Created thee bringin from not livin toward livin...** ¹² **all this were thy money - that thou might kill and heal to do all that thou loved - that thou might work and demolish - that thou might honour and abuse - that thou might ilivate and downbase - and as thou have neglected I Worship and I praise when I-man am Who gave thee lordship and also honour alongside persons who are beneath thy authority - thou cyaan escape from I anger that will come on thee.** ¹³ and if thou did JAH Accord and if thou lived frmed up in Him Command - Him will love thee-I that thou might be Feeling good with Him in Him Lordship - and that thou might be a partaker with persons who inherited a honoured country. ¹⁴ to Him have said - **If them ilivate I - I-man will bequeath them bein I-loved and honour - to I-man shall make them Feeling good in the Temple where prayer are prayed** - to JAH Who rule all have said - and **them shall be I-loved and chosen like unto a sacrifice.** ¹⁵ Don't neglect to do Work whereby welfare are done and a goodly thing that you might cross from death toward Life. ¹⁶ But persons who work goodly Work -

JAH shall keep them in all Him goodly Work - that them might be Him slaves like unto 'Iyob whom JAH kept from all the tribulation ¹⁷ JAH shall keep them in all goodly Work - that them might be Him slaves to Him like unto 'Abriham whom Him saved on the time him killed the kings - and like unto Mussie whom Him saved from Kenaniewon hand and Fer`on hand - in whom 'Abriham lived - and who were also disturbin him body evenin and mornin night and day that them might make him worship idols. ¹⁸ But when them took him toward the idols that were them money - him would indure the tribulation while him refused. ¹⁹ to 'Abriham who believed Him Beginnin from him childhood were to JAH Him trusted friend - and while him refused him would worship JAH Who Created him. ²⁰ As him totally love JAH - him didn't quit worshippin JAH up til him dead - and him didn't depart from Him LAW up til when him dead - and him taught him childran that them might keep JAH LAW. ²¹ and like unto them father 'Abriham kept Him LAW - them didn't depart from JAH LAW ~ like unto Him told to Angels sayin - **I-man have a friend in this world called 'Abriham** - 'Abriham childran Ya`iqob and Yis'haq - who are Him slaves because whom JAH spoke - didn't depart from JAH LAW. ²² JAH Who were praised alongside them and Who rule all said - **'Abriham are I friend ~ Yis'haq are I canfidante - and Ya`iqob are I friend whom I Reasonin loved.** ²³ But when Him totally loved 'Isra'iel childran - them lived when them Continually saddened Him - and Him lived when Him indured them and when Him fed them *menna* in wilderness. ²⁴ Them clothes didn't age - to them have been fed *menna* that are knowledge *'injera* - and them feet didn't awaken. ²⁵ But them reasonins would distance from JAH everytime ~ as them were who work sin Beginnin from Antiquity - them had no hope to be saved. ²⁶ Them became like unto a crooked bow - yet them didn't become like unto them fathers Yis'haq and 'Abriham and Ya`iqob who served JAH in them beautiful way of Life ~ them would sadden Him everytime by them idols on the mountains and the hills ~ them would eat on the mountain and at the caves and the trees roots. ²⁷ Them would slaughter a steer ~ them would sacrifice a sacrifice - and them would be Feeling good in them hands Work ~ them would eat the rest of the sacrifice ~ them would drink of them sacrifice - and them would play with demons while them sang. ²⁸ and demons would admire all them games and them songs to them - and them would work them drunkenness and adultery without measure - and them would do the robbery and greed that JAH don't love. ²⁹ to Kene`an idols - and to Midyam idols and to Be`al - and to 'Aphlon and Dagon and Seraphyon and 'Arthiemadies who are 'Eloflee idols... ³⁰ and to all peoples idols in them area - them would sacrifice; and all 'Isra'iel would worship idols like unto peoples worship idols by money that them sight up and heard ~ them would make them games and them songs and them bluster that peoples make. ³¹ All 'Isra'iel kindreds do likewise - who say 'We will worship JAH' - without keepin Him Command and Him LAW that Mussie told them in 'Oreet that them might keep JAH LAW and might distance from worshippin idols. ³² Lest them worship separated idols - apart from them fathers Creator Who fed them the honey found from Maga who fed them the plantation grain and sent them forth toward the Earth crops - and Who fed them the *menna...* ³³ Mussie commanded them sayin 'Don't worship' - to Him are them Creator - and to Him feed them who loved Him - and Him won't deprive them who loved Him and desired Him. ³⁴ But them didn't quit saddenin JAH - and them would sadden JAH on the time Him made them Feeling good. ³⁵ and on the time Him saddened them - them would cry toward Him - and Him would save them from the tribulation that found them - and them would again be totally Feeling good and would live many eras. ³⁶ and at that time them would totally return them heart toward sin that them might sadden JAH like unto formerly - and Him would arouse on them peoples in them area that them might destroy them - and them would worry and tax them. ³⁷ and again them would totally return and cry toward them Creator JAH. ³⁸ and Him would forgive them ~ it are because them fathers - Noh - Yis'haq and 'Abriham and Ya`iqob - who served JAH in them beautiful way of Life Iginnnin from Antiquity - to whom Him firmed up Him Oath - yet it aren't because them ras selves Work that Him forgive them. ³⁹ and Him loved persons who kept Him LAW lovin that them might multiply them childran like unto Heaven stars and sea sand. ⁴⁰ But on the time dead ones arose that them have like unto sea sand - them are sinner persons souls that will separate from 'Isra'iel childran and enter toward Gehannem. ⁴¹ As JAH have told 'Abriham - **Sight up toward Heaven at night and count Heaven stars as it were thou could count** - likewise as Him have told him - **Thy childran and righteous ones shall shine in Heaven like unto Heaven star**s - them are like unto stars that shine in Heaven - but what them have are kind persons souls birthed from 'Isra'iel. ⁴² and again as Him have told him - **Overstand toward the river edge and the sea - and sight up what are amidst the sand ~ count as it were thou could count - and thy sinner children are likewise - who will descend toward *Gehannem*** *on* **the time dead ones arose** - them are sinner persons souls. <sup>43</sup> and 'Abriham believed in JAH ~ because this thing it were counted to him bein Truth ~ him found him morale in this world - and after him wife Sora aged she birthed a child called Yis'haq. <sup>44</sup> to him have believed that persons who worked goodly Work shall arise and go toward the Kingdom of Heaven that live firmed up forever - and again him shall find a Kingdom in Heaven. <sup>45</sup> But to him have believed that persons who worked sin shall go toward *Gehannem* that live firmed up forever on the time dead ones arose - but that righteous ones who worked goodly Work shall reign with Him forever. <sup>46</sup> But to him have believed that it shall be judged forever to true without falsehood on persons who worked sin - to him shall find Life Kingdom in Heaven." make glory and praise enter to JAH to true without falsehood - and the first book that speak the Meqabyans thing were filled and fulfilled.

# The Book of Meqabyan II
## 1

<sup>1</sup> This are a book that speak that Meqabees found 'Isra'iel in Mesphiethomya that are Sorya part and killed them in them region beginnin from 'Iyabboq up til 'Iyerusaliem square - and that him destroyed the country. <sup>2</sup> Because Sorya and 'Edomyas persons and the 'Amalieqans were one with the Mo`ab man Meqabees who destroyed 'Iyerusaliem country - as them have camped beginnin from Semarya up til 'Iyerusaliem square and up til all she region - them killed in war without preservin persons who fled apart from a few persons. <sup>3</sup> and on the time 'Isra'iel childran wronged - Him aroused Mo`ab man Meqabees on them - and him killed them by a sword. <sup>4</sup> and because this thing JAH enemies the peoples bragged on Him honoured country - and them swore in them crime. <sup>5</sup> and 'Iloflee and 'Idomyas persons camped - as Him have sent them because them pretended JAH Word - them began to revenge and destroy JAH country. <sup>6</sup> and that Meqabees country are Riemat that are Mo`ab part - and him arose from him country in Power and them swore also with persons with him. <sup>7</sup> and them camped in Gielabuhie region that are Mesphiethomya lot up til Sorya that them might destroy JAH country - and there him begged the 'Amalieqans and 'Iloflans ~ him gave them much silver and gold and chariots and horses that them might be one with him in crime. <sup>8</sup> Them came together and crushed the fortress ~ persons who lived in she shed blood like unto Water. <sup>9</sup> and them made 'Iyerusaliem like unto a plant keepin hut - and him made a voice heard within she ~ him worked all the sin Work that JAH don't love - and them also defouled JAH country that were filled of praise and honour. <sup>10</sup> Them made thy friends flesh and thy slaves corpses food to wilderness beasts and Heaven birds. <sup>11</sup> and them robbed childran whose mother and father dead on them and widows - to without fearin JAH them have done like unto Satan taught them - and up til JAH Who examine kidneys and reasonins vexed - them took out the fetus in pregnant daughters belly. <sup>12</sup> Them returned toward them country while them were Feeling good because them worked evil Work on JAH kindreds - and them took the plunder that them captured from a honoured country. <sup>13</sup> on the time them returned and entered toward them houses them made joy and song and clappin.

## 2

<sup>1</sup> The prophet whom them call Re`ay told him thus: - "Today be Feeling good a little on the time when Feeling good joy were made ~ JAH Whom 'Isra'iel glorified have that Him might revenge and destroy thee in the chastisemant thou didn't doubt. <sup>2</sup> Will thou say - 'Mi horses are swift ~ because this mi will escape by runnin'? <sup>3</sup> As to I - I-man tell thee - Persons who will follow thee are swifter than vultures ~ thou won't escape from JAH Judgemant and destruction that shall come on thee. <sup>4</sup> Will thou say - 'Mi wear iron clothes - and spear flingin and bow stingin aren't able to mi'?; JAH Who honour 'Isra'iel said - **It aren't by spear flingin that I-man will revenge and destroy thee"** Him told him ~ **"I-man shall bring on thee heart sickness and itch and rheumatism sickness that were worse and firmer than spear flingin and bow stingin - yet it aren't by this that I-man shall revenge and destroy thee.** <sup>5</sup> **Thou have aroused I anger ~ I-man shall bring heart sickness on thee - and thou will lack one who help thee - and thou won't escape from I Authority up til I-man destroy thy name invocation from this world.** <sup>6</sup> **As thou have firmed up thy collar of reasonin - and as thou have ilivated thy ras self on I country - on the time I-man quickly did this thing like unto a eye wink - thou will know I that I-man were thy Creator ~ as thou are before I like unto grass before the wind that fire eat - and as thou are like unto the dust that winds spill and scattar from Earth - thou are like unto them alongside I.** <sup>7</sup> to **thou have aroused I anger - and to thou didn't know thy Creator - and I-man shall neglect all thy kindred - and neither will I-man preserve him who neared on thy fortress.** <sup>8</sup> and now return from all thy sin that thou worked ~ if thou return from thy sin and totally appease in mournin and sadness before JAH - and if thou

beg toward him in clean reasonin - JAH will forgive thee all thy sin that thou worked before Him" - him told him. <sup>9</sup> At that time Meqabees wore dust and mourned before JAH because him sin - to JAH have vexed on him. <sup>10</sup> to Him eyes are revealed - to Him don't withhold - and to Him ears are opened - to Him don't neglect - and to Him don't make the word Him spoke false - and to Him quickly do she at one time - to JAH knew lest Him preserve the chastisemant Him spoke by the prophet Word. <sup>11</sup> Him cast him clothes and wore sackcloth and sprinkled dust on him head and cried and wept before him Creator JAH because him sin that him worked.

## 3

<sup>1</sup> and the prophet came from Riemat and told him - to Riemat that are Mo`ab part are near to Sorya. <sup>2</sup> Him dug a pit and entered up til him neck and wept firm tears - and him entered repentance because him sin that him worked before JAH. <sup>3</sup> and JAH told the prophet thus: - **Return from Yihuda country Riemat toward the Mo`ab official Meqabees** Him told him. **Tell him - "JAH told thee thus" - Tell him - "Him told thee - I-man JAH Who am thy Creator sent thee by I Accord that thou might destroy I country - lest thou say - 'Mi destroyed the honoured country 'Iyerusaliem by mi Power firmness and mi army abundance' - yet it aren't thou who did this thing.** <sup>4</sup> to **she have saddened I by all she greed and she perfidy and she lustfulness.** <sup>5</sup> and **I-man neglected and cast she by thy hand - and now JAH forgave thee thy sin because thy childran whom thou birthed ~ it aren't because thou who firmed up thy collar of reasonin and say 'Mi incircled the country 'Iyerusaliem by mi authority firmness.'** <sup>6</sup> **As persons who doubt aren't disciplined to enter repentance - don't be a doubter - and now enter repentance bein disciplined in thy complete reasonin."** <sup>7</sup> However persons are admired who enter repentance in them complete reasonins and who don't again return toward thirst and sin by all that entered toward repentance because them sin. <sup>8</sup> Persons are admired who return toward them Creator JAH bein disciplined in mournin and sadness - in bowin and many pleas. Persons are admired who are disciplined and enter repentance - to Him have told them - **You are I moneys who entered repentance after you misled persons who entered repentance.** <sup>9</sup> Him told arrogant Meqabees on the time him returned toward Him in repentance after him misled - **I-man forgive thee thy sin because thy fright and thy alarm; to I-man am JAH thy Creator Who bring hardship on childran by a father sin up til seven generations if the child work the sin that the father worked - and Who do Charity up til ten thousand generations to persons who love I and keep I LAW.** <sup>10</sup> and **now I-man will firm up I Oath with thee because these thy childran whom thou birthed** - and JAH Who rule all and Who honoured 'Isra'iel said - **I-man will accept the repentance thou made because thy sin that thou worked.** <sup>11</sup> At that time him proceeded from the pit and bowed to the prophet ~ him swore sayin - "As mi have saddened JAH - make mi what thou loved - yet make JAH do mi thus lest mi separate from thee-I ~ as we have no Law - mi didn't live firmed up in Him Command like unto mi fathers ~ thou know that we fathers taught we and that we worship idols. <sup>12</sup> to mi are a sinner who lived firmed up in mi sin - who firmed up in mi collar of reasonin firmness and mi reasonin arrogance whereby mi saddened JAH Command - but up til now mi hadn't heard JAH servants the prophets Word - and mi didn't live firmed up in Him LAW and Him Command that Him commanded mi." <sup>13</sup> Him told him sayin - "As there are none from your kindred precedin you who trusted him sin - mi knew that the prophet raceived repentance today." <sup>14</sup> "But now quit thy worshippin idols and return toward knowin JAH that thou might have true repentance" him told him ~ him fell and bowed at the prophet feet - and the prophet lifted up and commanded him all the goodly Work that are due him. <sup>15</sup> and him returned toward him house doin also like unto JAH commanded him. <sup>16</sup> and that Meqabees returned him body toward worshippin JAH - and him destroyed from him house the idols and also the sorcery - persons who worship idols and pessimists and magicians. <sup>17</sup> and mornin and evenin like unto them fathers do - him would examine the childran him captured and brought from 'Iyerusaliem in all JAH Commands and Him Order and Him LAW. <sup>18</sup> and from the childran him captured - him appointed knowin ones on him house. <sup>19</sup> and again from the infants him appointed knowin childran who keep levelled childran who were small - who enter toward the beddin that them might teach them JAH LAW that 'Isra'iel childran do ~ him would hear from captured 'Isra'iel childran the Order and the LAW and the Nine Laws - that Mo`ab persons order and them mosques that them make were vain. <sup>20</sup> Him destroyed them mosques - them idols and them sorcery - and the sacrifice and the grapes sacrificed to the idols mornin and evenin from the goat kids and fattened sheeps flocks. <sup>21</sup> and him destroyed him idols whom him worship and beg and believe in all him Work while him sacrificed sacrifice afternoon and at noon - and to all priests told him - and him idols to whom him do them accord. <sup>22</sup> As it

would seem to him that them save him in all that them told - him wouldn't scorn all the thing them told him. ²³ But that Meqabees quit them Work. ²⁴ After him heard the Ra`ay thing - whom them call a prophet - him accomplished him Work in repentance ~ as 'Isra'iel childran would sadden Him at one time - and on the time Him chastised them in the tribulation - as them know and also cry toward JAH - all Him kindreds worked goodly Work more than 'Isra'iel childran in that season. ²⁵ on the time Him heard that them were seized and abused by peoples hand who firm up tribulation on them and that them cried toward Him - Him thought of them fathers oath and at that time Him would forgive them because them fathers Yis'haq - 'Abriham - and Ya`iqob. ²⁶ and on the time Him saved them - them would forget JAH Who saved them from tribulation - and them would return toward worshippin the idols. ²⁷ and at that time Him would arouse on them peoples who firm up tribulation on them - and on the time them firmed up tribulation on them and saddened them - them would cry toward JAH ~ as Him love them because them were Him Authority Creation - at that time Him would be nice and forgive them. ²⁸ and on the time Him kept them - them again returned toward sin that them might sadden Him by them hands Work that were firm and by worshippin idols in them councils. ²⁹ But Him would arouse on them Mo`ab and 'Iloflee - Sorya - Midyam and Gibts persons; and on the time them enemies defeated them - them would cry and weep ~ on the time them firmed up on them and taxed them and ruled them - JAH would arouse princes to them that Him might save them on the time Him loved.

## 4

¹ and in 'Iyasu time are a day when Him saved them. ² and in Giediewon time are a day when Him saved them. ³ and in Somson time and in Deebora and Bariq and Yodeet time are a day when Him saved them - and lodgin whether on male or on daughter - Him would arouse princes to them that them might save them from them enemies hands who firm up tribulation on them. ⁴ and like unto JAH loved - Him would save them from persons who firm up tribulation on them. ⁵ and them would be totally Feeling good in all the Work that Him accomplished to them ~ them would be Feeling good in them land seed and in multiplyin all them flocks in wilderness and them livestock. ⁶ and Him would bless them plants and them livestock to them - to Him sight them up in Eye of Mercy - and to Him wouldn't diminish them livestock on them - to them are kind persons childran and Him would totally love them. ⁷ But on the time them were evil in them Work - Him would cast them in them enemies hands. ⁸ and on the time Him destroyed them - them would seek Him in worship - and them would return from sin and march toward JAH in repentance. ⁹ and on the time them returned in them complete reasonin - Him would atone them sin to them ~ Him wouldn't think of them former sin on them - to Him know them that them were flesh and blood - to them have this world misleadin thoughts on them - and to them have demons in them. ¹⁰ But on the time that Meqabees heard this Order that JAH worked in Him worshippin place the Temple - him were slain in repentance. ¹¹ After him sight up and heard this - him didn't scorn workin goodly Work; him didn't scorn workin all the goodly Work that 'Isra'iel childran work on the time JAH forgave them - and after them trespassed from Him LAW - them weep and would cry on the time JAH whipped them - and again Him would forgive them - and them would keep Him LAW. ¹² and Meqabees likewise would straighten up him Work - and him would keep Him LAW - and him would live firmed up in 'Isra'iel Creator JAH Command. ¹³ At that time after him heard all the Work whereby 'Isra'iel childran boast - Him would boast like unto them in keepin JAH LAW. ¹⁴ Him would urge him kindred and childran that them might live firmed up in JAH Command and all Him LAW. ¹⁵ and him would forbid the order that 'Isra'iel forbid - and him would hear and keep the Law that 'Isra'iel keep - and when him kindred are another Mo`ab man - him would forbid the food that 'Isra'iel forbid. ¹⁶ and him would send forth tithes ~ him would give all that were first birthed and that him owned from him cows and him sheeps and him donkeys - and returnin him face toward 'Iyerusaliem him would sacrifice the sacrifice that 'Isra'iel sacrifice. ¹⁷ Him would sacrifice sin and vow sacrifice - a sacrifice whereby welfare are done and a accord sacrifice - and the Itinual sacrifice. ¹⁸ and him would give him first crops - and him would gush and pour the grapes that 'Isra'iel pour - and him would give this to him priest whom him I-pointed - and likewise him would do all that 'Isra'iel do - and him would sweeten him ishence. ¹⁹ Him built a candlestick and a bowl and a seat and a tent and the four links of rings - and diluted oil to the Hola of Holas lamps - and the curtain that 'Isra'iel make in the Hola of Holas on the time them served JAH. ²⁰ and like unto them worked goodly Work on the time them lived firmed up in Him Order and Him LAW and on the time JAH didn't neglect and cast them in them enemies hands - Meqabees also would work goodly Work like unto them. ²¹ Him would beg toward 'Isra'iel Creator JAH everytime that Him might be him Teacher and lest Him separate him

from 'Isra'iel childran whom Him chose and who did Him Accord. ²² and again him would beg Him that Him might give him childran in Tsiyon and a house in 'Iyerusaliem - that Him might give them Heavenly Seed of Virtue in Tsiyon and a Heavenly House of Soul in 'Iyerusaliem - and that Him might save him from the destruction spoken by the prophet tongue - that Him might accept him repentance in all the mournin him wept before JAH bein sad and enterin repentance... ²³ and lest Him destroy childran in this world on him - and that Him might keep him in him proceedin and enterin. ²⁴ Kindreds from Mo`ab peoples beneath Meqabees Authority were Feeling good that them might believe - to them chief live firmed up in straight Work - and them would check up him judgemant and fulfill him accord - and them would scorn them country language and them country justice ~ them would overstand that Meqabees Work surpassed and were straight. ²⁵ and them would come and hear Meqabees charity and Truth judgemants. ²⁶ Him had much money ~ him had daughter slaves and male slaves and camels and donkeys - and him had five hundred horses that wear breastplates ~ him would totally defeat the 'Amalieqans and 'Iloflans and Sorya persons - but formerly when him worshipped idols him lived when them defeated him. ²⁷ Him prevailed - yet but from him worshippin JAH onward - when him went toward battle there are none who defeated him. ²⁸ But them would come in them idols Power that them might fight him - and them would call them idols names and curse him - however there were none who defeat him - to him have made him faith on him Creator JAH. ²⁹ and when him did thus and when him defeated him enemies - him lived when him ruled peoples in him Authority. ³⁰ Him would revenge and destroy wronged persons enemy to them ~ him would judge Truth to a child whose mother and father dead on him. ³¹ and him would raceive widows in them trouble time - and him would give from him food and satta them who hungered - and him would clothe the naked from him clothes. ³² and him would be Feeling good in him hands Work - and him would give from the money him had without begrudgin - and him would give tithes to the Temple ~ Meqabees dead havin lived in Feeling good joy when him did this.

## 5

¹ and him dead quittin him childran who were small - and them grew up like unto them father taught them ~ them kept them house Order - and them would keep all them kindred - and them wouldn't make poor ones cry - nor widows nor a child whose mother and father dead on him. ² Them would fear JAH - and them would give them money alms to poor ones - and them would keep all the trust them father told them - and them would calm the child whose mother and father dead on them and widows in them trouble time - and them would be them mother and father ~ them would make them cast from persons hand who wrong them - and calm them from all the disturbance and sadness that found them. ³ Them lived five years while them did thus. ⁴ After this the Keledans king Tseerutsaydan came ~ him destroyed all them country - and him captured Meqabees childran and destroyed all them villages. ⁵ and him plundered all them money ~ them lived firmed up in all evil Work and sin - in adultery - insult and greed and not thinkin of them Creator - yet persons who don't live firmed up in JAH LAW and Him Command and who worship idols seized them also and took them toward them country. ⁶ Them eat what a beast bit and the blood and the carcass - and what a scavenger beat and cast - all that JAH don't love - yet them have no order from all the true Commands written in 'Oreet. ⁷ Them don't know JAH them Creator - Who sent them forth from them mothers wombs and fed them by what are due - were them Medicine. ⁸ Them marry from them aunt and them father wife - them step mother - and them go toward robbery and evil thing and sin and adultery - yet them have no order in Judgemant time - and them work all evil Work and them marry them aunts and them sistren and them have no LAW. ⁹ and all them roads are dark and slippery - and them Work are sin and adultery. ¹⁰ But those Meqabees childran would keep in all them Order ~ them wouldn't eat what a scavenger beat nor what dead and lodged ~ them wouldn't work all the Work that the Keledans childran work - to them many Works are evil that weren't written in this book - that sinners work - and doubters and criminals - betrayers totally filled of robbery and sin and pagans childran. ¹¹ All the Work them Creator JAH love aren't there alongside them. ¹² and again them would worship a idol called Bi'iel Fiegor ~ them would trust it like unto them Creator JAH when it were deaf and dumb. to it are the idol that a person hand worked - to it are the person hand Work that a smith worked who work silver and gold - that have no breath nor knowledge - and it had nothing that it sight up nor hear. ¹³ It don't eat nor drink. ¹⁴ It don't kill nor save. ¹⁵ It don't plant nor uproot. ¹⁶ It don't harm it enemy nor benefit it friend. ¹⁷ It don't impoverish nor honour. ¹⁸ It will be a hindrance to mislead the Keledans persons who were lazy - yet it don't chastise nor forgive.

## 6

¹ JAH enemy Tseerutsaydan who were arrogant appointed them who veil and falsehood priests to him idols. ² Him would sacrifice to them

and pour the grapes to them. ³ and it would seem to him that them eat and drink. ⁴ and while it dawned him would give them cows and donkeys and heifers - and him would sacrifice mornin and evenin - and him would eat from that defouled sacrifice. ⁵ and again him would disturb and obligate other persons that them might sacrifice to him idols - yet it weren't that only them do it. ⁶ on the time them sight up Meqabees childran that them were handsome and that them worship them Creator JAH - the idols priests loved that them might mislead them to sacrifice and to eat from that hated sacrifice - but these honoured Meqabees childran refused them. ⁷ As them keep them father command - and as them have firmed up in workin goodly Work - and as them totally fear JAH - it failed them to agree... ⁸ on the time them bound them and insulted them and robbed them. ⁹ Them told to the king Tseerutsaydan that them refused sacrifice and bowin to him idols. ¹⁰ and because this thing the king vexed ~ him were sad and commanded that them might bring them - and them brought and stood them before him - and the king told them to him idols - "Sacrifice a sacrifice to mi idols." ¹¹ and them spoke and told him - "An I won't answer thee in this thing - and I won't sacrifice to thy defouled idols." ¹² Him frightened them by Works that abounded - yet him couldn't able to them - to them have disciplined them reasonins believin in JAH. ¹³ Him flamed a fire and cast them in fire - and them gave them bodies to JAH. ¹⁴ After them dead them arose and were sight up to him at night drawin them swords when him had reclined on him lordship throne - and him totally feared. ¹⁵ "Mi sirs - tell mi alright - what should mi do to you? Don't take mi body in death - that mi might do all thou commanded mi." ¹⁶ Them told him all that are due to him while them said - "Think that JAH were thy Creator - and JAH are there Who shall dismiss from this thy kingdom where thou are arrogant - and Who shall lower thee toward *Gehannem* of fire with thy father Deeyablos ~ when I worshipped I Creator JAH without a iniquity livin that I wronged thee - and when I bowed to Him in fearin Him JAH-ness that also. ¹⁷ to Him are Who Created all - Earth and Heaven and sea and all that are within she. ¹⁸ and to Him are Who Created moon and Sun and stars - and to Him Who Created all the Creation are JAH. ¹⁹ to there are no other creator withou Him in Earth nor Heaven - to Him are Who able to all - and to there are nothing that fail Him. As Him are Who kill and Who save - Who whip in tribulation and Who forgive - when I bowed to Him in fearin JAH - like unto thou burned I in fire - thou will finish thy hardship by that" them told him. ²⁰ "As Him are Who rule Earth and Heaven - there are none who escape from Him Authority. ²¹ There are none from the Creation Him Created who departed from Him Command - apart from thou who are a criminal - and criminals like unto thee whose reasonins thy father Satan hid - and thou and those thy priests and thy idols will descend together toward *Gehannem* where are no exits up til Eternity. ²² Thy teacher are Satan who taught thee this evil Work that thou might do a evil thing on I - yet as it aren't only thou who do this - you will descend toward *Gehannem* together. ²³ to thou make thy ras self like unto thy Creator JAH - yet thou didn't know JAH Who Created thee. ²⁴ and thou are arrogant in thy idols and thy hand Work up til JAH make thee wretched ~ Him shall canvict thee on all thy sin and iniquity that thou worked in this world.

## 7

¹ Woe to you who don't know JAH Who Created you - to thy idols who are like unto thee - and to thee - and to you have that you might regret a regrets that won't profit on the time you were sad bein seized in *See'ol* difficulty - and woe to thee - to you who don't keep Him Word and Him LAW. ² You will have no exit from she up til Eternity - thy priests and thou who sacrifice to them like unto your Creator JAH - to thy idols who have no breath nor soul - who won't revenge and destroy him who did a evil thing on them - nor do a goodly thing to him who did a goodly thing to them. ³ Woe to you who sacrifice to them - to them are a person hands Work where Satan live - lodgin there to mislead lazy ones reasonin like unto thee - that him might lower you toward *Gehannem* of fire - and the priests who serve demons commanded to you and your idols. ⁴ As you don't know that there are nothing that will profit you - you wrong and err. ⁵ As to the animals that JAH Created to be food to you - and dogs and beasts - them are better than you - to besides one death there are no more candemnation on them. ⁶ But as you will dead and raceive hardship in *Gehannem fire* where are no exits up til Eternity - animals are better." ⁷ Havin spoken this - them went and were hidden from him. ⁸ But that Tseerutsaydan lodged when him trembled - seized by a firm fright - and fright didn't quit him up til it dawned.

## 8

¹ and him lived firmed up in reasonin malice and arrogance. ² and as iron have been called firm - like unto Dan'iel sight it up on him kingdom - him turned in peoples countries in him area. ³ Him lived firmed up in evil and all him laziness and in disturbin persons. ⁴ and him totally

destroy what I spoke formerly - and him eat a person money. ⁵ to him are diligent to evil like unto him father Deeyablos who firmed up him collar of reasonin - and him destroy what remained with him army. ⁶ Him say - "Mi era became like unto the Sun era" - yet him don't know JAH that Him were him Creator. ⁷ and in him reasonin him think that the Sun are found from him. ⁸ Him arise in Power - him camp in Tribe of Zablon lot and begin a formation in Meqiedonya - and him receive him food from Semarya - and them give him presents from Semarya. ⁹ Him camp in nomads region - and him reach up til Seedona - and him cast a tax on 'Akayya - and him elevate him collar of reasonin up til the flowin sea - and him return and send messengers up til Hindekie sea. ¹⁰ and likewise him elevate him collar of reasonin up til Heaven. ¹¹ Him live firmed up in bein arrogant and in evil - yet him don't have humblin him ras self. ¹² and him path are toward darkness and slipperiness - and toward crime and bein arrogant - and toward sheddin blood and tribulation. ¹³ and all him Work are what JAH hate ~ him do like unto robbery and evil and sin teacher Deeyablos taught him ~ him make a child cry whose mother and father dead on him - and him aren't nice to a poor one. ¹⁴ and him defeated and destroyed peoples kings by him authority. ¹⁵ and him ruled enemies chiefs - and him ruled many peoples - and him taxed them like unto him loved. ¹⁶ Even if him destroyed - him didn't quit ~ there are no person whom him didn't snatch Beginnin from Tersies sea up til 'Iyareeko sea. ¹⁷ Him would bow to idols ~ him would eat what dead and lodged - the blood - what a sword bloated and cut - and what were sacrificed to idols ~ all him Work are without justice - yet him have no justice ~ as him have been who alarm peoples beneath him authority - him would tax them tax like unto him loved. ¹⁸ As him do all that him loved before him - there are no fearin JAH before him - and him live in malice before JAH Who Created him. ¹⁹ Him didn't do it like unto him Creator - and like unto him did a evil thing on him companion on the time him vexed and seized him - JAH shall also pay him hardship. ²⁰ As JAH have said - **I-man shall revenge and destroy sinner persons who don't live by I Command - that I-man might destroy them name invocation from this world** - like unto Him destroyed peoples who were precedin him - Him shall revenge and destroy him on the time when Him destroy. ²¹ and like unto evil persons did evil things - them shall raceive them hardship. ²² But bein commanded from JAH - goodly Work shall follow persons who work goodly Work. ²³ to like unto 'Iyasu destroyed the five Kene`an kings in cave in one day - and like unto him made Sun stand in Geba`on by him prayer that him might destroy them armies - Sun have stood amidst Heaven up til him destroyed 'Ewiewon and Kenaniewon - Fierziewon and Kiethiewon and 'Iyabusiewon armies - and like unto him killed around twenty thousand persons at one time - and like unto him killed them - and like unto him bound them makin foot from neck - and like unto him killed them in cave by spear - and like unto him fitted a stone on them... ²⁴ Tribulation like unto this shall find all persons who sadden JAH in them evil Work.

## 9

¹ "O thou weak man who aren't JAH - why are thou proud? thou who are sight up today bein a man are Earth ashes tomorrow - and thou will totally be worms in thy grave. ² to thy teacher are Deeyablos who return all persons sin hardship toward him ras self because him misled I father 'Adam - and *See'ol* will find thee again - and she will find persons who work thy sin. ³ to in firmin up him collar of reasonin and makin him ras self proud - like unto him refused to bow to 'Adam whom the Creator Created... ⁴ thou also have refused to bow to thy Creator JAH like unto thy teacher Deeyablos did. ⁵ Like unto thy precedin fathers - who don't know them Creator JAH in worship - will go toward *Gehannem* - thou also will go toward *Gehannem*. ⁶ Like unto Him revenged and destroyed them because them evil Work that them worked in this world - and like unto them descended toward *Gehannem*... ⁷ thou also will descend toward *Gehannem* like unto them. ⁸ As thou have aroused Him anger - and as thou have neglected to worship JAH Who gave thee Authority on the five kingdoms - do it seem to thee that thou will escape from JAH Authority? ⁹ Thou don't do thus that thou do Him Accord - thus Him examined thee - but if thou work goodly Work in this world - JAH will accomplish all thy Work to thee-I - and Him will accomplish and bless all the Work thou seized in thy hand to thee-I - and Him will subject thy Antiquity of enemies and thy day enemies to thee-I. ¹⁰ Thou will be Feeling good in thy enterins and thy proceedins and in thy child birthed from thy nature - and in thy flocks and thy fatnesses - and in all Work where thou placed thy hand - and in all that thou thought in thy heart ~ as Authority have been given thee-I from alongside JAH that thou might do thus and might work and plant and demolish - all will be commanded to thee-I. ¹¹ However if thou won't hear JAH Word nor live firmed up in Him LAW - like unto criminals who were precedin thee - and who don't worship JAH by what are due - and who didn't believe firmed up in HIM straight LAW - there are nothing whereby thou will escape from JAH Authority - to JAH Judgemant are Truth. ¹² All are

totally revealed before Him - yet there are nothing hidden from before Him. [13] Him are Who seize the kings Authority and Who overturn powerful ones thrones. [14] Him are Who Ilivate them who were downbased and Who lift up them who fell. [15] Him are Who loose them who were bound and Who arouse them who dead ~ as pardon dew are found from alongside Him - on the time Him loved Him shall arouse persons whose flesh were demolished and rotten and were like unto dust. [16] and havin aroused and judged persons who worked evil Work - Him will take them toward *Gehannem* - to them have saddened Him. [17] to them are who demolished JAH Order and Him LAW - and Him will destroy them child from this world. [18] As kind persons Work are more difficult than sinner persons Work - sinner persons don't love that them might live in kind persons counsel. [19] Like unto Heavens were distanced from Earth - likewise kind persons Work were distanced from evil persons Work. [20] But sinner persons Work are robbery and sin - adultery and iniquity - greed and perfidy Work ~ it are bein drunk in iniquity and robbin a person money. [21] It are quickly goin toward sheddin a person blood - and it are goin toward destruction that don't benefit - and it are makin a child weep whose mother and father dead on him ~ it are eatin blood and what dead and lodged - and it are eatin camel and boar flesh - and it are goin toward a daughter in she blood before she are cleansed - and toward a daughter in childbirth. [22] All this are sinner persons Work ~ she are Satan trap that were a wide and prepared path - and that take toward *Gehannem* that live firmed up forever - and toward *See'ol*. [23] But righteous ones path that were totally narrow are what take toward welfare - and innocence and humbleness - and Inity and Love - and prayer and fast - and flesh purity - toward keepin from what don't benefit - from eatin what a sword bloated and cut and what dead and lodged - and from goin toward a youtmon wife and from adultery. [24] Them keep from what weren't commanded by LAW - from eatin disgustin food and from all hated Work - and from all the Work that JAH don't love - to sinner persons do all this. [25] As to kind persons - them distance from all the Work that JAH don't love. [26] Him love them and shall keep them from all them tribulation like unto Trust money. [27] to them keep Him Order and Him LAW and all that Him love - but Satan rule sinner persons.

## 10

[1] Fear JAH Who Created you and kept you up til today - yet you the nobles and the kings - don't go on Satan path. [2] Live in the LAW and Command of JAH Who rule all - yet don't go on Satan path. [3] As on the time 'Isra'iel childran came toward 'Amalieq that them might inherit Kiethiewon and Kenaniewon and Fierziewon country - Siefor child Balaq and Bele`am... [4] whom thou cursed are cursed - and him whom thou blessed blessed ~ don't go on Satan road - to him have said - "An mi will give thee much silver and gold that honour thee - that thou might curse to mi and - and havin cursed - that thou might destroy to mi." [5] and to Bele`am have come makin him sorcery reward a morale - and to Siefor child Balaq have shown him the place where 'Isra'iel childran camped. [6] to him have done him pessimism - and to him have sacrificed him sacrifice - and to him have slaughtered from him fattened cows and sheeps - and to him have loved that him might curse and destroy 'Isra'iel childran. [7] Him returned a curse toward a bless - yet but as JAH didn't love that him might curse them by Him Word - don't go on Satan road. [8] "As thou are the kindred that JAH chose - as thou are JAH Lodgin that shall come from Heaven - make persons be cursed who curse thee-I - and make persons who bless thee-I be blessed" him said. [9] on the time him blessed them before him - after this Siefor child Balaq were sad - and him totally vexed and commanded that him might curse them. [10] to the kindred that JAH blessed have come toward this country - and Bele`am told him - "Mi won't curse 'Isra'iel whom JAH blessed." [11] and Siefor child Balaq told Bele`am - "As to mi - mi had loved that thou might curse to mi ~ thou blessed them before mi - yet but thou didn't curse them ~ if thou had cursed to mi and told mi 'Give mi' - as to mi - mi would have given thee a house full of silver and gold - but thou totally blessed them - and thou didn't do a goodly thing to mi - and mi won't do a goodly thing to thee." [12] Bele`am said - "What JAH told mi **Speak** with mi tongue - mi will speak it - yet as to mi - mi cyaan dare to ignore JAH thing. [13] Lest mi curse a blessed kindred - as JAH shall vex on mi if mi love money - as to mi - mi don't love money more than mi soul. [14] As JAH have told them father Ya`iqob - make **persons who bless thee-I be blessed and make persons who curse thee-I be cursed** - lest mi curse blessed Ya`iqob - as to mi - mi don't love money more than mi soul" him said - and as JAH have told him - **Him who bless thee-I are blessed...** [15] and **a person who curse thee-I unjustly are cursed** - accomplish thy path and thy Work that JAH might love thee. [16] and don't be like unto former persons who saddened JAH in them sin and whom Him neglected - and there are them whom Him destroyed in Destruction Water. [17] and there are them whom Him destroyed by them haters hands ~ there are them whom Him destroyed by them enemies hands - bringin enemies who were evil persons who

firmed up tribulation on them - and them captured them lords with them priests and them prophets. [18] and them delivered them toward the foreign country them don't know ~ them totally captured them - and them plundered them livestocks on them and destroyed them country. [19] to them have demolished the honoured country 'Iyerusaliem fences and ramparts - and them made 'Iyerusaliem like unto a field. [20] and the priests were capture - and the LAW were demolished - and warriors fought in war and fell. [21] and widows were capture ~ as them have been capture - them wept to them ras selves - yet them didn't weep to them husbands who dead. [22] and the childran wept - and elders shamed - and them weren't nice to neither a grey haired person nor a elder. [23] Them destroyed all them found in the country - yet them weren't nice to beauties nor to them in LAW ~ as JAH have vexed on Him kindreds on the time Him loved that Him might beforehand destroy Him Lodgin the Temple - them captured and took them toward the country them don't know and toward peoples. [24] As them sadden them Creator everytime - because this thing on the time JAH neglected 'Isra'iel childran - JAH made 'Iyerusaliem to be ploughed like unto a field. [25] to Him are nice to them because them fathers - but Him didn't destroy them at one time ~ as Him love them fathers Yis'haq and 'Abriham and Ya`iqob who reigned to true and lived firmed up in straight LAW before them Creator - it are because them fathers kindness - yet it aren't because them ras selves kindness that him forgive them. [26] and Him I-pointed them on honours that were twofold - and them found two Kingdoms - on Earth and in Heaven. [27] and you the kings and the nobles who live in this passin world - like unto your fathers who lived firmed up in Work that are due and who were precedin you likewise inherited the Kingdom of Heaven - and like unto them names were beautiful to a child childran - think of them. [28] and thou - straighten up thy Work - that Him might straighten up thy Kingdom to thee - and that thy name might be called in goodly invocation like unto the kind kings who were precedin thee who served JAH in them beautiful lifestyle.

## 11

[1] Think of JAH slave Mussie who weren't annoyed when him kept around this kindred in him humbleness and him prayer and whom not even one person destroyed - and him begged toward JAH in him innocence to him sista and bredda who backbit him and loved that JAH might destroy them while him said - "As them have wronged Thee-I - Lord - pardon and don't neglect thy kindreds" - and him atoned them sin to them - yet Him thought of JAH servant Mussie who weren't annoyed. [2] "To I-man have wronged Thee-I - and forgive I Thy slave who am a sinner - to Thou are Merciful - and to Thou are a Pardoner - and forgive them them sin." [3] and Mussie likewise atoned them sin to him sista and bredda who backbit him. [4] and because this thing him were called innocent. [5] and JAH totally loved him more than all the priests childran who were him bredren - to Him I-point the priests - and JAH made him like unto Him Ras Self alongside them. [6] But Him also sank beneath Earth Qorie childran who challenged ~ Him lowered them toward *See'ol* with them livestocks and them tents when them said "We are there - we are there in flesh and soul" ~ as him Creator JAH have loved him - and as him didn't depart from Him Command - all the word him spoke would be done to him like unto JAH Word. [7] and unless thou demolished JAH Command likewise - JAH will do thy accord to thee-I and will love thy thing to thee-I - and Him will keep thy Kingdom to thee-I. [8] and 'Asaf and Qorie childran who departed from Mussie command grumbled on him because him told them - "Straighten up your reasonins to be ruled to JAH." [9] Them grumbled sayin - "How about aren't we Liewee childran who work priesthood Work in Tent that were special?" [10] Them went and smoked up ishence seizin them censers that them might smoke up - but JAH didn't accept them plea - and them were burnt by the fire in them censers - and them melted like unto the wax that fire melt - and not even one person remained from them ~ as Him have said - **Them censers were honoured by them bodies bein burnt** - apart from them censers that entered toward JAH Lodgin to JAH Command - neither them clothes nor them bones remained. [11] Because this thing JAH told 'Aron and Mussie - **Gather them censers toward the Tent ~ make it be a instrumant to I Lodgin wherefor I-man prepared all I-ginnin from outside up til within.** [12] and him prepared the honoured Tent instrumants ~ him prepared the rings and the joiners - *Keerubiel* picture sea. [13] Him worked the cups - the curtains - the Tent area grounds to the mobilisation - the altar and the jugs whereby them sacrifice in the Tent that were special. [14] Them sacrificed the sacrifice that them sacrifice by them accord - the sacrifice whereby welfare are made - the sacrifice whereby Him atone sin - and the vow sacrifice and the mornin and the evenin sacrifice. [15] All that Him commanded to Mussie - him commanded them in the Tent that were special - that them might work Work in she. [16] Them didn't scorn bein ruled to them Creator JAH - that Him Name might be praised by them in the LAW Lodgin Tent of them Creator JAH Who gave them a promise that Him might give them to give them them fathers

inheritance that produce honey and milk that Him swore to 'Abriham. [17] Them didn't scorn bein ruled to them Creator JAH - Who swore to Yis'haq and firmed up Him Worship to Ya`iqob... [18] and Who firmed up to 'Aron and Mussie the Tent where Him Worship are kept... [19] and Who firmed up Him Worship to both 'Elyas and Samu'iel in the Temple and Tent that Selomon worked up til it became JAH Lodgin in 'Iyerusaliem - and up til JAH Name Lodgin became JAH Lodgin that honoured 'Isra'iel. [20] to she are a supplication - and to she are a sin atonemant where it are overturned to them who live in innocence and to the priests. [21] and to she are a place to persons who do Him Accord where Him will hear them pleas... [22] and JAH LAW Canstruction that honoured 'Isra'iel. [23] to she are where sacrifice are sacrificed and where Ishence are smoked up that JAH Who honoured 'Isra'iel be in goodly Fragrance. [24] and Him would speak bein on the joiner where Him forgive in the Tent that were special ~ JAH Light would be revealed to Ya`iqob childran whom Him chose and to friends who live firmed up in Him LAW and Him Command. [25] But persons who ignored JAH LAW will be like unto Qorie childran whom Earth sank - and likewise sinner persons have that them might enter toward *Gehannem* that have no exits up til Eternity.

## 12

[1] You who didn't keep the LAW Him commanded you in Tent - woe to you 'Isra'iel nobles who also didn't do Him Accord - yet you did your ras selves accord - and this are bein arrogant and pride - greed and adultery - drink and bein drunk - and swearin in lie. [2] and **because this thing I anger - like unto chaff are burnt before a fire - and like unto fire burn the mountain - and like unto a whirl wind spill the crushed chaff from Earth and scattar it toward Heaven - lest it trace be found in it place - I anger will destroy you like unto that.** [3] JAH Who honoured 'Isra'iel said - **I-man shall likewise destroy all persons who work sin** - and think of JAH Who rule all and to Whom nothing fail. [4] Him love persons who love Him - and to persons who live firmed up in Him Command - Him will atone them iniquity and them sin to them ~ don't be dull and stingy of heart by not believin. [5] and make your reasonins straight to be ruled to JAH - and believe in Him that you might firm up your bodies - and **I-man shall save you from your enemy hand in your tribulation day.** [6] and **in your plea time I-man tell you - Check - I-man am there with you in Support ~ I-man shall save you from your enemy hand ~ as you have believed in I - and as you have done I Command - and as you didn't depart from I LAW - and as you have loved what I-man love** - JAH Who rule all said - **I-man won't neglect you on your tribulation day.** [7] Him love them who love Him - to Him are a Pardoner - and to Him are nice - and Him keep persons who keep Him LAW - like unto a trust money. [8] Him return Him anger to them many times ~ because Him were who know them that them are flesh and blood - as Him are a Pardoner - Him didn't destroy all in Him chastisemant - and on the time them souls were separated from them flesh - them will return toward them Earthliness. [9] As Him have Created them bringin from not livin toward livin - them won't know the place where them live up til JAH love that Him might bring them from not livin toward livin ~ again Him separated them souls from them flesh - and Earth nature returned toward it Earthliness. [10] and again Him Accord shall bring them from not livin toward livin." [11] But Tseerutsaydan who denied JAH multiplied bein arrogant before JAH ~ him made him ras self lofty up til the day that him loved on the time him quit Him. [12] "An mi era became like unto Heaven era - and mi are who send forth Sun - and mi won't dead up til Eternity" him said. [13] and before him finished speakin this thing the Angel of Death whose name are called Thilimyakos alit and struck him heart ~ him dead in that hour ~ as him didn't praise him Creator - him were separated from him beautiful lifestyle and him perished arisin from him arrogance abundance and him Work evil. [14] But when the Keledans king army had camped in the city and the country squares lovin to fight him - on the time him dead - them proceeded and destroyed him country ~ them plundered all him livestock - and them didn't preserve a elder who near and sight up ramparts. [15] Them plundered all him money - and them took him tiny money - and them burned him country in fire and returned toward them country.

## 13

[1] But these five Meqabees childran who believed gave them bodies to death refusin to eat the sacrifice to idols. [2] to them have known that pretendin with JAH surpass from pretendin with persons - and JAH anger from the king anger. [3] Havin known that this world will totally pass and that the Feeling good joy won't live firmed up forever - them gave them bodies to fire that them might be saved from fire in Heaven. [4] and as them have known that bein made Feeling good in Garden one day are better than livin many eras in this world - and that findin Thy Pardon one hour Lord - are better than many eras - them gave them bodies to fire. [5] What are I era? Like unto a shadow - like unto passin

wax melt and perish on a fire edge - aren't it like unto that? [6] But Thou Lord live forever - and Thy Era aren't fulfilled - and Thy Name invocation are to a child childran. [7] and Meqabees childran thought that it seemed all this ~ refusin to eat a disgustin sacrifice them chose believin in JAH. [8] Knowin that them will arise with persons who dead - and meanin because JAH - knowin that Judgemant shall be judged after Resurrection of Council - because this thing them gave them bodies to martyrdom. [9] You persons who don't know nor believe persons who dead risin - knowin that the Life them find later will surpass from this them passin Earthly Life - arisin from these five Meqabees childran who gave them bodies together to the death and whose appearance were handsome - after this them knew Resurrection. [10] Because them believed in Him knowin that all shall pass - and because them didn't bow to idols - because them didn't eat a disgustin sacrifice that don't give Support - them gave them bodies to death that them might find thanks from JAH. [11] to because this thing knowin that Him will make them Feeling good in flesh and soul in later era - them didn't know this world flavour and death tribulation a serious thing to them who have child and wife - and knowin that Resurrection be made in flesh and soul on the Day of Advent - them gave them bodies to death. [12] and knowin that persons who kept JAH LAW - with the nobles and the kings who believed JAH Word and were nice... [13] shall live reignin to a child childran many eras in Kingdom of Heaven where are no sadness and tribulation nor death - and knowin in them reasonins what will be done later - like unto wax melt amidst a fire - because this thing them gave them bodies to death. [14] Believin that them faces will shine seven hands more than the Sun - and that them will be Feeling good in Him Love on the time all arose in flesh and soul - them gave them bodies to death.

## 14

[1] But the Samrans and 'Ayhuds thing - the Seduqans who don't believe persons who dead risin - and the Fereesans thing quite totally sadden I - and it help I to I reasonin ~ "We will dead tomorrow" 'Ayhuds say - "Make we eat and drink ~ we will dead tomorrow ~ there are no Feeling good joy we will sight up in grave." [2] But the Samrans say - "As we flesh will be dust - it won't arise. [3] Because she were invisible like unto wind and like unto iyunder voice - check - she are here - and because she were what them don't call and invisible - as soul won't arise if flesh dead - on the time Resurrection are done we will believe we souls arisin. [4] But as beasts will eat she and as worms will eat she in the grave - we flesh are sight up alongside all ~ she will become dust and ashes. [5] and those beasts who ate she will become dust - to them have been like unto grass - and to them have become dust like unto them weren't Created - and to them trace won't be found - but we flesh won't arise." [6] and the Fereesans say - "We believe as to persons who dead arisin - however Him will bring and Inite souls with another flesh that are in Heaven - that aren't on Earth ~ where will demolished and rotten fleshes be found?" [7] But the Seduqans say - "After we soul proceeded from we flesh - we won't arise with persons who dead - and flesh and soul have no arisin after them dead - and after we dead we won't arise." [8] and because this thing them totally err - and as them speak insult on JAH Lordship - them thing sadden I. [9] As them didn't believe JAH Who honour them - them have no hope to be saved - however them have no hope to dead and arise and be saved. [10] O 'Ayhudan who are blind of reasonin - when thou are whom Him Created bringin from not livin toward livin - and scorned like unto spit - will thou make JAH ignorant - Who made thee a person? Will it fail JAH Who Created thee in Him Example and Him Appearance to arouse Initin thy flesh and thy soul? [11] As thou won't escape from JAH Authority - don't think a thing that are thus ~ thou will arise without thou lovin - to there are the hardship thou will raceive in *See'ol* where thou were seized on the time thou dead - and it shall be judged on thee without thou lovin. [12] to the sin found from demons that demons place in thy reasonin are worked alongside thee after thou were birthed from thy mother womb - and to she are worked abundantly on the time thou grew up. [13] Them place she in thy body on the time thou dead - and she will bring hardship on them on the time them worked she. [14] Like unto there are sin in them collar of reasonin - as there are persons who work sin bein seized by she - she kindreds will present demons. [15] All sinner persons souls shall come from Heaven edge where them are - and thy sin likewise shall introduce thee toward *Gehannem* pullin and bringin thy soul from where thou are. [16] and after thy flesh lived separate from thy soul - JAH Charity dew shall arouse thee bein seven fold like unto I father 'Adam flesh. [17] Thou who live in grave - thou also err in thy error - yet make it not seem to thee that thou only mislead the others ~ thou say - "The arisin that persons who dead shall arise aren't there" - that them might depart from JAH Command and err. [18] Him shall arouse thee that Him might give thee thy hardship like unto thy Work that thou worked - yet who shall quit thee that thou might remain bein dust? [19] But at that time - whether wind in wind be thy nature - or if Water in Water be thy nature - or if

Earth in Earth be thy nature - or if fire in fire be thy nature - it shall come. [20] and if a soul that lodged in thee be what lived in *See'ol* - she shall come. [21] and righteous ones souls that live in Garden in joy shall come. [22] But thou 'Ayhudan - Samran - Fereesan - Seduqan - will live in *See'ol* up til it are judged on thee. [23] At that time thou will sight up that JAH shall pay thee the hardship like unto thy sin because thou misled persons. [24] "Persons who dead won't arise ~ as we will dead - make we eat and drink" - and because thou sat in Mussie chair and misled by thy words while thou said - "Persons who dead won't arise" - thou will sight up that Him shall pay thee thy hardship. [25] and without thy knowin *'Oreet* Book - and when thou teach the books word - because this thing thou erred ~ it would be better had thou remained without learnin from thy misleadin a person. [26] It would have been better if thou didn't know the books word - when thou promulgate JAH kindreds in evil teachin and thy worthless words. [27] to JAH don't favour havin sight up a face - and to Him shall give the grace and glory Him prepared to Him friends - persons who teach goodly Work - but thou have that thou might raceive thy reward like unto thy Work and the things that thou spoke. [28] But there are nothing whereby thou will escape from JAH Authority Who shall judge on thee - and Him have that Him might pay thee like unto thy Work - to them whom thou taught and thou together will receive a sentance. [29] Know that persons who dead shall arise - and if them are persons who kept Him LAW them shall arise - and like unto Earth send forth grass on the time rain rained - as Him Command shall send them forth from a grave - it aren't possible to it to remain demolished and rotten. [30] Like unto moist wood drink dew and send forth leaves on the time Him satta she rain to Earth - like unto wheat bear forth fruit - and like unto grain produce buds - like unto it aren't possible to she to withhold that she might prevent she fruit if JAH loved... [31] and like unto it aren't possible to a daughter who canceived to close and prevent she womb on the time labour seized she - like unto it aren't possible to she to escape without birthin... [32] as dew have alit toward she bein commanded from JAH - at that time she shall produce them at one time - yet after she heard JAH Word - a grave also likewise cyaan prevent the persons gathered alongside she from arisin. [33] and fleshes shall be gathered in the place where them corpses fell - and them places where souls live shall be opened - and souls shall return toward the flesh where them were formerly separated. [34] and on the time a drum were beaten - persons who dead shall quickly arise like unto a eye wink - and havin arisen them shall stand before JAH - and Him shall give them them reward like unto them hand Work. [35] At that time thou will sight up that thou arise with dead ones - and thou will marvel at all the Work thou worked in this world - and on the time thou sight up all thy sins written before thee - at that time thou will regret a useless regret. [36] Thou know that thou will arise with dead ones and that thou will raceive thy hardship like unto the Work that thou worked.

## 15

[1] But persons who found them reward by them goodly Work shall be Feeling good at that time ~ persons who ignored while them said - "Persons who dead won't arise" shall be sad at that time on the time them sight up that persons who dead arose with them evil Work that don't benefit. [2] That - them Work that them worked shall canvict them - and them ras selves shall know that it canvict them without one livin who will dispute them. [3] on the day when Judgemant and mournin are done - on the day when JAH shall come - on the day when Definite Judgemant are judged - persons who forgot JAH LAW shall stand in the place where them stand. [4] on the day when there shall be total darkness - and on the day when mist are pulled - on the day when flashes are sight up and when lightnin are heard... [5] and on the day when quakes and fright and heatwave and sleet frost are made... [6] on the day when a evil person who worked evil Work raceive hardship - and on the day when a clean person raceive him reward like unto him worked clean Work - and on the day when persons who forgot JAH LAW raceive the hardship like unto a sinner person worked sin - them shall stand in the place where them stand. [7] to on the day when a master aren't more honoured than him slave - and on the time when a mistress aren't more honoured than she slave... [8] and on the time when the king aren't more honoured than a poor one - and on the time when a elder aren't more honoured than a infant - on the time when a father aren't more honoured than him child - and on the time when a mother aren't more honoured than she child... [9] on the time when a wealthy one aren't more honoured than a poor one - and on the time when a arrogant one aren't more honoured than a downbased one - and on the time when the great aren't more honoured than the small - she are the day when Judgemant are judged - to she are the day when them raceive sentance and hardship - and to she are the day when all will raceive hardship like unto them worked sin. [10] and to she are the day when persons who worked goodly Work raceive them reward - and to she are the day when persons who worked sin raceive hardship. [11] and as she are the day when persons who found them reward are made Feeling good - persons who forgot

JAH LAW shall stand in the place where them stand. Persons who make liars - who digest books while them said - "Persons who dead won't arise" - them shall sight up Resurrection. [12] At that time this world sinners - who didn't work goodly Work in this world - shall weep on them sin that them worked - because sadness found them without calmin. [13] and all likewise - kind persons who worked goodly Work - them Feeling good joy won't be fulfilled up til Eternity - to them have worked goodly Work when them were in this world. [14] to them have known that them will arise after them dead - and them didn't depart from them Creator LAW. [15] Because them didn't depart from Him LAW - them shall inherit two welfares ~ Him multiplied them seed in this world - and Him honoured them childran. [16] Him bequeathed them the Kingdom of Heaven where shall be found the welfare him swore to them fathers on the time when persons who dead arise - and on the time when rich ones become poor. [17] Persons shall weep who worked sin - who don't believe persons who dead arisin - who don't keep JAH LAW - and who don't think of Arisin Day. [18] At that time them will sight up the tribulation that shall find them and shall have no endin - and where are no calmin nor welfare - and it have the sadness that have no rest nor calmin in them reasonin. [19] and a fire that don't perish and worms that don't sleep shall find them. [20] and in the place where are them flesh are fire - sulphur - whirl wind - frost - hail - sleet ~ all this shall rain over them. [21] to persons who don't believe persons who dead arisin - there are fire of *Gehannem on* them.

## 16

[1] Thou - please think of what are on thy flesh - and thy feet and thy hands nails - and thy head hair - to them proceed quickly on the time thou cut them ~ know Resurrection by this - that thou have a reasonin - and that thou have religion and knowledge. [2] Thy feet and thy hands nails and thy head hair - thou say - "Where do these come from?" ~ aren't it JAH Who prepared it that them might proceed - that thou know arisin that shall be done on thy flesh that aren't on another flesh - that thou might know that thou will arise after thou dead? [3] Because thou misled persons while thou said - "There are no Resurrection of the dead ones" - on the time when dead ones arise thou will raceive thy hardship like unto thou worked sin and iniquity. [4] and as even what thou planted now won't remain refusin that it might grow - whether it be wheat or barley - thou will sight she up on the time the day arrived when thou raceive thy hardship. [5] and again - the plant thou planted won't say - "I-man won't grow" - and be it a fig wood or a grape vine - it fruit and it leaf won't be changed. [6] If thou plant grapes - it won't be changed that it might be a fig - and if thou plant figs - it won't be changed that it might be grapes - and if thou sow wheat it won't be changed that it might be barley. [7] All - in each of the seeds - in each of it kinds - each of the fruits - each of the woods - each of the leaves - each of the roots - send forth fruit havin raceived Pardon Dew blessin by what are found from JAH - yet if thou sow barley also it won't be changed that it might be wheat. [8] and all likewise - that a grave might produce flesh and soul - she shall produce persons like unto JAH sowed on she ~ the flesh and soul that JAH sowed shall arise bein Inited - yet persons who worked goodly Work won't be changed in persons who worked evil Work - and persons who worked evil Work also won't be changed in persons who worked goodly Work. [9] on the time the hour arrived when a drum are beaten - persons who dead shall arise by the Pardon Dew found from JAH ~ persons who worked goodly Work shall arise in Life Resurrection - and them reward are the Garden where are Feeling good joy that JAH prepared to kind persons - where are no tribulation nor disease - and that are clean ones lodgin where them won't again dead after this. [10] But persons who worked evil Work shall arise a Definite Judgemant arisin - and with Deeyablos who misled them... [11] and with him armies - demons who don't love that even one person might be saved from all 'Adam childran... [12] them shall descend toward *Gehannem* that were darkness edge - where are tooth grindin and mournin - where are no charity nor pardon - and where are no exits up til Eternity - that are beneath *See'ol* forever. to them didn't work goodly Work in this world when them were in them flesh. [13] Because this thing it shall be judged on them on the time when flesh and soul arise bein Inited. [14] Woe to persons who don't believe the flesh and soul arisin whereby JAH show Him miracles abundance together. [15] and all and each one shall raceive him reward like unto him Work and him hands weariness.

## 17

[1] A wheat kernel won't grow nor bear fruit unless she were demolished. But if a wheat kernel are demolished she will send roots toward Earth ~ she will send forth leaves ~ there will be buds ~ it will bear fruit. [2] You know that the one wheat kernel will become many kernels. [3] and all likewise - this kernel grow risin up from Water and wind and Earth dew - to wheat cyaan bear fruit without Sun - but Sun are because fire stead. [4] and wind are because a soul stead - and wheat cyaan bear fruit without wind - and the Water give Earth to drink and satta she. [5] and

after Earth that are ashes drank Water - she produce roots - and she tips are lofty upward ~ she bear fruit around what JAH blessed she. **6** But a wheat kernel are 'Adam example - in whom lodged a resonatin soul that JAH Created - and likewise a grape wood drink Water and send forth roots - and the thin root kinds drink Water. **7** to Pardon Dew found from JAH give to drink vines tips that were long - and it send the Water upward toward the leaf tips ~ it bud up from the Sun heat - and by JAH Accord it bear fruit. **8** It shall be a goodly fragrance that make a reasonin Feeling good - and on the time them ate it - it shall satta like unto Water that don't make thirsty and grain that don't make hungry - and on the time them immersed it - it will be the cluster blood. **9** and like unto it were told in Psalm sayin - "Grapes make a person reasonin Feeling good" - on the time them drank it - it make a person heart Feeling good - and on the time a person who came loose opened him mouth and drank it - him are drunk ~ him drink and fill in him lungs - and the blood flow toward him heart. **10** As grapes drunkenness totally mislead - and as it deprive him him mind - it make the pit and the cliff like unto a wide meadow - and him don't know obstacles and thorns on him feet and hands. **11** JAH did thus on she fruit and grape wood that Him Name might be praised by persons who believe dead persons arisin and who do Him Accord. **12** in the Kingdom of Heaven Him shall make persons Feeling good who believe persons who dead arisin.

## 18

**1** You persons who don't believe persons who dead arisin - around what error you err! and on the time them took you toward the place you don't know - you will regret a useless regrets - and because you didn't believe the arisin that persons who dead shall arise Inited in soul and flesh - and on the time persons cast you toward *Gehannem*... **2** if you work whether the good or the evil - you will raceive your reward like unto your Work - to you have misled them companions reasonin while you said - "We know that persons who dead - who were dust and ashes - won't arise." **3** As them death have no exit - and as them have no Power to them chastisemant that shall come on them - and as them weren't firm in them tribulation - because this thing them mislead them companions ~ to them have that them might stand in JAH Square. **4** on the time Him vexed on them in Him wrath them will totally fear ~ because them didn't know that them were Created bringin from not livin toward livin - as them speak JAH LAW without knowin - it shall be judged on them all because them worked evil. **5** Them don't know *Gehannem* where them will go - to because them were angry and because them were crooked in them Work - them teach to them companions like unto them reasonin thirst measure - and to them are evil ones who teach a crooked thing while them said - "There are no Resurrection of dead ones." **6** At that time them shall know that persons who dead shall arise - and them shall know that it shall be judged on them because them didn't believe the persons who dead arisin that are to all 'Adam childran. **7** to all I are 'Adam childran - and to I have dead because 'Adam - and to death judgemant have found I all from alongside JAH because I father 'Adam error. **8** I will again arise there with I father 'Adam that I might raceive I hardship by I Work that I worked - to the world have been ruled to death by I father 'Adam ignorance. **9** By 'Adam infringin JAH Command - because this thing I raceived hardship ~ I flesh in grave melted like unto wax - and I bodies perished. **10** and Earth drank I marrow ~ I perished and I attractiveness perished in grave - and I flesh were buried in grave - and I beautiful words were buried in Earth. **11** and worms proceeded from I shinin eyes - and I features perished in grave and became dust. **12** Where are youtmons features attractiveness - who were attractive - whose stance were handsome and whose word thing succeeded? How about where are warriors firmness? **13** Where are the kings armies - or how about the nobles lordship? Where are adornin in horses and adornin in silver and gold and adornin in shinin weapons? Didn't it perish? **14** Where are sweet grape drink - and how about food flavour?

## 19

**1** O Earth who gathered the nobles and the kings and rich ones and elders and daughters who were attractive and beauties who were attractive - woe arisin from thee-I. **2** O Earth who gathered persons who were warriors - them who have attractiveness - and them who were fine of leg - and them who have reasonin and knowledge - and them whose words have words that were beautiful like unto a hummin harp and like unto a lyre and a violin beat... **3** and them who have a tune that make Feeling good like unto grape drink make Feeling good - and them whose eyes shine like unto a mornin star... **4** and them who sketch what were firm like unto them right hands lift up what are given and withheld and like unto them were - and them whose feet were beautiful to sight up - and them who run like unto rushin wheels - woe arisin from thee-I. **5** O death who separated attractive persons souls from them flesh - woe arisin from thee-I - to thou have been sent by JAH Accord. **6** As thou have gathered many persons whom JAH produced from thee-I and returned toward thee-I - thou Earth - woe arisin from thee-I ~ I were

found from thee-I ~ I returned toward thee-I by Accord of JAH ~ I were Feeling good over thee-I by JAH Accord. **7** Thou became a carpet to I corpses ~ I recurred over thee-I - and I were buried within thee-I ~ I ate thy fruit - and thou ate I flesh. **8** and I drank the Water found from thy springs - and thou drank I blood springs ~ I ate the fruit found from thy Earthliness - and thou ate I body flesh. **9** Like unto JAH commanded thee-I to be I food - I ate grain from thy Earthliness that have beautiful dew - and thou raceived I fleh attractiveness and made it dust to thy food like unto JAH commanded thee-I. **10** O death who gathered the nobles and the kings who were powerful - woe arisin from thee-I ~ thou didn't fear arisin from them famousness and them frightenin - like unto JAH Who Created them commanded thee-I ~ o death - woe arisin from thee-I - and thou didn't scorn the sufferah. **11** and thou weren't nice to persons whose features are beautiful - and thou didn't quit powerful ones and warriors ~ thou didn't quit poor nor rich ones - neither kind nor evil ones - neither childran nor elders - neither daughters nor males. **12** Thou didn't quit persons who think a goodly thing and who didn't depart from the LAW - and thou didn't quit them who were like unto animals in them Work - who think a evil thing - who were totally beautiful in them features attractiveness - in them thing flavour and in them words ~ o death - woe arisin from thee-I. **13** Thou didn't quit persons whose words were angry and whose mouths were full of curses ~ thou gathered persons who live in darkness and in light and them souls in thy places ~ o death - woe arisin from thee-I. **14** and Earth gathered the persons flesh who live whether in cave or in Earth - up til a drum are beaten and persons who dead arise. **15** As persons who dead shall arise quickly like unto a eye wink by JAH Command and on a drum bein beaten - persons who worked evil Work shall raceive them hardship in them sin abundance measure that them worked it - and persons who worked goodly Work shall be Feeling good.

## 20

**1** and believe I that all I Work that I worked in this world won't remain nor be hidden on the time I stood before Him fearin and tremblin. **2** and on the time I didn't seize provisions to I path - and on the time I won't have clothes to I bodies... **3** on the time I won't have a staff to I hands nor shoes to I feet... **4** and on the time I won't know the paths where demons take I - whether it be slippery or smooth - or be it dark - and whether it be thorns or nettles - or whether it be a Water depth or a pit depth - believe I that I Work that I worked in this world won't remain nor be hidden. **5** I won't know the demons who take I - and I won't hear them thing. **6** As them are black ones - and as them lead I toward darkness - I don't sight up them faces. **7** and like unto the prophet spoke sayin - "On the time I soul were separated from I flesh - Lord I Lord - Thou know I path - and them hid a trap on that path where I-man went - and I-man sight up returnin toward the right ~ I-man lacked one who know I - and I-man have nothing there whereby I-man will escape" - as them take I toward darkness - I won't sight up them faces. **8** As him know that demons ridicule on him - and as them will lead him toward the path him don't know - him speakin this are because this - and if him return leftward and rightward - there are no person who know him. **9** Him are alone amidst demons - and yet there are none who know him. **10** Angels of Light who are subtle are who are sent toward kind persons that them might raceive righteous ones souls - and might take toward a Light place - toward the Garden - where welfare are found. **11** Demons and Angels of darkness are who are sent that them might raceive them and might take them toward *Gehannem* that were prepared to them that them might raceive them hardship by them sin that them worked. **12** Woe to sinner persons souls who take them toward destruction - who have no welfare nor rest - nor escapin from the tribulation that found them - nor proceedin from *Gehannem* up til Eternity. **13** As them have lived firmed up in Qayel Work - and as them have perished by Bele`am iniquity price - and as them have lacked what them will do - woe to sinner persons - to them pretext to raceive interest and presents that in downgression them might take a foreigner money that weren't them money. **14** Them shall raceive them hardship in *Gehannem* by them sin that them worked.

## 21

**1** Where are persons who gather a foreigner money that weren't them hands Work nor them money? **2** to them take a person money for free - and to them shll be gathered without knowin the day when them dead that shall arrive on them - however them quit them money for a foreigner. **3** to like unto them fathers - them are sinners kindreds who worry and seize sinners like unto them whether it be by theft or by robbery - and them childran won't be Feeling good by them fathers money. **4** As them have gathered to them in downgression - and as it are like unto misty urine and like unto the smoke that wind scattar and like unto wiltin grass - and like unto wax that melt arisin from before a fire - as sinners glory shall perish like unto that - there are none whom them fathers money will benefit ~ like unto Daweet spoke sayin - "I-man sight up a sinner man... **5** bein honoured and famed like unto a cordia and like unto a cypress - but on the time I-man returned I-man lacked him ~ I-man searched and didn't find him place" - there are none whom them fathers money will profit nor benefit. <sup>6</sup> Because them gathered a person money in downggression - it seemin to them that them won't dead - like unto persons who wrong them companions won't boast - sinner persons destruction are likewise at one time. <sup>7</sup> You lazy ones - think that you will perish and that your money will perish with you - and if your silver and your gold abound it shall be rusted. <sup>8</sup> and if you birth many childran them shall be to many graves - and if you work many houses them shall be demolished. <sup>9</sup> to you didn't fulfill your Creator JAH Accord - and if you multiply livestock them shall be for your enemies capture - and all the money you seized in your hands won't be found - to it have been what weren't blessed. <sup>10</sup> Whether it be in house or in forest - and be it in wilderness or a pasture place - and be it in grape threshinfloor or in grain threshinfloor - it won't be found. <sup>11</sup> Because you didn't keep JAH Command - as JAH won't save you with all your house hold from the tribulation - there shall be sadness on you arisin from all your enemies - yet you won't be Feeling good in your childran birthed from your nature. <sup>12</sup> But from Him plenty - Him won't trouble persons who kept Him Order and Him LAW ~ Him give all who begged Him - yet Him bless them childran birthed from them nature and also them land fruit to them. <sup>13</sup> and Him make them rulers on all peoples in them area that them might rule lest them be who are ruled - and Him give them all Him plenty in them pasture place. <sup>14</sup> Him bless to them all them seized in them hand - all them field fruit - and all them livestocks places - and Him make them Feeling good in them childran birthed from them nature. <sup>15</sup> and Him don't diminish them livestocks on them ~ Him save them from all them tribulation and from weariness and illness and destruction - and from them enemy them don't know and from him them know. <sup>16</sup> and Him will dispute to them in Judgemant time - and Him shall save them from a evil thing and from tribulation and from all who dispute them ~ in the first era if a priest lived who work the Tent Work - who keep the LAW and keep the Tent Order and live firmed up in JAH Accord - by the first Order and all the LAW as them would give him the tithe and what were birthed first Beginnin from man up til livestock - Him would save them from all the tribulation. <sup>17</sup> Like unto Mussie commanded Newie child 'Iyasu - there was a country of sanctuary in all them country ~ by not knowin and by knowin up til them judged judgemant on whom them canvicted and to whom them acquitted... <sup>18</sup> if a person lived who killed a soul - him would be measured there that him might be saved. <sup>19</sup> Him told them - "Examine in your reasonins that him have a quarrel with him formerly - and be it by axe or be it by a stone or be it by wood - as it have fallen from him hand by not knowin - if him say "That person on whom it fell dead on mi" - examine and save him ~ if him did it in not knowin make him be saved. <sup>20</sup> But if him do it knowin - him will raceive him hardship like unto him sin - and there are none who will pardon him; but if him kill him in not knowin - as him have done it in not knowin - examine and save him lest him dead. <sup>21</sup> Him worked to them that them might distance from all the sin - yet Mussie would work like unto this to 'Isra'iel childran lest them depart from JAH LAW. <sup>22</sup> Him commanded them that 'Adam childran - who live firmed up in JAH Command from worshippin idols and eatin what dead and lodged and what a sword bloated and cut - and who distance from all evil work like unto him worked to them - that them might work it and might totally distance from all that aren't due. <sup>23</sup> Him commanded them lest them depart from the Command Him worked to them in the Tent example in Heaven - that them might save them bodies and might find them lodgin with them fathers. <sup>24</sup> As them have been birthed from Siet and 'Adam who did JAH Accord - persons who believed in JAH Word and lived firmed up in Him Command will be called kind persons childran. <sup>25</sup> As I are 'Adam childran - as Him have Created I in Him Example and Him Appearance that I might work all goodly Work that make JAH Feeling good - Him won't scorn it. <sup>26</sup> As Him totally won't separate Him friends - if I work goodly Work - I shall inherit the Kingdom of Heaven where are welfare with persons who work goodly Work. <sup>27</sup> Him totally love persons who beg him cleanly - and Him hear them in them prayer - and Him accept the repentance of persons who are disciplined and enter repentance ~ Him give firmness and Power to persons who keep Him Order and Him LAW and Him Command. <sup>28</sup> Persons who did Him Accord shall be Feeling good with Him in Him Kingdom forever - and whether them be persons who preceded or who arose later - them will present praise to Him Beginnin from today up til Eternity. Make glory due to JAH forever - and the secand Meqabyan arrived and were fulfilled.

# The Book of Meqabyan III
## 1

<sup>1</sup> Kristos shall rejoice Gibts persons - because Him shall come toward them in later era that Him will revenge and destroy Deeyablos - who wronged them who were kindly and innocent - and who misled persons - and who hate him Creator Work. <sup>2</sup> Him shall revenge and destroy him ~ Him shall return him lordship toward wretchedness and bein downbased - to him have been arrogant in him reasonin. <sup>3</sup> Him shall return him lordship toward bein downbased - to him have said - "As mi will enter toward the sea midst - and as mi will proceed toward Heaven - and as mi will sight up depths - and as mi will grasp and seize 'Adam childran like unto bird chicks - who are it who are loftier than mi? <sup>4</sup> Because mi became by them reason that mi might distance them from the straight LAW of JAH - as mi will strengthen on persons who live in this world unless them did JAH Accord - there are none who will depose mi from mi authority" him said. <sup>5</sup> "To mi will be a reason to return them toward a path that were smooth to go toward *Gehannem* with mi. <sup>6</sup> Persons who loved Him and kept Him LAW hate mi because this thing - but persons who departed from them Lord LAW and who erred will come toward mi and love mi and keep mi oath ~ as mi will make them reasonin evil and change them thoughts lest them return toward them Creator JAH - them will do mi command like unto mi commanded them. <sup>7</sup> and on the time mi showed them this world money - mi will mislead them reasonin from straight LAW - and on the time mi showed them beautiful and attractive daughters - mi will distance them by these from straight LAW. <sup>8</sup> and on the time mi showed them shinin Hindekie jewels and silver and gold - mi will distance them by this also from straight LAW that them might return toward mi Work. <sup>9</sup> and on the time mi showed them thin clothes and red silk and white silk - and linens and white silk - mi will distance them by this also from straight LAW - and mi will return them toward mi thoughts ~ on the time mi multiplied money and livestocks like unto sand and showed them - by this also mi will return them toward mi Work. <sup>10</sup> and on the time mi showed them jealousy done in arrogance because daughters and because anger and quarrels - by all this mi will return them toward mi Work. <sup>11</sup> and on the time mi showed them signs - mi will lodge in them companions reasonin - and mi will lodge a sign thing that were to each of the ras selves in them reasonin - and mi showed them words signs and misled them. <sup>12</sup> and to persons in whom mi lodged mi lodgin - mi will show them signs - and be it in stars gait - or be it in cloud proceedin or in fire flickerin - or be it in beasts and birds cries - as them are mi lodgins - and mi will lodge signs in them reasonin on them by all this. <sup>13</sup> Them will speak and give signs to them companions - and like unto those them naysayers told them - mi will precede and be a sign to them. <sup>14</sup> Mi will do them words signs to them - that persons who examined them might be misled - and that them might give a wage to magicians - and that them might tell to them companions sayin - 'There are no savants like unto so-an-so and so-an-so to whom it are done like unto them spoke - and who know prophecy - and who separate good and evil - and to whom all are like unto them spoke - and to whom it are done like unto them word.' <sup>15</sup> Mi will be Feeling good on the time them spoke this - that persons who perish and err by mi might totally abound and that 'Adam childran might perish - to JAH have downbased mi from mi rank because them father 'Adam - on mi sayin 'Mi won't bow to 'Adam who are downbased to mi.' <sup>16</sup> and mi will take toward destruction all him childran who live firmed up in mi command ~ mi have a Oath from JAH Who Created mi - that all persons whom mi misled might descend toward *Gehannem* with mi. <sup>17</sup> and on the time Him multiplied Him anger on mi - and on the time Him commanded that them might bind and cast mi toward *Gehannem* - on the time mi Creator commanded sayin thus - mi interceded with mi Lord ~ mi interceded before Him while mi said - 'As Thou have vexed on mi - and as Thou have admonished mi by Thy chastisemant - and as Thou have chastised mi by Thy wrath - Lord mi Lord - adjourn mi that mi might speak one thing before Thee-I.' <sup>18</sup> and mi Lord answered to mi sayin - **Speak - I-man will hear thee** ~ at that time mi began mi plea toward Him sayin - 'After mi were downbased from mi rank - make the persons whom mi misled be like unto mi in *Gehannem* where mi will raceive tribulation. <sup>19</sup> and make them be to Thy Lordship who refused mi - who didn't err by mi - who didn't keep mi command - that them might do Thy Command and might fulfill Thy Accord and might keep Thy Word - on the time them didn't err by mi like unto mi misled them havin refused like unto mi taught them - and on the time Thou loved mi - make them take the crown Thou gave to mi. <sup>20</sup> Give them the crown of the authorities called Satans who were sent with mi ~ seat them on mi throne on Thy Right that were a wilderness from mi and mi hosts. <sup>21</sup> and make them praise Thee-I like unto Thou loved - and make them be like unto mi hosts and like unto mi ~ because Thou hated mi and loved them who were Created from ashes and Earth - as mi authority have perished - and as them authority have been lofty - make them praise Thee-I like unto Thou loved.' <sup>22</sup> Mi Lord answered to mi sayin - **As thou have misled them while them sight up and while them heard -**

if thou misled them without them lovin I Order - make them be to thee like unto thy accord and like unto thy word. **23** If them quit the Books Word and I Command and came toward thee - and if thou misled them while them destruction also saddened mi - make them raceive tribulation in *Gehannem* like unto thee - Him told mi. **24** You will raceive tribulation in *Gehannem* up til the Eternity - yet you will have no exits from *Gehannem* up til the Eternity - to them whom thou misled nor to thee.

## 2

**1** But I-man shall bequeath thy throne in lordship to them whom it failed thee to mislead - like unto I slave 'Iyob ~ JAH Who rule all said - I-man will give the Kingdom of Heaven to persons whom it failed thee to mislead. **2** and mi provoke on 'Adam childran in all ~ if it were possible to mi to mislead them - mi won't quit them that them might firm up in goodly Work ~ to mi provoke on all 'Adam childran - and mi sweeten this world Feeling good joy to them. **3** Be it by lovin drink and food and clothes - or by lovin things - or by withholdin and givin... **4** or be it by lovin to hear and sight up - or be it by lovin to caress and go - or be it by multiplyin arrogance and things - or be it by lovin dreams and slumber... **5** or be it by multiplyin drunkenness and drink - or be it by multiplyin insults and anger - be it by speakin games and useless things... **6** or be it by quarrels and by backbitin them companion - or be it by sightin up this world daughters who were attractive - be it by smellin perfumes fragrance that mislead them... **7** mi hate them by all this lest them able to be saved ~ mi distance them from JAH LAW that them might enter with mi toward the destruction whereby mi were downbased from mi rank." **8** and the prophet told him - "Thou who destroy persons - perish ~ on the time thou departed from JAH LAW and committed crime in thy reasonin firmness and thy arrogance - and by saddenin thy Creator and not worshippin thy Creator in thy reasonin firmness - will thou thus be arrogant on JAH Creation? **9** on the time thy Creator vexed on thee - Him downbased thee from thy rank because thy evil Work ~ why do thou take 'Adam toward sin - him whom thy Creator Created from Earth - whom Him made like unto Him loved - and whom Him placed to Him praise?" him told him. **10** "On the time thou - who are subtle and were Created from wind and fire - were arrogant in sayin 'Mi are the Creator'... **11** on the time thou boasted - as JAH have sight up thy evil Work and thou have denied JAH with thy hosts - Him Created 'Adam who will praise because thy stead - that him might praise Him Name without diminishin. **12** As thou have made thy ras self prouder than all Angels hosts who are like unto thee - because thy arrogance JAH Created 'Adam with him childran that them might praise JAH Name because the praise that thou praise with thy hosts whom Him scorned. **13** and because this thing JAH destroyed thee separatin from all Angels chiefs like unto thee - and thy hosts Created in one counsel with thee - and thou - you proceeded and erred from JAH praise because your useless reasonin arrogance and because your reasonin firmness - and you were arrogant on your Creator - that aren't on another. **14** Because this thing Him Created 'Adam from Earth that Him might be praised by downbased persons - and Him gave him a Command and Law sayin **Don't eat** lest him eat from fig fruit. **15** and Him I-pointed him on all the Creation Him Created ~ Him notified him sayin - **Don't eat from one fig fruit that bring death - lest thou bring death on thy ras self - yet eat fruit from all the woods amidst the Garden.** **16** and on the time thou heard this Word - thou lodged perfidy in him arisin from the thing thou spoke in thy tongue to Hiewan who were found from 'Adam side bone. **17** Thou misled 'Adam who were clean - a firm perfidy that thou might make him a Law demolisher like unto thee. **18** on the time thou misled Hiewan - who were Created bein like unto a innocent dove and who don't know thy malice - thou made she betray by thy thing that succeeded and thy crooked word - and after thou misled that Hiewan who were Created beforehand - she also went and misled JAH Creation 'Adam who were Created from Earth beforehand. **19** and thou made him betray a disturbance that aren't by thy arrogance - and thou made him to deny that him might deny him Creator Word - and thou destroyed 'Adam in thy arrogance. **20** and in thy malice thou distanced him from him Creator Love - and by thy reason thou sent him way from the Garden where Feeling good joy are - and by thy hindrance thou made him quit the Garden food. **21** to Beginnin from Antiquity thou have quarreled with the innocent Creation 'Adam that thou might lower him toward *See'ol* where thou will raceive hardship - and that thou might send him way from the Love that brought him and Created him from not livin toward true livin - and by thy false thing thou made him thirst a drink from the Garden. **22** and when him are Earthly - Him made him a subtle Angel who totally praise him Creator in him flesh and him soul and him reasonin. **23** and Him Created many thoughts to him - like unto harps praise in each of them styles.

## 3

**1** But Him Created one thought to thee - that thou might totally praise while thou were sent toward where thy Creator sent thee. **2** But to 'Adam were given five thoughts that were evil and five thoughts that were goodly - ten thoughts. **3** and again him have many thoughts like unto sea waves - and like unto a whirl wind that scattar dust liftin up from Earth - and like unto the sea waves that shake - and arisin from him unnumbered thoughts abundance in him heart like unto unnumbered rain drops - 'Adam thoughts are like unto that. **4** But thy thought are one ~ as thou aren't fleshly - thou have no other thought. **5** But thou lodged in snake reasonin ~ in evil perfidy thou destroyed 'Adam who were one limb - and Hiewan heard the snake thing - and havin heard - she did like unto she commanded she. **6** After she ate a fig fruit - she came and misled JAH first Creation 'Adam - and she brought death on him and on she childran because she infringed she Creator Command. **7** Them proceeded from the Garden to JAH by Him true Judgemant ~ Him calmed them in the land where them were sent by them childran birthed from them nature and by them crops found from Earth - yet Him didn't distance them from the Garden quarrelin. **8** and on the time thou expelled them straight from the Garden - that them might plant plants and childran to be calmed and to renew them reasonin in the Earth fruit that Earth prepared from she Earthliness - and that them might be calmed by Earth fruit and the Garden fruit that JAH gave them... **9** JAH gave them woods more verdant than the Garden woods - and Hiewan and 'Adam - whom thou sent way from the Garden on them eatin it - were totally calmed from sadness. **10** As JAH know to calm Him Creation - them reasonins are calmed because them childran and because the crops found from Earth. **11** As them have been sent toward this world that grow nettles and thorns - them firm up them reasonins in Water and grain.

## 4

**1** The Lord have that Him might ransom 'Adam - and Him shall shame thee ~ Him will save a sheep from a wolf mouth ('Adam from Deeyablos). **2** However thou will go toward *Gehannem* seizin with thee the persons whom thou ruled. **3** Persons who kept them Creator JAH LAW shall be Feeling good with them Creator JAH Who hid them from evil Work that Him might make them Him fortune - and that them might praise Him with honoured Angels who didn't infringe them Creator JAH LAW like unto thee. **4** But JAH - Who chose and gave thee more than all Angels like unto thee that thou might praise Him with Him servant Angels - withheld from thee a lofty throne in thy arrogance. **5** But thou became famous and were called one who love godhood - and thy hosts were called demons. **6** But persons who loved JAH shall be Him kindreds like unto honoured Angels - and the *Surafiel* and *Keerubiel* who praise Him streach forth them wings and praise without slackness. **7** But in thy arrogance and thy laziness thou destroyed thy praise that thou might praise Him everytime with thy host and thy kindreds Created in thy features. **8** Lest the praise of JAH - Who Created thee makin a tenth tribe - be diminished on the time thou forgot the praise of JAH Who Created thee - it havin seemed to thee that it aren't posssible to Him to Create a Creation like unto thee - and lest the praise of JAH - Who Created thee - be diminished on the time thou were separated from thy bredren Inity - Him Created 'Adam because thy stead. **9** But in thy reasonin arrogance thou neglected the praise of JAH Who Created thee - and Him vexed on thee ~ Him ridiculed thee - and Him bound and banished thee in *Gehannem* with thy hosts also. **10** Him brought Soil from Earth with Him glorified Hands - and addin fire and Water and wind - Him Created 'Adam in Him Example and Him Features. **11** Him I-pointed him on all the Creation Him Created in Him Authority - that Him praise might be filled by the praise thou would praise Him ~ 'Adam praise became one with Angels praise - and them praise were level. **12** But in thy collar of reasonin firmness and thy arrogance thou were downbased from thy rank - and havin departed from JAH Lordship - Who Created thee - thou destroyed thy ras self. **13** Know that Him praise weren't diminished - to JAH have Created 'Adam who praised Him in him reasonin counsel lest Him JAH-ness praise be diminished. **14** to Him know all before it are done - and Him knew thee before Him Created thee that thou will demolish Him Command ~ as there are a counsel hidden alongside Him before Him Created the world - on the time thou denied Him - Him Created Him slave 'Adam in Him Features and Him Example. **15** Like unto Selomon spoke sayin - 'Before hills were Created and before the world succeeded bein Created - and before winds that are Earth grounations were Created... **16** and before Him firmed up hills and mountains grounations - and before this world Work firmed up - and before moon and Sun light shone - before eras and stars caretakin were known... **17** and before daylight and night alternated - and before the sea were delineated by sand - before all the Created Creation were Created... **18** and before all sight up today were sight up - before all the names called today were called - Him Created I Selomon' - Angels like unto you and thou and Him slave 'Adam were in JAH Reasonin. **19** Him

Created 'Adam that Him glorified Name might be praised on the time thou mutinied - and that Him might be praised by Him downbased slave 'Adam who were Created from Earth on the time thou were arrogant. [20] to bein in Heaven JAH hear poor ones plea - and Him love downbased persons praise. [21] Him love to save havin lodged in persons who fear Him - yet as Him don't love horse Power - and as Him don't step meanin to the lap of a concubine - JAH shall ignore arrogant ones thing. [22] and them shall weep while them cried because them sin that them worked. [23] It failed thee to plead in repentance. [24] But 'Adam who were Created from Earth returned in repentance while him totally wept before JAH because him sin. [25] But in thy collar of reasonin firmness and thy heart arrogance thou didn't know Love Work and thou didn't know repentance ~ it failed thee to plead before thy Creator JAH in repentance and mournin and sadness. [26] But that 'Adam who are ashes and Earth returned toward repentance in mournin and sadness - and him returned toward humbleness and Love Work. [27] But thou didn't downbase thy reasonin and thy ras self to JAH Who Created thee. [28] As to 'Adam - him downbased him ras self and pleaded on the iniquity him wronged ~ him weren't proud. [29] As thou have totally produced crime - it were found from thee - yet it aren't him who produced that error ~ in thy arrogance thou took him with thee toward thy destruction. [30] Before him Created you both - as Him have known you that you were sinners - and as Him have known your Works - Him know that this that were done were in thy heart arrogance. [31] But Him returned that 'Adam - who were without arrogance or malice - in repentance mournin and sadness. [32] to a person who wrong and don't plead in repentance have multiplied him iniquity more than him earlier iniquity - but in thy heart arrogance it failed thee to plead in repentance - but a person who plead and weep enterin repentance before Him Creator JAH... [33] him entered repentance to true - and him found Work whereby him will be saved that him might fear him Lord Heart - and him pleaded before him Creator - to him have pleaded before Him in bowin and much repentance - and arisin from the earlier tribulation the Lord shall lighten him sin to him lest Him vex on Him slave - and Him will forgive him him former sin. [34] If him didn't return toward him former sin and if him did this - this are perfect repentance ~ 'Adam didn't forget to think of him Creator nor to implore him Creator JAH in repentance. [35] and thou - plea in repentance toward thy Creator JAH - and don't wrong them because them were flesh and blood - to JAH Who Created them know them weakness - and don't wrong the persons Him Created by Him Authority. [36] and after them soul were separated from them flesh - them flesh shall be dust up til the day that JAH love.

## 5

[1] Know JAH WHo Created thee-I ~ as JAH have Created thee-I in Him Features and Him Example when thou are Earth - don't forget JAH Who firmed thee-I up and saved thee-I and Whom 'Isra'iel glorified ~ Him placed thee-I in Garden that thou might be Feeling good and might dig Earth. [2] on the time thou demolished Him Command - Him sent thee way from the Garden toward this world that Him cursed because thee - that grow nettles and thorns. [3] to *thou are Earth - and to she are Earth - to thou are dust - and to she are dust - to thou are Soil - and to she are Soil - to thou are fed the grain found from she - and to thou will return toward she* - to thou will be Soil up til Him love that Him might raise thee - and to Him shall examine thee the sin thou worked and all the iniquity. [4] Know what thou will answer Him at that time ~ think of the good and evil thou worked in this world ~ examine whether the evil would abound or whether the good would abound ~ try. [5] If thou work a goodly thing - it are a goodly thing to thee-I that thou might be Feeling good on the day when persons who dead will arise. [6] But if thou work evil Work - woe to thee - to thou will receive thy hardship like unto thy hands Work and like unto thy reasonin evil ~ to if thou work a evil thing on thy companion and if thou didn't fear JAH - thou will receive thy hardship. [7] and if thou betray thy companion and if thou call JAH Name and swear in lie - as thou will receive thy hardship like unto thy Work - woe to thee. [8] and thou tell thy false thing to thy companion simulatin Truth - but thou know that thou spoke a lie. [9] and thou persuade the persons with thee thy false thing simulatin Truth - and thou multiply false things that weren't Truth - and thou will receive thy hardship like unto thy sin ~ thou deny thy companion while thou tell thy companion 'mi will give thee' what thou won't give him. [10] and on the time thou said 'Mi will give' in thy pure reasonin - demons make application to thee like unto dogs - and them make thee forget all - and if thou withhold or if thou love that thou might give - them don't know the person to whom them gather - yet as Him have said - **Them shall fatten** - this world money appetise thee that thou might fatten the money that won't benefit thee and that thou won't eat. [11] and again - as Him have said - **'Adam liar childran make a balance false ~ as to them - them go from robbery toward robbery** - this world money appetise thee. [12] O persons - don't make hope in distortin scales and balances - and in stealin a person money - and in makin a person money

one in downgression - and in infringin your companions money - and in stealin him field - in all the lies you do to your ras selves profit that aren't to your companions. [13] If you do this you will raceive your hardship like unto your Work. [14] O persons - be fed by your hands Work that were straight - yet don't desire robbery ~ don't love that you might totally rob and eat a person money without justice by what aren't due. [15] and if you eat it - it won't satta you ~ on the time you dead you will quit it to another - yet even if you fatten - it won't benefit you. [16] and if your money abound - don't distort your reasonins ~ as sinner persons money are like unto the smoke that proceed from a griddle and the wind take it - better than sinner persons money are the little money them accumulated in Truth.

## 6

[1] Think of the day when you will dead ~ on the time your souls were separated from your flesh - and on the time you quit your money to another - and on the time you went on the path you don't know - think of the tribulation that shall come on you. [2] and the demons that will raceive you are evil - and them features are ugly - and them are frightenin in them splendour - and them won't hear your words - and you won't hear them words. [3] and because you didn't do your Creator JAH Accord - them won't hear you in your plea on the time you begged them ~ because this thing them will totally frighten you. [4] But persons who fulfilled JAH Accord have no fear - to demons fear them. But demons shall ridicule sinner persons souls on them. [5] But kind persons souls shall be Feeling good on Angels in Feeling good joy - to them shall totally make them Feeling good because them scorned this world - but angels who are evil shall raceive sinner persons souls. [6] Pardon Angels shall raceive kind persons and righteous ones souls - to them are sent from JAH that them might calm righteous ones souls ~ as Angels that were evil are sent from Deeyablos that them might ridicule on sinner persons souls - demons shall raceive sinner persons souls. [7] Sinner persons - woe to you ~ weep to your ras selves before the day when you dead arrive on you ~ on the time you reach toward JAH... [8] enter repentance in your era that are there before your era pass - that you might live in Feeling goodness and joy without tribulation nor disease - yet as after you dead your era won't return that passed - weep. [9] Lest it be on you toward a vain accord that distance from JAH - in your firm criticism make lovin to be lavished and food and Feeling good joy not be found in you ~ as a body that are sated without measure won't think of JAH Name - Deeyablos wealth shall lodge on it - yet as the Hola Spirit won't lodge in it - make lovin the Feeling good joy not be found in you. [10] Like unto Mussie spoke - Mussie havin said - "Ya`iqob ate and were sated and fattened and tall and wide - and JAH Who Created him were separated from him. [11] and him lifestyle distanced from JAH" - as a body that were sated without measure nor moderation won't think of JAH Name - make lovin Feeling good joy not be found alongside you ~ as belly satiety without measure are bein like unto a boar and like unto a wanderin horse - make drinkin and eatin without measure and adultery not be found in you. [12] But a person who eat in measure shall live firmed up in JAH Support - and him shall live firmed up like unto the horizon and like unto a tower that have a stone fence; a person who forgot JAH LAW shall flee without one livin who chase him. [13] A kind person shall live in bein raspected like unto a lion. [14] But persons who don't love JAH won't keep Him LAW - and them reasonins aren't straight. [15] and JAH shall bring sadness and alarm on them when them are in this world - and bein seized in tremblin and fright - and bein seized in the tribulations without number by them money bein snatched - bein bound by them hands in chains from them masters hands... [16] lest them be who rested from the tribulation - and lest them lifestyle be in Feeling good joy - lest them rest when them are in alarmin tribulations that are on each of them ras selves - Him shall bring sadness and alarm on them.

## 7

[1] But like unto Daweet spoke sayin - "I-man believed in JAH ~ I-man won't fear havin said - 'What would a person make I?'" - there are no fright and alarm on persons who believed in JAH. [2] and again like unto him spoke sayin - "If warriors surround I - I-man believed in Him ~ I-man begged JAH one thing ~ I-man seek that" - persons who believed in Him have no fright on them ~ a person who believed in Him shall live in Life forever - and him won't fear arisin from a evil thing. [3] Who are a person who shamed believin in JAH? how about who ignored Him to a desire? [4] As Him have said - **I-man love him who loved I - and I-man shall honour him who glorified I ~ I-man shall keep him who returned toward I in repentance** - who are a person who shamed believin in Him? [5] Judge Truth and save the widow body ~ save them that JAH might save you from all that oppose you in evil thing ~ keep them ~ as kind persons childran are honoured - them are given makin a profit - and yet Him shall save your childran after you - to them won't be troubled to grain.

## 8

[1] 'Iyob believed in JAH ~ as him didn't neglect to praise him Creator JAH - JAH saved him from all the tribulation that 'Adam childran enemy Deeyablos brought on him ~ him said - "JAH gave ~ JAH withheld ~ it happened like unto JAH loved on I - and make JAH Name be praised by all on Earth and in Heaven" - yet as him didn't sadden him reasonin - JAH saved him. [2] and on the time JAH sight up 'Iyob that him heart were cleansed from sin - Him raceived him in much honour. [3] and Him gave him money that abounded more than him money that preceded ~ to him have totally indured him tribulation - and Him cured him from him wounds because him indurin all the tribulation that arrived on him. [4] and if you like unto him indure the tribulation arisin from demons sent toward you - you will be admired. [5] Indure the tribulation ~ that JAH might be to you a fortress Refuge from persons who hate you - and that Him might be a fortress Refuge to your childran childran and to your childran after you - don't sadden your reasonins arisin from the tribulation that came on you ~ believe in Him - and Him shall be a fortress Refuge to you. [6] Beg Him ~ Him will hear you ~ make hope - and Him will forgive you ~ beg Him - and Him will be a Father to you; [7] Think of Merdokyos and 'Astier - Yodeet and Giediewon and Deebora and Bariq and Yoftahie and Somson... [8] and other persons like unto them who were disciplined to believe in JAH and whose enemies didn't defeat them. [9] to JAH are True - and to Him don't favour havin sight up a face - but persons raceived hardship who love that them might work sin on them ras selves ~ all persons who fear Him and keep Him LAW shall keep bodies - and Him shall give them bein I-loved and honour. [10] Him shall make them Feeling good in them proceedin and them enterin - in them Life and them death - and in them arisin and sittin ~ to Him save - and Him seclude. [11] to Him sadden - and Him pardon. [12] to Him make poor - and Him honour ~ Him make wretched - and as Him honour - Him make them Feeling good.

## 9

[1] and whether it be what are in Heaven - or whether it be what are on Earth - and be it either subtle or stout - everything n all Him money live bein firmed up in Him Order. [2] There are nothing that departed from JAH LAW and Him Order - Who Created all the world ~ be it a vulture track that fly in Heaven - Him command toward it destination where Him loved. [3] and Him command a Earth snake path that live in cave toward where Him loved - and a boat path that go on sea - apart from only JAH there are none who know it path. [4] and apart from only JAH - there are none who know the path where a soul go on the time it were separated from it flesh - be it a righteous or a sinner soul. [5] Who know where it will turn - that it would turn in wilderness or on a mountain? or that it would fly like unto a bird - that it would be like unto Heaven dew that alight on a mountain... [6] or that it would be like unto deep wind - or that it would be like unto lightnin that straighten up it path... [7] or that it would be like unto stars that shine amidst the deep - or that it would be like unto sand on a sea shore that are piled amidst the deep... [8] or that it would be like unto a horizon stone that firmed up on the sea deep edge - or like unto a wood that give she beautiful fruit that grew by a Water spout... [9] or that it would be that I likened unto the reed that heat of the Sun burnt - and that wind lift and take toward another place where it didn't grow - and whose trace aren't found... [10] or that it would be like unto misty urine whose trace aren't found - who know JAH Work? who are Him counsellors? how about with whom did Him counsel? [11] As JAH Thoughts are hidden from persons - who will examine and know Him Work? [12] As Him have Created Earth on Water - and as Him have firmed she up without stakes - there are none who examine and know JAH Counsel or Him Wisdom - and Him Created Heaven in Him perfect Wisdom and firmed it up in winds - and Him streached forth a lofty cosmos like unto a tent. [13] Him commanded clouds that them might rain rain on Earth - and Him grow grass - and Him grow fruits without number to be food to persons - that I might believe in JAH and be Feeling good in Inity. [14] JAH are Who give 'Adam childran the Feeling good joy and all the fatness and all the satiety ~ JAH are Who give that them might satta and praise JAH Who gave them fruit from Earth... [15] and Who dressed them in beautiful robes - Who gave them all the I-loved plenty - the Feeling goodness and the joy that are given to persons who fulfill JAH Accord. [16] Him give bein I-loved and honour in the house Him prepared and in the Kingdom of Heaven to them fathers who keep JAH LAW. [17] Him give bein I-loved and honour in the place Him prepared and in the Kingdom of Heaven to them fathers who lived firmed up in Him Worship and Him LAW - and who didn't depart from Him LAW - whom Him famed and raised that them might keep Him Order and Him LAW - and I-man sight up what JAH do to Him friends in this world by weakenin them enemies and by keepin them bodies. [18] I-man sight up that Him give them all them begged Him and that Him fulfill them accord to them ~ don't depart from JAH - and fulfill JAH Accord. [19] Don't depart from Him Command and Him LAW - lest Him vex on you and lest Him destroy you at one time - and lest Him vex and whip you in the tribulation from where you lived formerly - lest you depart from your fathers Order where you were formerly - and lest uour lodgin be in Gehannem where are no exits up til the Eternity. [20] Keep your Creator JAH LAW when your soul are separated from your flesh that Him might do goodly Work to you on the time you stood before JAH. [21] to Earth and Heaven Kingdoms are to Him - and to Kingdom and capability are to Him - and to bein nice and pardonin are only to Him. [22] As Him make rich and Him make poor - as Him make wretched and Him honour - keep JAH LAW. [23] and Daweet spoke because Him while him said - "Man seem vain - and him era pass like unto a shadow." [24] Him spoke because Him sayin - "But Lord - Thou live forever - and Thy Name Invocation are to a child childran." [25] and again him said - "Thy Kingdom are all the world Kingdom - and Thy Rulership are to a child childran" ~ Thou returned a kingdom to Daweet bringin from Sa'ol. [26] But there are none who will I-point Thee-I ~ there are none who can dismiss ~ Thou sight up all - yet there are none who can sight up Thee-I. [27] and Thy kingdom won't perish forever to a child children ~ there are none who will rule Him - but Him rule all ~ Him sight up all - but there are none who sight Him up. [28] As Him have Created man in Him Features and in Him example that them might praise Him and might know Him Worship in straight reasonin without doubt - Him examine and know what kidneys smoked up and what a reasonin transported. [29] Yet them bow to stone - to wood - and to silver and gold that a person hand worked. [30] and them sacrifice to them up til them sacrifice smoke proceed toward Heaven - that them sin might live firmed up before JAH - but yet them refused to worship JAH Who Created them ~ Him shall downcuse them because all them sin that them worked in worshippin them idols. [31] Them learned bowin to idols and all stained Work that aren't due - naysayin by stars - sorcery - worshippin idols - evil accord - and all the Work that JAH don't love - yet them didn't keep JAH Command that them learned. [32] As them didn't love to worship JAH that them might save them bodies from sin and iniquity by Him servants the Angels and by money that them praise before JAH - them work all this in lackin goodly Work. [33] and on the time them all arose together from the graves where them were buried and where them bodies perished - them souls shall stand empty before JAH - and them souls lived in the Kingdom of Heaven prepared to kind persons. [34] But sinner persons souls shall live in *Gehannem* - and on the time graves were opened - persons who dead shall arise - and souls shall return toward the flesh that them were separated formerly. [35] Like unto them were bithed in them nakedness from them mother belly - them shall stand in them nakedness before JAH - and them sins that them worked Beginnin from them infancy up til that time shall be revealed. [36] Them shall raceive them sin hardship on them bodies - and whether them little or much sin - them shall raceive them hardship like unto them sin.

## 10

[1] to the blood of soul found from JAH shall lodge in them like unto it lodged in them formerly - and if you didn't believe persons who dead arisin - hear that Creations shall arise in rainy season without bein birthed from them mother nor father. [2] and Him command them formerly by Him Word that them dead. [3] and them flesh bein demolished and rotten and again renewed - them shall arise like unto Him loved. [4] and again on the time rain alit and on the time it sated Earth - them shall live havin arisin like unto them were Created formerly. [5] As them who are everlivin in bloodly soul and who live in this world and them whom Water produce have been Created - Him havin said make **them be Created** - and as JAH Authority lodge on the Water - she give them a bloodly soul by Him Authority and by Him Word. [6] As them are Created by Him Authority and by Him Word without a father nor mother - thou blind of reasonin who say "Persons who dead won't arise" - if thou have knowledge or Wisdom - how will thou say persons who dead won't arise by them Creator JAH Word? [7] As persons who dead - who were ashes and dust in grave - shall arise by JAH Word - as to thou - enter repentance and return toward thy religion. [8] Like unto Him Word spoke formerly - them shall arise by the Pardon Dew found from JAH - and that Word shall turn all the world and arouse the persons who dead like unto Him loved. [9] and know that thou will arise and stand before Him - and make it not seem to thee in thy reasonin dullness that thou will remain in grave. [10] It aren't thus ~ thou will arise and raceive thy hardship like unto the Work measure that thou worked - whether it be goodly or evil - yet make it not seem to thee that thou will remain - to this Day are the day when them will raceive hardship. [11] and in Resurrection time thou will raceive thy hardship by all thy sin that thou worked ~ thou will finish thy sin hardship that were written Beginnin from thy infancy up til that time - and thou have no reason that thou will pretext on thy sin like unto this world Work that thou might deny thy sin. [12] Like unto thou make thy false word truth before thee - and like unto thou make the lie thing that thou spoke truth - thou have no reason that thou will pretext like unto

this world Work. ¹³ Because it were that she know on thee all thy evil Work thou worked - and because it were that she will reveal on thee before she Creator JAH - as JAH Word shall lodge on thee and speak on thee - thou have no reason on what thou pretext. ¹⁴ Thou will shame there because thy sin that thou worked ~ it are that thou might be thanked with persons who are thanke on them beautiful Work - yet lest thou shame before man and Angels on the day when Judgement are judged - quickly enter repentance in this world before thou arrive toward there. ¹⁵ Persons who praise JAH with Angels shall raceive them reward from them Creator without shamin - and them shall be Feeling good in the Kingdom of Heaven - however unless thou worked goodly Work when thou are in thy flesh in Life - thou have no fortune with righteous ones. ¹⁶ As thou weren't prepared when thou have knowledge and when thou have this world where thou enter repentance - there shall be a useless regret on thee - and to thou didn't give a morsel to the hungry when thou have money. ¹⁷ and to thou didn't clothe the naked when thou have clothes - and to thou didn't save the wronged when thou have Authority. ¹⁸ to thou didn't teach the sinner person when thou have knowledge - that him might return and enter repentance - and that JAH might forgive him him sin that him formerly worked in ignorance - and to thou didn't fight with demons who quarrel with thee when thou have Power that thou able to prevail. ¹⁹ and to thou didn't fast nor pray when thou have firmness that thou might weaken thy infancy Power that are on flesh - and that thou might subject thy ras self to Rightness that aren't favorin on flesh... ²⁰ that aren't favorin Feeling good joy when it are in this world in beautiful drink and sweet food - and that aren't adornin in thin clothes and silver and gold... ²¹ and as thou didn't fast nor pray when thou have firmness that thou might subject thy ras self to Rightness that aren't adornin in honoured Hindekie jewels called emerald and phazyon - there shall be a useless regret on thee ~ this aren't a person ornamant that are due. ²² As to a person ornamant - it are purity - Wisdom - knowledge - lovin one another by what are due without envyin nor jealousy nor doubtin nor quarrels ~ while thou loved thy companion like unto thy ras self... ²³ and without thy doin a evil thing on a person who did a evil thing on thee-I - it are lovin one another by what are due - that thou might enter toward the Kingdom of Heaven that are given to person who indured the tribulation - that Him might give thee the honoured Kingdom of Heaven and thy reward on makin hope in the Kingdom of Heaven in Resurrection time with honoured persons in knowledge and Wisdom. ²⁴ and don't say "After we dead we won't arise" - to Deeyablos cut off hope of persons who speak and think this lest them be saved in Resurrection time ~ them will know that them have hardship on them on the time Advent arrived on them ~ in Resurrection time persons will be totally sad who worked sin in not knowin that Him might think of them sin on them - to them didn't believe in Him that them will arise on that Day. ²⁵ Because this thing them shall be reproached like unto them Work evil measure that them worked in this world - and them shall sight up the Resurrection that them denied whereby them will arise together in flesh. ²⁶ Them shall weep at that time because them didn't work goodly Work ~ it would have been better to them if them wept in this world if it are possible to them lest them be who weep in *Gehannem*. ²⁷ If I didn't weep in this world by I accord - demons will make I weep without I accord in *Gehannem* ~ if I didn't enter repentance in this world - I prepare worthless and useless cries and mournin in *Gehannem*. ²⁸ Prepare goodly Work - that you might cross from death toward Life - and that you might go from this passin world toward the Kingdom of Heaven - and that you might sight up the Kingdom of Heaven Light that surpass light in this world. ²⁹ Refuse Feeling good joy that are in this world - that thou might be Feeling good without measure in the Kingdom of Heaven in Feeling good joy that aren't fulfilled Beginnin from today up til the Eternity with persons who believe persons who dead arisin. Make Glory and praise due JAH forever - and the third book that speak the Meqabyans thing were fulfilled.

# The Book of Job

## 1

¹ There was a man in the land of Uz, whose name was Job. That man was blameless and upright, and one who feared God,ª and turned away from evil. ² There were born to him seven sons and three daughters. ³ His possessions also were seven thousand sheep, three thousand camels, five hundred yoke of oxen, five hundred female donkeys, and a very great household; so that this man was the greatest of all the children of the east. ⁴ His sons went and held a feast in the house of each one on his birthday; and they sent and called for their three sisters to eat and to drink with them. ⁵ It was so, when the days of their feasting had run their course, that Job sent and sanctified them, and rose up early in the morning, and offered burnt offerings according to the number of them all. For Job said, "It may be that my sons have sinned, and renounced God in their hearts." Job did so continually. ⁶ Now on the day when God's sons came to present themselves before Yahweh,ᵇ Satan also came among them. ⁷ Yahweh said to Satan, "Where have you come from?" Then Satan answered Yahweh, and said, "From going back and forth in the earth, and from walking up and down in it." ⁸ Yahweh said to Satan, "Have you considered my servant, Job? For there is no one like him in the earth, a blameless and an upright man, one who fears God, and turns away from evil." ⁹ Then Satan answered Yahweh, and said, "Does Job fear God for nothing? ¹⁰ Haven't you made a hedge around him, and around his house, and around all that he has, on every side? You have blessed the work of his hands, and his substance is increased in the land. ¹¹ But stretch out your hand now, and touch all that he has, and he will renounce you to your face." ¹² Yahweh said to Satan, "Behold,ᶜ all that he has is in your power. Only on himself don't stretch out your hand." So Satan went out from the presence of Yahweh. ¹³ It fell on a day when his sons and his daughters were eating and drinking wine in their oldest brother's house, ¹⁴ that a messenger came to Job, and said, "The oxen were plowing, and the donkeys feeding beside them, ¹⁵ and the Sabeans attacked, and took them away. Yes, they have killed the servants with the edge of the sword, and I alone have escaped to tell you." ¹⁶ While he was still speaking, another also came and said, "The fire of God has fallen from the sky, and has burned up the sheep and the servants, and consumed them, and I alone have escaped to tell you." ¹⁷ While he was still speaking, another also came and said, "The Chaldeans made three bands, and swept down on the camels, and have taken them away, yes, and killed the servants with the edge of the sword; and I alone have escaped to tell you." ¹⁸ While he was still speaking, there came also another, and said, "Your sons and your daughters were eating and drinking wine in their oldest brother's house, ¹⁹ and behold, there came a great wind from the wilderness, and struck the four corners of the house, and it fell on the young men, and they are dead. I alone have escaped to tell you." ²⁰ Then Job arose, and tore his robe, and shaved his head, and fell down on the ground, and worshiped. ²¹ He said, "Naked I came out of my mother's womb, and naked will I return there. Yahweh gave, and Yahweh has taken away. Blessed be Yahweh's name." ²² In all this, Job didn't sin, nor charge God with wrongdoing.

## 2

¹ Again, on the day when God's sons came to present themselves before Yahweh, Satan came also among them to present himself before Yahweh. ² Yahweh said to Satan, "Where have you come from?" Satan answered Yahweh, and said, "From going back and forth in the earth, and from walking up and down in it." ³ Yahweh said to Satan, "Have you considered my servant Job? For there is no one like him in the earth, a blameless and an upright man, one who fears God, and turns away from evil. He still maintains his integrity, although you incited me against him, to ruin him without cause." ⁴ Satan answered Yahweh, and said, "Skin for skin. Yes, all that a man has he will give for his life. ⁵ But stretch out your hand now, and touch his bone and his flesh, and he will renounce you to your face." ⁶ Yahweh said to Satan, "Behold, he is in your hand. Only spare his life." ⁷ So Satan went out from the presence of Yahweh, and struck Job with painful sores from the sole of his foot to his head. ⁸ He took for himself a potsherd to scrape himself with, and he sat among the ashes. ⁹ Then his wife said to him, "Do you still maintain your integrity? Renounce God, and die." ¹⁰ But he said to her, "You speak as one of the foolish women would speak. What? Shall we receive good at the hand of God, and shall we not receive evil?" In all this Job didn't sin with his lips. ¹¹ Now when Job's three friends heard of all this evil that had come on him, they each came from his own place: Eliphaz the Temanite, Bildad the Shuhite, and Zophar the Naamathite; and they made an appointment together to come to sympathize with him and to comfort him. ¹² When they lifted up their eyes from a distance, and didn't recognize him, they raised their voices, and wept; and they each tore his robe, and sprinkled dust on their heads toward the sky. ¹³ So they sat down with him on the ground seven days and seven nights, and no one spoke a word to him, for they saw that his grief was very great.

## 3

¹ After this Job opened his mouth, and cursed the day of his birth. ² Job answered: ³"Let the day perish in which I was born, the night which

---

ª *1:1* The Hebrew word rendered "God" is "אֱלֹהִים" (Elohim).

ᵇ *1:6* "Yahweh" is God's proper Name, sometimes rendered "LORD" (all caps) in other translations.

ᶜ *1:12* "Behold", from "הִנֵּה", means look at, take notice, observe, see, or gaze at. It is often used as an interjection.

said, 'There is a boy conceived.' ⁴ Let that day be darkness. Don't let God from above seek for it, neither let the light shine on it. ⁵ Let darkness and the shadow of death claim it for their own. Let a cloud dwell on it. Let all that makes the day black terrify it. ⁶ As for that night, let thick darkness seize on it. Let it not rejoice among the days of the year. Let it not come into the number of the months. ⁷ Behold, let that night be barren. Let no joyful voice come therein. ⁸ Let them curse it who curse the day, who are ready to rouse up leviathan. ⁹ Let the stars of its twilight be dark. Let it look for light, but have none, neither let it see the eyelids of the morning, ¹⁰ because it didn't shut up the doors of my mother's womb, nor did it hide trouble from my eyes. ¹¹"Why didn't I die from the womb? Why didn't I give up the spirit when my mother bore me? ¹² Why did the knees receive me? Or why the breast, that I should nurse? ¹³ For now I should have lain down and been quiet. I should have slept, then I would have been at rest, ¹⁴ with kings and counselors of the earth, who built up waste places for themselves; ¹⁵ or with princes who had gold, who filled their houses with silver; ¹⁶ or as a hidden untimely birth I had not been, as infants who never saw light. ¹⁷ There the wicked cease from troubling. There the weary are at rest. ¹⁸ There the prisoners are at ease together. They don't hear the voice of the taskmaster. ¹⁹ The small and the great are there. The servant is free from his master. ²⁰"Why is light given to him who is in misery, life to the bitter in soul, ²¹ who long for death, but it doesn't come; and dig for it more than for hidden treasures, ²² who rejoice exceedingly, and are glad, when they can find the grave? ²³ Why is light given to a man whose way is hidden, whom God has hedged in? ²⁴ For my sighing comes before I eat. My groanings are poured out like water. ²⁵ For the thing which I fear comes on me, that which I am afraid of comes to me. ²⁶ I am not at ease, neither am I quiet, neither do I have rest; but trouble comes."

## 4

¹ Then Eliphaz the Temanite answered, ²"If someone ventures to talk with you, will you be grieved? But who can withhold himself from speaking? ³ Behold, you have instructed many, you have strengthened the weak hands. ⁴ Your words have supported him who was falling, you have made the feeble knees firm. ⁵ But now it has come to you, and you faint. It touches you, and you are troubled. ⁶ Isn't your piety your confidence? Isn't the integrity of your ways your hope? ⁷"Remember, now, whoever perished, being innocent? Or where were the upright cut off? ⁸ According to what I have seen, those who plow iniquity and sow trouble, reap the same. ⁹ By the breath of God they perish. By the blast of his anger are they consumed. ¹⁰ The roaring of the lion, and the voice of the fierce lion, the teeth of the young lions, are broken. ¹¹ The old lion perishes for lack of prey. The cubs of the lioness are scattered abroad. ¹²"Now a thing was secretly brought to me. My ear received a whisper of it. ¹³ In thoughts from the visions of the night, when deep sleep falls on men, ¹⁴ fear came on me, and trembling, which made all my bones shake. ¹⁵ Then a spirit passed before my face. The hair of my flesh stood up. ¹⁶ It stood still, but I couldn't discern its appearance. A form was before my eyes. Silence, then I heard a voice, saying, ¹⁷'Shall mortal man be more just than God? Shall a man be more pure than his Maker? ¹⁸ Behold, he puts no trust in his servants. He charges his angels with error. ¹⁹ How much more those who dwell in houses of clay, whose foundation is in the dust, who are crushed before the moth! ²⁰ Between morning and evening they are destroyed. They perish forever without any regarding it. ²¹ Isn't their tent cord plucked up within them? They die, and that without wisdom.'

## 5

¹"Call now; is there any who will answer you? To which of the holy ones will you turn? ² For resentment kills the foolish man, and jealousy kills the simple. ³ I have seen the foolish taking root, but suddenly I cursed his habitation. ⁴ His children are far from safety. They are crushed in the gate. Neither is there any to deliver them, ⁵ whose harvest the hungry eat up, and take it even out of the thorns. The snare gapes for their substance. ⁶ For affliction doesn't come out of the dust, neither does trouble spring out of the ground; ⁷ but man is born to trouble, as the sparks fly upward. ⁸"But as for me, I would seek God. I would commit my cause to God, ⁹ who does great things that can't be fathomed, marvelous things without number; ¹⁰ who gives rain on the earth, and sends waters on the fields; ¹¹ so that he sets up on high those who are low, those who mourn are exalted to safety. ¹² He frustrates the plans of the crafty, so that their hands can't perform their enterprise. ¹³ He takes the wise in their own craftiness; the counsel of the cunning is carried headlong. ¹⁴ They meet with darkness in the day time, and grope at noonday as in the night. ¹⁵ But he saves from the sword of their mouth, even the needy from the hand of the mighty. ¹⁶ So the poor has hope, and injustice shuts her mouth. ¹⁷"Behold, happy is the man whom God corrects. Therefore do not despise the chastening of the Almighty. ¹⁸ For he wounds and binds up. He injures and his hands make whole. ¹⁹ He will deliver you in six troubles; yes, in seven no evil will touch you. ²⁰ In famine he will redeem you from death; in war, from the power of the sword. ²¹ You will be hidden from the scourge of the tongue, neither will you be afraid of destruction when it comes. ²² You will laugh at destruction and famine, neither will you be afraid of the animals of the earth. ²³ For you will be allied with the stones of the field. The animals of the field will be at peace with you. ²⁴ You will know that your tent is in peace. You will visit your fold, and will miss nothing. ²⁵ You will know also that your offspringᵃ will be great, your offspring as the grass of the earth. ²⁶ You will come to your grave in a full age, like a shock of grain comes in its season. ²⁷ Behold, we have researched it. It is so. Hear it, and know it for your good."

## 6

¹ Then Job answered, ²"Oh that my anguish were weighed, and all my calamity laid in the balances! ³ For now it would be heavier than the sand of the seas, therefore my words have been rash. ⁴ For the arrows of the Almighty are within me. My spirit drinks up their poison. The terrors of God set themselves in array against me. ⁵ Does the wild donkey bray when he has grass? Or does the ox low over his fodder? ⁶ Can that which has no flavor be eaten without salt? Or is there any taste in the white of an egg? ⁷ My soul refuses to touch them. They are as loathsome food to me. ⁸"Oh that I might have my request, that God would grant the thing that I long for, ⁹ even that it would please God to crush me; that he would let loose his hand, and cut me off! ¹⁰ Let it still be my consolation, yes, let me exult in pain that doesn't spare, that I have not denied the words of the Holy One. ¹¹ What is my strength, that I should wait? What is my end, that I should be patient? ¹² Is my strength the strength of stones? Or is my flesh of bronze? ¹³ Isn't it that I have no help in me, that wisdom is driven away from me? ¹⁴"To him who is ready to faint, kindness should be shown from his friend; even to him who forsakes the fear of the Almighty. ¹⁵ My brothers have dealt deceitfully as a brook, as the channel of brooks that pass away; ¹⁶ which are black by reason of the ice, in which the snow hides itself. ¹⁷ In the dry season, they vanish. When it is hot, they are consumed out of their place. ¹⁸ The caravans that travel beside them turn away. They go up into the waste, and perish. ¹⁹ The caravans of Tema looked. The companies of Sheba waited for them. ²⁰ They were distressed because they were confident. They came there, and were confounded. ²¹ For now you are nothing. You see a terror, and are afraid. ²² Did I ever say, 'Give to me'? or, 'Offer a present for me from your substance'? ²³ or, 'Deliver me from the adversary's hand'? or, 'Redeem me from the hand of the oppressors'? ²⁴"Teach me, and I will hold my peace. Cause me to understand my error. ²⁵ How forcible are words of uprightness! But your reproof, what does it reprove? ²⁶ Do you intend to reprove words, since the speeches of one who is desperate are as wind? ²⁷ Yes, you would even cast lots for the fatherless, and make merchandise of your friend. ²⁸ Now therefore be pleased to look at me, for surely I will not lie to your face. ²⁹ Please return. Let there be no injustice. Yes, return again. My cause is righteous. ³⁰ Is there injustice on my tongue? Can't my taste discern mischievous things?

## 7

¹"Isn't a man forced to labor on earth? Aren't his days like the days of a hired hand? ² As a servant who earnestly desires the shadow, as a hireling who looks for his wages, ³ so I am made to possess months of misery, wearisome nights are appointed to me. ⁴ When I lie down, I say, 'When will I arise, and the night be gone?' I toss and turn until the dawning of the day. ⁵ My flesh is clothed with worms and clods of dust. My skin closes up, and breaks out afresh. ⁶ My days are swifter than a weaver's shuttle, and are spent without hope. ⁷ Oh remember that my life is a breath. My eye will no more see good. ⁸ The eye of him who sees me will see me no more. Your eyes will be on me, but I will not be. ⁹ As the cloud is consumed and vanishes away, so he who goes down to Sheolᵇ will come up no more. ¹⁰ He will return no more to his house, neither will his place know him any more. ¹¹"Therefore I will not keep silent. I will speak in the anguish of my spirit. I will complain in the bitterness of my soul. ¹² Am I a sea, or a sea monster, that you put a guard over me? ¹³ When I say, 'My bed will comfort me. My couch will ease my complaint,' ¹⁴ then you scare me with dreams and terrify me through visions, ¹⁵ so that my soul chooses strangling, death rather than my bones. ¹⁶ I loathe my life. I don't want to live forever. Leave me alone, for my days are but a breath. ¹⁷ What is man, that you should magnify him, that you should set your mind on him, ¹⁸ that you should visit him every morning, and test him every moment? ¹⁹ How long will you not look away from me, nor leave me alone until I swallow down my spittle? ²⁰ If I have sinned, what do I do to you, you

---

ᵃ 5:25 or, seed

ᵇ 7:9 Sheol is the place of the dead.

watcher of men? Why have you set me as a mark for you, so that I am a burden to myself? <sup>21</sup> Why do you not pardon my disobedience, and take away my iniquity? For now will I lie down in the dust. You will seek me diligently, but I will not be."

## 8

<sup>1</sup> Then Bildad the Shuhite answered, <sup>2</sup>"How long will you speak these things? Shall the words of your mouth be a mighty wind? <sup>3</sup> Does God pervert justice? Or does the Almighty pervert righteousness? <sup>4</sup> If your children have sinned against him, he has delivered them into the hand of their disobedience. <sup>5</sup> If you want to seek God diligently, make your supplication to the Almighty. <sup>6</sup> If you were pure and upright, surely now he would awaken for you, and make the habitation of your righteousness prosperous. <sup>7</sup> Though your beginning was small, yet your latter end would greatly increase. <sup>8</sup>"Please inquire of past generations. Find out about the learning of their fathers. <sup>9</sup>(For we are but of yesterday, and know nothing, because our days on earth are a shadow.) <sup>10</sup> Shall they not teach you, tell you, and utter words out of their heart? <sup>11</sup>"Can the papyrus grow up without mire? Can the rushes grow without water? <sup>12</sup> While it is yet in its greenness, not cut down, it withers before any other reed. <sup>13</sup> So are the paths of all who forget God. The hope of the godless man will perish, <sup>14</sup> whose confidence will break apart, whose trust is a spider's web. <sup>15</sup> He will lean on his house, but it will not stand. He will cling to it, but it will not endure. <sup>16</sup> He is green before the sun. His shoots go out along his garden. <sup>17</sup> His roots are wrapped around the rock pile. He sees the place of stones. <sup>18</sup> If he is destroyed from his place, then it will deny him, saying, 'I have not seen you.' <sup>19</sup> Behold, this is the joy of his way. Out of the earth, others will spring. <sup>20</sup>"Behold, God will not cast away a blameless man, neither will he uphold the evildoers. <sup>21</sup> He will still fill your mouth with laughter, your lips with shouting. <sup>22</sup> Those who hate you will be clothed with shame. The tent of the wicked will be no more."

## 9

<sup>1</sup> Then Job answered, <sup>2</sup>"Truly I know that it is so, but how can man be just with God? <sup>3</sup> If he is pleased to contend with him, he can't answer him one time in a thousand. <sup>4</sup> God is wise in heart, and mighty in strength. Who has hardened himself against him and prospered? <sup>5</sup> He removes the mountains, and they don't know it, when he overturns them in his anger. <sup>6</sup> He shakes the earth out of its place. Its pillars tremble. <sup>7</sup> He commands the sun and it doesn't rise, and seals up the stars. <sup>8</sup> He alone stretches out the heavens, and treads on the waves of the sea. <sup>9</sup> He makes the Bear, Orion, and the Pleiades, and the rooms of the south. <sup>10</sup> He does great things past finding out; yes, marvelous things without number. <sup>11</sup> Behold, he goes by me, and I don't see him. He passes on also, but I don't perceive him. <sup>12</sup> Behold, he snatches away. Who can hinder him? Who will ask him, 'What are you doing?' <sup>13</sup>"God will not withdraw his anger. The helpers of Rahab stoop under him. <sup>14</sup> How much less will I answer him, and choose my words to argue with him? <sup>15</sup> Though I were righteous, yet I wouldn't answer him. I would make supplication to my judge. <sup>16</sup> If I had called, and he had answered me, yet I wouldn't believe that he listened to my voice. <sup>17</sup> For he breaks me with a storm, and multiplies my wounds without cause. <sup>18</sup> He will not allow me to catch my breath, but fills me with bitterness. <sup>19</sup> If it is a matter of strength, behold, he is mighty! If of justice, 'Who,' says he, 'will summon me?' <sup>20</sup> Though I am righteous, my own mouth will condemn me. Though I am blameless, it will prove me perverse. <sup>21</sup> I am blameless. I don't respect myself. I despise my life. <sup>22</sup>"It is all the same. Therefore I say he destroys the blameless and the wicked. <sup>23</sup> If the scourge kills suddenly, he will mock at the trial of the innocent. <sup>24</sup> The earth is given into the hand of the wicked. He covers the faces of its judges. If not he, then who is it? <sup>25</sup>"Now my days are swifter than a runner. They flee away. They see no good. <sup>26</sup> They have passed away as the swift ships, as the eagle that swoops on the prey. <sup>27</sup> If I say, 'I will forget my complaint, I will put off my sad face, and cheer up,' <sup>28</sup> I am afraid of all my sorrows. I know that you will not hold me innocent. <sup>29</sup> I will be condemned. Why then do I labor in vain? <sup>30</sup> If I wash myself with snow, and cleanse my hands with lye, <sup>31</sup> yet you will plunge me in the ditch. My own clothes will abhor me. <sup>32</sup> For he is not a man, as I am, that I should answer him, that we should come together in judgment. <sup>33</sup> There is no umpire between us, that might lay his hand on us both. <sup>34</sup> Let him take his rod away from me. Let his terror not make me afraid; <sup>35</sup> then I would speak, and not fear him, for I am not so in myself.

## 10

<sup>1</sup>"My soul is weary of my life. I will give free course to my complaint. I will speak in the bitterness of my soul. <sup>2</sup> I will tell God, 'Do not condemn me. Show me why you contend with me. <sup>3</sup> Is it good to you that you should oppress, that you should despise the work of your

hands, and smile on the counsel of the wicked? <sup>4</sup> Do you have eyes of flesh? Or do you see as man sees? <sup>5</sup> Are your days as the days of mortals, or your years as man's years, <sup>6</sup> that you inquire after my iniquity, and search after my sin? <sup>7</sup> Although you know that I am not wicked, there is no one who can deliver out of your hand. <sup>8</sup>"Your hands have framed me and fashioned me altogether, yet you destroy me. <sup>9</sup> Remember, I beg you, that you have fashioned me as clay. Will you bring me into dust again? <sup>10</sup> Haven't you poured me out like milk, and curdled me like cheese? <sup>11</sup> You have clothed me with skin and flesh, and knit me together with bones and sinews. <sup>12</sup> You have granted me life and loving kindness. Your visitation has preserved my spirit. <sup>13</sup> Yet you hid these things in your heart. I know that this is with you: <sup>14</sup> if I sin, then you mark me. You will not acquit me from my iniquity. <sup>15</sup> If I am wicked, woe to me. If I am righteous, I still will not lift up my head, being filled with disgrace, and conscious of my affliction. <sup>16</sup> If my head is held high, you hunt me like a lion. Again you show yourself powerful to me. <sup>17</sup> You renew your witnesses against me, and increase your indignation on me. Changes and warfare are with me. <sup>18</sup>"Why, then, have you brought me out of the womb? I wish I had given up the spirit, and no eye had seen me. <sup>19</sup> I should have been as though I had not been. I should have been carried from the womb to the grave. <sup>20</sup> Aren't my days few? Stop! Leave me alone, that I may find a little comfort, <sup>21</sup> before I go where I will not return from, to the land of darkness and of the shadow of death; <sup>22</sup> the land dark as midnight, of the shadow of death, without any order, where the light is as midnight.'"

## 11

<sup>1</sup> Then Zophar, the Naamathite, answered, <sup>2</sup>"Shouldn't the multitude of words be answered? Should a man full of talk be justified? <sup>3</sup> Should your boastings make men hold their peace? When you mock, will no man make you ashamed? <sup>4</sup> For you say, 'My doctrine is pure. I am clean in your eyes.' <sup>5</sup> But oh that God would speak, and open his lips against you, <sup>6</sup> that he would show you the secrets of wisdom! For true wisdom has two sides. Know therefore that God exacts of you less than your iniquity deserves. <sup>7</sup>"Can you fathom the mystery of God? Or can you probe the limits of the Almighty? <sup>8</sup> They are high as heaven. What can you do? They are deeper than Sheol.<sup>a</sup> What can you know? <sup>9</sup> Its measure is longer than the earth, and broader than the sea. <sup>10</sup> If he passes by, or confines, or convenes a court, then who can oppose him? <sup>11</sup> For he knows false men. He sees iniquity also, even though he doesn't consider it. <sup>12</sup> An empty-headed man becomes wise when a man is born as a wild donkey's colt. <sup>13</sup>"If you set your heart aright, stretch out your hands toward him. <sup>14</sup> If iniquity is in your hand, put it far away. Don't let unrighteousness dwell in your tents. <sup>15</sup> Surely then you will lift up your face without spot. Yes, you will be steadfast, and will not fear, <sup>16</sup> for you will forget your misery. You will remember it like waters that have passed away. <sup>17</sup> Life will be clearer than the noonday. Though there is darkness, it will be as the morning. <sup>18</sup> You will be secure, because there is hope. Yes, you will search, and will take your rest in safety. <sup>19</sup> Also you will lie down, and no one will make you afraid. Yes, many will court your favor. <sup>20</sup> But the eyes of the wicked will fail. They will have no way to flee. Their hope will be the giving up of the spirit."

## 12

<sup>1</sup> Then Job answered, <sup>2</sup>"No doubt, but you are the people, and wisdom will die with you. <sup>3</sup> But I have understanding as well as you; I am not inferior to you. Yes, who doesn't know such things as these? <sup>4</sup> I am like one who is a joke to his neighbor, I, who called on God, and he answered. The just, the blameless man is a joke. <sup>5</sup> In the thought of him who is at ease there is contempt for misfortune. It is ready for them whose foot slips. <sup>6</sup> The tents of robbers prosper. Those who provoke God are secure, who carry their god in their hands. <sup>7</sup>"But ask the animals now, and they will teach you; the birds of the sky, and they will tell you. <sup>8</sup> Or speak to the earth, and it will teach you. The fish of the sea will declare to you. <sup>9</sup> Who doesn't know that in all these, Yahweh's hand has done this, <sup>10</sup> in whose hand is the life of every living thing, and the breath of all mankind? <sup>11</sup> Doesn't the ear try words, even as the palate tastes its food? <sup>12</sup> With aged men is wisdom, in length of days understanding. <sup>13</sup>"With God is wisdom and might. He has counsel and understanding. <sup>14</sup> Behold, he breaks down, and it can't be built again. He imprisons a man, and there can be no release. <sup>15</sup> Behold, he withholds the waters, and they dry up. Again, he sends them out, and they overturn the earth. <sup>16</sup> With him is strength and wisdom. The deceived and the deceiver are his. <sup>17</sup> He leads counselors away stripped. He makes judges fools. <sup>18</sup> He loosens the bond of kings. He binds their waist with a belt. <sup>19</sup> He leads priests away stripped, and overthrows the mighty. <sup>20</sup> He removes the speech of those who are trusted, and takes away the understanding of the elders. <sup>21</sup> He pours contempt on princes, and loosens the belt of the strong. <sup>22</sup> He uncovers deep things out of

darkness, and brings out to light the shadow of death. [23] He increases the nations, and he destroys them. He enlarges the nations, and he leads them captive. [24] He takes away understanding from the chiefs of the people of the earth, and causes them to wander in a wilderness where there is no way. [25] They grope in the dark without light. He makes them stagger like a drunken man.

## 13

[1]"Behold, my eye has seen all this. My ear has heard and understood it. [2] What you know, I know also. I am not inferior to you. [3]"Surely I would speak to the Almighty. I desire to reason with God. [4] But you are forgers of lies. You are all physicians of no value. [5] Oh that you would be completely silent! Then you would be wise. [6] Hear now my reasoning. Listen to the pleadings of my lips. [7] Will you speak unrighteously for God, and talk deceitfully for him? [8] Will you show partiality to him? Will you contend for God? [9] Is it good that he should search you out? Or as one deceives a man, will you deceive him? [10] He will surely reprove you if you secretly show partiality. [11] Won't his majesty make you afraid and his dread fall on you? [12] Your memorable sayings are proverbs of ashes. Your defenses are defenses of clay. [13]"Be silent! Leave me alone, that I may speak. Let come on me what will. [14] Why should I take my flesh in my teeth, and put my life in my hand? [15] Behold, he will kill me. I have no hope. Nevertheless, I will maintain my ways before him. [16] This also will be my salvation, that a godless man will not come before him. [17] Listen carefully to my speech. Let my declaration be in your ears. [18] See now, I have set my cause in order. I know that I am righteous. [19] Who is he who will contend with me? For then would I hold my peace and give up the spirit. [20]"Only don't do two things to me, then I will not hide myself from your face: [21] withdraw your hand far from me, and don't let your terror make me afraid. [22] Then call, and I will answer, or let me speak, and you answer me. [23] How many are my iniquities and sins? Make me know my disobedience and my sin. [24] Why do you hide your face, and consider me your enemy? [25] Will you harass a driven leaf? Will you pursue the dry stubble? [26] For you write bitter things against me, and make me inherit the iniquities of my youth. [27] You also put my feet in the stocks, and mark all my paths. You set a bound to the soles of my feet, [28] though I am decaying like a rotten thing, like a garment that is moth-eaten.

## 14

[1]"Man, who is born of a woman, is of few days, and full of trouble. [2] He grows up like a flower, and is cut down. He also flees like a shadow, and doesn't continue. [3] Do you open your eyes on such a one, and bring me into judgment with you? [4] Who can bring a clean thing out of an unclean? Not one. [5] Seeing his days are determined, the number of his months is with you, and you have appointed his bounds that he can't pass. [6] Look away from him, that he may rest, until he accomplishes, as a hireling, his day. [7]"For there is hope for a tree if it is cut down, that it will sprout again, that the tender branch of it will not cease. [8] Though its root grows old in the earth, and its stock dies in the ground, [9] yet through the scent of water it will bud, and sprout boughs like a plant. [10] But man dies, and is laid low. Yes, man gives up the spirit, and where is he? [11] As the waters fail from the sea, and the river wastes and dries up, [12] so man lies down and doesn't rise. Until the heavens are no more, they will not awake, nor be roused out of their sleep. [13]"Oh that you would hide me in Sheol,[a] that you would keep me secret until your wrath is past, that you would appoint me a set time and remember me! [14] If a man dies, will he live again? I would wait all the days of my warfare, until my release should come. [15] You would call, and I would answer you. You would have a desire for the work of your hands. [16] But now you count my steps. Don't you watch over my sin? [17] My disobedience is sealed up in a bag. You fasten up my iniquity. [18]"But the mountain falling comes to nothing. The rock is removed out of its place. [19] The waters wear the stones. The torrents of it wash away the dust of the earth. So you destroy the hope of man. [20] You forever prevail against him, and he departs. You change his face, and send him away. [21] His sons come to honor, and he doesn't know it. They are brought low, but he doesn't perceive it of them. [22] But his flesh on him has pain, and his soul within him mourns."

## 15

[1] Then Eliphaz the Temanite answered, [2]"Should a wise man answer with vain knowledge, and fill himself with the east wind? [3] Should he reason with unprofitable talk, or with speeches with which he can do no good? [4] Yes, you do away with fear, and hinder devotion before God. [5] For your iniquity teaches your mouth, and you choose the language of the crafty. [6] Your own mouth condemns you, and not I. Yes, your own lips testify against you. [7]"Are you the first man who was born? Or were you brought out before the hills? [8] Have you heard the secret counsel of God? Do you limit wisdom to yourself? [9] What do you know

that we don't know? What do you understand which is not in us? [10] With us are both the gray-headed and the very aged men, much older than your father. [11] Are the consolations of God too small for you, even the word that is gentle toward you? [12] Why does your heart carry you away? Why do your eyes flash, [13] that you turn your spirit against God, and let such words go out of your mouth? [14] What is man, that he should be clean? What is he who is born of a woman, that he should be righteous? [15] Behold, he puts no trust in his holy ones. Yes, the heavens are not clean in his sight; [16] how much less one who is abominable and corrupt, a man who drinks iniquity like water! [17]"I will show you, listen to me; that which I have seen I will declare [18](which wise men have told by their fathers, and have not hidden it; [19] to whom alone the land was given, and no stranger passed among them): [20] the wicked man writhes in pain all his days, even the number of years that are laid up for the oppressor. [21] A sound of terrors is in his ears. In prosperity the destroyer will come on him. [22] He doesn't believe that he will return out of darkness. He is waited for by the sword. [23] He wanders abroad for bread, saying, 'Where is it?' He knows that the day of darkness is ready at his hand. [24] Distress and anguish make him afraid. They prevail against him, as a king ready to the battle. [25] Because he has stretched out his hand against God, and behaves himself proudly against the Almighty, [26] he runs at him with a stiff neck, with the thick shields of his bucklers, [27] because he has covered his face with his fatness, and gathered fat on his thighs. [28] He has lived in desolate cities, in houses which no one inhabited, which were ready to become heaps. [29] He will not be rich, neither will his substance continue, neither will their possessions be extended on the earth. [30] He will not depart out of darkness. The flame will dry up his branches. He will go away by the breath of God's mouth. [31] Let him not trust in emptiness, deceiving himself, for emptiness will be his reward. [32] It will be accomplished before his time. His branch will not be green. [33] He will shake off his unripe grape as the vine, and will cast off his flower as the olive tree. [34] For the company of the godless will be barren, and fire will consume the tents of bribery. [35] They conceive mischief and produce iniquity. Their heart prepares deceit."

## 16

[1] Then Job answered, [2]"I have heard many such things. You are all miserable comforters! [3] Shall vain words have an end? Or what provokes you that you answer? [4] I also could speak as you do. If your soul were in my soul's place, I could join words together against you, and shake my head at you, [5] but I would strengthen you with my mouth. The solace of my lips would relieve you. [6]"Though I speak, my grief is not subsided. Though I forbear, what am I eased? [7] But now, God, you have surely worn me out. You have made all my company desolate. [8] You have shriveled me up. This is a witness against me. My leanness rises up against me. It testifies to my face. [9] He has torn me in his wrath and persecuted me. He has gnashed on me with his teeth. My adversary sharpens his eyes on me. [10] They have gaped on me with their mouth. They have struck me on the cheek reproachfully. They gather themselves together against me. [11] God delivers me to the ungodly, and casts me into the hands of the wicked. [12] I was at ease, and he broke me apart. Yes, he has taken me by the neck, and dashed me to pieces. He has also set me up for his target. [13] His archers surround me. He splits my kidneys apart, and does not spare. He pours out my bile on the ground. [14] He breaks me with breach on breach. He runs at me like a giant. [15] I have sewed sackcloth on my skin, and have thrust my horn in the dust. [16] My face is red with weeping. Deep darkness is on my eyelids, [17] although there is no violence in my hands, and my prayer is pure. [18]"Earth, don't cover my blood. Let my cry have no place to rest. [19] Even now, behold, my witness is in heaven. He who vouches for me is on high. [20] My friends scoff at me. My eyes pour out tears to God, [21] that he would maintain the right of a man with God, of a son of man with his neighbor! [22] For when a few years have come, I will go the way of no return.

## 17

[1]"My spirit is consumed. My days are extinct and the grave is ready for me. [2] Surely there are mockers with me. My eye dwells on their provocation. [3]"Now give a pledge. Be collateral for me with yourself. Who is there who will strike hands with me? [4] For you have hidden their heart from understanding, therefore you will not exalt them. [5] He who denounces his friends for plunder, even the eyes of his children will fail. [6]"But he has made me a byword of the people. They spit in my face. [7] My eye also is dim by reason of sorrow. All my members are as a shadow. [8] Upright men will be astonished at this. The innocent will stir himself up against the godless. [9] Yet the righteous will hold to his way. He who has clean hands will grow stronger and stronger. [10] But as for you all, come back. I will not find a wise man among you. [11]

My days are past. My plans are broken off, as are the thoughts of my heart. ¹² They change the night into day, saying 'The light is near' in the presence of darkness. ¹³ If I look for Sheol<sup>a</sup> as my house, if I have spread my couch in the darkness, ¹⁴ if I have said to corruption, 'You are my father,' and to the worm, 'My mother,' and 'My sister,' ¹⁵ where then is my hope? As for my hope, who will see it? ¹⁶ Shall it go down with me to the gates of Sheol,<sup>b</sup> or descend together into the dust?"

## 18

¹ Then Bildad the Shuhite answered, ²"How long will you hunt for words? Consider, and afterwards we will speak. ³ Why are we counted as animals, which have become unclean in your sight? ⁴ You who tear yourself in your anger, will the earth be forsaken for you? Or will the rock be removed out of its place? ⁵"Yes, the light of the wicked will be put out. The spark of his fire won't shine. ⁶ The light will be dark in his tent. His lamp above him will be put out. ⁷ The steps of his strength will be shortened. His own counsel will cast him down. ⁸ For he is cast into a net by his own feet, and he wanders into its mesh. ⁹ A snare will take him by the heel. A trap will catch him. ¹⁰ A noose is hidden for him in the ground, a trap for him on the path. ¹¹ Terrors will make him afraid on every side, and will chase him at his heels. ¹² His strength will be famished. Calamity will be ready at his side. ¹³ The members of his body will be devoured. The firstborn of death will devour his members. ¹⁴ He will be rooted out of the security of his tent. He will be brought to the king of terrors. ¹⁵ There will dwell in his tent that which is none of his. Sulfur will be scattered on his habitation. ¹⁶ His roots will be dried up beneath. His branch will be cut off above. ¹⁷ His memory will perish from the earth. He will have no name in the street. ¹⁸ He will be driven from light into darkness, and chased out of the world. ¹⁹ He will have neither son nor grandson among his people, nor any remaining where he lived. ²⁰ Those who come after will be astonished at his day, as those who went before were frightened. ²¹ Surely such are the dwellings of the unrighteous. This is the place of him who doesn't know God."

## 19

¹ Then Job answered, ²"How long will you torment me, and crush me with words? ³ You have reproached me ten times. You aren't ashamed that you attack me. ⁴ If it is true that I have erred, my error remains with myself. ⁵ If indeed you will magnify yourselves against me, and plead against me my reproach, ⁶ know now that God has subverted me, and has surrounded me with his net. ⁷"Behold, I cry out of wrong, but I am not heard. I cry for help, but there is no justice. ⁸ He has walled up my way so that I can't pass, and has set darkness in my paths. ⁹ He has stripped me of my glory, and taken the crown from my head. ¹⁰ He has broken me down on every side, and I am gone. He has plucked my hope up like a tree. ¹¹ He has also kindled his wrath against me. He counts me among his adversaries. ¹² His troops come on together, build a siege ramp against me, and encamp around my tent. ¹³"He has put my brothers far from me. My acquaintances are wholly estranged from me. ¹⁴ My relatives have gone away. My familiar friends have forgotten me. ¹⁵ Those who dwell in my house and my maids consider me a stranger. I am an alien in their sight. ¹⁶ I call to my servant, and he gives me no answer. I beg him with my mouth. ¹⁷ My breath is offensive to my wife. I am loathsome to the children of my own mother. ¹⁸ Even young children despise me. If I arise, they speak against me. ¹⁹ All my familiar friends abhor me. They whom I loved have turned against me. ²⁰ My bones stick to my skin and to my flesh. I have escaped by the skin of my teeth. ²¹"Have pity on me. Have pity on me, you my friends, for the hand of God has touched me. ²² Why do you persecute me as God, and are not satisfied with my flesh? ²³"Oh that my words were now written! Oh that they were inscribed in a book! ²⁴ That with an iron pen and lead they were engraved in the rock forever! ²⁵ But as for me, I know that my Redeemer lives. In the end, he will stand upon the earth. ²⁶ After my skin is destroyed, then I will see God in my flesh, ²⁷ whom I, even I, will see on my side. My eyes will see, and not as a stranger. "My heart is consumed within me. ²⁸ If you say, 'How we will persecute him!' because the root of the matter is found in me, ²⁹ be afraid of the sword, for wrath brings the punishments of the sword, that you may know there is a judgment."

## 20

¹ Then Zophar the Naamathite answered, ²"Therefore my thoughts answer me, even by reason of my haste that is in me. ³ I have heard the reproof which puts me to shame. The spirit of my understanding answers me. ⁴ Don't you know this from old time, since man was placed on earth, ⁵ that the triumphing of the wicked is short, the joy of the godless but for a moment? ⁶ Though his height mount up to the heavens, and his head reach to the clouds, ⁷ yet he will perish forever like his own dung. Those who have seen him will say, 'Where is he?' ⁸ He will

fly away as a dream, and will not be found. Yes, he will be chased away like a vision of the night. ⁹ The eye which saw him will see him no more, neither will his place see him any more. ¹⁰ His children will seek the favor of the poor. His hands will give back his wealth. ¹¹ His bones are full of his youth, but youth will lie down with him in the dust. ¹²"Though wickedness is sweet in his mouth, though he hide it under his tongue, ¹³ though he spare it, and will not let it go, but keep it still within his mouth, ¹⁴ yet his food in his bowels is turned. It is cobra venom within him. ¹⁵ He has swallowed down riches, and he will vomit them up again. God will cast them out of his belly. ¹⁶ He will suck cobra venom. The viper's tongue will kill him. ¹⁷ He will not look at the rivers, the flowing streams of honey and butter. ¹⁸ He will restore that for which he labored, and will not swallow it down. He will not rejoice according to the substance that he has gotten. ¹⁹ For he has oppressed and forsaken the poor. He has violently taken away a house, and he will not build it up. ²⁰"Because he knew no quietness within him, he will not save anything of that in which he delights. ²¹ There was nothing left that he didn't devour, therefore his prosperity will not endure. ²² In the fullness of his sufficiency, distress will overtake him. The hand of everyone who is in misery will come on him. ²³ When he is about to fill his belly, God will cast the fierceness of his wrath on him. It will rain on him while he is eating. ²⁴ He will flee from the iron weapon. The bronze arrow will strike him through. ²⁵ He draws it out, and it comes out of his body. Yes, the glittering point comes out of his liver. Terrors are on him. ²⁶ All darkness is laid up for his treasures. An unfanned fire will devour him. It will consume that which is left in his tent. ²⁷ The heavens will reveal his iniquity. The earth will rise up against him. ²⁸ The increase of his house will depart. They will rush away in the day of his wrath. ²⁹ This is the portion of a wicked man from God, the heritage appointed to him by God."

## 21

¹ Then Job answered, ²"Listen diligently to my speech. Let this be your consolation. ³ Allow me, and I also will speak. After I have spoken, mock on. ⁴ As for me, is my complaint to man? Why shouldn't I be impatient? ⁵ Look at me, and be astonished. Lay your hand on your mouth. ⁶ When I remember, I am troubled. Horror takes hold of my flesh. ⁷"Why do the wicked live, become old, yes, and grow mighty in power? ⁸ Their child is established with them in their sight, their offspring before their eyes. ⁹ Their houses are safe from fear, neither is the rod of God upon them. ¹⁰ Their bulls breed without fail. Their cows calve, and don't miscarry. ¹¹ They send out their little ones like a flock. Their children dance. ¹² They sing to the tambourine and harp, and rejoice at the sound of the pipe. ¹³ They spend their days in prosperity. In an instant they go down to Sheol.<sup>c</sup> ¹⁴ They tell God, 'Depart from us, for we don't want to know about your ways. ¹⁵ What is the Almighty, that we should serve him? What profit should we have, if we pray to him?' ¹⁶ Behold, their prosperity is not in their hand. The counsel of the wicked is far from me. ¹⁷"How often is it that the lamp of the wicked is put out, that their calamity comes on them, that God distributes sorrows in his anger? ¹⁸ How often is it that they are as stubble before the wind, as chaff that the storm carries away? ¹⁹ You say, 'God lays up his iniquity for his children.' Let him recompense it to himself, that he may know it. ²⁰ Let his own eyes see his destruction. Let him drink of the wrath of the Almighty. ²¹ For what does he care for his house after him, when the number of his months is cut off? ²²"Shall any teach God knowledge, since he judges those who are high? ²³ One dies in his full strength, being wholly at ease and quiet. ²⁴ His pails are full of milk. The marrow of his bones is moistened. ²⁵ Another dies in bitterness of soul, and never tastes of good. ²⁶ They lie down alike in the dust. The worm covers them. ²⁷"Behold, I know your thoughts, the plans with which you would wrong me. ²⁸ For you say, 'Where is the house of the prince? Where is the tent in which the wicked lived?' ²⁹ Haven't you asked wayfaring men? Don't you know their evidences, ³⁰ that the evil man is reserved to the day of calamity, that they are led out to the day of wrath? ³¹ Who will declare his way to his face? Who will repay him what he has done? ³² Yet he will be borne to the grave. Men will keep watch over the tomb. ³³ The clods of the valley will be sweet to him. All men will draw after him, as there were innumerable before him. ³⁴ So how can you comfort me with nonsense, because in your answers there remains only falsehood?"

## 22

¹ Then Eliphaz the Temanite answered, ²"Can a man be profitable to God? Surely he who is wise is profitable to himself. ³ Is it any pleasure to the Almighty that you are righteous? Or does it benefit him that you make your ways perfect? ⁴ Is it for your piety that he reproves you, that he enters with you into judgment? ⁵ Isn't your wickedness great? Neither is there any end to your iniquities. ⁶ For you have taken pledges

---

<sup>a</sup> *17:13* Sheol is the place of the dead.

<sup>b</sup> *17:16* Sheol is the place of the dead.

<sup>c</sup> *21:13* Sheol is the place of the dead.

from your brother for nothing, and stripped the naked of their clothing. [7] You haven't given water to the weary to drink, and you have withheld bread from the hungry. [8] But as for the mighty man, he had the earth. The honorable man, he lived in it. [9] You have sent widows away empty, and the arms of the fatherless have been broken. [10] Therefore snares are around you. Sudden fear troubles you, [11] or darkness, so that you can not see, and floods of waters cover you. [12]"Isn't God in the heights of heaven? See the height of the stars, how high they are! [13] You say, 'What does God know? Can he judge through the thick darkness? [14] Thick clouds are a covering to him, so that he doesn't see. He walks on the vault of the sky.' [15] Will you keep the old way, which wicked men have trodden, [16] who were snatched away before their time, whose foundation was poured out as a stream, [17] who said to God, 'Depart from us!' and, 'What can the Almighty do for us?' [18] Yet he filled their houses with good things, but the counsel of the wicked is far from me. [19] The righteous see it, and are glad. The innocent ridicule them, [20] saying, 'Surely those who rose up against us are cut off. The fire has consumed their remnant.' [21]"Acquaint yourself with him now, and be at peace. By it, good will come to you. [22] Please receive instruction from his mouth, and lay up his words in your heart. [23] If you return to the Almighty, you will be built up, if you put away unrighteousness far from your tents. [24] Lay your treasure in the dust, the gold of Ophir among the stones of the brooks. [25] The Almighty will be your treasure, and precious silver to you. [26] For then you will delight yourself in the Almighty, and will lift up your face to God. [27] You will make your prayer to him, and he will hear you. You will pay your vows. [28] You will also decree a thing, and it will be established to you. Light will shine on your ways. [29] When they cast down, you will say, 'be lifted up.' He will save the humble person. [30] He will even deliver him who is not innocent. Yes, he will be delivered through the cleanness of your hands."

## 23

[1] Then Job answered, [2]"Even today my complaint is rebellious. His hand is heavy in spite of my groaning. [3] Oh that I knew where I might find him! That I might come even to his seat! [4] I would set my cause in order before him, and fill my mouth with arguments. [5] I would know the words which he would answer me, and understand what he would tell me. [6] Would he contend with me in the greatness of his power? No, but he would listen to me. [7] There the upright might reason with him, so I should be delivered forever from my judge. [8]"If I go east, he is not there. If I go west, I can't find him. [9] He works to the north, but I can't see him. He turns south, but I can't catch a glimpse of him. [10] But he knows the way that I take. When he has tried me, I will come out like gold. [11] My foot has held fast to his steps. I have kept his way, and not turned away. [12] I haven't gone back from the commandment of his lips. I have treasured up the words of his mouth more than my necessary food. [13] But he stands alone, and who can oppose him? What his soul desires, even that he does. [14] For he performs that which is appointed for me. Many such things are with him. [15] Therefore I am terrified at his presence. When I consider, I am afraid of him. [16] For God has made my heart faint. The Almighty has terrified me. [17] Because I was not cut off before the darkness, neither did he cover the thick darkness from my face.

## 24

[1]"Why aren't times laid up by the Almighty? Why don't those who know him see his days? [2] There are people who remove the landmarks. They violently take away flocks, and feed them. [3] They drive away the donkey of the fatherless, and they take the widow's ox for a pledge. [4] They turn the needy out of the way. The poor of the earth all hide themselves. [5] Behold, as wild donkeys in the desert, they go out to their work, seeking diligently for food. The wilderness yields them bread for their children. [6] They cut their food in the field. They glean the vineyard of the wicked. [7] They lie all night naked without clothing, and have no covering in the cold. [8] They are wet with the showers of the mountains, and embrace the rock for lack of a shelter. [9] There are those who pluck the fatherless from the breast, and take a pledge of the poor, [10] so that they go around naked without clothing. Being hungry, they carry the sheaves. [11] They make oil within the walls of these men. They tread wine presses, and suffer thirst. [12] From out of the populous city, men groan. The soul of the wounded cries out, yet God doesn't regard the folly. [13]"These are of those who rebel against the light. They don't know its ways, nor stay in its paths. [14] The murderer rises with the light. He kills the poor and needy. In the night he is like a thief. [15] The eye also of the adulterer waits for the twilight, saying, 'No eye will see me.' He disguises his face. [16] In the dark they dig through houses. They shut themselves up in the daytime. They don't know the light. [17] For the morning is to all of them like thick darkness, for they know the terrors

of the thick darkness. [18]"They are foam on the surface of the waters. Their portion is cursed in the earth. They don't turn into the way of the vineyards. [19] Drought and heat consume the snow waters, so does Sheol[a] those who have sinned. [20] The womb will forget him. The worm will feed sweetly on him. He will be no more remembered. Unrighteousness will be broken as a tree. [21] He devours the barren who don't bear. He shows no kindness to the widow. [22] Yet God preserves the mighty by his power. He rises up who has no assurance of life. [23] God gives them security, and they rest in it. His eyes are on their ways. [24] They are exalted; yet a little while, and they are gone. Yes, they are brought low, they are taken out of the way as all others, and are cut off as the tops of the ears of grain. [25] If it isn't so now, who will prove me a liar, and make my speech worth nothing?"

## 25

[1] Then Bildad the Shuhite answered, [2]"Dominion and fear are with him. He makes peace in his high places. [3] Can his armies be counted? On whom does his light not arise? [4] How then can man be just with God? Or how can he who is born of a woman be clean? [5] Behold, even the moon has no brightness, and the stars are not pure in his sight; [6] How much less man, who is a worm, and the son of man, who is a worm!"

## 26

[1] Then Job answered, [2]"How have you helped him who is without power! How have you saved the arm that has no strength! [3] How have you counseled him who has no wisdom, and plentifully declared sound knowledge! [4] To whom have you uttered words? Whose spirit came out of you? [5]"The departed spirits tremble, those beneath the waters and all that live in them. [6] Sheol[b] is naked before God, and Abaddon[c] has no covering. [7] He stretches out the north over empty space, and hangs the earth on nothing. [8] He binds up the waters in his thick clouds, and the cloud is not burst under them. [9] He encloses the face of his throne, and spreads his cloud on it. [10] He has described a boundary on the surface of the waters, and to the confines of light and darkness. [11] The pillars of heaven tremble and are astonished at his rebuke. [12] He stirs up the sea with his power, and by his understanding he strikes through Rahab. [13] By his Spirit the heavens are garnished. His hand has pierced the swift serpent. [14] Behold, these are but the outskirts of his ways. How small a whisper do we hear of him! But the thunder of his power who can understand?"

## 27

[1] Job again took up his parable, and said, [2]"As God lives, who has taken away my right, the Almighty, who has made my soul bitter [3](for the length of my life is still in me, and the spirit of God is in my nostrils); [4] surely my lips will not speak unrighteousness, neither will my tongue utter deceit. [5] Far be it from me that I should justify you. Until I die I will not put away my integrity from me. [6] I hold fast to my righteousness, and will not let it go. My heart will not reproach me so long as I live. [7]"Let my enemy be as the wicked. Let him who rises up against me be as the unrighteous. [8] For what is the hope of the godless, when he is cut off, when God takes away his life? [9] Will God hear his cry when trouble comes on him? [10] Will he delight himself in the Almighty, and call on God at all times? [11] I will teach you about the hand of God. I will not conceal that which is with the Almighty. [12] Behold, all of you have seen it yourselves; why then have you become altogether vain? [13]"This is the portion of a wicked man with God, the heritage of oppressors, which they receive from the Almighty. [14] If his children are multiplied, it is for the sword. His offspring will not be satisfied with bread. [15] Those who remain of him will be buried in death. His widows will make no lamentation. [16] Though he heap up silver as the dust, and prepare clothing as the clay; [17] he may prepare it, but the just will put it on, and the innocent will divide the silver. [18] He builds his house as the moth, as a booth which the watchman makes. [19] He lies down rich, but he will not do so again. He opens his eyes, and he is not. [20] Terrors overtake him like waters. A storm steals him away in the night. [21] The east wind carries him away, and he departs. It sweeps him out of his place. [22] For it hurls at him, and does not spare, as he flees away from his hand. [23] Men will clap their hands at him, and will hiss him out of his place.

## 28

[1]"Surely there is a mine for silver, and a place for gold which they refine. [2] Iron is taken out of the earth, and copper is smelted out of the ore. [3] Man sets an end to darkness, and searches out, to the furthest bound, the stones of obscurity and of thick darkness. [4] He breaks open a shaft away from where people live. They are forgotten by the foot. They hang far from men, they swing back and forth. [5] As for the earth, out of it comes bread. Underneath it is turned up as it were by fire. [6] Sapphires come from its rocks. It has dust of gold. [7] That path no bird of prey knows, neither has the falcon's eye seen it. [8] The proud animals

---

[a] *24:19* Sheol is the place of the dead.

[b] *26:6* Sheol is the place of the dead.

[c] *26:6* Abaddon means Destroyer.

have not trodden it, nor has the fierce lion passed by there. <sup>9</sup> He puts his hand on the flinty rock, and he overturns the mountains by the roots. <sup>10</sup> He cuts out channels among the rocks. His eye sees every precious thing. <sup>11</sup> He binds the streams that they don't trickle. The thing that is hidden he brings out to light. <sup>12</sup>"But where will wisdom be found? Where is the place of understanding? <sup>13</sup> Man doesn't know its price, and it isn't found in the land of the living. <sup>14</sup> The deep says, 'It isn't in me.' The sea says, 'It isn't with me.' <sup>15</sup> It can't be gotten for gold, neither will silver be weighed for its price. <sup>16</sup> It can't be valued with the gold of Ophir, with the precious onyx, or the sapphire.<sup>a</sup> <sup>17</sup> Gold and glass can't equal it, neither will it be exchanged for jewels of fine gold. <sup>18</sup> No mention will be made of coral or of crystal. Yes, the price of wisdom is above rubies. <sup>19</sup> The topaz of Ethiopia will not equal it. It won't be valued with pure gold. <sup>20</sup> Where then does wisdom come from? Where is the place of understanding? <sup>21</sup> Seeing it is hidden from the eyes of all living, and kept close from the birds of the sky. <sup>22</sup> Destruction and Death say, 'We have heard a rumor of it with our ears.' <sup>23</sup>"God understands its way, and he knows its place. <sup>24</sup> For he looks to the ends of the earth, and sees under the whole sky. <sup>25</sup> He establishes the force of the wind. Yes, he measures out the waters by measure. <sup>26</sup> When he made a decree for the rain, and a way for the lightning of the thunder, <sup>27</sup> then he saw it, and declared it. He established it, yes, and searched it out. <sup>28</sup> To man he said, 'Behold, the fear of the Lord,<sup>b</sup> that is wisdom. To depart from evil is understanding.'"

## 29

<sup>1</sup> Job again took up his parable, and said, <sup>2</sup>"Oh that I were as in the months of old, as in the days when God watched over me; <sup>3</sup> when his lamp shone on my head, and by his light I walked through darkness, <sup>4</sup> as I was in my prime, when the friendship of God was in my tent, <sup>5</sup> when the Almighty was yet with me, and my children were around me, <sup>6</sup> when my steps were washed with butter, and the rock poured out streams of oil for me, <sup>7</sup> when I went out to the city gate, when I prepared my seat in the street. <sup>8</sup> The young men saw me and hid themselves. The aged rose up and stood. <sup>9</sup> The princes refrained from talking, and laid their hand on their mouth. <sup>10</sup> The voice of the nobles was hushed, and their tongue stuck to the roof of their mouth. <sup>11</sup> For when the ear heard me, then it blessed me, and when the eye saw me, it commended me, <sup>12</sup> because I delivered the poor who cried, and the fatherless also, who had no one to help him, <sup>13</sup> the blessing of him who was ready to perish came on me, and I caused the widow's heart to sing for joy. <sup>14</sup> I put on righteousness, and it clothed me. My justice was as a robe and a diadem. <sup>15</sup> I was eyes to the blind, and feet to the lame. <sup>16</sup> I was a father to the needy. I researched the cause of him whom I didn't know. <sup>17</sup> I broke the jaws of the unrighteous and plucked the prey out of his teeth. <sup>18</sup> Then I said, 'I will die in my own house, I will count my days as the sand. <sup>19</sup> My root is spread out to the waters. The dew lies all night on my branch. <sup>20</sup> My glory is fresh in me. My bow is renewed in my hand.' <sup>21</sup>"Men listened to me, waited, and kept silence for my counsel. <sup>22</sup> After my words they didn't speak again. My speech fell on them. <sup>23</sup> They waited for me as for the rain. Their mouths drank as with the spring rain. <sup>24</sup> I smiled on them when they had no confidence. They didn't reject the light of my face. <sup>25</sup> I chose out their way, and sat as chief. I lived as a king in the army, as one who comforts the mourners.

## 30

<sup>1</sup>"But now those who are younger than I have me in derision, whose fathers I considered unworthy to put with my sheep dogs. <sup>2</sup> Of what use is the strength of their hands to me, men in whom ripe age has perished? <sup>3</sup> They are gaunt from lack and famine. They gnaw the dry ground, in the gloom of waste and desolation. <sup>4</sup> They pluck salt herbs by the bushes. The roots of the broom tree are their food. <sup>5</sup> They are driven out from among men. They cry after them as after a thief, <sup>6</sup> so that they live in frightful valleys, and in holes of the earth and of the rocks. <sup>7</sup> They bray among the bushes. They are gathered together under the nettles. <sup>8</sup> They are children of fools, yes, children of wicked men. They were flogged out of the land. <sup>9</sup>"Now I have become their song. Yes, I am a byword to them. <sup>10</sup> They abhor me, they stand aloof from me, and don't hesitate to spit in my face. <sup>11</sup> For he has untied his cord, and afflicted me; and they have thrown off restraint before me. <sup>12</sup> On my right hand rise the rabble. They thrust aside my feet. They cast their ways of destruction up against me. <sup>13</sup> They mar my path. They promote my destruction without anyone's help. <sup>14</sup> As through a wide breach they come. They roll themselves in amid the ruin. <sup>15</sup> Terrors have turned on me. They chase my honor as the wind. My welfare has passed away as a cloud. <sup>16</sup>"Now my soul is poured out within me. Days of affliction have taken hold of me. <sup>17</sup> In the night season my bones are pierced in me, and the pains that gnaw me take no rest. <sup>18</sup> My garment is disfigured by great force. It binds me about as the collar of my tunic. <sup>19</sup> He has

cast me into the mire. I have become like dust and ashes. <sup>20</sup> I cry to you, and you do not answer me. I stand up, and you gaze at me. <sup>21</sup> You have turned to be cruel to me. With the might of your hand you persecute me. <sup>22</sup> You lift me up to the wind, and drive me with it. You dissolve me in the storm. <sup>23</sup> For I know that you will bring me to death, to the house appointed for all living. <sup>24</sup>"However doesn't one stretch out a hand in his fall? Or in his calamity therefore cry for help? <sup>25</sup> Didn't I weep for him who was in trouble? Wasn't my soul grieved for the needy? <sup>26</sup> When I looked for good, then evil came. When I waited for light, darkness came. <sup>27</sup> My heart is troubled, and doesn't rest. Days of affliction have come on me. <sup>28</sup> I go mourning without the sun. I stand up in the assembly, and cry for help. <sup>29</sup> I am a brother to jackals, and a companion to ostriches. <sup>30</sup> My skin grows black and peels from me. My bones are burned with heat. <sup>31</sup> Therefore my harp has turned to mourning, and my pipe into the voice of those who weep.

## 31

<sup>1</sup>"I made a covenant with my eyes; how then should I look lustfully at a young woman? <sup>2</sup> For what is the portion from God above, and the heritage from the Almighty on high? <sup>3</sup> Is it not calamity to the unrighteous, and disaster to the workers of iniquity? <sup>4</sup> Doesn't he see my ways, and count all my steps? <sup>5</sup>"If I have walked with falsehood, and my foot has hurried to deceit <sup>6</sup>(let me be weighed in an even balance, that God may know my integrity); <sup>7</sup> if my step has turned out of the way, if my heart walked after my eyes, if any defilement has stuck to my hands, <sup>8</sup> then let me sow, and let another eat. Yes, let the produce of my field be rooted out. <sup>9</sup>"If my heart has been enticed to a woman, and I have laid wait at my neighbor's door, <sup>10</sup> then let my wife grind for another, and let others sleep with her. <sup>11</sup> For that would be a heinous crime. Yes, it would be an iniquity to be punished by the judges, <sup>12</sup> for it is a fire that consumes to destruction, and would root out all my increase. <sup>13</sup>"If I have despised the cause of my male servant or of my female servant, when they contended with me, <sup>14</sup> what then will I do when God rises up? When he visits, what will I answer him? <sup>15</sup> Didn't he who made me in the womb make him? Didn't one fashion us in the womb? <sup>16</sup>"If I have withheld the poor from their desire, or have caused the eyes of the widow to fail, <sup>17</sup> or have eaten my morsel alone, and the fatherless has not eaten of it <sup>18</sup>(no, from my youth he grew up with me as with a father, I have guided her from my mother's womb); <sup>19</sup> if I have seen any perish for want of clothing, or that the needy had no covering; <sup>20</sup> if his heart hasn't blessed me, if he hasn't been warmed with my sheep's fleece; <sup>21</sup> if I have lifted up my hand against the fatherless, because I saw my help in the gate; <sup>22</sup> then let my shoulder fall from the shoulder blade, and my arm be broken from the bone. <sup>23</sup> For calamity from God is a terror to me. Because of his majesty, I can do nothing. <sup>24</sup>"If I have made gold my hope, and have said to the fine gold, 'You are my confidence;' <sup>25</sup> If I have rejoiced because my wealth was great, and because my hand had gotten much; <sup>26</sup> if I have seen the sun when it shined, or the moon moving in splendor, <sup>27</sup> and my heart has been secretly enticed, and my hand threw a kiss from my mouth; <sup>28</sup> this also would be an iniquity to be punished by the judges, for I would have denied the God who is above. <sup>29</sup>"If I have rejoiced at the destruction of him who hated me, or lifted up myself when evil found him <sup>30</sup>(I have certainly not allowed my mouth to sin by asking his life with a curse); <sup>31</sup> if the men of my tent have not said, 'Who can find one who has not been filled with his meat?' <sup>32</sup>(the foreigner has not camped in the street, but I have opened my doors to the traveler); <sup>33</sup> if like Adam I have covered my transgressions, by hiding my iniquity in my heart, <sup>34</sup> because I feared the great multitude, and the contempt of families terrified me, so that I kept silence, and didn't go out of the door— <sup>35</sup> oh that I had one to hear me! Behold, here is my signature! Let the Almighty answer me! Let the accuser write my indictment! <sup>36</sup> Surely I would carry it on my shoulder, and I would bind it to me as a crown. <sup>37</sup> I would declare to him the number of my steps. I would go near to him like a prince. <sup>38</sup> If my land cries out against me, and its furrows weep together; <sup>39</sup> if I have eaten its fruits without money, or have caused its owners to lose their life, <sup>40</sup> let briers grow instead of wheat, and stinkweed instead of barley." The words of Job are ended.

## 32

<sup>1</sup> So these three men ceased to answer Job, because he was righteous in his own eyes. <sup>2</sup> Then the wrath of Elihu the son of Barachel, the Buzite, of the family of Ram, was kindled against Job. His wrath was kindled because he justified himself rather than God. <sup>3</sup> Also his wrath was kindled against his three friends, because they had found no answer, and yet had condemned Job. <sup>4</sup> Now Elihu had waited to speak to Job, because they were older than he. <sup>5</sup> When Elihu saw that there was no answer in the mouth of these three men, his wrath was kindled. <sup>6</sup> Elihu the son of Barachel the Buzite answered, "I am young, and you are very

---

<sup>a</sup> *28:16* or, lapis lazuli

<sup>b</sup> *28:28* The word translated "Lord" is "Adonai."

old. Therefore I held back, and didn't dare show you my opinion. ⁷ I said, 'Days should speak, and multitude of years should teach wisdom.' ⁸ But there is a spirit in man, and the Spirit[a] of the Almighty gives them understanding. ⁹ It is not the great who are wise, nor the aged who understand justice. ¹⁰ Therefore I said, 'Listen to me; I also will show my opinion.' ¹¹"Behold, I waited for your words, and I listened for your reasoning, while you searched out what to say. ¹² Yes, I gave you my full attention, but there was no one who convinced Job, or who answered his words, among you. ¹³ Beware lest you say, 'We have found wisdom. God may refute him, not man;' ¹⁴ for he has not directed his words against me; neither will I answer him with your speeches. ¹⁵"They are amazed. They answer no more. They don't have a word to say. ¹⁶ Shall I wait, because they don't speak, because they stand still, and answer no more? ¹⁷ I also will answer my part, and I also will show my opinion. ¹⁸ For I am full of words. The spirit within me constrains me. ¹⁹ Behold, my breast is as wine which has no vent; like new wineskins it is ready to burst. ²⁰ I will speak, that I may be refreshed. I will open my lips and answer. ²¹ Please don't let me respect any man's person, neither will I give flattering titles to any man. ²² For I don't know how to give flattering titles, or else my Maker would soon take me away.

## 33

¹"However, Job, please hear my speech, and listen to all my words. ² See now, I have opened my mouth. My tongue has spoken in my mouth. ³ My words will utter the uprightness of my heart. That which my lips know they will speak sincerely. ⁴ The Spirit of God has made me, and the breath of the Almighty gives me life. ⁵ If you can, answer me. Set your words in order before me, and stand up. ⁶ Behold, I am toward God even as you are. I am also formed out of the clay. ⁷ Behold, my terror will not make you afraid, neither will my pressure be heavy on you. ⁸"Surely you have spoken in my hearing, I have heard the voice of your words, saying, ⁹'I am clean, without disobedience. I am innocent, neither is there iniquity in me. ¹⁰ Behold, he finds occasions against me. He counts me for his enemy. ¹¹ He puts my feet in the stocks. He marks all my paths.' ¹²"Behold, I will answer you. In this you are not just, for God is greater than man. ¹³ Why do you strive against him, because he doesn't give account of any of his matters? ¹⁴ For God speaks once, yes twice, though man pays no attention. ¹⁵ In a dream, in a vision of the night, when deep sleep falls on men, in slumbering on the bed, ¹⁶ then he opens the ears of men, and seals their instruction, ¹⁷ that he may withdraw man from his purpose, and hide pride from man. ¹⁸ He keeps back his soul from the pit, and his life from perishing by the sword. ¹⁹"He is chastened also with pain on his bed, with continual strife in his bones, ²⁰ so that his life abhors bread, and his soul dainty food. ²¹ His flesh is so consumed away that it can't be seen. His bones that were not seen stick out. ²² Yes, his soul draws near to the pit, and his life to the destroyers. ²³"If there is beside him an angel, an interpreter, one among a thousand, to show to man what is right for him, ²⁴ then God is gracious to him, and says, 'Deliver him from going down to the pit, I have found a ransom.' ²⁵ His flesh will be fresher than a child's. He returns to the days of his youth. ²⁶ He prays to God, and he is favorable to him, so that he sees his face with joy. He restores to man his righteousness. ²⁷ He sings before men, and says, 'I have sinned, and perverted that which was right, and it didn't profit me. ²⁸ He has redeemed my soul from going into the pit. My life will see the light.' ²⁹"Behold, God does all these things, twice, yes three times, with a man, ³⁰ to bring back his soul from the pit, that he may be enlightened with the light of the living. ³¹ Mark well, Job, and listen to me. Hold your peace, and I will speak. ³² If you have anything to say, answer me. Speak, for I desire to justify you. ³³ If not, listen to me. Hold your peace, and I will teach you wisdom."

## 34

¹ Moreover Elihu answered, ²"Hear my words, you wise men. Give ear to me, you who have knowledge. ³ For the ear tries words, as the palate tastes food. ⁴ Let us choose for us that which is right. Let us know among ourselves what is good. ⁵ For Job has said, 'I am righteous, God has taken away my right. ⁶ Notwithstanding my right I am considered a liar. My wound is incurable, though I am without disobedience.' ⁷ What man is like Job, who drinks scorn like water, ⁸ who goes in company with the workers of iniquity, and walks with wicked men? ⁹ For he has said, 'It profits a man nothing that he should delight himself with God.' ¹⁰"Therefore listen to me, you men of understanding: far be it from God, that he should do wickedness, from the Almighty, that he should commit iniquity. ¹¹ For the work of a man he will render to him, and cause every man to find according to his ways. ¹² Yes surely, God will not do wickedly, neither will the Almighty pervert justice. ¹³ Who put him in charge of the earth? Or who has appointed him over the whole world? ¹⁴ If he set his heart on himself, if he gathered to himself his

spirit and his breath, ¹⁵ all flesh would perish together, and man would turn again to dust. ¹⁶"If now you have understanding, hear this. Listen to the voice of my words. ¹⁷ Should even one who hates justice govern? Will you condemn him who is righteous and mighty, ¹⁸ who says to a king, 'Vile!' or to nobles, 'Wicked!'? ¹⁹ He doesn't respect the persons of princes, nor respect the rich more than the poor, for they all are the work of his hands. ²⁰ In a moment they die, even at midnight. The people are shaken and pass away. The mighty are taken away without a hand. ²¹"For his eyes are on the ways of a man. He sees all his goings. ²² There is no darkness, nor thick gloom, where the workers of iniquity may hide themselves. ²³ For he doesn't need to consider a man further, that he should go before God in judgment. ²⁴ He breaks mighty men in pieces in ways past finding out, and sets others in their place. ²⁵ Therefore he takes knowledge of their works. He overturns them in the night, so that they are destroyed. ²⁶ He strikes them as wicked men in the open sight of others; ²⁷ because they turned away from following him, and wouldn't pay attention to any of his ways, ²⁸ so that they caused the cry of the poor to come to him. He heard the cry of the afflicted. ²⁹ When he gives quietness, who then can condemn? When he hides his face, who then can see him? He is over a nation or a man alike, ³⁰ that the godless man may not reign, that there be no one to ensnare the people. ³¹"For has any said to God, 'I am guilty, but I will not offend any more. ³² Teach me that which I don't see. If I have done iniquity, I will do it no more'? ³³ Shall his recompense be as you desire, that you refuse it? For you must choose, and not I. Therefore speak what you know. ³⁴ Men of understanding will tell me, yes, every wise man who hears me: ³⁵'Job speaks without knowledge. His words are without wisdom.' ³⁶ I wish that Job were tried to the end, because of his answering like wicked men. ³⁷ For he adds rebellion to his sin. He claps his hands among us, and multiplies his words against God."

## 35

¹ Moreover Elihu answered, ²"Do you think this to be your right, or do you say, 'My righteousness is more than God's,' ³ that you ask, 'What advantage will it be to you? What profit will I have, more than if I had sinned?' ⁴ I will answer you, and your companions with you. ⁵ Look to the skies, and see. See the skies, which are higher than you. ⁶ If you have sinned, what effect do you have against him? If your transgressions are multiplied, what do you do to him? ⁷ If you are righteous, what do you give him? Or what does he receive from your hand? ⁸ Your wickedness may hurt a man as you are, and your righteousness may profit a son of man. ⁹"By reason of the multitude of oppressions they cry out. They cry for help by reason of the arm of the mighty. ¹⁰ But no one says, 'Where is God my Maker, who gives songs in the night, ¹¹ who teaches us more than the animals of the earth, and makes us wiser than the birds of the sky?' ¹² There they cry, but no one answers, because of the pride of evil men. ¹³ Surely God will not hear an empty cry, neither will the Almighty regard it. ¹⁴ How much less when you say you don't see him. The cause is before him, and you wait for him! ¹⁵ But now, because he has not visited in his anger, neither does he greatly regard arrogance, ¹⁶ therefore Job opens his mouth with empty talk, and he multiplies words without knowledge."

## 36

¹ Elihu also continued, and said, ²"Bear with me a little, and I will show you; for I still have something to say on God's behalf. ³ I will get my knowledge from afar, and will ascribe righteousness to my Maker. ⁴ For truly my words are not false. One who is perfect in knowledge is with you. ⁵"Behold, God is mighty, and doesn't despise anyone. He is mighty in strength of understanding. ⁶ He doesn't preserve the life of the wicked, but gives justice to the afflicted. ⁷ He doesn't withdraw his eyes from the righteous, but with kings on the throne, he sets them forever, and they are exalted. ⁸ If they are bound in fetters, and are taken in the cords of afflictions, ⁹ then he shows them their work, and their transgressions, that they have behaved themselves proudly. ¹⁰ He also opens their ears to instruction, and commands that they return from iniquity. ¹¹ If they listen and serve him, they will spend their days in prosperity, and their years in pleasures. ¹² But if they don't listen, they will perish by the sword; they will die without knowledge. ¹³"But those who are godless in heart lay up anger. They don't cry for help when he binds them. ¹⁴ They die in youth. Their life perishes among the unclean. ¹⁵ He delivers the afflicted by their affliction, and opens their ear in oppression. ¹⁶ Yes, he would have allured you out of distress, into a wide place, where there is no restriction. That which is set on your table would be full of fatness. ¹⁷"But you are full of the judgment of the wicked. Judgment and justice take hold of you. ¹⁸ Don't let riches entice you to wrath, neither let the great size of a bribe turn you aside. ¹⁹ Would your wealth sustain you in distress, or all the might of your strength? ²⁰ Don't desire the night, when people are cut off in their place. ²¹ Take heed, don't regard iniquity; for you have chosen this

ᵃ 32:8 or, breath

rather than affliction. ²² Behold, God is exalted in his power. Who is a teacher like him? ²³ Who has prescribed his way for him? Or who can say, 'You have committed unrighteousness'? ²⁴"Remember that you magnify his work, about which men have sung. ²⁵ All men have looked on it. Man sees it afar off. ²⁶ Behold, God is great, and we don't know him. The number of his years is unsearchable. ²⁷ For he draws up the drops of water, which distill in rain from his vapor, ²⁸ which the skies pour down and which drop on man abundantly. ²⁹ Indeed, can anyone understand the spreading of the clouds and the thunderings of his pavilion? ³⁰ Behold, he spreads his light around him. He covers the bottom of the sea. ³¹ For by these he judges the people. He gives food in abundance. ³² He covers his hands with the lightning, and commands it to strike the mark. ³³ Its noise tells about him, and the livestock also, concerning the storm that comes up.

## 37

¹"Yes, at this my heart trembles, and is moved out of its place. ² Hear, oh, hear the noise of his voice, the sound that goes out of his mouth. ³ He sends it out under the whole sky, and his lightning to the ends of the earth. ⁴ After it a voice roars. He thunders with the voice of his majesty. He doesn't hold back anything when his voice is heard. ⁵ God thunders marvelously with his voice. He does great things, which we can't comprehend. ⁶ For he says to the snow, 'Fall on the earth,' likewise to the shower of rain, and to the showers of his mighty rain. ⁷ He seals up the hand of every man, that all men whom he has made may know it. ⁸ Then the animals take cover, and remain in their dens. ⁹ Out of its room comes the storm, and cold out of the north. ¹⁰ By the breath of God, ice is given, and the width of the waters is frozen. ¹¹ Yes, he loads the thick cloud with moisture. He spreads abroad the cloud of his lightning. ¹² It is turned around by his guidance, that they may do whatever he commands them on the surface of the habitable world, ¹³ whether it is for correction, or for his land, or for loving kindness, that he causes it to come. ¹⁴"Listen to this, Job. Stand still, and consider the wondrous works of God. ¹⁵ Do you know how God controls them, and causes the lightning of his cloud to shine? ¹⁶ Do you know the workings of the clouds, the wondrous works of him who is perfect in knowledge? ¹⁷ You whose clothing is warm when the earth is still by reason of the south wind? ¹⁸ Can you, with him, spread out the sky, which is strong as a cast metal mirror? ¹⁹ Teach us what we will tell him, for we can't make our case by reason of darkness. ²⁰ Will it be told him that I would speak? Or should a man wish that he were swallowed up? ²¹ Now men don't see the light which is bright in the skies, but the wind passes, and clears them. ²² Out of the north comes golden splendor. With God is awesome majesty. ²³ We can't reach the Almighty. He is exalted in power. In justice and great righteousness, he will not oppress. ²⁴ Therefore men revere him. He doesn't regard any who are wise of heart."

## 38

¹ Then Yahweh answered Job out of the whirlwind, ²"Who is this who darkens counsel by words without knowledge? ³ Brace yourself like a man, for I will question you, then you answer me! ⁴"Where were you when I laid the foundations of the earth? Declare, if you have understanding. ⁵ Who determined its measures, if you know? Or who stretched the line on it? ⁶ What were its foundations fastened on? Or who laid its cornerstone, ⁷ when the morning stars sang together, and all the sons of God shouted for joy? ⁸"Or who shut up the sea with doors, when it broke out of the womb, ⁹ when I made clouds its garment, and wrapped it in thick darkness, ¹⁰ marked out for it my bound, set bars and doors, ¹¹ and said, 'You may come here, but no further. Your proud waves shall be stopped here'? ¹²"Have you commanded the morning in your days, and caused the dawn to know its place, ¹³ that it might take hold of the ends of the earth, and shake the wicked out of it? ¹⁴ It is changed as clay under the seal, and presented as a garment. ¹⁵ From the wicked, their light is withheld. The high arm is broken. ¹⁶"Have you entered into the springs of the sea? Or have you walked in the recesses of the deep? ¹⁷ Have the gates of death been revealed to you? Or have you seen the gates of the shadow of death? ¹⁸ Have you comprehended the earth in its width? Declare, if you know it all. ¹⁹"What is the way to the dwelling of light? As for darkness, where is its place, ²⁰ that you should take it to its bound, that you should discern the paths to its house? ²¹ Surely you know, for you were born then, and the number of your days is great! ²² Have you entered the storehouses of the snow, or have you seen the storehouses of the hail, ²³ which I have reserved against the time of trouble, against the day of battle and war? ²⁴ By what way is the lightning distributed, or the east wind scattered on the earth? ²⁵ Who has cut a channel for the flood water, or the path for the thunderstorm, ²⁶ to cause it to rain on a land where there is no man, no one on the wilderness, in which there is no man, ²⁷ to satisfy the waste and desolate ground, to cause the tender grass to grow? ²⁸ Does the rain have a father? Or who fathers the drops of dew? ²⁹ Whose womb did the ice come out of? Who has given birth to the

gray frost of the sky? ³⁰ The waters become hard like stone, when the surface of the deep is frozen. ³¹"Can you bind the cluster of the Pleiades, or loosen the cords of Orion? ³² Can you lead the constellations out in their season? Or can you guide the Bear with her cubs? ³³ Do you know the laws of the heavens? Can you establish its dominion over the earth? ³⁴"Can you lift up your voice to the clouds, that abundance of waters may cover you? ³⁵ Can you send out lightnings, that they may go? Do they report to you, 'Here we are'? ³⁶ Who has put wisdom in the inward parts? Or who has given understanding to the mind? ³⁷ Who can count the clouds by wisdom? Or who can pour out the containers of the sky, ³⁸ when the dust runs into a mass, and the clods of earth stick together? ³⁹"Can you hunt the prey for the lioness, or satisfy the appetite of the young lions, ⁴⁰ when they crouch in their dens, and lie in wait in the thicket? ⁴¹ Who provides for the raven his prey, when his young ones cry to God, and wander for lack of food?

## 39

¹"Do you know the time when the mountain goats give birth? Do you watch when the doe bears fawns? ² Can you count the months that they fulfill? Or do you know the time when they give birth? ³ They bow themselves. They bear their young. They end their labor pains. ⁴ Their young ones become strong. They grow up in the open field. They go out, and don't return again. ⁵"Who has set the wild donkey free? Or who has loosened the bonds of the swift donkey, ⁶ whose home I have made the wilderness, and the salt land his dwelling place? ⁷ He scorns the tumult of the city, neither does he hear the shouting of the driver. ⁸ The range of the mountains is his pasture. He searches after every green thing. ⁹"Will the wild ox be content to serve you? Or will he stay by your feeding trough? ¹⁰ Can you hold the wild ox in the furrow with his harness? Or will he till the valleys after you? ¹¹ Will you trust him, because his strength is great? Or will you leave to him your labor? ¹² Will you confide in him, that he will bring home your seed, and gather the grain of your threshing floor? ¹³"The wings of the ostrich wave proudly, but are they the feathers and plumage of love? ¹⁴ For she leaves her eggs on the earth, warms them in the dust, ¹⁵ and forgets that the foot may crush them, or that the wild animal may trample them. ¹⁶ She deals harshly with her young ones, as if they were not hers. Though her labor is in vain, she is without fear, ¹⁷ because God has deprived her of wisdom, neither has he imparted to her understanding. ¹⁸ When she lifts up herself on high, she scorns the horse and his rider. ¹⁹"Have you given the horse might? Have you clothed his neck with a quivering mane? ²⁰ Have you made him to leap as a locust? The glory of his snorting is awesome. ²¹ He paws in the valley, and rejoices in his strength. He goes out to meet the armed men. ²² He mocks at fear, and is not dismayed, neither does he turn back from the sword. ²³ The quiver rattles against him, the flashing spear and the javelin. ²⁴ He eats up the ground with fierceness and rage, neither does he stand still at the sound of the trumpet. ²⁵ As often as the trumpet sounds he snorts, 'Aha!' He smells the battle afar off, the thunder of the captains, and the shouting. ²⁶"Is it by your wisdom that the hawk soars, and stretches her wings toward the south? ²⁷ Is it at your command that the eagle mounts up, and makes his nest on high? ²⁸ On the cliff he dwells and makes his home, on the point of the cliff and the stronghold. ²⁹ From there he spies out the prey. His eyes see it afar off. ³⁰ His young ones also suck up blood. Where the slain are, there he is."

## 40

¹ Moreover Yahweh answered Job, ²"Shall he who argues contend with the Almighty? He who argues with God, let him answer it." ³ Then Job answered Yahweh, ⁴"Behold, I am of small account. What will I answer you? I lay my hand on my mouth. ⁵ I have spoken once, and I will not answer; Yes, twice, but I will proceed no further." ⁶ Then Yahweh answered Job out of the whirlwind: ⁷"Now brace yourself like a man. I will question you, and you will answer me. ⁸ Will you even annul my judgment? Will you condemn me, that you may be justified? ⁹ Or do you have an arm like God? Can you thunder with a voice like him? ¹⁰"Now deck yourself with excellency and dignity. Array yourself with honor and majesty. ¹¹ Pour out the fury of your anger. Look at everyone who is proud, and bring him low. ¹² Look at everyone who is proud, and humble him. Crush the wicked in their place. ¹³ Hide them in the dust together. Bind their faces in the hidden place. ¹⁴ Then I will also admit to you that your own right hand can save you. ¹⁵"See now behemoth, which I made as well as you. He eats grass as an ox. ¹⁶ Look now, his strength is in his thighs. His force is in the muscles of his belly. ¹⁷ He moves his tail like a cedar. The sinews of his thighs are knit together. ¹⁸ His bones are like tubes of bronze. His limbs are like bars of iron. ¹⁹ He is the chief of the ways of God. He who made him gives him his sword. ²⁰ Surely the mountains produce food for him, where all the animals of the field play. ²¹ He lies under the lotus trees, in the covert of the reed, and the marsh. ²² The lotuses cover him with their shade. The willows of the brook surround him. ²³ Behold, if a river

overflows, he doesn't tremble. He is confident, though the Jordan swells even to his mouth. <sup>24</sup> Shall any take him when he is on the watch, or pierce through his nose with a snare?

## 41

<sup>1</sup>"Can you draw out Leviathan<sup>a</sup> with a fish hook, or press down his tongue with a cord? <sup>2</sup> Can you put a rope into his nose, or pierce his jaw through with a hook? <sup>3</sup> Will he make many petitions to you, or will he speak soft words to you? <sup>4</sup> Will he make a covenant with you, that you should take him for a servant forever? <sup>5</sup> Will you play with him as with a bird? Or will you bind him for your girls? <sup>6</sup> Will traders barter for him? Will they part him among the merchants? <sup>7</sup> Can you fill his skin with barbed irons, or his head with fish spears? <sup>8</sup> Lay your hand on him. Remember the battle, and do so no more. <sup>9</sup> Behold, the hope of him is in vain. Won't one be cast down even at the sight of him? <sup>10</sup> None is so fierce that he dare stir him up. Who then is he who can stand before me? <sup>11</sup> Who has first given to me, that I should repay him? Everything under the heavens is mine. <sup>12</sup>"I will not keep silence concerning his limbs, nor his mighty strength, nor his goodly frame. <sup>13</sup> Who can strip off his outer garment? Who will come within his jaws? <sup>14</sup> Who can open the doors of his face? Around his teeth is terror. <sup>15</sup> Strong scales are his pride, shut up together with a close seal. <sup>16</sup> One is so near to another, that no air can come between them. <sup>17</sup> They are joined to one another. They stick together, so that they can't be pulled apart. <sup>18</sup> His sneezing flashes out light. His eyes are like the eyelids of the morning. <sup>19</sup> Out of his mouth go burning torches. Sparks of fire leap out. <sup>20</sup> Out of his nostrils a smoke goes, as of a boiling pot over a fire of reeds. <sup>21</sup> His breath kindles coals. A flame goes out of his mouth. <sup>22</sup> There is strength in his neck. Terror dances before him. <sup>23</sup> The flakes of his flesh are joined together. They are firm on him. They can't be moved. <sup>24</sup> His heart is as firm as a stone, yes, firm as the lower millstone. <sup>25</sup> When he raises himself up, the mighty are afraid. They retreat before his thrashing. <sup>26</sup> If one attacks him with the sword, it can't prevail; nor the spear, the dart, nor the pointed shaft. <sup>27</sup> He counts iron as straw, and bronze as rotten wood. <sup>28</sup> The arrow can't make him flee. Sling stones are like chaff to him. <sup>29</sup> Clubs are counted as stubble. He laughs at the rushing of the javelin. <sup>30</sup> His undersides are like sharp potsherds, leaving a trail in the mud like a threshing sledge. <sup>31</sup> He makes the deep to boil like a pot. He makes the sea like a pot of ointment. <sup>32</sup> He makes a path shine after him. One would think the deep had white hair. <sup>33</sup> On earth there is not his equal, that is made without fear. <sup>34</sup> He sees everything that is high. He is king over all the sons of pride."

## 42

<sup>1</sup> Then Job answered Yahweh: <sup>2</sup>"I know that you can do all things, and that no purpose of yours can be restrained. <sup>3</sup> You asked, 'Who is this who hides counsel without knowledge?' therefore I have uttered that which I didn't understand, things too wonderful for me, which I didn't know. <sup>4</sup> You said, 'Listen, now, and I will speak; I will question you, and you will answer me.' <sup>5</sup> I had heard of you by the hearing of the ear, but now my eye sees you. <sup>6</sup> Therefore I abhor myself, and repent in dust and ashes." <sup>7</sup> It was so, that after Yahweh had spoken these words to Job, Yahweh said to Eliphaz the Temanite, "My wrath is kindled against you, and against your two friends; for you have not spoken of me the thing that is right, as my servant Job has. <sup>8</sup> Now therefore, take to yourselves seven bulls and seven rams, and go to my servant Job, and offer up for yourselves a burnt offering; and my servant Job shall pray for you, for I will accept him, that I not deal with you according to your folly. For you have not spoken of me the thing that is right, as my servant Job has." <sup>9</sup> So Eliphaz the Temanite and Bildad the Shuhite and Zophar the Naamathite went and did what Yahweh commanded them, and Yahweh accepted Job. <sup>10</sup> Yahweh restored Job's prosperity when he prayed for his friends. Yahweh gave Job twice as much as he had before. <sup>11</sup> Then all his brothers, all his sisters, and all those who had been of his acquaintance before, came to him and ate bread with him in his house. They comforted him, and consoled him concerning all the evil that Yahweh had brought on him. Everyone also gave him a piece of money,<sup>b</sup> and everyone a ring of gold. <sup>12</sup> So Yahweh blessed the latter end of Job more than his beginning. He had fourteen thousand sheep, six thousand camels, one thousand yoke of oxen, and a thousand female donkeys. <sup>13</sup> He had also seven sons and three daughters. <sup>14</sup> He called the name of the first, Jemimah; and the name of the second, Keziah; and the name of the third, Keren Happuch. <sup>15</sup> In all the land were no women found so beautiful as the daughters of Job. Their father gave them an inheritance among their brothers. <sup>16</sup> After this Job lived one

hundred forty years, and saw his sons, and his sons' sons, to four generations. <sup>17</sup> So Job died, being old and full of days.

# The Psalms
## 1

**Book 1**
<sup>1</sup> Blessed is the man who doesn't walk in the counsel of the wicked, nor stand on the path of sinners, nor sit in the seat of scoffers; <sup>2</sup> but his delight is in Yahweh's<sup>c</sup> law. On his law he meditates day and night. <sup>3</sup> He will be like a tree planted by the streams of water, that produces its fruit in its season, whose leaf also does not wither. Whatever he does shall prosper. <sup>4</sup> The wicked are not so, but are like the chaff which the wind drives away. <sup>5</sup> Therefore the wicked shall not stand in the judgment, nor sinners in the congregation of the righteous. <sup>6</sup> For Yahweh knows the way of the righteous, but the way of the wicked shall perish.

## 2

<sup>1</sup> Why do the nations rage, and the peoples plot a vain thing? <sup>2</sup> The kings of the earth take a stand, and the rulers take counsel together, against Yahweh, and against his Anointed,<sup>d</sup> saying, <sup>3</sup>"Let's break their bonds apart, and cast their cords from us." <sup>4</sup> He who sits in the heavens will laugh. The Lord<sup>e</sup> will have them in derision. <sup>5</sup> Then he will speak to them in his anger, and terrify them in his wrath: <sup>6</sup>"Yet I have set my King on my holy hill of Zion." <sup>7</sup> I will tell of the decree: Yahweh said to me, "You are my son. Today I have become your father. <sup>8</sup> Ask of me, and I will give the nations for your inheritance, the uttermost parts of the earth for your possession. <sup>9</sup> You shall break them with a rod of iron. You shall dash them in pieces like a potter's vessel." <sup>10</sup> Now therefore be wise, you kings. Be instructed, you judges of the earth. <sup>11</sup> Serve Yahweh with fear, and rejoice with trembling. <sup>12</sup> Give sincere homage to the Son,<sup>f</sup> lest he be angry, and you perish on the way, for his wrath will soon be kindled. Blessed are all those who take refuge in him.

## 3

A Psalm by David, when he fled from Absalom his son.
<sup>1</sup> Yahweh, how my adversaries have increased! Many are those who rise up against me. <sup>2</sup> Many there are who say of my soul, "There is no help for him in God."<sup>g</sup> Selah. <sup>3</sup> But you, Yahweh, are a shield around me, my glory, and the one who lifts up my head. <sup>4</sup> I cry to Yahweh with my voice, and he answers me out of his holy hill. Selah. <sup>5</sup> I laid myself down and slept. I awakened, for Yahweh sustains me. <sup>6</sup> I will not be afraid of tens of thousands of people who have set themselves against me on every side. <sup>7</sup> Arise, Yahweh! Save me, my God! For you have struck all of my enemies on the cheek bone. You have broken the teeth of the wicked. <sup>8</sup> Salvation belongs to Yahweh. May your blessing be on your people. Selah.

## 4

For the Chief Musician; on stringed instruments. A Psalm by David.
<sup>1</sup> Answer me when I call, God of my righteousness. Give me relief from my distress. Have mercy on me, and hear my prayer. <sup>2</sup> You sons of men, how long shall my glory be turned into dishonor? Will you love vanity and seek after falsehood? Selah. <sup>3</sup> But know that Yahweh has set apart for himself him who is godly; Yahweh will hear when I call to him. <sup>4</sup> Stand in awe, and don't sin. Search your own heart on your bed, and be still. Selah. <sup>5</sup> Offer the sacrifices of righteousness. Put your trust in Yahweh. <sup>6</sup> Many say, "Who will show us any good?" Yahweh, let the light of your face shine on us. <sup>7</sup> You have put gladness in my heart, more than when their grain and their new wine are increased. <sup>8</sup> In peace I will both lay myself down and sleep, for you alone, Yahweh, make me live in safety.

## 5

For the Chief Musician, with the flutes. A Psalm by David.
<sup>1</sup> Give ear to my words, Yahweh. Consider my meditation. <sup>2</sup> Listen to the voice of my cry, my King and my God, for I pray to you. <sup>3</sup> Yahweh, in the morning you will hear my voice. In the morning I will lay my requests before you, and will watch expectantly. <sup>4</sup> For you are not a God who has pleasure in wickedness. Evil can't live with you. <sup>5</sup> The arrogant will not stand in your sight. You hate all workers of iniquity. <sup>6</sup> You will destroy those who speak lies. Yahweh abhors the bloodthirsty and deceitful man. <sup>7</sup> But as for me, in the abundance of your loving kindness I will come into your house. I will bow toward your holy temple in reverence of you. <sup>8</sup> Lead me, Yahweh, in your

---

<sup>a</sup> *41:1* Leviathan is a name for a crocodile or similar creature.
<sup>b</sup> *42:11* literally, kesitah, a unit of money, probably silver
<sup>c</sup> *1:2* "Yahweh" is God's proper Name, sometimes rendered "LORD" (all caps) in other translations.
<sup>d</sup> *2:2* The word "Anointed" is the same as the word for "Messiah" or "Christ"
<sup>e</sup> *2:4* The word translated "Lord" is "Adonai."
<sup>f</sup> *2:12* or, Kiss the son
<sup>g</sup> *3:2* The Hebrew word rendered "God" is "אֱלֹהִים" (Elohim).

righteousness because of my enemies. Make your way straight before my face. ⁹ For there is no faithfulness in their mouth. Their heart is destruction. Their throat is an open tomb. They flatter with their tongue. ¹⁰ Hold them guilty, God. Let them fall by their own counsels. Thrust them out in the multitude of their transgressions, for they have rebelled against you. ¹¹ But let all those who take refuge in you rejoice. Let them always shout for joy, because you defend them. Let them also who love your name be joyful in you. ¹² For you will bless the righteous. Yahweh, you will surround him with favor as with a shield.

## 6

For the Chief Musician; on stringed instruments, upon the eight-stringed lyre. A Psalm by David.
¹ Yahweh, don't rebuke me in your anger, neither discipline me in your wrath. ² Have mercy on me, Yahweh, for I am faint. Yahweh, heal me, for my bones are troubled. ³ My soul is also in great anguish. But you, Yahweh—how long? ⁴ Return, Yahweh. Deliver my soul, and save me for your loving kindness' sake. ⁵ For in death there is no memory of you. In Sheol,ᵃ who shall give you thanks? ⁶ I am weary with my groaning. Every night I flood my bed. I drench my couch with my tears. ⁷ My eye wastes away because of grief. It grows old because of all my adversaries. ⁸ Depart from me, all you workers of iniquity, for Yahweh has heard the voice of my weeping. ⁹ Yahweh has heard my supplication. Yahweh accepts my prayer. ¹⁰ May all my enemies be ashamed and dismayed. They shall turn back, they shall be disgraced suddenly.

## 7

A meditation by David, which he sang to Yahweh, concerning the words of Cush, the Benjamite.
¹ Yahweh, my God, I take refuge in you. Save me from all those who pursue me, and deliver me, ² lest they tear apart my soul like a lion, ripping it in pieces, while there is no one to deliver. ³ Yahweh, my God, if I have done this, if there is iniquity in my hands, ⁴ if I have rewarded evil to him who was at peace with me (yes, I have plundered him who without cause was my adversary), ⁵ let the enemy pursue my soul, and overtake it; yes, let him tread my life down to the earth, and lay my glory in the dust. Selah. ⁶ Arise, Yahweh, in your anger. Lift up yourself against the rage of my adversaries. Awake for me. You have commanded judgment. ⁷ Let the congregation of the peoples surround you. Rule over them on high. ⁸ Yahweh administers judgment to the peoples. Judge me, Yahweh, according to my righteousness, and to my integrity that is in me. ⁹ Oh let the wickedness of the wicked come to an end, but establish the righteous; their minds and hearts are searched by the righteous God. ¹⁰ My shield is with God, who saves the upright in heart. ¹¹ God is a righteous judge, yes, a God who has indignation every day. ¹² If a man doesn't repent, he will sharpen his sword; he has bent and strung his bow. ¹³ He has also prepared for himself the instruments of death. He makes ready his flaming arrows. ¹⁴ Behold,ᵇ he travails with iniquity. Yes, he has conceived mischief, and brought out falsehood. ¹⁵ He has dug a hole, and has fallen into the pit which he made. ¹⁶ The trouble he causes shall return to his own head. His violence shall come down on the crown of his own head. ¹⁷ I will give thanks to Yahweh according to his righteousness, and will sing praise to the name of Yahweh Most High.

## 8

For the Chief Musician; on an instrument of Gath. A Psalm by David.
¹ Yahweh, our Lord, how majestic is your name in all the earth! You have set your glory above the heavens! ² From the lips of babes and infants you have established strength, because of your adversaries, that you might silence the enemy and the avenger. ³ When I consider your heavens, the work of your fingers, the moon and the stars, which you have ordained, ⁴ what is man, that you think of him? What is the son of man, that you care for him? ⁵ For you have made him a little lower than the angels,ᶜ and crowned him with glory and honor. ⁶ You make him ruler over the works of your hands. You have put all things under his feet: ⁷ All sheep and cattle, yes, and the animals of the field, ⁸ the birds of the sky, the fish of the sea, and whatever passes through the paths of the seas. ⁹ Yahweh, our Lord, how majestic is your name in all the earth!

## 9

For the Chief Musician. Set to "The Death of the Son." A Psalm by David.
¹ I will give thanks to Yahweh with my whole heart. I will tell of all your marvelous works. ² I will be glad and rejoice in you. I will sing praise to your name, O Most High. ³ When my enemies turn back, they stumble and perish in your presence. ⁴ For you have maintained my just cause. You sit on the throne judging righteously. ⁵ You have rebuked the nations. You have destroyed the wicked. You have blotted out their name forever and ever. ⁶ The enemy is overtaken by endless ruin. The very memory of the cities which you have overthrown has perished. ⁷ But Yahweh reigns forever. He has prepared his throne for judgment. ⁸ He will judge the world in righteousness. He will administer judgment to the peoples in uprightness. ⁹ Yahweh will also be a high tower for the oppressed; a high tower in times of trouble. ¹⁰ Those who know your name will put their trust in you, for you, Yahweh, have not forsaken those who seek you. ¹¹ Sing praises to Yahweh, who dwells in Zion, and declare among the people what he has done. ¹² For he who avenges blood remembers them. He doesn't forget the cry of the afflicted. ¹³ Have mercy on me, Yahweh. See my affliction by those who hate me, and lift me up from the gates of death, ¹⁴ that I may show all of your praise. I will rejoice in your salvation in the gates of the daughter of Zion. ¹⁵ The nations have sunk down in the pit that they made. In the net which they hid, their own foot is taken. ¹⁶ Yahweh has made himself known. He has executed judgment. The wicked is snared by the work of his own hands. Meditation. Selah. ¹⁷ The wicked shall be turned back to Sheol,ᵈ even all the nations that forget God. ¹⁸ For the needy shall not always be forgotten, nor the hope of the poor perish forever. ¹⁹ Arise, Yahweh! Don't let man prevail. Let the nations be judged in your sight. ²⁰ Put them in fear, Yahweh. Let the nations know that they are only men. Selah.

## 10

¹ Why do you stand far off, Yahweh? Why do you hide yourself in times of trouble? ² In arrogance, the wicked hunt down the weak. They are caught in the schemes that they devise. ³ For the wicked boasts of his heart's cravings. He blesses the greedy and condemns Yahweh. ⁴ The wicked, in the pride of his face, has no room in his thoughts for God. ⁵ His ways are prosperous at all times. He is arrogant, and your laws are far from his sight. As for all his adversaries, he sneers at them. ⁶ He says in his heart, "I shall not be shaken. For generations I shall have no trouble." ⁷ His mouth is full of cursing, deceit, and oppression. Under his tongue is mischief and iniquity. ⁸ He lies in wait near the villages. From ambushes, he murders the innocent. His eyes are secretly set against the helpless. ⁹ He lurks in secret as a lion in his ambush. He lies in wait to catch the helpless. He catches the helpless when he draws him in his net. ¹⁰ The helpless are crushed. They collapse. They fall under his strength. ¹¹ He says in his heart, "God has forgotten. He hides his face. He will never see it."
¹² Arise, Yahweh! God, lift up your hand! Don't forget the helpless. ¹³ Why does the wicked person condemn God, and say in his heart, "God won't call me into account"? ¹⁴ But you do see trouble and grief. You consider it to take it into your hand. You help the victim and the fatherless. ¹⁵ Break the arm of the wicked. As for the evil man, seek out his wickedness until you find none. ¹⁶ Yahweh is King forever and ever! The nations will perish out of his land. ¹⁷ Yahweh, you have heard the desire of the humble. You will prepare their heart. You will cause your ear to hear, ¹⁸ to judge the fatherless and the oppressed, that man who is of the earth may terrify no more.

## 11

For the Chief Musician. By David. ¹ In Yahweh, I take refuge. How can you say to my soul, "Flee as a bird to your mountain"? ² For, behold, the wicked bend their bows. They set their arrows on the strings, that they may shoot in darkness at the upright in heart. ³ If the foundations are destroyed, what can the righteous do? ⁴ Yahweh is in his holy temple. Yahweh is on his throne in heaven. His eyes observe. His eyes examine the children of men. ⁵ Yahweh examines the righteous, but his soul hates the wicked and him who loves violence. ⁶ On the wicked he will rain blazing coals; fire, sulfur, and scorching wind shall be the portion of their cup. ⁷ For Yahweh is righteous. He loves righteousness. The upright shall see his face.

## 12

For the Chief Musician; upon an eight-stringed lyre. A Psalm of David.
¹ Help, Yahweh; for the godly man ceases. For the faithful fail from among the children of men. ² Everyone lies to his neighbor. They speak with flattering lips, and with a double heart. ³ May Yahweh cut off all flattering lips, and the tongue that boasts, ⁴ who have said, "With our tongue we will prevail. Our lips are our own. Who is lord over us?" ⁵ "Because of the oppression of the weak and because of the groaning of the needy, I will now arise," says Yahweh; "I will set him in safety from those who malign him." ⁶ Yahweh's words are flawless words, as silver refined in a clay furnace, purified seven times. ⁷ You will keep them, Yahweh. You will preserve them from this generation forever. ⁸

---

ᵃ 6:5 Sheol is the place of the dead.
ᵇ 7:14 "Behold", from "הִנֵּה", means look at, take notice, observe, see, or gaze at. It is often used as an interjection.
ᶜ 8:5 Hebrew: Elohim. The word Elohim, used here, usually means "God", but can also mean "gods", "princes", or "angels". The Septuagint reads "angels" here. See also the quote from the Septuagint in Hebrews 2:7.
ᵈ 9:17 Sheol is the place of the dead.

The wicked walk on every side, when what is vile is exalted among the sons of men.

## 13

For the Chief Musician. A Psalm by David.

[1] How long, Yahweh? Will you forget me forever? How long will you hide your face from me? [2] How long shall I take counsel in my soul, having sorrow in my heart every day? How long shall my enemy triumph over me? [3] Behold, and answer me, Yahweh, my God. Give light to my eyes, lest I sleep in death; [4] lest my enemy say, "I have prevailed against him;" lest my adversaries rejoice when I fall. [5] But I trust in your loving kindness. My heart rejoices in your salvation. [6] I will sing to Yahweh, because he has been good to me.

## 14

For the Chief Musician. By David.

[1] The fool has said in his heart, "There is no God." They are corrupt. They have done abominable deeds. There is no one who does good. [2] Yahweh looked down from heaven on the children of men, to see if there were any who understood, who sought after God. [3] They have all gone aside. They have together become corrupt. There is no one who does good, no, not one. [4] Have all the workers of iniquity no knowledge, who eat up my people as they eat bread, and don't call on Yahweh? [5] There they were in great fear, for God is in the generation of the righteous. [6] You frustrate the plan of the poor, because Yahweh is his refuge. [7] Oh that the salvation of Israel would come out of Zion! When Yahweh restores the fortunes of his people, then Jacob shall rejoice, and Israel shall be glad.

## 15

A Psalm by David.

[1] Yahweh, who shall dwell in your sanctuary? Who shall live on your holy hill? [2] He who walks blamelessly and does what is right, and speaks truth in his heart; [3] he who doesn't slander with his tongue, nor does evil to his friend, nor casts slurs against his fellow man; [4] in whose eyes a vile man is despised, but who honors those who fear Yahweh; he who keeps an oath even when it hurts, and doesn't change; [5] he who doesn't lend out his money for usury, nor take a bribe against the innocent. He who does these things shall never be shaken.

## 16

A Poem by David.

[1] Preserve me, God, for I take refuge in you. [2] My soul, you have said to Yahweh, "You are my Lord. Apart from you I have no good thing." [3] As for the saints who are in the earth, they are the excellent ones in whom is all my delight. [4] Their sorrows shall be multiplied who give gifts to another god. Their drink offerings of blood I will not offer, nor take their names on my lips. [5] Yahweh assigned my portion and my cup. You made my lot secure. [6] The lines have fallen to me in pleasant places. Yes, I have a good inheritance. [7] I will bless Yahweh, who has given me counsel. Yes, my heart instructs me in the night seasons. [8] I have set Yahweh always before me. Because he is at my right hand, I shall not be moved. [9] Therefore my heart is glad, and my tongue rejoices. My body shall also dwell in safety. [10] For you will not leave my soul in Sheol,[a] neither will you allow your holy one to see corruption. [11] You will show me the path of life. In your presence is fullness of joy. In your right hand there are pleasures forever more.

## 17

A Prayer by David.

[1] Hear, Yahweh, my righteous plea. Give ear to my prayer that doesn't go out of deceitful lips. [2] Let my sentence come out of your presence. Let your eyes look on equity. [3] You have proved my heart. You have visited me in the night. You have tried me, and found nothing. I have resolved that my mouth shall not disobey. [4] As for the deeds of men, by the word of your lips, I have kept myself from the ways of the violent. [5] My steps have held fast to your paths. My feet have not slipped. [6] I have called on you, for you will answer me, God. Turn your ear to me. Hear my speech. [7] Show your marvelous loving kindness, you who save those who take refuge by your right hand from their enemies. [8] Keep me as the apple of your eye. Hide me under the shadow of your wings, [9] from the wicked who oppress me, my deadly enemies, who surround me. [10] They close up their callous hearts. With their mouth they speak proudly. [11] They have now surrounded us in our steps. They set their eyes to cast us down to the earth. [12] He is like a lion that is greedy of his prey, as it were a young lion lurking in secret places. [13] Arise, Yahweh, confront him. Cast him down. Deliver my soul from the wicked by your sword, [14] from men by your hand, Yahweh, from men of the world, whose portion is in this life. You fill the belly of your cherished ones. Your sons have plenty, and they store up wealth for

their children. [15] As for me, I shall see your face in righteousness. I shall be satisfied, when I awake, with seeing your form.

## 18

For the Chief Musician. By David the servant of Yahweh, who spoke to Yahweh the words of this song in the day that Yahweh delivered him from the hand of all his enemies, and from the hand of Saul. He said,

[1] I love you, Yahweh, my strength. [2] Yahweh is my rock, my fortress, and my deliverer; my God, my rock, in whom I take refuge; my shield, and the horn of my salvation, my high tower. [3] I call on Yahweh, who is worthy to be praised; and I am saved from my enemies. [4] The cords of death surrounded me. The floods of ungodliness made me afraid. [5] The cords of Sheol[b] were around me. The snares of death came on me. [6] In my distress I called on Yahweh, and cried to my God. He heard my voice out of his temple. My cry before him came into his ears. [7] Then the earth shook and trembled. The foundations also of the mountains quaked and were shaken, because he was angry. [8] Smoke went out of his nostrils. Consuming fire came out of his mouth. Coals were kindled by it. [9] He bowed the heavens also, and came down. Thick darkness was under his feet. [10] He rode on a cherub, and flew. Yes, he soared on the wings of the wind. [11] He made darkness his hiding place, his pavilion around him, darkness of waters, thick clouds of the skies. [12] At the brightness before him his thick clouds passed, hailstones and coals of fire. [13] Yahweh also thundered in the sky. The Most High uttered his voice: hailstones and coals of fire. [14] He sent out his arrows, and scattered them. He routed them with great lightning bolts. [15] Then the channels of waters appeared. The foundations of the world were laid bare at your rebuke, Yahweh, at the blast of the breath of your nostrils. [16] He sent from on high. He took me. He drew me out of many waters. [17] He delivered me from my strong enemy, from those who hated me; for they were too mighty for me. [18] They came on me in the day of my calamity, but Yahweh was my support. [19] He brought me out also into a large place. He delivered me, because he delighted in me. [20] Yahweh has rewarded me according to my righteousness. According to the cleanness of my hands, he has recompensed me. [21] For I have kept the ways of Yahweh, and have not wickedly departed from my God. [22] For all his ordinances were before me. I didn't put away his statutes from me. [23] I was also blameless with him. I kept myself from my iniquity. [24] Therefore Yahweh has rewarded me according to my righteousness, according to the cleanness of my hands in his eyesight. [25] With the merciful you will show yourself merciful. With the perfect man, you will show yourself perfect. [26] With the pure, you will show yourself pure. With the crooked you will show yourself shrewd. [27] For you will save the afflicted people, but the arrogant eyes you will bring down. [28] For you will light my lamp, Yahweh. My God will light up my darkness. [29] For by you, I advance through a troop. By my God, I leap over a wall. [30] As for God, his way is perfect. Yahweh's word is tried. He is a shield to all those who take refuge in him. [31] For who is God, except Yahweh? Who is a rock, besides our God, [32] the God who arms me with strength, and makes my way perfect? [33] He makes my feet like deer's feet, and sets me on my high places. [34] He teaches my hands to war, so that my arms bend a bow of bronze. [35] You have also given me the shield of your salvation. Your right hand sustains me. Your gentleness has made me great. [36] You have enlarged my steps under me, My feet have not slipped. [37] I will pursue my enemies, and overtake them. I won't turn away until they are consumed. [38] I will strike them through, so that they will not be able to rise. They shall fall under my feet. [39] For you have armed me with strength to the battle. You have subdued under me those who rose up against me. [40] You have also made my enemies turn their backs to me, that I might cut off those who hate me. [41] They cried, but there was no one to save; even to Yahweh, but he didn't answer them. [42] Then I beat them small as the dust before the wind. I cast them out as the mire of the streets. [43] You have delivered me from the strivings of the people. You have made me the head of the nations. A people whom I have not known shall serve me. [44] As soon as they hear of me they shall obey me. The foreigners shall submit themselves to me. [45] The foreigners shall fade away, and shall come trembling out of their strongholds. [46] Yahweh lives! Blessed be my rock. Exalted be the God of my salvation, [47] even the God who executes vengeance for me, and subdues peoples under me. [48] He rescues me from my enemies. Yes, you lift me up above those who rise up against me. You deliver me from the violent man. [49] Therefore I will give thanks to you, Yahweh, among the nations, and will sing praises to your name. [50] He gives great deliverance to his king, and shows loving kindness to his anointed, to David and to his offspring,[c] forever more.

---

[a] *16:10* Sheol is the place of the dead.

[b] *18:5* Sheol is the place of the dead.

[c] *18:50* or, seed

## 19

For the Chief Musician. A Psalm by David.

[1] The heavens declare the glory of God. The expanse shows his handiwork. [2] Day after day they pour out speech, and night after night they display knowledge. [3] There is no speech nor language where their voice is not heard. [4] Their voice has gone out through all the earth, their words to the end of the world. In them he has set a tent for the sun, [5] which is as a bridegroom coming out of his room, like a strong man rejoicing to run his course. [6] His going out is from the end of the heavens, his circuit to its ends. There is nothing hidden from its heat. [7] Yahweh's law is perfect, restoring the soul. Yahweh's covenant is sure, making wise the simple. [8] Yahweh's precepts are right, rejoicing the heart. Yahweh's commandment is pure, enlightening the eyes. [9] The fear of Yahweh is clean, enduring forever. Yahweh's ordinances are true, and righteous altogether. [10] They are more to be desired than gold, yes, than much fine gold, sweeter also than honey and the extract of the honeycomb. [11] Moreover your servant is warned by them. In keeping them there is great reward. [12] Who can discern his errors? Forgive me from hidden errors. [13] Keep back your servant also from presumptuous sins. Let them not have dominion over me. Then I will be upright. I will be blameless and innocent of great transgression. [14] Let the words of my mouth and the meditation of my heart be acceptable in your sight, Yahweh, my rock, and my redeemer.

## 20

For the Chief Musician. A Psalm by David.

[1] May Yahweh answer you in the day of trouble. May the name of the God of Jacob set you up on high, [2] send you help from the sanctuary, grant you support from Zion, [3] remember all your offerings, and accept your burned sacrifice. Selah. [4] May he grant you your heart's desire, and fulfill all your counsel. [5] We will triumph in your salvation. In the name of our God, we will set up our banners. May Yahweh grant all your requests. [6] Now I know that Yahweh saves his anointed. He will answer him from his holy heaven, with the saving strength of his right hand. [7] Some trust in chariots, and some in horses, but we trust in the name of Yahweh our God. [8] They are bowed down and fallen, but we rise up, and stand upright. [9] Save, Yahweh! Let the King answer us when we call!

## 21

For the Chief Musician. A Psalm by David.

[1] The king rejoices in your strength, Yahweh! How greatly he rejoices in your salvation! [2] You have given him his heart's desire, and have not withheld the request of his lips. Selah. [3] For you meet him with the blessings of goodness. You set a crown of fine gold on his head. [4] He asked life of you and you gave it to him, even length of days forever and ever. [5] His glory is great in your salvation. You lay honor and majesty on him. [6] For you make him most blessed forever. You make him glad with joy in your presence. [7] For the king trusts in Yahweh. Through the loving kindness of the Most High, he shall not be moved. [8] Your hand will find out all of your enemies. Your right hand will find out those who hate you. [9] You will make them as a fiery furnace in the time of your anger. Yahweh will swallow them up in his wrath. The fire shall devour them. [10] You will destroy their descendants from the earth, their posterity from among the children of men. [11] For they intended evil against you. They plotted evil against you which cannot succeed. [12] For you will make them turn their back, when you aim drawn bows at their face. [13] Be exalted, Yahweh, in your strength, so we will sing and praise your power.

## 22

For the Chief Musician; set to "The Doe of the Morning." A Psalm by David.

[1] My God, my God, why have you forsaken me? Why are you so far from helping me, and from the words of my groaning? [2] My God, I cry in the daytime, but you don't answer; in the night season, and am not silent. [3] But you are holy, you who inhabit the praises of Israel. [4] Our fathers trusted in you. They trusted, and you delivered them. [5] They cried to you, and were delivered. They trusted in you, and were not disappointed. [6] But I am a worm, and no man; a reproach of men, and despised by the people. [7] All those who see me mock me. They insult me with their lips. They shake their heads, saying, [8]"He trusts in Yahweh. Let him deliver him. Let him rescue him, since he delights in him." [9] But you brought me out of the womb. You made me trust while at my mother's breasts. [10] I was thrown on you from my mother's womb. You are my God since my mother bore me. [11] Don't be far from me, for trouble is near. For there is no one to help. [12] Many bulls have surrounded me. Strong bulls of Bashan have encircled me. [13] They open their mouths wide against me, lions tearing prey and roaring. [14] I am poured out like water. All my bones are out of joint. My heart is like wax. It is melted within me. [15] My strength is dried up like a potsherd. My tongue sticks to the roof of my mouth. You have brought me into the dust of death. [16] For dogs have surrounded me. A company of evildoers have enclosed me. They have pierced my hands and feet.[a] [17] I can count all of my bones. They look and stare at me. [18] They divide my garments among them. They cast lots for my clothing. [19] But don't be far off, Yahweh. You are my help. Hurry to help me! [20] Deliver my soul from the sword, my precious life from the power of the dog. [21] Save me from the lion's mouth! Yes, you have rescued me from the horns of the wild oxen. [22] I will declare your name to my brothers. Among the assembly, I will praise you. [23] You who fear Yahweh, praise him! All you descendants of Jacob, glorify him! Stand in awe of him, all you descendants of Israel! [24] For he has not despised nor abhorred the affliction of the afflicted, neither has he hidden his face from him; but when he cried to him, he heard. [25] My praise of you comes in the great assembly. I will pay my vows before those who fear him. [26] The humble shall eat and be satisfied. They shall praise Yahweh who seek after him. Let your hearts live forever. [27] All the ends of the earth shall remember and turn to Yahweh. All the relatives of the nations shall worship before you. [28] For the kingdom is Yahweh's. He is the ruler over the nations. [29] All the rich ones of the earth shall eat and worship. All those who go down to the dust shall bow before him, even he who can't keep his soul alive. [30] Posterity shall serve him. Future generations shall be told about the Lord. [31] They shall come and shall declare his righteousness to a people that shall be born, for he has done it.

## 23

A Psalm by David.

[1] Yahweh is my shepherd; I shall lack nothing. [2] He makes me lie down in green pastures. He leads me beside still waters. [3] He restores my soul. He guides me in the paths of righteousness for his name's sake. [4] Even though I walk through the valley of the shadow of death, I will fear no evil, for you are with me. Your rod and your staff, they comfort me. [5] You prepare a table before me in the presence of my enemies. You anoint my head with oil. My cup runs over. [6] Surely goodness and loving kindness shall follow me all the days of my life, and I will dwell in Yahweh's house forever.

## 24

A Psalm by David.

[1] The earth is Yahweh's, with its fullness; the world, and those who dwell in it. [2] For he has founded it on the seas, and established it on the floods. [3] Who may ascend to Yahweh's hill? Who may stand in his holy place? [4] He who has clean hands and a pure heart; who has not lifted up his soul to falsehood, and has not sworn deceitfully. [5] He shall receive a blessing from Yahweh, righteousness from the God of his salvation. [6] This is the generation of those who seek Him, who seek your face—even Jacob. Selah. [7] Lift up your heads, you gates! Be lifted up, you everlasting doors, and the King of glory will come in. [8] Who is the King of glory? Yahweh strong and mighty, Yahweh mighty in battle. [9] Lift up your heads, you gates; yes, lift them up, you everlasting doors, and the King of glory will come in. [10] Who is this King of glory? Yahweh of Armies is the King of glory! Selah.

## 25

By David.

[1] To you, Yahweh, I lift up my soul. [2] My God, I have trusted in you. Don't let me be shamed. Don't let my enemies triumph over me. [3] Yes, no one who waits for you will be shamed. They will be shamed who deal treacherously without cause. [4] Show me your ways, Yahweh. Teach me your paths. [5] Guide me in your truth, and teach me, for you are the God of my salvation. I wait for you all day long. [6] Yahweh, remember your tender mercies and your loving kindness, for they are from old times. [7] Don't remember the sins of my youth, nor my transgressions. Remember me according to your loving kindness, for your goodness' sake, Yahweh. [8] Good and upright is Yahweh, therefore he will instruct sinners in the way. [9] He will guide the humble in justice. He will teach the humble his way. [10] All the paths of Yahweh are loving kindness and truth to such as keep his covenant and his testimonies. [11] For your name's sake, Yahweh, pardon my iniquity, for it is great. [12] What man is he who fears Yahweh? He shall instruct him in the way that he shall choose. [13] His soul shall dwell at ease. His offspring will inherit the land. [14] The friendship of Yahweh is with those who fear him. He will show them his covenant. [15] My eyes are ever on Yahweh, for he will pluck my feet out of the net. [16] Turn to me, and have mercy on me, for I am desolate and afflicted. [17] The troubles of my heart are enlarged. Oh bring me out of my distresses. [18] Consider my affliction and my travail. Forgive all my sins. [19] Consider my enemies, for they are many. They hate me with cruel hatred. [20] Oh keep my soul, and deliver me. Let me not be disappointed, for I take refuge in you. [21] Let

---

[a] 22:16 So Dead Sea Scrolls. Masoretic Text reads, "Like a lion, they pin my hands and feet."

integrity and uprightness preserve me, for I wait for you. [22] God, redeem Israel out of all his troubles.

## 26

By David.

[1] Judge me, Yahweh, for I have walked in my integrity. I have trusted also in Yahweh without wavering. [2] Examine me, Yahweh, and prove me. Try my heart and my mind. [3] For your loving kindness is before my eyes. I have walked in your truth. [4] I have not sat with deceitful men, neither will I go in with hypocrites. [5] I hate the assembly of evildoers, and will not sit with the wicked. [6] I will wash my hands in innocence, so I will go about your altar, Yahweh, [7] that I may make the voice of thanksgiving to be heard and tell of all your wondrous deeds. [8] Yahweh, I love the habitation of your house, the place where your glory dwells. [9] Don't gather my soul with sinners, nor my life with bloodthirsty men [10] in whose hands is wickedness; their right hand is full of bribes. [11] But as for me, I will walk in my integrity. Redeem me, and be merciful to me. [12] My foot stands in an even place. In the congregations I will bless Yahweh.

## 27

By David.

[1] Yahweh is my light and my salvation. Whom shall I fear? Yahweh is the strength of my life. Of whom shall I be afraid? [2] When evildoers came at me to eat up my flesh, even my adversaries and my foes, they stumbled and fell. [3] Though an army should encamp against me, my heart shall not fear. Though war should rise against me, even then I will be confident. [4] One thing I have asked of Yahweh, that I will seek after: that I may dwell in Yahweh's house all the days of my life, to see Yahweh's beauty, and to inquire in his temple. [5] For in the day of trouble, he will keep me secretly in his pavilion. In the secret place of his tabernacle, he will hide me. He will lift me up on a rock. [6] Now my head will be lifted up above my enemies around me. I will offer sacrifices of joy in his tent. I will sing, yes, I will sing praises to Yahweh. [7] Hear, Yahweh, when I cry with my voice. Have mercy also on me, and answer me. [8] When you said, "Seek my face," my heart said to you, "I will seek your face, Yahweh." [9] Don't hide your face from me. Don't put your servant away in anger. You have been my help. Don't abandon me, neither forsake me, God of my salvation. [10] When my father and my mother forsake me, then Yahweh will take me up. [11] Teach me your way, Yahweh. Lead me in a straight path, because of my enemies. [12] Don't deliver me over to the desire of my adversaries, for false witnesses have risen up against me, such as breathe out cruelty. [13] I am still confident of this: I will see the goodness of Yahweh in the land of the living. [14] Wait for Yahweh. Be strong, and let your heart take courage. Yes, wait for Yahweh.

## 28

By David.

[1] To you, Yahweh, I call. My rock, don't be deaf to me, lest, if you are silent to me, I would become like those who go down into the pit. [2] Hear the voice of my petitions, when I cry to you, when I lift up my hands toward your Most Holy Place. [3] Don't draw me away with the wicked, with the workers of iniquity who speak peace with their neighbors, but mischief is in their hearts. [4] Give them according to their work, and according to the wickedness of their doings. Give them according to the operation of their hands. Bring back on them what they deserve. [5] Because they don't respect the works of Yahweh, nor the operation of his hands, he will break them down and not build them up. [6] Blessed be Yahweh, because he has heard the voice of my petitions. [7] Yahweh is my strength and my shield. My heart has trusted in him, and I am helped. Therefore my heart greatly rejoices. With my song I will thank him. [8] Yahweh is their strength. He is a stronghold of salvation to his anointed. [9] Save your people, and bless your inheritance. Be their shepherd also, and bear them up forever.

## 29

A Psalm by David.

[1] Ascribe to Yahweh, you sons of the mighty, ascribe to Yahweh glory and strength. [2] Ascribe to Yahweh the glory due to his name. Worship Yahweh in holy array. [3] Yahweh's voice is on the waters. The God of glory thunders, even Yahweh on many waters. [4] Yahweh's voice is powerful. Yahweh's voice is full of majesty. [5] Yahweh's voice breaks the cedars. Yes, Yahweh breaks in pieces the cedars of Lebanon. [6] He makes them also to skip like a calf; Lebanon and Sirion like a young, wild ox. [7] Yahweh's voice strikes with flashes of lightning. [8] Yahweh's voice shakes the wilderness. Yahweh shakes the wilderness of Kadesh. [9] Yahweh's voice makes the deer calve, and strips the forests bare. In his temple everything says, "Glory!" [10] Yahweh sat enthroned at the Flood. Yes, Yahweh sits as King forever. [11] Yahweh will give strength to his people. Yahweh will bless his people with peace.

## 30

A Psalm. A Song for the Dedication of the Temple. By David.

[1] I will extol you, Yahweh, for you have raised me up, and have not made my foes to rejoice over me. [2] Yahweh my God, I cried to you, and you have healed me. [3] Yahweh, you have brought up my soul from Sheol.[a] You have kept me alive, that I should not go down to the pit. [4] Sing praise to Yahweh, you saints of his. Give thanks to his holy name. [5] For his anger is but for a moment. His favor is for a lifetime. Weeping may stay for the night, but joy comes in the morning. [6] As for me, I said in my prosperity, "I shall never be moved." [7] You, Yahweh, when you favored me, made my mountain stand strong; but when you hid your face, I was troubled. [8] I cried to you, Yahweh. I made supplication to the Lord: [9] "What profit is there in my destruction, if I go down to the pit? Shall the dust praise you? Shall it declare your truth? [10] Hear, Yahweh, and have mercy on me. Yahweh, be my helper." [11] You have turned my mourning into dancing for me. You have removed my sackcloth, and clothed me with gladness, [12] to the end that my heart may sing praise to you, and not be silent. Yahweh my God, I will give thanks to you forever!

## 31

For the Chief Musician. A Psalm by David.

[1] In you, Yahweh, I take refuge. Let me never be disappointed. Deliver me in your righteousness. [2] Bow down your ear to me. Deliver me speedily. Be to me a strong rock, a house of defense to save me. [3] For you are my rock and my fortress, therefore for your name's sake lead me and guide me. [4] Pluck me out of the net that they have laid secretly for me, for you are my stronghold. [5] Into your hand I commend my spirit. You redeem me, Yahweh, God of truth. [6] I hate those who regard lying vanities, but I trust in Yahweh. [7] I will be glad and rejoice in your loving kindness, for you have seen my affliction. You have known my soul in adversities. [8] You have not shut me up into the hand of the enemy. You have set my feet in a large place. [9] Have mercy on me, Yahweh, for I am in distress. My eye, my soul, and my body waste away with grief. [10] For my life is spent with sorrow, my years with sighing. My strength fails because of my iniquity. My bones are wasted away. [11] Because of all my adversaries I have become utterly contemptible to my neighbors, a horror to my acquaintances. Those who saw me on the street fled from me. [12] I am forgotten from their hearts like a dead man. I am like broken pottery. [13] For I have heard the slander of many, terror on every side, while they conspire together against me, they plot to take away my life. [14] But I trust in you, Yahweh. I said, "You are my God." [15] My times are in your hand. Deliver me from the hand of my enemies, and from those who persecute me. [16] Make your face to shine on your servant. Save me in your loving kindness. [17] Let me not be disappointed, Yahweh, for I have called on you. Let the wicked be disappointed. Let them be silent in Sheol.[b] [18] Let the lying lips be mute, which speak against the righteous insolently, with pride and contempt. [19] Oh how great is your goodness, which you have laid up for those who fear you, which you have worked for those who take refuge in you, before the sons of men! [20] In the shelter of your presence you will hide them from the plotting of man. You will keep them secretly in a dwelling away from the strife of tongues. [21] Praise be to Yahweh, for he has shown me his marvelous loving kindness in a strong city. [22] As for me, I said in my haste, "I am cut off from before your eyes." Nevertheless you heard the voice of my petitions when I cried to you. [23] Oh love Yahweh, all you his saints! Yahweh preserves the faithful, and fully recompenses him who behaves arrogantly. [24] Be strong, and let your heart take courage, all you who hope in Yahweh.

## 32

By David. A contemplative psalm.

[1] Blessed is he whose disobedience is forgiven, whose sin is covered. [2] Blessed is the man to whom Yahweh doesn't impute iniquity, in whose spirit there is no deceit. [3] When I kept silence, my bones wasted away through my groaning all day long. [4] For day and night your hand was heavy on me. My strength was sapped in the heat of summer. Selah. [5] I acknowledged my sin to you. I didn't hide my iniquity. I said, I will confess my transgressions to Yahweh, and you forgave the iniquity of my sin. Selah. [6] For this, let everyone who is godly pray to you in a time when you may be found. Surely when the great waters overflow, they shall not reach to him. [7] You are my hiding place. You will preserve me from trouble. You will surround me with songs of deliverance. Selah. [8] I will instruct you and teach you in the way which you shall go. I will counsel you with my eye on you. [9] Don't be like the horse, or like the mule, which have no understanding, who are controlled by bit and bridle, or else they will not come near to you. [10] Many sorrows come to the wicked, but loving kindness shall surround

---

[a] *30:3* Sheol is the place of the dead.

[b] *31:17* Sheol is the place of the dead.

him who trusts in Yahweh. [11] Be glad in Yahweh, and rejoice, you righteous! Shout for joy, all you who are upright in heart!

## 33

[1] Rejoice in Yahweh, you righteous! Praise is fitting for the upright. [2] Give thanks to Yahweh with the lyre. Sing praises to him with the harp of ten strings. [3] Sing to him a new song. Play skillfully with a shout of joy! [4] For Yahweh's word is right. All his work is done in faithfulness. [5] He loves righteousness and justice. The earth is full of the loving kindness of Yahweh. [6] By Yahweh's word, the heavens were made: all their army by the breath of his mouth. [7] He gathers the waters of the sea together as a heap. He lays up the deeps in storehouses. [8] Let all the earth fear Yahweh. Let all the inhabitants of the world stand in awe of him. [9] For he spoke, and it was done. He commanded, and it stood firm. [10] Yahweh brings the counsel of the nations to nothing. He makes the thoughts of the peoples to be of no effect. [11] The counsel of Yahweh stands fast forever, the thoughts of his heart to all generations. [12] Blessed is the nation whose God is Yahweh, the people whom he has chosen for his own inheritance. [13] Yahweh looks from heaven. He sees all the sons of men. [14] From the place of his habitation he looks out on all the inhabitants of the earth, [15] he who fashions all of their hearts; and he considers all of their works. [16] There is no king saved by the multitude of an army. A mighty man is not delivered by great strength. [17] A horse is a vain thing for safety, neither does he deliver any by his great power. [18] Behold, Yahweh's eye is on those who fear him, on those who hope in his loving kindness, [19] to deliver their soul from death, to keep them alive in famine. [20] Our soul has waited for Yahweh. He is our help and our shield. [21] For our heart rejoices in him, because we have trusted in his holy name. [22] Let your loving kindness be on us, Yahweh, since we have hoped in you.

## 34

By David; when he pretended to be insane before Abimelech, who drove him away, and he departed.

[1] [a] I will bless Yahweh at all times. His praise will always be in my mouth. [2] My soul shall boast in Yahweh. The humble shall hear of it and be glad. [3] Oh magnify Yahweh with me. Let's exalt his name together. [4] I sought Yahweh, and he answered me, and delivered me from all my fears. [5] They looked to him, and were radiant. Their faces shall never be covered with shame. [6] This poor man cried, and Yahweh heard him, and saved him out of all his troubles. [7] Yahweh's angel encamps around those who fear him, and delivers them. [8] Oh taste and see that Yahweh is good. Blessed is the man who takes refuge in him. [9] Oh fear Yahweh, you his saints, for there is no lack with those who fear him. [10] The young lions do lack, and suffer hunger, but those who seek Yahweh shall not lack any good thing. [11] Come, you children, listen to me. I will teach you the fear of Yahweh. [12] Who is someone who desires life, and loves many days, that he may see good? [13] Keep your tongue from evil, and your lips from speaking lies. [14] Depart from evil, and do good. Seek peace, and pursue it. [15] Yahweh's eyes are toward the righteous. His ears listen to their cry. [16] Yahweh's face is against those who do evil, to cut off their memory from the earth. [17] The righteous cry, and Yahweh hears, and delivers them out of all their troubles. [18] Yahweh is near to those who have a broken heart, and saves those who have a crushed spirit. [19] Many are the afflictions of the righteous, but Yahweh delivers him out of them all. [20] He protects all of his bones. Not one of them is broken. [21] Evil shall kill the wicked. Those who hate the righteous shall be condemned. [22] Yahweh redeems the soul of his servants. None of those who take refuge in him shall be condemned.

## 35

By David.

[1] Contend, Yahweh, with those who contend with me. Fight against those who fight against me. [2] Take hold of shield and buckler, and stand up for my help. [3] Brandish the spear and block those who pursue me. Tell my soul, "I am your salvation." [4] Let those who seek after my soul be disappointed and brought to dishonor. Let those who plot my ruin be turned back and confounded. [5] Let them be as chaff before the wind, Yahweh's angel driving them on. [6] Let their way be dark and slippery, Yahweh's angel pursuing them. [7] For without cause they have hidden their net in a pit for me. Without cause they have dug a pit for my soul. [8] Let destruction come on him unawares. Let his net that he has hidden catch himself. Let him fall into that destruction. [9] My soul shall be joyful in Yahweh. It shall rejoice in his salvation. [10] All my bones shall say, "Yahweh, who is like you, who delivers the poor from him who is too strong for him; yes, the poor and the needy from him who robs him?" [11] Unrighteous witnesses rise up. They ask me about things that I don't know about. [12] They reward me evil for good, to the bereaving of my soul. [13] But as for me, when they were sick, my clothing was

sackcloth. I afflicted my soul with fasting. My prayer returned into my own bosom. [14] I behaved myself as though it had been my friend or my brother. I bowed down mourning, as one who mourns his mother. [15] But in my adversity, they rejoiced, and gathered themselves together. The attackers gathered themselves together against me, and I didn't know it. They tore at me, and didn't cease. [16] Like the profane mockers in feasts, they gnashed their teeth at me. [17] Lord, how long will you look on? Rescue my soul from their destruction, my precious life from the lions. [18] I will give you thanks in the great assembly. I will praise you among many people. [19] Don't let those who are my enemies wrongfully rejoice over me; neither let those who hate me without a cause wink their eyes. [20] For they don't speak peace, but they devise deceitful words against those who are quiet in the land. [21] Yes, they opened their mouth wide against me. They said, "Aha! Aha! Our eye has seen it!" [22] You have seen it, Yahweh. Don't keep silent. Lord, don't be far from me. [23] Wake up! Rise up to defend me, my God! My Lord, contend for me! [24] Vindicate me, Yahweh my God, according to your righteousness. Don't let them gloat over me. [25] Don't let them say in their heart, "Aha! That's the way we want it!" Don't let them say, "We have swallowed him up!" [26] Let them be disappointed and confounded together who rejoice at my calamity. Let them be clothed with shame and dishonor who magnify themselves against me. [27] Let those who favor my righteous cause shout for joy and be glad. Yes, let them say continually, "May Yahweh be magnified, who has pleasure in the prosperity of his servant!" [28] My tongue shall talk about your righteousness and about your praise all day long.

## 36

For the Chief Musician. By David, the servant of Yahweh.

[1] A revelation is within my heart about the disobedience of the wicked: There is no fear of God before his eyes. [2] For he flatters himself in his own eyes, too much to detect and hate his sin. [3] The words of his mouth are iniquity and deceit. He has ceased to be wise and to do good. [4] He plots iniquity on his bed. He sets himself in a way that is not good. He doesn't abhor evil. [5] Your loving kindness, Yahweh, is in the heavens. Your faithfulness reaches to the skies. [6] Your righteousness is like the mountains of God. Your judgments are like a great deep. Yahweh, you preserve man and animal. [7] How precious is your loving kindness, God! The children of men take refuge under the shadow of your wings. [8] They shall be abundantly satisfied with the abundance of your house. You will make them drink of the river of your pleasures. [9] For with you is the spring of life. In your light we will see light. [10] Oh continue your loving kindness to those who know you, your righteousness to the upright in heart. [11] Don't let the foot of pride come against me. Don't let the hand of the wicked drive me away. [12] There the workers of iniquity are fallen. They are thrust down, and shall not be able to rise.

## 37

By David.

[1] Don't fret because of evildoers, neither be envious against those who work unrighteousness. [2] For they shall soon be cut down like the grass, and wither like the green herb. [3] Trust in Yahweh, and do good. Dwell in the land, and enjoy safe pasture. [4] Also delight yourself in Yahweh, and he will give you the desires of your heart. [5] Commit your way to Yahweh. Trust also in him, and he will do this: [6] he will make your righteousness shine out like light, and your justice as the noon day sun. [7] Rest in Yahweh, and wait patiently for him. Don't fret because of him who prospers in his way, because of the man who makes wicked plots happen. [8] Cease from anger, and forsake wrath. Don't fret; it leads only to evildoing. [9] For evildoers shall be cut off, but those who wait for Yahweh shall inherit the land. [10] For yet a little while, and the wicked will be no more. Yes, though you look for his place, he isn't there. [11] But the humble shall inherit the land, and shall delight themselves in the abundance of peace. [12] The wicked plots against the just, and gnashes at him with his teeth. [13] The Lord will laugh at him, for he sees that his day is coming. [14] The wicked have drawn out the sword, and have bent their bow, to cast down the poor and needy, to kill those who are upright on the path. [15] Their sword shall enter into their own heart. Their bows shall be broken. [16] Better is a little that the righteous has, than the abundance of many wicked. [17] For the arms of the wicked shall be broken, but Yahweh upholds the righteous. [18] Yahweh knows the days of the perfect. Their inheritance shall be forever. [19] They shall not be disappointed in the time of evil. In the days of famine they shall be satisfied. [20] But the wicked shall perish. The enemies of Yahweh shall be like the beauty of the fields. They will vanish— vanish like smoke. [21] The wicked borrow, and don't pay back, but the righteous give generously. [22] For such as are blessed by him shall inherit the land. Those who are cursed by him shall be cut off. [23] A man's steps are established by Yahweh. He delights in his way. [24] Though he stumble,

---

[a] *34:1* Psalm 34 is an acrostic poem, with each verse starting with a letter of the alphabet (ordered from Alef to Tav).

The Psalms | 303

he shall not fall, for Yahweh holds him up with his hand. ²⁵ I have been young, and now am old, yet I have not seen the righteous forsaken, nor his children begging for bread. ²⁶ All day long he deals graciously, and lends. His offspring is blessed. ²⁷ Depart from evil, and do good. Live securely forever. ²⁸ For Yahweh loves justice, and doesn't forsake his saints. They are preserved forever, but the children of the wicked shall be cut off. ²⁹ The righteous shall inherit the land, and live in it forever. ³⁰ The mouth of the righteous talks of wisdom. His tongue speaks justice. ³¹ The law of his God is in his heart. None of his steps shall slide. ³² The wicked watch the righteous, and seek to kill him. ³³ Yahweh will not leave him in his hand, nor condemn him when he is judged. ³⁴ Wait for Yahweh, and keep his way, and he will exalt you to inherit the land. When the wicked are cut off, you shall see it. ³⁵ I have seen the wicked in great power, spreading himself like a green tree in its native soil. ³⁶ But he passed away, and behold, he was not. Yes, I sought him, but he could not be found. ³⁷ Mark the perfect man, and see the upright, for there is a future for the man of peace. ³⁸ As for transgressors, they shall be destroyed together. The future of the wicked shall be cut off. ³⁹ But the salvation of the righteous is from Yahweh. He is their stronghold in the time of trouble. ⁴⁰ Yahweh helps them and rescues them. He rescues them from the wicked and saves them, because they have taken refuge in him.

## 38

A Psalm by David, for a memorial.

¹ Yahweh, don't rebuke me in your wrath, neither chasten me in your hot displeasure. ² For your arrows have pierced me, your hand presses hard on me. ³ There is no soundness in my flesh because of your indignation, neither is there any health in my bones because of my sin. ⁴ For my iniquities have gone over my head. As a heavy burden, they are too heavy for me. ⁵ My wounds are loathsome and corrupt because of my foolishness. ⁶ I am in pain and bowed down greatly. I go mourning all day long. ⁷ For my waist is filled with burning. There is no soundness in my flesh. ⁸ I am faint and severely bruised. I have groaned by reason of the anguish of my heart. ⁹ Lord, all my desire is before you. My groaning is not hidden from you. ¹⁰ My heart throbs. My strength fails me. As for the light of my eyes, it has also left me. ¹¹ My lovers and my friends stand aloof from my plague. My kinsmen stand far away. ¹² They also who seek after my life lay snares. Those who seek my hurt speak mischievous things, and meditate deceits all day long. ¹³ But I, as a deaf man, don't hear. I am as a mute man who doesn't open his mouth. ¹⁴ Yes, I am as a man who doesn't hear, in whose mouth are no reproofs. ¹⁵ For I hope in you, Yahweh. You will answer, Lord my God. ¹⁶ For I said, "Don't let them gloat over me, or exalt themselves over me when my foot slips." ¹⁷ For I am ready to fall. My pain is continually before me. ¹⁸ For I will declare my iniquity. I will be sorry for my sin. ¹⁹ But my enemies are vigorous and many. Those who hate me without reason are numerous. ²⁰ They who render evil for good are also adversaries to me, because I follow what is good. ²¹ Don't forsake me, Yahweh. My God, don't be far from me. ²² Hurry to help me, Lord, my salvation.

## 39

For the Chief Musician. For Jeduthun. A Psalm by David.

¹ I said, "I will watch my ways, so that I don't sin with my tongue. I will keep my mouth with a bridle while the wicked is before me." ² I was mute with silence. I held my peace, even from good. My sorrow was stirred. ³ My heart was hot within me. While I meditated, the fire burned. I spoke with my tongue: ⁴"Yahweh, show me my end, what is the measure of my days. Let me know how frail I am. ⁵ Behold, you have made my days hand widths. My lifetime is as nothing before you. Surely every man stands as a breath." Selah. ⁶"Surely every man walks like a shadow. Surely they busy themselves in vain. He heaps up, and doesn't know who shall gather. ⁷ Now, Lord, what do I wait for? My hope is in you. ⁸ Deliver me from all my transgressions. Don't make me the reproach of the foolish. ⁹ I was mute. I didn't open my mouth, because you did it. ¹⁰ Remove your scourge away from me. I am overcome by the blow of your hand. ¹¹ When you rebuke and correct man for iniquity, you consume his wealth like a moth. Surely every man is but a breath." Selah. ¹²"Hear my prayer, Yahweh, and give ear to my cry. Don't be silent at my tears. For I am a stranger with you, a foreigner, as all my fathers were. ¹³ Oh spare me, that I may recover strength, before I go away and exist no more."

## 40

For the Chief Musician. A Psalm by David.

¹ I waited patiently for Yahweh. He turned to me, and heard my cry. ² He brought me up also out of a horrible pit, out of the miry clay. He set my feet on a rock, and gave me a firm place to stand. ³ He has put a new song in my mouth, even praise to our God. Many shall see it, and fear, and shall trust in Yahweh. ⁴ Blessed is the man who makes Yahweh his trust, and doesn't respect the proud, nor such as turn away to lies. ⁵ Many, Yahweh, my God, are the wonderful works which you have done, and your thoughts which are toward us. They can't be declared back to you. If I would declare and speak of them, they are more than can be counted. ⁶ Sacrifice and offering you didn't desire. You have opened my ears. You have not required burnt offering and sin offering. ⁷ Then I said, "Behold, I have come. It is written about me in the book in the scroll. ⁸ I delight to do your will, my God. Yes, your law is within my heart." ⁹ I have proclaimed glad news of righteousness in the great assembly. Behold, I will not seal my lips, Yahweh, you know. ¹⁰ I have not hidden your righteousness within my heart. I have declared your faithfulness and your salvation. I have not concealed your loving kindness and your truth from the great assembly. ¹¹ Don't withhold your tender mercies from me, Yahweh. Let your loving kindness and your truth continually preserve me. ¹² For innumerable evils have surrounded me. My iniquities have overtaken me, so that I am not able to look up. They are more than the hairs of my head. My heart has failed me. ¹³ Be pleased, Yahweh, to deliver me. Hurry to help me, Yahweh. ¹⁴ Let them be disappointed and confounded together who seek after my soul to destroy it. Let them be turned backward and brought to dishonor who delight in my hurt. ¹⁵ Let them be desolate by reason of their shame that tell me, "Aha! Aha!" ¹⁶ Let all those who seek you rejoice and be glad in you. Let such as love your salvation say continually, "Let Yahweh be exalted!" ¹⁷ But I am poor and needy. May the Lord think about me. You are my help and my deliverer. Don't delay, my God.

## 41

For the Chief Musician. A Psalm by David.

¹ Blessed is he who considers the poor. Yahweh will deliver him in the day of evil. ² Yahweh will preserve him, and keep him alive. He shall be blessed on the earth, and he will not surrender him to the will of his enemies. ³ Yahweh will sustain him on his sickbed, and restore him from his bed of illness. ⁴ I said, "Yahweh, have mercy on me! Heal me, for I have sinned against you." ⁵ My enemies speak evil against me: "When will he die, and his name perish?" ⁶ If he comes to see me, he speaks falsehood. His heart gathers iniquity to itself. When he goes abroad, he tells it. ⁷ All who hate me whisper together against me. They imagine the worst for me. ⁸"An evil disease", they say, "has afflicted him. Now that he lies he shall rise up no more." ⁹ Yes, my own familiar friend, in whom I trusted, who ate bread with me, has lifted up his heel against me. ¹⁰ But you, Yahweh, have mercy on me, and raise me up, that I may repay them. ¹¹ By this I know that you delight in me, because my enemy doesn't triumph over me. ¹² As for me, you uphold me in my integrity, and set me in your presence forever. ¹³ Blessed be Yahweh, the God of Israel, from everlasting and to everlasting! Amen and amen.

## 42

**Book 2**

For the Chief Musician. A contemplation by the sons of Korah.

¹ As the deer pants for the water brooks, so my soul pants after you, God.ᵃ ² My soul thirsts for God, for the living God. When shall I come and appear before God? ³ My tears have been my food day and night, while they continually ask me, "Where is your God?" ⁴ These things I remember, and pour out my soul within me, how I used to go with the crowd, and led them to God's house, with the voice of joy and praise, a multitude keeping a holy day. ⁵ Why are you in despair, my soul? Why are you disturbed within me? Hope in God! For I shall still praise him for the saving help of his presence. ⁶ My God, my soul is in despair within me. Therefore I remember you from the land of the Jordan, the heights of Hermon, from the hill Mizar. ⁷ Deep calls to deep at the noise of your waterfalls. All your waves and your billows have swept over me. ⁸ Yahwehᵇ will command his loving kindness in the daytime. In the night his song shall be with me: a prayer to the God of my life. ⁹ I will ask God, my rock, "Why have you forgotten me? Why do I go mourning because of the oppression of the enemy?" ¹⁰ As with a sword in my bones, my adversaries reproach me, while they continually ask me, "Where is your God?" ¹¹ Why are you in despair, my soul? Why are you disturbed within me? Hope in God! For I shall still praise him, the saving help of my countenance, and my God.

## 43

¹ Vindicate me, God, and plead my cause against an ungodly nation. Oh, deliver me from deceitful and wicked men. ² For you are the God of my strength. Why have you rejected me? Why do I go mourning because of the oppression of the enemy? ³ Oh, send out your light and your truth. Let them lead me. Let them bring me to your holy hill, to

---

ᵃ *42:1* The Hebrew word rendered "God" is "אֱלֹהִים" (Elohim).

ᵇ *42:8* "Yahweh" is God's proper Name, sometimes rendered "LORD" (all caps) in other translations.

your tents. [4] Then I will go to the altar of God, to God, my exceeding joy. I will praise you on the harp, God, my God. [5] Why are you in despair, my soul? Why are you disturbed within me? Hope in God! For I shall still praise him: my Savior, my helper, and my God.

## 44

For the Chief Musician. By the sons of Korah. A contemplative psalm.
[1] We have heard with our ears, God; our fathers have told us what work you did in their days, in the days of old. [2] You drove out the nations with your hand, but you planted them. You afflicted the peoples, but you spread them abroad. [3] For they didn't get the land in possession by their own sword, neither did their own arm save them; but your right hand, your arm, and the light of your face, because you were favorable to them. [4] God, you are my King. Command victories for Jacob! [5] Through you, we will push down our adversaries. Through your name, we will tread down those who rise up against us. [6] For I will not trust in my bow, neither will my sword save me. [7] But you have saved us from our adversaries, and have shamed those who hate us. [8] In God we have made our boast all day long. We will give thanks to your name forever. Selah. [9] But now you rejected us, and brought us to dishonor, and don't go out with our armies. [10] You make us turn back from the adversary. Those who hate us take plunder for themselves. [11] You have made us like sheep for food, and have scattered us among the nations. [12] You sell your people for nothing, and have gained nothing from their sale. [13] You make us a reproach to our neighbors, a scoffing and a derision to those who are around us. [14] You make us a byword among the nations, a shaking of the head among the peoples. [15] All day long my dishonor is before me, and shame covers my face, [16] at the taunt of one who reproaches and verbally abuses, because of the enemy and the avenger. [17] All this has come on us, yet we haven't forgotten you. We haven't been false to your covenant. [18] Our heart has not turned back, neither have our steps strayed from your path, [19] though you have crushed us in the haunt of jackals, and covered us with the shadow of death. [20] If we have forgotten the name of our God, or spread out our hands to a strange god, [21] won't God search this out? For he knows the secrets of the heart. [22] Yes, for your sake we are killed all day long. We are regarded as sheep for the slaughter. [23] Wake up! Why do you sleep, Lord?[a] Arise! Don't reject us forever. [24] Why do you hide your face, and forget our affliction and our oppression? [25] For our soul is bowed down to the dust. Our body clings to the earth. [26] Rise up to help us. Redeem us for your loving kindness' sake.

## 45

For the Chief Musician. Set to "The Lilies." A contemplation by the sons of Korah. A wedding song.
[1] My heart overflows with a noble theme. I recite my verses for the king. My tongue is like the pen of a skillful writer. [2] You are the most excellent of the sons of men. Grace has anointed your lips, therefore God has blessed you forever. [3] Strap your sword on your thigh, O mighty one, in your splendor and your majesty. [4] In your majesty ride on victoriously on behalf of truth, humility, and righteousness. Let your right hand display awesome deeds. [5] Your arrows are sharp. The nations fall under you, with arrows in the heart of the king's enemies. [6] Your throne, God, is forever and ever. A scepter of equity is the scepter of your kingdom. [7] You have loved righteousness, and hated wickedness. Therefore God, your God, has anointed you with the oil of gladness above your fellows. [8] All your garments smell like myrrh, aloes, and cassia. Out of ivory palaces stringed instruments have made you glad. [9] Kings' daughters are among your honorable women. At your right hand the queen stands in gold of Ophir. [10] Listen, daughter, consider, and turn your ear. Forget your own people, and also your father's house. [11] So the king will desire your beauty, honor him, for he is your lord. [12] The daughter of Tyre comes with a gift. The rich among the people entreat your favor. [13] The princess inside is all glorious. Her clothing is interwoven with gold. [14] She shall be led to the king in embroidered work. The virgins, her companions who follow her, shall be brought to you. [15] With gladness and rejoicing they shall be led. They shall enter into the king's palace. [16] Your sons will take the place of your fathers. You shall make them princes in all the earth. [17] I will make your name to be remembered in all generations. Therefore the peoples shall give you thanks forever and ever.

## 46

For the Chief Musician. By the sons of Korah. According to Alamoth.[b]
[1] God is our refuge and strength, a very present help in trouble. [2] Therefore we won't be afraid, though the earth changes, though the mountains are shaken into the heart of the seas; [3] though its waters roar and are troubled, though the mountains tremble with their swelling.

Selah. [4] There is a river, the streams of which make the city of God glad, the holy place of the tents of the Most High. [5] God is within her. She shall not be moved. God will help her at dawn. [6] The nations raged. The kingdoms were moved. He lifted his voice and the earth melted. [7] Yahweh of Armies is with us. The God of Jacob is our refuge. Selah. [8] Come, see Yahweh's works, what desolations he has made in the earth. [9] He makes wars cease to the end of the earth. He breaks the bow, and shatters the spear. He burns the chariots in the fire. [10] "Be still, and know that I am God. I will be exalted among the nations. I will be exalted in the earth." [11] Yahweh of Armies is with us. The God of Jacob is our refuge. Selah.

## 47

For the Chief Musician. A Psalm by the sons of Korah.
[1] Oh clap your hands, all you nations. Shout to God with the voice of triumph! [2] For Yahweh Most High is awesome. He is a great King over all the earth. [3] He subdues nations under us, and peoples under our feet. [4] He chooses our inheritance for us, the glory of Jacob whom he loved. Selah. [5] God has gone up with a shout, Yahweh with the sound of a trumpet. [6] Sing praises to God! Sing praises! Sing praises to our King! Sing praises! [7] For God is the King of all the earth. Sing praises with understanding. [8] God reigns over the nations. God sits on his holy throne. [9] The princes of the peoples are gathered together, the people of the God of Abraham. For the shields of the earth belong to God. He is greatly exalted!

## 48

A Song. A Psalm by the sons of Korah.
[1] Great is Yahweh, and greatly to be praised, in the city of our God, in his holy mountain. [2] Beautiful in elevation, the joy of the whole earth, is Mount Zion, on the north sides, the city of the great King. [3] God has shown himself in her citadels as a refuge. [4] For, behold, the kings assembled themselves, they passed by together. [5] They saw it, then they were amazed. They were dismayed. They hurried away. [6] Trembling took hold of them there, pain, as of a woman in travail. [7] With the east wind, you break the ships of Tarshish. [8] As we have heard, so we have seen, in the city of Yahweh of Armies, in the city of our God. God will establish it forever. Selah. [9] We have thought about your loving kindness, God, in the middle of your temple. [10] As is your name, God, so is your praise to the ends of the earth. Your right hand is full of righteousness. [11] Let Mount Zion be glad! Let the daughters of Judah rejoice because of your judgments. [12] Walk about Zion, and go around her. Number its towers. [13] Notice her bulwarks. Consider her palaces, that you may tell it to the next generation. [14] For this God is our God forever and ever. He will be our guide even to death.

## 49

For the Chief Musician. A Psalm by the sons of Korah.
[1] Hear this, all you peoples. Listen, all you inhabitants of the world, [2] both low and high, rich and poor together. [3] My mouth will speak words of wisdom. My heart will utter understanding. [4] I will incline my ear to a proverb. I will solve my riddle on the harp. [5] Why should I fear in the days of evil, when iniquity at my heels surrounds me? [6] Those who trust in their wealth, and boast in the multitude of their riches— [7] none of them can by any means redeem his brother, nor give God a ransom for him. [8] For the redemption of their life is costly, no payment is ever enough, [9] that he should live on forever, that he should not see corruption. [10] For he sees that wise men die; likewise the fool and the senseless perish, and leave their wealth to others. [11] Their inward thought is that their houses will endure forever, and their dwelling places to all generations. They name their lands after themselves. [12] But man, despite his riches, doesn't endure. He is like the animals that perish. [13] This is the destiny of those who are foolish, and of those who approve their sayings. Selah. [14] They are appointed as a flock for Sheol.[c] Death shall be their shepherd. The upright shall have dominion over them in the morning. Their beauty shall decay in Sheol,[d] far from their mansion. [15] But God will redeem my soul from the power of Sheol,[e] for he will receive me. Selah. [16] Don't be afraid when a man is made rich, when the glory of his house is increased; [17] for when he dies he will carry nothing away. His glory won't descend after him. [18] Though while he lived he blessed his soul— and men praise you when you do well for yourself— [19] he shall go to the generation of his fathers. They shall never see the light. [20] A man who has riches without understanding, is like the animals that perish.

## 50

A Psalm by Asaph.
[1] The Mighty One, God, Yahweh, speaks, and calls the earth from sunrise to sunset. [2] Out of Zion, the perfection of beauty, God shines

---

[a] 44:23 The word translated "Lord" is "Adonai."

[b] 46:0 Alamoth is a musical term.

[c] 49:14 Sheol is the place of the dead.

[d] 49:14 Sheol is the place of the dead.

[e] 49:15 Sheol is the place of the dead.

out. <sup>3</sup> Our God comes, and does not keep silent. A fire devours before him. It is very stormy around him. <sup>4</sup> He calls to the heavens above, to the earth, that he may judge his people: <sup>5</sup>"Gather my saints together to me, those who have made a covenant with me by sacrifice." <sup>6</sup> The heavens shall declare his righteousness, for God himself is judge. Selah. <sup>7</sup>"Hear, my people, and I will speak. Israel, I will testify against you. I am God, your God. <sup>8</sup> I don't rebuke you for your sacrifices. Your burnt offerings are continually before me. <sup>9</sup> I have no need for a bull from your stall, nor male goats from your pens. <sup>10</sup> For every animal of the forest is mine, and the livestock on a thousand hills. <sup>11</sup> I know all the birds of the mountains. The wild animals of the field are mine. <sup>12</sup> If I were hungry, I would not tell you, for the world is mine, and all that is in it. <sup>13</sup> Will I eat the meat of bulls, or drink the blood of goats? <sup>14</sup> Offer to God the sacrifice of thanksgiving. Pay your vows to the Most High. <sup>15</sup> Call on me in the day of trouble. I will deliver you, and you will honor me." <sup>16</sup> But to the wicked God says, "What right do you have to declare my statutes, that you have taken my covenant on your lips, <sup>17</sup> since you hate instruction, and throw my words behind you? <sup>18</sup> When you saw a thief, you consented with him, and have participated with adulterers. <sup>19</sup>"You give your mouth to evil. Your tongue frames deceit. <sup>20</sup> You sit and speak against your brother. You slander your own mother's son. <sup>21</sup> You have done these things, and I kept silent. You thought that I was just like you. I will rebuke you, and accuse you in front of your eyes. <sup>22</sup>"Now consider this, you who forget God, lest I tear you into pieces, and there be no one to deliver. <sup>23</sup> Whoever offers the sacrifice of thanksgiving glorifies me, and prepares his way so that I will show God's salvation to him."

## 51

For the Chief Musician. A Psalm by David, when Nathan the prophet came to him, after he had gone in to Bathsheba.

<sup>1</sup> Have mercy on me, God, according to your loving kindness. According to the multitude of your tender mercies, blot out my transgressions. <sup>2</sup> Wash me thoroughly from my iniquity. Cleanse me from my sin. <sup>3</sup> For I know my transgressions. My sin is constantly before me. <sup>4</sup> Against you, and you only, I have sinned, and done that which is evil in your sight, so you may be proved right when you speak, and justified when you judge. <sup>5</sup> Behold, I was born in iniquity. My mother conceived me in sin. <sup>6</sup> Behold, you desire truth in the inward parts. You teach me wisdom in the inmost place. <sup>7</sup> Purify me with hyssop, and I will be clean. Wash me, and I will be whiter than snow. <sup>8</sup> Let me hear joy and gladness, that the bones which you have broken may rejoice. <sup>9</sup> Hide your face from my sins, and blot out all of my iniquities. <sup>10</sup> Create in me a clean heart, O God. Renew a right spirit within me. <sup>11</sup> Don't throw me from your presence, and don't take your Holy Spirit from me. <sup>12</sup> Restore to me the joy of your salvation. Uphold me with a willing spirit. <sup>13</sup> Then I will teach transgressors your ways. Sinners will be converted to you. <sup>14</sup> Deliver me from the guilt of bloodshed, O God, the God of my salvation. My tongue will sing aloud of your righteousness. <sup>15</sup> Lord, open my lips. My mouth will declare your praise. <sup>16</sup> For you don't delight in sacrifice, or else I would give it. You have no pleasure in burnt offering. <sup>17</sup> The sacrifices of God are a broken spirit. O God, you will not despise a broken and contrite heart. <sup>18</sup> Do well in your good pleasure to Zion. Build the walls of Jerusalem. <sup>19</sup> Then you will delight in the sacrifices of righteousness, in burnt offerings and in whole burnt offerings. Then they will offer bulls on your altar.

## 52

For the Chief Musician. A contemplation by David, when Doeg the Edomite came and told Saul, "David has come to Ahimelech's house."

<sup>1</sup> Why do you boast of mischief, mighty man? God's loving kindness endures continually. <sup>2</sup> Your tongue plots destruction, like a sharp razor, working deceitfully. <sup>3</sup> You love evil more than good, lying rather than speaking the truth. Selah. <sup>4</sup> You love all devouring words, you deceitful tongue. <sup>5</sup> God will likewise destroy you forever. He will take you up, and pluck you out of your tent, and root you out of the land of the living. Selah. <sup>6</sup> The righteous also will see it, and fear, and laugh at him, saying, <sup>7</sup>"Behold, this is the man who didn't make God his strength, but trusted in the abundance of his riches, and strengthened himself in his wickedness." <sup>8</sup> But as for me, I am like a green olive tree in God's house. I trust in God's loving kindness forever and ever. <sup>9</sup> I will give you thanks forever, because you have done it. I will hope in your name, for it is good, in the presence of your saints.

## 53

For the Chief Musician. To the tune of "Mahalath." A contemplation by David.

<sup>1</sup> The fool has said in his heart, "There is no God." They are corrupt, and have done abominable iniquity. There is no one who does good. <sup>2</sup>

God looks down from heaven on the children of men, to see if there are any who understood, who seek after God. <sup>3</sup> Every one of them has gone back. They have become filthy together. There is no one who does good, no, not one. <sup>4</sup> Have the workers of iniquity no knowledge, who eat up my people as they eat bread, and don't call on God? <sup>5</sup> There they were in great fear, where no fear was, for God has scattered the bones of him who encamps against you. You have put them to shame, because God has rejected them. <sup>6</sup> Oh that the salvation of Israel would come out of Zion! When God brings back his people from captivity, then Jacob shall rejoice, and Israel shall be glad.

## 54

For the Chief Musician. On stringed instruments. A contemplation by David, when the Ziphites came and said to Saul, "Isn't David hiding himself among us?"

<sup>1</sup> Save me, God, by your name. Vindicate me in your might. <sup>2</sup> Hear my prayer, God. Listen to the words of my mouth. <sup>3</sup> For strangers have risen up against me. Violent men have sought after my soul. They haven't set God before them. Selah. <sup>4</sup> Behold, God is my helper. The Lord is the one who sustains my soul. <sup>5</sup> He will repay the evil to my enemies. Destroy them in your truth. <sup>6</sup> With a free will offering, I will sacrifice to you. I will give thanks to your name, Yahweh, for it is good. <sup>7</sup> For he has delivered me out of all trouble. My eye has seen triumph over my enemies.

## 55

For the Chief Musician. On stringed instruments. A contemplation by David.

<sup>1</sup> Listen to my prayer, God.

Don't hide yourself from my supplication. <sup>2</sup> Attend to me, and answer me. I am restless in my complaint, and moan <sup>3</sup> because of the voice of the enemy, because of the oppression of the wicked. For they bring suffering on me. In anger they hold a grudge against me. <sup>4</sup> My heart is severely pained within me. The terrors of death have fallen on me. <sup>5</sup> Fearfulness and trembling have come on me. Horror has overwhelmed me. <sup>6</sup> I said, "Oh that I had wings like a dove! Then I would fly away, and be at rest. <sup>7</sup> Behold, then I would wander far off. I would lodge in the wilderness." Selah. <sup>8</sup>"I would hurry to a shelter from the stormy wind and storm." <sup>9</sup> Confuse them, Lord, and confound their language, for I have seen violence and strife in the city. <sup>10</sup> Day and night they prowl around on its walls. Malice and abuse are also within her. <sup>11</sup> Destructive forces are within her. Threats and lies don't depart from her streets. <sup>12</sup> For it was not an enemy who insulted me, then I could have endured it. Neither was it he who hated me who raised himself up against me, then I would have hidden myself from him. <sup>13</sup> But it was you, a man like me, my companion, and my familiar friend. <sup>14</sup> We took sweet fellowship together. We walked in God's house with company. <sup>15</sup> Let death come suddenly on them. Let them go down alive into Sheol.<sup>a</sup> For wickedness is among them, in their dwelling. <sup>16</sup> As for me, I will call on God. Yahweh will save me. <sup>17</sup> Evening, morning, and at noon, I will cry out in distress. He will hear my voice. <sup>18</sup> He has redeemed my soul in peace from the battle that was against me, although there are many who oppose me. <sup>19</sup> God, who is enthroned forever, will hear and answer them. Selah. They never change and don't fear God. <sup>20</sup> He raises his hands against his friends. He has violated his covenant. <sup>21</sup> His mouth was smooth as butter, but his heart was war. His words were softer than oil, yet they were drawn swords. <sup>22</sup> Cast your burden on Yahweh and he will sustain you. He will never allow the righteous to be moved. <sup>23</sup> But you, God, will bring them down into the pit of destruction. Bloodthirsty and deceitful men shall not live out half their days, but I will trust in you.

## 56

For the Chief Musician. To the tune of "Silent Dove in Distant Lands." A poem by David, when the Philistines seized him in Gath.

<sup>1</sup> Be merciful to me, God, for man wants to swallow me up. All day long, he attacks and oppresses me. <sup>2</sup> My enemies want to swallow me up all day long, for they are many who fight proudly against me. <sup>3</sup> When I am afraid, I will put my trust in you. <sup>4</sup> In God, I praise his word. In God, I put my trust. I will not be afraid. What can flesh do to me? <sup>5</sup> All day long they twist my words. All their thoughts are against me for evil. <sup>6</sup> They conspire and lurk, watching my steps. They are eager to take my life. <sup>7</sup> Shall they escape by iniquity? In anger cast down the peoples, God. <sup>8</sup> You count my wanderings. You put my tears into your container. Aren't they in your book? <sup>9</sup> Then my enemies shall turn back in the day that I call. I know this: that God is for me. <sup>10</sup> In God, I will praise his word. In Yahweh, I will praise his word. <sup>11</sup> I have put my trust in God. I will not be afraid. What can man do to me? <sup>12</sup> Your vows are on me, God. I will give thank offerings to you. <sup>13</sup> For you have delivered my

<sup>a</sup> 55:15 Sheol is the place of the dead.

soul from death, and prevented my feet from falling, that I may walk before God in the light of the living.

## 57

For the Chief Musician. To the tune of "Do Not Destroy." A poem by David, when he fled from Saul, in the cave.

[1] Be merciful to me, God, be merciful to me, for my soul takes refuge in you. Yes, in the shadow of your wings, I will take refuge, until disaster has passed. [2] I cry out to God Most High, to God who accomplishes my requests for me. [3] He will send from heaven, and save me, he rebukes the one who is pursuing me. Selah. God will send out his loving kindness and his truth. [4] My soul is among lions. I lie among those who are set on fire, even the sons of men, whose teeth are spears and arrows, and their tongue a sharp sword. [5] Be exalted, God, above the heavens! Let your glory be above all the earth! [6] They have prepared a net for my steps. My soul is bowed down. They dig a pit before me. They fall into the middle of it themselves. Selah. [7] My heart is steadfast, God. My heart is steadfast. I will sing, yes, I will sing praises. [8] Wake up, my glory! Wake up, lute and harp! I will wake up the dawn. [9] I will give thanks to you, Lord, among the peoples. I will sing praises to you among the nations. [10] For your great loving kindness reaches to the heavens, and your truth to the skies. [11] Be exalted, God, above the heavens. Let your glory be over all the earth.

## 58

For the Chief Musician. To the tune of "Do Not Destroy." A poem by David.

[1] Do you indeed speak righteousness, silent ones? Do you judge blamelessly, you sons of men? [2] No, in your heart you plot injustice. You measure out the violence of your hands in the earth. [3] The wicked go astray from the womb. They are wayward as soon as they are born, speaking lies. [4] Their poison is like the poison of a snake, like a deaf cobra that stops its ear, [5] which doesn't listen to the voice of charmers, no matter how skillful the charmer may be. [6] Break their teeth, God, in their mouth. Break out the great teeth of the young lions, Yahweh. [7] Let them vanish like water that flows away. When they draw the bow, let their arrows be made blunt. [8] Let them be like a snail which melts and passes away, like the stillborn child, who has not seen the sun. [9] Before your pots can feel the heat of the thorns, he will sweep away the green and the burning alike. [10] The righteous shall rejoice when he sees the vengeance. He shall wash his feet in the blood of the wicked, [11] so that men shall say, "Most certainly there is a reward for the righteous. Most certainly there is a God who judges the earth."

## 59

For the Chief Musician. To the tune of "Do Not Destroy." A poem by David, when Saul sent, and they watched the house to kill him.

[1] Deliver me from my enemies, my God. Set me on high from those who rise up against me. [2] Deliver me from the workers of iniquity. Save me from the bloodthirsty men. [3] For, behold, they lie in wait for my soul. The mighty gather themselves together against me, not for my disobedience, nor for my sin, Yahweh. [4] I have done no wrong, yet they are ready to attack me. Rise up, behold, and help me! [5] You, Yahweh God of Armies, the God of Israel, rouse yourself to punish the nations. Show no mercy to the wicked traitors. Selah. [6] They return at evening, howling like dogs, and prowl around the city. [7] Behold, they spew with their mouth. Swords are in their lips, "For", they say, "who hears us?" [8] But you, Yahweh, laugh at them. You scoff at all the nations. [9] Oh, my Strength, I watch for you, for God is my high tower. [10] My God will go before me with his loving kindness. God will let me look at my enemies in triumph. [11] Don't kill them, or my people may forget. Scatter them by your power, and bring them down, Lord our shield. [12] For the sin of their mouth, and the words of their lips, let them be caught in their pride, for the curses and lies which they utter. [13] Consume them in wrath. Consume them, and they will be no more. Let them know that God rules in Jacob, to the ends of the earth. Selah. [14] At evening let them return. Let them howl like a dog, and go around the city. [15] They shall wander up and down for food, and wait all night if they aren't satisfied. [16] But I will sing of your strength. Yes, I will sing aloud of your loving kindness in the morning. For you have been my high tower, a refuge in the day of my distress. [17] To you, my strength, I will sing praises. For God is my high tower, the God of my mercy.

## 60

For the Chief Musician. To the tune of "The Lily of the Covenant." A teaching poem by David, when he fought with Aram Naharaim and with Aram Zobah, and Joab returned, and killed twelve thousand of Edom in the Valley of Salt.

[1] God, you have rejected us. You have broken us down. You have been angry. Restore us, again. [2] You have made the land tremble. You have torn it. Mend its fractures, for it quakes. [3] You have shown your people hard things. You have made us drink the wine that makes us stagger. [4] You have given a banner to those who fear you, that it may be displayed because of the truth. Selah. [5] So that your beloved may be delivered, save with your right hand, and answer us. [6] God has spoken from his sanctuary: "I will triumph. I will divide Shechem, and measure out the valley of Succoth. [7] Gilead is mine, and Manasseh is mine. Ephraim also is the defense of my head. Judah is my scepter. [8] Moab is my wash basin. I will throw my sandal on Edom. I shout in triumph over Philistia." [9] Who will bring me into the strong city? Who has led me to Edom? [10] Haven't you, God, rejected us? You don't go out with our armies, God. [11] Give us help against the adversary, for the help of man is vain. [12] Through God we will do valiantly, for it is he who will tread down our adversaries.

## 61

For the Chief Musician. For a stringed instrument. By David.

[1] Hear my cry, God. Listen to my prayer. [2] From the end of the earth, I will call to you when my heart is overwhelmed. Lead me to the rock that is higher than I. [3] For you have been a refuge for me, a strong tower from the enemy. [4] I will dwell in your tent forever. I will take refuge in the shelter of your wings. Selah. [5] For you, God, have heard my vows. You have given me the heritage of those who fear your name. [6] You will prolong the king's life. His years will be for generations. [7] He shall be enthroned in God's presence forever. Appoint your loving kindness and truth, that they may preserve him. [8] So I will sing praise to your name forever, that I may fulfill my vows daily.

## 62

For the Chief Musician. To Jeduthun. A Psalm by David.

[1] My soul rests in God alone. My salvation is from him. [2] He alone is my rock, my salvation, and my fortress. I will never be greatly shaken. [3] How long will you assault a man? Would all of you throw him down, like a leaning wall, like a tottering fence? [4] They fully intend to throw him down from his lofty place. They delight in lies. They bless with their mouth, but they curse inwardly. Selah. [5] My soul, wait in silence for God alone, for my expectation is from him. [6] He alone is my rock and my salvation, my fortress. I will not be shaken. [7] My salvation and my honor is with God. The rock of my strength, and my refuge, is in God. [8] Trust in him at all times, you people. Pour out your heart before him. God is a refuge for us. Selah. [9] Surely men of low degree are just a breath, and men of high degree are a lie. In the balances they will go up. They are together lighter than a breath. [10] Don't trust in oppression. Don't become vain in robbery. If riches increase, don't set your heart on them. [11] God has spoken once; twice I have heard this, that power belongs to God. [12] Also to you, Lord, belongs loving kindness, for you reward every man according to his work.

## 63

A Psalm by David, when he was in the desert of Judah.

[1] God, you are my God. I will earnestly seek you. My soul thirsts for you. My flesh longs for you, in a dry and weary land, where there is no water. [2] So I have seen you in the sanctuary, watching your power and your glory. [3] Because your loving kindness is better than life, my lips shall praise you. [4] So I will bless you while I live. I will lift up my hands in your name. [5] My soul shall be satisfied as with the richest food. My mouth shall praise you with joyful lips, [6] when I remember you on my bed, and think about you in the night watches. [7] For you have been my help. I will rejoice in the shadow of your wings. [8] My soul stays close to you. Your right hand holds me up. [9] But those who seek my soul to destroy it shall go into the lower parts of the earth. [10] They shall be given over to the power of the sword. They shall be jackal food. [11] But the king shall rejoice in God. Everyone who swears by him will praise him, for the mouth of those who speak lies shall be silenced.

## 64

For the Chief Musician. A Psalm by David.

[1] Hear my voice, God, in my complaint. Preserve my life from fear of the enemy. [2] Hide me from the conspiracy of the wicked, from the noisy crowd of the ones doing evil; [3] who sharpen their tongue like a sword, and aim their arrows, deadly words, [4] to shoot innocent men from ambushes. They shoot at him suddenly and fearlessly. [5] They encourage themselves in evil plans. They talk about laying snares secretly. They say, "Who will see them?" [6] They plot injustice, saying, "We have made a perfect plan!" Surely man's mind and heart are cunning. [7] But God will shoot at them. They will be suddenly struck down with an arrow. [8] Their own tongues shall ruin them. All who see them will shake their heads. [9] All mankind shall be afraid. They shall declare the work of God, and shall wisely ponder what he has done. [10] The righteous shall be glad in Yahweh, and shall take refuge in him. All the upright in heart shall praise him!

## 65

For the Chief Musician. A Psalm by David. A song.

[1] Praise waits for you, God, in Zion. Vows shall be performed to you. [2] You who hear prayer, all men will come to you. [3] Sins overwhelmed me, but you atoned for our transgressions. [4] Blessed is the one whom you choose and cause to come near, that he may live in your courts. We

will be filled with the goodness of your house, your holy temple. <sup>5</sup> By awesome deeds of righteousness, you answer us, God of our salvation. You who are the hope of all the ends of the earth, of those who are far away on the sea. <sup>6</sup> By your power, you form the mountains, having armed yourself with strength. <sup>7</sup> You still the roaring of the seas, the roaring of their waves, and the turmoil of the nations. <sup>8</sup> They also who dwell in faraway places are afraid at your wonders. You call the morning's dawn and the evening with songs of joy. <sup>9</sup> You visit the earth, and water it. You greatly enrich it. The river of God is full of water. You provide them grain, for so you have ordained it. <sup>10</sup> You drench its furrows. You level its ridges. You soften it with showers. You bless it with a crop. <sup>11</sup> You crown the year with your bounty. Your carts overflow with abundance. <sup>12</sup> The wilderness grasslands overflow. The hills are clothed with gladness. <sup>13</sup> The pastures are covered with flocks. The valleys also are clothed with grain. They shout for joy! They also sing.

## 66

For the Chief Musician. A song. A Psalm.

<sup>1</sup> Make a joyful shout to God, all the earth! <sup>2</sup> Sing to the glory of his name! Offer glory and praise! <sup>3</sup> Tell God, "How awesome are your deeds! Through the greatness of your power, your enemies submit themselves to you. <sup>4</sup> All the earth will worship you, and will sing to you; they will sing to your name." Selah. <sup>5</sup> Come, and see God's deeds— awesome work on behalf of the children of men. <sup>6</sup> He turned the sea into dry land. They went through the river on foot. There, we rejoiced in him. <sup>7</sup> He rules by his might forever. His eyes watch the nations. Don't let the rebellious rise up against him. Selah. <sup>8</sup> Praise our God, you peoples! Make the sound of his praise heard, <sup>9</sup> who preserves our life among the living, and doesn't allow our feet to be moved. <sup>10</sup> For you, God, have tested us. You have refined us, as silver is refined. <sup>11</sup> You brought us into prison. You laid a burden on our backs. <sup>12</sup> You allowed men to ride over our heads. We went through fire and through water, but you brought us to the place of abundance. <sup>13</sup> I will come into your temple with burnt offerings. I will pay my vows to you, <sup>14</sup> which my lips promised, and my mouth spoke, when I was in distress. <sup>15</sup> I will offer to you burnt offerings of fat animals, with the offering of rams, I will offer bulls with goats. Selah. <sup>16</sup> Come and hear, all you who fear God. I will declare what he has done for my soul. <sup>17</sup> I cried to him with my mouth. He was extolled with my tongue. <sup>18</sup> If I cherished sin in my heart, the Lord wouldn't have listened. <sup>19</sup> But most certainly, God has listened. He has heard the voice of my prayer. <sup>20</sup> Blessed be God, who has not turned away my prayer, nor his loving kindness from me.

## 67

For the Chief Musician. With stringed instruments. A Psalm. A song.

<sup>1</sup> May God be merciful to us, bless us, and cause his face to shine on us. Selah. <sup>2</sup> That your way may be known on earth, and your salvation among all nations, <sup>3</sup> let the peoples praise you, God. Let all the peoples praise you. <sup>4</sup> Oh let the nations be glad and sing for joy, for you will judge the peoples with equity, and govern the nations on earth. Selah. <sup>5</sup> Let the peoples praise you, God. Let all the peoples praise you. <sup>6</sup> The earth has yielded its increase. God, even our own God, will bless us. <sup>7</sup> God will bless us. All the ends of the earth shall fear him.

## 68

For the Chief Musician. A Psalm by David. A song.

<sup>1</sup> Let God arise! Let his enemies be scattered! Let them who hate him also flee before him. <sup>2</sup> As smoke is driven away, so drive them away. As wax melts before the fire, so let the wicked perish at the presence of God. <sup>3</sup> But let the righteous be glad. Let them rejoice before God. Yes, let them rejoice with gladness. <sup>4</sup> Sing to God! Sing praises to his name! Extol him who rides on the clouds: to Yah, his name! Rejoice before him! <sup>5</sup> A father of the fatherless, and a defender of the widows, is God in his holy habitation. <sup>6</sup> God sets the lonely in families. He brings out the prisoners with singing, but the rebellious dwell in a sun-scorched land. <sup>7</sup> God, when you went out before your people, when you marched through the wilderness... Selah. <sup>8</sup> The earth trembled. The sky also poured down rain at the presence of the God of Sinai— at the presence of God, the God of Israel. <sup>9</sup> You, God, sent a plentiful rain. You confirmed your inheritance when it was weary. <sup>10</sup> Your congregation lived therein. You, God, prepared your goodness for the poor. <sup>11</sup> The Lord announced the word. The ones who proclaim it are a great company. <sup>12</sup> "Kings of armies flee! They flee!" She who waits at home divides the plunder, <sup>13</sup> while you sleep among the camp fires, the wings of a dove sheathed with silver, her feathers with shining gold. <sup>14</sup> When the Almighty scattered kings in her, it snowed on Zalmon. <sup>15</sup> The mountains of Bashan are majestic mountains. The mountains of Bashan are rugged. <sup>16</sup> Why do you look in envy, you rugged mountains, at the mountain where God chooses to reign? Yes, Yahweh will dwell there forever. <sup>17</sup> The chariots of God are tens of thousands and thousands of thousands. The Lord is among them, from Sinai, into the sanctuary. <sup>18</sup> You have ascended on high. You have led away captives. You have

received gifts among people, yes, among the rebellious also, that Yah God might dwell there. <sup>19</sup> Blessed be the Lord, who daily bears our burdens, even the God who is our salvation. Selah. <sup>20</sup> God is to us a God of deliverance. To Yahweh, the Lord, belongs escape from death. <sup>21</sup> But God will strike through the head of his enemies, the hairy scalp of such a one as still continues in his guiltiness. <sup>22</sup> The Lord said, "I will bring you again from Bashan, I will bring you again from the depths of the sea, <sup>23</sup> that you may crush them, dipping your foot in blood, that the tongues of your dogs may have their portion from your enemies." <sup>24</sup> They have seen your processions, God, even the processions of my God, my King, into the sanctuary. <sup>25</sup> The singers went before, the minstrels followed after, among the ladies playing with tambourines, <sup>26</sup> "Bless God in the congregations, even the Lord in the assembly of Israel!" <sup>27</sup> There is little Benjamin, their ruler, the princes of Judah, their council, the princes of Zebulun, and the princes of Naphtali. <sup>28</sup> Your God has commanded your strength. Strengthen, God, that which you have done for us. <sup>29</sup> Because of your temple at Jerusalem, kings shall bring presents to you. <sup>30</sup> Rebuke the wild animal of the reeds, the multitude of the bulls with the calves of the peoples. Trample under foot the bars of silver. Scatter the nations who delight in war. <sup>31</sup> Princes shall come out of Egypt. Ethiopia shall hurry to stretch out her hands to God. <sup>32</sup> Sing to God, you kingdoms of the earth! Sing praises to the Lord—Selah— <sup>33</sup> to him who rides on the heaven of heavens, which are of old; behold, he utters his voice, a mighty voice. <sup>34</sup> Ascribe strength to God! His excellency is over Israel, his strength is in the skies. <sup>35</sup> You are awesome, God, in your sanctuaries. The God of Israel gives strength and power to his people. Praise be to God!

## 69

For the Chief Musician. To the tune of "Lilies." By David.

<sup>1</sup> Save me, God, for the waters have come up to my neck! <sup>2</sup> I sink in deep mire, where there is no foothold. I have come into deep waters, where the floods overflow me. <sup>3</sup> I am weary with my crying. My throat is dry. My eyes fail looking for my God. <sup>4</sup> Those who hate me without a cause are more than the hairs of my head. Those who want to cut me off, being my enemies wrongfully, are mighty. I have to restore what I didn't take away. <sup>5</sup> God, you know my foolishness. My sins aren't hidden from you. <sup>6</sup> Don't let those who wait for you be shamed through me, Lord Yahweh of Armies. Don't let those who seek you be brought to dishonor through me, God of Israel. <sup>7</sup> Because for your sake, I have borne reproach. Shame has covered my face. <sup>8</sup> I have become a stranger to my brothers, an alien to my mother's children. <sup>9</sup> For the zeal of your house consumes me. The reproaches of those who reproach you have fallen on me. <sup>10</sup> When I wept and I fasted, that was to my reproach. <sup>11</sup> When I made sackcloth my clothing, I became a byword to them. <sup>12</sup> Those who sit in the gate talk about me. I am the song of the drunkards. <sup>13</sup> But as for me, my prayer is to you, Yahweh, in an acceptable time. God, in the abundance of your loving kindness, answer me in the truth of your salvation. <sup>14</sup> Deliver me out of the mire, and don't let me sink. Let me be delivered from those who hate me, and out of the deep waters. <sup>15</sup> Don't let the flood waters overwhelm me, neither let the deep swallow me up. Don't let the pit shut its mouth on me. <sup>16</sup> Answer me, Yahweh, for your loving kindness is good. According to the multitude of your tender mercies, turn to me. <sup>17</sup> Don't hide your face from your servant, for I am in distress. Answer me speedily! <sup>18</sup> Draw near to my soul and redeem it. Ransom me because of my enemies. <sup>19</sup> You know my reproach, my shame, and my dishonor. My adversaries are all before you. <sup>20</sup> Reproach has broken my heart, and I am full of heaviness. I looked for some to take pity, but there was none; for comforters, but I found none. <sup>21</sup> They also gave me poison for my food. In my thirst, they gave me vinegar to drink. <sup>22</sup> Let their table before them become a snare. May it become a retribution and a trap. <sup>23</sup> Let their eyes be darkened, so that they can't see. Let their backs be continually bent. <sup>24</sup> Pour out your indignation on them. Let the fierceness of your anger overtake them. <sup>25</sup> Let their habitation be desolate. Let no one dwell in their tents. <sup>26</sup> For they persecute him whom you have wounded. They tell of the sorrow of those whom you have hurt. <sup>27</sup> Charge them with crime upon crime. Don't let them come into your righteousness. <sup>28</sup> Let them be blotted out of the book of life, and not be written with the righteous. <sup>29</sup> But I am in pain and distress. Let your salvation, God, protect me. <sup>30</sup> I will praise the name of God with a song, and will magnify him with thanksgiving. <sup>31</sup> It will please Yahweh better than an ox, or a bull that has horns and hoofs. <sup>32</sup> The humble have seen it, and are glad. You who seek after God, let your heart live. <sup>33</sup> For Yahweh hears the needy, and doesn't despise his captive people. <sup>34</sup> Let heaven and earth praise him; the seas, and everything that moves therein. <sup>35</sup> For God will save Zion, and build the cities of Judah. They shall settle there, and own it. <sup>36</sup> The children also of his servants shall inherit it. Those who love his name shall dwell therein.

## 70

For the Chief Musician. By David. A reminder.

[1] Hurry, God, to deliver me. Come quickly to help me, Yahweh. [2] Let them be disappointed and confounded who seek my soul. Let those who desire my ruin be turned back in disgrace. [3] Let them be turned because of their shame who say, "Aha! Aha!" [4] Let all those who seek you rejoice and be glad in you. Let those who love your salvation continually say, "Let God be exalted!" [5] But I am poor and needy. Come to me quickly, God. You are my help and my deliverer. Yahweh, don't delay.

## 71

[1] In you, Yahweh, I take refuge. Never let me be disappointed. [2] Deliver me in your righteousness, and rescue me. Turn your ear to me, and save me. [3] Be to me a rock of refuge to which I may always go. Give the command to save me, for you are my rock and my fortress. [4] Rescue me, my God, from the hand of the wicked, from the hand of the unrighteous and cruel man. [5] For you are my hope, Lord Yahweh, my confidence from my youth. [6] I have relied on you from the womb. You are he who took me out of my mother's womb. I will always praise you. [7] I am a marvel to many, but you are my strong refuge. [8] My mouth shall be filled with your praise, with your honor all day long. [9] Don't reject me in my old age. Don't forsake me when my strength fails. [10] For my enemies talk about me. Those who watch for my soul conspire together, [11] saying, "God has forsaken him. Pursue and take him, for no one will rescue him." [12] God, don't be far from me. My God, hurry to help me. [13] Let my accusers be disappointed and consumed. Let them be covered with disgrace and scorn who want to harm me. [14] But I will always hope, and will add to all of your praise. [15] My mouth will tell about your righteousness, and of your salvation all day, though I don't know its full measure. [16] I will come with the mighty acts of the Lord Yahweh. I will make mention of your righteousness, even of yours alone. [17] God, you have taught me from my youth. Until now, I have declared your wondrous works. [18] Yes, even when I am old and gray-haired, God, don't forsake me, until I have declared your strength to the next generation, your might to everyone who is to come. [19] God, your righteousness also reaches to the heavens. You have done great things. God, who is like you? [20] You, who have shown us many and bitter troubles, you will let me live. You will bring us up again from the depths of the earth. [21] Increase my honor and comfort me again. [22] I will also praise you with the harp for your faithfulness, my God. I sing praises to you with the lyre, Holy One of Israel. [23] My lips shall shout for joy! My soul, which you have redeemed, sings praises to you! [24] My tongue will also talk about your righteousness all day long, for they are disappointed, and they are confounded, who want to harm me.

## 72

By Solomon.

[1] God, give the king your justice; your righteousness to the royal son. [2] He will judge your people with righteousness, and your poor with justice. [3] The mountains shall bring prosperity to the people. The hills bring the fruit of righteousness. [4] He will judge the poor of the people. He will save the children of the needy, and will break the oppressor in pieces. [5] They shall fear you while the sun endures; and as long as the moon, throughout all generations. [6] He will come down like rain on the mown grass, as showers that water the earth. [7] In his days, the righteous shall flourish, and abundance of peace, until the moon is no more. [8] He shall have dominion also from sea to sea, from the River to the ends of the earth. [9] Those who dwell in the wilderness shall bow before him. His enemies shall lick the dust. [10] The kings of Tarshish and of the islands will bring tribute. The kings of Sheba and Seba shall offer gifts. [11] Yes, all kings shall fall down before him. All nations shall serve him. [12] For he will deliver the needy when he cries; the poor, who has no helper. [13] He will have pity on the poor and needy. He will save the souls of the needy. [14] He will redeem their soul from oppression and violence. Their blood will be precious in his sight. [15] He will live; and Sheba's gold will be given to him. Men will pray for him continually. They will bless him all day long. [16] Abundance of grain shall be throughout the land. Its fruit sways like Lebanon. Let it flourish, thriving like the grass of the field. [17] His name endures forever. His name continues as long as the sun. Men shall be blessed by him. All nations will call him blessed. [18] Praise be to Yahweh God, the God of Israel, who alone does marvelous deeds. [19] Blessed be his glorious name forever! Let the whole earth be filled with his glory! Amen and amen. [20] This ends the prayers by David, the son of Jesse.

## 73

**Book 3**

A Psalm by Asaph.

[1] Surely God[a] is good to Israel, to those who are pure in heart. [2] But as for me, my feet were almost gone. My steps had nearly slipped. [3] For I was envious of the arrogant, when I saw the prosperity of the wicked. [4] For there are no struggles in their death, but their strength is firm. [5] They are free from burdens of men, neither are they plagued like other men. [6] Therefore pride is like a chain around their neck. Violence covers them like a garment. [7] Their eyes bulge with fat. Their minds pass the limits of conceit. [8] They scoff and speak with malice. In arrogance, they threaten oppression. [9] They have set their mouth in the heavens. Their tongue walks through the earth. [10] Therefore their people return to them, and they drink up waters of abundance. [11] They say, "How does God know? Is there knowledge in the Most High?" [12] Behold, these are the wicked. Being always at ease, they increase in riches. [13] Surely I have cleansed my heart in vain, and washed my hands in innocence, [14] For all day long I have been plagued, and punished every morning. [15] If I had said, "I will speak thus", behold, I would have betrayed the generation of your children. [16] When I tried to understand this, it was too painful for me— [17] until I entered God's sanctuary, and considered their latter end. [18] Surely you set them in slippery places. You throw them down to destruction. [19] How they are suddenly destroyed! They are completely swept away with terrors. [20] As a dream when one wakes up, so, Lord,[b] when you awake, you will despise their fantasies. [21] For my soul was grieved. I was embittered in my heart. [22] I was so senseless and ignorant. I was a brute beast before you. [23] Nevertheless, I am continually with you. You have held my right hand. [24] You will guide me with your counsel, and afterward receive me to glory. [25] Whom do I have in heaven? There is no one on earth whom I desire besides you. [26] My flesh and my heart fails, but God is the strength of my heart and my portion forever. [27] For, behold, those who are far from you shall perish. You have destroyed all those who are unfaithful to you. [28] But it is good for me to come close to God. I have made the Lord Yahweh[c] my refuge, that I may tell of all your works.

## 74

A contemplation by Asaph.

[1] God, why have you rejected us forever? Why does your anger smolder against the sheep of your pasture? [2] Remember your congregation, which you purchased of old, which you have redeemed to be the tribe of your inheritance: Mount Zion, in which you have lived. [3] Lift up your feet to the perpetual ruins, all the evil that the enemy has done in the sanctuary. [4] Your adversaries have roared in the middle of your assembly. They have set up their standards as signs. [5] They behaved like men wielding axes, cutting through a thicket of trees. [6] Now they break all its carved work down with hatchet and hammers. [7] They have burned your sanctuary to the ground. They have profaned the dwelling place of your Name. [8] They said in their heart, "We will crush them completely." They have burned up all the places in the land where God was worshiped. [9] We see no miraculous signs. There is no longer any prophet, neither is there among us anyone who knows how long. [10] How long, God, shall the adversary reproach? Shall the enemy blaspheme your name forever? [11] Why do you draw back your hand, even your right hand? Take it from your chest and consume them! [12] Yet God is my King of old, working salvation throughout the earth. [13] You divided the sea by your strength. You broke the heads of the sea monsters in the waters. [14] You broke the heads of Leviathan in pieces. You gave him as food to people and desert creatures. [15] You opened up spring and stream. You dried up mighty rivers. [16] The day is yours, the night is also yours. You have prepared the light and the sun. [17] You have set all the boundaries of the earth. You have made summer and winter. [18] Remember this, that the enemy has mocked you, Yahweh. Foolish people have blasphemed your name. [19] Don't deliver the soul of your dove to wild beasts. Don't forget the life of your poor forever. [20] Honor your covenant, for haunts of violence fill the dark places of the earth. [21] Don't let the oppressed return ashamed. Let the poor and needy praise your name. [22] Arise, God! Plead your own cause. Remember how the foolish man mocks you all day. [23] Don't forget the voice of your adversaries. The tumult of those who rise up against you ascends continually.

## 75

For the Chief Musician. To the tune of "Do Not Destroy." A Psalm by Asaph. A song.

[1] We give thanks to you, God. We give thanks, for your Name is near. Men tell about your wondrous works. [2] When I choose the appointed time, I will judge blamelessly. [3] The earth and all its inhabitants quake. I firmly hold its pillars. Selah. [4] I said to the arrogant, "Don't boast!" I

---

[a] *73:1* The Hebrew word rendered "God" is אֱלֹהִים (Elohim).

[b] *73:20* The word translated "Lord" is "Adonai."

[c] *73:28* "Yahweh" is God's proper Name, sometimes rendered "LORD" (all caps) in other translations.

said to the wicked, "Don't lift up the horn. [5] Don't lift up your horn on high. Don't speak with a stiff neck." [6] For neither from the east, nor from the west, nor yet from the south, comes exaltation. [7] But God is the judge. He puts down one, and lifts up another. [8] For in Yahweh's hand there is a cup, full of foaming wine mixed with spices. He pours it out. Indeed the wicked of the earth drink and drink it to its very dregs. [9] But I will declare this forever: I will sing praises to the God of Jacob. [10] I will cut off all the horns of the wicked, but the horns of the righteous shall be lifted up.

## 76

For the Chief Musician. On stringed instruments. A Psalm by Asaph. A song.

[1] In Judah, God is known. His name is great in Israel. [2] His tabernacle is also in Salem. His dwelling place in Zion. [3] There he broke the flaming arrows of the bow, the shield, and the sword, and the weapons of war. Selah. [4] Glorious are you, and excellent, more than mountains of game. [5] Valiant men lie plundered, they have slept their last sleep. None of the men of war can lift their hands. [6] At your rebuke, God of Jacob, both chariot and horse are cast into a dead sleep. [7] You, even you, are to be feared. Who can stand in your sight when you are angry? [8] You pronounced judgment from heaven. The earth feared, and was silent, [9] when God arose to judgment, to save all the afflicted ones of the earth. Selah. [10] Surely the wrath of man praises you. The survivors of your wrath are restrained. [11] Make vows to Yahweh your God, and fulfill them! Let all of his neighbors bring presents to him who is to be feared. [12] He will cut off the spirit of princes. He is feared by the kings of the earth.

## 77

For the Chief Musician. To Jeduthun. A Psalm by Asaph.

[1] My cry goes to God! Indeed, I cry to God for help, and for him to listen to me. [2] In the day of my trouble I sought the Lord. My hand was stretched out in the night, and didn't get tired. My soul refused to be comforted. [3] I remember God, and I groan. I complain, and my spirit is overwhelmed. Selah. [4] You hold my eyelids open. I am so troubled that I can't speak. [5] I have considered the days of old, the years of ancient times. [6] I remember my song in the night. I consider in my own heart; my spirit diligently inquires: [7]"Will the Lord reject us forever? Will he be favorable no more? [8] Has his loving kindness vanished forever? Does his promise fail for generations? [9] Has God forgotten to be gracious? Has he, in anger, withheld his compassion?" Selah. [10] Then I thought, "I will appeal to this: the years of the right hand of the Most High." [11] I will remember Yah's deeds; for I will remember your wonders of old. [12] I will also meditate on all your work, and consider your doings. [13] Your way, God, is in the sanctuary. What god is great like God? [14] You are the God who does wonders. You have made your strength known among the peoples. [15] You have redeemed your people with your arm, the sons of Jacob and Joseph. Selah. [16] The waters saw you, God. The waters saw you, and they writhed. The depths also convulsed. [17] The clouds poured out water. The skies resounded with thunder. Your arrows also flashed around. [18] The voice of your thunder was in the whirlwind. The lightnings lit up the world. The earth trembled and shook. [19] Your way was through the sea, your paths through the great waters. Your footsteps were not known. [20] You led your people like a flock, by the hand of Moses and Aaron.

## 78

A contemplation by Asaph.

[1] Hear my teaching, my people. Turn your ears to the words of my mouth. [2] I will open my mouth in a parable. I will utter dark sayings of old, [3] which we have heard and known, and our fathers have told us. [4] We will not hide them from their children, telling to the generation to come the praises of Yahweh, his strength, and his wondrous deeds that he has done. [5] For he established a covenant in Jacob, and appointed a teaching in Israel, which he commanded our fathers, that they should make them known to their children; [6] that the generation to come might know, even the children who should be born; who should arise and tell their children, [7] that they might set their hope in God, and not forget God's deeds, but keep his commandments, [8] and might not be as their fathers— a stubborn and rebellious generation, a generation that didn't make their hearts loyal, whose spirit was not steadfast with God. [9] The children of Ephraim, being armed and carrying bows, turned back in the day of battle. [10] They didn't keep God's covenant, and refused to walk in his law. [11] They forgot his doings, his wondrous deeds that he had shown them. [12] He did marvelous things in the sight of their fathers, in the land of Egypt, in the field of Zoan. [13] He split the sea, and caused them to pass through. He made the waters stand as a heap. [14] In the daytime he also led them with a cloud, and all night with a light of fire. [15] He split rocks in the wilderness, and gave them drink abundantly as out of the depths. [16] He brought streams also out of the rock, and caused waters to run down like rivers. [17] Yet they still went on to sin against him, to rebel against the Most High in the desert. [18] They tempted God

in their heart by asking food according to their desire. [19] Yes, they spoke against God. They said, "Can God prepare a table in the wilderness? [20] Behold, he struck the rock, so that waters gushed out, and streams overflowed. Can he give bread also? Will he provide meat for his people?" [21] Therefore Yahweh heard, and was angry. A fire was kindled against Jacob, anger also went up against Israel, [22] because they didn't believe in God, and didn't trust in his salvation. [23] Yet he commanded the skies above, and opened the doors of heaven. [24] He rained down manna on them to eat, and gave them food from the sky. [25] Man ate the bread of angels. He sent them food to the full. [26] He caused the east wind to blow in the sky. By his power he guided the south wind. [27] He also rained meat on them as the dust, winged birds as the sand of the seas. [28] He let them fall in the middle of their camp, around their habitations. [29] So they ate, and were well filled. He gave them their own desire. [30] They didn't turn from their cravings. Their food was yet in their mouths, [31] when the anger of God went up against them, killed some of their strongest, and struck down the young men of Israel. [32] For all this they still sinned, and didn't believe in his wondrous works. [33] Therefore he consumed their days in vanity, and their years in terror. [34] When he killed them, then they inquired after him. They returned and sought God earnestly. [35] They remembered that God was their rock, the Most High God, their redeemer. [36] But they flattered him with their mouth, and lied to him with their tongue. [37] For their heart was not right with him, neither were they faithful in his covenant. [38] But he, being merciful, forgave iniquity, and didn't destroy them. Yes, many times he turned his anger away, and didn't stir up all his wrath. [39] He remembered that they were but flesh, a wind that passes away, and doesn't come again. [40] How often they rebelled against him in the wilderness, and grieved him in the desert! [41] They turned again and tempted God, and provoked the Holy One of Israel. [42] They didn't remember his hand, nor the day when he redeemed them from the adversary; [43] how he set his signs in Egypt, his wonders in the field of Zoan, [44] he turned their rivers into blood, and their streams, so that they could not drink. [45] He sent among them swarms of flies, which devoured them; and frogs, which destroyed them. [46] He also gave their increase to the caterpillar, and their labor to the locust. [47] He destroyed their vines with hail, their sycamore fig trees with frost. [48] He also gave over their livestock to the hail, and their flocks to hot thunderbolts. [49] He threw on them the fierceness of his anger, wrath, indignation, and trouble, and a band of angels of evil. [50] He made a path for his anger. He didn't spare their soul from death, but gave their life over to the pestilence, [51] and struck all the firstborn in Egypt, the chief of their strength in the tents of Ham. [52] But he led out his own people like sheep, and guided them in the wilderness like a flock. [53] He led them safely, so that they weren't afraid, but the sea overwhelmed their enemies. [54] He brought them to the border of his sanctuary, to this mountain, which his right hand had taken. [55] He also drove out the nations before them, allotted them for an inheritance by line, and made the tribes of Israel to dwell in their tents. [56] Yet they tempted and rebelled against the Most High God, and didn't keep his testimonies, [57] but turned back, and dealt treacherously like their fathers. They were twisted like a deceitful bow. [58] For they provoked him to anger with their high places, and moved him to jealousy with their engraved images. [59] When God heard this, he was angry, and greatly abhorred Israel, [60] so that he abandoned the tent of Shiloh, the tent which he placed among men, [61] and delivered his strength into captivity, his glory into the adversary's hand. [62] He also gave his people over to the sword, and was angry with his inheritance. [63] Fire devoured their young men. Their virgins had no wedding song. [64] Their priests fell by the sword, and their widows couldn't weep. [65] Then the Lord awakened as one out of sleep, like a mighty man who shouts by reason of wine. [66] He struck his adversaries backward. He put them to a perpetual reproach. [67] Moreover he rejected the tent of Joseph, and didn't choose the tribe of Ephraim, [68] But chose the tribe of Judah, Mount Zion which he loved. [69] He built his sanctuary like the heights, like the earth which he has established forever. [70] He also chose David his servant, and took him from the sheepfolds; [71] from following the ewes that have their young, he brought him to be the shepherd of Jacob, his people, and Israel, his inheritance. [72] So he was their shepherd according to the integrity of his heart, and guided them by the skillfulness of his hands.

## 79

A Psalm by Asaph.

[1] God, the nations have come into your inheritance. They have defiled your holy temple. They have laid Jerusalem in heaps. [2] They have given the dead bodies of your servants to be food for the birds of the sky, the flesh of your saints to the animals of the earth. [3] They have shed their blood like water around Jerusalem. There was no one to bury them. [4] We have become a reproach to our neighbors, a scoffing and derision to those who are around us. [5] How long, Yahweh? Will you be angry forever? Will your jealousy burn like fire? [6] Pour out your wrath on the

nations that don't know you, on the kingdoms that don't call on your name, [7] for they have devoured Jacob, and destroyed his homeland. [8] Don't hold the iniquities of our forefathers against us. Let your tender mercies speedily meet us, for we are in desperate need. [9] Help us, God of our salvation, for the glory of your name. Deliver us, and forgive our sins, for your name's sake. [10] Why should the nations say, "Where is their God?" Let it be known among the nations, before our eyes, that vengeance for your servants' blood is being poured out. [11] Let the sighing of the prisoner come before you. According to the greatness of your power, preserve those who are sentenced to death. [12] Pay back to our neighbors seven times into their bosom their reproach with which they have reproached you, Lord. [13] So we, your people and sheep of your pasture, will give you thanks forever. We will praise you forever, to all generations.

## 80

For the Chief Musician. To the tune of "The Lilies of the Covenant." A Psalm by Asaph.

[1] Hear us, Shepherd of Israel, you who lead Joseph like a flock, you who sit above the cherubim, shine out. [2] Before Ephraim, Benjamin, and Manasseh, stir up your might! Come to save us! [3] Turn us again, God. Cause your face to shine, and we will be saved. [4] Yahweh God of Armies, how long will you be angry against the prayer of your people? [5] You have fed them with the bread of tears, and given them tears to drink in large measure. [6] You make us a source of contention to our neighbors. Our enemies laugh among themselves. [7] Turn us again, God of Armies. Cause your face to shine, and we will be saved. [8] You brought a vine out of Egypt. You drove out the nations, and planted it. [9] You cleared the ground for it. It took deep root, and filled the land. [10] The mountains were covered with its shadow. Its boughs were like God's cedars. [11] It sent out its branches to the sea, its shoots to the River. [12] Why have you broken down its walls, so that all those who pass by the way pluck it? [13] The boar out of the wood ravages it. The wild animals of the field feed on it. [14] Turn again, we beg you, God of Armies. Look down from heaven, and see, and visit this vine, [15] the stock which your right hand planted, the branch that you made strong for yourself. [16] It's burned with fire. It's cut down. They perish at your rebuke. [17] Let your hand be on the man of your right hand, on the son of man whom you made strong for yourself. [18] So we will not turn away from you. Revive us, and we will call on your name. [19] Turn us again, Yahweh God of Armies. Cause your face to shine, and we will be saved.

## 81

For the Chief Musician. On an instrument of Gath. By Asaph.

[1] Sing aloud to God, our strength! Make a joyful shout to the God of Jacob! [2] Raise a song, and bring here the tambourine, the pleasant lyre with the harp. [3] Blow the trumpet at the New Moon, at the full moon, on our feast day. [4] For it is a statute for Israel, an ordinance of the God of Jacob. [5] He appointed it in Joseph for a covenant, when he went out over the land of Egypt, I heard a language that I didn't know. [6]"I removed his shoulder from the burden. His hands were freed from the basket. [7] You called in trouble, and I delivered you. I answered you in the secret place of thunder. I tested you at the waters of Meribah." Selah. [8]"Hear, my people, and I will testify to you, Israel, if you would listen to me! [9] There shall be no strange god in you, neither shall you worship any foreign god. [10] I am Yahweh, your God, who brought you up out of the land of Egypt. Open your mouth wide, and I will fill it. [11] But my people didn't listen to my voice. Israel desired none of me. [12] So I let them go after the stubbornness of their hearts, that they might walk in their own counsels. [13] Oh that my people would listen to me, that Israel would walk in my ways! [14] I would soon subdue their enemies, and turn my hand against their adversaries. [15] The haters of Yahweh would cringe before him, and their punishment would last forever. [16] But he would have also fed them with the finest of the wheat. I will satisfy you with honey out of the rock."

## 82

A Psalm by Asaph.

[1] God presides in the great assembly. He judges among the gods. [2]"How long will you judge unjustly, and show partiality to the wicked?" Selah. [3]"Defend the weak, the poor, and the fatherless. Maintain the rights of the poor and oppressed. [4] Rescue the weak and needy. Deliver them out of the hand of the wicked." [5] They don't know, neither do they understand. They walk back and forth in darkness. All the foundations of the earth are shaken. [6] I said, "You are gods, all of you are sons of the Most High. [7] Nevertheless you shall die like men, and fall like one of the rulers." [8] Arise, God, judge the earth, for you inherit all of the nations.

## 83

A song. A Psalm by Asaph.

[1] God, don't keep silent. Don't keep silent, and don't be still, God. [2] For, behold, your enemies are stirred up. Those who hate you have lifted up their heads. [3] They conspire with cunning against your people.

They plot against your cherished ones. [4]"Come," they say, "let's destroy them as a nation, that the name of Israel may be remembered no more." [5] For they have conspired together with one mind. They form an alliance against you. [6] The tents of Edom and the Ishmaelites; Moab, and the Hagrites; [7] Gebal, Ammon, and Amalek; Philistia with the inhabitants of Tyre; [8] Assyria also is joined with them. They have helped the children of Lot. Selah. [9] Do to them as you did to Midian, as to Sisera, as to Jabin, at the river Kishon; [10] who perished at Endor, who became as dung for the earth. [11] Make their nobles like Oreb and Zeeb, yes, all their princes like Zebah and Zalmunna, [12] who said, "Let's take possession of God's pasture lands." [13] My God, make them like tumbleweed, like chaff before the wind. [14] As the fire that burns the forest, as the flame that sets the mountains on fire, [15] so pursue them with your tempest, and terrify them with your storm. [16] Fill their faces with confusion, that they may seek your name, Yahweh. [17] Let them be disappointed and dismayed forever. Yes, let them be confounded and perish; [18] that they may know that you alone, whose name is Yahweh, are the Most High over all the earth.

## 84

For the Chief Musician. On an instrument of Gath. A Psalm by the sons of Korah.

[1] How lovely are your dwellings, Yahweh of Armies! [2] My soul longs, and even faints for the courts of Yahweh. My heart and my flesh cry out for the living God. [3] Yes, the sparrow has found a home, and the swallow a nest for herself, where she may have her young, near your altars, Yahweh of Armies, my King, and my God. [4] Blessed are those who dwell in your house. They are always praising you. Selah. [5] Blessed are those whose strength is in you, who have set their hearts on a pilgrimage. [6] Passing through the valley of Weeping, they make it a place of springs. Yes, the autumn rain covers it with blessings. [7] They go from strength to strength. Every one of them appears before God in Zion. [8] Yahweh, God of Armies, hear my prayer. Listen, God of Jacob. Selah. [9] Behold, God our shield, look at the face of your anointed. [10] For a day in your courts is better than a thousand. I would rather be a doorkeeper in the house of my God, than to dwell in the tents of wickedness. [11] For Yahweh God is a sun and a shield. Yahweh will give grace and glory. He withholds no good thing from those who walk blamelessly. [12] Yahweh of Armies, blessed is the man who trusts in you.

## 85

For the Chief Musician. A Psalm by the sons of Korah.

[1] Yahweh, you have been favorable to your land. You have restored the fortunes of Jacob. [2] You have forgiven the iniquity of your people. You have covered all their sin. Selah. [3] You have taken away all your wrath. You have turned from the fierceness of your anger. [4] Turn us, God of our salvation, and cause your indignation toward us to cease. [5] Will you be angry with us forever? Will you draw out your anger to all generations? [6] Won't you revive us again, that your people may rejoice in you? [7] Show us your loving kindness, Yahweh. Grant us your salvation. [8] I will hear what God, Yahweh, will speak, for he will speak peace to his people, his saints; but let them not turn again to folly. [9] Surely his salvation is near those who fear him, that glory may dwell in our land. [10] Mercy and truth meet together. Righteousness and peace have kissed each other. [11] Truth springs out of the earth. Righteousness has looked down from heaven. [12] Yes, Yahweh will give that which is good. Our land will yield its increase. [13] Righteousness goes before him, and prepares the way for his steps.

## 86

A Prayer by David.

[1] Hear, Yahweh, and answer me, for I am poor and needy. [2] Preserve my soul, for I am godly. You, my God, save your servant who trusts in you. [3] Be merciful to me, Lord, for I call to you all day long. [4] Bring joy to the soul of your servant, for to you, Lord, do I lift up my soul. [5] For you, Lord, are good, and ready to forgive, abundant in loving kindness to all those who call on you. [6] Hear, Yahweh, my prayer. Listen to the voice of my petitions. [7] In the day of my trouble I will call on you, for you will answer me. [8] There is no one like you among the gods, Lord, nor any deeds like your deeds. [9] All nations you have made will come and worship before you, Lord. They shall glorify your name. [10] For you are great, and do wondrous things. You are God alone. [11] Teach me your way, Yahweh. I will walk in your truth. Make my heart undivided to fear your name. [12] I will praise you, Lord my God, with my whole heart. I will glorify your name forever more. [13] For your loving kindness is great toward me. You have delivered my soul from

the lowest Sheol.[a] [14] God, the proud have risen up against me. A company of violent men have sought after my soul, and they don't hold regard for you before them. [15] But you, Lord, are a merciful and gracious God, slow to anger, and abundant in loving kindness and truth. [16] Turn to me, and have mercy on me! Give your strength to your servant. Save the son of your servant. [17] Show me a sign of your goodness, that those who hate me may see it, and be shamed, because you, Yahweh, have helped me, and comforted me.

## 87

A Psalm by the sons of Korah; a Song.

[1] His foundation is in the holy mountains. [2] Yahweh loves the gates of Zion more than all the dwellings of Jacob. [3] Glorious things are spoken about you, city of God. Selah. [4] I will record Rahab[b] and Babylon among those who acknowledge me. Behold, Philistia, Tyre, and also Ethiopia: "This one was born there." [5] Yes, of Zion it will be said, "This one and that one was born in her;" the Most High himself will establish her. [6] Yahweh will count, when he writes up the peoples, "This one was born there." Selah. [7] Those who sing as well as those who dance say, "All my springs are in you."

## 88

A Song. A Psalm by the sons of Korah. For the Chief Musician. To the tune of "The Suffering of Affliction." A contemplation by Heman, the Ezrahite.

[1] Yahweh, the God of my salvation, I have cried day and night before you. [2] Let my prayer enter into your presence. Turn your ear to my cry. [3] For my soul is full of troubles. My life draws near to Sheol.[c] [4] I am counted among those who go down into the pit. I am like a man who has no help, [5] set apart among the dead, like the slain who lie in the grave, whom you remember no more. They are cut off from your hand. [6] You have laid me in the lowest pit, in the darkest depths. [7] Your wrath lies heavily on me. You have afflicted me with all your waves. Selah. [8] You have taken my friends from me. You have made me an abomination to them. I am confined, and I can't escape. [9] My eyes are dim from grief. I have called on you daily, Yahweh. I have spread out my hands to you. [10] Do you show wonders to the dead? Do the departed spirits rise up and praise you? Selah. [11] Is your loving kindness declared in the grave? Or your faithfulness in Destruction? [12] Are your wonders made known in the dark? Or your righteousness in the land of forgetfulness? [13] But to you, Yahweh, I have cried. In the morning, my prayer comes before you. [14] Yahweh, why do you reject my soul? Why do you hide your face from me? [15] I am afflicted and ready to die from my youth up. While I suffer your terrors, I am distracted. [16] Your fierce wrath has gone over me. Your terrors have cut me off. [17] They came around me like water all day long. They completely engulfed me. [18] You have put lover and friend far from me, and my friends into darkness.

## 89

A contemplation by Ethan, the Ezrahite.

[1] I will sing of the loving kindness of Yahweh forever. With my mouth, I will make known your faithfulness to all generations. [2] I indeed declare, "Love stands firm forever. You established the heavens. Your faithfulness is in them." [3] "I have made a covenant with my chosen one, I have sworn to David, my servant, [4] 'I will establish your offspring forever, and build up your throne to all generations.'" Selah. [5] The heavens will praise your wonders, Yahweh, your faithfulness also in the assembly of the holy ones. [6] For who in the skies can be compared to Yahweh? Who among the sons of the heavenly beings is like Yahweh, [7] a very awesome God in the council of the holy ones, to be feared above all those who are around him? [8] Yahweh, God of Armies, who is a mighty one, like you? Yah, your faithfulness is around you. [9] You rule the pride of the sea. When its waves rise up, you calm them. [10] You have broken Rahab in pieces, like one of the slain. You have scattered your enemies with your mighty arm. [11] The heavens are yours. The earth also is yours, the world and its fullness. You have founded them. [12] You have created the north and the south. Tabor and Hermon rejoice in your name. [13] You have a mighty arm. Your hand is strong, and your right hand is exalted. [14] Righteousness and justice are the foundation of your throne. Loving kindness and truth go before your face. [15] Blessed are the people who learn to acclaim you. They walk in the light of your presence, Yahweh. [16] In your name they rejoice all day. In your righteousness, they are exalted. [17] For you are the glory of their strength. In your favor, our horn will be exalted. [18] For our shield belongs to Yahweh, our king to the Holy One of Israel. [19] Then you spoke in vision to your saints, and said, "I have given strength to the warrior. I have exalted a young man from the people. [20] I have found David, my servant. I have anointed him with my holy oil, [21] with whom my hand shall be established. My arm will also strengthen him. [22] No enemy will tax him. No wicked man will oppress him. [23] I will beat down his adversaries before him, and strike those who hate him. [24] But my faithfulness and my loving kindness will be with him. In my name, his horn will be exalted. [25] I will set his hand also on the sea, and his right hand on the rivers. [26] He will call to me, 'You are my Father, my God, and the rock of my salvation!' [27] I will also appoint him my firstborn, the highest of the kings of the earth. [28] I will keep my loving kindness for him forever more. My covenant will stand firm with him. [29] I will also make his offspring endure forever, and his throne as the days of heaven. [30] If his children forsake my law, and don't walk in my ordinances; [31] if they break my statutes, and don't keep my commandments; [32] then I will punish their sin with the rod, and their iniquity with stripes. [33] But I will not completely take my loving kindness from him, nor allow my faithfulness to fail. [34] I will not break my covenant, nor alter what my lips have uttered. [35] Once I have sworn by my holiness, I will not lie to David. [36] His offspring will endure forever, his throne like the sun before me. [37] It will be established forever like the moon, the faithful witness in the sky." Selah. [38] But you have rejected and spurned. You have been angry with your anointed. [39] You have renounced the covenant of your servant. You have defiled his crown in the dust. [40] You have broken down all his hedges. You have brought his strongholds to ruin. [41] All who pass by the way rob him. He has become a reproach to his neighbors. [42] You have exalted the right hand of his adversaries. You have made all of his enemies rejoice. [43] Yes, you turn back the edge of his sword, and haven't supported him in battle. [44] You have ended his splendor, and thrown his throne down to the ground. [45] You have shortened the days of his youth. You have covered him with shame. Selah. [46] How long, Yahweh? Will you hide yourself forever? Will your wrath burn like fire? [47] Remember how short my time is, for what vanity you have created all the children of men! [48] What man is he who shall live and not see death, who shall deliver his soul from the power of Sheol?[d] Selah. [49] Lord, where are your former loving kindnesses, which you swore to David in your faithfulness? [50] Remember, Lord, the reproach of your servants, how I bear in my heart the taunts of all the mighty peoples, [51] With which your enemies have mocked, Yahweh, with which they have mocked the footsteps of your anointed one. [52] Blessed be Yahweh forever more. Amen, and Amen.

## 90

### Book 4

A Prayer by Moses, the man of God.[e]

[1] Lord,[f] you have been our dwelling place for all generations. [2] Before the mountains were born, before you had formed the earth and the world, even from everlasting to everlasting, you are God. [3] You turn man to destruction, saying, "Return, you children of men." [4] For a thousand years in your sight are just like yesterday when it is past, like a watch in the night. [5] You sweep them away as they sleep. In the morning they sprout like new grass. [6] In the morning it sprouts and springs up. By evening, it is withered and dry. [7] For we are consumed in your anger. We are troubled in your wrath. [8] You have set our iniquities before you, our secret sins in the light of your presence. [9] For all our days have passed away in your wrath. We bring our years to an end as a sigh. [10] The days of our years are seventy, or even by reason of strength eighty years; yet their pride is but labor and sorrow, for it passes quickly, and we fly away. [11] Who knows the power of your anger, your wrath according to the fear that is due to you? [12] So teach us to count our days, that we may gain a heart of wisdom. [13] Relent, Yahweh![g] How long? Have compassion on your servants! [14] Satisfy us in the morning with your loving kindness, that we may rejoice and be glad all our days. [15] Make us glad for as many days as you have afflicted us, for as many years as we have seen evil. [16] Let your work appear to your servants, your glory to their children. [17] Let the favor of the Lord our God be on us. Establish the work of our hands for us. Yes, establish the work of our hands.

## 91

[1] He who dwells in the secret place of the Most High will rest in the shadow of the Almighty. [2] I will say of Yahweh, "He is my refuge and my fortress; my God, in whom I trust." [3] For he will deliver you from the snare of the fowler, and from the deadly pestilence. [4] He will cover you with his feathers. Under his wings you will take refuge. His faithfulness is your shield and rampart. [5] You shall not be afraid of the

---

[a] *86:13* Sheol is the place of the dead.
[b] *87:4* Rahab is a reference to Egypt.
[c] *88:3* Sheol is the place of the dead.
[d] *89:48* Sheol is the place of the dead.
[e] *90:0* The Hebrew word rendered "God" is "אֱלֹהִים" (Elohim).
[f] *90:1* The word translated "Lord" is "Adonai."
[g] *90:13* "Yahweh" is God's proper Name, sometimes rendered "LORD" (all caps) in other translations.

terror by night, nor of the arrow that flies by day, [6] nor of the pestilence that walks in darkness, nor of the destruction that wastes at noonday. [7] A thousand may fall at your side, and ten thousand at your right hand; but it will not come near you. [8] You will only look with your eyes, and see the recompense of the wicked. [9] Because you have made Yahweh your refuge, and the Most High your dwelling place, [10] no evil shall happen to you, neither shall any plague come near your dwelling. [11] For he will put his angels in charge of you, to guard you in all your ways. [12] They will bear you up in their hands, so that you won't dash your foot against a stone. [13] You will tread on the lion and cobra. You will trample the young lion and the serpent underfoot. [14] "Because he has set his love on me, therefore I will deliver him. I will set him on high, because he has known my name. [15] He will call on me, and I will answer him. I will be with him in trouble. I will deliver him, and honor him. [16] I will satisfy him with long life, and show him my salvation."

## 92

A Psalm. A song for the Sabbath day.

[1] It is a good thing to give thanks to Yahweh, to sing praises to your name, Most High, [2] to proclaim your loving kindness in the morning, and your faithfulness every night, [3] with the ten-stringed lute, with the harp, and with the melody of the lyre. [4] For you, Yahweh, have made me glad through your work. I will triumph in the works of your hands. [5] How great are your works, Yahweh! Your thoughts are very deep. [6] A senseless man doesn't know, neither does a fool understand this: [7] though the wicked spring up as the grass, and all the evildoers flourish, they will be destroyed forever more. [8] But you, Yahweh, are on high forever more. [9] For behold, your enemies, Yahweh, for behold, your enemies shall perish. All the evildoers will be scattered. [10] But you have exalted my horn like that of the wild ox. I am anointed with fresh oil. [11] My eye has also seen my enemies. My ears have heard of the wicked enemies who rise up against me. [12] The righteous shall flourish like the palm tree. He will grow like a cedar in Lebanon. [13] They are planted in Yahweh's house. They will flourish in our God's courts. [14] They will still produce fruit in old age. They will be full of sap and green, [15] to show that Yahweh is upright. He is my rock, and there is no unrighteousness in him.

## 93

[1] Yahweh reigns! He is clothed with majesty! Yahweh is armed with strength. The world also is established. It can't be moved. [2] Your throne is established from long ago. You are from everlasting. [3] The floods have lifted up, Yahweh, the floods have lifted up their voice. The floods lift up their waves. [4] Above the voices of many waters, the mighty breakers of the sea, Yahweh on high is mighty. [5] Your statutes stand firm. Holiness adorns your house, Yahweh, forever more.

## 94

[1] Yahweh, you God to whom vengeance belongs, you God to whom vengeance belongs, shine out. [2] Rise up, you judge of the earth. Pay back the proud what they deserve. [3] Yahweh, how long will the wicked, how long will the wicked triumph? [4] They pour out arrogant words. All the evildoers boast. [5] They break your people in pieces, Yahweh, and afflict your heritage. [6] They kill the widow and the alien, and murder the fatherless. [7] They say, "Yah will not see, neither will Jacob's God consider." [8] Consider, you senseless among the people; you fools, when will you be wise? [9] He who implanted the ear, won't he hear? He who formed the eye, won't he see? [10] He who disciplines the nations, won't he punish? He who teaches man knows. [11] Yahweh knows the thoughts of man, that they are futile. [12] Blessed is the man whom you discipline, Yah, and teach out of your law, [13] that you may give him rest from the days of adversity, until the pit is dug for the wicked. [14] For Yahweh won't reject his people, neither will he forsake his inheritance. [15] For judgment will return to righteousness. All the upright in heart shall follow it. [16] Who will rise up for me against the wicked? Who will stand up for me against the evildoers? [17] Unless Yahweh had been my help, my soul would have soon lived in silence. [18] When I said, "My foot is slipping!" Your loving kindness, Yahweh, held me up. [19] In the multitude of my thoughts within me, your comforts delight my soul. [20] Shall the throne of wickedness have fellowship with you, which brings about mischief by statute? [21] They gather themselves together against the soul of the righteous, and condemn the innocent blood. [22] But Yahweh has been my high tower, my God, the rock of my refuge. [23] He has brought on them their own iniquity, and will cut them off in their own wickedness. Yahweh, our God, will cut them off.

## 95

[1] Oh come, let's sing to Yahweh. Let's shout aloud to the rock of our salvation! [2] Let's come before his presence with thanksgiving. Let's extol him with songs! [3] For Yahweh is a great God, a great King above all gods. [4] In his hand are the deep places of the earth. The heights of the mountains are also his. [5] The sea is his, and he made it. His hands formed the dry land. [6] Oh come, let's worship and bow down. Let's kneel before Yahweh, our Maker, [7] for he is our God. We are the people of his pasture, and the sheep in his care. Today, oh that you would hear his voice! [8] Don't harden your heart, as at Meribah, as in the day of Massah in the wilderness, [9] when your fathers tempted me, tested me, and saw my work. [10] Forty long years I was grieved with that generation, and said, "They are a people who err in their heart. They have not known my ways." [11] Therefore I swore in my wrath, "They won't enter into my rest."

## 96

[1] Sing to Yahweh a new song! Sing to Yahweh, all the earth. [2] Sing to Yahweh! Bless his name! Proclaim his salvation from day to day! [3] Declare his glory among the nations, his marvelous works among all the peoples. [4] For Yahweh is great, and greatly to be praised! He is to be feared above all gods. [5] For all the gods of the peoples are idols, but Yahweh made the heavens. [6] Honor and majesty are before him. Strength and beauty are in his sanctuary. [7] Ascribe to Yahweh, you families of nations, ascribe to Yahweh glory and strength. [8] Ascribe to Yahweh the glory due to his name. Bring an offering, and come into his courts. [9] Worship Yahweh in holy array. Tremble before him, all the earth. [10] Say among the nations, "Yahweh reigns." The world is also established. It can't be moved. He will judge the peoples with equity. [11] Let the heavens be glad, and let the earth rejoice. Let the sea roar, and its fullness! [12] Let the field and all that is in it exult! Then all the trees of the woods shall sing for joy [13] before Yahweh; for he comes, for he comes to judge the earth. He will judge the world with righteousness, the peoples with his truth.

## 97

[1] Yahweh reigns! Let the earth rejoice! Let the multitude of islands be glad! [2] Clouds and darkness are around him. Righteousness and justice are the foundation of his throne. [3] A fire goes before him, and burns up his adversaries on every side. [4] His lightning lights up the world. The earth sees, and trembles. [5] The mountains melt like wax at the presence of Yahweh, at the presence of the Lord of the whole earth. [6] The heavens declare his righteousness. All the peoples have seen his glory. [7] Let all them be shamed who serve engraved images, who boast in their idols. Worship him, all you gods![a] [8] Zion heard and was glad. The daughters of Judah rejoiced because of your judgments, Yahweh. [9] For you, Yahweh, are most high above all the earth. You are exalted far above all gods. [10] You who love Yahweh, hate evil! He preserves the souls of his saints. He delivers them out of the hand of the wicked. [11] Light is sown for the righteous, and gladness for the upright in heart. [12] Be glad in Yahweh, you righteous people! Give thanks to his holy Name.

## 98

A Psalm.

[1] Sing to Yahweh a new song, for he has done marvelous things! His right hand and his holy arm have worked salvation for him. [2] Yahweh has made known his salvation. He has openly shown his righteousness in the sight of the nations. [3] He has remembered his loving kindness and his faithfulness toward the house of Israel. All the ends of the earth have seen the salvation of our God. [4] Make a joyful noise to Yahweh, all the earth! Burst out and sing for joy, yes, sing praises! [5] Sing praises to Yahweh with the harp, with the harp and the voice of melody. [6] With trumpets and sound of the ram's horn, make a joyful noise before the King, Yahweh. [7] Let the sea roar with its fullness; the world, and those who dwell therein. [8] Let the rivers clap their hands. Let the mountains sing for joy together. [9] Let them sing before Yahweh, for he comes to judge the earth. He will judge the world with righteousness, and the peoples with equity.

## 99

[1] Yahweh reigns! Let the peoples tremble. He sits enthroned among the cherubim. Let the earth be moved. [2] Yahweh is great in Zion. He is high above all the peoples. [3] Let them praise your great and awesome name. He is Holy! [4] The King's strength also loves justice. You establish equity. You execute justice and righteousness in Jacob. [5] Exalt Yahweh our God. Worship at his footstool. He is Holy! [6] Moses and Aaron were among his priests, Samuel was among those who call on his name. They called on Yahweh, and he answered them. [7] He spoke to them in the pillar of cloud. They kept his testimonies, the statute that he gave them. [8] You answered them, Yahweh our God. You are a God who forgave them, although you took vengeance for their doings. [9] Exalt Yahweh, our God. Worship at his holy hill, for Yahweh, our God, is holy!

---

[a] *97:7 LXX reads "angels" instead of "gods".*

## 100

A Psalm of thanksgiving.

[1] Shout for joy to Yahweh, all you lands! [2] Serve Yahweh with gladness. Come before his presence with singing. [3] Know that Yahweh, he is God. It is he who has made us, and we are his. We are his people, and the sheep of his pasture. [4] Enter into his gates with thanksgiving, and into his courts with praise. Give thanks to him, and bless his name. [5] For Yahweh is good. His loving kindness endures forever, his faithfulness to all generations.

## 101

A Psalm by David.

[1] I will sing of loving kindness and justice. To you, Yahweh, I will sing praises. [2] I will be careful to live a blameless life. When will you come to me? I will walk within my house with a blameless heart. [3] I will set no vile thing before my eyes. I hate the deeds of faithless men. They will not cling to me. [4] A perverse heart will be far from me. I will have nothing to do with evil. [5] I will silence whoever secretly slanders his neighbor. I won't tolerate one who is arrogant and conceited. [6] My eyes will be on the faithful of the land, that they may dwell with me. He who walks in a perfect way, he will serve me. [7] He who practices deceit won't dwell within my house. He who speaks falsehood won't be established before my eyes. [8] Morning by morning, I will destroy all the wicked of the land, to cut off all the workers of iniquity from Yahweh's city.

## 102

A Prayer of the afflicted, when he is overwhelmed and pours out his complaint before Yahweh.

[1] Hear my prayer, Yahweh! Let my cry come to you. [2] Don't hide your face from me in the day of my distress. Turn your ear to me. Answer me quickly in the day when I call. [3] For my days consume away like smoke. My bones are burned as a torch. [4] My heart is blighted like grass, and withered, for I forget to eat my bread. [5] By reason of the voice of my groaning, my bones stick to my skin. [6] I am like a pelican of the wilderness. I have become as an owl of the waste places. [7] I watch, and have become like a sparrow that is alone on the housetop. [8] My enemies reproach me all day. Those who are mad at me use my name as a curse. [9] For I have eaten ashes like bread, and mixed my drink with tears, [10] because of your indignation and your wrath; for you have taken me up and thrown me away. [11] My days are like a long shadow. I have withered like grass. [12] But you, Yahweh, will remain forever; your renown endures to all generations. [13] You will arise and have mercy on Zion, for it is time to have pity on her. Yes, the set time has come. [14] For your servants take pleasure in her stones, and have pity on her dust. [15] So the nations will fear Yahweh's name, all the kings of the earth your glory. [16] For Yahweh has built up Zion. He has appeared in his glory. [17] He has responded to the prayer of the destitute, and has not despised their prayer. [18] This will be written for the generation to come. A people which will be created will praise Yah, [19] for he has looked down from the height of his sanctuary. From heaven, Yahweh saw the earth, [20] to hear the groans of the prisoner, to free those who are condemned to death, [21] that men may declare Yahweh's name in Zion, and his praise in Jerusalem, [22] when the peoples are gathered together, the kingdoms, to serve Yahweh. [23] He weakened my strength along the course. He shortened my days. [24] I said, "My God, don't take me away in the middle of my days. Your years are throughout all generations. [25] Of old, you laid the foundation of the earth. The heavens are the work of your hands. [26] They will perish, but you will endure. Yes, all of them will wear out like a garment. You will change them like a cloak, and they will be changed. [27] But you are the same. Your years will have no end. [28] The children of your servants will continue. Their offspring will be established before you."

## 103

By David.

[1] Praise Yahweh, my soul! All that is within me, praise his holy name! [2] Praise Yahweh, my soul, and don't forget all his benefits, [3] who forgives all your sins, who heals all your diseases, [4] who redeems your life from destruction, who crowns you with loving kindness and tender mercies, [5] who satisfies your desire with good things, so that your youth is renewed like the eagle's. [6] Yahweh executes righteous acts, and justice for all who are oppressed. [7] He made known his ways to Moses, his deeds to the children of Israel. [8] Yahweh is merciful and gracious, slow to anger, and abundant in loving kindness. [9] He will not always accuse; neither will he stay angry forever. [10] He has not dealt with us according to our sins, nor repaid us for our iniquities. [11] For as the heavens are high above the earth, so great is his loving kindness toward those who fear him. [12] As far as the east is from the west, so far has he removed our transgressions from us. [13] Like a father has compassion on his children, so Yahweh has compassion on those who fear him. [14] For he knows how we are made. He remembers that we are dust. [15] As for man, his days are like grass. As a flower of the field, so he flourishes. [16] For the wind passes over it, and it is gone. Its place remembers it no more. [17] But Yahweh's loving kindness is from everlasting to everlasting with those who fear him, his righteousness to children's children, [18] to those who keep his covenant, to those who remember to obey his precepts. [19] Yahweh has established his throne in the heavens. His kingdom rules over all. [20] Praise Yahweh, you angels of his, who are mighty in strength, who fulfill his word, obeying the voice of his word. [21] Praise Yahweh, all you armies of his, you servants of his, who do his pleasure. [22] Praise Yahweh, all you works of his, in all places of his dominion. Praise Yahweh, my soul!

## 104

[1] Bless Yahweh, my soul. Yahweh, my God, you are very great. You are clothed with honor and majesty. [2] He covers himself with light as with a garment. He stretches out the heavens like a curtain. [3] He lays the beams of his rooms in the waters. He makes the clouds his chariot. He walks on the wings of the wind. [4] He makes his messengers[a] winds, and his servants flames of fire. [5] He laid the foundations of the earth, that it should not be moved forever. [6] You covered it with the deep as with a cloak. The waters stood above the mountains. [7] At your rebuke they fled. At the voice of your thunder they hurried away. [8] The mountains rose, the valleys sank down, to the place which you had assigned to them. [9] You have set a boundary that they may not pass over, that they don't turn again to cover the earth. [10] He sends springs into the valleys. They run among the mountains. [11] They give drink to every animal of the field. The wild donkeys quench their thirst. [12] The birds of the sky nest by them. They sing among the branches. [13] He waters the mountains from his rooms. The earth is filled with the fruit of your works. [14] He causes the grass to grow for the livestock, and plants for man to cultivate, that he may produce food out of the earth: [15] wine that makes the heart of man glad, oil to make his face to shine, and bread that strengthens man's heart. [16] Yahweh's trees are well watered, the cedars of Lebanon, which he has planted, [17] where the birds make their nests. The stork makes its home in the cypress trees. [18] The high mountains are for the wild goats. The rocks are a refuge for the rock badgers. [19] He appointed the moon for seasons. The sun knows when to set. [20] You make darkness, and it is night, in which all the animals of the forest prowl. [21] The young lions roar after their prey, and seek their food from God. [22] The sun rises, and they steal away, and lie down in their dens. [23] Man goes out to his work, to his labor until the evening. [24] Yahweh, how many are your works! In wisdom, you have made them all. The earth is full of your riches. [25] There is the sea, great and wide, in which are innumerable living things, both small and large animals. [26] There the ships go, and leviathan, whom you formed to play there. [27] These all wait for you, that you may give them their food in due season. [28] You give to them; they gather. You open your hand; they are satisfied with good. [29] You hide your face; they are troubled. You take away their breath; they die and return to the dust. [30] You send out your Spirit and they are created. You renew the face of the ground. [31] Let Yahweh's glory endure forever. Let Yahweh rejoice in his works. [32] He looks at the earth, and it trembles. He touches the mountains, and they smoke. [33] I will sing to Yahweh as long as I live. I will sing praise to my God while I have any being. [34] Let my meditation be sweet to him. I will rejoice in Yahweh. [35] Let sinners be consumed out of the earth. Let the wicked be no more. Bless Yahweh, my soul. Praise Yah!

## 105

[1] Give thanks to Yahweh! Call on his name! Make his doings known among the peoples. [2] Sing to him, sing praises to him! Tell of all his marvelous works. [3] Glory in his holy name. Let the heart of those who seek Yahweh rejoice. [4] Seek Yahweh and his strength. Seek his face forever more. [5] Remember his marvelous works that he has done: his wonders, and the judgments of his mouth, [6] you offspring of Abraham, his servant, you children of Jacob, his chosen ones. [7] He is Yahweh, our God. His judgments are in all the earth. [8] He has remembered his covenant forever, the word which he commanded to a thousand generations, [9] the covenant which he made with Abraham, his oath to Isaac, [10] and confirmed it to Jacob for a statute; to Israel for an everlasting covenant, [11] saying, "To you I will give the land of Canaan, the lot of your inheritance," [12] when they were but a few men in number, yes, very few, and foreigners in it. [13] They went about from nation to nation, from one kingdom to another people. [14] He allowed no one to do them wrong. Yes, he reproved kings for their sakes, [15] "Don't touch my anointed ones! Do my prophets no harm!" [16] He called for a famine on the land. He destroyed the food supplies. [17] He sent a man before them. Joseph was sold for a slave. [18] They bruised his feet with shackles. His neck was locked in irons, [19] until the time that his word happened, and Yahweh's word proved him true. [20] The king sent and

---

[a] 104:4 or, angels

freed him, even the ruler of peoples, and let him go free. ²¹ He made him lord of his house, and ruler of all of his possessions, ²² to discipline his princes at his pleasure, and to teach his elders wisdom. ²³ Israel also came into Egypt. Jacob lived in the land of Ham. ²⁴ He increased his people greatly, and made them stronger than their adversaries. ²⁵ He turned their heart to hate his people, to conspire against his servants. ²⁶ He sent Moses, his servant, and Aaron, whom he had chosen. ²⁷ They performed miracles among them, and wonders in the land of Ham. ²⁸ He sent darkness, and made it dark. They didn't rebel against his words. ²⁹ He turned their waters into blood, and killed their fish. ³⁰ Their land swarmed with frogs, even in the rooms of their kings. ³¹ He spoke, and swarms of flies came, and lice in all their borders. ³² He gave them hail for rain, with lightning in their land. ³³ He struck their vines and also their fig trees, and shattered the trees of their country. ³⁴ He spoke, and the locusts came with the grasshoppers, without number. ³⁵ They ate up every plant in their land, and ate up the fruit of their ground. ³⁶ He struck also all the firstborn in their land, the first fruits of all their manhood. ³⁷ He brought them out with silver and gold. There was not one feeble person among his tribes. ³⁸ Egypt was glad when they departed, for the fear of them had fallen on them. ³⁹ He spread a cloud for a covering, fire to give light in the night. ⁴⁰ They asked, and he brought quails, and satisfied them with the bread of the sky. ⁴¹ He opened the rock, and waters gushed out. They ran as a river in the dry places. ⁴² For he remembered his holy word, and Abraham, his servant. ⁴³ He brought his people out with joy, his chosen with singing. ⁴⁴ He gave them the lands of the nations. They took the labor of the peoples in possession, ⁴⁵ that they might keep his statutes, and observe his laws. Praise Yah!

## 106

¹ Praise Yahweh! Give thanks to Yahweh, for he is good, for his loving kindness endures forever. ² Who can utter the mighty acts of Yahweh, or fully declare all his praise? ³ Blessed are those who keep justice. Blessed is one who does what is right at all times. ⁴ Remember me, Yahweh, with the favor that you show to your people. Visit me with your salvation, ⁵ that I may see the prosperity of your chosen, that I may rejoice in the gladness of your nation, that I may glory with your inheritance. ⁶ We have sinned with our fathers. We have committed iniquity. We have done wickedly. ⁷ Our fathers didn't understand your wonders in Egypt. They didn't remember the multitude of your loving kindnesses, but were rebellious at the sea, even at the Red Sea. ⁸ Nevertheless he saved them for his name's sake, that he might make his mighty power known. ⁹ He rebuked the Red Sea also, and it was dried up; so he led them through the depths, as through a desert. ¹⁰ He saved them from the hand of him who hated them, and redeemed them from the hand of the enemy. ¹¹ The waters covered their adversaries. There was not one of them left. ¹² Then they believed his words. They sang his praise. ¹³ They soon forgot his works. They didn't wait for his counsel, ¹⁴ but gave in to craving in the desert, and tested God in the wasteland. ¹⁵ He gave them their request, but sent leanness into their soul. ¹⁶ They envied Moses also in the camp, and Aaron, Yahweh's saint. ¹⁷ The earth opened and swallowed up Dathan, and covered the company of Abiram. ¹⁸ A fire was kindled in their company. The flame burned up the wicked. ¹⁹ They made a calf in Horeb, and worshiped a molten image. ²⁰ Thus they exchanged their glory for an image of a bull that eats grass. ²¹ They forgot God, their Savior, who had done great things in Egypt, ²² wondrous works in the land of Ham, and awesome things by the Red Sea. ²³ Therefore he said that he would destroy them, had Moses, his chosen, not stood before him in the breach, to turn away his wrath, so that he wouldn't destroy them. ²⁴ Yes, they despised the pleasant land. They didn't believe his word, ²⁵ but murmured in their tents, and didn't listen to Yahweh's voice. ²⁶ Therefore he swore to them that he would overthrow them in the wilderness, ²⁷ that he would overthrow their offspring among the nations, and scatter them in the lands. ²⁸ They joined themselves also to Baal Peor, and ate the sacrifices of the dead. ²⁹ Thus they provoked him to anger with their deeds. The plague broke in on them. ³⁰ Then Phinehas stood up and executed judgment, so the plague was stopped. ³¹ That was credited to him for righteousness, for all generations to come. ³² They angered him also at the waters of Meribah, so that Moses was troubled for their sakes; ³³ because they were rebellious against his spirit, he spoke rashly with his lips. ³⁴ They didn't destroy the peoples, as Yahweh commanded them, ³⁵ but mixed themselves with the nations, and learned their works. ³⁶ They served their idols, which became a snare to them. ³⁷ Yes, they sacrificed their sons and their daughters to demons. ³⁸ They shed innocent blood, even the blood of their sons and of their daughters, whom they sacrificed to the idols of Canaan. The land was polluted with blood. ³⁹ Thus they were defiled with their works, and prostituted themselves in their deeds. ⁴⁰ Therefore Yahweh burned with anger against his people. He abhorred his inheritance. ⁴¹ He gave them into the hand of the nations. Those who hated them ruled over them. ⁴² Their enemies also oppressed them. They were brought into subjection under their hand. ⁴³ He rescued them many times, but they were rebellious in their counsel, and were brought low in their iniquity. ⁴⁴ Nevertheless he regarded their distress, when he heard their cry. ⁴⁵ He remembered for them his covenant, and repented according to the multitude of his loving kindnesses. ⁴⁶ He made them also to be pitied by all those who carried them captive. ⁴⁷ Save us, Yahweh, our God, gather us from among the nations, to give thanks to your holy name, to triumph in your praise! ⁴⁸ Blessed be Yahweh, the God of Israel, from everlasting even to everlasting! Let all the people say, "Amen." Praise Yah!

## 107

**Book 5**

¹ Give thanks to Yahweh,ᵃ for he is good, for his loving kindness endures forever. ² Let the redeemed by Yahweh say so, whom he has redeemed from the hand of the adversary, ³ and gathered out of the lands, from the east and from the west, from the north and from the south. ⁴ They wandered in the wilderness in a desert way. They found no city to live in. ⁵ Hungry and thirsty, their soul fainted in them. ⁶ Then they cried to Yahweh in their trouble, and he delivered them out of their distresses. ⁷ He led them also by a straight way, that they might go to a city to live in. ⁸ Let them praise Yahweh for his loving kindness, for his wonderful deeds to the children of men! ⁹ For he satisfies the longing soul. He fills the hungry soul with good. ¹⁰ Some sat in darkness and in the shadow of death, being bound in affliction and iron, ¹¹ because they rebelled against the words of God,ᵇ and condemned the counsel of the Most High. ¹² Therefore he brought down their heart with labor. They fell down, and there was no one to help. ¹³ Then they cried to Yahweh in their trouble, and he saved them out of their distresses. ¹⁴ He brought them out of darkness and the shadow of death, and broke away their chains. ¹⁵ Let them praise Yahweh for his loving kindness, for his wonderful deeds to the children of men! ¹⁶ For he has broken the gates of bronze, and cut through bars of iron. ¹⁷ Fools are afflicted because of their disobedience, and because of their iniquities. ¹⁸ Their soul abhors all kinds of food. They draw near to the gates of death. ¹⁹ Then they cry to Yahweh in their trouble, and he saves them out of their distresses. ²⁰ He sends his word, and heals them, and delivers them from their graves. ²¹ Let them praise Yahweh for his loving kindness, for his wonderful deeds to the children of men! ²² Let them offer the sacrifices of thanksgiving, and declare his deeds with singing. ²³ Those who go down to the sea in ships, who do business in great waters, ²⁴ these see Yahweh's deeds, and his wonders in the deep. ²⁵ For he commands, and raises the stormy wind, which lifts up its waves. ²⁶ They mount up to the sky; they go down again to the depths. Their soul melts away because of trouble. ²⁷ They reel back and forth, and stagger like a drunken man, and are at their wits' end. ²⁸ Then they cry to Yahweh in their trouble, and he brings them out of their distress. ²⁹ He makes the storm a calm, so that its waves are still. ³⁰ Then they are glad because it is calm, so he brings them to their desired haven. ³¹ Let them praise Yahweh for his loving kindness, for his wonderful deeds for the children of men! ³² Let them exalt him also in the assembly of the people, and praise him in the seat of the elders. ³³ He turns rivers into a desert, water springs into a thirsty ground, ³⁴ and a fruitful land into a salt waste, for the wickedness of those who dwell in it. ³⁵ He turns a desert into a pool of water, and a dry land into water springs. ³⁶ There he makes the hungry live, that they may prepare a city to live in, ³⁷ sow fields, plant vineyards, and reap the fruits of increase. ³⁸ He blesses them also, so that they are multiplied greatly. He doesn't allow their livestock to decrease. ³⁹ Again, they are diminished and bowed down through oppression, trouble, and sorrow. ⁴⁰ He pours contempt on princes, and causes them to wander in a trackless waste. ⁴¹ Yet he lifts the needy out of their affliction, and increases their families like a flock. ⁴² The upright will see it, and be glad. All the wicked will shut their mouths. ⁴³ Whoever is wise will pay attention to these things. They will consider the loving kindnesses of Yahweh.

## 108

A Song. A Psalm by David.

¹ My heart is steadfast, God. I will sing and I will make music with my soul. ² Wake up, harp and lyre! I will wake up the dawn. ³ I will give thanks to you, Yahweh, among the nations. I will sing praises to you among the peoples. ⁴ For your loving kindness is great above the heavens. Your faithfulness reaches to the skies. ⁵ Be exalted, God, above the heavens! Let your glory be over all the earth. ⁶ That your beloved may be delivered, save with your right hand, and answer us. ⁷

---

ᵃ *107:1* "Yahweh" is God's proper Name, sometimes rendered "LORD" (all caps) in other translations.

ᵇ *107:11* The Hebrew word rendered "God" is "אֱלֹהִים" (Elohim).

God has spoken from his sanctuary: "In triumph, I will divide Shechem, and measure out the valley of Succoth. **8** Gilead is mine. Manasseh is mine. Ephraim also is my helmet. Judah is my scepter. **9** Moab is my wash pot. I will toss my sandal on Edom. I will shout over Philistia." **10** Who will bring me into the fortified city? Who will lead me to Edom? **11** Haven't you rejected us, God? You don't go out, God, with our armies. **12** Give us help against the enemy, for the help of man is vain. **13** Through God, we will do valiantly, for it is he who will tread down our enemies.

## 109

For the Chief Musician. A Psalm by David.

**1** God of my praise, don't remain silent, **2** for they have opened the mouth of the wicked and the mouth of deceit against me. They have spoken to me with a lying tongue. **3** They have also surrounded me with words of hatred, and fought against me without a cause. **4** In return for my love, they are my adversaries; but I am in prayer. **5** They have rewarded me evil for good, and hatred for my love. **6** Set a wicked man over him. Let an adversary stand at his right hand. **7** When he is judged, let him come out guilty. Let his prayer be turned into sin. **8** Let his days be few. Let another take his office. **9** Let his children be fatherless, and his wife a widow. **10** Let his children be wandering beggars. Let them be sought from their ruins. **11** Let the creditor seize all that he has. Let strangers plunder the fruit of his labor. **12** Let there be no one to extend kindness to him, neither let there be anyone to have pity on his fatherless children. **13** Let his posterity be cut off. In the generation following let their name be blotted out. **14** Let the iniquity of his fathers be remembered by Yahweh. Don't let the sin of his mother be blotted out. **15** Let them be before Yahweh continually, that he may cut off their memory from the earth; **16** because he didn't remember to show kindness, but persecuted the poor and needy man, the broken in heart, to kill them. **17** Yes, he loved cursing, and it came to him. He didn't delight in blessing, and it was far from him. **18** He clothed himself also with cursing as with his garment. It came into his inward parts like water, like oil into his bones. **19** Let it be to him as the clothing with which he covers himself, for the belt that is always around him. **20** This is the reward of my adversaries from Yahweh, of those who speak evil against my soul. **21** But deal with me, Yahweh the Lord,[a] for your name's sake, because your loving kindness is good, deliver me; **22** for I am poor and needy. My heart is wounded within me. **23** I fade away like an evening shadow. I am shaken off like a locust. **24** My knees are weak through fasting. My body is thin and lacks fat. **25** I have also become a reproach to them. When they see me, they shake their head. **26** Help me, Yahweh, my God. Save me according to your loving kindness; **27** that they may know that this is your hand; that you, Yahweh, have done it. **28** They may curse, but you bless. When they arise, they will be shamed, but your servant shall rejoice. **29** Let my adversaries be clothed with dishonor. Let them cover themselves with their own shame as with a robe. **30** I will give great thanks to Yahweh with my mouth. Yes, I will praise him among the multitude. **31** For he will stand at the right hand of the needy, to save him from those who judge his soul.

## 110

A Psalm by David.

**1** Yahweh says to my Lord, "Sit at my right hand, until I make your enemies your footstool for your feet." **2** Yahweh will send out the rod of your strength out of Zion. Rule among your enemies. **3** Your people offer themselves willingly in the day of your power, in holy array. Out of the womb of the morning, you have the dew of your youth. **4** Yahweh has sworn, and will not change his mind: "You are a priest forever in the order of Melchizedek." **5** The Lord is at your right hand. He will crush kings in the day of his wrath. **6** He will judge among the nations. He will heap up dead bodies. He will crush the ruler of the whole earth. **7** He will drink of the brook on the way; therefore he will lift up his head.

## 111

**1** Praise Yah![b] I will give thanks to Yahweh with my whole heart, in the council of the upright, and in the congregation. **2** Yahweh's works are great, pondered by all those who delight in them. **3** His work is honor and majesty. His righteousness endures forever. **4** He has caused his wonderful works to be remembered. Yahweh is gracious and merciful. **5** He has given food to those who fear him. He always remembers his covenant. **6** He has shown his people the power of his works, in giving them the heritage of the nations. **7** The works of his hands are truth and justice. All his precepts are sure. **8** They are established forever and ever. They are done in truth and uprightness. **9** He has sent redemption to his people. He has ordained his covenant forever. His name is holy

and awesome! **10** The fear of Yahweh is the beginning of wisdom. All those who do his work have a good understanding. His praise endures forever!

## 112

**1** Praise Yah![c] Blessed is the man who fears Yahweh, who delights greatly in his commandments. **2** His offspring will be mighty in the land. The generation of the upright will be blessed. **3** Wealth and riches are in his house. His righteousness endures forever. **4** Light dawns in the darkness for the upright, gracious, merciful, and righteous. **5** It is well with the man who deals graciously and lends. He will maintain his cause in judgment. **6** For he will never be shaken. The righteous will be remembered forever. **7** He will not be afraid of evil news. His heart is steadfast, trusting in Yahweh. **8** His heart is established. He will not be afraid in the end when he sees his adversaries. **9** He has dispersed, he has given to the poor. His righteousness endures forever. His horn will be exalted with honor. **10** The wicked will see it, and be grieved. He shall gnash with his teeth, and melt away. The desire of the wicked will perish.

## 113

**1** Praise Yah! Praise, you servants of Yahweh, praise Yahweh's name. **2** Blessed be Yahweh's name, from this time forward and forever more. **3** From the rising of the sun to its going down, Yahweh's name is to be praised. **4** Yahweh is high above all nations, his glory above the heavens. **5** Who is like Yahweh, our God, who has his seat on high, **6** who stoops down to see in heaven and in the earth? **7** He raises up the poor out of the dust, and lifts up the needy from the ash heap, **8** that he may set him with princes, even with the princes of his people. **9** He settles the barren woman in her home as a joyful mother of children. Praise Yah!

## 114

**1** When Israel went out of Egypt, the house of Jacob from a people of foreign language, **2** Judah became his sanctuary, Israel his dominion. **3** The sea saw it, and fled. The Jordan was driven back. **4** The mountains skipped like rams, the little hills like lambs. **5** What was it, you sea, that you fled? You Jordan, that you turned back? **6** You mountains, that you skipped like rams? You little hills, like lambs? **7** Tremble, you earth, at the presence of the Lord, at the presence of the God of Jacob, **8** who turned the rock into a pool of water, the flint into a spring of waters.

## 115

**1** Not to us, Yahweh, not to us, but to your name give glory, for your loving kindness, and for your truth's sake. **2** Why should the nations say, "Where is their God, now?" **3** But our God is in the heavens. He does whatever he pleases. **4** Their idols are silver and gold, the work of men's hands. **5** They have mouths, but they don't speak. They have eyes, but they don't see. **6** They have ears, but they don't hear. They have noses, but they don't smell. **7** They have hands, but they don't feel. They have feet, but they don't walk, neither do they speak through their throat. **8** Those who make them will be like them; yes, everyone who trusts in them. **9** Israel, trust in Yahweh! He is their help and their shield. **10** House of Aaron, trust in Yahweh! He is their help and their shield. **11** You who fear Yahweh, trust in Yahweh! He is their help and their shield. **12** Yahweh remembers us. He will bless us. He will bless the house of Israel. He will bless the house of Aaron. **13** He will bless those who fear Yahweh, both small and great. **14** May Yahweh increase you more and more, you and your children. **15** Blessed are you by Yahweh, who made heaven and earth. **16** The heavens are Yahweh's heavens, but he has given the earth to the children of men. **17** The dead don't praise Yah, nor any who go down into silence, **18** but we will bless Yah, from this time forward and forever more. Praise Yah!

## 116

**1** I love Yahweh, because he listens to my voice, and my cries for mercy. **2** Because he has turned his ear to me, therefore I will call on him as long as I live. **3** The cords of death surrounded me, the pains of Sheol[d] got a hold of me. I found trouble and sorrow. **4** Then I called on Yahweh's name: "Yahweh, I beg you, deliver my soul." **5** Yahweh is gracious and righteous. Yes, our God is merciful. **6** Yahweh preserves the simple. I was brought low, and he saved me. **7** Return to your rest, my soul, for Yahweh has dealt bountifully with you. **8** For you have delivered my soul from death, my eyes from tears, and my feet from falling. **9** I will walk before Yahweh in the land of the living. **10** I believed, therefore I said, "I was greatly afflicted." **11** I said in my haste, "All people are liars." **12** What will I give to Yahweh for all his benefits toward me? **13** I will take the cup of salvation, and call on Yahweh's name. **14** I will pay my vows to Yahweh, yes, in the presence of all his people. **15** Precious in Yahweh's sight is the death of his saints. **16**

---

Yahweh, truly I am your servant. I am your servant, the son of your servant girl. You have freed me from my chains. [17] I will offer to you the sacrifice of thanksgiving, and will call on Yahweh's name. [18] I will pay my vows to Yahweh, yes, in the presence of all his people, [19] in the courts of Yahweh's house, in the middle of you, Jerusalem. Praise Yah!

## 117

[1] Praise Yahweh, all you nations! Extol him, all you peoples! [2] For his loving kindness is great toward us. Yahweh's faithfulness endures forever. Praise Yah!

## 118

[1] Give thanks to Yahweh, for he is good, for his loving kindness endures forever. [2] Let Israel now say that his loving kindness endures forever. [3] Let the house of Aaron now say that his loving kindness endures forever. [4] Now let those who fear Yahweh say that his loving kindness endures forever. [5] Out of my distress, I called on Yah. Yah answered me with freedom. [6] Yahweh is on my side. I will not be afraid. What can man do to me? [7] Yahweh is on my side among those who help me. Therefore I will look in triumph at those who hate me. [8] It is better to take refuge in Yahweh, than to put confidence in man. [9] It is better to take refuge in Yahweh, than to put confidence in princes. [10] All the nations surrounded me, but in Yahweh's name I cut them off. [11] They surrounded me, yes, they surrounded me. In Yahweh's name I indeed cut them off. [12] They surrounded me like bees. They are quenched like the burning thorns. In Yahweh's name I cut them off. [13] You pushed me back hard, to make me fall, but Yahweh helped me. [14] Yah is my strength and song. He has become my salvation. [15] The voice of rejoicing and salvation is in the tents of the righteous. "The right hand of Yahweh does valiantly. [16] The right hand of Yahweh is exalted! The right hand of Yahweh does valiantly!" [17] I will not die, but live, and declare Yah's works. [18] Yah has punished me severely, but he has not given me over to death. [19] Open to me the gates of righteousness. I will enter into them. I will give thanks to Yah. [20] This is the gate of Yahweh; the righteous will enter into it. [21] I will give thanks to you, for you have answered me, and have become my salvation. [22] The stone which the builders rejected has become the cornerstone.[a] [23] This is Yahweh's doing. It is marvelous in our eyes. [24] This is the day that Yahweh has made. We will rejoice and be glad in it! [25] Save us now, we beg you, Yahweh! Yahweh, we beg you, send prosperity now. [26] Blessed is he who comes in Yahweh's name! We have blessed you out of Yahweh's house. [27] Yahweh is God, and he has given us light. Bind the sacrifice with cords, even to the horns of the altar. [28] You are my God, and I will give thanks to you. You are my God, I will exalt you. [29] Oh give thanks to Yahweh, for he is good, for his loving kindness endures forever.

## 119

ALEPH
[1] Blessed are those whose ways are blameless, who walk according to Yahweh's law. [2] Blessed are those who keep his statutes, who seek him with their whole heart. [3] Yes, they do nothing wrong. They walk in his ways. [4] You have commanded your precepts, that we should fully obey them. [5] Oh that my ways were steadfast to obey your statutes! [6] Then I wouldn't be disappointed, when I consider all of your commandments. [7] I will give thanks to you with uprightness of heart, when I learn your righteous judgments. [8] I will observe your statutes. Don't utterly forsake me.
BETH
[9] How can a young man keep his way pure? By living according to your word. [10] With my whole heart I have sought you. Don't let me wander from your commandments. [11] I have hidden your word in my heart, that I might not sin against you. [12] Blessed are you, Yahweh. Teach me your statutes. [13] With my lips, I have declared all the ordinances of your mouth. [14] I have rejoiced in the way of your testimonies, as much as in all riches. [15] I will meditate on your precepts, and consider your ways. [16] I will delight myself in your statutes. I will not forget your word.
GIMEL
[17] Do good to your servant. I will live and I will obey your word. [18] Open my eyes, that I may see wondrous things out of your law. [19] I am a stranger on the earth. Don't hide your commandments from me. [20] My soul is consumed with longing for your ordinances at all times. [21] You have rebuked the proud who are cursed, who wander from your commandments. [22] Take reproach and contempt away from me, for I have kept your statutes. [23] Though princes sit and slander me, your servant will meditate on your statutes. [24] Indeed your statutes are my delight, and my counselors.
DALETH
[25] My soul is laid low in the dust. Revive me according to your word! [26] I declared my ways, and you answered me. Teach me your statutes.

[27] Let me understand the teaching of your precepts! Then I will meditate on your wondrous works. [28] My soul is weary with sorrow; strengthen me according to your word. [29] Keep me from the way of deceit. Grant me your law graciously! [30] I have chosen the way of truth. I have set your ordinances before me. [31] I cling to your statutes, Yahweh. Don't let me be disappointed. [32] I run in the path of your commandments, for you have set my heart free.
HE
[33] Teach me, Yahweh, the way of your statutes. I will keep them to the end. [34] Give me understanding, and I will keep your law. Yes, I will obey it with my whole heart. [35] Direct me in the path of your commandments, for I delight in them. [36] Turn my heart toward your statutes, not toward selfish gain. [37] Turn my eyes away from looking at worthless things. Revive me in your ways. [38] Fulfill your promise to your servant, that you may be feared. [39] Take away my disgrace that I dread, for your ordinances are good. [40] Behold, I long for your precepts! Revive me in your righteousness.
VAV
[41] Let your loving kindness also come to me, Yahweh, your salvation, according to your word. [42] So I will have an answer for him who reproaches me, for I trust in your word. [43] Don't snatch the word of truth out of my mouth, for I put my hope in your ordinances. [44] So I will obey your law continually, forever and ever. [45] I will walk in liberty, for I have sought your precepts. [46] I will also speak of your statutes before kings, and will not be disappointed. [47] I will delight myself in your commandments, because I love them. [48] I reach out my hands for your commandments, which I love. I will meditate on your statutes.
ZAYIN
[49] Remember your word to your servant, because you gave me hope. [50] This is my comfort in my affliction, for your word has revived me. [51] The arrogant mock me excessively, but I don't swerve from your law. [52] I remember your ordinances of old, Yahweh, and have comforted myself. [53] Indignation has taken hold on me, because of the wicked who forsake your law. [54] Your statutes have been my songs in the house where I live. [55] I have remembered your name, Yahweh, in the night, and I obey your law. [56] This is my way, that I keep your precepts.
HETH
[57] Yahweh is my portion. I promised to obey your words. [58] I sought your favor with my whole heart. Be merciful to me according to your word. [59] I considered my ways, and turned my steps to your statutes. [60] I will hurry, and not delay, to obey your commandments. [61] The ropes of the wicked bind me, but I won't forget your law. [62] At midnight I will rise to give thanks to you, because of your righteous ordinances. [63] I am a friend of all those who fear you, of those who observe your precepts. [64] The earth is full of your loving kindness, Yahweh. Teach me your statutes.
TETH
[65] You have treated your servant well, according to your word, Yahweh. [66] Teach me good judgment and knowledge, for I believe in your commandments. [67] Before I was afflicted, I went astray; but now I observe your word. [68] You are good, and do good. Teach me your statutes. [69] The proud have smeared a lie upon me. With my whole heart, I will keep your precepts. [70] Their heart is as callous as the fat, but I delight in your law. [71] It is good for me that I have been afflicted, that I may learn your statutes. [72] The law of your mouth is better to me than thousands of pieces of gold and silver.
YODH
[73] Your hands have made me and formed me. Give me understanding, that I may learn your commandments. [74] Those who fear you will see me and be glad, because I have put my hope in your word. [75] Yahweh, I know that your judgments are righteous, that in faithfulness you have afflicted me. [76] Please let your loving kindness be for my comfort, according to your word to your servant. [77] Let your tender mercies come to me, that I may live; for your law is my delight. [78] Let the proud be disappointed, for they have overthrown me wrongfully. I will meditate on your precepts. [79] Let those who fear you turn to me. They will know your statutes. [80] Let my heart be blameless toward your decrees, that I may not be disappointed.
KAPF
[81] My soul faints for your salvation. I hope in your word. [82] My eyes fail for your word. I say, "When will you comfort me?" [83] For I have become like a wineskin in the smoke. I don't forget your statutes. [84] How many are the days of your servant? When will you execute judgment on those who persecute me? [85] The proud have dug pits for me, contrary to your law. [86] All of your commandments are faithful. They persecute me wrongfully. Help me! [87] They had almost wiped me from the earth, but I didn't forsake your precepts. [88] Preserve my life

according to your loving kindness, so I will obey the statutes of your mouth.

LAMEDH

[89] Yahweh, your word is settled in heaven forever. [90] Your faithfulness is to all generations. You have established the earth, and it remains. [91] Your laws remain to this day, for all things serve you. [92] Unless your law had been my delight, I would have perished in my affliction. [93] I will never forget your precepts, for with them, you have revived me. [94] I am yours. Save me, for I have sought your precepts. [95] The wicked have waited for me, to destroy me. I will consider your statutes. [96] I have seen a limit to all perfection, but your commands are boundless.

MEM

[97] How I love your law! It is my meditation all day. [98] Your commandments make me wiser than my enemies, for your commandments are always with me. [99] I have more understanding than all my teachers, for your testimonies are my meditation. [100] I understand more than the aged, because I have kept your precepts. [101] I have kept my feet from every evil way, that I might observe your word. [102] I have not turned away from your ordinances, for you have taught me. [103] How sweet are your promises to my taste, more than honey to my mouth! [104] Through your precepts, I get understanding; therefore I hate every false way.

NUN

[105] Your word is a lamp to my feet, and a light for my path. [106] I have sworn, and have confirmed it, that I will obey your righteous ordinances. [107] I am afflicted very much. Revive me, Yahweh, according to your word. [108] Accept, I beg you, the willing offerings of my mouth. Yahweh, teach me your ordinances. [109] My soul is continually in my hand, yet I won't forget your law. [110] The wicked have laid a snare for me, yet I haven't gone astray from your precepts. [111] I have taken your testimonies as a heritage forever, for they are the joy of my heart. [112] I have set my heart to perform your statutes forever, even to the end.

SAMEKH

[113] I hate double-minded men, but I love your law. [114] You are my hiding place and my shield. I hope in your word. [115] Depart from me, you evildoers, that I may keep the commandments of my God. [116] Uphold me according to your word, that I may live. Let me not be ashamed of my hope. [117] Hold me up, and I will be safe, and will have respect for your statutes continually. [118] You reject all those who stray from your statutes, for their deceit is in vain. [119] You put away all the wicked of the earth like dross. Therefore I love your testimonies. [120] My flesh trembles for fear of you. I am afraid of your judgments.

AYIN

[121] I have done what is just and righteous. Don't leave me to my oppressors. [122] Ensure your servant's well-being. Don't let the proud oppress me. [123] My eyes fail looking for your salvation, for your righteous word. [124] Deal with your servant according to your loving kindness. Teach me your statutes. [125] I am your servant. Give me understanding, that I may know your testimonies. [126] It is time to act, Yahweh, for they break your law. [127] Therefore I love your commandments more than gold, yes, more than pure gold. [128] Therefore I consider all of your precepts to be right. I hate every false way.

PE

[129] Your testimonies are wonderful, therefore my soul keeps them. [130] The entrance of your words gives light. It gives understanding to the simple. [131] I opened my mouth wide and panted, for I longed for your commandments. [132] Turn to me, and have mercy on me, as you always do to those who love your name. [133] Establish my footsteps in your word. Don't let any iniquity have dominion over me. [134] Redeem me from the oppression of man, so I will observe your precepts. [135] Make your face shine on your servant. Teach me your statutes. [136] Streams of tears run down my eyes, because they don't observe your law.

TZADHE

[137] You are righteous, Yahweh. Your judgments are upright. [138] You have commanded your statutes in righteousness. They are fully trustworthy. [139] My zeal wears me out, because my enemies ignore your words. [140] Your promises have been thoroughly tested, and your servant loves them. [141] I am small and despised. I don't forget your precepts. [142] Your righteousness is an everlasting righteousness. Your law is truth. [143] Trouble and anguish have taken hold of me. Your commandments are my delight. [144] Your testimonies are righteous forever. Give me understanding, that I may live.

QOPH

[145] I have called with my whole heart. Answer me, Yahweh! I will keep your statutes. [146] I have called to you. Save me! I will obey your statutes. [147] I rise before dawn and cry for help. I put my hope in your words. [148] My eyes stay open through the night watches, that I might meditate on your word. [149] Hear my voice according to your loving kindness. Revive me, Yahweh, according to your ordinances. [150] They

draw near who follow after wickedness. They are far from your law. [151] You are near, Yahweh. All your commandments are truth. [152] Of old I have known from your testimonies, that you have founded them forever.

RESH

[153] Consider my affliction, and deliver me, for I don't forget your law. [154] Plead my cause, and redeem me! Revive me according to your promise. [155] Salvation is far from the wicked, for they don't seek your statutes. [156] Great are your tender mercies, Yahweh. Revive me according to your ordinances. [157] Many are my persecutors and my adversaries. I haven't swerved from your testimonies. [158] I look at the faithless with loathing, because they don't observe your word. [159] Consider how I love your precepts. Revive me, Yahweh, according to your loving kindness. [160] All of your words are truth. Every one of your righteous ordinances endures forever.

SIN AND SHIN

[161] Princes have persecuted me without a cause, but my heart stands in awe of your words. [162] I rejoice at your word, as one who finds great plunder. [163] I hate and abhor falsehood. I love your law. [164] Seven times a day, I praise you, because of your righteous ordinances. [165] Those who love your law have great peace. Nothing causes them to stumble. [166] I have hoped for your salvation, Yahweh. I have done your commandments. [167] My soul has observed your testimonies. I love them exceedingly. [168] I have obeyed your precepts and your testimonies, for all my ways are before you.

TAV

[169] Let my cry come before you, Yahweh. Give me understanding according to your word. [170] Let my supplication come before you. Deliver me according to your word. [171] Let my lips utter praise, for you teach me your statutes. [172] Let my tongue sing of your word, for all your commandments are righteousness. [173] Let your hand be ready to help me, for I have chosen your precepts. [174] I have longed for your salvation, Yahweh. Your law is my delight. [175] Let my soul live, that I may praise you. Let your ordinances help me. [176] I have gone astray like a lost sheep. Seek your servant, for I don't forget your commandments.

# 120

A Song of Ascents.

[1] In my distress, I cried to Yahweh. He answered me. [2] Deliver my soul, Yahweh, from lying lips, from a deceitful tongue. [3] What will be given to you, and what will be done more to you, you deceitful tongue? [4] Sharp arrows of the mighty, with coals of juniper. [5] Woe is me, that I live in Meshech, that I dwell among the tents of Kedar! [6] My soul has had her dwelling too long with him who hates peace. [7] I am for peace, but when I speak, they are for war.

# 121

A Song of Ascents.

[1] I will lift up my eyes to the hills. Where does my help come from? [2] My help comes from Yahweh, who made heaven and earth. [3] He will not allow your foot to be moved. He who keeps you will not slumber. [4] Behold, he who keeps Israel will neither slumber nor sleep. [5] Yahweh is your keeper. Yahweh is your shade on your right hand. [6] The sun will not harm you by day, nor the moon by night. [7] Yahweh will keep you from all evil. He will keep your soul. [8] Yahweh will keep your going out and your coming in, from this time forward, and forever more.

# 122

A Song of Ascents. By David.

[1] I was glad when they said to me, "Let's go to Yahweh's house!" [2] Our feet are standing within your gates, Jerusalem! [3] Jerusalem is built as a city that is compact together, [4] where the tribes go up, even Yah's tribes, according to an ordinance for Israel, to give thanks to Yahweh's name. [5] For there are set thrones for judgment, the thrones of David's house. [6] Pray for the peace of Jerusalem. Those who love you will prosper. [7] Peace be within your walls, and prosperity within your palaces. [8] For my brothers' and companions' sakes, I will now say, "Peace be within you." [9] For the sake of the house of Yahweh our God, I will seek your good.

# 123

A Song of Ascents.

[1] I lift up my eyes to you, you who sit in the heavens. [2] Behold, as the eyes of servants look to the hand of their master, as the eyes of a maid to the hand of her mistress, so our eyes look to Yahweh, our God, until he has mercy on us. [3] Have mercy on us, Yahweh, have mercy on us, for we have endured much contempt. [4] Our soul is exceedingly filled with the scoffing of those who are at ease, with the contempt of the proud.

# 124

A Song of Ascents. By David.

[1] If it had not been Yahweh who was on our side, let Israel now say, [2] if it had not been Yahweh who was on our side, when men rose up

against us, ³ then they would have swallowed us up alive, when their wrath was kindled against us, ⁴ then the waters would have overwhelmed us, the stream would have gone over our soul. ⁵ Then the proud waters would have gone over our soul. ⁶ Blessed be Yahweh, who has not given us as a prey to their teeth. ⁷ Our soul has escaped like a bird out of the fowler's snare. The snare is broken, and we have escaped. ⁸ Our help is in Yahweh's name, who made heaven and earth.

## 125

A Song of Ascents.
¹ Those who trust in Yahweh are as Mount Zion, which can't be moved, but remains forever. ² As the mountains surround Jerusalem, so Yahweh surrounds his people from this time forward and forever more. ³ For the scepter of wickedness won't remain over the allotment of the righteous, so that the righteous won't use their hands to do evil. ⁴ Do good, Yahweh, to those who are good, to those who are upright in their hearts. ⁵ But as for those who turn away to their crooked ways, Yahweh will lead them away with the workers of iniquity. Peace be on Israel.

## 126

A Song of Ascents.
¹ When Yahweh brought back those who returned to Zion, we were like those who dream. ² Then our mouth was filled with laughter, and our tongue with singing. Then they said among the nations, "Yahweh has done great things for them." ³ Yahweh has done great things for us, and we are glad. ⁴ Restore our fortunes again, Yahweh, like the streams in the Negev. ⁵ Those who sow in tears will reap in joy. ⁶ He who goes out weeping, carrying seed for sowing, will certainly come again with joy, carrying his sheaves.

## 127

A Song of Ascents. By Solomon.
¹ Unless Yahweh builds the house, they who build it labor in vain. Unless Yahweh watches over the city, the watchman guards it in vain. ² It is vain for you to rise up early, to stay up late, eating the bread of toil, for he gives sleep to his loved ones. ³ Behold, children are a heritage of Yahweh. The fruit of the womb is his reward. ⁴ As arrows in the hand of a mighty man, so are the children of youth. ⁵ Happy is the man who has his quiver full of them. They won't be disappointed when they speak with their enemies in the gate.

## 128

A Song of Ascents.
¹ Blessed is everyone who fears Yahweh,
who walks in his ways. ² For you will eat the labor of your hands. You will be happy, and it will be well with you. ³ Your wife will be as a fruitful vine in the innermost parts of your house, your children like olive shoots around your table. ⁴ Behold, this is how the man who fears Yahweh is blessed. ⁵ May Yahweh bless you out of Zion, and may you see the good of Jerusalem all the days of your life. ⁶ Yes, may you see your children's children. Peace be upon Israel.

## 129

A Song of Ascents.
¹ Many times they have afflicted me from my youth up. Let Israel now say: ² many times they have afflicted me from my youth up, yet they have not prevailed against me. ³ The plowers plowed on my back. They made their furrows long. ⁴ Yahweh is righteous. He has cut apart the cords of the wicked. ⁵ Let them be disappointed and turned backward, all those who hate Zion. ⁶ Let them be as the grass on the housetops, which withers before it grows up, ⁷ with which the reaper doesn't fill his hand, nor he who binds sheaves, his bosom. ⁸ Neither do those who go by say, "The blessing of Yahweh be on you. We bless you in Yahweh's name."

## 130

A Song of Ascents.
¹ Out of the depths I have cried to you, Yahweh. ² Lord, hear my voice. Let your ears be attentive to the voice of my petitions. ³ If you, Yah, kept a record of sins, Lord, who could stand? ⁴ But there is forgiveness with you, therefore you are feared. ⁵ I wait for Yahweh. My soul waits. I hope in his word. ⁶ My soul longs for the Lord more than watchmen long for the morning, more than watchmen for the morning. ⁷ Israel, hope in Yahweh, for there is loving kindness with Yahweh. Abundant redemption is with him. ⁸ He will redeem Israel from all their sins.

## 131

A Song of Ascents. By David.
¹ Yahweh, my heart isn't arrogant, nor my eyes lofty; nor do I concern myself with great matters, or things too wonderful for me. ² Surely I have stilled and quieted my soul, like a weaned child with his mother, like a weaned child is my soul within me. ³ Israel, hope in Yahweh, from this time forward and forever more.

## 132

A Song of Ascents.
¹ Yahweh, remember David and all his affliction, ² how he swore to Yahweh, and vowed to the Mighty One of Jacob: ³ "Surely I will not come into the structure of my house, nor go up into my bed; ⁴ I will not give sleep to my eyes, or slumber to my eyelids, ⁵ until I find out a place for Yahweh, a dwelling for the Mighty One of Jacob." ⁶ Behold, we heard of it in Ephrathah. We found it in the field of Jaar. ⁷ "We will go into his dwelling place. We will worship at his footstool." ⁸ Arise, Yahweh, into your resting place, you, and the ark of your strength. ⁹ Let your priests be clothed with righteousness. Let your saints shout for joy! ¹⁰ For your servant David's sake, don't turn away the face of your anointed one. ¹¹ Yahweh has sworn to David in truth. He will not turn from it: "I will set the fruit of your body on your throne. ¹² If your children will keep my covenant, my testimony that I will teach them, their children also will sit on your throne forever more." ¹³ For Yahweh has chosen Zion. He has desired it for his habitation. ¹⁴ "This is my resting place forever. I will live here, for I have desired it. ¹⁵ I will abundantly bless her provision. I will satisfy her poor with bread. ¹⁶ I will also clothe her priests with salvation. Her saints will shout aloud for joy. ¹⁷ I will make the horn of David to bud there. I have ordained a lamp for my anointed. ¹⁸ I will clothe his enemies with shame, but on himself, his crown will shine."

## 133

A Song of Ascents. By David.
¹ See how good and how pleasant it is for brothers to live together in unity! ² It is like the precious oil on the head, that ran down on the beard, even Aaron's beard, that came down on the edge of his robes, ³ like the dew of Hermon, that comes down on the hills of Zion; for there Yahweh gives the blessing, even life forever more.

## 134

A Song of Ascents.
¹ Look! Praise Yahweh, all you servants of Yahweh, who stand by night in Yahweh's house! ² Lift up your hands in the sanctuary. Praise Yahweh! ³ May Yahweh bless you from Zion, even he who made heaven and earth.

## 135

¹ Praise Yah! Praise Yahweh's name! Praise him, you servants of Yahweh, ² you who stand in Yahweh's house, in the courts of our God's house. ³ Praise Yah, for Yahweh is good. Sing praises to his name, for that is pleasant. ⁴ For Yah has chosen Jacob for himself, Israel for his own possession. ⁵ For I know that Yahweh is great, that our Lord is above all gods. ⁶ Whatever Yahweh pleased, that he has done, in heaven and in earth, in the seas and in all deeps. ⁷ He causes the clouds to rise from the ends of the earth. He makes lightnings with the rain. He brings the wind out of his treasuries. ⁸ He struck the firstborn of Egypt, both of man and animal. ⁹ He sent signs and wonders into the middle of you, Egypt, on Pharaoh, and on all his servants. ¹⁰ He struck many nations, and killed mighty kings— ¹¹ Sihon king of the Amorites, Og king of Bashan, and all the kingdoms of Canaan— ¹² and gave their land for a heritage, a heritage to Israel, his people. ¹³ Your name, Yahweh, endures forever; your renown, Yahweh, throughout all generations. ¹⁴ For Yahweh will judge his people and will have compassion on his servants. ¹⁵ The idols of the nations are silver and gold, the work of men's hands. ¹⁶ They have mouths, but they can't speak. They have eyes, but they can't see. ¹⁷ They have ears, but they can't hear, neither is there any breath in their mouths. ¹⁸ Those who make them will be like them, yes, everyone who trusts in them. ¹⁹ House of Israel, praise Yahweh! House of Aaron, praise Yahweh! ²⁰ House of Levi, praise Yahweh! You who fear Yahweh, praise Yahweh! ²¹ Blessed be Yahweh from Zion, who dwells in Jerusalem. Praise Yah!

## 136

¹ Give thanks to Yahweh, for he is good, for his loving kindness endures forever. ² Give thanks to the God of gods, for his loving kindness endures forever. ³ Give thanks to the Lord of lords, for his loving kindness endures forever; ⁴ to him who alone does great wonders, for his loving kindness endures forever; ⁵ to him who by understanding made the heavens, for his loving kindness endures forever; ⁶ to him who spread out the earth above the waters, for his loving kindness endures forever; ⁷ to him who made the great lights, for his loving kindness endures forever; ⁸ the sun to rule by day, for his loving kindness endures forever; ⁹ the moon and stars to rule by night, for his loving kindness endures forever; ¹⁰ to him who struck down the Egyptian firstborn, for his loving kindness endures forever; ¹¹ and brought out Israel from among them, for his loving kindness endures forever; ¹² with a strong hand, and with an outstretched arm, for his loving kindness endures forever; ¹³ to him who divided the Red Sea apart, for his loving kindness endures forever; ¹⁴ and made Israel to pass through the middle of it, for his loving kindness endures forever; ¹⁵ but overthrew Pharaoh and his

army in the Red Sea, for his loving kindness endures forever; [16] to him who led his people through the wilderness, for his loving kindness endures forever; [17] to him who struck great kings, for his loving kindness endures forever; [18] and killed mighty kings, for his loving kindness endures forever; [19] Sihon king of the Amorites, for his loving kindness endures forever; [20] Og king of Bashan, for his loving kindness endures forever; [21] and gave their land as an inheritance, for his loving kindness endures forever; [22] even a heritage to Israel his servant, for his loving kindness endures forever; [23] who remembered us in our low estate, for his loving kindness endures forever; [24] and has delivered us from our adversaries, for his loving kindness endures forever; [25] who gives food to every creature, for his loving kindness endures forever. [26] Oh give thanks to the God of heaven, for his loving kindness endures forever.

## 137

[1] By the rivers of Babylon, there we sat down. Yes, we wept, when we remembered Zion. [2] On the willows in that land, we hung up our harps. [3] For there, those who led us captive asked us for songs. Those who tormented us demanded songs of joy: "Sing us one of the songs of Zion!" [4] How can we sing Yahweh's song in a foreign land? [5] If I forget you, Jerusalem, let my right hand forget its skill. [6] Let my tongue stick to the roof of my mouth if I don't remember you, if I don't prefer Jerusalem above my chief joy. [7] Remember, Yahweh, against the children of Edom in the day of Jerusalem, who said, "Raze it! Raze it even to its foundation!" [8] Daughter of Babylon, doomed to destruction, he will be happy who repays you, as you have done to us. [9] Happy shall he be, who takes and dashes your little ones against the rock.

## 138

By David.

[1] I will give you thanks with my whole heart. Before the gods,[a] I will sing praises to you. [2] I will bow down toward your holy temple, and give thanks to your Name for your loving kindness and for your truth; for you have exalted your Name and your Word above all. [3] In the day that I called, you answered me. You encouraged me with strength in my soul. [4] All the kings of the earth will give you thanks, Yahweh, for they have heard the words of your mouth. [5] Yes, they will sing of the ways of Yahweh, for Yahweh's glory is great! [6] For though Yahweh is high, yet he looks after the lowly; but he knows the proud from afar. [7] Though I walk in the middle of trouble, you will revive me. You will stretch out your hand against the wrath of my enemies. Your right hand will save me. [8] Yahweh will fulfill that which concerns me. Your loving kindness, Yahweh, endures forever. Don't forsake the works of your own hands.

## 139

For the Chief Musician. A Psalm by David.

[1] Yahweh, you have searched me, and you know me. [2] You know my sitting down and my rising up. You perceive my thoughts from afar. [3] You search out my path and my lying down, and are acquainted with all my ways. [4] For there is not a word on my tongue, but behold, Yahweh, you know it altogether. [5] You hem me in behind and before. You laid your hand on me. [6] This knowledge is beyond me. It's lofty. I can't attain it. [7] Where could I go from your Spirit? Or where could I flee from your presence? [8] If I ascend up into heaven, you are there. If I make my bed in Sheol,[b] behold, you are there! [9] If I take the wings of the dawn, and settle in the uttermost parts of the sea, [10] even there your hand will lead me, and your right hand will hold me. [11] If I say, "Surely the darkness will overwhelm me. The light around me will be night," [12] even the darkness doesn't hide from you, but the night shines as the day. The darkness is like light to you. [13] For you formed my inmost being. You knit me together in my mother's womb. [14] I will give thanks to you, for I am fearfully and wonderfully made. Your works are wonderful. My soul knows that very well. [15] My frame wasn't hidden from you, when I was made in secret, woven together in the depths of the earth. [16] Your eyes saw my body. In your book they were all written, the days that were ordained for me, when as yet there were none of them. [17] How precious to me are your thoughts, God! How vast is their sum! [18] If I would count them, they are more in number than the sand. When I wake up, I am still with you. [19] If only you, God, would kill the wicked. Get away from me, you bloodthirsty men! [20] For they speak against you wickedly. Your enemies take your name in vain. [21] Yahweh, don't I hate those who hate you? Am I not grieved with those who rise up against you? [22] I hate them with perfect hatred. They have become my enemies. [23] Search me, God, and know my heart. Try me, and know my thoughts. [24] See if there is any wicked way in me, and lead me in the everlasting way.

## 140

For the Chief Musician. A Psalm by David.

[1] Deliver me, Yahweh, from evil men. Preserve me from violent men: [2] those who devise mischief in their hearts. They continually gather themselves together for war. [3] They have sharpened their tongues like a serpent. Viper's poison is under their lips. Selah. [4] Yahweh, keep me from the hands of the wicked. Preserve me from the violent men who have determined to trip my feet. [5] The proud have hidden a snare for me, they have spread the cords of a net by the path. They have set traps for me. Selah. [6] I said to Yahweh, "You are my God." Listen to the cry of my petitions, Yahweh. [7] Yahweh, the Lord, the strength of my salvation, you have covered my head in the day of battle. [8] Yahweh, don't grant the desires of the wicked. Don't let their evil plans succeed, or they will become proud. Selah. [9] As for the head of those who surround me, let the mischief of their own lips cover them. [10] Let burning coals fall on them. Let them be thrown into the fire, into miry pits, from where they never rise. [11] An evil speaker won't be established in the earth. Evil will hunt the violent man to overthrow him. [12] I know that Yahweh will maintain the cause of the afflicted, and justice for the needy. [13] Surely the righteous will give thanks to your name. The upright will dwell in your presence.

## 141

A Psalm by David.

[1] Yahweh, I have called on you. Come to me quickly! Listen to my voice when I call to you. [2] Let my prayer be set before you like incense; the lifting up of my hands like the evening sacrifice. [3] Set a watch, Yahweh, before my mouth. Keep the door of my lips. [4] Don't incline my heart to any evil thing, to practice deeds of wickedness with men who work iniquity. Don't let me eat of their delicacies. [5] Let the righteous strike me, it is kindness; let him reprove me, it is like oil on the head; don't let my head refuse it; Yet my prayer is always against evil deeds. [6] Their judges are thrown down by the sides of the rock. They will hear my words, for they are well spoken. [7] "As when one plows and breaks up the earth, our bones are scattered at the mouth of Sheol."[c] [8] For my eyes are on you, Yahweh, the Lord. I take refuge in you. Don't leave my soul destitute. [9] Keep me from the snare which they have laid for me, from the traps of the workers of iniquity. [10] Let the wicked fall together into their own nets while I pass by.

## 142

A contemplation by David, when he was in the cave. A Prayer.

[1] I cry with my voice to Yahweh. With my voice, I ask Yahweh for mercy. [2] I pour out my complaint before him. I tell him my troubles. [3] When my spirit was overwhelmed within me, you knew my route. On the path in which I walk, they have hidden a snare for me. [4] Look on my right, and see; for there is no one who is concerned for me. Refuge has fled from me. No one cares for my soul. [5] I cried to you, Yahweh. I said, "You are my refuge, my portion in the land of the living." [6] Listen to my cry, for I am in desperate need. Deliver me from my persecutors, for they are too strong for me. [7] Bring my soul out of prison, that I may give thanks to your name. The righteous will surround me, for you will be good to me.

## 143

A Psalm by David.

[1] Hear my prayer, Yahweh. Listen to my petitions. In your faithfulness and righteousness, relieve me. [2] Don't enter into judgment with your servant, for in your sight no man living is righteous. [3] For the enemy pursues my soul. He has struck my life down to the ground. He has made me live in dark places, as those who have been long dead. [4] Therefore my spirit is overwhelmed within me. My heart within me is desolate. [5] I remember the days of old. I meditate on all your doings. I contemplate the work of your hands. [6] I spread out my hands to you. My soul thirsts for you, like a parched land. Selah. [7] Hurry to answer me, Yahweh. My spirit fails. Don't hide your face from me, so that I don't become like those who go down into the pit. [8] Cause me to hear your loving kindness in the morning, for I trust in you. Cause me to know the way in which I should walk, for I lift up my soul to you. [9] Deliver me, Yahweh, from my enemies. I flee to you to hide me. [10] Teach me to do your will, for you are my God. Your Spirit is good. Lead me in the land of uprightness. [11] Revive me, Yahweh, for your name's sake. In your righteousness, bring my soul out of trouble. [12] In your loving kindness, cut off my enemies, and destroy all those who afflict my soul, for I am your servant.

## 144

By David.

[1] Blessed be Yahweh, my rock, who trains my hands to war, and my fingers to battle— [2] my loving kindness, my fortress, my high tower,

---

[a] *138:1* The word elohim, used here, usually means "God" but can also mean "gods", "princes", or "angels".

[b] *139:8* Sheol is the place of the dead.

[c] *141:7* Sheol is the place of the dead.

my deliverer, my shield, and he in whom I take refuge, who subdues my people under me. ³ Yahweh, what is man, that you care for him? Or the son of man, that you think of him? ⁴ Man is like a breath. His days are like a shadow that passes away. ⁵ Part your heavens, Yahweh, and come down. Touch the mountains, and they will smoke. ⁶ Throw out lightning, and scatter them. Send out your arrows, and rout them. ⁷ Stretch out your hand from above, rescue me, and deliver me out of great waters, out of the hands of foreigners, ⁸ whose mouths speak deceit, whose right hand is a right hand of falsehood. ⁹ I will sing a new song to you, God. On a ten-stringed lyre, I will sing praises to you. ¹⁰ You are he who gives salvation to kings, who rescues David, his servant, from the deadly sword. ¹¹ Rescue me, and deliver me out of the hands of foreigners, whose mouths speak deceit, whose right hand is a right hand of falsehood. ¹² Then our sons will be like well-nurtured plants, our daughters like pillars carved to adorn a palace. ¹³ Our barns are full, filled with all kinds of provision. Our sheep produce thousands and ten thousands in our fields. ¹⁴ Our oxen will pull heavy loads. There is no breaking in, and no going away, and no outcry in our streets. ¹⁵ Happy are the people who are in such a situation. Happy are the people whose God is Yahweh.

## 145

A praise psalm by David.ᵃ
¹ I will exalt you, my God, the King. I will praise your name forever and ever. ² Every day I will praise you. I will extol your name forever and ever. ³ Great is Yahweh, and greatly to be praised! His greatness is unsearchable. ⁴ One generation will commend your works to another, and will declare your mighty acts. ⁵ I will meditate on the glorious majesty of your honor, on your wondrous works. ⁶ Men will speak of the might of your awesome acts. I will declare your greatness. ⁷ They will utter the memory of your great goodness, and will sing of your righteousness. ⁸ Yahweh is gracious, merciful, slow to anger, and of great loving kindness. ⁹ Yahweh is good to all. His tender mercies are over all his works. ¹⁰ All your works will give thanks to you, Yahweh. Your saints will extol you. ¹¹ They will speak of the glory of your kingdom, and talk about your power, ¹² to make known to the sons of men his mighty acts, the glory of the majesty of his kingdom. ¹³ Your kingdom is an everlasting kingdom. Your dominion endures throughout all generations. Yahweh is faithful in all his words, and loving in all his deeds.ᵇ ¹⁴ Yahweh upholds all who fall, and raises up all those who are bowed down. ¹⁵ The eyes of all wait for you. You give them their food in due season. ¹⁶ You open your hand, and satisfy the desire of every living thing. ¹⁷ Yahweh is righteous in all his ways, and gracious in all his works. ¹⁸ Yahweh is near to all those who call on him, to all who call on him in truth. ¹⁹ He will fulfill the desire of those who fear him. He also will hear their cry, and will save them. ²⁰ Yahweh preserves all those who love him, but he will destroy all the wicked. ²¹ My mouth will speak the praise of Yahweh. Let all flesh bless his holy name forever and ever.

## 146

¹ Praise Yah! Praise Yahweh, my soul. ² While I live, I will praise Yahweh. I will sing praises to my God as long as I exist. ³ Don't put your trust in princes, in a son of man in whom there is no help. ⁴ His spirit departs, and he returns to the earth. In that very day, his thoughts perish. ⁵ Happy is he who has the God of Jacob for his help, whose hope is in Yahweh, his God, ⁶ who made heaven and earth, the sea, and all that is in them; who keeps truth forever; ⁷ who executes justice for the oppressed; who gives food to the hungry. Yahweh frees the prisoners. ⁸ Yahweh opens the eyes of the blind. Yahweh raises up those who are bowed down. Yahweh loves the righteous. ⁹ Yahweh preserves the foreigners. He upholds the fatherless and widow, but he turns the way of the wicked upside down. ¹⁰ Yahweh will reign forever; your God, O Zion, to all generations. Praise Yah!

## 147

¹ Praise Yah, for it is good to sing praises to our God; for it is pleasant and fitting to praise him. ² Yahweh builds up Jerusalem. He gathers together the outcasts of Israel. ³ He heals the broken in heart, and binds up their wounds. ⁴ He counts the number of the stars. He calls them all by their names. ⁵ Great is our Lord, and mighty in power. His understanding is infinite. ⁶ Yahweh upholds the humble. He brings the wicked down to the ground. ⁷ Sing to Yahweh with thanksgiving. Sing praises on the harp to our God, ⁸ who covers the sky with clouds, who prepares rain for the earth, who makes grass grow on the mountains. ⁹ He provides food for the livestock, and for the young ravens when they call. ¹⁰ He doesn't delight in the strength of the horse. He takes no pleasure in the legs of a man. ¹¹ Yahweh takes pleasure in those who fear him, in those who hope in his loving kindness. ¹² Praise Yahweh, Jerusalem! Praise your God, Zion! ¹³ For he has strengthened the bars of your gates. He has blessed your children within you. ¹⁴ He makes peace in your borders. He fills you with the finest of the wheat. ¹⁵ He sends out his commandment to the earth. His word runs very swiftly. ¹⁶ He gives snow like wool, and scatters frost like ashes. ¹⁷ He hurls down his hail like pebbles. Who can stand before his cold? ¹⁸ He sends out his word, and melts them. He causes his wind to blow, and the waters flow. ¹⁹ He shows his word to Jacob, his statutes and his ordinances to Israel. ²⁰ He has not done this for just any nation. They don't know his ordinances. Praise Yah!

## 148

¹ Praise Yah! Praise Yahweh from the heavens! Praise him in the heights! ² Praise him, all his angels! Praise him, all his army! ³ Praise him, sun and moon! Praise him, all you shining stars! ⁴ Praise him, you heavens of heavens, you waters that are above the heavens. ⁵ Let them praise Yahweh's name, for he commanded, and they were created. ⁶ He has also established them forever and ever. He has made a decree which will not pass away. ⁷ Praise Yahweh from the earth, you great sea creatures, and all depths, ⁸ lightning and hail, snow and clouds, stormy wind, fulfilling his word, ⁹ mountains and all hills, fruit trees and all cedars, ¹⁰ wild animals and all livestock, small creatures and flying birds, ¹¹ kings of the earth and all peoples, princes and all judges of the earth, ¹² both young men and maidens, old men and children. ¹³ Let them praise Yahweh's name, for his name alone is exalted. His glory is above the earth and the heavens. ¹⁴ He has lifted up the horn of his people, the praise of all his saints, even of the children of Israel, a people near to him. Praise Yah!

## 149

¹ Praise Yahweh! Sing to Yahweh a new song, his praise in the assembly of the saints. ² Let Israel rejoice in him who made them. Let the children of Zion be joyful in their King. ³ Let them praise his name in the dance! Let them sing praises to him with tambourine and harp! ⁴ For Yahweh takes pleasure in his people. He crowns the humble with salvation. ⁵ Let the saints rejoice in honor. Let them sing for joy on their beds. ⁶ May the high praises of God be in their mouths, and a two-edged sword in their hand, ⁷ to execute vengeance on the nations, and punishments on the peoples; ⁸ to bind their kings with chains, and their nobles with fetters of iron; ⁹ to execute on them the written judgment. All his saints have this honor. Praise Yah!

## 150

¹ Praise Yah! Praise God in his sanctuary! Praise him in his heavens for his acts of power! ² Praise him for his mighty acts! Praise him according to his excellent greatness! ³ Praise him with the sounding of the trumpet! Praise him with harp and lyre! ⁴ Praise him with tambourine and dancing! Praise him with stringed instruments and flute! ⁵ Praise him with loud cymbals! Praise him with resounding cymbals! ⁶ Let everything that has breath praise Yah! Praise Yah!

# Psalm 151

*Psalm 151* is recognized as Deuterocanonical Scripture by the Greek Orthodox and Russian Orthodox Churches.

## 151

This Psalm is a genuine one of David, though extra,ᶜ composed when he fought in single combat with Goliath. ¹ I was small among my brothers, and youngest in my father's house. I tended my father's sheep. ² My hands formed a musical instrument, and my fingers tuned a lyre. ³ Who shall tell my Lord? The Lord himself, he himself hears. ⁴ He sent forth his angel and took me from my father's sheep, and he anointed me with his anointing oil. ⁵ My brothers were handsome and tall; but the Lord didn't take pleasure in them. ⁶ I went out to meet the Philistine, and he cursed me by his idols. ⁷ But I drew his own sword and beheaded him, and removed reproach from the children of Israel.

# The Proverbs

**I–XXIV. Tegsats (Reproof)**

## 1

¹ The proverbs of Solomon, the son of David, king of Israel: ² to know wisdom and instruction; to discern the words of understanding; ³ to receive instruction in wise dealing, in righteousness, justice, and equity; ⁴ to give prudence to the simple, knowledge and discretion to the young man— ⁵ that the wise man may hear, and increase in learning; that the man of understanding may attain to sound counsel; ⁶ to understand a proverb and parables, the words and riddles of the wise. ⁷ The fear of

---

ᵃ *145:0* This is an acrostic psalm, with every verse (including the second half of verse 13) starting with a consecutive letter of the Hebrew alphabet.

ᵇ *145:13* Some manuscripts omit these last two lines.

ᶜ *1:0* or, supernumerary

Yahweh[a] is the beginning of knowledge, but the foolish despise wisdom and instruction. **8** My son, listen to your father's instruction, and don't forsake your mother's teaching; **9** for they will be a garland to grace your head, and chains around your neck. **10** My son, if sinners entice you, don't consent. **11** If they say, "Come with us. Let's lie in wait for blood. Let's lurk secretly for the innocent without cause. **12** Let's swallow them up alive like Sheol,[b] and whole, like those who go down into the pit. **13** We'll find all valuable wealth. We'll fill our houses with plunder. **14** You shall cast your lot among us. We'll all have one purse"— **15** my son, don't walk on the path with them. Keep your foot from their path, **16** for their feet run to evil. They hurry to shed blood. **17** For the net is spread in vain in the sight of any bird; **18** but these lay in wait for their own blood. They lurk secretly for their own lives. **19** So are the ways of everyone who is greedy for gain. It takes away the life of its owners. **20** Wisdom calls aloud in the street. She utters her voice in the public squares. **21** She calls at the head of noisy places. At the entrance of the city gates, she utters her words: **22**"How long, you simple ones, will you love simplicity? How long will mockers delight themselves in mockery, and fools hate knowledge? **23** Turn at my reproof. Behold,[c] I will pour out my spirit on you. I will make known my words to you. **24** Because I have called, and you have refused; I have stretched out my hand, and no one has paid attention; **25** but you have ignored all my counsel, and wanted none of my reproof; **26** I also will laugh at your disaster. I will mock when calamity overtakes you, **27** when calamity overtakes you like a storm, when your disaster comes on like a whirlwind, when distress and anguish come on you. **28** Then they will call on me, but I will not answer. They will seek me diligently, but they will not find me, **29** because they hated knowledge, and didn't choose the fear of Yahweh. **30** They wanted none of my counsel. They despised all my reproof. **31** Therefore they will eat of the fruit of their own way, and be filled with their own schemes. **32** For the backsliding of the simple will kill them. The careless ease of fools will destroy them. **33** But whoever listens to me will dwell securely, and will be at ease, without fear of harm."

## 2

**1** My son, if you will receive my words, and store up my commandments within you, **2** so as to turn your ear to wisdom, and apply your heart to understanding; **3** yes, if you call out for discernment, and lift up your voice for understanding; **4** if you seek her as silver, and search for her as for hidden treasures; **5** then you will understand the fear of Yahweh, and find the knowledge of God.[d] **6** For Yahweh gives wisdom. Out of his mouth comes knowledge and understanding. **7** He lays up sound wisdom for the upright. He is a shield to those who walk in integrity, **8** that he may guard the paths of justice, and preserve the way of his saints. **9** Then you will understand righteousness and justice, equity and every good path. **10** For wisdom will enter into your heart. Knowledge will be pleasant to your soul. **11** Discretion will watch over you. Understanding will keep you, **12** to deliver you from the way of evil, from the men who speak perverse things, **13** who forsake the paths of uprightness, to walk in the ways of darkness, **14** who rejoice to do evil, and delight in the perverseness of evil, **15** who are crooked in their ways, and wayward in their paths, **16** to deliver you from the strange woman, even from the foreigner who flatters with her words, **17** who forsakes the friend of her youth, and forgets the covenant of her God; **18** for her house leads down to death, her paths to the departed spirits. **19** None who go to her return again, neither do they attain to the paths of life. **20** Therefore walk in the way of good men, and keep the paths of the righteous. **21** For the upright will dwell in the land. The perfect will remain in it. **22** But the wicked will be cut off from the land. The treacherous will be rooted out of it.

## 3

**1** My son, don't forget my teaching, but let your heart keep my commandments, **2** for they will add to you length of days, years of life, and peace. **3** Don't let kindness and truth forsake you. Bind them around your neck. Write them on the tablet of your heart. **4** So you will find favor, and good understanding in the sight of God and man. **5** Trust in Yahweh with all your heart, and don't lean on your own understanding. **6** In all your ways acknowledge him, and he will make your paths straight. **7** Don't be wise in your own eyes. Fear Yahweh, and depart from evil. **8** It will be health to your body, and nourishment to your bones. **9** Honor Yahweh with your substance, with the first fruits of all your increase; **10** so your barns will be filled with plenty, and your vats will overflow with new wine. **11** My son, don't despise Yahweh's discipline, neither be weary of his correction; **12** for whom Yahweh

loves, he corrects, even as a father reproves the son in whom he delights. **13** Happy is the man who finds wisdom, the man who gets understanding. **14** For her good profit is better than getting silver, and her return is better than fine gold. **15** She is more precious than rubies. None of the things you can desire are to be compared to her. **16** Length of days is in her right hand. In her left hand are riches and honor. **17** Her ways are ways of pleasantness. All her paths are peace. **18** She is a tree of life to those who lay hold of her. Happy is everyone who retains her. **19** By wisdom Yahweh founded the earth. By understanding, he established the heavens. **20** By his knowledge, the depths were broken up, and the skies drop down the dew. **21** My son, let them not depart from your eyes. Keep sound wisdom and discretion, **22** so they will be life to your soul, and grace for your neck. **23** Then you shall walk in your way securely. Your foot won't stumble. **24** When you lie down, you will not be afraid. Yes, you will lie down, and your sleep will be sweet. **25** Don't be afraid of sudden fear, neither of the desolation of the wicked, when it comes; **26** for Yahweh will be your confidence, and will keep your foot from being taken. **27** Don't withhold good from those to whom it is due, when it is in the power of your hand to do it. **28** Don't say to your neighbor, "Go, and come again; tomorrow I will give it to you," when you have it by you. **29** Don't devise evil against your neighbor, since he dwells securely by you. **30** Don't strive with a man without cause, if he has done you no harm. **31** Don't envy the man of violence. Choose none of his ways. **32** For the perverse is an abomination to Yahweh, but his friendship is with the upright. **33** Yahweh's curse is in the house of the wicked, but he blesses the habitation of the righteous. **34** Surely he mocks the mockers, but he gives grace to the humble. **35** The wise will inherit glory, but shame will be the promotion of fools.

## 4

**1** Listen, sons, to a father's instruction. Pay attention and know understanding; **2** for I give you sound learning. Don't forsake my law. **3** For I was a son to my father, tender and an only child in the sight of my mother. **4** He taught me, and said to me: "Let your heart retain my words. Keep my commandments, and live. **5** Get wisdom. Get understanding. Don't forget, and don't deviate from the words of my mouth. **6** Don't forsake her, and she will preserve you. Love her, and she will keep you. **7** Wisdom is supreme. Get wisdom. Yes, though it costs all your possessions, get understanding. **8** Esteem her, and she will exalt you. She will bring you to honor when you embrace her. **9** She will give to your head a garland of grace. She will deliver a crown of splendor to you." **10** Listen, my son, and receive my sayings. The years of your life will be many. **11** I have taught you in the way of wisdom. I have led you in straight paths. **12** When you go, your steps will not be hampered. When you run, you will not stumble. **13** Take firm hold of instruction. Don't let her go. Keep her, for she is your life. **14** Don't enter into the path of the wicked. Don't walk in the way of evil men. **15** Avoid it, and don't pass by it. Turn from it, and pass on. **16** For they don't sleep unless they do evil. Their sleep is taken away, unless they make someone fall. **17** For they eat the bread of wickedness and drink the wine of violence. **18** But the path of the righteous is like the dawning light that shines more and more until the perfect day. **19** The way of the wicked is like darkness. They don't know what they stumble over. **20** My son, attend to my words. Turn your ear to my sayings. **21** Let them not depart from your eyes. Keep them in the center of your heart. **22** For they are life to those who find them, and health to their whole body. **23** Keep your heart with all diligence, for out of it is the wellspring of life. **24** Put away from yourself a perverse mouth. Put corrupt lips far from you. **25** Let your eyes look straight ahead. Fix your gaze directly before you. **26** Make the path of your feet level. Let all of your ways be established. **27** Don't turn to the right hand nor to the left. Remove your foot from evil.

## 5

**1** My son, pay attention to my wisdom. Turn your ear to my understanding, **2** that you may maintain discretion, that your lips may preserve knowledge. **3** For the lips of an adulteress drip honey. Her mouth is smoother than oil, **4** but in the end she is as bitter as wormwood, and as sharp as a two-edged sword. **5** Her feet go down to death. Her steps lead straight to Sheol.[e] **6** She gives no thought to the way of life. Her ways are crooked, and she doesn't know it. **7** Now therefore, my sons, listen to me. Don't depart from the words of my mouth. **8** Remove your way far from her. Don't come near the door of her house, **9** lest you give your honor to others, and your years to the cruel one; **10** lest strangers feast on your wealth, and your labors enrich

[a] 1:7 "Yahweh" is God's proper Name, sometimes rendered "LORD" (all caps) in other translations.

[b] 1:12 Sheol is the place of the dead.
[c] 1:23 "Behold", from "הִנֵּה", means look at, take notice, observe, see, or gaze at. It is often used as an interjection.
[d] 2:5 The Hebrew word rendered "God" is "אֱלֹהִים" (Elohim).

[e] 5:5 Sheol is the place of the dead.

another man's house. ¹¹ You will groan at your latter end, when your flesh and your body are consumed, ¹² and say, "How I have hated instruction, and my heart despised reproof. ¹³ I haven't obeyed the voice of my teachers, nor turned my ear to those who instructed me! ¹⁴ I have come to the brink of utter ruin, among the gathered assembly." ¹⁵ Drink water out of your own cistern, running water out of your own well. ¹⁶ Should your springs overflow in the streets, streams of water in the public squares? ¹⁷ Let them be for yourself alone, not for strangers with you. ¹⁸ Let your spring be blessed. Rejoice in the wife of your youth. ¹⁹ A loving doe and a graceful deer— let her breasts satisfy you at all times. Be captivated always with her love. ²⁰ For why should you, my son, be captivated with an adulteress? Why embrace the bosom of another? ²¹ For the ways of man are before Yahweh's eyes. He examines all his paths. ²² The evil deeds of the wicked ensnare him. The cords of his sin hold him firmly. ²³ He will die for lack of instruction. In the greatness of his folly, he will go astray.

## 6

¹ My son, if you have become collateral for your neighbor, if you have struck your hands in pledge for a stranger, ² you are trapped by the words of your mouth; you are ensnared with the words of your mouth. ³ Do this now, my son, and deliver yourself, since you have come into the hand of your neighbor. Go, humble yourself. Press your plea with your neighbor. ⁴ Give no sleep to your eyes, nor slumber to your eyelids. ⁵ Free yourself, like a gazelle from the hand of the hunter, like a bird from the snare of the fowler. ⁶ Go to the ant, you sluggard. Consider her ways, and be wise; ⁷ which having no chief, overseer, or ruler, ⁸ provides her bread in the summer, and gathers her food in the harvest. ⁹ How long will you sleep, sluggard? When will you arise out of your sleep? ¹⁰ A little sleep, a little slumber, a little folding of the hands to sleep— ¹¹ so your poverty will come as a robber, and your scarcity as an armed man. ¹² A worthless person, a man of iniquity, is he who walks with a perverse mouth, ¹³ who winks with his eyes, who signals with his feet, who motions with his fingers, ¹⁴ in whose heart is perverseness, who devises evil continually, who always sows discord. ¹⁵ Therefore his calamity will come suddenly. He will be broken suddenly, and that without remedy. ¹⁶ There are six things which Yahweh hates; yes, seven which are an abomination to him: ¹⁷ arrogant eyes, a lying tongue, hands that shed innocent blood, ¹⁸ a heart that devises wicked schemes, feet that are swift in running to mischief, ¹⁹ a false witness who utters lies, and he who sows discord among brothers. ²⁰ My son, keep your father's commandment, and don't forsake your mother's teaching. ²¹ Bind them continually on your heart. Tie them around your neck. ²² When you walk, it will lead you. When you sleep, it will watch over you. When you awake, it will talk with you. ²³ For the commandment is a lamp, and the law is light. Reproofs of instruction are the way of life, ²⁴ to keep you from the immoral woman, from the flattery of the wayward wife's tongue. ²⁵ Don't lust after her beauty in your heart, neither let her captivate you with her eyelids. ²⁶ For a prostitute reduces you to a piece of bread. The adulteress hunts for your precious life. ²⁷ Can a man scoop fire into his lap, and his clothes not be burned? ²⁸ Or can one walk on hot coals, and his feet not be scorched? ²⁹ So is he who goes in to his neighbor's wife. Whoever touches her will not be unpunished. ³⁰ Men don't despise a thief if he steals to satisfy himself when he is hungry, ³¹ but if he is found, he shall restore seven times. He shall give all the wealth of his house. ³² He who commits adultery with a woman is void of understanding. He who does it destroys his own soul. ³³ He will get wounds and dishonor. His reproach will not be wiped away. ³⁴ For jealousy arouses the fury of the husband. He won't spare in the day of vengeance. ³⁵ He won't regard any ransom, neither will he rest content, though you give many gifts.

## 7

¹ My son, keep my words. Lay up my commandments within you. ² Keep my commandments and live! Guard my teaching as the apple of your eye. ³ Bind them on your fingers. Write them on the tablet of your heart. ⁴ Tell wisdom, "You are my sister." Call understanding your relative, ⁵ that they may keep you from the strange woman, from the foreigner who flatters with her words. ⁶ For at the window of my house, I looked out through my lattice. ⁷ I saw among the simple ones. I discerned among the youths a young man void of understanding, ⁸ passing through the street near her corner, he went the way to her house, ⁹ in the twilight, in the evening of the day, in the middle of the night and in the darkness. ¹⁰ Behold, there a woman met him with the attire of a prostitute, and with crafty intent. ¹¹ She is loud and defiant. Her feet don't stay in her house. ¹² Now she is in the streets, now in the squares, and lurking at every corner. ¹³ So she caught him, and kissed him. With an impudent face she said to him: ¹⁴"Sacrifices of peace offerings are with me. Today I have paid my vows. ¹⁵ Therefore I came

out to meet you, to diligently seek your face, and I have found you. ¹⁶ I have spread my couch with carpets of tapestry, with striped cloths of the yarn of Egypt. ¹⁷ I have perfumed my bed with myrrh, aloes, and cinnamon. ¹⁸ Come, let's take our fill of loving until the morning. Let's solace ourselves with loving. ¹⁹ For my husband isn't at home. He has gone on a long journey. ²⁰ He has taken a bag of money with him. He will come home at the full moon." ²¹ With persuasive words, she led him astray. With the flattering of her lips, she seduced him. ²² He followed her immediately, as an ox goes to the slaughter, as a fool stepping into a noose. ²³ Until an arrow strikes through his liver, as a bird hurries to the snare, and doesn't know that it will cost his life. ²⁴ Now therefore, sons, listen to me. Pay attention to the words of my mouth. ²⁵ Don't let your heart turn to her ways. Don't go astray in her paths, ²⁶ for she has thrown down many wounded. Yes, all her slain are a mighty army. ²⁷ Her house is the way to Sheol,ᵃ going down to the rooms of death.

## 8

¹ Doesn't wisdom cry out? Doesn't understanding raise her voice? ² On the top of high places by the way, where the paths meet, she stands. ³ Beside the gates, at the entry of the city, at the entry doors, she cries aloud: ⁴"I call to you men! I send my voice to the sons of mankind. ⁵ You simple, understand prudence! You fools, be of an understanding heart! ⁶ Hear, for I will speak excellent things. The opening of my lips is for right things. ⁷ For my mouth speaks truth. Wickedness is an abomination to my lips. ⁸ All the words of my mouth are in righteousness. There is nothing crooked or perverse in them. ⁹ They are all plain to him who understands, right to those who find knowledge. ¹⁰ Receive my instruction rather than silver, knowledge rather than choice gold. ¹¹ For wisdom is better than rubies. All the things that may be desired can't be compared to it. ¹²"I, wisdom, have made prudence my dwelling. Find out knowledge and discretion. ¹³ The fear of Yahweh is to hate evil. I hate pride, arrogance, the evil way, and the perverse mouth. ¹⁴ Counsel and sound knowledge are mine. I have understanding and power. ¹⁵ By me kings reign, and princes decree justice. ¹⁶ By me princes rule, nobles, and all the righteous rulers of the earth. ¹⁷ I love those who love me. Those who seek me diligently will find me. ¹⁸ With me are riches, honor, enduring wealth, and prosperity. ¹⁹ My fruit is better than gold, yes, than fine gold, my yield than choice silver. ²⁰ I walk in the way of righteousness, in the middle of the paths of justice, ²¹ that I may give wealth to those who love me. I fill their treasuries. ²²"Yahweh possessed me in the beginning of his work, before his deeds of old. ²³ I was set up from everlasting, from the beginning, before the earth existed. ²⁴ When there were no depths, I was born, when there were no springs abounding with water. ²⁵ Before the mountains were settled in place, before the hills, I was born; ²⁶ while as yet he had not made the earth, nor the fields, nor the beginning of the dust of the world. ²⁷ When he established the heavens, I was there. When he set a circle on the surface of the deep, ²⁸ when he established the clouds above, when the springs of the deep became strong, ²⁹ when he gave to the sea its boundary, that the waters should not violate his commandment, when he marked out the foundations of the earth, ³⁰ then I was the craftsman by his side. I was a delight day by day, always rejoicing before him, ³¹ rejoicing in his whole world. My delight was with the sons of men. ³²"Now therefore, my sons, listen to me, for blessed are those who keep my ways. ³³ Hear instruction, and be wise. Don't refuse it. ³⁴ Blessed is the man who hears me, watching daily at my gates, waiting at my door posts. ³⁵ For whoever finds me finds life, and will obtain favor from Yahweh. ³⁶ But he who sins against me wrongs his own soul. All those who hate me love death."

## 9

¹ Wisdom has built her house. She has carved out her seven pillars. ² She has prepared her meat. She has mixed her wine. She has also set her table. ³ She has sent out her maidens. She cries from the highest places of the city: ⁴"Whoever is simple, let him turn in here!" As for him who is void of understanding, she says to him, ⁵"Come, eat some of my bread, Drink some of the wine which I have mixed! ⁶ Leave your simple ways, and live. Walk in the way of understanding." ⁷ One who corrects a mocker invites insult. One who reproves a wicked man invites abuse. ⁸ Don't reprove a scoffer, lest he hate you. Reprove a wise person, and he will love you. ⁹ Instruct a wise person, and he will be still wiser. Teach a righteous person, and he will increase in learning. ¹⁰ The fear of Yahweh is the beginning of wisdom. The knowledge of the Holy One is understanding. ¹¹ For by me your days will be multiplied. The years of your life will be increased. ¹² If you are wise, you are wise for yourself. If you mock, you alone will bear it. ¹³ The foolish woman is loud, undisciplined, and knows nothing. ¹⁴ She sits at the door of her house, on a seat in the high places of the city, ¹⁵ to call

ᵃ 7:27 Sheol is the place of the dead.

to those who pass by, who go straight on their ways, [16]"Whoever is simple, let him turn in here." As for him who is void of understanding, she says to him, [17]"Stolen water is sweet. Food eaten in secret is pleasant." [18] But he doesn't know that the departed spirits are there, that her guests are in the depths of Sheol.[a]

## 10

[1] The proverbs of Solomon. A wise son makes a glad father; but a foolish son brings grief to his mother. [2] Treasures of wickedness profit nothing, but righteousness delivers from death. [3] Yahweh will not allow the soul of the righteous to go hungry, but he thrusts away the desire of the wicked. [4] He becomes poor who works with a lazy hand, but the hand of the diligent brings wealth. [5] He who gathers in summer is a wise son, but he who sleeps during the harvest is a son who causes shame. [6] Blessings are on the head of the righteous, but violence covers the mouth of the wicked. [7] The memory of the righteous is blessed, but the name of the wicked will rot. [8] The wise in heart accept commandments, but a chattering fool will fall. [9] He who walks blamelessly walks surely, but he who perverts his ways will be found out. [10] One who winks with the eye causes sorrow, but a chattering fool will fall. [11] The mouth of the righteous is a spring of life, but violence covers the mouth of the wicked. [12] Hatred stirs up strife, but love covers all wrongs. [13] Wisdom is found on the lips of him who has discernment, but a rod is for the back of him who is void of understanding. [14] Wise men lay up knowledge, but the mouth of the foolish is near ruin. [15] The rich man's wealth is his strong city. The destruction of the poor is their poverty. [16] The labor of the righteous leads to life. The increase of the wicked leads to sin. [17] He is in the way of life who heeds correction, but he who forsakes reproof leads others astray. [18] He who hides hatred has lying lips. He who utters a slander is a fool. [19] In the multitude of words there is no lack of disobedience, but he who restrains his lips does wisely. [20] The tongue of the righteous is like choice silver. The heart of the wicked is of little worth. [21] The lips of the righteous feed many, but the foolish die for lack of understanding. [22] Yahweh's blessing brings wealth, and he adds no trouble to it. [23] It is a fool's pleasure to do wickedness, but wisdom is a man of understanding's pleasure. [24] What the wicked fear will overtake them, but the desire of the righteous will be granted. [25] When the whirlwind passes, the wicked is no more; but the righteous stand firm forever. [26] As vinegar to the teeth, and as smoke to the eyes, so is the sluggard to those who send him. [27] The fear of Yahweh prolongs days, but the years of the wicked shall be shortened. [28] The prospect of the righteous is joy, but the hope of the wicked will perish. [29] The way of Yahweh is a stronghold to the upright, but it is a destruction to the workers of iniquity. [30] The righteous will never be removed, but the wicked will not dwell in the land. [31] The mouth of the righteous produces wisdom, but the perverse tongue will be cut off. [32] The lips of the righteous know what is acceptable, but the mouth of the wicked is perverse.

## 11

[1] A false balance is an abomination to Yahweh, but accurate weights are his delight. [2] When pride comes, then comes shame, but with humility comes wisdom. [3] The integrity of the upright shall guide them, but the perverseness of the treacherous shall destroy them. [4] Riches don't profit in the day of wrath, but righteousness delivers from death. [5] The righteousness of the blameless will direct his way, but the wicked shall fall by his own wickedness. [6] The righteousness of the upright shall deliver them, but the unfaithful will be trapped by evil desires. [7] When a wicked man dies, hope perishes, and expectation of power comes to nothing. [8] A righteous person is delivered out of trouble, and the wicked takes his place. [9] With his mouth the godless man destroys his neighbor, but the righteous will be delivered through knowledge. [10] When it goes well with the righteous, the city rejoices. When the wicked perish, there is shouting. [11] By the blessing of the upright, the city is exalted, but it is overthrown by the mouth of the wicked. [12] One who despises his neighbor is void of wisdom, but a man of understanding holds his peace. [13] One who brings gossip betrays a confidence, but one who is of a trustworthy spirit is one who keeps a secret. [14] Where there is no wise guidance, the nation falls, but in the multitude of counselors there is victory. [15] He who is collateral for a stranger will suffer for it, but he who refuses pledges of collateral is secure. [16] A gracious woman obtains honor, but violent men obtain riches. [17] The merciful man does good to his own soul, but he who is cruel troubles his own flesh. [18] Wicked people earn deceitful wages, but one who sows righteousness reaps a sure reward. [19] He who is truly righteous gets life. He who pursues evil gets death. [20] Those who are perverse in heart are an abomination to Yahweh, but those whose ways are blameless are his delight. [21] Most certainly, the evil man will not be unpunished, but the offspring[b] of the righteous will be delivered. [22] Like a gold ring in a pig's snout, is a beautiful woman who lacks discretion. [23] The desire of the righteous is only good. The expectation of the wicked is wrath. [24] There is one who scatters, and increases yet more. There is one who withholds more than is appropriate, but gains poverty. [25] The liberal soul shall be made fat. He who waters shall be watered also himself. [26] People curse someone who withholds grain, but blessing will be on the head of him who sells it. [27] He who diligently seeks good seeks favor, but he who searches after evil, it shall come to him. [28] He who trusts in his riches will fall, but the righteous shall flourish as the green leaf. [29] He who troubles his own house shall inherit the wind. The foolish shall be servant to the wise of heart. [30] The fruit of the righteous is a tree of life. He who is wise wins souls. [31] Behold, the righteous shall be repaid in the earth, how much more the wicked and the sinner!

## 12

[1] Whoever loves correction loves knowledge, but he who hates reproof is stupid. [2] A good man shall obtain favor from Yahweh, but he will condemn a man of wicked plans. [3] A man shall not be established by wickedness, but the root of the righteous shall not be moved. [4] A worthy woman is the crown of her husband, but a disgraceful wife is as rottenness in his bones. [5] The thoughts of the righteous are just, but the advice of the wicked is deceitful. [6] The words of the wicked are about lying in wait for blood, but the speech of the upright rescues them. [7] The wicked are overthrown, and are no more, but the house of the righteous shall stand. [8] A man shall be commended according to his wisdom, but he who has a warped mind shall be despised. [9] Better is he who is little known, and has a servant, than he who honors himself and lacks bread. [10] A righteous man respects the life of his animal, but the tender mercies of the wicked are cruel. [11] He who tills his land shall have plenty of bread, but he who chases fantasies is void of understanding. [12] The wicked desires the plunder of evil men, but the root of the righteous flourishes. [13] An evil man is trapped by sinfulness of lips, but the righteous shall come out of trouble. [14] A man shall be satisfied with good by the fruit of his mouth. The work of a man's hands shall be rewarded to him. [15] The way of a fool is right in his own eyes, but he who is wise listens to counsel. [16] A fool shows his annoyance the same day, but one who overlooks an insult is prudent. [17] He who is truthful testifies honestly, but a false witness lies. [18] There is one who speaks rashly like the piercing of a sword, but the tongue of the wise heals. [19] Truth's lips will be established forever, but a lying tongue is only momentary. [20] Deceit is in the heart of those who plot evil, but joy comes to the promoters of peace. [21] No mischief shall happen to the righteous, but the wicked shall be filled with evil. [22] Lying lips are an abomination to Yahweh, but those who do the truth are his delight. [23] A prudent man keeps his knowledge, but the hearts of fools proclaim foolishness. [24] The hands of the diligent ones shall rule, but laziness ends in slave labor. [25] Anxiety in a man's heart weighs it down, but a kind word makes it glad. [26] A righteous person is cautious in friendship, but the way of the wicked leads them astray. [27] The slothful man doesn't roast his game, but the possessions of diligent men are prized. [28] In the way of righteousness is life; in its path there is no death.

## 13

[1] A wise son listens to his father's instruction, but a scoffer doesn't listen to rebuke. [2] By the fruit of his lips, a man enjoys good things, but the unfaithful crave violence. [3] He who guards his mouth guards his soul. One who opens wide his lips comes to ruin. [4] The soul of the sluggard desires, and has nothing, but the desire of the diligent shall be fully satisfied. [5] A righteous man hates lies, but a wicked man brings shame and disgrace. [6] Righteousness guards the way of integrity, but wickedness overthrows the sinner. [7] There are some who pretend to be rich, yet have nothing. There are some who pretend to be poor, yet have great wealth. [8] The ransom of a man's life is his riches, but the poor hear no threats. [9] The light of the righteous shines brightly, but the lamp of the wicked is snuffed out. [10] Pride only breeds quarrels, but wisdom is with people who take advice. [11] Wealth gained dishonestly dwindles away, but he who gathers by hand makes it grow. [12] Hope deferred makes the heart sick, but when longing is fulfilled, it is a tree of life. [13] Whoever despises instruction will pay for it, but he who respects a command will be rewarded. [14] The teaching of the wise is a spring of life, to turn from the snares of death. [15] Good understanding wins favor, but the way of the unfaithful is hard. [16] Every prudent man acts from knowledge, but a fool exposes folly. [17] A wicked messenger falls into trouble, but a trustworthy envoy gains healing. [18] Poverty and shame come to him who refuses discipline, but he who heeds correction shall be honored. [19] Longing fulfilled is sweet to the soul, but fools detest turning from evil. [20] One who walks with wise men grows wise, but a companion of fools suffers harm. [21] Misfortune pursues sinners, but

---

[a] 9:18 Sheol is the place of the dead.

[b] 11:21 or, seed

prosperity rewards the righteous. ²² A good man leaves an inheritance to his children's children, but the wealth of the sinner is stored for the righteous. ²³ An abundance of food is in poor people's fields, but injustice sweeps it away. ²⁴ One who spares the rod hates his son, but one who loves him is careful to discipline him. ²⁵ The righteous one eats to the satisfying of his soul, but the belly of the wicked goes hungry.

## 14

¹ Every wise woman builds her house, but the foolish one tears it down with her own hands. ² He who walks in his uprightness fears Yahweh, but he who is perverse in his ways despises him. ³ The fool's talk brings a rod to his back, but the lips of the wise protect them. ⁴ Where no oxen are, the crib is clean, but much increase is by the strength of the ox. ⁵ A truthful witness will not lie, but a false witness pours out lies. ⁶ A scoffer seeks wisdom, and doesn't find it, but knowledge comes easily to a discerning person. ⁷ Stay away from a foolish man, for you won't find knowledge on his lips. ⁸ The wisdom of the prudent is to think about his way, but the folly of fools is deceit. ⁹ Fools mock at making atonement for sins, but among the upright there is good will. ¹⁰ The heart knows its own bitterness and joy; he will not share these with a stranger. ¹¹ The house of the wicked will be overthrown, but the tent of the upright will flourish. ¹² There is a way which seems right to a man, but in the end it leads to death. ¹³ Even in laughter the heart may be sorrowful, and mirth may end in heaviness. ¹⁴ The unfaithful will be repaid for his own ways; likewise a good man will be rewarded for his ways. ¹⁵ A simple man believes everything, but the prudent man carefully considers his ways. ¹⁶ A wise man fears and shuns evil, but the fool is hot headed and reckless. ¹⁷ He who is quick to become angry will commit folly, and a crafty man is hated. ¹⁸ The simple inherit folly, but the prudent are crowned with knowledge. ¹⁹ The evil bow down before the good, and the wicked at the gates of the righteous. ²⁰ The poor person is shunned even by his own neighbor, but the rich person has many friends. ²¹ He who despises his neighbor sins, but he who has pity on the poor is blessed. ²² Don't they go astray who plot evil? But love and faithfulness belong to those who plan good. ²³ In all hard work there is profit, but the talk of the lips leads only to poverty. ²⁴ The crown of the wise is their riches, but the folly of fools crowns them with folly. ²⁵ A truthful witness saves souls, but a false witness is deceitful. ²⁶ In the fear of Yahweh is a secure fortress, and he will be a refuge for his children. ²⁷ The fear of Yahweh is a fountain of life, turning people from the snares of death. ²⁸ In the multitude of people is the king's glory, but in the lack of people is the destruction of the prince. ²⁹ He who is slow to anger has great understanding, but he who has a quick temper displays folly. ³⁰ The life of the body is a heart at peace, but envy rots the bones. ³¹ He who oppresses the poor shows contempt for his Maker, but he who is kind to the needy honors him. ³² The wicked is brought down in his calamity, but in death, the righteous has a refuge. ³³ Wisdom rests in the heart of one who has understanding, and is even made known in the inward part of fools. ³⁴ Righteousness exalts a nation, but sin is a disgrace to any people. ³⁵ The king's favor is toward a servant who deals wisely, but his wrath is toward one who causes shame.

## 15

¹ A gentle answer turns away wrath, but a harsh word stirs up anger. ² The tongue of the wise commends knowledge, but the mouths of fools gush out folly. ³ Yahweh's eyes are everywhere, keeping watch on the evil and the good. ⁴ A gentle tongue is a tree of life, but deceit in it crushes the spirit. ⁵ A fool despises his father's correction, but he who heeds reproof shows prudence. ⁶ In the house of the righteous is much treasure, but the income of the wicked brings trouble. ⁷ The lips of the wise spread knowledge; not so with the heart of fools. ⁸ The sacrifice made by the wicked is an abomination to Yahweh, but the prayer of the upright is his delight. ⁹ The way of the wicked is an abomination to Yahweh, but he loves him who follows after righteousness. ¹⁰ There is stern discipline for one who forsakes the way. Whoever hates reproof shall die. ¹¹ Sheolᵃ and Abaddon are before Yahweh— how much more then the hearts of the children of men! ¹² A scoffer doesn't love to be reproved; he will not go to the wise. ¹³ A glad heart makes a cheerful face, but an aching heart breaks the spirit. ¹⁴ The heart of one who has understanding seeks knowledge, but the mouths of fools feed on folly. ¹⁵ All the days of the afflicted are wretched, but one who has a cheerful heart enjoys a continual feast. ¹⁶ Better is little, with the fear of Yahweh, than great treasure with trouble. ¹⁷ Better is a dinner of herbs, where love is, than a fattened calf with hatred. ¹⁸ A wrathful man stirs up contention, but one who is slow to anger appeases strife. ¹⁹ The way of the sluggard is like a thorn patch, but the path of the upright is a highway. ²⁰ A wise son makes a father glad, but a foolish man despises

his mother. ²¹ Folly is joy to one who is void of wisdom, but a man of understanding keeps his way straight. ²² Where there is no counsel, plans fail; but in a multitude of counselors they are established. ²³ Joy comes to a man with the reply of his mouth. How good is a word at the right time! ²⁴ The path of life leads upward for the wise, to keep him from going downward to Sheol.ᵇ ²⁵ Yahweh will uproot the house of the proud, but he will keep the widow's borders intact. ²⁶ Yahweh detests the thoughts of the wicked, but the thoughts of the pure are pleasing. ²⁷ He who is greedy for gain troubles his own house, but he who hates bribes will live. ²⁸ The heart of the righteous weighs answers, but the mouth of the wicked gushes out evil. ²⁹ Yahweh is far from the wicked, but he hears the prayer of the righteous. ³⁰ The light of the eyes rejoices the heart. Good news gives health to the bones. ³¹ The ear that listens to reproof lives, and will be at home among the wise. ³² He who refuses correction despises his own soul, but he who listens to reproof gets understanding. ³³ The fear of Yahweh teaches wisdom. Before honor is humility.

## 16

¹ The plans of the heart belong to man, but the answer of the tongue is from Yahweh. ² All the ways of a man are clean in his own eyes, but Yahweh weighs the motives. ³ Commit your deeds to Yahweh, and your plans shall succeed. ⁴ Yahweh has made everything for its own end— yes, even the wicked for the day of evil. ⁵ Everyone who is proud in heart is an abomination to Yahweh; they shall certainly not be unpunished. ⁶ By mercy and truth iniquity is atoned for. By the fear of Yahweh men depart from evil. ⁷ When a man's ways please Yahweh, he makes even his enemies to be at peace with him. ⁸ Better is a little with righteousness, than great revenues with injustice. ⁹ A man's heart plans his course, but Yahweh directs his steps. ¹⁰ Inspired judgments are on the lips of the king. He shall not betray his mouth. ¹¹ Honest balances and scales are Yahweh's; all the weights in the bag are his work. ¹² It is an abomination for kings to do wrong, for the throne is established by righteousness. ¹³ Righteous lips are the delight of kings. They value one who speaks the truth. ¹⁴ The king's wrath is a messenger of death, but a wise man will pacify it. ¹⁵ In the light of the king's face is life. His favor is like a cloud of the spring rain. ¹⁶ How much better it is to get wisdom than gold! Yes, to get understanding is to be chosen rather than silver. ¹⁷ The highway of the upright is to depart from evil. He who keeps his way preserves his soul. ¹⁸ Pride goes before destruction, and an arrogant spirit before a fall. ¹⁹ It is better to be of a lowly spirit with the poor, than to divide the plunder with the proud. ²⁰ He who heeds the Word finds prosperity. Whoever trusts in Yahweh is blessed. ²¹ The wise in heart shall be called prudent. Pleasantness of the lips promotes instruction. ²² Understanding is a fountain of life to one who has it, but the punishment of fools is their folly. ²³ The heart of the wise instructs his mouth, and adds learning to his lips. ²⁴ Pleasant words are a honeycomb, sweet to the soul, and health to the bones. ²⁵ There is a way which seems right to a man, but in the end it leads to death. ²⁶ The appetite of the laboring man labors for him, for his mouth urges him on. ²⁷ A worthless man devises mischief. His speech is like a scorching fire. ²⁸ A perverse man stirs up strife. A whisperer separates close friends. ²⁹ A man of violence entices his neighbor, and leads him in a way that is not good. ³⁰ One who winks his eyes to plot perversities, one who compresses his lips, is bent on evil. ³¹ Gray hair is a crown of glory. It is attained by a life of righteousness. ³² One who is slow to anger is better than the mighty; one who rules his spirit, than he who takes a city. ³³ The lot is cast into the lap, but its every decision is from Yahweh.

## 17

¹ Better is a dry morsel with quietness, than a house full of feasting with strife. ² A servant who deals wisely will rule over a son who causes shame, and shall have a part in the inheritance among the brothers. ³ The refining pot is for silver, and the furnace for gold, but Yahweh tests the hearts. ⁴ An evildoer heeds wicked lips. A liar gives ear to a mischievous tongue. ⁵ Whoever mocks the poor reproaches his Maker. He who is glad at calamity shall not be unpunished. ⁶ Children's children are the crown of old men; the glory of children are their parents. ⁷ Excellent speech isn't fitting for a fool, much less do lying lips fit a prince. ⁸ A bribe is a precious stone in the eyes of him who gives it; wherever he turns, he prospers. ⁹ He who covers an offense promotes love; but he who repeats a matter separates best friends. ¹⁰ A rebuke enters deeper into one who has understanding than a hundred lashes into a fool. ¹¹ An evil man seeks only rebellion; therefore a cruel messenger shall be sent against him. ¹² Let a bear robbed of her cubs meet a man, rather than a fool in his folly. ¹³ Whoever rewards evil for good, evil shall not depart from his house. ¹⁴ The beginning of strife is like breaching a dam, therefore stop contention before quarreling

---

ᵃ *15:11 Sheol is the place of the dead.*

ᵇ *15:24 Sheol is the place of the dead.*

breaks out. [15] He who justifies the wicked, and he who condemns the righteous, both of them alike are an abomination to Yahweh. [16] Why is there money in the hand of a fool to buy wisdom, since he has no understanding? [17] A friend loves at all times; and a brother is born for adversity. [18] A man void of understanding strikes hands, and becomes collateral in the presence of his neighbor. [19] He who loves disobedience loves strife. One who builds a high gate seeks destruction. [20] One who has a perverse heart doesn't find prosperity, and one who has a deceitful tongue falls into trouble. [21] He who becomes the father of a fool grieves. The father of a fool has no joy. [22] A cheerful heart makes good medicine, but a crushed spirit dries up the bones. [23] A wicked man receives a bribe in secret, to pervert the ways of justice. [24] Wisdom is before the face of one who has understanding, but the eyes of a fool wander to the ends of the earth. [25] A foolish son brings grief to his father, and bitterness to her who bore him. [26] Also to punish the righteous is not good, nor to flog officials for their integrity. [27] He who spares his words has knowledge. He who is even tempered is a man of understanding. [28] Even a fool, when he keeps silent, is counted wise. When he shuts his lips, he is thought to be discerning.

## 18

[1] A man who isolates himself pursues selfishness, and defies all sound judgment. [2] A fool has no delight in understanding, but only in revealing his own opinion. [3] When wickedness comes, contempt also comes, and with shame comes disgrace. [4] The words of a man's mouth are like deep waters. The fountain of wisdom is like a flowing brook. [5] To be partial to the faces of the wicked is not good, nor to deprive the innocent of justice. [6] A fool's lips come into strife, and his mouth invites beatings. [7] A fool's mouth is his destruction, and his lips are a snare to his soul. [8] The words of a gossip are like dainty morsels: they go down into a person's innermost parts. [9] One who is slack in his work is brother to him who is a master of destruction. [10] Yahweh's name is a strong tower: the righteous run to him, and are safe. [11] The rich man's wealth is his strong city, like an unscalable wall in his own imagination. [12] Before destruction the heart of man is proud, but before honor is humility. [13] He who answers before he hears, that is folly and shame to him. [14] A man's spirit will sustain him in sickness, but a crushed spirit, who can bear? [15] The heart of the discerning gets knowledge. The ear of the wise seeks knowledge. [16] A man's gift makes room for him, and brings him before great men. [17] He who pleads his cause first seems right— until another comes and questions him. [18] The lot settles disputes, and keeps strong ones apart. [19] A brother offended is more difficult than a fortified city. Disputes are like the bars of a fortress. [20] A man's stomach is filled with the fruit of his mouth. With the harvest of his lips he is satisfied. [21] Death and life are in the power of the tongue; those who love it will eat its fruit. [22] Whoever finds a wife finds a good thing, and obtains favor of Yahweh. [23] The poor plead for mercy, but the rich answer harshly. [24] A man of many companions may be ruined, but there is a friend who sticks closer than a brother.

## 19

[1] Better is the poor who walks in his integrity than he who is perverse in his lips and is a fool. [2] It isn't good to have zeal without knowledge, nor being hasty with one's feet and missing the way. [3] The foolishness of man subverts his way; his heart rages against Yahweh. [4] Wealth adds many friends, but the poor is separated from his friend. [5] A false witness shall not be unpunished. He who pours out lies shall not go free. [6] Many will entreat the favor of a ruler, and everyone is a friend to a man who gives gifts. [7] All the relatives of the poor shun him; how much more do his friends avoid him! He pursues them with pleas, but they are gone. [8] He who gets wisdom loves his own soul. He who keeps understanding shall find good. [9] A false witness shall not be unpunished. He who utters lies shall perish. [10] Delicate living is not appropriate for a fool, much less for a servant to have rule over princes. [11] The discretion of a man makes him slow to anger. It is his glory to overlook an offense. [12] The king's wrath is like the roaring of a lion, but his favor is like dew on the grass. [13] A foolish son is the calamity of his father. A wife's quarrels are a continual dripping. [14] House and riches are an inheritance from fathers, but a prudent wife is from Yahweh. [15] Slothfulness casts into a deep sleep. The idle soul shall suffer hunger. [16] He who keeps the commandment keeps his soul, but he who is contemptuous in his ways shall die. [17] He who has pity on the poor lends to Yahweh; he will reward him. [18] Discipline your son, for there is hope; don't be a willing party to his death. [19] A hot-tempered man must pay the penalty, for if you rescue him, you must do it again. [20] Listen to counsel and receive instruction, that you may be wise in your latter end. [21] There are many plans in a man's heart, but Yahweh's counsel will prevail. [22] That which makes a man to be desired is his kindness. A poor man is better than a liar. [23] The fear of Yahweh leads to life, then contentment; he rests and will not be touched by trouble. [24] The sluggard buries his hand in the dish; he will not so much as bring it to his mouth again. [25] Flog a scoffer, and the simple will learn prudence; rebuke one who has understanding,

and he will gain knowledge. [26] He who robs his father and drives away his mother is a son who causes shame and brings reproach. [27] If you stop listening to instruction, my son, you will stray from the words of knowledge. [28] A corrupt witness mocks justice, and the mouth of the wicked gulps down iniquity. [29] Penalties are prepared for scoffers, and beatings for the backs of fools.

## 20

[1] Wine is a mocker and beer is a brawler. Whoever is led astray by them is not wise. [2] The terror of a king is like the roaring of a lion. He who provokes him to anger forfeits his own life. [3] It is an honor for a man to keep aloof from strife, but every fool will be quarreling. [4] The sluggard will not plow by reason of the winter; therefore he shall beg in harvest, and have nothing. [5] Counsel in the heart of man is like deep water, but a man of understanding will draw it out. [6] Many men claim to be men of unfailing love, but who can find a faithful man? [7] A righteous man walks in integrity. Blessed are his children after him. [8] A king who sits on the throne of judgment scatters away all evil with his eyes. [9] Who can say, "I have made my heart pure. I am clean and without sin"? [10] Differing weights and differing measures, both of them alike are an abomination to Yahweh. [11] Even a child makes himself known by his doings, whether his work is pure, and whether it is right. [12] The hearing ear, and the seeing eye, Yahweh has made even both of them. [13] Don't love sleep, lest you come to poverty. Open your eyes, and you shall be satisfied with bread. [14] "It's no good, it's no good," says the buyer; but when he is gone his way, then he boasts. [15] There is gold and abundance of rubies, but the lips of knowledge are a rare jewel. [16] Take the garment of one who puts up collateral for a stranger; and hold him in pledge for a wayward woman. [17] Fraudulent food is sweet to a man, but afterwards his mouth is filled with gravel. [18] Plans are established by advice; by wise guidance you wage war! [19] He who goes about as a tale-bearer reveals secrets; therefore don't keep company with him who opens wide his lips. [20] Whoever curses his father or his mother, his lamp shall be put out in blackness of darkness. [21] An inheritance quickly gained at the beginning won't be blessed in the end. [22] Don't say, "I will pay back evil." Wait for Yahweh, and he will save you. [23] Yahweh detests differing weights, and dishonest scales are not pleasing. [24] A man's steps are from Yahweh; how then can man understand his way? [25] It is a snare to a man to make a rash dedication, then later to consider his vows. [26] A wise king winnows out the wicked, and drives the threshing wheel over them. [27] The spirit of man is Yahweh's lamp, searching all his innermost parts. [28] Love and faithfulness keep the king safe. His throne is sustained by love. [29] The glory of young men is their strength. The splendor of old men is their gray hair. [30] Wounding blows cleanse away evil, and beatings purge the innermost parts.

## 21

[1] The king's heart is in Yahweh's hand like the watercourses. He turns it wherever he desires. [2] Every way of a man is right in his own eyes, but Yahweh weighs the hearts. [3] To do righteousness and justice is more acceptable to Yahweh than sacrifice. [4] A high look and a proud heart, the lamp of the wicked, is sin. [5] The plans of the diligent surely lead to profit; and everyone who is hasty surely rushes to poverty. [6] Getting treasures by a lying tongue is a fleeting vapor for those who seek death. [7] The violence of the wicked will drive them away, because they refuse to do what is right. [8] The way of the guilty is devious, but the conduct of the innocent is upright. [9] It is better to dwell in the corner of the housetop than to share a house with a contentious woman. [10] The soul of the wicked desires evil; his neighbor finds no mercy in his eyes. [11] When the mocker is punished, the simple gains wisdom. When the wise is instructed, he receives knowledge. [12] The Righteous One considers the house of the wicked, and brings the wicked to ruin. [13] Whoever stops his ears at the cry of the poor, he will also cry out, but shall not be heard. [14] A gift in secret pacifies anger, and a bribe in the cloak, strong wrath. [15] It is joy to the righteous to do justice; but it is a destruction to the workers of iniquity. [16] The man who wanders out of the way of understanding shall rest in the assembly of the departed spirits. [17] He who loves pleasure will be a poor man. He who loves wine and oil won't be rich. [18] The wicked is a ransom for the righteous, the treacherous for the upright. [19] It is better to dwell in a desert land, than with a contentious and fretful woman. [20] There is precious treasure and oil in the dwelling of the wise, but a foolish man swallows it up. [21] He who follows after righteousness and kindness finds life, righteousness, and honor. [22] A wise man scales the city of the mighty, and brings down the strength of its confidence. [23] Whoever guards his mouth and his tongue keeps his soul from troubles. [24] The proud and arrogant man— "Scoffer" is his name— he works in the arrogance of pride. [25] The desire of the sluggard kills him, for his hands refuse to labor. [26] There are those who covet greedily all day long; but the righteous give and don't withhold. [27] The sacrifice of the wicked is an abomination— how much more, when he brings it with a wicked mind! [28] A false witness will perish. A man who listens speaks to eternity. [29] A wicked man

hardens his face; but as for the upright, he establishes his ways. <sup>30</sup> There is no wisdom nor understanding nor counsel against Yahweh. <sup>31</sup> The horse is prepared for the day of battle; but victory is with Yahweh.

## 22

<sup>1</sup> A good name is more desirable than great riches, and loving favor is better than silver and gold. <sup>2</sup> The rich and the poor have this in common: Yahweh is the maker of them all. <sup>3</sup> A prudent man sees danger and hides himself; but the simple pass on, and suffer for it. <sup>4</sup> The result of humility and the fear of Yahweh is wealth, honor, and life. <sup>5</sup> Thorns and snares are in the path of the wicked; whoever guards his soul stays far from them. <sup>6</sup> Train up a child in the way he should go, and when he is old he will not depart from it. <sup>7</sup> The rich rule over the poor. The borrower is servant to the lender. <sup>8</sup> He who sows wickedness reaps trouble, and the rod of his fury will be destroyed. <sup>9</sup> He who has a generous eye will be blessed, for he shares his food with the poor. <sup>10</sup> Drive out the mocker, and strife will go out; yes, quarrels and insults will stop. <sup>11</sup> He who loves purity of heart and speaks gracefully is the king's friend. <sup>12</sup> Yahweh's eyes watch over knowledge, but he frustrates the words of the unfaithful. <sup>13</sup> The sluggard says, "There is a lion outside! I will be killed in the streets!" <sup>14</sup> The mouth of an adulteress is a deep pit. He who is under Yahweh's wrath will fall into it. <sup>15</sup> Folly is bound up in the heart of a child; the rod of discipline drives it far from him. <sup>16</sup> Whoever oppresses the poor for his own increase and whoever gives to the rich, both come to poverty. <sup>17</sup> Turn your ear, and listen to the words of the wise. Apply your heart to my teaching. <sup>18</sup> For it is a pleasant thing if you keep them within you, if all of them are ready on your lips. <sup>19</sup> I teach you today, even you, so that your trust may be in Yahweh. <sup>20</sup> Haven't I written to you thirty excellent things of counsel and knowledge, <sup>21</sup> To teach you truth, reliable words, to give sound answers to the ones who sent you? <sup>22</sup> Don't exploit the poor because he is poor; and don't crush the needy in court; <sup>23</sup> for Yahweh will plead their case, and plunder the life of those who plunder them. <sup>24</sup> Don't befriend a hot-tempered man. Don't associate with one who harbors anger, <sup>25</sup> lest you learn his ways and ensnare your soul. <sup>26</sup> Don't you be one of those who strike hands, of those who are collateral for debts. <sup>27</sup> If you don't have means to pay, why should he take away your bed from under you? <sup>28</sup> Don't move the ancient boundary stone which your fathers have set up. <sup>29</sup> Do you see a man skilled in his work? He will serve kings. He won't serve obscure men.

## 23

<sup>1</sup> When you sit to eat with a ruler, consider diligently what is before you; <sup>2</sup> put a knife to your throat if you are a man given to appetite. <sup>3</sup> Don't be desirous of his dainties, since they are deceitful food. <sup>4</sup> Don't weary yourself to be rich. In your wisdom, show restraint. <sup>5</sup> Why do you set your eyes on that which is not? For it certainly sprouts wings like an eagle and flies in the sky. <sup>6</sup> Don't eat the food of him who has a stingy eye, and don't crave his delicacies, <sup>7</sup> for as he thinks about the cost, so he is. "Eat and drink!" he says to you, but his heart is not with you. <sup>8</sup> You will vomit up the morsel which you have eaten and waste your pleasant words. <sup>9</sup> Don't speak in the ears of a fool, for he will despise the wisdom of your words. <sup>10</sup> Don't move the ancient boundary stone. Don't encroach on the fields of the fatherless, <sup>11</sup> for their Defender is strong. He will plead their case against you. <sup>12</sup> Apply your heart to instruction, and your ears to the words of knowledge. <sup>13</sup> Don't withhold correction from a child. If you punish him with the rod, he will not die. <sup>14</sup> Punish him with the rod, and save his soul from Sheol.<sup>a</sup> <sup>15</sup> My son, if your heart is wise, then my heart will be glad, even mine. <sup>16</sup> Yes, my heart will rejoice when your lips speak what is right. <sup>17</sup> Don't let your heart envy sinners, but rather fear Yahweh all day long. <sup>18</sup> Indeed surely there is a future hope, and your hope will not be cut off. <sup>19</sup> Listen, my son, and be wise, and keep your heart on the right path! <sup>20</sup> Don't be among ones drinking too much wine, or those who gorge themselves on meat; <sup>21</sup> for the drunkard and the glutton shall become poor; and drowsiness clothes them in rags. <sup>22</sup> Listen to your father who gave you life, and don't despise your mother when she is old. <sup>23</sup> Buy the truth, and don't sell it. Get wisdom, discipline, and understanding. <sup>24</sup> The father of the righteous has great joy. Whoever fathers a wise child delights in him. <sup>25</sup> Let your father and your mother be glad! Let her who bore you rejoice! <sup>26</sup> My son, give me your heart; and let your eyes keep in my ways. <sup>27</sup> For a prostitute is a deep pit; and a wayward wife is a narrow well. <sup>28</sup> Yes, she lies in wait like a robber, and increases the unfaithful among men. <sup>29</sup> Who has woe? Who has sorrow? Who has strife? Who has complaints? Who has needless bruises? Who has bloodshot eyes? <sup>30</sup> Those who stay long at the wine; those who go to seek out mixed wine. <sup>31</sup> Don't look at the wine when it is red, when it sparkles in the cup, when it goes down smoothly. <sup>32</sup> In the end, it bites like a snake, and poisons like a viper. <sup>33</sup> Your eyes will see strange things, and your mind will imagine confusing things. <sup>34</sup> Yes, you will be as he who lies down in the middle of the sea, or as he who lies on top of the rigging: <sup>35</sup>"They hit me, and I was not hurt! They beat me, and I don't feel it! When will I wake up? I can do it again. I will look for more."

## 24

<sup>1</sup> Don't be envious of evil men, neither desire to be with them; <sup>2</sup> for their hearts plot violence and their lips talk about mischief. <sup>3</sup> Through wisdom a house is built; by understanding it is established; <sup>4</sup> by knowledge the rooms are filled with all rare and beautiful treasure. <sup>5</sup> A wise man has great power. A knowledgeable man increases strength, <sup>6</sup> for by wise guidance you wage your war, and victory is in many advisors. <sup>7</sup> Wisdom is too high for a fool. He doesn't open his mouth in the gate. <sup>8</sup> One who plots to do evil will be called a schemer. <sup>9</sup> The schemes of folly are sin. The mocker is detested by men. <sup>10</sup> If you falter in the time of trouble, your strength is small. <sup>11</sup> Rescue those who are being led away to death! Indeed, hold back those who are staggering to the slaughter! <sup>12</sup> If you say, "Behold, we didn't know this," doesn't he who weighs the hearts consider it? He who keeps your soul, doesn't he know it? Shall he not render to every man according to his work? <sup>13</sup> My son, eat honey, for it is good, the droppings of the honeycomb, which are sweet to your taste; <sup>14</sup> so you shall know wisdom to be to your soul. If you have found it, then there will be a reward: Your hope will not be cut off. <sup>15</sup> Don't lay in wait, wicked man, against the habitation of the righteous. Don't destroy his resting place; <sup>16</sup> for a righteous man falls seven times and rises up again, but the wicked are overthrown by calamity. <sup>17</sup> Don't rejoice when your enemy falls. Don't let your heart be glad when he is overthrown, <sup>18</sup> lest Yahweh see it, and it displease him, and he turn away his wrath from him. <sup>19</sup> Don't fret yourself because of evildoers, neither be envious of the wicked; <sup>20</sup> for there will be no reward to the evil man. The lamp of the wicked will be snuffed out. <sup>21</sup> My son, fear Yahweh and the king. Don't join those who are rebellious, <sup>22</sup> for their calamity will rise suddenly. Who knows what destruction may come from them both? <sup>23</sup> These also are sayings of the wise: To show partiality in judgment is not good. <sup>24</sup> He who says to the wicked, "You are righteous," peoples will curse him, and nations will abhor him— <sup>25</sup> but it will go well with those who convict the guilty, and a rich blessing will come on them. <sup>26</sup> An honest answer is like a kiss on the lips. <sup>27</sup> Prepare your work outside, and get your fields ready. Afterwards, build your house. <sup>28</sup> Don't be a witness against your neighbor without cause. Don't deceive with your lips. <sup>29</sup> Don't say, "I will do to him as he has done to me; I will repay the man according to his work." <sup>30</sup> I went by the field of the sluggard, by the vineyard of the man void of understanding. <sup>31</sup> Behold, it was all grown over with thorns. Its surface was covered with nettles, and its stone wall was broken down. <sup>32</sup> Then I saw, and considered well. I saw, and received instruction: <sup>33</sup> a little sleep, a little slumber, a little folding of the hands to sleep, <sup>34</sup> so your poverty will come as a robber and your want as an armed man.

### XXV-XXXI. Metsihafe Tibeb (The Books of Wisdom)

## 25

<sup>1</sup> These also are proverbs of Solomon, which the men of Hezekiah king of Judah copied out. <sup>2</sup> It is the glory of God to conceal a thing, but the glory of kings is to search out a matter. <sup>3</sup> As the heavens for height, and the earth for depth, so the hearts of kings are unsearchable. <sup>4</sup> Take away the dross from the silver, and material comes out for the refiner. <sup>5</sup> Take away the wicked from the king's presence, and his throne will be established in righteousness. <sup>6</sup> Don't exalt yourself in the presence of the king, or claim a place among great men; <sup>7</sup> for it is better that it be said to you, "Come up here," than that you should be put lower in the presence of the prince, whom your eyes have seen. <sup>8</sup> Don't be hasty in bringing charges to court. What will you do in the end when your neighbor shames you? <sup>9</sup> Debate your case with your neighbor, and don't betray the confidence of another, <sup>10</sup> lest one who hears it put you to shame, and your bad reputation never depart. <sup>11</sup> A word fitly spoken is like apples of gold in settings of silver. <sup>12</sup> As an earring of gold, and an ornament of fine gold, so is a wise reprover to an obedient ear. <sup>13</sup> As the cold of snow in the time of harvest, so is a faithful messenger to those who send him; for he refreshes the soul of his masters. <sup>14</sup> As clouds and wind without rain, so is he who boasts of gifts deceptively. <sup>15</sup> By patience a ruler is persuaded. A soft tongue breaks the bone. <sup>16</sup> Have you found honey? Eat as much as is sufficient for you, lest you eat too much, and vomit it. <sup>17</sup> Let your foot be seldom in your neighbor's house, lest he be weary of you, and hate you. <sup>18</sup> A man who gives false testimony against his neighbor is like a club, a sword, or a sharp arrow. <sup>19</sup> Confidence in someone unfaithful in time of trouble is like a bad tooth or a lame foot. <sup>20</sup> As one who takes away a garment in cold

---

<sup>a</sup> *23:14* Sheol is the place of the dead.

weather, or vinegar on soda, so is one who sings songs to a heavy heart. <sup>21</sup> If your enemy is hungry, give him food to eat. If he is thirsty, give him water to drink; <sup>22</sup> for you will heap coals of fire on his head, and Yahweh will reward you. <sup>23</sup> The north wind produces rain; so a backbiting tongue brings an angry face. <sup>24</sup> It is better to dwell in the corner of the housetop than to share a house with a contentious woman. <sup>25</sup> Like cold water to a thirsty soul, so is good news from a far country. <sup>26</sup> Like a muddied spring and a polluted well, so is a righteous man who gives way before the wicked. <sup>27</sup> It is not good to eat much honey, nor is it honorable to seek one's own honor. <sup>28</sup> Like a city that is broken down and without walls is a man whose spirit is without restraint.

## 26

<sup>1</sup> Like snow in summer, and as rain in harvest, so honor is not fitting for a fool. <sup>2</sup> Like a fluttering sparrow, like a darting swallow, so the undeserved curse doesn't come to rest. <sup>3</sup> A whip is for the horse, a bridle for the donkey, and a rod for the back of fools! <sup>4</sup> Don't answer a fool according to his folly, lest you also be like him. <sup>5</sup> Answer a fool according to his folly, lest he be wise in his own eyes. <sup>6</sup> One who sends a message by the hand of a fool is cutting off feet and drinking violence. <sup>7</sup> Like the legs of the lame that hang loose, so is a parable in the mouth of fools. <sup>8</sup> As one who binds a stone in a sling, so is he who gives honor to a fool. <sup>9</sup> Like a thorn bush that goes into the hand of a drunkard, so is a parable in the mouth of fools. <sup>10</sup> As an archer who wounds all, so is he who hires a fool or he who hires those who pass by. <sup>11</sup> As a dog that returns to his vomit, so is a fool who repeats his folly. <sup>12</sup> Do you see a man wise in his own eyes? There is more hope for a fool than for him. <sup>13</sup> The sluggard says, "There is a lion in the road! A fierce lion roams the streets!" <sup>14</sup> As the door turns on its hinges, so does the sluggard on his bed. <sup>15</sup> The sluggard buries his hand in the dish. He is too lazy to bring it back to his mouth. <sup>16</sup> The sluggard is wiser in his own eyes than seven men who answer with discretion. <sup>17</sup> Like one who grabs a dog's ears is one who passes by and meddles in a quarrel not his own. <sup>18</sup> Like a madman who shoots torches, arrows, and death, <sup>19</sup> is the man who deceives his neighbor and says, "Am I not joking?" <sup>20</sup> For lack of wood a fire goes out. Without gossip, a quarrel dies down. <sup>21</sup> As coals are to hot embers, and wood to fire, so is a contentious man to kindling strife. <sup>22</sup> The words of a whisperer are as dainty morsels, they go down into the innermost parts. <sup>23</sup> Like silver dross on an earthen vessel are the lips of a fervent one with an evil heart. <sup>24</sup> A malicious man disguises himself with his lips, but he harbors evil in his heart. <sup>25</sup> When his speech is charming, don't believe him, for there are seven abominations in his heart. <sup>26</sup> His malice may be concealed by deception, but his wickedness will be exposed in the assembly. <sup>27</sup> Whoever digs a pit shall fall into it. Whoever rolls a stone, it will come back on him. <sup>28</sup> A lying tongue hates those it hurts; and a flattering mouth works ruin.

## 27

<sup>1</sup> Don't boast about tomorrow; for you don't know what a day may bring. <sup>2</sup> Let another man praise you, and not your own mouth; a stranger, and not your own lips. <sup>3</sup> A stone is heavy, and sand is a burden; but a fool's provocation is heavier than both. <sup>4</sup> Wrath is cruel, and anger is overwhelming; but who is able to stand before jealousy? <sup>5</sup> Better is open rebuke than hidden love. <sup>6</sup> The wounds of a friend are faithful, although the kisses of an enemy are profuse. <sup>7</sup> A full soul loathes a honeycomb; but to a hungry soul, every bitter thing is sweet. <sup>8</sup> As a bird that wanders from her nest, so is a man who wanders from his home. <sup>9</sup> Perfume and incense bring joy to the heart; so does earnest counsel from a man's friend. <sup>10</sup> Don't forsake your friend and your father's friend. Don't go to your brother's house in the day of your disaster. A neighbor who is near is better than a distant brother. <sup>11</sup> Be wise, my son, and bring joy to my heart, then I can answer my tormentor. <sup>12</sup> A prudent man sees danger and takes refuge; but the simple pass on, and suffer for it. <sup>13</sup> Take his garment when he puts up collateral for a stranger. Hold it for a wayward woman! <sup>14</sup> He who blesses his neighbor with a loud voice early in the morning, it will be taken as a curse by him. <sup>15</sup> A continual dropping on a rainy day and a contentious wife are alike: <sup>16</sup> restraining her is like restraining the wind, or like grasping oil in his right hand. <sup>17</sup> Iron sharpens iron; so a man sharpens his friend's countenance. <sup>18</sup> Whoever tends the fig tree shall eat its fruit. He who looks after his master shall be honored. <sup>19</sup> Like water reflects a face, so a man's heart reflects the man. <sup>20</sup> Sheol<sup>a</sup> and Abaddon are never satisfied; and a man's eyes are never satisfied. <sup>21</sup> The crucible is for silver, and the furnace for gold; but man is refined by his praise. <sup>22</sup> Though you grind a fool in a mortar with a pestle along with grain, yet his foolishness will not be removed from him. <sup>23</sup> Know well the state of your flocks, and pay attention to your herds, <sup>24</sup> for riches are not forever, nor does the crown endure to all generations. <sup>25</sup> The hay is removed, and the new growth appears, the grasses of the hills are gathered in. <sup>26</sup> The lambs are for your clothing, and the goats are the price of a field. <sup>27</sup> There will be plenty of goats' milk for your food, for your family's food, and for the nourishment of your servant girls.

## 28

<sup>1</sup> The wicked flee when no one pursues; but the righteous are as bold as a lion. <sup>2</sup> In rebellion, a land has many rulers, but order is maintained by a man of understanding and knowledge. <sup>3</sup> A needy man who oppresses the poor is like a driving rain which leaves no crops. <sup>4</sup> Those who forsake the law praise the wicked; but those who keep the law contend with them. <sup>5</sup> Evil men don't understand justice; but those who seek Yahweh understand it fully. <sup>6</sup> Better is the poor who walks in his integrity than he who is perverse in his ways, and he is rich. <sup>7</sup> Whoever keeps the law is a wise son; but he who is a companion of gluttons shames his father. <sup>8</sup> He who increases his wealth by excessive interest gathers it for one who has pity on the poor. <sup>9</sup> He who turns away his ear from hearing the law, even his prayer is an abomination. <sup>10</sup> Whoever causes the upright to go astray in an evil way, he will fall into his own trap; but the blameless will inherit good. <sup>11</sup> The rich man is wise in his own eyes; but the poor who has understanding sees through him. <sup>12</sup> When the righteous triumph, there is great glory; but when the wicked rise, men hide themselves. <sup>13</sup> He who conceals his sins doesn't prosper, but whoever confesses and renounces them finds mercy. <sup>14</sup> Blessed is the man who always fears; but one who hardens his heart falls into trouble. <sup>15</sup> As a roaring lion or a charging bear, so is a wicked ruler over helpless people. <sup>16</sup> A tyrannical ruler lacks judgment. One who hates ill-gotten gain will have long days. <sup>17</sup> A man who is tormented by blood guilt will be a fugitive until death. No one will support him. <sup>18</sup> Whoever walks blamelessly is kept safe; but one with perverse ways will fall suddenly. <sup>19</sup> One who works his land will have an abundance of food; but one who chases fantasies will have his fill of poverty. <sup>20</sup> A faithful man is rich with blessings; but one who is eager to be rich will not go unpunished. <sup>21</sup> To show partiality is not good, yet a man will do wrong for a piece of bread. <sup>22</sup> A stingy man hurries after riches, and doesn't know that poverty waits for him. <sup>23</sup> One who rebukes a man will afterward find more favor than one who flatters with the tongue. <sup>24</sup> Whoever robs his father or his mother and says, "It's not wrong," is a partner with a destroyer. <sup>25</sup> One who is greedy stirs up strife; but one who trusts in Yahweh will prosper. <sup>26</sup> One who trusts in himself is a fool; but one who walks in wisdom is kept safe. <sup>27</sup> One who gives to the poor has no lack; but one who closes his eyes will have many curses. <sup>28</sup> When the wicked rise, men hide themselves; but when they perish, the righteous thrive.

## 29

<sup>1</sup> He who is often rebuked and stiffens his neck will be destroyed suddenly, with no remedy. <sup>2</sup> When the righteous thrive, the people rejoice; but when the wicked rule, the people groan. <sup>3</sup> Whoever loves wisdom brings joy to his father; but a companion of prostitutes squanders his wealth. <sup>4</sup> The king by justice makes the land stable, but he who takes bribes tears it down. <sup>5</sup> A man who flatters his neighbor spreads a net for his feet. <sup>6</sup> An evil man is snared by his sin, but the righteous can sing and be glad. <sup>7</sup> The righteous care about justice for the poor. The wicked aren't concerned about knowledge. <sup>8</sup> Mockers stir up a city, but wise men turn away anger. <sup>9</sup> If a wise man goes to court with a foolish man, the fool rages or scoffs, and there is no peace. <sup>10</sup> The bloodthirsty hate a man of integrity; and they seek the life of the upright. <sup>11</sup> A fool vents all of his anger, but a wise man brings himself under control. <sup>12</sup> If a ruler listens to lies, all of his officials are wicked. <sup>13</sup> The poor man and the oppressor have this in common: Yahweh gives sight to the eyes of both. <sup>14</sup> The king who fairly judges the poor, his throne shall be established forever. <sup>15</sup> The rod of correction gives wisdom, but a child left to himself causes shame to his mother. <sup>16</sup> When the wicked increase, sin increases; but the righteous will see their downfall. <sup>17</sup> Correct your son, and he will give you peace; yes, he will bring delight to your soul. <sup>18</sup> Where there is no revelation, the people cast off restraint; but one who keeps the law is blessed. <sup>19</sup> A servant can't be corrected by words. Though he understands, yet he will not respond. <sup>20</sup> Do you see a man who is hasty in his words? There is more hope for a fool than for him. <sup>21</sup> He who pampers his servant from youth will have him become a son in the end. <sup>22</sup> An angry man stirs up strife, and a wrathful man abounds in sin. <sup>23</sup> A man's pride brings him low, but one of lowly spirit gains honor. <sup>24</sup> Whoever is an accomplice of a thief is an enemy of his own soul. He takes an oath, but dares not testify. <sup>25</sup> The fear of man proves to be a snare, but whoever puts his trust in Yahweh is kept safe. <sup>26</sup> Many seek the ruler's favor, but a man's justice comes from Yahweh. <sup>27</sup> A dishonest man detests the righteous, and the upright in their ways detest the wicked.

<sup>a</sup> 27:20 Sheol is the place of the dead.

## 30

¹ The words of Agur the son of Jakeh, the revelation: the man says to Ithiel, to Ithiel and Ucal: ²"Surely I am the most ignorant man, and don't have a man's understanding. ³ I have not learned wisdom, neither do I have the knowledge of the Holy One. ⁴ Who has ascended up into heaven, and descended? Who has gathered the wind in his fists? Who has bound the waters in his garment? Who has established all the ends of the earth? What is his name, and what is his son's name, if you know? ⁵"Every word of God is flawless. He is a shield to those who take refuge in him. ⁶ Don't you add to his words, lest he reprove you, and you be found a liar. ⁷"Two things I have asked of you. Don't deny me before I die. ⁸ Remove far from me falsehood and lies. Give me neither poverty nor riches. Feed me with the food that is needful for me, ⁹ lest I be full, deny you, and say, 'Who is Yahweh?' or lest I be poor, and steal, and so dishonor the name of my God. ¹⁰"Don't slander a servant to his master, lest he curse you, and you be held guilty. ¹¹ There is a generation that curses their father, and doesn't bless their mother. ¹² There is a generation that is pure in their own eyes, yet are not washed from their filthiness. ¹³ There is a generation, oh how lofty are their eyes! Their eyelids are lifted up. ¹⁴ There is a generation whose teeth are like swords, and their jaws like knives, to devour the poor from the earth, and the needy from among men. ¹⁵"The leech has two daughters: 'Give, give.' "There are three things that are never satisfied; four that don't say, 'Enough!': ¹⁶ Sheol,ᵃ the barren womb, the earth that is not satisfied with water, and the fire that doesn't say, 'Enough!' ¹⁷"The eye that mocks at his father, and scorns obedience to his mother, the ravens of the valley shall pick it out, the young eagles shall eat it. ¹⁸"There are three things which are too amazing for me, four which I don't understand: ¹⁹ The way of an eagle in the air, the way of a serpent on a rock, the way of a ship in the middle of the sea, and the way of a man with a maiden. ²⁰"So is the way of an adulterous woman: She eats and wipes her mouth, and says, 'I have done nothing wrong.' ²¹"For three things the earth trembles, and under four, it can't bear up: ²² For a servant when he is king, a fool when he is filled with food, ²³ for an unloved woman when she is married, and a servant who is heir to her mistress. ²⁴"There are four things which are little on the earth, but they are exceedingly wise: ²⁵ The ants are not a strong people, yet they provide their food in the summer. ²⁶ The hyraxes are but a feeble folk, yet make they their houses in the rocks. ²⁷ The locusts have no king, yet they advance in ranks. ²⁸ You can catch a lizard with your hands, yet it is in kings' palaces. ²⁹"There are three things which are stately in their march, four which are stately in going: ³⁰ The lion, which is mightiest among animals, and doesn't turn away for any; ³¹ the greyhound; the male goat; and the king against whom there is no rising up. ³²"If you have done foolishly in lifting up yourself, or if you have thought evil, put your hand over your mouth. ³³ For as the churning of milk produces butter, and the wringing of the nose produces blood, so the forcing of wrath produces strife."

## 31

¹ The words of King Lemuel—the revelation which his mother taught him: ²"Oh, my son! Oh, son of my womb! Oh, son of my vows! ³ Don't give your strength to women, nor your ways to that which destroys kings. ⁴ It is not for kings, Lemuel, it is not for kings to drink wine, nor for princes to say, 'Where is strong drink?' ⁵ lest they drink, and forget the law, and pervert the justice due to anyone who is afflicted. ⁶ Give strong drink to him who is ready to perish, and wine to the bitter in soul. ⁷ Let him drink, and forget his poverty, and remember his misery no more. ⁸ Open your mouth for the mute, in the cause of all who are left desolate. ⁹ Open your mouth, judge righteously, and serve justice to the poor and needy." ¹⁰ ᵇWho can find a worthy woman? For her value is far above rubies. ¹¹ The heart of her husband trusts in her. He shall have no lack of gain. ¹² She does him good, and not harm, all the days of her life. ¹³ She seeks wool and flax, and works eagerly with her hands. ¹⁴ She is like the merchant ships. She brings her bread from afar. ¹⁵ She rises also while it is yet night, gives food to her household, and portions for her servant girls. ¹⁶ She considers a field, and buys it. With the fruit of her hands, she plants a vineyard. ¹⁷ She arms her waist with strength, and makes her arms strong. ¹⁸ She perceives that her merchandise is profitable. Her lamp doesn't go out by night. ¹⁹ She lays her hands to the distaff, and her hands hold the spindle. ²⁰ She opens her arms to the poor; yes, she extends her hands to the needy. ²¹ She is not afraid of the snow for her household, for all her household are clothed with scarlet. ²² She makes for herself carpets of tapestry. Her clothing is fine linen and purple. ²³ Her husband is respected in the gates, when he sits among the elders of the land. ²⁴ She makes linen garments and sells them, and delivers sashes to the merchant. ²⁵ Strength and dignity are her clothing. She laughs at the time to come. ²⁶ She opens her mouth with wisdom. Kind instruction is on her tongue. ²⁷ She looks well to the ways of her household, and doesn't eat the bread of idleness. ²⁸ Her children rise up and call her blessed. Her husband also praises her: ²⁹"Many women do noble things, but you excel them all." ³⁰ Charm is deceitful, and beauty is vain; but a woman who fears Yahweh, she shall be praised. ³¹ Give her of the fruit of her hands! Let her works praise her in the gates!

# The Wisdom of Solomon

The *Wisdom of Solomon* is recognized as Deuterocanonical Scripture by the Roman Catholic, Greek Orthodox, and Russian Orthodox Churches.

## 1

¹ Love righteousness, all you who are judges of the earth. Think of the Lordᶜ with a good mind. Seek him in singleness of heart, ² because he is found by those who don't put him to the test, and is manifested to those who trust him. ³ for crooked thoughts separate from God. His Power convicts when it is tested, and exposes the foolish; ⁴ because wisdom will not enter into a soul that devises evil, nor dwell in a body that is enslaved by sin. ⁵ For a holy spirit of discipline will flee deceit, and will depart from thoughts that are without understanding, and will be ashamed when unrighteousness has come in. ⁶ Forᵈ wisdom is a spirit who loves man, and she will not hold aᵉ blasphemer guiltless for his lips, because God is witness of his inmost self, and is a true overseer of his heart, and a hearer of his tongue. ⁷ Because the spirit of the Lord has filledᶠ the world, and that which holds all things together knows what is said. ⁸ Therefore no one who utters unrighteous things will be unseen; neither will Justice, when it convicts, pass him by. ⁹ For in his counsels the ungodly will be searched out, and the sound of his words will come to the Lord to bring his lawless deeds to conviction; ¹⁰ because a jealous ear listens to all things, and the noise of murmurings is not hidden. ¹¹ Beware then of unprofitable murmuring, and keep your tongue from slander; because no secret utterance will go on its way void, and a lying mouth destroys a soul. ¹² Don't court death in the error of your life. Don't draw destruction upon yourselves by the works of your hands; ¹³ because God didn't make death, neither does he delight when the living perish. ¹⁴ For he created all things that they might have being. The generative powers of the world are wholesome, and there is no poison of destruction in them, nor has Hadesᵍ royal dominion upon earth; ¹⁵ for righteousness is immortal, ¹⁶ but ungodly men by their hands and their words summon death; deeming him a friend theyʰ pined away. They made a covenant with him, because they are worthy to belong with him.

## 2

¹ For they saidⁱ within themselves, with unsound reasoning, "Our life is short and sorrowful. There is no healing when a man comes to his end, and no one was ever known whoʲ was released from Hades. ² Because we were born by mere chance, and hereafter we will be as though we had never been, because the breath in our nostrils is smoke, and reason is a spark kindled by the beating of our heart, ³ which being extinguished, the body will be turned into ashes, and the spirit will be dispersed as thin air. ⁴ Our name will be forgotten in time. No one will remember our works. Our life will pass away as the traces of a cloud, and will be scattered as is a mist, when it is chased by the rays of the sun, andᵏ overcome by its heat. ⁵ For our allotted time is the passing of a shadow, and our end doesn't retreat, because it is securely sealed, and no oneˡ turns it back. ⁶"Come therefore and let's enjoy the good things that exist. Let's use the creation earnestly as in our youth. ⁷ Let's fill ourselves with costly wine and perfumes, and let no spring flower pass us by. ⁸ Let's crown ourselves with rosebuds before they wither. ⁹ Let none of us go without his share in our proud revelry. Let's leave tokens of mirth everywhere, because this is our portion, and this is our lot. ¹⁰ Let's oppress the righteous poor. Let's not spare the widow, nor regard the gray hair of the old man. ¹¹ But let our strength be a law of righteousness; for that which is weak is proven useless. ¹² But let's lie in wait for the righteous man, because he annoys us, is contrary to our works, reproaches us with sins against the law, and charges us with sins against our training. ¹³ He professes to have knowledge of God, and calls himself a child of the Lord. ¹⁴ He became to us a reproof of our

---

ᵃ *30:16* Sheol is the place of the dead.
ᵇ *31:10* Proverbs 31:10-31 form an acrostic, with each verse starting with each letter

of the Hebrew alphabet, in order.
ᶜ *1:1* Gr. in goodness.
ᵈ *1:6* Some authorities read the spirit of wisdom is loving to man.

ᵉ *1:6* Or, reviler
ᶠ *1:7* Gr. the inhabited earth.
ᵍ *1:14* Or, a royal house
ʰ *1:16* Or, were consumed with love of him
ⁱ *2:1* Or, among

ʲ *2:1* Or, returned out of Hades
ᵏ *2:4* Gr. weighed down.
ˡ *2:5* Or, comes again

thoughts. ¹⁵ He is grievous to us even to look at, because his life is unlike other men's, and his paths are strange. ¹⁶ We were regarded by him as something worthless, and he abstains from our ways as from uncleanness. He calls the latter end of the righteous happy. He boasts that God is his father. ¹⁷ Let's see if his words are true. Let's test what will happen at the end of his life. ¹⁸ For if the righteous man is God's son, he will uphold him, and he will deliver him out of the hand of his adversaries. ¹⁹ Let's test him with insult and torture, that we may find out how gentle he is, and test his patience. ²⁰ Let's condemn him to a shameful death, for he will be protected, according to his words." ²¹ Thus they reasoned, and they were led astray; for their wickedness blinded them, ²² and they didn't know the mysteries of God, neither did they hope for wages of holiness, nor did they discern that there is a prize for blameless souls. ²³ Because God created man for incorruption, and made him an image of his own everlastingness; ²⁴ but death entered into the world by the envy of the devil, and those who belong to him experience it.

**3**

¹ But the souls of the righteous are in the hand of God, and no torment will touch them. ² In the eyes of the foolish they seemed to have died. Their departure was considered a disaster, ³ and their travel away from us ruin, but they are in peace. ⁴ For even if in the sight of men they are punished, their hope is full of immortality. ⁵ Having borne a little chastening, they will receive great good; because God tested them, and found them worthy of himself. ⁶ He tested them like gold in the furnace, and he accepted them as a whole burnt offering. ⁷ In the time of their visitation they will shine. They will run back and forth like sparks among stubble. ⁸ They will judge nations and have dominion over peoples. The Lord will reign over them forever. ⁹ Those who trust him will understand truth. The faithful will live with him in love, because grace and mercy are with his chosen ones. ¹⁰ But the ungodly will be punished even as their reasoning deserves, those who neglected righteousness and revolted from the Lord; ¹¹ for he who despises wisdom and discipline is miserable. Their hope is void and their toils unprofitable. Their works are useless. ¹² Their wives are foolish and their children are wicked. ¹³ Their descendants are cursed. For the barren woman who is undefiled is happy, she who has not conceived in transgression. She will have fruit when God examines souls. ¹⁴ So is the eunuch which has done no lawless deed with his hands, nor imagined wicked things against the Lord; for a precious gift will be given to him for his faithfulness, and a delightful inheritance in the Lord's sanctuary. ¹⁵ For good labors have fruit of great renown. The root of understanding can't fail. ¹⁶ But children of adulterers will not come to maturity. The seed of an unlawful union will vanish away. ¹⁷ For if they live long, they will not be esteemed, and in the end, their old age will be without honor. ¹⁸ If they die young, they will have no hope, nor consolation in the day of judgment. ¹⁹ For the end of an unrighteous generation is always grievous.

**4**

¹ It is better to be childless with virtue, for immortality is in the memory of virtue, because it is recognized both before God and before men. ² When it is present, people imitate it. They long after it when it has departed. Throughout all time it marches, crowned in triumph, victorious in the competition for the prizes that are undefiled. ³ But the multiplying brood of the ungodly will be of no profit, and their illegitimate offshoots won't take deep root, nor will they establish a sure hold. ⁴ For even if they grow branches and flourish for a season, standing unsure, they will be shaken by the wind. They will be uprooted by the violence of winds. ⁵ Their branches will be broken off before they come to maturity. Their fruit will be useless, never ripe to eat, and fit for nothing. ⁶ For unlawfully conceived children are witnesses of wickedness against parents when they are investigated. ⁷ But a righteous man, even if he dies before his time, will be at rest. ⁸ For honorable old age is not that which stands in length of time, nor is its measure given by number of years, ⁹ but understanding is gray hair to men, and an unspotted life is ripe old age. ¹⁰ Being found well-pleasing to God, someone was loved. While living among sinners he was transported. ¹¹ He was caught away, lest evil should change his understanding, or guile deceive his soul. ¹² For the fascination of wickedness obscures the things which are good, and the whirl of desire perverts an innocent mind. ¹³ Being made perfect quickly, he filled a long time; ¹⁴ for his soul was pleasing to the Lord. Therefore he hurried out of the midst of wickedness. ¹⁵ But the peoples saw and didn't understand, not considering this, that grace and mercy are with his chosen, and that he visits his holy ones; ¹⁶ but a righteous man who is

dead will condemn the ungodly who are living, and youth who is quickly perfected will condemn the many years of an unrighteous man's old age. ¹⁷ For the ungodly will see a wise man's end, and won't understand what the Lord planned for him, and why he safely kept him. ¹⁸ They will see, and they will despise; but the Lord will laugh them to scorn. After this, they will become a dishonored carcass and a reproach among the dead forever; ¹⁹ because he will dash them speechless to the ground, and will shake them from the foundations. They will lie utterly waste. They will be in anguish and their memory will perish. ²⁰ They will come with coward fear when their sins are counted. Their lawless deeds will convict them to their face.

**5**

¹ Then the righteous man will stand in great boldness before the face of those who afflicted him, and those who make his labors of no account. ² When they see him, they will be troubled with terrible fear, and will be amazed at the marvel of salvation. ³ They will speak among themselves repenting, and for distress of spirit they will groan, "This was he whom we used to hold in derision, as a parable of reproach. ⁴ We fools considered his life madness, and his end without honor. ⁵ How was he counted among sons of God? How is his lot among saints? ⁶ Truly we went astray from the way of truth. The light of righteousness didn't shine for us. The sun didn't rise for us. ⁷ We[a] took our fill of the paths of lawlessness and destruction. We traveled through trackless deserts, but we didn't know the Lord's way. ⁸ What did our arrogance profit us? What good have riches and boasting brought us? ⁹ Those things all passed away as a shadow, like a rumor that runs by, ¹⁰ like a ship passing through the billowy water, which, when it has gone by, there is no trace to be found, no pathway of its keel in the waves. ¹¹ Or it is like when a bird flies through the air, no evidence of its passage is found, but the light wind, lashed with the stroke of its pinions, and torn apart with the violent rush of the moving wings, is passed through. Afterwards no sign of its coming remains. ¹² Or it is like when an arrow is shot at a mark, the air it divided closes up again immediately, so that men don't know where it passed through. ¹³ So we also, as soon as we were born, ceased to be; and we had no sign of virtue to show, but we were utterly consumed in our wickedness." ¹⁴ Because the hope of the ungodly man is like chaff carried by the wind, and[b] as[c] foam vanishing before a tempest; and is scattered like smoke by the wind, and passes by as the remembrance of a guest who stays just a day. ¹⁵ But the

righteous live forever. Their reward is in the Lord, and the care for them with the Most High. ¹⁶ Therefore they will receive the crown of royal dignity and the diadem of beauty from the Lord's hand, because he will cover them with his right hand, and he will shield them with his arm. ¹⁷ He will take his zeal as complete armor, and will make the whole creation his weapons to punish his enemies: ¹⁸ He will put on righteousness as a breastplate, and will wear impartial judgment as a helmet. ¹⁹ He will take holiness as an invincible shield. ²⁰ He will sharpen stern wrath for a sword. The universe will go with him to fight against his frenzied foes. ²¹ Shafts of lightning will fly with true aim. They will leap to the mark from the clouds, as from a well-drawn bow. ²² Hailstones full of wrath will be hurled as from a catapult. The water of the sea will be angered against them. Rivers will sternly overwhelm them. ²³ A mighty wind will encounter them. It will winnow them away like a tempest. So lawlessness will make all the land desolate. Their evil-doing will overturn the thrones of princes.

**6**

¹ Hear therefore, you kings, and understand. Learn, you judges of the ends of the earth. ² Give ear, you rulers who have dominion over many people, and make your boast[d] in multitudes of nations, ³ because your dominion was given to you from the Lord, and your sovereignty from the Most High. He will search out your works, and will inquire about your plans, ⁴ because being officers of his kingdom, you didn't judge rightly, nor did you keep the law, nor did you walk according to God's counsel. ⁵ He will come upon you awfully and swiftly, because a stern judgment comes on those who are in high places. ⁶ For the man of low

---

ᵃ *5:7* See Proverbs 14:14.
ᵇ *5:14* Gr. like foam chased to thinness: or, as thin foam chased.

ᶜ *5:14* Most Greek authorities read hoar frost: some authorities, perhaps rightly, a spider's web.

ᵈ *6:2* Or, in the multitudes of your nations

estate may be pardoned in mercy, but mighty men will be mightily tested. [7] For the Sovereign Lord of all will not be impressed with anyone, neither will he show deference to greatness; because it is he who made both small and great, and cares about them all; [8] but the scrutiny that comes upon the powerful is strict. [9] Therefore, my words are to you, O princes, that you may learn wisdom and not fall away. [10] For those who have kept the things that are holy in holiness will be made holy. Those who have been taught them will find what to say in defense. [11] Therefore set your desire on my words. Long for them, and you princes will be instructed. [12] Wisdom is radiant and doesn't fade away; and is easily seen by those who love her, and found by those who seek her. [13] She anticipates those who desire her, making herself known. [14] He who rises up early to seek her won't have difficulty, for he will find her sitting at his gates. [15] For to think upon her is perfection of understanding, and he who watches for her will quickly be free from care; [16] because she herself goes around, seeking those who are worthy of her, and in their paths she appears to them graciously, and in every purpose she meets them. [17] For her true beginning is desire for instruction; and desire for instruction is love. [18] And love is observance of her laws. To give heed to her laws confirms immortality. [19] Immortality brings closeness to God. [20] So then desire for wisdom promotes to a kingdom. [21] If therefore you delight in thrones and sceptres, you princes of peoples, honor wisdom, that you may reign forever. [22] But what wisdom is, and how she came into being, I will declare. I won't hide mysteries from you; but I will explore from her first beginning, bring the knowledge of her into clear light, and I will not pass by the truth. [23] Indeed, I won't travel with consuming envy, because envy will have no fellowship with wisdom. [24] But a multitude of wise men is salvation to the world, and an understanding king is stability for his people. [25] Therefore be instructed by my words, and you will profit.

## 7

[1] I myself am also[a] mortal, like everyone else, and am a descendant of one formed first and born of the earth. [2] I molded into flesh in the time of ten months in my mother's womb, being compacted in blood from the seed of man and pleasure of marriage. [3] I also, when I was born, drew in the common air, and fell upon the kindred earth, uttering, like all, for my first voice, the same cry. [4] I was nursed with care in swaddling clothes. [5] For no king had a different beginning, [6] but all men have one entrance into life, and a common departure. [7] For this cause I prayed, and understanding was given to me. I asked, and a spirit of wisdom came to me. [8] I preferred her before sceptres and thrones. I considered riches nothing in comparison to her. [9] Neither did I liken to her any priceless gem, because all gold in her presence is a little sand, and silver will be considered as clay before her. [10] I loved her more than health and beauty, and I chose to have her rather than light, because her bright shining is never laid to sleep. [11] All good things came to me with her, and innumerable riches are in her hands. [12] And I rejoiced over them all because wisdom leads them; although I didn't know that she was their mother. [13] As I learned without guile, I impart without grudging. I don't hide her riches. [14] For she is a treasure for men that doesn't fail, and those who use it obtain friendship with God, commended by the gifts which they present through discipline. [15] But may God grant that I may speak his judgment, and to conceive thoughts worthy of what has been given me; because he is one who guides even wisdom and who corrects the wise. [16] For both we and our words are in his hand, with all understanding and skill in various crafts. [17] For he himself gave me an unerring knowledge of the things that are, to know the structure of the universe and the operation of the elements; [18] the beginning, end, and middle of times; the alternations of the solstices and the changes of seasons; [19] the circuits of years and the positions of stars; [20] the natures of living creatures and the raging of wild beasts; the violence of[b] winds and the thoughts of men; the diversities of plants and the virtues of roots. [21] All things that are either secret or manifest I learned, [22] for wisdom, that is the architect of all things, taught me. For there is in her a spirit that is quick to understand, holy, unique, manifold, subtle, freely moving, clear in utterance, unpolluted, distinct, invulnerable, loving what is good, keen, unhindered, [23] beneficent, loving toward man, steadfast, sure, free from care, all-powerful, all-surveying, and penetrating through all spirits that are quick to understand, pure, most subtle. [24] For wisdom is more mobile than any motion. Yes, she pervades and penetrates all things by reason of her purity. [25] For she is a breath of the power of God, and a pure emanation of the glory of the Almighty. Therefore nothing defiled can find entrance into her. [26] For she is a reflection of everlasting light, an unspotted mirror of the working of God, and an image of his goodness. [27] Although she is one, she has power to do all things. Remaining in

herself, she renews all things. From generation to generation passing into holy souls, she makes friends of God and prophets. [28] For God loves nothing as much as one who dwells with wisdom. [29] For she is fairer than the sun, and above all the constellations of the stars. She is better than light. [30] For daylight yields to night, but evil does not prevail against wisdom.

## 8

[1] But she reaches from one end to the other with full strength, and orders all things well. [2] I loved her and sought her from my youth. I sought to take her for my bride. I became enamoured by her beauty. [3] She glorifies her noble birth by living with God. The Sovereign Lord of all loves her. [4] For she is initiated into the knowledge of God, and she chooses his works. [5] But if riches are a desired possession in life, what is richer than wisdom, which makes all things? [6] And if understanding is effective, who more than[c] wisdom is an architect of the things that exist? [7] If a man loves righteousness, the fruits of wisdom's labor[d] are virtues, for she teaches soberness, understanding, righteousness, and courage. There is nothing in life more profitable for people than these. [8] And if anyone longs for wide experience, she knows the things of old, and infers the things to come. She understands subtleties of speeches and interpretations of dark sayings. She foresees signs and wonders, and the issues of seasons and times. [9] Therefore I determined to take her to live with me, knowing that she is one who would give me good counsel, and encourage me in cares and grief. [10] Because of her, I will have glory among multitudes, and honor in the sight of elders, though I am young. [11] I will be found keen when I give judgment. I will be admired in the presence of rulers. [12] When I am silent, they will wait for me. When I open my lips, they will heed what I say. If I continue speaking, they will put their hands on their mouths. [13] Because of her, I will have immortality, and leave behind an eternal memory to those who come after me. [14] I will govern peoples. Nations will be subjected to me. [15] Dreaded monarchs will fear me when they hear of me. Among the people, I will show myself to be good, and courageous in war. [16] When I come into my house, I will find rest with her. For conversation with her has no bitterness, and living with her has no pain, but gladness and joy. [17] When I considered these things in myself, and thought in my heart how immortality is in kinship to wisdom, [18] and in her friendship is good delight, and in the labors of her hands is wealth that doesn't fail, and understanding is in her companionship, and great renown in having fellowship with her words, I went about seeking how to take her to myself. [19] Now I was a clever child, and received a good soul. [20] Or rather, being good, I came into an undefiled body. [21] But perceiving that I could not otherwise possess wisdom unless God gave her to me— yes, and to know and understand by whom the grace is given— I pleaded with the Lord and implored him, and with my whole heart I said:

## 9

[1] "O God of my ancestors and Lord of mercy, who made all things by your word; [2] and by your wisdom you formed man, that he should have dominion over the creatures that were made by you, [3] and rule the world in holiness and righteousness, and execute judgment in uprightness of soul, [4] give me wisdom, her who sits by you on your thrones. Don't reject me from among your[e] servants, [5] because I am your servant and the son of your handmaid, a weak and short-lived man, with little power to understand judgment and laws. [6] For even if a man is perfect among the sons of men, if the wisdom that comes from you is not with him, he will count for nothing. [7] You chose me to be king of your people, and a judge for your sons and daughters. [8] You gave a command to build a sanctuary on your holy mountain, and[f] an altar in the city where you live, a copy of the holy tent which you prepared from the beginning. [9] Wisdom is with you and knows your works, and was present when you were making the world, and understands what is pleasing in your eyes, and what is right according to your commandments. [10] Send her from the holy heavens, and ask her to come from the throne of your glory, that being present with me she may work, and I may learn what pleases you well. [11] For she knows all things and understands, and she will guide me prudently in my actions. She will guard me in her glory. [12] So my works will be acceptable. I will judge your people righteously, and I will be worthy of my father's[g] throne. [13] For what man will know the counsel of God? Or who will conceive what the Lord wills? [14] For the thoughts of mortals are unstable, and our plans are prone to fail. [15] For a corruptible body weighs down the soul. The earthy tent burdens a mind that is full of cares. [16] We can hardly guess the things that are on earth, and we find the things that are close at hand with labor; but who has traced out the things that are in the heavens? [17] Who gained knowledge of your counsel, unless you gave wisdom, and sent your holy spirit from on high? [18] It was thus that the ways of those who are

---

[a] 7:1 Many authorities read a mortal man.

[b] 7:20 Or, spirits
[c] 8:6 Gr. she.

[d] 8:7 Gr. her labors
[e] 9:4 Or, children

[f] 9:8 Or, a place of sacrifice
[g] 9:12 Gr. thrones.

on earth were corrected, and men were taught the things that are pleasing to you. They were saved through wisdom."

## 10

[1] Wisdom[a] guarded to the end the first formed father of the world, who was created alone, and delivered him out of his own transgression, [2] and gave him strength to rule over all things. [3] But when an unrighteous man fell away from her in his anger, he perished himself in the rage with which he killed his brother. [4] When for his cause the earth was drowning with a flood, wisdom again saved it, guiding the righteous man's course by a paltry piece of wood. [5] Moreover, when nations consenting together in wickedness had been confounded, wisdom[b] knew the righteous man, and preserved him blameless to God, and kept him strong when his heart yearned toward his child. [6] While the ungodly were perishing, wisdom[c] delivered a righteous man, when he fled from the fire that descended out of heaven on the five cities. [7] To whose wickedness a smoking waste still witnesses, and plants bearing fair fruit that doesn't ripen, a disbelieving soul has a memorial: a standing pillar of salt. [8] For having passed wisdom by, not only were they disabled from recognising the things which are good, but they also left behind them for their life a monument of their folly, to the end that where they stumbled, they might fail even to be unseen; [9] but wisdom delivered those who waited on her out of troubles. [10] When a righteous man was a fugitive from a brother's wrath,[d] wisdom guided him in straight paths. She showed him God's kingdom, and gave him knowledge of holy things. She prospered him in his toils, and multiplied the fruits of his labor. [11] When in their covetousness men dealt harshly with him, she stood by him and made him rich. [12] She guarded him from enemies, and she kept him safe from those who lay in wait. Over his severe conflict, she watched as judge, that he might know that godliness is more powerful than every one. [13] When a righteous man was sold,[e] wisdom didn't forsake him, but she delivered him from sin. She went down with him into a dungeon, [14] and in bonds she didn't depart from him, until she brought him the sceptre of a kingdom, and authority over those that dealt like a tyrant with him. She also showed those who had mockingly accused him to be false, and gave him eternal glory. [15] Wisdom[f] delivered a holy people and a blameless seed from a nation of oppressors. [16] She entered into the soul of a servant of the Lord, and withstood terrible kings in wonders and signs. [17] She rendered to holy men a reward of their toils. She guided them along a marvelous way, and became to them a covering in the day-time, and a starry flame through the night. [18] She brought them over the Red sea, and led them through much water; [19] but she drowned their enemies, and she cast them up from the bottom of the deep. [20] Therefore the righteous plundered the ungodly, and they sang praise to your holy name, O Lord, and extolled with one accord your hand that fought for them, [21] because wisdom opened the mouth of the mute, and made the tongues of babes to speak clearly.

## 11

[1] Wisdom prospered their works in the hand of a holy prophet. [2] They traveled through a desert without inhabitant, and they pitched their tents in trackless regions. [3] They withstood enemies and repelled foes. [4] They thirsted, and they called upon you, and water was given to them out of the[g] flinty rock, and healing of their thirst out of the hard stone. [5] For by what things their foes were punished, by these they in their need were benefited. [6] When enemies were troubled with clotted blood instead of a river's ever-flowing fountain, [7] to rebuke the decree for the slaying of babies, you gave them abundant water beyond all hope, [8] having shown by the thirst which they had suffered how you punished the adversaries. [9] For when they were tried, although chastened in mercy, they learned how the ungodly were tormented, being judged with wrath. [10] For you tested these as a father admonishing them; but you searched out those as a stern king condemning them. [11] Yes and whether they were far off or near, they were equally distressed; [12] for a double grief seized them, and a groaning at the memory of things past. [13] For when they heard that through their own punishments the others benefited, they recognized the Lord. [14] For him who long before was thrown out and exposed they stopped mocking. In the end of what happened, they marveled, having thirsted in another manner than the righteous. [15] But in return for the senseless imaginings of their unrighteousness, wherein they were led astray to worship irrational reptiles and wretched vermin, you sent upon them a multitude of irrational creatures to punish them, [16] that they might learn that by what things a man sins, by these he is punished. [17] For your all-powerful hand that created the world out of formless matter didn't lack means to send upon them a multitude of bears, fierce lions, [18] or newly-created and unknown wild beasts, full of rage, either breathing out a blast of fiery breath, or belching out smoke, or flashing dreadful sparks from their eyes; [19] which had power not only to consume them by their violence, but to destroy them even by the terror of their sight. [20] Yes and without these they might have fallen by a single breath, being pursued by Justice, and scattered abroad by the breath of your power; but you arranged all things by measure, number, and weight. [21] For to be greatly strong is yours at all times. Who could withstand the might of your arm? [22] Because the whole world before you is as a grain in a balance, and as a drop of dew that comes down upon the earth in the morning. [23] But you have mercy on all men, because you have power to do all things, and you overlook the sins of men to the end that they may repent. [24] For you love all things that are, and abhor none of the things which you made; For you never would have formed anything if you hated it. [25] How would anything have endured unless you had willed it? Or that which was not called by you, how would it have been preserved? [26] But you spare all things, because they are yours, O Sovereign Lord, you who love the living.

## 12

[1] For your incorruptible spirit is in all things. [2] Therefore you convict little by little those who fall from the right way, and, putting them in remembrance by the things wherein they sin, you admonish them, that escaping from their wickedness they may believe in you, O Lord. [3] For truly the old inhabitants of your holy land, [4] hating them because they practiced detestable works of enchantments and unholy rites— [5] merciless slaughters of children and sacrificial banquets of men's flesh and of blood— [6] allies in an impious fellowship, and murderers of their own helpless babes, it was your counsel to destroy by the hands of our fathers; [7] that the land which in your sight is most precious of all might receive a worthy colony of God's servants.[h] [8] Nevertheless you even spared these as men, and you sent hornets[i] as forerunners of your army, to cause them to perish little by little. [9] Not that you were unable to subdue the ungodly under the hand of the righteous in battle, or by terrible beasts or by a stern word to make away with them at once, [10] but judging them little by little you gave them a chance to repent, not being ignorant that their nature by birth was evil, their wickedness inborn, and that their manner of thought would never be changed. [11] For they were a cursed seed from the beginning. It wasn't through fear of any that you left them unpunished for their sins. [12] For who will say, "What have you done?" Or "Who will withstand your judgment?" Who will accuse you for the perishing of nations which you caused? Or who will come and stand before you as an avenger for unrighteous men? [13] For there isn't any God beside you that cares for all, that you might show that you didn't judge unrighteously. [14] No king or prince will be able to confront you about those whom you have punished. [15] But being righteous, you rule all things righteously, deeming it a thing alien from your power to condemn one who doesn't deserve to be punished. [16] For your strength is the source of righteousness, and your sovereignty over all makes you to forbear all. [17] For when men don't believe that you are perfect in power, you show your strength, and, in dealing with those who think this, you confuse their boldness. [18] But you, being sovereign in strength, judge in gentleness, and with great forbearance you govern us; for the power is yours whenever you desire it. [19] But you taught your people by such works as these, how the righteous must be kind. You made your sons to have good hope, because you give repentance when men have sinned. [20] For if on those who were enemies of your servants[j] and deserving of death, you took vengeance with so great deliberation and indulgence, giving them times and opportunities when they might escape from their wickedness, [21] with how great care you judged your sons, to whose fathers you gave oaths and covenants of good promises! [22] Therefore while you chasten us, you scourge our enemies ten thousand times more, to the intent that we may ponder your goodness when we judge, and when we are judged may look for mercy. [23] Therefore also the unrighteous that lived in a life of folly, you tormented through their own abominations. [24] For truly they went astray very far in the ways of error, Taking as gods those animals[k] which even among their enemies were held in dishonor, deceived like foolish babes. [25] Therefore, as to unreasoning children, you sent your judgment to mock them. [26] But those who would not be admonished by mild correction will experience the deserved judgment of God. [27] For through the sufferings they were indignant of, being punished in these creatures which they supposed to be gods, they saw and recognized as the true God him whom they previously refused to know. Therefore also the result of extreme condemnation came upon them.

---

[a] 10:1 Gr. She.
[b] 10:5 Gr. she
[c] 10:6 Gr. she
[d] 10:10 Gr. she.

[e] 10:13 Gr. she.
[f] 10:15 Gr. she.
[g] 11:4 See Deuteronomy 8:15; Psalms 114:8.

[h] 12:7 Or, children
[i] 12:8 Or, wasps
[j] 12:20 Or, children

[k] 12:24 Gr. living creatures: and so elsewhere in this book.

## 13

[1] For truly all men who had no perception of God were foolish by nature, and didn't gain power to know him who exists from the good things that are seen. They didn't recognize the architect from his works. [2] But they thought that either fire, or wind, or swift air, or circling stars, or raging water, or luminaries of heaven were gods that rule the world. [3] If it was through delight in their beauty that they took them to be gods, let them know how much better their Sovereign Lord is than these, for the first author of beauty created them. [4] But if it was through astonishment at their power and influence, then let them understand from them how much more powerful he who formed them is. [5] For from the greatness of the beauty of created things, mankind forms the corresponding perception of their Maker.[a] [6] But yet for these men there is but small blame, for they too perhaps go astray while they are seeking God and desiring to find him. [7] For they diligently search while living among his works, and they trust their sight that the things that they look at are beautiful. [8] But again even they are not to be excused. [9] For if they had power to know so much, that they should be able to explore the world, how is it that they didn't find the Sovereign Lord sooner? [10] But they were miserable, and their hopes were in dead things, who called them gods which are works of men's hands, gold and silver, skillfully made, and likenesses of animals, or a useless stone, the work of an ancient hand. [11] Yes and some[b] woodcutter might saw down a tree that is easily moved, skillfully strip away all its bark, and fashion it in attractive form, make a useful vessel to serve his life's needs. [12] Burning the scraps from his handiwork to cook his food, he eats his fill. [13] Taking a discarded scrap which served no purpose, a crooked piece of wood and full of knots, he carves it with the diligence of his idleness, and shapes it by the skill of his idleness. He shapes it in the image of a man, [14] or makes it like some worthless animal, smearing it with something red, painting it red, and smearing over every stain in it. [15] Having made a worthy chamber for it, he sets it in a wall, securing it with iron. [16] He plans for it that it may not fall down, knowing that it is unable to help itself (for truly it is an image, and needs help). [17] When he makes his prayer concerning goods and his marriage and children, he is not ashamed to speak to that which has no life. [18] Yes, for health, he calls upon that which is weak. For life, he implores that which is dead. For aid, he supplicates that which has no experience. For a good journey, he asks that which can't so much as move a step. [19] And for profit in business and good success of his hands, he asks ability from that which has hands with no ability.

## 14

[1] Again, one preparing to sail, and about to journey over raging waves, calls upon a piece of wood more fragile than the vessel that carries him. [2] For the hunger for profit planned it, and wisdom was the craftsman who built it. [3] Your providence, O Father, guides it along, because even in the sea you gave a way, and in the waves a sure path, [4] showing that you can save out of every danger, that even a man without skill may put to sea. [5] It is your will that the works of your wisdom should not be ineffective. Therefore men also entrust their lives to a little piece of wood, and passing through the surge on a raft come safely to land. [6] For[c] in the old time also, when proud giants were perishing, the hope of the world, taking refuge on a raft, your hand guided the seed of generations of the race of men. [7] For blessed is wood through which comes righteousness; [8] but the idol made with hands is accursed, itself and he that made it; because his was the working, and the corruptible thing was called a god. [9] For both the ungodly and his ungodliness are alike hateful to God; [10] for truly the deed will be punished together with him who committed it. [11] Therefore also there will be a visitation among the idols of the nation, because, though formed of things which God created, they were made an abomination, stumbling blocks to the souls of men, and a snare to the feet of the foolish. [12] For the devising of idols was the beginning of fornication, and the invention of them the corruption of life. [13] For they didn't exist from the beginning, and they won't exist forever. [14] For by the boastfulness of men they entered into the world, and therefore a speedy end was planned for them. [15] For a father worn with untimely grief, making an image of the child quickly taken away, now honored him as a god which was then a dead human being, and delivered to those that were under him mysteries and solemn rites. [16] Afterward the ungodly custom, in process of time grown strong, was kept as a law, and the engraved images received worship by the commandments of princes. [17] And when men could not honor them in presence because they lived far off, imagining the likeness from afar, they made a visible image of the king whom they honored, that by their zeal they might flatter the absent as if present. [18] But worship was raised to a yet higher pitch, even by those who didn't know him, urged forward by the ambition of the architect; [19] for he, wishing perhaps to please his ruler, used his art to force the likeness toward a greater beauty. [20] So the multitude, allured by reason of the grace of his handiwork, now consider an object of devotion him that a little before was honored as a man. [21] And this became an ambush, because men, in bondage either to calamity or to tyranny, invested stones and stocks with the Name that shouldn't be shared. [22] Afterward it was not enough for them to go astray concerning the knowledge of God, but also, while they live in a great war of ignorance, they call a multitude of evils peace. [23] For either slaughtering children in solemn rites, or celebrating secret mysteries, or holding frenzied revels of strange customs, [24] no longer do they guard either life or purity of marriage, but one brings upon another either death by treachery, or anguish by adultery. [25] And all things confusedly are filled with blood and murder, theft and deceit, corruption, faithlessness, tumult, perjury, [26] confusion about what is good, forgetfulness of favors, ingratitude for benefits, defiling of souls, confusion of sex, disorder in marriage, adultery and wantonness. [27] For the worship of idols that may not be named [*] is a beginning and cause and end of every evil. [28] For their worshipers either make merry to madness, or prophesy lies, or live unrighteously, or lightly commit perjury. [29] For putting their trust in lifeless idols, when they have sworn a wicked oath, they expect not to suffer harm. [30] But on both counts, the just doom will pursue them, because they had evil thoughts of God by giving heed to idols, and swore unrighteously in deceit through contempt for holiness. [31] For it is not the power of things by which men swear, but it is the just penalty for those who sin that always visits the transgression of the unrighteous.

## 15

[1] But you, our God, are gracious and true, patient, and in mercy ordering all things. [2] For even if we sin, we are yours, knowing your dominion; but we will not sin, knowing that we have been accounted yours. [3] For to be acquainted with you is[d] perfect righteousness, and to know your dominion is the root of immortality. [4] For we weren't led astray by any evil plan of men's, nor yet by painters' fruitless labor, a form stained with varied colors, [5] the sight of which leads fools into[e] lust. Their desire is for the breathless form of a dead image. [6] Lovers of evil things, and worthy of such hopes, are those who make, desire, and worship them. [7] For a potter, kneading soft earth, laboriously molds each article for our service. He fashions out of the same clay both the vessels that minister to clean uses, and those of a contrary sort, all in like manner. What shall be the use of each article of either sort, the potter is the judge. [8] Also, laboring to an evil end, he molds a vain god out of the same clay, he who, having but a little before been made of earth, after a short space goes his way to the earth out of which he was taken, when he is required to render back the[f] soul which was lent him. [9] However he has anxious care, not because his powers must fail, nor because his span of life is short; But he compares himself with goldsmiths and silversmiths, and he imitates molders in[g] brass, and considers it great that he molds counterfeit gods. [10] His heart is ashes. His hope is of less value than earth. His life is of less honor than clay, [11] because he was ignorant of him who molded him, and of him that inspired into him[h] an active[i] soul, and breathed into him a vital spirit. [12] But[j] he accounted our life to be a game, and our[k] lifetime a festival for profit; for, he says, one must get gain however one can, even if it is by evil. [13] For this man, beyond all others, knows that he sins, out of earthy matter making brittle vessels and engraved images. [14] But most foolish and more miserable than a baby, are the enemies of your people, who oppressed them; [15] because they even considered all the idols of the nations to be gods, which have neither the use of eyes for seeing, nor nostrils for drawing breath, nor ears to hear, nor fingers for handling, and their feet are helpless for walking. [16] For a man made them, and one whose own spirit is borrowed molded them; for no one has power as a man to mold a god like himself. [17] But, being mortal, he makes a dead thing by the work of lawless hands; for he is better than the objects of his worship, since he indeed had life, but they never did. [18] Yes, and they worship the creatures that are most hateful, for, being compared as to lack of sense, these are worse than all others; [19] Neither, as seen beside other creatures, are they beautiful, so that one should desire them, but they have escaped both the praise of God and his blessing.

---

[a] 13:5 Gr. is the first maker of them seen.

[b] 13:11 Gr. carpenter who is a woodcutter.

[c] 14:6 The Greek text here may be corrupt.

[*] 14:27 Exodus 23:13; Psalms 16:4; Hosea 2:17; Wisdom 14:21

[d] 15:3 Gr. entire.

[e] 15:5 Some authorities read reproach.

[f] 15:8 Or, life

[g] 15:9 Or, copper

[h] 15:11 Gr. a soul that moves to activity.

[i] 15:11 Or, life

[j] 15:12 Some authorities read they accounted.

[k] 15:12 Or, way of life

## 16

[1] For this cause, they were deservedly punished through creatures like those which they worship, and tormented through a multitude of vermin. [2] Instead of this punishment, you, giving benefits to your people, prepared quails for food, a delicacy to satisfy the desire of their appetite, [3] to the end that your enemies, desiring food, might for the hideousness of the creatures sent among them, loathe even the necessary appetite; but these, your people, having for a short time suffered lack, might even partake of delicacies. [4] For it was necessary that inescapable lack should come upon those oppressors, but that to these it should only be showed how their enemies were tormented. [5] For even when terrible raging of wild beasts came upon your people, and they were perishing by the bites of crooked serpents, your wrath didn't continue to the uttermost; [6] but for admonition were they troubled for a short time, having a token of salvation to put them in remembrance of the commandment of your law; [7] for he who turned toward it was not saved because of that which was seen, but because of you, the Savior of all. [8] Yes, and in this you persuaded our enemies that you are he who delivers out of every evil. [9] For the bites of locusts and flies truly killed them. No healing for their life was found, because they were worthy to be punished by such things. [10] But your children weren't overcome by the very fangs of venomous dragons, for your mercy passed by where they were and healed them. [11] For they were bitten to put them in remembrance of your oracles, and were quickly saved, lest, falling into deep forgetfulness, they should become unable to respond to your kindness. [12] For truly it was neither herb nor poultice that cured them, but your word, O Lord, which heals all people. [13] For you have authority over life and death, and you lead down to the gates of Hades, and lead up again. [14] But though a man kills by his wickedness, he can't retrieve the spirit that has departed or release the imprisoned soul. [15] But it is not possible to escape your hand; [16] for ungodly men, refusing to know you, were scourged in the strength of your arm, pursued with strange rains and hails and relentless storms, and utterly consumed with fire. [17] For, what was most marvelous, in the water which quenches all things, the fire burned hotter; for the world fights for the righteous. [18] For at one time the flame was restrained, that it might not burn up the creatures sent against the ungodly, but that these themselves as they looked might see that they were chased by the judgment of God. [19] At another time even in the midst of water it burns more intensely than fire, that it may destroy the produce of an unrighteous land. [20] Instead of these things, you gave your people angels' food to eat, and you provided ready-to-eat bread for them from heaven without toil, having the virtue of every pleasant flavor, and agreeable to every taste. [21] For your nature showed your sweetness toward your children, while that bread, serving the desire of the eater, changed itself according to every man's choice. [22] But snow and ice endured fire, and didn't melt, that people might know that fire was destroying the fruits of the enemies, burning in the hail and flashing in the rains; [23] and that this fire, again, in order that righteous people may be nourished, has even forgotten its own power. [24] For the creation, ministering to you, its maker, strains its force against the unrighteous for punishment and in kindness, slackens it on behalf of those who trust in you. [25] Therefore at that time also, converting itself into all forms, it ministered to your all-nourishing bounty, according to the desire of those who had need, [26] that your children, whom you loved, O Lord, might learn that it is not the growth of crops that nourishes a man, but that your word preserves those who trust you. [27] For that which was not destroyed by fire, melted away when it was simply warmed by a faint sunbeam, [28] that it might be known that we must rise before the sun to give you thanks, and must pray to you at the dawning of the light; [29] for the hope of the unthankful will melt as the winter's hoar frost, and will flow away as water that has no use.

## 17

[1] For your judgments are great, and hard to interpret; therefore undisciplined souls went astray. [2] For when lawless men had supposed that they held a holy nation in their power, they, prisoners of darkness, and bound in the fetters of a long night, kept close beneath their roofs, lay exiled from the eternal providence. [3] For while they thought that they were unseen in their secret sins, they were divided from one another by a dark curtain of forgetfulness, stricken with terrible awe, and very troubled by apparitions. [4] For neither did the dark recesses that held them guard them from fears, but terrifying sounds rang around them, and dismal phantoms appeared with unsmiling faces. [5] And no power of fire prevailed to give light, neither were the brightest flames of the stars strong enough to illuminate that gloomy night; [6] but only the glimmering of a self-kindled fire appeared to them, full of fear. In terror, they considered the things which they saw to be worse than that sight, on which they could not gaze. [7] The mockeries of their magic arts were powerless, now, and a shameful rebuke of their boasted understanding: [8] For those who promised to drive away terrors and disorders from a sick soul, these were sick with a ludicrous fearfulness.

[9] For even if no troubling thing frighted them, yet, scared with the creeping of vermin and hissing of serpents, [10] they perished trembling in fear, refusing even to look at the air, which could not be escaped on any side. [11] For wickedness, condemned by a witness within, is a coward thing, and, being pressed hard by conscience, always has added forecasts of the worst. [12] For fear is nothing else but a surrender of the help which reason offers; [13] and from within, the expectation of being less prefers ignorance of the cause that brings the torment. [14] But they, all through the night which was powerless indeed, and which came upon them out of the recesses of powerless Hades, sleeping the same sleep, [15] now were haunted by monstrous apparitions, and now were paralyzed by their soul's surrendering; for sudden and unexpected fear came upon them. [16] So then whoever it might be, sinking down in his place, was kept captive, shut up in that prison which was not barred with iron; [17] for whether he was a farmer, or a shepherd, or a laborer whose toils were in the wilderness, he was overtaken, and endured that inescapable sentence; for they were all bound with one chain of darkness. [18] Whether there was a whistling wind, or a melodious sound of birds among the spreading branches, or a measured fall of water running violently, [19] or a harsh crashing of rocks hurled down, or the swift course of animals bounding along unseen, or the voice of wild beasts harshly roaring, or an echo rebounding from the hollows of the mountains, all these things paralyzed them with terror. [20] For the whole world was illuminated with clear light, and was occupied with unhindered works, [21] while over them alone was spread a heavy night, an image of the darkness that should afterward receive them; but to themselves, they were heavier than darkness.

## 18

[1] But for your holy ones there was great light. Their enemies, hearing their voice but not seeing their form, counted it a happy thing that they too had suffered, [2] yet for that they do not hurt them, though wronged by them before, they are thankful; and because they had been at variance with them, they begged for pardon. [3] Therefore you provided a burning pillar of fire, to be a guide for your people's unknown journey, and a harmless sun for their glorious exile. [4] For the Egyptians well deserved to be deprived of light and imprisoned by darkness, they who had imprisoned your children, through whom the incorruptible light of the law was to be given to the race of men. [5] After they had taken counsel to kill the babes of the holy ones, and when a single child had been abandoned and saved to convict them of their sin, you took away from them their multitude of children, and destroyed all their army together in a mighty flood. [6] Our fathers were made aware of that night beforehand, that, having sure knowledge, they might be cheered by the oaths which they had trusted. [7] Salvation of the righteous and destruction of the enemies was expected by your people. [8] For as you took vengeance on the adversaries, by the same means, calling us to yourself, you glorified us. [9] For holy children of good men offered sacrifice in secret, and with one consent they agreed to the covenant of the divine law, that they would partake alike in the same good things and the same perils, the fathers already leading the sacred songs of praise. [10] But the discordant cry of the enemies echoed back, and a pitiful voice of lamentation for children was spread abroad. [11] Both servant and master were punished with the same just doom, and the commoner suffering the same as king; [12] Yes, they all together, under one form of death, had corpses without number. For the living were not sufficient even to bury them, Since at a single stroke, their most cherished offspring was consumed. [13] For while they were disbelieving all things by reason of the enchantments, upon the destruction of the firstborn they confessed the people to be God's children. [14] For while peaceful silence wrapped all things, and night in her own swiftness was half spent, [15] your all-powerful word leaped from heaven, from the royal throne, a stern warrior, into the midst of the doomed land, [16] bearing as a sharp sword your authentic commandment, and standing, it filled all things with death, and while it touched the heaven it stood upon the earth. [17] Then immediately apparitions in dreams terribly troubled them, and unexpected fears came upon them. [18] And each, one thrown here half dead, another there, made known why he was dying; [19] for the dreams, disturbing them, forewarned them of this, that they might not perish without knowing why they were afflicted. [20] The experience of death also touched the righteous, and a multitude were destroyed in the wilderness, but the wrath didn't last long. [21] For a blameless man hurried to be their champion, bringing the weapon of his own ministry, prayer, and the atoning sacrifice of incense. He withstood the indignation and set an end to the calamity, showing that he was your servant. [22] And he overcame the anger, not by strength of body, not by force of weapons, but by his word, he subdued the avenger by bringing to remembrance oaths and covenants made with the fathers. [23] For when the dead had already fallen in heaps one upon another, he intervened and stopped the wrath, and cut off its way to the living. [24] For the whole world was pictured on his long robe, and the glories of

the fathers were upon the engraving of the four rows of precious stones, and your majesty was upon the diadem on his head. ²⁵ The destroyer yielded to these, and they feared; for it was enough only to test the wrath.

## 19

¹ But indignation without mercy came upon the ungodly to the end; for God also foreknew their future, ² how, having changed their minds to let your people go, and having sped them eagerly on their way, they would change their minds and pursue them. ³ For while they were yet in the midst of their mourning, and lamenting at the graves of the dead, they made another foolish decision, and pursued as fugitives those whom they had begged to leave and driven out. ⁴ For the doom which they deserved was drawing them to this end, and it made them forget the things that had happened to them, that they might fill up the punishment which was yet lacking from their torments, ⁵ and that your people might journey on by a marvelous road, but they themselves might find a strange death. ⁶ For the whole creation, each part in its diverse kind, was made new again, complying with your commandments, that your servants might be kept unharmed. ⁷ Then the cloud that overshadowed the camp was seen, and dry land rising up out of what had been water, out of the Red sea an unhindered highway, and a grassy plain out of the violent surge, ⁸ by which they passed over with all their army, these who were covered with your hand, having seen strange marvels. ⁹ For like horses they roamed at large, and they skipped about like lambs, praising you, O Lord, who was their deliverer. ¹⁰ For they still remembered the things that happened in the time of their sojourning, how instead of bearing cattle, the land brought forth lice, and instead of fish, the river spewed out a multitude of frogs. ¹¹ But afterwards, they also saw a new kind of birds, when, led on by desire, they asked for luxurious dainties; ¹² for, to comfort them, quails came up for them from the sea. ¹³ Punishments came upon the sinners, not without the signs that were given beforehand by the violence of the thunder, for they justly suffered through their own wickednesses, for the hatred which they practiced toward guests was grievous indeed. ¹⁴ For while the others didn't receive the strangers when they came to them, the Egyptians made slaves of guests who were their benefactors. ¹⁵ And not only so, but while punishment of some sort will come upon the former, since they received as enemies those who were aliens; ¹⁶ because these first welcomed with feastings, and then afflicted with dreadful toils, those who had already shared with them in the same rights. ¹⁷ And moreover they were stricken with loss of sight (even as were those others at the righteous man's doors), when, being surrounded with yawning darkness, they each looked for the passage through his own door. ¹⁸ For as the notes of a lute vary the character of the rhythm, even so the elements, changing their order one with another, continuing always in its sound, as may clearly be conjectured from the sight of the things that have happened. ¹⁹ For creatures of the dry land were turned into creatures of the waters, and creatures that swim moved upon the land. ²⁰ Fire kept the mastery of its own power in water, and water forgot its quenching nature. ²¹ On the contrary, flames didn't consume flesh of perishable creatures that walked among them, neither did they melt the crystalline grains of ambrosial food that were melted easily. ²² For in all things, O Lord, you magnified your people, and you glorified them and didn't lightly regard them, standing by their side in every time and place.

# Ecclesiastes or, The Preacher
## 1

¹ The words of the Preacher, the son of David, king in Jerusalem: ² "Vanity of vanities," says the Preacher; "Vanity of vanities, all is vanity." ³ What does man gain from all his labor in which he labors under the sun? ⁴ One generation goes, and another generation comes; but the earth remains forever. ⁵ The sun also rises, and the sun goes down, and hurries to its place where it rises. ⁶ The wind goes toward the south, and turns around to the north. It turns around continually as it goes, and the wind returns again to its courses. ⁷ All the rivers run into the sea, yet the sea is not full. To the place where the rivers flow, there they flow again. ⁸ All things are full of weariness beyond uttering. The eye is not satisfied with seeing, nor the ear filled with hearing. ⁹ That which has been is that which shall be, and that which has been done is that which shall be done; and there is no new thing under the sun. ¹⁰ Is there a thing of which it may be said, "Behold,ᵃ this is new"? It has been long ago, in the ages which were before us. ¹¹ There is no memory of the former; neither shall there be any memory of the latter that are to come, among those that shall come after. ¹² I, the Preacher,

was king over Israel in Jerusalem. ¹³ I applied my heart to seek and to search out by wisdom concerning all that is done under the sky. It is a heavy burden that Godᵇ has given to the sons of men to be afflicted with. ¹⁴ I have seen all the works that are done under the sun; and behold, all is vanity and a chasing after wind. ¹⁵ That which is crooked can't be made straight; and that which is lacking can't be counted. ¹⁶ I said to myself, "Behold, I have obtained for myself great wisdom above all who were before me in Jerusalem. Yes, my heart has had great experience of wisdom and knowledge." ¹⁷ I applied my heart to know wisdom, and to know madness and folly. I perceived that this also was a chasing after wind. ¹⁸ For in much wisdom is much grief; and he who increases knowledge increases sorrow.

## 2

¹ I said in my heart, "Come now, I will test you with mirth; therefore enjoy pleasure;" and behold, this also was vanity. ² I said of laughter, "It is foolishness;" and of mirth, "What does it accomplish?" ³ I searched in my heart how to cheer my flesh with wine, my heart yet guiding me with wisdom, and how to lay hold of folly, until I might see what it was good for the sons of men that they should do under heaven all the days of their lives. ⁴ I made myself great works. I built myself houses. I planted myself vineyards. ⁵ I made myself gardens and parks, and I planted trees in them of all kinds of fruit. ⁶ I made myself pools of water, to water the forest where trees were grown. ⁷ I bought male servants and female servants, and had servants born in my house. I also had great possessions of herds and flocks, above all who were before me in Jerusalem. ⁸ I also gathered silver and gold for myself, and the treasure of kings and of the provinces. I got myself male and female singers, and the delights of the sons of men: musical instruments of all sorts. ⁹ So I was great, and increased more than all who were before me in Jerusalem. My wisdom also remained with me. ¹⁰ Whatever my eyes desired, I didn't keep from them. I didn't withhold my heart from any joy, for my heart rejoiced because of all my labor, and this was my portion from all my labor. ¹¹ Then I looked at all the works that my hands had worked, and at the labor that I had labored to do; and behold, all was vanity and a chasing after wind, and there was no profit under the sun. ¹² I turned myself to consider wisdom, madness, and folly; for what can the king's successor do? Just that which has been done long ago. ¹³ Then I saw that wisdom excels folly, as far as light excels darkness. ¹⁴ The wise man's eyes are in his head, and the fool walks in darkness—and yet I perceived that one event happens to them all. ¹⁵ Then I said in my heart, "As it happens to the fool, so will it happen even to me; and why was I then more wise?" Then I said in my heart that this also is vanity. ¹⁶ For of the wise man, even as of the fool, there is no memory forever, since in the days to come all will have been long forgotten. Indeed, the wise man must die just like the fool! ¹⁷ So I hated life, because the work that is worked under the sun was grievous to me; for all is vanity and a chasing after wind. ¹⁸ I hated all my labor in which I labored under the sun, because I must leave it to the man who comes after me. ¹⁹ Who knows whether he will be a wise man or a fool? Yet he will have rule over all of my labor in which I have labored, and in which I have shown myself wise under the sun. This also is vanity. ²⁰ Therefore I began to cause my heart to despair concerning all the labor in which I had labored under the sun. ²¹ For there is a man whose labor is with wisdom, with knowledge, and with skillfulness; yet he shall leave it for his portion to a man who has not labored for it. This also is vanity and a great evil. ²² For what does a man have of all his labor and of the striving of his heart, in which he labors under the sun? ²³ For all his days are sorrows, and his travail is grief; yes, even in the night his heart takes no rest. This also is vanity. ²⁴ There is nothing better for a man than that he should eat and drink, and make his soul enjoy good in his labor. This also I saw, that it is from the hand of God. ²⁵ For who can eat, or who can have enjoyment, more than I? ²⁶ For to the man who pleases him, God gives wisdom, knowledge, and joy; but to the sinner he gives travail, to gather and to heap up, that he may give to him who pleases God. This also is vanity and a chasing after wind.

## 3

¹ For everything there is a season, and a time for every purpose under heaven: ² a time to be born, and a time to die; a time to plant, and a time to pluck up that which is planted; ³ a time to kill, and a time to heal; a time to break down, and a time to build up; ⁴ a time to weep, and a time to laugh; a time to mourn, and a time to dance; ⁵ a time to cast away stones, and a time to gather stones together; a time to embrace, and a time to refrain from embracing; ⁶ a time to seek, and a time to lose; a time to keep, and a time to cast away; ⁷ a time to tear, and a time to sew; a time to keep silence, and a time to speak; ⁸ a time to love, and a time to hate; a time for war, and a time for peace. ⁹ What profit has he who

---

ᵃ *1:10* "Behold", from "הִנֵּה", means look at, take notice, observe, see, or gaze at. It is often used as an interjection.

ᵇ *1:13* The Hebrew word rendered "God" is "אֱלֹהִ֑ים" (Elohim).

works in that in which he labors? ¹⁰ I have seen the burden which God has given to the sons of men to be afflicted with. ¹¹ He has made everything beautiful in its time. He has also set eternity in their hearts, yet so that man can't find out the work that God has done from the beginning even to the end. ¹² I know that there is nothing better for them than to rejoice, and to do good as long as they live. ¹³ Also that every man should eat and drink, and enjoy good in all his labor, is the gift of God. ¹⁴ I know that whatever God does, it shall be forever. Nothing can be added to it, nor anything taken from it; and God has done it, that men should fear before him. ¹⁵ That which is has been long ago, and that which is to be has been long ago. God seeks again that which is passed away. ¹⁶ Moreover I saw under the sun, in the place of justice, that wickedness was there; and in the place of righteousness, that wickedness was there. ¹⁷ I said in my heart, "God will judge the righteous and the wicked; for there is a time there for every purpose and for every work." ¹⁸ I said in my heart, "As for the sons of men, God tests them, so that they may see that they themselves are like animals. ¹⁹ For that which happens to the sons of men happens to animals. Even one thing happens to them. As the one dies, so the other dies. Yes, they have all one breath; and man has no advantage over the animals, for all is vanity. ²⁰ All go to one place. All are from the dust, and all turn to dust again. ²¹ Who knows the spirit of man, whether it goes upward, and the spirit of the animal, whether it goes downward to the earth?" ²² Therefore I saw that there is nothing better than that a man should rejoice in his works, for that is his portion; for who can bring him to see what will be after him?

## 4

¹ Then I returned and saw all the oppressions that are done under the sun: and behold, the tears of those who were oppressed, and they had no comforter; and on the side of their oppressors there was power; but they had no comforter. ² Therefore I praised the dead who have been long dead more than the living who are yet alive. ³ Yes, better than them both is him who has not yet been, who has not seen the evil work that is done under the sun. ⁴ Then I saw all the labor and achievement that is the envy of a man's neighbor. This also is vanity and a striving after wind. ⁵ The fool folds his hands together and ruins himself. ⁶ Better is a handful, with quietness, than two handfuls with labor and chasing after wind. ⁷ Then I returned and saw vanity under the sun. ⁸ There is one who is alone, and he has neither son nor brother. There is no end to all of his labor, neither are his eyes satisfied with wealth. "For whom then do I labor and deprive my soul of enjoyment?" This also is vanity. Yes, it is a miserable business. ⁹ Two are better than one, because they have a good reward for their labor. ¹⁰ For if they fall, the one will lift up his fellow; but woe to him who is alone when he falls, and doesn't have another to lift him up. ¹¹ Again, if two lie together, then they have warmth; but how can one keep warm alone? ¹² If a man prevails against one who is alone, two shall withstand him; and a threefold cord is not quickly broken. ¹³ Better is a poor and wise youth than an old and foolish king who doesn't know how to receive admonition any more. ¹⁴ For out of prison he came out to be king; yes, even in his kingdom he was born poor. ¹⁵ I saw all the living who walk under the sun, that they were with the youth, the other, who succeeded him. ¹⁶ There was no end of all the people, even of all them over whom he was—yet those who come after shall not rejoice in him. Surely this also is vanity and a chasing after wind.

## 5

¹ Guard your steps when you go to God's house; for to draw near to listen is better than to give the sacrifice of fools, for they don't know that they do evil. ² Don't be rash with your mouth, and don't let your heart be hasty to utter anything before God; for God is in heaven, and you on earth. Therefore let your words be few. ³ For as a dream comes with a multitude of cares, so a fool's speech with a multitude of words. ⁴ When you vow a vow to God, don't defer to pay it; for he has no pleasure in fools. Pay that which you vow. ⁵ It is better that you should not vow, than that you should vow and not pay. ⁶ Don't allow your mouth to lead you into sin. Don't protest before the messenger that this was a mistake. Why should God be angry at your voice, and destroy the work of your hands? ⁷ For in the multitude of dreams there are vanities, as well as in many words; but you must fear God. ⁸ If you see the oppression of the poor, and the violent taking away of justice and righteousness in a district, don't marvel at the matter, for one official is eyed by a higher one, and there are officials over them. ⁹ Moreover the profit of the earth is for all. The king profits from the field. ¹⁰ He who loves silver shall not be satisfied with silver, nor he who loves abundance, with increase. This also is vanity. ¹¹ When goods increase, those who eat them are increased; and what advantage is there to its owner, except to feast on them with his eyes? ¹² The sleep of a laboring man is sweet, whether he eats little or much; but the abundance of the rich will not allow him to sleep. ¹³ There is a grievous evil which I have seen under the sun: wealth kept by its owner to his harm. ¹⁴ Those riches

perish by misfortune, and if he has fathered a son, there is nothing in his hand. ¹⁵ As he came out of his mother's womb, naked shall he go again as he came, and shall take nothing for his labor, which he may carry away in his hand. ¹⁶ This also is a grievous evil, that in all points as he came, so shall he go. And what profit does he have who labors for the wind? ¹⁷ All his days he also eats in darkness, he is frustrated, and has sickness and wrath. ¹⁸ Behold, that which I have seen to be good and proper is for one to eat and to drink, and to enjoy good in all his labor, in which he labors under the sun, all the days of his life which God has given him; for this is his portion. ¹⁹ Every man also to whom God has given riches and wealth, and has given him power to eat of it, and to take his portion, and to rejoice in his labor—this is the gift of God. ²⁰ For he shall not often reflect on the days of his life, because God occupies him with the joy of his heart.

## 6

¹ There is an evil which I have seen under the sun, and it is heavy on men: ² a man to whom God gives riches, wealth, and honor, so that he lacks nothing for his soul of all that he desires, yet God gives him no power to eat of it, but an alien eats it. This is vanity, and it is an evil disease. ³ If a man fathers a hundred children, and lives many years, so that the days of his years are many, but his soul is not filled with good, and moreover he has no burial, I say that a stillborn child is better than he; ⁴ for it comes in vanity, and departs in darkness, and its name is covered with darkness. ⁵ Moreover it has not seen the sun nor known it. This has rest rather than the other. ⁶ Yes, though he live a thousand years twice told, and yet fails to enjoy good, don't all go to one place? ⁷ All the labor of man is for his mouth, and yet the appetite is not filled. ⁸ For what advantage has the wise more than the fool? What has the poor man, that knows how to walk before the living? ⁹ Better is the sight of the eyes than the wandering of the desire. This also is vanity and a chasing after wind. ¹⁰ Whatever has been, its name was given long ago; and it is known what man is; neither can he contend with him who is mightier than he. ¹¹ For there are many words that create vanity. What does that profit man? ¹² For who knows what is good for man in life, all the days of his vain life which he spends like a shadow? For who can tell a man what will be after him under the sun?

## 7

¹ A good name is better than fine perfume; and the day of death better than the day of one's birth. ² It is better to go to the house of mourning than to go to the house of feasting; for that is the end of all men, and the living should take this to heart. ³ Sorrow is better than laughter; for by the sadness of the face the heart is made good. ⁴ The heart of the wise is in the house of mourning; but the heart of fools is in the house of mirth. ⁵ It is better to hear the rebuke of the wise than for a man to hear the song of fools. ⁶ For as the crackling of thorns under a pot, so is the laughter of the fool. This also is vanity. ⁷ Surely extortion makes the wise man foolish; and a bribe destroys the understanding. ⁸ Better is the end of a thing than its beginning. The patient in spirit is better than the proud in spirit. ⁹ Don't be hasty in your spirit to be angry, for anger rests in the bosom of fools. ¹⁰ Don't say, "Why were the former days better than these?" For you do not ask wisely about this. ¹¹ Wisdom is as good as an inheritance. Yes, it is more excellent for those who see the sun. ¹² For wisdom is a defense, even as money is a defense; but the excellency of knowledge is that wisdom preserves the life of him who has it. ¹³ Consider the work of God, for who can make that straight which he has made crooked? ¹⁴ In the day of prosperity be joyful, and in the day of adversity consider; yes, God has made the one side by side with the other, to the end that man should not find out anything after him. ¹⁵ All this I have seen in my days of vanity: there is a righteous man who perishes in his righteousness, and there is a wicked man who lives long in his evildoing. ¹⁶ Don't be overly righteous, neither make yourself overly wise. Why should you destroy yourself? ¹⁷ Don't be too wicked, neither be foolish. Why should you die before your time? ¹⁸ It is good that you should take hold of this. Yes, also don't withdraw your hand from that; for he who fears God will come out of them all. ¹⁹ Wisdom is a strength to the wise man more than ten rulers who are in a city. ²⁰ Surely there is not a righteous man on earth who does good and doesn't sin. ²¹ Also don't take heed to all words that are spoken, lest you hear your servant curse you; ²² for often your own heart knows that you yourself have likewise cursed others. ²³ All this I have proved in wisdom. I said, "I will be wise;" but it was far from me. ²⁴ That which is, is far off and exceedingly deep. Who can find it out? ²⁵ I turned around, and my heart sought to know and to search out, and to seek wisdom and the scheme of things, and to know that wickedness is stupidity, and that foolishness is madness. ²⁶ I find more bitter than death the woman whose heart is snares and traps, whose hands are chains. Whoever pleases God shall escape from her; but the sinner will be ensnared by her. ²⁷ "Behold, I have found this," says the Preacher, "to one another, to find an explanation ²⁸ which my soul still seeks, but I have not found. I have found one man among a thousand, but I have

not found a woman among all those. ²⁹ Behold, I have only found this: that God made mankind upright; but they search for many inventions."

# 8

¹ Who is like the wise man? And who knows the interpretation of a thing? A man's wisdom makes his face shine, and the hardness of his face is changed. ² I say, "Keep the king's command!" because of the oath to God. ³ Don't be hasty to go out of his presence. Don't persist in an evil thing, for he does whatever pleases him, ⁴ for the king's word is supreme. Who can say to him, "What are you doing?" ⁵ Whoever keeps the commandment shall not come to harm, and his wise heart will know the time and procedure. ⁶ For there is a time and procedure for every purpose, although the misery of man is heavy on him. ⁷ For he doesn't know that which will be; for who can tell him how it will be? ⁸ There is no man who has power over the spirit to contain the spirit; neither does he have power over the day of death. There is no discharge in war; neither shall wickedness deliver those who practice it. ⁹ All this I have seen, and applied my mind to every work that is done under the sun. There is a time in which one man has power over another to his hurt. ¹⁰ So I saw the wicked buried. Indeed they came also from holiness. They went and were forgotten in the city where they did this. This also is vanity. ¹¹ Because sentence against an evil work is not executed speedily, therefore the heart of the sons of men is fully set in them to do evil. ¹² Though a sinner commits crimes a hundred times, and lives long, yet surely I know that it will be better with those who fear God, who are reverent before him. ¹³ But it shall not be well with the wicked, neither shall he lengthen days like a shadow, because he doesn't fear God. ¹⁴ There is a vanity which is done on the earth, that there are righteous men to whom it happens according to the work of the wicked. Again, there are wicked men to whom it happens according to the work of the righteous. I said that this also is vanity. ¹⁵ Then I commended mirth, because a man has no better thing under the sun than to eat, to drink, and to be joyful: for that will accompany him in his labor all the days of his life which God has given him under the sun. ¹⁶ When I applied my heart to know wisdom, and to see the business that is done on the earth (even though eyes see no sleep day or night), ¹⁷ then I saw all the work of God, that man can't find out the work that is done under the sun, because however much a man labors to seek it out, yet he won't find it. Yes even though a wise man thinks he can comprehend it, he won't be able to find it.

# 9

¹ For all this I laid to my heart, even to explore all this: that the righteous, and the wise, and their works, are in the hand of God; whether it is love or hatred, man doesn't know it; all is before them. ² All things come alike to all. There is one event to the righteous and to the wicked; to the good, to the clean, to the unclean, to him who sacrifices, and to him who doesn't sacrifice. As is the good, so is the sinner; he who takes an oath, as he who fears an oath. ³ This is an evil in all that is done under the sun, that there is one event to all. Yes also, the heart of the sons of men is full of evil, and madness is in their heart while they live, and after that they go to the dead. ⁴ For to him who is joined with all the living there is hope; for a living dog is better than a dead lion. ⁵ For the living know that they will die, but the dead don't know anything, neither do they have any more a reward; for their memory is forgotten. ⁶ Also their love, their hatred, and their envy has perished long ago; neither do they any longer have a portion forever in anything that is done under the sun. ⁷ Go your way—eat your bread with joy, and drink your wine with a merry heart; for God has already accepted your works. ⁸ Let your garments be always white, and don't let your head lack oil. ⁹ Live joyfully with the wife whom you love all the days of your life of vanity, which he has given you under the sun, all your days of vanity, for that is your portion in life, and in your labor in which you labor under the sun. ¹⁰ Whatever your hand finds to do, do it with your might; for there is no work, nor plan, nor knowledge, nor wisdom, in Sheol,ᵃ where you are going. ¹¹ I returned and saw under the sun that the race is not to the swift, nor the battle to the strong, neither yet bread to the wise, nor yet riches to men of understanding, nor yet favor to men of skill; but time and chance happen to them all. ¹² For man also doesn't know his time. As the fish that are taken in an evil net, and as the birds that are caught in the snare, even so are the sons of men snared in an evil time, when it falls suddenly on them. ¹³ I have also seen wisdom under the sun in this way, and it seemed great to me. ¹⁴ There was a little city, and few men within it; and a great king came against it, besieged it, and built great bulwarks against it. ¹⁵ Now a poor wise man was found in it, and he by his wisdom delivered the city; yet no man remembered that same poor man. ¹⁶ Then I said, "Wisdom is better than strength." Nevertheless the poor man's wisdom is despised, and his words are not heard. ¹⁷ The words of the wise heard

in quiet are better than the cry of him who rules among fools. ¹⁸ Wisdom is better than weapons of war; but one sinner destroys much good.

# 10

¹ Dead flies cause the oil of the perfumer to produce an evil odor; so does a little folly outweigh wisdom and honor. ² A wise man's heart is at his right hand, but a fool's heart at his left. ³ Yes also when the fool walks by the way, his understanding fails him, and he says to everyone that he is a fool. ⁴ If the spirit of the ruler rises up against you, don't leave your place; for gentleness lays great offenses to rest. ⁵ There is an evil which I have seen under the sun, the sort of error which proceeds from the ruler. ⁶ Folly is set in great dignity, and the rich sit in a low place. ⁷ I have seen servants on horses, and princes walking like servants on the earth. ⁸ He who digs a pit may fall into it; and whoever breaks through a wall may be bitten by a snake. ⁹ Whoever carves out stones may be injured by them. Whoever splits wood may be endangered by it. ¹⁰ If the ax is blunt, and one doesn't sharpen the edge, then he must use more strength; but skill brings success. ¹¹ If the snake bites before it is charmed, then is there no profit for the charmer's tongue. ¹² The words of a wise man's mouth are gracious; but a fool is swallowed by his own lips. ¹³ The beginning of the words of his mouth is foolishness; and the end of his talk is mischievous madness. ¹⁴ A fool also multiplies words. Man doesn't know what will be; and that which will be after him, who can tell him? ¹⁵ The labor of fools wearies every one of them; for he doesn't know how to go to the city. ¹⁶ Woe to you, land, when your king is a child, and your princes eat in the morning! ¹⁷ Happy are you, land, when your king is the son of nobles, and your princes eat in due season, for strength, and not for drunkenness! ¹⁸ By slothfulness the roof sinks in; and through idleness of the hands the house leaks. ¹⁹ A feast is made for laughter, and wine makes the life glad; and money is the answer for all things. ²⁰ Don't curse the king, no, not in your thoughts; and don't curse the rich in your bedroom, for a bird of the sky may carry your voice, and that which has wings may tell the matter.

# 11

¹ Cast your bread on the waters; for you shall find it after many days. ² Give a portion to seven, yes, even to eight; for you don't know what evil will be on the earth. ³ If the clouds are full of rain, they empty themselves on the earth; and if a tree falls toward the south, or toward the north, in the place where the tree falls, there it shall be. ⁴ He who observes the wind won't sow; and he who regards the clouds won't reap. ⁵ As you don't know what is the way of the wind, nor how the bones grow in the womb of her who is with child; even so you don't know the work of God who does all. ⁶ In the morning sow your seed, and in the evening don't withhold your hand; for you don't know which will prosper, whether this or that, or whether they both will be equally good. ⁷ Truly the light is sweet, and it is a pleasant thing for the eyes to see the sun. ⁸ Yes, if a man lives many years, let him rejoice in them all; but let him remember the days of darkness, for they shall be many. All that comes is vanity. ⁹ Rejoice, young man, in your youth, and let your heart cheer you in the days of your youth, and walk in the ways of your heart, and in the sight of your eyes; but know that for all these things God will bring you into judgment. ¹⁰ Therefore remove sorrow from your heart, and put away evil from your flesh; for youth and the dawn of life are vanity.

# 12

¹ Remember also your Creator in the days of your youth, before the evil days come, and the years draw near, when you will say, "I have no pleasure in them;" ² Before the sun, the light, the moon, and the stars are darkened, and the clouds return after the rain; ³ in the day when the keepers of the house shall tremble, and the strong men shall bow themselves, and the grinders cease because they are few, and those who look out of the windows are darkened, ⁴ and the doors shall be shut in the street; when the sound of the grinding is low, and one shall rise up at the voice of a bird, and all the daughters of music shall be brought low; ⁵ yes, they shall be afraid of heights, and terrors will be on the way; and the almond tree shall blossom, and the grasshopper shall be a burden, and desire shall fail; because man goes to his everlasting home, and the mourners go about the streets; ⁶ before the silver cord is severed, or the golden bowl is broken, or the pitcher is broken at the spring, or the wheel broken at the cistern, ⁷ and the dust returns to the earth as it was, and the spirit returns to God who gave it. ⁸ "Vanity of vanities," says the Preacher. "All is vanity!" ⁹ Further, because the Preacher was wise, he still taught the people knowledge. Yes, he pondered, sought out, and set in order many proverbs. ¹⁰ The Preacher sought to find out acceptable words, and that which was written blamelessly, words of truth. ¹¹ The words of the wise are like goads; and like nails well fastened are words from the masters of assemblies, which are given

---

ᵃ *9:10 Sheol is the place of the dead.*

from one shepherd. ¹² Furthermore, my son, be admonished: of making many books there is no end; and much study is a weariness of the flesh. ¹³ This is the end of the matter. All has been heard. Fear God and keep his commandments; for this is the whole duty of man. ¹⁴ For God will bring every work into judgment, with every hidden thing, whether it is good, or whether it is evil.

# The Song of Songs, or Song of Solomon

## 1

¹ The Song of songs, which is Solomon's.

*Beloved*

² Let him kiss me with the kisses of his mouth; for your love is better than wine. ³ Your oils have a pleasing fragrance. Your name is oil poured out, therefore the virgins love you. ⁴ Take me away with you. Let's hurry. The king has brought me into his rooms.

*Friends*

We will be glad and rejoice in you. We will praise your love more than wine!

*Beloved*

They are right to love you. ⁵ I am dark, but lovely, you daughters of Jerusalem, like Kedar's tents, like Solomon's curtains. ⁶ Don't stare at me because I am dark, because the sun has scorched me. My mother's sons were angry with me. They made me keeper of the vineyards. I haven't kept my own vineyard. ⁷ Tell me, you whom my soul loves, where you graze your flock, where you rest them at noon; for why should I be as one who is veiled beside the flocks of your companions?

*Lover*

⁸ If you don't know, most beautiful among women, follow the tracks of the sheep. Graze your young goats beside the shepherds' tents. ⁹ I have compared you, my love, to a steed in Pharaoh's chariots. ¹⁰ Your cheeks are beautiful with earrings, your neck with strings of jewels.

*Friends*

¹¹ We will make you earrings of gold, with studs of silver.

*Beloved*

¹² While the king sat at his table, my perfume spread its fragrance. ¹³ My beloved is to me a sachet of myrrh, that lies between my breasts. ¹⁴ My beloved is to me a cluster of henna blossoms from the vineyards of En Gedi.

*Lover*

¹⁵ Behold,[a] you are beautiful, my love. Behold, you are beautiful. Your eyes are like doves.

*Beloved*

¹⁶ Behold, you are beautiful, my beloved, yes, pleasant; and our couch is verdant.

*Lover*

¹⁷ The beams of our house are cedars. Our rafters are firs.

## 2

*Beloved*

¹ I am a rose of Sharon, a lily of the valleys.

*Lover*

² As a lily among thorns, so is my love among the daughters.

*Beloved*

³ As the apple tree among the trees of the wood, so is my beloved among the sons. I sat down under his shadow with great delight, his fruit was sweet to my taste. ⁴ He brought me to the banquet hall. His banner over me is love. ⁵ Strengthen me with raisins, refresh me with apples; for I am faint with love.

⁶ His left hand is under my head. His right hand embraces me. ⁷ I adjure you, daughters of Jerusalem, by the roes, or by the hinds of the field, that you not stir up, nor awaken love, until it so desires. ⁸ The voice of my beloved! Behold, he comes, leaping on the mountains, skipping on the hills. ⁹ My beloved is like a roe or a young deer. Behold, he stands behind our wall! He looks in at the windows. He glances through the lattice. ¹⁰ My beloved spoke, and said to me, "Rise up, my love, my beautiful one, and come away. ¹¹ For behold, the winter is past. The rain is over and gone. ¹² The flowers appear on the earth. The time of the singing has come, and the voice of the turtledove is heard in our land. ¹³ The fig tree ripens her green figs. The vines are in blossom. They give out their fragrance. Arise, my love, my beautiful one, and come away."

*Lover*

¹⁴ My dove in the clefts of the rock, in the hiding places of the mountainside, let me see your face. Let me hear your voice; for your voice is sweet and your face is lovely. ¹⁵ Catch for us the foxes, the little foxes that plunder the vineyards; for our vineyards are in blossom.

*Beloved*

¹⁶ My beloved is mine, and I am his. He browses among the lilies. ¹⁷ Until the day is cool, and the shadows flee away, turn, my beloved, and be like a roe or a young deer on the mountains of Bether.

## 3

¹ By night on my bed, I sought him whom my soul loves. I sought him, but I didn't find him. ² I will get up now, and go about the city; in the streets and in the squares I will seek him whom my soul loves. I sought him, but I didn't find him. ³ The watchmen who go about the city found me; "Have you seen him whom my soul loves?" ⁴ I had scarcely passed from them, when I found him whom my soul loves. I held him, and would not let him go, until I had brought him into my mother's house, into the room of her who conceived me. ⁵ I adjure you, daughters of Jerusalem, by the roes, or by the hinds of the field, that you not stir up nor awaken love, until it so desires. ⁶ Who is this who comes up from the wilderness like pillars of smoke, perfumed with myrrh and frankincense, with all spices of the merchant? ⁷ Behold, it is Solomon's carriage! Sixty mighty men are around it, of the mighty men of Israel. ⁸ They all handle the sword, and are expert in war. Every man has his sword on his thigh, because of fear in the night. ⁹ King Solomon made himself a carriage of the wood of Lebanon. ¹⁰ He made its pillars of silver, its bottom of gold, its seat of purple, the middle of it being paved with love, from the daughters of Jerusalem. ¹¹ Go out, you daughters of Zion, and see King Solomon, with the crown with which his mother has crowned him, in the day of his weddings, in the day of the gladness of his heart.

## 4

*Lover*

¹ Behold, you are beautiful, my love. Behold, you are beautiful. Your eyes are like doves behind your veil. Your hair is as a flock of goats, that descend from Mount Gilead. ² Your teeth are like a newly shorn flock, which have come up from the washing, where every one of them has twins. None is bereaved among them. ³ Your lips are like scarlet thread. Your mouth is lovely. Your temples are like a piece of a pomegranate behind your veil. ⁴ Your neck is like David's tower built for an armory, on which a thousand shields hang, all the shields of the mighty men. ⁵ Your two breasts are like two fawns that are twins of a roe, which feed among the lilies. ⁶ Until the day is cool, and the shadows flee away, I will go to the mountain of myrrh, to the hill of frankincense. ⁷ You are all beautiful, my love. There is no spot in you. ⁸ Come with me from Lebanon, my bride, with me from Lebanon. Look from the top of Amana, from the top of Senir and Hermon, from the lions' dens, from the mountains of the leopards. ⁹ You have ravished my heart, my sister, my bride. You have ravished my heart with one of your eyes, with one chain of your neck. ¹⁰ How beautiful is your love, my sister, my bride! How much better is your love than wine, the fragrance of your perfumes than all kinds of spices! ¹¹ Your lips, my bride, drip like the honeycomb. Honey and milk are under your tongue. The smell of your garments is like the smell of Lebanon. ¹² My sister, my bride, is a locked up garden; a locked up spring, a sealed fountain. ¹³ Your shoots are an orchard of pomegranates, with precious fruits, henna with spikenard plants, ¹⁴ spikenard and saffron, calamus and cinnamon, with every kind of incense tree; myrrh and aloes, with all the best spices, ¹⁵ a fountain of gardens, a well of living waters, flowing streams from Lebanon.

*Beloved*

¹⁶ Awake, north wind, and come, you south! Blow on my garden, that its spices may flow out. Let my beloved come into his garden, and taste his precious fruits.

## 5

*Lover*

¹ I have come into my garden, my sister, my bride. I have gathered my myrrh with my spice; I have eaten my honeycomb with my honey; I have drunk my wine with my milk.

*Friends*

Eat, friends! Drink, yes, drink abundantly, beloved.

*Beloved*

² I was asleep, but my heart was awake. It is the voice of my beloved who knocks: "Open to me, my sister, my love, my dove, my undefiled; for my head is filled with dew, and my hair with the dampness of the night." ³ I have taken off my robe. Indeed, must I put it on? I have washed my feet. Indeed, must I soil them? ⁴ My beloved thrust his hand in through the latch opening. My heart pounded for him. ⁵ I rose up to open for my beloved. My hands dripped with myrrh, my fingers with liquid myrrh, on the handles of the lock. ⁶ I opened to my beloved; but my beloved left, and had gone away. My heart went out when he spoke. I looked for him, but I didn't find him. I called him, but he didn't answer. ⁷ The watchmen who go about the city found me. They beat

---

[a] *1:15* "Behold", from "הִנֵּה", means look at, take notice, observe, see, or gaze at. It is often used as an interjection.

me. They bruised me. The keepers of the walls took my cloak away from me. [8] I adjure you, daughters of Jerusalem, If you find my beloved, that you tell him that I am faint with love.

*Friends*

[9] How is your beloved better than another beloved, you fairest among omen?

How is your beloved better than another beloved, that you do so adjure us?

*Beloved*

[10] My beloved is white and ruddy. The best among ten thousand. [11] His head is like the purest gold. His hair is bushy, black as a raven. [12] His eyes are like doves beside the water brooks, washed with milk, mounted like jewels. [13] His cheeks are like a bed of spices with towers of perfumes. His lips are like lilies, dropping liquid myrrh. [14] His hands are like rings of gold set with beryl. His body is like ivory work overlaid with sapphires. [15] His legs are like pillars of marble set on sockets of fine gold. His appearance is like Lebanon, excellent as the cedars. [16] His mouth is sweetness; yes, he is altogether lovely. This is my beloved, and this is my friend, daughters of Jerusalem.

## 6

*Friends*

[1] Where has your beloved gone, you fairest among women? Where has your beloved turned, that we may seek him with you?

*Beloved*

[2] My beloved has gone down to his garden, to the beds of spices, to pasture his flock in the gardens, and to gather lilies. [3] I am my beloved's, and my beloved is mine. He browses among the lilies.

*Lover*

[4] You are beautiful, my love, as Tirzah, lovely as Jerusalem, awesome as an army with banners. [5] Turn away your eyes from me, for they have overcome me. Your hair is like a flock of goats, that lie along the side of Gilead. [6] Your teeth are like a flock of ewes, which have come up from the washing, of which every one has twins; not one is bereaved among them. [7] Your temples are like a piece of a pomegranate behind your veil. [8] There are sixty queens, eighty concubines, and virgins without number. [9] My dove, my perfect one, is unique. She is her mother's only daughter. She is the favorite one of her who bore her. The daughters saw her, and called her blessed. The queens and the concubines saw her, and they praised her. [10] Who is she who looks out as the morning, beautiful as the moon, clear as the sun, and awesome as an army with banners? [11] I went down into the nut tree grove, to see the green plants of the valley, to see whether the vine budded, and the pomegranates were in flower. [12] Without realizing it, my desire set me with my royal people's chariots.

*Friends*

[13] Return, return, Shulammite! Return, return, that we may gaze at you.

*Lover*

Why do you desire to gaze at the Shulammite, as at the dance of Mahanaim?

## 7

[1] How beautiful are your feet in sandals, prince's daughter! Your rounded thighs are like jewels, the work of the hands of a skillful workman. [2] Your body is like a round goblet, no mixed wine is wanting. Your waist is like a heap of wheat, set about with lilies. [3] Your two breasts are like two fawns, that are twins of a roe. [4] Your neck is like an ivory tower. Your eyes are like the pools in Heshbon by the gate of Bathrabbim. Your nose is like the tower of Lebanon which looks toward Damascus. [5] Your head on you is like Carmel. The hair of your head like purple. The king is held captive in its tresses. [6] How beautiful and how pleasant you are, love, for delights! [7] This, your stature, is like a palm tree, your breasts like its fruit. [8] I said, "I will climb up into the palm tree. I will take hold of its fruit." Let your breasts be like clusters of the vine, the smell of your breath like apples. [9] Your mouth is like the best wine, that goes down smoothly for my beloved, gliding through the lips of those who are asleep.

*Beloved*

[10] I am my beloved's. His desire is toward me. [11] Come, my beloved! Let's go out into the field. Let's lodge in the villages. [12] Let's go early up to the vineyards. Let's see whether the vine has budded, its blossom is open,

and the pomegranates are in flower. There I will give you my love. [13] The mandrakes produce fragrance. At our doors are all kinds of

precious fruits, new and old, which I have stored up for you, my beloved.

## 8

[1] Oh that you were like my brother, who nursed from the breasts of my mother! If I found you outside, I would kiss you; yes, and no one would despise me. [2] I would lead you, bringing you into the house of my mother, who would instruct me. I would have you drink spiced wine, of the juice of my pomegranate. [3] His left hand would be under my head. His right hand would embrace me. [4] I adjure you, daughters of Jerusalem, that you not stir up, nor awaken love, until it so desires.

*Friends*

[5] Who is this who comes up from the wilderness, leaning on her beloved?

*Beloved*

Under the apple tree I awakened you. There your mother conceived you. There she was in labor and bore you. [6] Set me as a seal on your heart, as a seal on your arm; for love is strong as death. Jealousy is as cruel as Sheol.[a] Its flashes are flashes of fire, a very flame of Yah.[b] [7] Many waters can't quench love, neither can floods drown it. If a man would give all the wealth of his house for love, he would be utterly scorned.

*Brothers*

[8] We have a little sister. She has no breasts. What shall we do for our sister in the day when she is to be spoken for? [9] If she is a wall, we will build on her a turret of silver. If she is a door, we will enclose her with boards of cedar.

*Beloved*

[10] I am a wall, and my breasts like towers, then I was in his eyes like one who found peace. [11] Solomon had a vineyard at Baal Hamon. He leased out the vineyard to keepers. Each was to bring a thousand shekels[c] of silver for its fruit. [12] My own vineyard is before me. The thousand are for you, Solomon, two hundred for those who tend its fruit.

*Lover*

[13] You who dwell in the gardens, with friends in attendance, let me hear your voice! Beloved [14] Come away, my beloved! Be like a gazelle or a young stag on the mountains of spices!

# The Wisdom of Jesus the Son of Sirach, or Ecclesiasticus

*The Wisdom of Jesus the Son of Sirach*, also called *Ecclesiasticus*, is recognized as Deuterocanonical Scripture by the Roman Catholic, Greek Orthodox, and Russian Orthodox Churches.

## 1

[1] All wisdom comes from the Lord, and is with him forever. [2] Who can count the sand of the seas, the drops of rain, and the days of eternity? [3] Who will search out the height of the sky, the breadth of the earth, the deep, and wisdom? [4] Wisdom has been created before all things, and the understanding of prudence from everlasting. [5] [d] [6] To whom has the root of wisdom been revealed? Who has known her shrewd counsels? [7] [e] [8] There is one wise, greatly to be feared, sitting upon his throne: the Lord. [9] He created her. He saw and measured her. He poured her out upon all his works. [10] She is with all flesh according to his gift. He gave her freely to those who love him. [11] The fear of the Lord is glory, exultation, gladness, and a crown of rejoicing. [12] The fear of the Lord will delight the heart, and will give gladness, joy, and length of days. [13] Whoever fears the Lord, it will go well with him at the last. He will be blessed in the day of his death. [14] To fear the Lord is the beginning of wisdom. It was created together with the faithful in the womb. [15] She[f] laid an eternal foundation with men. She will be trusted among their offspring. [16] To fear the Lord is the fullness of wisdom. She inebriates men with her fruits. [17] She will fill all her house with desirable things, and her storehouses with her produce. [18] The fear of the Lord is the crown of wisdom, making peace and[g] perfect health to flourish.[h] [19] He both saw and measured her. He rained down skill and knowledge of understanding, and exalted the honor of those who hold her fast. [20] To fear the Lord is the root of wisdom. Her branches are length of days. [21]

---

[a] *8:6* Sheol is the place of the dead.

[b] *8:6* "Yah" is a short form of "Yahweh", which is God's proper Name, sometimes rendered "LORD" (all caps) in other translations.

[c] *8:11* A shekel is about 10 grams or about 0.35 ounces, so 1000 shekels is about 10 kilograms or about 22 pounds.

[d] *1:5* Verse 5 is omitted by the best authorities: The source of wisdom is God's word in the

highest heaven, and her ways are the eternal commandments.

[e] *1:7* Verse 7 is omitted by the best authorities: To whom was the knowledge of wisdom manifested? Who has understood her abundant experience?

[f] *1:15* Gr. nested.

[g] *1:18* Gr. health of cure.

[h] *1:18* The remainder of this verse is omitted by the best authorities: Both are gifts of God for peace; glory opens out for those who love him. He saw her and took her measure.

[a] 22 Unjust wrath can never be justified, for his wrath tips the scale to his downfall. 23 A man that is patient will resist for a season, and afterward gladness will spring up to him. 24 He will hide his words until the right moment, and the lips of many will tell of his understanding. 25 A wise saying is in the treasures of wisdom; but godliness is an abomination to a sinner. 26 If you desire wisdom, keep the commandments and the Lord will give her to you freely; 27 for the fear of the Lord is wisdom and instruction. Faith and humility are his good pleasure. 28 Don't disobey the fear of the Lord. Don't come to him with a double heart. 29 Don't be a hypocrite in men's sight. Keep watch over your lips. 30 Don't exalt yourself, lest you fall and bring dishonor upon your soul. The Lord will reveal your secrets and will cast you down in the midst of the congregation, because you didn't come to the fear of the Lord and your heart was full of deceit.

## 2

1 My son, if you come to serve the Lord, prepare your soul for temptation. 2 Set your heart aright, constantly endure, and don't make haste in time of calamity. 3 Cling to him, and don't depart, that you may be increased at your latter end. 4 Accept whatever is brought upon you, and be patient when you suffer humiliation. 5 For gold is tried in the fire, and acceptable men in the furnace of humiliation. 6 Put your trust in him, and he will help you. Make your ways straight, and set your hope on him. 7 All you who fear the Lord, wait for his mercy. Don't turn aside, lest you fall. 8 All you who fear the Lord, put your trust in him, and your reward will not fail. 9 All you who fear the Lord, hope for good things, and for eternal gladness and mercy. 10 Look at the generations of old, and see: Who ever put his trust in the Lord, and was ashamed? Or who remained in his fear, and was forsaken? Or who called upon him, and he neglected him? 11 For the Lord is full of compassion and mercy. He forgives sins and saves in time of affliction. 12 Woe to fearful hearts, to faint hands, and to the sinner who goes two ways! 13 Woe to the faint heart! For it doesn't believe. Therefore it won't be defended. 14 Woe to you who have lost your patience! And what will you all do when the Lord visits you? 15 Those who fear the Lord will not disobey his words. Those who love him will keep his ways. 16 Those who fear the Lord will seek his good pleasure. Those who love him will be filled with the law. 17 Those who fear the Lord will prepare their hearts, and will humble their souls in his sight. 18 We will fall into the hands of the Lord, and not into the hands of men; for as his majesty is, so also is his mercy.

## 3

1 Hear me, your father, O my children, and do what you hear, that you all may be safe. 2 For the Lord honors the father over the children, and has confirmed the judgment of the mother over her sons. 3 He who honors his father will make atonement for sins. 4 He who gives glory to his mother is as one who lays up treasure. 5 Whoever honors his father will have joy in his own children. He will be heard in the day of his prayer. 6 He who gives glory to his father will have length of days. He who listens to the Lord will bring rest to his mother, 7 [b] and will serve under his parents, as to masters. 8 Honor your father in deed and word, that a blessing may come upon you from him. 9 For the blessing of the father establishes the houses of children, but the curse of the mother roots out the foundations. 10 Don't glorify yourself in the dishonor of your father, for your father's dishonor is no glory to you. 11 For the glory of a man is from the honor of his father, and a mother in dishonor is a reproach to her children. 12 My son, help your father in his old age, and don't grieve him as long as he lives. 13 If he fails in understanding, have patience with him. Don't dishonor him in your full strength. 14 For the kindness to your father will not be forgotten. Instead of sins it will be added to build you up. 15 In the day of your affliction it will be remembered for you, as fair weather upon ice, so your sins will also melt away. 16 He who forsakes his father is as a blasphemer. He who provokes his mother is cursed by the Lord. 17 My son, go on with your business in humility; so you will be loved by an acceptable man. 18 The greater you are, humble yourself the more, and you will find favor before the Lord. 19 [c] 20 For the power of the Lord is great, and he is glorified by those who are lowly. 21 Don't seek things that are too hard for you, and don't search out things that are above your strength. 22 Think about the things that have been commanded you, for you have no need of the things that are secret. 23 Don't be overly busy in tasks that are beyond you, for more things are shown to you than men can understand. 24 For the conceit of many has led them astray. Evil opinion has caused their judgment to slip. 25 [d] There is no light without eyes. There is no wisdom without knowledge. 26 A stubborn heart will do

badly at the end. He who loves danger will perish in it. 27 A stubborn heart will be burdened with troubles. The sinner will heap sin upon sins. 28 The calamity of the proud has no healing, for a weed of wickedness has taken root in him. 29 The heart of the prudent will understand a proverb. A wise man desires the ear of a listener. 30 Water will quench a flaming fire; almsgiving will make atonement for sins. 31 He who repays good turns is mindful of that which comes afterward. In the time of his falling he will find a support.

## 4

1 My son, don't deprive the poor of his living. Don't make the needy eyes wait long. 2 Don't make a hungry soul sorrowful, or provoke a man in his distress. 3 Don't add more trouble to a heart that is provoked. Don't put off giving to him who is in need. 4 Don't reject a supliant in his affliction. Don't turn your face away from a poor man. 5 Don't turn your eye away from one who asks. Give no occasion to a man to curse you. 6 For if he curses you in the bitterness of his soul, he who made him will hear his supplication. 7 Endear yourself to the assembly. Bow your head to a great man. 8 Incline your ear to a poor man. Answer him with peaceful words in humility. 9 Deliver him who is wronged from the hand of him who wrongs him; Don't be hesitant in giving judgment. 10 Be as a father to the fatherless, and like a husband to their mother. So you will be as a son of the Most High, and he will love you more than your mother does. 11 Wisdom exalts her sons, and takes hold of those who seek her. 12 He who loves her loves life. Those who seek her early will be filled with gladness. 13 He who holds her fast will inherit glory. Where[e] he enters, the Lord will bless. 14 Those who serve her minister to the Holy One. The Lord loves those who love her. 15 He who listens to her will judge the nations. He who heeds her will dwell securely. 16 If he trusts her, he will inherit her, and his generations will possess her. 17 For at the first she will walk with him in crooked ways, and will bring fear and dread upon him, and torment him with her discipline, until she may trust his soul, and try him by her judgments. 18 Then she will return him again to the straight way, and will gladden him, and reveal to him her secrets. 19 If he goes astray, she will forsake him, and hand him over to his fall. 20 Watch for the opportunity, and beware of evil. Don't be ashamed of your soul. 21 For there is a shame that brings sin, and there is a shame that is glory and grace. 22 Don't show partiality, discrediting your soul. Don't revere any man to your falling. 23 Don't refrain from speaking when it is for safety. [f] Don't hide your wisdom for the sake of seeming fair. 24 For wisdom will be known by speech, and instruction by the word of the tongue. 25 Don't speak against the truth and be shamed for your ignorance. 26 Don't be ashamed to confess your sins. Don't fight the river's current. 27 Don't lay yourself down for a fool to tread upon. Don't be partial to one who is mighty. 28 Strive for the truth to death, and the Lord God will fight for you. 29 Don't be hasty with your tongue, or slack and negligent in your deeds. 30 Don't be like a lion in your house, or suspicious of your servants. 31 Don't let your hand be stretched out to receive, and closed when you should repay.

## 5

1 Don't set your heart upon your goods. Don't say, "They are sufficient for me." 2 Don't follow your own mind and your strength to walk in the desires of your heart. 3 Don't say, "Who will have dominion over me?" for the Lord will surely take vengeance on you. 4 Don't say, "I sinned, and what happened to me?" for the Lord is patient. 5 Don't be so confident of atonement that you add sin upon sins. 6 Don't say, "His compassion is great. He will be pacified for the multitude of my sins," for mercy and wrath are with him, and his indignation will rest on sinners. 7 Don't wait to turn to the Lord. Don't put off from day to day; for suddenly the wrath of the Lord will come on you, and you will perish in the time of vengeance. 8 Don't set your heart upon unrighteous gains, for you will profit nothing in the day of calamity. 9 Don't winnow with every wind. Don't walk in every path. This is what the sinner who has a double tongue does. 10 Be steadfast in your understanding. Let your speech be consistent. 11 Be swift to hear and answer with patience. 12 If you have understanding, answer your neighbor; but if not, put your hand over your mouth. 13 Glory and dishonor is in talk. A man's tongue may be his downfall. 14 Don't be called a whisperer. Don't lie in wait with your tongue; for shame is on the thief, and an evil condemnation is on him who has a double tongue. 15 Don't be ignorant in a great or small matter.

## 6

1 Don't become an enemy instead of a friend; for an evil name will inherit shame and reproach. So it is with the sinner who has a double tongue. 2 Don't exalt yourself in the counsel of your soul, that your soul

---

[a] 1:21 Verse 21 is omitted by the best authorities: The fear of the Lord drives away sins. Where it resides, it will turn away all anger.

[b] 3:7 Some manuscripts add those who fear the Lord honor their father,

[c] 3:19 Some manuscripts add Many are lofty and renowned,

but he reveals his secrets to the humble.

[d] 3:25 Some manuscripts omit verse 25.

[e] 4:13 Or, she

[f] 4:23 Some manuscripts omit this line.

not be torn in pieces like a bull. ³ You will eat up your leaves, destroy your fruit, and leave yourself like a dry tree. ⁴ A wicked soul will destroy him who has it, and will make him a laughing stock to his enemies. ⁵ Sweet words will multiply a man's friends. A gracious tongue will multiply courtesies. ⁶ Let those that are at peace with you be many, but your advisers one of a thousand. ⁷ If you want to gain a friend, get him in a time of testing, and don't be in a hurry to trust him. ⁸ For there is a friend just for an occasion. He won't continue in the day of your affliction. ⁹ And there is a friend who turns into an enemy. He will discover strife to your reproach. ¹⁰ And there is a friend who is a companion at the table, but he won't continue in the day of your affliction. ¹¹ In your prosperity he will be as yourself, and will be bold over your servants. ¹² If you are brought low, he will be against you, and will hide himself from your face. ¹³ Separate yourself from your enemies, and beware of your friends. ¹⁴ A faithful friend is a strong defense. He who has found him has found a treasure. ¹⁵ There is nothing that can be taken in exchange for a faithful friend. His excellency is beyond price. ¹⁶ A faithful friend is a life-saving medicine. Those who fear the Lord will find him. ¹⁷ He who fears the Lord directs his friendship properly; for as he is, so is his neighbor also. ¹⁸ My son, gather instruction from your youth up. Even when you have gray hair you will find wisdom. ¹⁹ Come to her as one who plows and sows and wait for her good fruit; for your toil will be little in her cultivation, and you will soon eat of her fruit. ²⁰ How exceedingly harsh she is to the unlearned! He who is without understanding will not remain in her. ²¹ She will rest upon him as a mighty stone of trial. He won't hesitate to cast her from him. ²² For wisdom is according to her name. She isn't manifest to many. ²³ Give ear, my son, and accept my judgment. Don't refuse my counsel. ²⁴ Bring your feet into her fetters, and your neck into her chain. ²⁵ Put your shoulder under her and bear her. Don't be grieved with her bonds. ²⁶ Come to her with all your soul. Keep her ways with your whole power. ²⁷ Search and seek, and she will be made known to you. When you get hold of her, don't let her go. ²⁸ For at the last you will find her rest; and she will be turned for you into gladness. ²⁹ Her fetters will be to you for a covering of strength, and her chains for a robe of glory. ³⁰ For there is a golden ornament upon her, and her bands are * a purple cord. ³¹ You shall put her on as a robe of glory, and shall put her on as a crown of rejoicing. ³² My son, if you are willing, you will be instructed. If you will yield your soul, you will be prudent. ³³ If you love to hear, you will receive. If you incline your ear, you will be wise. ³⁴ Stand in the multitude of the elders. Attach yourself to whomever is wise. ³⁵ Be willing to listen to every godly discourse. Don't let the proverbs of understanding escape you. ³⁶ If you see a man of understanding, get to him early. Let your foot wear out the steps of his doors. ³⁷ Let your mind dwell on the ordinances of the Lord and meditate continually on his commandments. He will establish your heart and your desire for wisdom will be given to you.

## 7

¹ Do no evil, so no evil will overtake you. ² Depart from wrong, and it will turn away from you. ³ My son, don't sow upon the furrows of unrighteousness, and you won't reap them sevenfold. ⁴ Don't seek preeminence from the Lord, nor the seat of honor from the king. ⁵ Don't justify yourself in the presence of the Lord, and don't display your wisdom before the king. ⁶ Don't seek to be a judge, lest you not be able to take away iniquities, lest perhaps you fear the person of a mighty man, and lay a stumbling block in the way of your uprightness. ⁷ Don't sin against the multitude of the city. Don't disgrace yourself in the crowd. ⁸ Don't commit a sin twice, for even in one you will not be unpunished. ⁹ Don't say, "He will look upon the multitude of my gifts. When I make an offering to the Most High God, he will accept it." ¹⁰ Don't be faint-hearted in your prayer. Don't neglect to give alms. ¹¹ Don't laugh a man to scorn when he is in the bitterness of his soul, for there is one who humbles and exalts. ¹² Don't deviseᵃ a lie against your brother, or do the same to a friend. ¹³ Refuse to utter a lie, for that habit results in no good. ¹⁴ Don't babble in the assembly of elders. Don't repeat your words in your prayer. ¹⁵ Don't hate hard labor or farm work, which the Most High has created. ¹⁶ Don't number yourself among the multitude of sinners. Remember that wrath will not wait. ¹⁷ Humble your soul greatly, for the punishment of the ungodly man is fire and the worm. ¹⁸ Don't exchange a friend for something, neither a true brother for the gold of Ophir. ¹⁹ Don't deprive yourself of a wise and good wife, for her grace is worth more than gold. ²⁰ Don't abuse a servant who works faithfully, or a hireling who gives you his life. ²¹ Let your soul love a wise servant. Don't defraud him of liberty. ²² Do you have cattle? Look after them. If they are profitable to you, let them stay by you. ²³ Do you have children? Correct them, and make them obedient from their youth. ²⁴ Do you have daughters? Take care of their bodies, and don't be overly indulgent toward them. ²⁵ Give your daughter in marriage, and you will have accomplished a great matter. Give her to a man of understanding. ²⁶ Do you have a wife who pleases you? Don't cast her out. ᵇ But don't trust yourself to one who is hateful. ²⁷ Honor your father with your whole heart, and don't forget the birth pangs of your mother. ²⁸ Remember that you were born of them. What will you repay them for the things that they have done for you? ²⁹ Fear the Lord with all your soul; and revere his priests. ³⁰ With all your strength love him who made you. Don't forsake his ministers. ³¹ Fear the Lord and honor the priest. Give him his portion, even as it is commanded you: the first fruits, the trespass offering, the gift of the shoulders, the sacrifice of sanctification, and the first fruits of holy things. ³² Also stretch out your hand to the poor man, that your blessing may be complete. ³³ A gift has grace in the sight of every living man. Don't withhold grace for a dead man. ³⁴ Don't avoid those who weep, and mourn with those who mourn. ³⁵ Don't be slow to visit a sick man, for by such things you will gain love. ³⁶ In all your words, remember eternity, and you will never sin.

## 8

¹ Don't contend with a mighty man, lest perhaps you fall into his hands. ² Don't strive with a rich man, lest perhaps he overpower you; for gold has destroyed many, and turned away the hearts of kings. ³ Don't argue with a loudmouthed man. Don't heap wood upon his fire. ⁴ Don't make fun of a rude man, lest your ancestors be dishonored. ⁵ Don't reproach a man when he turns from sin. Remember that we are all worthy of punishment. ⁶ Don't dishonor a man in his old age, for some of us are also growing old. ⁷ Don't rejoice over anyone's death. Remember that we all die. ⁸ Don't neglect the discourse of the wise. Be conversant with their proverbs; for from them you will learn discipline and how to serve great men. ⁹ Don't miss the discourse of the aged, for they also learned from their parents, because from them you will learn understanding, and to give an answer in time of need. ¹⁰ Don't kindle the coals of a sinner, lest you be burned with the flame of his fire. ¹¹ Don't rise up from the presence of an insolent man, lest he lie in wait as an ambush for your mouth. ¹² Don't lend to a man who is stronger than you; and if you lend, count it as a loss. ¹³ Don't be surety beyond your means. If you give surety, think as one who will have to pay. ¹⁴ Don't go to law with a judge; for according to his honor they will give judgment for him. ¹⁵ Don't travel with a reckless man, lest he be burdensome to you; for he will do as he pleases, and you will perish with his folly. ¹⁶ Don't fight with a wrathful man. Don't travel with him through the desert, for blood is as nothing in his sight. Where there is no help, he will overthrow you. ¹⁷ Don't consult with a fool, for he will not be able to keep a secret. ¹⁸ Do no secret thing before a stranger, for you don't know what it will cause. ¹⁹ Don't open your heart to every man. Don't let him return you a favor.

## 9

¹ Don't be jealous over the wife of your bosom, and don't teach her an evil lesson against yourself. ² Don't give your soul to a woman and let her trample down your strength. ³ Don't go to meet a woman who plays the prostitute, lest perhaps you fall into her snares. ⁴ Don't associate with a woman who is a singer, lest perhaps you be caught by her tricks. ⁵ Don't gaze at a virgin, lest perhaps you stumble and incur penalties for her. ⁶ Don't give your soul to prostitutes, that you not lose your inheritance. ⁷ Don't look around in the streets of the city. Don't wander in its deserted places. ⁸ Turn your eye away from a beautiful woman, and don't gaze at another's beauty. Many have been led astray by the beauty of a woman; and with this, passion is kindled like a fire. ⁹ Don't dine at all with a woman who has a husband, or revel with her at wine,ᶜ lest perhaps your soul turn away to her, and with your spirit you slide into destruction. ¹⁰ Don't forsake an old friend; for a new one is not comparable to him. A new friend is like new wine: if it becomes old, you will drink it with gladness. ¹¹ Don't envy the success of a sinner; for you don't know what his end will be. ¹² Don't delight in the delights of the ungodly. Remember they will not go unpunished toᵈ the grave. ¹³ Keep yourself far from the man who hasᵉ power to kill, and you will not be troubled by the fear of death. If you come to him, commit no fault, lest he take away your life. Know surely that you go about in the midst of snares, and walk upon the battlements of a city. ¹⁴ As well as you can, aim to know your neighbors, and take counsel with the wise. ¹⁵ Let your conversation be with men of understanding. Let all your discourse be in the law of the Most High. ¹⁶ Let righteous people be companions at your table. Let your glorying be in the fear of the Lord. ¹⁷ A work is commended because of the skill of the artisan; so he who rules the people will be considered wise for his speech. ¹⁸ A

---

* 6:30 Numbers 15:38

ᵃ 7:12 Gr. Don't plow

ᵇ 7:26 Many authorities omit this line

ᶜ 9:9 The preceding line of this verse is omitted by the best authorities.

ᵈ 9:12 Gr. Hades.

ᵉ 9:13 Or, authority

loudmouthed man is dangerous in his city. He who is reckless in his speech will be hated.

## 10

¹ A wise judge will instruct his people. The government of a man of understanding will be well ordered. ² As is the judge of his people, so are his officials. As the city's ruler is, so are all those who dwell in it. ³ An undisciplined king will destroy his people. A city will be established through the understanding of the powerful. ⁴ The government of the earth is in the Lord's hand. In due time, he will raise up over it the right person at the right time. ⁵ A man's prosperity is in the Lord's hand. He will lay his honor upon the person of the scribe. ⁶ Don't be angry with your neighbor for every wrong. Do nothing by works of violence. ⁷ Pride is hateful before the Lord and men. Arrogance is abhorrent in the judgment of both. ⁸ Sovereignty is transferred from nation to nation because of injustice, violence, and greed for money. ⁹ Why are dirt and ashes proud?ᵃ Because in life, my body decays. ¹⁰ A long disease mocks the physician. The king of today will die tomorrow. ¹¹ For when a man is dead, he will inherit maggots, vermin, and worms. ¹² It is the beginning of pride when a man departs from the Lord. His heart has departed from him who made him. ¹³ For the beginning of pride is sin. He who keeps it will pour out abomination. For this cause the Lord brought upon them strange calamities and utterly overthrew them. ¹⁴ The Lord cast down the thrones of rulers and set the lowly in their place. ¹⁵ The Lord plucked up the roots of nations and planted the lowly in their place. ¹⁶ The Lord overthrew the lands of nations and destroyed them to the foundations of the earth. ¹⁷ He took some of them away and destroyed them, and made their memory to cease from the earth. ¹⁸ Pride has not been created for men, nor wrathful anger for the offspring of women. ¹⁹ Whose offspring has honor? Human offspring who fear the Lord. Whose offspring has no honor? Human offspring who break the commandments. ²⁰ In the midst of kindred he who rules them has honor. Those who fear the Lord have honor in his eyes. ²¹ ᵇ ²² The rich man, the honorable, and the poor all glory in the fear of the Lord. ²³ It is not right to dishonor a poor man who has understanding. It is not fitting to glorify a man who is a sinner. ²⁴ The prince, the judge, and the mighty man will be honored. There is not one of them greater than he who fears the Lord. ²⁵ Free men will minister to a wise servant. A man who has knowledge will not complain. ²⁶ Don't flaunt your wisdom in doing your work. Don't boast in the time of your distress. ²⁷ Better is he who labors and abounds in all things, than he who boasts and lacks bread. ²⁸ My son, glorify your soul in humility, and ascribe to yourself honor according to your worthiness. ²⁹ Who will justify him who sins against his own soul? Who will honor him who dishonors his own life? ³⁰ A poor man is honored for his knowledge. A rich man is honored for his riches. ³¹ But he who is honored in poverty, how much more in riches? He who is dishonored in riches, how much more in poverty?

## 11

¹ The wisdom of the lowly will lift up his head, and make him sit in the midst of great men. ² Don't commend a man for his good looks. Don't abhor a man for his outward appearance. ³ The bee is little among flying creatures, but what it produces is the best of confections. ⁴ Don't boast about the clothes you wear, and don't exalt yourself in the day of honor; for the Lord's works are wonderful, and his works are hidden among men. ⁵ Manyᶜ kings have sat down upon the ground, but one who was never thought of has worn a crown. ⁶ Many mighty men have been greatly disgraced. Men of renown have been delivered into other men's hands. ⁷ Don't blame before you investigate. Understand first, and then rebuke. ⁸ Don't answer before you have heard. Don't interrupt while someone else is speaking. ⁹ Don't argue about a matter that doesn't concern you. Don't sit with sinners when they judge. ¹⁰ My son, don't be busy about many matters; for if you meddle much, you will not be unpunished. If you pursue, you will not overtake, and you will not escape by fleeing. ¹¹ There is one who toils, labors, and hurries, and is even more behind. ¹² There is one who is sluggish, and needs help, lacking in strength, and who abounds in poverty, but the Lord's eyes looked upon him for good, and he raised him up from his low condition, ¹³ and lifted up his head so that many marveled at him. ¹⁴ Good things and bad, life and death, poverty and riches, are from the Lord. ¹⁵⁻¹⁶ ᵈ ¹⁷ The Lord's gift remains with the godly. His good pleasure will prosper forever. ¹⁸ One grows rich by his diligence and self-denial, and this is the portion of his reward: ¹⁹ when he says, "I have found rest, and now I will eat of my goods!" he doesn't know how much time will pass until he leaves them to others and dies. ²⁰ Be steadfast in your covenant and be doing it, and grow old in your work. ²¹ Don't marvel at the works of a sinner, but trust the Lord and stay in your labor; for it is an easy thing in the sight of the Lord to swiftly and suddenly make a poor man rich. ²² The Lord's blessing is in the reward of the godly. He makes his blessing flourish in an hour that comes swiftly. ²³ Don't say, "What use is there of me? What further good things can be mine?" ²⁴ Don't say, "I have enough. What harm could happen to me now?" ²⁵ In the day of good things, bad things are forgotten. In the day of bad things, a man will not remember things that are good. ²⁶ For it is an easy thing in the sight of the Lord to reward a man in the day of death according to his ways. ²⁷ The affliction of an hour causes delights to be forgotten. In the end, a man's deeds are revealed. ²⁸ Call no man happy before his death. A man will be known in his children. ²⁹ Don't bring every man into your house, for many are the tricks of a deceitful man. ³⁰ Like a decoy partridge in a cage, so is the heart of a proud man. Like a spy, he looks for your weakness. ³¹ For he lies in wait to turn things that are good into evil, and assigns blame in things that are praiseworthy. ³² From a spark of fire, a heap of many coals is kindled, and a sinful man lies in wait to shed blood. ³³ Take heed of an evil-doer, for he plans wicked things, lest perhaps he ruin your reputation forever. ³⁴ Receive a stranger into your house, and he will distract you with arguments and estrange you from your own family.

## 12

¹ If you do good, know to whom you do it, and your good deeds will have thanks. ² Do good to a godly man, and you will find a reward— if not from him, then from the Most High. ³ No good will come to him who continues to do evil, nor to him who gives no alms. ⁴ Give to the godly man, and don't help the sinner. ⁵ Do good to one who is lowly. Don't give to an ungodly man. Keep back his bread, and don't give it to him, lest he subdue you with it; for you would receive twice as much evil for all the good you would have done to him. ⁶ For the Most High also hates sinners, and will repay vengeance to the ungodly.ᵉ ⁷ Give to the good man, and don't help the sinner. ⁸ A man's friend won't beᶠ fully tried in prosperity. His enemy won't be hidden in adversity. ⁹ In a man's prosperity, his enemies are grieved. In his adversity, even his friend leaves. ¹⁰ Never trust your enemy, for his wickedness is like corrosion in copper. ¹¹ Though he humbles himself and walks bowed down, still be careful and beware of him. You will be to him as one who has wiped a mirror, to be sure it doesn't completely tarnish. ¹² Don't set him next to you, lest he overthrow you and stand in your place. Don't let him sit on your right hand, lest he seek to take your seat, and at the last you acknowledge my words, and be pricked with my sayings. ¹³ Who will pity a charmer that is bitten by a snake, or any who come near wild beasts? ¹⁴ Even so, who will pity him who goes to a sinner, and is associated with him in his sins? ¹⁵ For a while he will stay with you, and if you falter, he will not stay. ¹⁶ The enemy will speak sweetly with his lips, and in his heart plan to throw you into a pit. The enemy may weep with his eyes, but if he finds opportunity, he will want more blood. ¹⁷ If adversity meets you, you will find him there before you. Pretending to help you, he will trip you. ¹⁸ He will shake his head, clap his hands, whisper much, and change his countenance.

## 13

¹ He who touches pitch will be defiled. He who has fellowship with a proud man will become like him. ² Don't take up a burden above your strength. Have no fellowship with one who is mightier and richer than yourself. What fellowship would the earthen pot have with the kettle? The kettle will strike, and the pot will be dashed in pieces. ³ The rich man does a wrong and threatens. The poor is wronged and apologizes. ⁴ If you are profitable, he will exploit you. If you are in need, he will forsake you. ⁵ If you own something, he will live with you. He will drain your resources and will not be sorry. ⁶ Does he need you? Then he will deceive you, smile at you, and give you hope. He will speak kindly to you and say, "What do you need?" ⁷ He will shame you by his delicacies until he has made you bare twice or thrice, and in the end he will laugh you to scorn. Afterward he will see you, will forsake you, and shake his head at you. ⁸ Beware that you are not deceived and brought low in your enjoyment. ⁹ If a mighty man invites you, be reserved, and he will invite you more. ¹⁰ Don't press him, lest you be thrust back. Don't stand far off, lest you be forgotten. ¹¹ Don't try to speak with him as an equal, and don't believe his many words; for he will test you with much talk, and will examine you in a smiling manner. ¹² He who doesn't keep secrets to himself is unmerciful. He won't hesitate to harm and to bind. ¹³ Keep them to yourself and be careful,

---

ᵃ *10:9* Two lines of this verse are here omitted by the best authorities.
ᵇ *10:21* Verse 21 is omitted by the best authorities: Fear of the Lord is the beginning of acceptance, but obstinance and pride are the beginning of rejection.
ᶜ *11:5* Gr. tyrants
ᵈ *11:15-16* Verses 15 and 16 are omitted by the best authorities.
ᵉ *12:6* The remainder of this verse is omitted by the best authorities.
ᶠ *12:8* Or, punished

for you walk[a] in danger of falling. ¹⁴ ᵇ ¹⁵ Every living creature loves its own kind, and every man loves his neighbor. ¹⁶ All flesh associates with their own kind. A man will stick to people like himself. ¹⁷ What fellowship would the wolf have with the lamb? So is the sinner to the godly. ¹⁸ What peace is there between a hyena and a dog? What peace is there between a rich man and the poor? ¹⁹ Wild donkeys are the prey of lions in the wilderness; likewise poor men are feeding grounds for the rich. ²⁰ Lowliness is an abomination to a proud man; likewise a poor man is an abomination to the rich. ²¹ When a rich man is shaken, he is supported by his friends, but when the humble is down, he is pushed away even by his friends. ²² When a rich man falls, there are many helpers. He speaks things not to be spoken, and men justify him. A humble man falls, and men rebuke him. He utters wisdom, and is not listened to. ²³ A rich man speaks, and all keep silence. They extol what he says to the clouds. A poor man speaks, and they say, "Who is this?" If he stumbles, they will help to overthrow him. ²⁴ Riches are good if they have no sin. Poverty is evil only in the opinion of the ungodly. ²⁵ The heart of a man changes his countenance, whether it is for good or for evil.[c] ²⁶ A cheerful countenance is a sign of a prosperous heart. Devising proverbs takes strenuous thinking.

## 14

¹ Blessed is the man who has not slipped with his mouth, and doesn't suffer from sorrow for sins. ² Blessed is he whose soul does not condemn him, and who has not given up hope. ³ Riches are not appropriate for a stingy person. What would a miser do with money? ⁴ He who gathers by denying himself gathers for others. Others will revel in his goods. ⁵ If one is mean to himself, to whom will he be good? He won't enjoy his possessions. ⁶ There is none more evil than he who is grudging to himself. This is a punishment for his wickedness. ⁷ Even if he does good, he does it in forgetfulness. In the end, he reveals his wickedness. ⁸ A miser is evil. He turns away and disregards souls. ⁹ A covetous man's eye is not satisfied with his portion. Wicked injustice dries up his soul. ¹⁰ A miser begrudges bread, and it is lacking at his table. ¹¹ My son, according to what you have, treat yourself well, and bring worthy offerings to the Lord. ¹² Remember that death will not wait, and that the covenant of Hades hasn't been shown to you. ¹³ Do good to your friends before you die. According to your ability, reach out and give to them. ¹⁴ Don't deprive yourself of a good day. Don't let your share of a desired good pass you by. ¹⁵ Won't you leave your labors to another, and your toils be divided by lot? ¹⁶ Give, take, and treat yourself well, because there is no seeking of luxury in Hades. ¹⁷ All flesh grows old like a garment, for the covenant from the beginning is, "You must die!" ¹⁸ Like the leaves flourishing on a thick tree, some it sheds, and some grow, so also are the generations of flesh and blood: one comes to an end and another is born. ¹⁹ Every work rots and falls away, and its builder will depart with it. ²⁰ Blessed is the man who meditates on wisdom, and who reasons by his understanding. ²¹ He who considers her ways in his heart will also have knowledge of her secrets. ²² Go after her like a hunter, and lie in wait in her paths. ²³ He who peers in at her windows will also listen at her doors. ²⁴ He who lodges close to her house will also fasten a nail in her walls. ²⁵ He will pitch his tent near at hand to her, and will lodge in a lodging where good things are. ²⁶ He will set his children under her shelter, and will rest under her branches. ²⁷ By her he will be covered from heat, and will lodge in her glory.

## 15

¹ He who fears the Lord will do this. He who has possession of the law will obtain her. ² She will meet him like a mother, and receive him like a wife married in her virginity. ³ She will feed him with bread of understanding and give him water of wisdom to drink. ⁴ He will be stayed upon her, and will not be moved. He will rely upon her, and will not be confounded. ⁵ She will exalt him above his neighbors. She will open his mouth in the midst of the congregation. ⁶ He will inherit joy, a crown of gladness, and an everlasting name. ⁷ Foolish men will not obtain her. Sinners will not see her. ⁸ She is far from pride. Liars will not remember her. ⁹ Praise is not attractive in the mouth of a sinner; for it was not sent to him from the Lord. ¹⁰ For praise will be spoken in wisdom; The Lord will prosper it. ¹¹ Don't say, "It is through the Lord that I fell away;" for you shall not do the things that he hates. ¹² Don't say, "It is he that caused me to err;" for he has no need of a sinful man. ¹³ The Lord hates every abomination; and those who fear him don't love

them. ¹⁴ He himself made man from the beginning and left him in the hand of his own counsel. ¹⁵ If you choose, you can keep the commandments. To be faithful is a matter of your choice. ¹⁶ He has set fire and water before you. You will stretch forth your hand to whichever you desire. ¹⁷ Before man is life and death. Whichever he likes, it will be given to him. ¹⁸ For the wisdom of the Lord is great. He is mighty in power, and sees all things. ¹⁹ His eyes are upon those who fear him. He knows every act of man. ²⁰ He has not commanded any man to be ungodly. He has not given any man license to sin.

## 16

¹ Don't desire a multitude of unprofitable children, neither delight in ungodly sons. ² If they multiply, don't delight in them unless the fear of the Lord is in them. ³ Don't trust in their life. Don't rely on their numbers; for one can be better than a thousand, and to die childless than to have ungodly children. ⁴ For from one who has understanding, a city will be populated, but a race of wicked men will be made desolate. ⁵ I have seen many such things with my eyes. My ear has heard mightier things than these. ⁶ In a congregation of sinners, a fire will be kindled. In a disobedient nation, wrath is kindled. ⁷ He was not pacified toward the giants of old time, who revolted in their strength. ⁸ He didn't spare Lot's neighbors, whom he abhorred for their pride. ⁹ He didn't pity the people of perdition who were taken away in their sins, ¹⁰ or in like manner, the six hundred thousand footmen who were gathered together in the hardness of their hearts. ¹¹ Even if there is one stiff-necked person, it is a marvel if he will be unpunished; for mercy and wrath are both with him who is mighty to forgive, and he pours out wrath. ¹² As his mercy is great, so is his correction also. He judges a man according to his works. ¹³ The sinner will not escape with plunder. The perseverance of the godly will not be frustrated. ¹⁴ He will make room for every work of mercy. Each man will receive according to his works. ¹⁵⁻¹⁶ ᵈ ¹⁷ Don't say, "I will be hidden from the Lord," and "Who will remember me from on high?" I will not be known among so many people, for what is my soul in a boundless creation? ¹⁸ Behold, the heaven, the heaven of heavens, the deep, and the earth, will be moved when he visits. ¹⁹ The mountains and the foundations of the earth together are shaken with trembling when he looks at them. ²⁰ No heart will think about these things. Who could comprehend his ways? ²¹ Like a tempest which no man can see, so, the majority of his works are[e] hidden. ²² Who will declare his works of righteousness? Who will wait for them? For his covenant is afar off.[f] ²³ He who is lacking in[g] understanding thinks about these things. An unwise and erring man thinks foolishly. ²⁴ My son, listen to me, learn knowledge, and heed my words with your heart. ²⁵ I will impart instruction with precision, and declare knowledge exactly. ²⁶ In the judgment of the Lord are his works from the beginning. From the making of them he determined their boundaries. ²⁷ He arranged his works for all time, and their beginnings to their generations. They aren't hungry or weary, and they don't cease from their works. ²⁸ No one pushes aside his neighbor. They will never disobey his word. ²⁹ After this also the Lord looked at the earth and filled it with his blessings. ³⁰ All manner of living things covered its surface, and they return into it.

## 17

¹ The Lord created mankind out of earth, and turned them back to it again. ² He gave them days by number, and a set time, and gave them authority over the things that are on it. ³ He endowed them with strength proper to them, and made them according to his own image. ⁴ He put the fear of man upon all flesh, and gave him dominion over beasts and birds. ⁵ ʰ ⁶ He gave them counsel, tongue, eyes, ears, and heart to have understanding. ⁷ He filled them with the knowledge of wisdom, and showed them good and evil. ⁸ He set his eye upon their hearts, to show them the majesty of his works. ⁹ ⁱ ¹⁰ And they will praise his holy name, ʲ that they may declare the majesty of his works. ¹¹ He added to them knowledge, and gave them a law of life for a heritage. ¹² He made an everlasting covenant with them, and showed them his decrees. ¹³ Their eyes saw the majesty of his glory. Their ears heard the glory of his voice. ¹⁴ He said to them, "Beware of all unrighteousness." So he gave them commandment, each man concerning his neighbor. ¹⁵ Their ways are ever before him. They will not be hidden from his eyes. ¹⁶ ᵏ ¹⁷ ˡFor every nation he appointed a ruler, but Israel is the Lord's portion. ¹⁸ ᵐ ¹⁹ All their works are as clear as the sun before him. His eyes are

---

ᵃ *13:13* Gr. along with.

ᵇ *13:14* The remainder of verse 13, and verse 14, are omitted by the best authorities.

ᶜ *13:25* The remainder of this verse is omitted by the best authorities.

ᵈ *16:15-16* Verses 15 and 16 are omitted by the best authorities.

ᵉ *16:21* Gr. among hidden things.

ᶠ *16:22* The remainder of this verse is omitted by the best authorities.

ᵍ *16:23* Gr. heart.

ʰ *17:5* Verse 5 is omitted by the best authorities.

ⁱ *17:9* Verse 9 is omitted by the best authorities.

ʲ *17:10* This line is added by the best authorities.

ᵏ *17:16* Verses 16,18, and 21 are omitted by the best authorities.

ˡ *17:17* The preceding part of this verse is omitted by the best authorities.

ᵐ *17:18* Verses 16,18, and 21 are omitted by the best authorities.

continually upon their ways. ²⁰ Their iniquities are not hidden from him. All their sins are before the Lord. ²¹ ᵃ ²² With him the alms of a man is as a signet. He will keep a man's kindness as the pupil of the eye.ᵇ ²³ Afterwards he will rise up and repay them, and render their repayment upon their head. ²⁴ However to those who repent he grants a return. He comforts those who are losing hope. ²⁵ Return to the Lord, and forsake sins. Make your prayer before his face offend less. ²⁶ Turn again to the Most High, and turn away from iniquity.ᶜ Greatly hate the abominable thing. ²⁷ Who will give praise to the Most High in Hades, in place of the living who return thanks? ²⁸ Thanksgiving perishes from the dead, as from one who doesn't exist. He who is in life and health will praise the Lord. ²⁹ How great is the mercy of the Lord, and his forgiveness to those who turn to him! ³⁰ For humans are not capable of everything, because the son of man is not immortal. ³¹ What is brighter than the sun? Yet even this can be eclipsed. So flesh and blood devise evil. ³² He looks upon the power of the height of heaven, while all men are earth and ashes.

## 18

¹ He who lives forever created the whole universe. ² The Lord alone is just. ³ ᵈ ⁴ He has given power to declare his works to no one. Who could trace out his mighty deeds? ⁵ Who could measure the strength of his majesty? Who could also proclaim his mercies? ⁶ As for the wondrous works of the Lord, it is not possible to take from them nor add to them, neither is it possible to explore them. ⁷ When a man has finished, then he is just at the beginning. When he stops, then he will be perplexed. ⁸ What is mankind, and what purpose do they serve? What is their good, and what is their evil? ⁹ The number of man's days at the most are a hundred years. ¹⁰ As a drop of water from the sea, and a pebble from the sand, so are a few years in the day of eternity. ¹¹ For this cause the Lord was patient over them, and poured out his mercy upon them. ¹² He saw and perceived their end, that it is evil. Therefore he multiplied his forgiveness. ¹³ The mercy of a man is on his neighbor; but the mercy of the Lord is on all flesh: reproving, chastening, teaching, and bringing back, as a shepherd does his flock. ¹⁴ He has mercy on those who accept chastening, and that diligently seek after his judgments. ¹⁵ My son, don't add reproach to your good deeds, and no harsh words in any of your giving. ¹⁶ Doesn't the dew relieve the scorching heat? So a word is better than a gift. ¹⁷ Behold, isn't a word better than a gift? Both are with a gracious person. ¹⁸ A fool is ungracious and abusive. The gift of an grudging person consumes the eyes. ¹⁹ Learn before you speak. Take care of your health before you get sick. ²⁰ Before judgment, examine yourself, and in the hour of scrutiny you will find forgiveness. ²¹ Humble yourself before you get sick. In the time of sins, repent. ²² Let nothing hinder you to pay your vow in due time. Don't wait until death to be released. ²³ Before you make a vow, prepare yourself. Don't be like a man who tests the Lord. ²⁴ Think about the wrath coming in the days of the end, and the time of vengeance, when he turns away his face. ²⁵ In the days of fullness remember the time of hunger. Remember poverty and lack in the days of wealth. ²⁶ From morning until evening, the time changes. All things are speedy before the Lord. ²⁷ A wise man is cautious in everything. In days of sinning, he will beware of offense.ᵉ ²⁸ Every man of understanding knows wisdom. He will give thanks to him who found her. ²⁹ They who were of understanding in sayings also became wise themselves, and poured out apt proverbs. ³⁰ Don't go after your lusts. Restrain your appetites. ³¹ If you give fully to your soul the delight of her desire, she will make youᶠ the laughing stock of your enemies. ³² Don't make merry in much luxury, and don't be tied to its expense. ³³ Don't be made a beggar by banqueting with borrowed money when you have nothing in your purse.ᵍ

## 19

¹ A worker who is a drunkard will not become rich. He who despises small things will fall little by little. ² Wine and women will make men of understanding go astray. He who joins with prostitutes is reckless. ³ Decay and worms will have him as their heritage. A reckless soul will be taken away. ⁴ He who is hasty to trust is shallow-hearted. He who sins offends against his own soul. ⁵ He who rejoices in wickedness will be condemned.ʰ ⁶ ⁱ He who hates gossip has less wickedness. ⁷ Never repeat what is told you, and you won't lose anything. ⁸ Whether it is of friend or foe, don't tell it. Unless it is a sin to you, don't reveal it. ⁹ For

if he has heard you and observed you, when the time comes, he will hate you. ¹⁰ Have you heard something? Let it die with you. Be brave: it will not make you burst! ¹¹ A fool will travail in pain with a word, as a woman in labor with a child. ¹² As an arrow that sticks in the flesh of the thigh, so is gossip in a fool. ¹³ Question a friend; it may be he didn't do it. If he did something, it may be that he may do it no more. ¹⁴ Question your neighbor; it may be he didn't say it. If he has said it, it may be that he may not say it again. ¹⁵ Question a friend; for many times there is slander. Don't trust every word. ¹⁶ There is one who slips, and not from the heart. Who is he who hasn't sinned with his tongue? ¹⁷ Reprove your neighbor before you threaten him; and give place to the law of the Most High. ¹⁸⁻¹⁹ ʲ ²⁰ All wisdom is the fear of the Lord. In all wisdom is the doing of the law. ²¹ ᵏ ²² The knowledge of wickedness is not wisdom. The prudence of sinners is not counsel. ²³ There is a wickedness, and it is an abomination. There is a fool lacking in wisdom. ²⁴ Better is one who has little understanding, and fears God, than one who has much intelligence and transgresses the law. ²⁵ There is an exquisite subtlety, and it is unjust. And there is one who perverts favor to gain a judgment.ˡ ²⁶ There is one who does wickedly, who hangs down his head with mourning; but inwardly he is full of deceit, ²⁷ bowing down his face, and pretending to be deaf in one ear. Where he isn't known, he will take advantage of you. ²⁸ And if for lack of power he is hindered from sinning, if he finds opportunity, he will do mischief. ²⁹ A man will be known by his appearance. One who has understanding will be known by his face when you meet him. ³⁰ A man's attire, grinning laughter, and the way he walks show what he is.

## 20

¹ There is a reproof that is not timely; and there is a person who is wise enough to keep silent. ² How good is it to reprove, rather than to be angry. He who confesses will be kept back from harm. ³ ᵐ ⁴ As is the lust of a eunuch to deflower a virgin, so is he who executes judgments with violence. ⁵ There is one who keeps silent and is found wise; and there is one who is hated for his much talk. ⁶ There is one who keeps silent, for he has no answer to make; And there is one who keeps silent, knowing when to speak. ⁷ A wise man will be silent until his time has come, but the braggart and fool will miss his time. ⁸ He who uses many words will be abhorred. He who takes authority for himself will be hated in it. ⁹ There is a prosperity that a man finds in misfortunes; and there is a gain that turns to loss. ¹⁰ There is a gift that will not profit you; and there is a gift that pays back double. ¹¹ There are losses because of glory; and there is one who has lifted up his head from a low estate. ¹² There is one who buys much for a little, and pays for it again sevenfold. ¹³ He who is wise in words will make himself beloved; but the pleasantries of fools will be wasted. ¹⁴ The gift of a fool will not profit you,ⁿ for he looks for repayment many times instead of one. ¹⁵ He will give little and insult much. He will open his mouth like a crier. Today he will lend, and tomorrow he will ask for it back. Such a one is a hateful man. ¹⁶ The fool will say, "I have no friend, and I have no thanks for my good deeds. Those who eat my bread have an evil tongue." ¹⁷ How often, and of how many, will he be laughed to scorn!ᵒ ¹⁸ A slip on a pavement is better than a slip with the tongue. So the fall of the wicked will come speedily. ¹⁹ A man without grace is a tale out of season. It will be continually in the mouth of the ignorant. ²⁰ A parable from a fool's mouth will be rejected; for he won't tell it at the proper time. ²¹ There is one who is hindered from sinning through lack. When he rests, he will not be troubled. ²² There is one who destroys his soul through bashfulness. By a foolish countenance, he will destroy it. ²³ There is one who for bashfulness makes promises to his friend; and he makes him his enemy for nothing. ²⁴ A lie is an ugly blot on a person. It will be continually in the mouth of the ignorant. ²⁵ A thief is better than a man who is continually lying, but they both will inherit destruction. ²⁶ The destination of a liar is dishonor. His shame is with him continually. ²⁷ He who is wise in words will advance himself. And one who is prudent will please great men. ²⁸ He who tills his land will raise his harvest high. He who pleases great men will get pardon for iniquity. ²⁹ Favors and gifts blind the eyes of the wise, and as a muzzle on the mouth, turn away reproofs. ³⁰ Wisdom that is hidden, and treasure that is out of sight— what profit is in either of them? ³¹ Better is a man who hides his folly than a man who hides his wisdom. ³² ᵖ

---

ᵃ 17:21 Verses 16,18, and 21 are omitted by the best authorities.
ᵇ 17:22 The remainder of this verse is omitted by the best authorities.
ᶜ 17:26 A line is here omitted by the best authorities.
ᵈ 18:3 The remainder of verse 2, and verse 3, are omitted by the best authorities.

ᵉ 18:27 The remainder of this verse is omitted by the best authorities.
ᶠ 18:31 Or, a rejoicing to
ᵍ 18:33 The remainder of this verse is omitted by the best authorities.
ʰ 19:5 The remainder of this verse is omitted by the best authorities.

ⁱ 19:6 The preceding part of this verse is omitted by the best authorities.
ʲ 19:18-19 Verses 18 and 19 are omitted by the best authorities.
ᵏ 19:21 The remainder of verse 20 and verse 21 are omitted by the best authorities.
ˡ 19:25 The remainder of this verse is omitted by the best authorities.

ᵐ 20:3 Verse 3 is omitted by the best authorities.
ⁿ 20:14 A line of this verse is here omitted by the best authorities.
ᵒ 20:17 The latter part of verse 17 is omitted by the best authorities.
ᵖ 20:32 Verse 32 is omitted by the best authorities.

## 21

¹ My son, have you sinned? Do it no more; and ask forgiveness for your past sins. ² Flee from sin as from the face of a snake; for if you go near, it will bite you. Its teeth are like lion's teeth, slaying people's souls. ³ All iniquity is as a two-edged sword. Its stroke has no healing. ⁴ Terror and violence will waste away riches. So the house of an arrogant man will be laid waste. ⁵ Supplication from a poor man's mouth reaches to the ears of[a] God, and his judgment comes speedily. ⁶ One who hates reproof is in the path of the sinner. He who fears the Lord will repent in his heart. ⁷ He who is mighty in tongue is known far away; but the man of understanding knows when he slips. ⁸ He who builds his house with other men's money is like one who gathers stones for his own tomb. ⁹ The congregation of wicked men is as a bundle of tow with a flame of fire at the end of them. ¹⁰ The way of sinners is paved with stones; and at the end of it is the pit of Hades. ¹¹ He who keeps the law becomes master of its intent. The fulfilment of the fear of the Lord is wisdom. ¹² He who is not clever will not be instructed. There is a cleverness which makes bitterness abound. ¹³ The knowledge of a wise man will be made to abound as a flood, and his counsel as a fountain of life. ¹⁴ The inward parts of a fool are like a broken vessel. He will hold no knowledge. ¹⁵ If a man of knowledge hears a wise word, he will commend it and add to it. The wanton man hears it, and it displeases him, so he throws it away behind his back. ¹⁶ The chatter of a fool is like a burden in the way, but grace will be found on the lips of the wise. ¹⁷ The utterance of the prudent man will be sought for in the congregation. They will ponder his words in their heart. ¹⁸ As a house that is destroyed, so is wisdom to a fool. The knowledge of an unwise man is talk without sense.[b] ¹⁹ Instruction is as fetters on the feet of an unwise man, and as manacles on the right hand. ²⁰ A fool lifts up his voice with laughter, but a clever man smiles quietly. ²¹ Instruction is to a prudent man as an ornament of gold, and as a bracelet upon his right arm. ²² The foot of a fool rushes into a house, but a man of experience will be ashamed of entering. ²³ A foolish man peers into the door of a house, but a man who is instructed will stand outside. ²⁴ It is rude for someone to listen at a door, but a prudent person will be grieved with the disgrace. ²⁵ The lips of strangers will be grieved at these things, but the words of prudent men will be weighed in the balance. ²⁶ The heart of fools is in their mouth, but the mouth of wise men is their heart. ²⁷ When the ungodly curses an adversary, he curses his own soul. ²⁸ A whisperer defiles his own soul, and will be hated wherever he travels.

## 22

¹ A slothful man is compared to a stone that is defiled. Everyone will at hiss at him in his disgrace. ² A slothful man is compared to the filth of a dunghill. Anyone who picks it up will shake it out of his hand. ³ An undisciplined child is a disgrace to his father, and a foolish daughter is born to his loss. ⁴ A prudent daughter will inherit a husband of her own. She who brings shame is the grief of her father. ⁵ She who is arrogant brings shame on father and husband. She will be despised by both of them. ⁶ Ill-timed conversation is like music in mourning, but stripes and correction are wisdom in every season. ⁷ He who teaches a fool is like one who glues potsherds together, even like one who wakes a sleeper out of a deep sleep. ⁸ He who teaches a fool is as one who teaches a man who slumbers. In the end he will say, "What is it?" ⁹ ¹⁰ [c] ¹¹ Weep for the dead, for he lacks light. Weep for a fool, for he lacks understanding. Weep more sweetly for the dead, because he has found rest, but the life of the fool is worse than death. ¹² Mourning for the dead lasts seven days, but for a fool and an ungodly man, it lasts all the days of his life. ¹³ Don't talk much with a foolish man, and don't go to one who has no understanding. Beware of him, lest you have trouble and be defiled in his onslaught. Turn away from him, and you will find rest, and you won't be wearied in his madness. ¹⁴ What would be heavier than lead? What is its name, but "Fool"? ¹⁵ Sand, salt, and a mass of iron is easier to bear than a man without understanding. ¹⁶ Timber girded and bound into a building will not be released with shaking. So a heart established in due season on well advised counsel will not be afraid. ¹⁷ A heart settled upon a thoughtful understanding is as an ornament of plaster on a polished wall. ¹⁸ Fences set on a high place will not stand against the wind; so a fearful heart in the imagination of a fool will not stand against any fear. ¹⁹ He who pricks the eye will make tears fall. He who pricks the heart makes it show feeling. ²⁰ Whoever casts a stone at birds scares them away. He who insults a friend will dissolve friendship. ²¹ If you have drawn a sword against a friend, don't despair, for there may be a way back. ²² If you have opened your mouth against a friend, don't

be afraid, for there may be reconciliation, unless it is for insulting, arrogance, disclosing of a secret, or a treacherous blow— for these things any friend will flee. ²³ Gain trust with your neighbor in his poverty, that in his prosperity you may have gladness. Stay steadfast to him in the time of his affliction, that you may be heir with him in his inheritance.[d] ²⁴ Before fire is the vapor and smoke of a furnace, so insults precede bloodshed. ²⁵ I won't be ashamed to shelter a friend. I won't hide myself from his face. ²⁶ If any evil happens to me because of him, everyone who hears it will beware of him. ²⁷ Who will set a watch over my mouth, and a seal of shrewdness upon my lips, that I may not fall from it, and that my tongue may not destroy me?

## 23

¹ O Lord, Father and Master of my life, don't abandon me to their counsel. Don't let me fall because of them. ² Who will set scourges over my thought, and a discipline of wisdom over my heart, that they spare me not for my errors, and not overlook their sins? ³ Otherwise my errors might be multiplied, and my sins abound, I fall before my adversaries, and my enemy rejoice over me.[e] ⁴ O Lord, Father and God of my life, don't give me a haughty eyes,[f] ⁵ and turn away evil desire from me.[g] ⁶ Let neither gluttony nor lust overtake me. Don't give me over to a shameless mind. ⁷ Listen, my children, to the discipline of the mouth. He who keeps it will not be caught. ⁸ The sinner will be overpowered through his lips. By them, the insulter and the arrogant will stumble. ⁹ Don't accustom your mouth to an oath, and don't be accustomed to naming the Holy One, ¹⁰ for as a servant who is continually scourged will not lack bruises, so he also who swears and continually utters the Name will not be cleansed from sin. ¹¹ A man of many oaths will be filled with iniquity. The scourge will not depart from his house. If he offends, his sin will be upon him. If he disregards it, he has sinned doubly. If he has sworn falsely, he will not be justified, for his house will be filled with calamities. ¹² There is a manner of speech that is clothed with death. Let it not be found in the heritage of Jacob, for all these things will be far from the godly, and they will not wallow in sins. ¹³ Don't accustom your mouth to gross rudeness, for it involves sinful speech. ¹⁴ Remember your father and your mother, for you sit in the midst of great men, that you be not forgetful before them, and become a fool by your bad habit; so you may wish that you had not been born, and curse the day of your birth. ¹⁵ A man who is accustomed to abusive language won't be corrected all the days of his life. ¹⁶ Two sorts of people multiply sins, and the third will bring wrath: a hot passion, like a burning fire, will not be quenched until it is consumed; a fornicator in the body of his flesh will never cease until he has burned out the fire. ¹⁷ All bread is sweet to a fornicator. He will not cease until he dies. ¹⁸ A man who goes astray from his own marriage bed says in his heart, "Who sees me? Darkness is around me, and the walls hide me. No one sees me. Of whom am I afraid? The Most High will not remember my sins." ¹⁹ The eyes of men are his terror. He doesn't know that the eyes of the Lord are ten thousand times brighter than the sun, seeing all the ways of men, and looking into secret places. ²⁰ All things were known to him before they were created, and also after they were completed. ²¹ This man will be punished in the streets of the city. He will be seized where he least expects it. ²² So also is a wife who leaves her husband, and produces an heir by another man. ²³ For first, she was disobedient in the law of the Most High. Second, she trespassed against her own husband. Third, she played the adulteress in fornication, and had children by another man. ²⁴ She shall be brought out into the congregation. Her punishment will extend to her children. ²⁵ Her children will not take root. Her branches will bear no fruit. ²⁶ She will leave her memory for a curse. Her reproach won't be blotted out. ²⁷ And those who are left behind will know that there is nothing better than the fear of the Lord, and nothing sweeter than to heed the commandments of the Lord. ²⁸ [h]

## 24

¹ Wisdom will praise her own soul, and will proclaim her glory in the midst of her people. ² She will open her mouth in the congregation of the Most High, and proclaim her glory in the presence of his power. ³ "I came out of the mouth of the Most High, and covered the earth as a mist. ⁴ I lived in high places, and my throne is in the pillar of the cloud. ⁵ Alone I surrounded the circuit of heaven, and walked in the depth of the abyss. ⁶ In the waves of the sea, and in all the earth, and in every people and nation, I obtained a possession. ⁷ With all these I sought rest. In whose inheritance shall I lodge? ⁸ Then the Creator of all things gave me a command. He who created me made my tent to rest, and said, 'Let

---

[a] 21:5 Gr. him.
[b] 21:18 Gr. unexamined words.
[c] 22:9-10 Verses 9 and 10 are omitted by the best authorities.
[d] 22:23 The remainder of this verse is omitted by the best authorities.
[e] 23:3 The remainder of this verse is omitted by the best authorities.
[f] 23:4 The remainder of this verse is omitted by the best authorities.
[g] 23:5 The remainder of this verse is omitted by the best authorities.
[h] 23:28 Verse 28 is omitted by the best authorities.

your dwelling be in Jacob, and your inheritance in Israel.' **9** He created me from the beginning, before the ages. For all ages, I will not cease to exist. **10** In the holy tabernacle, I ministered before him. So I was established in Zion. **11** In the beloved city, likewise he gave me rest. In Jerusalem was my domain. **12** I took root in a people that was honored, even in the portion of the Lord's own inheritance. **13** I was exalted like a cedar in Lebanon, And like a cypress tree on the mountains of Hermon. **14** I was exalted like a palm tree on the sea shore, like rose bushes in Jericho, and like a fair olive tree in the plain. I was exalted like a plane tree. **15** Like cinnamon and aspalathus, I have given a scent to perfumes. Like choice myrrh, I spread abroad a pleasant fragrance, likeᵃ galbanum, onycha, stacte, and as the smell of frankincense in the tabernacle. **16** Like the terebinth, I stretched out my branches. My branches are glorious and graceful. **17** Like the vine, I put forth grace. My flowers are the fruit of glory and riches. **18** ᵇ **19**"Come to me, all you who desire me, and be filled with my fruits. **20** For my memory is sweeter than honey, and my inheritance than the honeycomb. **21** Those who eat me will be hungry for more. Those who drink me will be thirsty for more. **22** He who obeys me will not be ashamed. Those who work with me will not sin." **23** All these things are the book of the covenant of the Most High God, the law which Moses commanded us for an inheritance for the assemblies of Jacob. **24** ᶜ **25** It is he who makes wisdom abundant, as Pishon, and as Tigris in the days of first fruits. **26** He makes understanding full as the Euphrates, and as the Jordan in the days of harvest, **27** who makes instruction shine forth as the light, as Gihon in the days of vintage. **28** The first man didn't know her perfectly. In like manner, the last has not explored her. **29** For her thoughts are filled from the sea, and her counsels from the great deep. **30** I came out as a canal stream from a river, and as an irrigation ditch into a garden. **31** I said, "I will water my garden, and will drench my garden bed." Behold, my stream became a river, and my river became a sea. **32** I will yet bring instruction to light as the morning, and will make these things clear from far away. **33** I will continue to pour out teaching like prophecy, and leave it to all generations. **34** See that I have not labored for myself only, but for all those who diligently seek wisdom.

## 25

**1** I enjoy three things, and they are beautiful before the Lord and men: the agreement of kindred, the friendship of neighbors, and a woman and her husband who walk together in agreement. **2** But my soul hates three sorts of people, and I am greatly offended at their life: a poor man who is arrogant, a rich man who is a liar, and an old fool who is an adulterer. **3** If you gathered nothing in your youth, how could you find anything in your old age? **4** How beautiful a thing is judgment in the gray-haired, and for elders to know good counsel! **5** How beautiful is the wisdom of old men, and understanding and counsel to men who are in honor! **6** Much experience is the crown of the aged. Their glory is the fear of the Lord. **7** There are nine things that I have thought of, and in my heart counted happy, and the tenth I will utter with my tongue: a man who has joy with his children, and a man who lives and sees the fall of his enemies. **8** Happy is he who dwells with a wife of understanding, he who has not slipped with his tongue, and he who has not served a man who is unworthy of him. **9** Happy is he who has found prudence, and he who speaks in the ears of those who listen. **10** How great is he who has found wisdom! Yet is there none above him who fears the Lord. **11** The fear of the Lord surpasses all things. To whom shall he who holds it be likened? **12** ᵈ **13** Any wound but a wound of the heart! Any wickedness but the wickedness of a woman! **14** Any calamity but a calamity from those who hate me! Any vengeance but the vengeance of enemies! **15** There is no venom worse than a snake's venom. There is no wrath worse than an enemy's wrath. **16** I would rather dwell with a lion and a dragon than keep house with a wicked woman. **17** The wickedness of a woman changes her appearance, and darkens her countenance like that of a bear. **18** Her husband will sit among his neighbors, and when he hears it, he sighs bitterly. **19** All malice is small compared to the malice of a woman. Let the portion of a sinner fall on her. **20** As walking up a sandy hill is to the feet of the aged, so is a wife full of words to a quiet man. **21** Don't be ensnared by a woman's beauty. Don't desire a woman for her beauty. **22** There is anger, impudence, and great reproach if a woman supports her husband. **23** A wicked woman is abasement of heart, sadness of countenance, and a wounded heart. A woman who won't make her husband happy is like hands that hang down, and weak knees. **24** The beginning of sin came from a woman. Because of her, we all die. **25** Don't give water an outlet, and don't give a wicked woman freedom of speech. **26** If she doesn't go as you direct, cut her away from your flesh.ᵉ

## 26

**1** Happy is the husband of a good wife. The number of his days will be doubled. **2** A faithful wife gives joy to her husband. He will fulfill his years in peace. **3** A good wife is a great gift. She will be given to those who fear the Lord. **4** Whether a man is rich or poor, a good heart makes a cheerful face at all times. **5** Of three things my heart was afraid, and concerning the fourthᶠ kind I made supplication: The slander of a city, the assembly of a mob, and a false accusation. All these are more grievous than death. **6** A grief of heart and sorrow is a woman who is jealous of another woman. Her tongue-lashing makes it known to all. **7** A wicked woman is like a chafing yoke. He who takes hold of her is like one who grasps a scorpion. **8** A drunken woman causes great wrath. She will not cover her own shame. **9** The fornication of a woman is in the lifting up of her eyes; it will be known by her eyelids. **10** Keep strict watch on a headstrong daughter, lest she find liberty for herself, and use it. **11** Watch out for an impudent eye, and don't be surprised if it sins against you. **12** She will open her mouth like a thirsty traveller, and drink from every water that is near. She will sit down at every post, and open her quiver to any arrow. **13** The grace of a wife will delight her husband. Her knowledge will strengthenᵍ his bones. **14** A silent woman is a gift of the Lord. There is nothing worth so much as a well-instructed soul. **15** A modest woman is grace upon grace. There are no scales that can weigh the value of a self-controlled soul. **16** As the sun when it arises in the highest places of the Lord, so is the beauty of a good wife in her well-organized home. **17** As the lamp that shines upon the holy lampstand, so is the beauty of the face on a well-proportioned body. **18** As the golden pillars are upon a base of silver, so are beautiful feet with the breasts of one who is steadfast. **19⁻27** ʰ **28** For two things my heart is grieved, and for the third anger comes upon me: a warrior who suffers for poverty, men of understanding who are counted as garbage, and one who turns back from righteousness to sin— the Lord will prepare him for the sword! **29** It is difficult for a merchant to keep himself from wrong doing, and for a retailer to be acquitted of sin.

## 27

**1** Many have sinned for profit. He who seeks to multiply wealth will turn his eye away. **2** As a nail will stick fast between the joinings of stones, so sin will thrust itself in between buying and selling. **3** Unless a person holds on diligently to the fear of the Lord, his house will be overthrown quickly. **4** In the shaking of a sieve, the refuse remains, so does the filth of man in his thoughts. **5** The furnace tests the potter's vessels; so the test of a person is in his thoughts. **6** The fruit of a tree discloses its cultivation, so is the utterance of the thought of a person's heart. **7** Praise no man before you hear his thoughts, for this is how people are tested. **8** If you follow righteousness, you will obtain it, and put it on like a long robe of glory. **9** Birds will return to their own kind, so truth will return to those who practice it. **10** The lion lies in wait for prey. So does sin for those who do evil. **11** The discourse of a godly man is always wise, but the fool changes like the moon. **12** Limit your time among people void of understanding, but persevere among the thoughtful. **13** The talk of fools is offensive. Their laughter is wantonly sinful. **14** Their talk with much swearing makes hair stand upright. Their strife makes others plug their ears. **15** The strife of the proud leads to bloodshed. Their abuse of each other is a grievous thing to hear. **16** He who reveals secrets destroys trust, and will not find a close friend. **17** Love a friend, and keep faith with him; but if you reveal his secrets, you shall not follow him; **18** for as a man has destroyed his enemy, so you have destroyed the friendship of your neighbor. **19** As a bird which you have released out of your hand, so you have let your neighbor go, and you will not catch him again. **20** Don't pursue him, for he has gone far away, and has escaped like a gazelle out of the snare. **21** For a wound may be bound up, and after abuse there may be reconciliation; but he who reveals secrets is without hope. **22** One who winks the eye contrives evil things; and those who know him will keep their distance. **23** When you are present, he will speak sweetly, and will admire your words; but afterward he will twist his speech and set a trap in your words. **24** I have hated many things, but nothing like him. The Lord will hate him. **25** One who casts a stone straight up casts it on his own head. A deceitful blow opens wounds. **26** He who digs a pit will fall into it. He who sets a snare will be caught in it. **27** He who does evil things, they will roll back upon him, and he will not know where they came from. **28** Mockery and reproach are from the arrogant. Vengeance lies in wait for them like a lion. **29** Those who rejoice at the fall of the godly will be caught in a snare. Anguish will consume them before they die. **30** Wrath and anger, these also are abominations. A sinner will possess them.

---

ᵃ *24:15* See Exodus 30:34.
ᵇ *24:18* Verse 18 is omitted by the best authorities.

ᶜ *24:24* Verse 24 is omitted by the best authorities.
ᵈ *25:12* Verse 12 is omitted by the best authorities.

ᵉ *25:26* The remainder of this verse is omitted by the best authorities.
ᶠ *26:5* Gr. countenance.

ᵍ *26:13* or, fatten
ʰ *26:19-27* Verses 19- 27 are omitted by the best authorities.

## 28

[1] He who takes vengeance will find vengeance from the Lord, and he will surely make his sins firm. [2] Forgive your neighbor the hurt that he has done, and then your sins will be pardoned when you pray. [3] Does anyone harbor anger against another and expect healing from the Lord? [4] Upon a man like himself he has no mercy, and does he make supplication for his own sins? [5] He himself, being flesh, nourishes wrath. Who will make atonement for his sins? [6] Remember your last end, and stop enmity. Remember corruption and death, and be true to the commandments. [7] Remember the commandments, and don't be angry with your neighbor. Remember the covenant of the Highest, and overlook ignorance. [8] Abstain from strife, and you will diminish your sins, for a passionate man will kindle strife. [9] A man who is a sinner will trouble friends and sow discord among those who are at peace. [10] As is the fuel of the fire, so it will burn; and as the stoutness of the strife is, so it will burn. As is the strength of the man, so will be his wrath; and as is his wealth, so he will exalt his anger. [11] A contention begun in haste kindles a fire; and hasty fighting sheds blood. [12] If you blow on a spark, it will burn; and if you spit upon it, it will be quenched. Both of these come out of your mouth. [13] Curse the whisperer and double-tongued, for he has destroyed many who were at peace. [14] A slanderer has shaken many, and dispersed them from nation to nation. It has pulled down strong cities and overthrown the houses of great men. [15] A slanderer has cast out brave women and deprived them of their labors. [16] He who listens to it will not find rest, nor will he live quietly. [17] The stroke of a whip makes a mark in the flesh, but the stroke of a tongue will break bones. [18] Many have fallen by the edge of the sword, yet not so many as those who have fallen because of the tongue. [19] Happy is he who is sheltered from it, who has not passed through its wrath, who has not drawn its yoke, and has not been bound with its bands. [20] For its yoke is a yoke of iron, and its bands are bands of brass. [21] Its death is an evil death, and Hades is better than it. [22] It will not have rule over godly men. They will not be burned in its flame. [23] Those who forsake the Lord will fall into it. It will burn among them, and won't be quenched. It will be sent against them like a lion. It will destroy them like a leopard. [24] As you hedge your possession about with thorns, and secure your silver and your gold, [25] so make a balance and a weight for your words, and make a door and a bar for your mouth. [26] Take heed lest you slip with it, lest you fall before one who lies in wait.

## 29

[1] He who shows mercy will lend to his neighbor. He who strengthens him with his hand keeps the commandments. [2] Lend to your neighbor in time of his need. Repay your neighbor on time. [3] Confirm your word, and keep faith with him; and at all seasons you will find what you need. [4] Many have considered a loan to be a windfall, and have given trouble to those who helped them. [5] Until he has received, he will kiss a man's hands. For his neighbor's money he will speak submissively. Then when payment is due, he will prolong the time, return excuses, and complain about the season. [6] If he prevails, the creditor will hardly receive half; and he will count it as a windfall. If not, he has deprived him of his money, and he has gotten him for an enemy without cause. He will pay him with cursing and railing. Instead of honor, he will pay him disgrace. [7] Many on account of fraud have turned away. They are afraid of being defrauded for nothing. [8] However be patient with a man in poor estate. Don't keep him waiting for your alms. [9] Help a poor man for the commandment's sake. According to his need don't send him empty away. [10] Lose your money for a brother and a friend. Don't let it rust under a stone and be lost. [11] Allocate your treasure according to the commandments of the Most High and it will profit you more than gold. [12] Store up almsgiving in your store-chambers and it will deliver you out of all affliction. [13] It will fight for you against your enemy better than a mighty shield and a ponderous spear. [14] A good man will be surety for his neighbor. He who has lost shame will fail him. [15] Don't forget the kindness of your guarantor, for he has given his life for you. [16] A sinner will waste the property of his guarantor. [17] He who is thankless will fail him who delivered him. [18] Being surety has undone many who were prospering and shaken them as a wave of the sea. It has driven mighty men from their homes. They wandered among foreign nations. [19] A sinner who falls into suretiship and undertakes contracts for work will fall into lawsuits. [20] Help your neighbor according to your power, and be careful not to fall yourself. [21] The essentials of life are water, bread, a garment, and a house for privacy. [22] Better is the life of a poor man under a shelter of logs than sumptuous fare in another man's house. [23] With little or with much, be well satisfied.[a] [24] It is a miserable life to go from house to house. Where you are a guest, you dare not open your mouth. [25] You will entertain, serve

drinks, and have no thanks. In addition to this, you will hear bitter words. [26] "Come here, you sojourner, set a table, and if you have anything in your hand, feed me with it." [27] "Leave, you sojourner, for an honored guest is here. My brother has come to be my guest. I need my house." [28] These things are grievous to a man of understanding: The scolding about lodging and the insults of creditors.

## 30

[1] He who loves his son will continue to lay stripes upon him, that he may have joy from him in the end. [2] He who chastises his son will have profit from him, and will brag about him among his acquaintants. [3] He who teaches his son will provoke his enemy to jealousy. Before friends, he will rejoice in him. [4] His father dies, and is as though he had not died; for he has left one behind him like himself. [5] In his life, he saw his son and rejoiced. When he died, it was without regret. [6] He left behind him an avenger against his enemies, and one to repay kindness to his friends. [7] He who makes too much of his son will bind up his wounds. His heart will be troubled at every cry. [8] An unbroken horse becomes stubborn. An unrestrained son becomes headstrong. [9] Pamper your child, and he will make you afraid. Play with him, and he will grieve you. [10] Don't laugh with him, lest you have sorrow with him, and you gnash your teeth in the end. [11] Give him no liberty in his youth, and don't ignore his follies.[b] [12] [c]Bow down his neck in his youth, and beat him on the sides while he is a child, lest he become stubborn, and be disobedient to you, and there be sorrow to your soul.[d] [13] Chastise your son, and give him work, lest his shameless behavior be an offense to you. [14] Better is a poor man who is healthy and fit, than a rich man who is afflicted in his body. [15] Health and fitness are better than all gold, and a strong body better than wealth without measure. [16] There is no wealth better than health of body. There is no gladness above the joy of the heart. [17] Death is better than a bitter life, and eternal rest than a continual sickness. [18] Good things poured out upon a mouth that is closed are like food offerings laid upon a grave. [19] What does an offering profit an idol? For it can't eat or smell. So is he who is punished by the Lord, [20] seeing with his eyes and groaning, like a eunuch embracing a virgin and groaning. [21] Don't give your soul to sorrow. Don't afflict yourself deliberately. [22] Gladness of heart is the life of a man. Cheerfulness of a man lengthens his days. [23] Love your own soul, and comfort your heart. Remove sorrow far from you, for sorrow has destroyed many, and there is no profit in it. [24] Envy and wrath shorten life. Anxiety brings old age before its time. [25] Those who are cheerful and merry will benefit from their food.

## 31

[1] Wakefulness that comes from riches consumes the flesh, and anxiety about it takes away sleep. [2] Wakeful anxiety will crave slumber. In a severe disease, sleep will be broken. [3] A rich man toils in gathering money together. When he rests, he is filled with his good things. [4] A poor man toils in lack of substance. When he rests, he becomes needy. [5] He who loves gold won't be justified. He who follows destruction will himself have his fill of it. [6] Many have been given over to ruin for the sake of gold. Their destruction meets them face to face. [7] It is a stumbling block to those who sacrifice to it. Every fool will be taken by it. [8] Blessed is the rich person who is found blameless, and who doesn't go after gold. [9] Who is he, that we may call him blessed? For he has done wonderful things among his people. [10] Who has been tried by it, and found perfect? Then let him boast. Who has had the power to transgress, and has not transgressed? And to do evil, and has not done it? [11] His prosperity will be made sure. The congregation will proclaim his alms. [12] Do you sit at a great table? Don't be greedy on it. Don't say, "There is a lot of food on it!" [13] Remember that a greedy eye is a wicked thing. What has been created more greedy than an eye? Therefore it sheds tears from every face. [14] Don't stretch your hand wherever it looks. Don't thrust yourself with it into the dish. [15] Consider your neighbor's feelings by your own. Be discreet in every point. [16] Eat like a human being those things which are set before you. Don't eat greedily, lest you be hated. [17] Be first to stop for manners' sake. Don't be insatiable, lest you offend. [18] And if you sit among many, Don't reach out your hand before them. [19] How sufficient to a well-mannered man is a very little. He doesn't breathe heavily in his bed. [20] Healthy sleep comes from moderate eating. He rises early, and his wits are with him. The pain of wakefulness, colic, and griping are with an insatiable man. [21] And if you have been forced to eat, rise up in the middle of it, and you shall have rest. [22] Hear me, my son, and don't despise me, and in the end you will appreciate my words. In all your works be skillful, and no disease will come to you. [23] People bless him who is liberal with his food. The testimony of his excellence will be believed. [24] The city will murmur at him who is a stingy with his food. The testimony of his

[a] 29:23 The remainder of this verse is omitted by the best authorities.

[b] 30:11 This line and the previous two lines are absent from some older MSS.

[c] 30:12 These three lines are absent from the oldest MSS.

[d] 30:12 These three lines are absent from the oldest MSS.

stinginess will be accurate. ²⁵ Don't show yourself valiant in wine, for wine has destroyed many. ²⁶ The furnace tests the temper of steel by dipping; so does wine test hearts in the quarreling of the proud. ²⁷ Wine is as good as life to men, if you drink it in moderation. What life is there to a man who is without wine? It has been created to make men glad. ²⁸ Wine drunk in season and in moderation is joy of heart and gladness of soul: ²⁹ Wine drunk excessively is bitterness of soul, with provocation and conflict. ³⁰ Drunkenness increases the rage of a fool to his hurt. It diminishes strength and adds wounds. ³¹ Don't rebuke your neighbor at a banquet of wine. Don't despise him in his mirth. Don't speak a word of reproach to him. Don't distress him by making demands of him.

## 32

¹ Have they made you ruler of a feast? Don't be lifted up. Be among them as one of them. Take care of them first, and then sit down. ² And when you have done all your duties, take your place, that you may be gladdened on their account, and receive a wreath for your good service. ³ Speak, you who are older, for it's your right, but with sound knowledge; and don't interrupt the music. ⁴ Don't pour out talk where there is a performance of music. Don't display your wisdom at the wrong time. ⁵ As a ruby signet in a setting of gold, so is a music concert at a wine banquet. ⁶ As an emerald signet in a work of gold, so is musical melody with pleasant wine. ⁷ Speak, young man, if you are obliged to, but no more than twice, and only if asked. ⁸ Sum up your speech, many things in few words. Be as one who knows and yet holds his tongue. ⁹ When among great men, don't behave as their equal. When another is speaking, don't babble. ¹⁰ Lightning speeds before thunder. Approval goes before one who is modest. ¹¹ Rise up in good time, and don't be last. Go home quickly and don't loiter ¹² Amuse yourself there and do what is in your heart. Don't sin by proud speech. ¹³ For these things bless your Maker, who gives you to drink freely of his good things. ¹⁴ He who fears the Lord will receive discipline. Those who seek him early will find favor. ¹⁵ He who seeks the law shall be filled with it, but the hypocrite will stumble at it. ¹⁶ Those who fear the Lord will find true judgment, and will kindle righteous acts like a light. ¹⁷ A sinful man shuns reproof, and will find a judgment according to his will. ¹⁸ A sensible person won't neglect a thought. An insolent and proud man won't crouch in fear, even after he has done a thing by himself without counsel. ¹⁹ Do nothing without counsel, but when you have acted, don't regret it. ²⁰ Don't go in a way of conflict. Don't stumble in stony places. ²¹ Don't be overconfident on a smooth road. ²² Beware of your own children. ²³ In every work guard your own soul, for this is the keeping of the commandments. ²⁴ He who believes the law gives heed to the commandment. He who trusts in the Lord will suffer no loss.

## 33

¹ No evil will happen to him who fears the Lord, but in trials once and again he will deliver him. ² A wise man will not hate the law, but he who is a hypocrite about it is like a boat in a storm. ³ A man of understanding will put his trust in the law. And the law is faithful to him, as when one asks a divine oracle. ⁴ Prepare your speech, and so you will be heard. Bind up instruction, and make your answer. ⁵ The heart of a fool is like a cartwheel. His thoughts are like a rolling axle. ⁶ A stallion horse is like a mocking friend. He neighs under every one who sits upon him. ⁷ Why does one day excel another, when all the light of every day in the year is from the sun? ⁸ They were distinguished by the Lord's knowledge, and he varied seasons and feasts. ⁹ Some of them he exalted and hallowed, and some of them he has made ordinary days. ¹⁰ And all men are from the ground. Adam was created from dust. ¹¹ In the abundance of his knowledge the Lord distinguished them, and made their ways different. ¹² Some of them he blessed and exalted, and some of them he made holy and brought near to himself. Some of them he cursed and brought low, and overthrew them from their place. ¹³ As the clay of the potter in his hand, all his ways are according to his good pleasure, so men are in the hand of him who made them, to render to them according to his judgment. ¹⁴ Good is the opposite of evil, and life is the opposite of death; soª the sinner is the opposite of the godly. ¹⁵ Look upon all the works of the Most High like this, they come in pairs, one against another. ¹⁶ I was the last on watch, like one who gleans after the grape gatherers. ¹⁷ By the Lord's blessing I arrived before them, and filled my winepress like one who gathers grapes. ¹⁸ Consider that I labored not for myself alone, but for all those who seek instruction. ¹⁹ Hear me, you great men of the people, and listen with your ears, you rulers of the congregation. ²⁰ To son and wife, to brother and friend, don't give power over yourself while you live, and don't give your goods to another, lest you regret it and must ask for them. ²¹ While you still live and breath is in you, don't give yourself over to anybody. ²² For it is better that your children should ask from you than that you should look to the hand of your children. ²³ Excel in all your works. Don't bring a stain on your honor. ²⁴ In the day that you end the days of your life, in the time of death, distribute your inheritance. ²⁵ Fodder, a stick, and burdens are for a donkey. Bread, discipline, and work are for a servant. ²⁶ Set your slave to work, and you will find rest. Leave his hands idle, and he will seek liberty. ²⁷ Yoke and whip will bow the neck. For an evil slave there are racks and tortures. ²⁸ Send him to labor, that he not be idle, for idleness teaches much mischief. ²⁹ Set him to work, as is fit for him. If he doesn't obey, make his fetters heavy. ³⁰ Don't be excessive toward any. Do nothing unjust. ³¹ If you have a slave, treat him like yourself, because you have bought him with blood. ³² If you have a slave, treat him like yourself. For like your own soul, you will need him. If you treat him ill, and he departs and runs away, ³³ which way will you go to seek him?

## 34

¹ Vain and false hopes are for a man void of understanding. Dreams give wings to fools. ² As one who grasps at a shadow and follows after the wind, so is he who sets his mind on dreams. ³ The vision of dreams is a reflection, the likeness of a face near a face. ⁴ From an unclean thing what can be cleansed? From that which is false what can be true? ⁵ Divinations, and soothsayings, and dreams, are vain. The heart has fantasies like a woman in labor. ⁶ If they are not sent in a visitation from the Most High, don't give your heart to them. ⁷ For dreams have led many astray. They have failed by putting their hope in them. ⁸ Without lying the law will be fulfilled. Wisdom is complete in a faithful mouth. ⁹ A well-instructed man knows many things. He who has much experience will declare understanding. ¹⁰ He who has no experience knows few things. But he who has traveled increases cleverness. ¹¹ I have seen many things in my travels. My understanding is more than my words. ¹² I was often in danger even to death. I was preserved because of these experiences. ¹³ The spirit of those who fear the Lord will live, for their hope is in him who saves them. ¹⁴ Whoever fears the Lord won't be afraid, and won't be a coward, for he is his hope. ¹⁵ Blessed is the soul of him who fears the Lord. To whom does he give heed? Who is his support? ¹⁶ The eyes of the Lord are on those who love him, a mighty protection and strong support, a cover from the hot blast, a shade from the noonday sun, a guard from stumbling, and a help from falling. ¹⁷ He raises up the soul, and enlightens the eyes. He gives health, life, and blessing. ¹⁸ He who sacrifices a thing wrongfully gotten, his offering is made in mockery. The mockeries of wicked men are not acceptable. ¹⁹ The Most High has no pleasure in the offerings of the ungodly, Neither is he pacified for sins by the multitude of sacrifices. ²⁰ Like one who kills a son before his father's eyes is he who brings a sacrifice from the goods of the poor. ²¹ The bread of the needy is the life of the poor. He who deprives him of it is a man of blood. ²² Like one who murders his neighbor is he who takes away his living. Like a shedder of blood is he who deprives a hireling of his hire. ²³ When one builds, and another pulls down, what profit do they have but toil? ²⁴ When one prays, and another curses, whose voice will the Lord listen to? ²⁵ He who washes himself after touching a dead body, and touches it again, what does he gain by his washing? ²⁶ Even so a man fasting for his sins, and going again, and doing the same, who will listen to his prayer? What profit does he have in his humiliation?

## 35

¹ He who keeps the law multiplies offerings. He who heeds the commandments sacrifices a peace offering. ² He who returns a kindness offers fine flour. He who gives alms sacrifices a thank offering. ³ To depart from wickedness pleases the Lord. To depart from unrighteousness is an atoning sacrifice. ⁴ See that you don't appear in the presence of the Lord empty. ⁵ For all these things are done because of the commandment. ⁶ The offering of the righteous enriches the altar. The sweet fragrance of it is before the Most High. ⁷ The sacrifice of a righteous man is acceptable. It won't be forgotten. ⁸ Glorify the Lord with generosity. Don't reduce the first fruits of your hands. ⁹ In every gift show a cheerful countenance, And dedicate your tithe with gladness. ¹⁰ Give to the Most High according as he has given. As your hand has found, give generously. ¹¹ For the Lord repays, and he will repay you sevenfold. ¹² Don't plan to bribe him with gifts, for he will not receive them. Don't set your mind on an unrighteous sacrifice. For the Lord is the judge, and with him is no respect of persons. ¹³ He won't accept any person against a poor man. He will listen to the prayer of him who is wronged. ¹⁴ He will in no way despise the supplication of the fatherless or the widow, when she pours out her tale. ¹⁵ Don't the tears of the widow run down her cheek? Isn't her cry against him who has caused them to fall? ¹⁶ He who serves God according to his good pleasure will be accepted. His supplication will reach to the clouds. ¹⁷

ª *33:14* A line of this verse is here omitted by the best authorities.

The prayer of the humble pierces the clouds. until it comes near, he will not be comforted. He won't depart until the Most High visits and he judges righteously and executes judgment. [18] And the Lord will not be slack, neither will he be patient toward them, until he has crushed the loins of the unmerciful. He will repay vengeance to the heathen until he has taken away the multitude of the arrogant and broken in pieces the sceptres of the unrighteous, [19] until he has rendered to every man according to his deeds, and repaid the works of men according to their plans, until he has judged the cause of his people, and he will make them rejoice in his mercy. [20] Mercy is as welcome in the time of his affliction, as clouds of rain in the time of drought.

## 36

[1] Have mercy upon us, O Lord the God of all, and look at us with favor; [2] and send your fear upon all the nations.[a] [3] Lift up your hand against the foreign nations and let them see your mighty power. [4] As you showed your holiness in us before them, so be magnified in them before us. [5] Let them know you, as we also have known you, that there is no God but only you, O God. [6] Show new signs, and work various wonders. Glorify your hand and your right arm.[b] [7] Raise up indignation and pour out wrath. Take away the adversary and destroy the enemy. [8] Hasten the time and remember your oath. Let them declare your mighty works. [9] Let him who escapes be devoured by raging fire. May those who harm your people find destruction. [10] Crush the heads of the rulers of the enemies who say, "There is no one but ourselves." [11] Gather all the tribes of Jacob together, and[c] take them for your inheritance, as from the beginning. [12] O Lord, have mercy upon the people that is called by your name, and upon Israel, whom you likened to a firstborn. [13] Have compassion upon the city of your sanctuary, Jerusalem, the place of your rest. [14] Fill Zion. Exalt your oracles and fill your people with your glory. [15] Give testimony to those who were your creatures in the beginning, and fulfill the prophecies that have been spoken in your name. [16] Reward those who wait for you, and men will put their trust in your prophets. [17] Listen, O Lord, to the prayer of your servants, according to the blessing of Aaron concerning your people; and all those who are on the earth will know that you are the Lord, the[d] eternal God. [18] The belly will eat any food, but one food is better than another. [19] The mouth tastes meats taken in hunting, so does an understanding heart detect false speech. [20] A contrary heart will cause heaviness. A man of experience will pay him back. [21] A woman will receive any man, but one daughter is better than another. [22] The beauty of a woman cheers the countenance. A man desires nothing more. [23] If kindness and humility are on her tongue, her husband is not like other sons of men. [24] He who gets a wife gets his richest treasure, a help meet for him and a pillar of support. [25] Where no hedge is, the property will be plundered. He who has no wife will mourn as he wanders. [26] For who would trust a nimble robber who skips from city to city? Even so, who would trust a man who has no nest, and lodges wherever he finds himself at nightfall?

## 37

[1] Every friend will say, "I also am his friend"; but there is a friend which is only a friend in name. [2] Isn't there a grief in it even to death when a companion and friend is turned into an enemy? [3] O wicked imagination, why were you formed to cover the dry land with deceit? [4] There is a companion who rejoices in the gladness of a friend, but in time of affliction will be against him. [5] There is a companion who for the belly's sake labors with his friend, yet in the face of battle will carry his buckler. [6] Don't forget a friend in your soul. Don't be unmindful of him in your riches. [7] Every counselor extols counsel, but some give counsel in their own interest. [8] Let your soul beware of a counselor, and know in advance what is his interest (for he will take counsel for himself), lest he cast the lot against you, [9] and say to you, "Your way is good." Then he will stand near you, to see what will happen to you. [10] Don't take counsel with one who looks askance at you. Hide your counsel from those who are jealous of you. [11] Don't consult with a woman about her rival, with a coward about war, with a merchant about business, with a buyer about selling, with an envious man about thankfulness, with an unmerciful man about kindliness, with a sluggard about any kind of work, with a hireling in your house about finishing his work, or with an idle servant about much business. Pay no attention to these in any matter of counsel. [12] But rather be continually with a godly man, whom you know to be a keeper of the commandments, who in his soul is as your own soul, and who will grieve with you, if you fail. [13] Make the counsel of your heart stand, for there is no one more faithful to you than it. [14] For a man's soul is sometimes inclined to inform him better than seven watchmen who sit on high on a watch-tower. [15] Above all this ask the Most High that he may direct your way in truth. [16] Let

reason be the beginning of every work. Let counsel go before every action. [17] As a token of the changing of the heart, [18] four kinds of things rise up: good and evil, life and death. That which rules over them continually is the tongue. [19] There is one who is clever and the instructor of many, and yet is unprofitable to his own soul. [20] There is one who is subtle in words, and is hated. He will be destitute of all food. [21] For grace was not given to him from the Lord, because he is deprived of all wisdom. [22] There is one who is wise to his own soul, and the fruits of his understanding are trustworthy in the mouth. [23] A wise man will instruct his own people. The fruits of his understanding are trustworthy. [24] A wise man will be filled with blessing. All those who see him will call him happy. [25] The life of a man is counted by days. The days of Israel are innumerable. [26] The wise man will inherit confidence among his people. His name will live forever. [27] My son, test your soul in your life. See what is evil for it, and don't give in to it. [28] For not all things are profitable for all men. Not every soul has pleasure in everything. [29] Don't be insatiable in any luxury. Don't be greedy in the things that you eat. [30] For overeating brings disease, and gluttony causes nausea. [31] Because of gluttony, many have perished, but he who takes heed shall prolong his life.

## 38

[1] Honor a physician according to your need with the honors due to him, for truly the Lord has created him. [2] For healing comes from the Most High, and he shall receive a gift from the king. [3] The skill of the physician will lift up his head. He will be admired in the sight of great men. [4] The Lord created medicines out of the earth. A prudent man will not despise them. [5] Wasn't water made sweet with wood, that its power might be known? [6] He gave men skill that he might be glorified in his marvelous works. [7] With them he heals and takes away pain. [8] With these, the pharmacist makes a mixture. God's works won't be brought to an end. From him, peace is upon the face of the earth. [9] My son, in your sickness don't be negligent, but pray to the Lord, and he will heal you. [10] Put away wrong doing, and direct your hands in righteousness. Cleanse your heart from all sin. [11] Give a sweet savor and a memorial of fine flour, and pour oil on your offering, according to your means. [12] Then give place to the physician, for truly the Lord has created him. Don't let him leave you, for you need him. [13] There is a time when in recovery is in their hands. [14] For they also shall ask the Lord to prosper them in diagnosis and in healing for the maintenance of life. [15] He who sins before his Maker, let him fall into the hands of the physician. [16] My son, let your tears fall over the dead, and as one who suffers grievously, begin lamentation. Wind up his body with due honor. Don't neglect his burial. [17] Make bitter weeping and make passionate wailing. Let your mourning be according to his merit, for one day or two, lest you be spoken evil of; and so be comforted for your sorrow. [18] For from sorrow comes death. Sorrow of heart saps one's strength. [19] In calamity, sorrow also remains. A poor man's life is grievous to the heart. [20] Don't give your heart to sorrow. Put it away, remembering the end. [21] Don't forget it, for there is no returning again. You do him no good, and you would harm yourself. [22] Remember his end, for so also will yours be: yesterday for me, and today for you. [23] When the dead is at rest, let his remembrance rest. Be comforted for him when his spirit departs from him. [24] The wisdom of the scribe comes by the opportunity of leisure. He who has little business can become wise. [25] How could he become wise who holds the plow, who glories in the shaft of the goad, who drives oxen and is occupied in their labors, and who mostly talks about bulls? [26] He will set his heart upon turning his furrows. His lack of sleep is to give his heifers their fodder. [27] So is every craftsman and master artisan who passes his time by night as by day, those who cut engravings of signets. His diligence is to make great variety. He sets his heart to preserve likeness in his portraiture, and is careful to finish his work. [28] So too is the smith sitting by the anvil and considering the unwrought iron. The smoke of the fire will waste his flesh. He toils in the heat of the furnace. The noise of the hammer deafens his ear. His eyes are upon the pattern of the object. He will set his heart upon perfecting his works. He will be careful to adorn them perfectly. [29] So is the potter sitting at his work and turning the wheel around with his feet, who is always anxiously set at his work. He produces his handiwork in quantity. [30] He will fashion the clay with his arm and will bend its strength in front of his feet. He will apply his heart to finish the glazing. He will be careful to clean the kiln. [31] All these put their trust in their hands. Each becomes skillful in his own work. [32] Without these no city would be inhabited. Men wouldn't reside as foreigners or walk up and down there. [33] They won't be sought for in the council of the people. They won't mount on high in the assembly. They won't sit on the seat of the judge. They won't understand the covenant of judgment.

---

[a] *36:2* The remainder of this verse is omitted by the best authorities.

[b] *36:6* The remainder of this verse is omitted by the best authorities.

[c] *36:11* The ancient authorities read I took them for my

inheritance: but the Greek text is here very confused.

[d] *36:17* Gr. God of the ages.

Neither will they declare instruction and judgment. They won't be found where parables are. [34] But they will maintain the fabric of the age. Their prayer is in the handiwork of their craft.

## 39

[1] Not so he who has applied his soul and meditates in the law of the Most High. He will seek out the wisdom of all the ancients and will be occupied with prophecies. [2] He will keep the sayings of the men of renown and will enter in amidst the subtleties of parables. [3] He will seek out the hidden meaning of proverbs and be conversant in the dark sayings of parables. [4] He will serve among great men and appear before him who rules. He will travel through the land of foreign nations, for he has learned what is good and evil among men. [5] He will apply his heart to return early to the Lord who made him, and will make supplication before the Most High, and will open his mouth in prayer, and will ask for pardon for his sins. [6] If the great Lord wills, he will be filled with the spirit of understanding; he will pour forth the words of his wisdom and in prayer give thanks to the Lord. [7] He will direct his counsel and knowledge, and he will meditate in his secrets. [8] He will show the instruction which he has been taught and will glory in the law of the covenant of the Lord. [9] Many will commend his understanding. So long as the world endures, it won't be blotted out. His memory won't depart. His name will live from generation to generation. [10] Nations will declare his wisdom. The congregation will proclaim his praise. [11] If he continues, he will leave a greater name than a thousand. If he finally rests, it is enough for him. [12] Yet more I will utter, which I have thought about. I am filled like the full moon. [13] Listen to me, you holy children, and bud forth like a rose growing by a brook of water. [14] Give a sweet fragrance like frankincense. Put forth flowers like a lily. Scatter a sweet smell and sing a song of praise. Bless the Lord for all his works! [15] Magnify his name and give utterance to his praise with the songs on your lips and with harps! Say this when you utter his praise: [16] All the works of the Lord are exceedingly good, and every command will be done in its time. [17] No one can say, "What is this?" "Why is that?" for at the proper time they will all be sought out. At his word, the waters stood as a heap, as did the reservoirs of water at the word of his mouth. [18] At his command all his good pleasure is fulfilled. There is no one who can hinder his salvation. [19] The works of all flesh are before him. It's impossible to be hidden from his eyes. [20] He sees from everlasting to everlasting. There is nothing too wonderful for him. [21] No one can say, "What is this?" "Why is that?" for all things are created for their own uses. [22] His blessing covered the dry land as a river and saturated it as a flood. [23] As he has made the waters salty, so the heathen will inherit his wrath. [24] His ways are plain to the holy. They are stumbling blocks to the wicked. [25] Good things are created from the beginning for the good. So are evil things for sinners. [26] The main things necessary for the life of man are water, fire, iron, salt, wheat flour, and honey, milk, the blood of the grape, oil, and clothing. [27] All these things are for good to the godly, but for sinners, they will be turned into evils. [28] There are winds that are created for vengeance, and in their fury they lay on their scourges heavily. In the time of reckoning, they pour out their strength, and will appease the wrath of him who made them. [29] Fire, hail, famine, and death— all these are created for vengeance— [30] wild beasts' teeth, scorpions, adders, and a sword punishing the ungodly to destruction. [31] They will rejoice in his commandment, and will be made ready upon earth when needed. In their seasons, they won't disobey his command. [32] Therefore from the beginning I was convinced, and I thought it through and left it in writing: [33] All the works of the Lord are good. He will supply every need in its time. [34] No one can say, "This is worse than that," for they will all be well approved in their time. [35] Now with all your hearts and voices, sing praises and bless the Lord's name!

## 40

[1] Great travail is created for every man. A heavy yoke is upon the sons of Adam, from the day of their coming forth from their mother's womb, until the day for their burial in the mother of all things. [2] The expectation of things to come, and the day of death, trouble their thoughts, and cause fear in their hearts. [3] From him who sits on a throne of glory, even to him who is humbled in earth and ashes, [4] from him who wears purple and a crown, even to him who is clothed in burlap, [5] there is wrath, jealousy, trouble, unrest, fear of death, anger, and strife. In the time of rest upon his bed, his night sleep changes his knowledge. [6] He gets little or no rest, and afterward in his sleep, as in a day of keeping watch, he is troubled in the vision of his heart, as one who has escaped from the front of battle. [7] In the very time of his deliverance, he awakens, and marvels that the fear is nothing. [8] To all creatures, human and animal, and upon sinners sevenfold more, [9] come death, bloodshed, strife, sword, calamities, famine, suffering, and plague. [10]

All these things were created for the wicked, and because of them the flood came. [11] All things that are of the earth turn to the earth again. All things that are of the waters return into the sea. [12] All bribery and injustice will be blotted out. Good faith will stand forever. [13] The goods of the unjust will be dried up like a river, and like a great thunder in rain will go off in noise. [14] In opening his hands, a man will be made glad; so lawbreakers will utterly fail. [15] The children of the ungodly won't grow many branches, and are as unhealthy roots on a sheer rock. [16] The reeds by every water or river bank will be plucked up before all grass. [17] Kindness is like a garden of blessings. Almsgiving endures forever. [18] The life of one who labors and is content will be made sweet. He who finds a treasure is better than both. [19] Children and the building of a city establish a name. A blameless wife is better than both. [20] Wine and music rejoice the heart. The love of wisdom is better than both. [21] The pipe and the lute make pleasant melody. A pleasant tongue is better than both. [22] Your eye desires grace and beauty, but the green shoots of grain more than both. [23] A friend and a companion is always welcome, and a wife with her husband is better than both. [24] Relatives and helpers are for a time of affliction, but almsgiving rescues better than both. [25] Gold and silver will make the foot stand sure, and counsel is esteemed better than both. [26] Riches and strength will lift up the heart. The fear of the Lord is better than both. There is nothing lacking in the fear of the Lord. In it, there is no need to seek help. [27] The fear of the Lord is like a garden of blessing and covers a man more than any glory. [28] My son, don't lead a beggar's life. It is better to die than to beg. [29] A man who looks to the table of another, his life is not to be considered a life. He will pollute his soul with another person's food, but a wise and well-instructed person will beware of that. [30] Begging will be sweet in the mouth of the shameless, but it kindles a fire in his belly.

## 41

[1] O death, how bitter is the memory of you to a man who is at peace in his possessions, to the man who has nothing to distract him and has prosperity in all things, and who still has strength to enjoy food! [2] O death, your sentence is acceptable to a man who is needy and who fails in strength, who is in extreme old age, is distracted about all things, is perverse, and has lost patience! [3] Don't be afraid of the sentence of death. Remember those who have been before you and who come after. This is the sentence from the Lord over all flesh. [4] And why do you refuse when it is the good pleasure of the Most High? Whether life lasts ten, or a hundred, or a thousand years, there is no inquiry about life in Hades.[a] [5] The children of sinners are abominable children and they frequent the dwellings of the ungodly. [6] The inheritance of sinners' children will perish and with their posterity will be a perpetual disgrace. [7] Children will complain of an ungodly father, because they suffer disgrace because of him. [8] Woe to you, ungodly men, who have forsaken the law of the Most High God![b] [9] If you are born, you will be born to a curse. If you die, a curse will be your portion. [10] All things that are of the earth will go back to the earth; so the ungodly will go from a curse to perdition. [11] The mourning of men is about their bodies; but the evil name of sinners will be blotted out. [12] Have regard for your name, for it continues with you longer than a thousand great treasures of gold. [13] A good life has its number of days, but a good name continues forever. [14] My children, follow instruction in peace. But wisdom that is hidden and a treasure that is not seen, what benefit is in them both? [15] Better is a man who hides his foolishness than a man who hides his wisdom. [16] Therefore show respect for my words; for it is not good to retain every kind of shame. Not everything is approved by all in good faith. [17] Be ashamed of sexual immorality before father and mother, of a lie before a prince and a mighty man, [18] of an offense before a judge and ruler, of iniquity before the congregation and the people, of unjust dealing before a partner and friend, [19] and of theft in the place where you sojourn. Be ashamed in regard of the truth of God and his covenant, of leaning on your elbow at dinner, of contemptuous behavior in the matter of giving and taking, [20] of silence before those who greet you, of looking at a woman who is a prostitute, [21] of turning away your face from a kinsman, of taking away a portion or a gift, of gazing at a woman who has a husband, [22] of meddling with his maid— and don't come near her bed, of abusive speech to friends—and after you have given, don't insult, [23] of repeating and speaking what you have heard, and of revealing of secrets. [24] So you will be ashamed of the right things and find favor in the sight of every man.

## 42

[1] Don't be ashamed of these things, and don't sin to save face: [2] of the law of the Most High and his covenant, of judgment to do justice to the ungodly, [3] of reckoning with a partner and with travellers, of a gift from the inheritance of friends, [4] of exactness of scales and weights, of

---

[a] 41:4 or, the place of the dead or, Sheol    [b] 41:8 The remainder of this verse is omitted by the best authorities.

getting much or little, ⁵ of bargaining dealing with merchants, of frequent correction of children, and of making the back of an evil slave to bleed. ⁶ A seal is good where an evil wife is. Where there are many hands, lock things up. ⁷ Whatever you hand over, let it be by number and weight. In giving and receiving, let all be in writing. ⁸ Don't be ashamed to instruct the unwise and foolish, and one of extreme old age who contends with those who are young. So you will be well instructed indeed and approved in the sight of every living man. ⁹ A daughter is a secret cause of wakefulness to a father. Care for her takes away sleep— in her youth, lest she pass the flower of her age; when she is married, lest she should be hated; ¹⁰ in her virginity, lest she should be defiled and be with child in her father's house; when she has a husband, lest she should transgress; and when she is married, lest she should be barren. ¹¹ Keep a strict watch over a headstrong daughter, lest she make you a laughingstock to your enemies, a byword in the city and notorious among the people, and shame you in public. ¹² Don't gaze at every beautiful body. Don't sit in the midst of women. ¹³ For from garments comes a moth, and from a woman comes a woman's wickedness. ¹⁴ Better is the wickedness of a man than a pleasant woman, a woman who puts you to shame and disgrace. ¹⁵ I will make mention now of the works of the Lord, and will declare the things that I have seen. The Lord's works are in his words. ¹⁶ The sun that gives light looks at all things. The Lord's work is full of his glory. ¹⁷ The Lord has not given power to the saints to declare all his marvelous works, which the Almighty Lord firmly settled, that the universe might be established in his glory. ¹⁸ He searches out the deep and the heart. He has understanding of their secrets. For the Most High knows all knowledge. He sees the signs of the world. ¹⁹ He declares the things that are past and the things that shall be, and reveals the traces of hidden things. ²⁰ No thought escapes him. There is not a word hidden from him. ²¹ He has ordered the mighty works of his wisdom. He is from everlasting to everlasting. Nothing has been added to them, nor diminished from them. He had no need of any counselor. ²² How desirable are all his works! One may see this even in a spark. ²³ All these things live and remain forever in all manner of uses. They are all obedient. ²⁴ All things are in pairs, one opposite the other. He has made nothing imperfect. ²⁵ One thing establishes the good things of another. Who could ever see enough of his glory?

## 43

¹ The pride of the heavenly heights is the clear sky, the appearance of heaven, in the spectacle of its glory. ² The sun, when it appears, bringing tidings as it rises, is a marvelous instrument, the work of the Most High. ³ At noon, it dries up the land. Who can stand against its burning heat? ⁴ A man tending a furnace is in burning heat, but the sun three times more, burning up the mountains, breathing out fiery vapors, and sending out bright beams, it blinds the eyes. ⁵ Great is the Lord who made it. At his word, he hastens on its course. ⁶ The moon marks the changing seasons, declares times, and is a sign for the world. ⁷ From the moon is the sign of feast days, a light that wanes when it completes its course. ⁸ The month is called after its name, increasing wonderfully in its changing— an instrument of the army on high, shining in the structure of heaven, ⁹ the beauty of heaven, the glory of the stars, an ornament giving light in the highest places of the Lord. ¹⁰ At the word of the Holy One, they will stand in due order. They won't faint in their watches. ¹¹ Look at the rainbow, and praise him who made it. It is exceedingly beautiful in its brightness. ¹² It encircles the sky with its glorious circle. The hands of the Most High have stretched it out. ¹³ By his commandment, he makes the snow fall and swiftly sends the lightnings of his judgment. ¹⁴ Therefore the storehouses are opened, and clouds fly out like birds. ¹⁵ By his mighty power, he makes the clouds strong and the hailstones are broken in pieces. ¹⁶ At his appearing, the mountains will be shaken. At his will, the south wind will blow. ¹⁷ The voice of his thunder rebukes the earth. So does the northern storm and the whirlwind. Like birds flying down, he sprinkles the snow. It falls down like the lighting of locusts. ¹⁸ The eye is dazzled at the beauty of its whiteness. The heart is amazed as it falls. ¹⁹ He also pours out frost on the earth like salt. When it freezes, it has points like thorns. ²⁰ The cold north wind blows and ice freezes on the water. It settles on every pool of water. The water puts it on like it was a breastplate. ²¹ It will devour the mountains, burn up the wilderness, and consume the green grass like fire. ²² A mist coming speedily heals all things. A dew coming after heat brings cheerfulness. ²³ By his counsel, he has calmed the deep and planted islands in it. ²⁴ Those who sail on the sea tell of its dangers. We marvel when we hear it with our ears. ²⁵ There are also those strange and wondrous works in it— variety of all that has life and the huge creatures of the sea. ²⁶ Because of him, his messengers succeed. By his word, all things hold together. ²⁷ We may say many things, but couldn't say enough. The summary of our words is, "He is everything!" ²⁸ How could we have strength to glorify him? For he is himself the greater than all his works. ²⁹ The Lord is awesome and exceedingly great! His

power is marvelous! ³⁰ Glorify the Lord and exalt him as much as you can! For even yet, he will surpass that. When you exalt him, summon your full strength. Don't be weary, because you can't praise him enough. ³¹ Who has seen him, that he may describe him? Who can magnify him as he is? ³² Many things greater than these are hidden, for we have seen just a few of his works. ³³ For the Lord made all things. He gave wisdom to the godly.

## 44

¹ Let us now praise famous men, our ancestors in their generations. ² The Lord created great glory in them— his mighty power from the beginning. ³ Some ruled in their kingdoms and were men renowned for their power, giving counsel by their understanding. Some have spoken in prophecies, ⁴ leaders of the people by their counsels, and by their understanding, giving instruction for the people. Their words in their instruction were wise. ⁵ Some composed musical tunes, and set forth verses in writing, ⁶ rich men endowed with ability, living peaceably in their homes. ⁷ All these were honored in their generations, and were outstanding in their days. ⁸ Some of them have left a name behind them, so that others declare their praises. ⁹ But of others, there is no memory. They perished as though they had not been. They become as though they had not been born, they and their children after them. ¹⁰ But these were men of mercy, whose righteous deeds have not been forgotten. ¹¹ A good inheritance remains with their offspring. Their children are within the covenant. ¹² Their offspring stand fast, with their children, for their sakes. ¹³ Their offspring will remain forever. Their glory won't be blotted out. ¹⁴ Their bodies were buried in peace. Their name lives to all generations. ¹⁵ People will declare their wisdom. The congregation proclaims their praise. ¹⁶ Enoch pleased the Lord, and was taken up, an example of repentance to all generations. ¹⁷ Noah was found perfect and righteous. In the season of wrath, he kept the race alive. Therefore a remnant was left on the earth when the flood came. ¹⁸ Everlasting covenants were made with him, that all flesh should no more be blotted out by a flood. ¹⁹ Abraham was a great father of a multitude of nations. There was none found like him in glory, ²⁰ who kept the law of the Most High, and was taken into covenant with him. In his flesh he established the covenant. When he was tested, he was found faithful. ²¹ Therefore he assured him by an oath that the nations would be blessed through his offspring, that he would multiply him like the dust of the earth, exalt his offspring like the stars, and cause them to inherit from sea to sea, and from the Euphrates River to the utmost parts of the earth. ²² In Isaac also, he established the same assurance for Abraham his father's sake, the blessing of all men, and the covenant. ²³ He made it rest upon the head of Jacob. He acknowledged him in his blessings, gave to him by inheritance, and divided his portions. He distributed them among twelve tribes.

## 45

¹ He brought out of him a man of mercy, who found favor in the sight of all people, a man loved by God and men, even Moses, whose memory is blessed. ² He made him equal to the glory of the saints, and magnified him in the fears of his enemies. ³ By his words he caused the wonders to cease. God glorified him in the sight of kings. He gave him commandments for his people and showed him part of his glory. ⁴ He sanctified him in his faithfulness and meekness. He chose him out of all people. ⁵ He made him to hear his voice, led him into the thick darkness, and gave him commandments face to face, even the law of life and knowledge, that he might teach Jacob the covenant, and Israel his judgments. ⁶ He exalted Aaron, a holy man like Moses, even his brother, of the tribe of Levi. ⁷ He established an everlasting covenant with him, and gave him the priesthood of the people. He blessed him with stateliness, and dressed him in a glorious robe. ⁸ He clothed him in perfect splendor, and strengthened him with symbols of authority: the linen trousers, the long robe, and the ephod. ⁹ He encircled him with pomegranates; with many golden bells around him, to make a sound as he went, to make a sound that might be heard in the temple, for a reminder for the children of his people; ¹⁰ with a holy garment, with gold, blue, and purple, the work of the embroiderer; with an oracle of judgment—Urim and Thummim; ¹¹ with twisted scarlet, the work of the craftsman; with precious stones engraved like a signet, in a setting of gold, the work of the jeweller, for a reminder engraved in writing, after the number of the tribes of Israel; ¹² with a crown of gold upon the mitre, having engraved on it, as on a signet, "HOLINESS", an ornament of honor, the work of an expert, the desires of the eyes, goodly and beautiful. ¹³ Before him there never have been anything like it. No stranger put them on, but only his sons and his offspring perpetually. ¹⁴ His sacrifices shall be wholly burned, twice every day continually. ¹⁵ Moses consecrated him, and anointed him with holy oil. It was an everlasting covenant with him and to his offspring, all the days of heaven, to minister to the Lord, to serve as a priest, and to bless his people in his name. ¹⁶ He chose him out of all living to offer sacrifice to the Lord— incense, and a sweet fragrance, for a memorial, to make

atonement for your people. [17] He gave to him in his commandments, authority in the covenants of judgments, to teach Jacob the testimonies, and to enlighten Israel in his law. [18] Strangers conspired against him and envied him in the wilderness: Dathan and Abiram with their company, and the congregation of Korah, with wrath and anger. [19] The Lord saw it, and it displeased him. In the wrath of his anger, they were destroyed. He did wonders upon them, to consume them with flaming fire. [20] He added glory to Aaron, and gave him a heritage. He divided to him the first fruits of the increase, and prepared bread of first fruits in abundance. [21] For they eat the sacrifices of the Lord, which he gave to him and to his offspring. [22] However, in the land of the people, he has no inheritance, and he has no portion among the people, for the Lord himself is your portion and inheritance. [23] Phinehas the son of Eleazar is the third in glory, in that he was zealous in the fear of the Lord, and stood fast when the people turned away, and he made atonement for Israel. [24] Therefore, a covenant of peace was established for him, that he should be leader of the sanctuary and of his people, that he and his offspring should have the dignity of the priesthood forever. [25] Also he made a covenant with David the son of Jesse, of the tribe of Judah. The inheritance of the king is his alone from son to son. So the inheritance of Aaron is also to his seed. [26] May God give you wisdom in your heart to judge his people in righteousness, that their good things may not be abolished, and that their glory may endure for all their generations.

## 46

[1] Joshua the son of Nun was valiant in war, and was the successor of Moses in prophecies. He was made great according to his name for the saving of[a] God's elect, to take vengeance on the enemies that rose up against them, that he might give Israel their inheritance. [2] How was he glorified in the lifting up his hands, and in stretching out his sword against the cities! [3] Who before him stood so firm? For the Lord himself brought his enemies to him. [4] Didn't the sun go back by his hand? Didn't one day become as two? [5] He called upon the Most High, the Mighty One, when his foes pressed in all around him, and the great Lord heard him. [6] With hailstones of mighty power, he caused war to break violently upon the nation, and[b] on the slope he destroyed those who resisted, so that the nations might know his armor, how he fought in the sight of the Lord; for he followed the Mighty One. [7] Also in the time of Moses, he did a work of mercy— he and Caleb the son of Jephunneh— in that they withstood the adversary, hindered the people from sin, and stilled their wicked complaining. [8] And of six hundred thousand people on foot, they two alone were preserved to bring them into their inheritance, into a land flowing with milk and honey. [9] The Lord gave strength to Caleb, and it remained with him to his old age, so that he entered the hill country, and his offspring obtained it for an inheritance, [10] that all the children of Israel might see that it is good to follow the Lord. [11] Also the judges, every one by his name, all whose hearts didn't engage in immorality, and who didn't turn away from the Lord— may their memory be blessed! [12] May their bones flourish again out of their place. May the name of those who have been honored be renewed in their children. [13] Samuel, the prophet of the Lord, loved by his Lord, established a kingdom and anointed princes over his people. [14] By the law of the Lord he judged the congregation, and the Lord watched over Jacob. [15] By his faithfulness he was proved to be a prophet. By his words he was known to be faithful in vision. [16] When his enemies pressed on him on every side, he called upon the Lord, the Mighty One, with the offering of the suckling lamb. [17] Then the Lord thundered from heaven. He made his voice heard with a mighty sound. [18] He utterly destroyed the rulers of the Tyrians and all the princes of the Philistines. [19] Before the time of his age-long sleep, he testified in the sight of the lord and his anointed, "I have not taken any man's goods, so much as a sandal;" and no one accused him. [20] Even after he fell asleep, he prophesied, and showed the king his end, and lifted up his voice from the earth in prophecy, to blot out the wickedness of the people.

## 47

[1] After him, Nathan rose up to prophesy in the days of David. [2] As is the fat when it is separated from the peace offering, so was David separated from the children of Israel. [3] He played with lions as with kids, and with bears as with lambs of the flock. [4] In his youth didn't he kill a giant, and take away reproach from the people when he lifted up his hand with a sling stone, and beat down the boasting Goliath? [5] For he called upon the Most High Lord, and he gave him strength in his right hand to kill a man mighty in war, to exalt the horn of his people. [6] So they glorified him for his tens of thousands, and praised him for the blessings of the Lord, in that a glorious diadem was given to him. [7]

For he destroyed the enemies on every side, and defeated the Philistines his adversaries. He broke their horn in pieces to this day. [8] In every work of his he gave thanks to the Holy One Most High with words of glory. He sang praise with his whole heart, and loved him who made him. [9] He set singers before the altar, to make sweet melody by their music.[c] [10] He gave beauty to the feasts, and set in order the seasons to completion while they praised his holy name, and the sanctuary resounded from early morning. [11] The Lord took away his sins, and exalted his horn forever. He gave him a covenant of kings, and a glorious throne in Israel. [12] After him a wise son rose up, who because of him lived in security. [13] Solomon reigned in days of peace. God gave him rest all around, that he might set up a house for his name, and prepare a sanctuary forever. [14] How wise you were made in your youth, and filled as a river with understanding! [15] Your influence covered the earth, and you filled it with parables and riddles. [16] Your name reached to the far away islands, and you were loved for your peace. [17] For your songs, proverbs, parables, and interpretations, the countries marveled at you. [18] By the name of the Lord God, who is called the God of Israel, you gathered gold like tin, and multiplied silver like lead. [19] You bowed your loins to women, and in your body you were brought into subjection. [20] You blemished your honor, and defiled your offspring, to bring wrath upon your children. I was grieved for your folly, [21] because the sovereignty was divided, and a disobedient kingdom ruled out of Ephraim. [22] But the Lord will never forsake his mercy. He won't destroy any of his works, nor blot out the posterity of his elect. He won't take away the offspring of him who loved him. He gave a remnant to Jacob, and to David a root from his own family. [23] So Solomon rested with his fathers. Of his offspring, he left behind him Rehoboam, the foolishness of the people, and one who lacked understanding, who made the people revolt by his counsel. Also Jeroboam the son of Nebat, who made Israel to sin, and gave a way of sin to Ephraim. [24] Their sins were multiplied exceedingly, until they were removed from their land. [25] For they sought out all manner of wickedness, until vengeance came upon them.

## 48

[1] Then Elijah arose, the prophet like fire. His word burned like a torch. [2] He brought a famine upon them, and by his zeal made them few in number. [3] By the word of the Lord he shut up the heavens. He brought down fire three times. [4] How you were glorified, O Elijah, in your wondrous deeds! Whose glory is like yours? [5] You raised up a dead man from death, from Hades, by the word of the Most High. [6] You brought down kings to destruction, and honorable men from their sickbeds. [7] You heard rebuke in Sinai, and judgments of vengeance in Horeb. [8] You anointed kings for retribution, and prophets to succeed after you. [9] You were taken up in a tempest of fire, in a chariot of fiery horses. [10] You were recorded for reproofs in their seasons, to pacify anger, before it broke out into wrath, to turn the heart of the father to the son, and to restore the tribes of Jacob. [11] Blessed are those who saw you, and those who have been beautified with love; for we also shall surely live. [12] Elijah was wrapped in a whirlwind. Elisha was filled with his spirit. In his days he was not moved by the fear of any ruler, and no one brought him into subjection. [13] Nothing was too hard for him. When he was buried, his body prophesied. [14] As in his life he did wonders, so his works were also marvelous in death. [15] For all this the people didn't repent. They didn't depart from their sins, until they were carried away as a plunder from their land, and were scattered through all the earth. The people were left very few in number, but with a ruler from the house of David. [16] Some of them did that which was right, but some multiplied sins. [17] Hezekiah fortified his city, and brought water into its midst. He tunneled through rock with iron, and built cisterns for water. [18] In his days Sennacherib invaded, and sent Rabshakeh, and departed. He lifted up his hand against Zion, and boasted great things in his arrogance. [19] Then their hearts and their hands were shaken, and they were in pain, as women in labor. [20] But they called upon the Lord who is merciful, spreading out their hands to him. The Holy One quickly heard them out of Heaven, and delivered them by the hand of Isaiah. [21] He struck the camp of the Assyrians, and his angel utterly destroyed them. [22] For Hezekiah did that which was pleasing to the Lord, and was strong in the ways of his ancestor David, which Isaiah the prophet commanded, who was great and faithful in his vision. [23] In his days the sun went backward. He prolonged the life of the king. [24] He saw by an excellent spirit what would come to pass in the future; and he comforted those who mourned in Zion. [25] He showed the things that would happen through the end of time, and the hidden things before they came.

## 49

[1] The memory of Josiah is like the composition of incense prepared by the work of the perfumer. It will be sweet as honey in every mouth, and

---

[a] 46:1 Gr. his.
[b] 46:6 See Joshua 10:11

[c] 47:9 The remainder of this verse is omitted by the best authorities.

like music at a banquet of wine. ² He did what was right in the reforming of the people, and took away the abominations of iniquity. ³ He set his heart right toward the Lord. In lawless days, he made godliness prevail. ⁴ Except David, Hezekiah, and Josiah, all were wicked, because they abandoned the law of the Most High. The kings of Judah came to an end. ⁵ They gave their power to others, and their glory to a foreign nation. ⁶ They set the chosen city of the sanctuary on fire and made her streets desolate, as it was written by the hand of Jeremiah. ⁷ For they mistreated him; yet he was sanctified in the womb to be a prophet, to root out, to afflict, to destroy and likewise to build and to plant. ⁸ Ezekiel saw the vision of glory, which God showed him on the chariot of the cherubim. ⁹ For truly he remembered the enemies in rainstorm, and to do good to those who directed their ways aright. ¹⁰ Also of the twelve prophets,ᵃ may their bones flourish again out of their place. He comforted the people of Jacob, and delivered them by confident hope. ¹¹ How shall we magnify Zerubbabel? He was like a signet ring on the right hand. ¹² So was Jesus the son of Josedek, who in their days built the house, and exalted aᵇ people holy to the Lord, prepared for everlasting glory. ¹³ Also of Nehemiah the memory is great. He raised up for us fallen walls, set up the gates and bars, and rebuilt our houses. ¹⁴ No man was created upon the earth like Enoch, for he was taken up from the earth. ¹⁵ Nor was there a man born like Joseph, a leader of his kindred, a supporter of the people. Even his bones were cared for. ¹⁶ Shem and Seth were honored among men, but above every living thing in the creation was Adam.

## 50

¹ It was Simon, the son of Onias, the high priest, who in his life repaired the house, and in his days strengthened the temple. ² The foundation was built by him to the height of the double walls, the lofty retaining walls of the temple enclosure. ³ In his days, a water cistern was dug, the brazen vessel like the sea in circumference. ⁴ He planned to save his people from ruin, and fortified the city against siege. ⁵ How glorious he was when the people gathered around him as he came out of the house of the veil! ⁶ He was like the morning star among clouds, like the full moon, ⁷ like the sun shining on the temple of the Most High, like the rainbow shining in clouds of glory, ⁸ like roses in the days of first fruits, like lilies by a water spring, like the shoot of the frankincense tree in summer time, ⁹ like fire and incense in the censer, like a vessel of beaten gold adorned with all kinds of precious stones, ¹⁰ like an olive tree loaded with fruit, and like a cypress growing high among the clouds. ¹¹ When he put on his glorious robe, and clothed himself in perfect splendor, ascending to the holy altar, he made the court of the sanctuary glorious. ¹² When he received the portions out of the priests' hands, as he stood by the hearth of the altar, with his kindred like a garland around him, he was like a young cedar in Lebanon surrounded by the trunks of palm trees. ¹³ All the sons of Aaron in their glory, held the Lord's offering in their hands before all the congregation of Israel. ¹⁴ Finishing the service at the altars, that he might arrange the offering of the Most High, the Almighty, ¹⁵ he stretched out his hand to the cup of libation, and poured out the cup of the grape. He poured it out at the foot of the altar, a sweet smelling fragrance to the Most High, the King of all. ¹⁶ Then the sons of Aaron shouted. They sounded the trumpets of beaten work. They made a great fanfare to be heard, for a reminder before the Most High. ¹⁷ Then all the people together hurried, and fell down to the ground on their faces to worship their Lord, the Almighty, God Most High. ¹⁸ The singers also praised him with their voices. There was a sweet melody in the whole house. ¹⁹ And the people implored the Lord Most High, in prayer before him who is merciful, until the worship of the Lord was finished, and so they accomplished his service. ²⁰ Then he went down, and lifted up his hands over the whole congregation of the children of Israel, to give blessing to the Lord with his lips, and to glory in his name. ²¹ He bowed himself down in worship the second time, to declare the blessing from the Most High. ²² Now bless the God of all, who everywhere does great things, who exalts our days from the womb, and deals with us according to his mercy. ²³ May he grant us joyfulness of heart, and that peace may be in our days in Israel for the days of eternity, ²⁴ to entrust his mercy with us, and let him deliver us in his time! ²⁵ With two nations my soul is vexed, and the third is no nation: ²⁶ Those who sit on the mountain ofᶜ Samaria, the Philistines, and the foolish people who live in Shechem. ²⁷ I have written in this book the instruction of understanding and knowledge, I Jesus, the son of Sirach Eleazar, of Jerusalem, who out of his heart poured forth wisdom. ²⁸ Blessed is he who will exercise these things. He who lays them up in his heart will become wise. ²⁹ For if he does

them, he will be strong in all things, for the light of the Lord is his guide.ᵈ

## 51

A Prayer of Jesus the son of Sirach. ¹ I will give thanks to you, O Lord, O King, and will praise you, O God my Savior. I give thanks to your name, ² for you have been my protector and helper, and delivered my body out of destruction, and out of the snare of a slanderous tongue, from lips that fabricate lies. You were my helper before those who stood by, ³ and delivered me, according to the abundance of your mercy and of your name, from the gnashings of teeth ready to devour, out of the hand of those seeking my life, out of the many afflictions I endured, ⁴ from the choking of a fire on every side, and out of the midst of fire that I hadn't kindled, ⁵ out of the depth of the belly of Hades, from an unclean tongue, and from lying words— ⁶ the slander of an unrighteous tongue to the king. My soul drew near to death. My life was near to Hades. ⁷ They surrounded me on every side. There was no one to help me. I was looking for human help, and there was none. ⁸ Then I remembered your mercy, O Lord, and your working which has been from everlasting, how you deliver those who wait for you, and save them out of the hand of their enemies. ⁹ I lifted up my prayer from the earth, and prayed for deliverance from death. ¹⁰ I called upon the Lord, the Father of my Lord, that he would not forsake me in the days of affliction, in the time when there was no help against the proud. ¹¹ I will praise your name continually. I will sing praise with thanksgiving. My prayer was heard. ¹² You saved me from destruction and delivered me from the evil time. Therefore I will give thanks and praise to you, and bless the name of the Lord. ¹³ When I was yet young, before I went abroad, I sought wisdom openly in my prayer. ¹⁴ Before the temple I asked for her. I will seek her out even to the end. ¹⁵ From the first flower to the ripening grape my heart delighted in her. My foot walked in uprightness. From my youth I followed her steps. ¹⁶ I inclined my ear a little, and received her, and found for myself much instruction. ¹⁷ I profited in her. I will give glory to him who gives me wisdom. ¹⁸ For I determined to practice her. I was zealous for that which is good. I will never be put to shame. ¹⁹ My soul has wrestled with her. In my conduct I was exact. I spread out my hands to the heaven above, and bewailed my ignorances of her. ²⁰ I directed my soul to her. In purity I found her. I got myself a heart joined with her from the beginning. Therefore I won't be forsaken. ²¹ My belly also was troubled to seek her. Therefore I have gained a good possession. ²² The Lord gave me a tongue for my reward. I will praise him with it. ²³ Draw near to me, all you who are uneducated, and live in the house of instruction. ²⁴ Why therefore are you all lacking in these things, and your souls are very thirsty? ²⁵ I opened my mouth and spoke, "Get her for yourselves without money." ²⁶ Put your neck under the yoke, and let your soul receive instruction. She is near to find. ²⁷ See with your eyes how that I labored just a little and found for myself much rest. ²⁸ Get instruction with a great sum of silver, and gain much gold by her. ²⁹ May your soul rejoice in his mercy, and may you all not be put to shame in praising him. ³⁰ Work your work before the time comes, and in his time he will give you your reward.

# The Book of the Prophet Isaiah

## 1

¹ The vision of Isaiah the son of Amoz, which he saw concerning Judah and Jerusalem, in the days of Uzziah, Jotham, Ahaz, and Hezekiah, kings of Judah. ² Hear, heavens, and listen, earth; for Yahwehᵉ has spoken: "I have nourished and brought up children and they have rebelled against me. ³ The ox knows his owner, and the donkey his master's crib; but Israel doesn't know. My people don't consider." ⁴ Ah sinful nation, a people loaded with iniquity, offspringᶠ of evildoers, children who deal corruptly! They have forsaken Yahweh. They have despised the Holy One of Israel. They are estranged and backward. ⁵ Why should you be beaten more, that you revolt more and more? The whole head is sick, and the whole heart faint. ⁶ From the sole of the foot even to the head there is no soundness in it, but wounds, welts, and open sores. They haven't been closed, bandaged, or soothed with oil. ⁷ Your country is desolate. Your cities are burned with fire. Strangers devour your land in your presence and it is desolate, as overthrown by strangers. ⁸ The daughter of Zion is left like a shelter in a vineyard, like a hut in a field of melons, like a besieged city. ⁹ Unless Yahweh of Armies had left to us a very small remnant, we would have been as Sodom. We would have been like Gomorrah. ¹⁰ Hear Yahweh's word, you rulers of Sodom! Listen to the law of our God,ᵍ you people of

---

Gomorrah! [11]"What are the multitude of your sacrifices to me?", says Yahweh. "I have had enough of the burnt offerings of rams and the fat of fed animals. I don't delight in the blood of bulls, or of lambs, or of male goats. [12] When you come to appear before me, who has required this at your hand, to trample my courts? [13] Bring no more vain offerings. Incense is an abomination to me. New moons, Sabbaths, and convocations— I can't stand evil assemblies. [14] My soul hates your New Moons and your appointed feasts. They are a burden to me. I am weary of bearing them. [15] When you spread out your hands, I will hide my eyes from you. Yes, when you make many prayers, I will not hear. Your hands are full of blood. [16] Wash yourselves. Make yourself clean. Put away the evil of your doings from before my eyes. Cease to do evil. [17] Learn to do well. Seek justice. Relieve the oppressed. Defend the fatherless. Plead for the widow." [18]"Come now, and let's reason together," says Yahweh: "Though your sins are as scarlet, they shall be as white as snow. Though they are red like crimson, they shall be as wool. [19] If you are willing and obedient, you will eat the good of the land; [20] but if you refuse and rebel, you will be devoured with the sword; for Yahweh's mouth has spoken it." [21] How the faithful city has become a prostitute! She was full of justice. Righteousness lodged in her, but now there are murderers. [22] Your silver has become dross, your wine mixed with water. [23] Your princes are rebellious and companions of thieves. Everyone loves bribes and follows after rewards. They don't defend the fatherless, neither does the cause of the widow come to them. [24] Therefore the Lord,[a] Yahweh of Armies, the Mighty One of Israel, says: "Ah, I will get relief from my adversaries, and avenge myself on my enemies. [25] I will turn my hand on you, thoroughly purge away your dross, and will take away all your tin.[b] [26] I will restore your judges as at the first, and your counselors as at the beginning. Afterward you shall be called 'The city of righteousness, a faithful town.' [27] Zion shall be redeemed with justice, and her converts with righteousness. [28] But the destruction of transgressors and sinners shall be together, and those who forsake Yahweh shall be consumed. [29] For they shall be ashamed of the oaks which you have desired, and you shall be confounded for the gardens that you have chosen. [30] For you shall be as an oak whose leaf fades, and as a garden that has no water. [31] The strong will be like tinder, and his work like a spark. They will both burn together, and no one will quench them."

## 2

[1] This is what Isaiah the son of Amoz saw concerning Judah and Jerusalem. [2] It shall happen in the latter days, that the mountain of Yahweh's house shall be established on the top of the mountains, and shall be raised above the hills; and all nations shall flow to it. [3] Many peoples shall go and say, "Come, let's go up to the mountain of Yahweh, to the house of the God of Jacob; and he will teach us of his ways, and we will walk in his paths." For the law shall go out of Zion, and Yahweh's word from Jerusalem. [4] He will judge between the nations, and will decide concerning many peoples. They shall beat their swords into plowshares, and their spears into pruning hooks. Nation shall not lift up sword against nation, neither shall they learn war any more. [5] House of Jacob, come, and let's walk in the light of Yahweh. [6] For you have forsaken your people, the house of Jacob, because they are filled from the east, with those who practice divination like the Philistines, and they clasp hands with the children of foreigners. [7] Their land is full of silver and gold, neither is there any end of their treasures. Their land also is full of horses, neither is there any end of their chariots. [8] Their land also is full of idols. They worship the work of their own hands, that which their own fingers have made. [9] Man is brought low, and mankind is humbled; therefore don't forgive them. [10] Enter into the rock, and hide in the dust, from before the terror of Yahweh, and from the glory of his majesty. [11] The lofty looks of man will be brought low, the arrogance of men will be bowed down, and Yahweh alone will be exalted in that day. [12] For there will be a day of Yahweh of Armies for all that is proud and arrogant, and for all that is lifted up, and it shall be brought low— [13] for all the cedars of Lebanon, that are high and lifted up, for all the oaks of Bashan, [14] for all the high mountains, for all the hills that are lifted up, [15] for every lofty tower, for every fortified wall, [16] for all the ships of Tarshish, and for all pleasant imagery. [17] The loftiness of man shall be bowed down, and the arrogance of men shall be brought low; and Yahweh alone shall be exalted in that day. [18] The idols shall utterly pass away. [19] Men shall go into the caves of the rocks, and into the holes of the earth, from before the terror of Yahweh, and from the glory of his majesty, when he arises to shake the earth mightily. [20] In that day, men shall cast away their idols of silver and their idols of gold, which have been made for themselves to worship,

to the moles and to the bats, [21] to go into the caverns of the rocks, and into the clefts of the ragged rocks, from before the terror of Yahweh, and from the glory of his majesty, when he arises to shake the earth mightily. [22] Stop trusting in man, whose breath is in his nostrils; for of what account is he?

## 3

[1] For, behold,[c] the Lord, Yahweh of Armies, takes away from Jerusalem and from Judah supply and support, the whole supply of bread, and the whole supply of water; [2] the mighty man, the man of war, the judge, the prophet, the diviner, the elder, [3] the captain of fifty, the honorable man, the counselor, the skilled craftsman, and the clever enchanter. [4] I will give boys to be their princes, and children shall rule over them. [5] The people will be oppressed, everyone by another, and everyone by his neighbor. The child will behave himself proudly against the old man, and the wicked against the honorable. [6] Indeed a man shall take hold of his brother in the house of his father, saying, "You have clothing, you be our ruler, and let this ruin be under your hand." [7] In that day he will cry out, saying, "I will not be a healer; for in my house is neither bread nor clothing. You shall not make me ruler of the people." [8] For Jerusalem is ruined, and Judah is fallen; because their tongue and their doings are against Yahweh, to provoke the eyes of his glory. [9] The look of their faces testify against them. They parade their sin like Sodom. They don't hide it. Woe to their soul! For they have brought disaster upon themselves. [10] Tell the righteous that it will be well with them, for they will eat the fruit of their deeds. [11] Woe to the wicked! Disaster is upon them, for the deeds of their hands will be paid back to them. [12] As for my people, children are their oppressors, and women rule over them. My people, those who lead you cause you to err, and destroy the way of your paths. [13] Yahweh stands up to contend, and stands to judge the peoples. [14] Yahweh will enter into judgment with the elders of his people and their leaders: "It is you who have eaten up the vineyard. The plunder of the poor is in your houses. [15] What do you mean that you crush my people, and grind the face of the poor?" says the Lord, Yahweh of Armies. [16] Moreover Yahweh said, "Because the daughters of Zion are arrogant, and walk with outstretched necks and flirting eyes, walking daintily as they go, jingling ornaments on their feet; [17] therefore the Lord brings sores on the crown of the head of the women of Zion, and Yahweh will make their scalps bald." [18] In that day the Lord will take away the beauty of their anklets, the headbands, the crescent necklaces, [19] the earrings, the bracelets, the veils, [20] the headdresses, the ankle chains, the sashes, the perfume containers, the charms, [21] the signet rings, the nose rings, [22] the fine robes, the capes, the cloaks, the purses, [23] the hand mirrors, the fine linen garments, the tiaras, and the shawls. [24] It shall happen that instead of sweet spices, there shall be rottenness; instead of a belt, a rope; instead of well set hair, baldness; instead of a robe, a wearing of sackcloth; and branding instead of beauty. [25] Your men shall fall by the sword, and your mighty in the war. [26] Her gates shall lament and mourn. She shall be desolate and sit on the ground.

## 4

[1] Seven women shall take hold of one man in that day, saying, "We will eat our own bread, and wear our own clothing. Just let us be called by your name. Take away our reproach." [2] In that day, Yahweh's branch will be beautiful and glorious, and the fruit of the land will be the beauty and glory of the survivors of Israel. [3] It will happen that he who is left in Zion and he who remains in Jerusalem shall be called holy, even everyone who is written among the living in Jerusalem, [4] when the Lord shall have washed away the filth of the daughters of Zion, and shall have purged the blood of Jerusalem from within it, by the spirit of justice and by the spirit of burning. [5] Yahweh will create over the whole habitation of Mount Zion and over her assemblies, a cloud and smoke by day, and the shining of a flaming fire by night, for over all the glory will be a canopy. [6] There will be a pavilion for a shade in the daytime from the heat, and for a refuge and for a shelter from storm and from rain.

## 5

[1] Let me sing for my well beloved a song of my beloved about his vineyard.
My beloved had a vineyard on a very fruitful hill. [2] He dug it up, gathered out its stones, planted it with the choicest vine, built a tower in the middle of it, and also cut out a wine press in it. He looked for it to yield grapes, but it yielded wild grapes. [3]"Now, inhabitants of Jerusalem and men of Judah, please judge between me and my vineyard. [4] What could have been done more to my vineyard, that I have not done in it? Why, when I looked for it to yield grapes, did it

---

[a] *1:24* The word translated "Lord" is "Adonai."
[b] *1:25* tin is a metal that is separated from silver during the refining and purification process.
[c] *3:1* "Behold", from "הִנֵּה", means look at, take notice, observe, see, or gaze at. It is often used as an interjection.

yield wild grapes? ⁵ Now I will tell you what I will do to my vineyard. I will take away its hedge, and it will be eaten up. I will break down its wall, and it will be trampled down. ⁶ I will lay it a wasteland. It won't be pruned or hoed, but it will grow briers and thorns. I will also command the clouds that they rain no rain on it." ⁷ For the vineyard of Yahweh of Armies is the house of Israel, and the men of Judah his pleasant plant. He looked for justice, but behold, oppression, for righteousness, but behold, a cry of distress. ⁸ Woe to those who join house to house, who lay field to field, until there is no room, and you are made to dwell alone in the middle of the land! ⁹ In my ears, Yahweh of Armies says: "Surely many houses will be desolate, even great and beautiful, unoccupied. ¹⁰ For ten acresª of vineyard shall yield one bath,ᵇ and a homerᶜ of seed shall yield an ephah."ᵈ ¹¹ Woe to those who rise up early in the morning, that they may follow strong drink, who stay late into the night, until wine inflames them! ¹² The harp, lyre, tambourine, and flute, with wine, are at their feasts; but they don't respect the work of Yahweh, neither have they considered the operation of his hands. ¹³ Therefore my people go into captivity for lack of knowledge. Their honorable men are famished, and their multitudes are parched with thirst. ¹⁴ Therefore Sheolᵉ has enlarged its desire, and opened its mouth without measure; and their glory, their multitude, their pomp, and he who rejoices among them, descend into it. ¹⁵ So man is brought low, mankind is humbled, and the eyes of the arrogant ones are humbled; ¹⁶ but Yahweh of Armies is exalted in justice, and God the Holy One is sanctified in righteousness. ¹⁷ Then the lambs will graze as in their pasture, and strangers will eat the ruins of the rich. ¹⁸ Woe to those who draw iniquity with cords of falsehood, and wickedness as with cart rope, ¹⁹ who say, "Let him make haste, let him hasten his work, that we may see it; let the counsel of the Holy One of Israel draw near and come, that we may know it!" ²⁰ Woe to those who call evil good, and good evil; who put darkness for light, and light for darkness; who put bitter for sweet, and sweet for bitter! ²¹ Woe to those who are wise in their own eyes, and prudent in their own sight! ²² Woe to those who are mighty to drink wine, and champions at mixing strong drink; ²³ who acquit the guilty for a bribe, but deny justice for the innocent! ²⁴ Therefore as the tongue of fire devours the stubble, and as the dry grass sinks down in the flame, so their root shall be as rottenness, and their blossom shall go up as dust, because they have rejected the law of Yahweh of Armies, and despised the word of the Holy One of Israel. ²⁵ Therefore Yahweh's anger burns against his people, and he has stretched out his hand against them and has struck them. The mountains tremble, and their dead bodies are as refuse in the middle of the streets. For all this, his anger is not turned away, but his hand is still stretched out. ²⁶ He will lift up a banner to the nations from far away, and he will whistle for them from the end of the earth. Behold, they will come speedily and swiftly. ²⁷ No one shall be weary nor stumble among them; no one shall slumber nor sleep, neither shall the belt of their waist be untied, nor the strap of their sandals be broken, ²⁸ whose arrows are sharp, and all their bows bent. Their horses' hoofs will be like flint, and their wheels like a whirlwind. ²⁹ Their roaring will be like a lioness. They will roar like young lions. Yes, they shall roar, and seize their prey and carry it off, and there will be no one to deliver. ³⁰ They will roar against them in that day like the roaring of the sea. If one looks to the land, behold, darkness and distress. The light is darkened in its clouds.

## 6

¹ In the year that King Uzziah died, I saw the Lord sitting on a throne, high and lifted up; and his train filled the temple. ² Above him stood the seraphim. Each one had six wings. With two he covered his face. With two he covered his feet. With two he flew. ³ One called to another, and said, "Holy, holy, holy, is Yahweh of Armies! The whole earth is full of his glory!" ⁴ The foundations of the thresholds shook at the voice of him who called, and the house was filled with smoke. ⁵ Then I said, "Woe is me! For I am undone, because I am a man of unclean lips and I live among a people of unclean lips, for my eyes have seen the King, Yahweh of Armies!" ⁶ Then one of the seraphim flew to me, having a live coal in his hand, which he had taken with the tongs from off the altar. ⁷ He touched my mouth with it, and said, "Behold, this has touched your lips; and your iniquity is taken away, and your sin forgiven." ⁸ I heard the Lord's voice, saying, "Whom shall I send, and who will go for us?" Then I said, "Here I am. Send me!" ⁹ He said, "Go, and tell this people, 'You hear indeed, but don't understand. You see indeed, but don't perceive.' ¹⁰ Make the heart of this people fat. Make

their ears heavy, and shut their eyes; lest they see with their eyes, hear with their ears, understand with their heart, and turn again, and be healed." ¹¹ Then I said, "Lord, how long?" He answered, "Until cities are waste without inhabitant, houses without man, the land becomes utterly waste, ¹² and Yahweh has removed men far away, and the forsaken places are many within the land. ¹³ If there is a tenth left in it, that also will in turn be consumed, as a terebinth, and as an oak whose stump remains when they are cut down, so the holy seed is its stump."

## 7

¹ In the days of Ahaz the son of Jotham, the son of Uzziah, king of Judah, Rezin the king of Syria and Pekah the son of Remaliah, king of Israel, went up to Jerusalem to war against it, but could not prevail against it. ² David's house was told, "Syria is allied with Ephraim." His heart trembled, and the heart of his people, as the trees of the forest tremble with the wind. ³ Then Yahweh said to Isaiah, "Go out now to meet Ahaz, you, and Shearjashub your son, at the end of the conduit of the upper pool, on the highway of the fuller's field. ⁴ Tell him, 'Be careful, and keep calm. Don't be afraid, neither let your heart be faint because of these two tails of smoking torches, for the fierce anger of Rezin and Syria, and of the son of Remaliah. ⁵ Because Syria, Ephraim, and the son of Remaliah, have plotted evil against you, saying, ⁶"Let's go up against Judah, and tear it apart, and let's divide it among ourselves, and set up a king within it, even the son of Tabeel." ⁷ This is what the Lord Yahweh says: "It shall not stand, neither shall it happen." ⁸ For the head of Syria is Damascus, and the head of Damascus is Rezin. Within sixty-five years Ephraim shall be broken in pieces, so that it shall not be a people. ⁹ The head of Ephraim is Samaria, and the head of Samaria is Remaliah's son. If you will not believe, surely you shall not be established.'" ¹⁰ Yahweh spoke again to Ahaz, saying, ¹¹"Ask a sign of Yahweh your God; ask it either in the depth, or in the height above." ¹² But Ahaz said, "I won't ask. I won't tempt Yahweh." ¹³ He said, "Listen now, house of David. Is it not enough for you to try the patience of men, that you will try the patience of my God also? ¹⁴ Therefore the Lord himself will give you a sign. Behold, the virgin will conceive, and bear a son, and shall call his name Immanuel.ᶠ ¹⁵ He shall eat butter and honey when he knows to refuse the evil and choose the good. ¹⁶ For before the child knows to refuse the evil and choose the good, the land whose two kings you abhor shall be forsaken. ¹⁷ Yahweh will bring on you, on your people, and on your father's house days that have not come, from the day that Ephraim departed from Judah, even the king of Assyria. ¹⁸ It will happen in that day that Yahweh will whistle for the fly that is in the uttermost part of the rivers of Egypt, and for the bee that is in the land of Assyria. ¹⁹ They shall come, and shall all rest in the desolate valleys, in the clefts of the rocks, on all thorn hedges, and on all pastures. ²⁰ In that day the Lord will shave with a razor that is hired in the parts beyond the River, even with the king of Assyria, the head and the hair of the feet; and it shall also consume the beard. ²¹ It shall happen in that day that a man shall keep alive a young cow, and two sheep. ²² It shall happen, that because of the abundance of milk which they shall give he shall eat butter, for everyone will eat butter and honey that is left within the land. ²³ It will happen in that day that every place where there were a thousand vines worth a thousand silver shekels,ᵍ will be for briers and thorns. ²⁴ People will go there with arrows and with bow, because all the land will be briers and thorns. ²⁵ All the hills that were cultivated with the hoe, you shall not come there for fear of briers and thorns; but it shall be for the sending out of oxen, and for sheep to tread on."

## 8

¹ Yahweh said to me, "Take a large tablet, and write on it with a man's pen, 'For Maher Shalal Hash Baz';ʰ ² and I will take for myself faithful witnesses to testify: Uriah the priest, and Zechariah the son of Jeberechiah." ³ I went to the prophetess, and she conceived, and bore a son. Then Yahweh said to me, "Call his name 'Maher Shalal Hash Baz.' ⁴ For before the child knows how to say, 'My father' and 'My mother,' the riches of Damascus and the plunder of Samaria will be carried away by the king of Assyria." ⁵ Yahweh spoke to me yet again, saying, ⁶"Because this people has refused the waters of Shiloah that go softly, and rejoice in Rezin and Remaliah's son; ⁷ now therefore, behold, the Lord brings upon them the mighty flood waters of the River: the king of Assyria and all his glory. It will come up over all its channels, and go over all its banks. ⁸ It will sweep onward into Judah. It will overflow and pass through. It will reach even to the neck. The stretching out of

---

ª 5:10 literally, ten yokes, or the amount of land that ten yokes of oxen can plow in one day, which is about 10 acres or 4 hectares.
ᵇ 5:10 1 bath is about 22 liters or 5.8 U. S. gallons

ᶜ 5:10 1 homer is about 220 liters or 6 bushels
ᵈ 5:10 1 ephah is about 22 liters or 0.6 bushels or about 2 pecks—only one tenth of what was sown.

ᵉ 5:14 Sheol is the place of the dead.
ᶠ 7:14 "Immanuel" means "God with us".
ᵍ 7:23 A shekel is about 10 grams or about 0.35 ounces, so

1000 shekels is about 10 kilograms or 22 pounds.
ʰ 8:1 "Maher Shalal Hash Baz" means "quick to the plunder, swift to the prey".

its wings will fill the width of your land, O Immanuel. ⁹ Make an uproar, you peoples, and be broken in pieces! Listen, all you from far countries: dress for battle, and be shattered! Dress for battle, and be shattered! ¹⁰ Take counsel together, and it will be brought to nothing; speak the word, and it will not stand, for God is with us." ¹¹ For Yahweh spoke this to me with a strong hand, and instructed me not to walk in the way of this people, saying, ¹²"Don't call a conspiracy all that this people call a conspiracy. Don't fear their threats or be terrorized. ¹³ Yahweh of Armies is who you must respect as holy. He is the one you must fear. He is the one you must dread. ¹⁴ He will be a sanctuary, but for both houses of Israel, he will be a stumbling stone and a rock that makes them fall. For the people of Jerusalem, he will be a trap and a snare. ¹⁵ Many will stumble over it, fall, be broken, be snared, and be captured." ¹⁶ Wrap up the covenant. Seal the law among my disciples. ¹⁷ I will wait for Yahweh, who hides his face from the house of Jacob, and I will look for him. ¹⁸ Behold, I and the children whom Yahweh has given me are for signs and for wonders in Israel from Yahweh of Armies, who dwells in Mount Zion. ¹⁹ When they tell you, "Consult with those who have familiar spirits and with the wizards, who chirp and who mutter," shouldn't a people consult with their God? Should they consult the dead on behalf of the living? ²⁰ Turn to the law and to the covenant! If they don't speak according to this word, surely there is no morning for them. ²¹ They will pass through it, very distressed and hungry. It will happen that when they are hungry, they will worry, and curse their king and their God. They will turn their faces upward, ²² then look to the earth and see distress, darkness, and the gloom of anguish. They will be driven into thick darkness.

# 9

¹ But there shall be no more gloom for her who was in anguish. In the former time, he brought into contempt the land of Zebulun and the land of Naphtali; but in the latter time he has made it glorious, by the way of the sea, beyond the Jordan, Galilee of the nations. ² The people who walked in darkness have seen a great light. The light has shined on those who lived in the land of the shadow of death. ³ You have multiplied the nation. You have increased their joy. They rejoice before you according to the joy in harvest, as men rejoice when they divide the plunder. ⁴ For the yoke of his burden, and the staff of his shoulder, the rod of his oppressor, you have broken as in the day of Midian. ⁵ For all the armor of the armed man in the noisy battle, and the garments rolled in blood, will be for burning, fuel for the fire. ⁶ For a child is born to us. A son is given to us; and the government will be on his shoulders. His name will be called Wonderful Counselor, Mighty God, Everlasting Father, Prince of Peace. ⁷ Of the increase of his government and of peace there shall be no end, on David's throne, and on his kingdom, to establish it, and to uphold it with justice and with righteousness from that time on, even forever. The zeal of Yahweh of Armies will perform this. ⁸ The Lord sent a word into Jacob, and it falls on Israel. ⁹ All the people will know, including Ephraim and the inhabitants of Samaria, who say in pride and in arrogance of heart, ¹⁰"The bricks have fallen, but we will build with cut stone. The sycamore fig trees have been cut down, but we will put cedars in their place." ¹¹ Therefore Yahweh will set up on high against him the adversaries of Rezin, and will stir up his enemies, ¹² The Syrians in front, and the Philistines behind; and they will devour Israel with open mouth. For all this, his anger is not turned away, but his hand is stretched out still. ¹³ Yet the people have not turned to him who struck them, neither have they sought Yahweh of Armies. ¹⁴ Therefore Yahweh will cut off from Israel head and tail, palm branch and reed, in one day. ¹⁵ The elder and the honorable man is the head, and the prophet who teaches lies is the tail. ¹⁶ For those who lead this people lead them astray; and those who are led by them are destroyed. ¹⁷ Therefore the Lord will not rejoice over their young men, neither will he have compassion on their fatherless and widows; for everyone is profane and an evildoer, and every mouth speaks folly. For all this his anger is not turned away, but his hand is stretched out still. ¹⁸ For wickedness burns like a fire. It devours the briers and thorns; yes, it kindles in the thickets of the forest, and they roll upward in a column of smoke. ¹⁹ Through Yahweh of Armies' wrath, the land is burned up; and the people are the fuel for the fire. No one spares his brother. ²⁰ One will devour on the right hand, and be hungry; and he will eat on the left hand, and they will not be satisfied. Everyone will eat the flesh of his own arm: ²¹ Manasseh eating Ephraim and Ephraim eating Manasseh, and they together will be against Judah. For all this his anger is not turned away, but his hand is stretched out still.

# 10

¹ Woe to those who decree unrighteous decrees, and to the writers who write oppressive decrees ² to deprive the needy of justice, and to rob the poor among my people of their rights, that widows may be their plunder, and that they may make the fatherless their prey! ³ What will you do in the day of visitation, and in the desolation which will come from afar? To whom will you flee for help? Where will you leave your wealth? ⁴ They will only bow down under the prisoners, and will fall under the slain. For all this his anger is not turned away, but his hand is stretched out still. ⁵ Alas Assyrian, the rod of my anger, the staff in whose hand is my indignation! ⁶ I will send him against a profane nation, and against the people who anger me I will give him a command to take the plunder and to take the prey, and to tread them down like the mire of the streets. ⁷ However, he doesn't mean so, neither does his heart think so; but it is in his heart to destroy, and to cut off not a few nations. ⁸ For he says, "Aren't all of my princes kings? ⁹ Isn't Calno like Carchemish? Isn't Hamath like Arpad? Isn't Samaria like Damascus?" ¹⁰ As my hand has found the kingdoms of the idols, whose engraved images exceeded those of Jerusalem and of Samaria, ¹¹ shall I not, as I have done to Samaria and her idols, so do to Jerusalem and her idols? ¹² Therefore it will happen that when the Lord has performed his whole work on Mount Zion and on Jerusalem, I will punish the fruit of the willful proud heart of the king of Assyria, and the insolence of his arrogant looks. ¹³ For he has said, "By the strength of my hand I have done it, and by my wisdom, for I have understanding. I have removed the boundaries of the peoples, and have robbed their treasures. Like a valiant man I have brought down their rulers. ¹⁴ My hand has found the riches of the peoples like a nest, and like one gathers eggs that are abandoned, I have gathered all the earth. There was no one who moved their wing, or that opened their mouth, or chirped." ¹⁵ Should an ax brag against him who chops with it? Should a saw exalt itself above him who saws with it? As if a rod should lift those who lift it up, or as if a staff should lift up someone who is not wood. ¹⁶ Therefore the Lord, Yahweh of Armies, will send among his fat ones leanness; and under his glory a burning will be kindled like the burning of fire. ¹⁷ The light of Israel will be for a fire, and his Holy One for a flame; and it will burn and devour his thorns and his briers in one day. ¹⁸ He will consume the glory of his forest and of his fruitful field, both soul and body. It will be as when a standard bearer faints. ¹⁹ The remnant of the trees of his forest shall be few, so that a child could write their number. ²⁰ It will come to pass in that day that the remnant of Israel, and those who have escaped from the house of Jacob will no more again lean on him who struck them, but shall lean on Yahweh, the Holy One of Israel, in truth. ²¹ A remnant will return, even the remnant of Jacob, to the mighty God. ²² For though your people, Israel, are like the sand of the sea, only a remnant of them will return. A destruction is determined, overflowing with righteousness. ²³ For the Lord, Yahweh of Armies, will make a full end, and that determined, throughout all the earth. ²⁴ Therefore the Lord, Yahweh of Armies, says, "My people who dwell in Zion, don't be afraid of the Assyrian, though he strike you with the rod, and lift up his staff against you, as Egypt did. ²⁵ For yet a very little while, and the indignation against you will be accomplished, and my anger will be directed to his destruction." ²⁶ Yahweh of Armies will stir up a scourge against him, as in the slaughter of Midian at the rock of Oreb. His rod will be over the sea, and he will lift it up like he did against Egypt. ²⁷ It will happen in that day that his burden will depart from off your shoulder, and his yoke from off your neck, and the yoke shall be destroyed because of the anointing oil. ²⁸ He has come to Aiath. He has passed through Migron. At Michmash he stores his baggage. ²⁹ They have gone over the pass. They have taken up their lodging at Geba. Ramah trembles. Gibeah of Saul has fled. ³⁰ Cry aloud with your voice, daughter of Gallim! Listen, Laishah! You poor Anathoth! ³¹ Madmenah is a fugitive. The inhabitants of Gebim flee for safety. ³² This very day he will halt at Nob. He shakes his hand at the mountain of the daughter of Zion, the hill of Jerusalem. ³³ Behold, the Lord, Yahweh of Armies, will lop the boughs with terror. The tall will be cut down, and the lofty will be brought low. ³⁴ He will cut down the thickets of the forest with iron, and Lebanon will fall by the Mighty One.

# 11

¹ A shoot will come out of the stock of Jesse, and a branch out of his roots will bear fruit. ² Yahweh's Spirit will rest on him: the spirit of wisdom and understanding, the spirit of counsel and might, the spirit of knowledge and of the fear of Yahweh. ³ His delight will be in the fear of Yahweh. He will not judge by the sight of his eyes, neither decide by the hearing of his ears; ⁴ but he will judge the poor with righteousness, and decide with equity for the humble of the earth. He will strike the earth with the rod of his mouth; and with the breath of his lips he will kill the wicked. ⁵ Righteousness will be the belt around his waist, and faithfulness the belt around his waist. ⁶ The wolf will live with the lamb, and the leopard will lie down with the young goat, the calf, the young lion, and the fattened calf together; and a little child will lead them. ⁷ The cow and the bear will graze. Their young ones will lie down together. The lion will eat straw like the ox. ⁸ The nursing child will play near a cobra's hole, and the weaned child will put his hand on the viper's den. ⁹ They will not hurt nor destroy in all my holy mountain; for the earth will be full of the knowledge of Yahweh, as the waters cover the sea. ¹⁰ It will happen in that day that the nations will

seek the root of Jesse, who stands as a banner of the peoples; and his resting place will be glorious. [11] It will happen in that day that the Lord will set his hand again the second time to recover the remnant that is left of his people from Assyria, from Egypt, from Pathros, from Cush, from Elam, from Shinar, from Hamath, and from the islands of the sea. [12] He will set up a banner for the nations, and will assemble the outcasts of Israel, and gather together the dispersed of Judah from the four corners of the earth. [13] The envy also of Ephraim will depart, and those who persecute Judah will be cut off. Ephraim won't envy Judah, and Judah won't persecute Ephraim. [14] They will fly down on the shoulders of the Philistines on the west. Together they will plunder the children of the east. They will extend their power over Edom and Moab, and the children of Ammon will obey them. [15] Yahweh will utterly destroy the tongue of the Egyptian sea; and with his scorching wind he will wave his hand over the River, and will split it into seven streams, and cause men to march over in sandals. [16] There will be a highway for the remnant that is left of his people from Assyria, like there was for Israel in the day that he came up out of the land of Egypt.

## 12

[1] In that day you will say, "I will give thanks to you, Yahweh; for though you were angry with me, your anger has turned away and you comfort me. [2] Behold, God is my salvation. I will trust, and will not be afraid; for Yah, Yahweh, is my strength and song; and he has become my salvation." [3] Therefore with joy you will draw water out of the wells of salvation. [4] In that day you will say, "Give thanks to Yahweh! Call on his name! Declare his doings among the peoples! Proclaim that his name is exalted! [5] Sing to Yahweh, for he has done excellent things! Let this be known in all the earth! [6] Cry aloud and shout, you inhabitant of Zion, for the Holy One of Israel is great among you!"

## 13

[1] The burden of Babylon, which Isaiah the son of Amoz saw. [2] Set up a banner on the bare mountain! Lift up your voice to them! Wave your hand, that they may go into the gates of the nobles. [3] I have commanded my consecrated ones; yes, I have called my mighty men for my anger, even my proudly exulting ones. [4] The noise of a multitude is in the mountains, as of a great people; the noise of an uproar of the kingdoms of the nations gathered together! Yahweh of Armies is mustering the army for the battle. [5] They come from a far country, from the uttermost part of heaven, even Yahweh, and the weapons of his indignation, to destroy the whole land. [6] Wail, for Yahweh's day is at hand! It will come as destruction from the Almighty. [7] Therefore all hands will be feeble, and everyone's heart will melt. [8] They will be dismayed. Pangs and sorrows will seize them. They will be in pain like a woman in labor. They will look in amazement one at another. Their faces will be faces of flame. [9] Behold, the day of Yahweh comes, cruel, with wrath and fierce anger; to make the land a desolation, and to destroy its sinners out of it. [10] For the stars of the sky and its constellations will not give their light. The sun will be darkened in its going out, and the moon will not cause its light to shine. [11] I will punish the world for their evil, and the wicked for their iniquity. I will cause the arrogance of the proud to cease, and will humble the arrogance of the terrible. [12] I will make people more rare than fine gold, even a person than the pure gold of Ophir. [13] Therefore I will make the heavens tremble, and the earth will be shaken out of its place in Yahweh of Armies' wrath, and in the day of his fierce anger. [14] It will happen that like a hunted gazelle and like sheep that no one gathers, they will each turn to their own people, and will each flee to their own land. [15] Everyone who is found will be thrust through. Everyone who is captured will fall by the sword. [16] Their infants also will be dashed in pieces before their eyes. Their houses will be ransacked, and their wives raped. [17] Behold, I will stir up the Medes against them, who will not value silver, and as for gold, they will not delight in it. [18] Their bows will dash the young men in pieces; and they shall have no pity on the fruit of the womb. Their eyes will not spare children. [19] Babylon, the glory of kingdoms, the beauty of the Chaldeans' pride, will be like when God overthrew Sodom and Gomorrah. [20] It will never be inhabited, neither will it be lived in from generation to generation. The Arabian will not pitch a tent there, neither will shepherds make their flocks lie down there. [21] But wild animals of the desert will lie there, and their houses will be full of jackals. Ostriches will dwell there, and wild goats will frolic there. [22] Hyenas will cry in their fortresses, and jackals in the pleasant palaces. Her time is near to come, and her days will not be prolonged.

## 14

[1] For Yahweh will have compassion on Jacob, and will yet choose Israel, and set them in their own land. The foreigner will join himself with them, and they will unite with the house of Jacob. [2] The peoples will take them, and bring them to their place. The house of Israel will possess them in Yahweh's land for servants and for handmaids. They will take as captives those whose captives they were; and they shall rule over their oppressors. [3] It will happen in the day that Yahweh will give you rest from your sorrow, from your trouble, and from the hard service in which you were made to serve, [4] that you will take up this parable against the king of Babylon, and say, "How the oppressor has ceased! The golden city has ceased!" [5] Yahweh has broken the staff of the wicked, the scepter of the rulers, [6] who struck the peoples in wrath with a continual stroke, who ruled the nations in anger, with a persecution that no one restrained. [7] The whole earth is at rest, and is quiet. They break out in song. [8] Yes, the cypress trees rejoice with you, with the cedars of Lebanon, saying, "Since you are humbled, no lumberjack has come up against us." [9] Sheol[a] from beneath has moved for you to meet you at your coming. It stirs up the departed spirits for you, even all the rulers of the earth. It has raised up from their thrones all the kings of the nations. [10] They all will answer and ask you, "Have you also become as weak as we are? Have you become like us?" [11] Your pomp is brought down to Sheol,[b] with the sound of your stringed instruments. Maggots are spread out under you, and worms cover you. [12] How you have fallen from heaven, shining one, son of the dawn! How you are cut down to the ground, who laid the nations low! [13] You said in your heart, "I will ascend into heaven! I will exalt my throne above the stars of God! I will sit on the mountain of assembly, in the far north! [14] I will ascend above the heights of the clouds! I will make myself like the Most High!" [15] Yet you shall be brought down to Sheol,[c] to the depths of the pit. [16] Those who see you will stare at you. They will ponder you, saying, "Is this the man who made the earth to tremble, who shook kingdoms, [17] who made the world like a wilderness, and overthrew its cities, who didn't release his prisoners to their home?" [18] All the kings of the nations sleep in glory, everyone in his own house. [19] But you are cast away from your tomb like an abominable branch, clothed with the slain who are thrust through with the sword, who go down to the stones of the pit; like a dead body trodden under foot. [20] You will not join them in burial, because you have destroyed your land. You have killed your people. The offspring of evildoers will not be named forever. [21] Prepare for slaughter of his children because of the iniquity of their fathers, that they not rise up and possess the earth, and fill the surface of the world with cities. [22] "I will rise up against them," says Yahweh of Armies, "and cut off from Babylon name and remnant, and son and son's son," says Yahweh. [23] "I will also make it a possession for the porcupine, and pools of water. I will sweep it with the broom of destruction," says Yahweh of Armies. [24] Yahweh of Armies has sworn, saying, "Surely, as I have thought, so shall it happen; and as I have purposed, so shall it stand: [25] that I will break the Assyrian in my land, and tread him under foot on my mountains. Then his yoke will leave them, and his burden leave their shoulders. [26] This is the plan that is determined for the whole earth. This is the hand that is stretched out over all the nations. [27] For Yahweh of Armies has planned, and who can stop it? His hand is stretched out, and who can turn it back?" [28] This burden was in the year that King Ahaz died. [29] Don't rejoice, O Philistia, all of you, because the rod that struck you is broken; for out of the serpent's root an adder will emerge, and his fruit will be a fiery flying serpent. [30] The firstborn of the poor will eat, and the needy will lie down in safety; and I will kill your root with famine, and your remnant will be killed. [31] Howl, gate! Cry, city! You are melted away, Philistia, all of you; for smoke comes out of the north, and there is no straggler in his ranks. [32] What will they answer the messengers of the nation? That Yahweh has founded Zion, and in her the afflicted of his people will take refuge.

## 15

[1] The burden of Moab. For in a night, Ar of Moab is laid waste, and brought to nothing. For in a night Kir of Moab is laid waste, and brought to nothing. [2] They have gone up to Bayith, and to Dibon, to the high places, to weep. Moab wails over Nebo and over Medeba. Baldness is on all of their heads. Every beard is cut off. [3] In their streets, they clothe themselves in sackcloth. In their streets and on their housetops, everyone wails, weeping abundantly. [4] Heshbon cries out with Elealeh. Their voice is heard even to Jahaz. Therefore the armed men of Moab cry aloud. Their souls tremble within them. [5] My heart cries out for Moab! Her nobles flee to Zoar, to Eglath Shelishiyah; for they go up by the ascent of Luhith with weeping; for on the way to Horonaim, they raise up a cry of destruction. [6] For the waters of Nimrim will be desolate; for the grass has withered away, the tender grass fails, there is no green thing. [7] Therefore they will carry away the abundance they have gotten, and that which they have stored up, over the brook of the willows. [8] For the cry has gone around the borders of Moab, its wailing to Eglaim, and its wailing to Beer Elim. [9] For the waters of Dimon are

---

full of blood; for I will bring yet more on Dimon, a lion on those of Moab who escape, and on the remnant of the land.

## 16

¹ Send the lambs for the ruler of the land from Selah to the wilderness, to the mountain of the daughter of Zion. ² For it will be that as wandering birds, as a scattered nest, so will the daughters of Moab be at the fords of the Arnon. ³ Give counsel! Execute justice! Make your shade like the night in the middle of the noonday! Hide the outcasts! Don't betray the fugitive! ⁴ Let my outcasts dwell with you! As for Moab, be a hiding place for him from the face of the destroyer. For the extortioner is brought to nothing. Destruction ceases. The oppressors are consumed out of the land. ⁵ A throne will be established in loving kindness. One will sit on it in truth, in the tent of David, judging, seeking justice, and swift to do righteousness. ⁶ We have heard of the pride of Moab, that he is very proud; even of his arrogance, his pride, and his wrath. His boastings are nothing. ⁷ Therefore Moab will wail for Moab. Everyone will wail. You will mourn for the raisin cakes of Kir Hareseth, utterly stricken. ⁸ For the fields of Heshbon languish with the vine of Sibmah. The lords of the nations have broken down its choice branches, which reached even to Jazer, which wandered into the wilderness. Its shoots were spread abroad. They passed over the sea. ⁹ Therefore I will weep with the weeping of Jazer for the vine of Sibmah. I will water you with my tears, Heshbon, and Elealeh: for on your summer fruits and on your harvest the battle shout has fallen. ¹⁰ Gladness is taken away, and joy out of the fruitful field; and in the vineyards there will be no singing, neither joyful noise. Nobody will tread out wine in the presses. I have made the shouting stop. ¹¹ Therefore my heart sounds like a harp for Moab, and my inward parts for Kir Heres. ¹² It will happen that when Moab presents himself, when he wearies himself on the high place, and comes to his sanctuary to pray, that he will not prevail. ¹³ This is the word that Yahweh spoke concerning Moab in time past. ¹⁴ But now Yahweh has spoken, saying, "Within three years, as a worker bound by contract would count them, the glory of Moab shall be brought into contempt, with all his great multitude; and the remnant will be very small and feeble."

## 17

¹ The burden of Damascus. "Behold, Damascus is taken away from being a city, and it will be a ruinous heap. ² The cities of Aroer are forsaken. They will be for flocks, which shall lie down, and no one shall make them afraid. ³ The fortress shall cease from Ephraim, and the kingdom from Damascus, and the remnant of Syria. They will be as the glory of the children of Israel," says Yahweh of Armies. ⁴"It will happen in that day that the glory of Jacob will be made thin, and the fatness of his flesh will become lean. ⁵ It will be like when the harvester gathers the wheat, and his arm reaps the grain. Yes, it will be like when one gleans grain in the valley of Rephaim. ⁶ Yet gleanings will be left there, like the shaking of an olive tree, two or three olives in the top of the uppermost bough, four or five in the outermost branches of a fruitful tree," says Yahweh, the God of Israel. ⁷ In that day, people will look to their Maker, and their eyes will have respect for the Holy One of Israel. ⁸ They will not look to the altars, the work of their hands; neither shall they respect that which their fingers have made, either the Asherah poles or the incense altars. ⁹ In that day, their strong cities will be like the forsaken places in the woods and on the mountain top, which were forsaken from before the children of Israel; and it will be a desolation. ¹⁰ For you have forgotten the God of your salvation, and have not remembered the rock of your strength. Therefore you plant pleasant plants, and set out foreign seedlings. ¹¹ In the day of your planting, you hedge it in. In the morning, you make your seed blossom, but the harvest flees away in the day of grief and of desperate sorrow. ¹² Ah, the uproar of many peoples who roar like the roaring of the seas; and the rushing of nations that rush like the rushing of mighty waters! ¹³ The nations will rush like the rushing of many waters, but he will rebuke them, and they will flee far off, and will be chased like the chaff of the mountains before the wind, and like the whirling dust before the storm. ¹⁴ At evening, behold, terror! Before the morning, they are no more. This is the portion of those who plunder us, and the lot of those who rob us.

## 18

¹ Ah, the land of the rustling of wings, which is beyond the rivers of Ethiopia; ² that sends ambassadors by the sea, even in vessels of papyrus on the waters, saying, "Go, you swift messengers, to a nation tall and smooth, to a people awesome from their beginning onward, a nation that measures out and treads down, whose land the rivers divide!" ³ All you inhabitants of the world, and you dwellers on the earth, when a banner is lifted up on the mountains, look! When the trumpet is blown, listen! ⁴ For Yahweh said to me, "I will be still, and I will see in my dwelling place, like clear heat in sunshine, like a cloud of dew in the heat of harvest." ⁵ For before the harvest, when the blossom is over, and the flower becomes a ripening grape, he will cut off the sprigs with pruning hooks, and he will cut down and take away the spreading branches. ⁶ They will be left together for the ravenous birds of the mountains, and for the animals of the earth. The ravenous birds will eat them in the summer, and all the animals of the earth will eat them in the winter. ⁷ In that time, a present will be brought to Yahweh of Armies from a people tall and smooth, even from a people awesome from their beginning onward, a nation that measures out and treads down, whose land the rivers divide, to the place of the name of Yahweh of Armies, Mount Zion.

## 19

¹ The burden of Egypt. "Behold, Yahweh rides on a swift cloud, and comes to Egypt. The idols of Egypt will tremble at his presence; and the heart of Egypt will melt within it. ² I will stir up the Egyptians against the Egyptians, and they will fight everyone against his brother, and everyone against his neighbor; city against city, and kingdom against kingdom. ³ The spirit of the Egyptians will fail within them. I will destroy their counsel. They will seek the idols, the charmers, those who have familiar spirits, and the wizards. ⁴ I will give over the Egyptians into the hand of a cruel lord. A fierce king will rule over them," says the Lord, Yahweh of Armies. ⁵ The waters will fail from the sea, and the river will be wasted and become dry. ⁶ The rivers will become foul. The streams of Egypt will be diminished and dried up. The reeds and flags will wither away. ⁷ The meadows by the Nile, by the brink of the Nile, and all the sown fields of the Nile, will become dry, be driven away, and be no more. ⁸ The fishermen will lament, and all those who fish in the Nile will mourn, and those who spread nets on the waters will languish. ⁹ Moreover those who work in combed flax, and those who weave white cloth, will be confounded. ¹⁰ The pillars will be broken in pieces. All those who work for hire will be grieved in soul. ¹¹ The princes of Zoan are utterly foolish. The counsel of the wisest counselors of Pharaoh has become stupid. How do you say to Pharaoh, "I am the son of the wise, the son of ancient kings"? ¹² Where then are your wise men? Let them tell you now; and let them know what Yahweh of Armies has purposed concerning Egypt. ¹³ The princes of Zoan have become fools. The princes of Memphis are deceived. They have caused Egypt to go astray, those who are the cornerstone of her tribes. ¹⁴ Yahweh has mixed a spirit of perverseness in the middle of her; and they have caused Egypt to go astray in all of its works, like a drunken man staggers in his vomit. ¹⁵ Neither shall there be any work for Egypt, which head or tail, palm branch or rush, may do. ¹⁶ In that day the Egyptians will be like women. They will tremble and fear because of the shaking of Yahweh of Armies's hand, which he shakes over them. ¹⁷ The land of Judah will become a terror to Egypt. Everyone to whom mention is made of it will be afraid, because of the plans of Yahweh of Armies, which he determines against it. ¹⁸ In that day, there will be five cities in the land of Egypt that speak the language of Canaan, and swear to Yahweh of Armies. One will be called "The city of destruction." ¹⁹ In that day, there will be an altar to Yahweh in the middle of the land of Egypt, and a pillar to Yahweh at its border. ²⁰ It will be for a sign and for a witness to Yahweh of Armies in the land of Egypt; for they will cry to Yahweh because of oppressors, and he will send them a savior and a defender, and he will deliver them. ²¹ Yahweh will be known to Egypt, and the Egyptians will know Yahweh in that day. Yes, they will worship with sacrifice and offering, and will vow a vow to Yahweh, and will perform it. ²² Yahweh will strike Egypt, striking and healing. They will return to Yahweh, and he will be entreated by them, and will heal them. ²³ In that day there will be a highway out of Egypt to Assyria, and the Assyrian shall come into Egypt, and the Egyptian into Assyria; and the Egyptians will worship with the Assyrians. ²⁴ In that day, Israel will be the third with Egypt and with Assyria, a blessing within the earth; ²⁵ because Yahweh of Armies has blessed them, saying, "Blessed be Egypt my people, Assyria the work of my hands, and Israel my inheritance."

## 20

¹ In the year that Tartan came to Ashdod, when Sargon the king of Assyria sent him, and he fought against Ashdod and took it; ² at that time Yahweh spoke by Isaiah the son of Amoz, saying, "Go, and loosen the sackcloth from off your waist, and take your sandals from off your feet." He did so, walking naked and barefoot. ³ Yahweh said, "As my servant Isaiah has walked naked and barefoot three years for a sign and a wonder concerning Egypt and concerning Ethiopia, ⁴ so the king of Assyria will lead away the captives of Egypt and the exiles of Ethiopia, young and old, naked and barefoot, and with buttocks uncovered, to the shame of Egypt. ⁵ They will be dismayed and confounded, because of Ethiopia their expectation, and of Egypt their glory. ⁶ The inhabitants of this coast land will say in that day, 'Behold, this is our expectation, where we fled for help to be delivered from the king of Assyria. And we, how will we escape?'"

## 21

¹ The burden of the wilderness of the sea. As whirlwinds in the South sweep through, it comes from the wilderness, from an awesome land. ² A grievous vision is declared to me. The treacherous man deals treacherously, and the destroyer destroys. Go up, Elam; attack! I have stopped all of Media's sighing. ³ Therefore my thighs are filled with anguish. Pains have seized me, like the pains of a woman in labor. I am in so much pain that I can't hear. I am so dismayed that I can't see. ⁴ My heart flutters. Horror has frightened me. The twilight that I desired has been turned into trembling for me. ⁵ They prepare the table. They set the watch. They eat. They drink. Rise up, you princes, oil the shield! ⁶ For the Lord said to me, "Go, set a watchman. Let him declare what he sees. ⁷ When he sees a troop, horsemen in pairs, a troop of donkeys, a troop of camels, he shall listen diligently with great attentiveness." ⁸ He cried like a lion: "Lord, I stand continually on the watchtower in the daytime, and every night I stay at my post. ⁹ Behold, here comes a troop of men, horsemen in pairs." He answered, "Fallen, fallen is Babylon; and all the engraved images of her gods are broken to the ground. ¹⁰ You are my threshing, and the grain of my floor!" That which I have heard from Yahweh of Armies, the God of Israel, I have declared to you. ¹¹ The burden of Dumah. One calls to me out of Seir, "Watchman, what of the night? Watchman, what of the night?" ¹² The watchman said, "The morning comes, and also the night. If you will inquire, inquire. Come back again." ¹³ The burden on Arabia. You will lodge in the thickets in Arabia, you caravans of Dedanites. ¹⁴ They brought water to him who was thirsty. The inhabitants of the land of Tema met the fugitives with their bread. ¹⁵ For they fled away from the swords, from the drawn sword, from the bent bow, and from the heat of battle. ¹⁶ For the Lord said to me, "Within a year, as a worker bound by contract would count it, all the glory of Kedar will fail, ¹⁷ and the residue of the number of the archers, the mighty men of the children of Kedar, will be few; for Yahweh, the God of Israel, has spoken it."

## 22

¹ The burden of the valley of vision. What ails you now, that you have all gone up to the housetops? ² You that are full of shouting, a tumultuous city, a joyous town, your slain are not slain with the sword, neither are they dead in battle. ³ All your rulers fled away together. They were bound by the archers. All who were found by you were bound together. They fled far away. ⁴ Therefore I said, "Look away from me. I will weep bitterly. Don't labor to comfort me for the destruction of the daughter of my people. ⁵ For it is a day of confusion, and of treading down, and of perplexity from the Lord, Yahweh of Armies, in the valley of vision, a breaking down of the walls, and a crying to the mountains." ⁶ Elam carried his quiver, with chariots of men and horsemen; and Kir uncovered the shield. ⁷ Your choicest valleys were full of chariots, and the horsemen set themselves in array at the gate. ⁸ He took away the covering of Judah; and you looked in that day to the armor in the house of the forest. ⁹ You saw the breaches of David's city, that they were many; and you gathered together the waters of the lower pool. ¹⁰ You counted the houses of Jerusalem, and you broke down the houses to fortify the wall. ¹¹ You also made a reservoir between the two walls for the water of the old pool. But you didn't look to him who had done this, neither did you have respect for him who planned it long ago. ¹² In that day, the Lord, Yahweh of Armies, called to weeping, to mourning, to baldness, and to dressing in sackcloth; ¹³ and behold, there is joy and gladness, killing cattle and killing sheep, eating meat and drinking wine: "Let's eat and drink, for tomorrow we will die." ¹⁴ Yahweh of Armies revealed himself in my ears, "Surely this iniquity will not be forgiven you until you die," says the Lord, Yahweh of Armies. ¹⁵ The Lord, Yahweh of Armies says, "Go, get yourself to this treasurer, even to Shebna, who is over the house, and say, ¹⁶'What are you doing here? Who has you here, that you have dug out a tomb here?' Cutting himself out a tomb on high, chiseling a habitation for himself in the rock!" ¹⁷ Behold, Yahweh will overcome you and hurl you away violently. Yes, he will grasp you firmly. ¹⁸ He will surely wind you around and around, and throw you like a ball into a large country. There you will die, and there the chariots of your glory will be, you disgrace of your lord's house. ¹⁹ I will thrust you from your office. You will be pulled down from your station. ²⁰ It will happen in that day that I will call my servant Eliakim the son of Hilkiah, ²¹ and I will clothe him with your robe, and strengthen him with your belt. I will commit your government into his hand; and he will be a father to the inhabitants of Jerusalem, and to the house of Judah. ²² I will lay the key of David's house on his shoulder. He will open, and no one will shut. He will shut, and no one will open. ²³ I will fasten him like a nail in a sure place. He will be for a throne of glory to his father's house. ²⁴ They will hang on him all the glory of his father's house, the offspring and the issue, every small vessel, from the cups even to all the pitchers. ²⁵"In that day," says Yahweh of Armies, "the nail that was fastened in a sure place will give way. It will be cut down

and fall. The burden that was on it will be cut off, for Yahweh has spoken it."

## 23

¹ The burden of Tyre. Howl, you ships of Tarshish! For it is laid waste, so that there is no house, no entering in. From the land of Kittim it is revealed to them. ² Be still, you inhabitants of the coast, you whom the merchants of Sidon that pass over the sea have replenished. ³ On great waters, the seed of the Shihor, the harvest of the Nile, was her revenue. She was the market of nations. ⁴ Be ashamed, Sidon; for the sea has spoken, the stronghold of the sea, saying, "I have not travailed, nor given birth, neither have I nourished young men, nor brought up virgins." ⁵ When the report comes to Egypt, they will be in anguish at the report of Tyre. ⁶ Pass over to Tarshish! Wail, you inhabitants of the coast! ⁷ Is this your joyous city, whose antiquity is of ancient days, whose feet carried her far away to travel? ⁸ Who has planned this against Tyre, the giver of crowns, whose merchants are princes, whose traders are the honorable of the earth? ⁹ Yahweh of Armies has planned it, to stain the pride of all glory, to bring into contempt all the honorable of the earth. ¹⁰ Pass through your land like the Nile, daughter of Tarshish. There is no restraint any more. ¹¹ He has stretched out his hand over the sea. He has shaken the kingdoms. Yahweh has ordered the destruction of Canaan's strongholds. ¹² He said, "You shall rejoice no more, you oppressed virgin daughter of Sidon. Arise, pass over to Kittim. Even there you will have no rest." ¹³ Behold, the land of the Chaldeans. This people didn't exist. The Assyrians founded it for those who dwell in the wilderness. They set up their towers. They overthrew its palaces. They made it a ruin. ¹⁴ Howl, you ships of Tarshish, for your stronghold is laid waste! ¹⁵ It will come to pass in that day that Tyre will be forgotten seventy years, according to the days of one king. After the end of seventy years it will be to Tyre like in the song of the prostitute. ¹⁶ Take a harp; go about the city, you prostitute that has been forgotten. Make sweet melody. Sing many songs, that you may be remembered. ¹⁷ It will happen after the end of seventy years that Yahweh will visit Tyre. She will return to her wages, and will play the prostitute with all the kingdoms of the world on the surface of the earth. ¹⁸ Her merchandise and her wages will be holiness to Yahweh. It will not be treasured nor laid up; for her merchandise will be for those who dwell before Yahweh, to eat sufficiently, and for durable clothing.

## 24

¹ Behold, Yahweh makes the earth empty, makes it waste, turns it upside down, and scatters its inhabitants. ² It will be as with the people, so with the priest; as with the servant, so with his master; as with the maid, so with her mistress; as with the buyer, so with the seller; as with the creditor, so with the debtor; as with the taker of interest, so with the giver of interest. ³ The earth will be utterly emptied and utterly laid waste; for Yahweh has spoken this word. ⁴ The earth mourns and fades away. The world languishes and fades away. The lofty people of the earth languish. ⁵ The earth also is polluted under its inhabitants, because they have transgressed the laws, violated the statutes, and broken the everlasting covenant. ⁶ Therefore the curse has devoured the earth, and those who dwell therein are found guilty. Therefore the inhabitants of the earth are burned, and few men are left. ⁷ The new wine mourns. The vine languishes. All the merry-hearted sigh. ⁸ The mirth of tambourines ceases. The sound of those who rejoice ends. The joy of the harp ceases. ⁹ They will not drink wine with a song. Strong drink will be bitter to those who drink it. ¹⁰ The confused city is broken down. Every house is shut up, that no man may come in. ¹¹ There is a crying in the streets because of the wine. All joy is darkened. The mirth of the land is gone. ¹² The city is left in desolation, and the gate is struck with destruction. ¹³ For it will be so within the earth among the peoples, as the shaking of an olive tree, as the gleanings when the vintage is done. ¹⁴ These shall lift up their voice. They will shout for the majesty of Yahweh. They cry aloud from the sea. ¹⁵ Therefore glorify Yahweh in the east, even the name of Yahweh, the God of Israel, in the islands of the sea! ¹⁶ From the uttermost part of the earth have we heard songs. Glory to the righteous! But I said, "I pine away! I pine away! woe is me!" The treacherous have dealt treacherously. Yes, the treacherous have dealt very treacherously. ¹⁷ Fear, the pit, and the snare are on you who inhabit the earth. ¹⁸ It will happen that he who flees from the noise of the fear will fall into the pit; and he who comes up out of the middle of the pit will be taken in the snare; for the windows on high are opened, and the foundations of the earth tremble. ¹⁹ The earth is utterly broken. The earth is torn apart. The earth is shaken violently. ²⁰ The earth will stagger like a drunken man, and will sway back and forth like a hammock. Its disobedience will be heavy on it, and it will fall and not rise again. ²¹ It will happen in that day that Yahweh will punish the army of the high ones on high, and the kings of the earth on the earth. ²² They will be gathered together, as prisoners are gathered in the pit, and will be shut up in the prison; and after many days they will be visited. ²³ Then the moon will be confounded, and the sun ashamed; for

Yahweh of Armies will reign on Mount Zion and in Jerusalem; and glory will be before his elders.

## 25

¹ Yahweh, you are my God. I will exalt you! I will praise your name, for you have done wonderful things, things planned long ago, in complete faithfulness and truth. ² For you have made a city into a heap, a fortified city into a ruin, a palace of strangers to be no city. It will never be built. ³ Therefore a strong people will glorify you. A city of awesome nations will fear you. ⁴ For you have been a stronghold to the poor, a stronghold to the needy in his distress, a refuge from the storm, a shade from the heat, when the blast of the dreaded ones is like a storm against the wall. ⁵ As the heat in a dry place you will bring down the noise of strangers; as the heat by the shade of a cloud, the song of the dreaded ones will be brought low. ⁶ In this mountain, Yahweh of Armies will make all peoples a feast of choice meat,ᵃ a feast of choice wines, of choice meat full of marrow, of well refined choice wines. ⁷ He will destroy in this mountain the surface of the covering that covers all peoples, and the veil that is spread over all nations. ⁸ He has swallowed up death forever! The Lord Yahweh will wipe away tears from off all faces. He will take the reproach of his people away from off all the earth, for Yahweh has spoken it. ⁹ It shall be said in that day, "Behold, this is our God! We have waited for him, and he will save us! This is Yahweh! We have waited for him. We will be glad and rejoice in his salvation!" ¹⁰ For Yahweh's hand will rest in this mountain. Moab will be trodden down in his place, even like straw is trodden down in the water of the dunghill. ¹¹ He will spread out his hands in the middle of it, like one who swims spreads out hands to swim, but his pride will be humbled together with the craft of his hands. ¹² He has brought the high fortress of your walls down, laid low, and brought to the ground, even to the dust.

## 26

¹ In that day, this song will be sung in the land of Judah: "We have a strong city. God appoints salvation for walls and bulwarks. ² Open the gates, that the righteous nation may enter: the one which keeps faith. ³ You will keep whoever's mind is steadfast in perfect peace, because he trusts in you. ⁴ Trust in Yahweh forever; for in Yah, Yahweh, is an everlasting Rock. ⁵ For he has brought down those who dwell on high, the lofty city. He lays it low. He lays it low even to the ground. He brings it even to the dust. ⁶ The foot shall tread it down, even the feet of the poor and the steps of the needy." ⁷ The way of the just is uprightness. You who are upright make the path of the righteous level. ⁸ Yes, in the way of your judgments, Yahweh, we have waited for you. Your name and your renown are the desire of our soul. ⁹ With my soul I have desired you in the night. Yes, with my spirit within me I will seek you earnestly; for when your judgments are in the earth, the inhabitants of the world learn righteousness. ¹⁰ Let favor be shown to the wicked, yet he will not learn righteousness. In the land of uprightness he will deal wrongfully, and will not see Yahweh's majesty. ¹¹ Yahweh, your hand is lifted up, yet they don't see; but they will see your zeal for the people and be disappointed. Yes, fire will consume your adversaries. ¹² Yahweh, you will ordain peace for us, for you have also done all our work for us. ¹³ Yahweh our God, other lords besides you have had dominion over us, but we will only acknowledge your name. ¹⁴ The dead shall not live. The departed spirits shall not rise. Therefore you have visited and destroyed them, and caused all memory of them to perish. ¹⁵ You have increased the nation, O Yahweh. You have increased the nation! You are glorified! You have enlarged all the borders of the land. ¹⁶ Yahweh, in trouble they have visited you. They poured out a prayer when your chastening was on them. ¹⁷ Just as a woman with child, who draws near the time of her delivery, is in pain and cries out in her pangs, so we have been before you, Yahweh. ¹⁸ We have been with child. We have been in pain. We gave birth, it seems, only to wind. We have not worked any deliverance in the earth; neither have the inhabitants of the world fallen. ¹⁹ Your dead shall live. Their dead bodies shall arise. Awake and sing, you who dwell in the dust; for your dew is like the dew of herbs, and the earth will cast out the departed spirits. ²⁰ Come, my people, enter into your rooms, and shut your doors behind you. Hide yourself for a little moment, until the indignation is past. ²¹ For, behold, Yahweh comes out of his place to punish the inhabitants of the earth for their iniquity. The earth also will disclose her blood, and will no longer cover her slain.

## 27

¹ In that day, Yahweh with his hard and great and strong sword will punish leviathan, the fleeing serpent, and leviathan, the twisted serpent; and he will kill the dragon that is in the sea. ² In that day, sing to her, "A pleasant vineyard! ³ I, Yahweh, am its keeper. I will water it every moment. Lest anyone damage it, I will keep it night and day. ⁴ Wrath

is not in me, but if I should find briers and thorns, I would do battle! I would march on them and I would burn them together. ⁵ Or else let him take hold of my strength, that he may make peace with me. Let him make peace with me." ⁶ In days to come, Jacob will take root. Israel will blossom and bud. They will fill the surface of the world with fruit. ⁷ Has he struck them as he struck those who struck them? Or are they killed like those who killed them were killed? ⁸ In measure, when you send them away, you contend with them. He has removed them with his rough blast in the day of the east wind. ⁹ Therefore by this the iniquity of Jacob will be forgiven, and this is all the fruit of taking away his sin: that he makes all the stones of the altar as chalk stones that are beaten in pieces, so that the Asherah poles and the incense altars shall rise no more. ¹⁰ For the fortified city is solitary, a habitation deserted and forsaken, like the wilderness. The calf will feed there, and there he will lie down, and consume its branches. ¹¹ When its boughs are withered, they will be broken off. The women will come and set them on fire, for they are a people of no understanding. Therefore he who made them will not have compassion on them, and he who formed them will show them no favor. ¹² It will happen in that day that Yahweh will thresh from the flowing stream of the Euphrates to the brook of Egypt; and you will be gathered one by one, children of Israel. ¹³ It will happen in that day that a great trumpet will be blown; and those who were ready to perish in the land of Assyria, and those who were outcasts in the land of Egypt, shall come; and they will worship Yahweh in the holy mountain at Jerusalem.

## 28

¹ Woe to the crown of pride of the drunkards of Ephraim, and to the fading flower of his glorious beauty, which is on the head of the fertile valley of those who are overcome with wine! ² Behold, the Lord has one who is mighty and strong. Like a storm of hail, a destroying storm, and like a storm of mighty waters overflowing, he will cast them down to the earth with his hand. ³ The crown of pride of the drunkards of Ephraim will be trodden under foot. ⁴ The fading flower of his glorious beauty, which is on the head of the fertile valley, shall be like the first-ripe fig before the summer, which someone picks and eats as soon as he sees it. ⁵ In that day, Yahweh of Armies will become a crown of glory and a diadem of beauty to the residue of his people, ⁶ and a spirit of justice to him who sits in judgment, and strength to those who turn back the battle at the gate. ⁷ They also reel with wine, and stagger with strong drink. The priest and the prophet reel with strong drink. They are swallowed up by wine. They stagger with strong drink. They err in vision. They stumble in judgment. ⁸ For all tables are completely full of filthy vomit and filthiness. ⁹ Whom will he teach knowledge? To whom will he explain the message? Those who are weaned from the milk, and drawn from the breasts? ¹⁰ For it is precept on precept, precept on precept; line on line, line on line; here a little, there a little. ¹¹ But he will speak to this nation with stammering lips and in another language, ¹² to whom he said, "This is the resting place. Give rest to the weary," and "This is the refreshing;" yet they would not hear. ¹³ Therefore Yahweh's word will be to them precept on precept, precept on precept; line on line, line on line; here a little, there a little; that they may go, fall backward, be broken, be snared, and be taken. ¹⁴ Therefore hear Yahweh's word, you scoffers, that rule this people in Jerusalem: ¹⁵"Because you have said, 'We have made a covenant with death, and we are in agreement with Sheol.ᵇ When the overflowing scourge passes through, it won't come to us; for we have made lies our refuge, and we have hidden ourselves under falsehood.'" ¹⁶ Therefore the Lord Yahweh says, "Behold, I lay in Zion for a foundation a stone, a tried stone, a precious cornerstone of a sure foundation. He who believes shall not act hastily. ¹⁷ I will make justice the measuring line, and righteousness the plumb line. The hail will sweep away the refuge of lies, and the waters will overflow the hiding place. ¹⁸ Your covenant with death shall be annulled, and your agreement with Sheolᶜ shall not stand. When the overflowing scourge passes through, then you will be trampled down by it. ¹⁹ As often as it passes through, it will seize you; for morning by morning it will pass through, by day and by night; and it will be nothing but terror to understand the message." ²⁰ For the bed is too short to stretch out on, and the blanket is too narrow to wrap oneself in. ²¹ For Yahweh will rise up as on Mount Perazim. He will be angry as in the valley of Gibeon; that he may do his work, his unusual work, and bring to pass his act, his extraordinary act. ²² Now therefore don't be scoffers, lest your bonds be made strong; for I have heard a decree of destruction from the Lord, Yahweh of Armies, on the whole earth. ²³ Give ear, and hear my voice! Listen, and hear my speech! ²⁴ Does he who plows to sow plow continually? Does he keep turning the soil and breaking the clods? ²⁵ When he has leveled its surface, doesn't he plant the dill, and scatter the cumin seed, and put in the wheat in

---

ᵃ 25:6 literally, fat things

ᵇ 28:15 Sheol is the place of the dead.

ᶜ 28:18 Sheol is the place of the dead.

rows, the barley in the appointed place, and the spelt in its place? ²⁶ For his God instructs him in right judgment and teaches him. ²⁷ For the dill isn't threshed with a sharp instrument, neither is a cart wheel turned over the cumin; but the dill is beaten out with a stick, and the cumin with a rod. ²⁸ Bread flour must be ground; so he will not always be threshing it. Although he drives the wheel of his threshing cart over it, his horses don't grind it. ²⁹ This also comes out from Yahweh of Armies, who is wonderful in counsel, and excellent in wisdom.

## 29

¹ Woe to Ariel! Ariel, the city where David encamped! Add year to year; let the feasts come around; ² then I will distress Ariel, and there will be mourning and lamentation. She shall be to me as an altar hearth.ᵃ ³ I will encamp against you all around you, and will lay siege against you with posted troops. I will raise siege works against you. ⁴ You will be brought down, and will speak out of the ground. Your speech will mumble out of the dust. Your voice will be as of one who has a familiar spirit, out of the ground, and your speech will whisper out of the dust. ⁵ But the multitude of your foes will be like fine dust, and the multitude of the ruthless ones like chaff that blows away. Yes, it will be in an instant, suddenly. ⁶ She will be visited by Yahweh of Armies with thunder, with earthquake, with great noise, with whirlwind and storm, and with the flame of a devouring fire. ⁷ The multitude of all the nations that fight against Ariel, even all who fight against her and her stronghold, and who distress her, will be like a dream, a vision of the night. ⁸ It will be like when a hungry man dreams, and behold, he eats; but he awakes, and his hunger isn't satisfied; or like when a thirsty man dreams, and behold, he drinks; but he awakes, and behold, he is faint, and he is still thirsty. The multitude of all the nations that fight against Mount Zion will be like that. ⁹ Pause and wonder! Blind yourselves and be blind! They are drunken, but not with wine; they stagger, but not with strong drink. ¹⁰ For Yahweh has poured out on you a spirit of deep sleep, and has closed your eyes, the prophets; and he has covered your heads, the seers. ¹¹ All vision has become to you like the words of a book that is sealed, which men deliver to one who is educated, saying, "Read this, please;" and he says, "I can't, for it is sealed;" ¹² and the book is delivered to one who is not educated, saying, "Read this, please;" and he says, "I can't read." ¹³ The Lord said, "Because this people draws near with their mouth and honors me with their lips, but they have removed their heart far from me, and their fear of me is a commandment of men which has been taught; ¹⁴ therefore, behold, I will proceed to do a marvelous work among this people, even a marvelous work and a wonder; and the wisdom of their wise men will perish, and the understanding of their prudent men will be hidden." ¹⁵ Woe to those who deeply hide their counsel from Yahweh, and whose deeds are in the dark, and who say, "Who sees us?" and "Who knows us?" ¹⁶ You turn things upside down! Should the potter be thought to be like clay, that the thing made should say about him who made it, "He didn't make me;" or the thing formed say of him who formed it, "He has no understanding"? ¹⁷ Isn't it yet a very little while, and Lebanon will be turned into a fruitful field, and the fruitful field will be regarded as a forest? ¹⁸ In that day, the deaf will hear the words of the book, and the eyes of the blind will see out of obscurity and out of darkness. ¹⁹ The humble also will increase their joy in Yahweh, and the poor among men will rejoice in the Holy One of Israel. ²⁰ For the ruthless is brought to nothing, and the scoffer ceases, and all those who are alert to do evil are cut off— ²¹ who cause a person to be indicted by a word, and lay a snare for one who reproves in the gate, and who deprive the innocent of justice with false testimony. ²² Therefore Yahweh, who redeemed Abraham, says concerning the house of Jacob: "Jacob shall no longer be ashamed, neither shall his face grow pale. ²³ But when he sees his children, the work of my hands, in the middle of him, they will sanctify my name. Yes, they will sanctify the Holy One of Jacob, and will stand in awe of the God of Israel. ²⁴ They also who err in spirit will come to understanding, and those who grumble will receive instruction."

## 30

¹ "Woe to the rebellious children", says Yahweh, "who take counsel, but not from me; and who make an alliance, but not with my Spirit, that they may add sin to sin; ² who set out to go down into Egypt without asking for my advice, to strengthen themselves in the strength of Pharaoh, and to take refuge in the shadow of Egypt! ³ Therefore the strength of Pharaoh will be your shame, and the refuge in the shadow of Egypt your confusion. ⁴ For their princes are at Zoan, and their ambassadors have come to Hanes. ⁵ They shall all be ashamed because of a people that can't profit them, that are not a help nor profit, but a shame, and also a reproach." ⁶ The burden of the animals of the South. Through the land of trouble and anguish, of the lioness and the lion, the viper and fiery flying serpent, they carry their riches on the shoulders of young donkeys, and their treasures on the humps of camels, to an

unprofitable people. ⁷ For Egypt helps in vain, and to no purpose; therefore I have called her Rahab who sits still. ⁸ Now go, write it before them on a tablet, and inscribe it in a book, that it may be for the time to come forever and ever. ⁹ For it is a rebellious people, lying children, children who will not hear Yahweh's law; ¹⁰ who tell the seers, "Don't see!" and the prophets, "Don't prophesy to us right things. Tell us pleasant things. Prophesy deceits. ¹¹ Get out of the way. Turn away from the path. Cause the Holy One of Israel to cease from before us." ¹² Therefore the Holy One of Israel says, "Because you despise this word, and trust in oppression and perverseness, and rely on it, ¹³ therefore this iniquity shall be to you like a breach ready to fall, swelling out in a high wall, whose breaking comes suddenly in an instant. ¹⁴ He will break it as a potter's vessel is broken, breaking it in pieces without sparing, so that there won't be found among the broken pieces a piece good enough to take fire from the hearth, or to dip up water out of the cistern." ¹⁵ For thus said the Lord Yahweh, the Holy One of Israel, "You will be saved in returning and rest. Your strength will be in quietness and in confidence." You refused, ¹⁶ but you said, "No, for we will flee on horses;" therefore you will flee; and, "We will ride on the swift;" therefore those who pursue you will be swift. ¹⁷ One thousand will flee at the threat of one. At the threat of five, you will flee until you are left like a beacon on the top of a mountain, and like a banner on a hill. ¹⁸ Therefore Yahweh will wait, that he may be gracious to you; and therefore he will be exalted, that he may have mercy on you, for Yahweh is a God of justice. Blessed are all those who wait for him. ¹⁹ For the people will dwell in Zion at Jerusalem. You will weep no more. He will surely be gracious to you at the voice of your cry. When he hears you, he will answer you. ²⁰ Though the Lord may give you the bread of adversity and the water of affliction, yet your teachers won't be hidden any more, but your eyes will see your teachers; ²¹ and when you turn to the right hand, and when you turn to the left, your ears will hear a voice behind you, saying, "This is the way. Walk in it." ²² You shall defile the overlaying of your engraved images of silver, and the plating of your molten images of gold. You shall cast them away as an unclean thing. You shall tell it, "Go away!" ²³ He will give the rain for your seed, with which you will sow the ground; and bread of the increase of the ground will be rich and plentiful. In that day, your livestock will feed in large pastures. ²⁴ The oxen likewise and the young donkeys that till the ground will eat savory feed, which has been winnowed with the shovel and with the fork. ²⁵ There will be brooks and streams of water on every lofty mountain and on every high hill in the day of the great slaughter, when the towers fall. ²⁶ Moreover the light of the moon will be like the light of the sun, and the light of the sun will be seven times brighter, like the light of seven days, in the day that Yahweh binds up the fracture of his people, and heals the wound they were struck with. ²⁷ Behold, Yahweh's name comes from far away, burning with his anger, and in thick rising smoke. His lips are full of indignation. His tongue is as a devouring fire. ²⁸ His breath is as an overflowing stream that reaches even to the neck, to sift the nations with the sieve of destruction. A bridle that leads to ruin will be in the jaws of the peoples. ²⁹ You will have a song, as in the night when a holy feast is kept, and gladness of heart, as when one goes with a flute to come to Yahweh's mountain, to Israel's Rock. ³⁰ Yahweh will cause his glorious voice to be heard, and will show the descent of his arm, with the indignation of his anger and the flame of a devouring fire, with a blast, storm, and hailstones. ³¹ For through Yahweh's voice the Assyrian will be dismayed. He will strike him with his rod. ³² Every stroke of the rod of punishment, which Yahweh will lay on him, will be with the sound of tambourines and harps. He will fight with them in battles, brandishing weapons. ³³ For his burning place has long been ready. Yes, it is prepared for the king. He has made its pyre deep and large with fire and much wood. Yahweh's breath, like a stream of sulfur, kindles it.

## 31

¹ Woe to those who go down to Egypt for help, and rely on horses, and trust in chariots because they are many, and in horsemen because they are very strong, but they don't look to the Holy One of Israel, and they don't seek Yahweh! ² Yet he also is wise, and will bring disaster, and will not call back his words, but will arise against the house of the evildoers, and against the help of those who work iniquity. ³ Now the Egyptians are men, and not God; and their horses flesh, and not spirit. When Yahweh stretches out his hand, both he who helps shall stumble, and he who is helped shall fall, and they all shall be consumed together. ⁴ For Yahweh says to me, "As the lion and the young lion growling over his prey, if a multitude of shepherds is called together against him, will not be dismayed at their voice, nor abase himself for their noise, so Yahweh of Armies will come down to fight on Mount Zion and on its heights. ⁵ As birds hovering, so Yahweh of Armies will protect

ᵃ 29:2 or, Ariel

Jerusalem. He will protect and deliver it. He will pass over and preserve it." ⁶ Return to him from whom you have deeply revolted, children of Israel. ⁷ For in that day everyone shall cast away his idols of silver and his idols of gold—sin which your own hands have made for you. ⁸ "The Assyrian will fall by the sword, not of man; and the sword, not of mankind, shall devour him. He will flee from the sword, and his young men will become subject to forced labor. ⁹ His rock will pass away by reason of terror, and his princes will be afraid of the banner," says Yahweh, whose fire is in Zion, and his furnace in Jerusalem.

## 32

¹ Behold, a king shall reign in righteousness, and princes shall rule in justice. ² A man shall be as a hiding place from the wind, and a covert from the storm, as streams of water in a dry place, as the shade of a large rock in a weary land. ³ The eyes of those who see will not be dim, and the ears of those who hear will listen. ⁴ The heart of the rash will understand knowledge, and the tongue of the stammerers will be ready to speak plainly. ⁵ The fool will no longer be called noble, nor the scoundrel be highly respected. ⁶ For the fool will speak folly, and his heart will work iniquity, to practice profanity, and to utter error against Yahweh, to make empty the soul of the hungry, and to cause the drink of the thirsty to fail. ⁷ The ways of the scoundrel are evil. He devises wicked plans to destroy the humble with lying words, even when the needy speaks right. ⁸ But the noble devises noble things, and he will continue in noble things. ⁹ Rise up, you women who are at ease! Hear my voice! You careless daughters, give ear to my speech! ¹⁰ For days beyond a year you will be troubled, you careless women; for the vintage will fail. The harvest won't come. ¹¹ Tremble, you women who are at ease! Be troubled, you careless ones! Strip yourselves, make yourselves naked, and put sackcloth on your waist. ¹² Beat your breasts for the pleasant fields, for the fruitful vine. ¹³ Thorns and briers will come up on my people's land; yes, on all the houses of joy in the joyous city. ¹⁴ For the palace will be forsaken. The populous city will be deserted. The hill and the watchtower will be for dens forever, a delight for wild donkeys, a pasture of flocks, ¹⁵ until the Spirit is poured on us from on high, and the wilderness becomes a fruitful field, and the fruitful field is considered a forest. ¹⁶ Then justice will dwell in the wilderness; and righteousness will remain in the fruitful field. ¹⁷ The work of righteousness will be peace, and the effect of righteousness, quietness and confidence forever. ¹⁸ My people will live in a peaceful habitation, in safe dwellings, and in quiet resting places, ¹⁹ though hail flattens the forest, and the city is leveled completely. ²⁰ Blessed are you who sow beside all waters, who send out the feet of the ox and the donkey.

## 33

¹ Woe to you who destroy, but you weren't destroyed, and who betray, but nobody betrayed you! When you have finished destroying, you will be destroyed; and when you have finished betrayal, you will be betrayed. ² Yahweh, be gracious to us. We have waited for you. Be our strength every morning, our salvation also in the time of trouble. ³ At the noise of the thunder, the peoples have fled. When you lift yourself up, the nations are scattered. ⁴ Your plunder will be gathered as the caterpillar gathers. Men will leap on it as locusts leap. ⁵ Yahweh is exalted, for he dwells on high. He has filled Zion with justice and righteousness. ⁶ There will be stability in your times, abundance of salvation, wisdom, and knowledge. The fear of Yahweh is your treasure. ⁷ Behold, their valiant ones cry outside; the ambassadors of peace weep bitterly. ⁸ The highways are desolate. The traveling man ceases. The covenant is broken. He has despised the cities. He doesn't respect man. ⁹ The land mourns and languishes. Lebanon is confounded and withers away. Sharon is like a desert, and Bashan and Carmel are stripped bare. ¹⁰ "Now I will arise," says Yahweh. "Now I will lift myself up. Now I will be exalted. ¹¹ You will conceive chaff. You will give birth to stubble. Your breath is a fire that will devour you. ¹² The peoples will be like the burning of lime, like thorns that are cut down and burned in the fire. ¹³ Hear, you who are far off, what I have done; and, you who are near, acknowledge my might." ¹⁴ The sinners in Zion are afraid. Trembling has seized the godless ones. Who among us can live with the devouring fire? Who among us can live with everlasting burning? ¹⁵ He who walks righteously and speaks blamelessly, he who despises the gain of oppressions, who gestures with his hands, refusing to take a bribe, who stops his ears from hearing of bloodshed, and shuts his eyes from looking at evil— ¹⁶ he will dwell on high. His place of defense will be the fortress of rocks. His bread will be supplied. His waters will be sure. ¹⁷ Your eyes will see the king in his beauty. They will see a distant land. ¹⁸ Your heart will meditate on the terror. Where is he who counted? Where is he who weighed? Where is he who counted the towers? ¹⁹ You will no longer see the fierce people, a people

of a deep speech that you can't comprehend, with a strange language that you can't understand. ²⁰ Look at Zion, the city of our appointed festivals. Your eyes will see Jerusalem, a quiet habitation, a tent that won't be removed. Its stakes will never be plucked up, nor will any of its cords be broken. ²¹ But there Yahweh will be with us in majesty, a place of wide rivers and streams, in which no galley with oars will go, neither will any gallant ship pass by there. ²² For Yahweh is our judge. Yahweh is our lawgiver. Yahweh is our king. He will save us. ²³ Your rigging is untied. They couldn't strengthen the foot of their mast. They couldn't spread the sail. Then the prey of a great plunder was divided. The lame took the prey. ²⁴ The inhabitant won't say, "I am sick." The people who dwell therein will be forgiven their iniquity.

## 34

¹ Come near, you nations, to hear! Listen, you peoples. Let the earth and all it contains hear, the world, and everything that comes from it. ² For Yahweh is enraged against all the nations, and angry with all their armies. He has utterly destroyed them. He has given them over for slaughter. ³ Their slain will also be cast out, and the stench of their dead bodies will come up. The mountains will melt in their blood. ⁴ All of the army of the sky will be dissolved. The sky will be rolled up like a scroll, and all its armies will fade away, as a leaf fades from off a vine or a fig tree. ⁵ For my sword has drunk its fill in the sky. Behold, it will come down on Edom, and on the people of my curse, for judgment. ⁶ Yahweh's sword is filled with blood. It is covered with fat, with the blood of lambs and goats, with the fat of the kidneys of rams; for Yahweh has a sacrifice in Bozrah, and a great slaughter in the land of Edom. ⁷ The wild oxen will come down with them, and the young bulls with the mighty bulls; and their land will be drunken with blood, and their dust made greasy with fat. ⁸ For Yahweh has a day of vengeance, a year of recompense for the cause of Zion. ⁹ Its streams will be turned into pitch, its dust into sulfur, and its land will become burning pitch. ¹⁰ It won't be quenched night or day. Its smoke will go up forever. From generation to generation, it will lie waste. No one will pass through it forever and ever. ¹¹ But the pelican and the porcupine will possess it. The owl and the raven will dwell in it. He will stretch the line of confusion over it, and the plumb line of emptiness. ¹² They shall call its nobles to the kingdom, but none shall be there; and all its princes shall be nothing. ¹³ Thorns will come up in its palaces, nettles and thistles in its fortresses; and it will be a habitation of jackals, a court for ostriches. ¹⁴ The wild animals of the desert will meet with the wolves, and the wild goat will cry to his fellow. Yes, the night creatureᵃ shall settle there, and shall find herself a place of rest. ¹⁵ The arrow snake will make her nest there, and lay, hatch, and gather under her shade. Yes, the kites will be gathered there, every one with her mate. ¹⁶ Search in the book of Yahweh, and read: not one of these will be missing. None will lack her mate. For my mouth has commanded, and his Spirit has gathered them. ¹⁷ He has cast the lot for them, and his hand has divided it to them with a measuring line. They shall possess it forever. From generation to generation they will dwell in it.

## 35

¹ The wilderness and the dry land will be glad. The desert will rejoice and blossom like a rose. ² It will blossom abundantly, and rejoice even with joy and singing. Lebanon's glory will be given to it, the excellence of Carmel and Sharon. They will see Yahweh's glory, the excellence of our God. ³ Strengthen the weak hands, and make the feeble knees firm. ⁴ Tell those who have a fearful heart, "Be strong! Don't be afraid! Behold, your God will come with vengeance, God's retribution. He will come and save you. ⁵ Then the eyes of the blind will be opened, and the ears of the deaf will be unstopped. ⁶ Then the lame man will leap like a deer, and the tongue of the mute will sing; for waters will break out in the wilderness, and streams in the desert. ⁷ The burning sand will become a pool, and the thirsty ground springs of water. Grass with reeds and rushes will be in the habitation of jackals, where they lay. ⁸ A highway will be there, a road, and it will be called "The Holy Way". The unclean shall not pass over it, but it will be for those who walk in the Way. Wicked fools shall not go there. ⁹ No lion will be there, nor will any ravenous animal go up on it. They will not be found there; but the redeemed will walk there. ¹⁰ Then Yahweh's ransomed ones will return, and come with singing to Zion; and everlasting joy will be on their heads. They will obtain gladness and joy, and sorrow and sighing will flee away."

## 36

¹ Now in the fourteenth year of King Hezekiah, Sennacherib king of Assyria attacked all of the fortified cities of Judah and captured them. ² The king of Assyria sent Rabshakeh from Lachish to Jerusalem to King Hezekiah with a large army. He stood by the aqueduct from the

upper pool in the fuller's field highway. ³ Then Eliakim the son of Hilkiah, who was over the household, and Shebna the scribe, and Joah, the son of Asaph the recorder came out to him. ⁴ Rabshakeh said to them, "Now tell Hezekiah, 'The great king, the king of Assyria, says, "What confidence is this in which you trust? ⁵ I say that your counsel and strength for the war are only vain words. Now in whom do you trust, that you have rebelled against me? ⁶ Behold, you trust in the staff of this bruised reed, even in Egypt, which if a man leans on it, it will go into his hand and pierce it. So is Pharaoh king of Egypt to all who trust in him. ⁷ But if you tell me, 'We trust in Yahweh our God,' isn't that he whose high places and whose altars Hezekiah has taken away, and has said to Judah and to Jerusalem, 'You shall worship before this altar'?" ⁸ Now therefore, please make a pledge to my master the king of Assyria, and I will give you two thousand horses, if you are able on your part to set riders on them. ⁹ How then can you turn away the face of one captain of the least of my master's servants, and put your trust in Egypt for chariots and for horsemen? ¹⁰ Have I come up now without Yahweh against this land to destroy it? Yahweh said to me, "Go up against this land, and destroy it."'" ¹¹ Then Eliakim, Shebna and Joah said to Rabshakeh, "Please speak to your servants in Aramaic, for we understand it. Don't speak to us in the Jews' language in the hearing of the people who are on the wall." ¹² But Rabshakeh said, "Has my master sent me only to your master and to you, to speak these words, and not to the men who sit on the wall, who will eat their own dung and drink their own urine with you?" ¹³ Then Rabshakeh stood, and called out with a loud voice in the Jews' language, and said, "Hear the words of the great king, the king of Assyria! ¹⁴ The king says, 'Don't let Hezekiah deceive you; for he will not be able to deliver you. ¹⁵ Don't let Hezekiah make you trust in Yahweh, saying, "Yahweh will surely deliver us. This city won't be given into the hand of the king of Assyria."' ¹⁶ Don't listen to Hezekiah, for the king of Assyria says, 'Make your peace with me, and come out to me; and each of you eat from his vine, and each one from his fig tree, and each one of you drink the waters of his own cistern; ¹⁷ until I come and take you away to a land like your own land, a land of grain and new wine, a land of bread and vineyards. ¹⁸ Beware lest Hezekiah persuade you, saying, "Yahweh will deliver us." Have any of the gods of the nations delivered their lands from the hand of the king of Assyria? ¹⁹ Where are the gods of Hamath and Arpad? Where are the gods of Sepharvaim? Have they delivered Samaria from my hand? ²⁰ Who are they among all the gods of these countries that have delivered their country out of my hand, that Yahweh should deliver Jerusalem out of my hand?'" ²¹ But they remained silent, and said nothing in reply, for the king's commandment was, "Don't answer him." ²² Then Eliakim the son of Hilkiah, who was over the household, and Shebna the scribe, and Joah, the son of Asaph the recorder, came to Hezekiah with their clothes torn, and told him the words of Rabshakeh.

# 37

¹ When King Hezekiah heard it, he tore his clothes, covered himself with sackcloth, and went into Yahweh's house. ² He sent Eliakim, who was over the household, and Shebna the scribe, and the elders of the priests, covered with sackcloth, to Isaiah the prophet, the son of Amoz. ³ They said to him, "Hezekiah says, 'Today is a day of trouble, and of rebuke, and of rejection; for the children have come to the birth, and there is no strength to give birth. ⁴ It may be Yahweh your God will hear the words of Rabshakeh, whom the king of Assyria his master has sent to defy the living God, and will rebuke the words which Yahweh your God has heard. Therefore lift up your prayer for the remnant that is left.'" ⁵ So the servants of King Hezekiah came to Isaiah. ⁶ Isaiah said to them, "Tell your master, 'Yahweh says, "Don't be afraid of the words that you have heard, with which the servants of the king of Assyria have blasphemed me. ⁷ Behold, I will put a spirit in him and he will hear news, and will return to his own land. I will cause him to fall by the sword in his own land."'" ⁸ So Rabshakeh returned, and found the king of Assyria warring against Libnah, for he heard that he had departed from Lachish. ⁹ He heard news concerning Tirhakah king of Ethiopia, "He has come out to fight against you." When he heard it, he sent messengers to Hezekiah, saying, ¹⁰"Thus you shall speak to Hezekiah king of Judah, saying, 'Don't let your God in whom you trust deceive you, saying, "Jerusalem won't be given into the hand of the king of Assyria." ¹¹ Behold, you have heard what the kings of Assyria have done to all lands, by destroying them utterly. Shall you be delivered? ¹² Have the gods of the nations delivered them, which my fathers have destroyed, Gozan, Haran, Rezeph, and the children of Eden who were in Telassar? ¹³ Where is the king of Hamath, and the king of Arpad, and the king of the city of Sepharvaim, of Hena, and Ivvah?'" ¹⁴ Hezekiah received the letter from the hand of the

messengers and read it. Then Hezekiah went up to Yahweh's house, and spread it before Yahweh. ¹⁵ Hezekiah prayed to Yahweh, saying, ¹⁶"Yahweh of Armies, the God of Israel, who is enthroned among the cherubim, you are the God, even you alone, of all the kingdoms of the earth. You have made heaven and earth. ¹⁷ Turn your ear, Yahweh, and hear. Open your eyes, Yahweh, and behold. Hear all of the words of Sennacherib, who has sent to defy the living God. ¹⁸ Truly, Yahweh, the kings of Assyria have destroyed all the countries and their land, ¹⁹ and have cast their gods into the fire; for they were no gods, but the work of men's hands, wood and stone; therefore they have destroyed them. ²⁰ Now therefore, Yahweh our God, save us from his hand, that all the kingdoms of the earth may know that you are Yahweh, even you only." ²¹ Then Isaiah the son of Amoz sent to Hezekiah, saying, "Yahweh, the God of Israel says, 'Because you have prayed to me against Sennacherib king of Assyria, ²² this is the word which Yahweh has spoken concerning him: The virgin daughter of Zion has despised you and ridiculed you. The daughter of Jerusalem has shaken her head at you. ²³ Whom have you defied and blasphemed? Against whom have you exalted your voice and lifted up your eyes on high? Against the Holy One of Israel. ²⁴ By your servants, you have defied the Lord, and have said, "With the multitude of my chariots I have come up to the height of the mountains, to the innermost parts of Lebanon. I will cut down its tall cedars and its choice cypress trees. I will enter into its farthest height, the forest of its fruitful field. ²⁵ I have dug and drunk water, and with the sole of my feet I will dry up all the rivers of Egypt." ²⁶"Have you not heard how I have done it long ago, and formed it in ancient times? Now I have brought it to pass, that it should be yours to destroy fortified cities, turning them into ruinous heaps. ²⁷ Therefore their inhabitants had little power. They were dismayed and confounded. They were like the grass of the field, and like the green herb, like the grass on the housetops, and like a field before its crop has grown. ²⁸ But I know your sitting down, your going out, your coming in, and your raging against me. ²⁹ Because of your raging against me, and because your arrogance has come up into my ears, therefore I will put my hook in your nose and my bridle in your lips, and I will turn you back by the way by which you came. ³⁰"This shall be the sign to you: You will eat this year that which grows of itself, and in the second year that which springs from it; and in the third year sow and reap and plant vineyards, and eat their fruit. ³¹ The remnant that is escaped of the house of Judah will again take root downward, and bear fruit upward. ³² For out of Jerusalem a remnant will go out, and survivors will escape from Mount Zion. The zeal of Yahweh of Armies will perform this.' ³³"Therefore Yahweh says concerning the king of Assyria, 'He will not come to this city, nor shoot an arrow there, neither will he come before it with shield, nor cast up a mound against it. ³⁴ He will return the way that he came, and he won't come to this city,' says Yahweh. ³⁵'For I will defend this city to save it, for my own sake, and for my servant David's sake.'" ³⁶ Then Yahweh's angel went out and struck one hundred and eighty-five thousand men in the camp of the Assyrians. When men arose early in the morning, behold, these were all dead bodies. ³⁷ So Sennacherib king of Assyria departed, went away, returned to Nineveh, and stayed there. ³⁸ As he was worshiping in the house of Nisroch his god, Adrammelech and Sharezer his sons struck him with the sword; and they escaped into the land of Ararat. Esar Haddon his son reigned in his place.

# 38

¹ In those days Hezekiah was sick and near death. Isaiah the prophet, the son of Amoz, came to him, and said to him, "Yahweh says, 'Set your house in order, for you will die, and not live.'" ² Then Hezekiah turned his face to the wall and prayed to Yahweh, ³ and said, "Remember now, Yahweh, I beg you, how I have walked before you in truth and with a perfect heart, and have done that which is good in your sight." Then Hezekiah wept bitterly. ⁴ Then Yahweh's word came to Isaiah, saying, ⁵"Go, and tell Hezekiah, 'Yahweh, the God of David your father, says, "I have heard your prayer. I have seen your tears. Behold, I will add fifteen years to your life. ⁶ I will deliver you and this city out of the hand of the king of Assyria, and I will defend this city. ⁷ This shall be the sign to you from Yahweh, that Yahweh will do this thing that he has spoken. ⁸ Behold, I will cause the shadow on the sundial, which has gone down on the sundial of Ahaz with the sun, to return backward ten steps."'" So the sun returned ten steps on the sundial on which it had gone down. ⁹ The writing of Hezekiah king of Judah, when he had been sick, and had recovered of his sickness: ¹⁰ I said, "In the middle of my life I go into the gates of Sheol.ᵃ I am deprived of the residue of my years." ¹¹ I said, "I won't see Yah, Yah in the land of the living. I will see man no more with the inhabitants of the world. ¹² My dwelling is removed, and is carried away from me like a shepherd's tent. I have rolled up my life like a weaver. He will cut me

---

ᵃ *38:10* Sheol is the place of the dead.

off from the loom. From day even to night you will make an end of me. [13] I waited patiently until morning. He breaks all my bones like a lion. From day even to night you will make an end of me. [14] I chattered like a swallow or a crane. I moaned like a dove. My eyes weaken looking upward. Lord, I am oppressed. Be my security." [15] What will I say? He has both spoken to me, and himself has done it. I will walk carefully all my years because of the anguish of my soul. [16] Lord, men live by these things; and my spirit finds life in all of them. You restore me, and cause me to live. [17] Behold, for peace I had great anguish, but you have in love for my soul delivered it from the pit of corruption; for you have cast all my sins behind your back. [18] For Sheol[a] can't praise you. Death can't celebrate you. Those who go down into the pit can't hope for your truth. [19] The living, the living, he shall praise you, as I do today. The father shall make known your truth to the children. [20] Yahweh will save me. Therefore we will sing my songs with stringed instruments all the days of our life in Yahweh's house. [21] Now Isaiah had said, "Let them take a cake of figs, and lay it for a poultice on the boil, and he shall recover." [22] Hezekiah also had said, "What is the sign that I will go up to Yahweh's house?"

## 39

[1] At that time, Merodach-baladan the son of Baladan, king of Babylon, sent letters and a present to Hezekiah, for he heard that he had been sick, and had recovered. [2] Hezekiah was pleased with them, and showed them the house of his precious things, the silver, the gold, the spices, and the precious oil, and all the house of his armor, and all that was found in his treasures. There was nothing in his house, nor in all his dominion, that Hezekiah didn't show them. [3] Then Isaiah the prophet came to King Hezekiah, and asked him, "What did these men say? From where did they come to you?" Hezekiah said, "They have come from a country far from me, even from Babylon." [4] Then he asked, "What have they seen in your house?" Hezekiah answered, "They have seen all that is in my house. There is nothing among my treasures that I have not shown them." [5] Then Isaiah said to Hezekiah, "Hear the word of Yahweh of Armies: [6] 'Behold, the days are coming when all that is in your house, and that which your fathers have stored up until today, will be carried to Babylon. Nothing will be left,' says Yahweh. [7] 'They will take away your sons who will issue from you, whom you shall father, and they will be eunuchs in the king of Babylon's palace.'" [8] Then Hezekiah said to Isaiah, "Yahweh's word which you have spoken is good." He said moreover, "For there will be peace and truth in my days."

## 40

[1] "Comfort, comfort my people," says your God. [2] "Speak comfortably to Jerusalem, and call out to her that her warfare is accomplished, that her iniquity is pardoned, that she has received of Yahweh's hand double for all her sins." [3] The voice of one who calls out, "Prepare the way of Yahweh in the wilderness! Make a level highway in the desert for our God. [4] Every valley shall be exalted, and every mountain and hill shall be made low. The uneven shall be made level, and the rough places a plain. [5] Yahweh's glory shall be revealed, and all flesh shall see it together; for the mouth of Yahweh has spoken it." [6] The voice of one saying, "Cry out!" One said, "What shall I cry?" "All flesh is like grass, and all its glory is like the flower of the field. [7] The grass withers, the flower fades, because Yahweh's breath blows on it. Surely the people are like grass. [8] The grass withers, the flower fades; but the word of our God stands forever." [9] You who tell good news to Zion, go up on a high mountain. You who tell good news to Jerusalem, lift up your voice with strength! Lift it up! Don't be afraid! Say to the cities of Judah, "Behold, your God!" [10] Behold, the Lord Yahweh will come as a mighty one, and his arm will rule for him. Behold, his reward is with him, and his recompense before him. [11] He will feed his flock like a shepherd. He will gather the lambs in his arm, and carry them in his bosom. He will gently lead those who have their young. [12] Who has measured the waters in the hollow of his hand, and marked off the sky with his span, and calculated the dust of the earth in a measuring basket, and weighed the mountains in scales, and the hills in a balance? [13] Who has directed Yahweh's Spirit, or has taught him as his counselor? [14] Who did he take counsel with, and who instructed him, and taught him in the path of justice, and taught him knowledge, and showed him the way of understanding? [15] Behold, the nations are like a drop in a bucket, and are regarded as a speck of dust on a balance. Behold, he lifts up the islands like a very little thing. [16] Lebanon is not sufficient to burn, nor its animals sufficient for a burnt offering. [17] All the nations are like nothing before him. They are regarded by him as less than nothing, and vanity. [18] To whom then will you liken God? Or what likeness will you compare to him? [19] A workman has cast an image, and the goldsmith overlays it with gold, and casts silver chains for it. [20] He who is too

impoverished for such an offering chooses a tree that will not rot. He seeks a skillful workman to set up a carved image for him that will not be moved. [21] Haven't you known? Haven't you heard? Haven't you been told from the beginning? Haven't you understood from the foundations of the earth? [22] It is he who sits above the circle of the earth, and its inhabitants are like grasshoppers; who stretches out the heavens like a curtain, and spreads them out like a tent to dwell in, [23] who brings princes to nothing, who makes the judges of the earth meaningless. [24] They are planted scarcely. They are sown scarcely. Their stock has scarcely taken root in the ground. He merely blows on them, and they wither, and the whirlwind takes them away as stubble. [25] "To whom then will you liken me? Who is my equal?" says the Holy One. [26] Lift up your eyes on high, and see who has created these, who brings out their army by number. He calls them all by name. By the greatness of his might, and because he is strong in power, not one is lacking. [27] Why do you say, Jacob, and speak, Israel, "My way is hidden from Yahweh, and the justice due me is disregarded by my God"? [28] Haven't you known? Haven't you heard? The everlasting God, Yahweh, the Creator of the ends of the earth, doesn't faint. He isn't weary. His understanding is unsearchable. [29] He gives power to the weak. He increases the strength of him who has no might. [30] Even the youths faint and get weary, and the young men utterly fall; [31] but those who wait for Yahweh will renew their strength. They will mount up with wings like eagles. They will run, and not be weary. They will walk, and not faint.

## 41

[1] "Keep silent before me, islands, and let the peoples renew their strength. Let them come near, then let them speak. Let's meet together for judgment. [2] Who has raised up one from the east? Who called him to his feet in righteousness? He hands over nations to him and makes him rule over kings. He gives them like the dust to his sword, like the driven stubble to his bow. [3] He pursues them and passes by safely, even by a way that he had not gone with his feet. [4] Who has worked and done it, calling the generations from the beginning? I, Yahweh, the first, and with the last, I am he." [5] The islands have seen, and fear. The ends of the earth tremble. They approach, and come. [6] Everyone helps his neighbor. They say to their brothers, "Be strong!" [7] So the carpenter encourages the goldsmith. He who smooths with the hammer encourages him who strikes the anvil, saying of the soldering, "It is good;" and he fastens it with nails, that it might not totter. [8] "But you, Israel, my servant, Jacob whom I have chosen, the offspring of Abraham my friend, [9] you whom I have taken hold of from the ends of the earth, and called from its corners, and said to you, 'You are my servant. I have chosen you and have not cast you away.' [10] Don't you be afraid, for I am with you. Don't be dismayed, for I am your God. I will strengthen you. Yes, I will help you. Yes, I will uphold you with the right hand of my righteousness. [11] Behold, all those who are incensed against you will be disappointed and confounded. Those who strive with you will be like nothing, and shall perish. [12] You will seek them, and won't find them, even those who contend with you. Those who war against you will be as nothing, as a nonexistent thing. [13] For I, Yahweh your God, will hold your right hand, saying to you, 'Don't be afraid. I will help you.' [14] Don't be afraid, you worm Jacob, and you men of Israel. I will help you," says Yahweh. "Your Redeemer is the Holy One of Israel. [15] Behold, I have made you into a new sharp threshing instrument with teeth. You will thresh the mountains, and beat them small, and will make the hills like chaff. [16] You will winnow them, and the wind will carry them away, and the whirlwind will scatter them. You will rejoice in Yahweh. You will glory in the Holy One of Israel. [17] The poor and needy seek water, and there is none. Their tongue fails for thirst. I, Yahweh, will answer them. I, the God of Israel, will not forsake them. [18] I will open rivers on the bare heights, and springs in the middle of the valleys. I will make the wilderness a pool of water, and the dry land springs of water. [19] I will put cedar, acacia, myrtle, and oil trees in the wilderness. I will set cypress trees, pine, and box trees together in the desert; [20] that they may see, know, consider, and understand together, that Yahweh's hand has done this, and the Holy One of Israel has created it. [21] Produce your cause," says Yahweh. "Bring out your strong reasons!" says the King of Jacob. [22] "Let them announce and declare to us what will happen! Declare the former things, what they are, that we may consider them, and know the latter end of them; or show us things to come. [23] Declare the things that are to come hereafter, that we may know that you are gods. Yes, do good, or do evil, that we may be dismayed, and see it together. [24] Behold, you are nothing, and your work is nothing. He who chooses you is an abomination. [25] "I have raised up one from the north, and he has come, from the rising of the sun, one who calls on my name, and he shall come on rulers as on mortar, and as the potter treads clay. [26] Who has declared

---

[a] *38:18* Sheol is the place of the dead.

it from the beginning, that we may know? and before, that we may say, 'He is right'? Surely, there is no one who declares. Surely, there is no one who shows. Surely, there is no one who hears your words. <sup>27</sup> I am the first to say to Zion, 'Behold, look at them;' and I will give one who brings good news to Jerusalem. <sup>28</sup> When I look, there is no man, even among them there is no counselor who, when I ask, can answer a word. <sup>29</sup> Behold, all of their deeds are vanity and nothing. Their molten images are wind and confusion.

## 42

<sup>1</sup>"Behold, my servant, whom I uphold, my chosen, in whom my soul delights: I have put my Spirit on him. He will bring justice to the nations. <sup>2</sup> He will not shout, nor raise his voice, nor cause it to be heard in the street. <sup>3</sup> He won't break a bruised reed. He won't quench a dimly burning wick. He will faithfully bring justice. <sup>4</sup> He will not fail nor be discouraged, until he has set justice in the earth, and the islands wait for his law." <sup>5</sup> God Yahweh, he who created the heavens and stretched them out, he who spread out the earth and that which comes out of it, he who gives breath to its people and spirit to those who walk in it, says: <sup>6</sup>"I, Yahweh, have called you in righteousness. I will hold your hand. I will keep you, and make you a covenant for the people, as a light for the nations, <sup>7</sup> to open the blind eyes, to bring the prisoners out of the dungeon, and those who sit in darkness out of the prison. <sup>8</sup>"I am Yahweh. That is my name. I will not give my glory to another, nor my praise to engraved images. <sup>9</sup> Behold, the former things have happened and I declare new things. I tell you about them before they come up." <sup>10</sup> Sing to Yahweh a new song, and his praise from the end of the earth, you who go down to the sea, and all that is therein, the islands and their inhabitants. <sup>11</sup> Let the wilderness and its cities raise their voices, with the villages that Kedar inhabits. Let the inhabitants of Sela sing. Let them shout from the top of the mountains! <sup>12</sup> Let them give glory to Yahweh, and declare his praise in the islands. <sup>13</sup> Yahweh will go out like a mighty man. He will stir up zeal like a man of war. He will raise a war cry. Yes, he will shout aloud. He will triumph over his enemies. <sup>14</sup>"I have been silent a long time. I have been quiet and restrained myself. Now I will cry out like a travailing woman. I will both gasp and pant. <sup>15</sup> I will destroy mountains and hills, and dry up all their herbs. I will make the rivers islands, and will dry up the pools. <sup>16</sup> I will bring the blind by a way that they don't know. I will lead them in paths that they don't know. I will make darkness light before them, and crooked places straight. I will do these things, and I will not forsake them. <sup>17</sup>"Those who trust in engraved images, who tell molten images, 'You are our gods,' will be turned back. They will be utterly disappointed. <sup>18</sup>"Hear, you deaf, and look, you blind, that you may see. <sup>19</sup> Who is blind, but my servant? Or who is as deaf as my messenger whom I send? Who is as blind as he who is at peace, and as blind as Yahweh's servant? <sup>20</sup> You see many things, but don't observe. His ears are open, but he doesn't listen. <sup>21</sup> It pleased Yahweh, for his righteousness' sake, to magnify the law and make it honorable. <sup>22</sup> But this is a robbed and plundered people. All of them are snared in holes, and they are hidden in prisons. They have become captives, and no one delivers, and a plunder, and no one says, 'Restore them!' <sup>23</sup> Who is there among you who will give ear to this? Who will listen and hear for the time to come? <sup>24</sup> Who gave Jacob as plunder, and Israel to the robbers? Didn't Yahweh, he against whom we have sinned? For they would not walk in his ways, and they disobeyed his law. <sup>25</sup> Therefore he poured the fierceness of his anger on him, and the strength of battle. It set him on fire all around, but he didn't know. It burned him, but he didn't take it to heart."

## 43

<sup>1</sup> But now Yahweh who created you, Jacob, and he who formed you, Israel, says: "Don't be afraid, for I have redeemed you. I have called you by your name. You are mine. <sup>2</sup> When you pass through the waters, I will be with you, and through the rivers, they will not overflow you. When you walk through the fire, you will not be burned, and flame will not scorch you. <sup>3</sup> For I am Yahweh your God, the Holy One of Israel, your Savior. I have given Egypt as your ransom, Ethiopia and Seba in your place. <sup>4</sup> Since you have been precious and honored in my sight, and I have loved you, therefore I will give people in your place, and nations instead of your life. <sup>5</sup> Don't be afraid, for I am with you. I will bring your offspring from the east, and gather you from the west. <sup>6</sup> I will tell the north, 'Give them up!' and tell the south, 'Don't hold them back! Bring my sons from far away, and my daughters from the ends of the earth— <sup>7</sup> everyone who is called by my name, and whom I have created for my glory, whom I have formed, yes, whom I have made.'" <sup>8</sup> Bring out the blind people who have eyes, and the deaf who have ears. <sup>9</sup> Let all the nations be gathered together, and let the peoples be assembled. Who among them can declare this, and show us former things? Let them bring their witnesses, that they may be justified, or let them hear, and say, "That is true." <sup>10</sup>"You are my witnesses," says Yahweh, "With my servant whom I have chosen; that you may know

and believe me, and understand that I am he. Before me there was no God formed, neither will there be after me. <sup>11</sup> I myself am Yahweh. Besides me, there is no savior. <sup>12</sup> I have declared, I have saved, and I have shown, and there was no strange god among you. Therefore you are my witnesses", says Yahweh, "and I am God. <sup>13</sup> Yes, since the day was, I am he. There is no one who can deliver out of my hand. I will work, and who can hinder it?" <sup>14</sup> Yahweh, your Redeemer, the Holy One of Israel says: "For your sake, I have sent to Babylon, and I will bring all of them down as fugitives, even the Chaldeans, in the ships of their rejoicing. <sup>15</sup> I am Yahweh, your Holy One, the Creator of Israel, your King." <sup>16</sup> Yahweh, who makes a way in the sea, and a path in the mighty waters, <sup>17</sup> who brings out the chariot and horse, the army and the mighty man (they lie down together, they shall not rise; they are extinct, they are quenched like a wick) says: <sup>18</sup>"Don't remember the former things, and don't consider the things of old. <sup>19</sup> Behold, I will do a new thing. It springs out now. Don't you know it? I will even make a way in the wilderness, and rivers in the desert. <sup>20</sup> The animals of the field, the jackals and the ostriches, shall honor me, because I give water in the wilderness and rivers in the desert, to give drink to my people, my chosen, <sup>21</sup> the people which I formed for myself, that they might declare my praise. <sup>22</sup> Yet you have not called on me, Jacob; but you have been weary of me, Israel. <sup>23</sup> You have not brought me any of your sheep for burnt offerings, neither have you honored me with your sacrifices. I have not burdened you with offerings, nor wearied you with frankincense. <sup>24</sup> You have bought me no sweet cane with money, nor have you filled me with the fat of your sacrifices, but you have burdened me with your sins. You have wearied me with your iniquities. <sup>25</sup> I, even I, am he who blots out your transgressions for my own sake; and I will not remember your sins. <sup>26</sup> Put me in remembrance. Let us plead together. Declare your case, that you may be justified. <sup>27</sup> Your first father sinned, and your teachers have transgressed against me. <sup>28</sup> Therefore I will profane the princes of the sanctuary; and I will make Jacob a curse, and Israel an insult."

## 44

<sup>1</sup> Yet listen now, Jacob my servant, and Israel, whom I have chosen. <sup>2</sup> This is what Yahweh who made you, and formed you from the womb, who will help you says: "Don't be afraid, Jacob my servant; and you, Jeshurun, whom I have chosen. <sup>3</sup> For I will pour water on him who is thirsty, and streams on the dry ground. I will pour my Spirit on your descendants, and my blessing on your offspring; <sup>4</sup> and they will spring up among the grass, as willows by the watercourses. <sup>5</sup> One will say, 'I am Yahweh's.' Another will be called by the name of Jacob; and another will write with his hand 'to Yahweh,' and honor the name of Israel." <sup>6</sup> This is what Yahweh, the King of Israel, and his Redeemer, Yahweh of Armies, says: "I am the first, and I am the last; and besides me there is no God. <sup>7</sup> Who is like me? Who will call, and will declare it, and set it in order for me, since I established the ancient people? Let them declare the things that are coming, and that will happen. <sup>8</sup> Don't fear, neither be afraid. Haven't I declared it to you long ago, and shown it? You are my witnesses. Is there a God besides me? Indeed, there is not. I don't know any other Rock." <sup>9</sup> Everyone who makes a carved image is vain. The things that they delight in will not profit. Their own witnesses don't see, nor know, that they may be disappointed. <sup>10</sup> Who has fashioned a god, or molds an image that is profitable for nothing? <sup>11</sup> Behold, all his fellows will be disappointed; and the workmen are mere men. Let them all be gathered together. Let them stand up. They will fear. They will be put to shame together. <sup>12</sup> The blacksmith takes an ax, works in the coals, fashions it with hammers, and works it with his strong arm. He is hungry, and his strength fails; he drinks no water, and is faint. <sup>13</sup> The carpenter stretches out a line. He marks it out with a pencil. He shapes it with planes. He marks it out with compasses, and shapes it like the figure of a man, with the beauty of a man, to reside in a house. <sup>14</sup> He cuts down cedars for himself, and takes the cypress and the oak, and strengthens for himself one among the trees of the forest. He plants a cypress tree, and the rain nourishes it. <sup>15</sup> Then it will be for a man to burn; and he takes some of it and warms himself. Yes, he burns it and bakes bread. Yes, he makes a god and worships it; he makes it a carved image, and falls down to it. <sup>16</sup> He burns part of it in the fire. With part of it, he eats meat. He roasts a roast and is satisfied. Yes, he warms himself and says, "Aha! I am warm. I have seen the fire." <sup>17</sup> The rest of it he makes into a god, even his engraved image. He bows down to it and worships, and prays to it, and says, "Deliver me, for you are my god!" <sup>18</sup> They don't know, neither do they consider, for he has shut their eyes, that they can't see, and their hearts, that they can't understand. <sup>19</sup> No one thinks, neither is there knowledge nor understanding to say, "I have burned part of it in the fire. Yes, I have also baked bread on its coals. I have roasted meat and eaten it. Shall I make the rest of it into an abomination? Shall I bow down to a tree trunk?" <sup>20</sup> He feeds on ashes. A deceived heart has turned him aside; and he can't deliver his soul, nor say, "Isn't there a lie in my right hand?" <sup>21</sup> Remember these

things, Jacob and Israel, for you are my servant. I have formed you. You are my servant. Israel, you will not be forgotten by me. [22] I have blotted out, as a thick cloud, your transgressions, and, as a cloud, your sins. Return to me, for I have redeemed you. [23] Sing, you heavens, for Yahweh has done it! Shout, you lower parts of the earth! Break out into singing, you mountains, O forest, all of your trees, for Yahweh has redeemed Jacob, and will glorify himself in Israel. [24] Yahweh, your Redeemer, and he who formed you from the womb says: "I am Yahweh, who makes all things; who alone stretches out the heavens; who spreads out the earth by myself; [25] who frustrates the signs of the liars, and makes diviners mad; who turns wise men backward, and makes their knowledge foolish; [26] who confirms the word of his servant, and performs the counsel of his messengers; who says of Jerusalem, 'She will be inhabited;' and of the cities of Judah, 'They will be built,' and 'I will raise up its waste places;' [27] who says to the deep, 'Be dry,' and 'I will dry up your rivers,' [28] who says of Cyrus, 'He is my shepherd, and shall perform all my pleasure,' even saying of Jerusalem, 'She will be built;' and of the temple, 'Your foundation will be laid.'"

## 45

[1] Yahweh says to his anointed, to Cyrus, whose right hand I have held to subdue nations before him and strip kings of their armor, to open the doors before him, and the gates shall not be shut: [2]"I will go before you and make the rough places smooth. I will break the doors of bronze in pieces and cut apart the bars of iron. [3] I will give you the treasures of darkness and hidden riches of secret places, that you may know that it is I, Yahweh, who calls you by your name, even the God of Israel. [4] For Jacob my servant's sake, and Israel my chosen, I have called you by your name. I have given you a title, though you have not known me. [5] I am Yahweh, and there is no one else. Besides me, there is no God. I will strengthen[a] you, though you have not known me, [6] that they may know from the rising of the sun, and from the west, that there is no one besides me. I am Yahweh, and there is no one else. [7] I form the light and create darkness. I make peace and create calamity. I am Yahweh, who does all these things. [8] Rain, you heavens, from above, and let the skies pour down righteousness. Let the earth open, that it may produce salvation, and let it cause righteousness to spring up with it. I, Yahweh, have created it. [9] Woe to him who strives with his Maker— a clay pot among the clay pots of the earth! Shall the clay ask him who fashions it, 'What are you making?' or your work, 'He has no hands'? [10] Woe to him who says to a father, 'What have you become the father of?' or to a mother, 'What have you given birth to?'" [11] Yahweh, the Holy One of Israel and his Maker says: "You ask me about the things that are to come, concerning my sons, and you command me concerning the work of my hands! [12] I have made the earth, and created man on it. I, even my hands, have stretched out the heavens. I have commanded all their army. [13] I have raised him up in righteousness, and I will make all his ways straight. He shall build my city, and he shall let my exiles go free, not for price nor reward," says Yahweh of Armies. [14] Yahweh says: "The labor of Egypt, and the merchandise of Ethiopia, and the Sabeans, men of stature, will come over to you, and they will be yours. They will go after you. They shall come over in chains. They will bow down to you. They will make supplication to you: 'Surely God is in you; and there is no one else. There is no other god. [15] Most certainly you are a God who has hidden yourself, God of Israel, the Savior.'" [16] They will be disappointed, yes, confounded, all of them. Those who are makers of idols will go into confusion together. [17] Israel will be saved by Yahweh with an everlasting salvation. You will not be disappointed nor confounded to ages everlasting. [18] For Yahweh who created the heavens, the God who formed the earth and made it, who established it and didn't create it a waste, who formed it to be inhabited says: "I am Yahweh. There is no other. [19] I have not spoken in secret, in a place of the land of darkness. I didn't say to the offspring of Jacob, 'Seek me in vain.' I, Yahweh, speak righteousness. I declare things that are right. [20]"Assemble yourselves and come. Draw near together, you who have escaped from the nations. Those have no knowledge who carry the wood of their engraved image, and pray to a god that can't save. [21] Declare and present it. Yes, let them take counsel together. Who has shown this from ancient time? Who has declared it of old? Haven't I, Yahweh? There is no other God besides me, a just God and a Savior. There is no one besides me. [22]"Look to me, and be saved, all the ends of the earth; for I am God, and there is no other. [23] I have sworn by myself. The word has gone out of my mouth in righteousness, and will not be revoked, that to me every knee shall bow, every tongue shall take an oath. [24] They will say of me, 'There is righteousness and strength only in Yahweh.'" Even to him will men come. All those who raged against him will be disappointed. [25] All the offspring of Israel will be justified in Yahweh, and will rejoice!

## 46

[1] Bel bows down. Nebo stoops. Their idols are carried by animals, and on the livestock. The things that you carried around are heavy loads, a burden for the weary. [2] They stoop and they bow down together. They could not deliver the burden, but they have gone into captivity. [3]"Listen to me, house of Jacob, and all the remnant of the house of Israel, that have been carried from their birth, that have been carried from the womb. [4] Even to old age I am he, and even to gray hairs I will carry you. I have made, and I will bear. Yes, I will carry, and will deliver. [5]"To whom will you compare me, and consider my equal, and compare me, as if we were the same? [6] Some pour out gold from the bag, and weigh silver in the balance. They hire a goldsmith, and he makes it a god. They fall down— yes, they worship. [7] They bear it on their shoulder. They carry it, and set it in its place, and it stands there. It cannot move from its place. Yes, one may cry to it, yet it can not answer. It cannot save him out of his trouble. [8]"Remember this, and show yourselves men. Bring it to mind again, you transgressors. [9] Remember the former things of old; for I am God, and there is no other. I am God, and there is none like me. [10] I declare the end from the beginning, and from ancient times things that are not yet done. I say: My counsel will stand, and I will do all that I please. [11] I call a ravenous bird from the east, the man of my counsel from a far country. Yes, I have spoken. I will also bring it to pass. I have planned. I will also do it. [12] Listen to me, you stubborn-hearted, who are far from righteousness! [13] I bring my righteousness near. It is not far off, and my salvation will not wait. I will grant salvation to Zion, my glory to Israel.

## 47

[1]"Come down and sit in the dust, virgin daughter of Babylon. Sit on the ground without a throne, daughter of the Chaldeans. For you will no longer be called tender and delicate. [2] Take the millstones and grind flour. Remove your veil, lift up your skirt, uncover your legs, and wade through the rivers. [3] Your nakedness will be uncovered. Yes, your shame will be seen. I will take vengeance, and will spare no one." [4] Our Redeemer, Yahweh of Armies is his name, is the Holy One of Israel. [5]"Sit in silence, and go into darkness, daughter of the Chaldeans. For you shall no longer be called the mistress of kingdoms. [6] I was angry with my people. I profaned my inheritance and gave them into your hand. You showed them no mercy. You laid a very heavy yoke on the aged. [7] You said, 'I will be a princess forever,' so that you didn't lay these things to your heart, nor did you remember the results. [8]"Now therefore hear this, you who are given to pleasures, who sit securely, who say in your heart, 'I am, and there is no one else besides me. I won't sit as a widow, neither will I know the loss of children.' [9] But these two things will come to you in a moment in one day: the loss of children and widowhood. They will come on you in their full measure, in the multitude of your sorceries, and the great abundance of your enchantments. [10] For you have trusted in your wickedness. You have said, 'No one sees me.' Your wisdom and your knowledge has perverted you. You have said in your heart, 'I am, and there is no one else besides me.' [11] Therefore disaster will come on you. You won't know when it dawns. Mischief will fall on you. You won't be able to put it away. Desolation will come on you suddenly, which you don't understand. [12]"Stand now with your enchantments and with the multitude of your sorceries, in which you have labored from your youth, as if you might profit, as if you might prevail. [13] You are wearied in the multitude of your counsels. Now let the astrologers, the stargazers, and the monthly prognosticators stand up and save you from the things that will happen to you. [14] Behold, they are like stubble. The fire will burn them. They won't deliver themselves from the power of the flame. It won't be a coal to warm at or a fire to sit by. [15] The things that you labored in will be like this: those who have trafficked with you from your youth will each wander in his own way. There will be no one to save you.

## 48

[1]"Hear this, house of Jacob, you who are called by the name of Israel, and have come out of the waters of Judah. You swear by Yahweh's name, and make mention of the God of Israel, but not in truth, nor in righteousness— [2] for they call themselves citizens of the holy city, and rely on the God of Israel; Yahweh of Armies is his name. [3] I have declared the former things from of old. Yes, they went out of my mouth, and I revealed them. I did them suddenly, and they happened. [4] Because I knew that you are obstinate, and your neck is an iron sinew, and your brow bronze; [5] therefore I have declared it to you from of old; before it came to pass I showed it to you; lest you should say, 'My idol has done them. My engraved image and my molten image has commanded them.' [6] You have heard it. Now see all this. And you, won't you declare it? "I have shown you new things from this time, even hidden things, which you have not known. [7] They are created now, and not

from of old. Before today, you didn't hear them, lest you should say, 'Behold, I knew them.' [8] Yes, you didn't hear. Yes, you didn't know. Yes, from of old your ear was not opened, for I knew that you dealt very treacherously, and were called a transgressor from the womb. [9] For my name's sake, I will defer my anger, and for my praise, I hold it back for you so that I don't cut you off. [10] Behold, I have refined you, but not as silver. I have chosen you in the furnace of affliction. [11] For my own sake, for my own sake, I will do it; for how would my name be profaned? I will not give my glory to another. [12] "Listen to me, O Jacob, and Israel my called: I am he. I am the first. I am also the last. [13] Yes, my hand has laid the foundation of the earth, and my right hand has spread out the heavens. when I call to them, they stand up together. [14] "Assemble yourselves, all of you, and hear! Who among them has declared these things? He whom Yahweh loves will do what he likes to Babylon, and his arm will be against the Chaldeans. [15] I, even I, have spoken. Yes, I have called him. I have brought him and he shall make his way prosperous. [16] "Come near to me and hear this: "From the beginning I have not spoken in secret; from the time that it happened, I was there." Now the Lord Yahweh has sent me with his Spirit. [17] Yahweh, your Redeemer, the Holy One of Israel, says: "I am Yahweh your God, who teaches you to profit, who leads you by the way that you should go. [18] Oh that you had listened to my commandments! Then your peace would have been like a river and your righteousness like the waves of the sea. [19] Your offspring also would have been as the sand and the descendants of your body like its grains. His name would not be cut off nor destroyed from before me." [20] Leave Babylon! Flee from the Chaldeans! With the sound of joyful shouting announce this, tell it even to the end of the earth; say, "Yahweh has redeemed his servant Jacob!" [21] They didn't thirst when he led them through the deserts. He caused the waters to flow out of the rock for them. He also split the rock and the waters gushed out. [22] "There is no peace", says Yahweh, "for the wicked."

## 49

[1] Listen, islands, to me. Listen, you peoples, from afar: Yahweh has called me from the womb; from the inside of my mother, he has mentioned my name. [2] He has made my mouth like a sharp sword. He has hidden me in the shadow of his hand. He has made me a polished shaft. He has kept me close in his quiver. [3] He said to me, "You are my servant, Israel, in whom I will be glorified." [4] But I said, "I have labored in vain. I have spent my strength in vain for nothing; yet surely the justice due to me is with Yahweh, and my reward with my God." [5] Now Yahweh, he who formed me from the womb to be his servant, says to bring Jacob again to him, and to gather Israel to him, for I am honorable in Yahweh's eyes, and my God has become my strength. [6] Indeed, he says, "It is too light a thing that you should be my servant to raise up the tribes of Jacob, and to restore the preserved of Israel. I will also give you as a light to the nations, that you may be my salvation to the end of the earth." [7] Yahweh, the Redeemer of Israel, and his Holy One, says to him whom man despises, to him whom the nation abhors, to a servant of rulers: "Kings shall see and rise up, princes, and they shall worship, because of Yahweh who is faithful, even the Holy One of Israel, who has chosen you." [8] Yahweh says, "I have answered you in an acceptable time. I have helped you in a day of salvation. I will preserve you and give you for a covenant of the people, to raise up the land, to make them inherit the desolate heritage, [9] saying to those who are bound, 'Come out!'; to those who are in darkness, 'Show yourselves!' "They shall feed along the paths, and their pasture shall be on all treeless heights. [10] They shall not hunger nor thirst; neither shall the heat nor sun strike them, for he who has mercy on them will lead them. He will guide them by springs of water. [11] I will make all my mountains a road, and my highways shall be exalted. [12] Behold, these shall come from afar, and behold, these from the north and from the west, and these from the land of Sinim." [13] Sing, heavens, and be joyful, earth! Break out into singing, mountains! For Yahweh has comforted his people, and will have compassion on his afflicted. [14] But Zion said, "Yahweh has forsaken me, and the Lord has forgotten me." [15] "Can a woman forget her nursing child, that she should not have compassion on the son of her womb? Yes, these may forget, yet I will not forget you! [16] Behold, I have engraved you on the palms of my hands. Your walls are continually before me. [17] Your children hurry. Your destroyers and those who devastated you will leave you. [18] Lift up your eyes all around, and see: all these gather themselves together, and come to you. As I live," says Yahweh, "you shall surely clothe yourself with them all as with an ornament, and dress yourself with them, like a bride. [19] "For, as for your waste and your desolate places, and your land that has been destroyed, surely now that land will be too small for the inhabitants, and those who swallowed you up will be far away. [20] The children of your bereavement will say in your ears, 'This place is too small for me. Give me a place to live in.' [21] Then you will say in your heart, 'Who has conceived these for me, since I have been bereaved of my children and

am alone, an exile, and wandering back and forth? Who has brought these up? Behold, I was left alone. Where were these?'" [22] The Lord Yahweh says, "Behold, I will lift up my hand to the nations, and lift up my banner to the peoples. They shall bring your sons in their bosom, and your daughters shall be carried on their shoulders. [23] Kings shall be your foster fathers, and their queens your nursing mothers. They will bow down to you with their faces to the earth, and lick the dust of your feet. Then you will know that I am Yahweh; and those who wait for me won't be disappointed." [24] Shall the plunder be taken from the mighty, or the lawful captives be delivered? [25] But Yahweh says, "Even the captives of the mighty shall be taken away, and the plunder retrieved from the fierce, for I will contend with him who contends with you and I will save your children. [26] I will feed those who oppress you with their own flesh; and they will be drunk on their own blood, as with sweet wine. Then all flesh shall know that I, Yahweh, am your Savior and your Redeemer, the Mighty One of Jacob."

## 50

[1] Yahweh says, "Where is the bill of your mother's divorce, with which I have put her away? Or to which of my creditors have I sold you? Behold, you were sold for your iniquities, and your mother was put away for your transgressions. [2] Why, when I came, was there no one? When I called, why was there no one to answer? Is my hand shortened at all, that it can't redeem? Or have I no power to deliver? Behold, at my rebuke I dry up the sea. I make the rivers a wilderness. Their fish stink because there is no water, and die of thirst. [3] I clothe the heavens with blackness. I make sackcloth their covering." [4] The Lord Yahweh has given me the tongue of those who are taught, that I may know how to sustain with words him who is weary. He awakens morning by morning, he awakens my ear to hear as those who are taught. [5] The Lord Yahweh has opened my ear. I was not rebellious. I have not turned back. [6] I gave my back to those who beat me, and my cheeks to those who plucked off the hair. I didn't hide my face from shame and spitting. [7] For the Lord Yahweh will help me. Therefore I have not been confounded. Therefore I have set my face like a flint, and I know that I won't be disappointed. [8] He who justifies me is near. Who will bring charges against me? Let us stand up together. Who is my adversary? Let him come near to me. [9] Behold, the Lord Yahweh will help me! Who is he who will condemn me? Behold, they will all grow old like a garment. The moths will eat them up. [10] Who among you fears Yahweh and obeys the voice of his servant? He who walks in darkness and has no light, let him trust in Yahweh's name, and rely on his God. [11] Behold, all you who kindle a fire, who adorn yourselves with torches around yourselves, walk in the flame of your fire, and among the torches that you have kindled. You will have this from my hand: you will lie down in sorrow.

## 51

[1] "Listen to me, you who follow after righteousness, you who seek Yahweh. Look to the rock you were cut from, and to the quarry you were dug from. [2] Look to Abraham your father, and to Sarah who bore you; for when he was but one I called him, I blessed him, and made him many. [3] For Yahweh has comforted Zion. He has comforted all her waste places, and has made her wilderness like Eden, and her desert like the garden of Yahweh. Joy and gladness will be found in them, thanksgiving, and the voice of melody. [4] "Listen to me, my people; and hear me, my nation, for a law will go out from me, and I will establish my justice for a light to the peoples. [5] My righteousness is near. My salvation has gone out, and my arms will judge the peoples. The islands will wait for me, and they will trust my arm. [6] Lift up your eyes to the heavens, and look at the earth beneath; for the heavens will vanish away like smoke, and the earth will wear out like a garment. Its inhabitants will die in the same way, but my salvation will be forever, and my righteousness will not be abolished. [7] "Listen to me, you who know righteousness, the people in whose heart is my law. Don't fear the reproach of men, and don't be dismayed at their insults. [8] For the moth will eat them up like a garment, and the worm will eat them like wool; but my righteousness will be forever, and my salvation to all generations." [9] Awake, awake, put on strength, arm of Yahweh! Awake, as in the days of old, the generations of ancient times. Isn't it you who cut Rahab in pieces, who pierced the monster? [10] Isn't it you who dried up the sea, the waters of the great deep; who made the depths of the sea a way for the redeemed to pass over? [11] Those ransomed by Yahweh will return, and come with singing to Zion. Everlasting joy shall be on their heads. They will obtain gladness and joy. Sorrow and sighing shall flee away. [12] "I, even I, am he who comforts you. Who are you, that you are afraid of man who shall die, and of the son of man who will be made as grass? [13] Have you forgotten Yahweh your Maker, who stretched out the heavens, and laid the foundations of the earth? Do you live in fear continually all day because of the fury of the oppressor, when he prepares to destroy? Where is the fury of the oppressor? [14] The captive exile will speedily be freed. He will not die

and go down into the pit. His bread won't fail. [15] For I am Yahweh your God, who stirs up the sea so that its waves roar. Yahweh of Armies is his name. [16] I have put my words in your mouth and have covered you in the shadow of my hand, that I may plant the heavens, and lay the foundations of the earth, and tell Zion, 'You are my people.'" [17] Awake, awake! Stand up, Jerusalem, you who have drunk from Yahweh's hand the cup of his wrath. You have drunken the bowl of the cup of staggering, and drained it. [18] There is no one to guide her among all the sons to whom she has given birth; and there is no one who takes her by the hand among all the sons whom she has brought up. [19] These two things have happened to you— who will grieve with you?— desolation and destruction, and famine and the sword. How can I comfort you? [20] Your sons have fainted. They lie at the head of all the streets, like an antelope in a net. They are full of Yahweh's wrath, the rebuke of your God. [21] Therefore now hear this, you afflicted, and drunken, but not with wine: [22] Your Lord Yahweh, your God who pleads the cause of his people, says, "Behold, I have taken out of your hand the cup of staggering, even the bowl of the cup of my wrath. You will not drink it any more. [23] I will put it into the hand of those who afflict you, who have said to your soul, 'Bow down, that we may walk over you;' and you have laid your back as the ground, like a street to those who walk over."

## 52

[1] Awake, awake! Put on your strength, Zion. Put on your beautiful garments, Jerusalem, the holy city, for from now on the uncircumcised and the unclean will no more come into you. [2] Shake yourself from the dust! Arise, sit up, Jerusalem! Release yourself from the bonds of your neck, captive daughter of Zion! [3] For Yahweh says, "You were sold for nothing; and you will be redeemed without money." [4] For the Lord Yahweh says: "My people went down at the first into Egypt to live there; and the Assyrian has oppressed them without cause. [5]"Now therefore, what do I do here," says Yahweh, "seeing that my people are taken away for nothing? Those who rule over them mock," says Yahweh, "and my name is blasphemed continually all day long. [6] Therefore my people shall know my name. Therefore they shall know in that day that I am he who speaks. Behold, it is I." [7] How beautiful on the mountains are the feet of him who brings good news, who publishes peace, who brings good news, who proclaims salvation, who says to Zion, "Your God reigns!" [8] Your watchmen lift up their voice. Together they sing; for they shall see eye to eye when Yahweh returns to Zion. [9] Break out into joy! Sing together, you waste places of Jerusalem; for Yahweh has comforted his people. He has redeemed Jerusalem. [10] Yahweh has made his holy arm bare in the eyes of all the nations. All the ends of the earth have seen the salvation of our God. [11] Depart! Depart! Go out from there! Touch no unclean thing! Go out from among her! Cleanse yourselves, you who carry Yahweh's vessels. [12] For you shall not go out in haste, neither shall you go by flight; for Yahweh will go before you, and the God of Israel will be your rear guard. [13] Behold, my servant will deal wisely. He will be exalted and lifted up, and will be very high. [14] Just as many were astonished at you— his appearance was marred more than any man, and his form more than the sons of men— [15] so he will cleanse[a] many nations. Kings will shut their mouths at him; for they will see that which had not been told them, and they will understand that which they had not heard.

## 53

[1] Who has believed our message? To whom has Yahweh's arm been revealed? [2] For he grew up before him as a tender plant, and as a root out of dry ground. He has no good looks or majesty. When we see him, there is no beauty that we should desire him. [3] He was despised and rejected by men, a man of suffering and acquainted with disease. He was despised as one from whom men hide their face; and we didn't respect him. [4] Surely he has borne our sickness and carried our suffering; yet we considered him plagued, struck by God, and afflicted. [5] But he was pierced for our transgressions. He was crushed for our iniquities. The punishment that brought our peace was on him; and by his wounds we are healed. [6] All we like sheep have gone astray. Everyone has turned to his own way; and Yahweh has laid on him the iniquity of us all. [7] He was oppressed, yet when he was afflicted he didn't open his mouth. As a lamb that is led to the slaughter, and as a sheep that before its shearers is silent, so he didn't open his mouth. [8] He was taken away by oppression and judgment. As for his generation, who considered that he was cut off out of the land of the living and stricken for the disobedience of my people? [9] They made his grave with the wicked, and with a rich man in his death, although he had done no violence, nor was any deceit in his mouth. [10] Yet it pleased Yahweh to bruise him. He has caused him to suffer. When you make his soul an offering for sin, he will see his offspring. He will prolong his days and

Yahweh's pleasure will prosper in his hand. [11] After the suffering of his soul, he will see the light[b] and be satisfied. My righteous servant will justify many by the knowledge of himself; and he will bear their iniquities. [12] Therefore I will give him a portion with the great. He will divide the plunder with the strong, because he poured out his soul to death and was counted with the transgressors; yet he bore the sins of many and made intercession for the transgressors.

## 54

[1]"Sing, barren, you who didn't give birth! Break out into singing, and cry aloud, you who didn't travail with child! For more are the children of the desolate than the children of the married wife," says Yahweh. [2]"Enlarge the place of your tent, and let them stretch out the curtains of your habitations; don't spare; lengthen your cords, and strengthen your stakes. [3] For you will spread out on the right hand and on the left; and your offspring will possess the nations and settle in desolate cities. [4]"Don't be afraid, for you will not be ashamed. Don't be confounded, for you will not be disappointed. For you will forget the shame of your youth. You will remember the reproach of your widowhood no more. [5] For your Maker is your husband; Yahweh of Armies is his name. The Holy One of Israel is your Redeemer. He will be called the God of the whole earth. [6] For Yahweh has called you as a wife forsaken and grieved in spirit, even a wife of youth, when she is cast off," says your God. [7]"For a small moment I have forsaken you, but I will gather you with great mercies. [8] In overflowing wrath I hid my face from you for a moment, but with everlasting loving kindness I will have mercy on you," says Yahweh your Redeemer. [9]"For this is like the waters of Noah to me; for as I have sworn that the waters of Noah will no more go over the earth, so I have sworn that I will not be angry with you, nor rebuke you. [10] For the mountains may depart, and the hills be removed, but my loving kindness will not depart from you, and my covenant of peace will not be removed," says Yahweh who has mercy on you. [11]"You afflicted, tossed with storms, and not comforted, behold, I will set your stones in beautiful colors, and lay your foundations with sapphires. [12] I will make your pinnacles of rubies, your gates of sparkling jewels, and all your walls of precious stones. [13] All your children will be taught by Yahweh, and your children's peace will be great. [14] You will be established in righteousness. You will be far from oppression, for you will not be afraid, and far from terror, for it shall not come near you. [15] Behold, they may gather together, but not by me. Whoever gathers together against you will fall because of you. [16]"Behold, I have created the blacksmith who fans the coals into flame, and forges a weapon for his work; and I have created the destroyer to destroy. [17] No weapon that is formed against you will prevail; and you will condemn every tongue that rises against you in judgment. This is the heritage of Yahweh's servants, and their righteousness is of me," says Yahweh.

## 55

[1]"Hey! Come, everyone who thirsts, to the waters! Come, he who has no money, buy, and eat! Yes, come, buy wine and milk without money and without price. [2] Why do you spend money for that which is not bread, and your labor for that which doesn't satisfy? Listen diligently to me, and eat that which is good, and let your soul delight itself in richness. [3] Turn your ear, and come to me. Hear, and your soul will live. I will make an everlasting covenant with you, even the sure mercies of David. [4] Behold, I have given him for a witness to the peoples, a leader and commander to the peoples. [5] Behold, you shall call a nation that you don't know; and a nation that didn't know you shall run to you, because of Yahweh your God, and for the Holy One of Israel; for he has glorified you." [6] Seek Yahweh while he may be found. Call on him while he is near. [7] Let the wicked forsake his way, and the unrighteous man his thoughts. Let him return to Yahweh, and he will have mercy on him, to our God, for he will freely pardon. [8]"For my thoughts are not your thoughts, and your ways are not my ways," says Yahweh. [9]"For as the heavens are higher than the earth, so are my ways higher than your ways, and my thoughts than your thoughts. [10] For as the rain comes down and the snow from the sky, and doesn't return there, but waters the earth, and makes it grow and bud, and gives seed to the sower and bread to the eater; [11] so is my word that goes out of my mouth: it will not return to me void, but it will accomplish that which I please, and it will prosper in the thing I sent it to do. [12] For you shall go out with joy, and be led out with peace. The mountains and the hills will break out before you into singing; and all the trees of the fields will clap their hands. [13] Instead of the thorn the cypress tree will come up; and instead of the brier the myrtle tree will come up. It will make a name for Yahweh, for an everlasting sign that will not be cut off."

---

[a] 52:15 or, sprinkle

[b] 53:11 So read the Dead Sea Scrolls and Septuagint.

Masoretic Text omits "the light".

## 56

[1] Yahweh says: "Maintain justice and do what is right, for my salvation is near and my righteousness will soon be revealed. [2] Blessed is the man who does this, and the son of man who holds it fast; who keeps the Sabbath without profaning it and keeps his hand from doing any evil." [3] Let no foreigner who has joined himself to Yahweh speak, saying, "Yahweh will surely separate me from his people." Do not let the eunuch say, "Behold, I am a dry tree." [4] For Yahweh says, "To the eunuchs who keep my Sabbaths, choose the things that please me, and hold fast to my covenant, [5] I will give them in my house and within my walls a memorial and a name better than of sons and of daughters. I will give them an everlasting name that will not be cut off. [6] Also the foreigners who join themselves to Yahweh to serve him, and to love Yahweh's name, to be his servants, everyone who keeps the Sabbath from profaning it, and holds fast my covenant, [7] I will bring these to my holy mountain, and make them joyful in my house of prayer. Their burnt offerings and their sacrifices will be accepted on my altar; for my house will be called a house of prayer for all peoples." [8] The Lord Yahweh, who gathers the outcasts of Israel, says, "I will yet gather others to him, in addition to his own who are gathered." [9] All you animals of the field, come to devour, all you animals in the forest. [10] His watchmen are blind. They are all without knowledge. They are all mute dogs. They can't bark— dreaming, lying down, loving to slumber. [11] Yes, the dogs are greedy. They can never have enough. They are shepherds who can't understand. They have all turned to their own way, each one to his gain, from every quarter. [12] "Come," they say, "I will get wine, and we will fill ourselves with strong drink; and tomorrow will be as today, great beyond measure."

## 57

[1] The righteous perish, and no one lays it to heart. Merciful men are taken away, and no one considers that the righteous is taken away from the evil. [2] He enters into peace. They rest in their beds, each one who walks in his uprightness. [3] "But draw near here, you sons of a sorceress, you offspring of adulterers and prostitutes. [4] Whom do you mock? Against whom do you make a wide mouth and stick out your tongue? Aren't you children of disobedience and offspring of falsehood, [5] you who inflame yourselves among the oaks, under every green tree; who kill the children in the valleys, under the clefts of the rocks? [6] Among the smooth stones of the valley is your portion. They, they are your lot. You have even poured a drink offering to them. You have offered an offering. Shall I be appeased for these things? [7] On a high and lofty mountain you have set your bed. You also went up there to offer sacrifice. [8] You have set up your memorial behind the doors and the posts, for you have exposed yourself to someone besides me, and have gone up. You have enlarged your bed and made you a covenant with them. You loved what you saw on their bed. [9] You went to the king with oil, increased your perfumes, sent your ambassadors far off, and degraded yourself even to Sheol.[a] [10] You were wearied with the length of your ways; yet you didn't say, 'It is in vain.' You found a reviving of your strength; therefore you weren't faint. [11] "Whom have you dreaded and feared, so that you lie, and have not remembered me, nor laid it to your heart? Haven't I held my peace for a long time, and you don't fear me? [12] I will declare your righteousness; and as for your works, they will not benefit you. [13] When you cry, let those whom you have gathered deliver you, but the wind will take them. A breath will carry them all away, but he who takes refuge in me will possess the land, and will inherit my holy mountain." [14] He will say, "Build up, build up, prepare the way! Remove the stumbling-block out of the way of my people." [15] For the high and lofty One who inhabits eternity, whose name is Holy, says: "I dwell in the high and holy place, with him also who is of a contrite and humble spirit, to revive the spirit of the humble, and to revive the heart of the contrite. [16] For I will not contend forever, neither will I always be angry; for the spirit would faint before me, and the souls whom I have made. [17] I was angry because of the iniquity of his covetousness and struck him. I hid myself and was angry; and he went on backsliding in the way of his heart. [18] I have seen his ways, and will heal him. I will lead him also, and restore comforts to him and to his mourners. [19] I create the fruit of the lips: Peace, peace, to him who is far off and to him who is near," says Yahweh; "and I will heal them." [20] But the wicked are like the troubled sea; for it can't rest and its waters cast up mire and mud. [21] "There is no peace", says my God, "for the wicked."

## 58

[1] "Cry aloud! Don't spare! Lift up your voice like a trumpet! Declare to my people their disobedience, and to the house of Jacob their sins. [2] Yet they seek me daily, and delight to know my ways. As a nation that did righteousness, and didn't forsake the ordinance of their God, they ask of me righteous judgments. They delight to draw near to God. [3] 'Why have we fasted,' they say, 'and you don't see? Why have we afflicted our soul, and you don't notice?' "Behold, in the day of your fast you find pleasure, and oppress all your laborers. [4] Behold, you fast for strife and contention, and to strike with the fist of wickedness. You don't fast today so as to make your voice to be heard on high. [5] Is this the fast that I have chosen? A day for a man to humble his soul? Is it to bow down his head like a reed, and to spread sackcloth and ashes under himself? Will you call this a fast, and an acceptable day to Yahweh? [6] "Isn't this the fast that I have chosen: to release the bonds of wickedness, to undo the straps of the yoke, to let the oppressed go free, and that you break every yoke? [7] Isn't it to distribute your bread to the hungry, and that you bring the poor who are cast out to your house? When you see the naked, that you cover him; and that you not hide yourself from your own flesh? [8] Then your light will break out as the morning, and your healing will appear quickly; then your righteousness shall go before you, and Yahweh's glory will be your rear guard. [9] Then you will call, and Yahweh will answer. You will cry for help, and he will say, 'Here I am.' "If you take away from among you the yoke, finger pointing, and speaking wickedly; [10] and if you pour out your soul to the hungry, and satisfy the afflicted soul, then your light will rise in darkness, and your obscurity will be as the noonday; [11] and Yahweh will guide you continually, satisfy your soul in dry places, and make your bones strong. You will be like a watered garden, and like a spring of water whose waters don't fail. [12] Those who will be of you will build the old waste places. You will raise up the foundations of many generations. You will be called Repairer of the Breach, Restorer of Paths with Dwellings. [13] "If you turn away your foot from the Sabbath, from doing your pleasure on my holy day, and call the Sabbath a delight, and the holy of Yahweh honorable, and honor it, not doing your own ways, nor finding your own pleasure, nor speaking your own words, [14] then you will delight yourself in Yahweh, and I will make you to ride on the high places of the earth, and I will feed you with the heritage of Jacob your father;" for Yahweh's mouth has spoken it.

## 59

[1] Behold, Yahweh's hand is not shortened, that it can't save; nor his ear dull, that it can't hear. [2] But your iniquities have separated you and your God, and your sins have hidden his face from you, so that he will not hear. [3] For your hands are defiled with blood, and your fingers with iniquity. Your lips have spoken lies. Your tongue mutters wickedness. [4] No one sues in righteousness, and no one pleads in truth. They trust in vanity and speak lies. They conceive mischief and give birth to iniquity. [5] They hatch adders' eggs and weave the spider's web. He who eats of their eggs dies; and that which is crushed breaks out into a viper. [6] Their webs won't become garments. They won't cover themselves with their works. Their works are works of iniquity, and acts of violence are in their hands. [7] Their feet run to evil, and they hurry to shed innocent blood. Their thoughts are thoughts of iniquity. Desolation and destruction are in their paths. [8] They don't know the way of peace; and there is no justice in their ways. They have made crooked paths for themselves; whoever goes in them doesn't know peace. [9] Therefore justice is far from us, and righteousness doesn't overtake us. We look for light, but see darkness; for brightness, but we walk in obscurity. [10] We grope for the wall like the blind. Yes, we grope as those who have no eyes. We stumble at noon as if it were twilight. Among those who are strong, we are like dead men. [11] We all roar like bears and moan sadly like doves. We look for justice, but there is none, for salvation, but it is far off from us. [12] For our transgressions are multiplied before you, and our sins testify against us; for our transgressions are with us, and as for our iniquities, we know them: [13] transgressing and denying Yahweh, and turning away from following our God, speaking oppression and revolt, conceiving and uttering from the heart words of falsehood. [14] Justice is turned away backward, and righteousness stands far away; for truth has fallen in the street, and uprightness can't enter. [15] Yes, truth is lacking; and he who departs from evil makes himself a prey. Yahweh saw it, and it displeased him that there was no justice. [16] He saw that there was no man, and wondered that there was no intercessor. Therefore his own arm brought salvation to him; and his righteousness sustained him. [17] He put on righteousness as a breastplate, and a helmet of salvation on his head. He put on garments of vengeance for clothing, and was clad with zeal as a mantle. [18] According to their deeds, he will repay as appropriate: wrath to his adversaries, recompense to his enemies. He will repay the islands their due. [19] So they will fear Yahweh's name from the west, and his glory from the rising of the sun; for he will come as a rushing stream, which Yahweh's breath drives. [20] "A Redeemer will come to Zion, and to those who turn from disobedience in Jacob," says Yahweh.

[a] 57:9 Sheol is the place of the dead.

²¹"As for me, this is my covenant with them," says Yahweh. "My Spirit who is on you, and my words which I have put in your mouth shall not depart out of your mouth, nor out of the mouth of your offspring, nor out of the mouth of your offspring's offspring," says Yahweh, "from now on and forever."

## 60

¹"Arise, shine; for your light has come, and Yahweh's glory has risen on you! ² For behold, darkness will cover the earth, and thick darkness the peoples; but Yahweh will arise on you, and his glory shall be seen on you. ³ Nations will come to your light, and kings to the brightness of your rising. ⁴"Lift up your eyes all around, and see: they all gather themselves together. They come to you. Your sons will come from far away, and your daughters will be carried in arms. ⁵ Then you shall see and be radiant, and your heart will thrill and be enlarged; because the abundance of the sea will be turned to you. The wealth of the nations will come to you. ⁶ A multitude of camels will cover you, the dromedaries of Midian and Ephah. All from Sheba will come. They will bring gold and frankincense, and will proclaim the praises of Yahweh. ⁷ All the flocks of Kedar will be gathered together to you. The rams of Nebaioth will serve you. They will be accepted as offerings on my altar; and I will beautify my glorious house. ⁸"Who are these who fly as a cloud, and as the doves to their windows? ⁹ Surely the islands will wait for me, and the ships of Tarshish first, to bring your sons from far away, their silver and their gold with them, for the name of Yahweh your God, and for the Holy One of Israel, because he has glorified you. ¹⁰"Foreigners will build up your walls, and their kings will serve you; for in my wrath I struck you, but in my favor I have had mercy on you. ¹¹ Your gates also shall be open continually; they shall not be shut day nor night, that men may bring to you the wealth of the nations, and their kings led captive. ¹² For that nation and kingdom that will not serve you shall perish; yes, those nations shall be utterly wasted. ¹³"The glory of Lebanon shall come to you, the cypress tree, the pine, and the box tree together, to beautify the place of my sanctuary; and I will make the place of my feet glorious. ¹⁴ The sons of those who afflicted you will come bowing to you; and all those who despised you will bow themselves down at the soles of your feet. They will call you Yahweh's City, the Zion of the Holy One of Israel. ¹⁵"Whereas you have been forsaken and hated, so that no one passed through you, I will make you an eternal excellency, a joy of many generations. ¹⁶ You will also drink the milk of the nations, and will nurse from royal breasts. Then you will know that I, Yahweh, am your Savior, your Redeemer, the Mighty One of Jacob. ¹⁷ For bronze I will bring gold; for iron I will bring silver; for wood, bronze, and for stones, iron. I will also make peace your governor, and righteousness your ruler. ¹⁸ Violence shall no more be heard in your land, nor desolation or destruction within your borders; but you will call your walls Salvation, and your gates Praise. ¹⁹ The sun will be no more your light by day, nor will the brightness of the moon give light to you, but Yahweh will be your everlasting light, and your God will be your glory. ²⁰ Your sun will not go down any more, nor will your moon withdraw itself; for Yahweh will be your everlasting light, and the days of your mourning will end. ²¹ Then your people will all be righteous. They will inherit the land forever, the branch of my planting, the work of my hands, that I may be glorified. ²² The little one will become a thousand, and the small one a strong nation. I, Yahweh, will do this quickly in its time."

## 61

¹ The Lord Yahweh's Spirit is on me, because Yahweh has anointed me to preach good news to the humble. He has sent me to bind up the broken hearted, to proclaim liberty to the captives and release to those who are bound,ᵃ ² to proclaim the year of Yahweh's favor and the day of vengeance of our God, to comfort all who mourn, ³ to provide for those who mourn in Zion, to give to them a garland for ashes, the oil of joy for mourning, the garment of praise for the spirit of heaviness, that they may be called trees of righteousness, the planting of Yahweh, that he may be glorified. ⁴ They will rebuild the old ruins. They will raise up the former devastated places. They will repair the ruined cities that have been devastated for many generations. ⁵ Strangers will stand and feed your flocks. Foreigners will work your fields and your vineyards. ⁶ But you will be called Yahweh's priests. Men will call you the servants of our God. You will eat the wealth of the nations. You will boast in their glory. ⁷ Instead of your shame you will have double. Instead of dishonor, they will rejoice in their portion. Therefore in their land they will possess double. Everlasting joy will be to them. ⁸"For I, Yahweh, love justice. I hate robbery and iniquity. I will give them their reward in truth and I will make an everlasting covenant with them. ⁹ Their offspring will be known among the nations, and their offspring among the peoples. All who see them will acknowledge them, that they are the offspring which Yahweh has blessed." ¹⁰ I will greatly rejoice in Yahweh! My soul will be joyful in my God, for he has clothed me with the garments of salvation. He has covered me with the robe of righteousness, as a bridegroom decks himself with a garland and as a bride adorns herself with her jewels. ¹¹ For as the earth produces its bud, and as the garden causes the things that are sown in it to spring up, so the Lord Yahweh will cause righteousness and praise to spring up before all the nations.

## 62

¹ For Zion's sake I will not hold my peace, and for Jerusalem's sake I will not rest, until her righteousness shines out like the dawn, and her salvation like a burning lamp. ² The nations will see your righteousness, and all kings your glory. You will be called by a new name, which Yahweh's mouth will name. ³ You will also be a crown of beauty in Yahweh's hand, and a royal diadem in your God's hand. ⁴ You will not be called Forsaken any more, nor will your land be called Desolate any more; but you will be called Hephzibah,ᵇ and your land Beulah;ᶜ for Yahweh delights in you, and your land will be married. ⁵ For as a young man marries a virgin, so your sons will marry you. As a bridegroom rejoices over his bride, so your God will rejoice over you. ⁶ I have set watchmen on your walls, Jerusalem. They will never be silent day nor night. You who call on Yahweh, take no rest, ⁷ and give him no rest until he establishes, and until he makes Jerusalem a praise in the earth. ⁸ Yahweh has sworn by his right hand, and by the arm of his strength, "Surely I will no more give your grain to be food for your enemies, and foreigners will not drink your new wine, for which you have labored, ⁹ but those who have harvested it will eat it, and praise Yahweh. Those who have gathered it will drink it in the courts of my sanctuary." ¹⁰ Go through, go through the gates! Prepare the way of the people! Build up, build up the highway! Gather out the stones! Lift up a banner for the peoples. ¹¹ Behold, Yahweh has proclaimed to the end of the earth: "Say to the daughter of Zion, 'Behold, your salvation comes! Behold, his reward is with him, and his recompense before him!'" ¹² They will call them "The Holy People, Yahweh's Redeemed". You will be called "Sought Out, A City Not Forsaken".

## 63

¹ Who is this who comes from Edom, with dyed garments from Bozrah? Who is this who is glorious in his clothing, marching in the greatness of his strength? "It is I who speak in righteousness, mighty to save." ² Why is your clothing red, and your garments like him who treads in the wine vat? ³"I have trodden the wine press alone. Of the peoples, no one was with me. Yes, I trod them in my anger and trampled them in my wrath. Their lifeblood is sprinkled on my garments, and I have stained all my clothing. ⁴ For the day of vengeance was in my heart, and the year of my redeemed has come. ⁵ I looked, and there was no one to help; and I wondered that there was no one to uphold. Therefore my own arm brought salvation to me. My own wrath upheld me. ⁶ I trod down the peoples in my anger and made them drunk in my wrath. I poured their lifeblood out on the earth." ⁷ I will tell of the loving kindnesses of Yahweh and the praises of Yahweh, according to all that Yahweh has given to us, and the great goodness toward the house of Israel, which he has given to them according to his mercies, and according to the multitude of his loving kindnesses. ⁸ For he said, "Surely, they are my people, children who will not deal falsely;" so he became their Savior. ⁹ In all their affliction he was afflicted, and the angel of his presence saved them. In his love and in his pity he redeemed them. He bore them, and carried them all the days of old. ¹⁰ But they rebelled and grieved his Holy Spirit. Therefore he turned and became their enemy, and he himself fought against them. ¹¹ Then he remembered the days of old, Moses and his people, saying, "Where is he who brought them up out of the sea with the shepherds of his flock? Where is he who put his Holy Spirit among them?" ¹² Who caused his glorious arm to be at Moses' right hand? Who divided the waters before them, to make himself an everlasting name? ¹³ Who led them through the depths, like a horse in the wilderness, so that they didn't stumble? ¹⁴ As the livestock that go down into the valley, Yahweh's Spirit caused them to rest. So you led your people to make yourself a glorious name. ¹⁵ Look down from heaven, and see from the habitation of your holiness and of your glory. Where are your zeal and your mighty acts? The yearning of your heart and your compassion is restrained toward me. ¹⁶ For you are our Father, though Abraham doesn't know us, and Israel does not acknowledge us. You, Yahweh, are our Father. Our Redeemer from everlasting is your name. ¹⁷ O Yahweh, why do you make us wander from your ways, and harden our heart from your fear? Return for your servants' sake, the tribes of your inheritance. ¹⁸ Your holy people possessed it but a little while. Our adversaries have trodden down your sanctuary. ¹⁹ We have

---

ᵃ 61:1 LXX and DSS add: recovery of sight to the blind

ᵇ 62:4 Hephzibah means "I delight in her".

ᶜ 62:4 Beulah means "married"

become like those over whom you never ruled, like those who were not called by your name.

## 64

¹ Oh that you would tear the heavens, that you would come down, that the mountains might quake at your presence— ² as when fire kindles the brushwood, and the fire causes the water to boil. Make your name known to your adversaries, that the nations may tremble at your presence! ³ When you did awesome things which we didn't look for, you came down, and the mountains quaked at your presence. ⁴ For from of old men have not heard, nor perceived by the ear, nor has the eye seen a God besides you, who works for him who waits for him. ⁵ You meet him who rejoices and does righteousness, those who remember you in your ways. Behold, you were angry, and we sinned. We have been in sin for a long time. Shall we be saved? ⁶ For we have all become like one who is unclean, and all our righteousness is like a polluted garment. We all fade like a leaf; and our iniquities, like the wind, take us away. ⁷ There is no one who calls on your name, who stirs himself up to take hold of you; for you have hidden your face from us, and have consumed us by means of our iniquities. ⁸ But now, Yahweh, you are our Father. We are the clay and you our potter. We all are the work of your hand. ⁹ Don't be furious, Yahweh. Don't remember iniquity forever. Look and see, we beg you, we are all your people. ¹⁰ Your holy cities have become a wilderness. Zion has become a wilderness, Jerusalem a desolation. ¹¹ Our holy and our beautiful house where our fathers praised you is burned with fire. All our pleasant places are laid waste. ¹² Will you hold yourself back for these things, Yahweh? Will you keep silent and punish us very severely?

## 65

¹"I am inquired of by those who didn't ask. I am found by those who didn't seek me. I said, 'See me, see me,' to a nation that was not called by my name. ² I have spread out my hands all day to a rebellious people, who walk in a way that is not good, after their own thoughts; ³ a people who provoke me to my face continually, sacrificing in gardens, and burning incense on bricks; ⁴ who sit among the graves, and spend nights in secret places; who eat pig's meat, and broth of abominable things is in their vessels; ⁵ who say, 'Stay by yourself, don't come near to me, for I am holier than you.' These are smoke in my nose, a fire that burns all day. ⁶"Behold, it is written before me: I will not keep silence, but will repay, yes, I will repay into their bosom ⁷ your own iniquities and the iniquities of your fathers together", says Yahweh, "who have burned incense on the mountains, and blasphemed me on the hills. Therefore I will first measure their work into their bosom." ⁸ Yahweh says, "As the new wine is found in the cluster, and one says, 'Don't destroy it, for a blessing is in it:' so I will do for my servants' sake, that I may not destroy them all. ⁹ I will bring offspring out of Jacob, and out of Judah an inheritor of my mountains. My chosen will inherit it, and my servants will dwell there. ¹⁰ Sharon will be a fold of flocks, and the valley of Achor a place for herds to lie down in, for my people who have sought me. ¹¹"But you who forsake Yahweh, who forget my holy mountain, who prepare a table for Fortune, and who fill up mixed wine to Destiny; ¹² I will destine you to the sword, and you will all bow down to the slaughter; because when I called, you didn't answer. When I spoke, you didn't listen; but you did that which was evil in my eyes, and chose that in which I didn't delight." ¹³ Therefore the Lord Yahweh says, "Behold, my servants will eat, but you will be hungry; behold, my servants will drink, but you will be thirsty. Behold, my servants will rejoice, but you will be disappointed. ¹⁴ Behold, my servants will sing for joy of heart, but you will cry for sorrow of heart, and will wail for anguish of spirit. ¹⁵ You will leave your name for a curse to my chosen, and the Lord Yahweh will kill you. He will call his servants by another name, ¹⁶ so that he who blesses himself in the earth will bless himself in the God of truth; and he who swears in the earth will swear by the God of truth; because the former troubles are forgotten, and because they are hidden from my eyes. ¹⁷ "For, behold, I create new heavens and a new earth; and the former things will not be remembered, nor come into mind. ¹⁸ But be glad and rejoice forever in that which I create; for, behold, I create Jerusalem to be a delight, and her people a joy. ¹⁹ I will rejoice in Jerusalem, and delight in my people; and the voice of weeping and the voice of crying will be heard in her no more. ²⁰"No more will there be an infant who only lives a few days, nor an old man who has not filled his days; for the child will die one hundred years old, and the sinner being one hundred years old will be accursed. ²¹ They will build houses and inhabit them. They will plant vineyards and eat their fruit. ²² They will not build and another inhabit. They will not plant and another eat; for the days of my people will be like the days of a tree, and my chosen will long enjoy the work of their hands. ²³ They will not labor in vain nor give birth for calamity; for they are the

offspring of Yahweh's blessed and their descendants with them. ²⁴ It will happen that before they call, I will answer; and while they are yet speaking, I will hear. ²⁵ The wolf and the lamb will feed together. The lion will eat straw like the ox. Dust will be the serpent's food. They will not hurt nor destroy in all my holy mountain," says Yahweh.

## 66

¹ Yahweh says: "Heaven is my throne, and the earth is my footstool. What kind of house will you build to me? Where will I rest? ² For my hand has made all these things, and so all these things came to be," says Yahweh: "but I will look to this man, even to he who is poor and of a contrite spirit, and who trembles at my word. ³ He who kills an ox is as he who kills a man; he who sacrifices a lamb, as he who breaks a dog's neck; he who offers an offering, as he who offers pig's blood; he who burns frankincense, as he who blesses an idol. Yes, they have chosen their own ways, and their soul delights in their abominations. ⁴ I also will choose their delusions, and will bring their fears on them, because when I called, no one answered; when I spoke, they didn't listen, but they did that which was evil in my eyes, and chose that in which I didn't delight." ⁵ Hear Yahweh's word, you who tremble at his word: "Your brothers who hate you, who cast you out for my name's sake, have said, 'Let Yahweh be glorified, that we may see your joy;' but it is those who shall be disappointed. ⁶ A voice of tumult from the city, a voice from the temple, a voice of Yahweh that repays his enemies what they deserve. ⁷"Before she travailed, she gave birth. Before her pain came, she delivered a son. ⁸ Who has heard of such a thing? Who has seen such things? Shall a land be born in one day? Shall a nation be born at once? For as soon as Zion travailed, she gave birth to her children. ⁹ Shall I bring to the birth, and not cause to be delivered?" says Yahweh. "Shall I who cause to give birth shut the womb?" says your God. ¹⁰"Rejoice with Jerusalem, and be glad for her, all you who love her. Rejoice for joy with her, all you who mourn over her; ¹¹ that you may nurse and be satisfied at the comforting breasts; that you may drink deeply, and be delighted with the abundance of her glory." ¹² For Yahweh says, "Behold, I will extend peace to her like a river, and the glory of the nations like an overflowing stream, and you will nurse. You will be carried on her side, and will be dandled on her knees. ¹³ As one whom his mother comforts, so I will comfort you. You will be comforted in Jerusalem." ¹⁴ You will see it, and your heart shall rejoice, and your bones will flourish like the tender grass. Yahweh's hand will be known among his servants; and he will have indignation against his enemies. ¹⁵ For, behold, Yahweh will come with fire, and his chariots will be like the whirlwind; to render his anger with fierceness, and his rebuke with flames of fire. ¹⁶ For Yahweh will execute judgment by fire and by his sword on all flesh; and those slain by Yahweh will be many. ¹⁷"Those who sanctify themselves and purify themselves to go to the gardens, following one in the middle, eating pig's meat, abominable things, and the mouse, they shall come to an end together," says Yahweh. ¹⁸"For I know their works and their thoughts. The time comes that I will gather all nations and languages, and they will come, and will see my glory. ¹⁹ "I will set a sign among them, and I will send those who escape of them to the nations, to Tarshish, Pul, and Lud, who draw the bow, to Tubal and Javan, to far-away islands, who have not heard my fame, nor have seen my glory; and they shall declare my glory among the nations. ²⁰ They shall bring all your brothers out of all the nations for an offering to Yahweh, on horses, in chariots, in litters, on mules, and on camels, to my holy mountain Jerusalem, says Yahweh, as the children of Israel bring their offering in a clean vessel into Yahweh's house. ²¹ Of them I will also select priests and Levites," says Yahweh. ²²"For as the new heavens and the new earth, which I will make, shall remain before me," says Yahweh, "so your offspring and your name shall remain. ²³ It shall happen that from one new moon to another, and from one Sabbath to another, all flesh will come to worship before me," says Yahweh. ²⁴ "They will go out, and look at the dead bodies of the men who have transgressed against me; for their worm will not die, nor will their fire be quenched, and they will be loathsome to all mankind."

# The Book of Jeremiah

## 1

¹ The words of Jeremiah the son of Hilkiah, one of the priests who were in Anathoth in the land of Benjamin. ² Yahweh'sᵃ word came to him in the days of Josiah the son of Amon, king of Judah, in the thirteenth year of his reign. ³ It came also in the days of Jehoiakim the son of Josiah, king of Judah, to the end of the eleventh year of Zedekiah, the son of Josiah, king of Judah, to the carrying away of Jerusalem captive in the fifth month. ⁴ Now Yahweh's word came to me, saying, ⁵"Before I

ᵃ 1:2 "Yahweh" is God's proper Name, sometimes | rendered "LORD" (all caps) in other translations.

formed you in the womb, I knew you. Before you were born, I sanctified you. I have appointed you a prophet to the nations." ⁶ Then I said, "Ah, Lordᵃ Yahweh! Behold,ᵇ I don't know how to speak; for I am a child." ⁷ But Yahweh said to me, "Don't say, 'I am a child;' for you must go to whomever I send you, and you must say whatever I command you. ⁸ Don't be afraid because of them, for I am with you to rescue you," says Yahweh. ⁹ Then Yahweh stretched out his hand and touched my mouth. Then Yahweh said to me, "Behold, I have put my words in your mouth. ¹⁰ Behold, I have today set you over the nations and over the kingdoms, to uproot and to tear down, to destroy and to overthrow, to build and to plant." ¹¹ Moreover Yahweh's word came to me, saying, "Jeremiah, what do you see?" I said, "I see a branch of an almond tree." ¹² Then Yahweh said to me, "You have seen well; for I watch over my word to perform it." ¹³ Yahweh's word came to me the second time, saying, "What do you see?" I said, "I see a boiling cauldron; and it is tipping away from the north." ¹⁴ Then Yahweh said to me, "Out of the north, evil will break out on all the inhabitants of the land. ¹⁵ For behold, I will call all the families of the kingdoms of the north," says Yahweh. "They will come, and they will each set his throne at the entrance of the gates of Jerusalem, and against all its walls all around, and against all the cities of Judah. ¹⁶ I will utter my judgments against them concerning all their wickedness, in that they have forsaken me, and have burned incense to other gods, and worshiped the works of their own hands. ¹⁷"You therefore put your belt on your waist, arise, and say to them all that I command you. Don't be dismayed at them, lest I dismay you before them. ¹⁸ For behold, I have made you today a fortified city, an iron pillar, and bronze walls against the whole land— against the kings of Judah, against its princes, against its priests, and against the people of the land. ¹⁹ They will fight against you, but they will not prevail against you; for I am with you", says Yahweh, "to rescue you."

## 2

¹ Yahweh's word came to me, saying, ²"Go and proclaim in the ears of Jerusalem, saying, 'Yahweh says, "I remember for you the kindness of your youth, your love as a bride, how you went after me in the wilderness, in a land that was not sown. ³ Israel was holiness to Yahweh, the first fruits of his increase. All who devour him will be held guilty. Evil will come on them,"' says Yahweh." ⁴ Hear Yahweh's word, O house of Jacob, and all the families of the house of Israel! ⁵ Yahweh says, "What unrighteousness have your fathers found in me, that they have gone far from me, and have walked after worthless vanity, and have become worthless? ⁶ They didn't say, 'Where is Yahweh who brought us up out of the land of Egypt, who led us through the wilderness, through a land of deserts and of pits, through a land of drought and of the shadow of death, through a land that no one passed through, and where no man lived?' ⁷ I brought you into a plentiful land to eat its fruit and its goodness; but when you entered, you defiled my land, and made my heritage an abomination. ⁸ The priests didn't say, 'Where is Yahweh?' and those who handle the law didn't know me. The rulers also transgressed against me, and the prophets prophesied by Baal and followed things that do not profit. ⁹"Therefore I will yet contend with you," says Yahweh, "and I will contend with your children's children. ¹⁰ For pass over to the islands of Kittim, and see. Send to Kedar, and consider diligently, and see if there has been such a thing. ¹¹ Has a nation changed its gods, which really are no gods? But my people have changed their glory for that which doesn't profit. ¹²"Be astonished, you heavens, at this and be horribly afraid. Be very desolate," says Yahweh. ¹³"For my people have committed two evils: they have forsaken me, the spring of living waters, and cut out cisterns for themselves: broken cisterns that can't hold water. ¹⁴ Is Israel a slave? Is he born into slavery? Why has he become a captive? ¹⁵ The young lions have roared at him and raised their voices. They have made his land waste. His cities are burned up, without inhabitant. ¹⁶ The children also of Memphis and Tahpanhes have broken the crown of your head. ¹⁷"Haven't you brought this on yourself, in that you have forsaken Yahweh your God,ᶜ when he led you by the way? ¹⁸ Now what do you gain by going to Egypt, to drink the waters of the Shihor? Or why do you go on the way to Assyria, to drink the waters of the River?ᵈ ¹⁹"Your own wickedness will correct you, and your backsliding will rebuke you. Know therefore and see that it is an evil and bitter thing, that you have forsaken Yahweh your God, and that my fear is not in you," says the Lord, Yahweh of Armies. ²⁰"For long ago I broke off your yoke, and burst your bonds. You said, 'I will not serve;' for on every high hill and under every green tree you bowed yourself, playing the prostitute. ²¹ Yet I had planted you a noble vine, a pure and faithful

seed. How then have you turned into the degenerate branches of a foreign vine to me? ²² For though you wash yourself with lye, and use much soap, yet your iniquity is marked before me," says the Lord Yahweh. ²³"How can you say, 'I am not defiled. I have not gone after the Baals'? See your way in the valley. Know what you have done. You are a swift dromedary traversing her ways, ²⁴ a wild donkey used to the wilderness, that sniffs the wind in her craving. When she is in heat, who can turn her away? All those who seek her will not weary themselves. In her month, they will find her. ²⁵"Keep your feet from being bare, and your throat from thirst. But you said, 'It is in vain. No, for I have loved strangers, and I will go after them.' ²⁶ As the thief is ashamed when he is found, so the house of Israel is ashamed— they, their kings, their princes, their priests, and their prophets, ²⁷ who tell wood, 'You are my father,' and a stone, 'You have given birth to me,' for they have turned their back to me, and not their face, but in the time of their trouble they will say, 'Arise, and save us!' ²⁸"But where are your gods that you have made for yourselves? Let them arise, if they can save you in the time of your trouble, for you have as many gods as you have towns, O Judah. ²⁹"Why will you contend with me? You all have transgressed against me," says Yahweh. ³⁰"I have struck your children in vain. They received no correction. Your own sword has devoured your prophets, like a destroying lion. ³¹ Generation, consider Yahweh's word. Have I been a wilderness to Israel? Or a land of thick darkness? Why do my people say, 'We have broken loose. We will come to you no more'? ³²"Can a virgin forget her ornaments, or a bride her attire? Yet my people have forgotten me for days without number. ³³ How well you prepare your way to seek love! Therefore you have even taught the wicked women your ways. ³⁴ Also the blood of the souls of the innocent poor is found in your skirts. You didn't find them breaking in, but it is because of all these things. ³⁵"Yet you said, 'I am innocent. Surely his anger has turned away from me.' "Behold, I will judge you, because you say, 'I have not sinned.' ³⁶ Why do you go about so much to change your ways? You will be ashamed of Egypt also, as you were ashamed of Assyria. ³⁷ You will also leave that place with your hands on your head; for Yahweh has rejected those in whom you trust, and you won't prosper with them.

## 3

¹"They say, 'If a man puts away his wife, and she goes from him, and becomes another man's, should he return to her again?' Wouldn't that land be greatly polluted? But you have played the prostitute with many lovers; yet return again to me," says Yahweh. ²"Lift up your eyes to the bare heights, and see! Where have you not been lain with? You have sat waiting for them by the road, as an Arabian in the wilderness. You have polluted the land with your prostitution and with your wickedness. ³ Therefore the showers have been withheld and there has been no latter rain; yet you have had a prostitute's forehead and you refused to be ashamed. ⁴ Will you not from this time cry to me, 'My Father, you are the guide of my youth!'? ⁵"Will he retain his anger forever? Will he keep it to the end?' Behold, you have spoken and have done evil things, and have had your way." ⁶ Moreover, Yahweh said to me in the days of Josiah the king, "Have you seen that which backsliding Israel has done? She has gone up on every high mountain and under every green tree, and has played the prostitute there. ⁷ I said after she had done all these things, 'She will return to me;' but she didn't return, and her treacherous sister Judah saw it. ⁸ I saw when, for this very cause, that backsliding Israel had committed adultery, I had put her away and given her a certificate of divorce, yet treacherous Judah, her sister, had no fear, but she also went and played the prostitute. ⁹ Because she took her prostitution lightly, the land was polluted, and she committed adultery with stones and with wood. ¹⁰ Yet for all this her treacherous sister, Judah, has not returned to me with her whole heart, but only in pretense," says Yahweh. ¹¹ Yahweh said to me, "Backsliding Israel has shown herself more righteous than treacherous Judah. ¹² Go, and proclaim these words toward the north, and say, 'Return, you backsliding Israel,' says Yahweh; 'I will not look in anger on you, for I am merciful,' says Yahweh. 'I will not keep anger forever. ¹³ Only acknowledge your iniquity, that you have transgressed against Yahweh your God, and have scattered your ways to the strangers under every green tree, and you have not obeyed my voice,'" says Yahweh. ¹⁴"Return, backsliding children," says Yahweh, "for I am a husband to you. I will take one of you from a city, and two from a family, and I will bring you to Zion. ¹⁵ I will give you shepherds according to my heart, who will feed you with knowledge and understanding. ¹⁶ It will come to pass, when you are multiplied and increased in the land in those days," says Yahweh, "they will no longer say, 'the ark of Yahweh's

---

ᵃ 1:6 The word translated "Lord" is "Adonai."
ᵇ 1:6 "Behold", from "הִנֵּה", means look at, take notice,

observe, see, or gaze at. It is often used as an interjection.

ᶜ 2:17 The Hebrew word rendered "God" is "אֱלֹהִים" (Elohim).
ᵈ 2:18 i.e., the Euphrates River

covenant!' It will not come to mind. They won't remember it. They won't miss it, nor will another be made. [17] At that time they will call Jerusalem 'Yahweh's Throne;' and all the nations will be gathered to it, to Yahweh's name, to Jerusalem. They will no longer walk after the stubbornness of their evil heart. [18] In those days the house of Judah will walk with the house of Israel, and they will come together out of the land of the north to the land that I gave for an inheritance to your fathers. [19] "But I said, 'How I desire to put you among the children, and give you a pleasant land, a goodly heritage of the armies of the nations!' and I said, 'You shall call me "My Father", and shall not turn away from following me.' [20] "Surely as a wife treacherously departs from her husband, so you have dealt treacherously with me, house of Israel," says Yahweh. [21] A voice is heard on the bare heights, the weeping and the petitions of the children of Israel; because they have perverted their way, they have forgotten Yahweh their God. [22] Return, you backsliding children, and I will heal your backsliding. "Behold, we have come to you; for you are Yahweh our God. [23] Truly help from the hills, the tumult on the mountains, is in vain. Truly the salvation of Israel is in Yahweh our God. [24] But the shameful thing has devoured the labor of our fathers from our youth, their flocks and their herds, their sons and their daughters. [25] Let us lie down in our shame, and let our confusion cover us; for we have sinned against Yahweh our God, we and our fathers, from our youth even to this day. We have not obeyed Yahweh our God's voice."

## 4

[1] "If you will return, Israel," says Yahweh, "if you will return to me, and if you will put away your abominations out of my sight; then you will not be removed; [2] and you will swear, 'As Yahweh lives,' in truth, in justice, and in righteousness. The nations will bless themselves in him, and they will glory in him." [3] For Yahweh says to the men of Judah and to Jerusalem, "Break up your fallow ground, and don't sow among thorns. [4] Circumcise yourselves to Yahweh, and take away the foreskins of your heart, you men of Judah and inhabitants of Jerusalem; lest my wrath go out like fire, and burn so that no one can quench it, because of the evil of your doings. [5] Declare in Judah, and publish in Jerusalem; and say, 'Blow the trumpet in the land!' Cry aloud and say, 'Assemble yourselves! Let's go into the fortified cities!' [6] Set up a standard toward Zion. Flee for safety! Don't wait; for I will bring evil from the north, and a great destruction." [7] A lion has gone up from his thicket, and a destroyer of nations. He is on his way. He has gone out from his place, to make your land desolate, that your cities be laid waste, without inhabitant. [8] For this, clothe yourself with sackcloth, lament and wail; for the fierce anger of Yahweh hasn't turned back from us. [9] "It will happen at that day," says Yahweh, "that the heart of the king will perish, along with the heart of the princes. The priests will be astonished, and the prophets will wonder." [10] Then I said, "Ah, Lord Yahweh! Surely you have greatly deceived this people and Jerusalem, saying, 'You will have peace;' whereas the sword reaches to the heart." [11] At that time it will be said to this people and to Jerusalem, "A hot wind blows from the bare heights in the wilderness toward the daughter of my people, not to winnow, nor to cleanse. [12] A full wind from these will come for me. Now I will also utter judgments against them." [13] Behold, he will come up as clouds, and his chariots will be as the whirlwind. His horses are swifter than eagles. Woe to us! For we are ruined. [14] Jerusalem, wash your heart from wickedness, that you may be saved. How long will your evil thoughts lodge within you? [15] For a voice declares from Dan, and publishes evil from the hills of Ephraim: [16] "Tell the nations, behold, publish against Jerusalem, 'Watchers come from a far country, and raise their voice against the cities of Judah. [17] As keepers of a field, they are against her all around, because she has been rebellious against me,'" says Yahweh. [18] "Your way and your doings have brought these things to you. This is your wickedness, for it is bitter, for it reaches to your heart." [19] My anguish, my anguish! I am pained at my very heart! My heart trembles within me. I can't hold my peace, because you have heard, O my soul, the sound of the trumpet, the alarm of war. [20] Destruction on destruction is decreed, for the whole land is laid waste. Suddenly my tents are destroyed, and my curtains gone in a moment. [21] How long will I see the standard and hear the sound of the trumpet? [22] "For my people are foolish. They don't know me. They are foolish children, and they have no understanding. They are skillful in doing evil, but they don't know how to do good." [23] I saw the earth and, behold, it was waste and void, and the heavens, and they had no light. [24] I saw the mountains, and behold, they trembled, and all the hills moved back and forth. [25] I saw, and behold, there was no man, and all the birds of the sky had fled. [26] I saw, and behold, the fruitful field was a wilderness, and all its cities were broken down at the presence of Yahweh, before his fierce anger. [27] For Yahweh says, "The whole land will be a desolation; yet I will not make a full end. [28] For this the earth will mourn, and the heavens above be black, because I have spoken it. I have planned it, and I have not repented, neither will

I turn back from it." [29] Every city flees for the noise of the horsemen and archers. They go into the thickets and climb up on the rocks. Every city is forsaken, and not a man dwells therein. [30] You, when you are made desolate, what will you do? Though you clothe yourself with scarlet, though you deck yourself with ornaments of gold, though you enlarge your eyes with makeup, you make yourself beautiful in vain. Your lovers despise you. They seek your life. [31] For I have heard a voice as of a woman in travail, the anguish as of her who gives birth to her first child, the voice of the daughter of Zion, who gasps for breath, who spreads her hands, saying, "Woe is me now! For my soul faints before the murderers."

## 5

[1] "Run back and forth through the streets of Jerusalem, and see now, and know, and seek in its wide places, if you can find a man, if there is anyone who does justly, who seeks truth, then I will pardon her. [2] Though they say, 'As Yahweh lives,' surely they swear falsely." [3] O Yahweh, don't your eyes look on truth? You have stricken them, but they were not grieved. You have consumed them, but they have refused to receive correction. They have made their faces harder than a rock. They have refused to return. [4] Then I said, "Surely these are poor. They are foolish; for they don't know Yahweh's way, nor the law of their God. [5] I will go to the great men and will speak to them, for they know the way of Yahweh, and the law of their God." But these with one accord have broken the yoke, and burst the bonds. [6] Therefore a lion out of the forest will kill them. A wolf of the evenings will destroy them. A leopard will watch against their cities. Everyone who goes out there will be torn in pieces, because their transgressions are many and their backsliding has increased. [7] "How can I pardon you? Your children have forsaken me, and sworn by what are no gods. When I had fed them to the full, they committed adultery, and assembled themselves in troops at the prostitutes' houses. [8] They were as fed horses roaming at large. Everyone neighed after his neighbor's wife. [9] Shouldn't I punish them for these things?" says Yahweh. "Shouldn't my soul be avenged on such a nation as this? [10] "Go up on her walls, and destroy, but don't make a full end. Take away her branches, for they are not Yahweh's. [11] For the house of Israel and the house of Judah have dealt very treacherously against me," says Yahweh. [12] They have denied Yahweh, and said, "It is not he. Evil won't come on us. We won't see sword or famine. [13] The prophets will become wind, and the word is not in them. Thus it will be done to them." [14] Therefore Yahweh, the God of Armies says, "Because you speak this word, behold, I will make my words in your mouth fire, and this people wood, and it will devour them. [15] Behold, I will bring a nation on you from far away, house of Israel," says Yahweh. "It is a mighty nation. It is an ancient nation, a nation whose language you don't know and don't understand what they say. [16] Their quiver is an open tomb. They are all mighty men. [17] They will eat up your harvest and your bread, which your sons and your daughters should eat. They will eat up your flocks and your herds. They will eat up your vines and your fig trees. They will beat down your fortified cities in which you trust with the sword. [18] "But even in those days," says Yahweh, "I will not make a full end of you. [19] It will happen when you say, 'Why has Yahweh our God done all these things to us?' Then you shall say to them, 'Just as you have forsaken me and served foreign gods in your land, so you will serve strangers in a land that is not yours.' [20] "Declare this in the house of Jacob, and publish it in Judah, saying, [21] "Hear this now, foolish people without understanding, who have eyes, and don't see, who have ears, and don't hear: [22] Don't you fear me?' says Yahweh. 'Won't you tremble at my presence, who have placed the sand for the bound of the sea by a perpetual decree, that it can't pass it? Though its waves toss themselves, yet they can't prevail. Though they roar, they still can't pass over it.' [23] "But this people has a revolting and a rebellious heart. They have revolted and gone. [24] They don't say in their heart, 'Let's now fear Yahweh our God, who gives rain, both the former and the latter, in its season, who preserves to us the appointed weeks of the harvest.' [25] "Your iniquities have turned away these things, and your sins have withheld good from you. [26] For wicked men are found among my people. They watch, as fowlers lie in wait. They set a trap. They catch men. [27] As a cage is full of birds, so are their houses full of deceit. Therefore they have become great, and grew rich. [28] They have grown fat. They shine; yes, they excel in deeds of wickedness. They don't plead the cause, the cause of the fatherless, that they may prosper; and they don't defend the rights of the needy. [29] "Shouldn't I punish for these things?" says Yahweh. "Shouldn't my soul be avenged on such a nation as this? [30] "An astonishing and horrible thing has happened in the land. [31] The prophets prophesy falsely, and the priests rule by their own authority; and my people love to have it so. What will you do in the end of it?

## 6

[1] "Flee for safety, you children of Benjamin, out of the middle of Jerusalem! Blow the trumpet in Tekoa and raise up a signal on Beth

Haccherem, for evil looks out from the north with a great destruction. [2] I will cut off the beautiful and delicate one, the daughter of Zion. [3] Shepherds with their flocks will come to her. They will pitch their tents against her all around. They will feed everyone in his place." [4]"Prepare war against her! Arise! Let's go up at noon. Woe to us! For the day declines, for the shadows of the evening are stretched out. [5] Arise! Let's go up by night, and let's destroy her palaces." [6] For Yahweh of Armies said, "Cut down trees, and cast up a mound against Jerusalem. This is the city to be visited. She is filled with oppression within herself. [7] As a well produces its waters, so she produces her wickedness. Violence and destruction is heard in her. Sickness and wounds are continually before me. [8] Be instructed, Jerusalem, lest my soul be alienated from you, lest I make you a desolation, an uninhabited land." [9] Yahweh of Armies says, "They will thoroughly glean the remnant of Israel like a vine. Turn again your hand as a grape gatherer into the baskets." [10] To whom should I speak and testify, that they may hear? Behold, their ear is uncircumcised, and they can't listen. Behold, Yahweh's word has become a reproach to them. They have no delight in it. [11] Therefore I am full of Yahweh's wrath. I am weary with holding it in. "Pour it out on the children in the street, and on the assembly of young men together; for even the husband with the wife will be taken, the aged with him who is full of days. [12] Their houses will be turned to others, their fields and their wives together; for I will stretch out my hand on the inhabitants of the land, says Yahweh. [13]"For from their least even to their greatest, everyone is given to covetousness. From the prophet even to the priest, everyone deals falsely. [14] They have healed also the hurt of my people superficially, saying, 'Peace, peace!' when there is no peace. [15] Were they ashamed when they had committed abomination? No, they were not at all ashamed, neither could they blush. Therefore they will fall among those who fall. When I visit them, they will be cast down," says Yahweh. [16] Yahweh says, "Stand in the ways and see, and ask for the old paths, 'Where is the good way?' and walk in it, and you will find rest for your souls. But they said, 'We will not walk in it.' [17] I set watchmen over you, saying, 'Listen to the sound of the trumpet!' But they said, 'We will not listen!' [18] Therefore hear, you nations, and know, congregation, what is among them. [19] Hear, earth! Behold, I will bring evil on this people, even the fruit of their thoughts, because they have not listened to my words; and as for my law, they have rejected it. [20] To what purpose does frankincense from Sheba come to me, and the sweet cane from a far country? Your burnt offerings are not acceptable, and your sacrifices are not pleasing to me." [21] Therefore Yahweh says, "Behold, I will lay stumbling blocks before this people. The fathers and the sons together will stumble against them. The neighbor and his friend will perish." [22] Yahweh says, "Behold, a people comes from the north country. A great nation will be stirred up from the uttermost parts of the earth. [23] They take hold of bow and spear. They are cruel, and have no mercy. Their voice roars like the sea, and they ride on horses, everyone set in array, as a man to the battle, against you, daughter of Zion." [24] We have heard its report. Our hands become feeble. Anguish has taken hold of us, and pains as of a woman in labor. [25] Don't go out into the field or walk by the way; for the sword of the enemy and terror are on every side. [26] Daughter of my people, clothe yourself with sackcloth, and wallow in ashes! Mourn, as for an only son, most bitter lamentation, for the destroyer will suddenly come on us. [27]"I have made you a tester of metals and a fortress among my people, that you may know and try their way. [28] They are all grievous rebels, going around to slander. They are bronze and iron. All of them deal corruptly. [29] The bellows blow fiercely. The lead is consumed in the fire. In vain they go on refining, for the wicked are not plucked away. [30] Men will call them rejected silver, because Yahweh has rejected them."

# 7

[1] The word that came to Jeremiah from Yahweh, saying, [2]"Stand in the gate of Yahweh's house, and proclaim this word there, and say, 'Hear Yahweh's word, all you of Judah, who enter in at these gates to worship Yahweh.'" [3] Yahweh of Armies, the God of Israel says, "Amend your ways and your doings, and I will cause you to dwell in this place. [4] Don't trust in lying words, saying, 'Yahweh's temple, Yahweh's temple, Yahweh's temple, are these.' [5] For if you thoroughly amend your ways and your doings, if you thoroughly execute justice between a man and his neighbor; [6] if you don't oppress the foreigner, the fatherless, and the widow, and don't shed innocent blood in this place, and don't walk after other gods to your own hurt, [7] then I will cause you to dwell in this place, in the land that I gave to your fathers, from of old even forever more. [8] Behold, you trust in lying words that can't profit. [9] Will you steal, murder, commit adultery, swear falsely, burn incense to Baal, and walk after other gods that you have not known, [10] then come and stand before me in this house, which is called by my name, and say, 'We are delivered,' that you may do all these abominations? [11] Has this house, which is called by my name, become a den of robbers in your eyes? Behold, I myself have seen it," says Yahweh. [12]"But go now to my place which was in Shiloh, where I caused my name to dwell at the first, and see what I did to it for the wickedness of my people Israel. [13] Now, because you have done all these works," says Yahweh, "and I spoke to you, rising up early and speaking, but you didn't hear; and I called you, but you didn't answer; [14] therefore I will do to the house which is called by my name, in which you trust, and to the place which I gave to you and to your fathers, as I did to Shiloh. [15] I will cast you out of my sight, as I have cast out all your brothers, even the whole offspring[a] of Ephraim. [16]"Therefore don't pray for this people. Don't lift up a cry or prayer for them or make intercession to me; for I will not hear you. [17] Don't you see what they do in the cities of Judah and in the streets of Jerusalem? [18] The children gather wood, and the fathers kindle the fire, and the women knead the dough, to make cakes to the queen of the sky, and to pour out drink offerings to other gods, that they may provoke me to anger. [19] Do they provoke me to anger?" says Yahweh. "Don't they provoke themselves, to the confusion of their own faces?" [20] Therefore the Lord Yahweh says: "Behold, my anger and my wrath will be poured out on this place, on man, on animal, on the trees of the field, and on the fruit of the ground; and it will burn and will not be quenched." [21] Yahweh of Armies, the God of Israel says: "Add your burnt offerings to your sacrifices and eat meat. [22] For I didn't speak to your fathers or command them in the day that I brought them out of the land of Egypt concerning burnt offerings or sacrifices; [23] but this thing I commanded them, saying, 'Listen to my voice, and I will be your God, and you shall be my people. Walk in all the way that I command you, that it may be well with you.' [24] But they didn't listen or turn their ear, but walked in their own counsels and in the stubbornness of their evil heart, and went backward, and not forward. [25] Since the day that your fathers came out of the land of Egypt to this day, I have sent to you all my servants the prophets, daily rising up early and sending them. [26] Yet they didn't listen to me or incline their ear, but made their neck stiff. They did worse than their fathers. [27]"You shall speak all these words to them, but they will not listen to you. You shall also call to them, but they will not answer you. [28] You shall tell them, 'This is the nation that has not listened to Yahweh their God's voice, nor received instruction. Truth has perished, and is cut off from their mouth.' [29] Cut off your hair, and throw it away, and take up a lamentation on the bare heights; for Yahweh has rejected and forsaken the generation of his wrath. [30]"For the children of Judah have done that which is evil in my sight," says Yahweh. "They have set their abominations in the house which is called by my name, to defile it. [31] They have built the high places of Topheth, which is in the valley of the son of Hinnom, to burn their sons and their daughters in the fire, which I didn't command, nor did it come into my mind. [32] Therefore behold, the days come", says Yahweh, "that it will no more be called 'Topheth' or 'The valley of the son of Hinnom', but 'The valley of Slaughter'; for they will bury in Topheth until there is no place to bury. [33] The dead bodies of this people will be food for the birds of the sky, and for the animals of the earth. No one will frighten them away. [34] Then I will cause to cease from the cities of Judah and from the streets of Jerusalem the voice of mirth and the voice of gladness, the voice of the bridegroom and the voice of the bride; for the land will become a waste."

# 8

[1]"At that time," says Yahweh, "they will bring the bones of the kings of Judah, the bones of his princes, the bones of the priests, the bones of the prophets, and the bones of the inhabitants of Jerusalem, out of their graves. [2] They will spread them before the sun, the moon, and all the army of the sky, which they have loved, which they have served, after which they have walked, which they have sought, and which they have worshiped. They will not be gathered or be buried. They will be like dung on the surface of the earth. [3] Death will be chosen rather than life by all the residue that remain of this evil family, that remain in all the places where I have driven them," says Yahweh of Armies. [4]"Moreover you shall tell them, 'Yahweh says: "'Do men fall, and not rise up again? Does one turn away, and not return? [5] Why then have the people of Jerusalem fallen back by a perpetual backsliding? They cling to deceit. They refuse to return. [6] I listened and heard, but they didn't say what is right. No one repents of his wickedness, saying, "What have I done?" Everyone turns to his course, as a horse that rushes headlong in the battle. [7] Yes, the stork in the sky knows her appointed times. The turtledove, the swallow, and the crane observe the time of their coming; but my people don't know Yahweh's law. [8]"How do you say, "We are wise, and Yahweh's law is with us"? But, behold, the false pen of the scribes has made that a lie. [9] The wise men are disappointed. They are

dismayed and trapped. Behold, they have rejected Yahweh's word. What kind of wisdom is in them? ¹⁰ Therefore I will give their wives to others and their fields to those who will possess them. For everyone from the least even to the greatest is given to covetousness; from the prophet even to the priest everyone deals falsely. ¹¹ They have healed the hurt of the daughter of my people slightly, saying, "Peace, peace," when there is no peace. ¹² Were they ashamed when they had committed abomination? No, they were not at all ashamed. They couldn't blush. Therefore they will fall among those who fall. In the time of their visitation they will be cast down, says Yahweh. ¹³"I will utterly consume them, says Yahweh. No grapes will be on the vine, no figs on the fig tree, and the leaf will fade. The things that I have given them will pass away from them.'" ¹⁴"Why do we sit still? Assemble yourselves! Let's enter into the fortified cities, and let's be silent there; for Yahweh our God has put us to silence, and given us poisoned water to drink, because we have sinned against Yahweh. ¹⁵ We looked for peace, but no good came; and for a time of healing, and behold, dismay! ¹⁶ The snorting of his horses is heard from Dan. The whole land trembles at the sound of the neighing of his strong ones; for they have come, and have devoured the land and all that is in it, the city and those who dwell therein." ¹⁷"For, behold, I will send serpents, adders among you, which will not be charmed; and they will bite you," says Yahweh. ¹⁸ Oh that I could comfort myself against sorrow! My heart is faint within me. ¹⁹ Behold, the voice of the cry of the daughter of my people from a land that is very far off: "Isn't Yahweh in Zion? Isn't her King in her?" "Why have they provoked me to anger with their engraved images, and with foreign idols?" ²⁰"The harvest is past. The summer has ended, and we are not saved." ²¹ For the hurt of the daughter of my people, I am hurt. I mourn. Dismay has taken hold of me. ²² Is there no balm in Gilead? Is there no physician there? Why then isn't the health of the daughter of my people recovered?

## 9

¹ Oh that my head were waters, and my eyes a spring of tears, that I might weep day and night for the slain of the daughter of my people! ² Oh that I had in the wilderness a lodging place of wayfaring men, that I might leave my people and go from them! For they are all adulterers, an assembly of treacherous men. ³"They bend their tongue, as their bow, for falsehood. They have grown strong in the land, but not for truth; for they proceed from evil to evil, and they don't know me," says Yahweh. ⁴"Everyone beware of his neighbor, and don't trust in any brother; for every brother will utterly supplant, and every neighbor will go around like a slanderer. ⁵ Friends deceive each other, and will not speak the truth. They have taught their tongue to speak lies. They weary themselves committing iniquity. ⁶ Your habitation is in the middle of deceit. Through deceit, they refuse to know me," says Yahweh. ⁷ Therefore Yahweh of Armies says, "Behold, I will melt them and test them; for how should I deal with the daughter of my people? ⁸ Their tongue is a deadly arrow. It speaks deceit. One speaks peaceably to his neighbor with his mouth, but in his heart, he waits to ambush him. ⁹ Shouldn't I punish them for these things?" says Yahweh. "Shouldn't my soul be avenged on a nation such as this? ¹⁰ I will weep and wail for the mountains, and lament for the pastures of the wilderness, because they are burned up, so that no one passes through; Men can't hear the voice of the livestock. Both the birds of the sky and the animals have fled. They are gone. ¹¹"I will make Jerusalem heaps, a dwelling place of jackals. I will make the cities of Judah a desolation, without inhabitant." ¹² Who is wise enough to understand this? Who is he to whom the mouth of Yahweh has spoken, that he may declare it? Why has the land perished and burned up like a wilderness, so that no one passes through? ¹³ Yahweh says, "Because they have forsaken my law which I set before them, and have not obeyed my voice or walked in my ways, ¹⁴ but have walked after the stubbornness of their own heart and after the Baals, which their fathers taught them." ¹⁵ Therefore Yahweh of Armies, the God of Israel, says, "Behold, I will feed them, even this people, with wormwood and give them poisoned water to drink. ¹⁶ I will scatter them also among the nations, whom neither they nor their fathers have known. I will send the sword after them, until I have consumed them." ¹⁷ Yahweh of Armies says, "Consider, and call for the mourning women, that they may come. Send for the skillful women, that they may come. ¹⁸ Let them make haste and take up a wailing for us, that our eyes may run down with tears and our eyelids gush out with waters. ¹⁹ For a voice of wailing is heard out of Zion, 'How we are ruined! We are greatly confounded because we have forsaken the land, because they have cast down our dwellings.'" ²⁰ Yet hear Yahweh's word, you women. Let your ear receive the word of his mouth. Teach your daughters wailing. Everyone teach her neighbor a lamentation. ²¹ For death has come up into our windows. It has entered into our palaces to cut off the children from outside, and the young men from the streets. ²² Speak, "Yahweh says, "'The dead bodies of men will fall as dung on the open field, and as the handful after the harvester.

No one will gather them.'" ²³ Yahweh says, "Don't let the wise man glory in his wisdom. Don't let the mighty man glory in his might. Don't let the rich man glory in his riches. ²⁴ But let him who glories glory in this, that he has understanding, and knows me, that I am Yahweh who exercises loving kindness, justice, and righteousness in the earth, for I delight in these things," says Yahweh. ²⁵"Behold, the days come," says Yahweh, "that I will punish all those who are circumcised only in their flesh: ²⁶ Egypt, Judah, Edom, the children of Ammon, Moab, and all who have the corners of their hair cut off, who dwell in the wilderness, for all the nations are uncircumcised, and all the house of Israel are uncircumcised in heart."

## 10

¹ Hear the word which Yahweh speaks to you, house of Israel! ² Yahweh says, "Don't learn the way of the nations, and don't be dismayed at the signs of the sky; for the nations are dismayed at them. ³ For the customs of the peoples are vanity; for one cuts a tree out of the forest, the work of the hands of the workman with the ax. ⁴ They deck it with silver and with gold. They fasten it with nails and with hammers, so that it can't move. ⁵ They are like a palm tree, of turned work, and don't speak. They must be carried, because they can't move. Don't be afraid of them; for they can't do evil, neither is it in them to do good." ⁶ There is no one like you, Yahweh. You are great, and your name is great in might. ⁷ Who shouldn't fear you, King of the nations? For it belongs to you. Because among all the wise men of the nations, and in all their royal estate, there is no one like you. ⁸ But they are together brutish and foolish, instructed by idols! It is just wood. ⁹ There is silver beaten into plates, which is brought from Tarshish, and gold from Uphaz, the work of the engraver and of the hands of the goldsmith. Their clothing is blue and purple. They are all the work of skillful men. ¹⁰ But Yahweh is the true God. He is the living God, and an everlasting King. At his wrath, the earth trembles. The nations aren't able to withstand his indignation. ¹¹"You shall say this to them: 'The gods that have not made the heavens and the earth will perish from the earth, and from under the heavens.'" ¹² God has made the earth by his power. He has established the world by his wisdom, and by his understanding has he stretched out the heavens. ¹³ When he utters his voice, the waters in the heavens roar, and he causes the vapors to ascend from the ends of the earth. He makes lightnings for the rain, and brings the wind out of his treasuries. ¹⁴ Every man has become brutish and without knowledge. Every goldsmith is disappointed by his engraved image; for his molten image is falsehood, and there is no breath in them. ¹⁵ They are vanity, a work of delusion. In the time of their visitation they will perish. ¹⁶ The portion of Jacob is not like these; for he is the maker of all things; and Israel is the tribe of his inheritance. Yahweh of Armies is his name. ¹⁷ Gather up your wares out of the land, you who live under siege. ¹⁸ For Yahweh says, "Behold, I will sling out the inhabitants of the land at this time, and will distress them, that they may feel it." ¹⁹ Woe is me because of my injury! My wound is serious; but I said, "Truly this is my grief, and I must bear it." ²⁰ My tent has been destroyed, and all my cords are broken. My children have gone away from me, and they are no more. There is no one to spread my tent any more, to set up my curtains. ²¹ For the shepherds have become brutish, and have not inquired of Yahweh. Therefore they have not prospered, and all their flocks have scattered. ²² The voice of news, behold, it comes, and a great commotion out of the north country, to make the cities of Judah a desolation, a dwelling place of jackals. ²³ Yahweh, I know that the way of man is not in himself. It is not in man who walks to direct his steps. ²⁴ Yahweh, correct me, but gently; not in your anger, lest you reduce me to nothing. ²⁵ Pour out your wrath on the nations that don't know you, and on the families that don't call on your name; for they have devoured Jacob. Yes, they have devoured him, consumed him, and have laid waste his habitation.

## 11

¹ The word that came to Jeremiah from Yahweh, saying, ²"Hear the words of this covenant, and speak to the men of Judah, and to the inhabitants of Jerusalem; ³ and say to them, Yahweh, the God of Israel says: 'Cursed is the man who doesn't hear the words of this covenant, ⁴ which I commanded your fathers in the day that I brought them out of the land of Egypt, out of the iron furnace,' saying, 'Obey my voice and do them, according to all which I command you; so you shall be my people, and I will be your God; ⁵ that I may establish the oath which I swore to your fathers, to give them a land flowing with milk and honey,' as it is today." Then I answered, and said, "Amen, Yahweh." ⁶ Yahweh said to me, "Proclaim all these words in the cities of Judah, and in the streets of Jerusalem, saying, 'Hear the words of this covenant, and do them. ⁷ For I earnestly protested to your fathers in the day that I brought them up out of the land of Egypt, even to this day, rising early and protesting, saying, "Obey my voice." ⁸ Yet they didn't obey, nor turn their ear, but everyone walked in the stubbornness of their evil heart. Therefore I brought on them all the words of this

covenant, which I commanded them to do, but they didn't do them.'" ⁹ Yahweh said to me, "A conspiracy is found among the men of Judah, and among the inhabitants of Jerusalem. ¹⁰ They have turned back to the iniquities of their forefathers, who refused to hear my words. They have gone after other gods to serve them. The house of Israel and the house of Judah have broken my covenant which I made with their fathers. ¹¹ Therefore Yahweh says, 'Behold, I will bring evil on them which they will not be able to escape; and they will cry to me, but I will not listen to them. ¹² Then the cities of Judah and the inhabitants of Jerusalem will go and cry to the gods to which they offer incense, but they will not save them at all in the time of their trouble. ¹³ For according to the number of your cities are your gods, Judah; and according to the number of the streets of Jerusalem you have set up altars to the shameful thing, even altars to burn incense to Baal.' ¹⁴"Therefore don't pray for this people. Don't lift up cry or prayer for them; for I will not hear them in the time that they cry to me because of their trouble. ¹⁵ What has my beloved to do in my house, since she has behaved lewdly with many, and the holy flesh has passed from you? When you do evil, then you rejoice." ¹⁶ Yahweh called your name, "A green olive tree, beautiful with goodly fruit." With the noise of a great roar he has kindled fire on it, and its branches are broken. ¹⁷ For Yahweh of Armies, who planted you, has pronounced evil against you, because of the evil of the house of Israel and of the house of Judah, which they have done to themselves in provoking me to anger by offering incense to Baal. ¹⁸ Yahweh gave me knowledge of it, and I knew it. Then you showed me their doings. ¹⁹ But I was like a gentle lamb that is led to the slaughter. I didn't know that they had devised plans against me, saying, "Let's destroy the tree with its fruit, and let's cut him off from the land of the living, that his name may be no more remembered." ²⁰ But, Yahweh of Armies, who judges righteously, who tests the heart and the mind, I will see your vengeance on them; for to you I have revealed my cause. ²¹"Therefore Yahweh says concerning the men of Anathoth, who seek your life, saying, 'You shall not prophesy in Yahweh's name, that you not die by our hand'— ²² therefore Yahweh of Armies says, 'Behold, I will punish them. The young men will die by the sword. Their sons and their daughters will die by famine. ²³ There will be no remnant to them, for I will bring evil on the men of Anathoth, even the year of their visitation.'"

## 12

¹ You are righteous, Yahweh, when I contend with you; yet I would like to plead a case with you. Why does the way of the wicked prosper? Why are they all at ease who deal very treacherously? ² You have planted them. Yes, they have taken root. They grow. Yes, they produce fruit. You are near in their mouth, and far from their heart. ³ But you, Yahweh, know me. You see me, and test my heart toward you. Pull them out like sheep for the slaughter, and prepare them for the day of slaughter. ⁴ How long will the land mourn, and the herbs of the whole country wither? Because of the wickedness of those who dwell therein, the animals and birds are consumed; because they said, "He won't see our latter end." ⁵"If you have run with the footmen, and they have wearied you, then how can you contend with horses? Though in a land of peace you are secure, yet how will you do in the pride of the Jordan? ⁶ For even your brothers, and the house of your father, even they have dealt treacherously with you! Even they have cried aloud after you! Don't believe them, though they speak beautiful words to you. ⁷"I have forsaken my house. I have cast off my heritage. I have given the dearly beloved of my soul into the hand of her enemies. ⁸ My heritage has become to me as a lion in the forest. She has uttered her voice against me. Therefore I have hated her. ⁹ Is my heritage to me as a speckled bird of prey? Are the birds of prey against her all around? Go, assemble all the animals of the field. Bring them to devour. ¹⁰ Many shepherds have destroyed my vineyard. They have trodden my portion under foot. They have made my pleasant portion a desolate wilderness. ¹¹ They have made it a desolation. It mourns to me, being desolate. The whole land is made desolate, because no one cares. ¹² Destroyers have come on all the bare heights in the wilderness; for the sword of Yahweh devours from the one end of the land even to the other end of the land. No flesh has peace. ¹³ They have sown wheat, and have reaped thorns. They have exhausted themselves, and profit nothing. You will be ashamed of your fruits, because of Yahweh's fierce anger." ¹⁴ Yahweh says, "Concerning all my evil neighbors, who touch the inheritance which I have caused my people Israel to inherit: Behold, I will pluck them up from off their land, and will pluck up the house of Judah from among them. ¹⁵ It will happen that after I have plucked them up, I will return and have compassion on them. I will bring them again, every man to his heritage, and every man to his land. ¹⁶ It will happen, if they will diligently learn the ways of my people, to swear by my name, 'As Yahweh lives;' even as they taught my people to swear by Baal, then they will be built up in the middle of my people. ¹⁷ But if they will not

hear, then I will pluck up that nation, plucking up and destroying it," says Yahweh.

## 13

¹ Yahweh said to me, "Go, and buy yourself a linen belt, and put it on your waist, and don't put it in water." ² So I bought a belt according to Yahweh's word, and put it on my waist. ³ Yahweh's word came to me the second time, saying, ⁴"Take the belt that you have bought, which is on your waist, and arise, go to the Euphrates, and hide it there in a cleft of the rock." ⁵ So I went and hid it by the Euphrates, as Yahweh commanded me. ⁶ After many days, Yahweh said to me, "Arise, go to the Euphrates, and take the belt from there, which I commanded you to hide there." ⁷ Then I went to the Euphrates, and dug, and took the belt from the place where I had hidden it; and behold, the belt was ruined. It was profitable for nothing. ⁸ Then Yahweh's word came to me, saying, ⁹"Yahweh says, 'In this way I will ruin the pride of Judah, and the great pride of Jerusalem. ¹⁰ This evil people, who refuse to hear my words, who walk in the stubbornness of their heart, and have gone after other gods to serve them and to worship them, will even be as this belt, which is profitable for nothing. ¹¹ For as the belt clings to the waist of a man, so I have caused the whole house of Israel and the whole house of Judah to cling to me,' says Yahweh; 'that they may be to me for a people, for a name, for praise, and for glory; but they would not hear.' ¹²"Therefore you shall speak to them this word: 'Yahweh, the God of Israel says, "Every container should be filled with wine."' They will tell you, 'Do we not certainly know that every container should be filled with wine?' ¹³ Then tell them, 'Yahweh says, "Behold, I will fill all the inhabitants of this land, even the kings who sit on David's throne, the priests, the prophets, and all the inhabitants of Jerusalem, with drunkenness. ¹⁴ I will dash them one against another, even the fathers and the sons together," says Yahweh: "I will not pity, spare, or have compassion, that I should not destroy them."'" ¹⁵ Hear, and give ear. Don't be proud, for Yahweh has spoken. ¹⁶ Give glory to Yahweh your God, before he causes darkness, and before your feet stumble on the dark mountains, and while you look for light, he turns it into the shadow of death, and makes it deep darkness. ¹⁷ But if you will not hear it, my soul will weep in secret for your pride. My eye will weep bitterly, and run down with tears, because Yahweh's flock has been taken captive. ¹⁸ Say to the king and to the queen mother, "Humble yourselves. Sit down, for your crowns have come down, even the crown of your glory. ¹⁹ The cities of the South are shut up, and there is no one to open them. Judah is carried away captive: all of them. They are wholly carried away captive. ²⁰ Lift up your eyes, and see those who come from the north. Where is the flock that was given to you, your beautiful flock? ²¹ What will you say when he sets over you as head those whom you have yourself taught to be friends to you? Won't sorrows take hold of you, as of a woman in travail? ²² If you say in your heart, "Why have these things come on me?" Your skirts are uncovered because of the greatness of your iniquity, and your heels suffer violence. ²³ Can the Ethiopian change his skin, or the leopard his spots? Then may you also do good, who are accustomed to do evil. ²⁴"Therefore I will scatter them as the stubble that passes away by the wind of the wilderness. ²⁵ This is your lot, the portion measured to you from me," says Yahweh, "because you have forgotten me, and trusted in falsehood." ²⁶ Therefore I will also uncover your skirts on your face, and your shame will appear. ²⁷ I have seen your abominations, even your adulteries and your neighing, the lewdness of your prostitution, on the hills in the field. Woe to you, Jerusalem! You will not be made clean. How long will it yet be?"

## 14

¹ This is Yahweh's word that came to Jeremiah concerning the drought: ²"Judah mourns, and its gates languish. They sit in black on the ground. The cry of Jerusalem goes up. ³ Their nobles send their little ones to the waters. They come to the cisterns, and find no water. They return with their vessels empty. They are disappointed and confounded, and cover their heads. ⁴ Because of the ground which is cracked, because no rain has been in the land, the plowmen are disappointed. They cover their heads. ⁵ Yes, the doe in the field also calves and forsakes her young, because there is no grass. ⁶ The wild donkeys stand on the bare heights. They pant for air like jackals. Their eyes fail, because there is no vegetation. ⁷ Though our iniquities testify against us, work for your name's sake, Yahweh; for our rebellions are many. We have sinned against you. ⁸ You hope of Israel, its Savior in the time of trouble, why should you be as a foreigner in the land, and as a wayfaring man who turns aside to stay for a night? ⁹ Why should you be like a scared man, as a mighty man who can't save? Yet you, Yahweh, are in the middle of us, and we are called by your name. Don't leave us. ¹⁰ Yahweh says to this people: "Even so they have loved to wander. They have not restrained their feet. Therefore Yahweh does not accept them. Now he will remember their iniquity, and punish them for their sins." ¹¹ Yahweh said to me, "Don't pray for this people for their good. ¹² When they fast,

I will not hear their cry; and when they offer burnt offering and meal offering, I will not accept them; but I will consume them by the sword, by famine, and by pestilence." [13] Then I said, "Ah, Lord Yahweh! Behold, the prophets tell them, 'You will not see the sword, neither will you have famine; but I will give you assured peace in this place.'" [14] Then Yahweh said to me, "The prophets prophesy lies in my name. I didn't send them. I didn't command them. I didn't speak to them. They prophesy to you a lying vision, divination, and a thing of nothing, and the deceit of their own heart. [15] Therefore Yahweh says concerning the prophets who prophesy in my name, but I didn't send them, yet they say, 'Sword and famine will not be in this land.' Those prophets will be consumed by sword and famine. [16] The people to whom they prophesy will be cast out in the streets of Jerusalem because of the famine and the sword. They will have no one to bury them—them, their wives, their sons, or their daughters, for I will pour their wickedness on them. [17] "You shall say this word to them: "'Let my eyes run down with tears night and day, and let them not cease; for the virgin daughter of my people is broken with a great breach, with a very grievous wound. [18] If I go out into the field, then behold, the slain with the sword! If I enter into the city, then behold, those who are sick with famine! For both the prophet and the priest go about in the land, and have no knowledge.'" [19] Have you utterly rejected Judah? Has your soul loathed Zion? Why have you struck us, and there is no healing for us? We looked for peace, but no good came; and for a time of healing, and behold, dismay! [20] We acknowledge, Yahweh, our wickedness, and the iniquity of our fathers; for we have sinned against you. [21] Do not abhor us, for your name's sake. Do not disgrace the throne of your glory. Remember, and don't break your covenant with us. [22] Are there any among the vanities of the nations that can cause rain? Or can the sky give showers? Aren't you he, Yahweh our God? Therefore we will wait for you; for you have made all these things.

## 15

[1] Then Yahweh said to me, "Though Moses and Samuel stood before me, yet my mind would not turn toward this people. Cast them out of my sight, and let them go out! [2] It will happen when they ask you, 'Where shall we go out?' then you shall tell them, 'Yahweh says: "Such as are for death, to death; such as are for the sword, to the sword; such as are for the famine, to the famine; and such as are for captivity, to captivity."' [3] "I will appoint over them four kinds," says Yahweh: "the sword to kill, the dogs to tear, the birds of the sky, and the animals of the earth, to devour and to destroy. [4] I will cause them to be tossed back and forth among all the kingdoms of the earth, because of Manasseh, the son of Hezekiah, king of Judah, for that which he did in Jerusalem. [5] For who will have pity on you, Jerusalem? Who will mourn you? Who will come to ask of your welfare? [6] You have rejected me," says Yahweh. "You have gone backward. Therefore I have stretched out my hand against you and destroyed you. I am weary of showing compassion. [7] I have winnowed them with a fan in the gates of the land. I have bereaved them of children. I have destroyed my people. They didn't return from their ways. [8] Their widows are increased more than the sand of the seas. I have brought on them against the mother of the young men a destroyer at noonday. I have caused anguish and terrors to fall on her suddenly. [9] She who has borne seven languishes. She has given up the spirit. Her sun has gone down while it was yet day. She has been disappointed and confounded. I will deliver their residue to the sword before their enemies," says Yahweh. [10] Woe is me, my mother, that you have borne me, a man of strife, and a man of contention to the whole earth! I have not lent, neither have men lent to me; yet every one of them curses me. [11] Yahweh said, "Most certainly I will strengthen you for good. Most certainly I will cause the enemy to make supplication to you in the time of evil and in the time of affliction. [12] Can one break iron, even iron from the north, and bronze? [13] I will give your substance and your treasures for a plunder without price, and that for all your sins, even in all your borders. [14] I will make them to pass with your enemies into a land which you don't know; for a fire is kindled in my anger, which will burn on you." [15] Yahweh, you know. Remember me, visit me, and avenge me of my persecutors. You are patient, so don't take me away. Know that for your sake I have suffered reproach. [16] Your words were found, and I ate them. Your words were to me a joy and the rejoicing of my heart, for I am called by your name, Yahweh, God of Armies. [17] I didn't sit in the assembly of those who make merry and rejoice. I sat alone because of your hand, for you have filled me with indignation. [18] Why is my pain perpetual, and my wound incurable, which refuses to be healed? Will you indeed be to me as a deceitful brook, like waters that fail? [19] Therefore Yahweh says, "If you return, then I will bring you again, that you may stand before me; and if you take out the precious from the vile, you will be as my mouth. They will return to you, but you will not return to them. [20] I will make you to this people a fortified bronze wall. They will fight against you, but they will not prevail against you; for I am with you to save you and

to deliver you," says Yahweh. [21] "I will deliver you out of the hand of the wicked, and I will redeem you out of the hand of the terrible."

## 16

[1] Then Yahweh's word came to me, saying, [2] "You shall not take a wife, neither shall you have sons or daughters, in this place." [3] For Yahweh says concerning the sons and concerning the daughters who are born in this place, and concerning their mothers who bore them, and concerning their fathers who became their father in this land: [4] "They will die grievous deaths. They will not be lamented, neither will they be buried. They will be as dung on the surface of the ground. They will be consumed by the sword and by famine. Their dead bodies will be food for the birds of the sky and for the animals of the earth." [5] For Yahweh says, "Don't enter into the house of mourning. Don't go to lament. Don't bemoan them, for I have taken away my peace from this people," says Yahweh, "even loving kindness and tender mercies. [6] Both great and small will die in this land. They will not be buried. Men won't lament for them, cut themselves, or make themselves bald for them. [7] Men won't break bread for them in mourning, to comfort them for the dead. Men won't give them the cup of consolation to drink for their father or for their mother. [8] You shall not go into the house of feasting to sit with them, to eat and to drink." [9] For Yahweh of Armies, the God of Israel says: "Behold, I will cause to cease out of this place, before your eyes and in your days, the voice of mirth and the voice of gladness, the voice of the bridegroom and the voice of the bride. [10] It will happen, when you tell this people all these words, and they ask you, 'Why has Yahweh pronounced all this great evil against us?' or 'What is our iniquity?' or 'What is our sin that we have committed against Yahweh our God?' [11] then you shall tell them, 'Because your fathers have forsaken me,' says Yahweh, 'and have walked after other gods, have served them, have worshiped them, have forsaken me, and have not kept my law. [12] You have done evil more than your fathers, for behold, you each walk after the stubbornness of his evil heart, so that you don't listen to me. [13] Therefore I will cast you out of this land into the land that you have not known, neither you nor your fathers. There you will serve other gods day and night, for I will show you no favor.' [14] "Therefore behold, the days come," says Yahweh, "that it will no more be said, 'As Yahweh lives, who brought up the children of Israel out of the land of Egypt;' [15] but, 'As Yahweh lives, who brought up the children of Israel from the land of the north, and from all the countries where he had driven them.' I will bring them again into their land that I gave to their fathers. [16] "Behold, I will send for many fishermen," says Yahweh, "and they will fish them up. Afterward I will send for many hunters, and they will hunt them from every mountain, from every hill, and out of the clefts of the rocks. [17] For my eyes are on all their ways. They are not hidden from my face. Their iniquity isn't concealed from my eyes. [18] First I will recompense their iniquity and their sin double, because they have polluted my land with the carcasses of their detestable things, and have filled my inheritance with their abominations." [19] Yahweh, my strength, my stronghold, and my refuge in the day of affliction, the nations will come to you from the ends of the earth, and will say, "Our fathers have inherited nothing but lies, vanity and things in which there is no profit. [20] Should a man make to himself gods which yet are no gods?" [21] "Therefore behold, I will cause them to know, this once I will cause them to know my hand and my might. Then they will know that my name is Yahweh."

## 17

[1] "The sin of Judah is written with a pen of iron, and with the point of a diamond. It is engraved on the tablet of their heart, and on the horns of your altars. [2] Even their children remember their altars and their Asherah poles by the green trees on the high hills. [3] My mountain in the field, I will give your substance and all your treasures for a plunder, and your high places, because of sin, throughout all your borders. [4] You, even of yourself, will discontinue from your heritage that I gave you. I will cause you to serve your enemies in the land which you don't know, for you have kindled a fire in my anger which will burn forever." [5] Yahweh says: "Cursed is the man who trusts in man, relies on strength of flesh, and whose heart departs from Yahweh. [6] For he will be like a bush in the desert, and will not see when good comes, but will inhabit the parched places in the wilderness, an uninhabited salt land. [7] "Blessed is the man who trusts in Yahweh, and whose confidence is in Yahweh. [8] For he will be as a tree planted by the waters, who spreads out its roots by the river, and will not fear when heat comes, but its leaf will be green, and will not be concerned in the year of drought. It won't cease from yielding fruit. [9] The heart is deceitful above all things and it is exceedingly corrupt. Who can know it? [10] "I, Yahweh, search the mind. I try the heart, even to give every man according to his ways, according to the fruit of his doings." [11] As the partridge that sits on eggs which she has not laid, so is he who gets riches, and not by right. In the middle of his days, they will leave him. At his end, he will be a fool. [12] A glorious throne, set on high from the beginning, is the place of our

sanctuary. [13] Yahweh, the hope of Israel, all who forsake you will be disappointed. Those who depart from me will be written in the earth, because they have forsaken Yahweh, the spring of living waters. [14] Heal me, O Yahweh, and I will be healed. Save me, and I will be saved; for you are my praise. [15] Behold, they ask me, "Where is Yahweh's word? Let it be fulfilled now." [16] As for me, I have not hurried from being a shepherd after you. I haven't desired the woeful day. You know. That which came out of my lips was before your face. [17] Don't be a terror to me. You are my refuge in the day of evil. [18] Let them be disappointed who persecute me, but don't let me be disappointed. Let them be dismayed, but don't let me be dismayed. Bring on them the day of evil, and destroy them with double destruction. [19] Yahweh said this to me: "Go and stand in the gate of the children of the people, through which the kings of Judah come in and by which they go out, and in all the gates of Jerusalem. [20] Tell them, 'Hear Yahweh's word, you kings of Judah, all Judah, and all the inhabitants of Jerusalem, that enter in by these gates: [21] Yahweh says, "Be careful, and bear no burden on the Sabbath day, nor bring it in by the gates of Jerusalem. [22] Don't carry a burden out of your houses on the Sabbath day. Don't do any work, but make the Sabbath day holy, as I commanded your fathers. [23] But they didn't listen. They didn't turn their ear, but made their neck stiff, that they might not hear, and might not receive instruction. [24] It will happen, if you diligently listen to me," says Yahweh, "to bring in no burden through the gates of this city on the Sabbath day, but to make the Sabbath day holy, to do no work therein; [25] then there will enter in by the gates of this city kings and princes sitting on David's throne, riding in chariots and on horses, they and their princes, the men of Judah and the inhabitants of Jerusalem; and this city will remain forever. [26] They will come from the cities of Judah, and from the places around Jerusalem, from the land of Benjamin, from the lowland, from the hill country, and from the South, bringing burnt offerings, sacrifices, meal offerings, and frankincense, and bringing sacrifices of thanksgiving to Yahweh's house. [27] But if you will not listen to me to make the Sabbath day holy, and not to bear a burden and enter in at the gates of Jerusalem on the Sabbath day, then I will kindle a fire in its gates, and it will devour the palaces of Jerusalem. It will not be quenched."'"

## 18

[1] The word which came to Jeremiah from Yahweh, saying, [2]"Arise, and go down to the potter's house, and there I will cause you to hear my words."

[3] Then I went down to the potter's house, and behold, he was making something on the wheels. [4] When the vessel that he made of the clay was marred in the hand of the potter, he made it again another vessel, as seemed good to the potter to make it. [5] Then Yahweh's word came to me, saying, [6]"House of Israel, can't I do with you as this potter?" says Yahweh. "Behold, as the clay in the potter's hand, so are you in my hand, house of Israel. [7] At the instant I speak concerning a nation, and concerning a kingdom, to pluck up and to break down and to destroy it, [8] if that nation, concerning which I have spoken, turns from their evil, I will repent of the evil that I thought to do to them. [9] At the instant I speak concerning a nation, and concerning a kingdom, to build and to plant it, [10] if they do that which is evil in my sight, that they not obey my voice, then I will repent of the good with which I said I would benefit them. [11]"Now therefore, speak to the men of Judah, and to the inhabitants of Jerusalem, saying, 'Yahweh says: "Behold, I frame evil against you, and devise a plan against you. Everyone return from his evil way now, and amend your ways and your doings."' [12] But they say, 'It is in vain; for we will walk after our own plans, and we will each follow the stubbornness of his evil heart.'" [13] Therefore Yahweh says: "Ask now among the nations, 'Who has heard such things?' The virgin of Israel has done a very horrible thing. [14] Will the snow of Lebanon fail from the rock of the field? Will the cold waters that flow down from afar be dried up? [15] For my people have forgotten me. They have burned incense to false gods. They have been made to stumble in their ways in the ancient paths, to walk in byways, in a way not built up, [16] to make their land an astonishment, and a perpetual hissing. Everyone who passes by it will be astonished, and shake his head. [17] I will scatter them as with an east wind before the enemy. I will show them the back, and not the face, in the day of their calamity. [18] Then they said, "Come! Let's devise plans against Jeremiah; for the law won't perish from the priest, nor counsel from the wise, nor the word from the prophet. Come, and let's strike him with the tongue, and let's not give heed to any of his words." [19] Give heed to me, Yahweh, and listen to the voice of those who contend with me. [20] Should evil be recompensed for good? For they have dug a pit for my soul. Remember how I stood before you to speak good for them, to turn away your wrath from them. [21] Therefore deliver up their children to the famine, and give them over to the power

of the sword. Let their wives become childless and widows. Let their men be killed and their young men struck by the sword in battle. [22] Let a cry be heard from their houses when you bring a troop suddenly on them; for they have dug a pit to take me and hidden snares for my feet. [23] Yet, Yahweh, you know all their counsel against me to kill me. Don't forgive their iniquity. Don't blot out their sin from your sight, Let them be overthrown before you. Deal with them in the time of your anger.

## 19

[1] Thus said Yahweh, "Go, and buy a potter's earthen container, and take some of the elders of the people and of the elders of the priests; [2] and go out to the valley of the son of Hinnom, which is by the entry of the gate Harsith, and proclaim there the words that I will tell you. [3] Say, 'Hear Yahweh's word, kings of Judah and inhabitants of Jerusalem: Yahweh of Armies, the God of Israel says, "Behold, I will bring evil on this place, which whoever hears, his ears will tingle. [4] Because they have forsaken me, and have defiled this place, and have burned incense in it to other gods that they didn't know—they, their fathers, and the kings of Judah—and have filled this place with the blood of innocents, [5] and have built the high places of Baal to burn their children in the fire for burnt offerings to Baal, which I didn't command, nor speak, which didn't even enter into my mind. [6] Therefore, behold, the days come," says Yahweh, "that this place will no more be called 'Topheth', nor 'The Valley of the son of Hinnom', but 'The valley of Slaughter'. [7]"'I will make the counsel of Judah and Jerusalem void in this place. I will cause them to fall by the sword before their enemies, and by the hand of those who seek their life. I will give their dead bodies to be food for the birds of the sky and for the animals of the earth. [8] I will make this city an astonishment and a hissing. Everyone who passes by it will be astonished and hiss because of all its plagues. [9] I will cause them to eat the flesh of their sons and the flesh of their daughters. They will each eat the flesh of his friend in the siege and in the distress with which their enemies, and those who seek their life, will distress them.'" [10]"Then you shall break the container in the sight of the men who go with you, [11] and shall tell them, 'Yahweh of Armies says: "Even so I will break this people and this city as one breaks a potter's vessel, that can't be made whole again. They will bury in Topheth until there is no place to bury. [12] This is what I will do to this place," says Yahweh, "and to its inhabitants, even making this city as Topheth. [13] The houses of Jerusalem and the houses of the kings of Judah, which are defiled, will be as the place of Topheth, even all the houses on whose roofs they have burned incense to all the army of the sky and have poured out drink offerings to other gods."'" [14] Then Jeremiah came from Topheth, where Yahweh had sent him to prophesy, and he stood in the court of Yahweh's house, and said to all the people: [15]"Yahweh of Armies, the God of Israel says, 'Behold, I will bring on this city and on all its towns all the evil that I have pronounced against it, because they have made their neck stiff, that they may not hear my words.'"

## 20

[1] Now Pashhur, the son of Immer the priest, who was chief officer in Yahweh's house, heard Jeremiah prophesying these things. [2] Then Pashhur struck Jeremiah the prophet and put him in the stocks that were in the upper gate of Benjamin, which was in Yahweh's house. [3] On the next day, Pashhur released Jeremiah out of the stocks. Then Jeremiah said to him, "Yahweh has not called your name Pashhur, but Magormissabib.[a] [4] For Yahweh says, 'Behold, I will make you a terror to yourself and to all your friends. They will fall by the sword of their enemies, and your eyes will see it. I will give all Judah into the hand of the king of Babylon, and he will carry them captive to Babylon, and will kill them with the sword. [5] Moreover I will give all the riches of this city, and all its gains, and all its precious things, yes, I will give all the treasures of the kings of Judah into the hand of their enemies. They will make them captives, take them, and carry them to Babylon. [6] You, Pashhur, and all who dwell in your house will go into captivity. You will come to Babylon, and there you will die, and there you will be buried, you, and all your friends, to whom you have prophesied falsely.'" [7] Yahweh, you have persuaded me, and I was persuaded. You are stronger than I, and have prevailed. I have become a laughingstock all day. Everyone mocks me. [8] For as often as I speak, I cry out; I cry, "Violence and destruction!" because Yahweh's word has been made a reproach to me, and a derision, all day. [9] If I say that I will not make mention of him, or speak any more in his name, then there is in my heart as it were a burning fire shut up in my bones. I am weary with holding it in. I can't. [10] For I have heard the defaming of many: "Terror on every side! Denounce, and we will denounce him!" say all my familiar friends, those who watch for my fall. "Perhaps he will be persuaded, and we will prevail against him, and we will take our revenge on him." [11] But Yahweh is with me as an awesome mighty one.

---

[a] 20:3 "Magormissabib" means "surrounded by terror"

Therefore my persecutors will stumble, and they won't prevail. They will be utterly disappointed because they have not dealt wisely, even with an everlasting dishonor which will never be forgotten. ¹² But Yahweh of Armies, who tests the righteous, who sees the heart and the mind, let me see your vengeance on them, for I have revealed my cause to you. ¹³ Sing to Yahweh! Praise Yahweh, for he has delivered the soul of the needy from the hand of evildoers. ¹⁴ Cursed is the day in which I was born. Don't let the day in which my mother bore me be blessed. ¹⁵ Cursed is the man who brought news to my father, saying, "A boy is born to you," making him very glad. ¹⁶ Let that man be as the cities which Yahweh overthrew, and didn't repent. Let him hear a cry in the morning, and shouting at noontime, ¹⁷ because he didn't kill me from the womb. So my mother would have been my grave, and her womb always great. ¹⁸ Why did I come out of the womb to see labor and sorrow, that my days should be consumed with shame?

## 21

¹ The word which came to Jeremiah from Yahweh, when King Zedekiah sent to him Pashhur the son of Malchijah, and Zephaniah the son of Maaseiah, the priest, saying, ²"Please inquire of Yahweh for us; for Nebuchadnezzar king of Babylon makes war against us. Perhaps Yahweh will deal with us according to all his wondrous works, that he may withdraw from us." ³ Then Jeremiah said to them, "Tell Zedekiah: ⁴'Yahweh, the God of Israel says, "Behold, I will turn back the weapons of war that are in your hands, with which you fight against the king of Babylon, and against the Chaldeans who besiege you outside the walls; and I will gather them into the middle of this city. ⁵ I myself will fight against you with an outstretched hand and with a strong arm, even in anger, in wrath, and in great indignation. ⁶ I will strike the inhabitants of this city, both man and animal. They will die of a great pestilence. ⁷ Afterward," says Yahweh, "I will deliver Zedekiah king of Judah, his servants, and the people, even those who are left in this city from the pestilence, from the sword, and from the famine, into the hand of Nebuchadnezzar king of Babylon, and into the hand of their enemies, and into the hand of those who seek their life. He will strike them with the edge of the sword. He will not spare them, have pity, or have mercy."' ⁸"You shall say to this people, 'Yahweh says: "Behold, I set before you the way of life and the way of death. ⁹ He who remains in this city will die by the sword, by the famine, and by the pestilence, but he who goes out and passes over to the Chaldeans who besiege you, he will live, and he will escape with his life. ¹⁰ For I have set my face on this city for evil, and not for good," says Yahweh. "It will be given into the hand of the king of Babylon, and he will burn it with fire."' ¹¹"Concerning the house of the king of Judah, hear Yahweh's word: ¹² House of David, Yahweh says, 'Execute justice in the morning, and deliver him who is robbed out of the hand of the oppressor, lest my wrath go out like fire, and burn so that no one can quench it, because of the evil of your doings. ¹³ Behold, I am against you, O inhabitant of the valley, and of the rock of the plain,' says Yahweh. 'You that say, "Who would come down against us?" or, "Who would enter into our homes?" ¹⁴ I will punish you according to the fruit of your doings,' says Yahweh; 'and I will kindle a fire in her forest, and it will devour all that is around her.'"

## 22

¹ Yahweh said, "Go down to the house of the king of Judah, and speak this word there: ²'Hear Yahweh's word, king of Judah, who sits on David's throne—you, your servants, and your people who enter in by these gates. ³ Yahweh says: "Execute justice and righteousness, and deliver him who is robbed out of the hand of the oppressor. Do no wrong. Do no violence to the foreigner, the fatherless, or the widow. Don't shed innocent blood in this place. ⁴ For if you do this thing indeed, then kings sitting on David's throne will enter in by the gates of this house, riding in chariots and on horses—they, their servants, and their people. ⁵ But if you will not hear these words, I swear by myself," says Yahweh, "that this house will become a desolation."'" ⁶ For Yahweh says concerning the house of the king of Judah: "You are Gilead to me, the head of Lebanon. Yet surely I will make you a wilderness, cities which are not inhabited. ⁷ I will prepare destroyers against you, everyone with his weapons, and they will cut down your choice cedars, and cast them into the fire. ⁸"Many nations will pass by this city, and they will each ask his neighbor, 'Why has Yahweh done this to this great city?' ⁹ Then they will answer, 'Because they abandoned the covenant of Yahweh their God, worshiped other gods, and served them.'" ¹⁰ Don't weep for the dead. Don't bemoan him; but weep bitterly for him who goes away, for he will return no more, and not see his native country. ¹¹ For Yahweh says touching Shallum the son of Josiah, king of Judah, who reigned instead of Josiah his father, and who went out of this place: "He won't return there any more. ¹² But he will die in the place where they have led him captive. He will see this land no more." ¹³"Woe to him who builds his house by unrighteousness, and his rooms by injustice; who uses his neighbor's

service without wages, and doesn't give him his hire; ¹⁴ who says, 'I will build myself a wide house and spacious rooms,' and cuts out windows for himself, with a cedar ceiling, and painted with red. ¹⁵"Should you reign because you strive to excel in cedar? Didn't your father eat and drink, and do justice and righteousness? Then it was well with him. ¹⁶ He judged the cause of the poor and needy; so then it was well. Wasn't this to know me?" says Yahweh. ¹⁷ But your eyes and your heart are only for your covetousness, for shedding innocent blood, for oppression, and for doing violence." ¹⁸ Therefore Yahweh says concerning Jehoiakim the son of Josiah, king of Judah: "They won't lament for him, saying, 'Ah my brother!' or, 'Ah sister!' They won't lament for him, saying 'Ah lord!' or, 'Ah his glory!' ¹⁹ He will be buried with the burial of a donkey, drawn and cast out beyond the gates of Jerusalem." ²⁰"Go up to Lebanon, and cry out. Lift up your voice in Bashan, and cry from Abarim; for all your lovers have been destroyed. ²¹ I spoke to you in your prosperity, but you said, 'I will not listen.' This has been your way from your youth, that you didn't obey my voice. ²² The wind will feed all your shepherds, and your lovers will go into captivity. Surely then you will be ashamed and confounded for all your wickedness. ²³ Inhabitant of Lebanon, who makes your nest in the cedars, how greatly to be pitied you will be when pangs come on you, the pain as of a woman in travail! ²⁴"As I live," says Yahweh, "though Coniah the son of Jehoiakim king of Judah were the signet on my right hand, I would still pluck you from there. ²⁵ I would give you into the hand of those who seek your life, and into the hand of them of whom you are afraid, even into the hand of Nebuchadnezzar king of Babylon, and into the hand of the Chaldeans. ²⁶ I will cast you out with your mother who bore you into another country, where you were not born; and there you will die. ²⁷ But to the land to which their soul longs to return, there they will not return." ²⁸ Is this man Coniah a despised broken vessel? Is he a vessel in which no one delights? Why are they cast out, he and his offspring, and cast into a land which they don't know? ²⁹ O earth, earth, earth, hear Yahweh's word! ³⁰ Yahweh says, "Record this man as childless, a man who will not prosper in his days; for no more will a man of his offspring prosper, sitting on David's throne and ruling in Judah."

## 23

¹"Woe to the shepherds who destroy and scatter the sheep of my pasture!" says Yahweh. ² Therefore Yahweh, the God of Israel, says against the shepherds who feed my people: "You have scattered my flock, driven them away, and have not visited them. Behold, I will visit on you the evil of your doings," says Yahweh. ³"I will gather the remnant of my flock out of all the countries where I have driven them, and will bring them again to their folds; and they will be fruitful and multiply. ⁴ I will set up shepherds over them who will feed them. They will no longer be afraid or dismayed, neither will any be lacking," says Yahweh. ⁵"Behold, the days come," says Yahweh, "that I will raise to David a righteous Branch; and he will reign as king and deal wisely, and will execute justice and righteousness in the land. ⁶ In his days Judah will be saved, and Israel will dwell safely. This is his name by which he will be called: Yahweh our righteousness. ⁷"Therefore, behold, the days come," says Yahweh, "that they will no more say, 'As Yahweh lives, who brought up the children of Israel out of the land of Egypt;' ⁸ but, 'As Yahweh lives, who brought up and who led the offspring of the house of Israel out of the north country, and from all the countries where I had driven them.' Then they will dwell in their own land." ⁹ Concerning the prophets: My heart within me is broken. All my bones shake. I am like a drunken man, and like a man whom wine has overcome, because of Yahweh, and because of his holy words. ¹⁰"For the land is full of adulterers; for because of the curse the land mourns. The pastures of the wilderness have dried up. Their course is evil, and their might is not right; ¹¹ for both prophet and priest are profane. Yes, in my house I have found their wickedness," says Yahweh. ¹² Therefore their way will be to them as slippery places in the darkness. They will be driven on, and fall therein; for I will bring evil on them, even the year of their visitation," says Yahweh. ¹³"I have seen folly in the prophets of Samaria. They prophesied by Baal, and caused my people Israel to err. ¹⁴ In the prophets of Jerusalem I have also seen a horrible thing: they commit adultery and walk in lies. They strengthen the hands of evildoers, so that no one returns from his wickedness. They have all become to me as Sodom, and its inhabitants as Gomorrah." ¹⁵ Therefore Yahweh of Armies says concerning the prophets: "Behold, I will feed them with wormwood, and make them drink poisoned water; for from the prophets of Jerusalem ungodliness has gone out into all the land." ¹⁶ Yahweh of Armies says, "Don't listen to the words of the prophets who prophesy to you. They teach you vanity. They speak a vision of their own heart, and not out of the mouth of Yahweh. ¹⁷ They say continually to those who despise me, 'Yahweh has said, "You will have peace;"' and to everyone who walks in the stubbornness of his own heart they say, 'No evil will come on you.' ¹⁸

For who has stood in the council of Yahweh, that he should perceive and hear his word? Who has listened to my word, and heard it? ¹⁹ Behold, Yahweh's storm, his wrath, has gone out. Yes, a whirling storm! It will burst on the head of the wicked. ²⁰ Yahweh's anger will not return until he has executed and performed the intents of his heart. In the latter days, you will understand it perfectly. ²¹ I didn't send these prophets, yet they ran. I didn't speak to them, yet they prophesied. ²² But if they had stood in my council, then they would have caused my people to hear my words, and would have turned them from their evil way, and from the evil of their doings. ²³"Am I a God at hand," says Yahweh, "and not a God afar off? ²⁴ Can anyone hide himself in secret places so that I can't see him?" says Yahweh. "Don't I fill heaven and earth?" says Yahweh. ²⁵"I have heard what the prophets have said, who prophesy lies in my name, saying, 'I had a dream! I had a dream!' ²⁶ How long will this be in the heart of the prophets who prophesy lies, even the prophets of the deceit of their own heart? ²⁷ They intend to cause my people to forget my name by their dreams which they each tell his neighbor, as their fathers forgot my name because of Baal. ²⁸ The prophet who has a dream, let him tell a dream; and he who has my word, let him speak my word faithfully. What is the straw to the wheat?" says Yahweh. ²⁹"Isn't my word like fire?" says Yahweh; "and like a hammer that breaks the rock in pieces? ³⁰"Therefore behold, I am against the prophets," says Yahweh, "who each steal my words from his neighbor. ³¹ Behold, I am against the prophets," says Yahweh, "who use their tongues, and say, 'He says.' ³² Behold, I am against those who prophesy lying dreams," says Yahweh, "who tell them, and cause my people to err by their lies, and by their vain boasting; yet I didn't send them or command them. They don't profit this people at all," says Yahweh. ³³"When this people, or the prophet, or a priest, asks you, saying, 'What is the message from Yahweh?' Then you shall tell them, '"What message? I will cast you off," says Yahweh.' ³⁴ As for the prophet, the priest, and the people, who say, 'The message from Yahweh,' I will even punish that man and his household. ³⁵ You will say everyone to his neighbor, and everyone to his brother, 'What has Yahweh answered?' and, 'What has Yahweh said?' ³⁶ You will mention the message from Yahweh no more, for every man's own word has become his message; for you have perverted the words of the living God, of Yahweh of Armies, our God. ³⁷ You will say to the prophet, 'What has Yahweh answered you?' and, 'What has Yahweh spoken?' ³⁸ Although you say, 'The message from Yahweh,' therefore Yahweh says: 'Because you say this word, "The message from Yahweh," and I have sent to you, telling you not to say, "The message from Yahweh," ³⁹ therefore behold, I will utterly forget you, and I will cast you off with the city that I gave to you and to your fathers, away from my presence. ⁴⁰ I will bring an everlasting reproach on you, and a perpetual shame, which will not be forgotten.'"

## 24

¹ Yahweh showed me, and behold, two baskets of figs were set before Yahweh's temple, after Nebuchadnezzar king of Babylon had carried away captive Jeconiah the son of Jehoiakim, king of Judah, and the princes of Judah, with the craftsmen and smiths, from Jerusalem, and had brought them to Babylon. ² One basket had very good figs, like the figs that are first-ripe; and the other basket had very bad figs, which could not be eaten, they were so bad. ³ Then Yahweh asked me, "What do you see, Jeremiah?" I said, "Figs. The good figs are very good, and the bad are very bad, so bad that they can't be eaten." ⁴ Yahweh's word came to me, saying, ⁵"Yahweh, the God of Israel says: 'Like these good figs, so I will regard the captives of Judah, whom I have sent out of this place into the land of the Chaldeans, as good. ⁶ For I will set my eyes on them for good, and I will bring them again to this land. I will build them, and not pull them down. I will plant them, and not pluck them up. ⁷ I will give them a heart to know me, that I am Yahweh. They will be my people, and I will be their God; for they will return to me with their whole heart. ⁸"'As the bad figs, which can't be eaten, they are so bad,' surely Yahweh says, 'So I will give up Zedekiah the king of Judah, and his princes, and the remnant of Jerusalem who remain in this land, and those who dwell in the land of Egypt. ⁹ I will even give them up to be tossed back and forth among all the kingdoms of the earth for evil, to be a reproach and a proverb, a taunt and a curse, in all places where I will drive them. ¹⁰ I will send the sword, the famine, and the pestilence among them, until they are consumed from off the land that I gave to them and to their fathers.'"

## 25

¹ The word that came to Jeremiah concerning all the people of Judah, in the fourth year of Jehoiakim the son of Josiah, king of Judah (this was the first year of Nebuchadnezzar king of Babylon), ² which Jeremiah the prophet spoke to all the people of Judah, and to all the inhabitants of Jerusalem: ³ From the thirteenth year of Josiah the son of Amon, king of Judah, even to this day, these twenty-three years, Yahweh's word has come to me, and I have spoken to you, rising up early and speaking; but you have not listened. ⁴ Yahweh has sent to you all his servants the prophets, rising up early and sending them (but you have not listened or inclined your ear to hear), ⁵ saying, "Return now everyone from his evil way, and from the evil of your doings, and dwell in the land that Yahweh has given to you and to your fathers, from of old and even forever more. ⁶ Don't go after other gods to serve them or worship them, and don't provoke me to anger with the work of your hands; then I will do you no harm." ⁷"Yet you have not listened to me," says Yahweh, "that you may provoke me to anger with the work of your hands to your own hurt." ⁸ Therefore Yahweh of Armies says: "Because you have not heard my words, ⁹ behold, I will send and take all the families of the north," says Yahweh, "and I will send to Nebuchadnezzar the king of Babylon, my servant, and will bring them against this land, and against its inhabitants, and against all these nations around. I will utterly destroy them, and make them an astonishment, and a hissing, and perpetual desolations. ¹⁰ Moreover I will take from them the voice of mirth and the voice of gladness, the voice of the bridegroom and the voice of the bride, the sound of the millstones, and the light of the lamp. ¹¹ This whole land will be a desolation, and an astonishment; and these nations will serve the king of Babylon seventy years. ¹²"It will happen, when seventy years are accomplished, that I will punish the king of Babylon and that nation," says Yahweh, "for their iniquity. I will make the land of the Chaldeans desolate forever. ¹³ I will bring on that land all my words which I have pronounced against it, even all that is written in this book, which Jeremiah has prophesied against all the nations. ¹⁴ For many nations and great kings will make bondservants of them, even of them. I will recompense them according to their deeds, and according to the work of their hands." ¹⁵ For Yahweh, the God of Israel, says to me: "Take this cup of the wine of wrath from my hand, and cause all the nations to whom I send you to drink it. ¹⁶ They will drink, and reel back and forth, and be insane, because of the sword that I will send among them." ¹⁷ Then I took the cup at Yahweh's hand, and made all the nations to drink, to whom Yahweh had sent me: ¹⁸ Jerusalem, and the cities of Judah, with its kings and its princes, to make them a desolation, an astonishment, a hissing, and a curse, as it is today; ¹⁹ Pharaoh king of Egypt, with his servants, his princes, and all his people; ²⁰ and all the mixed people, and all the kings of the land of Uz, all the kings of the Philistines, Ashkelon, Gaza, Ekron, and the remnant of Ashdod; ²¹ Edom, Moab, and the children of Ammon; ²² and all the kings of Tyre, all the kings of Sidon, and the kings of the isle which is beyond the sea; ²³ Dedan, Tema, Buz, and all who have the corners of their beard cut off; ²⁴ and all the kings of Arabia, all the kings of the mixed people who dwell in the wilderness; ²⁵ and all the kings of Zimri, all the kings of Elam, and all the kings of the Medes; ²⁶ and all the kings of the north, far and near, one with another; and all the kingdoms of the world, which are on the surface of the earth. The king of Sheshach will drink after them. ²⁷"You shall tell them, 'Yahweh of Armies, the God of Israel says: "Drink, and be drunk, vomit, fall, and rise no more, because of the sword which I will send among you."' ²⁸ It shall be, if they refuse to take the cup at your hand to drink, then you shall tell them, 'Yahweh of Armies says: "You shall surely drink. ²⁹ For, behold, I begin to work evil at the city which is called by my name; and should you be utterly unpunished? You will not be unpunished; for I will call for a sword on all the inhabitants of the earth, says Yahweh of Armies."' ³⁰"Therefore prophesy against them all these words, and tell them, "'Yahweh will roar from on high, and utter his voice from his holy habitation. He will mightily roar against his fold. He will give a shout, as those who tread grapes, against all the inhabitants of the earth. ³¹ A noise will come even to the end of the earth; for Yahweh has a controversy with the nations. He will enter into judgment with all flesh. As for the wicked, he will give them to the sword,'" says Yahweh." ³² Yahweh of Armies says, "Behold, evil will go out from nation to nation, and a great storm will be raised up from the uttermost parts of the earth." ³³ The slain of Yahweh will be at that day from one end of the earth even to the other end of the earth. They won't be lamented. They won't be gathered or buried. They will be dung on the surface of the ground. ³⁴ Wail, you shepherds, and cry. Wallow in dust, you leader of the flock; for the days of your slaughter and of your dispersions have fully come, and you will fall like fine pottery. ³⁵ The shepherds will have no way to flee. The leader of the flock will have no escape. ³⁶ A voice of the cry of the shepherds, and the wailing of the leader of the flock, for Yahweh destroys their pasture. ³⁷ The peaceful folds are brought to silence because of the fierce anger of Yahweh. ³⁸ He has left his covert, as the lion; for their land has become an astonishment because of the fierceness of the oppression, and because of his fierce anger.

## 26

¹ In the beginning of the reign of Jehoiakim the son of Josiah, king of Judah, this word came from Yahweh: ²"Yahweh says: 'Stand in the court of Yahweh's house, and speak to all the cities of Judah which

come to worship in Yahweh's house, all the words that I command you to speak to them. Don't omit a word. ³ It may be they will listen, and every man turn from his evil way, that I may relent from the evil which I intend to do to them because of the evil of their doings.'" ⁴ You shall tell them, "Yahweh says: 'If you will not listen to me, to walk in my law which I have set before you, ⁵ to listen to the words of my servants the prophets whom I send to you, even rising up early and sending them—but you have not listened— ⁶ then I will make this house like Shiloh, and will make this city a curse to all the nations of the earth.'"

⁷ The priests and the prophets and all the people heard Jeremiah speaking these words in Yahweh's house. ⁸ When Jeremiah had finished speaking all that Yahweh had commanded him to speak to all the people, the priests and the prophets and all the people seized him, saying, "You shall surely die! ⁹ Why have you prophesied in Yahweh's name, saying, 'This house will be like Shiloh, and this city will be desolate, without inhabitant'?" All the people were crowded around Jeremiah in Yahweh's house. ¹⁰ When the princes of Judah heard these things, they came up from the king's house to Yahweh's house; and they sat in the entry of the new gate of Yahweh's house. ¹¹ Then the priests and the prophets spoke to the princes and to all the people, saying, "This man is worthy of death, for he has prophesied against this city, as you have heard with your ears." ¹² Then Jeremiah spoke to all the princes and to all the people, saying, "Yahweh sent me to prophesy against this house and against this city all the words that you have heard. ¹³ Now therefore amend your ways and your doings, and obey Yahweh your God's voice; then Yahweh will relent from the evil that he has pronounced against you. ¹⁴ But as for me, behold, I am in your hand. Do with me what is good and right in your eyes. ¹⁵ Only know for certain that if you put me to death, you will bring innocent blood on yourselves, on this city, and on its inhabitants; for in truth Yahweh has sent me to you to speak all these words in your ears." ¹⁶ Then the princes and all the people said to the priests and to the prophets: "This man is not worthy of death; for he has spoken to us in the name of Yahweh our God." ¹⁷ Then certain of the elders of the land rose up, and spoke to all the assembly of the people, saying, ¹⁸"Micah the Morashtite prophesied in the days of Hezekiah king of Judah; and he spoke to all the people of Judah, saying, 'Yahweh of Armies says: "'Zion will be plowed as a field, and Jerusalem will become heaps, and the mountain of the house as the high places of a forest.' ¹⁹ Did Hezekiah king of Judah and all Judah put him to death? Didn't he fear Yahweh, and entreat the favor of Yahweh, and Yahweh relented of the disaster which he had pronounced against them? We would commit great evil against our own souls that way!" ²⁰ There was also a man who prophesied in Yahweh's name, Uriah the son of Shemaiah of Kiriath Jearim; and he prophesied against this city and against this land according to all the words of Jeremiah. ²¹ When Jehoiakim the king, with all his mighty men and all the princes heard his words, the king sought to put him to death; but when Uriah heard it, he was afraid, and fled, and went into Egypt. ²² Then Jehoiakim the king sent Elnathan the son of Achbor and certain men with him into Egypt. ²³ They fetched Uriah out of Egypt and brought him to Jehoiakim the king, who killed him with the sword and cast his dead body into the graves of the common people. ²⁴ But the hand of Ahikam the son of Shaphan was with Jeremiah, so that they didn't give him into the hand of the people to put him to death.

## 27

¹ In the beginning of the reign of Jehoiakim the son of Josiah, king of Judah, this word came to Jeremiah from Yahweh, saying, ² Yahweh says to me: "Make bonds and bars, and put them on your neck. ³ Then send them to the king of Edom, to the king of Moab, to the king of the children of Ammon, to the king of Tyre, and to the king of Sidon, by the hand of the messengers who come to Jerusalem to Zedekiah king of Judah. ⁴ Give them a command to their masters, saying, 'Yahweh of Armies, the God of Israel says, "You shall tell your masters: ⁵'I have made the earth, the men, and the animals that are on the surface of the earth by my great power and by my outstretched arm. I give it to whom it seems right to me. ⁶ Now I have given all these lands into the hand of Nebuchadnezzar the king of Babylon, my servant. I have also given the animals of the field to him to serve him. ⁷ All the nations will serve him, his son, and his son's son, until the time of his own land comes. Then many nations and great kings will make him their bondservant. ⁸"'"It will happen that I will punish the nation and the kingdom which will not serve the same Nebuchadnezzar king of Babylon, and that will not put their neck under the yoke of the king of Babylon,' says Yahweh, 'with the sword, with famine, and with pestilence, until I have consumed them by his hand. ⁹ But as for you, don't listen to your prophets, to your diviners, to your dreams, to your soothsayers, or to your sorcerers, who speak to you, saying, "You shall not serve the king of Babylon;" ¹⁰ for they prophesy a lie to you, to remove you far from your land, so that I would drive you out, and you would perish. ¹¹ But the nation that brings their neck under the yoke of the king of Babylon

and serves him, that nation I will let remain in their own land,' says Yahweh; 'and they will till it and dwell in it.'"'" ¹² I spoke to Zedekiah king of Judah according to all these words, saying, "Bring your necks under the yoke of the king of Babylon, and serve him and his people, and live. ¹³ Why will you die, you and your people, by the sword, by the famine, and by the pestilence, as Yahweh has spoken concerning the nation that will not serve the king of Babylon? ¹⁴ Don't listen to the words of the prophets who speak to you, saying, 'You shall not serve the king of Babylon;' for they prophesy a lie to you. ¹⁵ For I have not sent them," says Yahweh, "but they prophesy falsely in my name; that I may drive you out, and that you may perish, you, and the prophets who prophesy to you." ¹⁶ Also I spoke to the priests and to all this people, saying, Yahweh says, "Don't listen to the words of your prophets who prophesy to you, saying, 'Behold, the vessels of Yahweh's house will now shortly be brought again from Babylon;' for they prophesy a lie to you. ¹⁷ Don't listen to them. Serve the king of Babylon, and live. Why should this city become a desolation? ¹⁸ But if they are prophets, and if Yahweh's word is with them, let them now make intercession to Yahweh of Armies, that the vessels which are left in Yahweh's house, in the house of the king of Judah, and at Jerusalem, don't go to Babylon. ¹⁹ For Yahweh of Armies says concerning the pillars, concerning the sea, concerning the bases, and concerning the rest of the vessels that are left in this city, ²⁰ which Nebuchadnezzar king of Babylon didn't take when he carried away captive Jeconiah the son of Jehoiakim, king of Judah, from Jerusalem to Babylon, and all the nobles of Judah and Jerusalem— ²¹ yes, Yahweh of Armies, the God of Israel, says concerning the vessels that are left in Yahweh's house, and in the house of the king of Judah, and at Jerusalem: ²²'They will be carried to Babylon, and there they will be, until the day that I visit them,' says Yahweh; 'then I will bring them up, and restore them to this place.'"

## 28

¹ That same year, in the beginning of the reign of Zedekiah king of Judah, in the fourth year, in the fifth month, Hananiah the son of Azzur, the prophet, who was of Gibeon, spoke to me in Yahweh's house, in the presence of the priests and of all the people, saying, ²"Yahweh of Armies, the God of Israel, says, 'I have broken the yoke of the king of Babylon. ³ Within two full years I will bring again into this place all the vessels of Yahweh's house that Nebuchadnezzar king of Babylon took away from this place and carried to Babylon. ⁴ I will bring again to this place Jeconiah the son of Jehoiakim, king of Judah, with all the captives of Judah, who went to Babylon,' says Yahweh; 'for I will break the yoke of the king of Babylon.'" ⁵ Then the prophet Jeremiah said to the prophet Hananiah in the presence of the priests, and in the presence of all the people who stood in Yahweh's house, ⁶ even the prophet Jeremiah said, "Amen! May Yahweh do so. May Yahweh perform your words which you have prophesied, to bring again the vessels of Yahweh's house, and all those who are captives, from Babylon to this place. ⁷ Nevertheless listen now to this word that I speak in your ears, and in the ears of all the people: ⁸ The prophets who have been before me and before you of old prophesied against many countries, and against great kingdoms, of war, of evil, and of pestilence. ⁹ As for the prophet who prophesies of peace, when the word of the prophet happens, then the prophet will be known, that Yahweh has truly sent him." ¹⁰ Then Hananiah the prophet took the bar from off the prophet Jeremiah's neck, and broke it. ¹¹ Hananiah spoke in the presence of all the people, saying, "Yahweh says: 'Even so I will break the yoke of Nebuchadnezzar king of Babylon from off the neck of all the nations within two full years.'" Then the prophet Jeremiah went his way. ¹² Then Yahweh's word came to Jeremiah, after Hananiah the prophet had broken the bar from off the neck of the prophet Jeremiah, saying, ¹³"Go, and tell Hananiah, saying, 'Yahweh says, "You have broken the bars of wood, but you have made in their place bars of iron." ¹⁴ For Yahweh of Armies, the God of Israel says, "I have put a yoke of iron on the neck of all these nations, that they may serve Nebuchadnezzar king of Babylon; and they will serve him. I have also given him the animals of the field."'" ¹⁵ Then the prophet Jeremiah said to Hananiah the prophet, "Listen, Hananiah! Yahweh has not sent you, but you make this people trust in a lie. ¹⁶ Therefore Yahweh says, 'Behold, I will send you away from off the surface of the earth. This year you will die, because you have spoken rebellion against Yahweh.'" ¹⁷ So Hananiah the prophet died the same year in the seventh month. 29¹ Now these are the words of the letter that Jeremiah the prophet sent from Jerusalem to the residue of the elders of the captivity, and to the priests, to the prophets, and to all the people whom Nebuchadnezzar had carried away captive from Jerusalem to Babylon, ²(after Jeconiah the king, the queen mother, the eunuchs, the princes of Judah and Jerusalem, the craftsmen, and the smiths had departed from Jerusalem), ³ by the hand of Elasah the son of Shaphan and Gemariah the son of Hilkiah, (whom Zedekiah king of Judah sent to Babylon to Nebuchadnezzar king of Babylon). It said: ⁴

Yahweh of Armies, the God of Israel, says to all the captives whom I have caused to be carried away captive from Jerusalem to Babylon: [5]"Build houses and dwell in them. Plant gardens and eat their fruit. [6] Take wives and father sons and daughters. Take wives for your sons, and give your daughters to husbands, that they may bear sons and daughters. Multiply there, and don't be diminished. [7] Seek the peace of the city where I have caused you to be carried away captive, and pray to Yahweh for it; for in its peace you will have peace." [8] For Yahweh of Armies, the God of Israel says: "Don't let your prophets who are among you and your diviners deceive you. Don't listen to your dreams which you cause to be dreamed. [9] For they prophesy falsely to you in my name. I have not sent them," says Yahweh. [10] For Yahweh says, "After seventy years are accomplished for Babylon, I will visit you and perform my good word toward you, in causing you to return to this place. [11] For I know the thoughts that I think toward you," says Yahweh, "thoughts of peace, and not of evil, to give you hope and a future. [12] You shall call on me, and you shall go and pray to me, and I will listen to you. [13] You shall seek me and find me, when you search for me with all your heart. [14] I will be found by you," says Yahweh, "and I will turn again your captivity, and I will gather you from all the nations, and from all the places where I have driven you, says Yahweh. I will bring you again to the place from where I caused you to be carried away captive." [15] Because you have said, "Yahweh has raised us up prophets in Babylon," [16] Yahweh says concerning the king who sits on David's throne, and concerning all the people who dwell in this city, your brothers who haven't gone with you into captivity, [17] Yahweh of Armies says: "Behold, I will send on them the sword, the famine, and the pestilence, and will make them like rotten figs that can't be eaten, they are so bad. [18] I will pursue after them with the sword, with the famine, and with the pestilence, and will deliver them to be tossed back and forth among all the kingdoms of the earth, to be an object of horror, an astonishment, a hissing, and a reproach among all the nations where I have driven them, [19] because they have not listened to my words," says Yahweh, "with which I sent to them my servants the prophets, rising up early and sending them; but you would not hear," says Yahweh. [20] Hear therefore Yahweh's word, all you captives whom I have sent away from Jerusalem to Babylon. [21] Yahweh of Armies, the God of Israel, says concerning Ahab the son of Kolaiah, and concerning Zedekiah the son of Maaseiah, who prophesy a lie to you in my name: "Behold, I will deliver them into the hand of Nebuchadnezzar king of Babylon; and he will kill them before your eyes. [22] A curse will be taken up about them by all the captives of Judah who are in Babylon, saying, 'Yahweh make you like Zedekiah and like Ahab, whom the king of Babylon roasted in the fire;' [23] because they have done foolish things in Israel, and have committed adultery with their neighbors' wives, and have spoken words in my name falsely, which I didn't command them. I am he who knows, and am witness," says Yahweh. [24] Concerning Shemaiah the Nehelamite you shall speak, saying, [25]"Yahweh of Armies, the God of Israel, says, 'Because you have sent letters in your own name to all the people who are at Jerusalem, and to Zephaniah the son of Maaseiah, the priest, and to all the priests, saying, [26]"Yahweh has made you priest in the place of Jehoiada the priest, that there may be officers in Yahweh's house, for every man who is crazy and makes himself a prophet, that you should put him in the stocks and in shackles. [27] Now therefore, why have you not rebuked Jeremiah of Anathoth, who makes himself a prophet to you, [28] because he has sent to us in Babylon, saying, The captivity is long. Build houses, and dwell in them. Plant gardens, and eat their fruit?"'" [29] Zephaniah the priest read this letter in the hearing of Jeremiah the prophet. [30] Then Yahweh's word came to Jeremiah, saying, [31]"Send to all of the captives, saying, 'Yahweh says concerning Shemaiah the Nehelamite: "Because Shemaiah has prophesied to you, and I didn't send him, and he has caused you to trust in a lie," [32] therefore Yahweh says, "Behold, I will punish Shemaiah the Nehelamite and his offspring. He will not have a man to dwell among this people. He won't see the good that I will do to my people," says Yahweh, "because he has spoken rebellion against Yahweh.""'

## 30

[1] The word that came to Jeremiah from Yahweh, saying, [2]"Yahweh, the God of Israel, says, 'Write all the words that I have spoken to you in a book. [3] For, behold, the days come,' says Yahweh, 'that I will reverse the captivity of my people Israel and Judah,' says Yahweh. 'I will cause them to return to the land that I gave to their fathers, and they will possess it.'" [4] These are the words that Yahweh spoke concerning Israel and concerning Judah. [5] For Yahweh says: "We have heard a voice of trembling; a voice of fear, and not of peace. [6] Ask now, and see whether a man travails with child. Why do I see every man with his hands on his waist, as a woman in travail, and all faces are turned pale? [7] Alas, for that day is great, so that none is like it! It is even the time of Jacob's trouble; but he will be saved out of it. [8] It will come to pass in that day,

says Yahweh of Armies, that I will break his yoke from off your neck, and will burst your bonds. Strangers will no more make them their bondservants; [9] but they will serve Yahweh their God, and David their king, whom I will raise up to them. [10] Therefore don't be afraid, O Jacob my servant, says Yahweh. Don't be dismayed, Israel. For, behold, I will save you from afar, and save your offspring from the land of their captivity. Jacob will return, and will be quiet and at ease. No one will make him afraid. [11] For I am with you, says Yahweh, to save you; for I will make a full end of all the nations where I have scattered you, but I will not make a full end of you; but I will correct you in measure, and will in no way leave you unpunished." [12] For Yahweh says, "Your hurt is incurable. Your wound is grievous. [13] There is no one to plead your cause, that you may be bound up. You have no healing medicines. [14] All your lovers have forgotten you. They don't seek you. For I have wounded you with the wound of an enemy, with the chastisement of a cruel one, for the greatness of your iniquity, because your sins were increased. [15] Why do you cry over your injury? Your pain is incurable. For the greatness of your iniquity, because your sins have increased, I have done these things to you. [16] Therefore all those who devour you will be devoured. All your adversaries, everyone of them, will go into captivity. Those who plunder you will be plunder. I will make all who prey on you become prey. [17] For I will restore health to you, and I will heal you of your wounds," says Yahweh, "because they have called you an outcast, saying, 'It is Zion, whom no man seeks after.'" [18] Yahweh says: "Behold, I will reverse the captivity of Jacob's tents, and have compassion on his dwelling places. The city will be built on its own hill, and the palace will be inhabited in its own place. [19] Thanksgiving will proceed out of them with the voice of those who make merry. I will multiply them, and they will not be few; I will also glorify them, and they will not be small. [20] Their children also will be as before, and their congregation will be established before me. I will punish all who oppress them. [21] Their prince will be one of them, and their ruler will proceed from among them. I will cause him to draw near, and he will approach me; for who is he who has had boldness to approach me?" says Yahweh. [22]"You shall be my people, and I will be your God. [23] Behold, Yahweh's storm, his wrath, has gone out, a sweeping storm; it will burst on the head of the wicked. [24] The fierce anger of Yahweh will not return until he has accomplished, and until he has performed the intentions of his heart. In the latter days you will understand it."

## 31

[1]"At that time," says Yahweh, "I will be the God of all the families of Israel, and they will be my people." [2] Yahweh says, "The people who survive the sword found favor in the wilderness; even Israel, when I went to cause him to rest." [3] Yahweh appeared of old to me, saying, "Yes, I have loved you with an everlasting love. Therefore I have drawn you with loving kindness. [4] I will build you again, and you will be built, O virgin of Israel. You will again be adorned with your tambourines, and will go out in the dances of those who make merry. [5] Again you will plant vineyards on the mountains of Samaria. The planters will plant, and will enjoy its fruit. [6] For there will be a day that the watchmen on the hills of Ephraim cry, 'Arise! Let's go up to Zion to Yahweh our God.'" [7] For Yahweh says, "Sing with gladness for Jacob, and shout for the chief of the nations. Publish, praise, and say, 'Yahweh, save your people, the remnant of Israel!' [8] Behold, I will bring them from the north country, and gather them from the uttermost parts of the earth, along with the blind and the lame, the woman with child and her who travails with child together. They will return as a great company. [9] They will come with weeping. I will lead them with petitions. I will cause them to walk by rivers of waters, in a straight way in which they won't stumble; for I am a father to Israel. Ephraim is my firstborn. [10]"Hear Yahweh's word, you nations, and declare it in the distant islands. Say, 'He who scattered Israel will gather him, and keep him, as a shepherd does his flock.' [11] For Yahweh has ransomed Jacob, and redeemed him from the hand of him who was stronger than he. [12] They will come and sing in the height of Zion, and will flow to the goodness of Yahweh, to the grain, to the new wine, to the oil, and to the young of the flock and of the herd. Their soul will be as a watered garden. They will not sorrow any more at all. [13] Then the virgin will rejoice in the dance, the young men and the old together; for I will turn their mourning into joy, and will comfort them, and make them rejoice from their sorrow. [14] I will satiate the soul of the priests with fatness, and my people will be satisfied with my goodness," says Yahweh. [15] Yahweh says: "A voice is heard in Ramah, lamentation and bitter weeping, Rachel weeping for her children. She refuses to be comforted for her children, because they are no more." [16] Yahweh says: "Refrain your voice from weeping, and your eyes from tears, for your work will be rewarded," says Yahweh. "They will come again from the land of the enemy. [17] There is hope for your latter end," says Yahweh. "Your children will come again to their own territory. [18]"I have surely heard Ephraim grieving thus, 'You have chastised me, and I was chastised, as an untrained calf. Turn me, and I

will be turned, for you are Yahweh my God. ¹⁹ Surely after that I was turned. I repented. After that I was instructed. I struck my thigh. I was ashamed, yes, even confounded, because I bore the reproach of my youth.' ²⁰ Is Ephraim my dear son? Is he a darling child? For as often as I speak against him, I still earnestly remember him. Therefore my heart yearns for him. I will surely have mercy on him," says Yahweh. ²¹"Set up road signs. Make guideposts. Set your heart toward the highway, even the way by which you went. Turn again, virgin of Israel. Turn again to these your cities. ²² How long will you go here and there, you backsliding daughter? For Yahweh has created a new thing in the earth: a woman will encompass a man." ²³ Yahweh of Armies, the God of Israel, says: "Yet again they will use this speech in the land of Judah and in its cities, when I reverse their captivity: 'Yahweh bless you, habitation of righteousness, mountain of holiness.' ²⁴ Judah and all its cities will dwell therein together, the farmers, and those who go about with flocks. ²⁵ For I have satiated the weary soul, and I have replenished every sorrowful soul." ²⁶ On this I awakened, and saw; and my sleep was sweet to me. ²⁷"Behold, the days come," says Yahweh, "that I will sow the house of Israel and the house of Judah with the seed of man and with the seed of animal. ²⁸ It will happen that, like as I have watched over them to pluck up and to break down and to overthrow and to destroy and to afflict, so I will watch over them to build and to plant," says Yahweh. ²⁹"In those days they will say no more, "'The fathers have eaten sour grapes, and the children's teeth are set on edge.' ³⁰ But everyone will die for his own iniquity. Every man who eats the sour grapes, his teeth will be set on edge. ³¹"Behold, the days come," says Yahweh, "that I will make a new covenant with the house of Israel, and with the house of Judah, ³² not according to the covenant that I made with their fathers in the day that I took them by the hand to bring them out of the land of Egypt, which covenant of mine they broke, although I was a husband to them," says Yahweh. ³³"But this is the covenant that I will make with the house of Israel after those days," says Yahweh: "I will put my law in their inward parts, and I will write it in their heart. I will be their God, and they shall be my people. ³⁴ They will no longer each teach his neighbor, and every man teach his brother, saying, 'Know Yahweh;' for they will all know me, from their least to their greatest," says Yahweh, "for I will forgive their iniquity, and I will remember their sin no more." ³⁵ Yahweh, who gives the sun for a light by day, and the ordinances of the moon and of the stars for a light by night, who stirs up the sea, so that its waves roar— Yahweh of Armies is his name, says: ³⁶"If these ordinances depart from before me," says Yahweh, "then the offspring of Israel also will cease from being a nation before me forever." ³⁷ Yahweh says: "If heaven above can be measured, and the foundations of the earth searched out beneath, then I will also cast off all the offspring of Israel for all that they have done," says Yahweh. ³⁸"Behold, the days come," says Yahweh, "that the city will be built to Yahweh from the tower of Hananel to the gate of the corner. ³⁹ The measuring line will go out further straight onward to the hill Gareb, and will turn toward Goah. ⁴⁰ The whole valley of the dead bodies and of the ashes, and all the fields to the brook Kidron, to the corner of the horse gate toward the east, will be holy to Yahweh. It will not be plucked up or thrown down any more forever."

## 32

¹ This is the word that came to Jeremiah from Yahweh in the tenth year of Zedekiah king of Judah, which was the eighteenth year of Nebuchadnezzar. ² Now at that time the king of Babylon's army was besieging Jerusalem. Jeremiah the prophet was shut up in the court of the guard, which was in the king of Judah's house. ³ For Zedekiah king of Judah had shut him up, saying, "Why do you prophesy, and say, 'Yahweh says, "Behold, I will give this city into the hand of the king of Babylon, and he will take it; ⁴ and Zedekiah king of Judah won't escape out of the hand of the Chaldeans, but will surely be delivered into the hand of the king of Babylon, and will speak with him mouth to mouth, and his eyes will see his eyes; ⁵ and he will bring Zedekiah to Babylon, and he will be there until I visit him," says Yahweh, "though you fight with the Chaldeans, you will not prosper"'?" ⁶ Jeremiah said, "Yahweh's word came to me, saying, ⁷'Behold, Hanamel the son of Shallum your uncle will come to you, saying, "Buy my field that is in Anathoth; for the right of redemption is yours to buy it."'" ⁸"So Hanamel my uncle's son came to me in the court of the guard according to Yahweh's word, and said to me, 'Please buy my field that is in Anathoth, which is in the land of Benjamin; for the right of inheritance is yours, and the redemption is yours. Buy it for yourself.' "Then I knew that this was Yahweh's word. ⁹ I bought the field that was in Anathoth of Hanamel my uncle's son, and weighed him the money, even seventeen shekelsᵃ of silver. ¹⁰ I signed the deed, sealed it, called witnesses, and weighed the money in the balances to him. ¹¹ So I took

the deed of the purchase, both that which was sealed, containing the terms and conditions, and that which was open; ¹² and I delivered the deed of the purchase to Baruch the son of Neriah, the son of Mahseiah, in the presence of Hanamel my uncle's son, and in the presence of the witnesses who signed the deed of the purchase, before all the Jews who sat in the court of the guard. ¹³"I commanded Baruch before them, saying, ¹⁴ Yahweh of Armies, the God of Israel, says: 'Take these deeds, this deed of the purchase which is sealed, and this deed which is open, and put them in an earthen vessel, that they may last many days.' ¹⁵ For Yahweh of Armies, the God of Israel says: 'Houses and fields and vineyards will yet again be bought in this land.' ¹⁶ Now after I had delivered the deed of the purchase to Baruch the son of Neriah, I prayed to Yahweh, saying, ¹⁷"Ah Lord Yahweh! Behold, you have made the heavens and the earth by your great power and by your outstretched arm. There is nothing too hard for you. ¹⁸ You show loving kindness to thousands, and repay the iniquity of the fathers into the bosom of their children after them. The great, the mighty God, Yahweh of Armies is your name: ¹⁹ great in counsel, and mighty in work; whose eyes are open to all the ways of the children of men, to give everyone according to his ways, and according to the fruit of his doings; ²⁰ who performed signs and wonders in the land of Egypt, even to this day, both in Israel and among other men; and made yourself a name, as it is today; ²¹ and brought your people Israel out of the land of Egypt with signs, with wonders, with a strong hand, with an outstretched arm, and with great terror; ²² and gave them this land, which you swore to their fathers to give them, a land flowing with milk and honey. ²³ They came in and possessed it, but they didn't obey your voice and didn't walk in your law. They have done nothing of all that you commanded them to do. Therefore you have caused all this evil to come upon them. ²⁴"Behold, siege ramps have been built against the city to take it. The city is given into the hand of the Chaldeans who fight against it, because of the sword, of the famine, and of the pestilence. What you have spoken has happened. Behold, you see it. ²⁵ You have said to me, Lord Yahweh, 'Buy the field for money, and call witnesses;' whereas the city is given into the hand of the Chaldeans." ²⁶ Then Yahweh's word came to Jeremiah, saying, ²⁷"Behold, I am Yahweh, the God of all flesh. Is there anything too hard for me? ²⁸ Therefore Yahweh says: Behold, I will give this city into the hand of the Chaldeans, and into the hand of Nebuchadnezzar king of Babylon, and he will take it. ²⁹ The Chaldeans, who fight against this city, will come and set this city on fire, and burn it with the houses on whose roofs they have offered incense to Baal, and poured out drink offerings to other gods, to provoke me to anger. ³⁰"For the children of Israel and the children of Judah have done only that which was evil in my sight from their youth; for the children of Israel have only provoked me to anger with the work of their hands, says Yahweh. ³¹ For this city has been to me a provocation of my anger and of my wrath from the day that they built it even to this day, so that I should remove it from before my face, ³² because of all the evil of the children of Israel and of the children of Judah, which they have done to provoke me to anger—they, their kings, their princes, their priests, their prophets, the men of Judah, and the inhabitants of Jerusalem. ³³ They have turned their backs to me, and not their faces. Although I taught them, rising up early and teaching them, yet they have not listened to receive instruction. ³⁴ But they set their abominations in the house which is called by my name, to defile it. ³⁵ They built the high places of Baal, which are in the valley of the son of Hinnom, to cause their sons and their daughters to pass through fire to Molech, which I didn't command them; neither did it come into my mind, that they should do this abomination, to cause Judah to sin." ³⁶ Now therefore Yahweh, the God of Israel, says concerning this city, about which you say, "It is given into the hand of the king of Babylon by the sword, by the famine, and by the pestilence:" ³⁷"Behold, I will gather them out of all the countries where I have driven them in my anger, and in my wrath, and in great indignation; and I will bring them again to this place. I will cause them to dwell safely. ³⁸ Then they will be my people, and I will be their God. ³⁹ I will give them one heart and one way, that they may fear me forever, for their good and the good of their children after them. ⁴⁰ I will make an everlasting covenant with them, that I will not turn away from following them, to do them good. I will put my fear in their hearts, that they may not depart from me. ⁴¹ Yes, I will rejoice over them to do them good, and I will plant them in this land assuredly with my whole heart and with my whole soul." ⁴² For Yahweh says: "Just as I have brought all this great evil on this people, so I will bring on them all the good that I have promised them. ⁴³ Fields will be bought in this land, about which you say, 'It is desolate, without man or animal. It is given into the hand of the Chaldeans.' ⁴⁴ Men will buy fields for money, sign the deeds, seal them, and call witnesses, in the land of Benjamin,

ᵃ 32:9 A shekel is about 10 grams or about 0.35 ounces.

and in the places around Jerusalem, in the cities of Judah, in the cities of the hill country, in the cities of the lowland, and in the cities of the South; for I will cause their captivity to be reversed," says Yahweh.

## 33

¹ Moreover Yahweh's word came to Jeremiah the second time, while he was still locked up in the court of the guard, saying, ²"Yahweh who does it, Yahweh who forms it to establish it—Yahweh is his name, says: ³'Call to me, and I will answer you, and will show you great and difficult things, which you don't know.' ⁴ For Yahweh, the God of Israel, says concerning the houses of this city and concerning the houses of the kings of Judah, which are broken down to make a defense against the mounds and against the sword: ⁵'While men come to fight with the Chaldeans, and to fill them with the dead bodies of men, whom I have killed in my anger and in my wrath, and for all whose wickedness I have hidden my face from this city, ⁶ behold, I will bring it health and healing, and I will cure them; and I will reveal to them abundance of peace and truth. ⁷ I will restore the fortunes of Judah and Israel, and will build them as at the first. ⁸ I will cleanse them from all their iniquity by which they have sinned against me. I will pardon all their iniquities by which they have sinned against me and by which they have transgressed against me. ⁹ This city will be to me for a name of joy, for praise, and for glory, before all the nations of the earth, which will hear all the good that I do to them, and will fear and tremble for all the good and for all the peace that I provide to it.'" ¹⁰ Yahweh says: "Yet again there will be heard in this place, about which you say, 'It is waste, without man and without animal, even in the cities of Judah, and in the streets of Jerusalem, that are desolate, without man and without inhabitant and without animal,' ¹¹ the voice of joy and the voice of gladness, the voice of the bridegroom and the voice of the bride, the voice of those who say, 'Give thanks to Yahweh of Armies, for Yahweh is good, for his loving kindness endures forever;' who bring thanksgiving into Yahweh's house. For I will cause the captivity of the land to be reversed as at the first," says Yahweh. ¹² Yahweh of Armies says: "Yet again there will be in this place, which is waste, without man and without animal, and in all its cities, a habitation of shepherds causing their flocks to lie down. ¹³ In the cities of the hill country, in the cities of the lowland, in the cities of the South, in the land of Benjamin, in the places around Jerusalem, and in the cities of Judah, the flocks will again pass under the hands of him who counts them," says Yahweh. ¹⁴"Behold, the days come," says Yahweh, "that I will perform that good word which I have spoken concerning the house of Israel and concerning the house of Judah. ¹⁵"In those days and at that time, I will cause a Branch of righteousness to grow up to David. He will execute justice and righteousness in the land. ¹⁶ In those days Judah will be saved, and Jerusalem will dwell safely. This is the name by which she will be called: Yahweh our righteousness." ¹⁷ For Yahweh says: "David will never lack a man to sit on the throne of the house of Israel. ¹⁸ The Levitical priests won't lack a man before me to offer burnt offerings, to burn meal offerings, and to do sacrifice continually." ¹⁹ Yahweh's word came to Jeremiah, saying, ²⁰"Yahweh says: 'If you can break my covenant of the day and my covenant of the night, so that there will not be day and night in their time, ²¹ then my covenant could also be broken with David my servant, that he won't have a son to reign on his throne; and with the Levitical priests, my ministers. ²² As the army of the sky can't be counted, and the sand of the sea can't be measured, so I will multiply the offspring of David my servant and the Levites who minister to me.'" ²³ Yahweh's word came to Jeremiah, saying, ²⁴"Don't consider what this people has spoken, saying, 'Has Yahweh cast off the two families which he chose?' Thus they despise my people, that they should be no more a nation before them." ²⁵ Yahweh says: "If my covenant of day and night fails, if I have not appointed the ordinances of heaven and earth, ²⁶ then I will also cast away the offspring of Jacob, and of David my servant, so that I will not take of his offspring to be rulers over the offspring of Abraham, Isaac, and Jacob; for I will cause their captivity to be reversed and will have mercy on them."

## 34

¹ The word which came to Jeremiah from Yahweh, when Nebuchadnezzar king of Babylon, with all his army, all the kingdoms of the earth that were under his dominion, and all the peoples, were fighting against Jerusalem and against all its cities, saying: ²"Yahweh, the God of Israel, says, 'Go, and speak to Zedekiah king of Judah, and tell him, Yahweh says, "Behold, I will give this city into the hand of the king of Babylon and he will burn it with fire. ³ You won't escape out of his hand, but will surely be taken and delivered into his hand. Your eyes will see the eyes of the king of Babylon, and he will speak with you mouth to mouth. You will go to Babylon."' ⁴"Yet hear Yahweh's word, O Zedekiah king of Judah. Yahweh says concerning you, 'You won't die by the sword. ⁵ You will die in peace; and with the burnings of your fathers, the former kings who were before you, so they

will make a burning for you. They will lament you, saying, "Ah Lord!" for I have spoken the word,' says Yahweh." ⁶ Then Jeremiah the prophet spoke all these words to Zedekiah king of Judah in Jerusalem, ⁷ when the king of Babylon's army was fighting against Jerusalem and against all the cities of Judah that were left, against Lachish and against Azekah; for these alone remained of the cities of Judah as fortified cities. ⁸ The word came to Jeremiah from Yahweh, after King Zedekiah had made a covenant with all the people who were at Jerusalem, to proclaim liberty to them, ⁹ that every man should let his male servant, and every man his female servant, who is a Hebrew or a Hebrewess, go free, that no one should make bondservants of them, of a Jew his brother. ¹⁰ All the princes and all the people obeyed who had entered into the covenant, that everyone should let his male servant and everyone his female servant go free, that no one should make bondservants of them any more. They obeyed and let them go, ¹¹ but afterwards they turned, and caused the servants and the handmaids whom they had let go free to return, and brought them into subjection for servants and for handmaids. ¹² Therefore Yahweh's word came to Jeremiah from Yahweh, saying, ¹³"Yahweh, the God of Israel, says: 'I made a covenant with your fathers in the day that I brought them out of the land of Egypt, out of the house of bondage, saying: ¹⁴ At the end of seven years, every man of you shall release his brother who is a Hebrew, who has been sold to you, and has served you six years. You shall let him go free from you. But your fathers didn't listen to me, and didn't incline their ear. ¹⁵ You had now turned, and had done that which is right in my eyes, in every man proclaiming liberty to his neighbor. You had made a covenant before me in the house which is called by my name; ¹⁶ but you turned and profaned my name, and every man caused his servant and every man his handmaid, whom you had let go free at their pleasure, to return. You brought them into subjection, to be to you for servants and for handmaids.'" ¹⁷ Therefore Yahweh says: "You have not listened to me, to proclaim liberty, every man to his brother, and every man to his neighbor. Behold, I proclaim to you a liberty," says Yahweh, "to the sword, to the pestilence, and to the famine. I will make you be tossed back and forth among all the kingdoms of the earth. ¹⁸ I will give the men who have transgressed my covenant, who have not performed the words of the covenant which they made before me when they cut the calf in two and passed between its parts: ¹⁹ the princes of Judah, the princes of Jerusalem, the eunuchs, the priests, and all the people of the land, who passed between the parts of the calf. ²⁰ I will even give them into the hand of their enemies and into the hand of those who seek their life. Their dead bodies will be food for the birds of the sky and for the animals of the earth. ²¹"I will give Zedekiah king of Judah and his princes into the hands of their enemies, into the hands of those who seek their life and into the hands of the king of Babylon's army, who has gone away from you. ²² Behold, I will command," says Yahweh, "and cause them to return to this city. They will fight against it, take it, and burn it with fire. I will make the cities of Judah a desolation, without inhabitant."

## 35

¹ The word which came to Jeremiah from Yahweh in the days of Jehoiakim the son of Josiah, king of Judah, saying, ²"Go to the house of the Rechabites, and speak to them, and bring them into Yahweh's house, into one of the rooms, and give them wine to drink." ³ Then I took Jaazaniah the son of Jeremiah, the son of Habazziniah, with his brothers, all his sons, and the whole house of the Rechabites; ⁴ and I brought them into Yahweh's house, into the room of the sons of Hanan the son of Igdaliah, the man of God, which was by the room of the princes, which was above the room of Maaseiah the son of Shallum, the keeper of the threshold. ⁵ I set before the sons of the house of the Rechabites bowls full of wine, and cups; and I said to them, "Drink wine!" ⁶ But they said, "We will drink no wine; for Jonadab the son of Rechab, our father, commanded us, saying, 'You shall drink no wine, neither you nor your children, forever. ⁷ You shall not build a house, sow seed, plant a vineyard, or have any; but all your days you shall dwell in tents, that you may live many days in the land in which you live as nomads.' ⁸ We have obeyed the voice of Jonadab the son of Rechab, our father, in all that he commanded us, to drink no wine all our days, we, our wives, our sons, or our daughters; ⁹ and not to build houses for ourselves to dwell in. We have no vineyard, field, or seed; ¹⁰ but we have lived in tents, and have obeyed, and done according to all that Jonadab our father commanded us. ¹¹ But when Nebuchadnezzar king of Babylon came up into the land, we said, 'Come! Let's go to Jerusalem for fear of the army of the Chaldeans, and for fear of the army of the Syrians; so we will dwell at Jerusalem.'" ¹² Then Yahweh's word came to Jeremiah, saying, ¹³"Yahweh of Armies, the God of Israel, says: 'Go and tell the men of Judah and the inhabitants of Jerusalem, "Will you not receive instruction to listen to my words?" says Yahweh. ¹⁴"The words of Jonadab the son of Rechab that he commanded his sons, not to drink wine, are performed; and to

this day they drink none, for they obey their father's commandment; but I have spoken to you, rising up early and speaking, and you have not listened to me. ¹⁵ I have sent also to you all my servants the prophets, rising up early and sending them, saying, 'Every one of you must return now from his evil way, amend your doings, and don't go after other gods to serve them. Then you will dwell in the land which I have given to you and to your fathers;' but you have not inclined your ear, nor listened to me. ¹⁶ The sons of Jonadab the son of Rechab have performed the commandment of their father which he commanded them, but this people has not listened to me.'" ¹⁷"Therefore Yahweh, the God of Armies, the God of Israel, says: 'Behold, I will bring on Judah and on all the inhabitants of Jerusalem all the evil that I have pronounced against them, because I have spoken to them, but they have not heard; and I have called to them, but they have not answered.'" ¹⁸ Jeremiah said to the house of the Rechabites, "Yahweh of Armies, the God of Israel, says: 'Because you have obeyed the commandment of Jonadab your father, and kept all his precepts, and done according to all that he commanded you,' ¹⁹ therefore Yahweh of Armies, the God of Israel, says: 'Jonadab the son of Rechab will not lack a man to stand before me forever.'"

## 36

¹ In the fourth year of Jehoiakim the son of Josiah, king of Judah, this word came to Jeremiah from Yahweh, saying, ²"Take a scroll of a book, and write in it all the words that I have spoken to you against Israel, against Judah, and against all the nations, from the day I spoke to you, from the days of Josiah even to this day. ³ It may be that the house of Judah will hear all the evil which I intend to do to them, that they may each return from his evil way; that I may forgive their iniquity and their sin." ⁴ Then Jeremiah called Baruch the son of Neriah; and Baruch wrote from the mouth of Jeremiah all Yahweh's words, which he had spoken to him, on a scroll of a book. ⁵ Jeremiah commanded Baruch, saying, "I am restricted. I can't go into Yahweh's house. ⁶ Therefore you go, and read from the scroll which you have written from my mouth, Yahweh's words, in the ears of the people in Yahweh's house on the fast day. Also you shall read them in the ears of all Judah who come out of their cities. ⁷ It may be they will present their supplication before Yahweh, and will each return from his evil way; for Yahweh has pronounced great anger and wrath against this people." ⁸ Baruch the son of Neriah did according to all that Jeremiah the prophet commanded him, reading in the book Yahweh's words in Yahweh's house. ⁹ Now in the fifth year of Jehoiakim the son of Josiah, king of Judah, in the ninth month, all the people in Jerusalem and all the people who came from the cities of Judah to Jerusalem, proclaimed a fast before Yahweh. ¹⁰ Then Baruch read the words of Jeremiah from the book in Yahweh's house, in the room of Gemariah the son of Shaphan the scribe, in the upper court, at the entry of the new gate of Yahweh's house, in the ears of all the people. ¹¹ When Micaiah the son of Gemariah, the son of Shaphan, had heard out of the book all Yahweh's words, ¹² he went down into the king's house, into the scribe's room; and behold, all the princes were sitting there, Elishama the scribe, Delaiah the son of Shemaiah, Elnathan the son of Achbor, Gemariah the son of Shaphan, Zedekiah the son of Hananiah, and all the princes. ¹³ Then Micaiah declared to them all the words that he had heard, when Baruch read the book in the ears of the people. ¹⁴ Therefore all the princes sent Jehudi the son of Nethaniah, the son of Shelemiah, the son of Cushi, to Baruch, saying, "Take in your hand the scroll in which you have read in the ears of the people, and come." So Baruch the son of Neriah took the scroll in his hand, and came to them. ¹⁵ They said to him, "Sit down now, and read it in our hearing." So Baruch read it in their hearing. ¹⁶ Now when they had heard all the words, they turned in fear one toward another, and said to Baruch, "We will surely tell the king of all these words." ¹⁷ They asked Baruch, saying, "Tell us now, how did you write all these words at his mouth?" ¹⁸ Then Baruch answered them, "He dictated all these words to me with his mouth, and I wrote them with ink in the book." ¹⁹ Then the princes said to Baruch, "You and Jeremiah go hide. Don't let anyone know where you are." ²⁰ They went in to the king into the court, but they had laid up the scroll in the room of Elishama the scribe. Then they told all the words in the hearing of the king. ²¹ So the king sent Jehudi to get the scroll, and he took it out of the room of Elishama the scribe. Jehudi read it in the hearing of the king, and in the hearing of all the princes who stood beside the king. ²² Now the king was sitting in the winter house in the ninth month, and there was a fire in the brazier burning before him. ²³ When Jehudi had read three or four columns, the king cut it with the penknife, and cast it into the fire that was in the brazier, until all the scroll was consumed in the fire that was in the brazier. ²⁴ The king and his servants who heard all these words were not afraid, and didn't tear their garments. ²⁵ Moreover Elnathan and Delaiah and Gemariah had made intercession to the king that he would not burn the scroll; but he would not listen to them. ²⁶ The king commanded Jerahmeel the king's

son, and Seraiah the son of Azriel, and Shelemiah the son of Abdeel, to arrest Baruch the scribe and Jeremiah the prophet; but Yahweh hid them. ²⁷ Then Yahweh's word came to Jeremiah, after the king had burned the scroll, and the words which Baruch wrote at the mouth of Jeremiah, saying, ²⁸"Take again another scroll, and write in it all the former words that were in the first scroll, which Jehoiakim the king of Judah has burned. ²⁹ Concerning Jehoiakim king of Judah you shall say, 'Yahweh says: "You have burned this scroll, saying, 'Why have you written therein, saying, "The king of Babylon will certainly come and destroy this land, and will cause to cease from there man and animal"?'" ³⁰ Therefore Yahweh says concerning Jehoiakim king of Judah: "He will have no one to sit on David's throne. His dead body will be cast out in the day to the heat, and in the night to the frost. ³¹ I will punish him, his offspring, and his servants for their iniquity. I will bring on them, on the inhabitants of Jerusalem, and on the men of Judah, all the evil that I have pronounced against them, but they didn't listen."'" ³² Then Jeremiah took another scroll, and gave it to Baruch the scribe, the son of Neriah, who wrote therein from the mouth of Jeremiah all the words of the book which Jehoiakim king of Judah had burned in the fire; and many similar words were added to them.

## 37

¹ Zedekiah the son of Josiah reigned as king instead of Coniah the son of Jehoiakim, whom Nebuchadnezzar king of Babylon made king in the land of Judah. ² But neither he, nor his servants, nor the people of the land, listened to Yahweh's words, which he spoke by the prophet Jeremiah. ³ Zedekiah the king sent Jehucal the son of Shelemiah and Zephaniah the son of Maaseiah, the priest, to the prophet Jeremiah, saying, "Pray now to Yahweh our God for us." ⁴ Now Jeremiah came in and went out among the people, for they had not put him into prison. ⁵ Pharaoh's army had come out of Egypt; and when the Chaldeans who were besieging Jerusalem heard news of them, they withdrew from Jerusalem. ⁶ Then Yahweh's word came to the prophet Jeremiah, saying, ⁷"Yahweh, the God of Israel, says, 'You shall tell the king of Judah, who sent you to me to inquire of me: "Behold, Pharaoh's army, which has come out to help you, will return to Egypt into their own land. ⁸ The Chaldeans will come again, and fight against this city. They will take it and burn it with fire."' ⁹"Yahweh says, 'Don't deceive yourselves, saying, "The Chaldeans will surely depart from us;" for they will not depart. ¹⁰ For though you had struck the whole army of the Chaldeans who fight against you, and only wounded men remained among them, they would each rise up in his tent and burn this city with fire.'" ¹¹ When the army of the Chaldeans had withdrawn from Jerusalem for fear of Pharaoh's army, ¹² then Jeremiah went out of Jerusalem to go into the land of Benjamin, to receive his portion there, in the middle of the people. ¹³ When he was in Benjamin's gate, a captain of the guard was there, whose name was Irijah, the son of Shelemiah, the son of Hananiah; and he seized Jeremiah the prophet, saying, "You are defecting to the Chaldeans!" ¹⁴ Then Jeremiah said, "That is false! I am not defecting to the Chaldeans." But he didn't listen to him; so Irijah seized Jeremiah, and brought him to the princes. ¹⁵ The princes were angry with Jeremiah, and struck him, and put him in prison in the house of Jonathan the scribe; for they had made that the prison. ¹⁶ When Jeremiah had come into the dungeon house and into the cells, and Jeremiah had remained there many days, ¹⁷ then Zedekiah the king sent and had him brought out. The king asked him secretly in his house, "Is there any word from Yahweh?" Jeremiah said, "There is." He also said, "You will be delivered into the hand of the king of Babylon." ¹⁸ Moreover Jeremiah said to King Zedekiah, "How have I sinned against you, against your servants, or against this people, that you have put me in prison? ¹⁹ Now where are your prophets who prophesied to you, saying, 'The king of Babylon will not come against you, nor against this land'? ²⁰ Now please hear, my lord the king: please let my supplication be presented before you, that you not cause me to return to the house of Jonathan the scribe, lest I die there." ²¹ Then Zedekiah the king commanded, and they committed Jeremiah into the court of the guard. They gave him daily a loaf of bread out of the bakers' street, until all the bread in the city was gone. Thus Jeremiah remained in the court of the guard.

## 38

¹ Shephatiah the son of Mattan, Gedaliah the son of Pashhur, Jucal the son of Shelemiah, and Pashhur the son of Malchijah heard the words that Jeremiah spoke to all the people, saying, ²"Yahweh says, 'He who remains in this city will die by the sword, by the famine, and by the pestilence, but he who goes out to the Chaldeans will live. He will escape with his life and he will live.' ³ Yahweh says, 'This city will surely be given into the hand of the army of the king of Babylon, and he will take it.'" ⁴ Then the princes said to the king, "Please let this man be put to death, because he weakens the hands of the men of war who remain in this city, and the hands of all the people, in speaking such words to them; for this man doesn't seek the welfare of this people, but

harm." ⁵ Zedekiah the king said, "Behold, he is in your hand; for the king can't do anything to oppose you." ⁶ Then they took Jeremiah and threw him into the dungeon of Malchijah the king's son, that was in the court of the guard. They let down Jeremiah with cords. In the dungeon there was no water, but mire; and Jeremiah sank in the mire. ⁷ Now when Ebedmelech the Ethiopian, a eunuch, who was in the king's house, heard that they had put Jeremiah in the dungeon (the king was then sitting in Benjamin's gate), ⁸ Ebedmelech went out of the king's house, and spoke to the king, saying, ⁹"My lord the king, these men have done evil in all that they have done to Jeremiah the prophet, whom they have cast into the dungeon. He is likely to die in the place where he is, because of the famine; for there is no more bread in the city." ¹⁰ Then the king commanded Ebedmelech the Ethiopian, saying, "Take from here thirty men with you, and take up Jeremiah the prophet out of the dungeon, before he dies." ¹¹ So Ebedmelech took the men with him, and went into the house of the king under the treasury, and took from there rags and worn-out garments, and let them down by cords into the dungeon to Jeremiah. ¹² Ebedmelech the Ethiopian said to Jeremiah, "Now put these rags and worn-out garments under your armpits under the cords." Jeremiah did so. ¹³ So they lifted Jeremiah up with the cords, and took him up out of the dungeon; and Jeremiah remained in the court of the guard. ¹⁴ Then Zedekiah the king sent and took Jeremiah the prophet to himself into the third entry that is in Yahweh's house. Then the king said to Jeremiah, "I will ask you something. Hide nothing from me." ¹⁵ Then Jeremiah said to Zedekiah, "If I declare it to you, will you not surely put me to death? If I give you counsel, you will not listen to me." ¹⁶ So Zedekiah the king swore secretly to Jeremiah, saying, "As Yahweh lives, who made our souls, I will not put you to death, neither will I give you into the hand of these men who seek your life." ¹⁷ Then Jeremiah said to Zedekiah, "Yahweh, the God of Armies, the God of Israel, says: 'If you will go out to the king of Babylon's princes, then your soul will live, and this city will not be burned with fire. You will live, along with your house. ¹⁸ But if you will not go out to the king of Babylon's princes, then this city will be given into the hand of the Chaldeans, and they will burn it with fire, and you won't escape out of their hand.'" ¹⁹ Zedekiah the king said to Jeremiah, "I am afraid of the Jews who have defected to the Chaldeans, lest they deliver me into their hand, and they mock me." ²⁰ But Jeremiah said, "They won't deliver you. Obey, I beg you, Yahweh's voice, in that which I speak to you; so it will be well with you, and your soul will live. ²¹ But if you refuse to go out, this is the word that Yahweh has shown me: ²²'Behold, all the women who are left in the king of Judah's house will be brought out to the king of Babylon's princes, and those women will say, "Your familiar friends have turned on you, and have prevailed over you. Your feet are sunk in the mire, they have turned away from you." ²³ They will bring out all your wives and your children to the Chaldeans. You won't escape out of their hand, but will be taken by the hand of the king of Babylon. You will cause this city to be burned with fire.'" ²⁴ Then Zedekiah said to Jeremiah, "Let no man know of these words, and you won't die. ²⁵ But if the princes hear that I have talked with you, and they come to you, and tell you, 'Declare to us now what you have said to the king; don't hide it from us, and we will not put you to death; also tell us what the king said to you;' ²⁶ then you shall tell them, 'I presented my supplication before the king, that he would not cause me to return to Jonathan's house, to die there.'" ²⁷ Then all the princes came to Jeremiah, and asked him; and he told them according to all these words that the king had commanded. So they stopped speaking with him, for the matter was not perceived. ²⁸ So Jeremiah stayed in the court of the guard until the day that Jerusalem was taken.

## 39

¹ In the ninth year of Zedekiah king of Judah, in the tenth month, Nebuchadnezzar king of Babylon and all his army came against Jerusalem, and besieged it. ² In the eleventh year of Zedekiah, in the fourth month, the ninth day of the month, a breach was made in the city. ³ All the princes of the king of Babylon came in, and sat in the middle gate: Nergal Sharezer, Samgarnebo, Sarsechim the Rabsaris, Nergal Sharezer the Rabmag, with all the rest of the princes of the king of Babylon. ⁴ When Zedekiah the king of Judah and all the men of war saw them, then they fled and went out of the city by night, by the way of the king's garden, through the gate between the two walls; and he went out toward the Arabah. ⁵ But the army of the Chaldeans pursued them, and overtook Zedekiah in the plains of Jericho. When they had taken him, they brought him up to Nebuchadnezzar king of Babylon to Riblah in the land of Hamath; and he pronounced judgment on him. ⁶ Then the king of Babylon killed Zedekiah's sons in Riblah before his eyes. The king of Babylon also killed all the nobles of Judah. ⁷ Moreover he put out Zedekiah's eyes and bound him in fetters, to carry him to Babylon. ⁸ The Chaldeans burned the king's house and the people's houses with fire and broke down the walls of Jerusalem. ⁹ Then Nebuzaradan the captain of the guard carried away captive into Babylon the rest of the people who remained in the city, the deserters also who fell away to him, and the rest of the people who remained. ¹⁰ But Nebuzaradan the captain of the guard left of the poor of the people, who had nothing, in the land of Judah, and gave them vineyards and fields at the same time. ¹¹ Now Nebuchadnezzar king of Babylon commanded Nebuzaradan the captain of the guard concerning Jeremiah, saying, ¹²"Take him and take care of him. Do him no harm; but do to him even as he tells you." ¹³ So Nebuzaradan the captain of the guard, Nebushazban, Rabsaris, and Nergal Sharezer, Rabmag, and all the chief officers of the king of Babylon ¹⁴ sent and took Jeremiah out of the court of the guard, and committed him to Gedaliah the son of Ahikam, the son of Shaphan, that he should bring him home. So he lived among the people. ¹⁵ Now Yahweh's word came to Jeremiah while he was shut up in the court of the guard, saying, ¹⁶"Go, and speak to Ebedmelech the Ethiopian, saying, 'Yahweh of Armies, the God of Israel, says: "Behold, I will bring my words on this city for evil, and not for good; and they will be accomplished before you in that day. ¹⁷ But I will deliver you in that day," says Yahweh; "and you will not be given into the hand of the men of whom you are afraid. ¹⁸ For I will surely save you. You won't fall by the sword, but you will escape with your life, because you have put your trust in me," says Yahweh.'"

## 40

¹ The word which came to Jeremiah from Yahweh, after Nebuzaradan the captain of the guard had let him go from Ramah, when he had taken him being bound in chains among all the captives of Jerusalem and Judah who were carried away captive to Babylon. ² The captain of the guard took Jeremiah and said to him, "Yahweh your God pronounced this evil on this place; ³ and Yahweh has brought it, and done according as he spoke. Because you have sinned against Yahweh, and have not obeyed his voice, therefore this thing has come on you. ⁴ Now, behold, I release you today from the chains which are on your hand. If it seems good to you to come with me into Babylon, come, and I will take care of you; but if it seems bad to you to come with me into Babylon, don't. Behold, all the land is before you. Where it seems good and right to you to go, go there." ⁵ Now while he had not yet gone back, "Go back then," he said, "to Gedaliah the son of Ahikam, the son of Shaphan, whom the king of Babylon has made governor over the cities of Judah, and dwell with him among the people; or go wherever it seems right to you to go." So the captain of the guard gave him food and a present, and let him go. ⁶ Then Jeremiah went to Gedaliah the son of Ahikam to Mizpah, and lived with him among the people who were left in the land. ⁷ Now when all the captains of the forces who were in the fields, even they and their men, heard that the king of Babylon had made Gedaliah the son of Ahikam governor in the land, and had committed to him men, women, children, and of the poorest of the land, of those who were not carried away captive to Babylon, ⁸ then Ishmael the son of Nethaniah, and Johanan and Jonathan the sons of Kareah, and Seraiah the son of Tanhumeth, and the sons of Ephai the Netophathite, and Jezaniah the son of the Maacathite, they and their men came to Gedaliah to Mizpah. ⁹ Gedaliah the son of Ahikam the son of Shaphan swore to them and to their men, saying, "Don't be afraid to serve the Chaldeans. Dwell in the land, and serve the king of Babylon, and it will be well with you. ¹⁰ As for me, behold, I will dwell at Mizpah, to stand before the Chaldeans who will come to us; but you, gather wine and summer fruits and oil, and put them in your vessels, and dwell in your cities that you have taken." ¹¹ Likewise when all the Jews who were in Moab, and among the children of Ammon, and in Edom, and who were in all the countries, heard that the king of Babylon had left a remnant of Judah, and that he had set over them Gedaliah the son of Ahikam, the son of Shaphan, ¹² then all the Jews returned out of all places where they were driven, and came to the land of Judah, to Gedaliah, to Mizpah, and gathered very much wine and summer fruits. ¹³ Moreover Johanan the son of Kareah, and all the captains of the forces who were in the fields, came to Gedaliah to Mizpah, ¹⁴ and said to him, "Do you know that Baalis the king of the children of Ammon has sent Ishmael the son of Nethaniah to take your life?" But Gedaliah the son of Ahikam didn't believe them. ¹⁵ Then Johanan the son of Kareah spoke to Gedaliah in Mizpah secretly, saying, "Please let me go, and I will kill Ishmael the son of Nethaniah, and no man will know it. Why should he take your life, that all the Jews who are gathered to you should be scattered, and the remnant of Judah perish?" ¹⁶ But Gedaliah the son of Ahikam said to Johanan the son of Kareah, "You shall not do this thing, for you speak falsely of Ishmael."

## 41

¹ Now in the seventh month, Ishmael the son of Nethaniah, the son of Elishama, of the royal offspring and one of the chief officers of the king, and ten men with him, came to Gedaliah the son of Ahikam to Mizpah; and there they ate bread together in Mizpah. ² Then Ishmael the son of Nethaniah arose, and the ten men who were with him, and struck Gedaliah the son of Ahikam the son of Shaphan with the sword

and killed him, whom the king of Babylon had made governor over the land. ³ Ishmael also killed all the Jews who were with Gedaliah at Mizpah, and the Chaldean men of war who were found there. ⁴ The second day after he had killed Gedaliah, and no man knew it, ⁵ men came from Shechem, from Shiloh, and from Samaria, even eighty men, having their beards shaved and their clothes torn, and having cut themselves, with meal offerings and frankincense in their hand, to bring them to Yahweh's house. ⁶ Ishmael the son of Nethaniah went out from Mizpah to meet them, weeping all along as he went, and as he met them, he said to them, "Come to Gedaliah the son of Ahikam." ⁷ It was so, when they came into the middle of the city, that Ishmael the son of Nethaniah killed them, and cast them into the middle of the pit, he, and the men who were with him. ⁸ But ten men were found among those who said to Ishmael, "Don't kill us; for we have stores hidden in the field, of wheat, and of barley, and of oil, and of honey." So he stopped, and didn't kill them among their brothers. ⁹ Now the pit in which Ishmael cast all the dead bodies of the men whom he had killed, by the side of Gedaliah (this was that which Asa the king had made for fear of Baasha king of Israel), Ishmael the son of Nethaniah filled it with those who were killed. ¹⁰ Then Ishmael carried away captive all of the people who were left in Mizpah, even the king's daughters, and all the people who remained in Mizpah, whom Nebuzaradan the captain of the guard had committed to Gedaliah the son of Ahikam. Ishmael the son of Nethaniah carried them away captive, and departed to go over to the children of Ammon. ¹¹ But when Johanan the son of Kareah, and all the captains of the forces who were with him, heard of all the evil that Ishmael the son of Nethaniah had done, ¹² then they took all the men, and went to fight with Ishmael the son of Nethaniah, and found him by the great waters that are in Gibeon. ¹³ Now when all the people who were with Ishmael saw Johanan the son of Kareah, and all the captains of the forces who were with him, then they were glad. ¹⁴ So all the people who Ishmael had carried away captive from Mizpah turned about and came back, and went to Johanan the son of Kareah. ¹⁵ But Ishmael the son of Nethaniah escaped from Johanan with eight men, and went to the children of Ammon. ¹⁶ Then Johanan the son of Kareah and all the captains of the forces who were with him took all the remnant of the people whom he had recovered from Ishmael the son of Nethaniah, from Mizpah, after he had killed Gedaliah the son of Ahikam—the men of war, with the women, the children, and the eunuchs, whom he had brought back from Gibeon. ¹⁷ They departed and lived in Geruth Chimham, which is by Bethlehem, to go to enter into Egypt ¹⁸ because of the Chaldeans; for they were afraid of them, because Ishmael the son of Nethaniah had killed Gedaliah the son of Ahikam, whom the king of Babylon made governor over the land.

## 42

¹ Then all the captains of the forces, and Johanan the son of Kareah, and Jezaniah the son of Hoshaiah, and all the people from the least even to the greatest, came near, ² and said to Jeremiah the prophet, "Please let our supplication be presented before you, and pray for us to Yahweh your God, even for all this remnant, for we are left but a few of many, as your eyes see us, ³ that Yahweh your God may show us the way in which we should walk, and the things that we should do." ⁴ Then Jeremiah the prophet said to them, "I have heard you. Behold, I will pray to Yahweh your God according to your words; and it will happen that whatever thing Yahweh answers you, I will declare it to you. I will keep nothing back from you." ⁵ Then they said to Jeremiah, "May Yahweh be a true and faithful witness among us, if we don't do according to all the word with which Yahweh your God sends you to tell us. ⁶ Whether it is good, or whether it is bad, we will obey the voice of Yahweh our God, to whom we send you; that it may be well with us, when we obey the voice of Yahweh our God." ⁷ After ten days, Yahweh's word came to Jeremiah. ⁸ Then he called Johanan the son of Kareah, and all the captains of the forces who were with him, and all the people from the least even to the greatest, ⁹ and said to them, "Yahweh, the God of Israel, to whom you sent me to present your supplication before him, says: ¹⁰'If you will still live in this land, then I will build you, and not pull you down, and I will plant you, and not pluck you up; for I grieve over the distress that I have brought on you. ¹¹ Don't be afraid of the king of Babylon, of whom you are afraid. Don't be afraid of him,' says Yahweh, 'for I am with you to save you, and to deliver you from his hand. ¹² I will grant you mercy, that he may have mercy on you, and cause you to return to your own land. ¹³'"But if you say, "We will not dwell in this land," so that you don't obey Yahweh your God's voice, ¹⁴ saying, "No, but we will go into the land of Egypt, where we will see no war, nor hear the sound of the trumpet, nor have hunger of bread; and there we will dwell;"' ¹⁵ now therefore hear Yahweh's word, O remnant of Judah! Yahweh of Armies, the God of Israel, says, 'If you indeed set your faces to enter into Egypt, and go to live there, ¹⁶ then it will happen that the sword, which you fear, will overtake you there in the land of Egypt; and the famine, about which

you are afraid, will follow close behind you there in Egypt; and you will die there. ¹⁷ So will it be with all the men who set their faces to go into Egypt to live there. They will die by the sword, by the famine, and by the pestilence. None of them will remain or escape from the evil that I will bring on them.' ¹⁸ For Yahweh of Armies, the God of Israel, says: 'As my anger and my wrath has been poured out on the inhabitants of Jerusalem, so my wrath will be poured out on you, when you enter into Egypt; and you will be an object of horror, an astonishment, a curse, and a reproach; and you will see this place no more.' ¹⁹"Yahweh has spoken concerning you, remnant of Judah, 'Don't go into Egypt!' Know certainly that I have testified to you today. ²⁰ For you have dealt deceitfully against your own souls; for you sent me to Yahweh your God, saying, 'Pray for us to Yahweh our God; and according to all that Yahweh our God says, so declare to us, and we will do it.' ²¹ I have declared it to you today; but you have not obeyed Yahweh your God's voice in anything for which he has sent me to you. ²² Now therefore know certainly that you will die by the sword, by the famine, and by the pestilence in the place where you desire to go to live."

## 43

¹ When Jeremiah had finished speaking to all the people all the words of Yahweh their God, with which Yahweh their God had sent him to them, even all these words, ² then Azariah the son of Hoshaiah, Johanan the son of Kareah, and all the proud men spoke, saying to Jeremiah, "You speak falsely. Yahweh our God has not sent you to say, 'You shall not go into Egypt to live there;' ³ but Baruch the son of Neriah has turned you against us, to deliver us into the hand of the Chaldeans, that they may put us to death or carry us away captive to Babylon." ⁴ So Johanan the son of Kareah, and all the captains of the forces, and all the people, didn't obey Yahweh's voice, to dwell in the land of Judah. ⁵ But Johanan the son of Kareah and all the captains of the forces took all the remnant of Judah, who had returned from all the nations where they had been driven, to live in the land of Judah— ⁶ the men, the women, the children, the king's daughters, and every person who Nebuzaradan the captain of the guard had left with Gedaliah the son of Ahikam, the son of Shaphan; and Jeremiah the prophet, and Baruch the son of Neriah. ⁷ They came into the land of Egypt, for they didn't obey Yahweh's voice; and they came to Tahpanhes. ⁸ Then Yahweh's word came to Jeremiah in Tahpanhes, saying, ⁹"Take great stones in your hand and hide them in mortar in the brick work which is at the entry of Pharaoh's house in Tahpanhes, in the sight of the men of Judah. ¹⁰ Tell them, Yahweh of Armies, the God of Israel, says: 'Behold, I will send and take Nebuchadnezzar the king of Babylon, my servant, and will set his throne on these stones that I have hidden; and he will spread his royal pavilion over them. ¹¹ He will come, and will strike the land of Egypt; such as are for death will be put to death, and such as are for captivity to captivity, and such as are for the sword to the sword. ¹² I will kindle a fire in the houses of the gods of Egypt. He will burn them, and carry them away captive. He will array himself with the land of Egypt, as a shepherd puts on his garment; and he will go out from there in peace. ¹³ He will also break the pillars of Beth Shemesh that is in the land of Egypt; and he will burn the houses of the gods of Egypt with fire.'"

## 44

¹ The word that came to Jeremiah concerning all the Jews who lived in the land of Egypt, who lived at Migdol, and at Tahpanhes, and at Memphis, and in the country of Pathros, saying, ²"Yahweh of Armies, the God of Israel, says: 'You have seen all the evil that I have brought on Jerusalem, and on all the cities of Judah. Behold, today they are a desolation, and no man dwells in them, ³ because of their wickedness which they have committed to provoke me to anger, in that they went to burn incense, to serve other gods that they didn't know, neither they, nor you, nor your fathers. ⁴ However I sent to you all my servants the prophets, rising up early and sending them, saying, "Oh, don't do this abominable thing that I hate." ⁵ But they didn't listen and didn't incline their ear. They didn't turn from their wickedness, to stop burning incense to other gods. ⁶ Therefore my wrath and my anger was poured out, and was kindled in the cities of Judah and in the streets of Jerusalem; and they are wasted and desolate, as it is today.' ⁷"Therefore now Yahweh, the God of Armies, the God of Israel, says: 'Why do you commit great evil against your own souls, to cut off from yourselves man and woman, infant and nursing child out of the middle of Judah, to leave yourselves no one remaining, ⁸ in that you provoke me to anger with the works of your hands, burning incense to other gods in the land of Egypt where you have gone to live, that you may be cut off, and that you may be a curse and a reproach among all the nations of the earth? ⁹ Have you forgotten the wickedness of your fathers, the wickedness of the kings of Judah, the wickedness of their wives, your own wickedness, and the wickedness of your wives which they committed in the land of Judah and in the streets of Jerusalem? ¹⁰ They are not humbled even to this day, neither have they feared, nor walked in my

law, nor in my statutes, that I set before you and before your fathers.' ¹¹"Therefore Yahweh of Armies, the God of Israel, says: 'Behold, I will set my face against you for evil, even to cut off all Judah. ¹² I will take the remnant of Judah that have set their faces to go into the land of Egypt to live there, and they will all be consumed. They will fall in the land of Egypt. They will be consumed by the sword and by the famine. They will die, from the least even to the greatest, by the sword and by the famine. They will be an object of horror, an astonishment, a curse, and a reproach. ¹³ For I will punish those who dwell in the land of Egypt, as I have punished Jerusalem, by the sword, by the famine, and by the pestilence; ¹⁴ so that none of the remnant of Judah, who have gone into the land of Egypt to live there, will escape or be left to return into the land of Judah, to which they have a desire to return to dwell there; for no one will return except those who will escape.'" ¹⁵ Then all the men who knew that their wives burned incense to other gods, and all the women who stood by, a great assembly, even all the people who lived in the land of Egypt, in Pathros, answered Jeremiah, saying, ¹⁶"As for the word that you have spoken to us in Yahweh's name, we will not listen to you. ¹⁷ But we will certainly perform every word that has gone out of our mouth, to burn incense to the queen of the sky and to pour out drink offerings to her, as we have done, we and our fathers, our kings and our princes, in the cities of Judah and in the streets of Jerusalem; for then we had plenty of food, and were well, and saw no evil. ¹⁸ But since we stopped burning incense to the queen of the sky, and pouring out drink offerings to her, we have lacked all things, and have been consumed by the sword and by the famine." ¹⁹ The women said, "When we burned incense to the queen of the sky and poured out drink offerings to her, did we make her cakes to worship her, and pour out drink offerings to her, without our husbands?" ²⁰ Then Jeremiah said to all the people—to the men and to the women, even to all the people who had given him an answer, saying, ²¹"The incense that you burned in the cities of Judah, and in the streets of Jerusalem, you and your fathers, your kings and your princes, and the people of the land, didn't Yahweh remember them, and didn't it come into his mind? ²² Thus Yahweh could no longer bear it, because of the evil of your doings and because of the abominations which you have committed. Therefore your land has become a desolation, an astonishment, and a curse, without inhabitant, as it is today. ²³ Because you have burned incense and because you have sinned against Yahweh, and have not obeyed Yahweh's voice, nor walked in his law, nor in his statutes, nor in his testimonies; therefore this evil has happened to you, as it is today." ²⁴ Moreover Jeremiah said to all the people, including all the women, "Hear Yahweh's word, all Judah who are in the land of Egypt! ²⁵ Yahweh of Armies, the God of Israel, says, 'You and your wives have both spoken with your mouths, and with your hands have fulfilled it, saying, "We will surely perform our vows that we have vowed, to burn incense to the queen of the sky, and to pour out drink offerings to her." '"Establish then your vows, and perform your vows.' ²⁶"Therefore hear Yahweh's word, all Judah who dwell in the land of Egypt: 'Behold, I have sworn by my great name,' says Yahweh, 'that my name will no more be named in the mouth of any man of Judah in all the land of Egypt, saying, "As the Lord Yahweh lives." ²⁷ Behold, I watch over them for evil, and not for good; and all the men of Judah who are in the land of Egypt will be consumed by the sword and by the famine, until they are all gone. ²⁸ Those who escape the sword will return out of the land of Egypt into the land of Judah few in number. All the remnant of Judah, who have gone into the land of Egypt to live there, will know whose word will stand, mine or theirs. ²⁹"'This will be the sign to you,' says Yahweh, 'that I will punish you in this place, that you may know that my words will surely stand against you for evil.' ³⁰ Yahweh says, 'Behold, I will give Pharaoh Hophra king of Egypt into the hand of his enemies and into the hand of those who seek his life, just as I gave Zedekiah king of Judah into the hand of Nebuchadnezzar king of Babylon, who was his enemy and sought his life.'"

## 45

¹ The message that Jeremiah the prophet spoke to Baruch the son of Neriah, when he wrote these words in a book at the mouth of Jeremiah, in the fourth year of Jehoiakim the son of Josiah, king of Judah, saying, ²"Yahweh, the God of Israel, says to you, Baruch: ³'You said, "Woe is me now! For Yahweh has added sorrow to my pain! I am weary with my groaning, and I find no rest."' ⁴"You shall tell him, Yahweh says: 'Behold, that which I have built, I will break down, and that which I have planted I will pluck up; and this in the whole land. ⁵ Do you seek great things for yourself? Don't seek them; for, behold, I will bring evil on all flesh,' says Yahweh, 'but I will let you escape with your life wherever you go.'"

## 46

¹ Yahweh's word which came to Jeremiah the prophet concerning the nations. ² Of Egypt: concerning the army of Pharaoh Necoh king of Egypt, which was by the river Euphrates in Carchemish, which

Nebuchadnezzar king of Babylon struck in the fourth year of Jehoiakim the son of Josiah, king of Judah. ³"Prepare the buckler and shield, and draw near to battle! ⁴Harness the horses, and get up, you horsemen, and stand up with your helmets. Polish the spears, put on the coats of mail. ⁵ Why have I seen it? They are dismayed and are turned backward. Their mighty ones are beaten down, have fled in haste, and don't look back. Terror is on every side," says Yahweh. ⁶"Don't let the swift flee away, nor the mighty man escape. In the north by the river Euphrates they have stumbled and fallen. ⁷"Who is this who rises up like the Nile, like rivers whose waters surge? ⁸ Egypt rises up like the Nile, like rivers whose waters surge. He says, 'I will rise up. I will cover the earth. I will destroy cities and its inhabitants.' ⁹ Go up, you horses! Rage, you chariots! Let the mighty men go out: Cush and Put, who handle the shield; and the Ludim, who handle and bend the bow. ¹⁰ For that day is of the Lord, Yahweh of Armies, a day of vengeance, that he may avenge himself of his adversaries. The sword will devour and be satiated, and will drink its fill of their blood; for the Lord, Yahweh of Armies, has a sacrifice in the north country by the river Euphrates. ¹¹ Go up into Gilead, and take balm, virgin daughter of Egypt. You use many medicines in vain. There is no healing for you. ¹² The nations have heard of your shame, and the earth is full of your cry; for the mighty man has stumbled against the mighty, they both fall together." ¹³ The word that Yahweh spoke to Jeremiah the prophet, how that Nebuchadnezzar king of Babylon should come and strike the land of Egypt: ¹⁴"Declare in Egypt, publish in Migdol, and publish in Memphis and in Tahpanhes; say, 'Stand up, and prepare, for the sword has devoured around you.' ¹⁵ Why are your strong ones swept away? They didn't stand, because Yahweh pushed them. ¹⁶ He made many to stumble. Yes, they fell on one another. They said, 'Arise! Let's go again to our own people, and to the land of our birth, from the oppressing sword.' ¹⁷ They cried there, 'Pharaoh king of Egypt is but a noise; he has let the appointed time pass by.' ¹⁸"As I live," says the King, whose name is Yahweh of Armies, "surely like Tabor among the mountains, and like Carmel by the sea, so he will come. ¹⁹ You daughter who dwells in Egypt, furnish yourself to go into captivity; for Memphis will become a desolation, and will be burned up, without inhabitant. ²⁰"Egypt is a very beautiful heifer; but destruction out of the north has come. It has come. ²¹ Also her hired men in the middle of her are like calves of the stall, for they also are turned back. They have fled away together. They didn't stand, for the day of their calamity has come on them, the time of their visitation. ²² Its sound will go like the serpent, for they will march with an army, and come against her with axes, as wood cutters. ²³ They will cut down her forest," says Yahweh, "though it can't be searched; because they are more than the locusts, and are innumerable. ²⁴ The daughter of Egypt will be disappointed; she will be delivered into the hand of the people of the north." ²⁵ Yahweh of Armies, the God of Israel, says: "Behold, I will punish Amon of No, and Pharaoh, and Egypt, with her gods and her kings, even Pharaoh, and those who trust in him. ²⁶ I will deliver them into the hand of those who seek their lives, and into the hand of Nebuchadnezzar king of Babylon, and into the hand of his servants. Afterwards it will be inhabited, as in the days of old," says Yahweh. ²⁷"But don't you be afraid, Jacob my servant. Don't be dismayed, Israel; for, behold, I will save you from afar, and your offspring from the land of their captivity. Jacob will return, and will be quiet and at ease. No one will make him afraid. ²⁸ Don't be afraid, O Jacob my servant," says Yahweh, "for I am with you; for I will make a full end of all the nations where I have driven you, but I will not make a full end of you, but I will correct you in measure, and will in no way leave you unpunished."

## 47

¹ Yahweh's word that came to Jeremiah the prophet concerning the Philistines, before Pharaoh struck Gaza. ² Yahweh says: "Behold, waters rise up out of the north, and will become an overflowing stream, and will overflow the land and all that is therein, the city and those who dwell therein. The men will cry, and all the inhabitants of the land will wail. ³ At the noise of the stamping of the hoofs of his strong ones, at the rushing of his chariots, at the rumbling of his wheels, the fathers don't look back for their children because their hands are so feeble, ⁴ because of the day that comes to destroy all the Philistines, to cut off from Tyre and Sidon every helper who remains; for Yahweh will destroy the Philistines, the remnant of the isle of Caphtor. ⁵ Baldness has come on Gaza; Ashkelon is brought to nothing. You remnant of their valley, how long will you cut yourself? ⁶"You sword of Yahweh, how long will it be before you are quiet? Put yourself back into your scabbard; rest, and be still.' ⁷"How can you be quiet, since Yahweh has given you a command? Against Ashkelon, and against the seashore, there he has appointed it."

## 48

[1] Of Moab. Yahweh of Armies, the God of Israel, says: "Woe to Nebo! For it is laid waste. Kiriathaim is disappointed. It is taken. Misgab[a] is put to shame and broken down. [2] The praise of Moab is no more. In Heshbon they have devised evil against her: 'Come! Let's cut her off from being a nation.' You also, Madmen, will be brought to silence. The sword will pursue you. [3] The sound of a cry from Horonaim, desolation and great destruction! [4] Moab is destroyed. Her little ones have caused a cry to be heard. [5] For they will go up by the ascent of Luhith with continual weeping. For at the descent of Horonaim they have heard the distress of the cry of destruction. [6] Flee! Save your lives! Be like the juniper bush in the wilderness. [7] For, because you have trusted in your works and in your treasures, you also will be taken. Chemosh will go out into captivity, his priests and his princes together. [8] The destroyer will come on every city, and no city will escape; the valley also will perish, and the plain will be destroyed, as Yahweh has spoken. [9] Give wings to Moab, that she may fly and get herself away: and her cities will become a desolation, without anyone to dwell in them. [10] "Cursed is he who does the work of Yahweh negligently; and cursed is he who keeps back his sword from blood. [11] "Moab has been at ease from his youth, and he has settled on his dregs, and has not been emptied from vessel to vessel, neither has he gone into captivity; therefore his taste remains in him, and his scent is not changed. [12] Therefore behold, the days come," says Yahweh, "that I will send to him those who pour off, and they will pour him off; and they will empty his vessels, and break their containers in pieces. [13] Moab will be ashamed of Chemosh, as the house of Israel was ashamed of Bethel, their confidence. [14] "How do you say, 'We are mighty men, and valiant men for the war'? [15] Moab is laid waste, and they have gone up into his cities, and his chosen young men have gone down to the slaughter," says the King, whose name is Yahweh of Armies. [16] "The calamity of Moab is near to come, and his affliction hurries fast. [17] All you who are around him, bemoan him; and all you who know his name, say, 'How the strong staff is broken, the beautiful rod!' [18] "You daughter who dwells in Dibon, come down from your glory, and sit in thirst; for the destroyer of Moab has come up against you. He has destroyed your strongholds. [19] Inhabitant of Aroer, stand by the way and watch. Ask him who flees, and her who escapes; say, 'What has been done?' [20] Moab is disappointed; for it is broken down. Wail and cry! Tell it by the Arnon, that Moab is laid waste. [21] Judgment has come on the plain country— on Holon, on Jahzah, on Mephaath, [22] on Dibon, on Nebo, on Beth Diblathaim, [23] on Kiriathaim, on Beth Gamul, on Beth Meon, [24] on Kerioth, on Bozrah, and on all the cities of the land of Moab, far or near. [25] The horn of Moab is cut off, and his arm is broken," says Yahweh. [26] "Make him drunk, for he magnified himself against Yahweh. Moab will wallow in his vomit, and he also will be in derision. [27] For wasn't Israel a derision to you? Was he found among thieves? For as often as you speak of him, you shake your head. [28] You inhabitants of Moab, leave the cities, and dwell in the rock. Be like the dove that makes her nest over the mouth of the abyss. [29] "We have heard of the pride of Moab. He is very proud in his loftiness, his pride, his arrogance, and the arrogance of his heart. [30] I know his wrath," says Yahweh, "that it is nothing; his boastings have done nothing. [31] Therefore I will wail for Moab. Yes, I will cry out for all Moab. They will mourn for the men of Kir Heres. [32] With more than the weeping of Jazer I will weep for you, vine of Sibmah. Your branches passed over the sea. They reached even to the sea of Jazer. The destroyer has fallen on your summer fruits and on your vintage. [33] Gladness and joy is taken away from the fruitful field and from the land of Moab. I have caused wine to cease from the wine presses. No one will tread with shouting. The shouting will be no shouting. [34] From the cry of Heshbon even to Elealeh, even to Jahaz they have uttered their voice, from Zoar even to Horonaim, to Eglath Shelishiyah; for the waters of Nimrim will also become desolate. [35] Moreover I will cause to cease in Moab," says Yahweh, "him who offers in the high place, and him who burns incense to his gods. [36] Therefore my heart sounds for Moab like flutes, and my heart sounds like flutes for the men of Kir Heres. Therefore the abundance that he has gotten has perished. [37] For every head is bald, and every beard clipped. There are cuttings on all the hands, and sackcloth on the waist. [38] On all the housetops of Moab, and in its streets, there is lamentation everywhere; for I have broken Moab like a vessel in which no one delights," says Yahweh. [39] "How it is broken down! How they wail! How Moab has turned the back with shame! So will Moab become a derision and a terror to all who are around him." [40] For Yahweh says: "Behold, he will fly as an eagle, and will spread out his wings against Moab. [41] Kerioth is taken, and the strongholds are seized. The heart of the mighty men of Moab at that day will be as the heart of a woman in her pangs. [42] Moab will be destroyed from being a people, because he has magnified himself against Yahweh. [43] Terror, the pit, and the snare are on you, inhabitant of Moab," says Yahweh. [44] "He who flees from the terror will fall into the pit; and he who gets up out of the pit will be taken in the snare, for I will bring on him, even on Moab, the year of their visitation," says Yahweh. [45] "Those who fled stand without strength under the shadow of Heshbon; for a fire has gone out of Heshbon, and a flame from the middle of Sihon, and has devoured the corner of Moab, and the crown of the head of the tumultuous ones. [46] Woe to you, O Moab! The people of Chemosh are undone; for your sons are taken away captive, and your daughters into captivity. [47] "Yet I will reverse the captivity of Moab in the latter days," says Yahweh. Thus far is the judgment of Moab.

## 49

[1] Of the children of Ammon. Yahweh says: "Has Israel no sons? Has he no heir? Why then does Malcam possess Gad, and his people dwell in its cities? [2] Therefore behold, the days come," says Yahweh, "that I will cause an alarm of war to be heard against Rabbah of the children of Ammon, and it will become a desolate heap, and her daughters will be burned with fire; then Israel will possess those who possessed him," says Yahweh. [3] "Wail, Heshbon, for Ai is laid waste! Cry, you daughters of Rabbah! Clothe yourself in sackcloth. Lament, and run back and forth among the fences; for Malcam will go into captivity, his priests and his princes together. [4] Why do you boast in the valleys, your flowing valley, backsliding daughter? You trusted in her treasures, saying, 'Who will come to me?' [5] Behold, I will bring a terror on you," says the Lord, Yahweh of Armies, "from all who are around you. All of you will be driven completely out, and there will be no one to gather together the fugitives. [6] "But afterward I will reverse the captivity of the children of Ammon," says Yahweh. [7] Of Edom, Yahweh of Armies says: "Is wisdom no more in Teman? Has counsel perished from the prudent? Has their wisdom vanished? [8] Flee! Turn back! Dwell in the depths, inhabitants of Dedan; for I will bring the calamity of Esau on him when I visit him. [9] If grape gatherers came to you, would they not leave some gleaning grapes? If thieves came by night, wouldn't they steal until they had enough? [10] But I have made Esau bare, I have uncovered his secret places, and he will not be able to hide himself. His offspring is destroyed, with his brothers and his neighbors; and he is no more. [11] Leave your fatherless children. I will preserve them alive. Let your widows trust in me." [12] For Yahweh says: "Behold, they to whom it didn't pertain to drink of the cup will certainly drink; and are you he who will altogether go unpunished? You won't go unpunished, but you will surely drink. [13] For I have sworn by myself," says Yahweh, "that Bozrah will become an astonishment, a reproach, a waste, and a curse. All its cities will be perpetual wastes." [14] I have heard news from Yahweh, and an ambassador is sent among the nations, saying, "Gather yourselves together! Come against her! Rise up to the battle!" [15] "For, behold, I have made you small among the nations, and despised among men. [16] As for your terror, the pride of your heart has deceived you, O you who dwell in the clefts of the rock, who hold the height of the hill, though you should make your nest as high as the eagle, I will bring you down from there," says Yahweh. [17] "Edom will become an astonishment. Everyone who passes by it will be astonished, and will hiss at all its plagues. [18] As in the overthrow of Sodom and Gomorrah and its neighbor cities," says Yahweh, "no man will dwell there, neither will any son of man live therein. [19] "Behold, he will come up like a lion from the pride of the Jordan against the strong habitation; for I will suddenly make them run away from it, and whoever is chosen, I will appoint him over it. For who is like me? Who will appoint me a time? Who is the shepherd who will stand before me?" [20] Therefore hear the counsel of Yahweh, that he has taken against Edom, and his purposes that he has purposed against the inhabitants of Teman: Surely they will drag them away, the little ones of the flock. Surely he will make their habitation desolate over them. [21] The earth trembles at the noise of their fall; there is a cry, the noise which is heard in the Red Sea. [22] Behold, he will come up and fly as the eagle, and spread out his wings against Bozrah. The heart of the mighty men of Edom at that day will be as the heart of a woman in her pangs. [23] Of Damascus: "Hamath and Arpad are confounded, for they have heard evil news. They have melted away. There is sorrow on the sea. It can't be quiet. [24] Damascus has grown feeble, she turns herself to flee, and trembling has seized her. Anguish and sorrows have taken hold of her, as of a woman in travail. [25] How is the city of praise not forsaken, the city of my joy? [26] Therefore her young men will fall in her streets, and all the men of war will be brought to silence in that day," says Yahweh of Armies. [27] "I will kindle a fire in the wall of Damascus, and it will devour the palaces of Ben Hadad." [28] Of Kedar, and of the kingdoms of Hazor, which Nebuchadnezzar king of Babylon struck, Yahweh says: "Arise, go up to Kedar, and destroy the children of the east. [29] They will take their tents and their

flocks. they will carry away for themselves their curtains, all their vessels, and their camels; and they will cry to them, 'Terror on every side!' ³⁰ Flee! Wander far off! Dwell in the depths, you inhabitants of Hazor," says Yahweh; "for Nebuchadnezzar king of Babylon has taken counsel against you, and has conceived a purpose against you. ³¹ Arise! Go up to a nation that is at ease, that dwells without care," says Yahweh; "that has neither gates nor bars, that dwells alone. ³² Their camels will be a booty, and the multitude of their livestock a plunder. I will scatter to all winds those who have the corners of their beards cut off; and I will bring their calamity from every side of them," says Yahweh. ³³ Hazor will be a dwelling place of jackals, a desolation forever. No man will dwell there, neither will any son of man live therein." ³⁴ Yahweh's word that came to Jeremiah the prophet concerning Elam, in the beginning of the reign of Zedekiah king of Judah, saying, ³⁵"Yahweh of Armies says: 'Behold, I will break the bow of Elam, the chief of their might. ³⁶ I will bring on Elam the four winds from the four quarters of the sky, and will scatter them toward all those winds. There will be no nation where the outcasts of Elam will not come. ³⁷ I will cause Elam to be dismayed before their enemies, and before those who seek their life. I will bring evil on them, even my fierce anger,' says Yahweh; 'and I will send the sword after them, until I have consumed them. ³⁸ I will set my throne in Elam, and will destroy from there king and princes,' says Yahweh. ³⁹'But it will happen in the latter days that I will reverse the captivity of Elam,' says Yahweh."

## 50

¹ The word that Yahweh spoke concerning Babylon, concerning the land of the Chaldeans, by Jeremiah the prophet. ²"Declare among the nations and publish, and set up a standard; publish, and don't conceal; say, 'Babylon has been taken, Bel is disappointed, Merodach is dismayed! Her images are disappointed. Her idols are dismayed.' ³ For a nation comes up out of the north against her, which will make her land desolate, and no one will dwell in it. They have fled. They are gone, both man and animal. ⁴"In those days, and in that time," says Yahweh, "the children of Israel will come, they and the children of Judah together; they will go on their way weeping, and will seek Yahweh their God. ⁵ They will inquire concerning Zion with their faces turned toward it, saying, 'Come, and join yourselves to Yahweh in an everlasting covenant that will not be forgotten.' ⁶ My people have been lost sheep. Their shepherds have caused them to go astray. They have turned them away on the mountains. They have gone from mountain to hill. They have forgotten their resting place. ⁷ All who found them have devoured them. Their adversaries said, 'We are not guilty, because they have sinned against Yahweh, the habitation of righteousness, even Yahweh, the hope of their fathers.' ⁸"Flee out of the middle of Babylon! Go out of the land of the Chaldeans, and be as the male goats before the flocks. ⁹ For, behold, I will stir up and cause to come up against Babylon a company of great nations from the north country; and they will set themselves in array against her. She will be taken from there. Their arrows will be as of an expert mighty man. None of them will return in vain. ¹⁰ Chaldea will be a prey. All who prey on her will be satisfied," says Yahweh. ¹¹"Because you are glad, because you rejoice, O you who plunder my heritage, because you are wanton as a heifer that treads out the grain, and neigh as strong horses, ¹² your mother will be utterly disappointed. She who bore you will be confounded. Behold, she will be the least of the nations, a wilderness, a dry land, and a desert. ¹³ Because of Yahweh's wrath she won't be inhabited, but she will be wholly desolate. Everyone who goes by Babylon will be astonished, and hiss at all her plagues. ¹⁴ Set yourselves in array against Babylon all around, all you who bend the bow; shoot at her. Spare no arrows, for she has sinned against Yahweh. ¹⁵ Shout against her all around. She has submitted herself. Her bulwarks have fallen. Her walls have been thrown down, for it is the vengeance of Yahweh. Take vengeance on her. As she has done, do to her. ¹⁶ Cut off the sower from Babylon, and him who handles the sickle in the time of harvest. For fear of the oppressing sword, they will each return to their own people, and they will each flee to their own land. ¹⁷"Israel is a hunted sheep. The lions have driven him away. First, the king of Assyria devoured him, and now at last Nebuchadnezzar king of Babylon has broken his bones." ¹⁸ Therefore Yahweh of Armies, the God of Israel, says: "Behold, I will punish the king of Babylon and his land, as I have punished the king of Assyria. ¹⁹ I will bring Israel again to his pasture, and he will feed on Carmel and Bashan. His soul will be satisfied on the hills of Ephraim and in Gilead. ²⁰ In those days, and in that time," says Yahweh, "the iniquity of Israel will be sought for, and there will be none, also the sins of Judah, and they won't be found; for I will pardon them whom I leave as a remnant. ²¹"Go up against the land of Merathaim, even against it, and against the inhabitants of Pekod. Kill and utterly destroy after them," says Yahweh, "and do according to all that I have commanded you. ²² A sound of battle is in the land, and of great destruction. ²³ How the hammer of the whole earth is cut apart and broken! How Babylon has become a desolation among the nations! ²⁴ I have laid a snare for you, and you are also taken, Babylon, and you weren't aware. You are found, and also caught, because you have fought against Yahweh. ²⁵ Yahweh has opened his armory, and has brought out the weapons of his indignation; for the Lord, Yahweh of Armies, has a work to do in the land of the Chaldeans. ²⁶ Come against her from the farthest border. Open her storehouses. Cast her up as heaps. Destroy her utterly. Let nothing of her be left. ²⁷ Kill all her bulls. Let them go down to the slaughter. Woe to them! For their day has come, the time of their visitation. ²⁸ Listen to those who flee and escape out of the land of Babylon, to declare in Zion the vengeance of Yahweh our God, the vengeance of his temple. ²⁹"Call together the archers against Babylon, all those who bend the bow. Encamp against her all around. Let none of it escape. Pay her back according to her work. According to all that she has done, do to her; for she has been proud against Yahweh, against the Holy One of Israel. ³⁰ Therefore her young men will fall in her streets. All her men of war will be brought to silence in that day," says Yahweh. ³¹"Behold, I am against you, you proud one," says the Lord, Yahweh of Armies; "for your day has come, the time that I will visit you. ³² The proud one will stumble and fall, and no one will raise him up. I will kindle a fire in his cities, and it will devour all who are around him." ³³ Yahweh of Armies says: "The children of Israel and the children of Judah are oppressed together. All who took them captive hold them fast. They refuse to let them go. ³⁴ Their Redeemer is strong. Yahweh of Armies is his name. He will thoroughly plead their cause, that he may give rest to the earth, and disquiet the inhabitants of Babylon. ³⁵"A sword is on the Chaldeans," says Yahweh, "and on the inhabitants of Babylon, on her princes, and on her wise men. ³⁶ A sword is on the boasters, and they will become fools. A sword is on her mighty men, and they will be dismayed. ³⁷ A sword is on their horses, on their chariots, and on all the mixed people who are in the middle of her; and they will become as women. A sword is on her treasures, and they will be robbed. ³⁸ A drought is on her waters, and they will be dried up; for it is a land of engraved images, and they are mad over idols. ³⁹ Therefore the wild animals of the desert with the wolves will dwell there. The ostriches will dwell therein. It will be inhabited no more forever, neither will it be lived in from generation to generation. ⁴⁰ As when God overthrew Sodom and Gomorrah and its neighbor cities," says Yahweh, "so no man will dwell there, neither will any son of man live therein. ⁴¹"Behold, a people comes from the north. A great nation and many kings will be stirred up from the uttermost parts of the earth. ⁴² They take up bow and spear. They are cruel, and have no mercy. Their voice roars like the sea. They ride on horses, everyone set in array, as a man to the battle, against you, daughter of Babylon. ⁴³ The king of Babylon has heard the news of them, and his hands become feeble. Anguish has taken hold of him, pains as of a woman in labor. ⁴⁴ Behold, the enemy will come up like a lion from the thickets of the Jordan against the strong habitation; for I will suddenly make them run away from it. Whoever is chosen, I will appoint him over it, for who is like me? Who will appoint me a time? Who is the shepherd who can stand before me?" ⁴⁵ Therefore hear the counsel of Yahweh that he has taken against Babylon; and his purposes that he has purposed against the land of the Chaldeans: Surely they will drag them away, even the little ones of the flock. Surely he will make their habitation desolate over them. ⁴⁶ The earth trembles at the noise of the taking of Babylon. The cry is heard among the nations.

## 51

¹ Yahweh says: "Behold, I will raise up against Babylon, and against those who dwell in Lebkamai, a destroying wind. ² I will send to Babylon strangers, who will winnow her. They will empty her land; for in the day of trouble they will be against her all around. ³ Against him who bends, let the archer bend his bow, also against him who lifts himself up in his coat of mail. Don't spare her young men! Utterly destroy all her army! ⁴ They will fall down slain in the land of the Chaldeans, and thrust through in her streets. ⁵ For Israel is not forsaken, nor Judah, by his God, by Yahweh of Armies; though their land is full of guilt against the Holy One of Israel. ⁶"Flee out of the middle of Babylon! Everyone save his own life! Don't be cut off in her iniquity, for it is the time of Yahweh's vengeance. He will render to her a recompense. ⁷ Babylon has been a golden cup in Yahweh's hand, who made all the earth drunk. The nations have drunk of her wine; therefore the nations have gone mad. ⁸ Babylon has suddenly fallen and been destroyed! Wail for her! Take balm for her pain. Perhaps she may be healed. ⁹"We would have healed Babylon, but she is not healed. Forsake her, and let's each go into his own country; for her judgment reaches to heaven, and is lifted up even to the skies. ¹⁰'Yahweh has produced our righteousness. Come, and let's declare in Zion the work of Yahweh our God.' ¹¹"Make the arrows sharp! Hold the shields firmly! Yahweh has stirred up the spirit of the kings of the Medes, because his purpose is against Babylon, to destroy it; for it is the

vengeance of Yahweh, the vengeance of his temple. ¹² Set up a standard against the walls of Babylon! Make the watch strong! Set the watchmen, and prepare the ambushes; for Yahweh has both purposed and done that which he spoke concerning the inhabitants of Babylon. ¹³ You who dwell on many waters, abundant in treasures, your end has come, the measure of your covetousness. ¹⁴ Yahweh of Armies has sworn by himself, saying, 'Surely I will fill you with men, as with locusts, and they will lift up a shout against you.' ¹⁵"He has made the earth by his power. He has established the world by his wisdom. By his understanding he has stretched out the heavens. ¹⁶ When he utters his voice, there is a roar of waters in the heavens, and he causes the vapors to ascend from the ends of the earth. He makes lightning for the rain, and brings the wind out of his treasuries. ¹⁷"Every man has become stupid and without knowledge. Every goldsmith is disappointed by his image, for his molten images are falsehood, and there is no breath in them. ¹⁸ They are vanity, a work of delusion. In the time of their visitation, they will perish. ¹⁹ The portion of Jacob is not like these, for he formed all things, including the tribe of his inheritance. Yahweh of Armies is his name. ²⁰"You are my battle ax and weapons of war. With you I will break the nations into pieces. With you I will destroy kingdoms. ²¹ With you I will break in pieces the horse and his rider. ²² With you I will break in pieces the chariot and him who rides therein. With you I will break in pieces man and woman. With you I will break in pieces the old man and the youth. With you I will break in pieces the young man and the virgin. ²³ With you I will break in pieces the shepherd and his flock. With you I will break in pieces the farmer and his yoke. With you I will break in pieces governors and deputies. ²⁴"I will render to Babylon and to all the inhabitants of Chaldea all their evil that they have done in Zion in your sight," says Yahweh. ²⁵"Behold, I am against you, destroying mountain," says Yahweh, "which destroys all the earth. I will stretch out my hand on you, roll you down from the rocks, and will make you a burned mountain. ²⁶ They won't take a cornerstone from you, nor a stone for foundations; but you will be desolate forever," says Yahweh. ²⁷"Set up a standard in the land! Blow the trumpet among the nations! Prepare the nations against her! Call together against her the kingdoms of Ararat, Minni, and Ashkenaz! Appoint a marshal against her! Cause the horses to come up as the swarming locusts! ²⁸ Prepare against her the nations, the kings of the Medes, its governors, and all its deputies, and all the land of their dominion! ²⁹ The land trembles and is in pain; for the purposes of Yahweh against Babylon stand, to make the land of Babylon a desolation, without inhabitant. ³⁰ The mighty men of Babylon have stopped fighting, they remain in their strongholds. Their might has failed. They have become as women. Her dwelling places are set on fire. Her bars are broken. ³¹ One runner will run to meet another, and one messenger to meet another, to show the king of Babylon that his city is taken on every quarter. ³² So the passages are seized. They have burned the reeds with fire. The men of war are frightened." ³³ For Yahweh of Armies, the God of Israel says: "The daughter of Babylon is like a threshing floor at the time when it is trodden. Yet a little while, and the time of harvest comes for her." ³⁴"Nebuchadnezzar the king of Babylon has devoured me. He has crushed me. He has made me an empty vessel. He has, like a monster, swallowed me up. He has filled his mouth with my delicacies. He has cast me out. ³⁵ May the violence done to me and to my flesh be on Babylon!" the inhabitant of Zion will say; and, "May my blood be on the inhabitants of Chaldea!" will Jerusalem say. ³⁶ Therefore Yahweh says: "Behold, I will plead your cause, and take vengeance for you. I will dry up her sea, and make her fountain dry. ³⁷ Babylon will become heaps, a dwelling place for jackals, an astonishment, and a hissing, without inhabitant. ³⁸ They will roar together like young lions. They will growl as lions' cubs. ³⁹ When they are inflamed, I will make their feast, and I will make them drunk, that they may rejoice, and sleep a perpetual sleep, and not wake up," says Yahweh. ⁴⁰"I will bring them down like lambs to the slaughter, like rams with male goats. ⁴¹"How Sheshach is taken! How the praise of the whole earth is seized! How Babylon has become a desolation among the nations! ⁴² The sea has come up on Babylon. She is covered with the multitude of its waves. ⁴³ Her cities have become a desolation, a dry land, and a desert, a land in which no man dwells. No son of man passes by it. ⁴⁴ I will execute judgment on Bel in Babylon, and I will bring out of his mouth that which he has swallowed up. The nations will not flow any more to him. Yes, the wall of Babylon will fall. ⁴⁵"My people, go away from the middle of her, and each of you save yourselves from Yahweh's fierce anger. ⁴⁶ Don't let your heart faint. Don't fear for the news that will be heard in the land. For news will come one year, and after that in another year news will come, and violence in the land, ruler against ruler. ⁴⁷ Therefore behold, the days come that I will execute judgment on the engraved images of Babylon; and her whole land will be confounded. All her slain will fall in the middle of her. ⁴⁸ Then the heavens and the earth, and all that is therein,

will sing for joy over Babylon; for the destroyers will come to her from the north," says Yahweh. ⁴⁹"As Babylon has caused the slain of Israel to fall, so the slain of all the land will fall at Babylon. ⁵⁰ You who have escaped the sword, go! Don't stand still! Remember Yahweh from afar, and let Jerusalem come into your mind." ⁵¹"We are confounded because we have heard reproach. Confusion has covered our faces, for strangers have come into the sanctuaries of Yahweh's house." ⁵²"Therefore behold, the days come," says Yahweh, "that I will execute judgment on her engraved images; and through all her land the wounded will groan. ⁵³ Though Babylon should mount up to the sky, and though she should fortify the height of her strength, yet destroyers will come to her from me," says Yahweh. ⁵⁴"The sound of a cry comes from Babylon, and of great destruction from the land of the Chaldeans! ⁵⁵ For Yahweh lays Babylon waste, and destroys out of her the great voice! Their waves roar like many waters. The noise of their voice is uttered. ⁵⁶ For the destroyer has come on her, even on Babylon. Her mighty men are taken. Their bows are broken in pieces, for Yahweh is a God of retribution. He will surely repay. ⁵⁷ I will make her princes, her wise men, her governors, her deputies, and her mighty men drunk. They will sleep a perpetual sleep, and not wake up," says the King, whose name is Yahweh of Armies. ⁵⁸ Yahweh of Armies says: "The wide walls of Babylon will be utterly overthrown. Her high gates will be burned with fire. The peoples will labor for vanity, and the nations for the fire; and they will be weary." ⁵⁹ The word which Jeremiah the prophet commanded Seraiah the son of Neriah, the son of Mahseiah, when he went with Zedekiah the king of Judah to Babylon in the fourth year of his reign. Now Seraiah was chief quartermaster. ⁶⁰ Jeremiah wrote in a book all the evil that should come on Babylon, even all these words that are written concerning Babylon. ⁶¹ Jeremiah said to Seraiah, "When you come to Babylon, then see that you read all these words, ⁶² and say, 'Yahweh, you have spoken concerning this place, to cut it off, that no one will dwell in it, neither man nor animal, but that it will be desolate forever.' ⁶³ It will be, when you have finished reading this book, that you shall bind a stone to it, and cast it into the middle of the Euphrates. ⁶⁴ Then you shall say, 'Thus will Babylon sink, and will not rise again because of the evil that I will bring on her; and they will be weary.'" Thus far are the words of Jeremiah.

## 52

¹ Zedekiah was twenty-one years old when he began to reign. He reigned eleven years in Jerusalem. His mother's name was Hamutal the daughter of Jeremiah of Libnah. ² He did that which was evil in Yahweh's sight, according to all that Jehoiakim had done. ³ For through Yahweh's anger this happened in Jerusalem and Judah, until he had cast them out from his presence. Zedekiah rebelled against the king of Babylon. ⁴ In the ninth year of his reign, in the tenth month, in the tenth day of the month, Nebuchadnezzar king of Babylon came, he and all his army, against Jerusalem, and encamped against it; and they built forts against it round about. ⁵ So the city was besieged to the eleventh year of King Zedekiah. ⁶ In the fourth month, in the ninth day of the month, the famine was severe in the city, so that there was no bread for the people of the land. ⁷ Then a breach was made in the city, and all the men of war fled, and went out of the city by night by the way of the gate between the two walls, which was by the king's garden. Now the Chaldeans were against the city all around. The men of war went toward the Arabah, ⁸ but the army of the Chaldeans pursued the king, and overtook Zedekiah in the plains of Jericho; and all his army was scattered from him. ⁹ Then they took the king, and carried him up to the king of Babylon to Riblah in the land of Hamath; and he pronounced judgment on him. ¹⁰ The king of Babylon killed the sons of Zedekiah before his eyes. He also killed all the princes of Judah in Riblah. ¹¹ He put out the eyes of Zedekiah; and the king of Babylon bound him in fetters, and carried him to Babylon, and put him in prison until the day of his death. ¹² Now in the fifth month, in the tenth day of the month, which was the nineteenth year of King Nebuchadnezzar, king of Babylon, Nebuzaradan the captain of the guard, who stood before the king of Babylon, came into Jerusalem. ¹³ He burned Yahweh's house, and the king's house; and all the houses of Jerusalem, even every great house, he burned with fire. ¹⁴ All the army of the Chaldeans, who were with the captain of the guard, broke down all the walls of Jerusalem all around. ¹⁵ Then Nebuzaradan the captain of the guard carried away captive of the poorest of the people, and the rest of the people who were left in the city, and those who fell away, who defected to the king of Babylon, and the rest of the multitude. ¹⁶ But Nebuzaradan the captain of the guard left of the poorest of the land to be vineyard keepers and farmers. ¹⁷ The Chaldeans broke the pillars of bronze that were in Yahweh's house and the bases and the bronze sea that were in Yahweh's house in pieces, and carried all of their bronze to Babylon. ¹⁸ They also took away the pots, the shovels, the snuffers, the basins, the spoons, and all the vessels of bronze with which they ministered. ¹⁹ The captain of the guard took away the cups, the fire pans, the basins,

the pots, the lamp stands, the spoons, and the bowls; that which was of gold, as gold, and that which was of silver, as silver. ²⁰ They took the two pillars, the one sea, and the twelve bronze bulls that were under the bases, which King Solomon had made for Yahweh's house. The bronze of all these vessels was without weight. ²¹ As for the pillars, the height of the one pillar was eighteen cubits;ᵃ and a line of twelve cubits encircled it; and its thickness was four fingers. It was hollow. ²² A capital of bronze was on it; and the height of the one capital was five cubits,ᵇ with network and pomegranates on the capital all around, all of bronze. The second pillar also had the same, with pomegranates. ²³ There were ninety-six pomegranates on the sides; all the pomegranates were one hundred on the network all around. ²⁴ The captain of the guard took Seraiah the chief priest, and Zephaniah the second priest, and the three keepers of the threshold, ²⁵ and out of the city he took an officer who was set over the men of war; and seven men of those who saw the king's face, who were found in the city; and the scribe of the captain of the army, who mustered the people of the land; and sixty men of the people of the land, who were found in the middle of the city. ²⁶ Nebuzaradan the captain of the guard took them, and brought them to the king of Babylon to Riblah. ²⁷ The king of Babylon struck them, and put them to death at Riblah in the land of Hamath. So Judah was carried away captive out of his land. ²⁸ This is the number of the people whom Nebuchadnezzar carried away captive: in the seventh year, three thousand twenty-three Jews; ²⁹ in the eighteenth year of Nebuchadnezzar, he carried away captive from Jerusalem eight hundred thirty-two persons; ³⁰ in the twenty-third year of Nebuchadnezzar, Nebuzaradan the captain of the guard carried away captive of the Jews seven hundred forty-five people. All the people numbered four thousand six hundred. ³¹ In the thirty-seventh year of the captivity of Jehoiachin king of Judah, in the twelfth month, in the twenty-fifth day of the month, Evilmerodach king of Babylon, in the first year of his reign, lifted up the head of Jehoiachin king of Judah, and released him from prison. ³² He spoke kindly to him, and set his throne above the throne of the kings who were with him in Babylon, ³³ and changed his prison garments. Jehoiachin ate bread before him continually all the days of his life. ³⁴ For his allowance, there was a continual allowance given him by the king of Babylon, every day a portion until the day of his death, all the days of his life.

# The Lamentations of Jeremiah

## 1

¹ How the city sits solitary, that was full of people! She has become as a widow, who was great among the nations! She who was a princess among the provinces has become a slave! ² She weeps bitterly in the night. Her tears are on her cheeks. Among all her lovers she has no one to comfort her. All her friends have dealt treacherously with her. They have become her enemies. ³ Judah has gone into captivity because of affliction and because of great servitude. She dwells among the nations. She finds no rest. All her persecutors overtook her in her distress. ⁴ The roads to Zion mourn, because no one comes to the solemn assembly. All her gates are desolate. Her priests sigh. Her virgins are afflicted, and she herself is in bitterness. ⁵ Her adversaries have become the head. Her enemies prosper; for Yahwehᶜ has afflicted her for the multitude of her transgressions. Her young children have gone into captivity before the adversary. ⁶ All majesty has departed from the daughter of Zion. Her princes have become like deer that find no pasture. They have gone without strength before the pursuer. ⁷ Jerusalem remembers in the days of her affliction and of her miseries all her pleasant things that were from the days of old; when her people fell into the hand of the adversary, and no one helped her. The adversaries saw her. They mocked at her desolations. ⁸ Jerusalem has grievously sinned. Therefore she has become unclean. All who honored her despise her, because they have seen her nakedness. Yes, she sighs and turns backward. ⁹ Her filthiness was in her skirts. She didn't remember her latter end. Therefore she has come down astoundingly. She has no comforter. "See, Yahweh, my affliction; for the enemy has magnified himself." ¹⁰ The adversary has spread out his hand on all her pleasant things; for she has seen that the nations have entered into her sanctuary, concerning whom you commanded that they should not enter into your assembly. ¹¹ All her people sigh. They seek bread. They have given their pleasant things for food to refresh their soul. "Look, Yahweh, and see, for I have become despised." ¹²"Is it nothing to you, all you who pass by? Look, and see if there is any sorrow like my sorrow, which is brought on me, with which Yahweh has afflicted me in the day of his fierce anger. ¹³"From on high has he sent fire into my bones, and it prevails against them. He has spread a net for my feet. He has turned me back. He has made me desolate and I faint all day long. ¹⁴"The yoke of my transgressions is bound by his hand. They are knit together. They have come up on my neck. He made my strength fail. The Lordᵈ has delivered me into their hands, against whom I am not able to stand. ¹⁵"The Lord has set at nothing all my mighty men within me. He has called a solemn assembly against me to crush my young men. The Lord has trodden the virgin daughter of Judah as in a wine press. ¹⁶"For these things I weep. My eye, my eye runs down with water, because the comforter who should refresh my soul is far from me. My children are desolate, because the enemy has prevailed." ¹⁷ Zion spreads out her hands. There is no one to comfort her. Yahweh has commanded concerning Jacob, that those who are around him should be his adversaries. Jerusalem is among them as an unclean thing. ¹⁸"Yahweh is righteous, for I have rebelled against his commandment. Please hear all you peoples, and see my sorrow. My virgins and my young men have gone into captivity. ¹⁹"I called for my lovers, but they deceived me. My priests and my elders gave up the spirit in the city, while they sought food for themselves to refresh their souls. ²⁰"Look, Yahweh; for I am in distress. My heart is troubled. My heart turns over within me, for I have grievously rebelled. Abroad, the sword bereaves. At home, it is like death. ²¹"They have heard that I sigh. There is no one to comfort me. All my enemies have heard of my trouble. They are glad that you have done it. You will bring the day that you have proclaimed, and they will be like me. ²²"Let all their wickedness come before you. Do to them as you have done to me for all my transgressions. For my sighs are many, and my heart is faint.

## 2

¹ How has the Lord covered the daughter of Zion with a cloud in his anger! He has cast the beauty of Israel down from heaven to the earth, and hasn't remembered his footstool in the day of his anger. ² The Lord has swallowed up all the dwellings of Jacob without pity. He has thrown down in his wrath the strongholds of the daughter of Judah. He has brought them down to the ground. He has profaned the kingdom and its princes. ³ He has cut off all the horn of Israel in fierce anger. He has drawn back his right hand from before the enemy. He has burned up Jacob like a flaming fire, which devours all around. ⁴ He has bent his bow like an enemy. He has stood with his right hand as an adversary. He has killed all that were pleasant to the eye. In the tent of the daughter of Zion, he has poured out his wrath like fire. ⁵ The Lord has become as an enemy. He has swallowed up Israel. He has swallowed up all her palaces. He has destroyed his strongholds. He has multiplied mourning and lamentation in the daughter of Judah. ⁶ He has violently taken away his tabernacle, as if it were a garden. He has destroyed his place of assembly. Yahweh has caused solemn assembly and Sabbath to be forgotten in Zion. In the indignation of his anger, he has despised the king and the priest. ⁷ The Lord has cast off his altar. He has abhorred his sanctuary. He has given the walls of her palaces into the hand of the enemy. They have made a noise in Yahweh's house, as in the day of a solemn assembly. ⁸ Yahweh has purposed to destroy the wall of the daughter of Zion. He has stretched out the line. He has not withdrawn his hand from destroying; He has made the rampart and wall lament. They languish together. ⁹ Her gates have sunk into the ground. He has destroyed and broken her bars. Her king and her princes are among the nations where the law is not. Yes, her prophets find no vision from Yahweh. ¹⁰ The elders of the daughter of Zion sit on the ground. They keep silence. They have cast up dust on their heads. They have clothed themselves with sackcloth. The virgins of Jerusalem hang down their heads to the ground. ¹¹ My eyes fail with tears. My heart is troubled. My bile is poured on the earth, because of the destruction of the daughter of my people, because the young children and the infants swoon in the streets of the city. ¹² They ask their mothers, "Where is grain and wine?" when they swoon as the wounded in the streets of the city, when their soul is poured out into their mothers' bosom. ¹³ What shall I testify to you? What shall I liken to you, daughter of Jerusalem? What shall I compare to you, that I may comfort you, virgin daughter of Zion? For your breach is as big as the sea. Who can heal you? ¹⁴ Your prophets have seen false and foolish visions for you. They have not uncovered your iniquity, to reverse your captivity, but have seen for you false revelations and causes of banishment. ¹⁵ All that pass by clap their hands at you. They hiss and wag their head at the daughter of Jerusalem, saying, "Is this the city that men called 'The perfection of

---

ᵃ 52:21 A cubit is the length from the tip of the middle finger to the elbow on a man's arm, or about 18 inches or 46 centimeters.

ᵇ 52:22 A cubit is the length from the tip of the middle finger to the elbow on a man's arm, or about 18 inches or 46 centimeters.

ᶜ 1:5 "Yahweh" is God's proper Name, sometimes rendered "LORD" (all caps) in other translations.

ᵈ 1:14 The word translated "Lord" is "Adonai."

beauty, the joy of the whole earth'?" ¹⁶ All your enemies have opened their mouth wide against you. They hiss and gnash their teeth. They say, "We have swallowed her up. Certainly this is the day that we looked for. We have found it. We have seen it." ¹⁷ Yahweh has done that which he planned. He has fulfilled his word that he commanded in the days of old. He has thrown down, and has not pitied. He has caused the enemy to rejoice over you. He has exalted the horn of your adversaries. ¹⁸ Their heart cried to the Lord. O wall of the daughter of Zion, let tears run down like a river day and night. Give yourself no relief. Don't let your eyes rest. ¹⁹ Arise, cry out in the night, at the beginning of the watches! Pour out your heart like water before the face of the Lord. Lift up your hands toward him for the life of your young children, who faint for hunger at the head of every street. ²⁰"Look, Yahweh, and see to whom you have done thus! Should the women eat their offspring, the children that they held and bounced on their knees? Should the priest and the prophet be killed in the sanctuary of the Lord? ²¹"The youth and the old man lie on the ground in the streets. My virgins and my young men have fallen by the sword. You have killed them in the day of your anger. You have slaughtered, and not pitied. ²²"You have called, as in the day of a solemn assembly, my terrors on every side. There was no one that escaped or remained in the day of Yahweh's anger. My enemy has consumed those whom I have cared for and brought up.

## 3

¹ I am the man who has seen affliction by the rod of his wrath. ² He has led me and caused me to walk in darkness, and not in light. ³ Surely he turns his hand against me again and again all day long. ⁴ He has made my flesh and my skin old. He has broken my bones. ⁵ He has built against me, and surrounded me with bitterness and hardship. ⁶ He has made me dwell in dark places, as those who have been long dead. ⁷ He has walled me about, so that I can't go out. He has made my chain heavy. ⁸ Yes, when I cry, and call for help, he shuts out my prayer. ⁹ He has walled up my ways with cut stone. He has made my paths crooked. ¹⁰ He is to me as a bear lying in wait, as a lion in hiding. ¹¹ He has turned away my path, and pulled me in pieces. He has made me desolate. ¹² He has bent his bow, and set me as a mark for the arrow. ¹³ He has caused the shafts of his quiver to enter into my kidneys. ¹⁴ I have become a derision to all my people, and their song all day long. ¹⁵ He has filled me with bitterness. He has stuffed me with wormwood. ¹⁶ He has also broken my teeth with gravel. He has covered me with ashes. ¹⁷ You have removed my soul far away from peace. I forgot prosperity. ¹⁸ I said, "My strength has perished, along with my expectation from Yahweh." ¹⁹ Remember my affliction and my misery, the wormwood and the bitterness. ²⁰ My soul still remembers them, and is bowed down within me. ²¹ This I recall to my mind; therefore I have hope. ²² It is because of Yahweh's loving kindnesses that we are not consumed, because his mercies don't fail. ²³ They are new every morning. Great is your faithfulness. ²⁴"Yahweh is my portion," says my soul. "Therefore I will hope in him." ²⁵ Yahweh is good to those who wait for him, to the soul who seeks him. ²⁶ It is good that a man should hope and quietly wait for the salvation of Yahweh. ²⁷ It is good for a man that he bear the yoke in his youth. ²⁸ Let him sit alone and keep silence, because he has laid it on him. ²⁹ Let him put his mouth in the dust, if it is so that there may be hope. ³⁰ Let him give his cheek to him who strikes him. Let him be filled full of reproach. ³¹ For the Lord will not cast off forever. ³² For though he causes grief, yet he will have compassion according to the multitude of his loving kindnesses. ³³ For he does not afflict willingly, nor grieve the children of men. ³⁴ To crush under foot all the prisoners of the earth, ³⁵ to turn away the right of a man before the face of the Most High, ³⁶ to subvert a man in his cause, the Lord doesn't approve. ³⁷ Who is he who says, and it comes to pass, when the Lord doesn't command it? ³⁸ Doesn't evil and good come out of the mouth of the Most High? ³⁹ Why should a living man complain, a man for the punishment of his sins? ⁴⁰ Let us search and try our ways, and turn again to Yahweh. ⁴¹ Let's lift up our heart with our hands to Godᵃ in the heavens. ⁴²"We have transgressed and have rebelled. You have not pardoned. ⁴³"You have covered us with anger and pursued us. You have killed. You have not pitied. ⁴⁴ You have covered yourself with a cloud, so that no prayer can pass through. ⁴⁵ You have made us an off-scouring and refuse in the middle of the peoples. ⁴⁶"All our enemies have opened their mouth wide against us. ⁴⁷ Terror and the pit have come on us, devastation and destruction." ⁴⁸ My eye runs down with streams of water, for the destruction of the daughter of my people. ⁴⁹ My eye pours down and doesn't cease, without any intermission, ⁵⁰ until Yahweh looks down, and sees from heaven. ⁵¹ My eye affects my soul, because of all the daughters of my city. ⁵² They have chased me

relentlessly like a bird, those who are my enemies without cause. ⁵³ They have cut off my life in the dungeon, and have cast a stone on me. ⁵⁴ Waters flowed over my head. I said, "I am cut off." ⁵⁵ I called on your name, Yahweh, out of the lowest dungeon. ⁵⁶ You heard my voice: "Don't hide your ear from my sighing, and my cry." ⁵⁷ You came near in the day that I called on you. You said, "Don't be afraid." ⁵⁸ Lord, you have pleaded the causes of my soul. You have redeemed my life. ⁵⁹ Yahweh, you have seen my wrong. Judge my cause. ⁶⁰ You have seen all their vengeance and all their plans against me. ⁶¹ You have heard their reproach, Yahweh, and all their plans against me, ⁶² the lips of those that rose up against me, and their plots against me all day long. ⁶³ You see their sitting down and their rising up. I am their song. ⁶⁴ You will pay them back, Yahweh, according to the work of their hands. ⁶⁵ You will give them hardness of heart, your curse to them. ⁶⁶ You will pursue them in anger, and destroy them from under the heavens of Yahweh.

## 4

¹ How the gold has become dim! The most pure gold has changed! The stones of the sanctuary are poured out at the head of every street. ² The precious sons of Zion, comparable to fine gold, how they are esteemed as earthen pitchers, the work of the hands of the potter! ³ Even the jackals offer their breast. They nurse their young ones. But the daughter of my people has become cruel, like the ostriches in the wilderness. ⁴ The tongue of the nursing child clings to the roof of its mouth for thirst. The young children ask for bread, and no one breaks it for them. ⁵ Those who ate delicacies are desolate in the streets. Those who were brought up in purple embrace dunghills. ⁶ For the iniquity of the daughter of my people is greater than the sin of Sodom, which was overthrown as in a moment. No hands were laid on her. ⁷ Her nobles were purer than snow. They were whiter than milk. They were more ruddy in body than rubies. Their polishing was like sapphire. ⁸ Their appearance is blacker than a coal. They are not known in the streets. Their skin clings to their bones. It is withered. It has become like wood. ⁹ Those who are killed with the sword are better than those who are killed with hunger; for these pine away, stricken through, for lack of the fruits of the field. ¹⁰ The hands of the pitiful women have boiled their own children. They were their food in the destruction of the daughter of my people. ¹¹ Yahweh has accomplished his wrath. He has poured out his fierce anger. He has kindled a fire in Zion, which has devoured its foundations. ¹² The kings of the earth didn't believe, neither did all the inhabitants of the world, that the adversary and the enemy would enter into the gates of Jerusalem. ¹³ It is because of the sins of her prophets and the iniquities of her priests, that have shed the blood of the just in the middle of her. ¹⁴ They wander as blind men in the streets. They are polluted with blood, So that men can't touch their garments. ¹⁵"Go away!" they cried to them. "Unclean! Go away! Go away! Don't touch! When they fled away and wandered, men said among the nations, "They can't live here any more." ¹⁶ Yahweh's anger has scattered them. He will not pay attention to them any more. They didn't respect the persons of the priests. They didn't favor the elders. ¹⁷ Our eyes still fail, looking in vain for our help. In our watching we have watched for a nation that could not save. ¹⁸ They hunt our steps, so that we can't go in our streets. Our end is near. Our days are fulfilled, for our end has come. ¹⁹ Our pursuers were swifter than the eagles of the sky. They chased us on the mountains. They set an ambush for us in the wilderness. ²⁰ The breath of our nostrils, the anointed of Yahweh, was taken in their pits; of whom we said, his shadow we will live among the nations. ²¹ Rejoice and be glad, daughter of Edom, who dwells in the land of Uz. The cup will pass through to you also. You will be drunken, and will make yourself naked. ²² The punishment of your iniquity is accomplished, daughter of Zion. He will no more carry you away into captivity. He will visit your iniquity, daughter of Edom. He will uncover your sins.

## 5

¹ Remember, Yahweh, what has come on us. Look, and see our reproach. ² Our inheritance has been turned over to strangers, our houses to aliens. ³ We are orphans and fatherless. Our mothers are as widows. ⁴ We must pay for water to drink. Our wood is sold to us. ⁵ Our pursuers are on our necks. We are weary, and have no rest. ⁶ We have given our hands to the Egyptians, and to the Assyrians, to be satisfied with bread. ⁷ Our fathers sinned, and are no more. We have borne their iniquities. ⁸ Servants rule over us. There is no one to deliver us out of their hand. ⁹ We get our bread at the peril of our lives, because of the sword in the wilderness. ¹⁰ Our skin is black like an oven, because of the burning heat of famine. ¹¹ They ravished the women in Zion, the virgins in the cities of Judah. ¹² Princes were hanged up by their hands.

---

ᵃ *3:41 The Hebrew word rendered "God" is "אֱלֹהִים" (Elohim).*

The faces of elders were not honored. ¹³ The young men carry millstones. The children stumbled under loads of wood. ¹⁴ The elders have ceased from the gate, and the young men from their music. ¹⁵ The joy of our heart has ceased. Our dance is turned into mourning. ¹⁶ The crown has fallen from our head. Woe to us, for we have sinned! ¹⁷ For this our heart is faint. For these things our eyes are dim: ¹⁸ for the mountain of Zion, which is desolate. The foxes walk on it. ¹⁹ You, Yahweh, remain forever. Your throne is from generation to generation. ²⁰ Why do you forget us forever, and forsake us for so long a time? ²¹ Turn us to yourself, Yahweh, and we will be turned. Renew our days as of old. ²² But you have utterly rejected us. You are very angry against us.

# The Book of Baruch

The book of *Baruch* is recognized as Deuterocanonical Scripture by the Roman Catholic, Greek Orthodox, and Russian Orthodox Churches. In some Bibles, Baruch chapter **6** is listed as a separate book called *The Letter of Jeremiah*, reflecting its separation from Baruch in some copies of the Greek Septuagint.

## 1

¹ These are the words of the book which Baruch the son of Nerias, the son of Maaseas, the son of Sedekias, the son of Asadias, the son of Helkias, wrote in Babylon, ² in the fifth year, in the seventh day of the month, at the time when the Chaldeans took Jerusalem and burned it with fire. ³ Baruch read the words of this book in the hearing of Jechonias the son of Joakim king of Judah, and in the hearing of all the people who came to hear the book, ⁴ and in the hearing of the mighty men, and of the kings' sons, and in the hearing of the elders, and in the hearing of all the people, from the least to the greatest, even of all those who lived at Babylon by the river Sud. ⁵ Then they wept, fasted,ᵃ and prayed before the Lord. ⁶ They also made a collection of money according to every man's ability; ⁷ and they sent it to Jerusalem to Joakim the high priest, the son of Helkias, the son of Salom, and to the priests and to all the people who were found with him at Jerusalem, ⁸ at the same time when he took the vessels of the house of the Lord, that had been carried out of the temple, to return them into the land of Judah, the tenth day of Sivan—silver vessels which Sedekias the son of Josias king of Judah had made, ⁹ after Nabuchodonosor king of Babylon had carried away Jechonias, the princes, the captives, the mighty men, and the people of the land from Jerusalem, and brought them to Babylon. ¹⁰ And they said: Behold, we have sent you money; therefore buy with the money burnt offerings, sin offerings, and incense, and prepare an oblation, and offer upon the altar of the Lord our God; ¹¹ and pray for the life of Nabuchodonosor king of Babylon, and for the life of Baltasar his son, that their days may beᵇ as the days of heaven above the earth. ¹² The Lord will give us strength and light to our eyes. We will live under the shadow of Nabuchodonosor king of Babylon and under the shadow of Baltasar his son, and we shall serve them many days, and find favor in their sight. ¹³ Pray for us also to the Lord our God, for we have sinned against the Lord our God. To this day the wrath of the Lord and his indignation is not turned from us. ¹⁴ You shall read this book which we have sent to you, to make confession in the house of the Lord upon the day of the feast and on the days of the solemn assembly. ¹⁵ You shall say: To the Lord our God belongs righteousness, but to us confusion of face, as at this day—to the men of Judah, to the inhabitants of Jerusalem, ¹⁶ to our kings, to our princes, to our priests, to our prophets, and to our fathers, ¹⁷ because we have sinned before the Lord. ¹⁸ We have disobeyed him and have not listened to the voice of the Lord our God, to walk in the commandments of the Lord that he has set before us. ¹⁹ Since the day that the Lord brought our fathers out of the land of Egypt to this present day, we have been disobedient to the Lord our God, and we have been negligent in not listening to his voice. ²⁰ Therefore the plagues have clung to us, along with the curse which the Lord declared through Moses his servant in the day that he brought our fathers out of the land of Egypt to give us a land that flows with milk and honey, as at this day. ²¹ Nevertheless we didn't listen to the voice of the Lord our God, according to all the words of the prophets whom he sent to us, ²² but we each walked in the imagination of his own wicked heart, to serve strange gods and to do what is evil in the sight of the Lord our God.

## 2

¹ Therefore the Lord has made good his word which he pronounced against us, and against our judges who judged Israel, and against our kings, and against our princes, and against the men of Israel and Judah, ² to bring upon us great plagues such as never happened before under the whole heaven,ᶜ as it came to pass in Jerusalem, according to the things that are written in the law of Moses, ³ that we should each eat the flesh of our own son, and each eat the flesh of our own daughter. ⁴ Moreover he has given them to be in subjection to all the kingdoms that are around us, to be a reproach and a desolation among all the people around us, where the Lord has scattered them. ⁵ Thus they were cast down and not exalted, because we sinned against the Lord our God in not listening to his voice. ⁶ To the Lord our God belongs righteousness, but to us and to our fathers confusion of face, as at this day. ⁷ All these plagues have come upon us which the Lord has pronounced against us. ⁸ Yet have we not entreated the favor of the Lord by everyone turning from the thoughts of his wicked heart. ⁹ Therefore the Lord has kept watch over the plagues. The Lord has brought them upon us, for the Lord is righteous in all his works which he has commanded us. ¹⁰ Yet we have not listened to his voice, to walk in the commandments of the Lord that he has set before us. ¹¹ And now, O Lord, you God of Israel who have brought your people out of the land of Egypt with a mighty hand, with signs, with wonders, with great power, and with a high arm, and have gotten yourself a name, as at this day: ¹² O Lord our God, we have sinned. We have been ungodly. We have done wrong in all your ordinances. ¹³ Let your wrath turn from us, for we are but a few left among the heathen where you have scattered us. ¹⁴ Hear our prayer, O Lord, and our petition, and deliver us for your own sake. Give us favor in the sight of those who have led us away captive, ¹⁵ that all the earth may know that you are the Lord our God, because Israel and his posterity is called by your name. ¹⁶ O Lord, look down from your holy house and consider us. Incline your ear, O Lord, and hear. ¹⁷ Open your eyes, and see; for the dead that are in Hades, whose breath is taken from their bodies, will give to the Lord neither glory nor righteousness; ¹⁸ but the soul who is greatly vexed, who goes stooping and feeble, and the eyes that fail, and the hungry soul, will declare your glory and righteousness, O Lord. ¹⁹ For we do not present our supplication before you, O Lord our God, for the righteousness of our fathers and of our kings. ²⁰ For you have sent your wrath and your indignation upon us, as you have spoken by your servants the prophets, saying, ²¹ "The Lord says, 'Bow your shoulders to serve the king of Babylon, and remain in the land that I gave to your fathers. ²² But if you won't hear the voice of the Lord to serve the king of Babylon, ²³ I will cause to cease out of the cities of Judah and from the region near Jerusalem the voice of mirth, the voice of gladness, voice of the bridegroom, and the voice of the bride. The whole land will be desolate without inhabitant.'" ²⁴ But we wouldn't listen to your voice, to serve the king of Babylon. Therefore you have made good your words that you spoke by your servants the prophets, that the bones of our kings and the bones of our fathers would be taken out of their places. ²⁵ Behold, they are cast out to the heat by day and to the frost by night. They died in great miseries by famine, by sword, and byᵈ pestilence. ²⁶ You have made the house that is called by your name as it is today because of the wickedness of the house of Israel and the house of Judah. ²⁷ Yet, O Lord our God, you have dealt with us after all your kindness and according to all your great mercy, ²⁸ as you spoke by your servant Moses in the day when you commanded him to write your law in the presence of the children of Israel, saying, ²⁹ "If you won't hear my voice, surely this very great multitude will be turned into a small number among the nations where I will scatter them. ³⁰ For I know that they will not hear me, because they are a stiff-necked people; but in the land of their captivity they will take it to heart, ³¹ and will know that I am the Lord their God. I will give them a heart and ears to hear. ³² Then they will praise me in the land of their captivity, and think about my name, ³³ and will return from their stiff neck and from their wicked deeds; for they will remember the way of their fathers who sinned before the Lord. ³⁴ I will bring them again into the land which I promised to their fathers, to Abraham, to Isaac, and to Jacob, and they will rule over it. I will increase them, and they won't be diminished. ³⁵ And I will make an everlasting covenant with them to be their God, and they will be my people. I will no more remove my people Israel out of the land that I have given them."

## 3

¹ O Lord Almighty, you God of Israel, the soul in anguish and the troubled spirit cries to you. ² Hear, O Lord, and have mercy; for you are a merciful God. Yes, have mercy upon us, because we have sinned before you. ³ For you are enthroned forever, and we keep perishing. ⁴ O Lord Almighty, you God of Israel, hear now the prayer of the dead Israelites, and of the children of those who were sinners before you, who didn't listen to the voice of you their God; because of this, these plagues cling to us. ⁵ Don't remember the iniquities of our fathers, but remember your power and your name at this time. ⁶ For you are the Lord our God, and we will praise you, O Lord. ⁷ For this cause, you have put your fear in our hearts, to the intent that we should call upon

---

ᵃ *1:5 Another reading is, and vowed vows.*

ᵇ *1:11 See Deuteronomy 11:21.*

ᶜ *2:2 Another reading is, even as he has done.*

ᵈ *2:25 See Jeremiah 32:36.*

your name. We will praise you in our captivity, for we have called to mind all the iniquity of our fathers who sinned before you. ⁸ Behold, we are yet this day in our captivity where you have scattered us, for a reproach and a curse, and to be subject to penalty according to all the iniquities of our fathers who departed from the Lord our God. ⁹ Hear, O Israel, the commandments of life! Give ear to understand wisdom! ¹⁰ How is it, O Israel, that you are in your enemies' land, that you have become old in a strange country, that you are defiled with the dead, ¹¹ that you are counted with those who are in Hades? ¹² You have forsaken the fountain of wisdom. ¹³ If you had walked in the way of God, you would have dwelled in peace forever. ¹⁴ Learn where there is wisdom, where there is strength, and where there is understanding, that you may also know where there is length of days and life, where there is the light of the eyes and peace. ¹⁵ Who has found out her place? Who has come into her treasuries? ¹⁶ Where are the princes of the heathen, and those who ruled the beasts that are on the earth, ¹⁷ those who had their pastime with the fowls of the air, and those who hoarded up silver and gold, in which people trust, and of their getting there is no end? ¹⁸ For those who diligently sought silver, and were so anxious, and whose works are past finding out, ¹⁹ they have vanished and gone down to Hades, and others have come up in their place. ²⁰ Younger men have seen the light and lived upon the earth, but they haven't known the way of knowledge, ²¹ nor understood its paths. Their children haven't embraced it. They are far off from their way. ²² It has not been heard of in Canaan, neither has it been seen in Teman. ²³ The sons also of Agar who seek understanding, which are in the land, the merchants of Merran and Teman, and the authors of fables, and the searchers out of understanding—none of these have known the way of wisdom or remembered her paths. ²⁴ O Israel, how great is the house of God! How large is the place of his possession! ²⁵ It is great and has no end. It is high and unmeasurable. ²⁶ Giants were born that were famous of old, great of stature, and expert in war. ²⁷ God didn't choose these, nor did he give the way of knowledge to them, ²⁸ so they perished, because they had no wisdom. They perished through their own foolishness. ²⁹ Who has gone up into heaven, taken her, and brought her down from the clouds? ³⁰ Who has gone over the sea, found her, and will bring her for choice gold? ³¹ There is no one who knows her way, nor any who comprehend her path. ³² But he that knows all things knows her, he found her out with his understanding. He who prepared the earth for all time has filled it with four-footed beasts. ³³ It is he who sends forth the light, and it goes. He called it, and it obeyed him with fear. ³⁴ The stars shone in their watches, and were glad. When he called them, they said, "Here we are." They shone with gladness to him who made them. ³⁵ This is our God. No other can be compared to him. ³⁶ He has found out all the way of knowledge, and has given it to Jacob his servant and to Israel who is loved by him. ³⁷ Afterward she appeared upon earth, and lived with men.

# 4

¹ This is the book of God's commandments and the law that endures forever. All those who hold it fast will live, but those who leave it will die. ² Turn, O Jacob, and take hold of it. Walk toward the shining of its light. ³ Don't give your glory to another, nor the things that are to your advantage to a foreign nation. ⁴ O Israel, we are happy; for the things that are pleasing to God are made known to us. ⁵ Be of good cheer, my people, the memorial of Israel. ⁶ You were not sold to the nations for destruction, but because you moved God to wrath, you were delivered to your adversaries. ⁷ For you provoked him who made you by sacrificing to demons and not to God. ⁸ You forgot the everlasting God who brought you up. You also grieved Jerusalem, who nursed you. ⁹ For she saw the wrath that came upon you from God, and said, "Listen, you who dwell near Zion; for God has brought upon me great mourning. ¹⁰ For I have seen the captivity of my sons and daughters, which the Everlasting has brought upon them. ¹¹ For with joy I nourished them, but sent them away with weeping and mourning. ¹² Let no man rejoice over me, a widow and forsaken by many. For the sins of my children, I am left desolate, because they turned away from the law of God ¹³ and had no regard for his statutes. They didn't walk in the ways of God's commandments or tread in the paths of discipline in his righteousness. ¹⁴ Let those who dwell near Zion come and remember the captivity of my sons and daughters, which the Everlasting has brought upon them. ¹⁵ For he has brought a nation upon them from afar, a shameless nation with a strange language, who didn't respect old men or pity children. ¹⁶ They have carried away the dear beloved sons of the widow, and left her who was alone desolate of her daughters." ¹⁷ But I—how can I help you? ¹⁸ For he who brought these calamities upon you will deliver you from the hand of your enemies. ¹⁹ Go your way, O my children. Go your way, for I am left desolate. ²⁰ I have put off the garment of peace, and put on the sackcloth of my petition. I will cry to the Everlasting as long as I live. ²¹ Take courage, my children. Cry to God, and he will deliver you from the power and hand of the enemies.

²² For I have trusted in the Everlasting, that he will save you; and joy has come to me from the Holy One, because of the mercy that will soon come to you from your Everlasting Savior. ²³ For I sent you out with mourning and weeping, but God will give you to me again with joy and gladness forever. ²⁴ For as now those who dwell near Zion have seen your captivity, so they will shortly see your salvation from our God which will come upon you with great glory and brightness of the Everlasting. ²⁵ My children, suffer patiently the wrath that has come upon you from God, for your enemy has persecuted you; but shortly you will see his destruction and will tread upon their necks. ²⁶ My delicate ones have traveled rough roads. They were taken away like a flock carried off by enemies. ²⁷ Take courage, my children, and cry to God; for you will be remembered by him who has brought this upon you. ²⁸ For as it was your decision to go astray from God, return and seek him ten times more. ²⁹ For he who brought these calamities upon you will bring you everlasting joy again with your salvation. ³⁰ Take courage, O Jerusalem, for he who called you by name will comfort you. ³¹ Miserable are those who afflicted you and rejoiced at your fall. ³² Miserable are the cities which your children served. Miserable is she who received your sons. ³³ For as she rejoiced at your fall and was glad of your ruin, so she will be grieved at her own desolation. ³⁴ And I will take away her pride in her great multitude and her boasting will be turned into mourning. ³⁵ For fire will come upon her from the Everlasting for many days; and she will be inhabited by demons for a long time. ³⁶ O Jerusalem, look around you toward the east, and behold the joy that comes to you from God. ³⁷ Behold, your sons come, whom you sent away. They come gathered together from the east to the west at the word of the Holy One, rejoicing in the glory of God.

# 5

¹ Take off the garment of your mourning and affliction, O Jerusalem, and put on forever the beauty of the glory from God. ² Put on the robe of the righteousness from God. Set on your head a diadem of the glory of the Everlasting. ³ For God will show your splendor everywhere under heaven. ⁴ For your name will be called by God forever "Righteous Peace, Godly Glory". ⁵ Arise, O Jerusalem, and stand upon the height. Look around you toward the east and see your children gathered from the going down of the sun to its rising at the word of the Holy One, rejoicing that God has remembered them. ⁶ For they went from you on foot, being led away by their enemies, but God brings them in to you carried on high with glory, on a royal throne. ⁷ For God has appointed that every high mountain and the everlasting hills should be made low, and the valleys filled up to make the ground level, that Israel may go safely in the glory of God. ⁸ Moreover the woods and every sweet smelling tree have shaded Israel by the commandment of God. ⁹ For God will lead Israel with joy in the light of his glory with the mercy and righteousness that come from him.

# The Letter of Jeremiah
## 6

¹ A copy of a letter that Jeremy sent to those who were to be led captives into Babylon by the king of the Babylonians, to give them the message that God commanded him. ² Because of the sins which you have committed before God, you will be led away captives to Babylon by Nabuchodonosor king of the Babylonians. ³ So when you come to Babylon, you will remain there many years, and for a long season, even for seven generations. After that, I will bring you out peacefully from there. ⁴ But now you will see in Babylon gods of silver, gold, wood carried on shoulders, which cause the nations to fear. ⁵ Beware therefore that you in no way become like these foreigners. Don't let fear take hold of you because of them when you see the multitude before them and behind them, worshiping them. ⁶ But say in your hearts, "O Lord, we must worship you." ⁷ For my angel is with you, and I myself care for your souls. ⁸ For their tongue is polished by the workman, and they themselves are overlaid with gold and with silver; yet they are only fake, and can't speak. ⁹ And taking gold, as if it were for a virgin who loves to be happy, they make crowns for the heads of their gods. ¹⁰ Sometimes also the priests take gold and silver from their gods, and spend it on themselves. ¹¹ They will even give some of it to the common prostitutes. They dress them like men with garments, even the gods of silver, gods of gold, and gods of wood. ¹² Yet these gods can't save themselves from rust and moths, even though they are covered with purple garments. ¹³ They wipe their faces because of the dust of the temple, which is thick upon them. ¹⁴ And he who can't put to death one who offends against him holds a sceptre, as though he were judge of a country. ¹⁵ He has also a dagger in his right hand, and an axe, but can't deliver himself from war and robbers. ¹⁶ By this they are known not to be gods. Therefore don't fear them. ¹⁷ For like a vessel that a man uses is worth nothing when it is broken, even so it is with their gods. When they are set up in the temples, their eyes are full of dust through the feet

of those who come in. [18] As the courts are secured on every side upon him who offends the king, as being committed to suffer death, even so the priests secure their temples with doors, with locks, and bars, lest they be carried off by robbers. [19] They light candles for them, yes, more than for themselves, even though they can't see one. [20] They are like one of the beams of the temple. Men say their hearts are eaten out when things creeping out of the earth devour both them and their clothing. They don't feel it [21] when their faces are blackened through the smoke that comes out of the temple. [22] Bats, swallows, and birds land on their bodies and heads. So do the cats. [23] By this you may know that they are no gods. Therefore don't fear them. [24] Notwithstanding the gold with which they are covered to make them beautiful, unless someone wipes off the tarnish, they won't shine; for they didn't even feel it when they were molten. [25] Things in which there is no breath are bought at any cost. [26] Having no feet, they are carried upon shoulders. By this, they declare to men that they are worth nothing. [27] Those who serve them are also ashamed, for if they fall to the ground at any time, they can't rise up again by themselves. If they are bowed down, they can't make themselves straight; but the offerings are set before them, as if they were dead men. [28] And the things that are sacrificed to them, their priests sell and spend. In like manner, their wives also lay up part of it in salt; but to the poor and to the impotent they give none of it. [29] The menstruous woman and the woman in childbed touch their sacrifices, knowing therefore by these things that they are no gods. Don't fear them. [30] For how can they be called gods? Because women set food before the gods of silver, gold, and wood. [31] And in their temples the priests sit on seats, having their clothes torn and their heads and beards shaven, and nothing on their heads. [32] They roar and cry before their gods, as men do at the feast when one is dead. [33] The priests also take off garments from them and clothe their wives and children with them. [34] Whether it is evil or good what one does to them, they are not able to repay it. They can't set up a king or put him down. [35] In like manner, they can neither give riches nor money. Though a man make a vow to them and doesn't keep it, they will never exact it. [36] They can save no man from death. They can't deliver the weak from the mighty. [37] They can't restore a blind man to his sight, or deliver anyone who is in distress. [38] They can show no mercy to the widow, or do good to the fatherless. [39] They are like the stones that are cut out of the mountain, these gods of wood that are overlaid with gold and with silver. Those who minister to them will be confounded. [40] How could a man then think or say that they are gods, when even the Chaldeans themselves dishonor them? [41] If they shall see one mute who can't speak, they bring him and ask him to call upon Bel, as though he were able to understand. [42] Yet they can't perceive this themselves, and forsake them; for they have no understanding. [43] The women also with cords around them sit in the ways, burning bran for incense; but if any of them, drawn by someone who passes by, lies with him, she reproaches her fellow, that she was not thought as worthy as herself and her cord wasn't broken. [44] Whatever is done among them is false. How could a man then think or say that they are gods? [45] They are fashioned by carpenters and goldsmiths. They can be nothing else than what the workmen make them to be. [46] And they themselves who fashioned them can never continue long. How then should the things that are fashioned by them? [47] For they have left lies and reproaches to those who come after. [48] For when there comes any war or plague upon them, the priests consult with themselves, where they may be hidden with them. [49] How then can't men understand that they are no gods, which can't save themselves from war or from plague? [50] For seeing they are only wood and overlaid with gold and silver, it will be known hereafter that they are false. [51] It will be manifest to all nations and kings that they are no gods, but the works of men's hands, and that there is no work of God in them. [52] Who then may not know that they are not gods? [53] For they can't set up a king in a land or give rain to men. [54] They can't judge their own cause, or redress a wrong, being unable; for they are like crows between heaven and earth. [55] For even when fire falls upon the house of gods of wood overlaid with gold or with silver, their priests will flee away, and escape, but they themselves will be burned apart like beams. [56] Moreover they can't withstand any king or enemies. How could a man then admit or think that they are gods? [57] Those gods of wood overlaid with silver or with gold aren't able to escape from thieves or robbers. [58] The gold, silver, and garments with which they are clothed—those who are strong will take from them, and go away with them. They won't be able to help themselves. [59] Therefore it is better to be a king who shows his manhood, or else a vessel in a house profitable for whatever the owner needs, than such false gods—or even a door in a house, to keep the things safe that are in it, than such false gods; or better to be a pillar of wood in a palace than such false gods. [60] For sun, moon, and stars, being bright and sent to do their jobs, are obedient. [61] Likewise also the lightning when it flashes is beautiful to see. In the same way, the wind also blows in every country. [62] And when God

commands the clouds to go over the whole world, they do as they are told. [63] And the fire sent from above to consume mountains and woods does as it is commanded; but these are to be compared to them neither in show nor power. [64] Therefore a man shouldn't think or say that they are gods, seeing they aren't able to judge causes or to do good to men. [65] Knowing therefore that they are no gods, don't fear them. [66] For they can neither curse nor bless kings. [67] They can't show signs in the heavens among the nations, or shine as the sun, or give light as the moon. [68] The beasts are better than they; for they can get under a covert, and help themselves. [69] In no way then is it manifest to us that they are gods. Therefore don't fear them. [70] For as a scarecrow in a garden of cucumbers that keeps nothing, so are their gods of wood overlaid with gold and silver. [71] Likewise also their gods of wood overlaid with gold and with silver, are like a white thorn in an orchard that every bird sits upon. They are also like a dead body that is thrown out into the dark. [72] You will know them to be no gods by the bright purple that rots upon them. They themselves will be consumed afterwards, and will be a reproach in the country. [73] Better therefore is the just man who has no idols; for he will be far from reproach.

# 4 Baruch, or Paralipomena of Jeremiah

## 1

[1] It came to pass, when the children of Israel were taken captive by the king of the Chaldeans, that God spoke to Jeremiah saying: Jeremiah, my chosen [one] *[servant]*, arise and depart from this city, you and Baruch, since I am going to destroy it because of the multitude of the sins of those who dwell in it. [2] For your prayers are like a solid pillar in its midst, and like an indestructible wall surrounding it. [3] Now, then, arise and depart before the host of the Chaldeans surrounds it. [4] And Jeremiah answered, saying: I beseech you, Lord, permit me, your servant, to speak in your presence. [5] And the Lord said to him: Speak, my chosen [one] *[servant]* Jeremiah. [6] And Jeremiah spoke, saying: Lord Almighty, would you deliver the chosen city into the hands of the Chaldeans, so that the king with the multitude of his people might boast and say: "I have prevailed over the holy city of God"? [7] No, my Lord, but if it is your will, let it be destroyed by your hands. [8] And the Lord said to Jeremiah: Since you are my chosen one, arise and depart form this city, you and Baruch, for I am going to destroy it because of the multitude of the sins of those who dwell in it. [9] For neither the king nor his host will be able to enter it unless I first open its gates. [10] Arise, then, and go to Baruch, and tell him these words. [11] And when you have arisen at the sixth hour of the night, go out on the city walls and I will show you that unless I first destroy the city, they cannot enter it. [12] When the Lord had said this, he departed from Jeremiah.

## 2

[1] And Jeremiah ran and told these things to Baruch; and as they went into the temple of God, Jeremiah tore his garments and put dust on his head and entered the holy place of God. [2] And when Baruch saw him with dust sprinkled on his head and his garments torn, he cried out in a loud voice, saying: Father Jeremiah, what are you doing? What sin has the people committed? [3] (For whenever the people sinned, Jeremiah would sprinkle dust on his head and would pray for the people until their sin was forgiven.) [4] So Baruch asked him, saying: Father, what is this? [5] And Jeremiah said to him: Refrain from rending your garments — rather, let us rend our hearts! And let us not draw water for the trough, but let us weep and fill them with tears! For the Lord will not have mercy on this people. [6] And Baruch said: Father Jeremiah, what has happened? [7] And Jeremiah said: God is delivering the city into the hands of the king of the Chaldeans, to take the people captive into Babylon. [8] And when Baruch heard these things, he also tore his garments and said: Father Jeremiah, who has made this known to you? [9] And Jeremiah said to him: Stay with me awhile, until the sixth hour of the night, so that you may know that this word is true. [10] Therefore they both remained in the altar-area weeping, and their garments were torn.

## 3

[1] And when the hour of the night arrived, as the Lord had told Jeremiah they came up together on the walls of the city, Jeremiah and Baruch. [2] And behold, there came a sound of trumpets; and angels emerged from heaven holding torches in their hands, and they set them on the walls of the city. [3] And when Jeremiah and Baruch saw them, they wept, saying: Now we know that the word is true! [4] And Jeremiah besought the angels, saying: I beseech you, do not destroy the city yet, until I say something to the Lord. [5] And the Lord spoke to the angels, saying: Do not destroy the city until I speak to my chosen one, Jeremiah. [6] Then Jeremiah spoke, saying: I beg you, Lord, bid me to speak in your presence. [7] And the Lord said: Speak, my chosen [one] *[servant]* Jeremiah. [8] And Jeremiah said: Behold, Lord, now we know that you

are delivering the city into the hands of its enemies, and they will take the people away to Babylon. What do you want me to do with the holy vessels of the temple service? [10] And the Lord said to him: Take them and consign them to the earth, saying: Hear, Earth, the voice of your creator who formed you in the abundance of waters, who sealed you with seven seals for seven epochs, and after this you will receive your ornaments (?) — [11] Guard the vessels of the temple service until the gathering of the beloved. [12] And Jeremiah spoke, saying: I beseech you, Lord, show me what I should do for Abimelech the Ethiopian, for he has done many kindnesses to your servant Jeremiah. [13] For he pulled me out of the miry pit; and I do not wish that he should see the destruction and desolation of this city, but that you should be merciful to him and that he should not be grieved. [14] And the Lord said to Jeremiah: Send him to the vineyard of Agrippa, and I will hide him in the shadow of the mountain until I cause the people to return to the city. [15] And you, Jeremiah, go with your people into Babylon and stay with them, preaching to them, until I cause them to return to the city. [16] But leave Baruch here until I speak with him. [17] When he had said these things, the Lord ascended from Jeremiah into heaven. [18] But Jeremiah and Baruch entered the holy place, and taking the vessels of the temple service, they consigned them to the earth as the Lord had told them. [19] And immediately the earth swallowed them. [20] And they both sat down and wept. [21] And when morning came, Jeremiah sent Abimelech, saying: Take a basket and go to the estate of Agrippa by the mountain road, and bring back some figs to give to the sick among the people; for the favor of the Lord is on you and his glory is on your head. [22] And when he had said this, Jeremiah sent him away; and Abimelech went as he told him.

## 4

[1] And when morning came, behold the host of the Chaldeans surrounded the city. [2] And the great angel trumpeted, saying: Enter the city, host of the Chaldeans; for behold, the gate is opened for you. [3] Therefore let the king enter, with his multitudes, and let him take all the people captive. [4] But taking the keys of the temple, Jeremiah went outside the city and threw them away in the presence of the sun, saying: I say to you, Sun, take the keys of the temple of God and guard them until the day in which the Lord asks you for them. [5] For we have not been found worthy to keep them, for we have become unfaithful guardians. [6] While Jeremiah was still weeping for the people, they brought him out with the people and dragged them into Babylon. [7] But Baruch put dust on his head and sat and wailed this lamentation, saying: Why has Jerusalem been devastated? Because of the sins of the beloved people she was delivered into the hands of enemies — because of our sins and those of the people. [8] But let not the lawless ones boast and say: "We were strong enough to take the city of God by our might;" but it was delivered to you because of our sins. [9] And God will pity us and cause us to return to our city, but you will not survive! [10] Blessed are our fathers, Abraham, Isaac and Jacob, for they departed from this world and did not see the destruction of this city. [11] When he had said this, Baruch departed from the city, weeping and saying: Grieving because of you, Jerusalem, I went out from you. [12] And he remained sitting in a tomb, while the angels came to him and explained to him everything that the Lord revealed to him through them.

## 5

[1] But Abimelech took the figs in the burning heat; and coming upon a tree, he sat under its shade to rest a bit. [2] And leaning his head on the basket of figs, he fell asleep and slept for 66 years; and he was not awakened from his slumber. [3] And afterward, when he awoke from his sleep, he said: I slept sweetly for a little while, but my head is heavy because I did not get enough sleep. [4] Then he uncovered the basket of figs and found them dripping milk. [5] And he said: I would like to sleep a little longer, because my head is heavy. But I am afraid that I might fall asleep and be late in awakening and my father Jeremiah would think badly of me; for if he were not in a hurry, he would not have sent me today at daybreak. [6] So I will get up, and proceed in the burning heat; for isn't there heat, isn't there toil every day? [7] So he got up and took the basket of figs and placed it on his shoulders, and he entered into Jerusalem and did not recognize it — neither his own house, nor the place — nor did he find his own family or any of his acquaintances. [8] And he said: The Lord be blessed, for a great trance has come over me today! [9] This is not the city Jerusalem — and I have lost my way because I came by the mountain road when I arose from my sleep; and since my head was heavy because I did not get enough sleep, I lost my way. [10] It will seem incredible to Jeremiah that I lost my way! [11] And he departed from the city; and as he searched he saw the landmarks of the city, and he said: Indeed, this is the city; I lost my way. [12] And again he returned to the city and searched, and found no one of his own people; and he said: The Lord be blessed, for a great trance has come over me! [13] And again he departed from the city, and he stayed grieving, not knowing where he should go. [14] And he put down the basket, saying: I will sit here until the Lord takes this trance from me. [15] And as he sat, he saw an old man coming from the field; and Abimelech said to him: I say to you, old man, what city is this? [16] And he said to him: It is Jerusalem. [17] And Abimelech said to him: Where is Jeremiah the priest, and Baruch the secretary, and all the people of this city, for I could not find them? [18] And the old man said to him: Are you not from this city, seeing that you remember Jeremiah today, because you are asking about him after such a long time? [19] For Jeremiah is in Babylon with the people; for they were taken captive by king Nebuchadnezzar, and Jeremiah is with them to preach the good news to them and to teach them the word. [20] As soon as Abimelech heard this from the old man, he said: If you were not an old man, and if it were not for the fact that it is not lawful for a man to upbraid one older than himself, I would laugh at you and say that you are out of your mind — since you say that the people have been taken captive into Babylon. [21] Even if the heavenly torrents had descended on them, there has not yet been time for them to go into Babylon! [22] For how much time has passed since my father Jeremiah sent me to the estate of Agrippa to bring a few figs, so that I might give them to the sick among the people? [23] And I went and got them, and when I came to a certain tree in the burning heat, I sat to rest a little; and I leaned my head on the basket and fell asleep. [24] And when I awoke I uncovered the basket of figs, supposing that I was late; and I found the figs dripping milk, just as I had collected them. [25] But you claim that the people have been taken captive into Babylon. [26] But that you might know, take the figs and see! [27] And he uncovered the basket of figs for the old man, and he saw them dripping milk. [28] And when the old man saw them, he said: O my son, you are a righteous man, and God did not want you to see the desolation of the city, so he brought this trance upon you. [29] For behold it is 66 years today since the people were taken captive into Babylon. [30] But that you might learn, my son, that what I tell you is true — look into the field and see that the ripening of the crops has not appeared. [31] And notice that the figs are not in season, and be enlightened. [32] Then Abimelech cried out in a loud voice, saying: I bless you, God of heaven and earth, the Rest of the souls of the righteous in every place! [33] Then he said to the old man: What month is this? [34] And he said: Nisan (which is Abib). [35] And taking some of figs, he gave them to the old man and said to him: May God illumine your way to the city above, Jerusalem.

## 6

[1] After this, Abimelech went out of the city and prayed to the Lord. [2] And behold, an angel of the Lord came and took him by the right hand and brought him back to where Baruch was sitting, and he found him in a tomb. [3] And when they saw each other, they both wept and kissed each other. [4] But when Baruch looked up he saw with his own eyes the figs that were covered in Abimelech's basket. [5] And lifting his eyes to heaven, he prayed, saying: [6] You are the God who gives a reward to those who love you. Prepare yourself, my heart, and rejoice and be glad while you are in your tabernacle, saying to your fleshly house, "your grief has been changed to joy;" for the Sufficient One is coming and will deliver you in your tabernacle — for there is no sin in you. [7] Revive in your tabernacle, in your virginal faith, and believe that you will live! [8] Look at this basket of figs — for behold, they are 66 years old and have not become shrivelled or rotten, but they are dripping milk. [9] So it will be with you, my flesh, if you do what is commanded you by the angel of righteousness. [10] He who preserved the basket of figs, the same will again preserve you by his power. [11] When Baruch had said this, he said to Abimelech: Stand up and let us pray that the Lord may make known to us how we shall be able to send to Jeremiah in Babylon the report about the shelter provided for you on the way. [12] And Baruch prayed, saying: Lord God, our strength is the elect light which comes forth from your mouth. [13] We beseech and beg of your goodness — you whose great name no one is able to know — hear the voice of your servants and let knowledge come into our hearts. [14] What shall we do, and how shall we send this report to Jeremiah in Babylon? [15] And while Baruch was still praying, behold an angel of the Lord came and said all these words to Baruch: Agent of the light, do not be anxious about how you will send to Jeremiah; for an eagle is coming to you at the hour of light tomorrow, and you will direct him to Jeremiah. [16] Therefore, write in a letter: Say to the children of Israel: Let the stranger who comes among you be set apart and let 15 days go by; and after this I will lead you into your city, says the Lord. [17] He who is not separated from Babylon will not enter into the city; and I will punish them by keeping them from being received back by the Babylonians, says the Lord. [18] And when the angel had said this, he departed from Baruch. [19] And Baruch sent to the market of the gentiles and got papyrus and ink and wrote a letter as follows: Baruch, the servant of God, writes to Jeremiah in the captivity of Babylon: [20] Greetings! Rejoice, for God has not allowed us to depart from this body grieving for the city which was laid waste and outraged. [21] Wherefore the Lord has had compassion on our

tears, and has remembered the covenant which he established with our fathers Abraham, Isaac and Jacob. [22] And he sent his angel to me, and he told me these words which I send to you. [23] These, then, are the words which the Lord, the God of Israel, spoke, who led us out of Egypt, out of the great furnace: Because you did not keep my ordinances, but your heart was lifted up, and you were haughty before me, in anger and wrath I delivered you to the furnace in Babylon. [24] If, therefore, says the Lord, you listen to my voice, from the mouth of Jeremiah my servant, I will bring the one who listens up from Babylon; but the one who does not listen will become a stranger to Jerusalem and to Babylon. [25] And you will test them by means of the water of the Jordan; whoever does not listen will be exposed — this is the sign of the great seal.

## 7

[1] And Baruch got up and departed from the tomb and found the eagle sitting outside the tomb. [2] And the eagle said to him in a human voice: Hail, Baruch, steward of the faith. [3] And Baruch said to him: You who speak are chosen from among all the birds of heaven, for this is clear from the gleam of your eyes; tell me, then, what are you doing here? [4] And the eagle said to him: I was sent here so that you might through me send whatever message you want. [5] And Baruch said to him: Can you carry this message to Jeremiah in Babylon? [6] And the eagle said to him: Indeed, it was for this reason I was sent. [7] And Baruch took the letter, and 15 figs from Abimelech's basket, and tied them to the eagle's neck and said to him: I say to you, king of the birds, go in peace with good health and carry the message for me. [8] Do not be like the raven which Noah sent out and which never came back to him in the ark; but be like the dove which, the third time, brought a report to the righteous one. [9] So you also, take this good message to Jeremiah and to those in bondage with him, that it may be well with you-take this papyrus to the people and to the chosen one of God. [10] Even if all the birds of heaven surround you and want to fight with you, struggle — the Lord will give you strength. [11] And do not turn aside to the right or to the left, but straight as a speeding arrow, go in the power of God, and the glory of the Lord will be with you the entire way. [12] Then the eagle took flight and went away to Babylon, having the letter tied to his neck; and when he arrived he rested on a post outside the city in a desert place. [13] And he kept silent until Jeremiah came along, for he and some of the people were coming out to bury a corpse outside the city. [14] (For Jeremiah had petitioned king Nebuchadnezzar, saying: "Give me a place where I may bury those of my people who have died;" and the king gave it to him.) [15] And as they were coming out with the body, and weeping, they came to where the eagle was. [16] And the eagle cried out in a loud voice, saying: I say to you, Jeremiah the chosen [one] *[servant]* of God, go and gather together the people and come here so that they may hear a letter which I have brought to you from Baruch and Abimelech. [17] And when Jeremiah heard this, he glorified God; and he went and gathered together the people along with their wives and children, and he came to where the eagle was. [18] And the eagle came down on the corpse, and it revived. [19] (Now this took place so that they might believe.) [20] And all the people were astounded at what had happened, and said: This is the God who appeared to our fathers in the wilderness through Moses, and now he has appeared to us through the eagle. [21] And the eagle said: I say to you, Jeremiah, come, untie this letter and read it to the people — So he untied the letter and read it to the people. [22] And when the people heard it, they wept and put dust on their heads, and they said to Jeremiah: Deliver us and tell us what to do that we may once again enter our city. [23] And Jeremiah answered and said to them: Do whatever you heard from the letter, and the Lord will lead us into our city. [24] And Jeremiah wrote a letter to Baruch, saying thus: My beloved son, do not be negligent in your prayers, beseeching God on our behalf, that he might direct our way until we come out of the jurisdiction of this lawless king. [25] For you have been found righteous before God, and he did not let you come here, lest you see the affliction which has come upon the people at the hands of the Babylonians. [26] For it is like a father with an only son, who is given over for punishment; and those who see his father and console him cover his face, lest he see how his son is being punished, and be even more ravaged by grief. [27] For thus God took pity on you and did not let you enter Babylon lest you see the affliction of the people. [28] For since we came here, grief has not left us, for 66 years today. [29] For many times when I went out I found some of the people hung up by king Nebuchadnezzar, crying and saying: "Have mercy on us, God-ZAR!" [30] When I heard this, I grieved and cried with two-fold mourning, not only because they were hung up, but because they were calling on a foreign God, saying "Have mercy on us." [31] But I remembered days of festivity which we celebrated in Jerusalem before our captivity; and when I remembered, I groaned, and returned to my house wailing and weeping. [32] Now, then, pray in the place where you are — you and Abimelech — for this people, that they may listen to my voice and to the decrees of my mouth, so that we may depart from here.

[33] For I tell you that the entire time that we have spent here they have kept us in subjection, saying: Recite for us a song from the songs of Zion — the song of your God. *Psalm 3-4* [34] And we reply to them: How shall we sing for you since we are in a foreign land? [35] And after this, Jeremiah tied the letter to the eagle's neck, saying: Go in peace, and may the Lord watch over both of us. [36] And the eagle took flight and came to Jerusalem and gave the letter to Baruch; and when he had untied it he read it and kissed it and wept when he heard about the distresses and afflictions of the people. [37] But Jeremiah took the figs and distributed them to the sick among the people, and he kept teaching them to abstain from the pollutions of the gentiles of Babylon.

## 8

[1] And the day came in which the Lord brought the people out of Babylon. [2] And the Lord said to Jeremiah: Rise up — you and the people — and come to the Jordan and say to the people: Let anyone who desires the Lord forsake the works of Babylon. [3] As for the men who took wives from them and the women who took husbands from them — those who listen to you shall cross over, and you take them into Jerusalem; but those who do not listen to you, do not lead them there. [4] And Jeremiah spoke these words to the people, and they arose and came to the Jordan to cross over. [5] As he told them the words that the Lord had spoken to him, half of those who had taken spouses from them did not wish to listen to Jeremiah, but said to him: We will never forsake our wives, but we will bring them back with us into our city. [6] So they crossed the Jordan and came to Jerusalem. [7] And Jeremiah and Baruch and Abimelech stood up and said: No man joined with Babylonians shall enter this city! [8] And they said to one another: Let us arise and return to Babylon to our place — And they departed. [9] But while they were coming to Babylon, the Babylonians came out to meet them, saying: You shall not enter our city, for you hated us and you left us secretly; therefore you cannot come in with us. [10] For we have taken a solemn oath together in the name of our god to receive neither you nor your children, since you left us secretly. [11] And when they heard this, they returned and came to a desert place some distance from Jerusalem and built a city for themselves and named it 'SAMARIA.' [12] And Jeremiah sent to them, saying: Repent, for the angel of righteousness is coming and will lead you to your exalted place.

## 9

[1] Now those who were with Jeremiah were rejoicing and offering sacrifices on behalf of the people for nine days. [2] But on the tenth, Jeremiah alone offered sacrifice. [3] And he prayed a prayer, saying: Holy, holy, holy, fragrant aroma of the living trees, true light that enlightens me until I ascend to you; [4] For your mercy, I beg you — for the sweet voice of the two seraphim, I beg — for another fragrant aroma. [5] And may Michael, archangel of righteousness, who opens the gates to the righteous, be my guardian (?) until he causes the righteous to enter. [6] I beg you, almighty Lord of all creation, unbegotten and incomprehensible, in whom all judgment was hidden before these things came into existence. [7] When Jeremiah had said this, and while he was standing in the altar-area with Baruch and Abimelech, he became as one whose soul had departed. [8] And Baruch and Abimelech were weeping and crying out in a loud voice: Woe to us! For our father Jeremiah has left us — the priest of God has departed! [9] And all the people heard their weeping and they all ran to them and saw Jeremiah lying on the ground as if dead. [10] And they tore their garments and put dust on their heads and wept bitterly. [11] And after this they prepared to bury him. [12] And behold, there came a voice saying: Do not bury the one who yet lives, for his soul is returning to his body! [13] And when they heard the voice they did not bury him, but stayed around his tabernacle for three days saying, "when will he arise?" [14] And after three days his soul came back into his body and he raised his voice in the midst of them all and said: Glorify God with one voice! All of you glorify God and the son of God who awakens us — messiah Jesus — the light of all the ages, the inextinguishable lamp, the life of faith. [15] But after these times there shall be 477 years more and he comes to earth. [16] And the tree of life planted in the midst of paradise will cause all the unfruitful trees to bear fruit, and will grow and sprout forth. [17] And the trees that had sprouted and became haughty and said: "We have supplied our power (?) to the air," he will cause them to wither, with the grandeur of their branches, and he will cause them to be judged — that firmly rooted tree! [18] And what is crimson will become white as wool — the snow will be blackened — the sweet waters will become salty, and the salty sweet, in the intense light of the joy of God. [19] And he will bless the isles so that they become fruitful by the word of the mouth of his messiah. [20] For he shall come, and he will go out and choose for himself twelve apostles to proclaim the news among the nations– he whom I have seen adorned by his father and coming into the world on the Mount of Olives — and he shall fill the hungry souls. [21] When Jeremiah was saying this concerning the son of God — that he is coming into the world — the people became very angry and said:

This is a repetition of the words spoken by Isaiah son of Amos, when he said: I saw God and the son of God. ²² Come, then, and let us not kill him by the same sort of death with which we killed Isaiah, but let us stone him with stones. ²³ And Baruch and Abimelech were greatly grieved because they wanted to hear in full the mysteries that he had seen. ²⁴ But Jeremiah said to them: Be silent and weep not, for they cannot kill me until I describe for you everything I saw. ²⁵ And he said to them: Bring a stone here to me. ²⁶ And he set it up and said: Light of the ages, make this stone to become like me in appearance, until I have described to Baruch and Abimelech everything I saw. ²⁷ Then the stone, by God's command, took on the appearance of Jeremiah. ²⁸ And they were stoning the stone, supposing that it was Jeremiah! ²⁹ But Jeremiah delivered to Baruch and to Abimelech all the mysteries he had seen, and forthwith he stood in the midst of the people desiring to complete his ministry. ³⁰ Then the stone cried out, saying: O foolish children of Israel, why do you stone me, supposing that I am Jeremiah? Behold, Jeremiah is standing in your midst! ³¹ And when they saw him, immediately they rushed upon him with many stones, and his ministry was fulfilled. ³² And when Baruch and Abimelech came, they buried him, and taking the stone they placed it on his tomb and inscribed it thus: This is the stone that was the ally of Jeremiah.

# The Book of Ezekiel

## 1

¹ Now in the thirtieth year, in the fourth month, in the fifth day of the month, as I was among the captives by the river Chebar, the heavens were opened, and I saw visions of God.ᵃ ² In the fifth of the month, which was the fifth year of King Jehoiachin's captivity, ³ Yahweh'sᵇ word came to Ezekiel the priest, the son of Buzi, in the land of the Chaldeans by the river Chebar; and Yahweh's hand was there on him. ⁴ I looked, and behold,ᶜ a stormy wind came out of the north: a great cloud, with flashing lightning, and a brightness around it, and out of the middle of it as it were glowing metal, out of the middle of the fire. ⁵ Out of its center came the likeness of four living creatures. This was their appearance: They had the likeness of a man. ⁶ Everyone had four faces, and each one of them had four wings. ⁷ Their feet were straight feet. The sole of their feet was like the sole of a calf's foot; and they sparkled like burnished bronze. ⁸ They had the hands of a man under their wings on their four sides. The four of them had their faces and their wings like this: ⁹ Their wings were joined to one another. They didn't turn when they went. Each one went straight forward. ¹⁰ As for the likeness of their faces, they had the face of a man. The four of them had the face of a lion on the right side. The four of them had the face of an ox on the left side. The four of them also had the face of an eagle. ¹¹ Such were their faces. Their wings were spread out above. Two wings of each one touched another, and two covered their bodies. ¹² Each one went straight forward. Where the spirit was to go, they went. They didn't turn when they went. ¹³ As for the likeness of the living creatures, their appearance was like burning coals of fire, like the appearance of torches. The fire went up and down among the living creatures. The fire was bright, and lightning went out of the fire. ¹⁴ The living creatures ran and returned as the appearance of a flash of lightning. ¹⁵ Now as I saw the living creatures, behold, there was one wheel on the earth beside the living creatures, for each of the four faces of it. ¹⁶ The appearance of the wheels and their work was like a beryl. The four of them had one likeness. Their appearance and their work was as it were a wheel within a wheel. ¹⁷ When they went, they went in their four directions. They didn't turn when they went. ¹⁸ As for their rims, they were high and dreadful; and the four of them had their rims full of eyes all around. ¹⁹ When the living creatures went, the wheels went beside them. When the living creatures were lifted up from the earth, the wheels were lifted up. ²⁰ Wherever the spirit was to go, they went. The spirit was to go there. The wheels were lifted up beside them; for the spirit of the living creature was in the wheels. ²¹ When those went, these went. When those stood, these stood. When those were lifted up from the earth, the wheels were lifted up beside them; for the spirit of the living creature was in the wheels. ²² Over the head of the living creature there was the likeness of an expanse, like an awesome crystal to look at, stretched out over their heads above. ²³ Under the expanse, their wings were straight, one toward the other. Each one had two which covered on this side, and each one had two which covered their bodies on that side. ²⁴ When they went, I heard the noise of their wings like the noise of great waters, like the voice of the Almighty, a noise of tumult

like the noise of an army. When they stood, they let down their wings. ²⁵ There was a voice above the expanse that was over their heads. When they stood, they let down their wings. ²⁶ Above the expanse that was over their heads was the likeness of a throne, as the appearance of a sapphireᵈ stone. On the likeness of the throne was a likeness as the appearance of a man on it above. ²⁷ I saw as it were glowing metal, as the appearance of fire within it all around, from the appearance of his waist and upward; and from the appearance of his waist and downward I saw as it were the appearance of fire, and there was brightness around him. ²⁸ As the appearance of the rainbow that is in the cloud in the day of rain, so was the appearance of the brightness all around. This was the appearance of the likeness of Yahweh's glory. When I saw it, I fell on my face, and I heard a voice of one that spoke.

## 2

¹ He said to me, "Son of man, stand on your feet, and I will speak with you." ² The Spirit entered into me when he spoke to me, and set me on my feet; and I heard him who spoke to me. ³ He said to me, "Son of man, I send you to the children of Israel, to a nation of rebels who have rebelled against me. They and their fathers have transgressed against me even to this very day. ⁴ The children are impudent and stiff-hearted. I am sending you to them, and you shall tell them, 'This is what the Lordᵉ Yahweh says.' ⁵ They, whether they will hear, or whether they will refuse—for they are a rebellious house—yet they will know that there has been a prophet among them. ⁶ You, son of man, don't be afraid of them, neither be afraid of their words, though briers and thorns are with you, and you dwell among scorpions. Don't be afraid of their words, nor be dismayed at their looks, though they are a rebellious house. ⁷ You shall speak my words to them, whether they will hear or whether they will refuse; for they are most rebellious. ⁸ But you, son of man, hear what I tell you. Don't be rebellious like that rebellious house. Open your mouth, and eat that which I give you." ⁹ When I looked, behold, a hand was stretched out to me; and behold, a scroll of a book was in it. ¹⁰ He spread it before me. It was written within and without; and lamentations, mourning, and woe were written in it.

## 3

¹ He said to me, "Son of man, eat what you find. Eat this scroll, and go, speak to the house of Israel." ² So I opened my mouth, and he caused me to eat the scroll. ³ He said to me, "Son of man, eat this scroll that I give you and fill your belly and your bowels with it." Then I ate it. It was as sweet as honey in my mouth. ⁴ He said to me, "Son of man, go to the house of Israel, and speak my words to them. ⁵ For you are not sent to a people of a strange speech and of a hard language, but to the house of Israel— ⁶ not to many peoples of a strange speech and of a hard language, whose words you can't understand. Surely, if I sent you to them, they would listen to you. ⁷ But the house of Israel will not listen to you, for they will not listen to me; for all the house of Israel are obstinateᶠ and hard-hearted. ⁸ Behold, I have made your face hard against their faces, and your forehead hard against their foreheads. ⁹ I have made your forehead as a diamond, harder than flint. Don't be afraid of them, neither be dismayed at their looks, though they are a rebellious house." ¹⁰ Moreover he said to me, "Son of man, receive in your heart and hear with your ears all my words that I speak to you. ¹¹ Go to them of the captivity, to the children of your people, and speak to them, and tell them, 'This is what the Lord Yahweh says,' whether they will hear, or whether they will refuse." ¹² Then the Spirit lifted me up, and I heard behind me the voice of a great rushing, saying, "Blessed be Yahweh's glory from his place." ¹³ I heard the noise of the wings of the living creatures as they touched one another, and the noise of the wheels beside them, even the noise of a great rushing. ¹⁴ So the Spirit lifted me up, and took me away; and I went in bitterness, in the heat of my spirit; and Yahweh's hand was strong on me. ¹⁵ Then I came to them of the captivity at Tel Aviv who lived by the river Chebar, and to where they lived; and I sat there overwhelmed among them seven days. ¹⁶ At the end of seven days, Yahweh's word came to me, saying, ¹⁷ "Son of man, I have made you a watchman to the house of Israel. Therefore hear the word from my mouth, and warn them from me. ¹⁸ When I tell the wicked, 'You will surely die;' and you give him no warning, nor speak to warn the wicked from his wicked way, to save his life, that wicked man will die in his iniquity; but I will require his blood at your hand. ¹⁹ Yet if you warn the wicked, and he doesn't turn from his wickedness, nor from his wicked way, he will die in his iniquity; but you have delivered your soul." ²⁰ "Again, when a righteous man turns from his righteousness and commits iniquity, and I lay a stumbling block before him, he will die. Because you have not given him warning,

ᵃ 1:1 The Hebrew word rendered "God" is "אֱלֹהִים" (Elohim).
ᵇ 1:3 "Yahweh" is God's proper Name, sometimes

rendered "LORD" (all caps) in other translations.
ᶜ 1:4 "Behold", from "הִנֵּה", means look at, take notice,

observe, see, or gaze at. It is often used as an interjection.
ᵈ 1:26 or, lapis lazuli
ᵉ 2:4 The word translated "Lord" is "Adonai."

ᶠ 3:7 Literally, have a hard forehead

he will die in his sin, and his righteous deeds which he has done will not be remembered; but I will require his blood at your hand. ²¹ Nevertheless if you warn the righteous man, that the righteous not sin, and he does not sin, he will surely live, because he took warning; and you have delivered your soul." ²² Yahweh's hand was there on me; and he said to me, "Arise, go out into the plain, and I will talk with you there." ²³ Then I arose, and went out into the plain, and behold, Yahweh's glory stood there, like the glory which I saw by the river Chebar. Then I fell on my face. ²⁴ Then the Spirit entered into me and set me on my feet. He spoke with me, and said to me, "Go, shut yourself inside your house. ²⁵ But you, son of man, behold, they will put ropes on you, and will bind you with them, and you will not go out among them. ²⁶ I will make your tongue stick to the roof of your mouth so that you will be mute and will not be able to correct them, for they are a rebellious house. ²⁷ But when I speak with you, I will open your mouth, and you shall tell them, 'This is what the Lord Yahweh says.' He who hears, let him hear; and he who refuses, let him refuse; for they are a rebellious house."

## 4

¹ "You also, son of man, take a tile, and lay it before yourself, and portray on it a city, even Jerusalem. ² Lay siege against it, build forts against it, and cast up a mound against it. Also set camps against it and plant battering rams against it all around. ³ Take for yourself an iron pan and set it for a wall of iron between you and the city. Then set your face toward it. It will be besieged, and you shall lay siege against it. This shall be a sign to the house of Israel. ⁴ "Moreover lie on your left side, and lay the iniquity of the house of Israel on it. According to the number of the days that you shall lie on it, you shall bear their iniquity. ⁵ For I have appointed the years of their iniquity to be to you a number of days, even three hundred ninety days. So you shall bear the iniquity of the house of Israel. ⁶ "Again, when you have accomplished these, you shall lie on your right side, and shall bear the iniquity of the house of Judah. I have appointed forty days, each day for a year, to you. ⁷ You shall set your face toward the siege of Jerusalem, with your arm uncovered; and you shall prophesy against it. ⁸ Behold, I put ropes on you, and you shall not turn yourself from one side to the other, until you have accomplished the days of your siege. ⁹ "Take for yourself also wheat, barley, beans, lentils, millet, and spelt, and put them in one vessel. Make bread of it. According to the number of the days that you will lie on your side, even three hundred ninety days, you shall eat of it. ¹⁰ Your food which you shall eat shall be by weight, twenty shekels[a] a day. From time to time you shall eat it. ¹¹ You shall drink water by measure, the sixth part of a hin.[b] From time to time you shall drink. ¹² You shall eat it as barley cakes, and you shall bake it in their sight with dung that comes out of man." ¹³ Yahweh said, "Even thus will the children of Israel eat their bread unclean, among the nations where I will drive them." ¹⁴ Then I said, "Ah Lord Yahweh! Behold, my soul has not been polluted; for from my youth up even until now I have not eaten of that which dies of itself, or is torn of animals. No abominable meat has come into my mouth!" ¹⁵ Then he said to me, "Behold, I have given you cow's dung for man's dung, and you shall prepare your bread on it." ¹⁶ Moreover he said to me, "Son of man, behold, I will break the staff of bread in Jerusalem. They will eat bread by weight, and with fearfulness. They will drink water by measure, and in dismay; ¹⁷ that they may lack bread and water, be dismayed one with another, and pine away in their iniquity.

## 5

¹ "You, son of man, take a sharp sword. You shall take it as a barber's razor to yourself, and shall cause it to pass over your head and over your beard. Then take balances to weigh and divide the hair. ² A third part you shall burn in the fire in the middle of the city, when the days of the siege are fulfilled. You shall take a third part, and strike with the sword around it. A third part you shall scatter to the wind, and I will draw out a sword after them. ³ You shall take a small number of these and bind them in the folds of your robe. ⁴ Of these again you shall take, and cast them into the middle of the fire, and burn them in the fire. From it a fire will come out into all the house of Israel. ⁵ "The Lord Yahweh says: 'This is Jerusalem. I have set her in the middle of the nations, and countries are around her. ⁶ She has rebelled against my ordinances in doing wickedness more than the nations, and against my statutes more than the countries that are around her; for they have rejected my ordinances, and as for my statutes, they have not walked in them.' ⁷ "Therefore the Lord Yahweh says: 'Because you are more turbulent than the nations that are around you, and have not walked in my statutes, neither have kept my ordinances, neither have followed the ordinances of the nations that are around you; ⁸ therefore the Lord Yahweh says: 'Behold, I, even I, am against you; and I will execute judgments among you in the sight of the nations. ⁹ I will do in you that which I have not done, and which I will not do anything like it any more, because of all your abominations. ¹⁰ Therefore the fathers will eat the sons within you, and the sons will eat their fathers. I will execute judgments on you; and I will scatter the whole remnant of you to all the winds. ¹¹ Therefore as I live,' says the Lord Yahweh, 'surely, because you have defiled my sanctuary with all your detestable things, and with all your abominations, therefore I will also diminish you. My eye won't spare, and I will have no pity. ¹² A third part of you will die with the pestilence, and they will be consumed with famine within you. A third part will fall by the sword around you. A third part I will scatter to all the winds, and will draw out a sword after them. ¹³ "Thus my anger will be accomplished, and I will cause my wrath toward them to rest, and I will be comforted. They will know that I, Yahweh, have spoken in my zeal, when I have accomplished my wrath on them. ¹⁴ "Moreover I will make you a desolation and a reproach among the nations that are around you, in the sight of all that pass by. ¹⁵ So it will be a reproach and a taunt, an instruction and an astonishment, to the nations that are around you, when I execute judgments on you in anger and in wrath, and in wrathful rebukes—I, Yahweh, have spoken it— ¹⁶ when I send on them the evil arrows of famine that are for destruction, which I will send to destroy you. I will increase the famine on you and will break your staff of bread. ¹⁷ I will send on you famine and evil animals, and they will bereave you. Pestilence and blood will pass through you. I will bring the sword on you. I, Yahweh, have spoken it.'"

## 6

¹ Yahweh's word came to me, saying, ² "Son of man, set your face toward the mountains of Israel, and prophesy to them, ³ and say, 'You mountains of Israel, hear the word of the Lord Yahweh! The Lord Yahweh says to the mountains and to the hills, to the watercourses and to the valleys: "Behold, I, even I, will bring a sword on you, and I will destroy your high places. ⁴ Your altars will become desolate, and your incense altars will be broken. I will cast down your slain men before your idols. ⁵ I will lay the dead bodies of the children of Israel before their idols. I will scatter your bones around your altars. ⁶ In all your dwelling places, the cities will be laid waste and the high places will be desolate, so that your altars may be laid waste and made desolate, and your idols may be broken and cease, and your incense altars may be cut down, and your works may be abolished. ⁷ The slain will fall among you, and you will know that I am Yahweh. ⁸ "Yet I will leave a remnant, in that you will have some that escape the sword among the nations, when you are scattered through the countries. ⁹ Those of you that escape will remember me among the nations where they are carried captive, how I have been broken with their lewd heart, which has departed from me, and with their eyes, which play the prostitute after their idols. Then they will loathe themselves in their own sight for the evils which they have committed in all their abominations. ¹⁰ They will know that I am Yahweh. I have not said in vain that I would do this evil to them."' ¹¹ "The Lord Yahweh says: 'Strike with your hand, and stamp with your foot, and say, "Alas!", because of all the evil abominations of the house of Israel; for they will fall by the sword, by the famine, and by the pestilence. ¹² He who is far off will die of the pestilence. He who is near will fall by the sword. He who remains and is besieged will die by the famine. Thus I will accomplish my wrath on them. ¹³ You will know that I am Yahweh when their slain men are among their idols around their altars, on every high hill, on all the tops of the mountains, under every green tree, and under every thick oak—the places where they offered pleasant aroma to all their idols. ¹⁴ I will stretch out my hand on them and make the land desolate and waste, from the wilderness toward Diblah, throughout all their habitations. Then they will know that I am Yahweh.'"

## 7

¹ Moreover Yahweh's word came to me, saying, ² "You, son of man, the Lord Yahweh says to the land of Israel, 'An end! The end has come on the four corners of the land. ³ Now the end is on you, and I will send my anger on you, and will judge you according to your ways. I will bring on you all your abominations. ⁴ My eye will not spare you, neither will I have pity; but I will bring your ways on you, and your abominations will be among you. Then you will know that I am Yahweh.' ⁵ "The Lord Yahweh says: 'A disaster! A unique disaster! Behold, it comes. ⁶ An end has come. The end has come! It awakes against you. Behold, it comes. ⁷ Your doom has come to you, inhabitant of the land! The time has come! The day is near, a day of tumult, and not of joyful shouting, on the mountains. ⁸ Now I will shortly pour out my wrath on you, and accomplish my anger against you, and will judge you according to your ways. I will bring on you all your abominations. ⁹ My eye won't spare, neither will I have pity. I will punish you

---

[a] *4:10* A shekel is about 10 grams or about 0.35 ounces.

[b] *4:11* A hin is about 6.5 liters or 1.7 gallons.

according to your ways. Your abominations will be among you. Then you will know that I, Yahweh, strike. ¹⁰ "Behold, the day! Behold, it comes! Your doom has gone out. The rod has blossomed. Pride has budded. ¹¹ Violence has risen up into a rod of wickedness. None of them will remain, nor of their multitude, nor of their wealth. There will be nothing of value among them. ¹² The time has come! The day draws near. Don't let the buyer rejoice, nor the seller mourn; for wrath is on all its multitude. ¹³ For the seller won't return to that which is sold, although they are still alive; for the vision concerns the whole multitude of it. None will return. None will strengthen himself in the iniquity of his life. ¹⁴ They have blown the trumpet, and have made all ready; but no one goes to the battle, for my wrath is on all its multitude. ¹⁵ "The sword is outside, and the pestilence and the famine within. He who is in the field will die by the sword. He who is in the city will be devoured by famine and pestilence. ¹⁶ But of those who escape, they will escape and will be on the mountains like doves of the valleys, all of them moaning, everyone in his iniquity. ¹⁷ All hands will be feeble, and all knees will be weak as water. ¹⁸ They will also clothe themselves with sackcloth, and horror will cover them. Shame will be on all faces, and baldness on all their heads. ¹⁹ They will cast their silver in the streets, and their gold will be as an unclean thing. Their silver and their gold won't be able to deliver them in the day of Yahweh's wrath. They won't satisfy their souls or fill their bellies; because it has been the stumbling block of their iniquity. ²⁰ As for the beauty of his ornament, he set it in majesty; but they made the images of their abominations and their detestable things therein. Therefore I have made it to them as an unclean thing. ²¹ I will give it into the hands of the strangers for a prey, and to the wicked of the earth for a plunder; and they will profane it. ²² I will also turn my face from them, and they will profane my secret place. Robbers will enter into it, and profane it. ²³ "Make chains, for the land is full of bloody crimes, and the city is full of violence. ²⁴ Therefore I will bring the worst of the nations, and they will possess their houses. I will also make the pride of the strong to cease. Their holy places will be profaned. ²⁵ Destruction comes! They will seek peace, and there will be none. ²⁶ Mischief will come on mischief, and rumor will be on rumor. They will seek a vision of the prophet; but the law will perish from the priest, and counsel from the elders. ²⁷ The king will mourn, and the prince will be clothed with desolation. The hands of the people of the land will be troubled. I will do to them after their way, and according to their own judgments I will judge them. Then they will know that I am Yahweh.'"

## 8

¹ In the sixth year, in the sixth month, in the fifth day of the month, as I sat in my house, and the elders of Judah sat before me, the Lord Yahweh's hand fell on me there. ² Then I saw, and behold, a likeness as the appearance of fire—from the appearance of his waist and downward, fire, and from his waist and upward, as the appearance of brightness, as it were glowing metal. ³ He stretched out the form of a hand, and took me by a lock of my head; and the Spirit lifted me up between earth and the sky, and brought me in the visions of God to Jerusalem, to the door of the gate of the inner court that looks toward the north, where there was the seat of the image of jealousy, which provokes to jealousy. ⁴ Behold, the glory of the God of Israel was there, according to the appearance that I saw in the plain. ⁵ Then he said to me, "Son of man, lift up your eyes now the way toward the north." So I lifted up my eyes the way toward the north, and saw, northward of the gate of the altar this image of jealousy in the entry. ⁶ He said to me, "Son of man, do you see what they do? Even the great abominations that the house of Israel commit here, that I should go far off from my sanctuary? But you will again see yet other great abominations." ⁷ He brought me to the door of the court; and when I looked, behold, a hole in the wall. ⁸ Then he said to me, "Son of man, dig now in the wall." When I had dug in the wall, I saw a door. ⁹ He said to me, "Go in, and see the wicked abominations that they do here." ¹⁰ So I went in and looked, and saw every form of creeping things, abominable animals, and all the idols of the house of Israel, portrayed around on the wall. ¹¹ Seventy men of the elders of the house of Israel stood before them. In the middle of them Jaazaniah the son of Shaphan stood, every man with his censer in his hand; and the smell of the cloud of incense went up. ¹² Then he said to me, "Son of man, have you seen what the elders of the house of Israel do in the dark, every man in his rooms of imagery? For they say, 'Yahweh doesn't see us. Yahweh has forsaken the land.'" ¹³ He said also to me, "You will again see more of the great abominations which they do." ¹⁴ Then he brought me to the door of the gate of Yahweh's house which was toward the north; and I saw the women sit there weeping for Tammuz. ¹⁵ Then he said to me, "Have you seen this, son of man? You will again see yet greater abominations than these." ¹⁶ He brought me into the inner court of Yahweh's house; and I saw at

the door of Yahweh's temple, between the porch and the altar, there were about twenty-five men with their backs toward Yahweh's temple and their faces toward the east. They were worshiping the sun toward the east. ¹⁷ Then he said to me, "Have you seen this, son of man? Is it a light thing to the house of Judah that they commit the abominations which they commit here? For they have filled the land with violence, and have turned again to provoke me to anger. Behold, they put the branch to their nose. ¹⁸ Therefore I will also deal in wrath. My eye won't spare, neither will I have pity. Though they cry in my ears with a loud voice, yet I will not hear them."

## 9

¹ Then he cried in my ears with a loud voice, saying, "Cause those who are in charge of the city to draw near, each man with his destroying weapon in his hand." ² Behold, six men came from the way of the upper gate, which lies toward the north, every man with his slaughter weapon in his hand. One man in the middle of them was clothed in linen, with a writer's inkhorn by his side. They went in, and stood beside the bronze altar. ³ The glory of the God of Israel went up from the cherub, whereupon it was, to the threshold of the house; and he called to the man clothed in linen, who had the writer's inkhorn by his side. ⁴ Yahweh said to him, "Go through the middle of the city, through the middle of Jerusalem, and set a mark on the foreheads of the men that sigh and that cry over all the abominations that are done within it." ⁵ To the others he said in my hearing, "Go through the city after him, and strike. Don't let your eye spare, neither have pity. ⁶ Kill utterly the old man, the young man, the virgin, little children and women; but don't come near any man on whom is the mark. Begin at my sanctuary." Then they began at the old men who were before the house. ⁷ He said to them, "Defile the house, and fill the courts with the slain. Go out!" They went out, and struck in the city. ⁸ While they were killing, and I was left, I fell on my face, and cried, and said, "Ah Lord Yahweh! Will you destroy all the residue of Israel in your pouring out of your wrath on Jerusalem?" ⁹ Then he said to me, "The iniquity of the house of Israel and Judah is exceedingly great, and the land is full of blood, and the city full of perversion; for they say, 'Yahweh has forsaken the land, and Yahweh doesn't see.' ¹⁰ As for me also, my eye won't spare, neither will I have pity, but I will bring their way on their head." ¹¹ Behold, the man clothed in linen, who had the inkhorn by his side, reported the matter, saying, "I have done as you have commanded me."

## 10

¹ Then I looked, and see, in the expanse that was over the head of the cherubim there appeared above them as it were a sapphire[a] stone, as the appearance of the likeness of a throne. ² He spoke to the man clothed in linen, and said, "Go in between the whirling wheels, even under the cherub, and fill both your hands with coals of fire from between the cherubim, and scatter them over the city." He went in as I watched. ³ Now the cherubim stood on the right side of the house when the man went in; and the cloud filled the inner court. ⁴ Yahweh's glory mounted up from the cherub, and stood over the threshold of the house; and the house was filled with the cloud, and the court was full of the brightness of Yahweh's glory. ⁵ The sound of the wings of the cherubim was heard even to the outer court, as the voice of God Almighty when he speaks. ⁶ It came to pass, when he commanded the man clothed in linen, saying, "Take fire from between the whirling wheels, from between the cherubim," that he went in and stood beside a wheel. ⁷ The cherub stretched out his hand from between the cherubim to the fire that was between the cherubim, and took some of it, and put it into the hands of him who was clothed in linen, who took it and went out. ⁸ The form of a man's hand appeared here in the cherubim under their wings. ⁹ I looked, and behold, there were four wheels beside the cherubim, one wheel beside one cherub, and another wheel beside another cherub. The appearance of the wheels was like a beryl stone. ¹⁰ As for their appearance, the four of them had one likeness, like a wheel within a wheel. ¹¹ When they went, they went in their four directions. They didn't turn as they went, but to the place where the head looked they followed it. They didn't turn as they went. ¹² Their whole body, including their backs, their hands, their wings, and the wheels, were full of eyes all around, even the wheels that the four of them had. ¹³ As for the wheels, they were called in my hearing, "the whirling wheels". ¹⁴ Every one of them had four faces. The first face was the face of the cherub. The second face was the face of a man. The third face was the face of a lion. The fourth was the face of an eagle. ¹⁵ The cherubim mounted up. This is the living creature that I saw by the river Chebar. ¹⁶ When the cherubim went, the wheels went beside them; and when the cherubim lifted up their wings to mount up from the earth, the wheels also didn't turn from beside them. ¹⁷ When they stood, these stood. When they mounted up, these mounted up with them; for the spirit of the living creature was in them. ¹⁸ Yahweh's glory went out

from over the threshold of the house and stood over the cherubim. ¹⁹ The cherubim lifted up their wings and mounted up from the earth in my sight when they went out, with the wheels beside them. Then they stood at the door of the east gate of Yahweh's house; and the glory of the God of Israel was over them above. ²⁰ This is the living creature that I saw under the God of Israel by the river Chebar; and I knew that they were cherubim. ²¹ Every one had four faces, and every one four wings. The likeness of the hands of a man was under their wings. ²² As for the likeness of their faces, they were the faces which I saw by the river Chebar, their appearances and themselves. They each went straight forward.

# 11

¹ Moreover the Spirit lifted me up and brought me to the east gate of Yahweh's house, which looks eastward. Behold, twenty-five men were at the door of the gate; and I saw among them Jaazaniah the son of Azzur, and Pelatiah the son of Benaiah, princes of the people. ² He said to me, "Son of man, these are the men who devise iniquity, and who give wicked counsel in this city; ³ who say, 'The time is not near to build houses. This is the cauldron, and we are the meat.' ⁴ Therefore prophesy against them. Prophesy, son of man." ⁵ Yahweh's Spirit fell on me, and he said to me, "Speak, 'Yahweh says: "Thus you have said, house of Israel; for I know the things that come into your mind. ⁶ You have multiplied your slain in this city, and you have filled its streets with the slain." ⁷ "Therefore the Lord Yahweh says: "Your slain whom you have laid in the middle of it, they are the meat, and this is the cauldron; but you will be brought out of the middle of it. ⁸ You have feared the sword; and I will bring the sword on you," says the Lord Yahweh. ⁹ "I will bring you out of the middle of it, and deliver you into the hands of strangers, and will execute judgments among you. ¹⁰ You will fall by the sword. I will judge you in the border of Israel. Then you will know that I am Yahweh. ¹¹ This will not be your cauldron, neither will you be the meat in the middle of it. I will judge you in the border of Israel. ¹² You will know that I am Yahweh, for you have not walked in my statutes. You have not executed my ordinances, but have done after the ordinances of the nations that are around you."'" ¹³ When I prophesied, Pelatiah the son of Benaiah died. Then I fell down on my face, and cried with a loud voice, and said, "Ah Lord Yahweh! Will you make a full end of the remnant of Israel?" ¹⁴ Yahweh's word came to me, saying, ¹⁵ "Son of man, your brothers, even your brothers, the men of your relatives, and all the house of Israel, all of them, are the ones to whom the inhabitants of Jerusalem have said, 'Go far away from Yahweh. This land has been given to us for a possession.' ¹⁶ "Therefore say, 'The Lord Yahweh says: "Whereas I have removed them far off among the nations, and whereas I have scattered them among the countries, yet I will be to them a sanctuary for a little while in the countries where they have come."' ¹⁷ "Therefore say, 'The Lord Yahweh says: "I will gather you from the peoples, and assemble you out of the countries where you have been scattered, and I will give you the land of Israel." ¹⁸ "'They will come there, and they will take away all its detestable things and all its abominations from there. ¹⁹ I will give them one heart, and I will put a new spirit within them. I will take the stony heart out of their flesh, and will give them a heart of flesh, ²⁰ that they may walk in my statutes, and keep my ordinances, and do them. They will be my people, and I will be their God. ²¹ But as for them whose heart walks after the heart of their detestable things and their abominations, I will bring their way on their own heads,' says the Lord Yahweh." ²² Then the cherubim lifted up their wings, and the wheels were beside them. The glory of the God of Israel was over them above. ²³ Yahweh's glory went up from the middle of the city, and stood on the mountain which is on the east side of the city. ²⁴ The Spirit lifted me up, and brought me in the vision by the Spirit of God into Chaldea, to the captives. So the vision that I had seen went up from me. ²⁵ Then I spoke to the captives all the things that Yahweh had shown me.

# 12

¹ Yahweh's word also came to me, saying, ² "Son of man, you dwell in the middle of the rebellious house, who have eyes to see, and don't see, who have ears to hear, and don't hear; for they are a rebellious house. ³ "Therefore, you son of man, prepare your baggage for moving, and move by day in their sight. You shall move from your place to another place in their sight. It may be they will consider, though they are a rebellious house. ⁴ You shall bring out your baggage by day in their sight, as baggage for moving. You shall go out yourself at evening in their sight, as when men go out into exile. ⁵ Dig through the wall in their sight, and carry your baggage out that way. ⁶ In their sight you shall bear it on your shoulder, and carry it out in the dark. You shall cover your face, so that you don't see the land, for I have set you for a sign to the house of Israel." ⁷ I did so as I was commanded. I brought out my baggage by day, as baggage for moving, and in the evening I dug through the wall with my hand. I brought it out in the dark, and bore it on my shoulder in their sight. ⁸ In the morning, Yahweh's word

came to me, saying, ⁹ "Son of man, hasn't the house of Israel, the rebellious house, said to you, 'What are you doing?' ¹⁰ "Say to them, 'The Lord Yahweh says: "This burden concerns the prince in Jerusalem, and all the house of Israel among whom they are."' ¹¹ "Say, 'I am your sign. As I have done, so will it be done to them. They will go into exile, into captivity. ¹² "'The prince who is among them will bear his baggage on his shoulder in the dark, and will go out. They will dig through the wall to carry things out that way. He will cover his face, because he will not see the land with his eyes. ¹³ I will also spread my net on him, and he will be taken in my snare. I will bring him to Babylon to the land of the Chaldeans; yet he will not see it, though he will die there. ¹⁴ I will scatter toward every wind all who are around him to help him, and all his bands. I will draw out the sword after them. ¹⁵ "'They will know that I am Yahweh when I disperse them among the nations and scatter them through the countries. ¹⁶ But I will leave a few men of them from the sword, from the famine, and from the pestilence, that they may declare all their abominations among the nations where they come. Then they will know that I am Yahweh.'" ¹⁷ Moreover Yahweh's word came to me, saying, ¹⁸ "Son of man, eat your bread with quaking, and drink your water with trembling and with fearfulness. ¹⁹ Tell the people of the land, 'The Lord Yahweh says concerning the inhabitants of Jerusalem and the land of Israel: "They will eat their bread with fearfulness and drink their water in dismay, that her land may be desolate, and all that is therein, because of the violence of all those who dwell therein. ²⁰ The cities that are inhabited will be laid waste, and the land will be a desolation. Then you will know that I am Yahweh."'" ²¹ Yahweh's word came to me, saying, ²² "Son of man, what is this proverb that you have in the land of Israel, saying, 'The days are prolonged, and every vision fails'? ²³ Tell them therefore, 'The Lord Yahweh says: "I will make this proverb to cease, and they will no more use it as a proverb in Israel;"' but tell them, "'The days are at hand, and the fulfillment of every vision. ²⁴ For there will be no more any false vision nor flattering divination within the house of Israel. ²⁵ For I am Yahweh. I will speak, and the word that I speak will be performed. It will be no more deferred; for in your days, rebellious house, I will speak the word and will perform it," says the Lord Yahweh.'" ²⁶ Again Yahweh's word came to me, saying, ²⁷ "Son of man, behold, they of the house of Israel say, 'The vision that he sees is for many days to come, and he prophesies of times that are far off.' ²⁸ "Therefore tell them, 'The Lord Yahweh says: "None of my words will be deferred any more, but the word which I speak will be performed," says the Lord Yahweh.'"

# 13

¹ Yahweh's word came to me, saying, ² "Son of man, prophesy against the prophets of Israel who prophesy, and say to those who prophesy out of their own heart, 'Hear Yahweh's word: ³ The Lord Yahweh says, "Woe to the foolish prophets, who follow their own spirit, and have seen nothing! ⁴ Israel, your prophets have been like foxes in the waste places. ⁵ You have not gone up into the gaps or built up the wall for the house of Israel, to stand in the battle in Yahweh's day. ⁶ They have seen falsehood and lying divination, who say, 'Yahweh says;' but Yahweh has not sent them. They have made men to hope that the word would be confirmed. ⁷ Haven't you seen a false vision, and haven't you spoken a lying divination, in that you say, 'Yahweh says;' but I have not spoken?" ⁸ "'Therefore the Lord Yahweh says: "Because you have spoken falsehood and seen lies, therefore, behold, I am against you," says the Lord Yahweh. ⁹ "My hand will be against the prophets who see false visions and who utter lying divinations. They will not be in the council of my people, neither will they be written in the writing of the house of Israel, neither will they enter into the land of Israel. Then you will know that I am the Lord Yahweh." ¹⁰ "'Because, even because they have seduced my people, saying, "Peace;" and there is no peace. When one builds up a wall, behold, they plaster it with whitewash. ¹¹ Tell those who plaster it with whitewash that it will fall. There will be an overflowing shower; and you, great hailstones, will fall. A stormy wind will tear it. ¹² Behold, when the wall has fallen, won't it be said to you, "Where is the plaster with which you have plastered it?" ¹³ "'Therefore the Lord Yahweh says: "I will even tear it with a stormy wind in my wrath. There will be an overflowing shower in my anger, and great hailstones in wrath to consume it. ¹⁴ So I will break down the wall that you have plastered with whitewash, and bring it down to the ground, so that its foundation will be uncovered. It will fall, and you will be consumed in the middle of it. Then you will know that I am Yahweh. ¹⁵ Thus I will accomplish my wrath on the wall, and on those who have plastered it with whitewash. I will tell you, 'The wall is no more, nor those who plastered it— ¹⁶ to wit, the prophets of Israel who prophesy concerning Jerusalem, and who see visions of peace for her, and there is no peace,'" says the Lord Yahweh.'" ¹⁷ You, son of man, set your face against the daughters of your people, who prophesy out of their own heart; and prophesy against them, ¹⁸ and say, "The Lord Yahweh says: 'Woe to the women who sew magic bands on all elbows and make

veils for the head of persons of every stature to hunt souls! Will you hunt the souls of my people and save souls alive for yourselves? ¹⁹ You have profaned me among my people for handfuls of barley and for pieces of bread, to kill the souls who should not die and to save the souls alive who should not live, by your lying to my people who listen to lies.' ²⁰"Therefore the Lord Yahweh says: 'Behold, I am against your magic bands, with which you hunt the souls to make them fly, and I will tear them from your arms. I will let the souls fly free, even the souls whom you ensnare like birds. ²¹ I will also tear your veils and deliver my people out of your hand; and they will no longer be in your hand to be ensnared. Then you will know that I am Yahweh. ²² Because with lies you have grieved the heart of the righteous, whom I have not made sad; and strengthened the hands of the wicked, that he should not return from his wicked way, and be saved alive. ²³ Therefore you shall no more see false visions nor practice divination. I will deliver my people out of your hand. Then you will know that I am Yahweh.'"

## 14

¹ Then some of the elders of Israel came to me and sat before me. ² Yahweh's word came to me, saying, ³"Son of man, these men have taken their idols into their heart, and put the stumbling block of their iniquity before their face. Should I be inquired of at all by them? ⁴ Therefore speak to them and tell them, 'The Lord Yahweh says: "Every man of the house of Israel who takes his idols into his heart and puts the stumbling block of his iniquity before his face then comes to the prophet, I Yahweh will answer him there according to the multitude of his idols, ⁵ that I may take the house of Israel in their own heart, because they are all estranged from me through their idols."' ⁶"Therefore tell the house of Israel, 'The Lord Yahweh says: "Return, and turn yourselves from your idols! Turn away your faces from all your abominations. ⁷"""For everyone of the house of Israel, or of the strangers who live in Israel, who separates himself from me and takes his idols into his heart, and puts the stumbling block of his iniquity before his face, and comes to the prophet to inquire for himself of me, I Yahweh will answer him by myself. ⁸ I will set my face against that man and will make him an astonishment, for a sign and a proverb, and I will cut him off from among my people. Then you will know that I am Yahweh. ⁹"""If the prophet is deceived and speaks a word, I, Yahweh, have deceived that prophet, and I will stretch out my hand on him, and will destroy him from among my people Israel. ¹⁰ They will bear their iniquity. The iniquity of the prophet will be even as the iniquity of him who seeks him, ¹¹ that the house of Israel may no more go astray from me, neither defile themselves any more with all their transgressions; but that they may be my people, and I may be their God," says the Lord Yahweh.'" ¹² Yahweh's word came to me, saying, ¹³"Son of man, when a land sins against me by committing a trespass, and I stretch out my hand on it, and break the staff of its bread and send famine on it, and cut off from it man and animal— ¹⁴ though these three men, Noah, Daniel, and Job, were in it, they would deliver only their own souls by their righteousness," says the Lord Yahweh. ¹⁵"If I cause evil animals to pass through the land, and they ravage it and it is made desolate, so that no man may pass through because of the animals— ¹⁶ though these three men were in it, as I live," says the Lord Yahweh, "they would deliver neither sons nor daughters. They only would be delivered, but the land would be desolate. ¹⁷Or if I bring a sword on that land, and say, 'Sword, go through the land, so that I cut off from it man and animal'— ¹⁸ though these three men were in it, as I live," says the Lord Yahweh, "they would deliver neither sons nor daughters, but they only would be delivered themselves. ¹⁹Or if I send a pestilence into that land, and pour out my wrath on it in blood, to cut off from it man and animal— ²⁰ though Noah, Daniel, and Job, were in it, as I live," says the Lord Yahweh, "they would deliver neither son nor daughter; they would deliver only their own souls by their righteousness." ²¹ For the Lord Yahweh says: "How much more when I send my four severe judgments on Jerusalem—the sword, the famine, the evil animals, and the pestilence—to cut off from it man and animal! ²² Yet, behold, there will be left a remnant in it that will be carried out, both sons and daughters. Behold, they will come out to you, and you will see their way and their doings. Then you will be comforted concerning the evil that I have brought on Jerusalem, even concerning all that I have brought on it. ²³ They will comfort you, when you see their way and their doings; then you will know that I have not done all that I have done in it without cause," says the Lord Yahweh.

## 15

¹ Yahweh's word came to me, saying, ²"Son of man, what is the vine tree more than any tree, the vine branch which is among the trees of the forest? ³ Will wood be taken of it to make anything? Will men take a pin of it to hang any vessel on it? ⁴ Behold, it is cast into the fire for fuel; the fire has devoured both its ends, and the middle of it is burned. Is it profitable for any work? ⁵ Behold, when it was whole, it was suitable for no work. How much less, when the fire has devoured it, and

it has been burned, will it yet be suitable for any work?" ⁶ Therefore the Lord Yahweh says: "As the vine wood among the trees of the forest, which I have given to the fire for fuel, so I will give the inhabitants of Jerusalem. ⁷ I will set my face against them. They will go out from the fire, but the fire will still devour them. Then you will know that I am Yahweh, when I set my face against them. ⁸ I will make the land desolate, because they have acted unfaithfully," says the Lord Yahweh.

## 16

¹ Again Yahweh's word came to me, saying, ²"Son of man, cause Jerusalem to know her abominations; ³ and say, 'The Lord Yahweh says to Jerusalem: "Your origin and your birth is of the land of the Canaanite. An Amorite was your father, and your mother was a Hittite. ⁴ As for your birth, in the day you were born your navel was not cut. You weren't washed in water to cleanse you. You weren't salted at all, nor wrapped in blankets at all. ⁵ No eye pitied you, to do any of these things to you, to have compassion on you; but you were cast out in the open field, because you were abhorred in the day that you were born. ⁶"""When I passed by you, and saw you wallowing in your blood, I said to you, 'Though you are in your blood, live!' Yes, I said to you, 'Though you are in your blood, live!' ⁷ I caused you to multiply as that which grows in the field, and you increased and grew great, and you attained to excellent beauty. Your breasts were formed, and your hair grew; yet you were naked and bare. ⁸"""Now when I passed by you, and looked at you, behold, your time was the time of love; and I spread my garment over you and covered your nakedness. Yes, I pledged myself to you and entered into a covenant with you," says the Lord Yahweh, "and you became mine. ⁹"""Then I washed you with water. Yes, I thoroughly washed away your blood from you, and I anointed you with oil. ¹⁰ I clothed you also with embroidered work and put leather sandals on you. I dressed you with fine linen and covered you with silk. ¹¹ I decked you with ornaments, put bracelets on your hands, and put a chain on your neck. ¹² I put a ring on your nose, earrings in your ears, and a beautiful crown on your head. ¹³ Thus you were decked with gold and silver. Your clothing was of fine linen, silk, and embroidered work. You ate fine flour, honey, and oil. You were exceedingly beautiful, and you prospered to royal estate. ¹⁴ Your renown went out among the nations for your beauty; for it was perfect, through my majesty which I had put on you," says the Lord Yahweh. ¹⁵"""But you trusted in your beauty, and played the prostitute because of your renown, and poured out your prostitution on everyone who passed by. It was his. ¹⁶ You took some of your garments, and made for yourselves high places decked with various colors, and played the prostitute on them. This shouldn't happen, neither shall it be. ¹⁷ You also took your beautiful jewels of my gold and of my silver, which I had given you, and made for yourself images of men, and played the prostitute with them. ¹⁸ You took your embroidered garments, covered them, and set my oil and my incense before them. ¹⁹ My bread also which I gave you, fine flour, oil, and honey, with which I fed you, you even set it before them for a pleasant aroma; and so it was," says the Lord Yahweh. ²⁰"""Moreover you have taken your sons and your daughters, whom you have borne to me, and you have sacrificed these to them to be devoured. Was your prostitution a small matter, ²¹ that you have slain my children and delivered them up, in causing them to pass through the fire to them? ²² In all your abominations and your prostitution you have not remembered the days of your youth, when you were naked and bare, and were wallowing in your blood. ²³"""It has happened after all your wickedness—woe, woe to you!" says the Lord Yahweh— ²⁴"that you have built for yourselves a vaulted place, and have made yourselves a lofty place in every street. ²⁵ You have built your lofty place at the head of every way, and have made your beauty an abomination, and have opened your feet to everyone who passed by, and multiplied your prostitution. ²⁶ You have also committed sexual immorality with the Egyptians, your neighbors, great of flesh; and have multiplied your prostitution, to provoke me to anger. ²⁷ See therefore, I have stretched out my hand over you, and have diminished your portion, and delivered you to the will of those who hate you, the daughters of the Philistines, who are ashamed of your lewd way. ²⁸ You have played the prostitute also with the Assyrians, because you were insatiable; yes, you have played the prostitute with them, and yet you weren't satisfied. ²⁹ You have moreover multiplied your prostitution to the land of merchants, to Chaldea; and yet you weren't satisfied with this. ³⁰"""How weak is your heart," says the Lord Yahweh, "since you do all these things, the work of an impudent prostitute; ³¹ in that you build your vaulted place at the head of every way, and make your lofty place in every street, and have not been as a prostitute, in that you scorn pay. ³²"""Adulterous wife, who takes strangers instead of her husband! ³³ People give gifts to all prostitutes; but you give your gifts to all your lovers, and bribe them, that they may come to you on every side for your prostitution. ³⁴ You are different from other women in your prostitution, in that no one follows you to play the prostitute; and

whereas you give hire, and no hire is given to you, therefore you are different." ³⁵"Therefore, prostitute, hear Yahweh's word: ³⁶'The Lord Yahweh says, "Because your filthiness was poured out, and your nakedness uncovered through your prostitution with your lovers; and because of all the idols of your abominations, and for the blood of your children, that you gave to them; ³⁷ therefore see, I will gather all your lovers, with whom you have taken pleasure, and all those whom you have loved, with all those whom you have hated. I will even gather them against you on every side, and will uncover your nakedness to them, that they may see all your nakedness. ³⁸ I will judge you as women who break wedlock and shed blood are judged; and I will bring on you the blood of wrath and jealousy. ³⁹ I will also give you into their hand, and they will throw down your vaulted place, and break down your lofty places. They will strip you of your clothes and take your beautiful jewels. They will leave you naked and bare. ⁴⁰ They will also bring up a company against you, and they will stone you with stones, and thrust you through with their swords. ⁴¹ They will burn your houses with fire, and execute judgments on you in the sight of many women. I will cause you to cease from playing the prostitute, and you will also give no hire any more. ⁴² So I will cause my wrath toward you to rest, and my jealousy will depart from you. I will be quiet, and will not be angry any more. ⁴³"'"Because you have not remembered the days of your youth, but have raged against me in all these things; therefore, behold, I also will bring your way on your head," says the Lord Yahweh: "and you shall not commit this lewdness with all your abominations. ⁴⁴"'"Behold, everyone who uses proverbs will use this proverb against you, saying, 'As is the mother, so is her daughter.' ⁴⁵ You are the daughter of your mother, who loathes her husband and her children; and you are the sister of your sisters, who loathed their husbands and their children. Your mother was a Hittite, and your father an Amorite. ⁴⁶ Your elder sister is Samaria, who dwells at your left hand, she and her daughters; and your younger sister, who dwells at your right hand, is Sodom with her daughters. ⁴⁷ Yet you have not walked in their ways, nor done their abominations; but soon you were more corrupt than they in all your ways. ⁴⁸ As I live," says the Lord Yahweh, "Sodom your sister has not done, she nor her daughters, as you have done, you and your daughters. ⁴⁹"'"Behold, this was the iniquity of your sister Sodom: pride, fullness of bread, and prosperous ease was in her and in her daughters. She also didn't strengthen the hand of the poor and needy. ⁵⁰ They were arrogant and committed abomination before me. Therefore I took them away when I saw it. ⁵¹ Samaria hasn't committed half of your sins; but you have multiplied your abominations more than they, and have justified your sisters by all your abominations which you have done. ⁵² You also bear your own shame yourself, in that you have given judgment for your sisters; through your sins that you have committed more abominable than they, they are more righteous than you. Yes, be also confounded, and bear your shame, in that you have justified your sisters. ⁵³"'"I will reverse their captivity, the captivity of Sodom and her daughters, and the captivity of Samaria and her daughters, and the captivity of your captives among them; ⁵⁴ that you may bear your own shame, and may be ashamed because of all that you have done, in that you are a comfort to them. ⁵⁵ Your sisters, Sodom and her daughters, will return to their former estate; and Samaria and her daughters will return to their former estate; and you and your daughters will return to your former estate. ⁵⁶ For your sister Sodom was not mentioned by your mouth in the day of your pride, ⁵⁷ before your wickedness was uncovered, as at the time of the reproach of the daughters of Syria, and of all who are around her, the daughters of the Philistines, who despise you all around. ⁵⁸ You have borne your lewdness and your abominations," says Yahweh. ⁵⁹"'For the Lord Yahweh says: "I will also deal with you as you have done, who have despised the oath in breaking the covenant. ⁶⁰ Nevertheless I will remember my covenant with you in the days of your youth, and I will establish an everlasting covenant with you. ⁶¹ Then you will remember your ways and be ashamed when you receive your sisters, your elder sisters and your younger; and I will give them to you for daughters, but not by your covenant. ⁶² I will establish my covenant with you. Then you will know that I am Yahweh; ⁶³ that you may remember, and be confounded, and never open your mouth any more because of your shame, when I have forgiven you all that you have done," says the Lord Yahweh.'"

## 17

¹ Yahweh's word came to me, saying, ²"Son of man, tell a riddle, and speak a parable to the house of Israel; ³ and say, 'The Lord Yahweh says: "A great eagle with great wings and long feathers, full of feathers which had various colors, came to Lebanon and took the top of the cedar. ⁴ He cropped off the topmost of its young twigs, and carried it to a land of traffic. He planted it in a city of merchants. ⁵"'"He also took

some of the seed of the land and planted it in fruitful soil. He placed it beside many waters. He set it as a willow tree. ⁶ It grew and became a spreading vine of low stature, whose branches turned toward him, and its roots were under him. So it became a vine, produced branches, and shot out sprigs. ⁷"'"There was also another great eagle with great wings and many feathers. Behold, this vine bent its roots toward him, and shot out its branches toward him, from the ground where it was planted, that he might water it. ⁸ It was planted in a good soil by many waters, that it might produce branches and that it might bear fruit, that it might be a good vine."' ⁹"Say, 'The Lord Yahweh says: "Will it prosper? Won't he pull up its roots and cut off its fruit, that it may wither, that all its fresh springing leaves may wither? It can't be raised from its roots by a strong arm or many people. ¹⁰ Yes, behold, being planted, will it prosper? Won't it utterly wither when the east wind touches it? It will wither in the ground where it grew."'" ¹¹ Moreover Yahweh's word came to me, saying, ¹²"Say now to the rebellious house, 'Don't you know what these things mean?' Tell them, 'Behold, the king of Babylon came to Jerusalem, and took its king, and its princes, and brought them to him to Babylon. ¹³ He took one of the royal offspring,ᵃ and made a covenant with him. He also brought him under an oath, and took away the mighty of the land, ¹⁴ that the kingdom might be brought low, that it might not lift itself up, but that by keeping his covenant it might stand. ¹⁵ But he rebelled against him in sending his ambassadors into Egypt, that they might give him horses and many people. Will he prosper? Will he who does such things escape? Will he break the covenant, and still escape? ¹⁶"'As I live,' says the Lord Yahweh, 'surely in the place where the king dwells who made him king, whose oath he despised, and whose covenant he broke, even with him in the middle of Babylon he will die. ¹⁷ Pharaoh with his mighty army and great company won't help him in the war, when they cast up mounds and build forts to cut off many persons. ¹⁸ For he has despised the oath by breaking the covenant; and behold, he had given his hand, and yet has done all these things. He won't escape.' ¹⁹"Therefore the Lord Yahweh says: 'As I live, I will surely bring on his own head my oath that he has despised and my covenant that he has broken. ²⁰ I will spread my net on him, and he will be taken in my snare. I will bring him to Babylon, and will enter into judgment with him there for his trespass that he has trespassed against me. ²¹ All his fugitives in all his bands will fall by the sword, and those who remain will be scattered toward every wind. Then you will know that I, Yahweh, have spoken it.' ²²"The Lord Yahweh says: 'I will also take some of the lofty top of the cedar, and will plant it. I will crop off from the topmost of its young twigs a tender one, and I will plant it on a high and lofty mountain. ²³ I will plant it in the mountain of the height of Israel; and it will produce boughs, and bear fruit, and be a good cedar. Birds of every kind will dwell in the shade of its branches. ²⁴ All the trees of the field will know that I, Yahweh, have brought down the high tree, have exalted the low tree, have dried up the green tree, and have made the dry tree flourish. "'I, Yahweh, have spoken and have done it."

## 18

¹ Yahweh's word came to me again, saying, ²"What do you mean, that you use this proverb concerning the land of Israel, saying, 'The fathers have eaten sour grapes, and the children's teeth are set on edge'? ³"As I live," says the Lord Yahweh, "you shall not use this proverb any more in Israel. ⁴ Behold, all souls are mine; as the soul of the father, so also the soul of the son is mine. The soul who sins, he shall die. ⁵"But if a man is just, and does that which is lawful and right, ⁶ and has not eaten on the mountains, hasn't lifted up his eyes to the idols of the house of Israel, hasn't defiled his neighbor's wife, hasn't come near a woman in her impurity, ⁷ and has not wronged any, but has restored to the debtor his pledge, has taken nothing by robbery, has given his bread to the hungry, and has covered the naked with a garment; ⁸ he who hasn't lent to them with interest, hasn't taken any increase from them, who has withdrawn his hand from iniquity, has executed true justice between man and man, ⁹ has walked in my statutes, and has kept my ordinances, to deal truly; he is just, he shall surely live," says the Lord Yahweh. ¹⁰"If he fathers a son who is a robber who sheds blood, and who does any one of these things, ¹¹ or who does not do any of those things but has eaten at the mountain shrines and defiled his neighbor's wife, ¹² has wronged the poor and needy, has taken by robbery, has not restored the pledge, and has lifted up his eyes to the idols, has committed abomination, ¹³ has lent with interest, and has taken increase from the poor, shall he then live? He shall not live. He has done all these abominations. He shall surely die. His blood will be on him. ¹⁴"Now, behold, if he fathers a son who sees all his father's sins which he has done, and fears, and doesn't do likewise, ¹⁵ who hasn't eaten on the mountains, hasn't lifted up his eyes to the idols of the house of Israel, hasn't defiled his neighbor's wife, ¹⁶ hasn't wronged any, hasn't taken

anything to pledge, hasn't taken by robbery, but has given his bread to the hungry, and has covered the naked with a garment; ¹⁷ who has withdrawn his hand from the poor, who hasn't received interest or increase, has executed my ordinances, has walked in my statutes; he shall not die for the iniquity of his father. He shall surely live. ¹⁸ As for his father, because he cruelly oppressed, robbed his brother, and did that which is not good among his people, behold, he will die in his iniquity. ¹⁹"Yet you say, 'Why doesn't the son bear the iniquity of the father?' When the son has done that which is lawful and right, and has kept all my statutes, and has done them, he will surely live. ²⁰ The soul who sins, he shall die. The son shall not bear the iniquity of the father, neither shall the father bear the iniquity of the son. The righteousness of the righteous shall be on him, and the wickedness of the wicked shall be on him. ²¹"But if the wicked turns from all his sins that he has committed, and keeps all my statutes, and does that which is lawful and right, he shall surely live. He shall not die. ²² None of his transgressions that he has committed will be remembered against him. In his righteousness that he has done, he shall live. ²³ Have I any pleasure in the death of the wicked?" says the Lord Yahweh, "and not rather that he should return from his way, and live? ²⁴"But when the righteous turns away from his righteousness, and commits iniquity, and does according to all the abominations that the wicked man does, should he live? None of his righteous deeds that he has done will be remembered. In his trespass that he has trespassed, and in his sin that he has sinned, in them he shall die. ²⁵"Yet you say, 'The way of the Lord is not equal.' Hear now, house of Israel: Is my way not equal? Aren't your ways unequal? ²⁶ When the righteous man turns away from his righteousness, and commits iniquity, and dies in it, then he dies in his iniquity that he has done. ²⁷ Again, when the wicked man turns away from his wickedness that he has committed, and does that which is lawful and right, he will save his soul alive. ²⁸ Because he considers, and turns away from all his transgressions that he has committed, he shall surely live. He shall not die. ²⁹ Yet the house of Israel says, 'The way of the Lord is not fair.' House of Israel, aren't my ways fair? Aren't your ways unfair? ³⁰"Therefore I will judge you, house of Israel, everyone according to his ways," says the Lord Yahweh. "Return, and turn yourselves from all your transgressions, so iniquity will not be your ruin. ³¹ Cast away from you all your transgressions in which you have transgressed; and make yourself a new heart and a new spirit. For why will you die, house of Israel? ³² For I have no pleasure in the death of him who dies," says the Lord Yahweh. "Therefore turn yourselves, and live!

## 19

¹"Moreover, take up a lamentation for the princes of Israel, ² and say, 'What was your mother? A lioness. She couched among lions, in the middle of the young lions she nourished her cubs. ³ She brought up one of her cubs. He became a young lion. He learned to catch the prey. He devoured men. ⁴ The nations also heard of him. He was taken in their pit; and they brought him with hooks to the land of Egypt. ⁵"Now when she saw that she had waited, and her hope was lost, then she took another of her cubs, and made him a young lion. ⁶ He went up and down among the lions. He became a young lion. He learned to catch the prey. He devoured men. ⁷ He knew their palaces, and laid waste their cities. The land was desolate with its fullness, because of the noise of his roaring. ⁸ Then the nations attacked him on every side from the provinces. They spread their net over him. He was taken in their pit. ⁹ They put him in a cage with hooks, and brought him to the king of Babylon. They brought him into strongholds, so that his voice should no more be heard on the mountains of Israel. ¹⁰"Your mother was like a vine in your blood, planted by the waters. It was fruitful and full of branches by reason of many waters. ¹¹ It had strong branches for the scepters of those who ruled. Their stature was exalted among the thick boughs. They were seen in their height with the multitude of their branches. ¹² But it was plucked up in fury. It was cast down to the ground, and the east wind dried up its fruit. Its strong branches were broken off and withered. The fire consumed them. ¹³ Now it is planted in the wilderness, in a dry and thirsty land. ¹⁴ Fire has gone out of its branches. It has devoured its fruit, so that there is in it no strong branch to be a scepter to rule.' This is a lamentation, and shall be for a lamentation."

## 20

¹ In the seventh year, in the fifth month, the tenth day of the month, some of the elders of Israel came to inquire of Yahweh, and sat before me. ² Yahweh's word came to me, saying, ³"Son of man, speak to the elders of Israel, and tell them, 'The Lord Yahweh says: "Is it to inquire of me that you have come? As I live," says the Lord Yahweh, "I will not be inquired of by you."' ⁴"Will you judge them, son of man? Will

you judge them? Cause them to know the abominations of their fathers. ⁵ Tell them, 'The Lord Yahweh says: "In the day when I chose Israel, and swore to the offspring of the house of Jacob, and made myself known to them in the land of Egypt, when I swore to them, saying, 'I am Yahweh your God;' ⁶ in that day I swore to them to bring them out of the land of Egypt into a land that I had searched out for them, flowing with milk and honey, which is the glory of all lands. ⁷ I said to them, 'Each of you throw away the abominations of his eyes. Don't defile yourselves with the idols of Egypt. I am Yahweh your God.' ⁸"But they rebelled against me and wouldn't listen to me. They didn't all throw away the abominations of their eyes. They also didn't forsake the idols of Egypt. Then I said I would pour out my wrath on them, to accomplish my anger against them in the middle of the land of Egypt. ⁹ But I worked for my name's sake, that it should not be profaned in the sight of the nations among which they were, in whose sight I made myself known to them in bringing them out of the land of Egypt. ¹⁰ So I caused them to go out of the land of Egypt and brought them into the wilderness. ¹¹ I gave them my statutes and showed them my ordinances, which if a man does, he will live in them. ¹² Moreover also I gave them my Sabbaths, to be a sign between me and them, that they might know that I am Yahweh who sanctifies them. ¹³"But the house of Israel rebelled against me in the wilderness. They didn't walk in my statutes, and they rejected my ordinances, which if a man keeps, he shall live in them. They greatly profaned my Sabbaths. Then I said I would pour out my wrath on them in the wilderness, to consume them. ¹⁴ But I worked for my name's sake, that it should not be profaned in the sight of the nations, in whose sight I brought them out. ¹⁵ Moreover also I swore to them in the wilderness that I would not bring them into the land which I had given them, flowing with milk and honey, which is the glory of all lands, ¹⁶ because they rejected my ordinances, and didn't walk in my statutes, and profaned my Sabbaths; for their heart went after their idols. ¹⁷ Nevertheless my eye spared them, and I didn't destroy them. I didn't make a full end of them in the wilderness. ¹⁸ I said to their children in the wilderness, 'Don't walk in the statutes of your fathers. Don't observe their ordinances or defile yourselves with their idols. ¹⁹ I am Yahweh your God. Walk in my statutes, keep my ordinances, and do them. ²⁰ Make my Sabbaths holy. They shall be a sign between me and you, that you may know that I am Yahweh your God.' ²¹"But the children rebelled against me. They didn't walk in my statutes, and didn't keep my ordinances to do them, which if a man does, he shall live in them. They profaned my Sabbaths. Then I said I would pour out my wrath on them, to accomplish my anger against them in the wilderness. ²² Nevertheless I withdrew my hand and worked for my name's sake, that it should not be profaned in the sight of the nations, in whose sight I brought them out. ²³ Moreover I swore to them in the wilderness, that I would scatter them among the nations and disperse them through the countries, ²⁴ because they had not executed my ordinances, but had rejected my statutes, and had profaned my Sabbaths, and their eyes were after their fathers' idols. ²⁵ Moreover also I gave them statutes that were not good, and ordinances in which they couldn't live. ²⁶ I polluted them in their own gifts, in that they caused all that opens the womb to pass through the fire, that I might make them desolate, to the end that they might know that I am Yahweh."' ²⁷"Therefore, son of man, speak to the house of Israel, and tell them, 'The Lord Yahweh says: "Moreover, in this your fathers have blasphemed me, in that they have committed a trespass against me. ²⁸ For when I had brought them into the land which I swore to give to them, then they saw every high hill and every thick tree, and they offered there their sacrifices, and there they presented the provocation of their offering. There they also made their pleasant aroma, and there they poured out their drink offerings. ²⁹ Then I said to them, 'What does the high place where you go mean?' So its name is called Bamahª to this day."' ³⁰"Therefore tell the house of Israel, 'The Lord Yahweh says: "Do you pollute yourselves in the way of your fathers? Do you play the prostitute after their abominations? ³¹ When you offer your gifts, when you make your sons pass through the fire, do you pollute yourselves with all your idols to this day? Should I be inquired of by you, house of Israel? As I live, says the Lord Yahweh, I will not be inquired of by you! ³²"That which comes into your mind will not be at all, in that you say, 'We will be as the nations, as the families of the countries, to serve wood and stone.' ³³ As I live," says the Lord Yahweh, "surely with a mighty hand, with an outstretched arm, and with wrath poured out, I will be king over you. ³⁴ I will bring you out from the peoples, and will gather you out of the countries in which you are scattered with a mighty hand, with an outstretched arm, and with wrath poured out. ³⁵ I will bring you into the wilderness of the peoples, and there I will enter into judgment with you face to face. ³⁶ Just as I

---

ª *20:29* "Bamah" means "High Place".

entered into judgment with your fathers in the wilderness of the land of Egypt, so I will enter into judgment with you," says the Lord Yahweh. [37]"I will cause you to pass under the rod, and I will bring you into the bond of the covenant. [38] I will purge out from among you the rebels and those who disobey me. I will bring them out of the land where they live, but they shall not enter into the land of Israel. Then you will know that I am Yahweh." [39]"As for you, house of Israel, the Lord Yahweh says: "Go, everyone serve his idols, and hereafter also, if you will not listen to me; but you shall no more profane my holy name with your gifts and with your idols. [40] For in my holy mountain, in the mountain of the height of Israel," says the Lord Yahweh, "there all the house of Israel, all of them, shall serve me in the land. There I will accept them, and there I will require your offerings and the first fruits of your offerings, with all your holy things. [41] I will accept you as a pleasant aroma when I bring you out from the peoples and gather you out of the countries in which you have been scattered. I will be sanctified in you in the sight of the nations. [42] You will know that I am Yahweh when I bring you into the land of Israel, into the country which I swore to give to your fathers. [43] There you will remember your ways, and all your deeds in which you have polluted yourselves. Then you will loathe yourselves in your own sight for all your evils that you have committed. [44] You will know that I am Yahweh, when I have dealt with you for my name's sake, not according to your evil ways, nor according to your corrupt doings, you house of Israel," says the Lord Yahweh.'" [45] Yahweh's word came to me, saying, [46]"Son of man, set your face toward the south, and preach toward the south, and prophesy against the forest of the field in the south. [47] Tell the forest of the south, 'Hear Yahweh's word: The Lord Yahweh says, "Behold, I will kindle a fire in you, and it will devour every green tree in you, and every dry tree. The burning flame will not be quenched, and all faces from the south to the north will be burned by it. [48] All flesh will see that I, Yahweh, have kindled it. It will not be quenched."'" [49] Then I said, "Ah Lord Yahweh! They say of me, 'Isn't he a speaker of parables?'"

## 21

[1] Yahweh's word came to me, saying, [2]"Son of man, set your face toward Jerusalem, and preach toward the sanctuaries, and prophesy against the land of Israel. [3] Tell the land of Israel, 'Yahweh says: "Behold, I am against you, and will draw my sword out of its sheath, and will cut off from you the righteous and the wicked. [4] Seeing then that I will cut off from you the righteous and the wicked, therefore my sword will go out of its sheath against all flesh from the south to the north. [5] All flesh will know that I, Yahweh, have drawn my sword out of its sheath. It will not return any more.'" [6]"Therefore sigh, you son of man. You shall sigh before their eyes with a broken heart[a] and with bitterness. [7] It shall be, when they ask you, 'Why do you sigh?' that you shall say, 'Because of the news, for it comes! Every heart will melt, all hands will be feeble, every spirit will faint, and all knees will be weak as water. Behold, it comes, and it shall be done, says the Lord Yahweh.'" [8] Yahweh's word came to me, saying, [9]"Son of man, prophesy, and say, 'Yahweh says: "A sword! A sword! It is sharpened, and also polished. [10] It is sharpened that it may make a slaughter. It is polished that it may be as lightning. Should we then make mirth? The rod of my son condemns every tree. [11] It is given to be polished, that it may be handled. The sword is sharpened. Yes, it is polished to give it into the hand of the killer.'" [12] Cry and wail, son of man; for it is on my people. It is on all the princes of Israel. They are delivered over to the sword with my people. Therefore beat your thigh. [13]"For there is a trial. What if even the rod that condemns will be no more?" says the Lord Yahweh. [14]"You therefore, son of man, prophesy, and strike your hands together. Let the sword be doubled the third time, the sword of the fatally wounded. It is the sword of the great one who is fatally wounded, which enters into their rooms. [15] I have set the threatening sword against all their gates, that their heart may melt, and their stumblings be multiplied. Ah! It is made as lightning. It is pointed for slaughter. [16] Gather yourselves together. Go to the right. Set yourselves in array. Go to the left, wherever your face is set. [17] I will also strike my hands together, and I will cause my wrath to rest. I, Yahweh, have spoken it." [18] Yahweh's word came to me again, saying, [19]"Also, you son of man, appoint two ways, that the sword of the king of Babylon may come. They both will come out of one land, and mark out a place. Mark it out at the head of the way to the city. [20] You shall appoint a way for the sword to come to Rabbah of the children of Ammon, and to Judah in Jerusalem the fortified. [21] For the king of Babylon stood at the parting of the way, at the head of the two ways, to use divination. He shook the arrows back and forth. He consulted the teraphim.[b] He looked in the liver. [22] In his right hand was the lot for Jerusalem, to set battering rams,

to open the mouth in the slaughter, to lift up the voice with shouting, to set battering rams against the gates, to cast up mounds, and to build forts. [23] It will be to them as a false divination in their sight, who have sworn oaths to them; but he brings iniquity to memory, that they may be taken. [24]"Therefore the Lord Yahweh says: 'Because you have caused your iniquity to be remembered, in that your transgressions are uncovered, so that in all your doings your sins appear; because you have come to memory, you will be taken with the hand. [25]"You, deadly wounded wicked one, the prince of Israel, whose day has come, in the time of the iniquity of the end, [26] the Lord Yahweh says: "Remove the turban, and take off the crown. This will not be as it was. Exalt that which is low, and humble that which is high. [27] I will overturn, overturn, overturn it. This also will be no more, until he comes whose right it is; and I will give it.'" [28]"You, son of man, prophesy and say, 'The Lord Yahweh says this concerning the children of Ammon, and concerning their reproach: "A sword! A sword is drawn! It is polished for the slaughter, to cause it to devour, that it may be as lightning; [29] while they see for you false visions, while they divine lies to you, to lay you on the necks of the wicked who are deadly wounded, whose day has come in the time of the iniquity of the end. [30] Cause it to return into its sheath. In the place where you were created, in the land of your birth, I will judge you. [31] I will pour out my indignation on you. I will blow on you with the fire of my wrath. I will deliver you into the hand of brutish men, skillful to destroy. [32] You will be for fuel to the fire. Your blood will be in the middle of the land. You will be remembered no more; for I, Yahweh, have spoken it."'"

## 22

[1] Moreover Yahweh's word came to me, saying, [2]"You, son of man, will you judge? Will you judge the bloody city? Then cause her to know all her abominations. [3] You shall say, 'The Lord Yahweh says: "A city that sheds blood within herself, that her time may come, and that makes idols against herself to defile her! [4] You have become guilty in your blood that you have shed, and are defiled in your idols which you have made! You have caused your days to draw near, and have come to the end of your years. Therefore I have made you a reproach to the nations, and a mocking to all the countries. [5] Those who are near and those who are far from you will mock you, you infamous one, full of tumult. [6]"Behold, the princes of Israel, everyone according to his power, have been in you to shed blood. [7] In you have they treated father and mother with contempt.[c] Among you they have oppressed the foreigner. In you they have wronged the fatherless and the widow. [8] You have despised my holy things, and have profaned my Sabbaths. [9] Slanderous men have been in you to shed blood. In you they have eaten on the mountains. They have committed lewdness among you. [10] In you have they uncovered their fathers' nakedness. In you have they humbled her who was unclean in her impurity. [11] One has committed abomination with his neighbor's wife, and another has lewdly defiled his daughter-in-law. Another in you has humbled his sister, his father's daughter. [12] In you have they taken bribes to shed blood. You have taken interest and increase, and you have greedily gained of your neighbors by oppression, and have forgotten me," says the Lord Yahweh. [13]"Behold, therefore I have struck my hand at your dishonest gain which you have made, and at the blood which has been shed within you. [14] Can your heart endure, or can your hands be strong, in the days that I will deal with you? I, Yahweh, have spoken it, and will do it. [15] I will scatter you among the nations, and disperse you through the countries. I will purge your filthiness out of you. [16] You will be profaned in yourself in the sight of the nations. Then you will know that I am Yahweh."'" [17] Yahweh's word came to me, saying, [18]"Son of man, the house of Israel has become dross to me. All of them are bronze, tin, iron, and lead in the middle of the furnace. They are the dross of silver. [19] Therefore the Lord Yahweh says: 'Because you have all become dross, therefore, behold, I will gather you into the middle of Jerusalem. [20] As they gather silver, bronze, iron, lead, and tin into the middle of the furnace, to blow the fire on it, to melt it, so I will gather you in my anger and in my wrath, and I will lay you there and melt you. [21] Yes, I will gather you, and blow on you with the fire of my wrath, and you will be melted in the middle of it. [22] As silver is melted in the middle of the furnace, so you will be melted in the middle of it; and you will know that I, Yahweh, have poured out my wrath on you.'" [23] Yahweh's word came to me, saying, [24]"Son of man, tell her, 'You are a land that is not cleansed nor rained on in the day of indignation.' [25] There is a conspiracy of her prophets within it, like a roaring lion ravening the prey. They have devoured souls. They take treasure and precious things. They have made many widows within it. [26] Her priests have done violence to my law and have profaned my holy things. They have

[a] 21:6 literally, the breaking of your thighs

[b] 21:21 teraphim were household idols that may have been associated with

inheritance rights to the household property.

[c] 22:7 Literally, made light of father and mother.

made no distinction between the holy and the common, neither have they caused men to discern between the unclean and the clean, and have hidden their eyes from my Sabbaths. So I am profaned among them. ²⁷ Her princes within it are like wolves ravening the prey, to shed blood and to destroy souls, that they may get dishonest gain. ²⁸ Her prophets have plastered for them with whitewash, seeing false visions, and divining lies to them, saying, 'The Lord Yahweh says,' when Yahweh has not spoken. ²⁹ The people of the land have used oppression and exercised robbery. Yes, they have troubled the poor and needy, and have oppressed the foreigner wrongfully. ³⁰"I sought for a man among them who would build up the wall and stand in the gap before me for the land, that I would not destroy it; but I found no one. ³¹ Therefore I have poured out my indignation on them. I have consumed them with the fire of my wrath. I have brought their own way on their heads," says the Lord Yahweh.

## 23

¹ Yahweh's word came again to me, saying, ²"Son of man, there were two women, the daughters of one mother. ³ They played the prostitute in Egypt. They played the prostitute in their youth. Their breasts were fondled there, and their youthful nipples were caressed there. ⁴ Their names were Oholah the elder, and Oholibah her sister. They became mine, and they bore sons and daughters. As for their names, Samaria is Oholah, and Jerusalem Oholibah. ⁵"Oholah played the prostitute when she was mine. She doted on her lovers, on the Assyrians her neighbors, ⁶ who were clothed with blue—governors and rulers, all of them desirable young men, horsemen riding on horses. ⁷ She gave herself as a prostitute to them, all of them the choicest men of Assyria. She defiled herself with the idols of whomever she lusted after. ⁸ She hasn't left her prostitution since leaving Egypt; for in her youth they lay with her. They caressed her youthful nipples and they poured out their prostitution on her. ⁹"Therefore I delivered her into the hand of her lovers, into the hand of the Assyrians on whom she doted. ¹⁰ These uncovered her nakedness. They took her sons and her daughters, and they killed her with the sword. She became a byword among women; for they executed judgments on her. ¹¹"Her sister Oholibah saw this, yet she was more corrupt in her lusting than she, and in her prostitution which was more depraved than the prostitution of her sister. ¹² She lusted after the Assyrians, governors and rulers—her neighbors, clothed most gorgeously, horsemen riding on horses, all of them desirable young men. ¹³ I saw that she was defiled. They both went the same way. ¹⁴"She increased her prostitution; for she saw men portrayed on the wall, the images of the Chaldeans portrayed with red, ¹⁵ dressed with belts on their waists, with flowing turbans on their heads, all of them looking like princes, after the likeness of the Babylonians in Chaldea, the land of their birth. ¹⁶ As soon as she saw them, she lusted after them and sent messengers to them into Chaldea. ¹⁷ The Babylonians came to her into the bed of love, and they defiled her with their prostitution. She was polluted with them, and her soul was alienated from them. ¹⁸ So she uncovered her prostitution and uncovered her nakedness. Then my soul was alienated from her, just like my soul was alienated from her sister. ¹⁹ Yet she multiplied her prostitution, remembering the days of her youth, in which she had played the prostitute in the land of Egypt. ²⁰ She lusted after their lovers, whose flesh is as the flesh of donkeys, and whose issue is like the issue of horses. ²¹ Thus you called to memory the lewdness of your youth, in the caressing of your nipples by the Egyptians because of your youthful breasts. ²²"Therefore, Oholibah, the Lord Yahweh says: 'Behold, I will raise up your lovers against you, from whom your soul is alienated, and I will bring them against you on every side: ²³ the Babylonians and all the Chaldeans, Pekod, Shoa, Koa, and all the Assyrians with them; all of them desirable young men, governors and rulers, princes and men of renown, all of them riding on horses. ²⁴ They will come against you with weapons, chariots, and wagons, and with a company of peoples. They will set themselves against you with buckler, shield, and helmet all around. I will commit the judgment to them, and they will judge you according to their judgments. ²⁵ I will set my jealousy against you, and they will deal with you in fury. They will take away your nose and your ears. Your remnant will fall by the sword. They will take your sons and your daughters; and the rest of you will be devoured by the fire. ²⁶ They will also strip you of your clothes and take away your beautiful jewels. ²⁷ Thus I will make your lewdness to cease from you, and remove your prostitution from the land of Egypt, so that you will not lift up your eyes to them, nor remember Egypt any more.' ²⁸"For the Lord Yahweh says: 'Behold, I will deliver you into the hand of them whom you hate, into the hand of them from whom your soul is alienated. ²⁹ They will deal with you in hatred, and will take away all your labor, and will leave you naked and bare. The nakedness of your prostitution will be uncovered, both your lewdness and your prostitution. ³⁰ These things will be done to you because you have played the prostitute after the nations, and because you are polluted with their idols. ³¹ You have

walked in the way of your sister; therefore I will give her cup into your hand.' ³²"The Lord Yahweh says: 'You will drink of your sister's cup, which is deep and large. You will be ridiculed and held in derision. It contains much. ³³ You will be filled with drunkenness and sorrow, with the cup of astonishment and desolation, with the cup of your sister Samaria. ³⁴ You will even drink it and drain it out. You will gnaw the broken pieces of it, and will tear your breasts; for I have spoken it,' says the Lord Yahweh. ³⁵"Therefore the Lord Yahweh says: 'Because you have forgotten me and cast me behind your back, therefore you also bear your lewdness and your prostitution.'" ³⁶ Yahweh said moreover to me: "Son of man, will you judge Oholah and Oholibah? Then declare to them their abominations. ³⁷ For they have committed adultery, and blood is in their hands. They have committed adultery with their idols. They have also caused their sons, whom they bore to me, to pass through the fire to them to be devoured. ³⁸ Moreover this they have done to me: they have defiled my sanctuary in the same day, and have profaned my Sabbaths. ³⁹ For when they had slain their children to their idols, then they came the same day into my sanctuary to profane it; and behold, they have done this in the middle of my house. ⁴⁰"Furthermore you sisters have sent for men who come from far away, to whom a messenger was sent, and behold, they came; for whom you washed yourself, painted your eyes, decorated yourself with ornaments, ⁴¹ and sat on a stately bed, with a table prepared before it, whereupon you set my incense and my oil. ⁴²"The voice of a multitude being at ease was with her. With men of the common sort were brought drunkards from the wilderness; and they put bracelets on their hands, and beautiful crowns on their heads. ⁴³ Then I said of her who was old in adulteries, 'Now they will play the prostitute with her, and she with them.' ⁴⁴ They went in to her, as they go in to a prostitute. So they went in to Oholah and to Oholibah, the lewd women. ⁴⁵ Righteous men will judge them with the judgment of adulteresses and with the judgment of women who shed blood, because they are adulteresses, and blood is in their hands. ⁴⁶"For the Lord Yahweh says: 'I will bring up a mob against them, and will give them to be tossed back and forth and robbed. ⁴⁷ The company will stone them with stones and dispatch them with their swords. They will kill their sons and their daughters, and burn up their houses with fire. ⁴⁸"Thus I will cause lewdness to cease out of the land, that all women may be taught not to be lewd like you. ⁴⁹ They will recompense your lewdness on you, and you will bear the sins of your idols. Then you will know that I am the Lord Yahweh.'"

## 24

¹ Again, in the ninth year, in the tenth month, in the tenth day of the month, Yahweh's word came to me, saying, ²"Son of man, write the name of the day, this same day. The king of Babylon drew close to Jerusalem this same day. ³ Utter a parable to the rebellious house, and tell them, 'The Lord Yahweh says, "Put the cauldron on the fire. Put it on, and also pour water into it. ⁴ Gather its pieces into it, even every good piece: the thigh and the shoulder. Fill it with the choice bones. ⁵ Take the choice of the flock, and also a pile of wood for the bones under the cauldron. Make it boil well. Yes, let its bones be boiled within it." ⁶"Therefore the Lord Yahweh says: "Woe to the bloody city, to the cauldron whose rust is in it, and whose rust hasn't gone out of it! Take out of it piece after piece without casting lots for it. ⁷"For the blood she shed is in the middle of her. She set it on the bare rock. She didn't pour it on the ground, to cover it with dust. ⁸ That it may cause wrath to come up to take vengeance, I have set her blood on the bare rock, that it should not be covered." ⁹"Therefore the Lord Yahweh says: "Woe to the bloody city! I also will make the pile great. ¹⁰ Heap on the wood. Make the fire hot. Boil the meat well. Make the broth thick, and let the bones be burned. ¹¹ Then set it empty on its coals, that it may be hot, and its bronze may burn, and that its filthiness may be molten in it, that its rust may be consumed. ¹² She is weary with toil; yet her great rust, rust by fire, doesn't leave her. ¹³"In your filthiness is lewdness. Because I have cleansed you and you weren't cleansed, you won't be cleansed from your filthiness any more, until I have caused my wrath toward you to rest. ¹⁴"I, Yahweh, have spoken it. It will happen, and I will do it. I won't go back. I won't spare. I won't repent. According to your ways and according to your doings, they will judge you," says the Lord Yahweh.'" ¹⁵ Also Yahweh's word came to me, saying, ¹⁶"Son of man, behold, I will take away from you the desire of your eyes with one stroke; yet you shall neither mourn nor weep, neither shall your tears run down. ¹⁷ Sigh, but not aloud. Make no mourning for the dead. Bind your headdress on you, and put your sandals on your feet. Don't cover your lips, and don't eat mourner's bread." ¹⁸ So I spoke to the people in the morning, and at evening my wife died. So I did in the morning as I was commanded. ¹⁹ The people asked me, "Won't you tell us what these things mean to us, that you act like this?" ²⁰ Then I said to them, "Yahweh's word came to me, saying, ²¹'Speak to the house of Israel, "The Lord Yahweh says: 'Behold, I will profane my sanctuary, the pride of your power, the desire of your eyes, and that which your

soul pities; and your sons and your daughters whom you have left behind will fall by the sword. ²² You will do as I have done. You won't cover your lips or eat mourner's bread. ²³ Your turbans will be on your heads, and your sandals on your feet. You won't mourn or weep; but you will pine away in your iniquities, and moan one toward another. ²⁴ Thus Ezekiel will be a sign to you; according to all that he has done, you will do. When this comes, then you will know that I am the Lord Yahweh.'"'" ²⁵"You, son of man, shouldn't it be in the day when I take from them their strength, the joy of their glory, the desire of their eyes, and that whereupon they set their heart—their sons and their daughters— ²⁶ that in that day he who escapes will come to you, to cause you to hear it with your ears? ²⁷ In that day your mouth will be opened to him who has escaped, and you will speak and be no more mute. So you will be a sign to them. Then they will know that I am Yahweh."

## 25

¹ Yahweh's word came to me, saying, ²"Son of man, set your face toward the children of Ammon, and prophesy against them. ³ Tell the children of Ammon, 'Hear the word of the Lord Yahweh! The Lord Yahweh says, "Because you said, 'Aha!' against my sanctuary when it was profaned, and against the land of Israel when it was made desolate, and against the house of Judah when they went into captivity, ⁴ therefore, behold, I will deliver you to the children of the east for a possession. They will set their encampments in you and make their dwellings in you. They will eat your fruit and they will drink your milk. ⁵ I will make Rabbah a stable for camels and the children of Ammon a resting place for flocks. Then you will know that I am Yahweh." ⁶ For the Lord Yahweh says: "Because you have clapped your hands, stamped with the feet, and rejoiced with all the contempt of your soul against the land of Israel, ⁷ therefore, behold, I have stretched out my hand on you, and will deliver you for a plunder to the nations. I will cut you off from the peoples, and I will cause you to perish out of the countries. I will destroy you. Then you will know that I am Yahweh." ⁸"The Lord Yahweh says: "Because Moab and Seir say, 'Behold, the house of Judah is like all the nations,' ⁹ therefore, behold, I will open the side of Moab from the cities, from his cities which are on its frontiers, the glory of the country, Beth Jeshimoth, Baal Meon, and Kiriathaim, ¹⁰ to the children of the east, to go against the children of Ammon; and I will give them for a possession, that the children of Ammon may not be remembered among the nations. ¹¹ I will execute judgments on Moab. Then they will know that I am Yahweh." ¹²"The Lord Yahweh says: "Because Edom has dealt against the house of Judah by taking vengeance, and has greatly offended, and taken revenge on them," ¹³ therefore the Lord Yahweh says, "I will stretch out my hand on Edom, and will cut off man and animal from it; and I will make it desolate from Teman. They will fall by the sword even to Dedan. ¹⁴ I will lay my vengeance on Edom by the hand of my people Israel. They will do in Edom according to my anger and according to my wrath. Then they will know my vengeance," says the Lord Yahweh. ¹⁵"The Lord Yahweh says: "Because the Philistines have taken revenge, and have taken vengeance with contempt of soul to destroy with perpetual hostility," ¹⁶ therefore the Lord Yahweh says, "Behold, I will stretch out my hand on the Philistines, and I will cut off the Cherethites, and destroy the remnant of the sea coast. ¹⁷ I will execute great vengeance on them with wrathful rebukes. Then they will know that I am Yahweh, when I lay my vengeance on them."'"

## 26

¹ In the eleventh year, in the first of the month, Yahweh's word came to me, saying, ²"Son of man, because Tyre has said against Jerusalem, 'Aha! She is broken! She who was the gateway of the peoples has been returned to me. I will be replenished, now that she is laid waste;' ³ therefore the Lord Yahweh says, 'Behold, I am against you, Tyre, and will cause many nations to come up against you, as the sea causes its waves to come up. ⁴ They will destroy the walls of Tyre, and break down her towers. I will also scrape her dust from her, and make her a bare rock. ⁵ She will be a place for the spreading of nets in the middle of the sea; for I have spoken it,' says the Lord Yahweh. 'She will become plunder for the nations. ⁶ Her daughters who are in the field will be slain with the sword. Then they will know that I am Yahweh.' ⁷"For the Lord Yahweh says: 'Behold, I will bring on Tyre Nebuchadnezzar king of Babylon, king of kings, from the north, with horses, with chariots, with horsemen, and an army with many people. ⁸ He will kill your daughters in the field with the sword. He will make forts against you, cast up a mound against you, and raise up the buckler against you. ⁹ He will set his battering engines against your walls, and with his axes he will break down your towers. ¹⁰ By reason of the abundance of his horses, their dust will cover you. Your walls will shake at the noise of the horsemen, of the wagons, and of the chariots, when he enters into your gates, as men enter into a city which is broken open. ¹¹ He will tread down all your streets with the hoofs of his horses.

He will kill your people with the sword. The pillars of your strength will go down to the ground. ¹² They will make a plunder of your riches and make a prey of your merchandise. They will break down your walls and destroy your pleasant houses. They will lay your stones, your timber, and your dust in the middle of the waters. ¹³ I will cause the noise of your songs to cease. The sound of your harps won't be heard any more. ¹⁴ I will make you a bare rock. You will be a place for the spreading of nets. You will be built no more; for I Yahweh have spoken it,' says the Lord Yahweh. ¹⁵"The Lord Yahweh says to Tyre: 'Won't the islands shake at the sound of your fall, when the wounded groan, when the slaughter is made within you? ¹⁶ Then all the princes of the sea will come down from their thrones, and lay aside their robes, and strip off their embroidered garments. They will clothe themselves with trembling. They will sit on the ground, and will tremble every moment, and be astonished at you. ¹⁷ They will take up a lamentation over you, and tell you, "How you are destroyed, who were inhabited by seafaring men, the renowned city, who was strong in the sea, she and her inhabitants, who caused their terror to be on all who lived there!" ¹⁸ Now the islands will tremble in the day of your fall. Yes, the islands that are in the sea will be dismayed at your departure.' ¹⁹"For the Lord Yahweh says: 'When I make you a desolate city, like the cities that are not inhabited, when I bring up the deep on you, and the great waters cover you, ²⁰ then I will bring you down with those who descend into the pit, to the people of old time, and will make you dwell in the lower parts of the earth, in the places that are desolate of old, with those who go down to the pit, that you be not inhabited; and I will set glory in the land of the living. ²¹ I will make you a terror, and you will no more have any being. Though you are sought for, yet you will never be found again,' says the Lord Yahweh."

## 27

¹ Yahweh's word came again to me, saying, ²"You, son of man, take up a lamentation over Tyre; ³ and tell Tyre, 'You who dwell at the entry of the sea, who are the merchant of the peoples to many islands, the Lord Yahweh says: "You, Tyre, have said, 'I am perfect in beauty.' ⁴ Your borders are in the heart of the seas. Your builders have perfected your beauty. ⁵ They have made all your planks of cypress trees from Senir. They have taken a cedar from Lebanon to make a mast for you. ⁶ They have made your oars of the oaks of Bashan. They have made your benches of ivory inlaid in cypress wood from the islands of Kittim. ⁷ Your sail was of fine linen with embroidered work from Egypt, that it might be to you for a banner. Blue and purple from the islands of Elishah was your awning. ⁸ The inhabitants of Sidon and Arvad were your rowers. Your wise men, Tyre, were in you. They were your pilots. ⁹ The old men of Gebal and its wise men were your repairers of ship seams in you. All the ships of the sea with their mariners were in you to deal in your merchandise. ¹⁰"Persia, Lud, and Put were in your army, your men of war. They hung the shield and helmet in you. They showed your beauty. ¹¹ The men of Arvad with your army were on your walls all around, and valiant men were in your towers. They hung their shields on your walls all around. They have perfected your beauty. ¹²"Tarshish was your merchant by reason of the multitude of all kinds of riches. They traded for your wares with silver, iron, tin, and lead. ¹³"Javan, Tubal, and Meshech were your traders. They traded the persons of men and vessels of bronze for your merchandise. ¹⁴"They of the house of Togarmah traded for your wares with horses, war horses, and mules. ¹⁵"The men of Dedan traded with you. Many islands were the market of your hand. They brought you horns of ivory and ebony in exchange. ¹⁶"Syria was your merchant by reason of the multitude of your handiworks. They traded for your wares with emeralds, purple, embroidered work, fine linen, coral, and rubies. ¹⁷"Judah and the land of Israel were your traders. They traded wheat of Minnith, confections, honey, oil, and balm for your merchandise. ¹⁸"Damascus was your merchant for the multitude of your handiworks by reason of the multitude of all kinds of riches, with the wine of Helbon, and white wool. ¹⁹"Vedan and Javan traded with yarn for your wares; wrought iron, cassia, and calamus were among your merchandise. ²⁰"Dedan was your merchant in precious saddle blankets for riding. ²¹"Arabia and all the princes of Kedar were your favorite dealers in lambs, rams, and goats. In these, they were your merchants. ²²"The traders of Sheba and Raamah were your traders. They traded for your wares with the best of all spices, all precious stones, and gold. ²³"Haran, Canneh, Eden, the traders of Sheba, Asshur and Chilmad, were your traders. ²⁴ These were your traders in choice wares, in wrappings of blue and embroidered work, and in cedar chests of rich clothing bound with cords, among your merchandise. ²⁵"The ships of Tarshish were your caravans for your merchandise. You were replenished and made very glorious in the heart of the seas. ²⁶ Your rowers have brought you into great waters. The east wind has broken you in the heart of the seas. ²⁷ Your riches, your wares, your merchandise, your mariners, your pilots, your repairers of ship seams,

the dealers in your merchandise, and all your men of war who are in you, with all your company which is among you, will fall into the heart of the seas in the day of your ruin. ²⁸ At the sound of the cry of your pilots, the pasture lands will shake. ²⁹ All who handle the oars, the mariners and all the pilots of the sea, will come down from their ships. They will stand on the land, ³⁰ and will cause their voice to be heard over you, and will cry bitterly. They will cast up dust on their heads. They will wallow in the ashes. ³¹ They will make themselves bald for you, and clothe themselves with sackcloth. They will weep for you in bitterness of soul, with bitter mourning. ³² In their wailing they will take up a lamentation for you, and lament over you, saying, 'Who is there like Tyre, like her who is brought to silence in the middle of the sea?' ³³ When your wares came from the seas, you filled many peoples. You enriched the kings of the earth with the multitude of your riches and of your merchandise. ³⁴ In the time that you were broken by the seas, in the depths of the waters, your merchandise and all your company fell within you. ³⁵ All the inhabitants of the islands are astonished at you, and their kings are horribly afraid. They are troubled in their face. ³⁶ The merchants among the peoples hiss at you. You have come to a terrible end, and you will be no more.""""

## 28

¹ Yahweh's word came again to me, saying, ²"Son of man, tell the prince of Tyre, 'The Lord Yahweh says: "Because your heart is lifted up, and you have said, 'I am a god, I sit in the seat of God, in the middle of the seas;' yet you are man, and no god, though you set your heart as the heart of a god— ³ behold, you are wiser than Daniel. There is no secret that is hidden from you. ⁴ By your wisdom and by your understanding you have gotten yourself riches, and have gotten gold and silver into your treasuries. ⁵ By your great wisdom and by your trading you have increased your riches, and your heart is lifted up because of your riches— ⁶ "therefore the Lord Yahweh says: "Because you have set your heart as the heart of God, ⁷ therefore, behold, I will bring strangers on you, the terrible of the nations. They will draw their swords against the beauty of your wisdom. They will defile your brightness. ⁸ They will bring you down to the pit. You will die the death of those who are slain in the heart of the seas. ⁹ Will you yet say before him who kills you, 'I am God'? But you are man, and not God, in the hand of him who wounds you. ¹⁰ You will die the death of the uncircumcised by the hand of strangers; for I have spoken it," says the Lord Yahweh.'" ¹¹ Moreover Yahweh's word came to me, saying, ¹²"Son of man, take up a lamentation over the king of Tyre, and tell him, 'The Lord Yahweh says: "You were the seal of full measure, full of wisdom, and perfect in beauty. ¹³ You were in Eden, the garden of God. Every precious stone adorned you: ruby, topaz, emerald, chrysolite, onyx, jasper, sapphire,ᵃ turquoise, and beryl. Gold work of tambourines and of pipes was in you. They were prepared in the day that you were created. ¹⁴ You were the anointed cherub who covers. Then I set you up on the holy mountain of God. You have walked up and down in the middle of the stones of fire. ¹⁵ You were perfect in your ways from the day that you were created, until unrighteousness was found in you. ¹⁶ By the abundance of your commerce, your insides were filled with violence, and you have sinned. Therefore I have cast you as profane out of God's mountain. I have destroyed you, covering cherub, from the middle of the stones of fire. ¹⁷ Your heart was lifted up because of your beauty. You have corrupted your wisdom by reason of your splendor. I have cast you to the ground. I have laid you before kings, that they may see you. ¹⁸ By the multitude of your iniquities, in the unrighteousness of your commerce, you have profaned your sanctuaries. Therefore I have brought out a fire from the middle of you. It has devoured you. I have turned you to ashes on the earth in the sight of all those who see you. ¹⁹ All those who know you among the peoples will be astonished at you. You have become a terror, and you will exist no more."'" ²⁰ Yahweh's word came to me, saying, ²¹"Son of man, set your face toward Sidon, and prophesy against it, ²² and say, 'The Lord Yahweh says: "Behold, I am against you, Sidon. I will be glorified among you. Then they will know that I am Yahweh, when I have executed judgments in her, and am sanctified in her. ²³ For I will send pestilence into her, and blood into her streets. The wounded will fall within her, with the sword on her on every side. Then they will know that I am Yahweh. ²⁴ "There will no longer be a pricking brier to the house of Israel, nor a hurting thorn of any that are around them that scorned them. Then they will know that I am the Lord Yahweh." ²⁵ "The Lord Yahweh says: "When I have gathered the house of Israel from the peoples among whom they are scattered, and am shown as holy among them in the sight of the nations, then they will dwell in their own land which I gave to my servant Jacob. ²⁶ They will dwell in it securely. Yes, they will build houses, plant vineyards, and will dwell securely when I have executed judgments on all those around them who

have treated them with contempt. Then they will know that I am Yahweh their God."" **29**¹ In the tenth year, in the tenth month, on the twelfth day of the month, Yahweh's word came to me, saying, ²"Son of man, set your face against Pharaoh king of Egypt, and prophesy against him and against all Egypt. ³ Speak and say, 'The Lord Yahweh says: "Behold, I am against you, Pharaoh king of Egypt, the great monster that lies in the middle of his rivers, that has said, 'My river is my own, and I have made it for myself.' ⁴ I will put hooks in your jaws, and I will make the fish of your rivers stick to your scales. I will bring you up out of the middle of your rivers, with all the fish of your rivers which stick to your scales. ⁵ I'll cast you out into the wilderness, you and all the fish of your rivers. You'll fall on the open field. You won't be brought together or gathered. I have given you for food to the animals of the earth and to the birds of the sky. ⁶ "All the inhabitants of Egypt will know that I am Yahweh, because they have been a staff of reed to the house of Israel. ⁷ When they took hold of you by your hand, you broke and tore all their shoulders. When they leaned on you, you broke and paralyzed all of their thighs." ⁸ "Therefore the Lord Yahweh says: "Behold, I will bring a sword on you, and will cut off man and animal from you. ⁹ The land of Egypt will be a desolation and a waste. Then they will know that I am Yahweh. ""Because he has said, 'The river is mine, and I have made it,' ¹⁰ therefore, behold, I am against you, and against your rivers. I will make the land of Egypt an utter waste and desolation, from the tower of Seveneh even to the border of Ethiopia. ¹¹ No foot of man will pass through it, nor will any animal foot pass through it. It won't be inhabited for forty years. ¹² I will make the land of Egypt a desolation in the middle of the countries that are desolate. Her cities among the cities that are laid waste will be a desolation forty years. I will scatter the Egyptians among the nations, and will disperse them through the countries." ¹³ "For the Lord Yahweh says: "At the end of forty years I will gather the Egyptians from the peoples where they were scattered. ¹⁴ I will reverse the captivity of Egypt, and will cause them to return into the land of Pathros, into the land of their birth. There they will be a lowly kingdom. ¹⁵ It will be the lowest of the kingdoms. It won't lift itself up above the nations any more. I will diminish them so that they will no longer rule over the nations. ¹⁶ It will no longer be the confidence of the house of Israel, bringing iniquity to memory, when they turn to look after them. Then they will know that I am the Lord Yahweh."" ¹⁷ It came to pass in the twenty-seventh year, in the first month, in the first day of the month, Yahweh's word came to me, saying, ¹⁸"Son of man, Nebuchadnezzar king of Babylon caused his army to serve a great service against Tyre. Every head was made bald, and every shoulder was worn; yet he had no wages, nor did his army, from Tyre, for the service that he had served against it. ¹⁹ Therefore the Lord Yahweh says: 'Behold, I will give the land of Egypt to Nebuchadnezzar king of Babylon. He will carry off her multitude, take her plunder, and take her prey. That will be the wages for his army. ²⁰ I have given him the land of Egypt as his payment for which he served, because they worked for me,' says the Lord Yahweh. ²¹"In that day I will cause a horn to sprout for the house of Israel, and I will open your mouth among them. Then they will know that I am Yahweh."

## 30

¹ Yahweh's word came again to me, saying, ²"Son of man, prophesy, and say, 'The Lord Yahweh says: "Wail, 'Alas for the day!' ³ For the day is near, even Yahweh's day is near. It will be a day of clouds, a time of the nations. ⁴ A sword will come on Egypt, and anguish will be in Ethiopia, when the slain fall in Egypt. They take away her multitude, and her foundations are broken down. ⁵ "Ethiopia, Put, Lud, all the mixed people, Cub, and the children of the land that is allied with them, will fall with them by the sword." ⁶ "Yahweh says: "They also who uphold Egypt will fall. The pride of her power will come down. They will fall by the sword in it from the tower of Seveneh," says the Lord Yahweh. ⁷ "They will be desolate in the middle of the countries that are desolate. Her cities will be among the cities that are wasted. ⁸ They will know that I am Yahweh when I have set a fire in Egypt, and all her helpers are destroyed. ⁹ "In that day messengers will go out from before me in ships to make the careless Ethiopians afraid. There will be anguish on them, as in the day of Egypt; for, behold, it comes." ¹⁰ "The Lord Yahweh says: "I will also make the multitude of Egypt to cease, by the hand of Nebuchadnezzar king of Babylon. ¹¹ He and his people with him, the terrible of the nations, will be brought in to destroy the land. They will draw their swords against Egypt, and fill the land with the slain. ¹² I will make the rivers dry, and will sell the land into the hand of evil men. I will make the land desolate, and all that is therein, by the hand of foreigners. I, Yahweh, have spoken it." ¹³ "The Lord Yahweh says: "I will also destroy the idols, and I will cause the images to cease from Memphis. There will be no more a prince from the land

---

ᵃ 28:13 or, lapis lazuli

of Egypt. I will put a fear in the land of Egypt. ¹⁴ I will make Pathros desolate, and will set a fire in Zoan, and will execute judgments on No. ¹⁵ I will pour my wrath on Sin, the stronghold of Egypt. I will cut off the multitude of No. ¹⁶ I will set a fire in Egypt Sin will be in great anguish. No will be broken up. Memphis will have adversaries in the daytime. ¹⁷ The young men of Aven and of Pibeseth will fall by the sword. They will go into captivity. ¹⁸ At Tehaphnehes also the day will withdraw itself, when I break the yokes of Egypt there. The pride of her power will cease in her. As for her, a cloud will cover her, and her daughters will go into captivity. ¹⁹ Thus I will execute judgments on Egypt. Then they will know that I am Yahweh.'"" ²⁰ In the eleventh year, in the first month, in the seventh day of the month, Yahweh's word came to me, saying, ²¹"Son of man, I have broken the arm of Pharaoh king of Egypt. Behold, it has not been bound up, to apply medicines, to put a bandage to bind it, that it may become strong to hold the sword. ²² Therefore the Lord Yahweh says: 'Behold, I am against Pharaoh king of Egypt, and will break his arms, the strong arm, and that which was broken. I will cause the sword to fall out of his hand. ²³ I will scatter the Egyptians among the nations, and will disperse them through the countries. ²⁴ I will strengthen the arms of the king of Babylon, and put my sword in his hand; but I will break the arms of Pharaoh, and he will groan before the king of Babylon with the groaning of a mortally wounded man. ²⁵ I will hold up the arms of the king of Babylon, but the arms of Pharaoh will fall down. Then they will know that I am Yahweh when I put my sword into the hand of the king of Babylon, and he stretches it out on the land of Egypt. ²⁶ I will scatter the Egyptians among the nations and disperse them through the countries. Then they will know that I am Yahweh.'"

## 31

¹ In the eleventh year, in the third month, in the first day of the month, Yahweh's word came to me, saying, ²"Son of man, tell Pharaoh king of Egypt and his multitude: 'Whom are you like in your greatness? ³ Behold, the Assyrian was a cedar in Lebanon with beautiful branches, and with a forest-like shade, of high stature; and its top was among the thick boughs. ⁴ The waters nourished it. The deep made it to grow. Its rivers ran all around its plantation. It sent out its channels to all the trees of the field. ⁵ Therefore its stature was exalted above all the trees of the field; and its boughs were multiplied. Its branches became long by reason of many waters, when it spread them out. ⁶ All the birds of the sky made their nests in its boughs. Under its branches, all the animals of the field gave birth to their young. All great nations lived under its shadow. ⁷ Thus it was beautiful in its greatness, in the length of its branches; for its root was by many waters. ⁸ The cedars in the garden of God could not hide it. The cypress trees were not like its branches. The pine trees were not like its branches; nor was any tree in the garden of God like it in its beauty. ⁹ I made it beautiful by the multitude of its branches, so that all the trees of Eden, that were in the garden of God, envied it.' ¹⁰"Therefore thus said the Lord Yahweh: 'Because he is exalted in stature, and he has set his top among the thick branches, and his heart is lifted up in his height, ¹¹ I will deliver him into the hand of the mighty one of the nations. He will surely deal with him. I have driven him out for his wickedness. ¹² Foreigners, the tyrants of the nations, have cut him off and have left him. His branches have fallen on the mountains and in all the valleys, and his boughs are broken by all the watercourses of the land. All the peoples of the earth have gone down from his shadow and have left him. ¹³ All the birds of the sky will dwell on his ruin, and all the animals of the field will be on his branches, ¹⁴ to the end that none of all the trees by the waters exalt themselves in their stature, and don't set their top among the thick boughs. Their mighty ones don't stand up on their height, even all who drink water; for they are all delivered to death, to the lower parts of the earth, among the children of men, with those who go down to the pit.' ¹⁵"The Lord Yahweh says: 'In the day when he went down to Sheol,ᵃ I caused a mourning. I covered the deep for him, and I restrained its rivers. The great waters were stopped. I caused Lebanon to mourn for him, and all the trees of the field fainted for him. ¹⁶ I made the nations to shake at the sound of his fall, when I cast him down to Sheolᵇ with those who descend into the pit. All the trees of Eden, the choice and best of Lebanon, all that drink water, were comforted in the lower parts of the earth. ¹⁷ They also went down into Sheol with him to those who are slain by the sword; yes, those who were his arm, who lived under his shadow in the middle of the nations. ¹⁸"'To whom are you thus like in glory and in greatness among the trees of Eden? Yet you will be brought down with the trees of Eden to the lower parts of the earth. You will lie in the middle of the uncircumcised, with those who are slain by the sword. "'This is Pharaoh and all his multitude,' says the Lord Yahweh."

## 32

¹ In the twelfth year, in the twelfth month, in the first day of the month, "Yahweh's word came to me, saying, ²'Son of man, take up a lamentation over Pharaoh king of Egypt, and tell him, "You were likened to a young lion of the nations; yet you are as a monster in the seas. You broke out with your rivers, and troubled the waters with your feet, and fouled their rivers." ³ The Lord Yahweh says: "I will spread out my net on you with a company of many peoples. They will bring you up in my net. ⁴ I will leave you on the land. I will cast you out on the open field, and will cause all the birds of the sky to settle on you. I will satisfy the animals of the whole earth with you. ⁵ I will lay your flesh on the mountains, and fill the valleys with your height. ⁶ I will also water the land in which you swim with your blood, even to the mountains. The watercourses will be full of you. ⁷ When I extinguish you, I will cover the heavens and make its stars dark. I will cover the sun with a cloud, and the moon won't give its light. ⁸ I will make all the bright lights of the sky dark over you, and set darkness on your land," says the Lord Yahweh. ⁹"I will also trouble the hearts of many peoples, when I bring your destruction among the nations, into the countries which you have not known. ¹⁰ Yes, I will make many peoples amazed at you, and their kings will be horribly afraid for you, when I brandish my sword before them. They will tremble at every moment, every man for his own life, in the day of your fall." ¹¹ For the Lord Yahweh says: "The sword of the king of Babylon will come on you. ¹² I will cause your multitude to fall by the swords of the mighty. They are all the ruthless of the nations. They will bring the pride of Egypt to nothing, and all its multitude will be destroyed. ¹³ I will destroy also all its animals from beside many waters. The foot of man won't trouble them any more, nor will the hoofs of animals trouble them. ¹⁴ Then I will make their waters clear, and cause their rivers to run like oil," says the Lord Yahweh. ¹⁵"When I make the land of Egypt desolate and waste, a land destitute of that of which it was full, when I strike all those who dwell therein, then they will know that I am Yahweh. ¹⁶""This is the lamentation with which they will lament. The daughters of the nations will lament with this. They will lament with it over Egypt, and over all her multitude," says the Lord Yahweh.'" ¹⁷ Also in the twelfth year, in the fifteenth day of the month, Yahweh's word came to me, saying, ¹⁸"Son of man, wail for the multitude of Egypt, and cast them down, even her and the daughters of the famous nations, to the lower parts of the earth, with those who go down into the pit. ¹⁹ Whom do you pass in beauty? Go down, and be laid with the uncircumcised. ²⁰ They will fall among those who are slain by the sword. She is delivered to the sword. Draw her away with all her multitudes. ²¹ The strong among the mighty will speak to him out of the middle of Sheolᶜ with those who help him. They have gone down. The uncircumcised lie still, slain by the sword. ²²"Asshur is there with all her company. Her graves are all around her. All of them are slain, fallen by the sword, ²³ whose graves are set in the uttermost parts of the pit, and her company is around her grave, all of them slain, fallen by the sword, who caused terror in the land of the living. ²⁴"There is Elam and all her multitude around her grave; all of them slain, fallen by the sword, who have gone down uncircumcised into the lower parts of the earth, who caused their terror in the land of the living, and have borne their shame with those who go down to the pit. ²⁵ They have made Elam a bed among the slain with all her multitude. Her graves are around her, all of them uncircumcised, slain by the sword; for their terror was caused in the land of the living, and they have borne their shame with those who go down to the pit. He is put among those who are slain. ²⁶"There is Meshech, Tubal, and all their multitude. Their graves are around them, all of them uncircumcised, slain by the sword; for they caused their terror in the land of the living. ²⁷ They will not lie with the mighty who are fallen of the uncircumcised, who have gone down to Sheol with their weapons of war and have laid their swords under their heads. Their iniquities are on their bones; for they were the terror of the mighty in the land of the living. ²⁸"But you will be broken among the uncircumcised, and will lie with those who are slain by the sword. ²⁹"There is Edom, her kings, and all her princes, who in their might are laid with those who are slain by the sword. They will lie with the uncircumcised, and with those who go down to the pit. ³⁰"There are the princes of the north, all of them, and all the Sidonians, who have gone down with the slain. They are put to shame in the terror which they caused by their might. They lie uncircumcised with those who are slain by the sword, and bear their shame with those who go down to the pit. ³¹"Pharaoh will see them and will be comforted over all his multitude, even Pharaoh and all his army, slain by the sword," says the Lord Yahweh. ³²"For I have put his terror in the land of the living. He will be laid among the uncircumcised, with

---

ᵃ *31:15 Sheol is the place of the dead.*

ᵇ *31:16 Sheol is the place of the dead.*

ᶜ *32:21 Sheol is the place of the dead.*

those who are slain by the sword, even Pharaoh and all his multitude," says the Lord Yahweh.

## 33

¹ Yahweh's word came to me, saying, ²"Son of man, speak to the children of your people, and tell them, 'When I bring the sword on a land, and the people of the land take a man from among them, and set him for their watchman, ³ if, when he sees the sword come on the land, he blows the trumpet and warns the people, ⁴ then whoever hears the sound of the trumpet and doesn't heed the warning, if the sword comes and takes him away, his blood will be on his own head. ⁵ He heard the sound of the trumpet and didn't take warning. His blood will be on him; whereas if he had heeded the warning, he would have delivered his soul. ⁶ But if the watchman sees the sword come and doesn't blow the trumpet, and the people aren't warned, and the sword comes and takes any person from among them, he is taken away in his iniquity, but his blood I will require at the watchman's hand.' ⁷So you, son of man, I have set you a watchman to the house of Israel. Therefore hear the word from my mouth, and give them warnings from me. ⁸ When I tell the wicked, 'O wicked man, you will surely die,' and you don't speak to warn the wicked from his way, that wicked man will die in his iniquity, but I will require his blood at your hand. ⁹ Nevertheless, if you warn the wicked of his way to turn from it, and he doesn't turn from his way; he will die in his iniquity, but you have delivered your soul. ¹⁰"You, son of man, tell the house of Israel: 'You say this, "Our transgressions and our sins are on us, and we pine away in them. How then can we live?"' ¹¹ Tell them, "'As I live," says the Lord Yahweh, "I have no pleasure in the death of the wicked, but that the wicked turn from his way and live. Turn, turn from your evil ways! For why will you die, house of Israel?" ¹²"You, son of man, tell the children of your people, 'The righteousness of the righteous will not deliver him in the day of his disobedience. And as for the wickedness of the wicked, he will not fall by it in the day that he turns from his wickedness; neither will he who is righteous be able to live by it in the day that he sins. ¹³ When I tell the righteous that he will surely live, if he trusts in his righteousness and commits iniquity, none of his righteous deeds will be remembered; but he will die in his iniquity that he has committed. ¹⁴ Again, when I say to the wicked, "You will surely die," if he turns from his sin and does that which is lawful and right, ¹⁵ if the wicked restore the pledge, give again that which he had taken by robbery, walk in the statutes of life, committing no iniquity, he will surely live. He will not die. ¹⁶ None of his sins that he has committed will be remembered against him. He has done that which is lawful and right. He will surely live. ¹⁷"'Yet the children of your people say, "The way of the Lord is not fair;" but as for them, their way is not fair. ¹⁸ When the righteous turns from his righteousness and commits iniquity, he will even die therein. ¹⁹ When the wicked turns from his wickedness and does that which is lawful and right, he will live by it. ²⁰ Yet you say, "The way of the Lord is not fair." House of Israel, I will judge every one of you after his ways.'" ²¹ In the twelfth year of our captivity, in the tenth month, in the fifth day of the month, one who had escaped out of Jerusalem came to me, saying, "The city has been defeated!" ²² Now Yahweh's hand had been on me in the evening, before he who had escaped came; and he had opened my mouth until he came to me in the morning; and my mouth was opened, and I was no longer mute. ²³ Yahweh's word came to me, saying, ²⁴"Son of man, those who inhabit the waste places in the land of Israel speak, saying, 'Abraham was one, and he inherited the land; but we are many. The land is given us for inheritance.' ²⁵ Therefore tell them, 'The Lord Yahweh says: "You eat with the blood, and lift up your eyes to your idols, and shed blood. So should you possess the land? ²⁶ You stand on your sword, you work abomination, and every one of you defiles his neighbor's wife. So should you possess the land?"' ²⁷"You shall tell them, 'The Lord Yahweh says: "As I live, surely those who are in the waste places will fall by the sword. I will give whoever is in the open field to the animals to be devoured, and those who are in the strongholds and in the caves will die of the pestilence. ²⁸ I will make the land a desolation and an astonishment. The pride of her power will cease. The mountains of Israel will be desolate, so that no one will pass through. ²⁹ Then they will know that I am Yahweh, when I have made the land a desolation and an astonishment because of all their abominations which they have committed."' ³⁰"As for you, son of man, the children of your people talk about you by the walls and in the doors of the houses, and speak to one another, everyone to his brother, saying, 'Please come and hear what the word is that comes out from Yahweh.' ³¹ They come to you as the people come, and they sit before you as my people, and they hear your words, but don't do them; for with their mouth they show much love, but their heart goes after their gain. ³² Behold, you are to them as a very lovely song of one who has a pleasant voice, and can play well on an instrument; for they hear your words, but they don't do them. ³³"When this comes to pass—behold, it comes—then they will know that a prophet has been among them."

## 34

¹ Yahweh's word came to me, saying, ²"Son of man, prophesy against the shepherds of Israel. Prophesy, and tell them, even the shepherds, 'The Lord Yahweh says: "Woe to the shepherds of Israel who feed themselves! Shouldn't the shepherds feed the sheep? ³ You eat the fat. You clothe yourself with the wool. You kill the fatlings, but you don't feed the sheep. ⁴ You haven't strengthened the diseased. You haven't healed that which was sick. You haven't bound up that which was broken. You haven't brought back that which was driven away. You haven't sought that which was lost, but you have ruled over them with force and with rigor. ⁵ They were scattered, because there was no shepherd. They became food to all the animals of the field, and were scattered. ⁶ My sheep wandered through all the mountains and on every high hill. Yes, my sheep were scattered on all the surface of the earth. There was no one who searched or sought." ⁷"Therefore, you shepherds, hear Yahweh's word: ⁸"As I live," says the Lord Yahweh, "surely because my sheep became a prey, and my sheep became food to all the animals of the field, because there was no shepherd, and my shepherds didn't search for my sheep, but the shepherds fed themselves, and didn't feed my sheep, ⁹ therefore, you shepherds, hear Yahweh's word!" ¹⁰ The Lord Yahweh says: "Behold, I am against the shepherds. I will require my sheep at their hand, and cause them to cease from feeding the sheep. The shepherds won't feed themselves any more. I will deliver my sheep from their mouth, that they may not be food for them." ¹¹"For the Lord Yahweh says: "Behold, I myself, even I, will search for my sheep, and will seek them out. ¹² As a shepherd seeks out his flock in the day that he is among his sheep that are scattered abroad, so I will seek out my sheep. I will deliver them out of all places where they have been scattered in the cloudy and dark day. ¹³ I will bring them out from the peoples, and gather them from the countries, and will bring them into their own land. I will feed them on the mountains of Israel, by the watercourses, and in all the inhabited places of the country. ¹⁴ I will feed them with good pasture, and their fold will be on the mountains of the height of Israel. There they will lie down in a good fold. They will feed on rich pasture on the mountains of Israel. ¹⁵ I myself will be the shepherd of my sheep, and I will cause them to lie down," says the Lord Yahweh. ¹⁶"I will seek that which was lost, and will bring back that which was driven away, and will bind up that which was broken, and will strengthen that which was sick; but I will destroy the fat and the strong. I will feed them in justice.'" ¹⁷"As for you, O my flock, the Lord Yahweh says: 'Behold, I judge between sheep and sheep, the rams and the male goats. ¹⁸ Does it seem a small thing to you to have fed on the good pasture, but you must tread down with your feet the residue of your pasture? And to have drunk of the clear waters, but must you foul the residue with your feet? ¹⁹ As for my sheep, they eat that which you have trodden with your feet, and they drink that which you have fouled with your feet.' ²⁰"Therefore the Lord Yahweh says to them: 'Behold, I, even I, will judge between the fat sheep and the lean sheep. ²¹ Because you thrust with side and with shoulder, and push all the diseased with your horns, until you have scattered them abroad, ²² therefore I will save my flock, and they will no more be a prey. I will judge between sheep and sheep. ²³ I will set up one shepherd over them, and he will feed them, even my servant David. He will feed them, and he will be their shepherd. ²⁴ I, Yahweh, will be their God, and my servant David prince among them. I, Yahweh, have spoken it. ²⁵"'I will make with them a covenant of peace, and will cause evil animals to cease out of the land. They will dwell securely in the wilderness and sleep in the woods. ²⁶ I will make them and the places around my hill a blessing. I will cause the shower to come down in its season. There will be showers of blessing. ²⁷ The tree of the field will yield its fruit, and the earth will yield its increase, and they will be secure in their land. Then they will know that I am Yahweh, when I have broken the bars of their yoke, and have delivered them out of the hand of those who made slaves of them. ²⁸ They will no more be a prey to the nations, neither will the animals of the earth devour them; but they will dwell securely, and no one will make them afraid. ²⁹ I will raise up to them a plantation for renown, and they will no more be consumed with famine in the land, and not bear the shame of the nations any more. ³⁰ They will know that I, Yahweh, their God am with them, and that they, the house of Israel, are my people, says the Lord Yahweh. ³¹ You my sheep, the sheep of my pasture, are men, and I am your God,' says the Lord Yahweh."

## 35

¹ Moreover Yahweh's word came to me, saying, ²"Son of man, set your face against Mount Seir, and prophesy against it, ³ and tell it, 'The Lord Yahweh says: "Behold, I am against you, Mount Seir, and I will stretch out my hand against you. I will make you a desolation and an astonishment. ⁴ I will lay your cities waste, and you will be desolate. Then you will know that I am Yahweh. ⁵"'"Because you have had a perpetual hostility, and have given over the children of Israel to the

power of the sword in the time of their calamity, in the time of the iniquity of the end, [6] therefore, as I live," says the Lord Yahweh, "I will prepare you for blood, and blood will pursue you. Since you have not hated blood, therefore blood will pursue you. [7] Thus I will make Mount Seir an astonishment and a desolation. I will cut off from it him who passes through and him who returns. [8] I will fill its mountains with its slain. The slain with the sword will fall in your hills and in your valleys and in all your watercourses. [9] I will make you a perpetual desolation, and your cities will not be inhabited. Then you will know that I am Yahweh. [10]"Because you have said, 'These two nations and these two countries will be mine, and we will possess it,' although Yahweh was there, [11] therefore, as I live," says the Lord Yahweh, "I will do according to your anger, and according to your envy which you have shown out of your hatred against them; and I will make myself known among them when I judge you. [12] You will know that I, Yahweh, have heard all your insults which you have spoken against the mountains of Israel, saying, 'They have been laid desolate. They have been given to us to devour.' [13] You have magnified yourselves against me with your mouth, and have multiplied your words against me. I have heard it." [14] The Lord Yahweh says: "When the whole earth rejoices, I will make you desolate. [15] As you rejoiced over the inheritance of the house of Israel because it was desolate, so I will do to you. You will be desolate, Mount Seir, and all Edom, even all of it. Then they will know that I am Yahweh.'"

## 36

[1] You, son of man, prophesy to the mountains of Israel, and say, "You mountains of Israel, hear Yahweh's word. [2] The Lord Yahweh says: 'Because the enemy has said against you, "Aha!" and, "The ancient high places are ours in possession!"' [3] therefore prophesy, and say, 'The Lord Yahweh says: "Because, even because they have made you desolate, and swallowed you up on every side, that you might be a possession to the residue of the nations, and you are taken up in the lips of talkers, and the evil report of the people;" [4] therefore, you mountains of Israel, hear the word of the Lord Yahweh: The Lord Yahweh says to the mountains and to the hills, to the watercourses and to the valleys, to the desolate wastes and to the cities that are forsaken, which have become a prey and derision to the residue of the nations that are all around; [5] therefore the Lord Yahweh says: "Surely in the fire of my jealousy I have spoken against the residue of the nations, and against all Edom, that have appointed my land to themselves for a possession with the joy of all their heart, with despite of soul, to cast it out for a prey."' [6] Therefore prophesy concerning the land of Israel, and tell the mountains, the hills, the watercourses and the valleys, 'The Lord Yahweh says: "Behold, I have spoken in my jealousy and in my wrath, because you have borne the shame of the nations." [7] Therefore the Lord Yahweh says: "I have sworn, 'Surely the nations that are around you will bear their shame.' [8]"But you, mountains of Israel, you shall shoot out your branches and yield your fruit to my people Israel; for they are at hand to come. [9] For, behold, I am for you, and I will come to you, and you will be tilled and sown. [10] I will multiply men on you, all the house of Israel, even all of it. The cities will be inhabited and the waste places will be built. [11] I will multiply man and animal on you. They will increase and be fruitful. I will cause you to be inhabited as you were before, and you will do better than at your beginnings. Then you will know that I am Yahweh. [12] Yes, I will cause men to walk on you, even my people Israel. They will possess you, and you will be their inheritance, and you will never again bereave them of their children." [13]"The Lord Yahweh says: "Because they say to you, 'You are a devourer of men, and have been a bereaver of your nation;' [14] therefore you shall devour men no more, and not bereave your nation any more," says the Lord Yahweh. [15]"I won't let you hear the shame of the nations any more. You won't bear the reproach of the peoples any more, and you won't cause your nation to stumble any more," says the Lord Yahweh.'" [16] Moreover Yahweh's word came to me, saying, [17]"Son of man, when the house of Israel lived in their own land, they defiled it by their ways and by their deeds. Their way before me was as the uncleanness of a woman in her impurity. [18] Therefore I poured out my wrath on them for the blood which they had poured out on the land, and because they had defiled it with their idols. [19] I scattered them among the nations, and they were dispersed through the countries. I judged them according to their way and according to their deeds. [20] When they came to the nations where they went, they profaned my holy name, in that men said of them, 'These are Yahweh's people, and have left his land.' [21] But I had respect for my holy name, which the house of Israel had profaned among the nations where they went. [22]"Therefore tell the house of Israel, 'The Lord Yahweh says: "I don't do this for your sake, house of Israel, but for my holy name, which you have profaned among the nations where you went. [23] I will sanctify my great name, which has been profaned among the nations, which you have profaned among them. Then the nations will know that I am Yahweh," says the Lord

Yahweh, "when I am proven holy in you before their eyes. [24]"For I will take you from among the nations and gather you out of all the countries, and will bring you into your own land. [25] I will sprinkle clean water on you, and you will be clean. I will cleanse you from all your filthiness and from all your idols. [26] I will also give you a new heart, and I will put a new spirit within you. I will take away the stony heart out of your flesh, and I will give you a heart of flesh. [27] I will put my Spirit within you, and cause you to walk in my statutes. You will keep my ordinances and do them. [28] You will dwell in the land that I gave to your fathers. You will be my people, and I will be your God. [29] I will save you from all your uncleanness. I will call for the grain and will multiply it, and lay no famine on you. [30] I will multiply the fruit of the tree and the increase of the field, that you may receive no more the reproach of famine among the nations. [31]"Then you will remember your evil ways, and your deeds that were not good; and you will loathe yourselves in your own sight for your iniquities and for your abominations. [32] I don't do this for your sake," says the Lord Yahweh. "Let it be known to you. Be ashamed and confounded for your ways, house of Israel." [33]"The Lord Yahweh says: "In the day that I cleanse you from all your iniquities, I will cause the cities to be inhabited and the waste places will be built. [34] The land that was desolate will be tilled instead of being a desolation in the sight of all who passed by. [35] They will say, 'This land that was desolate has become like the garden of Eden. The waste, desolate, and ruined cities are fortified and inhabited.' [36] Then the nations that are left around you will know that I, Yahweh, have built the ruined places and planted that which was desolate. I, Yahweh, have spoken it, and I will do it." [37]"The Lord Yahweh says: "For this, moreover, I will be inquired of by the house of Israel, to do it for them: I will increase them with men like a flock. [38] As the flock for sacrifice, as the flock of Jerusalem in her appointed feasts, so the waste cities will be filled with flocks of men. Then they will know that I am Yahweh.'"

## 37

[1] Yahweh's hand was on me, and he brought me out in Yahweh's Spirit, and set me down in the middle of the valley; and it was full of bones. [2] He caused me to pass by them all around; and behold, there were very many in the open valley, and behold, they were very dry. [3] He said to me, "Son of man, can these bones live?" I answered, "Lord Yahweh, you know." [4] Again he said to me, "Prophesy over these bones, and tell them, 'You dry bones, hear Yahweh's word. [5] The Lord Yahweh says to these bones: "Behold, I will cause breath to enter into you, and you will live. [6] I will lay sinews on you, and will bring up flesh on you, and cover you with skin, and put breath in you, and you will live. Then you will know that I am Yahweh."'" [7] So I prophesied as I was commanded. As I prophesied, there was a noise, and behold, there was an earthquake. Then the bones came together, bone to its bone. [8] I saw, and, behold, there were sinews on them, and flesh came up, and skin covered them above; but there was no breath in them. [9] Then he said to me, "Prophesy to the wind, prophesy, son of man, and tell the wind, 'The Lord Yahweh says: "Come from the four winds, breath, and breathe on these slain, that they may live."'" [10] So I prophesied as he commanded me, and the breath came into them, and they lived, and stood up on their feet, an exceedingly great army. [11] Then he said to me, "Son of man, these bones are the whole house of Israel. Behold, they say, 'Our bones are dried up, and our hope is lost. We are completely cut off.' [12] Therefore prophesy, and tell them, 'The Lord Yahweh says: "Behold, I will open your graves, and cause you to come up out of your graves, my people; and I will bring you into the land of Israel. [13] You will know that I am Yahweh, when I have opened your graves and caused you to come up out of your graves, my people. [14] I will put my Spirit in you, and you will live. Then I will place you in your own land; and you will know that I, Yahweh, have spoken it and performed it," says Yahweh.'" [15] Yahweh's word came again to me, saying, [16]"You, son of man, take one stick and write on it, 'For Judah, and for the children of Israel his companions.' Then take another stick, and write on it, 'For Joseph, the stick of Ephraim, and for all the house of Israel his companions.' [17] Then join them for yourself to one another into one stick, that they may become one in your hand. [18]"When the children of your people speak to you, saying, 'Won't you show us what you mean by these?' [19] tell them, 'The Lord Yahweh says: "Behold, I will take the stick of Joseph, which is in the hand of Ephraim, and the tribes of Israel his companions; and I will put them with it, with the stick of Judah, and make them one stick, and they will be one in my hand. [20] The sticks on which you write will be in your hand before their eyes." [21] Say to them, 'The Lord Yahweh says: "Behold, I will take the children of Israel from among the nations where they have gone, and will gather them on every side, and bring them into their own land. [22] I will make them one nation in the land, on the mountains of Israel. One king will be king to them all. They will no longer be two nations. They won't be divided into two kingdoms any more at all. [23] They

won't defile themselves any more with their idols, nor with their detestable things, nor with any of their transgressions; but I will save them out of all their dwelling places in which they have sinned, and will cleanse them. So they will be my people, and I will be their God. [24]"My servant David will be king over them. They all will have one shepherd. They will also walk in my ordinances and observe my statutes, and do them. [25] They will dwell in the land that I have given to Jacob my servant, in which your fathers lived. They will dwell therein, they, and their children, and their children's children, forever. David my servant will be their prince forever. [26] Moreover I will make a covenant of peace with them. It will be an everlasting covenant with them. I will place them, multiply them, and will set my sanctuary among them forever more. [27] My tent also will be with them. I will be their God, and they will be my people. [28] The nations will know that I am Yahweh who sanctifies Israel, when my sanctuary is among them forever more.""

## 38

[1] Yahweh's word came to me, saying, [2]"Son of man, set your face toward Gog, of the land of Magog, the prince of Rosh, Meshech, and Tubal, and prophesy against him, [3] and say, 'The Lord Yahweh says: "Behold, I am against you, Gog, prince of Rosh, Meshech, and Tubal. [4] I will turn you around, and put hooks into your jaws, and I will bring you out, with all your army, horses and horsemen, all of them clothed in full armor, a great company with buckler and shield, all of them handling swords; [5] Persia, Cush, and Put with them, all of them with shield and helmet; [6] Gomer, and all his hordes; the house of Togarmah in the uttermost parts of the north, and all his hordes—even many peoples with you. [7]"Be prepared, yes, prepare yourself, you, and all your companies who are assembled to you, and be a guard to them. [8] After many days you will be visited. In the latter years you will come into the land that is brought back from the sword, that is gathered out of many peoples, on the mountains of Israel, which have been a continual waste; but it is brought out of the peoples and they will dwell securely, all of them. [9] You will ascend. You will come like a storm. You will be like a cloud to cover the land, you and all your hordes, and many peoples with you." [10]"The Lord Yahweh says: "It will happen in that day that things will come into your mind, and you will devise an evil plan. [11] You will say, 'I will go up to the land of unwalled villages. I will go to those who are at rest, who dwell securely, all of them dwelling without walls, and having neither bars nor gates, [12] to take the plunder and to take prey; to turn your hand against the waste places that are inhabited, and against the people who are gathered out of the nations, who have gotten livestock and goods, who dwell in the middle of the earth.' [13] Sheba, Dedan, and the merchants of Tarshish, with all its young lions, will ask you, 'Have you come to take the plunder? Have you assembled your company to take the prey, to carry away silver and gold, to take away livestock and goods, to take great plunder?'" [14]"Therefore, son of man, prophesy, and tell Gog, 'The Lord Yahweh says: "In that day when my people Israel dwells securely, will you not know it? [15] You will come from your place out of the uttermost parts of the north, you, and many peoples with you, all of them riding on horses, a great company and a mighty army. [16] You will come up against my people Israel as a cloud to cover the land. It will happen in the latter days that I will bring you against my land, that the nations may know me when I am sanctified in you, Gog, before their eyes." [17]"The Lord Yahweh says: "Are you he of whom I spoke in old time by my servants the prophets of Israel, who prophesied in those days for years that I would bring you against them? [18] It will happen in that day, when Gog comes against the land of Israel," says the Lord Yahweh, "that my wrath will come up into my nostrils. [19] For in my jealousy and in the fire of my wrath I have spoken. Surely in that day there will be a great shaking in the land of Israel, [20] so that the fish of the sea, the birds of the sky, the animals of the field, all creeping things who creep on the earth, and all the men who are on the surface of the earth will shake at my presence. Then the mountains will be thrown down, the steep places will fall, and every wall will fall to the ground. [21] I will call for a sword against him to all my mountains," says the Lord Yahweh. "Every man's sword will be against his brother. [22] I will enter into judgment with him with pestilence and with blood. I will rain on him, on his hordes, and on the many peoples who are with him, torrential rains with great hailstones, fire, and sulfur. [23] I will magnify myself and sanctify myself, and I will make myself known in the eyes of many nations. Then they will know that I am Yahweh.'"

## 39

[1]"You, son of man, prophesy against Gog, and say, 'The Lord Yahweh says: "Behold, I am against you, Gog, prince of Rosh, Meshech, and Tubal. [2] I will turn you around, will lead you on, and will cause you to come up from the uttermost parts of the north; and I will bring you onto the mountains of Israel. [3] I will strike your bow out of your left hand, and will cause your arrows to fall out of your right hand. [4] You will fall on the mountains of Israel, you, and all your hordes, and the peoples who are with you. I will give you to the ravenous birds of every sort and to the animals of the field to be devoured. [5] You will fall on the open field, for I have spoken it," says the Lord Yahweh. [6]"I will send a fire on Magog and on those who dwell securely in the islands. Then they will know that I am Yahweh. [7]"I will make my holy name known among my people Israel. I won't allow my holy name to be profaned any more. Then the nations will know that I am Yahweh, the Holy One in Israel. [8] Behold, it comes, and it will be done," says the Lord Yahweh. "This is the day about which I have spoken. [9]"Those who dwell in the cities of Israel will go out and will make fires of the weapons and burn them, both the shields and the bucklers, the bows and the arrows, and the war clubs and the spears, and they will make fires with them for seven years; [10] so that they will take no wood out of the field, and not cut down any out of the forests; for they will make fires with the weapons. They will plunder those who plundered them, and rob those who robbed them," says the Lord Yahweh. [11]"It will happen in that day, that I will give to Gog a place for burial in Israel, the valley of those who pass through on the east of the sea; and it will stop those who pass through. They will bury Gog and all his multitude there, and they will call it 'The valley of Hamon Gog'. [12]"The house of Israel will be burying them for seven months, that they may cleanse the land. [13] Yes, all the people of the land will bury them; and they will become famous in the day that I will be glorified," says the Lord Yahweh. [14]"They will set apart men of continual employment who will pass through the land. Those who pass through will go with those who bury those who remain on the surface of the land, to cleanse it. After the end of seven months they will search. [15] Those who search through the land will pass through; and when anyone sees a man's bone, then he will set up a sign by it, until the undertakers have buried it in the valley of Hamon Gog. [16] Hamonah will also be the name of a city. Thus will they cleanse the land.'" [17]"You, son of man, the Lord Yahweh says: 'Speak to the birds of every sort, and to every animal of the field, "Assemble yourselves, and come; gather yourselves on every side to my sacrifice that I sacrifice for you, even a great sacrifice on the mountains of Israel, that you may eat meat and drink blood. [18] You shall eat the flesh of the mighty, and drink the blood of the princes of the earth, of rams, of lambs, and of goats, of bulls, all of them fatlings of Bashan. [19] You shall eat fat until you are full, and drink blood until you are drunk, of my sacrifice which I have sacrificed for you. [20] You shall be filled at my table with horses and charioteers, with mighty men, and with all men of war," says the Lord Yahweh.' [21]"I will set my glory among the nations. Then all the nations will see my judgment that I have executed, and my hand that I have laid on them. [22] So the house of Israel will know that I am Yahweh their God, from that day and forward. [23] The nations will know that the house of Israel went into captivity for their iniquity, because they trespassed against me, and I hid my face from them; so I gave them into the hand of their adversaries, and they all fell by the sword. [24] I did to them according to their uncleanness and according to their transgressions. I hid my face from them. [25]"Therefore the Lord Yahweh says: 'Now I will reverse the captivity of Jacob and have mercy on the whole house of Israel. I will be jealous for my holy name. [26] They will forget their shame and all their trespasses by which they have trespassed against me, when they dwell securely in their land. No one will make them afraid [27] when I have brought them back from the peoples, gathered them out of their enemies' lands, and am shown holy among them in the sight of many nations. [28] They will know that I am Yahweh their God, in that I caused them to go into captivity among the nations, and have gathered them to their own land. Then I will leave none of them captive any more. [29] I won't hide my face from them any more, for I have poured out my Spirit on the house of Israel,' says the Lord Yahweh."

## 40

[1] In the twenty-fifth year of our captivity, in the beginning of the year, in the tenth day of the month, in the fourteenth year after the city was struck, in the same day, Yahweh's hand was on me, and he brought me there. [2] In the visions of God he brought me into the land of Israel, and set me down on a very high mountain, on which was something like the frame of a city to the south. [3] He brought me there; and, behold, there was a man whose appearance was like the appearance of bronze, with a line of flax in his hand and a measuring reed; and he stood in the gate. [4] The man said to me, "Son of man, see with your eyes, and hear with your ears, and set your heart on all that I will show you; for you have been brought here so that I may show them to you. Declare all that you see to the house of Israel." [5] Behold, there was a wall on the outside of

the house all around, and in the man's hand a measuring reed six cubits[a] long, of a cubit and a hand width each. So he measured the thickness of the building, one reed; and the height, one reed. **6** Then he came to the gate which looks toward the east, and went up its steps. He measured the threshold of the gate, one reed wide; and the other threshold, one reed wide. **7** Every lodge was one reed long and one reed wide. Between the lodges was five cubits. The threshold of the gate by the porch of the gate toward the house was one reed. **8** He measured also the porch of the gate toward the house, one reed. **9** Then he measured the porch of the gate, eight cubits; and its posts, two cubits; and the porch of the gate was toward the house. **10** The side rooms of the gate eastward were three on this side, and three on that side. The three of them were of one measure. The posts had one measure on this side and on that side. **11** He measured the width of the opening of the gate, ten cubits; and the length of the gate, thirteen cubits; **12** and a border before the lodges, one cubit on this side, and a border, one cubit on that side; and the side rooms, six cubits on this side, and six cubits on that side. **13** He measured the gate from the roof of the one side room to the roof of the other, a width of twenty-five cubits, door against door. **14** He also made posts, sixty cubits; and the court reached to the posts, around the gate. **15** From the forefront of the gate at the entrance to the forefront of the inner porch of the gate were fifty cubits. **16** There were closed windows to the side rooms, and to their posts within the gate all around, and likewise to the arches. Windows were around inward. Palm trees were on each post. **17** Then he brought me into the outer court. Behold, there were rooms and a pavement made for the court all around. Thirty rooms were on the pavement. **18** The pavement was by the side of the gates, corresponding to the length of the gates, even the lower pavement. **19** Then he measured the width from the forefront of the lower gate to the forefront of the inner court outside, one hundred cubits, both on the east and on the north. **20** He measured the length and width of the gate of the outer court which faces toward the north. **21** The lodges of it were three on this side and three on that side. Its posts and its arches were the same as the measure of the first gate: its length was fifty cubits, and the width twenty-five cubits. **22** Its windows, its arches, and its palm trees were the same as the measure of the gate which faces toward the east. They went up to it by seven steps. Its arches were before them. **23** There was a gate to the inner court facing the other gate, on the north and on the east. He measured one hundred cubits from gate to gate. **24** He led me toward the south; and behold, there was a gate toward the south. He measured its posts and its arches according to these measurements. **25** There were windows in it and in its arches all around, like the other windows: the length was fifty cubits, and the width twenty-five cubits. **26** There were seven steps to go up to it, and its arches were before them. It had palm trees, one on this side, and another on that side, on its posts. **27** There was a gate to the inner court toward the south. He measured one hundred cubits from gate to gate toward the south. **28** Then he brought me to the inner court by the south gate. He measured the south gate according to these measurements; **29** with its lodges, its posts, and its arches, according to these measurements. There were windows in it and in its arches all around. It was fifty cubits long, and twenty-five cubits wide. **30** There were arches all around, twenty-five cubits long and five cubits wide. **31** Its arches were toward the outer court. Palm trees were on its posts. The ascent to it had eight steps. **32** He brought me into the inner court toward the east. He measured the gate according to these measurements; **33** with its lodges, its posts, and its arches, according to these measurements. There were windows in it and in its arches all around. It was fifty cubits long, and twenty-five cubits wide. **34** Its arches were toward the outer court. Palm trees were on its posts on this side and on that side. The ascent to it had eight steps. **35** He brought me to the north gate, and he measured it according to these measurements— **36** its lodges, its posts, and its arches. There were windows in it all around. The length was fifty cubits and the width twenty-five cubits. **37** Its posts were toward the outer court. Palm trees were on its posts on this side and on that side. The ascent to it had eight steps. **38** A room with its door was by the posts at the gates. They washed the burnt offering there. **39** In the porch of the gate were two tables on this side and two tables on that side, on which to kill the burnt offering, the sin offering, and the trespass offering. **40** On the one side outside, as one goes up to the entry of the gate toward the north, were two tables; and on the other side, which belonged to the porch of the gate, were two tables. **41** Four tables were on this side, and four tables on that side, by the side of the gate: eight tables, on which they killed the sacrifices. **42** There were four cut stone tables for the burnt offering, a cubit and a half long, a cubit and a half wide, and one cubit high. They

laid the instruments with which they killed the burnt offering and the sacrifice on them. **43** The hooks, a hand width long, were fastened within all around. The meat of the offering was on the tables. **44** Outside of the inner gate were rooms for the singers in the inner court, which was at the side of the north gate. They faced toward the south. One at the side of the east gate faced toward the north. **45** He said to me, "This room, which faces toward the south, is for the priests who perform the duty of the house. **46** The room which faces toward the north is for the priests who perform the duty of the altar. These are the sons of Zadok, who from among the sons of Levi come near to Yahweh to minister to him." **47** He measured the court, one hundred cubits long and one hundred cubits wide, square. The altar was before the house. **48** Then he brought me to the porch of the house, and measured each post of the porch, five cubits on this side, and five cubits on that side. The width of the gate was three cubits on this side and three cubits on that side. **49** The length of the porch was twenty cubits and the width eleven cubits, even by the steps by which they went up to it. There were pillars by the posts, one on this side, and another on that side.

# 41

**1** He brought me to the nave and measured the posts, six cubits wide on the one side and six cubits wide on the other side, which was the width of the tent. **2** The width of the entrance was ten cubits,[b] and the sides of the entrance were five cubits on the one side, and five cubits on the other side. He measured its length, forty cubits, and the width, twenty cubits. **3** Then he went inward and measured each post of the entrance, two cubits; and the entrance, six cubits; and the width of the entrance, seven cubits. **4** He measured its length, twenty cubits, and the width, twenty cubits, before the nave. He said to me, "This is the most holy place." **5** Then he measured the wall of the house, six cubits; and the width of every side room, four cubits, all around the house on every side. **6** The side rooms were in three stories, one over another, and thirty in each story. They entered into the wall which belonged to the house for the side rooms all around, that they might be supported and not penetrate the wall of the house. **7** The side rooms were wider as they encircled the house higher and higher; for the encircling of the house went higher and higher around the house. Therefore the width of the house increased upward; and so one went up from the lowest level to the highest through the middle level. **8** I saw also that the house had a raised base all around. The foundations of the side rooms were a full reed of six great cubits. **9** The thickness of the outer wall of the side rooms was five cubits. That which was left was the place of the side rooms that belonged to the house. **10** Between the rooms was a width of twenty cubits around the house on every side. **11** The doors of the side rooms were toward an open area that was left, one door toward the north, and another door toward the south. The width of the open area was five cubits all around. **12** The building that was before the separate place at the side toward the west was seventy cubits wide; and the wall of the building was five cubits thick all around, and its length ninety cubits. **13** So he measured the temple, one hundred cubits long; and the separate place, and the building, with its walls, one hundred cubits long; **14** also the width of the face of the temple, and of the separate place toward the east, one hundred cubits. **15** He measured the length of the building before the separate place which was at its back, and its galleries on the one side and on the other side, one hundred cubits from the inner temple, and the porches of the court, **16** the thresholds, and the closed windows, and the galleries around on their three stories, opposite the threshold, with wood ceilings all around, and from the ground up to the windows, (now the windows were covered), **17** to the space above the door, even to the inner house, and outside, and by all the wall all around inside and outside, by measure. **18** It was made with cherubim and palm trees. A palm tree was between cherub and cherub, and every cherub had two faces, **19** so that there was the face of a man toward the palm tree on the one side, and the face of a young lion toward the palm tree on the other side. It was made like this through all the house all around. **20** Cherubim and palm trees were made from the ground to above the door. The wall of the temple was like this. **21** The door posts of the nave were squared. As for the face of the nave, its appearance was as the appearance of the temple. **22** The altar was of wood, three cubits high, and its length two cubits. Its corners, its base, and its walls were of wood. He said to me, "This is the table that is before Yahweh." **23** The temple and the sanctuary had two doors. **24** The doors had two leaves each, two turning leaves: two for the one door, and two leaves for the other. **25** There were made on them, on the doors of the nave, cherubim and palm trees, like those made on the walls. There was a threshold of wood on the face of the porch outside. **26** There

---

were closed windows and palm trees on the one side and on the other side, on the sides of the porch. This is how the side rooms of the temple and the thresholds were arranged.

## 42

¹ Then he brought me out into the outer court, the way toward the north. Then he brought me into the room that was opposite the separate place, and which was opposite the building toward the north. ² Facing the length of one hundred cubitsᵃ was the north door, and the width was fifty cubits. ³ Opposite the twenty cubits which belonged to the inner court, and opposite the pavement which belonged to the outer court, was gallery against gallery in the three stories. ⁴ Before the rooms was a walk of ten cubits' width inward, a way of one cubit; and their doors were toward the north. ⁵ Now the upper rooms were shorter; for the galleries took away from these more than from the lower and the middle in the building. ⁶ For they were in three stories, and they didn't have pillars as the pillars of the courts. Therefore the uppermost was set back more than the lowest and the middle from the ground. ⁷ The wall that was outside by the side of the rooms, toward the outer court before the rooms, was fifty cubits long. ⁸ For the length of the rooms that were in the outer court was fifty cubits. Behold, those facing the temple were one hundred cubits. ⁹ From under these rooms was the entry on the east side, as one goes into them from the outer court. ¹⁰ In the thickness of the wall of the court toward the east, before the separate place, and before the building, there were rooms. ¹¹ The way before them was like the appearance of the rooms which were toward the north. Their length and width were the same. All their exits had the same arrangement and doors. ¹² Like the doors of the rooms that were toward the south was a door at the head of the way, even the way directly before the wall toward the east, as one enters into them. ¹³ Then he said to me, "The north rooms and the south rooms, which are opposite the separate place, are the holy rooms, where the priests who are near to Yahweh shall eat the most holy things. There they shall lay the most holy things, with the meal offering, the sin offering, and the trespass offering; for the place is holy. ¹⁴ When the priests enter in, then they shall not go out of the holy place into the outer court until they lay their garments in which they minister there; for they are holy. Then they shall put on other garments, and shall approach that which is for the people." ¹⁵ Now when he had finished measuring the inner house, he brought me out by the way of the gate which faces toward the east, and measured it all around. ¹⁶ He measured on the east side with the measuring reed five hundred reeds, with the measuring reed all around. ¹⁷ He measured on the north side five hundred reeds with the measuring reed all around. ¹⁸ He measured on the south side five hundred reeds with the measuring reed. ¹⁹ He turned about to the west side, and measured five hundred reeds with the measuring reed. ²⁰ He measured it on the four sides. It had a wall around it, the length five hundred cubits, and the width five hundred cubits, to make a separation between that which was holy and that which was common.

## 43

¹ Afterward he brought me to the gate, even the gate that looks toward the east. ² Behold, the glory of the God of Israel came from the way of the east. His voice was like the sound of many waters; and the earth was illuminated with his glory. ³ It was like the appearance of the vision which I saw, even according to the vision that I saw when I came to destroy the city; and the visions were like the vision that I saw by the river Chebar; and I fell on my face. ⁴ Yahweh's glory came into the house by the way of the gate which faces toward the east. ⁵ The Spirit took me up and brought me into the inner court; and behold, Yahweh's glory filled the house. ⁶ I heard one speaking to me out of the house, and a man stood by me. ⁷ He said to me, "Son of man, this is the place of my throne and the place of the soles of my feet, where I will dwell among the children of Israel forever. The house of Israel will no more defile my holy name, neither they nor their kings, by their prostitution and by the dead bodies of their kings in their high places; ⁸ in their setting of their threshold by my threshold and their door post beside my door post. There was a wall between me and them; and they have defiled my holy name by their abominations which they have committed. Therefore I have consumed them in my anger. ⁹ Now let them put away their prostitution, and the dead bodies of their kings far from me. Then I will dwell among them forever. ¹⁰"You, son of man, show the house to the house of Israel, that they may be ashamed of their iniquities; and let them measure the pattern. ¹¹ If they are ashamed of all that they have done, make known to them the form of the house, its fashion, its exits, its entrances, its structure, all its ordinances, all its

forms, and all its laws; and write it in their sight, that they may keep the whole form of it, and all its ordinances, and do them. ¹²"This is the law of the house. On the top of the mountain the whole limit around it shall be most holy. Behold, this is the law of the house. ¹³"These are the measurements of the altar by cubits (the cubitᵇ is a cubit and a hand width): the bottom shall be a cubit, and the width a cubit, and its border around its edge a span;ᶜ and this shall be the base of the altar. ¹⁴ From the bottom on the ground to the lower ledge shall be two cubits, and the width one cubit; and from the lesser ledge to the greater ledge shall be four cubits, and the width a cubit. ¹⁵ The upper altar shall be four cubits; and from the altar hearth and upward there shall be four horns. ¹⁶ The altar hearth shall be twelve cubits long by twelve wide, square in its four sides. ¹⁷ The ledge shall be fourteen cubits long by fourteen wide in its four sides; and the border about it shall be half a cubit; and its bottom shall be a cubit around; and its steps shall look toward the east." ¹⁸ He said to me, "Son of man, the Lord Yahweh says: 'These are the ordinances of the altar in the day when they make it, to offer burnt offerings on it, and to sprinkle blood on it. ¹⁹ You shall give to the Levitical priests who are of the offspring of Zadok, who are near to me, to minister to me,' says the Lord Yahweh, 'a young bull for a sin offering. ²⁰ You shall take of its blood and put it on its four horns, and on the four corners of the ledge, and on the border all around. You shall cleanse it and make atonement for it that way. ²¹ You shall also take the bull of the sin offering, and it shall be burned in the appointed place of the house, outside of the sanctuary. ²²"On the second day you shall offer a male goat without defect for a sin offering; and they shall cleanse the altar, as they cleansed it with the bull. ²³ When you have finished cleansing it, you shall offer a young bull without defect and a ram out of the flock without defect. ²⁴ You shall bring them near to Yahweh, and the priests shall cast salt on them, and they shall offer them up for a burnt offering to Yahweh. ²⁵"Seven days you shall prepare every day a goat for a sin offering. They shall also prepare a young bull and a ram out of the flock, without defect. ²⁶ Seven days shall they make atonement for the altar and purify it. So shall they consecrate it. ²⁷ When they have accomplished the days, it shall be that on the eighth day and onward, the priests shall make your burnt offerings on the altar and your peace offerings. Then I will accept you,' says the Lord Yahweh."

## 44

¹ Then he brought me back by the way of the outer gate of the sanctuary, which looks toward the east; and it was shut. ² Yahweh said to me, "This gate shall be shut. It shall not be opened, no man shall enter in by it; for Yahweh, the God of Israel, has entered in by it. Therefore it shall be shut. ³ As for the prince, he shall sit in it as prince to eat bread before Yahweh. He shall enter by the way of the porch of the gate, and shall go out the same way." ⁴ Then he brought me by the way of the north gate before the house; and I looked, and behold, Yahweh's glory filled Yahweh's house; so I fell on my face. ⁵ Yahweh said to me, "Son of man, mark well, and see with your eyes, and hear with your ears all that I tell you concerning all the ordinances of Yahweh's house and all its laws; and mark well the entrance of the house, with every exit of the sanctuary. ⁶ You shall tell the rebellious, even the house of Israel, 'The Lord Yahweh says: "You house of Israel, let that be enough of all your abominations, ⁷ in that you have brought in foreigners, uncircumcised in heart and uncircumcised in flesh, to be in my sanctuary, to profane it, even my house, when you offer my bread, the fat and the blood; and they have broken my covenant, to add to all your abominations. ⁸ You have not performed the duty of my holy things; but you have set performers of my duty in my sanctuary for yourselves." ⁹ The Lord Yahweh says, "No foreigner, uncircumcised in heart and uncircumcised in flesh, shall enter into my sanctuary, of any foreigners who are among the children of Israel. ¹⁰"""But the Levites who went far from me when Israel went astray, who went astray from me after their idols, they will bear their iniquity. ¹¹ Yet they shall be ministers in my sanctuary, having oversight at the gates of the house, and ministering in the house. They shall kill the burnt offering and the sacrifice for the people, and they shall stand before them to minister to them. ¹² Because they ministered to them before their idols, and became a stumbling block of iniquity to the house of Israel, therefore I have lifted up my hand against them," says the Lord Yahweh, "and they will bear their iniquity. ¹³ They shall not come near to me, to execute the office of priest to me, nor to come near to any of my holy things, to the things that are most holy; but they will bear their shame and their abominations which they have committed. ¹⁴ Yet I will make them performers of the duty of the house, for all its service and for all that

---

ᵃ *42:2* A cubit is the length from the tip of the middle finger to the elbow on a man's arm, or about 18 inches or 46 centimeters.

ᵇ *43:13* A normal cubit is the length from the tip of the middle finger to the elbow on a man's arm, or about 18 inches or 46 centimeters. A hand

width is about 4.3 inches or 11 cm.
ᶜ *43:13* A span is the length from the tip of a man's thumb to the tip of his little finger

when his hand is stretched out (about half a cubit, or 9 inches, or 22.8 cm.)

will be done therein. ¹⁵"""But the Levitical priests, the sons of Zadok, who performed the duty of my sanctuary when the children of Israel went astray from me, shall come near to me to minister to me. They shall stand before me to offer to me the fat and the blood," says the Lord Yahweh. ¹⁶"They shall enter into my sanctuary, and they shall come near to my table, to minister to me, and they shall keep my instruction. ¹⁷"""It will be that when they enter in at the gates of the inner court, they shall be clothed with linen garments. No wool shall come on them while they minister in the gates of the inner court, and within. ¹⁸ They shall have linen turbans on their heads, and shall have linen trousers on their waists. They shall not clothe themselves with anything that makes them sweat. ¹⁹ When they go out into the outer court, even into the outer court to the people, they shall put off their garments in which they minister and lay them in the holy rooms. They shall put on other garments, that they not sanctify the people with their garments. ²⁰"""They shall not shave their heads, or allow their locks to grow long. They shall only cut off the hair of their heads. ²¹ None of the priests shall drink wine when they enter into the inner court. ²² They shall not take for their wives a widow, or her who is put away; but they shall take virgins of the offspring of the house of Israel, or a widow who is the widow of a priest. ²³ They shall teach my people the difference between the holy and the common, and cause them to discern between the unclean and the clean. ²⁴"""In a controversy they shall stand to judge. They shall judge it according to my ordinances. They shall keep my laws and my statutes in all my appointed feasts. They shall make my Sabbaths holy. ²⁵"""They shall go in to no dead person to defile themselves; but for father, or for mother, or for son, or for daughter, for brother, or for sister who has had no husband, they may defile themselves. ²⁶ After he is cleansed, they shall reckon to him seven days. ²⁷ In the day that he goes into the sanctuary, into the inner court, to minister in the sanctuary, he shall offer his sin offering," says the Lord Yahweh. ²⁸"""They shall have an inheritance: I am their inheritance; and you shall give them no possession in Israel. I am their possession. ²⁹ They shall eat the meal offering, and the sin offering, and the trespass offering; and every devoted thing in Israel shall be theirs. ³⁰ The first of all the first fruits of every thing, and every offering of everything, of all your offerings, shall be for the priest. You shall also give to the priests the first of your dough, to cause a blessing to rest on your house. ³¹ The priests shall not eat of anything that dies of itself or is torn, whether it is bird or animal.

## 45

¹"""Moreover, when you divide by lot the land for inheritance, you shall offer an offering to Yahweh, a holy portion of the land. The length shall be the length of twenty-five thousand reeds, and the width shall be ten thousand. It shall be holy in all its border all around. ² Of this there shall be a five hundred by five hundred square for the holy place, and fifty cubitsᵃ for its pasture lands all around. ³ Of this measure you shall measure a length of twenty-five thousand, and a width of ten thousand. In it shall be the sanctuary, which is most holy. ⁴ It is a holy portion of the land; it shall be for the priests, the ministers of the sanctuary, who come near to minister to Yahweh. It shall be a place for their houses and a holy place for the sanctuary. ⁵ Twenty-five thousand cubits in length and ten thousand in width shall be for the Levites, the ministers of the house, as a possession for themselves, for twenty rooms. ⁶"""You shall appoint the possession of the city five thousand cubits wide and twenty-five thousand long, side by side with the offering of the holy portion. It shall be for the whole house of Israel. ⁷"""What is for the prince shall be on the one side and on the other side of the holy allotment and of the possession of the city, in front of the holy allotment and in front of the possession of the city, on the west side westward, and on the east side eastward, and in length corresponding to one of the portions, from the west border to the east border. ⁸ In the land it shall be to him for a possession in Israel. My princes shall no more oppress my people, but they shall give the land to the house of Israel according to their tribes." ⁹"The Lord Yahweh says: "Enough you, princes of Israel! Remove violence and plunder, and execute justice and righteousness! Stop dispossessing my people!" says the Lord Yahweh. ¹⁰"You shall have just balances, a just ephah,ᵇ and a just bath. ¹¹ The ephah and the bath shall be of one measure, that the bath may contain one tenth of a homer,ᶜ and the ephah one tenth of a homer. Its measure shall be the same as the homer. ¹² The shekelᵈ shall be twenty gerahs.ᵉ

Twenty shekels plus twenty-five shekels plus fifteen shekels shall be your mina.ᶠ ¹³"""This is the offering that you shall offer: the sixth part of an ephah from a homer of wheat, and you shall give the sixth part of an ephah from a homer of barley, ¹⁴ and the set portion of oil, of the bath of oil, one tenth of a bath out of the cor, which is ten baths, even a homer (for ten baths are a homer),ᵍ ¹⁵ and one lamb of the flock out of two hundred, from the well-watered pastures of Israel—for a meal offering, for a burnt offering, and for peace offerings, to make atonement for them," says the Lord Yahweh. ¹⁶"All the people of the land shall give to this offering for the prince in Israel. ¹⁷ It shall be the prince's part to give the burnt offerings, the meal offerings, and the drink offerings, in the feasts, and on the new moons, and on the Sabbaths, in all the appointed feasts of the house of Israel. He shall prepare the sin offering, the meal offering, the burnt offering, and the peace offerings, to make atonement for the house of Israel." ¹⁸"""The Lord Yahweh says: "In the first month, on the first day of the month, you shall take a young bull without defect, and you shall cleanse the sanctuary. ¹⁹ The priest shall take of the blood of the sin offering and put it on the door posts of the house, and on the four corners of the ledge of the altar, and on the posts of the gate of the inner court. ²⁰ So you shall do on the seventh day of the month for everyone who errs, and for him who is simple. So you shall make atonement for the house. ²¹"""In the first month, on the fourteenth day of the month, you shall have the Passover, a feast of seven days; unleavened bread shall be eaten. ²² On that day the prince shall prepare for himself and for all the people of the land a bull for a sin offering. ²³ The seven days of the feast he shall prepare a burnt offering to Yahweh, seven bulls and seven rams without defect daily the seven days; and a male goat daily for a sin offering. ²⁴ He shall prepare a meal offering, an ephahʰ for a bull, an ephah for a ram, and a hinⁱ of oil to an ephah. ²⁵"""In the seventh month, on the fifteenth day of the month, during the feast, he shall do like that for seven days. He shall make the same provision for sin offering, the burnt offering, the meal offering, and the oil."

## 46

¹"""The Lord Yahweh says: "The gate of the inner court that looks toward the east shall be shut the six working days; but on the Sabbath day it shall be opened, and on the day of the new moon it shall be opened. ² The prince shall enter by the way of the porch of the gate outside, and shall stand by the post of the gate; and the priests shall prepare his burnt offering and his peace offerings, and he shall worship at the threshold of the gate. Then he shall go out, but the gate shall not be shut until the evening. ³ The people of the land shall worship at the door of that gate before Yahweh on the Sabbaths and on the new moons. ⁴ The burnt offering that the prince shall offer to Yahweh shall be on the Sabbath day, six lambs without defect and a ram without defect; ⁵ and the meal offering shall be an ephah for the ram, and the meal offering for the lambs as he is able to give, and a hinʲ of oil to an ephah.ᵏ ⁶ On the day of the new moon it shall be a young bull without defect, six lambs, and a ram. They shall be without defect. ⁷ He shall prepare a meal offering: an ephah for the bull, and an ephah for the ram, and for the lambs according as he is able, and a hin of oil to an ephah. ⁸ When the prince enters, he shall go in by the way of the porch of the gate, and he shall go out by its way. ⁹"""But when the people of the land come before Yahweh in the appointed feasts, he who enters by the way of the north gate to worship shall go out by the way of the south gate; and he who enters by the way of the south gate shall go out by the way of the north gate. He shall not return by the way of the gate by which he came in, but shall go out straight before him. ¹⁰ The prince shall go in with them when they go in. When they go out, he shall go out. ¹¹"""In the feasts and in the appointed holidays, the meal offering shall be an ephahˡ for a bull, and an ephah for a ram, and for the lambs as he is able to give, and a hin of oil to an ephah. ¹² When the prince prepares a free will offering, a burnt offering or peace offerings as a free will offering to Yahweh, one shall open for him the gate that looks toward the east; and he shall prepare his burnt offering and his peace offerings, as he does on the Sabbath day. Then he shall go out; and after his going out one shall shut the gate. ¹³"""You shall prepare a lamb a year old without defect for a burnt offering to Yahweh daily. Morning by morning you shall prepare it. ¹⁴ You shall prepare a meal offering with it morning by morning, the sixth part of an ephah,ᵐ and the third part of a hin of oil to moisten the fine flour; a meal offering to Yahweh continually by a

---

ᵃ *45:2* A cubit is the length from the tip of the middle finger to the elbow on a man's arm, or about 18 inches or 46 centimeters.
ᵇ *45:10* 1 ephah is about 22 liters or about 2/3 of a bushel
ᶜ *45:11* 1 homer is about 220 liters or 6 bushels

ᵈ *45:12* A shekel is about 10 grams or about 0.35 ounces.
ᵉ *45:12* a gerah is about 0.5 grams or about 7.7 grains
ᶠ *45:12* A mina is about 600 grams or 1.3 U. S. pounds.
ᵍ *45:14* 1 cor is the same as 1 homer in volume, and is about 211 liters, 55.9 gallons, or 6

bushels. 1 bath is about 21.1 liters, 5.59 gallons, or 2.4 pecks.
ʰ *45:24* 1 ephah is about 22 liters or about 2/3 of a bushel
ⁱ *45:24* A hin is about 6.5 liters or 1.7 gallons.
ʲ *46:5* A hin is about 6.5 liters or 1.7 gallons.

ᵏ *46:5* 1 ephah is about 22 liters or about 2/3 of a bushel
ˡ *46:11* 1 ephah is about 22 liters or about 2/3 of a bushel
ᵐ *46:14* 1 ephah is about 22 liters or about 2/3 of a bushel

perpetual ordinance. ¹⁵ Thus they shall prepare the lamb, the meal offering, and the oil, morning by morning, for a continual burnt offering." ¹⁶ "The Lord Yahweh says: "If the prince gives a gift to any of his sons, it is his inheritance. It shall belong to his sons. It is their possession by inheritance. ¹⁷ But if he gives of his inheritance a gift to one of his servants, it shall be his to the year of liberty; then it shall return to the prince; but as for his inheritance, it shall be for his sons. ¹⁸ Moreover the prince shall not take of the people's inheritance, to thrust them out of their possession. He shall give inheritance to his sons out of his own possession, that my people not each be scattered from his possession."''' ¹⁹ Then he brought me through the entry, which was at the side of the gate, into the holy rooms for the priests, which looked toward the north. Behold, there was a place on the back part westward. ²⁰ He said to me, "This is the place where the priests shall boil the trespass offering and the sin offering, and where they shall bake the meal offering, that they not bring them out into the outer court, to sanctify the people." ²¹ Then he brought me out into the outer court and caused me to pass by the four corners of the court; and behold, in every corner of the court there was a court. ²² In the four corners of the court there were courts enclosed, forty cubits[a] long and thirty wide. These four in the corners were the same size. ²³ There was a wall around in them, around the four, and boiling places were made under the walls all around. ²⁴ Then he said to me, "These are the boiling houses, where the ministers of the house shall boil the sacrifice of the people."

## 47

¹ He brought me back to the door of the temple; and behold, waters flowed out from under the threshold of the temple eastward, for the front of the temple faced toward the east. The waters came down from underneath, from the right side of the temple, on the south of the altar. ² Then he brought me out by the way of the gate northward, and led me around by the way outside to the outer gate, by the way of the gate that looks toward the east. Behold, waters ran out on the right side. ³ When the man went out eastward with the line in his hand, he measured one thousand cubits,[b] and he caused me to pass through the waters, waters that were to the ankles. ⁴ Again he measured one thousand, and caused me to pass through the waters, waters that were to the knees. Again he measured one thousand, and caused me to pass through waters that were to the waist. ⁵ Afterward he measured one thousand; and it was a river that I could not pass through, for the waters had risen, waters to swim in, a river that could not be walked through. ⁶ He said to me, "Son of man, have you seen this?" Then he brought me and caused me to return to the bank of the river. ⁷ Now when I had returned, behold, on the bank of the river were very many trees on the one side and on the other. ⁸ Then he said to me, "These waters flow out toward the eastern region and will go down into the Arabah. Then they will go toward the sea and flow into the sea which will be made to flow out; and the waters will be healed. ⁹ It will happen that every living creature which swarms, in every place where the rivers come, will live. Then there will be a very great multitude of fish; for these waters have come there, and the waters of the sea will be healed, and everything will live wherever the river comes. ¹⁰ It will happen that fishermen will stand by it. From En Gedi even to En Eglaim will be a place for the spreading of nets. Their fish will be after their kinds, as the fish of the great sea, exceedingly many. ¹¹ But its swamps and marshes will not be healed. They will be given up to salt. ¹² By the river banks, on both sides, will grow every tree for food, whose leaf won't wither, neither will its fruit fail. It will produce new fruit every month, because its waters issue out of the sanctuary. Its fruit will be for food, and its leaf for healing." ¹³ The Lord Yahweh says: "This shall be the border by which you shall divide the land for inheritance according to the twelve tribes of Israel. Joseph shall have two portions. ¹⁴ You shall inherit it, one as well as another; for I swore to give it to your fathers. This land will fall to you for inheritance. ¹⁵ "This shall be the border of the land: "On the north side, from the great sea, by the way of Hethlon, to the entrance of Zedad; ¹⁶ Hamath, Berothah, Sibraim (which is between the border of Damascus and the border of Hamath), to Hazer Hatticon, which is by the border of Hauran. ¹⁷ The border from the sea shall be Hazar Enon at the border of Damascus; and on the north northward is the border of Hamath. This is the north side. ¹⁸ "The east side, between Hauran, Damascus, Gilead, and the land of Israel, shall be the Jordan; from the north border to the east sea you shall measure. This is the east side. ¹⁹ "The south side southward shall be from Tamar as far as the waters of Meriboth Kadesh, to the brook, to the great sea. This is the south side southward. ²⁰ "The west side shall be the great sea, from the south border as far as opposite the entrance of Hamath. This is the west side. ²¹ "So you shall divide this land to yourselves according to the tribes of Israel. ²² You shall

divide it by lot for an inheritance to you and to the aliens who live among you, who will father children among you. Then they shall be to you as the native-born among the children of Israel. They shall have inheritance with you among the tribes of Israel. ²³ In whatever tribe the stranger lives, there you shall give him his inheritance," says the Lord Yahweh.

## 48

¹ "Now these are the names of the tribes: From the north end, beside the way of Hethlon to the entrance of Hamath, Hazar Enan at the border of Damascus, northward beside Hamath (and they shall have their sides east and west), Dan, one portion. ² "By the border of Dan, from the east side to the west side, Asher, one portion. ³ "By the border of Asher, from the east side even to the west side, Naphtali, one portion. ⁴ "By the border of Naphtali, from the east side to the west side, Manasseh, one portion. ⁵ "By the border of Manasseh, from the east side to the west side, Ephraim, one portion. ⁶ "By the border of Ephraim, from the east side even to the west side, Reuben, one portion. ⁷ "By the border of Reuben, from the east side to the west side, Judah, one portion. ⁸ "By the border of Judah, from the east side to the west side, shall be the offering which you shall offer, twenty-five thousand reeds in width, and in length as one of the portions, from the east side to the west side; and the sanctuary shall be in the middle of it. ⁹ "The offering that you shall offer to Yahweh shall be twenty-five thousand reeds in length, and ten thousand in width. ¹⁰ For these, even for these, shall be the holy offering: toward the north twenty-five thousand in length, and toward the west ten thousand in width, and toward the east ten thousand in width, and toward the south twenty-five thousand in length; and the sanctuary of Yahweh shall be in the middle of it. ¹¹ It shall be for the priests who are sanctified of the sons of Zadok, who have kept my instruction, who didn't go astray when the children of Israel went astray, as the Levites went astray. ¹² It shall be to them an offering from the offering of the land, a most holy thing, by the border of the Levites. ¹³ "Alongside the border of the priests, the Levites shall have twenty-five thousand cubits in length and ten thousand in width. All the length shall be twenty-five thousand, and the width ten thousand. ¹⁴ They shall sell none of it, nor exchange it, nor shall the first fruits of the land be alienated, for it is holy to Yahweh. ¹⁵ "The five thousand cubits that are left in the width, in front of the twenty-five thousand, shall be for common use, for the city, for dwelling and for pasture lands; and the city shall be in the middle of it. ¹⁶ These shall be its measurements: the north side four thousand and five hundred, and the south side four thousand and five hundred, and on the east side four thousand and five hundred, and the west side four thousand and five hundred. ¹⁷ The city shall have pasture lands: toward the north two hundred fifty, and toward the south two hundred fifty, and toward the east two hundred fifty, and toward the west two hundred fifty. ¹⁸ The remainder of the length, alongside the holy offering, shall be ten thousand eastward and ten thousand westward; and it shall be alongside the holy offering. Its increase shall be for food to those who labor in the city. ¹⁹ Those who labor in the city, out of all the tribes of Israel, shall cultivate it. ²⁰ All the offering shall be a square of twenty-five thousand by twenty-five thousand. You shall offer it as a holy offering, with the possession of the city. ²¹ "The remainder shall be for the prince, on the one side and on the other of the holy offering and of the possession of the city; in front of the twenty-five thousand of the offering toward the east border, and westward in front of the twenty-five thousand toward the west border, alongside the portions, it shall be for the prince. The holy offering and the sanctuary of the house shall be in the middle of it. ²² Moreover, from the possession of the Levites, and from the possession of the city, being in the middle of that which is the prince's, between the border of Judah and the border of Benjamin, shall be for the prince. ²³ "As for the rest of the tribes: from the east side to the west side, Benjamin, one portion. ²⁴ "By the border of Benjamin, from the east side to the west side, Simeon, one portion. ²⁵ "By the border of Simeon, from the east side to the west side, Issachar, one portion. ²⁶ "By the border of Issachar, from the east side to the west side, Zebulun, one portion. ²⁷ "By the border of Zebulun, from the east side to the west side, Gad, one portion. ²⁸ "By the border of Gad, at the south side southward, the border shall be even from Tamar to the waters of Meribath Kadesh, to the brook, to the great sea. ²⁹ "This is the land which you shall divide by lot to the tribes of Israel for inheritance, and these are their several portions, says the Lord Yahweh. ³⁰ "These are the exits of the city: On the north side four thousand five hundred reeds by measure; ³¹ and the gates of the city shall be named after the tribes of Israel, three gates northward: the gate of Reuben, one; the gate of Judah, one; the gate of Levi, one. ³² "At the east side four thousand five hundred reeds, and

---

[a] 46:22 A cubit is the length from the tip of the middle finger to the elbow on a man's arm, or about 18 inches or 46 centimeters.

[b] 47:3 A cubit is the length from the tip of the middle finger to the elbow on a man's arm, or about 18 inches or 46 centimeters.

three gates: even the gate of Joseph, one; the gate of Benjamin, one; the gate of Dan, one. <sup>33</sup>"At the south side four thousand five hundred reeds by measure, and three gates: the gate of Simeon, one; the gate of Issachar, one; the gate of Zebulun, one. <sup>34</sup>"At the west side four thousand five hundred reeds, with their three gates: the gate of Gad, one; the gate of Asher, one; the gate of Naphtali, one.
<sup>35</sup>"It shall be eighteen thousand reeds in circumference; and the name of the city from that day shall be, 'Yahweh is there.'

# The Book of Daniel
## 1

<sup>1</sup> In the third year of the reign of Jehoiakim king of Judah, Nebuchadnezzar king of Babylon came to Jerusalem and besieged it. <sup>2</sup> The Lord<sup>a</sup> gave Jehoiakim king of Judah into his hand, with some of the vessels of the house of God;<sup>b</sup> and he carried them into the land of Shinar to the house of his god. He brought the vessels into the treasure house of his god. <sup>3</sup> The king spoke to Ashpenaz, the master of his eunuchs, that he should bring in some of the children of Israel, even of the royal offspring<sup>c</sup> and of the nobles: <sup>4</sup> youths in whom was no defect, but well-favored, skillful in all wisdom, endowed with knowledge, understanding science, and who had the ability to stand in the king's palace; and that he should teach them the learning and the language of the Chaldeans. <sup>5</sup> The king appointed for them a daily portion of the king's delicacies and of the wine which he drank, and that they should be nourished three years, that at its end they should stand before the king. <sup>6</sup> Now among these of the children of Judah were Daniel, Hananiah, Mishael, and Azariah. <sup>7</sup> The prince of the eunuchs gave names to them: to Daniel he gave the name Belteshazzar; to Hananiah, Shadrach; to Mishael, Meshach; and to Azariah, Abednego. <sup>8</sup> But Daniel purposed in his heart that he would not defile himself with the king's delicacies, nor with the wine which he drank. Therefore he requested of the prince of the eunuchs that he might not defile himself. <sup>9</sup> Now God made Daniel find kindness and compassion in the sight of the prince of the eunuchs. <sup>10</sup> The prince of the eunuchs said to Daniel, "I fear my lord the king, who has appointed your food and your drink. For why should he see your faces worse looking than the youths who are of your own age? Then you would endanger my head with the king." <sup>11</sup> Then Daniel said to the steward whom the prince of the eunuchs had appointed over Daniel, Hananiah, Mishael, and Azariah: <sup>12</sup>"Test your servants, I beg you, ten days; and let them give us vegetables to eat and water to drink. <sup>13</sup> Then let our faces be examined before you, and the face of the youths who eat of the king's delicacies; and as you see, deal with your servants." <sup>14</sup> So he listened to them in this matter, and tested them for ten days. <sup>15</sup> At the end of ten days, their faces appeared fairer and they were fatter in flesh than all the youths who ate of the king's delicacies. <sup>16</sup> So the steward took away their delicacies and the wine that they were given to drink, and gave them vegetables. <sup>17</sup> Now as for these four youths, God gave them knowledge and skill in all learning and wisdom; and Daniel had understanding in all visions and dreams. <sup>18</sup> At the end of the days which the king had appointed for bringing them in, the prince of the eunuchs brought them in before Nebuchadnezzar. <sup>19</sup> The king talked with them; and among them all was found no one like Daniel, Hananiah, Mishael, and Azariah. Therefore stood they before the king. <sup>20</sup> In every matter of wisdom and understanding concerning which the king inquired of them, he found them ten times better than all the magicians and enchanters who were in all his realm. <sup>21</sup> Daniel continued even to the first year of King Cyrus.

## 2

<sup>1</sup> In the second year of the reign of Nebuchadnezzar, Nebuchadnezzar dreamed dreams; and his spirit was troubled, and his sleep went from him. <sup>2</sup> Then the king commanded that the magicians, the enchanters, the sorcerers, and the Chaldeans be called to tell the king his dreams. So they came in and stood before the king. <sup>3</sup> The king said to them, "I have dreamed a dream, and my spirit is troubled to know the dream." <sup>4</sup> Then the Chaldeans spoke to the king in the Syrian language, "O king, live forever! Tell your servants the dream, and we will show the interpretation." <sup>5</sup> The king answered the Chaldeans, "The thing has gone from me. If you don't make known to me the dream and its interpretation, you will be cut in pieces, and your houses will be made a dunghill. <sup>6</sup> But if you show the dream and its interpretation, you will receive from me gifts, rewards, and great honor. Therefore show me the dream and its interpretation." <sup>7</sup> They answered the second time and said, "Let the king tell his servants the dream, and we will show the interpretation." <sup>8</sup> The king answered, "I know of a certainty that you are trying to gain time, because you see the thing has gone from me. <sup>9</sup>

But if you don't make known to me the dream, there is but one law for you; for you have prepared lying and corrupt words to speak before me, until the situation changes. Therefore tell me the dream, and I will know that you can show me its interpretation." <sup>10</sup> The Chaldeans answered the king and said, "There is not a man on the earth who can show the king's matter, because no king, lord, or ruler has asked such a thing of any magician, enchanter, or Chaldean. <sup>11</sup> It is a rare thing that the king requires, and there is no other who can show it before the king except the gods, whose dwelling is not with flesh." <sup>12</sup> Because of this, the king was angry and very furious, and commanded that all the wise men of Babylon be destroyed. <sup>13</sup> So the decree went out, and the wise men were to be slain. They sought Daniel and his companions to be slain. <sup>14</sup> Then Daniel returned answer with counsel and prudence to Arioch the captain of the king's guard, who had gone out to kill the wise men of Babylon. <sup>15</sup> He answered Arioch the king's captain, "Why is the decree so urgent from the king?" Then Arioch made the thing known to Daniel. <sup>16</sup> Daniel went in, and desired of the king that he would appoint him a time, and he would show the king the interpretation. <sup>17</sup> Then Daniel went to his house and made the thing known to Hananiah, Mishael, and Azariah, his companions: <sup>18</sup> that they would desire mercies of the God of heaven concerning this secret, that Daniel and his companions would not perish with the rest of the wise men of Babylon. <sup>19</sup> Then the secret was revealed to Daniel in a vision of the night. Then Daniel blessed the God of heaven. <sup>20</sup> Daniel answered, "Blessed be the name of God forever and ever; for wisdom and might are his. <sup>21</sup> He changes the times and the seasons. He removes kings and sets up kings. He gives wisdom to the wise, and knowledge to those who have understanding. <sup>22</sup> He reveals the deep and secret things. He knows what is in the darkness, and the light dwells with him. <sup>23</sup> I thank you and praise you, O God of my fathers, who have given me wisdom and might, and have now made known to me what we desired of you; for you have made known to us the king's matter." <sup>24</sup> Therefore Daniel went in to Arioch, whom the king had appointed to destroy the wise men of Babylon. He went and said this to him: "Don't destroy the wise men of Babylon. Bring me in before the king, and I will show to the king the interpretation." <sup>25</sup> Then Arioch brought in Daniel before the king in haste, and said this to him: "I have found a man of the children of the captivity of Judah who will make known to the king the interpretation." <sup>26</sup> The king answered Daniel, whose name was Belteshazzar, "Are you able to make known to me the dream which I have seen, and its interpretation?" <sup>27</sup> Daniel answered before the king, and said, "The secret which the king has demanded can't be shown to the king by wise men, enchanters, magicians, or soothsayers; <sup>28</sup> but there is a God in heaven who reveals secrets, and he has made known to King Nebuchadnezzar what will be in the latter days. Your dream and the visions of your head on your bed are these: <sup>29</sup>"As for you, O king, your thoughts came on your bed, what should happen hereafter; and he who reveals secrets has made known to you what will happen. <sup>30</sup> But as for me, this secret is not revealed to me for any wisdom that I have more than any living, but to the intent that the interpretation may be made known to the king, and that you may know the thoughts of your heart. <sup>31</sup>"You, O king, saw, and behold,<sup>d</sup> a great image. This image, which was mighty, and whose brightness was excellent, stood before you; and its appearance was terrifying. <sup>32</sup> As for this image, its head was of fine gold, its chest and its arms of silver, its belly and its thighs of bronze, <sup>33</sup> its legs of iron, its feet part of iron and part of clay. <sup>34</sup> You saw until a stone was cut out without hands, which struck the image on its feet that were of iron and clay, and broke them in pieces. <sup>35</sup> Then the iron, the clay, the bronze, the silver, and the gold were broken in pieces together, and became like the chaff of the summer threshing floors. The wind carried them away, so that no place was found for them. The stone that struck the image became a great mountain and filled the whole earth. <sup>36</sup>"This is the dream; and we will tell its interpretation before the king. <sup>37</sup> You, O king, are king of kings, to whom the God of heaven has given the kingdom, the power, the strength, and the glory. <sup>38</sup> Wherever the children of men dwell, he has given the animals of the field and the birds of the sky into your hand, and has made you rule over them all. You are the head of gold. <sup>39</sup>"After you, another kingdom will arise that is inferior to you; and another third kingdom of bronze, which will rule over all the earth. <sup>40</sup> The fourth kingdom will be strong as iron, because iron breaks in pieces and subdues all things; and as iron that crushes all these, it will break in pieces and crush. <sup>41</sup> Whereas you saw the feet and toes, part of potters' clay and part of iron, it will be a divided kingdom; but there will be in it of the strength of the iron, because you saw the iron mixed with miry clay. <sup>42</sup> As the toes of the feet were part of iron, and part of clay, so the kingdom will be partly strong and partly brittle. <sup>43</sup> Whereas

<sup>a</sup> 1:2 The word translated "Lord" is "Adonai."

<sup>b</sup> 1:2 The Hebrew word rendered "God" is "אֱלֹהִים" (Elohim).

<sup>c</sup> 1:3 or, seed
<sup>d</sup> 2:31 "Behold", from "הִנֵּה", means look at, take notice,

observe, see, or gaze at. It is often used as an interjection.

you saw the iron mixed with miry clay, they will mingle themselves with the seed of men; but they won't cling to one another, even as iron does not mix with clay. [44]"In the days of those kings the God of heaven will set up a kingdom which will never be destroyed, nor will its sovereignty be left to another people; but it will break in pieces and consume all these kingdoms, and it will stand forever. [45] Because you saw that a stone was cut out of the mountain without hands, and that it broke in pieces the iron, the bronze, the clay, the silver, and the gold, the great God has made known to the king what will happen hereafter. The dream is certain, and its interpretation sure." [46] Then King Nebuchadnezzar fell on his face, worshiped Daniel, and commanded that they should offer an offering and sweet odors to him. [47] The king answered to Daniel, and said, "Of a truth your God is the God of gods, and the Lord of kings, and a revealer of secrets, since you have been able to reveal this secret." [48] Then the king made Daniel great and gave him many great gifts, and made him rule over the whole province of Babylon and to be chief governor over all the wise men of Babylon. [49] Daniel requested of the king, and he appointed Shadrach, Meshach, and Abednego over the affairs of the province of Babylon, but Daniel was in the king's gate.

## 3

[1] Nebuchadnezzar the king made an image of gold, whose height was sixty cubits[a] and its width six cubits. He set it up in the plain of Dura, in the province of Babylon. [2] Then Nebuchadnezzar the king sent to gather together the local governors, the deputies, and the governors, the judges, the treasurers, the counselors, the sheriffs, and all the rulers of the provinces, to come to the dedication of the image which Nebuchadnezzar the king had set up. [3] Then the local governors, the deputies, and the governors, the judges, the treasurers, the counselors, the sheriffs, and all the rulers of the provinces were gathered together to the dedication of the image that Nebuchadnezzar the king had set up; and they stood before the image that Nebuchadnezzar had set up. [4] Then the herald cried aloud, "To you it is commanded, peoples, nations, and languages, [5] that whenever you hear the sound of the horn, flute, zither, lyre, harp, pipe, and all kinds of music, you fall down and worship the golden image that Nebuchadnezzar the king has set up. [6] Whoever doesn't fall down and worship shall be cast into the middle of a burning fiery furnace the same hour." [7] Therefore at that time, when all the peoples heard the sound of the horn, flute, zither, lyre, harp, pipe, and all kinds of music, all the peoples, the nations, and the languages fell down and worshiped the golden image that Nebuchadnezzar the king had set up. [8] Therefore at that time certain Chaldeans came near and brought accusation against the Jews. [9] They answered Nebuchadnezzar the king, "O king, live for ever! [10] You, O king, have made a decree that every man who hears the sound of the horn, flute, zither, lyre, harp, pipe, and all kinds of music shall fall down and worship the golden image; [11] and whoever doesn't fall down and worship shall be cast into the middle of a burning fiery furnace. [12] There are certain Jews whom you have appointed over the affairs of the province of Babylon: Shadrach, Meshach, and Abednego. These men, O king, have not respected you. They don't serve your gods, and don't worship the golden image which you have set up." [13] Then Nebuchadnezzar in rage and fury commanded that Shadrach, Meshach, and Abednego be brought. Then these men were brought before the king. [14] Nebuchadnezzar answered them, "Is it true, Shadrach, Meshach, and Abednego, that you don't serve my gods and you don't worship the golden image which I have set up? [15] Now if you are ready whenever you hear the sound of the horn, flute, zither, lyre, harp, pipe, and all kinds of music to fall down and worship the image which I have made, good; but if you don't worship, you shall be cast the same hour into the middle of a burning fiery furnace. Who is that god who will deliver you out of my hands?" [16] Shadrach, Meshach, and Abednego answered the king, "Nebuchadnezzar, we have no need to answer you in this matter. [17] If it happens, our God whom we serve is able to deliver us from the burning fiery furnace; and he will deliver us out of your hand, O king. [18] But if not, let it be known to you, O king, that we will not serve your gods or worship the golden image which you have set up." [19] Then Nebuchadnezzar was full of fury, and the form of his appearance was changed against Shadrach, Meshach, and Abednego. He spoke, and commanded that they should heat the furnace seven times more than it was usually heated. [20] He commanded certain mighty men who were in his army to bind Shadrach, Meshach, and Abednego, and to cast them into the burning fiery furnace. [21] Then these men were bound in their pants, their tunics, and their mantles, and their other clothes, and were cast into the middle of the burning fiery furnace. [22] Therefore because the king's commandment was urgent and the furnace exceedingly hot, the flame of the fire killed those men who took up Shadrach, Meshach, and Abednego. [23] These three men, Shadrach, Meshach, and Abednego, fell down bound into the middle of the burning fiery furnace. [24] Then Nebuchadnezzar the king was astonished and rose up in haste. He spoke and said to his counselors, "Didn't we cast three men bound into the middle of the fire?" They answered the king, "True, O king." [25] He answered, "Look, I see four men loose, walking in the middle of the fire, and they are unharmed. The appearance of the fourth is like a son of the gods.[b]" [26] Then Nebuchadnezzar came near to the mouth of the burning fiery furnace. He spoke and said, "Shadrach, Meshach, and Abednego, you servants of the Most High God, come out, and come here!" Then Shadrach, Meshach, and Abednego came out of the middle of the fire. [27] The local governors, the deputies, and the governors, and the king's counselors, being gathered together, saw these men, that the fire had no power on their bodies. The hair of their head wasn't singed. Their pants weren't changed. The smell of fire wasn't even on them. [28] Nebuchadnezzar spoke and said, "Blessed be the God of Shadrach, Meshach, and Abednego, who has sent his angel and delivered his servants who trusted in him, and have changed the king's word, and have yielded their bodies, that they might not serve nor worship any god except their own God. [29] Therefore I make a decree that every people, nation, and language which speak anything evil against the God of Shadrach, Meshach, and Abednego shall be cut in pieces, and their houses shall be made a dunghill; because there is no other god who is able to deliver like this." [30] Then the king promoted Shadrach, Meshach, and Abednego in the province of Babylon.

## 4

[1] Nebuchadnezzar the king, to all the peoples, nations, and languages, who dwell in all the earth: Peace be multiplied to you. [2] It has seemed good to me to show the signs and wonders that the Most High God has worked toward me. [3] How great are his signs! How mighty are his wonders! His kingdom is an everlasting kingdom. His dominion is from generation to generation. [4] I, Nebuchadnezzar, was at rest in my house, and flourishing in my palace. [5] I saw a dream which made me afraid; and the thoughts on my bed and the visions of my head troubled me. [6] Therefore I made a decree to bring in all the wise men of Babylon before me, that they might make known to me the interpretation of the dream. [7] Then the magicians, the enchanters, the Chaldeans, and the soothsayers came in; and I told them the dream, but they didn't make known to me its interpretation. [8] But at last, Daniel came in before me, whose name was Belteshazzar according to the name of my god, and in whom is the spirit of the holy gods. I told the dream before him, saying, [9]"Belteshazzar, master of the magicians, because I know that the spirit of the holy gods is in you and no secret troubles you, tell me the visions of my dream that I have seen, and its interpretation. [10] These were the visions of my head on my bed: I saw, and behold, a tree in the middle of the earth; and its height was great. [11] The tree grew and was strong. Its height reached to the sky and its sight to the end of all the earth. [12] Its leaves were beautiful, and it had much fruit, and in it was food for all. The animals of the field had shade under it, and the birds of the sky lived in its branches, and all flesh was fed from it. [13]"I saw in the visions of my head on my bed, and behold, a holy watcher came down from the sky. [14] He cried aloud and said this: 'Cut down the tree, and cut off its branches! Shake off its leaves and scatter its fruit! Let the animals get away from under it and the birds from its branches. [15] Nevertheless leave the stump of its roots in the earth, even with a band of iron and bronze, in the tender grass of the field; and let it be wet with the dew of the sky. Let his portion be with the animals in the grass of the earth. [16] Let his heart be changed from man's, and let an animal's heart be given to him. Then let seven times pass over him. [17]"'The sentence is by the decree of the watchers and the demand by the word of the holy ones, to the intent that the living may know that the Most High rules in the kingdom of men, and gives it to whomever he will, and sets up over it the lowest of men.' [18]"This dream I, King Nebuchadnezzar, have seen; and you, Belteshazzar, declare the interpretation, because all the wise men of my kingdom are not able to make known to me the interpretation; but you are able, for the spirit of the holy gods is in you." [19] Then Daniel, whose name was Belteshazzar, was stricken mute for a while, and his thoughts troubled him. The king answered, "Belteshazzar, don't let the dream or the interpretation, trouble you." Belteshazzar answered, "My lord, may the dream be for those who hate you, and its interpretation to your adversaries. [20] The tree that you saw, which grew and was strong, whose height reached to the sky and its sight to all the earth; [21] whose leaves were beautiful and its fruit plentiful, and in it was food for all; under which the animals of the field lived, and on whose branches the birds of the sky had their habitation—

---

[a] *3:1* A cubit is the length from the tip of the middle finger to the elbow on a man's arm, or about 18 inches or 46 centimeters.
[b] *3:25* Or, the Son of God.

²² it is you, O king, that have grown and become strong; for your greatness has grown, and reaches to the sky, and your dominion to the end of the earth. ²³"Whereas the king saw a holy watcher coming down from the sky and saying, 'Cut down the tree, and destroy it; nevertheless leave the stump of its roots in the earth, even with a band of iron and bronze, in the tender grass of the field, and let it be wet with the dew of the sky. Let his portion be with the animals of the field, until seven times pass over him.' ²⁴"This is the interpretation, O king, and it is the decree of the Most High, which has come on my lord the king: ²⁵ You will be driven from men and your dwelling shall be with the animals of the field. You will be made to eat grass as oxen, and will be wet with the dew of the sky, and seven times shall pass over you, until you know that the Most High rules in the kingdom of men, and gives it to whomever he will. ²⁶ Whereas it was commanded to leave the stump of the roots of the tree, your kingdom shall be sure to you after you know that Heaven rules. ²⁷ Therefore, O king, let my counsel be acceptable to you, and break off your sins by righteousness, and your iniquities by showing mercy to the poor. Perhaps there may be a lengthening of your tranquility." ²⁸ All this came on the King Nebuchadnezzar. ²⁹ At the end of twelve months he was walking in the royal palace of Babylon. ³⁰ The king spoke and said, "Is not this great Babylon, which I have built for the royal dwelling place by the might of my power and for the glory of my majesty?" ³¹ While the word was in the king's mouth, a voice came from the sky, saying, "O King Nebuchadnezzar, to you it is spoken: 'The kingdom has departed from you. ³² You shall be driven from men, and your dwelling shall be with the animals of the field. You shall be made to eat grass like oxen. Seven times shall pass over you, until you know that the Most High rules in the kingdom of men, and gives it to whomever he will.'" ³³ This was fulfilled the same hour on Nebuchadnezzar. He was driven from men and ate grass like oxen; and his body was wet with the dew of the sky until his hair had grown like eagles' feathers, and his nails like birds' claws. ³⁴ At the end of the days I, Nebuchadnezzar, lifted up my eyes to heaven, and my understanding returned to me; and I blessed the Most High, and I praised and honored him who lives forever, for his dominion is an everlasting dominion, and his kingdom from generation to generation. ³⁵ All the inhabitants of the earth are reputed as nothing; and he does according to his will in the army of heaven, and among the inhabitants of the earth; and no one can stop his hand, or ask him, "What are you doing?" ³⁶ At the same time my understanding returned to me; and for the glory of my kingdom, my majesty and brightness returned to me. My counselors and my lords sought me; and I was established in my kingdom, and excellent greatness was added to me. ³⁷ Now I, Nebuchadnezzar, praise and extol and honor the King of heaven; for all his works are truth, and his ways justice; and those who walk in pride he is able to abase.

# 5

¹ Belshazzar the king made a great feast to a thousand of his lords, and drank wine before the thousand. ² Belshazzar, while he tasted the wine, commanded that the golden and silver vessels which Nebuchadnezzar his father had taken out of the temple which was in Jerusalem be brought to him, that the king and his lords, his wives and his concubines, might drink from them. ³ Then they brought the golden vessels that were taken out of the temple of God's house which was at Jerusalem; and the king and his lords, his wives and his concubines, drank from them. ⁴ They drank wine, and praised the gods of gold, and of silver, of bronze, of iron, of wood, and of stone. ⁵ In the same hour, the fingers of a man's hand came out and wrote near the lamp stand on the plaster of the wall of the king's palace. The king saw the part of the hand that wrote. ⁶ Then the king's face was changed in him, and his thoughts troubled him; and the joints of his thighs were loosened, and his knees struck one against another. ⁷ The king cried aloud to bring in the enchanters, the Chaldeans, and the soothsayers. The king spoke and said to the wise men of Babylon, "Whoever reads this writing and shows me its interpretation shall be clothed with purple, and have a chain of gold about his neck, and shall be the third ruler in the kingdom." ⁸ Then all the king's wise men came in; but they could not read the writing, and couldn't make known to the king the interpretation. ⁹ Then King Belshazzar was greatly troubled, and his face was changed in him, and his lords were perplexed. ¹⁰ The queen by reason of the words of the king and his lords came into the banquet house. The queen spoke and said, "O king, live forever; don't let your thoughts trouble you, nor let your face be changed. ¹¹ There is a man in your kingdom in whom is the spirit of the holy gods; and in the days of your father, light and understanding and wisdom, like the wisdom of the gods, were found in him. The king, Nebuchadnezzar, your father— yes, the king, your father—made him master of the magicians, enchanters, Chaldeans, and soothsayers, ¹² because an excellent spirit, knowledge, understanding, interpreting of dreams, showing of dark sentences, and dissolving of doubts were found in the same Daniel,

whom the king named Belteshazzar. Now let Daniel be called, and he will show the interpretation." ¹³ Then Daniel was brought in before the king. The king spoke and said to Daniel, "Are you that Daniel of the children of the captivity of Judah, whom the king my father brought out of Judah? ¹⁴ I have heard of you, that the spirit of the gods is in you and that light, understanding, and excellent wisdom are found in you. ¹⁵ Now the wise men, the enchanters, have been brought in before me, that they should read this writing, and make known to me its interpretation; but they could not show the interpretation of the thing. ¹⁶ But I have heard of you, that you can give interpretations and dissolve doubts. Now if you can read the writing and make known to me its interpretation, you shall be clothed with purple, and have a chain of gold around your neck, and shall be the third ruler in the kingdom." ¹⁷ Then Daniel answered before the king, "Let your gifts be to yourself, and give your rewards to another. Nevertheless, I will read the writing to the king, and make known to him the interpretation. ¹⁸"To you, O king, the Most High God gave Nebuchadnezzar your father the kingdom, and greatness, and glory, and majesty. ¹⁹ Because of the greatness that he gave him, all the peoples, nations, and languages trembled and feared before him. He killed whom he wanted to, and he kept alive whom he wanted to. He raised up whom he wanted to, and he put down whom he wanted to. ²⁰ But when his heart was lifted up, and his spirit was hardened so that he dealt proudly, he was deposed from his kingly throne, and they took his glory from him. ²¹ He was driven from the sons of men, and his heart was made like the animals', and his dwelling was with the wild donkeys. He was fed with grass like oxen, and his body was wet with the dew of the sky, until he knew that the Most High God rules in the kingdom of men, and that he sets up over it whomever he will. ²²"You, his son, Belshazzar, have not humbled your heart, though you knew all this, ²³ but have lifted up yourself against the Lord of heaven; and they have brought the vessels of his house before you, and you and your lords, your wives, and your concubines, have drunk wine from them. You have praised the gods of silver and gold, of bronze, iron, wood, and stone, which don't see, or hear, or know; and you have not glorified the God in whose hand your breath is, and whose are all your ways. ²⁴ Then the part of the hand was sent from before him, and this writing was inscribed. ²⁵"This is the writing that was inscribed: 'MENE, MENE, TEKEL, UPHARSIN.' ²⁶"This is the interpretation of the thing: MENE: God has counted your kingdom, and brought it to an end. ²⁷ TEKEL: you are weighed in the balances, and are found wanting. ²⁸ PERES: your kingdom is divided, and given to the Medes and Persians." ²⁹ Then Belshazzar commanded, and they clothed Daniel with purple, and put a chain of gold about his neck, and made proclamation concerning him, that he should be the third ruler in the kingdom. ³⁰ In that night Belshazzar the Chaldean King was slain. ³¹ Darius the Mede received the kingdom, being about sixty-two years old.

# 6

¹ It pleased Darius to set over the kingdom one hundred twenty local governors, who should be throughout the whole kingdom; ² and over them three presidents, of whom Daniel was one, that these local governors might give account to them, and that the king should suffer no loss. ³ Then this Daniel was distinguished above the presidents and the local governors, because an excellent spirit was in him; and the king thought to set him over the whole realm. ⁴ Then the presidents and the local governors sought to find occasion against Daniel as touching the kingdom; but they could find no occasion or fault, because he was faithful. There wasn't any error or fault found in him. ⁵ Then these men said, "We won't find any occasion against this Daniel, unless we find it against him concerning the law of his God." ⁶ Then these presidents and local governors assembled together to the king, and said this to him, "King Darius, live forever! ⁷ All the presidents of the kingdom, the deputies and the local governors, the counselors and the governors, have consulted together to establish a royal statute and to make a strong decree, that whoever asks a petition of any god or man for thirty days, except of you, O king, he shall be cast into the den of lions. ⁸ Now, O king, establish the decree and sign the writing, that it not be changed, according to the law of the Medes and Persians, which doesn't alter." ⁹ Therefore King Darius signed the writing and the decree. ¹⁰ When Daniel knew that the writing was signed, he went into his house (now his windows were open in his room toward Jerusalem) and he kneeled on his knees three times a day, and prayed, and gave thanks before his God, as he did before. ¹¹ Then these men assembled together, and found Daniel making petition and supplication before his God. ¹² Then they came near, and spoke before the king concerning the king's decree: "Haven't you signed a decree that every man who makes a petition to any god or man within thirty days, except to you, O king, shall be cast into the den of lions?" The king answered, "This thing is true, according to the law of the Medes and Persians, which doesn't alter." ¹³ Then they answered and said before the king, "That Daniel, who is of the children

of the captivity of Judah, doesn't respect you, O king, nor the decree that you have signed, but makes his petition three times a day." ¹⁴ Then the king, when he heard these words, was very displeased, and set his heart on Daniel to deliver him; and he labored until the going down of the sun to rescue him. ¹⁵ Then these men assembled together to the king, and said to the king, "Know, O king, that it is a law of the Medes and Persians, that no decree nor statute which the king establishes may be changed." ¹⁶ Then the king commanded, and they brought Daniel and cast him into the den of lions. The king spoke and said to Daniel, "Your God whom you serve continually, he will deliver you." ¹⁷ A stone was brought, and laid on the mouth of the den; and the king sealed it with his own signet, and with the signet of his lords; that nothing might be changed concerning Daniel. ¹⁸ Then the king went to his palace, and passed the night fasting. No musical instruments were brought before him; and his sleep fled from him. ¹⁹ Then the king arose very early in the morning, and went in haste to the den of lions. ²⁰ When he came near to the den to Daniel, he cried with a troubled voice. The king spoke and said to Daniel, "Daniel, servant of the living God, is your God, whom you serve continually, able to deliver you from the lions?" ²¹ Then Daniel said to the king, "O king, live forever! ²² My God has sent his angel, and has shut the lions' mouths, and they have not hurt me, because innocence was found in me before him; and also before you, O king, I have done no harm." ²³ Then the king was exceedingly glad, and commanded that they should take Daniel up out of the den. So Daniel was taken up out of the den, and no kind of harm was found on him, because he had trusted in his God. ²⁴ The king commanded, and they brought those men who had accused Daniel, and they cast them into the den of lions—them, their children, and their wives; and the lions mauled them, and broke all their bones in pieces before they came to the bottom of the den. ²⁵ Then King Darius wrote to all the peoples, nations, and languages who dwell in all the earth: "Peace be multiplied to you. ²⁶ "I make a decree that in all the dominion of my kingdom men tremble and fear before the God of Daniel. "For he is the living God, and steadfast forever. His kingdom is that which will not be destroyed. His dominion will be even to the end. ²⁷ He delivers and rescues. He works signs and wonders in heaven and in earth, who has delivered Daniel from the power of the lions." ²⁸ So this Daniel prospered in the reign of Darius and in the reign of Cyrus the Persian.

## 7

¹ In the first year of Belshazzar king of Babylon, Daniel had a dream and visions of his head while on his bed. Then he wrote the dream and told the sum of the matters. ² Daniel spoke and said, "I saw in my vision by night, and, behold, the four winds of the sky broke out on the great sea. ³ Four great animals came up from the sea, different from one another. ⁴ "The first was like a lion, and had eagle's wings. I watched until its wings were plucked, and it was lifted up from the earth and made to stand on two feet as a man. A man's heart was given to it. ⁵ "Behold, there was another animal, a second, like a bear. It was raised up on one side, and three ribs were in its mouth between its teeth. They said this to it: 'Arise! Devour much flesh!' ⁶ "After this I saw, and behold, another, like a leopard, which had on its back four wings of a bird. The animal also had four heads; and dominion was given to it. ⁷ "After this I saw in the night visions, and, behold, there was a fourth animal, awesome, powerful, and exceedingly strong. It had great iron teeth. It devoured and broke in pieces, and stamped the residue with its feet. It was different from all the animals that were before it. It had ten horns. ⁸ "I considered the horns, and behold, there came up among them another horn, a little one, before which three of the first horns were plucked up by the roots; and behold, in this horn were eyes like the eyes of a man, and a mouth speaking arrogantly. ⁹ "I watched until thrones were placed, and one who was Ancient of Days sat. His clothing was white as snow, and the hair of his head like pure wool. His throne was fiery flames, and its wheels burning fire. ¹⁰ A fiery stream issued and came out from before him. Thousands of thousands ministered to him. Ten thousand times ten thousand stood before him. The judgment was set. The books were opened. ¹¹ "I watched at that time because of the voice of the arrogant words which the horn spoke. I watched even until the animal was slain, and its body destroyed, and it was given to be burned with fire. ¹² As for the rest of the animals, their dominion was taken away; yet their lives were prolonged for a season and a time. ¹³ "I saw in the night visions, and behold, there came with the clouds of the sky one like a son of man, and he came even to the Ancient of Days, and they brought him near before him. ¹⁴ Dominion was given him, and glory, and a kingdom, that all the peoples, nations, and languages should serve him. His dominion is an everlasting dominion, which will not pass away, and his kingdom one that will not be destroyed. ¹⁵ "As for me, Daniel, my spirit was grieved within my body, and the visions of my head troubled me. ¹⁶ I came near to one of those who stood by, and asked him the truth concerning all this. "So he told me, and made me know the interpretation of the things. ¹⁷ 'These great animals, which

are four, are four kings, who will arise out of the earth. ¹⁸ But the saints of the Most High will receive the kingdom, and possess the kingdom forever, even forever and ever.' ¹⁹ "Then I desired to know the truth concerning the fourth animal, which was different from all of them, exceedingly terrible, whose teeth were of iron, and its nails of bronze; which devoured, broke in pieces, and stamped the residue with its feet; ²⁰ and concerning the ten horns that were on its head, and the other horn which came up, and before which three fell, even that horn that had eyes and a mouth that spoke arrogantly, whose look was more stout than its fellows. ²¹ I saw, and the same horn made war with the saints, and prevailed against them, ²² until the Ancient of Days came, and judgment was given to the saints of the Most High, and the time came that the saints possessed the kingdom. ²³ "So he said, 'The fourth animal will be a fourth kingdom on earth, which will be different from all the kingdoms, and will devour the whole earth, and will tread it down and break it in pieces. ²⁴ As for the ten horns, ten kings will arise out of this kingdom. Another will arise after them; and he will be different from the former, and he will put down three kings. ²⁵ He will speak words against the Most High, and will wear out the saints of the Most High. He will plan to change the times and the law; and they will be given into his hand until a time and times and half a time. ²⁶ "But the judgment will be set, and they will take away his dominion, to consume and to destroy it to the end. ²⁷ The kingdom and the dominion, and the greatness of the kingdoms under the whole sky, will be given to the people of the saints of the Most High. His kingdom is an everlasting kingdom, and all dominions will serve and obey him.' ²⁸ "Here is the end of the matter. As for me, Daniel, my thoughts troubled me greatly, and my face was changed in me; but I kept the matter in my heart."

## 8

¹ In the third year of the reign of King Belshazzar, a vision appeared to me, even to me, Daniel, after that which appeared to me at the first. ² I saw the vision. Now it was so, that when I saw, I was in the citadel of Susa, which is in the province of Elam. I saw in the vision, and I was by the river Ulai. ³ Then I lifted up my eyes and saw, and, behold, a ram which had two horns stood before the river. The two horns were high, but one was higher than the other, and the higher came up last. ⁴ I saw the ram pushing westward, northward, and southward. No animals could stand before him. There wasn't any who could deliver out of his hand, but he did according to his will, and magnified himself. ⁵ As I was considering, behold, a male goat came from the west over the surface of the whole earth, and didn't touch the ground. The goat had a notable horn between his eyes. ⁶ He came to the ram that had the two horns, which I saw standing before the river, and ran on him in the fury of his power. ⁷ I saw him come close to the ram, and he was moved with anger against him, and struck the ram, and broke his two horns. There was no power in the ram to stand before him; but he cast him down to the ground and trampled on him. There was no one who could deliver the ram out of his hand. ⁸ The male goat magnified himself exceedingly. When he was strong, the great horn was broken; and instead of it there came up four notable horns toward the four winds of the sky. ⁹ Out of one of them came out a little horn which grew exceedingly great—toward the south, and toward the east, and toward the glorious land. ¹⁰ It grew great, even to the army of the sky; and it cast down some of the army and of the stars to the ground and trampled on them. ¹¹ Yes, it magnified itself, even to the prince of the army; and it took away from him the continual burnt offering, and the place of his sanctuary was cast down. ¹² The army was given over to it together with the continual burnt offering through disobedience. It cast down truth to the ground, and it did its pleasure and prospered. ¹³ Then I heard a holy one speaking; and another holy one said to that certain one who spoke, "How long will the vision about the continual burnt offering, and the disobedience that makes desolate, to give both the sanctuary and the army to be trodden under foot be?" ¹⁴ He said to me, "To two thousand and three hundred evenings and mornings. Then the sanctuary will be cleansed." ¹⁵ When I, even I Daniel, had seen the vision, I sought to understand it. Then behold, there stood before me someone with the appearance of a man. ¹⁶ I heard a man's voice between the banks of the Ulai, which called and said, "Gabriel, make this man understand the vision." ¹⁷ So he came near where I stood; and when he came, I was frightened, and fell on my face; but he said to me, "Understand, son of man, for the vision belongs to the time of the end." ¹⁸ Now as he was speaking with me, I fell into a deep sleep with my face toward the ground; but he touched me and set me upright. ¹⁹ He said, "Behold, I will make you know what will be in the latter time of the indignation, for it belongs to the appointed time of the end. ²⁰ The ram which you saw, that had the two horns, they are the kings of Media and Persia. ²¹ The rough male goat is the king of Greece. The great horn that is between his eyes is the first king. ²² As for that which was broken, in the place where four stood up, four kingdoms will stand up out of the nation, but not with his power. ²³ "In the latter time of their kingdom,

when the transgressors have come to the full, a king of fierce face, and understanding riddles, will stand up. [24] His power will be mighty, but not by his own power. He will destroy awesomely, and will prosper in what he does. He will destroy the mighty ones and the holy people. [25] Through his policy he will cause deceit to prosper in his hand. He will magnify himself in his heart, and he will destroy many in their security. He will also stand up against the prince of princes; but he will be broken without human hands. [26]"The vision of the evenings and mornings which has been told is true; but seal up the vision, for it belongs to many days to come." [27] I, Daniel, fainted, and was sick for some days. Then I rose up and did the king's business. I wondered at the vision, but no one understood it.

# 9

[1] In the first year of Darius the son of Ahasuerus, of the offspring of the Medes, who was made king over the realm of the Chaldeans— [2] in the first year of his reign I, Daniel, understood by the books the number of the years about which Yahweh's[a] word came to Jeremiah the prophet for the accomplishing of the desolations of Jerusalem, even seventy years. [3] I set my face to the Lord God, to seek by prayer and petitions, with fasting and sackcloth and ashes. [4] I prayed to Yahweh my God, and made confession, and said, "Oh, Lord, the great and dreadful God, who keeps covenant and loving kindness with those who love him and keep his commandments, [5] we have sinned, and have dealt perversely, and have done wickedly, and have rebelled, even turning aside from your precepts and from your ordinances. [6] We haven't listened to your servants the prophets, who spoke in your name to our kings, our princes, and our fathers, and to all the people of the land. [7]"Lord, righteousness belongs to you, but to us confusion of face, as it is today; to the men of Judah, and to the inhabitants of Jerusalem, and to all Israel, who are near and who are far off, through all the countries where you have driven them, because of their trespass that they have trespassed against you. [8] Lord, to us belongs confusion of face, to our kings, to our princes, and to our fathers, because we have sinned against you. [9] To the Lord our God belong mercies and forgiveness, for we have rebelled against him. [10] We haven't obeyed Yahweh our God's voice, to walk in his laws, which he set before us by his servants the prophets. [11] Yes, all Israel have transgressed your law, turning aside, that they should not obey your voice. "Therefore the curse and the oath written in the law of Moses the servant of God has been poured out on us, for we have sinned against him. [12] He has confirmed his words, which he spoke against us and against our judges who judged us, by bringing on us a great evil; for under the whole sky, such has not been done as has been done to Jerusalem. [13] As it is written in the law of Moses, all this evil has come on us. Yet we have not entreated the favor of Yahweh our God, that we should turn from our iniquities and have discernment in your truth. [14] Therefore Yahweh has watched over the evil, and brought it on us; for Yahweh our God is righteous in all his works which he does, and we have not obeyed his voice. [15]"Now, Lord our God, who has brought your people out of the land of Egypt with a mighty hand, and have gotten yourself renown, as it is today, we have sinned. We have done wickedly. [16] Lord, according to all your righteousness, please let your anger and your wrath be turned away from your city Jerusalem, your holy mountain; because for our sins and for the iniquities of our fathers, Jerusalem and your people have become a reproach to all who are around us. [17]"Now therefore, our God, listen to the prayer of your servant and to his petitions, and cause your face to shine on your sanctuary that is desolate, for the Lord's sake. [18] My God, turn your ear and hear. Open your eyes and see our desolations, and the city which is called by your name; for we do not present our petitions before you for our righteousness, but for your great mercies' sake. [19] Lord, hear. Lord, forgive. Lord, listen and do. Don't defer, for your own sake, my God, because your city and your people are called by your name." [20] While I was speaking, praying, and confessing my sin and the sin of my people Israel, and presenting my supplication before Yahweh my God for the holy mountain of my God— [21] yes, while I was speaking in prayer—the man Gabriel, whom I had seen in the vision at the beginning, being caused to fly swiftly, touched me about the time of the evening offering. [22] He instructed me and talked with me, and said, "Daniel, I have now come to give you wisdom and understanding. [23] At the beginning of your petitions the commandment went out, and I have come to tell you, for you are greatly beloved. Therefore consider the matter and understand the vision. [24]"Seventy weeks are decreed on your people and on your holy city, to finish disobedience, to make an end of sins, to make reconciliation for iniquity, to bring in everlasting righteousness, to seal up vision and

prophecy, and to anoint the most holy. [25]"Know therefore and discern that from the going out of the commandment to restore and build Jerusalem to the Anointed One,[b] the prince, will be seven weeks and sixty-two weeks. It will be built again, with street and moat, even in troubled times. [26] After the sixty-two weeks the Anointed One[c] will be cut off, and will have nothing. The people of the prince who come will destroy the city and the sanctuary. Its end will be with a flood, and war will be even to the end. Desolations are determined. [27] He will make a firm covenant with many for one week. In the middle of the week he will cause the sacrifice and the offering to cease. On the wing of abominations will come one who makes desolate; and even to the decreed full end, wrath will be poured out on the desolate."

# 10

[1] In the third year of Cyrus king of Persia a message was revealed to Daniel, whose name was called Belteshazzar; and the message was true, even a great warfare. He understood the message, and had understanding of the vision. [2] In those days I, Daniel, was mourning three whole weeks. [3] I ate no pleasant food. No meat or wine came into my mouth. I didn't anoint myself at all, until three whole weeks were fulfilled. [4] In the twenty-fourth day of the first month, as I was by the side of the great river, which is Hiddekel,[d] [5] I lifted up my eyes and looked, and behold, there was a man clothed in linen, whose waist was adorned with pure gold of Uphaz. [6] His body also was like beryl, and his face as the appearance of lightning, and his eyes as flaming torches. His arms and his feet were like burnished bronze. The voice of his words was like the voice of a multitude. [7] I, Daniel, alone saw the vision, for the men who were with me didn't see the vision, but a great quaking fell on them, and they fled to hide themselves. [8] So I was left alone and saw this great vision. No strength remained in me; for my face grew deathly pale, and I retained no strength. [9] Yet I heard the voice of his words. When I heard the voice of his words, then I fell into a deep sleep on my face, with my face toward the ground. [10] Behold, a hand touched me, which set me on my knees and on the palms of my hands. [11] He said to me, "Daniel, you greatly beloved man, understand the words that I speak to you, and stand upright, for I have been sent to you, now." When he had spoken this word to me, I stood trembling. [12] Then he said to me, "Don't be afraid, Daniel; for from the first day that you set your heart to understand, and to humble yourself before your God, your words were heard. I have come for your words' sake. [13] But the prince of the kingdom of Persia withstood me twenty-one days; but, behold, Michael, one of the chief princes, came to help me because I remained there with the kings of Persia. [14] Now I have come to make you understand what will happen to your people in the latter days, for the vision is yet for many days." [15] When he had spoken these words to me, I set my face toward the ground and was mute. [16] Behold, one in the likeness of the sons of men touched my lips. Then I opened my mouth, and spoke and said to him who stood before me, "My lord, by reason of the vision my sorrows have overtaken me, and I retain no strength. [17] For how can the servant of this my lord talk with this my lord? For as for me, immediately there remained no strength in me. There was no breath left in me." [18] Then one like the appearance of a man touched me again, and he strengthened me. [19] He said, "Greatly beloved man, don't be afraid. Peace be to you. Be strong. Yes, be strong." When he spoke to me, I was strengthened, and said, "Let my lord speak, for you have strengthened me." [20] Then he said, "Do you know why I have come to you? Now I will return to fight with the prince of Persia. When I go out, behold, the prince of Greece will come. [21] But I will tell you that which is inscribed in the writing of truth. There is no one who holds with me against these but Michael your prince.

# 11

[1]"As for me, in the first year of Darius the Mede, I stood up to confirm and strengthen him. [2]"Now I will show you the truth. Behold, three more kings will stand up in Persia. The fourth will be far richer than all of them. When he has grown strong through his riches, he will stir up all against the realm of Greece. [3] A mighty king will stand up, who will rule with great dominion, and do according to his will. [4] When he stands up, his kingdom will be broken and will be divided toward the four winds of the sky, but not to his posterity, nor according to his dominion with which he ruled; for his kingdom will be plucked up, even for others besides these. [5]"The king of the south will be strong. One of his princes will become stronger than him, and have dominion. His dominion will be a great dominion. [6] At the end of years they will join themselves together; and the daughter of the king of the south will come to the king of the north to make an agreement, but she will not retain the strength of her arm. He will also not stand, nor will his arm; but she will be

---

[a] 9:2 "Yahweh" is God's proper Name, sometimes rendered "LORD" (all caps) in other translations.

[b] 9:25 "Anointed One" can also be translated "Messiah" (same as "Christ").

[c] 9:26 "Anointed One" can also be translated "Messiah" (same as "Christ").

[d] 10:4 or, Tigris River

given up, with those who brought her, and he who became the father of her, and he who strengthened her in those times. ⁷But out of a shoot from her roots one will stand up in his place, who will come to the army and will enter into the fortress of the king of the north, and will deal against them and will prevail. ⁸ He will also carry their gods with their molten images, and with their goodly vessels of silver and of gold, captive into Egypt. He will refrain some years from the king of the north. ⁹ He will come into the realm of the king of the south, but he will return into his own land. ¹⁰ His sons will wage war, and will assemble a multitude of great forces which will come on, and overflow, and pass through. They will return and wage war, even to his fortress. ¹¹"The king of the south will be moved with anger and will come out and fight with him, even with the king of the north. He will send out a great multitude, and the multitude will be given into his hand. ¹² The multitude will be carried off, and his heart will be exalted. He will cast down tens of thousands, but he won't prevail. ¹³ The king of the north will return, and will send out a multitude greater than the former. He will come on at the end of the times, even of years, with a great army and with abundant supplies. ¹⁴"In those times many will stand up against the king of the south. Also the children of the violent among your people will lift themselves up to establish the vision, but they will fall. ¹⁵ So the king of the north will come and cast up a mound, and take a well-fortified city. The forces of the south won't stand, neither will his select troops, neither will there be any strength to stand. ¹⁶ But he who comes against him will do according to his own will, and no one will stand before him. He will stand in the glorious land, and destruction will be in his hand. ¹⁷ He will set his face to come with the strength of his whole kingdom, and with him equitable conditions. He will perform them. He will give him the daughter of women, to destroy the kingdom, but she will not stand, and won't be for him. ¹⁸ After this he will turn his face to the islands, and will take many, but a prince will cause the reproach offered by him to cease. Yes, moreover, he will cause his reproach to turn on him. ¹⁹ Then he will turn his face toward the fortresses of his own land; but he will stumble and fall, and won't be found. ²⁰"Then one who will cause a tax collector to pass through the kingdom to maintain its glory will stand up in his place; but within few days he shall be destroyed, not in anger, and not in battle. ²¹"In his place a contemptible person will stand up, to whom they had not given the honor of the kingdom; but he will come in time of security, and will obtain the kingdom by flatteries. ²² The overwhelming forces will be overwhelmed from before him, and will be broken. Yes, also the prince of the covenant. ²³ After the treaty made with him he will work deceitfully; for he will come up and will become strong with few people. ²⁴ In time of security he will come even on the fattest places of the province. He will do that which his fathers have not done, nor his fathers' fathers. He will scatter among them prey, plunder, and wealth. Yes, he will devise his plans against the strongholds, but only for a time. ²⁵ "He will stir up his power and his courage against the king of the south with a great army; and the king of the south will wage war in battle with an exceedingly great and mighty army, but he won't stand; for they will devise plans against him. ²⁶ Yes, those who eat of his delicacies will destroy him, and his army will be swept away. Many will fall down slain. ²⁷ As for both these kings, their hearts will be to do evil, and they will speak lies at one table; but it won't prosper, for the end will still be at the appointed time. ²⁸ Then he will return into his land with great wealth. His heart will be against the holy covenant. He will take action, and return to his own land. ²⁹ "He will return at the appointed time and come into the south; but it won't be in the latter time as it was in the former. ³⁰ For ships of Kittim will come against him. Therefore he will be grieved, and will return, and have indignation against the holy covenant, and will take action. He will even return, and have regard to those who forsake the holy covenant. ³¹"Forces from him will profane the sanctuary, even the fortress, and will take away the continual burnt offering. Then they will set up the abomination that makes desolate. ³² He will corrupt those who do wickedly against the covenant by flatteries; but the people who know their God will be strong and take action. ³³"Those who are wise among the people will instruct many; yet they will fall by the sword and by flame, by captivity and by plunder, many days. ³⁴ Now when they fall, they will be helped with a little help; but many will join themselves to them with flatteries. ³⁵ Some of those who are wise will fall—to refine them, and to purify, and to make them white, even to the time of the end, because it is yet for the time appointed. ³⁶"The king will do according to his will. He will exalt himself and magnify himself above every god, and will speak marvelous things against the God of gods. He will prosper until the indignation is accomplished, for that which is determined will be done.

³⁷ He won't regard the gods of his fathers, or the desire of women, or regard any god; for he will magnify himself above all. ³⁸ But in their place he will honor the god of fortresses. He will honor a god whom his fathers didn't know with gold, silver, and with precious stones and pleasant things. ³⁹ He will deal with the strongest fortresses by the help of a foreign god. He will increase with glory whoever acknowledges him. He will cause them to rule over many, and will divide the land for a price. ⁴⁰"At the time of the end the king of the south will contend with him; and the king of the north will come against him like a whirlwind, with chariots, with horsemen, and with many ships. He will enter into the countries, and will overflow and pass through. ⁴¹ He will enter also into the glorious land, and many countries will be overthrown; but these will be delivered out of his hand: Edom, Moab, and the chief of the children of Ammon. ⁴² He will also stretch out his hand on the countries. The land of Egypt won't escape. ⁴³ But he will have power over the treasures of gold and of silver, and over all the precious things of Egypt. The Libyans and the Ethiopians will follow his steps. ⁴⁴ But news out of the east and out of the north will trouble him; and he will go out with great fury to destroy and utterly to sweep away many. ⁴⁵ He will plant the tents of his palace between the sea and the glorious holy mountain; yet he will come to his end, and no one will help him.

## 12

¹"At that time Michael will stand up, the great prince who stands for the children of your people; and there will be a time of trouble, such as never was since there was a nation even to that same time. At that time your people will be delivered, everyone who is found written in the book. ² Many of those who sleep in the dust of the earth will awake, some to everlasting life, and some to shame and everlasting contempt. ³ Those who are wise will shine as the brightness of the expanse. Those who turn many to righteousness will shine as the stars forever and ever. ⁴ But you, Daniel, shut up the words and seal the book, even to the time of the end. Many will run back and forth, and knowledge will be increased." ⁵ Then I, Daniel, looked, and behold, two others stood, one on the river bank on this side, and the other on the river bank on that side. ⁶ One said to the man clothed in linen, who was above the waters of the river, "How long will it be to the end of these wonders?" ⁷ I heard the man clothed in linen, who was above the waters of the river, when he held up his right hand and his left hand to heaven, and swore by him who lives forever that it will be for a time, times, and a half; and when they have finished breaking in pieces the power of the holy people, all these things will be finished. ⁸ I heard, but I didn't understand. Then I said, "My lord, what will be the outcome of these things?" ⁹ He said, "Go your way, Daniel; for the words are shut up and sealed until the time of the end. ¹⁰ Many will purify themselves, and make themselves white, and be refined, but the wicked will do wickedly; and none of the wicked will understand, but those who are wise will understand. ¹¹"From the time that the continual burnt offering is taken away and the abomination that makes desolate set up, there will be one thousand two hundred ninety days. ¹² Blessed is he who waits, and comes to the one thousand three hundred thirty-five days. ¹³"But go your way until the end; for you will rest, and will stand in your inheritance at the end of the days."

## The Book of Daniel with Greek Portions
### 1

¹ In the third year of the reign of Jehoiakim king of Judah, Nebuchadnezzar king of Babylon came to Jerusalem and besieged it. ² The Lordᵃ gave Jehoiakim king of Judah into his hand, with part of the vessels of the house of God;ᵇ and he carried them into the land of Shinar to the house of his god. He brought the vessels into the treasure house of his god. ³ The king spoke to Ashpenaz the master of his eunuchs, that he should bring in some of the children of Israel, even of the royal offspringᶜ and of the nobles— ⁴ youths in whom was no defect, but well-favored, and skillful in all wisdom, and endowed with knowledge, and understanding science, and who had the ability to serve in the king's palace; and that he should teach them the learning and the language of the Chaldeans. ⁵ The king appointed for them a daily portion of the king's delicacies, and of the wine which he drank, and that they should be nourished three years; that at its end they should serve the king. ⁶ Now among these were of the children of Judah: Daniel, Hananiah, Mishael, and Azariah. ⁷ The prince of the eunuchs gave names to them: to Daniel he gave the name Belteshazzar; to Hananiah, Shadrach; to Mishael, Meshach; and to Azariah, Abednego. ⁸ But Daniel purposed in his heart that he would not defile himself with the king's delicacies, nor with the wine which he drank. Therefore he

---

ᵃ *1:2* The word translated "Lord" is "Adonai."

ᵇ *1:2* The Hebrew word rendered "God" is "אֱלֹהִים" (Elohim).

ᶜ *1:3* or, seed

requested of the prince of the eunuchs that he might not defile himself. [9] Now God made Daniel find kindness and compassion in the sight of the prince of the eunuchs. [10] The prince of the eunuchs said to Daniel, "I fear my lord the king, who has appointed your food and your drink. For why should he see your faces worse looking than the youths who are of your own age? Then you would endanger my head with the king." [11] Then Daniel said to the steward whom the prince of the eunuchs had appointed over Daniel, Hananiah, Mishael, and Azariah: [12]"Test your servants, I beg you, ten days; and let them give us vegetables to eat and water to drink. [13] Then let our faces be examined before you, and the face of the youths who eat of the king's delicacies; and as you see, deal with your servants." [14] So he listened to them in this matter, and tested them for ten days. [15] At the end of ten days, their faces appeared fairer, and they were fatter in flesh, than all the youths who ate of the king's delicacies. [16] So the steward took away their delicacies, and the wine that they would drink, and gave them vegetables. [17] Now as for these four youths, God gave them knowledge and skill in all learning and wisdom; and Daniel had understanding in all visions and dreams. [18] At the end of the days which the king had appointed for bringing them in, the prince of the eunuchs brought them in before Nebuchadnezzar. [19] The king talked with them; and among them all was found no one like Daniel, Hananiah, Mishael, and Azariah. Therefore they served the king. [20] In every matter of wisdom and understanding concerning which the king inquired of them, he found them ten times better than all the magicians and enchanters who were in all his realm. [21] Daniel continued serving even to the first year of King Cyrus.

## 2

[1] In the second year of the reign of Nebuchadnezzar, Nebuchadnezzar dreamed dreams; and his spirit was troubled, and his sleep went from him. [2] Then the king commanded that the magicians, the enchanters, the sorcerers, and the Chaldeans be called to tell the king his dreams. So they came in and stood before the king. [3] The king said to them, "I have dreamed a dream, and my spirit is troubled to know the dream." [4] Then the Chaldeans spoke to the king in the Syrian language, "O king, live forever! Tell your servants the dream, and we will show the interpretation." [5] The king answered the Chaldeans, "The thing has gone from me. If you don't make known to me the dream and its interpretation, you will be cut in pieces, and your houses will be made a dunghill. [6] But if you show the dream and its interpretation, you will receive from me gifts, rewards, and great honor. Therefore show me the dream and its interpretation." [7] They answered the second time and said, "Let the king tell his servants the dream, and we will show the interpretation." [8] The king answered, "I know of a certainty that you are trying to gain time, because you see the thing has gone from me. [9] But if you don't make known to me the dream, there is but one law for you; for you have prepared lying and corrupt words to speak before me, until the situation changes. Therefore tell me the dream, and I will know that you can show me its interpretation." [10] The Chaldeans answered before the king, and said, "There is not a man on the earth who can show the king's matter, because no king, lord, or ruler, has asked such a thing of any magician, enchanter, or Chaldean. [11] It is a rare thing that the king requires, and there is no other who can show it before the king, except the gods, whose dwelling is not with flesh." [12] Because of this, the king was angry and very furious, and commanded that all the wise men of Babylon be destroyed. [13] So the decree went out, and the wise men were to be slain. They sought Daniel and his companions to be slain. [14] Then Daniel returned answer with counsel and prudence to Arioch the captain of the king's guard, who had gone out to kill the wise men of Babylon. [15] He answered Arioch the king's captain, "Why is the decree so urgent from the king?" Then Arioch made the thing known to Daniel. [16] Daniel went in, and desired of the king that he would appoint him a time, and he would show the king the interpretation. [17] Then Daniel went to his house and made the thing known to Hananiah, Mishael, and Azariah, his companions, [18] that they would desire mercies of the God of heaven concerning this secret, and that Daniel and his companions would not perish with the rest of the wise men of Babylon. [19] Then the secret was revealed to Daniel in a vision of the night. Then Daniel blessed the God of heaven. [20] Daniel answered, "Blessed be the name of God forever and ever; for wisdom and might are his. [21] He changes the times and the seasons. He removes kings and sets up kings. He gives wisdom to the wise, and knowledge to those who have understanding. [22] He reveals the deep and secret things. He knows what is in the darkness, and the light dwells with him. [23] I thank you and praise you, O God of my fathers, who have given me wisdom and might, and have now made known to me what we desired of you; for you have made known to us the king's matter." [24] Therefore Daniel went in to Arioch, whom the king had appointed to destroy the wise men of Babylon. He went and said this to him: "Don't destroy the wise men of Babylon. Bring me in before the king, and I will show to the king the interpretation." [25] Then Arioch brought in Daniel before the king in haste, and said this to him: "I have found a man of the children of the captivity of Judah who will make known to the king the interpretation." [26] The king answered Daniel, whose name was Belteshazzar, "Are you able to make known to me the dream which I have seen, and its interpretation?" [27] Daniel answered before the king, and said, "The secret which the king has demanded can't be shown to the king by wise men, enchanters, magicians, or soothsayers; [28] but there is a God in heaven who reveals secrets, and he has made known to King Nebuchadnezzar what will be in the latter days. Your dream, and the visions of your head on your bed, are these: [29]"As for you, O king, your thoughts came on your bed, what should happen hereafter; and he who reveals secrets has made known to you what will happen. [30] But as for me, this secret is not revealed to me for any wisdom that I have more than any living, but to the intent that the interpretation may be made known to the king, and that you may know the thoughts of your heart. [31]"You, O king, saw, and behold,[a] a great image. This image, which was mighty, and whose brightness was excellent, stood before you; and its appearance was terrifying. [32] As for this image, its head was of fine gold, its chest and its arms of silver, its belly and its thighs of bronze, [33] its legs of iron, its feet part of iron, and part of clay. [34] You saw until a stone was cut out without hands, which struck the image on its feet that were of iron and clay, and broke them in pieces. [35] Then the iron, the clay, the bronze, the silver, and the gold were broken in pieces together, and became like the chaff of the summer threshing floors. The wind carried them away, so that no place was found for them. The stone that struck the image became a great mountain, and filled the whole earth. [36]"This is the dream; and we will tell its interpretation before the king. [37] You, O king, are king of kings, to whom the God of heaven has given the kingdom, the power, the strength, and the glory. [38] Wherever the children of men dwell, he has given the animals of the field and the birds of the sky into your hand, and has made you rule over them all. You are the head of gold. [39]"After you, another kingdom will arise that is inferior to you; and a third kingdom of bronze, which will rule over all the earth. [40] The fourth kingdom will be strong as iron, because iron breaks in pieces and subdues all things; and as iron that crushes all these, it will break in pieces and crush. [41] Whereas you saw the feet and toes, part of potters' clay, and part of iron, it will be a divided kingdom; but there will be in it of the strength of the iron, because you saw the iron mixed with miry clay. [42] As the toes of the feet were part of iron, and part of clay, so the kingdom will be partly strong, and partly brittle. [43] Whereas you saw the iron mixed with miry clay, they will mingle themselves with the seed of men; but they won't cling to one another, even as iron does not mix with clay. [44]"In the days of those kings the God of heaven will set up a kingdom which will never be destroyed, nor will its sovereignty be left to another people; but it will break in pieces and consume all these kingdoms, and it will stand forever. [45] Because you saw that a stone was cut out of the mountain without hands, and that it broke in pieces the iron, the bronze, the clay, the silver, and the gold. The great God has made known to the king what will happen hereafter. The dream is certain, and its interpretation sure." [46] Then King Nebuchadnezzar fell on his face, worshiped Daniel, and commanded that they should offer an offering and sweet odors to him. [47] The king answered to Daniel, and said, "Of a truth your God is the God of gods, and the Lord of kings, and a revealer of secrets, since you have been able to reveal this secret." [48] Then the king made Daniel great, and gave him many great gifts, and made him rule over the whole province of Babylon, and to be chief governor over all the wise men of Babylon. [49] Daniel requested of the king, and he appointed Shadrach, Meshach, and Abednego over the affairs of the province of Babylon; but Daniel was in the king's gate.

## 3

[1] Nebuchadnezzar the king made an image of gold, whose height was sixty cubits,[b] and its width six cubits. He set it up in the plain of Dura, in the province of Babylon. [2] Then Nebuchadnezzar the king sent to gather together the local governors, the deputies, and the governors, the judges, the treasurers, the counselors, the sheriffs, and all the rulers of the provinces, to come to the dedication of the image which Nebuchadnezzar the king had set up. [3] Then the local governors, the deputies, and the governors, the judges, the treasurers, the counselors, the sheriffs, and all the rulers of the provinces, were gathered together to the dedication of the image that Nebuchadnezzar the king had set up; and they stood before the image that Nebuchadnezzar had set up. [4] Then

---

[a] *2:31* "Behold", from "הִנֵּה", means look at, take notice, observe, see, or gaze at. It is often used as an interjection.

[b] *3:1* A cubit is the length from the tip of the middle finger to the elbow on a man's arm, or about 18 inches or 46 centimeters.

the herald cried aloud, "To you it is commanded, peoples, nations, and languages, [5] that whenever you hear the sound of the horn, flute, zither, lyre, harp, pipe, and all kinds of music, you fall down and worship the golden image that Nebuchadnezzar the king has set up. [6] Whoever doesn't fall down and worship shall be cast into the middle of a burning fiery furnace the same hour." [7] Therefore at that time, when all the peoples heard the sound of the horn, flute, zither, lyre, harp, pipe, and all kinds of music, all the peoples, the nations, and the languages, fell down and worshiped the golden image that Nebuchadnezzar the king had set up. [8] Therefore at that time certain Chaldeans came near, and brought accusation against the Jews. [9] They answered Nebuchadnezzar the king, "O king, live for ever! [10] You, O king, have made a decree that every man who hears the sound of the horn, flute, zither, lyre, harp, pipe, and all kinds of music shall fall down and worship the golden image; [11] and whoever doesn't fall down and worship shall be cast into the middle of a burning fiery furnace. [12] There are certain Jews whom you have appointed over the affairs of the province of Babylon: Shadrach, Meshach, and Abednego. These men, O king, have not respected you. They don't serve your gods, and don't worship the golden image which you have set up." [13] Then Nebuchadnezzar in rage and fury commanded that Shadrach, Meshach, and Abednego be brought. Then these men were brought before the king. [14] Nebuchadnezzar answered them, "Is it on purpose, Shadrach, Meshach, and Abednego, that you don't serve my god, nor worship the golden image which I have set up? [15] Now if you are ready whenever you hear the sound of the horn, flute, zither, lyre, harp, pipe, and all kinds of music to fall down and worship the image which I have made, good; but if you don't worship, you shall be cast the same hour into the middle of a burning fiery furnace. Who is that god who will deliver you out of my hands?" [16] Shadrach, Meshach, and Abednego answered the king, "Nebuchadnezzar, we have no need to answer you in this matter. [17] If it happens, our God whom we serve is able to deliver us from the burning fiery furnace; and he will deliver us out of your hand, O king. [18] But if not, let it be known to you, O king, that we will not serve your gods or worship the golden image which you have set up." [19] Then Nebuchadnezzar was full of fury, and the form of his appearance was changed against Shadrach, Meshach, and Abednego. He spoke, and commanded that they should heat the furnace seven times more than it was usually heated. [20] He commanded certain mighty men who were in his army to bind Shadrach, Meshach, and Abednego, and to cast them into the burning fiery furnace. [21] Then these men were bound in their pants, their tunics, their mantles, and their other clothes, and were cast into the middle of the burning fiery furnace. [22] Therefore because the king's commandment was urgent, and the furnace exceedingly hot, the flame of the fire killed those men who took up Shadrach, Meshach, and Abednego. [23] These three men, Shadrach, Meshach, and Abednego, fell down bound into the middle of the burning fiery furnace.

# The Song of the Three Holy Children[a], or The Prayer of Azariah

**Continuation of Daniel with Greek Portions**

## 3

[24] They walked in the midst of the fire, praising God, and blessing the Lord. [25] Then Azarias stood, and prayed like this. Opening his mouth in the midst of the fire he said, [26]"Blessed are you, O Lord, you God of our fathers! Your name is worthy to be praised and glorified for evermore; [27] for you are righteous in all the things that you have done. Yes, all your works are true. Your ways are right, and all your judgments are truth. [28] In all the things that you have brought upon us, and upon the holy city of our fathers, Jerusalem, you have executed true judgments. For according to truth and justice you have brought all these things upon us because of our sins. [29] For we have sinned and committed iniquity in departing from you. [30] In all things we have trespassed, and not obeyed your commandments or kept them. We haven't done as you have commanded us, that it might go well with us. [31] Therefore all that you have brought upon us, and everything that you have done to us, you have done in true judgment. [32] You delivered us into the hands of lawless enemies, most hateful rebels, and to an unjust king who is the most wicked in all the world. [33] And now we can't open our mouth. Shame and reproach have come on your servants and those who worship you. [34] Don't utterly deliver us up, for your name's sake. Don't annul your covenant. [35] Don't cause your mercy to depart from us, for the sake of Abraham who is loved by you, and for the sake of

Isaac your servant, and Israel your holy one, [36] to whom you promised that you would multiply their offspring as the stars of the sky, and as the sand that is on the sea shore. [37] For we, O Lord, have become less than any nation, and are brought low this day in all the world because of our sins. [38] There isn't at this time prince, or prophet, or leader, or burnt offering, or sacrifice, or oblation, or incense, or place to offer before you, and to find mercy. [39] Nevertheless in a contrite heart and a humble spirit let us be accepted, [40] like the burnt offerings of rams and bullocks, and like ten thousands of fat lambs. So let our sacrifice be in your sight this day, that we may wholly go after you, for they shall not be ashamed who put their trust in you. [41] And now we follow you with all our heart. We fear you, and seek your face. [42] Put us not to shame; but deal with us after your kindness, and according to the multitude of your mercy. [43] Deliver us also according to your marvelous works, and give glory to your name, O Lord. Let all those who harm your servants be confounded. [44] Let them be ashamed of all their power and might, and let their strength be broken. [45] Let them know that you are the Lord, the only God, and glorious over the whole world." [46] The king's servants who put them in didn't stop making the furnace hot with naphtha, pitch, tinder, and small wood, [47] so that the flame streamed out forty nine cubits above the furnace. [48] It spread and burned those Chaldeans whom it found around the furnace. [49] But the angel of the Lord came down into the furnace together with Azarias and his fellows, and he struck the flame of the fire out of the furnace, [50] and made the midst of the furnace as it had been a moist whistling wind, so that the fire didn't touch them at all. It neither hurt nor troubled them. [51] Then the three, as out of one mouth, praised, glorified, and blessed God in the furnace, saying, [52]"Blessed are you, O Lord, you God of our fathers, to be praised and exalted above all forever! [53] Blessed is your glorious and holy name, to be praised and exalted above all forever! [54] Blessed are you in the temple of your holy glory, to be praised and glorified above all forever! [55] Blessed are you who see the depths and sit upon the cherubim, to be praised and exalted above all forever. [56] Blessed are you on the throne of your kingdom, to be praised and extolled above all forever! [57] Blessed are you in the firmament of heaven, to be praised and glorified forever! [58] O all you works of the Lord, bless the Lord! Praise and exalt him above all forever! [59] O you heavens, bless the Lord! Praise and exalt him above all for ever! [60] O you angels of the Lord, bless the Lord! Praise and exalt him above all forever! [61] O all you waters that are above the sky, bless the Lord! Praise and exalt him above all forever! [62] O all you powers of the Lord, bless the Lord! Praise and exalt him above all forever! [63] O you sun and moon, bless the Lord! Praise and exalt him above all forever! [64] O you stars of heaven, bless the Lord! Praise and exalt him above all forever! [65] O every shower and dew, bless the Lord! Praise and exalt him above all forever! [66] O all you winds, bless the Lord! Praise and exalt him above all forever! [67] O you fire and heat, bless the Lord! Praise and exalt him above all forever! [68] O you dews and storms of snow, bless the Lord! Praise and exalt him above all forever! [69] O you nights and days, bless the Lord! Praise and exalt him above all forever! [70] O you light and darkness, bless the Lord! Praise and exalt him above all forever! [71] O you cold and heat, bless the Lord! Praise and exalt him above all forever! [72] O you frost and snow, bless the Lord! Praise and exalt him above all forever! [73] O you lightnings and clouds, bless the Lord! Praise and exalt him above all forever! [74] O let the earth bless the Lord! Let it praise and exalt him above all forever! [75] O you mountains and hills, bless the Lord! Praise and exalt him above all forever! [76] O all you things that grow on the earth, bless the Lord! Praise and exalt him above all forever! [77] [b]O sea and rivers, bless the Lord! Praise and exalt him above all forever! [78] O you springs, bless the Lord! Praise and exalt him above all forever! [79] O you whales and all that move in the waters, bless the Lord! Praise and exalt him above all forever! [80] O all you birds of the air, bless the Lord! Praise and exalt him above all forever! [81] O all you beasts and cattle, bless the Lord! Praise and exalt him above all forever! [82] O you children of men, bless the Lord! Praise and exalt him above all forever! [83] O let Israel bless the Lord! Praise and exalt him above all forever. [84] O you priests of the Lord, bless the Lord! Praise and exalt him above all forever! [85] O you servants of the Lord, bless the Lord! Praise and exalt him above all forever! [86] O you spirits and souls of the righteous, bless the Lord! Praise and exalt him above all forever! [87] O you who are holy and humble of heart, bless the Lord! Praise and exalt him above all forever! [88] O Hananiah, Mishael, and Azariah, bless the Lord! Praise and exalt him above all forever; for he has rescued us from Hades, and saved us from the hand of death! He has delivered us out of the midst of the furnace and burning flame. He has delivered us out of the midst

---

[a] *3:24 The Song of the Three Holy Children* is an addition to *Daniel* found in the Greek Septuagint but not found in the traditional Hebrew text of *Daniel*. This portion is recognized as Deuterocanonical Scripture by the Roman Catholic, Greek Orthodox, and Russian Orthodox Churches. It is found inserted between Daniel 3:23 and Daniel 3:24 of the traditional Hebrew Bible. Here, the verses after 23 from the Hebrew Bible are numbered starting at 91 to make room for these verses.
[b] *3:77 Some authorities transpose this verse and the next one.*

of the fire. ⁸⁹ O give thanks to the Lord, for he is good; for his mercy is forever. ⁹⁰ O all you who worship the Lord, bless the God of gods, praise him, and give him thanks; for his mercy is forever!"

**Deliverance from the Furnace**

⁹¹ ᵃ Then Nebuchadnezzar the king was astonished and rose up in haste. He spoke and said to his counselors, "Didn't we cast three men bound into the middle of the fire?" They answered the king, "True, O king." ⁹² He answered, "Look, I see four men loose, walking in the middle of the fire, and they are unharmed. The appearance of the fourth is like a son of the gods." ⁹³ Then Nebuchadnezzar came near to the mouth of the burning fiery furnace. He spoke and said, "Shadrach, Meshach, and Abednego, you servants of the Most High God, come out, and come here!" Then Shadrach, Meshach, and Abednego came out of the middle of the fire. ⁹⁴ The local governors, the deputies, and the governors, and the king's counselors, being gathered together, saw these men, that the fire had no power on their bodies. The hair of their head wasn't singed. Their pants weren't changed. The smell of fire wasn't even on them. ⁹⁵ Nebuchadnezzar spoke and said, "Blessed be the God of Shadrach, Meshach, and Abednego, who has sent his angel and delivered his servants who trusted in him, and have changed the king's word, and have yielded their bodies, that they might not serve nor worship any god, except their own God. ⁹⁶ Therefore I make a decree, that every people, nation, and language, who speak anything evil against the God of Shadrach, Meshach, and Abednego, shall be cut in pieces, and their houses shall be made a dunghill, because there is no other god who is able to deliver like this." ⁹⁷ Then the king promoted Shadrach, Meshach, and Abednego in the province of Babylon.

# 4

¹ Nebuchadnezzar the king, to all the peoples, nations, and languages, who dwell in all the earth: Peace be multiplied to you. ² It has seemed good to me to show the signs and wonders that the Most High God has worked toward me. ³ How great are his signs! How mighty are his wonders! His kingdom is an everlasting kingdom. His dominion is from generation to generation. ⁴ I, Nebuchadnezzar, was at rest in my house, and flourishing in my palace. ⁵ I saw a dream which made me afraid; and the thoughts on my bed and the visions of my head troubled me. ⁶ Therefore I made a decree to bring in all the wise men of Babylon before me, that they might make known to me the interpretation of the dream. ⁷ Then the magicians, the enchanters, the Chaldeans, and the soothsayers came in; and I told the dream before them; but they didn't make known to me its interpretation. ⁸ But at the last Daniel came in before me, whose name was Belteshazzar, according to the name of my god, and in whom is the spirit of the holy gods. I told the dream before him, saying, ⁹"Belteshazzar, master of the magicians, because I know that the spirit of the holy gods is in you, and no secret troubles you, tell me the visions of my dream that I have seen, and its interpretation. ¹⁰ These were the visions of my head on my bed: I saw, and behold, a tree in the middle of the earth; and its height was great. ¹¹ The tree grew, and was strong, and its height reached to the sky, and its sight to the end of all the earth. ¹² Its leaves were beautiful, and it had much fruit, and in it was food for all. The animals of the field had shade under it, and the birds of the sky lived in its branches, and all flesh was fed from it. ¹³"I saw in the visions of my head on my bed, and behold, a watcher and a holy one came down from the sky. ¹⁴ He cried aloud, and said this, 'Cut down the tree and cut off its branches! Shake off its leaves and scatter its fruit! Let the animals get away from under it, and the fowls from its branches. ¹⁵ Nevertheless leave the stump of its roots in the earth, even with a band of iron and bronze, in the tender grass of the field; and let it be wet with the dew of the sky. Let his portion be with the animals in the grass of the earth. ¹⁶ Let his heart be changed from man's, and let an animal's heart be given to him. Then let seven times pass over him. ¹⁷"'The sentence is by the decree of the watchers, and the demand by the word of the holy ones, to the intent that the living may know that the Most High rules in the kingdom of men, and gives it to whomever he will, and sets up over it the lowest of men.' ¹⁸"This dream I, King Nebuchadnezzar, have seen; and you, Belteshazzar, declare the interpretation, because all the wise men of my kingdom are not able to make known to me the interpretation; but you are able, for the spirit of the holy gods is in you." ¹⁹ Then Daniel, whose name was Belteshazzar, was stricken mute for a while, and his thoughts troubled him. The king answered, "Belteshazzar, don't let the dream, or the interpretation, trouble you." Belteshazzar answered, "My lord, may the dream be for those who hate you, and its interpretation to your adversaries. ²⁰ The tree that you saw, which grew and was strong, whose height reached to the sky, and its sight to all the earth; ²¹ whose leaves were beautiful, and its fruit plentiful, and in it was food for all; under which the animals of the field lived, and on whose branches the birds

of the sky had their habitation— ²² it is you, O king, who have grown and become strong; for your greatness has grown, and reaches to the sky, and your dominion to the end of the earth. ²³"Whereas the king saw a watcher and a holy one coming down from the sky, and saying, 'Cut down the tree, and destroy it; nevertheless leave the stump of its roots in the earth, even with a band of iron and bronze, in the tender grass of the field, and let it be wet with the dew of the sky. Let his portion be with the animals of the field, until seven times pass over him.' ²⁴"This is the interpretation, O king, and it is the decree of the Most High, which has come on my lord the king: ²⁵ that you shall be driven from men, and your dwelling shall be with the animals of the field. You shall be made to eat grass as oxen, and shall be wet with the dew of the sky, and seven times shall pass over you; until you know that the Most High rules in the kingdom of men, and gives it to whomever he will. ²⁶ Their command to leave the stump of the roots of the tree means your kingdom will be sure to you, after you will have known that the heavens do rule. ²⁷ Therefore, O king, let my counsel be acceptable to you, and break off your sins by righteousness, and your iniquities by showing mercy to the poor. Perhaps there may be a lengthening of your tranquility." ²⁸ All this came on the King Nebuchadnezzar. ²⁹ At the end of twelve months he was walking in the royal palace of Babylon. ³⁰ The king spoke and said, "Is not this great Babylon, which I have built for the royal dwelling place, by the might of my power and for the glory of my majesty?" ³¹ While the word was in the king's mouth, a voice came from the sky, saying, "O King Nebuchadnezzar, to you it is spoken: 'The kingdom has departed from you. ³² You shall be driven from men, and your dwelling shall be with the animals of the field. You shall be made to eat grass as oxen. Seven times shall pass over you, until you know that the Most High rules in the kingdom of men, and gives it to whomever he will.'" ³³ This was fulfilled the same hour on Nebuchadnezzar. He was driven from men, and ate grass as oxen, and his body was wet with the dew of the sky, until his hair had grown like eagles' feathers, and his nails like birds' claws. ³⁴ At the end of the days I, Nebuchadnezzar, lifted up my eyes to heaven, and my understanding returned to me, and I blessed the Most High, and I praised and honored him who lives forever. For his dominion is an everlasting dominion, and his kingdom from generation to generation. ³⁵ All the inhabitants of the earth are reputed as nothing; and he does according to his will in the army of heaven, and among the inhabitants of the earth; and no one can stop his hand, or ask him, "What are you doing?" ³⁶ At the same time my understanding returned to me; and for the glory of my kingdom, my majesty and brightness returned to me. My counselors and my lords sought me; and I was established in my kingdom, and excellent greatness was added to me. ³⁷ Now I, Nebuchadnezzar, praise and extol and honor the King of heaven; for all his works are right and his ways just; and those who walk in pride he is able to humble.

# 5

¹ Belshazzar the king made a great feast to a thousand of his lords, and drank wine before the thousand. ² Belshazzar, while he tasted the wine, commanded that the golden and silver vessels which Nebuchadnezzar his father had taken out of the temple which was in Jerusalem be brought to him, that the king and his lords, his wives and his concubines, might drink from them. ³ Then they brought the golden vessels that were taken out of the temple of God's house which was at Jerusalem; and the king and his lords, his wives and his concubines, drank from them. ⁴ They drank wine, and praised the gods of gold, and of silver, of bronze, of iron, of wood, and of stone. ⁵ In the same hour, the fingers of a man's hand came out and wrote near the lamp stand on the plaster of the wall of the king's palace. The king saw the part of the hand that wrote. ⁶ Then the king's face was changed in him, and his thoughts troubled him; and the joints of his thighs were loosened, and his knees struck one against another. ⁷ The king cried aloud to bring in the enchanters, the Chaldeans, and the soothsayers. The king spoke and said to the wise men of Babylon, "Whoever reads this writing and shows me its interpretation shall be clothed with purple, and have a chain of gold about his neck, and shall be the third ruler in the kingdom." ⁸ Then all the king's wise men came in; but they could not read the writing and couldn't make known to the king the interpretation. ⁹ Then King Belshazzar was greatly troubled. His face was changed in him, and his lords were perplexed. ¹⁰ The queen by reason of the words of the king and his lords came into the banquet house. The queen spoke and said, "O king, live forever; don't let your thoughts trouble you, nor let your face be changed. ¹¹ There is a man in your kingdom in whom is the spirit of the holy gods. In the days of your father, light, understanding, and wisdom like the wisdom of the gods were found in him. The king, Nebuchadnezzar, your father—yes, the king, your

father—made him master of the magicians, enchanters, Chaldeans, and soothsayers [12] because an excellent spirit, knowledge, understanding, interpreting of dreams, showing of dark sentences, and dissolving of doubts were found in the same Daniel, whom the king named Belteshazzar. Now let Daniel be called, and he will show the interpretation." [13] Then Daniel was brought in before the king. The king spoke and said to Daniel, "Are you that Daniel of the children of the captivity of Judah, whom the king my father brought out of Judah? [14] I have heard of you, that the spirit of the gods is in you, and that light, understanding, and excellent wisdom are found in you. [15] Now the wise men, the enchanters, have been brought in before me to read this writing, and make known to me its interpretation; but they could not show the interpretation of the thing. [16] But I have heard of you, that you can give interpretations and dissolve doubts. Now if you can read the writing, and make known to me its interpretation, you shall be clothed with purple, and have a chain of gold around your neck, and shall be the third ruler in the kingdom." [17] Then Daniel answered the king, "Let your gifts be to yourself, and give your rewards to another. Nevertheless, I will read the writing to the king, and make known to him the interpretation. [18]"To you, king, the Most High God gave Nebuchadnezzar your father the kingdom, and greatness, and glory, and majesty. [19] Because of the greatness that he gave him, all the peoples, nations, and languages trembled and feared before him. He killed whom he wanted to, and he kept alive whom he wanted to. He raised up whom he wanted to, and he put down whom he wanted to. [20] But when his heart was lifted up, and his spirit was hardened so that he dealt proudly, he was deposed from his kingly throne, and they took his glory from him. [21] He was driven from the sons of men and his heart was made like the animals', and his dwelling was with the wild donkeys. He was fed with grass like oxen, and his body was wet with the dew of the sky, until he knew that the Most High God rules in the kingdom of men, and that he sets up over it whomever he will. [22]"You, his son, Belshazzar, have not humbled your heart, though you knew all this, [23] but have lifted up yourself against the Lord of heaven; and they have brought the vessels of his house before you, and you and your lords, your wives, and your concubines, have drunk wine from them. You have praised the gods of silver, gold, bronze, iron, wood, and stone, which don't see, hear, or know; and you have not glorified the God in whose hand is your breath and whose are all your ways. [24] Then the part of the hand was sent from before him, and this writing was inscribed. [25]"This is the writing that was inscribed: 'MENE, MENE, TEKEL, UPHARSIN.' [26]"This is the interpretation of the thing: MENE: God has counted your kingdom, and brought it to an end. [27] TEKEL: you are weighed in the balances, and are found wanting. [28] PERES: your kingdom is divided, and given to the Medes and Persians." [29] Then Belshazzar commanded, and they clothed Daniel with purple, and put a chain of gold about his neck, and proclaimed that he should be the third highest ruler in the kingdom. [30] In that night Belshazzar the Chaldean King was slain. [31] Darius the Mede received the kingdom, being about sixty-two years old.

## 6

[1] It pleased Darius to set over the kingdom one hundred twenty local governors, who should be throughout the whole kingdom; [2] and over them three presidents, of whom Daniel was one; that these local governors might give account to them, and that the king should suffer no loss. [3] Then this Daniel was distinguished above the presidents and the local governors, because an excellent spirit was in him; and the king thought to set him over the whole realm. [4] Then the presidents and the local governors sought to find occasion against Daniel as touching the kingdom; but they could find no occasion or fault, because he was faithful. There wasn't any error or fault found in him. [5] Then these men said, "We won't find any occasion against this Daniel, unless we find it against him concerning the law of his God." [6] Then these presidents and local governors assembled together to the king, and said this to him, "King Darius, live forever! [7] All the presidents of the kingdom, the deputies and the local governors, the counselors and the governors, have consulted together to establish a royal statute, and to make a strong decree, that whoever asks a petition of any god or man for thirty days, except of you, O king, he shall be cast into the den of lions. [8] Now, O king, establish the decree, and sign the writing, that it not be changed, according to the law of the Medes and Persians, which doesn't alter." [9] Therefore King Darius signed the writing and the decree. [10] When Daniel knew that the writing was signed, he went into his house (now his windows were open in his room toward Jerusalem) and he kneeled on his knees three times a day, and prayed, and gave thanks before his God, as he did before. [11] Then these men assembled together, and found Daniel making petition and supplication before his God. [12] Then they came near, and spoke before the king concerning the king's decree: "Haven't you signed a decree that every man who makes a petition to any god or man within thirty days, except to you, O king, shall be cast

into the den of lions?" The king answered, "This thing is true, according to the law of the Medes and Persians, which doesn't alter." [13] Then they answered and said before the king, "That Daniel, who is of the children of the captivity of Judah, doesn't respect you, O king, nor the decree that you have signed, but makes his petition three times a day." [14] Then the king, when he heard these words, was very displeased, and set his heart on Daniel to deliver him; and he labored until the going down of the sun to rescue him. [15] Then these men assembled together to the king, and said to the king, "Know, O king, that it is a law of the Medes and Persians, that no decree nor statute which the king establishes may be changed." [16] Then the king commanded, and they brought Daniel, and cast him into the den of lions. The king spoke and said to Daniel, "Your God whom you serve continually, he will deliver you." [17] A stone was brought, and laid on the mouth of the den; and the king sealed it with his own signet, and with the signet of his lords, that nothing might be changed concerning Daniel. [18] Then the king went to his palace, and passed the night fasting. No musical instruments were brought before him; and his sleep fled from him. [19] Then the king arose very early in the morning, and went in haste to the den of lions. [20] When he came near to the den to Daniel, he cried with a troubled voice. The king spoke and said to Daniel, "Daniel, servant of the living God, is your God, whom you serve continually, able to deliver you from the lions?" [21] Then Daniel said to the king, "O king, live forever! [22] My God has sent his angel, and has shut the lions' mouths, and they have not hurt me; because I am innocent in his sight. Also before you, O king, I have done no harm." [23] Then the king was exceedingly glad, and commanded that they should take Daniel up out of the den. So Daniel was taken up out of the den, and no kind of harm was found on him, because he had trusted in his God. [24] The king commanded, and they brought those men who had accused Daniel, and they cast them into the den of lions— them, their children, and their wives; and the lions mauled them and broke all their bones in pieces before they came to the bottom of the den. [25] Then King Darius wrote to all the peoples, nations, and languages, who dwell in all the earth: "Peace be multiplied to you. [26]"I make a decree that in all the dominion of my kingdom men tremble and fear before the God of Daniel; "for he is the living God, and steadfast forever. His kingdom is that which will not be destroyed. His dominion will be even to the end. [27] He delivers and rescues. He works signs and wonders in heaven and in earth, who has delivered Daniel from the power of the lions." [28] So this Daniel prospered in the reign of Darius, and in the reign of Cyrus the Persian.

## 7

[1] In the first year of Belshazzar king of Babylon, Daniel had a dream and visions of his head on his bed. Then he wrote the dream and told the sum of the matters. [2] Daniel spoke and said, "I saw in my vision by night and behold, the four winds of the sky broke out on the great sea. [3] Four great animals came up from the sea, different from one another. [4]"The first was like a lion, and had eagle's wings. I watched until its wings were plucked, and it was lifted up from the earth, and made to stand on two feet as a man. A man's heart was given to it. [5]"Behold, there was another animal, a second, like a bear. It was raised up on one side, and three ribs were in its mouth between its teeth. They said this to it: 'Arise! Devour much flesh!' [6]"After this I saw, and behold, another, like a leopard, which had on its back four wings of a bird. The animal also had four heads; and dominion was given to it. [7]"After this I saw in the night visions, and, behold, there was a fourth animal, awesome and powerful, and exceedingly strong. It had great iron teeth. It devoured and broke in pieces, and stamped the residue with its feet. It was different from all the animals that were before it. It had ten horns. [8]"I considered the horns, and behold, another horn came up among them, a little one, before which three of the first horns were plucked up by the roots: and behold, in this horn were eyes like the eyes of a man, and a mouth speaking great things. [9]"I watched until thrones were placed, and one who was Ancient of Days sat. His clothing was white as snow, and the hair of his head like pure wool. His throne was fiery flames, and its wheels burning fire. [10] A fiery stream issued and came out from before him. Thousands of thousands ministered to him. Ten thousand times ten thousand stood before him. The judgment was set. The books were opened. [11]"I watched at that time because of the voice of the great words which the horn spoke. I watched even until the animal was slain, its body destroyed, and it was given to be burned with fire. [12] As for the rest of the animals, their dominion was taken away; yet their lives were prolonged for a season and a time. [13]"I saw in the night visions, and behold, one like a son of man came with the clouds, and he came to the Ancient of Days, and they brought him near before him. [14] Dominion was given him, with glory and a kingdom, that all the peoples, nations, and languages should serve him. His dominion is an everlasting dominion, which will not pass away, and his kingdom will not be destroyed. [15]"As for me, Daniel, my spirit was grieved within my body, and the visions of my head troubled me. [16] I came near to one

of those who stood by, and asked him the truth concerning all this. "So he told me, and made me know the interpretation of the things. ¹⁷·These great animals, which are four, are four kings, who will arise out of the earth. ¹⁸ But the saints of the Most High will receive the kingdom, and possess the kingdom forever, even forever and ever.' ¹⁹"Then I desired to know the truth concerning the fourth animal, which was different from all of them, exceedingly terrible, whose teeth were of iron, and its nails of bronze; which devoured, broke in pieces, and stamped the residue with its feet; ²⁰ and concerning the ten horns that were on its head, and the other horn which came up, and before which three fell, even that horn that had eyes, and a mouth that spoke great things, whose look was more stout than its fellows. ²¹ I saw, and the same horn made war with the saints and prevailed against them ²² until the Ancient of Days came, and judgment was given to the saints of the Most High, and the time came that the saints possessed the kingdom. ²³"So he said, 'The fourth animal will be a fourth kingdom on earth, which will be different from all the kingdoms, and will devour the whole earth, and will tread it down, and break it in pieces. ²⁴ As for the ten horns, ten kings will arise out of this kingdom. Another will arise after them; and he will be different from the former, and he will put down three kings. ²⁵ He will speak words against the Most High, and will wear out the saints of the Most High. He will plan to change the times and the law; and they will be given into his hand until a time and times and half a time. ²⁶"But the judgment will be set, and they will take away his dominion, to consume and to destroy it to the end. ²⁷ The kingdom and the dominion, and the greatness of the kingdoms under the whole sky, will be given to the people of the saints of the Most High. His kingdom is an everlasting kingdom, and all dominions will serve and obey him.' ²⁸"Here is the end of the matter. As for me, Daniel, my thoughts troubled me greatly, and my face was changed in me; but I kept the matter in my heart."

# 8

¹ In the third year of the reign of King Belshazzar, a vision appeared to me, even to me, Daniel, after that which appeared to me at the first. ² I saw the vision. Now it was so, that when I saw, I was in the citadel of Susa, which is in the province of Elam. I saw in the vision, and I was by the river Ulai. ³ Then I lifted up my eyes, and saw, and behold, a ram which had two horns stood before the river. The two horns were high; but one was higher than the other, and the higher came up last. ⁴ I saw the ram pushing westward, northward, and southward. No animals could stand before him. There wasn't anyone who could deliver out of his hand; but he did according to his will, and magnified himself. ⁵ As I was considering, behold, a male goat came from the west over the surface of the whole earth, and didn't touch the ground. The goat had a notable horn between his eyes. ⁶ He came to the ram that had the two horns, which I saw standing before the river, and ran on him in the fury of his power. ⁷ I saw him come close to the ram, and he was moved with anger against him, and struck the ram, and broke his two horns. There was no power in the ram to stand before him; but he cast him down to the ground, and trampled on him. There was no one who could deliver the ram out of his hand. ⁸ The male goat magnified himself exceedingly. When he was strong, the great horn was broken; and instead of it there came up four notable horns toward the four winds of the sky. ⁹ Out of one of them came out a little horn, which grew exceedingly great, toward the south, and toward the east, and toward the glorious land. ¹⁰ It grew great, even to the army of the sky; and it cast down some of the army and of the stars to the ground, and trampled on them. ¹¹ Yes, it magnified itself, even to the prince of the army; and it took away from him the continual burnt offering, and the place of his sanctuary was cast down. ¹² The army was given over to it together with the continual burnt offering through disobedience. It cast down truth to the ground, and it did its pleasure and prospered. ¹³ Then I heard a holy one speaking; and another holy one said to that certain one who spoke, "How long will the vision about the continual burnt offering, and the disobedience that makes desolate, to give both the sanctuary and the army to be trodden under foot be?" ¹⁴ He said to me, "To two thousand and three hundred evenings and mornings. Then the sanctuary will be cleansed." ¹⁵ When I, even I Daniel, had seen the vision, I sought to understand it. Then behold, there stood before me something like the appearance of a man. ¹⁶ I heard a man's voice between the banks of the Ulai, which called, and said, "Gabriel, make this man understand the vision." ¹⁷ So he came near where I stood; and when he came, I was frightened, and fell on my face; but he said to me, "Understand, son of man; for the vision belongs to the time of the end." ¹⁸ Now as he was speaking with me, I fell into a deep sleep with my face toward the ground; but he touched me, and set me upright. ¹⁹ He said, "Behold, I will make you know what will be in the latter time of the indignation; for it belongs to the appointed time

of the end. ²⁰ The ram which you saw, that had the two horns, they are the kings of Media and Persia. ²¹ The rough male goat is the king of Greece. The great horn that is between his eyes is the first king. ²² As for that which was broken, in the place where four stood up, four kingdoms will stand up out of the nation, but not with his power. ²³"In the latter time of their kingdom, when the transgressors have come to the full, a king of fierce face, and understanding dark sentences, will stand up. ²⁴ His power will be mighty, but not by his own power. He will destroy awesomely, and will prosper in what he does. He will destroy the mighty ones and the holy people. ²⁵ Through his policy he will cause deceit to prosper in his hand. He will magnify himself in his heart, and he will destroy many in their security. He will also stand up against the prince of princes; but he will be broken without human power. ²⁶"The vision of the evenings and mornings which has been told is true; but seal up the vision, for it belongs to many days to come." ²⁷ I, Daniel, fainted, and was sick for some days. Then I rose up, and did the king's business. I wondered at the vision, but no one understood it.

# 9

¹ In the first year of Darius the son of Ahasuerus, of the offspring of the Medes, who was made king over the realm of the Chaldeans, ² in the first year of his reign I, Daniel, understood by the books the number of the years about which Yahweh'sᵃ word came to Jeremiah the prophet, for the accomplishing of the desolations of Jerusalem, even seventy years. ³ I set my face to the Lord God, to seek by prayer and petitions, with fasting in sackcloth and ashes. ⁴ I prayed to Yahweh my God, and made confession, and said, "Oh, Lord, the great and dreadful God, who keeps covenant and loving kindness with those who love him and keep his commandments, ⁵ we have sinned, and have dealt perversely, and have done wickedly, and have rebelled, even turning aside from your precepts and from your ordinances. ⁶ We haven't listened to your servants the prophets, who spoke in your name to our kings, our princes, and our fathers, and to all the people of the land. ⁷"Lord, righteousness belongs to you, but to us confusion of face, as it is today—to the men of Judah, and to the inhabitants of Jerusalem, and to all Israel, who are near, and who are far off, through all the countries where you have driven them, because of their trespass that they have trespassed against you. ⁸ Lord, to us belongs confusion of face, to our kings, to our princes, and to our fathers, because we have sinned against you. ⁹ To the Lord our God belong mercies and forgiveness; for we have rebelled against him. ¹⁰ We haven't obeyed Yahweh our God's voice, to walk in his laws, which he set before us by his servants the prophets. ¹¹ Yes, all Israel have transgressed your law, turning aside, that they wouldn't obey your voice. "Therefore the curse and the oath written in the law of Moses the servant of God has been poured out on us; for we have sinned against him. ¹² He has confirmed his words, which he spoke against us, and against our judges who judged us, by bringing on us a great evil; for under the whole sky, such has not been done as has been done to Jerusalem. ¹³ As it is written in the law of Moses, all this evil has come on us. Yet we have not entreated the favor of Yahweh our God, that we should turn from our iniquities and have discernment in your truth. ¹⁴ Therefore Yahweh has watched over the evil, and brought it on us; for Yahweh our God is righteous in all his works which he does, and we have not obeyed his voice. ¹⁵"Now, Lord our God, who has brought your people out of the land of Egypt with a mighty hand, and have gotten yourself renown, as it is today, we have sinned. We have done wickedly. ¹⁶ Lord, according to all your righteousness, please let your anger and your wrath be turned away from your city Jerusalem, your holy mountain, because for our sins, and for the iniquities of our fathers, Jerusalem and your people have become a reproach to all who are around us. ¹⁷"Now therefore, our God, listen to the prayer of your servant, and to his petitions, and cause your face to shine on your sanctuary that is desolate, for the Lord's sake. ¹⁸ My God, turn your ear and hear. Open your eyes and see our desolations and the city which is called by your name; for we don't present our petitions before you for our righteousness, but for your great mercies' sake. ¹⁹ Lord, hear. Lord, forgive. Lord, listen and do. Don't defer, for your own sake, my God, because your city and your people are called by your name." ²⁰ While I was speaking, praying, and confessing my sin and the sin of my people Israel, and presenting my supplication before Yahweh my God for the holy mountain of my God— ²¹ yes, while I was speaking in prayer, the man Gabriel, whom I had seen in the vision at the beginning, being caused to fly swiftly, touched me about the time of the evening offering. ²² He instructed me and talked with me, and said, "Daniel, I have now come to give you wisdom and understanding. ²³ At the beginning of your petitions the commandment went out and I have come to tell you, for you are greatly beloved. Therefore consider the matter and understand the vision. ²⁴"Seventy weeks are decreed on your people

ᵃ 9:2 "Yahweh" is God's proper Name, sometimes rendered "LORD" (all caps) in other translations.

and on your holy city, to finish disobedience, to put an end to sin, to make reconciliation for iniquity, to bring in everlasting righteousness, to seal up vision and prophecy, and to anoint the most holy. ²⁵"Know therefore and discern that from the going out of the commandment to restore and to build Jerusalem to the Anointed One,ᵃ the prince, will be seven weeks and sixty-two weeks. It will be built again with street and moat, even in troubled times. ²⁶ After the sixty-two weeks the Anointed Oneᵇ will be cut off and will have nothing. The people of the prince who come will destroy the city and the sanctuary. Its end will be with a flood, and war will be even to the end. Desolations are determined. ²⁷ He will make a firm covenant with many for one week. In the middle of the week he will cause the sacrifice and the offering to cease. On the wing of abominations will come one who makes desolate. Even to the full end that is decreed, wrath will be poured out on the desolate."

## 10

¹ In the third year of Cyrus king of Persia a revelation was revealed to Daniel, whose name was called Belteshazzar. The revelation was true, even a great warfare. He understood the revelation, and had understanding of the vision. ² In those days I, Daniel, was mourning three whole weeks. ³ I ate no pleasant bread. No meat or wine came into my mouth. I didn't anoint myself at all, until three whole weeks were fulfilled. ⁴ In the twenty-fourth day of the first month, as I was by the side of the great river, which is Hiddekel, ⁵ I lifted up my eyes and looked, and behold, there was a man clothed in linen, whose thighs were adorned with pure gold of Uphaz. ⁶ His body also was like beryl, and his face like the appearance of lightning, and his eyes like flaming torches. His arms and his feet were like burnished bronze. The voice of his words was like the voice of a multitude. ⁷ I, Daniel, alone saw the vision; for the men who were with me didn't see the vision; but a great quaking fell on them, and they fled to hide themselves. ⁸ So I was left alone, and saw this great vision. No strength remained in me; for my face grew deathly pale, and I retained no strength. ⁹ Yet I heard the voice of his words. When I heard the voice of his words, then I fell into a deep sleep on my face, with my face toward the ground. ¹⁰ Behold, a hand touched me, which set me on my knees and on the palms of my hands. ¹¹ He said to me, "Daniel, you greatly beloved man, understand the words that I speak to you. Stand upright, for I have been sent to you, now." When he had spoken this word to me, I stood trembling. ¹² Then he said to me, "Don't be afraid, Daniel; for from the first day that you set your heart to understand, and to humble yourself before your God, your words were heard. I have come for your words' sake. ¹³ But the prince of the kingdom of Persia withstood me twenty-one days; but, behold, Michael, one of the chief princes, came to help me because I remained there with the kings of Persia. ¹⁴ Now I have come to make you understand what will happen to your people in the latter days; for the vision is yet for many days." ¹⁵ When he had spoken these words to me, I set my face toward the ground, and was mute. ¹⁶ Behold, one in the likeness of the sons of men touched my lips. Then I opened my mouth, and spoke and said to him who stood before me, "My lord, by reason of the vision my sorrows have overtaken me, and I retain no strength. ¹⁷ For how can the servant of my lord talk with my lord? For as for me, immediately there remained no strength in me. There was no breath left in me." ¹⁸ Then one like the appearance of a man touched me again, and he strengthened me. ¹⁹ He said, "Greatly beloved man, don't be afraid. Peace be to you. Be strong. Yes, be strong." When he spoke to me, I was strengthened, and said, "Let my lord speak; for you have strengthened me." ²⁰ Then he said, "Do you know why I have come to you? Now I will return to fight with the prince of Persia. When I go out, behold, the prince of Greece will come. ²¹ But I will tell you what is inscribed in the writing of truth. There is no one who supports me against these except Michael, your prince.

## 11

¹"As for me, in the first year of Darius the Mede, I stood up to confirm and strengthen him. ²"Now I will show you the truth. Behold, three more kings will stand up in Persia. The fourth will be far richer than all of them. When he has grown strong through his riches, he will stir up all against the realm of Greece. ³ A mighty king will stand up who will rule with great dominion, and do according to his will. ⁴ When he stands up, his kingdom will be broken, and will be divided toward the four winds of the sky, but not to his posterity, nor according to his dominion with which he ruled; for his kingdom will be plucked up, even for others besides these. ⁵"The king of the south will be strong. One of his princes will become stronger than him and have dominion. His dominion will be a great dominion. ⁶ At the end of years they will join themselves together. The daughter of the king of the south will come to the king of the north to make an agreement, but she will not retain the strength of

her arm. He will also not stand, nor will his arm; but she will be given up, with those who brought her and he who became her father, and he who strengthened her in those times. ⁷"But out of a shoot from her roots one will stand up in his place who will come to the army and will enter into the fortress of the king of the north, and will deal against them and will prevail. ⁸ He will also carry their gods, with their molten images and their precious vessels of silver and of gold, captive into Egypt. He will refrain some years from the king of the north. ⁹ He will come into the realm of the king of the south, but he will return into his own land. ¹⁰ His sons will wage war and will assemble a multitude of great forces which will keep coming and overflow and pass through. They will return and wage war, even to his fortress. ¹¹"The king of the south will be moved with anger and will come out and fight with him, even with the king of the north. He will send out a great multitude, and the multitude will be given into his hand. ¹² The multitude will be lifted up, and his heart will be exalted. He will cast down tens of thousands, but he won't prevail. ¹³ The king of the north will return, and will send out a multitude greater than the former. He will come on at the end of the times, even of years, with a great army and with abundant supplies. ¹⁴"In those times many will stand up against the king of the south. Also the children of the violent among your people will lift themselves up to establish the vision; but they will fall. ¹⁵ So the king of the north will come and cast up a mound, and take a well-fortified city. The forces of the south won't stand, neither will his chosen people, neither will there be any strength to stand. ¹⁶ But he who comes against him will do according to his own will, and no one will stand before him. He will stand in the glorious land, and destruction will be in his hand. ¹⁷ He will set his face to come with the strength of his whole kingdom, and with him equitable conditions. He will perform them. He will give him the daughter of women to corrupt her; but she will not stand, and won't be for him. ¹⁸ After this he will turn his face to the islands, and will take many; but a prince will cause the reproach offered by him to cease. Yes, moreover, he will cause his reproach to turn on him. ¹⁹ Then he will turn his face toward the fortresses of his own land; but he will stumble and fall, and won't be found. ²⁰"Then one who will cause a tax collector to pass through the kingdom to maintain its glory will stand up in his place; but within few days he shall be destroyed, not in anger, and not in battle. ²¹"In his place, a contemptible person will stand up, to whom they had not given the honor of the kingdom; but he will come in time of security, and will obtain the kingdom by flatteries. ²² The overwhelming forces will be overwhelmed from before him, and will be broken. Yes, also the prince of the covenant. ²³ After the treaty is made with him, he will work deceitfully; for he will come up, and will become strong with a small people. ²⁴ In time of security, he will come even on the fattest places of the province. He will do that which his fathers have not done, nor his fathers' fathers. He will scatter among them prey, plunder, and substance. Yes, he will devise his plans against the strongholds, even for a time. ²⁵"He will stir up his power and his courage against the king of the south with a great army; and the king of the south will wage war in battle with an exceedingly great and mighty army; but he won't stand, for they will devise plans against him. ²⁶ Yes, those who eat of his delicacies will destroy him, and his army will be swept away. Many will fall down slain. ²⁷ As for both these kings, their hearts will be to do mischief, and they will speak lies at one table; but it won't prosper, for the end will still be at the appointed time. ²⁸ Then he will return into his land with great wealth. His heart will be against the holy covenant. He will take action and return to his own land. ²⁹"He will return at the appointed time and come into the south; but it won't be in the latter time as it was in the former. ³⁰ For ships of Kittim will come against him. Therefore he will be grieved, and will return, and have indignation against the holy covenant, and will take action. He will even return, and have regard to those who forsake the holy covenant. ³¹"Forces will stand on his part and they will profane the sanctuary, even the fortress, and will take away the continual burnt offering. Then they will set up the abomination that makes desolate. ³² He will corrupt those who do wickedly against the covenant by flatteries; but the people who know their God will be strong and take action. ³³"Those who are wise among the people will instruct many; yet they will fall by the sword and by flame, by captivity and by plunder, many days. ³⁴ Now when they fall, they will be helped with a little help; but many will join themselves to them with flatteries. ³⁵ Some of those who are wise will fall, to refine them, and to purify, and to make them white, even to the time of the end; because it is yet for the appointed time. ³⁶"The king will do according to his will. He will exalt himself, and magnify himself above every god, and will speak marvelous things against the God of gods. He will prosper until the indignation is

---

ᵃ 9:25 "Anointed One" can also be translated "Messiah" (same as "Christ").

ᵇ 9:26 "Anointed One" can also be translated "Messiah" (same as "Christ").

accomplished; for what is determined will be done. ³⁷ He won't regard the gods of his fathers, or the desire of women, or regard any god; for he will magnify himself above all. ³⁸ But in his place he will honor the god of fortresses. He will honor a god whom his fathers didn't know with gold, silver, precious stones, and pleasant things. ³⁹ He will deal with the strongest fortresses by the help of a foreign god. He will increase with glory whoever acknowledges him. He will cause them to rule over many, and will divide the land for a price. ⁴⁰ "At the time of the end, the king of the south will contend with him; and the king of the north will come against him like a whirlwind, with chariots, with horsemen, and with many ships. He will enter into the countries, and will overflow and pass through. ⁴¹ He will enter also into the glorious land, and many countries will be overthrown; but these will be delivered out of his hand: Edom, Moab, and the chief of the children of Ammon. ⁴² He will also stretch out his hand against the countries. The land of Egypt won't escape. ⁴³ But he will have power over the treasures of gold and of silver, and over all the precious things of Egypt. The Libyans and the Ethiopians will be at his steps. ⁴⁴ But news out of the east and out of the north will trouble him; and he will go out with great fury to destroy and utterly to sweep away many. ⁴⁵ He will plant the tents of his palace between the sea and the glorious holy mountain; yet he will come to his end, and no one will help him.

## 12

¹ "At that time Michael will stand up, the great prince who stands for the children of your people. There will be a time of trouble, such as never was since there was a nation even to that same time. At that time, your people will be delivered—everyone who is found written in the book. ² Many of those who sleep in the dust of the earth will awake, some to everlasting life, and some to shame and everlasting contempt. ³ Those who are wise will shine as the brightness of the expanse. Those who turn many to righteousness will shine like the stars forever and ever. ⁴ But you, Daniel, shut up the words and seal the book, even to the time of the end. Many will run back and forth, and knowledge will be increased."

⁵ Then I, Daniel, looked, and behold, two others stood, one on the river bank on this side, and the other on the river bank on that side. ⁶ One said to the man clothed in linen, who was above the waters of the river, "How long will it be to the end of these wonders?" ⁷ I heard the man clothed in linen, who was above the waters of the river, when he held up his right hand and his left hand to heaven, and swore by him who lives forever that it will be for a time, times, and a half; and when they have finished breaking in pieces the power of the holy people, all these things will be finished. ⁸ I heard, but I didn't understand. Then I said, "My lord, what will be the outcome of these things?" ⁹ He said, "Go your way, Daniel; for the words are shut up and sealed until the time of the end. ¹⁰ Many will purify themselves, make themselves white, and be refined; but the wicked will do wickedly. None of the wicked will understand; but those who are wise will understand. ¹¹ "From the time that the continual burnt offering is taken away and the abomination that makes desolate set up, there will be one thousand two hundred ninety days. ¹² Blessed is he who waits and comes to the one thousand three hundred thirty-five days. ¹³ "But go your way until the end; for you will rest and will stand in your inheritance at the end of the days."

## The History of Susanna
## 13

¹ ᵃA man lived in Babylon, and his name was Joakim. ² He took a wife, whose name was Susanna, the daughter of Helkias, a very fair woman, and one who feared the Lord. ³ Her parents were also righteous, and taught their daughter according to the law of Moses. ⁴ Now Joakim was a great rich man, and had a beautiful garden next to his house. The Jews used to come to him, because he was more honorable than all others. ⁵ The same year, two of the elders of the people were appointed to be judges, such as the Lord spoke of, that wickedness came from Babylon from elders who were judges, who were supposed to govern the people. ⁶ These were often at Joakim's house. All that had any lawsuits came to them. ⁷ When the people departed away at noon, Susanna went into her husband's garden to walk. ⁸ The two elders saw her going in every day and walking; and they were inflamed with lust for her. ⁹ They perverted their own mind and turned away their eyes, that they might not look to heaven, nor remember just judgments. ¹⁰ And although they both were wounded with lust for her, yet dared not show the other his grief. ¹¹ For they were ashamed to declare their lust, what they desired to do with her. ¹² Yet they watched eagerly from day to day to see her. ¹³ The one said to the other, "Let's go home, now; for it is dinner time."

¹⁴ So when they had gone out, they parted company, and turning back again, they came to the same place. After they had asked one another the cause, they acknowledged their lust. Then they appointed a time both together, when they might find her alone. ¹⁵ It happened, as they watched on an opportune day, she went in as before with only two maids, and she desired to wash herself in the garden; for it was hot. ¹⁶ There was nobody there except the two elders who had hid themselves and watched her. ¹⁷ Then she said to her maids, "Bring me olive oil and ointment, and shut the garden doors, that I may wash myself." ¹⁸ They did as she asked them and shut the garden doors, and went out themselves at the side doors to fetch the things that she had commanded them. They didn't see the elders, because they were hidden. ¹⁹ Now when the maids had gone out, the two elders rose up and ran to her, saying, ²⁰ "Behold, the garden doors are shut, that no man can see us, and we are in love with you. Therefore consent to us, and lie with us. ²¹ If you will not, we will testify against you, that a young man was with you; therefore you sent your maids away from you." ²² Then Susanna sighed, and said, "I am trapped; for if I do this thing, it is death to me. If I don't do it, I can't escape your hands. ²³ It is better for me to fall into your hands, and not do it, than to sin in the sight of the Lord." ²⁴ With that Susanna cried with a loud voice; and the two elders cried out against her. ²⁵ Then one of them ran and opened the garden doors. ²⁶ So when the servants of the house heard the cry in the garden, they rushed in at the side door to see what had happened to her. ²⁷ But when the elders had told their tale, the servants were greatly ashamed; for there was never such a report made of Susanna. ²⁸ It came to pass on the next day, when the people assembled to her husband Joakim, the two elders came full of their wicked intent against Susanna to put her to death, ²⁹ and said before the people, "Send for Susanna, the daughter of Helkias, Joakim's wife." So they sent; ³⁰ and she came with her father and mother, her children, and all her kindred. ³¹ Now Susanna was a very delicate woman, and beautiful to behold. ³² These wicked men commanded her to be unveiled, for she was veiled, that they might be filled with her beauty. ³³ Therefore her friends and all who saw her wept. ³⁴ Then the two elders stood up in the midst of the people and laid their hands upon her head. ³⁵ She, weeping, looked up toward heaven; for her heart trusted in the Lord. ³⁶ The elders said, "As we walked in the garden alone, this woman came in with two maids, shut the garden doors, and sent the maids away. ³⁷ Then a young man who was hidden there came to her and lay with her. ³⁸ And we, being in a corner of the garden, saw this wickedness and ran to them. ³⁹ And when we saw them together, we couldn't hold the man; for he was stronger than we, and opened the doors, and leaped out. ⁴⁰ But having taken this woman, we asked who the young man was, but she would not tell us. We testify these things. ⁴¹ Then the assembly believed them, as those who were elders of the people and judges; so they condemned her to death. ⁴² Then Susanna cried out with a loud voice, and said, "O everlasting God, you know the secrets, and know all things before they happen. ⁴³ You know that they have testified falsely against me. Behold, I must die, even though I never did such things as these men have maliciously invented against me." ⁴⁴ The Lord heard her voice. ⁴⁵ Therefore when she was led away to be put to death, God raised up the holy spirit of a young youth, whose name was Daniel. ⁴⁶ He cried with a loud voice, "I am clear from the blood of this woman!" ⁴⁷ Then all the people turned them toward him, and said, "What do these words that you have spoken mean?" ⁴⁸ So he, standing in the midst of them, said, "Are you all such fools, you sons of Israel, that without examination or knowledge of the truth you have condemned a daughter of Israel? ⁴⁹ Return again to the place of judgment; for these have testified falsely against her." ⁵⁰ Therefore all the people turned again in haste, and the elders said to him, "Come, sit down among us, and show it to us, seeing God has given you the honor of an elder." ⁵¹ Then Daniel said to them, "Put them far apart from each another, and I will examine them." ⁵² So when they were put apart one from another, he called one of them, and said to him, "O you who have become old in wickedness, now your sins have returned which you have committed before, ⁵³ in pronouncing unjust judgment,

condemning the innocent, and letting the guilty go free; although the Lord says, 'You shall not kill the innocent and righteous.' ⁵⁴ Now then, if you saw her, tell me, under which tree did you see them companying together?" He answered, "Under a mastick tree." ⁵⁵ And Daniel said, "You have certainly lied against your own head; for even now the angel of God has received the sentence of God and will cut you in two." ⁵⁶ So he put him aside, and commanded to bring the other, and said to him, "O you seed of Canaan, and not of Judah, beauty has deceived you, and lust has perverted your heart. ⁵⁷ Thus you have dealt with the daughters of Israel, and they for fear were intimate with you; but the daughter of Judah would not tolerate your wickedness. ⁵⁸ Now therefore tell me, under which tree did you take them being intimate together?" He answered, "Under an evergreen oak tree." ⁵⁹ Then Daniel said to him, "You have also certainly lied against your own head; for the angel of God waits with the sword to cut you in two, that he may destroy you." ⁶⁰ With that, all the assembly cried out with a loud voice, and blessed God, who saves those who hope in him. ⁶¹ Then they arose against the two elders, for Daniel had convicted them of false testimony out of their own mouth. ⁶² According to the law of Moses they did to them what they maliciously intended to do to their neighbor. They put them to death, and the innocent blood was saved the same day. ⁶³ Therefore Helkias and his wife praised God for their daughter Susanna, with Joakim her husband, and all the kindred, because there was no dishonesty found in her. ⁶⁴ And from that day forth, Daniel had a great reputation in the sight of the people.

# Bel and the Dragon

## 14

¹ ᵃKing Astyages was gathered to his fathers, and Cyrus the Persian received his kingdom. ² Daniel lived with the king, and was honored above all his friends. ³ Now the Babylonians had an idol called Bel, and every day twelve great measures of fine flour, forty sheep, and six firkinsᵇ of wine were spent on it. ⁴ The king honored it and went daily to worship it; but Daniel worshiped his own God. The king said to him, "Why don't you worship Bel?" ⁵ He said, "Because I may not honor idols made with hands, but only the living God, who has created the sky and the earth, and has sovereignty over all flesh." ⁶ Then the king said to him, "Don't you think that Bel is a living god? Don't you see how much he eats and drinks every day?" ⁷ Then Daniel laughed, and said, "O king, don't be deceived; for this is just clay inside, and brass outside, and never ate or drank anything." ⁸ So the king was angry, and called for his priests, and said to them, "If you don't tell me who this is who devours these expenses, you shall die. ⁹ But if you can show me that Bel devours them, then Daniel shall die; for he has spoken blasphemy against Bel." Daniel said to the king, "Let it be according to your word." ¹⁰ Now there were seventy priests of Bel, besides their wives and children. The king went with Daniel into Bel's temple. ¹¹ So Bel's priests said, "Behold, we will leave; but you, O king, set out the food, and mix the wine and set it out, shut the door securely, and seal it with your own signet. ¹² When you come in the morning, if you don't find that Bel has eaten everything, we will suffer death, or else Daniel, who speaks falsely against us." ¹³ They weren't concerned, for under the table they had made a secret entrance, by which they entered in continually, and consumed those things. ¹⁴ It happened, when they had gone out, the king set the food before Bel. Now Daniel had commanded his servants to bring ashes, and they scattered them all over the temple in the presence of the king alone. Then they went out, shut the door, sealed it with the king's signet, and so departed. ¹⁵ Now in the night, the priests came with their wives and children, as they usually did, and ate and drank it all. ¹⁶ In the morning, the king arose, and Daniel with him. ¹⁷ The king said, "Daniel, are the seals whole?" He said, "Yes, O king, they are whole." ¹⁸ And as soon as he had opened the door, the king looked at the table, and cried with a loud voice, "You are great, O Bel, and with you is no deceit at all!" ¹⁹ Then Daniel laughed, and held the king that he should not go in, and said, "Behold now the pavement, and mark well whose footsteps these are." ²⁰ The king said, "I see the footsteps of men, women, and children." Then the king was angry, ²¹ and took the priests with their wives and children, who showed him the secret doors, where they came in and consumed the things that were on the table. ²² Therefore the king killed them, and delivered Bel into Daniel's power, who overthrew it and its temple. ²³ In that same place

there was a great dragon which the people of Babylon worshiped. ²⁴ The king said to Daniel, "Will you also say that this is of brass? Behold, he lives, eats and drinks. You can't say that he is no living god. Therefore worship him." ²⁵ Then Daniel said, "I will worship the Lord my God; for he is a living God. ²⁶ But allow me, O king, and I will kill this dragon without sword or staff." The king said, "I allow you." ²⁷ Then Daniel took pitch, fat, and hair, and melted them together, and made lumps of them. He put these in the dragon's mouth, so the dragon ate and burst apart. Daniel said, "Behold, these are the gods you all worship." ²⁸ When the people of Babylon heard that, they took great indignation, and conspired against the king, saying, "The king has become a Jew. He has pulled down Bel, slain the dragon, and put the priests to the sword." ²⁹ So they came to the king, and said, "Deliver Daniel to us, or else we will destroy you and your house." ³⁰ Now when the king saw that they trapped him, being constrained, the king delivered Daniel to them. ³¹ They cast him into the lion's den, where he was six days. ³² There were seven lions in the den, and they had been giving them two carcasses and two sheep every day, which then were not given to them, intending that they would devour Daniel. ³³ Now there was in Jewry the prophet Habakkuk,ᶜ who had made stew, and had broken bread into a bowl. He was going into the field to bring it to the reapers. ³⁴ But the angel of the Lord said to Habakkuk, "Go carry the dinner that you have into Babylon to Daniel, in the lions' den." ³⁵ Habakkuk said, "Lord, I never saw Babylon. I don't know where the den is." ³⁶ Then the angel of the Lord took him by the crown, and lifted him up by the hair of his head, and with the blast of his breath set him in Babylon over the den. ³⁷ Habakkuk cried, saying, "O Daniel, Daniel, take the dinner which God has sent you." ³⁸ Daniel said, "You have remembered me, O God! You haven't forsaken those who love you!" ³⁹ So Daniel arose and ate; and the angel of God set Habakkuk in his own place again immediately. ⁴⁰ On the seventh day, the king came to mourn for Daniel. When he came to the den, he looked in, and, behold, Daniel was sitting. ⁴¹ Then the king cried with a loud voice, saying, "Great are you, O Lord, you God of Daniel, and there is none other beside you!" ⁴² So he drew him out, and cast those that were the cause of his destruction into the den; and they were devoured in a moment before his face.

# The Book of Hosea

## 1

¹ Yahweh'sᵈ word that came to Hosea the son of Beeri, in the days of Uzziah, Jotham, Ahaz, and Hezekiah, kings of Judah, and in the days of Jeroboam the son of Joash, king of Israel. ² When Yahweh spoke at first by Hosea, Yahweh said to Hosea, "Go, take for yourself a wife of prostitution and children of unfaithfulness; for the land commits great adultery, forsaking Yahweh." ³ So he went and took Gomer the daughter of Diblaim; and she conceived, and bore him a son. ⁴ Yahweh said to him, "Call his name Jezreel, for yet a little while, and I will avenge the blood of Jezreel on the house of Jehu, and will cause the kingdom of the house of Israel to cease. ⁵ It will happen in that day that I will break the bow of Israel in the valley of Jezreel." ⁶ She conceived again, and bore a daughter. Then he said to him, "Call her name Lo-Ruhamah,ᵉ for I will no longer have mercy on the house of Israel, that I should in any way pardon them. ⁷ But I will have mercy on the house of Judah, and will save them by Yahweh their God,ᶠ and will not save them by bow, sword, battle, horses, or horsemen." ⁸ Now when she had weaned Lo-Ruhamah, she conceived, and bore a son. ⁹ He said, "Call his name Lo-Ammi,ᵍ for you are not my people, and I will not be yours. ¹⁰ Yet the number of the children of Israel will be as the sand of the sea, which can't be measured or counted; and it will come to pass that, in the place where it was said to them, 'You are not my people,' they will

---

ᵃ *14:1 Bel and the Dragon* is translated from chapter 14 of *Daniel* in the Greek Septuagint. It is not found in the traditional Hebrew text of *Daniel. Bel and the Dragon* is recognized as Deuterocanonical Scripture by

the Roman Catholic, Greek Orthodox, and Russian Orthodox Churches.
ᵇ *14:3* a firkin is about 41 liters or 11 gallons.
ᶜ *14:33* Gr. Ambakoum.

ᵈ *1:1* "Yahweh" is God's proper Name, sometimes rendered "LORD" (all caps) in other translations.
ᵉ *1:6* Lo-Ruhamah means "not loved".

ᶠ *1:7* The Hebrew word rendered "God" is "אֱלֹהִים" (Elohim).
ᵍ *1:9* Lo-Ammi means "not my people".

be called 'sons of the living God.' [11] The children of Judah and the children of Israel will be gathered together, and they will appoint themselves one head, and will go up from the land; for great will be the day of Jezreel.

## 2

[1]"Say to your brothers, 'My people!'[a] and to your sisters, 'My loved one!'[b] [2] Contend with your mother! Contend, for she is not my wife, neither am I her husband; and let her put away her prostitution from her face, and her adulteries from between her breasts; [3] lest I strip her naked, and make her bare as in the day that she was born, and make her like a wilderness, and set her like a dry land, and kill her with thirst. [4] Indeed, on her children I will have no mercy, for they are children of unfaithfulness. [5] For their mother has played the prostitute. She who conceived them has done shamefully; for she said, 'I will go after my lovers, who give me my bread and my water, my wool and my flax, my oil and my drink.' [6] Therefore behold,[c] I will hedge up your way with thorns, and I will build a wall against her, that she can't find her way. [7] She will follow after her lovers, but she won't overtake them; and she will seek them, but won't find them. Then she will say, 'I will go and return to my first husband, for then it was better with me than now.' [8] For she didn't know that I gave her the grain, the new wine, and the oil, and multiplied to her silver and gold, which they used for Baal. [9] Therefore I will take back my grain in its time, and my new wine in its season, and will pluck away my wool and my flax which should have covered her nakedness. [10] Now I will uncover her lewdness in the sight of her lovers, and no one will deliver her out of my hand. [11] I will also cause all her celebrations to cease: her feasts, her new moons, her Sabbaths, and all her solemn assemblies. [12] I will lay waste her vines and her fig trees, about which she has said, 'These are my wages that my lovers have given me,' and I will make them a forest, and the animals of the field shall eat them. [13] I will visit on her the days of the Baals, to which she burned incense when she decked herself with her earrings and her jewels, and went after her lovers and forgot me," says Yahweh. [14]"Therefore behold, I will allure her, and bring her into the wilderness, and speak tenderly to her. [15] I will give her vineyards from there, and the valley of Achor for a door of hope; and she will respond there as in the days of her youth, and as in the day when she came up out of the land of Egypt. [16] It will be in that day," says Yahweh, "that you will call me 'my husband,' and no longer call me 'my master.' [17] For I will take away the names of the Baals out of her mouth, and they will no longer be mentioned by name. [18] In that day I will make a covenant for them with the animals of the field, and with the birds of the sky, and with the creeping things of the ground. I will break the bow, the sword, and the battle out of the land, and will make them lie down safely. [19] I will betroth you to me forever. Yes, I will betroth you to me in righteousness, in justice, in loving kindness, and in compassion. [20] I will even betroth you to me in faithfulness; and you shall know Yahweh. [21] It will happen in that day, that I will respond," says Yahweh. "I will respond to the heavens, and they will respond to the earth; [22] and the earth will respond to the grain, and the new wine, and the oil; and they will respond to Jezreel. [23] I will sow her to me in the earth; and I will have mercy on her who had not obtained mercy; and I will tell those who were not my people, 'You are my people;' and they will say, 'You are My God!'"

## 3

[1] Yahweh said to me, "Go again, love a woman loved by another, and an adulteress, even as Yahweh loves the children of Israel, though they turn to other gods, and love cakes of raisins." [2] So I bought her for myself for fifteen pieces of silver and a homer[d] and a half of barley. [3] I said to her, "You shall stay with me many days. You shall not play the prostitute, and you shall not be with any other man. I will also be so toward you." [4] For the children of Israel shall live many days without king, without prince, without sacrifice, without sacred stone, and without ephod or idols. [5] Afterward the children of Israel shall return and seek Yahweh their God, and David their king, and shall come with trembling to Yahweh and to his blessings in the last days.

## 4

[1] Hear Yahweh's word, you children of Israel, for Yahweh has a charge against the inhabitants of the land: "Indeed there is no truth, nor goodness, nor knowledge of God in the land. [2] There is cursing, lying, murder, stealing, and committing adultery; they break boundaries, and bloodshed causes bloodshed. [3] Therefore the land will mourn, and everyone who dwells in it will waste away, with all living things in her, even the animals of the field and the birds of the sky; yes, the fish of the sea also die. [4]"Yet let no man bring a charge, neither let any man accuse; for your people are like those who bring charges against a priest. [5] You will stumble in the day, and the prophet will also stumble

with you in the night; and I will destroy your mother. [6] My people are destroyed for lack of knowledge. Because you have rejected knowledge, I will also reject you, that you may be no priest to me. Because you have forgotten your God's law, I will also forget your children. [7] As they were multiplied, so they sinned against me. I will change their glory into shame. [8] They feed on the sin of my people, and set their heart on their iniquity. [9] It will be like people, like priest; and I will punish them for their ways, and will repay them for their deeds. [10] They will eat, and not have enough. They will play the prostitute, and will not increase; because they have abandoned listening to Yahweh. [11] Prostitution, wine, and new wine take away understanding. [12] My people consult with their wooden idol, and answer to a stick of wood. Indeed the spirit of prostitution has led them astray, and they have been unfaithful to their God. [13] They sacrifice on the tops of the mountains, and burn incense on the hills, under oaks, poplars, and terebinths, because its shade is good. Therefore your daughters play the prostitute, and your brides commit adultery. [14] I will not punish your daughters when they play the prostitute, nor your brides when they commit adultery; because the men consort with prostitutes, and they sacrifice with the shrine prostitutes; so the people without understanding will come to ruin. [15]"Though you, Israel, play the prostitute, yet don't let Judah offend; and don't come to Gilgal, neither go up to Beth Aven, nor swear, 'As Yahweh lives.' [16] For Israel has behaved extremely stubbornly, like a stubborn heifer. Then how will Yahweh feed them like a lamb in a meadow? [17] Ephraim is joined to idols. Leave him alone! [18] Their drink has become sour. They play the prostitute continually. Her rulers dearly love their shameful way. [19] The wind has wrapped her up in its wings; and they shall be disappointed because of their sacrifices.

## 5

[1]"Listen to this, you priests! Listen, house of Israel, and give ear, house of the king! For the judgment is against you; for you have been a snare at Mizpah, and a net spread on Tabor. [2] The rebels are deep in slaughter, but I discipline all of them. [3] I know Ephraim, and Israel is not hidden from me; for now, Ephraim, you have played the prostitute. Israel is defiled. [4] Their deeds won't allow them to turn to their God, for the spirit of prostitution is within them, and they don't know Yahweh. [5] The pride of Israel testifies to his face. Therefore Israel and Ephraim will stumble in their iniquity. Judah also will stumble with them. [6] They will go with their flocks and with their herds to seek Yahweh, but they won't find him. He has withdrawn himself from them. [7] They are unfaithful to Yahweh; for they have borne illegitimate children. Now the new moon will devour them with their fields. [8]"Blow the cornet in Gibeah, and the trumpet in Ramah! Sound a battle cry at Beth Aven, behind you, Benjamin! [9] Ephraim will become a desolation in the day of rebuke. Among the tribes of Israel, I have made known that which will surely be. [10] The princes of Judah are like those who remove a landmark. I will pour out my wrath on them like water. [11] Ephraim is oppressed, he is crushed in judgment, because he is intent in his pursuit of idols. [12] Therefore I am to Ephraim like a moth, and to the house of Judah like rottenness. [13]"When Ephraim saw his sickness, and Judah his wound, then Ephraim went to Assyria, and sent to King Jareb: but he is not able to heal you, neither will he cure you of your wound. [14] For I will be to Ephraim like a lion, and like a young lion to the house of Judah. I myself will tear in pieces and go away. I will carry off, and there will be no one to deliver. [15] I will go and return to my place, until they acknowledge their offense, and seek my face. In their affliction they will seek me earnestly."

## 6

[1]"Come! Let's return to Yahweh; for he has torn us to pieces, and he will heal us; he has injured us, and he will bind up our wounds. [2] After two days he will revive us. On the third day he will raise us up, and we will live before him. [3] Let's acknowledge Yahweh. Let's press on to know Yahweh. As surely as the sun rises, Yahweh will appear. He will come to us like the rain, like the spring rain that waters the earth." [4]"Ephraim, what shall I do to you? Judah, what shall I do to you? For your love is like a morning cloud, and like the dew that disappears early. [5] Therefore I have cut them to pieces with the prophets; I killed them with the words of my mouth. Your judgments are like a flash of lightning. [6] For I desire mercy, and not sacrifice; and the knowledge of God more than burnt offerings. [7] But they, like Adam, have broken the covenant. They were unfaithful to me there. [8] Gilead is a city of those who work iniquity; it is stained with blood. [9] As gangs of robbers wait to ambush a man, so the company of priests murder on the path toward Shechem, committing shameful crimes. [10] In the house of Israel I have seen a horrible thing. There is prostitution in Ephraim. Israel is defiled.

---

¹¹"Also, Judah, there is a harvest appointed for you, when I restore the fortunes of my people.

## 7

¹ When I would heal Israel, then the iniquity of Ephraim is uncovered, also the wickedness of Samaria; for they commit falsehood, and the thief enters in, and the gang of robbers ravages outside. ² They don't consider in their hearts that I remember all their wickedness. Now their own deeds have engulfed them. They are before my face. ³ They make the king glad with their wickedness, and the princes with their lies. ⁴ They are all adulterers. They are burning like an oven that the baker stops stirring, from the kneading of the dough, until it is leavened. ⁵ On the day of our king, the princes made themselves sick with the heat of wine. He joined his hand with mockers. ⁶ For they have prepared their heart like an oven, while they lie in wait. Their anger smolders all night. In the morning it burns as a flaming fire. ⁷ They are all hot as an oven, and devour their judges. All their kings have fallen. There is no one among them who calls to me. ⁸ Ephraim mixes himself among the nations. Ephraim is a pancake not turned over. ⁹ Strangers have devoured his strength, and he doesn't realize it. Indeed, gray hairs are here and there on him, and he doesn't realize it. ¹⁰ The pride of Israel testifies to his face; yet they haven't returned to Yahweh their God, nor sought him, for all this. ¹¹"Ephraim is like an easily deceived dove, without understanding. They call to Egypt. They go to Assyria. ¹² When they go, I will spread my net on them. I will bring them down like the birds of the sky. I will chastise them, as their congregation has heard. ¹³ Woe to them! For they have wandered from me. Destruction to them! For they have trespassed against me. Though I would redeem them, yet they have spoken lies against me. ¹⁴ They haven't cried to me with their heart, but they howl on their beds. They assemble themselves for grain and new wine. They turn away from me. ¹⁵ Though I have taught and strengthened their arms, yet they plot evil against me. ¹⁶ They return, but not to the Most High. They are like a faulty bow. Their princes will fall by the sword for the rage of their tongue. This will be their derision in the land of Egypt.

## 8

¹"Put the trumpet to your lips! Something like an eagle is over Yahweh's house, because they have broken my covenant and rebelled against my law. ² They cry to me, 'My God, we, Israel, acknowledge you!' ³ Israel has cast off that which is good. The enemy will pursue him. ⁴ They have set up kings, but not by me. They have made princes, and I didn't approve. Of their silver and their gold they have made themselves idols, that they may be cut off. ⁵ Let Samaria throw out his calf idol! My anger burns against them! How long will it be until they are capable of purity? ⁶ For this is even from Israel! The workman made it, and it is no God; indeed, the calf of Samaria shall be broken in pieces. ⁷ For they sow the wind, and they will reap the whirlwind. He has no standing grain. The stalk will yield no head. If it does yield, strangers will swallow it up. ⁸ Israel is swallowed up. Now they are among the nations like a worthless thing. ⁹ For they have gone up to Assyria, like a wild donkey wandering alone. Ephraim has hired lovers for himself. ¹⁰ But although they sold themselves among the nations, I will now gather them; and they begin to waste away because of the oppression of the king of mighty ones. ¹¹ Because Ephraim has multiplied altars for sinning, they became for him altars for sinning. ¹² I wrote for him the many things of my law, but they were regarded as a strange thing. ¹³ As for the sacrifices of my offerings, they sacrifice meat and eat it, but Yahweh doesn't accept them. Now he will remember their iniquity, and punish their sins. They will return to Egypt. ¹⁴ For Israel has forgotten his Maker and built palaces; and Judah has multiplied fortified cities; but I will send a fire on his cities, and it will devour its fortresses."

## 9

¹ Don't rejoice, Israel, to jubilation like the nations; for you were unfaithful to your God. You love the wages of a prostitute at every grain threshing floor. ² The threshing floor and the wine press won't feed them, and the new wine will fail her. ³ They won't dwell in Yahweh's land; but Ephraim will return to Egypt, and they will eat unclean food in Assyria. ⁴ They won't pour out wine offerings to Yahweh, neither will they be pleasing to him. Their sacrifices will be to them like the bread of mourners; all who eat of it will be polluted; for their bread will be for their appetite. It will not come into Yahweh's house. ⁵ What will you do in the day of solemn assembly, and in the day of the feast of Yahweh? ⁶ For, behold, when they flee destruction, Egypt will gather them up. Memphis will bury them. Nettles will possess their pleasant things of silver. Thorns will be in their tents. ⁷ The days of visitation have come. The days of reckoning have come. Israel will consider the prophet to be a fool, and the man who is inspired to be insane, because of the abundance of your sins, and because your hostility is great. ⁸ A prophet watches over Ephraim with my God. A fowler's snare is on all of his paths, and hostility in the house of his God. ⁹ They have deeply

corrupted themselves, as in the days of Gibeah. He will remember their iniquity. He will punish them for their sins. ¹⁰ I found Israel like grapes in the wilderness. I saw your fathers as the first ripe in the fig tree at its first season; but they came to Baal Peor, and consecrated themselves to the shameful thing, and became abominable like that which they loved. ¹¹ As for Ephraim, their glory will fly away like a bird. There will be no birth, no one with child, and no conception. ¹² Though they bring up their children, yet I will bereave them, so that not a man shall be left. Indeed, woe also to them when I depart from them! ¹³ I have seen Ephraim, like Tyre, planted in a pleasant place; but Ephraim will bring out his children to the murderer. ¹⁴ Give them—Yahweh what will you give? Give them a miscarrying womb and dry breasts. ¹⁵"All their wickedness is in Gilgal; for there I hated them. Because of the wickedness of their deeds, I will drive them out of my house! I will love them no more. All their princes are rebels. ¹⁶ Ephraim is struck. Their root has dried up. They will bear no fruit. Even though they give birth, yet I will kill the beloved ones of their womb." ¹⁷ My God will cast them away, because they didn't listen to him; and they will be wanderers among the nations.

## 10

¹ Israel is a luxuriant vine that produces his fruit. According to the abundance of his fruit he has multiplied his altars. As their land has prospered, they have adorned their sacred stones. ² Their heart is divided. Now they will be found guilty. He will demolish their altars. He will destroy their sacred stones. ³ Surely now they will say, "We have no king; for we don't fear Yahweh; and the king, what can he do for us?" ⁴ They make promises, swearing falsely in making covenants. Therefore judgment springs up like poisonous weeds in the furrows of the field. ⁵ The inhabitants of Samaria will be in terror for the calves of Beth Aven, for its people will mourn over it, along with its priests who rejoiced over it, for its glory, because it has departed from it. ⁶ It also will be carried to Assyria for a present to a great king. Ephraim will receive shame, and Israel will be ashamed of his own counsel. ⁷ Samaria and her king float away like a twig on the water. ⁸ The high places also of Aven, the sin of Israel, will be destroyed. The thorn and the thistle will come up on their altars. They will tell the mountains, "Cover us!" and the hills, "Fall on us!" ⁹"Israel, you have sinned from the days of Gibeah. There they remained. The battle against the children of iniquity doesn't overtake them in Gibeah. ¹⁰ When it is my desire, I will chastise them; and the nations will be gathered against them when they are bound to their two transgressions. ¹¹ Ephraim is a trained heifer that loves to thresh, so I will put a yoke on her beautiful neck. I will set a rider on Ephraim. Judah will plow. Jacob will break his clods. ¹² Sow to yourselves in righteousness, reap according to kindness. Break up your fallow ground, for it is time to seek Yahweh, until he comes and rains righteousness on you. ¹³ You have plowed wickedness. You have reaped iniquity. You have eaten the fruit of lies, for you trusted in your way, in the multitude of your mighty men. ¹⁴ Therefore a battle roar will arise among your people, and all your fortresses will be destroyed, as Shalman destroyed Beth Arbel in the day of battle. The mother was dashed in pieces with her children. ¹⁵ So Bethel will do to you because of your great wickedness. At daybreak the king of Israel will be destroyed.

## 11

¹"When Israel was a child, then I loved him, and called my son out of Egypt. ² They called to them, so they went from them. They sacrificed to the Baals, and burned incense to engraved images. ³ Yet I taught Ephraim to walk. I took them by their arms, but they didn't know that I healed them. ⁴ I drew them with cords of a man, with ties of love; and I was to them like those who lift up the yoke on their necks; and I bent down to him and I fed him. ⁵"They won't return into the land of Egypt; but the Assyrian will be their king, because they refused to repent. ⁶ The sword will fall on their cities, and will destroy the bars of their gates, and will put an end to their plans. ⁷ My people are determined to turn from me. Though they call to the Most High, he certainly won't exalt them. ⁸"How can I give you up, Ephraim? How can I hand you over, Israel? How can I make you like Admah? How can I make you like Zeboiim? My heart is turned within me, my compassion is aroused. ⁹ I will not execute the fierceness of my anger. I will not return to destroy Ephraim, for I am God, and not man—the Holy One among you. I will not come in wrath. ¹⁰ They will walk after Yahweh, who will roar like a lion; for he will roar, and the children will come trembling from the west. ¹¹ They will come trembling like a bird out of Egypt, and like a dove out of the land of Assyria; and I will settle them in their houses," says Yahweh. ¹² Ephraim surrounds me with falsehood, and the house of Israel with deceit. Judah still strays from God, and is unfaithful to the Holy One.

## 12

¹ Ephraim feeds on wind, and chases the east wind. He continually multiplies lies and desolation. They make a covenant with Assyria, and

oil is carried into Egypt. ² Yahweh also has a controversy with Judah, and will punish Jacob according to his ways; according to his deeds he will repay him. ³ In the womb he took his brother by the heel, and in his manhood he contended with God. ⁴ Indeed, he struggled with the angel, and prevailed; he wept, and made supplication to him. He found him at Bethel, and there he spoke with us— ⁵ even Yahweh, the God of Armies. Yahweh is his name of renown! ⁶ Therefore turn to your God. Keep kindness and justice, and wait continually for your God. ⁷ A merchant has dishonest scales in his hand. He loves to defraud. ⁸ Ephraim said, "Surely I have become rich. I have found myself wealth. In all my wealth they won't find in me any iniquity that is sin." ⁹ "But I am Yahweh your God from the land of Egypt. I will yet again make you dwell in tents, as in the days of the solemn feast. ¹⁰ I have also spoken to the prophets, and I have multiplied visions; and by the ministry of the prophets I have used parables. ¹¹ If Gilead is wicked, surely they are worthless. In Gilgal they sacrifice bulls. Indeed, their altars are like heaps in the furrows of the field. ¹² Jacob fled into the country of Aram. Israel served to get a wife. For a wife he tended flocks and herds. ¹³ By a prophet Yahweh brought Israel up out of Egypt, and by a prophet he was preserved. ¹⁴ Ephraim has bitterly provoked anger. Therefore his blood will be left on him, and his Lordᵃ will repay his contempt.

## 13

¹ When Ephraim spoke, there was trembling. He exalted himself in Israel, but when he became guilty through Baal, he died. ² Now they sin more and more, and have made themselves molten images of their silver, even idols according to their own understanding, all of them the work of the craftsmen. They say of them, 'They offer human sacrifice and kiss the calves.' ³ Therefore they will be like the morning mist, like the dew that passes away early, like the chaff that is driven with the whirlwind out of the threshing floor, and like the smoke out of the chimney. ⁴ "Yet I am Yahweh your God from the land of Egypt; and you shall acknowledge no god but me, and besides me there is no savior. ⁵ I knew you in the wilderness, in the land of great drought. ⁶ According to their pasture, so were they filled; they were filled, and their heart was exalted. Therefore they have forgotten me. ⁷ Therefore I am like a lion to them. Like a leopard, I will lurk by the path. ⁸ I will meet them like a bear that is bereaved of her cubs, and will tear the covering of their heart. There I will devour them like a lioness. The wild animal will tear them. ⁹ You are destroyed, Israel, because you are against me, against your helper. ¹⁰ Where is your king now, that he may save you in all your cities? And your judges, of whom you said, 'Give me a king and princes'? ¹¹ I have given you a king in my anger, and have taken him away in my wrath. ¹² The guilt of Ephraim is stored up. His sin is stored up. ¹³ The sorrows of a travailing woman will come on him. He is an unwise son, for when it is time, he doesn't come to the opening of the womb. ¹⁴ I will ransom them from the power of Sheol.ᵇ I will redeem them from death! Death, where are your plagues? Sheol, where is your destruction? "Compassion will be hidden from my eyes. ¹⁵ Though he is fruitful among his brothers, an east wind will come, the breath of Yahweh coming up from the wilderness; and his spring will become dry, and his fountain will be dried up. He will plunder the storehouse of treasure. ¹⁶ Samaria will bear her guilt, for she has rebelled against her God. They will fall by the sword. Their infants will be dashed in pieces, and their pregnant women will be ripped open."

## 14

¹ Israel, return to Yahweh your God; for you have fallen because of your sin. ² Take words with you, and return to Yahweh. Tell him, "Forgive all our sins, and accept that which is good; so we offer bulls as we vowed of our lips. ³ Assyria can't save us. We won't ride on horses; neither will we say any more to the work of our hands, 'Our gods!' for in you the fatherless finds mercy." ⁴ "I will heal their waywardness. I will love them freely; for my anger is turned away from them. ⁵ I will be like the dew to Israel. He will blossom like the lily, and send down his roots like Lebanon. ⁶ His branches will spread, and his beauty will be like the olive tree, and his fragrance like Lebanon. ⁷ Men will dwell in his shade. They will revive like the grain, and blossom like the vine. Their fragrance will be like the wine of Lebanon. ⁸ Ephraim, what have I to do any more with idols? I answer, and will take care of him. I am like a green cypress tree; from me your fruit is found." ⁹ Who is wise, that he may understand these things? Who is prudent, that he may know them? For the ways of Yahweh are right, and the righteous walk in them, but the rebellious stumble in them.

# The Book of Joel

## 1

¹ Yahweh'sᶜ word that came to Joel, the son of Pethuel. ² Hear this, you elders, and listen, all you inhabitants of the land! Has this ever happened in your days, or in the days of your fathers? ³ Tell your children about it, and have your children tell their children, and their children, another generation. ⁴ What the swarming locust has left, the great locust has eaten. What the great locust has left, the grasshopper has eaten. What the grasshopper has left, the caterpillar has eaten. ⁵ Wake up, you drunkards, and weep! Wail, all you drinkers of wine, because of the sweet wine, for it is cut off from your mouth. ⁶ For a nation has come up on my land, strong, and without number. His teeth are the teeth of a lion, and he has the fangs of a lioness. ⁷ He has laid my vine waste, and stripped my fig tree. He has stripped its bark, and thrown it away. Its branches are made white. ⁸ Mourn like a virgin dressed in sackcloth for the husband of her youth! ⁹ The meal offering and the drink offering are cut off from Yahweh's house. The priests, Yahweh's ministers, mourn. ¹⁰ The field is laid waste. The land mourns, for the grain is destroyed, The new wine has dried up, and the oil languishes. ¹¹ Be confounded, you farmers! Wail, you vineyard keepers, for the wheat and for the barley; for the harvest of the field has perished. ¹² The vine has dried up, and the fig tree withered— the pomegranate tree, the palm tree also, and the apple tree, even all of the trees of the field are withered; for joy has withered away from the sons of men. ¹³ Put on sackcloth and mourn, you priests! Wail, you ministers of the altar. Come, lie all night in sackcloth, you ministers of my God,ᵈ for the meal offering and the drink offering are withheld from your God's house. ¹⁴ Sanctify a fast. Call a solemn assembly. Gather the elders and all the inhabitants of the land to the house of Yahweh, your God, and cry to Yahweh. ¹⁵ Alas for the day! For the day of Yahweh is at hand, and it will come as destruction from the Almighty. ¹⁶ Isn't the food cut off before our eyes, joy and gladness from the house of our God? ¹⁷ The seeds rot under their clods. The granaries are laid desolate. The barns are broken down, for the grain has withered. ¹⁸ How the animals groan! The herds of livestock are perplexed, because they have no pasture. Yes, the flocks of sheep are made desolate. ¹⁹ Yahweh, I cry to you, for the fire has devoured the pastures of the wilderness, and the flame has burned all the trees of the field. ²⁰ Yes, the animals of the field pant to you, for the water brooks have dried up, and the fire has devoured the pastures of the wilderness.

## 2

¹ Blow the trumpet in Zion, and sound an alarm in my holy mountain! Let all the inhabitants of the land tremble, for the day of Yahweh comes, for it is close at hand: ² A day of darkness and gloominess, a day of clouds and thick darkness. As the dawn spreading on the mountains, a great and strong people; there has never been the like, neither will there be any more after them, even to the years of many generations. ³ A fire devours before them, and behind them, a flame burns. The land is as the garden of Eden before them, and behind them, a desolate wilderness. Yes, and no one has escaped them. ⁴ Their appearance is as the appearance of horses, and they run as horsemen. ⁵ Like the noise of chariots on the tops of the mountains, they leap, like the noise of a flame of fire that devours the stubble, like a strong people set in battle array. ⁶ At their presence the peoples are in anguish. All faces have grown pale. ⁷ They run like mighty men. They climb the wall like warriors. They each march in his line, and they don't swerve off course. ⁸ One doesn't jostle another. They each march in their own path. They burst through the defenses and don't break ranks. ⁹ They rush on the city. They run on the wall. They climb up into the houses. They enter in at the windows like thieves. ¹⁰ The earth quakes before them. The heavens tremble. The sun and the moon are darkened, and the stars withdraw their shining. ¹¹ Yahweh thunders his voice before his army, for his forces are very great; for he is strong who obeys his command; for the day of Yahweh is great and very awesome, and who can endure it? ¹² "Yet even now," says Yahweh, "turn to me with all your heart, and with fasting, and with weeping, and with mourning." ¹³ Tear your heart and not your garments, and turn to Yahweh, your God; for he is gracious and merciful, slow to anger, and abundant in loving kindness, and relents from sending calamity. ¹⁴ Who knows? He may turn and relent, and leave a blessing behind him, even a meal offering and a drink offering to Yahweh, your God. ¹⁵ Blow the trumpet in Zion! Sanctify a fast. Call a solemn assembly. ¹⁶ Gather the people. Sanctify the assembly. Assemble the elders. Gather the children, and those who nurse from breasts. Let the bridegroom go out of his room, and the bride out of her chamber. ¹⁷ Let the priests, the ministers of Yahweh, weep

---

ᵃ *12:14* The word translated "Lord" is "Adonai."
ᵇ *13:14* Sheol is the place of the dead.

ᶜ *1:1* "Yahweh" is God's proper Name, sometimes rendered "LORD" (all caps) in other translations.

ᵈ *1:13* The Hebrew word rendered "God" is "אֱלֹהִים" (Elohim).

between the porch and the altar, and let them say, "Spare your people, Yahweh, and don't give your heritage to reproach, that the nations should rule over them. Why should they say among the peoples, 'Where is their God?'" [18] Then Yahweh was jealous for his land, and had pity on his people. [19] Yahweh answered his people, "Behold,[a] I will send you grain, new wine, and oil, and you will be satisfied with them; and I will no more make you a reproach among the nations. [20] But I will remove the northern army far away from you, and will drive it into a barren and desolate land, its front into the eastern sea, and its back into the western sea; and its stench will come up, and its bad smell will rise." Surely he has done great things. [21] Land, don't be afraid. Be glad and rejoice, for Yahweh has done great things. [22] Don't be afraid, you animals of the field; for the pastures of the wilderness spring up, for the tree bears its fruit. The fig tree and the vine yield their strength. [23]"Be glad then, you children of Zion, and rejoice in Yahweh, your God; for he gives you the early rain in just measure, and he causes the rain to come down for you, the early rain and the latter rain, as before. [24] The threshing floors will be full of wheat, and the vats will overflow with new wine and oil. [25] I will restore to you the years that the swarming locust has eaten, the great locust, the grasshopper, and the caterpillar, my great army, which I sent among you. [26] You will have plenty to eat and be satisfied, and will praise the name of Yahweh, your God, who has dealt wondrously with you; and my people will never again be disappointed. [27] You will know that I am among Israel, and that I am Yahweh, your God, and there is no one else; and my people will never again be disappointed. [28]"It will happen afterward, that I will pour out my Spirit on all flesh; and your sons and your daughters will prophesy. Your old men will dream dreams. Your young men will see visions. [29] And also on the servants and on the handmaids in those days, I will pour out my Spirit. [30] I will show wonders in the heavens and in the earth: blood, fire, and pillars of smoke. [31] The sun will be turned into darkness, and the moon into blood, before the great and terrible day of Yahweh comes. [32] It will happen that whoever will call on Yahweh's name shall be saved; for in Mount Zion and in Jerusalem there will be those who escape, as Yahweh has said, and among the remnant, those whom Yahweh calls.

## 3

[1]"For, behold, in those days, and in that time, when I restore the fortunes of Judah and Jerusalem, [2] I will gather all nations, and will bring them down into the valley of Jehoshaphat; and I will execute judgment on them there for my people, and for my heritage, Israel, whom they have scattered among the nations. They have divided my land, [3] and have cast lots for my people, and have given a boy for a prostitute, and sold a girl for wine, that they may drink. [4]"Yes, and what are you to me, Tyre and Sidon, and all the regions of Philistia? Will you repay me? And if you repay me, I will swiftly and speedily return your repayment on your own head. [5] Because you have taken my silver and my gold, and have carried my finest treasures into your temples, [6] and have sold the children of Judah and the children of Jerusalem to the sons of the Greeks, that you may remove them far from their border. [7] Behold, I will stir them up out of the place where you have sold them, and will return your repayment on your own head; [8] and I will sell your sons and your daughters into the hands of the children of Judah, and they will sell them to the men of Sheba, to a faraway nation, for Yahweh has spoken it." [9] Proclaim this among the nations: "Prepare for war! Stir up the mighty men. Let all the warriors draw near. Let them come up. [10] Beat your plowshares into swords, and your pruning hooks into spears. Let the weak say, 'I am strong.' [11] Hurry and come, all you surrounding nations, and gather yourselves together." Cause your mighty ones to come down there, Yahweh. [12]"Let the nations arouse themselves, and come up to the valley of Jehoshaphat; for there I will sit to judge all the surrounding nations. [13] Put in the sickle; for the harvest is ripe. Come, tread, for the wine press is full, the vats overflow, for their wickedness is great." [14] Multitudes, multitudes in the valley of decision! For the day of Yahweh is near in the valley of decision. [15] The sun and the moon are darkened, and the stars withdraw their shining. [16] Yahweh will roar from Zion, and thunder from Jerusalem; and the heavens and the earth will shake; but Yahweh will be a refuge to his people, and a stronghold to the children of Israel. [17]"So you will know that I am Yahweh, your God, dwelling in Zion, my holy mountain. Then Jerusalem will be holy, and no strangers will pass through her any more. [18] It will happen in that day, that the mountains will drop down sweet wine, the hills will flow with milk, all the brooks of Judah will flow with waters; and a fountain will flow out from Yahweh's house,

and will water the valley of Shittim. [19] Egypt will be a desolation and Edom will be a desolate wilderness, for the violence done to the children of Judah, because they have shed innocent blood in their land. [20] But Judah will be inhabited forever, and Jerusalem from generation to generation. [21] I will cleanse their blood that I have not cleansed, for Yahweh dwells in Zion."

# The Book of Amos

## 1

[1] The words of Amos, who was among the herdsmen of Tekoa, which he saw concerning Israel in the days of Uzziah king of Judah and in the days of Jeroboam the son of Joash, king of Israel, two years before the earthquake. [2] He said: "Yahweh[b] will roar from Zion, and utter his voice from Jerusalem; and the pastures of the shepherds will mourn, and the top of Carmel will wither." [3] Yahweh says: "For three transgressions of Damascus, yes, for four, I will not turn away its punishment, because they have threshed Gilead with threshing instruments of iron; [4] but I will send a fire into the house of Hazael, and it will devour the palaces of Ben Hadad. [5] I will break the bar of Damascus, and cut off the inhabitant from the valley of Aven, and him who holds the scepter from the house of Eden; and the people of Syria shall go into captivity to Kir," says Yahweh. [6] Yahweh says: "For three transgressions of Gaza, yes, for four, I will not turn away its punishment, because they carried away captive the whole community, to deliver them up to Edom; [7] but I will send a fire on the wall of Gaza, and it will devour its palaces. [8] I will cut off the inhabitant from Ashdod, and him who holds the scepter from Ashkelon; and I will turn my hand against Ekron; and the remnant of the Philistines will perish," says the Lord[c] Yahweh. [9] Yahweh says: "For three transgressions of Tyre, yes, for four, I will not turn away its punishment; because they delivered up the whole community to Edom, and didn't remember the brotherly covenant; [10] but I will send a fire on the wall of Tyre, and it will devour its palaces." [11] Yahweh says: "For three transgressions of Edom, yes, for four, I will not turn away its punishment, because he pursued his brother with the sword and cast off all pity, and his anger raged continually, and he kept his wrath forever; [12] but I will send a fire on Teman, and it will devour the palaces of Bozrah." [13] Yahweh says: "For three transgressions of the children of Ammon, yes, for four, I will not turn away its punishment, because they have ripped open the pregnant women of Gilead, that they may enlarge their border. [14] But I will kindle a fire in the wall of Rabbah, and it will devour its palaces, with shouting in the day of battle, with a storm in the day of the whirlwind; [15] and their king will go into captivity, he and his princes together," says Yahweh.

## 2

[1] Yahweh says: "For three transgressions of Moab, yes, for four, I will not turn away its punishment, because he burned the bones of the king of Edom into lime; [2] but I will send a fire on Moab, and it will devour the palaces of Kerioth; and Moab will die with tumult, with shouting, and with the sound of the trumpet; [3] and I will cut off the judge from among them, and will kill all its princes with him," says Yahweh. [4] Yahweh says: "For three transgressions of Judah, yes, for four, I will not turn away its punishment, because they have rejected Yahweh's law, and have not kept his statutes, and their lies have led them astray, after which their fathers walked; [5] but I will send a fire on Judah, and it will devour the palaces of Jerusalem." [6] Yahweh says: "For three transgressions of Israel, yes, for four, I will not turn away its punishment, because they have sold the righteous for silver, and the needy for a pair of sandals; [7] They trample the heads of the poor into the dust of the earth and deny justice to the oppressed. A man and his father use the same maiden, to profane my holy name. [8] They lay themselves down beside every altar on clothes taken in pledge. In the house of their God[d] they drink the wine of those who have been fined. [9] Yet I destroyed the Amorite before them, whose height was like the height of the cedars, and he was strong as the oaks; yet I destroyed his fruit from above, and his roots from beneath. [10] Also I brought you up out of the land of Egypt and led you forty years in the wilderness, to possess the land of the Amorite. [11] I raised up some of your sons for prophets, and some of your young men for Nazirites. Isn't this true, you children of Israel?" says Yahweh. [12]"But you gave the Nazirites wine to drink, and commanded the prophets, saying, 'Don't prophesy!' [13] Behold,[e] I will crush you in your place, as a cart crushes that is full of grain. [14] Flight will perish from the swift. The strong won't strengthen

---

[a] *2:19* "Behold", from "הִנֵּה", means look at, take notice, observe, see, or gaze at. It is often used as an interjection.

[b] *1:2* "Yahweh" is God's proper Name, sometimes rendered "LORD" (all caps) in other translations.

[c] *1:8* The word translated "Lord" is "Adonai."
[d] *2:8* The Hebrew word rendered "God" is "אֱלֹהִים" (Elohim).

[e] *2:13* "Behold", from "הִנֵּה", means look at, take notice, observe, see, or gaze at. It is often used as an interjection.

his force. The mighty won't deliver himself. [15] He who handles the bow won't stand. He who is swift of foot won't escape. He who rides the horse won't deliver himself. [16] He who is courageous among the mighty will flee away naked on that day," says Yahweh.

## 3

[1] Hear this word that Yahweh has spoken against you, children of Israel, against the whole family which I brought up out of the land of Egypt, saying: [2]"I have only chosen you of all the families of the earth. Therefore I will punish you for all of your sins." [3] Do two walk together, unless they have agreed? [4] Will a lion roar in the thicket, when he has no prey? Does a young lion cry out of his den, if he has caught nothing? [5] Can a bird fall in a trap on the earth, where no snare is set for him? Does a snare spring up from the ground, when there is nothing to catch? [6] Does the trumpet alarm sound in a city, without the people being afraid? Does evil happen to a city, and Yahweh hasn't done it? [7] Surely the Lord Yahweh will do nothing, unless he reveals his secret to his servants the prophets. [8] The lion has roared. Who will not fear? The Lord Yahweh has spoken. Who can but prophesy? [9] Proclaim in the palaces at Ashdod, and in the palaces in the land of Egypt, and say, "Assemble yourselves on the mountains of Samaria, and see what unrest is in her, and what oppression is among them." [10]"Indeed they don't know to do right," says Yahweh, "Who hoard plunder and loot in their palaces." [11] Therefore the Lord Yahweh says: "An adversary will overrun the land; and he will pull down your strongholds, and your fortresses will be plundered." [12] Yahweh says: "As the shepherd rescues out of the mouth of the lion two legs, or a piece of an ear, so shall the children of Israel be rescued who sit in Samaria on the corner of a couch, and on the silken cushions of a bed." [13]"Listen, and testify against the house of Jacob," says the Lord Yahweh, the God of Armies. [14]"For in the day that I visit the transgressions of Israel on him, I will also visit the altars of Bethel; and the horns of the altar will be cut off, and fall to the ground. [15] I will strike the winter house with the summer house; and the houses of ivory will perish, and the great houses will have an end," says Yahweh.

## 4

[1] Listen to this word, you cows of Bashan, who are on the mountain of Samaria, who oppress the poor, who crush the needy, who tell their husbands, "Bring us drinks!" [2] The Lord Yahweh has sworn by his holiness, "Behold, the days shall come on you that they will take you away with hooks, and the last of you with fish hooks. [3] You will go out at the breaks in the wall, everyone straight before her; and you will cast yourselves into Harmon," says Yahweh. [4]"Go to Bethel, and sin; to Gilgal, and sin more. Bring your sacrifices every morning, your tithes every three days, [5] offer a sacrifice of thanksgiving of that which is leavened, and proclaim free will offerings and brag about them; for this pleases you, you children of Israel," says the Lord Yahweh. [6]"I also have given you cleanness of teeth in all your cities, and lack of bread in every town; yet you haven't returned to me," says Yahweh. [7]"I also have withheld the rain from you, when there were yet three months to the harvest; and I caused it to rain on one city, and caused it not to rain on another city. One field was rained on, and the field where it didn't rain withered. [8] So two or three cities staggered to one city to drink water, and were not satisfied; yet you haven't returned to me," says Yahweh. [9]"I struck you with blight and mildew many times in your gardens and your vineyards, and the swarming locusts have devoured your fig trees and your olive trees; yet you haven't returned to me," says Yahweh. [10]"I sent plagues among you like I did Egypt. I have slain your young men with the sword, and have carried away your horses. I filled your nostrils with the stench of your camp, yet you haven't returned to me," says Yahweh. [11]"I have overthrown some of you, as when God overthrew Sodom and Gomorrah, and you were like a burning stick plucked out of the fire; yet you haven't returned to me," says Yahweh. [12]"Therefore I will do this to you, Israel; because I will do this to you, prepare to meet your God, Israel. [13] For, behold, he who forms the mountains, creates the wind, declares to man what is his thought, who makes the morning darkness, and treads on the high places of the earth: Yahweh, the God of Armies, is his name."

## 5

[1] Listen to this word which I take up for a lamentation over you, O house of Israel: [2]"The virgin of Israel has fallen; She shall rise no more. She is cast down on her land; there is no one to raise her up." [3] For the Lord Yahweh says: "The city that went out a thousand shall have a hundred left, and that which went out one hundred shall have ten left to the house of Israel." [4] For Yahweh says to the house of Israel: "Seek me, and you will live; [5] but don't seek Bethel, nor enter into Gilgal, and don't pass to Beersheba; for Gilgal shall surely go into captivity, and Bethel shall come to nothing. [6] Seek Yahweh, and you will live, lest he break out like fire in the house of Joseph, and it devour, and there be no one to quench it in Bethel. [7] You who turn justice to wormwood, and cast down righteousness to the earth! [8] Seek him who made the Pleiades

and Orion, and turns the shadow of death into the morning, and makes the day dark with night; who calls for the waters of the sea, and pours them out on the surface of the earth, Yahweh is his name, [9] who brings sudden destruction on the strong, so that destruction comes on the fortress. [10] They hate him who reproves in the gate, and they abhor him who speaks blamelessly. [11] Therefore, because you trample on the poor and take taxes from him of wheat, you have built houses of cut stone, but you will not dwell in them. You have planted pleasant vineyards, but you shall not drink their wine. [12] For I know how many are your offenses, and how great are your sins— you who afflict the just, who take a bribe, and who turn away the needy in the courts. [13] Therefore a prudent person keeps silent in such a time, for it is an evil time. [14] Seek good, and not evil, that you may live; and so Yahweh, the God of Armies, will be with you, as you say. [15] Hate evil, love good, and establish justice in the courts. It may be that Yahweh, the God of Armies, will be gracious to the remnant of Joseph." [16] Therefore Yahweh, the God of Armies, the Lord, says: "Wailing will be in all the wide ways. They will say in all the streets, 'Alas! Alas!' They will call the farmer to mourning, and those who are skillful in lamentation to wailing. [17] In all vineyards there will be wailing, for I will pass through the middle of you," says Yahweh. [18]"Woe to you who desire the day of Yahweh! Why do you long for the day of Yahweh? It is darkness, and not light. [19] As if a man fled from a lion, and a bear met him; or he went into the house and leaned his hand on the wall, and a snake bit him. [20] Won't the day of Yahweh be darkness, and not light? Even very dark, and no brightness in it? [21] I hate, I despise your feasts, and I can't stand your solemn assemblies. [22] Yes, though you offer me your burnt offerings and meal offerings, I will not accept them; neither will I regard the peace offerings of your fat animals. [23] Take away from me the noise of your songs! I will not listen to the music of your harps. [24] But let justice roll on like rivers, and righteousness like a mighty stream. [25]"Did you bring to me sacrifices and offerings in the wilderness forty years, house of Israel? [26] You also carried the tent of your king and the shrine of your images, the star of your god, which you made for yourselves. [27] Therefore I will cause you to go into captivity beyond Damascus," says Yahweh, whose name is the God of Armies.

## 6

[1] Woe to those who are at ease in Zion, and to those who are secure on the mountain of Samaria, the notable men of the chief of the nations, to whom the house of Israel come! [2] Go to Calneh, and see. From there go to Hamath the great. Then go down to Gath of the Philistines. Are they better than these kingdoms? Is their border greater than your border? [3] Alas for you who put far away the evil day, and cause the seat of violence to come near, [4] who lie on beds of ivory, and stretch themselves on their couches, and eat the lambs out of the flock, and the calves out of the middle of the stall, [5] who strum on the strings of a harp, who invent for themselves instruments of music, like David; [6] who drink wine in bowls, and anoint themselves with the best oils, but they are not grieved for the affliction of Joseph. [7] Therefore they will now go captive with the first who go captive. The feasting and lounging will end. [8]"The Lord Yahweh has sworn by himself," says Yahweh, the God of Armies: "I abhor the pride of Jacob, and detest his fortresses. Therefore I will deliver up the city with all that is in it. [9] It will happen that if ten men remain in one house, they will die. [10]"When a man's relative carries him, even he who burns him, to bring bodies out of the house, and asks him who is in the innermost parts of the house, 'Is there yet any with you?' And he says, 'No;' then he will say, 'Hush! Indeed we must not mention Yahweh's name.' [11]"For, behold, Yahweh commands, and the great house will be smashed to pieces, and the little house into bits. [12] Do horses run on the rocky crags? Does one plow there with oxen? But you have turned justice into poison, and the fruit of righteousness into bitterness, [13] you who rejoice in a thing of nothing, who say, 'Haven't we taken for ourselves horns by our own strength?' [14] For, behold, I will raise up against you a nation, house of Israel," says Yahweh, the God of Armies; "and they will afflict you from the entrance of Hamath to the brook of the Arabah."

## 7

[1] Thus the Lord Yahweh showed me: behold, he formed locusts in the beginning of the shooting up of the latter growth; and behold, it was the latter growth after the king's harvest. [2] When they finished eating the grass of the land, then I said, "Lord Yahweh, forgive, I beg you! How could Jacob stand? For he is small." [3] Yahweh relented concerning this. "It shall not be," says Yahweh. [4] Thus the Lord Yahweh showed me: behold, the Lord Yahweh called for judgment by fire; and it dried up the great deep, and would have devoured the land. [5] Then I said, "Lord Yahweh, stop, I beg you! How could Jacob stand? For he is small." [6] Yahweh relented concerning this. "This also shall not be," says the Lord Yahweh. [7] Thus he showed me: behold, the Lord stood beside a wall made by a plumb line, with a plumb line in his hand. [8] Yahweh

said to me, "Amos, what do you see?" I said, "A plumb line." Then the Lord said, "Behold, I will set a plumb line in the middle of my people Israel. I will not again pass by them any more. [9] The high places of Isaac will be desolate, the sanctuaries of Israel will be laid waste; and I will rise against the house of Jeroboam with the sword." [10] Then Amaziah the priest of Bethel sent to Jeroboam king of Israel, saying, "Amos has conspired against you in the middle of the house of Israel. The land is not able to bear all his words. [11] For Amos says, 'Jeroboam will die by the sword, and Israel shall surely be led away captive out of his land.'" [12] Amaziah also said to Amos, "You seer, go, flee away into the land of Judah, and there eat bread, and prophesy there, [13] but don't prophesy again any more at Bethel; for it is the king's sanctuary, and it is a royal house!" [14] Then Amos answered Amaziah, "I was no prophet, neither was I a prophet's son, but I was a herdsman, and a farmer of sycamore figs; [15] and Yahweh took me from following the flock, and Yahweh said to me, 'Go, prophesy to my people Israel.' [16] Now therefore listen to Yahweh's word: 'You say, Don't prophesy against Israel, and don't preach against the house of Isaac.' [17] Therefore Yahweh says: 'Your wife shall be a prostitute in the city, and your sons and your daughters shall fall by the sword, and your land shall be divided by line; and you yourself shall die in a land that is unclean, and Israel shall surely be led away captive out of his land.'"

## 8

[1] Thus the Lord Yahweh showed me: behold, a basket of summer fruit. [2] He said, "Amos, what do you see?" I said, "A basket of summer fruit." Then Yahweh said to me, "The end has come on my people Israel. I will not again pass by them any more. [3] The songs of the temple will be wailing in that day," says the Lord Yahweh. "The dead bodies will be many. In every place they will throw them out with silence. [4] Hear this, you who desire to swallow up the needy, and cause the poor of the land to fail, [5] saying, 'When will the new moon be gone, that we may sell grain? And the Sabbath, that we may market wheat, making the ephah[a] small, and the shekel[b] large, and dealing falsely with balances of deceit; [6] that we may buy the poor for silver, and the needy for a pair of sandals, and sell the sweepings with the wheat?'" [7] Yahweh has sworn by the pride of Jacob, "Surely I will never forget any of their works. [8] Won't the land tremble for this, and everyone mourn who dwells in it? Yes, it will rise up wholly like the River; and it will be stirred up and sink again, like the River of Egypt. [9] It will happen in that day," says the Lord Yahweh, "that I will cause the sun to go down at noon, and I will darken the earth in the clear day. [10] I will turn your feasts into mourning, and all your songs into lamentation; and I will make you wear sackcloth on all your bodies, and baldness on every head. I will make it like the mourning for an only son, and its end like a bitter day. [11] Behold, the days come," says the Lord Yahweh, "that I will send a famine in the land, not a famine of bread, nor a thirst for water, but of hearing Yahweh's words. [12] They will wander from sea to sea, and from the north even to the east; they will run back and forth to seek Yahweh's word, and will not find it. [13] In that day the beautiful virgins and the young men will faint for thirst. [14] Those who swear by the sin of Samaria, and say, 'As your god, Dan, lives,' and, 'As the way of Beersheba lives,' they will fall, and never rise up again."

## 9

[1] I saw the Lord standing beside the altar, and he said, "Strike the tops of the pillars, that the thresholds may shake. Break them in pieces on the head of all of them. I will kill the last of them with the sword. Not one of them will flee away. Not one of them will escape. [2] Though they dig into Sheol,[c] there my hand will take them; and though they climb up to heaven, there I will bring them down. [3] Though they hide themselves in the top of Carmel, I will search and take them out from there; and though they be hidden from my sight in the bottom of the sea, there I will command the serpent, and it will bite them. [4] Though they go into captivity before their enemies, there I will command the sword, and it will kill them. I will set my eyes on them for evil, and not for good. [5] For the Lord, Yahweh of Armies, is he who touches the land and it melts, and all who dwell in it will mourn; and it will rise up wholly like the River, and will sink again, like the River of Egypt. [6] It is he who builds his rooms in the heavens, and has founded his vault on the earth; he who calls for the waters of the sea, and pours them out on the surface of the earth—Yahweh is his name. [7] Are you not like the children of the Ethiopians to me, children of Israel?" says Yahweh. "Haven't I brought up Israel out of the land of Egypt, and the Philistines from Caphtor, and the Syrians from Kir? [8] Behold, the eyes of the Lord Yahweh are on the sinful kingdom, and I will destroy it from off the surface of the earth, except that I will not utterly destroy the house of

Jacob," says Yahweh. [9] "For behold, I will command, and I will sift the house of Israel among all the nations as grain is sifted in a sieve, yet not the least kernel will fall on the earth. [10] All the sinners of my people will die by the sword, who say, 'Evil won't overtake nor meet us.' [11] In that day I will raise up the tent of David who is fallen and close up its breaches, and I will raise up its ruins, and I will build it as in the days of old, [12] that they may possess the remnant of Edom and all the nations who are called by my name," says Yahweh who does this. [13] "Behold, the days come," says Yahweh, "that the plowman shall overtake the reaper, and the one treading grapes him who sows seed; and sweet wine will drip from the mountains, and flow from the hills. [14] I will bring my people Israel back from captivity, and they will rebuild the ruined cities, and inhabit them; and they will plant vineyards, and drink wine from them. They shall also make gardens, and eat their fruit. [15] I will plant them on their land, and they will no more be plucked up out of their land which I have given them," says Yahweh your God.

# The Book of Obadiah
## 1

[1] The vision of Obadiah. This is what the Lord[d] Yahweh[e] says about Edom. We have heard news from Yahweh, and an ambassador is sent among the nations, saying, "Arise, and let's rise up against her in battle. [2] Behold,[f] I have made you small among the nations. You are greatly despised. [3] The pride of your heart has deceived you, you who dwell in the clefts of the rock, whose habitation is high, who says in his heart, 'Who will bring me down to the ground?' [4] Though you mount on high as the eagle, and though your nest is set among the stars, I will bring you down from there," says Yahweh. [5] "If thieves came to you, if robbers by night—oh, what disaster awaits you—wouldn't they only steal until they had enough? If grape pickers came to you, wouldn't they leave some gleaning grapes? [6] How Esau will be ransacked! How his hidden treasures are sought out! [7] All the men of your alliance have brought you on your way, even to the border. The men who were at peace with you have deceived you, and prevailed against you. Friends who eat your bread lay a snare under you. There is no understanding in him." [8] "Won't I in that day", says Yahweh, "destroy the wise men out of Edom, and understanding out of the mountain of Esau? [9] Your mighty men, Teman, will be dismayed, to the end that everyone may be cut off from the mountain of Esau by slaughter. [10] For the violence done to your brother Jacob, shame will cover you, and you will be cut off forever. [11] In the day that you stood on the other side, in the day that strangers carried away his substance and foreigners entered into his gates and cast lots for Jerusalem, even you were like one of them. [12] But don't look down on your brother in the day of his disaster, and don't rejoice over the children of Judah in the day of their destruction. Don't speak proudly in the day of distress. [13] Don't enter into the gate of my people in the day of their calamity. Don't look down on their affliction in the day of their calamity, neither seize their wealth on the day of their calamity. [14] Don't stand in the crossroads to cut off those of his who escape. Don't deliver up those of his who remain in the day of distress. [15] For the day of Yahweh is near all the nations! As you have done, it will be done to you. Your deeds will return upon your own head. [16] For as you have

drunk on my holy mountain, so all the nations will drink continually. Yes, they will drink, swallow down, and will be as though they had not been. [17] But in Mount Zion, there will be those who escape, and it will be holy. The house of Jacob will possess their possessions. [18] The house of Jacob will be a fire, the house of Joseph a flame, and the house of Esau for stubble. They will burn among them and devour them. There will not be any remaining to the house of Esau." Indeed, Yahweh has spoken. [19] Those of the South will possess the mountain of Esau, and those of the lowland, the Philistines. They will possess the field of Ephraim, and the field of Samaria. Benjamin will possess Gilead. [20] The captives of this army of the children of Israel, who are among the Canaanites, will possess even to Zarephath; and the captives of

a 8:5 1 ephah is about 22 liters or about 2/3 of a bushel.

b 8:5 a normal shekel is about 10 grams or about 0.35 ounces.

c 9:2 Sheol is the place of the dead.

d 1:1 The word translated "Lord" is "Adonai."

e 1:1 "Yahweh" is God's proper Name, sometimes rendered "LORD" (all caps) in other translations.

f 1:2 "Behold", from "הִנֵּה", means look at, take notice, observe, see, or gaze at. It is often used as an interjection.

Jerusalem, who are in Sepharad, will possess the cities of the Negev. ²¹ Saviors will go up on Mount Zion to judge the mountains of Esau, and the kingdom will be Yahweh's.

# The Book of Jonah
## 1

¹ Now Yahweh'sᵃ word came to Jonah the son of Amittai, saying, ²"Arise, go to Nineveh, that great city, and preach against it, for their wickedness has come up before me." ³ But Jonah rose up to flee to Tarshish from the presence of Yahweh. He went down to Joppa, and found a ship going to Tarshish; so he paid its fare, and went down into it, to go with them to Tarshish from the presence of Yahweh. ⁴ But Yahweh sent out a great wind on the sea, and there was a mighty storm on the sea, so that the ship was likely to break up. ⁵ Then the mariners were afraid, and every man cried to his god. They threw the cargo that was in the ship into the sea to lighten the ship. But Jonah had gone down into the innermost parts of the ship and he was laying down, and was fast asleep. ⁶ So the ship master came to him, and said to him, "What do you mean, sleeper? Arise, call on your God!ᵇ Maybe your Godᶜ will notice us, so that we won't perish." ⁷ They all said to each other, "Come! Let's cast lots, that we may know who is responsible for this evil that is on us." So they cast lots, and the lot fell on Jonah. ⁸ Then they asked him, "Tell us, please, for whose cause this evil is on us. What is your occupation? Where do you come from? What is your country? Of what people are you?" ⁹ He said to them, "I am a Hebrew, and I fear Yahweh, the Godᵈ of heaven, who has made the sea and the dry land." ¹⁰ Then the men were exceedingly afraid, and said to him, "What have you done?" For the men knew that he was fleeing from the presence of Yahweh, because he had told them. ¹¹ Then they said to him, "What shall we do to you, that the sea may be calm to us?" For the sea grew more and more stormy. ¹² He said to them, "Take me up, and throw me into the sea. Then the sea will be calm for you; for I know that because of me this great storm is on you." ¹³ Nevertheless the men rowed hard to get them back to the land; but they could not, for the sea grew more and more stormy against them. ¹⁴ Therefore they cried to Yahweh, and said, "We beg you, Yahweh, we beg you, don't let us die for this man's life, and don't lay on us innocent blood; for you, Yahweh, have done as it pleased you." ¹⁵ So they took up Jonah and threw him into the sea; and the sea ceased its raging. ¹⁶ Then the men feared Yahweh exceedingly; and they offered a sacrifice to Yahweh and made vows. ¹⁷ Yahweh prepared a huge fish to swallow up Jonah, and Jonah was in the belly of the fish three days and three nights.

## 2

¹ Then Jonah prayed to Yahweh, his God, out of the fish's belly. ² He said, "I called because of my affliction to Yahweh. He answered me. Out of the belly of Sheolᵉ I cried. You heard my voice. ³ For you threw me into the depths, in the heart of the seas. The flood was all around me. All your waves and your billows passed over me. ⁴ I said, 'I have been banished from your sight; yet I will look again toward your holy temple.' ⁵ The waters surrounded me, even to the soul. The deep was around me. The weeds were wrapped around my head. ⁶ I went down to the bottoms of the mountains. The earth barred me in forever; yet you have brought my life up from the pit, Yahweh my God. ⁷"When my soul fainted within me, I remembered Yahweh. My prayer came in to you, into your holy temple. ⁸ Those who regard vain idols forsake their own mercy. ⁹ But I will sacrifice to you with the voice of thanksgiving. I will pay that which I have vowed. Salvation belongs to Yahweh." ¹⁰ Then Yahweh spoke to the fish, and it vomited out Jonah on the dry land.

## 3

¹ Yahweh's word came to Jonah the second time, saying, ²"Arise, go to Nineveh, that great city, and preach to it the message that I give you."

³ So Jonah arose, and went to Nineveh, according to Yahweh's word. Now Nineveh was an exceedingly great city, three days' journey across. ⁴ Jonah began to enter into the city a day's journey, and he cried out, and said, "In forty days, Nineveh will be overthrown!" ⁵ The people of Nineveh believed God; and they proclaimed a fast and put on sackcloth, from their greatest even to their least. ⁶ The news reached the king of Nineveh, and he arose from his throne, took off his royal robe, covered himself with sackcloth, and sat in ashes. ⁷ He made a proclamation and published through Nineveh by the decree of the king and his nobles, saying, "Let neither man nor animal, herd nor flock, taste anything; let them not feed, nor drink water; ⁸ but let them be covered with sackcloth, both man and animal, and let them cry mightily to God. Yes, let them turn everyone from his evil way and from the violence that is in his hands. ⁹ Who knows whether God will not turn and relent, and turn away from his fierce anger, so that we might not perish?" ¹⁰ God saw their works, that they turned from their evil way. God relented of the disaster which he said he would do to them, and he didn't do it.

## 4

¹ But it displeased Jonah exceedingly, and he was angry. ² He prayed to Yahweh, and said, "Please, Yahweh, wasn't this what I said when I was still in my own country? Therefore I hurried to flee to Tarshish, for I knew that you are a gracious God and merciful, slow to anger, and abundant in loving kindness, and you relent of doing harm. ³ Therefore now, Yahweh, take, I beg you, my life from me, for it is better for me to die than to live." ⁴ Yahweh said, "Is it right for you to be angry?" ⁵ Then Jonah went out of the city and sat on the east side of the city, and there made himself a booth and sat under it in the shade, until he might see what would become of the city. ⁶ Yahweh God prepared a vine and made it to come up over Jonah, that it might be a shade over his head to deliver him from his discomfort. So Jonah was exceedingly glad because of the vine. ⁷ But God prepared a worm at dawn the next day, and it chewed on the vine so that it withered. ⁸ When the sun arose, God prepared a sultry east wind; and the sun beat on Jonah's head, so that he was faint and requested for himself that he might die. He said, "It is better for me to die than to live." ⁹ God said to Jonah, "Is it right for you to be angry about the vine?" He said, "I am right to be angry, even to death." ¹⁰ Yahweh said, "You have been concerned for the vine, for which you have not labored, neither made it grow; which came up in a night and perished in a night. ¹¹ Shouldn't I be concerned for Nineveh, that great city, in which are more than one hundred twenty thousand persons who can't discern between their right hand and their left hand, and also many animals?"

# The Book of Micah
## 1

¹ Yahweh'sᶠ word that came to Micah of Morasheth in the days of Jotham, Ahaz, and Hezekiah, kings of Judah, which he saw concerning Samaria and Jerusalem. ² Hear, you peoples, all of you! Listen, O earth, and all that is therein. Let the Lordᵍ Yahweh be witness against you, the Lord from his holy temple. ³ For behold,ʰ Yahweh comes out of his place, and will come down and tread on the high places of the earth. ⁴ The mountains melt under him, and the valleys split apart like wax before the fire, like waters that are poured down a steep place. ⁵"All this is for the disobedience of Jacob, and for the sins of the house of Israel. What is the disobedience of Jacob? Isn't it Samaria? And what are the high places of Judah? Aren't they Jerusalem? ⁶ Therefore I will make Samaria like a rubble heap of the field, like places for planting vineyards; and I will pour down its stones into the valley, and I will uncover its foundations. ⁷ All her idols will be beaten to pieces, and all her temple gifts will be burned with fire, and I will destroy all her images; for of the hire of a prostitute has she gathered them, and to the hire of a prostitute shall they return." ⁸ For this I will lament and wail. I will go stripped and naked. I will howl like the jackals and mourn like the ostriches. ⁹ For her wounds are incurable; for it has come even to Judah. It reaches to the gate of my people, even to Jerusalem. ¹⁰ Don't tell it in Gath. Don't weep at all. At Beth Ophrahⁱ I have rolled myself in the dust. ¹¹ Pass on, inhabitant of Shaphir, in nakedness and shame. The inhabitant of Zaanan won't come out. The wailing of Beth Ezel will take from you his protection. ¹² For the inhabitant of Maroth waits anxiously for good, because evil has come down from Yahweh to the gate of Jerusalem. ¹³ Harness the chariot to the swift steed, inhabitant

ᵃ 1:1 "Yahweh" is God's proper Name, sometimes rendered "LORD" (all caps) in other translations.
ᵇ 1:6 or, gods
ᶜ 1:6 or, gods
ᵈ 1:9 The Hebrew word rendered "God" is "אֱלֹהִים" (Elohim).
ᵉ 2:2 Sheol is the place of the dead.
ᶠ 1:1 "Yahweh" is God's proper Name, sometimes rendered "LORD" (all caps) in other translations.
ᵍ 1:2 The word translated "Lord" is "Adonai."
ʰ 1:3 "Behold", from "הִנֵּה", means look at, take notice, observe, see, or gaze at. It is often used as an interjection.
ⁱ 1:10 Beth Ophrah means literally "House of Dust."

of Lachish. She was the beginning of sin to the daughter of Zion; for the transgressions of Israel were found in you. [14] Therefore you will give a parting gift to Moresheth Gath. The houses of Achzib will be a deceitful thing to the kings of Israel. [15] I will yet bring a conqueror to you, inhabitants of Mareshah. The glory of Israel will come to Adullam. [16] Shave your heads, and cut off your hair for the children of your delight. Enlarge your baldness like the vulture, for they have gone into captivity from you!

## 2

[1] Woe to those who devise iniquity and work evil on their beds! When the morning is light, they practice it, because it is in the power of their hand. [2] They covet fields and seize them, and houses, then take them away. They oppress a man and his house, even a man and his heritage. [3] Therefore Yahweh says: "Behold, I am planning against these people a disaster, from which you will not remove your necks, neither will you walk haughtily, for it is an evil time. [4] In that day they will take up a parable against you, and lament with a doleful lamentation, saying, 'We are utterly ruined! My people's possession is divided up. Indeed he takes it from me and assigns our fields to traitors!'" [5] Therefore you will have no one who divides the land by lot in Yahweh's assembly. [6]"Don't prophesy!"—they prophesy— "Don't prophesy about these things. Disgrace won't overtake us." [7] Shall it be said, O house of Jacob, "Is Yahweh's Spirit angry? Are these his doings? Don't my words do good to him who walks blamelessly?" [8] But lately my people have risen up as an enemy. You strip the robe and clothing from those who pass by without a care, returning from battle. [9] You drive the women of my people out from their pleasant houses; from their young children you take away my blessing forever. [10] Arise, and depart! For this is not your resting place, because of uncleanness that destroys, even with a grievous destruction. [11] If a man walking in a spirit of falsehood lies, saying, "I will prophesy to you of wine and of strong drink," he would be the prophet of this people. [12] I will surely assemble all of you, Jacob. I will surely gather the remnant of Israel. I will put them together as the sheep of Bozrah, as a flock in the middle of their pasture. They will swarm with people. [13] He who breaks open the way goes up before them. They break through the gate, and go out. Their king passes on before them, with Yahweh at their head.

## 3

[1] I said, "Please listen, you heads of Jacob, and rulers of the house of Israel: Isn't it for you to know justice? [2] You who hate the good, and love the evil; who tear off their skin, and their flesh from off their bones; [3] who also eat the flesh of my people, and peel their skin from off them, and break their bones, and chop them in pieces, as for the pot, and as meat within the cauldron. [4] Then they will cry to Yahweh, but he will not answer them. Yes, he will hide his face from them at that time, because they made their deeds evil." [5] Yahweh says concerning the prophets who lead my people astray—for those who feed their teeth, they proclaim, "Peace!" and whoever doesn't provide for their mouths, they prepare war against him: [6]"Therefore night is over you, with no vision, and it is dark to you, that you may not divine; and the sun will go down on the prophets, and the day will be black over them. [7] The seers shall be disappointed, and the diviners confounded. Yes, they shall all cover their lips, for there is no answer from God."[a] [8] But as for me, I am full of power by Yahweh's Spirit, and of judgment, and of might, to declare to Jacob his disobedience, and to Israel his sin. [9] Please listen to this, you heads of the house of Jacob, and rulers of the house of Israel, who abhor justice, and pervert all equity, [10] who build up Zion with blood, and Jerusalem with iniquity. [11] Her leaders judge for bribes, and her priests teach for a price, and her prophets of it tell fortunes for money; yet they lean on Yahweh, and say, "Isn't Yahweh among us? No disaster will come on us." [12] Therefore Zion for your sake will be plowed like a field, and Jerusalem will become heaps of rubble, and the mountain of the temple like the high places of a forest.

## 4

[1] But in the latter days, it will happen that the mountain of Yahweh's temple will be established on the top of the mountains, and it will be exalted above the hills; and peoples will stream to it. [2] Many nations will go and say, "Come! Let's go up to the mountain of Yahweh, and to the house of the God of Jacob; and he will teach us of his ways, and we will walk in his paths." For the law will go out of Zion, and Yahweh's word from Jerusalem; [3] and he will judge between many peoples, and will decide concerning strong nations afar off. They will beat their swords into plowshares, and their spears into pruning hooks. Nation will not lift up sword against nation, neither will they learn war any more. [4] But every man will sit under his vine and under his fig tree. No one will make them afraid, for the mouth of Yahweh of Armies has

spoken. [5] Indeed all the nations may walk in the name of their gods, but we will walk in the name of Yahweh our God forever and ever. [6]"In that day," says Yahweh, "I will assemble that which is lame, and I will gather that which is driven away, and that which I have afflicted; [7] and I will make that which was lame a remnant, and that which was cast far off a strong nation: and Yahweh will reign over them on Mount Zion from then on, even forever." [8] You, tower of the flock, the hill of the daughter of Zion, to you it will come. Yes, the former dominion will come, the kingdom of the daughter of Jerusalem. [9] Now why do you cry out aloud? Is there no king in you? Has your counselor perished, that pains have taken hold of you as of a woman in travail? [10] Be in pain, and labor to give birth, daughter of Zion, like a woman in travail; for now you will go out of the city, and will dwell in the field, and will come even to Babylon. There you will be rescued. There Yahweh will redeem you from the hand of your enemies. [11] Now many nations have assembled against you, that say, "Let her be defiled, and let our eye gloat over Zion." [12] But they don't know the thoughts of Yahweh, neither do they understand his counsel; for he has gathered them like the sheaves to the threshing floor. [13] Arise and thresh, daughter of Zion, for I will make your horn iron, and I will make your hoofs bronze. You will beat in pieces many peoples. I will devote their gain to Yahweh, and their substance to the Lord of the whole earth.

## 5

[1] Now you shall gather yourself in troops, daughter of troops. He has laid siege against us. They will strike the judge of Israel with a rod on the cheek. [2] But you, Bethlehem Ephrathah, being small among the clans of Judah, out of you one will come out to me who is to be ruler in Israel; whose goings out are from of old, from ancient times. [3] Therefore he will abandon them until the time that she who is in labor gives birth. Then the rest of his brothers will return to the children of Israel. [4] He shall stand, and shall shepherd in the strength of Yahweh, in the majesty of the name of Yahweh his God. They will live, for then he will be great to the ends of the earth. [5] He will be our peace when Assyria invades our land and when he marches through our fortresses, then we will raise against him seven shepherds, and eight leaders of men. [6] They will rule the land of Assyria with the sword, and the land of Nimrod in its gates. He will deliver us from the Assyrian, when he invades our land, and when he marches within our border. [7] The remnant of Jacob will be among many peoples like dew from Yahweh, like showers on the grass, that don't wait for man nor wait for the sons of men. [8] The remnant of Jacob will be among the nations, among many peoples, like a lion among the animals of the forest, like a young lion among the flocks of sheep; who, if he goes through, treads down and tears in pieces, and there is no one to deliver. [9] Let your hand be lifted up above your adversaries, and let all of your enemies be cut off. [10]"It will happen in that day", says Yahweh, "that I will cut off your horses from among you and will destroy your chariots. [11] I will cut off the cities of your land and will tear down all your strongholds. [12] I will destroy witchcraft from your hand. You shall have no soothsayers. [13] I will cut off your engraved images and your pillars from among you; and you shall no more worship the work of your hands. [14] I will uproot your Asherah poles from among you; and I will destroy your cities. [15] I will execute vengeance in anger and wrath on the nations that didn't listen."

## 6

[1] Listen now to what Yahweh says: "Arise, plead your case before the mountains, and let the hills hear what you have to say. [2] Hear, you mountains, Yahweh's indictment, and you enduring foundations of the earth; for Yahweh has a case against his people, and he will contend with Israel. [3] My people, what have I done to you? How have I burdened you? Answer me! [4] For I brought you up out of the land of Egypt, and redeemed you out of the house of bondage. I sent before you Moses, Aaron, and Miriam. [5] My people, remember now what Balak king of Moab devised, and what Balaam the son of Beor answered him from Shittim to Gilgal, that you may know the righteous acts of Yahweh." [6] How shall I come before Yahweh, and bow myself before the exalted God? Shall I come before him with burnt offerings, with calves a year old? [7] Will Yahweh be pleased with thousands of rams? With tens of thousands of rivers of oil? Shall I give my firstborn for my disobedience? The fruit of my body for the sin of my soul? [8] He has shown you, O man, what is good. What does Yahweh require of you, but to act justly, to love mercy, and to walk humbly with your God? [9] Yahweh's voice calls to the city— and wisdom fears your name— "Listen to the rod, and he who appointed it. [10] Are there yet treasures of wickedness in the house of the wicked, and a short ephah[b] that is accursed? [11] Shall I tolerate dishonest scales, and a bag of deceitful

---

[a] *3:7* The Hebrew word rendered "God" is "אֱלֹהִים" (Elohim).

[b] *6:10* An ephah is a measure of volume (about 22 liters or about 2/3 of a bushel), and a short ephah is made smaller than a full ephah for the purpose of cheating customers.

weights? [12] Her rich men are full of violence, her inhabitants speak lies, and their tongue is deceitful in their speech. [13] Therefore I also have struck you with a grievous wound. I have made you desolate because of your sins. [14] You shall eat, but not be satisfied. Your hunger will be within you. You will store up, but not save, and that which you save I will give up to the sword. [15] You will sow, but won't reap. You will tread the olives, but won't anoint yourself with oil; and crush grapes, but won't drink the wine. [16] For the statutes of Omri are kept, and all the works of Ahab's house. You walk in their counsels, that I may make you a ruin, and your inhabitants a hissing. You will bear the reproach of my people."

## 7

[1] Misery is mine! Indeed, I am like one who gathers the summer fruits, as gleanings of the vineyard. There is no cluster of grapes to eat. My soul desires to eat the early fig. [2] The godly man has perished out of the earth, and there is no one upright among men. They all lie in wait for blood; every man hunts his brother with a net. [3] Their hands are on that which is evil to do it diligently. The ruler and judge ask for a bribe. The powerful man dictates the evil desire of his soul. Thus they conspire together. [4] The best of them is like a brier. The most upright is worse than a thorn hedge. The day of your watchmen, even your visitation, has come; now is the time of their confusion. [5] Don't trust in a neighbor. Don't put confidence in a friend. With the woman lying in your embrace, be careful of the words of your mouth! [6] For the son dishonors the father, the daughter rises up against her mother, the daughter-in-law against her mother-in-law; a man's enemies are the men of his own house. [7] But as for me, I will look to Yahweh. I will wait for the God of my salvation. My God will hear me. [8] Don't rejoice against me, my enemy. When I fall, I will arise. When I sit in darkness, Yahweh will be a light to me. [9] I will bear the indignation of Yahweh, because I have sinned against him, until he pleads my case and executes judgment for me. He will bring me out to the light. I will see his righteousness. [10] Then my enemy will see it, and shame will cover her who said to me, "Where is Yahweh your God?" My eyes will see her. Now she will be trodden down like the mire of the streets. [11] A day to build your walls! In that day, he will extend your boundary. [12] In that day they will come to you from Assyria and the cities of Egypt, and from Egypt even to the River, and from sea to sea, and mountain to mountain. [13] Yet the land will be desolate because of those who dwell therein, for the fruit of their doings. [14] Shepherd your people with your staff, the flock of your heritage, who dwell by themselves in a forest. Let them feed in the middle of fertile pasture land, in Bashan and Gilead, as in the days of old. [15] "As in the days of your coming out of the land of Egypt, I will show you marvelous things." [16] The nations will see and be ashamed of all their might. They will lay their hand on their mouth. Their ears will be deaf. [17] They will lick the dust like a serpent. Like crawling things of the earth, they will come trembling out of their dens. They will come with fear to Yahweh our God, and will be afraid because of you. [18] Who is a God like you, who pardons iniquity, and passes over the disobedience of the remnant of his heritage? He doesn't retain his anger forever, because he delights in loving kindness. [19] He will again have compassion on us. He will tread our iniquities under foot. You will cast all their sins into the depths of the sea. [20] You will give truth to Jacob, and mercy to Abraham, as you have sworn to our fathers from the days of old.

## The Book of Nahum
### 1

[1] A revelation about Nineveh. The book of the vision of Nahum the Elkoshite. [2] Yahweh[a] is a jealous God[b] and avenges. Yahweh avenges and is full of wrath. Yahweh takes vengeance on his adversaries, and he maintains wrath against his enemies. [3] Yahweh is slow to anger, and great in power, and will by no means leave the guilty unpunished. Yahweh has his way in the whirlwind and in the storm, and the clouds are the dust of his feet. [4] He rebukes the sea and makes it dry, and dries up all the rivers. Bashan and Carmel languish. The flower of Lebanon languishes. [5] The mountains quake before him, and the hills melt away. The earth trembles at his presence, yes, the world, and all who dwell in it. [6] Who can stand before his indignation? Who can endure the fierceness of his anger? His wrath is poured out like fire, and the rocks are broken apart by him. [7] Yahweh is good, a stronghold in the day of trouble; and he knows those who take refuge in him. [8] But with an overflowing flood, he will make a full end of her place, and will pursue his enemies into darkness. [9] What do you plot against Yahweh? He will make a full end. Affliction won't rise up the second time. [10] For entangled like thorns, and drunken as with their drink, they are consumed utterly like dry stubble. [11] One has gone out of you who devises evil against Yahweh, who counsels wickedness. [12] Yahweh says: "Though they are in full strength and likewise many, even so they will be cut down and pass away. Though I have afflicted you, I will afflict you no more. [13] Now I will break his yoke from off you, and will burst your bonds apart." [14] Yahweh has commanded concerning you: "No more descendants will bear your name. Out of the house of your gods, I will cut off the engraved image and the molten image. I will make your grave, for you are vile." [15] Behold,[c] on the mountains the feet of him who brings good news, who publishes peace! Keep your feasts, Judah! Perform your vows, for the wicked one will no more pass through you. He is utterly cut off.

### 2

[1] He who dashes in pieces has come up against you. Keep the fortress! Watch the way! Strengthen your waist! Fortify your power mightily! [2] For Yahweh restores the excellency of Jacob, as the excellency of Israel, for the destroyers have destroyed them and ruined their vine branches. [3] The shield of his mighty men is made red. The valiant men are in scarlet. The chariots flash with steel in the day of his preparation, and the pine spears are brandished. [4] The chariots rage in the streets. They rush back and forth in the wide ways. Their appearance is like torches. They run like the lightnings. [5] He summons his picked troops. They stumble on their way. They dash to its wall, and the protective shield is put in place. [6] The gates of the rivers are opened, and the palace is dissolved. [7] It is decreed: she is uncovered, she is carried away; and her servants moan as with the voice of doves, beating on their breasts. [8] But Nineveh has been from of old like a pool of water, yet they flee away. "Stop! Stop!" they cry, but no one looks back. [9] Take the plunder of silver. Take the plunder of gold, for there is no end of treasure, an abundance of every precious thing. [10] She is empty, void, and waste. The heart melts, the knees knock together, their bodies and faces have grown pale. [11] Where is the den of the lions, and the feeding place of the young lions, where the lion and the lioness walked with the lion's cubs, and no one made them afraid? [12] The lion tore in pieces enough for his cubs, and strangled prey for his lionesses, and filled his caves with the kill and his dens with prey. [13] "Behold, I am against you," says Yahweh of Armies, "and I will burn her chariots in the smoke, and the sword will devour your young lions; and I will cut off your prey from the earth, and the voice of your messengers will no longer be heard."

### 3

[1] Woe to the bloody city! It is all full of lies and robbery—no end to the prey. [2] The noise of the whip, the noise of the rattling of wheels, prancing horses, and bounding chariots, [3] the horseman charging, and the flashing sword, the glittering spear, and a multitude of slain, and a great heap of corpses, and there is no end of the bodies. They stumble on their bodies [4] because of the multitude of the prostitution of the alluring prostitute, the mistress of witchcraft, who sells nations through her prostitution, and families through her witchcraft. [5] "Behold, I am against you," says Yahweh of Armies, "and I will lift your skirts over your face. I will show the nations your nakedness, and the kingdoms your shame. [6] I will throw abominable filth on you and make you vile, and will make you a spectacle. [7] It will happen that all those who look at you will flee from you, and say, 'Nineveh is laid waste! Who will mourn for her?' Where will I seek comforters for you?" [8] Are you better than No-Amon,[d] who was situated among the rivers,[e] who had the waters around her, whose rampart was the sea, and her wall was of the sea? [9] Cush and Egypt were her boundless strength. Put and Libya were her helpers. [10] Yet was she carried away. She went into captivity. Her young children also were dashed in pieces at the head of all the streets, and they cast lots for her honorable men, and all her great men were bound in chains. [11] You also will be drunken. You will be hidden. You also will seek a stronghold because of the enemy. [12] All your fortresses will be like fig trees with the first-ripe figs. If they are shaken, they fall into the mouth of the eater. [13] Behold, your troops among you are women. The gates of your land are set wide open to your enemies. The fire has devoured your bars. [14] Draw water for the siege. Strengthen your fortresses. Go into the clay, and tread the mortar. Make the brick kiln strong. [15] There the fire will devour you. The sword will cut you off. It will devour you like the grasshopper. Multiply like grasshoppers. Multiply like the locust. [16] You have increased your merchants more than the stars of the skies. The grasshopper strips and flees away. [17] Your guards are like the locusts, and your officials like the swarms of locusts, which settle on the walls on a cold day, but when the sun

---

[a] *1:2* "Yahweh" is God's proper Name, sometimes rendered "LORD" (all caps) in other translations.

[b] *1:2* The Hebrew word rendered "God" is "אֱלֹהִים" (Elohim).

[c] *1:15* "Behold", from "הִנֵּה", means look at, take notice, observe, see, or gaze at. It is often used as an interjection.

[d] *3:8* or, Thebes

[e] *3:8* or, Nile

appears, they flee away, and their place is not known where they are. [18] Your shepherds slumber, king of Assyria. Your nobles lie down. Your people are scattered on the mountains, and there is no one to gather them. [19] There is no healing your wound, for your injury is fatal. All who hear the report of you clap their hands over you, for who hasn't felt your endless cruelty?

# The Book of Habakkuk

## 1

[1] The revelation which Habakkuk the prophet saw. [2] Yahweh,[a] how long will I cry, and you will not hear? I cry out to you "Violence!" and will you not save? [3] Why do you show me iniquity, and look at perversity? For destruction and violence are before me. There is strife, and contention rises up. [4] Therefore the law is paralyzed, and justice never prevails; for the wicked surround the righteous; therefore justice comes out perverted. [5]"Look among the nations, watch, and wonder marvelously; for I am working a work in your days which you will not believe though it is told you. [6] For, behold,[b] I am raising up the Chaldeans, that bitter and hasty nation who march through the width of the earth, to possess dwelling places that are not theirs. [7] They are feared and dreaded. Their judgment and their dignity proceed from themselves. [8] Their horses also are swifter than leopards, and are more fierce than the evening wolves. Their horsemen press proudly on. Yes, their horsemen come from afar. They fly as an eagle that hurries to devour. [9] All of them come for violence. Their hordes face forward. They gather prisoners like sand. [10] Yes, they scoff at kings, and princes are a derision to them. They laugh at every stronghold, for they build up an earthen ramp and take it. [11] Then they sweep by like the wind and go on. They are indeed guilty, whose strength is their god." [12] Aren't you from everlasting, Yahweh my God,[c] my Holy One? We will not die. Yahweh, you have appointed them for judgment. You, Rock, have established him to punish. [13] You who have purer eyes than to see evil, and who cannot look on perversity, why do you tolerate those who deal treacherously and keep silent when the wicked swallows up the man who is more righteous than he, [14] and make men like the fish of the sea, like the creeping things that have no ruler over them? [15] He takes up all of them with the hook. He catches them in his net and gathers them in his dragnet. Therefore he rejoices and is glad. [16] Therefore he sacrifices to his net and burns incense to his dragnet, because by them his life is luxurious and his food is good. [17] Will he therefore continually empty his net, and kill the nations without mercy?

## 2

[1] I will stand at my watch and set myself on the ramparts, and will look out to see what he will say to me, and what I will answer concerning my complaint. [2] Yahweh answered me, "Write the vision, and make it plain on tablets, that he who runs may read it. [3] For the vision is yet for the appointed time, and it hurries toward the end, and won't prove false. Though it takes time, wait for it, because it will surely come. It won't delay. [4] Behold, his soul is puffed up. It is not upright in him, but the righteous will live by his faith. [5] Yes, moreover, wine is treacherous: an arrogant man who doesn't stay at home, who enlarges his desire as Sheol;[d] he is like death and can't be satisfied, but gathers to himself all nations and heaps to himself all peoples. [6] Won't all these take up a parable against him, and a taunting proverb against him, and say, 'Woe to him who increases that which is not his, and who enriches himself by extortion! How long?' [7] Won't your debtors rise up suddenly, and wake up those who make you tremble, and you will be their victim? [8] Because you have plundered many nations, all the remnant of the peoples will plunder you because of men's blood, and for the violence done to the land, to the city and to all who dwell in it. [9] Woe to him who gets an evil gain for his house, that he may set his nest on high, that he may be delivered from the hand of evil! [10] You have devised shame to your house by cutting off many peoples, and have sinned against your soul. [11] For the stone will cry out of the wall, and the beam out of the woodwork will answer it. [12] Woe to him who builds a town with blood, and establishes a city by iniquity! [13] Behold, isn't it from Yahweh of Armies that the peoples labor for the fire, and the nations weary themselves for vanity? [14] For the earth will be filled with the knowledge of Yahweh's glory, as the waters cover the sea. [15]"Woe to him who gives his neighbor drink, pouring your inflaming wine until they are drunk, so that you may gaze at their naked bodies! [16] You are filled with shame, and not glory. You will also drink and be exposed!

The cup of Yahweh's right hand will come around to you, and disgrace will cover your glory. [17] For the violence done to Lebanon will overwhelm you, and the destruction of the animals will terrify you, because of men's blood and for the violence done to the land, to every city and to those who dwell in them. [18]"What value does the engraved image have, that its maker has engraved it; the molten image, even the teacher of lies, that he who fashions its form trusts in it, to make mute idols? [19] Woe to him who says to the wood, 'Awake!' or to the mute stone, 'Arise!' Shall this teach? Behold, it is overlaid with gold and silver, and there is no breath at all within it. [20] But Yahweh is in his holy temple. Let all the earth be silent before him!"

## 3

[1] A prayer of Habakkuk, the prophet, set to victorious music. [2] Yahweh, I have heard of your fame. I stand in awe of your deeds, Yahweh. Renew your work in the middle of the years. In the middle of the years make it known. In wrath, you remember mercy. [3] God came from Teman, the Holy One from Mount Paran. Selah. His glory covered the heavens, and his praise filled the earth. [4] His splendor is like the sunrise. Rays shine from his hand, where his power is hidden. [5] Plague went before him, and pestilence followed his feet. [6] He stood, and shook the earth. He looked, and made the nations tremble. The ancient mountains were crumbled. The age-old hills collapsed. His ways are eternal. [7] I saw the tents of Cushan in affliction. The dwellings of the land of Midian trembled. [8] Was Yahweh displeased with the rivers? Was your anger against the rivers, or your wrath against the sea, that you rode on your horses, on your chariots of salvation? [9] You uncovered your bow. You called for your sworn arrows. Selah. You split the earth with rivers. [10] The mountains saw you, and were afraid. The storm of waters passed by. The deep roared and lifted up its hands on high. [11] The sun and moon stood still in the sky at the light of your arrows as they went, at the shining of your glittering spear. [12] You marched through the land in wrath. You threshed the nations in anger. [13] You went out for the salvation of your people, for the salvation of your anointed. You crushed the head of the land of wickedness. You stripped them head to foot. Selah. [14] You pierced the heads of his warriors with their own spears. They came as a whirlwind to scatter me, gloating as if to devour the wretched in secret. [15] You trampled the sea with your horses, churning mighty waters. [16] I heard, and my body trembled. My lips quivered at the voice. Rottenness enters into my bones, and I tremble in my place because I must wait quietly for the day of trouble, for the coming up of the people who invade us. [17] For even though the fig tree doesn't flourish, nor fruit be in the vines, the labor of the olive fails, the fields yield no food, the flocks are cut off from the fold, and there is no herd in the stalls, [18] yet I will rejoice in Yahweh. I will be joyful in the God of my salvation! [19] Yahweh, the Lord,[e] is my strength. He makes my feet like deer's feet, and enables me to go in high places. For the music director, on my stringed instruments.

# The Book of Zephaniah

## 1

[1] Yahweh's[f] word which came to Zephaniah, the son of Cushi, the son of Gedaliah, the son of Amariah, the son of Hezekiah, in the days of Josiah, the son of Amon, king of Judah. [2] I will utterly sweep away everything from the surface of the earth, says Yahweh. [3] I will sweep away man and animal. I will sweep away the birds of the sky, the fish of the sea, and the heaps of rubble with the wicked. I will cut off man from the surface of the earth, says Yahweh. [4] I will stretch out my hand against Judah and against all the inhabitants of Jerusalem. I will cut off the remnant of Baal from this place—the name of the idolatrous and pagan priests, [5] those who worship the army of the sky on the housetops, those who worship and swear by Yahweh and also swear by Malcam, [6] those who have turned back from following Yahweh, and those who haven't sought Yahweh nor inquired after him. [7] Be silent at the presence of the Lord[g] Yahweh, for the day of Yahweh is at hand. For Yahweh has prepared a sacrifice. He has consecrated his guests. [8] It will happen in the day of Yahweh's sacrifice that I will punish the princes, the king's sons, and all those who are clothed with foreign clothing. [9] In that day, I will punish all those who leap over the threshold, who fill their master's house with violence and deceit. [10] In that day, says Yahweh, there will be the noise of a cry from the fish gate, a wailing from the second quarter, and a great crashing from the hills. [11] Wail, you inhabitants of Maktesh, for all the people of Canaan

---

[a] *1:2* "Yahweh" is God's proper Name, sometimes rendered "LORD" (all caps) in other translations.
[b] *1:6* "Behold", from "הִנֵּה", means look at, take notice,

observe, see, or gaze at. It is often used as an interjection.
[c] *1:12* The Hebrew word rendered "God" is "אֱלֹהִים" (Elohim).

[d] *2:5* Sheol is the place of the dead.
[e] *3:19* The word translated "Lord" is "Adonai."
[f] *1:1* "Yahweh" is God's proper Name, sometimes rendered

"LORD" (all caps) in other translations.
[g] *1:7* The word translated "Lord" is "Adonai."

are undone! All those who were loaded with silver are cut off. ¹² It will happen at that time, that I will search Jerusalem with lamps, and I will punish the men who are settled on their dregs, who say in their heart, "Yahweh will not do good, neither will he do evil." ¹³ Their wealth will become a plunder, and their houses a desolation. Yes, they will build houses, but won't inhabit them. They will plant vineyards, but won't drink their wine. ¹⁴ The great day of Yahweh is near. It is near and hurries greatly, the voice of the day of Yahweh. The mighty man cries there bitterly. ¹⁵ That day is a day of wrath, a day of distress and anguish, a day of trouble and ruin, a day of darkness and gloom, a day of clouds and blackness, ¹⁶ a day of the trumpet and alarm against the fortified cities and against the high battlements. ¹⁷ I will bring such distress on men that they will walk like blind men because they have sinned against Yahweh. Their blood will be poured out like dust and their flesh like dung. ¹⁸ Neither their silver nor their gold will be able to deliver them in the day of Yahweh's wrath, but the whole land will be devoured by the fire of his jealousy; for he will make an end, yes, a terrible end, of all those who dwell in the land.

## 2

¹ Gather yourselves together, yes, gather together, you nation that has no shame, ² before the appointed time when the day passes as the chaff, before the fierce anger of Yahweh comes on you, before the day of Yahweh's anger comes on you. ³ Seek Yahweh, all you humble of the land, who have kept his ordinances. Seek righteousness. Seek humility. It may be that you will be hidden in the day of Yahweh's anger. ⁴ For Gaza will be forsaken, and Ashkelon a desolation. They will drive out Ashdod at noonday, and Ekron will be rooted up. ⁵ Woe to the inhabitants of the sea coast, the nation of the Cherethites! Yahweh's word is against you, Canaan, the land of the Philistines. I will destroy you until there is no inhabitant. ⁶ The sea coast will be pastures, with cottages for shepherds and folds for flocks. ⁷ The coast will be for the remnant of the house of Judah. They will find pasture. In the houses of Ashkelon, they will lie down in the evening, for Yahweh, their God,ᵃ will visit them and restore them. ⁸ I have heard the reproach of Moab and the insults of the children of Ammon, with which they have reproached my people and magnified themselves against their border. ⁹ Therefore, as I live, says Yahweh of Armies, the God of Israel, surely Moab will be as Sodom, and the children of Ammon as Gomorrah, a possession of nettles and salt pits, and a perpetual desolation. The remnant of my people will plunder them, and the survivors of my nation will inherit them. ¹⁰ This they will have for their pride, because they have reproached and magnified themselves against the people of Yahweh of Armies. ¹¹ Yahweh will be awesome to them, for he will famish all the gods of the land. Men will worship him, everyone from his place, even all the shores of the nations. ¹² You Cushites also, you will be killed by my sword. ¹³ He will stretch out his hand against the north, destroy Assyria, and will make Nineveh a desolation, as dry as the wilderness. ¹⁴ Herds will lie down in the middle of her, all kinds of animals. Both the pelican and the porcupine will lodge in its capitals. Their calls will echo through the windows. Desolation will be in the thresholds, for he has laid bare the cedar beams. ¹⁵ This is the joyous city that lived carelessly, that said in her heart, "I am, and there is no one besides me." How she has become a desolation, a place for animals to lie down in! Everyone who passes by her will hiss and shake their fists.

## 3

¹ Woe to her who is rebellious and polluted, the oppressing city! ² She didn't obey the voice. She didn't receive correction. She didn't trust in Yahweh. She didn't draw near to her God. ³ Her princes within her are roaring lions. Her judges are evening wolves. They leave nothing until the next day. ⁴ Her prophets are arrogant and treacherous people. Her priests have profaned the sanctuary. They have done violence to the law. ⁵ Yahweh, within her, is righteous. He will do no wrong. Every morning he brings his justice to light. He doesn't fail, but the unjust know no shame. ⁶ I have cut off nations. Their battlements are desolate. I have made their streets waste, so that no one passes by. Their cities are destroyed, so that there is no man, so that there is no inhabitant. ⁷ I said, "Just fear me. Receive correction," so that her dwelling won't be cut off, according to all that I have appointed concerning her. But they rose early and corrupted all their doings. ⁸"Therefore wait for me", says Yahweh, "until the day that I rise up to the prey, for my determination is to gather the nations, that I may assemble the kingdoms to pour on them my indignation, even all my fierce anger, for all the earth will be devoured with the fire of my jealousy. ⁹ For then I will purify the lips of the peoples, that they may all call on Yahweh's name, to serve him shoulder to shoulder. ¹⁰ From beyond the rivers of Cush, my worshipers, even the daughter of my dispersed people, will bring my offering. ¹¹ In that day you will not be disappointed for all your doings in which you have transgressed against me; for then I will take away out from among you your proudly exulting ones, and you will no more be arrogant in my holy mountain. ¹² But I will leave among you an afflicted and poor people, and they will take refuge in Yahweh's name. ¹³ The remnant of Israel will not do iniquity nor speak lies, neither will a deceitful tongue be found in their mouth, for they will feed and lie down, and no one will make them afraid." ¹⁴ Sing, daughter of Zion! Shout, Israel! Be glad and rejoice with all your heart, daughter of Jerusalem. ¹⁵ Yahweh has taken away your judgments. He has thrown out your enemy. The King of Israel, Yahweh, is among you. You will not be afraid of evil any more. ¹⁶ In that day, it will be said to Jerusalem, "Don't be afraid, Zion. Don't let your hands be weak." ¹⁷ Yahweh, your God, is among you, a mighty one who will save. He will rejoice over you with joy. He will calm you in his love. He will rejoice over you with singing. ¹⁸ I will remove those who grieve about the appointed feasts from you. They are a burden and a reproach to you. ¹⁹ Behold,ᵇ at that time I will deal with all those who afflict you; and I will save those who are lame and gather those who were driven away. I will give them praise and honor, whose shame has been in all the earth. ²⁰ At that time I will bring you in, and at that time I will gather you; for I will give you honor and praise among all the peoples of the earth when I restore your fortunes before your eyes, says Yahweh.

# The Book of Haggai

## 1

¹ In the second year of Darius the king, in the sixth month, in the first day of the month, Yahweh'sᶜ word came by Haggai the prophet, to Zerubbabel the son of Shealtiel, governor of Judah, and to Joshua the son of Jehozadak, the high priest, saying, ²"This is what Yahweh of Armies says: These people say, 'The time hasn't yet come, the time for Yahweh's house to be built.'" ³ Then Yahweh's word came by Haggai the prophet, saying, ⁴"Is it a time for you yourselves to dwell in your paneled houses, while this house lies waste? ⁵ Now therefore this is what Yahweh of Armies says: 'Consider your ways. ⁶ You have sown much, and bring in little. You eat, but you don't have enough. You drink, but you aren't filled with drink. You clothe yourselves, but no one is warm; and he who earns wages earns wages to put them into a bag with holes in it.' ⁷"This is what Yahweh of Armies says: 'Consider your ways. ⁸ Go up to the mountain, bring wood, and build the house. I will take pleasure in it, and I will be glorified," says Yahweh. ⁹"You looked for much, and, behold,ᵈ it came to little; and when you brought it home, I blew it away. Why?" says Yahweh of Armies, "Because of my house that lies waste, while each of you is busy with his own house. ¹⁰ Therefore for your sake the heavens withhold the dew, and the earth withholds its fruit. ¹¹ I called for a drought on the land, on the mountains, on the grain, on the new wine, on the oil, on that which the ground produces, on men, on livestock, and on all the labor of the hands." ¹² Then Zerubbabel the son of Shealtiel and Joshua the son of Jehozadak, the high priest, with all the remnant of the people, obeyed Yahweh their God'sᵉ voice, and the words of Haggai the prophet, as Yahweh their God had sent him; and the people feared Yahweh. ¹³ Then Haggai, Yahweh's messenger, spoke Yahweh's message to the people, saying, "I am with you," says Yahweh. ¹⁴ Yahweh stirred up the spirit of Zerubbabel the son of Shealtiel, governor of Judah, and the spirit of Joshua the son of Jehozadak, the high priest, and the spirit of all the remnant of the people; and they came and worked on the house of Yahweh of Armies, their God, ¹⁵ in the twenty-fourth day of the month, in the sixth month, in the second year of Darius the king.

## 2

¹ In the seventh month, in the twenty-first day of the month, Yahweh's word came by Haggai the prophet, saying, ²"Speak now to Zerubbabel the son of Shealtiel, governor of Judah, and to Joshua the son of Jehozadak, the high priest, and to the remnant of the people, saying, ³"Who is left among you who saw this house in its former glory? How do you see it now? Isn't it in your eyes as nothing? ⁴ Yet now be strong, Zerubbabel,' says Yahweh. 'Be strong, Joshua son of Jehozadak, the high priest. Be strong, all you people of the land,' says Yahweh, 'and work, for I am with you,' says Yahweh of Armies. ⁵ This is the word that I covenanted with you when you came out of Egypt, and my Spirit

ᵃ *2:7* The Hebrew word rendered "God" is "אֱלֹהִים" (Elohim).
ᵇ *3:19* "Behold", from "הִנֵּה", means look at, take notice,

observe, see, or gaze at. It is often used as an interjection.
ᶜ *1:1* "Yahweh" is God's proper Name, sometimes

rendered "LORD" (all caps) in other translations.
ᵈ *1:9* "Behold", from "הִנֵּה", means look at, take notice,

observe, see, or gaze at. It is often used as an interjection.
ᵉ *1:12* The Hebrew word rendered "God" is "אֱלֹהִים" (Elohim).

lived among you. 'Don't be afraid.' ⁶ For this is what Yahweh of Armies says: 'Yet once more, it is a little while, and I will shake the heavens, the earth, the sea, and the dry land; ⁷ and I will shake all nations. The treasure of all nations will come, and I will fill this house with glory, says Yahweh of Armies. ⁸ The silver is mine, and the gold is mine,' says Yahweh of Armies. ⁹ 'The latter glory of this house will be greater than the former,' says Yahweh of Armies; 'and in this place I will give peace,' says Yahweh of Armies." ¹⁰ In the twenty-fourth day of the ninth month, in the second year of Darius, Yahweh's word came by Haggai the prophet, saying, ¹¹ "Yahweh of Armies says: Ask now the priests concerning the law, saying, ¹² 'If someone carries holy meat in the fold of his garment, and with his fold touches bread, stew, wine, oil, or any food, will it become holy?'" The priests answered, "No." ¹³ Then Haggai said, "If one who is unclean by reason of a dead body touches any of these, will it be unclean?" The priests answered, "It will be unclean." ¹⁴ Then Haggai answered, "'So is this people, and so is this nation before me,' says Yahweh; 'and so is every work of their hands. That which they offer there is unclean. ¹⁵ Now, please consider from this day and backward, before a stone was laid on a stone in Yahweh's temple. ¹⁶ Through all that time, when one came to a heap of twenty measures, there were only ten. When one came to the wine vat to draw out fifty, there were only twenty. ¹⁷ I struck you with blight, mildew, and hail in all the work of your hands; yet you didn't turn to me,' says Yahweh. ¹⁸ 'Consider, please, from this day and backward, from the twenty-fourth day of the ninth month, since the day that the foundation of Yahweh's temple was laid, consider it. ¹⁹ Is the seed yet in the barn? Yes, the vine, the fig tree, the pomegranate, and the olive tree haven't produced. From today I will bless you.'" ²⁰ Yahweh's word came the second time to Haggai in the twenty-fourth day of the month, saying, ²¹ "Speak to Zerubbabel, governor of Judah, saying, 'I will shake the heavens and the earth. ²² I will overthrow the throne of kingdoms. I will destroy the strength of the kingdoms of the nations. I will overthrow the chariots and those who ride in them. The horses and their riders will come down, everyone by the sword of his brother. ²³ In that day, says Yahweh of Armies, I will take you, Zerubbabel my servant, the son of Shealtiel,' says Yahweh, 'and will make you like a signet ring, for I have chosen you,' says Yahweh of Armies."

## The Book of Zechariah

### 1

¹ In the eighth month, in the second year of Darius, Yahweh's[a] word came to the prophet Zechariah the son of Berechiah, the son of Iddo, saying, ² "Yahweh was very displeased with your fathers. ³ Therefore tell them, Yahweh of Armies says: 'Return to me,' says Yahweh of Armies, 'and I will return to you,' says Yahweh of Armies. ⁴ Don't you be like your fathers, to whom the former prophets proclaimed, saying: Yahweh of Armies says, 'Return now from your evil ways and from your evil doings;' but they didn't hear nor listen to me, says Yahweh. ⁵ Your fathers, where are they? And the prophets, do they live forever? ⁶ But my words and my decrees, which I commanded my servants the prophets, didn't they overtake your fathers? "Then they repented and said, 'Just as Yahweh of Armies determined to do to us, according to our ways and according to our practices, so he has dealt with us.'" ⁷ On the twenty-fourth day of the eleventh month, which is the month Shebat, in the second year of Darius, Yahweh's word came to the prophet Zechariah the son of Berechiah, the son of Iddo, saying, ⁸ "I had a vision in the night, and behold,[b] a man riding on a red horse, and he stood among the myrtle trees that were in a ravine; and behind him there were red, brown, and white horses. ⁹ Then I asked, 'My lord, what are these?'" The angel who talked with me said to me, "I will show you what these are." ¹⁰ The man who stood among the myrtle trees answered, "They are the ones Yahweh has sent to go back and forth through the earth." ¹¹ They reported to Yahweh's angel who stood among the myrtle trees, and said, "We have walked back and forth through the earth, and behold, all the earth is at rest and in peace." ¹² Then Yahweh's angel replied, "O Yahweh of Armies, how long will you not have mercy on Jerusalem and on the cities of Judah, against which you have had indignation these seventy years?" ¹³ Yahweh answered the angel who talked with me with kind and comforting words. ¹⁴ So the angel who talked with me said to me, "Proclaim, saying, 'Yahweh of Armies says: "I am jealous for Jerusalem and for Zion with a great jealousy. ¹⁵ I am very angry with the nations that are at ease; for I was but a little displeased, but they added to the calamity." ¹⁶ Therefore Yahweh says: "I have returned to Jerusalem with mercy. My house shall be built in it," says Yahweh of Armies, "and a line shall be stretched out over Jerusalem."' ¹⁷ "Proclaim further, saying,

'Yahweh of Armies says: "My cities will again overflow with prosperity, and Yahweh will again comfort Zion, and will again choose Jerusalem."'" ¹⁸ I lifted up my eyes and saw, and behold, four horns. ¹⁹ I asked the angel who talked with me, "What are these?" He answered me, "These are the horns which have scattered Judah, Israel, and Jerusalem." ²⁰ Yahweh showed me four craftsmen. ²¹ Then I asked, "What are these coming to do?" He said, "These are the horns which scattered Judah, so that no man lifted up his head; but these have come to terrify them, to cast down the horns of the nations that lifted up their horn against the land of Judah to scatter it."

### 2

¹ I lifted up my eyes, and saw, and behold, a man with a measuring line in his hand. ² Then I asked, "Where are you going?" He said to me, "To measure Jerusalem, to see what is its width and what is its length." ³ Behold, the angel who talked with me went out, and another angel went out to meet him, ⁴ and said to him, "Run, speak to this young man, saying, 'Jerusalem will be inhabited as villages without walls, because of the multitude of men and livestock in it. ⁵ For I,' says Yahweh, 'will be to her a wall of fire around it, and I will be the glory in the middle of her. ⁶ Come! Come! Flee from the land of the north,' says Yahweh; 'for I have spread you abroad as the four winds of the sky,' says Yahweh. ⁷ 'Come, Zion! Escape, you who dwell with the daughter of Babylon.' ⁸ For Yahweh of Armies says: 'For honor he has sent me to the nations which plundered you; for he who touches you touches the apple of his eye. ⁹ For, behold, I will shake my hand over them, and they will be a plunder to those who served them; and you will know that Yahweh of Armies has sent me. ¹⁰ Sing and rejoice, daughter of Zion! For behold, I come and I will dwell within you,' says Yahweh. ¹¹ Many nations shall join themselves to Yahweh in that day, and shall be my people; and I will dwell among you, and you shall know that Yahweh of Armies has sent me to you. ¹² Yahweh will inherit Judah as his portion in the holy land, and will again choose Jerusalem. ¹³ Be silent, all flesh, before Yahweh; for he has roused himself from his holy habitation!"

### 3

¹ He showed me Joshua the high priest standing before Yahweh's angel, and Satan standing at his right hand to be his adversary. ² Yahweh said to Satan, "Yahweh rebuke you, Satan! Yes, Yahweh who has chosen Jerusalem rebuke you! Isn't this a burning stick plucked out of the fire?" ³ Now Joshua was clothed with filthy garments, and was standing before the angel. ⁴ He answered and spoke to those who stood before him, saying, "Take the filthy garments off him." To him he said, "Behold, I have caused your iniquity to pass from you, and I will clothe you with rich clothing." ⁵ I said, "Let them set a clean turban on his head." So they set a clean turban on his head, and clothed him; and Yahweh's angel was standing by. ⁶ Yahweh's angel solemnly assured Joshua, saying, ⁷ "Yahweh of Armies says: 'If you will walk in my ways, and if you will follow my instructions, then you also shall judge my house, and shall also keep my courts, and I will give you a place of access among these who stand by. ⁸ Hear now, Joshua the high priest, you and your fellows who sit before you, for they are men who are a sign; for, behold, I will bring out my servant, the Branch. ⁹ For, behold, the stone that I have set before Joshua: on one stone are seven eyes; behold, I will engrave its inscription,' says Yahweh of Armies, 'and I will remove the iniquity of that land in one day. ¹⁰ In that day,' says Yahweh of Armies, 'you will invite every man his neighbor under the vine and under the fig tree.'"

### 4

¹ The angel who talked with me came again and wakened me, as a man who is wakened out of his sleep. ² He said to me, "What do you see?" I said, "I have seen, and behold, a lamp stand all of gold, with its bowl on the top of it, and its seven lamps on it; there are seven pipes to each of the lamps which are on the top of it; ³ and two olive trees by it, one on the right side of the bowl, and the other on the left side of it." ⁴ I answered and spoke to the angel who talked with me, saying, "What are these, my lord?" ⁵ Then the angel who talked with me answered me, "Don't you know what these are?" I said, "No, my lord." ⁶ Then he answered and spoke to me, saying, "This is Yahweh's word to Zerubbabel, saying, 'Not by might, nor by power, but by my Spirit,' says Yahweh of Armies. ⁷ Who are you, great mountain? Before Zerubbabel you are a plain; and he will bring out the capstone with shouts of 'Grace, grace, to it!'" ⁸ Moreover Yahweh's word came to me, saying, ⁹ "The hands of Zerubbabel have laid the foundation of this house. His hands shall also finish it; and you will know that Yahweh of Armies has sent me to you. ¹⁰ Indeed, who despises the day of small things? For these seven shall rejoice, and shall see the plumb line in the hand of Zerubbabel. These are Yahweh's eyes, which run back and

---

[a] 1:1 "Yahweh" is God's proper Name, sometimes rendered "LORD" (all caps) in other translations.

[b] 1:8 "Behold", from "הִנֵּה", means look at, take notice, observe, see, or gaze at. It is often used as an interjection.

forth through the whole earth." [11] Then I asked him, "What are these two olive trees on the right side of the lamp stand and on the left side of it?" [12] I asked him the second time, "What are these two olive branches, which are beside the two golden spouts that pour the golden oil out of themselves?" [13] He answered me, "Don't you know what these are?" I said, "No, my lord." [14] Then he said, "These are the two anointed ones who stand by the Lord[a] of the whole earth."

## 5

[1] Then again I lifted up my eyes and saw, and behold, a flying scroll. [2] He said to me, "What do you see?" I answered, "I see a flying scroll; its length is twenty cubits,[b] and its width ten cubits." [3] Then he said to me, "This is the curse that goes out over the surface of the whole land, for everyone who steals shall be cut off according to it on the one side; and everyone who swears falsely shall be cut off according to it on the other side. [4] I will cause it to go out," says Yahweh of Armies, "and it will enter into the house of the thief, and into the house of him who swears falsely by my name; and it will remain in the middle of his house, and will destroy it with its timber and its stones." [5] Then the angel who talked with me came forward and said to me, "Lift up now your eyes and see what this is that is appearing." [6] I said, "What is it?" He said, "This is the ephah[c] basket that is appearing." He said moreover, "This is their appearance in all the land— [7] and behold, a lead cover weighing one talent[d] was lifted up—and there was a woman sitting in the middle of the ephah[e] basket." [8] He said, "This is Wickedness;" and he threw her down into the middle of the ephah basket; and he threw the lead weight on its mouth. [9] Then I lifted up my eyes and saw, and behold, there were two women; and the wind was in their wings. Now they had wings like the wings of a stork, and they lifted up the ephah basket between earth and the sky. [10] Then I said to the angel who talked with me, "Where are these carrying the ephah basket?" [11] He said to me, "To build her a house in the land of Shinar. When it is prepared, she will be set there in her own place."

## 6

[1] Again I lifted up my eyes, and saw, and behold, four chariots came out from between two mountains; and the mountains were mountains of bronze. [2] In the first chariot were red horses. In the second chariot were black horses. [3] In the third chariot were white horses. In the fourth chariot were dappled horses, all of them powerful. [4] Then I asked the angel who talked with me, "What are these, my lord?" [5] The angel answered me, "These are the four winds of the sky, which go out from standing before the Lord of all the earth. [6] The one with the black horses goes out toward the north country; and the white went out after them; and the dappled went out toward the south country." [7] The strong went out, and sought to go so that they might walk back and forth through the earth. He said, "Go around and through the earth!" So they walked back and forth through the earth. [8] Then he called to me, and spoke to me, saying, "Behold, those who go toward the north country have quieted my spirit in the north country." [9] Yahweh's word came to me, saying, [10]"Take of them of the captivity, even of Heldai, of Tobijah, and of Jedaiah; and come the same day, and go into the house of Josiah the son of Zephaniah, where they have come from Babylon. [11] Yes, take silver and gold, and make crowns, and set them on the head of Joshua the son of Jehozadak, the high priest; [12] and speak to him, saying, 'Yahweh of Armies says, "Behold, the man whose name is the Branch! He will grow up out of his place; and he will build Yahweh's temple. [13] He will build Yahweh's temple. He will bear the glory, and will sit and rule on his throne. He will be a priest on his throne. The counsel of peace will be between them both. [14] The crowns shall be to Helem, to Tobijah, to Jedaiah, and to Hen the son of Zephaniah, for a memorial in Yahweh's temple. [15] Those who are far off shall come and build in Yahweh's temple; and you shall know that Yahweh of Armies has sent me to you. This will happen, if you will diligently obey Yahweh your God's voice."'"[f]

## 7

[1] In the fourth year of King Darius, Yahweh's word came to Zechariah in the fourth day of the ninth month, the month of Chislev. [2] The people of Bethel sent Sharezer and Regem Melech and their men to entreat Yahweh's favor, [3] and to speak to the priests of the house of Yahweh of Armies and to the prophets, saying, "Should I weep in the fifth month, separating myself, as I have done these so many years?" [4] Then the word of Yahweh of Armies came to me, saying, [5]"Speak to all the people of the land and to the priests, saying, 'When you fasted and mourned in the fifth and in the seventh month for these seventy years, did you at all fast to me, really to me? [6] When you eat and when you

drink, don't you eat for yourselves and drink for yourselves? [7] Aren't these the words which Yahweh proclaimed by the former prophets when Jerusalem was inhabited and in prosperity, and its cities around her, and the South and the lowland were inhabited?'" [8] Yahweh's word came to Zechariah, saying, [9]"Thus has Yahweh of Armies spoken, saying, 'Execute true judgment, and show kindness and compassion every man to his brother. [10] Don't oppress the widow, the fatherless, the foreigner, nor the poor; and let none of you devise evil against his brother in your heart.' [11] But they refused to listen, and turned their backs, and stopped their ears, that they might not hear. [12] Yes, they made their hearts as hard as flint, lest they might hear the law and the words which Yahweh of Armies had sent by his Spirit by the former prophets. Therefore great wrath came from Yahweh of Armies. [13] It has come to pass that, as he called and they refused to listen, so they will call and I will not listen," said Yahweh of Armies; [14]"but I will scatter them with a whirlwind among all the nations which they have not known. Thus the land was desolate after them, so that no man passed through nor returned; for they made the pleasant land desolate."

## 8

[1] The word of Yahweh of Armies came to me. [2] Yahweh of Armies says: "I am jealous for Zion with great jealousy, and I am jealous for her with great wrath." [3] Yahweh says: "I have returned to Zion, and will dwell in the middle of Jerusalem. Jerusalem shall be called 'The City of Truth;' and the mountain of Yahweh of Armies, 'The Holy Mountain.'" [4] Yahweh of Armies says: "Old men and old women will again dwell in the streets of Jerusalem, every man with his staff in his hand because of their old age. [5] The streets of the city will be full of boys and girls playing in its streets." [6] Yahweh of Armies says: "If it is marvelous in the eyes of the remnant of this people in those days, should it also be marvelous in my eyes?" says Yahweh of Armies. [7] Yahweh of Armies says: "Behold, I will save my people from the east country and from the west country. [8] I will bring them, and they will dwell within Jerusalem. They will be my people, and I will be their God, in truth and in righteousness." [9] Yahweh of Armies says: "Let your hands be strong, you who hear in these days these words from the mouth of the prophets who were in the day that the foundation of the house of Yahweh of Armies was laid, even the temple, that it might be built. [10] For before those days there was no wages for man nor any wages for an animal, neither was there any peace to him who went out or came in, because of the adversary. For I set all men everyone against his neighbor. [11] But now I will not be to the remnant of this people as in the former days," says Yahweh of Armies. [12]"For the seed of peace and the vine will yield its fruit, and the ground will give its increase, and the heavens will give their dew. I will cause the remnant of this people to inherit all these things. [13] It shall come to pass that, as you were a curse among the nations, house of Judah and house of Israel, so I will save you, and you shall be a blessing. Don't be afraid. Let your hands be strong." [14] For Yahweh of Armies says: "As I thought to do evil to you when your fathers provoked me to wrath," says Yahweh of Armies, "and I didn't repent, [15] so again I have thought in these days to do good to Jerusalem and to the house of Judah. Don't be afraid. [16] These are the things that you shall do: speak every man the truth with his neighbor. Execute the judgment of truth and peace in your gates, [17] and let none of you devise evil in your hearts against his neighbor, and love no false oath; for all these are things that I hate," says Yahweh. [18] The word of Yahweh of Armies came to me. [19] Yahweh of Armies says: "The fasts of the fourth, fifth, seventh, and tenth months shall be for the house of Judah joy, gladness, and cheerful feasts. Therefore love truth and peace." [20] Yahweh of Armies says: "Many peoples and the inhabitants of many cities will yet come. [21] The inhabitants of one will go to another, saying, 'Let's go speedily to entreat the favor of Yahweh, and to seek Yahweh of Armies. I will go also.' [22] Yes, many peoples and strong nations will come to seek Yahweh of Armies in Jerusalem and to entreat the favor of Yahweh." [23] Yahweh of Armies says: "In those days, ten men out of all the languages of the nations will take hold of the skirt of him who is a Jew, saying, 'We will go with you, for we have heard that God is with you.'"

## 9

[1] A revelation. Yahweh's word is against the land of Hadrach, and will rest upon Damascus— for the eye of man and of all the tribes of Israel is toward Yahweh— [2] and Hamath, also, which borders on it, Tyre and Sidon, because they are very wise. [3] Tyre built herself a stronghold, and heaped up silver like the dust, and fine gold like the mire of the streets. [4] Behold, the Lord will dispossess her, and he will strike her power in

---

[a] *4:14* The word translated "Lord" is "Adonai."
[b] *5:2* A cubit is the length from the tip of the middle finger to the elbow on a man's arm, or

about 18 inches or 46 centimeters.
[c] *5:6* An ephah is a measure of volume of about 22 liters, 5.8

U. S. gallons, or about 2/3 of a bushel.
[d] *5:7* A talent is about 30 kilograms or 66 pounds.

[e] *5:7* 1 ephah is about 22 liters or about 2/3 of a bushel
[f] *6:15* The Hebrew word rendered "God" is "אֱלֹהִים" (Elohim).

the sea; and she will be devoured with fire. [5] Ashkelon will see it, and fear; Gaza also, and will writhe in agony; as will Ekron, for her expectation will be disappointed; and the king will perish from Gaza, and Ashkelon will not be inhabited. [6] Foreigners will dwell in Ashdod, and I will cut off the pride of the Philistines. [7] I will take away his blood out of his mouth, and his abominations from between his teeth; and he also will be a remnant for our God; and he will be as a chieftain in Judah, and Ekron as a Jebusite. [8] I will encamp around my house against the army, that no one pass through or return; and no oppressor will pass through them any more: for now I have seen with my eyes. [9] Rejoice greatly, daughter of Zion! Shout, daughter of Jerusalem! Behold, your King comes to you! He is righteous, and having salvation; lowly, and riding on a donkey, even on a colt, the foal of a donkey. [10] I will cut off the chariot from Ephraim and the horse from Jerusalem. The battle bow will be cut off; and he will speak peace to the nations. His dominion will be from sea to sea, and from the River to the ends of the earth. [11] As for you also, because of the blood of your covenant, I have set free your prisoners from the pit in which is no water. [12] Turn to the stronghold, you prisoners of hope! Even today I declare that I will restore double to you. [13] For indeed I bend Judah as a bow for me. I have loaded the bow with Ephraim. I will stir up your sons, Zion, against your sons, Greece, and will make you like the sword of a mighty man. [14] Yahweh will be seen over them. His arrow will flash like lightning. The Lord Yahweh will blow the trumpet, and will go with whirlwinds of the south. [15] Yahweh of Armies will defend them. They will destroy and overcome with sling stones. They will drink, and roar as through wine. They will be filled like bowls, like the corners of the altar. [16] Yahweh their God will save them in that day as the flock of his people; for they are like the jewels of a crown, lifted on high over his land. [17] For how great is his goodness, and how great is his beauty! Grain will make the young men flourish, and new wine the virgins.

## 10

[1] Ask of Yahweh rain in the spring time, Yahweh who makes storm clouds, and he gives rain showers to everyone for the plants in the field. [2] For the teraphim[a] have spoken vanity, and the diviners have seen a lie; and they have told false dreams. They comfort in vain. Therefore they go their way like sheep. They are oppressed, because there is no shepherd. [3] My anger is kindled against the shepherds, and I will punish the male goats, for Yahweh of Armies has visited his flock, the house of Judah, and will make them as his majestic horse in the battle. [4] From him will come the cornerstone, from him the tent peg, from him the battle bow, from him every ruler together. [5] They will be as mighty men, treading down muddy streets in the battle. They will fight, because Yahweh is with them. The riders on horses will be confounded. [6] "I will strengthen the house of Judah, and I will save the house of Joseph. I will bring them back, for I have mercy on them. They will be as though I had not cast them off, for I am Yahweh their God, and I will hear them. [7] Ephraim will be like a mighty man, and their heart will rejoice as through wine. Yes, their children will see it and rejoice. Their heart will be glad in Yahweh. [8] I will signal for them and gather them, for I have redeemed them. They will increase as they were before. [9] I will sow them among the peoples. They will remember me in far countries. They will live with their children and will return. [10] I will bring them again also out of the land of Egypt, and gather them out of Assyria. I will bring them into the land of Gilead and Lebanon; and there won't be room enough for them. [11] He will pass through the sea of affliction, and will strike the waves in the sea, and all the depths of the Nile will dry up; and the pride of Assyria will be brought down, and the scepter of Egypt will depart. [12] I will strengthen them in Yahweh. They will walk up and down in his name," says Yahweh.

## 11

[1] Open your doors, Lebanon, that the fire may devour your cedars. [2] Wail, cypress tree, for the cedar has fallen, because the stately ones are destroyed. Wail, you oaks of Bashan, for the strong forest has come down. [3] A voice of the wailing of the shepherds! For their glory is destroyed—a voice of the roaring of young lions! For the pride of the Jordan is ruined. [4] Yahweh my God says: "Feed the flock of slaughter. [5] Their buyers slaughter them and go unpunished. Those who sell them say, 'Blessed be Yahweh, for I am rich;' and their own shepherds don't pity them. [6] For I will no more pity the inhabitants of the land," says Yahweh; "but, behold, I will deliver every one of the men into his neighbor's hand and into the hand of his king. They will strike the land, and out of their hand I will not deliver them." [7] So I fed the flock to be slaughtered, especially the oppressed of the flock. I took for myself two staffs. The one I called "Favor" and the other I called "Union", and I fed the flock. [8] I cut off the three shepherds in one month; for my soul

was weary of them, and their soul also loathed me. [9] Then I said, "I will not feed you. That which dies, let it die; and that which is to be cut off, let it be cut off; and let those who are left eat each other's flesh." [10] I took my staff Favor and cut it apart, that I might break my covenant that I had made with all the peoples. [11] It was broken in that day; and thus the poor of the flock that listened to me knew that it was Yahweh's word. [12] I said to them, "If you think it best, give me my wages; and if not, keep them." So they weighed for my wages thirty pieces of silver. [13] Yahweh said to me, "Throw it to the potter—the handsome price that I was valued at by them!" I took the thirty pieces of silver and threw them to the potter in Yahweh's house. [14] Then I cut apart my other staff, Union, that I might break the brotherhood between Judah and Israel. [15] Yahweh said to me, "Take for yourself yet again the equipment of a foolish shepherd. [16] For, behold, I will raise up a shepherd in the land who will not visit those who are cut off, neither will seek those who are scattered, nor heal that which is broken, nor feed that which is sound; but he will eat the meat of the fat sheep, and will tear their hoofs in pieces. [17] Woe to the worthless shepherd who leaves the flock! The sword will strike his arm and his right eye. His arm will be completely withered, and his right eye will be totally blinded!"

## 12

[1] A revelation of Yahweh's word concerning Israel: Yahweh, who stretches out the heavens and lays the foundation of the earth, and forms the spirit of man within him says: [2] "Behold, I will make Jerusalem a cup of reeling to all the surrounding peoples, and it will also be on Judah in the siege against Jerusalem. [3] It will happen in that day that I will make Jerusalem a burdensome stone for all the peoples. All who burden themselves with it will be severely wounded, and all the nations of the earth will be gathered together against it. [4] In that day," says Yahweh, "I will strike every horse with terror and his rider with madness. I will open my eyes on the house of Judah, and will strike every horse of the peoples with blindness. [5] The chieftains of Judah will say in their heart, 'The inhabitants of Jerusalem are my strength in Yahweh of Armies their God.' [6] In that day I will make the chieftains of Judah like a pan of fire among wood, and like a flaming torch among sheaves. They will devour all the surrounding peoples on the right hand and on the left; and Jerusalem will yet again dwell in their own place, even in Jerusalem. [7] Yahweh also will save the tents of Judah first, that the glory of David's house and the glory of the inhabitants of Jerusalem not be magnified above Judah. [8] In that day Yahweh will defend the inhabitants of Jerusalem. He who is feeble among them at that day will be like David, and David's house will be like God, like Yahweh's angel before them. [9] It will happen in that day, that I will seek to destroy all the nations that come against Jerusalem. [10] I will pour on David's house and on the inhabitants of Jerusalem the spirit of grace and of supplication. They will look to me[b] whom they have pierced; and they shall mourn for him as one mourns for his only son, and will grieve bitterly for him as one grieves for his firstborn. [11] In that day there will be a great mourning in Jerusalem, like the mourning of Hadadrimmon in the valley of Megiddo. [12] The land will mourn, every family apart; the family of David's house apart, and their wives apart; the family of the house of Nathan apart, and their wives apart; [13] the family of the house of Levi apart, and their wives apart; the family of the Shimeites apart, and their wives apart; [14] all the families who remain, every family apart, and their wives apart.

## 13

[1] "In that day there will be a fountain opened to David's house and to the inhabitants of Jerusalem, for sin and for uncleanness. [2] It will come to pass in that day, says Yahweh of Armies, that I will cut off the names of the idols out of the land, and they will be remembered no more. I will also cause the prophets and the spirit of impurity to pass out of the land. [3] It will happen that when anyone still prophesies, then his father and his mother who bore him will tell him, 'You must die, because you speak lies in Yahweh's name;' and his father and his mother who bore him will stab him when he prophesies. [4] It will happen in that day that the prophets will each be ashamed of his vision when he prophesies; they won't wear a hairy mantle to deceive, [5] but he will say, 'I am no prophet, I am a tiller of the ground; for I have been made a bondservant from my youth.' [6] One will say to him, 'What are these wounds between your arms?' Then he will answer, 'Those with which I was wounded in the house of my friends.' [7] "Awake, sword, against my shepherd, and against the man who is close to me," says Yahweh of Armies. "Strike the shepherd, and the sheep will be scattered; and I will turn my hand against the little ones. [8] It shall happen that in all the land," says Yahweh, "two parts in it will be cut off and die; but the third will be left in it. [9] I will bring the third part into the fire, and will refine them

---

[a] *10:2* teraphim were household idols that may have been associated with inheritance rights to the household property.

[b] *12:10* After "me", the Hebrew has the two letters "Aleph Tav" (the first and last letters of the Hebrew alphabet), not as a word, but as a grammatical marker.

as silver is refined, and will test them like gold is tested. They will call on my name, and I will hear them. I will say, 'It is my people;' and they will say, 'Yahweh is my God.'"

## 14

[1] Behold, a day of Yahweh comes, when your plunder will be divided within you. [2] For I will gather all nations against Jerusalem to battle; and the city will be taken, the houses rifled, and the women ravished. Half of the city will go out into captivity, and the rest of the people will not be cut off from the city. [3] Then Yahweh will go out and fight against those nations, as when he fought in the day of battle. [4] His feet will stand in that day on the Mount of Olives, which is before Jerusalem on the east; and the Mount of Olives will be split in two from east to west, making a very great valley. Half of the mountain will move toward the north, and half of it toward the south. [5] You shall flee by the valley of my mountains, for the valley of the mountains shall reach to Azel. Yes, you shall flee, just like you fled from before the earthquake in the days of Uzziah king of Judah. Yahweh my God will come, and all the holy ones with you.[a] [6] It will happen in that day that there will not be light, cold, or frost. [7] It will be a unique day which is known to Yahweh—not day, and not night; but it will come to pass that at evening time there will be light. [8] It will happen in that day that living waters will go out from Jerusalem, half of them toward the eastern sea, and half of them toward the western sea. It will be so in summer and in winter. [9] Yahweh will be King over all the earth. In that day Yahweh will be one, and his name one. [10] All the land will be made like the Arabah, from Geba to Rimmon south of Jerusalem; and she will be lifted up and will dwell in her place, from Benjamin's gate to the place of the first gate, to the corner gate, and from the tower of Hananel to the king's wine presses. [11] Men will dwell therein, and there will be no more curse; but Jerusalem will dwell safely. [12] This will be the plague with which Yahweh will strike all the peoples who have fought against Jerusalem: their flesh will consume away while they stand on their feet, and their eyes will consume away in their sockets, and their tongue will consume away in their mouth. [13] It will happen in that day that a great panic from Yahweh will be among them; and they will each seize the hand of his neighbor, and his hand will rise up against the hand of his neighbor. [14] Judah also will fight at Jerusalem; and the wealth of all the surrounding nations will be gathered together: gold, silver, and clothing, in great abundance. [15] A plague like this will fall on the horse, on the mule, on the camel, on the donkey, and on all the animals that will be in those camps. [16] It will happen that everyone who is left of all the nations that came against Jerusalem will go up from year to year to worship the King, Yahweh of Armies, and to keep the feast of booths. [17] It will be that whoever of all the families of the earth doesn't go up to Jerusalem to worship the King, Yahweh of Armies, on them there will be no rain. [18] If the family of Egypt doesn't go up and doesn't come, neither will it rain on them. This will be the plague with which Yahweh will strike the nations that don't go up to keep the feast of booths. [19] This will be the punishment of Egypt and the punishment of all the nations that don't go up to keep the feast of booths. [20] In that day there will be inscribed on the bells of the horses, "HOLY TO YAHWEH"; and the pots in Yahweh's house will be like the bowls before the altar. [21] Yes, every pot in Jerusalem and in Judah will be holy to Yahweh of Armies; and all those who sacrifice will come and take of them, and cook in them. In that day there will no longer be a Canaanite[b] in the house of Yahweh of Armies.

# The Book of Malachi

## 1

[1] A revelation, Yahweh's[c] word to Israel by Malachi. [2] "I have loved you," says Yahweh. Yet you say, "How have you loved us?" "Wasn't Esau Jacob's brother?" says Yahweh, "Yet I loved Jacob; [3] but Esau I hated, and made his mountains a desolation, and gave his heritage to the jackals of the wilderness." [4] Whereas Edom says, "We are beaten down, but we will return and build the waste places," Yahweh of Armies says, "They shall build, but I will throw down; and men will call them 'The Wicked Land,' even the people against whom Yahweh shows wrath forever." [5] Your eyes will see, and you will say, "Yahweh is great—even beyond the border of Israel!" [6] "A son honors his father, and a servant his master. If I am a father, then where is my honor? And if I am a master, where is the respect due me?" says Yahweh of Armies to you priests who despise my name. "You say, 'How have we despised your name?' [7] You offer polluted bread on my altar. You say, 'How have we polluted you?' In that you say, 'Yahweh's table is contemptible.' [8] When you offer the blind for sacrifice, isn't that evil? And when you offer the lame and sick, isn't that evil? Present it now to your governor! Will he be pleased with you? Or will he accept your person?" says Yahweh of Armies. [9] "Now, please entreat the favor of God,[d] that he may be gracious to us. With this, will he accept any of you?" says Yahweh of Armies. [10] "Oh that there were one among you who would shut the doors, that you might not kindle fire on my altar in vain! I have no pleasure in you," says Yahweh of Armies, "neither will I accept an offering at your hand. [11] For from the rising of the sun even to its going down, my name is great among the nations, and in every place incense will be offered to my name, and a pure offering; for my name is great among the nations," says Yahweh of Armies. [12] "But you profane it when you say, 'Yahweh's table is polluted, and its fruit, even its food, is contemptible.' [13] You say also, 'Behold,[e] what a weariness it is!' And you have sniffed at it", says Yahweh of Armies; "and you have brought that which was taken by violence, the lame, and the sick; thus you bring the offering. Should I accept this at your hand?" says Yahweh. [14] "But the deceiver is cursed who has in his flock a male, and vows and sacrifices to the Lord[f] a defective thing; for I am a great King," says Yahweh of Armies, "and my name is awesome among the nations."

## 2

[1] "Now, you priests, this commandment is for you. [2] If you will not listen, and if you will not take it to heart, to give glory to my name," says Yahweh of Armies, "then I will send the curse on you, and I will curse your blessings. Indeed, I have cursed them already, because you do not take it to heart. [3] Behold, I will rebuke your offspring,[g] and will spread dung on your faces, even the dung of your feasts; and you will be taken away with it. [4] You will know that I have sent this commandment to you, that my covenant may be with Levi," says Yahweh of Armies. [5] "My covenant was with him of life and peace; and I gave them to him that he might be reverent toward me; and he was reverent toward me, and stood in awe of my name. [6] The law of truth was in his mouth, and unrighteousness was not found in his lips. He walked with me in peace and uprightness, and turned many away from iniquity. [7] For the priest's lips should keep knowledge, and they should seek the law at his mouth; for he is the messenger of Yahweh of Armies. [8] But you have turned away from the path. You have caused many to stumble in the law. You have corrupted the covenant of Levi," says Yahweh of Armies. [9] "Therefore I have also made you contemptible and wicked before all the people, according to the way you have not kept my ways, but have had respect for persons in the law. [10] Don't we all have one father? Hasn't one God created us? Why do we deal treacherously every man against his brother, profaning the covenant of our fathers? [11] Judah has dealt treacherously, and an abomination is committed in Israel and in Jerusalem; for Judah has profaned the holiness of Yahweh which he loves, and has married the daughter of a foreign god. [12] Yahweh will cut off the man who does this, him who wakes and him who answers, out of the tents of Jacob and him who offers an offering to Yahweh of Armies. [13] "This again you do: you cover Yahweh's altar with tears, with weeping, and with sighing, because he doesn't regard the offering any more, neither receives it with good will at your hand. [14] Yet you say, 'Why?' Because Yahweh has been witness between you and the wife of your youth, against whom you have dealt treacherously, though she is your companion and the wife of your covenant. [15] Did he not make you one, although he had the residue of the Spirit? Why one? He sought godly offspring. Therefore take heed to your spirit, and let no one deal treacherously against the wife of his youth. [16] One who hates and divorces", says Yahweh, the God of Israel, "covers his garment with violence!" says Yahweh of Armies. "Therefore pay attention to your spirit, that you don't be unfaithful. [17] You have wearied Yahweh with your words. Yet you say, 'How have we wearied him?' In that you say, 'Everyone who does evil is good in Yahweh's sight, and he delights in them;' or 'Where is the God of justice?'

## 3

[1] "Behold, I send my messenger, and he will prepare the way before me! The Lord, whom you seek, will suddenly come to his temple. Behold, the messenger of the covenant, whom you desire, is coming!" says Yahweh of Armies. [2] "But who can endure the day of his coming? And who will stand when he appears? For he is like a refiner's fire, and like launderers' soap; [3] and he will sit as a refiner and purifier of silver, and he will purify the sons of Levi, and refine them as gold and silver; and

---

[a] 14:5 Septuagint reads "him" instead of "you".

[b] 14:21 or, merchant

[c] 1:1 "Yahweh" is God's proper Name, sometimes rendered "LORD" (all caps) in other translations.

[d] 1:9 The Hebrew word rendered "God" is "אֱלֹהִים" (Elohim).

[e] 1:13 "Behold", from "הִנֵּה", means look at, take notice, observe, see, or gaze at. It is often used as an interjection.

[f] 1:14 The word translated "Lord" is "Adonai."

[g] 2:3 or, seed

they shall offer to Yahweh offerings in righteousness. [4] Then the offering of Judah and Jerusalem will be pleasant to Yahweh as in the days of old and as in ancient years. [5] I will come near to you to judgment. I will be a swift witness against the sorcerers, against the adulterers, against the perjurers, and against those who oppress the hireling in his wages, the widow, and the fatherless, and who deprive the foreigner of justice, and don't fear me," says Yahweh of Armies. [6]"For I, Yahweh, don't change; therefore you, sons of Jacob, are not consumed. [7] From the days of your fathers you have turned away from my ordinances and have not kept them. Return to me, and I will return to you," says Yahweh of Armies. "But you say, 'How shall we return?' [8] Will a man rob God? Yet you rob me! But you say, 'How have we robbed you?' In tithes and offerings. [9] You are cursed with the curse; for you rob me, even this whole nation. [10] Bring the whole tithe into the storehouse, that there may be food in my house, and test me now in this," says Yahweh of Armies, "if I will not open you the windows of heaven, and pour you out a blessing, that there will not be enough room for. [11] I will rebuke the devourer for your sakes, and he shall not destroy the fruits of your ground; neither shall your vine cast its fruit before its time in the field," says Yahweh of Armies. [12]"All nations shall call you blessed, for you will be a delightful land," says Yahweh of Armies. [13]"Your words have been harsh against me," says Yahweh. "Yet you say, 'What have we spoken against you?' [14] You have said, 'It is vain to serve God,' and 'What profit is it that we have followed his instructions and that we have walked mournfully before Yahweh of Armies? [15] Now we call the proud happy; yes, those who work wickedness are built up; yes, they tempt God, and escape.' [16] Then those who feared Yahweh spoke one with another; and Yahweh listened and heard, and a book of memory was written before him for those who feared Yahweh and who honored his name. [17] They shall be mine," says Yahweh of Armies, "my own possession in the day that I make. I will spare them, as a man spares his own son who serves him. [18] Then you shall return and discern between the righteous and the wicked, between him who serves God and him who doesn't serve him.

4

[1] "For behold, the day comes, burning like a furnace, when all the proud and all who work wickedness will be stubble. The day that comes will burn them up," says Yahweh of Armies, "so that it will leave them neither root nor branch. [2] But to you who fear my name shall the sun of righteousness arise with healing in its wings. You will go out and leap like calves of the stall. [3] You shall tread down the wicked; for they will be ashes under the soles of your feet in the day that I make," says Yahweh of Armies.
[4] "Remember the law of Moses my servant, which I commanded to him in Horeb for all Israel, even statutes and ordinances.
[5] Behold, I will send you Elijah the prophet before the great and terrible day of Yahweh comes. [6] He will turn the hearts of the fathers to the children and the hearts of the children to their fathers, lest I come and strike the earth with a curse."

# THE NEW TESTAMENT

## The Good News According to Matthew

1

[1] The book of the genealogy of Jesus Christ,[a] the son of David, the son of Abraham. [2] Abraham became the father of Isaac. Isaac became the father of Jacob. Jacob became the father of Judah and his brothers. [3] Judah became the father of Perez and Zerah by Tamar. Perez became the father of Hezron. Hezron became the father of Ram. [4] Ram became the father of Amminadab. Amminadab became the father of Nahshon. Nahshon became the father of Salmon. [5] Salmon became the father of Boaz by Rahab. Boaz became the father of Obed by Ruth. Obed became the father of Jesse. [6] Jesse became the father of King David. David the king[b] became the father of Solomon by her who had been Uriah's wife. [7] Solomon became the father of Rehoboam. Rehoboam became the father of Abijah. Abijah became the father of Asa. [8] Asa became the father of Jehoshaphat. Jehoshaphat became the father of Joram. Joram became the father of Uzziah. [9] Uzziah became the father of Jotham. Jotham became the father of Ahaz. Ahaz became the father of Hezekiah. [10] Hezekiah became the father of Manasseh. Manasseh became the father of Amon. Amon became the father of Josiah. [11] Josiah became the father of Jechoniah and his brothers at the time of the exile to Babylon. [12] After the exile to Babylon, Jechoniah became the father of Shealtiel. Shealtiel became the father of Zerubbabel. [13] Zerubbabel became the father of Abiud. Abiud became the father of Eliakim. Eliakim became the father of Azor. [14] Azor became the father of Zadok. Zadok became the father of Achim. Achim became the father of Eliud. [15] Eliud became the father of Eleazar. Eleazar became the father of Matthan. Matthan became the father of Jacob. [16] Jacob became the father of Joseph, the husband of Mary, from whom was born Jesus,[c] who is called Christ. [17] So all the generations from Abraham to David are fourteen generations; from David to the exile to Babylon fourteen generations; and from the carrying away to Babylon to the Christ, fourteen generations. [18] Now the birth of Jesus Christ was like this: After his mother, Mary, was engaged to Joseph, before they came together, she was found pregnant by the Holy Spirit. [19] Joseph, her husband, being a righteous man, and not willing to make her a public example, intended to put her away secretly. [20] But when he thought about these things, behold,[d] an angel of the Lord appeared to him in a dream, saying, "Joseph, son of David, don't be afraid to take to yourself Mary as your wife, for that which is conceived in her is of the Holy Spirit. [21] She shall give birth to a son. You shall name him Jesus,[e] for it is he who shall save his people from their sins." [22] Now all this has happened that it might be fulfilled which was spoken by the Lord through the prophet, saying, [23]"Behold, the virgin shall be with child, and shall give birth to a son. They shall call his name Immanuel," which is, being interpreted, "God with us."* [24] Joseph arose from his sleep, and did as the angel of the Lord commanded him, and took his wife to himself; [25] and didn't know her sexually until she had given birth to her firstborn son. He named him Jesus.

2

[1] Now when Jesus was born in Bethlehem of Judea in the days of King Herod, behold, wise men[f] from the east came to Jerusalem, saying, [2]"Where is he who is born King of the Jews? For we saw his star in the east, and have come to worship him." [3] When King Herod heard it, he was troubled, and all Jerusalem with him. [4] Gathering together all the chief priests and scribes of the people, he asked them where the Christ would be born. [5] They said to him, "In Bethlehem of Judea, for this is written through the prophet, [6]'You Bethlehem, land of Judah, are in no way least among the princes of Judah; for out of you shall come a governor who shall shepherd my people, Israel.'"* [7] Then Herod secretly called the wise men, and learned from them exactly what time the star appeared. [8] He sent them to Bethlehem, and said, "Go and search diligently for the young child. When you have found him, bring me word, so that I also may come and worship him." [9] They, having heard the king, went their way; and behold, the star, which they saw in the east, went before them until it came and stood over where the young child was. [10] When they saw the star, they rejoiced with exceedingly great joy. [11] They came into the house and saw the young child with Mary, his mother, and they fell down and worshiped him. Opening their treasures, they offered to him gifts: gold, frankincense, and myrrh. [12] Being warned in a dream not to return to Herod, they went back to their

---

[a] *1:1* Messiah (Hebrew) and Christ (Greek) both mean "Anointed One"
[b] *1:6* NU omits "the king".
[c] *1:16* "Jesus" means "Salvation".

[d] *1:20* "Behold", from "ἰδού", means look at, take notice, observe, see, or gaze at. It is often used as an interjection.
[e] *1:21* "Jesus" means "Salvation".

* *1:23* Isaiah 7:14
[f] *2:1* The word for "wise men" (magoi) can also mean teachers, scientists, physicians, astrologers, seers, interpreters of dreams, or sorcerers.

* *2:6* Micah 5:2

own country another way. [13] Now when they had departed, behold, an angel of the Lord appeared to Joseph in a dream, saying, "Arise and take the young child and his mother, and flee into Egypt, and stay there until I tell you, for Herod will seek the young child to destroy him." [14] He arose and took the young child and his mother by night and departed into Egypt, [15] and was there until the death of Herod, that it might be fulfilled which was spoken by the Lord through the prophet, saying, "Out of Egypt I called my son."* [16] Then Herod, when he saw that he was mocked by the wise men, was exceedingly angry, and sent out and killed all the male children who were in Bethlehem and in all the surrounding countryside, from two years old and under, according to the exact time which he had learned from the wise men. [17] Then that which was spoken by Jeremiah the prophet was fulfilled, saying, [18]"A voice was heard in Ramah, lamentation, weeping and great mourning, Rachel weeping for her children; she wouldn't be comforted, because they are no more."* [19] But when Herod was dead, behold, an angel of the Lord appeared in a dream to Joseph in Egypt, saying, [20]"Arise and take the young child and his mother, and go into the land of Israel, for those who sought the young child's life are dead." [21] He arose and took the young child and his mother, and came into the land of Israel. [22] But when he heard that Archelaus was reigning over Judea in the place of his father, Herod, he was afraid to go there. Being warned in a dream, he withdrew into the region of Galilee, [23] and came and lived in a city called Nazareth; that it might be fulfilled which was spoken through the prophets that he will be called a Nazarene.

## 3

[1] In those days, John the Baptizer came, preaching in the wilderness of Judea, saying, [2]"Repent, for the Kingdom of Heaven is at hand!" [3] For this is he who was spoken of by Isaiah the prophet, saying, "The voice of one crying in the wilderness, make the way of the Lord ready! Make his paths straight!"* [4] Now John himself wore clothing made of camel's hair with a leather belt around his waist. His food was locusts and wild honey. [5] Then people from Jerusalem, all of Judea, and all the region around the Jordan went out to him. [6] They were baptized by him in the Jordan, confessing their sins. [7] But when he saw many of the Pharisees and Sadducees coming for his baptism, he said to them, "You offspring of vipers, who warned you to flee from the wrath to come? [8] Therefore produce fruit worthy of repentance! [9] Don't think to yourselves, 'We have Abraham for our father,' for I tell you that God is able to raise up children to Abraham from these stones. [10] Even now the ax lies at the root of the trees. Therefore every tree that doesn't produce good fruit is cut down, and cast into the fire. [11]"I indeed baptize you in water for repentance, but he who comes after me is mightier than I, whose sandals I am not worthy to carry. He will baptize you in the Holy Spirit.ᵃ [12] His winnowing fork is in his hand, and he will thoroughly cleanse his threshing floor. He will gather his wheat into the barn, but the chaff he will burn up with unquenchable fire." [13] Then Jesus came from Galilee to the Jordanᵇ to John, to be baptized by him. [14] But John would have hindered him, saying, "I need to be baptized by you, and you come to me?" [15] But Jesus, answering, said to him, "Allow it now, for this is the fitting way for us to fulfill all righteousness." Then he allowed him. [16] Jesus, when he was baptized, went up directly from the water: and behold, the heavens were opened to him. He saw the Spirit of God descending as a dove, and coming on him. [17] Behold, a voice out of the heavens said, "This is my beloved Son, with whom I am well pleased."

## 4

[1] Then Jesus was led up by the Spirit into the wilderness to be tempted by the devil. [2] When he had fasted forty days and forty nights, he was hungry afterward. [3] The tempter came and said to him, "If you are the Son of God, command that these stones become bread." [4] But he answered, "It is written, 'Man shall not live by bread alone, but by every word that proceeds out of God's mouth.'"* [5] Then the devil took him into the holy city. He set him on the pinnacle of the temple, [6] and said to him, "If you are the Son of God, throw yourself down, for it is written, 'He will command his angels concerning you,' and, 'On their hands they will bear you up, so that you don't dash your foot against a stone.'"* [7] Jesus said to him, "Again, it is written, 'You shall not test the Lord, your God.'"* [8] Again, the devil took him to an exceedingly high mountain, and showed him all the kingdoms of the world and their glory. [9] He said to him, "I will give you all of these things, if you will fall down and worship me." [10] Then Jesus said to him, "Get behind me,ᶜ Satan! For it is written, 'You shall worship the Lord your God, and you

shall serve him only.'" * [11] Then the devil left him, and behold, angels came and served him. [12] Now when Jesus heard that John was delivered up, he withdrew into Galilee. [13] Leaving Nazareth, he came and lived in Capernaum, which is by the sea, in the region of Zebulun and Naphtali, [14] that it might be fulfilled which was spoken through Isaiah the prophet, saying, [15]"The land of Zebulun and the land of Naphtali, toward the sea, beyond the Jordan, Galilee of the Gentiles, [16] the people who sat in darkness saw a great light; to those who sat in the region and shadow of death, to them light has dawned."* [17] From that time, Jesus began to preach, and to say, "Repent! For the Kingdom of Heaven is at hand." [18] Walking by the sea of Galilee, heᵈ saw two brothers: Simon, who is called Peter, and Andrew, his brother, casting a net into the sea; for they were fishermen. [19] He said to them, "Come after me, and I will make you fishers for men." [20] They immediately left their nets and followed him. [21] Going on from there, he saw two other brothers, James the son of Zebedee, and John his brother, in the boat with Zebedee their father, mending their nets. He called them. [22] They immediately left the boat and their father, and followed him. [23] Jesus went about in all Galilee, teaching in their synagogues, preaching the Good News of the Kingdom, and healing every disease and every sickness among the people. [24] The report about him went out into all Syria. They brought to him all who were sick, afflicted with various diseases and torments, possessed with demons, epileptics, and paralytics; and he healed them. [25] Great multitudes from Galilee, Decapolis, Jerusalem, Judea, and from beyond the Jordan followed him.

## 5

[1] Seeing the multitudes, he went up onto the mountain. When he had sat down, his disciples came to him. [2] He opened his mouth and taught them, saying, [3] "Blessed are the poor in spirit, for theirs is the Kingdom of Heaven.* [4] Blessed are those who mourn, for they shall be comforted.* [5] Blessed are the gentle, for they shall inherit the earth.e* [6] Blessed are those who hunger and thirst for righteousness, for they shall be filled. [7] Blessed are the merciful, for they shall obtain mercy. [8] Blessed are the pure in heart, for they shall see God. [9] Blessed are the peacemakers, for they shall be called children of God. [10] Blessed are those who have been persecuted for righteousness' sake, for theirs is the Kingdom of Heaven. [11] "Blessed are you when people reproach you, persecute you, and say all kinds of evil against you falsely, for my sake. [12] Rejoice, and be exceedingly glad, for great is your reward in heaven. For that is how they persecuted the prophets who were before you. [13] "You are the salt of the earth, but if the salt has lost its flavor, with what will it be salted? It is then good for nothing, but to be cast out and trodden under the feet of men. [14] You are the light of the world. A city located on a hill can't be hidden. [15] Neither do you light a lamp and put it under a measuring basket, but on a stand; and it shines to all who are in the house. [16] Even so, let your light shine before men, that they may see your good works and glorify your Father who is in heaven. [17] "Don't think that I came to destroy the law or the prophets. I didn't come to destroy, but to fulfill. [18] For most certainly, I tell you, until heaven and earth pass away, not even one smallest letterᶠ or one tiny pen strokeᵍ shall in any way pass away from the law, until all things are accomplished. [19] Therefore, whoever shall break one of these least commandments and teach others to do so, shall be called least in the Kingdom of Heaven; but whoever shall do and teach them shall be called great in the Kingdom of Heaven. [20] For I tell you that unless your righteousness exceeds that of the scribes and Pharisees, there is no way you will enter into the Kingdom of Heaven. [21] "You have heard that it was said to the ancient ones, 'You shall not murder;'* and 'Whoever murders will be in danger of the judgment.' [22] But I tell you that everyone who is angry with his brother without a cause ʰ will be in danger of the judgment. Whoever says to his brother, 'Raca!' ⁱ will be in danger of the council. Whoever says, 'You fool!' will be in danger of the fire of Gehenna.ʲ [23] "If therefore you are offering your gift at the altar, and there remember that your brother has anything against you, [24] leave your gift there before the altar, and go your way. First be reconciled to your brother, and then come and offer your gift. [25] Agree with your adversary quickly while you are with him on the way; lest perhaps the prosecutor deliver you to the judge, and the judge deliver you to the officer, and you be cast into prison. [26] Most certainly I tell you, you shall by no means get out of there until you have paid the last

---

* 2:15 Hosea 11:1
* 2:18 Jeremiah 31:15
* 3:3 Isaiah 40:3
ᵃ 3:11 TR and NU add "and with fire"
ᵇ 3:13 i.e., the Jordan River
* 4:4 Deuteronomy 8:3
* 4:6 Psalms 91:11- 12

* 4:7 Deuteronomy 6:16
ᶜ 4:10 TR and NU read "Go away" instead of "Get behind me"
* 4:10 Deuteronomy 6:13
* 4:16 Isaiah 9:1- 2
ᵈ 4:18 TR reads "Jesus" instead of "he"

* 5:3 Isaiah 57:15; 66:2
* 5:4 Isaiah 61:2; 66:10,13
ᵉ 5:5 or, land.
* 5:5 Psalms 37:11
ᶠ 5:18 literally, iota
ᵍ 5:18 or, serif
* 5:21 Exodus 20:13

ʰ 5:22 NU omits "without a cause."
ⁱ 5:22 "Raca" is an Aramaic insult, related to the word for "empty" and conveying the idea of empty-headedness.
ʲ 5:22 or, Hell

penny.[a] 27 "You have heard that it was said, [b] 'You shall not commit adultery;'* 28 but I tell you that everyone who gazes at a woman to lust after her has committed adultery with her already in his heart. 29 If your right eye causes you to stumble, pluck it out and throw it away from you. For it is more profitable for you that one of your members should perish than for your whole body to be cast into Gehenna.[c] 30 If your right hand causes you to stumble, cut it off, and throw it away from you. For it is more profitable for you that one of your members should perish, than for your whole body to be cast into Gehenna.[d] 31 "It was also said, 'Whoever shall put away his wife, let him give her a writing of divorce,'* 32 but I tell you that whoever puts away his wife, except for the cause of sexual immorality, makes her an adulteress; and whoever marries her when she is put away commits adultery. 33 "Again you have heard that it was said to the ancient ones, 'You shall not make false vows, but shall perform to the Lord your vows,'* 34 but I tell you, don't swear at all: neither by heaven, for it is the throne of God; 35 nor by the earth, for it is the footstool of his feet; nor by Jerusalem, for it is the city of the great King. 36 Neither shall you swear by your head, for you can't make one hair white or black. 37 But let your 'Yes' be 'Yes' and your 'No' be 'No.' Whatever is more than these is of the evil one. 38 "You have heard that it was said, 'An eye for an eye, and a tooth for a tooth.'* 39 But I tell you, don't resist him who is evil; but whoever strikes you on your right cheek, turn to him the other also. 40 If anyone sues you to take away your coat, let him have your cloak also. 41 Whoever compels you to go one mile, go with him two. 42 Give to him who asks you, and don't turn away him who desires to borrow from you. 43 "You have heard that it was said, 'You shall love your neighbor* and hate your enemy.'[e] 44 But I tell you, love your enemies, bless those who curse you, do good to those who hate you, and pray for those who mistreat you and persecute you, 45 that you may be children of your Father who is in heaven. For he makes his sun to rise on the evil and the good, and sends rain on the just and the unjust. 46 For if you love those who love you, what reward do you have? Don't even the tax collectors do the same? 47 If you only greet your friends, what more do you do than others? Don't even the tax collectors[f] do the same? 48 Therefore you shall be perfect, just as your Father in heaven is perfect.

## 6

1 "Be careful that you don't do your charitable giving[g] before men, to be seen by them, or else you have no reward from your Father who is in heaven. 2 Therefore, when you do merciful deeds, don't sound a trumpet before yourself, as the hypocrites do in the synagogues and in the streets, that they may get glory from men. Most certainly I tell you, they have received their reward. 3 But when you do merciful deeds, don't let your left hand know what your right hand does, 4 so that your merciful deeds may be in secret, then your Father who sees in secret will reward you openly. 5 "When you pray, you shall not be as the hypocrites, for they love to stand and pray in the synagogues and in the corners of the streets, that they may be seen by men. Most certainly, I tell you, they have received their reward. 6 But you, when you pray, enter into your inner room, and having shut your door, pray to your Father who is in secret; and your Father who sees in secret will reward you openly. 7 In praying, don't use vain repetitions as the Gentiles do; for they think that they will be heard for their much speaking. 8 Therefore don't be like them, for your Father knows what things you need before you ask him. 9 Pray like this: "'Our Father in heaven, may your name be kept holy. 10 Let your Kingdom come. Let your will be done on earth as it is in heaven. 11 Give us today our daily bread. 12 Forgive us our debts, as we also forgive our debtors. 13 Bring us not into temptation, but deliver us from the evil one. For yours is the Kingdom, the power, and the glory forever. Amen.'[h] 14 "For if you forgive men their trespasses, your heavenly Father will also forgive you. 15 But if you don't forgive men their trespasses, neither will your Father forgive your trespasses. 16 "Moreover when you fast, don't be like the hypocrites, with sad faces. For they disfigure their faces that they may be seen by men to be fasting. Most certainly I tell you, they have received their reward. 17 But you, when you fast, anoint your head and wash your face, 18 so that you are not seen by men to be fasting, but by your Father who is in secret; and your Father, who sees in secret, will reward you. 19 "Don't lay up treasures for yourselves on the earth, where moth and rust consume, and where thieves break through and steal; 20 but lay up for yourselves treasures in heaven, where neither moth nor rust consume, and where thieves don't break through and steal; 21 for where your treasure is, there your heart will be also. 22 "The lamp of the body is the eye. If therefore your eye is sound, your whole body will be full of light. 23 But if your eye is evil, your whole body will be full of darkness. If therefore the light that is in you is darkness, how great is the darkness! 24 "No one can serve two masters, for either he will hate the one and love the other, or else he will be devoted to one and despise the other. You can't serve both God and Mammon. 25 Therefore I tell you, don't be anxious for your life: what you will eat, or what you will drink; nor yet for your body, what you will wear. Isn't life more than food, and the body more than clothing? 26 See the birds of the sky, that they don't sow, neither do they reap, nor gather into barns. Your heavenly Father feeds them. Aren't you of much more value than they? 27 "Which of you by being anxious, can add one moment[i] to his lifespan? 28 Why are you anxious about clothing? Consider the lilies of the field, how they grow. They don't toil, neither do they spin, 29 yet I tell you that even Solomon in all his glory was not dressed like one of these. 30 But if God so clothes the grass of the field, which today exists and tomorrow is thrown into the oven, won't he much more clothe you, you of little faith? 31 "Therefore don't be anxious, saying, 'What will we eat?', 'What will we drink?' or, 'With what will we be clothed?' 32 For the Gentiles seek after all these things; for your heavenly Father knows that you need all these things. 33 But seek first God's Kingdom and his righteousness; and all these things will be given to you as well. 34 Therefore don't be anxious for tomorrow, for tomorrow will be anxious for itself. Each day's own evil is sufficient.

## 7

1 "Don't judge, so that you won't be judged. 2 For with whatever judgment you judge, you will be judged; and with whatever measure you measure, it will be measured to you. 3 Why do you see the speck that is in your brother's eye, but don't consider the beam that is in your own eye? 4 Or how will you tell your brother, 'Let me remove the speck from your eye,' and behold, the beam is in your own eye? 5 You hypocrite! First remove the beam out of your own eye, and then you can see clearly to remove the speck out of your brother's eye. 6 "Don't give that which is holy to the dogs, neither throw your pearls before the pigs, lest perhaps they trample them under their feet, and turn and tear you to pieces. 7 "Ask, and it will be given you. Seek, and you will find. Knock, and it will be opened for you. 8 For everyone who asks receives. He who seeks finds. To him who knocks it will be opened. 9 Or who is there among you who, if his son asks him for bread, will give him a stone? 10 Or if he asks for a fish, who will give him a serpent? 11 If you then, being evil, know how to give good gifts to your children, how much more will your Father who is in heaven give good things to those who ask him! 12 Therefore, whatever you desire for men to do to you, you shall also do to them; for this is the law and the prophets. 13 "Enter in by the narrow gate; for the gate is wide and the way is broad that leads to destruction, and there are many who enter in by it. 14 How[j] narrow is the gate and the way is restricted that leads to life! There are few who find it. 15 "Beware of false prophets, who come to you in sheep's clothing, but inwardly are ravening wolves. 16 By their fruits you will know them. Do you gather grapes from thorns or figs from thistles? 17 Even so, every good tree produces good fruit, but the corrupt tree produces evil fruit. 18 A good tree can't produce evil fruit, neither can a corrupt tree produce good fruit. 19 Every tree that doesn't grow good fruit is cut down and thrown into the fire. 20 Therefore by their fruits you will know them. 21 "Not everyone who says to me, 'Lord, Lord,' will enter into the Kingdom of Heaven, but he who does the will of my Father who is in heaven. 22 Many will tell me in that day, 'Lord, Lord, didn't we prophesy in your name, in your name cast out demons, and in your name do many mighty works?' 23 Then I will tell them, 'I never knew you. Depart from me, you who work iniquity.' 24 "Everyone therefore who hears these words of mine and does them, I will liken him to a wise man who built his house on a rock. 25 The rain came down, the floods came, and the winds blew and beat on that house; and it didn't fall, for it was founded on the rock. 26 Everyone who hears these words of mine and doesn't do them will be like a foolish man who built his house on the sand. 27 The rain came down, the floods came, and the winds blew and beat on that house; and it fell—and its fall was great." 28 When Jesus had finished saying these

---

a 5:26 literally, kodrantes. A kodrantes was a small copper coin worth about 2 lepta (widow's mites)—not enough to buy very much of anything.
b 5:27 TR adds "to the ancients".
* 5:27 Exodus 20:14
c 5:29 or, Hell

d 5:30 or, Hell
* 5:31 Deuteronomy 24:1
* 5:33 Numbers 30:2; Deuteronomy 23:21; Ecclesiastes 5:4
* 5:38 Exodus 21:24; Leviticus 24:20; Deuteronomy 19:21
* 5:43 Leviticus 19:18

e 5:43 not in the Bible, but see Qumran Manual of Discipline Ix, 21- 26
f 5:47 NU reads "Gentiles" instead of "tax collectors".
g 6:1 NU reads "acts of righteousness" instead of "charitable giving"

h 6:13 NU omits "For yours is the Kingdom, the power, and the glory forever. Amen."
i 6:27 literally, cubit
j 7:14 TR reads "Because" instead of "How"

things, the multitudes were astonished at his teaching, **²⁹** for he taught them with authority, and not like the scribes.

## 8

**¹** When he came down from the mountain, great multitudes followed him. **²** Behold, a leper came to him and worshiped him, saying, "Lord, if you want to, you can make me clean." **³** Jesus stretched out his hand and touched him, saying, "I want to. Be made clean." Immediately his leprosy was cleansed. **⁴** Jesus said to him, "See that you tell nobody; but go, show yourself to the priest, and offer the gift that Moses commanded, as a testimony to them." **⁵** When he came into Capernaum, a centurion came to him, asking him for help, **⁶** saying, "Lord, my servant lies in the house paralyzed, grievously tormented." **⁷** Jesus said to him, "I will come and heal him." **⁸** The centurion answered, "Lord, I'm not worthy for you to come under my roof. Just say the word, and my servant will be healed. **⁹** For I am also a man under authority, having under myself soldiers. I tell this one, 'Go,' and he goes; and tell another, 'Come,' and he comes; and tell my servant, 'Do this,' and he does it." **¹⁰** When Jesus heard it, he marveled and said to those who followed, "Most certainly I tell you, I haven't found so great a faith, not even in Israel. **¹¹** I tell you that many will come from the east and the west, and will sit down with Abraham, Isaac, and Jacob in the Kingdom of Heaven, **¹²** but the children of the Kingdom will be thrown out into the outer darkness. There will be weeping and gnashing of teeth." **¹³** Jesus said to the centurion, "Go your way. Let it be done for you as you have believed." His servant was healed in that hour. **¹⁴** When Jesus came into Peter's house, he saw his wife's mother lying sick with a fever. **¹⁵** He touched her hand, and the fever left her. So she got up and served him.ᵃ **¹⁶** When evening came, they brought to him many possessed with demons. He cast out the spirits with a word, and healed all who were sick, **¹⁷** that it might be fulfilled which was spoken through Isaiah the prophet, saying, "He took our infirmities and bore our diseases."* **¹⁸** Now when Jesus saw great multitudes around him, he gave the order to depart to the other side. **¹⁹** A scribe came and said to him, "Teacher, I will follow you wherever you go." **²⁰** Jesus said to him, "The foxes have holes and the birds of the sky have nests, but the Son of Man has nowhere to lay his head." **²¹** Another of his disciples said to him, "Lord, allow me first to go and bury my father." **²²** But Jesus said to him, "Follow me, and leave the dead to bury their own dead." **²³** When he got into a boat, his disciples followed him. **²⁴** Behold, a violent storm came up on the sea, so much that the boat was covered with the waves; but he was asleep. **²⁵** The disciples came to him and woke him up, saying, "Save us, Lord! We are dying!" **²⁶** He said to them, "Why are you fearful, O you of little faith?" Then he got up, rebuked the wind and the sea, and there was a great calm. **²⁷** The men marveled, saying, "What kind of man is this, that even the wind and the sea obey him?" **²⁸** When he came to the other side, into the country of the Gergesenes,ᵇ two people possessed by demons met him there, coming out of the tombs, exceedingly fierce, so that nobody could pass that way. **²⁹** Behold, they cried out, saying, "What do we have to do with you, Jesus, Son of God? Have you come here to torment us before the time?" **³⁰** Now there was a herd of many pigs feeding far away from them. **³¹** The demons begged him, saying, "If you cast us out, permit us to go away into the herd of pigs." **³²** He said to them, "Go!" They came out and went into the herd of pigs; and behold, the whole herd of pigs rushed down the cliff into the sea and died in the water. **³³** Those who fed them fled and went away into the city and told everything, including what happened to those who were possessed with demons. **³⁴** Behold, all the city came out to meet Jesus. When they saw him, they begged that he would depart from their borders.

## 9

**¹** He entered into a boat and crossed over, and came into his own city. **²** Behold, they brought to him a man who was paralyzed, lying on a bed. Jesus, seeing their faith, said to the paralytic, "Son, cheer up! Your sins are forgiven you." **³** Behold, some of the scribes said to themselves, "This man blasphemes." **⁴** Jesus, knowing their thoughts, said, "Why do you think evil in your hearts? **⁵** For which is easier, to say, 'Your sins are forgiven;' or to say, 'Get up, and walk'? **⁶** But that you may know that the Son of Man has authority on earth to forgive sins—" (then he said to the paralytic), "Get up, and take up your mat, and go to your house." **⁷** He arose and departed to his house. **⁸** But when the multitudes saw it, they marveled and glorified God, who had given such authority to men. **⁹** As Jesus passed by from there, he saw a man called Matthew sitting at the tax collection office. He said to him, "Follow me." He got up and followed him. **¹⁰** As he sat in the house, behold, many tax collectors and sinners came and sat down with Jesus and his

disciples. **¹¹** When the Pharisees saw it, they said to his disciples, "Why does your teacher eat with tax collectors and sinners?" **¹²** When Jesus heard it, he said to them, "Those who are healthy have no need for a physician, but those who are sick do. **¹³** But you go and learn what this means: 'I desire mercy, and not sacrifice,'* for I came not to call the righteous, but sinners to repentance."ᶜ **¹⁴** Then John's disciples came to him, saying, "Why do we and the Pharisees fast often, but your disciples don't fast?" **¹⁵** Jesus said to them, "Can the friends of the bridegroom mourn as long as the bridegroom is with them? But the days will come when the bridegroom will be taken away from them, and then they will fast. **¹⁶** No one puts a piece of unshrunk cloth on an old garment; for the patch would tear away from the garment, and a worse hole is made. **¹⁷** Neither do people put new wine into old wine skins, or else the skins would burst, and the wine be spilled, and the skins ruined. No, they put new wine into fresh wine skins, and both are preserved." **¹⁸** While he told these things to them, behold, a ruler came and worshiped him, saying, "My daughter has just died, but come and lay your hand on her, and she will live." **¹⁹** Jesus got up and followed him, as did his disciples. **²⁰** Behold, a woman who had a discharge of blood for twelve years came behind him, and touched the fringeᵈ of his garment; **²¹** for she said within herself, "If I just touch his garment, I will be made well." **²²** But Jesus, turning around and seeing her, said, "Daughter, cheer up! Your faith has made you well." And the woman was made well from that hour. **²³** When Jesus came into the ruler's house and saw the flute players and the crowd in noisy disorder, **²⁴** he said to them, "Make room, because the girl isn't dead, but sleeping." They were ridiculing him. **²⁵** But when the crowd was sent out, he entered in, took her by the hand, and the girl arose. **²⁶** The report of this went out into all that land. **²⁷** As Jesus passed by from there, two blind men followed him, calling out and saying, "Have mercy on us, son of David!" **²⁸** When he had come into the house, the blind men came to him. Jesus said to them, "Do you believe that I am able to do this?" They told him, "Yes, Lord." **²⁹** Then he touched their eyes, saying, "According to your faith be it done to you." **³⁰** Then their eyes were opened. Jesus strictly commanded them, saying, "See that no one knows about this." **³¹** But they went out and spread abroad his fame in all that land. **³²** As they went out, behold, a mute man who was demon possessed was brought to him. **³³** When the demon was cast out, the mute man spoke. The multitudes marveled, saying, "Nothing like this has ever been seen in Israel!" **³⁴** But the Pharisees said, "By the prince of the demons, he casts out demons." **³⁵** Jesus went about all the cities and the villages, teaching in their synagogues and preaching the Good News of the Kingdom, and healing every disease and every sickness among the people. **³⁶** But when he saw the multitudes, he was moved with compassion for them because they were harassedᵉ and scattered, like sheep without a shepherd. **³⁷** Then he said to his disciples, "The harvest indeed is plentiful, but the laborers are few. **³⁸** Pray therefore that the Lord of the harvest will send out laborers into his harvest."

## 10

**¹** He called to himself his twelve disciples, and gave them authority over unclean spirits, to cast them out, and to heal every disease and every sickness. **²** Now the names of the twelve apostles are these. The first, Simon, who is called Peter; Andrew, his brother; James the son of Zebedee; John, his brother; **³** Philip; Bartholomew; Thomas; Matthew the tax collector; James the son of Alphaeus; Lebbaeus, who was also calledᶠ Thaddaeus; **⁴** Simon the Zealot; and Judas Iscariot, who also betrayed him. **⁵** Jesus sent these twelve out and commanded them, saying, "Don't go among the Gentiles, and don't enter into any city of the Samaritans. **⁶** Rather, go to the lost sheep of the house of Israel. **⁷** As you go, preach, saying, 'The Kingdom of Heaven is at hand!' **⁸** Heal the sick, cleanse the lepers,ᵍ and cast out demons. Freely you received, so freely give. **⁹** Don't take any gold, silver, or brass in your money belts. **¹⁰** Take no bag for your journey, neither two coats, nor sandals, nor staff: for the laborer is worthy of his food. **¹¹** Into whatever city or village you enter, find out who in it is worthy, and stay there until you go on. **¹²** As you enter into the household, greet it. **¹³** If the household is worthy, let your peace come on it, but if it isn't worthy, let your peace return to you. **¹⁴** Whoever doesn't receive you or hear your words, as you go out of that house or that city, shake the dust off your feet. **¹⁵** Most certainly I tell you, it will be more tolerable for the land of Sodom and Gomorrah in the day of judgment than for that city. **¹⁶** "Behold, I send you out as sheep among wolves. Therefore be wise as serpents and harmless as doves. **¹⁷** But beware of men, for they will deliver you up to councils, and in their synagogues they will scourge you. **¹⁸** Yes, and you will be brought before governors and kings for my sake, for a

---

ᵃ *8:15 TR reads "them" instead of "him"
* *8:17 Isaiah 53:4
ᵇ *8:28 NU reads "Gadarenes"
* *9:13 Hosea 6:6
ᶜ *9:13 NU omits "to repentance".
ᵈ *9:20 or, tassel
ᵉ *9:36 TR reads "weary" instead of "harassed"
ᶠ *10:3 NU omits "Lebbaeus, who was also called"
ᵍ *10:8 TR adds "raise the dead,"

testimony to them and to the nations. [19] But when they deliver you up, don't be anxious how or what you will say, for it will be given you in that hour what you will say. [20] For it is not you who speak, but the Spirit of your Father who speaks in you. [21] "Brother will deliver up brother to death, and the father his child. Children will rise up against parents and cause them to be put to death. [22] You will be hated by all men for my name's sake, but he who endures to the end will be saved. [23] But when they persecute you in this city, flee into the next, for most certainly I tell you, you will not have gone through the cities of Israel until the Son of Man has come. [24] "A disciple is not above his teacher, nor a servant above his lord. [25] It is enough for the disciple that he be like his teacher, and the servant like his lord. If they have called the master of the house Beelzebul,[a] how much more those of his household! [26] Therefore don't be afraid of them, for there is nothing covered that will not be revealed, or hidden that will not be known. [27] What I tell you in the darkness, speak in the light; and what you hear whispered in the ear, proclaim on the housetops. [28] Don't be afraid of those who kill the body, but are not able to kill the soul. Rather, fear him who is able to destroy both soul and body in Gehenna.[b] [29] "Aren't two sparrows sold for an assarion coin?[c] Not one of them falls to the ground apart from your Father's will. [30] But the very hairs of your head are all numbered. [31] Therefore don't be afraid. You are of more value than many sparrows. [32] Everyone therefore who confesses me before men, I will also confess him before my Father who is in heaven. [33] But whoever denies me before men, I will also deny him before my Father who is in heaven. [34] "Don't think that I came to send peace on the earth. I didn't come to send peace, but a sword. [35] For I came to set a man at odds against his father, and a daughter against her mother, and a daughter-in-law against her mother-in-law. [36] A man's foes will be those of his own household.* [37] He who loves father or mother more than me is not worthy of me; and he who loves son or daughter more than me isn't worthy of me. [38] He who doesn't take his cross and follow after me isn't worthy of me. [39] He who seeks his life will lose it; and he who loses his life for my sake will find it. [40] "He who receives you receives me, and he who receives me receives him who sent me. [41] He who receives a prophet in the name of a prophet will receive a prophet's reward. He who receives a righteous man in the name of a righteous man will receive a righteous man's reward. [42] Whoever gives one of these little ones just a cup of cold water to drink in the name of a disciple, most certainly I tell you, he will in no way lose his reward."

## 11

[1] When Jesus had finished directing his twelve disciples, he departed from there to teach and preach in their cities. [2] Now when John heard in the prison the works of Christ, he sent two of his disciples [3] and said to him, "Are you he who comes, or should we look for another?" [4] Jesus answered them, "Go and tell John the things which you hear and see: [5] the blind receive their sight, the lame walk, the lepers are cleansed, the deaf hear,* the dead are raised up, and the poor have good news preached to them.* [6] Blessed is he who finds no occasion for stumbling in me." [7] As these went their way, Jesus began to say to the multitudes concerning John, "What did you go out into the wilderness to see? A reed shaken by the wind? [8] But what did you go out to see? A man in soft clothing? Behold, those who wear soft clothing are in kings' houses. [9] But why did you go out? To see a prophet? Yes, I tell you, and much more than a prophet. [10] For this is he, of whom it is written, 'Behold, I send my messenger before your face, who will prepare your way before you.'* [11] Most certainly I tell you, among those who are born of women there has not arisen anyone greater than John the Baptizer; yet he who is least in the Kingdom of Heaven is greater than he. [12] From the days of John the Baptizer until now, the Kingdom of Heaven suffers violence, and the violent take it by force.[d] [13] For all the prophets and the law prophesied until John. [14] If you are willing to receive it, this is Elijah, who is to come. [15] He who has ears to hear, let him hear. [16] "But to what shall I compare this generation? It is like children sitting in the marketplaces, who call to their companions [17] and say, 'We played the flute for you, and you didn't dance. We mourned for you, and you didn't lament.' [18] For John came neither eating nor drinking, and they say, 'He has a demon.' [19] The Son of Man came eating and drinking, and they say, 'Behold, a gluttonous man and a drunkard, a friend of tax collectors and sinners!' But wisdom is justified by her children."[e] [20] Then he began to denounce the cities in which most of his mighty works had been done, because they didn't repent. [21] "Woe to you, Chorazin! Woe to you, Bethsaida! For if the mighty works had been done in Tyre and Sidon which were done in you, they would have

repented long ago in sackcloth and ashes. [22] But I tell you, it will be more tolerable for Tyre and Sidon on the day of judgment than for you. [23] You, Capernaum, who are exalted to heaven, you will go down to Hades.[f] For if the mighty works had been done in Sodom which were done in you, it would have remained until today. [24] But I tell you that it will be more tolerable for the land of Sodom on the day of judgment, than for you." [25] At that time, Jesus answered, "I thank you, Father, Lord of heaven and earth, that you hid these things from the wise and understanding, and revealed them to infants. [26] Yes, Father, for so it was well-pleasing in your sight. [27] All things have been delivered to me by my Father. No one knows the Son, except the Father; neither does anyone know the Father, except the Son and he to whom the Son desires to reveal him. [28] "Come to me, all you who labor and are heavily burdened, and I will give you rest. [29] Take my yoke upon you and learn from me, for I am gentle and humble in heart; and you will find rest for your souls. [30] For my yoke is easy, and my burden is light."

## 12

[1] At that time, Jesus went on the Sabbath day through the grain fields. His disciples were hungry and began to pluck heads of grain and to eat. [2] But the Pharisees, when they saw it, said to him, "Behold, your disciples do what is not lawful to do on the Sabbath." [3] But he said to them, "Haven't you read what David did when he was hungry, and those who were with him: [4] how he entered into God's house and ate the show bread, which was not lawful for him to eat, nor for those who were with him, but only for the priests?* [5] Or have you not read in the law that on the Sabbath day the priests in the temple profane the Sabbath and are guiltless? [6] But I tell you that one greater than the temple is here. [7] But if you had known what this means, 'I desire mercy, and not sacrifice,'* you wouldn't have condemned the guiltless. [8] For the Son of Man is Lord of the Sabbath." [9] He departed from there and went into their synagogue. [10] And behold, there was a man with a withered hand. They asked him, "Is it lawful to heal on the Sabbath day?" so that they might accuse him. [11] He said to them, "What man is there among you who has one sheep, and if this one falls into a pit on the Sabbath day, won't he grab on to it and lift it out? [12] Of how much more value then is a man than a sheep! Therefore it is lawful to do good on the Sabbath day." [13] Then he told the man, "Stretch out your hand." He stretched it out; and it was restored whole, just like the other. [14] But the Pharisees went out and conspired against him, how they might destroy him. [15] Jesus, perceiving that, withdrew from there. Great multitudes followed him; and he healed them all, [16] and commanded them that they should not make him known, [17] that it might be fulfilled which was spoken through Isaiah the prophet, saying, [18]"Behold, my servant whom I have chosen, my beloved in whom my soul is well pleased. I will put my Spirit on him. He will proclaim justice to the nations. [19] He will not strive, nor shout, neither will anyone hear his voice in the streets. [20] He won't break a bruised reed. He won't quench a smoking flax, until he leads justice to victory. [21] In his name, the nations will hope."* [22] Then one possessed by a demon, blind and mute, was brought to him; and he healed him, so that the blind and mute man both spoke and saw. [23] All the multitudes were amazed, and said, "Can this be the son of David?" [24] But when the Pharisees heard it, they said, "This man does not cast out demons except by Beelzebul, the prince of the demons." [25] Knowing their thoughts, Jesus said to them, "Every kingdom divided against itself is brought to desolation, and every city or house divided against itself will not stand. [26] If Satan casts out Satan, he is divided against himself. How then will his kingdom stand? [27] If I by Beelzebul cast out demons, by whom do your children cast them out? Therefore they will be your judges. [28] But if I by the Spirit of God cast out demons, then God's Kingdom has come upon you. [29] Or how can one enter into the house of the strong man and plunder his goods, unless he first bind the strong man? Then he will plunder his house. [30] "He who is not with me is against me, and he who doesn't gather with me, scatters. [31] Therefore I tell you, every sin and blasphemy will be forgiven men, but the blasphemy against the Spirit will not be forgiven men. [32] Whoever speaks a word against the Son of Man, it will be forgiven him; but whoever speaks against the Holy Spirit, it will not be forgiven him, either in this age, or in that which is to come. [33] "Either make the tree good and its fruit good, or make the tree corrupt and its fruit corrupt; for the tree is known by its fruit. [34] You offspring of vipers, how can you, being evil, speak good things? For out of the abundance of the heart, the mouth speaks. [35] The good man out of his good treasure[g] brings out good things, and the evil man out of his evil treasure brings out evil things. [36] I tell you that every idle word that men

---

[a] *10:25 Literally, Lord of the Flies, or the devil
[b] *10:28 or, Hell.
[c] *10:29 An assarion is a small coin worth one tenth of a drachma or a sixteenth of a

denarius. An assarion is approximately the wages of one half hour of agricultural labor.
* 10:36 Micah 7:6
* 11:5 Isaiah 35:5
* 11:5 Isaiah 61:1- 4

* 11:10 Malachi 3:1
[d] *11:12 or, plunder it.
[e] *11:19 NU reads "actions" instead of "children"
[f] *11:23 or, Hell
* 12:4 1 Samuel 21:3- 6

* 12:7 Hosea 6:6
* 12:21 Isaiah 42:1- 4
[g] *12:35 TR adds "of the heart"

speak, they will give account of it in the day of judgment. **37** For by your words you will be justified, and by your words you will be condemned." **38** Then certain of the scribes and Pharisees answered, "Teacher, we want to see a sign from you." **39** But he answered them, "An evil and adulterous generation seeks after a sign, but no sign will be given to it but the sign of Jonah the prophet. **40** For as Jonah was three days and three nights in the belly of the huge fish, so will the Son of Man be three days and three nights in the heart of the earth. **41** The men of Nineveh will stand up in the judgment with this generation and will condemn it, for they repented at the preaching of Jonah; and behold, someone greater than Jonah is here. **42** The Queen of the South will rise up in the judgment with this generation and will condemn it, for she came from the ends of the earth to hear the wisdom of Solomon; and behold, someone greater than Solomon is here. **43** "When an unclean spirit has gone out of a man, he passes through waterless places seeking rest, and doesn't find it. **44** Then he says, 'I will return into my house from which I came;' and when he has come back, he finds it empty, swept, and put in order. **45** Then he goes and takes with himself seven other spirits more evil than he is, and they enter in and dwell there. The last state of that man becomes worse than the first. Even so will it be also to this evil generation." **46** While he was yet speaking to the multitudes, behold, his mother and his brothers stood outside, seeking to speak to him. **47** One said to him, "Behold, your mother and your brothers stand outside, seeking to speak to you." **48** But he answered him who spoke to him, "Who is my mother? Who are my brothers?" **49** He stretched out his hand toward his disciples, and said, "Behold, my mother and my brothers! **50** For whoever does the will of my Father who is in heaven, he is my brother, and sister, and mother."

## 13

**1** On that day Jesus went out of the house and sat by the seaside. **2** Great multitudes gathered to him, so that he entered into a boat and sat; and all the multitude stood on the beach. **3** He spoke to them many things in parables, saying, "Behold, a farmer went out to sow. **4** As he sowed, some seeds fell by the roadside, and the birds came and devoured them. **5** Others fell on rocky ground, where they didn't have much soil, and immediately they sprang up, because they had no depth of earth. **6** When the sun had risen, they were scorched. Because they had no root, they withered away. **7** Others fell among thorns. The thorns grew up and choked them. **8** Others fell on good soil and yielded fruit: some one hundred times as much, some sixty, and some thirty. **9** He who has ears to hear, let him hear." **10** The disciples came, and said to him, "Why do you speak to them in parables?" **11** He answered them, "To you it is given to know the mysteries of the Kingdom of Heaven, but it is not given to them. **12** For whoever has, to him will be given, and he will have abundance; but whoever doesn't have, from him will be taken away even that which he has. **13** Therefore I speak to them in parables, because seeing they don't see, and hearing, they don't hear, neither do they understand. **14** In them the prophecy of Isaiah is fulfilled, which says, 'By hearing you will hear, and will in no way understand; Seeing you will see, and will in no way perceive; **15** for this people's heart has grown callous, their ears are dull of hearing, and they have closed their eyes; or else perhaps they might perceive with their eyes, hear with their ears, understand with their heart, and would turn again, and I would heal them.'* **16** "But blessed are your eyes, for they see; and your ears, for they hear. **17** For most certainly I tell you that many prophets and righteous men desired to see the things which you see, and didn't see them; and to hear the things which you hear, and didn't hear them. **18** "Hear, then, the parable of the farmer. **19** When anyone hears the word of the Kingdom and doesn't understand it, the evil one comes and snatches away that which has been sown in his heart. This is what was sown by the roadside. **20** What was sown on the rocky places, this is he who hears the word and immediately with joy receives it; **21** yet he has no root in himself, but endures for a while. When oppression or persecution arises because of the word, immediately he stumbles. **22** What was sown among the thorns, this is he who hears the word, but the cares of this age and the deceitfulness of riches choke the word, and he becomes unfruitful. **23** What was sown on the good ground, this is he who hears the word and understands it, who most certainly bears fruit and produces, some one hundred times as much, some sixty, and some thirty." **24** He set another parable before them, saying, "The Kingdom of Heaven is like a man who sowed good seed in his field, **25** but while people slept, his enemy came and sowed darnel weeds[a] also among the wheat, and went away. **26** But when the blade sprang up and produced grain, then the darnel weeds appeared also. **27** The servants of the householder came and said to him, 'Sir, didn't you sow good seed in your field? Where did these darnel weeds come from?' **28** "He said to them, 'An enemy has done this.' "The servants asked him, 'Do you want us to go and gather them up?' **29** "But he said, 'No, lest perhaps while you gather up the darnel weeds, you root up the wheat with them. **30** Let both grow together until the harvest, and in the harvest time I will tell the reapers, "First, gather up the darnel weeds, and bind them in bundles to burn them; but gather the wheat into my barn."'" **31** He set another parable before them, saying, "The Kingdom of Heaven is like a grain of mustard seed which a man took, and sowed in his field, **32** which indeed is smaller than all seeds. But when it is grown, it is greater than the herbs and becomes a tree, so that the birds of the air come and lodge in its branches." **33** He spoke another parable to them. "The Kingdom of Heaven is like yeast which a woman took and hid in three measures[b] of meal, until it was all leavened." **34** Jesus spoke all these things in parables to the multitudes; and without a parable, he didn't speak to them, **35** that it might be fulfilled which was spoken through the prophet, saying, "I will open my mouth in parables; I will utter things hidden from the foundation of the world."* **36** Then Jesus sent the multitudes away, and went into the house. His disciples came to him, saying, "Explain to us the parable of the darnel weeds of the field." **37** He answered them, "He who sows the good seed is the Son of Man, **38** the field is the world, the good seeds are the children of the Kingdom, and the darnel weeds are the children of the evil one. **39** The enemy who sowed them is the devil. The harvest is the end of the age, and the reapers are angels. **40** As therefore the darnel weeds are gathered up and burned with fire; so will it be at the end of this age. **41** The Son of Man will send out his angels, and they will gather out of his Kingdom all things that cause stumbling and those who do iniquity, **42** and will cast them into the furnace of fire. There will be weeping and gnashing of teeth. **43** Then the righteous will shine like the sun in the Kingdom of their Father. He who has ears to hear, let him hear. **44** "Again, the Kingdom of Heaven is like treasure hidden in the field, which a man found and hid. In his joy, he goes and sells all that he has and buys that field. **45** "Again, the Kingdom of Heaven is like a man who is a merchant seeking fine pearls, **46** who having found one pearl of great price, he went and sold all that he had and bought it. **47** "Again, the Kingdom of Heaven is like a dragnet that was cast into the sea and gathered some fish of every kind, **48** which, when it was filled, fishermen drew up on the beach. They sat down and gathered the good into containers, but the bad they threw away. **49** So it will be in the end of the world.[c] The angels will come and separate the wicked from among the righteous, **50** and will cast them into the furnace of fire. There will be weeping and gnashing of teeth." **51** Jesus said to them, "Have you understood all these things?" They answered him, "Yes, Lord." **52** He said to them, "Therefore every scribe who has been made a disciple in the Kingdom of Heaven is like a man who is a householder, who brings out of his treasure new and old things." **53** When Jesus had finished these parables, he departed from there. **54** Coming into his own country, he taught them in their synagogue, so that they were astonished and said, "Where did this man get this wisdom and these mighty works? **55** Isn't this the carpenter's son? Isn't his mother called Mary, and his brothers James, Joses, Simon, and Judas?[d] **56** Aren't all of his sisters with us? Where then did this man get all of these things?" **57** They were offended by him. But Jesus said to them, "A prophet is not without honor, except in his own country and in his own house." **58** He didn't do many mighty works there because of their unbelief.

## 14

**1** At that time, Herod the tetrarch heard the report concerning Jesus, **2** and said to his servants, "This is John the Baptizer. He is risen from the dead. That is why these powers work in him." **3** For Herod had arrested John, bound him, and put him in prison for the sake of Herodias, his brother Philip's wife. **4** For John said to him, "It is not lawful for you to have her." **5** When he would have put him to death, he feared the multitude, because they counted him as a prophet. **6** But when Herod's birthday came, the daughter of Herodias danced among them and pleased Herod. **7** Therefore he promised with an oath to give her whatever she should ask. **8** She, being prompted by her mother, said, "Give me here on a platter the head of John the Baptizer." **9** The king was grieved, but for the sake of his oaths and of those who sat at the table with him, he commanded it to be given, **10** and he sent and beheaded John in the prison. **11** His head was brought on a platter and given to the young lady; and she brought it to her mother. **12** His disciples came, took the body, and buried it. Then they went and told Jesus. **13** Now when Jesus heard this, he withdrew from there in a boat to a deserted place apart. When the multitudes heard it, they followed

---

* 13:15 Isaiah 6:9- 10
[a] *13:25* darnel is a weed grass (probably bearded darnel or lolium temulentum) that looks very much like wheat until it is mature, when the difference becomes very apparent.

[b] *13:33* literally, three sata. Three sata is about 39 liters or a bit more than a bushel
* 13:35 Psalms 78:2

[c] *13:49* or, end of the age.
[d] *13:55* or, Judah

him on foot from the cities. **14** Jesus went out, and he saw a great multitude. He had compassion on them and healed their sick. **15** When evening had come, his disciples came to him, saying, "This place is deserted, and the hour is already late. Send the multitudes away, that they may go into the villages, and buy themselves food." **16** But Jesus said to them, "They don't need to go away. You give them something to eat." **17** They told him, "We only have here five loaves and two fish." **18** He said, "Bring them here to me." **19** He commanded the multitudes to sit down on the grass; and he took the five loaves and the two fish, and looking up to heaven, he blessed, broke and gave the loaves to the disciples; and the disciples gave to the multitudes. **20** They all ate and were filled. They took up twelve baskets full of that which remained left over from the broken pieces. **21** Those who ate were about five thousand men, in addition to women and children. **22** Immediately Jesus made the disciples get into the boat and go ahead of him to the other side, while he sent the multitudes away. **23** After he had sent the multitudes away, he went up into the mountain by himself to pray. When evening had come, he was there alone. **24** But the boat was now in the middle of the sea, distressed by the waves, for the wind was contrary. **25** In the fourth watch of the night,[a] Jesus came to them, walking on the sea.* **26** When the disciples saw him walking on the sea, they were troubled, saying, "It's a ghost!" and they cried out for fear. **27** But immediately Jesus spoke to them, saying, "Cheer up! It is I![b] Don't be afraid." **28** Peter answered him and said, "Lord, if it is you, command me to come to you on the waters." **29** He said, "Come!" Peter stepped down from the boat and walked on the waters to come to Jesus. **30** But when he saw that the wind was strong, he was afraid, and beginning to sink, he cried out, saying, "Lord, save me!" **31** Immediately Jesus stretched out his hand, took hold of him, and said to him, "You of little faith, why did you doubt?" **32** When they got up into the boat, the wind ceased. **33** Those who were in the boat came and worshiped him, saying, "You are truly the Son of God!" **34** When they had crossed over, they came to the land of Gennesaret. **35** When the people of that place recognized him, they sent into all that surrounding region and brought to him all who were sick; **36** and they begged him that they might just touch the fringe[c] of his garment. As many as touched it were made whole.

## 15

**1** Then Pharisees and scribes came to Jesus from Jerusalem, saying, **2** "Why do your disciples disobey the tradition of the elders? For they don't wash their hands when they eat bread." **3** He answered them, "Why do you also disobey the commandment of God because of your tradition? **4** For God commanded, 'Honor your father and your mother,'* and, 'He who speaks evil of father or mother, let him be put to death.'* **5** But you say, 'Whoever may tell his father or his mother, "Whatever help you might otherwise have gotten from me is a gift devoted to God," **6** he shall not honor his father or mother.' You have made the commandment of God void because of your tradition. **7** You hypocrites! Well did Isaiah prophesy of you, saying, **8** 'These people draw near to me with their mouth, and honor me with their lips; but their heart is far from me. **9** And they worship me in vain, teaching as doctrine rules made by men.'"* **10** He summoned the multitude, and said to them, "Hear, and understand. **11** That which enters into the mouth doesn't defile the man; but that which proceeds out of the mouth, this defiles the man." **12** Then the disciples came and said to him, "Do you know that the Pharisees were offended when they heard this saying?" **13** But he answered, "Every plant which my heavenly Father didn't plant will be uprooted. **14** Leave them alone. They are blind guides of the blind. If the blind guide the blind, both will fall into a pit." **15** Peter answered him, "Explain the parable to us." **16** So Jesus said, "Do you also still not understand? **17** Don't you understand that whatever goes into the mouth passes into the belly and then out of the body? **18** But the things which proceed out of the mouth come out of the heart, and they defile the man. **19** For out of the heart come evil thoughts, murders, adulteries, sexual sins, thefts, false testimony, and blasphemies. **20** These are the things which defile the man; but to eat with unwashed hands doesn't defile the man." **21** Jesus went out from there and withdrew into the region of Tyre and Sidon. **22** Behold, a Canaanite woman came out from those borders and cried, saying, "Have mercy on me, Lord, you son of David! My daughter is severely possessed by a demon!" **23** But he answered her not a word. His disciples came and begged him, saying, "Send her away; for she cries after us." **24** But he answered, "I wasn't sent to anyone but the lost sheep of the house of Israel." **25** But she came and worshiped him, saying, "Lord, help me."

**26** But he answered, "It is not appropriate to take the children's bread and throw it to the dogs." **27** But she said, "Yes, Lord, but even the dogs eat the crumbs which fall from their masters' table." **28** Then Jesus answered her, "Woman, great is your faith! Be it done to you even as you desire." And her daughter was healed from that hour. **29** Jesus departed from there and came near to the sea of Galilee; and he went up on the mountain and sat there. **30** Great multitudes came to him, having with them the lame, blind, mute, maimed, and many others, and they put them down at his feet. He healed them, **31** so that the multitude wondered when they saw the mute speaking, the injured healed, the lame walking, and the blind seeing—and they glorified the God of Israel. **32** Jesus summoned his disciples and said, "I have compassion on the multitude, because they have continued with me now three days and have nothing to eat. I don't want to send them away fasting, or they might faint on the way." **33** The disciples said to him, "Where could we get so many loaves in a deserted place as to satisfy so great a multitude?" **34** Jesus said to them, "How many loaves do you have?" They said, "Seven, and a few small fish." **35** He commanded the multitude to sit down on the ground; **36** and he took the seven loaves and the fish. He gave thanks and broke them, and gave to the disciples, and the disciples to the multitudes. **37** They all ate and were filled. They took up seven baskets full of the broken pieces that were left over. **38** Those who ate were four thousand men, in addition to women and children. **39** Then he sent away the multitudes, got into the boat, and came into the borders of Magdala.

## 16

**1** The Pharisees and Sadducees came, and testing him, asked him to show them a sign from heaven. **2** But he answered them, "When it is evening, you say, 'It will be fair weather, for the sky is red.' **3** In the morning, 'It will be foul weather today, for the sky is red and threatening.' Hypocrites! You know how to discern the appearance of the sky, but you can't discern the signs of the times! **4** An evil and adulterous generation seeks after a sign, and there will be no sign given to it, except the sign of the prophet Jonah." He left them and departed. **5** The disciples came to the other side and had forgotten to take bread. **6** Jesus said to them, "Take heed and beware of the yeast of the Pharisees and Sadducees." **7** They reasoned among themselves, saying, "We brought no bread." **8** Jesus, perceiving it, said, "Why do you reason among yourselves, you of little faith, because you have brought no bread? **9** Don't you yet perceive or remember the five loaves for the five thousand, and how many baskets you took up, **10** or the seven loaves for the four thousand, and how many baskets you took up? **11** How is it that you don't perceive that I didn't speak to you concerning bread? But beware of the yeast of the Pharisees and Sadducees." **12** Then they understood that he didn't tell them to beware of the yeast of bread, but of the teaching of the Pharisees and Sadducees. **13** Now when Jesus came into the parts of Caesarea Philippi, he asked his disciples, saying, "Who do men say that I, the Son of Man, am?" **14** They said, "Some say John the Baptizer, some, Elijah, and others, Jeremiah or one of the prophets." **15** He said to them, "But who do you say that I am?" **16** Simon Peter answered, "You are the Christ, the Son of the living God." **17** Jesus answered him, "Blessed are you, Simon Bar Jonah, for flesh and blood has not revealed this to you, but my Father who is in heaven. **18** I also tell you that you are Peter,[d] and on this rock [e] I will build my assembly, and the gates of Hades[f] will not prevail against it. **19** I will give to you the keys of the Kingdom of Heaven, and whatever you bind on earth will have been bound in heaven; and whatever you release on earth will have been released in heaven." **20** Then he commanded the disciples that they should tell no one that he was Jesus the Christ. **21** From that time, Jesus began to show his disciples that he must go to Jerusalem and suffer many things from the elders, chief priests, and scribes, and be killed, and the third day be raised up. **22** Peter took him aside and began to rebuke him, saying, "Far be it from you, Lord! This will never be done to you." **23** But he turned and said to Peter, "Get behind me, Satan! You are a stumbling block to me, for you are not setting your mind on the things of God, but on the things of men." **24** Then Jesus said to his disciples, "If anyone desires to come after me, let him deny himself, take up his cross, and follow me. **25** For whoever desires to save his life will lose it, and whoever will lose his life for my sake will find it. **26** For what will it profit a man if he gains the whole world and forfeits his life? Or what will a man give in exchange for his life? **27** For the Son of Man will come in the glory of his Father with his angels, and then he will render to everyone according to his deeds. **28** Most certainly

---

I tell you, there are some standing here who will in no way taste of death until they see the Son of Man coming in his Kingdom."

## 17

[1] After six days, Jesus took with him Peter, James, and John his brother, and brought them up into a high mountain by themselves. [2] He was changed[a] before them. His face shone like the sun, and his garments became as white as the light. [3] Behold, Moses and Elijah appeared to them talking with him.

[4] Peter answered and said to Jesus, "Lord, it is good for us to be here. If you want, let's make three tents here: one for you, one for Moses, and one for Elijah." [5] While he was still speaking, behold, a bright cloud overshadowed them. Behold, a voice came out of the cloud, saying, "This is my beloved Son, in whom I am well pleased. Listen to him." [6] When the disciples heard it, they fell on their faces, and were very afraid. [7] Jesus came and touched them and said, "Get up, and don't be afraid." [8] Lifting up their eyes, they saw no one, except Jesus alone. [9] As they were coming down from the mountain, Jesus commanded them, saying, "Don't tell anyone what you saw, until the Son of Man has risen from the dead." [10] His disciples asked him, saying, "Then why do the scribes say that Elijah must come first?" [11] Jesus answered them, "Elijah indeed comes first, and will restore all things; [12] but I tell you that Elijah has come already, and they didn't recognize him, but did to him whatever they wanted to. Even so the Son of Man will also suffer by them." [13] Then the disciples understood that he spoke to them of John the Baptizer. [14] When they came to the multitude, a man came to him, kneeling down to him and saying, [15]"Lord, have mercy on my son, for he is epileptic and suffers grievously; for he often falls into the fire, and often into the water. [16] So I brought him to your disciples, and they could not cure him." [17] Jesus answered, "Faithless and perverse generation! How long will I be with you? How long will I bear with you? Bring him here to me." [18] Jesus rebuked the demon, and it went out of him, and the boy was cured from that hour. [19] Then the disciples came to Jesus privately, and said, "Why weren't we able to cast it out?" [20] He said to them, "Because of your unbelief. For most certainly I tell you, if you have faith as a grain of mustard seed, you will tell this mountain, 'Move from here to there,' and it will move; and nothing will be impossible for you. [21] But this kind doesn't go out except by prayer and fasting." [b] [22] While they were staying in Galilee, Jesus said to them, "The Son of Man is about to be delivered up into the hands of men, [23] and they will kill him, and the third day he will be raised up." They were exceedingly sorry. [24] When they had come to Capernaum, those who collected the didrachma coins[c] came to Peter, and said, "Doesn't your teacher pay the didrachma?" [25] He said, "Yes." When he came into the house, Jesus anticipated him, saying, "What do you think, Simon? From whom do the kings of the earth receive toll or tribute? From their children, or from strangers?" [26] Peter said to him, "From strangers." Jesus said to him, "Therefore the children are exempt. [27] But, lest we cause them to stumble, go to the sea, cast a hook, and take up the first fish that comes up. When you have opened its mouth, you will find a stater coin.[d] Take that, and give it to them for me and you."

## 18

[1] In that hour the disciples came to Jesus, saying, "Who then is greatest in the Kingdom of Heaven?" [2] Jesus called a little child to himself, and set him in the middle of them [3] and said, "Most certainly I tell you, unless you turn and become as little children, you will in no way enter into the Kingdom of Heaven. [4] Whoever therefore humbles himself as this little child is the greatest in the Kingdom of Heaven. [5] Whoever receives one such little child in my name receives me, [6] but whoever causes one of these little ones who believe in me to stumble, it would be better for him if a huge millstone were hung around his neck and that he were sunk in the depths of the sea. [7] "Woe to the world because of occasions of stumbling! For it must be that the occasions come, but woe to that person through whom the occasion comes! [8] If your hand or your foot causes you to stumble, cut it off and cast it from you. It is better for you to enter into life maimed or crippled, rather than having two hands or two feet to be cast into the eternal fire. [9] If your eye causes you to stumble, pluck it out and cast it from you. It is better for you to enter into life with one eye, rather than having two eyes to be cast into the Gehenna[e] of fire. [10] See that you don't despise one of these little ones, for I tell you that in heaven their angels always see the face of my Father who is in heaven. [11] For the Son of Man came to save that which was lost.[f] [12] "What do you think? If a man has one hundred sheep, and one of them goes astray, doesn't he leave the ninety-nine, go to the mountains, and seek that which has gone astray? [13] If he finds it, most certainly I tell you, he rejoices over it more than over the ninety-nine which have not gone astray. [14] Even so it is not the will of your Father who is in heaven that one of these little ones should perish. [15] "If your brother sins against you, go, show him his fault between you and him alone. If he listens to you, you have gained back your brother. [16] But if he doesn't listen, take one or two more with you, that at the mouth of two or three witnesses every word may be established.[*] [17] If he refuses to listen to them, tell it to the assembly. If he refuses to hear the assembly also, let him be to you as a Gentile or a tax collector. [18] Most certainly I tell you, whatever things you bind on earth will have been bound in heaven, and whatever things you release on earth will have been released in heaven. [19] Again, assuredly I tell you, that if two of you will agree on earth concerning anything that they will ask, it will be done for them by my Father who is in heaven. [20] For where two or three are gathered together in my name, there I am in the middle of them." [21] Then Peter came and said to him, "Lord, how often shall my brother sin against me, and I forgive him? Until seven times?" [22] Jesus said to him, "I don't tell you until seven times, but, until seventy times seven. [23] Therefore the Kingdom of Heaven is like a certain king who wanted to settle accounts with his servants. [24] When he had begun to settle, one was brought to him who owed him ten thousand talents.[g] [25] But because he couldn't pay, his lord commanded him to be sold, with his wife, his children, and all that he had, and payment to be made. [26] The servant therefore fell down and knelt before him, saying, 'Lord, have patience with me, and I will repay you all!' [27] The lord of that servant, being moved with compassion, released him and forgave him the debt. [28] "But that servant went out and found one of his fellow servants who owed him one hundred denarii,[h] and he grabbed him and took him by the throat, saying, 'Pay me what you owe!' [29] "So his fellow servant fell down at his feet and begged him, saying, 'Have patience with me, and I will repay you!' [30] He would not, but went and cast him into prison until he should pay back that which was due. [31] So when his fellow servants saw what was done, they were exceedingly sorry, and came and told their lord all that was done. [32] Then his lord called him in and said to him, 'You wicked servant! I forgave you all that debt because you begged me. [33] Shouldn't you also have had mercy on your fellow servant, even as I had mercy on you?' [34] His lord was angry, and delivered him to the tormentors until he should pay all that was due to him. [35] So my heavenly Father will also do to you, if you don't each forgive your brother from your hearts for his misdeeds."

## 19

[1] When Jesus had finished these words, he departed from Galilee and came into the borders of Judea beyond the Jordan. [2] Great multitudes followed him, and he healed them there. [3] Pharisees came to him, testing him and saying, "Is it lawful for a man to divorce his wife for any reason?" [4] He answered, "Haven't you read that he who made them from the beginning made them male and female,[*] [5] and said, 'For this cause a man shall leave his father and mother, and shall be joined to his wife; and the two shall become one flesh'?[*] [6] So that they are no more two, but one flesh. What therefore God has joined together, don't let man tear apart." [7] They asked him, "Why then did Moses command us to give her a certificate of divorce and divorce her?" [8] He said to them, "Moses, because of the hardness of your hearts, allowed you to divorce your wives, but from the beginning it has not been so. [9] I tell you that whoever divorces his wife, except for sexual immorality, and marries another, commits adultery; and he who marries her when she is divorced commits adultery." [10] His disciples said to him, "If this is the case of the man with his wife, it is not expedient to marry." [11] But he said to them, "Not all men can receive this saying, but those to whom it is given. [12] For there are eunuchs who were born that way from their mother's womb, and there are eunuchs who were made eunuchs by men; and there are eunuchs who made themselves eunuchs for the Kingdom of Heaven's sake. He who is able to receive it, let him receive it." [13] Then little children were brought to him that he should lay his hands on them and pray; and the disciples rebuked them. [14] But Jesus said, "Allow the little children, and don't forbid them to come to me;

---

for the Kingdom of Heaven belongs to ones like these." **15** He laid his hands on them, and departed from there. **16** Behold, one came to him and said, "Good teacher, what good thing shall I do, that I may have eternal life?" **17** He said to him, "Why do you call me good?ᵃ No one is good but one, that is, God. But if you want to enter into life, keep the commandments." **18** He said to him, "Which ones?" Jesus said, "'You shall not murder.' 'You shall not commit adultery.' 'You shall not steal.' 'You shall not offer false testimony.' **19** 'Honor your father and your mother.'* And, 'You shall love your neighbor as yourself.'"* **20** The young man said to him, "All these things I have observed from my youth. What do I still lack?" **21** Jesus said to him, "If you want to be perfect, go, sell what you have, and give to the poor, and you will have treasure in heaven; and come, follow me." **22** But when the young man heard this, he went away sad, for he was one who had great possessions. **23** Jesus said to his disciples, "Most certainly I say to you, a rich man will enter into the Kingdom of Heaven with difficulty. **24** Again I tell you, it is easier for a camel to go through a needle's eye than for a rich man to enter into God's Kingdom." **25** When the disciples heard it, they were exceedingly astonished, saying, "Who then can be saved?" **26** Looking at them, Jesus said, "With men this is impossible, but with God all things are possible." **27** Then Peter answered, "Behold, we have left everything and followed you. What then will we have?" **28** Jesus said to them, "Most certainly I tell you that you who have followed me, in the regeneration when the Son of Man will sit on the throne of his glory, you also will sit on twelve thrones, judging the twelve tribes of Israel. **29** Everyone who has left houses, or brothers, or sisters, or father, or mother, or wife, or children, or lands, for my name's sake, will receive one hundred times, and will inherit eternal life. **30** But many will be last who are first, and first who are last.

## 20

**1** "For the Kingdom of Heaven is like a man who was the master of a household, who went out early in the morning to hire laborers for his vineyard. **2** When he had agreed with the laborers for a denariusᵇ a day, he sent them into his vineyard. **3** He went out about the third hour,ᶜ and saw others standing idle in the marketplace. **4** He said to them, 'You also go into the vineyard, and whatever is right I will give you.' So they went their way. **5** Again he went out about the sixth and the ninth hour,ᵈ and did likewise. **6** About the eleventh hourᵉ he went out and found others standing idle. He said to them, 'Why do you stand here all day idle?' **7** "They said to him, 'Because no one has hired us.' "He said to them, 'You also go into the vineyard, and you will receive whatever is right.' **8** "When evening had come, the lord of the vineyard said to his manager, 'Call the laborers and pay them their wages, beginning from the last to the first.' **9** "When those who were hired at about the eleventh hour came, they each received a denarius. **10** When the first came, they supposed that they would receive more; and they likewise each received a denarius. **11** When they received it, they murmured against the master of the household, **12** saying, 'These last have spent one hour, and you have made them equal to us who have borne the burden of the day and the scorching heat!' **13** "But he answered one of them, 'Friend, I am doing you no wrong. Didn't you agree with me for a denarius? **14** Take that which is yours, and go your way. It is my desire to give to this last just as much as to you. **15** Isn't it lawful for me to do what I want to with what I own? Or is your eye evil, because I am good?' **16** So the last will be first, and the first last. For many are called, but few are chosen." **17** As Jesus was going up to Jerusalem, he took the twelve disciples aside, and on the way he said to them, **18** "Behold, we are going up to Jerusalem, and the Son of Man will be delivered to the chief priests and scribes, and they will condemn him to death, **19** and will hand him over to the Gentiles to mock, to scourge, and to crucify; and the third day he will be raised up." **20** Then the mother of the sons of Zebedee came to him with her sons, kneeling and asking a certain thing of him. **21** He said to her, "What do you want?" She said to him, "Command that these, my two sons, may sit, one on your right hand and one on your left hand, in your Kingdom." **22** But Jesus answered, "You don't know what you are asking. Are you able to drink the cup that I am about to drink, and be baptized with the baptism that I am baptized with?" They said to him, "We are able." **23** He said to them, "You will indeed drink my cup, and be baptized with the baptism that I am baptized with; but to sit on my right hand and on my left hand is not mine to give, but it is for whom it has been prepared by my Father." **24** When the ten heard it, they were indignant with the two brothers. **25**

But Jesus summoned them, and said, "You know that the rulers of the nations lord it over them, and their great ones exercise authority over them. **26** It shall not be so among you; but whoever desires to become great among you shall beᶠ your servant. **27** Whoever desires to be first among you shall be your bondservant, **28** even as the Son of Man came not to be served, but to serve, and to give his life as a ransom for many." **29** As they went out from Jericho, a great multitude followed him. **30** Behold, two blind men sitting by the road, when they heard that Jesus was passing by, cried out, "Lord, have mercy on us, you son of David!" **31** The multitude rebuked them, telling them that they should be quiet, but they cried out even more, "Lord, have mercy on us, you son of David!" **32** Jesus stood still and called them, and asked, "What do you want me to do for you?" **33** They told him, "Lord, that our eyes may be opened." **34** Jesus, being moved with compassion, touched their eyes; and immediately their eyes received their sight, and they followed him.

## 21

**1** When they came near to Jerusalem and came to Bethsphage,ᵍ to the Mount of Olives, then Jesus sent two disciples, **2** saying to them, "Go into the village that is opposite you, and immediately you will find a donkey tied, and a colt with her. Untie them and bring them to me. **3** If anyone says anything to you, you shall say, 'The Lord needs them,' and immediately he will send them." **4** All this was done that it might be fulfilled which was spoken through the prophet, saying, **5** "Tell the daughter of Zion, behold, your King comes to you, humble, and riding on a donkey, on a colt, the foal of a donkey."* **6** The disciples went and did just as Jesus commanded them, **7** and brought the donkey and the colt and laid their clothes on them; and he sat on them. **8** A very great multitude spread their clothes on the road. Others cut branches from the trees and spread them on the road. **9** The multitudes who went in front of him, and those who followed, kept shouting, "Hosannaʰ to the son of David! Blessed is he who comes in the name of the Lord! Hosanna in the highest!" * **10** When he had come into Jerusalem, all the city was stirred up, saying, "Who is this?" **11** The multitudes said, "This is the prophet, Jesus, from Nazareth of Galilee." **12** Jesus entered into the temple of God and drove out all of those who sold and bought in the temple, and overthrew the money changers' tables and the seats of those who sold the doves. **13** He said to them, "It is written, 'My house shall be called a house of prayer,'* but you have made it a den of robbers!"* **14** The lame and the blind came to him in the temple, and he healed them. **15** But when the chief priests and the scribes saw the wonderful things that he did, and the children who were crying in the temple and saying, "Hosanna to the son of David!" they were indignant, **16** and said to him, "Do you hear what these are saying?" Jesus said to them, "Yes. Did you never read, 'Out of the mouth of children and nursing babies, you have perfected praise'?"* **17** He left them and went out of the city to Bethany, and camped there. **18** Now in the morning, as he returned to the city, he was hungry. **19** Seeing a fig tree by the road, he came to it and found nothing on it but leaves. He said to it, "Let there be no fruit from you forever!" Immediately the fig tree withered away. **20** When the disciples saw it, they marveled, saying, "How did the fig tree immediately wither away?" **21** Jesus answered them, "Most certainly I tell you, if you have faith and don't doubt, you will not only do what was done to the fig tree, but even if you told this mountain, 'Be taken up and cast into the sea,' it would be done. **22** All things, whatever you ask in prayer, believing, you will receive." **23** When he had come into the temple, the chief priests and the elders of the people came to him as he was teaching, and said, "By what authority do you do these things? Who gave you this authority?" **24** Jesus answered them, "I also will ask you one question, which if you tell me, I likewise will tell you by what authority I do these things. **25** The baptism of John, where was it from? From heaven or from men?" They reasoned with themselves, saying, "If we say, 'From heaven,' he will ask us, 'Why then did you not believe him?' **26** But if we say, 'From men,' we fear the multitude, for all hold John as a prophet." **27** They answered Jesus, and said, "We don't know." He also said to them, "Neither will I tell you by what authority I do these things. **28** But what do you think? A man had two sons, and he came to the first, and said, 'Son, go work today in my vineyard.' **29** He answered, 'I will not,' but afterward he changed his mind, and went. **30** He came to the second, and said the same thing. He answered, 'I'm going, sir,' but he didn't go. **31** Which of the two did the will of his father?" They said to him, "The first." Jesus said to them, "Most certainly I tell you that the tax collectors and the prostitutes are

ᵃ *19:17* So MT and TR. NU reads "Why do you ask me about what is good?"
* *19:19* Exodus 20:12- 16; Deuteronomy 5:16- 20
* *19:19* Leviticus 19:18
ᵇ *20:2* A denarius is a silver Roman coin worth 1/25 th of a

Roman aureus. This was a common wage for a day of farm labor.
ᶜ *20:3* Time was measured from sunrise to sunset, so the third hour would be about 9:00 a.m.
ᵈ *20:5* noon and 3:00 p.m.

ᵉ *20:6* 5:00 p.m.
ᶠ *20:26* TR reads "let him be" instead of "shall be"
ᵍ *21:1* TR & NU read "Bethphage" instead of "Bethsphage"
* *21:5* Zechariah 9:9

ʰ *21:9* "Hosanna" means "save us" or "help us, we pray".
* *21:9* Psalms 118:26
* *21:13* Isaiah 56:7
* *21:13* Jeremiah 7:11
* *21:16* Psalms 8:2

entering into God's Kingdom before you. ³² For John came to you in the way of righteousness, and you didn't believe him; but the tax collectors and the prostitutes believed him. When you saw it, you didn't even repent afterward, that you might believe him. ³³ "Hear another parable. There was a man who was a master of a household who planted a vineyard, set a hedge about it, dug a wine press in it, built a tower, leased it out to farmers, and went into another country. ³⁴ When the season for the fruit came near, he sent his servants to the farmers to receive his fruit. ³⁵ The farmers took his servants, beat one, killed another, and stoned another. ³⁶ Again, he sent other servants more than the first; and they treated them the same way. ³⁷ But afterward he sent to them his son, saying, 'They will respect my son.' ³⁸ But the farmers, when they saw the son, said among themselves, 'This is the heir. Come, let's kill him and seize his inheritance.' ³⁹ So they took him and threw him out of the vineyard, then killed him. ⁴⁰ When therefore the lord of the vineyard comes, what will he do to those farmers?" ⁴¹ They told him, "He will miserably destroy those miserable men, and will lease out the vineyard to other farmers who will give him the fruit in its season." ⁴² Jesus said to them, "Did you never read in the Scriptures, 'The stone which the builders rejected was made the head of the corner. This was from the Lord. It is marvelous in our eyes'?* ⁴³ "Therefore I tell you, God's Kingdom will be taken away from you and will be given to a nation producing its fruit. ⁴⁴ He who falls on this stone will be broken to pieces, but on whomever it will fall, it will scatter him as dust." ⁴⁵ When the chief priests and the Pharisees heard his parables, they perceived that he spoke about them. ⁴⁶ When they sought to seize him, they feared the multitudes, because they considered him to be a prophet.

## 22

¹ Jesus answered and spoke to them again in parables, saying, ² "The Kingdom of Heaven is like a certain king, who made a wedding feast for his son, ³ and sent out his servants to call those who were invited to the wedding feast, but they would not come. ⁴ Again he sent out other servants, saying, 'Tell those who are invited, "Behold, I have prepared my dinner. My cattle and my fatlings are killed, and all things are ready. Come to the wedding feast!"' ⁵ But they made light of it, and went their ways, one to his own farm, another to his merchandise; ⁶ and the rest grabbed his servants, treated them shamefully, and killed them. ⁷ When the king heard that, he was angry, and sent his armies, destroyed those murderers, and burned their city. ⁸ "Then he said to his servants, 'The wedding is ready, but those who were invited weren't worthy. ⁹ Go therefore to the intersections of the highways, and as many as you may find, invite to the wedding feast.' ¹⁰ Those servants went out into the highways and gathered together as many as they found, both bad and good. The wedding was filled with guests. ¹¹ "But when the king came in to see the guests, he saw there a man who didn't have on wedding clothing, ¹² and he said to him, 'Friend, how did you come in here not wearing wedding clothing?' He was speechless. ¹³ Then the king said to the servants, 'Bind him hand and foot, take him away, and throw him into the outer darkness. That is where the weeping and grinding of teeth will be.' ¹⁴ For many are called, but few chosen." ¹⁵ Then the Pharisees went and took counsel how they might entrap him in his talk. ¹⁶ They sent their disciples to him, along with the Herodians, saying, "Teacher, we know that you are honest, and teach the way of God in truth, no matter whom you teach; for you aren't partial to anyone. ¹⁷ Tell us therefore, what do you think? Is it lawful to pay taxes to Caesar, or not?" ¹⁸ But Jesus perceived their wickedness, and said, "Why do you test me, you hypocrites? ¹⁹ Show me the tax money." They brought to him a denarius. ²⁰ He asked them, "Whose is this image and inscription?" ²¹ They said to him, "Caesar's." Then he said to them, "Give therefore to Caesar the things that are Caesar's, and to God the things that are God's." ²² When they heard it, they marveled, and left him and went away. ²³ On that day Sadducees (those who say that there is no resurrection) came to him. They asked him, ²⁴ saying, "Teacher, Moses said, 'If a man dies, having no children, his brother shall marry his wife and raise up offspringᵃ for his brother.' ²⁵ Now there were with us seven brothers. The first married and died, and having no offspring left his wife to his brother. ²⁶ In the same way, the second also, and the third, to the seventh. ²⁷ After them all, the woman died. ²⁸ In the resurrection therefore, whose wife will she be of the seven? For they all had her." ²⁹ But Jesus answered them, "You are mistaken, not

knowing the Scriptures, nor the power of God. ³⁰ For in the resurrection they neither marry nor are given in marriage, but are like God's angels in heaven. ³¹ But concerning the resurrection of the dead, haven't you read that which was spoken to you by God, saying, ³² 'I am the God of Abraham, and the God of Isaac, and the God of Jacob'?* God is not the God of the dead, but of the living." ³³ When the multitudes heard it, they were astonished at his teaching. ³⁴ But the Pharisees, when they heard that he had silenced the Sadducees, gathered themselves together. ³⁵ One of them, a lawyer, asked him a question, testing him. ³⁶ "Teacher, which is the greatest commandment in the law?" ³⁷ Jesus said to him, "'You shall love the Lord your God with all your heart, with all your soul, and with all your mind.'* ³⁸ This is the first and great commandment. ³⁹ A second likewise is this, 'You shall love your neighbor as yourself.'* ⁴⁰ The whole law and the prophets depend on these two commandments." ⁴¹ Now while the Pharisees were gathered together, Jesus asked them a question, ⁴² saying, "What do you think of the Christ? Whose son is he?" They said to him, "Of David." ⁴³ He said to them, "How then does David in the Spirit call him Lord, saying, ⁴⁴ 'The Lord said to my Lord, sit on my right hand, until I make your enemies a footstool for your feet'?* ⁴⁵ "If then David calls him Lord, how is he his son?" ⁴⁶ No one was able to answer him a word, neither did any man dare ask him any more questions from that day forward.

## 23

¹ Then Jesus spoke to the multitudes and to his disciples, ² saying, "The scribes and the Pharisees sit on Moses' seat. ³ All things therefore whatever they tell you to observe, observe and do, but don't do their works; for they say, and don't do. ⁴ For they bind heavy burdens that are grievous to be borne, and lay them on men's shoulders; but they themselves will not lift a finger to help them. ⁵ But they do all their works to be seen by men. They make their phylacteriesᵇ broad and enlarge the fringesᶜ of their garments, ⁶ and love the place of honor at feasts, the best seats in the synagogues, ⁷ the salutations in the marketplaces, and to be called 'Rabbi, Rabbi'ᵈ by men. ⁸ But you are not to be called 'Rabbi', for one is your teacher, the Christ, and all of you are brothers. ⁹ Call no man on the earth your father, for one is your Father, he who is in heaven. ¹⁰ Neither be called masters, for one is your master, the Christ. ¹¹ But he who is greatest among you will be your servant. ¹² Whoever exalts himself will be humbled, and whoever humbles himself will be exalted. ¹³ "Woe to you, scribes and Pharisees, hypocrites! For you devour widows' houses, and as a pretense you make long prayers. Therefore you will receive greater condemnation. ¹⁴ "But woe to you, scribes and Pharisees, hypocrites! Because you shut up the Kingdom of Heaven against men; for you don't enter in yourselves, neither do you allow those who are entering in to enter.ᵉ ¹⁵ Woe to you, scribes and Pharisees, hypocrites! For you travel around by sea and land to make one proselyte; and when he becomes one, you make him twice as much a son of Gehennaᶠ as yourselves. ¹⁶ "Woe to you, you blind guides, who say, 'Whoever swears by the temple, it is nothing; but whoever swears by the gold of the temple, he is obligated.' ¹⁷ You blind fools! For which is greater, the gold or the temple that sanctifies the gold? ¹⁸ And, 'Whoever swears by the altar, it is nothing; but whoever swears by the gift that is on it, he is obligated.' ¹⁹ You blind fools! For which is greater, the gift, or the altar that sanctifies the gift? ²⁰ He therefore who swears by the altar, swears by it and by everything on it. ²¹ He who swears by the temple, swears by it and by him who has been livingᵍ in it. ²² He who swears by heaven, swears by the throne of God and by him who sits on it. ²³ "Woe to you, scribes and Pharisees, hypocrites! For you tithe mint, dill, and cumin,ʰ and have left undone the weightier matters of the law: justice, mercy, and faith. But you ought to have done these, and not to have left the other undone. ²⁴ You blind guides, who strain out a gnat, and swallow a camel! ²⁵ "Woe to you, scribes and Pharisees, hypocrites! For you clean the outside of the cup and of the platter, but within they are full of extortion and unrighteousness.ⁱ ²⁶ You blind Pharisee, first clean the inside of the cup and of the platter, that its outside may become clean also. ²⁷ "Woe to you, scribes and Pharisees, hypocrites! For you are like whitened tombs, which outwardly appear beautiful, but inwardly are full of dead men's bones and of all uncleanness. ²⁸ Even so you also outwardly appear righteous to men, but inwardly you are full of hypocrisy and iniquity. ²⁹ "Woe to you, scribes and Pharisees, hypocrites! For you build the tombs of the prophets and decorate the

---

* 21:42 Psalms 118:22-23
ᵃ 22:24 or, seed
* 22:32 Exodus 3:6
* 22:37 Deuteronomy 6:5
* 22:39 Leviticus 19:18
* 22:44 Psalms 110:1
ᵇ 23:5 phylacteries (tefillin in Hebrew) are small leather pouches that some Jewish men

wear on their forehead and arm in prayer. They are used to carry a small scroll with some Scripture in it. See Deuteronomy 6:8.
ᶜ 23:5 or, tassels
ᵈ 23:7 NU omits the second "Rabbi".

ᵉ 23:14 Some Greek texts reverse the order of verses 13 and 14, and some omit verse 13, numbering verse 14 as 13. NU omits verse 14.
ᶠ 23:15 or, Hell
ᵍ 23:21 NU reads "lives"
ʰ 23:23 cumin is an aromatic seed from Cuminum cyminum,

resembling caraway in flavor and appearance. It is used as a spice.
ⁱ 23:25 TR reads "self-indulgence" instead of "unrighteousness"

tombs of the righteous, <sup>30</sup> and say, 'If we had lived in the days of our fathers, we wouldn't have been partakers with them in the blood of the prophets.' <sup>31</sup> Therefore you testify to yourselves that you are children of those who killed the prophets. <sup>32</sup> Fill up, then, the measure of your fathers. <sup>33</sup> You serpents, you offspring of vipers, how will you escape the judgment of Gehenna?ᵃ <sup>34</sup> Therefore, behold, I send to you prophets, wise men, and scribes. Some of them you will kill and crucify; and some of them you will scourge in your synagogues and persecute from city to city, <sup>35</sup> that on you may come all the righteous blood shed on the earth, from the blood of righteous Abel to the blood of Zachariah son of Barachiah, whom you killed between the sanctuary and the altar. <sup>36</sup> Most certainly I tell you, all these things will come upon this generation. <sup>37</sup> "Jerusalem, Jerusalem, who kills the prophets and stones those who are sent to her! How often I would have gathered your children together, even as a hen gathers her chicks under her wings, and you would not! <sup>38</sup> Behold, your house is left to you desolate. <sup>39</sup> For I tell you, you will not see me from now on, until you say, 'Blessed is he who comes in the name of the Lord!'"*

## 24

<sup>1</sup> Jesus went out from the temple, and was going on his way. His disciples came to him to show him the buildings of the temple. <sup>2</sup> But he answered them, "You see all of these things, don't you? Most certainly I tell you, there will not be left here one stone on another, that will not be thrown down." <sup>3</sup> As he sat on the Mount of Olives, the disciples came to him privately, saying, "Tell us, when will these things be? What is the sign of your coming, and of the end of the age?" <sup>4</sup> Jesus answered them, "Be careful that no one leads you astray. <sup>5</sup> For many will come in my name, saying, 'I am the Christ,' and will lead many astray. <sup>6</sup> You will hear of wars and rumors of wars. See that you aren't troubled, for all this must happen, but the end is not yet. <sup>7</sup> For nation will rise against nation, and kingdom against kingdom; and there will be famines, plagues, and earthquakes in various places. <sup>8</sup> But all these things are the beginning of birth pains. <sup>9</sup> "Then they will deliver you up to oppression and will kill you. You will be hated by all of the nations for my name's sake. <sup>10</sup> Then many will stumble, and will deliver up one another, and will hate one another. <sup>11</sup> Many false prophets will arise and will lead many astray. <sup>12</sup> Because iniquity will be multiplied, the love of many will grow cold. <sup>13</sup> But he who endures to the end will be saved. <sup>14</sup> This Good News of the Kingdom will be preached in the whole world for a testimony to all the nations, and then the end will come. <sup>15</sup> "When, therefore, you see the abomination of desolation,* which was spoken of through Daniel the prophet, standing in the holy place (let the reader understand), <sup>16</sup> then let those who are in Judea flee to the mountains. <sup>17</sup> Let him who is on the housetop not go down to take out the things that are in his house. <sup>18</sup> Let him who is in the field not return back to get his clothes. <sup>19</sup> But woe to those who are with child and to nursing mothers in those days! <sup>20</sup> Pray that your flight will not be in the winter nor on a Sabbath, <sup>21</sup> for then there will be great suffering,ᵇ such as has not been from the beginning of the world until now, no, nor ever will be. <sup>22</sup> Unless those days had been shortened, no flesh would have been saved. But for the sake of the chosen ones, those days will be shortened. <sup>23</sup> "Then if any man tells you, 'Behold, here is the Christ!' or, 'There!' don't believe it. <sup>24</sup> For false christs and false prophets will arise, and they will show great signs and wonders, so as to lead astray, if possible, even the chosen ones. <sup>25</sup> "Behold, I have told you beforehand. <sup>26</sup> "If therefore they tell you, 'Behold, he is in the wilderness,' don't go out; or 'Behold, he is in the inner rooms,' don't believe it. <sup>27</sup> For as the lightning flashes from the east, and is seen even to the west, so will the coming of the Son of Man be. <sup>28</sup> For wherever the carcass is, that is where the vulturesᶜ gather together. <sup>29</sup> "But immediately after the sufferingᵈ of those days, the sun will be darkened, the moon will not give its light, the stars will fall from the sky, and the powers of the heavens will be shaken;* <sup>30</sup> and then the sign of the Son of Man will appear in the sky. Then all the tribes of the earth will mourn, and they will see the Son of Man coming on the clouds of the sky with power and great glory. <sup>31</sup> He will send out his angels with a great sound of a trumpet, and they will gather together his chosen ones from the four winds, from one end of the sky to the other. <sup>32</sup> "Now from the fig tree learn this parable: When its branch has now become tender and produces its leaves, you know that the summer is near. <sup>33</sup> Even so you also, when you see all these things, know that he is near, even at the doors. <sup>34</sup> Most certainly I tell you, this generationᵉ will not pass away until all these things are accomplished. <sup>35</sup> Heaven and earth will pass

away, but my words will not pass away. <sup>36</sup> "But no one knows of that day and hour, not even the angels of heaven,ᶠ but my Father only. <sup>37</sup> As the days of Noah were, so will the coming of the Son of Man be. <sup>38</sup> For as in those days which were before the flood they were eating and drinking, marrying and giving in marriage, until the day that Noah entered into the ship, <sup>39</sup> and they didn't know until the flood came and took them all away, so will the coming of the Son of Man be. <sup>40</sup> Then two men will be in the field: one will be taken and one will be left. <sup>41</sup> Two women will be grinding at the mill: one will be taken and one will be left. <sup>42</sup> Watch therefore, for you don't know in what hour your Lord comes. <sup>43</sup> But know this, that if the master of the house had known in what watch of the night the thief was coming, he would have watched, and would not have allowed his house to be broken into. <sup>44</sup> Therefore also be ready, for in an hour that you don't expect, the Son of Man will come. <sup>45</sup> "Who then is the faithful and wise servant, whom his lord has set over his household, to give them their food in due season? <sup>46</sup> Blessed is that servant whom his lord finds doing so when he comes. <sup>47</sup> Most certainly I tell you that he will set him over all that he has. <sup>48</sup> But if that evil servant should say in his heart, 'My lord is delaying his coming,' <sup>49</sup> and begins to beat his fellow servants, and eat and drink with the drunkards, <sup>50</sup> the lord of that servant will come in a day when he doesn't expect it and in an hour when he doesn't know it, <sup>51</sup> and will cut him in pieces and appoint his portion with the hypocrites. That is where the weeping and grinding of teeth will be.

## 25

<sup>1</sup> "Then the Kingdom of Heaven will be like ten virgins who took their lamps and went out to meet the bridegroom. <sup>2</sup> Five of them were foolish, and five were wise. <sup>3</sup> Those who were foolish, when they took their lamps, took no oil with them, <sup>4</sup> but the wise took oil in their vessels with their lamps. <sup>5</sup> Now while the bridegroom delayed, they all slumbered and slept. <sup>6</sup> But at midnight there was a cry, 'Behold! The bridegroom is coming! Come out to meet him!' <sup>7</sup> Then all those virgins arose, and trimmed their lamps.ᵍ <sup>8</sup> The foolish said to the wise, 'Give us some of your oil, for our lamps are going out.' <sup>9</sup> But the wise answered, saying, 'What if there isn't enough for us and you? You go rather to those who sell, and buy for yourselves.' <sup>10</sup> While they went away to buy, the bridegroom came, and those who were ready went in with him to the wedding feast, and the door was shut. <sup>11</sup> Afterward the other virgins also came, saying, 'Lord, Lord, open to us.' <sup>12</sup> But he answered, 'Most certainly I tell you, I don't know you.' <sup>13</sup> Watch therefore, for you don't know the day nor the hour in which the Son of Man is coming. <sup>14</sup> "For it is like a man going into another country, who called his own servants and entrusted his goods to them. <sup>15</sup> To one he gave five talents,ʰ to another two, to another one, to each according to his own ability. Then he went on his journey. <sup>16</sup> Immediately he who received the five talents went and traded with them, and made another five talents. <sup>17</sup> In the same way, he also who got the two gained another two. <sup>18</sup> But he who received the one talent went away and dug in the earth and hid his lord's money. <sup>19</sup> "Now after a long time the lord of those servants came, and settled accounts with them. <sup>20</sup> He who received the five talents came and brought another five talents, saying, 'Lord, you delivered to me five talents. Behold, I have gained another five talents in addition to them.' <sup>21</sup> "His lord said to him, 'Well done, good and faithful servant. You have been faithful over a few things, I will set you over many things. Enter into the joy of your lord.' <sup>22</sup> "He also who got the two talents came and said, 'Lord, you delivered to me two talents. Behold, I have gained another two talents in addition to them.' <sup>23</sup> "His lord said to him, 'Well done, good and faithful servant. You have been faithful over a few things. I will set you over many things. Enter into the joy of your lord.' <sup>24</sup> "He also who had received the one talent came and said, 'Lord, I knew you that you are a hard man, reaping where you didn't sow, and gathering where you didn't scatter. <sup>25</sup> I was afraid, and went away and hid your talent in the earth. Behold, you have what is yours.' <sup>26</sup> "But his lord answered him, 'You wicked and slothful servant. You knew that I reap where I didn't sow, and gather where I didn't scatter. <sup>27</sup> You ought therefore to have deposited my money with the bankers, and at my coming I should have received back my own with interest. <sup>28</sup> Take away therefore the talent from him and give it to him who has the ten talents. <sup>29</sup> For to everyone who has will be given, and he will have abundance, but from him who doesn't have, even that which he has will be taken away. <sup>30</sup> Throw out the unprofitable servant into the outer darkness, where there will be weeping and gnashing of teeth.' <sup>31</sup> "But when the Son of Man comes in

ᵃ 23:33 or, Hell
* 23:39 Psalms 118:26
* 24:15 Daniel 9:27; 11:31; 12:11
ᵇ 24:21 or, oppression
ᶜ 24:28 or, eagles
ᵈ 24:29 or, oppression

* 24:29 Isaiah 13:10; 34:4
ᵉ 24:34 The word for "generation" (genea) can also be translated as "race."
ᶠ 24:36 NU adds "nor the son"
ᵍ 25:7 The end of the wick of an oil lamp needs to be cut off

periodically to avoid having it become clogged with carbon deposits. The wick height is also adjusted so that the flame burns evenly and gives good light without producing a lot of smoke.

ʰ 25:15 A talent is about 30 kilograms or 66 pounds (usually used to weigh silver unless otherwise specified) his glory, and all the holy angels with him, then he will sit on the throne of his glory. **32** Before him all the nations will be gathered, and he will separate them one from another, as a shepherd separates the sheep from the goats. **33** He will set the sheep on his right hand, but the goats on the left. **34** Then the King will tell those on his right hand, 'Come, blessed of my Father, inherit the Kingdom prepared for you from the foundation of the world; **35** for I was hungry and you gave me food to eat. I was thirsty and you gave me drink. I was a stranger and you took me in. **36** I was naked and you clothed me. I was sick and you visited me. I was in prison and you came to me.' **37** "Then the righteous will answer him, saying, 'Lord, when did we see you hungry and feed you, or thirsty and give you a drink? **38** When did we see you as a stranger and take you in, or naked and clothe you? **39** When did we see you sick or in prison and come to you?' **40** "The King will answer them, 'Most certainly I tell you, because you did it to one of the least of these my brothers,ᵃ you did it to me.' **41** Then he will say also to those on the left hand, 'Depart from me, you cursed, into the eternal fire which is prepared for the devil and his angels; **42** for I was hungry, and you didn't give me food to eat; I was thirsty, and you gave me no drink; **43** I was a stranger, and you didn't take me in; naked, and you didn't clothe me; sick, and in prison, and you didn't visit me.' **44** "Then they will also answer, saying, 'Lord, when did we see you hungry, or thirsty, or a stranger, or naked, or sick, or in prison, and didn't help you?' **45** "Then he will answer them, saying, 'Most certainly I tell you, because you didn't do it to one of the least of these, you didn't do it to me.' **46** These will go away into eternal punishment, but the righteous into eternal life."

## 26

**1** When Jesus had finished all these words, he said to his disciples, **2** "You know that after two days the Passover is coming, and the Son of Man will be delivered up to be crucified." **3** Then the chief priests, the scribes, and the elders of the people were gathered together in the court of the high priest, who was called Caiaphas. **4** They took counsel together that they might take Jesus by deceit and kill him. **5** But they said, "Not during the feast, lest a riot occur among the people." **6** Now when Jesus was in Bethany, in the house of Simon the leper, **7** a woman came to him having an alabaster jar of very expensive ointment, and she poured it on his head as he sat at the table. **8** But when his disciples saw this, they were indignant, saying, "Why this waste? **9** For this ointment might have been sold for much and given to the poor." **10** However, knowing this, Jesus said to them, "Why do you trouble the woman? She has done a good work for me. **11** For you always have the poor with you, but you don't always have me. **12** For in pouring this ointment on my body, she did it to prepare me for burial. **13** Most certainly I tell you, wherever this Good News is preached in the whole world, what this woman has done will also be spoken of as a memorial of her." **14** Then one of the twelve, who was called Judas Iscariot, went to the chief priests **15** and said, "What are you willing to give me if I deliver him to you?" So they weighed out for him thirty pieces of silver. **16** From that time he sought opportunity to betray him. **17** Now on the first day of unleavened bread, the disciples came to Jesus, saying to him, "Where do you want us to prepare for you to eat the Passover?" **18** He said, "Go into the city to a certain person, and tell him, 'The Teacher says, "My time is at hand. I will keep the Passover at your house with my disciples."'" **19** The disciples did as Jesus commanded them, and they prepared the Passover. **20** Now when evening had come, he was reclining at the table with the twelve disciples. **21** As they were eating, he said, "Most certainly I tell you that one of you will betray me." **22** They were exceedingly sorrowful, and each began to ask him, "It isn't me, is it, Lord?" **23** He answered, "He who dipped his hand with me in the dish will betray me. **24** The Son of Man goes even as it is written of him, but woe to that man through whom the Son of Man is betrayed! It would be better for that man if he had not been born." **25** Judas, who betrayed him, answered, "It isn't me, is it, Rabbi?" He said to him, "You said it." **26** As they were eating, Jesus took bread, gave thanks forᵇ it, and broke it. He gave to the disciples and said, "Take, eat; this is my body." **27** He took the cup, gave thanks, and gave to them, saying, "All of you drink it, **28** for this is my blood of the new covenant, which is poured out for many for the remission of sins. **29** But I tell you that I will not drink of this fruit of the vine from now on, until that day when I drink it anew with you in my Father's Kingdom." **30** When they had sung a hymn, they went out to the Mount of Olives. **31** Then Jesus said to them, "All of you will be made to stumble because of me tonight, for it is written, 'I will strike the shepherd, and the sheep of the flock will be scattered.'* **32** But after I am raised up, I will go before you into Galilee." **33** But Peter answered him, "Even if all will be made to stumble because of you, I will never be made to stumble." **34** Jesus said

to him, "Most certainly I tell you that tonight, before the rooster crows, you will deny me three times." **35** Peter said to him, "Even if I must die with you, I will not deny you." All of the disciples also said likewise. **36** Then Jesus came with them to a place called Gethsemane, and said to his disciples, "Sit here, while I go there and pray." **37** He took with him Peter and the two sons of Zebedee, and began to be sorrowful and severely troubled. **38** Then Jesus said to them, "My soul is exceedingly sorrowful, even to death. Stay here and watch with me." **39** He went forward a little, fell on his face, and prayed, saying, "My Father, if it is possible, let this cup pass away from me; nevertheless, not what I desire, but what you desire." **40** He came to the disciples and found them sleeping, and said to Peter, "What, couldn't you watch with me for one hour? **41** Watch and pray, that you don't enter into temptation. The spirit indeed is willing, but the flesh is weak." **42** Again, a second time he went away and prayed, saying, "My Father, if this cup can't pass away from me unless I drink it, your desire be done." **43** He came again and found them sleeping, for their eyes were heavy. **44** He left them again, went away, and prayed a third time, saying the same words. **45** Then he came to his disciples and said to them, "Are you still sleeping and resting? Behold, the hour is at hand, and the Son of Man is betrayed into the hands of sinners. **46** Arise, let's be going. Behold, he who betrays me is at hand." **47** While he was still speaking, behold, Judas, one of the twelve, came, and with him a great multitude with swords and clubs, from the chief priests and elders of the people. **48** Now he who betrayed him had given them a sign, saying, "Whoever I kiss, he is the one. Seize him." **49** Immediately he came to Jesus, and said, "Greetings, Rabbi!" and kissed him. **50** Jesus said to him, "Friend, why are you here?" Then they came and laid hands on Jesus, and took him. **51** Behold, one of those who were with Jesus stretched out his hand and drew his sword, and struck the servant of the high priest, and cut off his ear. **52** Then Jesus said to him, "Put your sword back into its place, for all those who take the sword will die by the sword. **53** Or do you think that I couldn't ask my Father, and he would even now send me more than twelve legions of angels? **54** How then would the Scriptures be fulfilled that it must be so?" **55** In that hour Jesus said to the multitudes, "Have you come out as against a robber with swords and clubs to seize me? I sat daily in the temple teaching, and you didn't arrest me. **56** But all this has happened that the Scriptures of the prophets might be fulfilled." Then all the disciples left him and fled. **57** Those who had taken Jesus led him away to Caiaphas the high priest, where the scribes and the elders were gathered together. **58** But Peter followed him from a distance to the court of the high priest, and entered in and sat with the officers, to see the end. **59** Now the chief priests, the elders, and the whole council sought false testimony against Jesus, that they might put him to death, **60** and they found none. Even though many false witnesses came forward, they found none. But at last two false witnesses came forward **61** and said, "This man said, 'I am able to destroy the temple of God, and to build it in three days.'" **62** The high priest stood up and said to him, "Have you no answer? What is this that these testify against you?" **63** But Jesus stayed silent. The high priest answered him, "I adjure you by the living God that you tell us whether you are the Christ, the Son of God." **64** Jesus said to him, "You have said so. Nevertheless, I tell you, after this you will see the Son of Man sitting at the right hand of Power, and coming on the clouds of the sky." **65** Then the high priest tore his clothing, saying, "He has spoken blasphemy! Why do we need any more witnesses? Behold, now you have heard his blasphemy. **66** What do you think?" They answered, "He is worthy of death!" **67** Then they spat in his face and beat him with their fists, and some slapped him, **68** saying, "Prophesy to us, you Christ! Who hit you?" **69** Now Peter was sitting outside in the court, and a maid came to him, saying, "You were also with Jesus, the Galilean!" **70** But he denied it before them all, saying, "I don't know what you are talking about." **71** When he had gone out onto the porch, someone else saw him and said to those who were there, "This man also was with Jesus of Nazareth." **72** Again he denied it with an oath, "I don't know the man." **73** After a little while those who stood by came and said to Peter, "Surely you are also one of them, for your speech makes you known." **74** Then he began to curse and to swear, "I don't know the man!" Immediately the rooster crowed. **75** Peter remembered the word which Jesus had said to him, "Before the rooster crows, you will deny me three times." Then he went out and wept bitterly.

## 27

**1** Now when morning had come, all the chief priests and the elders of the people took counsel against Jesus to put him to death. **2** They bound him, led him away, and delivered him up to Pontius Pilate, the governor.

---

ᵃ *25:40* The word for "brothers" here may be also correctly translated "brothers and sisters" or "siblings."

ᵇ *26:26* TR reads "blessed" instead of "gave thanks for"

* *26:31* Zechariah 13:7

³ Then Judas, who betrayed him, when he saw that Jesus was condemned, felt remorse, and brought back the thirty pieces of silver to the chief priests and elders, ⁴ saying, "I have sinned in that I betrayed innocent blood."

But they said, "What is that to us? You see to it." ⁵ He threw down the pieces of silver in the sanctuary and departed. Then he went away and hanged himself. ⁶ The chief priests took the pieces of silver and said, "It's not lawful to put them into the treasury, since it is the price of blood." ⁷ They took counsel, and bought the potter's field with them to bury strangers in. ⁸ Therefore that field has been called "The Field of Blood" to this day. ⁹ Then that which was spoken through Jeremiahª the prophet was fulfilled, saying, "They took the thirty pieces of silver, the price of him upon whom a price had been set, whom some of the children of Israel priced, ¹⁰ and they gave them for the potter's field, as the Lord commanded me."* ¹¹ Now Jesus stood before the governor; and the governor asked him, saying, "Are you the King of the Jews?" Jesus said to him, "So you say." ¹² When he was accused by the chief priests and elders, he answered nothing. ¹³ Then Pilate said to him, "Don't you hear how many things they testify against you?" ¹⁴ He gave him no answer, not even one word, so that the governor marveled greatly. ¹⁵ Now at the feast the governor was accustomed to release to the multitude one prisoner whom they desired. ¹⁶ They had then a notable prisoner called Barabbas. ¹⁷ When therefore they were gathered together, Pilate said to them, "Whom do you want me to release to you? Barabbas, or Jesus who is called Christ?" ¹⁸ For he knew that because of envy they had delivered him up. ¹⁹ While he was sitting on the judgment seat, his wife sent to him, saying, "Have nothing to do with that righteous man, for I have suffered many things today in a dream because of him." ²⁰ Now the chief priests and the elders persuaded the multitudes to ask for Barabbas and destroy Jesus. ²¹ But the governor answered them, "Which of the two do you want me to release to you?" They said, "Barabbas!" ²² Pilate said to them, "What then shall I do to Jesus who is called Christ?" They all said to him, "Let him be crucified!" ²³ But the governor said, "Why? What evil has he done?" But they cried out exceedingly, saying, "Let him be crucified!" ²⁴ So when Pilate saw that nothing was being gained, but rather that a disturbance was starting, he took water and washed his hands before the multitude, saying, "I am innocent of the blood of this righteous person. You see to it." ²⁵ All the people answered, "May his blood be on us and on our children!" ²⁶ Then he released Barabbas to them, but Jesus he flogged and delivered to be crucified. ²⁷ Then the governor's soldiers took Jesus into the Praetorium, and gathered the whole garrison together against him. ²⁸ They stripped him and put a scarlet robe on him. ²⁹ They braided a crown of thorns and put it on his head, and a reed in his right hand; and they kneeled down before him and mocked him, saying, "Hail, King of the Jews!" ³⁰ They spat on him, and took the reed and struck him on the head. ³¹ When they had mocked him, they took the robe off him, and put his clothes on him, and led him away to crucify him. ³² As they came out, they found a man of Cyrene, Simon by name, and they compelled him to go with them, that he might carry his cross. ³³ When they came to a place called "Golgotha", that is to say, "The place of a skull," ³⁴ they gave him sour wineᵇ to drink mixed with gall.ᶜ When he had tasted it, he would not drink. ³⁵ When they had crucified him, they divided his clothing among them, casting lots,ᵈ ³⁶ and they sat and watched him there. ³⁷ They set up over his head the accusation against him written, "THIS IS JESUS, THE KING OF THE JEWS." ³⁸ Then there were two robbers crucified with him, one on his right hand and one on the left. ³⁹ Those who passed by blasphemed him, wagging their heads ⁴⁰ and saying, "You who destroy the temple and build it in three days, save yourself! If you are the Son of God, come down from the cross!" ⁴¹ Likewise the chief priests also mocking with the scribes, the Pharisees,ᵉ and the elders, said, ⁴²"He saved others, but he can't save himself. If he is the King of Israel, let him come down from the cross now, and we will believe in him. ⁴³ He trusts in God. Let God deliver him now, if he wants him; for he said, 'I am the Son of God.'" ⁴⁴ The robbers also who were crucified with him cast on him the same reproach. ⁴⁵ Now from the sixth hourᶠ there was darkness over all the land until the ninth hour.ᵍ ⁴⁶ About the ninth hour Jesus cried with a loud voice, saying, "Eli, Eli, limaʰ sabachthani?" That is, "My God, my God, why have you forsaken me?"* ⁴⁷ Some of them who stood there, when they heard it, said, "This man is calling

Elijah." ⁴⁸ Immediately one of them ran and took a sponge, filled it with vinegar, put it on a reed, and gave him a drink. ⁴⁹ The rest said, "Let him be. Let's see whether Elijah comes to save him." ⁵⁰ Jesus cried again with a loud voice, and yielded up his spirit. ⁵¹ Behold, the veil of the temple was torn in two from the top to the bottom. The earth quaked and the rocks were split. ⁵² The tombs were opened, and many bodies of the saints who had fallen asleep were raised; ⁵³ and coming out of the tombs after his resurrection, they entered into the holy city and appeared to many. ⁵⁴ Now the centurion and those who were with him watching Jesus, when they saw the earthquake and the things that were done, were terrified, saying, "Truly this was the Son of God!" ⁵⁵ Many women were there watching from afar, who had followed Jesus from Galilee, serving him. ⁵⁶ Among them were Mary Magdalene, Mary the mother of James and Joses, and the mother of the sons of Zebedee. ⁵⁷ When evening had come, a rich man from Arimathaea named Joseph, who himself was also Jesus' disciple, came. ⁵⁸ This man went to Pilate and asked for Jesus' body. Then Pilate commanded the body to be given up. ⁵⁹ Joseph took the body and wrapped it in a clean linen cloth ⁶⁰ and laid it in his own new tomb, which he had cut out in the rock. Then he rolled a large stone against the door of the tomb, and departed. ⁶¹ Mary Magdalene was there, and the other Mary, sitting opposite the tomb. ⁶² Now on the next day, which was the day after the Preparation Day, the chief priests and the Pharisees were gathered together to Pilate, ⁶³ saying, "Sir, we remember what that deceiver said while he was still alive: 'After three days I will rise again.' ⁶⁴ Command therefore that the tomb be made secure until the third day, lest perhaps his disciples come at night and steal him away, and tell the people, 'He is risen from the dead;' and the last deception will be worse than the first." ⁶⁵ Pilate said to them, "You have a guard. Go, make it as secure as you can." ⁶⁶ So they went with the guard and made the tomb secure, sealing the stone.

## 28

¹ Now after the Sabbath, as it began to dawn on the first day of the week, Mary Magdalene and the other Mary came to see the tomb. ² Behold, there was a great earthquake, for an angel of the Lord descended from the sky and came and rolled away the stone from the door and sat on it. ³ His appearance was like lightning, and his clothing white as snow. ⁴ For fear of him, the guards shook, and became like dead men. ⁵ The angel answered the women, "Don't be afraid, for I know that you seek Jesus, who has been crucified. ⁶ He is not here, for he has risen, just like he said. Come, see the place where the Lord was lying. ⁷ Go quickly and tell his disciples, 'He has risen from the dead, and behold, he goes before you into Galilee; there you will see him.' Behold, I have told you." ⁸ They departed quickly from the tomb with fear and great joy, and ran to bring his disciples word. ⁹ As they went to tell his disciples, behold, Jesus met them, saying, "Rejoice!" They came and took hold of his feet, and worshiped him. ¹⁰ Then Jesus said to them, "Don't be afraid. Go tell my brothers ⁱ that they should go into Galilee, and there they will see me." ¹¹ Now while they were going, behold, some of the guards came into the city and told the chief priests all the things that had happened. ¹² When they were assembled with the elders and had taken counsel, they gave a large amount of silver to the soldiers, ¹³ saying, "Say that his disciples came by night and stole him away while we slept. ¹⁴ If this comes to the governor's ears, we will persuade him and make you free of worry." ¹⁵ So they took the money and did as they were told. This saying was spread abroad among the Jews, and continues until today. ¹⁶ But the eleven disciples went into Galilee, to the mountain where Jesus had sent them. ¹⁷ When they saw him, they bowed down to him; but some doubted. ¹⁸ Jesus came to them and spoke to them, saying, "All authority has been given to me in heaven and on earth. ¹⁹ Goʲ and make disciples of all nations, baptizing them in the name of the Father and of the Son and of the Holy Spirit, ²⁰ teaching them to observe all things that I commanded you. Behold, I am with you always, even to the end of the age." Amen.

## The Good News According to Mark
### 1

¹ The beginning of the Good News of Jesus Christ, the Son of God. ² As it is written in the prophets, "Behold,ᵏ I send my messenger before your face, who will prepare your way before you:* ³ the voice of one

---

ª *27:9* some manuscripts omit "Jeremiah"
* *27:10* Zechariah 11:12- 13; Jeremiah 19:1- 13; 32:6- 9
ᵇ *27:34* or, vinegar
ᶜ *27:34* Gall is a bitter-tasting, dark green oil from a wormwood plant that is alcoholic in its effect.

ᵈ *27:35* TR adds "that it might be fulfilled which was spoken by the prophet: 'They divided my garments among them, and for my clothing they cast lots;'" [see Psalms 22:18 and John 19:24]
ᵉ *27:41* TR omits "the Pharisees"

ᶠ *27:45* noon
ᵍ *27:45* 3:00 p.m.
ʰ *27:46* TR reads "lama" instead of "lima"
ⁱ *28:10* The word for "brothers" here may be also correctly translated "brothers and sisters" or "siblings."

ʲ *28:19* TR and NU add "therefore"
ᵏ *1:2* "Behold", from "ἰδού", means look at, take notice, observe, see, or gaze at. It is often used as an interjection.
* *1:2* Malachi 3:1

crying in the wilderness, 'Make ready the way of the Lord! Make his paths straight!'"* [4] John came baptizing[a] in the wilderness and preaching the baptism of repentance for forgiveness of sins. [5] All the country of Judea and all those of Jerusalem went out to him. They were baptized by him in the Jordan river, confessing their sins. [6] John was clothed with camel's hair and a leather belt around his waist. He ate locusts and wild honey. [7] He preached, saying, "After me comes he who is mightier than I, the strap of whose sandals I am not worthy to stoop down and loosen. [8] I baptized you in[b] water, but he will baptize you in the Holy Spirit." [9] In those days, Jesus came from Nazareth of Galilee, and was baptized by John in the Jordan. [10] Immediately coming up from the water, he saw the heavens parting and the Spirit descending on him like a dove. [11] A voice came out of the sky, "You are my beloved Son, in whom I am well pleased." [12] Immediately the Spirit drove him out into the wilderness. [13] He was there in the wilderness forty days, tempted by Satan. He was with the wild animals; and the angels were serving him. [14] Now after John was taken into custody, Jesus came into Galilee, preaching the Good News of God's Kingdom, [15] and saying, "The time is fulfilled, and God's Kingdom is at hand! Repent, and believe in the Good News." [16] Passing along by the sea of Galilee, he saw Simon and Andrew, the brother of Simon, casting a net into the sea, for they were fishermen. [17] Jesus said to them, "Come after me, and I will make you into fishers for men." [18] Immediately they left their nets, and followed him. [19] Going on a little further from there, he saw James the son of Zebedee, and John his brother, who were also in the boat mending the nets. [20] Immediately he called them, and they left their father, Zebedee, in the boat with the hired servants, and went after him. [21] They went into Capernaum, and immediately on the Sabbath day he entered into the synagogue and taught. [22] They were astonished at his teaching, for he taught them as having authority, and not as the scribes. [23] Immediately there was in their synagogue a man with an unclean spirit, and he cried out, [24] saying, "Ha! What do we have to do with you, Jesus, you Nazarene? Have you come to destroy us? I know who you are: the Holy One of God!" [25] Jesus rebuked him, saying, "Be quiet, and come out of him!" [26] The unclean spirit, convulsing him and crying with a loud voice, came out of him. [27] They were all amazed, so that they questioned among themselves, saying, "What is this? A new teaching? For with authority he commands even the unclean spirits, and they obey him!" [28] The report of him went out immediately everywhere into all the region of Galilee and its surrounding area. [29] Immediately, when they had come out of the synagogue, they came into the house of Simon and Andrew, with James and John. [30] Now Simon's wife's mother lay sick with a fever, and immediately they told him about her. [31] He came and took her by the hand and raised her up. The fever left her immediately,[c] and she served them. [32] At evening, when the sun had set, they brought to him all who were sick and those who were possessed by demons. [33] All the city was gathered together at the door. [34] He healed many who were sick with various diseases and cast out many demons. He didn't allow the demons to speak, because they knew him. [35] Early in the morning, while it was still dark, he rose up and went out, and departed into a deserted place, and prayed there. [36] Simon and those who were with him searched for him. [37] They found him and told him, "Everyone is looking for you." [38] He said to them, "Let's go elsewhere into the next towns, that I may preach there also, because I came out for this reason." [39] He went into their synagogues throughout all Galilee, preaching and casting out demons. [40] A leper came to him, begging him, kneeling down to him, and saying to him, "If you want to, you can make me clean." [41] Being moved with compassion, he stretched out his hand, and touched him, and said to him, "I want to. Be made clean." [42] When he had said this, immediately the leprosy departed from him and he was made clean. [43] He strictly warned him and immediately sent him out, [44] and said to him, "See that you say nothing to anybody, but go show yourself to the priest and offer for your cleansing the things which Moses commanded, for a testimony to them." [45] But he went out, and began to proclaim it much, and to spread about the matter, so that Jesus could no more openly enter into a city, but was outside in desert places. People came to him from everywhere.

## 2

[1] When he entered again into Capernaum after some days, it was heard that he was at home. [2] Immediately many were gathered together, so that there was no more room, not even around the door; and he spoke the word to them. [3] Four people came, carrying a paralytic to him. [4] When they could not come near to him for the crowd, they removed the roof where he was. When they had broken it up, they let down the mat that the paralytic was lying on. [5] Jesus, seeing their faith, said to the paralytic, "Son, your sins are forgiven you." [6] But there were some of the scribes sitting there and reasoning in their hearts, [7] "Why does this man speak blasphemies like that? Who can forgive sins but God alone?" [8] Immediately Jesus, perceiving in his spirit that they so reasoned within themselves, said to them, "Why do you reason these things in your hearts? [9] Which is easier, to tell the paralytic, 'Your sins are forgiven;' or to say, 'Arise, and take up your bed, and walk'? [10] But that you may know that the Son of Man has authority on earth to forgive sins"—he said to the paralytic— [11] "I tell you, arise, take up your mat, and go to your house." [12] He arose, and immediately took up the mat and went out in front of them all, so that they were all amazed and glorified God, saying, "We never saw anything like this!" [13] He went out again by the seaside. All the multitude came to him, and he taught them. [14] As he passed by, he saw Levi the son of Alphaeus sitting at the tax office. He said to him, "Follow me." And he arose and followed him. [15] He was reclining at the table in his house, and many tax collectors and sinners sat down with Jesus and his disciples, for there were many, and they followed him. [16] The scribes and the Pharisees, when they saw that he was eating with the sinners and tax collectors, said to his disciples, "Why is it that he eats and drinks with tax collectors and sinners?" [17] When Jesus heard it, he said to them, "Those who are healthy have no need for a physician, but those who are sick. I came not to call the righteous, but sinners to repentance." [18] John's disciples and the Pharisees were fasting, and they came and asked him, "Why do John's disciples and the disciples of the Pharisees fast, but your disciples don't fast?" [19] Jesus said to them, "Can the groomsmen fast while the bridegroom is with them? As long as they have the bridegroom with them, they can't fast. [20] But the days will come when the bridegroom will be taken away from them, and then they will fast in that day. [21] No one sews a piece of unshrunk cloth on an old garment, or else the patch shrinks and the new tears away from the old, and a worse hole is made. [22] No one puts new wine into old wineskins; or else the new wine will burst the skins, and the wine pours out, and the skins will be destroyed; but they put new wine into fresh wineskins." [23] He was going on the Sabbath day through the grain fields; and his disciples began, as they went, to pluck the ears of grain. [24] The Pharisees said to him, "Behold, why do they do that which is not lawful on the Sabbath day?" [25] He said to them, "Did you never read what David did when he had need and was hungry—he, and those who were with him? [26] How he entered into God's house at the time of Abiathar the high priest, and ate the show bread, which is not lawful to eat except for the priests, and gave also to those who were with him?" [27] He said to them, "The Sabbath was made for man, not man for the Sabbath. [28] Therefore the Son of Man is lord even of the Sabbath."

## 3

[1] He entered again into the synagogue, and there was a man there whose hand was withered. [2] They watched him, whether he would heal him on the Sabbath day, that they might accuse him. [3] He said to the man whose hand was withered, "Stand up." [4] He said to them, "Is it lawful on the Sabbath day to do good or to do harm? To save a life or to kill?" But they were silent. [5] When he had looked around at them with anger, being grieved at the hardening of their hearts, he said to the man, "Stretch out your hand." He stretched it out, and his hand was restored as healthy as the other. [6] The Pharisees went out, and immediately conspired with the Herodians against him, how they might destroy him. [7] Jesus withdrew to the sea with his disciples; and a great multitude followed him from Galilee, from Judea, [8] from Jerusalem, from Idumaea, beyond the Jordan, and those from around Tyre and Sidon. A great multitude, hearing what great things he did, came to him. [9] He spoke to his disciples that a little boat should stay near him because of the crowd, so that they wouldn't press on him. [10] For he had healed many, so that as many as had diseases pressed on him that they might touch him. [11] The unclean spirits, whenever they saw him, fell down before him and cried, "You are the Son of God!" [12] He sternly warned them that they should not make him known. [13] He went up into the mountain and called to himself those whom he wanted, and they went to him. [14] He appointed twelve, that they might be with him, and that he might send them out to preach [15] and to have authority to heal sicknesses and to cast out demons: [16] Simon (to whom he gave the name Peter); [17] James the son of Zebedee; and John, the brother of James, (whom he called Boanerges, which means, Sons of Thunder); [18] Andrew; Philip; Bartholomew; Matthew; Thomas; James, the son of Alphaeus; Thaddaeus; Simon the Zealot; [19] and Judas Iscariot, who also betrayed him. Then he came into a house. [20] The multitude came together again, so that they could not so much as eat bread. [21] When his friends heard it, they went out to seize him; for they said, "He is insane." [22] The scribes who came down from Jerusalem said, "He has Beelzebul," and, "By the prince of the demons he casts out the demons." [23] He summoned them and said to them in parables, "How

---

* 1:3 Isaiah 40:3
a 1:4 or, immersing

b 1:8 The Greek word (en) translated here as "in" could

also be translated as "with" in some contexts.

c 1:31 NU omits "immediately".

can Satan cast out Satan? <sup>24</sup> If a kingdom is divided against itself, that kingdom cannot stand. <sup>25</sup> If a house is divided against itself, that house cannot stand. <sup>26</sup> If Satan has risen up against himself, and is divided, he can't stand, but has an end. <sup>27</sup> But no one can enter into the house of the strong man to plunder unless he first binds the strong man; then he will plunder his house. <sup>28</sup> "Most certainly I tell you, all sins of the descendants of man will be forgiven, including their blasphemies with which they may blaspheme; <sup>29</sup> but whoever may blaspheme against the Holy Spirit never has forgiveness, but is subject to eternal condemnation."ᵃ <sup>30</sup>—because they said, "He has an unclean spirit." <sup>31</sup> His mother and his brothers came, and standing outside, they sent to him, calling him. <sup>32</sup> A multitude was sitting around him, and they told him, "Behold, your mother, your brothers, and your sistersᵇ are outside looking for you." <sup>33</sup> He answered them, "Who are my mother and my brothers?" <sup>34</sup> Looking around at those who sat around him, he said, "Behold, my mother and my brothers! <sup>35</sup> For whoever does the will of God is my brother, my sister, and mother."

<h2 style="text-align:center">4</h2>

<sup>1</sup> Again he began to teach by the seaside. A great multitude was gathered to him, so that he entered into a boat in the sea and sat down. All the multitude were on the land by the sea. <sup>2</sup> He taught them many things in parables, and told them in his teaching, <sup>3</sup> "Listen! Behold, the farmer went out to sow. <sup>4</sup> As he sowed, some seed fell by the road, and the birdsᶜ came and devoured it. <sup>5</sup> Others fell on the rocky ground, where it had little soil, and immediately it sprang up, because it had no depth of soil. <sup>6</sup> When the sun had risen, it was scorched; and because it had no root, it withered away. <sup>7</sup> Others fell among the thorns, and the thorns grew up and choked it, and it yielded no fruit. <sup>8</sup> Others fell into the good ground and yielded fruit, growing up and increasing. Some produced thirty times, some sixty times, and some one hundred times as much." <sup>9</sup> He said, "Whoever has ears to hear, let him hear." <sup>10</sup> When he was alone, those who were around him with the twelve asked him about the parables. <sup>11</sup> He said to them, "To you is given the mystery of God's Kingdom, but to those who are outside, all things are done in parables, <sup>12</sup> that 'seeing they may see and not perceive, and hearing they may hear and not understand, lest perhaps they should turn again, and their sins should be forgiven them.'"* <sup>13</sup> He said to them, "Don't you understand this parable? How will you understand all of the parables? <sup>14</sup> The farmer sows the word. <sup>15</sup> The ones by the road are the ones where the word is sown; and when they have heard, immediately Satan comes and takes away the word which has been sown in them. <sup>16</sup> These in the same way are those who are sown on the rocky places, who, when they have heard the word, immediately receive it with joy. <sup>17</sup> They have no root in themselves, but are short-lived. When oppression or persecution arises because of the word, immediately they stumble. <sup>18</sup> Others are those who are sown among the thorns. These are those who have heard the word, <sup>19</sup> and the cares of this age, and the deceitfulness of riches, and the lusts of other things entering in choke the word, and it becomes unfruitful. <sup>20</sup> Those which were sown on the good ground are those who hear the word, accept it, and bear fruit, some thirty times, some sixty times, and some one hundred times." <sup>21</sup> He said to them, "Is a lamp brought to be put under a basket ᵈ or under a bed? Isn't it put on a stand? <sup>22</sup> For there is nothing hidden except that it should be made known, neither was anything made secret but that it should come to light. <sup>23</sup> If any man has ears to hear, let him hear." <sup>24</sup> He said to them, "Take heed what you hear. With whatever measure you measure, it will be measured to you; and more will be given to you who hear. <sup>25</sup> For whoever has, to him more will be given; and he who doesn't have, even that which he has will be taken away from him." <sup>26</sup> He said, "God's Kingdom is as if a man should cast seed on the earth, <sup>27</sup> and should sleep and rise night and day, and the seed should spring up and grow, though he doesn't know how. <sup>28</sup> For the earth bears fruit by itself: first the blade, then the ear, then the full grain in the ear. <sup>29</sup> But when the fruit is ripe, immediately he puts in the sickle, because the harvest has come." <sup>30</sup> He said, "How will we liken God's Kingdom? Or with what parable will we illustrate it? <sup>31</sup> It's like a grain of mustard seed, which, when it is sown in the earth, though it is less than all the seeds that are on the earth, <sup>32</sup> yet when it is sown, grows up and becomes greater than all the herbs, and puts out great branches, so that the birds of the sky can lodge under its shadow." <sup>33</sup> With many such parables he spoke the word to them, as they were able to hear it. <sup>34</sup> Without a parable he didn't speak to them; but privately to his own disciples he explained everything. <sup>35</sup> On that day, when evening had come, he said to them, "Let's go over to the other side." <sup>36</sup> Leaving the multitude, they took him with them, even as he was, in the boat. Other small boats were also with him. <sup>37</sup> A big wind storm arose, and the waves beat into the boat,

so much that the boat was already filled. <sup>38</sup> He himself was in the stern, asleep on the cushion; and they woke him up and asked him, "Teacher, don't you care that we are dying?" <sup>39</sup> He awoke and rebuked the wind, and said to the sea, "Peace! Be still!" The wind ceased and there was a great calm. <sup>40</sup> He said to them, "Why are you so afraid? How is it that you have no faith?" <sup>41</sup> They were greatly afraid and said to one another, "Who then is this, that even the wind and the sea obey him?"

<h2 style="text-align:center">5</h2>

<sup>1</sup> They came to the other side of the sea, into the country of the Gadarenes. <sup>2</sup> When he had come out of the boat, immediately a man with an unclean spirit met him out of the tombs. <sup>3</sup> He lived in the tombs. Nobody could bind him any more, not even with chains, <sup>4</sup> because he had been often bound with fetters and chains, and the chains had been torn apart by him, and the fetters broken in pieces. Nobody had the strength to tame him. <sup>5</sup> Always, night and day, in the tombs and in the mountains, he was crying out, and cutting himself with stones. <sup>6</sup> When he saw Jesus from afar, he ran and bowed down to him, <sup>7</sup> and crying out with a loud voice, he said, "What have I to do with you, Jesus, you Son of the Most High God? I adjure you by God, don't torment me." <sup>8</sup> For he said to him, "Come out of the man, you unclean spirit!" <sup>9</sup> He asked him, "What is your name?" He said to him, "My name is Legion, for we are many." <sup>10</sup> He begged him much that he would not send them away out of the country. <sup>11</sup> Now on the mountainside there was a great herd of pigs feeding. <sup>12</sup> All the demons begged him, saying, "Send us into the pigs, that we may enter into them." <sup>13</sup> At once Jesus gave them permission. The unclean spirits came out and entered into the pigs. The herd of about two thousand rushed down the steep bank into the sea, and they were drowned in the sea. <sup>14</sup> Those who fed the pigs fled, and told it in the city and in the country. The people came to see what it was that had happened. <sup>15</sup> They came to Jesus, and saw him who had been possessed by demons sitting, clothed, and in his right mind, even him who had the legion; and they were afraid. <sup>16</sup> Those who saw it declared to them what happened to him who was possessed by demons, and about the pigs. <sup>17</sup> They began to beg him to depart from their region. <sup>18</sup> As he was entering into the boat, he who had been possessed by demons begged him that he might be with him. <sup>19</sup> He didn't allow him, but said to him, "Go to your house, to your friends, and tell them what great things the Lord has done for you and how he had mercy on you." <sup>20</sup> He went his way, and began to proclaim in Decapolis how Jesus had done great things for him, and everyone marveled. <sup>21</sup> When Jesus had crossed back over in the boat to the other side, a great multitude was gathered to him; and he was by the sea. <sup>22</sup> Behold, one of the rulers of the synagogue, Jairus by name, came; and seeing him, he fell at his feet <sup>23</sup> and begged him much, saying, "My little daughter is at the point of death. Please come and lay your hands on her, that she may be made healthy, and live." <sup>24</sup> He went with him, and a great multitude followed him, and they pressed upon him on all sides. <sup>25</sup> A certain woman who had a discharge of blood for twelve years, <sup>26</sup> and had suffered many things by many physicians, and had spent all that she had, and was no better, but rather grew worse, <sup>27</sup> having heard the things concerning Jesus, came up behind him in the crowd and touched his clothes. <sup>28</sup> For she said, "If I just touch his clothes, I will be made well." <sup>29</sup> Immediately the flow of her blood was dried up, and she felt in her body that she was healed of her affliction. <sup>30</sup> Immediately Jesus, perceiving in himself that the power had gone out from him, turned around in the crowd and asked, "Who touched my clothes?" <sup>31</sup> His disciples said to him, "You see the multitude pressing against you, and you say, 'Who touched me?'" <sup>32</sup> He looked around to see her who had done this thing. <sup>33</sup> But the woman, fearing and trembling, knowing what had been done to her, came and fell down before him, and told him all the truth. <sup>34</sup> He said to her, "Daughter, your faith has made you well. Go in peace, and be cured of your disease." <sup>35</sup> While he was still speaking, people came from the synagogue ruler's house, saying, "Your daughter is dead. Why bother the Teacher any more?" <sup>36</sup> But Jesus, when he heard the message spoken, immediately said to the ruler of the synagogue, "Don't be afraid, only believe." <sup>37</sup> He allowed no one to follow him except Peter, James, and John the brother of James. <sup>38</sup> He came to the synagogue ruler's house, and he saw an uproar, weeping, and great wailing. <sup>39</sup> When he had entered in, he said to them, "Why do you make an uproar and weep? The child is not dead, but is asleep." <sup>40</sup> They ridiculed him. But he, having put them all out, took the father of the child, her mother, and those who were with him, and went in where the child was lying. <sup>41</sup> Taking the child by the hand, he said to her, "Talitha cumi!" which means, being interpreted, "Girl, I tell you, get up!" <sup>42</sup> Immediately the girl rose up and walked, for she was twelve years old. They were amazed with great amazement. <sup>43</sup> He strictly ordered them that no one

---

ᵃ *3:29* NU reads, guilty of an eternal sin.
ᵇ *3:32* TR omits "your sisters"
ᶜ *4:4* TR adds "of the air"
* *4:12* Isaiah 6:9-10
ᵈ *4:21* literally, a modion, a dry measuring basket containing about a peck (about 9 liters)

should know this, and commanded that something should be given to her to eat.

## 6

¹ He went out from there. He came into his own country, and his disciples followed him. ² When the Sabbath had come, he began to teach in the synagogue, and many hearing him were astonished, saying, "Where did this man get these things?" and, "What is the wisdom that is given to this man, that such mighty works come about by his hands? ³ Isn't this the carpenter, the son of Mary and brother of James, Joses, Judah, and Simon? Aren't his sisters here with us?" So they were offended at him. ⁴ Jesus said to them, "A prophet is not without honor, except in his own country, and among his own relatives, and in his own house." ⁵ He could do no mighty work there, except that he laid his hands on a few sick people and healed them. ⁶ He marveled because of their unbelief. He went around the villages teaching. ⁷ He called to himself the twelve, and began to send them out two by two; and he gave them authority over the unclean spirits. ⁸ He commanded them that they should take nothing for their journey, except a staff only: no bread, no wallet, no money in their purse, ⁹ but to wear sandals, and not put on two tunics. ¹⁰ He said to them, "Wherever you enter into a house, stay there until you depart from there. ¹¹ Whoever will not receive you nor hear you, as you depart from there, shake off the dust that is under your feet for a testimony against them. Assuredly, I tell you, it will be more tolerable for Sodom and Gomorrah in the day of judgment than for that city!" ¹² They went out and preached that people should repent. ¹³ They cast out many demons, and anointed many with oil who were sick and healed them. ¹⁴ King Herod heard this, for his name had become known, and he said, "John the Baptizer has risen from the dead, and therefore these powers are at work in him." ¹⁵ But others said, "He is Elijah." Others said, "He is a prophet, or like one of the prophets." ¹⁶ But Herod, when he heard this, said, "This is John, whom I beheaded. He has risen from the dead." ¹⁷ For Herod himself had sent out and arrested John and bound him in prison for the sake of Herodias, his brother Philip's wife, for he had married her. ¹⁸ For John had said to Herod, "It is not lawful for you to have your brother's wife." ¹⁹ Herodias set herself against him and desired to kill him, but she couldn't, ²⁰ for Herod feared John, knowing that he was a righteous and holy man, and kept him safe. When he heard him, he did many things, and he heard him gladly. ²¹ Then a convenient day came when Herod on his birthday made a supper for his nobles, the high officers, and the chief men of Galilee. ²² When the daughter of Herodias herself came in and danced, she pleased Herod and those sitting with him. The king said to the young lady, "Ask me whatever you want, and I will give it to you." ²³ He swore to her, "Whatever you ask of me, I will give you, up to half of my kingdom." ²⁴ She went out and said to her mother, "What shall I ask?" She said, "The head of John the Baptizer." ²⁵ She came in immediately with haste to the king and requested, "I want you to give me right now the head of John the Baptizer on a platter." ²⁶ The king was exceedingly sorry, but for the sake of his oaths and of his dinner guests, he didn't wish to refuse her. ²⁷ Immediately the king sent out a soldier of his guard and commanded to bring John's head; and he went and beheaded him in the prison, ²⁸ and brought his head on a platter, and gave it to the young lady; and the young lady gave it to her mother. ²⁹ When his disciples heard this, they came and took up his corpse and laid it in a tomb. ³⁰ The apostles gathered themselves together to Jesus, and they told him all things, whatever they had done, and whatever they had taught. ³¹ He said to them, "Come away into a deserted place, and rest awhile." For there were many coming and going, and they had no leisure so much as to eat. ³² They went away in the boat to a deserted place by themselves. ³³ They[a] saw them going, and many recognized him and ran there on foot from all the cities. They arrived before them and came together to him. ³⁴ Jesus came out, saw a great multitude, and he had compassion on them because they were like sheep without a shepherd; and he began to teach them many things. ³⁵ When it was late in the day, his disciples came to him and said, "This place is deserted, and it is late in the day. ³⁶ Send them away, that they may go into the surrounding country and villages and buy themselves bread, for they have nothing to eat." ³⁷ But he answered them, "You give them something to eat." They asked him, "Shall we go and buy two hundred denarii[b] worth of bread and give them something to eat?" ³⁸ He said to them, "How many loaves do you have? Go see." When they knew, they said, "Five, and two fish." ³⁹ He commanded them that everyone should sit down in groups on the green grass. ⁴⁰ They sat down in ranks, by hundreds and by fifties. ⁴¹ He took the five loaves and the two fish; and looking up to heaven, he blessed and broke the loaves, and he gave to his disciples to set before them, and he divided the two fish among them all. ⁴² They all ate and were filled. ⁴³ They took up twelve baskets full of broken pieces and also of the fish. ⁴⁴ Those who ate the loaves were[c] five thousand men. ⁴⁵ Immediately he made his disciples get into the boat and go ahead to the other side, to Bethsaida, while he himself sent the multitude away. ⁴⁶ After he had taken leave of them, he went up the mountain to pray. ⁴⁷ When evening had come, the boat was in the middle of the sea, and he was alone on the land. ⁴⁸ Seeing them distressed in rowing, for the wind was contrary to them, about the fourth watch of the night he came to them, walking on the sea; * and he would have passed by them, ⁴⁹ but they, when they saw him walking on the sea, supposed that it was a ghost, and cried out; ⁵⁰ for they all saw him and were troubled. But he immediately spoke with them and said to them, "Cheer up! It is I![d] Don't be afraid." ⁵¹ He got into the boat with them; and the wind ceased, and they were very amazed among themselves, and marveled; ⁵² for they hadn't understood about the loaves, but their hearts were hardened. ⁵³ When they had crossed over, they came to land at Gennesaret and moored to the shore. ⁵⁴ When they had come out of the boat, immediately the people recognized him, ⁵⁵ and ran around that whole region, and began to bring those who were sick on their mats to where they heard he was. ⁵⁶ Wherever he entered—into villages, or into cities, or into the country—they laid the sick in the marketplaces and begged him that they might just touch the fringe[e] of his garment; and as many as touched him were made well.

## 7

¹ Then the Pharisees and some of the scribes gathered together to him, having come from Jerusalem. ² Now when they saw some of his disciples eating bread with defiled, that is unwashed, hands, they found fault. ³(For the Pharisees and all the Jews don't eat unless they wash their hands and forearms, holding to the tradition of the elders. ⁴ They don't eat when they come from the marketplace unless they bathe themselves, and there are many other things which they have received to hold to: washings of cups, pitchers, bronze vessels, and couches.) ⁵ The Pharisees and the scribes asked him, "Why don't your disciples walk according to the tradition of the elders, but eat their bread with unwashed hands?" ⁶ He answered them, "Well did Isaiah prophesy of you hypocrites, as it is written, 'This people honors me with their lips, but their heart is far from me. ⁷ They worship me in vain, teaching as doctrines the commandments of men.'* ⁸ "For you set aside the commandment of God, and hold tightly to the tradition of men—the washing of pitchers and cups, and you do many other such things." ⁹ He said to them, "Full well do you reject the commandment of God, that you may keep your tradition. ¹⁰ For Moses said, 'Honor your father and your mother;'* and, 'He who speaks evil of father or mother, let him be put to death.'* ¹¹ But you say, 'If a man tells his father or his mother, "Whatever profit you might have received from me is Corban,"'[f] that is to say, given to God, ¹² "then you no longer allow him to do anything for his father or his mother, ¹³ making void the word of God by your tradition which you have handed down. You do many things like this." ¹⁴ He called the multitude to himself and said to them, "Hear me, all of you, and understand. ¹⁵ There is nothing from outside of the man that going into him can defile him; but the things which proceed out of the man are those that defile the man. ¹⁶ If anyone has ears to hear, let him hear!"[g] ¹⁷ When he had entered into a house away from the multitude, his disciples asked him about the parable. ¹⁸ He said to them, "Are you also without understanding? Don't you perceive that whatever goes into the man from outside can't defile him, ¹⁹ because it doesn't go into his heart, but into his stomach, then into the latrine, making all foods clean?"[h] ²⁰ He said, "That which proceeds out of the man, that defiles the man. ²¹ For from within, out of the hearts of men, proceed evil thoughts, adulteries, sexual sins, murders, thefts, ²² covetings, wickedness, deceit, lustful desires, an evil eye, blasphemy, pride, and foolishness. ²³ All these evil things come from within and defile the man." ²⁴ From there he arose and went away into the borders of Tyre and Sidon. He entered into a house and didn't want anyone to know it, but he couldn't escape notice. ²⁵ For a woman whose little daughter had an unclean spirit, having heard of him, came and fell down at his feet. ²⁶ Now the woman was a Greek, a Syrophoenician by race. She begged him that he would cast the demon out of her daughter. ²⁷ But Jesus said to her, "Let the children be filled first, for it is not appropriate to take the children's bread and throw it to the dogs." ²⁸ But she answered him, "Yes, Lord. Yet even the dogs under the table eat the children's crumbs." ²⁹ He said to her, "For this saying, go your way.

---

[a] 6:33 TR reads "The multitudes" instead of "They"
[b] 6:37 200 denarii was about 7 or 8 months wages for an agricultural laborer.
[c] 6:44 TR adds "about"

* 6:48 See Job 9:8
[d] 6:50 or, "I AM!"
[e] 6:56 or, tassel
* 7:7 Isaiah 29:13
* 7:10 Exodus 20:12; Deuteronomy 5:16

* 7:10 Exodus 21:17; Leviticus 20:9
[f] 7:11 Corban is a Hebrew word for an offering devoted to God.
[g] 7:16 NU omits verse 16.

[h] 7:19 NU ends Jesus' direct quote and question after "latrine", ending the verse with "Thus he declared all foods clean."

The demon has gone out of your daughter." ³⁰ She went away to her house, and found the child having been laid on the bed, with the demon gone out. ³¹ Again he departed from the borders of Tyre and Sidon, and came to the sea of Galilee through the middle of the region of Decapolis. ³² They brought to him one who was deaf and had an impediment in his speech. They begged him to lay his hand on him. ³³ He took him aside from the multitude privately and put his fingers into his ears; and he spat and touched his tongue. ³⁴ Looking up to heaven, he sighed, and said to him, "Ephphatha!" that is, "Be opened!" ³⁵ Immediately his ears were opened, and the impediment of his tongue was released, and he spoke clearly. ³⁶ He commanded them that they should tell no one, but the more he commanded them, so much the more widely they proclaimed it. ³⁷ They were astonished beyond measure, saying, "He has done all things well. He makes even the deaf hear and the mute speak!"

## 8

¹ In those days, when there was a very great multitude, and they had nothing to eat, Jesus called his disciples to himself and said to them, ² "I have compassion on the multitude, because they have stayed with me now three days and have nothing to eat. ³ If I send them away fasting to their home, they will faint on the way, for some of them have come a long way." ⁴ His disciples answered him, "From where could one satisfy these people with bread here in a deserted place?" ⁵ He asked them, "How many loaves do you have?" They said, "Seven." ⁶ He commanded the multitude to sit down on the ground, and he took the seven loaves. Having given thanks, he broke them and gave them to his disciples to serve, and they served the multitude. ⁷ They also had a few small fish. Having blessed them, he said to serve these also. ⁸ They ate and were filled. They took up seven baskets of broken pieces that were left over. ⁹ Those who had eaten were about four thousand. Then he sent them away. ¹⁰ Immediately he entered into the boat with his disciples and came into the region of Dalmanutha. ¹¹ The Pharisees came out and began to question him, seeking from him a sign from heaven and testing him. ¹² He sighed deeply in his spirit and said, "Why does this generationᵃ seek a sign? Most certainly I tell you, no sign will be given to this generation." ¹³ He left them, and again entering into the boat, departed to the other side. ¹⁴ They forgot to take bread; and they didn't have more than one loaf in the boat with them. ¹⁵ He warned them, saying, "Take heed: beware of the yeast of the Pharisees and the yeast of Herod." ¹⁶ They reasoned with one another, saying, "It's because we have no bread." ¹⁷ Jesus, perceiving it, said to them, "Why do you reason that it's because you have no bread? Don't you perceive yet or understand? Is your heart still hardened? ¹⁸ Having eyes, don't you see? Having ears, don't you hear? Don't you remember? ¹⁹ When I broke the five loaves among the five thousand, how many baskets full of broken pieces did you take up?" They told him, "Twelve." ²⁰ "When the seven loaves fed the four thousand, how many baskets full of broken pieces did you take up?" They told him, "Seven." ²¹ He asked them, "Don't you understand yet?" ²² He came to Bethsaida. They brought a blind man to him and begged him to touch him. ²³ He took hold of the blind man by the hand, and brought him out of the village. When he had spat on his eyes, and laid his hands on him, he asked him if he saw anything. ²⁴ He looked up, and said, "I see men, but I see them like walking trees." ²⁵ Then again he laid his hands on his eyes. He looked intently, and was restored, and saw everyone clearly. ²⁶ He sent him away to his house, saying, "Don't enter into the village, nor tell anyone in the village." ²⁷ Jesus went out, with his disciples, into the villages of Caesarea Philippi. On the way he asked his disciples, "Who do men say that I am?" ²⁸ They told him, "John the Baptizer, and others say Elijah, but others, one of the prophets." ²⁹ He said to them, "But who do you say that I am?" Peter answered, "You are the Christ." ³⁰ He commanded them that they should tell no one about him. ³¹ He began to teach them that the Son of Man must suffer many things, and be rejected by the elders, the chief priests, and the scribes, and be killed, and after three days rise again. ³² He spoke to them openly. Peter took him and began to rebuke him. ³³ But he, turning around and seeing his disciples, rebuked Peter, and said, "Get behind me, Satan! For you have in mind not the things of God, but the things of men." ³⁴ He called the multitude to himself with his disciples and said to them, "Whoever wants to come after me, let him deny himself, and take up his cross, and follow me. ³⁵ For whoever wants to save his life will lose it; and whoever will lose his life for my sake and the sake of the Good News will save it. ³⁶ For what does it profit a man to gain the whole world and forfeit his life? ³⁷ For what will a man give in exchange for his life? ³⁸ For whoever will be ashamed of me and of my words in this adulterous and sinful generation, the Son of Man also will be ashamed of him when he comes in his Father's glory with the holy angels."

## 9

¹ He said to them, "Most certainly I tell you, there are some standing here who will in no way taste death until they see God's Kingdom come with power." ² After six days Jesus took with him Peter, James, and John, and brought them up onto a high mountain privately by themselves, and he was changed into another form in front of them. ³ His clothing became glistening, exceedingly white, like snow, such as no launderer on earth can whiten them. ⁴ Elijah and Moses appeared to them, and they were talking with Jesus. ⁵ Peter answered Jesus, "Rabbi, it is good for us to be here. Let's make three tents: one for you, one for Moses, and one for Elijah." ⁶ For he didn't know what to say, for they were very afraid. ⁷ A cloud came, overshadowing them, and a voice came out of the cloud, "This is my beloved Son. Listen to him." ⁸ Suddenly looking around, they saw no one with them any more, except Jesus only. ⁹ As they were coming down from the mountain, he commanded them that they should tell no one what things they had seen, until after the Son of Man had risen from the dead. ¹⁰ They kept this saying to themselves, questioning what the "rising from the dead" meant. ¹¹ They asked him, saying, "Why do the scribes say that Elijah must come first?" ¹² He said to them, "Elijah indeed comes first, and restores all things. How is it written about the Son of Man, that he should suffer many things and be despised? ¹³ But I tell you that Elijah has come, and they have also done to him whatever they wanted to, even as it is written about him." ¹⁴ Coming to the disciples, he saw a great multitude around them, and scribes questioning them. ¹⁵ Immediately all the multitude, when they saw him, were greatly amazed, and running to him, greeted him. ¹⁶ He asked the scribes, "What are you asking them?" ¹⁷ One of the multitude answered, "Teacher, I brought to you my son, who has a mute spirit; ¹⁸ and wherever it seizes him, it throws him down; and he foams at the mouth, grinds his teeth, and becomes rigid. I asked your disciples to cast it out, and they weren't able." ¹⁹ He answered him, "Unbelieving generation, how long shall I be with you? How long shall I bear with you? Bring him to me." ²⁰ They brought him to him, and when he saw him, immediately the spirit convulsed him and he fell on the ground, wallowing and foaming at the mouth. ²¹ He asked his father, "How long has it been since this has been happening to him?" He said, "From childhood. ²² Often it has cast him both into the fire and into the water to destroy him. But if you can do anything, have compassion on us and help us." ²³ Jesus said to him, "If you can believe, all things are possible to him who believes." ²⁴ Immediately the father of the child cried out with tears, "I believe. Help my unbelief!" ²⁵ When Jesus saw that a multitude came running together, he rebuked the unclean spirit, saying to him, "You mute and deaf spirit, I command you, come out of him, and never enter him again!" ²⁶ After crying out and convulsing him greatly, it came out of him. The boy became like one dead, so much that most of them said, "He is dead." ²⁷ But Jesus took him by the hand and raised him up; and he arose. ²⁸ When he had come into the house, his disciples asked him privately, "Why couldn't we cast it out?" ²⁹ He said to them, "This kind can come out by nothing but by prayer and fasting." ³⁰ They went out from there and passed through Galilee. He didn't want anyone to know it, ³¹ for he was teaching his disciples, and said to them, "The Son of Man is being handed over to the hands of men, and they will kill him; and when he is killed, on the third day he will rise again." ³² But they didn't understand the saying, and were afraid to ask him. ³³ He came to Capernaum, and when he was in the house he asked them, "What were you arguing among yourselves on the way?" ³⁴ But they were silent, for they had disputed with one another on the way about who was the greatest. ³⁵ He sat down and called the twelve; and he said to them, "If any man wants to be first, he shall be last of all, and servant of all." ³⁶ He took a little child and set him in the middle of them. Taking him in his arms, he said to them, ³⁷ "Whoever receives one such little child in my name receives me; and whoever receives me, doesn't receive me, but him who sent me." ³⁸ John said to him, "Teacher, we saw someone who doesn't follow us casting out demons in your name; and we forbade him, because he doesn't follow us." ³⁹ But Jesus said, "Don't forbid him, for there is no one who will do a mighty work in my name and be able quickly to speak evil of me. ⁴⁰ For whoever is not against us is on our side. ⁴¹ For whoever will give you a cup of water to drink in my name because you are Christ's, most certainly I tell you, he will in no way lose his reward. ⁴² "Whoever will cause one of these little ones who believe in me to stumble, it would be better for him if he were thrown into the sea with a millstone hung around his neck. ⁴³ If your hand causes you to stumble, cut it off. It is better for you to enter into life maimed, rather than having your two hands to go into Gehenna, ᵇ into the unquenchable fire, ⁴⁴ 'where their worm doesn't die, and the fire is not quenched.' *ᶜ ⁴⁵ If

---

ᵃ *8:12* The word translated "generation" here (genea)

could also be translated "people", "race", or "family".

ᵇ *9:43* or, Hell
* *9:44* Isaiah 66:24

ᶜ *9:44* NU omits verse 44.

your foot causes you to stumble, cut it off. It is better for you to enter into life lame, rather than having your two feet to be cast into Gehenna, [a] into the fire that will never be quenched— **46** 'where their worm doesn't die, and the fire is not quenched.' [b] **47** If your eye causes you to stumble, throw it out. It is better for you to enter into God's Kingdom with one eye, rather than having two eyes to be cast into the Gehenna[c] of fire, **48** 'where their worm doesn't die, and the fire is not quenched.' * **49** For everyone will be salted with fire, and every sacrifice will be seasoned with salt. **50** Salt is good, but if the salt has lost its saltiness, with what will you season it? Have salt in yourselves, and be at peace with one another."

## 10

**1** He arose from there and came into the borders of Judea and beyond the Jordan. Multitudes came together to him again. As he usually did, he was again teaching them. **2** Pharisees came to him testing him, and asked him, "Is it lawful for a man to divorce his wife?" **3** He answered, "What did Moses command you?" **4** They said, "Moses allowed a certificate of divorce to be written, and to divorce her." **5** But Jesus said to them, "For your hardness of heart, he wrote you this commandment. **6** But from the beginning of the creation, God made them male and female.* **7** For this cause a man will leave his father and mother, and will join to his wife, **8** and the two will become one flesh,* so that they are no longer two, but one flesh. **9** What therefore God has joined together, let no man separate." **10** In the house, his disciples asked him again about the same matter. **11** He said to them, "Whoever divorces his wife and marries another commits adultery against her. **12** If a woman herself divorces her husband and marries another, she commits adultery." **13** They were bringing to him little children, that he should touch them, but the disciples rebuked those who were bringing them. **14** But when Jesus saw it, he was moved with indignation and said to them, "Allow the little children to come to me! Don't forbid them, for God's Kingdom belongs to such as these. **15** Most certainly I tell you, whoever will not receive God's Kingdom like a little child, he will in no way enter into it." **16** He took them in his arms and blessed them, laying his hands on them. **17** As he was going out into the way, one ran to him, knelt before him, and asked him, "Good Teacher, what shall I do that I may inherit eternal life?" **18** Jesus said to him, "Why do you call me good? No one is good except one—God. **19** You know the commandments: 'Do not murder,' 'Do not commit adultery,' 'Do not steal,' 'Do not give false testimony,' 'Do not defraud,' 'Honor your father and mother.'"* **20** He said to him, "Teacher, I have observed all these things from my youth." **21** Jesus looking at him loved him, and said to him, "One thing you lack. Go, sell whatever you have and give to the poor, and you will have treasure in heaven; and come, follow me, taking up the cross." **22** But his face fell at that saying, and he went away sorrowful, for he was one who had great possessions. **23** Jesus looked around and said to his disciples, "How difficult it is for those who have riches to enter into God's Kingdom!" **24** The disciples were amazed at his words. But Jesus answered again, "Children, how hard it is for those who trust in riches to enter into God's Kingdom! **25** It is easier for a camel to go through a needle's eye than for a rich man to enter into God's Kingdom." **26** They were exceedingly astonished, saying to him, "Then who can be saved?" **27** Jesus, looking at them, said, "With men it is impossible, but not with God, for all things are possible with God." **28** Peter began to tell him, "Behold, we have left all and have followed you." **29** Jesus said, "Most certainly I tell you, there is no one who has left house, or brothers, or sisters, or father, or mother, or wife, or children, or land, for my sake, and for the sake of the Good News, **30** but he will receive one hundred times more now in this time: houses, brothers, sisters, mothers, children, and land, with persecutions; and in the age to come eternal life. **31** But many who are first will be last, and the last first." **32** They were on the way, going up to Jerusalem; and Jesus was going in front of them, and they were amazed; and those who followed were afraid. He again took the twelve, and began to tell them the things that were going to happen to him. **33** "Behold, we are going up to Jerusalem. The Son of Man will be delivered to the chief priests and the scribes. They will condemn him to death, and will deliver him to the Gentiles. **34** They will mock him, spit on him, scourge him, and kill him. On the third day he will rise again." **35** James and John, the sons of Zebedee, came near to him, saying, "Teacher, we want you to do for us whatever we will ask." **36** He said to them, "What do you want me to do for you?" **37** They said to him, "Grant to us that we may sit, one at your right hand and one at your left hand, in your glory." **38** But Jesus said to them, "You don't know what you are asking. Are you able

to drink the cup that I drink, and to be baptized with the baptism that I am baptized with?" **39** They said to him, "We are able." Jesus said to them, "You shall indeed drink the cup that I drink, and you shall be baptized with the baptism that I am baptized with; **40** but to sit at my right hand and at my left hand is not mine to give, but for whom it has been prepared." **41** When the ten heard it, they began to be indignant toward James and John. **42** Jesus summoned them and said to them, "You know that they who are recognized as rulers over the nations lord it over them, and their great ones exercise authority over them. **43** But it shall not be so among you, but whoever wants to become great among you shall be your servant. **44** Whoever of you wants to become first among you shall be bondservant of all. **45** For the Son of Man also came not to be served but to serve, and to give his life as a ransom for many." **46** They came to Jericho. As he went out from Jericho with his disciples and a great multitude, the son of Timaeus, Bartimaeus, a blind beggar, was sitting by the road. **47** When he heard that it was Jesus the Nazarene, he began to cry out and say, "Jesus, you son of David, have mercy on me!" **48** Many rebuked him, that he should be quiet, but he cried out much more, "You son of David, have mercy on me!" **49** Jesus stood still and said, "Call him." They called the blind man, saying to him, "Cheer up! Get up. He is calling you!" **50** He, casting away his cloak, sprang up, and came to Jesus. **51** Jesus asked him, "What do you want me to do for you?" The blind man said to him, "Rabboni,[d] that I may see again." **52** Jesus said to him, "Go your way. Your faith has made you well." Immediately he received his sight and followed Jesus on the way.

## 11

**1** When they came near to Jerusalem, to Bethsphage[e] and Bethany, at the Mount of Olives, he sent two of his disciples **2** and said to them, "Go your way into the village that is opposite you. Immediately as you enter into it, you will find a young donkey tied, on which no one has sat. Untie him and bring him. **3** If anyone asks you, 'Why are you doing this?' say, 'The Lord needs him;' and immediately he will send him back here." **4** They went away, and found a young donkey tied at the door outside in the open street, and they untied him. **5** Some of those who stood there asked them, "What are you doing, untying the young donkey?" **6** They said to them just as Jesus had said, and they let them go. **7** They brought the young donkey to Jesus and threw their garments on it, and Jesus sat on it. **8** Many spread their garments on the way, and others were cutting down branches from the trees and spreading them on the road. **9** Those who went in front and those who followed cried out, "Hosanna![f] Blessed is he who comes in the name of the Lord!* **10** Blessed is the kingdom of our father David that is coming in the name of the Lord! Hosanna in the highest!" **11** Jesus entered into the temple in Jerusalem. When he had looked around at everything, it being now evening, he went out to Bethany with the twelve. **12** The next day, when they had come out from Bethany, he was hungry. **13** Seeing a fig tree afar off having leaves, he came to see if perhaps he might find anything on it. When he came to it, he found nothing but leaves, for it was not the season for figs. **14** Jesus told it, "May no one ever eat fruit from you again!" and his disciples heard it. **15** They came to Jerusalem, and Jesus entered into the temple and began to throw out those who sold and those who bought in the temple, and overthrew the money changers' tables and the seats of those who sold the doves. **16** He would not allow anyone to carry a container through the temple. **17** He taught, saying to them, "Isn't it written, 'My house will be called a house of prayer for all the nations'?* But you have made it a den of robbers!"* **18** The chief priests and the scribes heard it, and sought how they might destroy him. For they feared him, because all the multitude was astonished at his teaching. **19** When evening came, he went out of the city. **20** As they passed by in the morning, they saw the fig tree withered away from the roots. **21** Peter, remembering, said to him, "Rabbi, look! The fig tree which you cursed has withered away." **22** Jesus answered them, "Have faith in God. **23** For most certainly I tell you, whoever may tell this mountain, 'Be taken up and cast into the sea,' and doesn't doubt in his heart, but believes that what he says is happening, he shall have whatever he says. **24** Therefore I tell you, all things whatever you pray and ask for, believe that you have received them, and you shall have them. **25** Whenever you stand praying, forgive, if you have anything against anyone; so that your Father, who is in heaven, may also forgive you your transgressions. **26** But if you do not forgive, neither will your Father in heaven forgive your transgressions."[g] **27** They came again to Jerusalem, and as he was walking in the temple, the chief priests, the scribes, and the elders came to him, **28** and they began saying to him, "By what authority do you do these things? Or who gave you this

---

[a] *9:45* or, Hell
[b] *9:46* NU omits verse 46.
[c] *9:47* or, Hell
* 9:48 Isaiah 66:24
* 10:6 Genesis 1:27
* 10:8 Genesis 2:24

* 10:19 Exodus 20:12- 16; Deuteronomy 5:16- 20
[d] *10:51* Rabboni is a transliteration of the Hebrew word for "great teacher."

[e] *11:1* TR & NU read "Bethphage" instead of "Bethsphage"
[f] *11:9* "Hosanna" means "save us" or "help us, we pray".
* 11:9 Psalms 118:25- 26

* 11:17 Isaiah 56:7
* 11:17 Jeremiah 7:11
[g] *11:26* NU omits verse 26.

authority to do these things?" **29** Jesus said to them, "I will ask you one question. Answer me, and I will tell you by what authority I do these things. **30** The baptism of John—was it from heaven, or from men? Answer me." **31** They reasoned with themselves, saying, "If we should say, 'From heaven;' he will say, 'Why then did you not believe him?' **32** If we should say, 'From men'"—they feared the people, for all held John to really be a prophet. **33** They answered Jesus, "We don't know." Jesus said to them, "Neither will I tell you by what authority I do these things."

## 12

**1** He began to speak to them in parables. "A man planted a vineyard, put a hedge around it, dug a pit for the wine press, built a tower, rented it out to a farmer, and went into another country. **2** When it was time, he sent a servant to the farmer to get from the farmer his share of the fruit of the vineyard. **3** They took him, beat him, and sent him away empty. **4** Again, he sent another servant to them; and they threw stones at him, wounded him in the head, and sent him away shamefully treated. **5** Again he sent another, and they killed him, and many others, beating some, and killing some. **6** Therefore still having one, his beloved son, he sent him last to them, saying, 'They will respect my son.' **7** But those farmers said among themselves, 'This is the heir. Come, let's kill him, and the inheritance will be ours.' **8** They took him, killed him, and cast him out of the vineyard. **9** What therefore will the lord of the vineyard do? He will come and destroy the farmers, and will give the vineyard to others. **10** Haven't you even read this Scripture: 'The stone which the builders rejected was made the head of the corner. **11** This was from the Lord. It is marvelous in our eyes'?"* **12** They tried to seize him, but they feared the multitude; for they perceived that he spoke the parable against them. They left him and went away. **13** They sent some of the Pharisees and the Herodians to him, that they might trap him with words. **14** When they had come, they asked him, "Teacher, we know that you are honest, and don't defer to anyone; for you aren't partial to anyone, but truly teach the way of God. Is it lawful to pay taxes to Caesar, or not? **15** Shall we give, or shall we not give?" But he, knowing their hypocrisy, said to them, "Why do you test me? Bring me a denarius, that I may see it." **16** They brought it. He said to them, "Whose is this image and inscription?" They said to him, "Caesar's." **17** Jesus answered them, "Render to Caesar the things that are Caesar's, and to God the things that are God's." They marveled greatly at him. **18** Some Sadducees, who say that there is no resurrection, came to him. They asked him, saying, **19** "Teacher, Moses wrote to us, 'If a man's brother dies and leaves a wife behind him, and leaves no children, that his brother should take his wife and raise up offspring for his brother.' **20** There were seven brothers. The first took a wife, and dying left no offspring. **21** The second took her, and died, leaving no children behind him. The third likewise; **22** and the seven took her and left no children. Last of all the woman also died. **23** In the resurrection, when they rise, whose wife will she be of them? For the seven had her as a wife." **24** Jesus answered them, "Isn't this because you are mistaken, not knowing the Scriptures nor the power of God? **25** For when they will rise from the dead, they neither marry nor are given in marriage, but are like angels in heaven. **26** But about the dead, that they are raised, haven't you read in the book of Moses about the Bush, how God spoke to him, saying, 'I am the God of Abraham, the God of Isaac, and the God of Jacob'?* **27** He is not the God of the dead, but of the living. You are therefore badly mistaken." **28** One of the scribes came and heard them questioning together, and knowing that he had answered them well, asked him, "Which commandment is the greatest of all?" **29** Jesus answered, "The greatest is: 'Hear, Israel, the Lord our God, the Lord is one. **30** You shall love the Lord your God with all your heart, with all your soul, with all your mind, and with all your strength.'* This is the first commandment. **31** The second is like this: 'You shall love your neighbor as yourself.'* There is no other commandment greater than these." **32** The scribe said to him, "Truly, teacher, you have said well that he is one, and there is none other but he; **33** and to love him with all the heart, with all the understanding, all the soul, and with all the strength, and to love his neighbor as himself, is more important than all whole burnt offerings and sacrifices." **34** When Jesus saw that he answered wisely, he said to him, "You are not far from God's Kingdom." No one dared ask him any question after that. **35** Jesus responded, as he taught in the temple, "How is it that the scribes say that the Christ is the son of David? **36** For David himself said in the Holy Spirit, 'The Lord said to my Lord, "Sit at my right hand, until I make

your enemies the footstool of your feet."'* **37** Therefore David himself calls him Lord, so how can he be his son?" The common people heard him gladly. **38** In his teaching he said to them, "Beware of the scribes, who like to walk in long robes, and to get greetings in the marketplaces, **39** and to get the best seats in the synagogues and the best places at feasts, **40** those who devour widows' houses, and for a pretense make long prayers. These will receive greater condemnation." **41** Jesus sat down opposite the treasury and saw how the multitude cast money into the treasury. Many who were rich cast in much. **42** A poor widow came and she cast in two small brass coins,ᵃ which equal a quadrans coin.ᵇ **43** He called his disciples to himself and said to them, "Most certainly I tell you, this poor widow gave more than all those who are giving into the treasury, **44** for they all gave out of their abundance, but she, out of her poverty, gave all that she had to live on."

## 13

**1** As he went out of the temple, one of his disciples said to him, "Teacher, see what kind of stones and what kind of buildings!" **2** Jesus said to him, "Do you see these great buildings? There will not be left here one stone on another, which will not be thrown down." **3** As he sat on the Mount of Olives opposite the temple, Peter, James, John, and Andrew asked him privately, **4** "Tell us, when will these things be? What is the sign that these things are all about to be fulfilled?" **5** Jesus, answering, began to tell them, "Be careful that no one leads you astray. **6** For many will come in my name, saying, 'I am he!'ᶜ and will lead many astray. **7** "When you hear of wars and rumors of wars, don't be troubled. For those must happen, but the end is not yet. **8** For nation will rise against nation, and kingdom against kingdom. There will be earthquakes in various places. There will be famines and troubles. These things are the beginning of birth pains. **9** "But watch yourselves, for they will deliver you up to councils. You will be beaten in synagogues. You will stand before rulers and kings for my sake, for a testimony to them. **10** The Good News must first be preached to all the nations. **11** When they lead you away and deliver you up, don't be anxious beforehand or premeditate what you will say, but say whatever will be given you in that hour. For it is not you who speak, but the Holy Spirit. **12** "Brother will deliver up brother to death, and the father his child. Children will rise up against parents and cause them to be put to death. **13** You will be hated by all men for my name's sake, but he who endures to the end will be saved. **14** "But when you see the abomination of desolation,* spoken of by Daniel the prophet, standing where it ought not" (let the reader understand), "then let those who are in Judea flee to the mountains, **15** and let him who is on the housetop not go down, nor enter in, to take anything out of his house. **16** Let him who is in the field not return back to take his cloak. **17** But woe to those who are with child and to those who nurse babies in those days! **18** Pray that your flight won't be in the winter. **19** For in those days there will be oppression, such as there has not been the like from the beginning of the creation which God created until now, and never will be. **20** Unless the Lord had shortened the days, no flesh would have been saved; but for the sake of the chosen ones, whom he picked out, he shortened the days. **21** Then if anyone tells you, 'Look, here is the Christ!' or, 'Look, there!' don't believe it. **22** For false christs and false prophets will arise and will show signs and wonders, that they may lead astray, if possible, even the chosen ones. **23** But you watch. "Behold, I have told you all things beforehand. **24** But in those days, after that oppression, the sun will be darkened, the moon will not give its light, **25** the stars will be falling from the sky, and the powers that are in the heavens will be shaken.* **26** Then they will see the Son of Man coming in clouds with great power and glory. **27** Then he will send out his angels, and will gather together his chosen ones from the four winds, from the ends of the earth to the ends of the sky. **28** "Now from the fig tree, learn this parable. When the branch has now become tender and produces its leaves, you know that the summer is near; **29** even so you also, when you see these things coming to pass, know that it is near, at the doors. **30** Most certainly I say to you, this generationᵈ will not pass away until all these things happen. **31** Heaven and earth will pass away, but my words will not pass away. **32** "But of that day or that hour no one knows—not even the angels in heaven, nor the Son, but only the Father. **33** Watch, keep alert, and pray; for you don't know when the time is. **34** "It is like a man traveling to another country, having left his house and given authority to his servants, and to each one his work, and also commanded the doorkeeper to keep watch. **35** Watch therefore, for you don't know when the lord of the house is coming—whether at evening, or at midnight, or when the

---

* 12:11 Psalms 118:22-23
* 12:26 Exodus 3:6
* 12:30 Deuteronomy 6:4-5
* 12:31 Leviticus 19:18
* 12:36 Psalms 110:1
ᵃ *12:42* literally, lepta (or widow's mites). Lepta are very

small brass coins worth half a quadrans each, which is a quarter of the copper assarion. Lepta are worth less than 1% of an agricultural worker's daily wages.

ᵇ *12:42* A quadrans is a coin worth about 1/64 of a denarius. A denarius is about one day's wages for an agricultural laborer.
ᶜ *13:6* or, "I AM!"

* 13:14 Daniel 9:17; 11:31; 12:11
* 13:25 Isaiah 13:10; 34:4
ᵈ *13:30* The word translated "generation" (genea) could also be translated "race", "family", or "people".

rooster crows, or in the morning; **36** lest, coming suddenly, he might find you sleeping. **37** What I tell you, I tell all: Watch!"

## 14

**1** It was now two days before the Passover and the Feast of Unleavened Bread, and the chief priests and the scribes sought how they might seize him by deception and kill him. **2** For they said, "Not during the feast, because there might be a riot among the people." **3** While he was at Bethany, in the house of Simon the leper, as he sat at the table, a woman came having an alabaster jar of ointment of pure nard—very costly. She broke the jar and poured it over his head. **4** But there were some who were indignant among themselves, saying, "Why has this ointment been wasted? **5** For this might have been sold for more than three hundred denarii[a] and given to the poor." So they grumbled against her. **6** But Jesus said, "Leave her alone. Why do you trouble her? She has done a good work for me. **7** For you always have the poor with you, and whenever you want to, you can do them good; but you will not always have me. **8** She has done what she could. She has anointed my body beforehand for the burying. **9** Most certainly I tell you, wherever this Good News may be preached throughout the whole world, that which this woman has done will also be spoken of for a memorial of her." **10** Judas Iscariot, who was one of the twelve, went away to the chief priests, that he might deliver him to them. **11** They, when they heard it, were glad, and promised to give him money. He sought how he might conveniently deliver him. **12** On the first day of unleavened bread, when they sacrificed the Passover, his disciples asked him, "Where do you want us to go and prepare that you may eat the Passover?" **13** He sent two of his disciples and said to them, "Go into the city, and there a man carrying a pitcher of water will meet you. Follow him, **14** and wherever he enters in, tell the master of the house, 'The Teacher says, "Where is the guest room, where I may eat the Passover with my disciples?"' **15** He will himself show you a large upper room furnished and ready. Get ready for us there." **16** His disciples went out, and came into the city, and found things as he had said to them, and they prepared the Passover. **17** When it was evening he came with the twelve. **18** As they sat and were eating, Jesus said, "Most certainly I tell you, one of you will betray me—he who eats with me." **19** They began to be sorrowful, and to ask him one by one, "Surely not I?" And another said, "Surely not I?" **20** He answered them, "It is one of the twelve, he who dips with me in the dish. **21** For the Son of Man goes as it is written about him, but woe to that man by whom the Son of Man is betrayed! It would be better for that man if he had not been born." **22** As they were eating, Jesus took bread, and when he had blessed it, he broke it and gave to them, and said, "Take, eat. This is my body." **23** He took the cup, and when he had given thanks, he gave to them. They all drank of it. **24** He said to them, "This is my blood of the new covenant, which is poured out for many. **25** Most certainly I tell you, I will no more drink of the fruit of the vine until that day when I drink it anew in God's Kingdom." **26** When they had sung a hymn, they went out to the Mount of Olives. **27** Jesus said to them, "All of you will be made to stumble because of me tonight, for it is written, 'I will strike the shepherd, and the sheep will be scattered.'[*] **28** However, after I am raised up, I will go before you into Galilee." **29** But Peter said to him, "Although all will be offended, yet I will not." **30** Jesus said to him, "Most certainly I tell you that you today, even this night, before the rooster crows twice, you will deny me three times." **31** But he spoke all the more, "If I must die with you, I will not deny you." They all said the same thing. **32** They came to a place which was named Gethsemane. He said to his disciples, "Sit here while I pray." **33** He took with him Peter, James, and John, and began to be greatly troubled and distressed. **34** He said to them, "My soul is exceedingly sorrowful, even to death. Stay here and watch." **35** He went forward a little, and fell on the ground, and prayed that if it were possible, the hour might pass away from him. **36** He said, "Abba,[b] Father, all things are possible to you. Please remove this cup from me. However, not what I desire, but what you desire." **37** He came and found them sleeping, and said to Peter, "Simon, are you sleeping? Couldn't you watch one hour? **38** Watch and pray, that you may not enter into temptation. The spirit indeed is willing, but the flesh is weak." **39** Again he went away and prayed, saying the same words. **40** Again he returned and found them sleeping, for their eyes were very heavy; and they didn't know what to answer him. **41** He came the third time and said to them, "Sleep on now, and take your rest. It is enough. The hour has come. Behold, the Son of Man is betrayed into the hands of sinners. **42** Arise! Let's get going. Behold, he who betrays me is at hand." **43** Immediately, while he was still speaking, Judas, one of the twelve, came—and with him a multitude with swords and clubs, from the chief priests, the scribes, and the elders. **44** Now he who betrayed him had given them a sign, saying,

"Whomever I will kiss, that is he. Seize him, and lead him away safely." **45** When he had come, immediately he came to him and said, "Rabbi! Rabbi!" and kissed him. **46** They laid their hands on him and seized him. **47** But a certain one of those who stood by drew his sword and struck the servant of the high priest, and cut off his ear. **48** Jesus answered them, "Have you come out, as against a robber, with swords and clubs to seize me? **49** I was daily with you in the temple teaching, and you didn't arrest me. But this is so that the Scriptures might be fulfilled." **50** They all left him, and fled. **51** A certain young man followed him, having a linen cloth thrown around himself over his naked body. The young men grabbed him, **52** but he left the linen cloth and fled from them naked. **53** They led Jesus away to the high priest. All the chief priests, the elders, and the scribes came together with him. **54** Peter had followed him from a distance, until he came into the court of the high priest. He was sitting with the officers, and warming himself in the light of the fire. **55** Now the chief priests and the whole council sought witnesses against Jesus to put him to death, and found none. **56** For many gave false testimony against him, and their testimony didn't agree with each other. **57** Some stood up and gave false testimony against him, saying, **58**"We heard him say, 'I will destroy this temple that is made with hands, and in three days I will build another made without hands.'" **59** Even so, their testimony didn't agree. **60** The high priest stood up in the middle, and asked Jesus, "Have you no answer? What is it which these testify against you?" **61** But he stayed quiet, and answered nothing. Again the high priest asked him, "Are you the Christ, the Son of the Blessed?" **62** Jesus said, "I am. You will see the Son of Man sitting at the right hand of Power, and coming with the clouds of the sky." **63** The high priest tore his clothes and said, "What further need have we of witnesses? **64** You have heard the blasphemy! What do you think?" They all condemned him to be worthy of death. **65** Some began to spit on him, and to cover his face, and to beat him with fists, and to tell him, "Prophesy!" The officers struck him with the palms of their hands. **66** As Peter was in the courtyard below, one of the maids of the high priest came, **67** and seeing Peter warming himself, she looked at him and said, "You were also with the Nazarene, Jesus!" **68** But he denied it, saying, "I neither know nor understand what you are saying." He went out on the porch, and the rooster crowed. **69** The maid saw him and began again to tell those who stood by, "This is one of them." **70** But he again denied it. After a little while again those who stood by said to Peter, "You truly are one of them, for you are a Galilean, and your speech shows it." **71** But he began to curse and to swear, "I don't know this man of whom you speak!" **72** The rooster crowed the second time. Peter remembered the words that Jesus said to him, "Before the rooster crows twice, you will deny me three times." When he thought about that, he wept.

## 15

**1** Immediately in the morning the chief priests, with the elders, scribes, and the whole council, held a consultation, bound Jesus, carried him away, and delivered him up to Pilate. **2** Pilate asked him, "Are you the King of the Jews?" He answered, "So you say." **3** The chief priests accused him of many things. **4** Pilate again asked him, "Have you no answer? See how many things they testify against you!" **5** But Jesus made no further answer, so that Pilate marveled. **6** Now at the feast he used to release to them one prisoner, whomever they asked of him. **7** There was one called Barabbas, bound with his fellow insurgents, men who in the insurrection had committed murder. **8** The multitude, crying aloud, began to ask him to do as he always did for them. **9** Pilate answered them, saying, "Do you want me to release to you the King of the Jews?" **10** For he perceived that for envy the chief priests had delivered him up. **11** But the chief priests stirred up the multitude, that he should release Barabbas to them instead. **12** Pilate again asked them, "What then should I do to him whom you call the King of the Jews?" **13** They cried out again, "Crucify him!" **14** Pilate said to them, "Why, what evil has he done?" But they cried out exceedingly, "Crucify him!" **15** Pilate, wishing to please the multitude, released Barabbas to them, and handed over Jesus, when he had flogged him, to be crucified. **16** The soldiers led him away within the court, which is the Praetorium; and they called together the whole cohort. **17** They clothed him with purple; and weaving a crown of thorns, they put it on him. **18** They began to salute him, "Hail, King of the Jews!" **19** They struck his head with a reed and spat on him, and bowing their knees, did homage to him. **20** When they had mocked him, they took the purple cloak off him, and put his own garments on him. They led him out to crucify him. **21** They compelled one passing by, coming from the country, Simon of Cyrene, the father of Alexander and Rufus, to go with them that he might bear his cross. **22** They brought him to the place called Golgotha, which is, being interpreted, "The place of a skull." **23** They offered him

---

[a] *14:5* 300 denarii was about a year's wages for an agricultural laborer.

[*] 14:27 Zechariah 13:7
[b] *14:36* Abba is a Greek spelling for the Aramaic word

for "Father" or "Daddy" used in a familiar, respectful, and loving way.

wine mixed with myrrh to drink, but he didn't take it. [24]Crucifying him, they parted his garments among them, casting lots on them, what each should take. [25] It was the third hour[a] when they crucified him. [26] The superscription of his accusation was written over him: "THE KING OF THE JEWS." [27] With him they crucified two robbers, one on his right hand, and one on his left. [28] The Scripture was fulfilled which says, "He was counted with transgressors."[b] [29] Those who passed by blasphemed him, wagging their heads and saying, "Ha! You who destroy the temple and build it in three days, [30] save yourself, and come down from the cross!" [31] Likewise, also the chief priests mocking among themselves with the scribes said, "He saved others. He can't save himself. [32] Let the Christ, the King of Israel, now come down from the cross, that we may see and believe him."[c] Those who were crucified with him also insulted him. [33] When the sixth hour[d] had come, there was darkness over the whole land until the ninth hour.[e] [34] At the ninth hour Jesus cried with a loud voice, saying, "Eloi, Eloi, lama sabachthani?" which is, being interpreted, "My God, my God, why have you forsaken me?" [*] [35] Some of those who stood by, when they heard it, said, "Behold, he is calling Elijah." [36] One ran, and filling a sponge full of vinegar, put it on a reed and gave it to him to drink, saying, "Let him be. Let's see whether Elijah comes to take him down." [37] Jesus cried out with a loud voice, and gave up the spirit. [38] The veil of the temple was torn in two from the top to the bottom. [39] When the centurion, who stood by opposite him, saw that he cried out like this and breathed his last, he said, "Truly this man was the Son of God!" [40] There were also women watching from afar, among whom were both Mary Magdalene and Mary the mother of James the less and of Joses, and Salome; [41] who, when he was in Galilee, followed him and served him; and many other women who came up with him to Jerusalem. [42] When evening had now come, because it was the Preparation Day, that is, the day before the Sabbath, [43] Joseph of Arimathaea, a prominent council member who also himself was looking for God's Kingdom, came. He boldly went in to Pilate, and asked for Jesus' body. [44] Pilate was surprised to hear that he was already dead; and summoning the centurion, he asked him whether he had been dead long. [45] When he found out from the centurion, he granted the body to Joseph. [46] He bought a linen cloth, and taking him down, wound him in the linen cloth and laid him in a tomb which had been cut out of a rock. He rolled a stone against the door of the tomb. [47] Mary Magdalene and Mary the mother of Joses, saw where he was laid.

## 16

[1] When the Sabbath was past, Mary Magdalene, and Mary the mother of James, and Salome bought spices, that they might come and anoint him. [2] Very early on the first day of the week, they came to the tomb when the sun had risen. [3] They were saying among themselves, "Who will roll away the stone from the door of the tomb for us?" [4] for it was very big. Looking up, they saw that the stone was rolled back. [5] Entering into the tomb, they saw a young man sitting on the right side, dressed in a white robe; and they were amazed. [6] He said to them, "Don't be amazed. You seek Jesus, the Nazarene, who has been crucified. He has risen! He is not here. See the place where they laid him! [7] But go, tell his disciples and Peter, 'He goes before you into Galilee. There you will see him, as he said to you.'" [8] They went out,[f] and fled from the tomb, for trembling and astonishment had come on them. They said nothing to anyone; for they were afraid.[g] [9] [h]Now when he had risen early on the first day of the week, he appeared first to Mary Magdalene, from whom he had cast out seven demons. [10] She went and told those who had been with him, as they mourned and wept. [11] When they heard that he was alive and had been seen by her, they disbelieved. [12] After these things he was revealed in another form to two of them as they walked, on their way into the country. [13] They went away and told it to the rest. They didn't believe them, either. [14] Afterward he was revealed to the eleven themselves as they sat at the table; and he rebuked them for their unbelief and hardness of heart, because they didn't believe those who had seen him after he had risen. [15] He said to them, "Go into all the world and preach the Good News to the whole creation. [16] He who believes and is baptized will be saved; but he who disbelieves will be condemned. [17] These signs will accompany those who believe: in my name they will cast out demons; they will speak with new languages; [18] they will take up serpents; and if they drink any deadly thing, it will in no way hurt them; they will lay hands on the sick, and they will recover." [19] So then the Lord,[i] after he had spoken to them, was received up into heaven and sat down at the right hand of God. [20] They went out and preached everywhere, the Lord working with them and confirming the word by the signs that followed. Amen.

# The Good News According to Luke

## 1

[1] Since many have undertaken to set in order a narrative concerning those matters which have been fulfilled among us, [2] even as those who from the beginning were eyewitnesses and servants of the word delivered them to us, [3] it seemed good to me also, having traced the course of all things accurately from the first, to write to you in order, most excellent Theophilus; [4] that you might know the certainty concerning the things in which you were instructed. [5] There was in the days of Herod, the king of Judea, a certain priest named Zacharias, of the priestly division of Abijah. He had a wife of the daughters of Aaron, and her name was Elizabeth. [6] They were both righteous before God, walking blamelessly in all the commandments and ordinances of the Lord. [7] But they had no child, because Elizabeth was barren, and they both were well advanced in years. [8] Now while he executed the priest's office before God in the order of his division [9] according to the custom of the priest's office, his lot was to enter into the temple of the Lord and burn incense. [10] The whole multitude of the people were praying outside at the hour of incense. [11] An angel of the Lord appeared to him, standing on the right side of the altar of incense. [12] Zacharias was troubled when he saw him, and fear fell upon him. [13] But the angel said to him, "Don't be afraid, Zacharias, because your request has been heard. Your wife, Elizabeth, will bear you a son, and you shall call his name John. [14] You will have joy and gladness, and many will rejoice at his birth. [15] For he will be great in the sight of the Lord, and he will drink no wine nor strong drink. He will be filled with the Holy Spirit, even from his mother's womb. [16] He will turn many of the children of Israel to the Lord their God. [17] He will go before him in the spirit and power of Elijah, 'to turn the hearts of the fathers to the children,'[*] and the disobedient to the wisdom of the just; to prepare a people prepared for the Lord." [18] Zacharias said to the angel, "How can I be sure of this? For I am an old man, and my wife is well advanced in years." [19] The angel answered him, "I am Gabriel, who stands in the presence of God. I was sent to speak to you and to bring you this good news. [20] Behold,[i] you will be silent and not able to speak until the day that these things will happen, because you didn't believe my words, which will be fulfilled in their proper time." [21] The people were waiting for Zacharias, and they marveled that he delayed in the temple. [22] When he came out, he could not speak to them. They perceived that he had seen a vision in the temple. He continued making signs to them, and remained mute. [23] When the days of his service were fulfilled, he departed to his house. [24] After these days Elizabeth his wife conceived, and she hid herself five months, saying, [25]"Thus has the Lord done to me in the days in which he looked at me, to take away my reproach among men." [26] Now in the sixth month, the angel Gabriel was sent from God to a city of Galilee named Nazareth, [27] to a virgin pledged to be married to a man whose name was Joseph, of David's house. The virgin's name was Mary. [28] Having come in, the angel said to her, "Rejoice, you highly favored one! The Lord is with you. Blessed are you among women!" [29] But when she saw him, she was greatly troubled at the saying, and considered what kind of salutation this might be. [30] The angel said to her, "Don't be afraid, Mary, for you have found favor with God. [31] Behold, you will conceive in your womb and give birth to a son, and shall name him 'Jesus.' [32] He will be great and will be called the Son of the Most High. The Lord God will give him the throne of his father David, [33] and he will reign over the house of Jacob forever. There will be no end to his Kingdom." [34] Mary said to the angel, "How can this be, seeing I am a virgin?" [35] The angel answered her, "The Holy Spirit will come on you, and the power of the Most High will overshadow you. Therefore also the holy one who is born from you will be called the Son of God. [36] Behold, Elizabeth your relative also has conceived a son in her old age; and this is the sixth month with her who was called barren. [37] For nothing spoken by God is impossible."[k] [38] Mary said,

---

[a] 15:25 9:00 a.m.
[b] 15:28 NU omits verse 28.
[c] 15:32 TR omits "him"
[d] 15:33 or, noon
[e] 15:33 3:00 p.m.
[*] 15:34 Psalms 22:1
[f] 16:8 TR adds "quickly"
[g] 16:8 One isolated manuscript omits verses 9- 20 but adds this "short ending of Mark" to the

end of verse 8: They told all that had been commanded them briefly to those around Peter. After that, Jesus himself sent them out, from east to west, with the sacred and imperishable proclamation of eternal salvation.
[h] 16:9 NU includes the text of verses 9- 20, but mentions in a

footnote that a few manuscripts omitted it. The translators of the World English Bible regard Mark 16:9- 20 as reliable based on an overwhelming majority of textual evidence, including not only the authoritative Greek Majority Text New Testament, but also the TR and many of

the manuscripts cited in the NU text.
[i] 16:19 NU adds "Jesus"
[*] 1:17 Malachi 4:6
[j] 1:20 "Behold", from "ἰδού", means look at, take notice, observe, see, or gaze at. It is often used as an interjection.
[k] 1:37 or, "For everything spoken by God is possible."

"Behold, the servant of the Lord; let it be done to me according to your word." Then the angel departed from her. <sup>39</sup> Mary arose in those days and went into the hill country with haste, into a city of Judah, <sup>40</sup> and entered into the house of Zacharias and greeted Elizabeth. <sup>41</sup> When Elizabeth heard Mary's greeting, the baby leaped in her womb; and Elizabeth was filled with the Holy Spirit. <sup>42</sup> She called out with a loud voice and said, "Blessed are you among women, and blessed is the fruit of your womb! <sup>43</sup> Why am I so favored, that the mother of my Lord should come to me? <sup>44</sup> For behold, when the voice of your greeting came into my ears, the baby leaped in my womb for joy! <sup>45</sup> Blessed is she who believed, for there will be a fulfillment of the things which have been spoken to her from the Lord!" <sup>46</sup> Mary said, "My soul magnifies the Lord. <sup>47</sup> My spirit has rejoiced in God my Savior, <sup>48</sup> for he has looked at the humble state of his servant. For behold, from now on, all generations will call me blessed. <sup>49</sup> For he who is mighty has done great things for me. Holy is his name. <sup>50</sup> His mercy is for generations and generations on those who fear him. <sup>51</sup> He has shown strength with his arm. He has scattered the proud in the imagination of their hearts. <sup>52</sup> He has put down princes from their thrones, and has exalted the lowly. <sup>53</sup> He has filled the hungry with good things. He has sent the rich away empty. <sup>54</sup> He has given help to Israel, his servant, that he might remember mercy, <sup>55</sup> as he spoke to our fathers, to Abraham and his offspring[a] forever." <sup>56</sup> Mary stayed with her about three months, and then returned to her house. <sup>57</sup> Now the time that Elizabeth should give birth was fulfilled, and she gave birth to a son. <sup>58</sup> Her neighbors and her relatives heard that the Lord had magnified his mercy toward her, and they rejoiced with her. <sup>59</sup> On the eighth day, they came to circumcise the child; and they would have called him Zacharias, after the name of his father. <sup>60</sup> His mother answered, "Not so; but he will be called John." <sup>61</sup> They said to her, "There is no one among your relatives who is called by this name." <sup>62</sup> They made signs to his father, what he would have him called. <sup>63</sup> He asked for a writing tablet, and wrote, "His name is John." They all marveled. <sup>64</sup> His mouth was opened immediately and his tongue freed, and he spoke, blessing God. <sup>65</sup> Fear came on all who lived around them, and all these sayings were talked about throughout all the hill country of Judea. <sup>66</sup> All who heard them laid them up in their heart, saying, "What then will this child be?" The hand of the Lord was with him. <sup>67</sup> His father Zacharias was filled with the Holy Spirit, and prophesied, saying, <sup>68</sup>"Blessed be the Lord, the God of Israel, for he has visited and redeemed his people; <sup>69</sup> and has raised up a horn of salvation for us in the house of his servant David <sup>70</sup>(as he spoke by the mouth of his holy prophets who have been from of old), <sup>71</sup> salvation from our enemies and from the hand of all who hate us; <sup>72</sup> to show mercy toward our fathers, to remember his holy covenant, <sup>73</sup> the oath which he swore to Abraham our father, <sup>74</sup> to grant to us that we, being delivered out of the hand of our enemies, should serve him without fear, <sup>75</sup> in holiness and righteousness before him all the days of our life. <sup>76</sup> And you, child, will be called a prophet of the Most High; for you will go before the face of the Lord to prepare his ways, <sup>77</sup> to give knowledge of salvation to his people by the remission of their sins, <sup>78</sup> because of the tender mercy of our God, by which the dawn from on high will visit us, <sup>79</sup> to shine on those who sit in darkness and the shadow of death; to guide our feet into the way of peace." <sup>80</sup> The child was growing and becoming strong in spirit, and was in the desert until the day of his public appearance to Israel.

## 2

<sup>1</sup> Now in those days, a decree went out from Caesar Augustus that all the world should be enrolled. <sup>2</sup> This was the first enrollment made when Quirinius was governor of Syria. <sup>3</sup> All went to enroll themselves, everyone to his own city. <sup>4</sup> Joseph also went up from Galilee, out of the city of Nazareth, into Judea, to David's city, which is called Bethlehem, because he was of the house and family of David, <sup>5</sup> to enroll himself with Mary, who was pledged to be married to him as wife, being pregnant. <sup>6</sup> While they were there, the day had come for her to give birth. <sup>7</sup> She gave birth to her firstborn son. She wrapped him in bands of cloth and laid him in a feeding trough, because there was no room for them in the inn. <sup>8</sup> There were shepherds in the same country staying in the field, and keeping watch by night over their flock. <sup>9</sup> Behold, an angel of the Lord stood by them, and the glory of the Lord shone around them, and they were terrified. <sup>10</sup> The angel said to them, "Don't be afraid, for behold, I bring you good news of great joy which will be to all the people. <sup>11</sup> For there is born to you today, in David's city, a Savior, who is Christ[b] the Lord. <sup>12</sup> This is the sign to you: you will find a baby wrapped in strips of cloth, lying in a feeding trough." <sup>13</sup> Suddenly, there was with the angel a multitude of the heavenly army praising God and saying, <sup>14</sup>"Glory to God in the highest, on earth peace,

good will toward men." <sup>15</sup> When the angels went away from them into the sky, the shepherds said to one another, "Let's go to Bethlehem, now, and see this thing that has happened, which the Lord has made known to us." <sup>16</sup> They came with haste and found both Mary and Joseph, and the baby was lying in the feeding trough. <sup>17</sup> When they saw it, they publicized widely the saying which was spoken to them about this child. <sup>18</sup> All who heard it wondered at the things which were spoken to them by the shepherds. <sup>19</sup> But Mary kept all these sayings, pondering them in her heart. <sup>20</sup> The shepherds returned, glorifying and praising God for all the things that they had heard and seen, just as it was told them. <sup>21</sup> When eight days were fulfilled for the circumcision of the child, his name was called Jesus, which was given by the angel before he was conceived in the womb. <sup>22</sup> When the days of their purification according to the law of Moses were fulfilled, they brought him up to Jerusalem to present him to the Lord <sup>23</sup>(as it is written in the law of the Lord, "Every male who opens the womb shall be called holy to the Lord"),* <sup>24</sup> and to offer a sacrifice according to that which is said in the law of the Lord, "A pair of turtledoves, or two young pigeons."* <sup>25</sup> Behold, there was a man in Jerusalem whose name was Simeon. This man was righteous and devout, looking for the consolation of Israel, and the Holy Spirit was on him. <sup>26</sup> It had been revealed to him by the Holy Spirit that he should not see death before he had seen the Lord's Christ.[c] <sup>27</sup> He came in the Spirit into the temple. When the parents brought in the child, Jesus, that they might do concerning him according to the custom of the law, <sup>28</sup> then he received him into his arms and blessed God, and said, <sup>29</sup>"Now you are releasing your servant, Master, according to your word, in peace; <sup>30</sup> for my eyes have seen your salvation, <sup>31</sup> which you have prepared before the face of all peoples; <sup>32</sup> a light for revelation to the nations, and the glory of your people Israel." <sup>33</sup> Joseph and his mother were marveling at the things which were spoken concerning him. <sup>34</sup> Simeon blessed them, and said to Mary, his mother, "Behold, this child is appointed for the falling and the rising of many in Israel, and for a sign which is spoken against. <sup>35</sup> Yes, a sword will pierce through your own soul, that the thoughts of many hearts may be revealed." <sup>36</sup> There was one Anna, a prophetess, the daughter of Phanuel, of the tribe of Asher (she was of a great age, having lived with a husband seven years from her virginity, <sup>37</sup> and she had been a widow for about eighty-four years), who didn't depart from the temple, worshiping with fastings and petitions night and day. <sup>38</sup> Coming up at that very hour, she gave thanks to the Lord, and spoke of him to all those who were looking for redemption in Jerusalem. <sup>39</sup> When they had accomplished all things that were according to the law of the Lord, they returned into Galilee, to their own city, Nazareth. <sup>40</sup> The child was growing, and was becoming strong in spirit, being filled with wisdom, and the grace of God was upon him. <sup>41</sup> His parents went every year to Jerusalem at the feast of the Passover. <sup>42</sup> When he was twelve years old, they went up to Jerusalem according to the custom of the feast; <sup>43</sup> and when they had fulfilled the days, as they were returning, the boy Jesus stayed behind in Jerusalem. Joseph and his mother didn't know it, <sup>44</sup> but supposing him to be in the company, they went a day's journey; and they looked for him among their relatives and acquaintances. <sup>45</sup> When they didn't find him, they returned to Jerusalem, looking for him. <sup>46</sup> After three days they found him in the temple, sitting in the middle of the teachers, both listening to them and asking them questions. <sup>47</sup> All who heard him were amazed at his understanding and his answers. <sup>48</sup> When they saw him, they were astonished; and his mother said to him, "Son, why have you treated us this way? Behold, your father and I were anxiously looking for you." <sup>49</sup> He said to them, "Why were you looking for me? Didn't you know that I must be in my Father's house?" <sup>50</sup> They didn't understand the saying which he spoke to them. <sup>51</sup> And he went down with them and came to Nazareth. He was subject to them, and his mother kept all these sayings in her heart. <sup>52</sup> And Jesus increased in wisdom and stature, and in favor with God and men.

## 3

<sup>1</sup> Now in the fifteenth year of the reign of Tiberius Caesar, Pontius Pilate being governor of Judea, and Herod being tetrarch of Galilee, and his brother Philip tetrarch of the region of Ituraea and Trachonitis, and Lysanias tetrarch of Abilene, <sup>2</sup> during the high priesthood of Annas and Caiaphas, the word of God came to John, the son of Zacharias, in the wilderness. <sup>3</sup> He came into all the region around the Jordan, preaching the baptism of repentance for remission of sins. <sup>4</sup> As it is written in the book of the words of Isaiah the prophet, "The voice of one crying in the wilderness, 'Make ready the way of the Lord. Make his paths straight. <sup>5</sup> Every valley will be filled. Every mountain and hill will be brought low. The crooked will become straight, and the rough ways smooth. <sup>6</sup> All flesh will see God's salvation.'"* <sup>7</sup> He said therefore

[a] *1:55* or, seed
[b] *2:11* "Christ" means "Anointed One".
* 2:23 Exodus 13:2,12
* 2:24 Leviticus 12:8
[c] *2:26* "Christ" (Greek) and "Messiah" (Hebrew) both mean "Anointed One"
* 3:6 Isaiah 40:3-5

to the multitudes who went out to be baptized by him, "You offspring of vipers, who warned you to flee from the wrath to come? [8] Therefore produce fruits worthy of repentance, and don't begin to say among yourselves, 'We have Abraham for our father;' for I tell you that God is able to raise up children to Abraham from these stones! [9] Even now the ax also lies at the root of the trees. Every tree therefore that doesn't produce good fruit is cut down and thrown into the fire." [10] The multitudes asked him, "What then must we do?" [11] He answered them, "He who has two coats, let him give to him who has none. He who has food, let him do likewise." [12] Tax collectors also came to be baptized, and they said to him, "Teacher, what must we do?" [13] He said to them, "Collect no more than that which is appointed to you." [14] Soldiers also asked him, saying, "What about us? What must we do?" He said to them, "Extort from no one by violence, neither accuse anyone wrongfully. Be content with your wages." [15] As the people were in expectation, and all men reasoned in their hearts concerning John, whether perhaps he was the Christ, [16] John answered them all, "I indeed baptize you with water, but he comes who is mightier than I, the strap of whose sandals I am not worthy to loosen. He will baptize you in the Holy Spirit and fire. [17] His winnowing fan is in his hand, and he will thoroughly cleanse his threshing floor, and will gather the wheat into his barn; but he will burn up the chaff with unquenchable fire." [18] Then with many other exhortations he preached good news to the people, [19] but Herod the tetrarch,[a] being reproved by him for Herodias, his brother's[b] wife, and for all the evil things which Herod had done, [20] added this also to them all, that he shut up John in prison. [21] Now when all the people were baptized, Jesus also had been baptized and was praying. The sky was opened, [22] and the Holy Spirit descended in a bodily form like a dove on him; and a voice came out of the sky, saying "You are my beloved Son. In you I am well pleased." [23] Jesus himself, when he began to teach, was about thirty years old, being the son (as was supposed) of Joseph, the son of Heli, [24] the son of Matthat, the son of Levi, the son of Melchi, the son of Jannai, the son of Joseph, [25] the son of Mattathias, the son of Amos, the son of Nahum, the son of Esli, the son of Naggai, [26] the son of Maath, the son of Mattathias, the son of Semein, the son of Joseph, the son of Judah, [27] the son of Joanan, the son of Rhesa, the son of Zerubbabel, the son of Shealtiel, the son of Neri, [28] the son of Melchi, the son of Addi, the son of Cosam, the son of Elmodam, the son of Er, [29] the son of Jose, the son of Eliezer, the son of Jorim, the son of Matthat, the son of Levi, [30] the son of Simeon, the son of Judah, the son of Joseph, the son of Jonan, the son of Eliakim, [31] the son of Melea, the son of Menan, the son of Mattatha, the son of Nathan, the son of David, [32] the son of Jesse, the son of Obed, the son of Boaz, the son of Salmon, the son of Nahshon, [33] the son of Amminadab, the son of Aram,[c] the son of Hezron, the son of Perez, the son of Judah, [34] the son of Jacob, the son of Isaac, the son of Abraham, the son of Terah, the son of Nahor, [35] the son of Serug, the son of Reu, the son of Peleg, the son of Eber, the son of Shelah, [36] the son of Cainan, the son of Arphaxad, the son of Shem, the son of Noah, the son of Lamech, [37] the son of Methuselah, the son of Enoch, the son of Jared, the son of Mahalaleel, the son of Cainan, [38] the son of Enos, the son of Seth, the son of Adam, the son of God.

## 4

[1] Jesus, full of the Holy Spirit, returned from the Jordan and was led by the Spirit into the wilderness [2] for forty days, being tempted by the devil. He ate nothing in those days. Afterward, when they were completed, he was hungry. [3] The devil said to him, "If you are the Son of God, command this stone to become bread." [4] Jesus answered him, saying, "It is written, 'Man shall not live by bread alone, but by every word of God.'"[*] [5] The devil, leading him up on a high mountain, showed him all the kingdoms of the world in a moment of time. [6] The devil said to him, "I will give you all this authority and their glory, for it has been delivered to me, and I give it to whomever I want. [7] If you therefore will worship before me, it will all be yours." [8] Jesus answered him, "Get behind me, Satan! For it is written, 'You shall worship the Lord your God, and you shall serve him only.'"[*] [9] He led him to Jerusalem and set him on the pinnacle of the temple, and said to him, "If you are the Son of God, cast yourself down from here, [10] for it is written, 'He will put his angels in charge of you, to guard you;' [11] and, 'On their hands they will bear you up, lest perhaps you dash your foot against a stone.'"[*] [12] Jesus answering, said to him, "It has been said, 'You shall not tempt the Lord your God.'"[*] [13] When the devil had completed every temptation, he departed from him until another time. [14] Jesus returned in the power of the Spirit into Galilee, and news about him spread through all the surrounding area. [15] He taught in their

synagogues, being glorified by all. [16] He came to Nazareth, where he had been brought up. He entered, as was his custom, into the synagogue on the Sabbath day, and stood up to read. [17] The book of the prophet Isaiah was handed to him. He opened the book, and found the place where it was written, [18] "The Spirit of the Lord is on me, because he has anointed me to preach good news to the poor. He has sent me to heal the broken hearted,[d] to proclaim release to the captives, recovering of sight to the blind, to deliver those who are crushed, [19] and to proclaim the acceptable year of the Lord."[*] [20] He closed the book, gave it back to the attendant, and sat down. The eyes of all in the synagogue were fastened on him. [21] He began to tell them, "Today, this Scripture has been fulfilled in your hearing." [22] All testified about him and wondered at the gracious words which proceeded out of his mouth; and they said, "Isn't this Joseph's son?" [23] He said to them, "Doubtless you will tell me this proverb, 'Physician, heal yourself! Whatever we have heard done at Capernaum, do also here in your hometown.'" [24] He said, "Most certainly I tell you, no prophet is acceptable in his hometown. [25] But truly I tell you, there were many widows in Israel in the days of Elijah, when the sky was shut up three years and six months, when a great famine came over all the land. [26] Elijah was sent to none of them, except to Zarephath, in the land of Sidon, to a woman who was a widow. [27] There were many lepers in Israel in the time of Elisha the prophet, yet not one of them was cleansed, except Naaman, the Syrian." [28] They were all filled with wrath in the synagogue as they heard these things. [29] They rose up, threw him out of the city, and led him to the brow of the hill that their city was built on, that they might throw him off the cliff. [30] But he, passing through the middle of them, went his way. [31] He came down to Capernaum, a city of Galilee. He was teaching them on the Sabbath day, [32] and they were astonished at his teaching, for his word was with authority. [33] In the synagogue there was a man who had a spirit of an unclean demon; and he cried out with a loud voice, [34] saying, "Ah! what have we to do with you, Jesus of Nazareth? Have you come to destroy us? I know who you are: the Holy One of God!" [35] Jesus rebuked him, saying, "Be silent and come out of him!" When the demon had thrown him down in the middle of them, he came out of him, having done him no harm. [36] Amazement came on all and they spoke together, one with another, saying, "What is this word? For with authority and power he commands the unclean spirits, and they come out!" [37] News about him went out into every place of the surrounding region. [38] He rose up from the synagogue and entered into Simon's house. Simon's mother-in-law was afflicted with a great fever, and they begged him to help her. [39] He stood over her and rebuked the fever, and it left her. Immediately she rose up and served them. [40] When the sun was setting, all those who had any sick with various diseases brought them to him; and he laid his hands on every one of them, and healed them. [41] Demons also came out of many, crying out and saying, "You are the Christ, the Son of God!" Rebuking them, he didn't allow them to speak, because they knew that he was the Christ. [42] When it was day, he departed and went into an uninhabited place and the multitudes looked for him, and came to him, and held on to him, so that he wouldn't go away from them. [43] But he said to them, "I must preach the good news of God's Kingdom to the other cities also. For this reason I have been sent." [44] He was preaching in the synagogues of Galilee.

## 5

[1] Now while the multitude pressed on him and heard the word of God, he was standing by the lake of Gennesaret. [2] He saw two boats standing by the lake, but the fishermen had gone out of them and were washing their nets. [3] He entered into one of the boats, which was Simon's, and asked him to put out a little from the land. He sat down and taught the multitudes from the boat. [4] When he had finished speaking, he said to Simon, "Put out into the deep and let down your nets for a catch." [5] Simon answered him, "Master, we worked all night and caught nothing; but at your word I will let down the net." [6] When they had done this, they caught a great multitude of fish, and their net was breaking. [7] They beckoned to their partners in the other boat, that they should come and help them. They came and filled both boats, so that they began to sink. [8] But Simon Peter, when he saw it, fell down at Jesus' knees, saying, "Depart from me, for I am a sinful man, Lord." [9] For he was amazed, and all who were with him, at the catch of fish which they had caught; [10] and so also were James and John, sons of Zebedee, who were partners with Simon. Jesus said to Simon, "Don't be afraid. From now on you will be catching people alive." [11] When they had brought their boats to land, they left everything, and followed him. [12] While he was in one of the cities, behold, there was a man full of leprosy. When he saw Jesus, he fell on his face and begged him, saying, "Lord, if you want to, you

---

[a] 3:19 a tetrarch is one of four governors of a province
[b] 3:19 TR reads "brother Philip's" instead of "brother's"

[c] 3:33 NU reads "Admin, the son of Arni" instead of "Aram"
[*] 4:4 Deuteronomy 8:3
[*] 4:8 Deuteronomy 6:13

[*] 4:11 Psalms 91:11- 12
[*] 4:12 Deuteronomy 6:16
[d] 4:18 NU omits "to heal the broken hearted"

[*] 4:19 Isaiah 61:1- 2

can make me clean." ¹³ He stretched out his hand and touched him, saying, "I want to. Be made clean." Immediately the leprosy left him. ¹⁴ He commanded him to tell no one, "But go your way and show yourself to the priest, and offer for your cleansing according to what Moses commanded, for a testimony to them." ¹⁵ But the report concerning him spread much more, and great multitudes came together to hear and to be healed by him of their infirmities. ¹⁶ But he withdrew himself into the desert and prayed. ¹⁷ On one of those days, he was teaching; and there were Pharisees and teachers of the law sitting by who had come out of every village of Galilee, Judea, and Jerusalem. The power of the Lord was with him to heal them. ¹⁸ Behold, men brought a paralyzed man on a cot, and they sought to bring him in to lay before Jesus. ¹⁹ Not finding a way to bring him in because of the multitude, they went up to the housetop and let him down through the tiles with his cot into the middle before Jesus. ²⁰ Seeing their faith, he said to him, "Man, your sins are forgiven you." ²¹ The scribes and the Pharisees began to reason, saying, "Who is this who speaks blasphemies? Who can forgive sins, but God alone?" ²² But Jesus, perceiving their thoughts, answered them, "Why are you reasoning so in your hearts? ²³ Which is easier to say, 'Your sins are forgiven you,' or to say, 'Arise and walk'? ²⁴ But that you may know that the Son of Man has authority on earth to forgive sins," he said to the paralyzed man, "I tell you, arise, take up your cot, and go to your house." ²⁵ Immediately he rose up before them, and took up that which he was laying on, and departed to his house, glorifying God. ²⁶ Amazement took hold on all, and they glorified God. They were filled with fear, saying, "We have seen strange things today." ²⁷ After these things he went out and saw a tax collector named Levi sitting at the tax office, and said to him, "Follow me!" ²⁸ He left everything, and rose up and followed him. ²⁹ Levi made a great feast for him in his house. There was a great crowd of tax collectors and others who were reclining with them. ³⁰ Their scribes and the Pharisees murmured against his disciples, saying, "Why do you eat and drink with the tax collectors and sinners?" ³¹ Jesus answered them, "Those who are healthy have no need for a physician, but those who are sick do. ³² I have not come to call the righteous, but sinners, to repentance." ³³ They said to him, "Why do John's disciples often fast and pray, likewise also the disciples of the Pharisees, but yours eat and drink?" ³⁴ He said to them, "Can you make the friends of the bridegroom fast while the bridegroom is with them? ³⁵ But the days will come when the bridegroom will be taken away from them. Then they will fast in those days." ³⁶ He also told a parable to them. "No one puts a piece from a new garment on an old garment, or else he will tear the new, and also the piece from the new will not match the old. ³⁷ No one puts new wine into old wine skins, or else the new wine will burst the skins, and it will be spilled and the skins will be destroyed. ³⁸ But new wine must be put into fresh wine skins, and both are preserved. ³⁹ No man having drunk old wine immediately desires new, for he says, 'The old is better.'"

# 6

¹ Now on the second Sabbath after the first, he was going through the grain fields. His disciples plucked the heads of grain and ate, rubbing them in their hands. ² But some of the Pharisees said to them, "Why do you do that which is not lawful to do on the Sabbath day?" ³ Jesus, answering them, said, "Haven't you read what David did when he was hungry, he and those who were with him, ⁴ how he entered into God's house, and took and ate the show bread, and gave also to those who were with him, which is not lawful to eat except for the priests alone?" ⁵ He said to them, "The Son of Man is lord of the Sabbath." ⁶ It also happened on another Sabbath that he entered into the synagogue and taught. There was a man there, and his right hand was withered. ⁷ The scribes and the Pharisees watched him, to see whether he would heal on the Sabbath, that they might find an accusation against him. ⁸ But he knew their thoughts; and he said to the man who had the withered hand, "Rise up and stand in the middle." He arose and stood. ⁹ Then Jesus said to them, "I will ask you something: Is it lawful on the Sabbath to do good, or to do harm? To save a life, or to kill?" ¹⁰ He looked around at them all, and said to the man, "Stretch out your hand." He did, and his hand was restored as sound as the other. ¹¹ But they were filled with rage, and talked with one another about what they might do to Jesus. ¹² In these days, he went out to the mountain to pray, and he continued all night in prayer to God. ¹³ When it was day, he called his disciples, and from them he chose twelve, whom he also named apostles: ¹⁴ Simon, whom he also named Peter; Andrew, his brother; James; John; Philip; Bartholomew; ¹⁵ Matthew; Thomas; James the son of Alphaeus; Simon who was called the Zealot; ¹⁶ Judas the son of James; and Judas Iscariot, who also became a traitor. ¹⁷ He came down with them and stood on a level place, with a crowd of his disciples and a great number of the

people from all Judea and Jerusalem and the sea coast of Tyre and Sidon, who came to hear him and to be healed of their diseases, ¹⁸ as well as those who were troubled by unclean spirits; and they were being healed. ¹⁹ All the multitude sought to touch him, for power came out of him and healed them all. ²⁰ He lifted up his eyes to his disciples, and said: "Blessed are you who are poor, for God's Kingdom is yours. ²¹ Blessed are you who hunger now, for you will be filled. Blessed are you who weep now, for you will laugh. ²² Blessed are you when men hate you, and when they exclude and mock you, and throw out your name as evil, for the Son of Man's sake. ²³ Rejoice in that day and leap for joy, for behold, your reward is great in heaven, for their fathers did the same thing to the prophets. ²⁴ "But woe to you who are rich! For you have received your consolation. ²⁵ Woe to you, you who are full now, for you will be hungry. Woe to you who laugh now, for you will mourn and weep. ²⁶ Woe,ᵃ whenᵇ men speak well of you, for their fathers did the same thing to the false prophets. ²⁷ "But I tell you who hear: love your enemies, do good to those who hate you, ²⁸ bless those who curse you, and pray for those who mistreat you. ²⁹ To him who strikes you on the cheek, offer also the other; and from him who takes away your cloak, don't withhold your coat also. ³⁰ Give to everyone who asks you, and don't ask him who takes away your goods to give them back again. ³¹ "As you would like people to do to you, do exactly so to them. ³² "If you love those who love you, what credit is that to you? For even sinners love those who love them. ³³ If you do good to those who do good to you, what credit is that to you? For even sinners do the same. ³⁴ If you lend to those from whom you hope to receive, what credit is that to you? Even sinners lend to sinners, to receive back as much. ³⁵ But love your enemies, and do good, and lend, expecting nothing back; and your reward will be great, and you will be children of the Most High; for he is kind toward the unthankful and evil. ³⁶ "Therefore be merciful, even as your Father is also merciful. ³⁷ Don't judge, and you won't be judged. Don't condemn, and you won't be condemned. Set free, and you will be set free. ³⁸ "Give, and it will be given to you: good measure, pressed down, shaken together, and running over, will be given to you.ᶜ For with the same measure you measure it will be measured back to you." ³⁹ He spoke a parable to them. "Can the blind guide the blind? Won't they both fall into a pit? ⁴⁰ A disciple is not above his teacher, but everyone when he is fully trained will be like his teacher. ⁴¹ Why do you see the speck of chaff that is in your brother's eye, but don't consider the beam that is in your own eye? ⁴² Or how can you tell your brother, 'Brother, let me remove the speck of chaff that is in your eye,' when you yourself don't see the beam that is in your own eye? You hypocrite! First remove the beam from your own eye, and then you can see clearly to remove the speck of chaff that is in your brother's eye. ⁴³ "For there is no good tree that produces rotten fruit, nor again a rotten tree that produces good fruit. ⁴⁴ For each tree is known by its own fruit. For people don't gather figs from thorns, nor do they gather grapes from a bramble bush. ⁴⁵ The good man out of the good treasure of his heart brings out that which is good, and the evil man out of the evil treasure of his heart brings out that which is evil, for out of the abundance of the heart, his mouth speaks. ⁴⁶ "Why do you call me, 'Lord, Lord,' and don't do the things which I say? ⁴⁷ Everyone who comes to me, and hears my words and does them, I will show you who he is like. ⁴⁸ He is like a man building a house, who dug and went deep and laid a foundation on the rock. When a flood arose, the stream broke against that house, and could not shake it, because it was founded on the rock. ⁴⁹ But he who hears and doesn't do, is like a man who built a house on the earth without a foundation, against which the stream broke, and immediately it fell; and the ruin of that house was great."

# 7

¹ After he had finished speaking in the hearing of the people, he entered into Capernaum. ² A certain centurion's servant, who was dear to him, was sick and at the point of death. ³ When he heard about Jesus, he sent to him elders of the Jews, asking him to come and save his servant. ⁴ When they came to Jesus, they begged him earnestly, saying, "He is worthy for you to do this for him, ⁵ for he loves our nation, and he built our synagogue for us." ⁶ Jesus went with them. When he was now not far from the house, the centurion sent friends to him, saying to him, "Lord, don't trouble yourself, for I am not worthy for you to come under my roof. ⁷ Therefore I didn't even think myself worthy to come to you; but say the word, and my servant will be healed. ⁸ For I also am a man placed under authority, having under myself soldiers. I tell this one, 'Go!' and he goes; and to another, 'Come!' and he comes; and to my servant, 'Do this,' and he does it." ⁹ When Jesus heard these things, he marveled at him, and turned and said to the multitude who followed him, "I tell you, I have not found such great faith, no, not in Israel." ¹⁰

---

ᵃ 6:26 TR adds "to you"
ᵇ 6:26 TR adds "all"

ᶜ 6:38 literally, into your bosom.

Those who were sent, returning to the house, found that the servant who had been sick was well. [11] Soon afterwards, he went to a city called Nain. Many of his disciples, along with a great multitude, went with him. [12] Now when he came near to the gate of the city, behold, one who was dead was carried out, the only born[a] son of his mother, and she was a widow. Many people of the city were with her. [13] When the Lord saw her, he had compassion on her and said to her, "Don't cry." [14] He came near and touched the coffin, and the bearers stood still. He said, "Young man, I tell you, arise!" [15] He who was dead sat up and began to speak. Then he gave him to his mother. [16] Fear took hold of all, and they glorified God, saying, "A great prophet has arisen among us!" and, "God has visited his people!" [17] This report went out concerning him in the whole of Judea and in all the surrounding region. [18] The disciples of John told him about all these things. [19] John, calling to himself two of his disciples, sent them to Jesus, saying, "Are you the one who is coming, or should we look for another?" [20] When the men had come to him, they said, "John the Baptizer has sent us to you, saying, 'Are you he who comes, or should we look for another?'" [21] In that hour he cured many of diseases and plagues and evil spirits; and to many who were blind he gave sight. [22] Jesus answered them, "Go and tell John the things which you have seen and heard: that the blind receive their sight, the lame walk, the lepers are cleansed, the deaf hear, the dead are raised up, and the poor have good news preached to them. [23] Blessed is he who finds no occasion for stumbling in me." [24] When John's messengers had departed, he began to tell the multitudes about John, "What did you go out into the wilderness to see? A reed shaken by the wind? [25] But what did you go out to see? A man clothed in soft clothing? Behold, those who are gorgeously dressed and live delicately are in kings' courts. [26] But what did you go out to see? A prophet? Yes, I tell you, and much more than a prophet. [27] This is he of whom it is written, 'Behold, I send my messenger before your face, who will prepare your way before you.'* [28] "For I tell you, among those who are born of women there is not a greater prophet than John the Baptizer; yet he who is least in God's Kingdom is greater than he." [29] When all the people and the tax collectors heard this, they declared God to be just, having been baptized with John's baptism. [30] But the Pharisees and the lawyers rejected the counsel of God, not being baptized by him themselves. [31] [b] "To what then should I compare the people of this generation? What are they like? [32] They are like children who sit in the marketplace and call to one another, saying, 'We piped to you, and you didn't dance. We mourned, and you didn't weep.' [33] For John the Baptizer came neither eating bread nor drinking wine, and you say, 'He has a demon.' [34] The Son of Man has come eating and drinking, and you say, 'Behold, a glutton and a drunkard, a friend of tax collectors and sinners!' [35] Wisdom is justified by all her children." [36] One of the Pharisees invited him to eat with him. He entered into the Pharisee's house and sat at the table. [37] Behold, a woman in the city who was a sinner, when she knew that he was reclining in the Pharisee's house, brought an alabaster jar of ointment. [38] Standing behind at his feet weeping, she began to wet his feet with her tears, and she wiped them with the hair of her head, kissed his feet, and anointed them with the ointment. [39] Now when the Pharisee who had invited him saw it, he said to himself, "This man, if he were a prophet, would have perceived who and what kind of woman this is who touches him, that she is a sinner." [40] Jesus answered him, "Simon, I have something to tell you." He said, "Teacher, say on." [41] "A certain lender had two debtors. The one owed five hundred denarii, and the other fifty. [42] When they couldn't pay, he forgave them both. Which of them therefore will love him most?" [43] Simon answered, "He, I suppose, to whom he forgave the most." He said to him, "You have judged correctly." [44] Turning to the woman, he said to Simon, "Do you see this woman? I entered into your house, and you gave me no water for my feet, but she has wet my feet with her tears, and wiped them with the hair of her head. [45] You gave me no kiss, but she, since the time I came in, has not ceased to kiss my feet. [46] You didn't anoint my head with oil, but she has anointed my feet with ointment. [47] Therefore I tell you, her sins, which are many, are forgiven, for she loved much. But one to whom little is forgiven, loves little." [48] He said to her, "Your sins are forgiven." [49] Those who sat at the table with him began to say to themselves, "Who is this who even forgives sins?" [50] He said to the woman, "Your faith has saved you. Go in peace."

# 8

[1] Soon afterwards, he went about through cities and villages, preaching and bringing the good news of God's Kingdom. With him were the twelve, [2] and certain women who had been healed of evil spirits and infirmities: Mary who was called Magdalene, from whom seven demons had gone out; [3] and Joanna, the wife of Chuzas, Herod's steward; Susanna; and many others who served them[c] from their possessions. [4] When a great multitude came together and people from every city were coming to him, he spoke by a parable: [5] "The farmer went out to sow his seed. As he sowed, some fell along the road, and it was trampled under foot, and the birds of the sky devoured it. [6] Other seed fell on the rock, and as soon as it grew, it withered away, because it had no moisture. [7] Other fell amid the thorns, and the thorns grew with it and choked it. [8] Other fell into the good ground and grew and produced one hundred times as much fruit." As he said these things, he called out, "He who has ears to hear, let him hear!" [9] Then his disciples asked him, "What does this parable mean?" [10] He said, "To you it is given to know the mysteries of God's Kingdom, but to the rest it is given in parables, that 'seeing they may not see, and hearing they may not understand.'* [11] "Now the parable is this: The seed is the word of God. [12] Those along the road are those who hear; then the devil comes and takes away the word from their heart, that they may not believe and be saved. [13] Those on the rock are they who, when they hear, receive the word with joy; but these have no root. They believe for a while, then fall away in time of temptation. [14] What fell among the thorns, these are those who have heard, and as they go on their way they are choked with cares, riches, and pleasures of life; and they bring no fruit to maturity. [15] Those in the good ground, these are those who with an honest and good heart, having heard the word, hold it tightly, and produce fruit with perseverance. [16] "No one, when he has lit a lamp, covers it with a container or puts it under a bed; but puts it on a stand, that those who enter in may see the light. [17] For nothing is hidden that will not be revealed, nor anything secret that will not be known and come to light. [18] Be careful therefore how you hear. For whoever has, to him will be given; and whoever doesn't have, from him will be taken away even that which he thinks he has." [19] His mother and brothers came to him, and they could not come near him for the crowd. [20] Some people told him, "Your mother and your brothers stand outside, desiring to see you." [21] But he answered them, "My mother and my brothers are these who hear the word of God and do it." [22] Now on one of those days, he entered into a boat, himself and his disciples, and he said to them, "Let's go over to the other side of the lake." So they launched out. [23] But as they sailed, he fell asleep. A wind storm came down on the lake, and they were taking on dangerous amounts of water. [24] They came to him and awoke him, saying, "Master, Master, we are dying!" He awoke and rebuked the wind and the raging of the water; then they ceased, and it was calm.* [25] He said to them, "Where is your faith?" Being afraid, they marveled, saying to one another, "Who is this then, that he commands even the winds and the water, and they obey him?" [26] Then they arrived at the country of the Gadarenes, which is opposite Galilee. [27] When Jesus stepped ashore, a certain man out of the city who had demons for a long time met him. He wore no clothes, and didn't live in a house, but in the tombs. [28] When he saw Jesus, he cried out and fell down before him, and with a loud voice said, "What do I have to do with you, Jesus, you Son of the Most High God? I beg you, don't torment me!" [29] For Jesus was commanding the unclean spirit to come out of the man. For the unclean spirit had often seized the man. He was kept under guard and bound with chains and fetters. Breaking the bonds apart, he was driven by the demon into the desert. [30] Jesus asked him, "What is your name?" He said, "Legion," for many demons had entered into him. [31] They begged him that he would not command them to go into the abyss. [32] Now there was there a herd of many pigs feeding on the mountain, and they begged him that he would allow them to enter into those. Then he allowed them. [33] The demons came out of the man and entered into the pigs, and the herd rushed down the steep bank into the lake and were drowned. [34] When those who fed them saw what had happened, they fled and told it in the city and in the country. [35] People went out to see what had happened. They came to Jesus and found the man from whom the demons had gone out, sitting at Jesus' feet, clothed and in his right mind; and they were afraid. [36] Those who saw it told them how he who had been possessed by demons was healed. [37] All the people of the surrounding country of the Gadarenes asked him to depart from them, for they were very much afraid. Then he entered into the boat and returned. [38] But the man from whom the demons had gone out begged him that he might go with him, but Jesus sent him away, saying, [39] "Return to your house, and declare what great things God has done for you." He went his way, proclaiming throughout the whole city what great things Jesus had done for him. [40] When Jesus returned, the multitude welcomed him, for they were all

---

[a] *7:12* The phrase "only born" is from the Greek word "μονογενη", which is sometimes translated "only begotten" or "one and only".

* 7:27 Malachi 3:1

[b] *7:31* TR adds "But the Lord said,"

[c] *8:3* TR reads "him" instead of "them"

* 8:10 Isaiah 6:9
* 8:24 See Psalms 107:29

waiting for him. ⁴¹ Behold, a man named Jairus came. He was a ruler of the synagogue. He fell down at Jesus' feet and begged him to come into his house, ⁴² for he had an only born[a] daughter, about twelve years of age, and she was dying. But as he went, the multitudes pressed against him. ⁴³ A woman who had a flow of blood for twelve years, who had spent all her living on physicians and could not be healed by any, ⁴⁴ came behind him and touched the fringe[b] of his cloak. Immediately the flow of her blood stopped. ⁴⁵ Jesus said, "Who touched me?" When all denied it, Peter and those with him said, "Master, the multitudes press and jostle you, and you say, 'Who touched me?'" ⁴⁶ But Jesus said, "Someone did touch me, for I perceived that power has gone out of me." ⁴⁷ When the woman saw that she was not hidden, she came trembling; and falling down before him declared to him in the presence of all the people the reason why she had touched him, and how she was healed immediately. ⁴⁸ He said to her, "Daughter, cheer up. Your faith has made you well. Go in peace." ⁴⁹ While he still spoke, one from the ruler of the synagogue's house came, saying to him, "Your daughter is dead. Don't trouble the Teacher." ⁵⁰ But Jesus hearing it, answered him, "Don't be afraid. Only believe, and she will be healed." ⁵¹ When he came to the house, he didn't allow anyone to enter in, except Peter, John, James, the father of the child, and her mother. ⁵² All were weeping and mourning her, but he said, "Don't weep. She isn't dead, but sleeping." ⁵³ They were ridiculing him, knowing that she was dead. ⁵⁴ But he put them all outside, and taking her by the hand, he called, saying, "Child, arise!" ⁵⁵ Her spirit returned, and she rose up immediately. He commanded that something be given to her to eat. ⁵⁶ Her parents were amazed, but he commanded them to tell no one what had been done.

## 9

¹ He called the twelve[c] together and gave them power and authority over all demons, and to cure diseases. ² He sent them out to preach God's Kingdom and to heal the sick. ³ He said to them, "Take nothing for your journey—no staffs, nor wallet, nor bread, nor money. Don't have two tunics each. ⁴ Into whatever house you enter, stay there, and depart from there. ⁵ As many as don't receive you, when you depart from that city, shake off even the dust from your feet for a testimony against them." ⁶ They departed and went throughout the villages, preaching the Good News and healing everywhere. ⁷ Now Herod the tetrarch heard of all that was done by him; and he was very perplexed, because it was said by some that John had risen from the dead, ⁸ and by some that Elijah had appeared, and by others that one of the old prophets had risen again. ⁹ Herod said, "I beheaded John, but who is this about whom I hear such things?" He sought to see him. ¹⁰ The apostles, when they had returned, told him what things they had done. He took them and withdrew apart to a desert region of[d] a city called Bethsaida. ¹¹ But the multitudes, perceiving it, followed him. He welcomed them, spoke to them of God's Kingdom, and he cured those who needed healing. ¹² The day began to wear away; and the twelve came and said to him, "Send the multitude away, that they may go into the surrounding villages and farms and lodge and get food, for we are here in a deserted place." ¹³ But he said to them, "You give them something to eat." They said, "We have no more than five loaves and two fish, unless we should go and buy food for all these people." ¹⁴ For they were about five thousand men. He said to his disciples, "Make them sit down in groups of about fifty each." ¹⁵ They did so, and made them all sit down. ¹⁶ He took the five loaves and the two fish, and looking up to the sky, he blessed them, broke them, and gave them to the disciples to set before the multitude. ¹⁷ They ate and were all filled. They gathered up twelve baskets of broken pieces that were left over. ¹⁸ As he was praying alone, the disciples were near him, and he asked them, "Who do the multitudes say that I am?" ¹⁹ They answered, "'John the Baptizer,' but others say, 'Elijah,' and others, that one of the old prophets has risen again." ²⁰ He said to them, "But who do you say that I am?" Peter answered, "The Christ of God." ²¹ But he warned them and commanded them to tell this to no one, ²² saying, "The Son of Man must suffer many things, and be rejected by the elders, chief priests, and scribes, and be killed, and the third day be raised up." ²³ He said to all, "If anyone desires to come after me, let him deny himself, take up his cross,[e] and follow me. ²⁴ For whoever desires to save his life will lose it, but whoever will lose his life for my sake will save it. ²⁵ For what does it profit a man if he gains the whole world, and loses or forfeits his own self? ²⁶ For whoever will be ashamed of me and of my words, of him will the Son of Man be ashamed when he comes in his glory, and the glory of the Father, and of the holy angels. ²⁷ But I tell you the truth: There are some of those who stand here who will in no way taste of death until they see God's Kingdom." ²⁸ About eight days after these sayings, he took with him Peter, John, and James, and went up onto the mountain to pray. ²⁹ As he was praying, the appearance of his face was altered, and his clothing became white and dazzling. ³⁰ Behold, two men were talking with him, who were Moses and Elijah, ³¹ who appeared in glory and spoke of his departure,[f] which he was about to accomplish at Jerusalem. ³² Now Peter and those who were with him were heavy with sleep, but when they were fully awake, they saw his glory, and the two men who stood with him. ³³ As they were parting from him, Peter said to Jesus, "Master, it is good for us to be here. Let's make three tents: one for you, one for Moses, and one for Elijah," not knowing what he said. ³⁴ While he said these things, a cloud came and overshadowed them, and they were afraid as they entered into the cloud. ³⁵ A voice came out of the cloud, saying, "This is my beloved Son. Listen to him!" ³⁶ When the voice came, Jesus was found alone. They were silent, and told no one in those days any of the things which they had seen. ³⁷ On the next day, when they had come down from the mountain, a great multitude met him. ³⁸ Behold, a man from the crowd called out, saying, "Teacher, I beg you to look at my son, for he is my only born[g] child. ³⁹ Behold, a spirit takes him, he suddenly cries out, and it convulses him so that he foams; and it hardly departs from him, bruising him severely. ⁴⁰ I begged your disciples to cast it out, and they couldn't." ⁴¹ Jesus answered, "Faithless and perverse generation, how long shall I be with you and bear with you? Bring your son here." ⁴² While he was still coming, the demon threw him down and convulsed him violently. But Jesus rebuked the unclean spirit, healed the boy, and gave him back to his father. ⁴³ They were all astonished at the majesty of God. But while all were marveling at all the things which Jesus did, he said to his disciples, ⁴⁴ "Let these words sink into your ears, for the Son of Man will be delivered up into the hands of men." ⁴⁵ But they didn't understand this saying. It was concealed from them, that they should not perceive it, and they were afraid to ask him about this saying. ⁴⁶ An argument arose among them about which of them was the greatest. ⁴⁷ Jesus, perceiving the reasoning of their hearts, took a little child, and set him by his side, ⁴⁸ and said to them, "Whoever receives this little child in my name receives me. Whoever receives me receives him who sent me. For whoever is least among you all, this one will be great." ⁴⁹ John answered, "Master, we saw someone casting out demons in your name, and we forbade him, because he doesn't follow with us." ⁵⁰ Jesus said to him, "Don't forbid him, for he who is not against us is for us." ⁵¹ It came to pass, when the days were near that he should be taken up, he intently set his face to go to Jerusalem ⁵² and sent messengers before his face. They went and entered into a village of the Samaritans, so as to prepare for him. ⁵³ They didn't receive him, because he was traveling with his face set toward Jerusalem. ⁵⁴ When his disciples, James and John, saw this, they said, "Lord, do you want us to command fire to come down from the sky and destroy them, just as Elijah did?" ⁵⁵ But he turned and rebuked them, "You don't know of what kind of spirit you are. ⁵⁶ For the Son of Man didn't come to destroy men's lives, but to save them." They went to another village. ⁵⁷ As they went on the way, a certain man said to him, "I want to follow you wherever you go, Lord." ⁵⁸ Jesus said to him, "The foxes have holes and the birds of the sky have nests, but the Son of Man has no place to lay his head." ⁵⁹ He said to another, "Follow me!" But he said, "Lord, allow me first to go and bury my father." ⁶⁰ But Jesus said to him, "Leave the dead to bury their own dead, but you go and announce God's Kingdom." ⁶¹ Another also said, "I want to follow you, Lord, but first allow me to say good-bye to those who are at my house." ⁶² But Jesus said to him, "No one, having put his hand to the plow and looking back, is fit for God's Kingdom."

## 10

¹ Now after these things, the Lord also appointed seventy others, and sent them two by two ahead of him[h] into every city and place where he was about to come. ² Then he said to them, "The harvest is indeed plentiful, but the laborers are few. Pray therefore to the Lord of the harvest, that he may send out laborers into his harvest. ³ Go your ways. Behold, I send you out as lambs among wolves. ⁴ Carry no purse, nor wallet, nor sandals. Greet no one on the way. ⁵ Into whatever house you enter, first say, 'Peace be to this house.' ⁶ If a son of peace is there, your peace will rest on him; but if not, it will return to you. ⁷ Remain in that same house, eating and drinking the things they give, for the laborer is worthy of his wages. Don't go from house to house. ⁸ Into whatever city you enter and they receive you, eat the things that are set before

---

[a] *8:42* The phrase "only born" is from the Greek word "μονογενη", which is sometimes translated "only begotten" or "one and only".

[b] *8:44* or, tassel

[c] *9:1* TR reads "his twelve disciples" instead of "the twelve"

[d] *9:10* NU omits "a desert region of".

[e] *9:23* TR, NU add "daily"

[f] *9:31* literally, "exodus"

[g] *9:38* The phrase "only born" is from the Greek word "μονογενη", which is sometimes translated "only begotten" or "one and only".

[h] *10:1* literally, "before his face"

you. ⁹ Heal the sick who are there and tell them, 'God's Kingdom has come near to you.' ¹⁰ But into whatever city you enter and they don't receive you, go out into its streets and say, ¹¹ 'Even the dust from your city that clings to us, we wipe off against you. Nevertheless know this, that God's Kingdom has come near to you.' ¹² I tell you, it will be more tolerable in that day for Sodom than for that city. ¹³ "Woe to you, Chorazin! Woe to you, Bethsaida! For if the mighty works had been done in Tyre and Sidon which were done in you, they would have repented long ago, sitting in sackcloth and ashes. ¹⁴ But it will be more tolerable for Tyre and Sidon in the judgment than for you. ¹⁵ You, Capernaum, who are exalted to heaven, will be brought down to Hades. ᵃ ¹⁶ Whoever listens to you listens to me, and whoever rejects you rejects me. Whoever rejects me rejects him who sent me." ¹⁷ The seventy returned with joy, saying, "Lord, even the demons are subject to us in your name!" ¹⁸ He said to them, "I saw Satan having fallen like lightning from heaven. ¹⁹ Behold, I give you authority to tread on serpents and scorpions, and over all the power of the enemy. Nothing will in any way hurt you. ²⁰ Nevertheless, don't rejoice in this, that the spirits are subject to you, but rejoice that your names are written in heaven." ²¹ In that same hour, Jesus rejoiced in the Holy Spirit, and said, "I thank you, O Father, Lord of heaven and earth, that you have hidden these things from the wise and understanding, and revealed them to little children. Yes, Father, for so it was well-pleasing in your sight." ²² Turning to the disciples, he said, "All things have been delivered to me by my Father. No one knows who the Son is, except the Father, and who the Father is, except the Son, and he to whomever the Son desires to reveal him." ²³ Turning to the disciples, he said privately, "Blessed are the eyes which see the things that you see, ²⁴ for I tell you that many prophets and kings desired to see the things which you see, and didn't see them, and to hear the things which you hear, and didn't hear them." ²⁵ Behold, a certain lawyer stood up and tested him, saying, "Teacher, what shall I do to inherit eternal life?" ²⁶ He said to him, "What is written in the law? How do you read it?" ²⁷ He answered, "You shall love the Lord your God with all your heart, with all your soul, with all your strength, and with all your mind;* and your neighbor as yourself."* ²⁸ He said to him, "You have answered correctly. Do this, and you will live." ²⁹ But he, desiring to justify himself, asked Jesus, "Who is my neighbor?" ³⁰ Jesus answered, "A certain man was going down from Jerusalem to Jericho, and he fell among robbers, who both stripped him and beat him, and departed, leaving him half dead. ³¹ By chance a certain priest was going down that way. When he saw him, he passed by on the other side. ³² In the same way a Levite also, when he came to the place and saw him, passed by on the other side. ³³ But a certain Samaritan, as he traveled, came where he was. When he saw him, he was moved with compassion, ³⁴ came to him, and bound up his wounds, pouring on oil and wine. He set him on his own animal, brought him to an inn, and took care of him. ³⁵ On the next day, when he departed, he took out two denarii, gave them to the host, and said to him, 'Take care of him. Whatever you spend beyond that, I will repay you when I return.' ³⁶ Now which of these three do you think seemed to be a neighbor to him who fell among the robbers?" ³⁷ He said, "He who showed mercy on him." Then Jesus said to him, "Go and do likewise." ³⁸ As they went on their way, he entered into a certain village, and a certain woman named Martha received him into her house. ³⁹ She had a sister called Mary, who also sat at Jesus' feet and heard his word. ⁴⁰ But Martha was distracted with much serving, and she came up to him, and said, "Lord, don't you care that my sister left me to serve alone? Ask her therefore to help me." ⁴¹ Jesus answered her, "Martha, Martha, you are anxious and troubled about many things, ⁴² but one thing is needed. Mary has chosen the good part, which will not be taken away from her."

# 11

¹ When he finished praying in a certain place, one of his disciples said to him, "Lord, teach us to pray, just as John also taught his disciples." ² He said to them, "When you pray, say, 'Our Father in heaven, may your name be kept holy. May your Kingdom come. May your will be done on earth, as it is in heaven. ³ Give us day by day our daily bread. ⁴ Forgive us our sins, for we ourselves also forgive everyone who is indebted to us. Bring us not into temptation, but deliver us from the evil one.'" ⁵ He said to them, "Which of you, if you go to a friend at midnight and tell him, 'Friend, lend me three loaves of bread, ⁶ for a friend of mine has come to me from a journey, and I have nothing to set before him,' ⁷ and he from within will answer and say, 'Don't bother me. The door is now shut, and my children are with me in bed. I can't get up and give it to you'? ⁸ I tell you, although he will not rise and give it to him because he is his friend, yet because of his persistence, he will get up and give him as many as he needs. ⁹ "I tell you, keep asking, and

it will be given you. Keep seeking, and you will find. Keep knocking, and it will be opened to you. ¹⁰ For everyone who asks receives. He who seeks finds. To him who knocks it will be opened. ¹¹ "Which of you fathers, if your son asks for bread, will give him a stone? Or if he asks for a fish, he won't give him a snake instead of a fish, will he? ¹² Or if he asks for an egg, he won't give him a scorpion, will he? ¹³ If you then, being evil, know how to give good gifts to your children, how much more will your heavenly Father give the Holy Spirit to those who ask him?" ¹⁴ He was casting out a demon, and it was mute. When the demon had gone out, the mute man spoke; and the multitudes marveled. ¹⁵ But some of them said, "He casts out demons by Beelzebul, the prince of the demons." ¹⁶ Others, testing him, sought from him a sign from heaven. ¹⁷ But he, knowing their thoughts, said to them, "Every kingdom divided against itself is brought to desolation. A house divided against itself falls. ¹⁸ If Satan also is divided against himself, how will his kingdom stand? For you say that I cast out demons by Beelzebul. ¹⁹ But if I cast out demons by Beelzebul, by whom do your children cast them out? Therefore they will be your judges. ²⁰ But if I by God's finger cast out demons, then God's Kingdom has come to you. ²¹ "When the strong man, fully armed, guards his own dwelling, his goods are safe. ²² But when someone stronger attacks him and overcomes him, he takes from him his whole armor in which he trusted, and divides his plunder. ²³ "He who is not with me is against me. He who doesn't gather with me scatters. ²⁴ The unclean spirit, when he has gone out of the man, passes through dry places, seeking rest; and finding none, he says, 'I will turn back to my house from which I came out.' ²⁵ When he returns, he finds it swept and put in order. ²⁶ Then he goes and takes seven other spirits more evil than himself, and they enter in and dwell there. The last state of that man becomes worse than the first." ²⁷ It came to pass, as he said these things, a certain woman out of the multitude lifted up her voice and said to him, "Blessed is the womb that bore you, and the breasts which nursed you!" ²⁸ But he said, "On the contrary, blessed are those who hear the word of God, and keep it." ²⁹ When the multitudes were gathering together to him, he began to say, "This is an evil generation. It seeks after a sign. No sign will be given to it but the sign of Jonah the prophet. ³⁰ For even as Jonah became a sign to the Ninevites, so the Son of Man will also be to this generation. ³¹ The Queen of the South will rise up in the judgment with the men of this generation and will condemn them, for she came from the ends of the earth to hear the wisdom of Solomon; and behold, one greater than Solomon is here. ³² The men of Nineveh will stand up in the judgment with this generation, and will condemn it, for they repented at the preaching of Jonah; and behold, one greater than Jonah is here. ³³ "No one, when he has lit a lamp, puts it in a cellar or under a basket, but on a stand, that those who come in may see the light. ³⁴ The lamp of the body is the eye. Therefore when your eye is good, your whole body is also full of light; but when it is evil, your body also is full of darkness. ³⁵ Therefore see whether the light that is in you isn't darkness. ³⁶ If therefore your whole body is full of light, having no part dark, it will be wholly full of light, as when the lamp with its bright shining gives you light." ³⁷ Now as he spoke, a certain Pharisee asked him to dine with him. He went in and sat at the table. ³⁸ When the Pharisee saw it, he marveled that he had not first washed himself before dinner. ³⁹ The Lord said to him, "Now you Pharisees cleanse the outside of the cup and of the platter, but your inward part is full of extortion and wickedness. ⁴⁰ You foolish ones, didn't he who made the outside make the inside also? ⁴¹ But give for gifts to the needy those things which are within, and behold, all things will be clean to you. ⁴² But woe to you Pharisees! For you tithe mint and rue and every herb, but you bypass justice and God's love. You ought to have done these, and not to have left the other undone. ⁴³ Woe to you Pharisees! For you love the best seats in the synagogues and the greetings in the marketplaces. ⁴⁴ Woe to you, scribes and Pharisees, hypocrites! For you are like hidden graves, and the men who walk over them don't know it." ⁴⁵ One of the lawyers answered him, "Teacher, in saying this you insult us also." ⁴⁶ He said, "Woe to you lawyers also! For you load men with burdens that are difficult to carry, and you yourselves won't even lift one finger to help carry those burdens. ⁴⁷ Woe to you! For you build the tombs of the prophets, and your fathers killed them. ⁴⁸ So you testify and consent to the works of your fathers. For they killed them, and you build their tombs. ⁴⁹ Therefore also the wisdom of God said, 'I will send to them prophets and apostles; and some of them they will kill and persecute, ⁵⁰ that the blood of all the prophets, which was shed from the foundation of the world, may be required of this generation, ⁵¹ from the blood of Abel to the blood of Zachariah, who perished between the altar and the sanctuary.' Yes, I tell you, it will be required of this generation. ⁵² Woe to you lawyers! For you took away the key of knowledge. You didn't

---

ᵃ *10:15* Hades is the lower realm of the dead, or Hell.

* 10:27 Deuteronomy 6:5
* 10:27 Leviticus 19:18

enter in yourselves, and those who were entering in, you hindered." **53** As he said these things to them, the scribes and the Pharisees began to be terribly angry, and to draw many things out of him, **54** lying in wait for him, and seeking to catch him in something he might say, that they might accuse him.

## 12

**1** Meanwhile, when a multitude of many thousands had gathered together, so much so that they trampled on each other, he began to tell his disciples first of all, "Beware of the yeast of the Pharisees, which is hypocrisy. **2** But there is nothing covered up that will not be revealed, nor hidden that will not be known. **3** Therefore whatever you have said in the darkness will be heard in the light. What you have spoken in the ear in the inner rooms will be proclaimed on the housetops. **4** "I tell you, my friends, don't be afraid of those who kill the body, and after that have no more that they can do. **5** But I will warn you whom you should fear. Fear him who after he has killed, has power to cast into Gehenna.ᵃ Yes, I tell you, fear him. **6** "Aren't five sparrows sold for two assaria coinsᵇ? Not one of them is forgotten by God. **7** But the very hairs of your head are all counted. Therefore don't be afraid. You are of more value than many sparrows. **8** "I tell you, everyone who confesses me before men, the Son of Man will also confess before the angels of God; **9** but he who denies me in the presence of men will be denied in the presence of God's angels. **10** Everyone who speaks a word against the Son of Man will be forgiven, but those who blaspheme against the Holy Spirit will not be forgiven. **11** When they bring you before the synagogues, the rulers, and the authorities, don't be anxious how or what you will answer or what you will say; **12** for the Holy Spirit will teach you in that same hour what you must say." **13** One of the multitude said to him, "Teacher, tell my brother to divide the inheritance with me." **14** But he said to him, "Man, who made me a judge or an arbitrator over you?" **15** He said to them, "Beware! Keep yourselves from covetousness, for a man's life doesn't consist of the abundance of the things which he possesses." **16** He spoke a parable to them, saying, "The ground of a certain rich man produced abundantly. **17** He reasoned within himself, saying, 'What will I do, because I don't have room to store my crops?' **18** He said, 'This is what I will do. I will pull down my barns, build bigger ones, and there I will store all my grain and my goods. **19** I will tell my soul, "Soul, you have many goods laid up for many years. Take your ease, eat, drink, and be merry."' **20** "But God said to him, 'You foolish one, tonight your soul is required of you. The things which you have prepared—whose will they be?' **21** So is he who lays up treasure for himself, and is not rich toward God." **22** He said to his disciples, "Therefore I tell you, don't be anxious for your life, what you will eat, nor yet for your body, what you will wear. **23** Life is more than food, and the body is more than clothing. **24** Consider the ravens: they don't sow, they don't reap, they have no warehouse or barn, and God feeds them. How much more valuable are you than birds! **25** Which of you by being anxious can add a cubitᶜ to his height? **26** If then you aren't able to do even the least things, why are you anxious about the rest? **27** Consider the lilies, how they grow. They don't toil, neither do they spin; yet I tell you, even Solomon in all his glory was not arrayed like one of these. **28** But if this is how God clothes the grass in the field, which today exists and tomorrow is cast into the oven, how much more will he clothe you, O you of little faith? **29** "Don't seek what you will eat or what you will drink; neither be anxious. **30** For the nations of the world seek after all of these things, but your Father knows that you need these things. **31** But seek God's Kingdom, and all these things will be added to you. **32** "Don't be afraid, little flock, for it is your Father's good pleasure to give you the Kingdom. **33** Sell what you have and give gifts to the needy. Make for yourselves purses which don't grow old, a treasure in the heavens that doesn't fail, where no thief approaches and no moth destroys. **34** For where your treasure is, there will your heart be also. **35** "Let your waist be dressed and your lamps burning. **36** Be like men watching for their lord when he returns from the wedding feast, that when he comes and knocks, they may immediately open to him. **37** Blessed are those servants whom the lord will find watching when he comes. Most certainly I tell you that he will dress himself, make them recline, and will come and serve them. **38** They will be blessed if he comes in the second or third watch and finds them so. **39** But know this, that if the master of the house had known in what hour the thief was coming, he would have watched and not allowed his house to be broken into. **40** Therefore be ready also, for the Son of Man is coming in an hour that you don't expect him." **41** Peter said to him, "Lord, are you telling this parable to us, or to everybody?" **42** The Lord said, "Who

then is the faithful and wise steward, whom his lord will set over his household, to give them their portion of food at the right times? **43** Blessed is that servant whom his lord will find doing so when he comes. **44** Truly I tell you that he will set him over all that he has. **45** But if that servant says in his heart, 'My lord delays his coming,' and begins to beat the menservants and the maidservants, and to eat and drink and to be drunken, **46** then the lord of that servant will come in a day when he isn't expecting him and in an hour that he doesn't know, and will cut him in two, and place his portion with the unfaithful. **47** That servant who knew his lord's will, and didn't prepare nor do what he wanted, will be beaten with many stripes, **48** but he who didn't know, and did things worthy of stripes, will be beaten with few stripes. To whomever much is given, of him will much be required; and to whom much was entrusted, of him more will be asked. **49** "I came to throw fire on the earth. I wish it were already kindled. **50** But I have a baptism to be baptized with, and how distressed I am until it is accomplished! **51** Do you think that I have come to give peace in the earth? I tell you, no, but rather division. **52** For from now on, there will be five in one house divided, three against two, and two against three. **53** They will be divided, father against son, and son against father; mother against daughter, and daughter against her mother; mother-in-law against her daughter-in-law, and daughter-in-law against her mother-in-law." * **54** He said to the multitudes also, "When you see a cloud rising from the west, immediately you say, 'A shower is coming,' and so it happens. **55** When a south wind blows, you say, 'There will be a scorching heat,' and it happens. **56** You hypocrites! You know how to interpret the appearance of the earth and the sky, but how is it that you don't interpret this time? **57** "Why don't you judge for yourselves what is right? **58** For when you are going with your adversary before the magistrate, try diligently on the way to be released from him, lest perhaps he drag you to the judge, and the judge deliver you to the officer, and the officer throw you into prison. **59** I tell you, you will by no means get out of there until you have paid the very last penny.ᵈ"

## 13

**1** Now there were some present at the same time who told him about the Galileans whose blood Pilate had mixed with their sacrifices. **2** Jesus answered them, "Do you think that these Galileans were worse sinners than all the other Galileans, because they suffered such things? **3** I tell you, no, but unless you repent, you will all perish in the same way. **4** Or those eighteen on whom the tower in Siloam fell and killed them—do you think that they were worse offenders than all the men who dwell in Jerusalem? **5** I tell you, no, but, unless you repent, you will all perish in the same way." **6** He spoke this parable. "A certain man had a fig tree planted in his vineyard, and he came seeking fruit on it and found none. **7** He said to the vine dresser, 'Behold, these three years I have come looking for fruit on this fig tree, and found none. Cut it down! Why does it waste the soil?' **8** He answered, 'Lord, leave it alone this year also, until I dig around it and fertilize it. **9** If it bears fruit, fine; but if not, after that, you can cut it down.'" **10** He was teaching in one of the synagogues on the Sabbath day. **11** Behold, there was a woman who had a spirit of infirmity eighteen years. She was bent over and could in no way straighten herself up. **12** When Jesus saw her, he called her and said to her, "Woman, you are freed from your infirmity." **13** He laid his hands on her, and immediately she stood up straight and glorified God. **14** The ruler of the synagogue, being indignant because Jesus had healed on the Sabbath, said to the multitude, "There are six days in which men ought to work. Therefore come on those days and be healed, and not on the Sabbath day!" **15** Therefore the Lord answered him, "You hypocrites! Doesn't each one of you free his ox or his donkey from the stall on the Sabbath and lead him away to water? **16** Ought not this woman, being a daughter of Abraham whom Satan had bound eighteen long years, be freed from this bondage on the Sabbath day?" **17** As he said these things, all his adversaries were disappointed; and all the multitude rejoiced for all the glorious things that were done by him. **18** He said, "What is God's Kingdom like? To what shall I compare it? **19** It is like a grain of mustard seed which a man took and put in his own garden. It grew and became a large tree, and the birds of the sky live in its branches." **20** Again he said, "To what shall I compare God's Kingdom? **21** It is like yeast, which a woman took and hid in three measures ᵉ of flour, until it was all leavened." **22** He went on his way through cities and villages, teaching, and traveling on to Jerusalem. **23** One said to him, "Lord, are they few who are saved?" He said to them, **24** "Strive to enter in by the narrow door, for many, I tell you, will seek to enter in and will not be able. **25** When once the master of the house

---

ᵃ *12:5* or, Hell
ᵇ *12:6* An assarion was a small copper coin worth about an hour's wages for an agricultural laborer.

ᶜ *12:25* A cubit is the length from the tip of the middle finger to the elbow on a man's arm, or about 18 inches or 46 centimeters.
* 12:53 Micah 7:6

ᵈ *12:59* literally, lepton. A lepton is a very small brass Jewish coin worth half a Roman quadrans each, which is worth a quarter of the copper assarion. Lepta are worth less

than 1% of an agricultural worker's daily wages.
ᵉ *13:21* literally, three sata. 3 sata is about 39 liters or a bit more than a bushel.

has risen up and has shut the door, and you begin to stand outside and to knock at the door, saying, 'Lord, Lord, open to us!' then he will answer and tell you, 'I don't know you or where you come from.' <sup>26</sup> Then you will begin to say, 'We ate and drank in your presence, and you taught in our streets.' <sup>27</sup> He will say, 'I tell you, I don't know where you come from. Depart from me, all you workers of iniquity.' <sup>28</sup> There will be weeping and gnashing of teeth when you see Abraham, Isaac, Jacob, and all the prophets in God's Kingdom, and yourselves being thrown outside. <sup>29</sup> They will come from the east, west, north, and south, and will sit down in God's Kingdom. <sup>30</sup> Behold, there are some who are last who will be first, and there are some who are first who will be last."

<sup>31</sup> On that same day, some Pharisees came, saying to him, "Get out of here and go away, for Herod wants to kill you." <sup>32</sup> He said to them, "Go and tell that fox, 'Behold, I cast out demons and perform cures today and tomorrow, and the third day I complete my mission. <sup>33</sup> Nevertheless I must go on my way today and tomorrow and the next day, for it can't be that a prophet would perish outside of Jerusalem.' <sup>34</sup> "Jerusalem, Jerusalem, you who kills the prophets and stones those who are sent to her! How often I wanted to gather your children together, like a hen gathers her own brood under her wings, and you refused! <sup>35</sup> Behold, your house is left to you desolate. I tell you, you will not see me until you say, 'Blessed is he who comes in the name of the Lord!'" *

## 14

<sup>1</sup> When he went into the house of one of the rulers of the Pharisees on a Sabbath to eat bread, they were watching him. <sup>2</sup> Behold, a certain man who had dropsy was in front of him. <sup>3</sup> Jesus, answering, spoke to the lawyers and Pharisees, saying, "Is it lawful to heal on the Sabbath?" <sup>4</sup> But they were silent. He took him, and healed him, and let him go. <sup>5</sup> He answered them, "Which of you, if your son<sup>a</sup> or an ox fell into a well, wouldn't immediately pull him out on a Sabbath day?" <sup>6</sup> They couldn't answer him regarding these things. <sup>7</sup> He spoke a parable to those who were invited, when he noticed how they chose the best seats, and said to them, <sup>8</sup> "When you are invited by anyone to a wedding feast, don't sit in the best seat, since perhaps someone more honorable than you might be invited by him, <sup>9</sup> and he who invited both of you would come and tell you, 'Make room for this person.' Then you would begin, with shame, to take the lowest place. <sup>10</sup> But when you are invited, go and sit in the lowest place, so that when he who invited you comes, he may tell you, 'Friend, move up higher.' Then you will be honored in the presence of all who sit at the table with you. <sup>11</sup> For everyone who exalts himself will be humbled, and whoever humbles himself will be exalted." <sup>12</sup> He also said to the one who had invited him, "When you make a dinner or a supper, don't call your friends, nor your brothers, nor your kinsmen, nor rich neighbors, or perhaps they might also return the favor, and pay you back. <sup>13</sup> But when you make a feast, ask the poor, the maimed, the lame, or the blind; <sup>14</sup> and you will be blessed, because they don't have the resources to repay you. For you will be repaid in the resurrection of the righteous." <sup>15</sup> When one of those who sat at the table with him heard these things, he said to him, "Blessed is he who will feast in God's Kingdom!" <sup>16</sup> But he said to him, "A certain man made a great supper, and he invited many people. <sup>17</sup> He sent out his servant at supper time to tell those who were invited, 'Come, for everything is ready now.' <sup>18</sup> They all as one began to make excuses. "The first said to him, 'I have bought a field, and I must go and see it. Please have me excused.' <sup>19</sup> "Another said, 'I have bought five yoke of oxen, and I must go try them out. Please have me excused.' <sup>20</sup> "Another said, 'I have married a wife, and therefore I can't come.' <sup>21</sup> "That servant came, and told his lord these things. Then the master of the house, being angry, said to his servant, 'Go out quickly into the streets and lanes of the city, and bring in the poor, maimed, blind, and lame.' <sup>22</sup> "The servant said, 'Lord, it is done as you commanded, and there is still room.' <sup>23</sup> "The lord said to the servant, 'Go out into the highways and hedges, and compel them to come in, that my house may be filled. <sup>24</sup> For I tell you that none of those men who were invited will taste of my supper. For many are called, but few are chosen.<sup>b</sup>'" <sup>25</sup> Now great multitudes were going with him. He turned and said to them, <sup>26</sup> "If anyone comes to me, and doesn't disregard<sup>c</sup> his own father, mother, wife, children, brothers, and sisters, yes, and his own life also, he can't be my disciple. <sup>27</sup> Whoever doesn't bear his own cross and come after me, can't be my disciple. <sup>28</sup> For which of you, desiring to build a tower, doesn't first sit down and count the cost, to see if he has enough to complete it? <sup>29</sup> Or perhaps, when he has laid a foundation and isn't able to finish, everyone who sees begins to mock him, <sup>30</sup> saying, 'This man began to build and wasn't able to finish.' <sup>31</sup> Or what king, as he goes to encounter another king in war, will not sit down first and consider

whether he is able with ten thousand to meet him who comes against him with twenty thousand? <sup>32</sup> Or else, while the other is yet a great way off, he sends an envoy and asks for conditions of peace. <sup>33</sup> So therefore, whoever of you who doesn't renounce all that he has, he can't be my disciple. <sup>34</sup> "Salt is good, but if the salt becomes flat and tasteless, with what do you season it? <sup>35</sup> It is fit neither for the soil nor for the manure pile. It is thrown out. He who has ears to hear, let him hear."

## 15

<sup>1</sup> Now all the tax collectors and sinners were coming close to him to hear him. <sup>2</sup> The Pharisees and the scribes murmured, saying, "This man welcomes sinners, and eats with them." <sup>3</sup> He told them this parable: <sup>4</sup> "Which of you men, if you had one hundred sheep and lost one of them, wouldn't leave the ninety-nine in the wilderness and go after the one that was lost, until he found it? <sup>5</sup> When he has found it, he carries it on his shoulders, rejoicing. <sup>6</sup> When he comes home, he calls together his friends and his neighbors, saying to them, 'Rejoice with me, for I have found my sheep which was lost!' <sup>7</sup> I tell you that even so there will be more joy in heaven over one sinner who repents, than over ninety-nine righteous people who need no repentance. <sup>8</sup> "Or what woman, if she had ten drachma<sup>d</sup> coins, if she lost one drachma coin, wouldn't light a lamp, sweep the house, and seek diligently until she found it? <sup>9</sup> When she has found it, she calls together her friends and neighbors, saying, 'Rejoice with me, for I have found the drachma which I had lost!' <sup>10</sup> Even so, I tell you, there is joy in the presence of the angels of God over one sinner repenting." <sup>11</sup> He said, "A certain man had two sons. <sup>12</sup> The younger of them said to his father, 'Father, give me my share of your property.' So he divided his livelihood between them. <sup>13</sup> Not many days after, the younger son gathered all of this together and traveled into a far country. There he wasted his property with riotous living. <sup>14</sup> When he had spent all of it, there arose a severe famine in that country, and he began to be in need. <sup>15</sup> He went and joined himself to one of the citizens of that country, and he sent him into his fields to feed pigs. <sup>16</sup> He wanted to fill his belly with the pods that the pigs ate, but no one gave him any. <sup>17</sup> But when he came to himself, he said, 'How many hired servants of my father's have bread enough to spare, and I'm dying with hunger! <sup>18</sup> I will get up and go to my father, and will tell him, "Father, I have sinned against heaven and in your sight. <sup>19</sup> I am no more worthy to be called your son. Make me as one of your hired servants."' <sup>20</sup> "He arose and came to his father. But while he was still far off, his father saw him and was moved with compassion, and ran, fell on his neck, and kissed him. <sup>21</sup> The son said to him, 'Father, I have sinned against heaven and in your sight. I am no longer worthy to be called your son.' <sup>22</sup> "But the father said to his servants, 'Bring out the best robe and put it on him. Put a ring on his hand and sandals on his feet. <sup>23</sup> Bring the fattened calf, kill it, and let's eat and celebrate; <sup>24</sup> for this, my son, was dead and is alive again. He was lost and is found.' Then they began to celebrate. <sup>25</sup> "Now his elder son was in the field. As he came near to the house, he heard music and dancing. <sup>26</sup> He called one of the servants to him and asked what was going on. <sup>27</sup> He said to him, 'Your brother has come, and your father has killed the fattened calf, because he has received him back safe and healthy.' <sup>28</sup> But he was angry and would not go in. Therefore his father came out and begged him. <sup>29</sup> But he answered his father, 'Behold, these many years I have served you, and I never disobeyed a commandment of yours, but you never gave me a goat, that I might celebrate with my friends. <sup>30</sup> But when this your son came, who has devoured your living with prostitutes, you killed the fattened calf for him.' <sup>31</sup> "He said to him, 'Son, you are always with me, and all that is mine is yours. <sup>32</sup> But it was appropriate to celebrate and be glad, for this, your brother, was dead, and is alive again. He was lost, and is found.'"

## 16

<sup>1</sup> He also said to his disciples, "There was a certain rich man who had a manager. An accusation was made to him that this man was wasting his possessions. <sup>2</sup> He called him, and said to him, 'What is this that I hear about you? Give an accounting of your management, for you can no longer be manager.' <sup>3</sup> "The manager said within himself, 'What will I do, seeing that my lord is taking away the management position from me? I don't have strength to dig. I am ashamed to beg. <sup>4</sup> I know what I will do, so that when I am removed from management, they may receive me into their houses.' <sup>5</sup> Calling each one of his lord's debtors to him, he said to the first, 'How much do you owe to my lord?' <sup>6</sup> He said, 'A hundred batos<sup>e</sup> of oil.' He said to him, 'Take your bill, and sit down quickly and write fifty.' <sup>7</sup> Then he said to another, 'How much do you owe?' He said, 'A hundred cors<sup>f</sup> of wheat.' He said to him, 'Take your bill, and write eighty.' <sup>8</sup> "His lord commended the dishonest

---

* 13:35 Psalms 118:26
<sup>a</sup> 14:5 TR reads "donkey" instead of "son"

<sup>b</sup> 14:24 RP MT includes the last sentence. TR, NU, and FH MT omit: For many are called, but few are chosen.

<sup>c</sup> 14:26 or, hate
<sup>d</sup> 15:8 A drachma coin was worth about 2 days wages for an agricultural laborer.

<sup>e</sup> 16:6 100 batos is about 395 liters or 104 U. S. gallons.
<sup>f</sup> 16:7 100 cors = about 2,110 liters or 600 bushels.

manager because he had done wisely, for the children of this world are, in their own generation, wiser than the children of the light. **9** I tell you, make for yourselves friends by means of unrighteous mammon, so that when you fail, they may receive you into the eternal tents. **10** He who is faithful in a very little is faithful also in much. He who is dishonest in a very little is also dishonest in much. **11** If therefore you have not been faithful in the unrighteous mammon, who will commit to your trust the true riches? **12** If you have not been faithful in that which is another's, who will give you that which is your own? **13** No servant can serve two masters, for either he will hate the one and love the other; or else he will hold to one and despise the other. You aren't able to serve God and Mammon."ᵃ **14** The Pharisees, who were lovers of money, also heard all these things, and they scoffed at him. **15** He said to them, "You are those who justify yourselves in the sight of men, but God knows your hearts. For that which is exalted among men is an abomination in the sight of God. **16** "The law and the prophets were until John. From that time the Good News of God's Kingdom is preached, and everyone is forcing his way into it. **17** But it is easier for heaven and earth to pass away than for one tiny stroke of a pen in the law to fall. **18** "Everyone who divorces his wife and marries another commits adultery. He who marries one who is divorced from a husband commits adultery. **19** "Now there was a certain rich man, and he was clothed in purple and fine linen, living in luxury every day. **20** A certain beggar, named Lazarus, was taken to his gate, full of sores, **21** and desiring to be fed with the crumbs that fell from the rich man's table. Yes, even the dogs came and licked his sores. **22** The beggar died, and he was carried away by the angels to Abraham's bosom. The rich man also died and was buried. **23** In Hades,ᵇ he lifted up his eyes, being in torment, and saw Abraham far off, and Lazarus at his bosom. **24** He cried and said, 'Father Abraham, have mercy on me, and send Lazarus, that he may dip the tip of his finger in water and cool my tongue! For I am in anguish in this flame.' **25** "But Abraham said, 'Son, remember that you, in your lifetime, received your good things, and Lazarus, in the same way, bad things. But here he is now comforted and you are in anguish. **26** Besides all this, between us and you there is a great gulf fixed, that those who want to pass from here to you are not able, and that no one may cross over from there to us.' **27** "He said, 'I ask you therefore, father, that you would send him to my father's house— **28** for I have five brothers—that he may testify to them, so they won't also come into this place of torment.' **29** "But Abraham said to him, 'They have Moses and the prophets. Let them listen to them.' **30** "He said, 'No, father Abraham, but if one goes to them from the dead, they will repent.' **31** "He said to him, 'If they don't listen to Moses and the prophets, neither will they be persuaded if one rises from the dead.'"

## 17

**1** He said to the disciples, "It is impossible that no occasions of stumbling should come, but woe to him through whom they come! **2** It would be better for him if a millstone were hung around his neck, and he were thrown into the sea, rather than that he should cause one of these little ones to stumble. **3** Be careful. If your brother sins against you, rebuke him. If he repents, forgive him. **4** If he sins against you seven times in the day, and seven times returns, saying, 'I repent,' you shall forgive him." **5** The apostles said to the Lord, "Increase our faith." **6** The Lord said, "If you had faith like a grain of mustard seed, you would tell this sycamore tree, 'Be uprooted and be planted in the sea,' and it would obey you. **7** But who is there among you, having a servant plowing or keeping sheep, that will say when he comes in from the field, 'Come immediately and sit down at the table'? **8** Wouldn't he rather tell him, 'Prepare my supper, clothe yourself properly, and serve me while I eat and drink. Afterward you shall eat and drink'? **9** Does he thank that servant because he did the things that were commanded? I think not. **10** Even so you also, when you have done all the things that are commanded you, say, 'We are unworthy servants. We have done our duty.'" **11** As he was on his way to Jerusalem, he was passing along the borders of Samaria and Galilee. **12** As he entered into a certain village, ten men who were lepers met him, who stood at a distance. **13** They lifted up their voices, saying, "Jesus, Master, have mercy on us!" **14** When he saw them, he said to them, "Go and show yourselves to the priests." As they went, they were cleansed. **15** One of them, when he saw that he was healed, turned back, glorifying God with a loud voice. **16** He fell on his face at Jesus' feet, giving him thanks; and he was a Samaritan. **17** Jesus answered, "Weren't the ten cleansed? But where are the nine? **18** Were there none found who returned to give glory to God, except this foreigner?" **19** Then he said to him, "Get up, and go your way. Your faith has healed you." **20** Being asked by the Pharisees when God's Kingdom would come, he answered them, "God's Kingdom doesn't come with observation; **21** neither will they say,

'Look, here!' or, 'Look, there!' for behold, God's Kingdom is within you." **22** He said to the disciples, "The days will come when you will desire to see one of the days of the Son of Man, and you will not see it. **23** They will tell you, 'Look, here!' or 'Look, there!' Don't go away or follow after them, **24** for as the lightning, when it flashes out of one part under the sky, shines to another part under the sky, so will the Son of Man be in his day. **25** But first, he must suffer many things and be rejected by this generation. **26** As it was in the days of Noah, even so it will also be in the days of the Son of Man. **27** They ate, they drank, they married, and they were given in marriage until the day that Noah entered into the ship, and the flood came and destroyed them all. **28** Likewise, even as it was in the days of Lot: they ate, they drank, they bought, they sold, they planted, they built; **29** but in the day that Lot went out from Sodom, it rained fire and sulfur from the sky and destroyed them all. **30** It will be the same way in the day that the Son of Man is revealed. **31** In that day, he who will be on the housetop and his goods in the house, let him not go down to take them away. Let him who is in the field likewise not turn back. **32** Remember Lot's wife! **33** Whoever seeks to save his life loses it, but whoever loses his life preserves it. **34** I tell you, in that night there will be two people in one bed. One will be taken and the other will be left. **35** There will be two grinding grain together. One will be taken and the other will be left." **36** ᶜ **37** They, answering, asked him, "Where, Lord?" He said to them, "Where the body is, there the vultures will also be gathered together."

## 18

**1** He also spoke a parable to them that they must always pray and not give up, **2** saying, "There was a judge in a certain city who didn't fear God and didn't respect man. **3** A widow was in that city, and she often came to him, saying, 'Defend me from my adversary!' **4** He wouldn't for a while; but afterward he said to himself, 'Though I neither fear God nor respect man, **5** yet because this widow bothers me, I will defend her, or else she will wear me out by her continual coming.'" **6** The Lord said, "Listen to what the unrighteous judge says. **7** Won't God avenge his chosen ones who are crying out to him day and night, and yet he exercises patience with them? **8** I tell you that he will avenge them quickly. Nevertheless, when the Son of Man comes, will he find faith on the earth?" **9** He also spoke this parable to certain people who were convinced of their own righteousness, and who despised all others: **10** "Two men went up into the temple to pray; one was a Pharisee, and the other was a tax collector. **11** The Pharisee stood and prayed by himself like this: 'God, I thank you that I am not like the rest of men: extortionists, unrighteous, adulterers, or even like this tax collector. **12** I fast twice a week. I give tithes of all that I get.' **13** But the tax collector, standing far away, wouldn't even lift up his eyes to heaven, but beat his chest, saying, 'God, be merciful to me, a sinner!' **14** I tell you, this man went down to his house justified rather than the other; for everyone who exalts himself will be humbled, but he who humbles himself will be exalted." **15** They were also bringing their babies to him, that he might touch them. But when the disciples saw it, they rebuked them. **16** Jesus summoned them, saying, "Allow the little children to come to me, and don't hinder them, for God's Kingdom belongs to such as these. **17** Most certainly, I tell you, whoever doesn't receive God's Kingdom like a little child, he will in no way enter into it." **18** A certain ruler asked him, saying, "Good Teacher, what shall I do to inherit eternal life?" **19** Jesus asked him, "Why do you call me good? No one is good, except one: God. **20** You know the commandments: 'Don't commit adultery,' 'Don't murder,' 'Don't steal,' 'Don't give false testimony,' 'Honor your father and your mother.'"* **21** He said, "I have observed all these things from my youth up." **22** When Jesus heard these things, he said to him, "You still lack one thing. Sell all that you have and distribute it to the poor. Then you will have treasure in heaven; then come, follow me." **23** But when he heard these things, he became very sad, for he was very rich. **24** Jesus, seeing that he became very sad, said, "How hard it is for those who have riches to enter into God's Kingdom! **25** For it is easier for a camel to enter in through a needle's eye than for a rich man to enter into God's Kingdom." **26** Those who heard it said, "Then who can be saved?" **27** But he said, "The things which are impossible with men are possible with God." **28** Peter said, "Look, we have left everything and followed you." **29** He said to them, "Most certainly I tell you, there is no one who has left house, or wife, or brothers, or parents, or children, for God's Kingdom's sake, **30** who will not receive many times more in this time, and in the world to come, eternal life." **31** He took the twelve aside and said to them, "Behold, we are going up to Jerusalem, and all the things that are written through the prophets concerning the Son of Man will be completed. **32** For he will be delivered up to the Gentiles, will be mocked, treated shamefully, and

---

ᵃ *16:13* "Mammon" refers to riches or a false god of wealth.
ᵇ *16:23* or, Hell

ᶜ *17:36* Some Greek manuscripts add: "Two will be

in the field: the one taken, and the other left."

* *18:20* Exodus 20:12-16; Deuteronomy 5:16-20

spit on. <sup>33</sup> They will scourge and kill him. On the third day, he will rise again." <sup>34</sup> They understood none of these things. This saying was hidden from them, and they didn't understand the things that were said. <sup>35</sup> As he came near Jericho, a certain blind man sat by the road, begging. <sup>36</sup> Hearing a multitude going by, he asked what this meant. <sup>37</sup> They told him that Jesus of Nazareth was passing by. <sup>38</sup> He cried out, "Jesus, you son of David, have mercy on me!" <sup>39</sup> Those who led the way rebuked him, that he should be quiet; but he cried out all the more, "You son of David, have mercy on me!" <sup>40</sup> Standing still, Jesus commanded him to be brought to him. When he had come near, he asked him, <sup>41</sup> "What do you want me to do?" He said, "Lord, that I may see again." <sup>42</sup> Jesus said to him, "Receive your sight. Your faith has healed you." <sup>43</sup> Immediately he received his sight and followed him, glorifying God. All the people, when they saw it, praised God.

## 19

<sup>1</sup> He entered and was passing through Jericho. <sup>2</sup> There was a man named Zacchaeus. He was a chief tax collector, and he was rich. <sup>3</sup> He was trying to see who Jesus was, and couldn't because of the crowd, because he was short. <sup>4</sup> He ran on ahead and climbed up into a sycamore tree to see him, for he was going to pass that way. <sup>5</sup> When Jesus came to the place, he looked up and saw him, and said to him, "Zacchaeus, hurry and come down, for today I must stay at your house." <sup>6</sup> He hurried, came down, and received him joyfully. <sup>7</sup> When they saw it, they all murmured, saying, "He has gone in to lodge with a man who is a sinner." <sup>8</sup> Zacchaeus stood and said to the Lord, "Behold, Lord, half of my goods I give to the poor. If I have wrongfully exacted anything of anyone, I restore four times as much." <sup>9</sup> Jesus said to him, "Today, salvation has come to this house, because he also is a son of Abraham. <sup>10</sup> For the Son of Man came to seek and to save that which was lost." <sup>11</sup> As they heard these things, he went on and told a parable, because he was near Jerusalem, and they supposed that God's Kingdom would be revealed immediately. <sup>12</sup> He said therefore, "A certain nobleman went into a far country to receive for himself a kingdom and to return. <sup>13</sup> He called ten servants of his and gave them ten mina coins, <sup>a</sup> and told them, 'Conduct business until I come.' <sup>14</sup> But his citizens hated him, and sent an envoy after him, saying, 'We don't want this man to reign over us.' <sup>15</sup> "When he had come back again, having received the kingdom, he commanded these servants, to whom he had given the money, to be called to him, that he might know what they had gained by conducting business. <sup>16</sup> The first came before him, saying, 'Lord, your mina has made ten more minas.' <sup>17</sup> "He said to him, 'Well done, you good servant! Because you were found faithful with very little, you shall have authority over ten cities.' <sup>18</sup> "The second came, saying, 'Your mina, Lord, has made five minas.' <sup>19</sup> "So he said to him, 'And you are to be over five cities.' <sup>20</sup> Another came, saying, 'Lord, behold, your mina, which I kept laid away in a handkerchief, <sup>21</sup> for I feared you, because you are an exacting man. You take up that which you didn't lay down, and reap that which you didn't sow.' <sup>22</sup> "He said to him, 'Out of your own mouth I will judge you, you wicked servant! You knew that I am an exacting man, taking up that which I didn't lay down and reaping that which I didn't sow. <sup>23</sup> Then why didn't you deposit my money in the bank, and at my coming, I might have earned interest on it?' <sup>24</sup> He said to those who stood by, 'Take the mina away from him and give it to him who has the ten minas.' <sup>25</sup> "They said to him, 'Lord, he has ten minas!' <sup>26</sup> 'For I tell you that to everyone who has, will more be given; but from him who doesn't have, even that which he has will be taken away from him. <sup>27</sup> But bring those enemies of mine who didn't want me to reign over them here, and kill them before me.'" <sup>28</sup> Having said these things, he went on ahead, going up to Jerusalem. <sup>29</sup> When he came near to Bethsphage<sup>b</sup> and Bethany, at the mountain that is called Olivet, he sent two of his disciples, <sup>30</sup> saying, "Go your way into the village on the other side, in which, as you enter, you will find a colt tied, which no man has ever sat upon. Untie it and bring it. <sup>31</sup> If anyone asks you, 'Why are you untying it?' say to him: 'The Lord needs it.'" <sup>32</sup> Those who were sent went away and found things just as he had told them. <sup>33</sup> As they were untying the colt, its owners said to them, "Why are you untying the colt?" <sup>34</sup> They said, "The Lord needs it." <sup>35</sup> Then they brought it to Jesus. They threw their cloaks on the colt and sat Jesus on them. <sup>36</sup> As he went, they spread their cloaks on the road. <sup>37</sup> As he was now getting near, at the descent of the Mount of Olives, the whole multitude of the disciples began to rejoice and praise God with a loud voice for all the mighty works which they had seen, <sup>38</sup> saying, "Blessed is the King who comes in the name of the Lord! * Peace in heaven, and glory in the highest!" <sup>39</sup> Some of the Pharisees from the multitude said to him, "Teacher, rebuke your disciples!" <sup>40</sup> He

answered them, "I tell you that if these were silent, the stones would cry out." <sup>41</sup> When he came near, he saw the city and wept over it, <sup>42</sup> saying, "If you, even you, had known today the things which belong to your peace! But now, they are hidden from your eyes. <sup>43</sup> For the days will come on you when your enemies will throw up a barricade against you, surround you, hem you in on every side, <sup>44</sup> and will dash you and your children within you to the ground. They will not leave in you one stone on another, because you didn't know the time of your visitation." <sup>45</sup> He entered into the temple and began to drive out those who bought and sold in it, <sup>46</sup> saying to them, "It is written, 'My house is a house of prayer,' * but you have made it a 'den of robbers'!" * <sup>47</sup> He was teaching daily in the temple, but the chief priests, the scribes, and the leading men among the people sought to destroy him. <sup>48</sup> They couldn't find what they might do, for all the people hung on to every word that he said.

## 20

<sup>1</sup> On one of those days, as he was teaching the people in the temple and preaching the Good News, the<sup>c</sup> priests and scribes came to him with the elders. <sup>2</sup> They asked him, "Tell us: by what authority do you do these things? Or who is giving you this authority?" <sup>3</sup> He answered them, "I also will ask you one question. Tell me: <sup>4</sup> the baptism of John, was it from heaven, or from men?" <sup>5</sup> They reasoned with themselves, saying, "If we say, 'From heaven,' he will say, 'Why didn't you believe him?' <sup>6</sup> But if we say, 'From men,' all the people will stone us, for they are persuaded that John was a prophet." <sup>7</sup> They answered that they didn't know where it was from. <sup>8</sup> Jesus said to them, "Neither will I tell you by what authority I do these things." <sup>9</sup> He began to tell the people this parable: "A <sup>d</sup> man planted a vineyard and rented it out to some farmers, and went into another country for a long time. <sup>10</sup> At the proper season, he sent a servant to the farmers to collect his share of the fruit of the vineyard. But the farmers beat him and sent him away empty. <sup>11</sup> He sent yet another servant, and they also beat him and treated him shamefully, and sent him away empty. <sup>12</sup> He sent yet a third, and they also wounded him and threw him out. <sup>13</sup> The lord of the vineyard said, 'What shall I do? I will send my beloved son. It may be that seeing him, they will respect him.' <sup>14</sup> "But when the farmers saw him, they reasoned among themselves, saying, 'This is the heir. Come, let's kill him, that the inheritance may be ours.' <sup>15</sup> Then they threw him out of the vineyard and killed him. What therefore will the lord of the vineyard do to them? <sup>16</sup> He will come and destroy these farmers, and will give the vineyard to others." When they heard that, they said, "May that never be!" <sup>17</sup> But he looked at them and said, "Then what is this that is written, 'The stone which the builders rejected was made the chief cornerstone'?* <sup>18</sup> Everyone who falls on that stone will be broken to pieces, but it will crush whomever it falls on to dust." <sup>19</sup> The chief priests and the scribes sought to lay hands on him that very hour, but they feared the people— for they knew he had spoken this parable against them. <sup>20</sup> They watched him and sent out spies, who pretended to be righteous, that they might trap him in something he said, so as to deliver him up to the power and authority of the governor. <sup>21</sup> They asked him, "Teacher, we know that you say and teach what is right, and aren't partial to anyone, but truly teach the way of God. <sup>22</sup> Is it lawful for us to pay taxes to Caesar, or not?" <sup>23</sup> But he perceived their craftiness, and said to them, "Why do you test me? <sup>24</sup> Show me a denarius. Whose image and inscription are on it?" They answered, "Caesar's." <sup>25</sup> He said to them, "Then give to Caesar the things that are Caesar's, and to God the things that are God's." <sup>26</sup> They weren't able to trap him in his words before the people. They marveled at his answer and were silent. <sup>27</sup> Some of the Sadducees came to him, those who deny that there is a resurrection. <sup>28</sup> They asked him, "Teacher, Moses wrote to us that if a man's brother dies having a wife, and he is childless, his brother should take the wife and raise up children for his brother. <sup>29</sup> There were therefore seven brothers. The first took a wife, and died childless. <sup>30</sup> The second took her as wife, and he died childless. <sup>31</sup> The third took her, and likewise the seven all left no children, and died. <sup>32</sup> Afterward the woman also died. <sup>33</sup> Therefore in the resurrection whose wife of them will she be? For the seven had her as a wife." <sup>34</sup> Jesus said to them, "The children of this age marry and are given in marriage. <sup>35</sup> But those who are considered worthy to attain to that age and the resurrection from the dead neither marry nor are given in marriage. <sup>36</sup> For they can't die any more, for they are like the angels and are children of God, being children of the resurrection. <sup>37</sup> But that the dead are raised, even Moses showed at the bush, when he called the Lord 'The God of Abraham, the God of Isaac, and the God of Jacob.' * <sup>38</sup> Now he is not the God of the dead, but of the living, for all are alive to him." <sup>39</sup> Some of the scribes answered, "Teacher, you

<sup>a</sup> 19:13 10 minas was more than 3 years' wages for an agricultural laborer.

<sup>b</sup> 19:29 TR, NU read "Bethpage" instead of "Bethsphage"
* 19:38 Psalms 118:26

* 19:46 Isaiah 56:7
* 19:46 Jeremiah 7:11
<sup>c</sup> 20:1 TR adds "chief"

<sup>d</sup> 20:9 NU (in brackets) and TR add "certain"
* 20:17 Psalms 118:22
* 20:37 Exodus 3:6

speak well." **40** They didn't dare to ask him any more questions. **41** He said to them, "Why do they say that the Christ is David's son? **42** David himself says in the book of Psalms, 'The Lord said to my Lord, "Sit at my right hand, **43** until I make your enemies the footstool of your feet."' * **44** "David therefore calls him Lord, so how is he his son?" **45** In the hearing of all the people, he said to his disciples, **46** "Beware of those scribes who like to walk in long robes, and love greetings in the marketplaces, the best seats in the synagogues, and the best places at feasts; **47** who devour widows' houses, and for a pretense make long prayers. These will receive greater condemnation."

## 21

**1** He looked up and saw the rich people who were putting their gifts into the treasury. **2** He saw a certain poor widow casting in two small brass coins.ᵃ **3** He said, "Truly I tell you, this poor widow put in more than all of them, **4** for all these put in gifts for God from their abundance, but she, out of her poverty, put in all that she had to live on." **5** As some were talking about the temple and how it was decorated with beautiful stones and gifts, he said, **6** "As for these things which you see, the days will come in which there will not be left here one stone on another that will not be thrown down." **7** They asked him, "Teacher, so when will these things be? What is the sign that these things are about to happen?" **8** He said, "Watch out that you don't get led astray, for many will come in my name, saying, 'I am heᵇ', and, 'The time is at hand.' Therefore don't follow them. **9** When you hear of wars and disturbances, don't be terrified, for these things must happen first, but the end won't come immediately." **10** Then he said to them, "Nation will rise against nation, and kingdom against kingdom. **11** There will be great earthquakes, famines, and plagues in various places. There will be terrors and great signs from heaven. **12** But before all these things, they will lay their hands on you and will persecute you, delivering you up to synagogues and prisons, bringing you before kings and governors for my name's sake. **13** It will turn out as a testimony for you. **14** Settle it therefore in your hearts not to meditate beforehand how to answer, **15** for I will give you a mouth and wisdom which all your adversaries will not be able to withstand or to contradict. **16** You will be handed over even by parents, brothers, relatives, and friends. They will cause some of you to be put to death. **17** You will be hated by all men for my name's sake. **18** And not a hair of your head will perish. **19** "By your endurance you will win your lives. **20** "But when you see Jerusalem surrounded by armies, then know that its desolation is at hand. **21** Then let those who are in Judea flee to the mountains. Let those who are in the middle of her depart. Let those who are in the country not enter therein. **22** For these are days of vengeance, that all things which are written may be fulfilled. **23** Woe to those who are pregnant and to those who nurse infants in those days! For there will be great distress in the land and wrath to this people. **24** They will fall by the edge of the sword, and will be led captive into all the nations. Jerusalem will be trampled down by the Gentiles until the times of the Gentiles are fulfilled. **25** "There will be signs in the sun, moon, and stars; and on the earth anxiety of nations, in perplexity for the roaring of the sea and the waves; **26** men fainting for fear and for expectation of the things which are coming on the world, for the powers of the heavens will be shaken. **27** Then they will see the Son of Man coming in a cloud with power and great glory. **28** But when these things begin to happen, look up and lift up your heads, because your redemption is near." **29** He told them a parable. "See the fig tree and all the trees. **30** When they are already budding, you see it and know by your own selves that the summer is already near. **31** Even so you also, when you see these things happening, know that God's Kingdom is near. **32** Most certainly I tell you, this generation will not pass away until all things are accomplished. **33** Heaven and earth will pass away, but my words will by no means pass away. **34** "So be careful, or your hearts will be loaded down with carousing, drunkenness, and cares of this life, and that day will come on you suddenly. **35** For it will come like a snare on all those who dwell on the surface of all the earth. **36** Therefore be watchful all the time, praying that you may be counted worthy to escape all these things that will happen, and to stand before the Son of Man." **37** Every day Jesus was teaching in the temple, and every night he would go out and spend the night on the mountain that is called Olivet. **38** All the people came early in the morning to him in the temple to hear him.

## 22

**1** Now the feast of unleavened bread, which is called the Passover, was approaching. **2** The chief priests and the scribes sought how they might put him to death, for they feared the people. **3** Satan entered into Judas, who was also called Iscariot, who was counted with the twelve. **4** He went away and talked with the chief priests and captains about how he might deliver him to them. **5** They were glad, and agreed to give him

money. **6** He consented and sought an opportunity to deliver him to them in the absence of the multitude. **7** The day of unleavened bread came, on which the Passover must be sacrificed. **8** Jesus sent Peter and John, saying, "Go and prepare the Passover for us, that we may eat." **9** They said to him, "Where do you want us to prepare?" **10** He said to them, "Behold, when you have entered into the city, a man carrying a pitcher of water will meet you. Follow him into the house which he enters. **11** Tell the master of the house, 'The Teacher says to you, "Where is the guest room, where I may eat the Passover with my disciples?"' **12** He will show you a large, furnished upper room. Make preparations there." **13** They went, found things as Jesus had told them, and they prepared the Passover. **14** When the hour had come, he sat down with the twelve apostles. **15** He said to them, "I have earnestly desired to eat this Passover with you before I suffer, **16** for I tell you, I will no longer by any means eat of it until it is fulfilled in God's Kingdom." **17** He received a cup, and when he had given thanks, he said, "Take this and share it among yourselves, **18** for I tell you, I will not drink at all again from the fruit of the vine, until God's Kingdom comes." **19** He took bread, and when he had given thanks, he broke and gave it to them, saying, "This is my body which is given for you. Do this in memory of me." **20** Likewise, he took the cup after supper, saying, "This cup is the new covenant in my blood, which is poured out for you. **21** But behold, the hand of him who betrays me is with me on the table. **22** The Son of Man indeed goes as it has been determined, but woe to that man through whom he is betrayed!" **23** They began to question among themselves which of them it was who would do this thing. **24** A dispute also arose among them, which of them was considered to be greatest. **25** He said to them, "The kings of the nations lord it over them, and those who have authority over them are called 'benefactors.' **26** But not so with you. Rather, the one who is greater among you, let him become as the younger, and one who is governing, as one who serves. **27** For who is greater, one who sits at the table, or one who serves? Isn't it he who sits at the table? But I am among you as one who serves. **28** "But you are those who have continued with me in my trials. **29** I confer on you a kingdom, even as my Father conferred on me, **30** that you may eat and drink at my table in my Kingdom. You will sit on thrones, judging the twelve tribes of Israel." **31** The Lord said, "Simon, Simon, behold, Satan asked to have all of you, that he might sift you as wheat, **32** but I prayed for you, that your faith wouldn't fail. You, when once you have turned again, establish your brothers."ᶜ **33** He said to him, "Lord, I am ready to go with you both to prison and to death!" **34** He said, "I tell you, Peter, the rooster will by no means crow today until you deny that you know me three times." **35** He said to them, "When I sent you out without purse, bag, and sandals, did you lack anything?" They said, "Nothing." **36** Then he said to them, "But now, whoever has a purse, let him take it, and likewise a bag. Whoever has none, let him sell his cloak, and buy a sword. **37** For I tell you that this which is written must still be fulfilled in me: 'He was counted with transgressors.'* For that which concerns me is being fulfilled." **38** They said, "Lord, behold, here are two swords." He said to them, "That is enough." **39** He came out and went, as his custom was, to the Mount of Olives. His disciples also followed him. **40** When he was at the place, he said to them, "Pray that you don't enter into temptation." **41** He was withdrawn from them about a stone's throw, and he knelt down and prayed, **42** saying, "Father, if you are willing, remove this cup from me. Nevertheless, not my will, but yours, be done." **43** An angel from heaven appeared to him, strengthening him. **44** Being in agony, he prayed more earnestly. His sweat became like great drops of blood falling down on the ground. **45** When he rose up from his prayer, he came to the disciples and found them sleeping because of grief, **46** and said to them, "Why do you sleep? Rise and pray that you may not enter into temptation." **47** While he was still speaking, a crowd appeared. He who was called Judas, one of the twelve, was leading them. He came near to Jesus to kiss him. **48** But Jesus said to him, "Judas, do you betray the Son of Man with a kiss?" **49** When those who were around him saw what was about to happen, they said to him, "Lord, shall we strike with the sword?" **50** A certain one of them struck the servant of the high priest, and cut off his right ear. **51** But Jesus answered, "Let me at least do this"—and he touched his ear and healed him. **52** Jesus said to the chief priests, captains of the temple, and elders, who had come against him, "Have you come out as against a robber, with swords and clubs? **53** When I was with you in the temple daily, you didn't stretch out your hands against me. But this is your hour, and the power of darkness." **54** They seized him and led him away, and brought him into the high priest's house. But Peter followed from a distance. **55** When they had kindled a fire in the middle of the courtyard and had sat down together, Peter sat

---

* *20:43* Psalms 110:1
ᵃ *21:2* literally, "two lepta." 2 lepta was about 1% of a day's

wages for an agricultural laborer.
ᵇ *21:8* or, I AM

ᶜ *22:32* The word for "brothers" here may be also

correctly translated "brothers and sisters" or "siblings."
* *22:37* Isaiah 53:12

among them. <sup>56</sup> A certain servant girl saw him as he sat in the light, and looking intently at him, said, "This man also was with him." <sup>57</sup> He denied Jesus, saying, "Woman, I don't know him." <sup>58</sup> After a little while someone else saw him and said, "You also are one of them!" But Peter answered, "Man, I am not!" <sup>59</sup> After about one hour passed, another confidently affirmed, saying, "Truly this man also was with him, for he is a Galilean!" <sup>60</sup> But Peter said, "Man, I don't know what you are talking about!" Immediately, while he was still speaking, a rooster crowed. <sup>61</sup> The Lord turned and looked at Peter. Then Peter remembered the Lord's word, how he said to him, "Before the rooster crows you will deny me three times." <sup>62</sup> He went out, and wept bitterly. <sup>63</sup> The men who held Jesus mocked him and beat him. <sup>64</sup> Having blindfolded him, they struck him on the face and asked him, "Prophesy! Who is the one who struck you?" <sup>65</sup> They spoke many other things against him, insulting him. <sup>66</sup> As soon as it was day, the assembly of the elders of the people were gathered together, both chief priests and scribes, and they led him away into their council, saying, <sup>67</sup>"If you are the Christ, tell us." But he said to them, "If I tell you, you won't believe, <sup>68</sup> and if I ask, you will in no way answer me or let me go. <sup>69</sup> From now on, the Son of Man will be seated at the right hand of the power of God." <sup>70</sup> They all said, "Are you then the Son of God?" He said to them, "You say it, because I am." <sup>71</sup> They said, "Why do we need any more witness? For we ourselves have heard from his own mouth!"

## 23

<sup>1</sup> The whole company of them rose up and brought him before Pilate. <sup>2</sup> They began to accuse him, saying, "We found this man perverting the nation, forbidding paying taxes to Caesar, and saying that he himself is Christ, a king." <sup>3</sup> Pilate asked him, "Are you the King of the Jews?" He answered him, "So you say." <sup>4</sup> Pilate said to the chief priests and the multitudes, "I find no basis for a charge against this man." <sup>5</sup> But they insisted, saying, "He stirs up the people, teaching throughout all Judea, beginning from Galilee even to this place." <sup>6</sup> But when Pilate heard Galilee mentioned, he asked if the man was a Galilean. <sup>7</sup> When he found out that he was in Herod's jurisdiction, he sent him to Herod, who was also in Jerusalem during those days. <sup>8</sup> Now when Herod saw Jesus, he was exceedingly glad, for he had wanted to see him for a long time, because he had heard many things about him. He hoped to see some miracle done by him. <sup>9</sup> He questioned him with many words, but he gave no answers. <sup>10</sup> The chief priests and the scribes stood, vehemently accusing him. <sup>11</sup> Herod with his soldiers humiliated him and mocked him. Dressing him in luxurious clothing, they sent him back to Pilate. <sup>12</sup> Herod and Pilate became friends with each other that very day, for before that they were enemies with each other. <sup>13</sup> Pilate called together the chief priests, the rulers, and the people, <sup>14</sup> and said to them, "You brought this man to me as one that perverts the people, and behold, having examined him before you, I found no basis for a charge against this man concerning those things of which you accuse him. <sup>15</sup> Neither has Herod, for I sent you to him, and see, nothing worthy of death has been done by him. <sup>16</sup> I will therefore chastise him and release him." <sup>17</sup> Now he had to release one prisoner to them at the feast.<sup>a</sup> <sup>18</sup> But they all cried out together, saying, "Away with this man! Release to us Barabbas!"— <sup>19</sup> one who was thrown into prison for a certain revolt in the city, and for murder. <sup>20</sup> Then Pilate spoke to them again, wanting to release Jesus, <sup>21</sup> but they shouted, saying, "Crucify! Crucify him!" <sup>22</sup> He said to them the third time, "Why? What evil has this man done? I have found no capital crime in him. I will therefore chastise him and release him." <sup>23</sup> But they were urgent with loud voices, asking that he might be crucified. Their voices and the voices of the chief priests prevailed. <sup>24</sup> Pilate decreed that what they asked for should be done. <sup>25</sup> He released him who had been thrown into prison for insurrection and murder, for whom they asked, but he delivered Jesus up to their will. <sup>26</sup> When they led him away, they grabbed one Simon of Cyrene, coming from the country, and laid the cross on him to carry it after Jesus. <sup>27</sup> A great multitude of the people followed him, including women who also mourned and lamented him. <sup>28</sup> But Jesus, turning to them, said, "Daughters of Jerusalem, don't weep for me, but weep for yourselves and for your children. <sup>29</sup> For behold, the days are coming in which they will say, 'Blessed are the barren, the wombs that never bore, and the breasts that never nursed.' <sup>30</sup> Then they will begin to tell the mountains, 'Fall on us!' and tell the hills, 'Cover us.'* <sup>31</sup> For if they do these things in the green tree, what will be done in the dry?" <sup>32</sup> There were also others, two criminals, led with him to be put to death. <sup>33</sup> When they came to the place that is called "The Skull", they crucified him there with the criminals, one on the right and the other on the left. <sup>34</sup> Jesus said, "Father, forgive them, for they don't know what they are doing." Dividing his garments among them, they cast lots. <sup>35</sup> The people stood

watching. The rulers with them also scoffed at him, saying, "He saved others. Let him save himself, if this is the Christ of God, his chosen one!" <sup>36</sup> The soldiers also mocked him, coming to him and offering him vinegar, <sup>37</sup> and saying, "If you are the King of the Jews, save yourself!" <sup>38</sup> An inscription was also written over him in letters of Greek, Latin, and Hebrew: "THIS IS THE KING OF THE JEWS." <sup>39</sup> One of the criminals who was hanged insulted him, saying, "If you are the Christ, save yourself and us!" <sup>40</sup> But the other answered, and rebuking him said, "Don't you even fear God, seeing you are under the same condemnation? <sup>41</sup> And we indeed justly, for we receive the due reward for our deeds, but this man has done nothing wrong." <sup>42</sup> He said to Jesus, "Lord, remember me when you come into your Kingdom." <sup>43</sup> Jesus said to him, "Assuredly I tell you, today you will be with me in Paradise." <sup>44</sup> It was now about the sixth hour,<sup>b</sup> and darkness came over the whole land until the ninth hour.<sup>c</sup> <sup>45</sup> The sun was darkened, and the veil of the temple was torn in two. <sup>46</sup> Jesus, crying with a loud voice, said, "Father, into your hands I commit my spirit!" Having said this, he breathed his last. <sup>47</sup> When the centurion saw what was done, he glorified God, saying, "Certainly this was a righteous man." <sup>48</sup> All the multitudes that came together to see this, when they saw the things that were done, returned home beating their chests. <sup>49</sup> All his acquaintances and the women who followed with him from Galilee stood at a distance, watching these things. <sup>50</sup> Behold, there was a man named Joseph, who was a member of the council, a good and righteous man <sup>51</sup>(he had not consented to their counsel and deed), from Arimathaea, a city of the Jews, who was also waiting for God's Kingdom. <sup>52</sup> This man went to Pilate, and asked for Jesus' body. <sup>53</sup> He took it down and wrapped it in a linen cloth, and laid him in a tomb that was cut in stone, where no one had ever been laid. <sup>54</sup> It was the day of the Preparation, and the Sabbath was drawing near. <sup>55</sup> The women who had come with him out of Galilee followed after, and saw the tomb and how his body was laid. <sup>56</sup> They returned and prepared spices and ointments. On the Sabbath they rested according to the commandment.

## 24

<sup>1</sup> But on the first day of the week, at early dawn, they and some others came to the tomb, bringing the spices which they had prepared. <sup>2</sup> They found the stone rolled away from the tomb. <sup>3</sup> They entered in, and didn't find the Lord Jesus' body. <sup>4</sup> While they were greatly perplexed about this, behold, two men stood by them in dazzling clothing. <sup>5</sup> Becoming terrified, they bowed their faces down to the earth. The men said to them, "Why do you seek the living among the dead? <sup>6</sup> He isn't here, but is risen. Remember what he told you when he was still in Galilee, <sup>7</sup> saying that the Son of Man must be delivered up into the hands of sinful men and be crucified, and the third day rise again?" <sup>8</sup> They remembered his words, <sup>9</sup> returned from the tomb, and told all these things to the eleven and to all the rest. <sup>10</sup> Now they were Mary Magdalene, Joanna, and Mary the mother of James. The other women with them told these things to the apostles. <sup>11</sup> These words seemed to them to be nonsense, and they didn't believe them. <sup>12</sup> But Peter got up and ran to the tomb. Stooping and looking in, he saw the strips of linen lying by themselves, and he departed to his home, wondering what had happened. <sup>13</sup> Behold, two of them were going that very day to a village named Emmaus, which was sixty stadia<sup>d</sup> from Jerusalem. <sup>14</sup> They talked with each other about all of these things which had happened. <sup>15</sup> While they talked and questioned together, Jesus himself came near, and went with them. <sup>16</sup> But their eyes were kept from recognizing him. <sup>17</sup> He said to them, "What are you talking about as you walk, and are sad?" <sup>18</sup> One of them, named Cleopas, answered him, "Are you the only stranger in Jerusalem who doesn't know the things which have happened there in these days?" <sup>19</sup> He said to them, "What things?" They said to him, "The things concerning Jesus the Nazarene, who was a prophet mighty in deed and word before God and all the people; <sup>20</sup> and how the chief priests and our rulers delivered him up to be condemned to death, and crucified him. <sup>21</sup> But we were hoping that it was he who would redeem Israel. Yes, and besides all this, it is now the third day since these things happened. <sup>22</sup> Also, certain women of our company amazed us, having arrived early at the tomb; <sup>23</sup> and when they didn't find his body, they came saying that they had also seen a vision of angels, who said that he was alive. <sup>24</sup> Some of us went to the tomb and found it just like the women had said, but they didn't see him." <sup>25</sup> He said to them, "Foolish people, and slow of heart to believe in all that the prophets have spoken! <sup>26</sup> Didn't the Christ have to suffer these things and to enter into his glory?" <sup>27</sup> Beginning from Moses and from all the prophets, he explained to them in all the Scriptures the things concerning himself. <sup>28</sup> They came near to the village where they were going, and he acted like he would go further. <sup>29</sup> They urged him, saying, "Stay with us, for it is

---

<sup>a</sup> *23:17* NU omits verse 17.
<sup>*</sup> 23:30 Hosea 10:8

<sup>b</sup> *23:44* Time was counted from sunrise, so the sixth hour was about noon.

<sup>c</sup> *23:44* 3:00 p.m.
<sup>d</sup> *24:13* 60 stadia = about 11 kilometers or about 7 miles.

almost evening, and the day is almost over." He went in to stay with them. [30] When he had sat down at the table with them, he took the bread and gave thanks. Breaking it, he gave it to them. [31] Their eyes were opened and they recognized him; then he vanished out of their sight. [32] They said to one another, "Weren't our hearts burning within us while he spoke to us along the way, and while he opened the Scriptures to us?" [33] They rose up that very hour, returned to Jerusalem, and found the eleven gathered together, and those who were with them, [34] saying, "The Lord is risen indeed, and has appeared to Simon!" [35] They related the things that happened along the way, and how he was recognized by them in the breaking of the bread. [36] As they said these things, Jesus himself stood among them, and said to them, "Peace be to you." [37] But they were terrified and filled with fear, and supposed that they had seen a spirit. [38] He said to them, "Why are you troubled? Why do doubts arise in your hearts? [39] See my hands and my feet, that it is truly me. Touch me and see, for a spirit doesn't have flesh and bones, as you see that I have." [40] When he had said this, he showed them his hands and his feet. [41] While they still didn't believe for joy, and wondered, he said to them, "Do you have anything here to eat?" [42] They gave him a piece of a broiled fish and some honeycomb. [43] He took them, and ate in front of them. [44] He said to them, "This is what I told you while I was still with you, that all things which are written in the law of Moses, the prophets, and the psalms concerning me must be fulfilled." [45] Then he opened their minds, that they might understand the Scriptures. [46] He said to them, "Thus it is written, and thus it was necessary for the Christ to suffer and to rise from the dead the third day, [47] and that repentance and remission of sins should be preached in his name to all the nations, beginning at Jerusalem. [48] You are witnesses of these things. [49] Behold, I send out the promise of my Father on you. But wait in the city of Jerusalem until you are clothed with power from on high." [50] He led them out as far as Bethany, and he lifted up his hands and blessed them. [51] While he blessed them, he withdrew from them and was carried up into heaven. [52] They worshiped him and returned to Jerusalem with great joy, [53] and were continually in the temple, praising and blessing God. Amen.

# The Good News According to John

## 1

[1] In the beginning was the Word, and the Word was with God, and the Word was God. [2] The same was in the beginning with God. [3] All things were made through him. Without him, nothing was made that has been made. [4] In him was life, and the life was the light of men. [5] The light shines in the darkness, and the darkness hasn't overcome[a] it. [6] There came a man sent from God, whose name was John. [7] The same came as a witness, that he might testify about the light, that all might believe through him. [8] He was not the light, but was sent that he might testify about the light. [9] The true light that enlightens everyone was coming into the world. [10] He was in the world, and the world was made through him, and the world didn't recognize him. [11] He came to his own, and those who were his own didn't receive him. [12] But as many as received him, to them he gave the right to become God's children, to those who believe in his name: [13] who were born, not of blood, nor of the will of the flesh, nor of the will of man, but of God. [14] The Word became flesh and lived among us. We saw his glory, such glory as of the only born[b] Son of the Father, full of grace and truth. [15] John testified about him. He cried out, saying, "This was he of whom I said, 'He who comes after me has surpassed me, for he was before me.'" [16] From his fullness we all received grace upon grace. [17] For the law was given through Moses. Grace and truth were realized through Jesus Christ.[c] [18] No one has seen God at any time. The only born[d] Son,[e] who is in the bosom of the Father, has declared him. [19] This is John's testimony, when the Jews sent priests and Levites from Jerusalem to ask him, "Who are you?" [20] He declared, and didn't deny, but he declared, "I am not the Christ." [21] They asked him, "What then? Are you Elijah?" He said, "I am not." "Are you the prophet?" He answered, "No." [22] They said therefore to him, "Who are you? Give us an answer to take back to those who sent us. What do you say about yourself?" [23] He said, "I am the voice of one crying in the wilderness, 'Make straight the way of the Lord,'* as Isaiah the prophet said." [24] The ones who had been sent were from the

Pharisees. [25] They asked him, "Why then do you baptize if you are not the Christ, nor Elijah, nor the prophet?" [26] John answered them, "I baptize in water, but among you stands one whom you don't know. [27] He is the one who comes after me, who is preferred before me, whose sandal strap I'm not worthy to loosen." [28] These things were done in Bethany beyond the Jordan, where John was baptizing. [29] The next day, he saw Jesus coming to him, and said, "Behold,[f] the Lamb of God, who takes away the sin of the world! [30] This is he of whom I said, 'After me comes a man who is preferred before me, for he was before me.' [31] I didn't know him, but for this reason I came baptizing in water, that he would be revealed to Israel." [32] John testified, saying, "I have seen the Spirit descending like a dove out of heaven, and it remained on him. [33] I didn't recognize him, but he who sent me to baptize in water said to me, 'On whomever you will see the Spirit descending and remaining on him is he who baptizes in the Holy Spirit.' [34] I have seen and have testified that this is the Son of God." [35] Again, the next day, John was standing with two of his disciples, [36] and he looked at Jesus as he walked, and said, "Behold, the Lamb of God!" [37] The two disciples heard him speak, and they followed Jesus. [38] Jesus turned and saw them following, and said to them, "What are you looking for?" They said to him, "Rabbi" (which is to say, being interpreted, Teacher), "where are you staying?" [39] He said to them, "Come and see." They came and saw where he was staying, and they stayed with him that day. It was about the tenth hour.[g] [40] One of the two who heard John and followed him was Andrew, Simon Peter's brother. [41] He first found his own brother, Simon, and said to him, "We have found the Messiah!" (which is, being interpreted, Christ[h]). [42] He brought him to Jesus. Jesus looked at him and said, "You are Simon the son of Jonah. You shall be called Cephas" (which is by interpretation, Peter).[i] [43] On the next day, he was determined to go out into Galilee, and he found Philip. Jesus said to him, "Follow me." [44] Now Philip was from Bethsaida, the city of Andrew and Peter. [45] Philip found Nathanael, and said to him, "We have found him of whom Moses in the law and also the prophets, wrote: Jesus of Nazareth, the son of Joseph." [46] Nathanael said to him, "Can any good thing come out of Nazareth?" Philip said to him, "Come and see." [47] Jesus saw Nathanael coming to him, and said about him, "Behold, an Israelite indeed, in whom is no deceit!" [48] Nathanael said to him, "How do you know me?" Jesus answered him, "Before Philip called you, when you were under the fig tree, I saw you." [49] Nathanael answered him, "Rabbi, you are the Son of God! You are King of Israel!" [50] Jesus answered him, "Because I told you, 'I saw you underneath the fig tree,' do you believe? You will see greater things than these!" [51] He said to him, "Most certainly, I tell you all, hereafter you will see heaven opened, and the angels of God ascending and descending on the Son of Man."

## 2

[1] The third day, there was a wedding in Cana of Galilee. Jesus' mother was there. [2] Jesus also was invited, with his disciples, to the wedding. [3] When the wine ran out, Jesus' mother said to him, "They have no wine." [4] Jesus said to her, "Woman, what does that have to do with you and me? My hour has not yet come." [5] His mother said to the servants, "Whatever he says to you, do it." [6] Now there were six water pots of stone set there after the Jews' way of purifying, containing two or three metretes[j] apiece. [7] Jesus said to them, "Fill the water pots with water." So they filled them up to the brim. [8] He said to them, "Now draw some out, and take it to the ruler of the feast." So they took it. [9] When the ruler of the feast tasted the water now become wine, and didn't know where it came from (but the servants who had drawn the water knew), the ruler of the feast called the bridegroom [10] and said to him, "Everyone serves the good wine first, and when the guests have drunk freely, then that which is worse. You have kept the good wine until now!" [11] This beginning of his signs Jesus did in Cana of Galilee, and revealed his glory; and his disciples believed in him. [12] After this, he went down to Capernaum, he, and his mother, his brothers, and his disciples; and they stayed there a few days. [13] The Passover of the Jews was at hand, and Jesus went up to Jerusalem. [14] He found in the temple those who sold oxen, sheep, and doves, and the changers of money sitting. [15] He made a whip of cords and drove all out of the temple, both the sheep and the oxen; and he poured out the changers' money and overthrew their tables. [16] To those who sold the doves, he said, "Take

---

[a] 1:5 The word translated "overcome" (κατέλαβεν) can also be translated "comprehended." It refers to getting a grip on an enemy to defeat him.
[b] 1:14 The phrase "only born" is from the Greek word "μονογενους", which is

sometimes translated "only begotten" or "one and only".
[c] 1:17 "Christ" means "Anointed One".
[d] 1:18 The phrase "only born" is from the Greek word "μονογενη", which is sometimes translated "only begotten" or "one and only".

[e] 1:18 NU reads "God"
* 1:23 Isaiah 40:3
[f] 1:29 "Behold", from "ἰδού", means look at, take notice, observe, see, or gaze at. It is often used as an interjection.
[g] 1:39 4:00 p.m.

[h] 1:41 "Messiah" (Hebrew) and "Christ" (Greek) both mean "Anointed One".
[i] 1:42 "Cephas" (Aramaic) and "Peter" (Greek) both mean "Rock".
[j] 2:6 2 to 3 metretes is about 20 to 30 U. S. Gallons, or 75 to 115 liters.

these things out of here! Don't make my Father's house a marketplace!" **17** His disciples remembered that it was written, "Zeal for your house will eat me up."* **18** The Jews therefore answered him, "What sign do you show us, seeing that you do these things?" **19** Jesus answered them, "Destroy this temple, and in three days I will raise it up." **20** The Jews therefore said, "It took forty-six years to build this temple! Will you raise it up in three days?" **21** But he spoke of the temple of his body. **22** When therefore he was raised from the dead, his disciples remembered that he said this, and they believed the Scripture and the word which Jesus had said. **23** Now when he was in Jerusalem at the Passover, during the feast, many believed in his name, observing his signs which he did. **24** But Jesus didn't entrust himself to them, because he knew everyone, **25** and because he didn't need for anyone to testify concerning man; for he himself knew what was in man.

**3**

**1** Now there was a man of the Pharisees named Nicodemus, a ruler of the Jews. **2** He came to Jesus by night and said to him, "Rabbi, we know that you are a teacher come from God, for no one can do these signs that you do, unless God is with him." **3** Jesus answered him, "Most certainly I tell you, unless one is born anew, **ᵃ** he can't see God's Kingdom." **4** Nicodemus said to him, "How can a man be born when he is old? Can he enter a second time into his mother's womb and be born?" **5** Jesus answered, "Most certainly I tell you, unless one is born of water and Spirit, he can't enter into God's Kingdom. **6** That which is born of the flesh is flesh. That which is born of the Spirit is spirit. **7** Don't marvel that I said to you, 'You must be born anew.' **8** The wind**ᵇ** blows where it wants to, and you hear its sound, but don't know where it comes from and where it is going. So is everyone who is born of the Spirit." **9** Nicodemus answered him, "How can these things be?" **10** Jesus answered him, "Are you the teacher of Israel, and don't understand these things? **11** Most certainly I tell you, we speak that which we know and testify of that which we have seen, and you don't receive our witness. **12** If I told you earthly things and you don't believe, how will you believe if I tell you heavenly things? **13** No one has ascended into heaven but he who descended out of heaven, the Son of Man, who is in heaven. **14** As Moses lifted up the serpent in the wilderness, even so must the Son of Man be lifted up, **15** that whoever believes in him should not perish, but have eternal life. **16** For God so loved the world, that he gave his only born**ᶜ** Son, that whoever believes in him should not perish, but have eternal life. **17** For God didn't send his Son into the world to judge the world, but that the world should be saved through him. **18** He who believes in him is not judged. He who doesn't believe has been judged already, because he has not believed in the name of the only born Son of God. **19** This is the judgment, that the light has come into the world, and men loved the darkness rather than the light, for their works were evil. **20** For everyone who does evil hates the light and doesn't come to the light, lest his works would be exposed. **21** But he who does the truth comes to the light, that his works may be revealed, that they have been done in God." **22** After these things, Jesus came with his disciples into the land of Judea. He stayed there with them and baptized. **23** John also was baptizing in Enon near Salim, because there was much water there. They came and were baptized; **24** for John was not yet thrown into prison. **25** Therefore a dispute arose on the part of John's disciples with some Jews about purification. **26** They came to John and said to him, "Rabbi, he who was with you beyond the Jordan, to whom you have testified, behold, he baptizes, and everyone is coming to him." **27** John answered, "A man can receive nothing unless it has been given him from heaven. **28** You yourselves testify that I said, 'I am not the Christ,' but, 'I have been sent before him.' **29** He who has the bride is the bridegroom; but the friend of the bridegroom, who stands and hears him, rejoices greatly because of the bridegroom's voice. Therefore my joy is made full. **30** He must increase, but I must decrease. **31** "He who comes from above is above all. He who is from the earth belongs to the earth and speaks of the earth. He who comes from heaven is above all. **32** What he has seen and heard, of that he testifies; and no one receives his witness. **33** He who has received his witness has set his seal to this, that God is true. **34** For he whom God has sent speaks the words of God; for God gives the Spirit without measure. **35** The Father loves the Son, and has given all things into his hand. **36** One who believes in the Son has eternal life, but one who disobeys**ᵈ** the Son won't see life, but the wrath of God remains on him."

**4**

**1** Therefore when the Lord knew that the Pharisees had heard that Jesus was making and baptizing more disciples than John **2** (although Jesus himself didn't baptize, but his disciples), **3** he left Judea and departed into Galilee. **4** He needed to pass through Samaria. **5** So he came to a city of Samaria called Sychar, near the parcel of ground that Jacob gave to his son Joseph. **6** Jacob's well was there. Jesus therefore, being tired from his journey, sat down by the well. It was about the sixth hour.**ᵉ** **7** A woman of Samaria came to draw water. Jesus said to her, "Give me a drink." **8** For his disciples had gone away into the city to buy food. **9** The Samaritan woman therefore said to him, "How is it that you, being a Jew, ask for a drink from me, a Samaritan woman?" (For Jews have no dealings with Samaritans.) **10** Jesus answered her, "If you knew the gift of God, and who it is who says to you, 'Give me a drink,' you would have asked him, and he would have given you living water." **11** The woman said to him, "Sir, you have nothing to draw with, and the well is deep. So where do you get that living water? **12** Are you greater than our father Jacob, who gave us the well and drank from it himself, as did his children and his livestock?" **13** Jesus answered her, "Everyone who drinks of this water will thirst again, **14** but whoever drinks of the water that I will give him will never thirst again; but the water that I will give him will become in him a well of water springing up to eternal life." **15** The woman said to him, "Sir, give me this water, so that I don't get thirsty, neither come all the way here to draw." **16** Jesus said to her, "Go, call your husband, and come here." **17** The woman answered, "I have no husband." Jesus said to her, "You said well, 'I have no husband,' **18** for you have had five husbands; and he whom you now have is not your husband. This you have said truly." **19** The woman said to him, "Sir, I perceive that you are a prophet. **20** Our fathers worshiped in this mountain, and you Jews say that in Jerusalem is the place where people ought to worship." **21** Jesus said to her, "Woman, believe me, the hour is coming when neither in this mountain nor in Jerusalem will you worship the Father. **22** You worship that which you don't know. We worship that which we know; for salvation is from the Jews. **23** But the hour comes, and now is, when the true worshipers will worship the Father in spirit and truth, for the Father seeks such to be his worshipers. **24** God is spirit, and those who worship him must worship in spirit and truth." **25** The woman said to him, "I know that Messiah is coming, he who is called Christ.**ᶠ** When he has come, he will declare to us all things." **26** Jesus said to her, "I am he, the one who speaks to you." **27** Just then, his disciples came. They marveled that he was speaking with a woman; yet no one said, "What are you looking for?" or, "Why do you speak with her?" **28** So the woman left her water pot, went away into the city, and said to the people, **29** "Come, see a man who told me everything that I have done. Can this be the Christ?" **30** They went out of the city, and were coming to him. **31** In the meanwhile, the disciples urged him, saying, "Rabbi, eat." **32** But he said to them, "I have food to eat that you don't know about." **33** The disciples therefore said to one another, "Has anyone brought him something to eat?" **34** Jesus said to them, "My food is to do the will of him who sent me and to accomplish his work. **35** Don't you say, 'There are yet four months until the harvest'? Behold, I tell you, lift up your eyes and look at the fields, that they are white for harvest already. **36** He who reaps receives wages and gathers fruit to eternal life, that both he who sows and he who reaps may rejoice together. **37** For in this the saying is true, 'One sows, and another reaps.' **38** I sent you to reap that for which you haven't labored. Others have labored, and you have entered into their labor." **39** From that city many of the Samaritans believed in him because of the word of the woman, who testified, "He told me everything that I have done." **40** So when the Samaritans came to him, they begged him to stay with them. He stayed there two days. **41** Many more believed because of his word. **42** They said to the woman, "Now we believe, not because of your speaking; for we have heard for ourselves, and know that this is indeed the Christ, the Savior of the world." **43** After the two days he went out from there and went into Galilee. **44** For Jesus himself testified that a prophet has no honor in his own country. **45** So when he came into Galilee, the Galileans received him, having seen all the things that he did in Jerusalem at the feast, for they also went to the feast. **46** Jesus came therefore again to Cana of Galilee, where he made the water into wine. There was a certain nobleman whose son was sick at Capernaum. **47** When he heard that Jesus had come out of Judea into Galilee, he went to him and begged him that he would come down and heal his son, for he was at the point of death. **48** Jesus therefore said to him, "Unless you see signs and wonders, you will in no way believe." **49** The nobleman

* 2:17 Psalms 69:9
**ᵃ** 3:3 The word translated "anew" here and in John 3:7 (ἄνωθεν) also means "again" and "from above".
**ᵇ** 3:8 The same Greek word (πνεῦμα) means wind, breath, and spirit.
**ᶜ** 3:16 The phrase "only born" is from the Greek word "μονογενη", which is sometimes translated "only begotten" or "one and only".
**ᵈ** 3:36 The same word can be translated "disobeys" or "disbelieves" in this context.
**ᵉ** 4:6 noon
**ᶠ** 4:25 "Messiah" (Hebrew) and "Christ" (Greek) both mean "Anointed One".

said to him, "Sir, come down before my child dies." ⁵⁰ Jesus said to him, "Go your way. Your son lives." The man believed the word that Jesus spoke to him, and he went his way. ⁵¹ As he was going down, his servants met him and reported, saying "Your child lives!" ⁵² So he inquired of them the hour when he began to get better. They said therefore to him, "Yesterday at the seventh hour,ᵃ the fever left him." ⁵³ So the father knew that it was at that hour in which Jesus said to him, "Your son lives." He believed, as did his whole house. ⁵⁴ This is again the second sign that Jesus did, having come out of Judea into Galilee.

## 5

¹ After these things, there was a feast of the Jews, and Jesus went up to Jerusalem. ² Now in Jerusalem by the sheep gate, there is a pool, which is called in Hebrew, "Bethesda", having five porches. ³ In these lay a great multitude of those who were sick, blind, lame, or paralyzed, waiting for the moving of the water; ⁴ for an angel went down at certain times into the pool and stirred up the water. Whoever stepped in first after the stirring of the water was healed of whatever disease he had.ᵇ ⁵ A certain man was there who had been sick for thirty-eight years. ⁶ When Jesus saw him lying there, and knew that he had been sick for a long time, he asked him, "Do you want to be made well?" ⁷ The sick man answered him, "Sir, I have no one to put me into the pool when the water is stirred up, but while I'm coming, another steps down before me." ⁸ Jesus said to him, "Arise, take up your mat, and walk." ⁹ Immediately, the man was made well, and took up his mat and walked. Now that day was a Sabbath. ¹⁰ So the Jews said to him who was cured, "It is the Sabbath. It is not lawful for you to carry the mat." ¹¹ He answered them, "He who made me well said to me, 'Take up your mat and walk.' " ¹² Then they asked him, "Who is the man who said to you, 'Take up your mat and walk'?" ¹³ But he who was healed didn't know who it was, for Jesus had withdrawn, a crowd being in the place. ¹⁴ Afterward Jesus found him in the temple and said to him, "Behold, you are made well. Sin no more, so that nothing worse happens to you." ¹⁵ The man went away, and told the Jews that it was Jesus who had made him well. ¹⁶ For this cause the Jews persecuted Jesus and sought to kill him, because he did these things on the Sabbath. ¹⁷ But Jesus answered them, "My Father is still working, so I am working, too." ¹⁸ For this cause therefore the Jews sought all the more to kill him, because he not only broke the Sabbath, but also called God his own Father, making himself equal with God. ¹⁹ Jesus therefore answered them, "Most certainly, I tell you, the Son can do nothing of himself, but what he sees the Father doing. For whatever things he does, these the Son also does likewise. ²⁰ For the Father has affection for the Son, and shows him all things that he himself does. He will show him greater works than these, that you may marvel. ²¹ For as the Father raises the dead and gives them life, even so the Son also gives life to whom he desires. ²² For the Father judges no one, but he has given all judgment to the Son, ²³ that all may honor the Son, even as they honor the Father. He who doesn't honor the Son doesn't honor the Father who sent him. ²⁴ "Most certainly I tell you, he who hears my word and believes him who sent me has eternal life, and doesn't come into judgment, but has passed out of death into life. ²⁵ Most certainly I tell you, the hour comes, and now is, when the dead will hear the Son of God's voice; and those who hear will live. ²⁶ For as the Father has life in himself, even so he gave to the Son also to have life in himself. ²⁷ He also gave him authority to execute judgment, because he is a son of man. ²⁸ Don't marvel at this, for the hour comes in which all who are in the tombs will hear his voice ²⁹ and will come out; those who have done good, to the resurrection of life; and those who have done evil, to the resurrection of judgment. ³⁰ I can of myself do nothing. As I hear, I judge; and my judgment is righteous, because I don't seek my own will, but the will of my Father who sent me. ³¹ "If I testify about myself, my witness is not valid. ³² It is another who testifies about me. I know that the testimony which he testifies about me is true. ³³ You have sent to John, and he has testified to the truth. ³⁴ But the testimony which I receive is not from man. However, I say these things that you may be saved. ³⁵ He was the burning and shining lamp, and you were willing to rejoice for a while in his light. ³⁶ But the testimony which I have is greater than that of John; for the works which the Father gave me to accomplish, the very works that I do, testify about me, that the Father has sent me. ³⁷ The Father himself, who sent me, has testified about me. You have neither heard his voice at any time, nor seen his form. ³⁸ You don't have his word living in you, because you don't believe him whom he sent. ³⁹ "You search the Scriptures, because you think that in them you have eternal life; and these are they which testify about me. ⁴⁰ Yet you will not come to me, that you may

have life. ⁴¹ I don't receive glory from men. ⁴² But I know you, that you don't have God's love in yourselves. ⁴³ I have come in my Father's name, and you don't receive me. If another comes in his own name, you will receive him. ⁴⁴ How can you believe, who receive glory from one another, and you don't seek the glory that comes from the only God? ⁴⁵ "Don't think that I will accuse you to the Father. There is one who accuses you, even Moses, on whom you have set your hope. ⁴⁶ For if you believed Moses, you would believe me; for he wrote about me. ⁴⁷ But if you don't believe his writings, how will you believe my words?"

## 6

¹ After these things, Jesus went away to the other side of the sea of Galilee, which is also called the Sea of Tiberias. ² A great multitude followed him, because they saw his signs which he did on those who were sick. ³ Jesus went up into the mountain, and he sat there with his disciples. ⁴ Now the Passover, the feast of the Jews, was at hand. ⁵ Jesus therefore, lifting up his eyes and seeing that a great multitude was coming to him, said to Philip, "Where are we to buy bread, that these may eat?" ⁶ He said this to test him, for he himself knew what he would do. ⁷ Philip answered him, "Two hundred denariiᶜ worth of bread is not sufficient for them, that every one of them may receive a little." ⁸ One of his disciples, Andrew, Simon Peter's brother, said to him, ⁹"There is a boy here who has five barley loaves and two fish, but what are these among so many?" ¹⁰ Jesus said, "Have the people sit down." Now there was much grass in that place. So the men sat down, in number about five thousand. ¹¹ Jesus took the loaves, and having given thanks, he distributed to the disciples, and the disciples to those who were sitting down, likewise also of the fish as much as they desired. ¹² When they were filled, he said to his disciples, "Gather up the broken pieces which are left over, that nothing be lost." ¹³ So they gathered them up, and filled twelve baskets with broken pieces from the five barley loaves, which were left over by those who had eaten. ¹⁴ When therefore the people saw the sign which Jesus did, they said, "This is truly the prophet who comes into the world." ¹⁵ Jesus therefore, perceiving that they were about to come and take him by force to make him king, withdrew again to the mountain by himself. ¹⁶ When evening came, his disciples went down to the sea. ¹⁷ They entered into the boat, and were going over the sea to Capernaum. It was now dark, and Jesus had not come to them. ¹⁸ The sea was tossed by a great wind blowing. ¹⁹ When therefore they had rowed about twenty-five or thirty stadia,ᵈ they saw Jesus walking on the sea* and drawing near to the boat; and they were afraid. ²⁰ But he said to them, "It is I.ᵉ Don't be afraid." ²¹ They were willing therefore to receive him into the boat. Immediately the boat was at the land where they were going. ²² On the next day, the multitude that stood on the other side of the sea saw that there was no other boat there, except the one in which his disciples had embarked, and that Jesus hadn't entered with his disciples into the boat, but his disciples had gone away alone. ²³ However, boats from Tiberias came near to the place where they ate the bread after the Lord had given thanks. ²⁴ When the multitude therefore saw that Jesus wasn't there, nor his disciples, they themselves got into the boats and came to Capernaum, seeking Jesus. ²⁵ When they found him on the other side of the sea, they asked him, "Rabbi, when did you come here?" ²⁶ Jesus answered them, "Most certainly I tell you, you seek me, not because you saw signs, but because you ate of the loaves and were filled. ²⁷ Don't work for the food which perishes, but for the food which remains to eternal life, which the Son of Man will give to you. For God the Father has sealed him." ²⁸ They said therefore to him, "What must we do, that we may work the works of God?" ²⁹ Jesus answered them, "This is the work of God, that you believe in him whom he has sent." ³⁰ They said therefore to him, "What then do you do for a sign, that we may see and believe you? What work do you do? ³¹ Our fathers ate the manna in the wilderness. As it is written, 'He gave them bread out of heavenᶠ to eat.'"* ³² Jesus therefore said to them, "Most certainly, I tell you, it wasn't Moses who gave you the bread out of heaven, but my Father gives you the true bread out of heaven. ³³ For the bread of God is that which comes down out of heaven and gives life to the world." ³⁴ They said therefore to him, "Lord, always give us this bread." ³⁵ Jesus said to them, "I am the bread of life. Whoever comes to me will not be hungry, and whoever believes in me will never be thirsty. ³⁶ But I told you that you have seen me, and yet you don't believe. ³⁷ All those whom the Father gives me will come to me. He who comes to me I will in no way throw out. ³⁸ For I have come down from heaven, not to do my own will, but the will of him who sent me. ³⁹ This is the will of my Father who sent me, that of all

---

ᵃ *4:52* 1:00 p.m.
ᵇ *5:4* NU omits from "waiting" in verse 3 to the end of verse 4.
ᶜ *6:7* A denarius was a silver coin worth about a day's wages for an agricultural laborer, so

200 denari would be between 6 and 7 month's pay.
ᵈ *6:19* 25 to 30 stadia is about 5 to 6 kilometers or about 3 to 4 miles
* 6:19 See Job 9:8

ᵉ *6:20* or, I AM
ᶠ *6:31* Greek and Hebrew use the same word for "heaven", "the heavens", "the sky", and "the air".

* 6:31 Exodus 16:4; Nehemiah 9:15; Psalms 78:24-25

he has given to me I should lose nothing, but should raise him up at the last day. [40] This is the will of the one who sent me, that everyone who sees the Son and believes in him should have eternal life; and I will raise him up at the last day." [41] The Jews therefore murmured concerning him, because he said, "I am the bread which came down out of heaven." [42] They said, "Isn't this Jesus, the son of Joseph, whose father and mother we know? How then does he say, 'I have come down out of heaven'?" [43] Therefore Jesus answered them, "Don't murmur among yourselves. [44] No one can come to me unless the Father who sent me draws him; and I will raise him up in the last day. [45] It is written in the prophets, 'They will all be taught by God.' [*] Therefore everyone who hears from the Father and has learned, comes to me. [46] Not that anyone has seen the Father, except he who is from God. He has seen the Father. [47] Most certainly, I tell you, he who believes in me has eternal life. [48] I am the bread of life. [49] Your fathers ate the manna in the wilderness and they died. [50] This is the bread which comes down out of heaven, that anyone may eat of it and not die. [51] I am the living bread which came down out of heaven. If anyone eats of this bread, he will live forever. Yes, the bread which I will give for the life of the world is my flesh." [52] The Jews therefore contended with one another, saying, "How can this man give us his flesh to eat?" [53] Jesus therefore said to them, "Most certainly I tell you, unless you eat the flesh of the Son of Man and drink his blood, you don't have life in yourselves. [54] He who eats my flesh and drinks my blood has eternal life, and I will raise him up at the last day. [55] For my flesh is food indeed, and my blood is drink indeed. [56] He who eats my flesh and drinks my blood lives in me, and I in him. [57] As the living Father sent me, and I live because of the Father, so he who feeds on me will also live because of me. [58] This is the bread which came down out of heaven—not as our fathers ate the manna and died. He who eats this bread will live forever." [59] He said these things in the synagogue, as he taught in Capernaum. [60] Therefore many of his disciples, when they heard this, said, "This is a hard saying! Who can listen to it?" [61] But Jesus knowing in himself that his disciples murmured at this, said to them, "Does this cause you to stumble? [62] Then what if you would see the Son of Man ascending to where he was before? [63] It is the spirit who gives life. The flesh profits nothing. The words that I speak to you are spirit, and are life. [64] But there are some of you who don't believe." For Jesus knew from the beginning who they were who didn't believe, and who it was who would betray him. [65] He said, "For this cause I have said to you that no one can come to me, unless it is given to him by my Father." [66] At this, many of his disciples went back and walked no more with him. [67] Jesus said therefore to the twelve, "You don't also want to go away, do you?" [68] Simon Peter answered him, "Lord, to whom would we go? You have the words of eternal life. [69] We have come to believe and know that you are the Christ, the Son of the living God." [70] Jesus answered them, "Didn't I choose you, the twelve, and one of you is a devil?" [71] Now he spoke of Judas, the son of Simon Iscariot, for it was he who would betray him, being one of the twelve.

## 7

[1] After these things, Jesus was walking in Galilee, for he wouldn't walk in Judea, because the Jews sought to kill him. [2] Now the feast of the Jews, the Feast of Booths, was at hand. [3] His brothers therefore said to him, "Depart from here and go into Judea, that your disciples also may see your works which you do. [4] For no one does anything in secret while he seeks to be known openly. If you do these things, reveal yourself to the world." [5] For even his brothers didn't believe in him. [6] Jesus therefore said to them, "My time has not yet come, but your time is always ready. [7] The world can't hate you, but it hates me, because I testify about it, that its works are evil. [8] You go up to the feast. I am not yet going up to this feast, because my time is not yet fulfilled." [9] Having said these things to them, he stayed in Galilee. [10] But when his brothers had gone up to the feast, then he also went up, not publicly, but as it were in secret. [11] The Jews therefore sought him at the feast, and said, "Where is he?" [12] There was much murmuring among the multitudes concerning him. Some said, "He is a good man." Others said, "Not so, but he leads the multitude astray." [13] Yet no one spoke openly of him for fear of the Jews. [14] But when it was now the middle of the feast, Jesus went up into the temple and taught. [15] The Jews therefore marveled, saying, "How does this man know letters, having never been educated?" [16] Jesus therefore answered them, "My teaching is not mine, but his who sent me. [17] If anyone desires to do his will, he will know about the teaching, whether it is from God or if I am speaking from myself. [18] He who speaks from himself seeks his own glory, but he who seeks the glory of him who sent him is true, and no unrighteousness is

in him. [19] Didn't Moses give you the law, and yet none of you keeps the law? Why do you seek to kill me?" [20] The multitude answered, "You have a demon! Who seeks to kill you?" [21] Jesus answered them, "I did one work and you all marvel because of it. [22] Moses has given you circumcision (not that it is of Moses, but of the fathers), and on the Sabbath you circumcise a boy. [23] If a boy receives circumcision on the Sabbath, that the law of Moses may not be broken, are you angry with me because I made a man completely healthy on the Sabbath? [24] Don't judge according to appearance, but judge righteous judgment." [25] Therefore some of them of Jerusalem said, "Isn't this he whom they seek to kill? [26] Behold, he speaks openly, and they say nothing to him. Can it be that the rulers indeed know that this is truly the Christ? [27] However, we know where this man comes from, but when the Christ comes, no one will know where he comes from." [28] Jesus therefore cried out in the temple, teaching and saying, "You both know me, and know where I am from. I have not come of myself, but he who sent me is true, whom you don't know. [29] I know him, because I am from him, and he sent me." [30] They sought therefore to take him; but no one laid a hand on him, because his hour had not yet come. [31] But of the multitude, many believed in him. They said, "When the Christ comes, he won't do more signs than those which this man has done, will he?" [32] The Pharisees heard the multitude murmuring these things concerning him, and the chief priests and the Pharisees sent officers to arrest him. [33] Then Jesus said, "I will be with you a little while longer, then I go to him who sent me. [34] You will seek me and won't find me. You can't come where I am." [35] The Jews therefore said among themselves, "Where will this man go that we won't find him? Will he go to the Dispersion among the Greeks and teach the Greeks? [36] What is this word that he said, 'You will seek me, and won't find me;' and 'Where I am, you can't come'?" [37] Now on the last and greatest day of the feast, Jesus stood and cried out, "If anyone is thirsty, let him come to me and drink! [38] He who believes in me, as the Scripture has said, from within him will flow rivers of living water." [39] But he said this about the Spirit, which those believing in him were to receive. For the Holy Spirit was not yet given, because Jesus wasn't yet glorified. [40] Many of the multitude therefore, when they heard these words, said, "This is truly the prophet." [41] Others said, "This is the Christ." But some said, "What, does the Christ come out of Galilee? [42] Hasn't the Scripture said that the Christ comes of the offspring[a] [*] of David, [*] and from Bethlehem, [*] the village where David was?" [43] So a division arose in the multitude because of him. [44] Some of them would have arrested him, but no one laid hands on him. [45] The officers therefore came to the chief priests and Pharisees; and they said to them, "Why didn't you bring him?" [46] The officers answered, "No man ever spoke like this man!" [47] The Pharisees therefore answered them, "You aren't also led astray, are you? [48] Have any of the rulers or any of the Pharisees believed in him? [49] But this multitude that doesn't know the law is cursed." [50] Nicodemus (he who came to him by night, being one of them) said to them, [51] "Does our law judge a man unless it first hears from him personally and knows what he does?" [52] They answered him, "Are you also from Galilee? Search and see that no prophet has arisen out of Galilee." [*] [53] Everyone went to his own house,

## 8

[1] but Jesus went to the Mount of Olives. [2] Now very early in the morning, he came again into the temple, and all the people came to him. He sat down and taught them. [3] The scribes and the Pharisees brought a woman taken in adultery. Having set her in the middle, [4] they told him, "Teacher, we found this woman in adultery, in the very act. [5] Now in our law, Moses commanded us to stone such women. [*] What then do you say about her?" [6] They said this testing him, that they might have something to accuse him of. But Jesus stooped down and wrote on the ground with his finger. [7] But when they continued asking him, he looked up and said to them, "He who is without sin among you, let him throw the first stone at her." [8] Again he stooped down and wrote on the ground with his finger. [9] They, when they heard it, being convicted by their conscience, went out one by one, beginning from the oldest, even to the last. Jesus was left alone with the woman where she was, in the middle. [10] Jesus, standing up, saw her and said, "Woman, where are your accusers? Did no one condemn you?" [11] She said, "No one, Lord." Jesus said, "Neither do I condemn you. Go your way. From now on, sin no more." [b] [12] Again, therefore, Jesus spoke to them, saying, "I am the light of the world. [*] He who follows me will not walk in the darkness, but will have the light of life." [13] The Pharisees therefore said to him, "You testify about yourself. Your testimony is not valid." [14] Jesus answered them, "Even if I testify about myself, my testimony is true,

---

[*] 6:45 Isaiah 54:13
[a] *7:42* or, seed
[*] 7:42 2 Samuel 7:12
[*] 7:42 Micah 5:2

[*] 7:52 See Isaiah 9:1; Matthew 4:13-16
[*] 8:5 Leviticus 20:10; Deuteronomy 22:22

[b] *8:11* NU includes John 7:53– John 8:11, but puts brackets around it to indicate that the textual critics had less

confidence that this was original.
[*] 8:12 Isaiah 60:1

for I know where I came from, and where I am going; but you don't know where I came from, or where I am going. [15] You judge according to the flesh. I judge no one. [16] Even if I do judge, my judgment is true, for I am not alone, but I am with the Father who sent me. [17] It's also written in your law that the testimony of two people is valid.* [18] I am one who testifies about myself, and the Father who sent me testifies about me." [19] They said therefore to him, "Where is your Father?" Jesus answered, "You know neither me nor my Father. If you knew me, you would know my Father also." [20] Jesus spoke these words in the treasury, as he taught in the temple. Yet no one arrested him, because his hour had not yet come. [21] Jesus said therefore again to them, "I am going away, and you will seek me, and you will die in your sins. Where I go, you can't come." [22] The Jews therefore said, "Will he kill himself, because he says, 'Where I am going, you can't come'?" [23] He said to them, "You are from beneath. I am from above. You are of this world. I am not of this world. [24] I said therefore to you that you will die in your sins; for unless you believe that I am[a] he, you will die in your sins." [25] They said therefore to him, "Who are you?" Jesus said to them, "Just what I have been saying to you from the beginning. [26] I have many things to speak and to judge concerning you. However, he who sent me is true; and the things which I heard from him, these I say to the world." [27] They didn't understand that he spoke to them about the Father. [28] Jesus therefore said to them, "When you have lifted up the Son of Man, then you will know that I am he, and I do nothing of myself, but as my Father taught me, I say these things. [29] He who sent me is with me. The Father hasn't left me alone, for I always do the things that are pleasing to him." [30] As he spoke these things, many believed in him. [31] Jesus therefore said to those Jews who had believed him, "If you remain in my word, then you are truly my disciples. [32] You will know the truth, and the truth will make you free." * [33] They answered him, "We are Abraham's offspring, and have never been in bondage to anyone. How do you say, 'You will be made free'?" [34] Jesus answered them, "Most certainly I tell you, everyone who commits sin is the bondservant of sin. [35] A bondservant doesn't live in the house forever. A son remains forever. [36] If therefore the Son makes you free, you will be free indeed. [37] I know that you are Abraham's offspring, yet you seek to kill me, because my word finds no place in you. [38] I say the things which I have seen with my Father; and you also do the things which you have seen with your father." [39] They answered him, "Our father is Abraham." Jesus said to them, "If you were Abraham's children, you would do the works of Abraham. [40] But now you seek to kill me, a man who has told you the truth which I heard from God. Abraham didn't do this. [41] You do the works of your father." They said to him, "We were not born of sexual immorality. We have one Father, God." [42] Therefore Jesus said to them, "If God were your father, you would love me, for I came out and have come from God. For I haven't come of myself, but he sent me. [43] Why don't you understand my speech? Because you can't hear my word. [44] You are of your father the devil, and you want to do the desires of your father. He was a murderer from the beginning, and doesn't stand in the truth, because there is no truth in him. When he speaks a lie, he speaks on his own; for he is a liar, and the father of lies. [45] But because I tell the truth, you don't believe me. [46] Which of you convicts me of sin? If I tell the truth, why do you not believe me? [47] He who is of God hears the words of God. For this cause you don't hear, because you are not of God." [48] Then the Jews answered him, "Don't we say well that you are a Samaritan, and have a demon?" [49] Jesus answered, "I don't have a demon, but I honor my Father and you dishonor me. [50] But I don't seek my own glory. There is one who seeks and judges. [51] Most certainly, I tell you, if a person keeps my word, he will never see death." [52] Then the Jews said to him, "Now we know that you have a demon. Abraham died, as did the prophets; and you say, 'If a man keeps my word, he will never taste of death.' [53] Are you greater than our father Abraham, who died? The prophets died. Who do you make yourself out to be?" [54] Jesus answered, "If I glorify myself, my glory is nothing. It is my Father who glorifies me, of whom you say that he is our God. [55] You have not known him, but I know him. If I said, 'I don't know him,' I would be like you, a liar. But I know him and keep his word. [56] Your father Abraham rejoiced to see my day. He saw it and was glad." [57] The Jews therefore said to him, "You are not yet fifty years old! Have you seen Abraham?" [58] Jesus said to them, "Most certainly, I tell you, before Abraham came into existence, I AM.*" [59] Therefore they took up stones to throw at him, but Jesus hid himself and went out of the temple, having gone through the middle of them, and so passed by.

## 9

[1] As he passed by, he saw a man blind from birth. [2] His disciples asked him, "Rabbi, who sinned, this man or his parents, that he was born

blind?" [3] Jesus answered, "This man didn't sin, nor did his parents, but that the works of God might be revealed in him. [4] I must work the works of him who sent me while it is day. The night is coming, when no one can work. [5] While I am in the world, I am the light of the world." [6] When he had said this, he spat on the ground, made mud with the saliva, anointed the blind man's eyes with the mud, [7] and said to him, "Go, wash in the pool of Siloam" (which means "Sent"). So he went away, washed, and came back seeing. [8] Therefore the neighbors and those who saw that he was blind before said, "Isn't this he who sat and begged?" [9] Others were saying, "It is he." Still others were saying, "He looks like him." He said, "I am he." [10] They therefore were asking him, "How were your eyes opened?" [11] He answered, "A man called Jesus made mud, anointed my eyes, and said to me, 'Go to the pool of Siloam and wash.' So I went away and washed, and I received sight." [12] Then they asked him, "Where is he?" He said, "I don't know." [13] They brought him who had been blind to the Pharisees. [14] It was a Sabbath when Jesus made the mud and opened his eyes. [15] Again therefore the Pharisees also asked him how he received his sight. He said to them, "He put mud on my eyes, I washed, and I see." [16] Some therefore of the Pharisees said, "This man is not from God, because he doesn't keep the Sabbath." Others said, "How can a man who is a sinner do such signs?" So there was division among them. [17] Therefore they asked the blind man again, "What do you say about him, because he opened your eyes?" He said, "He is a prophet." [18] The Jews therefore didn't believe concerning him, that he had been blind and had received his sight, until they called the parents of him who had received his sight, [19] and asked them, "Is this your son, whom you say was born blind? How then does he now see?" [20] His parents answered them, "We know that this is our son, and that he was born blind; [21] but how he now sees, we don't know; or who opened his eyes, we don't know. He is of age. Ask him. He will speak for himself." [22] His parents said these things because they feared the Jews; for the Jews had already agreed that if any man would confess him as Christ, he would be put out of the synagogue. [23] Therefore his parents said, "He is of age. Ask him." [24] So they called the man who was blind a second time, and said to him, "Give glory to God. We know that this man is a sinner." [25] He therefore answered, "I don't know if he is a sinner. One thing I do know: that though I was blind, now I see." [26] They said to him again, "What did he do to you? How did he open your eyes?" [27] He answered them, "I told you already, and you didn't listen. Why do you want to hear it again? You don't also want to become his disciples, do you?" [28] They insulted him and said, "You are his disciple, but we are disciples of Moses. [29] We know that God has spoken to Moses. But as for this man, we don't know where he comes from." [30] The man answered them, "How amazing! You don't know where he comes from, yet he opened my eyes. [31] We know that God doesn't listen to sinners, but if anyone is a worshiper of God and does his will, he listens to him.* [32] Since the world began it has never been heard of that anyone opened the eyes of someone born blind. [33] If this man were not from God, he could do nothing." [34] They answered him, "You were altogether born in sins, and do you teach us?" Then they threw him out. [35] Jesus heard that they had thrown him out, and finding him, he said, "Do you believe in the Son of God?" [36] He answered, "Who is he, Lord, that I may believe in him?" [37] Jesus said to him, "You have both seen him, and it is he who speaks with you." [38] He said, "Lord, I believe!" and he worshiped him. [39] Jesus said, "I came into this world for judgment, that those who don't see may see; and that those who see may become blind." [40] Those of the Pharisees who were with him heard these things, and said to him, "Are we also blind?" [41] Jesus said to them, "If you were blind, you would have no sin; but now you say, 'We see.' Therefore your sin remains.

## 10

[1] "Most certainly, I tell you, one who doesn't enter by the door into the sheep fold, but climbs up some other way, is a thief and a robber. [2] But one who enters in by the door is the shepherd of the sheep. [3] The gatekeeper opens the gate for him, and the sheep listen to his voice. He calls his own sheep by name and leads them out. [4] Whenever he brings out his own sheep, he goes before them; and the sheep follow him, for they know his voice. [5] They will by no means follow a stranger, but will flee from him; for they don't know the voice of strangers." [6] Jesus spoke this parable to them, but they didn't understand what he was telling them. [7] Jesus therefore said to them again, "Most certainly, I tell you, I am the sheep's door. [8] All who came before me are thieves and robbers, but the sheep didn't listen to them. [9] I am the door. If anyone enters in by me, he will be saved, and will go in and go out and will find pasture. [10] The thief only comes to steal, kill, and destroy. I came that they may have life, and may have it abundantly. [11] "I am the good

---

* 8:17 Deuteronomy 17:6; 19:15

[a] 8:24 or, I AM
* 8:32 Psalms 119:45

* 8:58 Exodus 3:14

* 9:31 Psalms 66:18; Proverbs 15:29; 28:9

shepherd.* The good shepherd lays down his life for the sheep. **12** He who is a hired hand, and not a shepherd, who doesn't own the sheep, sees the wolf coming, leaves the sheep, and flees. The wolf snatches the sheep and scatters them. **13** The hired hand flees because he is a hired hand and doesn't care for the sheep. **14** I am the good shepherd. I know my own, and I'm known by my own; **15** even as the Father knows me, and I know the Father. I lay down my life for the sheep. **16** I have other sheep which are not of this fold.* I must bring them also, and they will hear my voice. They will become one flock with one shepherd. **17** Therefore the Father loves me, because I lay down my life, * that I may take it again. **18** No one takes it away from me, but I lay it down by myself. I have power to lay it down, and I have power to take it again. I received this commandment from my Father." **19** Therefore a division arose again among the Jews because of these words. **20** Many of them said, "He has a demon and is insane! Why do you listen to him?" **21** Others said, "These are not the sayings of one possessed by a demon. It isn't possible for a demon to open the eyes of the blind, is it?"* **22** It was the Feast of the Dedication<sup>a</sup> at Jerusalem. **23** It was winter, and Jesus was walking in the temple, in Solomon's porch. **24** The Jews therefore came around him and said to him, "How long will you hold us in suspense? If you are the Christ, tell us plainly." **25** Jesus answered them, "I told you, and you don't believe. The works that I do in my Father's name, these testify about me. **26** But you don't believe, because you are not of my sheep, as I told you. **27** My sheep hear my voice, and I know them, and they follow me. **28** I give eternal life to them. They will never perish, and no one will snatch them out of my hand. **29** My Father who has given them to me is greater than all. No one is able to snatch them out of my Father's hand. **30** I and the Father are one." **31** Therefore the Jews took up stones again to stone him. **32** Jesus answered them, "I have shown you many good works from my Father. For which of those works do you stone me?" **33** The Jews answered him, "We don't stone you for a good work, but for blasphemy, because you, being a man, make yourself God." **34** Jesus answered them, "Isn't it written in your law, 'I said, you are gods'?* **35** If he called them gods, to whom the word of God came (and the Scripture can't be broken), **36** do you say of him whom the Father sanctified and sent into the world, 'You blaspheme,' because I said, 'I am the Son of God'? **37** If I don't do the works of my Father, don't believe me. **38** But if I do them, though you don't believe me, believe the works, that you may know and believe that the Father is in me, and I in the Father." **39** They sought again to seize him, and he went out of their hand. **40** He went away again beyond the Jordan into the place where John was baptizing at first, and he stayed there. **41** Many came to him. They said, "John indeed did no sign, but everything that John said about this man is true." **42** Many believed in him there.

# 11

**1** Now a certain man was sick, Lazarus from Bethany, of the village of Mary and her sister, Martha. **2** It was that Mary who had anointed the Lord with ointment and wiped his feet with her hair, whose brother Lazarus was sick. **3** The sisters therefore sent to him, saying, "Lord, behold, he for whom you have great affection is sick." **4** But when Jesus heard it, he said, "This sickness is not to death, but for the glory of God, that God's Son may be glorified by it." **5** Now Jesus loved Martha, and her sister, and Lazarus. **6** When therefore he heard that he was sick, he stayed two days in the place where he was. **7** Then after this he said to the disciples, "Let's go into Judea again." **8** The disciples asked him, "Rabbi, the Jews were just trying to stone you. Are you going there again?" **9** Jesus answered, "Aren't there twelve hours of daylight? If a man walks in the day, he doesn't stumble, because he sees the light of this world. **10** But if a man walks in the night, he stumbles, because the light isn't in him." **11** He said these things, and after that, he said to them, "Our friend Lazarus has fallen asleep, but I am going so that I may awake him out of sleep." **12** The disciples therefore said, "Lord, if he has fallen asleep, he will recover." **13** Now Jesus had spoken of his death, but they thought that he spoke of taking rest in sleep. **14** So Jesus said to them plainly then, "Lazarus is dead. **15** I am glad for your sakes that I was not there, so that you may believe. Nevertheless, let's go to him." **16** Thomas therefore, who is called Didymus,<sup>b</sup> said to his fellow disciples, "Let's also go, that we may die with him." **17** So when Jesus came, he found that he had been in the tomb four days already. **18** Now Bethany was near Jerusalem, about fifteen stadia<sup>c</sup> away. **19** Many of the Jews had joined the women around Martha and Mary, to console them concerning their brother. **20** Then when Martha heard that Jesus was coming, she went and met him, but Mary stayed in the house. **21** Therefore Martha said to Jesus, "Lord, if you would have been here, my brother wouldn't have died. **22** Even now I know that whatever you ask of God, God will give you." **23** Jesus said to her, "Your brother will rise again." **24** Martha said to him, "I know that he will rise again in the resurrection at the last day." **25** Jesus said to her, "I am the resurrection and the life. He who believes in me will still live, even if he dies. **26** Whoever lives and believes in me will never die. Do you believe this?" **27** She said to him, "Yes, Lord. I have come to believe that you are the Christ, God's Son, he who comes into the world." **28** When she had said this, she went away and called Mary, her sister, secretly, saying, "The Teacher is here and is calling you." **29** When she heard this, she arose quickly and went to him. **30** Now Jesus had not yet come into the village, but was in the place where Martha met him. **31** Then the Jews who were with her in the house and were consoling her, when they saw Mary, that she rose up quickly and went out, followed her, saying, "She is going to the tomb to weep there." **32** Therefore when Mary came to where Jesus was and saw him, she fell down at his feet, saying to him, "Lord, if you would have been here, my brother wouldn't have died." **33** When Jesus therefore saw her weeping, and the Jews weeping who came with her, he groaned in the spirit and was troubled, **34** and said, "Where have you laid him?" They told him, "Lord, come and see." **35** Jesus wept. **36** The Jews therefore said, "See how much affection he had for him!" **37** Some of them said, "Couldn't this man, who opened the eyes of him who was blind, have also kept this man from dying?" **38** Jesus therefore, again groaning in himself, came to the tomb. Now it was a cave, and a stone lay against it. **39** Jesus said, "Take away the stone." Martha, the sister of him who was dead, said to him, "Lord, by this time there is a stench, for he has been dead four days." **40** Jesus said to her, "Didn't I tell you that if you believed, you would see God's glory?" **41** So they took away the stone from the place where the dead man was lying.<sup>d</sup> Jesus lifted up his eyes and said, "Father, I thank you that you listened to me. **42** I know that you always listen to me, but because of the multitude standing around I said this, that they may believe that you sent me." **43** When he had said this, he cried with a loud voice, "Lazarus, come out!" **44** He who was dead came out, bound hand and foot with wrappings, and his face was wrapped around with a cloth. Jesus said to them, "Free him, and let him go." **45** Therefore many of the Jews who came to Mary and saw what Jesus did believed in him. **46** But some of them went away to the Pharisees and told them the things which Jesus had done. **47** The chief priests therefore and the Pharisees gathered a council, and said, "What are we doing? For this man does many signs. **48** If we leave him alone like this, everyone will believe in him, and the Romans will come and take away both our place and our nation." **49** But a certain one of them, Caiaphas, being high priest that year, said to them, "You know nothing at all, **50** nor do you consider that it is advantageous for us that one man should die for the people, and that the whole nation not perish." **51** Now he didn't say this of himself, but being high priest that year, he prophesied that Jesus would die for the nation, **52** and not for the nation only, but that he might also gather together into one the children of God who are scattered abroad. **53** So from that day forward they took counsel that they might put him to death. **54** Jesus therefore walked no more openly among the Jews, but departed from there into the country near the wilderness, to a city called Ephraim. He stayed there with his disciples. **55** Now the Passover of the Jews was at hand. Many went up from the country to Jerusalem before the Passover, to purify themselves. **56** Then they sought for Jesus and spoke with one another as they stood in the temple, "What do you think—that he isn't coming to the feast at all?" **57** Now the chief priests and the Pharisees had commanded that if anyone knew where he was, he should report it, that they might seize him.

# 12

**1** Then, six days before the Passover, Jesus came to Bethany, where Lazarus was, who had been dead, whom he raised from the dead. **2** So they made him a supper there. Martha served, but Lazarus was one of those who sat at the table with him. **3** Therefore Mary took a pound<sup>e</sup> of ointment of pure nard, very precious, and anointed Jesus' feet and wiped his feet with her hair. The house was filled with the fragrance of the ointment. **4** Then Judas Iscariot, Simon's son, one of his disciples, who would betray him, said, **5** "Why wasn't this ointment sold for three hundred denarii<sup>f</sup> and given to the poor?" **6** Now he said this, not because he cared for the poor, but because he was a thief, and having the money box, used to steal what was put into it. **7** But Jesus said, "Leave her

---

* 10:11 Isaiah 40:11; Ezekiel 34:11- 12,15,22
* 10:16 Isaiah 56:8
* 10:17 Isaiah 53:7- 8
* 10:21 Exodus 4:11
<sup>a</sup> 10:22 The "Feast of the Dedication" is the Greek name

for "Hanukkah", a celebration of the rededication of the Temple.
* 10:34 Psalms 82:6
<sup>b</sup> 11:16 "Didymus" means "Twin".

<sup>c</sup> 11:18 15 stadia is about 2.8 kilometers or 1.7 miles
<sup>d</sup> 11:41 NU omits "from the place where the dead man was lying."
<sup>e</sup> 12:3 a Roman pound of 12 ounces, or about 340 grams

<sup>f</sup> 12:5 300 denarii was about a year's wages for an agricultural laborer.

alone. She has kept this for the day of my burial. [8] For you always have the poor with you, but you don't always have me." [9] A large crowd therefore of the Jews learned that he was there; and they came, not for Jesus' sake only, but that they might see Lazarus also, whom he had raised from the dead. [10] But the chief priests conspired to put Lazarus to death also, [11] because on account of him many of the Jews went away and believed in Jesus. [12] On the next day a great multitude had come to the feast. When they heard that Jesus was coming to Jerusalem, [13] they took the branches of the palm trees and went out to meet him, and cried out, "Hosanna![a] Blessed is he who comes in the name of the Lord,* the King of Israel!" [14] Jesus, having found a young donkey, sat on it. As it is written, [15]"Don't be afraid, daughter of Zion. Behold, your King comes, sitting on a donkey's colt."* [16] His disciples didn't understand these things at first, but when Jesus was glorified, then they remembered that these things were written about him, and that they had done these things to him. [17] The multitude therefore that was with him when he called Lazarus out of the tomb and raised him from the dead was testifying about it. [18] For this cause also the multitude went and met him, because they heard that he had done this sign. [19] The Pharisees therefore said among themselves, "See how you accomplish nothing. Behold, the world has gone after him." [20] Now there were certain Greeks among those who went up to worship at the feast. [21] Therefore, these came to Philip, who was from Bethsaida of Galilee, and asked him, saying, "Sir, we want to see Jesus." [22] Philip came and told Andrew, and in turn, Andrew came with Philip, and they told Jesus. [23] Jesus answered them, "The time has come for the Son of Man to be glorified. [24] Most certainly I tell you, unless a grain of wheat falls into the earth and dies, it remains by itself alone. But if it dies, it bears much fruit. [25] He who loves his life will lose it. He who hates his life in this world will keep it to eternal life. [26] If anyone serves me, let him follow me. Where I am, there my servant will also be. If anyone serves me, the Father will honor him. [27] "Now my soul is troubled. What shall I say? 'Father, save me from this time'? But I came to this time for this cause. [28] Father, glorify your name!" Then a voice came out of the sky, saying, "I have both glorified it and will glorify it again." [29] Therefore the multitude who stood by and heard it said that it had thundered. Others said, "An angel has spoken to him." [30] Jesus answered, "This voice hasn't come for my sake, but for your sakes. [31] Now is the judgment of this world. Now the prince of this world will be cast out. [32] And I, if I am lifted up from the earth, will draw all people to myself." [33] But he said this, signifying by what kind of death he should die. [34] The multitude answered him, "We have heard out of the law that the Christ remains forever.* How do you say, 'The Son of Man must be lifted up'? Who is this Son of Man?" [35] Jesus therefore said to them, "Yet a little while the light is with you. Walk while you have the light, that darkness doesn't overtake you. He who walks in the darkness doesn't know where he is going. [36] While you have the light, believe in the light, that you may become children of light." Jesus said these things, and he departed and hid himself from them. [37] But though he had done so many signs before them, yet they didn't believe in him, [38] that the word of Isaiah the prophet might be fulfilled, which he spoke: "Lord, who has believed our report? To whom has the arm of the Lord been revealed?"* [39] For this cause they couldn't believe, for Isaiah said again: [40]"He has blinded their eyes and he hardened their heart, lest they should see with their eyes, and perceive with their heart, and would turn, and I would heal them."* [41] Isaiah said these things when he saw his glory, and spoke of him. * [42] Nevertheless, even many of the rulers believed in him, but because of the Pharisees they didn't confess it, so that they wouldn't be put out of the synagogue, [43] for they loved men's praise more than God's praise. [44] Jesus cried out and said, "Whoever believes in me, believes not in me, but in him who sent me. [45] He who sees me sees him who sent me. [46] I have come as a light into the world, that whoever believes in me may not remain in the darkness. [47] If anyone listens to my sayings and doesn't believe, I don't judge him. For I came not to judge the world, but to save the world. [48] He who rejects me, and doesn't receive my sayings, has one who judges him. The word that I spoke will judge him in the last day. [49] For I spoke not from myself, but the Father who sent me gave me a commandment, what I should say and what I should speak. [50] I know that his commandment is eternal life. The things therefore which I speak, even as the Father has said to me, so I speak."

## 13

[1] Now before the feast of the Passover, Jesus, knowing that his time had come that he would depart from this world to the Father, having loved his own who were in the world, he loved them to the end. [2] During supper, the devil having already put into the heart of Judas Iscariot, Simon's son, to betray him, [3] Jesus, knowing that the Father had given all things into his hands, and that he came from God and was going to God, [4] arose from supper, and laid aside his outer garments. He took a towel and wrapped a towel around his waist. [5] Then he poured water into the basin, and began to wash the disciples' feet and to wipe them with the towel that was wrapped around him. [6] Then he came to Simon Peter. He said to him, "Lord, do you wash my feet?" [7] Jesus answered him, "You don't know what I am doing now, but you will understand later." [8] Peter said to him, "You will never wash my feet!" Jesus answered him, "If I don't wash you, you have no part with me." [9] Simon Peter said to him, "Lord, not my feet only, but also my hands and my head!" [10] Jesus said to him, "Someone who has bathed only needs to have his feet washed, but is completely clean. You are clean, but not all of you." [11] For he knew him who would betray him; therefore he said, "You are not all clean." [12] So when he had washed their feet, put his outer garment back on, and sat down again, he said to them, "Do you know what I have done to you? [13] You call me, 'Teacher' and 'Lord.' You say so correctly, for so I am. [14] If I then, the Lord and the Teacher, have washed your feet, you also ought to wash one another's feet. [15] For I have given you an example, that you should also do as I have done to you. [16] Most certainly I tell you, a servant is not greater than his lord, neither is one who is sent greater than he who sent him. [17] If you know these things, blessed are you if you do them. [18] I don't speak concerning all of you. I know whom I have chosen; but that the Scripture may be fulfilled, 'He who eats bread with me has lifted up his heel against me.'* [19] From now on, I tell you before it happens, that when it happens, you may believe that I am he. [20] Most certainly I tell you, he who receives whomever I send, receives me; and he who receives me, receives him who sent me." [21] When Jesus had said this, he was troubled in spirit, and testified, "Most certainly I tell you that one of you will betray me." [22] The disciples looked at one another, perplexed about whom he spoke. [23] One of his disciples, whom Jesus loved, was at the table, leaning against Jesus' chest. [24] Simon Peter therefore beckoned to him, and said to him, "Tell us who it is of whom he speaks." [25] He, leaning back, as he was, on Jesus' chest, asked him, "Lord, who is it?" [26] Jesus therefore answered, "It is he to whom I will give this piece of bread when I have dipped it." So when he had dipped the piece of bread, he gave it to Judas, the son of Simon Iscariot. [27] After the piece of bread, then Satan entered into him. Then Jesus said to him, "What you do, do quickly." [28] Now nobody at the table knew why he said this to him. [29] For some thought, because Judas had the money box, that Jesus said to him, "Buy what things we need for the feast," or that he should give something to the poor. [30] Therefore having received that morsel, he went out immediately. It was night. [31] When he had gone out, Jesus said, "Now the Son of Man has been glorified, and God has been glorified in him. [32] If God has been glorified in him, God will also glorify him in himself, and he will glorify him immediately. [33] Little children, I will be with you a little while longer. You will seek me, and as I said to the Jews, 'Where I am going, you can't come,' so now I tell you. [34] A new commandment I give to you, that you love one another. Just as I have loved you, you also love one another. [35] By this everyone will know that you are my disciples, if you have love for one another." [36] Simon Peter said to him, "Lord, where are you going?" Jesus answered, "Where I am going, you can't follow now, but you will follow afterwards." [37] Peter said to him, "Lord, why can't I follow you now? I will lay down my life for you." [38] Jesus answered him, "Will you lay down your life for me? Most certainly I tell you, the rooster won't crow until you have denied me three times.

## 14

[1] "Don't let your heart be troubled. Believe in God. Believe also in me. [2] In my Father's house are many homes. If it weren't so, I would have told you. I am going to prepare a place for you. [3] If I go and prepare a place for you, I will come again and will receive you to myself; that where I am, you may be there also. [4] You know where I go, and you know the way."

[5] Thomas said to him, "Lord, we don't know where you are going. How can we know the way?" [6] Jesus said to him, "I am the way, the truth, and the life. No one comes to the Father, except through me. [7] If you had known me, you would have known my Father also. From now on, you know him and have seen him." [8] Philip said to him, "Lord, show us the Father, and that will be enough for us." [9] Jesus said to him, "Have I been with you such a long time, and do you not know me, Philip? He who has seen me has seen the Father. How do you say, 'Show us the Father'? [10] Don't you believe that I am in the Father, and the Father in me? The words that I tell you, I speak not from myself; but the Father who lives in me does his works. [11] Believe me that I am in the Father,

---

a *12:13* "Hosanna" means "save us" or "help us, we pray".

* 12:13 Psalms 118:25-26
* 12:15 Zechariah 9:9

* 12:34 Isaiah 9:7; Daniel 2:44; See Isaiah 53:8
* 12:38 Isaiah 53:1

* 12:40 Isaiah 6:10
* 12:41 Isaiah 6:1
* 13:18 Psalms 41:9

and the Father in me; or else believe me for the very works' sake. [12] Most certainly I tell you, he who believes in me, the works that I do, he will do also; and he will do greater works than these, because I am going to my Father. [13] Whatever you will ask in my name, I will do it, that the Father may be glorified in the Son. [14] If you will ask anything in my name, I will do it. [15] If you love me, keep my commandments. [16] I will pray to the Father, and he will give you another Counselor, [a] that he may be with you forever: [17] the Spirit of truth, whom the world can't receive, for it doesn't see him and doesn't know him. You know him, for he lives with you and will be in you. [18] I will not leave you orphans. I will come to you. [19] Yet a little while, and the world will see me no more; but you will see me. Because I live, you will live also. [20] In that day you will know that I am in my Father, and you in me, and I in you. [21] One who has my commandments and keeps them, that person is one who loves me. One who loves me will be loved by my Father, and I will love him, and will reveal myself to him." [22] Judas (not Iscariot) said to him, "Lord, what has happened that you are about to reveal yourself to us, and not to the world?" [23] Jesus answered him, "If a man loves me, he will keep my word. My Father will love him, and we will come to him and make our home with him. [24] He who doesn't love me doesn't keep my words. The word which you hear isn't mine, but the Father's who sent me. [25] "I have said these things to you while still living with you. [26] But the Counselor, the Holy Spirit, whom the Father will send in my name, will teach you all things, and will remind you of all that I said to you. [27] Peace I leave with you. My peace I give to you; not as the world gives, I give to you. Don't let your heart be troubled, neither let it be fearful. [28] You heard how I told you, 'I am going away, and I will come back to you.' If you loved me, you would have rejoiced because I said 'I am going to my Father;' for the Father is greater than I. [29] Now I have told you before it happens so that when it happens, you may believe. [30] I will no more speak much with you, for the prince of the world comes, and he has nothing in me. [31] But that the world may know that I love the Father, and as the Father commanded me, even so I do. Arise, let's go from here.

## 15

[1] "I am the true vine, and my Father is the farmer. [2] Every branch in me that doesn't bear fruit, he takes away. Every branch that bears fruit, he prunes, that it may bear more fruit. [3] You are already pruned clean because of the word which I have spoken to you. [4] Remain in me, and I in you. As the branch can't bear fruit by itself unless it remains in the vine, so neither can you, unless you remain in me. [5] I am the vine. You are the branches. He who remains in me and I in him bears much fruit, for apart from me you can do nothing. [6] If a man doesn't remain in me, he is thrown out as a branch and is withered; and they gather them, throw them into the fire, and they are burned. [7] If you remain in me, and my words remain in you, you will ask whatever you desire, and it will be done for you. [8] "In this my Father is glorified, that you bear much fruit; and so you will be my disciples. [9] Even as the Father has loved me, I also have loved you. Remain in my love. [10] If you keep my commandments, you will remain in my love, even as I have kept my Father's commandments and remain in his love. [11] I have spoken these things to you, that my joy may remain in you, and that your joy may be made full. [12] "This is my commandment, that you love one another, even as I have loved you. [13] Greater love has no one than this, that someone lay down his life for his friends. [14] You are my friends if you do whatever I command you. [15] No longer do I call you servants, for the servant doesn't know what his lord does. But I have called you friends, for everything that I heard from my Father, I have made known to you. [16] You didn't choose me, but I chose you and appointed you, that you should go and bear fruit, and that your fruit should remain; that whatever you will ask of the Father in my name, he may give it to you. [17] "I command these things to you, that you may love one another. [18] If the world hates you, you know that it has hated me before it hated you. [19] If you were of the world, the world would love its own. But because you are not of the world, since I chose you out of the world, therefore the world hates you. [20] Remember the word that I said to you: 'A servant is not greater than his lord.'[*] If they persecuted me, they will also persecute you. If they kept my word, they will also keep yours. [21] But they will do all these things to you for my name's sake, because they don't know him who sent me. [22] If I had not come and spoken to them, they would not have had sin; but now they have no excuse for their sin. [23] He who hates me, hates my Father also. [24] If I hadn't done among them the works which no one else did, they wouldn't have had sin. But now they have seen and also hated both me and my Father. [25] But this happened so that the word may be fulfilled which was written in their law, 'They hated me without a cause.'[*] [26] "When the Counselor[b]

has come, whom I will send to you from the Father, the Spirit of truth, who proceeds from the Father, he will testify about me. [27] You will also testify, because you have been with me from the beginning.

## 16

[1] "I have said these things to you so that you wouldn't be caused to stumble. [2] They will put you out of the synagogues. Yes, the time is coming that whoever kills you will think that he offers service to God. [3] They will do these things[c] because they have not known the Father nor me. [4] But I have told you these things so that when the time comes, you may remember that I told you about them. I didn't tell you these things from the beginning, because I was with you. [5] But now I am going to him who sent me, and none of you asks me, 'Where are you going?' [6] But because I have told you these things, sorrow has filled your heart. [7] Nevertheless I tell you the truth: It is to your advantage that I go away; for if I don't go away, the Counselor won't come to you. But if I go, I will send him to you. [8] When he has come, he will convict the world about sin, about righteousness, and about judgment; [9] about sin, because they don't believe in me; [10] about righteousness, because I am going to my Father, and you won't see me any more; [11] about judgment, because the prince of this world has been judged. [12] "I still have many things to tell you, but you can't bear them now. [13] However, when he, the Spirit of truth, has come, he will guide you into all truth, for he will not speak from himself; but whatever he hears, he will speak. He will declare to you things that are coming. [14] He will glorify me, for he will take from what is mine and will declare it to you. [15] All things that the Father has are mine; therefore I said that he takes[d] of mine and will declare it to you. [16] "A little while, and you will not see me. Again a little while, and you will see me." [17] Some of his disciples therefore said to one another, "What is this that he says to us, 'A little while, and you won't see me, and again a little while, and you will see me;' and, 'Because I go to the Father'?" [18] They said therefore, "What is this that he says, 'A little while'? We don't know what he is saying." [19] Therefore Jesus perceived that they wanted to ask him, and he said to them, "Do you inquire among yourselves concerning this, that I said, 'A little while, and you won't see me, and again a little while, and you will see me'? [20] Most certainly I tell you that you will weep and lament, but the world will rejoice. You will be sorrowful, but your sorrow will be turned into joy. [21] A woman, when she gives birth, has sorrow because her time has come. But when she has delivered the child, she doesn't remember the anguish any more, for the joy that a human being is born into the world. [22] Therefore you now have sorrow, but I will see you again, and your heart will rejoice, and no one will take your joy away from you. [23] "In that day you will ask me no questions. Most certainly I tell you, whatever you may ask of the Father in my name, he will give it to you. [24] Until now, you have asked nothing in my name. Ask, and you will receive, that your joy may be made full. [25] "I have spoken these things to you in figures of speech. But the time is coming when I will no more speak to you in figures of speech, but will tell you plainly about the Father. [26] In that day you will ask in my name; and I don't say to you that I will pray to the Father for you, [27] for the Father himself loves you, because you have loved me, and have believed that I came from God. [28] I came from the Father and have come into the world. Again, I leave the world and go to the Father." [29] His disciples said to him, "Behold, now you are speaking plainly, and using no figures of speech. [30] Now we know that you know all things, and don't need for anyone to question you. By this we believe that you came from God." [31] Jesus answered them, "Do you now believe? [32] Behold, the time is coming, yes, and has now come, that you will be scattered, everyone to his own place, and you will leave me alone. Yet I am not alone, because the Father is with me. [33] I have told you these things, that in me you may have peace. In the world you have trouble; but cheer up! I have overcome the world."

## 17

[1] Jesus said these things, then lifting up his eyes to heaven, he said, "Father, the time has come. Glorify your Son, that your Son may also glorify you; [2] even as you gave him authority over all flesh, so he will give eternal life to all whom you have given him. [3] This is eternal life, that they should know you, the only true God, and him whom you sent, Jesus Christ. [4] I glorified you on the earth. I have accomplished the work which you have given me to do. [5] Now, Father, glorify me with your own self with the glory which I had with you before the world existed. [6] "I revealed your name to the people whom you have given me out of the world. They were yours, and you have given them to me. They have kept your word. [7] Now they have known that all things whatever you have given me are from you, [8] for the words which you have given me I have given to them; and they received them, and knew

---

[a] 14:16 Greek παρακλητον: Counselor, Helper, Intercessor, Advocate, and Comforter.

[*] 15:20 John 13:16
[*] 15:25 Psalms 35:19; 69:4

[b] 15:26 Greek Parakletos: Counselor, Helper, Advocate, Intercessor, and Comforter.

[c] 16:3 TR adds "to you"
[d] 16:15 TR reads "will take" instead of "takes"

for sure that I came from you. They have believed that you sent me. [9] I pray for them. I don't pray for the world, but for those whom you have given me, for they are yours. [10] All things that are mine are yours, and yours are mine, and I am glorified in them. [11] I am no more in the world, but these are in the world, and I am coming to you. Holy Father, keep them through your name which you have given me, that they may be one, even as we are. [12] While I was with them in the world, I kept them in your name. I have kept those whom you have given me. None of them is lost except the son of destruction, that the Scripture might be fulfilled. [13] But now I come to you, and I say these things in the world, that they may have my joy made full in themselves. [14] I have given them your word. The world hated them because they are not of the world, even as I am not of the world. [15] I pray not that you would take them from the world, but that you would keep them from the evil one. [16] They are not of the world, even as I am not of the world. [17] Sanctify them in your truth. Your word is truth.* [18] As you sent me into the world, even so I have sent them into the world. [19] For their sakes I sanctify myself, that they themselves also may be sanctified in truth. [20] "Not for these only do I pray, but for those also who will believe in me through their word, [21] that they may all be one; even as you, Father, are in me, and I in you, that they also may be one in us; that the world may believe that you sent me. [22] The glory which you have given me, I have given to them, that they may be one, even as we are one, [23] I in them, and you in me, that they may be perfected into one, that the world may know that you sent me and loved them, even as you loved me. [24] Father, I desire that they also whom you have given me be with me where I am, that they may see my glory which you have given me, for you loved me before the foundation of the world. [25] Righteous Father, the world hasn't known you, but I knew you; and these knew that you sent me. [26] I made known to them your name, and will make it known; that the love with which you loved me may be in them, and I in them."

## 18

[1] When Jesus had spoken these words, he went out with his disciples over the brook Kidron, where there was a garden, into which he and his disciples entered. [2] Now Judas, who betrayed him, also knew the place, for Jesus often met there with his disciples. [3] Judas then, having taken a detachment of soldiers and officers from the chief priests and the Pharisees, came there with lanterns, torches, and weapons. [4] Jesus therefore, knowing all the things that were happening to him, went out and said to them, "Who are you looking for?" [5] They answered him, "Jesus of Nazareth." Jesus said to them, "I am he." Judas also, who betrayed him, was standing with them. [6] When therefore he said to them, "I am he," they went backward and fell to the ground. [7] Again therefore he asked them, "Who are you looking for?" They said, "Jesus of Nazareth." [8] Jesus answered, "I told you that I am he. If therefore you seek me, let these go their way," [9] that the word might be fulfilled which he spoke, "Of those whom you have given me, I have lost none."* [10] Simon Peter therefore, having a sword, drew it, struck the high priest's servant, and cut off his right ear. The servant's name was Malchus. [11] Jesus therefore said to Peter, "Put the sword into its sheath. The cup which the Father has given me, shall I not surely drink it?" [12] So the detachment, the commanding officer, and the officers of the Jews seized Jesus and bound him, [13] and led him to Annas first, for he was father-in-law to Caiaphas, who was high priest that year. [14] Now it was Caiaphas who advised the Jews that it was expedient that one man should perish for the people. [15] Simon Peter followed Jesus, as did another disciple. Now that disciple was known to the high priest, and entered in with Jesus into the court of the high priest; [16] but Peter was standing at the door outside. So the other disciple, who was known to the high priest, went out and spoke to her who kept the door, and brought in Peter. [17] Then the maid who kept the door said to Peter, "Are you also one of this man's disciples?" He said, "I am not." [18] Now the servants and the officers were standing there, having made a fire of coals, for it was cold. They were warming themselves. Peter was with them, standing and warming himself. [19] The high priest therefore asked Jesus about his disciples and about his teaching. [20] Jesus answered him, "I spoke openly to the world. I always taught in synagogues and in the temple, where the Jews always meet. I said nothing in secret. [21] Why do you ask me? Ask those who have heard me what I said to them. Behold, they know the things which I said." [22] When he had said this, one of the officers standing by slapped Jesus with his hand, saying, "Do you answer the high priest like that?" [23] Jesus answered him, "If I have spoken evil, testify of the evil; but if well, why do you beat me?" [24] Annas sent him bound to Caiaphas, the high priest. [25] Now Simon Peter was standing and warming himself. They said therefore to him, "You aren't also one of his disciples, are you?" He denied it and said, "I am not." [26] One of the servants of the high priest, being a relative of him whose ear Peter had cut off, said, "Didn't I see you in the garden with him?" [27] Peter therefore denied it again, and immediately the rooster crowed. [28] They led Jesus therefore from Caiaphas into the Praetorium. It was early, and they themselves didn't enter into the Praetorium, that they might not be defiled, but might eat the Passover. [29] Pilate therefore went out to them and said, "What accusation do you bring against this man?" [30] They answered him, "If this man weren't an evildoer, we wouldn't have delivered him up to you." [31] Pilate therefore said to them, "Take him yourselves, and judge him according to your law." Therefore the Jews said to him, "It is illegal for us to put anyone to death," [32] that the word of Jesus might be fulfilled, which he spoke, signifying by what kind of death he should die. [33] Pilate therefore entered again into the Praetorium, called Jesus, and said to him, "Are you the King of the Jews?" [34] Jesus answered him, "Do you say this by yourself, or did others tell you about me?" [35] Pilate answered, "I'm not a Jew, am I? Your own nation and the chief priests delivered you to me. What have you done?" [36] Jesus answered, "My Kingdom is not of this world. If my Kingdom were of this world, then my servants would fight, that I wouldn't be delivered to the Jews. But now my Kingdom is not from here." [37] Pilate therefore said to him, "Are you a king then?" Jesus answered, "You say that I am a king. For this reason I have been born, and for this reason I have come into the world, that I should testify to the truth. Everyone who is of the truth listens to my voice." [38] Pilate said to him, "What is truth?" When he had said this, he went out again to the Jews, and said to them, "I find no basis for a charge against him. [39] But you have a custom that I should release someone to you at the Passover. Therefore, do you want me to release to you the King of the Jews?" [40] Then they all shouted again, saying, "Not this man, but Barabbas!" Now Barabbas was a robber.

## 19

[1] So Pilate then took Jesus and flogged him. [2] The soldiers twisted thorns into a crown and put it on his head, and dressed him in a purple garment. [3] They kept saying, "Hail, King of the Jews!" and they kept slapping him. [4] Then Pilate went out again, and said to them, "Behold, I bring him out to you, that you may know that I find no basis for a charge against him." [5] Jesus therefore came out, wearing the crown of thorns and the purple garment. Pilate said to them, "Behold, the man!" [6] When therefore the chief priests and the officers saw him, they shouted, saying, "Crucify! Crucify!" Pilate said to them, "Take him yourselves and crucify him, for I find no basis for a charge against him." [7] The Jews answered him, "We have a law, and by our law he ought to die, because he made himself the Son of God." [8] When therefore Pilate heard this saying, he was more afraid. [9] He entered into the Praetorium again, and said to Jesus, "Where are you from?" But Jesus gave him no answer. [10] Pilate therefore said to him, "Aren't you speaking to me? Don't you know that I have power to release you and have power to crucify you?" [11] Jesus answered, "You would have no power at all against me, unless it were given to you from above. Therefore he who delivered me to you has greater sin." [12] At this, Pilate was seeking to release him, but the Jews cried out, saying, "If you release this man, you aren't Caesar's friend! Everyone who makes himself a king speaks against Caesar!" [13] When Pilate therefore heard these words, he brought Jesus out and sat down on the judgment seat at a place called "The Pavement", but in Hebrew, "Gabbatha." [14] Now it was the Preparation Day of the Passover, at about the sixth hour.[a] He said to the Jews, "Behold, your King!" [15] They cried out, "Away with him! Away with him! Crucify him!" Pilate said to them, "Shall I crucify your King?" The chief priests answered, "We have no king but Caesar!" [16] So then he delivered him to them to be crucified. So they took Jesus and led him away. [17] He went out, bearing his cross, to the place called "The Place of a Skull", which is called in Hebrew, "Golgotha", [18] where they crucified him, and with him two others, on either side one, and Jesus in the middle. [19] Pilate wrote a title also, and put it on the cross. There was written, "JESUS OF NAZARETH, THE KING OF THE JEWS." [20] Therefore many of the Jews read this title, for the place where Jesus was crucified was near the city; and it was written in Hebrew, in Latin, and in Greek. [21] The chief priests of the Jews therefore said to Pilate, "Don't write, 'The King of the Jews,' but, 'he said, "I am King of the Jews."'" [22] Pilate answered, "What I have written, I have written." [23] Then the soldiers, when they had crucified Jesus, took his garments and made four parts, to every soldier a part; and also the tunic. Now the tunic was without seam, woven from the top throughout. [24] Then they said to one another, "Let's not tear it, but cast lots for it to decide whose it will be," that the Scripture might be fulfilled, which says, "They parted my garments among them. They

---

\* 17:17 Psalms 119:142
\* 18:9 John 6:39

[a] 19:14 "the sixth hour" would have been 6:00 a.m. according to the Roman timekeeping system, or noon for the Jewish timekeeping system in use, then.

cast lots for my clothing."* Therefore the soldiers did these things. ²⁵ But standing by Jesus' cross were his mother, his mother's sister, Mary the wife of Clopas, and Mary Magdalene. ²⁶ Therefore when Jesus saw his mother, and the disciple whom he loved standing there, he said to his mother, "Woman, behold, your son!" ²⁷ Then he said to the disciple, "Behold, your mother!" From that hour, the disciple took her to his own home. ²⁸ After this, Jesus, seeing[a] that all things were now finished, that the Scripture might be fulfilled, said, "I am thirsty!" ²⁹ Now a vessel full of vinegar was set there; so they put a sponge full of the vinegar on hyssop, and held it at his mouth. ³⁰ When Jesus therefore had received the vinegar, he said, "It is finished!" Then he bowed his head and gave up his spirit. ³¹ Therefore the Jews, because it was the Preparation Day, so that the bodies wouldn't remain on the cross on the Sabbath (for that Sabbath was a special one), asked of Pilate that their legs might be broken and that they might be taken away. ³² Therefore the soldiers came and broke the legs of the first and of the other who was crucified with him; ³³ but when they came to Jesus and saw that he was already dead, they didn't break his legs. ³⁴ However, one of the soldiers pierced his side with a spear, and immediately blood and water came out. ³⁵ He who has seen has testified, and his testimony is true. He knows that he tells the truth, that you may believe. ³⁶ For these things happened that the Scripture might be fulfilled, "A bone of him will not be broken."* ³⁷ Again another Scripture says, "They will look on him whom they pierced."* ³⁸ After these things, Joseph of Arimathaea, being a disciple of Jesus, but secretly for fear of the Jews, asked of Pilate that he might take away Jesus' body. Pilate gave him permission. He came therefore and took away his body. ³⁹ Nicodemus, who at first came to Jesus by night, also came bringing a mixture of myrrh and aloes, about a hundred Roman pounds.[b] ⁴⁰ So they took Jesus' body, and bound it in linen cloths with the spices, as the custom of the Jews is to bury. ⁴¹ Now in the place where he was crucified there was a garden. In the garden was a new tomb in which no man had ever yet been laid. ⁴² Then, because of the Jews' Preparation Day (for the tomb was near at hand), they laid Jesus there.

## 20

¹ Now on the first day of the week, Mary Magdalene went early, while it was still dark, to the tomb, and saw that the stone had been taken away from the tomb. ² Therefore she ran and came to Simon Peter and to the other disciple whom Jesus loved, and said to them, "They have taken away the Lord out of the tomb, and we don't know where they have laid him!" ³ Therefore Peter and the other disciple went out, and they went toward the tomb. ⁴ They both ran together. The other disciple outran Peter and came to the tomb first. ⁵ Stooping and looking in, he saw the linen cloths lying there; yet he didn't enter in. ⁶ Then Simon Peter came, following him, and entered into the tomb. He saw the linen cloths lying, ⁷ and the cloth that had been on his head, not lying with the linen cloths, but rolled up in a place by itself. ⁸ So then the other disciple who came first to the tomb also entered in, and he saw and believed. ⁹ For as yet they didn't know the Scripture, that he must rise from the dead. ¹⁰ So the disciples went away again to their own homes. ¹¹ But Mary was standing outside at the tomb weeping. So as she wept, she stooped and looked into the tomb, ¹² and she saw two angels in white sitting, one at the head and one at the feet, where the body of Jesus had lain. ¹³ They asked her, "Woman, why are you weeping?" She said to them, "Because they have taken away my Lord, and I don't know where they have laid him." ¹⁴ When she had said this, she turned around and saw Jesus standing, and didn't know that it was Jesus. ¹⁵ Jesus said to her, "Woman, why are you weeping? Who are you looking for?" She, supposing him to be the gardener, said to him, "Sir, if you have carried him away, tell me where you have laid him, and I will take him away." ¹⁶ Jesus said to her, "Mary." She turned and said to him, "Rabboni!"[c] which is to say, "Teacher!"[d] ¹⁷ Jesus said to her, "Don't hold me, for I haven't yet ascended to my Father; but go to my brothers and tell them, 'I am ascending to my Father and your Father, to my God and your God.'" ¹⁸ Mary Magdalene came and told the disciples that she had seen the Lord, and that he had said these things to her. ¹⁹ When therefore it was evening on that day, the first day of the week, and when the doors were locked where the disciples were assembled, for fear of the Jews, Jesus came and stood in the middle and said to them, "Peace be to you." ²⁰ When he had said this, he showed them his hands and his side. The disciples therefore were glad when they saw the Lord. ²¹ Jesus therefore said to them again, "Peace be to you. As the Father has sent me, even so I send you." ²² When he had said this, he breathed on them, and said to them, "Receive the Holy Spirit! ²³ If you forgive anyone's sins, they have been forgiven them. If you retain anyone's sins, they have been retained." ²⁴ But Thomas, one of the twelve, called Didymus,[e] wasn't with them when Jesus came. ²⁵ The other disciples therefore said to him, "We have seen the Lord!" But he said to them, "Unless I see in his hands the print of the nails, put my finger into the print of the nails, and put my hand into his side, I will not believe." ²⁶ After eight days, again his disciples were inside and Thomas was with them. Jesus came, the doors being locked, and stood in the middle, and said, "Peace be to you." ²⁷ Then he said to Thomas, "Reach here your finger, and see my hands. Reach here your hand, and put it into my side. Don't be unbelieving, but believing." ²⁸ Thomas answered him, "My Lord and my God!" ²⁹ Jesus said to him, "Because you have seen me,[f] you have believed. Blessed are those who have not seen and have believed." ³⁰ Therefore Jesus did many other signs in the presence of his disciples, which are not written in this book; ³¹ but these are written that you may believe that Jesus is the Christ, the Son of God, and that believing you may have life in his name.

## 21

¹ After these things, Jesus revealed himself again to the disciples at the sea of Tiberias. He revealed himself this way. ² Simon Peter, Thomas called Didymus,[g] Nathanael of Cana in Galilee, and the sons of Zebedee, and two others of his disciples were together. ³ Simon Peter said to them, "I'm going fishing." They told him, "We are also coming with you." They immediately went out and entered into the boat. That night, they caught nothing. ⁴ But when day had already come, Jesus stood on the beach; yet the disciples didn't know that it was Jesus. ⁵ Jesus therefore said to them, "Children, have you anything to eat?" They answered him, "No." ⁶ He said to them, "Cast the net on the right side of the boat, and you will find some." They cast it therefore, and now they weren't able to draw it in for the multitude of fish. ⁷ That disciple therefore whom Jesus loved said to Peter, "It's the Lord!" So when Simon Peter heard that it was the Lord, he wrapped his coat around himself (for he was naked), and threw himself into the sea. ⁸ But the other disciples came in the little boat (for they were not far from the land, but about two hundred cubits[h] away), dragging the net full of fish. ⁹ So when they got out on the land, they saw a fire of coals there, with fish and bread laid on it. ¹⁰ Jesus said to them, "Bring some of the fish which you have just caught." ¹¹ Simon Peter went up, and drew the net to land, full of one hundred fifty-three great fish. Even though there were so many, the net wasn't torn. ¹² Jesus said to them, "Come and eat breakfast!" None of the disciples dared inquire of him, "Who are you?" knowing that it was the Lord. ¹³ Then Jesus came and took the bread, gave it to them, and the fish likewise. ¹⁴ This is now the third time that Jesus was revealed to his disciples after he had risen from the dead. ¹⁵ So when they had eaten their breakfast, Jesus said to Simon Peter, "Simon, son of Jonah, do you love me more than these?" He said to him, "Yes, Lord; you know that I have affection for you." He said to him, "Feed my lambs." ¹⁶ He said to him again a second time, "Simon, son of Jonah, do you love me?" He said to him, "Yes, Lord; you know that I have affection for you." He said to him, "Tend my sheep." ¹⁷ He said to him the third time, "Simon, son of Jonah, do you have affection for me?" Peter was grieved because he asked him the third time, "Do you have affection for me?" He said to him, "Lord, you know everything. You know that I have affection for you." Jesus said to him, "Feed my sheep. ¹⁸ Most certainly I tell you, when you were young, you dressed yourself and walked where you wanted to. But when you are old, you will stretch out your hands, and another will dress you and carry you where you don't want to go." ¹⁹ Now he said this, signifying by what kind of death he would glorify God. When he had said this, he said to him, "Follow me." ²⁰ Then Peter, turning around, saw a disciple following. This was the disciple whom Jesus loved, the one who had also leaned on Jesus' chest at the supper and asked, "Lord, who is going to betray you?" ²¹ Peter, seeing him, said to Jesus, "Lord, what about this man?" ²² Jesus said to him, "If I desire that he stay until I come, what is that to you? You follow me." ²³ This saying therefore went out among the brothers[i] that this disciple wouldn't die. Yet Jesus didn't say to him that he wouldn't die, but, "If I desire that he stay until I come, what is that to you?" ²⁴ This is the disciple who testifies about these things, and wrote these things. We know that his witness is true. ²⁵ There are also many other things which Jesus did, which if they would all be written, I suppose that even the world itself wouldn't have room for the books that would be written.

---

* 19:24 Psalms 22:18

[a] 19:28 NU, TR read "knowing" instead of "seeing"

* 19:36 Exodus 12:46; Numbers 9:12; Psalms 34:20

* 19:37 Zechariah 12:10

[b] 19:39 100 Roman pounds of 12 ounces each, or about 72 pounds, or 33 Kilograms.

[c] 20:16 Rabboni is a transliteration of the Hebrew word for "great teacher."

[d] 20:16 or, Master

[e] 20:24 or, Twin

[f] 20:29 TR adds "Thomas,"

[g] 21:2 or, Twin

[h] 21:8 200 cubits is about 100 yards or about 91 meters

[i] 21:23 The word for "brothers" here may be also correctly translated "brothers and sisters" or "siblings."

# The Acts of the Apostles

## 1

[1] The first book I wrote, Theophilus, concerned all that Jesus began both to do and to teach, [2] until the day in which he was received up, after he had given commandment through the Holy Spirit to the apostles whom he had chosen. [3] To these he also showed himself alive after he suffered, by many proofs, appearing to them over a period of forty days and speaking about God's Kingdom. [4] Being assembled together with them, he commanded them, "Don't depart from Jerusalem, but wait for the promise of the Father, which you heard from me. [5] For John indeed baptized in water, but you will be baptized in the Holy Spirit not many days from now." [6] Therefore, when they had come together, they asked him, "Lord, are you now restoring the kingdom to Israel?" [7] He said to them, "It isn't for you to know times or seasons which the Father has set within his own authority. [8] But you will receive power when the Holy Spirit has come upon you. You will be witnesses to me in Jerusalem, in all Judea and Samaria, and to the uttermost parts of the earth." [9] When he had said these things, as they were looking, he was taken up, and a cloud received him out of their sight. [10] While they were looking steadfastly into the sky as he went, behold,[a] two men stood by them in white clothing, [11] who also said, "You men of Galilee, why do you stand looking into the sky? This Jesus, who was received up from you into the sky, will come back in the same way as you saw him going into the sky." [12] Then they returned to Jerusalem from the mountain called Olivet, which is near Jerusalem, a Sabbath day's journey away. [13] When they had come in, they went up into the upper room where they were staying, that is Peter, John, James, Andrew, Philip, Thomas, Bartholomew, Matthew, James the son of Alphaeus, Simon the Zealot, and Judas the son of James. [14] All these with one accord continued steadfastly in prayer and supplication, along with the women and Mary the mother of Jesus, and with his brothers. [15] In these days, Peter stood up in the middle of the disciples (and the number of names was about one hundred twenty), and said, [16]"Brothers, it was necessary that this Scripture should be fulfilled, which the Holy Spirit spoke before by the mouth of David concerning Judas, who was guide to those who took Jesus. [17] For he was counted with us, and received his portion in this ministry. [18] Now this man obtained a field with the reward for his wickedness; and falling headlong, his body burst open and all his intestines gushed out. [19] It became known to everyone who lived in Jerusalem that in their language that field was called 'Akeldama,' that is, 'The field of blood.' [20] For it is written in the book of Psalms, 'Let his habitation be made desolate. Let no one dwell in it;'* and, 'Let another take his office.'* [21]"Of the men therefore who have accompanied us all the time that the Lord Jesus went in and out among us, [22] beginning from the baptism of John to the day that he was received up from us, of these one must become a witness with us of his resurrection." [23] They put forward two: Joseph called Barsabbas, who was also called Justus, and Matthias. [24] They prayed and said, "You, Lord, who know the hearts of all men, show which one of these two you have chosen [25] to take part in this ministry and apostleship from which Judas fell away, that he might go to his own place." [26] They drew lots for them, and the lot fell on Matthias; and he was counted with the eleven apostles.

## 2

[1] Now when the day of Pentecost had come, they were all with one accord in one place. [2] Suddenly there came from the sky a sound like the rushing of a mighty wind, and it filled all the house where they were sitting. [3] Tongues like fire appeared and were distributed to them, and one sat on each of them. [4] They were all filled with the Holy Spirit and began to speak with other languages, as the Spirit gave them the ability to speak. [5] Now there were dwelling in Jerusalem Jews, devout men, from every nation under the sky. [6] When this sound was heard, the multitude came together and were bewildered, because everyone heard them speaking in his own language. [7] They were all amazed and marveled, saying to one another, "Behold, aren't all these who speak Galileans? [8] How do we hear, everyone in our own native language? [9] Parthians, Medes, Elamites, and people from Mesopotamia, Judea, Cappadocia, Pontus, Asia, [10] Phrygia, Pamphylia, Egypt, the parts of Libya around Cyrene, visitors from Rome, both Jews and proselytes, [11] Cretans and Arabians—we hear them speaking in our languages the mighty works of God!" [12] They were all amazed and were perplexed, saying to one another, "What does this mean?" [13] Others, mocking, said, "They are filled with new wine." [14] But Peter, standing up with the eleven, lifted up his voice and spoke out to them, "You men of Judea and all you who dwell at Jerusalem, let this be known to you, and listen to my words. [15] For these aren't drunken, as you suppose, seeing it is only the third hour of the day.[b] [16] But this is what has been spoken through the prophet Joel: [17]'It will be in the last days, says God, that I will pour out my Spirit on all flesh. Your sons and your daughters will prophesy. Your young men will see visions. Your old men will dream dreams. [18] Yes, and on my servants and on my handmaidens in those days, I will pour out my Spirit, and they will prophesy. [19] I will show wonders in the sky above, and signs on the earth beneath: blood, and fire, and billows of smoke. [20] The sun will be turned into darkness, and the moon into blood, before the great and glorious day of the Lord comes. [21] It will be that whoever will call on the name of the Lord will be saved.'* [22]"Men of Israel, hear these words! Jesus of Nazareth, a man approved by God to you by mighty works and wonders and signs which God did by him among you, even as you yourselves know, [23] him, being delivered up by the determined counsel and foreknowledge of God, you have taken by the hand of lawless men, crucified and killed; [24] whom God raised up, having freed him from the agony of death, because it was not possible that he should be held by it. [25] For David says concerning him, 'I saw the Lord always before my face, for he is on my right hand, that I should not be moved. [26] Therefore my heart was glad, and my tongue rejoiced. Moreover my flesh also will dwell in hope, [27] because you will not leave my soul in Hades,[c] neither will you allow your Holy One to see decay. [28] You made known to me the ways of life. You will make me full of gladness with your presence.'* [29]"Brothers, I may tell you freely of the patriarch David, that he both died and was buried, and his tomb is with us to this day. [30] Therefore, being a prophet, and knowing that God had sworn with an oath to him that of the fruit of his body, according to the flesh, he would raise up the Christ[d] to sit on his throne, [31] he foreseeing this, spoke about the resurrection of the Christ, that his soul wasn't left in Hades,[e] and his flesh didn't see decay. [32] This Jesus God raised up, to which we all are witnesses. [33] Being therefore exalted by the right hand of God, and having received from the Father the promise of the Holy Spirit, he has poured out this which you now see and hear. [34] For David didn't ascend into the heavens, but he says himself, 'The Lord said to my Lord, "Sit by my right hand [35] until I make your enemies a footstool for your feet."'* [36]"Let all the house of Israel therefore know certainly that God has made him both Lord and Christ, this Jesus whom you crucified." [37] Now when they heard this, they were cut to the heart, and said to Peter and the rest of the apostles, "Brothers, what shall we do?" [38] Peter said to them, "Repent and be baptized, every one of you, in the name of Jesus Christ for the forgiveness of sins, and you will receive the gift of the Holy Spirit. [39] For the promise is to you and to your children, and to all who are far off, even as many as the Lord our God will call to himself." [40] With many other words he testified and exhorted them, saying, "Save yourselves from this crooked generation!" [41] Then those who gladly received his word were baptized. There were added that day about three thousand souls. [42] They continued steadfastly in the apostles' teaching and fellowship, in the breaking of bread, and prayer. [43] Fear came on every soul, and many wonders and signs were done through the apostles. [44] All who believed were together, and had all things in common. [45] They sold their possessions and goods, and distributed them to all, according as anyone had need. [46] Day by day, continuing steadfastly with one accord in the temple, and breaking bread at home, they took their food with gladness and singleness of heart, [47] praising God and having favor with all the people. The Lord added to the assembly day by day those who were being saved.

## 3

[1] Peter and John were going up into the temple at the hour of prayer, the ninth hour.[f] [2] A certain man who was lame from his mother's womb was being carried, whom they laid daily at the door of the temple which is called Beautiful, to ask gifts for the needy of those who entered into the temple. [3] Seeing Peter and John about to go into the temple, he asked to receive gifts for the needy. [4] Peter, fastening his eyes on him, with John, said, "Look at us." [5] He listened to them, expecting to receive something from them. [6] But Peter said, "I have no silver or gold, but what I have, that I give you. In the name of Jesus Christ of Nazareth, get up and walk!" [7] He took him by the right hand and raised him up. Immediately his feet and his ankle bones received strength. [8] Leaping up, he stood and began to walk. He entered with them into the temple, walking, leaping, and praising God. [9] All the people saw him walking and praising God. [10] They recognized him, that it was he who used to sit begging for gifts for the needy at the Beautiful Gate of the temple. They were filled with wonder and amazement at what had happened to him. [11] As the lame man who was healed held on to Peter and John, all

---

a *1:10* "Behold", from "ἰδού", means look at, take notice, observe, see, or gaze at. It is often used as an interjection.

* *1:20* Psalms 69:25
* *1:20* Psalms 109:8
b *2:15* about 9:00 a.m.
* *2:21* Joel 2:28- 32

c *2:27* or, Hell
* *2:28* Psalms 16:8- 11
d *2:30* "Christ" means "Anointed One".

e *2:31* or, Hell
* *2:35* Psalms 110:1
f *3:1* 3:00 p.m.

the people ran together to them in the porch that is called Solomon's, greatly wondering. ¹² When Peter saw it, he responded to the people, "You men of Israel, why do you marvel at this man? Why do you fasten your eyes on us, as though by our own power or godliness we had made him walk? ¹³ The God of Abraham, Isaac, and Jacob, the God of our fathers, has glorified his Servant Jesus, whom you delivered up and denied in the presence of Pilate, when he had determined to release him. ¹⁴ But you denied the Holy and Righteous One and asked for a murderer to be granted to you, ¹⁵ and killed the Prince of life, whom God raised from the dead, to which we are witnesses. ¹⁶ By faith in his name, his name has made this man strong, whom you see and know. Yes, the faith which is through him has given him this perfect soundness in the presence of you all. ¹⁷"Now, brothers,ᵃ I know that you did this in ignorance, as did also your rulers. ¹⁸ But the things which God announced by the mouth of all his prophets, that Christ should suffer, he thus fulfilled. ¹⁹"Repent therefore, and turn again, that your sins may be blotted out, so that there may come times of refreshing from the presence of the Lord, ²⁰ and that he may send Christ Jesus, who was ordained for you before, ²¹ whom heaven must receive until the times of restoration of all things, which God spoke long ago by the mouth of his holy prophets. ²² For Moses indeed said to the fathers, 'The Lord God will raise up a prophet for you from among your brothers, like me. You shall listen to him in all things whatever he says to you. ²³ It will be that every soul that will not listen to that prophet will be utterly destroyed from among the people.'* ²⁴ Yes, and all the prophets from Samuel and those who followed after, as many as have spoken, also told of these days. ²⁵ You are the children of the prophets, and of the covenant which God made with our fathers, saying to Abraham, 'All the families of the earth will be blessed through your offspring.'ᵇ* ²⁶ God, having raised up his servant Jesus, sent him to you first to bless you, in turning away every one of you from your wickedness."

# 4

¹ As they spoke to the people, the priests and the captain of the temple and the Sadducees came to them, ² being upset because they taught the people and proclaimed in Jesus the resurrection from the dead. ³ They laid hands on them, and put them in custody until the next day, for it was now evening. ⁴ But many of those who heard the word believed, and the number of the men came to be about five thousand. ⁵ In the morning, their rulers, elders, and scribes were gathered together in Jerusalem. ⁶ Annas the high priest was there, with Caiaphas, John, Alexander, and as many as were relatives of the high priest. ⁷ When they had stood Peter and John in the middle of them, they inquired, "By what power, or in what name, have you done this?" ⁸ Then Peter, filled with the Holy Spirit, said to them, "You rulers of the people and elders of Israel, ⁹ if we are examined today concerning a good deed done to a crippled man, by what means this man has been healed, ¹⁰ may it be known to you all, and to all the people of Israel, that in the name of Jesus Christ of Nazareth, whom you crucified, whom God raised from the dead, this man stands here before you whole in him. ¹¹ He is 'the stone which was regarded as worthless by you, the builders, which has become the head of the corner.'* ¹² There is salvation in no one else, for there is no other name under heaven that is given among men, by which we must be saved!" ¹³ Now when they saw the boldness of Peter and John, and had perceived that they were unlearned and ignorant men, they marveled. They recognized that they had been with Jesus. ¹⁴ Seeing the man who was healed standing with them, they could say nothing against it. ¹⁵ But when they had commanded them to go aside out of the council, they conferred among themselves, ¹⁶ saying, "What shall we do to these men? Because indeed a notable miracle has been done through them, as can be plainly seen by all who dwell in Jerusalem, and we can't deny it. ¹⁷ But so that this spreads no further among the people, let's threaten them, that from now on they don't speak to anyone in this name." ¹⁸ They called them, and commanded them not to speak at all nor teach in the name of Jesus. ¹⁹ But Peter and John answered them, "Whether it is right in the sight of God to listen to you rather than to God, judge for yourselves, ²⁰ for we can't help telling the things which we saw and heard." ²¹ When they had further threatened them, they let them go, finding no way to punish them, because of the people; for everyone glorified God for that which was done. ²² For the man on whom this miracle of healing was performed was more than forty years old. ²³ Being let go, they came to their own company and reported all that the chief priests and the elders had said to them. ²⁴ When they heard it, they lifted up their voice to God with one accord and said, "O Lord, you are God, who made the heaven, the earth, the sea, and all that is in them; ²⁵ who by the mouth of your

servant David, said, 'Why do the nations rage, and the peoples plot a vain thing? ²⁶ The kings of the earth take a stand, and the rulers plot together, against the Lord, and against his Christ.'ᶜ* ²⁷"For truly,ᵈ both Herod and Pontius Pilate, with the Gentiles and the people of Israel, were gathered together against your holy servant Jesus, whom you anointed, ²⁸ to do whatever your hand and your counsel foreordained to happen. ²⁹ Now, Lord, look at their threats, and grant to your servants to speak your word with all boldness, ³⁰ while you stretch out your hand to heal; and that signs and wonders may be done through the name of your holy Servant Jesus." ³¹ When they had prayed, the place was shaken where they were gathered together. They were all filled with the Holy Spirit, and they spoke the word of God with boldness. ³² The multitude of those who believed were of one heart and soul. Not one of them claimed that anything of the things which he possessed was his own, but they had all things in common. ³³ With great power, the apostles gave their testimony of the resurrection of the Lord Jesus. Great grace was on them all. ³⁴ For neither was there among them any who lacked, for as many as were owners of lands or houses sold them, and brought the proceeds of the things that were sold, ³⁵ and laid them at the apostles' feet; and distribution was made to each, according as anyone had need. ³⁶ Joses, who by the apostles was also called Barnabas (which is, being interpreted, Son of Encouragement), a Levite, a man of Cyprus by race, ³⁷ having a field, sold it and brought the money and laid it at the apostles' feet.

# 5

¹ But a certain man named Ananias, with Sapphira his wife, sold a possession, ² and kept back part of the price, his wife also being aware of it, then brought a certain part and laid it at the apostles' feet. ³ But Peter said, "Ananias, why has Satan filled your heart to lie to the Holy Spirit and to keep back part of the price of the land? ⁴ While you kept it, didn't it remain your own? After it was sold, wasn't it in your power? How is it that you have conceived this thing in your heart? You haven't lied to men, but to God." ⁵ Ananias, hearing these words, fell down and died. Great fear came on all who heard these things. ⁶ The young men arose and wrapped him up, and they carried him out and buried him. ⁷ About three hours later, his wife, not knowing what had happened, came in. ⁸ Peter answered her, "Tell me whether you sold the land for so much." She said, "Yes, for so much." ⁹ But Peter asked her, "How is it that you have agreed together to tempt the Spirit of the Lord? Behold, the feet of those who have buried your husband are at the door, and they will carry you out." ¹⁰ She fell down immediately at his feet and died. The young men came in and found her dead, and they carried her out and buried her by her husband. ¹¹ Great fear came on the whole assembly, and on all who heard these things. ¹² By the hands of the apostles many signs and wonders were done among the people. They were all with one accord in Solomon's porch. ¹³ None of the rest dared to join them; however, the people honored them. ¹⁴ More believers were added to the Lord, multitudes of both men and women. ¹⁵ They even carried out the sick into the streets and laid them on cots and mattresses, so that as Peter came by, at least his shadow might overshadow some of them. ¹⁶ The multitude also came together from the cities around Jerusalem, bringing sick people and those who were tormented by unclean spirits; and they were all healed. ¹⁷ But the high priest rose up, and all those who were with him (which is the sect of the Sadducees), and they were filled with jealousy ¹⁸ and laid hands on the apostles, then put them in public custody. ¹⁹ But an angel of the Lord opened the prison doors by night, and brought them out and said, ²⁰"Go stand and speak in the temple to the people all the words of this life." ²¹ When they heard this, they entered into the temple about daybreak and taught. But the high priest and those who were with him came and called the council together, with all the senate of the children of Israel, and sent to the prison to have them brought. ²² But the officers who came didn't find them in the prison. They returned and reported, ²³"We found the prison shut and locked, and the guards standing before the doors, but when we opened them, we found no one inside!" ²⁴ Now when the high priest, the captain of the temple, and the chief priests heard these words, they were very perplexed about them and what might become of this. ²⁵ One came and told them, "Behold, the men whom you put in prison are in the temple, standing and teaching the people." ²⁶ Then the captain went with the officers, and brought them without violence, for they were afraid that the people might stone them. ²⁷ When they had brought them, they set them before the council. The high priest questioned them, ²⁸ saying, "Didn't we strictly command you not to teach in this name? Behold, you have filled Jerusalem with your teaching, and intend to bring this man's blood on us." ²⁹ But Peter and the apostles

---

ᵃ *3:17* The word for "brothers" here may be also correctly translated "brothers and sisters" or "siblings."

* *3:23* Deuteronomy 18:15,18-19
ᵇ *3:25* or, seed
* *3:25* Genesis 22:18; 26:4

* *4:11* Psalms 118:22
ᶜ *4:26* Christ (Greek) and Messiah (Hebrew) both mean Anointed One.

* *4:26* Psalms 2:1-2
ᵈ *4:27* nu adds "in this city,"

answered, "We must obey God rather than men. ³⁰ The God of our fathers raised up Jesus, whom you killed, hanging him on a tree. ³¹ God exalted him with his right hand to be a Prince and a Savior, to give repentance to Israel, and remission of sins. ³² We are his witnesses of these things; and so also is the Holy Spirit, whom God has given to those who obey him." ³³ But they, when they heard this, were cut to the heart, and were determined to kill them. ³⁴ But one stood up in the council, a Pharisee named Gamaliel, a teacher of the law, honored by all the people, and commanded to put the apostles out for a little while. ³⁵ He said to them, "You men of Israel, be careful concerning these men, what you are about to do. ³⁶ For before these days Theudas rose up, making himself out to be somebody; to whom a number of men, about four hundred, joined themselves. He was slain; and all, as many as obeyed him, were dispersed and came to nothing. ³⁷ After this man, Judas of Galilee rose up in the days of the enrollment, and drew away some people after him. He also perished, and all, as many as obeyed him, were scattered abroad. ³⁸ Now I tell you, withdraw from these men and leave them alone. For if this counsel or this work is of men, it will be overthrown. ³⁹ But if it is of God, you will not be able to overthrow it, and you would be found even to be fighting against God!" ⁴⁰ They agreed with him. Summoning the apostles, they beat them and commanded them not to speak in the name of Jesus, and let them go. ⁴¹ They therefore departed from the presence of the council, rejoicing that they were counted worthy to suffer dishonor for Jesus' name. ⁴² Every day, in the temple and at home, they never stopped teaching and preaching Jesus, the Christ.

## 6

¹ Now in those days, when the number of the disciples was multiplying, a complaint arose from the Hellenists[a] against the Hebrews, because their widows were neglected in the daily service. ² The twelve summoned the multitude of the disciples and said, "It is not appropriate for us to forsake the word of God and serve tables. ³ Therefore, select from among you, brothers, seven men of good report, full of the Holy Spirit and of wisdom, whom we may appoint over this business. ⁴ But we will continue steadfastly in prayer and in the ministry of the word." ⁵ These words pleased the whole multitude. They chose Stephen, a man full of faith and of the Holy Spirit, Philip, Prochorus, Nicanor, Timon, Parmenas, and Nicolaus, a proselyte of Antioch, ⁶ whom they set before the apostles. When they had prayed, they laid their hands on them. ⁷ The word of God increased and the number of the disciples greatly multiplied in Jerusalem. A great company of the priests were obedient to the faith. ⁸ Stephen, full of faith and power, performed great wonders and signs among the people. ⁹ But some of those who were of the synagogue called "The Libertines", and of the Cyrenians, of the Alexandrians, and of those of Cilicia and Asia arose, disputing with Stephen. ¹⁰ They weren't able to withstand the wisdom and the Spirit by which he spoke. ¹¹ Then they secretly induced men to say, "We have heard him speak blasphemous words against Moses and God." ¹² They stirred up the people, the elders, and the scribes, and came against him and seized him, then brought him in to the council, ¹³ and set up false witnesses who said, "This man never stops speaking blasphemous words against this holy place and the law. ¹⁴ For we have heard him say that this Jesus of Nazareth will destroy this place, and will change the customs which Moses delivered to us." ¹⁵ All who sat in the council, fastening their eyes on him, saw his face like it was the face of an angel.

## 7

¹ The high priest said, "Are these things so?" ² He said, "Brothers and fathers, listen. The God of glory appeared to our father Abraham when he was in Mesopotamia, before he lived in Haran, ³ and said to him, 'Get out of your land and away from your relatives, and come into a land which I will show you.'* ⁴ Then he came out of the land of the Chaldaeans and lived in Haran. From there, when his father was dead, God moved him into this land where you are now living. ⁵ He gave him no inheritance in it, no, not so much as to set his foot on. He promised that he would give it to him for a possession, and to his offspring after him, when he still had no child. ⁶ God spoke in this way: that his offspring would live as aliens in a strange land, and that they would be enslaved and mistreated for four hundred years. ⁷'I will judge the nation to which they will be in bondage,' said God, 'and after that they will come out and serve me in this place.'* ⁸ He gave him the covenant of circumcision. So Abraham became the father of Isaac, and circumcised him the eighth day. Isaac became the father of Jacob, and Jacob became the father of the twelve patriarchs. ⁹"The patriarchs, moved with

jealousy against Joseph, sold him into Egypt. God was with him ¹⁰ and delivered him out of all his afflictions, and gave him favor and wisdom before Pharaoh, king of Egypt. He made him governor over Egypt and all his house. ¹¹ Now a famine came over all the land of Egypt and Canaan, and great affliction. Our fathers found no food. ¹² But when Jacob heard that there was grain in Egypt, he sent out our fathers the first time. ¹³ On the second time Joseph was made known to his brothers, and Joseph's family was revealed to Pharaoh. ¹⁴ Joseph sent and summoned Jacob his father and all his relatives, seventy-five souls. ¹⁵ Jacob went down into Egypt and he died, himself and our fathers; ¹⁶ and they were brought back to Shechem and laid in the tomb that Abraham bought for a price in silver from the children of Hamor of Shechem. ¹⁷"But as the time of the promise came close which God had sworn to Abraham, the people grew and multiplied in Egypt, ¹⁸ until there arose a different king who didn't know Joseph. ¹⁹ The same took advantage of our race and mistreated our fathers, and forced them to abandon their babies, so that they wouldn't stay alive. ²⁰ At that time Moses was born, and was exceedingly handsome to God. He was nourished three months in his father's house. ²¹ When he was abandoned, Pharaoh's daughter took him up and reared him as her own son. ²² Moses was instructed in all the wisdom of the Egyptians. He was mighty in his words and works. ²³ But when he was forty years old, it came into his heart to visit his brothers,[b] the children of Israel. ²⁴ Seeing one of them suffer wrong, he defended him and avenged him who was oppressed, striking the Egyptian. ²⁵ He supposed that his brothers understood that God, by his hand, was giving them deliverance; but they didn't understand. ²⁶"The day following, he appeared to them as they fought, and urged them to be at peace again, saying, 'Sirs, you are brothers. Why do you wrong one another?' ²⁷ But he who did his neighbor wrong pushed him away, saying, 'Who made you a ruler and a judge over us? ²⁸ Do you want to kill me as you killed the Egyptian yesterday?'* ²⁹ Moses fled at this saying, and became a stranger in the land of Midian, where he became the father of two sons. ³⁰"When forty years were fulfilled, an angel of the Lord appeared to him in the wilderness of Mount Sinai, in a flame of fire in a bush. ³¹ When Moses saw it, he wondered at the sight. As he came close to see, the voice of the Lord came to him, ³²'I am the God of your fathers: the God of Abraham, the God of Isaac, and the God of Jacob.'* Moses trembled and dared not look. ³³ The Lord said to him, 'Take off your sandals, for the place where you stand is holy ground. ³⁴ I have surely seen the affliction of my people who are in Egypt, and have heard their groaning. I have come down to deliver them. Now come, I will send you into Egypt.'* ³⁵"This Moses whom they refused, saying, 'Who made you a ruler and a judge?'—God has sent him as both a ruler and a deliverer by the hand of the angel who appeared to him in the bush. ³⁶ This man led them out, having worked wonders and signs in Egypt, in the Red Sea, and in the wilderness for forty years. ³⁷ This is that Moses who said to the children of Israel, 'The Lord our God will raise up a prophet for you from among your brothers, like me.'*[c] ³⁸ This is he who was in the assembly in the wilderness with the angel that spoke to him on Mount Sinai, and with our fathers, who received living revelations to give to us, ³⁹ to whom our fathers wouldn't be obedient, but rejected him and turned back in their hearts to Egypt, ⁴⁰ saying to Aaron, 'Make us gods that will go before us, for as for this Moses who led us out of the land of Egypt, we don't know what has become of him.'* ⁴¹ They made a calf in those days, and brought a sacrifice to the idol, and rejoiced in the works of their hands. ⁴² But God turned away and gave them up to serve the army of the sky,[d] as it is written in the book of the prophets, 'Did you offer to me slain animals and sacrifices forty years in the wilderness, O house of Israel? ⁴³ You took up the tabernacle of Moloch, the star of your god Rephan, the figures which you made to worship, so I will carry you away* beyond Babylon.' ⁴⁴"Our fathers had the tabernacle of the testimony in the wilderness, even as he who spoke to Moses commanded him to make it according to the pattern that he had seen; ⁴⁵ which also our fathers, in their turn, brought in with Joshua when they entered into the possession of the nations whom God drove out before the face of our fathers to the days of David, ⁴⁶ who found favor in the sight of God, and asked to find a habitation for the God of Jacob. ⁴⁷ But Solomon built him a house. ⁴⁸ However, the Most High doesn't dwell in temples made with hands, as the prophet says, ⁴⁹'heaven is my throne, and the earth a footstool for my feet. What kind of house will you build me?' says the Lord. 'Or what is the place of my rest? ⁵⁰ Didn't my hand make all these things?'* ⁵¹"You stiff-necked and uncircumcised in heart and ears, you always

---

[a] 6:1 The Hellenists used Greek language and culture, even though they were also of Hebrew descent.
* 7:3 Genesis 12:1
* 7:7 Genesis 15:13-14

[b] 7:23 The word for "brothers" here and where the context allows may be also correctly translated "brothers and sisters" or "siblings."
* 7:28 Exodus 2:14

* 7:32 Exodus 3:6
* 7:34 Exodus 3:5,7-8,10
[c] 7:37 TR adds "You shall listen to him."
* 7:37 Deuteronomy 18:15
* 7:40 Exodus 32:1

[d] 7:42 This idiom could also be translated "host of heaven", or "angelic beings", or "heavenly bodies."
* 7:43 Amos 5:25-27
* 7:50 Isaiah 66:1-2

resist the Holy Spirit! As your fathers did, so you do. ⁵² Which of the prophets didn't your fathers persecute? They killed those who foretold the coming of the Righteous One, of whom you have now become betrayers and murderers. ⁵³ You received the law as it was ordained by angels, and didn't keep it!" ⁵⁴ Now when they heard these things, they were cut to the heart, and they gnashed at him with their teeth. ⁵⁵ But he, being full of the Holy Spirit, looked up steadfastly into heaven and saw the glory of God, and Jesus standing on the right hand of God, ⁵⁶ and said, "Behold, I see the heavens opened and the Son of Man standing at the right hand of God!" ⁵⁷ But they cried out with a loud voice and stopped their ears, then rushed at him with one accord. ⁵⁸ They threw him out of the city and stoned him. The witnesses placed their garments at the feet of a young man named Saul. ⁵⁹ They stoned Stephen as he called out, saying, "Lord Jesus, receive my spirit!" ⁶⁰ He kneeled down and cried with a loud voice, "Lord, don't hold this sin against them!" When he had said this, he fell asleep.

## 8

¹ Saul was consenting to his death. A great persecution arose against the assembly which was in Jerusalem in that day. They were all scattered abroad throughout the regions of Judea and Samaria, except for the apostles. ² Devout men buried Stephen and lamented greatly over him. ³ But Saul ravaged the assembly, entering into every house and dragged both men and women off to prison. ⁴ Therefore those who were scattered abroad went around preaching the word. ⁵ Philip went down to the city of Samaria and proclaimed to them the Christ. ⁶ The multitudes listened with one accord to the things that were spoken by Philip when they heard and saw the signs which he did. ⁷ For unclean spirits came out of many of those who had them. They came out, crying with a loud voice. Many who had been paralyzed and lame were healed. ⁸ There was great joy in that city. ⁹ But there was a certain man, Simon by name, who used to practice sorcery in the city and amazed the people of Samaria, making himself out to be some great one, ¹⁰ to whom they all listened, from the least to the greatest, saying, "This man is that great power of God." ¹¹ They listened to him because for a long time he had amazed them with his sorceries. ¹² But when they believed Philip preaching good news concerning God's Kingdom and the name of Jesus Christ, they were baptized, both men and women. ¹³ Simon himself also believed. Being baptized, he continued with Philip. Seeing signs and great miracles occurring, he was amazed. ¹⁴ Now when the apostles who were at Jerusalem heard that Samaria had received the word of God, they sent Peter and John to them, ¹⁵ who, when they had come down, prayed for them, that they might receive the Holy Spirit; ¹⁶ for as yet he had fallen on none of them. They had only been baptized in the name of Christ Jesus. ¹⁷ Then they laid their hands on them, and they received the Holy Spirit. ¹⁸ Now when Simon saw that the Holy Spirit was given through the laying on of the apostles' hands, he offered them money, ¹⁹ saying, "Give me also this power, that whomever I lay my hands on may receive the Holy Spirit." ²⁰ But Peter said to him, "May your silver perish with you, because you thought you could obtain the gift of God with money! ²¹ You have neither part nor lot in this matter, for your heart isn't right before God. ²² Repent therefore of this, your wickedness, and ask God if perhaps the thought of your heart may be forgiven you. ²³ For I see that you are in the poison of bitterness and in the bondage of iniquity." ²⁴ Simon answered, "Pray for me to the Lord, that none of the things which you have spoken happen to me." ²⁵ They therefore, when they had testified and spoken the word of the Lord, returned to Jerusalem, and preached the Good News to many villages of the Samaritans. ²⁶ Then an angel of the Lord spoke to Philip, saying, "Arise, and go toward the south to the way that goes down from Jerusalem to Gaza. This is a desert." ²⁷ He arose and went; and behold, there was a man of Ethiopia, a eunuch of great authority under Candace, queen of the Ethiopians, who was over all her treasure, who had come to Jerusalem to worship. ²⁸ He was returning and sitting in his chariot, and was reading the prophet Isaiah. ²⁹ The Spirit said to Philip, "Go near, and join yourself to this chariot." ³⁰ Philip ran to him, and heard him reading Isaiah the prophet, and said, "Do you understand what you are reading?" ³¹ He said, "How can I, unless someone explains it to me?" He begged Philip to come up and sit with him. ³² Now the passage of the Scripture which he was reading was this, "He was led as a sheep to the slaughter. As a lamb before his shearer is silent, so he doesn't open his mouth. ³³ In his humiliation, his judgment was taken away. Who will declare His generation? For his life is taken from the earth."* ³⁴ The eunuch answered Philip, "Who is the prophet talking about?

About himself, or about someone else?" ³⁵ Philip opened his mouth, and beginning from this Scripture, preached to him about Jesus. ³⁶ As they went on the way, they came to some water; and the eunuch said, "Behold, here is water. What is keeping me from being baptized?" ³⁷ ᵃ ³⁸ He commanded the chariot to stand still, and they both went down into the water, both Philip and the eunuch, and he baptized him. ³⁹ When they came up out of the water, the Spirit of the Lord caught Philip away, and the eunuch didn't see him any more, for he went on his way rejoicing. ⁴⁰ But Philip was found at Azotus. Passing through, he preached the Good News to all the cities until he came to Caesarea.

## 9

¹ But Saul, still breathing threats and slaughter against the disciples of the Lord, went to the high priest ² and asked for letters from him to the synagogues of Damascus, that if he found any who were of the Way, whether men or women, he might bring them bound to Jerusalem. ³ As he traveled, he got close to Damascus, and suddenly a light from the sky shone around him. ⁴ He fell on the earth, and heard a voice saying to him, "Saul, Saul, why do you persecute me?" ⁵ He said, "Who are you, Lord?" The Lord said, "I am Jesus, whom you are persecuting.ᵇ ⁶ Butᶜ rise up and enter into the city, then you will be told what you must do." ⁷ The men who traveled with him stood speechless, hearing the sound, but seeing no one. ⁸ Saul arose from the ground, and when his eyes were opened, he saw no one. They led him by the hand and brought him into Damascus. ⁹ He was without sight for three days, and neither ate nor drank. ¹⁰ Now there was a certain disciple at Damascus named Ananias. The Lord said to him in a vision, "Ananias!" He said, "Behold, it's me, Lord." ¹¹ The Lord said to him, "Arise and go to the street which is called Straight, and inquire in the house of Judahᵈ for one named Saul, a man of Tarsus. For behold, he is praying, ¹² and in a vision he has seen a man named Ananias coming in and laying his hands on him, that he might receive his sight." ¹³ But Ananias answered, "Lord, I have heard from many about this man, how much evil he did to your saints at Jerusalem. ¹⁴ Here he has authority from the chief priests to bind all who call on your name." ¹⁵ But the Lord said to him, "Go your way, for he is my chosen vessel to bear my name before the nations and kings, and the children of Israel. ¹⁶ For I will show him how many things he must suffer for my name's sake." ¹⁷ Ananias departed and entered into the house. Laying his hands on him, he said, "Brother Saul, the Lord, who appeared to you on the road by which you came, has sent me that you may receive your sight and be filled with the Holy Spirit." ¹⁸ Immediately something like scales fell from his eyes, and he received his sight. He arose and was baptized. ¹⁹ He took food and was strengthened. Saul stayed several days with the disciples who were at Damascus. ²⁰ Immediately in the synagogues he proclaimed the Christ, that he is the Son of God. ²¹ All who heard him were amazed, and said, "Isn't this he who in Jerusalem made **havoc** of those who called on this name? And he had come here intending to bring them bound before the chief priests!" ²² But Saul increased more in strength, and confounded the Jews who lived at Damascus, proving that this is the Christ. ²³ When many days were fulfilled, the Jews conspired together to kill him, ²⁴ but their plot became known to Saul. They watched the gates both day and night that they might kill him, ²⁵ but his disciples took him by night and let him down through the wall, lowering him in a basket. ²⁶ When Saul had come to Jerusalem, he tried to join himself to the disciples; but they were all afraid of him, not believing that he was a disciple. ²⁷ But Barnabas took him and brought him to the apostles, and declared to them how he had seen the Lord on the way, and that he had spoken to him, and how at Damascus he had preached boldly in the name of Jesus. ²⁸ He was with them entering intoᵉ Jerusalem, ²⁹ preaching boldly in the name of the Lord Jesus.ᶠ He spoke and disputed against the Hellenists,ᵍ but they were seeking to kill him. ³⁰ When the brothersʰ knew it, they brought him down to Caesarea and sent him off to Tarsus. ³¹ So the assemblies throughout all Judea, Galilee, and Samaria had peace and were built up. They were multiplied, walking in the fear of the Lord and in the comfort of the Holy Spirit. ³² As Peter went throughout all those parts, he came down also to the saints who lived at Lydda. ³³ There he found a certain man named Aeneas, who had been bedridden for eight years because he was paralyzed. ³⁴ Peter said to him, "Aeneas, Jesus Christ heals you. Get up and make your bed!" Immediately he arose. ³⁵ All who lived at Lydda and in Sharon saw him, and they turned to the Lord. ³⁶ Now there was at Joppa a certain disciple named Tabitha, which when translated means Dorcas.ⁱ This woman was full of good works and acts of mercy which

---

* 8:33 Isaiah 53:7,8
ᵃ 8:37 TR adds Philip said, "If you believe with all your heart, you may." He answered, "I believe that Jesus Christ is the Son of God."

ᵇ 9:5 TR adds "It's hard for you to kick against the cattle prods."
ᶜ 9:6 TR omits "But"
ᵈ 9:11 or, Judas
ᵉ 9:28 TR and NU add "and going out"

ᶠ 9:29 TR and NU omit "Jesus" and reverse the order of verses 28 & 29.
ᵍ 9:29 The Hellenists were Hebrews who used Greek language and culture.

ʰ 9:30 The word for "brothers" here and where the context allows may also be correctly translated "brothers and sisters" or "siblings."
ⁱ 9:36 "Dorcas" is Greek for "Gazelle."

she did. **37** In those days, she became sick and died. When they had washed her, they laid her in an upper room. **38** As Lydda was near Joppa, the disciples, hearing that Peter was there, sent two men[a] to him, imploring him not to delay in coming to them. **39** Peter got up and went with them. When he had come, they brought him into the upper room. All the widows stood by him weeping, and showing the tunics and other garments which Dorcas had made while she was with them. **40** Peter sent them all out, and knelt down and prayed. Turning to the body, he said, "Tabitha, get up!" She opened her eyes, and when she saw Peter, she sat up. **41** He gave her his hand and raised her up. Calling the saints and widows, he presented her alive. **42** This became known throughout all Joppa, and many believed in the Lord. **43** He stayed many days in Joppa with a tanner named Simon.

## 10

**1** Now there was a certain man in Caesarea, Cornelius by name, a centurion of what was called the Italian Regiment, **2** a devout man, and one who feared God with all his house, who gave gifts for the needy generously to the people, and always prayed to God. **3** At about the ninth hour of the day,[b] he clearly saw in a vision an angel of God coming to him and saying to him, "Cornelius!" **4** He, fastening his eyes on him and being frightened, said, "What is it, Lord?" He said to him, "Your prayers and your gifts to the needy have gone up for a memorial before God. **5** Now send men to Joppa, and get Simon, who is also called Peter. **6** He is staying with a tanner named Simon, whose house is by the seaside.[c] **7** When the angel who spoke to him had departed, Cornelius called two of his household servants and a devout soldier of those who waited on him continually. **8** Having explained everything to them, he sent them to Joppa. **9** Now on the next day as they were on their journey and got close to the city, Peter went up on the housetop to pray at about noon. **10** He became hungry and desired to eat, but while they were preparing, he fell into a trance. **11** He saw heaven opened and a certain container descending to him, like a great sheet let down by four corners on the earth, **12** in which were all kinds of four-footed animals of the earth, wild animals, reptiles, and birds of the sky. **13** A voice came to him, "Rise, Peter, kill and eat!" **14** But Peter said, "Not so, Lord; for I have never eaten anything that is common or unclean." **15** A voice came to him again the second time, "What God has cleansed, you must not call unclean." **16** This was done three times, and immediately the thing was received up into heaven. **17** Now while Peter was very perplexed in himself what the vision which he had seen might mean, behold, the men who were sent by Cornelius, having made inquiry for Simon's house, stood before the gate, **18** and called and asked whether Simon, who was also called Peter, was lodging there. **19** While Peter was pondering the vision, the Spirit said to him, "Behold, three[d] men seek you. **20** But arise, get down, and go with them, doubting nothing; for I have sent them." **21** Peter went down to the men, and said, "Behold, I am he whom you seek. Why have you come?" **22** They said, "Cornelius, a centurion, a righteous man and one who fears God, and well spoken of by all the nation of the Jews, was directed by a holy angel to invite you to his house, and to listen to what you say." **23** So he called them in and provided a place to stay. On the next day Peter arose and went out with them, and some of the brothers from Joppa accompanied him. **24** On the next day they entered into Caesarea. Cornelius was waiting for them, having called together his relatives and his near friends. **25** When Peter entered, Cornelius met him, fell down at his feet, and worshiped him. **26** But Peter raised him up, saying, "Stand up! I myself am also a man." **27** As he talked with him, he went in and found many gathered together. **28** He said to them, "You yourselves know how it is an unlawful thing for a man who is a Jew to join himself or come to one of another nation, but God has shown me that I shouldn't call any man unholy or unclean. **29** Therefore I also came without complaint when I was sent for. I ask therefore, why did you send for me?" **30** Cornelius said, "Four days ago, I was fasting until this hour; and at the ninth hour,[e] I prayed in my house, and behold, a man stood before me in bright clothing **31** and said, 'Cornelius, your prayer is heard, and your gifts to the needy are remembered in the sight of God. **32** Send therefore to Joppa and summon Simon, who is also called Peter. He is staying in the house of a tanner named Simon, by the seaside. When he comes, he will speak to you.' **33** Therefore I sent to you at once, and it was good of you to come. Now therefore we are all here present in the sight of God to hear all things that have been commanded you by God." **34** Peter opened his mouth and said, "Truly I perceive that God doesn't show favoritism; **35** but in every nation he who fears him and works righteousness is acceptable to him. **36** The

word which he sent to the children of Israel, preaching good news of peace by Jesus Christ—he is Lord of all— **37** you yourselves know what happened, which was proclaimed throughout all Judea, beginning from Galilee, after the baptism which John preached; **38** how God anointed Jesus of Nazareth with the Holy Spirit and with power, who went about doing good and healing all who were oppressed by the devil, for God was with him. **39** We are witnesses of everything he did both in the country of the Jews and in Jerusalem; whom they also[f] killed, hanging him on a tree. **40** God raised him up the third day and gave him to be revealed, **41** not to all the people, but to witnesses who were chosen before by God, to us, who ate and drank with him after he rose from the dead. **42** He commanded us to preach to the people and to testify that this is he who is appointed by God as the Judge of the living and the dead. **43** All the prophets testify about him, that through his name everyone who believes in him will receive remission of sins." **44** While Peter was still speaking these words, the Holy Spirit fell on all those who heard the word. **45** They of the circumcision who believed were amazed, as many as came with Peter, because the gift of the Holy Spirit was also poured out on the Gentiles. **46** For they heard them speaking in other languages and magnifying God. Then Peter answered, **47**"Can anyone forbid these people from being baptized with water? They have received the Holy Spirit just like us." **48** He commanded them to be baptized in the name of Jesus Christ. Then they asked him to stay some days.

## 11

**1** Now the apostles and the brothers[g] who were in Judea heard that the Gentiles had also received the word of God. **2** When Peter had come up to Jerusalem, those who were of the circumcision contended with him, **3** saying, "You went in to uncircumcised men and ate with them!" **4** But Peter began, and explained to them in order, saying, **5**"I was in the city of Joppa praying, and in a trance I saw a vision: a certain container descending, like it was a great sheet let down from heaven by four corners. It came as far as me. **6** When I had looked intently at it, I considered, and saw the four-footed animals of the earth, wild animals, creeping things, and birds of the sky. **7** I also heard a voice saying to me, 'Rise, Peter, kill and eat!' **8** But I said, 'Not so, Lord, for nothing unholy or unclean has ever entered into my mouth.' **9** But a voice answered me the second time out of heaven, 'What God has cleansed, don't you call unclean.' **10** This was done three times, and all were drawn up again into heaven. **11** Behold, immediately three men stood before the house where I was, having been sent from Caesarea to me. **12** The Spirit told me to go with them without discriminating. These six brothers also accompanied me, and we entered into the man's house. **13** He told us how he had seen the angel standing in his house and saying to him, 'Send to Joppa and get Simon, who is called Peter, **14** who will speak to you words by which you will be saved, you and all your house.' **15** As I began to speak, the Holy Spirit fell on them, even as on us at the beginning. **16** I remembered the word of the Lord, how he said, 'John indeed baptized in water, but you will be baptized in the Holy Spirit.' **17** If then God gave to them the same gift as us when we believed in the Lord Jesus Christ, who was I, that I could withstand God?" **18** When they heard these things, they held their peace and glorified God, saying, "Then God has also granted to the Gentiles repentance to life!" **19** They therefore who were scattered abroad by the oppression that arose about Stephen traveled as far as Phoenicia, Cyprus, and Antioch, speaking the word to no one except to Jews only. **20** But there were some of them, men of Cyprus and Cyrene, who, when they had come to Antioch, spoke to the Hellenists,[h] preaching the Lord Jesus. **21** The hand of the Lord was with them, and a great number believed and turned to the Lord. **22** The report concerning them came to the ears of the assembly which was in Jerusalem. They sent out Barnabas to go as far as Antioch, **23** who, when he had come, and had seen the grace of God, was glad. He exhorted them all, that with purpose of heart they should remain near to the Lord. **24** For he was a good man, and full of the Holy Spirit and of faith, and many people were added to the Lord. **25** Barnabas went out to Tarsus to look for Saul. **26** When he had found him, he brought him to Antioch. For a whole year they were gathered together with the assembly, and taught many people. The disciples were first called Christians in Antioch. **27** Now in these days, prophets came down from Jerusalem to Antioch. **28** One of them named Agabus stood up and indicated by the Spirit that there should be a great famine all over the world, which also happened in the days of Claudius. **29** As any of the disciples had plenty, each determined to send relief to the

---

[a] *9:38* Reading from NU, TR; MT omits "two men"
[b] *10:3* 3:00 p.m.

[c] *10:6* TR adds "This one will tell you what it is necessary for you to do."
[d] *10:19* Reading from TR and NU. MT omits "three"

[e] *10:30* 3:00 p.m.
[f] *10:39* TR omits "also"
[g] *11:1* The word for "brothers" here and where context allows may also be correctly translated

"brothers and sisters" or "siblings."
[h] *11:20* A Hellenist is someone who keeps Greek customs and culture.

brothers who lived in Judea; [30] which they also did, sending it to the elders by the hands of Barnabas and Saul.

## 12

[1] Now about that time, King Herod stretched out his hands to oppress some of the assembly. [2] He killed James, the brother of John, with the sword. [3] When he saw that it pleased the Jews, he proceeded to seize Peter also. This was during the days of unleavened bread. [4] When he had arrested him, he put him in prison and delivered him to four squads of four soldiers each to guard him, intending to bring him out to the people after the Passover. [5] Peter therefore was kept in the prison, but constant prayer was made by the assembly to God for him. [6] The same night when Herod was about to bring him out, Peter was sleeping between two soldiers, bound with two chains. Guards in front of the door kept the prison. [7] And behold, an angel of the Lord stood by him, and a light shone in the cell. He struck Peter on the side and woke him up, saying, "Stand up quickly!" His chains fell off his hands. [8] The angel said to him, "Get dressed and put on your sandals." He did so. He said to him, "Put on your cloak and follow me." [9] And he went out and followed him. He didn't know that what was being done by the angel was real, but thought he saw a vision. [10] When they were past the first and the second guard, they came to the iron gate that leads into the city, which opened to them by itself. They went out and went down one street, and immediately the angel departed from him. [11] When Peter had come to himself, he said, "Now I truly know that the Lord has sent out his angel and delivered me out of the hand of Herod, and from everything the Jewish people were expecting." [12] Thinking about that, he came to the house of Mary, the mother of John who was called Mark, where many were gathered together and were praying. [13] When Peter knocked at the door of the gate, a servant girl named Rhoda came to answer. [14] When she recognized Peter's voice, she didn't open the gate for joy, but ran in and reported that Peter was standing in front of the gate. [15] They said to her, "You are crazy!" But she insisted that it was so. They said, "It is his angel." [16] But Peter continued knocking. When they had opened, they saw him and were amazed. [17] But he, beckoning to them with his hand to be silent, declared to them how the Lord had brought him out of the prison. He said, "Tell these things to James and to the brothers." Then he departed and went to another place. [18] Now as soon as it was day, there was no small stir among the soldiers about what had become of Peter. [19] When Herod had sought for him and didn't find him, he examined the guards, then commanded that they should be put to death. He went down from Judea to Caesarea, and stayed there. [20] Now Herod was very angry with the people of Tyre and Sidon. They came with one accord to him and, having made Blastus, the king's personal aide, their friend, they asked for peace, because their country depended on the king's country for food. [21] On an appointed day, Herod dressed himself in royal clothing, sat on the throne, and gave a speech to them. [22] The people shouted, "The voice of a god, and not of a man!" [23] Immediately an angel of the Lord struck him, because he didn't give God the glory. Then he was eaten by worms and died. [24] But the word of God grew and multiplied. [25] Barnabas and Saul returned to[a] Jerusalem when they had fulfilled their service, also taking with them John who was called Mark.

## 13

[1] Now in the assembly that was at Antioch there were some prophets and teachers: Barnabas, Simeon who was called Niger, Lucius of Cyrene, Manaen the foster brother of Herod the tetrarch, and Saul. [2] As they served the Lord and fasted, the Holy Spirit said, "Separate Barnabas and Saul for me, for the work to which I have called them." [3] Then, when they had fasted and prayed and laid their hands on them, they sent them away. [4] So, being sent out by the Holy Spirit, they went down to Seleucia. From there they sailed to Cyprus. [5] When they were at Salamis, they proclaimed God's word in the Jewish synagogues. They also had John as their attendant. [6] When they had gone through the island to Paphos, they found a certain sorcerer, a false prophet, a Jew whose name was Bar Jesus, [7] who was with the proconsul, Sergius Paulus, a man of understanding. This man summoned Barnabas and Saul, and sought to hear the word of God. [8] But Elymas the sorcerer (for so is his name by interpretation) withstood them, seeking to turn the proconsul away from the faith. [9] But Saul, who is also called Paul, filled with the Holy Spirit, fastened his eyes on him [10] and said, "You son of the devil, full of all deceit and all cunning, you enemy of all righteousness, will you not cease to pervert the right ways of the Lord? [11] Now, behold, the hand of the Lord is on you, and you will be blind, not seeing the sun for a season!" Immediately a mist and darkness fell

on him. He went around seeking someone to lead him by the hand. [12] Then the proconsul, when he saw what was done, believed, being astonished at the teaching of the Lord. [13] Now Paul and his company set sail from Paphos and came to Perga in Pamphylia. John departed from them and returned to Jerusalem. [14] But they, passing on from Perga, came to Antioch of Pisidia. They went into the synagogue on the Sabbath day and sat down. [15] After the reading of the law and the prophets, the rulers of the synagogue sent to them, saying, "Brothers, if you have any word of exhortation for the people, speak." [16] Paul stood up, and gesturing with his hand said, "Men of Israel, and you who fear God, listen. [17] The God of this people[b] chose our fathers, and exalted the people when they stayed as aliens in the land of Egypt, and with an uplifted arm, he led them out of it. [18] For a period of about forty years he put up with them in the wilderness. [19] When he had destroyed seven nations in the land of Canaan, he gave them their land for an inheritance for about four hundred fifty years. [20] After these things, he gave them judges until Samuel the prophet. [21] Afterward they asked for a king, and God gave to them Saul the son of Kish, a man of the tribe of Benjamin, for forty years. [22] When he had removed him, he raised up David to be their king, to whom he also testified, 'I have found David the son of Jesse, a man after my heart, who will do all my will.' [23] From this man's offspring, God has brought salvation[c] to Israel according to his promise, [24] before his coming, when John had first preached the baptism of repentance to Israel.[d] [25] As John was fulfilling his course, he said, 'What do you suppose that I am? I am not he. But behold, one comes after me, the sandals of whose feet I am not worthy to untie.' [26] "Brothers, children of the stock of Abraham, and those among you who fear God, the word of this salvation is sent out to you. [27] For those who dwell in Jerusalem, and their rulers, because they didn't know him, nor the voices of the prophets which are read every Sabbath, fulfilled them by condemning him. [28] Though they found no cause for death, they still asked Pilate to have him killed. [29] When they had fulfilled all things that were written about him, they took him down from the tree and laid him in a tomb. [30] But God raised him from the dead, [31] and he was seen for many days by those who came up with him from Galilee to Jerusalem, who are his witnesses to the people. [32] We bring you good news of the promise made to the fathers, [33] that God has fulfilled this to us, their children, in that he raised up Jesus. As it is also written in the second psalm, 'You are my Son. Today I have become your father.'* [34] "Concerning that he raised him up from the dead, now no more to return to corruption, he has spoken thus: 'I will give you the holy and sure blessings of David.'* [35] Therefore he says also in another psalm, 'You will not allow your Holy One to see decay.'* [36] For David, after he had in his own generation served the counsel of God, fell asleep, was laid with his fathers, and saw decay. [37] But he whom God raised up saw no decay. [38] Be it known to you therefore, brothers,[e] that through this man is proclaimed to you remission of sins; [39] and by him everyone who believes is justified from all things, from which you could not be justified by the law of Moses. [40] Beware therefore, lest that come on you which is spoken in the prophets: [41] 'Behold, you scoffers! Wonder and perish, for I work a work in your days, a work which you will in no way believe, if one declares it to you.'"* [42] So when the Jews went out of the synagogue, the Gentiles begged that these words might be preached to them the next Sabbath. [43] Now when the synagogue broke up, many of the Jews and of the devout proselytes followed Paul and Barnabas; who, speaking to them, urged them to continue in the grace of God. [44] The next Sabbath, almost the whole city was gathered together to hear the word of God. [45] But when the Jews saw the multitudes, they were filled with jealousy, and contradicted the things which were spoken by Paul, and blasphemed. [46] Paul and Barnabas spoke out boldly, and said, "It was necessary that God's word should be spoken to you first. Since indeed you thrust it from yourselves, and judge yourselves unworthy of eternal life, behold, we turn to the Gentiles. [47] For so has the Lord commanded us, saying, 'I have set you as a light for the Gentiles, that you should bring salvation to the uttermost parts of the earth.'"* [48] As the Gentiles heard this, they were glad and glorified the word of God. As many as were appointed to eternal life believed. [49] The Lord's word was spread abroad throughout all the region. [50] But the Jews stirred up the devout and prominent women and the chief men of the city, and stirred up a persecution against Paul and Barnabas, and threw them out of their borders. [51] But they shook off the dust of their feet against them, and came to Iconium. [52] The disciples were filled with joy and with the Holy Spirit.

---

[a] *12:25* TR reads "from" instead of "to"

[b] *13:17* TR, NU add "Israel"

[c] *13:23* TR, NU read "a Savior, Jesus" instead of "salvation"

[d] *13:24* TR, NU read "to all the people of Israel" instead of "to Israel"

* 13:33 Psalms 2:7

* 13:34 Isaiah 55:3

* 13:35 Psalms 16:10

[e] *13:38* The word for "brothers" here and where the context allows may also be

correctly translated "brothers and sisters" or "siblings."

* 13:41 Habakkuk 1:5

* 13:47 Isaiah 49:6

## 14

¹ In Iconium, they entered together into the synagogue of the Jews, and so spoke that a great multitude both of Jews and of Greeks believed. ² But the disbelieving[a] Jews stirred up and embittered the souls of the Gentiles against the brothers. ³ Therefore they stayed there a long time, speaking boldly in the Lord, who testified to the word of his grace, granting signs and wonders to be done by their hands. ⁴ But the multitude of the city was divided. Part sided with the Jews and part with the apostles. ⁵ When some of both the Gentiles and the Jews, with their rulers, made a violent attempt to mistreat and stone them, ⁶ they became aware of it and fled to the cities of Lycaonia, Lystra, Derbe, and the surrounding region. ⁷ There they preached the Good News. ⁸ At Lystra a certain man sat, impotent in his feet, a cripple from his mother's womb, who never had walked. ⁹ He was listening to Paul speaking, who, fastening eyes on him and seeing that he had faith to be made whole, ¹⁰ said with a loud voice, "Stand upright on your feet!" He leaped up and walked. ¹¹ When the multitude saw what Paul had done, they lifted up their voice, saying in the language of Lycaonia, "The gods have come down to us in the likeness of men!" ¹² They called Barnabas "Jupiter", and Paul "Mercury", because he was the chief speaker. ¹³ The priest of Jupiter, whose temple was in front of their city, brought oxen and garlands to the gates, and would have made a sacrifice along with the multitudes. ¹⁴ But when the apostles, Barnabas and Paul, heard of it, they tore their clothes and sprang into the multitude, crying out, ¹⁵"Men, why are you doing these things? We also are men of the same nature as you, and bring you good news, that you should turn from these vain things to the living God, who made the sky, the earth, the sea, and all that is in them; ¹⁶ who in the generations gone by allowed all the nations to walk in their own ways. ¹⁷ Yet he didn't leave himself without witness, in that he did good and gave you[b] rains from the sky and fruitful seasons, filling our hearts with food and gladness." ¹⁸ Even saying these things, they hardly stopped the multitudes from making a sacrifice to them. ¹⁹ But some Jews from Antioch and Iconium came there, and having persuaded the multitudes, they stoned Paul and dragged him out of the city, supposing that he was dead. ²⁰ But as the disciples stood around him, he rose up, and entered into the city. On the next day he went out with Barnabas to Derbe. ²¹ When they had preached the Good News to that city and had made many disciples, they returned to Lystra, Iconium, and Antioch, ²² strengthening the souls of the disciples, exhorting them to continue in the faith, and that through many afflictions we must enter into God's Kingdom. ²³ When they had appointed elders for them in every assembly, and had prayed with fasting, they commended them to the Lord on whom they had believed. ²⁴ They passed through Pisidia and came to Pamphylia. ²⁵ When they had spoken the word in Perga, they went down to Attalia. ²⁶ From there they sailed to Antioch, from where they had been committed to the grace of God for the work which they had fulfilled. ²⁷ When they had arrived and had gathered the assembly together, they reported all the things that God had done with them, and that he had opened a door of faith to the nations. ²⁸ They stayed there with the disciples for a long time.

## 15

¹ Some men came down from Judea and taught the brothers,[c] "Unless you are circumcised after the custom of Moses, you can't be saved." ² Therefore when Paul and Barnabas had no small discord and discussion with them, they appointed Paul, Barnabas, and some others of them to go up to Jerusalem to the apostles and elders about this question. ³ They, being sent on their way by the assembly, passed through both Phoenicia and Samaria, declaring the conversion of the Gentiles. They caused great joy to all the brothers. ⁴ When they had come to Jerusalem, they were received by the assembly and the apostles and the elders, and they reported everything that God had done with them. ⁵ But some of the sect of the Pharisees who believed rose up, saying, "It is necessary to circumcise them, and to command them to keep the law of Moses." ⁶ The apostles and the elders were gathered together to see about this matter. ⁷ When there had been much discussion, Peter rose up and said to them, "Brothers, you know that a good while ago God made a choice among you that by my mouth the nations should hear the word of the Good News and believe. ⁸ God, who knows the heart, testified about them, giving them the Holy Spirit, just like he did to us. ⁹ He made no distinction between us and them, cleansing their hearts by faith. ¹⁰ Now therefore why do you tempt God, that you should put a yoke on the neck of the disciples which neither our fathers nor we were able to bear? ¹¹ But we believe that we are saved through the grace of the Lord Jesus,[d]

just as they are." ¹² All the multitude kept silence, and they listened to Barnabas and Paul reporting what signs and wonders God had done among the nations through them. ¹³ After they were silent, James answered, "Brothers, listen to me. ¹⁴ Simeon has reported how God first visited the nations to take out of them a people for his name. ¹⁵ This agrees with the words of the prophets. As it is written, ¹⁶"After these things I will return. I will again build the tabernacle of David, which has fallen. I will again build its ruins. I will set it up ¹⁷ that the rest of men may seek after the Lord: all the Gentiles who are called by my name, says the Lord, who does all these things.'* ¹⁸"All of God's works are known to him from eternity. ¹⁹ Therefore my judgment is that we don't trouble those from among the Gentiles who turn to God, ²⁰ but that we write to them that they abstain from the pollution of idols, from sexual immorality, from what is strangled, and from blood. ²¹ For Moses from generations of old has in every city those who preach him, being read in the synagogues every Sabbath." ²² Then it seemed good to the apostles and the elders, with the whole assembly, to choose men out of their company, and send them to Antioch with Paul and Barnabas: Judas called Barsabbas, and Silas, chief men among the brothers.[e] ²³ They wrote these things by their hand: "The apostles, the elders, and the brothers, to the brothers who are of the Gentiles in Antioch, Syria, and Cilicia: greetings. ²⁴ Because we have heard that some who went out from us have troubled you with words, unsettling your souls, saying, 'You must be circumcised and keep the law,' to whom we gave no commandment; ²⁵ it seemed good to us, having come to one accord, to choose out men and send them to you with our beloved Barnabas and Paul, ²⁶ men who have risked their lives for the name of our Lord Jesus Christ. ²⁷ We have sent therefore Judas and Silas, who themselves will also tell you the same things by word of mouth. ²⁸ For it seemed good to the Holy Spirit, and to us, to lay no greater burden on you than these necessary things: ²⁹ that you abstain from things sacrificed to idols, from blood, from things strangled, and from sexual immorality, from which if you keep yourselves, it will be well with you. Farewell." ³⁰ So, when they were sent off, they came to Antioch. Having gathered the multitude together, they delivered the letter. ³¹ When they had read it, they rejoiced over the encouragement. ³² Judas and Silas, also being prophets themselves, encouraged the brothers with many words and strengthened them. ³³ After they had spent some time there, they were dismissed in peace from the brothers to the apostles. ³⁴ [f] ³⁵ But Paul and Barnabas stayed in Antioch, teaching and preaching the word of the Lord, with many others also. ³⁶ After some days Paul said to Barnabas, "Let's return now and visit our brothers in every city in which we proclaimed the word of the Lord, to see how they are doing." ³⁷ Barnabas planned to take John, who was called Mark, with them also. ³⁸ But Paul didn't think that it was a good idea to take with them someone who had withdrawn from them in Pamphylia, and didn't go with them to do the work. ³⁹ Then the contention grew so sharp that they separated from each other. Barnabas took Mark with him and sailed away to Cyprus, ⁴⁰ but Paul chose Silas and went out, being commended by the brothers to the grace of God. ⁴¹ He went through Syria and Cilicia, strengthening the assemblies.

## 16

¹ He came to Derbe and Lystra; and behold, a certain disciple was there, named Timothy, the son of a Jewess who believed, but his father was a Greek. ² The brothers who were at Lystra and Iconium gave a good testimony about him. ³ Paul wanted to have him go out with him, and he took and circumcised him because of the Jews who were in those parts, for they all knew that his father was a Greek. ⁴ As they went on their way through the cities, they delivered the decrees to them to keep which had been ordained by the apostles and elders who were at Jerusalem. ⁵ So the assemblies were strengthened in the faith, and increased in number daily. ⁶ When they had gone through the region of Phrygia and Galatia, they were forbidden by the Holy Spirit to speak the word in Asia. ⁷ When they had come opposite Mysia, they tried to go into Bithynia, but the Spirit didn't allow them. ⁸ Passing by Mysia, they came down to Troas. ⁹ A vision appeared to Paul in the night. There was a man of Macedonia standing, begging him and saying, "Come over into Macedonia and help us." ¹⁰ When he had seen the vision, immediately we sought to go out to Macedonia, concluding that the Lord had called us to preach the Good News to them. ¹¹ Setting sail therefore from Troas, we made a straight course to Samothrace, and the day following to Neapolis; ¹² and from there to Philippi, which is a city of Macedonia, the foremost of the district, a Roman colony. We were staying some days in this city. ¹³ On the Sabbath day we went outside

of the city by a riverside, where we supposed there was a place of prayer, and we sat down and spoke to the women who had come together. [14] A certain woman named Lydia, a seller of purple, of the city of Thyatira, one who worshiped God, heard us. The Lord opened her heart to listen to the things which were spoken by Paul. [15] When she and her household were baptized, she begged us, saying, "If you have judged me to be faithful to the Lord, come into my house and stay." So she persuaded us. [16] As we were going to prayer, a certain girl having a spirit of divination met us, who brought her masters much gain by fortune telling. [17] Following Paul and us, she cried out, "These men are servants of the Most High God, who proclaim to us a way of salvation!" [18] She was doing this for many days. But Paul, becoming greatly annoyed, turned and said to the spirit, "I command you in the name of Jesus Christ to come out of her!" It came out that very hour. [19] But when her masters saw that the hope of their gain was gone, they seized Paul and Silas and dragged them into the marketplace before the rulers. [20] When they had brought them to the magistrates, they said, "These men, being Jews, are agitating our city [21] and advocate customs which it is not lawful for us to accept or to observe, being Romans." [22] The multitude rose up together against them and the magistrates tore their clothes from them, then commanded them to be beaten with rods. [23] When they had laid many stripes on them, they threw them into prison, charging the jailer to keep them safely. [24] Having received such a command, he threw them into the inner prison and secured their feet in the stocks. [25] But about midnight Paul and Silas were praying and singing hymns to God, and the prisoners were listening to them. [26] Suddenly there was a great earthquake, so that the foundations of the prison were shaken; and immediately all the doors were opened, and everyone's bonds were loosened. [27] The jailer, being roused out of sleep and seeing the prison doors open, drew his sword and was about to kill himself, supposing that the prisoners had escaped. [28] But Paul cried with a loud voice, saying, "Don't harm yourself, for we are all here!" [29] He called for lights, sprang in, fell down trembling before Paul and Silas, [30] brought them out, and said, "Sirs, what must I do to be saved?" [31] They said, "Believe in the Lord Jesus Christ, and you will be saved, you and your household." [32] They spoke the word of the Lord to him, and to all who were in his house. [33] He took them the same hour of the night and washed their stripes, and was immediately baptized, he and all his household. [34] He brought them up into his house and set food before them, and rejoiced greatly with all his household, having believed in God. [35] But when it was day, the magistrates sent the sergeants, saying, "Let those men go." [36] The jailer reported these words to Paul, saying, "The magistrates have sent to let you go; now therefore come out and go in peace." [37] But Paul said to them, "They have beaten us publicly without a trial, men who are Romans, and have cast us into prison! Do they now release us secretly? No, most certainly, but let them come themselves and bring us out!" [38] The sergeants reported these words to the magistrates, and they were afraid when they heard that they were Romans, [39] and they came and begged them. When they had brought them out, they asked them to depart from the city. [40] They went out of the prison and entered into Lydia's house. When they had seen the brothers, they encouraged them, then departed.

## 17

[1] Now when they had passed through Amphipolis and Apollonia, they came to Thessalonica, where there was a Jewish synagogue. [2] Paul, as was his custom, went in to them; and for three Sabbath days reasoned with them from the Scriptures, [3] explaining and demonstrating that the Christ had to suffer and rise again from the dead, and saying, "This Jesus, whom I proclaim to you, is the Christ." [4] Some of them were persuaded and joined Paul and Silas: of the devout Greeks a great multitude, and not a few of the chief women. [5] But the unpersuaded Jews took along[a] some wicked men from the marketplace and gathering a crowd, set the city in an uproar. Assaulting the house of Jason, they sought to bring them out to the people. [6] When they didn't find them, they dragged Jason and certain brothers[b] before the rulers of the city, crying, "These who have turned the world upside down have come here also, [7] whom Jason has received. These all act contrary to the decrees of Caesar, saying that there is another king, Jesus!" [8] The multitude and the rulers of the city were troubled when they heard these things. [9] When they had taken security from Jason and the rest, they let them go. [10] The brothers immediately sent Paul and Silas away by night to Beroea. When they arrived, they went into the Jewish synagogue. [11] Now these were more noble than those in Thessalonica, in that they received the word with all readiness of mind, examining the Scriptures daily to see whether these things were so. [12] Many of them therefore believed; also of the prominent Greek women, and not a few men. [13]

But when the Jews of Thessalonica had knowledge that the word of God was proclaimed by Paul at Beroea also, they came there likewise, agitating the multitudes. [14] Then the brothers immediately sent out Paul to go as far as to the sea, and Silas and Timothy still stayed there. [15] But those who escorted Paul brought him as far as Athens. Receiving a commandment to Silas and Timothy that they should come to him very quickly, they departed. [16] Now while Paul waited for them at Athens, his spirit was provoked within him as he saw the city full of idols. [17] So he reasoned in the synagogue with the Jews and the devout persons, and in the marketplace every day with those who met him. [18] Some of the Epicurean and Stoic philosophers also[c] were conversing with him. Some said, "What does this babbler want to say?" Others said, "He seems to be advocating foreign deities," because he preached Jesus and the resurrection. [19] They took hold of him and brought him to the Areopagus, saying, "May we know what this new teaching is, which you are speaking about? [20] For you bring certain strange things to our ears. We want to know therefore what these things mean." [21] Now all the Athenians and the strangers living there spent their time in nothing else, but either to tell or to hear some new thing. [22] Paul stood in the middle of the Areopagus and said, "You men of Athens, I perceive that you are very religious in all things. [23] For as I passed along and observed the objects of your worship, I also found an altar with this inscription: 'TO AN UNKNOWN GOD.' What therefore you worship in ignorance, I announce to you. [24] The God who made the world and all things in it, he, being Lord of heaven and earth, doesn't dwell in temples made with hands. [25] He isn't served by men's hands, as though he needed anything, seeing he himself gives to all life and breath and all things. [26] He made from one blood every nation of men to dwell on all the surface of the earth, having determined appointed seasons and the boundaries of their dwellings, [27] that they should seek the Lord, if perhaps they might reach out for him and find him, though he is not far from each one of us. [28] 'For in him we live, move, and have our being.' As some of your own poets have said, 'For we are also his offspring.' [29] Being then the offspring of God, we ought not to think that the Divine Nature is like gold, or silver, or stone, engraved by art and design of man. [30] The times of ignorance therefore God overlooked. But now he commands that all people everywhere should repent, [31] because he has appointed a day in which he will judge the world in righteousness by the man whom he has ordained; of which he has given assurance to all men, in that he has raised him from the dead." [32] Now when they heard of the resurrection of the dead, some mocked; but others said, "We want to hear you again concerning this." [33] Thus Paul went out from among them. [34] But certain men joined with him and believed, including Dionysius the Areopagite, and a woman named Damaris, and others with them.

## 18

[1] After these things Paul departed from Athens and came to Corinth. [2] He found a certain Jew named Aquila, a man of Pontus by race, who had recently come from Italy with his wife Priscilla, because Claudius had commanded all the Jews to depart from Rome. He came to them, [3] and because he practiced the same trade, he lived with them and worked, for by trade they were tent makers. [4] He reasoned in the synagogue every Sabbath and persuaded Jews and Greeks. [5] When Silas and Timothy came down from Macedonia, Paul was compelled by the Spirit, testifying to the Jews that Jesus was the Christ. [6] When they opposed him and blasphemed, he shook out his clothing and said to them, "Your blood be on your own heads! I am clean. From now on, I will go to the Gentiles!" [7] He departed there and went into the house of a certain man named Justus, one who worshiped God, whose house was next door to the synagogue. [8] Crispus, the ruler of the synagogue, believed in the Lord with all his house. Many of the Corinthians, when they heard, believed and were baptized. [9] The Lord said to Paul in the night by a vision, "Don't be afraid, but speak and don't be silent; [10] for I am with you, and no one will attack you to harm you, for I have many people in this city." [11] He lived there a year and six months, teaching the word of God among them. [12] But when Gallio was proconsul of Achaia, the Jews with one accord rose up against Paul and brought him before the judgment seat, [13] saying, "This man persuades men to worship God contrary to the law." [14] But when Paul was about to open his mouth, Gallio said to the Jews, "If indeed it were a matter of wrong or of wicked crime, you Jews, it would be reasonable that I should bear with you; [15] but if they are questions about words and names and your own law, look to it yourselves. For I don't want to be a judge of these matters." [16] So he drove them from the judgment seat. [17] Then all the Greeks seized Sosthenes, the ruler of the synagogue, and beat him before the judgment seat. Gallio didn't care about any of these things.

[a] 17:5 TR reads "And the Jews who were unpersuaded, becoming envious and taking along" instead of "But the unpersuaded Jews took along"

[b] 17:6 The word for "brothers" here and where the context allows may be also correctly translated "brothers and sisters" or "siblings."

[c] 17:18 TR omits "also"

[18] Paul, having stayed after this many more days, took his leave of the brothers,[a] and sailed from there for Syria, together with Priscilla and Aquila. He shaved his head in Cenchreae, for he had a vow. [19] He came to Ephesus, and he left them there; but he himself entered into the synagogue and reasoned with the Jews. [20] When they asked him to stay with them a longer time, he declined; [21] but taking his leave of them, he said, "I must by all means keep this coming feast in Jerusalem, but I will return again to you if God wills." Then he set sail from Ephesus. [22] When he had landed at Caesarea, he went up and greeted the assembly, and went down to Antioch. [23] Having spent some time there, he departed and went through the region of Galatia and Phrygia, in order, establishing all the disciples. [24] Now a certain Jew named Apollos, an Alexandrian by race, an eloquent man, came to Ephesus. He was mighty in the Scriptures. [25] This man had been instructed in the way of the Lord; and being fervent in spirit, he spoke and taught accurately the things concerning Jesus, although he knew only the baptism of John. [26] He began to speak boldly in the synagogue. But when Priscilla and Aquila heard him, they took him aside, and explained to him the way of God more accurately. [27] When he had determined to pass over into Achaia, the brothers encouraged him; and wrote to the disciples to receive him. When he had come, he greatly helped those who had believed through grace; [28] for he powerfully refuted the Jews, publicly showing by the Scriptures that Jesus was the Christ.

## 19

[1] While Apollos was at Corinth, Paul, having passed through the upper country, came to Ephesus and found certain disciples. [2] He said to them, "Did you receive the Holy Spirit when you believed?" They said to him, "No, we haven't even heard that there is a Holy Spirit." [3] He said, "Into what then were you baptized?" They said, "Into John's baptism." [4] Paul said, "John indeed baptized with the baptism of repentance, saying to the people that they should believe in the one who would come after him, that is, in Christ Jesus."[b] [5] When they heard this, they were baptized in the name of the Lord Jesus. [6] When Paul had laid his hands on them, the Holy Spirit came on them and they spoke with other languages and prophesied. [7] They were about twelve men in all. [8] He entered into the synagogue and spoke boldly for a period of three months, reasoning and persuading about the things concerning God's Kingdom. [9] But when some were hardened and disobedient, speaking evil of the Way before the multitude, he departed from them and separated the disciples, reasoning daily in the school of Tyrannus. [10] This continued for two years, so that all those who lived in Asia heard the word of the Lord Jesus, both Jews and Greeks. [11] God worked special miracles by the hands of Paul, [12] so that even handkerchiefs or aprons were carried away from his body to the sick, and the diseases departed from them, and the evil spirits went out. [13] But some of the itinerant Jews, exorcists, took on themselves to invoke over those who had the evil spirits the name of the Lord Jesus, saying, "We adjure you by Jesus whom Paul preaches." [14] There were seven sons of one Sceva, a Jewish chief priest, who did this. [15] The evil spirit answered, "Jesus I know, and Paul I know, but who are you?" [16] The man in whom the evil spirit was leaped on them, overpowered them, and prevailed against them, so that they fled out of that house naked and wounded. [17] This became known to all, both Jews and Greeks, who lived at Ephesus. Fear fell on them all, and the name of the Lord Jesus was magnified. [18] Many also of those who had believed came, confessing and declaring their deeds. [19] Many of those who practiced magical arts brought their books together and burned them in the sight of all. They counted their price, and found it to be fifty thousand pieces of silver.[c] [20] So the word of the Lord was growing and becoming mighty. [21] Now after these things had ended, Paul determined in the Spirit, when he had passed through Macedonia and Achaia, to go to Jerusalem, saying, "After I have been there, I must also see Rome." [22] Having sent into Macedonia two of those who served him, Timothy and Erastus, he himself stayed in Asia for a while. [23] About that time there arose no small disturbance concerning the Way. [24] For a certain man named Demetrius, a silversmith who made silver shrines of Artemis, brought no little business to the craftsmen, [25] whom he gathered together with the workmen of like occupation, and said, "Sirs, you know that by this business we have our wealth. [26] You see and hear that not at Ephesus alone, but almost throughout all Asia, this Paul has persuaded and turned away many people, saying that they are no gods that are made with hands. [27] Not only is there danger that this our trade come into disrepute, but also that the temple of the great goddess Artemis will be counted as nothing and her majesty destroyed, whom all Asia and the world worships." [28] When they heard this they were filled with anger, and cried out, saying, "Great is Artemis of the Ephesians!" [29] The whole city was filled with confusion, and they rushed with one accord into the theater, having seized Gaius and Aristarchus, men of Macedonia, Paul's companions in travel. [30] When Paul wanted to enter in to the people, the disciples didn't allow him. [31] Certain also of the Asiarchs, being his friends, sent to him and begged him not to venture into the theater. [32] Some therefore cried one thing, and some another, for the assembly was in confusion. Most of them didn't know why they had come together. [33] They brought Alexander out of the multitude, the Jews putting him forward. Alexander beckoned with his hand, and would have made a defense to the people. [34] But when they perceived that he was a Jew, all with one voice for a time of about two hours cried out, "Great is Artemis of the Ephesians!" [35] When the town clerk had quieted the multitude, he said, "You men of Ephesus, what man is there who doesn't know that the city of the Ephesians is temple keeper of the great goddess Artemis, and of the image which fell down from Zeus? [36] Seeing then that these things can't be denied, you ought to be quiet and to do nothing rash. [37] For you have brought these men here, who are neither robbers of temples nor blasphemers of your goddess. [38] If therefore Demetrius and the craftsmen who are with him have a matter against anyone, the courts are open and there are proconsuls. Let them press charges against one another. [39] But if you seek anything about other matters, it will be settled in the regular assembly. [40] For indeed we are in danger of being accused concerning today's riot, there being no cause. Concerning it, we wouldn't be able to give an account of this commotion." [41] When he had thus spoken, he dismissed the assembly.

## 20

[1] After the uproar had ceased, Paul sent for the disciples, took leave of them, and departed to go into Macedonia. [2] When he had gone through those parts and had encouraged them with many words, he came into Greece. [3] When he had spent three months there, and a plot was made against him by Jews as he was about to set sail for Syria, he determined to return through Macedonia. [4] These accompanied him as far as Asia: Sopater of Beroea, Aristarchus and Secundus of the Thessalonians, Gaius of Derbe, Timothy, and Tychicus and Trophimus of Asia. [5] But these had gone ahead, and were waiting for us at Troas. [6] We sailed away from Philippi after the days of Unleavened Bread, and came to them at Troas in five days, where we stayed seven days. [7] On the first day of the week, when the disciples were gathered together to break bread, Paul talked with them, intending to depart on the next day; and continued his speech until midnight. [8] There were many lights in the upper room where we[d] were gathered together. [9] A certain young man named Eutychus sat in the window, weighed down with deep sleep. As Paul spoke still longer, being weighed down by his sleep, he fell down from the third floor and was taken up dead. [10] Paul went down and fell upon him, and embracing him said, "Don't be troubled, for his life is in him." [11] When he had gone up, had broken bread and eaten, and had talked with them a long while, even until break of day, he departed. [12] They brought the boy in alive, and were greatly comforted. [13] But we, going ahead to the ship, set sail for Assos, intending to take Paul aboard there; for he had so arranged, intending himself to go by land. [14] When he met us at Assos, we took him aboard and came to Mitylene. [15] Sailing from there, we came the following day opposite Chios. The next day we touched at Samos and stayed at Trogyllium, and the day after we came to Miletus. [16] For Paul had determined to sail past Ephesus, that he might not have to spend time in Asia; for he was hastening, if it were possible for him, to be in Jerusalem on the day of Pentecost. [17] From Miletus he sent to Ephesus and called to himself the elders of the assembly. [18] When they had come to him, he said to them, "You yourselves know, from the first day that I set foot in Asia, how I was with you all the time, [19] serving the Lord with all humility, with many tears, and with trials which happened to me by the plots of the Jews; [20] how I didn't shrink from declaring to you anything that was profitable, teaching you publicly and from house to house, [21] testifying both to Jews and to Greeks repentance toward God and faith toward our Lord Jesus.[e] [22] Now, behold, I go bound by the Spirit to Jerusalem, not knowing what will happen to me there; [23] except that the Holy Spirit testifies in every city, saying that bonds and afflictions wait for me. [24] But these things don't count; nor do I hold my life dear to myself, so that I may finish my race with joy, and the ministry which I received from the Lord Jesus, to fully testify to the Good News of the grace of God. [25] "Now, behold, I know that you all, among whom I went about preaching God's Kingdom, will see my face no more. [26] Therefore I

---

[a] 18:18 The word for "brothers" here and where the context allows may also be correctly translated "brothers and sisters" or "siblings."

[b] 19:4 NU omits Christ.
[c] 19:19 The 50,000 pieces of silver here probably referred to 50,000 drachmas. If so, the value of the burned books was

equivalent to about 160 man-years of wages for agricultural laborers
[d] 20:8 TR reads "they" instead of "we"

[e] 20:21 TR adds "Christ"

testify to you today that I am clean from the blood of all men, ²⁷ for I didn't shrink from declaring to you the whole counsel of God. ²⁸ Take heed, therefore, to yourselves and to all the flock, in which the Holy Spirit has made you overseers, to shepherd the assembly of the Lord and<sup>a</sup> God which he purchased with his own blood. ²⁹ For I know that after my departure, vicious wolves will enter in among you, not sparing the flock. ³⁰ Men will arise from among your own selves, speaking perverse things, to draw away the disciples after them. ³¹ Therefore watch, remembering that for a period of three years I didn't cease to admonish everyone night and day with tears. ³² Now, brothers,<sup>b</sup> I entrust you to God and to the word of his grace, which is able to build up and to give you the inheritance among all those who are sanctified. ³³ I coveted no one's silver, gold, or clothing. ³⁴ You yourselves know that these hands served my necessities, and those who were with me. ³⁵ In all things I gave you an example, that so laboring you ought to help the weak, and to remember the words of the Lord Jesus, that he himself said, 'It is more blessed to give than to receive.' " ³⁶ When he had spoken these things, he knelt down and prayed with them all. ³⁷ They all wept freely, and fell on Paul's neck and kissed him, ³⁸ sorrowing most of all because of the word which he had spoken, that they should see his face no more. Then they accompanied him to the ship.

## 21

¹ When we had departed from them and had set sail, we came with a straight course to Cos, and the next day to Rhodes, and from there to Patara. ² Having found a ship crossing over to Phoenicia, we went aboard and set sail. ³ When we had come in sight of Cyprus, leaving it on the left hand, we sailed to Syria and landed at Tyre, for the ship was there to unload her cargo. ⁴ Having found disciples, we stayed there seven days. These said to Paul through the Spirit that he should not go up to Jerusalem. ⁵ When those days were over, we departed and went on our journey. They all, with wives and children, brought us on our way until we were out of the city. Kneeling down on the beach, we prayed. ⁶ After saying goodbye to each other, we went on board the ship, and they returned home again. ⁷ When we had finished the voyage from Tyre, we arrived at Ptolemais. We greeted the brothers and stayed with them one day. ⁸ On the next day, we who were Paul's companions departed and came to Caesarea. We entered into the house of Philip the evangelist, who was one of the seven, and stayed with him. ⁹ Now this man had four virgin daughters who prophesied. ¹⁰ As we stayed there some days, a certain prophet named Agabus came down from Judea. ¹¹ Coming to us and taking Paul's belt, he bound his own feet and hands, and said, "The Holy Spirit says: 'So the Jews at Jerusalem will bind the man who owns this belt, and will deliver him into the hands of the Gentiles.'" ¹² When we heard these things, both we and the people of that place begged him not to go up to Jerusalem. ¹³ Then Paul answered, "What are you doing, weeping and breaking my heart? For I am ready not only to be bound, but also to die at Jerusalem for the name of the Lord Jesus." ¹⁴ When he would not be persuaded, we ceased, saying, "The Lord's will be done." ¹⁵ After these days we took up our baggage and went up to Jerusalem. ¹⁶ Some of the disciples from Caesarea also went with us, bringing one Mnason of Cyprus, an early disciple, with whom we would stay. ¹⁷ When we had come to Jerusalem, the brothers received us gladly. ¹⁸ The day following, Paul went in with us to James; and all the elders were present. ¹⁹ When he had greeted them, he reported one by one the things which God had worked among the Gentiles through his ministry. ²⁰ They, when they heard it, glorified God. They said to him, "You see, brother, how many thousands there are among the Jews of those who have believed, and they are all zealous for the law. ²¹ They have been informed about you, that you teach all the Jews who are among the Gentiles to forsake Moses, telling them not to circumcise their children and not to walk after the customs. ²² What then? The assembly must certainly meet, for they will hear that you have come. ²³ Therefore do what we tell you. We have four men who have taken a vow. ²⁴ Take them and purify yourself with them, and pay their expenses for them, that they may shave their heads. Then all will know that there is no truth in the things that they have been informed about you, but that you yourself also walk keeping the law. ²⁵ But concerning the Gentiles who believe, we have written our decision that they should observe no such thing, except that they should keep themselves from food offered to idols, from blood, from strangled things, and from sexual immorality." ²⁶ Then Paul took the men, and the next day purified himself and went with them into the temple, declaring the fulfillment of the days of purification, until the offering was offered for every one of them. ²⁷ When the seven days were almost completed, the Jews from Asia, when they saw him in the temple, stirred up all the multitude and laid hands on him, ²⁸ crying out, "Men of Israel, help! This is the man who teaches all men everywhere against the people, and the law, and this place. Moreover, he also brought Greeks into the temple and has defiled this holy place!" ²⁹ For they had seen Trophimus the Ephesian, with him in the city, and they supposed that Paul had brought him into the temple. ³⁰ All the city was moved and the people ran together. They seized Paul and dragged him out of the temple. Immediately the doors were shut. ³¹ As they were trying to kill him, news came up to the commanding officer of the regiment that all Jerusalem was in an uproar. ³² Immediately he took soldiers and centurions and ran down to them. They, when they saw the chief captain and the soldiers, stopped beating Paul. ³³ Then the commanding officer came near, arrested him, commanded him to be bound with two chains, and inquired who he was and what he had done. ³⁴ Some shouted one thing and some another, among the crowd. When he couldn't find out the truth because of the noise, he commanded him to be brought into the barracks. ³⁵ When he came to the stairs, he was carried by the soldiers because of the violence of the crowd; ³⁶ for the multitude of the people followed after, crying out, "Away with him!" ³⁷ As Paul was about to be brought into the barracks, he asked the commanding officer, "May I speak to you?" He said, "Do you know Greek? ³⁸ Aren't you then the Egyptian who before these days stirred up to sedition and led out into the wilderness the four thousand men of the Assassins?" ³⁹ But Paul said, "I am a Jew from Tarsus in Cilicia, a citizen of no insignificant city. I beg you, allow me to speak to the people." ⁴⁰ When he had given him permission, Paul, standing on the stairs, beckoned with his hand to the people. When there was a great silence, he spoke to them in the Hebrew language, saying,

## 22

¹ "Brothers and fathers, listen to the defense which I now make to you." ² When they heard that he spoke to them in the Hebrew language, they were even more quiet. He said, ³ "I am indeed a Jew, born in Tarsus of Cilicia, but brought up in this city at the feet of Gamaliel, instructed according to the strict tradition of the law of our fathers, being zealous for God, even as you all are today. ⁴ I persecuted this Way to the death, binding and delivering into prisons both men and women, ⁵ as also the high priest and all the council of the elders testify, from whom also I received letters to the brothers, and traveled to Damascus to bring them also who were there to Jerusalem in bonds to be punished. ⁶ "As I made my journey and came close to Damascus, about noon suddenly a great light shone around me from the sky. ⁷ I fell to the ground and heard a voice saying to me, 'Saul, Saul, why are you persecuting me?' ⁸ I answered, 'Who are you, Lord?' He said to me, 'I am Jesus of Nazareth, whom you persecute.' ⁹ "Those who were with me indeed saw the light and were afraid, but they didn't understand the voice of him who spoke to me. ¹⁰ I said, 'What shall I do, Lord?' The Lord said to me, 'Arise, and go into Damascus. There you will be told about all things which are appointed for you to do.' ¹¹ When I couldn't see for the glory of that light, being led by the hand of those who were with me, I came into Damascus. ¹² "One Ananias, a devout man according to the law, well reported of by all the Jews who lived in Damascus, ¹³ came to me, and standing by me said to me, 'Brother Saul, receive your sight!' In that very hour I looked up at him. ¹⁴ He said, 'The God of our fathers has appointed you to know his will, and to see the Righteous One, and to hear a voice from his mouth. ¹⁵ For you will be a witness for him to all men of what you have seen and heard. ¹⁶ Now why do you wait? Arise, be baptized, and wash away your sins, calling on the name of the Lord.' ¹⁷ "When I had returned to Jerusalem and while I prayed in the temple, I fell into a trance ¹⁸ and saw him saying to me, 'Hurry and get out of Jerusalem quickly, because they will not receive testimony concerning me from you.' ¹⁹ I said, 'Lord, they themselves know that I imprisoned and beat in every synagogue those who believed in you. ²⁰ When the blood of Stephen, your witness, was shed, I also was standing by, consenting to his death, and guarding the cloaks of those who killed him.' ²¹ "He said to me, 'Depart, for I will send you out far from here to the Gentiles.' " ²² They listened to him until he said that; then they lifted up their voice and said, "Rid the earth of this fellow, for he isn't fit to live!" ²³ As they cried out, threw off their cloaks, and threw dust into the air, ²⁴ the commanding officer commanded him to be brought into the barracks, ordering him to be examined by scourging, that he might know for what crime they shouted against him like that. ²⁵ When they had tied him up with thongs, Paul asked the centurion who stood by, "Is it lawful for you to scourge a man who is a Roman, and not found guilty?" ²⁶ When the centurion heard it, he went to the commanding officer and told him, "Watch what you are about to do, for this man is a Roman!" ²⁷ The commanding officer came and asked him, "Tell me, are you a Roman?" He said, "Yes." ²⁸ The commanding officer

---

<sup>a</sup> 20:28 TR, NU omit "the Lord and"

<sup>b</sup> 20:32 The word for "brothers" here and where the context allows may also be correctly translated "brothers and sisters" or "siblings."

answered, "I bought my citizenship for a great price." Paul said, "But I was born a Roman." [29] Immediately those who were about to examine him departed from him, and the commanding officer also was afraid when he realized that he was a Roman, because he had bound him. [30] But on the next day, desiring to know the truth about why he was accused by the Jews, he freed him from the bonds and commanded the chief priests and all the council to come together, and brought Paul down and set him before them.

## 23

[1] Paul, looking steadfastly at the council, said, "Brothers, I have lived before God in all good conscience until today." [2] The high priest, Ananias, commanded those who stood by him to strike him on the mouth. [3] Then Paul said to him, "God will strike you, you whitewashed wall! Do you sit to judge me according to the law, and command me to be struck contrary to the law?" [4] Those who stood by said, "Do you malign God's high priest?" [5] Paul said, "I didn't know, brothers, that he was high priest. For it is written, 'You shall not speak evil of a ruler of your people.'"* [6] But when Paul perceived that the one part were Sadducees and the other Pharisees, he cried out in the council, "Men and brothers, I am a Pharisee, a son of Pharisees. Concerning the hope and resurrection of the dead I am being judged!" [7] When he had said this, an argument arose between the Pharisees and Sadducees, and the crowd was divided. [8] For the Sadducees say that there is no resurrection, nor angel, nor spirit; but the Pharisees confess all of these. [9] A great clamor arose, and some of the scribes of the Pharisees' part stood up, and contended, saying, "We find no evil in this man. But if a spirit or angel has spoken to him, let's not fight against God!" [10] When a great argument arose, the commanding officer, fearing that Paul would be torn in pieces by them, commanded the soldiers to go down and take him by force from among them and bring him into the barracks. [11] The following night, the Lord stood by him and said, "Cheer up, Paul, for as you have testified about me at Jerusalem, so you must testify also at Rome." [12] When it was day, some of the Jews banded together and bound themselves under a curse, saying that they would neither eat nor drink until they had killed Paul. [13] There were more than forty people who had made this conspiracy. [14] They came to the chief priests and the elders, and said, "We have bound ourselves under a great curse to taste nothing until we have killed Paul. [15] Now therefore, you with the council inform the commanding officer that he should bring him down to you tomorrow, as though you were going to judge his case more exactly. We are ready to kill him before he comes near." [16] But Paul's sister's son heard they were lying in wait, and he came and entered into the barracks and told Paul. [17] Paul summoned one of the centurions and said, "Bring this young man to the commanding officer, for he has something to tell him." [18] So he took him and brought him to the commanding officer and said, "Paul, the prisoner, summoned me and asked me to bring this young man to you. He has something to tell you." [19] The commanding officer took him by the hand, and going aside, asked him privately, "What is it that you have to tell me?" [20] He said, "The Jews have agreed to ask you to bring Paul down to the council tomorrow, as though intending to inquire somewhat more accurately concerning him. [21] Therefore don't yield to them, for more than forty men lie in wait for him, who have bound themselves under a curse to neither eat nor drink until they have killed him. Now they are ready, looking for the promise from you." [22] So the commanding officer let the young man go, charging him, "Tell no one that you have revealed these things to me." [23] He called to himself two of the centurions, and said, "Prepare two hundred soldiers to go as far as Caesarea, with seventy horsemen and two hundred men armed with spears, at the third hour of the night."[a] [24] He asked them to provide mounts, that they might set Paul on one, and bring him safely to Felix the governor. [25] He wrote a letter like this: [26]"Claudius Lysias to the most excellent governor Felix: Greetings. [27]"This man was seized by the Jews, and was about to be killed by them when I came with the soldiers and rescued him, having learned that he was a Roman. [28] Desiring to know the cause why they accused him, I brought him down to their council. [29] I found him to be accused about questions of their law, but not to be charged with anything worthy of death or of imprisonment. [30] When I was told that the Jews lay in wait for the man, I sent him to you immediately, charging his accusers also to bring their accusations against him before you. Farewell." [31] So the soldiers, carrying out their orders, took Paul and brought him by night to Antipatris. [32] But on the next day they left the horsemen to go with him, and returned to the barracks. [33] When they came to Caesarea and delivered the letter to the governor, they also presented Paul to him. [34]

When the governor had read it, he asked what province he was from. When he understood that he was from Cilicia, he said, [35]"I will hear you fully when your accusers also arrive." He commanded that he be kept in Herod's palace.

## 24

[1] After five days, the high priest, Ananias, came down with certain elders and an orator, one Tertullus. They informed the governor against Paul. [2] When he was called, Tertullus began to accuse him, saying, "Seeing that by you we enjoy much peace, and that prosperity is coming to this nation by your foresight, [3] we accept it in all ways and in all places, most excellent Felix, with all thankfulness. [4] But that I don't delay you, I entreat you to bear with us and hear a few words. [5] For we have found this man to be a plague, an instigator of insurrections among all the Jews throughout the world, and a ringleader of the sect of the Nazarenes. [6] He even tried to profane the temple, and we arrested him.[b] [7] [c] [8] [d]By examining him yourself you may ascertain all these things of which we accuse him." [9] The Jews also joined in the attack, affirming that these things were so. [10] When the governor had beckoned to him to speak, Paul answered, "Because I know that you have been a judge of this nation for many years, I cheerfully make my defense, [11] seeing that you can verify that it is not more than twelve days since I went up to worship at Jerusalem. [12] In the temple they didn't find me disputing with anyone or stirring up a crowd, either in the synagogues or in the city. [13] Nor can they prove to you the things of which they now accuse me. [14] But this I confess to you, that according to the Way, which they call a sect, so I serve the God of our fathers, believing all things which are according to the law, and which are written in the prophets; [15] having hope toward God, which these also themselves look for, that there will be a resurrection of the dead, both of the just and unjust. [16] In this I also practice always having a conscience void of offense toward God and men. [17] Now after some years, I came to bring gifts for the needy to my nation, and offerings; [18] amid which certain Jews from Asia found me purified in the temple, not with a mob, nor with turmoil. [19] They ought to have been here before you and to make accusation if they had anything against me. [20] Or else let these men themselves say what injustice they found in me when I stood before the council, [21] unless it is for this one thing that I cried standing among them, 'Concerning the resurrection of the dead I am being judged before you today!'" [22] But Felix, having more exact knowledge concerning the Way, deferred them, saying, "When Lysias, the commanding officer, comes down, I will decide your case." [23] He ordered the centurion that Paul should be kept in custody and should have some privileges, and not to forbid any of his friends to serve him or to visit him. [24] After some days, Felix came with Drusilla his wife, who was a Jewess, and sent for Paul and heard him concerning the faith in Christ Jesus. [25] As he reasoned about righteousness, self-control, and the judgment to come, Felix was terrified, and answered, "Go your way for this time, and when it is convenient for me, I will summon you." [26] Meanwhile, he also hoped that money would be given to him by Paul, that he might release him. Therefore also he sent for him more often and talked with him. [27] But when two years were fulfilled, Felix was succeeded by Porcius Festus, and desiring to gain favor with the Jews, Felix left Paul in bonds.

## 25

[1] Festus therefore, having come into the province, after three days went up to Jerusalem from Caesarea. [2] Then the high priest and the principal men of the Jews informed him against Paul, and they begged him, [3] asking a favor against him, that he would summon him to Jerusalem, plotting to kill him on the way. [4] However Festus answered that Paul should be kept in custody at Caesarea, and that he himself was about to depart shortly. [5]"Let them therefore", he said, "that are in power among you go down with me, and if there is anything wrong in the man, let them accuse him." [6] When he had stayed among them more than ten days, he went down to Caesarea, and on the next day he sat on the judgment seat, and commanded Paul to be brought. [7] When he had come, the Jews who had come down from Jerusalem stood around him, bringing against him many and grievous charges which they could not prove, [8] while he said in his defense, "Neither against the law of the Jews, nor against the temple, nor against Caesar, have I sinned at all." [9] But Festus, desiring to gain favor with the Jews, answered Paul and said, "Are you willing to go up to Jerusalem and be judged by me there concerning these things?" [10] But Paul said, "I am standing before Caesar's judgment seat, where I ought to be tried. I have done no wrong to the Jews, as you also know very well. [11] For if I have done wrong and have committed anything worthy of death, I don't refuse to die; but

---

* 23:5 Exodus 22:28
[a] 23:23 about 9:00 p.m.

[b] 24:6 TR adds "We wanted to judge him according to our law,"

[c] 24:7 TR adds "but the commanding officer, Lysias, came by and with great

violence took him out of our hands,"

[d] 24:8 TR adds "commanding his accusers to come to you."

if none of those things is true that they accuse me of, no one can give me up to them. I appeal to Caesar!" ¹² Then Festus, when he had conferred with the council, answered, "You have appealed to Caesar. To Caesar you shall go." ¹³ Now when some days had passed, King Agrippa and Bernice arrived at Caesarea and greeted Festus. ¹⁴ As he stayed there many days, Festus laid Paul's case before the king, saying, "There is a certain man left a prisoner by Felix; ¹⁵ about whom, when I was at Jerusalem, the chief priests and the elders of the Jews informed me, asking for a sentence against him. ¹⁶ I answered them that it is not the custom of the Romans to give up any man to destruction before the accused has met the accusers face to face and has had opportunity to make his defense concerning the matter laid against him. ¹⁷ When therefore they had come together here, I didn't delay, but on the next day sat on the judgment seat and commanded the man to be brought. ¹⁸ When the accusers stood up, they brought no charges against him of such things as I supposed; ¹⁹ but had certain questions against him about their own religion and about one Jesus, who was dead, whom Paul affirmed to be alive. ²⁰ Being perplexed how to inquire concerning these things, I asked whether he was willing to go to Jerusalem and there be judged concerning these matters. ²¹ But when Paul had appealed to be kept for the decision of the emperor, I commanded him to be kept until I could send him to Caesar." ²² Agrippa said to Festus, "I also would like to hear the man myself." "Tomorrow," he said, "you shall hear him." ²³ So on the next day, when Agrippa and Bernice had come with great pomp, and they had entered into the place of hearing with the commanding officers and the principal men of the city, at the command of Festus, Paul was brought in. ²⁴ Festus said, "King Agrippa, and all men who are here present with us, you see this man about whom all the multitude of the Jews petitioned me, both at Jerusalem and here, crying that he ought not to live any longer. ²⁵ But when I found that he had committed nothing worthy of death, and as he himself appealed to the emperor, I determined to send him, ²⁶ of whom I have no certain thing to write to my lord. Therefore I have brought him out before you, and especially before you, King Agrippa, that, after examination I may have something to write. ²⁷ For it seems to me unreasonable, in sending a prisoner, not to also specify the charges against him."

## 26

¹ Agrippa said to Paul, "You may speak for yourself." Then Paul stretched out his hand, and made his defense. ²"I think myself happy, King Agrippa, that I am to make my defense before you today concerning all the things that I am accused by the Jews, ³ especially because you are expert in all customs and questions which are among the Jews. Therefore I beg you to hear me patiently. ⁴"Indeed, all the Jews know my way of life from my youth up, which was from the beginning among my own nation and at Jerusalem; ⁵ having known me from the first, if they are willing to testify, that after the strictest sect of our religion I lived a Pharisee. ⁶ Now I stand here to be judged for the hope of the promise made by God to our fathers, ⁷ which our twelve tribes, earnestly serving night and day, hope to attain. Concerning this hope I am accused by the Jews, King Agrippa! ⁸ Why is it judged incredible with you if God does raise the dead? ⁹"I myself most certainly thought that I ought to do many things contrary to the name of Jesus of Nazareth. ¹⁰ I also did this in Jerusalem. I both shut up many of the saints in prisons, having received authority from the chief priests; and when they were put to death I gave my vote against them. ¹¹ Punishing them often in all the synagogues, I tried to make them blaspheme. Being exceedingly enraged against them, I persecuted them even to foreign cities. ¹²"Whereupon as I traveled to Damascus with the authority and commission from the chief priests, ¹³ at noon, O king, I saw on the way a light from the sky, brighter than the sun, shining around me and those who traveled with me. ¹⁴ When we had all fallen to the earth, I heard a voice saying to me in the Hebrew language, 'Saul, Saul, why are you persecuting me? It is hard for you to kick against the goads.' ¹⁵"I said, 'Who are you, Lord?' "He said, 'I am Jesus, whom you are persecuting. ¹⁶ But arise, and stand on your feet, for I have appeared to you for this purpose: to appoint you a servant and a witness both of the things which you have seen and of the things which I will reveal to you; ¹⁷ delivering you from the people and from the Gentiles, to whom I send you, ¹⁸ to open their eyes, that they may turn from darkness to light and from the power of Satan to God, that they may receive remission of sins and an inheritance among those who are sanctified by faith in me.' ¹⁹"Therefore, King Agrippa, I was not disobedient to the heavenly vision, ²⁰ but declared first to them of Damascus, at Jerusalem, and throughout all the country of Judea, and also to the Gentiles, that they should repent and turn to God, doing works worthy of repentance. ²¹ For this reason the Jews seized me in the temple and tried to kill me. ²² Having therefore obtained the help

that is from God, I stand to this day testifying both to small and great, saying nothing but what the prophets and Moses said would happen, ²³ how the Christ must suffer, and how, by the resurrection of the dead, he would be first to proclaim light both to these people and to the Gentiles." ²⁴ As he thus made his defense, Festus said with a loud voice, "Paul, you are crazy! Your great learning is driving you insane!" ²⁵ But he said, "I am not crazy, most excellent Festus, but boldly declare words of truth and reasonableness. ²⁶ For the king knows of these things, to whom also I speak freely. For I am persuaded that none of these things is hidden from him, for this has not been done in a corner. ²⁷ King Agrippa, do you believe the prophets? I know that you believe." ²⁸ Agrippa said to Paul, "With a little persuasion are you trying to make me a Christian?" ²⁹ Paul said, "I pray to God, that whether with little or with much, not only you, but also all that hear me today, might become such as I am, except for these bonds." ³⁰ The king rose up with the governor and Bernice, and those who sat with them. ³¹ When they had withdrawn, they spoke to one another, saying, "This man does nothing worthy of death or of bonds." ³² Agrippa said to Festus, "This man might have been set free if he had not appealed to Caesar."

## 27

¹ When it was determined that we should sail for Italy, they delivered Paul and certain other prisoners to a centurion named Julius, of the Augustan band. ² Embarking in a ship of Adramyttium, which was about to sail to places on the coast of Asia, we put to sea, Aristarchus, a Macedonian of Thessalonica being with us. ³ The next day, we touched at Sidon. Julius treated Paul kindly and gave him permission to go to his friends and refresh himself. ⁴ Putting to sea from there, we sailed under the lee of Cyprus, because the winds were contrary. ⁵ When we had sailed across the sea which is off Cilicia and Pamphylia, we came to Myra, a city of Lycia. ⁶ There the centurion found a ship of Alexandria sailing for Italy, and he put us on board. ⁷ When we had sailed slowly many days, and had come with difficulty opposite Cnidus, the wind not allowing us further, we sailed under the lee of Crete, opposite Salmone. ⁸ With difficulty sailing along it we came to a certain place called Fair Havens, near the city of Lasea. ⁹ When much time had passed and the voyage was now dangerous because the Fast had now already gone by, Paul admonished them ¹⁰ and said to them, "Sirs, I perceive that the voyage will be with injury and much loss, not only of the cargo and the ship, but also of our lives." ¹¹ But the centurion gave more heed to the master and to the owner of the ship than to those things which were spoken by Paul. ¹² Because the haven was not suitable to winter in, the majority advised going to sea from there, if by any means they could reach Phoenix and winter there, which is a port of Crete, looking southwest and northwest. ¹³ When the south wind blew softly, supposing that they had obtained their purpose, they weighed anchor and sailed along Crete, close to shore. ¹⁴ But before long, a stormy wind beat down from shore, which is called Euroclydon.ª ¹⁵ When the ship was caught and couldn't face the wind, we gave way to it and were driven along. ¹⁶ Running under the lee of a small island called Clauda, we were able, with difficulty, to secure the boat. ¹⁷ After they had hoisted it up, they used cables to help reinforce the ship. Fearing that they would run aground on the Syrtis sand bars, they lowered the sea anchor, and so were driven along. ¹⁸ As we labored exceedingly with the storm, the next day they began to throw things overboard. ¹⁹ On the third day, they threw out the ship's tackle with their own hands. ²⁰ When neither sun nor stars shone on us for many days, and no small storm pressed on us, all hope that we would be saved was now taken away. ²¹ When they had been long without food, Paul stood up in the middle of them and said, "Sirs, you should have listened to me, and not have set sail from Crete and have gotten this injury and loss. ²² Now I exhort you to cheer up, for there will be no loss of life among you, but only of the ship. ²³ For there stood by me this night an angel, belonging to the God whose I am and whom I serve, ²⁴ saying, 'Don't be afraid, Paul. You must stand before Caesar. Behold, God has granted you all those who sail with you.' ²⁵ Therefore, sirs, cheer up! For I believe God, that it will be just as it has been spoken to me. ²⁶ But we must run aground on a certain island." ²⁷ But when the fourteenth night had come, as we were driven back and forth in the Adriatic Sea, about midnight the sailors surmised that they were drawing near to some land. ²⁸ They took soundings and found twenty fathoms.ᵇ After a little while, they took soundings again, and found fifteen fathoms.ᶜ ²⁹ Fearing that we would run aground on rocky ground, they let go four anchors from the stern, and wished for daylight. ³⁰ As the sailors were trying to flee out of the ship and had lowered the boat into the sea, pretending that they would lay out anchors from the bow, ³¹ Paul said to the centurion and to the soldiers, "Unless these stay in the ship, you can't be saved." ³² Then the soldiers cut away the ropes of the boat and let it fall off. ³³

---

ª *27:14* Or, "a northeaster".

ᵇ *27:28* 20 fathoms = 120 feet = 36.6 meters

ᶜ *27:28* 15 fathoms = 90 feet = 27.4 meters

While the day was coming on, Paul begged them all to take some food, saying, "Today is the fourteenth day that you wait and continue fasting, having taken nothing. <sup>34</sup> Therefore I beg you to take some food, for this is for your safety; for not a hair will perish from any of your heads." <sup>35</sup> When he had said this and had taken bread, he gave thanks to God in the presence of all; then he broke it and began to eat. <sup>36</sup> Then they all cheered up, and they also took food. <sup>37</sup> In all, we were two hundred seventy-six souls on the ship. <sup>38</sup> When they had eaten enough, they lightened the ship, throwing out the wheat into the sea. <sup>39</sup> When it was day, they didn't recognize the land, but they noticed a certain bay with a beach, and they decided to try to drive the ship onto it. <sup>40</sup> Casting off the anchors, they left them in the sea, at the same time untying the rudder ropes. Hoisting up the foresail to the wind, they made for the beach. <sup>41</sup> But coming to a place where two seas met, they ran the vessel aground. The bow struck and remained immovable, but the stern began to break up by the violence of the waves. <sup>42</sup> The soldiers' counsel was to kill the prisoners, so that none of them would swim out and escape. <sup>43</sup> But the centurion, desiring to save Paul, stopped them from their purpose, and commanded that those who could swim should throw themselves overboard first to go toward the land; <sup>44</sup> and the rest should follow, some on planks and some on other things from the ship. So they all escaped safely to the land.

## 28

<sup>1</sup> When we had escaped, then they[a] learned that the island was called Malta. <sup>2</sup> The natives showed us uncommon kindness; for they kindled a fire and received us all, because of the present rain and because of the cold. <sup>3</sup> But when Paul had gathered a bundle of sticks and laid them on the fire, a viper came out because of the heat and fastened on his hand. <sup>4</sup> When the natives saw the creature hanging from his hand, they said to one another, "No doubt this man is a murderer, whom, though he has escaped from the sea, yet Justice has not allowed to live." <sup>5</sup> However he shook off the creature into the fire, and wasn't harmed. <sup>6</sup> But they expected that he would have swollen or fallen down dead suddenly, but when they watched for a long time and saw nothing bad happen to him, they changed their minds and said that he was a god. <sup>7</sup> Now in the neighborhood of that place were lands belonging to the chief man of the island, named Publius, who received us and courteously entertained us for three days. <sup>8</sup> The father of Publius lay sick of fever and dysentery. Paul entered in to him, prayed, and laying his hands on him, healed him. <sup>9</sup> Then when this was done, the rest also who had diseases in the island came and were cured. <sup>10</sup> They also honored us with many honors; and when we sailed, they put on board the things that we needed. <sup>11</sup> After three months, we set sail in a ship of Alexandria which had wintered in the island, whose figurehead was "The Twin Brothers." <sup>12</sup> Touching at Syracuse, we stayed there three days. <sup>13</sup> From there we circled around and arrived at Rhegium. After one day, a south wind sprang up, and on the second day we came to Puteoli, <sup>14</sup> where we found brothers,[b] and were entreated to stay with them for seven days. So we came to Rome. <sup>15</sup> From there the brothers, when they heard of us, came to meet us as far as The Market of Appius and The Three Taverns. When Paul saw them, he thanked God and took courage. <sup>16</sup> When we entered into Rome, the centurion delivered the prisoners to the captain of the guard, but Paul was allowed to stay by himself with the soldier who guarded him. <sup>17</sup> After three days Paul called together those who were the leaders of the Jews. When they had come together, he said to them, "I, brothers, though I had done nothing against the people or the customs of our fathers, still was delivered prisoner from Jerusalem into the hands of the Romans, <sup>18</sup> who, when they had examined me, desired to set me free, because there was no cause of death in me. <sup>19</sup> But when the Jews spoke against it, I was constrained to appeal to Caesar, not that I had anything about which to accuse my nation. <sup>20</sup> For this cause therefore I asked to see you and to speak with you. For because of the hope of Israel I am bound with this chain." <sup>21</sup> They said to him, "We neither received letters from Judea concerning you, nor did any of the brothers come here and report or speak any evil of you. <sup>22</sup> But we desire to hear from you what you think. For, as concerning this sect, it is known to us that everywhere it is spoken against." <sup>23</sup> When they had appointed him a day, many people came to him at his lodging. He explained to them, testifying about God's Kingdom, and persuading them concerning Jesus, both from the law of Moses and from the prophets, from morning until evening. <sup>24</sup> Some believed the things which were spoken, and some disbelieved. <sup>25</sup> When they didn't agree among themselves, they departed after Paul had spoken one message: "The Holy Spirit spoke rightly through Isaiah the prophet to our fathers, <sup>26</sup> saying, 'Go to this people and say, in hearing, you will hear, but will in no way understand. In seeing, you will see, but will in no way perceive. <sup>27</sup> For this people's heart has grown callous. Their ears are dull of hearing. Their eyes they have closed. Lest they should see with their eyes, hear with their ears, understand with their heart, and would turn again, then I would heal them.'* <sup>28</sup>"Be it known therefore to you that the salvation of God is sent to the nations, and they will listen." <sup>29</sup> When he had said these words, the Jews departed, having a great dispute among themselves.[c] <sup>30</sup> Paul stayed two whole years in his own rented house and received all who were coming to him, <sup>31</sup> preaching God's Kingdom and teaching the things concerning the Lord Jesus Christ with all boldness, without hindrance.

# Paul's Letter to the Romans
## 1

<sup>1</sup> Paul, a servant of Jesus Christ,[d] called to be an apostle, set apart for the Good News of God, <sup>2</sup> which he promised before through his prophets in the holy Scriptures, <sup>3</sup> concerning his Son, who was born of the offspring[e] of David according to the flesh, <sup>4</sup> who was declared to be the Son of God with power according to the Spirit of holiness, by the resurrection from the dead, Jesus Christ our Lord, <sup>5</sup> through whom we received grace and apostleship for obedience of faith among all the nations for his name's sake; <sup>6</sup> among whom you are also called to belong to Jesus Christ; <sup>7</sup> to all who are in Rome, beloved of God, called to be saints: Grace to you and peace from God our Father and the Lord Jesus Christ. <sup>8</sup> First, I thank my God through Jesus Christ for all of you, that your faith is proclaimed throughout the whole world. <sup>9</sup> For God is my witness, whom I serve in my spirit in the Good News of his Son, how unceasingly I make mention of you always in my prayers, <sup>10</sup> requesting, if by any means now at last I may be prospered by the will of God to come to you. <sup>11</sup> For I long to see you, that I may impart to you some spiritual gift, to the end that you may be established; <sup>12</sup> that is, that I with you may be encouraged in you, each of us by the other's faith, both yours and mine. <sup>13</sup> Now I don't desire to have you unaware, brothers, that I often planned to come to you (and was hindered so far), that I might have some fruit among you also, even as among the rest of the Gentiles. <sup>14</sup> I am debtor both to Greeks and to foreigners, both to the wise and to the foolish. <sup>15</sup> So as much as is in me, I am eager to preach the Good News to you also who are in Rome. <sup>16</sup> For I am not ashamed of the Good News of Christ, because it is the power of God for salvation for everyone who believes, for the Jew first, and also for the Greek. <sup>17</sup> For in it is revealed God's righteousness from faith to faith. As it is written, "But the righteous shall live by faith."* <sup>18</sup> For the wrath of God is revealed from heaven against all ungodliness and unrighteousness of men who suppress the truth in unrighteousness, <sup>19</sup> because that which is known of God is revealed in them, for God revealed it to them. <sup>20</sup> For the invisible things of him since the creation of the world are clearly seen, being perceived through the things that are made, even his everlasting power and divinity, that they may be without excuse. <sup>21</sup> Because knowing God, they didn't glorify him as God, and didn't give thanks, but became vain in their reasoning, and their senseless heart was darkened. <sup>22</sup> Professing themselves to be wise, they became fools, <sup>23</sup> and traded the glory of the incorruptible God for the likeness of an image of corruptible man, and of birds, four-footed animals, and creeping things. <sup>24</sup> Therefore God also gave them up in the lusts of their hearts to uncleanness, that their bodies should be dishonored among themselves; <sup>25</sup> who exchanged the truth of God for a lie, and worshiped and served the creature rather than the Creator, who is blessed forever. Amen. <sup>26</sup> For this reason, God gave them up to vile passions. For their women changed the natural function into that which is against nature. <sup>27</sup> Likewise also the men, leaving the natural function of the woman, burned in their lust toward one another, men doing what is inappropriate with men, and receiving in themselves the due penalty of their error. <sup>28</sup> Even as they refused to have God in their knowledge, God gave them up to a reprobate mind, to do those things which are not fitting; <sup>29</sup> being filled with all unrighteousness, sexual immorality, wickedness, covetousness, malice; full of envy, murder, strife, deceit, evil habits, secret slanderers, <sup>30</sup> backbiters, hateful to God, insolent, arrogant, boastful, inventors of evil things, disobedient to parents, <sup>31</sup> without understanding, covenant breakers, without natural affection, unforgiving, unmerciful; <sup>32</sup> who, knowing the ordinance of God, that those who practice such things are worthy of death, not only do the same, but also approve of those who practice them.

---

[a] *28:1* NU reads "we"
[b] *28:14* The word for "brothers" here and where context allows may also be correctly translated "brothers and sisters" or "siblings."
* 28:27 Isaiah 6:9-10
[c] *28:29* NU omits verse 29.
[d] *1:1* "Christ" means "Anointed One".
[e] *1:3* or, seed
* 1:17 Habakkuk 2:4

## 2

[1] Therefore you are without excuse, O man, whoever you are who judge. For in that which you judge another, you condemn yourself. For you who judge practice the same things. [2] We know that the judgment of God is according to truth against those who practice such things. [3] Do you think this, O man who judges those who practice such things, and do the same, that you will escape the judgment of God? [4] Or do you despise the riches of his goodness, forbearance, and patience, not knowing that the goodness of God leads you to repentance? [5] But according to your hardness and unrepentant heart you are treasuring up for yourself wrath in the day of wrath, revelation, and of the righteous judgment of God, [6] who "will pay back to everyone according to their works:"* [7] to those who by perseverance in well-doing seek for glory, honor, and incorruptibility, eternal life; [8] but to those who are self-seeking and don't obey the truth, but obey unrighteousness, will be wrath, indignation, [9] oppression, and anguish on every soul of man who does evil, to the Jew first, and also to the Greek. [10] But glory, honor, and peace go to every man who does good, to the Jew first, and also to the Greek. [11] For there is no partiality with God. [12] For as many as have sinned without the law will also perish without the law. As many as have sinned under the law will be judged by the law. [13] For it isn't the hearers of the law who are righteous before God, but the doers of the law will be justified [14](for when Gentiles who don't have the law do by nature the things of the law, these, not having the law, are a law to themselves, [15] in that they show the work of the law written in their hearts, their conscience testifying with them, and their thoughts among themselves accusing or else excusing them) [16] in the day when God will judge the secrets of men, according to my Good News, by Jesus Christ. [17] Indeed you bear the name of a Jew, rest on the law, glory in God, [18] know his will, and approve the things that are excellent, being instructed out of the law, [19] and are confident that you yourself are a guide of the blind, a light to those who are in darkness, [20] a corrector of the foolish, a teacher of babies, having in the law the form of knowledge and of the truth. [21] You therefore who teach another, don't you teach yourself? You who preach that a man shouldn't steal, do you steal? [22] You who say a man shouldn't commit adultery, do you commit adultery? You who abhor idols, do you rob temples? [23] You who glory in the law, do you dishonor God by disobeying the law? [24] For "the name of God is blasphemed among the Gentiles because of you," * just as it is written. [25] For circumcision indeed profits, if you are a doer of the law, but if you are a transgressor of the law, your circumcision has become uncircumcision. [26] If therefore the uncircumcised keep the ordinances of the law, won't his uncircumcision be accounted as circumcision? [27] Won't those who are physically uncircumcised, but fulfill the law, judge you, who with the letter and circumcision are a transgressor of the law? [28] For he is not a Jew who is one outwardly, neither is that circumcision which is outward in the flesh; [29] but he is a Jew who is one inwardly, and circumcision is that of the heart, in the spirit, not in the letter; whose praise is not from men, but from God.

## 3

[1] Then what advantage does the Jew have? Or what is the profit of circumcision? [2] Much in every way! Because first of all, they were entrusted with the revelations of God. [3] For what if some were without faith? Will their lack of faith nullify the faithfulness of God? [4] May it never be! Yes, let God be found true, but every man a liar. As it is written, "that you might be justified in your words, and might prevail when you come into judgment."* [5] But if our unrighteousness commends the righteousness of God, what will we say? Is God unrighteous who inflicts wrath? I speak like men do. [6] May it never be! For then how will God judge the world? [7] For if the truth of God through my lie abounded to his glory, why am I also still judged as a sinner? [8] Why not (as we are slanderously reported, and as some affirm that we say), "Let's do evil, that good may come?" Those who say so are justly condemned. [9] What then? Are we better than they? No, in no way. For we previously warned both Jews and Greeks that they are all under sin. [10] As it is written, "There is no one righteous; no, not one. [11] There is no one who understands. There is no one who seeks after God. [12] They have all turned away. They have together become unprofitable. There is no one who does good, no, not so much as one."* [13]"Their throat is an open tomb. With their tongues they have used deceit."* "The poison of vipers is under their lips."* [14]"Their mouth is full of cursing and bitterness."* [15]"Their feet are swift to shed blood. [16] Destruction and misery are in their ways. [17] The way of peace, they haven't known."* [18]"There is no fear of God before their eyes."* [19] Now

we know that whatever things the law says, it speaks to those who are under the law, that every mouth may be closed, and all the world may be brought under the judgment of God. [20] Because by the works of the law, no flesh will be justified in his sight; for through the law comes the knowledge of sin. [21] But now apart from the law, a righteousness of God has been revealed, being testified by the law and the prophets; [22] even the righteousness of God through faith in Jesus Christ to all and on all those who believe. For there is no distinction, [23] for all have sinned, and fall short of the glory of God; [24] being justified freely by his grace through the redemption that is in Christ Jesus, [25] whom God sent to be an atoning sacrifice[a] through faith in his blood, for a demonstration of his righteousness through the passing over of prior sins, in God's forbearance; [26] to demonstrate his righteousness at this present time, that he might himself be just and the justifier of him who has faith in Jesus. [27] Where then is the boasting? It is excluded. By what kind of law? Of works? No, but by a law of faith. [28] We maintain therefore that a man is justified by faith apart from the works of the law. [29] Or is God the God of Jews only? Isn't he the God of Gentiles also? Yes, of Gentiles also, [30] since indeed there is one God who will justify the circumcised by faith and the uncircumcised through faith. [31] Do we then nullify the law through faith? May it never be! No, we establish the law.

## 4

[1] What then will we say that Abraham, our forefather, has found according to the flesh? [2] For if Abraham was justified by works, he has something to boast about, but not toward God. [3] For what does the Scripture say? "Abraham believed God, and it was accounted to him for righteousness."* [4] Now to him who works, the reward is not counted as grace, but as something owed. [5] But to him who doesn't work, but believes in him who justifies the ungodly, his faith is accounted for righteousness. [6] Even as David also pronounces blessing on the man to whom God counts righteousness apart from works: [7]"Blessed are they whose iniquities are forgiven, whose sins are covered. [8] Blessed is the man whom the Lord will by no means charge with sin." * [9] Is this blessing then pronounced only on the circumcised, or on the uncircumcised also? For we say that faith was accounted to Abraham for righteousness. [10] How then was it counted? When he was in circumcision, or in uncircumcision? Not in circumcision, but in uncircumcision. [11] He received the sign of circumcision, a seal of the righteousness of the faith which he had while he was in uncircumcision, that he might be the father of all those who believe, though they might be in uncircumcision, that righteousness might also be accounted to them. [12] He is the father of circumcision to those who not only are of the circumcision, but who also walk in the steps of that faith of our father Abraham, which he had in uncircumcision. [13] For the promise to Abraham and to his offspring that he would be heir of the world wasn't through the law, but through the righteousness of faith. [14] For if those who are of the law are heirs, faith is made void, and the promise is made of no effect. [15] For the law produces wrath; for where there is no law, neither is there disobedience. [16] For this cause it is of faith, that it may be according to grace, to the end that the promise may be sure to all the offspring, not to that only which is of the law, but to that also which is of the faith of Abraham, who is the father of us all. [17] As it is written, "I have made you a father of many nations."* This is in the presence of him whom he believed: God, who gives life to the dead, and calls the things that are not, as though they were. [18] Against hope, Abraham in hope believed, to the end that he might become a father of many nations, according to that which had been spoken, "So will your offspring be."* [19] Without being weakened in faith, he didn't consider his own body, already having been worn out, (he being about a hundred years old), and the deadness of Sarah's womb. [20] Yet, looking to the promise of God, he didn't waver through unbelief, but grew strong through faith, giving glory to God, [21] and being fully assured that what he had promised, he was also able to perform. [22] Therefore it also was "credited to him for righteousness."* [23] Now it was not written that it was accounted to him for his sake alone, [24] but for our sake also, to whom it will be accounted, who believe in him who raised Jesus our Lord from the dead, [25] who was delivered up for our trespasses, and was raised for our justification.

## 5

[1] Being therefore justified by faith, we have peace with God through our Lord Jesus Christ; [2] through whom we also have our access by faith into this grace in which we stand. We rejoice in hope of the glory of God. [3] Not only this, but we also rejoice in our sufferings, knowing that

---

* 2:6 Psalms 62:12; Proverbs 24:12
* 2:24 Isaiah 52:5; Ezekiel 36:22
* 3:4 Psalms 51:4

* 3:12 Psalms 14:1- 3; 53:1- 3; Ecclesiastes 7:20
* 3:13 Psalms 5:9
* 3:13 Psalms 140:3
* 3:14 Psalms 10:7

* 3:17 Isaiah 59:7- 8
* 3:18 Psalms 36:1
a 3:25 or, a propitiation
* 4:3 Genesis 15:6
* 4:8 Psalms 32:1- 2

* 4:17 Genesis 17:5
* 4:18 Genesis 15:5
* 4:22 Genesis 15:6

suffering produces perseverance; [4] and perseverance, proven character; and proven character, hope; [5] and hope doesn't disappoint us, because God's love has been poured into our hearts through the Holy Spirit who was given to us. [6] For while we were yet weak, at the right time Christ died for the ungodly. [7] For one will hardly die for a righteous man. Yet perhaps for a good person someone would even dare to die. [8] But God commends his own love toward us, in that while we were yet sinners, Christ died for us. [9] Much more then, being now justified by his blood, we will be saved from God's wrath through him. [10] For if while we were enemies, we were reconciled to God through the death of his Son, much more, being reconciled, we will be saved by his life. [11] Not only so, but we also rejoice in God through our Lord Jesus Christ, through whom we have now received the reconciliation. [12] Therefore, as sin entered into the world through one man, and death through sin, so death passed to all men because all sinned. [13] For until the law, sin was in the world; but sin is not charged when there is no law. [14] Nevertheless death reigned from Adam until Moses, even over those whose sins weren't like Adam's disobedience, who is a foreshadowing of him who was to come. [15] But the free gift isn't like the trespass. For if by the trespass of the one the many died, much more did the grace of God and the gift by the grace of the one man, Jesus Christ, abound to the many. [16] The gift is not as through one who sinned; for the judgment came by one to condemnation, but the free gift followed many trespasses to justification. [17] For if by the trespass of the one, death reigned through the one; so much more will those who receive the abundance of grace and of the gift of righteousness reign in life through the one, Jesus Christ. [18] So then as through one trespass, all men were condemned; even so through one act of righteousness, all men were justified to life. [19] For as through the one man's disobedience many were made sinners, even so through the obedience of the one, many will be made righteous. [20] The law came in that the trespass might abound; but where sin abounded, grace abounded more exceedingly, [21] that as sin reigned in death, even so grace might reign through righteousness to eternal life through Jesus Christ our Lord.

## 6

[1] What shall we say then? Shall we continue in sin, that grace may abound? [2] May it never be! We who died to sin, how could we live in it any longer? [3] Or don't you know that all of us who were baptized into Christ Jesus were baptized into his death? [4] We were buried therefore with him through baptism into death, that just as Christ was raised from the dead through the glory of the Father, so we also might walk in newness of life. [5] For if we have become united with him in the likeness of his death, we will also be part of his resurrection; [6] knowing this, that our old man was crucified with him, that the body of sin might be done away with, so that we would no longer be in bondage to sin. [7] For he who has died has been freed from sin. [8] But if we died with Christ, we believe that we will also live with him, [9] knowing that Christ, being raised from the dead, dies no more. Death no longer has dominion over him! [10] For the death that he died, he died to sin one time; but the life that he lives, he lives to God. [11] Thus consider yourselves also to be dead to sin, but alive to God in Christ Jesus our Lord. [12] Therefore don't let sin reign in your mortal body, that you should obey it in its lusts. [13] Also, do not present your members to sin as instruments of unrighteousness, but present yourselves to God as alive from the dead, and your members as instruments of righteousness to God. [14] For sin will not have dominion over you, for you are not under law, but under grace. [15] What then? Shall we sin because we are not under law but under grace? May it never be! [16] Don't you know that when you present yourselves as servants and obey someone, you are the servants of whomever you obey, whether of sin to death, or of obedience to righteousness? [17] But thanks be to God that, whereas you were bondservants of sin, you became obedient from the heart to that form of teaching to which you were delivered. [18] Being made free from sin, you became bondservants of righteousness. [19] I speak in human terms because of the weakness of your flesh; for as you presented your members as servants to uncleanness and to wickedness upon wickedness, even so now present your members as servants to righteousness for sanctification. [20] For when you were servants of sin, you were free from righteousness. [21] What fruit then did you have at that time in the things of which you are now ashamed? For the end of those things is death. [22] But now, being made free from sin and having become servants of God, you have your fruit of sanctification and the result of eternal life. [23] For the wages of sin is death, but the free gift of God is eternal life in Christ Jesus our Lord.

## 7

[1] Or don't you know, brothers[a] (for I speak to men who know the law), that the law has dominion over a man for as long as he lives? [2] For the woman that has a husband is bound by law to the husband while he lives, but if the husband dies, she is discharged from the law of the husband. [3] So then if, while the husband lives, she is joined to another man, she would be called an adulteress. But if the husband dies, she is free from the law, so that she is no adulteress, though she is joined to another man. [4] Therefore, my brothers, you also were made dead to the law through the body of Christ, that you would be joined to another, to him who was raised from the dead, that we might produce fruit to God. [5] For when we were in the flesh, the sinful passions which were through the law worked in our members to bring out fruit to death. [6] But now we have been discharged from the law, having died to that in which we were held; so that we serve in newness of the spirit, and not in oldness of the letter. [7] What shall we say then? Is the law sin? May it never be! However, I wouldn't have known sin except through the law. For I wouldn't have known coveting unless the law had said, "You shall not covet."[*] [8] But sin, finding occasion through the commandment, produced in me all kinds of coveting. For apart from the law, sin is dead. [9] I was alive apart from the law once, but when the commandment came, sin revived and I died. [10] The commandment which was for life, this I found to be for death; [11] for sin, finding occasion through the commandment, deceived me, and through it killed me. [12] Therefore the law indeed is holy, and the commandment holy, righteous, and good. [13] Did then that which is good become death to me? May it never be! But sin, that it might be shown to be sin, was producing death in me through that which is good; that through the commandment sin might become exceedingly sinful. [14] For we know that the law is spiritual, but I am fleshly, sold under sin. [15] For I don't understand what I am doing. For I don't practice what I desire to do; but what I hate, that I do. [16] But if what I don't desire, that I do, I consent to the law that it is good. [17] So now it is no more I that do it, but sin which dwells in me. [18] For I know that in me, that is, in my flesh, dwells no good thing. For desire is present with me, but I don't find it doing that which is good. [19] For the good which I desire, I don't do; but the evil which I don't desire, that I practice. [20] But if what I don't desire, that I do, it is no more I that do it, but sin which dwells in me. [21] I find then the law that, while I desire to do good, evil is present. [22] For I delight in God's law after the inward person, [23] but I see a different law in my members, warring against the law of my mind, and bringing me into captivity under the law of sin which is in my members. [24] What a wretched man I am! Who will deliver me out of the body of this death? [25] I thank God through Jesus Christ, our Lord! So then with the mind, I myself serve God's law, but with the flesh, sin's law.

## 8

[1] There is therefore now no condemnation to those who are in Christ Jesus, who don't walk according to the flesh, but according to the Spirit.[b] [2] For the law of the Spirit of life in Christ Jesus made me free from the law of sin and of death. [3] For what the law couldn't do, in that it was weak through the flesh, God did, sending his own Son in the likeness of sinful flesh and for sin, he condemned sin in the flesh, [4] that the ordinance of the law might be fulfilled in us who don't walk according to the flesh, but according to the Spirit. [5] For those who live according to the flesh set their minds on the things of the flesh, but those who live according to the Spirit, the things of the Spirit. [6] For the mind of the flesh is death, but the mind of the Spirit is life and peace; [7] because the mind of the flesh is hostile toward God, for it is not subject to God's law, neither indeed can it be. [8] Those who are in the flesh can't please God. [9] But you are not in the flesh but in the Spirit, if it is so that the Spirit of God dwells in you. But if any man doesn't have the Spirit of Christ, he is not his. [10] If Christ is in you, the body is dead because of sin, but the spirit is alive because of righteousness. [11] But if the Spirit of him who raised up Jesus from the dead dwells in you, he who raised up Christ Jesus from the dead will also give life to your mortal bodies through his Spirit who dwells in you. [12] So then, brothers, we are debtors, not to the flesh, to live after the flesh. [13] For if you live after the flesh, you must die; but if by the Spirit you put to death the deeds of the body, you will live. [14] For as many as are led by the Spirit of God, these are children of God. [15] For you didn't receive the spirit of bondage again to fear, but you received the Spirit of adoption, by whom we cry, "Abba![c] Father!" [16] The Spirit himself testifies with our spirit that we are children of God; [17] and if children, then heirs—heirs of God and joint heirs with Christ, if indeed we suffer with him, that we may also

---

[a] 7:1 The word for "brothers" here and where context allows may also be correctly translated "brothers and sisters" or "siblings."

[*] 7:7 Exodus 20:17; Deuteronomy 5:21
[b] 8:1 NU omits "who don't walk according to the flesh, but according to the Spirit"

[c] 8:15 Abba is an Aramaic word for "Father" or "Daddy", which can be used affectionately and respectfully

in prayer to our Father in heaven.

---

be glorified with him. **18** For I consider that the sufferings of this present time are not worthy to be compared with the glory which will be revealed toward us. **19** For the creation waits with eager expectation for the children of God to be revealed. **20** For the creation was subjected to vanity, not of its own will, but because of him who subjected it, in hope **21** that the creation itself also will be delivered from the bondage of decay into the liberty of the glory of the children of God. **22** For we know that the whole creation groans and travails in pain together until now. **23** Not only so, but ourselves also, who have the first fruits of the Spirit, even we ourselves groan within ourselves, waiting for adoption, the redemption of our body. **24** For we were saved in hope, but hope that is seen is not hope. For who hopes for that which he sees? **25** But if we hope for that which we don't see, we wait for it with patience. **26** In the same way, the Spirit also helps our weaknesses, for we don't know how to pray as we ought. But the Spirit himself makes intercession for us with groanings which can't be uttered. **27** He who searches the hearts knows what is on the Spirit's mind, because he makes intercession for the saints according to God. **28** We know that all things work together for good for those who love God, for those who are called according to his purpose. **29** For whom he foreknew, he also predestined to be conformed to the image of his Son, that he might be the firstborn among many brothers.[a] **30** Whom he predestined, those he also called. Whom he called, those he also justified. Whom he justified, those he also glorified. **31** What then shall we say about these things? If God is for us, who can be against us? **32** He who didn't spare his own Son, but delivered him up for us all, how would he not also with him freely give us all things? **33** Who could bring a charge against God's chosen ones? It is God who justifies. **34** Who is he who condemns? It is Christ who died, yes rather, who was raised from the dead, who is at the right hand of God, who also makes intercession for us. **35** Who shall separate us from the love of Christ? Could oppression, or anguish, or persecution, or famine, or nakedness, or peril, or sword? **36** Even as it is written, "For your sake we are killed all day long. We were accounted as sheep for the slaughter."* **37** No, in all these things we are more than conquerors through him who loved us. **38** For I am persuaded that neither death, nor life, nor angels, nor principalities, nor things present, nor things to come, nor powers, **39** nor height, nor depth, nor any other created thing will be able to separate us from God's love which is in Christ Jesus our Lord.

## 9

**1** I tell the truth in Christ. I am not lying, my conscience testifying with me in the Holy Spirit **2** that I have great sorrow and unceasing pain in my heart. **3** For I could wish that I myself were accursed from Christ for my brothers' sake, my relatives according to the flesh **4** who are Israelites; whose is the adoption, the glory, the covenants, the giving of the law, the service, and the promises; **5** of whom are the fathers, and from whom is Christ as concerning the flesh, who is over all, God, blessed forever. Amen. **6** But it is not as though the word of God has come to nothing. But it is not all Israel that are of Israel. **7** Neither, because they are Abraham's offspring, are they all children. But, "your offspring will be accounted as from Isaac."* **8** That is, it is not the children of the flesh who are children of God, but the children of the promise are counted as heirs. **9** For this is a word of promise: "At the appointed time I will come, and Sarah will have a son."* **10** Not only so, but Rebekah also conceived by one, by our father Isaac. **11** For being not yet born, neither having done anything good or bad, that the purpose of God according to election might stand, not of works, but of him who calls,[b] **12** it was said to her, "The elder will serve the younger."* **13** Even as it is written, "Jacob I loved, but Esau I hated."* **14** What shall we say then? Is there unrighteousness with God? May it never be! **15** For he said to Moses, "I will have mercy on whom I have mercy, and I will have compassion on whom I have compassion."* **16** So then it is not of him who wills, nor of him who runs, but of God who has mercy. **17** For the Scripture says to Pharaoh, "For this very purpose I caused you to be raised up, that I might show in you my power, and that my name might be proclaimed in all the earth."* **18** So then, he has mercy on whom he desires, and he hardens whom he desires. **19** You will say then to me, "Why does he still find fault? For who withstands his will?" **20** But indeed, O man, who are you to reply against God? Will the thing formed ask him who formed it, "Why did you make me like this?"* **21** Or hasn't the potter a right over the clay, from the same lump to make one part a vessel for honor, and another for dishonor? **22** What if God, willing to show his wrath and to make his power known, endured with much patience vessels of wrath prepared for destruction, **23** and that he might make known the riches of his glory on vessels of mercy, which he prepared beforehand for glory— **24** us, whom he also called, not from the Jews only, but also from the Gentiles? **25** As he says also in Hosea, "I will call them 'my people,' which were not my people; and her 'beloved,' who was not beloved."* **26** "It will be that in the place where it was said to them, 'You are not my people,' there they will be called 'children of the living God.'"* **27** Isaiah cries concerning Israel, "If the number of the children of Israel are as the sand of the sea, it is the remnant who will be saved; **28** for he will finish the work and cut it short in righteousness, because the Lord will make a short work upon the earth."* **29** As Isaiah has said before, "Unless the Lord of Armies[c] had left us a seed, we would have become like Sodom, and would have been made like Gomorrah."* **30** What shall we say then? That the Gentiles, who didn't follow after righteousness, attained to righteousness, even the righteousness which is of faith; **31** but Israel, following after a law of righteousness, didn't arrive at the law of righteousness. **32** Why? Because they didn't seek it by faith, but as it were by works of the law. They stumbled over the stumbling stone, **33** even as it is written, "Behold,[d] I lay in Zion a stumbling stone and a rock of offense; and no one who believes in him will be disappointed."*

## 10

**1** Brothers, my heart's desire and my prayer to God is for Israel, that they may be saved. **2** For I testify about them that they have a zeal for God, but not according to knowledge. **3** For being ignorant of God's righteousness, and seeking to establish their own righteousness, they didn't subject themselves to the righteousness of God. **4** For Christ is the fulfillment[e] of the law for righteousness to everyone who believes. **5** For Moses writes about the righteousness of the law, "The one who does them will live by them."* **6** But the righteousness which is of faith says this, "Don't say in your heart, 'Who will ascend into heaven?'* (that is, to bring Christ down); **7** or, 'Who will descend into the abyss?'* (that is, to bring Christ up from the dead.)" **8** But what does it say? "The word is near you, in your mouth and in your heart;"* that is, the word of faith which we preach: **9** that if you will confess with your mouth that Jesus is Lord and believe in your heart that God raised him from the dead, you will be saved. **10** For with the heart one believes resulting in righteousness; and with the mouth confession is made resulting in salvation. **11** For the Scripture says, "Whoever believes in him will not be disappointed."* **12** For there is no distinction between Jew and Greek; for the same Lord is Lord of all, and is rich to all who call on him. **13** For, "Whoever will call on the name of the Lord will be saved."* **14** How then will they call on him in whom they have not believed? How will they believe in him whom they have not heard? How will they hear without a preacher? **15** And how will they preach unless they are sent? As it is written: "How beautiful are the feet of those who preach the Good News of peace, who bring glad tidings of good things!"* **16** But they didn't all listen to the glad news. For Isaiah says, "Lord, who has believed our report?"* **17** So faith comes by hearing, and hearing by the word of God. **18** But I say, didn't they hear? Yes, most certainly, "Their sound went out into all the earth, their words to the ends of the world."* **19** But I ask, didn't Israel know? First Moses says, "I will provoke you to jealousy with that which is no nation. I will make you angry with a nation void of understanding."* **20** Isaiah is very bold and says, "I was found by those who didn't seek me. I was revealed to those who didn't ask for me."* **21** But about Israel he says, "All day long I stretched out my hands to a disobedient and contrary people."*

## 11

**1** I ask then, did God reject his people? May it never be! For I also am an Israelite, a descendant of Abraham, of the tribe of Benjamin. **2** God didn't reject his people, whom he foreknew. Or don't you know what the Scripture says about Elijah? How he pleads with God against Israel: **3** "Lord, they have killed your prophets. They have broken down your altars. I am left alone, and they seek my life."* **4** But how does God answer him? "I have reserved for myself seven thousand men who have

---

[a] *8:29* The word for "brothers" here and where context allows may also be correctly translated "brothers and sisters" or "siblings."
* *8:36* Psalms 44:22
* *9:7* Genesis 21:12
* *9:9* Genesis 18:10,14
[b] *9:11* NU puts the phrase "not of works, but of him who calls"

at the beginning of verse 12 instead of the end of verse 11.
* *9:12* Genesis 25:23
* *9:13* Malachi 1:2-3
* *9:15* Exodus 33:19
* *9:17* Exodus 9:16
* *9:20* Isaiah 29:16; 45:9
* *9:25* Hosea 2:23
* *9:26* Hosea 1:10
* *9:28* Isaiah 10:22-23

[c] *9:29* Greek: Sabaoth (or Hebrew: Tze'va'ot)
[d] *9:33* "Behold", from "ἰδοὺ", means look at, take notice, observe, see, or gaze at. It is often used as an interjection.
* *9:33* Isaiah 8:14; 28:16
[e] *10:4* or, completion, or end
* *10:5* Leviticus 18:5
* *10:6* Deuteronomy 30:12

* *10:7* Deuteronomy 30:13
* *10:8* Deuteronomy 30:14
* *10:11* Isaiah 28:16
* *10:13* Joel 2:32
* *10:15* Isaiah 52:7
* *10:16* Isaiah 53:1
* *10:18* Psalms 19:4
* *10:19* Deuteronomy 32:21
* *10:20* Isaiah 65:1
* *10:21* Isaiah 65:2
* *11:3* 1 Kings 19:10,14

not bowed the knee to Baal."* [5] Even so too at this present time also there is a remnant according to the election of grace. [6] And if by grace, then it is no longer of works; otherwise grace is no longer grace. But if it is of works, it is no longer grace; otherwise work is no longer work. [7] What then? That which Israel seeks for, that he didn't obtain, but the chosen ones obtained it, and the rest were hardened. [8] According as it is written, "God gave them a spirit of stupor, eyes that they should not see, and ears that they should not hear, to this very day." * [9] David says, "Let their table be made a snare, a trap, a stumbling block, and a retribution to them. [10] Let their eyes be darkened, that they may not see. Always keep their backs bent."* [11] I ask then, did they stumble that they might fall? May it never be! But by their fall salvation has come to the Gentiles, to provoke them to jealousy. [12] Now if their fall is the riches of the world, and their loss the riches of the Gentiles, how much more their fullness! [13] I speak to you who are Gentiles. Since then as I am an apostle to Gentiles, I glorify my ministry, [14] if by any means I may provoke to jealousy those who are my flesh, and may save some of them. [15] For if the rejection of them is the reconciling of the world, what would their acceptance be, but life from the dead? [16] If the first fruit is holy, so is the lump. If the root is holy, so are the branches. [17] But if some of the branches were broken off, and you, being a wild olive, were grafted in among them and became partaker with them of the root and of the richness of the olive tree, [18] don't boast over the branches. But if you boast, remember that it is not you who support the root, but the root supports you. [19] You will say then, "Branches were broken off, that I might be grafted in." [20] True; by their unbelief they were broken off, and you stand by your faith. Don't be conceited, but fear; [21] for if God didn't spare the natural branches, neither will he spare you. [22] See then the goodness and severity of God. Toward those who fell, severity; but toward you, goodness, if you continue in his goodness; otherwise you also will be cut off. [23] They also, if they don't continue in their unbelief, will be grafted in, for God is able to graft them in again. [24] For if you were cut out of that which is by nature a wild olive tree, and were grafted contrary to nature into a good olive tree, how much more will these, which are the natural branches, be grafted into their own olive tree? [25] For I don't desire you to be ignorant, brothers,[a] of this mystery, so that you won't be wise in your own conceits, that a partial hardening has happened to Israel, until the fullness of the Gentiles has come in, [26] and so all Israel will be saved. Even as it is written, "There will come out of Zion the Deliverer, and he will turn away ungodliness from Jacob. [27] This is my covenant with them, when I will take away their sins."* [28] Concerning the Good News, they are enemies for your sake. But concerning the election, they are beloved for the fathers' sake. [29] For the gifts and the calling of God are irrevocable. [30] For as you in time past were disobedient to God, but now have obtained mercy by their disobedience, [31] even so these also have now been disobedient, that by the mercy shown to you they may also obtain mercy. [32] For God has bound all to disobedience, that he might have mercy on all. [33] Oh the depth of the riches both of the wisdom and the knowledge of God! How unsearchable are his judgments, and his ways past tracing out! [34] "For who has known the mind of the Lord? Or who has been his counselor?"* [35] "Or who has first given to him, and it will be repaid to him again?"* [36] For of him and through him and to him are all things. To him be the glory for ever! Amen.

## 12

[1] Therefore I urge you, brothers, by the mercies of God, to present your bodies a living sacrifice, holy, acceptable to God, which is your spiritual service. [2] Don't be conformed to this world, but be transformed by the renewing of your mind, so that you may prove what is the good, well-pleasing, and perfect will of God. [3] For I say through the grace that was given me, to everyone who is among you, not to think of yourself more highly than you ought to think; but to think reasonably, as God has apportioned to each person a measure of faith. [4] For even as we have many members in one body, and all the members don't have the same function, [5] so we, who are many, are one body in Christ, and individually members of one another, [6] having gifts differing according to the grace that was given to us: if prophecy, let's prophesy according to the proportion of our faith; [7] or service, let's give ourselves to service; or he who teaches, to his teaching; [8] or he who exhorts, to his exhorting; he who gives, let him do it with generosity; he who rules, with diligence; he who shows mercy, with cheerfulness. [9] Let love be without hypocrisy. Abhor that which is evil. Cling to that which is good. [10] In love of the brothers be tenderly affectionate to one another; in honor prefer one another, [11] not lagging in diligence, fervent in spirit,

serving the Lord, [12] rejoicing in hope, enduring in troubles, continuing steadfastly in prayer, [13] contributing to the needs of the saints, and given to hospitality. [14] Bless those who persecute you; bless, and don't curse. [15] Rejoice with those who rejoice. Weep with those who weep. [16] Be of the same mind one toward another. Don't set your mind on high things, but associate with the humble. Don't be wise in your own conceits. [17] Repay no one evil for evil. Respect what is honorable in the sight of all men. [18] If it is possible, as much as it is up to you, be at peace with all men. [19] Don't seek revenge yourselves, beloved, but give place to God's wrath. For it is written, "Vengeance belongs to me; I will repay, says the Lord." * [20] Therefore "If your enemy is hungry, feed him. If he is thirsty, give him a drink; for in doing so, you will heap coals of fire on his head."* [21] Don't be overcome by evil, but overcome evil with good.

## 13

[1] Let every soul be in subjection to the higher authorities, for there is no authority except from God, and those who exist are ordained by God. [2] Therefore he who resists the authority withstands the ordinance of God; and those who withstand will receive to themselves judgment. [3] For rulers are not a terror to the good work, but to the evil. Do you desire to have no fear of the authority? Do that which is good, and you will have praise from the authority, [4] for he is a servant of God to you for good. But if you do that which is evil, be afraid, for he doesn't bear the sword in vain; for he is a servant of God, an avenger for wrath to him who does evil. [5] Therefore you need to be in subjection, not only because of the wrath, but also for conscience' sake. [6] For this reason you also pay taxes, for they are servants of God's service, continually doing this very thing. [7] Therefore give everyone what you owe: if you owe taxes, pay taxes; if customs, then customs; if respect, then respect; if honor, then honor. [8] Owe no one anything, except to love one another; for he who loves his neighbor has fulfilled the law. [9] For the commandments, "You shall not commit adultery," "You shall not murder," "You shall not steal,"[b] "You shall not covet," * and whatever other commandments there are, are all summed up in this saying, namely, "You shall love your neighbor as yourself."* [10] Love doesn't harm a neighbor. Love therefore is the fulfillment of the law. [11] Do this, knowing the time, that it is already time for you to awaken out of sleep, for salvation is now nearer to us than when we first believed. [12] The night is far gone, and the day is near. Let's therefore throw off the deeds of darkness, and let's put on the armor of light. [13] Let's walk properly, as in the day; not in reveling and drunkenness, not in sexual promiscuity and lustful acts, and not in strife and jealousy. [14] But put on the Lord Jesus Christ, and make no provision for the flesh, for its lusts.

## 14

[1] Now accept one who is weak in faith, but not for disputes over opinions. [2] One man has faith to eat all things, but he who is weak eats only vegetables. [3] Don't let him who eats despise him who doesn't eat. Don't let him who doesn't eat judge him who eats, for God has accepted him. [4] Who are you who judge another's servant? To his own lord he stands or falls. Yes, he will be made to stand, for God has power to make him stand. [5] One man esteems one day as more important. Another esteems every day alike. Let each man be fully assured in his own mind. [6] He who observes the day, observes it to the Lord; and he who does not observe the day, to the Lord he does not observe it. He who eats, eats to the Lord, for he gives God thanks. He who doesn't eat, to the Lord he doesn't eat, and gives God thanks. [7] For none of us lives to himself, and none dies to himself. [8] For if we live, we live to the Lord. Or if we die, we die to the Lord. If therefore we live or die, we are the Lord's. [9] For to this end Christ died, rose, and lived again, that he might be Lord of both the dead and the living. [10] But you, why do you judge your brother? Or you again, why do you despise your brother? For we will all stand before the judgment seat of Christ. [11] For it is written, "'As I live,' says the Lord, 'to me every knee will bow. Every tongue will confess to God.'"* [12] So then each one of us will give account of himself to God. [13] Therefore let's not judge one another any more, but judge this rather, that no man put a stumbling block in his brother's way, or an occasion for falling. [14] I know and am persuaded in the Lord Jesus that nothing is unclean of itself; except that to him who considers anything to be unclean, to him it is unclean. [15] Yet if because of food your brother is grieved, you walk no longer in love. Don't destroy with your food him for whom Christ died. [16] Then don't let your good be slandered, [17] for God's Kingdom is not eating and drinking, but righteousness, peace, and joy in the Holy Spirit. [18] For he who serves Christ in these things is acceptable to God and approved by

---

* 11:4 1 Kings 19:18
* 11:8 Deuteronomy 29:4; Isaiah 29:10
* 11:10 Psalms 69:22,23
[a] 11:25 The word for "brothers" here and where

context allows may also be correctly translated "brothers and sisters" or "siblings."
* 11:27 Isaiah 59:20- 21; 27:9; Jeremiah 31:33- 34
* 11:34 Isaiah 40:13

* 11:35 Job 41:11
* 12:19 Deuteronomy 32:35
* 12:20 Proverbs 25:21- 22
[b] 13:9 TR adds "You shall not give false testimony,"

* 13:9 Exodus 20:13- 15,17; Deuteronomy 5:17- 19,21
* 13:9 Leviticus 19:18
* 14:11 Isaiah 45:23

men. ¹⁹ So then, let's follow after things which make for peace, and things by which we may build one another up. ²⁰ Don't overthrow God's work for food's sake. All things indeed are clean, however it is evil for that man who creates a stumbling block by eating. ²¹ It is good to not eat meat, drink wine, nor do anything by which your brother stumbles, is offended, or is made weak. ²² Do you have faith? Have it to yourself before God. Happy is he who doesn't judge himself in that which he approves. ²³ But he who doubts is condemned if he eats, because it isn't of faith; and whatever is not of faith is sin. ²⁴ Now to him who is able to establish you according to my Good News and the preaching of Jesus Christ, according to the revelation of the mystery which has been kept secret through long ages, ²⁵ but now is revealed, and by the Scriptures of the prophets, according to the commandment of the eternal God, is made known for obedience of faith to all the nations; ²⁶ to the only wise God, through Jesus Christ, to whom be the glory forever! Amen.ᵃ

## 15

¹ Now we who are strong ought to bear the weaknesses of the weak, and not to please ourselves. ² Let each one of us please his neighbor for that which is good, to be building him up. ³ For even Christ didn't please himself. But, as it is written, "The reproaches of those who reproached you fell on me."* ⁴ For whatever things were written before were written for our learning, that through perseverance and through encouragement of the Scriptures we might have hope. ⁵ Now the God of perseverance and of encouragement grant you to be of the same mind with one another according to Christ Jesus, ⁶ that with one accord you may with one mouth glorify the God and Father of our Lord Jesus Christ. ⁷ Therefore accept one another, even as Christ also accepted you,ᵇ to the glory of God. ⁸ Now I say that Christ has been made a servant of the circumcision for the truth of God, that he might confirm the promises given to the fathers, ⁹ and that the Gentiles might glorify God for his mercy. As it is written, "Therefore I will give praise to you among the Gentiles and sing to your name."* ¹⁰ Again he says, "Rejoice, you Gentiles, with his people."* ¹¹ Again, "Praise the Lord, all you Gentiles! Let all the peoples praise him."* ¹² Again, Isaiah says, "There will be the root of Jesse, he who arises to rule over the Gentiles; in him the Gentiles will hope."* ¹³ Now may the God of hope fill you with all joy and peace in believing, that you may abound in hope in the power of the Holy Spirit. ¹⁴ I myself am also persuaded about you, my brothers,ᶜ that you yourselves are full of goodness, filled with all knowledge, able also to admonish others. ¹⁵ But I write the more boldly to you in part as reminding you, because of the grace that was given to me by God, ¹⁶ that I should be a servant of Christ Jesus to the Gentiles, serving as a priest of the Good News of God, that the offering up of the Gentiles might be made acceptable, sanctified by the Holy Spirit. ¹⁷ I have therefore my boasting in Christ Jesus in things pertaining to God. ¹⁸ For I will not dare to speak of any things except those which Christ worked through me for the obedience of the Gentiles, by word and deed, ¹⁹ in the power of signs and wonders, in the power of God's Spirit; so that from Jerusalem and around as far as to Illyricum, I have fully preached the Good News of Christ; ²⁰ yes, making it my aim to preach the Good News, not where Christ was already named, that I might not build on another's foundation. ²¹ But, as it is written, "They will see, to whom no news of him came. They who haven't heard will understand."* ²² Therefore also I was hindered these many times from coming to you, ²³ but now, no longer having any place in these regions, and having these many years a longing to come to you, ²⁴ whenever I travel to Spain, I will come to you. For I hope to see you on my journey, and to be helped on my way there by you, if first I may enjoy your company for a while. ²⁵ But now, I say, I am going to Jerusalem, serving the saints. ²⁶ For it has been the good pleasure of Macedonia and Achaia to make a certain contribution for the poor among the saints who are at Jerusalem. ²⁷ Yes, it has been their good pleasure, and they are their debtors. For if the Gentiles have been made partakers of their spiritual things, they owe it to them also to serve them in material things. ²⁸ When therefore I have accomplished this, and have sealed to them this fruit, I will go on by way of you to Spain. ²⁹ I know that when I come to you, I will come in the fullness of the blessing of the Good News of Christ. ³⁰ Now I beg you, brothers, by our Lord Jesus Christ and by the love of the Spirit, that you strive together with me in your prayers to God for me, ³¹ that I may be delivered from those who are disobedient

in Judea, and that my service which I have for Jerusalem may be acceptable to the saints, ³² that I may come to you in joy through the will of God, and together with you, find rest. ³³ Now the God of peace be with you all. Amen.

## 16

¹ I commend to you Phoebe, our sister, who is a servantᵈ of the assembly that is at Cenchreae, ² that you receive her in the Lord in a way worthy of the saints, and that you assist her in whatever matter she may need from you, for she herself also has been a helper of many, and of my own self. ³ Greet Prisca and Aquila, my fellow workers in Christ Jesus, ⁴ who risked their own necks for my life, to whom not only I give thanks, but also all the assemblies of the Gentiles. ⁵ Greet the assembly that is in their house. Greet Epaenetus, my beloved, who is the first fruits of Achaia to Christ. ⁶ Greet Mary, who labored much for us. ⁷ Greet Andronicus and Junia, my relatives and my fellow prisoners, who are notable among the apostles, who were also in Christ before me. ⁸ Greet Amplias, my beloved in the Lord. ⁹ Greet Urbanus, our fellow worker in Christ, and Stachys, my beloved. ¹⁰ Greet Apelles, the approved in Christ. Greet those who are of the household of Aristobulus. ¹¹ Greet Herodion, my kinsman. Greet them of the household of Narcissus, who are in the Lord. ¹² Greet Tryphaena and Tryphosa, who labor in the Lord. Greet Persis, the beloved, who labored much in the Lord. ¹³ Greet Rufus, the chosen in the Lord, and his mother and mine. ¹⁴ Greet Asyncritus, Phlegon, Hermes, Patrobas, Hermas, and the brothersᵉ who are with them. ¹⁵ Greet Philologus and Julia, Nereus and his sister, and Olympas, and all the saints who are with them. ¹⁶ Greet one another with a holy kiss. The assemblies of Christ greet you. ¹⁷ Now I beg you, brothers, look out for those who are causing the divisions and occasions of stumbling, contrary to the doctrine which you learned, and turn away from them. ¹⁸ For those who are such don't serve our Lord Jesus Christ, but their own belly; and by their smooth and flattering speech they deceive the hearts of the innocent. ¹⁹ For your obedience has become known to all. I rejoice therefore over you. But I desire to have you wise in that which is good, but innocent in that which is evil. ²⁰ And the God of peace will quickly crush Satan under your feet. The grace of our Lord Jesus Christ be with you. ²¹ Timothy, my fellow worker, greets you, as do Lucius, Jason, and Sosipater, my relatives. ²² I, Tertius, who write the letter, greet you in the Lord. ²³ Gaius, my host and host of the whole assembly, greets you. Erastus, the treasurer of the city, greets you, as does Quartus, the brother. ²⁴ The grace of our Lord Jesus Christ be with you all! Amen. ²⁵ ᶠ

## Paul's First Letter to the Corinthians
### 1

¹ Paul, called to be an apostle of Jesus Christᵍ through the will of God, and our brother Sosthenes, ² to the assembly of God which is at Corinth—those who are sanctified in Christ Jesus, called saints, with all who call on the name of our Lord Jesus Christ in every place, both theirs and ours: ³ Grace to you and peace from God our Father and the Lord Jesus Christ. ⁴ I always thank my God concerning you for the grace of God which was given you in Christ Jesus, ⁵ that in everything you were enriched in him, in all speech and all knowledge— ⁶ even as the testimony of Christ was confirmed in you— ⁷ so that you come behind in no gift, waiting for the revelation of our Lord Jesus Christ, ⁸ who will also confirm you until the end, blameless in the day of our Lord Jesus Christ. ⁹ God is faithful, through whom you were called into the fellowship of his Son, Jesus Christ our Lord. ¹⁰ Now I beg you, brothers,ʰ through the name of our Lord, Jesus Christ, that you all speak the same thing, and that there be no divisions among you, but that you be perfected together in the same mind and in the same judgment. ¹¹ For it has been reported to me concerning you, my brothers, by those who are from Chloe's household, that there are contentions among you. ¹² Now I mean this, that each one of you says, "I follow Paul," "I follow Apollos," "I follow Cephas," and, "I follow Christ." ¹³ Is Christ divided? Was Paul crucified for you? Or were you baptized into the name of Paul? ¹⁴ I thank God that I baptized none of you except Crispus and Gaius, ¹⁵ so that no one should say that I had baptized you into my own name. ¹⁶ (I also baptized the household of Stephanas; besides them,

---

ᵃ *14:26* TR places verses 24- 26 after Romans 16:24 as verses 25- 27.
* *15:3* Psalms 69:9
ᵇ *15:7* TR reads "us" instead of "you"
* 15:9 2 Samuel 22:50; Psalms 18:49
* 15:10 Deuteronomy 32:43

* 15:11 Psalms 117:1
* 15:12 Isaiah 11:10
ᶜ *15:14* The word for "brothers" here and where context allows may also be correctly translated "brothers and sisters" or "siblings."
* 15:21 Isaiah 52:15
ᵈ *16:1* or, deacon

ᵉ *16:14* The word for "brothers" here and where context allows may also be correctly translated "brothers and sisters" or "siblings."
ᶠ *16:25* TR places Romans 14:24- 26 at the end of Romans instead of at the end of chapter

14, and numbers these verses 16:25- 27.
ᵍ *1:1* "Christ" means "Anointed One".
ʰ *1:10* The word for "brothers" here and where context allows may also be correctly translated "brothers and sisters" or "siblings."

I don't know whether I baptized any other.) [17] For Christ sent me not to baptize, but to preach the Good News—not in wisdom of words, so that the cross of Christ wouldn't be made void. [18] For the word of the cross is foolishness to those who are dying, but to us who are being saved it is the power of God. [19] For it is written, "I will destroy the wisdom of the wise. I will bring the discernment of the discerning to nothing."* [20] Where is the wise? Where is the scribe? Where is the debater of this age? Hasn't God made foolish the wisdom of this world? [21] For seeing that in the wisdom of God, the world through its wisdom didn't know God, it was God's good pleasure through the foolishness of the preaching to save those who believe. [22] For Jews ask for signs, Greeks seek after wisdom, [23] but we preach Christ crucified, a stumbling block to Jews and foolishness to Greeks, [24] but to those who are called, both Jews and Greeks, Christ is the power of God and the wisdom of God; [25] because the foolishness of God is wiser than men, and the weakness of God is stronger than men. [26] For you see your calling, brothers, that not many are wise according to the flesh, not many mighty, and not many noble; [27] but God chose the foolish things of the world that he might put to shame those who are wise. God chose the weak things of the world that he might put to shame the things that are strong. [28] God chose the lowly things of the world, and the things that are despised, and the things that don't exist, that he might bring to nothing the things that exist, [29] that no flesh should boast before God. [30] Because of him, you are in Christ Jesus, who was made to us wisdom from God, and righteousness and sanctification, and redemption, [31] that, as it is written, "He who boasts, let him boast in the Lord."*

## 2

[1] When I came to you, brothers, I didn't come with excellence of speech or of wisdom, proclaiming to you the testimony of God. [2] For I determined not to know anything among you except Jesus Christ and him crucified. [3] I was with you in weakness, in fear, and in much trembling. [4] My speech and my preaching were not in persuasive words of human wisdom, but in demonstration of the Spirit and of power, [5] that your faith wouldn't stand in the wisdom of men, but in the power of God. [6] We speak wisdom, however, among those who are full grown, yet a wisdom not of this world nor of the rulers of this world who are coming to nothing. [7] But we speak God's wisdom in a mystery, the wisdom that has been hidden, which God foreordained before the worlds for our glory, [8] which none of the rulers of this world has known. For had they known it, they wouldn't have crucified the Lord of glory. [9] But as it is written, "Things which an eye didn't see, and an ear didn't hear, which didn't enter into the heart of man, these God has prepared for those who love him."* [10] But to us, God revealed them through the Spirit. For the Spirit searches all things, yes, the deep things of God. [11] For who among men knows the things of a man except the spirit of the man which is in him? Even so, no one knows the things of God except God's Spirit. [12] But we received not the spirit of the world, but the Spirit which is from God, that we might know the things that were freely given to us by God. [13] We also speak these things, not in words which man's wisdom teaches but which the Holy Spirit teaches, comparing spiritual things with spiritual things. [14] Now the natural man doesn't receive the things of God's Spirit, for they are foolishness to him; and he can't know them, because they are spiritually discerned. [15] But he who is spiritual discerns all things, and he himself is to be judged by no one. [16] "For who has known the mind of the Lord that he should instruct him?" * But we have Christ's mind.

## 3

[1] Brothers, I couldn't speak to you as to spiritual, but as to fleshly, as to babies in Christ. [2] I fed you with milk, not with solid food, for you weren't yet ready. Indeed, you aren't ready even now, [3] for you are still fleshly. For insofar as there is jealousy, strife, and factions among you, aren't you fleshly, and don't you walk in the ways of men? [4] For when one says, "I follow Paul," and another, "I follow Apollos," aren't you fleshly? [5] Who then is Apollos, and who is Paul, but servants through whom you believed, and each as the Lord gave to him? [6] I planted. Apollos watered. But God gave the increase. [7] So then neither he who plants is anything, nor he who waters, but God who gives the increase. [8] Now he who plants and he who waters are the same, but each will receive his own reward according to his own labor. [9] For we are God's fellow workers. You are God's farming, God's building. [10] According to the grace of God which was given to me, as a wise master builder I laid a foundation, and another builds on it. But let each man be careful how he builds on it. [11] For no one can lay any other foundation than that which has been laid, which is Jesus Christ. [12] But if anyone builds on the foundation with gold, silver, costly stones, wood, hay, or straw, [13] each man's work will be revealed. For the Day will declare it, because it is revealed in fire; and the fire itself will test what sort of work each

man's work is. [14] If any man's work remains which he built on it, he will receive a reward. [15] If any man's work is burned, he will suffer loss, but he himself will be saved, but as through fire. [16] Don't you know that you are God's temple and that God's Spirit lives in you? [17] If anyone destroys God's temple, God will destroy him; for God's temple is holy, which you are. [18] Let no one deceive himself. If anyone thinks that he is wise among you in this world, let him become a fool that he may become wise. [19] For the wisdom of this world is foolishness with God. For it is written, "He has taken the wise in their craftiness."* [20] And again, "The Lord knows the reasoning of the wise, that it is worthless."* [21] Therefore let no one boast in men. For all things are yours, [22] whether Paul, or Apollos, or Cephas, or the world, or life, or death, or things present, or things to come. All are yours, [23] and you are Christ's, and Christ is God's.

## 4

[1] So let a man think of us as Christ's servants and stewards of God's mysteries. [2] Here, moreover, it is required of stewards that they be found faithful. [3] But with me it is a very small thing that I should be judged by you, or by a human court. Yes, I don't even judge my own self. [4] For I know nothing against myself. Yet I am not justified by this, but he who judges me is the Lord. [5] Therefore judge nothing before the time, until the Lord comes, who will both bring to light the hidden things of darkness and reveal the counsels of the hearts. Then each man will get his praise from God. [6] Now these things, brothers, I have in a figure transferred to myself and Apollos for your sakes, that in us you might learn not to think beyond the things which are written, that none of you be puffed up against one another. [7] For who makes you different? And what do you have that you didn't receive? But if you did receive it, why do you boast as if you had not received it? [8] You are already filled. You have already become rich. You have come to reign without us. Yes, and I wish that you did reign, that we also might reign with you! [9] For I think that God has displayed us, the apostles, last of all, like men sentenced to death. For we are made a spectacle to the world, both to angels and men. [10] We are fools for Christ's sake, but you are wise in Christ. We are weak, but you are strong. You have honor, but we have dishonor. [11] Even to this present hour we hunger, thirst, are naked, are beaten, and have no certain dwelling place. [12] We toil, working with our own hands. When people curse us, we bless. Being persecuted, we endure. [13] Being defamed, we entreat. We are made as the filth of the world, the dirt wiped off by all, even until now. [14] I don't write these things to shame you, but to admonish you as my beloved children. [15] For though you have ten thousand tutors in Christ, you don't have many fathers. For in Christ Jesus, I became your father through the Good News. [16] I beg you therefore, be imitators of me. [17] Because of this I have sent Timothy to you, who is my beloved and faithful child in the Lord, who will remind you of my ways which are in Christ, even as I teach everywhere in every assembly. [18] Now some are puffed up, as though I were not coming to you. [19] But I will come to you shortly, if the Lord is willing. And I will know, not the word of those who are puffed up, but the power. [20] For God's Kingdom is not in word, but in power. [21] What do you want? Shall I come to you with a rod, or in love and a spirit of gentleness?

## 5

[1] It is actually reported that there is sexual immorality among you, and such sexual immorality as is not even named among the Gentiles, that one has his father's wife. [2] You are arrogant, and didn't mourn instead, that he who had done this deed might be removed from among you. [3] For I most certainly, as being absent in body but present in spirit, have already, as though I were present, judged him who has done this thing. [4] In the name of our Lord Jesus Christ, when you are gathered together with my spirit with the power of our Lord Jesus Christ, [5] you are to deliver such a one to Satan for the destruction of the flesh, that the spirit may be saved in the day of the Lord Jesus. [6] Your boasting is not good. Don't you know that a little yeast leavens the whole lump? [7] Purge out the old yeast, that you may be a new lump, even as you are unleavened. For indeed Christ, our Passover, has been sacrificed in our place. [8] Therefore let's keep the feast, not with old yeast, neither with the yeast of malice and wickedness, but with the unleavened bread of sincerity and truth. [9] I wrote to you in my letter to have no company with sexual sinners; [10] yet not at all meaning with the sexual sinners of this world, or with the covetous and extortionists, or with idolaters, for then you would have to leave the world. [11] But as it is, I wrote to you not to associate with anyone who is called a brother who is a sexual sinner, or covetous, or an idolater, or a slanderer, or a drunkard, or an extortionist. Don't even eat with such a person. [12] For what do I have to do with also judging those who are outside? Don't you judge those who are within?

---

* 1:19 Isaiah 29:14
* 1:31 Jeremiah 9:24
* 2:9 Isaiah 64:4
* 2:16 Isaiah 40:13
* 3:19 Job 5:13
* 3:20 Psalms 94:11

[13] But those who are outside, God judges. "Put away the wicked man from among yourselves."*

# 6

[1] Dare any of you, having a matter against his neighbor, go to law before the unrighteous, and not before the saints? [2] Don't you know that the saints will judge the world? And if the world is judged by you, are you unworthy to judge the smallest matters? [3] Don't you know that we will judge angels? How much more, things that pertain to this life? [4] If you have to judge things pertaining to this life, do you set them to judge who are of no account in the assembly? [5] I say this to move you to shame. Isn't there even one wise man among you who would be able to decide between his brothers? [6] But brother goes to law with brother, and that before unbelievers! [7] Therefore it is already altogether a defect in you that you have lawsuits one with another. Why not rather be wronged? Why not rather be defrauded? [8] No, but you yourselves do wrong and defraud, and that against your brothers. [9] Or don't you know that the unrighteous will not inherit God's Kingdom? Don't be deceived. Neither the sexually immoral, nor idolaters, nor adulterers, nor male prostitutes, nor homosexuals, [10] nor thieves, nor covetous, nor drunkards, nor slanderers, nor extortionists, will inherit God's Kingdom. [11] Some of you were such, but you were washed. You were sanctified. You were justified in the name of the Lord Jesus, and in the Spirit of our God. [12]"All things are lawful for me," but not all things are expedient. "All things are lawful for me," but I will not be brought under the power of anything. [13]"Foods for the belly, and the belly for foods," but God will bring to nothing both it and them. But the body is not for sexual immorality, but for the Lord, and the Lord for the body. [14] Now God raised up the Lord, and will also raise us up by his power. [15] Don't you know that your bodies are members of Christ? Shall I then take the members of Christ and make them members of a prostitute? May it never be! [16] Or don't you know that he who is joined to a prostitute is one body? For, "The two", he says, "will become one flesh."* [17] But he who is joined to the Lord is one spirit. [18] Flee sexual immorality! "Every sin that a man does is outside the body," but he who commits sexual immorality sins against his own body. [19] Or don't you know that your body is a temple of the Holy Spirit who is in you, whom you have from God? You are not your own, [20] for you were bought with a price. Therefore glorify God in your body and in your spirit, which are God's.

# 7

[1] Now concerning the things about which you wrote to me: it is good for a man not to touch a woman. [2] But, because of sexual immoralities, let each man have his own wife, and let each woman have her own husband. [3] Let the husband give his wife the affection owed her,[a] and likewise also the wife her husband. [4] The wife doesn't have authority over her own body, but the husband does. Likewise also the husband doesn't have authority over his own body, but the wife does. [5] Don't deprive one another, unless it is by consent for a season, that you may give yourselves to fasting and prayer, and may be together again, that Satan doesn't tempt you because of your lack of self-control. [6] But this I say by way of concession, not of commandment. [7] Yet I wish that all men were like me. However, each man has his own gift from God, one of this kind, and another of that kind. [8] But I say to the unmarried and to widows, it is good for them if they remain even as I am. [9] But if they don't have self-control, let them marry. For it's better to marry than to burn with passion. [10] But to the married I command—not I, but the Lord—that the wife not leave her husband [11](but if she departs, let her remain unmarried, or else be reconciled to her husband), and that the husband not leave his wife. [12] But to the rest I—not the Lord—say, if any brother has an unbelieving wife, and she is content to live with him, let him not leave her. [13] The woman who has an unbelieving husband, and he is content to live with her, let her not leave her husband. [14] For the unbelieving husband is sanctified in the wife, and the unbelieving wife is sanctified in the husband. Otherwise your children would be unclean, but now they are holy. [15] Yet if the unbeliever departs, let there be separation. The brother or the sister is not under bondage in such cases, but God has called us in peace. [16] For how do you know, wife, whether you will save your husband? Or how do you know, husband, whether you will save your wife? [17] Only, as the Lord has distributed to each man, as God has called each, so let him walk. So I command in all the assemblies. [18] Was anyone called having been circumcised? Let him not become uncircumcised. Has anyone been called in uncircumcision? Let him not be circumcised. [19] Circumcision is nothing, and uncircumcision is nothing, but what matters is keeping God's commandments. [20] Let each man stay in that calling in which he was called. [21] Were you called being a bondservant? Don't let that bother you, but if you get an opportunity to become free, use it. [22] For he who was called in the Lord being a bondservant is the Lord's free man. Likewise he who was called being free is Christ's bondservant. [23] You were bought with a price. Don't become bondservants of men. [24] Brothers, let each man, in whatever condition he was called, stay in that condition with God. [25] Now concerning virgins, I have no commandment from the Lord, but I give my judgment as one who has obtained mercy from the Lord to be trustworthy. [26] Therefore I think that because of the distress that is on us, it's good for a man to remain as he is. [27] Are you bound to a wife? Don't seek to be freed. Are you free from a wife? Don't seek a wife. [28] But if you marry, you have not sinned. If a virgin marries, she has not sinned. Yet such will have oppression in the flesh, and I want to spare you. [29] But I say this, brothers: the time is short. From now on, both those who have wives may be as though they had none; [30] and those who weep, as though they didn't weep; and those who rejoice, as though they didn't rejoice; and those who buy, as though they didn't possess; [31] and those who use the world, as not using it to the fullest. For the mode of this world passes away. [32] But I desire to have you to be free from cares. He who is unmarried is concerned for the things of the Lord, how he may please the Lord; [33] but he who is married is concerned about the things of the world, how he may please his wife. [34] There is also a difference between a wife and a virgin. The unmarried woman cares about the things of the Lord, that she may be holy both in body and in spirit. But she who is married cares about the things of the world—how she may please her husband. [35] This I say for your own benefit, not that I may ensnare you, but for that which is appropriate, and that you may attend to the Lord without distraction. [36] But if any man thinks that he is behaving inappropriately toward his virgin, if she is past the flower of her age, and if need so requires, let him do what he desires. He doesn't sin. Let them marry. [37] But he who stands steadfast in his heart, having no urgency, but has power over his own will, and has determined in his own heart to keep his own virgin, does well. [38] So then both he who gives his own virgin in marriage does well, and he who doesn't give her in marriage does better. [39] A wife is bound by law for as long as her husband lives; but if the husband is dead, she is free to be married to whomever she desires, only in the Lord. [40] But she is happier if she stays as she is, in my judgment, and I think that I also have God's Spirit.

# 8

[1] Now concerning things sacrificed to idols: We know that we all have knowledge. Knowledge puffs up, but love builds up. [2] But if anyone thinks that he knows anything, he doesn't yet know as he ought to know. [3] But anyone who loves God is known by him. [4] Therefore concerning the eating of things sacrificed to idols, we know that no idol is anything in the world, and that there is no other God but one. [5] For though there are things that are called "gods", whether in the heavens or on earth—as there are many "gods" and many "lords"— [6] yet to us there is one God, the Father, of whom are all things, and we for him; and one Lord, Jesus Christ, through whom are all things, and we live through him. [7] However, that knowledge isn't in all men. But some, with consciousness of an idol until now, eat as of a thing sacrificed to an idol, and their conscience, being weak, is defiled. [8] But food will not commend us to God. For neither, if we don't eat are we the worse, nor if we eat are we the better. [9] But be careful that by no means does this liberty of yours become a stumbling block to the weak. [10] For if a man sees you who have knowledge sitting in an idol's temple, won't his conscience, if he is weak, be emboldened to eat things sacrificed to idols? [11] And through your knowledge, he who is weak perishes, the brother for whose sake Christ died. [12] Thus, sinning against the brothers, and wounding their conscience when it is weak, you sin against Christ. [13] Therefore, if food causes my brother to stumble, I will eat no meat forever more, that I don't cause my brother to stumble.

# 9

[1] Am I not free? Am I not an apostle? Haven't I seen Jesus Christ, our Lord? Aren't you my work in the Lord? [2] If to others I am not an apostle, yet at least I am to you; for you are the seal of my apostleship in the Lord. [3] My defense to those who examine me is this: [4] Have we no right to eat and to drink? [5] Have we no right to take along a wife who is a believer, even as the rest of the apostles, and the brothers of the Lord, and Cephas? [6] Or have only Barnabas and I no right to not work? [7] What soldier ever serves at his own expense? Who plants a vineyard, and doesn't eat of its fruit? Or who feeds a flock, and doesn't drink from the flock's milk? [8] Do I speak these things according to the ways of men? Or doesn't the law also say the same thing? [9] For it is written in the law of Moses, "You shall not muzzle an ox while it treads out the grain."* Is it for the oxen that God cares, [10] or does he say it

---

* 5:13 Deuteronomy 17:7; 19:19; 21:21; 22:21; 24:7
* 6:16 Genesis 2:24

a 7:3 NU and TR have "what is owed her" instead of "the affection owed her".

* 9:9 Deuteronomy 25:4

assuredly for our sake? Yes, it was written for our sake, because he who plows ought to plow in hope, and he who threshes in hope should partake of his hope. ¹¹ If we sowed to you spiritual things, is it a great thing if we reap your fleshly things? ¹² If others partake of this right over you, don't we yet more? Nevertheless we didn't use this right, but we bear all things, that we may cause no hindrance to the Good News of Christ. ¹³ Don't you know that those who serve around sacred things eat from the things of the temple, and those who wait on the altar have their portion with the altar? ¹⁴ Even so the Lord ordained that those who proclaim the Good News should live from the Good News. ¹⁵ But I have used none of these things, and I don't write these things that it may be done so in my case; for I would rather die, than that anyone should make my boasting void. ¹⁶ For if I preach the Good News, I have nothing to boast about, for necessity is laid on me; but woe is to me if I don't preach the Good News. ¹⁷ For if I do this of my own will, I have a reward. But if not of my own will, I have a stewardship entrusted to me. ¹⁸ What then is my reward? That when I preach the Good News, I may present the Good News of Christ without charge, so as not to abuse my authority in the Good News. ¹⁹ For though I was free from all, I brought myself under bondage to all, that I might gain the more. ²⁰ To the Jews I became as a Jew, that I might gain Jews; to those who are under the law, as under the law,ᵃ that I might gain those who are under the law; ²¹ to those who are without law, as without law (not being without law toward God, but under law toward Christ), that I might win those who are without law. ²² To the weak I became as weak, that I might gain the weak. I have become all things to all men, that I may by all means save some. ²³ Now I do this for the sake of the Good News, that I may be a joint partaker of it. ²⁴ Don't you know that those who run in a race all run, but one receives the prize? Run like that, so that you may win. ²⁵ Every man who strives in the games exercises self-control in all things. Now they do it to receive a corruptible crown, but we an incorruptible. ²⁶ I therefore run like that, not aimlessly. I fight like that, not beating the air, ²⁷ but I beat my body and bring it into submission, lest by any means, after I have preached to others, I myself should be disqualified.

## 10

¹ Now I would not have you ignorant, brothers, that our fathers were all under the cloud, and all passed through the sea; ² and were all baptized into Moses in the cloud and in the sea; ³ and all ate the same spiritual food; ⁴ and all drank the same spiritual drink. For they drank of a spiritual rock that followed them, and the rock was Christ. ⁵ However with most of them, God was not well pleased, for they were overthrown in the wilderness. ⁶ Now these things were our examples, to the intent we should not lust after evil things as they also lusted. ⁷ Don't be idolaters, as some of them were. As it is written, "The people sat down to eat and drink, and rose up to play."* ⁸ Let's not commit sexual immorality, as some of them committed, and in one day twenty-three thousand fell. ⁹ Let's not test Christ,ᵇ as some of them tested, and perished by the serpents. ¹⁰ Don't grumble, as some of them also grumbled, and perished by the destroyer. ¹¹ Now all these things happened to them by way of example, and they were written for our admonition, on whom the ends of the ages have come. ¹² Therefore let him who thinks he stands be careful that he doesn't fall. ¹³ No temptation has taken you except what is common to man. God is faithful, who will not allow you to be tempted above what you are able, but will with the temptation also make the way of escape, that you may be able to endure it. ¹⁴ Therefore, my beloved, flee from idolatry. ¹⁵ I speak as to wise men. Judge what I say. ¹⁶ The cup of blessing which we bless, isn't it a sharing of the blood of Christ? The bread which we break, isn't it a sharing of the body of Christ? ¹⁷ Because there is one loaf of bread, we, who are many, are one body; for we all partake of the one loaf of bread. ¹⁸ Consider Israel according to the flesh. Don't those who eat the sacrifices participate in the altar? ¹⁹ What am I saying then? That a thing sacrificed to idols is anything, or that an idol is anything? ²⁰ But I say that the things which the Gentiles sacrifice, they sacrifice to demons and not to God, and I don't desire that you would have fellowship with demons. ²¹ You can't both drink the cup of the Lord and the cup of demons. You can't both partake of the table of the Lord and of the table of demons. ²² Or do we provoke the Lord to jealousy? Are we stronger than he? ²³"All things are lawful for me," but not all things are profitable. "All things are lawful for me," but not all things build up. ²⁴ Let no one seek his own, but each one his neighbor's good. ²⁵ Whatever is sold in the butcher shop, eat, asking no question for the sake of conscience, ²⁶ for "the earth is the Lord's, and its fullness."* ²⁷ But if one of those who don't believe invites you to a meal, and you are inclined to go, eat whatever is set before you, asking no questions for

the sake of conscience. ²⁸ But if anyone says to you, "This was offered to idols," don't eat it for the sake of the one who told you, and for the sake of conscience. For "the earth is the Lord's, with all its fullness." ²⁹ Conscience, I say, not your own, but the other's conscience. For why is my liberty judged by another conscience? ³⁰ If I partake with thankfulness, why am I denounced for something I give thanks for? ³¹ Whether therefore you eat or drink, or whatever you do, do all to the glory of God. ³² Give no occasion for stumbling, whether to Jews, to Greeks, or to the assembly of God; ³³ even as I also please all men in all things, not seeking my own profit, but the profit of the many, that they may be saved.

## 11

¹ Be imitators of me, even as I also am of Christ. ² Now I praise you, brothers, that you remember me in all things, and hold firm the traditions, even as I delivered them to you. ³ But I would have you know that the headᶜ of every man is Christ, and the headᵈ of the woman is man, and the headᵉ of Christ is God. ⁴ Every man praying or prophesying, having his head covered, dishonors his head. ⁵ But every woman praying or prophesying with her head uncovered dishonors her head. For it is one and the same thing as if she were shaved. ⁶ For if a woman is not covered, let her hair also be cut off. But if it is shameful for a woman to have her hair cut off or be shaved, let her be covered. ⁷ For a man indeed ought not to have his head covered, because he is the image and glory of God, but the woman is the glory of the man. ⁸ For man is not from woman, but woman from man; ⁹ for man wasn't created for the woman, but woman for the man. ¹⁰ For this cause the woman ought to have authority over her own head, because of the angels. ¹¹ Nevertheless, neither is the woman independent of the man, nor the man independent of the woman, in the Lord. ¹² For as woman came from man, so a man also comes through a woman; but all things are from God. ¹³ Judge for yourselves. Is it appropriate that a woman pray to God unveiled? ¹⁴ Doesn't even nature itself teach you that if a man has long hair, it is a dishonor to him? ¹⁵ But if a woman has long hair, it is a glory to her, for her hair is given to her for a covering. ¹⁶ But if any man seems to be contentious, we have no such custom, neither do God's assemblies. ¹⁷ But in giving you this command I don't praise you, because you come together not for the better but for the worse. ¹⁸ For first of all, when you come together in the assembly, I hear that divisions exist among you, and I partly believe it. ¹⁹ For there also must be factions among you, that those who are approved may be revealed among you. ²⁰ When therefore you assemble yourselves together, it is not the Lord's supper that you eat. ²¹ For in your eating each one takes his own supper first. One is hungry, and another is drunken. ²² What, don't you have houses to eat and to drink in? Or do you despise God's assembly and put them to shame who don't have enough? What shall I tell you? Shall I praise you? In this I don't praise you. ²³ For I received from the Lord that which also I delivered to you, that the Lord Jesus on the night in which he was betrayed took bread. ²⁴ When he had given thanks, he broke it and said, "Take, eat. This is my body, which is broken for you. Do this in memory of me." ²⁵ In the same way he also took the cup after supper, saying, "This cup is the new covenant in my blood. Do this, as often as you drink, in memory of me." ²⁶ For as often as you eat this bread and drink this cup, you proclaim the Lord's death until he comes. ²⁷ Therefore whoever eats this bread or drinks the Lord's cup in a way unworthy of the Lord will be guilty of the body and the blood of the Lord. ²⁸ But let a man examine himself, and so let him eat of the bread and drink of the cup. ²⁹ For he who eats and drinks in an unworthy way eats and drinks judgment to himself if he doesn't discern the Lord's body. ³⁰ For this cause many among you are weak and sickly, and not a few sleep. ³¹ For if we discerned ourselves, we wouldn't be judged. ³² But when we are judged, we are disciplined by the Lord, that we may not be condemned with the world. ³³ Therefore, my brothers, when you come together to eat, wait for one another. ³⁴ But if anyone is hungry, let him eat at home, lest your coming together be for judgment. The rest I will set in order whenever I come.

## 12

¹ Now concerning spiritual things, brothers, I don't want you to be ignorant. ² You know that when you were heathen,ᶠ you were led away to those mute idols, however you might be led. ³ Therefore I make known to you that no man speaking by God's Spirit says, "Jesus is accursed." No one can say, "Jesus is Lord," but by the Holy Spirit. ⁴ Now there are various kinds of gifts, but the same Spirit. ⁵ There are various kinds of service, and the same Lord. ⁶ There are various kinds of workings, but the same God who works all things in all. ⁷ But to each one is given the manifestation of the Spirit for the profit of all. ⁸ For to one is given through the Spirit the word of wisdom, and to another the

---

ᵃ 9:20 NU adds: though I myself am not under the law
* 10:7 Exodus 32:6

ᵇ 10:9 NU reads "the Lord" instead of "Christ".
* 10:26 Psalms 24:1

ᶜ 11:3 or, origin
ᵈ 11:3 or, origin
ᵉ 11:3 or, origin

ᶠ 12:2 or Gentiles

word of knowledge according to the same Spirit, [9] to another faith by the same Spirit, and to another gifts of healings by the same Spirit, [10] and to another workings of miracles, and to another prophecy, and to another discerning of spirits, to another different kinds of languages, and to another the interpretation of languages. [11] But the one and the same Spirit produces all of these, distributing to each one separately as he desires. [12] For as the body is one and has many members, and all the members of the body, being many, are one body; so also is Christ. [13] For in one Spirit we were all baptized into one body, whether Jews or Greeks, whether bond or free; and were all given to drink into one Spirit. [14] For the body is not one member, but many. [15] If the foot would say, "Because I'm not the hand, I'm not part of the body," it is not therefore not part of the body. [16] If the ear would say, "Because I'm not the eye, I'm not part of the body," it's not therefore not part of the body. [17] If the whole body were an eye, where would the hearing be? If the whole were hearing, where would the smelling be? [18] But now God has set the members, each one of them, in the body, just as he desired. [19] If they were all one member, where would the body be? [20] But now they are many members, but one body. [21] The eye can't tell the hand, "I have no need for you," or again the head to the feet, "I have no need for you." [22] No, much rather, those members of the body which seem to be weaker are necessary. [23] Those parts of the body which we think to be less honorable, on those we bestow more abundant honor; and our unpresentable parts have more abundant modesty, [24] while our presentable parts have no such need. But God composed the body together, giving more abundant honor to the inferior part, [25] that there should be no division in the body, but that the members should have the same care for one another. [26] When one member suffers, all the members suffer with it. When one member is honored, all the members rejoice with it. [27] Now you are the body of Christ, and members individually. [28] God has set some in the assembly: first apostles, second prophets, third teachers, then miracle workers, then gifts of healings, helps, governments, and various kinds of languages. [29] Are all apostles? Are all prophets? Are all teachers? Are all miracle workers? [30] Do all have gifts of healings? Do all speak with various languages? Do all interpret? [31] But earnestly desire the best gifts. Moreover, I show a most excellent way to you.

## 13

[1] If I speak with the languages of men and of angels, but don't have love, I have become sounding brass or a clanging cymbal. [2] If I have the gift of prophecy, and know all mysteries and all knowledge, and if I have all faith, so as to remove mountains, but don't have love, I am nothing. [3] If I give away all my goods to feed the poor, and if I give my body to be burned, but don't have love, it profits me nothing. [4] Love is patient and is kind. Love doesn't envy. Love doesn't brag, is not proud, [5] doesn't behave itself inappropriately, doesn't seek its own way, is not provoked, takes no account of evil; [6] doesn't rejoice in unrighteousness, but rejoices with the truth; [7] bears all things, believes all things, hopes all things, and endures all things. [8] Love never fails. But where there are prophecies, they will be done away with. Where there are various languages, they will cease. Where there is knowledge, it will be done away with. [9] For we know in part and we prophesy in part; [10] but when that which is complete has come, then that which is partial will be done away with. [11] When I was a child, I spoke as a child, I felt as a child, I thought as a child. Now that I have become a man, I have put away childish things. [12] For now we see in a mirror, dimly, but then face to face. Now I know in part, but then I will know fully, even as I was also fully known. [13] But now faith, hope, and love remain—these three. The greatest of these is love.

## 14

[1] Follow after love and earnestly desire spiritual gifts, but especially that you may prophesy. [2] For he who speaks in another language speaks not to men, but to God, for no one understands, but in the Spirit he speaks mysteries. [3] But he who prophesies speaks to men for their edification, exhortation, and consolation. [4] He who speaks in another language edifies himself, but he who prophesies edifies the assembly. [5] Now I desire to have you all speak with other languages, but even more that you would prophesy. For he is greater who prophesies than he who speaks with other languages, unless he interprets, that the assembly may be built up. [6] But now, brothers,[a] if I come to you speaking with other languages, what would I profit you unless I speak to you either by way of revelation, or of knowledge, or of prophesying, or of teaching? [7] Even lifeless things that make a sound, whether pipe or harp, if they didn't give a distinction in the sounds, how would it be known what is piped or harped? [8] For if the trumpet gave an uncertain sound, who would prepare himself for war? [9] So also you, unless you

uttered by the tongue words easy to understand, how would it be known what is spoken? For you would be speaking into the air. [10] There are, it may be, so many kinds of languages in the world, and none of them is without meaning. [11] If then I don't know the meaning of the language, I would be to him who speaks a foreigner, and he who speaks would be a foreigner to me. [12] So also you, since you are zealous for spiritual gifts, seek that you may abound to the building up of the assembly. [13] Therefore let him who speaks in another language pray that he may interpret. [14] For if I pray in another language, my spirit prays, but my understanding is unfruitful. [15] What should I do? I will pray with the spirit, and I will pray with the understanding also. I will sing with the spirit, and I will sing with the understanding also. [16] Otherwise, if you bless with the spirit, how will he who fills the place of the unlearned say the "Amen" at your giving of thanks, seeing he doesn't know what you say? [17] For you most certainly give thanks well, but the other person is not built up. [18] I thank my God, I speak with other languages more than you all. [19] However, in the assembly I would rather speak five words with my understanding, that I might instruct others also, than ten thousand words in another language. [20] Brothers, don't be children in thoughts, yet in malice be babies, but in thoughts be mature. [21] In the law it is written, "By men of strange languages and by the lips of strangers I will speak to this people. They won't even listen to me that way, says the Lord."[*] [22] Therefore other languages are for a sign, not to those who believe, but to the unbelieving; but prophesying is for a sign, not to the unbelieving, but to those who believe. [23] If therefore the whole assembly is assembled together and all speak with other languages, and unlearned or unbelieving people come in, won't they say that you are crazy? [24] But if all prophesy, and someone unbelieving or unlearned comes in, he is reproved by all, and he is judged by all. [25] And thus the secrets of his heart are revealed. So he will fall down on his face and worship God, declaring that God is among you indeed. [26] What is it then, brothers? When you come together, each one of you has a psalm, has a teaching, has a revelation, has another language, or has an interpretation. Let all things be done to build each other up. [27] If any man speaks in another language, let there be two, or at the most three, and in turn; and let one interpret. [28] But if there is no interpreter, let him keep silent in the assembly, and let him speak to himself and to God. [29] Let two or three of the prophets speak, and let the others discern. [30] But if a revelation is made to another sitting by, let the first keep silent. [31] For you all can prophesy one by one, that all may learn and all may be exhorted. [32] The spirits of the prophets are subject to the prophets, [33] for God is not a God of confusion but of peace, as in all the assemblies of the saints. [34] Let the wives be quiet in the assemblies, for it has not been permitted for them to be talking except in submission, as the law also says,[*] [35] if they desire to learn anything. "Let them ask their own husbands at home, for it is shameful for a wife to be talking in the assembly." [36] What!? Was it from you that the word of God went out? Or did it come to you alone? [37] If any man thinks himself to be a prophet or spiritual, let him recognize the things which I write to you, that they are the commandment of the Lord. [38] But if anyone is ignorant, let him be ignorant. [39] Therefore, brothers, desire earnestly to prophesy, and don't forbid speaking with other languages. [40] Let all things be done decently and in order.

## 15

[1] Now I declare to you, brothers, the Good News which I preached to you, which also you received, in which you also stand, [2] by which also you are saved, if you hold firmly the word which I preached to you— unless you believed in vain. [3] For I delivered to you first of all that which I also received: that Christ died for our sins according to the Scriptures, [4] that he was buried, that he was raised on the third day according to the Scriptures, [5] and that he appeared to Cephas, then to the twelve. [6] Then he appeared to over five hundred brothers at once, most of whom remain until now, but some have also fallen asleep. [7] Then he appeared to James, then to all the apostles, [8] and last of all, as to the child born at the wrong time, he appeared to me also. [9] For I am the least of the apostles, who is not worthy to be called an apostle, because I persecuted the assembly of God. [10] But by the grace of God I am what I am. His grace which was given to me was not futile, but I worked more than all of them; yet not I, but the grace of God which was with me. [11] Whether then it is I or they, so we preach, and so you believed. [12] Now if Christ is preached, that he has been raised from the dead, how do some among you say that there is no resurrection of the dead? [13] But if there is no resurrection of the dead, neither has Christ been raised. [14] If Christ has not been raised, then our preaching is in vain and your faith also is in vain. [15] Yes, we are also found false witnesses of God, because we testified about God that he raised up

---

[a] *14:6* The word for "brothers" here and where context allows may also be correctly translated "brothers and sisters" or "siblings."

[*] *14:21* Isaiah 28:11-12

[*] 14:34 Deuteronomy 27:9

Christ, whom he didn't raise up if it is true that the dead are not raised. **16** For if the dead aren't raised, neither has Christ been raised. **17** If Christ has not been raised, your faith is vain; you are still in your sins. **18** Then they also who are fallen asleep in Christ have perished. **19** If we have only hoped in Christ in this life, we are of all men most pitiable. **20** But now Christ has been raised from the dead. He became the first fruit of those who are asleep. **21** For since death came by man, the resurrection of the dead also came by man. **22** For as in Adam all die, so also in Christ all will be made alive. **23** But each in his own order: Christ the first fruits, then those who are Christ's at his coming. **24** Then the end comes, when he will deliver up the Kingdom to God the Father, when he will have abolished all rule and all authority and power. **25** For he must reign until he has put all his enemies under his feet. **26** The last enemy that will be abolished is death. **27** For, "He put all things in subjection under his feet."* But when he says, "All things are put in subjection", it is evident that he is excepted who subjected all things to him. **28** When all things have been subjected to him, then the Son will also himself be subjected to him who subjected all things to him, that God may be all in all. **29** Or else what will they do who are baptized for the dead? If the dead aren't raised at all, why then are they baptized for the dead? **30** Why do we also stand in jeopardy every hour? **31** I affirm, by the boasting in you which I have in Christ Jesus our Lord, I die daily. **32** If I fought with animals at Ephesus for human purposes, what does it profit me? If the dead are not raised, then "let's eat and drink, for tomorrow we die."* **33** Don't be deceived! "Evil companionships corrupt good morals." **34** Wake up righteously and don't sin, for some have no knowledge of God. I say this to your shame. **35** But someone will say, "How are the dead raised?" and, "With what kind of body do they come?" **36** You foolish one, that which you yourself sow is not made alive unless it dies. **37** That which you sow, you don't sow the body that will be, but a bare grain, maybe of wheat, or of some other kind. **38** But God gives it a body even as it pleased him, and to each seed a body of its own. **39** All flesh is not the same flesh, but there is one flesh of men, another flesh of animals, another of fish, and another of birds. **40** There are also celestial bodies and terrestrial bodies; but the glory of the celestial differs from that of the terrestrial. **41** There is one glory of the sun, another glory of the moon, and another glory of the stars; for one star differs from another star in glory. **42** So also is the resurrection of the dead. The body is sown perishable; it is raised imperishable. **43** It is sown in dishonor; it is raised in glory. It is sown in weakness; it is raised in power. **44** It is sown a natural body; it is raised a spiritual body. There is a natural body and there is also a spiritual body. **45** So also it is written, "The first man Adam became a living soul."* The last Adam became a life-giving spirit. **46** However, that which is spiritual isn't first, but that which is natural, then that which is spiritual. **47** The first man is of the earth, made of dust. The second man is the Lord from heaven. **48** As is the one made of dust, such are those who are also made of dust; and as is the heavenly, such are they also that are heavenly. **49** As we have borne the image of those made of dust, let's[a] also bear the image of the heavenly. **50** Now I say this, brothers,[b] that flesh and blood can't inherit God's Kingdom; neither does the perishable inherit imperishable. **51** Behold,[c] I tell you a mystery. We will not all sleep, but we will all be changed, **52** in a moment, in the twinkling of an eye, at the last trumpet. For the trumpet will sound and the dead will be raised incorruptible, and we will be changed. **53** For this perishable body must become imperishable, and this mortal must put on immortality. **54** But when this perishable body will have become imperishable, and this mortal will have put on immortality, then what is written will happen: "Death is swallowed up in victory."* **55** "Death, where is your sting? Hades,[d] where is your victory?"* **56** The sting of death is sin, and the power of sin is the law. **57** But thanks be to God, who gives us the victory through our Lord Jesus Christ. **58** Therefore, my beloved brothers, be steadfast, immovable, always abounding in the Lord's work, because you know that your labor is not in vain in the Lord.

## 16

**1** Now concerning the collection for the saints: as I commanded the assemblies of Galatia, you do likewise. **2** On the first day of every week, let each one of you save as he may prosper, that no collections are made when I come. **3** When I arrive, I will send whoever you approve with letters to carry your gracious gift to Jerusalem. **4** If it is appropriate for me to go also, they will go with me. **5** I will come to you when I have passed through Macedonia, for I am passing through Macedonia. **6** But

with you it may be that I will stay with you, or even winter with you, that you may send me on my journey wherever I go. **7** For I do not wish to see you now in passing, but I hope to stay a while with you, if the Lord permits. **8** But I will stay at Ephesus until Pentecost, **9** for a great and effective door has opened to me, and there are many adversaries. **10** Now if Timothy comes, see that he is with you without fear, for he does the work of the Lord, as I also do. **11** Therefore let no one despise him. But set him forward on his journey in peace, that he may come to me; for I expect him with the brothers. **12** Now concerning Apollos the brother, I strongly urged him to come to you with the brothers, but it was not at all his desire to come now; but he will come when he has an opportunity. **13** Watch! Stand firm in the faith! Be courageous! Be strong! **14** Let all that you do be done in love. **15** Now I beg you, brothers—you know the house of Stephanas, that it is the first fruits of Achaia, and that they have set themselves to serve the saints— **16** that you also be in subjection to such, and to everyone who helps in the work and labors. **17** I rejoice at the coming of Stephanas, Fortunatus, and Achaicus; for that which was lacking on your part, they supplied. **18** For they refreshed my spirit and yours. Therefore acknowledge those who are like that. **19** The assemblies of Asia greet you. Aquila and Priscilla greet you warmly in the Lord, together with the assembly that is in their house. **20** All the brothers greet you. Greet one another with a holy kiss. **21** This greeting is by me, Paul, with my own hand. **22** If any man doesn't love the Lord Jesus Christ, let him be cursed.[e] Come, Lord![f] **23** The grace of the Lord Jesus Christ be with you. **24** My love to all of you in Christ Jesus. Amen.

# Paul's Second Letter to the Corinthians

## 1

**1** Paul, an apostle of Christ[g] Jesus through the will of God, and Timothy our brother, to the assembly of God which is at Corinth, with all the saints who are in the whole of Achaia: **2** Grace to you and peace from God our Father and the Lord Jesus Christ. **3** Blessed be the God and Father of our Lord Jesus Christ, the Father of mercies and God of all comfort, **4** who comforts us in all our affliction, that we may be able to comfort those who are in any affliction, through the comfort with which we ourselves are comforted by God. **5** For as the sufferings of Christ abound to us, even so our comfort also abounds through Christ. **6** But if we are afflicted, it is for your comfort and salvation. If we are comforted, it is for your comfort, which produces in you the patient enduring of the same sufferings which we also suffer. **7** Our hope for you is steadfast, knowing that, since you are partakers of the sufferings, so you are also of the comfort. **8** For we don't desire to have you uninformed, brothers,[h] concerning our affliction which happened to us in Asia: that we were weighed down exceedingly, beyond our power, so much that we despaired even of life. **9** Yes, we ourselves have had the sentence of death within ourselves, that we should not trust in ourselves, but in God who raises the dead, **10** who delivered us out of so great a death, and does deliver, on whom we have set our hope that he will also still deliver us, **11** you also helping together on our behalf by your supplication; that, for the gift given to us by means of many, thanks may be given by many persons on your behalf. **12** For our boasting is this: the testimony of our conscience that in holiness and sincerity of God, not in fleshly wisdom but in the grace of God, we behaved ourselves in the world, and more abundantly toward you. **13** For we write no other things to you than what you read or even acknowledge, and I hope you will acknowledge to the end— **14** as also you acknowledged us in part—that we are your boasting, even as you also are ours, in the day of our Lord Jesus. **15** In this confidence, I was determined to come first to you, that you might have a second benefit, **16** and by you to pass into Macedonia, and again from Macedonia to come to you, and to be sent forward by you on my journey to Judea. **17** When I therefore planned this, did I show fickleness? Or the things that I plan, do I plan according to the flesh, that with me there should be the "Yes, yes" and the "No, no?" **18** But as God is faithful, our word toward you was not "Yes and no." **19** For the Son of God, Jesus Christ, who was preached among you by us—by me, Silvanus, and Timothy—was not "Yes and no," but in him is "Yes." **20** For however many are the promises of God, in him is the "Yes." Therefore also through him is the "Amen", to the glory of God through us. **21** Now he who establishes us with you in Christ and anointed us is God, **22** who also sealed us and

---

* 15:27 Psalms 8:6
* 15:32 Isaiah 22:13
* 15:45 Genesis 2:7
[a] *15:49* NU, TR read "we will" instead of "let's"
[b] *15:50* The word for "brothers" here and where

context allows may also be correctly translated "brothers and sisters" or "siblings."
[c] *15:51* "Behold", from "ἰδού", means look at, take notice, observe, see, or gaze at. It is often used as an interjection.

* 15:54 Isaiah 25:8
[d] *15:55* or, Hell
* 15:55 See Hosea 13:14
[e] *16:22* Greek: anathema.
[f] *16:22* Aramaic: Maranatha!
[g] *1:1* "Christ" means "Anointed One".

[h] *1:8* The word for "brothers" here and where context allows may also be correctly translated "brothers and sisters" or "siblings."

gave us the down payment of the Spirit in our hearts. ²³ But I call God for a witness to my soul, that to spare you, I didn't come to Corinth. ²⁴ We don't control your faith, but are fellow workers with you for your joy. For you stand firm in faith.

## 2

¹ But I determined this for myself, that I would not come to you again in sorrow. ² For if I make you grieve, then who will make me glad but he who is made to grieve by me? ³ And I wrote this very thing to you, so that when I came, I wouldn't have sorrow from them of whom I ought to rejoice; having confidence in you all that my joy would be shared by all of you. ⁴ For out of much affliction and anguish of heart I wrote to you with many tears, not that you should be made to grieve, but that you might know the love that I have so abundantly for you. ⁵ But if any has caused sorrow, he has caused sorrow not to me, but in part (that I not press too heavily) to you all. ⁶ This punishment which was inflicted by the many is sufficient for such a one; ⁷ so that, on the contrary, you should rather forgive him and comfort him, lest by any means such a one should be swallowed up with his excessive sorrow. ⁸ Therefore I beg you to confirm your love toward him. ⁹ For to this end I also wrote, that I might know the proof of you, whether you are obedient in all things. ¹⁰ Now I also forgive whomever you forgive anything. For if indeed I have forgiven anything, I have forgiven that one for your sakes in the presence of Christ, ¹¹ that no advantage may be gained over us by Satan, for we are not ignorant of his schemes. ¹² Now when I came to Troas for the Good News of Christ, and when a door was opened to me in the Lord, ¹³ I had no relief for my spirit, because I didn't find Titus my brother, but taking my leave of them, I went out into Macedonia. ¹⁴ Now thanks be to God who always leads us in triumph in Christ, and reveals through us the sweet aroma of his knowledge in every place. ¹⁵ For we are a sweet aroma of Christ to God in those who are saved and in those who perish: ¹⁶ to the one a stench from death to death, to the other a sweet aroma from life to life. Who is sufficient for these things? ¹⁷ For we are not as so many, peddling the word of God. But as of sincerity, but as of God, in the sight of God, we speak in Christ.

## 3

¹ Are we beginning again to commend ourselves? Or do we need, as do some, letters of commendation to you or from you? ² You are our letter, written in our hearts, known and read by all men, ³ being revealed that you are a letter of Christ, served by us, written not with ink, but with the Spirit of the living God; not in tablets of stone, but in tablets that are hearts of flesh. ⁴ Such confidence we have through Christ toward God, ⁵ not that we are sufficient of ourselves to account anything as from ourselves; but our sufficiency is from God, ⁶ who also made us sufficient as servants of a new covenant, not of the letter but of the Spirit. For the letter kills, but the Spirit gives life. ⁷ But if the service of death, written engraved on stones, came with glory, so that the children of Israel could not look steadfastly on the face of Moses for the glory of his face, which was passing away, ⁸ won't service of the Spirit be with much more glory? ⁹ For if the service of condemnation has glory, the service of righteousness exceeds much more in glory. ¹⁰ For most certainly that which has been made glorious has not been made glorious in this respect, by reason of the glory that surpasses. ¹¹ For if that which passes away was with glory, much more that which remains is in glory. ¹² Having therefore such a hope, we use great boldness of speech, ¹³ and not as Moses, who put a veil on his face so that the children of Israel wouldn't look steadfastly on the end of that which was passing away. ¹⁴ But their minds were hardened, for until this very day at the reading of the old covenant the same veil remains, because in Christ it passes away. ¹⁵ But to this day, when Moses is read, a veil lies on their heart. ¹⁶ But whenever someone turns to the Lord, the veil is taken away. ¹⁷ Now the Lord is the Spirit; and where the Spirit of the Lord is, there is liberty. ¹⁸ But we all, with unveiled face seeing the glory of the Lord as in a mirror, are transformed into the same image from glory to glory, even as from the Lord, the Spirit.

## 4

¹ Therefore, seeing we have this ministry, even as we obtained mercy, we don't faint. ² But we have renounced the hidden things of shame, not walking in craftiness nor handling the word of God deceitfully, but by the manifestation of the truth commending ourselves to every man's conscience in the sight of God. ³ Even if our Good News is veiled, it is veiled in those who are dying, ⁴ in whom the god of this world has blinded the minds of the unbelieving, that the light of the Good News of the glory of Christ, who is the image of God, should not dawn on them. ⁵ For we don't preach ourselves, but Christ Jesus as Lord, and ourselves as your servants for Jesus' sake, ⁶ seeing it is God who said, "Light will shine out of darkness,"* who has shone in our hearts to give

the light of the knowledge of the glory of God in the face of Jesus Christ. ⁷ But we have this treasure in clay vessels, that the exceeding greatness of the power may be of God and not from ourselves. ⁸ We are pressed on every side, yet not crushed; perplexed, yet not to despair; ⁹ pursued, yet not forsaken; struck down, yet not destroyed; ¹⁰ always carrying in the body the putting to death of the Lord Jesus, that the life of Jesus may also be revealed in our body. ¹¹ For we who live are always delivered to death for Jesus' sake, that the life also of Jesus may be revealed in our mortal flesh. ¹² So then death works in us, but life in you. ¹³ But having the same spirit of faith, according to that which is written, "I believed, and therefore I spoke."* We also believe, and therefore we also speak, ¹⁴ knowing that he who raised the Lord Jesus will raise us also with Jesus, and will present us with you. ¹⁵ For all things are for your sakes, that the grace, being multiplied through the many, may cause the thanksgiving to abound to the glory of God. ¹⁶ Therefore we don't faint, but though our outward person is decaying, yet our inward person is renewed day by day. ¹⁷ For our light affliction, which is for the moment, works for us more and more exceedingly an eternal weight of glory, ¹⁸ while we don't look at the things which are seen, but at the things which are not seen. For the things which are seen are temporal, but the things which are not seen are eternal.

## 5

¹ For we know that if the earthly house of our tent is dissolved, we have a building from God, a house not made with hands, eternal, in the heavens. ² For most certainly in this we groan, longing to be clothed with our habitation which is from heaven, ³ if indeed being clothed, we will not be found naked. ⁴ For indeed we who are in this tent do groan, being burdened, not that we desire to be unclothed, but that we desire to be clothed, that what is mortal may be swallowed up by life. ⁵ Now he who made us for this very thing is God, who also gave to us the down payment of the Spirit. ⁶ Therefore we are always confident and know that while we are at home in the body, we are absent from the Lord; ⁷ for we walk by faith, not by sight. ⁸ We are courageous, I say, and are willing rather to be absent from the body and to be at home with the Lord. ⁹ Therefore also we make it our aim, whether at home or absent, to be well pleasing to him. ¹⁰ For we must all be revealed before the judgment seat of Christ that each one may receive the things in the body according to what he has done, whether good or bad. ¹¹ Knowing therefore the fear of the Lord, we persuade men, but we are revealed to God, and I hope that we are revealed also in your consciences. ¹² For we are not commending ourselves to you again, but speak as giving you occasion of boasting on our behalf, that you may have something to answer those who boast in appearance and not in heart. ¹³ For if we are beside ourselves, it is for God. Or if we are of sober mind, it is for you. ¹⁴ For the love of Christ compels us; because we judge thus: that one died for all, therefore all died. ¹⁵ He died for all, that those who live should no longer live to themselves, but to him who for their sakes died and rose again. ¹⁶ Therefore we know no one according to the flesh from now on. Even though we have known Christ according to the flesh, yet now we know him so no more. ¹⁷ Therefore if anyone is in Christ, he is a new creation. The old things have passed away. Behold,ᵃ all things have become new. ¹⁸ But all things are of God, who reconciled us to himself through Jesus Christ, and gave to us the ministry of reconciliation; ¹⁹ namely, that God was in Christ reconciling the world to himself, not reckoning to them their trespasses, and having committed to us the word of reconciliation. ²⁰ We are therefore ambassadors on behalf of Christ, as though God were entreating by us: we beg you on behalf of Christ, be reconciled to God. ²¹ For him who knew no sin he made to be sin on our behalf, so that in him we might become the righteousness of God.

## 6

¹ Working together, we entreat also that you do not receive the grace of God in vain. ² For he says, "At an acceptable time I listened to you. In a day of salvation I helped you."* Behold, now is the acceptable time. Behold, now is the day of salvation. ³ We give no occasion of stumbling in anything, that our service may not be blamed, ⁴ but in everything commending ourselves as servants of God: in great endurance, in afflictions, in hardships, in distresses, ⁵ in beatings, in imprisonments, in riots, in labors, in watchings, in fastings, ⁶ in pureness, in knowledge, in perseverance, in kindness, in the Holy Spirit, in sincere love, ⁷ in the word of truth, in the power of God, by the armor of righteousness on the right hand and on the left, ⁸ by glory and dishonor, by evil report and good report, as deceivers and yet true, ⁹ as unknown and yet well known, as dying and behold—we live, as punished and not killed, ¹⁰ sorrowful yet always rejoicing, as poor yet making many rich, as having nothing and yet possessing all things. ¹¹ Our mouth is open to you, Corinthians. Our heart is enlarged. ¹² You are not restricted by us, but

---

* 4:6 Genesis 1:3
* 4:13 Psalms 116:10

ᵃ 5:17 "Behold", from "ἰδοὺ", means look at, take notice,

observe, see, or gaze at. It is often used as an interjection.

* 6:2 Isaiah 49:8

you are restricted by your own affections. [13] Now in return—I speak as to my children—you also open your hearts. [14] Don't be unequally yoked with unbelievers, for what fellowship do righteousness and iniquity have? Or what fellowship does light have with darkness? [15] What agreement does Christ have with Belial? Or what portion does a believer have with an unbeliever? [16] What agreement does a temple of God have with idols? For you are a temple of the living God. Even as God said, "I will dwell in them and walk in them. I will be their God and they will be my people."* [17] Therefore "'Come out from among them, and be separate,' says the Lord. 'Touch no unclean thing. I will receive you.* [18] I will be to you a Father. You will be to me sons and daughters,' says the Lord Almighty."*

## 7

[1] Having therefore these promises, beloved, let's cleanse ourselves from all defilement of flesh and spirit, perfecting holiness in the fear of God. [2] Open your hearts to us. We wronged no one. We corrupted no one. We took advantage of no one. [3] I say this not to condemn you, for I have said before that you are in our hearts to die together and live together. [4] Great is my boldness of speech toward you. Great is my boasting on your behalf. I am filled with comfort. I overflow with joy in all our affliction. [5] For even when we had come into Macedonia, our flesh had no relief, but we were afflicted on every side. Fightings were outside. Fear was inside. [6] Nevertheless, he who comforts the lowly, God, comforted us by the coming of Titus, [7] and not by his coming only, but also by the comfort with which he was comforted in you while he told us of your longing, your mourning, and your zeal for me, so that I rejoiced still more. [8] For though I grieved you with my letter, I do not regret it, though I did regret it. For I see that my letter made you grieve, though just for a while. [9] I now rejoice, not that you were grieved, but that you were grieved to repentance. For you were grieved in a godly way, that you might suffer loss by us in nothing. [10] For godly sorrow produces repentance leading to salvation, which brings no regret. But the sorrow of the world produces death. [11] For behold, this same thing, that you were grieved in a godly way, what earnest care it worked in you. Yes, what defense, indignation, fear, longing, zeal, and vindication! In everything you demonstrated yourselves to be pure in the matter. [12] So although I wrote to you, I wrote not for his cause that did the wrong, nor for his cause that suffered the wrong, but that your earnest care for us might be revealed in you in the sight of God. [13] Therefore we have been comforted. In our comfort we rejoiced the more exceedingly for the joy of Titus, because his spirit has been refreshed by you all. [14] For if in anything I have boasted to him on your behalf, I was not disappointed. But as we spoke all things to you in truth, so our glorying also which I made before Titus was found to be truth. [15] His affection is more abundantly toward you, while he remembers all of your obedience, how with fear and trembling you received him. [16] I rejoice that in everything I am confident concerning you.

## 8

[1] Moreover, brothers, we make known to you the grace of God which has been given in the assemblies of Macedonia, [2] how in a severe ordeal of affliction, the abundance of their joy and their deep poverty abounded to the riches of their generosity. [3] For according to their power, I testify, yes and beyond their power, they gave of their own accord, [4] begging us with much entreaty to receive this grace and the fellowship in the service to the saints. [5] This was not as we had expected, but first they gave their own selves to the Lord, and to us through the will of God. [6] So we urged Titus, that as he had made a beginning before, so he would also complete in you this grace. [7] But as you abound in everything—in faith, utterance, knowledge, all earnestness, and in your love to us—see that you also abound in this grace. [8] I speak not by way of commandment, but as proving through the earnestness of others the sincerity also of your love. [9] For you know the grace of our Lord Jesus Christ, that though he was rich, yet for your sakes he became poor, that you through his poverty might become rich. [10] I give advice in this: it is expedient for you who were the first to start a year ago, not only to do, but also to be willing. [11] But now complete the doing also, that as there was the readiness to be willing, so there may be the completion also out of your ability. [12] For if the readiness is there, it is acceptable according to what you have, not according to what you don't have. [13] For this is not that others may be eased and you distressed, [14] but for equality. Your abundance at this present time supplies their lack, that their abundance also may become a supply for your lack, that there may be equality. [15] As it is written, "He who gathered much had nothing left over, and he who gathered little had no lack."* [16] But thanks be to God, who puts the same earnest care for you into the heart of Titus. [17] For he indeed accepted our exhortation, but

being himself very earnest, he went out to you of his own accord. [18] We have sent together with him the brother whose praise in the Good News is known throughout all the assemblies. [19] Not only so, but he was also appointed by the assemblies to travel with us in this grace, which is served by us to the glory of the Lord himself, and to show our readiness. [20] We are avoiding this, that any man should blame us concerning this abundance which is administered by us. [21] Having regard for honorable things, not only in the sight of the Lord, but also in the sight of men. [22] We have sent with them our brother whom we have many times proved earnest in many things, but now much more earnest, by reason of the great confidence which he has in you. [23] As for Titus, he is my partner and fellow worker for you. As for our brothers, they are the apostles of the assemblies, the glory of Christ. [24] Therefore show the proof of your love to them before the assemblies, and of our boasting on your behalf.

## 9

[1] It is indeed unnecessary for me to write to you concerning the service to the saints, [2] for I know your readiness, of which I boast on your behalf to those of Macedonia, that Achaia has been prepared for the past year. Your zeal has stirred up very many of them. [3] But I have sent the brothers so that our boasting on your behalf may not be in vain in this respect, that, just as I said, you may be prepared, [4] lest by any means, if anyone from Macedonia comes there with me and finds you unprepared, we (to say nothing of you) would be disappointed in this confident boasting. [5] I thought it necessary therefore to entreat the brothers that they would go before to you and arrange ahead of time the generous gift that you promised before, that the same might be ready as a matter of generosity, and not of greediness. [6] Remember this: he who sows sparingly will also reap sparingly. He who sows bountifully will also reap bountifully. [7] Let each man give according as he has determined in his heart, not grudgingly or under compulsion, for God loves a cheerful giver. [8] And God is able to make all grace abound to you, that you, always having all sufficiency in everything, may abound to every good work. [9] As it is written, "He has scattered abroad. He has given to the poor. His righteousness remains forever."* [10] Now may he who supplies seed to the sower and bread for food, supply and multiply your seed for sowing, and increase the fruits of your righteousness, [11] you being enriched in everything for all generosity, which produces thanksgiving to God through us. [12] For this service of giving that you perform not only makes up for lack among the saints, but abounds also through much giving of thanks to God, [13] seeing that through the proof given by this service, they glorify God for the obedience of your confession to the Good News of Christ and for the generosity of your contribution to them and to all, [14] while they themselves also, with supplication on your behalf, yearn for you by reason of the exceeding grace of God in you. [15] Now thanks be to God for his unspeakable gift!

## 10

[1] Now I Paul, myself, entreat you by the humility and gentleness of Christ, I who in your presence am lowly among you, but being absent am bold toward you. [2] Yes, I beg you that I may not, when present, show courage with the confidence with which I intend to be bold against some, who consider us to be walking according to the flesh. [3] For though we walk in the flesh, we don't wage war according to the flesh; [4] for the weapons of our warfare are not of the flesh, but mighty before God to the throwing down of strongholds, [5] throwing down imaginations and every high thing that is exalted against the knowledge of God and bringing every thought into captivity to the obedience of Christ, [6] and being in readiness to avenge all disobedience when your obedience is made full. [7] Do you look at things only as they appear in front of your face? If anyone trusts in himself that he is Christ's, let him consider this again with himself, that even as he is Christ's, so we also are Christ's. [8] For even if I boast somewhat abundantly concerning our authority, which the Lord gave for building you up and not for casting you down, I will not be ashamed, [9] that I may not seem as if I desire to terrify you by my letters. [10] For, "His letters", they say, "are weighty and strong, but his bodily presence is weak, and his speech is despised." [11] Let such a person consider this, that what we are in word by letters when we are absent, such we are also in deed when we are present. [12] For we are not bold to number or compare ourselves with some of those who commend themselves. But they themselves, measuring themselves by themselves, and comparing themselves with themselves, are without understanding. [13] But we will not boast beyond proper limits, but within the boundaries with which God appointed to us, which reach even to you. [14] For we don't stretch ourselves too much, as though we didn't reach to you. For we came even as far as to you with the Good News of Christ, [15] not boasting beyond proper limits in other men's labors, but having hope that as your faith grows, we will be abundantly enlarged by you in our sphere of influence, [16] so as to preach the Good

---

* 6:16 Leviticus 26:12; Jeremiah 32:38; Ezekiel 37:27
* 6:17 Isaiah 52:11; Ezekiel 20:34,41
* 6:18 2 Samuel 7:14; 7:8
* 8:15 Exodus 16:18
* 9:9 Psalms 112:9

News even to the parts beyond you, not to boast in what someone else has already done. [17] But "he who boasts, let him boast in the Lord."* [18] For it isn't he who commends himself who is approved, but whom the Lord commends.

## 11

[1] I wish that you would bear with me in a little foolishness, but indeed you do bear with me. [2] For I am jealous over you with a godly jealousy. For I promised you in marriage to one husband, that I might present you as a pure virgin to Christ. [3] But I am afraid that somehow, as the serpent deceived Eve in his craftiness, so your minds might be corrupted from the simplicity that is in Christ. [4] For if he who comes preaches another Jesus whom we didn't preach, or if you receive a different spirit which you didn't receive, or a different "good news" which you didn't accept, you put up with that well enough. [5] For I reckon that I am not at all behind the very best apostles. [6] But though I am unskilled in speech, yet I am not unskilled in knowledge. No, in every way we have been revealed to you in all things. [7] Or did I commit a sin in humbling myself that you might be exalted, because I preached to you God's Good News free of charge? [8] I robbed other assemblies, taking wages from them that I might serve you. [9] When I was present with you and was in need, I wasn't a burden on anyone, for the brothers, when they came from Macedonia, supplied the measure of my need. In everything I kept myself from being burdensome to you, and I will continue to do so. [10] As the truth of Christ is in me, no one will stop me from this boasting in the regions of Achaia. [11] Why? Because I don't love you? God knows. [12] But what I do, that I will continue to do, that I may cut off opportunity from those who desire an opportunity, that in which they boast, they may be recognized just like us. [13] For such men are false apostles, deceitful workers, masquerading as Christ's apostles. [14] And no wonder, for even Satan masquerades as an angel of light. [15] It is no great thing therefore if his servants also masquerade as servants of righteousness, whose end will be according to their works. [16] I say again, let no one think me foolish. But if so, yet receive me as foolish, that I also may boast a little. [17] That which I speak, I don't speak according to the Lord, but as in foolishness, in this confidence of boasting. [18] Seeing that many boast after the flesh, I will also boast. [19] For you bear with the foolish gladly, being wise. [20] For you bear with a man if he brings you into bondage, if he devours you, if he takes you captive, if he exalts himself, or if he strikes you on the face. [21] To my shame, I speak as though we had been weak. Yet in whatever way anyone is bold (I speak in foolishness), I am bold also. [22] Are they Hebrews? So am I. Are they Israelites? So am I. Are they the offspring[a] of Abraham? So am I. [23] Are they servants of Christ? (I speak as one beside himself.) I am more so: in labors more abundantly, in prisons more abundantly, in stripes above measure, and in deaths often. [24] Five times I received forty stripes minus one from the Jews. [25] Three times I was beaten with rods. Once I was stoned. Three times I suffered shipwreck. I have been a night and a day in the deep. [26] I have been in travels often, perils of rivers, perils of robbers, perils from my countrymen, perils from the Gentiles, perils in the city, perils in the wilderness, perils in the sea, perils among false brothers; [27] in labor and travail, in watchings often, in hunger and thirst, in fastings often, and in cold and nakedness. [28] Besides those things that are outside, there is that which presses on me daily: anxiety for all the assemblies. [29] Who is weak, and I am not weak? Who is caused to stumble, and I don't burn with indignation? [30] If I must boast, I will boast of the things that concern my weakness. [31] The God and Father of the Lord Jesus Christ, he who is blessed forever more, knows that I don't lie. [32] In Damascus the governor under King Aretas guarded the Damascenes' city, desiring to arrest me. [33] I was let down in a basket through a window by the wall, and escaped his hands.

## 12

[1] It is doubtless not profitable for me to boast, but I will come to visions and revelations of the Lord. [2] I know a man in Christ who was caught up into the third heaven fourteen years ago—whether in the body, I don't know, or whether out of the body, I don't know; God knows. [3] I know such a man (whether in the body, or outside of the body, I don't know; God knows), [4] how he was caught up into Paradise and heard unspeakable words, which it is not lawful for a man to utter. [5] On behalf of such a one I will boast, but on my own behalf I will not boast, except in my weaknesses. [6] For if I would desire to boast, I will not be foolish; for I will speak the truth. But I refrain, so that no man may think more of me than that which he sees in me or hears from me. [7] By reason of the exceeding greatness of the revelations, that I should not be exalted excessively, a thorn in the flesh was given to me: a messenger of Satan to torment me, that I should not be exalted excessively. [8] Concerning

this thing, I begged the Lord three times that it might depart from me. [9] He has said to me, "My grace is sufficient for you, for my power is made perfect in weakness." Most gladly therefore I will rather glory in my weaknesses, that the power of Christ may rest on me. [10] Therefore I take pleasure in weaknesses, in injuries, in necessities, in persecutions, and in distresses, for Christ's sake. For when I am weak, then am I strong. [11] I have become foolish in boasting. You compelled me, for I ought to have been commended by you, for I am in no way inferior to the very best apostles, though I am nothing. [12] Truly the signs of an apostle were worked among you in all perseverance, in signs and wonders and mighty works. [13] For what is there in which you were made inferior to the rest of the assemblies, unless it is that I myself was not a burden to you? Forgive me this wrong! [14] Behold, this is the third time I am ready to come to you, and I will not be a burden to you; for I seek not your possessions, but you. For the children ought not to save up for the parents, but the parents for the children. [15] I will most gladly spend and be spent for your souls. If I love you more abundantly, am I loved the less? [16] Even so, I myself didn't burden you. But you might say that being crafty, I caught you with deception. [17] Did I take advantage of you by anyone of those whom I have sent to you? [18] I exhorted Titus, and I sent the brother with him. Did Titus take any advantage of you? Didn't we walk in the same spirit? Didn't we walk in the same steps? [19] Again, do you think that we are excusing ourselves to you? In the sight of God we speak in Christ. But all things, beloved, are for your edifying. [20] For I am afraid that perhaps when I come, I might find you not the way I want to, and that I might be found by you as you don't desire, that perhaps there would be strife, jealousy, outbursts of anger, factions, slander, whisperings, proud thoughts, or riots, [21] that again when I come my God would humble me before you, and I would mourn for many of those who have sinned before now, and not repented of the uncleanness, sexual immorality, and lustfulness which they committed.

## 13

[1] This is the third time I am coming to you. "At the mouth of two or three witnesses shall every word be established."* [2] I have warned previously, and I warn again, as when I was present the second time, so now, being absent, I write to those who have sinned before now and to all the rest that if I come again, I will not spare, [3] seeing that you seek a proof of Christ who speaks in me who is not weak, but is powerful in you. [4] For he was crucified through weakness, yet he lives through the power of God. For we also are weak in him, but we will live with him through the power of God toward you. [5] Examine your own selves, whether you are in the faith. Test your own selves. Or don't you know about your own selves, that Jesus Christ is in you?—unless indeed you are disqualified. [6] But I hope that you will know that we aren't disqualified. [7] Now I pray to God that you do no evil; not that we may appear approved, but that you may do that which is honorable, though we may seem to have failed. [8] For we can do nothing against the truth, but for the truth. [9] For we rejoice when we are weak and you are strong. We also pray for this: your becoming perfect. [10] For this cause I write these things while absent, that I may not deal sharply when present, according to the authority which the Lord gave me for building up and not for tearing down. [11] Finally, brothers, rejoice! Be perfected. Be comforted. Be of the same mind. Live in peace, and the God of love and peace will be with you. [12] Greet one another with a holy kiss. [13] All the saints greet you. [14] The grace of the Lord Jesus Christ, God's love, and the fellowship of the Holy Spirit be with you all. Amen.

# Paul's Letter to the Galatians
## 1

[1] Paul, an apostle—not from men, nor through man, but through Jesus Christ,[b] and God the Father, who raised him from the dead— [2] and all the brothers[c] who are with me, to the assemblies of Galatia: [3] Grace to you and peace from God the Father and our Lord Jesus Christ, [4] who gave himself for our sins, that he might deliver us out of this present evil age, according to the will of our God and Father— [5] to whom be the glory forever and ever. Amen. [6] I marvel that you are so quickly deserting him who called you in the grace of Christ to a different "good news", [7] but there isn't another "good news." Only there are some who trouble you and want to pervert the Good News of Christ. [8] But even though we, or an angel from heaven, should preach to you any "good news" other than that which we preached to you, let him be cursed. [9] As we have said before, so I now say again: if any man preaches to you any "good news" other than that which you received, let him be cursed. [10] For am I now seeking the favor of men, or of God? Or am I striving

---

* 10:17 Jeremiah 9:24
[a] 11:22 or, seed
* 13:1 Deuteronomy 19:15

[b] 1:1 "Christ" means "Anointed One".

[c] 1:2 The word for "brothers" here and where context allows may also be correctly translated

"brothers and sisters" or "siblings."

to please men? For if I were still pleasing men, I wouldn't be a servant of Christ. [11] But I make known to you, brothers, concerning the Good News which was preached by me, that it is not according to man. [12] For I didn't receive it from man, nor was I taught it, but it came to me through revelation of Jesus Christ. [13] For you have heard of my way of living in time past in the Jews' religion, how that beyond measure I persecuted the assembly of God and ravaged it. [14] I advanced in the Jews' religion beyond many of my own age among my countrymen, being more exceedingly zealous for the traditions of my fathers. [15] But when it was the good pleasure of God, who separated me from my mother's womb and called me through his grace, [16] to reveal his Son in me, that I might preach him among the Gentiles, I didn't immediately confer with flesh and blood, [17] nor did I go up to Jerusalem to those who were apostles before me, but I went away into Arabia. Then I returned to Damascus. [18] Then after three years I went up to Jerusalem to visit Peter, and stayed with him fifteen days. [19] But of the other apostles I saw no one except James, the Lord's brother. [20] Now about the things which I write to you, behold,[a] before God, I'm not lying. [21] Then I came to the regions of Syria and Cilicia. [22] I was still unknown by face to the assemblies of Judea which were in Christ, [23] but they only heard, "He who once persecuted us now preaches the faith that he once tried to destroy." [24] So they glorified God in me.

## 2

[1] Then after a period of fourteen years I went up again to Jerusalem with Barnabas, taking Titus also with me. [2] I went up by revelation, and I laid before them the Good News which I preach among the Gentiles, but privately before those who were respected, for fear that I might be running, or had run, in vain. [3] But not even Titus, who was with me, being a Greek, was compelled to be circumcised. [4] This was because of the false brothers secretly brought in, who stole in to spy out our liberty which we have in Christ Jesus, that they might bring us into bondage, [5] to whom we gave no place in the way of subjection, not for an hour, that the truth of the Good News might continue with you. [6] But from those who were reputed to be important—whatever they were, it makes no difference to me; God doesn't show partiality to man—they, I say, who were respected imparted nothing to me, [7] but to the contrary, when they saw that I had been entrusted with the Good News for the uncircumcised, even as Peter with the Good News for the circumcised— [8] for he who worked through Peter in the apostleship with the circumcised also worked through me with the Gentiles— [9] and when they perceived the grace that was given to me, James and Cephas and John, those who were reputed to be pillars, gave to Barnabas and me the right hand of fellowship, that we should go to the Gentiles, and they to the circumcision. [10] They only asked us to remember the poor—which very thing I was also zealous to do. [11] But when Peter came to Antioch, I resisted him to his face, because he stood condemned. [12] For before some people came from James, he ate with the Gentiles. But when they came, he drew back and separated himself, fearing those who were of the circumcision. [13] And the rest of the Jews joined him in his hypocrisy, so that even Barnabas was carried away with their hypocrisy. [14] But when I saw that they didn't walk uprightly according to the truth of the Good News, I said to Peter before them all, "If you, being a Jew, live as the Gentiles do, and not as the Jews do, why do you compel the Gentiles to live as the Jews do? [15] "We, being Jews by nature and not Gentile sinners, [16] yet knowing that a man is not justified by the works of the law but through faith in Jesus Christ, even we believed in Christ Jesus, that we might be justified by faith in Christ and not by the works of the law, because no flesh will be justified by the works of the law. [17] But if while we sought to be justified in Christ, we ourselves also were found sinners, is Christ a servant of sin? Certainly not! [18] For if I build up again those things which I destroyed, I prove myself a lawbreaker. [19] For I through the law died to the law, that I might live to God. [20] I have been crucified with Christ, and it is no longer I who live, but Christ lives in me. That life which I now live in the flesh, I live by faith in the Son of God, who loved me and gave himself up for me. [21] I don't reject the grace of God. For if righteousness is through the law, then Christ died for nothing!"

## 3

[1] Foolish Galatians, who has bewitched you not to obey the truth, before whose eyes Jesus Christ was openly portrayed among you as crucified? [2] I just want to learn this from you: Did you receive the Spirit by the works of the law, or by hearing of faith? [3] Are you so foolish? Having begun in the Spirit, are you now completed in the flesh? [4] Did you suffer so many things in vain, if it is indeed in vain? [5] He therefore who supplies the Spirit to you and does miracles among you, does he do it by the works of the law, or by hearing of faith? [6] Even so, Abraham "believed God, and it was counted to him for righteousness."[*] [7] Know therefore that those who are of faith are children of Abraham. [8] The Scripture, foreseeing that God would justify the Gentiles by faith, preached the Good News beforehand to Abraham, saying, "In you all the nations will be blessed."[*] [9] So then, those who are of faith are blessed with the faithful Abraham. [10] For as many as are of the works of the law are under a curse. For it is written, "Cursed is everyone who doesn't continue in all things that are written in the book of the law, to do them."[*] [11] Now that no man is justified by the law before God is evident, for, "The righteous will live by faith."[*] [12] The law is not of faith, but, "The man who does them will live by them."[*] [13] Christ redeemed us from the curse of the law, having become a curse for us. For it is written, "Cursed is everyone who hangs on a tree,"[*] [14] that the blessing of Abraham might come on the Gentiles through Christ Jesus, that we might receive the promise of the Spirit through faith. [15] Brothers, speaking of human terms, though it is only a man's covenant, yet when it has been confirmed, no one makes it void or adds to it. [16] Now the promises were spoken to Abraham and to his offspring.[b] He doesn't say, "To descendants[c]", as of many, but as of one, "To your offspring",[*] which is Christ. [17] Now I say this: A covenant confirmed beforehand by God in Christ, the law, which came four hundred thirty years after, does not annul, so as to make the promise of no effect. [18] For if the inheritance is of the law, it is no more of promise; but God has granted it to Abraham by promise. [19] Then why is there the law? It was added because of transgressions, until the offspring should come to whom the promise has been made. It was ordained through angels by the hand of a mediator. [20] Now a mediator is not between one, but God is one. [21] Is the law then against the promises of God? Certainly not! For if there had been a law given which could make alive, most certainly righteousness would have been of the law. [22] But the Scripture imprisoned all things under sin, that the promise by faith in Jesus Christ might be given to those who believe. [23] But before faith came, we were kept in custody under the law, confined for the faith which should afterwards be revealed. [24] So that the law has become our tutor to bring us to Christ, that we might be justified by faith. [25] But now that faith has come, we are no longer under a tutor. [26] For you are all children of God, through faith in Christ Jesus. [27] For as many of you as were baptized into Christ have put on Christ. [28] There is neither Jew nor Greek, there is neither slave nor free man, there is neither male nor female; for you are all one in Christ Jesus. [29] If you are Christ's, then you are Abraham's offspring and heirs according to promise.

## 4

[1] But I say that so long as the heir is a child, he is no different from a bondservant, though he is lord of all, [2] but is under guardians and stewards until the day appointed by the father. [3] So we also, when we were children, were held in bondage under the elemental principles of the world. [4] But when the fullness of the time came, God sent out his Son, born to a woman, born under the law, [5] that he might redeem those who were under the law, that we might receive the adoption as children. [6] And because you are children, God sent out the Spirit of his Son into your hearts, crying, "Abba,[d] Father!" [7] So you are no longer a bondservant, but a son; and if a son, then an heir of God through Christ. [8] However at that time, not knowing God, you were in bondage to those who by nature are not gods. [9] But now that you have come to know God, or rather to be known by God, why do you turn back again to the weak and miserable elemental principles, to which you desire to be in bondage all over again? [10] You observe days, months, seasons, and years. [11] I am afraid for you, that I might have wasted my labor for you. [12] I beg you, brothers, become as I am, for I also have become as you are. You did me no wrong, [13] but you know that because of weakness in the flesh I preached the Good News to you the first time. [14] That which was a temptation to you in my flesh, you didn't despise nor reject; but you received me as an angel of God, even as Christ Jesus. [15] What was the blessing you enjoyed? For I testify to you that, if possible, you would have plucked out your eyes and given them to me. [16] So then, have I become your enemy by telling you the truth? [17] They zealously seek you in no good way. No, they desire to alienate you, that you may seek them. [18] But it is always good to be zealous in a good cause, and not only when I am present with you. [19] My little children, of whom I am again in travail until Christ is formed in you— [20] but I could wish to be present with you now, and to change my tone, for I am perplexed about you. [21] Tell me, you that desire to be under the law,

---

[a] *1:20* "Behold", from "ἰδού", means look at, take notice, observe, see, or gaze at. It is often used as an interjection.
[*] 3:6 Genesis 15:6

[*] 3:8 Genesis 12:3; 18:18; 22:18
[*] 3:10 Deuteronomy 27:26
[*] 3:11 Habakkuk 2:4
[*] 3:12 Leviticus 18:5

[*] 3:13 Deuteronomy 21:23
[b] *3:16* or, seed
[c] *3:16* or, seeds
[*] 3:16 Genesis 12:7; 13:15; 24:7

[d] *4:6* Abba is a Greek spelling for the Aramaic word for "Father" or "Daddy" used in a familiar, respectful, and loving way.

don't you listen to the law? [22] For it is written that Abraham had two sons, one by the servant, and one by the free woman. [23] However, the son by the servant was born according to the flesh, but the son by the free woman was born through promise. [24] These things contain an allegory, for these are two covenants. One is from Mount Sinai, bearing children to bondage, which is Hagar. [25] For this Hagar is Mount Sinai in Arabia, and answers to the Jerusalem that exists now, for she is in bondage with her children. [26] But the Jerusalem that is above is free, which is the mother of us all. [27] For it is written, "Rejoice, you barren who don't bear. Break out and shout, you who don't travail. For the desolate women have more children than her who has a husband." * [28] Now we, brothers, as Isaac was, are children of promise. [29] But as then, he who was born according to the flesh persecuted him who was born according to the Spirit, so also it is now. [30] However, what does the Scripture say? "Throw out the servant and her son, for the son of the servant will not inherit with the son of the free woman."* [31] So then, brothers, we are not children of a servant, but of the free woman.

## 5

[1] Stand firm therefore in the liberty by which Christ has made us free, and don't be entangled again with a yoke of bondage. [2] Behold, I, Paul, tell you that if you receive circumcision, Christ will profit you nothing. [3] Yes, I testify again to every man who receives circumcision that he is a debtor to do the whole law. [4] You are alienated from Christ, you who desire to be justified by the law. You have fallen away from grace. [5] For we through the Spirit, by faith wait for the hope of righteousness. [6] For in Christ Jesus neither circumcision nor uncircumcision amounts to anything, but faith working through love. [7] You were running well! Who interfered with you that you should not obey the truth? [8] This persuasion is not from him who calls you. [9] A little yeast grows through the whole lump. [10] I have confidence toward you in the Lord that you will think no other way. But he who troubles you will bear his judgment, whoever he is. [11] But I, brothers, if I still preach circumcision, why am I still persecuted? Then the stumbling block of the cross has been removed. [12] I wish that those who disturb you would cut themselves off. [13] For you, brothers, were called for freedom. Only don't use your freedom as an opportunity for the flesh, but through love be servants to one another. [14] For the whole law is fulfilled in one word, in this: "You shall love your neighbor as yourself."* [15] But if you bite and devour one another, be careful that you don't consume one another. [16] But I say, walk by the Spirit, and you won't fulfill the lust of the flesh. [17] For the flesh lusts against the Spirit, and the Spirit against the flesh; and these are contrary to one another, that you may not do the things that you desire. [18] But if you are led by the Spirit, you are not under the law. [19] Now the deeds of the flesh are obvious, which are: adultery, sexual immorality, uncleanness, lustfulness, [20] idolatry, sorcery, hatred, strife, jealousies, outbursts of anger, rivalries, divisions, heresies, [21] envy, murders, drunkenness, orgies, and things like these; of which I forewarn you, even as I also forewarned you, that those who practice such things will not inherit God's Kingdom. [22] But the fruit of the Spirit is love, joy, peace, patience, kindness, goodness, faith,[a] [23] gentleness, and self-control. Against such things there is no law. [24] Those who belong to Christ have crucified the flesh with its passions and lusts. [25] If we live by the Spirit, let's also walk by the Spirit. [26] Let's not become conceited, provoking one another, and envying one another.

## 6

[1] Brothers, even if a man is caught in some fault, you who are spiritual must restore such a one in a spirit of gentleness, looking to yourself so that you also aren't tempted. [2] Bear one another's burdens, and so fulfill the law of Christ. [3] For if a man thinks himself to be something when he is nothing, he deceives himself. [4] But let each man examine his own work, and then he will have reason to boast in himself, and not in someone else. [5] For each man will bear his own burden. [6] But let him who is taught in the word share all good things with him who teaches. [7] Don't be deceived. God is not mocked, for whatever a man sows, that he will also reap. [8] For he who sows to his own flesh will from the flesh reap corruption. But he who sows to the Spirit will from the Spirit reap eternal life. [9] Let's not be weary in doing good, for we will reap in due season if we don't give up. [10] So then, as we have opportunity, let's do what is good toward all men, and especially toward those who are of the household of the faith. [11] See with what large letters I write to you with my own hand. [12] As many as desire to make a good impression in the flesh compel you to be circumcised, just so they may not be persecuted for the cross of Christ. [13] For even they who receive circumcision don't keep the law themselves, but they desire to have you circumcised, so that they may boast in your flesh. [14] But far be it from me to boast except in the cross of our Lord Jesus Christ, through which the world has been crucified to me, and I to the world. [15] For in Christ Jesus neither is circumcision anything, nor uncircumcision, but a new creation. [16] As many as walk by this rule, peace and mercy be on them, and on God's Israel. [17] From now on, let no one cause me any trouble, for I bear the marks of the Lord Jesus branded on my body. [18] The grace of our Lord Jesus Christ be with your spirit, brothers. Amen.

# Paul's Letter to the Ephesians
## 1

[1] Paul, an apostle of Christ[b] Jesus through the will of God, to the saints who are at Ephesus, and the faithful in Christ Jesus: [2] Grace to you and peace from God our Father and the Lord Jesus Christ. [3] Blessed be the God and Father of our Lord Jesus Christ, who has blessed us with every spiritual blessing in the heavenly places in Christ, [4] even as he chose us in him before the foundation of the world, that we would be holy and without defect before him in love, [5] having predestined us for adoption as children through Jesus Christ to himself, according to the good pleasure of his desire, [6] to the praise of the glory of his grace, by which he freely gave us favor in the Beloved. [7] In him we have our redemption through his blood, the forgiveness of our trespasses, according to the riches of his grace [8] which he made to abound toward us in all wisdom and prudence, [9] making known to us the mystery of his will, according to his good pleasure which he purposed in him [10] to an administration of the fullness of the times, to sum up all things in Christ, the things in the heavens and the things on the earth, in him. [11] We were also assigned an inheritance in him, having been foreordained according to the purpose of him who does all things after the counsel of his will, [12] to the end that we should be to the praise of his glory, we who had before hoped in Christ. [13] In him you also, having heard the word of the truth, the Good News of your salvation—in whom, having also believed, you were sealed with the promised Holy Spirit, [14] who is a pledge of our inheritance, to the redemption of God's own possession, to the praise of his glory. [15] For this cause I also, having heard of the faith in the Lord Jesus which is among you and the love which you have toward all the saints, [16] don't cease to give thanks for you, making mention of you in my prayers, [17] that the God of our Lord Jesus Christ, the Father of glory, may give to you a spirit of wisdom and revelation in the knowledge of him, [18] having the eyes of your hearts[c] enlightened, that you may know what is the hope of his calling, and what are the riches of the glory of his inheritance in the saints, [19] and what is the exceeding greatness of his power toward us who believe, according to that working of the strength of his might [20] which he worked in Christ when he raised him from the dead and made him to sit at his right hand in the heavenly places, [21] far above all rule, authority, power, dominion, and every name that is named, not only in this age, but also in that which is to come. [22] He put all things in subjection under his feet, and gave him to be head over all things for the assembly, [23] which is his body, the fullness of him who fills all in all.

## 2

[1] You were made alive when you were dead in transgressions and sins, [2] in which you once walked according to the course of this world, according to the prince of the power of the air, the spirit who now works in the children of disobedience. [3] We also all once lived among them in the lusts of our flesh, doing the desires of the flesh and of the mind, and were by nature children of wrath, even as the rest. [4] But God, being rich in mercy, for his great love with which he loved us, [5] even when we were dead through our trespasses, made us alive together with Christ— by grace you have been saved— [6] and raised us up with him, and made us to sit with him in the heavenly places in Christ Jesus, [7] that in the ages to come he might show the exceeding riches of his grace in kindness toward us in Christ Jesus; [8] for by grace you have been saved through faith, and that not of yourselves; it is the gift of God, [9] not of works, that no one would boast. [10] For we are his workmanship, created in Christ Jesus for good works, which God prepared before that we would walk in them. [11] Therefore remember that once you, the Gentiles in the flesh, who are called "uncircumcision" by that which is called "circumcision" (in the flesh, made by hands), [12] that you were at that time separate from Christ, alienated from the commonwealth of Israel, and strangers from the covenants of the promise, having no hope and without God in the world. [13] But now in Christ Jesus you who once were far off are made near in the blood of Christ. [14] For he is our peace, who made both one, and broke down the middle wall of separation, [15] having abolished in his flesh the hostility, the law of commandments contained in ordinances, that he might create in himself one new man

---

* 4:27 Isaiah 54:1
* 4:30 Genesis 21:10
* 5:14 Leviticus 19:18

[a] 5:22 or, faithfulness
[b] 1:1 "Christ" means "Anointed One".

[c] 1:18 TR reads "understanding" instead of "hearts"

of the two, making peace, [16] and might reconcile them both in one body to God through the cross, having killed the hostility through it. [17] He came and preached peace to you who were far off and to those who were near. [18] For through him we both have our access in one Spirit to the Father. [19] So then you are no longer strangers and foreigners, but you are fellow citizens with the saints and of the household of God, [20] being built on the foundation of the apostles and prophets, Christ Jesus himself being the chief cornerstone; [21] in whom the whole building, fitted together, grows into a holy temple in the Lord; [22] in whom you also are built together for a habitation of God in the Spirit.

## 3

[1] For this cause I, Paul, am the prisoner of Christ Jesus on behalf of you Gentiles, [2] if it is so that you have heard of the administration of that grace of God which was given me toward you, [3] how that by revelation the mystery was made known to me, as I wrote before in few words, [4] by which, when you read, you can perceive my understanding in the mystery of Christ, [5] which in other generations was not made known to the children of men, as it has now been revealed to his holy apostles and prophets in the Spirit, [6] that the Gentiles are fellow heirs and fellow members of the body, and fellow partakers of his promise in Christ Jesus through the Good News, [7] of which I was made a servant according to the gift of that grace of God which was given me according to the working of his power. [8] To me, the very least of all saints, was this grace given, to preach to the Gentiles the unsearchable riches of Christ, [9] and to make all men see what is the administration[a] of the mystery which for ages has been hidden in God, who created all things through Jesus Christ, [10] to the intent that now through the assembly the manifold wisdom of God might be made known to the principalities and the powers in the heavenly places, [11] according to the eternal purpose which he accomplished in Christ Jesus our Lord. [12] In him we have boldness and access in confidence through our faith in him. [13] Therefore I ask that you may not lose heart at my troubles for you, which are your glory. [14] For this cause, I bow my knees to the Father of our Lord Jesus Christ, [15] from whom every family in heaven and on earth is named, [16] that he would grant you, according to the riches of his glory, that you may be strengthened with power through his Spirit in the inner person, [17] that Christ may dwell in your hearts through faith, to the end that you, being rooted and grounded in love, [18] may be strengthened to comprehend with all the saints what is the width and length and height and depth, [19] and to know Christ's love which surpasses knowledge, that you may be filled with all the fullness of God. [20] Now to him who is able to do exceedingly abundantly above all that we ask or think, according to the power that works in us, [21] to him be the glory in the assembly and in Christ Jesus to all generations, forever and ever. Amen.

## 4

[1] I therefore, the prisoner in the Lord, beg you to walk worthily of the calling with which you were called, [2] with all lowliness and humility, with patience, bearing with one another in love, [3] being eager to keep the unity of the Spirit in the bond of peace. [4] There is one body and one Spirit, even as you also were called in one hope of your calling, [5] one Lord, one faith, one baptism, [6] one God and Father of all, who is over all and through all and in us all. [7] But to each one of us, the grace was given according to the measure of the gift of Christ. [8] Therefore he says, "When he ascended on high, he led captivity captive, and gave gifts to people."[*] [9] Now this, "He ascended", what is it but that he also first descended into the lower parts of the earth? [10] He who descended is the one who also ascended far above all the heavens, that he might fill all things. [11] He gave some to be apostles; and some, prophets; and some, evangelists; and some, shepherds[b] and teachers; [12] for the perfecting of the saints, to the work of serving, to the building up of the body of Christ, [13] until we all attain to the unity of the faith and of the knowledge of the Son of God, to a full grown man, to the measure of the stature of the fullness of Christ, [14] that we may no longer be children, tossed back and forth and carried about with every wind of doctrine, by the trickery of men, in craftiness, after the wiles of error; [15] but speaking truth in love, we may grow up in all things into him who is the head, Christ, [16] from whom all the body, being fitted and knit together through that which every joint supplies, according to the working in measure of each individual part, makes the body increase to the building up of itself in love. [17] This I say therefore, and testify in the Lord, that you no longer walk as the rest of the Gentiles also walk, in the futility of their mind, [18] being darkened in their understanding, alienated from the life of God because of the ignorance that is in them, because of the hardening of their hearts. [19] They, having become callous, gave themselves up to lust, to work all uncleanness with greediness. [20] But you didn't learn Christ that way, [21] if indeed you heard him and were taught in him, even as

truth is in Jesus: [22] that you put away, as concerning your former way of life, the old man that grows corrupt after the lusts of deceit, [23] and that you be renewed in the spirit of your mind, [24] and put on the new man, who in the likeness of God has been created in righteousness and holiness of truth. [25] Therefore, putting away falsehood, speak truth each one with his neighbor, for we are members of one another. [26] "Be angry, and don't sin."[*] Don't let the sun go down on your wrath, [27] and don't give place[c] to the devil. [28] Let him who stole steal no more; but rather let him labor, producing with his hands something that is good, that he may have something to give to him who has need. [29] Let no corrupt speech proceed out of your mouth, but only what is good for building others up as the need may be, that it may give grace to those who hear. [30] Don't grieve the Holy Spirit of God, in whom you were sealed for the day of redemption. [31] Let all bitterness, wrath, anger, outcry, and slander be put away from you, with all malice. [32] And be kind to one another, tender hearted, forgiving each other, just as God also in Christ forgave you.

## 5

[1] Be therefore imitators of God, as beloved children. [2] Walk in love, even as Christ also loved us and gave himself up for us, an offering and a sacrifice to God for a sweet-smelling fragrance. [3] But sexual immorality, and all uncleanness or covetousness, let it not even be mentioned among you, as becomes saints; [4] nor filthiness, nor foolish talking, nor jesting, which are not appropriate, but rather giving of thanks. [5] Know this for sure, that no sexually immoral person, nor unclean person, nor covetous man (who is an idolater), has any inheritance in the Kingdom of Christ and God. [6] Let no one deceive you with empty words, for because of these things the wrath of God comes on the children of disobedience. [7] Therefore don't be partakers with them. [8] For you were once darkness, but are now light in the Lord. Walk as children of light, [9] for the fruit of the Spirit is in all goodness and righteousness and truth, [10] proving what is well pleasing to the Lord. [11] Have no fellowship with the unfruitful deeds of darkness, but rather even reprove them. [12] For it is a shame even to speak of the things which are done by them in secret. [13] But all things, when they are reproved, are revealed by the light, for everything that reveals is light. [14] Therefore he says, "Awake, you who sleep, and arise from the dead, and Christ will shine on you." [15] Therefore watch carefully how you walk, not as unwise, but as wise, [16] redeeming the time, because the days are evil. [17] Therefore, don't be foolish, but understand what the will of the Lord is. [18] Don't be drunken with wine, in which is dissipation, but be filled with the Spirit, [19] speaking to one another in psalms, hymns, and spiritual songs; singing and making melody in your heart to the Lord; [20] giving thanks always concerning all things in the name of our Lord Jesus Christ to God, even the Father; [21] subjecting yourselves to one another in the fear of Christ. [22] Wives, be subject to your own husbands, as to the Lord. [23] For the husband is the head of the wife, as Christ also is the head of the assembly, being himself the savior of the body. [24] But as the assembly is subject to Christ, so let the wives also be to their own husbands in everything. [25] Husbands, love your wives, even as Christ also loved the assembly and gave himself up for her, [26] that he might sanctify her, having cleansed her by the washing of water with the word, [27] that he might present the assembly to himself gloriously, not having spot or wrinkle or any such thing, but that she should be holy and without defect. [28] Even so husbands also ought to love their own wives as their own bodies. He who loves his own wife loves himself. [29] For no man ever hated his own flesh, but nourishes and cherishes it, even as the Lord also does the assembly, [30] because we are members of his body, of his flesh and bones. [31] "For this cause a man will leave his father and mother and will be joined to his wife. Then the two will become one flesh."[*] [32] This mystery is great, but I speak concerning Christ and the assembly. [33] Nevertheless each of you must also love his own wife even as himself; and let the wife see that she respects her husband.

## 6

[1] Children, obey your parents in the Lord, for this is right. [2] "Honor your father and mother," which is the first commandment with a promise: [3] "that it may be well with you, and you may live long on the earth."[*] [4] You fathers, don't provoke your children to wrath, but nurture them in the discipline and instruction of the Lord. [5] Servants, be obedient to those who according to the flesh are your masters, with fear and trembling, in singleness of your heart, as to Christ, [6] not in the way of service only when eyes are on you, as men pleasers, but as servants of Christ, doing the will of God from the heart, [7] with good will doing service as to the Lord and not to men, [8] knowing that whatever good thing each one does, he will receive the same good again from the Lord, whether he is bound or free. [9] You masters, do the same things to them,

---

[a] *3:9* TR reads "fellowship" instead of "administration"

[*] *4:8* Psalms 68:18
[b] *4:11* or, pastors

[*] *4:26* Psalms 4:4
[c] *4:27* or, opportunity

[*] *5:31* Genesis 2:24
[*] *6:3* Deuteronomy 5:16

and give up threatening, knowing that he who is both their Master and yours is in heaven, and there is no partiality with him. [10] Finally, be strong in the Lord and in the strength of his might. [11] Put on the whole armor of God, that you may be able to stand against the wiles of the devil. [12] For our wrestling is not against flesh and blood, but against the principalities, against the powers, against the world's rulers of the darkness of this age, and against the spiritual forces of wickedness in the heavenly places. [13] Therefore put on the whole armor of God, that you may be able to withstand in the evil day, and having done all, to stand. [14] Stand therefore, having the utility belt of truth buckled around your waist, and having put on the breastplate of righteousness, [15] and having fitted your feet with the preparation of the Good News of peace, [16] above all, taking up the shield of faith, with which you will be able to quench all the fiery darts of the evil one. [17] And take the helmet of salvation, and the sword of the Spirit, which is the word[a] of God; [18] with all prayer and requests, praying at all times in the Spirit, and being watchful to this end in all perseverance and requests for all the saints. [19] Pray for me, that utterance may be given to me in opening my mouth, to make known with boldness the mystery of the Good News, [20] for which I am an ambassador in chains; that in it I may speak boldly, as I ought to speak. [21] But that you also may know my affairs, how I am doing, Tychicus, the beloved brother and faithful servant in the Lord, will make known to you all things. [22] I have sent him to you for this very purpose, that you may know our state and that he may comfort your hearts. [23] Peace be to the brothers, and love with faith, from God the Father and the Lord Jesus Christ. [24] Grace be with all those who love our Lord Jesus Christ with incorruptible love. Amen.

# Paul's Letter to the Philippians

## 1

[1] Paul and Timothy, servants of Jesus Christ,[b] to all the saints in Christ Jesus who are at Philippi, with the overseers[c] and servants:[d] [2] Grace to you and peace from God our Father and the Lord Jesus Christ. [3] I thank my God whenever I remember you, [4] always in every request of mine on behalf of you all, making my requests with joy, [5] for your partnership[e] in furtherance of the Good News from the first day until now; [6] being confident of this very thing, that he who began a good work in you will complete it until the day of Jesus Christ. [7] It is even right for me to think this way on behalf of all of you, because I have you in my heart, because both in my bonds and in the defense and confirmation of the Good News, you all are partakers with me of grace. [8] For God is my witness, how I long after all of you in the tender mercies of Christ Jesus. [9] This I pray, that your love may abound yet more and more in knowledge and all discernment, [10] so that you may approve the things that are excellent, that you may be sincere and without offense to the day of Christ, [11] being filled with the fruits of righteousness which are through Jesus Christ, to the glory and praise of God. [12] Now I desire to have you know, brothers,[f] that the things which happened to me have turned out rather to the progress of the Good News, [13] so that it became evident to the whole palace[g] guard, and to all the rest, that my bonds are in Christ, [14] and that most of the brothers in the Lord, being confident through my bonds, are more abundantly bold to speak the word of God without fear. [15] Some indeed preach Christ even out of envy and strife, and some also out of good will. [16] The former insincerely preach Christ from selfish ambition, thinking that they add affliction to my chains; [17] but the latter out of love, knowing that I am appointed for the defense of the Good News. [18] What does it matter? Only that in every way, whether in pretense or in truth, Christ is proclaimed. I rejoice in this, yes, and will rejoice. [19] For I know that this will turn out to my salvation through your prayers and the supply of the Spirit of Jesus Christ, [20] according to my earnest expectation and hope, that I will in no way be disappointed, but with all boldness, as always, now also Christ will be magnified in my body, whether by life or by death. [21] For to me to live is Christ, and to die is gain. [22] But if I live on in the flesh, this will bring fruit from my work; yet I don't know what I will choose. [23] But I am hard pressed between the two, having the desire to depart and be with Christ, which is far better. [24] Yet to remain in the flesh is more needful for your sake. [25] Having this confidence, I know that I will remain, yes, and remain with you all for your progress and joy in the faith, [26] that your boasting[h] may abound in Christ Jesus in me through my presence with you again. [27] Only let your way of life be worthy of the Good News of Christ, that whether I come and see you or am absent, I may hear of your state, that

you stand firm in one spirit, with one soul striving for the faith of the Good News; [28] and in nothing frightened by the adversaries, which is for them a proof of destruction, but to you of salvation, and that from God. [29] Because it has been granted to you on behalf of Christ, not only to believe in him, but also to suffer on his behalf, [30] having the same conflict which you saw in me and now hear is in me.

## 2

[1] If therefore there is any exhortation in Christ, if any consolation of love, if any fellowship of the Spirit, if any tender mercies and compassion, [2] make my joy full by being like-minded, having the same love, being of one accord, of one mind; [3] doing nothing through rivalry or through conceit, but in humility, each counting others better than himself; [4] each of you not just looking to his own things, but each of you also to the things of others. [5] Have this in your mind, which was also in Christ Jesus, [6] who, existing in the form of God, didn't consider equality with God a thing to be grasped, [7] but emptied himself, taking the form of a servant, being made in the likeness of men. [8] And being found in human form, he humbled himself, becoming obedient to the point of death, yes, the death of the cross. [9] Therefore God also highly exalted him, and gave to him the name which is above every name, [10] that at the name of Jesus every knee should bow, of those in heaven, those on earth, and those under the earth, [11] and that every tongue should confess that Jesus Christ is Lord, to the glory of God the Father. [12] So then, my beloved, even as you have always obeyed, not only in my presence, but now much more in my absence, work out your own salvation with fear and trembling. [13] For it is God who works in you both to will and to work for his good pleasure. [14] Do all things without complaining and arguing, [15] that you may become blameless and harmless, children of God without defect in the middle of a crooked and perverse generation, among whom you are seen as lights in the world, [16] holding up the word of life, that I may have something to boast in the day of Christ that I didn't run in vain nor labor in vain. [17] Yes, and if I am poured out on the sacrifice and service of your faith, I am glad and rejoice with you all. [18] In the same way, you also should be glad and rejoice with me. [19] But I hope in the Lord Jesus to send Timothy to you soon, that I also may be cheered up when I know how you are doing. [20] For I have no one else like-minded, who will truly care about you. [21] For they all seek their own, not the things of Jesus Christ. [22] But you know that he has proved himself. As a child serves a father, so he served with me in furtherance of the Good News. [23] Therefore I hope to send him at once, as soon as I see how it will go with me. [24] But I trust in the Lord that I myself also will come shortly. [25] But I thought it necessary to send to you Epaphroditus, my brother, fellow worker, fellow soldier, and your apostle and servant of my need, [26] since he longed for you all, and was very troubled because you had heard that he was sick. [27] For indeed he was sick nearly to death, but God had mercy on him, and not on him only, but on me also, that I might not have sorrow on sorrow. [28] I have sent him therefore the more diligently, that when you see him again, you may rejoice, and that I may be the less sorrowful. [29] Receive him therefore in the Lord with all joy, and hold such people in honor, [30] because for the work of Christ he came near to death, risking his life to supply that which was lacking in your service toward me.

## 3

[1] Finally, my brothers, rejoice in the Lord! To write the same things to you, to me indeed is not tiresome, but for you it is safe. [2] Beware of the dogs; beware of the evil workers; beware of the false circumcision. [3] For we are the circumcision, who worship God in the Spirit, and rejoice in Christ Jesus, and have no confidence in the flesh; [4] though I myself might have confidence even in the flesh. If any other man thinks that he has confidence in the flesh, I yet more: [5] circumcised the eighth day, of the stock of Israel, of the tribe of Benjamin, a Hebrew of Hebrews; concerning the law, a Pharisee; [6] concerning zeal, persecuting the assembly; concerning the righteousness which is in the law, found blameless. [7] However, I consider those things that were gain to me as a loss for Christ. [8] Yes most certainly, and I count all things to be a loss for the excellency of the knowledge of Christ Jesus, my Lord, for whom I suffered the loss of all things, and count them nothing but refuse, that I may gain Christ [9] and be found in him, not having a righteousness of my own, that which is of the law, but that which is through faith in Christ, the righteousness which is from God by faith, [10] that I may know him and the power of his resurrection, and the fellowship of his sufferings, becoming conformed to his death, [11] if by any means I may attain to the resurrection from the dead. [12] Not that I have already

---

[a] 6:17 from the Greek "ῥῆμα" (rhema), which means "spoken word"
[b] 1:1 "Christ" means "Anointed One".

[c] 1:1 or, superintendents, or bishops
[d] 1:1 Or, deacons
[e] 1:5 The word translated "partnership" (κοινωνία) also

means "fellowship" and "sharing".
[f] 1:12 The word for "brothers" here and where context allows may also be correctly translated

"brothers and sisters" or "siblings."
[g] 1:13 or, praetorian
[h] 1:26 or, rejoicing

obtained, or am already made perfect; but I press on, that I may take hold of that for which also I was taken hold of by Christ Jesus. [13] Brothers, I don't regard myself as yet having taken hold, but one thing I do: forgetting the things which are behind and stretching forward to the things which are before, [14] I press on toward the goal for the prize of the high calling of God in Christ Jesus. [15] Let us therefore, as many as are perfect, think this way. If in anything you think otherwise, God will also reveal that to you. [16] Nevertheless, to the extent that we have already attained, let's walk by the same rule. Let's be of the same mind. [17] Brothers, be imitators together of me, and note those who walk this way, even as you have us for an example. [18] For many walk, of whom I told you often, and now tell you even weeping, as the enemies of the cross of Christ, [19] whose end is destruction, whose god is the belly, and whose glory is in their shame, who think about earthly things. [20] For our citizenship is in heaven, from where we also wait for a Savior, the Lord Jesus Christ, [21] who will change the body of our humiliation to be conformed to the body of his glory, according to the working by which he is able even to subject all things to himself.

## 4

[1] Therefore, my brothers, beloved and longed for, my joy and crown, stand firm in the Lord in this way, my beloved. [2] I exhort Euodia, and I exhort Syntyche, to think the same way in the Lord. [3] Yes, I beg you also, true partner, help these women, for they labored with me in the Good News with Clement also, and the rest of my fellow workers, whose names are in the book of life. [4] Rejoice in the Lord always! Again I will say, "Rejoice!" [5] Let your gentleness be known to all men. The Lord is at hand. [6] In nothing be anxious, but in everything, by prayer and petition with thanksgiving, let your requests be made known to God. [7] And the peace of God, which surpasses all understanding, will guard your hearts and your thoughts in Christ Jesus. [8] Finally, brothers, whatever things are true, whatever things are honorable, whatever things are just, whatever things are pure, whatever things are lovely, whatever things are of good report: if there is any virtue and if there is anything worthy of praise, think about these things. [9] Do the things which you learned, received, heard, and saw in me, and the God of peace will be with you. [10] But I rejoice in the Lord greatly that now at length you have revived your thought for me; in which you did indeed take thought, but you lacked opportunity. [11] Not that I speak because of lack, for I have learned in whatever state I am, to be content in it. [12] I know how to be humbled, and I also know how to abound. In any and all circumstances I have learned the secret both to be filled and to be hungry, both to abound and to be in need. [13] I can do all things through Christ who strengthens me. [14] However you did well that you shared in my affliction. [15] You yourselves also know, you Philippians, that in the beginning of the Good News, when I departed from Macedonia, no assembly shared with me in the matter of giving and receiving but you only. [16] For even in Thessalonica you sent once and again to my need. [17] Not that I seek for the gift, but I seek for the fruit that increases to your account. [18] But I have all things and abound. I am filled, having received from Epaphroditus the things that came from you, a sweet-smelling fragrance, an acceptable and well-pleasing sacrifice to God. [19] My God will supply every need of yours according to his riches in glory in Christ Jesus. [20] Now to our God and Father be the glory forever and ever! Amen. [21] Greet every saint in Christ Jesus. The brothers who are with me greet you. [22] All the saints greet you, especially those who are of Caesar's household. [23] The grace of the Lord Jesus Christ be with you all. Amen.

# Paul's Letter to the Colossians

## 1

[1] Paul, an apostle of Christ[a] Jesus through the will of God, and Timothy our brother, [2] to the saints and faithful brothers[b] in Christ at Colossae: Grace to you and peace from God our Father and the Lord Jesus Christ. [3] We give thanks to God the Father of our Lord Jesus Christ, praying always for you, [4] having heard of your faith in Christ Jesus and of the love which you have toward all the saints, [5] because of the hope which is laid up for you in the heavens, of which you heard before in the word of the truth of the Good News [6] which has come to you, even as it is in all the world and is bearing fruit and growing, as it does in you also, since the day you heard and knew the grace of God in truth, [7] even as you learned from Epaphras our beloved fellow servant, who is a faithful servant of Christ on your[c] behalf, [8] who also declared to us your love in the Spirit. [9] For this cause, we also, since the day we heard this, don't cease praying and making requests for you, that you may be filled with the knowledge of his will in all spiritual wisdom and understanding, [10]

that you may walk worthily of the Lord, to please him in all respects, bearing fruit in every good work and increasing in the knowledge of God, [11] strengthened with all power, according to the might of his glory, for all endurance and perseverance with joy, [12] giving thanks to the Father, who made us fit to be partakers of the inheritance of the saints in light, [13] who delivered us out of the power of darkness, and translated us into the Kingdom of the Son of his love, [14] in whom we have our redemption,[d] the forgiveness of our sins. [15] He is the image of the invisible God, the firstborn of all creation. [16] For by him all things were created in the heavens and on the earth, visible things and invisible things, whether thrones or dominions or principalities or powers. All things have been created through him and for him. [17] He is before all things, and in him all things are held together. [18] He is the head of the body, the assembly, who is the beginning, the firstborn from the dead, that in all things he might have the preeminence. [19] For all the fullness was pleased to dwell in him, [20] and through him to reconcile all things to himself by him, whether things on the earth or things in the heavens, having made peace through the blood of his cross. [21] You, being in past times alienated and enemies in your mind in your evil deeds, [22] yet now he has reconciled in the body of his flesh through death, to present you holy and without defect and blameless before him, [23] if it is so that you continue in the faith, grounded and steadfast, and not moved away from the hope of the Good News which you heard, which is being proclaimed in all creation under heaven, of which I, Paul, was made a servant. [24] Now I rejoice in my sufferings for your sake, and fill up on my part that which is lacking of the afflictions of Christ in my flesh for his body's sake, which is the assembly, [25] of which I was made a servant according to the stewardship of God which was given me toward you to fulfill the word of God, [26] the mystery which has been hidden for ages and generations. But now it has been revealed to his saints, [27] to whom God was pleased to make known what are the riches of the glory of this mystery among the Gentiles, which is Christ in you, the hope of glory. [28] We proclaim him, admonishing every man and teaching every man in all wisdom, that we may present every man perfect in Christ Jesus; [29] for which I also labor, striving according to his working, which works in me mightily.

## 2

[1] For I desire to have you know how greatly I struggle for you and for those at Laodicea, and for as many as have not seen my face in the flesh; [2] that their hearts may be comforted, they being knit together in love, and gaining all riches of the full assurance of understanding, that they may know the mystery of God, both of the Father and of Christ, [3] in whom all the treasures of wisdom and knowledge are hidden. [4] Now I say this that no one may delude you with persuasiveness of speech. [5] For though I am absent in the flesh, yet I am with you in the spirit, rejoicing and seeing your order, and the steadfastness of your faith in Christ. [6] As therefore you received Christ Jesus the Lord, walk in him, [7] rooted and built up in him and established in the faith, even as you were taught, abounding in it in thanksgiving. [8] Be careful that you don't let anyone rob you through his philosophy and vain deceit, after the tradition of men, after the elemental spirits of the world, and not after Christ. [9] For in him all the fullness of the Deity dwells bodily, [10] and in him you are made full, who is the head of all principality and power. [11] In him you were also circumcised with a circumcision not made with hands, in the putting off of the body of the sins of the flesh, in the circumcision of Christ, [12] having been buried with him in baptism, in which you were also raised with him through faith in the working of God, who raised him from the dead. [13] You were dead through your trespasses and the uncircumcision of your flesh. He made you alive together with him, having forgiven us all our trespasses, [14] wiping out the handwriting in ordinances which was against us. He has taken it out of the way, nailing it to the cross. [15] Having stripped the principalities and the powers, he made a show of them openly, triumphing over them in it. [16] Let no one therefore judge you in eating or drinking, or with respect to a feast day or a new moon or a Sabbath day, [17] which are a shadow of the things to come; but the body is Christ's. [18] Let no one rob you of your prize by self-abasement and worshiping of the angels, dwelling in the things which he has not seen, vainly puffed up by his fleshly mind, [19] and not holding firmly to the Head, from whom all the body, being supplied and knit together through the joints and ligaments, grows with God's growth. [20] If you died with Christ from the elemental spirits of the world, why, as though living in the world, do you subject yourselves to ordinances, [21] "Don't handle, nor taste, nor touch" [22] (all of which perish with use), according to the precepts and doctrines of men? [23] These things indeed appear like wisdom in self-imposed

---

[a] *1:1* "Christ" means "Anointed One".

[b] *1:2* The word for "brothers" here and where context allows may also be correctly translated "brothers and sisters" or "siblings."

[c] *1:7* NU reads our

[d] *1:14* TR adds "through his blood,"

worship, humility, and severity to the body, but aren't of any value against the indulgence of the flesh.

## 3

¹ If then you were raised together with Christ, seek the things that are above, where Christ is, seated on the right hand of God. ² Set your mind on the things that are above, not on the things that are on the earth. ³ For you died, and your life is hidden with Christ in God. ⁴ When Christ, our life, is revealed, then you will also be revealed with him in glory. ⁵ Put to death therefore your members which are on the earth: sexual immorality, uncleanness, depraved passion, evil desire, and covetousness, which is idolatry. ⁶ For these things' sake the wrath of God comes on the children of disobedience. ⁷ You also once walked in those, when you lived in them, ⁸ but now you must put them all away: anger, wrath, malice, slander, and shameful speaking out of your mouth. ⁹ Don't lie to one another, seeing that you have put off the old man with his doings, ¹⁰ and have put on the new man, who is being renewed in knowledge after the image of his Creator, ¹¹ where there can't be Greek and Jew, circumcision and uncircumcision, barbarian, Scythian, bondservant, or free person; but Christ is all, and in all. ¹² Put on therefore, as God's chosen ones, holy and beloved, a heart of compassion, kindness, lowliness, humility, and perseverance; ¹³ bearing with one another, and forgiving each other, if any man has a complaint against any; even as Christ forgave you, so you also do. ¹⁴ Above all these things, walk in love, which is the bond of perfection. ¹⁵ And let the peace of God rule in your hearts, to which also you were called in one body, and be thankful. ¹⁶ Let the word of Christ dwell in you richly; in all wisdom teaching and admonishing one another with psalms, hymns, and spiritual songs, singing with grace in your heart to the Lord. ¹⁷ Whatever you do, in word or in deed, do all in the name of the Lord Jesus, giving thanks to God the Father through him. ¹⁸ Wives, be in subjection to your husbands, as is fitting in the Lord. ¹⁹ Husbands, love your wives, and don't be bitter against them. ²⁰ Children, obey your parents in all things, for this pleases the Lord. ²¹ Fathers, don't provoke your children, so that they won't be discouraged. ²² Servants, obey in all things those who are your masters according to the flesh, not just when they are looking, as men pleasers, but in singleness of heart, fearing God. ²³ And whatever you do, work heartily, as for the Lord and not for men, ²⁴ knowing that from the Lord you will receive the reward of the inheritance; for you serve the Lord Christ. ²⁵ But he who does wrong will receive again for the wrong that he has done, and there is no partiality.

## 4

¹ Masters, give to your servants that which is just and equal, knowing that you also have a Master in heaven. ² Continue steadfastly in prayer, watching in it with thanksgiving, ³ praying together for us also, that God may open to us a door for the word, to speak the mystery of Christ, for which I am also in bonds, ⁴ that I may reveal it as I ought to speak. ⁵ Walk in wisdom toward those who are outside, redeeming the time. ⁶ Let your speech always be with grace, seasoned with salt, that you may know how you ought to answer each one. ⁷ All my affairs will be made known to you by Tychicus, the beloved brother, faithful servant, and fellow bondservant in the Lord. ⁸ I am sending him to you for this very purpose, that he may know your circumstances and comfort your hearts, ⁹ together with Onesimus, the faithful and beloved brother, who is one of you. They will make known to you everything that is going on here. ¹⁰ Aristarchus, my fellow prisoner, greets you, and Mark the cousin of Barnabas (concerning whom you received instructions, "if he comes to you, receive him"), ¹¹ and Jesus who is called Justus. These are my only fellow workers for God's Kingdom who are of the circumcision, men who have been a comfort to me. ¹² Epaphras, who is one of you, a servant of Christ, salutes you, always striving for you in his prayers, that you may stand perfect and complete in all the will of God. ¹³ For I testify about him that he has great zeal for you, and for those in Laodicea, and for those in Hierapolis. ¹⁴ Luke the beloved physician and Demas greet you. ¹⁵ Greet the brothers who are in Laodicea, with Nymphas and the assembly that is in his house. ¹⁶ When this letter has been read among you, cause it to be read also in the assembly of the Laodiceans, and that you also read the letter from Laodicea. ¹⁷ Tell Archippus, "Take heed to the ministry which you have received in the Lord, that you fulfill it." ¹⁸ I, Paul, write this greeting with my own hand. Remember my chains. Grace be with you. Amen.

# Paul's First Letter to the Thessalonians

## 1

¹ Paul, Silvanus, and Timothy, to the assembly of the Thessalonians in God the Father and the Lord Jesus Christ:[a] Grace to you and peace from God our Father and the Lord Jesus Christ. ² We always give thanks to God for all of you, mentioning you in our prayers, ³ remembering without ceasing your work of faith and labor of love and perseverance of hope in our Lord Jesus Christ, before our God and Father. ⁴ We know, brothers[b] loved by God, that you are chosen, ⁵ and that our Good News came to you not in word only, but also in power, and in the Holy Spirit and with much assurance. You know what kind of men we showed ourselves to be among you for your sake. ⁶ You became imitators of us and of the Lord, having received the word in much affliction, with joy of the Holy Spirit, ⁷ so that you became an example to all who believe in Macedonia and in Achaia. ⁸ For from you the word of the Lord has been declared, not only in Macedonia and Achaia, but also in every place your faith toward God has gone out, so that we need not to say anything. ⁹ For they themselves report concerning us what kind of a reception we had from you, and how you turned to God from idols to serve a living and true God, ¹⁰ and to wait for his Son from heaven, whom he raised from the dead: Jesus, who delivers us from the wrath to come.

## 2

¹ For you yourselves know, brothers, our visit to you wasn't in vain, ² but having suffered before and been shamefully treated, as you know, at Philippi, we grew bold in our God to tell you the Good News of God in much conflict. ³ For our exhortation is not of error, nor of uncleanness, nor in deception. ⁴ But even as we have been approved by God to be entrusted with the Good News, so we speak—not as pleasing men, but God, who tests our hearts. ⁵ For neither were we at any time found using words of flattery, as you know, nor a cloak of covetousness (God is witness), ⁶ nor seeking glory from men (neither from you nor from others), when we might have claimed authority as apostles of Christ. ⁷ But we were gentle among you, like a nursing mother cherishes her own children. ⁸ Even so, affectionately longing for you, we were well pleased to impart to you not the Good News of God only, but also our own souls, because you had become very dear to us. ⁹ For you remember, brothers, our labor and travail; for working night and day, that we might not burden any of you, we preached to you the Good News of God. ¹⁰ You are witnesses with God how holy, righteously, and blamelessly we behaved ourselves toward you who believe. ¹¹ As you know, we exhorted, comforted, and implored every one of you, as a father does his own children, ¹² to the end that you should walk worthily of God, who calls you into his own Kingdom and glory. ¹³ For this cause we also thank God without ceasing that when you received from us the word of the message of God, you accepted it not as the word of men, but as it is in truth, God's word, which also works in you who believe. ¹⁴ For you, brothers, became imitators of the assemblies of God which are in Judea in Christ Jesus; for you also suffered the same things from your own countrymen, even as they did from the Jews ¹⁵ who killed both the Lord Jesus and their own prophets, and drove us out, and don't please God, and are contrary to all men, ¹⁶ forbidding us to speak to the Gentiles that they may be saved, to fill up their sins always. But wrath has come on them to the uttermost. ¹⁷ But we, brothers, being bereaved of you for a short season in presence, not in heart, tried even harder to see your face with great desire, ¹⁸ because we wanted to come to you—indeed, I, Paul, once and again—but Satan hindered us. ¹⁹ For what is our hope, or joy, or crown of rejoicing? Isn't it even you, before our Lord Jesus[c] at his coming? ²⁰ For you are our glory and our joy.

## 3

¹ Therefore when we couldn't stand it any longer, we thought it good to be left behind at Athens alone, ² and sent Timothy, our brother and God's servant in the Good News of Christ, to establish you and to comfort you concerning your faith, ³ that no one would be moved by these afflictions. For you know that we are appointed to this task. ⁴ For most certainly, when we were with you, we told you beforehand that we are to suffer affliction, even as it happened, and you know. ⁵ For this cause I also, when I couldn't stand it any longer, sent that I might know your faith, for fear that by any means the tempter had tempted you, and our labor would have been in vain. ⁶ But Timothy has just now come to us from you, and brought us glad news of your faith and love, and that you have good memories of us always, longing to see us, even as we also long to see you. ⁷ For this cause, brothers, we were comforted over you in all our distress and affliction through your faith. ⁸ For now we live, if you stand fast in the Lord. ⁹ For what thanksgiving can we

---

[a] *1:1* "Christ" means "Anointed One".

[b] *1:4* The word for "brothers" here and where context allows may also be correctly translated "brothers and sisters" or "siblings."

[c] *2:19* TR adds "Christ"

render again to God for you, for all the joy with which we rejoice for your sakes before our God, [10] night and day praying exceedingly that we may see your face and may perfect that which is lacking in your faith? [11] Now may our God and Father himself, and our Lord Jesus Christ, direct our way to you. [12] May the Lord make you to increase and abound in love toward one another and toward all men, even as we also do toward you, [13] to the end he may establish your hearts blameless in holiness before our God and Father at the coming of our Lord Jesus with all his saints.

## 4

[1] Finally then, brothers, we beg and exhort you in the Lord Jesus, that as you received from us how you ought to walk and to please God, that you abound more and more. [2] For you know what instructions we gave you through the Lord Jesus. [3] For this is the will of God: your sanctification, that you abstain from sexual immorality, [4] that each one of you know how to control his own body[a] in sanctification and honor, [5] not in the passion of lust, even as the Gentiles who don't know God, [6] that no one should take advantage of and wrong a brother or sister in this matter; because the Lord is an avenger in all these things, as also we forewarned you and testified. [7] For God called us not for uncleanness, but in sanctification. [8] Therefore he who rejects this doesn't reject man, but God, who has also given his Holy Spirit to you. [9] But concerning brotherly love, you have no need that one write to you. For you yourselves are taught by God to love one another, [10] for indeed you do it toward all the brothers who are in all Macedonia. But we exhort you, brothers, that you abound more and more; [11] and that you make it your ambition to lead a quiet life, and to do your own business, and to work with your own hands, even as we instructed you, [12] that you may walk properly toward those who are outside, and may have need of nothing. [13] But we don't want you to be ignorant, brothers, concerning those who have fallen asleep, so that you don't grieve like the rest, who have no hope. [14] For if we believe that Jesus died and rose again, even so God will bring with him those who have fallen asleep in Jesus. [15] For this we tell you by the word of the Lord, that we who are alive, who are left until the coming of the Lord, will in no way precede those who have fallen asleep. [16] For the Lord himself will descend from heaven with a shout, with the voice of the archangel and with God's trumpet. The dead in Christ will rise first, [17] then we who are alive, who are left, will be caught up together with them in the clouds to meet the Lord in the air. So we will be with the Lord forever. [18] Therefore comfort one another with these words.

## 5

[1] But concerning the times and the seasons, brothers, you have no need that anything be written to you. [2] For you yourselves know well that the day of the Lord comes like a thief in the night. [3] For when they are saying, "Peace and safety," then sudden destruction will come on them, like birth pains on a pregnant woman. Then they will in no way escape. [4] But you, brothers, aren't in darkness, that the day should overtake you like a thief. [5] You are all children of light and children of the day. We don't belong to the night, nor to darkness, [6] so then let's not sleep, as the rest do, but let's watch and be sober. [7] For those who sleep, sleep in the night; and those who are drunk are drunk in the night. [8] But since we belong to the day, let's be sober, putting on the breastplate of faith and love, and for a helmet, the hope of salvation. [9] For God didn't appoint us to wrath, but to the obtaining of salvation through our Lord Jesus Christ, [10] who died for us, that, whether we wake or sleep, we should live together with him. [11] Therefore exhort one another, and build each other up, even as you also do. [12] But we beg you, brothers, to know those who labor among you, and are over you in the Lord and admonish you, [13] and to respect and honor them in love for their work's sake. Be at peace among yourselves. [14] We exhort you, brothers: Admonish the disorderly; encourage the faint-hearted; support the weak; be patient toward all. [15] See that no one returns evil for evil to anyone, but always follow after that which is good for one another and for all. [16] Always rejoice. [17] Pray without ceasing. [18] In everything give thanks, for this is the will of God in Christ Jesus toward you. [19] Don't quench the Spirit. [20] Don't despise prophecies. [21] Test all things, and hold firmly that which is good. [22] Abstain from every form of evil. [23] May the God of peace himself sanctify you completely. May your whole spirit, soul, and body be preserved blameless at the coming of our Lord Jesus Christ. [24] He who calls you is faithful, who will also do it. [25] Brothers, pray for us. [26] Greet all the brothers with a holy kiss. [27] I solemnly command you by the Lord that this letter be read to all the holy brothers. [28] The grace of our Lord Jesus Christ be with you. Amen.

# Paul's Second Letter to the Thessalonians

## 1

[1] Paul, Silvanus, and Timothy, to the assembly of the Thessalonians in God our Father and the Lord Jesus Christ: [2] Grace to you and peace from God our Father and the Lord Jesus Christ. [3] We are bound to always give thanks to God for you, brothers,[b] even as it is appropriate, because your faith grows exceedingly, and the love of each and every one of you toward one another abounds, [4] so that we ourselves boast about you in the assemblies of God for your perseverance and faith in all your persecutions and in the afflictions which you endure. [5] This is an obvious sign of the righteous judgment of God, to the end that you may be counted worthy of God's Kingdom, for which you also suffer. [6] For it is a righteous thing with God to repay affliction to those who afflict you, [7] and to give relief to you who are afflicted with us when the Lord Jesus is revealed from heaven with his mighty angels in flaming fire, [8] punishing those who don't know God, and to those who don't obey the Good News of our Lord Jesus, [9] who will pay the penalty: eternal destruction from the face of the Lord and from the glory of his might, [10] when he comes in that day to be glorified in his saints and to be admired among all those who have believed, because our testimony to you was believed. [11] To this end we also pray always for you that our God may count you worthy of your calling, and fulfill every desire of goodness and work of faith with power, [12] that the name of our Lord Jesus[c] may be glorified in you, and you in him, according to the grace of our God and the Lord Jesus Christ.

## 2

[1] Now, brothers, concerning the coming of our Lord Jesus Christ and our gathering together to him, we ask you [2] not to be quickly shaken in your mind or troubled, either by spirit or by word or by letter as if from us, saying that the day of Christ has already come. [3] Let no one deceive you in any way. For it will not be unless the rebellion[d] comes first, and the man of sin is revealed, the son of destruction. [4] He opposes and exalts himself against all that is called God or that is worshiped, so that he sits as God in the temple of God, setting himself up as God. [5] Don't you remember that when I was still with you, I told you these things? [6] Now you know what is restraining him, to the end that he may be revealed in his own season. [7] For the mystery of lawlessness already works. Only there is one who restrains now, until he is taken out of the way. [8] Then the lawless one will be revealed, whom the Lord will kill with the breath of his mouth and destroy by the manifestation of his coming; [9] even he whose coming is according to the working of Satan with all power and signs and lying wonders, [10] and with all deception of wickedness for those who are being lost, because they didn't receive the love of the truth, that they might be saved. [11] Because of this, God sends them a powerful delusion, that they should believe a lie, [12] that they all might be judged who didn't believe the truth, but had pleasure in unrighteousness. [13] But we are bound to always give thanks to God for you, brothers loved by the Lord, because God chose you from the beginning for salvation through sanctification of the Spirit and belief in the truth, [14] to which he called you through our Good News, for the obtaining of the glory of our Lord Jesus Christ. [15] So then, brothers, stand firm and hold the traditions which you were taught by us, whether by word or by letter. [16] Now our Lord Jesus Christ himself, and God our Father, who loved us and gave us eternal comfort and good hope through grace, [17] comfort your hearts and establish you in every good work and word.

## 3

[1] Finally, brothers, pray for us, that the word of the Lord may spread rapidly and be glorified, even as also with you, [2] and that we may be delivered from unreasonable and evil men; for not all have faith. [3] But the Lord is faithful, who will establish you and guard you from the evil one. [4] We have confidence in the Lord concerning you, that you both do and will do the things we command. [5] May the Lord direct your hearts into God's love and into the perseverance of Christ. [6] Now we command you, brothers, in the name of our Lord Jesus Christ, that you withdraw yourselves from every brother who walks in rebellion and not after the tradition which they received from us. [7] For you know how you ought to imitate us. For we didn't behave ourselves rebelliously among you, [8] neither did we eat bread from anyone's hand without paying for it, but in labor and travail worked night and day, that we might not burden any of you. [9] This was not because we don't have the right, but to make ourselves an example to you, that you should imitate us. [10] For even when we were with you, we commanded you this: "If anyone is not willing to work, don't let him eat." [11] For we hear of some who walk among you in rebellion, who don't work at all, but are busybodies. [12] Now those who are that way, we command and exhort

---

[a] 4:4 literally, possess his own vessel

[b] 1:3 The word for "brothers" here and where context allows may also be correctly translated "brothers and sisters" or "siblings."

[c] 1:12 TR adds "Christ"

[d] 2:3 or, falling away, or, defection

in the Lord Jesus Christ, that they work with quietness and eat their own bread. [13] But you, brothers, don't be weary in doing what is right. [14] If any man doesn't obey our word in this letter, note that man and have no company with him, to the end that he may be ashamed. [15] Don't count him as an enemy, but admonish him as a brother. [16] Now may the Lord of peace himself give you peace at all times in all ways. The Lord be with you all. [17] I, Paul, write this greeting with my own hand, which is the sign in every letter. This is how I write. [18] The grace of our Lord Jesus Christ be with you all. Amen.

# Paul's First Letter to Timothy

## 1

[1] Paul, an apostle of Jesus Christ according to the commandment of God our Savior and the Lord Jesus Christ[a] our hope, [2] to Timothy, my true child in faith: Grace, mercy, and peace from God our Father and Christ Jesus our Lord. [3] As I urged you when I was going into Macedonia, stay at Ephesus that you might command certain men not to teach a different doctrine, [4] and not to pay attention to myths and endless genealogies, which cause disputes rather than God's stewardship, which is in faith. [5] But the goal of this command is love from a pure heart, a good conscience, and sincere faith, [6] from which things some, having missed the mark, have turned away to vain talking, [7] desiring to be teachers of the law, though they understand neither what they say nor about what they strongly affirm. [8] But we know that the law is good if a person uses it lawfully, [9] as knowing this, that law is not made for a righteous person, but for the lawless and insubordinate, for the ungodly and sinners, for the unholy and profane, for murderers of fathers and murderers of mothers, for manslayers, [10] for the sexually immoral, for homosexuals, for slave-traders, for liars, for perjurers, and for any other thing contrary to the sound doctrine, [11] according to the Good News of the glory of the blessed God, which was committed to my trust. [12] I thank him who enabled me, Christ Jesus our Lord, because he counted me faithful, appointing me to service, [13] although I used to be a blasphemer, a persecutor, and insolent. However, I obtained mercy because I did it ignorantly in unbelief. [14] The grace of our Lord abounded exceedingly with faith and love which is in Christ Jesus. [15] The saying is faithful and worthy of all acceptance, that Christ Jesus came into the world to save sinners, of whom I am chief. [16] However, for this cause I obtained mercy, that in me first, Jesus Christ might display all his patience for an example of those who were going to believe in him for eternal life. [17] Now to the King eternal, immortal, invisible, to God who alone is wise, be honor and glory forever and ever. Amen. [18] I commit this instruction to you, my child Timothy, according to the prophecies which were given to you before, that by them you may wage the good warfare, [19] holding faith and a good conscience, which some having thrust away made a shipwreck concerning the faith, [20] of whom are Hymenaeus and Alexander, whom I delivered to Satan that they might be taught not to blaspheme.

## 2

[1] I exhort therefore, first of all, that petitions, prayers, intercessions, and givings of thanks be made for all men, [2] for kings and all who are in high places, that we may lead a tranquil and quiet life in all godliness and reverence. [3] For this is good and acceptable in the sight of God our Savior, [4] who desires all people to be saved and come to full knowledge of the truth. [5] For there is one God and one mediator between God and men, the man Christ Jesus, [6] who gave himself as a ransom for all, the testimony at the proper time, [7] to which I was appointed a preacher and an apostle—I am telling the truth in Christ, not lying—a teacher of the Gentiles in faith and truth. [8] I desire therefore that the men in every place pray, lifting up holy hands without anger and doubting. [9] In the same way, that women also adorn themselves in decent clothing, with modesty and propriety, not[b] with braided hair, gold, pearls, or expensive clothing, [10] but with good works, which is appropriate for women professing godliness. [11] Let a woman learn in quietness with full submission. [12] But I don't permit a woman to teach, nor to exercise authority over a man, but to be in quietness. [13] For Adam was formed first, then Eve. [14] Adam wasn't deceived, but the woman, being deceived, has fallen into disobedience; [15] but she will be saved through her childbearing, if they continue in faith, love, and holiness with sobriety.

## 3

[1] This is a faithful saying: someone who seeks to be an overseer[c] desires a good work. [2] The overseer therefore must be without reproach, the husband of one wife, temperate, sensible, modest, hospitable, good at teaching; [3] not a drinker, not violent, not greedy for money, but gentle, not quarrelsome, not covetous; [4] one who rules his own house well, having children in subjection with all reverence; [5](for how could someone who doesn't know how to rule his own house take care of God's assembly?) [6] not a new convert, lest being puffed up he fall into the same condemnation as the devil. [7] Moreover he must have good testimony from those who are outside, to avoid falling into reproach and the snare of the devil. [8] Servants,[d] in the same way, must be reverent, not double-tongued, not addicted to much wine, not greedy for money, [9] holding the mystery of the faith in a pure conscience. [10] Let them also first be tested; then let them serve[e] if they are blameless. [11] Their wives in the same way must be reverent, not slanderers, temperate, and faithful in all things. [12] Let servants[f] be husbands of one wife, ruling their children and their own houses well. [13] For those who have served well[g] gain for themselves a good standing and great boldness in the faith which is in Christ Jesus. [14] These things I write to you, hoping to come to you shortly, [15] but if I wait long, that you may know how men ought to behave themselves in God's house, which is the assembly of the living God, the pillar and ground of the truth. [16] Without controversy, the mystery of godliness is great: God[h] was revealed in the flesh, justified in the spirit, seen by angels, preached among the nations, believed on in the world, and received up in glory.

## 4

[1] But the Spirit says expressly that in later times some will fall away from the faith, paying attention to seducing spirits and doctrines of demons, [2] through the hypocrisy of men who speak lies, branded in their own conscience as with a hot iron, [3] forbidding marriage and commanding to abstain from foods which God created to be received with thanksgiving by those who believe and know the truth. [4] For every creature of God is good, and nothing is to be rejected if it is received with thanksgiving. [5] For it is sanctified through the word of God and prayer. [6] If you instruct the brothers of these things, you will be a good servant of Christ Jesus, nourished in the words of the faith and of the good doctrine which you have followed. [7] But refuse profane and old wives' fables. Exercise yourself toward godliness. [8] For bodily exercise has some value, but godliness has value in all things, having the promise of the life which is now and of that which is to come. [9] This saying is faithful and worthy of all acceptance. [10] For to this end we both labor and suffer reproach, because we have set our trust in the living God, who is the Savior of all men, especially of those who believe. [11] Command and teach these things. [12] Let no man despise your youth; but be an example to those who believe, in word, in your way of life, in love, in spirit, in faith, and in purity. [13] Until I come, pay attention to reading, to exhortation, and to teaching. [14] Don't neglect the gift that is in you, which was given to you by prophecy with the laying on of the hands of the elders. [15] Be diligent in these things. Give yourself wholly to them, that your progress may be revealed to all. [16] Pay attention to yourself and to your teaching. Continue in these things, for in doing this you will save both yourself and those who hear you.

## 5

[1] Don't rebuke an older man, but exhort him as a father; the younger men as brothers; [2] the elder women as mothers; the younger as sisters, in all purity. [3] Honor widows who are widows indeed. [4] But if any widow has children or grandchildren, let them learn first to show piety toward their own family and to repay their parents, for this is[i] acceptable in the sight of God. [5] Now she who is a widow indeed and desolate, has her hope set on God and continues in petitions and prayers night and day. [6] But she who gives herself to pleasure is dead while she lives. [7] Also command these things, that they may be without reproach. [8] But if anyone doesn't provide for his own, and especially his own household, he has denied the faith and is worse than an unbeliever. [9] Let no one be enrolled as a widow under sixty years old, having been the wife of one man, [10] being approved by good works, if she has brought up children, if she has been hospitable to strangers, if she has washed the saints' feet, if she has relieved the afflicted, and if she has diligently followed every good work. [11] But refuse younger widows, for when they have grown wanton against Christ, they desire to marry, [12] having condemnation, because they have rejected their first pledge. [13] Besides, they also learn to be idle, going about from house to house.

---

[a] *1:1* NU reads Christ Jesus and omits the Lord.

[b] *2:9* The word for "not" is the negative particle "μη" which denies an expected idea, as opposed to the usual word for "not" (ου) which denies a fact. Thus "μη" in this context is denying an expected idea (that women can be properly dressed without good works).

[c] *3:1* or, superintendent, or bishop

[d] *3:8* or, Deacons.

[e] *3:10* or, serve as deacons

[f] *3:12* or, deacons

[g] *3:13* or, served well as deacons

[h] *3:16* NU replaces "God" with "who"

[i] *5:4* TR adds "good and"

Not only idle, but also gossips and busybodies, saying things which they ought not. [14] I desire therefore that the younger widows marry, bear children, rule the household, and give no occasion to the adversary for insulting. [15] For already some have turned away after Satan. [16] If any man or woman who believes has widows, let them relieve them, and don't let the assembly be burdened, that it might relieve those who are widows indeed. [17] Let the elders who rule well be counted worthy of double honor, especially those who labor in the word and in teaching. [18] For the Scripture says, "You shall not muzzle the ox when it treads out the grain."* And, "The laborer is worthy of his wages."* [19] Don't receive an accusation against an elder except at the word of two or three witnesses. [20] Those who sin, reprove in the sight of all, that the rest also may be in fear. [21] I command you in the sight of God, and the Lord Jesus Christ, and the chosen angels, that you observe these things without prejudice, doing nothing by partiality. [22] Lay hands hastily on no one. Don't be a participant in other people's sins. Keep yourself pure. [23] Be no longer a drinker of water only, but use a little wine for your stomach's sake and your frequent infirmities. [24] Some men's sins are evident, preceding them to judgment, and some also follow later. [25] In the same way also there are good works that are obvious, and those that are otherwise can't be hidden.

## 6

[1] Let as many as are bondservants under the yoke count their own masters worthy of all honor, that the name of God and the doctrine not be blasphemed. [2] Those who have believing masters, let them not despise them because they are brothers, but rather let them serve them, because those who partake of the benefit are believing and beloved. Teach and exhort these things. [3] If anyone teaches a different doctrine and doesn't consent to sound words, the words of our Lord Jesus Christ, and to the doctrine which is according to godliness, [4] he is conceited, knowing nothing, but obsessed with arguments, disputes, and word battles, from which come envy, strife, insulting, evil suspicions, [5] constant friction of people of corrupt minds and destitute of the truth, who suppose that godliness is a means of gain. Withdraw yourself from such.ᵃ [6] But godliness with contentment is great gain. [7] For we brought nothing into the world, and we certainly can't carry anything out. [8] But having food and clothing, we will be content with that. [9] But those who are determined to be rich fall into a temptation, a snare, and many foolish and harmful lusts, such as drown men in ruin and destruction. [10] For the love of money is a root of all kinds of evil. Some have been led astray from the faith in their greed, and have pierced themselves through with many sorrows. [11] But you, man of God, flee these things, and follow after righteousness, godliness, faith, love, perseverance, and gentleness. [12] Fight the good fight of faith. Take hold of the eternal life to which you were called, and you confessed the good confession in the sight of many witnesses. [13] I command you before God who gives life to all things, and before Christ Jesus who before Pontius Pilate testified the good confession, [14] that you keep the commandment without spot, blameless until the appearing of our Lord Jesus Christ, [15] which at the right time he will show, who is the blessed and only Ruler, the King of kings and Lord of lords. [16] He alone has immortality, dwelling in unapproachable light, whom no man has seen nor can see, to whom be honor and eternal power. Amen. [17] Charge those who are rich in this present age that they not be arrogant, nor have their hope set on the uncertainty of riches, but on the living God, who richly provides us with everything to enjoy; [18] that they do good, that they be rich in good works, that they be ready to distribute, willing to share; [19] laying up in store for themselves a good foundation against the time to come, that they may lay hold of eternal life. [20] Timothy, guard that which is committed to you, turning away from the empty chatter and oppositions of what is falsely called knowledge, [21] which some profess, and thus have wandered from the faith. Grace be with you. Amen.

# Paul's Second Letter to Timothy

## 1

[1] Paul, an apostle of Jesus Christᵇ through the will of God, according to the promise of the life which is in Christ Jesus, [2] to Timothy, my beloved child: Grace, mercy, and peace, from God the Father and Christ Jesus our Lord. [3] I thank God, whom I serve as my forefathers did, with a pure conscience. How unceasing is my memory of you in my petitions, night and day [4] longing to see you, remembering your tears, that I may be filled with joy; [5] having been reminded of the sincere faith that is in you, which lived first in your grandmother Lois and your mother Eunice and, I am persuaded, in you also. [6] For this cause, I remind you that you should stir up the gift of God which is in you

through the laying on of my hands. [7] For God didn't give us a spirit of fear, but of power, love, and self-control. [8] Therefore don't be ashamed of the testimony of our Lord, nor of me his prisoner; but endure hardship for the Good News according to the power of God, [9] who saved us and called us with a holy calling, not according to our works, but according to his own purpose and grace, which was given to us in Christ Jesus before times eternal, [10] but has now been revealed by the appearing of our Savior, Christ Jesus, who abolished death, and brought life and immortality to light through the Good News. [11] For this I was appointed as a preacher, an apostle, and a teacher of the Gentiles. [12] For this cause I also suffer these things. Yet I am not ashamed, for I know him whom I have believed, and I am persuaded that he is able to guard that which I have committed to him against that day. [13] Hold the pattern of sound words which you have heard from me, in faith and love which is in Christ Jesus. [14] That good thing which was committed to you, guard through the Holy Spirit who dwells in us. [15] This you know, that all who are in Asia turned away from me, of whom are Phygelus and Hermogenes. [16] May the Lord grant mercy to the house of Onesiphorus, for he often refreshed me, and was not ashamed of my chain, [17] but when he was in Rome, he sought me diligently and found me [18](the Lord grant to him to find the Lord's mercy in that day); and in how many things he served at Ephesus, you know very well.

## 2

[1] You therefore, my child, be strengthened in the grace that is in Christ Jesus. [2] The things which you have heard from me among many witnesses, commit the same things to faithful men who will be able to teach others also. [3] You therefore must endure hardship as a good soldier of Christ Jesus. [4] No soldier on duty entangles himself in the affairs of life, that he may please him who enrolled him as a soldier. [5] Also, if anyone competes in athletics, he isn't crowned unless he has competed by the rules. [6] The farmer who labors must be the first to get a share of the crops. [7] Consider what I say, and may the Lord give you understanding in all things. [8] Remember Jesus Christ, risen from the dead, of the offspringᶜ of David, according to my Good News, [9] in which I suffer hardship to the point of chains as a criminal. But God's word isn't chained. [10] Therefore I endure all things for the chosen ones' sake, that they also may obtain the salvation which is in Christ Jesus with eternal glory. [11] This saying is trustworthy: "For if we died with him, we will also live with him. [12] If we endure, we will also reign with him. If we deny him, he also will deny us. [13] If we are faithless, he remains faithful; for he can't deny himself." [14] Remind them of these things, charging them in the sight of the Lord that they don't argue about words to no profit, to the subverting of those who hear. [15] Give diligence to present yourself approved by God, a workman who doesn't need to be ashamed, properly handling the Word of Truth. [16] But shun empty chatter, for it will go further in ungodliness, [17] and those words will consume like gangrene, of whom is Hymenaeus and Philetus: [18] men who have erred concerning the truth, saying that the resurrection is already past, and overthrowing the faith of some. [19] However, God's firm foundation stands, having this seal: "The Lord knows those who are his,"* and, "Let every one who names the name of the Lordᵈ depart from unrighteousness." [20] Now in a large house there are not only vessels of gold and of silver, but also of wood and of clay. Some are for honor and some for dishonor. [21] If anyone therefore purges himself from these, he will be a vessel for honor, sanctified, and suitable for the master's use, prepared for every good work. [22] Flee from youthful lusts; but pursue righteousness, faith, love, and peace with those who call on the Lord out of a pure heart. [23] But refuse foolish and ignorant questionings, knowing that they generate strife. [24] The Lord's servant must not quarrel, but be gentle toward all, able to teach, patient, [25] in gentleness correcting those who oppose him. Perhaps God may give them repentance leading to a full knowledge of the truth, [26] and they may recover themselves out of the devil's snare, having been taken captive by him to do his will.

## 3

[1] But know this: that in the last days, grievous times will come. [2] For men will be lovers of self, lovers of money, boastful, arrogant, blasphemers, disobedient to parents, unthankful, unholy, [3] without natural affection, unforgiving, slanderers, without self-control, fierce, not lovers of good, [4] traitors, headstrong, conceited, lovers of pleasure rather than lovers of God, [5] holding a form of godliness but having denied its power. Turn away from these, also. [6] For some of these are people who creep into houses and take captive gullible women loaded down with sins, led away by various lusts, [7] always learning and never able to come to the knowledge of the truth. [8] Even as Jannes and Jambres opposed Moses, so these also oppose the truth, men corrupted

---

* 5:18 Deuteronomy 25:4
* 5:18 Luke 10:7; Leviticus 19:13

ᵃ 6:5 NU omits "Withdraw yourself from such."

ᵇ 1:1 "Christ" means "Anointed One".
ᶜ 2:8 or, seed

* 2:19 Numbers 16:5
ᵈ 2:19 TR reads "Christ" instead of "the Lord"

in mind, who concerning the faith are rejected. <sup>9</sup> But they will proceed no further. For their folly will be evident to all men, as theirs also came to be. <sup>10</sup> But you followed my teaching, conduct, purpose, faith, patience, love, steadfastness, <sup>11</sup> persecutions, and sufferings—those things that happened to me at Antioch, Iconium, and Lystra. I endured those persecutions. The Lord delivered me out of them all. <sup>12</sup> Yes, and all who desire to live godly in Christ Jesus will suffer persecution. <sup>13</sup> But evil men and impostors will grow worse and worse, deceiving and being deceived. <sup>14</sup> But you remain in the things which you have learned and have been assured of, knowing from whom you have learned them. <sup>15</sup> From infancy, you have known the holy Scriptures which are able to make you wise for salvation through faith which is in Christ Jesus. <sup>16</sup> Every Scripture is God-breathed and<sup>a</sup> profitable for teaching, for reproof, for correction, and for instruction in righteousness, <sup>17</sup> that each person who belongs to God may be complete, thoroughly equipped for every good work.

**4**

<sup>1</sup> I command you therefore before God and the Lord Jesus Christ, who will judge the living and the dead at his appearing and his Kingdom: <sup>2</sup> preach the word; be urgent in season and out of season; reprove, rebuke, and exhort with all patience and teaching. <sup>3</sup> For the time will come when they will not listen to the sound doctrine, but having itching ears, will heap up for themselves teachers after their own lusts, <sup>4</sup> and will turn away their ears from the truth, and turn away to fables. <sup>5</sup> But you be sober in all things, suffer hardship, do the work of an evangelist, and fulfill your ministry. <sup>6</sup> For I am already being offered, and the time of my departure has come. <sup>7</sup> I have fought the good fight. I have finished the course. I have kept the faith. <sup>8</sup> From now on, the crown of righteousness is stored up for me, which the Lord, the righteous judge, will give to me on that day; and not to me only, but also to all those who have loved his appearing. <sup>9</sup> Be diligent to come to me soon, <sup>10</sup> for Demas left me, having loved this present world, and went to Thessalonica; Crescens to Galatia; and Titus to Dalmatia. <sup>11</sup> Only Luke is with me. Take Mark and bring him with you, for he is useful to me for service. <sup>12</sup> But I sent Tychicus to Ephesus. <sup>13</sup> Bring the cloak that I left at Troas with Carpus when you come—and the books, especially the parchments. <sup>14</sup> Alexander the coppersmith did much evil to me. The Lord will repay him according to his deeds. <sup>15</sup> Beware of him, for he greatly opposed our words. <sup>16</sup> At my first defense, no one came to help me, but all left me. May it not be held against them. <sup>17</sup> But the Lord stood by me and strengthened me, that through me the message might be fully proclaimed, and that all the Gentiles might hear. So I was delivered out of the mouth of the lion. <sup>18</sup> And the Lord will deliver me from every evil work and will preserve me for his heavenly Kingdom. To him be the glory forever and ever. Amen. <sup>19</sup> Greet Prisca and Aquila, and the house of Onesiphorus. <sup>20</sup> Erastus remained at Corinth, but I left Trophimus at Miletus sick. <sup>21</sup> Be diligent to come before winter. Eubulus salutes you, as do Pudens, Linus, Claudia, and all the brothers. <sup>22</sup> The Lord Jesus Christ be with your spirit. Grace be with you. Amen.

## Paul's Letter to Titus
### 1

<sup>1</sup> Paul, a servant of God and an apostle of Jesus Christ,<sup>b</sup> according to the faith of God's chosen ones and the knowledge of the truth which is according to godliness, <sup>2</sup> in hope of eternal life, which God, who can't lie, promised before time began; <sup>3</sup> but in his own time revealed his word in the message with which I was entrusted according to the commandment of God our Savior, <sup>4</sup> to Titus, my true child according to a common faith: Grace, mercy, and peace from God the Father and the Lord Jesus Christ our Savior. <sup>5</sup> I left you in Crete for this reason, that you would set in order the things that were lacking and appoint elders in every city, as I directed you— <sup>6</sup> if anyone is blameless, the husband of one wife, having children who believe, who are not accused of loose or unruly behavior. <sup>7</sup> For the overseer must be blameless, as God's steward, not self-pleasing, not easily angered, not given to wine, not violent, not greedy for dishonest gain; <sup>8</sup> but given to hospitality, a lover of good, sober minded, fair, holy, self-controlled, <sup>9</sup> holding to the faithful word which is according to the teaching, that he may be able to exhort in the sound doctrine, and to convict those who contradict him. <sup>10</sup> For there are also many unruly men, vain talkers and deceivers, especially those of the circumcision, <sup>11</sup> whose mouths must be stopped: men who overthrow whole houses, teaching things which they ought not, for dishonest gain's sake. <sup>12</sup> One of them, a prophet of their own, said, "Cretans are always liars, evil beasts, and idle gluttons." <sup>13</sup> This testimony is true. For this cause, reprove them sharply, that they may be sound in the faith, <sup>14</sup> not paying attention to Jewish fables and

commandments of men who turn away from the truth. <sup>15</sup> To the pure, all things are pure, but to those who are defiled and unbelieving, nothing is pure; but both their mind and their conscience are defiled. <sup>16</sup> They profess that they know God, but by their deeds they deny him, being abominable, disobedient, and unfit for any good work.

**2**

<sup>1</sup> But say the things which fit sound doctrine, <sup>2</sup> that older men should be temperate, sensible, sober minded, sound in faith, in love, and in perseverance, <sup>3</sup> and that older women likewise be reverent in behavior, not slanderers nor enslaved to much wine, teachers of that which is good, <sup>4</sup> that they may train the young wives to love their husbands, to love their children, <sup>5</sup> to be sober minded, chaste, workers at home, kind, being in subjection to their own husbands, that God's word may not be blasphemed. <sup>6</sup> Likewise, exhort the younger men to be sober minded. <sup>7</sup> In all things show yourself an example of good works. In your teaching, show integrity, seriousness, incorruptibility, <sup>8</sup> and soundness of speech that can't be condemned, that he who opposes you may be ashamed, having no evil thing to say about us. <sup>9</sup> Exhort servants to be in subjection to their own masters and to be well-pleasing in all things, not contradicting, <sup>10</sup> not stealing, but showing all good fidelity, that they may adorn the doctrine of God, our Savior, in all things. <sup>11</sup> For the grace of God has appeared, bringing salvation to all men, <sup>12</sup> instructing us to the intent that, denying ungodliness and worldly lusts, we would live soberly, righteously, and godly in this present age; <sup>13</sup> looking for the blessed hope and appearing of the glory of our great God and Savior, Jesus Christ, <sup>14</sup> who gave himself for us, that he might redeem us from all iniquity and purify for himself a people for his own possession, zealous for good works. <sup>15</sup> Say these things and exhort and reprove with all authority. Let no one despise you.

**3**

<sup>1</sup> Remind them to be in subjection to rulers and to authorities, to be obedient, to be ready for every good work, <sup>2</sup> to speak evil of no one, not to be contentious, to be gentle, showing all humility toward all men. <sup>3</sup> For we were also once foolish, disobedient, deceived, serving various lusts and pleasures, living in malice and envy, hateful, and hating one another. <sup>4</sup> But when the kindness of God our Savior and his love toward mankind appeared, <sup>5</sup> not by works of righteousness which we did ourselves, but according to his mercy, he saved us through the washing of regeneration and renewing by the Holy Spirit, <sup>6</sup> whom he poured out on us richly through Jesus Christ our Savior; <sup>7</sup> that being justified by his grace, we might be made heirs according to the hope of eternal life. <sup>8</sup> This saying is faithful, and concerning these things I desire that you insist confidently, so that those who have believed God may be careful to maintain good works. These things are good and profitable to men; <sup>9</sup> but shun foolish questionings, genealogies, strife, and disputes about the law; for they are unprofitable and vain. <sup>10</sup> Avoid a factious man after a first and second warning, <sup>11</sup> knowing that such a one is perverted and sinful, being self-condemned. <sup>12</sup> When I send Artemas to you, or Tychicus, be diligent to come to me to Nicopolis, for I have determined to winter there. <sup>13</sup> Send Zenas the lawyer and Apollos on their journey speedily, that nothing may be lacking for them. <sup>14</sup> Let our people also learn to maintain good works to meet necessary needs, that they may not be unfruitful. <sup>15</sup> All who are with me greet you. Greet those who love us in faith. Grace be with you all. Amen.

## Paul's Letter to Philemon
### 1

<sup>1</sup> Paul, a prisoner of Christ<sup>c</sup> Jesus, and Timothy our brother, to Philemon, our beloved fellow worker, <sup>2</sup> to the beloved Apphia, to Archippus our fellow soldier, and to the assembly in your house: <sup>3</sup> Grace to you and peace from God our Father and the Lord Jesus Christ. <sup>4</sup> I thank my God always, making mention of you in my prayers, <sup>5</sup> hearing of your love and of the faith which you have toward the Lord Jesus and toward all the saints, <sup>6</sup> that the fellowship of your faith may become effective in the knowledge of every good thing which is in us in Christ Jesus. <sup>7</sup> For we have much joy and comfort in your love, because the hearts of the saints have been refreshed through you, brother. <sup>8</sup> Therefore though I have all boldness in Christ to command you that which is appropriate, <sup>9</sup> yet for love's sake I rather appeal to you, being such a one as Paul, the aged, but also a prisoner of Jesus Christ. <sup>10</sup> I appeal to you for my child Onesimus, whom I have become the father of in my chains,<sup>d</sup> <sup>11</sup> who once was useless to you, but now is useful to you and to me. <sup>12</sup> I am sending him back. Therefore receive him, that is, my own heart, <sup>13</sup> whom I desired to keep with me, that on your behalf he might serve me in my chains for the Good News. <sup>14</sup> But

<sup>a</sup> *3:16* or, Every writing inspired by God is

<sup>b</sup> *1:1* "Christ" means "Anointed One".

<sup>c</sup> *1:1* "Christ" means "Anointed One".

<sup>d</sup> *1:10* Onesimus means "useful".

I was willing to do nothing without your consent, that your goodness would not be as of necessity, but of free will. **15** For perhaps he was therefore separated from you for a while that you would have him forever, **16** no longer as a slave, but more than a slave, a beloved brother—especially to me, but how much rather to you, both in the flesh and in the Lord. **17** If then you count me a partner, receive him as you would receive me. **18** But if he has wronged you at all or owes you anything, put that to my account. **19** I, Paul, write this with my own hand: I will repay it (not to mention to you that you owe to me even your own self besides). **20** Yes, brother, let me have joy from you in the Lord. Refresh my heart in the Lord. **21** Having confidence in your obedience, I write to you, knowing that you will do even beyond what I say. **22** Also, prepare a guest room for me, for I hope that through your prayers I will be restored to you. **23** Epaphras, my fellow prisoner in Christ Jesus, greets you, **24** as do Mark, Aristarchus, Demas, and Luke, my fellow workers. **25** The grace of our Lord Jesus Christ be with your spirit. Amen.

# The Letter to the Hebrews

## 1

**1** God, having in the past spoken to the fathers through the prophets at many times and in various ways, **2** has at the end of these days spoken to us by his Son, whom he appointed heir of all things, through whom also he made the worlds. **3** His Son is the radiance of his glory, the very image of his substance, and upholding all things by the word of his power, who, when he had by himself purified us of our sins, sat down on the right hand of the Majesty on high, **4** having become as much better than the angels as the more excellent name he has inherited is better than theirs. **5** For to which of the angels did he say at any time, "You are my Son. Today I have become your father?"* and again, "I will be to him a Father, and he will be to me a Son?"* **6** When he again brings in the firstborn into the world he says, "Let all the angels of God worship him."* **7** Of the angels he says, "He makes his angels winds, and his servants a flame of fire."* **8** But of the Son he says, "Your throne, O God, is forever and ever. The scepter of uprightness is the scepter of your Kingdom. **9** You have loved righteousness and hated iniquity; therefore God, your God, has anointed you with the oil of gladness above your fellows."* **10** And, "You, Lord, in the beginning, laid the foundation of the earth. The heavens are the works of your hands. **11** They will perish, but you continue. They all will grow old like a garment does. **12** You will roll them up like a mantle, and they will be changed; but you are the same. Your years won't fail."* **13** But which of the angels has he told at any time, "Sit at my right hand, until I make your enemies the footstool of your feet?"* **14** Aren't they all serving spirits, sent out to do service for the sake of those who will inherit salvation?

## 2

**1** Therefore we ought to pay greater attention to the things that were heard, lest perhaps we drift away. **2** For if the word spoken through angels proved steadfast, and every transgression and disobedience received a just penalty, **3** how will we escape if we neglect so great a salvation—which at the first having been spoken through the Lord, was confirmed to us by those who heard, **4** God also testifying with them, both by signs and wonders, by various works of power, and by gifts of the Holy Spirit, according to his own will? **5** For he didn't subject the world to come, of which we speak, to angels. **6** But one has somewhere testified, saying, "What is man, that you think of him? Or the son of man, that you care for him? **7** You made him a little lower than the angels. You crowned him with glory and honor.ᵃ **8** You have put all things in subjection under his feet."* For in that he subjected all things to him, he left nothing that is not subject to him. But now we don't yet see all things subjected to him. **9** But we see him who has been made a little lower than the angels, Jesus, because of the suffering of death crowned with glory and honor, that by the grace of God he should taste of death for everyone. **10** For it became him, for whom are all things and through whom are all things, in bringing many children to glory, to make the author of their salvation perfect through sufferings. **11** For both he who sanctifies and those who are sanctified are all from one, for which cause he is not ashamed to call them brothers,ᵇ **12** saying, "I will declare your name to my brothers. Among the congregation I will sing your praise."* **13** Again, "I will put my trust in him." Again,

"Behold, here I am with the children whom God has given me."* **14** Since then the children have shared in flesh and blood, he also himself in the same way partook of the same, that through death he might bring to nothing him who had the power of death, that is, the devil, **15** and might deliver all of them who through fear of death were all their lifetime subject to bondage. **16** For most certainly, he doesn't give help to angels, but he gives help to the offspringᶜ of Abraham. **17** Therefore he was obligated in all things to be made like his brothers, that he might become a merciful and faithful high priest in things pertaining to God, to make atonement for the sins of the people. **18** For in that he himself has suffered being tempted, he is able to help those who are tempted.

## 3

**1** Therefore, holy brothers, partakers of a heavenly calling, consider the Apostle and High Priest of our confession: Jesus, **2** who was faithful to him who appointed him, as also Moses was in all his house. **3** For he has been counted worthy of more glory than Moses, because he who built the house has more honor than the house. **4** For every house is built by someone; but he who built all things is God. **5** Moses indeed was faithful in all his house as a servant, for a testimony of those things which were afterward to be spoken, **6** but Christᵈ is faithful as a Son over his house. We are his house, if we hold fast our confidence and the glorying of our hope firm to the end. **7** Therefore, even as the Holy Spirit says, "Today if you will hear his voice, **8** don't harden your hearts as in the rebellion, in the day of the trial in the wilderness, **9** where your fathers tested me and tried me, and saw my deeds for forty years. **10** Therefore I was displeased with that generation, and said, 'They always err in their heart, but they didn't know my ways.' **11** As I swore in my wrath, 'They will not enter into my rest.'"* **12** Beware, brothers, lest perhaps there might be in any one of you an evil heart of unbelief, in falling away from the living God; **13** but exhort one another day by day, so long as it is called "today", lest any one of you be hardened by the deceitfulness of sin. **14** For we have become partakers of Christ, if we hold the beginning of our confidence firm to the end, **15** while it is said, "Today if you will hear his voice, don't harden your hearts, as in the rebellion."* **16** For who, when they heard, rebelled? Wasn't it all those who came out of Egypt led by Moses? **17** With whom was he displeased forty years? Wasn't it with those who sinned, whose bodies fell in the wilderness? **18** To whom did he swear that they wouldn't enter into his rest, but to those who were disobedient? **19** We see that they weren't able to enter in because of unbelief.

## 4

**1** Let's fear therefore, lest perhaps anyone of you should seem to have come short of a promise of entering into his rest. **2** For indeed we have had good news preached to us, even as they also did, but the word they heard didn't profit them, because it wasn't mixed with faith by those who heard. **3** For we who have believed do enter into that rest, even as he has said, "As I swore in my wrath, they will not enter into my rest;"* although the works were finished from the foundation of the world. **4** For he has said this somewhere about the seventh day, "God rested on the seventh day from all his works;"* **5** and in this place again, "They will not enter into my rest."* **6** Seeing therefore it remains that some should enter into it, and they to whom the good news was preached before failed to enter in because of disobedience, **7** he again defines a certain day, "today", saying through David so long a time afterward (just as has been said), "Today if you will hear his voice, don't harden your hearts."* **8** For if Joshua had given them rest, he would not have spoken afterward of another day. **9** There remains therefore a Sabbath rest for the people of God. **10** For he who has entered into his rest has himself also rested from his works, as God did from his. **11** Let's therefore give diligence to enter into that rest, lest anyone fall after the same example of disobedience. **12** For the word of God is living and active, and sharper than any two-edged sword, piercing even to the dividing of soul and spirit, of both joints and marrow, and is able to discern the thoughts and intentions of the heart. **13** There is no creature that is hidden from his sight, but all things are naked and laid open before the eyes of him to whom we must give an account. **14** Having then a great high priest who has passed through the heavens, Jesus, the Son of God, let's hold tightly to our confession. **15** For we don't have a high priest who can't be touched with the feeling of our infirmities, but one who has been in all points tempted like we are, yet without sin. **16** Let's therefore draw near with boldness to the throne of grace, that we may receive mercy and may find grace for help in time of need.

---

* 1:5 Psalms 2:7
* 1:5 2 Samuel 7:14; 1 Chronicles 17:13
* 1:6 Deuteronomy 32:43 LXX
* 1:7 Psalms 104:4
* 1:9 Psalms 45:6- 7
* 1:12 Psalms 102:25- 27
* 1:13 Psalms 110:1
ᵃ 2:7 TR adds "and set him over the works of your hands"
* 2:8 Psalms 8:4- 6
ᵇ 2:11 The word for "brothers" here and where context allows may also be correctly translated "brothers and sisters" or "siblings."
* 2:12 Psalms 22:22
* 2:13 Isaiah 8:18
ᶜ 2:16 or, seed
ᵈ 3:6 "Christ" means "Anointed One".
* 3:11 Psalms 95:7- 11
* 3:15 Psalms 95:7- 8
* 4:3 Psalms 95:11
* 4:4 Genesis 2:2
* 4:5 Psalms 95:11
* 4:7 Psalms 95:7- 8

## 5

[1] For every high priest, being taken from among men, is appointed for men in things pertaining to God, that he may offer both gifts and sacrifices for sins. [2] The high priest can deal gently with those who are ignorant and going astray, because he himself is also surrounded with weakness. [3] Because of this, he must offer sacrifices for sins for the people, as well as for himself. [4] Nobody takes this honor on himself, but he is called by God, just like Aaron was. [5] So also Christ didn't glorify himself to be made a high priest, but it was he who said to him, "You are my Son. Today I have become your father."* [6] As he says also in another place, "You are a priest forever, after the order of Melchizedek."* [7] He, in the days of his flesh, having offered up prayers and petitions with strong crying and tears to him who was able to save him from death, and having been heard for his godly fear, [8] though he was a Son, yet learned obedience by the things which he suffered. [9] Having been made perfect, he became to all of those who obey him the author of eternal salvation, [10] named by God a high priest after the order of Melchizedek. [11] About him we have many words to say, and hard to interpret, seeing you have become dull of hearing. [12] For although by this time you should be teachers, you again need to have someone teach you the rudiments of the first principles of the revelations of God. You have come to need milk, and not solid food. [13] For everyone who lives on milk is not experienced in the word of righteousness, for he is a baby. [14] But solid food is for those who are full grown, who by reason of use have their senses exercised to discern good and evil.

## 6

[1] Therefore leaving the teaching of the first principles of Christ, let's press on to perfection—not laying again a foundation of repentance from dead works, of faith toward God, [2] of the teaching of baptisms, of laying on of hands, of resurrection of the dead, and of eternal judgment. [3] This will we do, if God permits. [4] For concerning those who were once enlightened and tasted of the heavenly gift, and were made partakers of the Holy Spirit, [5] and tasted the good word of God and the powers of the age to come, [6] and then fell away, it is impossible to renew them again to repentance; seeing they crucify the Son of God for themselves again, and put him to open shame. [7] For the land which has drunk the rain that comes often on it and produces a crop suitable for them for whose sake it is also tilled, receives blessing from God; [8] but if it bears thorns and thistles, it is rejected and near being cursed, whose end is to be burned. [9] But, beloved, we are persuaded of better things for you, and things that accompany salvation, even though we speak like this. [10] For God is not unrighteous, so as to forget your work and the labor of love which you showed toward his name, in that you served the saints, and still do serve them. [11] We desire that each one of you may show the same diligence to the fullness of hope even to the end, [12] that you won't be sluggish, but imitators of those who through faith and perseverance inherited the promises. [13] For when God made a promise to Abraham, since he could swear by no one greater, he swore by himself, [14] saying, "Surely blessing I will bless you, and multiplying I will multiply you."* [15] Thus, having patiently endured, he obtained the promise. [16] For men indeed swear by a greater one, and in every dispute of theirs the oath is final for confirmation. [17] In this way God, being determined to show more abundantly to the heirs of the promise the immutability of his counsel, interposed with an oath, [18] that by two immutable things, in which it is impossible for God to lie, we may have a strong encouragement, who have fled for refuge to take hold of the hope set before us. [19] This hope we have as an anchor of the soul, a hope both sure and steadfast and entering into that which is within the veil, [20] where as a forerunner Jesus entered for us, having become a high priest forever after the order of Melchizedek.

## 7

[1] For this Melchizedek, king of Salem, priest of God Most High, who met Abraham returning from the slaughter of the kings and blessed him, [2] to whom also Abraham divided a tenth part of all (being first, by interpretation, "king of righteousness", and then also "king of Salem", which means "king of peace", [3] without father, without mother, without genealogy, having neither beginning of days nor end of life, but made like the Son of God), remains a priest continually. [4] Now consider how great this man was, to whom even Abraham the patriarch gave a tenth out of the best plunder. [5] They indeed of the sons of Levi who receive the priest's office have a commandment to take tithes from the people according to the law, that is, of their brothers, though these have come out of the body of Abraham, [6] but he whose genealogy is not counted from them has accepted tithes from Abraham, and has blessed him who has the promises. [7] But without any dispute the lesser is blessed by the greater. [8] Here people who die receive tithes, but there one receives tithes of whom it is testified that he lives. [9] We can say that through Abraham even Levi, who receives tithes, has paid tithes, [10] for he was yet in the body of his father when Melchizedek met him. [11] Now if perfection was through the Levitical priesthood (for under it the people have received the law), what further need was there for another priest to arise after the order of Melchizedek, and not be called after the order of Aaron? [12] For the priesthood being changed, there is of necessity a change made also in the law. [13] For he of whom these things are said belongs to another tribe, from which no one has officiated at the altar. [14] For it is evident that our Lord has sprung out of Judah, about which tribe Moses spoke nothing concerning priesthood. [15] This is yet more abundantly evident, if after the likeness of Melchizedek there arises another priest, [16] who has been made, not after the law of a fleshly commandment, but after the power of an endless life; [17] for it is testified, "You are a priest forever, according to the order of Melchizedek."* [18] For there is an annulling of a foregoing commandment because of its weakness and uselessness [19](for the law made nothing perfect), and a bringing in of a better hope, through which we draw near to God. [20] Inasmuch as he was not made priest without the taking of an oath [21](for they indeed have been made priests without an oath), but he with an oath by him that says of him, "The Lord swore and will not change his mind, 'You are a priest forever, according to the order of Melchizedek.'"* [22] By so much, Jesus has become the guarantee of a better covenant. [23] Many, indeed, have been made priests, because they are hindered from continuing by death. [24] But he, because he lives forever, has his priesthood unchangeable. [25] Therefore he is also able to save to the uttermost those who draw near to God through him, seeing that he lives forever to make intercession for them. [26] For such a high priest was fitting for us: holy, guiltless, undefiled, separated from sinners, and made higher than the heavens; [27] who doesn't need, like those high priests, to offer up sacrifices daily, first for his own sins, and then for the sins of the people. For he did this once for all, when he offered up himself. [28] For the law appoints men as high priests who have weakness, but the word of the oath, which came after the law, appoints a Son forever who has been perfected.

## 8

[1] Now in the things which we are saying, the main point is this: we have such a high priest, who sat down on the right hand of the throne of the Majesty in the heavens, [2] a servant of the sanctuary and of the true tabernacle which the Lord pitched, not man. [3] For every high priest is appointed to offer both gifts and sacrifices. Therefore it is necessary that this high priest also have something to offer. [4] For if he were on earth, he would not be a priest at all, seeing there are priests who offer the gifts according to the law, [5] who serve a copy and shadow of the heavenly things, even as Moses was warned by God when he was about to make the tabernacle, for he said, "See, you shall make everything according to the pattern that was shown to you on the mountain."* [6] But now he has obtained a more excellent ministry, by as much as he is also the mediator of a better covenant, which on better promises has been given as law. [7] For if that first covenant had been faultless, then no place would have been sought for a second. [8] For finding fault with them, he said, "Behold,ᵃ the days are coming", says the Lord, "that I will make a new covenant with the house of Israel and with the house of Judah; [9] not according to the covenant that I made with their fathers in the day that I took them by the hand to lead them out of the land of Egypt; for they didn't continue in my covenant, and I disregarded them," says the Lord. [10]"For this is the covenant that I will make with the house of Israel after those days," says the Lord: "I will put my laws into their mind; I will also write them on their heart. I will be their God, and they will be my people. [11] They will not teach every man his fellow citizenᵇ and every man his brother, saying, 'Know the Lord,' for all will know me, from their least to their greatest. [12] For I will be merciful to their unrighteousness. I will remember their sins and lawless deeds no more."* [13] In that he says, "A new covenant", he has made the first obsolete. But that which is becoming obsolete and grows aged is near to vanishing away.

## 9

[1] Now indeed even the firstᶜ covenant had ordinances of divine service and an earthly sanctuary. [2] For a tabernacle was prepared. In the first part were the lamp stand, the table, and the show bread, which is called the Holy Place. [3] After the second veil was the tabernacle which is called the Holy of Holies, [4] having a golden altar of incense and the ark of the covenant overlaid on all sides with gold, in which was a golden pot holding the manna, Aaron's rod that budded, and the tablets of the

---

* 5:5 Psalms 2:7
* 5:6 Psalms 110:4
* 6:14 Genesis 22:17
* 7:17 Psalms 110:4

* 7:21 Psalms 110:4
* 8:5 Exodus 25:40
ᵃ 8:8 "Behold", from "ἰδού", means look at, take notice,

observe, see, or gaze at. It is often used as an interjection.
ᵇ 8:11 TR reads "neighbor" instead of "fellow citizen"

* 8:12 Jeremiah 31:31- 34
ᶜ 9:1 TR adds "tabernacle"

covenant; [5] and above it cherubim of glory overshadowing the mercy seat, of which things we can't speak now in detail. [6] Now these things having been thus prepared, the priests go in continually into the first tabernacle, accomplishing the services, [7] but into the second the high priest alone, once in the year, not without blood, which he offers for himself and for the errors of the people. [8] The Holy Spirit is indicating this, that the way into the Holy Place wasn't yet revealed while the first tabernacle was still standing. [9] This is a symbol of the present age, where gifts and sacrifices are offered that are incapable, concerning the conscience, of making the worshiper perfect, [10] being only (with foods and drinks and various washings) fleshly ordinances, imposed until a time of reformation. [11] But Christ having come as a high priest of the coming good things, through the greater and more perfect tabernacle, not made with hands, that is to say, not of this creation, [12] nor yet through the blood of goats and calves, but through his own blood, entered in once for all into the Holy Place, having obtained eternal redemption. [13] For if the blood of goats and bulls, and the ashes of a heifer sprinkling those who have been defiled, sanctify to the cleanness of the flesh, [14] how much more will the blood of Christ, who through the eternal Spirit offered himself without defect to God, cleanse your conscience from dead works to serve the living God? [15] For this reason he is the mediator of a new covenant, since a death has occurred for the redemption of the transgressions that were under the first covenant, that those who have been called may receive the promise of the eternal inheritance. [16] For where a last will and testament is, there must of necessity be the death of him who made it. [17] For a will is in force where there has been death, for it is never in force while he who made it lives. [18] Therefore even the first covenant has not been dedicated without blood. [19] For when every commandment had been spoken by Moses to all the people according to the law, he took the blood of the calves and the goats, with water and scarlet wool and hyssop, and sprinkled both the book itself and all the people, [20] saying, "This is the blood of the covenant which God has commanded you."* [21] He sprinkled the tabernacle and all the vessels of the ministry in the same way with the blood. [22] According to the law, nearly everything is cleansed with blood, and apart from shedding of blood there is no remission. [23] It was necessary therefore that the copies of the things in the heavens should be cleansed with these, but the heavenly things themselves with better sacrifices than these. [24] For Christ hasn't entered into holy places made with hands, which are representations of the true, but into heaven itself, now to appear in the presence of God for us; [25] nor yet that he should offer himself often, as the high priest enters into the holy place year by year with blood not his own, [26] or else he must have suffered often since the foundation of the world. But now once at the end of the ages, he has been revealed to put away sin by the sacrifice of himself. [27] Inasmuch as it is appointed for men to die once, and after this, judgment, [28] so Christ also, having been offered once to bear the sins of many, will appear a second time, not to deal with sin, but to save those who are eagerly waiting for him.

## 10

[1] For the law, having a shadow of the good to come, not the very image of the things, can never with the same sacrifices year by year, which they offer continually, make perfect those who draw near. [2] Or else wouldn't they have ceased to be offered, because the worshipers, having been once cleansed, would have had no more consciousness of sins? [3] But in those sacrifices there is a yearly reminder of sins. [4] For it is impossible that the blood of bulls and goats should take away sins. [5] Therefore when he comes into the world, he says, "You didn't desire sacrifice and offering, but you prepared a body for me. [6] You had no pleasure in whole burnt offerings and sacrifices for sin. [7] Then I said, 'Behold, I have come (in the scroll of the book it is written of me) to do your will, O God.'"* [8] Previously saying, "Sacrifices and offerings and whole burnt offerings and sacrifices for sin you didn't desire, neither had pleasure in them" (those which are offered according to the law), [9] then he has said, "Behold, I have come to do your will." He takes away the first, that he may establish the second, [10] by which will we have been sanctified through the offering of the body of Jesus Christ once for all. [11] Every priest indeed stands day by day serving and offering often the same sacrifices, which can never take away sins, [12] but he, when he had offered one sacrifice for sins forever, sat down on the right hand of God, [13] from that time waiting until his enemies are made the footstool of his feet. [14] For by one offering he has perfected forever those who are being sanctified. [15] The Holy Spirit also testifies to us, for after saying, [16]"This is the covenant that I will make with them after those days," says the Lord, "I will put my laws on their heart, I will also write them on their mind;"* then he says, [17]"I will remember their sins and their iniquities no more."* [18] Now where remission of these is, there is no more offering for sin. [19] Having therefore, brothers, boldness to enter into the holy place by the blood of Jesus, [20] by the way which he dedicated for us, a new and living way, through the veil, that is to say, his flesh, [21] and having a great priest over God's house, [22] let's draw near with a true heart in fullness of faith, having our hearts sprinkled from an evil conscience and having our body washed with pure water, [23] let's hold fast the confession of our hope without wavering; for he who promised is faithful. [24] Let's consider how to provoke one another to love and good works, [25] not forsaking our own assembling together, as the custom of some is, but exhorting one another, and so much the more as you see the Day approaching. [26] For if we sin willfully after we have received the knowledge of the truth, there remains no more a sacrifice for sins, [27] but a certain fearful expectation of judgment, and a fierceness of fire which will devour the adversaries. [28] A man who disregards Moses' law dies without compassion on the word of two or three witnesses. [29] How much worse punishment do you think he will be judged worthy of who has trodden under foot the Son of God, and has counted the blood of the covenant with which he was sanctified an unholy thing, and has insulted the Spirit of grace? [30] For we know him who said, "Vengeance belongs to me. I will repay," says the Lord.* Again, "The Lord will judge his people."* [31] It is a fearful thing to fall into the hands of the living God. [32] But remember the former days, in which, after you were enlightened, you endured a great struggle with sufferings: [33] partly, being exposed to both reproaches and oppressions, and partly, becoming partakers with those who were treated so. [34] For you both had compassion on me in my chains and joyfully accepted the plundering of your possessions, knowing that you have for yourselves a better possession and an enduring one in the heavens. [35] Therefore don't throw away your boldness, which has a great reward. [36] For you need endurance so that, having done the will of God, you may receive the promise. [37]"In a very little while, he who comes will come and will not wait. [38] But the righteous one will live by faith. If he shrinks back, my soul has no pleasure in him."* [39] But we are not of those who shrink back to destruction, but of those who have faith to the saving of the soul.

## 11

[1] Now faith is assurance of things hoped for, proof of things not seen. [2] For by this, the elders obtained approval. [3] By faith we understand that the universe has been framed by the word of God, so that what is seen has not been made out of things which are visible. [4] By faith Abel offered to God a more excellent sacrifice than Cain, through which he had testimony given to him that he was righteous, God testifying with respect to his gifts; and through it he, being dead, still speaks. [5] By faith Enoch was taken away, so that he wouldn't see death, and he was not found, because God translated him. For he has had testimony given to him that before his translation he had been well pleasing to God. [6] Without faith it is impossible to be well pleasing to him, for he who comes to God must believe that he exists, and that he is a rewarder of those who seek him. [7] By faith Noah, being warned about things not yet seen, moved with godly fear,[a] prepared a ship for the saving of his house, through which he condemned the world and became heir of the righteousness which is according to faith. [8] By faith Abraham, when he was called, obeyed to go out to the place which he was to receive for an inheritance. He went out, not knowing where he went. [9] By faith he lived as an alien in the land of promise, as in a land not his own, dwelling in tents with Isaac and Jacob, the heirs with him of the same promise. [10] For he was looking for the city which has foundations, whose builder and maker is God. [11] By faith even Sarah herself received power to conceive, and she bore a child when she was past age, since she counted him faithful who had promised. [12] Therefore as many as the stars of the sky in multitude, and as innumerable as the sand which is by the sea shore, were fathered by one man, and him as good as dead. [13] These all died in faith, not having received the promises, but having seen[b] them and embraced them from afar, and having confessed that they were strangers and pilgrims on the earth. [14] For those who say such things make it clear that they are seeking a country of their own. [15] If indeed they had been thinking of that country from which they went out, they would have had enough time to return. [16] But now they desire a better country, that is, a heavenly one. Therefore God is not ashamed of them, to be called their God, for he has prepared a city for them. [17] By faith, Abraham, being tested, offered up Isaac. Yes, he who had gladly received the promises was offering up his only born[c] son, [18] to

---

* 9:20 Exodus 24:8
* 10:7 Psalms 40:6- 8
* 10:16 Jeremiah 31:33
* 10:17 Jeremiah 31:34

* 10:30 Deuteronomy 32:35
* 10:30 Deuteronomy 32:36; Psalms 135:14
* 10:38 Habakkuk 2:3- 4

[a] 11:7 or, reverence
[b] 11:13 TR adds "and being convinced of"

[c] 11:17 The phrase "only born" is from the Greek word "μονογενη", which is

whom it was said, "Your offspring will be accounted as from Isaac," * [19] concluding that God is able to raise up even from the dead. Figuratively speaking, he also did receive him back from the dead. [20] By faith Isaac blessed Jacob and Esau, even concerning things to come. [21] By faith Jacob, when he was dying, blessed each of the sons of Joseph, and worshiped, leaning on the top of his staff. [22] By faith Joseph, when his end was near, made mention of the departure of the children of Israel, and gave instructions concerning his bones. [23] By faith Moses, when he was born, was hidden for three months by his parents, because they saw that he was a beautiful child; and they were not afraid of the king's commandment. [24] By faith Moses, when he had grown up, refused to be called the son of Pharaoh's daughter, [25] choosing rather to share ill treatment with God's people than to enjoy the pleasures of sin for a time, [26] considering the reproach of Christ greater riches than the treasures of Egypt; for he looked to the reward. [27] By faith he left Egypt, not fearing the wrath of the king; for he endured, as seeing him who is invisible. [28] By faith he kept the Passover and the sprinkling of the blood, that the destroyer of the firstborn should not touch them. [29] By faith they passed through the Red Sea as on dry land. When the Egyptians tried to do so, they were swallowed up. [30] By faith the walls of Jericho fell down after they had been encircled for seven days. [31] By faith Rahab the prostitute didn't perish with those who were disobedient, having received the spies in peace. [32] What more shall I say? For the time would fail me if I told of Gideon, Barak, Samson, Jephthah, David, Samuel, and the prophets— [33] who through faith subdued kingdoms, worked out righteousness, obtained promises, stopped the mouths of lions, * [34] quenched the power of fire, * escaped the edge of the sword, * from weakness were made strong, grew mighty in war, and caused foreign armies to flee. [35] Women received their dead by resurrection.* Others were tortured, not accepting their deliverance, that they might obtain a better resurrection. [36] Others were tried by mocking and scourging, yes, moreover by bonds and imprisonment. [37] They were stoned.* They were sawn apart. They were tempted. They were slain with the sword.* They went around in sheep skins and in goat skins; being destitute, afflicted, ill-treated— [38] of whom the world was not worthy—wandering in deserts, mountains, caves, and the holes of the earth. [39] These all, having been commended for their faith, didn't receive the promise, [40] God having provided some better thing concerning us, so that apart from us they should not be made perfect.

## 12

[1] Therefore let's also, seeing we are surrounded by so great a cloud of witnesses, lay aside every weight and the sin which so easily entangles us, and let's run with perseverance the race that is set before us, [2] looking to Jesus, the author and perfecter of faith, who for the joy that was set before him endured the cross, despising its shame, and has sat down at the right hand of the throne of God. [3] For consider him who has endured such contradiction of sinners against himself, that you don't grow weary, fainting in your souls. [4] You have not yet resisted to blood, striving against sin. [5] You have forgotten the exhortation which reasons with you as with children, "My son, don't take lightly the chastening of the Lord, nor faint when you are reproved by him; [6] for whom the Lord loves, he disciplines, and chastises every son whom he receives."* [7] It is for discipline that you endure. God deals with you as with children, for what son is there whom his father doesn't discipline? [8] But if you are without discipline, of which all have been made partakers, then you are illegitimate, and not children. [9] Furthermore, we had the fathers of our flesh to chasten us, and we paid them respect. Shall we not much rather be in subjection to the Father of spirits and live? [10] For they indeed for a few days disciplined us as seemed good to them, but he for our profit, that we may be partakers of his holiness. [11] All chastening seems for the present to be not joyous but grievous; yet afterward it yields the peaceful fruit of righteousness to those who have been trained by it. [12] Therefore lift up the hands that hang down and the feeble knees, * [13] and make straight paths for your feet,* so what is lame may not be dislocated, but rather be healed. [14] Follow after peace with all men, and the sanctification without which no man will see the Lord, [15] looking carefully lest there be any man who falls short of the grace of God, lest any root of bitterness springing up trouble you and many be defiled by it, [16] lest there be any sexually immoral person or profane person, like Esau, who sold his birthright for one meal. [17] For you know that even when he afterward desired to inherit the blessing, he was rejected, for he found no place for a change of mind though he sought it diligently with tears. [18] For you have not come to a

mountain that might be touched and that burned with fire, and to blackness, darkness, storm, [19] the sound of a trumpet, and the voice of words; which those who heard it begged that not one more word should be spoken to them, [20] for they could not stand that which was commanded, "If even an animal touches the mountain, it shall be stoned".ª* [21] So fearful was the appearance that Moses said, "I am terrified and trembling."* [22] But you have come to Mount Zion and to the city of the living God, the heavenly Jerusalem, and to innumerable multitudes of angels, [23] to the festal gathering and assembly of the firstborn who are enrolled in heaven, to God the Judge of all, to the spirits of just men made perfect, [24] to Jesus, the mediator of a new covenant,* and to the blood of sprinkling that speaks better than that of Abel. [25] See that you don't refuse him who speaks. For if they didn't escape when they refused him who warned on the earth, how much more will we not escape who turn away from him who warns from heaven, [26] whose voice shook the earth then, but now he has promised, saying, "Yet once more I will shake not only the earth, but also the heavens."* [27] This phrase, "Yet once more" signifies the removing of those things that are shaken, as of things that have been made, that those things which are not shaken may remain. [28] Therefore, receiving a Kingdom that can't be shaken, let's have grace, through which we serve God acceptably, with reverence and awe, [29] for our God is a consuming fire.*

## 13

[1] Let brotherly love continue. [2] Don't forget to show hospitality to strangers, for in doing so, some have entertained angels without knowing it. [3] Remember those who are in bonds, as bound with them, and those who are ill-treated, since you are also in the body. [4] Let marriage be held in honor among all, and let the bed be undefiled; but God will judge the sexually immoral and adulterers. [5] Be free from the love of money, content with such things as you have, for he has said, "I will in no way leave you, neither will I in any way forsake you."* [6] So that with good courage we say, "The Lord is my helper. I will not fear. What can man do to me?"* [7] Remember your leaders, men who spoke to you the word of God, and considering the results of their conduct, imitate their faith. [8] Jesus Christ is the same yesterday, today, and forever. [9] Don't be carried away by various and strange teachings, for it is good that the heart be established by grace, not by foods, through which those who were so occupied were not benefited. [10] We have an altar from which those who serve the holy tabernacle have no right to eat. [11] For the bodies of those animals, whose blood is brought into the holy place by the high priest as an offering for sin, are burned outside of the camp.* [12] Therefore Jesus also, that he might sanctify the people through his own blood, suffered outside of the gate. [13] Let's therefore go out to him outside of the camp, bearing his reproach. [14] For we don't have here an enduring city, but we seek that which is to come. [15] Through him, then, let's offer up a sacrifice of praise to God * continually, that is, the fruit of lips which proclaim allegiance to his name. [16] But don't forget to be doing good and sharing, for with such sacrifices God is well pleased. [17] Obey your leaders and submit to them, for they watch on behalf of your souls, as those who will give account, that they may do this with joy and not with groaning, for that would be unprofitable for you. [18] Pray for us, for we are persuaded that we have a good conscience, desiring to live honorably in all things. [19] I strongly urge you to do this, that I may be restored to you sooner. [20] Now may the God of peace, who brought again from the dead the great shepherd of the sheep with the blood of an eternal covenant, our Lord Jesus, [21] make you complete in every good work to do his will, working in you that which is well pleasing in his sight, through Jesus Christ, to whom be the glory forever and ever. Amen. [22] But I exhort you, brothers, endure the word of exhortation, for I have written to you in few words. [23] Know that our brother Timothy has been freed, with whom, if he comes shortly, I will see you. [24] Greet all of your leaders and all the saints. The Italians greet you. [25] Grace be with you all. Amen.

## The Letter from James

## 1

[1] James, a servant of God and of the Lord Jesus Christ,ᵇ to the twelve tribes which are in the Dispersion: Greetings. [2] Count it all joy, my

---

sometimes translated "only begotten" or "one and only".
* 11:18 Genesis 21:12
* 11:33 Daniel 6:22- 23
* 11:34 Daniel 3:1- 30
* 11:34 1 Kings 19:1- 3; 2 Kings 6:31— 7:20

* 11:35 1 Kings 17:17- 23; 2 Kings 4:32- 37
* 11:37 2 Chronicles 24:20- 21
* 11:37 Jeremiah 26:20- 23; 1 Kings 19:10
* 12:6 Proverbs 3:11- 12
* 12:12 Isaiah 35:3

* 12:13 Proverbs 4:26
ª *12:20* TR adds "or shot with an arrow"
* 12:20 Exodus 19:12- 13
* 12:21 Deuteronomy 9:19
* 12:24 Jeremiah 31:31
* 12:26 Haggai 2:6

* 12:29 Deuteronomy 4:24
* 13:5 Deuteronomy 31:6
* 13:6 Psalms 118:6- 7
* 13:11 Leviticus 16:27
* 13:15 Psalms 50:23
ᵇ *1:1* "Christ" means "Anointed One".

brothers,[a] when you fall into various temptations, ³ knowing that the testing of your faith produces endurance. ⁴ Let endurance have its perfect work, that you may be perfect and complete, lacking in nothing. ⁵ But if any of you lacks wisdom, let him ask of God, who gives to all liberally and without reproach, and it will be given to him. ⁶ But let him ask in faith, without any doubting, for he who doubts is like a wave of the sea, driven by the wind and tossed. ⁷ For that man shouldn't think that he will receive anything from the Lord. ⁸ He is a double-minded man, unstable in all his ways. ⁹ Let the brother in humble circumstances glory in his high position; ¹⁰ and the rich, in that he is made humble, because like the flower in the grass, he will pass away. ¹¹ For the sun arises with the scorching wind and withers the grass; and the flower in it falls, and the beauty of its appearance perishes. So the rich man will also fade away in his pursuits. ¹² Blessed is a person who endures temptation, for when he has been approved, he will receive the crown of life which the Lord promised to those who love him. ¹³ Let no man say when he is tempted, "I am tempted by God," for God can't be tempted by evil, and he himself tempts no one. ¹⁴ But each one is tempted when he is drawn away by his own lust and enticed. ¹⁵ Then the lust, when it has conceived, bears sin. The sin, when it is full grown, produces death. ¹⁶ Don't be deceived, my beloved brothers. ¹⁷ Every good gift and every perfect gift is from above, coming down from the Father of lights, with whom can be no variation nor turning shadow. ¹⁸ Of his own will he gave birth to us by the word of truth, that we should be a kind of first fruits of his creatures. ¹⁹ So, then, my beloved brothers, let every man be swift to hear, slow to speak, and slow to anger; ²⁰ for the anger of man doesn't produce the righteousness of God. ²¹ Therefore, putting away all filthiness and overflowing of wickedness, receive with humility the implanted word, which is able to save your souls.[b] ²² But be doers of the word, and not only hearers, deluding your own selves. ²³ For if anyone is a hearer of the word and not a doer, he is like a man looking at his natural face in a mirror; ²⁴ for he sees himself, and goes away, and immediately forgets what kind of man he was. ²⁵ But he who looks into the perfect law of freedom and continues, not being a hearer who forgets but a doer of the work, this man will be blessed in what he does. ²⁶ If anyone among you thinks himself to be religious while he doesn't bridle his tongue, but deceives his heart, this man's religion is worthless. ²⁷ Pure religion and undefiled before our God and Father is this: to visit the fatherless and widows in their affliction, and to keep oneself unstained by the world.

## 2

¹ My brothers, don't hold the faith of our glorious Lord Jesus Christ with partiality. ² For if a man with a gold ring, in fine clothing, comes into your synagogue,[c] and a poor man in filthy clothing also comes in, ³ and you pay special attention to him who wears the fine clothing and say, "Sit here in a good place;" and you tell the poor man, "Stand there," or "Sit by my footstool" ⁴ haven't you shown partiality among yourselves, and become judges with evil thoughts? ⁵ Listen, my beloved brothers. Didn't God choose those who are poor in this world to be rich in faith and heirs of the Kingdom which he promised to those who love him? ⁶ But you have dishonored the poor man. Don't the rich oppress you and personally drag you before the courts? ⁷ Don't they blaspheme the honorable name by which you are called? ⁸ However, if you fulfill the royal law according to the Scripture, "You shall love your neighbor as yourself,"* you do well. ⁹ But if you show partiality, you commit sin, being convicted by the law as transgressors. ¹⁰ For whoever keeps the whole law, and yet stumbles in one point, he has become guilty of all. ¹¹ For he who said, "Do not commit adultery,"* also said, "Do not commit murder."* Now if you do not commit adultery but do murder, you have become a transgressor of the law. ¹² So speak and so do as men who are to be judged by the law of freedom. ¹³ For judgment is without mercy to him who has shown no mercy. Mercy triumphs over judgment. ¹⁴ What good is it, my brothers, if a man says he has faith, but has no works? Can faith save him? ¹⁵ And if a brother or sister is naked and in lack of daily food, ¹⁶ and one of you tells them, "Go in peace. Be warmed and filled;" yet you didn't give them the things the body needs, what good is it? ¹⁷ Even so faith, if it has no works, is dead in itself. ¹⁸ Yes, a man will say, "You have faith, and I have works." Show me your faith without works, and I will show you my faith by my works. ¹⁹ You believe that God is one. You do well. The demons also believe—and shudder. ²⁰ But do you want to know, vain man, that faith apart from works is dead? ²¹ Wasn't Abraham our father justified by works, in that he offered up Isaac his son on the altar? ²² You see that faith worked with his works, and by works faith was perfected. ²³ So

the Scripture was fulfilled which says, "Abraham believed God, and it was accounted to him as righteousness,"* and he was called the friend of God. ²⁴ You see then that by works a man is justified, and not only by faith. ²⁵ In the same way, wasn't Rahab the prostitute also justified by works when she received the messengers and sent them out another way? ²⁶ For as the body apart from the spirit is dead, even so faith apart from works is dead.

## 3

¹ Let not many of you be teachers, my brothers, knowing that we will receive heavier judgment. ² For we all stumble in many things. Anyone who doesn't stumble in word is a perfect person, able to bridle the whole body also. ³ Indeed, we put bits into the horses' mouths so that they may obey us, and we guide their whole body. ⁴ Behold,[d] the ships also, though they are so big and are driven by fierce winds, are yet guided by a very small rudder, wherever the pilot desires. ⁵ So the tongue is also a little member, and boasts great things. See how a small fire can spread to a large forest! ⁶ And the tongue is a fire. The world of iniquity among our members is the tongue, which defiles the whole body, and sets on fire the course of nature, and is set on fire by Gehenna.[e] ⁷ For every kind of animal, bird, creeping thing, and sea creature is tamed, and has been tamed by mankind; ⁸ but nobody can tame the tongue. It is a restless evil, full of deadly poison. ⁹ With it we bless our God and Father, and with it we curse men who are made in the image of God. ¹⁰ Out of the same mouth comes blessing and cursing. My brothers, these things ought not to be so. ¹¹ Does a spring send out from the same opening fresh and bitter water? ¹² Can a fig tree, my brothers, yield olives, or a vine figs? Thus no spring yields both salt water and fresh water. ¹³ Who is wise and understanding among you? Let him show by his good conduct that his deeds are done in gentleness of wisdom. ¹⁴ But if you have bitter jealousy and selfish ambition in your heart, don't boast and don't lie against the truth. ¹⁵ This wisdom is not that which comes down from above, but is earthly, sensual, and demonic. ¹⁶ For where jealousy and selfish ambition are, there is confusion and every evil deed. ¹⁷ But the wisdom that is from above is first pure, then peaceful, gentle, reasonable, full of mercy and good fruits, without partiality, and without hypocrisy. ¹⁸ Now the fruit of righteousness is sown in peace by those who make peace.

## 4

¹ Where do wars and fightings among you come from? Don't they come from your pleasures that war in your members? ² You lust, and don't have. You murder and covet, and can't obtain. You fight and make war. You don't have, because you don't ask. ³ You ask, and don't receive, because you ask with wrong motives, so that you may spend it on your pleasures. ⁴ You adulterers and adulteresses, don't you know that friendship with the world is hostility toward God? Whoever therefore wants to be a friend of the world makes himself an enemy of God. ⁵ Or do you think that the Scripture says in vain, "The Spirit who lives in us yearns jealously"? ⁶ But he gives more grace. Therefore it says, "God resists the proud, but gives grace to the humble."* ⁷ Be subject therefore to God. Resist the devil, and he will flee from you. ⁸ Draw near to God, and he will draw near to you. Cleanse your hands, you sinners. Purify your hearts, you double-minded. ⁹ Lament, mourn, and weep. Let your laughter be turned to mourning and your joy to gloom. ¹⁰ Humble yourselves in the sight of the Lord, and he will exalt you. ¹¹ Don't speak against one another, brothers. He who speaks against a brother and judges his brother, speaks against the law and judges the law. But if you judge the law, you are not a doer of the law but a judge. ¹² Only one is the lawgiver, who is able to save and to destroy. But who are you to judge another? ¹³ Come now, you who say, "Today or tomorrow let's go into this city and spend a year there, trade, and make a profit." ¹⁴ Yet you don't know what your life will be like tomorrow. For what is your life? For you are a vapor that appears for a little time and then vanishes away. ¹⁵ For you ought to say, "If the Lord wills, we will both live, and do this or that." ¹⁶ But now you glory in your boasting. All such boasting is evil. ¹⁷ To him therefore who knows to do good and doesn't do it, to him it is sin.

## 5

¹ Come now, you rich, weep and howl for your miseries that are coming on you. ² Your riches are corrupted and your garments are moth-eaten. ³ Your gold and your silver are corroded, and their corrosion will be for a testimony against you and will eat your flesh like fire. You have laid up your treasure in the last days. ⁴ Behold, the wages of the laborers who mowed your fields, which you have kept back by fraud, cry out; and the cries of those who reaped have entered into the ears of the Lord

---

[a] *1:2* The word for "brothers" here and where context allows may also be correctly translated "brothers and sisters" or "siblings."

[b] *1:21* or, preserve your life.
[c] *2:2* or, meeting
* *2:8* Leviticus 19:18
* *2:11* Exodus 20:14; Deuteronomy 5:18

* *2:11* Exodus 20:13; Deuteronomy 5:17
* *2:23* Genesis 15:6
[d] *3:4* "Behold", from "ἰδοὺ", means look at, take notice,

observe, see, or gaze at. It is often used as an interjection.
[e] *3:6* or, Hell
* *4:6* Proverbs 3:34

of Armies.[a] [5] You have lived in luxury on the earth, and taken your pleasure. You have nourished your hearts as in a day of slaughter. [6] You have condemned and you have murdered the righteous one. He doesn't resist you. [7] Be patient therefore, brothers, until the coming of the Lord. Behold, the farmer waits for the precious fruit of the earth, being patient over it, until it receives the early and late rain. [8] You also be patient. Establish your hearts, for the coming of the Lord is at hand. [9] Don't grumble, brothers, against one another, so that you won't be judged. Behold, the judge stands at the door. [10] Take, brothers, for an example of suffering and of perseverance, the prophets who spoke in the name of the Lord. [11] Behold, we call them blessed who endured. You have heard of the perseverance of Job and have seen the Lord in the outcome, and how the Lord is full of compassion and mercy. [12] But above all things, my brothers, don't swear—not by heaven, or by the earth, or by any other oath; but let your "yes" be "yes", and your "no", "no", so that you don't fall into hypocrisy.[b] [13] Is any among you suffering? Let him pray. Is any cheerful? Let him sing praises. [14] Is any among you sick? Let him call for the elders of the assembly, and let them pray over him, anointing him with oil in the name of the Lord; [15] and the prayer of faith will heal him who is sick, and the Lord will raise him up. If he has committed sins, he will be forgiven. [16] Confess your sins to one another and pray for one another, that you may be healed. The insistent prayer of a righteous person is powerfully effective. [17] Elijah was a man with a nature like ours, and he prayed earnestly that it might not rain, and it didn't rain on the earth for three years and six months. [18] He prayed again, and the sky gave rain, and the earth produced its fruit. [19] Brothers, if any among you wanders from the truth and someone turns him back, [20] let him know that he who turns a sinner from the error of his way will save a soul from death and will cover a multitude of sins.

# Peter's First Letter

## 1

[1] Peter, an apostle of Jesus Christ,[c] to the chosen ones who are living as foreigners in the Dispersion in Pontus, Galatia, Cappadocia, Asia, and Bithynia, [2] according to the foreknowledge of God the Father, in sanctification of the Spirit, that you may obey Jesus Christ and be sprinkled with his blood: Grace to you and peace be multiplied. [3] Blessed be the God and Father of our Lord Jesus Christ, who according to his great mercy caused us to be born again to a living hope through the resurrection of Jesus Christ from the dead, [4] to an incorruptible and undefiled inheritance that doesn't fade away, reserved in Heaven for you, [5] who by the power of God are guarded through faith for a salvation ready to be revealed in the last time. [6] In this you greatly rejoice, though now for a little while, if need be, you have been grieved in various trials, [7] that the proof of your faith, which is more precious than gold that perishes, even though it is tested by fire, may be found to result in praise, glory, and honor at the revelation of Jesus Christ— [8] whom, not having known, you love. In him, though now you don't see him, yet believing, you rejoice greatly with joy that is unspeakable and full of glory, [9] receiving the result of your faith, the salvation of your souls. [10] Concerning this salvation, the prophets sought and searched diligently. They prophesied of the grace that would come to you, [11] searching for who or what kind of time the Spirit of Christ which was in them pointed to when he predicted the sufferings of Christ and the glories that would follow them. [12] To them it was revealed that they served not themselves, but you, in these things, which now have been announced to you through those who preached the Good News to you by the Holy Spirit sent out from heaven; which things angels desire to look into. [13] Therefore prepare your minds for action.[d] Be sober, and set your hope fully on the grace that will be brought to you at the revelation of Jesus Christ— [14] as children of obedience, not conforming yourselves according to your former lusts as in your ignorance, [15] but just as he who called you is holy, you yourselves also be holy in all of your behavior, [16] because it is written, "You shall be holy, for I am holy."[*] [17] If you call on him as Father, who without respect of persons judges according to each man's work, pass the time of your living as foreigners here in reverent fear, [18] knowing that you were redeemed, not with corruptible things like silver or gold, from the useless way of life handed down from your fathers, [19] but with precious blood, as of a lamb without blemish or spot, the blood of Christ, [20] who was

foreknown indeed before the foundation of the world, but was revealed in this last age for your sake, [21] who through him are believers in God, who raised him from the dead and gave him glory, so that your faith and hope might be in God. [22] Seeing you have purified your souls in your obedience to the truth through the Spirit in sincere brotherly affection, love one another from the heart fervently, [23] having been born again, not of corruptible seed, but of incorruptible, through the word of God, which lives and remains forever. [24] For, "All flesh is like grass, and all of man's glory like the flower in the grass. The grass withers, and its flower falls; [25] but the Lord's word endures forever."[*] This is the word of Good News which was preached to you.

## 2

[1] Putting away therefore all wickedness, all deceit, hypocrisies, envies, and all evil speaking, [2] as newborn babies, long for the pure spiritual milk, that with it you may grow, [3] if indeed you have tasted that the Lord is gracious. [4] Come to him, a living stone, rejected indeed by men, but chosen by God, precious. [5] You also as living stones are built up as a spiritual house, to be a holy priesthood, to offer up spiritual sacrifices, acceptable to God through Jesus Christ. [6] Because it is contained in Scripture, "Behold,[e] I lay in Zion a chief cornerstone, chosen and precious. He who believes in him will not be disappointed."[*] [7] For you who believe therefore is the honor, but for those who are disobedient, "The stone which the builders rejected has become the chief cornerstone,"[*] [8] and, "a stumbling stone and a rock of offense."[*] For they stumble at the word, being disobedient, to which also they were appointed. [9] But you are a chosen race, a royal priesthood, a holy nation, a people for God's own possession, that you may proclaim the excellence of him who called you out of darkness into his marvelous light. [10] In the past, you were not a people, but now are God's people, who had not obtained mercy, but now have obtained mercy. [11] Beloved, I beg you as foreigners and pilgrims to abstain from fleshly lusts which war against the soul, [12] having good behavior among the nations, so in that of which they speak against you as evildoers, they may see your good works and glorify God in the day of visitation. [13] Therefore subject yourselves to every ordinance of man for the Lord's sake: whether to the king, as supreme, [14] or to governors, as sent by him for vengeance on evildoers and for praise to those who do well. [15] For this is the will of God, that by well-doing you should put to silence the ignorance of foolish men. [16] Live as free people, yet not using your freedom for a cloak of wickedness, but as bondservants of God. [17] Honor all men. Love the brotherhood. Fear God. Honor the king. [18] Servants, be in subjection to your masters with all respect, not only to the good and gentle, but also to the wicked. [19] For it is commendable if someone endures pain, suffering unjustly, because of conscience toward God. [20] For what glory is it if, when you sin, you patiently endure beating? But if when you do well, you patiently endure suffering, this is commendable with God. [21] For you were called to this, because Christ also suffered for us, leaving you[f] an example, that you should follow his steps, [22] who didn't sin, "neither was deceit found in his mouth."[*] [23] When he was cursed, he didn't curse back. When he suffered, he didn't threaten, but committed himself to him who judges righteously. [24] He himself bore our sins in his body on the tree, that we, having died to sins, might live to righteousness. You were healed by his wounds.[g] [25] For you were going astray like sheep; but now you have returned to the Shepherd and Overseer[h] of your souls.

## 3

[1] In the same way, wives, be in subjection to your own husbands, so that, even if any don't obey the Word, they may be won by the behavior of their wives without a word, [2] seeing your pure behavior in fear. [3] Let your beauty come not from the outward adorning of braiding your hair, and of wearing gold ornaments or of putting on fine clothing, [4] but from the hidden person of the heart, in the incorruptible adornment of a gentle and quiet spirit, which is very precious in God's sight. [5] For this is how in the past the holy women who hoped in God also adorned themselves, being in subjection to their own husbands. [6] So Sarah obeyed Abraham, calling him lord, whose children you now are if you do well and are not put in fear by any terror. [7] You husbands, in the same way, live with your wives according to knowledge, giving honor to the woman as to the weaker vessel, as also being joint heirs of the grace of life, that your prayers may not be hindered. [8] Finally, all of you be like-minded, compassionate, loving as brothers, tenderhearted, courteous, [9] not rendering evil for evil or insult for insult; but instead

---

[a] 5:4 Greek: Sabaoth (or Hebrew: Tze'va'ot)
[b] 5:12 TR reads "under judgment" instead of "into hypocrisy"
[c] 1:1 "Christ" means "Anointed One".

[d] 1:13 literally, "gird up the waist of your mind" or "put on the belt of the waist of your mind"
[*] 1:16 Leviticus 11:44- 45
[*] 1:25 Isaiah 40:6- 8
[e] 2:6 "Behold", from "הִנֵּה" or "ἰδού", means look at, take

notice, observe, see, or gaze at. It is often used as an interjection.
[*] 2:6 Isaiah 28:16
[*] 2:7 Psalms 118:22
[*] 2:8 Isaiah 8:14
[f] 2:21 TR reads "us" instead of "you"

[*] 2:22 Isaiah 53:9
[g] 2:24 or, stripes
[h] 2:25 "Overseer" is from the Greek ἐπίσκοπον, which can mean overseer, curator, guardian, or superintendent.

blessing, knowing that you were called to this, that you may inherit a blessing. [10] For, "He who would love life and see good days, let him keep his tongue from evil and his lips from speaking deceit. [11] Let him turn away from evil and do good. Let him seek peace and pursue it. [12] For the eyes of the Lord are on the righteous, and his ears open to their prayer; but the face of the Lord is against those who do evil."* [13] Now who will harm you if you become imitators of that which is good? [14] But even if you should suffer for righteousness' sake, you are blessed. "Don't fear what they fear, neither be troubled."* [15] But sanctify the Lord God in your hearts. Always be ready to give an answer to everyone who asks you a reason concerning the hope that is in you, with humility and fear, [16] having a good conscience. Thus, while you are spoken against as evildoers, they may be disappointed who curse your good way of life in Christ. [17] For it is better, if it is God's will, that you suffer for doing what is right than for doing evil. [18] Because Christ also suffered for sins once, the righteous for the unrighteous, that he might bring you to God, being put to death in the flesh, but made alive in the Spirit, [19] in whom he also went and preached to the spirits in prison, [20] who before were disobedient when God waited patiently in the days of Noah while the ship was being built. In it, few, that is, eight souls, were saved through water. [21] This is a symbol of baptism, which now saves you—not the putting away of the filth of the flesh, but the answer of a good conscience toward God—through the resurrection of Jesus Christ, [22] who is at the right hand of God, having gone into heaven, angels and authorities and powers being made subject to him.

## 4

[1] Therefore, since Christ suffered for us in the flesh, arm yourselves also with the same mind; for he who has suffered in the flesh has ceased from sin, [2] that you no longer should live the rest of your time in the flesh for the lusts of men, but for the will of God. [3] For we have spent enough of our past time doing the desire of the Gentiles, and having walked in lewdness, lusts, drunken binges, orgies, carousings, and abominable idolatries. [4] They think it is strange that you don't run with them into the same excess of riot, speaking evil of you. [5] They will give account to him who is ready to judge the living and the dead. [6] For to this end the Good News was preached even to the dead, that they might be judged indeed as men in the flesh, but live as to God in the spirit. [7] But the end of all things is near. Therefore be of sound mind, self-controlled, and sober in prayer. [8] And above all things be earnest in your love among yourselves, for love covers a multitude of sins. [9] Be hospitable to one another without grumbling. [10] As each has received a gift, employ it in serving one another, as good managers of the grace of God in its various forms. [11] If anyone speaks, let it be as it were the very words of God. If anyone serves, let it be as of the strength which God supplies, that in all things God may be glorified through Jesus Christ, to whom belong the glory and the dominion forever and ever. Amen. [12] Beloved, don't be astonished at the fiery trial which has come upon you to test you, as though a strange thing happened to you. [13] But because you are partakers of Christ's sufferings, rejoice, that at the revelation of his glory you also may rejoice with exceeding joy. [14] If you are insulted for the name of Christ, you are blessed, because the Spirit of glory and of God rests on you. On their part he is blasphemed, but on your part he is glorified. [15] But let none of you suffer as a murderer, or a thief, or an evil doer, or a meddler in other men's matters. [16] But if one of you suffers for being a Christian, let him not be ashamed; but let him glorify God in this matter. [17] For the time has come for judgment to begin with the household of God. If it begins first with us, what will happen to those who don't obey the Good News of God? [18]"If it is hard for the righteous to be saved, what will happen to the ungodly and the sinner?"* [19] Therefore let them also who suffer according to the will of God in doing good entrust their souls to him, as to a faithful Creator.

## 5

[1] Therefore I exhort the elders among you, as a fellow elder and a witness of the sufferings of Christ, and who will also share in the glory that will be revealed: [2] shepherd the flock of God which is among you, exercising the oversight, not under compulsion, but voluntarily; not for dishonest gain, but willingly; [3] not as lording it over those entrusted to you, but making yourselves examples to the flock. [4] When the chief Shepherd is revealed, you will receive the crown of glory that doesn't fade away. [5] Likewise, you younger ones, be subject to the elder. Yes, all of you clothe yourselves with humility and subject yourselves to one another; for "God resists the proud, but gives grace to the humble."* [6] Humble yourselves therefore under the mighty hand of God, that he may exalt you in due time, [7] casting all your worries on him, because

he cares for you. [8] Be sober and self-controlled. Be watchful. Your adversary, the devil, walks around like a roaring lion, seeking whom he may devour. [9] Withstand him steadfast in your faith, knowing that your brothers who are in the world are undergoing the same sufferings. [10] But may the God of all grace, who called you to his eternal glory by Christ Jesus, after you have suffered a little while, perfect, establish, strengthen, and settle you. [11] To him be the glory and the power forever and ever. Amen. [12] Through Silvanus, our faithful brother, as I consider him, I have written to you briefly, exhorting and testifying that this is the true grace of God in which you stand. [13] She who is in Babylon, chosen together with you, greets you. So does Mark, my son. [14] Greet one another with a kiss of love. Peace be to all of you who are in Christ Jesus. Amen.

# Peter's Second Letter

## 1

[1] Simon Peter, a servant and apostle of Jesus Christ,[a] to those who have obtained a like precious faith with us in the righteousness of our God and Savior, Jesus Christ: [2] Grace to you and peace be multiplied in the knowledge of God and of Jesus our Lord, [3] seeing that his divine power has granted to us all things that pertain to life and godliness, through the knowledge of him who called us by his own glory and virtue, [4] by which he has granted to us his precious and exceedingly great promises; that through these you may become partakers of the divine nature, having escaped from the corruption that is in the world by lust. [5] Yes, and for this very cause adding on your part all diligence, in your faith supply moral excellence; and in moral excellence, knowledge; [6] and in knowledge, self-control; and in self-control, perseverance; and in perseverance, godliness; [7] and in godliness, brotherly affection; and in brotherly affection, love. [8] For if these things are yours and abound, they make you to not be idle or unfruitful in the knowledge of our Lord Jesus Christ. [9] For he who lacks these things is blind, seeing only what is near, having forgotten the cleansing from his old sins. [10] Therefore, brothers,[b] be more diligent to make your calling and election sure. For if you do these things, you will never stumble. [11] For thus you will be richly supplied with the entrance into the eternal Kingdom of our Lord and Savior, Jesus Christ. [12] Therefore I will not be negligent to remind you of these things, though you know them and are established in the present truth. [13] I think it right, as long as I am in this tent, to stir you up by reminding you, [14] knowing that the putting off of my tent comes swiftly, even as our Lord Jesus Christ made clear to me. [15] Yes, I will make every effort that you may always be able to remember these things even after my departure. [16] For we didn't follow cunningly devised fables when we made known to you the power and coming of our Lord Jesus Christ, but we were eyewitnesses of his majesty. [17] For he received from God the Father honor and glory when the voice came to him from the Majestic Glory, "This is my beloved Son, in whom I am well pleased."* [18] We heard this voice come out of heaven when we were with him on the holy mountain. [19] We have the more sure word of prophecy; and you do well that you heed it as to a lamp shining in a dark place, until the day dawns and the morning star arises in your hearts, [20] knowing this first, that no prophecy of Scripture is of private interpretation. [21] For no prophecy ever came by the will of man, but holy men of God spoke, being moved by the Holy Spirit.

## 2

[1] But false prophets also arose among the people, as false teachers will also be among you, who will secretly bring in destructive heresies, denying even the Master who bought them, bringing on themselves swift destruction. [2] Many will follow their immoral[c] ways, and as a result, the way of the truth will be maligned. [3] In covetousness they will exploit you with deceptive words: whose sentence now from of old doesn't linger, and their destruction will not slumber. [4] For if God didn't spare angels when they sinned, but cast them down to Tartarus,[d] and committed them to pits of darkness to be reserved for judgment; [5] and didn't spare the ancient world, but preserved Noah with seven others, a preacher of righteousness, when he brought a flood on the world of the ungodly, [6] and turning the cities of Sodom and Gomorrah into ashes, condemned them to destruction, having made them an example to those who would live in an ungodly way, [7] and delivered righteous Lot, who was very distressed by the lustful life of the wicked [8](for that righteous man dwelling among them was tormented in his righteous soul from day to day with seeing and hearing lawless deeds), [9] then the Lord knows how to deliver the godly out of temptation and

* 3:12 Psalms 34:12-16
* 3:14 Isaiah 8:12
* 4:18 Proverbs 11:31
* 5:5 Proverbs 3:34

[a] 1:1 "Christ" means "Anointed One".
[b] 1:10 The word for "brothers" here and where context allows may also be correctly translated

"brothers and sisters" or "siblings."
* 1:17 Matthew 17:5; Mark 9:7; Luke 9:35

[c] 2:2 TR reads "destructive" instead of "immoral"
[d] 2:4 Tartarus is another name for Hell

to keep the unrighteous under punishment for the day of judgment, [10] but chiefly those who walk after the flesh in the lust of defilement and despise authority. Daring, self-willed, they are not afraid to speak evil of dignitaries, [11] whereas angels, though greater in might and power, don't bring a slanderous judgment against them before the Lord. [12] But these, as unreasoning creatures, born natural animals to be taken and destroyed, speaking evil in matters about which they are ignorant, will in their destroying surely be destroyed, [13] receiving the wages of unrighteousness; people who count it pleasure to revel in the daytime, spots and defects, reveling in their deceit while they feast with you; [14] having eyes full of adultery, and who can't cease from sin, enticing unsettled souls, having a heart trained in greed, accursed children! [15] Forsaking the right way, they went astray, having followed the way of Balaam the son of Beor, who loved the wages of wrongdoing; [16] but he was rebuked for his own disobedience. A speechless donkey spoke with a man's voice and stopped the madness of the prophet. [17] These are wells without water, clouds driven by a storm, for whom the blackness of darkness has been reserved forever. [18] For, uttering great swelling words of emptiness, they entice in the lusts of the flesh, by licentiousness, those who are indeed escaping from those who live in error; [19] promising them liberty, while they themselves are bondservants of corruption; for a man is brought into bondage by whoever overcomes him. [20] For if, after they have escaped the defilement of the world through the knowledge of the Lord and Savior Jesus Christ, they are again entangled in it and overcome, the last state has become worse for them than the first. [21] For it would be better for them not to have known the way of righteousness, than after knowing it, to turn back from the holy commandment delivered to them. [22] But it has happened to them according to the true proverb, "The dog turns to his own vomit again,"[*] and "the sow that has washed to wallowing in the mire."

## 3

[1] This is now, beloved, the second letter that I have written to you; and in both of them I stir up your sincere mind by reminding you [2] that you should remember the words which were spoken before by the holy prophets and the commandment of us, the apostles of the Lord and Savior, [3] knowing this first, that in the last days mockers will come, walking after their own lusts [4] and saying, "Where is the promise of his coming? For, from the day that the fathers fell asleep, all things continue as they were from the beginning of the creation." [5] For they willfully forget that there were heavens from of old, and an earth formed out of water and amid water by the word of God, [6] by which means the world that existed then, being overflowed with water, perished. [7] But the heavens that exist now and the earth, by the same word have been stored up for fire, being reserved against the day of judgment and destruction of ungodly men. [8] But don't forget this one thing, beloved, that one day is with the Lord as a thousand years, and a thousand years as one day. [9] The Lord is not slow concerning his promise, as some count slowness; but he is patient with us, not wishing that anyone should perish, but that all should come to repentance. [10] But the day of the Lord will come as a thief in the night, in which the heavens will pass away with a great noise, and the elements will be dissolved with fervent heat; and the earth and the works that are in it will be burned up. [11] Therefore, since all these things will be destroyed like this, what kind of people ought you to be in holy living and godliness, [12] looking for and earnestly desiring the coming of the day of God, which will cause the burning heavens to be dissolved, and the elements will melt with fervent heat? [13] But, according to his promise, we look for new heavens and a new earth, in which righteousness dwells. [14] Therefore, beloved, seeing that you look for these things, be diligent to be found in peace, without defect and blameless in his sight. [15] Regard the patience of our Lord as salvation; even as our beloved brother Paul also, according to the wisdom given to him, wrote to you, [16] as also in all of his letters, speaking in them of these things. In those, there are some things that are hard to understand, which the ignorant and unsettled twist, as they also do to the other Scriptures, to their own destruction. [17] You therefore, beloved, knowing these things beforehand, beware, lest being carried away with the error of the wicked, you fall from your own steadfastness. [18] But grow in the grace and knowledge of our Lord and Savior Jesus Christ. To him be the glory both now and forever. Amen.

# John's First Letter

## 1

[1] That which was from the beginning, that which we have heard, that which we have seen with our eyes, that which we saw, and our hands touched, concerning the Word of life [2](and the life was revealed, and we have seen, and testify, and declare to you the life, the eternal life, which was with the Father, and was revealed to us); [3] that which we have seen and heard we declare to you, that you also may have fellowship with us. Yes, and our fellowship is with the Father and with his Son, Jesus Christ.[a] [4] And we write these things to you, that our joy may be fulfilled. [5] This is the message which we have heard from him and announce to you, that God is light, and in him is no darkness at all. [6] If we say that we have fellowship with him and walk in the darkness, we lie and don't tell the truth. [7] But if we walk in the light as he is in the light, we have fellowship with one another, and the blood of Jesus Christ his Son, cleanses us from all sin. [8] If we say that we have no sin, we deceive ourselves, and the truth is not in us. [9] If we confess our sins, he is faithful and righteous to forgive us the sins and to cleanse us from all unrighteousness. [10] If we say that we haven't sinned, we make him a liar, and his word is not in us.

## 2

[1] My little children, I write these things to you so that you may not sin. If anyone sins, we have a Counselor[b] with the Father, Jesus Christ, the righteous. [2] And he is the atoning sacrifice[c] for our sins, and not for ours only, but also for the whole world. [3] This is how we know that we know him: if we keep his commandments. [4] One who says, "I know him," and doesn't keep his commandments, is a liar, and the truth isn't in him. [5] But God's love has most certainly been perfected in whoever keeps his word. This is how we know that we are in him: [6] he who says he remains in him ought himself also to walk just like he walked. [7] Brothers, I write no new commandment to you, but an old commandment which you had from the beginning. The old commandment is the word which you heard from the beginning. [8] Again, I write a new commandment to you, which is true in him and in you, because the darkness is passing away and the true light already shines. [9] He who says he is in the light and hates his brother is in the darkness even until now. [10] He who loves his brother remains in the light, and there is no occasion for stumbling in him. [11] But he who hates his brother is in the darkness, and walks in the darkness, and doesn't know where he is going, because the darkness has blinded his eyes. [12] I write to you, little children, because your sins are forgiven you for his name's sake. [13] I write to you, fathers, because you know him who is from the beginning. I write to you, young men, because you have overcome the evil one. I write to you, little children, because you know the Father. [14] I have written to you, fathers, because you know him who is from the beginning. I have written to you, young men, because you are strong, and the word of God remains in you, and you have overcome the evil one. [15] Don't love the world or the things that are in the world. If anyone loves the world, the Father's love isn't in him. [16] For all that is in the world—the lust of the flesh, the lust of the eyes, and the pride of life—isn't the Father's, but is the world's. [17] The world is passing away with its lusts, but he who does God's will remains forever. [18] Little children, these are the end times, and as you heard that the Antichrist is coming, even now many antichrists have arisen. By this we know that it is the final hour. [19] They went out from us, but they didn't belong to us; for if they had belonged to us, they would have continued with us. But they left, that they might be revealed that none of them belong to us. [20] You have an anointing from the Holy One, and you all have knowledge.[d] [21] I have not written to you because you don't know the truth, but because you know it, and because no lie is of the truth. [22] Who is the liar but he who denies that Jesus is the Christ? This is the Antichrist, he who denies the Father and the Son. [23] Whoever denies the Son doesn't have the Father. He who confesses the Son has the Father also.[e] [24] Therefore, as for you, let that remain in you which you heard from the beginning. If that which you heard from the beginning remains in you, you also will remain in the Son, and in the Father. [25] This is the promise which he promised us, the eternal life. [26] These things I have written to you concerning those who would lead you astray. [27] As for you, the anointing which you received from him remains in you, and you don't need for anyone to teach you. But as his anointing teaches you concerning all things, and is true, and is no lie, and even as it taught you, you will remain in him. [28] Now, little children, remain in him, that when he appears, we may have boldness and not be ashamed before him at his coming. [29] If you know that he is righteous,

---

[*] 2:22 Proverbs 26:11
[a] 1:3 "Christ" means "Anointed One".

[b] 2:1 Greek παράκλητον: Counselor, Helper, Intercessor, Advocate, and Comforter.
[c] 2:2 "atoning sacrifice" is from the Greek "ἱλασμος", an

appeasing, propitiating, or the means of appeasement or propitiation—the sacrifice that turns away God's wrath because of our sin.

[d] 2:20 Or, "know what is true", or, "know all things"
[e] 2:23 MT omits: He who confesses the Son has the Father also.

you know that everyone who practices righteousness has been born of him.

## 3

[1] See how great a love the Father has given to us, that we should be called children of God! For this cause the world doesn't know us, because it didn't know him. [2] Beloved, now we are children of God. It is not yet revealed what we will be; but we know that when he is revealed, we will be like him, for we will see him just as he is. [3] Everyone who has this hope set on him purifies himself, even as he is pure. [4] Everyone who sins also commits lawlessness. Sin is lawlessness. [5] You know that he was revealed to take away our sins, and no sin is in him. [6] Whoever remains in him doesn't sin. Whoever sins hasn't seen him and doesn't know him. [7] Little children, let no one lead you astray. He who does righteousness is righteous, even as he is righteous. [8] He who sins is of the devil, for the devil has been sinning from the beginning. To this end the Son of God was revealed: that he might destroy the works of the devil. [9] Whoever is born of God doesn't commit sin, because his seed remains in him, and he can't sin, because he is born of God. [10] In this the children of God are revealed, and the children of the devil. Whoever doesn't do righteousness is not of God, neither is he who doesn't love his brother. [11] For this is the message which you heard from the beginning, that we should love one another— [12] unlike Cain, who was of the evil one and killed his brother. Why did he kill him? Because his deeds were evil, and his brother's righteous. [13] Don't be surprised, my brothers, if the world hates you. [14] We know that we have passed out of death into life, because we love the brothers. He who doesn't love his brother remains in death. [15] Whoever hates his brother is a murderer, and you know that no murderer has eternal life remaining in him. [16] By this we know love, because he laid down his life for us. And we ought to lay down our lives for the brothers. [17] But whoever has the world's goods and sees his brother in need, then closes his heart of compassion against him, how does God's love remain in him? [18] My little children, let's not love in word only, or with the tongue only, but in deed and truth. [19] And by this we know that we are of the truth and persuade our hearts before him, [20] because if our heart condemns us, God is greater than our heart, and knows all things. [21] Beloved, if our hearts don't condemn us, we have boldness toward God; [22] so whatever we ask, we receive from him, because we keep his commandments and do the things that are pleasing in his sight. [23] This is his commandment, that we should believe in the name of his Son, Jesus Christ, and love one another, even as he commanded. [24] He who keeps his commandments remains in him, and he in him. By this we know that he remains in us, by the Spirit which he gave us.

## 4

[1] Beloved, don't believe every spirit, but test the spirits, whether they are of God, because many false prophets have gone out into the world. [2] By this you know the Spirit of God: every spirit who confesses that Jesus Christ has come in the flesh is of God, [3] and every spirit who doesn't confess that Jesus Christ has come in the flesh is not of God; and this is the spirit of the Antichrist, of whom you have heard that it comes. Now it is in the world already. [4] You are of God, little children, and have overcome them, because greater is he who is in you than he who is in the world. [5] They are of the world. Therefore they speak of the world, and the world hears them. [6] We are of God. He who knows God listens to us. He who is not of God doesn't listen to us. By this we know the spirit of truth, and the spirit of error. [7] Beloved, let's love one another, for love is of God; and everyone who loves has been born of God and knows God. [8] He who doesn't love doesn't know God, for God is love. [9] By this God's love was revealed in us, that God has sent his only born[a] Son into the world that we might live through him. [10] In this is love, not that we loved God, but that he loved us, and sent his Son as the atoning sacrifice[b] for our sins. [11] Beloved, if God loved us in this way, we also ought to love one another. [12] No one has seen God at any time. If we love one another, God remains in us, and his love has been perfected in us. [13] By this we know that we remain in him and he in us, because he has given us of his Spirit. [14] We have seen and testify that the Father has sent the Son as the Savior of the world. [15] Whoever confesses that Jesus is the Son of God, God remains in him, and he in God. [16] We know and have believed the love which God has for us. God is love, and he who remains in love remains in God, and God remains in him. [17] In this, love has been made perfect among us, that we may have boldness in the day of judgment, because as he is, even so we are in this world. [18] There is no fear in love; but perfect love casts out fear, because fear has punishment. He who fears is not made perfect in love. [19] We love him,[c] because he first loved us. [20] If a man says, "I love God," and hates his brother, he is a liar; for he who doesn't love his brother whom he has seen, how can he love God whom he has not seen? [21] This commandment we have from him, that he who loves God should also love his brother.

## 5

[1] Whoever believes that Jesus is the Christ has been born of God. Whoever loves the Father also loves the child who is born of him. [2] By this we know that we love the children of God, when we love God and keep his commandments. [3] For this is loving God, that we keep his commandments. His commandments are not grievous. [4] For whatever is born of God overcomes the world. This is the victory that has overcome the world: your faith. [5] Who is he who overcomes the world, but he who believes that Jesus is the Son of God? [6] This is he who came by water and blood, Jesus Christ; not with the water only, but with the water and the blood. It is the Spirit who testifies, because the Spirit is the truth. [7] For there are three who testify:[d] [8] the Spirit, the water, and the blood; and the three agree as one. [9] If we receive the witness of men, the witness of God is greater; for this is God's testimony which he has testified concerning his Son. [10] He who believes in the Son of God has the testimony in himself. He who doesn't believe God has made him a liar, because he has not believed in the testimony that God has given concerning his Son. [11] The testimony is this: that God gave to us eternal life, and this life is in his Son. [12] He who has the Son has the life. He who doesn't have God's Son doesn't have the life. [13] These things I have written to you who believe in the name of the Son of God, that you may know that you have eternal life, and that you may continue to believe in the name of the Son of God. [14] This is the boldness which we have toward him, that if we ask anything according to his will, he listens to us. [15] And if we know that he listens to us, whatever we ask, we know that we have the petitions which we have asked of him. [16] If anyone sees his brother sinning a sin not leading to death, he shall ask, and God will give him life for those who sin not leading to death. There is sin leading to death. I don't say that he should make a request concerning this. [17] All unrighteousness is sin, and there is sin not leading to death. [18] We know that whoever is born of God doesn't sin, but he who was born of God keeps himself, and the evil one doesn't touch him. [19] We know that we are of God, and the whole world lies in the power of the evil one. [20] We know that the Son of God has come and has given us an understanding, that we know him who is true; and we are in him who is true, in his Son Jesus Christ. This is the true God and eternal life. [21] Little children, keep yourselves from idols.

# John's Second Letter
## 1

[1] The elder, to the chosen lady and her children, whom I love in truth, and not I only, but also all those who know the truth, [2] for the truth's sake, which remains in us, and it will be with us forever: [3] Grace, mercy, and peace will be with us, from God the Father and from the Lord Jesus Christ,[e] the Son of the Father, in truth and love. [4] I rejoice greatly that I have found some of your children walking in truth, even as we have been commanded by the Father. [5] Now I beg you, dear lady, not as though I wrote to you a new commandment, but that which we had from the beginning, that we love one another. [6] This is love, that we should walk according to his commandments. This is the commandment, even as you heard from the beginning, that you should walk in it. [7] For many deceivers have gone out into the world, those who don't confess that Jesus Christ came in the flesh. This is the deceiver and the Antichrist. [8] Watch yourselves, that we don't lose the things which we have accomplished, but that we receive a full reward. [9] Whoever transgresses and doesn't remain in the teaching of Christ doesn't have God. He who remains in the teaching has both the Father and the Son. [10] If anyone comes to you and doesn't bring this teaching, don't receive him into your house, and don't welcome him, [11] for he who welcomes him participates in his evil deeds. [12] Having many things to write to you, I don't want to do so with paper and ink, but I hope to come to you and to speak face to face, that our joy may be made full. [13] The children of your chosen sister greet you. Amen.

---

[a] *4:9* The phrase "only born" is from the Greek word "μονογενη", which is sometimes translated "only begotten" or "one and only".

[b] *4:10* "atoning sacrifice" is from the Greek "ιλασμος", an appeasing, propitiating, or the means of appeasement or propitiation—the sacrifice that turns away God's wrath because of our sin.

[c] *4:19* NU omits "him".

[d] *5:7* Only a few recent manuscripts add "in heaven: the Father, the Word, and the Holy Spirit; and these three are one. And there are three that testify on earth:"

[e] *1:3* "Christ" means "Anointed One".

## John's Third Letter

### 1

[1] The elder to Gaius the beloved, whom I love in truth. [2] Beloved, I pray that you may prosper in all things and be healthy, even as your soul prospers. [3] For I rejoiced greatly when brothers came and testified about your truth, even as you walk in truth. [4] I have no greater joy than this: to hear about my children walking in truth. [5] Beloved, you do a faithful work in whatever you accomplish for those who are brothers and strangers. [6] They have testified about your love before the assembly. You will do well to send them forward on their journey in a way worthy of God, [7] because for the sake of the Name they went out, taking nothing from the Gentiles. [8] We therefore ought to receive such, that we may be fellow workers for the truth. [9] I wrote to the assembly, but Diotrephes, who loves to be first among them, doesn't accept what we say. [10] Therefore, if I come, I will call attention to his deeds which he does, unjustly accusing us with wicked words. Not content with this, he doesn't receive the brothers himself, and those who would, he forbids and throws out of the assembly. [11] Beloved, don't imitate that which is evil, but that which is good. He who does good is of God. He who does evil hasn't seen God. [12] Demetrius has the testimony of all, and of the truth itself; yes, we also testify, and you know that our testimony is true. [13] I had many things to write to you, but I am unwilling to write to you with ink and pen; [14] but I hope to see you soon. Then we will speak face to face. Peace be to you. The friends greet you. Greet the friends by name.

## The Letter from Jude

### 1

[1] Jude,[a] a servant of Jesus Christ,[b] and brother of James, to those who are called, sanctified by God the Father, and kept for Jesus Christ: [2] May mercy, peace, and love be multiplied to you. [3] Beloved, while I was very eager to write to you about our common salvation, I was constrained to write to you exhorting you to contend earnestly for the faith which was once for all delivered to the saints. [4] For there are certain men who crept in secretly, even those who were long ago written about for this condemnation: ungodly men, turning the grace of our God into indecency, and denying our only Master, God, and Lord, Jesus Christ. [5] Now I desire to remind you, though you already know this, that the Lord, having saved a people out of the land of Egypt, afterward destroyed those who didn't believe. [6] Angels who didn't keep their first domain, but deserted their own dwelling place, he has kept in everlasting bonds under darkness for the judgment of the great day. [7] Even as Sodom and Gomorrah and the cities around them, having in the same way as these given themselves over to sexual immorality and gone after strange flesh, are shown as an example, suffering the punishment of eternal fire. [8] Yet in the same way, these also in their dreaming defile the flesh, despise authority, and slander celestial beings. [9] But Michael, the archangel, when contending with the devil and arguing about the body of Moses, dared not bring against him an abusive condemnation, but said, "May the Lord rebuke you!" [10] But these speak evil of whatever things they don't know. They are destroyed in these things that they understand naturally, like the creatures without reason. [11] Woe to them! For they went in the way of Cain, and ran riotously in the error of Balaam for hire, and perished in Korah's rebellion. [12] These are hidden rocky reefs in your love feasts when they feast with you, shepherds who without fear feed themselves; clouds without water, carried along by winds; autumn trees without fruit, twice dead, plucked up by the roots; [13] wild waves of the sea, foaming out their own shame; wandering stars, for whom the blackness of darkness has been reserved forever. [14] About these also Enoch, the seventh from Adam, prophesied, saying, "Behold,[c] the Lord came with ten thousands of his holy ones, [15] to execute judgment on all, and to convict all the ungodly of all their works of ungodliness which they have done in an ungodly way, and of all the hard things which ungodly sinners have spoken against him." [16] These are murmurers and complainers, walking after their lusts—and their mouth speaks proud things—showing respect of persons to gain advantage. [17] But you, beloved, remember the words which have been spoken before by the apostles of our Lord Jesus Christ. [18] They said to you, "In the last time there will be mockers, walking after their own ungodly lusts." [19] These are those who cause divisions and are sensual, not having the Spirit. [20] But you, beloved, keep building up yourselves on your most holy faith, praying in the Holy Spirit. [21] Keep yourselves in God's love, looking for the mercy of our Lord Jesus Christ to eternal life. [22] On some have compassion, making a distinction, [23] and some save, snatching them out of the fire with fear, hating even the clothing stained by the flesh. [24] Now to him who is able to keep them[d] from stumbling, and to present you faultless before the presence of his glory in great joy, [25] to God our Savior, who alone is wise, be glory and majesty, dominion and power, both now and forever. Amen.

## The Revelation to John

### 1

[1] This is the Revelation of Jesus Christ,[e] which God gave him to show to his servants the things which must happen soon, which he sent and made known by his angel[f] to his servant, John, [2] who testified to God's word and of the testimony of Jesus Christ, about everything that he saw. [3] Blessed is he who reads and those who hear the words of the prophecy, and keep the things that are written in it, for the time is near. [4] John, to the seven assemblies that are in Asia: Grace to you and peace from God, who is and who was and who is to come; and from the seven Spirits who are before his throne; [5] and from Jesus Christ, the faithful witness, the firstborn of the dead, and the ruler of the kings of the earth. To him who loves us, and washed us from our sins by his blood— [6] and he made us to be a Kingdom, priests[*] to his God and Father—to him be the glory and the dominion forever and ever. Amen. [7] Behold,[g] he is coming with the clouds, and every eye will see him, including those who pierced him. All the tribes of the earth will mourn over him. Even so, Amen. [8] "I am the Alpha and the Omega,[h]" says the Lord God,[i] "who is and who was and who is to come, the Almighty." [9] I John, your brother and partner with you in the oppression, Kingdom, and perseverance in Christ Jesus, was on the isle that is called Patmos because of God's Word and the testimony of Jesus Christ. [10] I was in the Spirit on the Lord's day, and I heard behind me a loud voice, like a trumpet [11] saying,[j] "What you see, write in a book and send to the seven assemblies:[k] to Ephesus, Smyrna, Pergamum, Thyatira, Sardis, Philadelphia, and to Laodicea." [12] I turned to see the voice that spoke with me. Having turned, I saw seven golden lamp stands. [13] And among the lamp stands was one like a son of man,[*] clothed with a robe reaching down to his feet, and with a golden sash around his chest. [14] His head and his hair were white as white wool, like snow. His eyes were like a flame of fire. [15] His feet were like burnished brass, as if it had been refined in a furnace. His voice was like the voice of many waters. [16] He had seven stars in his right hand. Out of his mouth proceeded a sharp two-edged sword. His face was like the sun shining at its brightest. [17] When I saw him, I fell at his feet like a dead man. He laid his right hand on me, saying, "Don't be afraid. I am the first and the last, [18] and the Living one. I was dead, and behold, I am alive forever and ever. Amen. I have the keys of Death and of Hades.[l] [19] Write therefore the things which you have seen, and the things which are, and the things which will happen hereafter. [20] The mystery of the seven stars which you saw in my right hand, and the seven golden lamp stands is this: The seven stars are the angels[m] of the seven assemblies. The seven lamp stands are seven assemblies.

### 2

[1] "To the angel of the assembly in Ephesus write: "He who holds the seven stars in his right hand, he who walks among the seven golden lamp stands says these things: [2] "I know your works, and your toil and perseverance, and that you can't tolerate evil men, and have tested those who call themselves apostles, and they are not, and found them false. [3] You have perseverance and have endured for my name's sake, and have [n] not grown weary. [4] But I have this against you, that you left your first love. [5] Remember therefore from where you have fallen, and repent and do the first works; or else I am coming to you swiftly, and will move your lamp stand out of its place, unless you repent. [6] But this you have, that you hate the works of the Nicolaitans, which I also hate. [7] He who has an ear, let him hear what the Spirit says to the assemblies. To him who overcomes I will give to eat from the tree of life, which is in the

---

[a] *1:1* or, Judah
[b] *1:1* "Christ" means "Anointed One".
[c] *1:14* "Behold", from "ἰδού", means look at, take notice, observe, see, or gaze at. It is often used as an interjection.
[d] *1:24* TR and NU read "you"

[e] *1:1* "Christ" means "Anointed One".
[f] *1:1* or, messenger (here and wherever angel is mentioned)
[*] 1:6 Exodus 19:6; Isaiah 61:6
[g] *1:7* "Behold", from "ἰδού", means look at, take notice, observe, see, or gaze at. It is often used as an interjection.

[h] *1:8* TR adds "the Beginning and the End"
[i] *1:8* TR omits "God"
[j] *1:11* TR adds "I am the Alpha and the Omega, the First and the Last."
[k] *1:11* TR adds "which are in Asia"
[*] 1:13 Daniel 7:13

[l] *1:18* or, Hell
[m] *1:20* or, messengers (here and wherever angels are mentioned)
[n] *2:3* TR adds "have labored and"

Paradise of my God. **8** "To the angel of the assembly in Smyrna write: "The first and the last, who was dead, and has come to life says these things: **9** "I know your works, oppression, and your poverty (but you are rich), and the blasphemy of those who say they are Jews, and they are not, but are a synagogue of Satan. **10** Don't be afraid of the things which you are about to suffer. Behold, the devil is about to throw some of you into prison, that you may be tested; and you will have oppression for ten days. Be faithful to death, and I will give you the crown of life. **11** He who has an ear, let him hear what the Spirit says to the assemblies. He who overcomes won't be harmed by the second death. **12** "To the angel of the assembly in Pergamum write: "He who has the sharp two-edged sword says these things: **13** "I know your works and where you dwell, where Satan's throne is. You hold firmly to my name, and didn't deny my faith in the days of Antipas my witness, my faithful one, who was killed among you, where Satan dwells. **14** But I have a few things against you, because you have there some who hold the teaching of Balaam, who taught Balak to throw a stumbling block before the children of Israel, to eat things sacrificed to idols, and to commit sexual immorality. **15** So also you likewise have some who hold to the teaching of the Nicolaitans.**ᵃ** **16** Repent therefore, or else I am coming to you quickly and I will make war against them with the sword of my mouth. **17** He who has an ear, let him hear what the Spirit says to the assemblies. To him who overcomes, to him I will give of the hidden manna, **ᵇ** and I will give him a white stone, and on the stone a new name written which no one knows but he who receives it. **18** "To the angel of the assembly in Thyatira write: "The Son of God, who has his eyes like a flame of fire, and his feet are like burnished brass, says these things: **19** "I know your works, your love, faith, service, patient endurance, and that your last works are more than the first. **20** But I have this against you, that you tolerate your**ᶜ** woman Jezebel, who calls herself a prophetess. She teaches and seduces my servants to commit sexual immorality and to eat things sacrificed to idols. **21** I gave her time to repent, but she refuses to repent of her sexual immorality. **22** Behold, I will throw her and those who commit adultery with her into a bed of great oppression, unless they repent of her works. **23** I will kill her children with Death, and all the assemblies will know that I am he who searches the minds and hearts. I will give to each one of you according to your deeds. **24** But to you I say, to the rest who are in Thyatira—as many as don't have this teaching, who don't know what some call 'the deep things of Satan'—to you I say, I am not putting any other burden on you. **25** Nevertheless, hold that which you have firmly until I come. **26** He who overcomes, and he who keeps my works to the end, to him I will give authority over the nations. **27** He will rule them with a rod of iron, shattering them like clay pots,**\*** as I also have received of my Father; **28** and I will give him the morning star. **29** He who has an ear, let him hear what the Spirit says to the assemblies.

### 3

**1** "And to the angel of the assembly in Sardis write: "He who has the seven Spirits of God and the seven stars says these things: "I know your works, that you have a reputation of being alive, but you are dead. **2** Wake up and strengthen the things that remain, which you were about to throw away,**ᵈ** for I have found no works of yours perfected before my God. **3** Remember therefore how you have received and heard. Keep it and repent. If therefore you won't watch, I will come as a thief, and you won't know what hour I will come upon you. **4** Nevertheless you have a few names in Sardis that didn't defile their garments. They will walk with me in white, for they are worthy. **5** He who overcomes will be arrayed in white garments, and I will in no way blot his name out of the book of life, and I will confess his name before my Father, and before his angels. **6** He who has an ear, let him hear what the Spirit says to the assemblies. **7** "To the angel of the assembly in Philadelphia write: "He who is holy, he who is true, he who has the key of David, he who opens and no one can shut, and who shuts and no one opens, says these things: **8** "I know your works (behold, I have set before you an open door, which no one can shut), that you have a little power, and kept my word, and didn't deny my name. **9** Behold, I make some of the synagogue of Satan, of those who say they are Jews, and they are not, but lie—behold, I will make them to come and worship before your feet, and to know that I have loved you. **10** Because you kept my command to endure, I also will keep you from the hour of testing which is to come on the whole world, to test those who dwell on the earth. **11** I am coming quickly! Hold firmly that which you have, so that no one takes your crown. **12** He who overcomes, I will make him a pillar in the temple of my God, and he will go out from there no more. I will write

on him the name of my God and the name of the city of my God, the new Jerusalem, which comes down out of heaven from my God, and my own new name. **13** He who has an ear, let him hear what the Spirit says to the assemblies. **14** "To the angel of the assembly in Laodicea write: "The Amen, the Faithful and True Witness, the Beginning**ᵉ** of God's creation, says these things: **15** "I know your works, that you are neither cold nor hot. I wish you were cold or hot. **16** So, because you are lukewarm, and neither hot nor cold, I will vomit you out of my mouth. **17** Because you say, 'I am rich, and have gotten riches, and have need of nothing,' and don't know that you are the wretched one, miserable, poor, blind, and naked; **18** I counsel you to buy from me gold refined by fire, that you may become rich; and white garments, that you may clothe yourself, and that the shame of your nakedness may not be revealed; and eye salve to anoint your eyes, that you may see. **19** As many as I love, I reprove and chasten. Be zealous therefore, and repent. **20** Behold, I stand at the door and knock. If anyone hears my voice and opens the door, then I will come in to him and will dine with him, and he with me. **21** He who overcomes, I will give to him to sit down with me on my throne, as I also overcame and sat down with my Father on his throne. **22** He who has an ear, let him hear what the Spirit says to the assemblies."

### 4

**1** After these things I looked and saw a door opened in heaven; and the first voice that I heard, like a trumpet speaking with me, was one saying, "Come up here, and I will show you the things which must happen after this." **2** Immediately I was in the Spirit. Behold, there was a throne set in heaven, and one sitting on the throne **3** that looked like a jasper stone and a sardius. There was a rainbow around the throne, like an emerald to look at. **4** Around the throne were twenty-four thrones. On the thrones were twenty-four elders sitting, dressed in white garments, with crowns of gold on their heads. **5** Out of the throne proceed lightnings, sounds, and thunders. There were seven lamps of fire burning before his throne, which are the seven Spirits of God. **6** Before the throne was something like a sea of glass, similar to crystal. In the middle of the throne, and around the throne were four living creatures full of eyes before and behind. **7** The first creature was like a lion, the second creature like a calf, the third creature had a face like a man, and the fourth was like a flying eagle. **8** The four living creatures, each one of them having six wings, are full of eyes around and within. They have no rest day and night, saying, "Holy, holy, holy**ᶠ** is the Lord God, the Almighty, who was and who is and who is to come!" **9** When the living creatures give glory, honor, and thanks to him who sits on the throne, to him who lives forever and ever, **10** the twenty-four elders fall down before him who sits on the throne and worship him who lives forever and ever, and throw their crowns before the throne, saying, **11**"Worthy are you, our Lord and God, the Holy One,**ᵍ** to receive the glory, the honor, and the power, for you created all things, and because of your desire they existed and were created!"

### 5

**1** I saw, in the right hand of him who sat on the throne, a book written inside and outside, sealed shut with seven seals. **2** I saw a mighty angel proclaiming with a loud voice, "Who is worthy to open the book, and to break its seals?" **3** No one in heaven above, or on the earth, or under the earth, was able to open the book or to look in it. **4** Then I wept much, because no one was found worthy to open the book or to look in it. **5** One of the elders said to me, "Don't weep. Behold, the Lion who is of the tribe of Judah, the Root of David, has overcome: he who opens the book and its seven seals." **6** I saw in the middle of the throne and of the four living creatures, and in the middle of the elders, a Lamb standing, as though it had been slain, having seven horns and seven eyes, which are the seven Spirits of God, sent out into all the earth. **7** Then he came, and he took it out of the right hand of him who sat on the throne. **8** Now when he had taken the book, the four living creatures and the twenty-four elders fell down before the Lamb, each one having a harp, and golden bowls full of incense, which are the prayers of the saints. **9** They sang a new song, saying, "You are worthy to take the book and to open its seals, for you were killed, and bought us for God with your blood out of every tribe, language, people, and nation, **10** and made us kings and priests to our God; and we will reign on the earth." **11** I looked, and I heard something like a voice of many angels around the throne, the living creatures, and the elders. The number of them was ten thousands of ten thousands, and thousands of thousands, **12** saying with a loud voice, "Worthy is the Lamb who has been killed to receive the power, wealth, wisdom, strength, honor, glory, and blessing!" **13** I heard every

---

**ᵃ** *2:15* TR reads "which I hate" instead of "likewise"
**ᵇ** *2:17* Manna is supernatural food, named after the Hebrew

for "What is it?". See Exodus 11:7-9.
**ᶜ** *2:20* TR, NU read "that" instead of "your"
**\*** 2:27 Psalms 2:9

**ᵈ** *3:2* NU & TR read "which were about to die" instead of "which you were about to throw away".
**ᵉ** *3:14* or, Source, or Head

**ᶠ** *4:8* Hodges/Farstad MT reads "holy" 9 times instead of 3.
**ᵍ** *4:11* TR omits "and God, the Holy One,"

created thing which is in heaven, on the earth, under the earth, on the sea, and everything in them, saying, "To him who sits on the throne and to the Lamb be the blessing, the honor, the glory, and the dominion, forever and ever! Amen!"[a] [14] The four living creatures said, "Amen!" Then the[b] elders fell down and worshiped.[c]

## 6

[1] I saw that the Lamb opened one of the seven seals, and I heard one of the four living creatures saying, as with a voice of thunder, "Come and see!" [2] Then a white horse appeared, and he who sat on it had a bow. A crown was given to him, and he came out conquering, and to conquer. [3] When he opened the second seal, I heard the second living creature saying, "Come!" [4] Another came out, a red horse. To him who sat on it was given power to take peace from the earth, and that they should kill one another. There was given to him a great sword. [5] When he opened the third seal, I heard the third living creature saying, "Come and see!" And behold, a black horse, and he who sat on it had a balance in his hand. [6] I heard a voice in the middle of the four living creatures saying, "A choenix[d] of wheat for a denarius, and three choenix of barley for a denarius! Don't damage the oil and the wine!" [7] When he opened the fourth seal, I heard the fourth living creature saying, "Come and see!" [8] And behold, a pale horse, and the name of he who sat on it was Death. Hades[e] followed with him. Authority over one fourth of the earth, to kill with the sword, with famine, with death, and by the wild animals of the earth was given to him. [9] When he opened the fifth seal, I saw underneath the altar the souls of those who had been killed for the Word of God, and for the testimony of the Lamb which they had. [10] They cried with a loud voice, saying, "How long, Master, the holy and true, until you judge and avenge our blood on those who dwell on the earth?" [11] A long white robe was given to each of them. They were told that they should rest yet for a while, until their fellow servants and their brothers,[f] who would also be killed even as they were, should complete their course. [12] I saw when he opened the sixth seal, and there was a great earthquake. The sun became black as sackcloth made of hair, and the whole moon became as blood. [13] The stars of the sky fell to the earth, like a fig tree dropping its unripe figs when it is shaken by a great wind. [14] The sky was removed like a scroll when it is rolled up. Every mountain and island was moved out of its place. [15] The kings of the earth, the princes, the commanding officers, the rich, the strong, and every slave and free person, hid themselves in the caves and in the rocks of the mountains. [16] They told the mountains and the rocks, "Fall on us, and hide us from the face of him who sits on the throne, and from the wrath of the Lamb, [17] for the great day of his wrath has come, and who is able to stand?"

## 7

[1] After this, I saw four angels standing at the four corners of the earth, holding the four winds of the earth, so that no wind would blow on the earth, or on the sea, or on any tree. [2] I saw another angel ascend from the sunrise, having the seal of the living God. He cried with a loud voice to the four angels to whom it was given to harm the earth and the sea, [3] saying, "Don't harm the earth, the sea, or the trees, until we have sealed the bondservants of our God on their foreheads!" [4] I heard the number of those who were sealed, one hundred forty-four thousand, sealed out of every tribe of the children of Israel: [5] of the tribe of Judah twelve thousand were sealed, of the tribe of Reuben twelve thousand, of the tribe of Gad twelve thousand, [6] of the tribe of Asher twelve thousand, of the tribe of Naphtali twelve thousand, of the tribe of Manasseh twelve thousand, [7] of the tribe of Simeon twelve thousand, of the tribe of Levi twelve thousand, of the tribe of Issachar twelve thousand, [8] of the tribe of Zebulun twelve thousand, of the tribe of Joseph twelve thousand, and of the tribe of Benjamin twelve thousand were sealed. [9] After these things I looked, and behold, a great multitude which no man could count, out of every nation and of all tribes, peoples, and languages, standing before the throne and before the Lamb, dressed in white robes, with palm branches in their hands. [10] They cried with a loud voice, saying, "Salvation be to our God, who sits on the throne, and to the Lamb!" [11] All the angels were standing around the throne, the elders, and the four living creatures; and they fell on their faces before his throne, and worshiped God, [12] saying, "Amen! Blessing, glory, wisdom, thanksgiving, honor, power, and might, be to our God forever and ever! Amen." [13] One of the elders answered, saying to me, "These who are arrayed in the white robes, who are they, and where did they come from?" [14] I told him, "My lord, you know." He said to me,

"These are those who came out of the great suffering.[g] They washed their robes and made them white in the Lamb's blood. [15] Therefore they are before the throne of God, and they serve him day and night in his temple. He who sits on the throne will spread his tabernacle over them. [16] They will never be hungry or thirsty any more. The sun won't beat on them, nor any heat; [17] for the Lamb who is in the middle of the throne shepherds them and leads them to springs of life-giving waters. And God will wipe away every tear from their eyes."

## 8

[1] When he opened the seventh seal, there was silence in heaven for about half an hour. [2] I saw the seven angels who stand before God, and seven trumpets were given to them. [3] Another angel came and stood over the altar, having a golden censer. Much incense was given to him, that he should add it to the prayers of all the saints on the golden altar which was before the throne. [4] The smoke of the incense, with the prayers of the saints, went up before God out of the angel's hand. [5] The angel took the censer, and he filled it with the fire of the altar, then threw it on the earth. Thunders, sounds, lightnings, and an earthquake followed. [6] The seven angels who had the seven trumpets prepared themselves to sound. [7] The first sounded, and there followed hail and fire, mixed with blood, and they were thrown to the earth. One third of the earth was burned up,[h] and one third of the trees were burned up, and all green grass was burned up. [8] The second angel sounded, and something like a great burning mountain was thrown into the sea. One third of the sea became blood, [9] and one third of the living creatures which were in the sea died. One third of the ships were destroyed. [10] The third angel sounded, and a great star fell from the sky, burning like a torch, and it fell on one third of the rivers, and on the springs of water. [11] The name of the star is "Wormwood." One third of the waters became wormwood. Many people died from the waters, because they were made bitter. [12] The fourth angel sounded, and one third of the sun was struck, and one third of the moon, and one third of the stars, so that one third of them would be darkened; and the day wouldn't shine for one third of it, and the night in the same way. [13] I saw, and I heard an eagle,[i] flying in mid heaven, saying with a loud voice, "Woe! Woe! Woe to those who dwell on the earth, because of the other blasts of the trumpets of the three angels, who are yet to sound!"

## 9

[1] The fifth angel sounded, and I saw a star from the sky which had fallen to the earth. The key to the pit of the abyss was given to him. [2] He opened the pit of the abyss, and smoke went up out of the pit, like the smoke from a[j] burning furnace. The sun and the air were darkened because of the smoke from the pit. [3] Then out of the smoke came locusts on the earth, and power was given to them, as the scorpions of the earth have power. [4] They were told that they should not hurt the grass of the earth, neither any green thing, neither any tree, but only those people who don't have God's seal on their foreheads. [5] They were given power, not to kill them, but to torment them for five months. Their torment was like the torment of a scorpion when it strikes a person. [6] In those days people will seek death, and will in no way find it. They will desire to die, and death will flee from them. [7] The shapes of the locusts were like horses prepared for war. On their heads were something like golden crowns, and their faces were like people's faces. [8] They had hair like women's hair, and their teeth were like those of lions. [9] They had breastplates like breastplates of iron. The sound of their wings was like the sound of many chariots and horses rushing to war. [10] They have tails like those of scorpions, with stingers. In their tails they have power to harm men for five months. [11] They have over them as king the angel of the abyss. His name in Hebrew is "Abaddon",[k] but in Greek, he has the name "Apollyon".[l] [12] The first woe is past. Behold, there are still two woes coming after this. [13] The sixth angel sounded. I heard a voice from the horns of the golden altar which is before God, [14] saying to the sixth angel who had the trumpet, "Free the four angels who are bound at the great river Euphrates!" [15] The four angels were freed who had been prepared for that hour and day and month and year, so that they might kill one third of mankind. [16] The number of the armies of the horsemen was two hundred million.[m] I heard the number of them. [17] Thus I saw the horses in the vision and those who sat on them, having breastplates of fiery red, hyacinth blue, and sulfur yellow; and the horses' heads resembled lions' heads. Out of their mouths proceed fire, smoke, and sulfur. [18] By these three plagues, one third of mankind was killed: by the fire, the smoke, and the sulfur, which proceeded out of their mouths.

---

[a] *5:13* TR omits "Amen!"

[b] *5:14* TR adds "twenty-four"

[c] *5:14* TR adds "the one living forever and ever"

[d] *6:6* A choenix is a dry volume measure that is a little more than a liter (a little more than a quart).

[e] *6:8* or, Hell

[f] *6:11* The word for "brothers" here and where context allows may also be correctly translated "brothers and sisters" or "siblings."

[g] *7:14* or, oppression

[h] *8:7* TR omits "One third of the earth was burned up"

[i] *8:13* TR reads "angel" instead of "eagle"

[j] *9:2* TR adds "great"

[k] *9:11* "Abaddon" is a Hebrew word that means "ruin",

[l] *9:11* "Apollyon" means "Destroyer".

[m] *9:16* literally, "ten thousands of ten thousands"

"destruction", or "the place of destruction"

**19** For the power of the horses is in their mouths and in their tails. For their tails are like serpents, and have heads; and with them they harm. **20** The rest of mankind, who were not killed with these plagues, didn't repent of the works of their hands, that they wouldn't worship demons, and the idols of gold, and of silver, and of brass, and of stone, and of wood, which can't see, hear, or walk. **21** They didn't repent of their murders, their sorceries,[a] their sexual immorality, or their thefts.

## 10

**1** I saw a mighty angel coming down out of the sky, clothed with a cloud. A rainbow was on his head. His face was like the sun, and his feet like pillars of fire. **2** He had in his hand a little open book. He set his right foot on the sea, and his left on the land. **3** He cried with a loud voice, as a lion roars. When he cried, the seven thunders uttered their voices. **4** When the seven thunders sounded, I was about to write; but I heard a voice from the sky saying, "Seal up the things which the seven thunders said, and don't write them." **5** The angel whom I saw standing on the sea and on the land lifted up his right hand to the sky **6** and swore by him who lives forever and ever, who created heaven and the things that are in it, the earth and the things that are in it, and the sea and the things that are in it, that there will no longer be delay, **7** but in the days of the voice of the seventh angel, when he is about to sound, then the mystery of God is finished, as he declared to his servants the prophets. **8** The voice which I heard from heaven, again speaking with me, said, "Go, take the book which is open in the hand of the angel who stands on the sea and on the land." **9** I went to the angel, telling him to give me the little book. He said to me, "Take it and eat it. It will make your stomach bitter, but in your mouth it will be as sweet as honey." **10** I took the little book out of the angel's hand, and ate it. It was as sweet as honey in my mouth. When I had eaten it, my stomach was made bitter. **11** They[b] told me, "You must prophesy again over many peoples, nations, languages, and kings."

## 11

**1** A reed like a rod was given to me. Someone said, "Rise and measure God's temple, and the altar, and those who worship in it. **2** Leave out the court which is outside of the temple, and don't measure it, for it has been given to the nations. They will tread the holy city under foot for forty-two months. **3** I will give power to my two witnesses, and they will prophesy one thousand two hundred sixty days, clothed in sackcloth." **4** These are the two olive trees and the two lamp stands, standing before the Lord of the earth. **5** If anyone desires to harm them, fire proceeds out of their mouth and devours their enemies. If anyone desires to harm them, he must be killed in this way. **6** These have the power to shut up the sky, that it may not rain during the days of their prophecy. They have power over the waters, to turn them into blood, and to strike the earth with every plague, as often as they desire. **7** When they have finished their testimony, the beast that comes up out of the abyss will make war with them, and overcome them, and kill them. **8** Their dead bodies will be in the street of the great city, which spiritually is called Sodom and Egypt, where also their Lord was crucified. **9** From among the peoples, tribes, languages, and nations, people will look at their dead bodies for three and a half days, and will not allow their dead bodies to be laid in a tomb. **10** Those who dwell on the earth will rejoice over them, and they will be glad. They will give gifts to one another, because these two prophets tormented those who dwell on the earth. **11** After the three and a half days, the breath of life from God entered into them, and they stood on their feet. Great fear fell on those who saw them. **12** I heard a loud voice from heaven saying to them, "Come up here!" They went up into heaven in a cloud, and their enemies saw them. **13** In that day there was a great earthquake, and a tenth of the city fell. Seven thousand people were killed in the earthquake, and the rest were terrified and gave glory to the God of heaven. **14** The second woe is past. Behold, the third woe comes quickly. **15** The seventh angel sounded, and great voices in heaven followed, saying, "The kingdom of the world has become the Kingdom of our Lord and of his Christ. He will reign forever and ever!" **16** The twenty-four elders, who sit on their thrones before God's throne, fell on their faces and worshiped God, **17** saying: "We give you thanks, Lord God, the Almighty, the one who is and who was,[c] because you have taken your great power and reigned. **18** The nations were angry, and your wrath came, as did the time for the dead to be judged, and to give your bondservants the prophets, their reward, as well as to the saints and those who fear your name, to the small and the great, and to destroy those who destroy the earth." **19** God's temple that is in heaven was opened, and the ark of the Lord's covenant was seen in his temple. Lightnings, sounds, thunders, an earthquake, and great hail followed.

## 12

**1** A great sign was seen in heaven: a woman clothed with the sun, and the moon under her feet, and on her head a crown of twelve stars. **2** She was with child. She cried out in pain, laboring to give birth. **3** Another sign was seen in heaven. Behold, a great red dragon, having seven heads and ten horns, and on his heads seven crowns. **4** His tail drew one third of the stars of the sky, and threw them to the earth. The dragon stood before the woman who was about to give birth, so that when she gave birth he might devour her child. **5** She gave birth to a son, a male child, who is to rule all the nations with a rod of iron. Her child was caught up to God and to his throne. **6** The woman fled into the wilderness, where she has a place prepared by God, that there they may nourish her one thousand two hundred sixty days. **7** There was war in the sky. Michael and his angels made war on the dragon. The dragon and his angels made war. **8** They didn't prevail. No place was found for them any more in heaven. **9** The great dragon was thrown down, the old serpent, he who is called the devil and Satan, the deceiver of the whole world. He was thrown down to the earth, and his angels were thrown down with him. **10** I heard a loud voice in heaven, saying, "Now the salvation, the power, and the Kingdom of our God, and the authority of his Christ has come; for the accuser of our brothers has been thrown down, who accuses them before our God day and night. **11** They overcame him because of the Lamb's blood, and because of the word of their testimony. They didn't love their life, even to death. **12** Therefore rejoice, heavens, and you who dwell in them. Woe to the earth and to the sea, because the devil has gone down to you, having great wrath, knowing that he has but a short time." **13** When the dragon saw that he was thrown down to the earth, he persecuted the woman who gave birth to the male child. **14** Two wings of the great eagle were given to the woman, that she might fly into the wilderness to her place, so that she might be nourished for a time, times, and half a time, from the face of the serpent. **15** The serpent spewed water out of his mouth after the woman like a river, that he might cause her to be carried away by the stream. **16** The earth helped the woman, and the earth opened its mouth and swallowed up the river which the dragon spewed out of his mouth. **17** The dragon grew angry with the woman, and went away to make war with the rest of her offspring,[d] who keep God's commandments and hold Jesus' testimony.

## 13

**1** Then I stood[e] on the sand of the sea. I saw a beast coming up out of the sea, having ten horns and seven heads. On his horns were ten crowns, and on his heads, blasphemous names. **2** The beast which I saw was like a leopard, and his feet were like those of a bear, and his mouth like the mouth of a lion. The dragon gave him his power, his throne, and great authority. **3** One of his heads looked like it had been wounded fatally. His fatal wound was healed, and the whole earth marveled at the beast. **4** They worshiped the dragon because he gave his authority to the beast; and they worshiped the beast, saying, "Who is like the beast? Who is able to make war with him?" **5** A mouth speaking great things and blasphemy was given to him. Authority to make war for forty-two months was given to him. **6** He opened his mouth for blasphemy against God, to blaspheme his name, his dwelling, and those who dwell in heaven. **7** It was given to him to make war with the saints and to overcome them. Authority over every tribe, people, language, and nation was given to him. **8** All who dwell on the earth will worship him, everyone whose name has not been written from the foundation of the world in the book of life of the Lamb who has been killed. **9** If anyone has an ear, let him hear. **10** If anyone is to go into captivity, he will go into captivity. If anyone is to be killed with the sword, he must be killed.[f] Here is the endurance and the faith of the saints. **11** I saw another beast coming up out of the earth. He had two horns like a lamb and it spoke like a dragon. **12** He exercises all the authority of the first beast in his presence. He makes the earth and those who dwell in it to worship the first beast, whose fatal wound was healed. **13** He performs great signs, even making fire come down out of the sky to the earth in the sight of people. **14** He deceives my own[g] people who dwell on the earth because of the signs he was granted to do in front of the beast, saying to those who dwell on the earth that they should make an image to the beast who had the sword wound and lived. **15** It was given to him to give breath to the image of the beast, that the image of the beast should both speak, and cause as many as wouldn't worship the image

---

[a] *9:21* The word for "sorceries" (pharmakeia) also implies the use of potions, poisons, and drugs
[b] *10:11* TR reads "He" instead of "They"
[c] *11:17* TR adds "and who is coming"
[d] *12:17* or, seed
[e] *13:1* NU reads he stood
[f] *13:10* TR reads "If anyone leads into captivity, into captivity he goes. If anyone will kill with the sword, he must be killed with a sword." instead of "If anyone is to go into captivity, he will go into captivity. If anyone is to be killed with the sword, he must be killed."
[g] *13:14* NU omits "my own"

of the beast to be killed. [16] He causes all, the small and the great, the rich and the poor, and the free and the slave, to be given marks on their right hands or on their foreheads; [17] and that no one would be able to buy or to sell unless he has that mark, which is the name of the beast or the number of his name. [18] Here is wisdom. He who has understanding, let him calculate the number of the beast, for it is the number of a man. His number is six hundred sixty-six.

## 14

[1] I saw, and behold, the Lamb standing on Mount Zion, and with him a number, one hundred forty-four thousand, having his name and the name of his Father written on their foreheads. [2] I heard a sound from heaven like the sound of many waters and like the sound of a great thunder. The sound which I heard was like that of harpists playing on their harps. [3] They sing a new song before the throne and before the four living creatures and the elders. No one could learn the song except the one hundred forty-four thousand, those who had been redeemed out of the earth. [4] These are those who were not defiled with women, for they are virgins. These are those who follow the Lamb wherever he goes. These were redeemed by Jesus from among men, the first fruits to God and to the Lamb. [5] In their mouth was found no lie, for they are blameless.[a] [6] I saw an angel flying in mid heaven, having an eternal Good News to proclaim to those who dwell on the earth—to every nation, tribe, language, and people. [7] He said with a loud voice, "Fear the Lord, and give him glory, for the hour of his judgment has come. Worship him who made the heaven, the earth, the sea, and the springs of waters!" [8] Another, a second angel, followed, saying, "Babylon the great has fallen, which has made all the nations to drink of the wine of the wrath of her sexual immorality." [9] Another angel, a third, followed them, saying with a great voice, "If anyone worships the beast and his image, and receives a mark on his forehead or on his hand, [10] he also will drink of the wine of the wrath of God, which is prepared unmixed in the cup of his anger. He will be tormented with fire and sulfur in the presence of the holy angels and in the presence of the Lamb. [11] The smoke of their torment goes up forever and ever. They have no rest day and night, those who worship the beast and his image, and whoever receives the mark of his name. [12] Here is the perseverance of the saints, those who keep the commandments of God and the faith of Jesus." [13] I heard a voice from heaven saying, "Write, 'Blessed are the dead who die in the Lord from now on.'" "Yes," says the Spirit, "that they may rest from their labors, for their works follow with them." [14] I looked, and saw a white cloud, and on the cloud one sitting like a son of man,* having on his head a golden crown, and in his hand a sharp sickle. [15] Another angel came out of the temple, crying with a loud voice to him who sat on the cloud, "Send your sickle and reap, for the hour to reap has come; for the harvest of the earth is ripe!" [16] He who sat on the cloud thrust his sickle on the earth, and the earth was reaped. [17] Another angel came out of the temple which is in heaven. He also had a sharp sickle. [18] Another angel came out from the altar, he who has power over fire, and he called with a great voice to him who had the sharp sickle, saying, "Send your sharp sickle and gather the clusters of the vine of the earth, for the earth's grapes are fully ripe!" [19] The angel thrust his sickle into the earth, and gathered the vintage of the earth and threw it into the great wine press of the wrath of God. [20] The wine press was trodden outside of the city, and blood came out of the wine press, up to the bridles of the horses, as far as one thousand six hundred stadia.[b]

## 15

[1] I saw another great and marvelous sign in the sky: seven angels having the seven last plagues, for in them God's wrath is finished. [2] I saw something like a sea of glass mixed with fire, and those who overcame the beast, his image,[c] and the number of his name, standing on the sea of glass, having harps of God. [3] They sang the song of Moses, the servant of God, and the song of the Lamb, saying, "Great and marvelous are your works, Lord God, the Almighty! Righteous and true are your ways, you King of the nations. [4] Who wouldn't fear you, Lord, and glorify your name? For you only are holy. For all the nations will come and worship before you. For your righteous acts have been revealed." [5] After these things I looked, and the temple of the tabernacle of the testimony in heaven was opened. [6] The seven angels who had the seven plagues came out, clothed with pure, bright linen, and wearing golden sashes around their chests. [7] One of the four living creatures gave to the seven angels seven golden bowls full of the wrath of God, who lives forever and ever. [8] The temple was filled with smoke from the glory of God and from his power. No one was able to enter into the temple until the seven plagues of the seven angels would be finished.

## 16

[1] I heard a loud voice out of the temple, saying to the seven angels, "Go and pour out the seven bowls of the wrath of God on the earth!" [2] The first went, and poured out his bowl into the earth, and it became a harmful and painful sore on the people who had the mark of the beast, and who worshiped his image. [3] The second angel poured out his bowl into the sea, and it became blood as of a dead man. Every living thing in the sea died. [4] The third poured out his bowl into the rivers and springs of water, and they became blood. [5] I heard the angel of the waters saying, "You are righteous, who are and who were, O Holy One, because you have judged these things. [6] For they poured out the blood of saints and prophets, and you have given them blood to drink. They deserve this." [7] I heard the altar saying, "Yes, Lord God, the Almighty, true and righteous are your judgments." [8] The fourth poured out his bowl on the sun, and it was given to him to scorch men with fire. [9] People were scorched with great heat, and people blasphemed the name of God who has the power over these plagues. They didn't repent and give him glory. [10] The fifth poured out his bowl on the throne of the beast, and his kingdom was darkened. They gnawed their tongues because of the pain, [11] and they blasphemed the God of heaven because of their pains and their sores. They still didn't repent of their works. [12] The sixth poured out his bowl on the great river, the Euphrates. Its water was dried up, that the way might be prepared for the kings that come from the sunrise.[d] [13] I saw coming out of the mouth of the dragon, and out of the mouth of the beast, and out of the mouth of the false prophet, three unclean spirits, something like frogs; [14] for they are spirits of demons, performing signs, which go out to the kings of the whole inhabited earth, to gather them together for the war of that great day of God the Almighty. [15] "Behold, I come like a thief. Blessed is he who watches, and keeps his clothes, so that he doesn't walk naked, and they see his shame." [16] He gathered them together into the place which is called in Hebrew, "Harmagedon". [17] The seventh poured out his bowl into the air. A loud voice came out of the temple of heaven, from the throne, saying, "It is done!" [18] There were lightnings, sounds, and thunders; and there was a great earthquake such as has not happened since there were men on the earth—so great an earthquake and so mighty. [19] The great city was divided into three parts, and the cities of the nations fell. Babylon the great was remembered in the sight of God, to give to her the cup of the wine of the fierceness of his wrath. [20] Every island fled away, and the mountains were not found. [21] Great hailstones, about the weight of a talent,[e] came down out of the sky on people. People blasphemed God because of the plague of the hail, for this plague was exceedingly severe.

## 17

[1] One of the seven angels who had the seven bowls came and spoke with me, saying, "Come here. I will show you the judgment of the great prostitute who sits on many waters, [2] with whom the kings of the earth committed sexual immorality. Those who dwell in the earth were made drunken with the wine of her sexual immorality." [3] He carried me away in the Spirit into a wilderness. I saw a woman sitting on a scarlet-colored beast, full of blasphemous names, having seven heads and ten horns. [4] The woman was dressed in purple and scarlet, and decked with gold and precious stones and pearls, having in her hand a golden cup full of abominations and the impurities of the sexual immorality of the earth. [5] And on her forehead a name was written, "MYSTERY, BABYLON THE GREAT, THE MOTHER OF THE PROSTITUTES AND OF THE ABOMINATIONS OF THE EARTH." [6] I saw the woman drunken with the blood of the saints and with the blood of the martyrs of Jesus. When I saw her, I wondered with great amazement. [7] The angel said to me, "Why do you wonder? I will tell you the mystery of the woman and of the beast that carries her, which has the seven heads and the ten horns. [8] The beast that you saw was, and is not; and is about to come up out of the abyss and to go into destruction. Those who dwell on the earth and whose names have not been written in the book of life from the foundation of the world will marvel when they see that the beast was, and is not, and shall be present.[f] [9] Here is the mind that has wisdom. The seven heads are seven mountains on which the woman sits. [10] They are seven kings. Five have fallen, the one is, and the other has not yet come. When he comes, he must continue a little while. [11] The beast that was, and is not, is himself also an eighth, and is of the seven; and he goes to destruction. [12] The ten horns that you saw are ten kings who have received no kingdom as yet, but they receive authority as kings with the beast for one hour. [13] These have one mind, and they give their power and authority to the beast. [14] These will war against the Lamb, and the Lamb will overcome them, for he is Lord of lords and King of kings; and those who are with him are called,

---

[a] *14:5* TR adds "before the throne of God"
* *14:14* Daniel 7:13

[b] *14:20* 1600 stadia = 296 kilometers or 184 miles
[c] *15:2* TR adds "his mark,"

[d] *16:12* or, east
[e] *16:21* A talent is about 30 kilograms or 66 pounds.

[f] *17:8* TR reads "yet is" instead of "shall be present"

chosen, and faithful." ¹⁵ He said to me, "The waters which you saw, where the prostitute sits, are peoples, multitudes, nations, and languages. ¹⁶ The ten horns which you saw, they and the beast will hate the prostitute, will make her desolate, will strip her naked, will eat her flesh, and will burn her utterly with fire. ¹⁷ For God has put in their hearts to do what he has in mind, to be of one mind, and to give their kingdom to the beast, until the words of God should be accomplished. ¹⁸ The woman whom you saw is the great city which reigns over the kings of the earth."

## 18

¹ After these things, I saw another angel coming down out of the sky, having great authority. The earth was illuminated with his glory. ² He cried with a mighty voice, saying, "Fallen, fallen is Babylon the great, and she has become a habitation of demons, a prison of every unclean spirit, and a prison of every unclean and hated bird! ³ For all the nations have drunk of the wine of the wrath of her sexual immorality, the kings of the earth committed sexual immorality with her, and the merchants of the earth grew rich from the abundance of her luxury." ⁴ I heard another voice from heaven, saying, "Come out of her, my people, that you have no participation in her sins, and that you don't receive of her plagues, ⁵ for her sins have reached to the sky, and God has remembered her iniquities. ⁶ Return to her just as she returned, and repay her double as she did, and according to her works. In the cup which she mixed, mix to her double. ⁷ However much she glorified herself and grew wanton, so much give her of torment and mourning. For she says in her heart, 'I sit a queen, and am no widow, and will in no way see mourning.' ⁸ Therefore in one day her plagues will come: death, mourning, and famine; and she will be utterly burned with fire, for the Lord God who has judged her is strong. ⁹ The kings of the earth who committed sexual immorality and lived wantonly with her will weep and wail over her, when they look at the smoke of her burning, ¹⁰ standing far away for the fear of her torment, saying, 'Woe, woe, the great city, Babylon, the strong city! For your judgment has come in one hour.' ¹¹ The merchants of the earth weep and mourn over her, for no one buys their merchandise any more: ¹² merchandise of gold, silver, precious stones, pearls, fine linen, purple, silk, scarlet, all expensive wood, every vessel of ivory, every vessel made of most precious wood, and of brass, and iron, and marble; ¹³ and cinnamon, incense, perfume, frankincense, wine, olive oil, fine flour, wheat, cattle, sheep, horses, chariots, and people's bodies and souls. ¹⁴ The fruits which your soul lusted after have been lost to you. All things that were dainty and sumptuous have perished from you, and you will find them no more at all. ¹⁵ The merchants of these things, who were made rich by her, will stand far away for the fear of her torment, weeping and mourning, ¹⁶ saying, 'Woe, woe, the great city, she who was dressed in fine linen, purple, and scarlet, and decked with gold and precious stones and pearls! ¹⁷ For in an hour such great riches are made desolate.' Every ship master, and everyone who sails anywhere, and mariners, and as many as gain their living by sea, stood far away, ¹⁸ and cried out as they looked at the smoke of her burning, saying, 'What is like the great city?' ¹⁹ They cast dust on their heads, and cried, weeping and mourning, saying, 'Woe, woe, the great city, in which all who had their ships in the sea were made rich by reason of her great wealth!' For she is made desolate in one hour. ²⁰"Rejoice over her, O heaven, you saints, apostles, and prophets, for God has judged your judgment on her." ²¹ A mighty angel took up a stone like a great millstone and cast it into the sea, saying, "Thus with violence will Babylon, the great city, be thrown down, and will be found no more at all. ²² The voice of harpists, minstrels, flute players, and trumpeters will be heard no more at all in you. No craftsman of whatever craft will be found any more at all in you. The sound of a mill will be heard no more at all in you. ²³ The light of a lamp will shine no more at all in you. The voice of the bridegroom and of the bride will be heard no more at all in you, for your merchants were the princes of the earth; for with your sorcery all the nations were deceived. ²⁴ In her was found the blood of prophets and of saints, and of all who have been slain on the earth."

## 19

¹ After these things I heard something like a loud voice of a great multitude in heaven, saying, "Hallelujah! Salvation, power, and glory belong to our God; ² for his judgments are true and righteous. For he has judged the great prostitute who corrupted the earth with her sexual immorality, and he has avenged the blood of his servants at her hand." ³ A second said, "Hallelujah! Her smoke goes up forever and ever." ⁴ The twenty-four elders and the four living creatures fell down and worshiped God who sits on the throne, saying, "Amen! Hallelujah!" ⁵ A voice came from the throne, saying, "Give praise to our God, all you

his servants, you who fear him, the small and the great!" ⁶ I heard something like the voice of a great multitude, and like the voice of many waters, and like the voice of mighty thunders, saying, "Hallelujah! For the Lord our God, the Almighty, reigns! ⁷ Let's rejoice and be exceedingly glad, and let's give the glory to him. For the wedding of the Lamb has come, and his wife has made herself ready." ⁸ It was given to her that she would array herself in bright, pure, fine linen, for the fine linen is the righteous acts of the saints. ⁹ He said to me, "Write, 'Blessed are those who are invited to the wedding supper of the Lamb.'" He said to me, "These are true words of God." ¹⁰ I fell down before his feet to worship him. He said to me, "Look! Don't do it! I am a fellow bondservant with you and with your brothers who hold the testimony of Jesus. Worship God, for the testimony of Jesus is the Spirit of Prophecy." ¹¹ I saw the heaven opened, and behold, a white horse, and he who sat on it is called Faithful and True. In righteousness he judges and makes war. ¹² His eyes are a flame of fire, and on his head are many crowns. He has names written and a name written which no one knows but he himself. ¹³ He is clothed in a garment sprinkled with blood. His name is called "The Word of God." ¹⁴ The armies which are in heaven, clothed in white, pure, fine linen, followed him on white horses. ¹⁵ Out of his mouth proceeds a sharp, double-edged sword that with it he should strike the nations. He will rule them with an iron rod.* He treads the wine press of the fierceness of the wrath of God, the Almighty. ¹⁶ He has on his garment and on his thigh a name written, "KING OF KINGS AND LORD OF LORDS." ¹⁷ I saw an angel standing in the sun. He cried with a loud voice, saying to all the birds that fly in the sky, "Come! Be gathered together to the great supper of God,ᵃ ¹⁸ that you may eat the flesh of kings, the flesh of captains, the flesh of mighty men, and the flesh of horses and of those who sit on them, and the flesh of all men, both free and slave, small and great." ¹⁹ I saw the beast, the kings of the earth, and their armies, gathered together to make war against him who sat on the horse and against his army. ²⁰ The beast was taken, and with him the false prophet who worked the signs in his sight, with which he deceived those who had received the mark of the beast and those who worshiped his image. These two were thrown alive into the lake of fire that burns with sulfur. ²¹ The rest were killed with the sword of him who sat on the horse, the sword which came out of his mouth. So all the birds were filled with their flesh.

## 20

¹ I saw an angel coming down out of heaven, having the key of the abyss and a great chain in his hand. ² He seized the dragon, the old serpent, who is the devil and Satan, who deceives the whole inhabited earth,ᵇ and bound him for a thousand years, ³ and cast him into the abyss, and shut it and sealed it over him, that he should deceive the nations no more until the thousand years were finished. After this, he must be freed for a short time. ⁴ I saw thrones, and they sat on them, and judgment was given to them. I saw the souls of those who had been beheaded for the testimony of Jesus and for the word of God, and such as didn't worship the beast nor his image, and didn't receive the mark on their forehead and on their hand. They lived and reigned with Christ for a thousand years. ⁵ The rest of the dead didn't live until the thousand years were finished. This is the first resurrection. ⁶ Blessed and holy is he who has part in the first resurrection. Over these, the second death has no power, but they will be priests of God and of Christ, and will reign with him one thousand years. ⁷ And after the thousand years, Satan will be released from his prison ⁸ and he will come out to deceive the nations which are in the four corners of the earth, Gog and Magog, to gather them together to the war, whose number is as the sand of the sea. ⁹ They went up over the width of the earth and surrounded the camp of the saints and the beloved city. Fire came down out of heaven from God and devoured them. ¹⁰ The devil who deceived them was thrown into the lake of fire and sulfur, where the beast and the false prophet are also. They will be tormented day and night forever and ever. ¹¹ I saw a great white throne and him who sat on it, from whose face the earth and the heaven fled away. There was found no place for them. ¹² I saw the dead, the great and the small, standing before the throne, and they opened books. Another book was opened, which is the book of life. The dead were judged out of the things which were written in the books, according to their works. ¹³ The sea gave up the dead who were in it. Death and Hadesᶜ gave up the dead who were in them. They were judged, each one according to his works. ¹⁴ Death and Hadesᵈ were thrown into the lake of fire. This is the second death, the lake of fire. ¹⁵ If anyone was not found written in the book of life, he was cast into the lake of fire.

* 19:15 Psalms 2:9    ᵃ 19:17 TR reads "supper of the great God" instead of "great supper of God"    ᵇ 20:2 TR and NU omit "who deceives the whole inhabited earth".    ᶜ 20:13 or, Hell    ᵈ 20:14 or, Hell

## 21

[1] I saw a new heaven and a new earth, for the first heaven and the first earth have passed away, and the sea is no more. [2] I saw the holy city, New Jerusalem, coming down out of heaven from God, prepared like a bride adorned for her husband. [3] I heard a loud voice out of heaven saying, "Behold, God's dwelling is with people; and he will dwell with them, and they will be his people, and God himself will be with them as their God. [4] He will wipe away every tear from their eyes. Death will be no more; neither will there be mourning, nor crying, nor pain any more. The first things have passed away." [5] He who sits on the throne said, "Behold, I am making all things new." He said, "Write, for these words of God are faithful and true." [6] He said to me, "I am the Alpha and the Omega, the Beginning and the End. I will give freely to him who is thirsty from the spring of the water of life. [7] He who overcomes, I will give him these things. I will be his God, and he will be my son. [8] But for the cowardly, unbelieving, sinners,[a] abominable, murderers, sexually immoral, sorcerers,[b] idolaters, and all liars, their part is in the lake that burns with fire and sulfur, which is the second death." [9] One of the seven angels who had the seven bowls which were loaded with the seven last plagues came, and he spoke with me, saying, "Come here. I will show you the bride, the Lamb's wife." [10] He carried me away in the Spirit to a great and high mountain, and showed me the holy city, Jerusalem, coming down out of heaven from God, [11] having the glory of God. Her light was like a most precious stone, like a jasper stone, clear as crystal; [12] having a great and high wall with twelve gates, and at the gates twelve angels, and names written on them, which are the names of the twelve tribes of the children of Israel. [13] On the east were three gates, and on the north three gates, and on the south three gates, and on the west three gates. [14] The wall of the city had twelve foundations, and on them twelve names of the twelve Apostles of the Lamb. [15] He who spoke with me had for a measure a golden reed to measure the city, its gates, and its walls. [16] The city is square. Its length is as great as its width. He measured the city with the reed: twelve thousand twelve stadia.[c] Its length, width, and height are equal. [17] Its wall is one hundred forty-four cubits,[d] by the measure of a man, that is, of an angel. [18] The construction of its wall was jasper. The city was pure gold, like pure glass. [19] The foundations of the city's wall were adorned with all kinds of precious stones. The first foundation was jasper, the second sapphire;[e] the third chalcedony, the fourth emerald, [20] the fifth sardonyx, the sixth sardius, the seventh chrysolite, the eighth beryl, the ninth topaz, the tenth chrysoprase, the eleventh jacinth, and the twelfth amethyst. [21] The twelve gates were twelve pearls. Each one of the gates was made of one pearl. The street of the city was pure gold, like transparent glass. [22] I saw no temple in it, for the Lord God the Almighty and the Lamb are its temple. [23] The city has no need for the sun or moon to shine, for the very glory of God illuminated it and its lamp is the Lamb. [24] The nations will walk in its light. The kings of the earth bring the glory and honor of the nations into it. [25] Its gates will in no way be shut by day (for there will be no night there), [26] and they shall bring the glory and the honor of the nations into it so that they may enter. [27] There will in no way enter into it anything profane, or one who causes an abomination or a lie, but only those who are written in the Lamb's book of life.

## 22

[1] He showed me a[f] river of water of life, clear as crystal, proceeding out of the throne of God and of the Lamb, [2] in the middle of its street. On this side of the river and on that was the tree of life, bearing twelve kinds of fruits, yielding its fruit every month. The leaves of the tree were for the healing of the nations. [3] There will be no curse any more. The throne of God and of the Lamb will be in it, and his servants will serve him. [4] They will see his face, and his name will be on their foreheads. [5] There will be no night, and they need no lamp light or sun light; for the Lord God will illuminate them. They will reign forever and ever. [6] He said to me, "These words are faithful and true. The Lord God of the spirits of the prophets sent his angel to show to his bondservants the things which must happen soon." [7] "Behold, I am coming soon! Blessed is he who keeps the words of the prophecy of this book." [8] Now I, John, am the one who heard and saw these things. When I heard and saw, I fell down to worship before the feet of the angel who had shown me these things. [9] He said to me, "You must not do that! I am a fellow bondservant with you and with your brothers, the prophets, and with those who keep the words of this book. Worship God." [10] He said to me, "Don't seal up the words of the prophecy of this book, for the time is at hand. [11] He who acts unjustly, let him act unjustly still. He who is filthy, let him be filthy still. He who is righteous, let him do righteousness still. He who is holy, let him be holy still." [12] "Behold, I am coming soon! My reward is with me, to repay to each man according to his work. [13] I am the Alpha and the Omega, the First and the Last, the Beginning and the End. [14] Blessed are those who do his commandments,[g] that they may have the right to the tree of life, and may enter in by the gates into the city. [15] Outside are the dogs, the sorcerers, the sexually immoral, the murderers, the idolaters, and everyone who loves and practices falsehood. [16] I, Jesus, have sent my angel to testify these things to you for the assemblies. I am the root and the offspring of David, the Bright and Morning Star." [17] The Spirit and the bride say, "Come!" He who hears, let him say, "Come!" He who is thirsty, let him come. He who desires, let him take the water of life freely. [18] I testify to everyone who hears the words of the prophecy of this book: if anyone adds to them, God will add to him the plagues which are written in this book. [19] If anyone takes away from the words of the book of this prophecy, God will take away his part from the tree[h] of life, and out of the holy city, which are written in this book. [20] He who testifies these things says, "Yes, I am coming soon." Amen! Yes, come, Lord Jesus! [21] The grace of the Lord Jesus Christ be with all the saints. Amen.

# The First Epistle of Clement to the Corinthians

## 1

[1] By reason of the sudden and repeated calamities and reverses which are befalling us, brethren, we consider that we have been somewhat tardy in giving heed to the matters of dispute that have arisen among you, dearly beloved, and to the detestable and unholy sedition, so alien and strange to the elect of God, which a few headstrong and self-willed persons have kindled to such a pitch of madness that your name, once revered and renowned and lovely in the sight of all men, hath been greatly reviled. [2] For who that had sojourned among you did not approve your most virtuous and steadfast faith? Who did not admire your sober and forbearing piety in Christ? Who did not publish abroad your magnificent disposition of hospitality? Who did not congratulate you on your perfect and sound knowledge? [3] For ye did all things without respect of persons, and ye walked after the ordinances of God, submitting yourselves to your rulers and rendering to the older men among you the honor which is their due. On the young too ye enjoined modest and seemly thoughts; and the women ye charged to perform all their duties in a blameless and seemly and pure conscience, cherishing their own husbands, as is meet; and ye taught them to keep in the rule of obedience, and to manage the affairs of their household in seemliness, with all discretion.

## 2

[1] And ye were all lowly in mind and free from arrogance, yielding rather than claiming submission, *more glad to give than to receive*, and content with the provisions which God supplieth. And giving heed unto His words, ye laid them up diligently in your hearts, and His sufferings were before your eyes. [2] Thus a profound and rich peace was given to all, and an insatiable desire of doing good. An abundant outpouring also of the Holy Spirit fell upon all; [3] and, being full of holy counsel, in excellent zeal and with a pious confidence ye stretched out your hands to Almighty God, supplicating Him to be propitious, if unwillingly ye had committed any sin. [4] Ye had conflict day and night for all the brotherhood, that the number of His elect might be saved with fearfulness and intentness of mind. [5] Ye were sincere and simple and free from malice one towards another. [6] Every sedition and every schism was abominable to you. Ye mourned over the transgressions of your neighbors: ye judged their shortcomings to be your own. [7] Ye repented not of any well-doing, but were *ready unto every good work*. [8] Being adorned with a most virtuous and honorable life, ye performed all your duties in the fear of Him. The commandments and the ordinances of the Lord were *written on the tablets of your hearts*.

## 3

[1] All glory and enlargement was given unto you, and that was fulfilled which is written *My beloved ate and drank and was enlarged and waxed fat and kicked.* [2] Hence come jealousy and envy, strife and sedition, persecution and tumult, war and captivity. [3] So men were stirred up, *the mean against the honorable*, the ill reputed against the highly reputed, the foolish against the wise, the *young against the elder*. [4] For this cause *righteousness* and peace *stand aloof*, while each man hath forsaken the fear of the Lord and become purblind in the faith of

---

[a] 21:8 TR and NU omit "sinners"

[b] 21:8 The word for "sorcerers" here also includes users of potions and drugs.

[c] 21:16 12,012 stadia = 2,221 kilometers or 1,380 miles. TR reads 12,000 stadia instead of 12,012 stadia.

[d] 21:17 144 cubits is about 65.8 meters or 216 feet

[e] 21:19 or, lapis lazuli

[f] 22:1 TR adds "pure"

[g] 22:14 NU reads "wash their robes" instead of "do his commandments".

[h] 22:19 TR reads "Book" instead of "tree"

Him, neither walketh in the ordinances of His commandments nor liveth according to that which becometh Christ, but each goeth after the lusts of his evil heart, seeing that they have conceived an unrighteous and ungodly jealousy, through which also *death entered into the world.*

## 4

**1** For so it is written, *And it came to pass after certain days that Cain brought of the fruits of the earth a sacrifice unto God, and Abel he also brought of the firstlings of the sheep and of their* fatness. **2** *And God looked upon Abel and upon his gifts, but unto Cain and unto his sacrifices He gave no heed.* **3** *And Cain sorrowed exceedingly, and his countenance fell.* **4** *And God said unto Cain, Wherefore art thou very sorrowful and wherefore did thy countenance fall? If thou hast offered aright and hast not divided aright, didst thou not sin? Hold thy peace.* **5** *Unto thee shall he turn, and thou shalt rule over him.* {This last phrase has also been translated: *Be at peace: thine offering returns to thyself, and thou shalt again possess it.*} **6** *And Cain said unto Abel his brother, Let us go over unto the plain. And it came to pass, while they Were in the plain, that Cain rose up against Abel his brother and slew him.* **7** Ye see, brethren, jealousy and envy wrought a brother's murder. **8** By reason of jealousy our father Jacob ran away from the face of Esau his brother. **9** Jealousy caused Joseph to be persecuted even unto death, and to come even unto bondage. **10** Jealousy compelled Moses to flee from the face of Pharaoh king of Egypt while it was said to him by his own countryman, *Who made thee a judge or a decider over us, Wouldest thou slay me, even as yesterday thou slewest the Egyptian?* **11** By reason of jealousy Aaron and Miriam were lodged outside the camp. **12** Jealousy brought Dathan and Abiram down alive to hades, because they made sedition against Moses the servant of God. **13** By reason of jealousy David was envied not only by the Philistines, but was persecuted also by Saul [king of Israel].

## 5

**1** But, to pass from the examples of ancient days, let us come to those champions who lived nearest to our time. Let us set before us the noble examples which belong to our generation. **2** By reason of jealousy and envy the greatest and most righteous pillars of the Church were persecuted, and contended even unto death. **3** Let us set before our eyes the good Apostles. **4** There was Peter who by reason of unrighteous jealousy endured not one not one but many labors, and thus having borne his testimony went to his appointed place of glory. **5** By reason of jealousy and strife Paul by his example pointed out the prize of patient endurance. After that he had been seven times in bonds, had been driven into exile, had been stoned, had preached in the East and in the West, he won the noble renown which was the reward of his faith, **6** having taught righteousness unto the whole world and having reached the farthest bounds of the West; and when he had borne his testimony before the rulers, so he departed from the world and went unto the holy place, having been found a notable pattern of patient endurance.

## 6

**1** Unto these men of holy lives was gathered a vast multitude of the elect, who through many indignities and tortures, being the victims of jealousy, set a brave example among ourselves. **2** By reason of jealousy women being persecuted, after that they had suffered cruel and unholy insults as Danaids and Dircae, safely reached the goal in the race of faith, and received a noble reward, feeble though they were in body. **3** Jealousy hath estranged wives from their husbands and changed the saying of our father Adam, *This now is bone of my bones and flesh of my flesh.* **4** Jealousy and strife have overthrown great cities and uprooted great nations.

## 7

**1** These things, dearly beloved, we write, not only as admonishing you, but also as putting ourselves in remembrance. For we are in the same lists, and the same contest awaiteth us. **2** Wherefore let us forsake idle and vain thoughts; and let us conform to the glorious and venerable rule which hath been handed down to us; **3** and let us see what is good and what is pleasant and what is acceptable in the sight of Him that made us. **4** Let us fix our eyes on the blood of Christ and understand how precious it is unto His Father, because being shed for our salvation it won for the whole world the grace of repentance. **5** Let us review all the generations in turn, and learn how from generation to generation the Master hath given a place for repentance unto them that desire to turn to Him. **6** Noah preached repentance, and they that obeyed were saved. **7** Jonah preached destruction unto the men of Nineveh; but they, repenting of their sins, obtained pardon of God by their supplications and received salvation, albeit they were aliens from God.

## 8

**1** The ministers of the grace of God through the Holy Spirit spake concerning repentance. **2** Yea and the Master of the universe Himself spake concerning repentance with an oath: **3** *for, as I live saith the Lord, I desire not the death of the sinner, so much as his repentance,* **4** and

He added also a merciful judgment: *Repent ye, O house of Israel, of your iniquity; say unto the sons of My people, Though your sins reach from the earth even unto the heaven, and though they be redder than scarlet and blacker than sackcloth, and ye turn unto Me with your whole heart and say Father, I will give ear unto you as unto a holy people.* **5** And in another place He saith on this wise, *Wash, be ye clean. Put away your iniquities from your souls out of My sight. Cease from your iniquities; learn to do good; seek out judgment; defend him that is wronged: give judgment for the orphan, and execute righteousness for the widow; and come and let us reason together, saith He; and though your sins be as crimson, I will make them white as snow; and though they be as scarlet, I will make them white as wool. And if ye be willing and will hearken unto Me, ye shall eat the good things of the earth; but if ye be not willing, neither hearken unto Me, a sword shall devour you; for the mouth of the Lord hath spoken these things.* **6** Seeing then that He desireth all His beloved to be partakers of repentance, He confirmed it by an act of His almighty will.

## 9

**1** Wherefore let us be obedient unto His excellent and glorious will; and presenting ourselves as suppliants of His mercy and goodness, let us fall down before Him and betake ourselves unto His compassions, forsaking the vain toil and the strife and the jealousy which leadeth unto death. **2** Let us fix our eyes on them that ministered perfectly unto His excellent glory. **3** Let us set before us Enoch, who being found righteous in obedience was translated, and his death was not found. **4** Noah, being found faithful, by his ministration preached regeneration unto the world, and through him the Master saved the living creatures that entered into the ark in concord.

## 10

**1** Abraham, who was called the 'friend,' was found faithful in that he rendered obedience unto the words of God. **2** He through obedience went forth from his land and from his kindred and from his father's house, that leaving a scanty land and a feeble kindred and a mean house he might inherit the promises of God. **3** For He saith unto him *Go forth from thy land and from thy kindred and from thy father's house unto the land which I shall show thee, and I will make thee into a great nation, and I will bless thee and will magnify thy name, and thou shalt be blessed. And I will bless them that bless thee, and I will curse them that curse thee; and in thee shall all the tribes of the earth be blessed.* **4** And again, when he was parted from Lot, God said unto him *Look up with thine eyes, and behold from the place where thou now art, unto the north and the south and the sunrise and the sea; for all the land which thou seest, I will give it unto thee and to thy seed for ever;* **5** *and I will make thy seed as the dust of the earth. If any man can count the dust of the earth, then shall thy seed also be counted.* **6** And again He saith; *God led Abraham forth and said unto him, Look up unto the heaven and count the stars, and see whether thou canst number them. So shall thy seed be. And Abraham believed God, and it was reckoned unto him for righteousness.* **7** For his faith and hospitality a son was given unto him in old age, and by obedience he offered him a sacrifice unto God on one of the mountains which He showed him.

## 11

**1** For his hospitality and godliness Lot was saved from Sodom, when all the country round about was judged by fire and brimstone; the Master having thus fore shown that He forsaketh not them which set their hope on Him, but appointeth unto punishment and torment them which swerve aside. **2** For when his wife had gone forth with him, being otherwise minded and not in accord, she was appointed for a sign hereunto, so that she became a pillar of salt unto this day, that it might be known unto all men that they which are double-minded and they which doubt concerning the power of God are set for a judgment and for a token unto all the generations.

## 12

**1** For her faith and hospitality Rahab the harlot was saved. **2** For when the spies were sent forth unto Jericho by Joshua the son of Nun, the king of the land perceived that they were come to spy out his country, and sent forth men to seize them, that being seized they might be put to death. **3** So the hospitable Rahab received them and hid them in the upper chamber under the flax stalks. **4** And when the messengers of the king came near and said, *The spies of our land entered in unto thee: bring them forth, for the king so ordereth:* then she answered, *The men truly, whom ye seek, entered in unto me, but they departed forthwith and are sojourning on the way;* and she pointed out to them the opposite road. **5** And she said unto the men, *Of a surety I perceive that the Lord your God delivereth this city unto you; for the fear and the dread of you is fallen upon the inhabitants thereof. When therefore it shall come to pass that ye take it, save me and the house of my father.* **6** And they said unto her, *It shall be even so as thou hast spoken unto us. Whensoever therefore thou perceivest that we are coming, thou shalt* *gather all thy folk beneath thy roof and they shall be saved; for as many as shall be found without the house shall perish.* ⁷ And moreover they gave her a sign, that she should hang out from her house a scarlet thread, thereby showing beforehand that through the blood of the Lord there shall be redemption unto all them that believe and hope on God. ⁸ Ye see, dearly beloved, not only faith, but prophecy, is found in the woman.

## 13

¹ Let us therefore be lowly minded, brethren, laying aside all arrogance and conceit and folly and anger, and let us do that which is written. For the Holy Ghost saith, *Let not the wise man boast in his wisdom, nor the strong in his strength, neither the rich in his riches; but he that boasteth let him boast in the Lord, that he may seek Him out, and do judgment and righteousness* most of all remembering the words of the Lord Jesus which He spake, teaching forbearance and long-suffering: ² for thus He spake *Have mercy, that ye may receive mercy: forgive, that it may be forgiven to you. As ye do, so shall it be done to you. As ye give, so shall it be given unto you. As ye judge, so shall ye be judged. As ye show kindness, so shall kindness be showed unto you. With what measure ye mete, it shall be measured withal to you.* ³ With this commandment and these precepts let us confirm ourselves, that we may walk in obedience to His hallowed words, with lowliness of mind. ⁴ For the holy word saith, *Upon whom shall I look, save upon him that is gentle and quiet and feareth Mine oracles?*

## 14

¹ Therefore it is right and proper, brethren, that we should be obedient unto God, rather than follow those who in arrogance and unruliness have set themselves up as leaders in abominable jealousy. ² For we shall bring upon us no common harm, but rather great peril, if we surrender ourselves recklessly to the purposes of men who launch out into strife and seditions, so as to estrange us from that which is right. ³ Let us be good one towards another according to the compassion and sweetness of Him that made us. For it is written: ⁴ *The good shall be dwellers in the land, and the innocent shall be left on it but they that transgress shall be destroyed utterly from it.* ⁵ And again He saith *I saw the ungodly lifted up on high and exalted as the cedars of Lebanon. And I passed by, and behold he was not; and sought out his place, and I found it not. Keep innocence and behold uprightness; for there is a remnant for the peaceful man.*

## 15

¹ Therefore let us cleave unto them that practice peace with godliness, and not unto them that desire peace with dissimulation. ² For He saith in a certain place *This people honoreth Me with their lips, but their heart is far from Me,* ³ and again, *they blessed with their mouth, but they cursed with their heart.* ⁴ And again He saith, *They loved Him with their mouth, and with their tongue they lied unto Him; and their heart was not upright with Him, neither were they steadfast in His covenant.* ⁵ *For this cause let the deceitful lips be made dumb which speak iniquity against the righteous.* And again *May the Lord utterly destroy all the deceitful lips, the tongue that speaketh proud things, even them that say, Let us magnify our tongue; our lips are our own; who is lord over us?* ⁶ *For the misery of the needy and for the groaning of the poor I will now arise, saith the Lord. I will set him in safety; I will deal boldly by him.*

## 16

¹ For Christ is with them that are lowly of mind, not with them that exalt themselves over the flock. ² The scepter of the majesty of God, even our Lord Jesus Christ, came not in the pomp of arrogance or of pride, though He might have done so, but in lowliness of mind, according as the Holy Spirit spake concerning Him. ³ For He saith *Lord, who believed our report? and to whom was the arm of the Lord revealed? We announced Him in His presence. As a child was He, as a root in a thirsty ground. There is no form in Him, neither glory. And we beheld Him, and He had no form nor comeliness, but His form was mean, lacking more than the form of men. He was a man of stripes and of toil, and knowing how to bear infirmity: for His face is turned away. He was dishonored and held of no account.* ⁴ *He beareth our sins and suffereth pain for our sakes: and we accounted Him to be in toil and in stripes and in affliction.* ⁵ *And He was wounded for our sins and hath been afflicted for our iniquities. The chastisement of our peace is upon Him. With His bruises we were healed.* ⁶ *We all went astray like sheep, each man went astray in his own path:* ⁷ *and the Lord delivered Him over for our sins. And He openeth not His mouth, because He is afflicted. As a sheep He was led to slaughter; and as a lamb before his shearer is dumb, so openeth He not His mouth. In His humiliation His judgment was taken away.* ⁸ *His generation who shall declare? For His life is taken away from the earth.* ⁹ *For the iniquities of my people He is come to death.* ¹⁰ *And I will give the wicked for His burial, and the rich for His death; for He wrought no iniquity, neither was guile found in His mouth. And the Lord desireth to cleanse Him from His stripes.* ¹¹ *If ye*

*offer for sin, your soul shall see along lived seed.* ¹² *And the Lord desireth to take away from the toil of His soul, to show Him light and to mould Him with understanding, to justify a Just One that is a good servant unto many. And He shall bear their sins.* ¹³ *Therefore He shall inherit many, and shall divide the spoils of the strong; because His soul was delivered unto death, and He was reckoned unto the transgressors;* ¹⁴ *and He bare the sins of many, and for their sins was He delivered up.* ¹⁵ And again He Himself saith; *But I am a worm and no man, a reproach of men and an outcast of the people.* ¹⁶ *All they that beheld me mocked at me; they spake with their lips; they wagged their heads, saying, He hoped on the Lord; let Him deliver him, or let Him save him, for He desireth him.* ¹⁷ Ye see, dearly beloved, what is the pattern that hath been given unto us; for, if the Lord was thus lowly of mind, what should we do, who through Him have been brought under the yoke of His grace?

## 17

¹ Let us be imitators also of them which went about in goatskins and sheepskins, preaching the coming of Christ. We mean Elijah and Elisha and likewise Ezekiel, the prophets, and besides them those men also that obtained a good report. ² Abraham obtained an exceeding good report and was called the friend of God; and looking steadfastly on the glory of God, he saith in lowliness of mind, *But I am dust and ashes.* ³ Moreover concerning Job also it is thus written; *And Job was righteous and unblamable, one that was true and honored God and abstained from all evil.* ⁴ Yet he himself accuseth himself saying, *No man from filth; no, not though his life be but for a day.* ⁵ Moses was called *faithful in all His house,* and through his ministration God judged Egypt with the plagues and the torments which befell them. Howbeit he also, though greatly glorified, yet spake no proud words, but said, when an oracle was given to him at the bush, *Who am I, that Thou sendest me?* ⁶ *Nay, I am feeble of speech and slow of tongue.* And again he saith, *But I am smoke from the pot.*

## 18

¹ But what must we say of David that obtained a good report? of whom God said, *I have found a man after My heart, David the son of Jesse: with eternal mercy have I anointed him.* ² Yet he too saith unto God *Have mercy upon me, O God, according to Thy great mercy; and according to the multitude of Thy compassions, blot out mine iniquity.* ³ *Wash me yet more from mine iniquity, and cleanse me from my sin. For I acknowledge mine iniquity, and my sin is ever before me. Against Thee only did I sin, and I wrought evil in Thy sight; that Thou mayest be justified in Thy words, and mayest conquer in Thy pleading.* ⁴ *For behold, in iniquities was I conceived, and in sins did my mother bear me. For behold Thou hast loved truth: the dark and hidden things of Thy wisdom hast Thou showed unto me.* ⁵ *Thou shalt sprinkle me with hyssop, and I shall be made clean. Thou shalt wash me, and I shall become whiter than snow.* ⁶ *Thou shalt make me to hear of joy and gladness. The bones which have been humbled shall rejoice.* ⁷ *Turn away Thy face from my sins, and blot out all mine iniquities.* ⁸ *Make a clean heart within me, O God, and renew a right spirit in mine inmost parts. Cast me not away from Thy presence, and take not Thy Holy Spirit from me.* ⁹ *Restore unto me the joy of Thy salvation, and strengthen me with a princely spirit.* ¹⁰ *I will teach sinners Thy ways, and godless men shall be converted unto Thee.* ¹¹ *Deliver me from blood guiltiness, O God, the God of my salvation. My tongue shall rejoice in Thy righteousness.* ¹² *Lord, Thou shalt open my mouth, and my lips shall declare Thy praise.* ¹³ *For, if Thou hadst desired sacrifice, I would have given it: in whole burnt offerings Thou wilt have no pleasure.* ¹⁴ *A sacrifice unto God is a contrite spirit; a contrite and humbled heart God will not despise.*

## 19

¹ The humility therefore and the submissiveness of so many and so great men, who have thus obtained a good report, hath through obedience made better not only us but also the generations which were before us, even them that received His oracles in fear and truth. ² Seeing then that we have been partakers of many great and glorious doings, let us hasten to return unto the goal of peace which hath been handed down to us from the beginning, and let us look steadfastly unto the Father and Maker of the whole world, and cleave unto His splendid and excellent gifts of peace and benefits. ³ Let us behold Him in our mind, and let us look with the eyes of our soul unto His long-suffering will. Let us note how free from anger He is towards all His creatures.

## 20

¹ The heavens are moved by His direction and obey Him in peace. ² Day and night accomplish the course assigned to them by Him, without hindrance one to another. ³ The sun and the moon and the dancing stars according to His appointment circle in harmony within the bounds assigned to them, without any swerving aside. ⁴ The earth, bearing fruit in fulfillment of His will at her proper seasons, putteth forth the food that supplieth abundantly both men and beasts and all living things

which are thereupon, making no dissension, neither altering anything which He hath decreed. **5** Moreover, the inscrutable depths of the abysses and the unutterable statutes of the nether regions are constrained by the same ordinances. **6** The basin of the boundless sea, gathered together by His workmanship *into it's reservoirs*, passeth not the barriers wherewith it is surrounded; but even as He ordered it, so it doeth. **7** For He said, *So far shalt thou come, and thy waves shall be broken within thee.* **8** The ocean which is impassable for men, and the worlds beyond it, are directed by the same ordinances of the Master. **9** The seasons of spring and summer and autumn and winter give way in succession one to another in peace. **10** The winds in their several quarters at their proper season fulfill their ministry without disturbance; and the ever flowing fountains, created for enjoyment and health, without fail give their breasts which sustain the life for men. Yea, the smallest of living things come together in concord and peace. **11** All these things the great Creator and Master of the universe ordered to be in peace and concord, doing good unto all things, but far beyond the rest unto us who have taken refuge in His compassionate mercies through our Lord Jesus Christ, **12** to whom be the glory and the majesty for ever and ever. Amen.

## 21

**1** Look ye, brethren, lest His benefits, which are many, turn unto judgment to all of us, if we walk not worthily of Him, and do those things which are good and well pleasing in His sight with concord. **2** For He saith in a certain place, *The Spirit of the Lord is a lamp searching the closets of the belly.* **3** Let us see how near He is, and how that nothing escapeth Him of our thoughts or our devices which we make. **4** It is right therefore that we should not be deserters from His will. **5** Let us rather give offense to foolish and senseless men who exalt themselves and boast in the arrogance of their words, than to God. **6** Let us fear the Lord Jesus [Christ], whose blood was given for us. Let us reverence our rulers; let us honor our elders; let us instruct our young men in the lesson of the fear of God. Let us guide our women toward that which is good: **7** let them show forth their lovely disposition of purity; let them prove their sincere affection of gentleness; let them make manifest the moderation of their tongue through their silence; let them show their love, not in factious preferences but without partiality towards all them that fear God, in holiness. Let our children be partakers of the instruction which is in Christ: **8** let them learn how lowliness of mind prevaileth with God, what power chaste love hath with God, how the fear of Him is good and great and saveth all them that walk therein in a pure mind with holiness. **9** For He is the searcher out of the intents and desires; whose breath is in us, and when He listeth, He shall take it away.

## 22

**1** Now all these things the faith which is in Christ confirmeth: for He Himself through the Holy Spirit thus invite thus: *Come, my children, hearken unto Me, I will teach you the fear of the Lord.* **2** *What man is he that desireth life and loveth to see good days?* **3** *Make thy tongue to cease from evil, and thy lips that they speak no guile.* **4** *Turn aside from evil and do good.* **5** *Seek peace and ensue it.* **6** *The eyes of the Lord are over the righteous, and His ears are turned to their prayers. But the face of the Lord is upon them that do evil, to destroy their memorial from the earth.* **7** *The righteous cried out, and the Lord heard him, and delivered him from all his troubles. Many are the troubles of the righteous, and the Lord shall deliver him from them all.* **8** And again *Many are the stripes of the sinner, but them that set their hope on the Lord mercy shall compass about.*

## 23

**1** The Father, who is pitiful in all things, and ready to do good, hath compassion on them that fear Him, and kindly and lovingly bestoweth His favors on them that draw nigh unto Him with a single mind. **2** Therefore let us not be double-minded, neither let our soul indulge in idle humors respecting His exceeding and glorious gifts. **3** Let this scripture be far from us where He saith *Wretched are the double-minded, Which doubt in their soul and say, These things we did hear in the days of our fathers also, and behold we have grown old, and none of these things hath befallen us.* **4** *Ye fools, compare yourselves unto a tree; take a vine. First it sheddeth its leaves, then a shoot cometh, then a leaf, then a flower, and after these a sour berry, then a full ripe grape.* Ye see that in a little time the fruit of the tree attaineth unto mellowness. **5** Of a truth quickly and suddenly shall His will be accomplished, the scripture also bearing witness to it, saying *He shall come quickly and shall not tarry; and the Lord shall come suddenly into His temple, even the Holy One, whom ye expect.*

## 24

**1** Let us understand, dearly beloved, how the Master continually showeth unto us the resurrection that shall be hereafter; whereof He made the Lord Jesus Christ the firstfruit, when He raised Him from the dead. **2** Let us behold, dearly beloved, the resurrection which happeneth

at its proper season. **3** Day and night show unto us the resurrection. The night falleth asleep, and day ariseth; the day departeth, and night cometh on. **4** Let us mark the fruits, how and in what manner the sowing taketh place. **5** *The sower goeth forth* and casteth into the earth each of the seeds; and these falling into the earth dry and bare decay: then out of their decay the mightiness of the Master's providence raiseth them up, and from being one they increase manifold and bear fruit.

## 25

**1** Let us consider the marvelous sign which is seen in the regions of the east, that is, in the parts about Arabia. **2** There is a bird, which is named the phoenix. This, being the only one of its kind, liveth for five hundred years; and when it hath now reached the time of its dissolution that it should die, it maketh for itself a coffin of frankincense and myrrh and the other spices, into the which in the fullness of time it entereth, and so it dieth. **3** But, as the flesh rotteth, a certain worm is engendered, which is nurtured from the moisture of the dead creature and putteth forth wings. Then, when it is grown lusty, it taketh up that coffin where are the bones of its parent, and carrying them journeyeth from the country of Arabia even unto Egypt, to the place called the City of the Sun; **4** and in the daytime in the sight of all, flying to the altar of the Sun, it layeth them thereupon; and this done, it setteth forth to return. **5** So the priests examine the registers of the times, and they find that it hath come when the five hundredth year is completed.

## 26

**1** Do we then think it to be a great and marvelous thing, if the Creator of the universe shall bring about the resurrection of them that have served Him with holiness in the assurance of a good faith, seeing that He showeth to us even by a bird the magnificence of His promise? **2** For He saith in a certain place *And Thou shalt raise me up, and I will praise Thee;* and; *I went to rest and slept, I was awaked, for Thou art with me.* **3** And again Job saith *And Thou shall raise this my flesh which hath endured all these things.*

## 27

**1** With this hope therefore let our souls be bound unto Him that is faithful in His promises and that is righteous in His judgments. **2** He that commanded not to lie, much more shall He Himself not lie: for nothing is impossible with God save to lie. **3** Therefore let our faith in Him be kindled within us, and let us understand that all things are nigh unto Him. **4** By a word of His majesty He compacted the universe; and by a word He can destroy it. **5** *Who shall say unto Him, What hast thou done? or who shall resist the might of His strength?* When He listeth, and as He listeth, He will do all things; and nothing shall pass away of those things that He hath decreed. **6** All things are in His sight, and nothing escapeth His counsel, **7** seeing that *The heavens declare the glory of God, and the firmament proclaimeth His handiwork. Day uttereth word unto day, and night proclaimeth knowledge unto night; and there are neither words nor speeches, whose voices are not heard.*

## 28

**1** Since therefore all things are seen and heard, let us fear Him and forsake the abominable lusts of evil works, that we maybe shielded by His mercy from the coming judgments. **2** For where can any of us escape from His strong hand? And what world will receive any of them that desert from His service? **3** For the holy writing saith in a certain place *Where shall I go, and where shall I be hidden from Thy face? If I ascend into the heaven, Thou art there; if I depart into the farthest parts of the earth, there is Thy right hand; if I make my bed in the depths, there is Thy Spirit.* **4** Whither then shall one depart, or where shall one flee, from Him that embraceth the universe?

## 29

**1** Let us therefore approach Him in holiness of soul, lifting up pure and undefiled hands unto Him, with love towards our gentle and compassionate Father who made us an elect portion unto Himself. **2** For thus it is written: *When the Most High divided the nations, when He dispersed the sons of Adam, He fixed the boundaries of the nations according to the number of the angels of God. His people Jacob became the portion of the Lord, and Israel the measurement of His inheritance.* **3** And in another place He saith, *Behold, the Lord taketh for Himself a nation out of the midst of the nations, as a man taketh the first fruits of his threshing floor; and the holy of holies shall come forth from that nation.*

## 30

**1** Seeing then that we are the special portion of a Holy God, let us do all things that pertain unto holiness, forsaking evil speakings, abominable and impure embraces, drunkennesses and tumults and hateful lusts, abominable adultery, hateful pride. **2** *For God*, He saith, *resisteth the proud, but giveth grace to the lowly.* **3** Let us therefore cleave unto those to whom grace is given from God. Let us clothe ourselves in concord, being lowlyminded and temperate, holding ourselves aloof from all back biting and evil speaking, being justified by works and not by words. [4] For He saith, *He that saith much shall hear also again. Doth the ready talker think to be righteous?* [5] *Blessed is the offspring of a woman that liveth but a short time. Be not thou abundant in words.* [6] Let our praise be with God, and not of ourselves: for God hateth them that praise themselves. [7] Let the testimony to our well doing be given by others, as it was given unto our fathers who were righteous. [8] Boldness and arrogance and daring are for them that are accursed of God; but forbearance and humility and gentleness are with them that are blessed of God.

## 31

[1] Let us therefore cleave unto His blessing, and let us see what are the ways of blessing. Let us study the records of the things that have happened from the beginning. [2] Wherefore was our father Abraham blessed? Was it not because he wrought righteousness and truth through faith? [3] Isaac with confidence, as knowing the future, was led a willing sacrifice. [4] Jacob with humility departed from his land because of his brother, and went unto Laban and served; and the twelve tribes of Israel were given unto him.

## 32

[1] If any man will consider them one by one in sincerity, he shall understand the magnificence of the gifts that are given by Him. [2] For of Jacob are all the priests and levites who minister unto the altar of God; of him is the Lord Jesus as concerning the flesh; of him are kings and rulers and governors in the line of Judah; yea and the rest of his tribes are held in no small honor, seeing that God promised saying, *Thy seed shall be as the stars of heaven.* [3] They all therefore were glorified and magnified, not through themselves or their own works or the righteous doing which they wrought, but through His will. [4] And so we, having been called through His will in Christ Jesus, are not justified through ourselves or through our own wisdom or understanding or piety or works which we wrought in holiness of heart, but through faith, whereby the Almighty God justified all men that have been from the beginning; to whom be the glory for ever and ever. Amen.

## 33

[1] What then must we do, brethren? Must we idly abstain from doing good, and forsake love? May the Master never allow this to befall us at least; but let us hasten with instancy and zeal to accomplish every good work. [2] For the Creator and Master of the universe Himself rejoiceth in His works. [3] For by His exceeding great might He established the heavens, and in His incomprehensible wisdom He set them in order. And the earth He separated from the water that surroundeth it, and He set it firm on the sure foundation of His own will; and the living creatures which walk upon it He commanded to exist by His ordinance. Having before created the sea and the living creatures therein, He enclosed it by His own power. [4] Above all, as the most excellent and exceeding great work of His intelligence, with His sacred and faultless hands He formed man in the impress of His own image. [5] For thus saith God *Let us make man after our image and after our likeness. And God made man; male and female made He them.* [6] So having finished all these things, He praised them and blessed them and said, *Increase and multiply.* [7] We have seen that all the righteous were adorned in good works. Yea, and the Lord Himself having adorned Himself with worlds rejoiced. [8] Seeing then that we have this pattern, let us conform ourselves with all diligence to His will; let us with all our strength work the work of righteousness.

## 34

[1] The good workman receiveth the bread of his work with boldness, but the slothful and careless dareth not look his employer in the face. [2] It is therefore needful that we should be zealous unto well doing, for of Him are all things: [3] since He forewarneth us saying, *Behold, the Lord, and His reward is before His face, to recompense each man according to his work.* [4] He exhorteth us therefore to believe on Him with our whole heart, and to be not idle nor careless unto every good work. [5] Let our boast and our confidence be in Him: let us submit ourselves to His will; let us mark the whole host of His angels, how they stand by and minister unto His will. [6] For the scripture saith, *Ten thousands of ten thousands stood by Him, and thousands of thousands ministered unto Him: and they cried aloud, Holy, holy, holy is the Lord of Sabaoth; all creation is full of His glory.* [7] Yea, and let us ourselves then, being gathered together in concord with intentness of heart, cry unto Him as from one mouth earnestly that we may be made partakers of His great and glorious promises. [8] For He saith, *Eye hath not seen and ear hath not heard, and it hath not entered into the heart of man what great things He hath prepared for them that patiently await Him.*

## 35

[1] How blessed and marvelous are the gifts of God, dearly beloved!! [2] Life in immortality, splendor in righteousness, truth in boldness, faith in confidence, temperance in sanctification! And all these things fall under our apprehension. [3] What then, think ye, are the things preparing for them that patiently await Him? The Creator and Father of the ages, the All holy One Himself knoweth their number and their beauty. [4] Let us therefore contend, that we may be found in the number of those that patiently await Him, to the end that we may be partakers of His promised gifts. [5] But how shall this be, dearly beloved? If our mind be fixed through faith towards God; if we seek out those things which are well pleasing and acceptable unto Him; if we accomplish such things as beseem His faultless will, and follow the way of truth, casting off from ourselves all unrighteousness and iniquity, covetousness, strifes, malignities and deceits, whisperings and backbitings, hatred of God, pride and arrogance, vainglory and inhospitality. [6] For they that do these things are hateful to God; and not only they that do them, but they also that consent unto them. [7] For the scripture saith, *But unto the sinner said God, Wherefore dost thou declare Mine ordinances, and takest My covenant upon thy lips?* [8] *Yet Thou didst hate instruction and didst cast away My words behind thee. If thou sawest a thief thou didst keep company with him, and with the adulterers thou didst set thy portion. Thy mouth multiplied wickedness and thy tongue wove deceit. Thou sattest and spakest against thy brother, and against the son of thy mother thou didst lay a stumbling block.* [9] *These things Thou hast done, and I kept silence. Thou thoughtest, unrighteous man, that I should be like unto thee.* [10] *I will convict thee and will set thee face to face with thyself.* [11] *Now understand ye these things, ye that forget God, lest at any time He seize you as a lion, and there be none to deliver.* [12] *The sacrifice of praise shall glorify Me, and there is the way wherein I will show him the salvation of God.*

## 36

[1] This is the way, dearly beloved, wherein we found our salvation, even Jesus Christ the High priest of our offerings, the Guardian and Helper of our weakness. [2] Through Him let us look steadfastly unto the heights of the heavens; through Him we behold as in a mirror His faultless and most excellent visage; through Him the eyes of our hearts were opened; through Him our foolish and darkened mind springeth up unto the light; through Him the Master willed that we should taste of the immortal knowledge *Who being the brightness of His majesty is so much greater than angels, as He hath inherited a more excellent name.* [3] For so it is written *Who maketh His angels spirits and His ministers aflame of fire* [4] but of His Son the Master said thus, *Thou art My Son, I this day have begotten thee. Ask of Me, and I will give Thee the Gentiles for Thine inheritance, and the ends of the earth for Thy possession.* [5] And again He saith unto Him *Sit Thou on My right hand, until I make Thine enemies a footstool for Thy feet.* [6] Who then are these enemies? They that are wicked and resist His will.

## 37

[1] Let us therefore enlist ourselves, brethren, with all earnestness in His faultless ordinances. [2] Let us mark the soldiers that are enlisted under our rulers, how exactly, how readily, how submissively, they execute the orders given them. [3] All are not prefects, nor rulers of thousands, nor rulers of hundreds, nor rulers of fifties, and so forth; but each man in his own rank executeth the orders given by the king and the governors. [4] The great without the small cannot exist, neither the small without the great. There is a certain mixture in all things, and therein is utility. [5] Let us take our body as an example. The head without the feet is nothing; so likewise the feet without the head are nothing: even the smallest limbs of our body are necessary and useful for the whole body: but all the members conspire and unite in subjection, that the whole body maybe saved.

## 38

[1] So in our case let the whole body be saved in Christ Jesus, and let each man be subject unto his neighbor, according as also he was appointed with his special grace. [2] Let not the strong neglect the weak; and let the weak respect the strong. Let the rich minister aid to the poor; and let the poor give thanks to God, because He hath given him one through whom his wants may be supplied. Let the wise display his wisdom, not in words, but in good works. He that is lowly in mind, let him not bear testimony to himself, but leave testimony to be borne to him by his neighbor. He that is pure in the flesh, let him be so, and not boast, knowing that it is Another who bestoweth his continence upon him. [3] Let us consider, brethren, of what matter we were made; who and what manner of beings we were, when we came into the world; from what a sepulchre and what darkness He that molded and created us brought us into His world, having prepared His benefits aforehand ere ever we were born. [4] Seeing therefore that we have all these things from Him, we ought in all things to give thanks to Him, to whom be the glory for ever and ever. Amen.

## 39

[1] Senseless and stupid and foolish and ignorant men jeer and mock at us, desiring that they themselves should be exalted in their imaginations.

[2] For what power hath a mortal? or what strength hath a child of earth? [3] For it is written; *There was no form before mine eyes; only I heard a breath and a voice.* [4] *What then? Shall a mortal be clean in the sight of the Lord; or shall a man be unblamable for his works? seeing that He is distrustful against His servants and noteth some perversity against His angels.* [5] *Nay, the heaven is not clean in His sight. Away then, ye that dwell in houses of clay, whereof, even of the same clay, we ourselves are made. He smote them like a moth, and from morn to even they are no more. Because they could not succor themselves, they perished.* [6] *He breathed on them and they died, because they had no wisdom.* [7] *But call thou, if perchance one shall obey thee, or if thou shalt see one of the holy angels. For wrath killeth the foolish man, and envy slayeth him that has gone astray.* [8] *And I have seen fools throwing out roots, but forthwith their habitation was eaten up.* [9] *Far be their sons from safety. May they be mocked at the gates of inferiors, and there shall be none to deliver them. For the things which are prepared for them, the righteous shall eat; but they themselves shall not be delivered from evils.*

## 40

[1] Forasmuch then as these things are manifest beforehand, and we have searched into the depths of the Divine knowledge, we ought to do all things in order, as many as the Master hath commanded us to perform at their appointed seasons. [2] Now the offerings and ministrations He commanded to be performed with care, and not to be done rashly or in disorder, but at fixed times and seasons. [3] And where and by whom He would have them performed, He Himself fixed by His supreme will: that all things being done with piety according to His good pleasure might be acceptable to His will. [4] They therefore that make their offerings at the appointed seasons are acceptable and blessed: for while they follow the institutions of the Master they cannot go wrong. [5] For unto the high priest his proper services have been assigned, and to the priests their proper office is appointed, and upon the levites their proper ministrations are laid. The layman is bound by the layman's ordinances.

## 41

[1] Let each of you, brethren, in his own order give thanks unto God, maintaining a good conscience and not transgressing the appointed rule of his service, but acting with all seemliness. [2] Not in every place, brethren, are the continual daily sacrifices offered, or the freewill offerings, or the sin offerings and the trespass offerings, but in Jerusalem alone. And even there the offering is not made in every place, but before the sanctuary in the court of the altar; and this too through the high priest and the afore said ministers, after that the victim to be offered hath been inspected for blemishes. [3] They therefore who do any thing contrary to the seemly ordinance of His will receive death as the penalty. [4] Ye see, brethren, in proportion as greater knowledge hath been vouchsafed unto us, so much the more are we exposed to danger.

## 42

[1] The Apostles received the Gospel for us from the Lord Jesus Christ; Jesus Christ was sent forth from God. [2] So then Christ is from God, and the Apostles are from Christ. Both therefore came of the will of God in the appointed order. [3] Having therefore received a charge, and having been fully assured through the resurrection of our Lord Jesus Christ and confirmed in the word of God with full assurance of the Holy Ghost, they went forth with the glad tidings that the kingdom of God should come. [4] So preaching everywhere in country and town, they appointed their firstfruits, when they had proved them by the Spirit, to be bishops and deacons unto them that should believe. [5] And this they did in no new fashion; for indeed it had been written concerning bishops and deacons from very ancient times; for thus saith the scripture in a certain place, *I will appoint their bishops in righteousness and their deacons in faith.*

## 43

[1] And what marvel, if they which were entrusted in Christ with such a work by God appointed the aforesaid persons? seeing that even the blessed Moses who was a *faithful servant in all His house* recorded for a sign in the sacred books all things that were enjoined upon him. And him also the rest of the prophets followed, bearing witness with him unto the laws that were ordained by him. [2] For he, when jealousy arose concerning the priesthood, and there was dissension among the tribes which of them was adorned with the glorious name, commanded the twelve chiefs of the tribes to bring to him rods inscribed with the name of each tribe. And he took them and tied them and sealed them with the signet rings of the chiefs of the tribes, and put them away in the tabernacle of the testimony on the table of God. [3] And having shut the tabernacle he sealed the keys and likewise also the doors. [4] And he said

unto them, Brethren, the tribe whose rod shall bud, this hath God chosen to be priests and ministers unto Him. [5] Now when morning came, he called together all Israel, even the six hundred thousand men, and showed the seals to the chiefs of the tribes and opened the tabernacle of the testimony and drew forth the rods. And the rod of Aaron was found not only with buds, but also bearing fruit. [6] What think ye, dearly beloved? Did not Moses know beforehand that this would come to pass? Assuredly he knew it. But that disorder might not arise in Israel, he did thus, to the end that the Name of the true and only God might be glorified: to whom he the glory for ever and ever. Amen...

## 44

[1] And our Apostles knew through our Lord Jesus Christ that there would be strife over the name of the bishop's office. [2] For this cause therefore, having received complete foreknowledge, they appointed the aforesaid persons, and afterwards they provided a continuance, that if these should fall asleep, other approved men should succeed to their ministration. Those therefore who were appointed by them, or afterward by other men of repute with the consent of the whole Church, and have ministered unblamably to the flock of Christ in lowliness of mind, peacefully and with all modesty, and for long time have borne a good report with all these men we consider to be unjustly thrust out from their ministration. [3] For it will be no light sin for us, if we thrust out those who have offered the gifts of the bishop's office unblamably and holily. [4] Blessed are those presbyters who have gone before, seeing that their departure was fruitful and ripe: for they have no fear lest any one should remove them from their appointed place. [5] For we see that ye have displaced certain persons, though they were living honorably, from the ministration which had been respected by them blamelessly.

## 45

[1] Be ye contentious, brethren, and jealous about the things that pertain unto salvation. [2] Ye have searched the scriptures, which are true, which were given through the Holy Ghost; [3] and ye know that nothing unrighteous or counterfeit is written in them. Ye will not find that righteous persons have been thrust out by holy men. [4] Righteous men were persecuted, but it was by the lawless; they were imprisoned, but it was by the unholy. They were stoned by transgressors: they were slain by those who had conceived a detestable and unrighteous jealousy. [5] Suffering these things, they endured nobly. [6] For what must we say, brethren? Was Daniel cast into the lions' den by them that feared God? [7] Or were Ananias and Azarias and Misael shut up in the furnace of fire by them that professed the excellent and glorious worship of the Most High? Far be this from our thoughts. Who then were they that did these things? Abominable men and full of all wickedness were stirred up to such a pitch of wrath, as to bring cruel suffering upon them that served God in a holy and blameless purpose, not knowing that the Most High is the champion and protector of them that in a pure conscience serve His excellent Name: unto whom be the glory for ever and ever. Amen. [8] But they that endured patiently in confidence inherited glory and honor; they were exalted, and had their names recorded by God in their memorial for ever and ever. Amen.

## 46

[1] To such examples as these therefore, brethren, we also ought to cleave.
[2] For it is written; *Cleave unto the saints, for they that cleave unto them shall be sanctified.* [3] And again He saith in another place; *With the guiltless man thou shalt be guiltless, and with the elect thou shalt be elect, and with the crooked thou shalt deal crookedly.* [4] Let us therefore cleave to the guiltless and righteous: and these are the elect of God. [5] Wherefore are there strifes and wraths and factions and divisions and war among you? [6] Have we not one God and one Christ and one Spirit of grace that was shed upon us? And is there not one calling in Christ? [7] Wherefore do we tear and rend asunder the members of Christ, and stir up factions against our own body, and reach such a pitch of folly, as to forget that we are members one of another? [8] Remember the words of Jesus our Lord: for He said, *Woe unto that man; it were good for him if he had not been born, rather than that at he should offend one of Mine elect. It were better for him that a millstone were hanged about him, and he be cast into the sea, than that he should pervert one of Mine elect.* [9] Your division hath perverted many; it hath brought many to despair, many to doubting, and all of us to sorrow. And your sedition still continueth.

## 47

[1] Take up the epistle of the blessed Paul the Apostle. [2] What wrote he first unto you in the beginning of the Gospel? [3] Of a truth he charged you in the Spirit concerning himself and Cephas and Apollos, because that even then ye had made parties. [4] Yet that making of parties brought less sin upon you; for ye were partisans of Apostles that were highly reputed, and of a man approved in their sight. [5] But now mark ye, who they are that have perverted you and diminished the glory of your renowned love for the brotherhood. [6] It is shameful, dearly beloved,

yes, utterly shameful and unworthy of your conduct in Christ, that it should be reported that the very steadfast and ancient Church of the Corinthians, for the sake of one or two persons, maketh sedition against its presbyters. [7] And this report hath reached not only us, but them also which differ from us, so that ye even heap blasphemies on the Name of the Lord by reason of your folly, and moreover create peril for yourselves.

## 48

[1] Let us therefore root this out quickly, and let us fall down before the Master and entreat Him with tears, that He may show Himself propitious and be reconciled unto us, and may restore us to the seemly and pure conduct which belongeth to our love of the brethren. [2] For this is a gate of righteousness opened unto life, as it is written; *Open me the gates of righteousness, that I may enter in thereby and preach the Lord.* [3] *This is the gate of the Lord; the righteous shall enter in thereby.* [4] Seeing then that many gates are opened, this is that gate which is in righteousness, even that which is in Christ, whereby all are blessed that have entered in and direct their path in holiness and righteousness, performing all things without confusion. [5] Let a man be faithful, let him be able to expound a deep saying, let him be wise in the discernment of words, let him be strenuous in deeds, let him be pure; [6] for so much the more ought he to be lowly in mind, in proportion as he seemeth to be the greater; and he ought to seek the common advantage of all, and not his own.

## 49

[1] Let him that hath love in Christ fulfill the commandments of Christ. [2] Who can declare the bond of the love of God? [3] Who is sufficient to tell the majesty of its beauty? [4] The height, where unto love exalteth, is unspeakable. [5] Love joineth us unto God; *love covereth a multitude of sins;* love endureth all things, is long-suffering in all things. There is nothing coarse, nothing arrogant in love. Love hath no divisions, love maketh no seditions, love doeth all things in concord. In love were all the elect of God made perfect; without love nothing is well pleasing to God: [6] in love the Master took us unto Himself; for the love which He had toward us, Jesus Christ our Lord hath given His blood for us by the will of God, and His flesh for our flesh and His life for our lives.

## 50

[1] Ye see, dearly beloved, how great and marvelous a thing is love, and there is no declaring its perfection. [2] Who is sufficient to be found therein, save those to whom God shall vouchsafe it? Let us therefore entreat and ask of His mercy, that we may be found blameless in love, standing apart from the factiousness of men. All the generations from Adam unto this day have passed away: but they that by God's grace were perfected in love dwell in the abode of the pious; and they shall be made manifest in the visitation of the Kingdom of God. [3] For it is written; *Enter into the closet for a very little while until Mine anger and Mine wrath shall pass away, and I will remember a good day and will raise you from your tombs.* [4] Blessed were we, dearly beloved, if we should be doing the commandments of God in concord of love, to the end that our sins may through love be forgiven us. [5] For it is written; *Blessed are they whose iniquities are forgiven, and whose sins are covered. Blessed is the man to whom the Lord shall impute no sin, neither is guile in his mouth.* [6] This declaration of blessedness was pronounced upon them that have been elected by God through Jesus Christ our Lord, to whom be the glory for ever and ever. Amen.

## 51

[1] For all our transgressions which we have committed through any of the wiles of the adversary, let us entreat that we may obtain forgiveness. Yea and they also, who set themselves up as leaders of faction and division, ought to look to the common ground of hope. [2] For such as walk in fear and love desire that they themselves should fall into suffering rather than their neighbors; and they pronounce condemnation against themselves rather than against the harmony which hath been handed down to us nobly and righteously. [3] For it is good for a man to make confession of his trespasses rather than to harden his heart, as the heart of those was hardened who made sedition against Moses the servant of God; whose condemnation was clearly manifest, [4] for they went down to hades alive, and *Death shall be their shepherd.* [5] Pharaoh and his host and all the rulers of Egypt, *their chariots and their horsemen,* were overwhelmed in the depths of the Red Sea, and perished for none other reason but because their foolish hearts were hardened after that the signs and the wonders had been wrought in the land of Egypt by the hand of Moses the servant of God.

## 52

[1] The Master, brethren, hath need of nothing at all. He desireth not anything of any man, save to confess unto Him. [2] For the elect David saith; *I will confess unto the Lord, and it shall please Him more than a young calf that groweth horns and hoofs. Let the poor see it, and*

*rejoice.* [3] For a sacrifice unto God is a broken spirit. **52:3** And again He saith; *Sacrifice to God a sacrifice of praise, and pay thy vows to the Most High: and call upon Me in the day of thine affliction, and I will deliver thee, and thou shalt glorify Me.* **52:4** For a sacrifice unto God is a broken spirit.

## 53

[1] For ye know, and know well, the sacred scriptures, dearly beloved, and ye have searched into the oracles of God. We write these things therefore to put you in remembrance. [2] When Moses went up into the mountain and had spent forty days and forty nights in fasting and humiliation, God said unto him; *Moses, Moses, come down , quickly hence, for My people whom thou leadest forth from the land of Egypt have wrought iniquity: they have transgressed quickly out of the way which thou didst command unto them: they have made for themselves molten images.* [3] And the Lord said unto him; *I have spoken unto thee once and twice, saying, I have seen this people, and behold it is stiff-necked. Let Me destroy them utterly, and I will blot out their name from under heaven, and I will make of thee a nation great and wonderful and numerous more than this.* [4] And Moses said; *Nay, not so, Lord Forgive this people their sin, or blot me also out of the book of the living.* [5] O mighty love! O unsurpassable perfection! The servant is bold with his Master; he asketh forgiveness for the multitude, or he demandeth that himself also be blotted out with them.

## 54

[1] Who therefore is noble among you? Who is compassionate? Who is fulfilled with love? [2] Let him say; If by reason of me there be faction and strife and divisions, I retire, I depart, whither ye will, and I do that which is ordered by the people: only let the flock of Christ be at peace with its duly appointed presbyters. [3] He that shall have done this, shall win for himself great renown in Christ, and every place will receive him: for *the earth is the Lord's and the fullness thereof.* [4] Thus have they done and will do, that live as citizens of that kingdom of God which bringeth no regrets.

## 55

[1] But, to bring forward examples of Gentiles also; many kings and rulers, when some season of pestilence pressed upon them, being taught by oracles have delivered themselves over to death, that they might rescue their fellow citizens through their own blood. Many have retired from their own cities, that they might have no more seditions. [2] We know that many among ourselves have delivered themselves to bondage, that they might ransom others. Many have sold themselves to slavery, and receiving the price paid for themselves have fed others. [3] Many women being strengthened through the grace of God have performed many manly deeds. [4] The blessed Judith, when the city was beleaguered, asked of the elders that she might be suffered to go forth into the camp of the aliens. [5] So she exposed herself to peril and went forth for love of her country and of her people which were beleaguered; and the Lord delivered Holophernes into the hand of a woman. [6] To no less peril did Esther also, who was perfect in faith, expose herself, that she might deliver the twelve tribes of Israel, when they were on the point to perish. For through her fasting and her humiliation she entreated the all seeing Master, the God of the ages; and He, seeing the humility of her soul, delivered the people for whose sake she encountered the peril.

## 56

[1] Therefore let us also make intercession for them that are in any transgression, that forbearance and humility may be given them, to the end that they may yield not unto us, but unto the will of God. For so shall the compassionate remembrance of them with God and the saints be fruitful unto them, and perfect. [2] Let us accept chastisement, whereat no man ought to be vexed, dearly beloved. The admonition which we give one to another is good and exceeding useful; for it joineth us unto the will of God. [3] For thus saith the holy word; *The Lord hath indeed chastened me, and hath not delivered me over unto death.* [4] *For whom the Lord loveth He chasteneth, and scourgeth every son whom He receiveth.* [5] *For the righteous,* it is said, *shall chasten me in mercy and shall reprove me, but let not the mercy of sinners anoint my head.* [6] And again He saith; *Blessed is the man whom the Lord hath reproved, and refuse not thou the admonition of the Almighty. For He causeth pain, and he restoreth again:* [7] *He hath smitten, and His hands have healed.* [8] *Six times shall He rescue thee from afflictions and at the seventh no evil shall touch thee.* [9] *In famine he shall deliver thee from death, and in war He shall release thee from the arm of the sword.* [10] *And from the scourge of the tongue He shall hide thee and thou shalt not be afraid when evils approach.* [11] *Thou shalt laugh at the unrighteous and wicked, and of the wild beasts thou shalt not be afraid.* [12] *For wild beasts shall be at peace with thee.* [13] *Then shalt thou know that thy house shall be at peace: and the abode of thy tabernacle shall not go wrong,* [14] *and thou shalt know that thy seed is many, and thy children as the plenteous herbage of the field.* [15] *And thou shalt come to the*

grave as ripe corn reaped in due season, or as the heap of the threshing floor gathered together at the right time. **16** Ye see, dearly beloved, how great protection there is for them that are chastened by the Master: for being a kind father He chasteneth us to the end that we may obtain mercy through His holy chastisement.

## 57

**1** Ye therefore that laid the foundation of the sedition, submit yourselves unto the presbyters and receive chastisement unto repentance, bending the knees of your heart. **2** Learn to submit yourselves, laying aside the arrogant and proud stubbornness of your tongue. For it is better for you to be found little in the flock of Christ and to have your name on God's roll, than to be had in exceeding honor and yet be cast out from the hope of Him. **3** For thus saith the All virtuous Wisdom; *Behold I will pour out for you a saying of My breath, and I will teach you My word.* **4** *Because I called and ye obeyed not, and I held out words and ye heeded not, but made My councils of none effect, and were disobedient unto My reproofs; therefore I also will laugh at your destruction, and will rejoice over you when ruin cometh upon you, and when confusion overtaketh you suddenly, and your overthrow is at hand like a whirlwind,* **5** *or when ye call upon Me, yet will I not here you. Evil men shall seek me and not find me: for they hated wisdom, and chose not the fear of the Lord, neither would they give head unto My councils, but mocked at My reproofs.* **6** *Therefore they shall eat the fruits of their own way, and shall be filled with their own ungodliness.* **7** *For because they wronged babes, they shall be slain, and inquisition shall destroy the ungodly. But he that heareth Me shall dwell safely trusting in hope, and shall be quiet from all fear of all evil.*

## 58

**1** Let us therefore be obedient unto His most holy and glorious Name, thereby escaping the threatenings which were spoken of old by the mouth of Wisdom against them which disobey, that we may dwell safely, trusting in the most holy Name of His majesty. **2** Receive our counsel, and ye shall have no occasion of regret. For as God liveth, and the Lord Jesus Christ liveth, and the Holy Spirit, who are the faith and the hope of the elect, so surely shall he, who with lowliness of mind and instant in gentleness hath without regretfulness performed the ordinances and commandments that are given by God, be enrolled and have a name among the number of them that are saved through Jesus Christ, through whom is the glory unto Him for ever and ever. Amen.

## 59

**1** But if certain persons should be disobedient unto the words spoken by Him through us, let them understand that they will entangle themselves in no slight transgression and danger; **2** but we shall be guiltless of this sin. And we will ask, with instancy of prayer and supplication, that the Creator of the universe may guard intact unto the end the number that hath been numbered of His elect throughout the whole world, through His beloved Son Jesus Christ, through whom He called us from darkness to light, from ignorance to the full knowledge of the glory of His Name. **3** [Grant unto us, Lord,] that we may set our hope on Thy Name which is the primal source of all creation, and open the eyes of our hearts, that we may know Thee, who alone abidest *Highest in the lofty, Holy in the holy;* who *layest low in the insolence of the proud,* who *settest the lowly on high,* and *bringest the lofty low;* who *makest rich and makest poor;* who *killest and makest alive;* who alone art the Benefactor of spirits and the God of all flesh; who *lookest into the abysses,* who scanest the works of man; the Succor of them that are in peril, the *Savior of them that are in despair*; The Creator and Overseer of every spirit; who multipliest the nations upon earth, and hast chosen out from all men those that love Thee through Jesus Christ, Thy beloved Son, through whom Thou didst instruct us, didst sanctify us, didst honor us. **4** We beseech Thee, Lord and Master, to be *our help and succor.* Save those among us who are in tribulation; have mercy on the lowly; lift up the fallen; show Thyself unto the needy; heal the ungodly; convert the wanderers of Thy people; feed the hungry; release our prisoners; raise up the weak; comfort the fainthearted. *Let all the Gentiles know that Thou art the God alone*, and Jesus Christ is Thy Son, and *we are Thy people and the sheep of Thy pasture.*

## 60

**1** Thou through Thine operations didst make manifest the everlasting fabric of the world. Thou, Lord, didst create the earth. Thou that art faithful throughout all generations, righteous in Thy judgments, marvelous in strength and excellence, Thou that art wise in creating and prudent in establishing that which Thou hast made, that art good in the things which are seen and faithful with them that trust on Thee, *pitiful and compassionate*, forgive us our iniquities and our unrighteousnesses and our transgressions and shortcomings. **2** Lay not to our account every sin of Thy servants and Thine handmaids, but cleanse us with the cleansing of Thy truth, and *guide our steps to walk in holiness* and righteousness and singleness *of heart* and *to do such things as are good and well pleasing in Thy sight* and in the sight of our rulers. **3** Yea,

Lord, *make Thy face to shine upon us* in peace for our good, that we may be sheltered *by Thy mighty hand and* delivered from every sin *by Thine uplifted arm.* And deliver us from them that hate us wrongfully. **4** Give concord and peace to us and to all that dwell on the earth, as Thou gavest to our fathers, *when they called on* Thee *in faith and truth* with holiness, [that we may be saved,] while we render obedience to Thine almighty and most excellent Name, and to our rulers and governors upon the earth.

## 61

**1** Thou, Lord and Master, hast given them the power of sovereignty through Thine excellent and unspeakable might, that we knowing the glory and honor which Thou hast given them may submit ourselves unto them, in nothing resisting Thy will. Grant unto them therefore, O Lord, health peace, concord, stability, that they may administer the government which Thou hast given them without failure. **2** For Thou, O heavenly Master, King of the ages, givest to the sons of men glory and honor and power over all things that are upon the earth. Do Thou, Lord, direct their counsel according to that which is good and well pleasing in Thy sight, that, administering in peace and gentleness with Godliness the power which Thou hast given them, they may obtain Thy favor. **3** O Thou, who alone art able to do these things and things far more exceeding good than these for us, we praise Thee through the High priest and Guardian of our souls, Jesus Christ, through whom be the glory and the majesty unto Thee both now and for all generations and for ever and ever. Amen.

## 62

**1** As touching those things which befit our religion and are most useful for a virtuous life to such as would guide [their steps] in holiness and righteousness, we have written fully unto you, brethren. **2** For concerning faith and repentance and genuine love and temperance and sobriety and patience we have handled every argument, putting you in remembrance, that ye ought to please Almighty God in righteousness and truth and long suffering with holiness, laying aside malice and pursuing concord in love and peace, being instant in gentleness; even as our fathers, of whom we spake before, pleased Him, being lowly minded toward their Father and God and Creator and towards all men. **3** And we have put you in mind of these things the more gladly, since we knew well that we were writing to men who are faithful and highly accounted and have diligently searched into the oracles of the teaching of God.

## 63

**1** Therefore it is right for us to give heed to so great and so many examples and to submit the neck and occupying the place of obedience to take our side with them that are the leaders of our souls, that ceasing from this foolish dissension we may attain unto the goal which lieth before us in truthfulness, keeping aloof from every fault. **2** For ye will give us great joy and gladness, if ye render obedience unto the things written by us through the Holy Spirit, and root out the unrighteous anger of your jealousy, according to the entreaty which we have made for peace and concord in this letter. **3** And we have also sent faithful and prudent men that have walked among us from youth unto old age unblamably, who shall also be witnesses between you and us. **4** And this we have done that ye might know that we have had, and still have, every solicitude that ye should be speedily at peace.

## 64

**1** Finally may the All seeing God and Master of spirits and Lord of all flesh, who chose the Lord Jesus Christ, and us through Him for a peculiar people, grant unto every soul that is called after His excellent and holy Name faith, fear, peace, patience, long-suffering, temperance, chastity and soberness, that they may be well pleasing unto His Name through our High priest and Guardian Jesus Christ, through whom unto Him be glory and majesty, might and honor, both now and for ever and ever. Amen.

## 65

**1** Now send ye back speedily unto us our messengers Claudius Ephebus and Valerius Bito, together with Fortunatus also, in peace and with joy, to the end that they may the more quickly report the peace and concord which is prayed for and earnestly desired by us, that we also may the more speedily rejoice over your good order. **2** The grace of our Lord Jesus Christ be with you and with all men in all places who have been called by God and through Him, through whom be glory and honor, power and greatness and eternal dominion, unto Him, from the ages past and forever and ever. Amen.

# Glossary

The following words used are not very common, either because they refer to ancient weights, measures, or money, or because they are in some way unique to the Bible.

**Abaddon** Abaddon is Hebrew for destruction.

**Abba** Abba is a Chaldee word for father, used in a respectful, affectionate, and familiar way, like papa, dad, or daddy. Often used in prayer to refer to our Father in Heaven.

**adultery** Adultery is having sexual intercourse with someone besides your own husband or wife. In the Bible, the only legitimate sexual intercourse is between a man and a woman who are married to each other.

**alpha** Alpha is the first letter of the Greek alphabet. It is sometimes used to mean the beginning or the first.

**amen** Amen means "So be it" or "I believe it is certainly so."

**angel** "Angel" literally means "messenger" or "envoy," and is usually used to refer to spiritual beings who normally are invisible to us, but can also appear as exceedingly strong creatures or as humans.

**Apollyon** Apollyon is Greek for destroyer.

**apostle** "Apostle" means a delegate, messenger, or one sent forth with orders. This term is applied in the New Testament in both a general sense connected with a ministry of establishing and strengthening church fellowships, as well as in a specific sense to "The **12** Apostles of the Lamb" (Revelation **21:14**). The former category applies to a specific ministry that continues in the Church (Ephesians **4:11-13**) and which includes many more than **12** people, while the latter refers to the apostles named in Matthew **10:2-4**, except with Judas Iscariot replaced by Matthias (Acts **1:26**).

**Armageddon** See Har-magedon.

**assarion** An assarion is a small Roman copper coin worth one tenth of a drachma, or about an hour's wages for an agricultural laborer.

**aureus** An aureus is a Roman gold coin, worth **25** silver denarii. An aureus weighed from **115** to **126.3** grains (**7.45** to **8.18** grams).

**baptize** Baptize means to immerse in, or wash with something, usually water. Baptism in the Holy Spirit, fire, the Body of Christ, and suffering are also mentioned in the New Testament, along with baptism in water. Baptism is not just to cleanse the body, but as an outward sign of an inward spiritual cleansing and commitment. Baptism is a sign of repentance, as practiced by John the Baptizer, and of faith in Jesus Christ, as practiced by Jesus' disciples.

**bath** A bath is a liquid measure of about **22** liters, **5.8** U. S. gallons, or **4.8** imperial gallons.

**batos** A batos is a liquid measure of about **39.5** liters, **10.4** U.S. gallons, or **8.7** imperial gallons.

**Beelzebul** literally, lord of the flies. A name used for the devil.

**Beersheba** Beersheba is Hebrew for "well of the oath" or "well of the seven." A city in Israel.

**behold** Look! See! Wow! Notice this! Lo!

**cherub** A cherub is a kind of angel with wings and hands that is associated with the throne room of God and guardian duty. See Ezekiel **10**.

**cherubim** Cherubim means more than one cherub or a mighty cherub.

**choenix** A choenix is a dry volume measure that is a little more than a liter (which is a little more than a quart). A choenix was the daily ration of grain for a soldier in some armies.

**concubine** a woman who is united to a man for the purpose of providing him with sexual pleasure and children, but not being honored as a full partner in marriage; a second-class wife. In Old Testament times (and in some places now), it was the custom of middle-eastern kings, chiefs, and wealthy men to marry multiple wives and concubines, but God commanded the Kings of Israel not to do so (Deuteronomy **17:17**) and Jesus encouraged people to either remain single or marry as God originally intended: one man married to one woman (Matthew **19:3-12**; 1 Corinthians **7:1-13**).

**cor** A cor is a dry measure of about **391** liters, **103** U. S. gallons, or **86** imperial gallons.

**corban** Corban is a Hebrew word for an offering devoted to God.

**crucify** Crucify means to execute someone by nailing them to a cross with metal spikes. Their hands are stretched out on the crossbeam with spikes driven through their wrists or hands. Their feet or ankles are attached to a cross with a metal spike. The weight of the victim's body tends to force the air out of his lungs. To rise up to breathe, the victim has to put weight on the wounds, and use a lot of strength. The victim is nailed to the cross while the cross is on the ground, then the cross is raised up and dropped into a hole, thus jarring the victim. Before crucifixion, the victim was usually whipped with a Roman cat of nine tails, which had bits of glass and metal tied to its ends. This caused chunks of flesh to be removed and open wounds to be placed against the raw wood of the cross. The victim was made to carry the heavy crossbeam of his cross from the place of judgment to the place of crucifixion, but often was physically unable after the scourging, so another person would be pressed into involuntary service to carry the cross for him. Roman crucifixion was generally done totally naked to maximize both shame and discomfort. Eventually, the pain, weakness, dehydration, and exhaustion of the muscles needed to breathe make breathing impossible, and the victim suffocates.

**cubit** A cubit is a unit of linear measure, from the elbow to the tip of the longest finger of a man. This unit is commonly converted to **0.46** meters or **18** inches, although that varies with height of the man doing the measurement. There is also a "long" cubit that is longer than a regular cubit by a handbreadth. (Ezekiel **43:13**)

**cummin** Cummin is an aromatic seed from Cuminum cyminum, resembling caraway in flavor and appearance. It is used as a spice.

**darnel** Darnel is a weed grass (probably bearded darnel or Lolium temulentum) that looks very much like wheat until it is mature, when the seeds reveal a great difference. Darnel seeds aren't good for much except as chicken feed or to burn to prevent the spread of this weed.

**denarii** denarii: plural form of denarius, a silver Roman coin worth about a day's wages for a laborer.

**denarius** A denarius is a silver Roman coin worth about a day's wages for an agricultural laborer. A denarius was worth **1/25** th of a Roman aureus.

**devil** The word "devil" comes from the Greek "diabolos," which means "one prone to slander; a liar." "Devil" is used to refer to a fallen angel, also called "Satan," who works to steal, kill, destroy, and do evil. The devil's doom is certain, and it is only a matter of time before he is thrown into the Lake of Fire, never to escape.

**didrachma** A didrachma is a Greek silver coin worth **2** drachmas, about as much as **2** Roman denarii, or about **2** days wages. It was commonly used to pay the half-shekel temple tax.

**disciple** a student who follows a teacher to learn both by precept and example.

**distaff** part of a spinning wheel used for twisting threads.

**drachma** A drachma is a Greek silver coin worth about one Roman denarius, or about a day's wages for an agricultural laborer.

**El-Elohe-Israel** El-Elohe-Israel means "God, the God of Israel" or "The God of Israel is mighty."

**ephah** An ephah is a measure of volume of about **22** liters, **5.8** U. S. gallons, **4.8** imperial gallons, or a bit more than half a bushel.

**Gehenna** Gehenna is one word used for Hell. It comes from the Hebrew Gey-Hinnom, literally "valley of Hinnom." This word originated as the name for a place south of the old city of Jerusalem where the city's rubbish was burned. At one time, live babies were thrown crying into the fire under the arms of the idol, Moloch, to die there. This place was so despised by the people after the righteous King Josiah abolished this hideous practice that it was made into a garbage heap. Bodies of diseased animals and executed criminals were thrown there and burned.

**gittith** Gittith is a musical term possibly meaning "an instrument of Gath."

**goad** a sharp, pointed prodding device used to motivate reluctant animals (such as oxen and mules) to move in the right direction.

**gospel** Gospel means "good news" or "glad tidings," specifically the Good News of Jesus' life, death, and resurrection for our salvation, healing, and provision; and the hope of eternal life that Jesus made available to us by God's grace.

**Hades** Hades: The nether realm of the disembodied spirits. Also known as "hell." See also "Sheol".

**Har-magedon** Har-magedon, also called Armegeddon, is most likely a reference to hill ("har") of Megiddo, near the Carmel Range in Israel. This area has a large valley plain with plenty of room for armies to maneuver.

**hin** A hin is a measure of volume of about about **6.5** liters or **1.7** gallons.

**homer** One homer is about **220** liters, **6.2** U. S. bushels, **6.1** imperial bushels, **58** U. S. gallons, or **48.4** imperial gallons.

**hypocrite** a stage actor; someone who pretends to be someone other than who they really are; a pretender; a dissembler

**Ishmael** Ishmael is the son of Abraham and Hagar. Ishmael literally means, "God hears."

**Jehovah** See "Yahweh."

**Jesus** "Jesus" is Greek for the Hebrew name "Yeshua," which is a short version of "Yehoshua," which comes from "Yoshia," which means "He will save."

**kodrantes** A kodrantes is a small coin worth one half of an Attic chalcus or two lepta. It is worth less than **2%** of a day's wages for an agricultural laborer.

**lepta** Lepta are very small, brass, Jewish coins worth half a Roman quadrans each, which is worth a quarter of the copper assarion. Lepta are worth less than **1%** of an agricultural worker's daily wages.

**leviathan** Leviathan is a poetic name for a large aquatic creature, possibly a crocodile or a dinosaur.

**mahalath** Mahalath is the name of a tune or a musical term.

**manna** Name for the food that God miraculously provided to the Israelites while they were wandering in the wilderness between Egypt and the promised land. From Hebrew man-hu (What is that?) or manan (to allot). See Exodus **16:14-35**.

**marriage** the union of a husband and a wife for the purpose of cohabitation, procreation, and to enjoy each other's company. God's plan for marriage is between one man and one woman (Mark **10:6-9**; 1 Corinthians **7**). Although there are many cases of a man marrying more than one woman in the Old Testament, being married to one wife is a requirement to serve in certain church leadership positions (1 Timothy **3:2,12**; Titus **1:5-6**).

**maschil** Maschil is a musical and literary term for "contemplation" or "meditative psalm."

**michtam** A michtam is a poem.

**mina** A mina is a Greek coin worth **100** Greek drachmas (or **100** Roman denarii), or about **100** day's wages for an agricultural laborer.

**myrrh** Myrrh is the fragrant substance that oozes out of the stems and branches of the low, shrubby tree commiphora myrrha or commiphora kataf native to the Arabian deserts and parts of Africa. The fragrant gum drops to the ground and hardens into an oily yellowish-brown resin. Myrrh was highly valued as a perfume, and as an ingredient in medicinal and ceremonial ointments.

**Nicolaitans** Nicolaitans were most likely Gnostics who taught the detestable lie that the physical and spiritual realms were entirely separate and that immorality in the physical realm wouldn't harm your spiritual health.

**omega** Omega is the last letter of the Greek alphabet. It is sometimes used to mean the last or the end.

**Peniel** Peniel is Hebrew for "face of God."

**phylactery** a leather container for holding a small scroll containing important Scripture passages that is worn on the arm or forehead in prayer. These phylacteries (tefillin in Hebrew) are still used by orthodox Jewish men. See Deuteronomy **6:8**.

**Praetorium** Praetorium: the Roman governor's residence and office building, and those who work there.

**quadrans** A quadrans is a Roman coin worth about **1/64** of a denarius. A denarius is about one day's wages for an agricultural laborer.

**rabbi** Rabbi is a transliteration of the Hebrew word for "my teacher," used as a title of respect for Jewish teachers.

**Rahab** Rahab is either (**1**) The prostitute who hid Joshua's **2** spies in Jericho (Joshua **2,6**) and later became an ancestor of Jesus (Matthew **1:5**) and an example of faith (Hebrews **11:31**; James **2:25**); or (**2**) Literally, "pride" or "arrogance" —possibly a reference to a large aquatic creature (Job **9:13**; **26:12**; Isaiah **51:9**) or symbolically referring to Egypt (Psalms **87:4**; **89:10**; Isaiah **30:7**).

**repent** to change one's mind; turn away from sin and turn toward God; to abhor one's past sins and determine to follow God.

**Rhabboni** Rhabboni: a transliteration of the Hebrew word for "great teacher."

**Sabbath** The seventh day of the week, set aside by God for man to rest.

**saints** The Greek word for "saints" literally means "holy ones." Saints are people set apart for service to God as holy and separate, living in righteousness. Used in the Bible to refer to all Christians and to all of those who worship Yahweh in Old Testament times.

**Samaritan** A Samaritan is a resident of Samaria. The Samaritans and the Jews generally detested each other during the time that Jesus walked among us.

**sanctify** To declare or set apart something as holy. To purify and separate a person from sin.

**sata** A sata is a dry measure of capacity approximately equal to **13** liters or **1.5** pecks.

**Satan** Satan means "accuser." This is one name for the devil, an enemy of God and God's people.

**scribe** A scribe is one who copies God's law. They were often respected as teachers and authorities on God's law.

**selah** Selah is a musical term indicating a pause or instrumental interlude for reflection.

**seraphim** Seraphim are **6**-winged angels. See Isaiah **6:2-6**.

**sexual immorality** The term "sexual immorality" in the New Testament comes from the Greek "porneia," which refers to any sexual activity besides that between a husband and his wife. In other words, prostitution (male or female), bestiality, homosexual activity, any sexual intercourse outside of marriage, and the production and consumption of pornography all are included in this term.

**shekel** A measure of weight, and when referring to that weight in gold, silver, or brass, of money. A shekel is approximately **16** grams, about a half an ounce, or **20** gerahs (Ezekiel **45:12**).

**Sheol** Sheol is the place of the dead. See also "Hades".

**Shibah** Shibah is Hebrew for "oath" or "seven." See Beersheba.

**shigionoth** Victorious music.

**soul** "Soul" refers to the emotions and intellect of a living person, as well as that person's very life. It is distinguished in the Bible from a person's spirit and body. (1 Thessalonians **5:23**, Hebrews **4:12**)

**span** A span is the length from the tip of a man's thumb to the tip of his little finger when his hand is stretched out (about half a cubit, or **9** inches, or **22.8** cm.)

**spirit** Spirit, breath, and wind all derive from the same Hebrew and Greek words. A person's spirit is the very essence of that person's life, which comes from God, who is a Spirit being (John **4:24**, Genesis **1:2**; **2:7**). The Bible distinguishes between a person's spirit, soul, and body (1 Thessalonians **5:23**, Hebrews **4:12**). Some beings may exist as spirits without necessarily having a visible body, such as angels and demons (Luke **9:39,1** John **4:1-3**).

**stadia** Stadia is plural for "stadion," a linear measure of about **184.9** meters or **606.6** feet (the length of the race course at Olympia).

**stater** A stater is a Greek silver coin equivalent to four Attic or two Alexandrian drachmas, or a Jewish shekel: just exactly enough to cover the half-shekel Temple Tax for two people.

**tabernacle** a dwelling place or place of worship, usually a tent.

**talent** A measure of weight or mass of **3000** shekels.

**Tartarus** Tartarus is the Greek name for an underworld for the wicked dead; another name for Gehenna or Hell.

**teraphim** Teraphim are household idols that may have been associated with inheritance rights to the household property.

**Yah** "Yah" is a shortened form of "Yahweh," which is God's proper name. This form is used occasionally in the Old Testament, mostly in the Psalms. See "Yahweh."

**Yahweh** "Yahweh" is God's proper name. In Hebrew, the four consonants roughly equivalent to YHWH were considered too holy to pronounce, so the Hebrew word for "Lord" (Adonai) was substituted when reading it aloud. When vowel points were added to the Hebrew Old Testament, the vowel points for "Adonai" were mixed with the consonants for "Yahweh," which if you pronounced it literally as written, would be pronounced "Yehovah" or "Jehovah." When the Old Testament was translated to Greek, the tradition of substituting "Lord" for God's proper name continued in the translation of God's name to "Lord" (Kurios). Some English Bibles translate God's proper name to "LORD" or "GOD" (usually with small capital letters), based on that same tradition. This can get really confusing, since two other words ("Adonai" and "Elohim") translate to "Lord" and "God," and they are sometimes used together. The ASV of **1901** (and some other translations) render YHWH as "Jehovah." The most probable pronunciation of God's proper name is "Yahweh." In Hebrew, the name "Yahweh" is related to the active declaration "I AM." See Exodus **3:13-14**. Since Hebrew has no tenses, the declaration "I AM" can also be interpreted as "I WAS" and "I WILL BE." Compare Revelation **1:8**.

**Zion** Zion is a name which originally referred one of the mountains of Jerusalem. It became a term synonymous with Jerusalem itself. The term "Heavenly Zion" is also used to refer the future dwelling place of God's people.

# Bonus Guide

Use your phone's camera to scan the QR code below or insert the web address in your browser: (peakquest.top/ethiopianbible-landing) … and **unlock your bonuses** on our website!

Made in the USA
Las Vegas, NV
20 September 2024

f5a12ed2-f4a8-479e-b360-3e9870db1515R01